THE
DESIGN
ENCYCLOPEDIA

MEL BYARS

John Wiley & Sons, Inc.
New York • Chichester • Brisbane • Toronto • Singapore

Published in the United States by John Wiley & Sons, Inc.,
605 Third Avenue, New York, NY 10158-0012

First published in the United Kingdom by Laurence King Publishing

This book was designed and produced by
Calmann & King Ltd, London
Designed by Karen Osborne, London
Printed in Spain

Consultants:
Arlette Barré-Despond, Design Historian, Paris
Stuart Durant, Kingston University, Kingston upon Thames
Milena Lamarová, Uměleckoprůmyslové Muzeum, Prague
David Revere McFadden, Decorative Arts Historian, New York
Gillian Naylor, Royal College of Art, London
Penny Sparke, Royal College of Art, London
Josef Straßer, Die Neue Sammlung, Munich

Library of Congress Cataloging in Publication
Data available

ISBN 0–471–02455–4

CONTENTS

Introduction

The Design Encyclopedia is intended to provide accurate and detailed information on people, firms, and materials, directly associated with the production of the decorative and applied arts in the past 125 years. Most of the entries are for designers of furniture, textiles, glass, metalware, wallpaper, and interiors as well as ceramists, industrial designers, and interior architects. There are no fine artists, photographers, architects, and graphic, fashion, and vehicle designers, except those active, if only peripherally, in the decorative and applied arts. The *Encyclopedia* covers decoration and design in Eastern and Western Europe, Japan, Australia, and North and South America. All of the important design-art organizations and groups, and manufacturers are discussed. Only prominent theoreticians, pedagogues, and schools have been included. There are some design stores listed, and some definitions of materials used in manufacturing and handicraft.

The aim of the book is to be as comprehensive as possible. However, some limits had to be imposed. The author received many helpful suggestions as to what could be left out, but had to be the final arbiter himself.

Organization

All the entries are organized alphabetically. In cases where there is a preposition as part of a person's family name, for example, Walter von Nessen, Nathalie du Pasquier, and Henry Clemens van de Velde, they are listed under 'v' for 'von Nessen,' 'd' for 'du Pasquier,' and 'v' for 'van de Velde.'

The entries for designers are divided into the following categories: general description and birthplace; education; general biography; exhibition activities and awards; and bibliography. There is no general bibliography. Individual bibliographies at the end of each entry are arranged chronologically by date of publication. These literature references serve both to validate most or all of the information given in the entry and, in numerous cases, to direct the reader to more complete information.

Since there appears to be no single comprehensive source where the titles, years, and locations of international expositions and specialized exhibitions are published, the lists in the back matter attempt to satisfy the absence. One-person and one-firm exhibitions have been included in the individual entries within the body of the encyclopedia itself.

Most of the institutions in non-English-language countries have not been translated into English. For example, while the Konstindustriskolan in Gothenburg and the Kungliga Konsthögskolan and the Konstfackskolan, both in Stockholm, may be translated respectively into the Royal Academy Art School, School of Arts and Crafts, and Swedish State School of Arts, Crafts and Design, it is often difficult to know to which school a reference is being made when the original name is not included with the translation. Occasionally it would have been helpful to offer translations in parentheses after difficult names, for example, Taideteollinen Korkeakoulu (Institute of Industrial Arts), Helsinki; these translations have not been provided in *The Design Encyclopedia* due to space limitations. References to exhibitions and institutions within all the entries are not abbreviated. There is no Key Guide included in this volume.

Russian proper names have been romanized from the Cyrillic alphabet according to the US Library of Congress system, with soft sounds indicated by an apostrophe, for example, Natal'ia Dan'ko. Bibliographical references have been retained as originally published.

Time Span

The *Encyclopedia*'s period of coverage spans design and decoration activities from approximately the last third of the 19th century to the immediate present. The words 'Modern' and 'Modernism,' frequently used in the *Encyclopedia*, are capitalized to indicate that 'Modern' no longer means 'contemporary,' 'up to date,' and 'now.'

The volume is an amalgamation of research, information, and criticism from a vast number of published sources and from personal communications with scholars and specialists which the author gathered from 1988–93. Due to the numerous examples in the bibliographic sources where data was in conflict – particularly dates – every effort was made to discover the correct information and put it right.

The author would particularly like to acknowledge the contributions of the seven advisors (Arlette Barré-Despond, Stuart Durant, Milena Lamarová, David Revere McFadden, Gillian Naylor, Penny Sparke, and Josef Straßer) who read through sections of the book, correcting and adding information, and suggesting further subjects for inclusion.

Mel Byars
New York City 1994

Acknowledgements

The author is grateful for the assistance, support, insights, and generosity of a large number of people, many of whom are mentioned below. He is particularly appreciative of his relationship with the staff of the Cooper-Hewitt National Museum of Design.

Nancy Aakre

Stanley Abercrombie

Paola Antonelli

Jean-François Barrielle

James Benjamin

Joel Berman

Susan Blair

Claire Bonney

Yvonne Brunhammer

Mathias Brüllmann

Barry Cenower

Peter Clark

Sophie Collins

Jacky Colliss Harvey

Gail Davidson

Guillemette Delaporte-Idrissi

Audrey Della Rossa

Isabelle Denamur

Giles Derain

Mary K. Doherty

Martin Eidelberg

Charles-Henri Flammarion

Marie-Françoise Flammarion

Russell Flinchum

Andrew Gary

Jane Havell

Loretta Kaufman

Stanley Kekwick

Joris Kila

Laurence King

Joanne Lightfoot

Marianne Loggia

Margaret Luchars

David Revere McFadden

Anne L. Miller

Wilfred Maurice Miller

Caroline Mortimer

Gillian Moss

Rex Nobles

Charlotte Nogard

Brad Nugent

Derek E. Ostergard

Dianne H. Pilgrim

Renata Rutledge

Deborah Sampson Shinn

Ronald-Cécil Sportes

Kevin Stayton

Angelique Sub-Sonderop

Timothy Sullivan

Suzanne Tise

Iren Tucker

John G. Tucker

Stephen Van Dyk

Neil Vaughn

Joanne Watkins

Pira Watkins

Leonard Webers

Christopher Wilk

Solveig Wilmering

Frances Wilson

A

Aalto, Aino (b. Aino Marsio 1894–1949)

▶ Finnish architect and designer; active Finland; wife of Alvar Aalto.

▶ Studied Helsingin Teknillinen Korkeakoulu, Helsinki.

▶ She and Alvar Aalto collaborated 1924–49; experimented by boiling pieces of birch in a saucepan in the rear of a local furniture store; worked together on other projects subsequently. On her own, she designed glass. She designed 1932 water-set (pitcher and drinking glasses) (oldest design in production at Iittala today) produced from 1933 by Karhula until the end of the 1950s, revived in the 1970s; in 1933, (with Alvar, Nils-Gustaf Hahl, and Marie Gullichsen) founded Artek. (Artek-affiliated firm Artek-Pascoe operated a shop in New York and distributed Aalto furniture in the USA.)

▶ Received second prize (water-set) in 1932 design competition sponsored by Karhula-Iittala glassworks; gold medal, 1936 (VI) Triennale di Milano. Work (water-set) shown at 1980 'Scandinavian Modern Design 1880–1980' exhibition, Cooper-Hewitt Museum, New York.

▶ Cat., David Revere McFadden (ed.), *Scandinavian Modern Design 1880–1980*, New York: Abrams, 1982:268, No. 115. Safu Grönstrand, *Alvar ja Aino Aalto Lasin Muotoilijoina*, Sävypaino: Iittala-Nuutajärvi, 1988. Elizabeth Gaynor, 'Around the Bend,' *Elle Decor*, October 1990:72.

Aalto, Hugo Alvar Henrik (1898–1976)

▶ Finnish architect, town planner, and designer of furniture, lighting, textiles, and glass; born Kuortane, near Jyväskylä; husband of Aino Marsio and Elissa Mäkiniemi Aalto.

▶ 1916–21, studied architecture, Helsingin Teknillinen Korkeakoulu, Helsinki, under Armas Lindgren and Lars Sonck.

▶ After his schooling he traveled widely in Central Europe, Scandinavia, and Italy; probably participated in planning the 1923 Gothenburg fair; except for minor previous works, was professionally active from the 1922 Tampere 'Industrial Exhibition'; in 1923, began an architecture practice in Jyväskylä, active 1927–33 in Turku, 1933–76 in Helsinki. He married architect Aino Marsio in 1924 and collaborated with her 1924–29, experimenting with wood. His 1929 exhibition (with Erik Bryggman) celebrating the 700th anniversary of Turku was the first complete public Modern structure in Scandinavia. His 1927–35 Viipuri Library and 1929–33 Sanatorium at Paimio were widely published examples of International Style architecture. An active and important designer for the Wohnbedarf store in Zürich, his entire bentwood furniture collection was included in the catalog *New Wooden Furniture: Aalto, Wohnbedarf* (1934) (designed by Herbert Bayer). In c1934, he furnished the new Corso theater, Zürich; influenced by the Bauhaus, some of his laminated-plywood chair designs were cantilevered like the bent-steel models of Marcel Breuer, Mies van der Rohe, Mart Stam; in 1928, purchased tubular-steel chairs by these designers for his apartment. His designs in turn were influential in Britain and the USA, inspiring others like Jack Pritchard of Isokon. His 1930 *Paimo* (or *Scroll*) chair was made from a single undulating plywood sheet for the 1929–33 Paimo Tuberculosis Sanatorium. Dubbed the first 'soft' chair in wood, it was manu-

factured at first by Huonekalu-ja Rakennus-työtehdas, Åbo (Finland), and subsequently by Artek. Many wooden Aalto chair designs followed. In 1933, he collaborated with Otto Korhonen in developing a solution for bending solid wood, resulting in the L-, Y-, and X-legged furniture; considered this solution to bentwood technology his single most important contribution to furniture design, calling it 'the little sister of the architectonic column'; 1935, met Marie Gullichsen and her industrialist husband Harry, who with Aalto and Aino established one of the first Modern home-furnishings shops in Helsinki. Gullichsen commissioned Aalto to design the 1934–35 Sunila Cellulose Factory, workers' housing, and Gullichsen's residence (the 1935 Villa Mairea). Established in Britain in 1934–35, Finmar was an importer and distributor of Aalto's furniture and furnishings. Aalto designed glass for Iittala in asymmetrical shapes and curves, of which his 1937 *Savoy* vase is the most famous. (The vase shape was said to reflect the fjord shorelines of Aalto's homeland.) In 1936, the Karhula-Iittala Glasbruk announced a design competition to find items to exhibit at the 1937 Paris 'Exposition Internationale des Arts et Techniques dans la Vie Moderne'; first-prize winner was Aalto's 1936 *Eskimoerindens skinnbuxa* ('leather trousers of an Eskimo woman') shape, the first of the glassware series that included the *Savoy* vase and was produced in clear and colored glass. Though a practitioner of the International Style, where other architects used ferro cement and stucco extensively, Aalto often used exposed brick; he advocated the use of natural materials and organic forms, promoting a humanistic tradition in architecture and design; in 1940, became a member of CIAM (Congrès Internationaux d'Architecture Moderne), which, along with Sigfried Giedion's approval of his work, gave Aalto prominence in the international avant-garde; 1940–49, was professor, College of Architecture, Massachusetts Institute of Technology; married architect Elissa Mäkiniemi in 1952 and collaborated with her 1952–76. After Aalto's death she finished work left incomplete. The little Aalto wrote is collected in Göran Schildt (ed.), *Alvar Aalto: Sketches* (1978).

▶ Architecture included 1923–25 Workers' Club and 1927–29 structure for the Patriots' Associations, both Jyväskylä; 1927–28 block of flats, Turku; 1929 exhibition (with Erik Bryggman) to commemorate the 700th anniversary of Turku; 1927–29 *Turun Sanomat* newspaper headquarters, Turku; 1927 and 1930–35 Municipal Library, Viipuri; 1928 and 1929–33 Sanitorium of Southwest Finland, Paimio; 1934–36 his own house, Helsinki; 1935–39 Cellulose Factory, Sunila; 1935–37 Finnish Pavilion, 1937 Paris 'Exposition Internationale des Arts et Techniques dans la Vie Moderne'; 1937–40 Terrace House, Kauttua; 1938 Blomberg Cinema, Helsinki; 1938 competition entry for University Library extension, Helsinki; Finnish pavilion, 1939 'New York World's Fair'; 1940 and 1950–52 Town Hall, Säynätsalo; 1940 Haka district competition entry; 1941 'Experimental City'; 1941 prototype houses; 1941–42 development plant for the Kokemäki valley; 1947–48 Baker House (senior students' dormitory), Massachusetts Institute of Technology; 1947 master plan for Imatra; 1950–55 regional plan for Lapland; 1950 and 1953–56 campus of the College of Education, Jyväskylä; 1955 'Interbau', Berlin;

Finnish pavilion, 1956 Biennale di Venezia; 1956 Maison Carré, Gazoches-sur-Buyonne (France); 1956–62 buildings for center of Seinäjoki; 1953 Vogelweidplatz, Vienna; 1958 and 1969–73 North Jutland Museum, Ålborg; 1958–62 apartment block, Neue Vahr, Bremen; 1958–62 culture center and 1959–62 parish community center, Wolfsburg (Germany); 1959 and 1960–62 Museum of Central Finland, Jyväskylä; 1964–69 Library of the Polytechnic, Otaniemi; 1967–70 Sports Institute of the College of Education, Jyväskylä; and 1971–73 Alvar Aalto Museum, Jyväskylä. Buildings after the war in Helsinki included 1959–73 different plans for the center of town; 1948 and 1952–56 National Pensions Institutions; 1952–55 Rautatalo Office Building; 1955–58 Cultural Center; 1959–62 Administration Building, Enso-Gutzeit Company; 1961 and 1963–65 Västmanland-Dala Students' Association headquarters, Uppsala (Sweden); 1962 Scandinavia House, Reykjavik; 1962–64 Scandinavian Bank Building; 1962 and 1966–69 University Bookshop; 1962 and 1967–71 Concert and Congress Hall; 1963–65 interior design of Institute of International Education, New York; 1965–68 Schönbühl apartment house, Lucerne; 1965–70 Library of Mount Angel Benedictine College, Mount Angel, Oregon; 1966–68 community center, Riola di Vergato (Italy); 1970 and 1973–75 'Finlandia' conference center and concert hall. Work completed after his death by Elissa Aalto included the extension to the Polytechnic in Otaniemi and the 1970–75 Lappia Cultural Center in Robaniemi; Essen (Germany) Opera House from 1959; Civic Center in Jyväskylä from 1964; 1950 church competition in Lahti begun 1970.

▶ Received honorary doctorate from Princeton University, 1947; Royal Gold Medal of Architecture, Britain, 1957; first, second, and third prizes, Finnish Pavilion Competition, 1939 'New York World's Fair'; first and second prizes (with A. Ervi and V. Rewell), Finnish Pavilion Competition, 1937 Paris 'Exposition Internationale des Arts et Techniques dans la Vie Moderne'; 1968 Royal Institute of British Architects gold medal. Appointed honorary member, Akademie der Künste, Berlin; from 1955, member of Academy of Finland. In 1947, elected Honorary Royal Designer for Industry, London.

▶ *Paimo* chair shown at November 1933 exhibition of Finnish design sponsored by *Architecture Review* at Fortnum and Mason, London. Work shown at a vast number of exhibitions including 1936 (VI) Triennale di Milano, 1954–57 USA 'Design in Scandinavia,' 1955 'H 55' Hälsingborg (Sweden), 1956 Berlin exhibition, 1958 Paris 'Formes Scandinaves,' 1961 Zürich/Amsterdam/London 'Finlandia,' 1968 Paris exhibition, 1970 'Modern Chairs 1918–1970' at Whitechapel Gallery, London, 1980 'Scandinavian Modern Design 1880–1980' exhibition, Cooper-Hewitt Museum, New York, 1983–84 'Design Since 1945' exhibition, Philadelphia Museum of Art. His work was the subject of 1938 (architecture and furniture) and 1984 (glassware and furniture) exhibitions, New York Museum of Modern Art.

▶ Giorgio Labò, *Alvar Aalto*, Milan, 1948. F. Gutheim, *Alvar Aalto*, New York and London, 1960. Karl Fleig, *Alvar Aalto 1922–62*, Zürich, 1963. Leonardo Mosso, *L'opera di Alvar Aalto*, Milan, 1965: *Alvar Aalto, I: 1922–62*, Zürich, 1963; *Alvar Aalto, II: 1963–70*, Zürich, 1971; *Alvar Aalto, III: Projekte und letzte Zeichnungen*, Zürich, 1978. Leonardo Mosso, 'Aalto' in Hatje (ed.), *Lexikon der modernen Architektur* (4), Munich/Zürich, 1969. Cat., *Modern Chairs 1918–1970*, London: Lund Humphries, 1971. 'Aalto: Interior Architecture, Furniture and Furnishings,' *Progressive Architecture*, April 1977:74–77. Göran Schildt (ed.), *Sketches: Alvar Aalto*, Cambridge: MIT, 1978. Paul David Pearson, *Alvar Aalto and the International Style*, New York, 1978. Malcolm Quantrill, *Alvar Aalto: A Critical Study*, New York, 1983. Göran Schildt, *Alvar Aalto, The Early Years*, New York: Rizzoli, 1984. Cat., *Der Kragstuhl*, Stuhlmuseum Burg Beverungen, Berlin: Alexander, 1986:12,130. Leonardo Mosso in Vittorio Magnago Lampugnani (ed.), *Encyclopedia of 20th-Century Architecture*, New York:

Abrams, 1986:9–13. Elizabeth Gaynor, 'Around the Bend,' *Elle Decor*, October 1990:72. Karl Fleig and Elissa Aalto, *Alvar Aalto: The Complete Work*, New York: Rizzoli, 1992.

Aarnio, Eero (1932–)

▶ Finnish interior and industrial designer.

▶ 1954–57, studied Taideteollinen oppilaitos, Helsinki.

▶ In 1962, he opened his own office in Kiittykumpu, Tontunmäki, working as an industrial and interior designer, specializing in furniture design in synthetic materials; is best known outside Finland for his chair designs; in 1960, began designing in plastics, executing two of the best known designs of the decade: the womb-like 1963 *Ball* (or *Globe*) fiberglass chair (produced from 1965) with its built-in telephone or stereo speakers, and 1968 *Gyro* (or *Pastille*) fiberglass chair, both produced by Asko of Lahti (Finland). *Mustang* chair of c1970 intended for contract interiors was renamed *Pony* by Stendig in the USA. Later he returned to more traditional materials, including his 1982 *Viking* dining table and chairs for Polardesign.

▶ *Pastille* chair received 1968 AID award. Work included in many exhibitions including 1966 (I) Genoa 'Eurodomus'; 1968 (II) Turin 'Eurodomus'; Triennali di Milano; 1959 Cantù International Furniture Fair; 1963 'Export Furniture Competition,' Helsinki; 1964 'Scandinavian Park Furniture Competition' (first prize); 1965 Cantù 'Furniture Competition' (first prize); 1967 Helsinki 'Steel Furniture Competition'; one-person exhibit at 1968 Helsinki and Stockholm 'Fiberglass Furniture Exhibition.' *Pastille* chair first shown at 1968 Cologne Furniture Fair; included in 1968 'Les Assises du siège contemporain', Paris Musée des Arts Décoratifs; 1970 'Modern Chairs, 1918–1970,' Whitechapel Gallery, London; 1983 'Scandinavian Modern Design: 1880–1980', Cooper-Hewitt Museum, New York; 1983–84 'Design Since 1945', Philadelphia Museum of Art; received 1969 USA 'Interior Design International Award.'

▶ Cat., *Les Assises du siège contemporain*, Paris: Musée des Arts Décoratifs, 1968. Simon Jervis, 'A Designer's Home Is His Showcase, Too,' *The New York Times*, 16 Dec. 1970. Cat., *Modern Chairs 1918–1970*, London: Lund Humphries, 1971. Eileene Harrison Beer, *Scandinavian Design: Objects of a Life Style*, New York, 1975:74,76–77,79. Cat., David Revere McFadden (ed.), *Scandinavian Modern Design 1880–1980*, New York: Abrams, 1982:261. Cat., Kathryn B. Hiesinger and George H. Marcus III (eds.), *Design Since 1945*, Philadelphia: Philadelphia Museum of Art, 1983. Charlotte Fiell and Peter Fiell, *Modern Furniture Classics Since 1945*, London: Thames and Hudson, 1991:87,88,107,114,137–38, Nos. 70,89.

Abdelkader, Abdi (1955–)

▶ Algerian designer; born Algiers.

▶ Studied École Nationale des Beaux-Arts, Algiers and École Nationale Supérieure des Arts Décoratifs, Paris.

▶ He was professor, École Nationale des Beaux-Arts in Algiers, where he established his own design studio; was briefly artistic director of Forum Design, Korea; designed furniture collections in Algiers and for the French embassy; furniture clients included Artistes et Modèles. He designed 1980 *Buffet Saha* sideboard sponsored by VIA (one of its first projects) and produced by Benoteau; taught at École Nationale Supérieure des Arts Décoratifs, Paris.

▶ Buffet shown at 1990 'Les années VIA' exhibition, Paris Musée des Arts Décoratifs.

▶ Cat., *Les années VIA*, Paris: Musée des Arts Décoratifs, 1990. 'Les Designers du soleil,' *Maison française décoration internationale*, June 1992.

Åberg, Gunhild (1939–)
▶ Danish ceramicist.
▶ Studied Kunsthåndvaerkerskolen, Copenhagen.
▶ Åberg, Jane Reumert, and Beate Andersen formed the workshop Strandstraede Keramik, Copenhagen. He executed designs for the Royal Copenhagen Porcelain Manufactory and for Dansk Designs.
▶ Work shown at 1975 Stockholm and Hälsingborg 'Dansk Kunsthaandvaerk'; 1975–77 'Dansk Miljø'; 1976 and 1977 Det Danske Kunstindustrimuseum, Copenhagen; 1981 Nordenfjeldske Kunstindustrimuseum, Trondheim; 1981 'Danish Ceramic Design,' University Park, Pennsylvania.
▶ Cat., David Revere McFadden (ed.), *Scandinavian Modern Design 1880–1980*, New York: Abrams, 1982:261.

Aberg, Margareta (1929–)
▶ Swedish designer; born Stockholm.
▶ Studied interior architecture and furniture design, Konstfackskolan, Stockholm.
▶ In 1956, she opened her own architecture studio with husband Rolf Aberg; designed *Salabim* cupboard of c1986 produced by Swedfun (Sweden); specialized in interior architecture and designed hospitals, hotels, and schools including the Bracke Osterjard Hospital, Gothenburg, for handicapped children.
▶ Robert A.M. Stern (ed.), *The International Design Yearbook*, New York: Abbeville, 1985/1986: No. 131.

Abraham, Jeanine
▶ French furniture designer.
▶ Studied École Nationale Supérieure des Beaux-Arts, Paris, and Centre Art et Technique.
▶ She was active in the 1950s; collaborated with René-Jean Caillette and Jacques Dumond in a studio where she met husband, Dutch architect and designer Dirk Jan Rol; collaborated with Rol in firm Abraham & Rol producing furniture for Meubles TV and the decoration of wood factory and stores Les Huchers Minvielle. According to Rol, he worked on the technical aspects and Abraham more on 'inventive' ideas. Their materials of choice included wood, aluminum, and rattan.
▶ Pascal Rénous, *Portraits de créateurs*, Paris: H. Vial, 1969. Yolande Amic, *Intérieurs: Le Mobilier français 1945–1965*, Paris: Regard/VIA, 1983.

Abramovitz, Gerald (1928–)
▶ South African architect and industrial designer; active Great Britain.
▶ 1949–51, studied architecture, University of Pretoria, and 1952–54, design, Royal College of Art, London.
▶ He specialized in seating, executing designs for Knoll, 1961,and Hille, 1966–67; designed children's play equipment, prefabricated housing parts, and kitchen appliances. His award-winning lighting was produced by Best and Lloyd.
▶ Based on his earlier piece for Knoll, 1963 armchair won 1963 international furniture design competition sponsored by *The Daily Mirror*; 1961 *Cantilever* desk lamp by Best and Lloyd received 1966 Design Centre Award.
▶ 'Design Centre Awards 1966: *Cantilever* Desk Lamp,' *Design*, No. 209, May 1966:40–41. Cat., Kathryn B. Hiesinger and George H. Marcus III (eds.), *Design Since 1945*, Philadelphia: Philadelphia Museum of Art, 1984.

Abson, Helen (1942–)
▶ Australian architect and designer; born Melbourne.
▶ Studied architecture, Melbourne University, to 1965.
▶ She practiced architecture for five years; established ZAB Design where she designed fabrics that exhibited a preoccupation for texture achieved through pattern and color, showing influences of ethnic textiles; designed *Shimmer Collection* of c1986.
▶ Robert A.M. Stern (ed.). *The International Design Yearbook*, New York: Abbeville, 1985/1986: nos. 330–32.

Acerbis
▶ Italian furniture manufacturer.
▶ The firm was founded in 1870 by a cabinetmaker, Acerbis, whose grandson Lodovico Acerbis (1939–, Albino), a student of the university in Milan, designed his first piece of furniture in 1956—a miniature table and chairs. His 1992 *Granducale* furniture collection was produced in homage to Kazimir Malevich. Designers included Giotto Stoppino.
▶ Received 1979 Premio Compasso d'Oro.
▶ 'Milan à l'heure de design,' *Maison et Jardin*, April 1992:124.

Acke, Johan Axel Gustaf (1859–1924)
▶ Swedish furniture designer.
▶ 1876–81, studied painting, Kungliga Konsthögskolan, Stockholm, and in Paris and Italy.
▶ Primarily a painter, he designed furniture in the Art Nouveau style.
▶ Cat., David Revere McFadden (ed.), *Scandinavian Modern Design 1880–1980*, New York: Abrams, 1982: 262.

Acking, Carl-Axel (1910–)
▶ Swedish architect and furniture designer.
▶ 1930–34, studied Konstfackskolan and 1934–39, Tekniska Skolan, Stockholm.
▶ In the 1930s, he worked as Gunnar Asplund's assistant; in 1939, set up his own design studio; 1943–64, taught at Konstfackskolan and 1964–76, Tekniska Skolan in Stockholm and the Tekniska Högskolan, Lund; was architect of Swedish Embassy, Tokyo, and interior designer of ships of North Star Line; designed (with others) 1955 'H 55' exhibition, Hälsingborg. In 1949, designed furnishings for Hotel Malmen, Stockholm; 1944 bentwood laminated chair by Avenska Möbelfabrikerna, 1944 telephone book for telephone commission of Sweden; was architect in charge of cathedral in Lund. His furniture was produced by the Kooperativa Förbundet, Stockholm; Nordiska Kompaniet, Stockholm; Svenka Möbelfabrikerna, Bodafors. Work included designs for wallpaper, textiles, and lighting.
▶ Received 1952 Lunning Prize. Work shown at Triennali di Milano, 1937 Paris 'Exposition Internationale des Arts et Techniques dans la Vie Moderne,' 1939 New York World's Fair, 1956 New York 'Lunning Prize Winners Exhibition,' 1986 'The Lunning Prize Exhibition,' Nationalmuseum, Stockholm.
▶ Cat., David Revere McFadden (ed.), *Scandinavian Modern Design 1880–1980*, New York: Abrams, 1982:262. Cat., *The Lunning Prize*, Stockholm: Nationalmuseum, 1986:42–45.

Adamovich, Mikhail Mikhailovich (1884–1947)
▶ Russian porcelain designer.
▶ 1894–1907, studied Stroganov School of Applied Art, Moscow.
▶ In 1909, he traveled to Italy; in the 1910s, was a decorative painter in Moscow and St. Petersburg; in 1914, was commissioned by the Greek government to design a mosaic for King George V's tomb; 1918–19 and 1921 was a designer, State Porcelain Factory, Petrograd (today St. Petersburg); 1924–37, was a designer, Volkhov and Dulevo ceramic factories.
▶ Cat., *Kunst und Revolution: Russische und Sowjetische Kunst 1910–1932*, Vienna: Österreichisches Museum für angewandte Kunst, 1988.

Adams, John (1882–1953)
▶ British ceramicist and designer; active London, Durban, and Poole, Dorset (England); husband of Gertrude Sharpe.
▶ Studied Hanley School of Art and 1908 Royal College of Art, London.
▶ He spent his early years in Stoke-on-Trent; from 1895–c1902, worked in the studio of Bernard Moore, which specialized in the production of plain and painted ceramics with effects through reduction-fired glazes; married Gertrude Sharpe, a fellow student at Royal College of Art; 1912–14, was head of School of Art at Durban Technical College; 1921–50, (with Cyril Carter and Harold Stabler) set up the firm Carter, Stabler and Adams, where Adams designed almost all the shapes for its decorative and

domestic ware, including the 1936 *Streamline* tableware; experimented with and produced high-temperature, crackle-finish, and other glazes.

▶ Cat., *Thirties: British Art and Design before the War*, London: Arts Council of Great Britain, Hayward Gallery, 1979:152,154, 284.

Adams-Teltscher, George (1903–51)

▶ Austrian theater and graphic designer; born near Vienna.
▶ 1919–20, studied applied arts in Vienna; 1920–23, Bauhaus, Weimar.
▶ He participated in the theater-design activities at the Bauhaus; in 1925, was a theater designer in Vienna and subsequently advertising graphic designer in Hamburg and Berlin; in 1934, emigrated to Barcelona and, in 1938, to London, where he taught until 1951.
▶ Lionel Richard, *Encyclopédie du Bauhaus*, Paris: Somogy, 1985:176.

Adeptus

▶ British furniture firm; located London.
▶ In *c*1969, Dennis Groves and Demetri Petrihelos established the firm Adeptus, the innovator of foam furniture. It closed in *c*1985.

Adie Brothers

▶ British silversmiths; located Birmingham.
▶ The firm was founded in 1879; produced Modern silver designs by Harold Stabler and Fernand Pire. One of its best known designs was Stabler's 1935 tea set, produced in smooth and rectangular forms with rectangular wooden handles and flat rectangular hinged lids and semicircular disk finials.
▶ Annelies Krekel-Aalberse, *Art Nouveau and Art Déco Silver*, New York: Abrams, 1989:35.

Adler, Friedrich (1878–1942?)

▶ German sculptor and designer; active Munich and Hamburg.
▶ Studied Debschitz-Schule (aka Lehr- und Versuchs-Ateliers für angewandte und freie Kunst), Munich.
▶ 1904–07, he taught at Debschitz-Schule, a private art school for training in the applied arts and crafts; 1907–33, at Kunstgewerbeschule, Hamburg; 1910–13, was director of master class in Nuremberg. Adler designed silver for P. Bruckmann & Söhne, Heilbronn. Work included jewelry, utensils, furniture, metalware, ceramics, stucco work, glass etching, and textiles. In the 1920s, he developed industrial-production methods based on batik techniques for Adler Textile Company, Hamburg (Ateha); designed for metalworkers O.G.F. Schmitt, Nuremberg; went from Jugendstil to abstract floral decoration and on to technological abstract ornamentation. He died at Auschwitz.
▶ Created entrance to Württemberg group at 1902 Turin 'Esposizione Internazionale d'Arte Decorativa Moderna.' Designed synagogue at 1914 Cologne 'Werkbund-ausstellung.'
▶ Hans Vollmer, *Allgemeines Lexikon der Bildenden Künstler*, Leipzig: Seemann, 1953. Fanelli, Giovanni, and Rosalia, *Il tessuto moderno*, Florence, 1976:166. Annelies Krekel-Aalberse, *Art Nouveau and Art Déco Silver*, New York: Abrams, 1989:133.

Adler, Rose (1892–1959)

▶ French decorative and bookbinding designer; born and active Paris.
▶ 1917–25, studied École de l'Union Centrale des Arts Décoratifs, Paris, under Andrée Langrand, and from 1923, under Henri Nouilhac.
▶ In 1923, when she was a student exhibitioner at Pavillon de Marsan at the Louvre, couturier Jacques Doucet bought three of her bindings; she worked for him until his death in 1929. A table commissioned by Doucet is today housed in the Virginia Museum of Fine Arts in Richmond, Virginia. Designing and occasionally executing furniture for Doucet and others, she produced small table-top accessories, including picture frames; worked in glass, metallized calfskins, reptile skins, and precious stones, using a style called *rythmes géométriques*; was greatly influenced by Pierre

Legrain, whom she met through Doucet and with whom she worked from 1923, incorporating abstract patterns and unusual materials; in 1931, became a member of UAM (Union des Artistes Modernes), showing her bindings and picture frames at its events. Mostly non-figurative and geometric with overlapping lettering, her bindings included those for *Calligrammes*, *Poèmes*, *Le Paysan de Paris*, *Beauté*, *Mon beau souci*, and *A.O. Barnabooth*. She created a wide range of objects, including jewelry, toiletry items, furniture, and clothing; when Doucet died, concentrated on work for private book collectors, libraries, and institutions, including the Bibliothèque Nationale, Fondation Littéraire Jacques Doucet, Victoria and Albert Museum, and New York Public Library; in 1947, became a member Société de la Reliure Moderne and showed work at its exhibitions.
▶ Work shown first at the student exhibition of École des Arts Décoratifs, 1923 Salon of the Société des Artistes Décorateurs, Paris. Work shown independently at Salons of the Société des Artistes Décorateurs from 1924–29, 1931 Paris 'Exposition Internationale du Livre,' events with the Chareau-Cournault-Garnier group in 1934, 1937 Paris 'Exposition Internationale des Arts et Techniques dans la Vie Moderne,' 1939 San Francisco 'Golden Gate International Exposition,' 1939 'New York World's Fair.' Bindings shown at 1949 (I) 'Formes Utiles' exhibition at the Pavillon de Marsan and 1956–57 (I) 'Triennale française d'Art Contemporain.'
▶ Rose Adler (presenter), 'Reliures,' *L'Art International d'aujourd-'hui*, No. 17, Paris: Charles Moreau. Gaston Quénioux, *Les Arts décoratifs modernes 1918–1925*, Paris, 1925:186. Rose Adler, *Reliures, présenté par Rose Adler*, Paris, 1929. Ernest de Crauzat, *La Reliure française de 1900 à 1925*, Vol. 2, Paris, 1932:147–53. Daniel Sickles, *Masterpieces of French Bindings*, New York 1947: 125. Yvonne Brunhammer, *The Nineteen Twenties Style*, London, 1966. Victor Arwas, *Art Déco*, Abrams, 1980. John F. Fleming and Priscilla Juvelis, *The Book Beautiful and the Binding as Art*, New York, Vol. 1, 1983:89; Vol. 2, 1985:6. Pierre Kjellberg, *Art Déco: les maîtres du Mobilier, le décor des Paquebots*, Paris: Amateur, 1986. Arlette Barré-Despond, *UAM*, Paris: Regard, 1986. Cat., *Les années UAM 1929–1958*, Paris: Musée des Arts Décoratifs, 1988:144. Alastair Duncan and Georges de Bartha, *Art Nouveau and Art Déco Bookbinding*, New York: Abrams, 1989:26–32,186.

Adlercreutz, Maria (1936–)

▶ Swedish textile designer.
▶ In 1971–72, she set up her own weaving workshop; in the 1970s, documented political events in her work.
▶ Cat., David Revere McFadden (ed.), *Scandinavian Modern Design 1880–1980*, New York: Abrams, 1982:262.

Adnet, Jacques (1900–84)

▶ French architect and decorator; born Chatillon-Coligny; active Paris.
▶ Studied École Nationale des Arts Décoratifs, Paris.
▶ He worked for Henri Rapin and Tony Selmersheim and, from 1920–22, for Maurice Dufrêne; designing accessories in metal and glass, executed sturdy Modern furniture designs, mixing them with traditional pieces, much like Jean-Michel Frank; used a logical, clear, refined approach; often collaborated with younger brother Jean Adnet; in 1922, became director of decorating studio La Maîtrise of Galeries Lafayette; designed the *salle commune* of the 1926 oceanliner *Île-de-France*; from 1928–1959, was director of design at Süe's and Mare's CAF (Compagnie des Arts français); designed furniture suites for the townhouse of Franck Jay Gould, apartment of Alice Cocéa, 1947 office of the French president Vincent Auriot's residence at Château de Rambouillet, and oceanliners of Ferdinand de Lesseps; in 1959, left CAF; in 1970, became director of École Nationale Supérieure des Arts Décoratifs, Paris; in the 1930s, often incorporated metal and glass into his furniture; applied a philosophy of stark Functionalism to all of his ensembles, including tubular chromed dressing tables, mobile drinks cabinets, and furniture in exotic woods, including bubenga

and white peroba. His kinetic and inventive lighting was based on severe geometric principles, with few concessions to ornamentation, showing the influence of contemporary *machinisme*. His 1929 table lamp with four lighted tubes in a square shape cantilevered from a marble base was widely published in journals and books, including Paul Frankl's *Form and Reform: A Practical Handbook of Modern Interiors* (New York: Harpers 1930); it was reproduced by Lumen Center 1988–91 and subsequently by Pentalux.
▶ Work shown at annual Salons through studio affiliations including La Maîtrise and Saddier et fils until 1928, when he took over CAF Furniture in both foreign and French stands, 1925 Paris 'Exposition Internationale des Arts Décoratifs et Industriels Modernes.' Received grand prize for architecture for St. Gobain pavilion (with René Coulon), 1937 Paris 'Exposition International des Arts et Techniques dans la Vie Moderne.'
▶ G. Henriot, *Luminaire Moderne*, 1937: Plate 9. *Ensembles Mobiliers*, Vol. II, Paris: Charles Moreau, 1937. Alastair Duncan, *Art Nouveau and Art Déco Lighting*, New York: Simon and Schuster, 1978:144. Pierre Kjellberg, *Art Déco: les maîtres du Mobilier, le décor des Paquebots*, Paris: Amateur, 1986:27–29.

Adnet, Jean
▶ French designer; active Paris; brother of Jacques Adnet.
▶ In 1928, Jean Adnet became director of the window-display department at Galeries Lafayette, where, in 1922, brother Jacques Adnet became director of its La Maîtrise decorating studio; they collaborated under the name 'JJ Adnet.'

ADSA Design Management
▶ French design group.
▶ In 1975, ADSA was founded by Marc Lebailly (president) and Maia Wodzislawska (vice-president); included designers Dominique Pierzo, Gil Adamy, Roger Tallon, and Pierre Paulin. Their work included different approaches to industrial design—heavy industry, transportation (Tallon and the TGV), and domestic and office furniture for banks, museums, cultural institutions, and others. Paulin's inexpensive 1980 outdoor chair *Dangari* in polypropylene, produced by Stamp, was a version of plastic stacking designs that became ubiquitous in the 1990s, reminiscent of early Thonet silhouettes in bentwood.
▶ Robert A.M. Stern (ed.), *The International Design Yearbook*, New York: Abbeville, 1985/1986: No. 16.

AEG (Allgemeine Elektrizitäts Gesellschaft)
▶ German electrical manufacturer; located Berlin.
▶ In 1883, Emil Rathenau (1838–1915) founded AEG to produce electrical products. Franz Schwechten designed the 1889 AEG factory on Ackerstrasse and the monumental 1896 portal on Brunnenstrasse and Alfred Messel the administration building of the late 1890s on the Friedrich-Karl-Ufer. Otto Eckmann designed AEG's catalogues and printed matter for the 1900 Paris 'Exposition universelle.' Peter Behrens was appointed artistic director in 1907. (Though credit for the appointment is generally given to Rathenau, Behrens said that the initiator was Paul Jordan, the director of AEG factories.) Behrens' AEG turbine factory in Berlin is considered a pioneering effort in Modern architecture, although even before the Behrens appointment the firm was noted for the technical qualities of its designs. Behrens created an 'intimate union' between the process and style of mass-produced goods and 'artistic and creative work' that would foster 'a general improvement in public taste.' Today an industrial giant, AEG is still noted for its high design standards.
▶ Karl Wilhelm, *Die AEG*, Berlin, 1931. Ernst Schulin, *Walter Rathenau—Gesamtausgabe*, Munich and Heidelberg, 1977. Tilman Buddensieg et al., *Industrie-Kultur, Peter Behrens und die AEG, 1907–1914*, Berlin: Mann, 1979. S. Anderson, 'Modern Architecture and Industry: Peter Behrens, the AEG, and Industrial Design,' *Oppositions*, No. 21, Summer 1980:78–93.

Aesthetic movement
▶ Based in Great Britain in the second half of the 19th century, the Aesthetic movement was never formally organized. Its exponents sought to rid themselves of the rigidness of Victorian design in favor of freer expression in the fine and decorative arts; some describe it as proto-Modern and include within it the Arts and Crafts movement led by William Morris, the neo-Queen Anne architecture of E.W. Godwin and Norman Shaw, Pre-Raphaelite art led by Dante Gabriel Rossetti and Edward Burne-Jones, the *japoniste* painting of James Abbott McNeill Whistler and Aubrey Beardsley, and literature of writers including Oscar Wilde. Philosophically, the movement owed much to the doctrine of 'art for art's sake,' a phrase coined by Walter Pater in 1868. In practical terms the eclecticism of the London 'International Exhibition on Industry and Art of 1862' was influential. Christopher Dresser's *The Art of Decorative Design* (London, 1862) might be thought of as the first of the Aesthetic movement pattern-books. The movement's designers included William Burges, Bruce Talbert, Christopher Dresser, Thomas Jekyll, Norman Shaw, A.H. Mackmurdo, E.W. Godwin, Lewis Day, and Walter Crane. The movement's influence spread to Europe, contributing to Art Nouveau and the Vienna Secession, and to America, influencing the work of Gustav Stickley, Louis Comfort Tiffany, and manufacturers, including the Herter Brothers.
▶ Elizabeth Aslin, *The Aesthetic Movement: Prelude to Art Nouveau*, London: Elek, 1969. Cat., Robin Spencer et al., *The Aesthetic Movement and the Cult of Japan*, London: The Fine Art Society, 1972. Mark Girouard, *Sweetness and Light: The 'Queen Anne' Movement, 1860–1900*, Oxford, 1977. Doreen Bolger Burke et al., *In Pursuit of Beauty: Americans and the Aesthetic Movement*, New York: Metropolitan Museum of Art and Rizzoli, 1986.

agitprop
▶ State-sponsored propagandist art in the Soviet Union in the years following the 1917 Communist Revolution. Short for 'Agitpropbyuro,' the Communist Party's Bureau for Agitation and Propaganda.
▶ Agitprop was emphatically focused on contemporary Russia, although artists incorporated themes and images from the past. Traditional distinctions between different art forms were blurred in the search for a revolutionary artistic synthesis. Since art was long thought to be a 'teacher of life' by Russians, it appeared to be appropriate to use the propagandistic functions of art at a time of social change. In 1918, Lenin presented a program, named 'monumental propaganda,' that became the basis for official art during the Revolutionary era. Agitprop forms had to be produced with little advance notice, in large quantities, and from expensive materials—resulting in the monumental forms characteristic of the revolutionary period. Agitprop influence could be seen in Imperial/State/Lamonosov porcelain, where, in 1918–22, there was a collision between the old and the new, represented notably in the work of Aria Lebedeva, Kasimir Malevich, and Nikolai Suetin. Credited with much of the agitprop porcelain of the period, Chekhonin executed brightly painted forms with colorful slogans on ceramic blanks originally intended for pre-Revolutionary china. On the ceramic pieces were applied the same slogans, illustrations, and quotations as those reproduced on posters, agitational reliefs, and festival decorations. Natan Al'tman designed Futurist agit-decorations for buildings and monuments in Uritskii Square in Petrograd (now St. Petersburg) in 1918 for the Revolution's first anniversary. In 1919–20, Vasilii Ermilov was involved in the design of various agitprop projects, including agit-posters, interiors of clubs, trains, and steamships. Agit-decorations were painted on the cars of touring railroad caravans, in an effort to produce popular support for the Revolution. Monuments included the 1918–19 *Monument to Liberty* (destroyed) by architect D. Osipov and sculptor Nikolai Andreev; 1920–25 *Monument to Marx* (unrealized) by sculptor S. Alyoshin and others and architects Alexandr and Viktor Vesnin; 1919 *Bakunin Monument* (unrealized) and 1920 *Labor Liberated* by Boris Korolyov; and a

relief portrait of Robespierre by Sarra Levedeva. Though construction was halted, Vladimir Tatlin's famous 1918 *Pamiatnik III—emu Internatsionalu (Monument to the Third International)* was a typically grandiose architectonic agitprop statement. Other notable agitprop practitioners were architects El Lissitzky and Nikolai Kolli and painter Gustav Klutsis.

▶ Cat., *Kunst und Revolution: Russische und Sowjetische Kunst 1910–1932*, Vienna: Österreichisches Museum für angewandte Kunst, 1988. Nina Lobanov-Rostovsky, *Revolutionary Ceramics*, London: Studio Vista, 1990. Selin Om Khan Magomedov, *Les Vhutemas*, Paris: Regard, 1990.

Agnoli, Tito (1931–)

▶ Italian designer and teacher; born Lima.
▶ Studied Politecnico di Milano to 1969.
▶ He was an assistant to Gio Ponti and Giancarlo De Carlo at the Facoltà di Architettura in Milan; he designed furniture (*843* table produced by Montina) and lighting; taught at the vocational school, Lissone; is active in his own design studio for clients including Arflex, O-Luce, Poltrona Frau, Pozzi, and Schiffini.
▶ Received a gold medal at Neocon in Chicago.
▶ Hans Wichmann, *Italien Design 1945 bis heute*, Munich: Die Neue Sammlung, 1988. *Modo*, No. 148, March–April 1993:115.

Agostoni, Egidio (1942–)

▶ Italian furniture designer; born Granaglione; active Bologna.
▶ He began his career as a professional designer in 1972; designed furniture for Ambos; became a member of ADI (Associazione per il Disegno Industriale).
▶ *ADI Annual 1976*, Milan: Associazione per il Disegno Industriale, 1976.

Aguesse, Henri

▶ French decorator and designer.
▶ At the 1927 competition of Union Centrale des Arts Décoratifs, he showed two dressing tables, one in white sycamore and the other in red *coquilles-d'œuf* synthetic lacquer and bent-metal tubing.
▶ Pierre Kjellberg, *Art Déco: les maîtres du Mobilier, le décor des Paquebots*, Paris: Amateur, 1986.

Ahlmann, Lis (1894–1979)

▶ Danish textile designer.
▶ A pioneer in textile design, Ahlmann shifted to commercial production in the 1950s; in 1953, became artistic consultant to C. Olesen of Copenhagen, where she collaborated with Børge Mogensen on furniture, furnishings, and upholstery weaves; in harmonizing colors, the patterns were interchangeable. She was known for her muted colors in plaids and stripes. Her designs were produced on simple power looms based on the principles of hand looms. Eventually, through Mogensen's intervention, she began executing weavings in bolder colorations on more sophisticated machinery.
▶ Bent Salicath and Arne Karlsen (eds.), *Modern Danish Textiles*, Copenhagen, 1959:12–15. Arne Karlsen, *Made in Denmark*, New York, 1960:72–79,122–23. Arne Karlsen, *Furniture Designed by Børge Mogensen*, Copenhagen, 1968. Thomas Mogensen, *Lis Ahlmann Tekstiler*, Copenhagen, 1974. Cat., Kathryn B. Hiesinger and George H. Marcus III (eds.), *Design Since 1945*, Philadelphia: Philadelphia Museum of Art, 1983.

Ahrén, Uno (1897–1977)

▶ Swedish architect and furniture designer.
▶ Ahrén was one of those responsible for bringing Modernism to Sweden and creating the style that became known as Swedish Modern; (with Sven Markelius) built a student union building for the 1930 'Stockholmsutstälining'; collaborated with Gunnar Asplund on the Exhibition; designed the 1929 Ford factory and 1930 cinema, both Sweden.
▶ Penny Sparke, *Introduction to Design and Culture in the Twentieth Century*, Allen and Unwin, 1986.

Aicher, Otl (1922–91)

▶ German industrial designer; born Ulm.
▶ 1946, studied sculpture at the Academy in Munich.
▶ In 1947, he established a graphics studio in Ulm; in 1967, in Munich, and in 1972, in Rotis, Allgau. In 1951, he became a founding member of Hochschule für Gestaltung, Ulm (Germany); 1954–66, taught in the communications department; 1962–64, was rector and guest lecturer at Yale University, New Haven, Connecticut and in Rio de Janeiro. He developed corporate identity programs for Braun, Lufthansa, ZDF, Erco lighting, Frankfurt airport, Dresdner Bank, Severin & Siedler publishers; worked at Braun with Fritz Eichler, Hans Gugelot, and Dieter Rams; 1967–72, was in charge of visuals for the Munich Olympics; in 1984, founded Institut für Analoge Studien, Rotis; 1968–87, wrote numerous books on design and drawing.
▶ H. Lindinger (ed.), *Hochschule für Gestaltung—Ulm*, Berlin, 1987.

Aida, Yüsuke (1931–)

▶ Japanese ceramics designer and industrial designer.
▶ Studied town planning, Chiba University, and ceramics under Ken Miyanohara.
▶ Working in the USA 1961–64, he was chief designer at Bennington Potters, Vermont, where he executed its 1961 *Classic* range of industrially produced tableware, still in production today; when he returned to Japan, reverted to studio pottery production; executed large ceramic wall panels for the Tourist Hotel, Nagoya, and the Osaka Ina building in the 1970s; 1972–74, was director of Japanese Designer Craftsman Association and, from 1976, its successor, Japan Craft Design Association.
▶ *Classic* tableware included in 1983–84 'Design Since 1945' exhibition, Philadelphia Museum of Art; work shown at 1982 'Contemporary Vessels: How to Pour' exhibition at Tokyo National Museum of Modern Art.
▶ Cat., *Contemporary Vessels: How to Pour*, Tokyo: Crafts Gallery, The National Museum of Modern Art, 1982. Cat., Kathryn B. Hiesinger and George H. Marcus III (eds.), *Design Since 1945*, Philadelphia: Philadelphia Museum of Art, 1983.

Airikka-Lammi, Anneli (1944–)

▶ Finnish textile designer.
▶ Studied Taideteollinen Korkeakoulu, Helsinki.
▶ Named 1982 textile artist of the year, Finland. Work shown in numerous exhibitions, including one-person shows.
▶ Robert A.M. Stern (ed.), *The International Design Yearbook*, New York: Abbeville, 1985/1986: No. 333.

AJS Aérolande

▶ French association of designers and architects.
▶ Active in Paris in the 1960s, the group was named 'A' for Jean Aubert, 'J' for Jean-Paul Jungman, and 'S' for Antoine Stinco. In 1968, they designed the first inflatable armchair in PVC, produced by Quasar's firm.

Akaba

▶ Spanish furniture firm; located San Sebastián.
▶ In 1983, Akaba was established by Txema García Amiano, who had previously worked at Enea. Critical of conservatism, Amiano set out to take risks and produced the 1986 *Frenesi* stool designed by Ramón Benedito. Akaba's first piece by Javier Mariscal was 1986 *Trampolín* chair (with Pepe Cortes); Mariscal's subsequent work included the 1986 *MOR* sofa. Akaba's line was thought by some to be frivolous.
▶ Mariscal's furniture pieces for Akaba were included in the 1987 'Nouvelles Tendences: avante-gardes de la fin du 20ème siècle' at Centre Georges Pompidou, Paris.
▶ Guy Julier, *New Spanish Design*, London: Thames & Hudson, 1991.

Akhrr
(Association of Artists of Revolutionary Russia)
▶ Russian organization; active Moscow.
▶ Active 1922–28, Akhrr opposed the avant-garde art movement; was the predecessor of Socialist Realism. From 1928, Akhr (Association of Artists of the Revolution) succeeded Akhrr.
▶ Cat., *Kunst und Revolution: Russische und Sowjetische Kunst 1910–1932*, Vienna: Österreichisches Museum für angewandte Kunst, 1988. Cat., *The Great Utopia: The Russian and Soviet Avant-Garde, 1915–1932*, New York: Guggenheim Musem, 1992.

Alavoine, L.
▶ French interior decorators; located Paris and New York.
▶ Active 1920–73, the firm was celebrated for its Louis-revival interiors and dramatic flair. Employing Jules Bouy from 1924–27, Alavoine prided itself on being able to produce decorations in any of the historicist styles popular at the time, including Tudor, Pompeiian, Georgian, and Turkish. From c1893, encouraged by the success of the 1893 Chicago exhibition, the firm opened studios and offices at 712 Fifth Avenue, New York with its façade by Lalique. Its staff designed and furnished the Manhattan apartment of the Worgelt family, today partially installed in the Brooklyn Museum. Armand Rateau was director 1905–14. The firm closed in 1972.
▶ Its heavy-handed Marie Antoinette room was shown at the 1893 Chicago 'World's Columbian Exposition' and published in *The Decorator and Furnisher*, New York, November 1893.
▶ Jessica Rutherford, *Art Nouveau, Art Deco and the Thirties: The Furniture Collections at Brighton Museum*, Brighton: The Royal Pavilion, Art Gallery and Museums, 1983:40. Pierre Kjellberg, *Art Déco: les maîtres du Mobilier, le décor des Paquebots*, Paris: Amateur, 1986:29–30. Stephen Calloway, *Twentieth-Century Decoration*, New York: Rizzoli, 1988:27,39.

Alberhill Pottery
▶ American ceramics manufactory; located Alberhill, California.
▶ In 1912, Alexander Robertson left Halcyon Art Pottery in Halcyon, California; was hired by James H. Hill, president of Alberhill Coal and Clay to experiment with Alberhill clays. The Alberhill-Corona district in the western part of Riverside County was one of the three most important clay-producing areas in California. While at Alberhill Pottery 1912–14, Robertson threw finely crafted art pottery in primarily unglazed models. The colors of his bisque vases were mostly light and ranged from the softest pink and white to red terracotta. Alberhill's output was small and exclusively the work of Robertson.
▶ Robertson received gold medal (for Alberhill Pottery work) at 1915 San Francisco 'Panama-Pacific International Exposition.'
▶ Andersen et al., *California Design 1910*, Salt Lake City: Peregrine Smith, 1980 (reprint of 1974 ed.).

Alberius, Olle (1926–)
▶ Swedish glassmaker.
▶ 1952–56, studied Konstfackskolan and Tekniska Skolan, Stockholm.
▶ 1957–63 worked for Syco, Strömstad; 1963–71, Rörstrands Porslinsfabriker, Lidköping; from 1971, Orrefors Glasbruk designing glassware and studio pieces. In his glass work at Orrefors in the 1960s, he returned to the Modernist forms of an earlier time.
▶ Work was subject of numerous exhibitions, beginning at the Artium in Gothenburg in 1968. Received 1968, 1974, 1975, and 1976 Bundespreis 'Die gute Industrieform,' Hanover fair; 1967, 1968, and 1969 diplomas at the fair in Faenza (Italy).
▶ Ann Marie Herlitz Gezelius, *Orrefors: A Swedish Glassplant*, Stockholm, 1984. Frederick Cooke, *Glass: Twentieth-Century Design*, New York: Dutton, 1986:86.

Albers, Anni Fleischmann (1899–)
▶ German textile designer, artist, designer for industrial production, and teacher; born Berlin; wife of Josef Albers.
▶ 1916–19, studied under Martin Brandenburg in Berlin; 1919–20, Kunstgewerbeschule, Hamburg; and 1920–22, Bauhaus,
Weimar and Dessau, under Georg Muche, Gunta Stölzl, and Paul Klee.
▶ 1922–29, she taught textile design at the Bauhaus, Weimar and Dessau; in 1925 married Josef Albers; was the first to experiment with weaving cellophane; 1930–33, worked independently in Dessau and Berlin; settling in the USA in 1933, was assistant professor of art at Black Mountain College, North Carolina, 1933–49; was active as a freelance textile designer; in 1949, moved with her husband to New Haven, Connecticut; was active in both handweaving and machine production, her designs sometimes reflecting the geometry of her husband's paintings; designed textiles for Knoll for more than 25 years from 1959, and, from 1978, for Sunar.
▶ Received 1961 gold medal for craftsmanship from American Institute of Architects.
▶ Anni Albers, *Anni Albers: Pictorial Weavings*, Cambridge, Mass.: MIT, 1959. Anni Albers: *On Designing*, Middletown, CT: Wesleyan University Press, 1962 and 1971. Anni Albers, *On Weaving*, Middletown, CT, 1965. Cat., Kathryn B. Hiesinger and George H. Marcus III (eds.), *Design Since 1945*, Philadelphia: Philadelphia Museum of Art, 1983. Cherie Fehrman and Kenneth Fehrman, *Postwar Interior Design: 1945–1960*, New York: Van Nostrand Reinhold, 1987. Cat., *Anni und Josef Albers. Eine Retrospektive*: Munich, Villa Stuck/Josef Albers Museum Bottrop, 1989. Matilda McQuaid, 'Anni Albers' in Mel Byars and Russell Flinchum (eds.), *50 American Designers, 1918–1968*, Washington: Preservation, 1994.

Albers, Josef (1888–1976)
▶ German painter, designer, theoretician, and teacher, born Bottrop, Westphalia; active Germany and USA; husband of Anni Fleischmann Albers.
▶ 1905–20, studied art in Buren, Berlin, Essen, and Munich, and 1920–23, Bauhaus, Dessau.
▶ In 1923, Albers began teaching at the Bauhaus, becoming a master in 1925; in 1923, taught the Bauhaus preliminary course in form (with Lázsló Moholy-Nagy) on which many design schools today base their courses; while at the Bauhaus, designed the innovative, widely published 1925 glass-and-metal tableware and, in 1927, some furniture models. Albers's 1923 vitrine in chrome, clear and opaque glass, and mirror was innovatory of its type. In 1925, he married Anni Fleischmann, whom he had met at the Bauhaus; in 1933, when the Nazis closed the Bauhaus in Berlin, was among the first of the Bauhaus teachers to emigrate to the USA; assisted through the financial generosity of Edward M.M. Warburg and Abby Aldrich Rockefeller on the instigation of Alfred H. Barr Jr., New York Museum of Modern Art director and on a non-quota visa guaranteed by Philip Johnson and Warburg; 1933–49, taught at Black Mountain College, an avant-garde school in North Carolina, and subsequently at Harvard University; 1950–60, was professor and chairman of the design department, Yale University. He is best known today for his color theories and minimalist color-interactive art, particularly in the *Homage to the Square* series of paintings and prints; published text and color plates entitled *Interaction of Color*.
▶ Living room installed at 1931 Berlin 'Deutsche Bauausstellung' and included in 1932 'The International Style: Architecture Since 1922' exhibition, New York Museum of Modern Art.
▶ Lionel Richard, *Encyclopédie du Bauhaus*, Paris: Somogy, 1985: 147. Cat., *Josef Albers*, New York: Guggenheim Museum, 1988. Alice Goldfarb Marquis, *Alfred H. Barr Jr.: Missionary for the Modern*, Chicago: Contemporary Books, 1989:182. Cat., *Anni und Josef Albers. Eine Retrospektive*, Villa Stuck München/Josef Albers Museum Bottrop, 1989.

Alberti, Damiano (1953–)
▶ Italian designer; born and active Bovisio, Milan.
▶ Alberti began his professional career as a designer in 1970; 1970–72, worked for Cucine Alberti on its kitchen systems; from 1972, worked in the studio of Rosselli on kitchen systems produced by Omfa in Treviso; designed the trademark and corporate-

identity program for the Microfar microfilm machine firm, Milan; became a member of ADI (Associazione per il Disegno Industriale).
► *ADI Annual 1976*, Milan: Associazione per il Disegno Industriale, 1976.

Alberti, Maurizio (1953–)
► Italian designer; born Milan.
► Studied Liceo Artistico di Brera, Milan, to 1970, and architecture, Politecnico di Milano.
► He worked as a graphic designer in various studios; in 1975, (with Giuseppe Bossi, Pierangelo Marucco, Francesco Roggero, and Bruno Rossio) founded studio Original Designers 6R5, Milan. Clients included Lanerossi, Sasatex, Taif, Bassetti, and Griso-Jover in Italy and Le Roi and Griffine Marechal in France. 6R5 designed tapestry murals for Printeco and wallpaper for a French firm. He was a member of ADI (Associazione per il Disegno Industriale).
► *ADI Annual 1976*, Milan: Associazione per il Disegno Industriale, 1976.

Albertus, Gundorph (1887–1970)
► Danish silversmith.
► Studied sculpture, Det Kongelige Danske Kunstakademi, Copenhagen.
► A brother-in-law of Georg Jensen, he joined the Jensen Sølvsmedie in 1911 as a chaser; 1926–54, was assistant director; designed *Mitra*, the company's first mass-produced stainless-steel flatware, and 1930 *Cactus* pattern, still in production.
► Work shown at events of the Salon d'Automne, Paris. Participated in many worldwide exhibitions; received gold medal, 1925 Paris 'Exposition Internationale des Arts Décoratifs et Industriels Modernes,' and diploma of honor, 1937 Paris 'Exposition Internationale des Arts et Techniques dans la Vie Moderne.'
► Cat., *Georg Jensen Silversmithy: 77 Artists, 75 Years*, Washington: Smithsonian Institution Press, 1980.

Albertus, Vilhelm (1878–1963)
► Danish silversmith; brother of Gundorph Albertus.
► Vilhelm worked for many years at the Georg Jensen Sølvsmedie.
► Cat., *Georg Jensen Silversmithy: 77 Artists, 75 Years*, Washington: Smithsonian Institution Press, 1980.

Albin-Guyot, Laura
► French bookbinder and photographer.
► In the late 1920s, Albin-Guyot used photography in her book covers and endpapers depicting micro-organisms, including plankton, algae, and bacteria printed in black and silver or brown and gold. Her style was influential on the work of Paul Bonet, whose Surrealist bindings were produced in c1933 for the works of André Breton and Paul Eluard. Albin-Guyot's covers for *Les Chansons de Bilitis* and *Le Trèfle noire* were bound by Michele Kieffer and for *L'Ombre de la croix* by Rose Adler. She photographed many of the leaders of the Art Déco movement.
► Rose Adler, *Reliure, Présenté par Rose Adler*, Paris, 1929: 5,7,24,33,43. Marie Michon, *Le Reliure française*, Paris, 1951: 133–34. Alastair Duncan and Georges de Bartha, *Art Nouveau and Art Déco Bookbinding*, New York: Abrams, 1989:186–87.

Albini, Franco (1905–77)
► Italian architect and designer; born Robbiate, Como.
► Studied architecture, Politecnico di Milano, to 1929.
► He worked as an architect, city planner, and interior, exhibition, furniture, and consumer-products designer; active in Gio Ponti's studio long after graduating in architecture; left in 1930 after meeting Edoardo Persico, who appeared to be more truly Rationalist, and (with Renato Camus and Giancarlo Palanti) set up his own studio, Milan; for a 1933 competition, designed a prototype transparent radio, housed between two sheets of Perspex. 1949–64, taught at Instituto Universitario di Architettura, Venice; 1954–55, Facoltà di Architettura, Turin; 1963–77, Politecnico di Milano (architectural composition); became a

member of CIAM (Congrès Internationaux d'Architecture Moderne), INU (Instituto Nazionale di Urbanistica), Accademia di San Luca, Instituto Scientifico of the CNR for Museography, ADI (Associazione per il Disegno Industriale), and honorary member of AIA (American Institute of Architects); in the prewar years, was a member of Rationalist groups, working in Milan and culturally supported by the journal *Casabella-continuá*, of which he was editor 1945–46. His 1940s and 1950s furniture clearly revealed his Rationalist leanings in its logical form and manufacturing process. His tension-wire suspension shelving was widely published. At *Casabella-continuá*, he expressed his theories, including an interest in novelty, uniqueness, mass production, and commonplace construction materials. In 1951, Franca Helg joined Albini's studio, which became Studio di Architettura Franco Albini e Franca Helg; accompanied him in his lecturing; this was an intense period of activity for them in interior design, architecture, town planning, and design. They co-designed furniture from the beginning of their association. Albini was the first architect-designer to work for Cassina. In 1962, Antonio Piva joined Albini's studio; in 1965, son Marco Albini joined the firm that became known as Marco Albini, Franca Helg, Antonio Piva, Architetti, after Albini's death.
► Work included 1957 La Rinascente department store in Rome and 1962 Milan subway interior; *Tensistructure* bookshelves, transparent radio, and a chair for Cassina; furniture in wood and metal included 1938–39 desk by Knoll/Gavina (produced from 1949), 1950 *Margherita* and *Gala* wicker armchairs, 1952 *Fiorenza* chair by Arflex, 1954 *Luisa* armchair, 1956 *PS16* rocking chair, 1968 lighting system (with Helg and Piva) by Sirrah. 1950–68, Poggi furniture company produced only Albini's designs. Other examples of his work produced by Bonacina, Arflex, Siemens, Fontana Arte, Sirrah, San Lorenzo.
► Received 1955, 1958, 1964 Premi Compasso d'Oro, 1971 Biscione d'Oro, and 1976 gold medal. In 1971, elected Honorary Royal Designer for Industry, London. As early as 1930, he participated in the third Monza 'Esposizione Biennale delle Arti Decorative e Industriali Moderne' as a Rationalist practitioner; designed 'Exhibition of Antique Goldsmithing and Jewelry' in plated tubular steel and glass and showed a bent tubular-steel upholstered chair at 1936 (VI) Triennale di Milano; with the Rationalists, showed work (homes, a man's room, living room in a villa, kitchen, bedroom, and bathroom) at 1936 (VI) Triennale di Milano; participated in the 1940 (VII) and 1948 (VIII) Triennali di Milano. Albini studio received 1955, 1958, 1964 Premio Compasso d'Oro; 1958 Premio Olivetti in Architecture; 1963 Premio IN-Arch Lazio. Work subject of 1981 exhibition, Rotonda della Bosana, Milan; included in 1983–84 'Design Since 1945' exhibition, Philadelphia Museum of Art. Work subject of 1989–91 'Franco Albini and his Studio: Architecture and Design 1930–1988' traveling exhibition, USA.
► Paolo Fossati, *Il design in Italia*, Turin, 1972:77–83,163–78. Barbie Campbell-Cole and Tim Benton (eds.), *Tubular Steel Furniture*, London: The Art Book Company, 1979:47. Andrea Branzi and Michele De Lucchi, *Design Italiano Degli Anni '50*, Milan: Editoriale Domus, 1980. *Franco Albini*, 1930–1970, London, 1981. Penny Sparke, *Design in Italy, 1870 to the Present*, New York: Abbeville, 1988. Cat., Franca Helg et al., *Franco Albini: Architecture and Design 1934–1977*, New York: Princeton Architectural Press, 1990. Charlotte Fiell and Peter Fiell, *Modern Furniture Classics Since 1945*, London: Thames and Hudson, 1991: 20,23,49,54.

Albini, Marco (1940–)
► Italian architect-designer; born Milan; son of Franco Albini.
► Studied architecture, Politecnico di Milano, to 1965.
► In 1965, he joined his father's architecture studio, Milan; was a member of Manager's Board of Documentation Center IN/ARCH, 1969–72, in charge of industrial design course at the art school in Venice and, 1971–73, at Instituto Universitario di Architettura, Venice; from 1980, was a researcher, Politecnico di Milano, where

he was in charge 1981–84 of the Architecture File and Projects section, Documentation Center; participated in numerous conferences in Italy and abroad.
▶ Fumio Shimizu and Matteo Thun (eds.), *The Descendants of Leonardo: The Italian Design*, Tokyo, 1987:330.

Albinson, Don (1915–)
▶ American furniture designer.
▶ Studied in Sweden, Cranbrook Academy of Art, Bloomfield Hills, Michigan, and Yale University.
▶ He collaborated with Charles Eames and George Nelson at Herman Miller. In Eames's Venice, California office, Albinson created the fiberglass shell, encouraged by Eames and often incorrectly credited solely to Eames; was instrumental in sculptor Harry Bertoia's joining the Eames design studio in California; 1964–71, was head of the design department at Knoll in New York. The 1965 stacking *Albinson Chair* produced by Knoll was similar to British designer Robin Day's extremely popular chair for Hille, although Albinson's was more sophisticated. After Knoll, he became a consultant designer to Westinghouse on office seating and furniture systems.
▶ Chairs shown at 1968 'Les Assises du siège contemporain' exhibition, Musée des Arts Décoratifs in Paris. Received 1967 American Architectural Design Award and 1967 AID Award, USA.
▶ Cat., *Les Assises du siège contemporain*, Paris: Musée des Arts Décoratifs, 1968. Cat., *Modern Chairs 1918–1970*, London: Lund Humphries, 1971.

Alchimia, Studio (Studio Alchymia)
▶ Italian design collaborative; located Milan.
▶ Founded in 1976, Alchimia was the proto-Memphis group that examined mass culture and communication, rather than the technological aspects of design; was a center for innovatory design made and sold rather than merely talked about. Members were known for recycling or transforming existing images, particularly famous works of art, as a form of commentary on the process of mass replication. Its membership came from late-1960s radical groups; included Donatella Biffi, Pier Carlo Bontempi, Carla Ceccariglia, Stefano Casciani, Rina Corti, Walter Garro, Bruno Gregori, Giorgio Gregori, Adriana Guerriero, Rainer Hegele, Jeremy King, Yumiko Kobajashi, Ewa Kulakowska, Mauro Panzeri, Patrizia Scarzella. When the Alchimia 1979 *Bau.Haus uno* and 1980 *Bau.Haus due* collections were shown along with recycled and repainted second-hand furniture, the Milan design establishment was shocked by the use of kitsch and popular-image metaphors. Alessandro Mendini, who brought international notice to Alchimia, created the particularly provocative 1981 *Mobile Infinito*. In 1984, Zabro furniture-production firm was established to unite the New Craft and industry. The group was placed in charge of art direction of the 1985 'Japanese Avant-Garde in the Future' festival, Genoa. Alchimia produced objects by Ettore Sottsass, Andrea Branzi, Alessandro Mendini, Michele De Lucchi, Franco Raggi, Daniela Puppa, Andrea Belloni, Paola Navone, Lapo Binazzi, Riccardo Dalisi, Trix and Robert Haussmann, and others.
▶ Works shown in its Alchimia Gallery. *Bau.Haus uno* (its first collection) and *Bau.Haus due* shown at 1979 (XVI) Triennale di Milano. Alchimia organized 1979 'Design Phenomene' exhibition in Linz and showed 'The Banal Object' at 1980 Biennale di Venezia. Group received 1981 Premio Compasso d'Oro (design research).
▶ Studio Alchimia, *Bauhaus collection 1980–1981*, Milan: Alchimia Editore, 1980. Penny Sparke, *Ettore Sottsass*, London: Design Council, 1982. *Michele De Lucchi*, The Hague: Uitgeverij Komplement, 1985. Pier Caro Bontempi, Giorgio Gregori, *Alchimia*, The Hague: Copi Den Haag, 1985. Guia Sambonet, *Alchimia 1977–78*, Turin: Allemandi, 1986. Stefano Casciani, *Disegni Alchimia 1982–87*, Turin, Allemandi, 1986. Fumio Shimizu and Matteo Thun (eds.), *The Descendants of Leonardo: The Italian Design*, Tokyo, 1987:322.

Aldridge, John (1905–)
▶ British painter and designer; active Great Bardfield, Essex.
▶ Studied classics, Oxford University.
▶ He was primarily a painter of still-life and landscape; illustrated books including *The Life of the Dead* (1933) by Laura Riding. His prints were included in the 1938 and 1939 editions of Curwen's *Contemporary Lithographs*. From the 1930s, he lived in Great Bardfield, Essex, where he met Eric Ravilious and Edward Bawden; in the 1960s, collaborated with Bawden on experimental hand-cut linoleum prints for commercial wallpaper produced by Cole and Son of London, who issued his wallpaper designs from the 1930s.
▶ Work subject of 1933, 1936, 1940, and 1947 exhibitions, Leicester Galleries and, from 1948, included regularly in exhibitions at the Royal Academy, London.
▶ Cat., *Thirties: British art and design before the war*, London: Arts Council of Great Britain, Hayward Gallery, 1979:127,284.

Alemagna, Renata (1948–)
▶ Italian furniture designer; born and active Milan.
▶ Active professionally from 1975, Alemagna designed furniture for clients including Parolini, Pozzi Figli di Cesare & Eugenio, De Gioanni, Pavus, Gnecchi, Face Standard. Alemagna was a member of ADI (Associazione per il Disegno Industriale).
▶ *ADI Annual 1976*, Milan: Associazione per il Disegno Industriale, 1976.

Alessandri, Marc (1932–)
▶ French designer; born Paris.
▶ Studied École Nationale des Beaux-Arts, Paris.
▶ In 1967, he set up his own architecture office L'Abaque (Abacus); designed numerous office interiors in France, Belgium, Spain, and Africa; in 1969, designed a range of ergonomic chairs, produced by Airborne; 1970–76, was president, Interior Architects Union; 1977–79, president of Société des Artistes Décorateurs; in 1979, became a founding member of VIA (Valorisation de l'innovation dans l'ameublement); from 1988, was a freelance designer associated with Asymétrie, Paris.
▶ Won 1982 Concours de mobilier de bureau sponsored by APCI, with entry produced by Knoll-France.

Alessi
▶ Italian domestic metal-products factory.
▶ Alessi was founded in 1921 by Giovanni Alessi. Its earliest products were coffee pots and trays. The firm was known as FAO (Fratelli Alessi Omegna) 1921–47, Alfra (Alessi Fratelli) 1947–68, and Ceselleria Alessi 1968–70. In c1935, Alessi's son Carlo began working as a designer at the firm; his most significant project was the 1945 *Bombé* coffee and tea set (discontinued in 1972 and put back into production in 1980); from 1945, he became the firm's general manager; shortly afterwards, began commissioning consultant-designers. From 1929, Alessi specialized in bar-counter and domestic tableware items, including bread baskets, teapots, egg cups, condiment sets, and cheese dishes. In 1932, under Carlo Alessi, the firm began to focus on the appearance of its wares. From 1935, more attention was paid to its industrial techniques in an attempt to turn away from its slow crafts approach. In 1950, with large US orders, it started mass production. The *Model No. 870* cocktail shaker designed by Luigi Massoni in the 1950s had sold one and a half million pieces by 1991. Carlo became president and brother Ettore Alessi vice-president. Producing numbered and signed pieces by international architects and designers, including Ettore Sottsass, the firm gained popularity in the 1970s. Its first cult object was 1978 espresso-coffee pot designed by Richard Sapper. The 1983 *Tea and Coffee Piazza* project initiated by Carlo Alessi's son Alberto, intended to create 'architecture in miniature' and in reality a clever publicity ploy, commissioned 11 architects: Robert Venturi, Michael Graves, Richard Meier, Stanley Tigerman, Aldo Rossi, Paolo Portoghesi, Alessandro Mendini, Hans Hollein, Charles Jencks, Oscar Blanca Tusquets, and Kasumasa Yamashita. Each set was made in a limited edition of 99 in silver (plus three artists' proofs in other metals); only Tusquets's service was avail-

able in silver-plated brass. The Eliel Saarinen set was made from a well-known example from the 1930s. The tremendous success of the venture prompted a wave of architect-designed goods from Alessi and other manufacturers. In 1991, designs by women on the theme of serving and offering began to be produced as part of a project coordinated by the Alessi Study Center in Milan set up in 1990 and directed by Laura Polinaro. In 1990, Alessi's ceramic line Tendentse was introduced. Alessofono, making brass musical instruments, was set up in the late 1980s. The Officina Alessi division produced limited editions of metalwares from 1982. 1,200 products were advertised in Alessi's 1991 catalog. Alessi acquired a wooden-products factory in 1989 and the Twergi range of wooden tabletops and kitchen-utensils was launched. Alberto Alessi's residence 'Casa della Felicità,' Lago d'Orta, was created as a laboratory and domicile for publicity purposes; it was designed by Alessandro Mendini, Francesco Mendini, and the Atelier Alchimia (Giorgio Gregori) with a tower by Aldo Rossi and with consultants Falvio Albanese and Alberto Gozzi on the wine cellar.

▶ Products included *Model No. 870* cocktail shaker designed by Luigi Massoni; 1978 espresso-coffee set by Richard Sapper; kettles by Robert Graves and Aldo Rossi; 1984–85 *Colore* range by Ettore Sottsass, Achile Castiglioni, Silvio Coppola, Giulio Confalonieri, and staff technicians; *Falstaf* cookware by Alessandro Mendini with knobs by Giorgio Gregori, Michael Graves, Arata Isozaki, Yuri Soloviev, and Philippe Starck; 1991 *Juicy Salif* lemon squeezer, 1991 *Hot Bertaa* kettle, and 1991 *Max le Chinois* colander, all by Starck; *Leina* fireplace poker and calipers by Pep Bonet; coffee mills (by Twergi division) by Riccardo Dalisi and Milton Glaser; 1992 *100-vases-by-100-designers* series; 1993 teapot by Frank Gehry.

▶ Products subject of 'Paesaggio Casalingo: La Produzione Alessi nell'industria dei casalinghi dal 1921 al 1980' exhibition originating at the 1979 (XVI) Triennale di Milano, 'Alessi/Mendini: Dix ans de collaboration' exhibition, Centre Georges Pompidou, Paris, 1990. Product designs by women coordinated by the Alessi Study Center first shown at 1991 Salone del Mobile in Milan.

▶ Cat., Alessandro Medini, *Paesaggio Casalingo: La produzione Alessi nell'industria dei casalinghi dal 1921 al 1980*, Milan: Editoriale Domus, 1979. Patricia Scarzella, *Tea and Coffee Piazza: 11 Servizi da tè e caffè . . .*, Crusinallo: Alessi, 1983. Arlene Hirst, *Metropolitan Home*, April 1990: 69. Lita Talarico, 'Alessi SpA,' *Graphis*, No. 272, Mar./Apr. 1991:61–77.

Alessi, Carlo (1916–)
▶ Italian entrepreneur; born Gravellona Toce.
▶ Studied Institute of Industrial Technology OMAR, Novara.
▶ In 1932 at age 16, he began working in the family firm Alessi.
▶ Receive first prize (export activities) from Chamber of Commerce and Industry, Novara Prefecture; Gold Mercury from European Commerce Committee; Premio Marazza (human relationships at the workplace).
▶ Fumio Shimizu and Matteo Thun (eds.), *The Descendants of Leonardo: The Italian Design*, Tokyo, 1987:331.
▶ See Alessi

Aliprandi, Dante
▶ Italian interior designer; active Milan.
▶ From 1957, Aliprandi was artistic director of Arredamenti 2A; occasionally collaborated with the Studi d'Architettura; 1964–66, artistic director of Xilometal, Milan; 1970–74, director general of Dado Industrial Design in Milan; from 1976, general manager and artistic director at Max Form; member of ADI (Associazione per il Disegno Industriale).
▶ Received silver medal at 1958 silver medal, 1960 gold medal, 1961 gold medal at national exhibition of interior design, Monza and 1975 Ape d'Oro prize for his proposal for the Instituto sul Lavoro. Participated in design of the Italy pavilion, 1962 international exhibition, Gent.
▶ *ADI Annual 1976*, Milan: Associazione per il Disegno Industriale, 1976.

Alix, Charlotte (1897–)
▶ French designer.
▶ 1925–27, Alix worked for the Baron de Rothschild; encouraged by her friend Gaston Roussel (director of the Laboratories Roussel, Paris), she pursued the study of new materials and forms; with his support, designed pieces produced by artisans in the Faubourg Saint-Antoine furniture-making area of Paris; from 1928, worked with Louis Sognot in the design office Bureau International des Arts français. Their first major commission was the 1929 Laboratoires Roussel, for which they designed furniture in bent-metal tubing and glass. They designed offices for *Le Semaine de Paris* newspaper (of which Robert Mallet-Stevens was overall architect), Polo de Bagatelle bar; interior of graphic artist Jean Carlu's residence, Paris; in 1929, became a members of UAM (Union des Artistes Modernes). Alix remained a member of the Salon d'Automne until 1952.
▶ Work (with Sognot) shown at Salons of the time, particularly at the Salon d'Automne, and, as members of UAM, at its exhibitions in the 1930s.
▶ Raymond Cogniat, Louis Sognot et Charlotte Alix, *Art et Décoration*, T. LIX, July–Dec. 1930. Cat., Aaron Lederfajn and Xavier Lenormand, *Le Louvre des Antiquaires présente: 1930 quand le meuble devient sculpture*, Paris, 1986. Arlette Barré-Despond, *UAM*, Paris: Regard, 1986:506–09. Pierre Kjellberg, *Art Déco: les maîtres du Mobilier, le décor des Paquebots*, Paris: Amateur, 1986.

Allard, René
▶ French architect, decorator, furniture designer; born Puy.
▶ 1920–23, Allard participated in the events of the Salon d'Automne, showing simple serially-produced furniture; until 1938, was an active member of the Société des Artistes Décorateurs.
▶ Pierre Kjellberg, *Art Déco: les maîtres du Mobilier, le décor des Paquebots*, Paris: Amateur, 1986:30.

Allen, Davis (1916–)
▶ American interior designer; born Ames, Iowa; active New York.
▶ 1934–36, studied Brown University, Providence, Rhode Island; returned home for a time; 1939, enrolled in Kungliga Tekniska Högskolan, Stockholm; met Aino and Alvar Aalto in Finland; 1940, enrolled in School of Architecture, Yale University, New Haven, Connecticut; served in World War II; interned at SOM (Skidmore, Owings and Merrill); 1946–47, returned to Yale; 1947, settled in New York and worked at Knoll Planning Unit as interior designer and briefly at Raymond Loewy's industrial-design office; subsequently for architects Harrison and Abramovitz, designing furnishings for General Assembly Building, United Nations, New York. In 1950, he was hired by architect Gordon Bunschaft at SOM, New York, as interior designer, with penthouse offices of 1954 Manufacturers Hanover Trust Building, New York, as his first important assignment. A vast number of Allen-designed or supervised interiors followed until the late 1980s. In 1965, he became associate partner and senior interior designer; in 1985, began semi-retirement. Designed furniture produced by Steelcase, GF, Stow and Davis, Berhardt, and Hickory Business Furniture, including the 1983 *Andover* chair versions by Stendig. Most of his furniture was originally designed for site-specific use for SOM architecture commissions.
▶ Elected to Hall of Fame, *Interiors* magazine.
▶ Maeve Slavin, *Davis Allen*, New York: Rizzoli, 1990.

Allier, Paul
▶ French painter and decorator; born Montpellier.
▶ 1913–19, Allier showed his furniture at the Salon d'Automne.
▶ Pierre Kjellberg, *Art Déco: les maîtres du Mobilier, le décor des Paquebots*, Paris: Amateur, 1986:30.

Alliot, Lucien (1877–)
▶ French sculptor and lighting designer.
▶ Studied sculpture under Barrias.
▶ Best known for 1905 *Violoncelliste* statue and 1920 *À l'Enface* park sculpture; rendered a number of small bronzes wired as lighting fixtures and finished in silver or *vert-de-gris*, having the stand-

ard theme of a draped *femme-fleur*, holding a light housed in a musical instrument.

▶ From 1903, showed busts, statuettes, and figural groups at Salons of the Société des Artistes français and, c1934–1939, was a juror on the Société's Salon committee.

▶ Alastair Duncan, *Art Nouveau and Art Déco Lighting*, New York: Simon & Schuster, 1978:69.

Alnas, Tormod   (1921–)

▶ Norwegian interior architect and furniture designer.

▶ Best known for his 1953 knock-down chair in bent metal and canvas for Asker Stålmøbelfabrikk.

▶ Fredrik Wildhagen, *Norge i Form*, Oslo: Stenersen, 1988:132.

Alons, Cor   (b. Cornelius Louis Alons 1892)

▶ Dutch interior architect and industrial designer; born Groningen.

▶ 1913–17, studied in drawing and painting department, Academie van Beeldende Kunsten, The Hague.

▶ 1917–21, worked as draftsman in Modern interior art department, H. Pander & Sons, The Hague, under architect Hendrik Wouda. 1919–20, taught evening furniture-drawing class, Patrimonium, The Hague. 1919, became member of VANK. 1921–23, worked as designer at painted- and stained-glass window firm G. van Geldermalsen, Rotterdam. 1922, designer at furniture firm LOV. 1923, traveled in France, Germany, and Hungary; designed stained-glass windows for Baarns Lyceum; settled in The Hague; became an independent interior architect and member of de Haagsche Kunstkring. 1923, designed pottery for NV De Duinvoet. A prolific interior designer, he participated with prominent Dutch architects. 1928, designed cutlery for Emailleerfabriek 'De IJsel'. 1928–36, active in own design office and showroom in own residence, The Hague. 1929–57, taught furniture construction, Academie van Beeldende Kunsten, The Hague, and, 1934, founded its interior-arts course. 1932–33, designed textiles of van den Bergh's firm in Oss. 1933, designed store front of decorative-arts shop De Kerhuil, Haarlem. 1935–40, designed tubular-steel furniture for Oostwoud Fabrieken, Kraneker. Stained-glass windows and bar of 1938 oceanliner *New Amsterdam*. 1942, became prisoner of the Germans and returned to the Netherlands. 1948, designed wooden furniture for C. den Boer. 1954, designed metal and glass furniture. 1962, honorary member of GKf. Died in The Hague.

▶ Work included in 1920 'Modern Interior Art' (stained-glass windows and decorative panels) organized by LOV in Oosterbeek; 1925 Paris 'Exhibition Internationale des Arts Décoratifs et Industriels Modernes'; 1927 one-person exhibition, The Hague; designed PTT pavilion, 'Jaarbeurs,' Utrecht; 1932 VANK exhibition (showing chrome-plated steel furniture by Ph. Dekker), Rotterdam; designed exhibition for 250th anniversary of Academie van Beeldende Kunsten, Pulchri Studio, The Hague; Dutch pavilion, 1937 Paris 'Exhibition Internationale des Arts et Techniques dans la Vie Moderne.'

▶ R.J. Risseeuw, 'Binnenhuiskunst: Een vraaggesprek met den binnenhuisarchitect Cor Alons,' *Op den Uitkijk, tijdschrift voor het Christelijk gezin*, No. 5, 1929: 469–74,504–08,532–35. P.J. Risseeuw, 'In gesprek met Cor Alons,' *Omtmoeting: Letterkundig en Algemeen Cultureel Maandblad*, No. 5, 1951:4–5,151–61. Cat., *Industrie U Vormgeving in Nederland 1850–1950*, Amsterdam: Stedelijk Museum, 1985. Marg van der Burgh, *Cor Alons: Binnenhuisarchitect en industrieel ontwerper 1892/1967*, Rotterdam: Uitgeverij 010, 1988.

Alring, Leif   (1936–)

▶ Danish designer.

▶ Studied Kunsthåndvaerkerskolen, Copenhagen.

▶ A qualified cabinetmaker, Alring designed carpets, furniture, and industrial goods; wrote regularly in the Danish press on technical matters; lectured widely in Scandinavia on plastics and their application to design; in 1964, experimented with plastics in attempting to form a one-piece chair. Several of his designs were manufactured under license by firms in Japan and elsewhere. His single-form plastic furniture model was the expanded-polystyrene *Series 261*.

▶ Received prizes at numerous competitions including 1966 annual prize of Danish Cabinetmakers Society and 1971 Bundespreis 'Die gute Industrieform,' Germany.

▶ Cat., Milena Lamarová, *Design a Plastické Hmoty*, Prague: Uměleckoprůmyslové Muzeum, 1972.

Altenloh, Robert

▶ Belgian silver designer; active Brussels.

▶ The firm E. Altenloh produced Modern silver objects in the 1920s to designs by Robert Altenloh.

▶ Work shown at 1910 Brussels 'Arts Industriels et des Métiers' and 1925 Paris 'Exposition Internationale des Arts Décoratifs et Industriels Modernes.'

▶ Annelies Krekel-Aalberse, *Art Nouveau and Art Déco Silver*, New York: Abrams, 1989:95.

Al'tman, Natan Isaevich   (1889–1970)

▶ Russian painter, sculptor, set designer, and propagandist; born Vinnitsa (now Ukraine).

▶ 1901–07, studied painting and sculpture, Odessa Art School; 1910–12, Mariia Vasil'eva's Russian Academy, Paris.

▶ In the early 1910s, he became interested in Cubism; 1912–17, contributed to the satirical magazine *Riab* (Ripple) in St. Petersburg; was active in the avant-garde group Union of Youth; in 1918, became a professor at Svomas, a member of Izo Nkp and designed agitprop decorations in Uritskii Square, Petrograd (now St. Petersburg) and elsewhere to celebrate the first anniversary of the October Revolution. Even though on the verge of collapse, the Soviet government provided Al'tman with 50,000 feet of canvas for his Futurist constructions and designs on the Winter Palace walls and General Staff arch. Al'tman made the Aleksandr column into a Futurist sculpture; in 1919, became a leading member of Komfut (Communist Futurism); in 1921, published his album of Lenin drawings and designed the décor for Vladimir Maiakovskii's play *Mystery-Bouffe*; 1929–35, lived in Paris. The 1933 monograph on Al'tman by Waldemar George and Il'ia Ehrenburg was published in Yiddish in Paris. He returned to Russia in 1935; settled in Leningrad (now St. Petersburg) in 1936; was active as a portraitist and still-life and landscape painter, sculptor, and set designer.

▶ Showed paintings, sculpture, and designs in many avant-garde exhibitions, including '0–10' and 'Jack of Diamonds.' Supporting the cause of Russo-Jewish artists, contributed to 1918 Moscow 'Exhibition of Paintings and Sculpture by Jewish Artists,' 1919 Petrograd 'First State Free Exhibition of Works of Art,' 1922 Berlin 'Erste Russische Kunstausstellung,' 1924 Venice 'Esposizione Internazionale,' 1925 Paris 'Exposition Internationale des Arts Décoratifs et Industriels Modernes.' Work subject of 1969 exhibition, Leningrad.

▶ Waldemar George and Il'ia Ehrenburg, monograph on Al'tman in Yiddish, Paris, 1933. M. Etkind, *Natan Altman*, Moscow, 1971. V. Petrov, 'O vystavke N.I. Altmana,' in D. Chebanova (ed.), *V.N. Petrov: Ocherki i issledovaniia*, Moscow, 1978:250–54. Stephanie Barron and Maurice Tuchman, *Avant-Garde Russia, 1919–1930, New Perspectives*, MIT, 1980. Nina Lobanov-Rostovsky, *Revolutionary Ceramics*, London: Studio Vista, 1990.

aluminum (aka aluminium)

▶ A silver-colored metal extracted from bauxite ore. Distinctive for its light weight it is frequently used in the manufacture of aircraft and in household utensils, cookware, and other domestic objects, including furniture. Fritz August Breuhaus de Groot, as the interior architect, and artist Arpke collaborated with Ludwig Dürr, the chief constructor at the Luftschiffbau-Zeppelin, to design the layout and decorations of the 1936 *Hindenburg* dirigible, using aluminum extensively. In 1930 in Los Angeles, American manufacturer Warren McArthur patented the use of aluminum in furniture. During the 1930s, it was incorporated into the furniture of Donald Deskey and Gerrit Rietveld, and wholly used in the 1938 *Landi* chair of Hans Coray. Alcoa (the Aluminum Company of America) promoted the use of aluminum in domestic accessories and functional household goods, from cookware to vases. Ernest Race in Britain reprocessed World War II surplus in his 1945 *BA* chair and other work. Aluminum is available in sheets, tubes, 'I's, 'T's, and angles and can be cast and extruded. The drawbacks of the metal include surface corrosion by a chalky oxidation (unless anodized) and its tendency to become scratched. Anodizing can be produced in colors and certain paints are appropriate finishes. Brightly colored domestic aluminum ware for the kitchen, including tumblers and water pitchers, was popular in the 1950s. Favored in domestic wares in the USA and France before World War II, after the war aluminum was incorporated into furniture by designers such as Charles Eames, Gae Aulenti, Andrew Morrison, Sylvain Dubuisson, Philippe Starck, and Bruce Hannah.

▶ John Fleming and Hugh Honour, *The Penguin Dictionary of Decorative Arts*, London: Penguin, 1989 (new ed.). Cat., *Aluminium: das Metall der Moderne*, Cologne: Kölnisches Stadtmuseum, 1991.

Alviar, Christopher (1961–)
▶ Filipino industrial designer; born Manila.
▶ Studied industrial design, University of Washington, to 1986.
▶ Alivar settled in the USA; designed for various firms as a freelance designer, including O'Brien International and Walter Dorwin Teague, before joining Ziba in 1987.
▶ He received IDSA's Merit Award in 1985 and 1986, and another IDSA award in 1988, for his electronic transparency-system work.
▶ Albrecht Bangert and Karl Michael Armer, *80s Style: Designs of the Decade*, New York: Abbeville, 1990:226.

Alvin
▶ American silversmiths.
▶ Founded in 1886, Alvin Manufacturing was established in Irvington, New Jersey by William H. Jamouneau, president until his retirement in 1898. The name was changed to Alvin-Beiderhase in 1895; was moved from New Jersey to Sag Harbor, Long Island, New York; in 1897, was purchased by Joseph Fahys and Co and operated as a branch of the firm c1898–1910; in 1919, changed name to Alvin Silver, becoming makers of sterling-silver flatware, hollow-ware, dresserware, silver-deposits ware, and plated-silver flatware. In 1928, certain assets, dies, and patterns were purchased by the Gorham company with its name changed to the Alvin Corporation. The firm exists today as a division of Gorham.
▶ Dorothy R. Rainwater, *Encyclopedia of American Silver Manufacturers*, New York: Crown, 1979. Annelies Krekel-Aalberse, *Art Nouveau and Art Déco Silver*, New York: Abrams, 1989:98.

Ambasz, Emilio (1943–)
▶ Argentine architect and designer; born Resistencia, Chaco; active New York.
▶ Studied Princeton University, New Jersey, to 1966.
▶ 1970–76, he was curator of design department, New York Museum of Modern Art, directing and installing numerous exhibits on architecture and industrial design; in 1976, set up his own studio office in New York, becoming active as architect and interior and industrial designer; was a co-founder of the Institute for Architecture and Urban Studies, New York, where he was president 1981–85; lecturing and writing widely, was president of the Architectural League of New York (1981–85) and taught at Hochschule für Gestaltung, Ulm (1966–67), and architecture at Princeton University (1967–69); designed buildings in Europe, Japan and the USA, including the Mycal Sanda Cultural Center, Japan, the Museum of American Folk Art, New York, and Houston Center Plaza, Houston, Texas; was a member of International Council, New York Museum of Modern Art, and coordinator of its architecture committee; patented a number of industrial and mechanical designs; was editor, *International Design Yearbook* (New York: Abbeville 1986–87). Designs included *Lumb-R* chair

by Cassina, 1980–82 *Liter* automobile engine for Cummins Engine Co., 1985 *Agamenone* lamp by Artemide, 1986 *Soffio* lighting system for Sirrah; (with Giancarlo Piretti) 1979 *Vertebra* seating system by Cassina, 1986 *Oseris* lamp, 1986 *Logotec* track lighting range for Erco. His architecture included 1982 Botanical Garden Conservatory, San Antonio, Texas.
▶ Organized 1972 'Italy: The New Domestic Landscape' exhibition, New York Museum of Modern Art. Represented USA at the 1976 Biennale di Venezia. Received numerous awards including 1976, 1980, and 1985 *Progressive Architecture* award, 1980 American National Industrial Design Award (*Logotec* lighting), 1983 (IV) Annual *Interiors* Award, 1977 gold medal (with Piretti) of the IBD-USA, 1979 SMAU Prize (Italy), 1981 and 1991 Compasso d'Oro (*Veterbra* and *Qualis* seating), 1988 National Glass Association Award for Excellence in Commercial Design, 1990 Quaternio Award, 1987 International Interior Design Award (UK), 1986 IDEA Award from IDSA, 1992 IDSA (*Handkerchief Television*). Prototype of the 'Library in the Garden' for 'Le Affinità Elettive' at the Palazzo della Triennale shown at 1985 Triennale di Milano. Exhibition, Axis Design and Architectural Gallery, Tokyo, 1985, Institute of Contemporary Art, Geneva, 1986.
▶ Cat., *Le Affinità Elettive*, Milan: Electa, 1985. Auction cat., *Asta di Modernariato 1900–1986, Auction 'Modernariato,'* Milan: Semenzato Nuova Geri, 8 Oct. 1986. Juli Capella and Quim Larrea, *Designed by Architects in the 1980s*, New York: Rizzoli, 1988:14–15. Hans Wichmann, *Italien Design 1945 bis heute*, Munich: Die Neue Sammlung, 1988.

American Designers' Gallery
▶ American artists' group.
▶ In 1928, American Designers' Gallery was formed in New York to foster the professional status of designers and to promote high aesthetic values in the Modern decorative arts. Its headquarters were located at the gallery of interior designer and decorator Paul Frankl. Members included Donald Deskey, Ruth Reeves, Joseph Urban, and Henry Varum Poor.
▶ First exhibition (15 designers in ten complete rooms and some displays), Chase National Bank building, New York, 1928; second exhibition 1929.
▶ Karen Davies (Lucic), *At Home in Manhattan*, New Haven: Yale, 1983:90–91. Mel Byars (intro.), 'What Makes American Design American?' in R.L. Leonard and C.A. Glassgold (eds.), *Modern American Design, by the American Union of Decorative Artists and Craftsmen*, New York: Acanthus Press, 1992 (reprint of 1930 edition).

American Encaustic Tiling
▶ American ceramics firm; located Zanesville, Ohio.
▶ One of the firms in the USA quick to take advantage of the varicolored local clays, American Encaustic Tiling was founded in 1875 by F.H. Hall with backing by Benedict Fischer and G.R. Lansing; in the forefront of tile manufacturing for more than 50 years, was incorporated in 1878 with a New York salesroom by the early 1880s; made glazed tiles from 1880, relief tiles from 1881, and white wall tiles from 1895; had its reputation established by the popularity of tiles; executed a large commission for encaustic tiles for new buildings constructed during the 1870s, including the state capitol, Albany, New York; 1890–92, greatly expanded its Zanesville, Ohio factory; in c1891, produced the illustrations of Walter Crane (from *The Baby's Own Aesop* of 1887) and, in the 1890s, William Morris patterns on tiles. Herman Mueller, a sculptor trained in Munich and Nuremberg, designed classical draped figures in pastoral scenes. Karl Langenbeck experimented with new glazes and Parian wares at the Zanesville firm. In 1894, they both left American Encaustic; formed Mosaic Tile, Zanesville. In 1908, Mueller established Mueller Mosaic, Trenton, New Jersey. American Encaustic was commissioned to supply the tiles for the Holland Tunnel, New York. The firm closed in 1935.
▶ Wares included in 1986–87 'In Pursuit of Beauty,' Metropolitan Museum of Art, New York.

▶ Doreen Bolger Burke et al., *In Pursuit of Beauty: Americans and the Aesthetic Movement*, New York: Metropolitan Museum of Art and Rizzoli, 1986:401, biblio.

American Society of Interior Designers (ASID)
▶ American professional association.
▶ American Society of Interior Designers (ASID) was founded in 1975 by the merger of National Society of Interior Designers (NSID) and American Institute of Interior Designs (AID). NSID was established in 1957 to align designers and decorators. AID was established in 1921 with 342 initial members. The ASID today works towards supporting high educational standards, generating publicity, encouraging standard business and professional practices, and establishing the parameters for licensing interior designers, an issue of some importance from the late 1980s.
▶ John Pile, *Dictionary of 20th-Century Design*, New York: Facts on File, 1990.

American Union of
Decorative Artists and Craftsmen (AUDAC)
▶ American artists' group.
▶ AUDAC was formed in New York in 1928 through an initial informal meeting of a group of designers including Kem Weber, Frederick Kiesler, Donald Deskey, and Lee Simonson and headed by Paul Frankl to promote Modern decorative art; considered to have been officially formed in 1930 with its first of only two exhibitions; grew to include more than 100 members in the arts, design, photography, and architecture, including William Lescaze, Gilbert, Rhode, Margaret Bourke-White, Joseph Urban, and Frank Lloyd Wright; dissolved possibly by *c*1932.
▶ Members' work subject of exhibitions, Grand Central Palace, New York, in 1930, and in Brooklyn Museum in 1931.
▶ Karen Davies (Lucic), *At Home in Manhattan*, New Haven: Yale, 1983:90–91. Mel Byars (introduction), 'What Makes American Design American?' in R.L. Leonard and C.A. Glassgold (eds.), *Modern American Design, by the American Union of Decorative Artists and Craftsmen*, New York: Acanthus Press, 1992 (reprint of 1930 edition).

Ammitzbøll, Anne   (1934–)
▶ Danish designer.
▶ Studied Finn Juhl School of Interior Design and Mulle Høyrup's experimental school for textile printing, Kokkedal.
▶ She designed children's clothing sold through her own shop; designed leather goods for Form & Farve, Copenhagen; in 1970, began working with Andreas Mikkelsen and, from 1978, for Georg Jensen Sølvsmedie.
▶ Cat., *Georg Jensen Silversmithy: 77 Artists, 75 Years*, Washington: Smithsonian Institution Press, 1980.

Ammundsen, Jens   (1944–)
▶ Danish architect and furniture designer.
▶ Studied Kunsthåndvaerkerskolen, Copenhagen, to 1966.
▶ His furniture designs were produced by Fritz Hansen.
▶ Frederik Sieck, *Nutidig Dansk Møbeldesign: en kortfattet illustreret beskrivelse*, Copenhagen: Bondo Gravesen; 1990 Busck edition in English.

Amstelhoek
▶ Dutch ceramics workshop; located Amsterdam.
▶ Willem Hoeker founded the Amstelhoek workshop in 1897 to produce Modern ceramics, metalwork and furniture. In 1899, Jan Eisenloeffel, who had worked as a draftsman in Hoeker's firm, became artistic director of the metalworking section. Simple in form with sparse geometrical ornament, handmade objects were decorated with enameled and pierced squares and rectangles. Spun pieces had concentric circles around the rim, reminiscent of Wiener Werkstätte work of Josef Hoffmann and Koloman Moser from 1903 onwards. Amstelhoek produced a 97-piece dinner service for the City Council of Amsterdam for Queen Wilhelmina's 1901 marriage. Eisenloeffel was not acknowledged for his Amstelhoek designs shown at 1900 Paris and 1902 Turin exhibitions,

and he soon left the firm; was succeeded by J. Blinxma. Amstelhoek's metalworking section closed in 1903.
▶ Wares shown at 1900 Paris 'Exhibition universelle,' from which Tiffany bought a number of pieces, and 1902 Turin 'Esposizione Internazionale d'Arte Decorativa Moderna,' receiving awards at both.
▶ Annelies Krekel-Aalberse, *Art Nouveau and Art Déco Silver*, New York: Abrams, 1989:176.

Andersen, Gunnar Aargaard   (1919–)
▶ Danish furniture designer.
▶ 1936–39 studied Kunsthåndværkerskolen; 1939–46 Det Kongelige Danske Kunstakademi, both Copenhagen.
▶ From 1972, he was a professor at Kunstakademiet; 1973–74, was vice-president of the Akademiet; designed furniture produced by Jensen Kjær, Rud. Rasmussen, and Fritz Hansen.
▶ Work first shown in 1939 at 'Kunstnernes Efterårshdstilling' and worldwide thereafter.
▶ Frederik Sieck, *Nutidig Dansk Møbeldesign: en kortfattet illustreret beskrivelse*, Copenhagen: Bondo Gravesen; 1990 Busck edition in English.

Andersen, Hans Munck   (1943–)
▶ Danish ceramicist.
▶ 1968, studied Kunsthåndvaerkerskolen; 1972–73 Kunstakademiets Arkitektskole, both Copenhagen.
▶ 1968–71, he was a designer for Royal Copenhagen Porcelain Manufactory; in 1973, set up own workshop, Rø, Bornholm Island.
▶ Work subject of 1971 and 1976 exhibitions, Royal Copenhagen Porcelain Manufactory. Work included in 1970 exhibition, Hetjen Museum, Düsseldorf; 1971 Faenza 'Concorso Internazionale della Ceramica'; 1975 and 1981 exhibitions, Bornholms Museum; 1979 exhibition, Galerie Inart in Amsterdam; 1980 'Danish Design Cavalcade,' Det Danske Kunstindustrimuseum, Copenhagen.
▶ Cat., David Revere McFadden (ed.), *Scandinavian Modern Design 1880–1980*, New York: Abrams, 1982:262.

Andersen, Ib Just   (1884–1943)
▶ Danish designer; active Copenhagen.
▶ Trained with Mogens Ballin and Peter Hertz.
▶ Originally a painter and sculptor, he established his own company, Just Andersen Pewter, in 1918; produced designs for the Georg Jensen Sølvsmedie. His wife Alba Lykke was a pupil of Jensen.
▶ Cat., *Georg Jensen Silversmithy: 77 Artists, 75 Years*, Washington: Smithsonian Institution Press, 1980. Annelies Krekel-Aalberse, *Art Nouveau and Art Déco Silver*, New York: Abrams, 1989:221.

Andersen, Knud Holst   (1935–)
▶ Danish designer.
▶ Apprenticed as a silversmith in Denmark; 1961–64, studied Tokyo University of Art; 1975, Royal College of Art, London.
▶ From 1973, he was associated with Georg Jensen Sølvsmedie.
▶ Silver and bronze hollow-ware shown at exhibitions in Denmark, Sweden, Germany, and France. Received 1973 Artist-Craftsman of the Year, Danish Society of Arts and Crafts.
▶ Cat., *Georg Jensen Silversmithy: 77 Artists, 75 Years*, Washington: Smithsonian Institution Press, 1980.

Andersen, Rigmor   (1903–)
▶ Danish designer.
▶ Studied architecture, Det Kongelige Danske Kunstakademi, Copenhagen; in 1944, in its furniture school.
▶ 1929–39, she worked with Kaare Klint; from 1944, taught at Det Kongelige Danske Kunstakademi.
▶ Received Knut V. Englehardt Memorial Prize and Eckersberg Medal (*Margrethe* flatware for Jensen). Work shown 1933, 1942 'Dansk Kunsthåndvaerk,' Nationalmuseum, Stockholm and 1980

'Georg Jensen Silversmithy: 77 Artists, 75 Years' exhibition, Smithsonian Institution.
▶ Cat., *Georg Jensen Silversmithy: 77 Artists, 75 Years*, Washington: Smithsonian Institution Press, 1980. Frederik Sieck, *Nutidig Dansk Møbeldesign: en kortfattet illustreret beskrivelse*, Copenhagen: Bondo Gravesen; 1990 Busck edition in English.

Andersen, Steffen (1936–)
▶ Danish designer.
▶ 1956–58, studied Guldsmedehøjskolen, Copenhagen.
▶ 1959–60, worked at Georg Jensen Silversmiths, London; 1961–71, in its design department, Copenhagen; 1971–75, the advertising department; from 1975, the hollow-ware department.
▶ Work included in 1980 'Georg Jensen Silversmithy: 77 Artists, 75 Years' exhibition, Smithsonian Institution.
▶ Cat., *Georg Jensen Silversmithy: 77 Artists, 75 Years*, Washington: Smithsonian Institution Press, 1980.

Anderson, Aagaard (1919–1983)
▶ Danish architect and designer; born Ordrup.
▶ 1936–39, studied Det Kongelige Danske Kunstakademi, Copenhagen; 1939–46, Kungliga Konsthögskolan, Stockholm.
▶ In 1951, he began to design furniture; 1951–75, worked for magazine *Mobilia*; was also active as fine artist. His chair sketch of 1952 for a cantilevered model and the prototype made from chicken wire and newspaper in 1953 clearly presaged Verner Panton's 1960 plastic chair of the same silhouette.
▶ Cat., *Der Kragstuhl*, Stuhlmuseum Burg Beverungen, Berlin: Alexander, 1986:118–19,130.

Anderson, K.
▶ Swedish silversmiths; located Stockholm.
▶ In c1908, K. Anderson began producing silver models in mainly traditional and ornamental types already considered out of fashion; became known for its Modern silver designed by architects Erik Ekeberg, Viking Göransson, and Hans Quinding.
▶ Annelies Krekel-Aalberse, *Art Nouveau and Art Déco Silver*, New York: Abrams, 1989:244,251.

Anderson, Winslow (1917–)
▶ American ceramicist and glassware designer; born Massachusetts.
▶ Studied New York State College of Ceramics, Alfred University, to 1946.
▶ In 1946, he joined Blenko Glass, Milton, West Virginia; not a glass blower himself, he designed simple silhouettes blown by others; worked closely with the factory craftspeople; was employed by Lenox China, Trenton, New Jersey, 1953–79; first a designer at Lenox, he became its design director.
▶ His Blenko bent-necked decanter (an accidental form due to overheating) won 1952 Good Design award, New York Museum of Modern Art and Chicago Merchandize Mart.
▶ Don Wallance, *Shaping America's Products*, New York: Reinhold, 1956:82,105,115–17. Cat., Kathryn B. Hiesinger and George H. Marcus III (eds.), *Design Since 1945*, Philadelphia: Philadelphia Museum of Art, 1983. Cherie Fehrman and Kenneth Fehrman, *Postwar Interior Design: 1945–1960*, New York: Van Nostrand Reinhold, 1987. Eason Eige and Rick Wilson, *Blenko Glass 1930–1953*, Marietta, Ohio: Antique Publications, 1987.

Andersson, John (1900–)
▶ Swedish ceramicist.
▶ He designed ceramics for Andersson & Johansson (today Höganäs), Höganäs, for whom he executed the 1955 *Old Höganäs* ceramic ovenproof tableware. The pieces were produced in traditional earthenware in olive-green, mustard-yellow, and manganese-brown associated with ceramic production at Höganäs since the last half of the 19th century. From c1969, the firm abandoned earthenware for nonporous wares.
▶ Erik Zahle (ed.), *A Treasury of Scandinavian Design*, New York, 1961:268, No. 295. Cat., Kathryn B. Hiesinger and George H. Marcus III (eds.), *Design Since 1945*, Philadelphia: Philadelphia Museum of Art, 1983.

Andrada, José de
▶ Brazilian designer; born São Paulo.
▶ Andrada showed his fabric designs printed by Atelier français at the 1920 Salon of Société des Artistes Décorateurs, Paris; at the 1921 Salon, showed wallpapers and a carved buffet; until 1938, appears to have participated in the events of the Société; designed in a very simple manner.
▶ Pierre Kjellberg, *Art Déco: les maîtres du Mobilier, le décor des Paquebots*, Paris: Amateur, 1986:30–31.

André, Émile (1871–1933)
▶ French architect and furniture designer; born Nancy.
▶ André was a founding member and the most notable architect of École de Nancy; advocated a union of the arts, designing furniture to coordinate with houses he built; showed architectural studies and photographs of his houses, apartment buildings, and stores. His most noteworthy architecture is 1903 house, 92 and 92 bis quai Claude-le-Lorrain, and 1903 house, 34 rue du Sergent-Blandan, both Nancy. Sons Jacques and Michel took over the family business; collaborated with Jean Prouvé, among others.
▶ Yvonne Brunhammer et al., *Art Nouveau Belgium, France*, Houston: Rice University, 1976, biblio. *Exposition École de Nancy*, 1903:7.

Andreasen, Jens (1924–)
▶ Danish designer.
▶ Studied Det Kongelige Danske Kunstakademi, Copenhagen.
▶ In 1978, he became associated with Georg Jensen Sølvsmedie.
▶ Won 1955 50th-anniversary competition (1954 coffee set) honoring Georg Jensen Sølvsmedie. Work included in 1980 'Georg Jensen Silversmithy: 77 Artists, 75 Years' exhibition, Smithsonian Institution.
▶ Cat., *Georg Jensen Silversmithy: 77 Artists, 75 Years*, Washington: Smithsonian Institution Press, 1980.

Angénieux
▶ French firm.
▶ Angénieux was founded in 1935 by Pierre Angénieux at Saint-Héand; in 1945, produced the *Rétrofocus* lens that was the decisive step towards the single-lens reflex camera. NASA used Angénieux lenses from 1964. In 1985, the firm produced zoom lens *DEM 180F2-3 APO* with automatic focusing from 1.8 meters to infinity, based on an Angénieux patent called DEM (Differential Element Movement).
▶ Agnés Lévitte and Margo Rouard, *100 quotidiens objets made in France*, Paris: APCI/Syros-Alternatives, 1987.

Ängman, Jacob (1876–1942)
▶ Swedish architect and furniture and silver designer; active Stockholm.
▶ 1893 and 1896–1903, studied Kungliga Tekniska Högskolan, Stockholm; 1903–04, in Germany.
▶ 1896–98, he worked at the Otto Meyer Bronze Casters works; in 1899, for the C.G. Hallberg bronze foundry, Stockholm; for a few months under Henry van de Velde at Theodore Müller's works, Weimar; 1903–04, with metal sculptor Otto Bommer in Berlin. 1904–07, he managed the engraving, casting, and metalwork department of Elmquist, Stockholm; 1907–42, worked at the Guldsmedsaktiebolaget (GAB), Stockholm, and became artistic director; 1919–20, worked with architect Gunnar Asplund on St. Peter's Church, Malmö. His simple forms had a contemporary appearance, though much of his silver was traditional.
▶ Silver for GAB shown for the first time abroad at 1925 Paris 'Exposition Internationale des Arts Décoratifs et Industriels Modernes.' Work included in 1927 exhibition of Danish wares, New York Metropolitan Museum of Art and subject of 1942 exhibition, Nationalmuseum, Stockholm.
▶ Åke Stavenow, *Silversmeden Jacob Ängman 1876–1942*, Stockholm: Nordisk Rotogravyr, 1955. Cat., David Revere McFadden

(ed.), *Scandinavian Modern Design 1880–1980*, New York: Abrams, 1982:262. Annelies Krekel-Aalberse, *Art Nouveau and Art Déco Silver*, New York: Abrams, 1989:243–46,251.

Annoni, Franco (1924–)
▶ Italian architect and designer; born and active Milan.
▶ Studied architecture, Politecnico di Milano to 1954; from 1956, Albo, Milan.
▶ An industrial and exhibition designer, his clients included Velca, Ampaglas, Reguitti, Stylresine, Mauri, and Madular. As a specialist in plastics, his designs included a motorcycle helmet by Kartell and furniture by SOLE. He became a member of ADI (Associazione per il Disegno Industriale).
▶ *ADI Annual 1976*, Milan: Associazione per il Disegno Industriale, 1976.

Anthoine-Legrain, Jacques (1907–)
▶ French bookbinder; stepson of Pierre Legrain; active Paris.
▶ Anthoine-Legrain made his debut in 1929, the year his step-father Pierre Legrain died; continued the family bindery business in Paris; designed covers including *Idylles* by Laurens in a geometric pattern with gold fillets and *L'Assassinat considéré comme un des beaux-arts* by Quincey, intended to reflect the author's style with titles reading from bottom to top.
▶ Cover of *Marrakech* commended at 1937 Paris 'Exposition Internationale des Arts Décoratifs et Industriels Modernes.'
▶ Georges Blaizot, *Masterpieces of French Modern Bindings*, Paris, 1947:110–17. *Catalogue de l'exposition de la reliure originale*, Paris: Société de la Reliure Originale, Bibliothèque Nationale, 1947. Thérèse Charpentier, *L'École de Nancy et la reliure d'art*, Paris, 1960:50. John F. Fleming and Priscilla Juvelis, *The Book Beautiful and the Binding as Art*, New York, Vol. 1, 1983:57; Vol. 2, 1985:19. Alastair Duncan and Georges de Bartha, *Art Nouveau and Art Déco Bookbinding*, New York: Abrams, 1989:23,24,116,117,192.

Anti-Design (or Radical-Design)
▶ Italian design movement.
▶ Anti-Design aligned itself with the European student unrest of the late 1960s and early 1970s and was inspired by Ettore Sottsass's 1966 exhibition of furniture in Milan. Members of the movement decided that Florence's industrial and cultural limitations were a handicap, and some moved to Milan, Rome, and Turin. The movement was characterized by idealism and irony. Rather than creating products, Anti-Design was a self-critical philosophy, typified by deliberate exploitation of bad taste. Writing, photography, and idealized architectural projects replaced the production of objects as a means of communicating ideas. Adherents related art to design politics and protested against limitations to political, social, and creative freedom. Many were interested in ecology and expressed themselves through natural materials. Influenced by Claes Oldenburg's soft sculptures, the movement's manifestations were seen in Gatti's, Paolini's, and Teodora's 1969 *Sacco* pellet-filled seat and De Pas's, Lomazzo's, and D'Urbino's 1970 *Joe* seat. The movement declared: 'The designer . . . is no longer the artist who helps us to make our homes beautiful, because they will never be beautiful, but the individual who moves on a dialectical as well as a formal plane and stimulates behavioral patterns which will contribute to full awareness, which is the sole premise required for a new equilibrium of values and finally for the evolution, or, if you will, the recovery of man himself.'
▶ A. De Angelis, 'Anti-Design,' in F. Raggi, 'Radical Story,' *Casabella*, No. 382 1973:39. Penny Sparke, *Ettore Sottsass*, London: Design Council, 1982. Cat., *Michele De Lucchi, A Friendly Image for the Electronic Age: Designs for Memphis*, Alchimia, Olivetti, Girmi, The Hague: Uitgeverij Komplement, 1985. Penny Sparke, *Design in Italy, 1870 to the Present*, New York: Abbeville, 1988.

ANVAR
(Agence pour la Valorisation de la Recherche Nationale)
▶ French government institution.
▶ Established in Paris in 1981, ANVAR supported design research and worked with industry.

APCI
(Agence pour la Promotion de la Création Industrielle)
▶ French government institution.
▶ APCI was founded in Paris in 1983 to support industrial and graphic design as they related to the human environment; published books and catalogs; participated (in conjunction with the Ministry of Culture, from which it receives funding) in sponsoring French and international competitions including 1982 'Concours de mobilier de bureau' (won by Norbert Scibilla, Serge Guillet, and Clen associates), 1985 'Concours pour les arts de la table' (won by Guy Boucher and Société Deshoulières), 1992 'Concours mobilier hospitalier' (won by Sylvain Dubuisson and Corona). Rules dictate that each competition be associated with an established manufacturer who will produce the winner's design.

Arabia
▶ Finnish ceramics firm; located near Helsinki.
▶ Arabia was established in 1873 as a subsidiary of Swedish firm Rörstrand Pottery; produced undecorated glazed stoneware table and kitchen wares at first; later began the production of bone china. The models and molds were from Sweden, and Rörstrand had a controlling interest until 1916. Its first permanent designer, Thure Öberg designed and painted some distinctive vases from 1895. Jac Ahrenberg was employed there. In 1922, when the factory was modernized, Arabia began production of Modern housewares forms; employed several young artists during the early 1920s, including Friedl Holzer-Kjellberg, Greta-Lisa Jäderholm-Snellman and decorators Svea Granlund and Olga Osol. Swedish artist Tyra Lundgren had a studio at Arabia. In 1929, the firm developed the world's largest tunnel kiln for firing household-ware. Its artists in the 1930s included Toino Muona, Aune Siimes, Michael Schilkin, and Birger Kaipiainen. Kurt Ekholm was artistic director 1932–48 and Kaj Frank 1945–78. Arabia helped establish Modern Scandinavian design. Studio potters, including Toino Muona and Kyllikki Salmenhaara, had a works studio. Arabia was taken over in 1947 by the Wärtsilä conglomerate. In 1946, designers Kaarina Aho and, in 1948, Ulla Procopé joined the firm. Its ware included the 1948 heat-proof earthenware cooking and tablewares (produced from 1953); 1957 *Liekki* or *Ruska* ware; 1960 wares designed by Procopé. In the 1960s, Wärtsilä decided to make the designers of its utility ware anonymous.
▶ Wares shown at 1878 Paris 'Exposition Universelle,' 1882 Moscow fair (gold medal), 1893 hygiene exhibition and medical congress in St. Petersburg (silver medals), 1900 Paris 'Exposition Universelle' (gold medal), 1929–30 'Exposición Internacional de Barcelona,' Barcelona (Spain) (grand prize); 1933 (V) Triennale di Milano (diploma of honor for the entire collection); 1951 (IX) Triennale di Milano.
▶ P. Aro, *Arabia Design*, Helsinki, 1958. Leena Maunula, 'A Hundred years of Arabia Dishes: Survey of utility ware models from Arabia since 1874,' *Ceramics and Glass*, Arabia, 1973. C. Marjut Kumela et al., *Arabia*, Helsinki: Uudenmaan Kirjapaino: 1987. Jennifer Hawkins Opie, *Scandinavia: Ceramics and Glass in the Twentieth Century*, New York: Rizzoli, 1989.

Arad, Ron (1951–)
▶ Israeli designer; born Tel Aviv; active London.
▶ 1971–73, studied Jerusalem Academy of Art; Architectural Association, London, under Peter Cook and Bernard Tschumi, to 1979.
▶ Arad worked with Cook at the Architectural Association on a design competition entry for a museum in Aachen; in 1974, settled in London. The high-tech *Kee Klamp* assembly system, incorrectly attributed to Arad, was designed by Stephen Povey and Dennis Groves in 1979. Arad joined Povey and Groves in 1980. After

working for a group of London architects, Arad set up the design firm One Off in 1981, whose logo was designed by Neville Brody. Arad's best known early piece was the 1985 *Rover Chair*, a salvaged automobile seat fitted to a custom-designed tubular-steel frame. These were necessarily individual pieces, since the 1960s model from which the seats were sourced was in dwindling supply. A double-seat or couch-like version followed. Arad produced lighting, including the *Aerial* light inspired by the post-apocalyptic *Mad Max* movies, but later moved from scavenging to new materials; his *Rocking Chair* of the late 1980s represented a more custom-made, refined approach. His 1985 *Well Tempered Chair* was made by Vitra Editions from four pieces of springy tempered steel folded and bolted into place. In 1986, Arad designed two fashion shops (Bazaar, London, and Equation, Bristol) and subsequently Michelle Ma Belle; the Milano Mon Amour shop, Milan; in 1986, Boutique Gauthier; and the executive offices of the clothing firm Bureaux with glass screens by Danny Lane. A 1988 British TV beer commercial featured the *Rover Chair*, as did Akai and Pernod commercials of 1989. The One Off workshop attracted collaborations, including with Caroline Thorman, John Mills, Simon Scott, and American-born designer Lane. Arad designed monumental and sculptural sheet-metal furniture for Sawaya & Moroni and Zeev Aram, and, 1990, for the Robin Wight house, London; mass-produced work, including the 1989 *Schizo* wooden chair and 1989 *Big Easy Red Volume I* vinyl chair produced by Moroso, Italy, and interior-design schemes, including the 1990 Opera House foyer, Tel Aviv.
▶ Work shown at British Furniture Manufacturers' stand, 1984 Salone del Mobile, Milan; Zeus stand, Salone del Mobile 1985–88; exhibitions at the Facsimile Gallery, Milan; 1986 exhibition, Totah Gallery, where *Shadow of Time* cone-shape clock-light shown; 1987 'Les Avante-Gardes de la fin du 20ème siècle,' Centre Georges Pompidou, Paris; 1988 London Metropolis exhibition, Institute of Contemporary Arts; 1989 'British Design,' Boymansvan Beuningen, Rotterdam; exhibitions in Spain, France, Germany, and Japan. Work was subject of 1986 exhibition, Galerie Yves Gastou, Paris; Facsimile Gallery, Milan, 1988; Arte et Industrie, New York, 1990; 1990 'Sticks and Stones' European travelling exhibition organized by Vitra Design Museum, Weil am Rhein; 'Ron Arad, New York,' L'Osservatoria, Milan; Röhsska Konstslöjdmuseet, Gothenburg, 1991.
▶ Deyan Sudjic, *Ron Arad, Restless Furniture*, New York: Rizzoli, 1989. Charlotte Fiell and Peter Fiell, *Modern Furniture Classics Since 1945*, London: Thames and Hudson, 1991:1,150,173,174,145, No. 133.

Arai, Junichi (1932–)
▶ Japanese textile designer and manufacturer; born Kiryu, Gunma.
▶ Arai specialized in deeply textured, sculptural fabrications in which he incorporated celluloid, aluminum tape, metallic filament, silk, and polyester; shifted to technological experimentation, maximizing the potential of punched cards used on jacquard looms by producing them by computer; created fabrics from yarns of different shrinkage rates and under extreme heat; lacerated film into complex weavings; heat-fixed synthetic fibers; supplied fabric designs to clients, including Issey Miyake and Comme des Garçons; closed his firm Anthologie in 1987; subsequently, was active as an independent designer through his Nuno shop, Tokyo.
▶ In 1987, elected Honorary Royal Designer of Industry, London. Work subject of 1993 'Hand and Technology' exhibition, Pacific Design Center, Los Angeles.
▶ Albrecht Bangert and Karl Michael Armer, *80s Style: Designs of the Decade*, New York: Abbeville, 1990:226.

Arbeitsgruppe 4
▶ Austrian art and architecture group.
▶ Active in Vienna from the late 1950s, Arbeitsgruppe was founded by Wilhelm Holzbauer, Friedrich Kurrent, and Johannes Spalt. Its furniture incorporated severe modular elements in vari-

ous bright colors and right-angle planes for their *Musikhaus 3/4* elements.
▶ Günther Feuerstein, *Vienna—Present and Past: Arts and Crafts—Applied Art—Design*, Vienna: Jugend und Volk, 1976:61.

Arbeitsrat für Kunst (Workers' Council for Art)
▶ German art and architecture group.
▶ The radical Arbeitsrat für Kunst was founded in 1918 under the leadership of Bruno Taut, quickly growing in membership to include sculptors Rudolf Belling, Oswald Herzog, and Gerhard Marks. Architects included Otto Bartning, Walter Gropius, Max Taut, and Erich Mendelsohn, and painters Ludwig Meidner, Max Pechstein, Karl Schmidt-Rottluff, and Lionel Feininger. Equivalent to the revolutionary workers' and soldiers' councils established in Germany in the chaotic aftermath of World War I, the group's original intention was to exert political influence through art, but this was not achieved. Its manifesto stated: 'Art and the people must form a unity. . . . From now on the artist alone, as molder of the sensibilities of the people, will be responsible for the visible fabric of the new state.' Gropius succeeded Taut as leader in 1919 and dropped the group's political aspirations, concentrating on the symbolic 'Bauprojekt.' Because of the scarcity of raw materials, hyperinflation, and severe political instability, no structures were realized, and the efforts of the group were directed towards publications and exhibitions. The first program of the Bauhaus, Weimar, of which Gropius became director in the same year, was similar to that of the Arbeitsrat. The group published *Ja! Stimmen des Arbeitsrates für Kunst in Berlin* (1919) and *Ruf zum Bauen* (1920); it disbanded in 1921 and was absorbed into the Novembergruppe.
▶ Its exhibitions included 1919 'Ausstellung für unbekannte Architekten,' 1920 exhibition of workers' and children's art, 1920 'Neues Bauen,' and contemporary German art exhibitions in Amsterdam and Antwerp.
▶ Iain Boyd Whyte in Magnago Lampugnani, *Encyclopedia of 20th-Century Architecture*, New York: Abrams, 1986:16.

Arbus, André (1903–69)
▶ French architect and decorator; born Toulouse.
▶ Studied École des Beaux-Arts, Toulouse.
▶ He was active in the workshop of his father and grandfather, both cabinetmakers; in 1925, became active in the Salons of the Société des Artistes Décorateurs and Salon d'Automne; in 1930, set up the shop Époque in Paris to show his work; settling in Paris in 1932, worked in the traditional modes of Émile-Jacque Ruhlmann, Süe et Mare, and Jules-Émile Leleu; designed furniture with elegant lines and volumes reflective of a kind of Mannerism. His satin-finished lacquer chairs of 1928 shown at the 1932 Salon of the Société des Artistes Décorateurs had Louis XV legs. He designed the *demeure* (lounge) on 1926 oceanliner *Île-de-France*. The influence of Ledoux's neoclassical forms were also evident, yet Arbus's lines were pure, lacked ornament, and gave an appearance of fragility. He compared the joints he used in his pieces to the joints in a human hand; antithetical to Le Corbusier, he used exotic and rare materials in his furniture, and on occasion incorporated the applied painting of Marc Saint-Saëns; after 1935, set up a new decoration department in the Palais de la Nouveauté, called Les Beaux Métiers. His architecture included 1937 Ministry of Agriculture building, Paris, and, after World War II, Médicis Room at the Château de Rambouillet, townhouse of Aimé Maeght on the Parc Monceau, and oceanliners, including *Bretagne, Provence*, and 1961 *France* (the smoking room in the first-class section). Mobilier National commissioned a desk design for US Ambassador W.H. Harriman in 1945. Architecture was important to Arbus, and he drew up plans for Crau, built 1942; Planier in Marseille, built 1950, and the new bridge in Martigues, built 1962.
▶ Furniture shown at the Salons of the Société des Artistes-Décorateurs, events of the Salon d'Automne, 1925 'Exposition Internationale des Arts Décoratifs et Industriels Modernes,' 1937 Paris 'Exposition Internationale des Arts et Techniques dans la Vie Moderne' (a suite and interior design for the 'Maison d'une famille

française'); 1939 'New York World's Fair' (in charge of French section). Received 1935 Blumenthal prize.

▶ Yolande Amic, *Mobilier français 1945–1964*, Paris: Regard, 1983. Pierre Kjellberg, *Art Déco: les maîtres du Mobilier, le décor des Paquebots*, Paris: Amateur, 1986:31–32.

Archigram (Britain)

▶ British architecture collaborative; active London.

▶ Theo Crosby, Warren Chalk, Peter Cook, Dennis Crompton, David Greene, Ron Herron, and Michael Webb established the publication *Archigram* in 1961 while working on the Euston Station underground redevelopment, London. The group, which adopted the name of its journal, had the stated intention of producing 'architecture by drawing.' It associated itself with pop culture and new technology, and wished to bring the materials of space exploration into the home to transform what it saw as the brutality and backwardness of the traditional metropolis; had an appreciable influence on Italian Radical Design of the 1960s. British critic Reyner Banham proselytized Archigram's views worldwide. Its predilection for the expendable was adopted by the Metabolism movement in Japan. Its most widely published project was Herron's 1964 *Walking City*; others included *Underwater Cities* and *Instant Cities*. From 1964, many of the group's ideas were published in their magazine in comic-strip form.

▶ Utopian projects included 1963 Fulham Study, 1964–66 *Plug-in City* (by Cook), 1964 *Walking City* (by Herron), 1966–67 *Cushicle* (by Webb), 1968 *Instant City* (by Cook), and 1968 *Inflatable Suit-Home* (by Greene). Showing for the first time, work was subject of 1963 'Living City' exhibition at the Institute of Contemporary Arts, London. Work included Archigram Capsule at 1970 'Japan World Exposition (Expo '70)'; 1971 project for a summer casino, Monte Carlo; 1971 exhibition of contemporary design in Britain, the Louvre, Paris; 1973 Malaysian Exhibition, Commonwealth Institute, London.

▶ Robert Maxwell in Vittorio Magnago Lampugnani, *Encyclopedia of 20th-Century Architecture*, New York: Abrams, 1986:16–17. Jonathan M. Woodham, *Twentieth-Century Ornament*, New York: Rizzoli, 1990:236–37.

Archigram (France)

▶ French design manufacturer.

▶ Archigram was founded in 1947 by Robert Sentou as a furniture manufacturer in Périgord; commissioned Charlotte Perriand and Roger Tallon, among others, as designers; had a workshop that was used to test new products and techniques, particularly the sophisticated use of various woods.

Archizoom Associati

▶ Italian design studio, specializing in product and architectural design and urban planning; located Florence; active 1966–74.

▶ Archizoom Associati was founded in Florence in 1966 by architects Andrea Branzi, Gilberto Corretti, Paolo Deganello, and Massimo Morozzi; in 1968, industrial designers Dario Bartolini and Lucia Bartolini joined the group. Archizoom was dedicated to bringing Anti-Design to furniture design; designed a number of visionary environments and fantasy furniture models, attempting to move Italian design away from consumerism and high style and arguing against tradition, familiarity, and comfort, as well as what it saw as the anti-humanism of Modernism. Its contemporary, Superstudio, took a similar line. The *Superonda* was Archizoom's version of the standard polyurethane foam sofa; highly graphic and assertive for its time, its silhouette undulated in waves. It described the *Safari* sofa as 'an imperial piece within the sordidness of your own home, a beautiful piece that you simply don't deserve. Clear out your lounges! Clear out your own lives!' The 1969 *Mies* chair produced by Poltronova was particularly daring in conception and starkly simple; it had a chromium frame supporting a stretched-rubber membrane, and while it paid homage to Ludwig Mies van der Rohe, was an essentially ironic example of Archizoom's 'counter-design.' The 1974 *AEO* chair produced by Cassina was radical, and the 1967 *Presagio di Rose*

bed tested conventional notions of good taste. The organization's archives are housed in the Archives of Communication, Institute for the History of Art, University of Parma.

▶ The group (with Superstudio) organized the 'Superarchitettura' exhibition, Pistoia in 1966 and Modena in 1967; 1967 'Dream Beds'; 1968 (II) 'Eurodomus' in Turin; 1968 'Teatro Domani,' Modena; 'Center for Electric Conspiracy,' 1968 (XIV) Triennale di Milano; 1969 'ICSID Design' exhibition, London; 1969 'Domus Design,' Rotterdam; 1969 Salone del Mobile, Milan; 1970 'No-Stop City,' the radical-architecture exhibition.

▶ Cat., *Modern Chairs 1918–1970*, London: Lund Humphries, 1971. *Italy: The New Domestic Landscape*, New York: Museum of Modern Art, 1972:101,103,108,232–39. 'Allestimento come informazione,' *Ottagono*, No. 34, September 1974:82–83. Andrea Branzi, *La Casa Calda: Esperienze del Nuovo Disegno Italiano*, Milan: Idea Books, 1982. Penny Sparke, *Ettore Sottsass*, London: Design Council, 1982. Hans Wichmann, *Italien Design 1945 bis heute*, Munich: Die Neue Sammlung, 1988. Jonathan M. Woodham, *Twentieth-Century Ornament*, New York: Rizzoli, 1990: 264–65.

Arens, Egmont   (1888–1966)

▶ American industrial designer and theoretician.

▶ Arens was sports editor on the Albuquerque *Tribune-Citizen* newspaper from 1916; in 1917, settled in New York, managing his own Washington Square bookstore; from 1918, printed newspapers under the name Flying Stag Press; with an interest in art, became editor of magazines *Creative Arts* and *Playboy* (the first American magazine specializing in Modern art—not the Hefner publication of today); subsequently, was editor of *Vanity Fair*; began his career as an industrial designer at advertising agency Earnest Elmo Calkins where, in 1929, he established an industrial styling department dedicated to what he termed 'consumer engineering'; was influential through his writings in the 1930s, which emphasized the relationship between marketing and design.

▶ Penny Sparke, *Introduction to Design and Culture in the Twentieth Century*, Allen and Unwin, 1986. Arthur J. Pulos, *American Design Ethic: A History of Industrial Design*, Cambridge: MIT, 1983.

Arequipa Pottery

▶ American ceramics studio; located Fairfax, California.

▶ Frederick H. Rhead joined Arequipa Sanatorium, Fairfax, California, as a ceramicist and instructor in 1911. Like Alexander Robertson at the Roblin Art Pottery and Halcyon Art Pottery, Rhead used California clays. Rhead had earlier worked at Weller Pottery in Zanesville, Ohio; employed many of their decorative techniques at Arequipa, including the squeeze-bag method of decoration, which was sometimes used to provide outlines for spaces into which colored glazes and slips were applied; Rhead left Arequipa in 1913 and was succeeded by Albert Solon, who greatly expanded its output. In 1916, F.H. Wilde succeeded Solon; introduced new glazes and attempted to shift Arequipa's production from artware to handmade tiles, particularly the Spanish type. The pottery closed in 1918 and the Sanatorium in 1957.

▶ Wares were shown at 1915 San Francisco 'Panama-Pacific International Exposition.'

▶ Paul Evans in Timothy J. Andersen et al., *California Design 1910*, Salt Lake City: Peregrine Smith, 1980:66–67.

Arflex

▶ Italian furniture manufacturer; located Limbiate.

▶ Pirelli employed Marco Zanuso in 1948 to explore the use of rubber in furniture design and manufacture and established Arflex in 1950 to produce furniture. Zanuso's 1951 *Lady* chair used rubber webbing and foam-rubber padding. The *Sleep-O-Matic* sofabed was introduced in 1954. Franco Albini designed the 1952 *Fiorenza* cross-legged armchair. Other Arflex consultant designers included Tito Agnoli, Carlo Bartoli, Lodovico Belgiojoso, Francesco Berarducci, F. Bini, Cini Boeri, Maurizio Calzavara, Erberto Carboni, Cesare Casati, V. Chiaia, Antonio A. Colombo, Joe Colombo,

Marcello Cuneo, Giancarlo De Carlo, E. Gentili, Martin Grierson, Laura Griziotti, A.A. Guerello, Roberto Lucci, Mario Maioli, Mario Marenco, L. Martellani, Roberto Menghi, Piero Menichetti, Giulio Minoletti, M. Napolitano, Herbert Ohl, Carlo Pagani, Enrico Perressutti, Gustavo Pulitzer, Ernesto N. Rogers, Alberto Rosselli, Carlo Santi, Annig Sarian, Pierluigi Spadolini, M. Tevarotto, Carla Venosta, and Guido Zimmerman. Alberto Burzio joined the firm in 1953 and later became general director; in 1964, became a member of ADI (Associazione per il Disegno Industriale) and, 1966—71, its committee director.

▶ *ADI Annual 1976*, Milan: Associazione per il Disegno Industriale, 1976. *Arflex 1951—1981*, Milan: Arflex, 1981. Cat., Leslie Jackson, *The New Look: Design in the Fifties*, New York: Thames and Hudson, 1991:126—27.

Argy-Rousseau, Gabriel   (aka Joseph-Gabriel Rousseau 1885—1953)

▶ French glassware designer; born Meslay-le-Vidame, Beauce.

▶ Studied École Breguet; 1902—06, École de Sèvres.

▶ At Sèvres, he was a fellow pupil of Jean Cros, son of Henri Cros, who developed the *pâte-de-verre* technique; in 1913, married Marianne Argyriadès, and began signing his name Gabriel Argy-Rousseau adding the first four letters of his wife's name to his own as a gesture of indebtedness to her moral support; in 1921, went into partnership with G.G. Moser-Millot, who financed Argy-Rousseau's atelier; made pieces in opaque *pâte-de-verre* and translucent *pâte-de-cristal* in animal, human, and abstract decorative motifs; from 1909, produced enameled scent bottles; in 1928, produced crystal sculptures based on H. Bourraire drawings and bases, bowls, plates, medallions, pendants, and *bonbonnières*. His Tanagra figurines were made in collaboration with Bourraire *c*1930 in clear crystal. As *pâte-de-verre* artists, Argy-Rousseau, Cros, and Françoise-Émile Décorchemont were in a class of their own.

▶ Showed work first in 1914, participating in the annual Salons of Société des Artistes français from 1919, Salon d'Automne from 1920, and Société des Artistes Décorateurs from 1920. At 1925 Paris 'Exposition Internationale des Arts Décoratifs et Industriels Modernes,' work shown at the Grand Palais and French Embassy and was a member of the jury for glass. Introduced glassware decorated with gold, platinum, silver, and enamel at the 1934 Salon.

▶ R. and L. Grover, *Carved and Decorated European Art Glass*, Rutland, Vermont: Tuttle, 1970:69. H. Hilschenz, *Das Glas des Jugendstils*, Munich, 1972:148—51. *L'Art Verrier*, Lausanne: Galerie des Arts Décoratifs, 1973:89—95. Duret Robert, *Connaissance des Arts*, No. 287, Jan. 1976:79—84. Sylvie Raulet, *Bijoux Art Déco*, Paris: Regard, 1984. Janine Block-Dermant (with preface and catalogue raisonné by Yves Delaborde), *G. Argy-Rousseau: Glassware as Art*, London: Thames and Hudson, 1991.

Arietti, Fabienne   (1956—)

▶ French designer.

▶ Studied École des Arts Appliqués et des Métiers d'Art, Paris.

▶ Arietti (with Dominique Maraval) designed wall decorations, advertising posters, and interiors for stores and hotels; in 1986, began collaborating with Thierry Husson. They designed 1986 *Babylone Chair* sponsored by VIA and produced by Édition AH!. A suite based on the *Babylone* motif was installed in the offices of French Minister of Culture and French National Assembly. In 1987, established Arietti & Husson to market furniture produced by Édition AH!, including pieces operated mechanically by folding and made of 'brutal' materials such as unfinished industrial steel and rough-hewn concrete.

▶ Received the young creators' prize for contemporary furniture (with Husson), 1987 Salon du Meuble, Paris.

▶ *Les Carnets du Design*, Paris: Mad-Cap Productions et APCI, 1986. Cat., *Les années VIA*, Paris: Musée des Arts Décoratifs, 1990.

Arman   (b. Armand Fernández   1928—)

▶ French sculptor; born Nice; active France and USA.

▶ In 1957, decided to be known by his first name, like friend and fellow *nouvel réaliste* Yves Klein; the 'd' was dropped as a result of a printer's error. Began with painterly experiments in three-dimensional assemblages, stamps, and drawn-on objects; in 1960, received international recognition with *Le Plein* (or *Full-Up*) installation (debris from the streets of Paris) at the Galerie Iris Clert, Paris, with a tin of sardines serving as the invitation; is best known for using junk, including the 1961 *Ascent to Heaven (Coupe)* sliced violin, and the welded mass of chromium hotel teapots, 1964 *Accumulation of Sliced Teapots*, and for embedding objects in clear lucite, including squeezed-out tubes of paint; became an American citizen in 1972. In 1990, he cancelled a retrospective at the Nice Musée d'Art Contemporain in protest at mayor Jacques Médecin's anti-Semitism and extreme right-wing sympathies; Médecin was forced to resign. He designed the 1972 *Demi-violin* neon light produced by Atelier A. Arman; designed 1990 44-piece range *Quatuor 84* porcelain dinnerware produced by Art Surface in two shades of gold, and, from 1991, jewelry produced by Movado.

▶ Work first shown in USA at William Seitz's 1961 'The Art of the Assemblage,' New York Museum of Modern Art, and 1961 one-person exhibition, Cordier-Warren Gallery, New York. *Demi-violin* light included in 1985 'Lumière je pense à vous' exhibition, Centre Georges Pompidou, Paris. Work was subject of 1991—92 'Arman, 1955—1991' exhibition, Houston Museum of Fine Arts.

▶ Cat., *Lumière je pense à vous*, Paris: Centre Georges Pompidou, 1985. Colette Gouvion, 'Porcelain: Today's Creations,' *Vogue Décoration*, No. 26, June/July 1990:174. Alison de Lima Greene, 'Arman Recasts Remnants of the Material World,' *The Journal of Art*, Dec. 1991:14.

Armstrong, John   (1893—1973)

▶ British painter, designer, and ceramicist.

▶ 1912—13, studied law, Oxford University; 1913—24, St. Johns Wood School of Art.

▶ In 1931, he executed designs for the ballet *Façade*; in 1933, became a member of artists' group Unit One; painted eight mural panels for Shell-Mex House, London; 1932—52, designed posters for Shell, costumes for Alexander Korda-produced films *The Private Life of Henry VIII* (1933), *The Scarlet Pimpernel* (1935), *Rembrandt* (1935), *Things to Come* (1935), and *I, Claudius* (1937); 1934 *Chevaux* ceramic dinnerware produced by A.J. Wilkinson, Burslem; created theater designs for the Old Vic/Sadler's Wells 1933—34; under Clarice Cliff's direction, designed 1934 tableware in the *Bizarreware* range for A.J. Wilkinson, Royal Staffordshire Pottery; 1940—44, active as an official war artist.

▶ Work subject of his first one-person exhibition, Leicester Gallery. In 1934, work shown with Unit One at the Mayor Gallery, Liverpool. His A.J. Wilkinson ceramics shown at 1934 'Modern Art for the Table,' Harrods department store, London.

▶ Cat., *Thirties: British art and design before the war*, London: Arts Council of Great Britain, Hayward Gallery, 1979:36,78,95, 133,168,212,214,279,281,284.

Arnal, François   (1924—)

▶ French painter and designer; born La Valette, Var.

▶ Arnal established Atelier A in 1969 to produce furniture designed by artists including Arman, Mark Brusse, Roy Adzak, Jean-Michel Sannejouand, César, Peter Klasen, and Arnal himself; produced 151 pieces by 40 artists. The enterprise was discontinued in 1975.

▶ Gilles de Bure, *Le Mobilier français 1965—1979*, Paris: Regard/VIA, 1983.

Arnaldi, Gianluigi   (1938—)

▶ Italian industrial designer; born Asmara, Eritrea.

▶ From 1955, he worked in the design department of Olivetti, designing its *P203* calculating machine and *Lexicon 83DL* typewriter; in 1973, set up his own design studio in Milan; became a

consultant to lighting manufacturers Arteluce; became a member of ADI (Associazione per il Disegno Industriale); began collaborating with Luigi Gaetani in the early 1980s; (with Gaetani) designed the *Daisy* lamp by PAF. Clients included Poltronova and the Design Centre.
► *ADI Annual 1976*, Milan: Associazione per il Disegno Industriale, 1976.

Arndt, Alfred (1898–1976)
► German architect and industrial designer.
► 1921–26, studied Bauhaus, Weimar and Dessau.
► In 1926, he practiced architecture in Thüringen; in 1929, returned to the Bauhaus as a teacher; until 1931, was in charge of the Bauhaus interior-design department, including the furniture workshop; 1929–31, was also head of the wall-painting workshop; designed furniture, including a cantilever chair; in 1933, when the Bauhaus closed, set up again as an architect, working in Probstzella and Jena; in 1948, fled Soviet-controlled East Germany to Darmstad in West Germany, where he was active as a painter and architect.
► Cat., *Alfred Arndt, Maler und Architekt*, Darmstadt: Bauhaus-Archiv, 1968. Hans M. Wingler, *The Bauhaus*, Cambridge: MIT, 1969. Lionel Richard, *Encyclopédie du Bauhaus*, Paris: Somogy, 1985:148. Cat., *Der Kragstuhl*, Stuhlmuseum Burg Beverungen, Berlin: Alexander, 1986:118–19,130.

Arnodin, Maïmé (1916–)
► French designer and entrepreneur.
► Studied engineering, École Centrale des Arts et Manufactures.
► 1951–57, she was active as a journalist and managed the fashion paper *Jardin des Modes*; 1958–60, was sales manager and advertising director, Au Printemps department store, Paris; 1961–67, ran her own *bureau de style* and promotion; 1968–88 (with Denise Fayolle), ran MAFIA (Maïmé Arnodin Fayolle International Associées), an advertising agency and product-design office; (with Fayolle) set up and became director of NOMAD (Nouvelle Organisation Maïmé and Denise), a communications agency; contributed to design consciousness in France and elsewhere.

Arnold, Eisenmöbelfabrik L. und C.
► German furniture manufacturer; located Württemberg.
► From 1871, the firm L. und C. Arnold manufactured furniture incorporating iron tubes; produced metal beds and tubular-steel tables and chairs, including the designs of the Rasch brothers and Arthur Korn. Mart Stam, who in 1926 built one of the first cantilever chairs from gas pipes with fittings, turned over production of the chair to Arnold, who began manufacturing it, with solid inlays, in 1927.
► Barbie Campbell-Cole and Tim Benton (eds.), *Tubular Steel Furniture*, London: The Art Book Company, 1979:13,19. Sonja Günther (introduction), *Thonet Tubular Steel Furniture Card Catalogue*, Weil am Rhein: Vitra Design Publications, 1989.

Arnold, Josef (1884–1960)
► German silversmith; active Hamburg.
► Trained with his father and at the silversmiths P. Bruckmann und Söhne in Heilbronn; studied under Paul Haustein, Stuttgart.
► He taught in Erbach and Hanau and, from 1921, in Hamburg; in 1931, set up his own workshop; like Christoph Kay and Otto Stüber, was active as a silversmith working in Hamburg in the 1920s and 1930s.
► Annelies Krekel-Aalberse, *Art Nouveau and Art Déco Silver*, New York: Abrams, 1989:145,251.

Aroldi, Corrado (1936–) and Danilo Aroldi (1925–)
► Italian designers born Casalmaggiore; brothers.
► The Aroldi brothers began their professional careers in 1960 in their own studio, Milan; designed 1970 *Periscopio* articulated table lamp produced by Stilnovo; became members of ADI (Associazione per il Disegno Industriale). Best known for the lighting and kitchens they designed for clients including Campi e Calegari, Luci, Pabis, Zetamobili, Tonon, and Delta.

► *Periscopio* lamp shown at 1985 'Lumière je pense à vous,' Centre Georges Pompidou, Paris.
►*ADI Annual 1976*, Milan: Associazione per il Disegno Industriale, 1976. Cat., *Lumière je pense à vous*, Paris: Centre Georges Pompidou, 1985. Hans Wichmann, *Italien Design 1945 bis heute*, Munich: Die Neue Sammlung, 1988.

Arp, Jean (aka Hans Arp 1886–1966)
► French sculptor, painter, poet, and glass designer; born Strasbourg; husband of Sophie Taeuber.
► 1904–08, studied in Weimar and Paris.
► Arp met Paul Klee, Vasilii Kandinski, and Robert Delaunay when he showed with the Blaue Reiter Group in Munich in its 1912 exhibition; in 1914, became one of the founders of Dada with Tzara, Janco, Ball, and Hulsenbeck; during World War I, met Max Ernst in Cologne; became a member of the circle in Paris which included Amedeo Modigliani, poet Max Jacob, Guillaume Apollinaire, and Pablo Picasso; married Swiss designer Sophie Taeuber in 1922; from 1916, (with Taeuber) collaborated closely with the Zürich Dada group and on several joint paintings and compositions in a Constructivist style; 1916–19, illustrated Dada publications and created his first abstract polychrome relief wood carving *Dada Relief*, 1916; 1919–20, worked with Max Ernst in Cologne and met Kurt Schwitters; 1926–28, (with Taeuber) collaborated with the de Stijl architect-designer Theo van Doesburg on the reconstruction of the Aubette dance hall and cinema in Strasbourg; 1927–40, lived in Meudon, near Paris, joining the Cercle et Carré in 1930 and Abstraction-Création in 1931; 1925–31, participated in Dada and Surrealism; in the 1930s, turned to sculpture, producing plant-like forms; during the 1940s, lived with his wife, Sonia Delaunay, and Alberto Magnelli in Grasse (France) and later in Switzerland; returning to Meudon in 1946, received notable commissions, including the relief for the 1958 Unesco building in Paris. His glass work was produced by Egidio Constantini in Venice.
► Janine Bloch-Dermant, *Le Guidargus de la Verrerie*, 1985:425. Ian Chilvers et al., *The Oxford Dictionary of Art*, Oxford and New York: OUP, 1988:25,486–87. Cat., *Applied Arts by Twentieth Century Artists*, Christie's Genève, 13 May 1991.

Arquitectonica
► American architecture and design practice; located Miami.
► Arquitectonica was founded in 1977 by Laurinda Spear, her husband Bernardo Fort-Brescia, and Hervin Romney (who left the partnership soon after); Spear was director. The pink house designed for Spear's parents gained publicity for the firm in the early 1980s. The 1978 Atlantis apartments and Palace buildings in Miami were two of the firm's better known works. Arquitectonica's Post-Modern style incorporating Russian Constructivism and De Stijl forms has been called 'romantic Modernism.' The firm's work included 1989 Banco de Credito, Lima.
► Work was subject of 'Arquitectonica: Yesterday, Today, Tomorrow' exhibition, traveling USA. Received design awards including from American Institute of Architects.
► Patricia Leigh Brown, 'Having a Wonderful Time in Miami,' *The New York Times*, 25 Oct. 1990:C1,6. *Arquitectonica*, Washington: AIA Press, 1991.

Arström, Folke (1907–)
► Swedish metalworker.
► Studied Kungliga Konsthögskolan, Stockholm.
► He opened his own design studio in 1934; in 1940, became head designer of Gense, for whom he designed the 1944 *Thebe* range of stainless-steel flatware, hoping to overcome consumer prejudice against the material. His 1956 *Focus de luxe* flatware pattern was particularly popular in the USA and helped establish stainless steel as a material appropriate for formal dining.
► Graham Hughes, *Modern Silver Throughout the World*, New York, 1967: Nos. 59,61. Jay Doblin, *One Hundred Great Product Designs*, New York, 1970: No. 79. Cat., Kathryn B. Hiesinger

and George H. Marcus III (eds.), *Design Since 1945*, Philadelphia: Philadelphia Museum of Art, 1983.

Art Déco

▶ International style of decorative art, design, and architecture.

▶ The term 'Art Déco' was derived in the 1960s from the name of the 1925 Paris 'Exposition Internationale des Arts Décoratifs et Industriels Modernes.' Other terms included Art Moderne, Jazz Moderne, and Déco or the Deco style. In 1908, couturier Paul Poiret showed dress designs in the portfolio *Les robes de Paul Poiret racontées par Paul Iribe* and the 1911 *Les choses de Paul Poiret vues par Georges Lepape* that presaged the Art Déco look. The 1925 exposition, originally planned for 1915, was one of the most influential ever in the applied arts; it included fashion, fabrics, interior decoration, furniture design, and architecture from Italy, Russia, Poland, the Netherlands, Austria, Britain, Spain, Belgium, Czechoslovakia, Japan, Denmark, Sweden, and, pre-eminently, France. The USA and Germany were absent. The Art Déco style first appeared in interiors, furniture, furnishings, and architecture in France; its popularity rapidly grew worldwide. Partly traditional and partly avant-garde, Art Déco amalgamated influences from various movements; these included Dada's machine aesthetic, Surrealism's interest in the subconscious, Cubism's and Fauvism's geometry and bold colors, the machine forms of Futurism, Constructivism, Vorticism, the Wiener Werkstätte and the Münchner Werkbund. Cubist Art Déco architecture came to be called the 'International Style,' coined from the 1932 'International Style' exhibition at the New York Museum of Modern Art; its leaders were Le Corbusier with his 1922 Villa Besno, Vaucresson (France), and Robert Mallet-Stevens, with his 1926–27 residential complex on the rue Mallet-Stevens, Auteuil, Paris. The more formal, traditionally oriented and luxurious aspects of the movement were seen in Pierre Patout's 'Pavillon du Collectionneur' at the 1925 exhibition. An idealistic approach was expressed in Pierre Chareau's and Bernard Bijvoet's 1928–32 Maison de Verre, Paris. Expressionism was seen in Germany in Bernhard Hoetger's 1929 Paula Modersohn-Becker house, Bremen. The influence of Frank Lloyd Wright's block-like structures showed up in the brick buildings of the School of Amsterdam, as seen in Pieter Kramer's 1926 Bijenkorf department store in The Hague and in the work of the De Stijl exponents. Expressed through color and ornamentation in the USA, the Art Déco style was seen in structures including William van Alen's 1928–30 Chrysler building, New York; William Lescaze's 1929–32 Philadelphia Savings Fund Society building, Philadelphia; and Raymond Hood's 1930 McGraw-Hill building, New York. Cubist forms were seen in Wells Coates's 1933 Lawn Road flats, London, and Guiseppe Terragni's 1928 apartment house, Como. The claim that Art Déco was essentially Cubism tamed is supported by the kitsch wares produced in the 1930s. Though largely rejecting abstract art, the middle classes of the 1920s and 1930s purchased Cubist-inspired wallpaper and linoleum in colors that originated in the garish palette of the Ballets Russes de Monte Carlo. Art Déco interiors paraphrased African art (in the furniture of Pierre Legrain), Egyptian temples and furniture (in George Coles's 1929 Carlton Cinema, Upton Park, Essex, England), animal-fantasy themes (Armand-Albert Rateau's 1912 Jean Lanvin apartment, Paris), native-American wares, Babylonian ziggurats, Mexican forms (in the silverware of Jean Puiforcat), and Pre-Columbian architecture (in the Mayan forms of Wright's 1920 Hollyhock House, Hollywood, California, Edward Sibbert's 1935 Kress building, New York, and Starrett and Van Vleck's 1930 Bloomingdale's store, New York); Jacques-Émile Ruhlmann's designs were derived from Louis XV and Louis Philippe styles of the late 18th century, and Süe et Mare's furniture was baroque in style.

▶ Yvonne Brunhammer, *Les années 25: Collections du Musée des Arts Décoratifs*, Paris: Musée des Arts Décoratifs, 1966. Cat., François Mathey, *Les années '25': Art Déco/Bauhaus/Stijl/Esprit Nouveau*, Paris: Musée des Arts Décoratifs, 1966. Bevis Hiller, *Art Déco*, Minneapolis, Minneapolis Institute of Arts, 1971. Cervin

Robinson and Rosemaire Haag Bletter, *Skyscraper Style*, New York, 1975. Bevis Hiller, *The Style of the Century, 1900–1980*, New York: Dutton, 1983. Norbert Mussler in Vittorio Magnago Lampugnani (ed.), *Encyclopedia of 20th-Century Architecture*, New York: Abrams, 1986:17–18. Robert Heide and John Gilman, *Popular Art Deco: Depression Era Style and Design*, New York: Abbeville, 1991.

Art Nouveau

▶ International style of design and architecture.

▶ Idiosyncratic and romantic, the Art Nouveau style derived from the vestiges of academic classicism of the École des Beaux-Arts, Paris, and from studies of plant forms. Between 1880 and 1910, the Art Nouveau movement was influential throughout Europe and, to a lesser degree, in the USA. It had a number of names: 'modern style' in Britain, 'Jugendstil' (from the Munich journal *Jugend*) in Germany; 'paling' (eel) style (based on Victor Horta's work), 'coup de fouet' (whiplash), and 'style des Vingt' (after the Belgian artists' group Les Vingt headed by Octave Maus); 'stile liberty' (after Liberty's in London) or 'stile floreale' in Italy; 'Sezessionsstil' (after the Vienna Secession group) in Austria; 'modernismo' in Spain; 'style Guimard' (after Métro-station architect Hector Guimard), 'style nouille' (noodle style), 'style 1900,' and 'art nouveau' (after Siegfried Bing's Paris shop La Maison de l'Art Nouveau) in France. Claiming to be anti-historicist, in truth the style owed much to the studies of ornamentation of earlier periods; a foretaste of Art Nouveau may be found in Eugène-Emmanuel Viollet-le-Duc's curvilinear metalwork of the 1860s and 1870s and in his brilliant coloring for the stenciled side chapels of Nôtre-Dame, Paris. Its exponents attempted to give value to the ornamental curved lines, possibly geometric in origin from Scotland or Austria, or floral from Belgium or France. The decorative arts first expressed the style in the 1880s in the designs of Arthur H. Mackmurdo and Henry van de Velde, glassware of Émile Gallé, textiles of William Morris, and furniture of Gustave Serrurier-Bovy. Architecture followed, notably with Victor Horta's 1892–93 Tassel house, Brussels, and August Endell's 1897–98 Elvira studio, Munich. A wide range of Art Nouveau architecture followed, including 1893–1900 houses by Paul Hankar, Brussels; Guimard's 1897–98 Castel Béranger; Horta's 1896–99 Maison du Peuple and 1895–1900 Hôtel Solvay, Brussels; structures by Kromhout, Sluyterman, and Wolf in the Netherlands; Henry van de Velde's 1900–02 Museum Folkwang and its interiors, Hagen (Germany); Antonio Gaudí's 1905–10 Casa Milà, Barcelona; and Otto Wagner's 1897 Karlsplatz Stadtbahn station, Vienna. The Art Nouveau style had little influence on subsequent architecture: Peter Behrens, Charles Rennie Mackintosh, and Josef Hoffmann adopted forms associated with the Modern Movement.

▶ F. Schmalenbach, *Jugendstil: Ein Beitrag zu Theorie und Geschichte der Flächenkunst*, Würzburg, 1934. Stephan Schudi Madsen, *Sources of Art Nouveau*, New York, 1956. Helmust (ed.), *Jugendstil: Der Weg ins 20. Jahrhundert*, Heidelberg, 1959. Peter Selz and Mildred Constantine (eds.), *Art Nouveau: Art and Design at the Turn of the Century*, New York: Museum of Modern Art, 1959. Robert Schmutzler, *Jugendstil—Art Nouveau*, Stuttgart, 1962. Frank Russell (ed.), *Art Nouveau Architecture*, London, 1979. Jean-Paul Bouillon, *Art Nouveau 1980–1914*, New York, 1985. Robert L. Delevoy and Barry Bergdoll in Vittorio Magnago Lampugnani (ed.), *Encyclopedia of 20th-Century Architecture*, New York: Abrams, 1986:19–21.

Art Silver Shop, The

▶ American metalsmithy; located Chicago.

▶ The Art Silver Shop was founded in 1912 by Edmund Boker and Ernest Gould. The name was changed in 1934 to Art Metal Studios.

▶ Annelies Krekel-Aalberse, *Art Nouveau and Art Déco Silver*, New York: Abrams, 1989:251.

Artek

See **Aalto, Hugo Alvar Henrik**

Artěl

▶ Czech cooperative and art studio; located Prague.

▶ Active from 1908, Artěl was founded by members of the young Czech avant-garde: Jaroslav Benda, Vratislav H. Brunner, Pavel Janák, Helena Johnová, Jan Konůpek, Marie Teinitzerová, Otakar Vondráček, and Aloie Dyk. Its manifesto declared it was 'against industrial stereotypes and surrogates . . . [and wish] to improve the sense of art and good taste in everyday life . . . from minor decorative objects to textiles, ceramics, furniture, bookbinding, and fashion . . .'; commissioned young designers, including Cubist architects, who worked in different studios and factories; 1911–14, was influenced by Cubism; published its work in magazine *Uměleckýměsíčník* (*Artistic Monthly*), in 1922, designed interiors of hotel Hviezdoslav in Štrbské Pleso (Slovakia), for which Vlastislav Hofman, Jaromír Krejčar, Ladislav Machoň, Otakar Novotný, and Rudolf Stockar designed furniture, textiles, and wall paintings; was unable to withstand the Great Depression and closed in 1934.

▶ Work shown at 1923 (I) Monza 'Esposizione Biennale delle Arti Decorative e Industriali Moderne'; 1928 'Contemporary Culture,' Brno; and others.

▶ A. Adlerová, *České užité umění 1918–1938*, Prague, 1983.

Arteluce

▶ Italian lighting firm.

▶ Gino Sarfatti founded Arteluce in 1939, at first producing lamps and lighting to his own designs; later commissioned other designers, including Vittoriano Vigano, Livio Castiglioni, Gianfranco Fratini, Ezio Didone, and Cini Boeri. The small firm achieved international renown in the 1950s and, continuing into the 1990s, produced imaginative lighting, including the *Donald* desk lamp and 1980 *Jill* halogen floor lamp, both designed by King and Miranda (with G. Arnaldi).

▶ Alfonso Grassi and Anty Pansera, *Atlante del Design Italiano 1940/80*, Milan: Fabbri, 1980.

Artemide

▶ Italian lighting and furniture manufacturer; located Pregnana Milanese.

▶ Studio Artemide was founded in 1959 by Ernesto Gismondi to produce lighting fixtures and plastic furniture; produced the 1966 *Demetrio 45* table in reinforced resin, followed by the *Stadio* range, both designed by Vico Magistretti. Its widely published 1969 *Boalum* snake-like tubular lighting designed by Gianfranco Frattini and Livio Castiglioni was over six feet (two meters) long. Gismondi gave Ettore Sottsass's fledgling Memphis group space in the Artemide showroom from 1981. Artemide's designers include Gismondi himself and Richard Sapper, Vico Magistretti, Antonio Citterio, Steven Lombardi, F.A. Porche, Gregory H. Tew, Angelo Mangiarotti, Ettore Sottsass, Michele De Lucchi, Giancarlo Fassina, Jean Jacques Villaret, Carlo Forcolini, Mario Botta, Enzo Mari, Mario Bellini, Luciano Vistosi, Lella and Massimo Vignelli, Emilio Ambasz, CP&PR Associati, Eric Gottein, Mitchell Mauk, Sergio Mazza, De Pas-D'Urbino-Lomazzi, Örni Halloween, and Mario Morenco. Sapper's 1978 *Tizio* lamp was its most popular product.

▶ Received numerous awards, including the 1967 Premio Compasso d'Oro; showed work at numerous international exhibitions, including 1972 'Italy: New Domestic Landscape,' New York Museum of Modern Art.

▶ Cat., Milena Lamarová, *Design a Plastické Hmoty*, Prague: Uměleckoprůmyslové Muzeum 1972:168.

Artificers' Guild

▶ British silversmiths; located London.

▶ Neil Dawson learned enameling from Alexander Fisher; in 1901, established the Artificers' Guild in London; his wife enameled most of its objects. Even though he bound himself to work exclusively for the Guild for five years, the operation hit financial difficulties in 1903, when the firm was taken over by Montague Fordham. Fordham, previously director of the Birmingham Guild of Handicraft, transferred the activities of the Artificers' Guild to the Montague Fordham Gallery, London; in 1900, bought the premises at Maddox Street that were known until 1906 as 'Montague Fordham, House Furnisher, Jeweller and Metalworker.' 1906–11, the firm was known as 'The Artificers Guild (late Montague Fordham) Art Metalworkers.' A former assistant of Dawson, Edward Spencer succeeded him as principal designer, combining silver with numerous other materials, including ivory, shagreen, coconut, mother-of-pearl, and wood. John Paul Cooper's and Henry Wilson's works were sold at the Guild. One of the few guilds to became a commercial success, it closed in 1942.

▶ Charlotte Gere, *American and European Jewelry 1830–1914*, New York: Crown, 1975:147. Annelies Krekel-Aalberse, *Art Nouveau and Art Déco Silver*, New York: Abrams, 1989:145,251.

Artifort

▶ Dutch furniture manufacturer; located Maastricht.

▶ Artifort used freelance designers, including Kho Liang Le and Pierre Paulin; produced chairs, settees, and tables; first used plastics in Paulin's 1965 *Chair 582* in tensioned rubber and latex foam and his 1965–66 *Armchair 303* in polyester fiberglass; produced Paulin's 1953 *Chair 157* in polyester, ABS, and elastomers and 1967 *F577* chair. In the mid-1960s, Paulin designed a succession of sculptural furniture forms composed of a tubular-steel structure covered in foam and upholstered in elasticized fabric. His ribbon-like 1965 *Chair 582,* produced by Artifort, was widely published. From 1962, British designer Geoffrey Harcourt designed seating for Artifort, which produced more than 20 models of his designs including the 1971 *Armchair 976* in polyester fiberglass. Gijs Bakker became one of its freelance designers in 1979.

▶ *Chair 582* shown at 1965 Utrecht Furniture Fairs and Paris Salon du Meuble. Paulin received 1969 USA Interior Design International Award for *Chair 582*. A 1983 retrospective of his work was mounted at the Paris Musée des Arts Décoratifs.

▶ Cat., *Les Assises du siège contemporain*, Paris: Musée des Arts Décoratifs, 1968. Cat., *Modern Chairs 1918–1970*, London: Lund Humphries, 1971. Cat., Milena Lamarová, *Design a Plastické Hmoty*, Prague: Uměleckoprůmyslové Muzeum, 1972:136.

Artigana Fiorentina Bigiotteria

▶ Italian jeweler; located Florence.

▶ The firm sold imported costume jewelry 1960–66; the only firm in Florence with its own galvanizing plastic laboratory, it produced 'classic' jewelry and costume jewelry; concentrated on enameled and metal goods from the 1970s.

▶ Deanna F. Cera (ed.), *Jewels of Fantasy: Costume Jewelry of the 20th Century*, New York: Abrams, 1992:302.

Arts and Crafts Exhibition Society
See Art-Workers' Guild

Arts and Crafts movement   (American)

▶ A style in interior furnishings and architecture in the USA.

▶ The Arts and Crafts movement in the USA, which lasted from c1875 to the 1910s, was more a mood than a definite style; it is sometimes regarded merely as a precursor of Modernism. Yet the Arts and Crafts movement, with its utopian ideals, was a call for reform of the way people lived and and the way they produced art. The misty, romantic photography of Edward Steichen and Alfred Stieglitz, and Edward Curtis, whose images were supposedly ennobling (though, to modern eyes, demeaningly synthetic) photographed native Americans. The photography all corresponded in idea and intention to the movement which included some of America's greatest artists, who produced works markedly different in form, subject matter, and idea from those of Britain and the rest of Europe. The finest exponents of the style include Charles and Henry Greene in California. The American Arts and Crafts style was popularized by periodicals like Elbert Hubbard's *Little Journeys* series and his journal *The Philistine*, Gustav Stickley's *The Craftsman*, and Adelaide Robineau's *Keramic Studio*. The movement's success was due in part to inexpensive wares, particularly those of the Stickleys, available to middle-class Americans. The use of the machine was far less contentious in the USA than in Britain, though for many American exponents it meant art in a folksy manner, associated with gardening, stenciling, and quilting, and a general rejection of European classicism. Frank Lloyd Wright, Japanese-style printmaker Arthur Wesley Dow, and others sought new ways of creating art and images to rival the best that Europe could produce. Art was to be placed in domestic settings and made available and usable, rather than enshrined. Some Americans thought that there could never be a break with Europe, and held on to European traditions through the American Renaissance movement, which proposed that the foundation of American art should be the importation or reproduction of 18th-century furniture, Old Master paintings, French châteaux, and *objets d'art*. Exponents of this position included Edith Wharton, John La Farge, Isabella Stewart Gardner, and Charles F. McKim. The American Renaissance and its after-effects in the 1920s and 1930s had a distinct American flavor while retaining its links with Europe. Popular taste about the time of World War I, which favored a more traditional and less severe style, brought an end to America's first exposure to Modernist design.

▶ The movement was the subject of the 1976 'The Arts and Crafts Movement in America, 1876–1916,' Princeton University Art Museum, and numerous important subsequent exhibitions.

▶ Gillian Naylor, *The Arts and Crafts Movement*, 1971. Cat., Robert Judson Clark (ed.), *The Arts and Crafts Movement in America, 1876–1916*, Princeton: Princeton University, 1976. David M. Cathers, *Furniture of the American Arts and Crafts Movement*, New York: The New American Library, 1981. Cat., Wendy Kaplan (ed.), 'The Art that Is Life': The Arts and Crafts Movement in America, 1875–1920, Boston: Museum of Fine Arts, 1987. Cat., Richard Guy Wilson (introduction), *From Architecture to Object: Masterworks of the Arts and Crafts Movement*, New York: Hirschl and Adler, 1989: 11–21. Cat., Leslie Greene Bowman, *American Arts and Crafts: Virtue in Design*, Los Angeles: Los Angeles County Museum of Art, 1990.

Arts and Crafts movement (British)

▶ A style in the decorative arts and architecture in Britain.

▶ The Arts and Crafts movement was a reaction against the proliferation, from the mid-19th century, of poorly designed cheap machine-made goods. The movement's leading figure, architect and social reformer William Morris, was inspired by the writings of A.W.N. Pugin and above all John Ruskin, who celebrated the dignity of the craftsman artisan. Morris led the practical revival of handcrafting, and his 1859 Red House at Bexleyheath, Kent, designed by Philip Webb, was the symbolic beginning of the movement. The Red House, in a simplified version of the Gothic Revival style, was offered as an epitome of good taste in contrast to the pretension of contemporary design. The Arts and Crafts philosophy encouraged collaboration; Webb and Morris designed wallpaper together. Extending his influence, Morris set up a group of architects and painters in the firm of Morris, Marshall, and Faulkner. Based on Henry Cole's Art Manufacturers, Morris's company produced tapestries, fabrics, wallpaper, and stained glass. A Socialist, Morris wrote *News from Nowhere* (1891), a utopian novel. Though intended for the middle classes, Morris's goods, with their handmade production based on medieval models, were expensive and exclusive. Influential groups grew from the foundations laid down by Morris, including the Century Guild of Arts founded in 1882 by Arthur Heygate Mackmurdo and his friends, and the St. George's Art Society founded in 1883 by, among others, William Richard Lethaby and Edward S. Prior. In 1884,the latter organization became the Art-Workers' Guild, from which the Arts and Crafts Exhibition Society was formed in 1888. Allied with the historicist aesthetic of the Pre-Raphaelites and adamantly against machine production, Walter Crane was the Society's first president. C.R. Ashbee, Prior, C.F.A. Voysey, Lethaby, Edwin Lutyens, and George Walton exhibited at the events of the Society; Charles Rennie Mackintosh and the Glasgow School were excluded because of their tolerance of machine-work. A landmark

for the movement was the founding in 1888 of Ashbee's Guild and School of Handicraft. No longer able to shun the machine and having decided publicly to use it as an ally, Ashbee used industrial-design methods. Arts and Crafts exponents were especially interested in house design. Site-specific furniture and furnishings were instrumental in the creation of the house as a total work of art. Ebenezer Howard's book *Tomorrow, A Peaceful Path to Social Reform* (1898; renamed *Garden Cities of Tomorrow*) initiated the Garden City movement, which grew out of the theories espoused by the Domestic Revival. The efforts of these crusaders resulted in a widespread rejection of 19th-century historicism and in an interest in high standards of taste augmented by machine production. Hermann Muthesius, who worked in England for a time, pursued the amalgamation of art, industry, and the machine in the Deutscher Werkbund. The Arts and Crafts movement prepared the way for both the Art Nouveau style, through its philosophy of design and ornamentation, and the Modern movement, through its rigorous discussions of design and architecture. Although the influence of the Arts and Crafts movement was far-reaching and exceptionally long-lived, its study has tended to be neglected through a historical preoccupation with Modernism, the International Style, and anti-ornamentation; yet Henry van de Velde, Muthesius, Adolf Loos, Walter Gropius, and other Modern movement pioneers acknowledged a debt to the British idea of an environment that served and expressed human needs.

▶ C.R. Ashbee, *Craftsman in Competitive Industry*, Essex House Press, 1908. Nikolaus Pevsner, *The Sources of Modern Architecture and Design*, London, 1968. P. Davey, *The Arts and Crafts Movement in Architecture*, London, 1980. Giulia Veronesi and Lampugnani in Vittorio Magnago Lampugnani (ed.), *Encyclopedia of 20th-Century Architecture*, New York: Abrams, 1986:22–23. Gillian Naylor, *The Arts and Crafts Movement*, London: Trefoil, 1990.

Art-Workers' Guild

▶ British craftsmen's fraternity; located London.

▶ The Art-Workers' Guild was founded in 1884 by members of St. George's Art Society, a group of architects and artists who were pupils and assistants of architect Richard Norman Shaw. Its founding members were W.R. Lethaby, Ernest Newton, Edward Prior, Mervyn Macartney, and Gerald Horsley. Another group, 'The Fifteen,' led by Lewis F. Day and Walter Crane, joined the group early on. All the leading members of the Craft Revival Movement became members, including Basil Champneys, Beresford Pite, C.F.A. Voysey, Harrison Townsend, Edwin Lutyens, Roger Fry, George Walton, Shaw, C.R. Ashbee, William Morris, and A.H. Mackmurdo. The Art-Workers' Guild provided a meeting place for lectures and discussions. An extension of Guild activities, the Arts and Crafts Exhibition Society was developed in 1888 by a group within the Art-Workers' Guild. With exhibitions in 1888, 1889, and 1890, quality began to decline after the 1890 event, and the events were held every third year until the beginning of World War I. The Guild (still in existence today) and the Exhibition Society contributed to the longevity of the Craft Movement in England.

▶ Isabelle Anscombe and Charlotte Gere, *Arts and Crafts in Britain and America*, New York: Rizzoli, 1978.

Arzberg, Porzellanfabrik

▶ German porcelain manufacturer.

▶ An industrial area for the production of porcelain was established in 1887 in Arzberg (Bavaria); in 1928, was named the Porzellanfabrik Arzberg; became known for its simple Functionalist tablewares, of which the widely published 1931 *Model 1382* porcelain dinnerware designed by Hermann Gretsch, in both plain white and with a thin red line, is an example. The service was used by the SS in the Nazi period. Arzberg's designers included Heinrich Löffelhardt, Hans Theo Baumann, Lutz Rabold, and Matteo Thun-Hohenstein.

▶ *Kunst der 20er und 30er Jahre*, vol. III, Berlin Sammlung Karl H. Bröhan. Cat., Wilhelm Siemen (ed.), *100 Jahre Porzellan-*

fabrik Arzberg. 1887–1987, Hohenberg a. d. Eger: Museum der Deutschen Porzellanindustrie, 1987.

Asbjørnsen, Svein   (1943–)
▶ Norwegian interior architect and furniture designer.
▶ Studied Statens Håndverks -og Kunstindustriskole, Oslo, to 1967.
▶ An NIL interior designer, he established the firm More Design team in Norway with Jan Lade in 1970. Their 1970 *Ecco* chair was produced by L.K. Hjelle Møbelfabrikk and *Split Returner* lounge chair of *c*1986 by Hag, Norway.
▶ More Design received 1971 Norwegian Design Prize (*Ecco* chair group) and first prize (*People Are Different* furniture), 1976 Nordic Furniture Competition. Asbjørnsen and Lade received first prize (*Split* furniture group), 1981 Nordic Furniture Competition.
▶ Robert A.M. Stern (ed.), *The International Design Yearbook*, New York: Abbeville, 1985/1986: Nos. 138–39. Fredrik Wildhagen, *Norge i Form*, Oslo: Stenersen, 1988.

Ascher, Zika   (1910–) and Lida Ascher
▶ Czech textile designers; husband and wife.
▶ They emigrated to England in the 1930s; in 1942, set up a screen-printing firm in London; with Zika as printer and Lida as designer, produced bold, vibrant prints in bright colors with black accents; became well known when they began commissioning Henri Matisse, Jean Cocteau, and Henry Moore to design scarves, known as Ascher Squares; produced fabrics for clothing designers including the 1952 cabbage-rose prints for Christian Dior.

Åse, Arne   (1940–)
▶ Norwegian ceramicist; active Oslo.
▶ 1965, studied Bergens Kunsthåndversskale, Bergen.
▶ From 1965, Åse taught at the Statens Håndverks -og Kunstindustriskole, Oslo, and was head of its ceramic department from 1975–86; in 1965, set up his own workshop, producing stoneware and porcelain; from 1986–87, professor, ceramics department, Bergens Kunsthåndversskole.
▶ Cat., David Revere McFadden (ed.), *Scandinavian Modern Design 1880–1980*, New York: Abrams, 1982:262. Fredrik Wildhagen, *Norge i Form*, Oslo: Stenersen, 1988:174. Jennifer Hawkins Opie, *Scandinavia: Ceramics and Glass in the Twentieth Century*, New York: Rizzoli, 1989.

Ashbee, Charles Robert   (1863–1942)
▶ British furniture, furnishings, and jewelry designer; born Isleworth.
▶ Studied Cambridge University and under architect G.F. Bodley.
▶ He became a designer, writer, and major force in the Arts and Crafts movement; strongly influenced by John Ruskin's and William Morris's Romantic anti-industrialism, in 1888 he founded the Guild and School of Handicraft, Toynbee Hall, London, where he lived; for the school, designed metalwork and furniture in a kind of light Morris style; translated and published Benvenuto Cellini's *Treatises* in 1898; moved the school and Guild to Essex House, Mile End, London, in 1890; in 1902, moved the Guild's workshops to the idyllic setting of Chipping Campden, in the Cotswolds, where the School of Arts and Crafts was active 1904–14; designed most of the Guild's work, although some pieces were designed by Hugh Seebohm. The Guild's two retail shops in London were a financial burden to Guild's activities. In 1907, a catalog was issued that offered silverwork and jewelry at cheap prices; in 1908, the Guild, unable to compete with commercial ventures such as Liberty, went into liquidation. Some of the craftsmen continued to work independently. Ashbee played a part in movements ranging from the conservation of historic buildings to early town planning; greatly influenced the designs of Liberty's jewelry and silverwork and the Vienna Secession; in 1909, published *Modern English Silverwork*; met Frank Lloyd Wright in 1910 in Chicago, with whose work and philosophy he was impressed. Ashbee wrote the introduction to Wright's 1911 photographic portfolio *Ausgeführte Bauten*; built in Budapest and Sicily; lectured in the USA; a prolific designer, built notable riverside houses in Chelsea, designed simple sturdy furniture, and rendered jewelry in a complicated Art Nouveau style (a term he would have rejected). His silver work consisted of both traditional and original vessels with dramatic, disproportionate, sweeping thin handles. After the death of Morris and the demise of Morris's Kelmscott Press, in 1898, Ashbee founded the Essex House Press, printing books by hand; giving up his practice, was a professor of English at Cairo University 1915–19; worked on restoring Jerusalem 1919–23.
▶ From 1888, he showed with the Arts and Crafts Exhibition Society and in the Vienna Secession exhibitions. His work was the subject of the 1981 'C.R. Ashbee and the Guild of Handicraft' at the Art Gallery and Museum, Cheltenham, 1981.
▶ C.R. Ashbee, *A Book of Cottages and Little Houses*, London, 1906. Charlotte Gere, *American and European Jewelry 1830–1914*, New York: Crown, 1975:147–48. Alistair Service, *Edwardian Architecture*, London, 1978. Cat., *C.R. Ashbee and the Guild of Handicraft*, Cheltenham, 1981. Alan Crawford, *C.R. Ashbee and the Guild of Handicraft*, Cheltenham, 1981. Alan Crawford, *C.R. Ashbee, Architect, Designer and Romantic Socialist*, New Haven: Yale, 1985. Annelies Krekel-Aalberse, *Art Nouveau and Art Déco Silver*, New York: Abrams, 1989:145,251.

Ashley, Laura   (b. Laura Mountney 1926–88)
▶ British fashion and fabric designer and entrepreneur; born Merthyr Tydfil.
▶ Ashley was the leading exponent of the 'cottagey' style associated with rural British design and chintz fabric. In 1953, she began making screen-printed linen tea-towels in her attic in London for herself and friends; encouraged by husband Bernard Ashley, set up textile printing firm Ashley-Mountney, active 1954–68 (1954–56 in Pimlico, London; 1956–61 in Kent; 1961–68 in Machynlleth, Wales) and Laura Ashley active from 1968; adapted 19th-century printed cotton fabrics for her dress designs. Her clothing line began with the 1961 cotton-drill apron. Eventually setting up shops worldwide, she transformed her hobby into a large enterprise, producing women's and children's wear and promoting a nostalgic, idealized vision of rural idyll that struck a chord with urban middle-class Britons in the 1960s and 1970s. She diversified into coordinated furnishing fabrics, wallpaper, and paint. The firm published numerous self-promotional books, including the *Laura Ashley Book of Interior Decoration* (1983) and annual catalogs. In the late 1980s, the firm began producing furniture in a similar historicist mode; by 1991, had 475 stores in 15 countries, selling 25,000 products including paint, perfume, furniture, women's clothing, and the floral chintzes for which it was best known. When Ashley died in 1988, her son Nick Ashley assumed control of the firm.
▶ Jonathan M. Woodham, *Twentieth-Century Ornament*, New York: Rizzoli, 1990:242–243,271. Charles Gandee, 'Nick Ashley: Life after Laura,' *House and Garden*, April 1991:212.

Asplund, Erik Gunnar   (1885–1940)
▶ Swedish architect and designer; active Stockholm.
▶ 1905–09 studied Kungliga Konsthögskolan, Stockholm, and privately under Begsten, Tengbom, Westman, and Österberg.
▶ Initially, he chose painting; in 1909, set up his own architecture office in Stockholm, designing primarily small houses and entering many competitions, winning those in 1912 and 1913 for schools (one of which was later built); 1912–13, was assistant lecturer in Stockholm and, 1917–18, special instructor in ornamental art; 1917–20, was editor of journal *Teknisk Tidskrift Arkitektur*; designed architecture and furniture 1911–30 in a neoclassical style then fashionable in Sweden; achieved some notoriety as a result of the designs for room sets for the 1917 exhibition at Liljevalchs Art Gallery in Stockholm; in 1920, visited the USA on research for public library for Stockholm City Council; designed furniture for the Nordiska Kompaniet and for the Stockholm City Hall, and for his own 1924–27 Stockholm City Library. The production of his 1925 *Senna Chair* and other models were revived in the 1980s by Cassina. As chief architect, he was the

creative force behind the 1930 'Stockholmsutstälaningen' exhibition organized by the Svenska Sljödföreningen (the equivalent to the Deutscher Werkbund) under its director Gregor Paulsson. Originally planned as a local event, this became an international exposition of the Modern movement by Asplund; his Paradiset Restaurant was considered by many to be the best building there. Asplund's exhibition buildings introduced Sweden to the International Style and the social ideals of the Svenska Sljödföreningen. He was professor of architecture at Kungliga Konsthögskolan, Stockholm, 1931–40; though identified with Modernism, was no radical and often produced simplified neoclassical forms incorporating decorative details and color influenced by the Scandinavian neo-classical and romantic revival. Architecture included 1917–18 Snellman Villa, Djursholm; 1918–20 Woodland Chapel, Stockholm; 1922–23 Skandia Cinema, Stockholm; 1924–27 Stockholm City Library; buildings at 1930 'Stockholmsutstälaningen'; 1933–35 Bredenberg store, Stockholm; 1933–37 State Bacteriological Laboratory, Stockholm; 1934–37 Gothenburg City Hall Extension; and 1935–40 Crematorium, Stockholm South Cemetery.

▶ Received 1913 first prize (extension to the Law Courts in Gothenburg; realized in 1937 after some controversy over façade style) and 1914 international competition (with Sigurd Lewerentz; layout of the Stockholm South Cemetery).

▶ Work shown at 1917 'Home' exhibition (room sets), Liljevalchs Art Gallery, Stockholm, and at 1925 Paris 'Exposition Internationale des Arts Décoratifs et Industriels Modernes.'

▶ Bruno Zevi, *E. Gunnar Asplund*, Milan, 1948. Gustav Holmdahl, Sven Ivar Lind, and Kjell Odeen (eds.), *Gunnar Asplund, Architect 1885–1940*, Stockholm, 1950. E. de Maré, *Gunnar Asplund: A Great Modern Architect*, London, 1955. Stuart Wrede, *The Architecture of Erik Gunnar Asplund*, Cambridge, MA, and London, 1980. Cat., David Revere McFadden (ed.), *Scandinavian Modern Design 1880–1980*, New York: Abrams, 1982:262. *Eric Gunnar Asplund: mobili*, Milan, Electa, 1985. Arnold Whittick in Vittorio Magnago Lampugnani (ed.), *Encyclopedia of 20th-Century Architecture*, New York: Abrams, 1986:22–23.

Associazione per il Disegno Industriale

▶ Italian professional designers' group.

▶ Associazione per il Disegno Industriale was founded in 1956 by Sergio Asti and others. Almost all important Italian industrial designers are members. Its awards competition, Premio Compasso d'Oro, was established in 1954 and placed under the aegis of ADI.

Asti, Sergio (1926–)

▶ Italian architect and designer; born and active Milan.

▶ Studied architecture, Politecnico di Milano, to 1953.

▶ He set up his own studio in Milan in 1953; 1956, became a founding member of ADI (Associazione per il Disegno Industriale); designed furniture, lighting, glassware, wood products, ceramics, electrical appliances, interiors, stores, and exhibitions; lectured widely. His designs included the 1956 kitchen system for Boffi, 1970 folding chair for Zanotta, 1956 soda syphon for Saccab. In 1953, he began experimenting in plastics; 1957–58, executed acrylic-resin lamp designs for Kartell, its first models to be produced in acrylics; designed the stainless-steel flatware for ICM, 1969–72 architectonic range of vases for Knoll, 1976 *Boca* flatware for Lauffer, 1961 *Marco* blown-glass vase for Salviati, 1974 TV-set and other appliances for Brionvega, 1978–79 *Glasses for Alice* glassware for Salviati, 1979 and 1981–82 cookware for Corning France, and 1975 ski-boots. Reflective of Josef Hoffmann motifs, his 1972 *Dada* tableware was produced by Ceramica Revelli in an anti-craft matt-white and black ceramic.

▶ Received a silver (1957 soda syphon by Saccab) and gold medal at 1957 (XI) Triennale di Milano, 1962 Compasso d'Oro (*Marco* vase), and numerous other awards. Work shown extensively including at 1951 (IX), 1954 (X), 1957 (XI), 1960 (XII), 1964 (XIII), 1968 (XIV) Triennali di Milano; 1968 (II) Turin 'Eurodomus'; 1959, 1963, 1971 exhibitions, New York Museum of Modern Art; 1961 Biennale di Venezia; 1971 exhibition, Victoria and Albert Museum; 1972 exhibition, Musée des Arts Décoratifs;

1983–84 'Design Since 1945' exhibition at the Philadelphia Museum of Art; and in Brussels, Copenhagen, Prague, Stockholm and Tokyo. Work was subject of 1970 exhibition, Design Research store, New York.

▶ 'Forme nuove per un'antica fornace,' *Domus*, No. 421, Dec. 1964:57–60. 'Segio Asti, tradition, recherches et dynamisme,' *L'Oeil* No. 190, Oct. 1970:60–67. 'Sergio Asti,' *Interiors*, Nov. 1970:120–21. Cat., Milena Lamarová, *Design a Plastické Hmoty*, Prague: Uměleckoprůmyslové Muzeum 1972. 'From Italy: New Vases for Knoll International,' *Domus*, No. 518, Jan. 1973:36–37. 'Le Design italien: Sergio Asti,' *L'Oeil*, Jan.–Feb. 1976:66–71. *ADI Annual 1976*, Milan: Associazione per il Disegno Industriale, 1976. 'Piccoli progetti ere ecologiche,' *Modo*, No. 54, Nov. 1982:46–48. Cat., Kathryn B. Hiesinger and George H. Marcus III (eds.), *Design Since 1945*, Philadelphia: Philadelphia Museum of Art, 1983. Hans Wichmann, *Italien Design 1945 bis heute*, Munich: Die Neue Sammlung, 1988.

Astori, Antonia (1940–)

▶ Italian designer; born Milan; sister of Enrico Astori.

▶ Studied industrial and visual design, Athenaeum, Lausanne, to 1966.

▶ From 1968, she designed for Driade, the firm she and brother Enrico Astori founded; designed single pieces and furniture groups and systems that were instrumental in forming Driade's design reputation; pursued a style said to be derived from De Stijl, particularly the paintings of Piet Mondriaan and designs of Gerrit Rietveld. Her first system was the 1968 Driade 1. Her best known furniture ranges included 1973 *Oikos* and *Kaos*, the former meticulously constructed of hand-coated particleboard and sold flatpacked. Designed *Bri* system with Enzo Mari and various shops in Paris, London, Brussels, and others. Fiorella Gussoni was her technical collaborator; collaborated on projects with Marithé and François Barband in Paris, Brussels, and Milan.

▶ 1980 *Astragale* table shown at 1991 'Mobili Italiani 1961–1991: Le Varie Età dei linguaggi' exhibition, Salone del Mobile, Milan. She won 1979 and 1981 Premi Compasso d'Oro.

▶ Robert A.M. Stern (ed.), *The International Design Yearbook*, New York: Abbeville, 1985/1986: Nos. 147–48. Fumio Shimizu and Matteo Thun (eds.), *The Descendants of Leonardo: The Italian Design*, Tokyo, 1987:336. *Mobili Italiani 1961–1991: Le Varie Età dei linguaggi*, Milan: Cosmit, 1992.

Astuguevielle, Christian (1946–)

▶ French designer; active in Paris

▶ His best known work involved antique chairs which he wrapped in rope and then painted.

▶ In 1989, work shown first time at Galerie Yves Gastou, Paris.

Asymétrie

▶ French cooperative group of designers.

▶ Furniture designer and interior architect Bernard Fric (1944–) established Asymétrie in 1984. For every program it supports, groups are organized by one or two people who are competent in various disciplines, including graphics, architecture, lighting, and scenic design. From 1988, Marc Alessandri was a freelance designer.

▶ Work subject of 'La fureur de lire' exhibition sponsored by French Ministry of Culture, Musée Louis Vuitton, Asnières, near Paris.

Atelier Martine
See Poiret, Paul

Atelier Vorsprung
See Frank, Beat

Athelia

▶ French design studio.

▶ Athelia was opened in 1928 as the design workshop of Trois-Quartiers department store, Paris; was managed by architect Robert Bloch; employed a group of designers who produced sober yet classical furniture and interiors, in some cases discreetly incorp-

orating metal and consistently paying great attention to detail. In the 1930s, Paul Delpuech succeeded Bloch as director.
▶ Pierre Kjellberg, *Art Déco: les maîtres du Mobilier, le décor des Paquebots*, Paris: Amateur, 1986:32.

Atika
▶ Design group; located Prague.
▶ Formed in 1987, Atika was aligned with the Anti-Design orientation of Archizoom, Alchimia, and Memphis in Italy. One of its goals was to support Post-Modernism, seeking an outlet for experimentation and new means of expression. Its expressive language used signs of symbolic meanings that referred to nature, society, and urban destruction. The designers worked mostly with wood, metal, and leather in a wide color range. Describing themselves as angry young designers, its members included Bohuslav Horák, Vít Cimbura, Jaroslav Šusta Jr., Jiří Pelcl, and Jiří Javůrek. Atika was dissolved in 1992.
▶ Albrecht Bangert and Karl Michael Armer, *80s Style: Designs of the Decade*, New York Abbeville, 1990:76,231. Cat., *Object Contra Design Atika*, Moravská Galerie v Brně, Prague: Forum Praha, 1992.

Auböck, Carl (1924—)
▶ Austrian architect and designer; born Vienna.
▶ Studied Technische Universität, Vienna, to 1949; 1952, Massachusetts Institute of Technology, Cambridge, Massachusetts.
▶ He designed furniture, ceramics, wood, and metal produced by the Auböck family firm, Vienna, founded by his father and still active on a craftsmanship basis, producing wooden and metal objects occasionally with leather and textiles, blending Scandinavian and Viennese styles. He designed many houses, exhibitions, scientific instruments, and buildings; interested in ergonomics and a crafts orientation, designed machinery, packaging, sporting goods, and scientific instruments for other firms. His 1957 *2060* cutlery service was produced by Neuzeughammer-Ambosswerk and 1963 microscope by Optische Werke C. Reichert. He designed glassware and enamel cooking wares for Culinar; taught at the Hochscule für angewandte Kunst in Vienna; was primarily engaged in object design; worked on chairs for serial production; designed ski books with improved fastenings, brightly colored ski wear, and ceramic and metal tableware, including 1990 oven-to-table ware.
▶ Jocelyn de Noblet, *Design*, Paris, 1974: 252. Günther Feuerstein, *Vienna—Present and Past: Arts and Crafts—Applied Art—Design*, Vienna: Jugend und Volk, 1976:61,76,78,79. Carl Auböck, 'Design für Überfluss, Design für Not,' in *Design ist unsichtbar*, Vienna, 1981:573—80. Cat., Kathryn B. Hiesinger and George H. Marcus III (eds.), *Design Since 1945*, Philadelphia: Philadelphia Museum of Art, 1983.

Aucoc, Maison
▶ French silversmiths; located Paris.
▶ The firm was established in Paris in 1821 by Casimir Aucoc. In 1854, Louis Aucoc succeeded his father as director of the firm and soon added jewelry to its inventory, although it was considered a sideline until 1900. In 1876, René Lalique was apprenticed to Louis Aucoc. When André Aucoc took over the direction of the firm, he concentrated on the reproduction of the work of famous silversmiths of the 18th and 19th centuries. In 1900, the firm produced works by Edouard Becker.
▶ Silverwares shown at 1902 St. Petersburg 'Comité français des Expositions à l'Étranger'; 1925 Paris 'Exposition Internationale des Arts Décoratifs et Industriels Modernes'; 1930 'Décor de la Table,' Musée Galliéra in Paris.
▶ Charlotte Gere, *American and European Jewelry 1830–1914*, New York: Crown, 1975:149. Annelies Krekel-Aalberse, *Art Nouveau and Art Déco Silver*, New York: Abrams, 1989:60,63,66,70, 247,251.

AUDAC
See American Union of Decorative Artists and Craftsmen

Audsley, George Ashdown (1838–1925) and Maurice Ashdown Audsley
▶ British architects and authors; born Elgin; active Liverpool.
▶ The Audsley brothers set up an architecture practice in Liverpool in 1856. Their ornamental work was derived from that of Christopher Dresser. They published books *The Sermon on the Mount* (1861), printed chromolithographically in the manner of Owen Jones's *Grammar of Ornament* (1856), *Outlines of Ornament in the Leading Styles* (1881), and *The Practical Decorator and Ornamentalist* (1892). George Audsley published *The Art of Chronolithography* (1883).
▶ Stuart Durant, *Ornament from the Industrial Revolution to Today*, Woodstock, NY: Overlook, 1986:45,320.

Aulenti, Gae (b. Gaetana Aulenti 1927—)
▶ Italian architect and designer; born Stella, near Udine; active Milan.
▶ Studied architecture, Politecnico di Milano, to 1954.
▶ She was a member of Movimento Studi per l'Architettura (MSA) (Movement for Architectural Studies) 1955—61; 1955—65, trained with the Ernesto N. Rogers architecture group; under Rogers as editor, was a member of the editorial department of *Casabella-continuità*; in 1960, became a member of ADI (Associazione per il Disegno Industriale), of which she was vice-president in 1966; 1964—69, taught at the Politecnico di Milano; in the late 1950s, became known as an exponent of the controversial Neo-Liberty style, illustrated by her 1961 *Sgarsul* bentwood rocking chair produced by Poltronova; from 1964, designed lighting for Francesconi, Martinelli, Candle, Artemide, Kartell, and Stilnovo; designed showrooms for Olivetti in Paris in 1967 and Buenos Aires in 1968, for Knoll in Boston in 1968 and in New York in 1970, and for Fiat in Turin, Brussels, and Zürich 1970—71; from 1965, worked as an architect and designer; an executive committee member of *Lotus International* from 1974; served on the editorial boards of its several architectural periodicals. Her architecture and industrial-design office was located in Milan, where she drew up stage designs from 1975 for operas with theatre director Luca Ronconi for his Laboratorio de Luca Ronconi in Prato (Italy), including *L'Anitra Selvatica*, Genoa, and *Wozzeck* at La Scala, Milan. 1976—79, she collaborated on research with members of the Laboratorio di Progettazione Teatrale in Prato; in 1980, was commissioned to design the architectural interiors of the Musée d'Orsay, Paris; worked on a project for the Musée d'Art Moderne, Centre Georges Pompidou, Paris. Her designs included the 1965 *Pipistrello* telescoping table lamp by Martinelli Luce, 1965 *Jumbo* coffee table by Knoll, 1973 *Faretti* lighting range by Zanotta, 1975 furniture collection by Knoll, 1975 *Alcindo* and 1975 *Patroclo* table lamps by Artemide, 1980 coffee service by Cleto Munari, 1980 *Tavolo con ruote* table by Fontana Arte, 1983 *Cardine* sawhorse-table by Zanotta, 1984 *706 Appia* table series by Zanotta, 1985 Fusital hardware-fittings, 1986 *0086* sofa by Maxalto.
▶ Work shown in Italy, America, and Japan, including one-person exhibitions. Participated in numerous Triennali di Milano, receiving award for her design of the Italian pavilion at its 1964 (XIII) secession. 'La Scatola Armonica' shown at 1985 Triennale di Milano. Received silver medal (*Faretti* range of lighting by Stilnovo) at the 1973 (XV) Triennale di Milano and 1977 Design Center Stuttgart Award (furniture collection by Knoll). In 1987, appointed Chevalier de la Légion d'honneur. Participated in National Conference of Design, Aspen, Colorado; convention of the American Society of Interior Designers (which elected her an honorary member); International Symposium of Interior Design, Medellin (Colombia).
▶ Cat., *Design Process Olivetti 1908–1978*, Los Angeles: Frederick S. Wight Art Gallery, 1979:254. Alfonso Grassi and Anty

Pansera, *Atlante del design italiano: 1940–1980*, Milan: Fabbri, 1980:157,166,179,188,176. P.-A. Croset, 'Aménagement intérieur del Museo d'Orsay,' *Casabella 46*, No. 482, 1982:48–61. Cat., Kathryn B. Hiesinger and George H. Marcus III (eds.), *Design Since 1945*, Philadelphia: Philadelphia Museum of Art, 1983. Cat., *Lumière je pense à vous*, Paris: Centre Georges Pompidou, 1985. P.-A. Croset and S. Milesi, 'Gae Aulenti, Piero Castiglioni, Italo Rota: Il nuovo allestimento del Museo Nazionale d'Arte Moderna nel Centre Georges Pompidou,' *Casabella 49*, No. 515, 1985:54–59. Gae Aulenti, 'Il progetto per il museo di Orsay: l'architettura come integrazione delle scelte,' *Urbanistica*, No. 81, 1985:30–43. Auction cat., *Asta di Modernariato 1900–1986, Auction 'Modernariato*,' Milan: Semenzato Nuova Geri, 8 Oct. 1986. Juli Capella and Quim Larrea, *Design by Architects in the 1980s*, New York: Rizzoli, 1988.

Aurdal, Synnøve Anker (1908–)
▶ Norwegian textile designer; born and active Kristiania (now Oslo).
▶ An exponent of the Norwegian weaving tradition and active from the early 1940s, Aurdal became known for her individualism and monumental compositions; said that her work was a visual expression of the amalgamation of colors, rhythms, music, and words; adopted the Norwegian landscape as a source of inspiration in her abstract patterns; in the 1960s, began experimenting with new materials and techniques, although she retained wool as a medium for its special color characteristics.
▶ Work shown at 1982 Biennale di Venezia (representing Norway).
▶ Cat., David Revere McFadden (ed.), *Scandinavian Modern Design 1880–1980*, New York: Abrams, 1982:262. Cat., Anne Wichstrøm, *Rooms with a View: Women's Art in Norway 1880–1990*, Oslo: The Royal Ministry of Foreign Affairs, 1990:32.

Aussourd, René (?–1968)
▶ French bookbinder and gilder; active Paris.
▶ Studied under uncle Charles Meunier.
▶ He worked for gilder Chambolle-Duru early on; in 1912, set up his own workshop in Paris; was fond of leaf, floral, Greek-key, and gold-fillet motifs; historicist designs included covers for *La Pière sur l'Acropole* and *Les Chansons de Bilitis*.
▶ Ernest de Crauzat, *La Reliure française de 1900 à 1925*, Vol. 2, Paris, 1932:48–49. Alastair Duncan and Georges de Bartha, *Art Nouveau and Art Déco Bookbinding*, New York: Abrams, 1989:33,187.

Avant-Première
See Rhinn, Eric

AVEM (Arte Vetraria Muranese)
▶ Italian glass manufacturer.
▶ Active in the 1940s and 1950s, the firm produced tableware, chandeliers, polychromed vases, and decorative objects. Designer Giulio Radi executed several pieces in opaque glass in odd shapes and often with metallic glazes and other surface effects.
▶ Cat., *Venini and Murano Renaissance: Italian Art Glass of the 1940s and 50s*, New York: Fifty/50, 1984.

Avril, Jean
▶ French designer; active Paris.
▶ Avril was the first to use lacquered cardboard in the design of a range of case goods, chairs, storage units, tables, and other pieces for children. The furniture was produced by Marty in 1967.
▶ Gilles de Bure, *Le Mobilier français 1965–1979*, Paris: Regard, 1983:30–32.

Awashima, Masakichi (1914–79)
▶ Japanese glassware designer.
▶ Studied design, Japan Art School, Tokyo.
▶ 1935–46, he worked for craftsman Kozo Kagami, who had studied glassmaking in Germany; 1946–50, was director of the industrial-art department of the Hoya glass factory; in 1950, established the Awashima Glass Design Research Institute; developing mold-blown techniques for mass production, in 1954, patented his *shizuku* ('dripping water') process for producing textured glasswares; putting the process to practical use, in 1956, established the Awashima glass company. Produced through advanced technology and in metal molds, the glassware produced by *shizuku* manifested the irregular forms of glass made in traditional ceramic molds.
▶ He received the 1956 Inventor's Prize from the Invention Society of Japan.
▶ Dorothy Blair, *A History of Glass in Japan*, New York: 1973: 254,298–99,319, plates 37,236. Cat., *Modern Japanese Glass*, Tokyo: The National Museum of Modern Art, 1982: Nos. 127–31. Cat., Kathryn B. Hiesinger and George H. Marcus III (eds.), *Design Since 1945*, Philadelphia: Philadelphia Museum of Art, 1983.

Awatsuji, Hiroshi (1929–)
▶ Japanese textile and graphic designer; born Kyoto.
▶ Studied Municipal College of Fine Arts, Kyoto, to 1950.
▶ From 1950, he worked as a textile designer for Kanebo; in c1955, set up his own studio; from 1964, collaborated with the Fujie textile company; on commission in 1971–72, designed furnishing fabrics for Tokyo Hotels, Ginza, and 1982 tapestries for IBM, Japan. From the mid-1960s, his bold and colorful printed textiles broke with traditional Japanese designs. His 1982 'art screens' in the form of roller screens drew upon popular advertising images.
▶ 'New Print Textile Designed by Hiroshi Awatsuji,' *Japan Interior Design*, No. 252, Mar. 1980:82–85. Chihaya Nakagawa, '"Art Screen" by Hiroshi Awatsuji,' *Japan Interior Design*, No. 280, July 1982:73–77. Cat., Kathryn B. Hiesinger and George H. Marcus III (eds.), *Design Since 1945*, Philadelphia: Philadelphia Museum of Art, 1983. Albrecht Bangert and Karl Michael Armer, *80s Style: Designs of the Decade*, New York; Abbeville, 1990:227.

Axén, Gunila (1941–)
▶ Swedish textile designer.
▶ Axén executed patterns for printed fabrics produced by Kooperativa Förbundet, Stockholm, from 1971, he was a member of 10-Gruppen.
▶ Cat., David Revere McFadden (ed.), *Scandinavian Modern Design 1880–1980*, New York: Abrams, 1982:262.

B

B2
▶ French design collaboration.
▶ B2's name was derived from the two Brunos who established the partnership. Founded in the 1980s by Bruno Berrione and Bruno Lefèbre, B2's work was dubbed 'from the school of Starck,' their design approach reflecting Philippe Starck's early simplicity. Its work was also compared to the furniture designs of Friso Kramer and Arne Jacobsen. Of note is B2's 1987 *Gúeridon et Chaise en Rondins*. Some of Berrione's and Lefèbre's prototype projects were financed by VIA.
▶ *Chaise* in wood sliced from a large tree trunk and bent sheet metal and tubular metal received 1987 VIA 'Appel Permanent' award.
▶ *Design d'Aujourd'hui*. Suzanne Tise, 'Innovators at the Museum,' *Vogue Décoration*, No. 26, June/July 1990:48.

Bablet, Paul (1889–)
▶ French jewelry designer; active Paris.
▶ Bablet showed his jewelry at the 1912 Paris Salon d'Automne, 1914 Salon of the Société des Artistes Décorateurs, and at exhibitions in New York, Zagreb, and Madrid, as well as Belgium and France. Participated in 1925 Paris 'Exposition Internationale des Arts Décoratifs et Industriels Modernes,' 1931 Paris 'Exposition Coloniale,' 1937 Paris 'Exposition Internationale des Arts et Techniques dans la Vie Moderne.'
▶ Sylvie Raulet, *Bijoux Art Déco*, Paris: Regard, 1984.

Baccarat
▶ French glassware manufacturer.
▶ The glass factory that became Baccarat was founded in 1765 by the Bishop de Montmorency-Laval of Metz. During the first years, Antoine Renaut ran the factory. In 1806, the company was bought by Lippman-Lippmann, a merchant from Verdun, and, 1808, he was joined by Duroux. Owner of the crystal factory of Vonèche in Belgium, d'Artiques bought the factory in 1816 and was exempted from tariffs by King Louis XVIII on condition that the factory produced at least 500 tons of crystal annually. In 1817, the company produced its first pieces from raw crystal. Becoming known as the Verrerie de Vonèche à Baccarat; in 1843, by royal decree, as the Compagnie des Verreries et Cristalleries de Baccarat; and, in 1841, as the Compagnie des Cristalleries de Baccarat. The factory became known for its opaline glassware, paperweights, and engraved rock crystal in the 19th century. By the early 20th century, Baccarat had distinguished patrons: Czar Nicholas II, the Shah of Iran, and other sovereigns purchased its wares. Baccarat was closed down by the Germans during World War I and assumed production again to full capacity in 1920. 1925–37, Georges Chevalier produced Modern models, often in geometric silhouettes. After World War II, the firm produced both traditional wares and contemporary pieces. In 1949, it opened a branch in New York. American teacher Van Day Truex collaborated with the firm as a designer for a time and designed its 1954 *Dionysos* decanter. The firm used other outside designers; sculptor Robert Rigot began with the firm in 1970, and Czech designer Yan Zoritchak began in 1972. Roberto Sambonet designed vases. Thomas Bastide became design director in 1983 and produced hundreds of designs.
▶ Won numerous awards including first at 1823 Paris 'Exposition Nationale' and showed engraved crystal inspired by rock crystal and in the *japoniste* taste at 1878 Paris 'Exposition Universelle.'
▶ Cat., *Verriers français contemporains: Art et industrie*, Paris: Musée des Arts Décoratifs, 1982. Jean-Louis Curtis, *Baccarat*, Paris: Regard, 1991.

Bach, Alfons (1904–)
▶ German industrial designer; husband of interior designer Anita Stewart Bach.
▶ Bach graduated from the Reimann School, Berlin; studied in Italy.
▶ Emigrated to the USA; had clients including Heywood Wakefield (furniture), Bigelow-Sanford (carpets), General Electric (electrical appliances); president, Industrial Designers Society of America; member, International Institute of Arts and Letters; national president, FIDSA.
▶ Work shown at Metropolitan Museum of Art, New York, 1934, 1936, and 1938; Philadelphia Arts Center; Newark Museum of Art. Work subject of one-person (painting) exhibitions at Babcock Gallery, New York, 1948, and Stamford (Connecticut) Museum, 1954. Received silver medal from Industrial Designers Institute.
▶ Alfons Bach Archive, Cooper-Hewitt Museum, New York.

Bäck, Göran (1923–)
▶ Finnish ceramicist.
▶ 1957–58, studied Höhr-Grenhausen, Germany.
▶ From 1948–86, worked at Arabia.
▶ Jennifer Hawkins Opie, *Scandinavia: Ceramics & Glass in the Twentieth Century*, New York: Rizzoli, 1989.

Backström, Monica (1939–)
▶ Swedish glassware designer; born Stockholm.
▶ Studied advertising and industrial design, Konstfackskolan and Tekniska Skolan, Stockholm.
▶ In 1965, she became a glassware designer for Boda. Her glass pieces often incorporated metal threads, nails, and small flakes. She sometimes applied enamel decoration to a silvered surface and executed large glass decorations for commercial and public buildings and Swedish oceanliners.
▶ 1978 bowl for Boda included in 1983–84 'Design Since 1945' exhibition at the Philadelphia Museum of Art.
▶ Lennart Lindkvist (ed.), *Design in Sweden*, Stockholm, 1972:16–18. Geoffrey Beard, *International Modern Glass*, London, 1976:112,139,329. Cat., Kathryn B. Hiesinger and George H. Marcus III (eds.), *Design Since 1945*, Philadelphia: Philadelphia Museum of Art, 1983. Jennifer Hawkins Opie, *Scandinavia: Ceramics and Glass in the Twentieth Century*, New York: Rizzoli, 1989.

Bäckström, Olof (1922–)
▶ Finnish engineer and industrial designer.
▶ Studied electrical engineering.

▶ He spent the first 11 years of his career as an engineer; turned to woodcarving and designing in 1954; created wooden household articles at first and, in c1960, cutlery; 1958–80, was an industrial designer at Fiskars, Helsinki, where his initial project was a Melamine tableware collection. Working on the project 1961–67, his popular ergonomic 1963 O-series orange-handled general-purpose scissors (produced from 1967) and pinking shears, both by Fiskars, were widely published. Though production models were with ABS-plastic handles, the prototype was carved in wood. Fiskars produced the scissors for Wilkinson Sword and sold licenses world-wide.

▶ Received silver medal (wooden domestic wares) 1957 (XI) Triennale di Milano and silver medal (camping flatware) at its 1960 (XII) session. Work included in 1958 'Formes Scandinaves,' Paris Musée des Arts Décoratifs, and 1961 Zürich/Amsterdam/London 'Finlandia' exhibition.

▶ Design, 13 Mar. 1952:8. Cat., David Revere McFadden (ed.), Scandinavian Modern Design 1880–1980, New York: Abrams, 1982:262. Cat., Kathryn B. Hiesinger and George H. Marcus III (eds.), Design Since 1945, Philadelphia: Philadelphia Museum of Art, 1983. Cherie Fehrman and Kenneth Fehrman, Postwar Interior Design, 1945–1960, New York: Van Nostrand Reinhold, 1987. Jeremy Myerson and Sylvia Katz, Conran Design Guides: Tableware, London: Conran Octopus, 1990:38,72.

Bacon, Francis H. (1856–1940)
▶ American furniture and interior designer; active Boston; brother of architect Henry Bacon.
▶ Studied Massachusetts Institute of Technology, Cambridge, Massachusetts to 1877 (USA).
▶ He traveled in Europe 1878–79; worked briefly as a draftsman in the offices of architects McKim, Mead and Bigelow, New York, and of architect and decorator Prentis Treadwell, Albany, NY; was a designer at furniture producer Herter Brothers, the firm commissioned to furnish the William H. Vanderbilt House in New York; 1881–83, worked on excavations at Assos (Turkey) for the Archaeological Institute of America; worked in the office of architect H.H. Richardson, Boston, before joining furniture firm A.H. Davenport, Boston, as its principal designer; 1885–1908, was a vice-president at Davenport, where he translated hand-crafted furniture and furnishings models into machine-produced wares; may have been responsible for introducing the Colonial Revival style of Davenport furniture designed by H.H. Richardson and probably designed some of the furniture for the 1886 John Jacob Glessner House in Chicago credited to Richardson; when Albert H. Davenport died, attempted without success to buy the company; from 1908, managed his own business.
▶ Work shown at 1986–87 'In Pursuit of Beauty' exhibition, Metropolitan Museum of Art, New York.
▶ Anne Farnam, 'A.H. Davenport and Company, Boston Furniture Makers,' Antiques, No. 109, May 1976:1048–55. Doreen Bolger Burke et al., In Pursuit of Beauty: Americans and the Aesthetic Movement, New York: Metropolitan Museum of Art and Rizzoli, 1986:418.

Bacon, Francis (1909–92)
▶ British painter and designer; born Dublin; active London.
▶ Moved to London in 1925; 1926–27, in Berlin and Paris; in 1930, showed his own design Modern furniture and carpets in his London studio, achieving modest notice; from 1929, had rugs woven to his designs and, the same year, began painting; in 1933, participated in a group exhibition. The grotesque nature of his paintings, his open homosexuality, heavy drinking, and dubious acquaintances made him a figure of some notoriety. With links to Surrealism, Picasso, and German Expressionism, he is best known for his images of screaming popes, contorted portraiture, and dismembered carcasses.
▶ Showed carpets and furniture in his own studio in 1930; set up 1934 'Transition Gallery' exhibition in London, which failed in 1937. In 1945, showed Three Studies for Figures at the Base of a Crucifixion at Lefevre Gallery, London. Work included in 1954

Biennale di Venezia. Work was subject of exhibition at Grand Palais, Paris, in 1971; Metropolitan Museum of Art, New York, in 1975; and traveled in 1989 to Hirschorn Museum, Washington; Los Angeles County Museum of Art; and New York Museum of Art.
▶ 'The 1930 Look in British Decoration,' The Studio, Aug. 1930. Cat., Thirties: British art and design before the war, London: Arts Council of Great Britain, Hayward Gallery, 1979. Michael Kimmelman, 'Francis Bacon, 82, Artist of the Macabre, Dies,' The New York Times, 29 April 1992:A1,D25.

Badovici, Jean (1893–1956)
▶ Hungarian; born Budapest
▶ 1917–19, studied École des Beaux-Arts under Julien Guadet and Jean-Baptiste Paulin, and École Spéciale d'Architecture, both Paris.
▶ When he met architect and designer Eileen Gray in Paris in c1918, he was penniless, studying for an architecture degree and working at odd jobs in the evening; lived with Greek journalist Christian Zervos. 1927–29, Gray outfitted her own house, named 'E 1027,' at Roquebrune-Cap-Martin with help of Badovici. (E 1027 represents 'E' for Eileen, '10' for 10th alphabet letter 'J' for Jean, '2' for 2nd letter 'B' for Badovici, '7' for 7th letter for Gray.) Clean and sparse, every area was multi-functional with collapsible furniture in tubular steel, glass, plate glass, and painted wood. He introduced Gray to the most important architects of the time and encouraged her to pursue architecture herself; was editor of avant-garde journal L'Architecture Vivante, which he and Zervos persuaded Albert Morancé to publish 1922–33 in 21 issues, including one devoted to Frank Lloyd Wright; wrote for Cahiers d'Art, the journal that Zervos began in 1926, and for Wendingen; (with Gray) visited numerous architecture exhibitions in Europe, including the 1927 'Deutscher Werkbund-Ausstellung,' Stuttgart, and 1931 Berlin 'Deutsche Bauausstellung'. In 1931, Gray designed Badovici's apartment in Paris, where his furniture and rugs were installed; the metal pieces for tables, stools, and chairs were produced by Alixia of Paris. Disliking Gray's shop Jean Désert, he refused to bring potential clients there. In 1932, she turned over 'E 1027' to Badovici and built the house 'Castellar,' in the Alpes-Maritimes, occupying it alone. In 1929, he and Gray traveled to Peru, and Badovici attended the 1933 CIAM (Congrès Internationaux d'Architecture Moderne) in Athens, when the Athens Charter was drafted. After World War II, she began to work on the reconstruction of the house 'Maubeuge' for Badovici, and gave up her studio, where some of Gray's furnishings were still installed. He renovated old houses in Vézelay, adding Modern architectural elements such as metallic beams and large bay windows. Le Corbusier and wife Yvonne were often guests in Vézelay and in Roquebrune on the Côte d'Azur. Le Corbusier, Gray, and Badovici later became estranged, although in 1950 Le Corbusier bought a property in Cap Martin near Gray's property in Roquebrune on which he later built a small one-room prefabricated house. Badovici spent most of the summer months with Gray in Roquebrune, where Gray lived with Louise Dany. Gray found his womanizing, heavy drinking, and friends tedious. In 1934, they traveled to Mexico and New York, where they visited the 1934 'Machine Art' exhibition, New York Museum of Modern Art, and architect and designer Frederick Kiesler. After World War II, Badovici became Adjunct Chief Architect of Reconstruction (with chief architect André Lurçat), Maubeuge and Solesmes (France); in 1955, joined UAM (Union des Artistes Modernes) but had little work. After Badovici's death, Le Corbusier arranged for Madame Schelbert to buy 'E 1027.' Originally Schelbert wanted to distroy the Gray furniture but kept the property, including the furniture, intact, until her death.
▶ Images of Badovici's flat by Gray shown at 1931 (II) UAM exhibition, Galerie Georges Petit, Paris. Work subject of 1956 exhibition sponsored by UAM, Pavillon Marsan, Paris.
▶ Jean Badovici, Les Grand Travaux de la ville de Lyon, Paris, 1920. Jean Badovici, Intérieurs de Süe et Mare, Paris, 1924. Jean

Badovici, 'A. et G. Perret,' *L'Architecture Vivante*, Summer 1925;17–23. Florence Camard, *Ruhlmann*, Paris: Regard, 1983. Arlette Barré-Despond, *UAM*, Paris: Regard, 1986. Peter Adam, *Eileen Gray, Architect/Designer*, New York: Abrams, 1987. Philippe Garner, *Eileen Gray: Design and Architecture, 1878–1976*, Cologne: Taschen, 1993.

Bagge, Eric Anthony   (1890–1978)

▶ French architect and interior decorator; born Antony, near Paris.

▶ Bagge designed furniture, wallpaper, fabrics, accessories, and silver. His furniture was produced in precious woods in geometric motifs (inspired by Cubist art) with ivory marquetry; in 1929, was in charge of the design of new exhibition space, Musée Galliéra, Paris; was a member of the Groupe des Architectes Modernes and of the French exhibitions committee of the Société d'Encouragement à l'Art et l'Industrie; from 1922, designed furniture for La Maîtrise decorating department of Galeries Lafayette department store, Paris, and for Paris furniture firms including Saddier frères, Mercier frères, and Dennery. His design for the grand suite of 1926 oceanliner *Île-de-France* was widely published. In the late 1920s, he designed a collection of fabrics and rugs in geometric motifs and in vivid and somber colors for Lucien Bouix. His elegant wallpapers were produced by Desfossés and by Karth. In 1929, he became artistic director, Palais du Marbre, Paris, the modern furniture store; in 1930, opened his own shop, where he sold furniture, furnishings, and lighting; as an architect, designed townhouses, stores, and the Church of Saint-Jacques, Montrouge, and pavilions at 1937 Paris 'Exposition Internationale des Arts et Techniques dans la Vie Moderne,' became director of the École Practique de Dessin de la Chambre Syndicale de la Bijouterie Joaillerie Orfèvrerie.

▶ Participated in Salons of Société des Artistes français from its beginning, events of the Salon d'Automne from 1919, Salons of Société des Artistes Décorateurs, and Salons of Union Centrale des Arts décoratifs. At the 1925 Paris 'Exposition Internationale des Arts Décoratifs et Industriels Modernes,' he designed the Hall of Jewelry at the Grand Palais, including other stands and the bedroom and bath of the French ambassador and other rooms in exhibitions for Les Gobelins and Beauvais.

▶ Victor Arwas, *Art Déco*, New York: Abrams, 1980. Sylvie Raulet, *Bijoux Art Déco*, Paris: Regard, 1984. Pierre Cabanne, *Encyclopédie Art Déco*, Paris: Somogy, 1986:117. Pierre Kjellberg, *Art Déco: les maîtres du Mobilier, le décor des Paquebots*, Paris: Amateur, 1986:33–34.

Baggs, Arthur Eugene
See Marblehead Pottery

Baguès Frères

▶ French designers; located Paris.

▶ The Baguès brothers had outlets in Brussels, London, and New York, with its main outlet in Paris, where it sold lighting (particularly Louis XIV and Empire styles), *objets d'art*, and ironwork; favored the use of glass crystal beads, as found in a luster designed for clothing designer Jeanne Lanvin, and topaz and amethyst stones; for the oceanliner *l'Atlantique* of 1932, produced four large reflecting vases for the lounge and, for the Crane showroom, Paris, by Charles Knight (with Jacques-Émile Ruhlmann), various accessories.

▶ Widely published pine-cone chandelier with five overlapping rows of weed pods in chromed metal bordered by crystal pearls shown at Pavillon de l'Elegance, 1925 Paris 'Exposition Internationale des Arts Décoratifs et Industriels Modernes.' Participated in 1934 Salon of Light, Paris, and 1937 Paris 'Exposition Internationale des Arts et Techniques dans la Vie Moderne.'

▶ Alastair Duncan, *Art Nouveau and Art Déco Lighting*, New York: Simon and Schuster, 1978:161–62.

Bahner, Franz

▶ German silversmiths; located Düsseldorf.

▶ The firm was founded in 1895 and specialized in silver flatware; commissioned designs by Peter Behrens in c1905, Henry van de Velde in 1905, Gerhard Duve in c1930, and Emil Lettré at the end of the 1930s; closed in the 1960s.

▶ Annelies Krekel-Aalberse, *Art Nouveau and Art Déco Silver*, New York: Abrams, 1989:132,251. Karl H. Bröhan (ed.), *Metallkunst*, Berlin: Bröhan-Museum, 1990:2–11.

Baier, Fred   (1949–)

▶ British furniture designer.

▶ Studied furniture, Birmingham Polytechnic to 1971; Royal College of Art, London, to 1975.

▶ A Craft Revivalist, Baier designed the anti-craft 1989 *Roll Top Drop Leaf Transforming Robot Desk*, a brightly colored object almost unrecognizable as a piece of furniture and based on 1950s Japanese science-fiction fantasies and images from the film *Forbidden Planet*. 1979–82, he taught at Brighton Polytechnic; from 1976–78, at Wendell Castle School, New York State; subsequently at Royal College of Art.

▶ Received 1971 bursary from Royal Society of Arts and 1976 award from Crafts Advisory Committee. Work shown at 1989 'British Design,' Boymansvan Beuningen, Rotterdam; Crafts Council, London, 1990.

▶ Frederique Huygen, *British Design: Image and Identity*, London: Thames and Hudson, 1989:128,133. Jonathan M. Woodham, *Twentieth-Century Ornament*, New York: Rizzoli, 1990. Charlotte Fiell and Peter Fiell, *Modern Furniture Classics Since 1945*, London: Thames and Hudson, 1991:149,174, No. 137.

Bailey, Banks and Biddle

▶ American jeweler and silversmiths; located Philadelphia.

▶ The firm Bailey and Kitchen was established in 1832 by Joseph Trowbridge Bailey and Andrew B. Kitchen in Philadelphia. Kitchen died in 1840, and the name was continued until 1846, when E.W. Bailey (brother of J.T. Bailey), Jeremiah Robbins, and James Gallagher formed the partnership Bailey and Company. In 1878, Joseph T. Bailey II, George Banks of J.E. Caldwell and Co, and Samuel Biddle of Robbins, Clark and Biddle formed the partnership Bailey, Banks and Biddle. The firm is still active in Philadelphia.

▶ Charlotte Gere, *American and European Jewelry 1830–1914*, New York: Crown, 1975:149. Dorothy T. Rainwater, *Encyclopedia of American Silver Manufacturers*, New York: Crown, 1979.

Baillie Scott, Mackay Hugh   (1865–1945)

▶ British architect and interior designer; born Ramsgate.

▶ Studied School of Art, Douglas, Isle of Man, where one of his teachers was Archibald Knox, with whom he designed stained glass and ironwork.

▶ On a visit to London, he decided to become an architect; 1886–89, was apprenticed to Bath city architect Charles E. Davis; in c1886, settled on the Isle of Man. Following Arts and Crafts ideals, most of his houses used traditional materials and forms. Showing some Art Nouveau motifs, his work was influenced by Ernest George and C.F.A. Voysey. Baillie Scott became known in Germany and Austria for his designs for the 1898 palace and furniture at Darmstadt for Grand Duke Louis IV of Hesse-Darmstadt; the furniture was made by C.R. Ashbee's Guild of Handicrafts. Since the Continental avant-garde idolized English gentlemen and their art, interest in Baillie Scott's picturesque ruralist style in flexibly planned interiors spread throughout Germany. His drawings for the competition 'Haus eines Kunstfreundes' ('House of an Art Lover') sponsored by *Innen-Dekoration* magazine spread Baillie Scott's fame further; the series editor was the influential Hermann Muthesius, the anglophile who influenced German taste for the Arts and Crafts style. Favorable publicity followed in *Kunst und Kunsthandwerk* (1901 and onwards), in *Deutsche Kunst und Dekoration* (1903 and onwards), and in *House Beautiful* (1904) in America. His practice extended to Switzerland, Poland, Russia, Italy,

Poland, and the USA. Notice of his work reached Romania, where he did work for Queen Marie for her forest eyrie 'Le Nid.' In 1903, he moved to Bedford (England) and built a pair of cottages at the 1905 Letchworth exhibition; in 1914, planned a garden city for Kharkov (Ukraine). The *Studio Yearbook of Decorative Art*, before its switch to Modernism in 1929, favored Baillie Scott's work. Strongly opposed to Modernism, he was greatly assisted by A. Edgar Beresford, his partner 1905–19; in 1919, resumed his practice in London, continuing to build small country houses.

▶ He showed his work with Macintosh at the 1902 exhibition of British decorative art in Hungary.

▶ M.H. Baillie Scott, *Haus eines Kunstfreundes*, Vol. I, Darmstadt and London, 1902. M.H. Baillie Scott, *Houses and Gardens*, London, 1906 (rev. ed. 1933). M.H. Baillie Scott, Raymond Unwin et al., *Town Planning and Modern Architecture in the Hampstead Garden Suburb*, London, 1909. M.H. Baillie Scott et al., *Garden Suburbs, Town Planning and Modern Architecture*, London, 1911. James D. Kornwulf, *M.H. Baillie Scott and the Arts and Crafts Movement: Pioneers of Modern Design*, Baltimore: Johns Hopkins, 1972. K. Medici Mall, *Das Landhaus Waldbühl von M.H. Baillie Scott: Ein Gesamtkunstwerk zwischen Neugotik und Jugendstil*, Bern, 1979. *British Art and Design 1900–1960*, London: Victoria and Albert Museum, 1983. Stuart Durant, *Ornament from the Industrial Revolution to Today*, Woodstock, NY: Overlook, 1986:216,223,224,229,231,237.

Bakelite

▶ Bakelite is a synthetic resin formed from simple chemical compounds. Named after its inventor Dr. Leo Baekeland, it was patented in 1907, when it began to be produced as the first totally synthetic plastic, in Yonkers, New York. Commercial production began in 1916. Bakelite is produced by combining phenol (a coaltar product) with a solution of formaldehyde. Unlike earlier plastics such as celluloid, Bakelite must be thermoformed and once hardened cannot be reformed. It created the plastics compression-molding industry; was often used generically in housings for electronic items, including radios in dark colors in Britain; was popular in brightly colored costume jewelry and radios in the USA; due to its brittleness, fell from popularity, although the term continues to be used generically for other hard plastics.

▶ John Kimberly Mumford, *The Story of Bakelite*, New York: Stillson, 1924. Michael Farr, *Design in British Industry: A Mid-Century Survey*, London: Cambridge, 1955:123.

Bakker, Gijs (1942–)

▶ Dutch sculptor and jewelry, furniture, and lighting designer; born Amersfoort.

▶ 1958–62 studied gold- and silversmithing, Instituut voor Kunstnijverheidsonderwijs, Amsterdam, and, 1962–63, Konstfack-skolan, Stockholm.

▶ 1963–66, he worked as a designer at Van Kempen and Begeer in Zeist; with wife Emmy van Leersum, became a leader in contemporary jewelry design. From the mid-1960s, they produced collars and bracelets in aluminum in their Atelier voor Sieraden, Utrecht; in the 1970s, extended their craft into art, performance, and sculpture. 1971–78, he taught at the Academie voor Beeldende Kunsten, Arnhem; in 1979, became a freelance designer for firms Bussum and Artifort, Maastricht; from 1972, designed furniture, including the 1974 *Strip* chair, 1979 *Finger* chair, and 1986 plywood-framed chair, and a number of product designs. In the mid-1980s, Bakker's massive jewelry pieces were composed of color photographs encased in plexiglas. 1985–87, he taught industrial design at Technische Hogeschool, Delft, and, in 1987, was senior lecturer at Akademie voor Industriële Vormgeving, Eindhoven, and became a partner in design studio BRS/Premsela/Vonk, Amsterdam.

▶ First jewelry exhibition organized by Riekje Swart in 1965. Work subject of 1974 exhibition, Kunsthistorisch Instituut, Groningen. Received 1983 architecture prize, foundation De Fantasie, Almere, executed in 1984, and 1988 Françoise van den Bosch prize for jewelry design.

▶ Cat., Gert Staal, *Gijs Bakker, vormgever: Solo voor een solist*, 's-Gravenhage: SDU uitgeverij, 1989.

Bakst, Léon (aka Léon Rozenberg; b. Lev Samuïlovitch Bakst 1886–1924)

▶ Russian theater designer and illustrator; born St. Petersburg; active Russia, France, and USA.

▶ Studied Academy of Art, St. Petersburg, under Chistakov and Venig; in Jean Léon Gérome's studio and at Académie Julian, both Paris; 1893–99, under A. Edelfelt in Paris.

▶ In the 1890s, he traveled in France, Germany, Belgium, Spain, and Italy; 1891–97, was a regular participant in exhibitions of Association of Russian Artists; illustrated several books; from the 1910s, designed for the theater and was a graphic designer and illustrator of works published in journals; painted portraits of Alexandre Benois in 1898 and V.V. Rozanov in 1901. Other works included portraits and decorative designs for 1906 revue *Zolotoïe rouno* (*The Golden Fleece*) and a portrait of Serge Diaghilev. In 1899, Bakst was one of the main organizers and founders of the Mire Iskasstv (World of Art) group and journal; 1906–09, taught at Y. Zvantseva's School for Painting and Drawing, St. Petersburg; from 1909 in Paris, introduced vibrant colors and oriental patterns into his sets and costumes for Diaghilev's Ballets Russes de Monte Carlo, including sets for *Carnaval* (1910) by Schumann, *Schéhérazade* (1910) by Rimski-Korsakov, *L'Oiseau de feu* (1910) by Stravinsky, *Spectre de la rose* (1911) by Weber, *Narcisse* (1911) by N. Tcherepnine, and *L'Après-Midi d'un faune* by Debussy; from 1914, was one of the leading stage, costume, and set designers not only for Diaghilev's Ballets Russes but for the Mariyinskii Theater in St. Petersburg, Alexandrinskii Theater, Paris Opéra, Ida Rubinstein's company, and others; was instrumental in transforming French and other Western concepts of interior design, particularly encouraging the use of bright color schemes; living for a time in the USA, designed stencilled mosaic-like patterns based on Russian folk art for the foyer, costumes, and stage sets of John and Alice Garrett's private theater at their 'Evergreen' residence in Baltimore. The theater was restored in the late 1980s. Some of his printed patterns on silk for a New York firm were based on Zuñi and Hopi designs.

▶ Cat., Victor Beyer, *Les Ballets Russes de S. de Diaghilev*, Strasbourg, 1969. Victor Arwas, *Art Déco*, Abrams, 1980. Hélène A. Borisova and Gregory Sterine, *Art Nouveau Russe*, Paris: Regard, 1987:367. Cat., *Kunst und Revolution: Russische und Sowjetische Kunst 1910–1932*, Vienna: Österreichisches Museum für angewandte Kunst, 1988.

Baldessari, Luciano (1896–1982)

▶ Italian designer; born Rovereto (then Hapsburg Empire).

▶ Studied Politecnico di Milano to 1922.

▶ As a young man, he participated with Futurist artist Fortunato Depero; at the beginning of his career in the 1920s, designed stage sets and was a painter. His widely published 1929 *Luminator torchère* was one of the few Rationalist designs for furniture or lighting put into production in Italy; inspired by German experimental work, was intended to be an abstraction of an 'illuminated mannequin' with the curved tubular steel representing arms; presaged later 'light sculptures.' Baldessari designed the offices (with Figini and Pollini) of De Angeli Frua; as an architect, was one of the least predictable exponents of Italian Rationalism. His architecture included the 1929–32 De Angeli Frua Press building (with Luigi Figini and Gino Pollini) in Milan; 1930 Craja bar, Piazza P. Ferrari, Milan; 1932–33 Cima chocolate factory (with Gio Ponti), Milan; Vesta Pavilion, 1933 (V) Triennale di Milano; 1951 (IX) Triennale; 1951, 1952, 1953, 1954 Breda Pavilion, International Trade Fair.

▶ His 1929 *Luminator torchère* was designed for the Barnocchi stand at the 1929 'Exposición Internacional de Barcelona.'

▶ Guilia Veronesi, *Luciano Baldessari Architetto*, Trent, Italy: Collana di Artisti Trentini, 1957. Lampugnani in Vittorio Magnago Lampugnani (ed.), *Encyclopedia of 20th-Century Architecture*, New York: Abrams, 1986:32. Penny Sparke, *Design in Italy, 1870 to the Present*, New York: Abbeville, 1988. Richard A. Etlin, *Modernism in Italian Architecture*, 1890–1940, Cambridge: MIT, 1991.

Baldi, Massimo (1962–)
► Italian designer; born and active Milan.
► Graduated Scuola Politecnica di Design, Milan.
► Active as a designer of furniture, lighting, and interior design and consultant to furniture manufacturers.
► *Modo*, No. 148, March–April 1993:116.

Baldwin, Billy (1903–84)
► American interior decorator; born Baltimore; active in New York.
► Studied Princeton University.
► Baldwin was already an interior decorator in Baltimore when, in 1935, Ruby Ross Wood invited him to join her in her decorating practice in New York. Accepted into the ranks of the city's powerful design figures, Baldwin's associates included Elsie de Wolfe. He lived in one of the townhouses on Sutton Place, whose façades interior decorator Dorothy Draper had painted black; in 1950, when Wood died, he became a partner of Edward Martin, designing residential interiors. His work depended heavily on the use of English and French antiques, detailing, and style. He became known for glossy brown walls and fabrics in cotton. The décor of the apartment of songwriter Cole Porter with its tubular-brass bookcases was widely published. Having set up his own business, his clients in the world of New York high society commissioned him to design their city apartments, country houses, and summer retreats. His work, combining antiques with modern elements, was regularly published.
► Stephen Calloway, *Twentieth-Century Decoration*, New York: Rizzoli, 1988:215–16. John Esten and Rose Bennett Gilbert, *Manhattan Style*, Boston: Little, Brown, 1990:10. Mark Hampton, *Legendary Decorators of the Twentieth Century*, New York: Doubleday, 1992.

Baldwin, James Benjamin (1913–)
► American interior designer; born Montgomery, Alabama.
► 1931–35, studied architecture at Princeton University; 1935–36, painting with Hans Hofmann in New York; 1936–38, at Graduate School of Architecture, Princeton University; 1938–39, Cranbrook Academy of Art, Bloomfield Hills, Michigan, under Eliel Saarinen.
► 1939–40, Baldwin worked with Eliel and Eero Saarinen; from 1941–1945, was partner of Harry Weese, Kenilworth, Illinois; from 1945–46, worked at architecture firm Skidmore, Ownings and Merrill, Chicago, where he was in charge of the interior design of 1947 Terrace Plaza Hotel, Cincinnati; in 1947, set up his own interior-design studio, designing residences in Chicago, New York, and Sarasota, Florida; from c1948–56, was partner of William Machado; from 1948–55, practiced in Montgomery; from 1956–63, practiced in Chicago; from 1963–73, practiced in New York. His work was simple and minimal. He worked with architects Edward Larrabee Barnes, I.M. Pei, and Louis Kahn on the interiors of their buildings; from 1973, practiced in East Hampton, New York, and Sarasota.
► With Harry Weese, received awards at 1940 'Organic Design in Home Furnishings' competition and exhibition, New York Museum of Modern Art.
► Robert Judson Clark et al., *The Cranbrook Vision*, New York: Abrams and Metropolitan Museum of Art, 1983.

Baleri, Enrico (1942–)
► Italian designer and entrepreneur; born Albino.
► Studied Facoltà di Architettura, Milan, not graduating.
► He designed the 1979 table system *Coloforte* for Knoll; was a founder of design companies Pluri in 1968 and Alias in 1979. At Alias, he was artistic director until 1983, when he set up Baleri Italia, producing the works of Philippe Starck, Alessandro Mendini, Hans Hollein, and others including himself; designed 1983 *Pauline* mirror by Baleri Italia; in 1986, he founded Studio Baleri & Associati.

► Albrecht Bangert and Karl Michael Armer, *80s Style: Designs of the Decade*, New York: Abbeville, 1990:227. *Modo*, No. 148, March–April 1993:116.

Ball, Douglas (1935–)
► Canadian industrial designer; born Peterborough, Ontario.
► Studied industrial design, Ontario College of Art, Toronto, to 1958.
► In the 1960s, he worked at Robin Bush Design Associates, Toronto; subsequently, set up his own industrial design studio, Montreal; from 1964, was active in product and corporate design for Sunar and, from 1979, was their director of design. His design work for Sunar, Waterloo, Ontario, was extensive, including office furniture and seating systems, 1969 *S System* steel desk and 1978 *Race* open-office system. Considered to be Canada's most successful industrial designer, he designed 1991 folding-table range produced by Vecta and transportation aids for the physically disadvantaged.
► Cat., *Seduced and Abandoned: Modern Furniture designers in Canada, the First Fifty Years*, Toronto: The Art Gallery at Harbourfront, 1986:23.

Balla, Giacomo (1871–1958)
► Italian artist and designer; born Turin.
► Studied Albertine Academy, Turin.
► His first painting was the *Street Light (Arc Lamp)* (dated 1909 but painted 1910–11), inspired by Filippo Tomasso Marinetti's *Let's Kill the Moonlight!* He taught painting to Gino Severini and Umberto Boccioni; in 1910, became a Futurist, signing the *Manifesto of Futurist Painters* and the *Technical Manifesto of Futurist Painting*, by which time he was already well known. His influences were the Pointillism of Pellizza da Volpedo and Segantini, the Initimism of Eugène Carrière, and the French Impressionists and Post-Impressionists. Traveling to Düsseldorf in 1912, he designed the Löwenstein house (destroyed) and returned in 1913 and 1914 to complete its furnishings and decoration, using the motif of bichrome, iridescent 'compenetrations'; in a dramatic gesture in 1913, placed all of his paintings up for auction, declaring, 'Balla is dead. Here the works of the late Balla are on sale'; designed Futurist clothing, arguing in his *Futurist Manifesto on Menswear* (1914) for practical clothing that would be 'dynamic,' 'strong-willed,' and 'violent'; fighting for a complete break with the past, expressed his manifesto on interior decoration in his Futurist House of c1918 in Rome, where his colorful painted and cut-out furniture was installed; designed the interior of Futurist-style 1921 Bal Tik-Tak dance-hall; at the end of the 1930s, broke from Futurism; designed many pieces of furniture, ceramics, and lighting in a highly developed abstract mode.
► With Fortunato Depero and Enrico Prampolini, he showed six large painted wall hangings at the 1925 Paris 'Exposition Internationale des Arts Décoratifs et Industriels Modernes.'
► Pontus Hulten (organizer), *Futurism and Futurism*, Milan: Fabbri, 1986.

Ballets Russes de Monte Carlo
See Diaghilev, Sergei Pavlovich

Ballin, Mogens (1871–1914)
► Danish painter and metalworker; active Copenhagen.
► Ballin's workshop made copper and pewter as well as silver objects. Georg Jensen worked for Ballin before setting up his own silversmithy; Ballin's and Thorwald Bindesbøll's influences appeared in his work. For the Ballin firm, Jensen produced his first jewelry designs after 1901; Ballin allowed him to exhibit under his own name. In Ballin's workshop in the 1900s–10s, he produced his own silver designs along with those of assistants Gudmund Hentze and Peter Hertz. Ballin's hollow-ware often bore the initials or signature of the designers. After Ballin's death, Hertz took over the management of the workshop.
► Annelies Krekel-Aalberse, *Art Nouveau and Art Déco Silver*, New York: Abrams, 1989:216,217,218,251.

Balzer, Gerd (1909–1986)
► German typographer, architect, and designer; born Rostock.
► 1929–33, studied Bauhaus, Dessau.
► He produced the 1929 precursor of the adjustable architect's lamp designed by Czech designer Josef Pohl. A similar lamp was produced by Körting und Mathieson as part of its Kandem range. Belzer and Pohl were given the task in 1932 of organizing Bauhaus students' works, which would result in a conference and a furniture-design competition. After the Bauhaus, he worked in the offices of several architects and, from 1933, for an architect in Rostock and, after World War II, in Hanover.
► Lionel Richard, *Encyclopédie du Bauhaus*, Paris: Somogy, 1985: 179. Cat., *The Bauhaus: Masters and Students*, New York: Barry Friedman, 1988. Cat., *Die Metallwerkstatt am Bauhaus*, Berlin: Bauhaus-Archiv, 1992:132,122,314,315.

bamboo
► Bamboo was first imported to the West from China in the 18th century. Desirable in England and America during the time of the Aesthetic Movement of the 1870s, 1880s, and afterwards, the use of bamboo became popular due to the interest in the Far East. Probably much of the bamboo furniture sold as being of Japanese origin was actually made in the West. Bamboo's special features include its light weight, low cost, and exotic associations; its rectilinearity was desirable to architects and designers towards the end of the 19th century. In some cases imitation bamboo was turned on a lathe and was used in the work of George Hunzinger of Brooklyn, New York.
► Doreen Bolger Burke et al., *In Pursuit of Beauty: Americans and the Aesthetic Movement*, New York: Metropolitan Museum of Art and Rizzoli, 1986:479. Carrie May Ashton, 'Popular Whims in Furniture,' *Interior Decorator*, Vol. 4, Aug. 1893:209–10. Gillian Walkling, 'Bamboo Furniture,' *Connoisseur*, Vol. 202, Oct. 1979:126–31.

Bandiera Cerantola, Marisa (1934–)
► Italian designer; born Bassano del Grappa.
► Bandiera Cerantola began her professional career in 1966. Clients for domestic furniture systems and textiles included Faram, Rossitex, Rossiflor, and Schio; pursued studies of visual perception and structural process; became a member of ADI (Associazione per il Disegno Industriale). Her textile patterns were geometric.
► *ADI Annual 1976*, Milan: Associazione per il Disegno Industriale, 1976.

Bandiera, Paolo (1937–)
► Italian designer; born in and active Treviso.
► Bandiera began his professional career in 1962; designed furniture for clients including Faram, Treviso, and Vidal Hermanos Santalò, Barcelona; collaborated with architect Umberto Facchini in Treviso on modular systems for offices, bathrooms, and domestic areas; became a member of ADI (Associazione per il Disegno Industriale).
► *ADI Annual 1976*, Milan: Associazione per il Disegno Industriale, 1976.

Banfi, Gianluigi
See BBPR

Bang and Olufsen
► Danish domestic electronics equipment manufacturer.
► In 1925, engineers Peter Bang and Svend Olufsen set up a workshop in the attic of the Olufsen family; began with a modest production of radios; in 1928, built a small factory, Stuer, Jutland, that could be converted into a school in case the manufacturing business failed; in 1929, were producing innovative equipment including an early radio with push-button tuning and the first mass-produced 5-valve radio. In 1930, their first radio-gramophone appeared. Bang and Olufsen were from the beginning concerned with sophisticated technology aligned with visual elegance. In the early 1960s, when transistors replaced valves, the firm offered an elegant and novel slim radio. The innovatory 1965 pick-up arm by E. Rorbaek Madsen was incorporated into the *Beogram 3000* turntable. Acton Bjørn designed the 1966 *Beolit 500* radio with its natural wood face and single row of black control buttons. Jakob Jensen designed the 1969 *Beogram 1200* component hi-fi group; 1976 *Beogram 4000*, the first electronic turntable with two separate arms; 1979 *Beocenter 7002* unit; 1980 *Beogram 8000* phonograph; *MX5000* television; and *VX5000* video-cassette recorder. The originality of Bang and Olufsen lies in its close collaboration with its designers and in its focus on good design, both of which are aligned from the first stages of product development with marketing and manufacturing. A complete overhaul of the firm's products was made in the late 1970s when the Japanese became competitors. Their designers included Ib Fabiansen, Lone Lindinger-Loewy, Gideon Loewy, Eric Madsen, Henning Moldenhawer, David Lewis, and Steve McGugan.
► Work was subject of 1990 exhibition, Paris Musée des Arts Décoratifs.
► Cat., Chantal Bizot, *Bang & Olufsen, Design et Technologie*, Paris: Musée des Arts Décoratifs, 1990.

Bang, Jacob E. (1899–1965)
► Danish sculptor, architect, and industrial designer.
► 1916–21, studied sculpture, Det Kongelige Danske Kunstakademi, Copenhagen.
► From 1925–42, he worked at Holmegård Glasvaerk, where he was artistic director 1928–42; 1942–57, worked in his own studio, designing ceramics for Nymølle and metalworks for F. Hingelberg and Pan Aluminium; from 1957, was artistic director of the Kastrup glassworks; 1965, merged with Holmegård; was a freelance designer at the Nymølle faïence factory, Pan Aluminium, and F. Hingelberg Sølvsmedie.
► Work included in the Triennali di Milano; 1954–57 'Design in Scandinavia' exhibition, USA; 1956–59 'Neue Form aus Dänemark,' Germany; 1958 'Formes Scandinaves,' Paris Musée des Arts Décoratifs; 1960–61 'The Arts of Denmark,' USA.
► Jacob E. Bang,' 'Lidt om Glasset i Hjemmet,' in Sigvard Bernadotte (ed.), *Moderne dansk boligkunst*, Vol. 1, Odense, 1946:255–60. *Glass 1959*, Corning, NY: The Corning Museum of Glass, 1959. Kastrup and Holmegaard Glassworks, *150 Years of Danish Glass*, 181–208. Erik Lassen and Mogens Schlüter, *Dansk Glas: 1925–1975*, Copenhagen, 1975:21–31,37–40. Cat., David Revere McFadden (ed.), *Scandinavian Modern Design 1880–1980*, New York: Abrams, 1982:262. Cat., Kathryn B. Hiesinger and George H. Marcus III (eds.), *Design Since 1945*, Philadelphia: Philadelphia Museum of Art, 1983.

Banham, P. Reyner (1920–1988)
► British architectural and design historian and critic.
► Banham wrote during the 1950s and 1960s about the Modern movement and its aftermath; was a key historian and critic of Modern in architecture and design; discussed design in relationship to mass culture; in 1956, (with Richard Hamilton and Eduardo Paolozzi) founded the Independent Group, British Pop Art association at the Institute of Contemporary Art, London; moved to Los Angeles; was appointed professor of art history, University of Los Angeles at Santa Cruz; was also the Bannister Fletcher Visiting Professor of Architectural History, University of London. His numerous publications included *Theory and Design in the First Machine Age* (1960), *The New Brutalism* (1966), and, following his appointment to the University of California at Los Angeles, *Scenes in American Deserts* (1982).
► Penny Sparke, *Design by Choice*, London: Academy Editions, 1981. Penny Sparke, *Introduction to Design and Culture in the Twentieth Century*, Allen and Unwin, 1986.

Bapst et Falize

▶ French goldsmiths and jewelers; located in Paris.

▶ In 1752, Georges-Michel Bapst became jeweler to King Louis XV and succeeded the directorship of his father-in-law Georges-Frédéric Stras's firm. (Stras was the inventor of 'strass,' the colorless glass paste used frequently for jewelry during the 18th and 19th centuries.) In 1797, Jacques Bapst (grandson of Georges-Michel) married Paul Nicholas Menière's daughter. A member of the 18th-century family of silversmiths, at the end of 1788, Menière acquired Boehmer et Bassange, jewelers to Marie-Antoinette. Jacques Bapst's sons Constant and Charles-Frédéric succeeded joint directorship and had as their first assignments to remake some of Emperor Napoleon I's regalia for Louis XVIII. Becoming known as Bapst frères, the firm produced the 1824 coronation regalia for Charles X. Joined by his nephew Alfred, Charles-Frédéric was director of the workshop for 50 years. The firm's impressive ensemble made from the diamonds in the crown of the Empress Eugénie was designed by Alfred, who along with Charles-Frédéric's sons Jules and Paul succeeded as directors in 1871. In 1879, Bapst et Falize was organized by representatives of two families of jewelers. Lucien Falize was the son of Alexis Falize, a jeweler who had set up the family firm in the Palais Royale in 1838. Influenced by Japanese art shown in London in 1862 and by Christofle's enamels, Alexis and Lucien Falize executed *cloisonné* jewelry during the late 1860s. Lucien collaborated with Emile Gallé and Paul Grandhomme; was a contributor to Siegfried Bing's book *Le Japon Artistique* (1888–91). The firm, after Lucien Falize's death in 1897, passed on to sons André, Pierre, and Jean.

▶ Bapst frères' work (diamond ensemble made from Empress Eugénie's crown) shown at 1867 Paris 'Exposition Universelle' and Falize frères' at 1900 Paris 'Exposition Universelle.'

▶ Charlotte Gere, *American and European Jewelry 1830–1914*, New York: Crown, 1975:149–50. Yvonne Brunhammer et al., *Art Nouveau Belgium, France*, Houston: Rice University, 1976, biblio.

Barbaglia, Mario (1950–)

▶ Italian architect and designer; born Milan.

▶ Studied architecture in Milan.

▶ In 1975, Barbaglia and Marco Colombo began collaborating as architects and on domestic and industrial designs; in 1984, became active in industrial design, beginning with commissions for PAF lighting; designed PAF's *Dove* table lamp.

▶ Hans Wichmann, *Italien Design 1945 bis heute*, Munich: Die Neue Sammlung, 1988.

Barbe, Pierre (1900–)

▶ French architect and designer.

▶ 1919–28, studied École des Beaux-Arts, Paris.

▶ In 1929, he became a founding member of UAM (Union des Artistes Modernes), secretary 1932–33, and participant in its group exhibitions until 1935; with Le Corbusier, he was a delegate at 1929 (II) in Frankfurt and 1930 (III) Brussels meeting of the CIAM (Congrès Internationaux d'Architecture Moderne). Until 1933, he was a member of CIRPAC (Comité International pour la Résolution des Problèmes de l'Architecture Contemporaine) and, in 1937, of the French section of CIAM. His work included numerous pieces of furniture in simple, sleek forms including tables in plate glass and bent-steel tubing seating; several post offices; 1926–39 thermoelectric plant for the Compagnie du Nord; 1929 Mimerel house (La Pacifique), Sanary-sur-Mer; 1929 interiors of Mme Dubonnet, Paris; 1931 furniture for vicomtesse de Noailles; 1930–34 Lambiotte townhouse, Neuilly.

▶ Received a silver medal at 1925 Paris 'Exposition Internationale des Arts Décoratifs et Industriels Modernes' and gold medal at 1936 (VI) Triennale di Milano for his 1930 townhouse, Neuilly; work shown at 1928 Salon of the Société des Artistes Décorateurs.

▶ Waldemar George, 'Meubles français: Les Meubles de Pierre Barbe,' *L'Amour de l'Art*, Feb. 1934. Arlette Barré-Despond, *UAM*, Paris: Regard, 1983. Jean-Baptiste Minnaert, *Pierre Barbe,*

architecte, Paris: Université de Paris, 1987. Cat., *Les années UAM 1929–1958*, Paris: Musée des Arts Décoratifs, 1988:146–47.

Barber, Wendy

▶ British ceramicist and textile designer.

▶ Studied in Sussex; 1960–65, Slade School of Fine Art, London.

▶ In 1981, she formed a partnership with John Hinchcliffe to design and produce textiles and ceramics; from 1983, worked on commissions.

▶ Barber and Hinchcliffe write and exhibit together.

▶ Robert A.M. Stern (ed.), *The International Design Yearbook*, New York: Abbeville, 1985/1986: No. 276.

Barbier, Philippe

▶ French designer; active Paris.

▶ Barbier designed the *Diabolo* stacking stool in colored ABS plastic produced by Barbier himself and, in 1969–70, by Galerie Péquignot.

▶ Gilles de Bure, *Le Mobilier français 1965–1979*, Paris: Regard, 1983:98.

Barbieri, Raul (1946–)

▶ Italian designer; born and active Milan.

▶ Studied architecture to 1973.

▶ 1970–73, he worked on the Olivetti account in the design studio of Ettore Sottsass; became a member of ADI (Associazione per il Disegno Industriale). Clients included Tronconi (lighting), Villa, and Mobilvetta.

▶ *ADI Annual 1976*, Milan: Associazione per il Disegno Industriale, 1976.

Barbini Glassworks

▶ Italian glass manufacturer.

▶ Alfredo Barbini, a descendant of glassmakers from the early 15th century, studied at Abate Zanetti (design school at Murano glass museum) from age ten; in 1930, began studying at Cristalleria, Murano, becoming a *maestro*; became *primo maestro* at Martinuzzi and Zecchin; worked with Cenedese in the late 1940s; created *masello* techniques – sculpting of solid piece of molten glass without molding and blowing; received 1955, Croce de Cavaliere al Merito from Italian government.

▶ Showed work independently at 1948 and 1950 Biennale di Venezia.

▶ Cat., *Venini and Murano Renaissance: Italian Art Glass of the 1940s and 50s*, New York: Fifty/50, 1984.

Barillet, Louis (1880–1948)

▶ French stained glass designer.

▶ Active in the 1920s–30s, Barillet received commissions from Modernist architects, including Robert Mallet-Stevens; 1920–45, was active in partnership with Jacques Le Chevallier in Paris; known for their geometrical approach, (with Le Chevallier) designed and produced the glass decoration in the windows of the 1928–29 offices of periodical *La Semaine à Paris* by Robert Mallet-Stevens in motifs portraying days of the week; (with Le Chevallier) commissions included the 1935 Capucins de Blois church; for the buildings on rue Mallet-Stevens in Neuilly, designed stained-glass windows for the stairwells and large bay windows; designed vigorous Cubist and Modern forms in clear and colored glass; in 1930, became a member of UAM (Union des Artistes Modernes), with which he exhibited until 1937; from 1945, was partner of Théodore Hansen. His 1932 Paris studio on Square Vergennes was designed by Mallet-Stevens.

▶ Robert Mallet-Stevens, *Les vitraux de Barillet*, Paris: Albert Morancé, 1926. Cat., Aaron Lederfajn and Xavier Lenormand, *Le Louvre des Antiquaires présente: 1930 quand le meuble devient sculpture*, Paris, 1986. Arlette Barré-Despond, *UAM*, Paris: Regard, 1986. Jean-François Pinchon (ed.), *Rob Mallet-Stevens, Architecture, Mobilier, Décoration*, Paris: Philippe Sers Editeur, 1986 (English ed., Cambridge: MIT, 1990). Cat., *Les années UAM 1929–1958*, Paris: Musée des Arts Décoratifs, 1988:148. Jonathan M. Woodham, *Twentieth-Century Ornament*, New York: Rizzoli, 1990:84.

Barker, Frederick

▶ British glassware designer and engraver.
▶ Studied Hornsey School of Art and Holloway Polytechnic.
▶ At the London Sand-Blast Decorative Glass Works, he treated the panels designed by Raymond McGrath and panels for RIBA building (by Juta); oceanliners *Queen Mary and Queen Elizabeth* in 1934, 1936, and 1938; 1935 *Orion*, and 1937 *Orcades*; from the 1930s to the 1980s, was engraver at T.W. Idle, London, and associate member of British Society of Master Glass Painters.
▶ Cat., *Thirties: British art and design before the war*, London: Arts Council of Great Britain, Hayward Gallery, 1979:143,284.

Barlach, Ernst (1870–1938)

▶ German sculptor, graphic artist, and ceramicist.
▶ Barlach began an association with R. Mutz with 1902 commemorative plaque for 25th anniversary of Hamburg museum; until 1904, modeled and relief-decorated ceramics, Mutz Workshop; from 1904, taught at Fachschule für Keramik, Höhr-Grenzhausen; collaborated with Richard Mutz in Berlin-Wilmersdorf; in 1906, returning from Russia, began producing sculptures for white porcelain and redware on theme of suffering peasants produced by Meissen; published *Keramik: Stoff und Form* (1908).
▶ Cat., W. Scheffler, *Werke um 1900*, Berlin: Kunstgewerbemuseum, 1966. K. Reutti, *Mutz-Keramik*, Hamburg: Ernst-Barlach-Hauses, 1966. Elisabeth Cameron, *Encyclopedia of Pottery and Porcelain*, London: Faber and Faber, 1986:36.

Barman, Christian (1898–1980)

▶ British writer and designer.
▶ Studied Liverpool University School of Architecture.
▶ In the 1930s, he was a product designer; 1935–41, succeeded G.W. Duncan as publicity officer (with Frank Pick) of London Passenger Transport Board in charge of visual public presentations; 1941–45, was assistant director of postwar building at Ministry of Works; 1947–62, ran Railway Design Panel; in 1953, became chief publicity officer at British Transport Commission; was commissioned by HMV to design 1934–36 electric iron and electric fan with innovatory streamlined housing; in the 1930s, executed other product designs; was editor of *Architects' Journal* and *Architectural Review* and author of numerous books on architecture, and, 1947–63, chief publicity officer of British Transport Commission; 1949–50, president of Society of Industrial Artists.
▶ In 1948, elected Royal Designer for Industry; in 1963, received Order of the British Empire.
▶ Michael Farr, *Design in British Industry: A Mid-Century Survey*, London: Cambridge, 1955:59. Cat., *Thirties: British art and design before the war*, London: Arts Council of Great Britain, Hayward Gallery, 1979:68,76,215,231,233,284. Fiona MacCarthy and Patrick Nuttgens, *An Eye for Industry*, London: Lund Humphries, 1986:26,81.

Barnack, Oscar (1879–1936)

▶ German industrial designer.
▶ Early 35mm cameras were unwieldy models that took a large number of pictures per roll of perforated cine film. Barnack designed the first Leica 35mm camera, which revolutionized still photography; his 1913 *UR* camera was put into production in 1918. Based on the *UR*, the Leica A, made by Leitz Wetzlar in Germany, had features including controls on the top of the body and a film winder on the right side. Convenient, practical, and attractive, it established 35mm photography as a standard.
▶ *The Camera*, London: Design Museum, 1989.

Barnard, Bishop and Barnards

▶ British manufacturer of iron and brass; located Norwich.
▶ Charles Barnard established a foundry in Norwich in 1826; joined forces with John Bishop in 1846. In 1859, the firm became known as Barnard, Bishop and Barnards reflecting the inclusion of Barnard's sons Charles and Godfrey; produced innovative agricultural and domestic products, including the 1838 self-rolling mangle, a so-called noiseless lawn mower, hot-water heating systems, and kitchen ranges. Barnard developed the machine-made wire netting commonly known as chicken wire, in production to this day. Moving to a new site in 1851, the Barnards began production of ornamental iron work. Barnard's chief craftsman Frank Ames and Norwich architect Thomas Jeckyll collaborated on the Norwich Gates, well received at the 1862 London exhibition and made as the 1863 wedding gift of the Gentlemen of Norfolk and Norwich to the Prince of Wales and Princess Alexandra, still standing at Sandringham. The zenith of Barnard's production was Jeckyll's 40-ton two-storey pavilion first shown at 1876 Philadelphia exhibition and purchased by Norwich City Council in 1888. Jeckyll designed cast-iron furniture and brass and cast-iron fireplace grates and surrounds. Barnard's also produced utilitarian metalwork, including manhole covers and grates.
▶ Received gold medal (slow-combustion stove) at 1878 Paris 'Exposition Universelle.' Work shown 1851 London 'Great Exhibition of the Works of Industry of All Nations' (wrought-iron hinge and door knocker), London 'International Exhibition of 1862' (Norwich Gates), 1876 Philadelphia 'Centennial Exposition' (pavilion by Jeckyll), 1878 Paris 'Exposition Universelle,' and in expositions until 1888.
▶ Doreen Bolger Burke et al., *In Pursuit of Beauty: Americans and the Aesthetic Movement*, New York: Metropolitan Museum of Art and Rizzoli, 1986:402.

Barnard, Jane (1902–)

▶ British silversmith; active London.
▶ Studied Central School of Arts and Crafts, London.
▶ In the 1920s and 1930s, she designed silver for father's firm Edward Barnard and Sons, London; produced smooth, round silhouettes embellished with blue enamel lines and edges. R.M.Y. Gleadowe also designed for the firm.
▶ Annelies Krekel-Aalberse, *Art Nouveau and Art Déco Silver*, New York: Abrams, 1989:35,251.

Barnes, Jhane (1954–)

▶ American textile and clothing designer; active New York and Japan.
▶ Studied Fashion Institute of Technology, New York.
▶ Internationally known for her clothing designs for men and women, Barnes began designing furnishing fabrics for Knoll in the late 1980s.
▶ In 1980, she was the first woman to receive a Coty Award for menswear. In 1981, received recognition from the Council of Fashion Designers.
▶ Timothy J. Ward, 'A 60s House Meets '90s Dreams,' *Metropolitan Home*, Sept./Oct. 1993:72–74.

Barnsley, Edward (1863–1926) and **Sidney Barnsley** (1865–1926)

▶ British architects, furniture designers, and craftsmen; brothers.
▶ Edward Barnsley worked with Gothic Revival architect J.D. Sedding and for a time with Norman Shaw; in 1895, (with brother Sidney Barnsley) set up a workshop in Pinbury, Gloucestershire, with Ernest Gimson. They focused on vernacular forms and traditional materials; in 1902, moved to Sapperton, Gloucestershire, and established the Cotswold School, specializing in simple handmade furniture. Production was carried on 1926–37 by Peter van der Waals, who had worked in the shop since 1901, in his shop in Chalford, Gloucestershire.
▶ William Lethaby, Alfred Powell, and Frederick Griggs, *Ernest Gimson, His Life and Work*, Shakespeare Head Press, 1924. Cat., *Thirties: British art and design before the war*, London: Arts Council of Great Britain, Hayward Gallery, 1979:284. Mary Comino, *Gimson and The Barnsleys, 'Wonderful furniture of a commonplace kind,'* Evans Brothers, 1980.

Barnsley, Ernest (1900–)

▶ British furniture maker and designer; born Pinbury, Gloucestershire; active Froxfield, Hampshire; son of Sidney Barnsley.
▶ In 1919, he became an apprentice to Geoffrey Lupton at Froxfield; in 1923, took over Lupton's furniture workshop, where he

worked until his retirement; based on the practice of his father and Ernest Gimson, designed historicist furniture, following 18th-century and some Arts and Crafts models; in the 1930s, collaborated with Francis Troup on furniture; in 1937, succeeding Peter van der Waals, became design adviser to Loughborough Training College; in 1945, became furniture design consultant to Rural Industries Bureau; was a member of Art-Workers' Guild.

▶ 1929–31 oak chest (produced by Herbert Upton) shown at 1979–80 'Thirties' exhibition at the Hayward Gallery, London. Appointed Commander of the British Empire in 1945.

▶ Cat., *Thirties: British art and design before the war*, London: Arts Council of Great Britain, Hayward Galley, 1979:72,83,84, 128,284,291.

Barovier, Angelo   (1927–)

▶ Italian glassware designer; active Murano; son of Ercole Barovier.

▶ A family member of a long line of Venetian glassmakers from the 13th century, Angelo Barovier, working with his father, produced vessels in elongated forms in *vetro a fili*, a technique of incorporating colored glass rods into bubbled and colored glass to form stripes; created glass sculptures in which constantly changing effects were created by the internal characteristics of patterns and light. His contribution to Venetian glass, it has been suggested, was greater than Paolo Venini's.

▶ Frederick Cooke, *Glass: Twentieth-Century Design*, New York: Dutton, 1986:96–99.

Barovier, Ercole   (1889–1974)

▶ Italian glassware designer: active Murano; father of Angelo Barovier; son of Benvenuto Barovier.

▶ In 1919, he established Artisti Barovier and, subsequently, Barovier e C.; like Paolo Venini and Giacomo Cappelin, was effective in reviving Murano glassmaking in the 1920s; served as chief designer, artist, and chemist and created more than 25,000 different models of decorative and functional pieces; formulated new color compounds; developed new techniques for textural surface effects and *vetro gemmato* (stony surface), *vetro barbarico* (applied rough surface), *vetro parabolico* (patchwork surface), and others; used subtle colors and open textures; (with son Angelo) produced vases and bottles in elongated forms in *vetro a fili* (glass with lines), where colored glass rods were embedded into colored, bubbled glass to form a stripe effect; in the early 1930s, developed the *vetro rugiada* (glass with a dew effect) technique, where small air bubbles created controlled texturing.

▶ Participated in XVII Biennale di Venezia and 'Esposizione Biennale delle Arti Decorative e Industriali Moderne.'

▶ Frederick Cooke, *Glass: Twentieth-Century Design*, New York: Dutton, 1986:96–99. Hans Wichmann, *Italien Design 1945 bis heute*, Munich: Die Neue Sammlung, 1988.

Barovier, Fratelli   (aka Barovier e Toso)

▶ Italian glassmakers; located in Murano.

▶ Benedetto, Benvenuto, and Giuseppe Barovier, members of a family with an illustrious tradition of glassmaking stretching back to the 14th century, established a factory in 1878 known as Fratelli Barovier, making beads and vessels in historicist 16th-century styles. In 1936, under the management of Ercole Barovier, son of Benvenuto, the firm became Barovier e Toso, under which name it operates today. Ercole's son Angelo Barovier, painter and glass designer, began at the firm in the late 1950s and, with Piero Toso, assumed management of the firm.

▶ Fratelli Barovier showed at several international exhibitions, including 1889 Paris 'Exposition Universelle' and 1891 London exhibition.

▶ Cat., *Venini and Murano Renaissance: Italian Art Glass of the 1940s and 50s*, New York: Fifty/50, 1984. John Fleming and Hugh Honour, *The Penguin Dictionary of Decorative Arts*, London: Penguin, 1989:63–64 (rev. ed.).

Barr Jr., Alfred Hamilton   (1902–81)

▶ American scholar, museum curator, and founder, New York Museum of Modern Art.

▶ Director of the New York Museum of Modern Art 1929–43, Barr introduced Modern European art, architecture, and design to the USA. He was responsible for mounting Henry-Russell Hitchcock's and Philip Johnson's 1932 'The International Style: Architecture Since 1922,' Johnson's 1934 'Machine Art' exhibitions, and numerous others.

▶ *Alfred H. Barr Jr.: A Memorial Tribute*, New York: Museum of Modern Art, 1981. Penny Sparke, *Introduction to Design and Culture in the Twentieth Century*, Allen and Unwin, 1986. Alice Goldfarb Marquis, *Alfred H. Barr Jr.: Missionary for the Modern*, Chicago: Contemporary Book, 1989.

Barrau, Gérard   (1945–)

▶ French industrial designer; active Paris.

▶ Studied École Nationale Supérieure des Arts Décoratifs, Paris.

▶ He was active in his own design office Architral; designed 1979 electrical switches produced by Legrand; specialized in chain-store layouts, including 30 stores for La FNAC (domestic hi-fi and electronic equipment); designed furniture for the shops of La Chemise Lacoste (clothing), 12 shop layouts for Darty (electric appliances); developed the design of stores for Grand Optical (quick-service eyeglasses).

▶ François Mathey, *Au bonheur des formes, le design français 1945 à 1992*, Paris: Regard, 1993:83,171–325.

Barrault, Jean-Louis

▶ French designer; active Paris.

▶ Barrault was a designer at Raymond Loewy's CEI (Compagnie de l'Esthétique Industrielle); product director, Harold Barnett group; in 1983, set up his own design office. His industrial-product designs included the 1968 all-plastic automobile *Méhari* produced by Citroën and 1986 mini-microwave oven by Moulinex; from 1986, was president of the French Industrial Designers Union (UFDI).

Barray, Jean-Paul   (1930–)

▶ French industrial designer and painter; active Paris.

▶ Studied École des Beaux-Arts and Atelier Le Corbusier-Wogensky, both Paris.

▶ In 1967, he opened his own office, Paris; was a consultant designer to the Bureau d'Études Technès, Maison Créa, and Daum; designed 1969 *Penta Chair* (with Kim Moltzer) in a thin zinc-plated frame with canvas seat, first mass-produced in 1970 by Wilhelm Bofinger, Stuttgart; taught at ENSCI (École Nationale de la Création Industrielle), Paris.

▶ Work shown at 1968 (XIV) Triennale di Milano; 1970 Cologne furniture fair; 1968 'Les Assises du siège contemporain' exhibition, Paris Musée des Arts Décoratifs; 1971 'Modern Chairs 1918–1970' exhibition, Whitechapel Gallery, London.

▶ See Museum of Modern Art.

▶ Cat., *Les Assises du siège contemporain*, Paris: Musée des Arts Décoratifs, 1968. Cat., *Modern Chairs 1918–1970*, London: Lund Humphries, 1971.

Barrese, Antonio   (1945–)

▶ Italian graphic designer; born and active Milan.

▶ Barrese began his professional career in 1965; was on the staff of MID Design 1964–70 and Gruppo Professionale PRO (aka Studio PRO); in 1980, set up his own studio; became a member of ADI (Associazione per il Disegno Industriale); (with I. Hosoe, A. Locatelli, R. Salmiraghi, and A. Torricelli) designed 1977–78 *Spazio* bus for Iveco Orlandi.

▶ See Studio PRO

▶ Alfonso Grassi and Anty Pansera, *Atlante del design italiano: 1940–1980*, Milan, 1980. Hans Wichmann, *Italien Design 1945 bis heute*, Munich: Die Neue Sammlung, 1988.

Barret, Maurice
▶ French interior architect.
▶ Barret was influenced by the architecture of Le Corbusier and interiors of Francis Jourdain; in 1934, became a member of the UAM (Union des Artistes Modernes); from 1933 to the 1950s, collaborated on the review *Le Décor d'aujourd'hui*, publishing his ideas on environments and Rational furnishings; for the journal *L'Architecture d'aujourd'hui*, wrote on the subject of school architecture and furniture; in 1937, built and designed all the furniture for a house in Villefranche-sur-Mer.
▶ From 1934, showed work at Salon des Arts Ménagers and 1936 Salon de l'Habitation (bedroom-studio). Participating in competitions for school furniture design for OTUA (Office Technique pour l'Utilisation de l'Acier), work shown at 1926 Salon d'Automne.
▶ Maurice Barret, 'Retour des USA,' *Mobilier et Décoration*, No. 4, 1956. Maurice Barret, 'Humanisme et architecture, l'avenir de la maison familiale,' *Le Décor d'aujourd'hui*, No. 39, 1947. Cat., *Les années UAM 1929–1958*, Paris: Musée des Arts Décoratifs, 1988:149.

Barron, Phyllis   (1890–1964)
▶ British textile designer; active London and Painswick, Gloucestershire.
▶ Studied drawing and painting, Slade School of Fine Art, London.
▶ Early on, she collected 19th-century French print-block textiles and began experimenting with textile printing and block cutting using 19th-century methods; printed textiles in her Hampstead studio; from the early 1920s, collaborated with Dorothy Larcher, forming Barron and Larcher. In 1930, they moved to Painswick, Gloucestershire, and printed dressmaking textiles and furnishing fabrics using both new and historic French blocks, rejecting aniline dyes; developed vegetable-dye solutions and revived discharge-printing techniques; were best known for fabrics that displayed bold monochromatic prints for furnishings in unbleached cottons and linens; sold through Footprints, London; (with Enid Marx) were the foremost exponents of the hand-block print in England during the first half of the 20th century; executed commissions including soft furnishings for the Duke of Westminster's yacht *The Flying Cloud* and the Senior Common Room of Girton College, Cambridge.
▶ *Phyllis Barron and Dorothy Larcher: Handblock Printed Textiles*, Bath: Crafts Study Centre, 1978. Cat., *Thirties: British art and design before the war*, London: Arts Council of Great Britain, Hayward Gallery, 1979:92,125,284, 296.

Bartels, Heiko   (1947–)
▶ German industrial designer.
▶ Bartels designed kitchen and camping equipment, automobiles, and motorcycles and, from 1974, lighting and interiors; in 1982 with designers Fischer, Hullmann, and Hüskes, set up the Kunstflug design group to produce their own lighting.
▶ Albrecht Bangert and Karl Michael Armer, *80s Style: Designs of the Decade*, New York: Abbeville, 1990:94,227.

Bartlmae, Kerstin   (1941–)
▶ Swedish industrial and furniture designer; born Stockholm; active Ulm (Germany) and Varese (Italy).
▶ 1956–57, studied ceramics and at art college in Stockholm; 1957, business school, Rapallo (Italy); 1958, art college, Florence; 1962, Hochschule für Gestaltung, Ulm.
▶ In 1961, she was an industrial ceramicist at Schwedische Form, Stockholm, and the Rörstrand porcelain factory, Lidköping; 1965–66, worked in a design office, Milan; 1968–69, worked at Institut für Produktgestaltung, Ulm, under Prof. Lindinger; in 1969, set up her own design office; 1970–80, was guest lecturer on product design, State Institute for Architecture and Town Planning, Antwerp and, in 1983, guest lecturer, Fachhochschule für Druck (Graphic Arts College), Stuttgart; from 1987, worked in her own Varese design office and was a guest lecturer on packaging design, graphic design department, Instituto Europea Design, Milan; wrote on

design and packaging and was a jury member of various design competitions. Designs included 1969–70 *1140* plastic wall scales by Soehnle Waagen; 1978 *TK-matic 9725* and *9725 L* fine drawing pencils, the first with an automatic lead feed; 1984–85 *Rolo* seating by Fröscher Sitform; 1986 *Lobby* seating by Casa Möbel-Werke.
▶ Cat., Design Center Stuttgart, *Women in Design: Careers and Life Histories Since 1900*, Stuttgart: Haus der Wirtschaft, 1989:64–67.

Bartning, Otto   (1883–1959)
▶ German architect and designer; born Karlsruhe.
▶ From 1904, studied Technische Hochschulen, Berlin–Charlottenburg; Hochschule, Karlsruhe, Berlin University.
▶ 1926–30, he was director of Hochschule für Handwerk und Baukunst, the successor of the Bauhaus in Weimar; designed industrial, public, and residential buildings, including Protestant churches and, early on, country houses in a version of architectural Expressionism; known for his churches, designed 1922 'Sternkirche,' steel church for the 1928 'Pressa' exhibition in Cologne, circular 1930 Church of the Resurrection, Essen, and, after World War II, prefabricated churches in timber.
▶ Otto Bartning, *Vom neuen Kirchenbau*, Berlin, 1919. Hans K.F. Mayer, *Der Baumeister Otto Bartning und die Wiederentdeckung des Raumes*, Heidelberg, 1951. Otto Bartning, *Was ist Bauen?*, Stuttgart, 1952. Otto Bartning, *Otto Bartning in kurzen Worten*, Hamburg, 1954. Otto Bartning, *Erde Geliebte*, Hamburg, 1955. Otto Bartning and W. Weyres, *Kirchen: Hanbuch für den Kirchenbau*, Munich, 1959. Vittorio Magnago Lampugnani (ed.), *Encyclopedia of 20th-Century Architecture*, New York: Abrams, 1986:22–23.

Bartoli, Carlo   (1931–)
▶ Italian architect, interior designer, and teacher; born Czechoslovakia; active Milan.
▶ Studied Politecnico di Milano to 1957.
▶ 1959–81, he was active in his own office for architecture, furniture, and industrial design, Milan, and from 1981, Monza; was an instructor of planning, High Course of Industrial Design, Florence; 1967–70, taught at the Corso Superiore di Disegno Industriale, Florence; became interested in plastic materials used for housing in 1966; designed 1966 *Gaia* chair in fiberglass (produced from 1967 by Arflex), 1969 *Bicia* armchair in fiberglass upholstered in leather by Arflex; became a member of ADI (Associazione per il Disegno Industriale). Clients included Arc Linea, UCG Confalonieri, Faver, Con & Con, Kartell, Oscam, Rossi di Albizzate, Tisettanta, and Gonfalonieri. From 1988, he taught at the ISA in Rome.
▶ Cat., *Modern Chairs 1918–1970*, London: Lund Humphries, 1971. Cat., Milena Lamarová, *Design a Plastické Hmoty*, Prague: Uměleckoprůmyslové Muzeum, 1972. *ADI Annual 1976*, Milan: Associazione per il Disegno Industriale, 1976. Alfonso Grassi and Anty Pansera, *Atlante del Design Italiano 1940–80*, Milan: Fabbri, 1980. Hans Wichmann, *Italien Design 1945 bis heute*, Munich: Die Neue Sammlung, 1988. *Modo*, No. 148, March–April 1993:116.

Bartolini, Dario   (1943–) and **Lucia Bartolini** (1944–)
▶ Italian industrial designers; born Florence.
▶ In 1968, the Bartolini brothers joined Archizoom Associati, Florence, founded in 1966 and active in industrial and architectural design and urban planning. They were members of the Archizoom team that designed 1969 *Mies* chair by Poltronova; became members of ADI (Associazione per il Disegno Industriale).
▶ Cat., *Modern Chairs 1918–1970*, London: Lund Humphries, 1971. *ADI Annual 1976*, Milan: Associazione per il Disegno Industriale, 1976.

Barwig, Franz   (1868–1931)
▶ Austrian designer.
▶ Studied sculpture, Kunstgewerbeschule, Vienna.
▶ He worked in bronze and wood and won numerous public commissions; though not himself a designer, had a great influence

on designers in Vienna; following his suicide, was honored with
a memorial service by the Vienna Secessionists.
▶ Hans Vollmer, *Allgemeines Lexikon der bildenden Künstler*, Vol.
I, Leipzig: Seemann, 1953:124. Auction catalog, Christie's New
York, 9 Dec. 1989.

Basile, Ernesto (1857–1932)
▶ Italian designer; born Palermo.
▶ Studied Università di Palermo.
▶ In 1881, he settled in Rome; in 1892, became professor, Università di Palermo; after 1893, taught at Università di Roma; designed
1883–84 Parliament Building, Rome, and 1899 Villino Florio,
Palermo; subsequently developed a style that combined his own
Neo-Norman approach with a highly refined version of Art Nouveau expressed in his 1903 Villino Basile, Palermo. Later on, classical traits appeared, as in the 1920–25 Instituto Provinciale Anti-
tubercolare and 1925 Albergo Diurno, both Palermo; this
approach was in opposition with the Italian Rationalist architecture of the 1920s. Active in the prevailing Stile Floreale, he
designed highly ornate, carved furniture for Ducrot in Sicily.
▶ *Ernesto Basile, Studi e schizzi*, Turin: Crudo, 1911. *Mobili e
Arredi di Ernesto Basile: nella produzione Ducrot*, Palermo:
Navecento, 1980. Cat., Paolo Portoghesi et al., *Ernesto Basile architetto*, Venice, 1980. Vittorio Magnago Lampugnani, *Encyclopedia
of 20th-Century Architecture*, New York: Abrams, 1986:34,168.
Cat., Gabriel P. Weisberg, *Stile Floreale: The Cult of Nature in
Italian Design*, Miami: The Wolfsonian Foundation, 1988.

Bastard, Georges (1881–1939)
▶ French tabletier, ceramicist, and glassware designer; born An-
derville, Oise.
▶ Studied École Nationale des Arts Décoratifs, Paris.
▶ Member of family of Paris tabletiers active from the 17th century, Bastard was director of École des Arts Décoratifs, Limoges
until 1938; in 1938, became director of Manufacture Nationale
de Porcelaine, Sèvres; from 1930, was a member of UAM (Union
des Artistes Modernes); collaborated with Jacques-Émile Ruhlmann and Pierre-Paul Montagnac.
▶ Showed work at Salons of the Société Nationale des Beaux-
Arts, events of Salon d'Automne from 1910–12; 1933 and 1934
events of Salon des Tuileries; 1925 Paris 'Exposition Internationale
des Arts Décoratifs et Industriels Modernes'; from 1930, UAM's
first three exhibitions. Work was subject of 1950 exhibition, Paris
Musée des Arts Décoratifs, and 1959 exhibition, Musée National
d'Art Antique, Lisbon.
▶ Gabrielle Rosenthal, 'Georges Bastard,' *L'Amour de l'Art*, No.
12, Dec. 1927. Cat., *Obras de Georges Bastard*, Lisbon: Musé
National d'Art Antique, 1959. Victor Arwas, *Art Déco*, Abrams,
1980. Sylvie Raulet, *Bijoux Arts Déco*, Paris: Regard, 1984. Arlette
Barré-Despond, *UAM*, Paris: Regard, 1986. Cat., *Les années UAM
1929–1958*, Paris: Musée des Arts Décoratifs, 1988:150.

Bastide, Thomas (1954–)
▶ French designer; born Biarritz.
▶ Studied École Supérieure d'Arts Graphiques, Penninghen
(France), École des Métiers d'Art, and industrial design, Philchuck
Glass School, Washington State (USA).
▶ Bastide joined Baccarat in 1981; became director of design in
1983, producing hundreds of designs for the firm, including 1986
Triangle drinking glass.
▶ *Les Carnets du Design*, Paris: Mad-Cap Productions et APCI,
1986:51. Jean-Louis Curtis, *Baccarat*, Paris: Regard, 1991.

Batchelder, Ernest Allen (1875–1957)
▶ American ceramicist; born Nashua, New Hampshire; active Pas-
adena, California.
▶ Studied Massachusetts Normal Art School to 1899.
▶ Teaching design theory and manual arts 1902–09, Batchelder
was director of art, Throop Polytechnic Institute, holding summer

classes at the Handicraft Guild Summer Schools in Minneapolis;
was influenced by the design theory of Denman W. Ross, the
Harvard University professor whose ideas were the basis of Batchelder's books *The Principles of Design* (1904) and *Design in Theory
and Practice* (1910); in 1905, traveled to centers of the Arts and
Crafts Movement in Europe; in 1909, established a pottery for
tile making on his own property in Pasadena; moved Batchelder
Tiles in 1916 to Los Angeles, where conveyor belts took sand-
pressed tiles into large kilns; in the early years, designed most of
the hand-molded tiles himself. Depicting California landscapes,
his work was almost entirely in brown with blue glaze rubbed
into and around reliefs of vines, peacocks and other animals,
flowers, and Viking ships. The firm closed in the 1930s. Batchelder
later occupied a small shop in Pasadena where he produced delicate slip-cast pottery.
▶ Paul Evans in Timothy J. Andersen et al., *California Design
1910*, Salt Lake City: Peregrine Smith, 1980:75.

Battersby, George Martin (1914–82)
▶ British collector, illustrator, and writer.
▶ Studied architecture, Regent Street Polytechnic; 1934–35,
Royal Academy of Dramatic Arts, both London.
▶ In the late 1920s, Battersby was a junior draftsman in studios
of decorators Gill and Reigate, London; worked briefly at Liberty's,
London; designed a 1938 production of *Hamlet* at the Old Vic
and sets for other productions; worked at couture house Bunny
Rogers; by the end of World War II, had become a collector of
Art Nouveau; from the late 1940s to 1951, was assistant set
designer to Cecil Beaton; 1948–51, (with Philip Dyer) worked on
backgrounds for Beaton's photographs for Modess advertisements; became active as an independent set designer; designed
interiors and painted murals for private clients; painted 1959
murals for Carlyle Hotel, New York; 1964 murals for First
National Bank of Wisconsin; designed interior schemes for Ken
Russell's 1965 BBC film on Claude Debussy; from mid-1960s,
operated Sphinx Studio with partner Paul Watson, whose suicide
ended the business; designed numerous exhibitions for Brighton
Museum including 1969 'The Jazz Age' and 1971 'Follies and
Fantasies'; sold his entire collection, except for minor gifts to Brighton Museum, in 1978; was best known for his books *The Decorative Twenties* (1966), *Art Nouveau* (1969), *The Decorative Thirties*
(1969), *Art Deco Fashion* (1974), *Trompe L'Œil* (1974).
▶ Work was subject of 1948 exhibition at Brook Street Gallery,
London; Sagittarius Gallery, New York, 1956; numerous sub-
sequent exhibitions including at Ebury Gallery, London, 1982.
Became known as collector and connoisseur with 1964 'Art Nou-
veau, The Collection of Martin Battersby' exhibition, Brighton
Museum. Received London *Evening Standard* Award for *Inter-
mezzo* (1974) opera production design.
▶ 'Sleight of Eye,' *Vogue*, 15 Feb. 1960. John Marley, 'Martin
Battersby,' *The Decorative Arts Society Journal*, No. 7, 1983. Jessica
Rutherford, *Art Nouveau, Art Deco and the Thirties: The Furniture
Collections at Brighton Museum*, Brighton: The Royal Pavilion, Art
Gallery and Museums, 1983:4. Philippe Garner, 'Martin Bat-
tersby: A Biography,' *The Decorative Twenties*, New York: Whit-
ney, 1988, 2nd. ed.

Bätzner, Helmut (1928–)
▶ German architect.
▶ Studied in Stuttgart.
▶ In 1960, he opened his own office in Karlsruhe; designed 1966
BA 1171 Chair in molded fiberglass produced by Wilhelm Bo-
finger, Stuttgart.
▶ Received 1966 Studio Rosenthal Prize (*BA 1171 Chair*); awards
for IBM office building, Berlin, 1960 Cologne University Library,
and 1963 Karlsruhe Theater. Work included in 1966 'Vijftig Jaar
Zitten,' Stedelijk Museum, Amsterdam, and 1968 'Les Assises du
siège contemporain' exhibition, Paris Musée des Arts Décoratifs.
▶ Cat., *Modern Chairs 1918–1970*, London: Lund Humphries,
1971.

Bauchet, François   (1948–)

▶ French sculptor and furniture designer; born Montluçon; active Saint-Étienne.

▶ Studied École des Beaux-Arts, Saint-Étienne.

▶ He taught at École des Beaux-Arts, Saint-Étienne, where his pupils included Eric Jourdan. His furniture designs and fine art were influenced by American minimalism. Initial designs in the early 1980s were for tables. He designed interiors commissioned by Fondation Cartier pour l'art contemporain in 1988; designed the lacquered chairs sponsored by VIA, which received its 1982 'L'Appel Permanent' award. Bauchet's minimalism was illustrated in his 1982 Cestaussi une chaise, 1987 Table Carrée, his undulating plastic forms in the 1987 Chaise Liliplon, 1988 Tabouret Foundation, and 1989 Cabinet, all produced by Néotù.

▶ Work included in exhibitions at Galerie Brune, Cosne-sur-Loire, 1977; Hôtel de Ville, Sancerre, 1977; Galerie Surface de Répration, Saint-Étienne, 1978; Galerie des Beaux Arts, Mâcon, 1979; Abbaye des Cordeliers, Châteauroux, 1979; 1982 Biennale de Paris; 1983 exhibition, VIA, Paris; 1983 Salon of the Société des Artistes Décorateurs. Became known through three 1987 exhibitions at Galerie Néotù, Paris; Octobre des Arts, Centre d'Art Plastique, Villefranche-sur-Saone; Gallery Arterieur, Berlin; Documenta 8, Kassel; Musée d'Aix les Bains. Work subject of 1988 exhibition, Centre d'Art Contemporain de Vassivière, near Limoges; 'Medium' exhibition, Fondation Cartier, Jouy-en-Josas; Paris Musée des Arts Décoratifs, and Artemide showroom, Milan; 'Les années 80,' Fondation Cartier. Work subject of 1989 exhibition, Galerie Néotù.

▶ Art Press, No. 63, 1982. 'Meubles au tire-ligne,' Décoration Internationale, No. 60, 1983. Christine Colin, 'Les français montent au créneau,' Cent Idées, No. 131, 1984. Cat., Jean-Claude Conesa, A Bruit Secret, Dunkerque: École des Beaux Arts, 1985. Cat., Hubert Besacier, Vivre en couleurs, Jouy-en-Josas: Fondation Cartier, 1985. Pierre Staudenmeyer, Cardinaux No. 1, Paris; Maeght, 1986. Pierre Staudenmeyer, Desco, Milan: Zeus, 1987. Christine Colin, Design d'Aujourdhui, Paris: Flammarion, 1988. Cat., François Bauchet Designer, Limoges: Centre d'Art Contemporain, 1988. Elisabeth Vedrenne, 'François Bauchet,' Beaux Arts, March 1989. Suzanne Tise, 'Innovators at the Museum,' Vogue Décoration, No. 26, June/July 1990:46.

Baudisch-Wittke, Gudrun   (b. Gudrun Baudisch 1907–82)

▶ Austrian ceramicist; born Vienna.

▶ 1922–26, studied ceramcis Österreichische Bundeslehranstalt für das Baufach und Kunstgewerbe, Graz, under Hans Adametz.

▶ The ceramic workshop of the Wiener Werkstätte was established in 1914; Baudisch-Wittke was a member 1916–30. In 1930, became active in her own workshop with Mario von Pontoni; in 1935, worked with others in the Austrian Pavilion at the world's exposition in Brussels; in 1936, moved to Berlin and, in 1945, to Hallstatt (Austria), where she established the workshop Hallstatt Keramik in 1947; produced numerous stucco ceilings for churches and other buildings.

▶ Günther Feuerstein, Vienna – Present and Past: Arts and Crafts – Applied Art – Design, Vienna: Jugend und Volk, 1976:35, 80. Otto Wutzel and Gudrun Baudisch, Keramik von der Wiener Werkstätte bis zur Keramik Hallstadt, Linz, 1980. Cat., Expressive Keramik der Wiener Werkstätte 1917–1930, Munich: Bayerische Vereinsbank, 1992:126–27.

Bauer, Karl Johann   (1877–1914)

▶ German designer and teacher; active Munich.

▶ Studied Debschitz-Schule (Lehr- und Versuchs-Atelier für Angewandte und freie Kunst), where he taught from 1904 onwards. Marga Jess was his pupil.

▶ Participated in 1914 Cologne 'Deutscher Werkbund-Ausstellung.'

▶ Annelies Krekel-Aalberse, Art Nouveau and Art Déco Silver, New York: Abrams, 1989:142,145,251.

Bauer, Leopold   (1872–1938)

▶ Austrian architect, artisan, and technical writer; born Jaegerndorf, Silesia.

▶ Studied Akademie der bildenden Künste, Vienna, under Karl von Hasenauer and Otto Wagner.

▶ From 1913, he was a professor, Akademie der bildenden Künste. Buildings included 1923–25 National Bank and British-Austrian Bank; Helden Church, Troppau; 1927–28, Weinstein department store; hunting lodge, Jaegerndorf; hotel, Graefenberg, Silesia; catholic church, Bielitz; caster Roster, Kolin, Bohemia. Published the Gesund wohnen und freudig arbeiten (1919).

▶ Hans Vollmer, Allgemeines Lexikon der Bildenden Künstler, Leipzig: Seemann, 1953. F. Fellner von Feldegg, Leopold Bauer: der Künstler und sein Werk, Vienna.

Bauer, Lisa   (1920–)

▶ Swedish glassware designer and graphic artist.

▶ 1937–42, studied Konstindustriskolan, Gothenburg, and Konstfackskolan and Tekniska Skolan, Stockholm.

▶ From 1969, she was a freelance designer for Kosta Boda glassworks, specializing in engraved designs for glass forms by Sigurd Persson.

▶ Cat., David Revere McFadden (ed.), Scandinavian Modern Design 1880–1980, New York: Abrams, 1982:262.

Bauhaus

▶ German architecture and design school; located Weimar 1919–25, Dessau 1925–32, and temporarily Berlin Oct. 1932–April 1933; directors Walter Gropius 1925–28, Hannes Meyer 1928–30, and Ludwig Mies van der Rohe 1930–32.

▶ The Staatliches Bauhaus in Weimar was founded in 1919 by the architect Walter Gropius. Gropius had taken over the Kunstgewerbeschule established earlier as the Hochschule für bildende Kunst by Henry van de Velde to improve standards of craftsmanship in the town, together with the old-established art school. The Bauhaus's first manifesto (1919), whose cover showed a woodcut by Lionel Feininger, proclaimed the unity of the arts through craftsmanship, stating, 'Architects, painters and sculptors, we must all return to the crafts!' To achieve this aim, Gropius organized a study program whose basic structure ultimately became adopted by numerous colleges of design worldwide after World War II. A preliminary or basic course, taken by all students, introduced them to a range of crafts and skills and to color, perception, materials, and form. Students then studied in specialized workshops; in Weimar, there were workshops for metalwork, cabinetmaking, glass painting, weaving, and ceramics. Gropius devised a system of dual control in the workshops, with an artist as a Formmeister (master of form) and a craftsperson as Lehrmeister (master of craft). Studies in color, perception, and form continued in challenging courses taught by Vasilii Kandinskii and Paul Klee, who attracted aspiring artists to the school. In the early period of the Bauhaus in Weimar, Johannes Itten, head of preliminary courses and an associate in the metalworking and glass-painting workshops, was the most influential personality there. His teaching, which aimed to 'release the forces of the soul,' and was related to the romantic idealism of German Expressionism, was in opposition to Gropius's pragmatic aim of establishing links with commerce and industry; Itten left in 1922. Other influences of the Bauhaus included Russian Constructivism and De Stijl artist Theo van Doesburg, who was at the school in Weimar in 1921. In 1923, Hungarian Constructivist László Moholy-Nagy ran the metal workshop and, with former student Josef Albers, the preliminary course. Moholy-Nagy was sympathetic with Gropius's Bauhaus credo, 'Art and Technology: a new unity,' the idea manifested in the Weimar exhibition of 1923 that included the show house Am Horn furnished by the workshop. Although the exhibition was successful and international recognition for the school had grown, the Weimar authorities demanded that it be closed for political and financial reasons. Moving to the industrial city Dessau, the school incorporated the local trade school, and a new 1925–26 building complex was designed by Gropius. He reorgan-

ized the workshops along 'type-forms' or prototypes for industrial production. Moholy-Nagy and Josef Albers jointly continued to run the preliminary course. Moholy-Nagy was in charge of the metal workshop and Georg Muche of the weaving workshops until 1925, when Gunta Stötzl took over. Other former students were in charge of other workshops, including Marcel Breuer of furniture, Herbert Bayer of printing, and Hinnerk Scheper of wall painting. The school's own journal *Bauhaus* published a series of books 1926–31. The ceramics workshop remained in Weimar, where Otto Bartning replaced Gropius as director. Distinguished Bauhaus students included Marianne Brandt, Gyula Pap, and Wilhelm Wagenfeld in metalworking; Anni Albers, Otti Berger, and Margaret Leichner in weaving; Alfred Arndt in furniture; and Joost Schmidt in typography. A Functionalist aesthetic was established at this time along with the production of furniture, textiles, lighting, and graphics, some examples of which became icons of the Modern movement. In Weimar and Dessau, the Bauhaus experimental theater was under the direction of Oscar Schlemmer from 1921; Klee and Kandinskii were staff members until 1931 and 1933, respectively. In 1927, an architecture department was set up and headed by architect and town planner Ludwig Hilberseimer. Gropius left the Bauhaus in 1928; his successor, radical Swiss architect Hannes Meyer, was summarily dismissed in 1930 because of left-wing convictions. Mies van der Rohe was put in charge and, with partner Lily Reich, attempted to established a new apolitical program focusing on *Bau und Ausbau* (building and development). The Nazis, already in control of Dessau city council, closed the school in 1932. Re-established in Berlin, the school operated from a former telephone factory for a further six months before being finally closed by the Nazis in 1933. Many of its staff emigrated to the USA, including Gropius, Breuer, Mies van der Rohe, Hilberseimer, Moholy-Nagy, and the Alberses.
► The Bauhaus (1919–28) was the subject of 1938 exhibition, New York Museum of Modern Art. 50th anniversary observed by the 1968 '50 Jahre Bauhaus' traveling exhibition.
► *Staatliches Bauhaus Weimar 1919–23*, Munich and Weimar, 1923. Walter Gropius, *Idee und Aufbau des Staatlichen Bauhauses*, Munich and Weimar, 1923. Herbert Bayer and Walter and Ilse Gropius (eds.), *Bauhaus 1919–1928*, New York, 1938. Hans M. Wingler, *Das Bauhaus 1919–1933, Weimar Dessau Berlin*, Cologne, 1962. Cat., *50 Jahre Bauhaus*, Stuttgart, 1968. Marcel Franciscono, *Walter Gropius and the Creation of the Bauhaus in Weimar*, Urbana, 1971. Lionel Richard, *Encyclopédie du Bauhaus*, Paris: Somogy, 1985. Wolfgang Pehnt in Vittorio Magnago Lampugnani (ed.), *Encyclopedia of 20th-Century Architecture*, New York: Abrams, 1986:35–37. Cat., *The Bauhaus: Masters and Students*, New York: Barry Friedman 1988. Cat., *Experiment Bauhaus*, Berlin: Bauhaus Dessau, 1988. Magdalena Droste, *Bauhaus*, Cologne: Taschen, 1990. Eckhard Neumann, *Bauhaus and Bauhaus People*, London: Chapman and Hall, 1993.

Baumann, Hans Theo   (1924–)
► Swiss ceramicist and glassware designer; active Germany.
► Studied in Dresden and Basel.
► Baumann was among Germany's leading postwar designers of ceramics and glassware; opening his own studio in 1955, designed ceramics for Rosenthal, Arzberg, Thomas, and Schönwald and glassware for Süssmuth, Rosenthal, Gral, Rheinkristall, Thomas, and Daum; designed furniture, lighting, and textiles, frequently incorporating his own particular round-geometric shapes, 1971 *Brasilia* coffee and tea services by Arzberg (similar to Hermann Gretsch's 1931 pattern, also by Arzberg), and porcelain dinnerware including 1970 *Form 3000*, 1972 *Delta*, and 1972 *Donau* by Arzberg; 1958 *Berlin* by Rosenthal; and *Rastergeschirr 2298* by Schönwald.
► Work subject of 1979–80 'Hans Theo Baumann Design' exhibition, Cologne Kunstgewerbemuseum.
► Cat., *Hans Theo Baumann Design*, Cologne: Kunstgewerbemuseum, 1979. Cat., Kathryn B. Hiesinger and George H. Marcus III (eds.), *Design Since 1945*, Philadelphia: Philadelphia Museum

of Art, 1983. Cherie Fehrman and Kenneth Fehrman, *Postwar Interior Design, 1945–1960*, New York: Van Nostrand Reinhold, 1987.

Bautte et Moynier
► Swiss watchmakers, jewelers, and enamelists; located Geneva.
► In the late 19th century, Jean-François Bautte established a firm specializing in very thin watches; also produced enameling and fine goldwork, rather than jewelry with precious stones. In the 19th century, the firm was known for producing and selling high quality 'Geneva' ornaments. A scathing critic of the work of London and Paris jewelers, John Ruskin, known to have purchased enameled pieces for his wife from this firm, described its wares of the 1840s, 'One went to Mr. Bautte's with awe, and of necessity as one did to one's bankers.'
► Cook and Wedderburn (eds.), John Ruskin, *Praeterita*, 1885–89 (new ed.). Charlotte Gere, *American and European Jewelry 1830–1914*, New York: Crown, 1975:150–51.

Bawden, Edward   (1903–)
► British painter, illustrator, and graphic designer.
► From 1919, studied Cambridge School of Art; 1922–25, Royal College of Art, London, under Paul Nash.
► Bawden was elected to the Seven and Five Society; 1928–29, collaborated with Eric Ravilious on murals for Morley College (destroyed during World War II and repainted by Bawden in 1958); designed advertising for clients including Westminster Bank and Shell-Mex and booklets for Fortnum and Mason; illustrated books for publishers including Faber and Faber, Nonesuch Press, and Kynoch Press; designed borders, endpapers, and wallpapers produced by Cole, posters (often reproduced by linoleum-cut printing) for London Passenger Transport Board, textiles for the Orient Steam Navigation; and decorated earthenware for Wedgwood. Commissions included murals for Hull University, Pilkington, British Petroleum, oceanliners, and the VIP lounge of the British Pavilion, 1967 Montreal 'Expo 67.' His tile decorations were installed on London Underground's Victoria Line.
► Douglas Percy Bliss, *Edward Bawden*, Godalming: Pendower, 1979. Cat., *Thirties: British art and design before the war*, London: Arts Council of Great Britain, Hayward Gallery, 1979:43,78,127, 165,178,201,214,220,280,285.

Baxter, George
► British glassware designer.
► Studied Guildford School of Art; from 1951, Royal College of Art, London.
► Hired by William Wilson, he joined the staff of Whitefriars Glass in 1954; produced a wide range of designs for both tablewares and ornamental glass; introduced innovative forms of molded glass based on themes from nature, including tree-bark and seashells.
► Frederick Cooke, *Glass: Twentieth-Century Design*, New York: Dutton, 1986:75.

Bayer
► German chemical manufacturer.
► The firm was founded by Friedrich Bayer in 1863 and became part of IG Farbenindustrie in 1925; produced colors, plastics, medicine, and other commercial chemical substances; 1951–72, was known as Farbenfabriken Bayer and, from 1971, as Bayer; sponsored design exhibitions; commissioned Joe Columbo and Verner Panton to design furniture. Olivier Mourgue designed the 1971 *Visiona 3* experimental seating.
► Cat., Milena Lamarová, *Design a Plastické Hmoty*, Prague: Uměleckoprůmyslové Muzeum, 1972:38.

B&B Italia
► Italian furniture manufacturer; located Novedrate, Como.
► Piero Ambrogio Busnelli and his brother Franco set up Fratelli Busnelli fu Giuseppe in 1953. Substituting polyurethane for latex rubber (discovered through the forming of toy ducks by Interplastic of London), Piero got the idea for cold molding furniture forms;

wishing to experiment further, left the family firm in 1966 and took ten employees to Plestem, a small plastics firm; set up a workshop in Meda, where designers included Paolo Caliari and Gianfranco Frattini; from the beginning, produced furniture in plastics; in partnership with Cesare Cassina, established C&B Italia in 1966 using new assembly-line methods executed by workers who were purposefully inexperienced in furniture production; Initial designers included Vico Magistretti, Paolo Caliari, Mario Bellini, and Tobia Scarpa. Its first furniture was the 1966 *Flower-pot holder* designed by Caliari, 1966 *Quattro Gatti* table by Bellini, 1966 *Amanta* armchair in Fiberlite by Bellini, 1966 *Coronado* by Scarpa, and *Serenza* divan-bed by Busnelli. It manufactured Gaetano Pesce's 1969 *Up* seating furniture in polyurethane and nylon jersey and Scarpa's 1971 *Bonanza* armchair in Duraplum and leather. In 1973, Busnelli bought out Cassina and changed the firm's name to B&B Italia. In 1975, the firm bought wooden-chair manufacturer Maspero and established Compagnia delle Filippine to produce rattan furniture; in 1981, the Office Furniture Division and Contract Division were established. Today, the firm claims to produce 80 per cent of polyurethane chairs worldwide. Other freelance designers included Carlo Bimbi and Nilo Gioacchini, Antonio Citterio and Paolo Nava, Gianfranco Ferré, Studio Kairos, Paolo Piva, Richard Sapper, Afra Scarpa, Kazuhide Takahama, and Marco Zanuso.

▶ Received International Design Prize (Bellini's *Quattro Gatti* tables). C&B's work shown at Salone del Mobile, Milan, from 1968; 1970 (III) 'Eurodomus,' Palazzo dell'Arte, Milan; Salon du Meuble, Paris, from 1969; 1972 (IV) 'Eurodomus,' Turin; Cologne furniture fair from 1973. Work included in 1972 'Design a Plastické Hmoty' exhibition, Uměleckoprůmyslové Muzeum, Prague.

▶ Cat., Milena Lamarová, *Design a Plastické Hmoty*, Prague: Uměleckoprůmyslové Muzeum, 1972:172:174. Mario Mastropietro et al., *Un'Industria per il Design: La ricerca, i designers, l'immagine B&B Italia*, Milan: Lybra Immagine, 1986.

BBPR

▶ Italian architecture, town planning, and design group.

▶ BBPR was formed in 1932 by Gianluigi Banfi, Lodovico Barbiano di Belgiojoso, Enrico Peressutti, and Ernesto N. Rogers. The firm began its activities in town planning (for the Valle d'Aosta in 1936–37 and tourist plan for the Island of Elba in 1936), architecture (1933 Villa Morpurgo in Opicina-Trieste and 1934 house of Ferrario in Milan), and interior design (1933 [V] Triennale pavilion, 1933 Marietti apartment, 1936 [VI] Triennale conference hall). It was a member of CIAM from 1935. During World War II, Rogers was interned in Switzerland, teaching architecture (Alberto Rosselli a student of his); Banfi died in Mauthausen concentration camp. BBPR, retaining its full name, continued after the war. 1955–63, Belgiojoso taught at Instituto di Architettura, Venice. 1950–62, Peressutti taught design in England and USA. Rogers taught at Facoltà di Architettura, Milan; was editor of *Casabella* from 1954–65; co-editor of *Domus* with Zanuso from 1946–47, and a writer. The group continued, taking in Aberico Bardiano as a member. Criticized after World War II for its rejection of Modernism, the group had always shown an awareness of historicist elements. Its architecture included 1937–38 Sanatorium in Legnano and 1940 Monastery of San Simpliciano (with E. Radice Rossati), the 1946 Memorial to concentration camp victims (Belgiojoso, Peressutti, and Rogers), 1950 INA-Casa quarter (with Franco Albini and Gianni Albricci) in the Cesate section, 1950–51 (completed 1958) 'Torre Velasca' skyscraper, 1954–56 restoration and layout of the museums of the Castello Sforzesco, 1954–58 Torre Velasca, and 1969 offices of the Chase Manhattan Bank, and 1958–59 office building of Immobiliare Cagisa in the Piazza Meda, all in Milan. Its design work included a 1950 electric clock for Solaroli, 1955 TV set for CGE Electric, 1956 *Spazio* and 1960 *Arco* metal office-furniture suites for Olivetti, and 1954–64 furniture for Arflex, including the 1954 *Elettra* suite. Belgiojoso, Peressutti, and Rogers designed glassware for Venini, including lighting in *c*1955.

▶ Work subject of 1982 'BBPR a Milano' exhibition, Milan.

▶ Enzo Paci, 'Continuità e coerenze dei BBPR,' *Zodiac*, No. 4, 1959:82–115. E, Bonfanti and M. Porta, *Città, museo e architettura: Il gruppo BBPR nella cultura architettonica italiana 1932–70*, Florence, 1973. Alfonso Grassi and Anty Pansera, *Atlante del Design Italiano 1940–80*, Milan: Fabbri, 1980. Andrea Branzi and Michele De Lucchi, *Design Italiano degli Anni '50*, Milano: Editoriale Domus, 1980. Antonio Piva (ed.), *BBPR a Milano*, Milan: Electa 1982. Cat., *Lumière je pense à vous*, Paris: Centre Georges Pompidou, 1985. Vittorio Magnago Lampugnani, *Encyclopedia of 20th-Century Architecture*, New York: Abrams, 1986:37–38.

B.d Ediciones de Diseño

▶ Spanish furniture and furnishings manufacturer.

▶ In 1972, Studio-PER members Oscar Tusquets, Lluís Clotet, Pep Bonet, Cristian Cirici, and Xavier Carulla with others formed B.d Ediciones de Diseño. The firm produced many of Tusquets's furniture and product designs and those of others considered too risky by other Spanish manufacturers at the time. The initials 'B.d' represented Boccaccio Diseño, referring to Oriol Regás, the firm's chief banker and entertainment tycoon, whose various enterprises were named 'Boccaccio.' B.d Ediciones de Diseño began as a retail sales showroom for furniture designed by Studio-PER members and for reproductions of pieces by Alvar Aalto, Eileen Gray, and Charles Rennie Mackintosh. Lectures and exhibitions were organized in the retail space and a public library set up to foster contemporary design in Barcelona. The firm is housed in Lluís Domènech i Montaner's 1898 Casa Thomas. Its products included the 1980 *Duplex* stool by Javier Mariscal (with Pepe Cortés), 1983 *Araña* lamp by Cortés and Mariscal, and 1988 *Coqueta* chair by Pete Sans.

▶ Guy Julier, *New Spanish Design*, New York: Rizzoli, 1991.

Beam, J. Wade (1944–)

▶ American designer.

▶ Studied School of Architecture, Clemson University, Charleston, South Carolina.

▶ He held key positions in sales and marketing, product research and development, and manufacturing for firms including Dunbar, Wrightline, and OSI; from 1973, was active in his own furniture-design and manufacturing firm in conjunction with an architecture and interior-design practice; became director of sales and marketing, Brueton Industries; designed the *Bearing Console*, *Reflections Mirror*, *Fushion Table*, and 1991 *Cristal* table produced by Brueton.

▶ Received three International Product Design Awards, ASID; two Roscoe Awards; Silver Production Design Award, IBD; and Product Design Award, Corporate Design and Realty.

Beaton, Cecil (1904–80)

▶ British photographer, interior designer, and stage designer.

▶ From 1922 studied Cambridge University.

▶ The house he occupied until 1945 at Ashcombe, Wiltshire, near friend Edith Olivier, was decorated with limited funds using exaggerated baroque furniture; the walls of the 'Circus Bedroom' were painted by visiting artist friends, including Rex Whistler and Oliver Messel, in a kind of Surrealistic overstatement. He published *The Book of Beauty* (1930) and memoirs in *Scrapbook* (1937); during most of the 1930s, worked in France and the USA as photographer for Condé Nast, publishers of *Vogue* and *Vanity Fair*; 1939–45, was a war photographer for the British Ministry of Information, working in Africa and India. In the 1950s, Beaton's house in Broadchalke, Wiltshire, was decorated by Felix Harbord, who used rich and grand furnishings, including wine velvet and leopard skin. In his later years, Beaton rented for a short time each year a suite at the St. Regis Hotel, New York, which he decorated, *Vogue* publishing the results. He designed sets and costumes for the films *Gigi* (1959) and *My Fair Lady* (1965), winning Academy Awards. Active as a set designer, he was assisted from the late 1940s by Martin Battersby and others.

▶ Appointed a Commander of the British Empire in 1957. Received the Légion d'Honneur in 1960.

▶ Cat., *Thirties: British art and design before the war*, London: Arts Council of Great Britain, Hayward Gallery, 1979:249,285. Hugo Vickers, *Cecil Beaton: A Biography*, New York: Donald I. Fine, 1987. Stephen Calloway, *Twentieth-Century Decoration*, New York: Rizzoli, 1988:152,280,282–83,319.

Beaux-Arts

▶ Style of architecture.

▶ The Beaux-Arts style was an architecture on a grand scale. The name is derived from the École des Beaux-Arts, Paris, where historical and eclectic ideas were taught during the 19th century and into the 20th century. The influence of Beaux-Arts design was felt in America during the early 19th century. Proponents of the Modern movement considered it decadent and retrograde.

Becca, Giuseppe   (1935–)

▶ Italian designer; born in Bologna; active Milan.

▶ From 1966, he designed exhibitions, ceramics, metalwork, and furniture; became a member of ADI (Associazione per il Disegno Industriale). Clients included Cava Ceramica (corporate image), Cava Inox (artistic direction), Sigma Tau, Coel Forni in Milan, Sideral (corporate image and ceramic design), and urban layouts for the towns of Rimini and Ferrara.

▶ *ADI Annual 1976*, Milan: Associazione per il Disegno Industriale, 1976.

Becchi, Alessandro   (1946–)

▶ Italian architect and designer; born and active Florence.

▶ Studied Instituto Statale d'Arte, Florence, to 1966.

▶ Active professionally from 1969, he founded Metaform industrial-design studio in Florence; collaborated with Graziano Giovannetti; executed a series of sofas in the 1970s, restating the standard convertible sofa; designed the frameless, soft-pad 1970 *Anfibio* sofabed by his own firm; became a member of ADI (Associazione per il Disegno Industriale). His furniture was produced by Giovannetti Collezioni. Clients included Emerson; B&B Italia; Art Museum, Jerusalem; Arflex; University of Illinois; and University of Texas.

▶ Received 1979 Premio Compasso d'Oro (*Anfibio* sofabed). Participated in 1975 'Desegno Italiano +' exhibition, São Paulo.

▶ 'The Anfibio Collection,' *Industrial Design*, Vol. 19, April 1972:28–29. *ADI Annual 1976*, Milan: Associazione per il Disegno Industriale, 1976. *Moderne Klassiker, Möbel, die Geschichte machen*, Hamburg, 1982:119. Cat., Kathryn B. Hiesinger and George H. Marcus III (eds.), *Design Since 1945*, Philadelphia: Philadelphia Museum of Art, 1983. Hans Wichmann, *Italien Design 1945 bis heute*, Munich: Die Neue Sammlung, 1988.

Bécheau, Vincent   (1955–) and Marie-Laure Bourgeois (1955–)

▶ French design collaborators; Bécheau born Périgueux; Bourgeois born Paris; both active Saint-Avit.

▶ Bourgeois studied architecture, Unité de Programme (UP6), Paris, 1981.

▶ Known for their manipulation of new material (known as 'third type') in furniture design. In 1982, two prototypes were selected for production by VIA. In 1983, their work won the *Progressive Architecture* competition, Chicago. In 1984, they designed the office of the Conseiller Artistique of Bordeaux; had a permanent installation realized at the Galerie Eric Fabre in Paris; opened a design office in Lille; in 1986, they won the Folies Siffait competition, Nantes; designed offices of the ADDC, Périgueux; in 1987, designed the reception hall of Font de Gaume les Elysées, Paris, and reception hall of FRAC Aquitaine, Dax; used sophisticated combinations of woods with kitsch, colorful corrugated plastic sheets, and high-tech substances with traditional materials.

▶ Work shown first time in 1983 at Galerie Ocheb et Nitro, Bordeaux, and in exhibitions including French Cultural Center, Belgrade, in 1983; Musée des Arts Décoratifs, Bordeaux, in 1983; École des Beaux-Arts, Dunkerque, in 1985. Work was subject of exhibitions at Galerie Néotù, Paris; 'Made in France,' Nantes, and Galerie de Brice d'Antras, Berlin, in 1986; Galerie BDX, Bordeaux, in 1988. Shiro Kuramata included the designers' work in his 1988 'In-Spiration' lighting exhibition for Yamagiwa, Tokyo.

▶ Christian Schlater, *Les années 80*, Paris: Flammarion, 1983. Sophie Anargyros, *Intérieurs 80*, Paris: Regard, 1983. *SD journal*, Tokyo, 1983. Sophie Anargyros, *Les années 80*, Paris: Rivages, 1986. *Wohnen von Sinnen*, Cologne: Dumont, 1986. Brochure, Christine Colin, *Vincent Bécheau, Marie-Laure Bourgeois, 1982 Mobilier 1987*, 1987.

Becker, Edmond-Henri   (1871–)

▶ French woodcarver; born Paris.

▶ Studied with Hiolon and Valton.

▶ Active at the beginning of the 20th century, he worked in collaboration with Parisian jeweler Boucheron, producing pieces that combined gold and enamel with ebony and other rare woods.

▶ Showed work at Salons of the Société des Artistes français from 1898 and others from *c*1900.

▶ Yvonne Brunhammer et al., *Art Nouveau Belgium, France*, Houston: Rice University, 1976, biblio.

Becker, Friedrich   (1922–)

▶ German goldsmith.

▶ A talented goldsmith who worked with precious stone, he produced ecclesiastical objects including a 1958 monstrance (a consecrated vessel holding the Host); from the late 1960s, designed kinetic jewelry and sculpture, including a geometric ring rotating on ball bearings; promoted the goldsmith's craft at a time when contemporary designers rejected the use of precious materials.

Becker, Martina   (1959–)

▶ German designer; born Giessen an der Lahn.

▶ Studied Hochschule für Gestaltung, Offenbach, to 1977.

▶ 1984–85, she worked at Mathias Hoffmann Design, Tübingen; designed 1987 vase collection for Wächtersbacher Keramik and 1986 *Karo* knock-down chair prototype; 1988–89, worked at Schlosser; from 1989, was an assistant to Professor Meru at Hochschule für Gestaltung, Linz.

▶ Cat., Design Center Stuttgart, *Women in Design: Careers and Life Histories Since 1900*, Stuttgart: Haus der Wirtschaft, 1989:70–71.

BecVar, Arthur N.

▶ American industrial designer.

▶ In the 1950s and 1960s, BecVar was manager of the major appliance division of General Electric, Louisville, Kentucky, responsible for industrial design.

Bedin, Martine   (1957–)

▶ French designer; born Bordeaux; active Paris, Florence, and Milan.

▶ From 1974, studied École d'architecture UP6, Paris, and 1978 in Florence.

▶ In 1978 in Italy, she met Adolfo Natalini and worked at Superstudio, Florence; discovered Radical Architecture; in 1979, built a small house for the 1979 (XVI) Triennale di Milano; worked with Ettore Sottsass from 1980–88 in the Memphis group, for which she designed 1981 *Super* multiple-light table lamps on wheels; 1980–81, was a correspondent for French journal *Architecture Interieur Crée*; in 1982, set up her own studio, Milan; from 1983, taught at École Camondo, Paris; designed 1987 salt and pepper shakers and 1988 tableware for Algorithme in Paris (produced by Nestor Perkal). Designs included 1985 *Gédéon* lamp (first prize at the lighting competition sponsored by APCI) and other models by Megalit; plaster lighting for Sedap; rugs for Élysée Éditions; buses for the city of Nîmes; faucets for Jacob Delafon (including 1985 *Skipper*); flatware for Sasaki. In 1986, she was artistic director of the domestic interiors department of Daniel Hechter; in 1987, designed a line of handbags for J. & F. Martell and baggage for Louis Vuitton; in 1988, designed the interior of a house near Toulouse; in 1990, laid out the bookstore of the Caisse nationale

des Monuments historiques (Hôtel de Sully), Paris; in 1992 with Piotr Serakowski and Mathilde Brétillot founded La Manufacture familiale, near Bordeaux, to produce furniture, mostly in wood. Works for Memphis included the 1981 *Super* table lamp, *Splendid* floor lamp, 1982 *Eastern* table lamps, 1984 *Charleston* floor lamp, 1985 *Olympia* table lamp, 1985 *Daisy* table lamp, 1985 *Cucumber* ceramic vase, 1986 *Paris* chair, and 1987 *Charlotte* sideboard.
▶ Received 1983 French Ministry of Culture award office lighting (*Gédéon*) competition. Showed work with the Memphis group at its first exhibition in 1981, Salone del Mobile, Milan; 1985 'Lumière je pense à vous,' Centre Georges Pompidou, Paris; 1988 'Design français 1960–1990: Trois décennies,' Centre Georges Pompidou; 1989 'L'Art de Vivre,' Cooper-Hewitt Museum, New York.
▶ Cat., *Lumière je pense à vous*, Paris: Centre Georges Pompidou, 1985. 'Martine Bedin,' *Intramuros*, No. 8, 1986. Cat., *Design français 1960–1990: Trois décennies*, Paris: APCI/Centre Georges Pompidou, 1988. Cat., Design Center Stuttgart, *Women in Design: Careers and Life Histories Since 1900*, Stuttgart: Haus der Wirtschaft, 1989:240–43. François Mathey, *Au bonheur des formes, le design français 1945 à 1992*, Paris: Regard, 1992.

Beene, Geoffrey (1927–)
▶ American fashion designer; born Haynesville, Louisiana.
▶ 1941–44, studied Tulane University in Louisiana; 1944–45, University of Southern California; 1949, Traphagen School of Fashion of Ethel Traphagen; 1949, Académie Julian, Paris.
▶ 1944–45, he was an assistant in the display department of I. Magnin in Los Angeles. 1949–50, he was a designer for Samuel Winston; 1950–57, at Harmay; 1958–62, at Teal Traina; and for Martini Designs and Abe Fetterman. In 1962, he set up his own design studio in New York; in 1969, the boutiques Beene Bazaar; and, in 1970, the Beenebag. He was a member of the Fashion Design Council of America. Known for quality rather than innovation, took a classic approach in the 1970s. He designed 1991 furniture that included the *Shoe-heel* stool and *Leg* table sold through his own outlet and 1993 *Drum* porcelain dinnerware by Swid Powell.
▶ Received 1964 and 1966 Coty American Fashion Critics Award, 1977 Hall of Fame, 1965 National Cotton Award, 1965 Nieman Marcus Award, and 1966 Ethel Traphagen Award.
▶ Ann Lee Morgan, *Contemporary Designers*, London: Macmillan, 1984:58–59. Wendy Goodman, 'Beene's New Line,' *House and Garden*, Aug. 1991:82.

Beese, Hedda (1944–)
▶ German product designer; born Guhrau; active London.
▶ Studied Pädigogische Hochschule (College of Education), Berlin; 1973–76, Central School of Arts and Crafts, London.
▶ She settled in London in 1968; in 1976, became active in industrial design; 1976–87, was joint manager, Moggridge Associates, London; from 1976, member of the board of directors, Design Developments, London; returned to Germany and, in 1987, set up Moggeridge's Design Drei division, Hanover; lectured at London Central School of Arts and Crafts; Royal College of Art, London; Newcastle Polytechnic; and DZ Design Centre, Bilboa, in 1987. She served as judge on many competition committees; became a member of Chartered Society of Designs; in 1983, of Chartered Society of Designers and Fellow of Royal Society of Arts, London; in 1988, of Verband Deutscher Industrie-Designer. Designs included 1986 *SL 48* solar lantern by BP Solar International, 1985 microwave by Hoover, 1986 *Venturer* telephone by Alcatel Bell, 1987 laboratory filter by Anotec Separations.
▶ Work included in 1980 'Designers in Britain,' Design Centre, London; 1981 '30 Ex-ILEA,' Whitechapel Gallery, London; 1981 'Designed in Britain, Made Abroad' and 1987 'Design It Again,' Design Centre, London and Glasgow.
▶ Received 1982 Design Council Award (STC Wide Area Radiopager), London; 1988 Design Innovation award, Haus Industrieform Essen (*SL 48* solar lantern); Best of Category Consumer Products, 1988 *ID* Magazine Annual.

▶ Liz McQuiston, *Women in Design: A Contemporary View*, New York: Rizzoli, 1988:10. Cat., Design Center Stuttgart, *Women in Design: Careers and Life Histories Since 1900*, Stuttgart: Haus der Wirtschaft, 1989:72–77. Albrecht Bangert and Karl Michael Armer, *80s Style: Designs of the Decade*. New York: Abbeville, 1990:227.

Beese, Lotte (1903–)
▶ German architect; wife of Mart Stam.
▶ Studied textile design and architecture, Bauhaus, Dessau.
▶ 1930–35, she lived in the Soviet Union; 1939–44, taught architecture, Amsterdam; subsequently, was active as an architect, Rotterdam; (with Stam) settled in Switzerland.
▶ Lionel Richard, *Encyclopédie du Bauhaus*, Paris: Somogy, 1985:180.

Begeer
▶ Dutch silversmiths; located Utrecht.
▶ C.J. Begeer founded the firm in 1868. In c1885, the firm's first Modern designs began to appear, for which Cornelis L.J. Begeer, who joined the family firm in 1888, was responsible. He left in 1904 to set up his own workshop, Stichtsche Zilverfabriek. At the turn of the century, it sold silver from the Wolfers factory in Brussels, which made both Modern and classic patterns. Cornelis's half-brother Carel J.A. Begeer set up his own workshop in the family firm's premises and produced the silver designs of Jan Eisenloeffel. The most important exponent of the geometrical style in the Netherlands, he signed a contract with Begeer in 1904 to put his designs into production. Even though his wares attracted much attention at exhibitions they were not commercially successful. A.F. Gips designed for the firm. The silver H.P. Berlage designed for the Kröller-Müllers was made by Begeer. In 1919, the C.J. Begeer firm merged with with former competitor J.M. van Kempen and jeweler J. Vos, becoming Van Kempen, Begeer & Vos, and then Zilverfabriek Voorschoten. The merger greatly diminished artistic development, until it was reorganized under the name Zilverfabriek Voorschoten in 1925 with Begeer as director. He met Christa Ehrlich at the 1927 Leipzig Europäisches Kunstgewerbe exhibition, where she had supervised the Austrian pavilion designed by Josef Hoffmann. Begeer persuaded Ehrlich to come to the Netherlands, where she produced outstanding designs in a Modern style.
▶ *Industry and Design in the Netherlands, 1850–1950*, Amsterdam: Stedelijk Museum, 1985. Annelies Krekel-Aalberse, *Art Nouveau and Art Déco Silver*, New York: Abrams, 1989:18,91, 177,251.

Begeer, Carel J.A. (1883–1956)
▶ Dutch silversmith; active Utrecht.
▶ Studied in Hanau.
▶ He set up his own workshop on the premises of the family firm, C.J. Begeer, in 1904, producing silver designs of Jan Eisenloeffel and other leading artists; in 1904, he took over the artistic direction of the firm from his half-brother Cornelis L.J. Begeer, who left the firm to set up his own workshop. Most of the wares of Carel were stamped with his own and the factory's mark. Begeer taught a drawing class, where Gerrit Rietveld rendered some medal designs. While Carel Begeer was at the firm, it sold silver by Georg Jensen, Josef Hoffmann, and Adolf von Mayrhofer, among others. Also a silversmith, Begeer did some experimentation of his own. Influenced by German silversmiths including Ernst Riegel, Begeer's work used less and less decoration. In 1919, the merger of competitor van Kempen and C.J. Begeer with the jeweler J. Vos further dampened artistic development. Carel became director of the merged and reorganized firms, in 1925 renamed Zilverfabriek Voorschoten.
▶ *Industry and Design in the Netherlands, 1850–1950*, Amsterdam: Stedelijk Museum, 1985. Annelies Krekel-Aalberse, *Art Nouveau and Art Déco Silver*, New York: Abrams, 1989:179–190,251.

Begeer, Cornelis L.J. (1868–)
▶ Dutch silversmith; active Utrecht.
▶ Studied Königliche Preussische Zeichenakademie, Hanau.

▶ In 1893, he visited the Chicago 'World's Columbian Exposition'; returning to the Netherlands with new ideas, executed designs inspired by nature, some of which were scarcely distinguishable from those of the Wolfers firm, Brussels, whose wares his family firm C.J. Begeer sold; was largely responsible for the appearance of the first Modern designs at C.J. Begeer, which he had joined in 1888; in 1904, left to set up his own workshop Stichtsche Zilverfabriek, producing mostly smaller objects. Half-brother Carel J.A. Begeer succeeded him as artistic director at C.J. Begeer.

▶ Showed silver at 1900 Paris 'Exposition Universelle.'

▶ *Industry and Design in the Netherlands, 1850–1950*, Amsterdam: Stedelijk Museum, 1985. Annelies Krekel-Aalberse, *Art Nouveau and Art Déco Silver*, New York: Abrams, 1989:179,251.

Behrens, Peter (1868–1940)

▶ German graphic artist, architect, and designer; born Hamburg.

▶ 1886–89, studied art school, Karlsruhe, and in Düsseldorf and Munich.

▶ In 1893, he joined the avant-garde group associated with the Munich Secession; in 1896, traveled in Italy; in 1898, studied industrial mass production; following the lead of the Wiener Werkstätte, in 1897 (with Hermann Obrist, Bruno Paul, Bernhard Pankok, and Richard Riemerschmid) founded Vereinigte Werkstätten für Kunst im Handwerk (United Workshops for Art in Hand-Work), aiming to sell everyday objects designed by Modern artists; inspired by English models, worked there as a painter and graphic designer. Early Jugendstil designs were replaced by a Cubist and Rationalist style that can be seen in his designs for the house in the Darmstadt artists' colony of 1901 and for the Pavilion of Decorative Arts at 1902 Turin 'Esposizione Internazionale d'Arte Decorativa Moderna.' In 1899, the Grand Duke Louis IV of Hesse-Darmstadt included Behrens in helping to form the art colony at Darmstadt. His first building was his 1901 house at Darmstardt, where he had an opportunity to employ his abilities as architect and designer of furniture, glass, ceramics, silver, and jewelry; in Darmstadt, designed silver flatware in the Secession style made by M.J. Rückert and a desk set by Martin Mayer. Ornamentation disappeared on his silverwork, especially that produced by Franz Bahner, Düsseldorf. Other silverwares were made by Bruckmann und Söhne, Heilbronn. Having left the artists' colony, he lived in Düsseldorf where he was director of the Kunstgewerbeschule 1904–07; (with Hermann Muthesius and others) founded the Deutscher Werkbund (German Work Association); on the invitation of AEG managing director Walter Rathenau, began to work in Berlin from 1908 on the corporate identity of the huge German industrial combine, for which Behrens produced architecture, graphics, kettles, electric fans, and clocks, the first time a firm had hired an artist to advise on all facets of industrial design; designed the seminal 1908–09 AEG turbine factory and several other buildings for AEG. Some porcelain designs were produced by Manufaktur Mehlem Gebr. Bauscher, Weiden, Bonn, and glass designs by Rheinische Glashütten, Köln-Ehrenfeld. For a time in 1910, Le Corbusier (1910–11), Gropius (1907–10), and Mies van der Rohe (1908–11) worked side by side in Behrens's office. In the 1910s, Behrens designed linoleum patterns for Delmenhorster Linoleum Fabrik, an early member of the Werkbund; from 1922, was director of both schools of architecture at Akademie der bildenden Künste, Vienna, and, from 1936, Preussische Akademie der Künste, Berlin; in 1926, designed the house 'New Ways,' Northampton (England); in 1932, collaborated with Ferdinand Wilm and others to form Gesellschaft für Goldschmiedekunst (Society for Goldsmiths' Work).

▶ Architecture included 1901 house, Darmstadt; 1905–06 Obenauer House, Saarbrücken; 1908–10 Cuno and Schroeder houses, Eppenhausen, near Hagen; 1908–09 turbine factory, 1910 high-tension plant, and 1910–11 small-motors factory for AEG, Berlin; 1910–11 district of flats for AEG workers, Henningsdorf, near Berlin; 1911–12 Mannesmann offices, Düsseldorf;

1911–12 German Embassy, St. Petersburg; 1920–25 technical administration building, Hoechst Dyeworks, Frankfurt; and 1913–20 offices of Continental Rubber, Hanover.

▶ Participated in 1910 Brussels 'Exposition Universelle et Internationale.'

▶ Peter Behrens, *Feste des Lebens und der Kunst*, Jena, 1900. *L'Art décoratif pour Tous*, 4 April 1902:7,9. Fritz Hoeber, *Peter Behrens*, Munich, 1913. Peter Behrens, *Beziehungen der künstlerischen und technischen Probleme*, Berlin, 1917. Peter Behrens, *Das Ethos und die Umlagerung der künstlerischen Probleme*, Darmstadt, 1920. Paul Joseph Cremers, *Peter Behrens, Sein Werk von 1909 bis zur Gegenwart*, Essen, 1928. K.M. Grimme, *Peter Behrens und seine Wiener akademische Meisterschule*, Vienna, 1930. Peter Behrens, 'Die Baugesinnung des Faschismus,' *Die Neue Linie*, Nov. 1933:11–13. Cat., *Peter Behrens (1868–1940)*, Pfalzgalerie Kaiserslautern, 1966–67. Tilman Buddensieg et al., *Industriekultur, Peter Behrens und die AEG, 1907–1914*, Cambridge: MIT, 1979. S. Anderson, 'Modern Architecture and Industry: Peter Behrens, the AEG, and Industrial Design,' *Oppositions*, No. 21, Summer 1980:78–93. Cat., *Peter Behrens und Nürnberg*, Nuremberg: Germanisches Nationalmuseum, 1980. Alan Windsor, *Peter Behrens, Architect and Designer, 1869–1940*, London, 1981. Vittorio Magnago Lampugnani, *Encyclopedia of 20th-Century Architecture*, New York: Abrams, 1986:39–41. Annelies Krekel-Aalberse, *Art Nouveau and Art Déco Silver*, New York: Abrams, 1989:129,132,138,251.

Bel Geddes, Norman
See Geddes, Norman Bel

Belgiojoso, Lodovico Barbiano di (1909–)

▶ Italian designer; born and active Milan.

▶ Studied Politecnico di Milano.

▶ Joined the Fascist Party in 1928; in 1932, began his professional career with the founding of the architecture design firm BBPR, Milan; 1955–63, taught at Instituto Universitario di Architettura, Venice, and, from 1963, Politecnico di Milano; (with others at BBPR) designed the *Spazio* and *Arco* office furniture ranges for Olivetti.

▶ Alfonso Grassi and Anty Pansera, *Atlante del Design Italiano 1940/1980*, Milano; Fabbri, 1980. Andrea Branzi and Michele De Lucchi, *Design Italiano degli Anni '50*, Milano: Editoriale Domus, 1980. Vittorio Magnago Lampugnani, *Encyclopedia of 20th-Century Architecture*, New York: Abrams, 1986:37–38,41. Richard A. Etlin, *Modernism in Italian Architecture, 1890–1940*, Cambridge: MIT, 1991:641.

▶ See BBPR

Bell, Cressida

▶ British textile designer; active London; granddaughter of Vanessa Bell.

▶ Studied St. Martin's School of Art, London, and Royal College of Art, London, to 1984.

▶ She set up her own studio in 1984, designing and hand-printing textiles; produced dress and furnishing fabrics, designed interiors, and decorated furniture; became a member of the Independent Designs Federation of London.

▶ Albrecht Bangert and Karl Michael Armer, *80s Style: Designs of the Decade*, New York: Abbeville, 1990:180,227.

Bell, Vanessa (b. Vanessa Stephen 1879–1961)

▶ British painter, muralist, and interior designer; sister of Virginia Woolf.

▶ 1901–04, studied Royal Academy Painting School, London, and Slade School of Art, London.

▶ 1913–19, (with Clive Grant) was a co-director of Roger Fry's Omega Workshops, where she painted furniture and screens and executed interior schemes, rugs, tableware, and printed textiles in a painterly style; (with Duncan Grant of Omega Workshops) executed interior-decoration schemes for others and for her house Charleston, near Firle, Sussex; designed embroideries executed by herself and Mary Hogarth and Grant's mother Bartle Grant; during the 1920s and 1930s, (with Grant) received commissions, including 1926 decorations of the Bell house, London; Mrs. St. John Hutchinson's house, London; and houses of Lady Dorothy Wellesley and Kenneth Clark. She lived with Grant at Charleston, where John Maynard Keynes wrote *The Economic Consequences of the Peace*; (with Grant) designed fabrics screened onto cotton, linen, and a satin-finished cotton-rayon; in 1932, was commissioned to design printed fabrics by Allan Walton; in 1933–34, decorated ceramic tableware by E. Brain; bookcovers for Hogarth Press; and, in 1934, tableware by A.J. Wilkinson, directed by Clarice Cliff. In 1940–43, she painted murals for Berwick Church, Sussex; became a member of AIA.

▶ Paintings were subject of 1937 exhibition, Lefevre Galleries, London, and included in 1912 Second Post-Impressionist Exhibition, London.

▶ Richard Shone, *Bloomsbury Portraits: Vanessa Bell, Duncan Grant, and their Circle*, London, 1976. Cat., *Thirties: British art and design before the war*, London: Arts Council of Great Britain, Hayward Gallery, 1979:81,84,91,92,95,96,126,131,133,157,174, 285. *British Art and Design, 1900–1960*, London: Victoria and Albert Museum, 1983. Frances Spalding, *Vanessa Bell*, London, 1983. Stephen Calloway, *Twentieth-Century Decoration*, New York: Rizzoli, 1988:148.

Bellefroid, G.M.E. (1893–1971)
▶ Dutch designer.
▶ Bellefroid designed pottery models and decoration 1929–46 at De Sphinx and the *Stramino* drinking glass set of *c*1939 for Kristalunie.
▶ See De Sphinx

Bellery-Desfontaines, Henri (1867–1909)
▶ French furniture designer; born Paris.
▶ An eclectic artist, he was an illustrator, decorator and designer of rugs, fabrics, bank notes, graphics, and posters; showing a predilection for the Middle Ages, designed a church in Cruse (France) based on the principles of Eugène-Emmanuel Viollet-le-Duc. Towards the end of his career, he developed a simple approach to his furniture design that was solidly architectonic, in a style between Le Style 1900 and Art Déco.
▶ Pierre Kjellberg, *Art Déco: les maîtres du Mobilier, le décor des Paquebots*, Paris: Amateur, 1986.

Belling, Charles (1884–
▶ British stove manufacturer; active Enfield, Middlesex.
▶ Charles Belling founded a stove-appliance factory in Enfield in 1912; made domestic heaters 1912–18. In 1919, the firm introduced the first domestic electric stove; in 1929, began producing the *Baby Belling* stove for which it was best known; in the early 1930s, was the first manufacturer in Britain of the white vitreous-enamel electric stove; ceased trading in 1992.
▶ *Issue 4*, London: Design Museum, Autumn 1990.

Bellini, Carlo (1960–)
▶ Italian architect and designer; born Perugia; active Milan.
▶ Studied architecture, Università di Milano, and engineering, Università di Perugia.
▶ With Marco Ferreri, he designed the widely published 1986 *Eddy* lamp produced by Luxo Italiana.
▶ Won 1984 'Consorso di design regione Toscana' competition.
▶ Albrecht Bangert and Karl Michael Armer, *80s Style: Designs of the Decade*, New York: Abbeville, 1990:94,227.

Bellini, Dario (1937–)
▶ Italian industrial designer; brother of Mario Bellini.
▶ Dario and Mario Bellini designed 1970 *Totem* hi-fi unit with detachable speakers produced by Brionvega from 1972.
▶ Jonathan M. Woodham, *Twentieth-Century Ornament*, New York: Rizzoli, 1990:258–59.

Bellini, Mario (1935–)
▶ Italian industrial designer; born and active Milan.
▶ Studied architecture, Politecnico di Milano, to 1959.

▶ 1959–62, he worked for La Rinascente department store; 1962–69, was a professor of industrial design at Instituto Superiore del Disegno Industriale, Venice; in 1962, opened his own office in Milan; a prolific designer, designed for B&B Italia, Cassina, Pedretti, C&B, BRAS, Poltrona Frau, Poggi, Bras, Bacci, Marcatré, and Rosenthal; a consultant designer to Olivetti since 1965, designed for Yamaha, Brionvega, Irradio, Minerva, Ideal Standard, and Vitra; designed lighting for Artemide, Flos, and Erco; executed designs for office machinery, furniture, kitchen systems, modular office furniture, TVs and hi-fis, and soda dispensers; designed automobiles for Renault; 1982–83, was professor of industrial design at Hochschule für angewandte Kunst, Vienna; 1983–85, at Domus Academy, Milan; 1986–91, was editor of *Domus*; in 1981, established the magazine *Album*; became a member of ADI (Associazione per il Disegno Industriale) and, 1969–71, its president; lectured at numerous European and American universities; became a member of the Scientific Council of the Design Division, 1983 (XVII) Triennale di Milano. Work included 1967 *Chair 832* in leather-covered injection-molded foam polyurethane, 1977–82 *Il Colonnato* marble table, 1977 *Cab* chair, 1982 *Victoria* sofa, 1982 *La Loggia* table, all by Cassina, 1973 *Divisumma* calculators by Olivetti, 1975 cassette deck by Yamaha, 1970 *Totem* audio unit by Brionvega, 1978 *Corium 1* leather-covered steel chair by Matteo Grassi, 1979 *Area 50* lighting range (Premio Compasso d'Oro winner), 1981 *Praxis* typewriters by Olivetti, 1986 *Eclipse* spotlight series by Erco, 1985 bracelet by Cleto Munari.
▶ Received seven Premi Compasso d'Oro, from 1962 to the late 1980s; Delta de Oro of Spain; 'Made in Germany' award; gold medal, 1968 'BIO' Industrial Design Biennale, Ljubljana; 1973 Bolaffi design award. Work shown in exhibitions in USA, Canada, Argentina, Brazil, England, France, Germany, Belgium, Italy, the Netherlands, and Russia, including 1972 'Italy: The New Domestic Landscape: Achievements and Problems of Italian Design' exhibition (showing his *Kar-a-Sutra* mobile environment), New York Museum of Modern Art, and 1983–84 'Design Since 1945,' Philadelphia Museum of Art. Work subject of 1987 exhibition, New York Museum of Modern Art.
▶ 'Mario Bellini per la Olivetti,' *Domus*, No. 494, Jan. 1971:32–42. *ADI Annual 1976*, Milan: Associazione per il Disegno Industriale, 1976. Cat., *Design Process Olivetti 1908–1978*, Los Angeles: Frederick S. Wight Art Gallery (University of California), 1979: 255–56. Alfonso Grassi and Anty Pansera, *Atlante del design italiano: 1940–1980*, Milan: Fabbri, 1980:277. 'Talking with Four Men Who Are Shaping Italian Design,' *Industrial Design*, Vol. 28, Sept.–Oct. 1981:30–35. Cat., Kathryn B. Hiesinger and George H. Marcus III (eds.), *Design Since 1945*, Philadelphia: Philadelphia Museum of Art, 1983. Robert A.M. Stern (ed.), *The International Design Yearbook*, New York: Abbeville, 1985/1986: No. 399. Cara McCarty, *Mario Bellini Designer*, New York: Museum of Modern Art, 1987. Juli Capella and Quim Larrea, *Designed by Architects in the 1980s*, New York: Rizzoli, 1988. Penny Sparke, *Design in Italy, 1870 to the Present*, New York: Abbeville, 1988.

Belotti, Giandomenico (1922–)
▶ Italian architect and designer; born Bergamo; active Milan.
▶ From 1938, studied sculpture with Marino Marini, Monza, Liceo Artistico di Brera, Milan, Politecnico di Milano, and Instituto Universitario di Architettura, Venice.
▶ Belotti was profoundly influenced by F. Marescotti. Designing residential, industrial and public buildings, his clients included public institutions and private firms. He was an industrial designer and urban planner; from 1979 for Alias, designed *Odessa* chair, nicknamed the *Spaghetti* chair when shown in New York; was known for creating furniture based on earlier 20th-century models, including chairs entitled *Omaggio a Chareau* and *Omaggio a Rietveld* made by Alias. Furniture designs for Alias included the 1979 *Spaghetti Chair*, *Spaghetti Stool*, and *Pardi* table, 1980 *Kiev*, *Spaghetti Armchair*, 1981 *Spaghetti Armrests*, *Tavolino*, and *Tadini* bookshelves, 1982 *Decimo* bed and *Outdoor Collection* of chairs,

chaises, and cart, 1984 *Tavolo Outdoor*, *Paludis* chair, *Alterego* wall cabinet, *Tavolo Forcolini*, *Carelli* cart series, *Twist* folding chair, *Omaggio a Man Ray* chair, *Omaggio a Theo Van Doesburg* chair, and *Omaggio a Gerrit Rietveld* chair, 1985 *Omaggio a Chareau* chair, *Fratus* table, *Ventura* shelving, *Wiener Collection*, *Tower* coat rack, and *Paludis Stool*, 1986 *Spaghetti Gemini* chair, *Paludis Gemini* chair, *Orsi* bed, *Iaia* sofa, and *Tavolo Restaurant*, 1987 *Trois Étoiles* chair, *Domestica* chair, *Four Balls* tables, and *Consolle*, and 1988 *Hoffmann*, *Moser*, and *Wagner* casegoods range.
► Robert A.M. Stern (ed.), *The International Design Yearbook*, New York: Abbeville, 1985/1986: No. 56.

Belperron, Suzanne
► French jewelry designer.
► Active in the 1920s and 1930s, Belperron produced numerous designs for sculptured jewelry for René Boivin's Paris shop; subsequently, opened her own Paris shop called Herz-Belperron. Her designs often featured glass encrusted with gemstones.
► Sylvie Raulet, *Bijoux Art Déco*, Paris: Regard, 1984. Melissa Gabardi, *Les Bijoux des Années 50*, Amateur, 1987.

Belvoir, Paul (1963–)
► British silversmith.
► Studied silversmithing, Medwick College of Design.
► He was commissioned by De Beers to design the trophy for 1986 King George VI and Queen Elizabeth Diamond Stakes Race.
► Received numerous awards including first prize in both silver design and craftsmanship at 1984 Goldsmiths' and Silversmiths' Art Council exhibition.

Bendixson, Frances (1934–)
► American jewelry designer; born Cambridge, Massachusetts; active Britain.
► Studied art history, Smith College, Massachusetts.
► Work shown in 1990 'Collecting for the Future: A Decade of Contemporary Acquisitions.' Work subject of 1985 exhibition. Both exhibitions, Victoria and Albert Museum, London.

Bendtsen, Niels (1943–)
► Danish architect and furniture designer.
► From 1977, he collaborated with Nina Koppel; designed furniture produced by Kebe and N. Eilersen.
► Work shown at Nordiska Galleriet, Stockholm, in 1977; Illums Bolighus in 1977; Design Research, New York; in Cologne in 1975; and in Paris in 1976.
► Frederik Sieck, *Nutidig Dansk Møbeldesign: -en kortfattet illustreret beskrivelse*, Copenhagen: Bondo Gravesen; 1990 Busck edition in English.

Bénédictus, Édouard (1878–1930)
► French painter, decorative designer, and scientist; born and active Paris.
► Benedictus designed fabrics and published a portfolio of abstract Art Moderne patterns used in decoration; regularly designed for textile firms Tassinari et Châtel and Brunet et Meunié; designed rugs and carpets; as a scientist, did research during World War I.
► Work shown at Salons of the Société des Artistes français, receiving various awards in 1899, 1902, 1907, and 1909, and shown in La Maitrîse's first important exhibition at 1922 Salon d'Automne.
► He was appointed Chevalier and Officier of the Légion d'Honneur.
► Victor Arwas, *Art Déco*, Abrams, 1980. Stuart Durant, *Ornament from the Industrial Revolution to Today*, Woodstock, NY: Overlook, 1986:204,240,260,268,278,280.

Benktzon, Maria (1946–)
► Swedish industrial designer.
► Studied Konstfackskolan and Tekniska Skolan, Stockholm.
► She worked at Ergonomi Design Gruppen, Stockholm, specializing in the design of technical products for people with disabilities.

► Cat., Kathryn B. Hiesinger and George H. Marcus III (eds.), *Design Since 1945*, Philadelphia: Philadelphia Museum of Art, 1983. Cat., *Gustavsberg 150 ar*, Stockholm: Nationalmuseum, 1975. Cat., *Aktuell Svensk Form*, Skien, Sweden: Ibsenhuset, 1982. Cat., David Revere McFadden (ed.), *Scandinavian Modern Design 1880–1980*, New York: Abrams, 1982:262.

Bennett Jr., John (1840–1907)
► American ceramicist; active New York.
► Trained at Staffordshire potteries.
► John Sparkes, head of the Lambeth School of Art in London, recommended Bennett to Henry Doulton, who hired him to set up a faïence department where he taught underglazing techniques to Doulton artisans. His work became known as 'Bennett ware.' Encouraged by his success at the 1876 Philadelphia exhibition, he left for New York in 1877; by 1879, had set up a studio. His pieces were sold at Tiffany and Co and Davis Collamore, New York, and Abram French, Boston. His motifs included flowers, grasses, apple, hawthorn and dogwood blossoms, peonies, roses, and asters in mustard yellow, lapis lazuli, Persian red, violet, and olive green with umber and gray shading. Bennett's work showed influences from British designers, including William Morris, and from Persian ceramics. 1878–79 Bennett was head of ceramics-painting classes at newly formed Society of Decorative Art, New York. Amateur ceramicists worldwide came to study his techniques.
► Pieces included in Doulton stand at 1876 Philadelphia 'Centennial Exposition.' Work shown frequently, especially in New York and Cincinnati.
► Edmund Grosse, *Sir Henry Doulton: The Man of Business as a Man of Imagination*, London, 1970:87. Doreen Bolger Burke et al., *In Pursuit of Beauty: Americans and the Aesthetic Movement*, New York: Metropolitan Museum of Art and Rizzoli, 1986:402–03.

Bennett, Ward (1917–)
► American artist, sculptor, and textile, jewelry, industrial, and interior designer; active New York and Paris.
► Studied with Constantin Brancusi, Paris, and Hans Hoffman and Louise Nevelson, New York.
► From 1930 (aged 13), he worked as a dress designer, sketch artist, and store-window decorator; in 1947, began as an interior designer with a penthouse for Harry Jason. His interior design work included corporate offices, banks, and residences in New York, London, Venice, Rome, and Neptuno (Italy). Best known for his industrial products, he designed furniture, textiles, and jewelry; in the 1970s and 1980s, created more than 100 designs for Brickel; in 1990, designed a 22-piece furniture collection produced by Geiger International to respond to the trend to smaller executive offices. His *Double Helix* stainless-steel flatware and *Sengai* crystal range of the late 1980s were produced by Sasaki.
► Robert A.M. Stern (ed.), *The International Design Yearbook*, New York: Abbeville, 1985/1986: No. 169. 'Celebrating Design Innovation,' *Designers West*, April 1991:30.

Benney, Gerald (1930–)
► British silversmith; born Hull.
► Studied Brighton College of Art and Royal College of Art, London.
► In 1955, he set up his own workshop; 1957–70, was a consultant to Viners for mass production items; in 1963, began his work for Reading Corporation's collection of civic-plate patterns; from 1970, produced a range of Beenham enamels; 1974–83, was professor of silversmithing, Royal College of Art.

Benois, Alexandr Nikolaevitch (1870–1960)
► Russian artist, illustrator, and set designer; active St. Petersburg and Paris.
► Studied Academy of Fine Art, St. Petersburg; 1890–94, University of St. Petersburg.
► He ran the art journal and organization *Mire Iskasstv*; illustrated books, created theatre sets, and rendered watercolors and gouaches with peasant subjects; illustrated Pushkin's poetry *The*

Bronze Horseman (1903–22), created sets for Wagner's opera *Twilight of the Gods* (1902), Stravinsky's *Petrouska* (1917–20), Molière's *Le mariage forcé*, Pushkin's *The Feast of the Time of the Plague* (1914). Benois's critical writings on art were influential in Russia at the beginning of the 20th century. In 1926, he settled in Paris.
► Hélène A. Borisova and Gregory Sterine, *Art Nouveau Russe*, Paris: Regard, 1987:367.

Benson, J.W.
► British retail jewelers; located London.
► The firm J.W. Benson was founded in 1874 at 25 Old Bond Street, London; in *c*1897, merged with Alfred Benson and Henry Webb, who had previously acquired well-known royal jewelers and goldsmiths Hunt and Roskell, 156 New Bond Street; is still in business.
► Charlotte Gere, *American and European Jewelry 1830–1914*, New York: Crown, 1975:151.

Benson, William Arthur Smith   (1854–1924)
► British designer, metalworker, and architect; born and active London.
► 1874–78, studied classics and philosophy, Oxford University.
► 1877–80, he was apprenticed to Basil Champneys; met Edward Burne-Jones in 1877 and William Morris in 1878; encouraged by the latter, set up his own workshop in 1880 and began producing metalwork; became the leading designer of Arts and Crafts metalwork, specializing in brass and copper; unlike Morris, was not averse to mechanical production and designed exclusively for it, including coat-stands, firescreens, chafing dishes, music stands, and electroplated kettles. His innovative designs included vacuum flasks and lighting. The only internationally recognized British lighting designer of his time, he showed models throughout Europe, especially at Siegfried Bing's shop L'Art Nouveau, Paris; in his catalogs, offered lighting models for each area of the house; in the 1880s, designed furniture for Art Nouveau cabinetmakers J.S. Henry, incorporating exotic-wood inlays and elaborate metal fittings; designed metal fireplaces and grates for Falkirk and Coalbrookdale iron firms; set up a factory and, in 1887, a London shop; assumed the directorship of Morris and Co when William Morris died in 1896. When Benson retired, the business closed. In 1884, he became a founding member of the Art-Workers' Guild; in 1888, Arts and Crafts Exhibition Society; in 1915, Design and Industries Association; published *Elements of Handicraft and Design* (1893), *Rudiments of Handicraft* (1919), and *Drawing, Its History and Uses* (1925).
► Work shown at 1895 Manchester Arts and Crafts Exhibition; Hirschwald Gallery, Berlin, 1899; Ashmolean Museum, Oxford, 1919.
► Alastair Duncan, *Art Nouveau and Art Déco Lighting*, Simon and Schuster, 1978:65. Cat., *W.A.S. Benson 1854–1924*, London: Haslam and Whiteway, 1981. *British Arts and Design, 1900–1960*, London: Victoria and Albert Museum, 1983.

Bepler, Emma   (1864–1947)
► American woodworker; active Cincinnati.
► 1881–84, studied drawing and decorative design, University of Cincinnati School of Design; 1886–87 and 1891–92, wood carving, Art Academy, Cincinnati, under Benn Pitman and, 1893–94, under William Fry.
► As a secondary figure in the art movement in Cincinnati, her woodcarvings were strongly influenced by teachers Pitman and Fry, who both emphasized the application of wood carvings to domestic interiors. 1906–47, she was a member of the Cincinnati Women's Art Club.
► Regularly showed drawings and painted textiles in annual exhibitions of University of Cincinnati School of Design. Received a prize for her china painting at 1904 St. Louis 'Louisiana Purchase Exposition.'
► Doreen Bolger Burke et al., *In Pursuit of Beauty: Americans and the Aesthetic Movement*, New York: Metropolitan Museum of Art

and Rizzoli, 1986:403. 'Woman Woodcarver, Artist, Dies at Eighty-Three,' *Cincinnati Times-Star*, Feb. 23, 1947. Anita J. Ellis, 'Cincinnati Art Furniture,' *Antiques*, No. 121, Apr. 1982:930–41.

Beran, Gustav   (1912–)
► Austrian designer; active Zeist (Netherlands).
► 1928–33, studied Kunstgewerbeschule, Vienna, under Josef Hoffmann and Eugen Mayer.
► Settling in the Netherlands, he was a designer 1934–41 for Holland's largest silverware producer Gerritsen & Van Kempen, Zeist, and, 1948–77, its artistic director.
► Representing Gerritsen & Van Kempen, work shown at 1937 Paris 'Exposition Internationale des Arts et Techniques dans la Vie Moderne.' Work subject of 1982 'Gustav Beran: Miniatures and Design' exhibition, Galerie Mara, Fribourg (Switzerland).
► *Gold und Silber, Uhren und Schmuck*, No. 1, Jan. 1963:30–31. Cat., *Gustav Beran: Miniatures and Design*, Fribourg: Galerie Mara, 1982. Cat., Kathryn B. Hiesinger and George H. Marcus III (eds.), *Design Since 1945*, Philadelphia: Philadelphia Museum of Art, 1983. Annelies Krekel-Aalberse, *Art Nouveau and Art Déco Silver*, New York: Abrams, 1989: 190,251.

Berchmans, Émile   (1867–1947)
► Belgian painter, decorator, illustrator, and poster artist; born Liège.
► Studied under his artist father and at the academy, Liège.
► He founded *Caprice Revue* with Rassenfosse, Donnay, and Maurice Siville; designed a poster for L'Art Indépendant group. In his bold lithographic work, he outlined his figures in black or white, and sometimes both.
► Work shown at La Libre Esthétique, Belgium, in 1895, 1896, and 1899 and with L'Art Indépendant, Paris.
► Yvonne Brunhammer et al., *Art Nouveau Belgium, France*, Houston: Rice University, 1976, biblio.

Berg, Franco Alberto   (1948–)
► German designer; active Brunswick.
► Studied University of Art, Brunswick, to 1978.
► In 1979, he set up the Berg Design Studio for product development in Brunswick; later moved to Hanover; worked on consumer goods. His 1984–85 *Argon*, *Radon*, and *Exnon* light sculptures were produced by Berg Licht und Objekt.
► Robert A.M. Stern (ed.), *The International Design Yearbook*, New York: Abbeville, 1985/1986: Nos. 209,212. Albrecht Bangert and Karl Michael Armer, *80s Style: Designs of the Decade*, New York: Abbeville, 1990:105,227.

Berg, G.A.   (1884–1957)
► Swedish furniture designer.
► Berg revived bentwood furniture in Sweden; founded a furniture store in Stockholm in the early 1930s; was a major influence behind the Modern movement in Sweden.
► Penny Sparke, *Introduction to Design and Culture in the Twentieth Century*, Allen and Unwin, 1986.

Berg, Sigrun   (1901–82)
► Norwegian textile designer.
► Active from the 1940s, Berg produced designs for De Forenede Ullvarefabrikker in 1957.
► Fredrik Wildhagen, *Norge i Form*, Oslo: Stenersen, 1988: 212,138.

Bergé, Henri
► French sculptor, painter, and glass designer.
► *c*1897–1914, Bergé was artistic director at Daum glassworks, Nancy; after 1908, made models for Almaric Walter's *pâte-de-verre* sculptures; became a member of the École de Nancy. His paintings were executed with flower motifs and landscapes.
► Yvonne Brunhammer et al., *Art Nouveau Belgium, France*, Houston: Rice University, 1976, biblio.

Berger, Artur (1892–1981)
▶ Austrian metalworker; active Vienna and Moscow.
▶ Studied Kunstgewerbeschule, Vienna, under Josef Hoffmann.
▶ He designed silver for the Wiener Werkstätte and, 1920–36, sets for more than 30 films; 1936–81, lived in Moscow.
▶ Werner J. Schweiger, *Wiener Werkstätte*, Vienna: Christian Brandstaetter, 1980:100,256,159. Annelies Krekel-Aalberse, *Art Nouveau and Art Déco Silver*, New York: Abrams, 1989:251.

Berger, Otti (1898–c1944)
▶ Croatian designer; born Zmajavac; active Dessau, Berlin, England, Prague, and Croatia.
▶ 1921–26, studied art academy, Zagreb; 1927–30, Bauhaus, Dessau, under Gunta Stölzl; 1929, in Sweden.
▶ In 1931, she became temporary head of the weaving department, Bauhaus, Dessau, replacing Anni Albers; in 1932, continued there under Lilly Reich; in 1933, set up her own workshop and laboratory in Berlin; collaborated with Gunta Stölzl and worked for various commercial firms in Germany, England, the Netherlands, and Czechoslovakia; in 1933, became a design consultant to Wohnbedarf department store, Zürich, which commissioned her to design textiles and wallcoverings for the Corso cinema and restaurant in Zürich, completed in 1934. In 1934, Wohnbedarf showed and sold her textiles and *Alvaräs* wooden furniture. In 1935, she designed curtain materials for de Ploeg in Bergeyk (Netherlands); settling in England, designed textiles for Helios, Bolton; refused a visa to the USA, went to Prague and then to Croatia; was imprisoned in a Nazi concentration camp, where she died in 1944 or 1945.
▶ Carpet of *c*1930 was shown at 1938 'Bauhaus 1919–1928' exhibition, New York Museum of Modern Art.
▶ Barbara von Lucadou, 'Otti Berger—Stoffe für die Zukunft' in cat., *Wechselwirkungen. Ungarische Avantgarde in der Weimarer Republik*, Kassel, 1986:301. Cat., *The Bauhaus: Masters and Students*, New York: Barry Friedman, 1988. Friederike Mehlau-Wiebking et al., *Schweizer Typenmöbel 1925–35*, Sigfried Giedion und die Wohnbedarf AG, Zürich, 1989. Hans Wichmann, *Von Morris bis Memphis. Textilien der Neuen Sammlung. Ende 19. bis Ende 20. Jahrhundert*, Basel: Birkhäuser, 1990:120,168,439.

Bergh, Hagbard Elis (1881–1954)
▶ Swedish metalworker and glassware designer; active Stockholm.
▶ 1897–99, studied Kungliga Konsthögskolan, Stockholm; 1899–1902, Konstfackskolan and Tekniska Skolan, Stockholm; 1905–06, studied architecture in Munich.
▶ From 1906–16, worked at Arv, Böhlmarks Lampfabric and Purkberg; from 1916–21, was director and artistic consultant at Herman Bermans Konstgiuteri metalworks, Stockholm; 1921–29, designed silver for C.G. Hallbergs Guldsmedsaktiebolag, along with Hakon Ahlberg, Sylvia Stave, and Edvin Ollers; designed simple, sober silver objects for Hallberg intended for mass production; is mainly known for his designs for Kosta Boda glassworks, 1929–50, where he was artistic director and, 1950–54, freelance designer. Work included architecture, lighting, and gold jewelry.
▶ Cat., David Revere McFadden (ed.), *Scandinavian Modern Design 1880–1980*, New York: Abrams, 1982:262. Sales catalog, *The Kosta Boda Book of Glass*, 1986:5. Jennifer Hawkins Opie, *Scandinavia: Ceramics and Glass in the Twentieth Century*, New York: Rizzoli, 1989. Annelies Krekel-Aalberse, *Art Nouveau and Art Déco Silver*, New York: Abrams, 1989:245–46,251.

Berghof, Norbert (1949–)
▶ German architect and designer.
▶ Studied School of Architecture, Technische Hochschule, Darmstadt.
▶ With Michael Landes and Wolfgang Rang, in 1981, he set up an architectural partnership. Their work included housing projects in Frankfurt, interior renovation, and graphic design. Their monumental 1985–86 *F1 Frankfurter Schrank* writing desk and 1986–

87 *Frankfurter Stuhl FIII* armchair were produced by Draenert Studio.
▶ Albrecht Bangert and Karl Michael Armer, *80s Style: Designs of the Decade*, New York: Abbeville, 1990:232,33,27.

Bergner, Léna Meyer (aka Helene Bergner 1906–81)
▶ German textile designer, active Germany, Russia, Mexico, and Switzerland; wife of Hannes Meyer.
▶ 1926–30, studied Bauhaus, Dessau.
▶ She took over the direction of the Bauhaus dyeing workshop; produced fabric, carpets, and wallpaper; in 1931, became director of the Ostpreussische Handweberei in Königsberg (today Kaliningrad, Russia), (with husband Meyer and a group of Bauhaus students) emigrated to the USSR, where her work was influenced by Russian avant-garde painters, including Liubov' Popova and Alexandra Exter; from 1939, lived in Mexico and, from 1949, in Lugano (Switzerland).
▶ Carpet of *c*1930 shown at 1938 'Bauhaus 1919–1928' exhibition, New York Museum of Modern Art.
▶ Cat., *Der Kragstuhl*, Stuhlmuseum Burg Beverungen, Berlin: Alexander, 1986:134. Cat., Gunta Stölzl, *Weberei am Bauhaus und aus eigener Werkstatt*, Berlin: Bauhaus-Archiv, 1987:159. Cat., *The Bauhaus: Masters and Students*, New York: Barry Friedman, 1988. Igor Golomstock, *Totalitarian Art in the Soviet Union, the Third Reich, Fascist Italy and the People's Republic of China*, New York: IconEditions 1990:67.

Bergslien, Gro Sommerfeldt (1940–)
▶ Norwegian textile and glassware designer.
▶ 1957–60, studied Statens Håndverks -og Kunstindustriskole, Oslo; 1960, studied weaving at Dannebrog Weavers and Material Printers, Amsterdam; in 1964, attended State School for teachers of drawing and woodwork, and in 1971, the Royal College of Art, London.
▶ In 1961, she was a textile designer at Plus, Fredrikstad, and, from 1964, a glassware designer at Hadeland's Glassverk; from *c*1964, was parttime designer of enamels, David-Andersen, Oslo.
▶ Cat., David Revere McFadden (ed.), *Scandinavian Modern Design 1880–1980*, New York: Abrams, 1982:262. Jennifer Hawkins Opie, *Scandinavia: Ceramics and Glass in the Twentieth Century*, New York: Rizzoli, 1989.

Bergsten, Carl (1879–1935)
▶ Swedish architect and furniture designer.
▶ 1901–03, studied architecture, Kungliga Konstkögskolan, Stockholm.
▶ He designed architecture and furniture at 1906 exhibition, Norrköping; was director of the Nordiska Kompaniet furniture department, Stockholm.
▶ Cat., David Revere McFadden (ed.), *Scandinavian Modern Design 1880–1980*, New York: Abrams, 1982:262.

Berlage, Hendrik Petrus (1856–1934)
▶ Dutch architect, theorist, and designer; born Amsterdam; active The Hague and Amsterdam.
▶ Studied briefly Academy of Fine Art, Amsterdam; 1875–78, Bauschule, Eidgenössische Technische Hochschule, Zürich under Gottfried Semper.
▶ In 1889, he set up his own architecture practice in Amsterdam; one of the first to abandon historicism, encouraged others through his writings to seek logical construction techniques and integrity of workmanship, calling it 'honest awareness of the problems of architecture'; he even considered it architecturally dishonest to plaster a wall. His attraction to the Romanesque was revealed in his wide unbroken wall surfaces and semi-circular arches, similar to features of the work of H.H. Richardson, Louis Sullivan, and Frank Lloyd Wright in the USA. He was instrumental in introducing Wright's work to Dutch and Swiss architects in 1912, after his visit to Austria in 1911. While the Modern movement was expressed through De Stijl in the Netherlands, Berlage's historicism strongly influenced the development of Dutch Expressionism, particularly through his 1903 Stock Exchange building,

Amsterdam, for which he designed furniture and many fittings. In 1911, he settled in The Hague. Of high technical quality, much of his furniture was bulky and made in the Amsterdam workshop Het Binnenhuis. He published *Een drietal lezingen in Amerika gehouden* (three lectures held in the United States) (Rotterdam: Brusse, 1913). He designed silver for Mr. and Mrs. Kröller-Müller, produced by C.J. Begeer, Utrecht, and by W. Voet, Haarlem, and austere, simple stained-glass vessels for Pantin and for Baccarat. Working at the Leerdam Glassworks, 1923–29 and 1931, Andries Copier was his apprentice; designed the canary-yellow pressed-glass service of *c*1924; proselytized the theories of Wright; admired Ludwig Mies van der Rohe and Gerrit Rietveld; in 1928, attended the CIAM (Congrès Internationaux d'Architecture Moderne) but did not join since its Modernism was in opposition to his own more traditional expression; 1928–30, designed for Rath & Doodeheefver wallpaper firm. Architecture included 1899–1900 Diamond-Workers' House, Amsterdam; 1897–1903 Stock Exchange (1897 competition winner), Amsterdam; 1912–13 Jahrhunderthalle, Breslau (now Wroclaw, Poland); 1914 Holland House, London.
▶ Hendrik Petrus Berlage, *Gedanken über den Stil in der Baukunst*, Leipzig, 1905. Hendrik Petrus, *Grundlagen und Entwicklung der Architektur*, Berlin and Rotterdam, 1908. Hendrik Petrus Berlage, *Studies over Bouwkunst, Stijl en Samenleving*, Rotterdam, 1910. Jan Gratama, *Dr. H.P. Berlage Bouwmeester*, Amsterdam, 1925. J. Havelaar, *Dr. H.P. Berlage*, Amsterdam, 1930. 'H.P. Berlage,' *Bouwkundig Weekblad Architectura*, No. 51 (special commemorative issue), 1934. Cat., *H.P. Berlage*, The Hague, 1975. Reyner Banham, *Theory and Design in the First Machine Age*, London, 1960. Pieter Singelenberg, *H.P. Berlage*, Amsterdam, 1969. Cat., *Industrie U Vormgeving in Nederland 1850–1950*, Amsterdam: Stedelijk Museum, 1985. Jacobus Johannes Vriend and Gerd Hatje in Vittorio Magnago Lampugnani, *Encyclopedia of 20th-Century Architecture*, New York: Abrams, 1986:44–45. Annelies Krekel-Aalberse, *Art Nouveau and Art Déco Silver*, New York: Abrams, 1989:251.

Berlinetta
▶ German design studio; located Berlin.
▶ The Berlinetta design office was set up in 1984 by John Hirschberg, Inge Sommer, Susanne Neubohn, and Christof Walther. In addition to furniture design, they were active in town planning and environmental issues.
▶ Received 1983 'Kitchens' second-prize competition of Design Plus, Frankfurt (Germany). Work included in 1982 '1 2, 3, . . . Egg Cup,' London and Berlin; 1984–85 'Shop of the East,' Berlin, Munich, and Hamburg; 1985 'The Art of Reading,' Frankfurt; 1985 'Berliner Zimmer: Exhibition for Interior Design,' Berlin; 1986 'Sentimental collages—living by senses' in Düsseldorf, 1986 'Explorations' in Stuttgart, 1986 'Women's Furniture,' Berlin; 1986 'Transit Berlin West—Furniture and Fashions from Berlin,' Berlin; 1986 'Between the Chairs: Objects for Living,' Bregenz (Austria); 1988 'Les Avantgardes du Mobilier: Berlin,' Centre Georges Pompidou and Galerie Néotù, Paris; 1988 'Prototypes for the Designwerkstatt' at Wertheim department store, Berlin, and 1989 'Internationalen Möbelmesse,' Cologne. Work subject of 1987 exhibition 'Berlinetta—Furniture 84–86,' Cologne.
▶ Cat., Design Center Stuttgart, *Women in Design: Careers and Life Histories Since 1900*, Stuttgart: Haus der Wirtschaft, 1989:78–80.

Bernadotte, Count Sigvard   (1907–)
▶ Swedish metal, furniture, textile, bookbinding, and theatre set designer; son of King Gustavus VI of Sweden.
▶ Studied Kungliga Konsthögskolan, Stockholm, to 1929.
▶ In 1930, he joined the Georg Jensen Sølvsmedie; the first designer in the Jensen workshop to break with the traditional naturalistic 'Jensen style,' preferred a more Modern, austere approach, that was severe, smooth and often had horizontal, vertical, or diagonal linear decoration, influenced by Johan Rohde. He is known for his 1939 *Bernadotte* silver flatware pattern. His

finest work was in tableware and larger pieces including jugs, bowls, and candlesticks. He served as a director at Jensen; opened a design studio, Copenhagen, in 1949 with Dutch architect Acton Bjørn, expanding later to Stockholm and New York; as an industrial designer, (with Bjørn) produced silver, furniture, textiles, plastics, camping, and heavy-machinery designs; in 1964, set up his own independent design studio; from 1967, was a director of the consulting firm Allied Industrial Designers, London.
▶ Sigvard Bernadotte (ed.), *Moderne dansk boligkunst*, Odense, 1946. Michael Farr, *Design in British Industry: A Mid-Century Survey*, London: Cambridge, 1955:41. Gotthard Johansson and Christian Ditlev Reventlow, *Sigvard Bernadotte sølvarbejder: 1930–1955*, Copenhagen: Georg Jensen, 1955. 'Designs from Abroad,' *Industrial Design*, Vol. 4, Feb. 1956:76–79. Cat., *Georg Jensen Silversmithy: 77 Artists, 75 Years*, Washington: Smithsonian Institution Press, 1980: Nos. 11–14. Jens Bernsen, *Design: The Problem Comes First*, Copenhagen, 1982:68–71. Cat., David Revere McFadden (ed.), *Scandinavian Modern Design 1880–1980*, New York: Abrams, 1982. Cat., Kathryn B. Hiesinger and George H. Marcus III (eds.), *Design Since 1945*, Philadelphia: Philadelphia Museum of Art, 1983. Cherie Fehrman and Kenneth Fehrman, *Postwar Interior Design, 1945–1960*, New York: Van Nostrand Reinhold, 1987.

Bernard, Oliver Percy   (1881–1939)
▶ British architect and designer; active Manchester, London, and Boston.
▶ He began his career working with a Manchester theatre, where he became a scenery painter; 1901–05, worked with scenery designer Walter Hann, London; in 1905, traveled to the USA with Thomas Ryan as a theatrical decorator; became a resident technician at Boston Opera House; returned to England after World War I and worked as a scenery designer and later chief architect for J. Lyon; designed sets for Drury Lane productions and interiors for theatres and cinemas; designed the decorations for 1924 Wembley 'Empire Exhibition'; was technical director for British pavilion, 1925 Paris 'Exposition Internationale des Arts Décoratifs et Industriels Modernes'; known for his steel furniture, produced by Pel, which was fashionable, inexpensive, and comparable with German models of the 1920s; 1931–33, was Pel's consultant designer; also designed for Pel's rival Cox; attracted to new materials like steel and glass, used them to great effect in commissions including 1929–30 Strand Palace Hotel, London, which may have been his earliest use of metal furniture; he placed two Thonet tubular-steel chairs in the foyer. Designed interiors for the 1929–30 Strand Palace Hotel, 1930 Cumberland Hotel, Regent Palace Hotel, 1932 Marble Arch Corner House, Oxford Street Corner House, and other Lyons restaurants; offices and shop interiors for Bakelite; and the Vickers Supermarine aviation works, Southampton.
▶ Cat., Dennis Sharp et al., *Pel and Tubular Steel Furniture of the Thirties*, London: Architectural Association, 1977. Cat., *Thirties: British art and design before the war*, London: Arts Council of Great Britain, Hayward Gallery, 1979:59,84.102,271,285. Barbie Campbell-Cole and Tim Benton (eds.), *Tubular Steel Furniture*, London: The Art Book Company, 1979:53.

Bernardaud, Porcelaines
▶ French ceramics firm; located Limoges.
▶ The firm was founded in 1863 by Pierre Guerry, who was joined in 1868 by brother-in-law Rémy Delinières. In 1895, Leonard Bernardaud became an associate and, in 1900, head of the firm. The firm is managed today by Pierre Bernardaud and sons Michel and Frédéric. Its best known designs included *Les anémones* pattern by Bernard Buffet, *Le coq* and *Les roses* patterns by Theo Van Dongen, a vase by Raymond Crevel, *Aries* shade by Raymond Loewy. Other designers included Marie-Christine Dorner, Roy Lichtenstein, George Segal, Cindy Sherman, Jean Tinguely, Joseph Kosuth, and César.
▶ Received silver medal for its square plate at 1889 Paris 'Exposition Universelle.'

Bernaux, Émile (1883–)
▶ French sculptor and furniture designer; born Paris.
▶ From 1909, Bernaux produced furniture with highly carved human, floral and fruit motifs.
▶ Work shown regularly at Salons of the Société des Artistes Décorateurs 1911–29, of which he was an active member until the end of the 1940s. Collaborated with architect Alfred Levard on a dining room at 1925 Paris 'Exposition Internationale des Arts Décoratifs et Industriel Modernes.'
▶ Maurice Dufrêne, *Emsembles Mobiliers, Exposition Internationale 1925*, Paris: Charles Moreau, 1925:76. Pierre Kjellberg, *Art Déco: les maîtres du Mobilier, le décor des Paquebots*, Paris: Amateur, 1986:35–36.

Bernini Mobili e Arredamenti
▶ Italian furniture manufacturer; located Carate Brianza.
▶ Bernini Mobili e Arredamenti first used plastics for furniture in 1964. Its designers included Rodolfo Benetto, Giotto Stoppino, Fabio Lenci, and Gianfranco Frattini. It produced Joe Colombo's 1969 mobile unit *Combicenter*, S. Coppola's and T. Kita's 1970 *Chair 622* in covered polyurethane for auditoria, T. Lenci's table-chair-tray set *230–232*, Rodolfo Benetto's 1971 flexible units *Quattroquarti 700* in ABS, and Gianfranco Frattini's *Screen 835*.
▶ The Colombo, Coppola/Kita, Lenci, and Benetto pieces were shown at 1972 'Design a Plastické Hmoty' exhibition, Uměleckoprůmyslové Muzeum, Prague.
▶ Cat., Milena Lamarová, *Design a Plastické Hmoty*, Prague: Uměleckoprůmyslové Muzeum, 1972:172.

Bernt (aka Bernt Petersen 1937–)
▶ Danish designer.
▶ Studied Kunsthåndvaerkerskolen, Copenhagen, to 1960, and Skolen for Brugskunst (formerly Det Tekniske Selskabs Skolen) to 1973.
▶ 1960–63, he worked with Hans J. Wegner; in 1963, set up studio where he designed furniture; undertook commissions including for 1972 Munich Olympic Games; taught and exhibited widely; in 1978, was a lecturer at Det Kongelige Danske Kunstakademi, Copenhagen; designed furniture produced by Wørts' Møbelsnedkeri, Odense Stole- og Møbelfabrik, and Søren Willadsens; designed the *CH 71* and *CH 72* plywood chairs by Carl Hansen, Denmark.
▶ Robert A.M. Stern (ed.), *The International Design Yearbook*, New York: Abbeville, 1985/1986: No. 96. Frederik Sieck, *Nutidig Dansk Møbeldesign: -en kortfattet illustreret beskrivelse*, Copenhagen: Bondo Gravesen; 1990 Busck edition in English.

Berry, Albert
▶ American metalworker.
▶ In the 1899 exhibition catalog of the Society of Arts and Crafts, Boston, Berry is listed as a silverware designer, Rhode Island School of Design, Providence. He subsequently lived in Alaska and, in 1918, moved to Seattle, where he set up Albert Berry's Craft Shop; produced imaginative hand-wrought designs such as lamps, incorporating various natural materials, including mica, shells, and even fossilized walrus tusks into copper. French Art Nouveau and German Jugendstil styles were reflected in his work. In addition to its own wares, the Berry shop carried native-American baskets and textiles.
▶ Work shown at 1899 exhibition, The Society of Arts and Crafts, Boston.
▶ Cat., *From Architecture to Object*, New York: Hirschl and Adler, 1989.

Berthet, Jean-Louis (1940–)
▶ French furniture designer.
▶ Studied École Nationale des Arts Décoratifs, Paris.
▶ He set up a research and design company in Paris, then in Avignon, followed by New York in 1986; 1974–77, was president of the Société des Artistes Décorateurs; designed the 1987 *Maestro* sofa; collaborated with Yves Pochy, Jean Crumière, and Gérard Sammut.

▶ Louis Bériot, *Berthet-Pochy architectes d'intérieur*, Paris: EPA, 1990.

Berthier, Marc (1935–)
▶ French designer.
▶ Berthier began working with Japanese and Italian manufacturers in 1976; designed the 1973 *Twentytube* children's furniture collection in lacquered tubes and linen, 1979 *Pliaviva* folding furniture series (with Alain Chauvel) produced by Magis, lighting by Holight, and furniture for Knoll; designed the 1985 *Kyoto* tea service in sanded melamine and silver-plated metal by Cité Future; designed 1985 *Magi's* office chair by Magis; designed 1970 polyester and fiberglass furniture by Ozoo et Dan; was a tutor, École Nationale Supérieure de Création Industrielle, Paris.
▶ Work shown at most Salons du Meuble, Paris. In 1975 with Daniel Pigeon, won the school-furniture competition sponsored by CCI (Centre de Création Industrielle).
▶ Gilles de Bure, *Le Mobilier français 1965–1979*, Paris: Regard/VIA, 1983. *Les Carnets du Design*, Paris: Mad-Cap Productions et APCI, 1986:19. François Mathey, *Au bonheur des formes, design français, 1945–1992*, Paris: Regard, 1992.

Bertoia, Harry (b. Arieto Bertoia   1915–78)
▶ Italian sculptor, printmaker and jewelry and furniture designer; born San Lorenzo, Udine; active USA.
▶ 1932–36 studied Cass Technical High School, Detroit; 1936, School of Arts and Crafts, Detroit; 1937–39, Cranbrook Academy of Art, Bloomfield, Michigan under Eliel Saarinen.
▶ Bertoia settled the USA in 1930; 1939–43, taught jewelry and metalworking at the Cranbrook Academy of Art in the metal workshop he set up there; produced jewelry and utilitarian metal objects; 1943–46, worked with Charles and Ray Eames at Eames's Evans Products, Venice, California; (with the Eameses) worked on molded-plywood technology and airplane and medical equipment for the war effort through the Evans firm; in the late 1940s, worked with the Eameses at Plyform Products Company, Venice, California. Eames used Bertoia's pioneering metal-basketwork seat design without acknowledging its source, and Bertoia left Eames's workshop in 1950 to become a designer for Knoll. Using the metal-wire basketwork technique, Bertoia designed his famous *Diamond Chair* range for Knoll, who put it into production 1952–53. The range included a pivoting lounge chair, small lounge chair, lounge chair with a back extension and footstool, side chair for adults and two sizes for children. From the mid-1950s, he was mainly active as a sculptor, producing metal pieces that moved with the wind, sometimes designed to produce percussive sounds. Eero Saarinen often used Bertoia's sculpture prominently in his buildings, including the chapel at the 1953–55 Massachusetts Institute of Technology, Cambridge, Massachusetts and 1958–63 Dulles International Airport, Virginia.
▶ Received 1955 Fine Arts Medal; 1956 Craftsmanship Medal; 1957 Graham Foundation Grant for European travel; 1963 AIA Fine Arts Medal, Pennsylvania chapter; 1973 gold medal, AIA.
▶ Cat., *Les Assises du siège contemporain*, Paris: Musée des Arts Décoratifs, 1968. June Kompass Nelson, *Harry Bertoia, Sculptor*, Detroit, 1970. Eric Larrabee and Massimo Vignelli, *Knoll Design*, New York: Abrams, 1981:66–71. Cat., *Modern Chairs 1918–1970*, London: Lund Humphries, 1971. Cat., *Knoll au Louvre*, Paris: Musée des Arts Décoratifs, 1972. Muriel Emanuel et al. (eds.), *Contemporary Artists*, New York: St Martin's, 1983:94–95. Charlotte Fiell and Peter Fiell, *Modern Furniture Classics Since 1945*, London: Thames and Hudson, 1991:15,19,20,21,50,51, 74, Nos. 11,33. David D.J. Rau, 'Harry Bertoia' in Mel Byars and Russell Flinchum (eds.), *50 American Designers, 1918–1968*, Washington: Preservation, 1994.

Bertoldi, Giorgio (1940–)
▶ Italian designer; born and active Venice.
▶ He designed glassware for Vistosi, the 1963–64 lamp for Tre Vi, public furniture for Malvestic, 1968 and 1972 kitchen systems for Noalex and Mobilgas, office schemes and modular domestic

storage systems for Longato Arredamenti; became a member of ADI (Associazione per il Disegno Industriale).

▶ Participated 1963 Triennale del Corso Superiore di Disegno Industriale, Venice.

▶ *ADI Annual 1976*, Milan: Associazione per il Disegno Industriale, 1976.

Bertoni, Maurizio (1946–)

▶ Italian designer; born Milan.

▶ Studied Accademia di Brera, Milan, and, 1967, Hochschule für Gestaltung, Ulm.

▶ He worked in the Peter Raacke Design Studio, Frankfurt, designing paper furniture, packaging, and domestic goods; from 1978, designed lighting for Castaldi Illuminazione and Firmen-Images.

▶ Hans Wichmann, *Design Italien 1945 bis heute*, Munich: Die Neue Sammlung, 1988.

Best, Robert Dudley (1892–1984)

▶ British lighting designer and manufacturer of lighting fittings and architectural metalwork.

▶ Studied School of Industrial Design, Düsseldorf.

▶ He worked in a studio in Paris; in 1925, became managing director of the family lighting business Best and Lloyd Smethwick; was introduced to Modern design through the work of Walter Gropius and the 1925 Paris 'Exposition Internationale des Arts Décoratifs et Industriels Modernes'; while on a trip to Zürich, was influenced by an electric lamp design he described as 'frankly mechanistic in appearance'; modified the model for the British market, resulting in the 1930 *Bestlite* lamp designed by R.D. Best and a milestone in British task lighting; was placed back into production in various sizes and models from the early 1990s. He became an early member of the Design and Industries Association (formed in 1915). Active before and after World War II, Best and Lloyd was known for its inexpensive lighting fixtures with high design standards.

▶ *Bestlite* table lamp included in 1979–80 'Thirties' exhibition, Hayward Gallery, London.

▶ Cat., *Thirties: British art and design before the war*, London: Arts Council of Great Britain, Hayward Gallery, 1979:231,233.

Bestagno, Vincenzo (1936–)

▶ Italian designer; active Verona.

▶ Active professionally from 1957, Bestagno was predominately involved with the interior design industry. His clients included Bernini, Archiutti, Mazzanica, and Cà d'Oro. He was a member of ADI (Associazione per il Disegno Industriale).

▶ *ADI Annual 1976*, Milan: Associazione per il Disegno Industriale, 1976.

Bettonica, Franco (1927–)

▶ Italian designer.

▶ In the 1960s with Mario Malocchi, Bettonica established Studio OPI. Clients included Cini and Nils.

▶ Cat., Kathryn B. Hiesinger and George H. Marcus III (eds.), *Design Since 1945*, Philadelphia: Philadelphia Museum of Art, 1983:232. Hans Wichmann, *Design Italien 1945 bis heute*, Munich: Die Neue Sammlung, 1988.

Beumers, Conrad Anton

▶ German silversmiths; located Düsseldorf.

▶ Conrad Anton Beumers founded the firm in 1858; produced silver designs by Hugo Leven and Paul Beumers. Emmy Roth trained under Anton Beumers in his workshop, which closed in 1928.

▶ Annelies Krekel-Aalberse, *Art Nouveau and Art Déco Silver*, New York: Abrams, 1989:145–245,252.

Bezalel School of Arts and Crafts

▶ Israeli design school, located Jerusalem.

▶ The school was founded in 1906, one of its aims being to propagate the ideals of Zionism through the production of a recognizably Jewish decorative style. Familiar symbols, the Star of David, and the menorah, were frequently incorporated into Bezalel designs; others included palm fronds along with the symbols of the Jewish state which was to be located in its traditional homeland in Palestine. Craftspeople from Middle-East communities taught traditional skills. The school's focus included metalwork, carpets, embroidery, cane furniture, inlaid-wood picture frames, damascene work, silver, and other media.

▶ Nurit Shilo-Cohen (ed.), *Bezalel 1906–1929*, Jerusalem: The Israel Museum, 1983.

Bézard, Aristide

▶ French ceramicist.

▶ Bézard made earthenware about 1902 with barbotine decoration at Marlotte, where a small factory for the production of decorated earthenware revetment tiles had been set up in the 1870s. Émile Moussaux, Bézard's associate, made *flambé* stoneware there. Bézard died in World War I. Moussaux closed the factory about 1930–32.

▶ Yvonne Brunhammer et al., *Art Nouveau Belgium, France*, Houston: Rice University, 1976, biblio.

Bialetti, Alfonso

▶ Italian designer.

▶ In the 1930s, Bialetti designed the *Moka Express* model, which marked a departure in coffeemaker design. In cast aluminum, it was rendered to reflect a kind of industrial solidity. Initially handmade, after World War II it was issued on a mass scale, becoming a tremendously popular household object. Bialetti's likeness in a caricature with moustache was applied to a facet on the bottom section of the pot.

▶ Penny Sparke, *Design in Italy, 1870 to the Present*, New York: Abbeville, 1988. Jeremy Myerson and Sylvia Katz, *Kitchenware*, London: Conran Octopus, 1990:56,61.

Bianchi, Bruno (1929–)

▶ Italian industrial designer; born Rome; active Gallarate.

▶ He began his professional career in 1959; became a member of ADI (Associazione per il Disegno Industriale). Designed washing machines, television sets, sound equipment, and professional photographic equipment. Clients included Autovox, Fiar CGE, Ire, Elemak, and Augusta. Was a consultant to Elemak, Augusta, and Fiar CGE.

▶ *ADI Annual 1976*, Milan: Associazione per il Disegno Industriale, 1976.

Bianchi, Giuliano (1944–)

▶ Italian industrial designer; born Brescello; active Gualtieri.

▶ He began his professional career in 1969, became a member of ADI (Associazione per il Disegno Industriale). Clients included Officine Bertoncini, Immergas, Ferrari, F.&T. Salotti, Ceramica Lux, Casalinghi Alvol, Suad, and Lima.

▶ *ADI Annual 1976*, Milan: Associazione per il Disegno Industriale, 1976.

Bianchi, Rodolfo (1948–)

▶ Italian furniture designer; born and active Milan.

▶ He began his professional career in 1974; became a member of ADI (Associazione per il Disegno Industriale). Known for his upholstered furniture for Themis, he designed furniture for Carlo Citterio.

▶ *ADI Annual 1976*, Milan: Associazione per il Disegno Industriale, 1976.

Bianconi, Fulvio (1915–)

▶ Italian illustrator, graphic and glass designer; born Padua.

▶ Studied Accademi di Belle Arti and Liceo Scientifico, Venice.

▶ He designed glass for Venini, Murano; particularly active in the 1950s; settled in Milan in 1939 and worked for Motta. Graphic clients included publishers Mondari and Garzanti; recording firms HMV, Pathé, and Columbia; Teatro Olimpico, Fiat, and Pirelli.

▶ A. Gatto, *Disegni di Bianconi*, Milan, 1959. Hans Wichmann, *Italien Design 1945 bis heute*, Munich: Die Neue Sammlung, 1988.

BIC
▶ French manufacturer.
▶ BIC was established in 1953 to produce disposable plastic products including razors, pens, and lighters; sold 12 million ballpoint pens each day worldwide. All products were designed in an in-house studio.

Bidasoa, Porcelanas del
▶ Spanish porcelain manufacturer.
▶ Porcelanas del Bidasoa worked with industrial designers and artists, including André Ricard, Salvador Dalí, and Raymond Loewy. It produced Javier Mariscal's 1988 *Florero* jar and Andres Nagel's 1988 tableware.
▶ Guy Julier, *New Spanish Design*, New York: Rizzoli, 1991.

Bigaux, Louis
▶ French architect and interior designer.
▶ Around 1900, Bigaux developed new concepts of form and decoration for interior decoration; gathered around himself a group of young disciples who contributed to his projects. His studio handled every aspect of the decorative arts, including painting, design, sculpture, and carpentry.
▶ At the 1900 Paris 'Exposition Universelle,' showed a luxurious interior, using the products of manufacturers who commissioned him to update their designs, in the pavilion that included bronzes by Eugène Bagués, wallpaper by Isidore Leroy, ceramics by Alexandre Bigot, furniture and paneling by Le Coeur, and marbles by Poincet.
▶ Yvonne Brunhammer et al., *Art Nouveau Belgium, France*, Houston: Rice University, 1976.

Bigot, Alexandre (1862–1927)
▶ French ceramicist; born Mer, Loir-et-Cher.
▶ Bigot discovered the stoneware and porcelain pieces of the Far East at 1889 Paris 'Exposition Universelle'; produced *flambé* stoneware and architectural products such as bricks, tiles, decorative panels, and other items; specializing in tile friezes, produced the designs of Guimard, Van de Velde, Roche, Jouve, Sauvage, Majorelle, de Baudot, Formigé, Lavirotte, and, for the Samaritaine department store, Frantz Jourdain; in 1897, sold work (sometimes with bronze mounts designed by Edward Colonna) at Bing's shop L'Art Nouveau, Paris; executed the ceramics for Lavirotte's building, and the vestibule of Guimard's Castel Béranger, both Paris. Bigot's catalog showed stoves and bathtubs. His shop closed in 1914.
▶ In 1894, first pieces (simple forms with yellow, green, and brown matt glazes) were shown. Received first prize at 1900 Paris 'Exposition Universelle' for his animal frieze, based on designs of Paul Jouve, installed at the Exhibition's huge gateway (architect René Binet). Work shown at Salon d'Automne.
▶ Yvonne Brunhammer et al., *Art Nouveau Belgium, France*, Houston: Rice University, 1976, biblio.

Bijoux Bozart
▶ Italian costume jeweler; located Milan.
▶ Bijoux Bozart was founded in Milan in 1956 by Emy and Giuseppe Manca. Its first customers were fashion houses in the 1960s. It later became identified with avant-garde body jewelry. Producing costume jewelry at first, its wares began to incorporate more precious materials from the 1970s. In 1982, the founders were joined by their son Maurizio Manca.
▶ Deanna F. Cera (ed.), *Jewels of Fantasy: Costume Jewelry of the 20th Century*, New York: Abrams, 1992:302.

Bijoux Cascio
▶ Italian costume jeweler; located Florence.
▶ The firm was founded in 1948 by Gaetano Cascio, whose meeting with G.B. Giorgini resulted from 1955 in the company's furnishing costume jewelry to fashion designers, American stores, and its fashion show début at the Palazzo Pitti with Schuberth. Cascio's son Riccardo expanded the business in the 1970s.

▶ Deanna F. Cera (ed.), *Jewels of Fantasy: Costume Jewelry of the 20th Century*, New York: Abrams, 1992:303.

Bijoux Elfe
▶ Italian costume jeweler; located Florence.
▶ Born in Florence, Elio Fedeli first represented Coppola and Parodi in Milan and, 1949–59, incorporated the Cesari costume jewelry firm in Rome. With Cinecittà, Cesare & Fedeli created jewelry for the film *Quo Vadis* (1951); Fedeli also designed jewelry and accessories for Dino De Laurentis's film *Ulysses* (1955). Moving to Florence, Fedeli founded Bijoux Elfe; designed pieces for the television ballets broadcast by Studio Uno, Rome; established a collaboration with fashion designer Emilio Pucci in Sala Bianca.
▶ Deanna F. Cera (ed.), *Jewels of Fantasy: Costume Jewelry of the 20th Century*, New York: Abrams, 1992:303.

Bijoux Fiaschi
▶ Italian costume jeweler; located Florence.
▶ Established in 1960, the firm established by Giancarlo Fiaschi sold its costume jewelry through Bijoux Cascio and Bijoux Elfe. He collaborated with avant-garde fashion designers, and, from 1966, his name became associated with other prestigious costume jewelers.
▶ Deanna F. Cera (ed.), *Jewels of Fantasy: Costume Jewelry of the 20th Century*, New York: Abrams, 1992:304.

Bijoux Sandra
▶ Italian costume jeweler; located Florence.
▶ Sandra Bartolomei was correspondent in Paris for the newspaper *Globe*; turned to creating imitation jewels as a hobby; began producing costume jewelry under the name Bijoux Sandra in 1949; setting up a studio in Florence, designed wares in the 1950s that showed a French influence; produced large chokers for Dior and Balenciaga and became known for her distinctive 19th-century-style necklaces; 1955–65, designed pieces that appeared in fashion shows at the Palazzo Pitti; became successful in the USA, Sweden, Norway, and Venezuela.
▶ Deanna F. Cera (ed.), *Jewels of Fantasy: Costume Jewelry of the 20th Century*, New York: Abrams, 1992:304.

Bijvoët, Bernard (1889–1979)
▶ Dutch architect; born Amsterdam; active Netherlands and France.
▶ Bijvoët and Johannes Duiker were partners in an architecture practice in Amsterdam. They designed 1926–28 Zonnestraal Sanatorium, Hilversum, known for its extensive use of glass and projecting terraced roofs. Meeting Pierre Chareau in Paris in 1919, Bijvoët left the Amsterdam practice in 1925; collaborated with Chareau on Jean Dalsace's 1928–32 Maison de Verre, rue Saint-Guillaume, Paris; in 1935, returned to Amsterdam to carry out Duiker's work after his death; 1937–40, worked with Eugène Beaudoin and Marcel Lods, practicing on his own until 1970 in the Netherlands.
▶ Johannes Duiker, *Hoogbouw*, Rotterdam, 1930. T. Boga (ed.), *B. Bijvoet & J. Duiker 1890–1935*, Zürich. R. Vickery, 'Bijvoet and Duiker,' *AA Quarterly*, Vol. 2, No. 1, 1970:4–10. 'Duiker 1' and 'Duiker 2' in *Forum*, Nov. 1971 and Jan. 1972. Vittorio Magnago Lampugnani (ed.), *Encyclopedia of 20th-Century Architecture*, New York: Abrams, 1986:85.

Bill, Max (1908–)
▶ Swiss industrial designer, sculptor, painter, architect, teacher, and writer; born Winterthur; active Zürich.
▶ 1924–27, studied silversmithing, Kunstgewerbeschule, Zürich; 1927–29, Bauhaus, Dessau.
▶ He moved to Zürich in 1929, active as an architect, painter, graphic designer, and, from 1932, sculptor; from 1936, a publicist; and, from 1944, a product designer. He was one of the architects of the SWB's (Schweizerischer Werkbund) 1930–32 Neubühl estate, near Zürich, a model for the Modern style; made contact with the staff of Wohnbedarf department store, Zürich; designed the store's letterhead, advertisements, flyers, invitation cards, and

1931 logo for its first branch store; in 1930, set up his architecture practice; 1930–62, was a member of SWB; 1932–36, member of the artists' group Abstraction-Création, Paris; in 1937, joined the Allianz (Association of Modern Swiss Artists); in 1939, joined CIAM; in 1939, joined UAM (Union des Artistes Modernes); in 1953, Institut d'Esthétique; in 1956, Deutscher Werkbund; in 1959, Bund Schweizer Architekten. From 1944, he was active as an industrial designer in Zürich; was responsible for Bundespreis 'Die gute Industrieform' exhibition; was a co-founder of Hochschule für Gestaltung, Ulm, where, 1951–56, he was rector and head of its architecture and 'Produktform' departments and, as a teacher, espoused Bauhaus theories and principles. The Ulm approach (as it became known) profoundly influenced postwar German designers and design, including Hans Gugelot and Dieter Rams. His best known structure was the 1953–55 building of Hochschule für Gestaltung, Ulm. Pursuing Functionalism, Bill's work was based on his idea of mathematical laws amalgamated with aesthetic standards. In 1956, he invited Tomás Maldonado to succeed him as director of the Ulm school; in 1957, set up his own studio in Zürich, where he became a painter and sculptor; 1961–64, was chief architect of the 'Educating and Creating' pavilion at 1964 Swiss National Exhibition, Lausanne; in 1964, an honorary member of the American Institute of Architects; 1967–71, member of the Swiss parliament; 1967–74, professor of environmental design at the Staatliche Hochschule für bildende Künste, Hamburg. His product designs included 1954 stacking chair, 1957 wall clock, and lighting.

▶ Received prix d'honneur (Swiss Pavilion) at 1936 (VI) Triennale di Milano; 1949 Kandinskii Prize, Paris; 1951 first prize, Biennale, São Paulo; 1966 gold medal, Italian Chamber of Deputies, Verucchio; 1968 art prize, City of Zürich. Industrial-design work subject of 1974 one-person traveling exhibition originating at Albright-Knox Art Gallery, Buffalo, New York.

▶ Max Bill (ed.), *Le Corbusier et P. Jeanneret, œuvre complète*, 1934–38; Zürich, 1939. Max Bill (ed.), *Moderne Schweizer Architektur*, Basel, 1942 and 1950. Max Bill, *Die gute Form*, Bern and Zürich, 1949. Max Bill (ed.), *Robert Maillart*, Zürich, 1949; London, 1969. Max Bill, *Form: A Balance Sheet of Mid-Twentieth Century Trends in Design*, Basel, 1952. Max Bill, 'The Bauhaus Idea: From Weimar to Ulm,' *The Architects' Year Book*, No. 5, 1953:29–32. Tomás Maldonado, *Max Bill*, Buenos Aires, 1955; Stuttgart, 1956. Margit Staber, *Max Bill*, London, 1964. Margit Staber, *Max Bill*, St. Gallen, 1971. Cat., *Max Bill*, Buffalo: Buffalo Fine Arts Academy and Albright-Knox Art Gallery, 1974. Eduard Hüttinger, *Max Bill*, Zürich, 1977; New York, 1978. Cat., Kathryn B. Hiesinger and George H., Marcus III (eds.), *Design Since 1945*, Philadelphia: Philadelphia Museum of Art, 1983. Eckhard Neumann (ed.), *Bauhaus und Bauhäusler*, Cologne, 1985. Cherie Fehrman and Kenneth Fehrman, *Postwar Interior Design, 1945–1960*, New York: Van Nostrand Reinhold, 1987. Friederike Mehlau-Wiebking et al., *Schweizer Typenmöbel 1925–35, Sigfried Giedion und die Wohnbedarf AG*, Zürich, 1989.

Billinghurst, A. Noel
See Graydon-Stannus, A.N.

Biloxi Art Pottery
See Ohr, George Edgar

Bimbi, Carlo   (1944–)
▶ Italian designer; born Volterra; active Florence.
▶ Graduated Instituto Europeo di Design in Florence.
▶ In 1960, he settled in Milan; 1968–69, he worked at Studio Nizzoli Associati, Milan; in 1970, (with Nilo Gioacchini and Gianni Ferrara) founded Gruppo Internotredici, where they executed industrial design for various clients, including machinery, domestic environmental unit, and furniture; became a member of ADI (Associazione per il Disegno Industriale); organized the 1984 exhibition 'Volterra, Cercase l'alabastro'; designed for Arketipo, B&B Italia, Ciatti, Guzzini, Metalmobile, Zucchetti Rubinetterie.

▶ Received first prizes at 1968 (VIII), 1969 (IX), and 1970 (X) Concorso Internazionale del Mobile, Trieste; first and second prizes (plastic furniture Abet-Print laminates) at Concorso Nazionale, Pesaro; first prize (alabaster objects) at 1972 exhibition, Volterra. Work shown at 1967 Montreal 'Universal and International Exhibition (Expo '67)'; 1972 'Italy: The New Domestic Landscape,' New York Museum of Modern Art; Gimbel's department store, Pittsburgh; Italian design pavilion, 1975 Salon d'Ameublement, Lausanne; 1973 'BIO 5' Industrial Design Biennale, Ljubljana. Designed the 100m² apartment for magazine *Rassegna* at 1971 (IX) Mostra Selettiva del Mobile, Cantù.

▶ *ADI Annual 1976*, Milan: Associazione per il Disegno Industriale, 1976. *Modo*, No. 148, March–April 1993:116.

Binazzi, Lapo   (1943–)
▶ Italian designer; born and active Florence.
▶ Studied architecture, Florence.
▶ In 1967, he was instrumental in the formation of the design group UFO and part of the original group that established Architettura Radicale; in 1968 with UFO, created large-scale objects located in unlikely areas in Florence, known as 'Transient Urbans'; in 1969, was active as an interior designer for various shops; wrote for journals, including *Domus* and *Modo*, and produced videos and films. His first architectural work was the 1971 house in Castel Rigone. In 1975, he founded an architecture and design studio in Florence, designing a number of lighting models, and designed ceramics for Eschanbach Porzellanen and silverware for Pampaloni.

▶ From 1968 with UFO, participated in exhibitions in Italy and abroad, including 1968 (XIV) and 1973 (XV) Triennali di Milano, 1971 Biennale de Paris, 1974 Contemporanea in Rome, 1976 International Biennale of Graphic Arts in Florence, 1978 Biennale di Venezia, 1981 New York 'Design by Circumstances,' 1978 Berlin 'Design als postulat,' and 1981 Hanover 'Provakationen,' 1987 Documenta 8 in Kassel. His work was the subject of the 1981 one-person exhibition at Alchimia in Florence.

▶ Andrea Branzi, *La Casa Calda: Esperienze del Nuovo Disegno Italiano*, Milan: Idea Books, 1982. *Modo*, No. 148, March–April 1993:116.

Binder, Wilhelm
▶ German silversmiths; located Schwäbisch-Gmünd.
▶ The Wilhelm Binder firm was founded in 1869 and, in the early 20th century, produced Modern silver hollow-ware and flatware designs.
▶ Annelies Krekel-Aalberse, *Art Nouveau and Art Déco Silver*, New York: Abrams, 1989:252. Cat., *Metallkunst*, Berlin: Bröhan Museum, 1990:45–47.

Bindesbøll, Thorvald   (1846–1908)
▶ Danish designer of furniture, ceramics, metalwork, and textiles; active Copenhagen.
▶ Studied architecture.
▶ From 1872, was active in architecture, decorative and monumental commissions, furniture design, embroidery, and book illustration; worked for J. Walmann Pottery, Utterslev Mark; Københavns Lervarefabrik ceramics factory from 1891–1902; for Mogens Ballin and A. Michelsen from c1898. His work combined influences of William Morris and Oriental art. His first silver designs dated from 1899 and were simple forms with strong abstract decoration. He derived some of his patterns from clouds and seaweed; in ceramics, furniture, and textiles, was the most important designer in Denmark from the 1890s onwards, having a great influence on an entire generation of young Danish artists with many imitators of his work, including Fr. Hegel who began working for Michelsen in 1906, Molger Kyster of Kolding, and, in his early work, Georg Jensen.

▶ Silver (by A. Michelsen) shown at 1900 Paris 'Exposition Universelle.'

▶ Karl J.V. Madsen, *Thorvald Bindes'bøll*, Copenhagen: Det Danske Kunstindustrimuseum, 1943. Charlotte Gere, *American and European Jewelry 1830–1914*, New York: Crown, 1975:151.

Cat., David Revere McFadden (ed.), *Scandinavian Modern Design 1880–1980*, New York: Abrams, 1982. Jennifer Hawkins Opie, *Scandinavia: Ceramics and Glass in the Twentieth Century*, New York: Rizzoli, 1989. Annelies Krekel-Aalberse, *Art Nouveau and Art Déco Silver*, New York: Abrams, 1989:252.

Binet, René (1866–1911)
▶ French architect and designer; active Paris.
▶ Studied École des Beaux-Arts, Paris, to 1892.
▶ In the late 1890s, he designed jewelry and silverware; was best known for the entrance to the 1900 Paris 'Exposition Universelle'; in 1905, designed sections of the Au Printemps department store, Paris, including fittings; published *Esquisses Décoration* (c1905).
▶ Bernard Marrey, *Les grands magasins*, Paris: Picard, 1979:263. René Julian, *Histoire de l'Architecture Moderne*, Paris: Sers, 1984. Stuart Durant, *Ornament from the Industrial Revolution to Today*, Woodstock, NY: Overlook, 1986:54,320.

Bing & Grøndahl Porcelaensfabrik
▶ Danish ceramics manufacturer.
▶ In 1853, Meyer Herman Bing and Jacob Herman Bing, paper and art dealers, and Frederik Vilhelm Grøndahl set up a factory; painter Peter Krohn was its artistic director 1853–85. By 1880, J.H. Bing's two sons Ludvig and Harald had joined the firm, with Ludwig as general manager and Harald in charge of technical developments. In 1885, Harald appointed Pietro Krohn artistic director, later succeeded by J.F. Willumsen. Krohn oversaw the production of the 1888 *Heron* dinner service, designed in a proto-Art Nouveau style. Some artists of the day worked for both Bing & Grøndahl and the Royal Danish Factory. The firm is noted for its figurines of women and children after models by Ingeborg Plockross-Irminger and also for the work of Jean Gauguin, son of Paul Gauguin. In the 1920s and 1930s, designers included Knud Kyhn, Axel Salto, Kai Nielsen, Ebbe Sadolin, Hans Tegner, and Kay Bojesen. After World War II, a new factory for dinnerware was built in Valby (Denmark), the original plant specializing in artware. The factory's designers later included Finn Juhl. In 1987, the firm merged with Royal Copenhagen.
▶ *Porcelaensfabrikken Bing & Grøndahl 1853–1928*, Copenhagen, 1928. Cat., *Porzellan-Kunst: Sammlung Karl H. Bröhan*, Berlin, 1969. Erik Larssen, *En københavnsk porcelaensfabriks historie: Bing & Grondahl 1853–1978*, Copenhagen, 1978. Jennifer Hawkins Opie, *Scandinavia: Ceramics and Glass in the Twentieth Century*, New York: Rizzoli, 1989.

Bing, Marcel (1875–1920)
▶ French designer; son of Siegfried Bing; born Paris.
▶ Studied École du Louvre, Paris.
▶ He designed bronze sculpture and jewelry for his father's shop L'Art Nouveau, Paris; on his father's death in 1905, took control of the business and moved it from 22 rue de Provence to 10 rue St.-Georges, dealing in Oriental and medieval antiques.
▶ He showed jewelry at the 1901 Paris Salon of the Société Nationale des Beaux-Arts.
▶ Yvonne Brunhammer et al., *Art Nouveau Belgium, France*, Houston: Rice University, 1976, biblio.

Bing, Siegfried (1838–1905)
▶ German writer and entrepreneur; born Hamburg; active Paris.
▶ He worked in a ceramics factory in Hamburg before the Franco-Prussian War; opened an oriental warehouse in Paris in 1877; became the friend of Louis Comfort Tiffany, whose glassware he sold; in 1895, opened the shop L'Art Nouveau, 22 rue de Provence, Paris, where he sold glass by Emile Gallé, René Lalique, and Karl Köpping. (The term 'Art Nouveau' originated from the name of Bing's shop.) Designer and decorator Alexandre Charpentier, designer and writer Eugène Gaillard, and ceramicist Auguste Delaherche were associated with the enterprise. Pierre Bonnard's stained-glass designs were made by Tiffany for the shop. Bing published *Le Japon Artistique* (1888–91) and *La Culture artistique en Amérique* (1896). John Getz opened a branch of Bing's firm in New York in 1887.

▶ Bing's Pavillon de l'Art Nouveau was built at 1900 Paris 'Exposition Universelle.'
▶ Julius Meier-Graefe, 'L'Art Nouveau: die Salons,' *Das Atelier*, No. 6, 15 March 1896. Cat., Gabriel P. Weisberg, *Art Nouveau Bing*, New York: Abrams, 1986. Annelies Krekel-Aalberse, *Art Nouveau and Art Déco Silver*, New York: Abrams, 1989:252. Nancy J. Troy, *Modernism and the Decorative Arts in France: Art Nouveau to Le Corbusier*, New Haven: Yale, 1991.

Bioli, Enzo (1932–)
▶ Italian designer and teacher; born and active Parma.
▶ He began his professional career in 1960, designing furniture, ceramics, and lighting; taught at Instituto d'Arte, Accademia Belle Arti, Parma; became a member of ADI (Associazione per il Disegno Industriale).
▶ *ADI Annual 1976*, Milan: Associazione per il Disegno Industriale, 1976.

Biondo, Francesco (1958–)
▶ Italian designer; born Gangi, Palermo.
▶ Studied architecture, Università di Palermo to 1983; 1983–84, Domus Academy, Milan.
▶ He was a consultant to a plastics firm; collaborated with Giovanni Levanti; in the early 1990s, designed African-inspired lamps.
▶ Fumio Shimizu and Matteo Thun (eds.), *The Descendants of Leonardo: The Italian Design*, Tokyo, 1987:326.

Birks, Henry
▶ Canadian jeweler and goldsmiths; located Montréal.
▶ Henry Birks, descended from a long line of Sheffield cutlers, established a business in Montréal in 1879; the firm grew into one of the largest jewelers in Canada, with over 200 employees by 1900. Birks's sons Gerald W., John Henry, and William Massey became partners; when Birks died in 1928, William became president of the enterprise. William's son Henry Gifford Birks became president in 1950. The firm is active today.
▶ Charlotte Gere, *American and European Jewelry 1830–1914*, New York: Crown, 1975:152. Mackenzie Porter, 'The House that Henry Birks Built,' *Maclean's Magazine*, Dec. 15, 1954.

Birmingham Guild of Handicraft
▶ British metal workshop; located Birmingham.
▶ The Birmingham Guild of Handicraft was established in 1890 to produce 'handmade articles superior in beauty of design and soundness of workmanship to those made by machinery.' The Guild is best known for works in precious and base metals. Montague Fordham became its first director; he was joined by other directors in 1895, when the Guild became a limited company. The Birmingham Guild expanded in 1895, with architect and silversmith Arthur Dixon and C. Napier-Clavering as its chief designers. In 1903, Fordham left to take over the Artificers' Guild. In 1910, the Guild was amalgamated with Gittins Craftsmen, Birmingham. Specializing in high-quality hand-made jewelry and other metalwork, its chief jewelry designer was H.R. Fowler. The production of jewelry at the Guild probably began with the Gittins merger. Despite its motto 'By Hammer and Hand,' it used machinery, including the lathe, and produced simple wares rather than luxury goods like those of the Guild of Handicraft, London. Its silverwork showed simple, honest forms, often incorporating cabochon semi-precious stones.
▶ Charlotte Gere, *American and European Jewelry 1830–1914*, New York: Crown, 1975:152–53. Cat., Alan Crawford (ed.), *By Hammer and Hand: The Arts and Crafts Movement in Birmingham*, Birmingham: Birmingham Museum and Art Gallery, 1984. Annelies Krekel-Aalberse, *Art Nouveau and Art Déco Silver*, New York: Abrams, 1989:24,28,252.

Biró, László (1889–1985)
▶ Hungarian sculptor, painter, journalist, and inventor.
▶ Biró (with brother György, an industrial chemist), wanting a pen that did not dry up for his art work, developed a fast-drying ink that fed a writing ball at the tip of a pen through capillary

action. Patented in 1938, his instrument was first manufactured by the Miles Martin Pen Company in Britain for World War II pilots, who used it to mark maps and charts at high altitude, where traditional pens leaked. Subsequently introduced to the consumer market, the ballpoint's success was established by Marcel Bich, who used clear acrylic plastics for the housing, and a tungsten-carbide ball. Assuming the patent, Bich first produced the disposable model, *Bic Crystal*, in 1958.

▶ Jeremy Myerson and Sylvia Katz, *Conran Design Guides: Home Office*, London: Conran Octopus, 1990:17,29,72.

Bitsch, Hans-Ullrich (1946–)

▶ German architect and interior and industrial designer; born Essen; active Düsseldorf.

▶ Studied architecture and design, Saarbrücken and Chicago.

▶ His clients included West Deutsche Rundfunk; designed 1988–89 confetti-like carpet in the *Dialog* carpet collection produced by Vorwerk.

▶ Albrecht Bangert and Karl Michael Armer, *80s Style: Designs of the Decade*, New York: Abbeville, 1990:191,227.

Bjørn, Acton (1910–92)

▶ Danish designer.

▶ Studied architecture and town planning.

▶ Bjørn became an industrial designer during World War II; in 1949, (with Sigvard Bernadotte) established Bernadotte and Bjørn, the first industrial-design firm in Denmark. Their clients and products were numerous, including metalworks, ceramics, industrial machinery, and office equipment. Bjørn's 1966 *Beolit 500* transistor radio, produced by Bang and Olufsen, was widely published.

▶ Received 1966 Danish ID award (*Beolit 500* radio).

▶ 'Designs from Abroad,' *Industrial Design*, Vol. 4, Feb. 1956:76–79. 'Acton Bjørn,' *Industrial Design*, Vol. 14, Oct. 1967:50–51. Jens Bernsen, *Design: The Problem Comes First*, Copenhagen, 1982:68–71. Cat., Kathryn B. Hiesinger and George H. Marcus III (eds.), *Design Since 1945*, Philadelphia: Philadelphia Museum of Art, 1983.

Bjørner, Annelise (1932–)

▶ Danish designer.

▶ Studied architecture and industrial design, Det Kongelige Danske Kunstakademi, Copenhagen, to 1957.

▶ She worked with architects Arne Karlsen, Mogens Koch, and Vilhelm Wohlert; collaborated with Rigmor Andersen on the *Margrethe* flatware pattern of *c*1968 by Georg Jensen; designed furniture produced by Karl Andersson and furniture for 1972 Munich Olympics.

▶ Received various awards (with Andersen), including 1968 Eckersberg Medal (*Margrethe* flatware), 1968 C.F. Hansen prize, 1968 Zacharias Jacobsens prize.

▶ Cat., *Georg Jensen Silversmithy: 77 Artists, 75 Years*, Washington: Smithsonian Institution Press, 1980. Frederik Sieck, *Nutidig Dansk Møbeldesign: -en kortfattet illustreret beskrivelse*, Copenhagen: Bondo Gravesen; 1990 Busck edition in English.

Bjørquist, Karin (1927–)

▶ Swedish ceramicist.

▶ 1945–50, studied Konstfackskolan and Tekniska Skolan, Stockholm, under Edgar Böckman.

▶ From 1950, she was assistant to Wilhelm Kåge at Gustavsberg ceramic factory, where she was a designer from 1950 and artistic director from 1980–88; in 1961, on Kåge's death, took over his studio.

▶ Received a gold medal at 1954 (X) Triennale di Milano and 1963 Lunning Prize.

▶ Cat., David Revere McFadden (ed.), *Scandinavian Modern Design 1880–1980*, New York: Abrams, 1982:262. Cat., *The Lunning Prize*, Stockholm: Nationalmuseum, 1986:138–41. Jennifer Hawkins Opie, *Scandinavia: Ceramics and Glass in the Twentieth Century*, New York: Rizzoli, 1989.

Black, Misha (1910–77)

▶ British industrial and exhibition designer; born Baku (Azerbaijan); active Britain.

▶ Black became an architect and designer in London in 1929, when he designed the Kardomah coffee shops in London and Manchester; 1933–39, was in partnership with Milner Gray in the Industrial Design Partnership, the first multi-skilled design group in England; designed radios and TV sets for E.K. Cole's Ekco firm, including the traditionally rendered 1938 *UAW 78* cabinet radio in exotic veneer; became an active member of the anti-war Artists' International Association; in 1938, became secretary of the MARS (Modern Architecture Research Group); 1940–45, was an exhibition designer for the Ministry of Information; in 1943, (with Milner Gray) set up the DRU (Design Research Unit); in 1945, (with Gray) co-founded DRG (Design Research Group); was chief exhibition designer of 1946 'Britain Can Make It' exhibition, Victoria and Albert Museum, London; designed the cars and stations of London Underground's Victoria Line, and interiors of London buses; specialized in corporate design, also designed interiors, furnishings, and engineering products; was effective as a design propagandist; 1959–75, was professor of industrial design, Royal College of Art, London, and pioneered design education.

▶ Knighted in 1972. Received a large number of honors and public and professional appointments, including Royal Designer for Industry in 1957.

▶ Avril Black, *Misha Black*, London: The Design Council, 1984. Fiona MacCarthy and Patrick Nuttgens, *An Eye for Industry*, London: Lund Humphries, 1986.

Black, Starr and Frost

▶ American jeweler and goldsmiths; located New York.

▶ The firm Marquand and Paulding was established in Savannah, Georgia, in 1801, by Isaac Marquand; moving to New York in 1810, became known as Marquand and Co; as Ball, Thomkins and Black in 1839; as Ball, Black and Co in 1951; and as Black, Starr and Frost in 1876. Ball, Black and Co was one of the oldest silver factories in the USA; was known as the 'Diamond Palace of Broadway.' In 1861, the Prince of Wales bought some pearls, and the *Quarterly Mirror of Fashion* showed some pieces by Ball, Black and Co. Its stock included imported jewelry and utilitarian goods. After producing commemorative pieces, the firm began to specialize in jewelry and accessories, later producing many designs in an Art Déco style. It merged with Gorham, the biggest silver factory in the USA, in 1929.

▶ Charlotte Gere, *American and European Jewelry 1830–1914*, New York: Crown, 1975:153. Sylvie Raulet, *Bijoux Art Déco*, Paris, Regard, 1984. Annelies Krekel-Aalberse, *Art Nouveau and Art Déco Silver*, New York: Abrams, 1989:252.

Blackband, William Thomas (1885–1949)

▶ British metalworker, active Birmingham.

▶ Studied Vittoria Street School for Jewellers and Silversmiths, Birmingham, and Central School of Arts and Crafts, London.

▶ He designed civic regalia and church plate in soft-finished historicist styles and a 1934–35 cup to commemorate the Silver Jubilee of King George V; was a teacher at Vittoria Street School and, 1924–46, succeeded Arthur Gaskin as headmaster there.

▶ Cat., *Thirties: British art and design before the war*, London: Arts Council of Great Britain, Hayward Gallery, 1979:139,285. Annelies Krekel-Aalberse, *Art Nouveau and Art Déco Silver*, New York: Abrams, 1989:252.

Blackman, Leo (1956–)

▶ American architect and industrial designer; born New York.

▶ Studied architecture, Columbia University, New York, to 1981.

▶ He designed furniture and lighting, including the *Quahog* lamp (with Lance Chantry).

▶ Work shown in gallery and museum exhibitions.

▶ Albrecht Bangert and Karl Michael Armer, *80s Style: Designs of the Decade*, New York: Abbeville, 1990:227.

Blaich, Robert (1931–)
▶ American industrial designer.
▶ In 1980 Blaich was appointed design director of Philips in the Netherlands, where he supervised 200 designers in 22 countries. Once described as 'the world's most influential product designer,' he at one time guided Charles Eames and George Nelson at Herman Miller in the USA. He asserted, 'You can be mass and class,' meaning excellence in design can exist with mass-produced goods.
▶ Arlene Hirst, *American Home*, April 1990:129.
▶ See Philips

Blanchetière, Henri (1881–1933)
▶ Bookbinder and publisher; active Paris.
▶ Studied École Estienne, Paris.
▶ He worked for Loric fils and for René Kieffer; in 1906, took over the bindery of Joseph Brétault, where he produced covers based on motifs from nature in an Art Nouveau style. His motifs were influenced by Marius-Michel. After World War I, Blanchetière turned to Modernism, illustrated in the patterns on *Les Climats, La Canne de Jaspe*, and *L'Age d'Or*.
▶ After 1900, showed covers at Salons in Paris.
▶ Ernest de Crauzat, *La Reliure française de 1900 à 1925*, Paris, Vol. 1, 1932:50–51; Vol. 2, 1932:58. Roger Devauchelle, *La Reliure en France de ses origines à nos jours*, Vol. 3, Paris, 1961: 127,136,244. John F. Fleming and Juvelis Priscilla, *The Book Beautiful and the Binding as Art*, Vol. 1, New York, 1983:61,108,178. Alastair Duncan and Georges de Bartha, *Art Nouveau and Art Déco Bookbinding*, New York: Abrams, 1989:36,187.

Blenko, William John (1854–1926)
▶ British glassmaker.
▶ Apprenticed in a London bottle factory at the age of 10, and studied French and chemistry at night school.
▶ In 1890, he introduced Norman slab-type stained glass for a Norfolk church; settled in Kokomo, Indiana, but returned to England when the business failed. In 1909, Blenko settled again in the USA at Point Marion, Pennsylvania, moving in 1911 to Clarksburg, West Virginia, near fine sand deposits. In 1913, he was forced to close his doors for the third time; developed a method of molding glass, assisted by son Walter Blenko; in the meantime, may have worked at Louis Tiffany's glassworks, Long Island, New York; in 1921, set up shop in a shack in Milton, West Virginia; founded Eureka Glass, which became Blenko Glass in 1930; in 1921, his son William H. Blenko Jr. joined the firm and helped produce blown sheet glass for use as stained-glass window material; recognized the need for utilitarian ware; his wife Marion Hunt, daughter of Pittsburgh stained-glass artists, ran the office. Orders began to come in: Blenko's stained glass was used in Liverpool Cathedral; Chartres Cathedral; St. John the Divine and St. Patrick's Cathedrals, New York; chapel of the Air Force Academy, Colorado; American Memorial Chapel, Meuse-Argonne (France). In 1926, a decision was made to produce decorative and utilitarian glassware, first for the Carbonnes store, Boston, which had been importing goods from Italy and Sweden. Swedish-American glassworkers and brothers Louis Miller and Axel Muller (who never Americanized his name) were hired. In 1932, Macy's in New York began selling Blenko glassware and, by 1935, major stores throughout the USA carried Blenko ware. In 1936, the firm received authorization to reproduce the glassware of Colonial Williamsburg, the restored British colony in Virginia. In 1946, Winslow Anderson was hired as its first designer. Makers of inexpensive glassware, Blenko produced free-blown forms in inventive Modern designs; made tall ribbed bottles, which took advantage of the plasticity of the molten medium; by 1987, had five staff designers.
▶ Wares shown at 1933–34 Chicago 'Century of Progress Exposition'; *Bent Decanter* by Anderson at 1952 Good Design exhibition, New York Museum of Modern Art and Chicago Merchandise Mart.
▶ Frederick Cooke, *Glass: Twentieth-Century Design*, New York: Dutton, 1986:99. Cherie Fehrman and Kenneth Fehrman, *Postwar*

Interior Design, 1945–1960, New York: Van Nostrand Reinhold, 1987. Eason Eige and Rick Wilson, *Blenko Glass 1930–1953*, Marielta, Ohio: Antique Publications, 1987.

Blet, Thierry
▶ French industrial designer.
▶ Studied École Camondo, Paris.
▶ With Catherine Le Teo, he formed the design team of Elixir. They designed a picnic-tableware set that won recognition in the 1986 competition sponsored by the APCI (Agence pour la Promotion de la Création Industrielle) and UGAP (Union des Groupements d'Achets Publics). He designed 1991 *Titiana* table lamp.
▶ *Les Carnets du Design*, Paris: Mad-Cap Productions et APCI, 1986:87.

Blinxma, Johannes (1872–1941)
▶ Dutch silversmith; active Amsterdam.
▶ Blinxma worked for Amstelhoek from 1902, where he was artistic director of the metalworking workshop, succeeding Jan Eisenloeffel; in 1904, opened his own workshop. His work was strongly influenced by Eisenloeffel, the most important exponent of the Dutch Modern style.
▶ Annelies Krekel-Aalberse, *Art Nouveau and Art Déco Silver*, New York: Abrams, 1989:252.

Bliss, George (?–1954) and **Arthur Bliss** (?–1960)
▶ American furniture makers; active Lake Placid area, New York.
▶ The brothers Bliss produced seating made from rough-hewn tree trunks and camping furnishings, furniture, and path railings, some in yellow birch.
▶ Craig Gilborn, *Adirondack Furniture and the Rustic Tradition*, New York: Abrams, 1987:317.

Bloc, André (1896–1966)
▶ French architect, sculptor, and theorist; born Algiers.
▶ He founded the international review *Architecture d'Aujourd'hui* in 1930 with Frantz and Francis Jourdain, Robert Mallet-Stevens, Pierre Chareau, and others; built his own 1949 house, Meudon, near Paris; 1956 villa (with Italian architect Vittoriano Viganó), Lac de Barde (Italy); 1960 summer house (with French architect Claude Parent), Antibes (France); founded sculptor-architects' association Groupe Espace.

Bloch-Eschwège
▶ French silversmiths, located Paris.
▶ Maison Henry Lageyre was founded in 1832; in 1921, it was succeeded by Bloch-Eschwège; produced Modern silver in the 1920s and 1930s.
▶ Silver works shown at 1930 Paris 'Décor de la Table,' Musée Galliéra.
▶ Annelies Krekel-Aalberse, *Art Nouveau and Art Déco Silver*, New York: Abrams, 1989:252.

Block, Robert
▶ French interior decorator and furniture designer.
▶ Block was artistic director of decorating firm Athélia, Paris; in the late 1920s, collaborated with Delpuech et Havard on the design of the restaurant Trois Quartiers.
▶ *Restaurants, dancing, cafés, bars*, Paris: Charles Moreau, 1929.

Block-Hellum, Charlotte (1911–)
▶ German ceramicist, metalworker, and enamelist; active Germany and Oslo.
▶ Studied Kunstgewerbeschule, Dresden, and pottery, Kunstgewerbeschule, Berlin.
▶ In 1946, she set up her own workshop in Oslo; from the 1960s, became a specialist in enamelwork.
▶ Cat., David Revere McFadden (ed.), *Scandinavian Modern Design 1880–1980*, New York: Abrams, 1982:262.

Blomberg, Hugo (1897–)
▶ Swedish engineer.
▶ Studied electrical engineering, Kungliga Tekniska Högskolan, Stockholm.

▶ In 1929, he joined Ericsson as head of its technical department; later became chief engineer and head of development; assisted by Ralph Lysell, conceived the *Ericofon* telephone that he, Lysell, and Gösta Thames designed and engineered 1940–54. The telephone was distinctive for its one-piece construction; it had fewer components and was lighter than earlier models.

▶ Hugo Blomberg, 'The Ericofon—The New Telephone Set,' *Ericsson Review*, Vol. 33, No. 4, 1956:99–109. Cat., Kathryn B. Hiesinger and George H. Marcus III (eds.), *Design Since 1945*, Philadelphia: Philadelphia Museum of Art, 1983.

Blomsted, Pauli   (1900–35)

▶ Finnish architect and designer.

▶ Blomsted was active in Funkis, a Finnish Functionalist group and counterpart to the German Bauhaus, although less doctrinaire; in his furniture designs, married natural materials such as wood with metal tubing; was rediscovered by Kenneth Smith in the early 1980s through archival material at Cranbrook Academy of Art, Bloomfield, Michigan, where Blomsted taught in the 1930s; designed furniture that was reissued by Smith's firm Arkitektura from the late 1980s.

Blount, Godfrey   (1859–1937)

▶ British artist and craftsman.

▶ Studied Cambridge University and Slade School of Fine Art, London.

▶ In 1896, he founded Haslemere Peasant Industries, producers of textiles and simple furniture. Subsequently, he founded the Peasant Arts Society; an early primer of the Arts and Crafts movement, published *Arbor Vitae: A book on the nature and development of imaginative design for the use of teachers, handicraftsmen and others* (1899). Other books included *For Our Country's Sake: An essay on the return to the land and the revival of country life and crafts* and *The Rustic Renaissance*.

▶ Stuart Durant, *Ornament from the Industrial Revolution to Today*, Woodstock, NY: Overlook, 1986:214,233,320–21.

Bluitgen, Ib   (1921–)

▶ Danish designer.

▶ Apprenticed at Georg Jensen Sølvsmedie; 1945–48, studied Det Kongelige Danske Kunstakademie, Copenhagen.

▶ 1948–61, he worked in Jensen's design department; subsequently, set up his own workshop producing hollow-ware and jewelry.

▶ Work shown in 1980 'Georg Jensen Silversmithy: 77 Artists, 75 Years' exhibition, Smithsonian Institution.

▶ Cat., *Georg Jensen Silversmithy: 77 Artists, 75 Years*, Washington: Smithsonian Institution Press, 1980.

Blümmel, Otto   (1881–1973)

▶ German architect, furniture designer, and painter; born Augsburg.

▶ Studied architecture, Technische Universität, and painting, Debschitz-Schule (Lehr- und Versuchs-Ateliers für angewandte und freie Kunst), both Munich.

▶ 1907–14, he was head of the design department, Vereinigte Werkstätten für Kunst im Handwerk, Munich, and designed furniture; 1916–20, was art master there; 1920–49, was director of Partenkirchner Schnitzschule; in 1925, established the Heimatmuseum while at the Museumsverein Werdenfels; wrote extensively.

▶ Received the order of the Verdienstkreuz am Bande, Germany.

Boake, George

▶ Canadian architect and designer; active Toronto.

▶ Boake was a partner in the firm Crang and Boake, Toronto; from the early 1950s, designed furniture for Metalsmiths, Toronto.

▶ Cat., *Seduced and Abandoned: Modern Furniture designers in Canada, the First Fifty Years*, Toronto: The Art Gallery at Harbourfront, 1986:14.

Boberg, Anna Katarina   (1864–1935)

▶ Swedish ceramicist and glassware and textile designer; active Stockholm; wife of Ferdinand Boberg.

▶ 1900–02, she designed ceramics for Rörstrand, Lidköping, and multi-colored art glass for the Reijmyre glassworks; was a textile designer for Handarbetets Vännar.

▶ Cat., David Revere McFadden (ed.), *Scandinavian Modern Design 1880–1980*, New York: Abrams, 1982:262.

Boberg, Ferdinand   (1860–1946)

▶ Swedish architect and designer; active Stockholm; husband of Anna Katarina Boberg.

▶ Boberg designed glass, ceramics, and textiles; became known for his furniture designs for the Swedish royal family; was one of the few designers to produce Modern silver in Sweden around 1900; used pine branches as decoration for his silverworks made by C.G. Hallberg, Stockholm.

▶ Swedish royal family's furniture shown at Swedish pavilion of the 1900 Paris 'Exposition Universelle.'

▶ Annelies Krekel-Aalberse, *Art Nouveau and Art Déco Silver*, New York: Abrams, 1989:244,252.

Bobergs Fajansfabrik

▶ Swedish ceramics firm.

▶ The factory for ceramic utilitarian wares was founded in 1874 by Erik Boberg; in 1910, enlarged to include art and decorative wares, in 1930, production included work by Ewald Dahlskog; in 1967, was bought by Steninge Keramik; closed in c1978–80.

▶ Jennifer Hawkins Opie, *Scandinavia: Ceramics and Glass in the Twentieth Century*, New York: Rizzoli, 1989.

Boccato, Marilena   (1941–)

▶ Italian designer; born Treviso; active Treviso and Padua.

▶ Boccato began professionally in 1967; collaborated with architects Gian Nicola Gigante and Antonio Zambusi; devised the *Programma Postumia* sliding-door system produced by Ca' Onorai; became a member of ADI (Associazione per il Disegno Industriale).

▶ *ADI Annual 1976*, Milan: Associazione per il Disegno Industriale, 1976.

Boch, Anna   (1848–1936)

▶ Belgian ceramicist; daughter of director of Boch ceramics factory.

▶ A painter, Boch became a member of Les Vingts (founded in Belgium in 1883 and succeeded by La Libre Esthétique in 1894) in 1886. She persuaded A.W. Finch to work at the Kéramis factory (the Boch ceramic branch in La Louvière, Belgium); decorated some ceramics there herself; designed *Die Kugel* dinner service in a single, spherical modular unit by Villeroy et Boch.

▶ Yvonne Brunhammer et al., *Art Nouveau Belgium, France*, Houston: Institute for the Arts, Rice University, 1976.

Boch Frères

See Villeroy et Boch

Boch, Helen von   (1938–)

▶ German ceramics designer; member of Boch family of ceramics and glassware producers.

▶ Boch collaborated with Federigo Fabbrini on the design of the 1973 *Sphere* stoneware and 1973 *Bomba* melamine-plastic dinner services by Villeroy et Boch. The pieces were designed to fit together into one transportable unit.

▶ 'Design in Action: Inner Beauty,' *Industrial Design*, Vol. 18, May 1971:34. Sylvia Katz, *Plastics: Designs and Materials*, London 1978:71–72. Cat., Kathryn B. Hiesinger and George H. Marcus III (eds.), *Design Since 1945*, Philadelphia: Philadelphia Museum of Art, 1983.

Bocker, Edmund   (1886–)

▶ American metalworker, active Chicago.

▶ With Ernest Gould, Bocker established the Chicago Art Silver Shop in 1912 at 11 E. Illinois Avenue, Chicago.

▶ Sharon S. Darling with Gail Farr Casterline, *Chicago Metalsmiths*, Chicago Historical Society, 1977.

Boda
See Kosta Boda

Boehm, Michael (1944–)
▶ German glassware and ceramics designer.
▶ 1959–62, studied Glasfachschule, Hadamar; 1962–66, Hochschule für Bildende Künste, Kassel.
▶ Boehm joined Rosenthal in 1966. His limited-edition *Reticelli* range illustrated his interest in Italian glass through the incorporation of cotton twist threads in the molten glass in a manner similar to 17th-century Venetian vessels. His Rosenthal stemware included the two-color *Sunflower* and 1976 *Papyrus* ranges. Boehm collaborated with Claus Josef Riedel to create the *Calyx* range, whose faint mold lines became a design feature.
▶ Frederick Cooke, *Glass: Twentieth-Century Design*, New York: Dutton, 1986:96. Cat., Kathryn B. Hiesinger and George H. Marcus III (eds.), *Design Since 1945*, Philadelphia: Philadelphia Museum of Art, 1983. *Mit Kunst leben*, Selb: Rosenthal: 52–53.

Boeri Mariani, Cini (1924–)
▶ Italian designer; born and active Milan.
▶ Studied architecture, Politecnico di Milano, to 1950.
▶ She worked as an interior and furniture designer in the studio of Marco Zanuso, Milan, 1952–63; in 1963, set up her own studio, specializing in civil and interior architecture and industrial design; was associated with ADI (Associazione per il Disegno Industriale); in 1979, formed Cini Boeri Associati, Milan; in the early 1970s, collaborated with Laura Griziotti on designs for Arflex. Her interior architecture was sparsely furnished; her furniture was multi-functional and expandable, often combining standardized fittings. She lectured and wrote widely; served as juror on several competition committees; began experimenting in plastics in 1966, her first designs being a 1966 set of luggage made of injection-molded ABS for Franzi. Her conservative approach can be seen in the 1983 *Malibu* table. The 1970–71 *Serpentone* foam-rubber seating system produced by Arflex offered both flexibility and an Anti-Design attitude. 1975–85, she designed showrooms for Knoll International in Los Angeles, Stuttgart, Paris, Milan, Foligno, and New York; in 1983, designed a series of prefabricated single-family houses for Misawa Company, Tokyo. Her clients included Artemide, Fiam, and Rosenthal; designed lighting for Stilnovo, Arflex, and, in the mid-1980s, Venini; 1980–83, taught architecture, planning, industrial design, and interior design at Politecnico di Milano and at universities and colleges in Spain, Brazil, and the USA, including the University of California at Berkeley; (with F. Angeli) published *The Human Dimensions of the House* (1980); (with Marisa Bertoldini) wrote 'La dimensione del domestico' in *La casa tra techniche e sogno* (1988). Work included 1968 *Cubetto* mobile storage unit by Arflex, 1970 *Luario* glass-chrome cantilevered table by Knoll, 1970–71 *Serpentone* foam-rubber seating system by Arflex, 1977 *Gradual System* sofa system by Knoll, 1980 *doubleface* bookshelf by Arflex, 1981 *Rever* door by Tre Più, 1983 *Pacific* sofa and loveseat by Arflex, 1983 *Malibu* table by Arflex, hardware fixtures by Fusital from 1980, 1984 *Chiara* lighting by Venini, 1986 *Brontes* lighting fixture by Artemide, 1986 *Past* modular sofa by Arflex, 1987 *Voyeur* screen by Fiam, and all-glass, one-piece 1987 *Ghost* chair (with Tomu Katayagi) by Fiam.
▶ At the Triennali di Milano, collaborated and showed furniture in the Arflex stand in 1965 (XIII) and subsequently, and at a vast number of exhibitions. Received a first prize, 1966 Milan 'Piastrella d'Oro Cedit ADI' competition; diploma of collaboration, 1968 (XIV) Triennale di Milano; 1970 mention and 1979 gold (1972 *Strips* seating) Premio Compasso d'Oro; 1978 and 1984 Roscoe Prize, New York City; a mention and a gold medal (1981 *Rever* door), 1984 'BIO 10' Industrial Design Biennale, Ljubljana; 1984 'Design 85' award, Design Center Stuttgart; 1985 German Selection award. Member of the organizing committee of the 1979 (XVI) Triennale di Milano.
▶ Cat., Milena Lamarová, *Design a Plastické Hmoty*, Prague: Uměleckoprůmyslové Muzeum, 1972. Cat., *Italy: The New Italian Landscape*, New York: The Museum of Modern Art, 1972:29,61,121.

ADI Annual 1976, Milan: Associazione per il Disegno Industriale, 1976. Alfonso Grassi and Anty Pansera, *Atlante del design italiano: 1940–1980*, Milan: Fabbri, 1980:162,165,176,187,278. Cat., Kathryn B. Hiesinger and George H. Marcus III (eds.), *Design Since 1945*, Philadelphia: Philadelphia Museum of Art, 1983. Robert A.M. Stern (ed.), *The International Design Yearbook*, New York: Abbeville, 1985/ 1986: Nos. 418–19. Cat., Design Center Stuttgart, *Women in Design: Careers and Life Histories Since 1900*, Stuttgart: Haus der Wirtschaft, 1989:276–83.

Bögel, Urike (1954–)
▶ German designer; born Blaubeuren, Ulm.
▶ 1974–79, studied product design, Fachhochschule für Gestaltung, Schwäbisch-Gmünd; 1979, Centro Internazionale della Ceramica, Rome.
▶ Bögel set up her own office in 1982 where she designed in glass, porcelain, ceramics, plastic, metal; became a member of VDID (Verband Deutscher Industrie-Designer). Work included the curvaceous 1980 *Tondo* drinking glass by Hutschenreuther, 1984 *Teaworld* tea service by Porzellanfabrik Arzberg, and 1989 *Club Cuisine* kitchen utensil series in ABS plastic by Buchsteiner.
▶ Cat., Design Center Stuttgart, *Women in Design: Careers and Life Histories Since 1900*, Stuttgart: Haus der Wirtschaft, 1989:84–87.

Bogler, Theodor (1897–1968)
▶ Germanceramicist.
▶ From 1919, studied Bauhaus, Weimar; subsequently, University of Munich.
▶ 1923–24 with Otto Lindig, Bogler shared supervision of the Production Workshop, Dornburg, near Weimar, the ceramics annex of the Bauhaus; designed 1923 mocha machine in ceramics for serial production. In 1925, his commercial work for the Velten factory, lasting a little over a year, resulted in numerous designs. He became a Benedictine monk in 1932; 1934–38, occasionally collaborated with the HB-Werkstätten of Hedwig Bollhagen, Marwitz, and, 1936–68, with Staatliche Majolika-Manufaktur Karlsruhe; abbot of the monastery of Maria Laach 1939–48, worked on the production of numerous catalogs, books, and religious objects.
▶ Earthenware kitchen containers by Velten-Vordamm ceramic factory shown at 1923 Bauhaus Exhibition.
▶ Cat., *50 Jahre Bauhaus*, Stuttgart, 1968. Lionel Richard, *Encyclopédie du Bauhaus*, Paris: Somogy, 1985:149. Cat., *The Bauhaus: Masters and Students*, New York: Barry Friedman, 1988. Cat., *Keramik und Bauhaus*, Berlin: Bauhaus-Archiv, 1989. Jonathan M. Woodham, *Twentieth-Century Ornament*, New York: Rizzoli, 1990:133.

Bogoslovskaia, Olga Vasil'evna (1905–)
▶ Russian textile designer.
▶ Studied art school, Mstera village, Ivanovo province, to 1929.
▶ She worked as a textile designer in the Krasnaïa Talka textile mill in Ivanovo province; 1931–33, was a designer in the Sosnevskii United textile mill in Ivanovo; participated in several Soviet exhibitions abroad.
▶ Cat., *Kunst und Revolution: Russische und Sowjetische Kunst 1910–1932*, Vienna: Österreichisches Museum für angewandte Kunst, 1988.

Bohlin, Jonas (1953–)
▶ Swedish designer; active Stockholm.
▶ 1976–81, studied High School of Arts and Crafts, Stockholm.
▶ Active from the 1980s, he specialized in interior architecture, stage arts, and furniture design, which included *Concave* lounge and *Zink* floor shelf.
▶ Robert A.M. Stern (ed.), *The International Design Yearbook*, New York: Abbeville, 1985/1986: No. 20.

Boiceau, Ernest (1881–1950)
▶ Swiss designer; active Paris.
▶ Studied drawing, painting, and architecture, École des Beaux-Arts, Paris.

▶ He became known for his tapestries and embroideries; in 1918, opened a shop in Paris, where he sold furnishing fabrics and embroidery; from 1926, decorated and furnished numerous apartments and townhouses in Switzerland, the USA, and France. Commissions included those for Cécile Sorel, Paris; Louise de Vilmorin, Varrières-le-Buisson; Jérôme and Jean Tharaud, Versailles; Hôtel de Wendel, and couture house of Worth, Paris.

▶ Work shown at 1928 and 1929 events of the Salon d'Automne. Work subject of 1982 exhibition, Galerie Eric Philippe, Paris.

▶ Pierre Kjellberg, *Art Déco: les maîtres du Mobilier, le décor des Paquebots*, Paris: Amateur, 1986:183−84.

Boileau, Louis-Hippolyte   (1878−1948)
▶ French architect and designer.
▶ In the late 1920s, Boileau designed the tea room of the Bon Marché department store and restaurant Prunier-Traktir (with Léon Carrière), Paris; used shades of green mosaics in a circular pattern applied to the façade.
▶ Participated in 1925 'Exposition Internationale des Arts Décoratifs et Industriels Modernes.'
▶ *Restaurants, dancing, cafés, bars*, Paris: Charles Moreau, No. 45−46, 1929. Paul Chemetov et al., *Banlieue*, Paris: Bordas, 1989.

Boillat, Enrico   (1921−)
▶ Italian lighting designer; born Marsala; active Milan.
▶ He began his professional career in 1956; using glass extensively, designed numerous lighting models for Zero Quattro, Milan; became a member of ADI (Associazione per il Disegno Industriale).
▶ *ADI Annual 1976*, Milan: Associazione per il Disegno Industriale, 1976.

Boin-Taburet
▶ French silversmiths.
▶ Founded in c1857, the firm sold the silver designs produced by Christopher Dresser in the last quarter of the 19th century.
▶ Work shown at exhibitions 1889−1937 and 1902 St. Petersburg 'Comité français des Expositions à l'Étranger.'
▶ Annelies Krekel-Aalberse, *Art Nouveau and Art Déco Silver*, New York: Abrams, 1989:21,247,252.

Boisselier, Philippe   (1942−)
▶ French designer.
▶ Studied decorative arts, École Boulle, Paris.
▶ In 1971, he set up his own studio as an interior architect; at the invitation of Denise Fayolle, executed a modular room design for 3 Suisses, a progressive French mail-order furniture and furnishings firm; in 1988, designed the exhibition of magazine *Intramuros* at the Salon du Meuble, Paris, and furniture for Unifor; became principal of École Camondo, Paris.

Boissevain, Antoinette   (1898−1973)
▶ Dutch painter, lighting designer and retailer; born The Hague; active London.
▶ From 1918, studied painting, Central School of Arts and Crafts, London.
▶ She settled in London in 1918; in 1924, took over the management of Merchant Adventurers, importers of china and glass from Europe. From 1930, they imported Wilhelm Gispen's *Giso* lighting range, first used on a contract for a yacht club, Burnham-on-Crouch, designed by Joseph Emberton. Merchant Adventurers began producing Gispen's lighting under license, and lighting of their own. Architectural commissions for their lighting fixtures included Shell-Mex House, Savoy Hotel, Harrods, and Bush House, all London. Boissevain and her husband were members of the Design and Industries Association.
▶ Cat., *Thirties: British art and design before the war*, London: Arts Council of Great Britain, Hayward Gallery, 1979:233,285.

Boivin, René
▶ French jewelry designer.
▶ Married to fashion designer Paul Poiret's sister, with whom he collaborated, Boivin opened a Paris shop in the early 1920s and featured Suzanne Belperron's designs; collaborated with Belperron

for ten years. With clients such as Louise de Vilmorin, who was helpful in promoting Boivin's ware, success was assured. He produced the designs of his daughters Juliette Moutard and Germaine Boivin. In 1976, jewelry designer Jacques Bernard became the firm's director.
▶ Work shown at 1937 Paris 'Exposition Internationale des Arts et Techniques dans la Vie Moderne' and 1946 Paris 'Exposition des Arts Décoratifs.'
▶ Sylvie Raulet, *Bijoux Art Déco*, Paris: Regard, 1984. Melissa Gabardi, *Les Bijoux des Années 50*, Paris: Amateur, 1987.

Bojesen, Kay   (1886−1958)
▶ Danish silversmith, ceramicist, and woodenware designer; active Copenhagen.
▶ 1907−10, trained with Georg Jensen; 1911, studied Royal Craft School of Precious Metals, Württemberg.
▶ He worked in Copenhagen and Paris before setting up his own workshop in 1913 in Copenhagen; a pioneer in the Danish Modern style, broke from Jensen's style in c1930 and pursued simple, undecorated forms that emphasized their mechanical production; in the 1930s, produced the designs of painters Lauritz Larsen and Svend Johansen and architects G.B. Petersen and Magnus Stephensen; 1930−31, was an art consultant to Bing & Grøndahl Porcelaensfabrik; designed stainless-steel tablewares for Universal Steel and, in Sweden, for Motala Verkstad; in an effort to promote Modern design, instigated the establishment of a permanent center for Danish crafts and mass-produced products, resulting in the opening in Copenhagen in 1931 of Den Permanente, one of the first design exhibition spaces in Europe; became known for his toy designs; in 1952, was appointed silversmith to the King of Denmark.
▶ Work subject of 1938 exhibition, Det Danske Kunstindustrimuseum, Copenhagen. Work shown at exhibitions including 1925 Paris 'Exposition Internationale des Arts Décoratifs et Industriels Modernes,' 1954−57 USA 'Design in Scandinavia,' 1958 Paris 'Formes Scandinaves.' Received grand prize and diploma of honor, 1951 (IX) Triennale di Milano, and diploma of honor (wooden objects), 1954 (X) Triennale di Milano.
▶ Edgar Kaufman, Jr., 'Kay Bojesen: Tableware to Toys,' *Interiors*, No. 112, Feb. 1953:64−67. Mary Lyon, 'Master Plays Wide Field,' *Craft Horizons*, Vol. 13, July 1953:26−31. Pierre Lübecker, *Applied Art by Kay Bojesen*, Copenhagen: National Association of Danish Handicraft, 1955. 'Kay Bohesen,' *Design Quarterly*, No. 39, 1957:2−5. Erik Zahle (ed.), *A Treasury of Scandinavian Design*, New York, 1961:269, Nos. 51,105,378−80. Cat., David Revere McFadden (ed.), *Scandinavian Modern Design 1880−1980*, New York: Abrams, 1982:262. Cat., Kathryn B. Hiesinger and George H. Marcus III (eds.), *Design Since 1945*, Philadelphia: Philadelphia Museum of Art, 1983. Annelies Krekel-Aalberse, *Art Nouveau and Art Déco Silver*, New York: Abrams, 1989:221,252.

Bolek, Hans   (1890−)
▶ Austrian architect and designer; active Vienna.
▶ Studied Kunstgewerbeschule, Vienna.
▶ He designed silver for Eduard Friedmann, Alfred Pollak, and Oskar Dietrich.
▶ Annelies Krekel-Aalberse, *Art Nouveau and Art Déco Silver*, New York: Abrams, 1989:252.

Bolidismo
▶ Italian design movement.
▶ Amalgamating retro-1950s and Streamline styling, Bolidismo was established in 1983 by a group of young architects practicing in Florence, including Massimo Iosa Ghini, Pierangelo Caramia, and Stephano Giavannoni. Examples of their approach can be seen in Caramia's 1987 *Arcadia Swing* glass and aluminum table made by XO and jewelry produced by Directory King Kong/Giavannoni.

Bolin, W.A.
▶ Swedish jewelers.
▶ Charles Bolin, a Swede, settled in St. Petersburg and married the daughter of a prominent jeweler, entering the jewelry business

in 1845, when (with brother Henrik) he set up a firm in St. Petersburg and later a branch in Moscow. The firm was appointed goldsmith and jeweler to the Russian Imperial Court. At the beginning of World War I, William Bolin settled in Stockholm, where he set up a branch at the request of King Gustav V. The business is still active today.

▶ Charlotte Gere, *American and European Jewelry 1830–1914*, New York: Crown, 1975:154.

Bollani, Eros   (1947–)

▶ Italian industrial designer; born Covo, Bologna; active Modena.

▶ Bollani began his professional career in 1974; subsequently, a member of ADI (Associazione per il Disegno Industriale). His Italian clients included G3 Ferrari electrical appliances, Caggiati Claudio bath and kitchen accessories, Laminart Pannelli, Simonini motor division of cross-country motorcycles, and Rampinelli REG Accessori for bicycles and motorcycles.

▶ *ADI Annual 1976*, Milan: Associazione per il Disegno Industriale, 1976.

Boltenstern, Erich   (1896–)

▶ Austrian architect and designer; born Vienna.

▶ 1918–22, studied Technische Hochschule, Vienna; 1922–28, Akademie der Künste, Berlin, under Hans Poelzig, and under Heiss and Jaksch in Vienna.

▶ 1929–34, he was an assistant at the Wiener Kunstgewerbeschule under Oskar Strnad; in 1930, began as an independent architect; associated with the Wiener Werkstätte; from 1952, taught at Technische Hochschule, Vienna.

▶ Günther Feuerstein, *Vienna—Present and Past: Arts and Crafts—Applied Art—Design*, Vienna: Jugend und Volk, 1976:49,61,80. Astrid Gmeiner and Gottfried Pirhofer, *Der Österreichische Werkbund*, Salzburg/Vienna: Residenz, 1985:223–24.

Bolz, Anne   (1958–)

▶ German designer; born Mömlingen.

▶ Studied product design, Hochschule für Gestaltung, Offenbach am Main, to 1980, and Mathias Hoffmann Furniture Design office, Tübingen, to 1986.

▶ In 1986, she worked as an independent consultant designer of furniture; in December 1988, became product coordinator at Eugen Schmidt, Darmstadt.

▶ Received 1987 Bayrischer Staatspreis für Nachwuchsdesigner (Bavarian State Prize for promising designers).

▶ Cat., *Bayerischer Staatspreis für Nachwuchsdesigner 1987*, Munich: Die Neue Sammlung, 1987:28. Cat., Design Center Stuttgart, *Women in Design: Careers and Life Histories Since 1900*, Stuttgart: Haus der Wirtschaft, 1989:88.

Bolze, Franz   (1902–76)

▶ German silversmith; active Bremen.

▶ One of many independent silversmiths working in prosperous North Germany in the 1920s and 1930s, Bolze worked as a silversmith in Bremen 1926–76; produced designs by sculptor Bernhard Hötger, including a 1927–28 mocha service.

▶ Annelies Krekel-Aalberse, *Art Nouveau and Art Déco Silver*, New York: Abrams, 1989:145,252.

Boman, Carl-Johan   (1883–1969)

▶ Finnish interior designer.

▶ 1906, studied Royal Institute of Decorative Arts, Berlin.

▶ 1906–11, he was director of the drafting office of Boman in Helsinki and, 1919–55, general director; 1955–59, active in his own office. The simplicity of his work can be seen in the 1962 *Boman I* chair made with a folding seat and sold by Schauman, Helsinki.

▶ His work was shown at exhibitions including the 1908 St. Petersburg, 1925 Monza 'Art and Design,' 1929 'Exposición Internacional de Barcelona,' 1951 (IX) Triennale di Milano where he won a gold medal, 1951 Concours International d'Invention in Paris where he won a silver medal, 1952 Brussels, 1952 Paris,

and 1954 (X) Triennale di Milano where he received the diploma of honor.

▶ Cat., *Modern Chairs 1918–1970*, London: Lund Humphries, 1971.

Bonacina, Mario   (1947–)

▶ Italian furniture designer.

▶ Founded in 1889, the Bonacina firm produced traditional wicker furniture, including Franco Albini's 1950 *Margherita* wicker armchair. Mario Bonacina began his professional career in 1966; became artistic director of the family firm; was a member of ADI (Associazione per il Disegno Industriale).

▶ *ADI Annual 1976*, Milan: Associazione per il Disegno Industriale, 1976. Cat., Leslie Jackson, *The New Look: Design in the Fifties*, New York: Thames and Hudson, 1991:126.

Bonaz, Maison Auguste

▶ French costume jeweler; located Oyonnax.

▶ The firm was founded in the mid-19th century by César Bonaz, who was commissioned by the citizens of Oyonnax to make horn combs as a gift to the Empress Eugénie on the occasion of her visit with Emperor Napoleon III. César's son Auguste Bonaz took over management of the firm; his widow Marguerite-Marie Bailly became manager and was later joined by her grandson Theo Bailly, who directed the firm until its closing in 1982.

▶ Deanna F. Cera (ed.), *Jewels of Fantasy: Costume Jewelry of the 20th Century*, New York: Abrams, 1992.

Bonderup, Claus   (1943–)

▶ Danish lighting designer.

▶ 1965–69, studied architecture and planning, Det Kongelige Danske Kunstakademi, Copenhagen, under Henning Larsen.

▶ He designed lighting fixtures for Focus Belysning, Holte, some in collaboration with Torsten Thorup, with whom he collaborated from 1968; 1969–70, worked in the office of architect Henning Larsen in Copenhagen; 1970–71, collaborated with architect Sergio Bernardes in Rio de Janeiro; 1971–73, worked with architects Vischer and Weber, Basel.

▶ Beach house shown at 1979 'Transformations of Modern Architecture,' New York Museum of Modern Art. Received 1982 Eckersberg medal.

▶ Cat., David Revere McFadden (ed.), *Scandinavian Modern Design 1880–1980*, New York: Abrams, 1982:262, No. 338.

Bonebakker en Zoon

▶ Dutch silversmiths; located Amsterdam.

▶ Bonebakker was founded as a silversmiths' workshop in 1853, headed by P. Pieterse and known for its high-quality hand-made silver. It commissioned others (including D.L. Bennewitz and T.G. Bentveld) to make its silverwares; in 1862, began employing craftspeople and apprentices; by 1898, had 38 foreign suppliers, although its most important clients were domestic. Frans Zwollo Sr. was an apprentice to his father at Bonebakker & Zoon 1888–93, after which he produced chased coins for the firm. From 1896, when he set up his own business, his most important client was Bonebakker, for which he produced rococo and neoclassical designs. The sculptor L.F. Edema van der Tuuk supplied the firm with drawings. Bonebakker imitated styles and plagiarized designs of competitors, including models of J. Eisenloeffel's work for Van Kempen and of Christopher Dresser; sold silverwares made by Wolfers Frères, Brussels; produced wares in the 1910s and 1920s with the plastic ornamentation of the Dutch Expressionist school of architecture in Amsterdam. The factory closed in 1952, although the shop still exists.

▶ *Industry and Design in the Netherlands 1850–1950*, Amsterdam: Stedelijk Museum, 1985. Annelies Krekel-Aalberse, *Art Nouveau and Art Déco Silver*, New York: Abrams, 1989:99,174, 175,252.

Bonet, Antonio　(1913–89)
See Ferrari-Hardoy, Jorge

Bonet, Paul　(1889–1971)
▶ French bookbinding designer; born and active Paris.
▶ 1904–06, he was an apprentice in an electrical shop, Paris; in 1909, became a sculptor of wooden fashion mannequins; first became involved in bookbinding in 1920, designing covers in sha-green for a friend's collection. He began to show his work in 1924; encouraged by Mattieu Gallerey, was introduced to Henri Clouzot, conservator of the Musée Galliéra; when his work was shown in the Salon at the end of 1925, decided to become a full-time bookbinding designer. 1927–29, his patron was R. Marty. Businessman Carlos R. Scherrer of Buenos Aires was a patron from 1928; in 1939, Scherrer fled to South America with his collection, which included 180 examples of Bonet's work. In 1931, Bonet's landmark bindings were produced by Ferdinand Giraldon with André Jeanne's gold fillet tooling. Bonet became known for his cover work in nickel, steel, platinum, duralumin, and gold, using silversmiths, jewelers and artists including Pierre Boit, Gustave Miklos, and Egouville; in the mid-1930s resumed mannequin making due to financial difficulties; worked on binding designs during World War II.
▶ Henri Clouzot, 'Paul Bonet: architecte de la reliure,' *Mobilier et décoration*, Feb. 1933:66–72. René Gaffe, *Connaissance de Paul Bonet*, Brussels, 1933. *Paul Bonet*, Paris: Blaizot, 1945. Georges Blaizot, *Masterpieces of French Modern Bindings*, New York, 1947. *Bibliothèque reliée par Paul Bonet*, Paris: Marcel Sautier, 1963. *Paul Bonet Carnets 1924–1971*, Paris, 1981. Alastair Duncan and Georges de Bartha, *Art Nouveau and Art Déco Bookbinding*, New York: Abrams, 1989:7,8,22,23,24,37–58,101,187.

Bonet, Pep　(1941–)
▶ Spanish designer; born Barcelona.
▶ 1965, studied Escuela Técnica Superior de Arquitectura, Barcelona.
▶ 1963–64, he worked in the office of architect José Antonio Coderch; in 1965, (with Cristián Circi, Oscar Tusquets Blanca, and Lluis Clotet) formed Studio PER. After 1972, the group began to design furniture and building components. 1975–78, Bonet was professor of design, Escuela Técnica Superior de Arquitectura, Barcelona, and, in 1981, at Washington University, St. Louis, Missouri. Work included 1980 towel rack by B.d Ediciones de Diseño, 1984 *Mantis* armchair by Levesta, 1986 chain-holder barrier by B.d Ediciones de Diseño, 1986 log tongs by Polinax, and 1986 *Albor* bookcase by B.d Ediciones de Diseño.
▶ He received the 1965, 1970, and 1972 FAD de Interiorismo, 1980 Premio FAD and Nacional de Restauración, 1967 and 1976 Delta de Oro of ADI/FAD, 1986 Delta de Plata of ADI/FAD.
▶ Robert A.M. Stern (ed.), *The International Design Yearbook*, New York: Abbeville, 1985/1986: No. 43. Juli Capella and Quim Larrea, *Design by Architects in the 1980s*, New York: Rizzoli, 1988.

Bonetti, Alfredo　(1938–)
▶ Italian designer; born Erba; active Milan.
▶ He began his professional career in 1966; subsequently, became a member of ADI (Associazione per il Disegno Industriale). His clients included Tecno, Gallotti e Radice, Riva foundry, and Fede Cheti.
▶ *ADI Annual 1976*, Milan: Associazione per il Disegno Industriale, 1976.

Bonetti, Mattia　(1953–)
▶ Italian furniture designer; born Lugano; active Paris.
▶ Studied Centro Scolastico per l'Industria Artistica, Italy.
▶ He worked as a color consultant to Rhône-Poulenc in Paris; was a stylist with Marie Berani; collaborated with designer Andrée Putman; in c1977, began collaborating with Elisabeth Garouste.
▶ Photography shown at Galerie Samia Saoumia, Paris; showed furniture and objects with Garouste et Jansen, Paris.

▶ Charlotte Fiell and Peter Fiell, *Modern Furniture Classics Since 1945*, London: Thames and Hudson, 1991:150,174,175, Nos. 141,143,139.
▶ See Garouste, Elizabeth and Bonetti, Mattia

Bonetto, Rodolfo　(1929–1991)
▶ Italian furniture and industrial designer; active Milan.
▶ He began his design career at the Pininfarina automobile body design firm; in 1958, founded his own studio; 1963–69, was a member of ADI (Associazione per il Disegno Industriale) advisory committee and participated in numerous other professional organizations; in 1963 and 1969, was a member of the guidance council of ADI at the ICSID (International Council of Societies of Industrial Design) from 1974, was a member of the committee on scientific education of the Instituto Superiore per le Industrie Artistiche, Rome; was a delegate at the 1972 event of ADI at Beda (Brussels), member of the executive board in 1971 and 1973, vice-president in 1973 and 1976 and president from 1981–83 of the ICSID; 1961–65, taught in the product-design department, Hochschule für Gestaltung, Ulm; 1971–73, taught at Instituto Superiore Disegno Industriale in Rome. He designed more than 400 products for clients including Driade, Brionvega, Valextra, and Bilumen. While manifesting the austere Functionalism of the Ulm school, his work exhibited humorous and ironic aspects, as illustrated by his 1971 *Boomerang* polyfoam chair and colorful 1969 *Quattroquarti* sectional table (produced 1970–78) by Bernini. Known for his use of plastic molding, his Fiat 132 Bellini molded interior was acclaimed. Work included 1962 sewing machine for Borletti, 1963 *Sfericlock* and timer for Veglia Borletti, 1966 soda dispenser for BRAS, 1968 espresso machine for Gaggia, 1969 canister radio for Autovox, 1971 television (with Naoki Matsunaga) for Voxson, 1977 air conditioner for Sime, 1971 auto parts for Shell, (with Matsunaga) heavy industrial machinery for Olivetti, and 1983 *Ala* table lamps by Fretelli Guzzini.
▶ Work shown in numerous exhibitions. Received 1964 (*Sfericlock*), 1967 (*Auctor* office machine by Olivetti), and 1980 (microfilm machine by BCM) Premio Compasso d'Oro, and four others.
▶ 'Rodolfo Bonetto, Designer Italiano,' *Domus*, No. 446, Jan. 1967:43–50. Cat., *Italy: The New Domestic Landscape*, New York: The Museum of Modern Art, 1972:28,33,49,71–72. Cat., *Design Process Olivetti*, Los Angeles: Frederick S. Wight Art Gallery (University of California), 1979:256. *ADI Annual 1976*, Milan: Associazione per il Disegno Industriale, 1976. Cat., Kathryn B. Hiesinger and George H. Marcus III (eds.), *Design Since 1945*, Philadelphia: Philadelphia Museum of Art, 1983. Gianni Pettena, *Rodolfo Bonetto*, Milan: Idea Books, 1992. *Modo*, No. 148, March–April 1993:116.

Bonfante, Egidio　(1922–)
▶ Italian architect and designer; born Treviso.
▶ Studied Accademia di Brera, Milan, and architecture, Politecnico di Milano.
▶ He was editor of *Posizione* (1942–43), *Numero* and *Il Ventaglio* (1946); was co-editor of *A. Arredamento* (1946), *Comunità* (1946–70), *Urbanistica* (1946–67); from 1948, worked for Olivetti; designed exhibitions, showrooms, exhibition catalogs, and advertising.
▶ Cat., *Design Process Olivetti 1908–1978*, Los Angeles: Frederick S. Wight Art Gallery (University of California), 1979:375. Hans Wichmann, *Italien Design 1945 bis heute*, Munich: Die Neue Sammlung, 1988.

Bonfanti, Lorenzo　(1949–)
▶ Italian industrial designer; born Brivio.
▶ He began his career in 1968 in the planning office Delchi; subsequently, became an independent designer; in 1977, (with Gianni Arduini and Gianfranco Salvemini) set up a design studio with clients Carrier, Gelman Elow Famak.
▶ Received 1984 Premio Compasso d'Oro (*FB 33* water purifier by Folletto).

▶ Hans Wichmann, *Italien Design 1945 bis heute*, Munich: Die Neue Sammlung, 1988.

Bonfanti, Renata (1929–)
▶ Italian textile designer; born Bassano del Grappa; active Mussolente.
▶ Bonfanti began her professional career in textile design in 1955; became a member of ADI (Associazione per il Disegno Industriale) in 1961.
▶ Received Premio Compasso d'Oro in 1956, 1960, and 1962 and first prize at the 1961 Concorso del Cotone.
▶ *ADI Annual 1976*, Milan: Associazione per il Disegno Industriale, 1976.

Bonfils, Robert (1886–1971)
▶ French graphic artist, painter, and designer; born Paris.
▶ From 1903, studied École Germain-Pilon and, from 1906, École Nationale des Beaux-Arts, both Paris.
▶ He worked for furniture designer Henri Hamm. Work included paintings, bookbindings, ceramics for Sèvres, silks for Bianchini-Frérier, wallpaper, and layouts for interior design. He designed the tea room of the Au Printemps department store, Paris, painting its walls with images of the seasons; from 1919, was professor of design at École Estienne.
▶ Work shown at Salons d'Automne 1909–1938, Salons des Tuileries to 1938, and Salons of the Société des Artistes Décorateurs from 1910. Showed first bookbinding *Clara d'Ellebeuse* at the 1913 Salon in Paris. An organizer of 1925 Paris 'Exposition Internationale des Arts Décoratifs et Industriels Modernes,' where he exhibited in nine categories, and designed one of the posters and the catalogue cover. Participated in 1937 Paris 'Exposition Internationale des Arts et Techniques dans la Vie Moderne,' 1939 New York 'World's Fair,' 1958 'Exposition Universelle et Internationale de Bruxelles.'
▶ Gaston Quénioux, *Les Arts décoratifs modernes 1918–1925*, Paris, 1925:338. Léon Deshairs, 'Robert Bonfils,' *Art et décoration*, Feb. 1929:33–43. Robert Burnand, 'Robert Bonfils: Peintre, Illustrateur, et Relieur,' *Byblis*, Summer 1929:49–51. Yvanhoe Rambosson, 'Les Reliures de Robert Bonfils,' *Mobilier et décoration*, Feb. 1932:71–74. '5 Relieurs,' *Mobilier et décoration*, April 1935:140–45. Georges Lecomte, 'Reliures modernes,' *Plaisir de France*, Dec. 1937:65–73. Thérèse Charpentier, *L'École de Nancy et la reliure d'art*, Paris, 1960:51. Roger Devauchelle, *La Reliure en France de ses origines à nos jours*, Vol. 3, Paris, 1961:245. Victor Arwas, *Art Déco*, New York: Abrams, 1980. Alastair Duncan and Georges de Bartha, *Art Nouveau and Art Déco Bookbinding*, New York: Abrams, 1989:17,21,59,61–64,187–88.

Bongard, Hermann (1921–)
▶ Norwegian graphic artist and glassware designer.
▶ 1938–41, studied lithography and commercial design, Statens Håndvaerks-og Kunstindustriskole, Oslo, under Sverre Pettersen and Per Krogh.
▶ He was known for his graphic design; 1947–55, produced crystal and glassware designs for Christiania Glasmagasin/Hadelands Glassverk under Sverre Pettersen; in imaginative silhouettes with engraved decoration, designed glassware, including 1954 *Ambassador* for Norwegian embassies; from 1955, was a consultant designer, executing glass, ceramic, textile, and silver designs and architectural decorations; from 1957–63, was advisor to Figgjo Fajanse, Stavanger; from the mid-1960s, specialized in graphics design; from 1966–68, was chief design advisor to J. W. Cappelens publishing firm; from 1968, taught in graphic design department, Statens Håndvaerks-og Kunstindustriskole.
▶ Received 1957 Lunning Prize and gold and silver medals at 1954 (X) Triennale di Milano. Work included in 1983–84 'Design Since 1945' exhibition, Philadelphia Museum of Art.
▶ 'Thirty-four Lunning Prize-Winners,' *Mobilia*, No. 146, Sept. 1967. *Tegneren Hermann Bongard*, Oslo: Kunstindustrimusset, 1971. Cat., Kathryn B. Hiesinger and George H. Marcus III (eds.), *Design Since 1945*, Philadelphia: Philadelphia Museum of Art,

1983. Cat., *The Lunning Prize*, Stockholm: Nationalmuseum, 1986:42–45. Fredrik Wildhagen, *Norge i Form*, Oslo: Stenersen, 1988:127. Jennifer Hawkins Opie, *Scandinavia: Ceramics and Glass in the Twentieth Century*, New York: Rizzoli, 1989.

Bonney, Thérèse (b. Mabel Bonney 1894–1978)
▶ American photographer; born Syracuse, New York.
▶ Studied University of California to 1916, Radcliff College, Cambridge, Massachusetts, to 1917, and, 1918–19, Sorbonne University, Paris.
▶ Bonney settled in Paris in 1918; from *c*1925, documented the decorative arts at Salon exhibitions, department stores, manufacturers, architects, and designers of furniture, ceramics, and jewelry; sold the photographic prints like a news service. In 1927, her Paris apartment was renovated by Gabriel Guévrékian. She attended and photographed the 1930 'Stockholmsutstäliningen' and traveled to the Netherlands, recording its contemporary architecture. She donated her photographs and furniture to the Caisse Nationale des Monuments Historiques et des Sites, Paris; the Cooper-Hewitt Museum, New York; the library of the University of California, Berkeley; and the New York Public Library.
▶ Photography subject of 1940 'War Comes to People: History Written with a Lens by Thérèse Bonney' exhibition, New York Museum of Modern Art; 1940 'To Whom the Wars Are Done,' concerning Finnish children in the Russian invasion of World War II; 1985 exhibition, Cooper-Hewitt Museum. Cooper-Hewitt photography shown at 1976 exhibition, International Center for Photography, New York.

Bonsiepe, Gui (1934–)
▶ Italian design; critic.
▶ 1955–59, studied Hochschule für Gestaltung, Ulm.
▶ 1960–68, he taught at Hochschule für Gestaltung, Ulm; when the school closed in 1968, left for South America, where he practiced industrial design; published *Teoria e Practica del Disegno Industriale* (1975).
▶ Penny Sparke, *Introduction to Design and Culture in the Twentieth Century*, Allen and Unwin, 1986.

Bontempi, Piercarlo (1954–)
▶ Italian architect; born Fornovo Taro.
▶ Studied architecture, Università di Firenze.
▶ He was an assistant to Adolfo Natalini; in 1980, joined Studio Alchimia; executed designs for Alessi; from 1980, specialized in architecture.
▶ Piercaro Bontempi, Giorgio Gregori, *Alchimia*, The Hague: Copi Den Haag, 1985. Kazuko Sato, *Alchimia*, Berlin: Taco, 1988.

Bonvallet, Lucien (1861–1919)
▶ French designer.
▶ Studied École Nationale des Arts Décoratifs, Paris, and under Lechevallier-Chevignard, director of the Sèvres porcelain works.
▶ He designed fabrics, lace, and furniture; from 1885, specialized in metal; became a master of copperware; designed mountings made by Ernest Cardeilhac for ceramics and glass by designers including Pierre Dalpayrat and Émile Gallé.
▶ In 1902, Bonvallet showed his *repoussé* copper and silver vases.
▶ Yvonne Brunhammer et al., *Art Nouveau Belgium, France*, Houston: Rice University, 1976, biblio.

Bookprinter, Anna Marie
See Valentien, Anna Marie

Boonzaauer, Karel (1948–)
▶ Dutch designer.
▶ Studied Academy of Modern Art, Utrecht.
▶ He worked for furniture manufacturer Pastoe for 10 years; from 1979, in partnership with Pierre Mazairac; was active in their studio specializing in product development and interior architecture. Their *MB* armchair of *c*1986 was produced by Metaform, Netherlands.
▶ Robert A.M. Stern (ed.), *The International Design Yearbook*, New York: Abbeville, 1985/1986: No. 19.

Boote, T. and R.

▶ British ceramics manufacturer; located Burslem, Staffordshire.

▶ The firm R. and R. Boote was founded in 1842 in Burslem; first produced encaustic tiles by the plastic-clay method; collaborating with Boulton and Worthington in 1863, patented the pressed-dust method, an inexpensive process that made encaustic tiles more widely available; produced Parian ware. It exhibited a copy of the Portland Vase at the 1851 London exhibition. By the last quarter of the 19th century, along with Minton and Maw, Boote became one of the largest producers of decorative tiles in Britain; in the 1880s, applied the illustrations of Walter Crane to a number of its tiles; at the end of the century, made encaustic and transfer-printed tiles along with numerous majolica tiles in Art Nouveau motifs. Its large white utilitarian tiles were used for public works, including the 1892–97 Blackwall Tunnel under the river Thames.

▶ Parian copy of the Portland Vase shown at 1851 London 'Great Exhibition of Works of Industry of All Nations.' Work included in 1986–87 'In Pursuit of Beauty' exhibition, Metropolitan Museum of Art, New York.

▶ Michael Messenger, 'Revival of a Medieval Technique: Encaustic Tiles in the Nineteenth Century,' *Country Life*, No. 163, Jan. 26, 1978:214–15. Jill and Brian Austwick, *The Decorated Tile: An Illustrated History of English Tile-making and Design*, London, 1980:67,86,100,130,154. Doreen Bolger Burke et al., *In Pursuit of Beauty: Americans and the Aesthetic Movement*, New York: Metropolitan Museum of Art and Rizzoli, 1986:404, biblio.

Booth, Charles   (1844–93)

▶ British stained-glass designer, born Liverpool; active New York, Orange, New Jersey, and London.

▶ Booth had a workshop in New York in the 1870s; in 1880, he returned to England, taking over the stained-glass workshop of George Edward Cook in London, but keeping the New York branch of his business. The workshops in England and America continued to operate after his death, to c1905. Incorporating some Modern Gothic motifs, his style was based on the geometric plant forms of Christopher Dresser and was typical of the 1870s Anglo-Japanese aesthetic. A number of his stained-glass windows were published, including those in the Jefferson Market Courthouse (by Stamford White, architect) and Calvary Church, both in New York.

▶ Work shown at 1986–87 'In Pursuit of Beauty' exhibition, Metropolitan Museum of Art, New York.

▶ Charles Booth, *Hints on Church and Domestic Windows, Plain and Decorated*, Orange, NJ: 1876. Martin Harrison, *Victorian Stained Glass*, London, 1980:57. James L. Sturm, *Stained Glass from Medieval Times to the Present: Treasures to Be Seen in New York*, New York, 1982:96,97,142. Doreen Bolger Burke et al., *In Pursuit of Beauty: Americans and the Aesthetic Movement*, New York: Metropolitan Museum of Art and Rizzoli, 1986:404.

Borbonese

▶ Italian costume jeweler; located Turin.

▶ Luciana Borbonese founded her firm in the mid-1930s by assuming the costume-jewelry and trimmings business of a relative. At first, Borbonese collaborated with dressmakers and reworked the themes they proposed. From the mid-1930s to the mid-1940s, Borbonese's wares were sold through the Turin headquarters of dressmakers such as Longo Comollo, San Lorenzo, and Rosa & Patriarca. Borbonese was joined by her son Umberto Ginestrone and, in the later 1950s, by painter Edoardo Calcagno, both costume jewelers.

▶ Deanna F. Cera (ed.), *Jewels of Fantasy: Costume Jewelry of the 20th Century*, New York: Abrams, 1992:305.

Borchert, Erich   (1907–44)

▶ German architect, town planner, and muralist; born Erfurt.

▶ Trained as a metal caster; 1926–29, studied Bauhaus, Dessau.

▶ He emigrated in 1929 to the Soviet Union, where he worked on the renovation of cities, in activities including architecture, town planning, and mural paintings, and as a graphic designer and painter.

▶ Lionel Richard, *Encyclopédie du Bauhaus*, Paris: Somogy, 1985:180.

Bordier, Primerose   (1929–)

▶ French textile designer; born and active Paris.

▶ Studied Atelier Charpentier, Paris.

▶ 1949–54, she worked as a textile designer; 1954–57, as a stylist at Cosserat; 1958–60, with the Boussac textile factory; 1958–60, at Au Printemps department store, Paris; in 1962, set up her own textile design studio CDM (Couleurs Dessins Modèles); designed tableware and houseware for Descamps.

▶ Appointed Chevalier of the Légion d'Honneur.

Borg, Olli   (1921–1979)

▶ Finnish interior and furniture designer.

▶ Studied Taideteollinen Korkeakoulu, Helsinki.

▶ 1947–50, he was an interior designer for Te-Ma; 1950–54, for Viljo Rewell; 1954–57, for Askon Tehtaat, Lahtis. He set up his own studio; in 1956, was head of industrial-design department, Taideteollinen Korkeakoulu.

▶ Work shown at 1954 (X) Triennale di Milano.

▶ Cat., David Revere McFadden (ed.), *Scandinavian Modern Design 1880–1980*, New York: Abrams, 1982:262.

Bornholm Glass Workshop

▶ Danish glassworks; located Bornholm Island.

▶ The glassworks was set up in 1978 in an abandoned herring smokehouse, Snogebaek, by Darryle Hinz and Charlie Meaker. Hinz moved his own workshop to Copenhagen and Meaker to England.

▶ Jennifer Hawkins Opie, *Scandinavia: Ceramics and Glass in the Twentieth Century*, New York: Rizzoli, 1989.

Borrelli, Corrado   (1947–)

▶ Italian industrial and graphic designer; born Trento; active Milan.

▶ Studied Corso Superiore di Disegno Industriale, Florence.

▶ From 1969, he worked in the studio of Marcello Nizzoli; 1971–73, in the studio of Giorgio Decursu, both Milan; was a consultant designer in graphics, electronics, and furniture for clients including Vittorio Bonacina (*Carlotta* bamboo chair) in Lurago d'Erba, Green Star Motor Oil in Bresso, Milan, and Reprorex, Milan; from 1974, was an industrial designer at Sogetel, designed the *Model 1475* television for AEG Telefunken; became a member of ADI (Associazione per il Disegno Industriale).

▶ *ADI Annual 1976*, Milan: Associazione per il Disegno Industriale, 1976.

Borsani, Osvaldo   (1911–)

▶ Italian furniture designer and architect; born Varedo, Switzerland; twin brother of Fulgenzio Borsani.

▶ 1937, studied architecture, Politecnico di Milano.

▶ He joined the Atelier Varedo; designed for A. and G. Pomodoro, Fontana, Sussu, Crippa, and Fabbri and executed wall-mounted bookshelf system in 1946; fastidious about his furniture designs, in 1954, with Fulgenzio Borsani, he established the furniture company Tecno out of his father's workshop Atelier Varedo and Arredamento Borsani. Tecno's products derived from technological research rather than styling. Borsani was best known for his 1954–55 *P40* articulated chaise longue and its mate, the 1955 *D70* sofa version. The rubber-armed chair was a sophisticated 'machine for sitting' that could, it was claimed, assume 486 positions. The *P40* chair was widely published.

▶ Participated in the 'Casa Minima' project (with architects Cairoli and G.B. Varisco) at 1933 (V) Triennale di Milano; showed *T95* desk at 1940 (VII) Triennale di Milano. Work shown at (X) and 1964 (XIII) Triennali di Milano (receiving prizes); 1968 'Les Assises du siège contemporain' exhibition at the Paris Musée des Arts Décoratifs; 1970 'Modern Chairs 1918–1970' exhibition,

Whitechapel Gallery, London. Received 1962 Premio Compasso d'Oro.
▶ Cat., *Modern Chairs 1918–1970*, London: Lund Humphries, 1971. Charlotte Fiell and Peter Fiell, *Modern Furniture Classics Since 1945*, London: Thames and Hudson, 1991:54,73,75, Nos. 25,41. 'Fulgenzio Borgani,' *Ottagano*, No. 105, Dec. 1992:61–64.

Bortnyik, Sándor (1893–1976)
▶ Hungarian artist and writer; born Marosvásárhely (now Tirgu Mures, Romania).
▶ Studied art, Budapest.
▶ 1918–22, he was active in avant-garde artistic circles; worked with Lajos Kassák on the revue *Ma*, to which Bortnyik contributed illustrations and geometric lino prints; in 1920, settled in Vienna; participated in the Russian revolution and the Budapest Commune. In 1922, broke his association with Kassák; in 1924, settled in Weimar, but was not connected with the Bauhaus there; in 1925, returned to Hungary, where he was active as an advertising graphic designer, theater designer, and journalist; 1928–38, was active in a studio he named the Hungarian Bauhaus; after World War II, became a teacher in the school of industrial design, Budapest, and subsequently at another applied-arts institution.
▶ Lionel Richard, *Encyclopédie du Bauhaus*, Paris: Somogy 1985:169–70.

Bortolotti, Ivana
▶ Italian designer.
▶ Studied European Institute of Design, Milan, under Roberto Lucci and Paolo Orlandini.
▶ She worked for Roberto Lucci and Paolo Orlandini; designed *c*1983 *Tenso* prototype chair for 'Seven Living Ideas Project' sponsored by B&B Italia Research Center and Instituto Europeo di Disegno, Italy.
▶ Robert A.M. Stern (ed.), *The International Design Yearbook*, New York: Abbeville, 1985/1986: Nos. 68–69.

Bosch, Stephan (1945–)
▶ Dutch architect; born Nijmegen; active Milan.
▶ Studied Royal Academy of Fine Art, the Netherlands.
▶ He participated in research concerning the Cuban Construction Center under architect W.P. Graatsma. In 1960, he was a sculptor and traveled in Africa and the USA, before turning to the design of objects and interiors; in 1971, settled in Milan, where he was a consultant to Braun; designed numerous exhibition stands and shop interiors; from 1975, concentrated on the production of heavy machinery; became a member of ADI (Associazione per il Disegno Industriale).
▶ *ADI Annual 1976*, Milan: Associazione per il Disegno Industriale, 1976.

Bose, Amar G. (1929–)
▶ American electronics entrepreneur and inventor; active Massachusetts.
▶ Bose began teaching electrical engineering at Massachusetts Institute of Technology in 1956; in 1964, founded the Bose Corporation, Farmingham, Massachusetts, with Sherwin Greenblatt to manufacture loudspeakers. His first loudspeaker, the Model 901, with a Saarinen-like pedestal, is still in production today.
▶ Barbara Mayer, 'Who's got the Button,' *Elle Decor*, November 1990:162.

Bossanyi, Ervin (1891–1975)
▶ Hungarian painter, sculptor, and stained-glass designer and maker; active Britain.
▶ Bossanyi settled in Britain in 1934. His commissions for stained glass included 1934 Senate House, London University; 1935 Beaux-Arts Exhibition in London; 1938 Uxbridge Underground Station; and 1938–41 Tate Gallery. Other commissions included stained glass for Canterbury Cathedral, Victoria and Albert Museum, the church at Port Sunlight, the Anglican Cathedral, Washington, Michaelhouse School Chapel, Durban, and York Minster. He was considered a radical exponent of stained glass.

▶ Cat., *Thirties: British art and design before the war*, London: Arts Council of Great Britain, Hayward Gallery, 1979:102,198,285.

Bossi, Giuseppe (1951–)
▶ Italian textile and graphic designer; born and active Milan.
▶ Studied architecture in Milan.
▶ He began working with the studio Designers 6R5 in 1973, producing designs for textiles and ceramics; in 1975, (with Pierangelo Marucco, Francesco Roggero, Maurizio Alberti, and Bruno Rossio) founded the studio Original Designers 6R5, Milan. The group designed textiles for Lanerossi, Sasatex, Taif, and Bassetti in Italy; Griso and Jover in Spain; tapestry producers Printeco and Sirpi in Italy; Le Roi, Griffine, Marechal, and wallpaper producers in France. He became a member of ADI (Associazione per il Disegno Industriale).
▶ *ADI Annual 1976*, Milan: Associazione per il Disegno Industriale, 1976.

Botta, Antonio (1931–)
▶ Italian designer; born Greve, Florence; active Florence.
▶ Botta began his professional career in 1971; designed lighting, domestic accessories, and toys produced by his own firm SDF Botta Felice Antonio, Florence; became a member of ADI (Associazione per il Disegno Industriale).
▶ *ADI Annual 1976*, Milan: Associazione per il Disegno Industriale, 1976.

Botta, Mario (1943–)
▶ Swiss architect and designer; born Mendrisio, Ticino; active Lugano.
▶ 1958–61, studied technical drafting; 1961–64, Liceo Artistico, Milan; 1964–69, Instituto Universitario di Architettura, Venice.
▶ Before his architectural studies, he built 1961–63 clergy house, Genestretta, which showed his early interest in geometrical forms with an emphasis on craftsmanship; 1958–61, was an apprentice building draftsman in the studio of architects Tita Carloni and Luigi Camenisch, Lugano; was influenced by the organic architecture espoused by Bruno Zevi in the 1950s in Italy; in 1965, did practical work in the studio of Le Corbusier, Paris, on a hospital project, and in the studio of Jullian de la Fuente and José Oubrerie, Venice. Botta's houses of the 1960s reflected the influence of Le Cobusier. In 1969, he met architect Louis Kahn in Venice; participated on the project for the new Palazzo dei Congressi Laurea all'UIA, Venice; in 1969, set up his own studio in Lugano, where he designed private, industrial, and public buildings in Switzerland; in 1969, was a visiting professor and member of institutions in Europe and USA; in 1976, was visiting professor at École Polytechnique Fédérale, Lausanne and, from 1983, professor there. Buildings included 1961–63 clergy house, Genestretta; 1972–77 school, Morbio Inferiore; 1965–67 house, Stabio; 1970–71 independent buildings, Cadenazzo; 1972–73 independent buildings, Riva San Vitale; 1975–76 striped house, Ligornetto; 1977–82 Staatsbank administration building, Fribourg; 1985 Ransila 1 Building, Lugano. Furniture produced by Alias included 1982 *Prima* side chair, 1982 *Seconda* armchair, 1983 *Terzo* table, 1984 *Quarta* chair, 1985 *Quinta* armchair, 1985 *Sesta* armchair, 1985 *Sesto* King and Queen chairs, 1986 *Tesi* table, 1987 *Latonda* armchair. 1985–86 *Shogun* lighting range and 1987 *Melanos* table lamp produced by Artemide. *Trasparenze* furniture container shown at 1985 Triennale di Milano.
▶ Italo Rota (ed.), *Mario Botta: Architetture e progetti negli anni '70*, Milan, 1979. *Mario Botta: Bâtiments et projets, 1978–1982*, Paris, 1982. Futagawa Yukio (ed.), *Architect Mario Botta*, Tokyo, 1984. *Le Affinità Elettive*, Milan: Electa, 1985. Auction cat., *Asta di Modernariato 1900–1986, Auction 'Modernariato,'* Milan: Semenzato Nuova Geri, 8 Oct. 1986. Juli Capella and Quim Larrea, *Design by Architects in the 1980s*, New York: Rizzoli, 1988.

Bottoni, Piero (1903–73)
▶ Italian architect and designer.
▶ A Rationalist architect, Bottoni designed the maid's room and bath of the Casa Elettrica (architects of which were fellow Gruppo

Sette members Luigi Figini and Gino Polini) for Montedison at the 1930 (IV) Exposition at Monza. It was the first truly public expression of Modern architecture in Italy and the prominently featured kitchen was influenced by German and American models. 1930–33, Bottoni collaborated on interiors with Giuseppe Terragni; was a member of MIAR (Movimento Italiano per l'Architettura Razionale); in 1933, editor of journal *Quadrante*. Bottoni and Enrico Griffini designed a housing development at the 1933 (V) Triennale di Milano. Bottoni's 1930s *Lira* plated tubular-steel chair with its prominent vertical wire splats was produced by Thonet and widely published; its production was revived in the 1980s by Zanotta. Bottoni designed the chair so that its tension wires suspended the seat on the frame in a technically and aesthetically sophisticated, if over-wrought, manner.

▶ Participated in 1928–31 Rational architecture exhibition, Rome; 1930 (IV) Monza 'Esposizione Biennale delle Arti Decorative e Industriali Moderne'; 1936 (VI) and 1947 (VI) Triennali di Milano.

▶ Barbie Campbell-Cole and Tim Benton (eds.), *Tubular Steel Furniture*, London: Art Book Company, 1979:47. Stefano Casciani, *Mobili come Architettura*, Milan, 1984:160. Penny Sparke, *Design in Italy, 1870 to the Present*, New York: Abbeville, 1988. Hans Wichmann, *Italien Design 1945 bis heute*, Munich: Die Neue Sammlung, 1988.

Botturi, Giuseppe   (1947–)

▶ Italian designer; born Cavriana; active Castiglione delle Stiviere.

▶ He began his professional career in 1974; became a member of ADI (Associazione per il Disegno Industriale). Clients included Arredamenti and Candle.

▶ He showed his paintings and sculpture in Roncoferraro.

▶ *ADI Annual 1976*, Milan: Associazione per il Disegno Industriale, 1976.

Boucher, Guy   (1935–1992)

▶ French designer.

▶ Studied engineering, Conservatoire National des Arts et Métiers, Paris, under Jean Prouvé.

▶ He was involved with advanced technology as well as artistic projects; one technical project was for Télémécanique; for Duralex-Saint Gobain, designed 1968 *SAFTBP12* dinnerware; designed 1983 *Service Antares* drinking glasses produced by Daum; in 1971, designed the first one-piece pocket lamp, produced by Mazda.

▶ Won French government sponsored APCI (Agence pour la Promotion de la Creation Industrielle) competition of 1986.

▶ *Les Carnets du Design*, Paris: Mad-Cap Productions et APCI, 1986:50. François Mathey, *Au bonheur des formes, design français 1945–1992*, Paris: Regard, 1992:123,339.

Boucher, Marcel

▶ American costume jeweler; located New York.

▶ Marcel Boucher was born in France, where he worked for Cartier; at the beginning of the 1920s, settled in the USA; in the early 1930s, designed shoe buckles for Mazer Bros., New York; established his own costume jewelry business in 1937 with 12 brooches, a line bought by Saks. The firm converted to the production of wartime materials during World War II; in 1949, Boucher hired Raymonde Semensohn as his assistant and engineer. Changing her name to Sandra Semensohn, she left for Tiffany's in 1958 but returned in 1961; in 1964, she married Boucher. After Boucher's death in 1965, she managed the firm, which became a subsidiary of watch manufacturer Dovorn Industries in 1972. In 1975, Sandra Boucher began designing costume jewelry for Ciner, New York.

▶ Deanna F. Cera (ed.), *Jewels of Fantasy: Costume Jewelry of the 20th Century*, New York: Abram, 1922.

Boucheron, Frédéric   (1830–1902)

▶ French jeweler, located Paris.

▶ 1844–45, apprenticed to Jules Chaise at the Palais Royal, Paris.

▶ Boucheron set up his own firm in 1858; by the mid-1860s, had become well known in the Palais Royal; in 1893 he moved to the luxurious Paris showroom where the firm is still active today. An expert in gemology, he employed artists Jules Brateau, Lucien Hirtz, Jules Debût, and sculptor Edouard Becker. Boucheron was succeeded by son Louis; he by his nephews Frédéric and Gérard. The first to combine rock crystal with precious stones, the firm is noted for its Art Déco jewelry of the 1930s. Its designers included Edmond-Henri Becker, René Lalique, and Paul Legrand. Its well-known pieces included 1889 *Question Mark* necklace, 1894 *Butterfly* brooch engraved by C. Bordinckx, 1925 pectoral ornament with sandstone mosaic by Hirtz, 1937 nail-head-shaped wristwatch. Numerous branches were opened abroad. From 1980, Alain Boucheron managed the firm.

▶ Lavish jewelry in innovative styles shown at 1876 Philadelphia 'Centennial Exhibition,' winning a first prize. Frequently at domestic and international expositions, work shown at 1867, 1889, and 1900 Paris 'Expositions Universelles.' Work subject of 1988 exhibition, Musée Jacquemart-André, Paris.

▶ Charlotte Gere, *American and European Jewelry 1830–1914*, New York: Crown, 1975:154–55. Sylvie Raulet, *Bijoux Art Déco*, Paris: Regard, 1984. Melissa Gabardi, *Les Bijoux des Années 50*, Amateur, 1987. Gilles Néret, *Boucheron: Histoire d'une dynastie de Joailliers*, Paris: Pont Royal, 1988. Katherine Purcell, *Boucheron: Histoire d'une dynastie de joailliers*, Fribourg: Office du Livre, 1988. Annelies Krekel-Aalberse, *Art Nouveau and Art Déco Silver*, New York: Abrams, 1989:623,66,252. Gilles Néret, *Boucheron: Le Joaillier du Temps*, Paris: Conti, 1992.

Bouchet, Léon-Émile   (c1880–1940)

▶ French decorator, furniture designer, and teacher; born Cannes; active Paris.

▶ Trained at furniture makers Carpezza and Carlhian, Paris.

▶ From 1898, he designed furniture for notable firms, including Bec and Le Confortable, and fabric for Bianchini-Férier; worked in a conservative Art Nouveau style inspired by Louis XVI models; during World War I, was in charge of the camouflage service; subsequently, adopted a Modern approach based on 18th- and 19th-century models; from 1913, taught at École Boulle, Paris; in c1926, became artistic director of G, E et J Dennery, Paris; worked with Epéaux and Soubrier; designed domestic interiors, offices, stores, and a suite on the 1930 oceanliner *Atlantique*.

▶ Work shown at all the Salons of the Société des Artistes Décorateurs, his most notable presentation being the *Bureau d'un homme d'affaires* at the 1929 session; Salon d'Automne; 1925 Paris 'Exposition Internationale des Arts Décoratifs et Industriels Modernes'; 1929 'Exposition de la Décoration française contemporaine.'

▶ *Ensembles Mobiliers*, Vol. II, Paris: Charles Moreau, 1937. Pierre Kjellberg, *Art Déco: les maîtres du Mobilier, le décor des Paquebots*, Paris: Amateur, 1986:36–37,223.

Bouilhet, Henri   (1931–)

▶ French architect and designer.

▶ Bouilhet designed *Géométrie* tea service produced by Christofle in c1970; became the artistic director of Christo.

Boulestin, X. Marcel

▶ French interior decorator; active London.

▶ Boulestin worked in Paris with novelist Colette and her husband Willy. Encouraged by friends including Max Beerbohm, Boulestin came to England in 1906 to pursue a literary career; in 1911, founded the shop Décoration Moderne, Elizabeth Street, London, one of the first small avant-garde decorator showrooms there; stocked furniture and furnishings from Paris, including the complete range of designs of Paul Poiret's Atelier Martine. Clients included Lady Curzon, the Baroness d'Erlanger, and Syrie Wellcome. The fashion for exotic wares declined after World War I

and Boulestin turned to the production of painted 'java paper' (silk glued to paper) lampshades; Décoration Moderne closed in 1921. Collaborating with friend Jean-Émile Laboureur; Boulestin became a restaurateur, hiring architect Clough Williams-Ellis and decorator Allan Walton for the 1925 Restaurant Français and 1927 Restaurant Boulestin. André Groult supervised the Restaurant Boulestin project, where circus-theme panels by Marie Laurencin and Laboureur and curtains by Raoul Dufy were installed.
► X.M. Boulestin, *Ease and Endurance*, London, 1948. William Gaunt, *The Studio*, 1928. Stephen Calloway, *Twentieth-Century Decoration*, New York: Rizzoli, 1988:63–64,109,137,167.

Boulle, École
See École Boulle

Bourgeois, Édouard-Joseph (aka Djo-Bourgeois; Georges Djo-Bourgeois 1898–1937)
► French architect and interior and furniture designer; born Bezons; active Paris.
► Studied École Spéciale d'Architecture, Paris, under Robert Mallet-Stevens, to 1922.
► In the early 1920s, he worked alongside Étienne Kohlmann and Maurice Matet for the Studium-Louvre, the decorating studio of Les Grands Magasins du Louvre, designing furniture and interiors. His architectural training spurred his interest in the spatial arrangement of moveable furniture. His furniture designs and interiors were geometric, austere, right-angled and enlivened by the bright colors in the curtains and rugs designed by his wife Elise Bourgeois and by Hélène Henry. He was attracted to innovative materials, including Terazolith composition rubber. Some of his furniture was produced with a lacquer finish. An early 1920s room setting included veneered pieces; from 1926, he used metal in his furniture, particularly aluminum with wood, and nickel-plated steel tubing. His interests included the design of kitchens and children's rooms. He renovated the apartment of Princess Faucigny-Lucinge in an old mansion, Île-St.-Louis, Paris. His architectural work included private homes and apartment buildings with some domestic architecture in the south of France, including the Lahy house, Saint Clair. In 1925, his personal style was shown fully formed in the interiors (with others) of the villa of the vicomte and vicomtesse de Noailles, Hyères. In 1929 for a townhouse in Paris, he designed the dining-room suite in aluminum, and executed the interiors for a number of apartments and shops. He is attributed with having designed accessories for Desny in Paris. Despite the Modernity of his work and closeness with Robert Mallet-Stevens, he did not join UAM (Union des Artistes Modernes).
► Work shown first at 1922 Salon d'Automne and regularly at Salons of the Société des Artistes Décorateurs from 1923. Designed office-library of Studium Louvre pavilion at 1925 Paris 'Exposition Internationale des Arts Décoratifs et Industriels Modernes.' 'Appartement d'un yachtman sur la Côte d'Azur' (completed posthumously by friends and colleagues) shown at pavilion of Société des Artistes Décorateurs, 1937 Paris 'Exposition Internationale des Arts et Techniques dans la Vie Moderne.'
► Léon Deshairs, *Modern French Decorative Art*, Paris: Albert Lévy. Victor Arwas, *Art Déco*, Abrams, 1980. A.H. Martinie, 'Djo-Bourgeois architecte et décorateur, *Art et décoration*, 1981. Pierre Kjellberg, *Art Déco: les maîtres du Mobilier, le décor des Paquebots*, Paris: Amateur, 1986:53–55.

Bourgeois, Elise
► French fabric designer.
► Bourgeois's printed curtain material, fabrics, and rugs were included in the interior architecture of husband Édouard-Joseph Bourgeois (Djo-Bourgeois). Her designs were bold, brightly colored, and geometric.

Bourgeois, Marie-Laure
See Bécheau, Vincent

Bourne, Agnes
► American furniture designer; active San Francisco.
► From the 1970s, she designed retail displays, theater sets, historical restorations, remodeling, and interiors; was an interior designer and manager of a shop, San Francisco; taught design at California College of Arts and Crafts; was co-author of a series of books on decorating. Her furniture designs included the *Chevy Chaise, Ham and Eggs* suite of tables and cubes, and the *Tao* chair.
► Ylanda Gault, 'The New American Entrepreneurs,' *Metropolis*, May 1991:65–66,68.

Boutet de Monvel, Bernard (1881–1949)
► French painter, watercolorist, and decorator; born and active Paris.
► Studied under Luc-Olivier Merson and Jean Dampt.
► He was best known for his portraits in a synthetic and elegant style (related to the arabesques of the Nabis and the geometry of neo-Cubism) of dandies, beauties, artists, and the *beau monde* of which he was a member. Subjects included his wife, Bernard Naudin, André Dunoyer de Segonzac, the maharajah of Kapurthala, Jean-Baptiste Boussingault, and himself. He illustrated books, participated in the Musée d'Art Contemporain of Süe et Mare at the 1925 exposition in Paris, and painted the countryside of Morocco.
► Work shown at 1910 Brussels 'Exposition Universelle et Internationale,' 1910 Humorists-group exhibition in Copenhagen, Salons of the Société Nationale des Beaux-Arts, Salons d'Automne; (with Süe et Mare) in Musée d'Art Contemporain at 1925 Paris 'Exposition Internationale des Arts Décoratifs et Industriels Modernes.'
► Cat., Aaron Lederfajn and Xavier Lenormand, *Le Louvre des Antiquaires présente: 1930 quand le meuble devient sculpture*, Paris, 1986. Pierre Cabanne, *Encyclopédie Art Déco*, Paris: Somogy, 1986:177.

Bouval, Maurice (?–c1920)
► French metalworker; born Toulouse.
► Studied under Alexandre Falguière.
► He made lamps and small bronze objects; often gilded his work, incorporating idealized Art Nouveau interpretations of the female form into utilitarian designs; adapted traditional sculpture into letter openers, inkwells, *garnitures de cheminée*, and other accessories. His bronzes were cast at the foundries of Colin, Jollet, and Thiebaut Frères. His motifs included nymphs, water lilies, poppies, and lotuses. Work included the *Ophelia* bust, *Le Secret* statuette, and *Dream* and *Obsession* candelabra. Lighting fixtures included sconces, table lamps, candelabra, and candlesticks.
► Work shown regularly at Salons of the Société des Artistes français, first as a sculptor and then as a designer in the decorative arts section, where his *Tristesse* bronze candlestick was shown at the 1897 event. Exhibiting at La Maison Goldscheider, pair of gilt-bronze flambeaux (produced by Goldscheider) shown at 1900 Paris 'Exposition Universelle.'
► Yvonne Brunhammer et al., *Art Nouveau Belgium, France*, Houston: Rice University, 1976, biblio. Alastair Duncan, *Art Nouveau and Art Déco Lighting*, New York: Simon and Schuster, 1978:69–70.

Bouy, Jules (1872–1937)
► French metalsmith; active Belgium and USA.
► Bouy established his first interior decoration firm in Belgium; in 1913, settled in New York; 1924–27, was associated with L. Alavoine, the Parisian decorating firm with an office in Manhattan; concurrently, was head of Ferrobrandt, New York, which produced his own designs and sold the metalwork of Edgar Brandt; by 1928, had set up his own firm, with fashionable clients including Agnes Miles Carpenter and Lizzie Bliss.
► *American Art Annual*, 1930:511. *The New York Times*, 29 June 1937:22. Karen Davies, *At Home in Manhattan: Modern Decorative Arts, 1925 to the Depression*, New Haven: Yale, 1983:74–75.

Boven, Gert   (1957–)
▶ Dutch lighting designer.
▶ Studied Akademie Industriële Vorgeving, Eindhoven.
▶ 1984–88, he was an associate designer, Neonis Design and Styling; in 1988, joined Lumiance Design Team.
▶ Received 1984 Kho Liang Ie Encouraging Award.

Bowlen, Nord   (1909–)
▶ American metalworker.
▶ Studied industrial design, Rhode Island School of Design.
▶ He was head of the design department, Lunt silversmiths, for over 25 years. His designs included the commercially unsuccessful 1954 *Contrast* sterling silver flatware with black injection molded nylon handles.
▶ 'Annual Design Review,' *Industrial Design*, Vol. 3, Dec. 1956: No. 148. Cat., Kathryn B. Hiesinger and George H. Marcus III (eds.), *Design Since 1945*, Philadelphia: Philadelphia Museum of Art, 1983.

Boyden, Frank S.   (1861–1943)
▶ American silversmith; active Chicago.
▶ With Fred G. Minuth, Boyden established Frank S. Boyden Company, Chicago, which in 1903 became Boyden-Minuth. The firm produced heavily embellished objects for ecclesiastical use and jewelry; until the 1950s, produced silver trophies; is still in operation.

Boyer, Michel
▶ French furniture designer; active Paris.
▶ Active in the 1950s and 1960s, Boyer specialized in the design of seating, most of which was produced by Airborne and Artifort.
▶ Gilles de Bure, *Le mobilier français 1965–1979*, Paris: Regard/VIA, 1983. François Mathey, *Au bonheur des formes, le design français 1945–1992*, Paris: Regard, 1992:257.

Boym, Constantin   (1955–)
▶ Russian furniture and product designer; born Moscow; active Boston, New York, and Milan.
▶ Studied Moscow Architectural Institute to 1978 and Domus Academy, Milan, to 1984.
▶ He settled in the USA, in 1981, working for several architectural firms in Boston, including Graham Gund Associates; in Milan 1984–86, collaborated with Matteo Thun, designing furniture, objects, interiors, and conceptual architecture; 1985–86, worked with Alessandro Mendini on Alberto Alessi's villa; returning to New York in 1986, set up his own studio and designed products and furniture for clients including Acerbis, Brickel, Detail, Elika, Formica, and Sasaki. His activities included interior and exhibition design and writing for magazines *Domus, Modo, Ufficiostile, Axis, FP, Interiors, ID, House and Garden*, and *Metropolis*. From 1986, he taught design at Parson School of Design, New York.
▶ Received 1988 and 1990 *ID* Design Review awards (range of clocks) and first prize in 1989 IDSA Design Competition (a writing instrument).

Boyton, Charles   (1885–1958)
▶ British silversmith; active London.
▶ Boyton at first worked in his family's firm; from the 1930s, made contemporary objects; in 1934, set up his own workshop for Modern silver. His work appeared to be influenced by Georg Jensen, including a cutlery set resembling Harald Nielsen's 1927 *Pyramid* pattern for Jensen.
▶ Annelies Krekel-Aalberse, *Art Nouveau and Art Déco Silver*, New York: Abrams, 1989:27,252.

Braakman, Cees
See UMS

Bracquemond, Félix-Henri   (1833–1914)
▶ French artist, etcher, ceramicist, and engraver; born Paris.
▶ Influenced by Katsuskika Hokusai whose discovery in the West heralded *japonisme* in France, Bracquemond became involved in executing woodcuts. His interest in ceramics began in the early 1860s when he decorated large earthenware plates for Joseph-Theodore Deck. Leaving the Sèvres porcelain works, he joined Charles Haviland's firm, becoming artistic director of its new studio, where he stayed until 1881; invited Ernest Chaplet to join the studio in 1875; created designs for use on ceramics; subsequently returned to engraving and began to write art criticism and to organize exhibitions; became a founding member of Société Nationale des Beaux-Arts; tried interior design around the turn of the century, collaborating with Alexandre Charpentier and Jules Chéret on a billiard room for Baron Vitta; designed enameled jewelry produced by Alexandre Riquet, bookbindings by Marius-Michel, and vases by Émile Müller.
▶ Baron Vitta billiard room shown at 1902 Paris Salon of the Société Nationale des Beaux-Arts.
▶ Yvonne Brunhammer et al., *Art Nouveau Belgium, France*, Houston: Rice University, 1976.

Braden, Nora   (1901–)
▶ British potter; active Brighton.
▶ 1919–21, studied Central School of Arts and Crafts and, from 1921, Royal College of Art, both London.
▶ 1925–28, she worked with Bernard Leach at St. Ives; met Katherine Pleydell-Bouverie, with whom she worked 1928–36 at her pottery at Coleshill, Wiltshire, where they produced a variety of ceramics with wood- and plant-ash glazes, issuing much of their finest work in the 1930s; destroyed much of her small output; in c1939, began teaching at Brighton Art School and discontinued her work as a potter.
▶ Cat., *Thirties: British art and design before the war*, London: Arts Council of Great Britain, Hayward Gallery, 1979:98,130, 286,299. Frederick Cooke, *Glass: Twentieth-Century Design*, New York: Dutton, 1986:104.

Bragdon, William Victor   (?–1959)
▶ American ceramic engineer; active Berkeley, California.
▶ Studied Alfred University, Alfred, New York, to 1908.
▶ From 1908, he taught at the University of Chicago and University City Porcelain Works, Missouri, under Taxile Doat; in 1915, settled in Berkeley, California, and began teaching at the California School of Arts and Crafts; in 1916, (with Chauncey R. Thomas) established California Faïence, producing art tiles and pottery until the 1930s; the firm's facilities were subsequently used by local artists and amateur decorators.
▶ Paul Evans in Timothy J. Andersen et al., *California Design 1910*, Salt Lake City: Peregrine Smith, 1980:76.

Brambilla, Enrico   (1943–)
▶ Italian industrial designer; born Bagnolomella; active Varese
▶ Brambilla began his professional career in 1971; designed domestic appliances, including refrigerators and washing machines, for clients including IRE, Cassinetta B., and Design Studio Broletto; became a member of ADI (Associazione per il Disegno Industriale).
▶ *ADI Annual 1976*, Milan: Associazione per il Disegno Industriale, 1976.

Brambilla, Giorgio   (1951–)
▶ Italian designer; born Desio, Milan; active Milan.
▶ Studied industrial design, Scuola Politecnica di Design, Milan.
▶ From 1974, he collaborated with Lorenzo Tosi, Fabio Stojan, and Anna Castelli in the studio Gruppo, Milan. They studied solar energy applications in housing at Montedison's office of accident prevention. Brambilla became a member of ADI (Associazione per il Disegno Industriale); (with Castelli) developed lightweight cardboard playground equipment.
▶ *ADI Annual 1976*, Milan: Associazione per il Disegno Industriale, 1976.

Brammer, Max   (1940–)
▶ Danish designer.
▶ Trained as a silversmith at Georg Jensen Sølvsmedie.
▶ He opened his own workshop in 1961.

Brandao, Marili

▶ Italian designer.
▶ Studied European Institute of Design, Milan, under Roberto Lucci and Paolo Orlandini.
▶ She designed c1986 *Tiete* adjustable divan for the 'Seven Living Ideas' project sponsored by B&B Italia Research Center and Instituto Europeo di Disegno, Italy.
▶ Robert A.M. Stern (ed.), *The International Design Yearbook*, New York: Abbeville, 1985/1986: No. 76.

Brandi, Ulrike   (1957–)

▶ German lighting designer; born Bevensen.
▶ From 1979, studied literature, Universität Hamburg; 1984–88, industrial design, Hochschule der bildenden Künste, Hamburg, under Dieter Rams, Achim Czemper, and Peter Raacke.
▶ In 1988, she became an independent consultant designer and lighting designer; designed the 1987 solar-powered light by Erco Leuchten and Mannesmann-DEMAG.
▶ Won the 1985 'Design Plus' competition (bedside table), Messe Frankfurt ; 1985 'Design Bourse' (chair design), Haus Industrieform Essen; Wilkhahn firm competition (chair design), 1986 competition (drawing instrument), 'Büro für das Existenzminimum'; 1987 'Design zur Zeit' competition (timepiece), Museum für Kunst und Gewerbe, Hamburg; 1988 competition, Österreichisches Instituts für Formgebung, Vienna.

Brandolini, Andreas   (1951–)

▶ German designer; born Taucha, Leipzig.
▶ 1973–79, studied architecture, Technische Universität, Berlin.
▶ From 1980, he worked as an industrial designer; lectured in industrial design, Hochschule der Künste, Berlin; Architectural Association, London; Hochschule für Gestaltung, Offenbach. In 1982–86 with Joachim B. Stanitzek, was active in an experimental studio in Berlin, designing under the name Bellefast (a play on words meaning 'instant beauty'). Their work included the 1984 *Hommage à Yuri Gagarin* lighting fixture and 1984 *Frühlingserwachen* coat rack. He opened Brandolini Büro für Gestaltung in 1986; from 1989, was full-time professor at the Hochschule der Bildenen Künste, Saarbrücken. Designed 1988–89, the *Bonanza* limited-production table.
▶ Work shown in Germany, Brazil, France, Italy, Britain, and the USA.
▶ Christian Borngraeber, *Prototypen: Avantgarde Design uit/aus Berlin*, Rotterdam: Uitgeverij 010, 1986. Albrecht Bangert and Karl Michael Armer, *80s Style: Designs of the Decade*, New York: Abbeville, 1990:86–87, 228. *Ottagono*, No. 100, 1991:1.

Brandt, Åsa   (1940–)

▶ Swedish glassware designer.
▶ 1962–67, studied Konstfackskolan and Tekniska Skolan, Stockholm; 1967, Gerrit Rietveld Akademie, Amsterdam, and Royal College of Art, London.
▶ In 1968, she set up her own workshop, Torshälla; (with Ulla Forsell and Eva Ullberg) set up the cooperative studio Freeblowers; became a member of the Konsthantverkarna, Stockholm.
▶ Her work was the subject of one-person exhibitions at the Varbergs Museum in 1980 and Konsthantverkarna in Stockholm, in 1972, 1978, and 1981.
▶ Cat., David Revere McFadden (ed.), *Scandinavian Modern Design 1880–1980*, New York: Abrams, 1982:263.

Brandt, Edgar-William   (1880–1960)

▶ French designer; born Paris.
▶ Studied École Nationale Professionelle de Vierzon, near Orléans.
▶ Beginning c1905, he executed lighting fixtures incorporating Daum glass with bronze; the partnership lasted into the 1930s. He established his own workshop in Auteuil, and, in 1919, on the site of his father's old ironworks, where he installed the newest equipment; Henri Favier designed the showroom, called La Maison d'un Ferronnier. Inspired by the Art Nouveau style, Brandt's metalwork was applied to dark, colorful, and even ornate ensembles

that lent a sense of dimension and space. Known for his wrought-iron work, Brandt gilded, silvered, and polished metals, marrying them with bronze and marble; designed the French Tomb of the Unknown soldier at the Arc de Triomphe, Paris, and the Amistice Monument in Rethondes. After 1925 his work became more geometric. In 1926, he moved his offices, gallery, and atelier to Paris; designed interiors, including those of apartments, offices, public spaces, and oceanliners; in 1925, opened a branch of his wrought iron business in New York, called Ferrobrandt and managed by Jules Bouy; in 1926, was commissioned to decorate the Cheney Stores, New York.
▶ Work shown at Salons of Société des Artistes français from 1900, Salon d'Automne from 1900, Salon des Beaux-Arts 1900–14, Salons of the Société des Artistes Décorateurs 1910, and most of the international exhibitions, winning numerous awards. At 1925 Paris 'Exposition Internationale des Arts Décoratifs et Industriels Modernes,' his wrought-iron metalwork was an essential part of many stands (including with Favier and Ventre and for the Hôtel du Collectionneur of Jacques-Émile Ruhlmann).
▶ Salon catalogs, Société des Artistes Décorateurs, 1910, 1911, 1919–22, 1924, 1926. Salon catalogs, Société des Artistes français, 1919–20. *Le Luminaire et les Moyens d'éclairages Nouveaux*, Paris: G. Janneau, 1st, 2nd, and 3rd series. Salon catalogs, Salon d'Automne, 1920–24, 1926, 1934. Cat., *The World of Art Deco*, New York, 1971: figs. 358–61. Cat., *Decorative Arts 1925 Style*, New York: Didier Aaron, 1979. Katherine Morrison McClinton, 'Edgar Brandt Art Déco Ironworker,' *The Connoisseur*, Sept. 1979:8–14. Victor Arwas, *Art Déco*, Abrams, 1980. Pierre Cabanne, *Encyclopédie Art Déco*, Paris: Somogy, 1986:177–79. Joan Kahr, 'Edgar Brandt and French Ironwork,' thesis, New York: Cooper-Hewitt/Parsons School of Design, 1988.

Brandt, Marianne   (1893–1983)

▶ German painter, designer, and metalworker; born Chemnitz; active Weimar, Chemnitz, Dresden, and Berlin.
▶ 1911 studied painting, Akademie der bildenden Künste, Weimar 1923–25, metalworking, Bauhaus, Weimar and Dessau.
▶ She set up her own studio in 1917; with Wilhelm Wagenfeld, became the best known pupil of the Bauhaus metalwork studio, directed by László Moholy-Nagy, whose Constructivist geometric forms inspired her and who was influential in turning her from an Arts and Crafts metalworker in 1924 into an industrial designer of lamps in 1925. Brandt's designs for domestic products were based on uncompromising geometric principles. She designed the 1928 *Kandem* night-light (with Hin Bredensieck) as a class project. At the Bauhaus, her colleagues included Christian Dell and Hans Pryzembel. Succeeding Moholy-Nagy, she was head of the Bauhaus metal workshop 1928–32; briefly in 1929, worked in the office of Walter Gropius in Berlin; became a consultant designer for various firms and a teacher. Manufacturers of her early lighting included Körting and Mathiesen. Until 1932, she worked at the Ruppelwerk metalworking factory, Gotha; from 1933, was unemployed, returning to Chemnitz and taking up painting; attempted to license the Wohnbedarf department store in Zürich to produce her bowls, ashtrays, dining utensils, and an egg cooker; 1949–51, taught in Dresden and, 1951–54, at Hochschule für Angewandte Kunst, Berlin; for a short period, was a freelance industrial designer before returning again to Chemnitz (then Karl-Marx-Stadt), devoting herself to painting and sculpture. Some of her designs are still produced, notably a tea set (originally designed in the 1930s) included in Alessi's Tea and Coffee Piazza project of 1983, the year she died.
▶ W. Scheidig, *Crafts of the Weimar Bauhaus*, London, 1967. Stephan Waetzold and Verena Haas, *Tendenzen der zwanziger Jahre*, 15, Berlin: Europäische Kunstausstellung, 1977. *Sammlungs Katalog*, Bauhaus-Archiv, Museum für Gestaltung, Berlin, 1981: pl. 193. Officina Alessi, *Tea and Coffee Piazza: 11 Servizi da tè e caffè . . .*, Milan: Crusinallo, 1983. F. Whitford, *Bauhaus*, London, 1984. Eckhard Neumann (ed.), *Bauhaus und Bauhäusler*, Cologne, 1985. Lionel Richard, *Encyclopédie du Bauhaus*, Paris: Somogy

1985:138,181. *Experiment Bauhaus*, Berlin: Bauhaus-Archiv Museum, 1988: plate 123. *Le Bauhaus dans les Collections de la République Démocratique Allemande*, Musées Royaux des Beaux Arts de Belgique, Brussels, 1988: plate 36. Cat., *The Bauhaus: Masters and Students*, New York: Barry Freidman, 1988. Friederike Mehlau-Wiebking et al., *Schweizer Typenmöbel 1925–35, Sigfried Giedion und die Wohnbedarf AG*, Zürich: gta, 1989. Christie's Bauhaus catalog, 1989. Cat., *Die Metallwerkstatt am Bauhaus*, Berlin: Bauhaus-Archiv, 1992.

Brandt, Paul-Émile
► Swiss silver and lacquer designer; born La Chaux-de-Fonds.
► Studied under Chaplin and Allard in Paris.
► He established a business in Paris, where he designed and produced a range of jewelry and watches in floral Art Nouveau motifs; combined gold, silver, platinum, and lacquer and produced silverware and boxes.
► Work shown at sessions of Salon d'Automne, Salons of Société des Artistes français, and 1925 Paris 'Exposition Internationale des Arts Décoratifs et Industriels Modernes.'
► Victor Arwas, *Art Déco*, New York: Abrams, 1980.

Brangwyn, Frank (1867–1956)
► British artist and designer; born Bruges (Belgium); active London.
► From 1882, through his friendship with Arthur H. Mackmurdo, he worked as a draftsman and designed tapestries for William Morris; in 1885, he rented a studio and showed his work for the first time at the Royal Academy; in 1895, executed murals for the entrance of and a frieze in Siegfried Bing's shop L'Art Nouveau, Paris; in 1900, designed a bedroom for E.J. Davies, the furniture of which was produced by Norman and Stacey, London. His designs, including furniture, textiles, and ceramics, illustrate his considerable knowledge of historical sources. The coromandel-like doors on his own print cabinet, published in the 1914 *Studio Year Book of Decorative Art*, reflect Far Eastern influences and are close to his contemporary painting style. After the 1914 murals for the San Francisco international exposition, many commissions followed in the USA. In *c*1927, he designed tableware for Doulton; painted 1928–32 *Empire Panels* murals for the House of Lords, rejected in 1930 and installed in 1934 in the Guildhall, Swansea; in 1930, designed two chenille carpets woven by James Templeton and hand-knotted Donegals produced by Alexander Morton; in 1932, painted a mural at Rockefeller Center, New York, where other muralists included Diego Rivera and Jose Maria Sert; in 1933, designed the new façade of the Rowley Gallery, London, using carved wood panels depicting craftsmen at work over Portland stone. In 1936, the Brangwyn Museum was opened in Bruges. On the walls of Skinners' Hall, London, he painted his 1937 *Education* and *Charity*. His work was revived following his 1952 Royal Academy exhibition, the first devoted to a living Academician.
► Work first shown at the Royal Academy, London, in 1885. Painting *Buccaneers* shown at 1893 Salon, Paris. Painted murals for 1914 San Francisco 'Panama-Pacific International Exposition.' Designed British exhibits at 1905 Biennale di Venezia. Knighted in 1941.
► Walter Shaw Sparrow, *Frank Brangwyn and His Work*, London: Kegan Paul, French and Trubner, 1910. Herbert Furst, *The Decorative Art of Frank Brangwyn*, London: Bodley Head, 1924. Rodney Brangwyn, *Brangwyn*, London: William Kimber, 1978. Cat., *Thirties: British art and design before the war*, London: Arts Council of Great Britain, Hayward Gallery, 1979:31,43,124,125,128,286. Cat., *The Art of Frank Brangwyn*, Brighton: Brighton Polytechnic and the Fine Art Society, 1980. *British Art and Design, 1900–1960*, London: Victoria and Albert Museum, 1983. Jessica Rutherford, *Art Nouveau, Art Deco and the Thirties: The Furniture Collections at Brighton Museum*, Brighton: The Royal Pavilion, Art Gallery and Museums, 1983:50,55.

Branzi, Andrea (1938–)
► Italian designer; born Florence; active Milan.
► Studied architecture and design, Florence, to 1966.
► He is known for his theoretical furniture; in 1966 (with Paolo Deganello and others) founded Archizoom Associati, the avant-garde group in Florence that brought the irony of Anti-Design of the 1960s to furniture design; participated in CDM (Consulenti Design Milano) firm, with whom he published the two-volume *Decorattivo 1* and *2* on environmental décor; in 1973, set up his studio, Milan; in the early 1980s, participated in the exhibitions of Studio Alchimia, the proto-Memphis group that explored metaphysical aspects of design; 1972–75, wrote on avant-garde architecture in *Casabella*; 1983–87, was managing editor of *Mode* and, for a time, president of *Domus*; (with Michele De Lucchi) organized the 1977 'Il design italiano degli anni 50,' the first major retrospective exhibition of Italian postwar design, at Naviglio, Milan, and co-wrote the catalogue; 1982–83, was professor at Instituto del Disegno Industriale, the architecture department of Università di Palermo; was visiting professor and lecturer at universities and schools in Italy, the Netherlands, France, Japan, Argentina, Brazil, and the USA; from 1983, was educational director, Domus Academy, Milan. His attempt to establish a new relationship between man and his possessions is the subject of his book *Domestic Animals* (1987), in which he suggests that it is valid to think of a sofa or a light fixture as a household pet. His other books included *The Colors of Energy* (1975), *Pre-Synthetic Colors* (1976), *Environmental Colors* (1977), *Moderno–Postmoderno–Millennario* (1980), *Good and the Metropolis*, *La Casa Calda: Esperienze del Nuovo Disegno Italiano* (1982), (with Michele De Lucci) *Il design italiano degli anni 50* (1979). For Memphis, work included 1982 *Gritti* bookcase, *Century* divan, and silver sauce boat, 1983 *Beach* chaise longue, 1985 *Magnolia* bookcase, 1987 *Andrea* chaise longue, and 1988 *Foglia* electroluminescent wall lamp. Other designs included the 1982 *Labrador* silver sauce dish by Rossi e Arcandi, 1985 *Animali Domestici* range of seating by Zabro, 1986 *Berlino* sofa by Zanotta, 1986 *Frande Tapetto Ibrido* range of tables by Zabro, and 1989 *Iudola* bench by Zanotta.
► Participated 1968 (XIV), 1979 (XVI), and 1983 (XVII) Triennali di Milano, was general coordinator of its (XV) session, and in the 1976, 1978, and 1980 Biennali di Venezia. Participated in Memphis's first exhibition in 1981. Received 1979 (primary design research) and 1987 Premi Compasso d'Oro. *Iudola* bench by Zanotta introduced at 1989 Salone del Mobile in Milan, and 1987 *Animali Domestici* shown at 1991 'Mobili Italiani 1961–1991: Le Varie Età dei linguaggi' exhibition, Milan. Work subject of exhibitions at New York Museum of Modern Art; Lijbanam Centrum, Rotterdam; CAYC, Buenos Aires; Musée St. Pierre, Lyons; Palazzo dei Diamanti, Ferrara; and included in numerous group exhibitions.
► Andrea Branzi and Michele De Lucchi, *Il design italiano degli anni 50*, Milan: Domus, 1979. Andrea Branzi, *Moderno Postmoderno millennario*, Milan: Studio Forma/Alchimia, 1980. Penny Sparke, *Ettore Sottsass Jnr*, London: Design Council, 1982. Andrea Branzi, *La Casa Calda: Esperienze del Nuovo Disegno Italiano*, Milan, 1982. 'Andrea Branzi,' *Intramuros*, No. 18, May–June 1988. Juli Capella and Quim Larrea, *Design by Architects in the 1980s*, New York: Rizzoli, 1988. Albrecht Bangert and Karl Michael Armer, *80s Style: Designs of the Decade*, New York: Abbeville, 1990: 121,136,228. Charlotte Fiell and Peter Fiell, *Modern Furniture Classics Since 1945*, London: Thames and Hudson, 1991:85,86, 116,118,147,148.

Brateau, Jules-Paul (1844–1923)
► French metalworker and jewelry designer; born Bourges.
► Studied École des Arts Décoratifs, Paris, under sculptor Auguste Nadaud, and under H.-S. Boudoncle.
► He became the primary designer at Boucheron and at Bapst et Falize, both Paris; collaborated with enameler Paul Grandhomme; at the end of the 19th century, contributed to the resurgence of interest in the art of pewter in France; made attractive and inex-

pensive objects in pewter; inspired by the work of Dammouse, designed delicate pieces in *pâte-de-verre* in *c*1910–12.
▶ Jewelry and pewter work shown at 1889 and 1900 Paris 'Expositions Universelles.'
▶ Yvonne Brunhammer et al., *Art Nouveau Belgium, France*, Houston: Rice University, 1976, biblio.

Brauckman, Cornelius (c1866–c1954)
▶ American ceramicist; born Missouri; active Los Angeles.
▶ Little is known of Brauckman and his ventures. In 1912, he established the Grand Feu Pottery in Los Angeles, but appears to have ceased commercial production around 1916.
▶ Received a gold medal at 1915 San Diego 'Panama-California Exposition.' Work shown at 1916 (I) Los Angeles 'Annual Arts and Crafts Salon.'
▶ Paul Evans in Timothy J. Andersen et al., *California Design 1910*, Salt Lake City: Peregrine Smith, 1980:76.

Brauer, Erich (1929–)
▶ Austrian painter and designer; born Vienna.
▶ Known as a 'fantastic' painter, Brauer's furniture combined fine art and utility.
▶ Günther Feuerstein, *Vienna—Present and Past: Arts and Crafts—Applied Art—Design*, Vienna: Jugend und Volk, 1976:61–62,80. Arik Brauer, *Werkverzeichnis*, Dortmund: Harenberg, 1984.

Braun
▶ German domestic appliance and sound equipment manufacturer; located Frankfurt.
▶ Braun was founded by Max Braun in Frankfurt in 1921; manufactured drive-belt connectors and scientific equipment; later began producing plastic components for radios and record-players. The factory was rebuilt in 1945, and in the 1950s Braun began to develop whole products, including flashlights and electric shavers. When Max Braun died in 1951, his sons Artur and Erwin assumed the management of the firm. Artur Braun embarked on a new design program emphasizing function and design, and hired Fritz Eichler, who worked with the teaching staff of the Hochschule für Gestaltung, Ulm. Eichler revised the entire Braun line, beginning with radios. The collaborative designs of Dieter Rams, Hans Gugelot, and Otl Aicher of the Ulm school manifest austere, unadorned forms. Rams, who joined the staff at Braun in 1955, became chief designer in 1961. Braun's 1955 *Phonosuper SK4* record player, designed by Eichler and Artur Braun, was the first of its products to speak the new design language. The Braun team produced geometrically proportioned, unadorned electronic products in white and gray cases punctuated with Swiss-type graphics. The influential Braun-Ulm design philosophy was carried through to every facet of the company's activities, including logo, advertising, and packaging. Braun's products sometimes looked better than they performed; the 1961 *HT1 Toaster* designed by Reinhold Weiss was not tall enough to toast the top section of a slice of bread. Cheap models from the Far East swamped the market in the early 1980s; Gillette acquired the firm in the late 1980s, and the firm gained global distribution.
▶ Work (1955 *Phonosuper SK4* record player) first shown at 1955 Düsseldorf exhibition; subsequent work shown at numerous design exhibitions and competitions. Received numerous awards, including Premio Compasso d'Oro and British Interplas.
▶ François Burkhardt and I. Franksen, *Dieter Rams*, Berlin: IDZ 1982. Cat., Kathryn B. Hiesinger and George H. Marcus III (eds.), *Design Since 1945*, Philadelphia: Philadelphia Museum of Art, 1983. Cat., *Donation Braun*, Munich: Die Neue Sammlung, 1985. 'The Radio,' London: Design Museum, 1989. Cat., Mehroder Weniger, *Braun-Design im Vergleich*, Hamburg: Museum für Kunst und Gewerbe, 1990.

Braunstein, Claude (1940–)
▶ French industrial designer; active Paris.
▶ Studied École des Arts Appliqués, Paris.
▶ 1964–70, he was director of product design, IBM; 1970–72, established the multi-disciplinary school of graphic, product, and

environmental design, Institut de l'Environment, Paris; 1970–75, worked for the public relations firm Signis; 1978–84, worked for PA Consulting International; in 1985, with Clément Rousseau, co-founded Plan créatif/Crabtree Hall.

Bredendieck, Hin (b. Heinrich Bredendieck 1904–)
▶ German designer; born Aurich, East Friesland.
▶ Studied Kunstgewerbeschule, Stuttgart and Hamburg.
▶ From 1927, he worked in the Bauhaus workshop, Dessau, designing furniture and, with Marianne Brandt, lamps, including the 1928 *Kandem* table fixture; 1931–32, worked in Herbert Bayer's and Lázsló Molholy-Nagy's studio in Berlin; in 1932, worked for lighting manufacturer BAG, Turgi (Switzerland); living in Oldenburg (Germany), designed fabric designs for furniture; with Sigfried Giedion, designed lamps, including the *Indi* lamp; 1935–37, was a furniture designer in Oldenburg; in 1937, settled in the USA, assuming the directorship of the basic design and metalworking workshops, New Bauhaus, Chicago; from 1939, worked as an independent designer, Chicago; 1945–52, taught product design, Institute of Design (the successor of the New Bauhaus), Chicago; 1949–54, was head of Lerner-Bredendieck Design, Chicago; 1952–73, was associate partner and active in the industrial-design department, Institute of Technology, Atlanta, becoming its head.
▶ Bredendieck and Giedion's *Indi* lamp shown at 1932 'Lichtausstellung,' Kunstgewerbe Museum, Zürich.
▶ Lionel Richard, *Encyclopédie du Bauhaus*, Paris: Somogy, 1985: 182. *New Bauhaus*, Berlin: Bauhaus-Archiv, 1987. Friederike Mehlau-Wiebking et al., *Schweizer Typenmöbel 1925–35, Sigfried Giedion und die Wohnbedarf AG*, Zürich: gta, 1989. Cat., *Die Metallwerkstatt am Bauhaus*, Berlin: Bauhaus-Archiv, 1992:184–91,315.

Breger, Carl-Arne (1932–)
▶ Swedish industrial designer; active Stockholm; husband of Bibi Breger.
▶ Studied Konstfackskolan and Tekniska Skolan, Stockholm.
▶ 1953–57, he worked at Gustavsberg, producing designs for tableware, sanitary fittings, and plastics. His 1959 square bucket was widely published. 1957–59, he was chief designer, Bernadotte & Björn studio, Stockholm; from 1959, with his wife had a studio with offices in Stockholm, Malmö, and Rome, where he designed the *Diavox* telephone produced by Ellemtel.
▶ Square bucket recognized as 'the best plastic product for the 1950–60 decade' by Swedish Plastic Association. Received 1975 Bundespreis 'Die gute Industrieform' (handsaw).
▶ *Gustavsberg 150 år*, Stockholm, 1975: Nos. 306,309–10,317. Carle-Arne Breger, 'The Story behind a Design,' *Tele*, No. 2, 1979:12–15. Cat., Kathryn B. Hiesinger and George H. Marcus III (eds.), *Design Since 1945*, Philadelphia: Philadelphia Museum of Art, 1983.

Breidfjord, Leifur (1945–)
▶ Icelandic stained-glass and textile designer.
▶ Breidfjord was a flat- and stained-glass designer and (with wife Sigridur Johannsdottir) a textile designer.
▶ Cat., David Revere McFadden (ed.), *Scandinavian Modern Design 1880–1980*, New York: Abrams, 1982:263.

Bremer Silberwarenfabrik
▶ German silversmiths; located Bremen.
▶ Bremer Silberwarenfabrik was founded in 1905; specialized in silver flatware; closed in 1981.
▶ Annelies Krekel-Aalberse, *Art Nouveau and Art Déco Silver*, New York: Abrams, 1989:221,252.

Bremer Werkstätte für Kunstgewerbliche Silberarbeiten
▶ German silversmiths; located Bremen.
▶ Bremer Werkstätte für Kunstgewerbliche Silberarbeiten (Bremen Workshop for Craft Silverwork) was founded in 1921; produced

items such as candelabra and bowls. Its designers included Wilhelm Schultze.

▶ Annelies Krekel-Aalberse, *Art Nouveau and Art Déco Silver*, New York: Abrams, 1989:145,252.

Bremers, Peter (1957–)

▶ Dutch artist and designer; born Maastricht.
▶ Studied Art Academy, Maastricht, to 1980.
▶ He first worked as a sculptor; subsequently executed furniture; designed 1986–87 table lamp produced in Corian synthetic marble by Galerie Néotù, and wrist-watch designs by Lincoln, Switzerland.
▶ Work shown at Galerie Néotù, Paris; Kortrijk Biennale; and in Marseilles, Berlin, and Arnhem.
▶ Albrecht Bangert and Karl Michael Armer, *80s Style: Designs of the Decade*, New York: Abbeville, 1990:111,228.

Bresciani, Franco (1952–)

▶ Italian designer; born Genoa; active Rome.
▶ He designed furniture and lighting for clients in Italy including Molteni, Poltrona Frau, Gabbianelli, Cucchiarelli, Pizzetti, Caleido, and Fratelli Guzzini. He designed the *Coral* range of furniture for WK Mobel, Germany, and graphics for American Export Lines and Shell, Italy; became a member of ADI (Associazione per il Disegno Industriale).
▶ Work shown widely in Italy, including the exposition, Urgnano.
▶ *ADI Annual 1976*, Milan: Associazione per il Disegno Industriale, 1976.

Bresler, Frank H.

▶ American furniture manufacturer and interior designer; active Milwaukee.
▶ The F.H. Bresler Company, Milwaukee, succeeding F.H. Durbin, was incorporated in 1900 by Frank H. Bresler, a business associate of George Mann Niedecken and a furniture maker, print dealer, and art importer. Bresler specialized in American Arts and Crafts products, Chinese ceramics, and Japanese prints; helped Niedecken realize his first interior design commissions; invested in the firm of Niedecken-Waldbridge, set up in 1907 and which, 1907–10, supervised the production of Frank Lloyd Wright furniture made by F.H. Bresler. The firm produced some of Wright's famous spindle-back chairs, including those for the 1908 Robert W. Evans house, Chicago. The firm continues today, specializing in custom framing.
▶ David A. Hanks, *The Decorative Designs of Frank Lloyd Wright*, New York: Dutton, 1979:202. Cat., Anne Yaffe Phillips, *From Architecture to Object*, New York: Hirschl and Adler, 1989:94,97.

Bresse, Edward H.

▶ British silversmith.
▶ Bresse worked in America, establishing a workshop in Chicago in 1921. His operation ceased in 1940.
▶ Sharon S. Darling and Gail Farr Casterline, *Chicago Metalsmiths*, Chicago Historical Society, 1977.

Breuer, Marcel Lajos (1902–81)

▶ Hungarian architect and industrial designer; born Pécs.
▶ 1920, studied Akademie der bildenden Künste, Vienna; 1920–24, Bauhaus, Weimar.
▶ He went to Vienna in 1920, intending to become a painter and sculptor; dissatisfied with the Akademie der bildenden Künste, enrolled at the Bauhaus, Weimar, becoming one of its best known students; following a period in Paris, returned in 1925 to the Bauhaus, Dessau, as director of its carpentry workshop until 1928; 1928–31, practiced architecture and design, Berlin; 1932–33, traveled throughout Europe and worked in Zürich. In 1921, his first chair in wood and woven upholstery (named the *Lattenstuhl* by Breuer) imitated Gerrit Rietveld's De Stijl furniture;

incorporating horsehair fabric woven in the Bauhaus weaving workshop, it was based on anatomical research. When the chair was shown in 1923, the enthusiastic reaction encouraged Breuer to continue research on seating models. It was illustrated in *Bauhausbücher 7*. Rietveld showed Breuer's furniture at the Bauhaus exhibition in the Netherlands, but by then the De Stijl influence was already strong among Bauhaus designers, clearly seen in Breuer's 1922 wood and canvas armchair. The design of the tubular-steel 1925 *Wassily* chair (originally named the *Club*) is related to the 1922 Breuer design. In 1925, according to Breuer, he bought his first bicycle and was so impressed by the lightness and strength of the frame that he visualized using tubular steel in furniture. The first experimental tubular-steel piece was this club-type armchair; the final design was not fully realized until 1926. It was the centerpiece at the Kunsthalle, Dessau (an exhibition where Breuer's other work was shown). Breuer described it in 1927 as 'my most extreme work both in its outward appearance and in its use of materials; it is the least artistic, the most logical, the least "cosy" and the most mechanical'; it was named *Wassily* because of Vasilii Kandinski's admiration of it. In the Bauhaus building, Dessau, Breuer's designs were used in the canteen (his stool), in the assembly hall (his linking auditorium chairs), and elsewhere (the first *Wassily* chair), all produced in tubular steel at Junkers, Dessau. The *Wassily* chair was first produced in Breuer's own workshop and, from 1929, by Standardmöbel Lengyel, Berlin. Early Breuer chairs were nickel plated, later ones chrome plated. One of the first designs to go into production independently of the Bauhaus was the *B32* side chair, manufactured first by Standardmöbel in 1927 and later by Thonet from c1928. It is closely related to his Bauhaus designs, particularly the chairs he designed for the Bauhaus auditorium in 1926. About 500 pieces were made in 1926 and 1000–1500 in 1927. In 1928, the firm Anton Lorenz, Berlin, took over production, becoming the first manufacturer to produce tubular-steel furniture on a commercial scale. It was used in Gropius's many interiors in the second half of the 1920s, including his own apartment. The 1928 *B32* chair was renamed *Cesca* (after Breuer's daughter Francesca) by furniture manufacturer Dino Gavina, who produced it from 1950 in his Foligno (Italy) factory purchased by Knoll Associates in 1968. Breuer designed the 1927 folding chair in tubular steel and iron-cloth; in 1928, set up practice as an architect, Berlin; designed the 1931 cantilever sofa and reclining chair on wheels of c1930 and, from 1932, aluminum furniture, some of whose frames were innovatively bent from a single thick sheet of aluminum; in 1932, completed his first building, the Harnischmacher house, Wiesbaden; moved to Britain in 1935 where, 1935–37, he was in practice with F.R.S. Yorke and designed bent-plywood furniture for Isokon, including the 1936 chaise longue; (with Yorke) designed houses at Angmering-on-Sea, West Sussex; Bristol; Eton, Berkshire; and Lee on the Solent, Hampshire; and the competition project 'A Garden City of the Future'; settled in the USA in 1937 where, 1937–46, he was a professor of architecture at Harvard University; 1937–41, collaborated with Walter Gropius in Massachusetts. His students included Florence Knoll, Philip Johnson, Edward Larrabee Barnes, Eliot Noyes, Paul Rudolph, and John Johansen. From 1946, when he gave up teaching and settled in New York, his interest shifted from furniture design to architecture; he established a New York practice (Marcel Breuer Associates) and executed numerous commissions. Some of his buildings were in reinforced concrete imprinted with wooden mold marks, illustrated by 1966 Whitney Museum of American Art, New York. He often incorporated local stone into his architecture; his New York office used a photograph of stones as wallpaper in the reception area.
▶ Buildings included 1932 Wohnbedarf furniture shop, Zürich; 1935–36 multiple housing (with A. and E. Roth) in the Doldertal, Zürich; his own 1947 house, New Canaan, Connecticut; 1953–58 UNESCO Headquarters (with Pier Luigi Nervi and Bernard Louis Zehrfuss), Paris; 1953–61 buildings at St. John's Abbey and University in Collegeville, Minnesota; 1956–61 campus at

University Heights, New York; 1960–60 IBM Research Center, La Gaude (France); 1963–66 Whitney Museum of American Art, New York; 1967–77 IBM buildings, Boca Raton, Florida; and 1970 Cleveland Museum of Art.

▶ Tubular-steel furniture by Standardmöbel used in Gropius's prefabricated house at 1927 Stuttgart 'Weissenhof-Siedlung.' Work subject of 1948 traveling exhibition organized by New York Museum of Modern Art, where his 'House in the Museum Garden' was installed in 1949 and where the 1981 'Marcel Breuer Furniture and Interiors' exhibition was organized; and 1972–73 'Marcel Breuer at the Metropolitan Museum of Art,' Metropolitan Museum of Art, New York.

▶ Marcel Breuer, 'Metallmöbel' in W. Gräff, *Innenräume*, Stuttgart, 1928:133–34. Peter Blake, *Marcel Breuer: Architect and Designer*, New York: An Architectural Record Book with the Museum of Modern Art, 1949. Michael Farr, *Design in British Industry: A Mid-Century Survey*, London: Cambridge, 1955. Peter Blake (ed.), *Sun and Shadow: The Philosophy of an Architect*, London, New York, and Toronto, 1956. Giulo Carlo Argan, *Marcel Breuer, Disegno industriale e architettura*, Milan, 1957. Cranston Jones (ed.), *Marcel Breuer, 1921–1961, Buildings and Projects*, London, 1962. Tician Papachristou, *Marcel Breuer: New Buildings and Projects*, New York: Praeger, 1970. Cat., Richard G. Stein, *A View of Marcel Breuer*, New York: Metropolitan Museum of Art, 1972. Cat., *Thirties: British art and design before the war*, London: Arts Council of Great Britain, Hayward Gallery, 1979:286,303. Jan van Geest and Otakar Máčel, *Stühle aus Stahl: Metallmöbel 1925–1940*, Cologne: König, 1980. Cat., Christopher Wilk, *Marcel Breuer Furniture and Interiors*, New York: Museum of Modern Art, 1981. Alfred Roth, 'Zum Tode des Architekten Marcel Breuer in Werk,' *Bauen und Wohnen*, Vol. 10, 1981. Peter Blake and Axel Menges in Vittorio Magnano Lampugnani (ed.), *Encyclopedia of 20th-Century Architecture*, New York: Abrams, 1986:53–55. Cat., *Der Kragstuhl*, Stuhlmuseum Burg Beverungen, Berlin: Alexander, 1986:118–19,130. Cat., Aaron Lederfajn and Xavier Lenormand, Lenormand, *Le Louvre des Antiquaires présente: 1930 quand le meuble devient sculpture*, Paris, 1986. Cat., *The Bauhaus: Masters and Students*, New York: Barry Friedman, 1988. Sonja Güntha (introduction), *Thonet Tubular Steel Furniture Card Catalogue*, Weil am Rhein: Vitra Design Publications, 1989. Otakar Máčel, 'Avant-garde Design and the Law-Litigation over the Cantilever Chair,' *Journal of Design History*, Vol. 3, Nos. 2 and 3, 1990:125. Magdalena Droste and Manfred Ludewig, *Marcel Breuer, Bauhaus-Archiv*, Cologne: Taschen, 1992.

Breuhaus de Groot, Fritz-August (1883–1960)
▶ German architect and designer; active Düsseldorf.
▶ Studied Technische Hochschule, Berlin-Charlottenburg, and Kunstgewerbeschule, Düsseldorf.
▶ He worked for Peter Behrens, his fellow student in Düsseldorf; after 1927, designed metalwork and silverwares for Württembergische Metallwarenfabrik (WMF). Hildegard Risch, a pupil of Karl Müller and collaborator of Eva Mascher-Elsässer, worked under Breuhaus. In the late 1920s, some of Breuhaus's tubular-steel chairs were produced by Thonet. Breuhaus, as interior architect, and artist Arpke collaborated with Ludwig Dürr, the chief constructor at the Luftschiffbau-Zeppelin, on the layout and decorations of the 1936 *Hindenburg* dirigible, making extensive use of aluminum. He also designed for trains and oceanliners, and his work included ceramics, wallpaper, and bookbindings.
▶ A tea service by Jan Eisenloeffel on Breuhaus's tea trolley produced by Vereinigte Werkstätten was published in *Dekorative Kunst* (1928).
▶ Barbie Campbell-Cole and Tim Benton (eds.), *Tubular Steel Furniture*, London: The Art Book Company, 1979. Annelies Krekel-Aalberse, *Art Nouveau and Art Déco Silver*, New York: Abrams, 1989:147,149,252. J. Gordon Vaeth, 'Zeppelin Decor: The Graf Zeppelin and the Hindenburg,' *Journal of Decorative and Propaganda Art*, No. 15, Winter/Spring 1990:53. Cat., *Metallkunst*, Berlin: Bröhan Museum, 1990:585–86.

Brionvega
▶ Italian manufacturer of sound equipment and televisions; located Milan.
▶ Brionvega was founded in Milan in 1945; specialized in radio sets at first; moved into TV sets in 1952, producing the first Italian TV set. In 1962, Marco Zanuso and Richard Sapper began a collaboration with the firm, when the *Doney 14* TV set was produced, marking the advent of Italy's first network TV company. The 1964 *TS502* table radio was an original design with two hinged compartments. Marco Zanuso designed its 1966 *Algol 11* transistorized portable TV set with an angled screen, 1966 *ts 502* portable tradio, and 1971 *Fd 1101* transistor radio. Brionvega's designers included Achille and Pier Giacomo Castiglioni, Franco Albini, Franca Helg, and Mario Bellini.
▶ Cat., Milena Lamarová, *Design a Plastické Hmoty*, Prague: Uměleckoprůmyslové Muzeum, 1972:42,44. Penny Sparke, *Design in Italy, 1870 to the Present*, New York: Abbeville, 1988.

British Committee on Art and Industry
See Gorell Committee

British Council for Art and Industry
See Council for Art and Industry

Brno Devětsil
▶ Czech literary, art, and design group.
▶ The Brno Devětsil group was active 1923–27 in Brno. Its members included Bedřich Véclavek, Zdeněk Rossmann, Jan Markalous, poet František Halas, and art-critic Artuš Černík.
▶ *Devětsil: The Czech Avant-Garde Art, Architecture and Design of the 1920s and 1930s*, Oxford: Museum of Modern Art, London: Design Museum, 1990:105.

Broadhead, Caroline (1950–)
▶ British jewelry designer.
▶ Studied Central School of Arts and Crafts, London.
▶ In her early work, she used colored ivory; in 1977, began making bound-thread necklaces; in 1978, created a wood- or silver-framed bracelet that held tufts of nylon through which the hand was pushed; prominent in the new jewelry movement active from c1968, she rejected precious materials for plastic, cloth, paper, and rubber; in the 1980s, produced a series of wearable objects that combined sculpture, clothing, and jewelry in a single object, such as her 1983 nylon monofilament necklace-headpiece veil.

Brocard, Philippe-Joseph (?–1896)
▶ French restaurateur, collector, and enameler.
▶ Brocard was influenced by the enameled decorations of the mosque lamps he saw at the Cluny Museum; painted designs in gold and enamel on white or lightly tinted glass; at first, he merely copied Egyptian and Persian lamps, vases, and bowls. Other influences on his work included Gallo-Roman, German, and Italian Renaissance glasswares. As its best exponent, he revived enameled glass in France. It has been suggested that Brocard introduced Émile Gallé to the art of enameled glass, while Gallé in turn introduced Brocard to naturalism. Around 1880, Brocard began using mistletoe, satinpod, and cornflower motifs. From 1884, he and his son produced glass with enameled decoration of gold, silver, platinum, and copper, signed 'Brocard et Fils.'
▶ Copies of Islamic models shown at 1867 and 1878 Paris 'Expositions Universelles.'
▶ Yvonne Brunhammer et al., *Art Nouveau Belgium, France*, Houston: Rice University, 1976, biblio. Cat., *Verriers français contemporains: Art et industrie*, Paris: Musée des Arts Décoratifs, 1982.

Brodt, Helen Tanner (1838–1908)
▶ American teacher, painter, and ceramics decorator; born Elmira, New York; active Oakland and Berkeley, California.
▶ She settled in Red Bluff, California, in 1863, where she taught school; by 1867, had moved to the San Francisco area, where she taught in Oakland public school, managing the art program 1872–

87; the painter Arthur F. Matthews was her student. She opened a studio in Oakland; by 1881, as evidenced by her *Oriental Fantasy* porcelain plate, was interested in china painting. The remainder of her career is unknown. Much of her work was lost in the 1906 San Francisco earthquake.

▶ Received award for china painting at 1884–85 New Orleans 'World's Industrial and Cotton Centennial Exposition.' Showed paintings at exhibitions of Mechanics' Institute, San Francisco, and a portrait at 1893 Chicago 'World's Columbian Exposition.' Work included in 1986–87 'In Pursuit of Beauty' exhibition, Metropolitan Museum of Art, New York.

▶ Cat., Phil Kovinick, 'Helen Tanner Brodt,' in *The Woman Artist in the American West, 1860–1960*, Fullerton, California: Muckenthaler Cultural Center, 1976:13. Chris Petteys, 'Brodt, Helen Tanner,' in *Dictionary of Women Artists: An International Dictionary of Women Artists Born Before 1900*, Boston, 1985:97. Doreen Bolger Burke et al., *In Pursuit of Beauty: Americans and the Aesthetic Movement*, New York: Metropolitan Museum of Art and Rizzoli, 1986:405.

Bromberg, Paul   (1893–1949)

▶ Dutch interior architect and theoretician; born Amsterdam.

▶ From 1908–09, active in Berlin; 1913, founded interior-architecture office in Amsterdam; 1913–18, designed and produced furniture; 1918, became head of Modern-decorative-arts and interior-design department, Metz & Co, Amsterdam, and designed several interiors and furniture designs for the firm from 1918–24; 1921, redecorated Metz store; from 1924, worked as an interior architect in Modern interiors department of Pander & Zoon, The Hague and Amsterdam, designing furniture and interiors of model houses and showrooms; 1927, decorated (with H.A. van Anrooy) interior of villa; 1930, decorated villa in Antwerp and house in Rotterdam; 1931–37, chair of Rotterdam section of VANK; decorated model house for 1931 Klein Zwitserland project (architect D. Roosenburg), The Hague; 1931, decorated model rooms of Pander's new building, The Hague, and houses in Rotterdam, Overschie, and Scheveningen (The Hague); 1940–45, stayed in the USA; 1945, returned to Amsterdam where he set up his own consultation office; died in Amsterdam.

▶ Work shown at 1918 'Tentoonstelling van Ambachts-, Nijverheids- en Volkskunst,' Rotterdam; 1919 exhibitions in Haarlem and at Stedelijk Museum, Amsterdam; 1923 Salon d'Automne, Paris; 1923 industrial-design exhibition (with Penaat), Kunstkring, Rotterdam; interiors at 1927 'Moderne Interieurs,' Stedelijk Museum. Organized 1919 traveling exhibition of Metz work throughout the Netherlands; 1935 and VANK exhibitions, Stedelijk Museum; 1939 'New York World's Fair.' Designed (with Arnold Pijpers and Leo Visser) 1928 'Hedendaagsche Huisinrichting' (Contemporary House Decoration), Enschede; VANK pavilion at 1932 (XXVI), Dept. of Economic stand at 1937 (XXXV), De Eland stand at 1938 (XXXVIII) annual exhibition Jaarbeurs, Utrecht.

▶ C. Brandes, 'Beschouwingen over binnenhuisarchitectuur en het werk van Paul Bromberg,' *Levende Kunst*, 1918:137–46. 'Inleiding tot de binnenhuiskunst van Paul Bromberg,' *Kunst in Arnhem*, No. 1, 1919:7,73–81. H.G. Cannegieter, 'Paul Bromberg,' *Morks Magazijn*, No. 39, 1937:280–94. Cat., *Industrie u Vormgeving in Nederland 1850–1950*, Amsterdam: Stedelijk Museum, 1985. Monique Teunissen, *Paul Bromberg: Binnenhuisarchitect en publicist 1893/1949*, Rotterdam: Uitgeverij 010, 1988.

Bromsgrove Guild of Applied Art

▶ British guild of crafts jewelers, located Bromsgrove, near Birmingham.

▶ Bromsgrove Guild of Applied Art was established in c1890 by Walter Gilbert, the sculptor, designer, and metalworker whose work was influenced by his better known cousin Alfred Gilbert. A number of Arts and Crafts designers worked for the Guild, including Benjamin Creswick, who had worked for A.H. Mackmurdo's Century Guild; Arthur Gaskin and his wife; and Joseph

A. Hodel, metalwork instructor at Liverpool School of Art and an established jewelry designer.

▶ Work shown at 1900 Paris 'Exposition Universelle.'

▶ Barbara J. Morrison, *Saga of the Guild of Decorative Art*, private press, 1969. Charlotte Gere, *American and European Jewelry 1830–1914*, New York: Crown, 1975:157. Cat., Alan Crawford, *By Hammer and Hand: The Arts and Crafts Movement in Birmingham*, Birmingham: Birmingham Museum and Art Gallery, 1984.

Bronzi, Francesco   (1934–)

▶ Italian designer; born Naples; active Rome.

▶ Bronzi began his professional career in 1968; became a member of ADI (Associazione per il Disegno Industriale). He designed furniture for clients including Dimension Design, Cooperativa 70, and Tarzia.

▶ *ADI Annual 1976*, Milan: Associazione per il Disegno Industriale, 1976.

Brookes and Adams

▶ British plastics manufacturer.

▶ Brookes and Adams introduced plastics for the first time in 1927, into lamps and lighting fixtures, using a substance called Bandalasta Ware. Marketed as 'both artistic and useful,' the shades and bases were molded from Bettle powders developed in Britain, which made it possible to create colorful forms, that in the case of the Bandalasta lamps created a warm glow. In the 1950s and 1960s, the firm produced plastic tableware and storage containers designed by Ronald Brookes.

▶ Jeremy Myerson and Sylvia Katz, *Conran Design Guides: Lamps and Lighting*, London: Conran Octopus, 1990:29.

Brouwer Jr., Theophilus Anthony   (?–1932)

▶ American ceramicist.

▶ Brouwer opened a small workshop known as Middle Lane Pottery in East Hampton, Long Island, New York; known for his luster and lusterless glazes, worked alone in throwing, turning, molding, and developing glaze technology. Characterized by surface iridescence and multiple color effects, his *Fire Painting* was the most famous of his five glazes. Brouwer, who was active as a painter, woodcarver, plaster modelmaker, and metalworker, built a new pottery in 1903 known as Brouwer Pottery in Westhampton, Long Island, where he perfected his *Flame* ware combining the five earlier glazes; he discontinued his ceramic work c1911 but continued to lecture and to sell his wares.

▶ Edwin AtLee Barber, *Marks of American Potters*, Philadelphia: Patterson and White, 1904:86. *American Art Pottery*, New York: Cooper-Hewitt Museum, 1987:72.

Brown, Barbara   (1932–)

▶ British textile and fashion designer.

▶ 1953–56 studied Canterbury College of Art and Royal College of Art, London.

▶ In bold Op-Art patterns, she executed a range of printed furnishing fabrics produced by Heal's in black and white, neutral, and narrow-ranged colors; taught at the Royal College of Art. As a consultant designer, she had clients in Britain, France, Italy, Germany, and the USA.

▶ Received 1968 and 1970 Council of Industrial Design awards (Heal's range).

▶ Cat., *Brown/Craven/Dodd: 3 Textile Designers*, Manchester: Whitworth Art Gallery, 1965:6–10. 'Furnishing Fabrics: Heal's Chevron, Complex and Extension,' *Design*, No. 233, May 1968:42–43. *Classics*, London: Heal and Son, Spring 1981: No. 119. Cat., Kathryn B. Hiesinger and George H. Marcus III (eds.), *Design Since 1945*, Philadelphia: Philadelphia Museum of Art, 1983.

Brown, Christopher   (aka Kit Brown)

▶ American furniture designer and maker.

▶ Active in upper New York State 1920–30, Brown made rustic furniture for E.A. Hoffman's Camp Hoff on the Lower St. Regis

Lake and for Margorie Merriweather Post at Camp Topridge (near Camp Hoff); worked in a rough-hewn style known today as Adirondack, named after the Adirondack Park in New York State. Brown's son James C. Brown also worked at the camp 1928–75.
► Craig Gilborn, *Adirondack Furniture and the Rustic Tradition*, New York: Abrams, 1987:317–18.

Brown, Eleanor McMillen (b. Eleanor Stockstrom 1890–1991)
► American interior decorator; born St. Louis, Missouri.
► Studied New York School of Fine and Applied Arts and Parsons School of Design, Paris, under William Odom.
► She began decorating in the office of Elsie Cobb Wilson; in her own studio developed the so-called McMillen Method of record-keeping. Clients included the Winthrop, Aldrich, Rockefeller, and Lorillard families; not afraid of making strong statements in her decorative schemes, she decorated the New York house of Mr. and Mrs. Henry Parish II in the late 1920s. Mrs. Parish (aka Sister Parish) later also became an interior decorator. Brown was a trustee of Parsons School and hired almost exclusively Parsons graduates. In 1926, she hired Grace Fakes and in the late 1930s Marian 'Tad' Morgan. Her firm became a training ground for young designers, including Nathalie Davenport, Mark Hampton, Kevin McNamara, and Albert Hadley. Her firm, McMillen, founded in the mid-1920s, is still in business, managed by Betty Sherrill.
► Mark Hampton, *House and Garden*, May 1990: 145–49,214. Mark Hampton, *Legendary Decorators of the Twentieth Century*, New York: Doubleday, 1992.

Brown, F. Gregory (1887–1948)
► British commercial artist and textile designer.
► Brown was apprenticed to an art metalworker in 1903 but turned from metalworking to illustration. As a commercial artist, his first important contact was from *TP's Weekly* and *TP's Magazine*. Brown's textile work, including his roller-printed 1931 *Leaping Deer with Hillocks and Trees*, was produced by William Foxton from 1920; his fabric designs, printed in black (a 1920s predilection) on linen, were published in the Design and Industries Association's yearbook *Design in Modern Industry*. His graphic-design clients included London and North East, Southern, and Great Western Railways, Mac Fisheries, Derry and Toms, Cadbury, Odhams Press, and Bobby's. In 1915, Brown became a founding member of the Design and Industries Association.
► Work shown at the Royal Academy in 1908. Foxton linen fabric designed by Brown received a gold medal for textiles at 1925 Paris 'Exposition Internationale des Arts Décoratifs et Industriels Modernes.'
► Cat., *Thirties: British art and design before the war*, London: Arts Council of Great Britain, Hayward Gallery, 1979:90,144, 216,286. *British Arts and Design, 1900–1960*, London: Victoria and Albert Museum, 1983. Jonathan M. Woodham, *Twentieth-Century Ornament*, New York: Rizzoli, 1990:107. Valerie Mendes, *The Victoria and Albert Museum's Textile Collection, British Textiles from 1900 to 1937*, London: Victoria and Albert Museum, 1992.

Brown, James C.
See Brown, Christopher

Brown, Tim (1962–)
► British industrial designer.
► Studied Newcastle upon Tyne Polytechnic and Royal College of Art, London.
► From 1987, he worked at Moggeridge Associates, London, where he designed office equipment and computer systems. Other designs included fax machines for Dancall, Sweden.
► Received Bursary Award (office-equipment designs), Royal Society of Arts.
► Albrecht Bangert and Karl Michael Armer, *80s Style: Designs of the Decade*, New York: Abbeville, 1990:228.

Brørby, Severin (1932–)
► Norwegian glassware designer.
► Studied Statens Handverks -og Kunstindustriskole, Oslo.
► Trained as an engraver, Brørby was a glassware designer at Hadelands Glassverk, Jevnaker, from 1956.
► Cat., David Revere McFadden (ed.), *Scandinavian Modern Design 1880–1980*, New York: Abrams, 1982:263. Fredrik Wildhagen, *Norge i Form*, Oslo: Stenersen, 1988:196.

Bruckmann und Söhne
► German silversmiths; located Heilbronn.
► Bruckmann und Söhne was founded in 1805; it trained its own designers, silversmiths, chasers, and engravers, and was the first firm of German silversmiths to introduce a steam engine in the 19th century, when it became that country's biggest silver factory. One of its founders, Peter Bruckmann, first president of the Deutscher Werkbund, produced the silver designs of leading German artists. Fritz Schmoll von Eisenwerth, while a teacher at the Debschitz-Schule in the 1910s, produced silver designs for the firm. Hans Christiansen's flatware design with abstract ornament and 1913 silverwork of Emanuel Josef Margold were produced by the firm. In 1923, Peter Bruckmann was succeeded by his son Dietrich, who had trained under Adolf von Mayrhofer at art school in Munich. 1924–27, Erna Zarges-Dürr was the first woman to work in its silversmiths' department. Greta Schröder and Paula Strauss produced silver designs there later. The firm closed in 1973.
► Wares were shown at 1910 Brussels 'Exposition Universelle et Internationale' by freelance artists Friedrich Adler, Franz Böres, et Friedrich Felger, Paul Haustein, Otto Rieth, Karl Wahl, and Bernhard Wenig, and staff designers Adolf Amberg, Hélène Brandt, Josef Lock, Karl Stock, and Karl Zeller.
► *Die Goldschmiedekunst*, 1911:18–26. Annelies Krekel-Aalberse, *Art Nouveau and Art Déco Silver*, New York: Abrams, 1989:131,133,134,135,139,252. Cat., *Metallkunst*, Berlin: Bröhan Museum, 1990:60–90.

Bruel, André (1895–)
► French bookbinder; born Saint-Sylvain d'Anjou.
► Studied Algiers and, from 1912, École Normale Supérieure.
► He worked for the bookbinder Légal in Algiers before setting up his own bindery in 1919; became one of the few provincial binders of renown. Usually in morocco or calf, his bindings featured heavy encrustations of metal and stones with colorful inlaid leathers. His covers included *Vie des martyrs*, *Le Feu*, and *Les Droits de l'homme et du citoyen*.
► Bindings shown at annual Paris Salons in the 1920s and at 1922 bookbinding exhibition, Galerie Reitlinger, Paris, and 1925 Paris 'Exposition Internationale des Arts Décoratifs et Industriels Modernes.' Work subject of 1927 exhibition, Galerie André, Paris.
► Ernest de Crauzat, *La Reliure française de 1900 à 1925*, Vol. 2, Paris, 1932:67–70. Gaston Derys, 'André Bruel,' *Mobilier et décoration*, Sept. 1932:410–13. Alastair Duncan and Georges de Bartha, *Art Nouveau and Art Déco Bookbinding*, New York: Abrams, 1989:18,60,188.

Brüel, Axel (1900–77)
► Danish ceramicist.
► 1928–56, Brüel produced ceramics in his own workshop; in 1956, became art consultant to porcelain manufacturer Denmark; used newer materials and techniques in his work, including heat-resistant cookware. The absence of handles on his 1957 *Thermodan* coffee service was practical thanks to its double-wall design.
► *Thermodan* shown at 1957 (XI) Triennale di Milano.
► Arne Karlsen, *Made in Denmark*, New York, 1960:64–71. Cat., Kathryn B. Hiesinger and George H. Marcus III (eds.), *Design Since 1945*, Philadelphia: Philadelphia Museum of Art, 1983.

Brukskunst
► Norwegian trade and art association.
► The purpose of the Brukskunst (Useful Art) was to produce practical and beautiful objects for everyday use by the masses. Its formation was inspired by the Deutscher Werkbund and other reform movements in Sweden and Britain. Its first exhibition was the 1920 'New Homes.' The movement faded out by the mid-1920s.
► Fredrik Wildhagen, *Norge i Form*, Oslo: Stenersen, 1988:76.

Brummer, Arttu   (1891–1951)
► Finnish interior and glassware designer.
► Brummer set up his own interior-design office in 1913; taught heraldry, composition, and furniture design, Taideteollinen Korkeakoulu, Helsinki, where he was director 1944–51; was a designer for the Riihimäki glassworks; in the 1930s, was editor of *Domus*, Milan; became chair of the Finnish association of designers ORNAMO and member of the administrative board of the Finnish Industrial Design Association and board of the Friends of Finnish Handicraft.
► Received a first prize at 1932 Karhula glass competition, and diploma of honor at 1937 Paris 'Exposition Internationale des Arts et Techniques dans la Vie Moderne.'
► Cat., *The Modern Spirit: Glass from Finland*, Riihimäki: The Finnish Glass Museum, 1985:38. Cat., David Revere McFadden (ed.), *Scandinavian Modern Design 1880–1980*, New York: Abrams, 1982:263.

Brummer, Eva   (1901–)
► Finnish textile designer.
► 1925 studied Taideteollisuuskeskuskoulu, Helsinki.
► She set up her own studio in 1929 with the intention of reviving traditional Finnish *rya* (or *ryijy*), a thick hand-knotted textile; at first, incorporated bright-colored, later more subdued, yarns into an unevenly cut pile, creating a relief; was associated throughout her career with the Friends of Finnish Handicraft.
► Received 1951 (IX) grand prize, 1954 (X) diploma of honor, and 1957 (XI) gold medal at Triennali di Milano.
► Oili Mäki (ed.), *Finnish Designers of Today*, Helsinki, 1954:14–18. Erik Zahle (ed.), *A Treasury of Scandinavian Design*, New York, 1961:270: No. 188. Anja Louhio, *Modern Finnish Rugs*, Helsinki, 1975:42–45. Cat., Kathryn B. Hiesinger and George H. Marcus III (eds.), *Design Since 1945*, Philadelphia: Philadelphia Museum of Art, 1983.

Brunati, Mario   (1931–)
► Italian designer; born and active Milan.
► He began his professional career in 1958; became a member of ADI (Associazione per il Disegno Industriale); had clients including Sormani from 1965, Moulton (bicycles) from 1960, Biotrading (packaging) in 1960, Avilla (furniture) from 1969.
► *ADI Annual 1976*, Milan: Associazione per il Disegno Industriale, 1976.

Bruni, Tat'iana Georgievna   (1902–)
► Russian stage designer.
► 1918–20, studied School of the Association for the Encouragement of the Arts, Petrograd (now St. Petersburg); 1920–26, Vkhutein, Petrograd/Leningrad, under O. Braz and N. Radlow.
► She produced her first stage designs in 1923; from 1927, participated in various exhibitions.
► Cat., *Kunst und Revolution: Russische und Sowjetische Kunst 1910–1932*, Vienna: Österreichisches Museum für angewandte Kunst, 1988. Cat., *The Great Utopia: The Russian and Soviet Avant-Garde, 1915–1932*, New York: Guggenheim Museum, 1992.

Brunner, Vratislav Hugo   (1886–1928)
► Czech designer and teacher, born Prague.
► 1903–06, studied Academy of Fine Arts, Prague, under V. Bukovac and M. Priner, and in Munich.
► In 1908, he became a member of Mánes Association of Plastic Artists; in 1908, became a co-founder of Artěl Cooperative and was a principal designer for toys, painted gingerbreads, souvenirs, painted glass, and other items there; in 1911, left Mánes and became an executive of newly formed Group of Plastic Artists; in 1912, studied in Leipzig, resigned from the Group and returned to Mánes; from 1919, was professor, School of Decorative Arts, Prague, becoming rector there in 1928; was active as a book designer for Kamila Neumannova's imprint Books by Good Authors, K.H. Hilar, and particularly for Aventinum; was an illustrator of magazines.
► Received grand prize and gold medal for book designs at 1925 Paris 'Exposition Internationale des Arts Décoratifs et Industriels Modernes.'
► Alexander von Vegesack et al., *Czech Cubism: Architecture, Furniture, and Decorative Arts, 1910–1925*, New York: Princeton Architectural Press, 1992.

Bryere, Joseph O.A.   (1860–1941)
► American furniture designer and maker, camp builder, carpenter, and tourist guide; born Quebec.
► Bryere first visited Raquette Lake, New York State, in *c*1880, and later settled there; 1883–86, was employed by Charles Durant as a carpenter and caretaker at Camp Fairview; 1886–90, worked at the camp of the Stott family on Bluff point; during the later 1880s, began building hotel Brightside-on-Raquette, Raquette Lake; in addition to being a carpenter, camp builder, and tourist guide, was a furniture designer and maker in a rough-hewn style known today as Adirondack, named after the Adirondack Park, New York State.
► Craig Gilborn, *Adirondack Furniture and the Rustic Tradition*, New York: Abrams, 1987:318.

Bryk, Rut   (1916–)
► Swedish ceramicist and graphic and textile designer.
► 1939, studied graphic design, Taideteollinen Korkeakoulu, Helsinki.
► In 1942, she worked for the pottery Arabia, Helsinki; from 1959, was freelance ceramics designer, Rosenthal, Selb; from 1960s, worked for Vassa Cotton Company.
► Received grand prize at 1951 (IX) Triennale and diploma of honor at its 1954 (X) session and 1968 Pro Finlandia Prize. In 1980, became the first Finnish woman to receive Order of Commandeur dans l'Ordre des Arts et des Lettres from the French Ministry of Culture and Communication. Work included in 1957 (XI) and 1960 (XII) Triennali di Milano and 1954–57 USA 'Design in Scandinavia.'
► Cat., David Revere McFadden (ed.), *Scandinavian Modern Design 1880–1980*, New York: Abrams, 1982:263. Jennifer Hawkins Opie, *Scandinavia: Ceramics and Glass in the Twentieth Century*, New York: Rizzoli, 1989.

Buadottir, Asgerdur Ester   (1920–)
► Icelandic textile designer.
► Work shown in international exhibitions. Received numerous awards.
► Cat., David Revere McFadden (ed.), *Scandinavian Modern Design 1880–1980*, New York: Abrams, 1982:263.

Buatta, Mario   (1936–)
► American interior designer; active New York.
► With an office in New York, Buatta (with Mark Hampton) designed the interiors of Blair House, Washington, America's government guest-house for visiting dignitaries. With décors that evoked 19th-century English interiors with their extensive use of flowered coated fabrics, he was dubbed 'Prince of Chintz.' His 1990 furniture collection was made by John Widdicomb; other clients for mass production goods included Fabriyaz (fabric), Revman Industries (bed linens), Thimbelina (needlepoint), Imperial-Sterlin (wallpaper), Aromatique (home fragrance), Sunweave/Vera Division (table linens), Frederick Cooper (lighting), Shyam Ahuja and Tianjin-Philadelphia Carpet (carpets), Framed Picture Enterprise (pictures).

Bücherer

▶ Swiss jeweler and clockmaker.

▶ Carl-Friedrich Bücherer opened a jewelry and clockmaker's shop in Lucerne in 1888. His son Carl was a jeweler; the other, Ernst, a clockmaker. Ernst was responsible for the international expansion of the firm in the 1930s. In the early 1950s, Ernst acquired a clockmaker's workshop in Bienne. Bücherer came to be second only to Rolex as the largest Swiss manufacturer of time-pieces. Carl's son Joerg Bücherer manages the firm today.

▶ Melissa Gabardi, *Les Bijoux des Années 50*, Paris: Amateur Somogy, 1987.

Bûcheron, Le

See Sylve, Le

Buckland, Wilfred

▶ American film set designer.

▶ Hired by Cecil B. De Mille, Buckland was the first stage designer to work in films. His glamorous bathroom set in De Mille's *Male and Female* (1919) featured Charles Ray's cut-glass bathtub for actress Gloria Swanson and was publicized as having cost $75,000. De Mille called Buckland 'the first man of a recognized ability to forsake the theater for the motion picture, and to him are attributed the first consistent and well-designed motion picture sets. He brought to the screen a knowledge of mood and a dramatic quality which until then had been totally lacking.'

▶ Howard Mandelbaun and Eric Myers, *Screen Deco: A Celebration of High Style in Hollywood*, New York: St. Martin's, 1985.

Bückling, Peer

▶ German designer.

▶ 1928, studied Bauhaus, Dessau.

▶ His 1928 wood chair produced at the Bauhaus furniture workshop, Dessau, had innovative L-shaped legs. Often attributed to Hannes Meyer, the chair was an attempt to create lightness with strength. Inexpensive, resilient, and easy to carry, it represents one of the first uses of plywood construction at the Bauhaus.

▶ Cat., *The Bauhaus: Masters and Students*, New York: Barry Friedman, 1988.

Bugatti, Carlo (1855–1940)

▶ Italian designer and maker of furniture; born and active Milan; father of Rembrandt Bugatti and Ettore Bugatti.

▶ Studied Accademia di Belle Arti di Brera, Milan.

▶ Bugatti worked most of his life in Milan; was active in several fields but best known as designer and maker of bizarre furnishings; later denied that he studied at Brera Academy in an attempt, some suggest, to present himself as self-taught; in 1880, designed his earliest known furniture for the marriage of his sister Luiga to artist Giovanni Segantini. His proto-Futuristic furniture of the 1880s shows influences from the fashionable Moorish and Japanese styles of the day. Breaking with traditional concepts of furniture, his often asymmetrical work was covered with parchment (sometimes painted), leather, metal inlays, beaten-copper plaques, dangling tassels, and exposed tacks. In 1900, he supplied furniture for the Khedive's palace, Istanbul; designed a room in *c*1901 in the house of Cyril Flowers, first Lord Battersea, in London. The Flowers room was something of a rarity, being a complete ensemble and décor treatment. In the 1890s, Bugatti turned from picturesque asymmetry towards more balanced geometrical shapes, culminating in his most notable achievement, the extravagant Snail Room installed with its site-specific furniture at the 1902 Turin exhibition, in which he combined rich inlaid and veneered woods, pewter and other metals, gilded and colored vellum, and formalized designs of birds, insects, and flowers. In 1904, he sold his furniture business to the firm De Becchi, Milan, and moved to Paris, where his last design work included silverware. The silver was cast and chased by the craftsmen of A.A. Hébrard, Paris, where he also exhibited them. He was mainly a painter in Paris. Bugatti's sons were successful in their own right, Rembrandt Bugatti as an *animalier* sculptor and Ettore (1881–1947) as painter and automobile designer. Carlo Bugatti's work

was rediscovered in the late 1960s and 1970s by show-business personalities wishing to furnish their residences eccentrically, although his furnishings have less impact out of their original designed context. Jean Bugatti (1909–39), like his father Ettore, was a sports and luxury automobile designer.

▶ Furniture group shown at 1888 Italian Exhibition at Earl's Court, London, 1898 Turin exhibition, and 1900 Paris 'Exposition Universelle.' Paintings and some furniture shown at 1907 Salon des Peintres Divisionistes, Paris. 'Snail Room' received a first prize at 1902 Turin 'Esposizione Internazionale d'Arte Decorativa Moderna.' Work subject of 1976 exhibition, Emporio Floreale, Rome, and 1983 exhibition, Hamburg.

▶ V. Rossi-Sacchetti, *Rembrandt Bugatti, Sculpteur, Carlo Bugatti et son Art*, Paris, 1907. L'Ebé Bugatti, *The Bugatti Story*, London, 1967. Simon Jervis, 'Carlo Bugatti,' *Arte Illustrata*, No. 3, 1970:80–87. Yvonne Brunhammer et al., *Art Nouveau Belgium, France*, Houston: Rice University, 1976, biblio. Cat., *Bugatti*, Rome: Emporio Floreale, 1976. Philippe Garner et al., *The Amazing Bugattis*, London: Design Council, 1979:12–30. Philippe De Jean, *Carlo—Rembrandt—Ettore—Jean Bugatti*, Paris: Regard, 1981:23–117. Cat., *Die Bugatti*, Hamburg, 1983. Jessica Rutherford, *Art Nouveau, Art Deco and the Thirties: The Furniture Collections at Brighton Museum*, Brighton: The Royal Pavilion, Art Gallery and Museums, 1983:27. Stephen Calloway, *Twentieth-Century Decoration*, New York: Rizzoli, 1988:78–79.

Bulgari, Sotirio (1857–1932)

▶ Greek jeweler; born Paramythia.

▶ Bulgari established himself in Rome in 1881, selling rings and modest jewels from a stall in front of the Academy of France building; after several years, was able to open a small shop not far from the present-day flagship store that was considerably enlarged in 1934. His sons Constantino and Giorgio joined the firm in 1889 and 1890 respectively; Constantino wrote *Argentieri, gemmari e orafi d'Italia*. Bugari is still a family-owned business, with branches worldwide.

▶ Melissa Gabardi, *Les Bijoux des Années 50*, Paris: Amateur, 1987. Charlotte Gere, *American and European Jewelry 1830–1914*, New York: Crown, 1975:158.

Bull

▶ French electronics firm.

▶ Bull was founded in 1933; became the first firm to make an electronic calculator, *Gamma 3*, in 1964, was amalgamated into General Electric; became part of the International CII group; in 1970, was sold to Honeywell; became a data-processing group. It designed, developed, produced, and marketed a full range of equipment and services.

Bülow-Hübe, Torun Vivianna (1927–)

▶ Swedish designer.

▶ Studied Konstfackskolan and Tekniska Skolan, Stockholm.

▶ 1951–56, she worked in her own studio in Stockholm; concentrated on wooden jewelry; in 1951, was commissioned by Orrefors to create silver jewelry; from 1967, collaborated in a business with Georg Jensen Sølvesmedie, for which she produced prototypes for jewelry and watches in gold, silver, and stainless steel; created porcelain and ceramics for Hutschenreuther and glassware for Glashütte Löhnberg; 1969–77, collaborated with Argentine sculptor Rainer Gualterio Anz; moving to Jakarta in 1978, became a diversified designer of a wide range of products including kitchen utensils, textiles, baskets, lamps, and office equipment.

▶ Received a silver medal at 1954 (X) and gold medal at 1960 (XII) Triennali di Milano. Received 1960 Lunning Prize and 1965 Swedish State's Grand Prix for Artists. In 1983, named 'Honorary Smith,' Association of Contemporary Swedish Silversmiths, Stockholm.

▶ Cat., *Georg Jensen Silversmithy: 77 Artists, 75 Years*, Washington: Smithsonian Institution Press, 1980. Cat., *The Lunning Prize*, Stockholm: Nationalmuseum, 1986:112–15.

Bunnell, Harry C.
▶ American furniture designer and maker; active Westport, New York.
▶ Bunnell began making chairs in c1904 in his own design for the porch and lawn, produced in a shop behind his house in Westport, New York. The chair had raked back and seat and wide, horizontal arms. He patented the original model, which became known as the *Westport* chair, along with at least four other versions that he designed and made up to c1925.
▶ Coy L. Ludwig, *The Arts and Crafts Movement in New York State 1890s–1920s*, Hamilton, New York: Gallery Association of New York State, 1983:31. Craig Gilborn, *Adirondack Furniture and the Rustic Tradition*, New York: Abrams, 1987:319.

Bunshaft, Gordon   (1909–90)
▶ American architect; born Buffalo, New York.
▶ Studied Massachusetts Institute of Technology, Cambridge, Massachusetts.
▶ Bunshaft joined the architecture firm Skidmore, Owings and Merrill, with which he was associated throughout his working life, when it opened its New York office in 1937. He was senior designer for the Venezuelan Pavilion at the 1939 'New York World's Fair.' His most successful buildings were corporate headquarters, including the 1952 Lever House and 1960 Pepsi-Cola Building, New York, 1960 Union Carbide Building, 1965 American Republic Life Building, Des Moines, and 1967 Marine Midland Building, New York. Known as an International Style architect, his buildings demanded compatible interior design; he was instrumental in creating a demand for the interiors that Florence Knoll of Knoll International executed for the firm. She and he established a powerful integrated design approach that became a standard and was widely imitated from the late 1950s onwards. The Functional approach to planning reached a peak with the 1960 Union Carbide Building, with interiors fully integrated with the external design. The office and its furnishings perfectly reflected the power of a major multinational corporation. The landscape-office layout demanded special furniture flexible enough to provide different design solutions for every office, while being mass-produced. Herman-Miller's designer Robert Probst solved the problem with the 1962 *Action Office 2*. Bunshaft was instrumental in changing the postwar skyline of cities worldwide. He also established a new style for suburban corporate campuses with long, low-profile buildings that clung to the landscape, such as the 1957 Connecticut General headquarters and 1963 Emhart, both near Hartford, Connecticut; 1958 Reynolds Metals in Richmond, Virginia; 1964 IBM in Armonk, New York; and 1970 American Can in Greenwich, Connecticut. His major institutional commissions included the 1962 Albright-Knox Gallery in Buffalo, New York; 1963 Beinecke Library at Yale University in New Haven, Connecticut; 1971 Lyndon B. Johnson Library in Austin, Texas; and 1974 Hirshhorn Museum in Washington, DC. His 'sky-slope' buildings in New York in the 1970s were not critically successful. The 1983 Haj Terminal and National Commercial Bank in Jeddah, completed after his retirement in 1979, restored his reputation somewhat, though his critical standing was low in the late stages of his career; not until 1988, a year before his death, was a monograph published on his work.
▶ Received 1988 Pritzker Prize (shared with Oscar Niemeyer), 1984 gold medal from American Academy of Arts and Letters, 12 American Institute of Architects Honor Awards for his buildings ranging from the 1952 Lever House to the 1983 National Commercial Bank in Jeddah.
▶ Carol Herselle Krinsky, *Gordon Bunshaft of Skidmore, Owings and Merrill*, Cambridge, MA: The Architectural History Foundations, 1988.

Burbidge, Pauline   (1950–)
▶ British designer; born Dorset.
▶ Studied Yeovil Technical College, London College of Fashion, and St. Martin's School of Art, London.

▶ She began designing clothes in 1972 for a small London firm, in which she was a partner 1973–76; began making quilts, including 1984–85 patchwork wall-hangings *Circular Series*; received awards; wrote; taught; became a consultant designer.
▶ Robert A.M. Stern (ed.), *The International Design Yearbook*, New York: Abbeville, 1985/1986: Nos. 362–65. Albrecht Bangert and Karl Michael Armer, *80s Style: Designs of the Decade*, New York: Abbeville, 1990:160,228.

Burckhardt, Ernst F.   (1900–58)
▶ Swiss architect; born Zürich; active Zürich and Britain.
▶ 1920–24, studied architecture, London.
▶ Burckhardt worked in 1923 in architecture office Gebruder Pfister, Zürich; 1922–24, designed theatre sets for two productions at the University of London, was active as set designer. His writings on theater architecture were numerous. In 1931, he was head of the Krater cabaret, Zürich; in 1924, set up an architecture practice, Zürich; in 1931, designed the first interiors for the Wohnbedarf department store, Zürich; in 1934, designed the renovation of the Corso theater, Zürich. He wrote for the *Neue Zürcher Zeitung* (1937); in 1944, began to contribute to the journal *Plan*, of which he was editor 1946–52. His buildings included the 1950 Zürcher Volkstheater and 1956 university theater, Durban. He designed exhibition buildings at the 1939 'Landesausstellung,' Zürich, and 1940 Triennale di Milano.
▶ In 1957, he and wife Elsa Burckhardt-Blum received honors for their work in the city of Zürich.
▶ *Schweizerische Bauzeitung*, 1958/42:633ff; 49:745ff. *Künstler-Lexikon der Schweiz, XX. Jahrhundert*, Frauenfeld, 1963–67, Vol. 1. Cat., *Um 1930 in Zürich*, Kunstgewerbemuseum der Stadt Zürich, 1977. Friederike Mehlau-Wiebking et al., *Schweizer Typenmöbel 1925–35, Sigfried Giedion und die Wohnbedarf AG*, Zürich: gta, 1989.

Bureau, Louis
▶ French decorator and furniture designer.
▶ In 1913, Michel Dufet established the decorating firm MAM (Mobilier Artistique Moderne), where Bureau was a designer. Subsequently, Bureau designed furniture produced by Guerin.
▶ *Ensembles Mobiliers*, Vol. II, Paris: Charles Moreau, 1937.

Burges, William   (1827–81)
▶ British architect, antiquary, and designer.
▶ Articled to the architect Edward Blore.
▶ He joined the office of architect Matthew Digby Wyatt in 1849; a friend of the Pre-Raphaelite painters, he became one of the most important Gothic-revival architects of the mid-19th century. Based on the French Gothic style of the 13th century, his work was based on a scholarly knowledge of the period; his interest in the arts of non-industrial cultures and his use of opium may have contributed to his style. The house he built for himself in London, the design for St. Finbar's Cathedral in Cork, and commissions from Lord Bute (the Cardiff Castle restoration, Castell Coch, and neo-Gothic marriage jewelry) reflected his wide interests in Gothic and French Renaissance architecture, antique metalwork and jewelry, archeology, and Indian and Japanese art. As early as 1858, he designed painted architectonic furniture with complex motifs. One piece of furniture showed his pet dogs. He designed stained glass, metalwork, ceramics, textiles, and jewelry. His jewelry was Gothic-inspired, apart from an Etruscan-style necklace and earrings. His article 'Antique Jewellery and its Revival' in *Gentleman's Magazine and Historical Review* (1862) showed his interest in Fortunato Piò Castellani's research into antique techniques. He designed metalwork, and possibly jewelry, for Hardman and Co; 1870–74, produced designs for wallpapers by Jeffrey and Co, some of which reached the USA, including in the late-1870s George Peabody Wetmore mansion in Newport, Rhode Island. He was one of the first in Britain to collect Japanese prints after seeing an 1862 exhibition of them in London. By the mid-1870s, his medievalism left him outside the architectural mainstream. Architecture included 1855 winning designs for Lille

Cathedral (unrealized); 1856 Crimea Memorial Church, Constantinople (now Istanbul) (unrealized); 1863 cathedral of St. Finbar Cork, Ireland; 1865 restoration of Cardiff Castle; 1875 Castell Coch, Wales; his own 1875–81 residence, London; and part of the 1874 commission to design Trinity College, Hartford, Connecticut.
▶ Furniture displayed at the Medieval Court, London 'International Exhibition of 1862.' Work included in 1986–87 'In Pursuit of Beauty' exhibition, New York Metropolitan Museum of Art.
▶ William Burges, *Art Applied to Industry*, Oxford and London, 1865. Charlotte Gere, *American and European Jewelry 1830–1914*, New York: Crown, 1975:158–59. J. Mordaunt Crook, *William Burges and the High Victorian Dream*, Chicago and London, 1981. Cat., Clive Wainwright and Charlotte Gere, *Architect Designers: Pugin to Mackintosh*, London: Fine Art Society, 1981. Doreen Bolger Burke et al., *In Pursuit of Beauty: Americans and the Aesthetic Movement*, New York: Metropolitan Museum of Art and Rizzoli, 1986:405–06, biblio.

Burgess, Paul (1961–)
▶ British designer, born Swindon.
▶ Studied print textiles, Camberwell School of Art and Royal College of Art, London.
▶ He executed textile collections for Extravert and Extetique/Amescote, one-off print designs, and window displays for the Next clothing chain.
▶ Received 1986 Drapers Record Award, 'Texprint 86' exhibition, London.
▶ Albrecht Bangert and Karl Michael Armer, *80s Style: Designs of the Decade*, New York: Abbeville, 1990:184,228.

Burkhalter, Jean (1895–1984)
▶ French furniture designer, painter, decorator, and ceramicist; born Auxerre.
▶ 1916–19, studied École Nationale des Arts Décoratifs, Paris.
▶ He designed furniture in metal and bent-metal tubing, often nickel plated; rendered furniture designs and prototypes for Primavera decorating studio of the Au Printemps department store, Paris; collaborated with Pierre Chareau and Robert Mallet-Stevens; employed new materials, including painted and chromed tubular steel, enameled sheet metal, and bakelite, in his furniture; designed ceramics produced by the Manufacture Nationale de Sèvres, silver accessories by Hénin, rugs and fabrics by the Boutique Pierre Chareau, furniture for the Maison de Verre (Pierre Chareau and Bernard Bijvöet, architects); in 1929, became a founding member of UAM (Union des Artistes Modernes), exhibiting at its events until 1937; collaborated with Jan and brother-in-law Joël Martel on 1932 monument to Claude Debussy; in 1935, became director of École Municipale des Arts Décoratifs, Auxerre, and, in 1946, of École Nationale des Arts Décoratifs, Limoges. His work was marketed by Les Fleurs de Nice and Primavera.
▶ From 1919, showed rugs, fabrics, enameled metal and goldwork, posters, bibelots, and tubular-steel furniture at Salons des Artistes Décorateurs. Designed dining room and domestic items, was a member of the jury of judges, received a grand prize at 1925 Paris 'Exposition Internationale des Arts Décoratfis et Industriels Modernes' and (with Joël and Jan Martel) designed the fountain of the commissariat of tourism there. Until 1937, showed at expositions of UAM, including ceramics and glassware in the UAM pavilion, 1937 Paris 'Exposition Internationale des Arts et Techniques dans la Vie Moderne.' Received 1924 Prix Blumenthal.
▶ Léon Moussinac, 'Jean Burkhalter,' *Art et Décoration*, Vol. LVII, 1930. Yvonne Brunhammer, *Le Cinquantenaire de l'exposition de 1925*, Paris: Musée des Arts Décoratifs, 1976:120. Pierre Cabanne, *Encyclopédie Art Déco*, Paris: Somogy, 1986:179. Pierre Kjellberg, *Art Déco: les maîtres du Mobilier, le décor des Paquebots*, Paris: Amateur, 1986:39–40. Arlette Barré-Despond, *UAM*, Paris: Regard, 1986. Cat., *Les années UAM 1929–1958*, Paris: Musée des Arts Décoratifs, 1988:156–57.

Burne-Jones, Edward (1838–1898)
▶ British artist and designer.
▶ Studied divinity, Oxford University, to 1856.
▶ With his friend William Morris, whom he met at Oxford, he discovered art, architecture, poetry, and the writings of John Ruskin and Thomas Carlyle. In 1856, Burne-Jones studied painting under Dante Gabriel Rossetti; he and Morris shared a house from 1856 until Morris's marriage to Jane Burden in 1859. In 1859, Philip Webb, Morris, Burne-Jones collaborated on much of the furniture for Morris's Red House, Bexleyheath, Kent, whose architect was Webb. In 1861, Burne-Jones became a partner with Webb, Rossetti, and Ford Madox Brown in the firm Marshall, Faulkner and Company. The firm's early commissions for stained-glass windows were designed by Marshall, Rossetti, Brown, Webb, Morris, and Burne-Jones. Morris taught embroidery to Burne-Jones's wife Georgiana, who later took charge of the firm's embroidery workshop. By the mid-1870s, the firm was in financial trouble; Morris bought his out his fellow partners and reorganized the firm as Morris and Company. Burne-Jones continued to work for Morris, designing the figurative tapestries produced by the firm. In 1883, John Ruskin commissioned Burne-Jones to execute designs for the Whitelands College cross medal. Burne-Jones's jewelry sketches showed delicate bird and leaf designs; the jewelry he designed for his wife and daughter was produced by Child and Child, London, or by Giuliano.
▶ Work shown at 1986–87 'In Pursuit of Beauty' exhibition, New York Metropolitan Museum of Art.
▶ Georgina Burne-Jones, *Memorials of Edward Burne-Jones*, London: Macmillan, 1904. Penelope Fitzgerald, *Edward Burne-Jones: A Biography*, London: Michael Joseph, 1975. Martin Harrison and Bill Walters, *Burne-Jones*, London: Barrie and Jenkins, 1973. Charlotte Gere, *American and European Jewelry 1830–1914*, New York: Crown, 1975:159. Doreen Bolger Burke et al., *In Pursuit of Beauty: Americans and the Aesthetic Movement*, New York: Metropolitan Museum of Art and Rizzoli, 1986: 455–56.

Burns, Mark A. (1950–)
▶ American ceramicist; born Springfield, Ohio.
▶ Studied with Howard Kottler and Patti Warashina, Dayton Art Institution, Dayton, Ohio, to 1972 and University of Washington in Seattle to 1974.
▶ Auction cat., 'Contemporary Works of Art,' Sotheby's New York, 14 March 1992.

Burri, Werner (1898–1972)
▶ Swiss ceramicist.
▶ 1921–25, studied Bauhaus, Weimar.
▶ 1928–31, he was head of design at ceramics firm Velten-Vordamm; 1932–33, worked in the workshop of Marcel Noverraz, Geneva; 1934–39, occasionally worked with HB-Werkstätten of Hedwig Bollhagen, Harwitz (Germany); 1961–63, taught at Keramische Fachschule, Bern.
▶ Cat., *The Bauhaus: Masters and Students*, New York: Barry Friedman, 1988. Cat., *Keramik und Bauhaus*, Berlin: Bauhaus-Archiv, 1989:262.

Burton, Scott (1939–89)
▶ American sculptor; born Greensboro, Alabama; active New York.
▶ 1957–59, studied painting, Leon Berkowitz, Washington, DC, and Hans Hofmann, Provincetown, Massachusetts; received bachelor's degree, Columbia University, New York, 1962, and master's degree, New York University, 1963.
▶ He worked for a time on the staff of the magazine *Art in America*; was considered a fine artist, and produced perfect sculpture that was indistinguishable from furniture in a variety of materials (stone, wood, metal plastic); produced 1972–75 *Bronze Chair* (a cast-bronze of a real Queen Anne-style chair), his first work, and 1976 *Lawn Chair* (an Adirondack-type chair), his first original chair design.

▶ Work shown first as a performance in 1971 'Eighteen Pieces,' Finch College, New York, with numerous exhibitions internationally following.

▶ Charles F. Stuckey, *Scott Burton Chairs*, Cleveland: Cleveland Art Center, Fort Worth: Forth Worth Art Museum, 1983. Brenda Richardson, *Scott Burton*, Baltimore: Baltimore Museum of Art, 1986. Jiri Svestka (ed.), *Scott Burton*, Düsseldorf: Kunstverein für die Rheinlande und Westfalen, 1989.

Burylin, Sergei Petrovich (1876–1942)
▶ Russian designer.
▶ From 1893, Burylin worked at Voznesenskii Textile Mill, Ivanovo-Vosnesensk; until 1930, was a designer at N. Zhiderev Factory, Ivanovo-Vosnesensk, and a textile designer for various textile mills. His widely published 1930 *Tractor* cotton printed fabric was produced in Ivanovo-Vosnesensk.
▶ Cat., *Kunst und Revolution: Russische und Sowjetische Kunst 1910–1932*, Vienna: Österreichisches Museum für angewandte Kunst, 1988. Jonathan M. Woodham, *Twentieth-Century Ornament*, New York: Rizzoli, 1990:119. Cat., *The Great Utopia: The Russian and Soviet Avant-Garde, 1915–1932*, New York: Guggenheim Museum, 1992.

Burzio, Alberto
See Arflex

Bush, Robin
▶ Canadian designer; active Toronto.
▶ He established Robin Bush Design Associates, Toronto. Its 1963 *Lollipop* tandem steel seating system was produced by the Canadian Office and School Furniture, Preston, Ontario, for the Lester B. Pearson International Airport, Toronto. In the 1960s, the firm's employees included Douglas Ball and Thomas Lamb.
▶ Cat., *Seduced and Abandoned: Modern Furniture designers in Canada, the First Fifty Years*, Toronto: The Art Gallery at Harbourfront, 1986.

Bush-Brown, Lydia (1887–)
▶ American textile artist; born Florence (Italy).
▶ Studied Pratt Institute, Brooklyn, New York.
▶ Middle Eastern crafts influenced her work; with images of trees (a favorite), abstract figures, animals, and natural forms, she called her wallhangings 'silk murals.'
▶ 'Modernistic Wall Hangings,' *Good Furniture Magazine*, Aug. 1928:108. Karen Davies, *At Home in Manhattan: Modern Decorative Arts, 1925 to the Depression*, New Haven: Yale, 1983:43.

Busnelli, Gruppo Industriale
▶ Italian furniture manufacturer; located Misinto.
▶ Busnelli specializes in upholstered furniture; began using plastics in its production in 1969; produced the *Zen* table and *Non-Stop* seat.
▶ Work shown at numerous exhibitions.
▶ Cat., Milena Lamarová, *Design a Plastické Hmoty*, Prague: Uměleckoprůmyslové Muzeum, 1972:172:176.
▶ See B&B Italia

Busquet, Édouard-Wilfrid
▶ French lighting designer.
▶ Busquet designed the original 1925 *Anglepoise* lamp, patented in 1927. (Its designer was unknown until the research of Eric Philippe in the 1970s.) It became one of the most practical and popular lighting fixtures of the period and was used by architects and interior designers including Marcel Breuer, Louis Sognot, Maurice Barret, Joubert and Petit, Lucien Rollin, Suzanne Guiguichon, Marcel Coard, and Jean Sedlak. The lamp was widely published in French periodicals 1938–39 without crediting the designer. Busquet's lamps were handmade to different specifications.
▶ Alastair Duncan, *Art Nouveau and Art Déco Lighting*, New York: Simon and Schuster, 1978:147. Cat., Aaron Lederfajn and Xavier Lenormand, *Le Louvre des Antiquaires présente: 1930 quand le meuble devient sculpture*, Paris, 1986.

Buthaud, René (1886–1987)
▶ French ceramicist; born Saintes.
▶ Studied École des Beaux-Arts, Bordeaux, and painting and gravure in Paris.
▶ Buthaud is considered by many to be the finest ceramicist of the Art Moderne period; in 1918, encouraged by Jean Dupas and Roger Bissiere, became a ceramicist; in 1923, set up ceramics factory Primavera, Sainte-Radegonde; developed a technique for a cracked-glaze surface; returned to Bordeaux and set up his own workshop. Maison Rouard in Paris was his primary sales outlet. He worked mostly in stoneware and faïence; treated his ceramic surfaces as a canvas; his most important commissions, in 1937, were for four monumental vases for Bordeaux Parc des Sports designed by Jacques d'Welles, and bas-reliefs of the Four Seasons for Bouscat town hall. In later years, he drew and painted on mirror-glass.
▶ Received grand prize, 1914 Prix de Rome, for gravure. Work shown in numerous exhibitions, including Salons of the Société des Artistes français from 1911; Salons d'Automne 1920–29; Salons of the Société des Artistes Décorateurs from 1920; 1925 'Exposition Internationale des Arts Décoratifs et Industriels Modernes'; 1928 exhibition, New York Metropolitan Museum of Art. Work subject of 1976 exhibition, Musée des Arts Décoratifs, Bordeaux. 1928–61, work shown regularly, Galerie Rouard, Paris.
▶ Cat., *Céramiques de René Buthaud*, Bordeaux: Musée des Arts Décoratifs, 1976. Cat., *Decorative Arts 1925 Style*, New York: Didier Aaron, 1979. Victor Arwas, *Art Déco*, Abrams, 1980. Auction Cat., Christie's, May 26, 1983: Lot 442.

Buti, Remo (1938–)
▶ Italian designer; born Florence.
▶ Studied architecture, Università di Firenze.
▶ In the late 1960s, he was active in the avant-garde architectural movement in Italy; in 1973, co-founded Global Tools; worked in a studio in Florence, where he designed furniture, ceramics, lamps, and jewelry for clients including Mark Cross, Takashemaya, Targetti; lectured on interior architecture and decoration at Università di Firenze. Worked for the communities of Florence, Prato, Livorno, for the Centro Moda di Firenze and the Bancadi Toscana; with Andrea Branzi, entered the competition for partial restoration of the Castel di Sangro. In c1986, he designed *Stars* sconces and floor lamps and *Iris* uplighter for Targetti Sankey.
▶ Projects shown at 1968 (XIV), 1979 (XVI), 1983 (XVII) Triennali di Milano and 1978 Biennale di Venezia. Won 1980 design competition for furnishing fabrics sponsored by journal *Jardin de Mode* and competition Construction et Humanism (with others), Cannes.
▶ Robert A.M. Stern (ed.), *The International Design Yearbook*, New York: Abbeville, 1985/1986: Nos. 208,211,229,232. Andrea Branzi, *La Casa Calda: Esperienze del Nuovo Disegno Italiano*, Milan: Idea Books, 1982. *Modo*, No. 148, March–April 1993:117.

Butler, Nick (1942–)
▶ British industrial designer.
▶ Studied Leeds College of Art and Royal College of Art, London.
▶ He worked under the guidance of Eliot Noyes on an IBM fellowship; in 1967, became a founding partner of BIB Design Consultants, where he designed Racal Decca radar and navigational products 1969–83, Ohmeda medical production, Dunhill pens and watches, the British Telecom *Tribune* telephone, JCB earth-moving equipment, the *Agenda* electronic diary, and Minolta cameras; was interested in combining product aesthetics with function and sound engineering principles; designed the Ferguson range of TV sets in 1986.
▶ Minolta *7000* camera design received best European camera award of 1985. Duracell flashlight product line received an award.
▶ Fiona MacCarthy and Patrick Nuttgens, *An Eye for Industry*, London: Lund Humphries, 1986.

Butterfield, Lindsay P. (1869–1948)

▶ British designer of textiles and wallpapers.

▶ Like C.F.A. Voysey, Butterfield produced textile designs for Alexander Morton in the 1890s, including the 1899 *Squill* and c1901 *Tudor* patterns. His subtly colored, flowing designs were made into woven wool and cotton reversible fabric (or double-cloth) in the 1890s and 1900s. In 1892, he worked at the same address as Harrison Townsend. From 1902, he had an exclusive arrangement to design tapestries for Morton, but also designed linens for G.A.P. Baker, textiles and wallpaper for Liberty, and wallpaper for Essex and Co and Sanderson. In *Floral Forms in Historic Designs* (1922), he showed 18 plates of objects from the Victoria and Albert Museum, London, and designs by William Morris and Voysey.

▶ *British Arts and Design, 1900–1960*, London: Victoria and Albert Museum, 1983. Simon Jervis, *The Penguin Dictionary of Design and Designers*, London: Penguin, 1984:94.

Byam, Wally

▶ American inventor and designer.

▶ Byam was a magazine publisher in the late 1920s, when he printed an article on the building of trailers; to correct errors in it, he wrote another article of his own and began selling instructional construction guides; in 1932, opened a facility in Jackson Center, Ohio, to manufacture trailers made of plywood; in 1934, coined the name 'Airstream' for a mobile home in the popular Streamline styling of the time, seen in Chrysler's 1934 *Airflow* automobile; in 1934, designed the *Airstream Clipper* mobile home (probably a reference to Igor Sikorsky's Clipper airships of the early 1930s), with a sleek aluminum-clad silhouette like a loaf of bread; with the shortage of aluminum for civilian uses during World War II, closed his shop, reopening in 1948; Americans took to the road in large numbers in *Airstreams*, and the Wally Byam Caravan Club was formed in 1955. Now a cult object, the trailer is still being manufactured.

▶ Diane di Costanzo, *Metropolitan Home*, November 1990:58B.

C

Caccia Dominioni, Luigi (1913–)

▶ Italian architect and designer; born Milan.
▶ Studied architecture, Politecnico di Milano, to 1936.
▶ In 1938, (with Pier Giacomo Castiglioni and brother Livio) he set up a studio in Milan; like others in Italy in the late 1950s, Caccia Dominioni sought to recover the representational value of the image in his architecture; designed interiors and restaurants; was an industrial designer. His work included ceramic tiles produced by the Cooperativa Ceramica, Imola, and collaborations with Castiglioni brothers, including first all-plastic 1940 radio by Phonola. Clients included Olivari. Architecture included 1954–55 villa and 1965 residential and office building, both Milan.
▶ G. Polin, 'Un architetto milanese tra regionalismo e sperimentazione: Luigi Caccia Dominioni,' *Casabella 46*, No. 508, 1984:40–51. Hans Wichmann, *Italien Design 1945 bis heute*, Munich: Die Neue Sammlung, 1988.
▶ See Castiglioni, Livio and Castiglioni, Pier Giacomo and Achille

Cadioli, Spartaco (1925–)

▶ Italian designer; born Mantua; active Cremona.
▶ Cadioli began his professional career in 1959, designing furniture, shelving systems, and stairways; became a member of ADI (Associazione per il Disegno Industriale). Clients included Pasini, Milan, and Artigianivari, Cremona.
▶ *ADI Annual 1976*, Milan: Associazione per il Disegno Industriale, 1976.

Cadovius, Poul (1911–)

▶ Danish furniture designer.
▶ He established furniture manufacturer Royal Systems in 1945; designed for Cado Center, Cadomus, France & Søn, Euroart, Barcelona, and La Boutique Dannoise, Paris.
▶ Received a silver medal at 1957 (XI) Triennale di Milano and numerous other awards.
▶ Frederik Sieck, *Nutidig Dansk Møbeldesign: -en kortfattet illustreret beskrivelse*, Copenhagen: Bondo Gravesen; 1990 Busck edition in English.

Caetani, Michelangelo (Duke of Sermoneta 1803–83)

▶ Italian antiquarian, painter, and jewelry designer.
▶ From 1828, Caetani was a collaborator, friend, and parton of Fortunato Piò Castellani and his sons; supported the Castellani firm with encouragement, money, and ideas in its archeological excavations and jewelry design. The Castellanis' jewelry in antique, neo-Gothic, and Italian medieval styles may have been designed by Caetani.
▶ Received a medal at the 1873 'Weltausstellung Wien' for his participation in the Castellanis' efforts.
▶ Charlotte Gere, *American and European Jewelry 1830–1914*, New York: Crown, 1975:160.
▶ See Castellani, Alessandro

CAF
See Compagnie des Arts français

Cagozzi, Alfonso (1942–)

▶ Italian designer; born Gualtieri; active Milan.
▶ Cagozzi began his professional career in 1967; subsequently, designed lighting for Philips; became a member of ADI (Associazione per il Disegno Industriale).
▶ *ADI Annual 1976*, Milan: Associazione per il Disegno Industriale, 1976.

Caillères, Jean-Pierre (1941–)

▶ French architect and designer.
▶ Studied architecture, École Nationale Supérieure des Beaux-Arts, Paris.
▶ He began his career in architecture and town planning; in 1979, set up his own studio Papyrus, specializing in the design of office, shop, and hotel interiors and furniture; in 1984 for ceramics firm Gien, designed the faïence dinner services *Dorique* in a skewed square form and the conical and triangular *Angles*; designed the 1983 *Equerre* armchair produced by Papyrus, 1989 *Genius* chair range by Sigebene, and dishes for the microwave oven by Pillivuyt; designed shops for Ercuis, Saint-Hilaire, Haviland, and Chromex.
▶ Won 1983 competition (1980 table by Papyrus) organized by VIA and Bloomingdale's and 1983 'Appel permanent' award (*Basculator* table) from VIA. Participated in first Triennale d'Art français Contemporain.
▶ Cat., *Les années VIA: 1980–1990*, Paris: Musée des Arts Décoratifs, 1990.

Caillette, René-Jean (1919–)

▶ French furniture and interior designer.
▶ Studied École des Arts Appliqués.
▶ In 1948, he became associated with Landault and other young designers who formed a group in Paris, and studied serially produced furniture; was active in the 1950s and 1960s, designing furniture in wood and rattan.
▶ Work shown regularly at Salons des Arts Ménagers and the Salons of the Sociéte des Artistes Décorateurs. Received awards including 1952 René Gabriel prize; 1957 (XI) Triennale di Milano (silver medal); 1958 'Exposition universelle et internationale de Bruxelles (Expo '58)' (grand prize); 1962 exposition (gold medal), Munich. Won 1982 Appel Spécifique award sponsored by VIA for *Primevère* chair produced by Collomb and *Trèfle* folding chair in lacquered steel tubing and Formica.
▶ Pascal Renous, *Portraits de créateurs*, Paris: H. Vial, 1969. Yolande Amic, *Intérieurs: Le Mobilier français, 1945–1964*, Paris: Regard/VIA, 1983:82. Cat., *Les années VIA 1980–1990*, Paris: Musée des Arts Décoratifs, 1990.

Calatrava, Santiago (1951–)

▶ Spanish architect, engineer, and furniture designer; born Valencia.
▶ Studied Escuela Técnica Superior de Arquitectura, Valencia, in Paris, and engineering, Federal Institute of Technology, Zürich.
▶ He taught at Zürich Federal Institute of Technology for three years, after which he opened his own architecture and engineering office; executed 1986 furniture designs, including his 1986–87

Espada DS-150 leather-and-metal chaise longue produced by de Sede, Switzerland, and 1990 *Montjuic* floor lamp produced by Artemide; was the architect of bridges in Spain, factory sheds in Germany, and train stations in Switzerland; (with architects Bruno Reichlin and Fabio Reinhart) was active in an architecture office in Switzerland.

▶ He participated in the 1968 (XIV) and 1973 (XV) Triennali di Milano and was general coordinator of its (XV) session and in the 1976, 1978 and 1980 Biennali di Venezia. He won first prize in the 1983 competition for the Zürich-Stadelhofen train station.
▶ Albrecht Bangert and Karl Michael Armer, *80s Style: Designs of the Decade*, New York: Abbeville, 1990:62–63,228.

Calder, Alexander (1898–1976)

▶ American sculptor, painter, and designer; born Philadelphia; son of sculptor Alexander Sterling Calder.
▶ 1915–18, studied Stevens Institute of Technology, Hoboken, New Jersey; 1923–25 painting, Art Students' League, New York, and under Boardman Robinson; 1926–27 art, Académie de la Grande Chaumière, Paris.
▶ In 1919, he worked as an engineer in Rutherford, New Jersey, and, 1919–23, as a draftsperson and engineer in West Coast logging camps; 1923–30, was active in New York, sketching for the *National Police Gazette* 1925–26; in 1926, traveled to England and Paris, where he produced his 1927–28 miniature circus and worked on wood sculpture; was best known for his 'mobiles'—hanging sculptures whose amorphic and biomorphic forms inspired many designers in the 1950s—and, subsequently, for his 'stabiles', which were anchored to the ground. His linear, wiry images were probably derived from artists Joan Miró and Paul Klee. In 1969, he designed porcelains for Sèvres and airplane fuselage motifs for Braniff Airlines; worked on stage designs, graphics, jewelry, and hand-made household objects; in his fine art, painted exclusively in black, red, yellow, and white.
▶ First shown in 1928 at Weyhe Gallery, New York, his work was subject of over 180 subsequent exhibitions. *Quick-silver fountain* installed alongside Picasso's *Guernica* and a painting by Joan Miró at Spanish pavilion, 1937 Paris 'Exposition Internationale des Arts et Techniques dans la Vie Moderne.' An international traveling exhibition of his utilitarian objects was organized in 1989–90.
▶ James Johnson Sweeney, *Calder*, Paris, 1971. Jean Lipman and Nancy Foot, *Calder's Circus*, New York, 1972. Muriel Emanuel et al. (eds.), *Contemporary Artists*, New York: St Martin's, 1983:664. Films include Hans Aerlis, *Alexander Calder*, Berlin, 1929; Agnes Rindge Claflin, *Alexander Calder: Sculpture and Constructions*, New York, 1944; Hans Richter, *Dreams That Money Can Buy*, New York, 1948; Burgess Meredith, *Works of Calder*, New York, 1951; Carlos Vilardebo, *Cirque Calder*, Paris, 1961; Hans Richter, *Alexander Calder: From the Circus to the Moon*, New York, 1963; Carlos Vilardebo, *Mobiles*, Paris, 1966; Robert Gardner, *The Great Sail*, New York, 1966; *Alexander Calder: The Creation of the Stabile*, New York, 1967; Charles Chaboud, *Calder: un Portrait*, Paris, 1969; and Carlos Vilardebo, *Les Gouaches de Sandy*, Paris, 1973.

Caldwell, J.E.

▶ American jewelers, antiquarians, and silversmiths; located Philadelphia.
▶ James E. Caldwell (1839–81) was born in New York; settling in Philadelphia, established the firm J.E. Caldwell and Co in 1839. 1843–48, when Caldwell and James M. Bennett were partners, the firm was known as Bennett and Caldwell. Caldwell's son J. Albert Caldwell directed the business 1881–1914; Albert's son J. Emott Caldwell directed the business until his death in 1919. It produced silver in the Art Nouveau style at the turn of the century; is one of the oldest jewelry and silver manufacturers and retail establishments extant in the USA.
▶ Joseph Hugh Green, *Jewelers to Philadelphia and the World, 125 Years on Chestnut Street*, Philadelphia: Newcomer Society of North America, 1965. Charlotte Gere, *American and European Jewelry 1830–1914*, New York: Crown, 1975:160–61. Annelies Krekel-Aalberse, *Art Nouveau and Art Déco Silver*, New York: Abrams, 1989:98,252.

California Drop Cloth

▶ American textile manufacturer; located Los Angeles.
▶ California Drop Cloth was founded in 1975 by Leonard Polikoff. Using pigments in a Jackson Pollock-like controlled splattering, artists-craftspeople created patterns on yard goods intended for upholstery, wallcovering, and floor covering. Custom colors could be ordered in some 70 patterns. Although the patterns appeared to be random, the effect was more or less predetermined. Other effects in the firm's range included abstracts, stripes, and foliage on colored backgrounds. The name of the firm derives from the similarity of its products to a house painter's cover cloth used to protect furniture and furnishings in a room.
▶ Les Gilbert, 'Happenings West: Drop Cloths Turn to Fabric Art,' *Home Fashions Textiles*, Vol. 1, June 1980:63,65. Cat., Kathryn B. Hiesinger and George H. Marcus III (eds.), *Design Since 1945*, Philadelphia: Philadelphia Museum of Art, 1983.

California Faience

▶ American ceramics manufactory; located Berkeley, California.
▶ In 1916, William V. Bragdon and Chauncey R. Thomas set up a collaboration to produce pottery in Berkeley, California, originally known as Thomas and Bragdon and in 1922 named The Tile Shop. Its tiles and a range of art pottery may have been named California Faience before 1924, when the firm took over the name. Dirk van Erp's hammered copperwares were applied with glazes by California Faience. Bragdon's and Thomas's production was mostly cast. Thomas was responsible for the technical aspects of pottery production, including mold making, and was in charge of the development of glazes, which were primarily matt, though with some high-gloss formulas. In 1930, art pottery production ended, although some pieces produced c1932 were shown at the Chicago fair. Bragdon bought out Thomas in c1932 and sold the manufactory in the early 1950s.
▶ Pottery of c1932 shown at 1933–34 Chicago 'A Century of Progress International Exhibition.'
▶ Waldemar F. Dietrich, *The Clay Resources and the Ceramic Industry of California, Bulletin 99*, Sacramento: California State Mining Bureau, 1928. Paul F. Evans, 'California Faience,' in *Art Pottery of the United States*, New York: Charles Scribner's Sons, 1974. Paul Evans in Timothy J. Andersen et al., *California Design 1910*, Salt Lake City: Peregrine Smith, 1980:73–74. Hazel V. Bray, *The Potter's Art in California, 1885–1955*, Oakland, California: Oakland Museum, 1980. *American Art Pottery*, New York: Cooper-Hewitt Museum, 1987:130.

Callegari, Wanda (1933–)

▶ Italian designer; born Piacenza; active Sesto S. Giovani.
▶ Callegari began her professional career in 1962; became a member of ADI (Associazione per il Disegno Industriale). Clients included seating manufacturer First, Mirabello di Cantù.
▶ *ADI Annual 1976*, Milan: Associazione per il Disegno Industriale, 1976.

Calm, Alice Charlotte (1897–)

▶ Austrian ceramicist; born Weinberg, near Prague.
▶ 1914, studied Kunstgewerbeschule, Vienna, under Oskar Strnad and Josef Hoffmann.
▶ From 1914, when the ceramics workshop of the Wiener Werkstätte was set up, Calm was active there; until 1953, lived in the Netherlands.
▶ Günther Feuerstein, *Vienna—Present and Past: Arts and Crafts—Applied Art—Design*, Vienna: Jugend und Volk, 1976: 35,80. Cat., *Expressive Keramik der Wiener Werkstätte 1917–1930*, Munich: Bayerische Vereinsbank, 1992:128.

Calò, Aldo   (1910–)

▶ Italian metalworker and teacher; born S. Cesario di Lecce; active Rome.

▶ In 1965, Calò organized the Corso Speciale Superiore di Disegno Industriale e Communicazioni Visive, Rome, where he was director until 1972; from 1973, worked in the office of the minister of public instruction on the organization and management of the Corso Superiore di Disegno Industriale, Rome; became a member of ADI (Associazione per il Disegno Industriale).

▶ Prototypes and projects included in various national and international exhibitions.

▶ *ADI Annual 1976*, Milan: Associazione per il Disegno Industriale, 1976.

Calzolari, Pier Paolo   (1944–)

▶ Italian artist and furniture designer.

▶ Calzolari was a conceptual artist aligned with the *arte povera* movement; executed furniture produced by Meta Memphis, including the 1989 *Pau* bench.

▶ Work shown at Persano Galleries, Turin, Galerie Sonnabend, Paris, and Gladstone Gallery, New York.

▶ Albrecht Bangert and Karl Michael Armer, *80s Style: Designs of the Decade*, New York: Abbeville, 1990:85,228.

Camardella De Oliveira, Sergio

▶ Brazilian designer; active Rio de Janeiro and Mestre (Italy).

▶ Studied Corso Speciale Superiore di Disegno Industriale and Università Internazionale dell'Arte, both Venice.

▶ He became a member of ADI (Associazione per il Disegno Industriale).

▶ *ADI Annual 1976*, Milan: Associazione per il Disegno Industriale, 1976.

Cammas, Fabienne   (1961–)

▶ French furniture designer.

▶ Studied École Nationale Supérieure des Arts Décoratifs, Paris, and engineering, INSA, Lyons.

▶ She turned from industrial design to become a teacher at Domus Academy, Milan; designed 1988 table for Giogetti with a circular moveable area and a tableware range for Alessi; (with Luc Jozancy and Jean-Yves Maurel) won 1986 picnic-tableware design competition sponsored by APCI (Agence pour la Promotion de la Création Industrielle) and UGAP (Union des Groupements d'Achats Publics).

▶ Participated in 1988 'A Tavola' exhibition, Centro Domus, directed by Vico Magistretti.

▶ *Les Carnets du Design*, Paris: Mad-Cap Productions et APCI, 1986:86.

Cammilli, Sergio   (1920–)

▶ Italian designer; active Agliana, Pistoia.

▶ Cammilli began his professional career in 1945; became a member of ADI (Associazione per il Disegno Industriale). His clients included Poltrona Frau and Francesconi lighting.

▶ *ADI Annual 1976*, Milan: Associazione per il Disegno Industriale, 1976.

Campi, Antonia   (1921–)

▶ Italian ceramics and industrial designer.

▶ Campi designed household objects and ceramics for clients including Ermenegildo Collini and Richard Ginori. Her scissors and poultry shears were widely published.

▶ Scissors received 1959 Premio Compasso d'Oro and poultry shears 1964 National Industrial Design Council of Canada award.

▶ Carlo Bestetti (ed.), *Forme nuove in Italia*, Rome, 1962:109. Cat., Kathryn B. Hiesinger and George H. Marcus III (eds.), *Design Since 1945*, Philadelphia: Philadelphia Museum of Art, 1983. Hans Wichmann, *Italien Design 1945 bis heute*, Munich: Die Neue Sammlung, 1988.

Canadian National Industrial Design Committee

▶ Canadian industrial design promotion organization.

▶ In 1947, the National Gallery of Canada organized a design-information office in Ottawa, one of its mandates being to provide photographs of items of Canadian design. It was called The Canadian Design Index. In 1948, some manufacturers, retailers, designers, and educators organized to form the Canadian National Industrial Design Committee, which promoted Canadian design through exhibitions, competitions, and booklets, which resulted in the establishment of the permanent Design Centre in 1953. In addition to its numerous exhibitions, it awarded an annual Design Merit Award to Industry, similar to the 'Good Design' labels of the New York Museum of Art of this period. The awards were given by a special jury of the National Industrial Design Committee, reviewing products selected for the Design Index. The Centre was funded by the Canadian government through the National Gallery of Canada, with financial support from firms.

▶ Michael Farr, *Design in British Industry: A Mid-Century Survey*, London: Cambridge, 1955.

Canal

▶ French architecture and design collaborative.

▶ Established in 1981 by architects Daniel Rubin, Patrick Rubin, and Annie Le Bot, the group designed furniture for public use in museums, stores, and work areas; designed offices for magazines *Actuel* in 1982 and *Libération* in 1987 and the Claude Montana shops; renovated the Centre National des Lettres and, in 1990–92, building of DMF (Direction des Musées de France). The group's 1984 *Frégate* chair, produced by SERQH, was designed for French minister of culture Jack Lang.

Canape, Georges   (1864–1940)

▶ French bookbinder and gilder; active Paris.

▶ In 1865, J. Canape set up a bindery in Paris. In 1884, Georges Canape took over his father's business; subsequently, set up a gilding department; practiced a restrained version of Art Nouveau; during World War I, produced covers for Jacques Doucet, designed by Pierre Legrain. William Augustus Spencer, Charles Miguet, Henri Vever, and L. Comar also collected Canape's work. Produced bindings by George Barbier, Robert Bonfils, Georges Lepape, Jules Chadel, Adolphe Giraldon, and Maurice Denis; in 1918, became president of the Syndicate of Patron Bookbinders. A. Corriez became a partner in the firm in 1927; after Corriez's death in 1937, Esparon purchased the bindery and Henri Mercher the gilding section.

▶ Work shown annually at Paris Salons. Legrain's bindings shown at 1919 Salon of Société des Artistes Décorateurs.

▶ Henri Nicolle, 'La Reliure moderne,' *Les Arts français: la reliure d'art*, No. 36, 1919:197. S.T. Prideaux, *Modern Bindings: Their Design and Decoration*, New York, 1906:97. Ernest de Crauzat, *La Reliure française de 1900 à 1925*, Paris, 1961. Vol. 1:61–62; Vol. 2. Roger Devauchelle, *La Reliure en France de ses origines à nos jours*, Vol. 3, Paris, 1961:127,148,153,158,246–47. John F. Fleming and Priscilla Juvelis, *The Book Beautiful and the Binding as Art*, Vol. 1, New York, 1983:35. Alastair Duncan and Georges de Bartha, *Art Nouveau and Art Déco Bookbinding*, New York: Abrams, 1989:16,17,19,21,61–64,188.

Canella, Guido   (1931–)

▶ Italian architect; born Bucharest; active Milan.

▶ Canella began his professional career in 1960, designing furniture and lighting; became a member of ADI (Associazione per il Disegno Industriale).

▶ *ADI Annual 1976*, Milan: Associazione per il Disegno Industriale, 1976.

Canesi

▶ Italian jeweler; located Milan.

▶ Canesi was founded in the 1950s by Gina and Giuseppe Canesi. Giuseppe Canesi had been a goldsmith; immediately after World War II, opened a studio in Milan, where his production was for commissions for Giuliano Fratti; through Gina Canesi, began receiving commissions from others; became one of the most respected jewelers in Italy in the 1950s and 1960s. Collaborating with the firm since the 1950s, Canesi's grandson Gianpiero Rossi became head of the firm in 1975. Its production is created mainly for fashion houses Fontana, Maria Antonelli, Enzo, Marucelli, and Veneziani.

▶ Necklace received first prize at 1957 Mostra dell'Accessorio.

▶ Deanna F. Cera (ed.), *Jewels of Fantasy: Costume Jewelry of the 20th Century*, New York: Abrams, 1992:305.

Canovas, Manuel (1935–)
▶ French textile designer; born Paris.

▶ Studied École des Beaux-Arts, Paris, to 1957, and Scuola di Belle Arti, Rome.

▶ His work was influenced by 1960s American, Mexican, and Japanese designs. He founded Les Tissus Manuel Canovas in 1963 to produce fabrics, wallpaper, and carpets sold through offices in USA, Europe, Australia, and Japan. Canovas designed a porcelain service for Puiforcat in the 1980s. The firm is a member of Comité Colbert. His daughter, Isabel Canovas, is a textile designer known for her fashion accessories.

▶ Work subject of 1987 exhibition, Paris Musée de la Mode.

Capey, Reco (1895–1961)
▶ British designer; born Burslem.

▶ Studied Royal College of Art, London, and in France, Italy, and Sweden.

▶ He designed pottery, glass, metal, textiles, and lacquer; as art director of Yardley 1928–38, was best known for his distinctive packaging designs; 1924–35, was chief instructor in design, Royal College of Art; 1938–41, president of the Arts and Crafts Exhibition Society; published *The Printing of Textiles* (1930).

▶ In 1937, elected Royal Designer for Industry.

▶ Cat., *Thirties: British art and design before the war*, London: Arts Council of Great Britain, Hayward Gallery, 1979:26,69, 71,141,154,257. Stuart Durant, *Ornament from the Industrial Revolution to Today*, Woodstock, NY: Overlook, 1986:254.

Capon, Eugène and G.-L.
▶ French metalworkers.

▶ Known for their chandeliers and sconces, vases, radiator covers, and other objects produced in brass, steel, and patinated and *martelé* bronze.

▶ In the 1920s, work shown in the Paris Salons. Lighting for the ensembles of Gallerey and Léon Jallot shown at 1923 Salon of Société des Artistes Décorateurs and 1925 Paris 'Exposition Internationale des Arts Décoratifs et Industriels Modernes.'

▶ Alastair Duncan, *Art Nouveau and Art Déco Lighting*, New York: Simon and Schuster, 1978:163. G. Janneau, *Le Luminaire et les Moyens d'éclairage Nouveaux*, first series, plates 25 and 26.

Cappelin, Giacomo (1887–1968)
▶ Italian glassware designer; active Murano.

▶ With Paolo Venini, Cappelin was a partner in Vetri Soffiati Muranesi Cappelin-Venini. Venini left to establish his own workshops in 1921 and 1925.

▶ Frederick Cooke, *Glass: Twentieth-Century Design*, New York: Dutton, 1986:96–97. Franco Deboni, *Venini Glass*, Basel: Wiese, 1990.

▶ See Venini, Paolo

Cappelli, Sergio (1948–)
▶ Italian designer; active Naples.

▶ From 1973, Cappelli collaborated with Patrizia Ranzo; became active in architecture and interior design, and industrial design, with clients including Abet Laminati, Alessi, Bardelli, Lapis, Ultima Edizione, and Cappellini International; in 1986, lectured on design, University of Illinois. Projects included the BMW showrooms in Avellino, Naples, and Caserta, Fiat showrooms, and so-called urban scenery and temporary architecture for 'Summer in Naples' and 'Piedigrotta' in Naples.

▶ Participated (with Ranzo) in 1981 Triennale di Milano; 'South Wave, Bari;' '1985 The Naturalist's House,' Naples; 1986 'Atelier Nouveau Competition of Tokyo.' Won WIDI Competition, California.

▶ Andrea Branzi, *La Casa Calda: Esperienze del Nuovo Disegno Italiano*, Milan: Idea Books, 1982. Fumio Shimizu and Matteo Thun (eds.), *The Descendants of Leonardo: The Italian Design*, Tokyo, 1987:323. *Modo*, No. 148, March–April 1993:117.

▶ See Ranzo, Patrizia

Cappellini International Interiors
▶ Italian furniture manufacturer.

▶ The firm was established in 1946; is directed by Giulio Cappellini. Designers included Jasper Morrison, Mark Newson, and Shiro Kuramata. Morrison's furniture collection was introduced at 1987 Salone del Mobile, Milan. Kuramata's 1970 wavy-silhouette cabinets with 18 drawers were widely published. Italian designers included Daniella Puppa, Franco Raggi, and Rodolfo Dordoni. Anna Gili designed the 1991 *Tonda* armchair.

▶ 'Milan à l'Heure du Design,' *Maison et Jardin*, April 1992:130.

Capriolo, Gigi (1940–)
▶ Italian designer; born and active Milan.

▶ Capriolo began her professional career in 1967; became a member of ADI (Associazione per il Disegno Industriale). Designing lighting, furniture, and shelving systems, clients in Italy included FLB, DID, Emmezeta, Gruppo Industriale Busnelli, Citterio, Fiarm, Temi, Arve, Complemento Idea, Bishop, Fian Forma Funzione, Nava, Elle, Giocarredo, Gallotti e Radice, Maya sanitary fixture, Jobs, and Elle 2 furniture.

▶ *ADI Annual 1976*, Milan: Associazione per il Disegno Industriale, 1976.

Carabin, François-Rupert (1862–1932)
▶ French furniture designer; born Alsace.

▶ Carabin carved cameos in Paris before learning woodcarving from a sculptor in 1873. One of his best-known sculptures is a 1896–97 figurine of Loïe Fuller, rendered more realistically than the Fuller images by Théodore Rivière, Raoul Larche, and Pierre Roche. A commission for a bookcase for collector Henry Montandon prompted his conclusion that furniture was not architecture but sculpture, where decoration becomes both sculptural and symbolic; used caryatids repeatedly in his work and, from 1899, the female form; from 1890, made jewelry, metalwork, and ceramics with Carriès; in 1914, became director of École des Arts Décoratifs, Strasbourg, where he followed German turn-of-the-century teaching methods.

▶ Work shown at Salon des Indépendants from its beginning in 1884.

▶ Yvonne Brunhammer et al., *Art Nouveau Belgium, France*, Houston: Rice University, 1976.

Caramia, Pierangelo (1957–)
▶ Italian designer; born Cisternino; active Milan and Paris.

▶ Studied architecture, Università di Firenze, to 1984, and Domus Academy, Milan, to 1986.

▶ In 1984, he became active as an architect and designer; from 1986, was a member of design group ELETTRA; associated himself with Massimo Iosa Ghini's Bolidismo movement, formed in 1983 and typified by 1950s shapes executed in luxury materials; in 1987, settled in France, collaborating on several projects with Philippe Starck; realized a number of design commissions in Paris and New York; taught at the École des Beaux Arts, Rennes; designed 1987 *Arcadia Wings* table by XO, which he compared to the Statue of Liberty, the Christ of São Paulo, and the Oscar statuette. Clients included Poltrona Frau, Alessi, and Arredaesse.

▶ Participated in numerous competitions and exhibitions. Work shown at 1992 'Nuovo Bel Design: 200 Nuovi Oggetti per la Casa,' Fiera di Milano.

▶ Fumio Shimizu and Matteo Thun (eds.), *The Descendants of Leonardo: The Italian Design*, Tokyo, 1987:323. *Modo*, No. 148, March–April 1993:117.

Carayon, Émile (1843–1909)

▶ French bookbinder; active Paris.

▶ Trained as a painter-decorator.

▶ In 1875, he set up a bindery in Paris; worked mainly in *cartonnage*, a technique developed in the late 18th century by Alexis-René Bradel whereby the cloth/leather casing is attached to end-papers rather than being sewn into the boards. Carayon's boards were painted by artists including Henriot, Louis Morin, and Théophile Robaudi. Marie Brisson, a student of Francisque Cuzin, became his assistant. With Cuzin and Champs from 1898, Carayon produced covers for publisher L. Conquet; by 1900, began producing formal leather bindings, some of which included modeled or incised pictorial panels by Gustave Guétant and Lucien Rudeaux.

▶ Work shown at 1894 'Exposition du Livre,' Paris.

▶ S.T. Prideaux, *Modern Bookbindings: Their Design and Decoration*, New York, 1906:95–97. Etienne Deville, *La Reliure française*, Vol. 1, Paris, 1930:41. Ernest de Crauzat, *La Reliure française de 1900 à 1925*, Vol. 1, Paris, 1932:51–53. Roger Devauchelle, *La Reliure en France de ses origines à nos jours*, Vol. 3, Paris, 1961:108–09,127. Alastair Duncan and Georges de Bartha, *Art Nouveau and Art Déco Bookbinding*, New York: Abrams, 1989:15,65,188.

Cardeilhac; Ernest Cardeilhac (1851–1904)

▶ French silversmiths; located Paris.

▶ Maison Cardeilhac was founded in Paris in 1804; registered its mark in 1817; for a number of years, specialized in flatware and cutlery. The founder's grandson, Ernest Cardeilhac, apprenticed under Harleux, added gold- and silversmithing. It frequently incorporated volutes and trefoils by Lucien Bonvallet, its most important designer. Around 1900, the firm was one of the important Paris workshops making Modern silver. With restrained naturalistic decoration, Cardeilhac's works incorporated ivory, wood, and different patinas. Ernest's sons Pierre and Jacques became directors of the firm in 1927. When Pierre died in 1944, Jacques managed the firm alone. It merged with Orfèvrerie Christofle in 1951.

▶ Ernest Cardeilhac showed his own wares and traditionally-chased silver designs by Bonvallet (including a chased chocolate pot with ivory handle and swizzle-stick) at 1900 Paris 'Exposition Universelle'; received a silver medal at the 1889 Paris 'Exposition Universelle.' Firm's works shown at 1925 Paris 'Exposition Internationale des Arts Décoratifs et Industriels Modernes' and 1930 'Décor de la Table,' Musée Galliéra, Paris.

▶ Yvonne Brunhammer et al., *Art Nouveau Belgium, France*, Houston: Rice University, 1976. Annelies Krekel-Aalberse, *Art Nouveau and Art Déco Silver*, New York: Abrams, 1989:57,59,63,64,252.

Carder, Frederick C. (1863–1963)

▶ British glassware designer; born Brockmoor, Staffordshire; active Britain and USA.

▶ Apprenticed in his father's pottery; studied chemistry and metallurgy, Dudley Mechanics' Institute, and Stourbridge School of Art, under John Northwood.

▶ Encouraged by Northwood, Carder joined the glass firm Stevens and Williams, Brierly Hill, in 1881 as designer in charge of applied decorations and shapes. In 1902, failing to get promotion to artistic director, he toured glassworks in Germany and Austria and urged Stevens and Williams to modernize their facilities and design new kilns; after a scouting trip to the USA, during which he visited the Corning Glassworks, Corning, New York, concluded that American production was as deficient as that in Britain. T.G. Hawkes was a small corning firm founded in 1880 that purchased its blanks from Corning Glassworks; its president Thomas G. Hawkes incorporated the S.W. Payne Foundry premises into his operation and established facilities to produce crystal and colored glass; Carder joined Hawkes in 1903 to found Steuben Glassworks, Corning, named after Steuben County, New York. Carder gave an interview to the local newspaper expressing disdain for the British glass industry and its trade unions. At Steuben, Carder recreated the moss agate glass developed by Northwood in the late 1880s, and Stevens and Williams's other techniques and patterns; also introduced new forms and processes, including a type of iridescent glass called 'Aurene'; initiated the production of cased (or cameo) glass, similar to late 18th-century Chinese models; retired in 1933, but continued to work in his own laboratory on vases produced by the lost-wax casting process. Carder is known as the father of Modern art glass in America.

▶ Robert F. Rockwell and Jack Lanahan, *Frederick Carder and his Steuben Glass 1903–33*, West Nyack, NY, 1968. Paul V. Gardner, *The Glass of Frederick Carder*, New York, 1971. James S. Plaut, *Steuben Glass*, New York, 1972. R.J. Charleston, *Masterpieces of Glass: A World History from the Corning Museum of Glass*, New York, 1980. Victor Arwas, *Glass: Art Nouveau to Art Deco*, London: Academy, 1987:244,247,296,298,300. Thomas Dimitroff, 'Frederick C. Carder' in Mel Byars and Russell Flinchum (eds.), *50 American Designers, 1918–1968*, Washington: Preservation, 1994.

Cardew, Michael (1901–83)

▶ British ceramicist.

▶ 1921–23 studied Oxford University.

▶ He learned to throw pottery from William Fishley Holland at the Braunton Pottery, North Devon, 1921–22; in 1923, met Bernard Leach and Shoji Hamada at St. Ives; in 1923, became Leach's first and best-known pupil; in 1926, acquired a traditional pottery set up at Winchcombe, Gloucestershire, where he revived English slipware; in 1929, moved to Wenford Bridge, Cornwall; 1942–45, taught pottery at Achimota College, Gold Coast (now Ghana); 1945–48, worked in his own pottery, Vumé-Dugamé (Lower Volta River); in 1948, returned to England; 1951–52, established the Pottery Training Centre, Abuja (Nigeria); up to the early 1980s, worked in his pottery, Wenford Bridge, Cornwall, traveled, and lectured.

▶ Garth Clark, *Michael Cardew*, London: Faber, 1978. Cat., *Thirties: British art and design before the war*, London: Arts Council of Great Britain, Hayward Gallery, 1979:98,130,286.

Cariboni, Giancarlo (1948–)

▶ Italian designer; active Bergamo.

▶ Cariboni began his professional career in 1970; designed furniture in marble and glass; became a member of ADI (Associazione per il Disegno Industriale). Clients included Acerbis.

▶ *ADI Annual 1976*, Milan: Associazione per il Disegno Industriale, 1976.

Carini, Giovanni (1944–)

▶ Italian designer; born and active Agliana, Pistoia.

▶ Studied Corso Superiore di Disegno Industriale, Florence, to 1965.

▶ Active from 1970, he designed domestic and office furniture and accessories for clients in Italy including Poltronova, Planula, C&B Italia, Marcatré, Porciani, Ugolini, Piemme, and Ciatti; became a member of ADI (Associazione per il Disegno Industriale).

▶ *ADI Annual 1976*, Milan: Associazione per il Disegno Industriale, 1976.

Carlman, C.F.

▶ Swedish silversmiths; located Stockholm.

▶ From the 1930s, when Sven Carlman became head of the family firm, C.F. Carlman produced silver designed by Per Sköld.

▶ Silver by Eric Lundqvist received a prize from Föreningen Svensk Hemslöjd (Swedish Handicraft Society) and shown at 1909 Stockholm decorative arts exhibition.

▶ Annelies Krekel-Aalberse, *Art Nouveau and Art Déco Silver*, New York: Abrams, 1989:244,252.

Carlson, William (1950–)

▶ American glass designer; born Dover, Ohio.

▶ Studied Cleveland Institute of Art, Cleveland, Ohio to 1976, and, New York State College of Ceramics, Alfred University, Alfred, New York.

▶ Auction cat., 'Contemporary Works of Art,' Sotheby's New York, 14 March 1992.

Carlsson, Daniel Johan (1853–1922)
▶ Swedish furniture designer and ceramicist.
▶ Carlsson collaborated with August Malmström and Magnus Isaeus on Viking-revival-style decorations for Gustavsberg pottery.
▶ Cat., David Revere McFadden (ed.), *Scandinavian Modern Design 1880–1980*, New York: Abrams, 1982:263.

Carnegie, Hattie (b. Henrietta Kanengeiser 1886–1956)
▶ Austrian clothing designer and costume jeweler; born Vienna; active New York.
▶ Her family settled in the USA when she was in her teens, and took the Carnegie name. In 1909, with a friend, she opened a small dress and hat shop, New York, known as Carnegie—Ladies' Hatter. In 1918, it became the Hattie Carnegie company and expanded to a number of shops. Threatened by the 1929 stock market crash, Carnegie launched a ready-to-wear line by talented young designers or copied from French originals. A number of her designers went on to their own successes, including Norman Norell from 1928, Pauline Trigère in the 1930s, Claire McCardell from 1939, and Halston in the 1950s. The firm also produced costume jewelry.
▶ Deanna F. Cera (ed.), *Jewels of Fantasy: Costume Jewelry of the 20th Century*, New York: Abrams, 1992.

Carr, Alwyn C.E. (1872–1940)
▶ British silversmith and enamelist; active London.
▶ Studied Sheffield School of Art.
▶ Carr met Omar Ramsden at Sheffield School of Art. After graduating, they traveled in Belgium, France, Italy, Switzerland, and Germany. Carr and Ramsden established a workshop in London in 1898, largely financed by Carr and named St. Dunstan, after the patron saint of silversmiths. They worked in a style influenced by the Arts and Crafts movement. It is probable that before World War I Carr was responsible for most of the output; the partnership was dissolved in 1919. Carr continued through the 1920s as a designer of wrought iron and silversmith.
▶ Charlotte Gere, *American and European Jewelry 1830–1914*, New York: Crown, 1975:161. Annelies Krekel-Aalberse, *Art Nouveau and Art Déco Silver*, New York: Abrams, 1989:22,26,27,252.

Carr, Temple St. Clair (1960–)
▶ American jewelry designer; born Virginia.
▶ She designed gold jewelry produced in Florence based on medieval and Renaissance styles and influenced by her study of the classics and interest in ancient coins and beads; in 1985, incorporated coins and beads into rings, earrings, necklaces, bracelets, and cufflinks; in her subsequent designs, used a variety of cabochon stones; produced rock crystal globes secured by gold wire and hung from leather or silk cords. Some designs were based on classical columns and spirals.
▶ Anne-Marie Schiro, *The New York Times*, January 27, 1991:30.

Carré, Alain (1945–)
▶ French industrial designer; active Paris.
▶ Studied École Nationale Supérieure des Arts Décoratifs, Paris.
▶ 1971–76, he was active in his own design office, Alain Carré Design, and was director of Pierre Cardin's design department; designed for a number of shops and restaurants, packaging, and products including Waterman pens and watches. In 1986, his agency was ranked among the top four design firms in France.
▶ Received 1987 silver medal (*Squale* prototype motorcycle by Suzuki), Société des Artistes Décorateurs.
▶ Cat., *Design français 1960–1990*, Paris, Centre Georges Pompidou/APCI, 1988. François Mathey, *Au bonheur des formes, design français 1945–1992*, Paris: Regard, 1992:120,133,313, 320,325,329,357–58.

Carrier-Belleuse, Albert-Ernest (1824–87)
▶ French ceramicist; born Anizy-le-Château; father-in-law of Joseph Chéret.
▶ Studied École des Beaux-Arts and École Royale Gratuite de Dessin.
▶ Carrier-Belleuse entered chaser Bauchery's studio in c1837 and subsequently the workshop of goldsmith Jacques-Henri Fauconnier; was one of the first jewelers to produce neo-Renaissance designs. When Fauconnier died in 1839, Carrier-Belleuse worked for his nephews, the brothers Fannière; met Péquegnot and Jules Salmson at the École des Beaux-Arts; became a freelance designer of metalwork for Barbedienne and for the porcelain factory of Michel Aaron; following Vechte, Arnoux, and Jeannest to England, he designed for Minton, Stoke-on-Trent; taught at schools of design in Hanley and in Stoke; on Jeannest's recommendation, designed majolica and Parian wares at Minton; while sending metalwork designs to Paris, also designed for Wedgwood and for William Brownfield; returning to Paris in 1855, became a successful sculptor as well as prolific designer. Clients included La Paiva in 1867; the Saïd Pasha, Viceroy of Egypt, in 1862; the Louvre, Christofle, Lucien Falize, Alphonse Fouquet, and Grohé.
▶ Work shown at 1855 'Exposition universelle des produits de l'agriculture, de l'industrie et des beaux-arts de Paris,' 1862 London 'International Exhibition of Industry and Art,' 1867 Paris 'Exposition Universelle.' Had his own stand at 1863 (I) exhibition, Union Centrale des Arts Décoratifs, Paris (the organization he founded with Klagmann).
▶ Albert-Ernest Carrier-Belleuse, *Études de figures appliquées à la décoration*, Paris, 1866. Albert-Ernest Carrier-Belleuse, *Application de la figure humaine à la décoration et à l'ornementation industrielle*, Paris, 1884. Simon Jervis, *Penguin Dictionary of Design and Designers*, London, 1984:99–100.

Carriès, Jean (1855–1894)
▶ French sculptor and ceramicist; born Lyons.
▶ Carriès executed his most important sculpture 1878–80 and 1888; influenced by the stoneware at the Japanese section of the 1878 Paris 'Exposition Universelle,' he moved to Saint-Amand-en-Puisaye, Nièvre, a small potters' village, to learn stoneware techniques. When he showed his pottery for the first time in his Paris studio in 1889, the Princess of Scey-Monbéliard commissioned a monumental doorway in glazed stoneware; with plans by Grasset, the project was a financial disaster for Carriès. His wares included Chinese and Japanese forms, pinched pots without handles, vases decorated with sculpture, and large pieces. He used glazes ranging from wood ash to copper base. His sculpture-ceramics were in the forms of masks, monsters, and *putti*.
▶ Work shown at 1892 Salon of the Société des Artistes français.
▶ Yvonne Brunhammer et al., *Art Nouveau Belgium, France*, Houston: Rice University, 1976.

Carter, Ronald (1926–)
▶ British furniture designer.
▶ Studied interior design, Birmingham College of Art, 1949, and furniture, Royal College of Art, London.
▶ 1952–53, he was a staff designer, Corning Glassworks, Corning, New York, before setting up his own business in London and Birmingham in 1954; 1956–74, taught at School of Furniture Design, Royal College of Art; 1960–68, was a partner in Design Partners; 1968–74, was a partner in Carter Freeman Associates; in 1974, set up his own practice; in 1980, became a director of Peter Miles Furniture; designed mass-production furniture for Stag, Consort, Habitat, and Peak and handmade furniture that combined machine methods for Gordon Russell; from 1980, was in partnership with Peter Miles of Miles/Carter. Carter's commissions included furniture for the BBC, Victoria and Albert Museum, and Terminal Four at Heathrow Airport. The *Hardwick* sofa of the late 1980s was widely published in a zebra printed fabric.
▶ Work (1984 *Liverpool* bench) shown at 1989 'British Design,' Museum Boymans-van Beuningen, Rotterdam, and exhibitions in San Francisco, Chicago, Cologne, Milan, Tokyo, Vienna, and Paris.

In 1974, appointed Royal Designer for Industry and honorary fellow, Royal College of Art, London.
▶ Robert A.M. Stern (ed.), *The International Design Yearbook*, New York: Abbeville, 1985/1986: No. 33. *Decorative Arts Today*, London: Bonhams, 1992: No. 48a.

Carter, Truda   (b. Gertrude Sharp; aka Gertrude Adams 1890–1958)
▶ British ceramic designer; wife of ceramicists John Adams and Cyril Carter.
▶ *c*1908–13, studied Royal College of Art, London.
▶ 1914–18, she taught art in Durban; in 1921, worked with husband John Adams for pottery Carter, Stabler and Adams in Poole, Dorset; 1921–39, created embroidery patterns based on Tudor and Jacobean models; 1932–58, with her second husband Cyril Carter, lived at Yaffle Hill (of which E. Maufe was architect), Broadstone, Dorset; she designed the furnishings, decorations, and color schemes. 1948–58, she was a design consultant to CSA.
▶ Cat., *Thirties: British art and design before the war*, London: Arts Council of Great Britain, Hayward Gallery, 1979:154,286.

Cartier
▶ French court jewelers; initially located Paris.
▶ Pierre Cartier was an apprentice at Picard, rue Montorgueil, Paris. His son Louis-François Cartier (1819–1904) took over Picard's atelier in 1847 and opened new quarters on rue Neuve-des-Petits-Champs in 1853; in 1859, opened a shop on boulevard des Italiens, where the international social élite were his customers. The success of Cartier during the Second Empire was assured through the patronage of Princess Mathilde Bonaparte, the German cousin of Napoleon III. The Franco-Prussian War of 1870–71 instigated prudent Louis-François to open a shop in London. In 1872, his son Alfred (1841–1925) became a partner in the firm; he had been working in the family business since 1864. In 1898, Cartier moved to rue de la Paix, where the fashionable jewelry shops in Paris were located. The sons assumed the management of various branches in France and abroad: Louis (1875–1942), Paris from 1898; Pierre (1878–1964), New York from 1908; Jacques (1884–1941), New Burlington Street (moving in 1904 to present address in New Bond Street), London, from 1902. The Cartier Fifth Avenue townhouse (built 1904) in New York was reputedly bought for a double-string of pearls in 1917 from Mrs. Morton F. Plant. The 1917 *Tank* watch was designed to honor the American Tank Corps of World War I. Creating a vast array of jewelry, clocks, and accessories for the dressing table and dinner table, staff designers' work was augmented by freelancers, including Jeanne Toussaint (from 1927). During the interwar Art Déco period, Cartier became known for its mantel clock with an invisible movement. The 1923 interlaced three-band ring was designed by Santos-Dumond (credited to Jean Cocteau) in three colors of gold, variously said to represent the three Cartier brothers or the three rings of Saturn. One of the first copies was given to Cocteau, who in turn commissioned one for Raymond Radiguet. Louis was regarded as the creative genius of the family and the one behind the firm's well-known Art Moderne creations. At the beginning of World War II, Louis joined his brother Pierre in New York in 1942, while Jacques lived in Saint-Moritz (Switzerland), leaving the shop in Paris in the hands of Jeanne Toussaint. The Duchess of Windsor commissioned many widely published designs. In 1972, French industrialist Robert Hocq acquired the Paris branch; in 1972, the London branch; and in 1976, the New York branch, creating Cartier International.
▶ Work shown at 1925 Paris 'Exposition Internationale des Arts Décoratifs et Industriels Modernes' and subject of 1992 'The Art of Cartier' at the Hermitage, St. Petersburg.
▶ Charlotte Gere, *American and European Jewelry 1830–1914*, New York: Crown, 1975:161–62. Sylvie Raulet, *Bijoux Art Déco*, Paris: Regard, 1984. Melissa Gabardi, *Les Bijoux des Années 50*, Paris: Amateur, 1987.

Cartwright, Ashley
▶ British furniture designer and maker.
▶ 1967–70, studied Kingston College of Art, Kingston-upon-Thames; subsequently, Royal College of Art, London.
▶ For a time, he worked with John Makepeace; in 1976, set up his own workshop. His furniture was produced by Tim Wells.
▶ Work shown in Britain, continental Europe, and Japan.
▶ Robert A.M. Stern (ed.), *The International Design Yearbook*, New York: Abbeville, 1985/1986: No. 184.

Carwardine, George   (1887–1948)
▶ British automobile engineer and lighting designer.
▶ As an automobile engineer, Carwardine specialized in suspension systems; was best known for 1934 *Anglepoise* articulated table lamp produced by Herbert Terry. Its design was based on the constant-tension principles of the human arm, although his original idea was to produce a simple, efficient lighting model made from basic metal components. The springs were the equivalent of the muscles in the human arm. It inspired Jacob Jacobsen's 1937 *Luxo* lamp; Jacobsen bought the patent and renamed the fixture, which was subsequently produced in Norway. Virtually unchanged, the lamp is still in production today worldwide. Carwardine was a director of the firm Cardine Associates, Bath.
▶ Jeremy Myerson and Sylvia Katz, *Conran Design Guides: Lamps and Lighting*, London: Conran Octopus, 1990:16,49,73.

Cary, Reuben   (1845–c1933)
▶ American furniture designer and maker; active New York State.
▶ In *c*1845, Cary's father settled in the Adirondacks area, New York State. In *c*1850, after living in a camp in Beach's Lake (called Brandreth Park after 1851), the family moved to Indian Lake and Long Lake. Cary was a guide for the Brandreth family; in 1880, was hired as gamekeeper and caretaker of their estate, which had several large cottages and service buildings; in the 1900s, was known as a carpenter and boat-builder. In 1874, Brandreth ordered 24 chairs from Cary, in vernacular designs with slatted backs, plain turned posts, and splint seats. Some of the rustic furniture in the cottages at Brandreth Park today may have been made by Cary.
▶ Craig Gilborn, *Adirondack Furniture and the Rustic Tradition*, New York: Abrams, 1987:319.

Casabella   (aka *Casa-Bella*)
▶ Italian architecture and design journal.
▶ *Casa-Bella* was founded in 1928 as an architecture-design journal in Italy; in the early years, was directed by Edoardo Persico and, after World War II, by Ernesto N. Rogers; under Rogers, it became a focal point for the new group of architect-editors, who included Vittorio Gregotti 1952–60, Gae Aulenti (under Rogers) in 1960, and Aldo Rossi 1955–64; 1970–76, it was directed by Alessandro Mendini, who promoted the efforts of the young avant-garde and pursued so-called Radical Design or Anti-Design. During the Mendini regime, its writers included Ettore Sottsass, Andrea Branzi, and Peter Cook. Tomás Maldonado succeeded Mendini 1976–81.
▶ Andrea Branzi, *La Casa Calda: Esperienze del Nuovo Disegno Italiano*, Milan: Idea Books, 1982.

Casas Mobilplast
▶ Spanish furniture manufacturer.
▶ The firm was founded by Oscar Tusquets Blanca, Lluís Clotet, Pep Bonet, and Cristian Cirici as an offshoot of the furniture workshop Casas of Carlos Riart; from 1961, produced non-Spanish design under license; in 1978, began production of its own collection. Initial production was of furniture in expanded polystyrene from Norway and, in 1968, through an agreement with C&B Italia, production began of furniture models in polyurethane. The firm's products included 1984 *Varius* polyurethane, metal, and leather armchair by Oscar Tusquets Blanca.

Casati, Cesare (1936–)

▶ Italian designer.

▶ With Emanuele Ponzio, Casati established Studio DA in 1965; designed interiors of hotels, banks, and other public buildings; had clients including Phoebus, Nai Ponteur, and Autovox.

▶ Hans Wichmann, *Italien Design 1945 bis heute*, Munich: Die Neue Sammlung, 1988.

Casati, Giorgio (1942–)

▶ Italian designer; born Giussano; active Milan.

▶ Casati was active from 1965 as an industrial designer; from 1967, was coordinator and organizer of the furniture-production committee of the Biennale dello Standard nell'Arredamento, Mariano; office of economic problems in furniture production at the Mariano, Cantù, and Lissone events; provincial office for the promotion of exported furniture of Brianza at the Como, Cantù, and Mariano events. In 1969, Casati and (with Marcello De Carli) proposed a school for professional design focusing on industrial furniture; designed 1969 tricolor plastic lamp (with E. Ponzio) produced by Maisa; in 1970, became a member of ADI (Associazione per il Disegno Industriale); in 1972, (with C. Conte, Leonardo Fiori, and C. Visani) developed a prefabricated system for the Edilizia Sociale e Scolastica building; from 1974, was active in textile-design education; from 1975, was a consultant on the Larco/System.

▶ Tricolor plastic lamp shown at 1985 'Lumière je pense à vous' exhibition, Centre Georges Pompidou, Paris.

▶ *ADI Annual 1976*, Milan: Associazione per il Disegno Industriale, 1976. Cat., *Lumière je pense à vous*, Paris: Centre Georges Pompidou, 1985.

Casciani, Stefano (1955–)

▶ Italian architect and designer; born Rome; active Rome and Milan.

▶ Studied architecture, Rome.

▶ He produced industrial designs for Instituto Superiore di Disegno Industriale; from 1979, associated with journal *Domus*; also wrote for *Modo* and *Raum*; working with Zanotta furniture company from 1980, taught architecture in Florence and Milan.

▶ Participated in 1980 Biennale di Venezia and 1981 Triennale di Milano.

▶ Robert A.M. Stern (ed.), *The International Design Yearbook*, New York: Abbeville, 1985/1986: No. 207.

Caseneuve, André

▶ French artist and designer; active Paris.

▶ Caseneuve was best known for 1967 *Luminescent Stones* lighting fixtures, simulating stones placed on the floor, produced by Atelier A.

Cassandre (b. Adolphe Jean Édouard-Marie Mouron 1901–68)

▶ French graphic, jewelry, and theatre set designer; born Kharkov (Ukraine); active Paris.

▶ Studied Cormon studio, École des Beaux-Arts; La Grande Chaumière; and Académie Julian, under Lucien Simon and René Menard; all Paris.

▶ Cassandre's family settled in Paris in 1915; a graphic artist, was best known for his posters, particularly those promoting oceanliners. His geometric style of poster art first appeared in 1925 for Bûcheron, but his name became known as a result of his 1927 poster *Étoile du Nord* and others, advertising the railway lines of the Compagnie des Chemins de Fer du Nord. He created jewelry designs in the late 1920s that were made by Georges Fouquet; (with Maurice Moyrand and Charles Loupot) formed AGI (Alliance Graphique Internationale), joined later by Loupot. They designed a large number of posters, including *L'Intran*, *Grand Fêtes de Paris*, 1934 *Pernod*, *Wagons-lits Cook*, *Nicolas*, *Triples*, 1935 *Normandie*, and 1934 *Dubo . . . Dubon . . . Dubonnet*. He traveled to America several times. His theatrical designs included 1929 production *Amphytrion 38* by Jean Giraudoux and Festival d'Aix-en-Provence (*Don Giovanni* and others). His sets

were in an elaborate monumental style, partly neo-classical and partly surrealistic. In 1930, he became a member of UAM (Union des Artistes Modernes); from the late 1920s to mid-1930s, designed three typefaces with friend Charles Peignot of type foundry Deberny & Peignot—1929 *Bifur*, 1930 *Acier Noir*, and 1936 *Peignot*; and, shortly before his death, 1968 *Cassandre*. When Moyrand died in an automobile accident in 1934, AGI was closed. About this time, Cassandre ran a small school of design, where pupils included Raymond Savignac, Bernard Villemot, and André François; 1934–35, taught at École des Arts Décoratifs, Paris; up to the end of 1939, limited his typography almost exclusively to capital letters, feeling they improved modularity and increased monumentality; in 1963, designed the monogram of Yves Saint Laurent. He committed suicide.

▶ Received a grand prize (poster design) at 1925 Paris 'Exposition Internationale des Arts Décoratifs et Industriels Modernes.'

▶ Sylvie Raulet, *Bijoux Art Déco*, Paris: Regard, 1984. Henri Mouron, *Cassandre*, Geneva: Skira, 1985. Pierre Cabanne, *Encyclopédie Art Déco*, Paris: Somogy, 1986:179–80. Arlette Barré-Despond, *UAM*, Paris: Regard, 1986. Cat., *Les années UAM 1929–1958*, Paris: Musée des Arts Décoratifs, 1988:160–61.

Cassina (Cassina Amadeo)

▶ Italian furniture manufacturer; located Meda, Milano.

▶ Founded in 1927 by brothers, Umberto Cassina (d. 1991) and Cesare Cassina (1908–81), the Cassina Amadeo company was initially a shop for craft production. In the early 1900s the family turned from producing chairs and barrels to upholstered furniture; used outside craftsmen extensively. Its early work was principally produced for shops in Milan and large-scale middlemen, and its designs were based on historicist 19th-century models. In the 1930s, the firm made armchairs and dining room sets for the Rinascente department store and Mobilificio di Fogliano, both Milan. In 1935, the firm's name changed to Figli di Amadeo Cassina. Focusing more on Rationalist models, a new workshop was built in 1937–39. In 1940, German and French machinery was installed, and Cassina began managing its own advertising and distribution. It belatedly moved into Modernist styles. Produced at first for single customer-decorators, contemporary pieces were put into limited production, although few were innovative. After World War II, Cassina expanded its production and distribution procedures. 1947–52, it produced large quantities of furniture for the Italian navy. From the 1950s, Cassina was an international success. The new generation of designers pushed the firm into the forefront of Modern design. There was a short collaboration with Paolo Buffa, and a successful collaboration with architect-designer Franco Albini. The most fruitful design arrangement was with Gio Ponti, with whom Cesare Cassina worked from 1950 on furniture including the *Distex* armchair and 1957 *Superleggera* side chair, an international success that established Cassina's reputation. Its relationship with Vico Magistretti began in 1960 and with Tobia Scarpa in 1963. From 1965, it reproduced vintage Modern designs, beginning with the 1920s furniture of Le Corbusier, Jeanneret, and Perriand. Later reproductions included the furniture of Frank Lloyd Wright, Gerrit Rietveld, Charles Rennie Mackintosh, and others. The firm was amalgamated into the Steelcase Group in the late 1980s.

▶ Pier Carlo Santini, *Gli anni del design italiano: Ritratto di Cesare Cassina*, Milan: Electa, 1981. Penny Sparke, *Design in Italy, 1870 to the Present*, New York: Abbeville, 1988. 'La saggezza di Umberto,' *Ottagono*, No. 104, Sept. 1992:61–64.

Casson, Dinah (1946–)

▶ British furniture and interior designer.

▶ In 1970, she set up her own design studio; from 1984, was a partner (with Roger Mann) in Casson, Mann Associates, whose work included the design of ice-cream shops, offices, books, door furniture, light fittings, and furniture; 1982–88, was a member of the Design Council where she was a juror on several occasions; from 1978, was a design instructor and, presently, a tutor at the Royal College of Art, London.

Castellani, Alessandro (1824–83) and Augusto Castellani (1829–1914)

▶ Italian goldsmiths, silversmiths, and antiquarians; active Rome.

▶ Fortunato Piò Castellani (1793–1865) began working in his father's jewelry workshop in Rome in 1814, producing jewelry in the manner of contemporary French work. From c1826, he began producing gold and filigree jewelry copied from early Roman pieces unearthed in archeological excavations. In 1836, through friend and patron Michelangelo Caetani, Duke of Sermoneta, Castellani was an advisor on the excavation of the Regulini Galassi tomb, which yielded much Etruscan metalwork; sought to discover the techniques of ancient goldsmiths so that he could copy their granulated decorations; found craftspeople in the small town of St. Angelo in Vado in the Marches using techniques similar to those of the Etruscans, and moved them to Rome to work for him. Castellani's sons Alessandro and Augusto assumed management of the family firm in 1851, although no work was done in the Rome workshop from 1848–58 due to the political situation in Italy. Authorities on classical and antique jewelry, the brothers furthered their father's efforts in popularizing the archeological style. Augusto's collection of antique jewelry formed the basis of Villa Giulia collection, Rome. A large amount of the firm's 60-year production exists today; its quality and aesthetic level vary. The earliest extant jewelry drawings date from c1870. Caetani's drawings for the jewelry ensemble designed for the Countess of Crawford date from 1860–70. Saulini produced cameos for which the Castellanis executed gold mounts in the 1860s. The period from 1858 to the 1870s was the most prolific for jewelry of high quality. They showed archeological-style jewelry from 1861 in London. Augusto read a paper on the classical revival and techniques at the Archaeological Association, London. The brothers' archeological style was widely imitated in France, Britain, America, and Italy.

▶ Etruscan-style work shown at London 'International Exhibition of 1862.'.

▶ Charlotte Gere, *American and European Jewelry 1830–1914*, New York: Crown, 1975:162–64.

Castelli, Anna (1954–)

▶ Italian designer; born and active Milan.

▶ Studied Scuola Politecnica di Disegno, Milan.

▶ Designing from 1974, she collaborated with Giorgio Brambilla, Fabio Stojan, and Lorenzo Tosi in the studio Gruppo, Milan; (with Bruno Munari and Brambilla) developed toys; while teaching at the Facoltà di Architettura of the Politecnico di Milano, participated in Montedison's office of accident prenvention; became a member of ADI (Associazione per il Disegno Industriale).

▶ *ADI Annual 1976*, Milan: Associazione per il Disegno Industriale, 1976.

Castelli, Clino Trini (1944–)

▶ Italian designer.

▶ In 1958, she began working at the Centro Stile, Fiat; from 1969, was a consultant at Olivetti with Ettore Sottsass; in 1967, (with Elio Fiorucci) founded Intrapresa Design; in 1969, returned to Olivetti to work on its corporate-identity program, and designed fabrics for Abet Print; in 1973, (with Andrea Branzi and Massimo Morozzi) organized the Centro Design Montefibre; (with Branzi, Morozzi, Sottsass, and Alessandro Mendini) established IVI Colourterminal, the first center in Europe for the promotion, documentation, and research of color. In 1976, set up the studio CDM with Alessandro Mendini, Gianni Cutolo, and Ettore Sottsass; in 1979, was a co-founder of Habitaco, owned by Fiat-Comind, where she became design coordinator; subsequently, worked for automobile firms and for 3M on lighting. Clients included Vitra, Herman Miller, Ermenegildo Zegna, Dartington Mills, Visconti di Modrone, Zanotta, Cassina, Sony, Canon, and Fiat.

▶ Andrea Branzi, *La Casa Calda: Esperienze del Nuovo Disegno Italiano*, Milan: Idea Books, 1982. *Modo*, No. 148, March–April 1993:117.

Castelli del Bue, Livia (1945–)

▶ Italian industrial designer; born Rome; active Milan.

▶ Castelli del Bue began her professional career in 1971; designed small domestic appliances, plastic kitchenware, and furniture. Her hair brushes were produced by Verbania. Clients in Italy included Dal Vera, Elco, Fanini, Fain, Merlett, Mazzucchelli, Gedy, BBB Bonacina, and Chicco Arisana; others included Domco Industries, Canada, and Meblo Jugoplastics, Yugoslovia (now Slovenia): became a member of ADI (Associazione per il Disegno Industriale).

▶ *ADI Annual 1976*, Milan: Associazione per il Disegno Industriale, 1976.

Castelli, Giulio (1920–)

▶ Italian engineer and developer; active Binasco.

▶ Studied Politecnico di Milano, under Giulio Natta.

▶ Castelli was a chemical engineer and technical consultant; (with Gillo Dorfles, Ignazio Gardella, Vico Magistretti, Bruno Munari, Pellizzari, Peressutti, Alberto Rosselli, and Steiner) was a member of the promotion committee of ADI (Associazione per il Disegno Industriale) and its president for four years; from 1962, was on the guidance committee of the Premio Compasso d'Oro of ADI, after which he founded and directed Kartell in Binasco, producers of technical articles, kitchenware, and plastic furniture and furnishings; hired Anna Castelli-Ferrieri and Ignazio Gardella as consultant designers at Kartell.

▶ Participated in 1972 'Italy: The New Domestic Landscape' exhibition, New York Museum of Modern Art.

▶ *ADI Annual 1976*, Milan: Associazione per il Disegno Industriale, 1976.

Castelli Ferrieri, Anna (1920–)

▶ Italian architect and designer; born and active Milan.

▶ 1938–42, studied architecture, Politecnico di Milano.

▶ In 1945, she became founding member, Movimento Studi per l'Architettura, Milan; 1946–47, editor of the journal *Casabella-Costruzioni*; in 1946, set up her own architecture office, Milan; 1959–73, was a partner of architect-designer Ignazio Gardella, working on public-housing and furniture projects; (with Gardella) designed pioneering plastic furniture for Kartell; in 1952, became member, Instituto Nazionale di Urbanistica; 1955–60, architecture correspondent, *Architectural Design*; in 1956, became a founding member of ADI (Associazione per il Disegno Industriale) and its president 1969–71; in 1965, became active as an industrial designer; from 1966 as a consultant designer at Kartell, became artistic director of its in-house design group Centrocappa; was a plastics technology expert, designing injection-molded plastic chairs, tables, and storage systems. Her *4870* stacking armchair, which did not camouflage its crudely mixed polymer material, was influential. Architecture includes 1984–85 Parish Center, Casate, and 1983–85 Castek office building, Milan. In 1990, she established ACF Officino, architecture and design group with Luca Piatti.

▶ Received awards at 1947 (VIII) (two gold medals) and 1950 (IX) (gold medal) Triennali di Milano; 1968 Oscar Plast; 1969 silver medal, Österreichisches Bauzentrum, Vienna; 1972 gold medal, Mostra Internazionale Arredamento, Monza; 1972 MACEF award, Mostra Articoli Casalinghi Ferramenta; 1973 Bundespreis 'Die gute Industrieform'; 1977 Smau award, Salone Internazionale Ufficio; 1979 Product Design Award, Resources Council; 1979 and 1987 Premio Compasso d'Oro and ten special mentions in 1970, 1972, 1979, and 1984; 1981 Design Award, American Societies of Industrial Design; 1982, Design Award, Möbelmesse, Cologne. Work shown at numerous exhibitions, beginning with 1968 'Design Italian Style,' Hallmark Gallery, New York.

▶ Alfonso Grassi and Anty Pansera, *Atlante del design italiano: 1940–80*, Milan: Fabbri, 1980. Andrea Branzi and Michele de Lucchi, *Design Italiano degli Anni '50*, Milan: Editoriale Domus, 1980. Fumio Shimizu and Matteo Thun (eds.), *The Descendants of Leonardo: The Italian Design*, Tokyo, 1987:333.

Castiglioni, Giorgina　(1943–)

▶ Italian designer; active Milan.

▶ Studied architecture, Politecnico di Milano, to 1969.

▶ Castiglioni began her professional career in 1971; became a member of ADI (Associazione per il Disegno Industriale). Designing furniture and lighting, clients in Italy included Audiomatic, Bilumen, Crien, Elle, Gufram, Kartell, Pedano, Sirrah, and Valenti; and Sirrah Iberica, Barcelona.

▶ Received first prize (plastic seating by Kartell) 1965 'Fiera di Trieste.' Participated in 1971 UCIMU competition of ADI.

▶ *ADI Annual 1976*, Milan: Associazione per il Disegno Industriale, 1976.

Castiglioni, Livio　(1911–79)

▶ Italian industrial designer; active Milan; brother of Pier Giacomo Castiglioni and Achille Castiglioni.

▶ Studied architecture, Politecnico di Milano, to 1936.

▶ In 1938, Castiglioni and his brother Pier Giacomo set up a studio with Luigi Caccia Dominioni, which closed in 1940. In 1940, they designed silver and aluminum flatware and the 1940 first Italian plastic (bakelite) *Model 547* radio by Phonola. 1940–60, Castiglioni was a consultant to Phonola and, 1960–64, consultant and agent to Brionvega; from 1946, collaborated on audio-visual technology with Radio Televisione Italiana, Montecatini Edison, Fiat, Eni, Italsider, Osram, the Eurodomus fair, La Rinascente department store, and Olivetti; (with Umberto Eco) designed the audio-visual presentations at the Italian pavilion, 1967 Montreal 'Universal and International Exhibition (Expo '67); (with Davide Boriani) designed the audio-visuals in the experimental section, 1970 (XXXV) Biennale di Venezia; until c1952, pursued lighting design, sometimes collaborating with brothers Pier Giacomo and Achille; in 1956, was active in the founding of ADI (Associazione per il Disegno Industriale), of which he was president 1959–60. His lighting work often incorporated industrial materials and new types of bulb, including his 1970 *Boalum* snake-like lighting (with Gianfranco Frattini) produced by Artemide.

▶ Received a gold medal (with others) at 1936 (VI) Triennale di Milano, grand prize (design) and gold medal (audio-visual environment) at 1940 (VII) Triennale, grand prize (audio-visual environment) at 1965 (XIII) Triennale, and 1968 gold medal for Pioneering Industrial Design. Jury member at 1954 (X) Triennale.

▶ Paolo Fossati, *Il design in italia*, Turin, 1972:122–27,224–33, plates 310–54. *ADI Annual 1976*, Milan: Associazione per il Disegno Industriale, 1976. Alfonso Grassi and Anty Pansera, *Atlante del design italiano: 1940–1980*, Milan: Fabbri, 1980:279. Andrea Branzi and Michele De Lucchi (eds.), *Il design italiano degli anni '50*, Milan, 1981. Daniele Baroni, *L'Oggetto lampada*, Milan, 1981:128–37, figs. 292–321. Cat., *Lumière je pense à vous*, Paris: Centre Georges Pompidou, 1985. Vittorio Gregotti (introduction), *Castiglioni*, Milan: Electa, 1985.

Castiglioni, Pier Giacomo　(1913–68)　and **Achille Castiglioni** (1918–)

▶ Italian designers; active Milan; brothers of Livio Castiglioni.

▶ Studied architecture, Politecnico di Milano, to 1937 and 1944 respectively.

▶ In 1938, Pier Giacomo Castiglioni and brother Livio set up a studio with Luigi Caccia Dominioni. They designed silver and aluminum flatware in 1940 and the first Italian plastic (bakelite) *Model 547* radio just before the studio was closed in 1940. In 1945, Pier Giacomo and Achille began collaborating separately from Livio, though participating with him occasionally. The prolific Castiglioni brothers were instrumental in founding the Triennale di Milano, the establishment of the Premio Compasso d'Oro in 1954, and the formation of ADI (Associazione per il Disegno Industriale) in 1956; collaborated on the journal *Stile Industria*; taught architecture in Milan and Turin, together and separately; worked together and collaborated with other designers. Their collaboration on exhibition and product design lasted 25 years. Using industrial materials, experimental forms, and advanced technology, they also produced lighting. The brothers' most notable interior design work was for the 1958 Radio Exhibition and 1962 Montecantini Pavilion, both at the Milan fairs. They went on to design plastics; ceramics; glassware; appliances for Nova Radio (1956 six-valve radio), Elettrodomestici, and Brionvega; metalware for Alessi; earphones for Phoebus Alter; and furniture for Kartell, Bernini, Beylerian, Zanotta, and Gavina. Other clients included Knoll, Lancia, Siemens, Gilardi e Barzaghi, Fonderie Perani, SLM, S. Giorgio, B&B Italia, Poggi, Ideal Standard, Bonacina, Bacci, Rem, and OMSA. 1965–77, Achille was head of the Facoltà di Architettura, Politecnico di Milano; in 1983, began working with Danese. His 1982 *Dry* flatware for Alessi proved popular.

▶ Their lighting included the 1949 *Turbino* desk lamp produced by Arreduluce, 1950 *Taraxacum* hanging lamp by Flos, 1951 hanging lamp by Castaldi, 1954 street lamp by Pollice, and 1955 *Luminator* indirect light by Gilardi. Their best known designs include 1956 *Spalter* vacuum cleaner by Rem, 1962 *Arco* lamp, 1972 *Toio* lamp by Flos adapted from an automobile headlight, 1957 *Messandro* stool designed with Pier Giacomo (a tractor seat, inspired by Marcel Duchamp's *Readymade*) by Zanotta from 1971, and 1979 *Cumano* folding metal tables by Zanotta. Achille's work included 1980–84 oil and vinegar flasks by Alessi, 1980 *Gibigiana* lamp by Flos, 1982 *Solone* table system by Marcatré, 1983 *Poltrona Imperiale* chair by Zanotta, 1983 *Paro* drinking glasses by Danese, 1983 *Rosacamuna* chair by Zanotta, 1985 *Grip* lamp by Flos, 1984 *Cinque C* hardware-fittings by Fusital, 1984 *Cot* bench by Zanotta, 1986 flagpoles by Zanotta, 1986 *Spluga* stool by Zanotta, 1986 *Ititti* bed (with Giancarlo Pozzi) by Interflex, and 1983 *Alberto* flowerpot holder by Zanotta.

▶ The brothers participated in Triennale di Milano from 1947 (VIII) to 1964 (XIII) and Achille Castiglioni alone afterwards, receiving 1955, 1960, 1962, 1964, 1967, 1969, 1984 Premi Compasso d'Oro (including five with Pier Giacomo); in 1986 elected Honorary Royal Designer for Industry, London. The 1984–86 'Achille Castiglioni' traveling exhibition originated at Triennale di Milano. The *Boalum* lighting (with Frattini) was included in 1984 'Design Since 1945' exhibition, Philadelphia Museum of Art, and 1985 'Lumière je pense à vous' exhibition, Centre Georges Pompidou, Paris. The 1961 *Sanluca* chair, their *Arco* floor lamp for Flos, and Pier Giacomo's and Gianfranco Frattini's 1970 *Boalum* snake lighting was included in 1991 'Mobili Italiani 1961–1991: Le Varie Età dei linguaggi' exhibition, Salone del Mobile, Milan.

▶ Agnoldomenico Pica, 'Piergiacomo Castiglioni,' *Domus*, No. 470, Jan. 1969:1–2. Vittorio Gregotti, 'Ricordo di Pier Giacomo Castiglioni,' *Ottagono*, No. 12, Jan. 1969:20–23. Paolo Fossati, *Il design in Italia*, Turin, 1972:122–27,224–33, plates 310–54. Andrea Branzi and Michele De Lucchi, *Design Italiano Degli Anni '50*, Milan: Editoriale Domus, 1980. Alfonso Grassi and Anty Pansera, *Atlante del design italiano: 1940–1980*, Milan: Fabbri, 1980: 279. Daniele Baroni, *L'Oggetto lampada*, Milan:, 1981:128–37, figs. 292–321. Cat., Kathryn B. Hiesinger and George H. Marcus III (eds.), *Design Since 1945*, Philadelphia: Philadelphia Museum of Art, 1983. Cat., *Lumière je pense à vous*, Paris: Centre Georges Pompidou, 1985. *Les Carnets du Design*, Paris: Mad-Cap Productions et APCI, 1986:47,68. Cat., *Achille Castiglioni*, Paris: Centre Georges Pompidou, 1986. Cherie Fehrman and Kenneth Fehrman, *Postwar Interior Design, 1945–1960*, New York: Van Nostrand Reinhold, 1987. Juli Capella and Quim Larrea, *Designed by Architects in the 1980s*, New York: Rizzoli, 1988.

Castle, Wendell　(1932–)

▶ American furniture designer; born Emporia, Kansas.

▶ Studied University of Kansas, Lawrence, Kansas, to 1961.

▶ In the early 1960s, designed and produced one-off furniture in provocative forms and pioneered a technique in which he used laminated wood in stacks that he carved into amorphic forms for use as chairs and other seating; designed the quirky 'Library of Dr. Caligari' installation in the residence of furniture collector

Peter Joseph, New York, who underwrote Castle's *Angel Chair* project.
▶ Work subject of 1991 USA traveling exhibition, including the American Crafts Museum, New York, and 1991 exhibition, Peter Joseph Gallery, New York, where his *Angel Chair* was introduced.
▶ *Furniture of Wendell Castle*, Wichita: Wichita Art Museum, 1969. *Wooden Works: Five Objects by Five Contemporary Craftsmen*, Washington: Renwick Gallery, 1972. *Fine Art of a Furniture Maker: Conversations with Wendell Castle*, Rochester: Memorial at Gallery of University of Rochester, 1981. Davira Spiro Taragin, *Furniture of Wendell Castle*, New York: Rizzoli 1989. Sara Medford, 'Art for Living, Wendell Castle,' *Metropolis*, October 1991:99. Auction cat., 'Contemporary Works of Art,' Sotheby's New York, 14 March 1992.

Caturegli, Beppe
▶ Italian architect and designer; born Pisa.
▶ Studied architecture, Università di Firenze.
▶ From 1982, he worked for Sottsass Associati, Milan; collaborated with Giovannella Formica.
▶ Received award in New Architecture Design competition.
▶ Fumio Shimizu and Matteo Thun (eds.), *The Descendants of Leonardo: The Italian Design*, Tokyo, 1987:325.

Caulkins, Horace James   (1850–1923)
▶ American inventor.
▶ Caulkins invented the gas-fired Revelation kiln installed in numerous art potteries in the USA; collaborated with Mary Chase Perry on porcelain decoration and production in Detroit.
▶ L.M. Pear, *The Pewabic Pottery: A History of its Products and its People*, Des Moines, 1976.

Caussé, Julien
▶ French metalworker; active Paris.
▶ His themes were primarily women and flowers. Best known for his *Fée des Glaces* (Ice Fairy) sculpture, his small bronzes included busts, statuettes, trays; he also produced bronze, stone, marble, and pewter sculptural lamps. Fond of allegorical and mythological titles, Caussé produced lamps in the form of young women.
▶ Small bronzes shown at Salons of the Société des Artistes français and Maison Eugène Blot.
▶ Alastair Duncan, *Art Nouveau and Art Déco Lighting*, New York: Simon and Schuster, 1978:70–71.

Cavaillon, Gaston
▶ French furniture designer.
▶ Cavaillon designed the *510* chair in *c*1945. 350,000 copies of the inexpensive chair, produced by Mullca, were sold to colleges, universities, and other institutions.

Cavart
▶ Italian design group.
▶ Active from 1973–76 in Padua, Cavart was founded by students Michele De Lucchi, Piero Brombin, Pierpaola Bortolami, Boris Premù, and Valerio Tridenti. The name derives from *cava* (quarry). Contemporary with Global Tools and the Anti-Design movement, the group organized events in and around the quarries of Florence, which served as natural amphitheaters. At one meeting, participants designed shirts on paper that they wore and, in 1975, copied Pablo Picasso's *Guernica* to show in the main squares of Milan, Venice, and Padua to protest the violation of human rights, particularly in Chile; this was destroyed in Bologna. In 1975, about 100 architects, artists, and students attended Cavart's 'Architettura Impossibile' meeting, where utopian structures were designed and in some cases built in the quarries at Monselice, near Padua. Cavart's films, happenings, performances, and contests were manifestations of the Anti-Design movement in Italy.
▶ 'Itinerario di Guernica,' *Casabella*, No. 406, 1975:10–13. Cat., *Michele De Lucchi*, The Hague: Uitgeverij Komplement, 1985.

Cazin, Michel   (1869–1917)
▶ French ceramicist; born Paris.
▶ He worked at the Fulham Pottery 1872–74; lived for a time in Paris, Bordeaux, and, from 1908, in London.
▶ Work shown at 1897 Salon of the Société Nationale des Beaux-Arts.
▶ *Europäische Keramik, 1880–1930: Sammlung Silzer*, Darmstadt: Hessissches Landesmuseum, 1986:77.

C&B Italia
▶ Italian furniture manufacturer; located Grisignano di Zocco.
▶ C&B Italia was founded in 1956 by the Cassina brothers and Piero Busnelli to produce contemporary furniture.
▶ See B&B Italia

CCI (Centre de Création Industrielle)
▶ French design organization.
▶ CCI was established in 1969 by François Mathey, Yolande Amic, and François Barré, and was modeled on the London and Brussels design centers. Mathey was chief curator at the Paris Musée des Arts Décoratifs when Barré proposed the idea of a French design center. Its first exhibition was 1969 'Qu'est ce que le design?,' where furniture designed by Roger Tallon, Charles Eames, Joe Colombo, and others was on display. Its 1971 'Le design français' exhibition was dedicated to young designers. CCI operated an information center for business people, students, and designers, and became a department of Centre Georges Pompidou, Paris.

CDM (Consulenti Design Milano)
▶ Italian design firm.
▶ Andrea Branzi, Gianni Cutolo, Alessandro Mendini, Clini Trini Castelli, and Ettore Sottsass founded CDM in 1973 with the intention of creating large-scale projects, such as corporate identity programs, landscapes, and advanced research. 1973–77, they collaborated in Centro Design Montefibre. Commissions included the landscape and corporate image of Leonardo da Vinci airport, Rome; information system for new Italian post offices; Louis Vuitton products; first center of Colorterminal creative colorimetrics; Piaggio Color System; and work on Centro Design Montefibre.
▶ Received 1979 Premio Compasso d'Oro for 'Fibermatching 25-Meracion.'
▶ Alfonso Grassi and Anty Pansera, *Atlante del design italiano: 1940–1980*, Milan, 1980:295. Andrea Branzi, *La Casa Calda: Esperienze del Nuovo Disegno Italiano*, Milan: Idea Books, 1982. Hans Wichmann, *Italien Design 1945 bis heute*, Munich: Die Neue Sammlung, 1988.

Ceccariglia, Carla   (1955–)
▶ Italian designer; born Rome; active Milan.
▶ Studied Industrial Design Institute of Art, Rome.
▶ She worked with Enzo Mari and on the staff of Decòro of the Centrodomus Studio 1979–80; joined Studio Alchimia in 1981; for Limonta, was in charge of textile design and clothing.
▶ Kazuko Sato, *Alchimia*, Berlin: Taco, 1988.

CEI (Compagnie de l'Esthétique Industrielle)
▶ French design firm.
▶ CEI was established by Raymond Loewy in 1951 in Paris; for 25 years was a diverse design firm; in 1982, was taken over by five of its former employees; mainly designs industrial products.

Celada, Gianni   (1935–)
▶ Italian designer; born and active Milan.
▶ Celada began his professional career in 1961; was artistic consultant, Fontana Arte, Corsico; became a member of ADI (Associazione per il Disegno Industriale). Designing furniture, lighting, and shelving systems, clients included Saint-Gobain, Cedit, Reflex-Vastill, Lar, and Giancarlo Pozzi.
▶ *ADI Annual 1976*, Milan: Associazione per il Disegno Industriale, 1976.

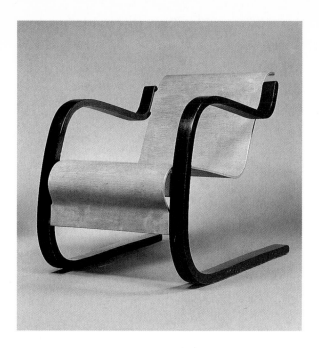

1 *31* armchair; birch plywood, painted bentwood, c1930–33. Designed by Alvar Aalto, produced by Artek, Helsinki. (The Metropolitan Museum of Art, New York, purchase, Robert and Meryl Meltzer gift, 1984)

2 Side chair; cherrywood, cane, c1925. Designed by Erich Dieckmann for the Staatlichen Hochschule für Handwerk und Baukunst, Munich. (Die Neue Sammlung, Staatliches Museum für angewandte Kunst, Munich)

3 *The Hunt; toile de Tournon* pattern printed on linen c1920. Designed by Raoul Dufy, produced by Bianchini-Férier, Lyons, France. (The Metropolitan Museum of Art, New York, purchase, Edward C. Moore Jr gift, 1923)

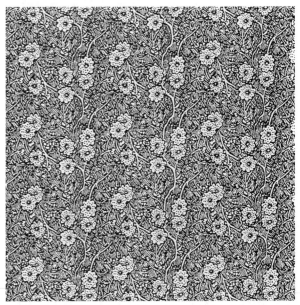

5 *S988* textile; printed cotton, c1972. Designed by Laura Ashley, produced by Laura Ashley Ltd. (The Metropolitan Museum of Art, New York, gift of Laura Ashley Shops Ltd, Toronto, 1977)

4 Fabric; linen and cotton, c1950. Designed and woven by Anni Albers. (The Metropolitan Museum of Art, New York, gift of Anni Albers, 1970)

6 *Gabon* fabric; printed in red, green, purple, and white on cotton, 1982. Designed by Nathalie du Pasquier, produced by Rainbow, Milan, Italy. (The Metropolitan Museum of Art, New York, gift of Geoffrey N. Bradfield, 1986)

7 Armchair; possibly
birch, 1901.
Designed and produced by
Mackay Hugh Baillie Scott.
(The Metropolitan Museum
of Art, New York,
The Cynthia Hazen Polsky
Fund, 1987)

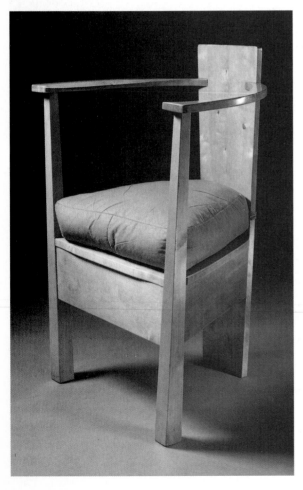

8 *Cobra* chair; wood,
parchment, gesso, gilt, 1902.
Designed by Carlo Bugatti
for the 'Camera del Bovolo'
('Snail Room') at the 1902
*'Esposizione Internazionale
d'Arte Decorativa
Moderna,'* Turin.
(The Brooklyn Museum,
Brooklyn, New York,
the Guennol Collection)

9 Armchair; oak, orange herringbone wool upholstery, 1922. Designed by Marcel Breuer, produced in the workshop of the Bauhaus, Weimar, Germany. (The Metropolitan Museum of Art, New York, purchase, Theodore Robert Gamble Jr gift, in honor of his mother Mrs Theodore Robert Gamble, and Lita Annenberg Hazen Charitable Trust gifts, 1983)

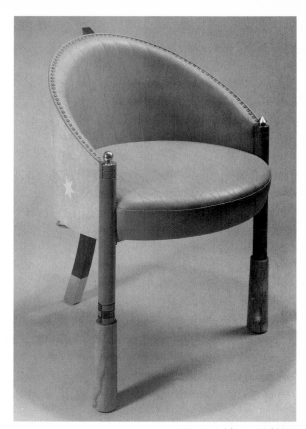

10 *Frankfurter Stuhl FIII* armchair; bird's-eye maple, leather, marble, ebony, lacquered wood, brass, 1986–7. Designed by Norbert Berghof, Michael Landes, and Wolfgang Rang, produced by Draenert Studio, Immenstaad/Bodensee, Germany, 1989. (The Metropolitan Museum of Art, New York, gift of Dr Peter Draenert, Immenstaad/Bodensee, 1988)

15 Lounge chair; wood,
fabric, 1938–9.
Designed by Franco Albini,
produced for Knoll,
Greenville, Pennsylvania,
from 1949. (Knoll)

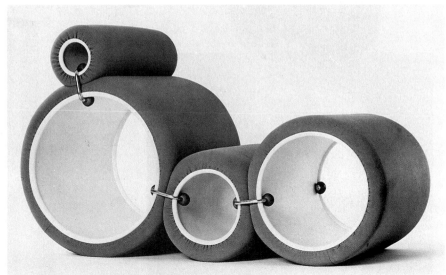

16 *Tube* chair (no. 0133);
plastic, polyurethane,
synthetic-knit fabric, 1969.
Designed by Joe Colombo,
produced by Flexform,
Meda, Italy.
(The Metropolitan Museum
of Art, New York, purchase,
Theodore Robert Gamble Jr
gift, in honor of his mother
Mrs Theodore Robert
Gamble, 1987)

17 *AEO* armchair;
lacquered steel, molded plastic,
canvas upholstery, 1974.
Designed by Archizoom
(Andrea Branzi, Gilberto
Corretti, Massimo Morozzi,
Paolo Deganello),
produced by Cassina, Milan.
(The Metropolitan Museum
of Art, New York, gift of
Cassina S.p.A., 1988)

18 *Vertebra* armchair;
polyurethane, leather,
metal, 1979.
Designed by Emilio Ambasz
and Giancarlo Piretti,
produced by Cassina, Milan.
(The Metropolitan Museum
of Art, New York,
gift of Open Ark,
The Netherlands, 1989)

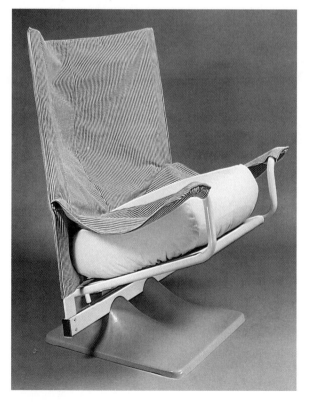

19 Radiator; glass, 1937.
Designed by René Coulon,
produced by Saint-Gobain,
Chapelle St.-Mesmin, France.
(Musée des Arts Décoratifs, Paris)

21 *Phonola* radio no. 573);
Bakelite, metal, 1939.
Designed by Livio and Pier
Giacomo Castiglioni with
Luigi Caccia Dominioni,
produced by Phonola
Radio Milan, Saronno, Italy.
(Die Neue Sammlung,
Staatliches Museum
für angewandte
Kunst, Munich)

20 Electric fan; black-
painted metal, brass, c1912.
Designed by Peter Behrens,
produced by AEG, Berlin.
(Die Neue Sammlung,
Staatliches Museum für
angewandte Kunst, Munich)

22 *Auto-Mat* wall clock
(no. 322/0389); metal,
glass, 1957.
Designed by Max Bill,
produced by Junghans,
Schramberg, Germany.
(Die Neue Sammlung,
Staatliches Museum für
angewandte Kunst, Munich)

23 *Landi-Stuhl*; aluminium,
rubber glides, 1938.
Designed by Hans Coray for
1938 Zürich 'Landesausstellung,'
produced by P. & W. Blattmann,
Metall- und Aluminium-Fabrik,
Wädenswill, Switzerland.
(Die Neue Sammlung,
Staatliches Museum für
angewandte Kunst, Munich)

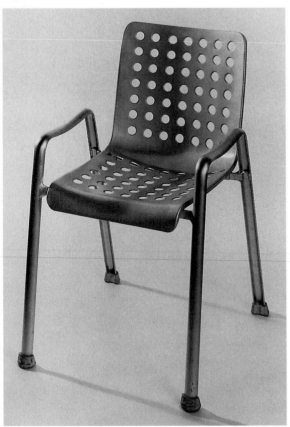

24 *S88* folding chair;
molded plywood,
black-painted tubular
steel, 1958. Designed by
Osvaldo Borsani,
produced by Tecno, Milan.
(The Brooklyn Museum,
Brooklyn New York, gift of
Barry Friedman)

25 *Seconda* armchair;
black- and grey-painted
steel, polyurethane, 1982.
Designed by Mario Botta,
produced by Alias,
Bergamo, Italy.
(The Metropolitan Museum
of Art, New York,
gift of ICF, 1988)

26 *Liliplon* side chair;
resin, steel, 1987.
Designed by
François Bauchet,
produced by Néotù, Paris.
(Cooper-Hewitt National
Museum of Design,
Smithsonian Institution/Art
Resource, New York,
gift of VIA France,
photography by John White)

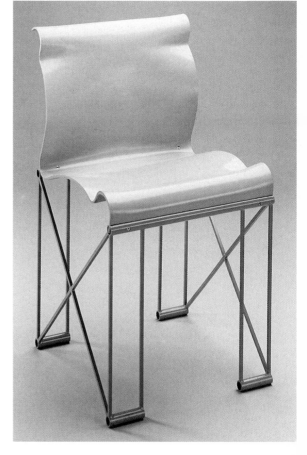

27 *Aino Aalto* plates (no. 2249);
centrifugal-cast clear glass, 1986,
based on 1932 design.
Designed by Aino Aalto, produced
by Ahlström/Iittala, Finland.
(Die Neue Sammlung, Staatliches
Museum für angewandte Kunst, Munich)

28 Wine pitcher; clear glass, silver-plated metal, ebony, 1881–2. Designed by Christopher Dresser, produced by Jonathan Wilson Hukin & John Thomas Heath, Birmingham, England. (Die Neue Sammlung, Staatliches Museum für angewandte Kunst, Munich)

29 *Rastergeschirr 2298* dinner service; white-glazed porcelain, 1972. Designed by Hans Theo Baumann, produced by Porzellanmanufaktur Schönwald, Schönwald, Germany. (Die Neue Sammlung, Staatliches Museum für angewandte Kunst, Munich)

31 Table lamp;
nickel-plated metal, c1926.
Designed and produced
by Desny, Paris.
(Die Neue Sammlung,
Staatliches Museum für
angewandte Kunst, Munich)

30 Table lamp; glass,
stoneware, 1895–1900.
Designed and produced by
Pierre-Adrien Dalpayrat
(base) and Louis Comfort
Tiffany (shade). (The
Metropolitan Museum of
Art, New York, gift of Ruth
and Frank Stanton, 1981)

32 *Anglepoise* adjustable
table lamp; black-painted
metal, Bakelite shade, 1932.
Designed by
George Carwardine,
produced by Herbert Terry
& Sons, Redditch, England.
(Die Neue Sammlung,
Staatliches Museum für
angewandte Kunst, Munich)

Cellini Shop, The

▶ American silversmiths; located Evanston, Illinois.
▶ The Cellini Shop was founded in 1914 by Ernest Gerlach. 1916–19, David and Walter Mulholland worked there, and, in the 1920s, Hans Gregg and Wilhelm Conrad from Germany were its most important artisans. In 1969, it was acquired by the Randahl Company.
▶ Annelies Krekel-Aalberse, *Art Nouveau and Art Déco Silver*, New York: Abrams, 1989:252.

celluloid

▶ Celluloid nitrate was the first plastic; a patent for its commercial application was applied for in 1865. In 1899, casein, a type of protein plastic, was produced in Germany and used for buttons and jewelry, thanks to its ability to hold bright colors. After World War I, cellulose acetate appeared and was used for fabrics, films, and, later, injection-molded toilet articles.
▶ Michael Farr, *Design in British Industry: A Mid-Century Survey*, London: Cambridge, 1955:123.

Cenedese

▶ Italian glass manufacturer.
▶ In 1945, Gino Cenedese opened a glass-making factory and achieved immediate recognition; developed a number of techniques for surfaces including *scavo* (rough, matt surface suggesting antiquity) and the application of minerals to surfaces. In the late 1940s, Alfredo Barbini worked for the firm. In the 1950s, Antonio da Ros designed transparent sculptural pieces and, from 1965, was chief designer.
▶ Cat., *Venini and Murano Renaissance: Italian Art Glass of the 1940s and 50s*, New York: Fifty/50, 1984.

Century Guild, The

▶ British cooperative; located London.
▶ The Century Guild was formed in 1882 by A.J. Mackmurdo and Selwyn Image and included Herbert P. Horne, sculptor Benjamin Creswick, stained-glass designer, enamelist, and metalworker Clement Heaton; and metalworkers George Esling and Kellock Brown. Others associated with the Guild were Heywood Sumner and William De Morgan. Members executed decorative work of all types, much of it shown as cooperative work. The Music Room, first mounted at the 1884 'Health Exhibition,' London, and with minor changes at the 1887 'Inventions Exhibition,' London, was designed and furnished by Guild members. The first issue of the Guild magazine *The Hobby Horse*, printed at the Chiswick Press, appeared in 1884; the next issue was in 1886. Successful until 1888, the Guild was less productive subsequently, although members continued to work together. Among the first of the crafts guilds, it exerted a great influence on the Craft Revival movement. Its stand at the 'Liverpool Exhibition' influenced interior decoration at the turn of the century.
▶ Isabelle Anscombe and Charlotte Gere, *Arts and Crafts in Britain and American*, Rizzoli, 1978:111.

Cerbaro, Carlo Antonio (1935–)

▶ Italian architect and designer; born and active Milan.
▶ Studied architecture to 1964.
▶ Cerbaro began his career in design in 1968. Executing designs for furniture, hardware, plastics, and lighting, clients in Italy included Porado Arredi (furnishings), Citterio Giulio (handles), Rossi Felice (furniture), Reggiani Goffredo (lighting), Santambrogio e De Berti (Italy), Fumagalli Arredamenti di Carlo (furniture), and Giuseppe Pozzi (furniture). He became a member of ADI (Associazione per il Disegno Industriale).
▶ *ADI Annual 1976*, Milan: Associazione per il Disegno Industriale, 1976.

Ceresolla, Claudio (1947–)

▶ Italian architect and designer; born and active Suzzara.
▶ Ceresolla began his professional career in 1974; designed the interior architecture of the firm Scaravelli e Baraldi; designed stage sets for a theatrical group in Suzzara and interior architecture,

lighting, furniture, and advertising layouts for various other clients; became a member of ADI (Associazione per il Disegno Industriale).
▶ *ADI Annual 1976*, Milan: Associazione per il Disegno Industriale, 1976.

Cerri, Pierluigi (1939–)

▶ Italian architect and industrial, graphic, and exhibition designer.
▶ Studied architecture, Politecnico di Milano.
▶ Cerri was a partner in the architecture firm Gregotti Associati; designed the 1976 Biennale di Venezia, for Electa publishing company, and for Palazzo Grassi, Venice; was a designer of books and art director of magazines *Rassegna* and *Casabella*, editor of the latter, and associated with the journal *Lotus International*; was responsible for the graphic design series *Pagina*; active as an exhibition designer, designed 1978 'Peter Behrens und die AEG' exhibition, Berlin; 1978 'Carrozzeria Italiana' exhibition, Turin and Rome; 1981 'Identité Italienne,' Centre Georges Pompidou, Paris; 1983 'Alexander Calder' exhibition, Turin; 1984 'Italian Design,' Stuttgart and Tokyo; 1984 'Venti Progetti per il futuro del Lingotto,' Turin; 1986 'Futurismo e Futurismi,' Venice. Industrial design clients included B&B Italia, Fiat, IBM, Molteni, Unifor, Missoni, and Marotto.
▶ *Okuspokus* armoire-vitrine shown at 1985 Triennale di Milano.
▶ Auction cat., *Asta di Modernariato 1900–1986, Auction 'Modernariato,'* Milan: Semenzato Nuova Geri, 8 Oct. 1986. Juli Capella and Quim Larrea, *Designed by Architects in the 1980s*, New York, Rizzoli, 1988.

Cerrutti, Antoinette

▶ French bookbinder and gilder; active Paris.
▶ 1925–31 studied bookbinding, École Nationale Supérieure des Arts Décoratifs, Paris, under Andrée Langrand.
▶ Binding books in her own library at first, she received commissions from collectors; in 1931, set up a bindery in Paris; used colored inlays and gold fillets. Influenced at first by Pierre Legrain's binding designs, her work by the early 1940s was more akin to Paul Bonet's. Reminiscent of his first irradiant designs of the 1930s yet airier and more lightly handled, her approach was applied to volumes including *Le Roman de Tristan et d'Iseult, L'Homme qui assassina*, and *Poèmes*.
▶ Bindings shown annually at Salons of Société des Artistes Décorateurs.
▶ Lucien Farnoux-Reynaud, 'La Reliure d'art: Triomphe du goût français,' *Mobilier et décoration*, Feb. 1938:74. Henri Colas, 'Les Reliures d'Antoinette Cerutti [sic],' *Mobilier et décoration*, Jan. 1948:31–37. Alastair Duncan and Georges de Bartha, *Art Nouveau and Art Déco Bookbinding*, New York: Abrams, 1989:188.

Cesana, Roberto (1930–)

▶ Italian industrial designer; born and active Milan.
▶ Best known for his sanitary fittings, his clients in Italy included Ceramica Dolomite, Veca, and Thema. He became a member of ADI (Associazione per il Disegno Industriale).
▶ *ADI Annual 1976*, Milan: Associazione per il Disegno Industriale, 1976.

César (aka César Baldaccini 1921–)

▶ French sculptor; born Marseilles; active in the south of France.
▶ Studied Écoles des Beaux-Arts, Marseilles and Paris.
▶ He was first recognized as an artist in the late 1950s with his assemblages of scrap from a suburban foundry; went on to compress old cars and combine other junk; in the 1960s, began to design in crystal, encouraged by Jacques Daum; in the 1970s and 1980s, experimented with synthetic materials; used expanding plastic-foam in his sculpture as well as in his furniture, including 1968 prototype lounge chair in expanded foam for Mobilier National and 1969 *César Chair* by Zol; best known in the applied arts for his carved wood chair in the shape of a hand; in 1965, made a 6ft (1.85m) enlargement of his thumb.

▶ Work first subject of exhibition in Paris in 1954. Represented in French Pavilion at 1956 Biennale di Venezia and 1959 Documenta II. In 1957, received first prize as a foreign sculptor, Carrara. Work shown worldwide including 1961 'Modern Jewellery Exhibition,' London, and experimental furniture at 1962 'Antagonisme II: l'objet' (organized by François Mathey) and 1968 'Les Assises du siège contemporain,' both Paris Musée des Arts Décoratifs. César Chair included in 1970 'International Furniture Exhibition,' Cologne, and 1970 'Modern Chairs 1918–1970' exhibition, Whitechapel Gallery, London. Work for Cristallerie Daum subject of exhibition, Musée des Arts Décoratifs, Paris, organized by François Mathey.

▶ Cat., Les Assises du siège contemporain, Paris: Musée des Arts Décoratifs, 1968. Cat., Modern Chairs 1918–1970, London: Lund Humphries, 1971. Cat., Verriers français contemporains: Art et industrie, Paris: Musée des Arts Décoratifs, 1982. Otto Hahn and César, Les Sept Vies de César. Stephen O'Shea, 'César in the Kitchen,' Elle Decor, Winter 1990:150–57.

Cetti Serbelloni, Francesco (1952–)
▶ Italian designer; born Appiano Gentile; active Milan.
▶ Cetti began his professional career in 1952; became a member of ADI (Associazione per il Disegno Industriale). Clients in Italy included Uvet Dimensioni, Collezione Delta, Salviati, Olivari, Giuseppe Rossi, Turri Giosuè and Cava Inox.
▶ ADI Annual 1976, Milan: Associazione per il Disegno Industriale, 1976.

Chabanne
▶ French metalworkers.
▶ The firm was founded by François Chabanne in 1912 in Thiers; in the beginning, produced cutlery. In 1924, the family of Brugere joined the firm, which was renamed Chabanne-Brugere. Production included the use of stainless steel from 1930 and silver from 1953.

Chadwick, Don (1936–)
▶ American furniture designer.
▶ Studied industrial design, University of California at Los Angeles.
▶ He worked for architect Victor Gruen; in 1964, set up his own practice in Los Angeles; designed 1979 C-Forms office desk system and 1974 modular curved seating system for Herman Miller; began collaborating with Bill Stumpf in the design firm Chadwick, Stumpf and Associates, Winona, Minnesota; the firm's ergonomic 1983 Equa flexing-plastic chair was produced by Herman Miller.

Chafik (1962–)
▶ Algerian designer; born Algiers; active Paris.
▶ Studied architecture, Paris-Tolbiac University.
▶ He designed the 1990 chairs Monsieur, Madame, Mademoiselle, and Culbuto; produced his furniture through his own firm, Univers Interieur.
▶ From 1991, work shown at Salon du Meuble, Paris. Received 1992 Grand Prix de la Critique.
▶ François Mathey, Au bonheur des formes, design français 1945–1992, Paris: Regard, 1992:265.

Chalon, Louis (1866–1916)
▶ French painter and designer; active Paris.
▶ Studied under Jules Lefebre and Boulanger.
▶ He began his career as a painter and illustrator, illuminating the works of Rabelais, Boccaccio, and Balzac; by 1900, had become an accomplished illustrator and rendered drawings for periodicals Figaro Illustré, L'Illustration, and La Vie Parisienne; was active as a gem-setter, couturier, ceramicist, and sculptor; about 1898, began designing lamps, inkwells, vases, clocks, and furniture; in 1898, was commissioned to produce a series of trompe-l'œil illustrations to mimic white-and-blue porcelain. He subsequently produced models for other objects, including a range of bronzes, frequently cast by Louchet. Chalon's portrait busts, clocks, inkwells, vase of the Hesperides, and silvered and chased watering-can exemplified

work that could have been mistaken for that of Théodore Rivière, Maurice Bouval, Jules Michelet, and Julien Caussé. Incorporating the popular femme-fleur theme, his lighting fixtures showed bronze nymphs, naiads holding torches, women with poppies, and flower coverings whose petals held electric bulbs and marble butterflies.
▶ From early 1880s, work shown at Salons of Société des Artistes français. Received awards at 1889 and 1900 Paris 'Expositions Universelles.'
▶ Yvonne Brunhammer. et al., Art Nouveau Belgium, France, Houston: Rice University, 1976. Alastair Duncan, Art Nouveau and Art Déco Lighting, New York: Simon and Schuster, 1978:71.

Chambellan, René
▶ French metalworker.
▶ Chambellan was known for his design of the dynamic wrought-iron and bronze ornamentation inside and outside the 1929 Chanin building, New York, whose architect was partnership Sloan and Robertson.
▶ Jonathan M. Woodham, Twentieth-Century Ornament, New York: Rizzoli, 1990:62,108.

Chambolle, Réné
▶ French bookbinder; son of Chambolle-Duru; active Paris.
▶ When his father retired in 1898, Chambolle became director of his father's bindery Chambolle-Duru, Paris; to the firm's historicist bindings, he added his own floral decorations, hinting at Art Nouveau.
▶ Josephine shown at 1900 Paris 'Exposition Universelle.' Work shown at 1904 St. Louis 'Louisiana Purchase Exposition.'
▶ Émile Bosquet, 'La Reliure française à l'exposition,' Art et décoration, July–Dec. 1900:52. S.T. Prideaux, Modern Bookbindings: Their Design and Decoration, New York, 1906:97. Ernest de Crauzat, La Reliure française de 1900 à 1925, Vol. 2, Paris, 1932:53–55. Roger Devauchele, La Reliure en France de ses origines à nos jours, Vol. 3, Paris, 1961:44–45,48,127. Alastair Duncan and Georges de Bartha, Art Nouveau and Art Déco Bookbinding, New York: Abrams, 1989:10,33,124.

Chambolle-Duru
▶ French bookbinder; father of René Chambolle; active Paris.
▶ Chambolle-Duru set up a bindery in Paris in 1873; produced plain leather bindings and developed the inexpensive faux des fermé technique; was a contemporary and equal of Georges Trautz, Marcellin Lortic, Francisque Cuzin, and Henri Marius-Michel; adopted the surname of binder Hippolyte Duru, to whom Chambolle had been apprenticed. In 1898, Chambolle-Duru's son assumed management of his bindery.
▶ Alastair Duncan and Georges de Bartha, Art Nouveau and Art Déco Bookbinding, New York: Abrams, 1989:189.

Champion, Georges (1889–1940)
▶ French decorator and furniture designer; born Chaumont; active Paris.
▶ A prolific furniture designer, from 1928 Champion was artistic director of Studio Gué, the decorating department of the firm Georges et Gaston Guérin, Paris; designed furniture in severe geometric forms and simple planes with contrasting colors, influenced by De Stijl; in 1930, opened Atelier 75; (with Jacques Guenne) managed the journal L'Art Vivant, which published the work of young artists.
▶ Dining rooms shown at 1929 Salon of the Société des Artistes Décorateurs; in the 1920s, at SAD and at events of Salon d'Automne; 1925 Paris 'Exposition Internationale des Arts Décoratifs et Industriels Modernes.' Received a gold medal at 1937 Paris 'Exposition Internationale des Arts et Techniques dans la Vie Moderne.'
▶ Ensembles Mobiliers, Vol. II, Paris: Charles Moreau, 1937, Ensembles Mobiliers, Vol. VI, Paris: Charles Moreau, 1945: Nos. 42–44. R. Moutard-Uldry, Dictionnaire des Artistes Décorateurs, Paris: Mobilier et Décoration, 1953–57, Sept./Oct. 1954. Pierre Kjellberg, Art Déco: les maîtres du Mobilier, le décor des Paquebots,

Paris: Amateur, 1986:41. *Meubles 1920–1937*, Paris: Musée d'Art Moderne, 1986.

Champney, John
▶ American furniture designer and maker, tourist guide, and caretaker; active West Parishville, New York.
▶ Champney lived just beyond the Adirondack Park in West Parishville, New York; a so-called Adirondack carpenter, worked on buildings in the Parishville area, including Colton, Moody, and Tupper Lake; drew his own patterns for furniture; glued strips of wood together to produce varied geometric designs when cut on a miter box; produced tables, cabinets, chest of drawers, and gun stocks; for local farmers, made axe helves, forward bobbies, sled platforms, and wagon tongues; 1912–17, served as guide and caretaker for Mrs. John Sprague, owner of a camp near Moody.
▶ Lecture by John Champney's daughter, Adirondack Museum, 14 July 1982. Craig Gilborn, *Adirondack Furniture and the Rustic Tradition*, New York: Abrams, 1987:320.

Chan, Kwok Hoi   (1939–87)
▶ Chinese architect and interior designer.
▶ Studied University of Architecture, Hong Kong.
▶ Interior design projects included furniture for Air India and the IBM offices in Hong Kong. 1966–68, Chan worked in a design studio, London, contributing to the interiors of the oceanliner *Queen Elizabeth II*; subsequently, designed for Spectrum, the Netherlands; designed the cantilever 1969 *Pussy-Cat Chair* in tubular steel with leather-covered thermoplastic material, *Alligator* lounge chair, *Chromatic* range, and *Zen* chair, all produced by Sièges Steiner.
▶ *Pussy-Cat Chair* was first shown at the 1969 (XV) Triennale di Milano.
▶ Cat., *Les Assises du siège contemporain*, Paris: Musée des Arts Décoratifs, 1968. Cat., *Modern Chairs 1918–1970*, London: Lund Humphries, 1971.

Chanaux, Adolphe   (1887–1965)
▶ French designer and interior decorator; active Paris.
▶ Studied École des Beaux-Arts, Paris.
▶ Known for his painstakingly matched and executed veneers in parchment, vellum, ivory, straw marquetry, and leather as well as shagreen, Chanaux first worked for André Groult from the late 1910s until 1924 or 1925; subsequently, left to work for Jacques-Émile Ruhlmann. Chairs designed by Chanaux for Groult with applied paintings by Marie Laurencin were entered (without attribution) in a competition of chair design organized by Pierre David-Weil at the Paris Musée des Arts Décoratifs in 1924. Certain pieces signed by Rhulmann also have the stamp of Chanaux. His association with Ruhlmann was not successful. For a time, he designed for Eugène Printz. In 1931, Jean-Michel Frank, searching for furnishings for his Paris apartment, met Chanaux. After a year of collaboration in a decorating business with workshops in La Ruche, Chanaux and Frank opened a Paris shop, 140 rue du Faubourg St.-Honoré, in 1932 and sold furniture, furnishings, and lighting that they designed and made, as well as those designed by friends and associates, including designer Emilio Terry, metalworkers Alberto and Diego Giacometti, and painter Christian Bérard. In 1941, Chanaux became artistic advisor at Guerlain, Paris.
▶ Through Ruhlmann, work shown at 1925 Paris 'Exposition Internationale des Arts Décoratifs et Industriels Modernes.'
▶ Léopold Diego Sanchez, *Jean-Michel Frank*, Paris: Regard, 1980. Pierre Kjellberg, *Art Déco: les maîtres du Mobilier, le décor des Paquebots*, Paris: Amateur, 1986:42. Stephen Calloway, 'Perfectly Frank,' *House and Garden*, Feb. 1990:180ff.

Chance, W.E.
▶ British glassware manufacturer; located Smethwick, West Midlands.
▶ Chance's pressed-glass wares were designed in the 1950s by Margaret Casson, who produced a number of models for water sets and buffet ware, including *Night Sky*.

▶ Frederick Cooke, *Glass: Twentieth-Century Design*, New York: Dutton, 1986:77.

Chantry, Lance   (1954–)
▶ American industrial designer; born Chicago.
▶ Chantry was consultant designer to electronic firms; used advanced electronics and robotics in his product and lighting designs; (with Leo Blackman) designed the *Quahog* lamp.
▶ Albrecht Bangert and Karl Michael Armer, *80s Style: Designs of the Decade*, New York: Abbeville, 1990:228.

Chaplet, Ernest   (1835–1909)
▶ French ceramicist; born Sèvres.
▶ From 1847, at the age of 12, worked at the ceramics factory at Sèvres, learning design, painting, and basic pottery techniques.
▶ 1857–74, he worked with Laurin, domestic pottery manufacturer; in 1871, perfected barbotine on terracotta at Bourg-la-Reine; in 1875, developed the technique at Haviland's studio, Auteuil, near Paris; in a Paris studio given to him by the Havilands, began applying Japanese and natural motifs on brown stoneware, a material he discovered in 1881 in Normandy. In 1884, the Haviland factory at Limoges produced porcelain pieces in this style using molds from Chaplet's workshop. In 1885, he began working with the *sang-de-boeuf* glaze of Chinese origin, applying it first to stoneware and then to porcelain; in 1887, began collaborating with Paul Gauguin and moved his studio to Choisy-le-Roi, where Émile Lenoble later practiced. Chaplet was in touch with the avant-garde and applied its ideas to ceramics. Towards the end of his life, was forced to abandon his work due to blindness.
▶ Yvonne Brunhammer et al., *Art Nouveau Belgium, France*, Houston: Rice University, 1976.

Charalambides-Divanis, Sonia   (1948–)
▶ Greek furniture designer; born Athens.
▶ 1966–72, studied architecture, École Nationale Supérieure des Beaux-Arts, Paris, and computer science, VIII University, Paris.
▶ 1972–77, she taught at École Spéciale d'Architecture, Paris, and in the computer science and linguistics department, VIII University; was engaged in research on design methods, computers in architecture, and design of the workplace at Institut de l'Environnement, Paris; in 1978, set up an architecture practice, Athens; 1978–85, was scientific collaborator, National University, Athens, where she taught from 1985; in 1981, began collaborating with architect Giorgos Parmenidis; they designed furniture and objects, including 1987 *First* one-piece tubular armchair and 1988 *Animate* birch and steel side chair, both by Tubecon.
▶ Cat., Design Center Stuttgart, *Women in Design: Careers and Life Histories Since 1900*, Stuttgart: Haus der Wirtschaft, 1989:252–55.

Chareau, Pierre Paul Constant   (1883–1950)
▶ French architect and decorator; born Bordeaux.
▶ Chareau worked *c*1900–14 for the British furniture firm of Waring and Gillow in Paris, before becoming an independent interior decorator; before 1914, was strongly influenced by English architecture and decoration. His furniture was generally site-specific, solving the requirements of a particular ensemble. He favored mahogany, rosewood, and sycamore for his furniture; while on leave during World War I, in 1917–18, designed a study and bedroom set for the Paris apartment of Annie Dalsace, a friend of his wife Dollie; the suites were shown at the 1919 Paris Salon. In 1918, he set up his own office where he designed interiors, furniture, and lighting and occasionally turned to architectural commissions; is best known for Jean and Annie Dalsace's 1928–32 office-residence 'Maison de Verre,' Paris, for which he designed the architecture and furniture with Dutch architect Bernard Bijvoët, whom he met at the 1925 Paris Exposition, and metalsmith Louis Dalbet; (with Bijvoët) collaborated on several other buildings. Built on an awkward site, the Dalsace house, with its exposed iron beams and glass cubes, was revolutionary in design and aesthetics, and a manifestation of Le Corbusier's notion of the house as a 'machine for living'. The glass tiles,

effectively concave lenses, transformed the internal lighting. The innovative flooring tiles with coin-shapes in linoleum were made by Pirelli. The house was on three levels, linked by sliding and revolving doors. Chareau's furniture was often mechanical, combining plain wrought-iron elements, and influenced by English 18th- and 19th-century styles, including Thomas Sheraton, chairs by whom could be found in Chareau's residence. His floor and table lamps and chandeliers were produced in wrought iron with slices of glass or alabaster and occasionally with cloth shades, such as the 1926 model he designed for Mme. Jacques Errers. He designed the salon in Robert Mallet-Stevens's house, Neuilly, in c1930, where his alabaster chandelier *La Religieuse* (first shown at 1924 Groupe des Cinq exhibition) was installed. He often used concealed lighting, as in the French pavilion at the 1925 Paris Exposition, with a domed cornice, and in 1928 reception rooms, Grand Hôtel, Tours, where illuminated ceiling tracks appeared; occasionally worked with lighting engineer André Salomon. With friends and associates Mallet-Stevens, Fernand Léger, and others, he collaborated on sets for Marcel L'Herbier's 1923 film *L'Inhumaine*. He was a member of Groupe des Cinq with Dominique, Pierre Legrain, Jean Puiforcat, and Raymond Templier. In 1924, he opened a shop, next to Jeanne Bucher's art gallery, in which, alongside a few original pieces, his catalogue of photographs by Thérèse Bonney illustrated his exhibition stands and interiors. By 1924, he had begun working with Louis Dalbet, the wrought-iron metalworker who made limited editions of Chareau's furniture models; designed furniture for 1925 studio-house designed by Le Corbusier for Jacques Lipschitz; in 1929, became a founding member of UAM (Union des Artistes Modernes) and of CIAM (Congrès Internationaux d'Architecture Moderne). In 1937, André de Heering began working with him in his office. His large collection of Modern art included the second painting sold by Piet Mondriaan, bought in 1928. In 1931, he joined the editorial board of journal *L'Architecture d'aujourd'hui*. In 1940 he settled in the USA; in 1941, worked for the cultural section of the French Embassy, organizing exhibitions of French art; designed the 1947 Quonset hut conversion for painter Robert Motherwell and opened an office in New York, though he had few commissions.

▶ Work included Hôtel Nord-Sud de Calvi in the 1920s; 1924 furniture, de Noailles villa, Hyères; sets for Marcel L'Herbier's films 1923 *L'Inhumaine* and 1926 *Le Vertige*; 1928 Club House (first architectural commission; with Bijvoët) for Émile Bernheim, St. Tropez; 1929 refurbishment of the reception rooms (with Bijvoët), Grand Hôtel, Tours; 1928–32 Maison de Verre (with Bijvoët and Dalbet), Paris; 1932–39 renovated offices, LTT telephone and telegraph company, Paris; 1937 country house of dancer Djémel Anik, near Rambouillet; office on the quai d'Orsay, Paris; 'Foyer du Soldat colonial,' Grand Palais, Paris; pavilion, Union des Artistes Modernes, and other exhibitions, 1937 Paris 'Exposition Internationale des Arts et Techniques dans la Vie Moderne'; commissioned by the French colonial administration, packing crates that soldiers overseas converted to 1939 furniture; weekend house, France; 1947 conversion of Quonset hut for Robert Motherwell, East Hampton, New York; one-room open-plan house for himself; 1948 'La Colline' residence (alterations) of Germaine Monteux and Nancy Laughlin.

▶ 1917–18 office and bedroom designs for Jean Dalsace shown at 1919 Salon d'Automne in Paris. Work shown in numerous exhibitions 1920s–1930s, including at Salons of Société des Artistes Décorateurs from 1922, 1925 Paris 'Exposition Internationale des Arts Décoratifs et Industriels Modernes' (office-library for French Embassy pavilion). In 1926 and 1927, work shown with Groupe des Cinq, Galerie Barbazanges, Paris; exhibitions of UAM from 1930; 1936 Salon d'Automne (demountable school furniture); 1934 and 1935 Paris Salons du Luminaire (with André Salomon on corner illumination).

▶ Pierre Chareau, *Meubles*, Paris: Moreau, 1929. René Herbst, *Un inventeur, l'architect Pierre Chareau*, Paris, 1954. 'Pierre Chareau with Bernard Bijvoët, Maison Dalsace ("Maison de Verre"),' *Global Architecture*, Tokyo, 1977. Alastair Duncan, *Art Nouveau and Art Déco Lighting*, New York: Simon and Schuster, 1978:148. Victor Arwas, *Art Déco*, Abrams, 1980. Marc Vellay and Kenneth Frampton, *Pierre Chareau architecte-meublier 1883–1950*, Paris: Regard, 1984. Pierre Cabanne, *Encyclopédie Art Déco*, Paris: Somogy, 1986:180–81. Pierre Kjellberg, *Art Déco: les maîtres du Mobilier, le décor des Paquebots*, Paris: Amateur, 1986:42–44. Brian Brace Taylor, *Pierre Chareau: Designer and Architect*, Cologne: Taschen, 1992.

Charles
▶ French metalworkers; located Paris.
▶ Ernest Charles founded Maison Ullmann, bronzier, in Paris in 1908. In 1920, Émile-Albert Charles took over management of the firm. In 1932, when he was joined by his son Pierre, the firm was named Charles Frères; became known for its bronze lighting fixtures and lighting sculptures in historicist models. In 1959, Émile Charles was joined was by sons Jean and Jacques. The best-known designs included lighting fixtures *Pineapple*, *Maize*, *Fir Cone*, *Lotus*, and *Medici Vases*. Jacques Charles designed 1965 *Ligne Inox* (*Stainless Steel Collection*), and, joining the firm in 1971, Chrystiane Charles (wife of Jean Charles) designed *Charles sculpte la lumière* collection. In 1982, architect Laurent Charles joined the firm and created *The New Light Sources* collection. Designers included Jacques Pierrejean, Zebulon, Arman, Didier La Mache, Christian Duc, Sylvain Dubuisson, Martine Bedin, and Jean-Charles de Castelbajac.
▶ Received Lampe d'Or de la Création awards at the 1978, 1981, and 1984 Salon International du Luminaire de Paris for *Colosseum* lamp and special mention at its 1992 session for *Stockholm* lamp of c1952.

Charpentier, Alexandre (1856–1909)
▶ French sculptor, medalist, designer, and decorator; born Paris.
▶ Charpentier was associated with Siegfried Bing and his shop L'Art Nouveau, Paris; active 1890–1902, was involved in both the fine and applied arts; (with Jean Dampt, Félix Aubert, Tony Selmersheim, and Etienne Moreau-Nélaton) formed Les Cinq (not Groupe des Cinq), a group renamed Les Six when Charles Plumet joined it and L'Art dans Tout when others were included, like Henri Sauvage. Charpentier designed furniture, interiors, metalwork, ceramics, lighting, and leather; was considered one of the best representatives of the Parisian style of Art Nouveau; designed numerous interiors, including dining room in mahogany, oak, and poplar with ceramics by Alexandre Bigot at Champrosay for Adrien Bénard, president of Société du Métropolitan, who commissioned Guimard to design the Paris Métro entrances. Charpentier collaborated with Félix-Henri Bracquemond and Jules Chéret on Baron Vitta's billiard room.
▶ In 1895, work shown in Brussels with Les Vingt and at 1899 Salon de la Libre Esthétique. Baron Vitta's billiard room shown at 1902 Salon of the Société Nationale des Beaux-Arts, Paris.
▶ Cat., Salon of the Société Nationale des Beaux-Arts, 1902. Yvonne Brunhammer et al., *Art Nouveau Belgium, France*, Houston: Rice University, 1976. Arlette Barré-Despond and Suzanne Tise, *Jourdain*, Paris: Regard, 1988.

Charpentier, Marcel (1888–1966)
▶ French furniture designer and maker; born Saint-Mandé; active Paris.
▶ Charpentier established a furniture firm in Paris; designed simple, massive pieces, sometimes lacquered; until the end of the 1940s, was a member of Société des Artistes Décorateurs.
▶ Bookcase (with Victor Courtray) shown at 1923 Salon d'Automne and a desk at 1923 Salon of Société des Artistes Décorateurs.
▶ Pierre Kjellberg, *Art Déco: les maîtres du Mobilier, le décor des paquebots*, Paris: Amateur, 1986:44.

Charpin, Pierre (1962–)
▶ French furniture designer.
▶ Studied École des Beaux-Arts, Bourges.

► Influenced by Ettore Sottsass and Alessandro Mendini, Charpin's work acknowledged the designs of the postwar Italians and Le Corbusier.

Chartered Society of Designers
► British design organization.
► The Society of Industrial Arts was founded in 1930 by Milner Gray and others as a professional association to advance and protect the interests of its members, as a forum for the exchange of ideas, and as an organization where standards of conduct and practice could be set down; played an important role in planning the 1951 London 'Festival of Britain' exhibition. Its membership grew in the 1950s and 1960s, and in 1976 it was incorporated under a Royal Charter with the Duke of Edinburgh as patron; in 1987, changed its name to the Chartered Society of Designers. Today the Society's 9,000 members are in product, graphic, interior, fashion, and textile design, design education, and design management.
► *Issue 4*, London: Design Museum, Autumn 1990.

Chase Brass and Copper
► American manufacturer of plumbing supplies.
► Established in 1876 in Waterbury, Connecticut, Chase produced industrial metal products. In *c*1927 Rodney Chase, son of the company's president, set up a speciality design division to produce domestic metal products from the mother firm's industrial forms. The objects included ashtrays, flatware, vases, lighting, and tea sets. The enterprise hired freelance designers Russell Wright, Walter von Nessen, Lurelle Guild, Ruth Gerth, Albert Reimann, and artist Rockwell Kent. Reimann sent his designs from Berlin. Chase's wholesale showroom was located in New York; the headquarters building in Waterbury was designed by Cass Gilbert. In the 1930s, Chase developed sophisticated advertising and marketing techniques. Production of the domestic line was discontinued in 1945.
► *Creative Art*, No. 9, 1931:475–82. Thomas M. Rosa, *Chase Chrome*, Stamford, Ct.: Robert Koch, 1978. Karen Davies, *At Home in Manhattan: Modern Decorative Arts, 1925 to the Depression*, New Haven: Yale, 1983:77. Judy Rudoe, *Decorative Arts 1850–1950: A Catalogue of the British Museum Collection*, London: British Museum, 1991:98.

Chase, William Merritt   (1849–1916)
► American artist and teacher; active New York.
► 1873–78 studied Munich.
► He settled in New York in 1878; subsequently, taught at Art Students' League, New York; in 1896, established the New York School of Fine and Applied Art (sometimes referred to as Chase School of Art), New York. Becoming known as America's most important art teacher at the time, he encouraged a lively approach and played a part in the infusion of fresh colorations in much of the best painting in America in the early 20th century. Chase's prolific work included still lifes, portraits, landscapes, and interiors. His students included Charles Demuth, Georgia O'Keefe, and Charles R. Sheeler. Chase offered courses in interior decoration from 1904. By this time, Frank Parsons was a faculty member, first as teacher of interior-design history, then as president of the New York School of Fine and Applied Art 1913–30. In 1940, the institution was renamed Parsons School of Design.
► Ian Chilvers, Harold Osborne, and Dennis Farr, *The Oxford Dictionary of Art*, Oxford: Oxford, 1988. John Esten and Rose Bennett Gilbert, *Manhattan Style*, Boston: Little, Brown, 1990:5.
► See Parsons, Frank Alvah

Chashnik, Il'ia Grigorievich
► Russian artist, architect, designer, and ceramicist; born Liuchite.
► 1916–19, studied Institute for Practical Art, Vitebsk (now Belo-russia), with Marc Chagall and Kazimir Malevich,
► Chasnik collaborated with Malevich; in 1919, became a founding member of Posnovis (later named Unovis), Vitebsk; within Malevich's group, worked closely with Vera Ermolaeva,

Lazar Khidekel, Gustav Klutcis, El Lissitzky, Nikolai Suetin, and Lev Yudin; in 1920, (with Lazar' Khidekel') edited Posnovis's journal *AERO*; in 1921, co-founded the journal *Unovis*; in 1922 (with Malevich group) moved to Inkhuk (Institute of Artistic Culture), Petrograd (now St. Petersburg), where he worked with Malevich on 'arkhitektony' and 'planity' (architecture constructions), on ceramic designs with Nikolai Suetin at Lomonosov State Porcelain Factory, and on his own Suprematist paintings; designed residential housing for Bolshevik factory, Leningrad (now St. Petersburg); from 1924, worked at Ginchuk as assistant to Malevich on architectural models; in 1925, was research associate at Decorative Institute; 1925–26, worked with Suetin and architect Aleksandr Nikolskii; in 1927, led the workshop of Izo RAM (Expressive Art of Working Youth); in 1923, was researcher at Museum of Painterly Culture, which closed that year.
► Work shown at 1923 'Exhibition of Paintings of Petrograd Artists of All Tendencies,' Petrograd.
► Stephanie Barron and Maurice Tuchman, *Avant-Garde Russia, 1919–1930*, New Perspectives, MIT, 1980. Cat., *Kunst und Revolution: Russische und Sowjetische Kunst 1910–1932*, Vienna: Österreichisches Museum für angewandte Kunst, 1988. Cat., *The Great Utopia: The Russian and Soviet Avant-Garde, 1915–1932*, New York: Guggenheim Museum, 1992.

Chauchet-Guilleré, Charlotte   (b. Charlotte Chauchet 1878–1964)
► French artist, decorator, and furniture designer; wife of René Guilleré.
► Studied painting under genre painter Gabriel Thurner.
► She was a painter and muralist; collaborated on interiors with architect Alfred Levard; was known for her robust forms and somber colors; in 1912, painted the frieze *Les Treilles (Vine Trellis)* in the dining room of cabinetmaket Mathieu Gallerey; 1913–39, was artistic director in Primavera workshop of the Au Printemps department store, Paris, established by husband Guilleré in the same year. When he died in 1931, she became director of Primavera; collaborated with Colette Guéden, who succeeded her in 1939.
► In the early 1910s, showed painting and decorative panels. From 1904 under Primavera at Société des Artistes Décorateurs, and from 1910 under own name, work shown regularly in Paris Salons, including dining room (with Marcel Guillemard) at 1922 Salon of Société des Artistes Décorateurs, pallisander work cabinet at 1924 Salon d'Automne, and bedroom at 1925 Paris 'Exposition Internationale des Arts Décoratifs et Industriels Modernes.'
► Léon Deshairs, *Modern French Decorative Art*, Paris: Albert Lévy. Pierre Kjellberg, *Art Déco: les maîtres du Mobilier, le décor des Paquebots*, Paris: Amateur, 1986:44,47. Maurice Dufrêne, *Ensembles Mobiliers, Exposition Internationale 1925*, Paris: Charles Moreau, 1925, Antique Collectors' Club edition 1989:126.

Chaumet
► French retail jeweler; located Paris.
► In 1780, Étienne Nitot set up a jewelry firm in Paris; as the royal jeweler and silversmith, designed and made Napoleon I's coronation sword; in 1815, turned over the business to Jean-Baptiste Fossin, who had been *chef d'atelier*, who set up shop in Paris. Fossin was successful throughout the Restoration period, receiving the *Brevet du Roi* recognition in 1830. His son Jules Fossin joined the firm in 1830, managing the business until 1862. With Prosper Morel, who had worked for Fossin, as its director from 1862, the firm became successful through its participation at universal exhibitions and patronage of Russian clients. In 1874, Morel's son-in-law Joseph Chaumet joined the firm and, in 1875, opened a branch in London; from 1889, was director of the firm. Marcel Chaumet succeeded his father. The firm is still in business today, no longer family controlled.
► Charlotte Gere, *American and European Jewelry 1830–1914*, New York: Crown, 1975:165–66. Sylvie Raulet, *Bijoux Art Déco*, Paris: Regard, 1984.

Cheesman, Kenneth (1900–64)

▶ British architect and interior designer; active London.

▶ He was chief draftsman c1929–30 in the office of architect Oliver P. Bernard; 1933–c50, was architect to glassmaker Pilkington; (with Sigmund Pollitzer) designed late-1930s Pilkington showrooms, London, and St. Helens, Lancashire. Much of Chessman's architecture incorporated decorative features by Pollitzer.

▶ Work included 1934 Kirk Sandall Hotel (interiors with Pollitzer; T.H. Johnson, architect), near Doncaster; 1934 British Vitrolite showroom, London; 1934 showrooms, Glasgow; 1935–36 Leeds; 1937 St. Helens; 1938 London; 1937 Glass Train; 1949 'Engineering and Marine Exhibition,' London; 1950 Selwyn House, London; 1951 'Festival of Britain.'

▶ Cat., *Thirties: British art and design before the war*, London: Arts Council of Great Britain, Hayward Gallery, 1979:102,271,286.

Chekhonin, Sergei Vasil'evich (1878–1936)

▶ Russian ceramicist and graphic artist; active St. Petersburg and Paris.

▶ 1896–97, studied School for the Association for the Encouragement of the Arts, St. Petersburg; 1897–1900 painting, Princess Maris Tenisheva's school, under Il'ia Repin.

▶ In 1904, he worked at Abramtsevo Ceramic Workshop of S. Mamontov; 1905–06, contributed caricatures and cartoons to revolutionary journals; in 1907, made a number of majolica panels for buildings in St. Petersburg at the Petr Vaulin ceramics factory, Kikerino, near St. Petersburg; in 1910, became member of V mire iskusstv (World of Art) and regularly contributed to its exhibitions until 1924; 1913–18, was a specialist consultant on artistic crafts to the Ministry of Agriculture and directed the school for decorative work on enamel at Rostov-Yaroslavkii; after the 1917 Revolution, 1918–23 and 1925–27, was artistic director of State Porcelain Factory, Petrograd/Leningrad; credited with much of the agitprop (or agitation-propaganda) porcelain of the period, he executed brightly painted forms with colorful slogans on ceramics blanks originally intended for pre-revolutionary ware; made no new shapes for porcelain but painted many plates, cups, and saucers himself and produced hundreds of compositions, drawings, monograms, and anniversary marks for Volkhov Factory, near Novgorod, where he was artistic director 1923–24; in 1928, settled in Paris, where he worked as a designer for cabaret 'Chauve-souris' of Nikita Baliev and for Vera Nemtchinova of Ballets Russes de Monte Carlo in 1929, and for *Vogue* magazine; designed jewelry, porcelain, and posters.

▶ Work shown at 1925 Paris 'Exposition Internationale des Arts Décoratifs et Industriels Modernes' and subject of 1928 exhibition, Paris.

▶ Cat., *Kunst und Revolution: Russische und Sowjetische Kunst 1910–1932*, Vienna: Österreichisches Museum für angewandte Kunst, 1988. Nina Lobanov-Rostovsky, *Revolutionary Ceramics*, London: Studio Vista, 1990.

Chelsea Keramic Art Works

▶ American pottery factory; located Chelsea, Massachusetts.

▶ Descended from at least five generations of potters, the Robertson family founded Chelsea Keramic Art Works, Chelsea, Massachusetts, in 1872. Born in Edinburgh, James Robertson (1810–80) learned mold-making techniques and modeling from his father, the head workman at Fife Pottery, Dysart; from 1826, worked for a number of ceramics factories, Scotland and England. Hugh Cornwall Robertson (1845–1908) became the primary artist at Chelsea Keramic Art Works. In 1853, James arrived at Roundabout (now Sayreville), New Jersey; 1853–58, worked first at James Carr ceramics factory, South Amboy, New Jersey, and subsequently at Speeler, Taylor and Bloor, Trenton, New Jersey; in c1859, moved to Boston. His son Hugh stayed behind as apprentice at Jersey City Pottery. In partnership, James and Nathaniel Plympton produced crockery from yellow and white New Jersey clays. In 1862, the partnership dissolved and Robertson became manager after it reverted to its former owner. In 1872, with his sons, he formed the Chelsea Keramic Art Works. In 1866,

James's son Alexander W. Robertson (1840–1925) produced simple brownware in Chelsea, Massachusetts, where a supply of fine, iron-content red clay was found. In c1868, brothers Hugh and Alexander Robertson began producing flower pots, ferneries, matchboxes, and other domestic accessories. After 1872, when James and his third son George W. Robertson (1840–1925) joined the firm, Chelsea's production turned to art pottery. 1872–80, when James died, the firm was named James Robertson and Sons, though the pottery was known as the Chelsea Keramic Art Works. James Robertson was best known as inventor of the first tile-pressing machine in the USA. Enthusiastic about the *sang-de-boeuf* glaze on Ming vases he had seen at 1876 Philadelphia 'Centennial Exposition,' Hugh experimented with various glazes, including deep blue, celadon green, mustard yellow, and rich brown colors. In a technique called *bourg-la-reine*, under-glaze painting with colored clays was developed at the firm. With his brothers' departure and his father's death, Hugh ran Chelsea Keramic Art Works; during the 1880s, searched for the secret of *sang-de-boeuf* glaze; finally succeeding produced about 300 pieces before the firm closed in 1889. Under different ownership and Hugh's management, the name was later changed to Dedham Pottery; in c1895 it moved to Dedham, Massachusetts, with blue and white crackleware (developed in 1886 by Robertson) as its specialty. Hugh's son and grandson managed Dedham Pottery (after Hugh's death attributed to lead poisoning) until it closed in 1943.

▶ James Robertson's and Nathaniel Plympton's pottery received third prize at 1860 (IX) 'Massachusetts Charitable Mechanics' Association Fair.' Hugh Robertson's glazes on examples of 'Twin Stars of Chelsea' and other wares received prizes at 1900 Paris 'Exposition Universelle,' 1904 St. Louis 'Louisiana Purchase Exposition,' and 1915 San Francisco 'Panama-Pacific International Exposition.'

▶ Jennie J. Young, *The Ceramic Art: A Compendium of the History and Manufacture of Pottery and Porcelain*, New York, 1879:459,468–70. Cat., Lloyd E. Hawes et al., *The Dedham Pottery and the Earlier Robertson's Chelsea Potteries*, Dedham, Mass.: Dedham Historical Society, 1968. Cat., Kirsten Hoving Keen, *American Art Pottery, 1875–1930*, Wilmington, Del.: Delaware Art Museum, 1978:22–23. *American Art Pottery*, New York: Cooper-Hewitt Museum, 1987. Doreen Bolger Burke et al., *In Pursuit of Beauty: Americans and the Aesthetic Movement*, New York: Metropolitan Museum of Art and Rizzoli, 1987:407–08. Anne Yaffe Phillips, *From Architecture to Object*, New York: Hirschl and Adler, 1989:25.

Chemetov, Paul (1928–)

▶ French architect and furniture designer; active Paris.

▶ 1947–59, studied École Nationale des Beaux-Arts, Paris, under André Lurçat.

▶ In 1961, he became a founding member of AUA (Agence d'Urbanisme et d'Architecture); specialized in low-cost housing in Parisian suburbs, as did the agency; designed new Ministry of Finance building, Paris; with Jean Deroche, was commissioned to work on the 1969 French Communist Party offices (Oscar Niemeyer architect), Paris; from 1977, taught architecture, École Nationale des Ponts et Chaussées; in 1987 with Borja Huidobro, designed two armchairs and table in wood, glass, and steel produced through VIA Carte Blanche; published (with others) *Banlieue* (1989).

▶ Received 1980 National Grand Prize for Architecture.

▶ *Dictionnaire encyclopédie de l'architecture moderne et contemporaine*, Paris: Philippe Sers/Vilo, 1987:75–76. Cat., *Les années VIA 1980–1990*, Paris: Musée des Arts Décoratifs, 1990: 90–91.

Cheney Brothers

▶ American textile manufacturers; located Manchester and Hartford, Connecticut.

▶ The achievement of Cheney Brothers in becoming one of the leading silk manufacturers in the USA was based on the business expertise of the family and a broad knowledge of technical processes. A prosperous farmer in Manchester, Connecticut, had eight sons, four of whom became involved in the speculative planting of imported Chinese mulberry trees and the silkworms that fed on them. Brothers Ralph (1806–97), Ward (1813–76), Rush (1815–82), and Frank Cheney (1817–1904) bought additional property in Burlington, New Jersey; in Georgia, and in Ohio, where they planted the trees; failed due to the depression of 1837, the high cost of labor, and the mulberry tree blight of 1844; since the brothers owned the Mount Nebo Silk Mills, Manchester, Connecticut, turned to producing silk thread commercially by importing Oriental raw silk, being the only silk mill in the USA to continue production into the later 19th century. In 1844, Ward Cheney learned the art of silk dyeing. In 1847, Frank Cheney patented silk sewing thread. Able to use the silk waste, the brothers produced silk ribbons, handkerchiefs and eventually other goods in addition to thread. Another brother Charles Cheney (1803–74) set up a mill in nearby Hartford, Connecticut, where there was a large workforce available. In c1854, the name was changed to the Cheney Brothers Silk Manufacturing Company and, in 1873, shortened to Cheney Brothers; Ward Cheney was its first president, succeeded 1876–82 by Rush Cheney and 1882–93 Frank Cheney. During the Civil War, the firm produced rifles for the Union Army. In 1861 and 1864, when heavy silk-import tariffs were levied, the domestic market was strengthened. By 1880, the firm led in the production of plush, velvet, printed, and jacquard silks. Candace Wheeler and her Associated Artists designed silk goods that were sophisticated and attractive. The firm's 1875 Cheney Block (its office building complex, Hartford) was designed by architect H.H. Richardson. Into the 20th century, the firm was still a leader in silk production, but excessive production and competition from producers of synthetic fabrics led to a decline in the firm's activities in the 1920s. It went bankrupt in the Depression, but the demand for parachutes and other military products for World War II extended its activities into the 1940s. 1955 saw the end of silk production in the USA, when Cheney Brothers was sold to J.P. Stevens.

▶ H.H. Manchester, *The Story of Silk and Cheney Silks*, South Manchester, Conn., and New York, 1916. Doreen Bolger Burke et al., *In Pursuit of Beauty: Americans and the Aesthetic Movement*, New York: Metropolitan Museum of Art and Rizzoli, 1987:408–09.

Chéret, Joseph (1838–94)

▶ French sculptor and ceramicist; born Paris; brother of poster designer Jules Chéret.

▶ Studied sculpture under Albert-Ernest Carrier-Belleuse.

▶ He designed models and decorations for ceramics produced Sèvres, where, in 1887, he succeed his father as artistic director of the modeling studio; in 1894, became a member of the Société Nationale des Beaux-Arts, Paris; made a number of centerpieces and plates in pewter and produced designs for Orfèvrerie Christofle, Grobé, and Baccarat; designed bronzes and electrified sconces produced by Soleau, Paris. Some of his bronzes produced ten years after his death still showed his signature, suggesting that Soleau may have recast a range of bronzes from maquettes still in the foundry.

▶ Work first shown at the 1863 Salon and at 1889 Paris 'Exposition Universelle' (gold medal for work for Maison Fourdinois). Recasts of lighting fixtures shown by Soleau at 1900 Paris 'Exposition Universelle.'

▶ Yvonne Brunhammer et al., *Art Nouveau Belgium, France*, Houston: Rice University, 1976. Alastair Duncan, *Art Nouveau and Art Déco Lighting*, New York: Simon and Schuster, 1978:72.

Chérif (b. Chérif Medjeber 1962–)

▶ Algerian furniture designer; active Paris.

▶ Studied architecture, École Nationale des Beaux-Arts, Algiers, to 1984, and École Nationale Supérieure des Arts Décoratifs, Paris, to 1989.

▶ In Algeria, he collaborated with Fernand Pouillon on several projects, including furnishings for a hotel in Algiers; settled in Paris in 1977; was the architect of a village in Algeria and a small building in the Arbalète; designed a rattan furniture collection by Chambon and a group of vases for En Attendant les Barbares. His furniture showed influences from primitive cultures.

▶ Work shown En Attendant les Barbares Gallery, Paris; included in the 1992 exhibition of European design 'Barcelone, Düsseldorf, Milan, Paris,' Centre Georges Pompidou, Paris, and with other North African artists, Institut du Monde Arabe, Paris, 1991.

▶ Cat., *Les années VIA 1980–1990*, Paris: Musée des Arts Décoratifs, 1990:187. François Mathey, *Au bonheur des formes, design français de 1945–1992*, Paris: Regard, 1992:265. 'Les Designers du soleil,' *Maison Française décoration internationale*, June 1992.

Chermayeff, Serge Ivan (b. Sergius Ivan Chermayeff 1900–)

▶ Russian architect and designer; born Grosny (now Azerbaijan); active Britain and USA.

▶ He settled in London in 1910, where, 1918–23, he was on the editorial staff of Amalgamated Press; 1922–24, worked in Argentina; 1924–27, was chief designer for the decorating firm E. Williams, London; 1928–31, (with Paul Follot) was joint director of Waring and Gillow's 'Modern Art Studio' department of French furniture, London, which he tried to reorganize in the image of a great department store of the type for which Paris had become known; in 1928, organized a seminal exhibition of French and English furniture at Waring's; in 1929, qualified as an architect; pioneered the acceptance of tubular-steel furniture in England; in 1930, designed early simple furniture produced by Waring and Gillow with geometric Art Déco decorations, some painted and silver-leafed, with incised wood or contrasting veneers; came to Modern architecture via interior and product design in the new style of the late 1920s. Typical of his interior designs is an all-metal and mirror bathroom in *The Studio Yearbook* (1930) with 'plymax' dado, 'plymax' and rubber floor, and polished and lacquered aluminum plumbing fixtures. In 1932, he founded the furniture retailer Plan; worked closely with manufacturers Walter Knoll and Franz Schuster, both Germany, from whom much of Plan's designs were derived; sold Plan in 1936. Chermayeff collaborated on lighting with Best and Lloyd on R.D. Best's *Bestlite*, producing the similar *Bestplan* lighting. In 1933, he began an architecture practice, with a house in Rugby as his first structure. By 1935, his architecture work included extensive use of his own furnishings, including clocks, rugs, textiles, radios, and furniture. He commissioned the 1938 *Recumbent Figure* sculpture by Henry Moore for the terrace of his own 1935–38 house overlooking the South Downs, Bentley Wood, near Halland, East Sussex; 1937–39, was a member of MARS (Modern Architectural Research Group); in the mid-1930s, pioneered Modern industrial design in Britain with his bakelite radio housings for Ekco, and designed bent-metal tubular furniture for Pel; gave Erich Mendelsohn a base in England when Mendelsohn was forced to leave Germany, resulting in their being partners in an uneasy relationship 1933–36, producing some of the most notable buildings of the period. Chermayeff's use of Samuely's structural engineering began a period coinciding with the British Modern movement in architecture. 1937–39, Chermayeff was again independent; moving to the USA in 1939, he first worked as an architect and town planner; succeeding László Moholy-Nagy in 1940, became head of department of design, Illinois Institute of Technology, Chicago; 1942–46, was director of department of art, Brooklyn College, New York; 1946–51, succeeded László Moholy-Nagy as president, Institute of Design, Chicago, which became a department of Armour Institute of Technology (renamed Illinois Institute of Technology); 1952–62, was professor of architecture, Harvard University, and, 1962–69, professor, Yale University; 1952–57, was a partner of Heywood Cutting, who had taught at the Chicago Institute of Design; while at Harvard, collaborated with Christopher Alexander and, at Yale, with Alexander Tzonis; during his time in the USA, designed textiles, interiors, and exhibitions and painted; (with Alexander) published the book *Community and Privacy: Toward a New Architecture of Humanism* (1963) and (with Tzonis) *The Shape of Community: Realization of Human Potential* (1971).

▶ In Britain, work included 1930 remodeled apartment, London, for himself; 1929–30 Cambridge Theatre, London; 1931–32 studios and fittings, BBC, London and 1934, Birmingham; 1933–34 (with Mendelsohn) Shrubs Wood; 1933–35 (with Mendelsohn) Earl De La Warr pavilion, Bexhill-on-Sea; 1936 (with Mendelsohn) house, Chalfont St. Giles; 1936 (with Mendelsohn) house, Chelsea; Ciro's shop, London; 1935–38 own house, Bentley Wood, near Halland; house, Rugby; furniture designs for Pel and Plan; radio cabinet designs for Ekco; 1936–38 research laboratories for ICI, Manchester; designs for ARP; from 1929, carpets woven in England by Wilton Royal Carpet, near Salisbury. In the USA, his work included 1942 Mayhew House, Oakland, California; 1942 Horn house, Redwood (Marin County), California; 1945–72 extension to own house, Truro, Massachusetts; 1954 and 1956 houses, Truro; and his own 1962–63 residence, New Haven, Connecticut.

▶ Came into prominence with furnishings for 1928–29 'Exhibition of Modern Furnishings,' London. His Plan furniture was shown in his 'Weekend House' installation, 1933 'British Industrial Art in Relationship to the Home' exhibition, London.

▶ 'Serge Chermayeff,' *Der Aufbau*, Sept. 1957:369–70. Serge Chermayeff and Christopher Alexander, *Community and Privacy*, London, 1962. Serge Chermayeff and Alexander Tzonis, *Shape of Community*, London, 1971. Cat., Dennis Sharp et al., *Pel and Tubular Steel Furniture in the Thirties*, London: Architectural Association, 1977. Cat., *Thirties: British art and design before the war*, London: Arts Council of Great Britain, Hayward Gallery, 1979: 42,52,54,55,73,84,86,87,146,147,148,192,194,196,198,205, 208,231,232,270,272,286,296. Barbie Campbell-Cole and Tim Benton (eds.), *Tubular Steel Furniture*, London: The Art Book Company, 1979:52–53. Victor Arwas, *Art Déco*, Abrams, 1980. Richard Plunz (ed.), *Design and the Public Good, the selected writings of Serge Chermayeff*, Cambridge, MA, 1983. Barbara Tilson in Vittorio Magnago Lampugani (ed.), *Encyclopedia of 20th-Century Architecture*, New York: Abrams, 1986:64. Barbara Tilson, *Erich Mendelsohn 1887–1953*, London: Modern British Architecture/A3 Times, 1987:59–67.

Cherner, Norman
▶ American designer.
▶ The hour-glass-shaped 1957 bent-plywood chair, incorrectly credited to Cherner in numerous sources, was produced by Plycraft of Massachusetts and actually designed by its president Paul Goodman. The chair is still in production today.
▶ *American Home*, Nov. 1992:35.

Chery, François
▶ French engineer and designer.
▶ Studied engineering, École des Arts et Métiers, Paris.
▶ Active from the 1960s, he worked at Peugeot Outillage, producers of tools, first as design engineer and then as director of research and development.
▶ Agnès Lévitte and Margo Rouard, *100 quotidiens objets made in France*, Paris: APCI/Syros-Alternatives, 1987:58.

Chessa, Paolo Antonio   (1922–)
▶ Italian architect and furniture, interior, and exhibition designer; born Milan; active Pescara.
▶ Studied architecture, Milan, to 1945.
▶ From 1945, he was a freelance architect and designer, Milan, taking on a number of small commissions and turning to furniture design in the late 1940s and early 1950s; is best known for his *Butterfly* chair in lacquered plywood components; subsequently, began producing plastic furniture designs for serial production. His ideas for kitchen furniture in 1955 were later taken up by others. 1945–47, he was editor of the journal *Domus;* from 1945 contributed to numerous magazines and journals; was an

instructor at the Politecnico di Milano. Architecture included Youth Hostel in the Park, Milan; Teatro Carlo Felice, Genoa; General Roca Hydro-Electric Centre, Rio Negro (Argentina); Chiavari Housing Block, Genoa; residential center, Montréal; three co-operative centers, Pakistan; Ethioplast building, Addis Ababa; and numerous industrial buildings.

▶ Work shown at 1979 exhibition '28/79 Architettura,' Palazzo delle Stelline, Milan.
▶ 'Il Carlo Felice di Genova,' *Domus*, No. 252, 1950. 'Centro Idroeletrica in Patagonia,' *Domus*, No. 256, 1951. Gustav Hassenpflug, *Stahlmöbel*, Düsseldorf, 1960. Pier Carlo Santini and Guiseppi Luigi Marini, *Catalogo Bolaffi dell'architettura italiana 1963–1966*, Turin, 1966. Anty Pansera, *Storia e cronaca della Triennale*, Milan, 1978.

Cheti, Fede   (1905–78)
▶ Italian textile designer; active Milan.
▶ In 1930, Cheti established her own firm in Milan. Discovered and encouraged by Gio Ponti, her textile fabrications became known outside Italy in the 1930s and 1940s and, in 1938, in the USA. Her oversized motifs, printed and painted chintzes and velvet and silk fabrics were popular in the 1950s. She produced fabrics designed by Ponti, René Gruau, Raoul Dufy, and Giorgio de Chirico.
▶ Work shown at 1930 (IV) Biennale di Monza and 1933 (V) Triennale di Milano; 1971 'Milano 70/70: Un secolo d'arte' exhibition, Milan; 1984 'Design Since 1945' exhibition, Philadelphia Museum of Art. Received first prize (art fabrics) at 1950 Biennale di Venezia.
▶ Cat., Museo Poldi Pezzoli, *Milano 70/70: Un secolo d'arte*, Vol. 2, 1971:195. Maria Vittoria Alfonsi, *Donne al vertice*, Milan, 1975:41–43. Cat., Kathryn B. Hiesinger and George H. Marcus III (eds.), *Design Since 1945*, Philadelphia: Philadelphia Museum of Art, 1983.

Cheuret, Albert
▶ French sculptor and designer; born Paris.
▶ Studied sculpture under Perrin and Philippe-Joseph-Henri Lemaire.
▶ He designed bronze and alabaster lighting fixtures in abstract and naturalistic forms and table top objects, clocks, and sculptures of birds.
▶ Work shown regularly at Salons of Société des Artistes français from 1907. Designed and executed the decoration of a shop at 1925 Paris 'Exposition Internationale des Arts Décoratifs et Industriels Modernes' (entire shop with lighting and bronzes displayed).
▶ Victor Arwas, *Art Déco*, New York: Abrams, 1980. Pierre Kjellberg, *Art Déco: les maîtres du Mobilier, le décor des Paquebots*, Paris: Amateur, 1986:47.

Cheval, Ferdinand   (aka Le Facteur Cheval 1836–1924)
▶ French postman, self-taught architect, and sculptor.
▶ In 1879, Cheval began building his *Palais idéal*, Hauterives, completed in 1910. The structure became his tomb; was indebted to European, African and Oriental architecture; contains labyrinths, galleries, and stairs; is a kind of international exposition unto itself. In 1969, André Malraux, French Minister of Culture, designated the *Palais idéal* an historic monument.
▶ *Dictionnaire de l'Art Moderne et Contemporaine*, Paris: Hazan, 1992. *Le Palais idéal du Facteur Cheval*, Paris: Moniteur, 1981.

Chevalier, Georges   (1894–1987)
▶ French designer; born Vitry-sur-Seine.
▶ Studied decorative art, fine art, and architecture.
▶ He worked with Maurice Dufrêne and Léon Bakst; with the latter, studied interior decoration and scenography; brought his interpretation of Cubism and orientalism to his work for Baccarat, for whom he worked from 1916. His prolific work for Baccarat included crystal table wares, vases, decanters, and their first purely decorative pieces, such as crystal animals. Many of his pieces are still in production today including 1937 *Panther*, 1947 *Cock*, 1949 *Stag's Head*, 1957 *Eagle*.

▶ Work shown at 1925 Paris 'Exposition Internationale des Arts Décoratifs et Industriels Modernes,' 1937 Paris 'Exposition Internationale des Arts et Techniques dans la Vie Moderne,' 1958 'Exposition Universelle et Internationale de Bruxelles.'

▶ Léon Deshairs, *Modern French Decorative Art*, Paris: Albert Lévy. Jean-Louis Curtis, *Baccarat*, Paris: Regard, 1991.

Chevallier, Jacques Le
See Le Chevallier, Jacques

Chicago Art Silver Shop
▶ American firm; located Chicago.

▶ Chicago Art Silver Shop was established in 1912 at 11 East Illinois Avenue, Chicago, by Edmund Boker and Ernest Gould; 1913–17, was located at 638 Lincoln Parkway; 1918–34, known as the Art Silver Shop at 17 North State Street; renamed Art Metal Studio, which it is today. Working in the French and Belgian Art Nouveau style, Boker (designer and chaser) and Gould (producer) made slender vases, tea services, and pitchers before *c*1914; worked in copper and bronze, often with silver overlay and floral patterns. The firm still produces some of Boker's handmade jewelry designs.

▶ Sharon S. Darling, *Chicago Metalsmiths: An Illustrated History*, Chicago: Chicago Historical Society, 1977.

Chiesa, Pietro (1892–1948)
▶ Italian furniture, glassware, and lighting designer; born Milan.

▶ Studied in Grenoble and Turin.

▶ He was an apprentice in the studio of Giovan Battista Gianotti, painter, furniture designer, and decorator; in 1921, opened Bottega di Pietro Chiesa, Milan; in 1927, (with Gio Ponti, Michele Marelli, Tomaso Buzzi, Emilio Lancia, and Paolo Venini) founded Il Labirinto, which produced high-quality glassware. In 1933, Ponti and Luigi Fontana founded Fontana Arte, which incorporated the Bottega di Pietro Chiesa. As Fontana Arte's artistic director, Chiesa became known for his innovative glass and wood-and-glass furniture; is possibly best known for his 1936 *Luminator* floor lamp produced in polished brass, one of his simpler pieces. The Fontana Arte factory was acquired by St. Gobain in 1945.

▶ Work shown at 1923 (I), 1925 (II), 1927 (III), and 1930 (IV) 'Esposizione Triennale delle Arti Decorative e Industriali Moderne' (Biennali di Monza); 1924 and 1926 Biennale di Venezia; 1925 Paris 'Exposition Internationale des Arts Décoratifs et Industriels Modernes'; 1929–30 'Exposición Internacional de Barcelona.'

▶ Moderne Klassiker: *Möbel, die Geschichte machen*, Hamburg, 1982:125. Cat., *Lumière je pense à vous*, Paris: Centre Georges Pompidou, 1985. Guglielmo Ulrich, *Arredamento movili e oggetti d'arte decorativa*, Milan: Edizioni Görlich. Irene Guttry and Maria Paola Maino, *Il mobile déco italiano*, Rome-Bari: Laterza, 1988.

Chiggio, Ennio (1938–)
▶ Italian industrial designer; born Naples; active Padua.

▶ He set up an independent studio in 1964; became a member of ADI (Associazione per il Disegno Industriale). Designing clocks, drawing boards, office furniture, and lighting, clients in Italy included Gaggia Elettromeccanica, Bieffe, Solari, Nikol Internazionale Arredamento, Lumenform, and Habitat IDS Arredamento.

▶ *ADI Annual 1976*, Milan: Associazione per il Disegno Industriale, 1976.

Chihuly, Dale (1941–)
▶ American glass designer; born Tacoma, Washington.

▶ Studied with Hope Foot, Warren Hill, Harvey Littleton, and Doris Breckway; University of Washington, Seattle, to 1965; University of Wisconsin, Madison, Wisconsin, to 1967; Rhode Island School of Design, Providence, Rhode Island, to 1968.

▶ Chihuly early on produced environmental glass and later major architectural installations; in *c*1965, was active briefly as an architect in Seattle; in 1968, became the first American glassblower to work at the Venini factory, Murano, his later work reflecting this influence; from 1968 for four summers, taught at Haystack

School, Maine; 1969–80, was chairperson of glass department, Rhode Island School of Design, and artist-in-residence from 1980; in 1971, established Pilchuck Glass School, Stanwood, Washington, on the forestry-research farm of John and Anne Gould Hauberg. Work included *Glass Forests* in the early 1970s, *Pilchuck Baskets* from the late 1970s, *Sea Forms* from 1980, *Macchia* groups from 1981, and *Navajo Cylinders*. Losing one eye in an automobile accident and thereby his depth perception, he began working with a group of artisan-craftspeople. From the early 1990s, his workshop was housed in a factory on the waterfront of Seattle. He designed 1991 sets and lighting for a production of *Pelléas et Mélisande* by the Seattle Opera Company.

▶ Auction cat., 'Contemporary Works of Art,' Sotheby's New York, 14 March 1992. Lloyd E. Herman, *Clearly Art: Pilchuck's Glass Legacy*, Bellingham, Washington: Whatcom Museum of Art, 1992.

Child and Child
▶ British silversmiths and jewelers; located London.

▶ Originally set up in Seville Street, London, in 1880, Child and Child moved to 35 Alfred Place West (now Thurloe Street), Kensington, in 1891; manufacturing jewelry and becoming known for their high-quality enamelwork as well as historicist 19th-century pieces, became jewelers by appointment to Princess (later Queen) Alexandra and Princess Christian; produced jewelry drawn by Edward Burne-Jones; closed in 1915–16.

▶ Charlotte Gere, *American and European Jewelry 1830–1914*, New York: Crown, 1975:167.

Chini, Galileo (1873–1954)
▶ Italian ceramicist.

▶ Originally a restorer, Chini opened a small factory in Faenza in 1896; became artistic director of L'Arte della Ceramica; produced conventional floral forms in china and glass.

▶ Penny Sparke, *Design in Italy, 1870 to the Present*, New York: Abbeville, 1988.

Chiozzi, Luciano (1943–)
▶ Italian architect, designer, and urban planner; born Varese; active Milan.

▶ Studied architecture, Politecnico di Milano, to 1969.

▶ He began his professional career in the studio CP & PR Associati with architects Luciano Chiozzi, Giorgio Pajetta, and Domenico Ronchi and designer Max Pajetta. Designing furniture, lighting, marble accessories, ceramics, and lighting, his clients included Cedit Ceramiche d'Italia, Fontana Arte, Ideal Standard, Trigano Italiana, Carrara e Matta, Salvarani, and Giuseppe Pozzi. He became a member of ADI (Associazione per il Disegno Industriale).

▶ *ADI Annual 1976*, Milan: Associazione per il Disegno Industriale, 1976.

Chiparus, Demêtre (1886–1947)
▶ Romanian sculptor; active Paris.

▶ Studied in Italy, and at École des Beaux-Arts, Paris, under Antonin Mercié and Jean Boucher.

▶ His best known work shows exotic dancers in carved ivory and highly worked bronze. The subject matter of these chryselephantine (Greek *chrysos* for gold; *elephantinos* referring to ivory) sculptures was taken from popular personalities of the day, including *The Sisters* from contemporary theater characters, and from the opera *Thaïs*. His early pieces on relatively simple bases were primarily cast by Etling, a 1920s–30s foundry in Paris and retailer of contemporary French domestic furnishings. Later sculptures were made in the foundry of LN & JL, the firm that appears to have made the elaborate stepped and zig-zag marble and onyx bases. Chiparus also designed a number of figures in polychrome ceramics made by Etling.

▶ 1914–28, 1942, and 1943, work shown at Salons of Société des Artistes français.

▶ Victor Arwas, *Art Déco*, Abrams, 1980. Auction cat., Christie's New York, 26 May 1983, Lots 455, 454, 459.

Chochol, Josef (1880–1956)

▶ Moravian architect, furniture designer, architectural theoretician; born Pisek (now Czech Republic).

▶ 1889–1904, studied Czech University of Technology, Prague 1908–09, Akademie der Bildenen Künste, Vienna, under Otto Wagner.

▶ He was a member of the Cubist group Skupina výtvarných umělcu; designed three Cubist houses in Prague-Vyšehrad. His Purist projects in Prague included the 1920–21 office block, 27 Jindřišska; Inženýrska komora; the union house, 19 Dittrichova St.; 1924 Barikádniku Bridge (demolished); and 1928–29 apartment buildings, 1–9 U vody St. His unrealized projects influenced by Russian Constructivism included a 1927 competition design for the bridge across the Nusle valley and 1927 design of the Osvobozené divadlo theater, which copied Barchin's design for 1925 Lenin cultural house, Ivanovo-Voznesensk (Russia). From 1923 until its close in 1931, he was a member of the Devětsil group. His 1930–31 house and interior, Neherovská St., Prague-Dejvice, had a built-in settee and bookcases produced in light wood and dining table and chair by the Vavrouš firm, Prague, 1934; there was a Morris-type chair and tubular bent-metal chairs.

▶ 1912–14, a number of Purist projects shown at 1921 exhibition of Tvrdošíjní group. Work shown at 1923 Bauhaus exhibition, Weimar.

▶ Cat., Devětsil: Czech Avant-Garde Art, Architecture, and Design of the 1920s and 30s, Oxford Museum of Modern Art Oxford and London Design Museum, 1990.

Choo, Chunghi (1938–)

▶ Korean metalworker and textile designer: born Inchon; active USA.

▶ Studied oriental painting, Ewha Women's University, Seoul, to 1961, Penland School of Crafts, Penland, North Carolina, 1961, Cranbrook Academy of Art, Bloomfield Hills, Michigan, 1965, and Tyler School of Art, Temple University, Elkins Park, Pennsylvania, 1971.

▶ She settled in the USA in 1961; taught at various institutions from 1968, including as professor and head of jewelry and metalsmithing, School of Art and Art History, University of Iowa. Her work was widely published, shown, and awarded.

Christensen, Kari (1938–)

▶ Norwegian ceramicist.

▶ 1961, studied Statens Håndverks -og Kunstindustriskole, Oslo; from 1963–65, Det Köngelige Danske Kunstakademi, Copenhagen.

▶ 1961–66, Christensen worked at Royal Copenhagen Porcelain manufactory; from 1966, worked in own workshop, Oslo; from c1966, taught, Statens Håndverks -og Kunstindustriskale, Oslo, and was professor there from c1986.

▶ Cat., David Revere McFadden ed., Scandinavian Modern Design 1880–1980, New York: Abrams, 1982:263. Jennifer Hawkins Opie, Scandinavia: Ceramics and Glass in the Twentieth Century, New York: Rizzoli, 1989.

Christiansen, Hans (1866–1945)

▶ German painter, designer, and silversmith; active Munich, Hamburg, Darmstadt, Wiesbaden and Paris.

▶ 1899–1902, Christiansen was a member of the Darmstadt artists' colony. He designed silver produced by E.L. Viëtor, Darmstadt, and Martin Mayer, Mainz; flatware by Bruckmann, Heilbronn; enameled boxes by Louis Kuppenheim, Pforzheim; and in c1903, porcelain by Krautheim und Aldelberg.

▶ Margret Zimmermann-Degen, Hans Christiansen, Königstein, 1985. Annelies Krekel-Aalberse, Art Nouveau and Art Déco Silver, New York: Abrams, 1989:252.

Christofle; Charles Christofle (1805–63)

▶ French silversmithy; located Paris.

▶ Charles Christofle established his jewelry firm in 1830; in 1845, opened a silver and gilt silversmithy, 56 rue de Bondy, near place de la République, Paris; an innovator, developed the techniques of electroplating and electroform (galvanoplastie), processes for which he bought the rights in 1842 and which eventually made him famous. Christofle used artists who were sympathetic to the process. In 1852, his son Paul and nephew Henri Bouilhet took over directorship of the firm. Bouilhet, with chief designer Ernest Reiber, produced objects of Oriental inspiration, including pieces with cloisonné enameling and several novel processes including new stamping methods and galvanoplasty for mass producing large-scale architectural ornaments and statues in a single piece. Technically, Christofle was at the forefront, using techniques such as mechanical damascening and electromagnetic engraving. The term 'christofle' has generically come to mean silverplating. Bouilhet's last years were devoted to writing the history Orfèvrerie française aux XVIIIe et XIXe siècles. King Louis-Philippe, Emperor Napoleon III, and his cousin Prince Joseph-Charles patronized Christofle. Before 1890, Christofle wares were in Louis XV and XVI styles and occasionally japonisme. About the turn of the century, it produced flatware for Maxim's restaurant. The Art Nouveau style began to appear in its wares in the 1890s; after World War I, becoming more adventuresome, Christofle began producing many models in the style 1925, including those by Luc Lanel for the 1935 oceanliner Normandie. Designers included Jean-Baptiste Carpeaux, Albert and Louis Carrier-Belleuse, Émile Reiber, and Charles Rossigneux in the 19th century , and Maurice Defrène, André Groult, Christian Fjerdingstad, Paul Follot, Luc Lanel, Louis Süe, André Mare, Gio Ponti, Jean Cocteau, Lino Sabattini, Jean-Michel Folon, Arman, and Tapio Wirkkala in the 20th century. The 1984 Aria silver-plated flatware design became the best selling flatware worldwide; was produced by the Christofle research team following an open design competition with over 3,000 entries. In 1986, Christofle created its first jewelry collection; is still in operation as an enterprise managed by descendants of Henri Bouilhet.

▶ Showed inlaid ironwood and ebony furniture with gilt bronze mounts and damascened object in the japoniste style at the Paris 1878 'Exposition Universelle.' Received a number of awards at exhibitions 1851–1937. Silver in the new heavy type of plate called 'Gallia Metal' designed by Eugène Bourgouin and chef de l'atelier shown at 1900 Paris 'Exposition Universelle.' Work subject of exhibitions 1981 'Christofle, 150 ans d'orfèvrerie,' Louvre des antiquaires, Paris; 1991 'Christofle, 150 ans d'orfèvrerie,' Château de Loches; 1992 'Christofle, une certaine idée de l'orfèvrerie, 1925–92,' Musée Mandet, Rion.

▶ Best-known wares include 1854 large electroplated dinner service for the Tuileries commission by Napoleon III, coffee set 'l'Union fait le Succès' design by Louis Carrier-Belleuse (grand prize at the 1880 'Exposition des Arts du métal' organized by the Union Centrale des Arts Décoratifs), and two 1869 galvanized copper monumental groups on the façade of the Opéra de Paris.

▶ Hugh Honour, Goldsmiths and Silversmiths, London, 1971. Yvonne Brunhammer et al., Art Nouveau Belgium, France, Houston: Rice University, 1976. Henri Bouilhet, Christofle, 150 ans d'orfèvrerie, Paris: Le Chêne, 1980. Annelies Krekel-Aalberse, Art Nouveau and Art Déco Silver, New York: Abrams, 1989:252. 'Christofle, 150 ans d'art et de rêve,' Les dossiers de l'Art, No. 2, July–Aug. 1991. Cat., Christofle, 150 ans d'orfèvrerie, Tours: Conseil Général d'Indre et Loire, 1991. Cat., Christofle, une certaine idée de l'orfèvrerie, Clermont Ferrand, 1992.

Ciaramitaro, Pietro (1950–)

▶ Italian industrial designer; born Trapani; active Modena.

▶ Studied Instituto Tecnico B. Amico, Trapani, to 1969, and Instituto Superiore di Scienza dell'Automobile di Modena.

▶ 1972–74, he collaborated in studio Bollani, Modena, specializing in thermoplastic, resin-based, metal-and-wood furniture and furnishings. Clients in Italy included Electromondial (furnishings), Caggiati (ecclesiastical furnishings), Simonini Moto (motorcycles), and G3 Ferrari (domestic electrical appliances). He became a member of ADI (Associazione per il Disegno Industriale); in 1976, joined studio Progettisti Designers Associati, Modena.

▶ Two-seat sports-car design shown at 1970 Salon, Turin. Collaborated (with Bollani and Ottonelli) in the 1972 cycle concours in Tokyo.
▶ *ADI Annual 1976*, Milan: Associazione per il Disegno Industriale, 1976.

Cibic, Aldo (1955–)
▶ Italian architect and designer; born Vicenza; active Milan.
▶ 1975–79, Cibic worked in his own studio on shop and office projects; in 1979, settled in Milan where he worked with Marco Zanini and Matteo Thun in Sottsass Associati from 1980; became active in industrial design, restoration, furniture design, interior design, and store design (Fiorucci and Esprit); had clients including Standard (objects and textiles), Cleto Munari (silver), Tissot (timepieces); was active at Memphis, where he designed the 1982 *Belvedere* console, 1985 *Sophia* desk, 1985 *Cabbage-Pepper-Radish* ceramic tea set, 1986 *Rio* tea cart, 1986 *Buenos Aires* floor lamp with Cesare Ongaro, 1987 *Andy* side table, 1987 *Sandy* bookcase, and 1987 *Louis* table; designed 1993 *Antologia* furniture range by Boffi.
▶ Work shown in numerous exhibitions.
▶ Fumio Shimizu and Matteo Thun (eds.), *The Descendants of Leonardo: The Italian Design*, Tokyo, 1987:323. *Modo*, No. 148, March–April 1993:118.

Cigler, Václav (1929–)
▶ Czech glass designer.
▶ Studied College of Applied Arts, Prague.
▶ From 1969 onwards, he was a tutor, College of Fine Arts, Bratislava (now Slovakia), where he became head of a workshop concerned with glass in architecture. His activities included plastics.
▶ Work shown extensively at glass exhibitions, Czechoslovakia, and in 1957 and 1960 in Milan, 1958 in São Paulo, 1958 Corning, New York, 1958 Brussels, and 1969 at the Museum of Contemporary Arts and Crafts in New York.
▶ Cat., Milena Lamarová, *Design a Plastické Hmoty*, Prague: Uměleckoprůmyslové Muzeum, 1972.

Cimini, Tommaso (1947–)
▶ Italian lighting designer; active Arluno.
▶ He worked as a technician at Artemide, Milan; from 1978, was an independent designer and producer of lighting, including *Elle 55* and 1977 *Daphne* lighting fixtures by Lumina.
▶ Fumio Shimizu and Matteo Thun (eds.), *The Descendants of Leonardo: The Italian Design*, Tokyo, 1987:336.

Cirici, Cristian (1941–)
▶ Spanish architect and designer; born Barcelona.
▶ Studied Escuela Técnica Superior de Arquitectura, Barcelona, to 1965.
▶ 1962–65, he worked in the office of architects Frederic Correa and Alfonso Milá and, in 1962, in the office of architects James Cubitt and Partners, London; in 1964, (with Pep Bonet, Lluís Clotet, and Oscar Tusquets Blanca) founded the Studio PER; 1975–78, Cirici was professor of design, Escuela Técnica Superior de Arquitectura; in 1981, visiting professor, Washington University, St. Louis, Missouri and, in 1983, at University of New Mexico, Albuquerque, New Mexico; 1974–77, was director of cultural activities, Colegio de Arquitectos de Cataluña y Baleares; 1980–82, was president of ADI/FAD. Work included 1986 hardware-fitting, 1986 *Armariu* cabinet, and 1986 audio stand, all by B.d Ediciones de Diseño.
▶ Received 1965, 1970, and 1972 Premio FAD de Interiorismo and 1980 Premio Nacional de Restauración.
▶ Juli Capella and Quim Larrea, *Designed by Architects in the 1980s*, New York: Rizzoli, 1988.

CIRVA (Centre International de Recherche sur le Verre)
▶ French glass workshop.
▶ CIRVA was established in 1986 as a glass workshop in Marseilles for artists, designers, and architects; is a unique structure in Europe that is neither school nor exhibition gallery and functions as a laboratory with a permanent team of technicians and engineers; has about 30 artists working on the premises each year; serves as an center for professional artists working in glass and provides information on techniques, materials, and industrial processes; is directed by Françoise Guichon. Artists working there have included Marc-Camille Chaimowicz, Eric Dietman, Gaetano Pesce, Marie-Christine Dorner, Sylvain Dubuisson, Olivier Gagnère, Piotr Kowalski, Elisabeth Garouste, Mattia Bonetti, and Bořek Šípek.
▶ Cat., *30 vases pour le CIRVA*, Marseilles: Michel Aveline/CIRVA, 1989.

Cissarz, Johann Vincenz (1873–1942)
▶ German architect, painter, graphic artist, silversmith, and wallpaper and furniture designer; active Dresden, Darmstadt, Stuttgart, and Frankfurt.
▶ Studied Academy, Dresden, under F.W. Pauwels.
▶ He was one of the first designers of the Dresdner Werkstätten für Handwerkkunst; 1903–07, was a member of the Darmstadt artists' colony; designed silver produced by E.L. Viëtor, Darmstadt; 1906–16, was teacher (later professor) at Lehr- und Versuchswerkstätten, Stuttgart and, from 1916, at Kunstgewerbeschule, Frankfurt.
▶ Annelies Krekel-Aalberse, *Art Nouveau and Art Déco Silver*, New York: Abrams, 1989:252.

Citterio, Antonio (1950–)
▶ Italian furniture designer; born Meda; active Milan.
▶ Studied architecture, Politecnico di Milano, to 1972.
▶ In 1967, Citterio began in industrial design; in 1972, set up a studio with Paolo Nava in Lissone, working together until 1981, collaborating on design and industrial strategy; worked with studio Gregotti Associati on the restoration of Brera Art Gallery, Milan; in 1973, began working with B&B Italia. Clients included Boffi, Xilitalia, Artwis, Paravicini, Flexform, Rivaplast, Vitra, Kartell, and Tisettanta, and Moroso. He became a member of ADI (Associazione per il Disegno Industriale); taught at Domus Academy, Milan. From 1987, his collaborator and wife was American designer Terry Dwan. The studio designed the partial restoration of Pinacothèque, Brera; showrooms of B&B Italia furniture firm, offices and showrooms of Vitra, Weil am Rhein (Germany) and Paris; office furniture system by Olivetti; 1992 commercial center near Milan; offices in Tokyo; and office (with studio Kita), Osaka. Work included 1980 *Diesis* sofa by B&B Italia, 1987 *Enea* lamp by Artemide, 1983 *Max* divan and 1985 *Phil* sofa by Flexform, 1986 *Sity* modular and stand-alone seating in variety of models (with Dwan) by B&B Italia. *Panca*, *Sento Muto* table, *Lunga* square armchair, *Tonda* round chair, 1981 *Ialea* chair and 1993 *Indo*, *Cina*, *Cubis*, and *Oriente* seating produced by B&B Italia.
▶ Received 1979 and 1987 Premio Compasso d'Oro. Work shown widely and included in 1985 group exhibitions, Hanover and Rome.
▶ *ADI Annual 1976*, Milan: Associazione per il Disegno Industriale, 1976. Andrea Branzi, *La Casa Calda: Esperienze del Nuovo Disegno Italiano*, Milan: Idea Books, 1982. Fumio Shimizu and Matteo Thun (eds.), *The Descendants of Leonardo: The Italian Design*, Tokyo, 1987:323. Juli Capella and Quim Larrea, *Designed by Architects in the 1980s*, New York: Rizzoli, 1988. Chantal Granier, 'Présence d'Esprit,' *Maison et Jardin*, April 1992:22.

Clapés, Jaime Tressera (1943–)
▶ Spanish architect and interior and furniture designer; born Barcelona.
▶ For 15 years, he worked as an architect and interior designer; subsequently pursued furniture, carpet, and lighting design; in 1986, set up his own studio; designed packaging for the 1992 Barcelona Olympic Games. His limited-production 1988–89 *Carlton House Butterfly* articulated desk was widely published.

▶ Received 1986 Casa Viva award (best design), Mogar Fair, Madrid, and best design award, 1987 'International Furniture Fair,' Valencia.
▶ Albrecht Bangert and Karl Michael Armer, *80s Style: Designs of the Decade*, New York: Abbeville, 1990:61,228.

Claude-Salvy, Mme.
▶ French decorator and furniture designer.
▶ Some of Claude-Salvy's furniture was produced by Paul Follot's decorating firm MAM (Mobilier Artistique Moderne), Paris.
▶ *Ensembles Mobiliers*, Vol. II, Paris: Charles Moreau, 1937.

Clemens, Roman
▶ Theater designer.
▶ 1927–31, studied Bauhaus, Dessau.
▶ From 1932, he was a theater designer in Zürich.
▶ Lionel Richard, *Encyclopédie du Bauhaus*, Paris: Somogy, 1985:183.

Clément, Raoul
▶ French decorator and furniture designer; active Paris.
▶ Active in the 1950s (possibly earlier), by 1954 Clément was a partner in Vérot et Clément, Paris.
▶ *Ensembles Mobiliers*, Paris: Charles Moreau, No. 8, 1954.

Clements, Eric (1925–)
▶ British silversmith.
▶ Studied Birmingham College of Art and, 1949–53, Royal College of Art, London.
▶ He was head of the Industrial Design School, Birmingham College of Art; from the 1950s, designed ceremonial silver and was a consultant designer to Mappin and Webb.

Clemmensen, Ebbe (1917–)
▶ Danish furniture designer.
▶ Studied Det Kongelige Danske Kunstakademi, Copenhagen, to 1941.
▶ Clemmensen collaborated with Poul Holsøe and Fritz Schlegel and, from 1946, with Karen Clemmensen; from 1964, taught at Kunstakademi; designed furniture produced by Fritz Hansen.
▶ Received the 1961 Eckersberg Medal (with Karen Clemmensen) and numerous other prizes.
▶ Frederik Sieck, *Nutidig Danks Møbeldesign: -en kortfattet illustreret beskrivelse*, Copenhagen: Bondo Gravesen; 1990 Busck edition in English.

Clemmensen, Karen (1917–)
▶ Danish furniture designer.
▶ 1939–41, studied under Professor K. Gottlob; 1942, Det Kongelige Danske Kunstakademi, Copenhagen; 1943–45, Stockholm; 1946 architecture, Copenhagen.
▶ Received the 1961 Eckersberg Medal (with Ebbe Clemmensen) and numerous other prizes.
▶ Frederik Sieck, *Nutidig Dansk Møbeldesign: -en kortfattet illustreret beskrivelse*, Copenhagen: Bondo Gravesen; 1990 Busck edition in English.

Clendinning, Max (1924–)
▶ British interior designer and architect; born Northern Ireland.
▶ Studied Architectural Association, London.
▶ Worked with architects Maxwell Fry, Jane Drew, and Denys Lasdun; became chiefly known for interior design that showed a predilection for a small amount of furniture, the use of white, and the use of plywood furniture; was widely known in the 1960s and involved with Crawley Civic Centre; designed a 1965 range of furniture for Liberty's.
▶ *Studio Dictionary of Design and Decoration*, New York: Viking, 1973:99–100.

Cliff, Clarice (1899–1972)
▶ British ceramic designer and painter; born Tunstall, Staffordshire.
▶ Before 1916, studied painting in evening classes, School of Art, Tunstall; 1924–25, evening classes, School of Art, Burslem, both

in Stoke-on-Trent; 1927, sculpture, Royal College of Art, London.
▶ In 1912, at the age of 13, she began work at earthenware potter Lingard Webster near her home in Staffordshire, learning freehand painting on pottery, and subsequently at Hollinshead and Kirkham, Tunstall, learning lithography, concurrently studying painting in evening classes at the School of Art, Tunstall; 1916–20 at Stoke-on-Trent, worked for local pottery manufacturer A.J. Wilkinson, the Royal Staffordshire potter, where she was associated with managing director Colley Shorter, whom she later married; subsequently, set up her own studio; *c*1924–27, having been given full rein by Shorter and decorating manager Jack Walker, executed hand-painted Art Déco and *ad hoc* patterns on old stock for Newport Pottery, one of Wilkinson's subsidiaries; 1929–35 at Newport, produced the *Bizarre* design pattern, which achieved instant success; to meet demand, hired young painters to follow her style. *Fantasque* and *Biarritz* patterns followed. At Wilkinson's, under the *Bizarre* name in 1934, she became artistic director for ceramics designed by Paul Nash, Laura Knight, Duncan Grant, and Vanessa Bell 1932–34; oversaw more than 150 employees in the decorating workshop. (Knight designed her own shapes for the *Circus* range as well as decorated them, although finished blanks were almost always sent to the artists.) Moving to Royal Staffordshire Pottery, Cliff painted the motifs executed by artists, including Graham Sutherland. Until 1963, she designed brilliantly colored motifs and geometrically shaped pottery.
▶ *Bizzare* ware exhibitions were held in London, throughout Britain, in Australia and New Zealand. Wilkinson's range of tableware by well-known designers under Cliff shown at 1934 'Modern Art for the Table,' Harrods department store, London. Cliff wares shown at 1979–80 'Thirties' exhibition at the Hayward Gallery, London.
▶ Cat., Thirties: *British art and design before the war*, London: Arts Council of Great Britain, Hayward Gallery, 1979:95,96,133, 153,287. Jeremy Myerson and Sylvia Katz, *Conran Design Guides: Tableware*, London: Conran Octopus, 1990.

Clotet, Lluís (1941–)
▶ Spanish architect and furniture designer; born Barcelona.
▶ Studied Escuela Técnica Superior de Arquitectura, Barcelona, to 1965.
▶ 1961–64, he worked in offices of Frederico Correa and Alfonso Milá; in 1964, (with Pep Bonet, Cristian Cirici and Oscar Tusquets Blanca) founded the Studio PER; until 1985, collaborated with Oscar Tusquets Blanca; was a founding partner of B.d Ediciones de Diseño, which produced some of his furniture and furnishings, including the 1986 *Zoraida* series of knock-down metal tables and pedestals; 1977–84, was professor, Escuela Técnica Superior de Arquitectura.
▶ Received 1965 and 1972 Premio FAD (best interior design), Barcelona; 1978 and 1978 Premio FAD de Arquitectura (best buildings); 1980 Premio FAD; 1980 Premio Nacional de Restauración; 1974, 1979, and 1980 Delta de Oro ADI/FAD de Diseño Industrial (best industrial design); 1985 Delta de Oro.
▶ Juli Capella and Quim Larrea, *Designed by Architects in the 1980s*, New York: Rizzoli, 1988. Albrecht Bangert and Karl Michael Armer, *80s Style: Designs of the Decade*, New York: Abbeville, 1990:228.

Coard, Marcel (1889–1975)
▶ French architect and furniture designer; active Paris.
▶ Studied architecture, École Nationale des Beaux-Arts, Paris.
▶ In 1919, he began working as an interior designer and opened his own shop in Paris, where he supplied antique furniture and reproductions and laid out classical interiors; worked for only a few clients, including couturier Jacques Doucet, for whom he designed and made furniture in simple forms; regularly used rare and unusual materials and appliqués, including shagreen, mirror-glass, mother-of-pearl, lapis lazuli, lacquer, and semi-precious stones; designed only one-off pieces and was one of the first to cover furniture surfaces with parchment, although Bugatti had

used the material at the turn of the century. Like Pierre Legrain and Jean Dunand, Coard's designs were inspired by Cubist forms and the art of West Africa and the South Pacific. His predilection for glass could be seen in *c*1920 in the interior design of a townhouse near Bois de Boulogne, Paris.

▶ Yvonne Brunhammer, *Le Cinquantenaire de l'exposition de 1925*, Paris: Musée des Arts Décoratifs, 1976:122. Victor Arwas, *Art Déco*, Abrams, 1980. Pierre Kjellberg, *Art Déco: les maîtres du Mobilier, le décor des Paquebots*, Paris: Amateur, 1986:47–48.

Coates, Nigel (1949–)

▶ British architect and furniture designer; born Malvern, Worcester-shire.

▶ 1969–71, studied Nottingham University, Nottingham; 1972–74, Architectural Association, London.

▶ He settled in London in 1971, working at the architects' department of Lambeth Town Hall; in 1985, (with Doug Branson) set up Branson Coates, producing domestic and commercial commissions for clients in Britain and Japan. Their commissions included designs of restaurants in London and the restaurants Bohemia, Caffé Bongo, and Metropolis in Japan and shops for clients Jasper Conran (1985 house, 1987 shop in Dublin, 1989 shop in Tokyo); 1988 Katharine Hamnett, Glasgow; 1988 Jigsaw shop, London. He worked regularly in Japan; commissions included mixed-use development, Tokyo; 1985 Metropole club/café; Noah's Ark restaurant; Hotel Marittimo, Otaru. From 1976, he taught at Architectural Association; was a founding member of group NATO (Narrative Architecture Today), collaborating with it on 1986 Caffé Bongo and 1986 Bohemia jazz club. Until the end of the 1980s, his furniture was only produced in Japan. His 1988 *Otaru* couch and chair, *Lips* sofa (based on Salvador Dalí original), *Tongue* chair, and other models were produced by SCP (Sheridan Coakley Products), London.

▶ Rick Poynor, *Nigel Coates: The City in Motion*, New York: Rizzoli, 1989. Albrecht Bangert and Karl Michael Armer, *80s Style: Designs of the Decade*, New York: Abbeville, 1990:228. *Contract*, July 1990:26. *Issue 5*, Design Museum, Winter 1990.

Coates, Wells Wintemute (1895–1958)

▶ Canadian architect and designer; born Tokyo; active Britain.

▶ 1913–15 and 1919–21, studied engineering, University of British Columbia, Vancouver, engineering, University of London, to 1924.

▶ His mother was an architecture pupil of Louis Sullivan and Frank Lloyd Wright in Chicago. 1924–27, he was a journalist, draftsperson, personal assistant, and lumberjack in Canada; 1923–26, worked with architects in London and Paris; in 1929, settled in London and began working on his own, first on interiors and later on architecture and industrial design; designed shop interiors for Cresta and others; from 1931, was a consultant to Jack Pritchard's Isokon, an association that produced innovative plywood furniture and Functionalist buildings; commissioned by Pritchard, introduced Britain to the International Style with his 1931–32 Lawn Road flats, Hampstead; was a member of Twentieth Century Group and Unit One; in 1933, became a founding member of the MARS (Modern Architecture Research Group); 1933–34, was in partnership with David Pleydell-Bouverie and, 1932–34, with Patrick Gwynne; from 1932, designed widely published radio sets for Ecko, the first truly Modern appliance designs in Britain. Coates's 1934 *AD65* circular plastic radio was also widely published and became the best known radio in Britain. Other Ekco products included 1946 *A22* radio and *Princess* portable radio. Though a restyled version of the cabinet was reissued after World War II, Coates completely redesigned the model, resulting in the 1947 *Princess* radio in colorful plastic with an adjustable clear handle; at this time, was designing aircraft interiors, continued in the 1950s by producing designs for TV cabinets; was an innovative and influential architect and designer in the 1930s, producing little after World War II, when he practiced in Vancouver and unsuccessfully pursued rail and ocean transporta-

tion studies and town planning and on aircraft interiors for De Havilland and BOAC.

▶ Work included 1932–34 Isokon flats, Lawn Road, Hampstead; designs for *Isotype* dwellings of *c*1932; 1934 'Sunspan' house (with Pleydell-Bouverie); furniture for Isokon from 1931; 1931–32 studios, control rooms, and effects suites and for 1935 BBC studios (with Raymond McGrath and Serge Chermayeff), Broadcasting House, London, and Newcastle; 1934 Embassy Court flats, Brighton; Ekco radio and radiogram housings, including 1934 Cole *AD65* radio in brown phenolic; 1934 heater for Lawn Road penthouse of Pritchard; *Flexunit* furniture of *c*1936 by P.E. Gane; *Thermovent* heater; 1937–39 flats, Palace Gate, London; Commander and Mrs. Gwynne's 1937–39 'The Homewood' residence (with Patrick Gwynne), Esher; steel furniture produced by Pel; shops and showrooms for Crysede, Silks Ltd., and Cresta Silks; Telekinema for the 1951 London 'Festival of Britain'; *Wingsail* catamaran; various one-off furniture models; and many unrealized projects and entries for design competitions (including flats for *News Chronicle* Schools Competition with Denys Lasdun).

▶ Participated in 1951 London 'Festival of Britain' exhibition. In 1938, elected Fellow of the Royal Institute of British Architects; in 1944, elected Royal Designer for Industry.

▶ Wells Coates, 'The Conditions for an Architecture for Today,' *Architectural Association Journal*, April 1938. J.M. Richards, 'Wells Coates 1893–1958,' *Architectural Review*, Vol. 124, Dec. 1958:357–60. 'Wells Coates 1895–1958: An Address to the 1957 Graduation Banquet, School of Architecture, University of British Columbia,' *Journal of the Royal Architectural Institute of Canada*, Vol. 36, June 1959:205–11. Cat., Dennis Sharp et al., *Pel and Tubular Steel Furniture in the Thirties*, London: Architectural Association, 1977. Sherban Cantacuzino, *Wells Coates: A Monograph*, London: Gordon Fraser, 1978. *Wells Coates, Architect and Designer*, Oxford: Oxford Polytechnic, 1979. Cat., *Thirties: British art and Design before the war*, London: Arts Council of Great Britain, Hayward Gallery, 1980. Cat., Kathryn B. Hiesinger and George H. Marcus III (eds.), *Design Since 1945*, Philadelphia: Philadelphia Museum of Art, 1983.

Cobden-Sanderson, Thomas James (1840–1922)

▶ British bookbinder and printer.

▶ Originally a lawyer, Cobden-Sanderson turned to handicrafts and, in 1884, opened a bindery specializing in limp bindings decorated with gold Art Nouveau-like motifs; from 1900, continued as a bookbinder at Doves Press, which he founded with Emery Walker. The term 'Arts and Crafts movement' was apparently coined by Cobden-Sanderson in his book *The Arts and Crafts Movement* (1905) (printed by Charles Whittingham at the Chiswick Press on handmade paper), although some credit the phrase to the Arts and Crafts Exhibition Society.

▶ M. Tidcombe, *The Bookbindings of T.J. Cobden-Sanderson*, London, 1984.

Cocchia, Fabrizio (1931–)

▶ Italian designer; born Naples; active Rome.

▶ Cocchia began his professional career in 1965; became a member of ADI (Associazione per il Disegno Industriale). Designing furniture and electrical appliances, clients included Triplex, Autovox, Sormani, Poltronova, and Pentastudio.

▶ *ADI Annual 1976*, Milan: Associazione per il Disegno Industriale, 1976.

Cocheco

▶ American textile manufacturer; located Dover, New Hamp-shire.

▶ In 1812, the Dover Cotton Factory was chartered by the New Hampshire legislature to produce calico fabrics; in 1822–23, expanded ambitiously, incorporating innovative architectural features into its plants; had financial difficulties and reformed as the Cocheco Manufacturing Co; produced cylinder-printed cotton fabric in large quantities throughout the 19th century, serving working- and middle-class markets; in the 1880s, printed fabric in more than 10,000 patterns, producing more than 50 million yards of cloth by 1892; had selling agents Lawrence and Co manage the pattern designs, packaging, pricing, and sales; hired mostly British skilled workers and managers. In 1909, Pacific Mills of Lawrence, Massachusetts, bought the firm. Cocheco produced printed cotton to *c*1913, and continued to manufacture goods until *c*1940.

▶ Doreen Bolger Burke et al., *In Pursuit of Beauty: Americans and the Aesthetic Movement*, New York: Metropolitan Museum of Art and Rizzoli, 1987:409–10.

Cocteau, Jean-Maurice-Clément-Eugène
(1889–1963)

▶ French poet, novelist, playwright, actor, cinematographer, sculptor, draftsperson, and decorative designer; born Maisons-Laffitte; active Paris.

▶ He became internationally well known for his avant-garde intellectual pursuits; was a friend of leading artists including Amedeo Modigliani; persuaded Pablo Picasso to collaborate with the Ballets Russes de Monte Carlo on *Parade*; though associated with Cubism and Surrealism, was himself of no school; was a prolific draftsman and poet and named his work 'graphic poetry'; with musicians Darius Milhaud and Jean Wiener, introduced jazz to France in the café Le Bœuf sur le toît, Paris, where intellectuals of the time met; was active in theater design with Sergei Diaghilev and composers Igor Stravinsky and Eric Satie and as a filmmaker, including his adaptation of *La Belle et la Bête* (1946) and three films on the role of the artist: *Le Sang d'un poète* (1930), *Orphée* (1950), and *Testament d'Orphée* (1960). Cocteau's nightclub in Paris was known as the Grand Écart. Active as a writer of poetry, novels (*Les Enfants Terribles*, 1923), and plays (adaptation of *Antigone*, 1928), he also produced a large number of paintings and drawings (including a large body of homosexual erotica); he practiced pottery 1957–63, working with Marie-Madeleine and Phillipe Madeline-Jolly; in 1960, gave friend François Hugo drawings and models from which a series of jewels was produced. Cocteau designed idiosyncratic ceramics and other jewelry, and silverware for Christofle.

▶ *Dictionnaire de l'Art Moderne et Contemporain*, Paris: Hazan, 1992.

CODIFA (Comité de Développement des Industries Françaises de l'Ameublement)

▶ French trade association.

▶ CODIFA was established in 1971 to represent the interests of the French furniture industry; promotes research, innovation, and modernization of manufacturing processes; assisted in the 1979 creation of VIA (Valorisation de l'Innovation dans l'Ameublement) and in its public relations and promotion of new French furniture.

Codman Jr., Ogden (1863–1951)

▶ American interior designer and architect; active New York.

▶ In contrast to the prevailing cluttered Edwardian interior, Codman introduced white paint, flowered fabrics, and airy rooms; with Edith Wharton, wrote the influential book *The Decoration of Houses* (1897). Codman's most important commission came in the winter of 1893 from Alice and Cornelius Vanderbilt II. The Breakers of 1895, as the Vanderbilt house in Newport, Rhode Island, became known, had Richard Morris Hunt as its architect. J. Allard, Parisian decorators, were assigned the first-floor reception areas. Codman's rooms, which inspired generations of designers, were light and informally elegant, with simple fabrics and cream-colored furniture and the first of many variations on neoclassical themes. In *c*1903 with Mrs. Wharton, he designed her house on Park Avenue, New York. He borrowed freely from 18th-century French, English, and American styles; preferred small rooms to grand ones, paneling to wallpaper, painted furniture to stained, and symmetry to asymmetry. He was hired by Elsie de Wolfe to help her design at the beginning of her career, though, like Wharton, she kept his collaboration a secret. Codman's work included the Lloyd Bryce Colonial Revival mansion, Roslyn, New York,

and Bayard Thayer house, Boston, now the Hampshire House restaurant. His masterpiece is considered to be 1929–31 La Leopolda, a large palazzo, Villefranche-sur-Mer, France, which he had built for himself and later rented to the Duke and Duchess of Windsor. Codman compiled a 36,000-entry index to French châteaux.

▶ Edith Wharton and Ogden Codman Jr., *The Decoration of Houses*, New York: Scribners, 1897. Cat., Pauline C. Metcalf, *Ogden Codman and the Decoration of Houses*, New York: National Academy of Design, 1988. Stephen Calloway, *Twentieth-Century Decoration*, New York: Rizzoli, 1988:61–62,80–81. Mitchell Owens, 'Let the Sunshine in,' *Elle Decor*, May 1990:28,32.

Cohn and Rosenberger; Coro

▶ American costume jeweler; located New York.

▶ Emanuel Cohn and Carl Rosenberger established a small store in 1901 on Broadway, New York, renamed Coro (from the first two letters of their names) in 1943. Its designers included Adolph Katz, who coordinated production of other designers. In 1929, the world's largest costume jewelry factory was opened in Providence, Rhode Island. 1930–60, was one of the most important and successful manufacturers of inexpensive costume jewelry; with showrooms throughout USA, was acquired by Richton International in 1957; today, operates under more than 50 trademarks including Coro, Vendome, and Oscar de la Renta.

▶ Deanna F. Cera (ed.), *Jewels of Fantasy: Costume Jewelry of the 20th Century*, New York: Abrams, 1992.

Cohr, Carl M.

▶ Danish silversmiths, located Fredericia.

▶ The firm Carl M. Cohr was founded in 1860; in 1907, commissioned architect Knud von Engelhardt to design flatware; after 1935, produced Modern hollow-ware patterns.

▶ Annelies Krekel-Aalberse, *Art Nouveau and Art Déco Silver*, New York: Abrams, 1989:220,252.

Colani, Luigi (1928–)

▶ German designer.

▶ Studied in Berlin and Paris, including classes in sculpture and aerodynamics.

▶ He designed speedboats, women's fashions, furniture, and ceramics. His 1970 *Drop* porcelain dinner service produced by Rosenthal had the teapot handle near the center of gravity to facilitate pouring, footed cups to prevent liquid from collecting in the saucer, and thin-walled porcelain to minimize heat loss. He designed the 1981 tea service produced by Melitta, 1981 *No1* and 1986 *441/432* writing instruments by Pelikan, and numerous other objects.

▶ *Drop* service received Bundespreis 'Die gute Industrieform,' 1972 Hanover fair.

▶ Cat., *Rosenthal: Hundert Jahre Porzellan*, Hanover, 1982:171–72, No. 102. 'Moderne Klassiker, pt. 13: Geschirr, Besteck, Glas,' *Schöner Wohnen*, Feb. 1982:174. Tommaso Trini, 'Il Design post-diluviano di Luigi Colani,' *Domus*, No. 636, Feb. 1983:48–49. Cat., Kathryn B. Hiesinger and George H. Marcus III (eds.), *Design Since 1945*, Philadelphia: Philadelphia Museum of Art, 1983.

Cole, Eric Kirkham (1901–65)

▶ British domestic electronics industrialist.

▶ In 1921, Cole founded Ekco Radio, Southend-on-Sea, Essex; first produced radio cabinets in wooden cases, resembling conventional furniture pieces; in the 1930s, was the first radio manufacturer in Britain to set up a plastics molding plant (Ekco Mouldings), although early bakelite cabinets were unsatisfactory and sold badly. Plastic models included 1930 *Ekco 313* and J.K. White 1932 *M25* radio receivers. Based on patterns for traditional wooden cabinets, they were visually unappealing. Cole commissioned designers including Serge Chermayeff and Wells Coates to produce a new line of radio sets. Coates designed inventive geometric and widely published plastic radio cabinets for the firm in the early 1930s; his stylish 1934 Ekco *AD65* radio was Cole's first break with the 'furniture style' tradition and became the most

popular wireless cabinet of the period in Britain, with its chrome grille, circular silhouette, and prominent dials. Ecko cabinets were produced in conservative finishes (black, brown, and walnut) compared to some contemporary American sets in brightly colored plastics with chrome trimming.
▶ Coates's concentric plastic and chrome *A22* model was shown at 1946 'Britain Can Make It' exhibition, Victoria and Albert Museum, London.
▶ Penny Sparke, *Introduction to Design and Culture in the Twentieth Century*, London: Allen and Unwin, 1986. *The Radio*, London, Design Museum, 1989.

Colefax, Sybil   (b. Sibyl Halsey c1875–1950)
▶ British collector and interior designer; active London.
▶ She established salons at Onslow Square and Argyll House; rivaled hostesses Lady Oxford, Lady Asquith, Lady Cunard, and Lady Ottoline Morrell; when her husband Arthur Colefax died in 1936, continued to entertain on a small scale at her home, Lord North Street, London; from 1922, cultivated the artists of the Bloomsbury circle, who treated her with disdain. In 1933, she began to work as an interior decorator. In 1936 at the Memoir Club, Virginia Woolf gave the paper 'Am I a Snob?' mocking Colefax's social pretensions, though they remained friends. As director of Colefax and Co, set up with John Fowler in 1934, she designed minutely detailed interiors in unconventional colors. Colefax was one of the 'lady decorators' in London between the wars, 'helping' with the decoration of wealthy friends' houses. John Fowler, a decorator of some prominence, had, before his partnership with Colefax, been active in his own shop, King's Road, London, near Lady Colefax's and Syrie Maugham's residences. Both Maugham and Colefax had courted him to join their firms.
▶ Cecil Beaton, *The Glass of Fashion*, London, 1954. J. Schulkind (ed.), *Moments of Being*, London, 1976. Alan and Veronica Palmer, *Who's Who in Bloomsbury*, New York: St. Martin's, 1987: 36–37. Stephen Calloway, *Twentieth-Century Decoration*, New York: Rizzoli, 1988:139,141,216, plate 326. Mark Hampton, *The Legendary Decorators of the Twentieth Century*, New York: Doubleday, 1992.

Colenbrander, Theodorus A.C.   (1841–1930)
▶ Dutch architect and ceramicist; born Doesburg.
▶ Colenbrander probably had his first lessons in architectural drawing in Doesburg; moving to Arnhem, worked with L.H. Eberson (later principal architect to King Willem III) and won architectural competitions, including 1867 town hall in Amsterdam; before he became the draftsperson for the Ministry of War in The Hague, designed a number of country houses in Arnhem; 1884–1889, was artistic advisor to and designer at art pottery Rozenburg, The Hague; became an interior designer to artists and wealthy clients; at the end of the century, designed carpets; from 1895, was designer and advisor to the carpet factory at Amersfoort and later at Deventer; shortly before World War I, returned to ceramics for Zuid-Holland at Gouda and again left due to artistic differences. In 1917, the ceramics factory RAM was established in Arnhem, founded by banker Charles Engelberts and art dealer Henri van Lerven, with the first vases being produced in 1921. Over a ten-year period, Colenbrander designed some 700 different decorations at RAM for over 60 new vase, plate, and bowl models. 1924–26, several thousand pieces of his were made. Except for a visit to Paris, he never left the Netherlands.
▶ *Industry and Design in the Netherlands, 1850–1950*, Amsterdam: Stedelijk Museum, 1985.

Coles, Peter   (1954–1985)
See Dumas, Rena

Collein, Lotte   (b. Lotte Gerson   1905–)
▶ German interior decorator; wife of architect Edmund Collein.
▶ 1927–30, studied fabric design and photography, Bauhaus, Dessau.

▶ She was active with her husband in interior design; after World War II, worked in the office of the minister of construction, East Berlin.
▶ Lionel Richard, *Encyclopédie du Bauhaus*, Paris: Somogy, 1985:183.

Collet, Julien
▶ French decorator and furniture designer.
▶ Studied École Boulle, Paris.
▶ Known for being an excellent technician, Collet was a decorator in a shop, impasse Charles-Petit, Paris.
▶ Work cabinet shown at 1927 exhibition, Palais Galliéra, and bureau at 1927 Salon of the Société des Artistes Décorateurs.
▶ Léon Deshairs, *Modern French Decorative Art*, Paris: Albert Lévy. Pierre Kjellberg, *Art Déco: les maîtres du Mobilier, le décor des Paquebots*, Paris: Amateur, 1986:185.

Collingwood
▶ British court jeweler; located London.
▶ Joseph Kitching established a jewelry store in London in 1817 patronized by Princess Charlotte, the Duke and Duchess of York, and the Duke of Gloucester; in 1834, moved to 46 Conduit Street, London; in 1837 when Queen Victoria ascended the throne, the firm received a royal warrant, which it held until 1963. In 1853, when Kitching retired, Henry Collingwood became director and was in turn followed by his son Robert Nelson Collingwood.
▶ Charlotte Gere, *American and European Jewelry 1830–1914*, New York: Crown, 1975:167.

Collinson and Lock
▶ British furniture manufacturer; located London.
▶ Frank G. Collinson and George James Lock formed a firm in 1870 to produce and market so-called art furniture. Illustrated by J. Moyr Smith, its first catalog *Sketches of Artistic Furniture* (1871) included designs by Smith and architect Thomas Edward Collcutt. Its stenciled, turned, and incised furniture included cabinets, sideboards, tables, chairs, wardrobes, and dressing tables. E.W. Godwin designed some of Collinson's furniture, including the 1873 *Lucretia* cabinet painted by Pre-Raphaelite artist Charles Fairfax Murray. The firm's commissions included the Savoy Theatre in 1881 and G.E. Street's Law Courts in 1874–82; during the 1870s, promoted ebonized furniture and Japanese lacquerwork, which it helped popularize in the USA. Some of the birds and female figures on its ebonized furniture were painted by Albert Moore. In 1885, sculptor Stephen Webb joined the firm as chief designer; he took his inspiration from French and Italian furniture. Seeking commissions from wealthy clients, the firm moved to Oxford Street, London, in c1885; in 1897, when George Lock withdrew his capital to set up his own business, bought by Gillow and Company.
▶ Collcutt's furniture shown at 1878 Paris 'Exposition Universelle' and Philadelphia 'Centennial Exposition.' Other models, including ebonized furniture painted by Albert Moore, shown at 1871 (II) and 1873 (III) London 'Annual International Exhibitions.'
▶ Julian Kinchin, 'Collinson and Lock,' *Connoisseur*, No. 201, May 1979:46–53. Doreen Bolger Burke et al., *In Pursuit of Beauty: Americans and the Aesthetic Movement*, New York: Metropolitan Museum of Art and Rizzoli, 1987:412.

Colombi, Alberto   (1941–)
▶ Italian designer; born and active Milan.
▶ Studied Politecnico di Milano to 1965.
▶ Colombi began his professional career in 1965; designed furniture, accessories, and interiors; in 1969, became a member of DAM (Designer Associati Milano) and later of ADI (Associazione per il Disegno Industriale).
▶ Received first prize (*DAM* fabric designs for Arredamento) at 1969 (I) Concorso Internazionale Arve Bayer; first prize (plastic-laminate designs; with architect P. Guzzetti) at 1973 (III) first Concorso Mia Abet Print; and first prize (furnishings for

Driade and Kartell for Casa Vacanza Mini Appartamenti) at open competition, 1974 Fiera Internazionale, Genoa.

▶ *ADI Annual 1976*, Milan: Associazione per il Disegno Industriale, 1976.

Colombini, Gino   (1915–)

▶ Italian industrial designer; born Milan.

▶ 1933–52, he worked in the studio of architect Franco Albini, where he designed furniture and commercial and domestic architecture; 1949–1961, headed the Kartell Samco technical department, Binasco; was a pioneer in high-quality plastic furniture manufactured in Italy. His interest in subtlety and precision was manifested in plastic items ranging from tureens and colanders to lemon squeezers and buckets, including a 1955 vertical-ribbed garbage can.

▶ Received Premio Compasso d'Oro 1955 (kitchen bucket), 1957, 1958 (lemon squeezer) 1959, and 1960. Work shown at 1979 'Design & design,' Palazzo delle Stelline, Milan, Italy.

▶ Gillo Dorfles, *Il disegno industriale e la sua estetica*, Bologna, 1963: figs. 113,136,138. Cat., *Design & design*, Milan: Palazzo delle Stelline, 1979:44,60,69,74. Cherie Fehrman and Kenneth Fehrman, *Postwar Interior Design, 1945–1960*, New York: Van Nostrand Reinhold, 1987. Jeremy Myerson and Sylvia Katz, *Conran Design Guides: Tableware*, London: Conran Octopus, 1990:38–39,72–73.

Colombo Ari, Antonio   (1946–)

▶ Italian designer; born and active Meda.

▶ Colombo Ari began his professional career in 1967; designed furniture in wood, metal, and glass; ceramics; and glassware; became a member of ADI (Associazione per il Disegno Industriale). Clients included Arflex (1970 research on seating, 1971 *Twin* table, 1974 *Tuli* table), Manifattura Isa (optical research in color and design), Selenova (research in lighting and furniture), Saint Gobain (marketing of crystal), Airborne (1975 *Sofone* furniture collection), Giancarlo Pozzi (furniture), Ceramiche Mauri, and IKS.

▶ *ADI Annual 1976*, Milan: Associazione per il Disegno Industriale, 1976.

Colombo, Joe   (b. Cesare Colombo   1930–71)

▶ Italian painter, sculptor, and designer; born Milan.

▶ Studied Accademia di Belle Arti di Brera, Milan, to 1949, and 1950–54, Politecnico di Milano.

▶ 1951–55, he was principally an avant-garde painter and sculptor; joined the Movimento Nucleare (founded 1951 by Enrico Baj and Sergio Dangelo) and Concrete art movement; in 1953, showed art at the jazz club Santa Tecla, Milan, for which he designed a ceiling; at the 1954 (X) Triennale di Milano, rendered three open-air rest areas with benches and 'television shrines,' where TV sets appeared as miniature theaters. His first architecture work was a condominium building in 1956. In 1959, he took on the family electrical equipment business; in 1962, opened his own design office, Milan. His first commissions included 1961 *Impronta* armchair, 1962 *Acrilica* lamp by O-Luce, 1963 *Minikitchen* by Boffi, and 1964 *Corsair* air-conditioning unit by Rheem-Safim. His range of objects included furniture, pottery, lighting, and electrical appliances. Among Italian designers of the 1955–65 decade, he was notable for his development of an elegant Functionalist furniture aesthetic. The 1965 *Spider* lamp, 1962 *Roll* chair, and 1963 *Elda* armchair exemplify his approach. Clients included Bernini, Candy, Comfort, Elco, Sormani, Stilnovo, O'Luce, and Italora. His 1965 *Chair 4860*, produced by Kartell in injection molded ABS plastic, was widely published; it was the first single-component chair with a molded-plastic seat and back. His 1968 *Poker* card table was produced by Zanotta and 1970 air conditioner by Candy. His 1970 *Boby* range of taborets in ABS plastics is still in production by Bieffeplast.

▶ Fine art shown with Movimento Nucleare group at 1952 exhibition, Amici della Francia; 1952 'Arte Organica Disintegrismo Macchinismo Arte Totale,' Saletta dell'Elicotero; 1953 exhibition, Galerie Saint Laurent, Brussels; 1954 exhibitions (with Baj), Ca'

Giustinian, Venice and Verviers. Work subject of 1984 'Joe Colombo' exhibition, Musée d'Art Moderne, Villeneuve d'Ascq (France); 1966 exhibition, Design Research, New York. Design work shown at 1965 Italian section, Kiel; 1966 'Vijftig Jaar Zitten,' Stedelijk Museum, Amsterdam; 1967 Montreal 'Universal and International Exhibition (Expo '67)'; 1968 'Les Assises du siège contemporain' exhibition (*Chair 4860*), Paris Musée des Arts Décoratifs; Italian Pavilion, 1968 'BIO 3' Industrial Design Biennale, Ljubljana; 1969 'Qu'est ce que le design?', Centre de Création Industrielle, Paris; 1970 'Modern Chairs 1918–1970' exhibition, Whitechapel Gallery, London; 1984 'Design Since 1945' exhibition, Philadelphia Museum of Art; Triennali di Milano from 1954 (X), winning three medals in 1964 (XIII). At 1972 'Italy: The New Domestic Landscape: Achievements and Problems of Italian Design,' New York Museum of Modern Art, Colombo (with Ignazia Favata) designed the prototype of 'Total Furnishing Unit' and 'Uniblock' furniture habitats. 1968 *Additional Chair* by Sormani shown at 1991 'Mobili Italiani 1961–1991: Le Varie Età dei linguaggi' exhibition, Milan. Received 1963 National Institute of Architecture IN/Arch Award (1963 Hotel Continental interiors, Sardinia); 1967 and 1968 ADI awards, USA; 1970 Premio Compasso d'Oro. Designed pavilion for Italian Association for Industrial Design, 1968 (II) Turin 'Eurodomus' and the 1969 'Visiona 69' for Bayer, Leverkusen. 1965 *Chair 4860* shown at 1967 Salone del Mobile, Milan and included in chair exhibitions.

▶ 'Una nuova concezione dell'arredamento: Joe Cesare Colombo,' *Lotus*, Vol. 3, 1966–67:176–95. Cat., *Les Assises du siège contemporain*, Paris: Musée des Arts Décoratifs, 1968. Cat., *Qu'est ce que le design?*, Paris, Centre de Création Industrielle, 1969:27. Cat., *Modern Chairs 1918–1970*, London: Lund Humphries, 1971. M. Pia Valota, 'Joe C. Colombo,' *Casabella*, Vol. 35, No. 358, 1971:46–48. Cat., *Milano 70/70: un secolo d'arte, Vol. 3, Dal 1946 al 1970*, Milan, 1972. Cat., *Italy: the New Domestic Landscape*, New York: The Museum of Modern Art, 1972. Cat., Milena Lamarová, *Design a Plastické Hmoty*, Prague: Uměleckoprůmyslové Muzeum, 1972. Alfonso Grassi and Anty Pansera, *Atlante del design italiano: 1940–1980*, Milan, 1980. Cat., Kathryn B. Hiesinger and George H. Marcus III (eds.), *Design Since 1945*, Philadelphia: Philadelphia Museum of Art, 1983. Ignazia Favata, *Joe Colombo, Designer 1930–1971*, Milan: Idea 1988.

Colombo, Marco   (1952–)

▶ Italian architect and designer; born Milan.

▶ In 1975, Colombo and Mario Barbaglia began collaborating as architects; in 1984, became active in industrial and exhibition design, when they began working for PAF on its *Studio* collection; designed PAF's 1984 *Dove* table lamp.

Colonna, Edward   (b. Edouard Klönne   1862–1948)

▶ German designer and decorator; born near Cologne.

▶ Studied architecture in Brussels to 1877.

▶ Moving to the USA in 1882, he worked for Associated Artists, a group of interior decorators headed by Louis Comfort Tiffany; participated in the interior design for real estate businessman Ogden Goelet and shipping magnate Charles Flint; 1884–85, worked for architect Bruce Price; in 1885, with Price's help, settled in Dayton, Ohio, and worked for Barney and Smith Manufacturing Company, where he designed railroad cars; while there, published the book *Essay on Broom-Corn* (1887) showing Art Nouveau work and designed furniture and *objets d'art*. The book presaged the work of Belgian artists, including Victor Horta and Henry van de Velde, and showed work resembling that of Chicago architect Louis Sullivan. He also published *Materiae Signa, Alchemistic Signs of Various Materials in Common Usage* (1887); was active in Cincinnati, Ohio, as well as Dayton; after a brief stay in Canada in 1888, became an architect in Montreal, primarily of railroad stations; moved to Paris, where 1898–1903 he worked for Siegfried Bing's L'Art Nouveau, designing jewelry, furniture, fabrics, porcelain table services, and vases; installed Bing's pavilion at 1900 Paris 'Exposition Universelle' with Georges de Feure and Eugène Gaillard; after Bing's store closed, returned to New York in 1905, where he became an antiques dealer and interior designer. In the 1920s, although his designs began to reflect fashionable French Art Déco geometry, this later work lacked the distinctive originality of that of the turn of the century. In 1923, he left the USA for France, settling in Nice.

▶ Work shown in Bing's pavilion at 1900 Paris 'Exhibition Universelle.' Work subject of exhibition, The Dayton Art Institute, Dayton, Ohio, 1983–84.

▶ Charlotte Gere, *American and European Jewelry 1830–1914*, New York: Crown, 1975:167–68. Yvonne Brunhammer et al., *Art Nouveau Belgium, France*, Houston: Rice University, 1976. Cat., Martin Eidelberg, *Edward Colonna*, The Dayton Art Institute, 1983. Annelies Krekel-Aalberse, *Art Nouveau and Art Déco Silver*, New York: Abrams, 1989:252.

Colotte, Aristide   (1885–1959)

▶ French glassware designer; born Baccarat.

▶ Studied École du Dessin, Cristallerie de Baccarat.

▶ From 1919, he worked as an engraver at Corbin; in c1920, began producing vessels and animal and human forms (including the head of Christ in c1928) by cutting solid blocks of crystal into geometric and figurative motifs; in c1925, became a molder, Cristallerie de Nancy, a rival of Daum, and produced several pieces signed with his name; with the aid of Henri Bossut, produced acid engraved work for Magasins Réunis; in 1926, established his own engraving workshop in Nancy known as Maison d'Art, where he specialized in custom work and Art Déco jewelry. In 1939, Bossut's and Colotte's collaboration was interrupted by World War II, in which Bossut died. Colotte's work included *pâte-de-verre*, engraving on metal, and jewelry.

▶ Work shown at sessions of Salon d'Automne and Société des Artistes Décorateurs. Received Meilleur Ouvrier de France medal (metal engravings) at 1925 Paris 'Exposition Internationale des Arts Décoratifs et Industriels Modernes.'

▶ Cat., *Verriers français contemporains: Art et industrie*, Paris: Musée des Arts Décoratifs, 1982. *Sammlung Bröhan Kunst der 20er und 30er Jahre*, Vol. III, Berlin, 1985:99. Janine Bloch-Dermant, *Le Verre en France d'Émile Gallé à nos jours*, Paris: 1986. Jean-Louis Curtis, *Baccarat*, Paris: Regard, 1992.

Colton, C.W.

▶ American furniture designer and maker; active Boonville, New York.

▶ Colton produced the furniture for numerous camps in the Adirondack Park area, New York State. From the 1880s, his shop was located in Boonville, New York.

▶ *Boonville Herald*, 23 June 1887. Craig Gilborn, *Adirondack Furniture and the Rustic Tradition*, New York: Abrams, 1987:321.

Colwell, David   (1944–)

▶ British industrial designer.

▶ Studied Royal College of Art, London.

▶ In 1968, he opened his own office, London; was a consultant to ICI Plastics. His range of objects included chairs and lighting. His 1968 *Contour Chair* was produced by 4's Company, London, from a molded acrylic sheet.

▶ *Contour Chair* first shown at 1968 'Prospex' exhibition, Royal College of Art, London, sponsored by ICI; 1968 London 'Décor International'; 1970 'Modern Chairs 1918–1970' exhibition, Whitechapel Gallery, London.

▶ Cat., *Modern Chairs 1918–1970*, London: Lund Humphries, 1971.

Colzani, Tarcisio   (1949–)

▶ Italian furniture designer; born and active Paina.

▶ Colzani began his professional career in 1975; became a member of ADI (Associazione per il Disegno Industriale); designed *Logico* seating furniture for Mobil Girgi and *Caris* component seating for Tremolada.

▶ *ADI Annual 1976*, Milan: Associazione per il Disegno Industriale, 1976.

Cometti, Giacomo   (1863–1938)

▶ Italian sculptor, craftsman, and designer.

▶ He turned from sculpture to the applied arts; by the time of the 1902 Turin exhibition, had established a successful workshop. Although he practiced in the prevailing Stile Floreale, his work was considered simple and geometric, showing German influence.

▶ Received honorable mention at 1900 Paris 'Exposition Universelle' and diploma of honor at 1902 Turin 'Esposizione Internazionale d'Arte Decorativa Moderna.'

▶ Cat., Gabriel P. Weisberg, *Stile Floreale: The Cult of Nature in Italian Design*, Miami: The Wolfsonian Foundation, 1988.

Comité Colbert

▶ French commercial association of manufacturers and merchants of luxury goods.

▶ Comité Colbert was established by Jean-Baptiste Colbert (1619–83), statesman and financier under Louis XIV, to encourage high standards in domestic luxury goods. The list of member companies varies from time to time. Comité Colbert awards prizes to promote the work of young artists designing for the luxury industries of France.

Comité Paris/Nancy (CPN)

▶ French designers' organization.

▶ CPN was established in 1923 to promote Modern Art and took a stand against the Art Déco idiom of the École de Nancy; organized conferences, and concerts performed by Darius Milhaud, Arthur Honegger, Francis Poulenc, Jacques Copeau, and others; in 1925, organized an exhibition with Jean and André Lurçat where Modern artists were invited to show work. It was divided into two sections: architecture in one and painting and sculpture in the other. Exhibitors included Walter Gropius, Ludwig Mies van der Rohe, Robert Mallet-Stevens, Le Corbusier, Pierre Chareau, Gabriel Guévrékian, Josef Frank, Josef Hoffmann, J.J.P. Oud, Theo van Doesburg, Georges Braque, Marc Chagall, André Derain, Henri Matisse, Amédée Ozenfant, Pascin, Henri Laurens, Jacques Lipchitz, and Aristide Maillol. Surrealist artists were not invited. After a period of conflict, CPN returned to the Nancy group with Jean Prouvé, Étienne Cournault, Jacques André, and others; had its last great year in 1926.

▶ Catherine Coley in *Le Pays Lorrain No. 1*, Nancy, June 1986.

Committee on Art and Industry
See Gorell Committee

Como, Patrizio   (1952–)

▶ Italian architect and furniture designer; active Milan.

▶ Studied Politecnico di Milano.

▶ He collaborated with Renata Calzi in Amalgama Studio Technico di Architettura, Milan; developed new design and furniture concepts.

▶ Fumio Shimizu and Matteo Thun (eds.), *The Descendants of Leonardo: The Italian Design*, Tokyo, 1987:322.

Compagnie des Arts français (CAF)

▶ French decorating firm, furniture maker, and shop; located Paris.

▶ Compagnie des Arts français was the successor to L'Atelier français, founded by Louis Süe and André Mare in 1919. In 1928, Jacques Adnet took over management of the firm at 116 rue du Faubourg-Saint-Honoré, Paris. In furniture, light woods were used, including sycamore and lemonwood, in simple shapes and a classic Modern style. CAF worked with painters, sculptors, and metalsmiths including Jean Lurçat and Jean Auricoste. Gilbert Poillerat and Richard Desvallières produced forged ironwork for the firm. A kind of artisans' collective, CAF was active 1919–59.

▶ Work included in the Pavillon Fontaine and Musée d'Art Contemporain by Süe and Mare at 1925 Paris 'Exposition Internationale des Arts Décoratifs et Industriels Modernes,' along with works of Jaulmes, Richard Desvallières, Paul Véra, Boutet de Monvel, Segonzac, Boussingault, André E. Marty, and Marinot.

▶ Yvonne Brunhammer, *Le Cinquantenaire de l'exposition de 1925*, Paris: Musée des Arts Décoratifs, 1976. Pierre Cabanne, *Encyclopédie Art Déco*, Paris: Somogy, 1986:183. Pierre Kjellberg, *Art Déco: les maîtres du Mobilier, le décor des Paquebots*, Paris: Amateur, 1986:48.

Compasso d'Oro (Premio Compasso d'Oro)

▶ Italian design prize.

▶ The Premio Compasso d'Oro for excellence in design and innovation was founded in 1954 by Aldo Borletti of La Rinascente department store, Milan. It was intended to encourage designers and manufacturers to reach high standards, particularly with ordinary domestic products. The award's early recipients included Gino Colombini's kitchen bucket in 1955 and his lemon squeezer in 1959, both produced by Kartell. The competition was held in 1954 (I), 1955 (II), 1956 (III), 1957 (IV), 1959 (V), 1960 (VI), 1962 (VII), 1964 (VIII), 1967 (IX), 1970 (X), 1979 (XI), 1981 (XII), 1984 (XIII), 1987 (XIV), 1989 (XV), 1991 (XVI).

▶ Penny Sparke, *Design in Italy, 1870 to the Present*, New York: Abbeville, 1988:116. Jeremy Myerson and Sylvia Katz, *Conran Design Guides: Tableware*, London: Conran Octopus, 1990:12.

Connell, G.L.

▶ British silversmiths; located London.

▶ G.L. Connell was founded before 1839; it manufactured silverwares and sold some foreign silver and designs made by William Hutton and A.E. Jones; at the turn of the century, produced wares in the Art Nouveau style.

▶ Annelies Krekel-Aalberse, *Art Nouveau and Art Déco Silver*, New York: Abrams, 1989:244,253.

Conran, Terence (1931–)

▶ British interior decorator, designer, and entrepreneur; born Esher, Surrey; active London.

▶ From 1947, studied textile design, Central School of Art and Design, London, under Eduardo Paolozzi.

▶ From c1950, he worked for Rayon Centre, London, and, 1951–52, as an interior designer for Dennis Lennon; designed 1955 'The Orrery' coffee-bar, London; in the late 1950s, was a freelance designer; in 1956 with John Stephenson, founded the Conran Design Group; was best known for his Habitat stores, the first of which was opened at 77 Fulham Road, London, in 1964, selling low-priced furniture and furnishings in a Modern style. Conran acquired Mothercare in 1982 and Heal's furniture store in 1983; in 1986, British Home Stores was added to these holdings to form the Storehouse Group, which had 1,000 retail outlets. In 1990, Terence Conran retired from its activities; in 1992, bought back The Conran Shop; opened several restaurants, including Neal Street Café and Bibendum; published *The House Book*, a best-selling guide to home design; as an architect, designed a hotel, Butlers Wharf, in the late 1980s. 1982–86, the Conran Foundation funded the Boilerhouse Project, which showed and promoted good design in a basement space in the Victoria and Albert Museum, London; in 1989, supported the establishment of the Design Museum, Butler's Wharf, London, first directed by Stephen Bayley. In the late 1980s, Conran acquired the Michelin building, London, from which he managed his activities.

▶ Barty Phillips, *Conran and the Habitat Store*, London: Weidenfeld and Nicolson, 1984. Arlene Hirst, *Metropolitan Home*, April 1990:108.

Consolidated Lamp and Glass

▶ American manufacturer; located Coraopolis, Pennsylvania.

▶ Consolidated's *Ruba Rombic* patterned glassware, patented in 1928, showed influences from European, and particularly Czech, Cubism. The pattern's name was derived from the first name of its designer Reuben Haley and the angular form of a rhomboid.

▶ *Official Gazette*, 10 April 1928:298. Hazel Marie Weatherman, *Colored Glass of the Depression Era 2*, Ozark, Mo.: Weatherman Glassbooks, 1974:48. Karen Davies, *At Home in Manhattan: Modern Decorative Arts, 1925 to the Depression*, New Haven: Yale, 1983.

Constructivism

▶ Russian movement in architecture, fine art, and design.

▶ The stylistic development of the Russian avant-garde up to the time of Kazimir Malevich's Suprematist compositions and Vladimir Tatlin's constructions paralleled the development of Modernism in Western Europe. In 1920, the advent of Constructivism was signaled by two manifestos: *The Program of the Group of Constructivists* by Alexei Gan, Aleksandr Rodchenko, and Varvara Stepanova, and *A Realistic Manifesto* by Antoine Pevsner and Naum Gabo. Constructivism had separate aspects: agitprop (or agitation-propaganda), expressed through revolutionary forms of street art and exhibitions; and building construction, expressed in a variety of ways from machine forms to biomorphic structures, including interlocking living units and access elements such as ramps and elevators. The further inclusion of elements outside the architectural norm (such as radio aerials, film-making equipment, and sky-signs) alienated the architect Nikolai Ladovskii (founder of the formalist group Asnova [New Association of Architects] in 1923), El Lissitzky (an important link between Constructivism and the European avant-garde), and Dutch Neo-plasticist leader Theo van Doesburg. Vladimir Tatlin's 1918 model for the *Monument to the Third International* was a manifestation of the success of Modern technology inspired by the Eiffel Tower, Paris, and influenced by the Futurist opera *Victory over the Sun* by Alexei Kruchenikh. The project was criticized by Gabo as being neither functional architecture nor pure art, but both. Although never built Tatlin's maquette was influential in turning numerous artists from fine art to industrial design. Several artist-designers wished to become known as Productivists rather than Constructivists, including Tatlin, Liubov' Popova, Rodchenko, Gan, and Stepanova. Much of Constructivism in Russia was not oriented towards production, but was rather a recreation of traditional Russian agrarian (but non-folkloric) forms as expressed by Konstantin Mel'nikov in his Mahorka pavilion, 1923 'All-Russia Agricultural and Craft Exhibition'; 1923 Sucharev Market, Moscow; and Russian Pavilion, 1925 Paris 'Exposition Internationale des Arts Décoratifs et Industriels Modernes.' Russian Constructivist architecture was pursued through two basic themes: utopian Socialist town planning (seen in N.A. Miliutin's model for a 'six-banded' linear city); and the new 'social condensers' (seen in workers' clubs and communal housing prototypes of Moisei Ginzburg's 1929 Narkomfin housing block, Moscow). Factions of the Constructivist movement were widely divergent; the Asmova group's Gestalt theories were incompatible with the Functionalist-oriented OCA (Association of Contemporary Architects), the group founded by Alekandr Vesnin in 1925. Constructivists were closer to European Functionalists, while Rationalists were more romantic, attempting to bring novelty to every project. In an effort to form a new architectural expression appropriate to the 1917 Revolution, Vesnin was one of the first to create the architectural language of Constructivism; a prime example, his 1923 project Leningradskaia Pravda building, Moscow, manifested the aesthetic of Constructivism in a unified whole, including signage, loudspeakers, elevator interiors, and advertising. Due to the essential underlying social theories of Russian Constructivism, its buildings were realized primarily through public works, including factories, workers' clubs, offices, department stores, plants, hospitals, and hydro-electric installations, including Viktor Vesnin's massive 1932 Dnieperstroi Dam. In the late 1920s, the influence of Constructivism began to be seen in structures by Walter Gropius and Hannes Meyer in Germany and Johannes Duiker, Johannes Brinkman, Cornelius van der Vlugt, and Mart Stam in the Netherlands, and in buildings in Czechoslovakia, Sweden, France, Switzerland, Britain, and the USA. Aspects of international Constructivism appeared in Pierre Chareau's and Bernard Bijvoët's 1928–32 Maison de Verre, Paris, and even Richard Rogers's studies of the early 1960s.

▶ Anatole Kopp, *Ville et révolution*, Paris, 1967. Vieri Quilici, *L'architettura del costruttivismo*, Bari, 1969. El Lissitzky, *Russia: An Architecture for World Revolution*, Cambridge, MA: 1970. O.A. Shvidkovsky, *Building in the USSR, 1917–1932*, London and New

York, 1971. Kenneth Frampton in Vittorio Magnago Lampugnani (ed.), *Encyclopedia of 20th-Century Architecture*, New York: Abrams, 1986:73–74. Jaroslav Andel et al., *Art into Life: Russian Constructivism 1914–1932*, New York: Rizzoli, 1990. Selim O. Khan-Magomedov, *Les Vhutemas*, Paris: Regard, 1990. Cat., *The Great Utopia: The Russian and Soviet Avant-Garde, 1915–1932*, New York: Guggenheim Musem, 1992.

Conte, Nereo   (1932–)

▶ Italian designer; born Pojana Maggiore; active Milan.
▶ Conte began his professional career in 1964 in the design studio of engineers C. Olivetti; designed children's toys; became a member of ADI (Associazione per il Disegno Industriale).
▶ *ADI Annual 1976*, Milan: Associazione per il Disegno Industriale, 1976.

Conterie e Cristallerie, Società Veneziana

▶ Italian jeweler; located Venice.
▶ In 1898, 17 firms were amalgamated as Società Veneziana per la Industria della Conterie, located from the beginning in Palazzo Trevisan, Fondamenta Navagero, Murano. In 1917, due to the invasion of Venetian territory, offices and storage houses were moved to Genoa; in 1920, returned to Venice having acquired an important crystal plant, Gablonz (now Jablonec, Czech Republic), resulting in the name Società Veneziana Conterie e Cristallerie; in the early 1960s, began to produce costume jewelry; production was discontinued in the 1970s.
▶ Deanna F. Cera (ed.) *Jewels of Fantasy: Costume Jewelry of the 20th Century*, New York: Abrams, 1992:308.

Conti, Flavio   (1943–)

▶ Italian architect and designer; born Legnago, Verona; active Milan.
▶ Studied architecture, Politecnico di Milano, to 1968.
▶ Conti began his professional career in 1969; from 1969, was an editor at journal *Arredamento-Interni*; from 1970, was editor and, from 1972, director of his own magazine; from 1973, was professor, Scuola Politecnica Design, Milan; worked out of his own studio in Milan; became a member of ADI (Associazione per il Disegno Industriale). Designing furniture, primarily knock-down and in wood, clients included Arcum, Former, Pedanoshop, Poggenpohl Italia, and Rosi Riparato.
▶ *ADI Annual 1976*, Milan: Associazione per il Disegno Industriale, 1976.

Coop Himmelblau

▶ Austrian architecture partnership; located Vienna.
▶ Wolf D. Prix, Helmut Swiczinsky, and Rainer Michael Holzer founded Coop Himmelblau in 1968. The group was influenced by Haus-Rucker-Co and Hans Hollein; at first was interested in pneumatic-space buildings; offered alternatives to standard concepts of town planning at its 1976 'Wiener Supersommer'. Its 1974 mobile kitchen elements were produced by Ewe-Küchen and 1988 *Vodöl* chair by Vitra. An early proponent of Deconstructivism before the term was coined, its so-called demonstration objects included 1977 Reiss Bar, Vienna; 'Humanic,' Mistelbach in 1979 and Vienna in 1981; 1980 Flammenflügel (Flamewing); and 1981 Roter Engel (Red Angel) Music Bar, Vienna. Its architecture included the 1993 new wing of the Akademie der bildenden Künste, Munich.
▶ Günther Feuerstein, *Vienna—Present and Past: Arts and Crafts—Applied Art—Design*, Vienna: Jugend und Volk, 1976: 35,80. *Coop Himmelblau, Architektur muss brennen*, Graz, 1980. Frank Werner in Vittorio Magnago Lampugnani (ed.), *Encyclopedia of 20th-Century Architecture*, New York: Abrams, 1986: 74–75. Philip Johnson and Mark Wigley, *Deconstructivist Architecture*, New York: Museum of Modern Art, 1988.

Cooper, John Paul   (1869–1933)

▶ British architect, silversmith, and jeweler; active London, Birmingham, and Westerham, Surrey.
▶ In 1887, Cooper was an apprentice to architect J.D. Sedding; in 1891, completed an apprenticeship under Henry Wilson, under whom Cooper's interest in metalworking was fostered; began silversmithing in 1897 specializing in unusual materials, especially shagreen, which he began using in 1903, before other Arts and Crafts practitioners or Clément Mère, Paris. From the turn of the century, Cooper's work was frequently published in reviews *The Studio* and *Art Journal*. Cooper set up a workshop in his house in Westerham, which he designed; from 1906, combined silver and copper in a Japanese metalworking technique; published book *Silverwork and Jewellery*. Strongly architectural in form, his work is often indistinguishable from Henry Wilson's; 1904–07, was head of the metalworking department, Birmingham Central School, where Robert Catterson-Smith was director, and where he was succeeded by his son Francis Cooper; after 1907, was active solely in silversmithing.
▶ *The Studio*, June 1900:48. Charlotte Gere, *American and European Jewelry 1830–1914*, New York: Crown, 1975:168–69. Annelies Krekel-Aalberse, *Art Nouveau and Art Déco Silver*, New York: Abrams, 1989:25,28,253.

Cooper, Susie   (1902–)

▶ British ceramicist; born Staffordshire; active Burslem.
▶ 1918–22, studied Burslem School of Art, under Gordon M. Forsyth.
▶ Starting her career in dress design, she took Gordon M. Forsyth's suggestion to pursue pottery; 1922–29, worked for decorating firm A.E. Gray as a decorator of ceramics, becoming the company's chief designer and the first woman in the potteries to be acknowledged as a designer with her name stamped on her wares; in 1929, set up Susie Cooper Pottery in a factory rented from Doulton; in 1931, moved to Crown Works, Burslem, where she remained for more than 50 years; bought blanks and designed her own shapes, both produced by various firms, until she made an arrangement with Wood and Sons to produce her goods; at first painted designs by hand; by 1933, used a lithographic-transfer process, and, employed over 40 painters. Her first major commission came from John Lewis in 1935, followed by those from Peter Jones, Harrods, Waring and Gillow, Selfridges, and Heal's. She designed the *Curlew* shape in c1933 and the *Kestrel* shape in c1935; in 1937–38, designed tableware for Imperial Airways. Known for her elegant and utilitarian shapes, she was a major innovator in domestic ceramics throughout the 1930s and beyond; produced tableware for the Royal Pavilion, 1951 'Festival of Britain' exhibition, London; produced bone china at Jason Works, Longton, which she acquired in 1950, renaming it Susie Cooper China. Bone china came to be her main product, and by the early 1960s, earthenware production virtually ended. In 1961, she merged with R.H. and S.L. Plant (Tuscan Works), and was in turn acquired by Wedgwood, where she remained as a senior designer and director until 1972. A prominent potter for six decades, her products received acclaim in Britain and abroad. In 1992, she produced new work to celebrate her 90th birthday.
▶ *Kestrel* shapes shown along with other work at British pavilion, 1937 Paris 'Exposition Internationale des Arts et Techniques dans la Vie Moderne.' Designed Royal Pavilion and Royal Society of Arts stand at 1951 London 'Festival of Britain.' In 1979, received the Order of the British Empire. In 1938, elected Fellow of the Royal Institute of British Architects and, in 1940, elected Royal Designer for Industry.
▶ *Susie Cooper: Elegance and Utility* (cat. of exhibition at Sanderson's, London), Barlaston: Wedgwood, 1978. Cat., *Thirties: British art and design before the war*, London: Arts Council of Great Britain, Hayward Gallery, 1979:95,152,287. Fiona MacCarthy and Patrick Nuttgens, *An Eye for Industry*, London: Lund Humphries, 1986. Adrian Woodhouse, *Susie Cooper*, Matlock: Trilby Books, 1992.

Cooperative Work's The Beautiful Room
See Krásná Jizba Družstevní Práce

Copeland, Elizabeth (1866–1957)
▶ American silversmith; born and active Boston.
▶ Copeland was best known for her *cloisonné* objects; learned enameling in Britain under Alexander Fisher; returned to USA and worked for Handicraft Shop, Boston, under the direction of Karl F. Leinonen; up to 1937, produced a variety of objects, including *cloisonné* silver coffers with naturalistic patterns made with a primitive look to emphasize their handmade quality.
▶ Annelies Krekel-Aalberse, *Art Nouveau and Art Déco Silver*, New York: Abrams, 1989:98,253.

Coper, Hans (1920–1981)
▶ British ceramicist; born Chemnitz (Germany).
▶ Studies textile engineering.
▶ In 1939, he settled in Britain; in 1946, discovered pottery in the London Albion Mews Pottery of Lucie Rie, with whom he became a collaborator. Influenced by Oriental techniques and models, he developed a distinctive style in his ceramics. In 1959, settled in Digswell, Hertfordshire. In 1962, his candlesticks were installed in Coventry Cathedral. He admired the work of sculptors Alberto Giacometti and Constantin Brancusi, Cycladic statuary, and primitive art; played a role in renewing ceramic art in England through his teaching efforts, 1961–69, at Camberwell School of Arts and Crafts; in 1966, moved to London and taught at Royal College of Art, 1966–75.
▶ From 1950 at Berkeley Galleries, London, work shown worldwide, frequently with Lucie Rie, including at 1955 exhibition, Röhsska Konstslöjdmuseet, Gothenburg; 1957 exhibition, University of Minnesota, Minneapolis; 1967 exhibition, Boymansvan Beuningen Museum, Rotterdam; and 1972 exhibition, Museum für Kunst und Gewerbe, Hamburg. Work shown at 1951 London 'Festival of Britain'; 1953 'Engelse Ceramiek,' Stedelijk Museum in Amsterdam; 1954 (X) Triennale di Milan (gold medal); 1959 'Ceramics International,' Syracuse, New York; 1969 exhibition (with Peter Collingwood), Victoria and Albert Museum, London; 1972 'International Ceramics,' Victoria and Albert Museum. Work subject of 1956 exhibition (first one-person show) at Bonnier's in New York; 1958 exhibition at Primavera, London; 1965 exhibition, Berkeley Galleries; 1980 retrospective, Hetjens Museum, Düsseldorf; and 1983–84 exhibitions, Sainsbury Centre, University of East Anglia, Norwich; Boymans-van Beuningen Museum; and Serpentine Gallery, London.
▶ Cat., *Nine Potters*, London: Fischer Fine Arts, 1986:8–15. *Collection Fina Gomez: 30 ans de céramique contemporaine*, Paris: Musée des Arts Décoratifs, 1991.

Copier, Andries Dirk (1901–c1990)
▶ Dutch glassware designer.
▶ In 1914, he became an apprentice at Glasfabriek Leerdam, the Netherlands, under Hendrikus Petrus Berlage and, in 1927, its general artistic director; his talents having been recognized by general manager P.M. Cochius, was sent to topographical school, Utrecht, as preparation for designing advertising materials for Leerdam. His *Unica* series (with glassblower Gerrit Vroegh) of one-of-a-kind glassware of *c*1925 continued to be produced until after World War II and, along with pieces produced by colleagues, brought distinction to Leerdam, which merged in the mid-1930s with Vereenigde to form Vereenigde Leerdam Glasfabriek. Copier's *Srica* range of table glass was artistically and commercially successful. From 1922, he designed glassware for himself; influenced by De Stijl from the late 1920s, he executed severe, unadorned forms, including the 1947 *Primula* pressed-glass tableware range and other designs in tumblers, pitchers, and stemware; from the beginning, was interested in Functionalist massproduced glass appropriate to the Modern movement. He designed the 1958 *Gourmet* set of glasses. In 1971, he left Leerdam; in 1977, (with glass blower Piet van Klei) worked on *Unica* again in De Oude Horn, Hessen, near Leerdam; in 1980, experi-

mented with etched and colored decorations and plastic forms in Murano and in the studio of Ann Wärff, Sweden; visited Spruce Pine, North Carolina, and worked with Harvey Littleton and Gary Beecham.
▶ Received silver medal (*Smeerwortel* set of glasses) at 1925 Paris 'Exposition Internationale des Arts Décoratifs et Industriels Modernes.' Work subject of first large-scale exhibition at 1927 Stuttgart 'Weissenhof-Siedlung'; 1963 exhibition, Museum Boymans-van Beuningen, Rotterdam; and 1982 exhibition, Gemeentemuseum, The Hague.
▶ Cat., *A.D. Copier, Glas*, Rotterdam: Museum Boymans-van Geuningen, 1963. Geoffrey Beard, *International Modern Glass*, London, 1976. Cat., *A.D. Copier*, The Hague: Gemeentemuseum, 1982. D.U. Kuyken-Schneider, 'The Old Man—Andries Dirk Copier,' *Neues Glas*, Feb. 1982:102–03. Cat., Kathryn B. Hiesinger and George H. Marcus III (eds.), *Design Since 1945*, Philadelphia: Philadelphia Museum of Art, 1983. Reino Liefkes, 'Master of Pure Form,' *Dutch Heights*, No. 1, Winter 1986/1987:8–41.

Coppens, Omer (1864–1926)
▶ Belgian artist.
▶ Coppens is best known for his paintings and engravings; created several ceramic pieces, some pewter, and bookbindings; was a founder of the group Pour l'Art, serving as president in the late 1890s; was a friend of Émile Gallé, dedicating one of his vases to him.
▶ Yvonne Brunhammer et al., *Art Nouveau Belgium, France*, Houston: Rice University, 1976.

Coppo Barberis, Liliana (1927–)
▶ Italian designer; born S. Giorgio Monferrato; active Casale Monferrato.
▶ Coppo Barberis became active as a designer in 1950; produced ceramic tableware designs produced by SIC; became a member of ADI (Associazione per il Disegno Industriale).
▶ *ADI Annual 1976*, Milan: Associazione per il Disegno Industriale, 1976.

Coppola e Toppo
▶ Italian costume jeweler; located Milan.
▶ Lyda Coppola studied Accademia di Belle Arti, Venice.
▶ Coppola was an apprentice to Ada Politzer in Milan, *c*1944, where she learned the basics of costume jewelry. She made her debut in Paris, setting up her firm in 1946; collaborated with Jacques Fath and Elsa Schiaparelli in 1948; added her husband's name Toppo to the firm name. From the late 1940s, developed a collection for the American market. Lyda Coppola retired in 1972 and the firm closed in 1986.
▶ Deanna F. Cera (ed.), *Jewels of Fantasy: Costume Jewelry of the 20th Century*, New York: Abrams, 1992:306.

Coppola, Silvio (1920–86)
▶ Italian architect, designer, graphic artist, and teacher; active Milan.
▶ Studied architecture, Politecnico di Milano.
▶ From 1947, he was active as a graphic designer; in 1960, began working in plastics, designing folding toys, book shelves, and various furniture pieces; designed buildings, including a department store, Baghdad, and buildings at the city university, Zaïre; was artistic director of Bernini (furniture, including the *Gru* seat made from a single bent metal tube), Cilsa (tiles), Tigamma (home furnishings), and Tessitura di Mompiano (textiles); was consultant designer to numerous Italian and foreign firms, including Bayer Italia, Montecatini, Monteshell, Cinzano, and Laminati Plastici; from 1967, (with Bruno Munari, Franco Grignani, Cofalonieri, Pino Tovaglia, and Mario Bellini) participated in the group Exhibition Design; from 1975, was professor of design, Accademia di Belle Arti, Carrara; became a member of ADI (Associazione per il Disegno Industriale), Architetti di Genoa, AGI (Alliance Graphique Internationale), and AIGA (American Institute of Graphic Art).

▶ Received awards including 1962 Palma d'Oro prize, 1966 and 1968 Rizzoli prize, 1968 Oscar Imballaggio prize, and 1967 Colonna Antonina prize.
▶ Cat., Milena Lamarová, *Design a Plastické Hmoty*, Prague: Um ěleckoprůmyslové Muzeum, 1972:106. *ADI Annual 1976*, Milan: Associazione per il Disegno Industriale, 1976. Moderne Klassiker: *Möbel, die Geschichte machen*, Hamburg, 1982:39.

Coray, Hans (1906–1991)
▶ Swiss designer and artist; born Wald, Zürich.
▶ Coray is best known for his 1938 *Landi* aluminum chair initially designed for use at 1939 Zürich 'Landesaustellung' or Swiss National Exhibition. Until the 1980s, when Zanotta began production, the chair was made solely by Swiss cookware manufacturer P. und W. Blattmann Wadenswil Metallwaren- und Aluminiumwarenfabrik. It weighed 2·9 kilograms (6·4 lbs) and was water-resistant. In the late 1940s, Coray designed furniture for the Wohnbedarf store, including aluminum chairs and tables; in the first half of the 1950s, was active as designer of various chairs, including upholstered, wire, and aluminum side chairs.
▶ Work subject of 'Hans Coray–Künstler und Entwerfer' exhibition at the Museum für Gestaltung, Kunstgewerbemuseum, Zürich, 1986.
▶ Cat., *Hans Coray–Künstler und Entwerfer,* Zürich: Museum für Gestaltung, 1986.

Corbani, Giovanni Dino (1933–)
▶ Italian textile designer; born Arcisate; active Monza.
▶ Corbani designed textiles for clients in Italy, including Fumagalli, Studio Castiglioni, Schmid, Radaelli, and Somma; was designer and director of Mambretti, Casletto; became a member of ADI (Associazione per il Disegno Industriale).
▶ *ADI Annual 1976*, Milan: Associazione per il Disegno Industriale, 1976.

Corette, Sylvia (1960–)
▶ French designer.
▶ Studied École Camondo, Paris.
▶ She was active in the design of the interiors of hotels, bars, and apartments; worked at firm Sleeping Concept on commissions for the city of Paris and subsequently for Protis on a collection of furniture. Her 1989 *Roxane princesse des djins* chair in aluminum and crushed velour was sponsored by VIA.
▶ Cat., *Les années VIA*, Paris: Musée des Arts Décoratifs, 1990.

Corning Glass Works
See Carder, Frederick C.

Coro
See Cohn and Rosenberger

Corretti, Gilberto (1941–)
▶ Italian designer; born and active Florence.
▶ 1966, graduated in architecture.
▶ Beginning his professional career in 1966, Corretti, with Andrea Branzi, Paolo Deganello, Massimo Morozzi, and Dario and Lucia Bartolini, founded the design studio Archizoom Associati in Florence. Archizoom's radical, Anti-Design 1974 *AEO* chair was produced by Cassina and *Arc 02* by Marcatré. Corretti was active as an industrial and graphic designer, and research consultant on industrial products; from 1985, taught at ISIA in Rome and Florence; design clients included Adica Pongo, Cassina, Cidue, Emme Edizioni, Marcatré, Mobel Racing, Planula, Prénatal. He became a member of ADI (Associazione per il Disegno Industriale).
▶ *ADI Annual 1976*, Milan: Associazione per il Disegno Industriale, 1976. *Modo*, No. 148, March–April 1993:119.

Cortes, Pepe (1945–)
▶ Spanish furniture and furnishing designer; born Barcelona.
▶ Cortes, with Javier Mariscal, executed numerous furniture, lighting, and interior designs. These included 1986–87 *Trampolin* chair produced by Akaba and *Araña* table lamp by BD.

▶ Albrecht Bangert and Karl Michael Armer, *80s Style: Designs of the Decade*, New York: Abbeville, 1990:40,116,228.

Cortesi, Angelo (1938–)
▶ Italian industrial designer; born Asola; active Milan.
▶ Cortesi began his professional career in 1966; in 1968, (with Carlo Ronchi and Patrizia Pataccini) set up Studio GPI; became a specialist in public areas and their equipment. Clients included DID (furniture and furnishing), Mostek, Texas (*Digitalclock* mini-computer), Plan (lighting), *First* (upholstered seating), Parker (writing pen), Video International (television camera, mini-computer, and microphone). He was artistic director of glass furniture manufacturer FIAM, Tavullia; from 1973, was a member of the organizing committee, ADI (Associazione per il Disegno Industriale) and its president in 1985–89 and from 1992; was on the jury of 1974 Concours International de Design Industriel Horloger, La Chaux-de-Fonds (France); 1975 'Abanguardia e Cultura Popolare' exhibition, Galleria d'Arte Moderna, Bologna; 1975 (XXXIII) Concorso Internazionale della Ceramica d'Arte Contemporanea, Faenza; 1975 'Concorso Ambienti per Soggiorno,' MIA, Monza; 'Concorso sui Monolocali,' 1975 Salone del Mobile, Milan, and conference on safety in the workplace and ergonomic concerns, Facoltà di Architettura, Pescara. Design clients included Seibu, Kartell, Tecno and Mitsukoshi.
▶ Received 1982 and 1984 Premio Compasso d'Oro; gold medal, 1981 'Bio 9,' Industrial Design Biennale, Ljubljana.
▶ *ADI Annual 1976*, Milan: Associazione per il Disegno Industriale, 1976. Alfonso Grassi and Anty Pansera, *Atlante del design italiano: 1940–1980*, Milan, 1980:296. Fumio Shimizu and Matteo Thun (eds.), *Descendants of Leonardo: The Italian Design*, Tokyo, 1987:336. Hans Wichmann, *Italien Design 1945 bis heute*, Munich: Die Deue Sammlung, 1988. *Modo*, No. 148, March–April 1993:118.

Coslin, Georges (1929–)
▶ Italian industrial designer; active Milan.
▶ Coslin began his professional career in 1960; became a member of ADI (Associazione per il Disegno Industriale). Designing kitchen systems, camping equipment, and domestic accessories, clients in Italy included Longato Arredamenti, Dada Cucine, and Liquigas Italiana.
▶ *ADI Annual 1976*, Milan: Associazione per il Disegno Industriale, 1976.

Cosserat, Kay (1947–)
▶ British textile designer.
▶ 1966–70, studied textiles, Goldsmiths' College, London; 1970–72, Royal College of Art, London.
▶ She became interested in knitting on flat-bed machines; in 1972, set up a weaving studio; knitted fabrics for James Drew and Christian Dior; in 1966, formed Cosserat Design with a factory located in Milton Keynes; worked on commissions for firms, including Jaeger; known for her adventurous color sense.
▶ Robert A.M. Stern (ed.), *The International Design Yearbook*, New York: Abbeville, 1985/1986.

Costa, Renato (1924–)
▶ Italian industrial designer; born Bologna; active Rome.
▶ Costa began his professional career in 1950. Clients included Cassina, Carugati, Cima (fiberglass boats), Caloi (furniture collections), Metallux (lighting), and RCA; in 1958, became a member of ADI (Associazione per il Disegno Industriale).
▶ *ADI Annual 1976*, Milan: Associazione per il Disegno Industriale, 1976.

Costard, Philippe (1960–)
▶ French industrial designer.
▶ Studied École Nationale Supérieure des Arts Décoratifs.
▶ Interested in the technological and marketing issues associated with mass-produced goods, Costard used computer-aided design in 1985 *Sillage* flatware.

▶ *Sillage* flatware received bronze medal for design, 1985 Salon of Société des Artistes Décorateurs; Janus award, Institut français de Design Industriel; 1985 Prix de la Création, Salon Bijorhca.
▶ *Les Carnets du Design*, Paris: Mad-Cap Productions et APCI, 1986:77.

Cottier, Daniel (1838–91)
▶ British stained glass designer, decorator, and art dealer; born Glasgow; active Glasgow, Edinburgh, London, New York, Sydney, and Melbourne.
▶ In the early 1850s, Cottier was an apprentice to stained glass producer David Kier in Glasgow; attended the lectures of and worked for John Ruskin and Ford Madox Brown in London; by 1862, had returned to Scotland, working for stained glass producers Field and Allan; was one of the first to design stained glass that diverged from the Gothic-revival style of the day; in 1864, (with Andrew Wells, formerly with Field and Allen) set up workshop, 40 George Street, Edinburgh; 1864–68, designed windows for the Cathedral of Saint Machar, Aberdeen; (with architects William Leiper and Alexander Thomson) collaborated on painted decorations, Dowanhill Church and United Presbyterian Church, Queen's Parish, both Glasgow; in 1869, set up Cottier and Company, Art Furniture Makers, Glass and Tile Painters, London, where Scottish architects John McKean Brydon, William Wallace, and Bruce J. Talbert were briefly partners. Cottier's staff designed the Colearn House, Auchterarder, Tayside, for which Talbert designed the dining room and its furniture, fireplace, and sideboard, and Cottier designed the allegorical stained-glass windows; in 1873, opened a branch at 144 Fifth Avenue, New York; sold furniture, Venetian glass, Oriental rugs, fabrics, faïence, lacquerwork, and bronzes. His furniture was produced in English, Japanese, and Queen-Anne styles. Cottier was one of the first to produce Aesthetic stained glass in the USA, where his earliest-known commission was 1878 window in Green Memorial Alcove, New York Society Library, of which Léon Marcotte was the decorator; produced stained-glass windows for H.H. Richardson's Trinity Church, Boston; Calvary Church, Gramercy Park, New York; Church of the Incarnation, New York; First Presbyterian Church, Brooklyn; Grace Church, Brooklyn; St. John's Church, Canadaigua, New York; private residences; and structures at Yale and Harvard Universities. In 1873, Cottier and John Lamb Lyon opened a branch in Sydney, and later Melbourne.
▶ Stained-glass window for Field and Allen shown at 1864 London 'Exhibition of Stained Glass and Mosaics,' Victoria and Albert Museum, London.
▶ *The New York Times*, 8 April 1891:5. 'The Late Daniel Cottier,' *Journal of Decorative Art and British Decorator*, No. 22, May 1902: 145. Mark Girouard, *Sweetness and Light: The 'Queen Anne' Movement, 1860–1900*, Oxford, 1977:210–12,241. Michael Donnelly, *Glasgow Stained Glass: A Preliminary Study*, Glasgow, 1981. James L. Sturm, *Stained Glass from Medieval Times to the Present: Treasures to Be Seen in New York*, New York, 1982. Doreen Bolger Burke et al., *In Pursuit of Beauty: Americans and the Aesthetic Movement*, New York: Metropolitan Museum of Art and Rizzoli, 1987:415.

Cottis, Jennifer (1946–)
▶ British industrial designer; born London.
▶ 1963–65, studied industrial design, Ealing Technical College; 1965–68, industrial design, Central School of Arts and Crafts, London.
▶ 1968–70, she was a staff designer, Parnals, Bristol, designing cookers, tumble dryers, and other electrical appliances; 1977–81, was a freelance consultant designer; 1981–83, worked for Herman Miller, Bath, designing and supervising the installation of materials-handling systems for clients in Europe, including Philips, Data General, and Digital Equipment; in 1983, became a member of Chartered Society of Designers and, in 1984, a fellow of the Royal Society of Arts; from 1983, was freelance consultant designer; 1984–87, was a member of Design Centre selection committee for domestic equipment; 1985–88, was a 'product group' member

of Chartered Society of Designers; from 1986, was a part-time lecturer in design and technology, Goldsmiths' College, London; in 1989, became a fellow of Chartered Society of Designers. Work included the 1987 *Neco System 4 Digital* DC motor controller, Normand Electrical; 1987 *Emerson* uninterruptible power supply unit, Emerson Electric Industrial Controls; 1987–88 *Multi-In-Feed* parcel sorting machine, Post Office Research Centre.
▶ Cat., Design Center Stuttgart, *Women in Design: Careers and Life Histories Since 1900*, Stuttgart: Haus der Wirtschaft, 1989:264–67.

Coulon, René-André (1907–)
▶ French furniture designer.
▶ Studied architecture to 1937.
▶ Coulon (with Jacques Adnet) incorporated tempered glass into his pieces, some of which were produced by Hagnauer, Vienna; designed furniture for rooms by Adnet for Saint-Gobain; in 1944, became a member of UAM (Union des Artistes Modernes); is best known for 1937 tempered-glass radiator produced by Saint-Gobain and for 1938 glass chair; was instrumental in establishing Saint-Gobain Institute of Iron and Steel Research and its laboratory; in 1955, associated with Ionel Schien and Yves Magnant.
▶ Radiator by Saint-Gobain and glass furniture shown in manufacturer's pavilion, which Coulon designed with Jacques Adnet, at 1937 Paris 'Exposition Internationale des Arts et Techniques dans la Vie Moderne,' where he showed a collection of glass furniture in UAM pavilion and collaborated with Robert Mallet-Stevens on the design of the Hygiène pavilion. Participated in the Salon des Arts Ménagers.
▶ Jean Favier, 'Le Pavillon de Saint-Gobain,' *La Construction Moderne*, No. 4, 24 Oct. 1937. Cat., *Verriers français contemporains: Art et industrie*, Paris: Musée des Arts Décoratifs, 1982. Cat., Aaron Lederfajn and Xavier Lenormand, *Le Louvre des Antiquaires présente: 1930 quand le meuble devient sculpture*, Paris, 1986. Cat., *Les années UAM 1929–1958*, Paris: Musée des Arts Décoratifs, 1988:166–67.

Council for Art and Industry
▶ British government-sponsored organization.
▶ In 1933, following the recommendations of the Gorell Committee, the British Board of Trade set up the Council for Art and Industry, with members from the industrial, commercial, artistic and design communities, and critics. In 1934, under Frank Pick, the council began to study the training and employment of designers in the pottery, textile, jewelry, metalsmithing, and other industries, and published the report *Design and the Designer in Industry* (1937); produced exhibitions, including those at and with the Victoria and Albert Museum, London, and studied art education in primary schools and adult visual education; in an effort to educate the general consumer, mounted exhibitions promoting inexpensive, well-designed products, including 1937 'The Working Class Home'; was responsible for the organization and selection of entries included in the British exhibition, 1937 Paris 'Exposition Internationale des Arts et Techniques dans la Vie Moderne.'
▶ Cat., *Thirties: British art and design before the war*, London: Arts Council of Great Britain, Hayward Gallery, 1979:304.

Counot-Blandin, Pierre
▶ French furniture designer.
▶ Counot-Blandin set up a workshop in 1911; produced furniture for oceanliners 1935 *Normandie* and 1927 *Liberté* and for Le Mobilier National, copies of which are still produced.

Courrèges, André (1923–)
▶ French couturier; active Paris.
▶ Studied École Supérieure du Vêtement, Paris, 1945, and École des Ponts et Chaussées, Paris.
▶ In 1950, he began his career as a cutter for Cristobal Balenciaga; in 1967, set up his own workshop; in 1965, had his first fashion show, featuring Futurist-looking clothing, mini-skirts, and

trousers in white and pastel shades; in 1987, set up an architecture and design office.
▶ Cat., *Design français, 1960–1990*, Paris: Centre Georges Pompidou/APCI, 1988.

Courtaulds
▶ British textile firm.
▶ Samuel Courtauld managed the Bocking silk mill in 1816; became principal founder of Courtaulds Ltd, which was incorporated in 1913 and became known for its production of crepe. It pioneered rayon made by the viscose process; in 1939, with ICI, began producing nylon; by 1940, as part of the conglomerate, was one of the largest textile firms worldwide; 1963, took over Edinburgh Weavers.
▶ Valerie Mendes, *The Victoria and Albert Museum's Textile Collection, British Textiles from 1900 to 1937*, London: Victoria and Albert Museum, 1992.

Courtois, Alice
▶ French decorator and furniture designer; active Paris.
▶ She rendered dramatic coromandel panels in black, white, and silver, and other stylish furniture in the Art Déco style; in her furniture designs, used rare woods in a highly geometric style.
▶ She participated in 1930 Salon d'Automne.
▶ Pierre Kjellberg, *Art Déco: les maîtres du Mobilier, le décor des Paquebots*, Paris: Amateur, 1986:48.

Coutellerie à Thiers, La
▶ French cutlery industry; located Thiers
▶ In 1272, a group of master cutlerysmiths established themselves in Thiers, which became the center for such activities in France. From the 14th century, the cutlery wares made in Thiers were exported to Spain and the Netherlands. By 1596, more than 170 workers were active in the area, and the number grew to 700 by 1615. Cutlery activities attracted other industries. Using the resources of the Durolle River on which the town is situated, electricity and gas motors aided the production of hand-forged, molded, and polished knives. Today in Thiers the workshops still produce cutlery along with surgical tools and vessels in stainless steel.

Cowan Pottery Studio
▶ American ceramics factory; located Rocky River, Ohio.
▶ R. Guy Cowan set up a ceramics studio in 1912, commissioning ceramic artists including Russell B. Aitken, Thelma Frazier, Arthur E. Baggs, Waylande Gregory, and Viktor Schreckengost. The firm produced both commercial and art pottery. In 1913, Richard O. Hummel joined the pottery, later becoming a chemist; glazed the work of other ceramicists and produced his own innovative, decorated forms, although never considering himself a ceramic artist.
▶ Wares first shown at annual exhibitions of industrial art, New York Metropolitan Museum of Art, in the 1920s–30s and at 1927 'Exposition of Art in Trade at Macy's,' Macy's department store, New York, and 1928 'Exposition of Art in Industry at Macy's.'
▶ Karen Davies, *At Home in Manhattan: Modern Decorative Arts, 1925 to the Depression*, New Haven: Yale, 1983:51.

Cox and Company
▶ British furniture manufacturer.
▶ Rowland Wilton Cox was general manager of Rotax Accessories, manufacturers of components for automobiles, London and Birmingham, until it was bought by Joseph Lucas in 1926. In 1927, Cox bought back the Birmingham plant. At the same time, Cox bought a car window manufacturer and car-hood manufacturer. The staff moved to new premises in South London. From 1929, when sales of automotive products declined, Cox pioneered the production in Britain of tubular-metal car seats and folding seats and tables for the garden. In 1930, sales manager Harry Taylor tried unsuccessfully to obtain rights to make Thonet tubular-steel furniture in England; Cox began producing a range of its own tubular-steel furniture to designs adapted from Thonet

models. In 1931, the Bobby's department store, Bournemouth, placed an order with Cox for 5,000 chairs and 2,500 tables for 'Dreamland' at Margate. Cox produced tubular-steel frames designed by Richter for Bath Cabinet Makers; in 1931–32, manufactured furniture that Raymond McGrath and Serge Chermayeff had designed for the new BBC studios, Broadcasting House, London; in 1933, after Oliver Bernard left competitor Pel, produced chairs for the Lyon's Corner Houses and 1933 winter garden of Cumberland Hotel. In 1934, Cox was involved in legal action with Pel over the production of the *RP6* stacking chair, the rights to which Pel had purchased from Austrian designer Bruno Pollock in 1934; Cox agreed to pay Pel a royalty. Cox's domestic furniture designs were never as sophisticated as Pel's, and it never hired a professional designer, its models being designed by Cox himself or adapted by his technical staff from the designs of other manufacturers. In 1935, Cox's first contract for tip-up auditorium seating came from the Royal Institute of British Architects for its Portland Place, London headquarters. In 1936, Cox moved to Watford. In 1939, the firm supplied aircraft assemblies and parts to Hawker Aircraft and Vickers, and until 1945 it moved over to the production of war materials, including aircraft-engine mountings, gun turrets and tanks.
▶ Cat., Dennis Sharp et al., *Pel and Tubular Steel Furniture of the Thirties*, London: Architectural Association, 1977. Barbie Campbell-Cole and Tim Benton (eds.), *Tubular Steel Furniture*, London: The Art Book Company, 1979:53.

Crabeth, Vennootschap
▶ Dutch glassmaker; active The Hague.
▶ Crabeth executed Theo van Doesburg's *Composition IV* triptych stained-glass window for 1917 Jan Wils townhouse, Alkmaar, and *Compositions II* and *V* for Menso Onnes's and J.J.P. Oud's Villa Allegonda, Katwijk aan Zees.
▶ Evert van Straaten, *Theo van Doesburg, Painter and Architect*, The Hague: SDU, 1988. Jonathan M. Woodham, *Twentieth-Century Ornament*, New York: Rizzoli, 1990:111.

Cranach, Wilhelm Lucas von   (1861–1918)
▶ German painter, jeweler, interior decorator, and designer.
▶ Studied Weimar and Paris.
▶ In 1893, he settled in Berlin, where he became a landscape and portrait painter. His Art Nouveau jewelry designs were more akin to French and Belgian than to German forms, with a decadence absent from the work of contemporaries such as René Lalique, Georges Fouquet, and Philippe Wolfers. Cranach claimed descent from his 16th-century painter namesake.
▶ Received gold medal at 1900 Paris 'Exposition Universelle.' Work shown at 1906 Berlin exhibition.
▶ W. Bode (ed.), *Werke moderner Goldschmiedekunst von W. Lucas von Cranach*, Leipzig, 1905. Charlotte Gere, *American and European Jewelry 1830–1914*, New York: Crown, 1975:169–70.

Cranbrook Academy of Art
▶ American design school; located Bloomfield Hills, Michigan.
▶ In 1927, the Cranbrook Foundation was established by newspaper publisher and arts patron George Gough Booth (1864–1949) as an education community that comprised four learning institutions and a church in Bloomfield Hills. Master craftspeople Tor Berglund, Arthur Nevill Kirk, and others set up studios for silver, iron, bookbinding, weaving, and cabinetry. Some worked with assistants and apprentices, following Booth's original concept for the institution, and in 1928 buildings for them to live and work were built. They were hired to teach at both the Cranbrook School and the Art School of the Detroit Society of Arts and Crafts. In 1932 Eliel Saarinen, previously a lecturer at the University of Michigan, became the first president of the formally established Cranbrook Academy of Art. Saarinen introduced full scholarships in architecture, painting, and sculpture which increased attendance during 1935–36. In 1942, the government of Michigan allowed the institution to grant graduate and undergraduate degrees according to certain newly established para-

meters. In 1946, Booth retired as chair due to illness. The first generation of faculty and students consisted mainly of Europeans, including Saarinen and his family: wife 'Loja,' daughter 'Pipsan,' and son Eero, and the second generation of Midwesterners such as Charles Eames and Florence Knoll. Other faculty students included silverware designer and sculptor Harry Bertoia, ceramicist Maija Grotell, sculptor Carl Milles, painter Zoltan Sepeshy, and others. Called by some America's democratic counterpart to the Bauhaus.

▶ Subject of 1984–85 exhibition, The Detroit Institute of Arts and traveling.

▶ Cat., Robert Judson Clark et al., Design in America: The Cranbrook Vision, 1925–1950, New York: Abrams, Detroit Institute of Arts, and Metropolitan Museum of Art, 1983.

Crane, Walter (1845–1915)

▶ British designer, artist, and writer; born Liverpool; son of portrait painter Thomas Crane (1808–59).

▶ 1859–62, apprenticed to woodcarver William J. Linton, London.

▶ By 1863, he had begun his long collaboration with publisher and printer Edmund Evans (1826–1906); from the 1860s, designed books; in the 1870s, was influenced by Japanese art, Edward Burne-Jones, Botticelli, and William Blake. His books were popular; The Baby's Opera: A Book of Old Rhymes with New Dresses (1877) sold over 40,000 copies. In original and pirated editions, his books were available in USA. American Encaustic Tiling Company, Zanesville, Ohio, produced transfer-printed tiles from the illustrations in The Baby's Own Æsop (1887). Helen Metcalf adapted his 1865–66 illustrations for her drawings for Jack and the Beanstalk (1874). Crane designed tiles for Maw, vases for Wedgwood, wallpapers for Jeffrey from 1874, a tapestry for Morris and Company, textiles for Wardle in the 1880s, carpets for Templeton's of Glasgow, and embroideries for the Royal School of Art Needlework; collaborated with William Morris and Thomas Jeckyll on the decoration of collector Alexander A. Ionides house, London; in the early 1870s, revived the art of decorative plasterwork; became a founder-member of the Art-Workers' Guild in 1884, serving as master from 1888–89; a Socialist from c1885, was founder-member and president of the Arts and Crafts Exhibition Society from its formation in 1888 until 1912 (excluding 1891–96); 1891–92, visited the USA and designed stained glass for Catharine Lorillard Wolfe house, Newport, Rhode Island and a church in Newark, New Jersey; designed two books for Houghton, Mifflin, Boston; and painted murals for the Women's Christian Temperance Building, Chicago. His work exerted an impact on graphic designers in the USA, including Will Bradley, Howard Pyle, and Edwin Austin Abbey. In the 1890s, Crane became director of design, Manchester School of Art, and briefly taught art, Reading College. In the 1890s, wrote numerous books on the decorative arts. He was one of the most versatile decorative artists of the late 19th century, designed stained glass, tiles and ceramics, wallpapers, embroideries, textiles, mosaics, and decorative plasterwork, his greatest contribution being in the graphic arts; by 1898, was already well known in Europe, when he was made principal, Royal College of Art, London. In 1895, his late work was on display at Siegfried Bing's shop L'Art Nouveau, Paris. As an honorary member of the Vienna Secession, he designed the 1898 cover for its review Jugend. Crane's style heralded continental Art Nouveau, of which he became a critic; his books and illustrations disseminated the Arts and Crafts style.

▶ Received a prize (wallpapers by Jeffrey) at 1876 Philadelphia 'Centennial Exposition,' where his embroidered screen with peacocks and portiers for Royal School of Art Needlework were included; 1905 gold medal from Royal Society of Arts. Work subject of 1891–96 exhibition, Fine Art Society, London, traveling to Chicago, St. Louis, Boston, Philadelphia, and Brooklyn. Work shown in Budapest in 1900; in Vienna in 1902; 1902 Turin 'Esposizione Internazionale d'Arte Decorativa Moderna.'

▶ P.G. Konody, The Art of Walter Crane, London, 1902. Russell Sturgis, 'English Decoration and Walter Crane,' Architectural Record, No. 12, Dec. 1902:685–91. Royal Institute of British Architects Journal, 3rd series 22, 1914–15:240,277,280. The New York Times, March 16, 1915:11. Gertrude C.E. Massé, A Bibliography of First Editions of Books Illustrated by Walter Crane, London, 1923. Isobel Spencer, Walter Crane, New York, 1975. Yvonne Brunhammer et al., Art Nouveau Belgium, France, Houston: Rice University, 1976. Doreen Bolger Burke et al., In Pursuit of Beauty: Americans and the Aesthetic Movement, New York: Metropolitan Museum of Art and Rizzoli, 1987:417.

Craven, Shirley (1934–)

▶ British textile designer.

▶ 1955–58, studied painting, sculpture, and textile design, Kingston upon Hull and Royal College of Art, London.

▶ From 1960, as consultant designer, she executed designs for printed fabrics produced by Hull Traders; in 1963, joined Hull Traders as director; when the firm closed in 1972, returned to painting and teaching.

▶ Received awards from Council of Industrial Design (fabrics by Hull Traders), including for Le Bosquet in 1961, Division, Sixty-Three, and Shape in 1964, and Simple Solar and Five in 1968.

▶ Cat., Brown/Craven/Dodd: 3 Textile Designers, Manchester: Whitworth Art Gallery, 1965:6–10. Ken Baynes, Industrial Design and the Community, London, 1967:57–59. 'Furnishing Fabrics: Hull Traders' Simple Solar, Five,' Design, No. 233, May 1968:30–31. Cat., Kathryn B. Hiesinger and George H. Marcus III (eds.), Design Since 1945, Philadelphia: Philadelphia Museum of Art, 1983.

Craver, Margaret Withers (1907–1991)

▶ American silversmith; born Kansas City, Missouri; active Boston.

▶ Studied Art School, University of Kansas City, Missouri; with Wilson Weir of Tiffany and with Stone Associates, Gardner, Massachusetts; with Leonard Heinrich, chief armor conservator of New York Metropolitan Museum of Art, from whom she learned toolmaking; and at Atelier Borgila of Baron Erik Fleming.

▶ Craver was one of the few women silversmiths to achieve international recognition; in her workshop in the 1940s and 1950s, revived hand-wrought silver hollow-ware. Her first major work in hollow-ware was a 1936 silver and ebony teapot, made under the direction of ecclesiastical metalworker Arthur Nevill Kirk, Detroit. Craver's work combined full, organic shapes with the influence of Art Moderne. Craver began her studies in metalsmithing in the 1930s, although the craft had long suffered from inadequate training due to the introduction of mechanized silver production in the 19th century. Returning to the USA in 1938 after her studies in Europe, Craver set up a workshop producing hollow-ware, sometimes decorated with enamel; she later worked at precious metal refiner Handy and Harmon to develop a program for rehabilitating veterans returning from World War II; while there, developed a program to train design teachers; most artists working today in American silversmithing were either trained at or learned from silversmithing conferences led by Craver and sponsored by Handy and Harmon. Craver revived the lost enreulle enameling technique and concentrated on jewelry in the latter part of her career.

▶ Work shown at numerous exhibitions including 1970 'Objects USA' and 1987 'The Eloquent Object.'

▶ Annelies Krekel-Aalberse, Art Nouveau and Art Déco Silver, New York: Abrams, 1989:124,253. Jeannine Falino, 'MFS Boston acquires Craver Silver Teapot,' Antiques and the Arts Weekly, 16 Feb. 1990:50. Jeannine Falino, 'Margaret Withers Craver' in Mel Byars and Russell Flinchum (eds.), 50 American Designers, 1918–1968, Washington: Preservation, 1994.

Créateurs et Industriels

▶ French fashion firm and furniture manufacturer; located Paris.

▶ Créateurs et Industriels was established in 1971 by Didier Grumbach and Andrée Putman. It helped young designers, including Valentino, Jean Muir, Jean-Claude de Castelbajac, Thierry Mugler, and Jean-Paul Gaultier to challenge the established cou-

ture houses; commissioned Marc Held to design 1971 table, bed, and desk, produced in polyester plastic.
▶ Held furniture shown at 1972 'Design a Plastické Hmoty,' Uměleckoprůmyslové Muzeum, Prague.
▶ Cat., Milena Lamarová, *Design a Plastické Hmoty*, Prague: Uměleckoprůmyslové Muzeum, 1972.

Creazioni Lisa
▶ Italian costume jeweler; located Florence.
▶ Lisa Battagli began to design and produce costume jewelry in 1960; achieving success in the high-fashion field at first, abandoned this exclusive outlet in favor of traditional boutiques until the end of the 1970s; at this time, began a collaboration with the ready-to-wear trade.
▶ Deanna F. Cera (ed.), *Jewels of Fantasy: Costume Jewelry of the 20th Century*, New York: Abrams, 1992:306.

Crémaillère, La
▶ French furnishings store and maker; located Paris.
▶ André Champetier de Ribes and Jacques Delore established La Crémaillère shop, 148 avenue Malakoff, Paris, in 1923, where they sold ceramics, glassware, silver, and various furnishings for domestic interiors. The design department was managed by Charles Goetz and Jacques Krauss. In 1930, André Renou joined the firm and, in 1941, became president and director general. Jean-Pierre Génisset joined the firm in 1933. Their collaboration lasted until 1965; their collaborative work was signed 'Renou et Génisset.' Renou's wife selected unusual objects for the firm. In 1937, the shop moved to 5 boulevard des Malesherbes, and, in 1967, to 74 boulevard des Malesherbes. Thérèse Bentz was one of its designers of tables and lamps and Germaine Montereau of fabrics, including table linen.
▶ Yolande Amic, *Intérieurs: Le Mobilier français 1945–1964*, Paris: Regard/VIA, 1983:44–45. Pierre Kjellberg, *Art Déco: les maîtres du Mobilier, le décor des Paquebots*, Paris: Amateur, 1986:48. Arlette Barré-Despond, *UAM*, Paris: Regard, 1986.
▶ See Renou, André

Crespin, Adolphe   (1859–1944)
▶ Belgian designer; born Anderlecht.
▶ Studied in Paris and Brussels.
▶ In 1889, he became professor of design at the art school in Schaerbeek (Netherlands), where he met architect Paul Hankar, with whom he collaborated. Hankar designed a bakery for a façade competition and Crespin the sgraffito murals that won a prize in 1896. Crespin designed an advertising poster for Hankar in 1894 and was one of the first Belgians to specialize in poster art; in collaboration with Edouard Duyck and alone, designed a number of notable posters.
▶ Crespin and Hankar designed the interior decoration for Salle d'Ethnographie, colonial section, 1897 Tervueren 'Exposition Internationale.'
▶ Yvonne Brunhammer et al., *Art Nouveau Belgium, France*, Houston: Rice University, 1976.

Cret, Paul Philippe   (1876–1945)
▶ French architect and designer; born Lyons.
▶ 1896, studied Atelier Pascal, École des Beaux-Arts, Paris; won Prix de Rougevin there.
▶ 1890, worked in uncle's architecture office, Lyons; designed 1941 Empire State Express Train of the New York Central Railroad and 1941 California Zephyr Train. Buildings included 1907 Pan American Union Building (with Albert Kelsey), Washington, DC; 1922 Detroit Institute of Arts; 1922 Delaware River Bridge (today, Benjamin Franklin Bridge), Philadelphia; 1929 Folger Shakespeare Library, Washington, DC; 1932 Federal Reserve Bank, Washington, DC.
▶ He designed a number of room settings for and was the director of the East Gallery of the 1935 'Contemporary American Industrial Art, 1934' exhibition, New York Metropolitan Museum of Art. Received Philadelphia (Bok) Award.

▶ Theo B. White (ed.), *Paul Philippe Cret: Architect and Teacher*, Philadelphia: Art Alliance, 1973. R. Craig Miller, *Modern Design 1890–1990*, New York: Abrams, 1990, notes.

Cretté, Georges   (1893–1969)
▶ French bookbinder and gilder; born Créteil; active Paris.
▶ Studied École Estienne, Paris, under Henri de Waroquier, Godefroy, and Masset, to 1911.
▶ He joined the Paris bindery of Henri Marius-Michel, designing in an Art Nouveau style like his employer; took over the firm when Marius-Michel died. Cretté's designs gradually became more geometric. His work was compared to Henri Creuzevault's. Known as the *maître des filets*, he was well established by 1930; bound lacquered volumes for François-Louis Schmied and Jean Dunand; remained active after World War II. Clients included Louis Barthou, Bussillet, J. André, Aubert, and Baron R. Gourgaud.
▶ Work shown as an independent binder at 1925 Paris 'Exposition Internationale des Arts Décoratifs et Industriels Modernes.'
▶ Gaston Quénioux, *Les Arts décoratifs modernes 1918–1925*, Paris, 1925:335. Georges Cretté, 'Distinctive Designs in Hand-Tooled Bookbindings,' *Creative Art*, Vol. 7, 1930:378–81. '5 Reliures,' *Mobilier et décoration*, April 1935: 140–45. Henri Colas, 'Les Reliures de Georges Cretté,' *Mobilier et décoration*, May 1946:40–45. René Chavance, 'Georges Cretté: artiste et artisan relieur,' *Mobilier et décoration*, May 1950:21–27. Jacques Guignard, 'Les Reliures de Georges Cretté,' *Mobilier et décoration*, Sept. 1954: 322–26. John F. Fleming and Priscilla Juvelis, *The Book Beautiful and the Binding as Art*, New York, Vol. 1, 1983:180; Vol. 2, 1985:2. Alastair Duncan and Georges de Bartha, *Art Nouveau and Art Déco Bookbinding*, New York: Abrams, 1989:7,8,17,20–21,23,24,66–67,93,160,163–65,189.

Creuzevault, Henri   (1905–1971)
▶ French bookbinder, designer, and gilder; born and active Paris; son of Louis-Lazare Creuzevault.
▶ Trained in glazing, painting, and drawing before apprenticeship in his father's workshop.
▶ 1918–20, Creuzevault was an apprentice gilder; subsequently, joined the family bindery, rue de Villejust, Paris; became known for his Modern designs produced through innovative techniques; from 1925, designed bindings that showed Art Déco motifs. In 1928, his brother joined the firm as his assistant. By 1934, the bindery was located at 159 rue du Faubourg St.-Honoré, Paris. Henri produced dynamic and lively designs for volumes including *Le Livre de la jungle* and *Les Carnets de voyage en Italie* (both c1926). His bindings showed two ribs (as opposed to the usual five) extending a half inch (1 cm.) from the spines. By the 1930s, his designs included sculptural or 'architectural' detailing, seen in volumes *La Bataille* (with gold and silver encrustations), *Le Pot au noir* (blind tooling and silver and aluminum features), and *La Rose de Bakawali* (with duco, or imitation lacquer). In 1937, he established a publishing firm; remained active and creative after World War II; in 1946, founded Société de la Reliure Originale; in the 1940s, became a member of UAM (Union des Artistes Modernes); in 1956 retiring from his book-binding business and from Groupe des Grand Reliures, purchased and managed an art gallery, avenue Matignon, Paris, and designed tapestries produced by Gobelins.
▶ Received grand prize and a gold medal at 1937 Paris 'Exposition Internationale des Arts et Techniques dans la Vie Moderne.' From 1947, work shown at exhibitions of La Reliure Originale. Work subject of 1984 'Henri Creuzevault, Naissance d'une reliure' exhibition, Musée des Arts Décoratifs, Bordeaux.
▶ Ernest de Crauzat, *La Reliure française de 1900 à 1925*, Vol. 2, Paris, 1932:54–56. Georges Lecomte, 'Reliures modernes,' *Plaisir de France*, Dec. 1937:72,73. Jacques Guignard 'Aspects de la reliure française et reliures modernes,' *Art et décoration*, April 1947:22,27. Roger Devauchelle, *La Reliure en France de ses origines à nos jours*, Vol. 3, Paris, 1961:171,202,210,228. John F. Fleming and Priscilla Juvelis, *The Book Beautiful and the Binding as Art*,

Vol. 1, 1983:24,28,79,153; Vol. 2, 1985:1,51. Cat., *Henri Creuzevault: naissance d'une reliure*, Bordeaux: Musée des Arts Décoratifs, Bordeaux, 1984. Avis Berman, 'Antiques: Bound for Glory: Rare Bookbindings of Art Déco Design,' *Architectural Digest*, May 1986: 188–93,234–35. Colette Creuzevault, *Henri Creuzevault 1905–1971*, Montfort, 1987. Cat., *Les années UAM 1929–1958*, Paris: Musée des Arts Décoratifs, 1988:170. Alastair Duncan and Georges de Bartha, *Art Nouveau and Art Déco Bookbinding*, New York: Abrams, 1989:8,21,23,24,66,78–83,189.

Creuzevault, Louis-Lazare (1879–1956)
▶ French bookbinder; born Bourgogne; active Paris; father of Henri Creuzevault.
▶ Apprenticed to Dode, Paris.
▶ In 1904, Creuzevault acquired Dode's Paris bindery. In Art Nouveau mode and including historicist designs, his work was in the mainstream of those practicing in Paris 1905–14. His son Henri put new life into the bindery.
▶ He showed bindings at the annual Salons in Paris.
▶ Alastair Duncan and Georges de Bartha, *Art Nouveau and Art Déco Bookbinding*, New York: Abrams, 1989:78,189.

Crevel, René (1900–35)
▶ French writer, painter, and jewelry designer; born in Rouen.
▶ Crevel belonged to the Surrealist group; was preoccupied in his writings with death and solitude; worked as a jewelry designer with Gérard Sandoz and assisted with the furniture for Sandoz's shop and apartment, rue Royale, Paris; painted portraits and bucolic and marine scenes, decorated panels, and designed wallpaper.
▶ Work shown at sessions of Salon d'Automne and Salons of Société des Artistes Décorateurs. Participated (with Paul Follot) in 1925 Paris 'Exposition International des Arts Décoratifs et Industriels Modernes' and with others showed textiles, tapestries, and *toiles* in the French Embassy pavilion.
▶ Yvonne Brunhammer, *Le Cinquantenaire de l'exposition de 1925*, Paris: Musée des Arts Décoratifs, 1976:122.

Crippa Guidetti, Pia Giuliana (1943–)
▶ Italian designer; born Ameno; active Milan.
▶ Crippa Guidetti began her professional career in 1969; became a member of ADI (Associazione per il Disegno Industriale). Designing lighting and furniture, clients in Italy included Lumi and Arredamento di Interni.
▶ *ADI Annual 1976*, Milan: Associazione per il Disegno Industriale, 1976.

Cristalleries de Saint-Louis
See Saint-Louis, Cristalleries de

Cristiani, Mario (1921–)
▶ Italian designer; born in and active Milan.
▶ Studied Accademia di Belle Arte di Brera, Milan, and Facoltà di Architettura, Politecnico di Milano.
▶ From 1957, he worked at La Rinascente department store, where he was manager of Centro Design in charge of the Settore furniture line; became a member of ADI (Associazione per il Disegno Industriale).
▶ Participated in 1951 (IX), 1957 (XI), and 1960 (XII) Triennali di Milano. *T92* folding table (with Eugenio Gerli) produced by Tecno received 1970 Premio Compasso d'Oro.
▶ *ADI Annual 1976*, Milan: Associazione per il Disegno Industriale, 1976.

Croce, Gaetano (1930–)
▶ Italian architect and industrial designer; born Rome; active Padua.
▶ Studied architecture.
▶ Croce began his professional career as architect and designer in 1960, became a member of ADI (Associazione per il Disegno Industriale). Clients in Italy included Officina Sordina, OMS Caselle di Selvazzano, EMMEGI, Monselice, and Limena (hospital and dental seating and equipment).

▶ *ADI Annual 1976*, Milan: Associazione per il Disegno Industriale, 1976.

Crochet, Jean-François
▶ French designer; active Italy.
▶ His 1988 *Antinea* spiral floor lamp for Terzani shown at 1991 'Mobili Italiani 1961–1991: Le Varie Età dei linguaggi' exhibition, Salone del Mobile, Milan.
▶ *Mobili Italiani 1961–1991: Le Varie Età dei linguaggi*, Milan: Cosmit, 1992.

Croix-Marie, Paul
▶ French sculptor; born Orléans.
▶ Primarily a sculptor in wood, Croix-Marie produced furniture for domestic interiors in ornately sculptured exotic woods.
▶ Pierre Kjellberg, *Art Déco: les maîtres du Mobilier, le décor des paquebots*, Paris: Amateur, 1986:48.

Cromie, Robert (1887–1971)
▶ British architect.
▶ Studied Architectural Association, London.
▶ He was an apprentice to architect A.J. Wood; became the first in Britain to use tubular-steel furniture on a large public scale, in the restaurant of 1929 Capital Cinema, Epsom, Surrey; was best known for his theater and cinema designs; was 'house architect' for the Ritz and Regal cinema chains.
▶ His work in the 1930s included Regal cinemas in Bexleyheath, Canterbury, Godalming, Kingston upon Thames, Margate, and Wimbledon; Ritz cinemas in Birkenhead, Chelmsford, Huddersfield, Oxford, Southend, and Turnbridge Wells; Paris cinemas in Regent St. (1938) and Drayton Gardens, London; Gaumont's Palace cinema in Hammersmith, London; 1937 Prince of Wales Theatre in London; Plaza, Rex, and Embassy cinemas; interiors of Oddenino's hotel in London and the nurses' training school in Hove.
▶ Work shown at 1979–80 'Thirties' exhibition, Hayward Gallery, London.
▶ Cat., *Thirties: British art and design before the war*, London: Arts Council of Great Britain, Hayward Gallery, 1979:272,273, 287. Barbie Campbell-Cole and Tim Benton (eds.), *Tubular Steel Furniture*, London: The Art Book Company, 1979:53.

Crompton, Rebecca (?–1947)
▶ British embroiderer.
▶ Trained in the Singer Machine Workroom with Dorothy Benson.
▶ She was a proponent of free machine embroidery in conjunction with hand techniques; lectured in Aberdeen, Dundee, Edinburgh, and Glasgow for the Needlework Development Scheme established in Scotland in 1934. Her work was widely published as examples of Modern embroidery. She was examiner and inspector of embroidery and women's crafts, Board of Education, and examiner in embroidery, Lancashire and Cheshire Institute (Advanced Section); contributed to *Modern Needlecraft* in 1932 (edited by Davide C. Minter), *Modern Design in Embroidery* (1936), and *A Plea for Freedom* (1936); (with Mary Hogarth, Kathleen Mann, and Molly Booker) was among the leading British embroiderers of the 1930s.
▶ Work shown at 1932 'Modern Embroidery' exhibition sponsored by British Institute of Industrial Art, Victoria and Albert Museum, London, and 1938 'Needlework Through the Ages' exhibition. 1930 white organdy panel of Diana shown at 1979–80 'Thirties' exhibition, Hayward Gallery, London.
▶ Cat., *Thirties: British art and design before the war*, London: Arts Council of Great Britain, Hayward Gallery, 1979:92,127,287–88.

Cros, Henry (1840–1907)
▶ French ceramicist, sculptor, and glass designer; born Narbonne.
▶ Studied École des Beaux-Arts, Paris, under François Jouffroy, Étex, and Valadon.
▶ He is credited with rediscovering the secret of making *pâte-de-verre*, a technique originally perfected by the ancient Egyptians;

first experimenting with wax, turned to *pâte-de-verre* after a long period of research; used powdered glass, mixed into a paste with flux and colored with metallic oxides; bonded the glass in molds at sufficiently high temperature for it to melt, but without sections of different colors running together; made mainly bas-reliefs and medals, with some masks, portraits, vases, and goblets; was active in research at the Sèvres factory.

▶ Powdered-glass sculpture shown at 1883 Paris Salon. Received gold medal (bas-relief *L'Histoire du Feu*) at the 1900 Paris 'Exposition Universelle.'

▶ Yvonne Brunhammer et al., *Art Nouveau Belgium, France*, Houston: Rice University, 1976. Cat., *Verriers français contemporains: Art et industrie*, Paris: Musée des Arts Décoratifs, 1982.

Crotti, Jean (1878–1958)
▶ Swiss painter and stained glass craftsman; active Paris.
▶ Crotti was married to Marcel Duchamp's sister, who was also a painter; practicing Cubism, was active in the Dada movement in Paris; towards the end of his life, created the *gemail* technique of assembling stained glass without leading.
▶ Cat., Aaron Lederfajn and Xavier Lenormand, *Le Louvre des Antiquaires présente: 1930 quand le meuble devient sculpture*, Paris, 1986.

Cumming, Rose (1877–1968)
▶ American interior decorator; born Australia; active New York.
▶ Cumming arrived in New York in 1917. Frank Crowninshield, editor of *Vanity Fair*, suggested that she become a decorator; she is said to have replied 'What is it?' Cumming worked briefly at the decorating studio Au Quatrième of Wanamaker's department store, New York; subsequently, opened a shop of her own on Madison Avenue. Her distinctive windows were noticed by the public and the press. Her house on East 53rd Street was fitted with theatrical mirrors and a great many black candles. The drawing room, shown in photographs of 1946, had Louis XV sofas and chairs with tattered original upholstery and walls covered with antique Chinese wallpaper. Furniture frames were white or natural wood. The house was neither heated in winter nor artificially cooled in summer. With tinted violet hair, her trademarks in design included silver-foil wrapping paper applied to walls, smoked mirrors, and full curtains in chintz fabrics vividly colored to her own specifications. Selling fabrics and furnishings after Cumming's taste, her firm continued in business after her death.
▶ Mark Hampton, *House and Garden*, May 1990: 145–49, 214. John Esten and Rose Bennett Gilbert, *Manhattan Style*, Boston: Little, Brown, 1990:8. Mark Hampton, *Legendary Decorators of the Twentieth Century*, New York: Doubleday, 1992.

Cuneo, Marcello (1933–)
▶ Italian designer; born Cagliari; active Peschiera Borromeo.
▶ Graduated from the Politecnico di Milano.
▶ Cuneo began his professional career in 1959; from 1962–70, collaborated with Gio Ponti; in 1971, set up his own design studio; was designer for the minister of Islamabad (Pakistan) and for De Bijenkorf, Eindhoven. His clients in Italy included Ampaglas (plastic accessories), Arflex (seating), Assioma, Gabbianelli (ceramics), La Linea (furniture in wood), Mobel Italia (seating in metal), and Valenti (lighting). He worked as consultant on prefabrication for Sculponia and FEAL. He was on the jury of the 1974 competition for industrial design in Faenza. His lighting was widely published. He was a member of ADI (Associazione per il Disegno Industriale).
▶ Received first prize (*Longobardo* lighting fixture) 1967 'Internazionale Andrea Palladio,' Venice, 1978 Bundespreis 'Die gute Industrieform' (desk chair for Comforto, Germany). Work shown at 1972 'Italy: The New Domestic Landscape' at the New York Museum of Modern Art.
▶ *ADI Annual 1976*, Milan: Associazione per il Disegno Industriale, 1976. Alfonso Grassi and Anty Pansera, *Atlante del design italiano: 1940–1980*, Milan, 1980: 297. *Modo*, No. 148, March–April 1993:118.

Cusi
▶ Italian jeweler; located Milan.
▶ Annibale Cusi (1863–1930) began as a jeweler in Milan, in 1886; had clientele including politicians, financiers, and wealthy industrialists; in 1915, was appointed the official royal jeweler of the Duke of Aoste and the Count of Turin; at the end of World War I, built the townhouse, via Clerici, Milan, in which his shop was housed; in 1929 when the casino at San Remo opened, opened a shop facing the grand staircase. Rinaldo Cusi succeeded his father in 1930. Ettore and Roberto Cusi succeeded their father Rinaldo in 1979. The two brothers managed the business separately, continuing with the family name. Ettore managed the shop on via Clerici, and Roberto on via Montenapoleone. In the 1950s, the Clerici atelier employed 50 people and three designers.
▶ Annibale Cusi received first prize (collar in 'platinuralium') at 1906 Milan 'Esposizione Internazionale.'
▶ Melissa Gabardi, *Les Bijoux des Années 50*, Paris: Amateur, 1987.

Cusimano, Angelo (1938–)
▶ Italian designer; born Tobruk (Libya); active Palermo.
▶ Studied architecture from 1958.
▶ He designed furniture from 1974, including a range of seating in laminated plastic, metal, and foam produced by Gufran, Torino; became a member of ADI (Associazione per il Disegno Industriale). Clients in Italy included Mediterranea Mobili, Dragna, Adile in Palermo, Francesconi, and Giovannetti.
▶ *ADI Annual 1976*, Milan: Associazione per il Disegno Industriale, 1976.

Custer, Walter (1909–)
▶ Swiss architect; born Rapperswil; active Zürich.
▶ Studied architecture, Eidgenössische Technische Hochschule, Zürich, under Otto Rudolf Salvisberg; 1931–32, Berlin, under Hans Poelzig.
▶ While still at technical school, he was hired to direct the technical activities of the Wohnbedarf department store, Zürich; while there, met Alvar Aalto, with whom he worked on Aalto's furniture prototypes until they were put into industrial production; in 1934, traveled through the Netherlands and Britain, looking for the appropriate hinge for Wohnbedarf's *incombi* model. Alvar and Aino Aalto invited him to work in their studio in Helsinki, where he worked on the competition design for the national post office building, Helsinki. Returning to Switzerland, he finished his studies at Eidgenössische Technische Hochschule; in 1935, worked in the office of German architect Werner M. Moser (later named Haefeli, Steiger und Moser); 1940–48, worked at the Central Studienbüro der Arbeitsgemeinschaft für Landesplanung and at the Büro für Regionalplanung, Kantonalem Hochbauamt Zürich der Orts-, Regional- und Landesplanung; 1948–51, traveled in Ceylon (now Sri Lanka), Nepal, and India, working on Swiss government development projects; in 1951, worked in Calcutta with Moser; from 1958, taught in the architecture department, Eidgenössische Technische Hochschule, Zürich.
▶ Huber et al. (eds.), *Urbanisationsprobleme in der Ersten und in der Dritten Welt: Festschrift für Walter Custer*, Zürich, 1979. Friederike Mehlau-Wiebking et al., *Schweizer Typenmöbel 1925–35, Sigfried Giedion und die Wohnbedarf AG*, Zürich: gta, 1989.

Cuttoli, Marie
▶ Entrepreneur; active Paris and North Africa.
▶ Cuttoli established the Myrbor shop and gallery, Paris, in the 1920s, where she produced and sold the rugs of Jean Lurçat, Le Corbusier, Fernand Léger, and others, some of which were made in Marrakesh; in 1929, commissioned architect Ernö Goldfinger to design the Paris shopfront and furniture, and the Marrakesh factory; neither was realized. André Lurçat subsequently designed the shop. She later occupied the 1929 apartment that Goldfinger had designed for interior-decorator De Verac. Le Corbusier's first tapestries of *c*1936 were produced by Cuttoli's workshop in Aubusson.

► Work shown on Myrbor stand, 1925 Paris 'Exposition Internationale des Arts Décoratifs et Industriels Modernes.'
► *Les Tapisseries de Le Corbusier*, Geneva and Paris, 1975. Cat., James Dunnett and Gavin Stamp, *Ernö Goldfinger*, London: Architectural Association, 1983:18.

Cuzner, Bernard (1877–1956)
► British silversmith and jeweler; born Warwickshire; active Birmingham.
► Studied Redditch School of Art and Birmingham Central School of Art, under Robert Catterson-Smith and Arthur Gaskin.
► He was apprentice to his watchmaker father in Warwickshire; worked for a Birmingham silver firm while taking night-classes at Redditch School of Art; 1896–1910, was apprentice to Catterson-Smith and Gaskin; working as an independent silversmith, began designing for Liberty around 1900 and subsequently for the Goldsmiths' and Silversmiths' Companies, London, and Elkington, Birmingham; may have worked for Birmingham Guild of Handicrafts; produced fine one-off pieces for private customers, churches, and government organizations, and simple designs for silver firms, establishing high standards for decoration and craftsmanship; 1910–42, was head of the metalwork department, Birmingham Central School of Art, where one of his pupils was Cyril James Shiner. Though his objects for Liberty were unattributed, they were identified as his when published in the art review *The Studio* and at exhibitions. He published *A Silversmith's Manual* (1935). One of his major commissions was the 1948 Olympic Torch for the Goldsmiths' Company.
► A reconstruction of Cuzner's workshop and a collection of his drawings for silverwork and jewelry are housed in Birmingham Museum of Science and Industry.
► Charlotte Gere, *American and European Jewelry 1830–1914*, New York: Crown, 1975:170–71. Cat., *Thirties: British art and design before the war*, London: Arts Council of Great Britain, Hayward Gallery, 1979:138,288,300. Annelies Krekel-Aalberse, *Art Nouveau and Art Déco Silver*, New York: Abrams, 1989:28,35,253.

Cyrén, Gunnar (1931–)
► Swedish glassware designer and metalworker.
► Studied gold- and silversmithing, Konstfackskolan and Tekniska Skolan, Stockholm, 1951–56 , and 1954, Kölner Werkschule, Cologne.
► In 1951, he received a goldsmith apprentice's diploma; 1959–70, he was a glassware designer at Orrefors Glasbruk; broke with the Orrefors house style of pure undecorated table and decorative wares, using the *graal* technique to produce 'anti-design' forms of which his 1967 *Pop* range of glasswares was an example; from 1970, was a freelance designer at Dansk Design; in 1975, worked independently as a silversmith and for Gävie; from 1976, concentrated on cutting, engraving, and acid-etched ornamentations. Work included cut-glass lighting, tableware, and one-off art glass.
► Received 1956 Medal for Proficiency and Industry, Society for Industrial Design, and 1966 Lunning Prize.
► 'Thirty-four Lunning Prize-Winners', *Mobilia*, No. 146, Sept. 1967. Eileene Harrison Beer, *Scandinavian Design: Objects of a Life Style*, New York, 1975:98–99. Cat., David Revere McFadden, *Scandinavian Modern Design: 1880–1980*, New York: Cooper-Hewitt Museum, 1982:263. Cat., *Aktuel Svensk Form*, Skien: Ibsenhuset, 1982:24–27. Cat., Kathryn B. Hiesinger and George

H. Marcus III (eds.), *Design Since 1945*, Philadelphia: Philadelphia Museum of Art, 1983. Frederick Cooke, *Glass: Twentieth-Century Design*, New York: Dutton, 1986:84–85–86. Cat., *The Lunning Prize*, Stockholm: Nationalmuseum, 1986: 166–69. Jennifer Hawkins Opie, *Scandinavia: Ceramics and Glass in the Twentieth Century*, New York: Rizzoli, 1989.

Czech Cubism
► Czech architectural movement.
► The influential architect and teacher Jan Kotěra's first generation of pupils (including Josef Chochol, Pavel Janák, and Josef Gočár) established the 1911 program of Czech Cubism, which encouraged the manipulation of plastic masses. They sought a new aesthetic language, expressing the spiritual and psychological through a rhythmic integration of triangles, crystals, and other 'privileged forms,' extending the aesthetic and philosophical intentions of Cubist painting and sculpture into architecture and utilitarian objects. The apartment houses and villas, tables and chairs, ceramics and metalwork these artists designed are startling even today. They applied three-dimensional surfaces to façades and included elements from disparate sources, including local architectural features (such as late-Gothic diamond vaults), the early 18th-century baroque (or pseudo-Gothic) forms of Giovanni Santini-Aichel, French Cubist art, and the aesthetics of the *Theorie der Einfühlung* of Munich scientists Theodor Lipps and Wilhelm Worringer. Czech Cubism culminated in 1914, when architects and artists in Prague collaborated with the journal *Der Sturm* in Germany (of which Herwarth Walden was chief editor), and with the building of the Czech Pavilion by Otakar Novotný at the 1914 Cologne 'Werkbund Ausstellung.'
► Subject of 'Czech Cubism: Architecture and Design, 1910–1925' traveling exhibition, organized by National Technical Museum and Uměleckoprůmyslové Muzeum, both Prague, and with the cooperation of Vitra Museum, Weil am Rhein.
► Vladimir Slapeta essay, *Czech Functionalism*, London: Architectural Association, 1987:8. Cat., Alexander von Vegesack et al., *Czech Cubism: Architecture, Furniture, and Decorative Arts, 1910–1925*, New York: Princeton Architectural Press/Vitra Design Museum, 1992.

Czeschka, Carl Otto (1878–1960)
► Austrian architect, painter, graphic designer, and designer of jewelry, embroidery, and stained glass; born Vienna; active Vienna and Hamburg.
► Studied Akademie der bildenden Künste and Kunstgewerbeschule, both Vienna.
► He joined Josef Hoffmann at the Wiener Werkstätte in 1905. Czechka and fellow Kunstgewerbeschule graduate Eduard Josef Wimmer-Wisgrill, who joined the Wiener Werkstätte in 1907, were effective in the introduction of ornamentation, Czeschka being the first to do so in silverware. Czeschka was a member of the Vienna Secession movement, formed in 1897–98; 1902–07, taught at Kunstgewerbeschule, Vienna; in 1907, left the Werkstätte and became professor, Kunstgewerbeschule, Hamburg, and continued to produce many designs for the Werkstätte.
► Charlotte Gere, *American and European Jewelry 1830–1914*, New York: Crown, 1975:172. Werner J. Schweiger, *Wiener Werkstätte*, Vienna: Brandstaetter, 1982:259–60. Annelies Krekel-Aalberse, *Art Nouveau and Art Déco Silver*, New York: Abrams, 1989:98,200,253.

D

Da Silva-Bruhns, Ivan (1881–1980)
▶ Brazilian painter, rug designer, and weaver; active Aisne (France) and Paris.
▶ Studied biology and medicine.
▶ Until 1918, he was active as a painter and sometime interior designer; began producing rugs in Paris in 1919, when he received a commission from Louis Majorelle; in 1922, set up a small weaving workshop and furnished small-scale watercolors to weavers; used the *point noué* technique in his geometrical interpretations of Near and Far Eastern rug and textile motifs, especially those of the Berbers and North Africans; commercially successful, had a small workshop in Aisne, where he wove rugs in Cubist, geometric, and African-inspired styles and in somber color, including brown, indigo, and black with white highlights; was an active member of Société des Artistes Décorateurs; opened a gallery, rue de l'Odéon, Paris, in 1925, moving to 79 rue du Faubourg Saint-Honoré in 1930; produced rugs for leading contemporary decorators and furnished the 1935 oceanliner *Normandie*; received rug commissions from Mobilier National; French embassies in Washington, Berlin, Warsaw, and League of Nations, Geneva. His work was much imitated. His rug production was disrupted by the outbreak of World War II, after which he returned to painting.
▶ In 1911, rugs first shown at event of Salon des Indépendants; subsequently, at Salons of Société Nationale des Beaux-Arts and sessions of Salons d'Automne, 1925 Paris 'Exposition Internationale des Arts Décoratifs et Industriels Modernes' (grand prize), 1931 'Exposition Coloniale,' and 1931 exhibition, Curtis Moffat Gallery, London, organized by *Vogue* editor Mage Garland.
▶ Peter Adam, *Eileen Gray, Architect/Designer*, New York: Abrams, 1987:182. Pierre Cabanne, *Encyclopédie Art Déco*, Paris: Somogy, 1986:183. Maurice Dufrêne, *Ensembles Mobiliers, Exposition Internationale* 1925, Paris: Charles Moreau, 1925, Antique Collectors' Club edition 1989:72.

Dahl, Birger (1916–)
▶ Norwegian interior architect and lighting designer.
▶ Studied Statens Håndverks -og Kunstindustriskole, Oslo.
▶ 1944–59, Dahl designed lighting fixtures for Sønnico Fabrikker, Oslo; was known for his aluminum lighting; was a consultant designer to Vallø wallpaper firm; from 1947, taught at Statens Håndverks -og Kunstindustriskole.
▶ Cat., David Revere McFadden (ed.), *Scandinavian Modern Design 1880–1980*, New York: Abrams, 1982:263. Fredrik Wildhagen, *Norge i Form*, Oslo: Stenersen, 1988:146.

Dahlerup, Jørgen (1930–)
▶ Danish metalworker.
▶ Studied sculpture and industrial design, Det Kongelige Danske Kunstakademi, Copenhagen; trained as a silversmith.
▶ His work included hollow-ware and religious objects.
▶ Work shown at 1980 'Georg Jensen Silversmithy: 77 Artists, 75 Years' exhibition, Smithsonian Institution, Washington.
▶ Cat., *Georg Jensen Silversmithy: 77 Artists, 75 Years*, Washington: Smithsonian Institution Press, 1980.

Dahlquist, Ibe (1924–)
▶ Swedish jewelry designer; active Stockholm.
▶ Studied Swedish School of Arts, Crafts, and Design, Stockholm.
▶ From 1965, she designed jewelry for the Georg Jensen Sølvsmedie.
▶ Cat., *Georg Jensen Silversmithy: 77 Artists, 75 Years*, Washington: Smithsonian Institution Press, 1980.

Dair, Thomas (1954–)
▶ American industrial designer; born Rome, New York.
▶ Studied industrial design, Syracuse University, Syracuse, New York, to 1977.
▶ He designed computer and medical products and, for Richmond Engineering Company, pressure vessels, mechanical equipment and systems for various industries; in 1979, was founding partner of Smart Design (formerly Davin Stowell Association), where he became executive vice-president. The firm's clients include Corning Glass, 3M, Knoll, Copco, Singer, Sanyei, Pottery Barn, and Kohler. Products included electrical appliances, sewing machines, and sunglasses. Dair taught product design, Parsons School of Design, New York; was a member of Industrial Designers Society of America.
▶ Received Annual *ID* Design Review Award.

Dal Lago, Adalberto (1937–)
▶ Italian architect and designer; born and active Milan.
▶ He was an assistant, Facoltà di Architettura, Politecnico di Milano from 1964–70 and subsequently chair of interior design and then of the elements of composition; published books on design and Modern architecture; (with architect Marco Zanuso) was commissioned by the European Council to publish a book on postwar European design; from 1968–75, was director of bimonthly architecture-design journal *Rassegnamodi*; became a member of ADI (Associazione per il Disegno Industriale). Designing a range of products from plastic furniture and electronics to lighting and laminate prints, clients included Rossiflor, IVM, Fantoni, Louis de Poortere, Pirelli, Piriv, Abet Laminati, Salvarani, Nonwoven, Anic, La Rinascente department store, Kartell, Reguitti, Misura Emme, Franceschini, Fanini Fain, Linoleum, SIR, and Lanerossi.
▶ Won the Nazionale SIR/In Arch competition (with others) for a proposal for an industrial-building enterprise.
▶ *ADI Annual 1976*, Milan: Associazione per il Disegno Industriale, 1976. *Modo*, No. 148, March–April 1993:118.

Dalí, Salvador (b. Salvador Felipe Jacinto Dalí y Domenech 1904–88)
▶ Spanish painter, sculptor, engraver, designer, book illustrator, and writer; born Figueras, Gerona.
▶ 1921–25, studied San Fernando Academy, Madrid; suspended for unorthodox behavior and, in 1926, dismissed for refusing to take the final examination.
▶ 1919–21, he worked as a book and magazine illustrator in Figueras; was an independent artist in Sitges 1925–30, in Paris 1930–40, in Pebble Beach, California 1940–48, and in Port-Lligat (Spain) from 1948; in Paris, he met fellow Spaniards Pablo Picasso,

Luis Buñuel, the Surrealists, and his future lifelong companion Gala, then wife of poet Paul Éluard; in 1929, became an official member of the Surrealist movement following his 1928 film with Buñuel, *Un Chien andalou*. His work was publicly acclaimed in his 1929 one-person exhibition, Galerie Goemans. In 1930, he married Gala Éluard. When his article on Surrealist objects was published in the third issue of *Le Surréalisme au Service de la Révolution*, object-making became integral to the Surrealists' activities. He returned with Gala to Port Lligat, Cadaqués (Spain), where he lived for the remainder of his life. His relations with other Surrealists grew distant during the 1930s. Dalí was the most successful of all propagandists for Surrealism, not merely as a style of painting or writing but as a way of life. Dalí's best-known decorative design was 1934 sofa for Edward James in the shape of Mae West's lips, realized in several copies by Green and Abbott, London, and by Jean-Michael Frank, Paris; it was reissued in a loose 1980 interpretation by Stendig and subsequently by others. It was derived from Dalí's idea that the mouth was an aesthetic form; he used it in his 1934 painting *Mae West* and 1934–35 drawing *The Birth of the Paranoiac Furniture*. Other works included 1936 lobster telephone and 1936 chair with hands for its back, both also for Edward James's residence, West Dean (England); Steuben glass (1938 and 1940); scarves for Simpsons of New York; and surrealist jewelry. Dalí was inspired by the writings of Sigmund Freud, including his theories of the unconscious. His 'Dream of Venus' exhibition was mounted at 1939 'New York World's Fair.' He thought he could conjure a fantasy of the unconscious through a series of controlled associations; while living in the USA, designed the dream sequence in the 1945 Alfred Hitchcock film *Spellbound*. From 1968, his glassware for Daum began with sculpture *Fleur du Mal* in *pâte-de-verre*. Later glass work included *Anti-fleur, Pégase, Poisson Malbranche*, and *Désir hyperrationnel*. In 1988, under different management, Daum revived production of Dalí's work, including *Venus aux trois tiroirs, Montre Molle* (the widely published melting clock on a clothes hanger), and *Débris d'une automobile donnant naissance à un cheval aveugle mordant un téléphone*.

▶ Work subject of 1929 exhibition, Galerie Goemans, Paris, where his work was first shown in 1925. Jewelry pieces subject of traveling exhibition organized in the late 1950s. 1936 *Hands Chair* shown at 1970 'Modern Chairs 1918–1970' exhibition, Whitechapel Gallery, London. Work subject of 1980 'Salvador Dalí rétrospective 1920–1980,' Centre Georges Pompidou, Musée National d'Art Moderne, Paris, and 1980 exhibition, Tate Gallery, London.

▶ Salvador Dalí, *The Secret Life of Salvador Dalí*, New York, 1942. Salvador Dalí, *Diary of a Genius*, London, 1966. Cat., *Modern Chairs 1918–1970*, London: Lund Humphries, 1971. Philip Purser, *The Extraordinary World of Edward James*, London, 1978. Léopold Diego Sanchez, *Jean-Michel Frank, Adolphe Chanaux*, Paris: Regard, 1980. *Salvador Dalí rétrospective 1920–1980*, Paris: Centre Georges Pompidou, Musée National d'Art Moderne, Paris, 1980. Simon Wilson, *Salvador Dalí*, London: Tate Gallery, 1980. Muriel Emanuel et al. (eds.), *Contemporary Artists*, New York: St Martin's, 1983:219–220. Jessica Rutherford, *Art Nouveau, Art Deco and the Thirties: The Furniture Collections at Brighton Museum*, Brighton: The Royal Pavilion, Art Gallery and Museums, 1983:59–60. Auction cat., Christie's New York, 9 December 1989. Auction cat., *Applied Arts of Twentieth Century Artists*, Christie's Geneva, 13 May 1991.

Dalisi, Riccardo (1931–)

▶ Italian architect and designer; born Potenza; active Naples.
▶ Studied architecture, Università di Napoli, to 1957.
▶ He was professor of architecture, university of Naples; in the 1970s, was identified with the ad-hoc Radical Architecture and Radical Group movements in Naples; organized working groups to participate in the poorer districts of Naples, who formed the nucleus of the debate on Anti-Design; in 1973, was a participant in the formation of Global Tools; subsequently, (with Filippo

Alison) organized Minimal Arts; published books including *Unforeseeable Architecture* (1970) which documents his university courses and *Gaudí, Furniture and Objects*, 1979; designed 1989 group of metal wire furniture produced by Zanotta and 1987–88 *Caffettiera Napoletana* coffee pot by Alessi; was credited with the revitalization of design research in southern Italy; had clients including Vanini, Zanotta, Zabro, Quartet, Baleri.

▶ Participated in three Triennali di Milano and two Biennali di Venezia. Received 1959 Arflex Domus-Premio and 1981 Premio Compasso d'Oro (design research on the Neopolitan coffee pot by Alessi).

▶ Andrea Branzi, *La Casa Calda: Experienze del Nuovo Disegno Italiano*, Milan: Idea Books, 1982. *Descendants of Leonardo da Vinci: The Italian Design*, Tokyo, 1987:336. Kazuko Sato, *Alchimia*, Berlin: Taco, 1988. Albrecht Bangert and Karl Michael Armer, *80s Style: Designs of the Decade*, New York: Abbeville, 1990:130–31,229. *Modo*, No. 148, March–April 1993:118.

Dallasta, Maurizio (1944–)

▶ Italian architect and designer; born Cotignola; active Milan.
▶ Studied architecture, Politecnico di Torino, to 1970.
▶ 1968–69, he worked in the studio of architect G. Silvestrini and, 1969–70, in studio Urbanistica Tordolo-Orsello, Turin; 1970–71, taught a course on research techniques, Technische Fachschule, Zürich and Lausanne; in 1973, contributed to the journal *Etas-Kompass*; in 1975, (with architect Davide Mercatali) worked on the 'Sistema Nomade' project; became a member of ADI (Associazione per il Disegno Industriale).
▶ Participated in 1971 (II) national convention on the development of the Po region.
▶ ADI *Annual 1976*, Milan: Associazione per il Disegno Industriale, 1976.

Dalmon, Gérard (1945–)

▶ French furniture designer and entrepreneur; active Paris and New York.
▶ Initially involved in the fields of chemical engineering and data processing in France, Dalmon began designing furniture in the early 1980s; (with Pierre Staudenmeyer) established Galerie Néotù, Paris, in 1984, and New York, in 1990. Incorporating inexpensive and unusual materials, his applied art included 1985 *Chaise YM*, 1986 lacquered pressed-board chair with animal hair, and 1989 *Bouton de porte* and *Poignée de porte* door handles, all produced by Néotù.
▶ Work shown at 1985 'Onze Lampes,' Galerie Néotù, Paris; 1985 Salon of Société des Artistes Décorateurs; 1985 'Un tapis n'est pas un tableau' exhibition, Galerie Néotù; 1986 exhibition, Galerie Théorème, Brussels; Galerie Lechanjour, Nice; Galerie Silicone, Nice; Shiseido department store, Tokyo; 1987 in Desco at Zeus, Milan; 1987 'Cent chaises,' Boulogne Billancourt (France); 1988 Paris and Cologne Furniture Fairs; 1988 'Design français,' Berlin decorative arts museum; 'Médium,' Fondation Cartier, Jouy-en-Josas (France); VIA exhibition, Netherlands; 1988 Salone del Mobile Italiano; 'Just Your Image' with Allessandro Mendini, Guerriero, and Dalisi, Milan.
▶ Sophie Anargyros, *Les années 80*, Paris: Rivages, 1986. *Design: actualités fin de siècle*, Cahiers du CCI, Paris: Centre Georges Pompidou. Cat., *Primitive Chairs*, Tokyo: Shiseido, 1986. Cat., *Médium*, Jouy-en-Josas: Fondation Cartier, 1988. Christine Colin, *Design d'Aujourd'hui*, Paris: Flammarion, 1988.

Dalpayrat, Pierre-Adrien (1844–1910)

▶ French porcelain painter and ceramicist; born Limoges.
▶ In 1867, Dalpayrat lived in Bordeaux and 1867–88, in Toulouse and Monte Carlo; after a short time in Limoges, in 1889, settled in Bourg-la-Reine, near Paris, where he specialized in stoneware, developing the color known as 'Dalpayrat rouge,' a copper-red glaze; by combining this color with others, made a marbleized effect, which he applied to Japanese-inspired forms in the shape of gourds and fruits and to figures and animals in high relief or sculpted forms; collaborated with Adèle Lesbros and Voisin to

produce reasonably priced stoneware; produced forms designed by Maurice Dufrêne for La Maison Moderne and by sculptors, including Constantin Meunier. Cardeilhac and others mounted several of his pieces in silver.

▶ 'Dalpayrat rouge' glaze shown at 1892 Paris Salon.

▶ Yvonne Brunhammer et al., *Art Nouveau Belgium, France*, Houston: Rice University, 1976.

Dalton, William Bower (1868–1965)

▶ British watercolorist and potter; active Kent and USA.

▶ Studied Manchester School of Art and Royal College of Art, London.

▶ 1899–1919, he was principal of Camberwell School of Arts and Crafts; during and after this time, was curator of South London Art Gallery; was a potter as well as a watercolorist and published three books on ceramic art; in 1909, designed and built his own residence in Kent; residing there until his workshop was burned during World War II; settled in the USA, where he continued to pot and paint; returned to England in 1965.

▶ Work shown with Red Rose Guild and at Colnaghi's, London; 1935 'English Pottery Old and New' exhibition, Victoria and Albert Museum, London; 1937 Paris 'Exposition Internationale des Arts et Techniques dans la Vie Moderne'; 1979–80 'Thirties' exhibition at the Hayward Gallery, London.

▶ Cat., *Thirties: British art and design before the war*, London: Arts Council of Great Britain, Hayward Gallery, 1979:98, 130,288.

Dammouse, Albert-Louis (1848–1926)

▶ French ceramicist; born Sèvres; son of sculptor and porcelain decorator Pierre-Adolphe Dammouse of the Sèvres factory.

▶ Studied École Nationale des Arts Décoratifs, Paris, and École des Beaux-Arts, Paris, under François Jouffroy.

▶ He was interested in technical problems and became apprentice of Marc-Louis Solon and then became Solon's collaborator. Solon introduced Dammouse to *pâtes d'application*, an under-glaze slip decoration. Working in Charles Haviland's workshop in Auteuil, Dammouse designed the form for the famous *Service aux Oiseaux* decorated with designs after Félix-Henri Bracquemond and made in a soft-paste porcelain; in 1892, (with brother Édouard-Alexandre Dammouse) set up a studio at Sèvres where they produced porcelain, earthenware, and stoneware in Japanese and Chinese inspired forms, at first monochromatic, then with painted foliage, algae, and flowers; was a master of the material by 1904; in 1897, encouraged by Ringel d'Illzach, turned to working in glass; probably influenced by Thesmar's enameled bowls, went on the develop *pâte d'émail*, a kind of cloisonné *pâte-de-verre*. Little is know about his technique. The number of colors may have determined the number of firings.

▶ Work shown at 1869, 1874, 1878, 1889, and 1900 (*pâte-de-verre* cups, bowls, and goblets) Paris 'Expositions Universelles.' On his death, retrospective mounted at Musée Galliéra, Paris.

▶ Yvonne Brunhammer et al., *Art Nouveau Belgium, France*, Houston: Rice University, 1976 Cat., *Verriers français contemporains: Art et industrie*, Paris: Musée des Arts Décoratifs, 1982.

Dammouse, Édouard-Alexandre (1850–1903)

▶ French ceramicist; born Paris; brother of Albert-Louis Dammouse; son of sculptor-decorator Pierre-Adolphe Dammouse of the Sèvres factory.

▶ Studied painting under Félix-Henri Bracquemond.

▶ At the Lurin factory, makers of ordinary domestic ceramics, he worked with Ernest Chaplet; when Chaplet and Dammouse's brother Albert-Louis went to Haviland's Auteuil workshop, he followed to become a member of the group of painters there, Les Cinq (Alexandre Charpentier, Jean-Auguste Dampt, Étienne Moreau-Nélaton, Charles Plumet, Henri Sauvage), not to be confused with Le Cinq (Le Groupe des Cinq) in Paris in the 1920s; worked in the Auteuil studio until it closed in 1881; with Chaplet, moved to the Haviland workshop, rue Blomet, in 1882, where he decorated stoneware in naturalistic and Japanese-derived styles;

when the rue Blomet studio closed in 1886, (with brother Albert-Louis) set up a workshop at Sèvres, where they produced objects in *pâte-de-verre* and later *pâte d'émail*.

▶ 1878–1900, work shown at Salons of Société des Artistes français.

▶ Yvonne Brunhammer et al., *Art Nouveau Belgium, France*, Houston: Rice University, 1976.

Damon

▶ French lighting designer and firm; located Paris.

▶ Active during the 1920s and 1930s, Damon was established at 4 avenue Pierre-Ier-de-Serbie, Paris; known for its particular use of glass in lighting fixtures, executed designs in white glass which created a dazzle effect without glare. Boris Lacroix designed for the firm, creating many lamps incorporating engraved mirror and frosted glass tubes. Pressed glass was dismissed as being appropriate only for architectural lighting fixtures. Damon manufactured glass enameled on the inside and frosted on the outside, creating a diffused light suitable for reading. The *verre émaillé difussants* were held by metal mountings that were often gilded or silvered bronze, chrome, or nickeled copper, and placed on black marbrite bases. Damon hired other designers, including Gorinthe, André Roy, André Basompierre, Jean Baignères, Georges Martin, and Daniel Stéphan (also a designer for DIM). Damon also sold standard lighting fixtures, such as illuminated vases, *bouts de table*, and *antéchambre lanternes*.

▶ Janneau, *Le Luminaire et les Moyens d'éclairage Nouveaux*, second series, plate 5. Alastair Duncan, *Art Nouveau and Art Déco Lighting*, New York: Simon and Schuster, 1978:164–65. Cat., Aaron Lederfajn and Xavier Lenormand, *Le Louvre des Antiquaires présente: 1930 quand le meuble devient sculpture*, Paris, 1986.

Dampt, Jean-Auguste (1854–1946)

▶ French sculptor and designer.

▶ Dampt executed Art Nouveau designs for furniture, interiors, goldsmiths' works, clock cases, electric lights, and jewelry; was a founder of Les Cinq, a group of designers and craftsmen, not to be confused with Le Cinq (Le Groupe des Cinq); was a member of artists' group L'Art dans Tout.

Danese

▶ Italian domestic goods manufacturer; located Milan.

▶ Produzioni Danese was founded in 1957 by Bruno Danese; began with the production of plastic tabletop items. Its freelance designers were Bruno Munari and Enzo Mari. In 1959, Edizioni Danese published the results of research in the 'phenomena of visual perception.' Munari's work for Danese included 1957 *Cubic Ashtray 2000B* in melamine and anodized aluminum, 1958 *Desk Set 2002* in melamine and aluminum, and 1961 *Triangular Lamp 2006* in blue opalescent fiberglass and anodized aluminum. Mari's work for Danese included 1967 *Everlasting Table Calendar 3079* (in French, English, German, and Italian versions), 1967 *Pencil Stand*, 1967 *Ashtray 3076*, 1969 *Set of Hemispherical Bowls 3089A–D*, and 1970 *Container 3008B*. Danese produces items in ceramics, woods, glass, plastics, and children's games and toys.

▶ Cat., Milena Lamarová, *Design a Plastické Hmoty*, Prague: Uměleckoprůmyslové Muzeum, 1972:178.

D'Aniello, Pierangela (1939–)

▶ Italian architect and industrial designer.

▶ Studied Politecnico di Milano.

▶ In 1966, she opened her own office in Milan; (with Aldo Jacober) designed 1966 *Trieste* folding chair, made by Alberto Bazzani. Work includes designs for furniture, tablewares, and power tools.

▶ Received first prize (*Trieste* chair) at 1969 Fiera di Trieste in Trieste and Premio Selettiva di Cantù at 1967 (XVIII) International Furniture Exhibition, Cantù.

▶ Cat., *Modern Chairs 1918–1970*, London: Lund Humphries, 1971. Hans Wichmann, *Italien Design 1945 bis heute*, Munich: Die Neue Sammlung, 1988.

Dansk International Designs
▶ See Quistgaard, Jens

Darmstadt Advisory Board for Design
▶ German promotional organization.
▶ In 1951, the Advisory Board for Design was established in Darmstadt to encourage good design in industry and thereby foster the local economy.

Darmstadt artists' colony
▶ Artists' activity at Hesse-Darmstadt seat of the Grand Duke.
▶ Ernst Ludwig was Grand Duke Louis IV of Hesse-Darmstadt 1892–1918, the last ruler of a formerly independent state that became part of the new German Empire in 1871. He learned about the English Arts and Crafts movement from M.H. Baillie Scott, who furnished two rooms in the palace at Darmstadt; C.R. Ashbee's Guild of Handicraft, London, made the furniture. The Grand Duke saw in the movement a practical way to foster the cultural and economic well-being of the duchy, and signed three-year contracts with numerous young artists, including Peter Behrens, Rudolf Bosselt, Paul Bürck, Hans Christiansen, Ludwig Habich, Patriz Huber, and Josef Maria Olbrich, to design, and direct the production of, goods by these craftspeople and workshops. The results were published and promoted by Alexander Koch through his journals *Innen-Dekoration* and *Deutsche Kunst und Dekoration*. 23 artists worked there at various times form 1899 to the end of the venture in 1914. There were two silversmiths, Ernst Riegel and Theodor Wende, although others designed for silver. Huber, Olbrich and Christiansen arrived in Darmstadt in 1899; Haustein in 1903; Müller in 1906; and Riegel in 1907. Margold and Wende were the last to arrive. Behrens had an opportunity to show his multiple talents in architecture and the design of furniture, silver, jewelry, glass, and porcelain. He taught the four-week 'Applied Art Master Course' in Nuremberg in 1901 and 1902 and left the colony in 1903. Courses were subsequently taught by Richard Riemerschmid, Paul Haustein, and Friederich Adler. Many of the artists who began their careers at Darmstadt went on to national and international renown.
▶ Participated in 1900 Paris 'Exposition Universelle.' Organized 1901 'A Document of German Art' (room settings in specially built houses by Olbrich and Behrens), Darmstadt. Subject of 1976–77 'Ein Dokument deutscher Kunst: Darmstadt 1901–1976,' Hessischen Landesmuseum, 1977.
▶ Cat., Gerhard Bott, *Kunsthandwerk um 1900: Jugendstil, art nouveau, modern style, nieuwe Kunst*, Darmstadt: Hessisches Landesmuseum, 1965. Cat., *Ein Dokument deutscher Kunst: Darmstadt 1901–1976*, Darmstadt: Hessisches Landesmuseum, 1976. Annelies Krekel-Aalberse, *Art Nouveau and Art Déco Silver*, New York: Abrams, 1989:131–35.

Darwin, Robin (1910–74)
▶ British educator; great-grandson of Charles Darwin; great-great-grandson of Josiah Wedgwood.
▶ Studied Cambridge University and Slade School of Art, London.
▶ During World War II, he served in the British camouflage directorate, where he met several of the artists and designers who were later to teach at Royal College of Art, London; 1945–46, was training officer of the newly formed Council of Industrial Design; in 1948, became rector of Royal College of Art, radically reorganizing the school in order to bring it up to date with contemporary industrial and technological methods; 1946–48, was professor of fine art, Durham University.
▶ Penny Sparke, *Introduction to Design and Culture in the Twentieth Century*, Allen and Unwin, 1986. Christopher Frayling, *The Royal College of Art: One Hundred and Fifty Years of Art and Design*, London: Barrie and Jenkins, 1987.

Dassi, Franco
▶ Italian industrial designer; active Parabiago.
▶ In 1955, Dassi began his professional career; is best known for his designs for small domestic electrical appliances; (with engineer Plinio Lojacono) collaborated on architecture and nautical inte-

riors; (with architect Giovanni Travasa) on interiors, kitchenware, and domestic electrical appliances; (with Giuseppe De Götzen) on domestic electrical appliances; with Vittorio Varo; and (with Centro Studi La Termozeta) on industrial electrical appliances; became a member of ADI (Associazione per il Disegno Industriale).
▶ *ADI Annual 1976*, Milan: Associazione per il Disegno Industriale, 1976.

Daum, Auguste (1853–1909),   Antonin Daum (1864–1930), and Paul Daum   (?–1943)
▶ French glassware designers and manufacturers; located Nancy.
▶ Jean Daum (1825–85) settled in Nancy 1875 after a series of unsuccessful business ventures and became the head of bottle factory Verrerie de Nancy in 1878; was joined there by his son Auguste in 1879 and Antonin in 1887. At first the Daums produced rather dull table and domestic glassware. Auguste was in charge of the firm's administrative and financial activities and Antonin, trained as an engineer, the production activities. They assembled a stable of designers, artists, and artisans. The factory gradually became known for its fine glassware with cut, etched, and gilt decorations in traditional styles. Beginning in 1890 and greatly influenced by Émile Gallé, with whom the brothers were on good terms, their objects were executed in the Art Nouveau style. In 1891, they opened a decoration studio directed by Eugène Damman, employing artists Émile Wirtz, Amalric Walter from 1906, Jacques Gruber 1894–1897, and Henri Bergé from 1900. Two specialities emerged: *berluzes* (vases with long necks) and lamps, produced mainly from 1893 in acid-etched cameo, often finished on an engraver's wheel, with decoration inspired by nature. Daum furnished the glass for Louis Majorelle's lamps and the metalwork for their own; the same arrangement was made with Edgar Brandt from 1905 and less frequently with André Groult. In 1906, Almaric Walter worked at Daum with *pâte-de-verre*. The firm closed during World War I; reopened in 1918, Daum's style changed radically. Under the direction of Paul Daum, the glasshouse attempted to satisfy the public demand for simpler designs, producing acid-etched, thick, colored glass vessels with geometric or stylized motifs. The technique required up to four acid baths for very deep etching. In 1925, Daum formed a partnership with nephews Paul and Henri Daum and son-in-law Pierre Froissart as fellow directors. The great depression of 1929 threatened the existence of the firm; the glass industry in France suffered particularly hard. Its art glass production dropped, replaced by its glass tableware. The Générale Transatlantique Compagnie commissioned 70,000 sets of crystal tableware for its 1935 oceanliner *Normandie*, prompting research into new techniques and designs. Paul Daum, arrested when the Germans occupied France during World War II, escaped, fought with the French Resistance, and was killed in 1943. In 1946, the firm reopened under Henri and Michel Daum. Various artists were commissioned to design models, including Salvador Dalí. The company, no longer in family hands, is still in operation, producing the work of designers such as Philippe Starck, Hilton McConnico, and Garouste and Bonnetti. In the 1980s, Daum produced McConnico's cactus *pâte-de-verre* and crystal wares and Starck's 1988 *Etrangetés Vase* series.
▶ Work shown at 1893 Chicago 'World's Columbian Exposition' and 1900 Paris 'Exposition Universelle.' Deeply etched glass first shown at 1925 Paris 'Exposition Internationale des Arts Décoratifs et Industriels Modernes.' Work shown regularly at Paris Salons including 1921, 1926, and 1932 sessions of Salon d'Automne.
▶ Yvonne Brunhammer et al., *Art Nouveau Belgium, France*, Houston: Rice University, 1967. R. & L. Grover, *Carved and Decorated European Art Glass*, Rutland, Vermont: Tuttle, 1970:70–71. *Le Modern Style*, Paris: Baschet, 1974:170–71,178,181. J. Bloch-Dermant, *L'Art du Verre en France: 1860–1914*, Paris, 1975:135–43. Alastair Duncan, *Art Nouveau and Art Déco Lighting*, New York: Simon and Schuster, 1978:73–74,165–66. *Éclairage de 1900 à nos jours*, Brussels: L'Écuyer, Nos. 38,72,75,87. Cat., *Verriers français contemporains: Art et industrie* Paris: Musée des Arts

Décoratifs, 1982. Clotilde Bacri: *Daum: Masters of French Decorative Glass*, New York: Rizzoli, 1993.

Davenport and Company, A.H.

▶ American furniture producers and interior decorators; located Boston and East Cambridge, Massachusetts.

▶ The firm began in 1842 as a 'furniture and feathers' business owned by Ezra H. Brabrook. Brabrook died in 1880, and the thriving firm was purchased by Albert H. Davenport (1845–1906), who had been bookkeeper since 1866. Davenport's cabinet shop, working department, and display of carpet, drapery, upholstery, wallpaper, and furniture were housed in a five-storey building, 96–98 Washington Street, Boston. Between 1875 and 1910, Davenport was one of the most important decorating firms in the USA; in 1883, expanded its quarters by acquiring 108 Cambridge Street, East Cambridge, and opening a New York office; was one of the few companies capable of supplying large amounts of deluxe furniture and interior-furnishing goods to the growing number of expensive public and private buildings of the day; it supplied 225 pieces of furniture and draperies for Hawaiian King Kalakaua's Iolani Palace in c1882, and furnished several rooms at the White House. Its wares were often specified by architects H.H. Richardson; Peabody and Stearns; McKim, Mead and White; and Shepley, Rutan and Coolidge. Davenport produced the dining furniture and chairs for 1886 John Jacob Glessner House, Chicago, designed by Charles Allerton Coolidge for architect H.H. Richardson. Francis H. Bacon was Davenport's principal designer, and vice-president 1885–1908, when the firm was sold. Irving and Casson took over the firm in 1914 and closed in 1973, its most productive period ending in the 1930s.

▶ The name 'davenport' came to be used generically for a large upholstered sofa convertible to a bed, from a product originally made by A.H. Davenport at the end of the 19th century.

▶ Anne Farnam, 'A.H. Davenport and Company, Boston Furniture Makers,' *Antiques*, No. 109, May 1976:1048–55. Anne Farnam, 'H.H. Richardson and A.H. Davenport: Architecture and Furniture as Big Business in America's Gilded Age,' in Paul B. Kebabian and William C. Lipke (ed.), *Tools and Technologies: America's Wooden Age*, Burlington, Vt., 1979:80–92. Doreen Bolger Burke et al., *In Pursuit of Beauty: Americans and the Aesthetic Movement*, New York: Metropolitan Museum of Art and Rizzoli, 1986:418.

Davey, Andy (1962–)

▶ British industrial designer.

▶ Studied Worthing College of Art and Royal College of Art, London, to 1987.

▶ In 1987, he began working for design consultancy Wharmby Associates, London, where he designed the 1988 *Taurus* telephone produced by Browns Holdings and made of black ABS plastic with a rubber cord; in 1990, Davey established own design studio TKO, Tokyo.

▶ Received 1989 Silver Award (*Taurus* telephone), Design and Art Directors Association.

▶ Jeremy Myerson and Sylvia Katz, *Conran Design Guides: Home Office*, London : Conran Octopus, 1990:33,73.

Davico, Aldo (1934–)

▶ Italian designer; born Cesana Torinese; active Torino.

▶ In 1965, he set up his own studio; 1961–65, was a consultant to Olivetti; became a member of ADI (Associazione per il Disegno Industriale); designed furniture; had clients including Art & Form and IMB industrial furniture.

▶ *ADI Annual 1976*, Milan: Associazione per il Disegno Industriale, 1976.

David, Salvadore (1859–1929)

▶ French bookbinder and gilder.

▶ David worked in the bindery of Léon Gruel; in 1855, set up his own workshop; in 1890 when his father died, took over management of the business at 12 rue Guénégaud, Paris, where he produced classically oriented covers; unsuccessful with commercial and library bindings; by 1900, became involved with *éditions de luxe*. Collectors of his work included Freund-Deschamps and René Descamps-Scrive. For the former, David produced bindings for *Mirages, La Mort du dauphin*, and *Les Liaisons dangereuses*; in 1907, moved shop to 49 rue le Peletier, Paris.

▶ Ernest de Crauzat, *La Reliure française de 1900 à 1925*, Vol. 2, Paris, 1932:55–56. Alastair Duncan and Georges de Bartha, *Art Nouveau and Art Deco Bookbinding*, New York: Abrams, 1989: 16,19,124,189–90.

David, Xavier (1940–)

▶ French designer; born Nevers, active Bologna and Paris.

▶ David began his professional career in 1965; in 1969 (with Gaetano Pesce and Beppe Vida) designed accessories, lighting, and inflatable seating; became a member of ADI (Associazione per il Disegno Industriale); designed *David* range of glass furniture produced by Glass Design Collection, Macherio (Italy); had clients in Italy including Gavina, Ny Form, Mari Arreda, Expansion Design, and Malferrari, and, in France, Souplina.

▶ *ADI Annual 1976*, Milan: Associazione per il Disegno Industriale, 1976.

David-Andersen, Arthur (1875–1970)

▶ Norwegian metalworker; active Oslo.

▶ The David-Andersen goldsmith workshop was founded in Oslo in 1876 by David Andersen; became famous for its high-quality enamel work. Arthur David-Andersen worked for the family firm. Its other designers included Harry Sørby, Johan Lund, Thorolf Holmboe, Ludvig Wittmann, and Johan Sirnes. Gustav Gaudernack worked for the firm 1891–1910.

▶ Annelies Krekel-Aalberse, *Art Nouveau and Art Déco Silver*, New York: Abrams, 1989:253. Fredrik Wildhagen, *Norge i Form*, Oslo: Stenersen, 1988:88. Cat., David Revere McFadden (ed.), *Scandinavian Modern Design 1880–1980*, New York: Abrams, 1982:263.

David-Andersen, Ivar (1903–)

▶ Norwegian metalworker; active Paris and Oslo.

▶ Apprenticed in family goldsmith workshop; studied Statens Håndverks -og Kunstindustriskole, Oslo, and sculpture in Paris under Ossip Zadkine.

▶ In the late 1920s, David-Andersen began as a designer; from the late 1930s, worked mainly as a manager in the family goldsmith workshop David-Andersen, Oslo, of which he became director in 1952.

▶ Cat., David Revere McFadden (ed.), *Scandinavian Modern Design 1880–1980*, New York: Abrams, 1982:263.

Davis, Owen William (1838–1913)

▶ British architect and designer.

▶ Studied architecture under James Kellaway Colling.

▶ He was an assistant to architect Matthew Digby Wyatt; was known for his ability to produce designs in fabrics and wallpaper in which the repeats were successfully camouflaged; designed wallpaper produced by Woollams; was a member of the school of designers who rejected medievalism. Work included furniture, carpets, and metalwork produced by major manufacturers.

▶ Stuart Durant, *Ornament from the Industrial Revolution to Today*, Woodstock, NY: Overlook, 1896:43,322.

Dawson, Nelson Ethelred (1859–1942) and Edith Dawson (b. Edith Robinson 1862–1928)

▶ Nelson Dawson: British architect, painter, and metalworker; Edith Dawson: artist and enamelist; both active London.

▶ Nelson Dawson trained as an architect in the office of his uncle; studied painting, South Kensington Schools; in 1891, attended lessons in enameling under Alexander Fisher.

▶ Dawson was more interested in painting and silversmithing than in architecture; met future wife Edith Robinson while working in an art shop, Scarborough, where her watercolors were for sale; in 1891, moved to London, where he began metalworking and attended Alexander Fisher enameling lectures; set up his own

workshop, where his wife executed most of the enameling and, after 1897, probably all of it; designed the metalwork crafted by apprentices in his studio; in 1901, founded the Artificers' Guild and was artistic director 1901–03; left when it was taken over by Montague Fordham, a prosperous businessman who had previously directed Birmingham Guild of Handicraft. The Dawsons' work was frequently published in *The Studio* and *Art Journal*. They developed a kind of architectonic style for silverwork that incorporated delicate enamels (often of flowers and birds); employed upwards of 20 craftspeople at one time, who executed commissions and prepared for exhibitions. Nelson Dawson abandoned metalworking altogether after 1914 and turned to painting.
▶ Work shown at 1893 Arts and Crafts Exhibition and subject of 1900 exhibition (125 pieces), Fine Art Society, London.
▶ Charlotte Gere, *American and European Jewelry 1830–1914*, New York: Crown, 1975:172. Toni Lesser Wolf, 'Women Jewelers of the British Arts and Crafts Movement,' *The Journal of Decorative and Propaganda Arts*, No. 14, Fall 1989:32–33. Annelies Krekel-Aalberse, *Art Nouveau and Art Déco Silver*, New York: Abrams, 1989:22,24,253.

Day, Lewis Foreman (1845–1910)
▶ British designer, writer, and teacher.
▶ In 1870, Day, an Arts and Crafts proponent, opened his own studio; in 1884, became a founding member of the Art-Workers' Guild and, in 1888, the Arts and Crafts Exhibition Society; produced designs for fabrics and wallpaper; published his first pattern book *Instances of Accessory Art* (1880) with a Japanese bent, and inexpensive books on ornamentation including *Ornamental Design* (4th ed., 1897), *Pattern Design* (3rd ed., 1923), and *The Planning of Ornament* (1887).
▶ Stuart Durant, *Ornament from the Industrial Revolution to Today*, Woodstock, NY: Overlook, 1986:322.

Day, Lucienne (1917–)
▶ British textile designer; born Surrey; wife of Robin Day.
▶ 1934–37, studied Croydon School of Art; 1937–40, Royal College of Art, London.
▶ 1942–47, she taught at Beckenham; in 1948, (with Robin Day) opened a design studio, when she began designing dress and furnishing fabrics, carpets, wallpapers, and table linens; designed for Alastair Morton's Edinburgh Weavers, Cavendish, Wilton Royal Carpets, John Lewis, Heal Fabrics (for 25 years); designed the wiry-lined *Calyx* pattern for 1951 London 'Festival of Britain' that was widely published and became an archetypal image of the 1950s; 1957–59, designed porcelain decorations for Rosenthal; moving towards a craft approach, from 1978, began to produce one-off mosaic tapestries while respecting both crafts methods and mass production; during the 1970s, produced unique abstract wall hangings that she named 'silk mosaics'; often collaborated with her husband producing stained glass (mainly for domestic use) and textiles and wallpapers for a number of companies; wrote design textbooks.
▶ Received first award of American Institute of Decorators for *Calyx* pattern, gold medal at 1951 (IX) and grand prize at 1954 (X) Triennali di Milano, and, in 1950s and 1960s, three awards from Council of Industrial Design.
▶ '8 British Designers,' *Design Quarterly*, No. 36, 1956:9–10. 'Furnishing Fabrics: Heal's Chevron, Complex and Extension,' *Design*, No. 233, May 1968:42–43. Fiona MacCarthy, *British Design since 1880*, London, 1982: figs.17,165. Cat., Kathryn B. Hiesinger and George H. Marcus III (eds.), *Design Since 1945*, Philadelphia: Philadelphia Museum of Art, 1983. Stuart Durant, *Ornament from the Industrial Revolution to Today*, Woodstock, NY: Overlook, 1986:288,291,294–95.

Day, Robin (1915–)
▶ British furniture designer; born High Wycombe; husband of Lucienne Day.
▶ 1930–33, studied local art school; 1934–38, Royal College of Art, London.

▶ In 1945, he became a freelance designer; in 1948, (with Lucienne Day) opened a design studio, often collaborating subsequently. His work was noticed by Hille at the 1948 international furniture design competition, New York Museum of Modern Art; the plywood cabinet at the exhibition (with Clive Latimer) was produced using a special technique which enabled it to be made with only two joints. The American firm Johnson-Carper Furniture, in reproducing the design, abandoned the original concept; the laminated wood became solid wood-and-joint construction, the tubular steel legs became separate legs, the sliding doors were hinged, and standardization and flexible interiors were eliminated. From 1949, Day was design consultant to Hille, designing contract furniture. His polypropylene 1963 *Mark II* or *Polyprop* chair produced by Hille and others sold more than 12 million copies. In 1962, Day became a consultant to the John Lewis department store chain. Work included pieces in the design section of 1951 'Festival of Britain', 1951 seating for Royal Festival Hall, London, interiors for the *Super VC10* and other aircraft, appliances for Pye, cutlery, carpets, and seating for many auditoria, including the Barbican Arts Centre, London, from 1968.
▶ Received gold metal at 1951 (IX) and silver medal at 1954 (IX) Triennali di Milano; first prize (with Clive Latimer; storage furniture) at 1948 'International Competition for Low Cost Furniture Design,' New York Museum of Modern Art; six Design Council awards. In 1959, elected Royal Designer for Industry.
▶ Edgar Kaufmann, Jr., *Prize Designs for Modern Furniture*, New York, 1950:34–41. Michael Farr, *Design in British Industry: A Mid-Century Survey*, London: Cambridge, 1955. Richard Carr, 'Design Analysis: Polypropylene Chair,' *Design*, No. 194, Feb. 1965:33–39. Sutherland Lyall, *Hille: 75 Years of British Furniture*, London, 1981. Fiona MacCarthy, *British Design since 1880*, London, 1982:figs. 146–47,169,178,183.

De Angelis, Almerico (1942–)
▶ Italian designer; born Naples.
▶ Studied architecture to 1969.
▶ He organized 1972 exhibition 'Naples and Its Region,' City Hall, Boston; in 1973, began the movement 'For eventual architecture' and, in 1974, the architectural journal *Che*; lectured in interior design and scenography at Facoltà di Architettura, Naples.
▶ Andrea Branzi, *La Casa Calda: Esperienze del Nuovo Disegno Italiano*, Milan: Idea Books, 1982.

de Bardyère, Georges (–1942)
▶ French decorator and furniture designer; born Wassy, Haute-Marne; active Paris.
▶ Bardyère was a decorator and furniture designer in Paris by 1912; designed classical furniture in a style similar to Léon Jallot's, and in the early Art Déco style; was fond of vegetal forms and the use of ivory.
▶ From 1919, work shown at Salons of the Société des Artistes Décorateurs and, from 1921, at Salon d'Automne.
▶ Pierre Kjellberg, *Art Déco: les maîtres du Mobilier, le décor des Paquebots*, Paris: Amateur, 1986:35.

De Barros Morais Caldas, Joaquim Manuel (1948–)
▶ Portugese designer; born Montalegre; active S. Stefano Roero (Italy).
▶ De Barros began his professional career in 1969; became a member of ADI (Associazione per il Disegno Industriale). His clients in Italy included Selenova (*Spot 2001* lighting system), Gufram (*Dog Wood* table and chairs), Ultravox (television sets), Seimart, and Coemi and, in Portugal, Plastidom, A. Campos, and EMHA.
▶ *ADI Annual 1976*, Milan: Associazione per il Disegno Industriale, 1976.

de Boer, Antoinette (1939–)
▶ German textile designer.
▶ 1957–61, studied Hochschule für Bildenden Künste, Hamburg, under Margret Hildebrand.

▶ In 1963, she became a textile designer for Stuttgarter Gardinenfabrik, where Margret Hildebrand was artistic director; from 1975, was artistic director of the firm; specializing in printed fabrics, attempted to relate fabric design to architecture; designed 1969 *Zazi* range, influenced by the shapes and colors of Italian design; in 1973, set up her design studio.

▶ 'Antoinette de Boer et ses dessins de tentures aux tendances nouvelles,' *Meubles et Décors*, Nov. 1969. 'Textil-Design ist keine Kunst,' *Meubles et Décors*, April 1976. Cat., Kathryn B. Hiesinger and George H. Marcus III (eds.), *Design Since 1945*, Philadelphia: Philadelphia Museum of Art, 1983. Hans Wichmann, *Von Morris bis Memphis, Textilien der Neuen Sammlung, Ende 19. bis Ende 20. Jahrhundert*, Basel: Birkhäuser, 1990:225,439.

de Carli, Carlo (1910–71

▶ Italian architect.

▶ De Carli's expressive furniture incorporated bent plywood, foam rubber, and steel rods; in the 1950s, along with Gianfranco Frattini and Ico Parisi, created ranges of furniture for Cassina.

▶ Penny Sparke, *Introduction to Design and Culture in the Twentieth Century*, Allen and Unwin, 1986. Cat., Leslie Jackson, *The New Look: Design in the Fifties*, New York: Thames and Hudson, 1991:126.

De Carlo, Giancarlo (1919–)

▶ Italian architect-designer; born Genoa; active Urbino.

▶ Studied engineering, Politecnico di Milano, and Instituto Universitario di Architettura, Venice.

▶ From 1955, he was professor of town planning, Instituto Universitario di Architettura, Venice; during the 1950s, became a member of Team X. His first major work was 1962–66 Students' Residence, Urbino. He designed 1970–74 first-phase Matteotti workers' housing (with Fausto Colombo and Valeria Fossati), Terni, a three-storey complex of varying floor-plans where each house had its own garden or terrace.

▶ Giancarlo De Carlo, *Questioni di architettura e urbanistica*, Urbino, 1965. 'G. De Carlo: La réconciliation de l'architecture et de la politique,' *L'Architecture d'aujourd'hui*, No. 177, Jan.–Feb. 1975:32–43. Axel Menges in Vittorio Magnago Lampugnani, *Encyclopedia of 20th-Century Architecture*, New York: Abrams, 1986:77.

de Castelbajac, Jean-Charles (1949–)

▶ French fashion designer; born Casablanca; active Paris.

▶ 1966–67, studied law, Faculté de Droit, Limoges.

▶ In 1968, (with mother Jeanne-Blanche de Castelbajac) founded Ko ready-to-wear fashion firm, Limoges; from 1968, worked as a freelance fashion designer for firms including Reynaud, Pierre d'Alby, Max Mara, Levi-Strauss, Jesus Jeans, Hilton, Ellesse, Carel shoes, Etam, Gadging, Julie Latour, Fusano, and Amaraggi; in 1973 in Paris, had his first fashion show; was primarily known for his women's clothing designs that incorporated canvas, blankets, plastic, automobile upholstery, parachute cloth, cheesecloth, and leather; in 1970 in Paris, established a line of women's clothing under his own name; 1975–76, set up boutiques in Paris, New York, and Tokyo; in 1978, became director of Société Jean-Charles de Castelbajac, Paris; designed costumes for films including *Violette et François* (1976), *Annie Hall* (1977), *Who Killed My Husband?* (1979), and TV series *Charlie's Angels* (1978–80); in 1976, designed stage costumes for musicians Rod Stewart, Elton John, and Talking Heads; from 1979, was active in interiors and furniture, designing the 1989 *Castelbajac* furniture range produced by Ligne Roset, which provided 14 mix-and-match polychrome cushions on sofas, all reversing to black leather on a black-leather frame, multi-colored seating including 1991 *My Funny Valentine* dining chairs in an array of bright-color combinations, and rugs for Ligne Roset.

▶ *My Funny Valentine* chairs shown at 1991 Salon du Meuble, Paris.

▶ 'Hot Properties,' *House and Garden*, May 1991:30. Anne Lee Morgan (ed.), *Contemporary Designers*, London: Macmillan, 1984:144.

de Coster, Germain (1895–)

▶ French designer and bookbinder; born Paris.

▶ Studied École Nationale Supérieure des Arts Décoratifs, Paris, under Jules Chadel, and Japanese wood-engraving under Yoshigiro Urishibora.

▶ From *c*1920, she was Chadel's assistant, designing book plates, bookbindings, and jewelry; from the early 1920s to 1961, was professor of decoration and gravure, Technical College of Applied Arts, Paris; from 1934, (with Hélène Dumas) collaborated on bookbindings for volumes, in some of which de Coster's illustrations appeared. Highly decorative in exotic skins and stones, the designs were executed by de Coster and produced by Dumas assisted by gilders Raymond Mondage and André Jeanne. De Coster's work included interior design, theater costumes, textiles, and posters.

▶ Work shown at Salons of Société des Artistes Décorateurs.

▶ Alastair Duncan and Georges de Bartha, *Art Nouveau and Art Déco Bookbinding*, New York: Abrams, 1989:24,190. Roger Devauchelle, *La Reliure en France de ses origines à nos jours*, Vol. 3, Paris, 1961:202,207,210,212,249–50. Henri Nicolle, 'La Reliure moderne,' *Les Arts français: la reliure d'art*, No. 36, 1919:11–12. Cat., *Reliure française contemporaine*, New York: The Grolier Club, 1987–88:34–39.

De Distel

▶ Dutch ceramics firm; located Amsterdam.

▶ In 1895, De Distel (The Thistle) was founded as a small ceramics firm by Jacobus Lob (1872–1942); employed artists as both designers and painters. In 1897, Plateelbakkerij De Distel was established to manufacture and sell art pottery, utility ware, tiles, ceramics for special occasions, and small sculpture. At De Distel from 1895 as a painter, Cornelis de Bruin became artistic director; designed décors on dark backgrounds in a Rosenburg style, tableaux with naturalistic pictures, tiles with Jugendstil motifs, and directed artists who both painted and designed ceramics in similar styles. J. Eisenloeffel was a designer 1900–08; Bert Nienhuis, a designer 1900–11, became head of the decoration department. At De Distel 1898–1923, Willem van Norden was head of the decoration department. The firm was sold to A. Goedewaagen II in 1924.

▶ Wares shown widely before World War I, including 1904 'Louisiana Purchase Exposition,' St. Louis.

▶ *Industry and Design in the Netherlands 1850–1950*, Amsterdam: Stedelijk Museum, 1985.

De Driehoek, Potterie
See **ESKAF**

de Felice, Marguerite

▶ French bookbinder, gilder, and leatherworker; active Neuilly, near Paris.

▶ Studied École Nationale Supérieure des Arts Décoratifs, Paris.

▶ She produced leather products in an Art Nouveau mode, including blotter ends, cushions, bags, menu holders, and decorated upholstery. Commissions declined during World War I, and at René Kieffer's suggestion she produced fantasy wrapping papers and book covers for *cartonnage*. In the 1920s, de Felice began to design bookbindings using the overlapping letters of the titles for decoration; from 1927, taught at École des Arts Décoratifs, Paris.

▶ Work shown regularly at Salons of Société des Artistes Décorateurs. Received gold medal (bindings) at 1925 Paris 'Exposition Internationale des Arts Décoratifs et Industriels Modernes.'

▶ Ernest de Crauzat, *La Reliure française de 1900 à 1925*, Vol. 2, Paris, 1932:145–47. Alastair Duncan and Georges de Bartha, *Art Nouveau and Art Déco Bookbinding*, New York: Abrams, 1989:190.

De Ferrari, Giorgio

▶ Italian designer; born Genoa; active Turin.

▶ Designing furniture, furnishings, and lighting, his clients in Italy included Elco, Gufram, Kartell, Lema, Stildomus, Veart, Colli, and Eroways. He was a member of ADI (Associazione per il Disegno Industriale).

▶ *ADI Annual 1976*, Milan: Associazione per il Disegno Industriale, 1976.

de Feure, Georges　(b. Georges Joseph van Sluijters 1868–1928)

▶ Dutch decorative artist, designer, painter, lithographer, and engraver; active Paris.

▶ De Feure was a Symbolist painter, watercolorist, illustrator, poster artist, and designer of Art Nouveau furniture, fabrics, stained glass, wallpaper, glassware, and ceramics; in 1890, moved to Paris, where he studied under Jules; came to public attention for the first time at his 1894 one-person exhibition in Paris; in 1894, designed furniture for Maison Fleury; in 1900, joined Siegfried Bing's shop L'Art Nouveau, Paris, and became head of the design department, designing with others the pavilion and the furnishings for the shop at the Paris Exposition Universelle; after World War I, became professor of decorative arts, École Nationale des Beaux-Arts, Paris; when public interest in the Art Nouveau style faded, moved to England, where he became a stage designer; returning to Paris, designed carpets, stained glass, decorative frescoes, lighting, mirrors, fabrics, with tapestries produced by Manufacture française de Tapis et Couverture, and, in 1924, all the furniture for Madeleine Vionnet's sumptuous fashion house, Paris, with 18 changing rooms, all differently arranged.

▶ Work shown at 1894 one-person exhibition, Paris, and at Salons of Société Nationale des Beaux-Arts from 1894, 1893 and 1894 salons of Rose et Croix and 1896 Munich Secession exposition. Designed and decorated pavilion of Roubaix et Tourcoing at 1925 Paris 'Exposition Internationale des Arts Décoratifs et Industriels Modernes.'

▶ Salon catalog, Société des Beaux-Arts, 1902. E. Mannoni, *Meubles et Ensembles: Style 1900*, Paris: C. Massin, 1968:5. Yvonne Brunhammer et al., *Art Nouveau Belgium, France*, Houston: Rice University, 1976. Alastair Duncan, *Art Nouveau and Art Déco Lighting*, New York: Simon and Schuster, 1978:74–75. *Éclairage de 1900 à nos Jours*, Brussels: L'Écuyer: Nos. 44,45,47. Cat., *Europa 1900*, Paris: Musée des Beaux-Arts, 1967: No. 342. Victor Arwas, *Art Déco*, Abrams, 1980.

De Genneper Molen

▶ Dutch furniture cooperative; located Gennep.

▶ In 1899, C.W. Steinmann founded De Genneper Molen as a sawmill and turnery on the river Niers to produce small items including curtain fittings; in c1917, began making furniture, which by 1924, formed the bulk of the firm's business. By 1927, its production included small tea tables, work tables, smoking tables, small wall cabinets, coat racks, lamps, umbrella stand, and curtain fittings. Factory manager and director C.R. Steinmann was also its furniture designer; in 1929, contracted P.E.L. Izeren, an author and teacher in Arnhem, who was a designer until at least 1938. At first symmetrical, Izeren's taut Cubist designs used woods and aluminum plymax. 1934–37, architect A.F. Schutte, as company manager, designed furniture and other items. After World War II, the firm shifted its production to wood boarding and paneling, with some piano benches. It went out of business in 1982.

▶ *Industry and Design in the Netherlands 1850/1950*, Amsterdam: Stedelijk Museum, 1985.

de Gramont, Arnaud　(1960–)

▶ French designer.

▶ Studied Camondo School, Paris.

▶ He worked with architect Ronald-Cecil Sportes on the interior of the Bastille Opera, Paris; in 1986, received a prize in Avis de Recherche competition sponsored by Paris Musée des Arts Décoratifs and Moving-Paris; also in 1986, designed starkly simple din-

nerware (segmented, with a section for sauces) made by Les Faïenceries de Mollins for Lauren G.

▶ *Les Carnets du Design*, Paris: Mad-Cap Productions et APCI, 1986:34.

de Gueltzl, Marco　(1962–1991)

▶ French sculptor and furniture and glass designer.

▶ Studied Otis Pearson School of Design, Los Angeles.

▶ He designed chandeliers, lamps, and furniture made in glass produced by Avant Scene. One of his last designs was 1989 large bureau and chair in sanded glass and *fer à béton*.

de Jarny, Paul Brindeau

▶ French designer; active Paris; brother of painter Edward de Jarny.

▶ He produced a wide range of domestic metalwork, including keys and key escutcheons, door handles, *portemanteaux*, and numerous lighting fixtures; an associate of Brandt and Schenck, showed brass, cast-iron, and wrought-iron lighting at Paris Salons over 30 years; none of his unsigned or crudely signed output has been identified. His Art Nouveau designs included themes from nature. Chandeliers and table lamps incorporated images of ivy, camellias, dandelions, mimosa, vines, and trees. He patented a twisted metal chain that supported his chandeliers.

▶ Metalware shown first at 1901 Salon of Société Nationale des Beaux-Arts. Participated almost annually in Salons into the 1930s, including Salon d'Automne from 1903 and Société des Artistes Décorateurs from 1904.

▶ Alastair Duncan, *Art Nouveau and Art Déco Lighting*, New York: Simon and Schuster, 1978:75. Salon catalogs, Salon d'Automne, 1903, 1905–09, 1922–23. Salon catalogs, Salon des Beaux-Arts, 1908–10, 1921. Salon catalogs, Société des Artistes Décorateurs, 1904, 1914, 1924.

de Klerk, Michel　(1884–1923)

▶ Dutch architect and designer; born Amsterdam.

▶ His 1913–19 Spaarndammerbuurt housing, Amsterdam, illustrated his eccentricity and lack of concern for function and construction; his idiosyncratic Amsterdam Arts and Crafts Expressionistic work was exemplified by 1913–17 Shipping Offices. He joined the practice of Hendrik Berlage and created closed and flattened forms in 1920–22 Amstellaan housing, Amsterdam South; was one of the architects of the School of Amsterdam, known for expressing Modern architecture through the use of brick shells rather than stucco as found elsewhere in Europe, as in his Zaanstraat apartments, Amsterdam, of c1920. He designed furniture for 1913 Dr. J. Polenaar residence, Amsterdam; 1915 directors' offices (with lighting produced by H.J. Winkelman), the Scheepvaarthuis; 1915 Mr. and Mrs. Polak-Krop residence (furniture produced by H.P. Mutters, The Hague), Steenwijk; 1916 't Woonhuys residence (furniture produced by Randoe), Haarlem. He was also a graphic artist.

▶ Work (living room furniture for 't Woonhuys) shown at 1925 Paris 'Exposition Internationale des Arts Décoratifs et Industriels Modernes.'

▶ Pieter Kramer, 'De Bauwwerken van Michel de Klerk,' *Wendingen*, Nos. 9–10, 1924. Suzanne Frank, 'Michel de Klerk's Design for Amsterdam's Spaarndammerbuurt,' *Nederlands Kunsthistorik Jaarboek*, Vol. 22, 1971:175–213. Helen Searing, 'With Red Flags Flying: Politics and Architecture in Amsterdam' in H. Millon and L. Nochlin (eds.), *Art and Architecture in the Service of Politics*, Cambridge, Massachusetts, 1978. Jonathan Woodham, *Twentieth-Century Ornament*, New York: Rizzoli, 1990:126–27.

de la Godelinais, Renan

▶ French decorator.

▶ De la Godelinais was student and collaborator of Jacques-Émile Ruhlmann, after whose death he continued to work for Porteneuve; in 1942, became *chargé de mission* of Musée des Arts et Traditions Populaires; in 1949, became a member of UAM (Union des Artistes Modernes); in 1948, was responsible for Centre de Documentation de l'Habitation, Pavillon de Marsan, Paris.

▶ Arlette Barré-Despond, *UAM*, Paris: Regard, 1986:522.

de Lanux, Eyre 'Lise' (b. Elizabeth de Lanux 1894–)
▶ American designer; active Paris and New York.
▶ Studied Art Students' League, New York.
▶ She adopted the name of her grandfather William Eyre as her professional name and became Eyre de Lanux in the 1920s; became a painter and later designed a small amount of uncompromising furniture, some in a Cubist style, along with geometric-patterned rugs during 1927–35 with Evelyn Wyld, who worked with Eileen Gray. De Lanux's pieces were shown with the work of Eileen Gray and Jean-Michel Frank in Paris salon exhibitions; were considered among the most sophisticated of the period, often using industrial products innovatively. She associated with André Gide, Ernest Hemingway, Henri Matisse, Picasso, and Bernard Berenson; was photographed by Man Ray, Berenice Abbott, and Arnold Genthe; in 1924, left her husband, writer and diplomat Pierre de Lanux, to live with Evelyn Wyld, with whom she worked; in 1929, moved to La Bastide Blanche and soon after to La Bastide Caillenco and opened the short-lived shop Décor in Cannes; designed interiors and lacquered furniture, some with the assistance of Seizo Sugawara; moved to Rome. In 1927, De Lanux designed a rug for the vicomte and vicomtesse de Noailles's villa, Hyères, and a 1928 monumental table of sandblasted glass supported by two stacks of glass blocks; contributed 'Letters of Elizabeth' to *Town and Country* magazine in the 1920s, and, in the 1960s, short stories for *The New Yorker*.
▶ In 1932, De Lanux and Wyld showed work at Salons des Artistes Décorateurs; took part in 1930 (I) exhibition of UAM (Union des Artistes Modernes); in 1931, showed carpet designs, Curtis Moffat Gallery, London.
▶ Cat., *Thirties: British art and design before the war*, London: Arts Council of Great Britain, Hayward Gallery, 1979:296. Philippe Garner, 'Introduction,' *Important 20th Century Furniture in a Philip Johnson Townhouse*, Sotheby's auction catalog, 6 May 1989. Peter Adam, *Eileen Gray, Architect/Designer*, New York: Abrams, 1987:181–82. Rita Rief, 'A "Lost" Designer Is Rediscovered,' *The New York Times*, May 4, 1989. Philippe Garner, *Eileen Gray: Design and Architecture, 1878–1976*, Cologne: Taschon, 1993.

de Léotard, Geneviève (1899–)
▶ French bookbinder and gilder; active Paris.
▶ From 1912, studied book composition and gilding, École des Arts Décoratifs, Paris, under Andrée Langrand and Mme. René Sergent.
▶ She worked for a short time with Pierre Legrain; in 1925, set up her own workshop; from 1927, taught gilding, École des Arts Décoratifs.
▶ Book work shown at École des Arts Décoratifs stand, annual Paris Salons. Received 1927 Prix Blumenthal.
▶ Léon Deshairs, *Les Arts Décoratifs modernes 1918–1925*, Paris, 1925:186. Philippe Dally, 'Les Téchniques modernes de la reliure,' *Art et décoration*, Jan. 1927:19,22. Rose Adler, *Reliures, présenté Rose Adler*, Paris, 1929, plates 17,23,34,44,48. Ernest de Crauzat, *La Reliure française de 1900 à 1925*, Vol. 2, Paris, 1932:158–59. Louis Barthou, 'L'Evolution artistique de la reliure,' *L'Illustration*, Christmas 1930. '5 Reliures,' *Mobilier et décoration*, April 1935: 141. Roger Devauchelle, *La Reliure en France de ses origines à nos jours*, Vol. 3, Paris, 1961:168,268. Alastair Duncan and Georges de Bartha, *Art Nouveau and Art Déco Bookbinding*, New York: Abrams, 1989:19,20,23,84–87,190.

de Looze, Hervé (1921–86)
▶ Belgian architect and industrial designer; born Brussels; active Paris.
▶ Studied under Victor Servranckx and Le Corbusier.
▶ In 1946, he became a member of UAM (Union des Artistes Modernes), of which he was secretary 1949–55; member of the selection committee, 'Formes Utiles' exhibition, of which he was the architect from 1951, secretary general in 1954, and president from 1969; was responsible for the steel-and-iron section, 1949–

50 (I) 'Formes Utiles' exhibition, Pavillon de Marsan; designed exposition entry, 1954 'Exposition Formes Utiles' of the Salon des Arts Ménagers, Paris.
▶ Sanitary and heating fixtures shown at 1956–67 (I) 'Triennale d'Art français Contemporain,' Paris. Responsible for sanitary features in first all-plastic (1956) house (with René Coulon) for Ionel Schein at 1956 Salon des Arts Ménagers, Paris.
▶ Cat., *Les années UAM 1929–1958*, Paris: Musée des Arts Décoratifs, 1988:218–19.

De Lorenzo, Laura (1951–)
▶ Italian architect-designer; active Rome.
▶ Studied architecture to 1977.
▶ From 1978, she collaborated with architect Stefano Stefani; was active in industrial and interior design, architecture, visual communication, and artistic research; in 1985, formed group Grafite with architects L. Leonori, F. Piferi, and S. Stefani, specializing in industrial design.
▶ Fumio Shimizu and Matteo Thun (eds). *The Descendants of Leonardo: The Italian Design*, Tokyo, 1987:324.

De Lucchi, Michele (1951–)
▶ Italian architect and designer; born Ferrara; active Milan.
▶ Studied Padua, 1975, and architecture, Università di Firenze, under Adolfo Natalini.
▶ He dabbled in new forms of art and film at Università di Firenze; in 1973, (with Piero Brombin, Pier Paola Bortolami, Boris Pastrovicchio, and Valerio Tridenti) founded the group Cavart, which played a leading role in Architettura Radicale, film-making, written works, and happenings; during this time, held the seminar 'Culturally Impossible Architecture' in the Monselice marble quarry near Padua; 1975–77, taught architecture, Università di Firenze; settling in Milan in 1978, joined Centrokappa, befriended Ettore Sottsass, and worked for Studio Alchimia in 1979; from 1978, assisted Sottsass in creating the first Memphis exhibition of 1981, to which he contributed some pieces; in 1979 (with Sottsass) became a consultant designer to Olivetti on its 1979 *Synthesis* office-furniture line; (with Sottsass) designed Olivetti's 1982 *Icarus* office-furniture range and collaborated at Sottsass Associati on the interiors of over 50 Fiorucci shops throughout Europe. His focus on the use of color could be seen in 1979 prototype household appliances for Girmi, the hi-fi sketches of 1981, and the Pensione Adriatico. He described his *Peter Pan* armchair as a 'chromatic experiment.' For Memphis's initial 1981 collection, he designed the *Pacific* armoire, *Atlantic* cabinet, *Kristall* side table, and *Oceanic* floor lamp. His most widely published Memphis piece was 1983 *First* chair. Other work included 1984 *Cadetti* tables and 1985 *Mist* table by Acerbis, 1985 *Witness* armchair by Massoli, 1985 rings by Cleto Munari (with Giancarlo Fassina), 1986–87 *Tomomeo* desk lamp by Artemide; designed metal furniture for Bieffeplast and Elam and wood furniture for ADL and T70; pursued a design approach that attempted to make household objects look more like toys; in the late 1980s, designed plastic tableware for Bodum, Switzerland. Other clients included Vistosi, RB Rossana, Girmi, Matau, Kumewa, Up & Up, Baldini, and Fontana Arte. In 1984, he set up his own studio; in the early 1990s, he founded Solid, a group of young international designers; taught at Domus Academy, Milan; Facoltà di Architettura, Palermo; and Cranbrook Academy of Art, Bloomfield Hills, Michigan. From the early 1990s, he was active in his own De Lucchi Group, Milan, with staff including Angelo Micheli, Nicholas Bewick, James Irvine, Geert Koster, and Ferruccio Laviani.
▶ Organized (with Andrea Branzi) 1977 'Italian Design of the Fifties' exhibition, Milan, resulting in their book *Il design italiano degli anni 50* (1979). Participated in 1979 (XVI) (prototype household appliances) and 1983 (XVII) Triennale di Milano. *Lido* sofa included in Memphis's first exhibition at 1981 Salone Del Mobile, Milan, and 1983 *First* chair in 1991 'Mobili Italiani 1961–1991: Le Varie Età dei linguaggi' exhibition, Salone del Mobile, Milan. Work subject of 1985 'A Friendly Image for the Electronic Age' exhibition organized by Ja-Vormgeving, Tilburg (Netherlands).

▶ Michele De Lucchi, 'Camin Elletrico,' *Modo*, No. 10, 1978: 73. Allessandro Mendini, 'Dear Michele De Lucchi,' *Domus*, No. 617, 1981:1. R. Sias, 'The New International Style o l'Ogetto Banale,' *Ufficio Style*, No. 6, 1982. R. Sias, 'Ufficia Stile Intervista: Michele De Lucchi,' *Ufficio Style*, No. 3, 1983. Michele De Lucchi, 'La Rivoluzione degli Accostamenti Cromatici,' *Interni*, No. 330, 1983:16—18. Barbara Radice, *Memphis: Richerche, Esperienze, Risultati, Fallimenti e Successi del Nuovo Design*, Milan: 1984. Cat., *Michele De Lucchi, A Friendly Image for the Electronic Age: Designs for Memphis Alchimia Olivetti Girmi*, The Hague: Uitgeverij Komplement, 1985. Fumio Shimizu and Matteo Thun (eds.), *The Descendants of Leonardo: The Italian Design*, Tokyo, 1987:324. Albrecht Bangert and Karl Michael Armer, *80s Style: Designs of the Decade*, New York: Abbeville, 1990:229.

de Mandrot, Hélène (?–1948)
▶ Swiss designer and arts patron; active Paris and Switzerland.
▶ In 1922, de Mandrot established a 'maison des artistes'; in 1927, began inviting artists, scientists, writers, and others to her medieval château, La Sarraz, north of Lake Geneva (Switzerland). Her intention was to create a center for the decorative and fine arts, music, and literature. She also sponsored a conference for film-makers, one of which was attended by Sergei Eisenstein. She was in charge of the Swiss pavilion, which included furniture, furnishings, rugs, and paintings, at 'Esposizione Biennale delle Arti Decorative e Industriali Moderne'; in 1928, hosted and was a major participant in the initial planning of first CIAM (Congrès Internationaux d'Architecture Moderne) at La Sarraz; in the 1920s in Paris designed rugs and collapsible furniture (produced by Jean Bonino, Paris) shown at Paris Salon d'Automne; commissioned Le Corbusier to design 1930–31 villa Le Pradet near Toulon, in stone and concrete with sculptures by Jacques Lipschitz on the terrace and lawn.
▶ Sigfried Giedion, *Space, Time and Architecture*, Cambridge: Harvard, 1982:696. Jacques Gubler, *Nationalisme et Internationalisme dans l'Architecture Moderne de la Suisse*, Geneva: Archigraphic, 1988:145.

De Mestral, Georges
▶ Swiss inventor.
▶ De Mestral invented the tape fastener known as Velcro (*Klettverschluss*, or 'burr-fastener'), with its fastener component of tiny hooked nylon filaments clinging to a fuzzy counterpart. The design, inspired by plant burrs in 1948, was patented in 1953.
▶ Velcro shown at 1991 'Schweizer Erfindungen' exhibition at Globus department store, Basel, 1991.

de Montaut, Adrienne Gorska (1899–1969)
See Gorska de Montaut, Adrienne

de Montaut, Pierre (1892–1947)
See Gorska de Montaut, Adrienne

De Morgan, William Frend (1839–1917)
▶ British painter, ceramicist, and tilemaker; born and active London.
▶ Studied at night classes, Cary's Art School, Bloomsbury, and, 1859, Royal Academy Schools.
▶ He began working for William Morris in c1862. Though he painted tiles, his major contribution was stained glass; he also worked independently for Morris in his own studio. In the late 1860s, he became interested in pottery and decorative tiles; in 1872, began firing tiles at his house, 30 Cheyne Row, Chelsea. More than 300 tile designs have been documented from 1872–81; they were made on blanks from Holland, Wedgwood, and the Architectural Pottery Company, Poole. He produced designs for fabrics and wallpaper; working in Chelsea 1872–81, he moved to Morris's Merton Abbey works in 1882. His most prolific period was whilst living in Fulham, 1888–98. His Hispano-Moresque lusterware and *Isnik* colored pottery reflect the powerful influence of Middle Eastern art; in the mid-1870s, he and Morris studied Islamic fabrics and pottery at South Kensington Museum (today

Victoria and Albert Museum). He produced decorative schemes with Halsey Ricardo for 12 oceanliners of the P&O line; his firm and partnership with Ricardo were dissolved in 1898. 1898–1907, he was active in a partnership with Frank Iles and the Passenger brothers; published the novels *Joseph Vance* (1906) and *Alice for Short* (1907), which began his late career as author.
▶ Cat., Martin Greenwood, *The Designs of William De Morgan*, Shepton Beauchamp: Dennis and Wiltshire, 1989.

de Noailles, vicomte Charles (1891–1981) and vicomtesse Marie-Laure de Noailles (1900–1970)
▶ French socialites, taste-makers, and patrons of the arts.
▶ The vicomte's interests centered on architecture and the decorative arts and the vicomtesse's on fine art. Commissioned in 1924, finished in 1933, and at the time one of the most radical Modern buildings in France, their villa in Hyères was built to the designs of Robert Mallet-Stevens and included his furniture and furnishings along with those of others, including Édouard-Joseph Bourgeois (Djo-bourgeois) (several bedrooms and living rooms), Pierre Chareau (a suspended bed and American-style open-air room on the roof), Gabriel Guévrékian (triangular Cubist garden), Théo van Doesburg (color scheme for a 'little flower room'), Jean-Michel Frank, and Eyre de Lanux. At the end of Guévrékian's garden was Jacques Lipschitz's *Joie de vivre* sculpture, cast by Jean Prouvé. Mallet-Stevens received the Hyères commission on the strength of his design for an aeroclub pavilion (with architect Paul Ruault, glassmaker Louis Barillet, and sculptor Henri Laurens) at 1922 Salon d'Automne, Paris, though he had no realized buildings; the vicomte disliked Le Corbusier's rudeness, Mies van der Rohe was not free, and the director of the Musée des Arts Décoratifs in Paris recommended Mallet-Stevens. Composed of Cubistic volumes, the house was used as a setting for Man Ray's film *Les Mystères du Château du Dé* (1928), with the vicomte's guests as its actors. The de Noailles entertained the cultural and artistic élite at Hyères. Additions to the house included a covered pool, squash court, gymnasium, bedrooms, and a studio in an enclosed courtyard lit from above by a monochrome stained-glass skylight at different levels by Louis Barillet, all resulting in a 60-room complex with dramatic views of the Mediterranean. Eight of the 15 guest bedrooms had porches for outdoor sleeping. Charles de Noailles commissioned a documentary film on the villa, directed by Jacques Manuel. Housed in the villa were the works of young contemporary artists, including Pablo Picasso, Christian Bérard, and Salvador Dalí, all of whom painted portraits of Marie-Laure. Abandoned for many years, the restoration of the house was begun in the late 1980s. The de Noailles' 18th-century Paris townhouse—the Hôtel Bischoffsheim, place des États Unis—contained rooms with period furniture, furnishings, and *boiserie* as well as some in contemporary styles of the 1920s, including the study with vellum walls and furnishings by Jean-Michel Frank.
▶ 'Une des maison-clés pour l'historie du goût au XXᵉ siècle,' *Connaissance des Arts*, Oct. 1964:68—91. Cécile Briolle et al., *Rob Mallet-Stevens, La Villa Noailles*, Paris: Parenthésis, 1900. Arlette Barré-Despond, *UAM*, Paris: Regard, 1986.

De Pas, Gionatan (1932–)
▶ Italian architect and designer; born and active Milan.
▶ De Pas, Donato D'Urbino, and Paolo Lomazzi set up a design studio in Milan in 1966 working on architecture, design, exhibitions, interior decoration, and town-planning projects. Their innovative 1967 *Blow* chair in inflatable clear plastic film and 1970 *Joe* seat in the form of a baseball glove were widely published. From the 1970s, they designed interchangeable and flexible units for modular seating, storage systems, and plastic and plywood furniture for BBB Bonacina, Driade, and Palina. More mainstream furniture and furnishings designs were produced for Zanotta, Poltronova, Forges, Gabbianelli, Marcatré, Hamano, Ligne Roset, Stilnovo, and Sirrah. De Pas became a member of ADI (Associazione per il Disegno Industriale). The group made the TV program *Dal cucchiaio alla città; il design italiano dal 1950 al 1980*. The group's work included 1967 *Blow* chair, 1970 *Joe* seat, 1972

multi-position lamp by Stilnova, 1972 *Flap* range of modular seating by BBB, 1975 *Jointed* modular-pillow range of seating, *Dado & Vite (Cube & Screw)* knock-down furniture by BBB, 1980 *Grand'Italia* sofa by Zanotta, 1981 *Dinamo* sofa by Zanotta, 1982 *Cloche* lamp by Sirrah, 1982 *Milano* sofa by Zanotta, 1983 *Sidone* lamp by Artemide, 1983 *ET* table by Zanotta, 1983 *Zona* sofa by Zanotta, 1984 *Mollo* bed by Cast Design, 1984 *Campo* armchair by Zanotta, 1984 *Palmira* side chair by Zanotta, 1984 *Wave* sofa by Zanotta, 1985 *Valentina* lamp by Valenti, 1985 *Iago* chair by Ligne Roset, 1986 *Airone* armchair by Poltronova, 1986 *Verbamis* armchairs by Matteo Grassi, and 1991 *Octopus* folding coat rack by Zerodisegno.

▶ Received 1979 Compasso d'Oro prize and award at 1979 'BIO 7' Industrial Design Biennale, Ljubljana.

▶ Cat., J. De Pas, D. D'Urbino, and P. Lomazzi, 'I nuostri buoni propositi,' in *Milano 70/70: Un secolo d'arte, Dal 1946 al 1970*, Vol. 3, Milan: Museo Poldi Pezzoli, 1972. Cat., *Italy: The New Domestic Landscape*, New York: Museum of Modern Art, 1972:34,44,57,95,114. Gerd Hatje, *New Furniture 11*, New York: 1973: Nos. 103,168–69,354–55. *ADI Annual 1976*, Milan: Associazione per il Disegno Industriale, 1976. Alfonso Grassi and Anty Pansera, *Atlante del design italiano: 1940–1980*, Milan, 1980:299. Andrea Branzi, *La Casa Calda: Esperienze del Nuovo Disegno Italiano*, Milan: Idea Books, 1982. Cat., Kathryn B. Hiesinger and George H. Marcus III (eds.), *Design Since 1945*, Philadelphia: Philadelphia Museum of Art, 1983. Juli Capella and Quim Larrea, *Designed by Architects in the 1980s*, New York: Rizzoli, 1988.

de Patta, Margaret (1907–)
▶ American jewelry designer.
▶ Studied Institute of Design, Chicago.
▶ She designed jewelry that was based on the principles and forms of abstract Constructivist sculpture.
▶ Penny Sparke, *Introduction to Design and Culture in the Twentieth Century*, Allen and Unwin, 1986.

De Ploeg
▶ Dutch fabric group; located Bergeyk.
▶ De Ploeg was founded in 1923 as Coöperatieve Productie- en Verbruiksvereeniging (Cooperative Production Association). Originally a kind of utopian agrarian colony at Best (Netherlands) from 1919, the initiators were C. Hijner and W. van Malsen. De Ploeg was to include farming and other activities appropriate to cooperative production. Intending to set up a colony for the production of vegetables and household textiles, van Malsen left in 1921 for Bergeyk and, in 1923, established De Ploeg. Its weaving mill and health resort were not profitable and were closed in 1925 and 1928, respectively. De Ploeg became successful with domestic goods and inexpensive textiles. In *c*1926, when trade in household textiles declined, it began to sell upholstery fabrications, and checked patterns produced by various other manufacturers; from *c*1928, had goods woven to its own designs. Freelance designs by friends of De Ploeg's staff made possible an unusually wide product range. By 1930, De Ploeg sold its textiles to arts and crafts shops and drapery goods and fabric stores. It ceased to be a cooperative in 1937. Spectrum was set up during World War II to make and sell arts and crafts products and to prevent workers being taken to Germany. After the war Spectrum became independent, and De Ploeg set up its own weaving works, with power looms added in 1950. Frit Wichard became its exclusive designer. The firm is still active.
▶ *Industry and Design in the Netherlands 1850–1950*, Amsterdam: Stedelijk Museum, 1985.

de Poorter, Christian (1946–)
▶ French designer; active Milan.
▶ Studied mechanical construction.
▶ In 1970, he worked in France on industrial aeronautics; 1971–74, was active in the studio of Rodolfo Bonetto, Milan; in 1974, set up his own studio in Milan; in 1973, became a member of

ADI (Associazione per il Disegno Industriale) and CSEI (Consul Supérieur d'Esthétique Industrielle), Paris.
▶ Received an honorable mention in the 1970 Prix Jacques Viénot competition.
▶ *ADI Annual 1976*, Milan: Associazione per il Disegno Industriale, 1976.

de Ribaucourt, Georges (1881–1907)
▶ French designer; born Soisy-sous-Montmorency.
▶ Studied École Nationale Supérieure des Arts Décoratifs, Paris, under Hector Lemaire.
▶ He began his career as an industrial artist, turning to jewelry design in 1902, when he entered and won first prize in the annual contest sponsored by *Revue de la Bijouterie, Joaillerie, Orfevrerie*.
▶ His rings (lent by Sarah Bernhardt) and a collection of objects in precious materials shown at 1902 Salon of Société des Artistes français.
▶ Yvonne Brunhammer et al., *Art Nouveau Belgium, France*, Houston: Rice University, 1976. *Revue de la Bijouterie, Joaillerie, Orfèvrerie*, No. 26, June 1902, p. 57; No. 27, July 1902, p. 87.

De Rossi, Pucci
See Rossi, Pucci De

De Rudder, Hélène (1870–)
▶ Belgian textile designer; born Ypres.
▶ Her embroidered panels were shown at 1895 Cercle Artistique et Littéraire, Brussels, and large embroidered panels after designs, by her husband, sculptor Isidore De Rudder, at Tervueren 1897 colonial exhibition.
▶ Yvonne Brunhammer et al., *Art Nouveau Belgium, France*, Houston: Rice University, 1976.

de Ruijter, Linda (1953–)
▶ Belgian industrial designer; born Antwerp.
▶ 1972–77, studied industrial design, Nationaal Hoger Instituut Voor Bouwkunst en Stedebouw, Antwerp.
▶ From 1979, she worked with IDEA and was a designer for Laurent David leather goods; designed 1986 *Unibind* sealing/binding machine by Peleman Saerens, 1987–88 plastic kitchenware (with IDEA) by DBP, 1988 *Fluo–Ottago–1952* luggage by Laurent David.
▶ Work shown at 1981 Fashion and Design exhibition, Design Center, Brussels.
▶ Cat., Design Center Stuttgart, *Women in Design: Careers and Life Histories Since 1900*, Stuttgart: Haus der Wirtschaft, 1989:220–21.

de Santillana, Ludovico (1931–)
▶ Italian architect, designer, teacher, and administrator; active Venice; son-in-law of Paolo Venini.
▶ Studied Instituto Universitario di Architettura, Venice, to 1955.
▶ 1959–68, he taught architectural design, Instituto Universitario di Architettura, Venice; was director of Venini International before, in 1959, (with wife Ginette Venini) took over the firm's management, on Paolo Venini's death. 1960 *Battuto* range (with Tobia Scarpa) was among de Santillana's first designs for the new administration at Venini. He designed 1963 *Faraono* eggs and 1969 vases, bowls, and accessories designed for Pierre Cardin; continuing the Venini tradition of producing new techniques and forms from the 1960s, hired consultant designers Tobia Scarpa, Tapio Wirkkala, Toni Zuccheri, Dale Chihuly, and Richard Marquis; in 1965, founded glassware manufacturers V-Linea and Ve-art, which used semi-automatic production techniques and mouth-blowing. In the 1970s and 1980s, in addition to traditional objects, these firms were known for their architectural lighting.
▶ *Venini Glass*, Washington, DC: Smithsonian Institution, 1981. Cat., Kathryn B. Hiesinger and George H. Marcus III (eds.), *Design Since 1945*, Philadelphia: Philadelphia Museum of Art, 1983:229.

De Sphinx
▶ Dutch glass, crystal, and ceramics firm; located Maastricht.

▶ Petrus L. Regout set up a glass cutting works in Maastricht in 1827 where he was originally a dealer in glass, crystal, and ceramics. From 1836, he manufactured ceramics, at first mainly inexpensive red-bodied *fayence commune*. In the 1840, the firm hired skilled British potters and began producing hard, white-bodied ceramics, similar to 18th-century Wedgwood wares, that it began exporting worldwide. In the second half the 19th century, Regout became the largest utility-ware firm in the Netherlands. At the peak of its success in 1913, the firm's 3,750 workers operated 43 kilns around the clock. Its products ranged from the inexpensive to the highest quality, and it made every imaginable object in ceramics, including music organ knobs. In 1899, the factory became known as the Kristal-, Glas- en Aardewerkfabrieken De Sphinx. 1917–34, J.H. Lint was its first designer and chief modeler. When joined by pictorial artist W.J. Rozendaal, chief designer 1924–29, Lint devoted himself to modeling. Sculptor Ch. H.M. Vos worked for the firm in 1929; he designed the firm's sphinx figurine. Designer of models and decorations G.M.E. Bellefroid, who worked for De Sphinx 1929–41 and in 1946, designed more than 30 services in the 1920s. He was interested in solving the technical problems of mechanized ceramic production; without changing the body shape, he would introduce new designs by varying spouts, handles, and lids. His most successful design was the 1934 *Maas* service for De Bijenkorf, the wholesale ceramics dealer; the sugar bowl had no handles. He left in 1946. There was no designer at De Sphinx until 1950, when Pierre Daems was hired. In 1958, the firm merged with Société Céramique in Maastricht.
▶ *Industry and Design in the Netherlands, 1850/1950*, Amsterdam: Stedelijk Museum, 1985:166–69.

De Stijl
▶ Dutch architecture, art, and design group and journal.
▶ The artists' group and journal *De Stijl* was founded in Leiden by Theo van Doesburg in 1917. Many of the visual characteristics of the group's production were derived from the paintings of Pieter Cornelis Mondriaan (Piet Mondrian), whose work was flat and geometric, rendered in primary colors, and arranged within a matrix. This approach was applied to architecture, furniture, textiles, interior decoration, graphics, and other media. The group felt a need to express a new, universal aesthetic appropriate to Modern life and technology and became effective in spreading its ideas on the design of interiors, typography, textiles, and furniture. The ideas of architects H.P. Berlage and Frank Lloyd Wright were also influential on De Stijl. The group's approach to form and color in domestic interiors, tiled floors, store-front lettering, and stained-glass windows was somewhat static and limiting until van Doesburg's introduction of dynamic diagonal lines. Van Doesburg taught briefly at the Bauhaus, Weimar; developed contacts with Constructivist El Lissitzky and László Moholy-Nagy. The 1923 exhibition, Galerie l'Effort Moderne, Paris, was the beginning of the organization's 'international phase' and produced a pronounced change in its membership, resulting in Mondriaan's withdrawal in 1925. From 1919 until the late 1920s, De Stijl member Bart van der Leck experimented with printed textiles. *De Stijl* was published 1917–28. The designer of the first issue, Vilmos Huszár, applied the group's principles to interiors and textiles. One of its best-known members, Gerrit Rietveld, produced a wide range of structures and furniture including the famous 1917–18 *Red/Blue* chair and the entire scheme of the canonical 1924 Schröder House (with Truss Schröder-Schräder), Utrecht. One of van Doesburg's more interesting works was 1926–28 Café l'Aubette, Strasbourg.
▶ Group's 1922 (first) exhibition of architectural designs shown in the Netherlands. A landmark event for the group, Van Doesburg collaborated with Cornelis van Eesteren and Gerrit Rietveld on models and architectural drawings. 1923 De Stijl architecture exhibition, Léonce Rosenberg's Galerie l'Effort Moderne, Paris. Subject of 1982 exhibition, Walker Art Center, Minneapolis, Minnesota.

▶ Hans L.C. Jaffé et al., *De Stijl: 1917–31*, Visions of Utopia, Abbeville, 1982. Vittorio Magnago Lampugnani (ed.), *Encyclopedia of 20th-Century Architecture*, New York: Abrams, 1986:318–20 passim.

De Vries, Derk Jan (1930–)
▶ Dutch designer; born Hilversum; active Netherlands and Milan.
▶ 1950–54, studied Academy of Industrial Design, Eindhoven 1954–58, Academy of Industrial Design, Amsterdam.
▶ 1954–58, he worked at Hiemstra & Evenblij, Amsterdam, designing projects for schools, the theater, hospitals, and civic and military marinas; in 1958, he was an advisor to Technische UNI, Amsterdam, and firm W.J. Stokvis-Reale Industria Metallurgica, Arnhem; 1960–68, designed sanitary fittings for public use; in 1969, was design consultant to Meroni-Maisa, Seveso; from 1969, was design consultant to Olivetti and Rinascente; in 1975, was designer at Arspect, Bergeyk (Netherlands); from 1987, became a member of KIO (Dutch industrial design organization) and ADI (Associazione per il Disegno Industriale), Milan, and committees of ICSID congress; taught at Rietveld Academy, Amsterdam, and Aive, Eindhoven.
▶ Received a gold medal at 1969 'Expo/Ct/69.'
▶ *ADI Annual 1976*, Milan: Associazione per il Disegno Industriale, 1976. Giancarlo Iliprandi and Pierluigi Molinari (eds.), *Industrial Designers Italiani*, Fagagna, 1985:90. Hans Wichmann, *Italien Design 1945 bis heute*, Munich: Die Neue Sammlung, 1988.

de Wolfe, Elsie (aka Lady Mendl 1865–1950)
▶ American interior designer; active New York, Paris, and Los Angeles.
▶ De Wolfe has been dubbed the first interior decorator in America; a trailblazer, went on the stage at a time when the profession of actress was not socially a desirable one; in 1892, (with long-time companion Elisabeth Marbury, a theatrical agent) moved into the small house in Irving Place, near Gramercy Park, New York, that originally did not belong to author Washington Irving, as often stated; the couple were given the nickname 'the Bachelors.' De Wolfe transformed the house from its dark Victorian clutter into the light colors and furnishings of the Louis XV and XVI periods; had walls and furniture painted white and installed numerous mirrors. In 1904, she retired from the stage and went into the business of helping people decorate their homes; (with architect Ogden Codman) worked on the architecture of the Irving Place house and renovated several New York brownstones. These properties included the townhouse, East 71st Street, that she bought in 1910 for a highly publicized professional experiment. The Colony Club, a women's organization, was founded in 1905 by de Wolfe's rich friends and a new building for it was built on Madison Avenue, designed by McKim, Mead and White. Stanford White persuaded the building committee to hire de Wolfe as decorator; she installed the indoor-outdoor effect of trelliswork. She decorated the private rooms of Henry Clay Frick on the second floor of his house, Fifth Avenue, New York, in 1913. For her Villa Trianon, Versailles, she created rooms of demure style and luxury. In 1926, she married British diplomat Sir Charles Mendl, becoming Lady Mendl. During World War II, they lived in a house in Beverly Hills, California, that had a primarily white décor, including a plethora of white flower-arrangements. Her book *The House in Good Taste* (1913) was ghost written by Ruby Ross Wood, who later became an interior decorator. De Wolfe's notable contributions to 20th-century decoration included trelliswork in interiors, leopard-printed velvet pillows, naïve painted furniture, *chinoiserie* accents, bold stripes, topiary plants, tarnished gilding, and mirrored walls.
▶ Elsie de Wolfe, *The House in Good Taste*, New York: The Century, 1913. Mark Hampton, *House and Garden*, May 1990:145–49,214. John Esten, Rose Bennett Gilbert, *Manhattan Style*, Boston: Little, Brown, 1990:2–3. N. Campbell and C. Seebohm, *Elsie de Wolfe*, New York: Panache-Potter, 1992.

Debain, Alphonse
▶ French metalworker.
▶ Debain's work at the 1900 Paris exhibition reflected the range of his work, which was produced in contemporary tastes from historical styles to Art Nouveau.
▶ Received gold medal at 1889 Paris 'Exposition Universelle.' Work shown at 1900 Paris 'Exposition Universelle.' *Repoussé* silver (designed by Piquemal and Valery-Bizouard) shown at 1901 Salon of the Société des Artistes français.
▶ Yvonne Brunhammer et al., *Art Nouveau Belgium, France*, Houston: Rice University, 1976.

Deboni, Franco (1950–)
▶ Italian architect and glassware designer; born Trieste; active Venice.
▶ Studied architecture and industrial design, Instituto Universitario di Architettura, Venice, to 1974.
▶ He worked for various firms in Italy and Yugoslavia; received a patent for a bookcase-component system. Clients included Ferro & Lazzarini (glassware) and Italianline. He was best known for his lighting in glass and a mushroom-shaped table lamp in marble; became a member of ADI (Associazione per il Disegno Industriale); was author of *Venini Glass* (1990) and the manager of an art auction house.
▶ *ADI Annual 1976*, Milan: Associazione per il Disegno Industriale, 1976.

Debschitz, Wilhelm von (1871–1948)
▶ German artist.
▶ Von Debschitz and Hermann Obrist founded the Lehr- und Versuchs-Ateliers für angewandte und freie Kunst, known as the Debschitz-Schule, in Munich in 1902. The institution was an innovatory private art school that trained in applied arts and crafts.
▶ Annelies Krekel-Aalberse, *Art Nouveau and Art Déco Silver*, New York: Abrams, 1989:129–30. Dagmar Rinker, *Die Lehr- und Versuch-Ateliers für angewandte und frei Kunst (Debschitz-Schule), München 1902–1914*, Munich: Tuduv, 1993.
▶ See Debschitz-Schule

Debschitz-Schule
▶ German school for applied arts; located Munich.
▶ Wilhelm von Debschitz and Hermann Obrist founded the Lehr-und Versuch-Ateliers für angewandte und freie Kunst, Munich, in 1902. Popularly known as the Debschitz-Schule, the institution was a private art school organized along new lines, offering instruction in applied arts and crafts; rather than copying models in its foundation courses, the school encouraged the students to use their powers of observation; established workshops taught by Eduard Steinicken and M.T. Wetzler; students included Josef Urban, Marga Jess, Gertraud von Schnellenbühel, Fritz Schmoll von Eisenwerth, Friedrich Adler, and Karl Johann Bauer.
▶ Students' work first shown in 1903.
▶ Beate Ziegert, 'The Debschitz School Munich 1902–1914,' Master's degree thesis, Syracuse: Syracuse University, 1985. Beate Ziegert, 'The Debschitz School Munich: 1902–1914,' *Design Issues*, Vol. 3, No. 1, Spring 1986:28–41. Annelies Krekel-Aalberse, *Art Nouveau and Art Déco Silver*, New York: Abrams, 1989:129–30. Dagmar Rinker, *Die Lehr- und Versuch-Ateliers für angewandte und freie Kunst (Debschitz-Schule), München 1902–1914*, Munich: Tuduv, 1993.

Debût, Jules (1838–1900)
▶ French jewelry designer; active Paris.
▶ Debût designed most of the jewelry shown by Boucheron in 1878 and some pieces for Sarah Bernhardt; until 1879, worked for Boucheron.
▶ Boucheron showed work including Debût's at 1900 Paris 'Exposition Universelle'.
▶ Charlotte Gere, *American and European Jewelry 1830–1914*, New York: Crown, 1975:155.

Decaux, Jean-Claude (1937–)
▶ French manufacturer; active Paris.
▶ In 1955, Decaux established a firm specializing in highway advertising; in 1964, turned to urban street advertising; created a bus shelter tested in cities including Lyons, Grenoble, and Poitiers; in 1972, established MUPI (Mobilier Urbain pour l'Information) and, in 1976, PISA (Point d'Information Service Animé); offered municipalities free street-information displays in exchange for rights to place MUPI mobile units and bus shelters; diversified into information columns, panels, lighting, and public toilets; in 1990, set up the design agency Decaux Design, working with Philippe Starck, Jean-Michel Wilmotte, Andrée Putman, and others.

Deck, Joseph-Theodore (1823–91)
▶ French art potter; born Guebwiller.
▶ Leaving his job as foreman of a Paris stove factory, he set up his own business in 1856 as ceramicist; was inspired by Persian and Near Eastern ceramics, especially cobalt blue and turquoise floral patterns. The ceramics of China fostered his interest in porcelain. He was the first French ceramicist to succeed with red *flambé* glazes, incised decoration on celadon glazes, imitation jade, and underglaze enamels; was inspired by a trip to Venice and began to use gold background underglazes; in Venice, discovered Japanese ceramics; in 1887, became director of the Sèvres factory; perfected *la grosse procelaine*, a name he coined for vases, sculptures, and outdoor objects covered with durable transparent glazes; was active in his studio, boulevard St.-Jacques, Paris, and at the Sèvres factory.
▶ Plates (with applied designs by Ranvier, Glück, Anker, Bracquemond, Harpignies, Raphaël Collin, and Reiber) shown at 1878 Paris 'Exposition Universelle.' Japanese-inspired ceramics shown at 1880 Salon of Union Centrale des Arts Décoratifs.
▶ Yvonne Brunhammer et al., *Art Nouveau Belgium, France*, Houston: Rice University, 1976.

Decœur, Émile (1876–1953)
▶ French decorator and ceramicist; born Paris.
▶ Apprenticed to Edmond Lachenal.
▶ He was allowed to place his signature jointly on Lachenal's pots; was associated for a short time with Fernand Rumèbe; in 1907 establishing his own workshop, Fontenay-aux-Roses, gave up faïence and specialized in stoneware; later worked in porcelain; in 1925 leaving the Art Nouveau style behind, increasingly favored simplification that evolved into absolutely plain, symmetrical forms; produced simple vases, dishes, and bowls enveloped in heavy, pale glazes of yellow, blue, green, white, and pink; 1942–48, was artistic consultant, Manufacture Nationale de Sèvres.
▶ Guillaume Janneau, *Émile Decœur*, Paris: La Connaissance, 1923. Yvonne Brunhammer et al., *Art Nouveau Belgium, France*, Houston: Rice University, 1976. Victor Arwas, *Art Déco*, Abrams, 1980. Pierre Cabanne, *Encyclopédie Art Déco*, Paris: Somogy, 1986:184.

Décoration Intérieure Moderne
▶ See DIM

Decorchemont, François-Émile (1880–1971)
▶ French painter, sculptor, ceramicist, and glass worker; born Conches.
▶ Studied École Nationale des Arts Décoratifs, Paris, to 1900.
▶ Initially known for his ceramics, in 1903, Decorchemont worked with his father, sculptor Émile Decorchemont, on glass experimentation in *pâtes-d'émail* and matt surfaces influenced by Albert-Louis Dammouse; 1901–1903, produced stoneware; from 1903, created very thin *pâte-de-verre* pieces that were slightly translucent with matt surfaces; 1907–08, created a true *pâte-de-verre* using colored-crystal powdered glass and metallic oxides that he bought at Cristalleries de St. Denis; at Daum in *c*1910, developed a denser colored, yet translucent, material. 1910–20, his work was influenced by Art Nouveau, realized as monumental, simplified, geometric flower, fruit, and animal motifs. In 1928, somber,

linear motifs were adopted. From 1933 to the beginning of World War II, he was active primarily in producing leaded-glass windows for churches, including Church of Sainte Odile, Paris.

▶ Work shown regularly at Salons of Société des Artistes français, Salon d'Automne, and Salon des Artistes Décorateurs, and included in Hôtel du Collectionneur and Rouart pavilion, 1925 Paris 'Exposition International des Arts Décoratifs et Industriels Modernes.'

▶ 'François Decorchemont, 1880–1971,' *Nouvelles de L'Eure*, No. 42–43, August 1971. Yvonne Brunhammer et al., *Art Nouveau Belgium, France*, Houston: Rice University, 1976. Victor Arwas, *Art Déco*, Abrams, 1980. Cat., *Verriers français contemporains: Art et industrie*, Paris: Musée des Arts Décoratifs, 1982. Cat., Aaron Lederfajn and Xavier Lenormand, *Le Louvre des Antiquaires présente: 1930 quand le meuble devient sculpture*, Paris, 1986. Pierre Cabanne, *Encyclopédie Art Déco*, Paris: Somogy, 1986:185.

Decursu, Giorgio (1927–)
▶ Italian industrial designer; born and active Milan.
▶ He began his professional career in 1955; 1956–66, collaborated with Marcello Nizzoli for clients including Olivetti, Agip, Faema, Laverda, and Olivari; in 1968, was a partner in studio Decursu, De Pas, D'Urbino & Lomazzi; from 1970, set up his own independent studio, Milan, designing a range of industrial products from furniture to heavy industrial equipment; became a member of ADI (Associazione per il Disegno Industriale). Borrelli Corrado worked in Decursu's studio 1971–73.
▶ Received first prize in 1972 Du Pont-Dacron Fiberfill competition; 1979 and 1989 Premio Compasso d'Oro.
▶ *ADI Annual 1976*, Milan: Associazione per il Disegno Industriale, 1976. *Modo*, No. 148, March–April 1993:117.

Dedham Pottery
See Chelsea Keramic Art Works

Deganello, Paolo (1940–)
▶ Italian architect and designer; born Este; active Milan.
▶ Studied architecture, Università di Firenze, to 1966.
▶ 1966–74, worked in the town-planning office of Calenzano, Florence; in 1966, (with Andrea Branzi, Gilberto Corretti, and Massimo Morozzi) founded studio Archizoom Associati, Milan, closing in 1974. Archizoom designed 1969 *Mies* chair produced by Poltronova. In 1966, he taught architecture, Università di Firenze; 1971–72 and 1974, Architectural Association, London; in 1976, university of Milan; was professor of design, ISIA, Rome; in 1975, (with Corretti, Franco Gatti, and Roberto Querci) founded Collettivo Tecnici Progettisti; in 1975, founded journal *Quaderni del Progetto* and wrote for *Casabella*, *IN*, *Rassegna*, *Domus*, *Urban Politics Problems*, *Modo*, and *Lotus*. Clients included Planula, Marcatré, Driade, Venini, Mega Editions (Tribu collection), Cidue, Cassina, Ycami Collection, Mclandia, Casigliani, and Vitra. His early 1980s furniture, especially pieces for Cassina, were associated with the 1950s revival style, including 1967 *Superonda* banquette, 1973 *A&O* armchair by Cassina, and 1982 *Torso* armchair, sofa, and bed for which he is best known. Work included *Palomar* coat rack by Ycami Collection, *Aurore* lamp by Venini, 1981 *Squash* sofa by Driade, *Duala* floor lamp by Ycami Collection, and 1985 *Articifi* table range by Cassina. He became a member of ADI (Associazione per il Disegno Industriale); in 1983, designed Schöner Wohnen, the interior design and housewares shop, Zürich, where his *Monument to the Snow* was mounted on the plaza in front of the store. From 1992, taught architecture at the Università di Firenze.
▶ Projects included in 'Design by Circumstance' exhibition, Clocktower, New York. Work shown at 1983 exhibition, Zürich. Participated in international exhibitions, competitions, and Triennali di Milano, including the 1979 (XVI) and 1983 (XVII) sessions. Work shown at 1987 'Les Avant-Gardes de la fin du 20ème siècle' exhibition, Centre Georges Pompidou, Paris, and 1987 'Documenta,' Kassel.

▶ *ADI Annual 1976*, Milan: Associazione per il Disegno Industriale, 1976. Paolo Deganello, 'Post-Modern Boulevard,' *Domus*, No. 614, Feb. 1981:9–10. 'Colloqui di Modo: Il progetto sulle spine,' *Modo*, No. 57, March 1983:26–30. Cristina Morozzi, 'Incastro simmetrico,' *Modo*, No. 56, Jan.–Feb. 1983:48–49. *Italianisches Mobeldesign Klassiker von 1945 bis 1985*, Munich: Bangert, 1985. Cat., *Nouvelles Tendances: Les avant-garde de la fin du 20ème siècle*, Paris: Centre Georges Pompidou, 1987. Andrea Branzi, 'Cose e case,' *Domus*, No. 699, Nov. 1988. Juli Capella and Quim Larrea, *Designed by Architects in the 1980s*, New York: Rizzoli, 1988.

Dehn, Jakki (1952–)
▶ British furniture designer.
▶ Studied furniture design Leeds Polytechnic, to 1974, and Royal College of Art, London.
▶ Work shown at 'Style 86' and 'Style 87,' London; 1990 '100 Designs,' Conran Habitat, New York; 1989 (I), 1990 (II), and 1991 (III) International Contemporary Furniture Fair, New York.
▶ *Decorative Arts Today*, London: Bonhams, 1992: No. 26a.

Del Marie, Félix (1889–1952)
▶ French painter and furniture designer; active Bécon-les-Bruyères.
▶ Known as a painter, he was an enthusiastic promulgator of Italian Futurism as espoused in his 1913 manifesto published in *Paris-Jour*; in 1922, became a follower of Piet Mondriaan and the De Stijl group and, in 1924, editor of journal *Vouloir*, which he turned into *Revue mensuelle d'Esthétique néo-plastique*; from 1925, designed interiors and furniture; designed chairs in two and three colors in the manner of Gerrit Rietveld and other models in bent tubular steel; worked in wrought iron, painted metal, and frosted and painted glass used in lighting; in 1951 with André Bloc, founded Groupe Espace.
▶ Pierre Kjellberg, *Art Déco: les maîtres du Mobilier, le décor des Paquebots*, Paris: Amateur, 1986:49.

Del Piero, Giorgio (1952–)
▶ Italian designer; born in Pordenone; active S. Giovanni al Natisone, Udine.
▶ In 1971, Del Piero and Alfredo Simonit became partners in a design studio, S. Giovanni al Natisone. In 1974, they set up studio A. Simonit & Del Piero. Clients included Artieri del Legno, lft, Mobel Italian, Nikol, Pallavisini, Montina, and Olivo Pietro. Del Piero became a member of ADI (Associazione per il Disegno Industriale)
▶ Designed an area (with Simonit) at the Italian furniture stand, 1972 (IV) 'Eurodomus,' Turin (Italy).
▶ *ADI Annual 1976*, Milan: Associazione per il Disegno Industriale, 1976.

Delaherche, Auguste (1857–1940)
▶ French ceramicist; born Beauvais.
▶ Studied École Nationale Supérieure des Arts Décoratifs, Paris.
▶ With Lechevallier-Chevignard, he helped restore the stained-glass windows of the church of Saint-Acceul, Ecouen; worked as a designer for religious jeweler Chartier 1883–86, created his first pots in salt-glazed stoneware inspired by folk pottery, producing them under the direction of Ludovic Pilleux at ceramics factory L'Italienne, near Goincourt; in 1887, bought Chaplet's workshop, rue Blomet, Paris; in 1894, moved to Armentières; abandoned modeled decoration for overflow glazes appropriate to the materials and to an unembellished form; began working in porcelain; from 1904, made only unique pieces, often in stoneware; with Chaplet, is recognized as being one of the most important ceramicists at the turn of the century. His work developed into a formal simplicity. He introduced ceramic work into architecture by modeling panels and borders into fireplaces. Siegfried Bing showed Delaherche's works at his shop L'Art Nouveau.
▶ Work shown at 1887 Salon of Union Centrale des Arts Décoratifs; received a gold medal at 1889 Paris 'Exposition Universelle,' where he showed decorated stoneware in gourd-shaped vases and pear-shaped cups, and vases with exaggerated handles.

▶ Yvonne Brunhammer et al., *Art Nouveau Belgium, France*, Houston: Rice University, 1976.

Delaunay, Marc
▶ French designer.
▶ Studied École Nationale des Arts Appliqués à l'Industrie, Paris.
▶ From 1968, he worked for the firm Guy Degrenne; designed picnic-tableware set, winning 1986 competition sponsored by APCI (Agence pour la Promotion et la Création Industrielle) and UGAP (Union des Groupements d'Achats Publics).
▶ *Les Carnets du Design*, Paris: Mad-Cap Productions et APCI, 1986:86.

Delaunay, Robert   (1885–1941)
▶ French painter and designer; born Paris; husband of Sonia Terk Delaunay.
▶ In 1902, Delaunay began as a scenery painter; in 1905, became a fine artist, at first influenced by neo-Impressionism and then Cubism; using Eugène Chevreul's theories of simultaneous contrasts of colors, painted a series of canvases that were prismatically brilliant and colorful, calling them 'simultaneous paintings.' Guillaume Apollinaire called the technique 'Orphism' in his book *Le Bestiaire* or *Cortège d'Orphée* (1911). He passed through a neo-Impressionist period during which he painted canvases including *Solar Disk* that presaged Futurism; some other works were more suggestive of Cubism. Delaunay's *Premier Disque* (1912) has been called the first French abstract painting. He influenced other artists of his generation; designed sets for Diaghilev's Ballets Russes de Monte Carlo.
▶ Work shown at Salons des Indépendants from 1904 and at Salon des Tuilleries. Painting of a woman and the Eiffel Tower shown at Mallet-Stevens hall, French Embassy, 1925 Paris 'Exposition Internationale des Arts Décoratifs et Industriels Modernes.'
▶ Victor Arwas, *Art Déco*, Abrams, 1980. Pontus Hulten, *Futurism and Futurisms*, New York: Abbeville, 1986. Rita Reif, '50 Paintings to Be Sold from Tremaine Estate,' *The New York Times*, 6 June 1991:C3.
▶ See Delaunay, Sonia

Delaunay, Sonia   (b. Sonia Terk 1885–1979)
▶ Russian painter and designer; born Gradzinssk (Ukraine); active Paris; wife of Robert Delaunay.
▶ Studied St. Petersburg to 1902; 1903–04, drawing and anatomy in Karlsruhe; 1905, painting, Académie de la Palette, Paris.
▶ She settled in Paris in 1905 and began designing fabrics, lampshades, wall textiles, mosaics, interior schemes, and painted an automobile in her characteristic syncopated geometric shapes; experimented with embroidery and fabric design and printing, transforming her rhythmical patterns from artist's canvas to fabrics; in 1913, made a patchwork quilt in geometric polychrome forms for her son's crib, the first of her 'Robes et Gilets Simultanés'; used *simultané* to indicate that a piece of clothing was to be considered as a whole and as a work of art, without focusing on its separate elements; studying color and materials, (with husband Robert Delaunay and Swiss writer Blaise Cendrars) investigated the Modern *simultané* movement influenced by Eugène Chevreul; including his book *On the Law of the Simultaneous Contrasts of Colors* (1839). Her collages and stenciled illustrations were published in *La Prose du Transsibérien et de la petite Jehanne de France* (1913) by Cendrars, who dedicated to her his so-called dress-poem 'Sur la robe elle a un corps' ('On the dress she has a body'), aptly summing up her theory of *simultané*. The book was six feet (two meters) long in an accordion format in different typographic styles and faces. In 1914, she opened a fashion workshop where she designed fabrics, shawls, and clothing for men and women; became attracted to working in ceramics after a trip to Portugal in 1915; in 1920, set up residence and workshop in an apartment, boulevard des Malesherbes, Paris; in 1922, designed bookstore Au Sans Pareil, Paris; published *Sonia Delaunay, ses peintures, ses objets, ses tissus simultanés, ses modes* (1925) with a preface by André Lhote: closely identified with Art Déco, designed interiors, clothing, and theatre and ballet sets and costumes emphasizing

bright solid colors. Her clothes were worn by writers, artists, and *beau monde* personalities. She designed fabrics for the film *Le Vertige* (1926) by Marcel L'Herbier and (with husband Robert) sets and costumes for the film *Le P'tit Parigot*. Her friends and associates included Walter Gropius, Marcel Breuer, Jean Arp, Sophie Taeuber-Arp, and Erich Mendelsohn. She designed furs for Jacques Heim and exhibited with him at 1925 Paris Exposition; like her husband, she executed designs for Diaghilev's Ballets Russes de Monte Carlo, including costumes for its 1918 revival of *Cleopatra*; concentrated on painting after the 1920s but continued with some fabrics; in 1927, arranged the conference 'L'influence de la peinture sur l'art vestimentaire' ('The influence of painting on the art of clothing') at the Sorbonne, Paris. Her activities were greatly diminished in 1929 due to the Great Depression; in 1930 for a short time, was a member of UAM (Union des Artistes Modernes); in 1931 turned exclusively to painting. In 1984, she designed a faïence dinner service produced by Les Faïenceries de Moustiers.
▶ Work shown at 1913 'Erster Deutsche Herbstsalon,' Galerie der Sturm, Berlin; in 1916, Nya Konstgallerien, Stockholm; in 1920, Galerie der Sturm, Berlin; (Boutique Simultanée and concrete trees with couturier Jacques Heim) on Alexandre III Bridge at 1925 Paris 'Exhibition Internationale des Arts Décoratifs et Industriels Modernes'; in 1938, Stedelijk Museum, Amsterdam; at 1945 'Art concret,' Galerie Drouin, Paris; in 1956, Galleria del Cavallino, Venice; in 1958, Stadlisches Kunsthaus, Bielefeld; at 1969 'Robert et Sonia Delaunay,' Musée des Beaux-Arts, Lyons; 1965 'Robert and Sonia Delaunay,' Musée d'Art Moderne, Paris; in 1969, Carnegie Institute, Pittsburgh; in 1969, National Gallery, Melbourne; in 1972, Musée d'Art Moderne de la Ville de Paris; in 1975, Galerie Gmurzynska, Cologne; in 1975, International Cultureel Centrum, Antwerp; and in 1980, Albright-Knox Art Gallery, Buffalo, New York. Office ensemble and the *Hommage à Blériot* (1914) painting (of husband Robert Delaunay) shown at 1930 (I) exhibition, UAM, Paris. Work subject of 1981 retrospective, Art Institute of Chicago, and 1985 one-person exhibition, Musée d'Art Moderne de la Ville de Paris. Collaborated with husband Robert on projects Palais des Chemins de Fer and Palais de l'Air, 1937 Paris 'Exposition Internationale des Arts et Techniques dans la Vie Moderne.' Neon-tube *Zig-Zag* sculpture received first prize in 1936 competition sponsored by Société d'Électricité de France.
▶ Work included 1912–13 Simultaneous dress-painting on a living form, 1914 posters for Pirelli and Dubonnet, 1918 Cleopatra costume, 1922–26 robe poems and clothings, 1925 decoration of Citroën B12 automobile, Boutique Simultanée (with Jacques Heim) on the Pont Alexandre III at the 1925 Paris 'Exposition Internationale des Arts Décoratifs et Industriels Modernes,' 1940s–1960s rhythm color series of paintings, graphics, and tapestries, 1959 playing cards produced in 1964 by Bielefelder Spielkarte Museum, 1967 decoration of Matra B530 automobile, 1975 UNESCO poster for International Women's Year, and ceramics.
▶ Cat., Madeleine Delpierre and Henriette Vanier (eds.), *Grands Couturiers Parisiens 1910–1939*, Paris, 1965. Cat., Bernard Dorival, *Sonia Delaunay*, Paris, 1965. Cat., Michael Hoog, *Sonia Delaunay*, London, 1969. Cat., Jacques Damase, *Sonia Delaunay: Rhythms and Colours*, Paris, 1971. Sonia Delaunay, *Rhythmes et Couleurs*, Paris: Hermann, 1974. Donata Devoti, *L'Arte del tessuto in Delaunay*, Milan, 1974. Germain Viatte, *Sonia Delaunay: noirs et blancs*, Paris, 1978. Victor Arwas, *Art Déco*, Abrams, 1980. Anne Lee Morgan (ed.), *Contemporary Designers*, London: Macmillan, 1984:148–49. Cat., *Delaunay*, Paris: Musées/SA-MAM, 1985. Pierre Cabanne, *Encyclopédie Art Déco*, Paris: Somogy, 1986:186–87. Cat., *Les années UAM 1929–1958*, Paris: Musée des Arts Décoratifs, 1988: 172–73. Jacques Damase, *Sonia Delaunay: Fashion and Fabrics*, New York: Abrams, 1991.

Delheid Frères
▶ Belgian silversmith; located Brussels.
▶ Before setting up his own workshop in Amsterdam in 1897, Frans Zwollo, the first teacher of 'art metalwork' in the

Netherlands, apprenticed at Delheid. The firm began producing Modern silver designs after 1925. About 1930, it made a number of fine objects in which silver was combined with wood and ivory from the Belgian Congo (now Zaïre). The angular forms appearing in its wares could be likened to French forms of the 1920s and the undulating curves to Streamline styling of the 1930s.

▶ Annelies Krekel-Aalberse, *Art Nouveau and Art Déco Silver*, New York: Abrams, 1989:95,174,253.

Delisle

▶ French lighting firm; located Paris.

▶ The firm was founded in 1895 by Henry Delisle in the Hôtel de Lamoignon, Paris, and moved in 1935 to the Hôtel de Canillac, rue du Parc Royal, where it is located today and managed by Jean-Michel Delisle. Its best-known fixtures include those at Versailles Palace's Grand Trianon; Geihinkan Palace, Tokyo; Florence Goubol Theatre, San Francisco Fine Art Museum; Hotel Plaza Athénée, New York, 1926 oceanliner *Île-de-France*, 1935 *Normandie*, and 1961 *France*. Christian Duc designed its 1987 spherical *Archéologie Future* lamp (with glass by Patrick Desserme and Bernard Pictet).

▶ Received awards at 1895 Paris 'Exposition Universelle,' 1937 Paris 'Exposition Internationale des Arts et Techniques dans la Vie Moderne,' and 1980, 1982, and 1988 Salon International du Luminaire, Paris.

Dell, Christian (1893–1974)

▶ German metalworker and designer; born Offenbach; active Hanau, Weimar, and Frankfurt.

▶ Studied Königliche Preussische Zeichenakademie, Hanau, and Kunstgewerbeschule, Weimar, under Henry van de Velde.

▶ 1922–25, he was active at the Bauhaus, Weimar, as *Handwerklicher Meister* of its metal workshop. His work represented the transition in the prevailing approach of the Wiener Werkstätte and the Dessau Bauhaus under the guidance of László Moholy-Nagy. Dell contended that a designer should not totally abandon historic styles, a point about which Dell and Moholy-Nagy differed; was successful in developing lighting design for mass production. Kaiser produced his lamp designs, including the range *Idell* (a play on *ideal*) that was plagiarized by Helo. 1926–33, he was in charge of the metal workshop of Frankfurter Kunstschule.

▶ *Sammlung Katalog*, Bauhaus-Archiv, Museum für Gestaltung, Berlin, 1981, pl. 188–89. Lionel Richard, *Encyclopédie du Bauhaus*, Paris: Somogy, 1985:150. *Experiment Bauhaus*, Bauhaus-Archiv Museum, Berlin, 1988:126. Cat., *The Bauhaus: Masters and Students*, New York: Barry Friedman 1988. Auction cat., Bauhaus sale, Christie's Amsterdam, Kaiser Idell catalog Lot No. 450, 26 Oct. 1989. Cat., *Die Metallwerkstatt am Bauhaus*, Berlin: Bauhaus-Archiv, 1992:192–207,316.

Della Chiesa, Ernesto (1923–)

▶ Italian designer; born Milan; active Cernusco sul Naviglio.

▶ He set up his own manufacturing firm Ernesto Della Chiesa; became a member of ADI (Associazione per il Disegno Industriale). Work included filing and bookcase systems for its Delso division.

▶ Received 1955, 1956, 1957, and 1960 Premio Compasso d'Oro (bookcase systems). Received first prize at Industrial Design Smau competition (special bookcase system).

▶ ADI *Annual 1976*, Milan: Associazone per il Disegno Industriale, 1976.

Della Robbia

▶ British art pottery company; located Birkenhead.

▶ Della Robbia, named for the Renaissance Florentine faïence artist Luca della Robbia, was founded in 1894 by sculptor Conrad Dressler and painter Harold Rathbone, a pupil of Ford Madox Brown; produced architectural decorative fittings and, early on, hollow-ware and painted sgraffito decoration; made low-relief plaques designed by Robert Anning Bell. Italian Carlo Manzoni, a designer at Della Robbia, came from Granville Pottery, Hanley, in *c*1897; other modelers and decorators came from local art schools. The firm closed in 1906.

▶ Isabelle Anscombe and Charlotte Gere, *Arts and Crafts in Britain and America*, New York: Rizzoli, 1978.

Dell'Oro, Luigi (1923–)

▶ Italian designer; born and active Lecco.

▶ While a member of architecture partnership Dell'Oro, Garatti & Rezzonico, he and others designed the Musei del Castello Sforzesco, Milan. In 1956, he and architect Rezzonico established a powdered-plastics facility, Garlate di Lecco and, 1961–67, were consultants to Oerre. 1958–65, he was president of Collegio Regionale Lombardo, Lecco; 1958–64, advisor to the organization of architects, Como, and, 1966–70, its president; 1971–73, advisor to CNA; 1973–76, designer at the firm Lamperti, Robbiate; became a member of ADI (Associazione per il Disegno Industriale).

▶ Participated in 1965 Quinquennale di Lecco; Vetri Jena stand, 1968 Salone del Mobile, Milan; Alpine architecture stand (with architect Giacomo Cereghini), 1966 Torino 'Salone Internazionale della Montagna.'

▶ ADI *Annual 1976*, Milan: Associazione per il Disegno Industriale, 1976.

Delorme, Raphael (1885–1962)

▶ French set designer and painter.

▶ Studied École des Beaux-Arts, Bordeaux.

▶ He became a stage designer in Paris, specializing in perspective effects; switching to easel painting, painted female nudes.

▶ Auction cat., Sotheby's New York, Lot No. 667A, 17 June 1989.

Delta Design

▶ French design firm.

▶ Delta Design was established in 1985 as a regional design studio active in the Rhône-Alpes; designs primarily products, including sports equipment such as *CBX4* sports helmet made of two semi-rigid ABS-polycarbonate half shells.

Demaria, Pierre (1896–)

▶ French painter and furniture designer.

▶ Primarily a painter, he designed furniture and ornate rugs in abstract geometric motifs; (with Édouard-Joseph Bourgeois) collaborated on kiosks and pavilions at 1925 Paris 'Exposition Internationale des Arts Décoratifs et Industriels Modernes.'

▶ Pierre Kjellberg, *Art Déco: les mâtres du Mobilier, le décor des Paquebots*, Paris: Amateur, 1986:49.

den Boon, Wim (1912–68)

▶ Dutch interior architect; born Waddinxveen (the Netherlands).

▶ 1924–29, studied Hogere Handelsschool, Rotterdam; 1941–45, interior design, Academie van Beeldende Kunsten, The Hague.

▶ 1924–29, worked as exhibition designer at Unilever; *c*1945, became a founding member with Hein Stolle and Pierre Kleykamp of Groep &; 1948, with Groep &, designed departure room of Schiphol airport, Amsterdam, and waiting room of Thomsen's harbor company; 1948–50, editor of magazine *Goed Wonen* that had its own furniture collection 'Groep &,' lectured widely in Holland, and designed interiors and architecture for showcase houses; 1950, set up (with Dora Mees and J.W. Jansen) group Mens en Huis and Groep & dissolved; 1950, became an interior architect in The Hague and designed upholstered and bamboo furniture for Jonkers; from the 1950s, was very active in interior design, architecture and rebuilding/reconstruction in the Netherlands; 1954, traveled to Morocco, Spain, and France to study architecture of Le Corbusier and Gaudí; 1955, traveled to Scandinavian countries to study architecture of Alvar Aalto. Den Boon archive housed in the Gemeentemuseum, The Hague.

▶ From 1946, was involved with competitions for furniture and interior design with Groep & and participated in its 1947 exhibition 'my home.' Participated (with Groep &) in 1949 Salon of Société des Artistes Décorateurs, Paris; 'Mens en Huis' exhibition of *c*1951, Stedelijk Museum, Amsterdam, and Gemeentemuseum,

The Hague; 1951 'woon goed,' Academie van Beeldende Kunsten, The Hague.

▶ D. Sliedregt, 'de ivoren toren, in memoriam Wim den Boon,' *Goed Wonen*, No. 11, 1968:7. P. Vöge and B. Westerveld, *Stoelen, Nederlandse ontwerpen 1945–1985*, Amsterdam, 1985. Peter Vöge, *Wim den Boon: Binnenhuisarchitect, 1912/1968*, Rotterdam: Uitgeverij 010, 1989.

Denis, Maurice (1870–1943)

▶ French artist and decorator; born Grandville.

▶ Studied Académie Julian and École des Beau-Arts, Paris.

▶ Denis met Roussel and Édouard Vuillard at school and became one of the chief exponents of Symbolism; after the meeting of Paul Sérusier and Paul Gauguin at café Brady, Paris, (with Ibels, Paul Ranson, Pierre Bonnard, and Sérusier) founded the Nabis group, 1888; became spokesperson and theoretician for the group; 1890, published his first theoretical article *Art et Critique*; painted canvases and murals (Hotel Morozov, Moscow, and Palais de Chaillot, Paris) and illustrated books by Paul Verlaine, André Gide, and others. Denis was a devout Catholic intent on reviving religious painting. His decorative work was primarily in the form of stained glass and wallpaper. In 1917, he painted frescoes in the Église de St. Paul, Geneva, and, in 1919, (with Georges Desvallières founded the Ateliers d'Art Sacré. His writings on art can be found in his books *Théories* (1912), *Nouvelles Théories* (1922), and his 1939 history of religious art. Denis's former home near Paris, the priory of St.-Germain-en-Laye, is today the Musée Symbolistes et Nabis.

▶ Yvonne Brunhammer et al., *Art Nouveau Belgium, France*, Houston: Rice University, 1976. Ivan Chilvers et al., *The Oxford Dictionary of Art*, Oxford: 1988:140. Claire Fresches-Thory, Antoine Terrasse, *The Nabis: Bonnard Vuillard and Their Circle*, New York: Abrams, 1991.

Dennery

▶ French furniture maker; located Paris.

▶ Dennery was founded in the Faubourg Saint-Antoine, Paris, by its director Léon-Émile Bouchet; from the 1920s, produced the furniture of Bouchet and Eric Bagge.

▶ Pierre Kjellberg, *Art Déco: les maîtres du Mobilier, le décor des Paquebots*, Paris: Amateur, 1986:71.

Denzel, Marianne (c1932–1971)

▶ Austrian industrial designer; born Vienna.

▶ Denzel designed hotel ceramics for Berndorf-Ranshofen and metalwares for Vereinigte Metallwerke Ranshofen-Berndorf.

▶ Günther Feuerstein, *Vienna—Present and Past: Arts and Crafts—Applied Art—Design*, Vienna: Jugend und Volk, 1976:76, 78, 80.

Depero, Fortunato (1892–1960)

▶ Italian artist and furniture designer; born Fondo, Trento.

▶ In 1907, he started as an artist; worked as a painter, sculptor, and writer, becoming a Social Realist and focusing on Symbolism; published booklet *Spezzature—Impressioni—Segni e ritmi (Breakings—Impressions—Signs and Rhythms)* (1913); in 1913, met the Futurists in Rome; 1925–26, was active in Paris and, 1928–30, in New York. From the early 1930s, his work became more elaborate, ambitious, and dramatic. His work included the manifesto *Futurist Reconstruction of the Universe* known as *Complessità plastica—gioco libero futurista—L'essere vivente-artificiale (Plastic Complexity—Free Futurist Play—The Living-Artificial Being)* (1915); architectural visions expressed in *Padiglioni plastici futuristi* and *Vegetazione a deformazione artificiale* (1916); stage set for *Mimismagia* (1916); Ballets Russes de Monte Carlo's 1916–17 sets for *Nightingale* and *Zoo* (both unrealized); late-1910s wall hangings (with wife Rosetta), furniture, advertising posters, and various applied art works; 1917 'constructions' including brightly colored objects in wood and cardboard; 1921–22 interiors and furnishings for the Devil's Cabaret in Hôtel Élite et des Étrangers, Rome; exhibition of a project for statue-building to hold Futurist theater-cabaret Polychrome Plastic-Luminous Glorification of F.R. Marinetti, 1923

(I) 'Internationale delle Arti Decorative et Industriali Moderne,' Monza; 1924 Tridentine Venice pavilion, Milan Trade Fair, with advertising stands; 1924 stand for his own Casa d'Arte Futurista; 1924 stand for Campari; 1929 interior of Enrico e Paglieri and 1930–31 Zucca Restaurants, both New York; 1924 comic-grotesque ballet *Anihccam of the Year 3000*; staging of *The New Babel* and costumes for *American Sketches*, both New York; writing of *L'Impero* (1925); Book Pavilion 1927 (III) 'Internationale delle Arti Decorative et Industriali Moderne,' Monza; magazine covers in the late 1920s and 1930s; famous bolted-book *Depero Futurista* (Dinamo-Azari, 1927); advertising designs for Campari and Verzocchi; 1932 theory of his work *Manifesto of Advertising Art*; as a journalist, contributions to newspapers and magazines; in Rovereto, 1932 almanac *Futurismo 1932—Anno X—W.E. Marinetti nel Trentino* and magazine *Dinamo Futurista*; 1932 free-word 'sound' book *New York—Film vissuto (New York—A Real-Life Film)* (never published); 1934 radio-poetry work *Radio Lyrics*; one-off furniture pieces from the 1930s through the 1950s.

▶ In 1914, work shown at Giuseppe Sprovieri's Galleria Futurista, participating in events with Giacomo Balla, Francesco Cangiullo, and Filippo Tommaso Marinetti; until 1935, continued to show with Futurists. Work shown at 1923 (I) Monza 'Esposizione Biennale delle Arti Decorative e Industriali Moderne,' 1928–30, in New York. Designed 1924 Tridentine Venice Pavilion, Milan Trade Fair. His furniture was subject of exhibition, 'Sedicesimo Salone del Mobile Triveneto,' Padua, 1990.

▶ Pontus Hulten (organizer), *Futurism and Futurisms*, New York: Abbeville, 1986. Mario Universo, *Fortunato Depero e il mobile Futurista*, Venice: Marsilio, 1990.

DePree, Dirk Jan (1891–1990)

▶ American furniture manufacturer; active Zealand, Michigan; son-in-law of Herman Miller.

▶ DePree founded Herman Miller, furniture manufacturers in 1923 using the name of his father-in-law, who was not otherwise associated with the firm. Before hiring Gilbert Rohde as design director in 1931, the firm produced historicist furniture models. An exponent of the Modern movement in Europe, Rohde persuaded DePree to produce some of his models; cautions, DePree continued simultaneously to issue traditional models. Finally embracing Modernism, DePree became an enthusiastic evangelist. When Rohde died in 1944, DePree hired George Nelson as design director. The firm became highly successful after World War II, when Nelson introduced DePree to Charles Eames, who became its most prominent consultant designer. Others followed Eames, including sculptor Isamu Noguchi and textile designer Alexander Girard. In the 1950s, DePree met Robert Propst, a Colorado sculptor and inventor. Their association resulted in the *Action Office* system, an open-office configuration of component desks, walls, and furniture that transformed the office environment and Herman Miller's fortunes. A highly effective salesperson (never designing furniture himself), DePree felt that a 'design custodianship' should exist, whereby all those in the firm were duty bound to support the success of a design when it was accepted for production. He devised an arrangement, still in place, for selling Herman Miller's line through representative firms that often also carried the furniture of other manufacturers; Herman Miller has no sales outlets of its own.

▶ Cat., *A Modern Consciousness: D. J. DuPree, Florence Knoll*, Washington, DC: Renwick Gallery, 1975. Ralph Caplan, *The Design of Herman Miller*, New York, 1976. 'Celebrating Design Design Innovation,' *Designers West*, April 1991:34.

Derain, Gilles (1944–)

▶ French designer; active Paris.

▶ An expert on the history of the decorative arts, Derain designed furniture, lighting, and accessories for Lumen and carpets for Géométrie Variable. His 1979 *Merci Chareau Pierre* (or *MCP*) lamp for Lumen Center sold 40,000 copies. In the 1980s, Derain designed jewelry for Gay Frères, Paris, combining gold and semi-precious stones; was the first French designer to be commissioned to design for Zanotta, Italy, designing its 1985 *Omega* metal pedestal; in 1991, set up own firm to manufacture desk accessories and furnishings. From 1992, his designs were produced by Pentalux.

▶ Work shown at 1989 'L'Art de Vivre' exhibition, Cooper-Hewitt Museum, New York; from 1989, Paris Salon du Meuble; from 1991, Euroluce di Milano.

▶ Cat., *L'Art de Vivre*, New York: Vendome, 1989. François Mathey, *Au bonheur des formes, design français 1945–1992*, Paris: Regard, 1992:150,302.

Derby Silver
▶ American silversmiths; located Derby, Connecticut.
▶ Derby Silver started production in 1873, specializing in affordable silverplated hollow-ware. Watson John Miller, who had managed his own silverplating factory in Middletown, Connecticut, took control of Derby Silver in 1879. Superintendent Thomas H. Newcomb and designer and master mechanic Henry Berry assisted Miller. Derby became known for its high-quality German (or nickel) silver, silver-copper alloy, zinc, and nickel used for the plating process; produced wares in the taste of the Aesthetic Movement, incorporating Japanese motifs, butterflies, cranes, and cattails; in 1933, was purchased by International Silver.
▶ *Victorian Silverplated Holloware*, Princeton, NJ, 1972:105–06, 109–56. Doreen Bolger Burke et al., *In Pursuit of Beauty: Americans and the Aesthetic Movement*, New York: Metropolitan Museum of Art and Rizzoli, 1986:419.

Design and Industries Association (DIA)
▶ British industrial-design organization.
▶ A group of British artists and craftsmen who had attended the 1914 Cologne 'Deutscher Werkbund-Ausstellung' were encouraged to persuade the Board of Trade to establish a similar design-reform organization in Britain. An exhibition took place and with it was published the pamphlet *Design and Industry: a proposal for the foundation of a Design and Industries Association*. In 1915, the Design and Industries Association was formed to encourage private individuals, manufacturers, and retailers to insist on high standards of design in British industry; initial membership was 199. The first Council included James Morton, H.H. Peach, Frank Pick, and Sir Frank Warner from the industrial sector, C.G. Brewer, B.J. Fletcher, Ambrose Heal, C.H. St. John Hornsby, E.F. Jackson, W.R. Lethaby, and Harold Stabler from art and architecture. The Association was allotted a section to show articles of good design from retail stores at the 1916 'Arts and Crafts Exhibition,' Burlington House, London. Its membership grew from 292 in 1916 to 602 in 1928. Its small journal was begun in 1916 with articles attacking poor design and inferior craftsmanship. From 1922, the Association began to publish well-written and illustrated Yearbooks, modeled on the Werkbund Yearbooks. The Association showed its members' works in the British Section (organized by H.H. Peach), 1927 Leipzig 'Europäisches Kunstgewerbe' and in exhibits in the British provinces. From the early 1930s, it focused on raising the quality and lowering the price of consumer goods; chaired by Frank Pick, members W.F. Crittall, Jack Pritchard, Maxwell Fry, and John Gloag developed the 'DIA Plan'; in 1932, published the periodical *Design for Industry*, renamed *Design for Today*; published 1936–38 *Trend in Design of Everyday Things*, discontinued due to lack of public interest. Indirectly encouraged by the Association was the 1933 London 'British Industrial Art in Relation to the Home' exhibition sponsored by *Country Life*. The Birmingham branch sponsored the 1934 'Midlands Industrial Art Exhibition.' From 1935, the organization sponsored exhibitions in large shops and department stores; goods selected by the Association from the stores' stocks were displayed at events held at Bowman's, Harrods, Peter Jones and Whiteleys in London, Furlong's in Woolwich, Kendall Milne in Manchester, Dunn's in Bromley, Jones's in Bristol, and Rowntree's in Scarborough. In 1933 and 1934, model home exhibitions were mounted. Most of the DIA's activities were curtailed by the threat of war 1938, although exhibitions dealing with housing

and domestic design were sent to army camps, art galleries, and schools. The DIA was incorporated; it sponsored the 1953 London 'Register Your Choice' exhibition at the Charing Cross underground station, where commuters voted 60–40 per cent for a contemporary (Modern) over a reproduction (historicist) room. The DIA is still active today as a forum for discussion.

▶ Michael Farr, *Design in British Industry: A Mid-Century Survey*, London: Cambridge, 1955:192–98. Cat., *Thirties: British art and design before the war*, London: Arts Council of Great Britain, Hayward Gallery, 1979:304.

Design Centrum České Republiky
(The Design Center of the Czech Republic)
▶ Czech design association; located Brno.
▶ The organization was established in 1990 to assist in the improvement of design standards in Czech industry; published the magazine *Trend*; organized competitions and exhibitions; annually selects best products.

Design Group Italia
▶ Italian design cooperative studio.
▶ In 1968, Marco del Corno and others set up Design Group Italia, an industrial design studio. Its work included electronic equipment, telephones and recording instruments. Projects included the *Pulsar* electronic telephone for Sip. Product clients included Vetta Cycling Products, Jacuzzi, Resinart Plastics, Magis, Tupperware. Packaging clients included Ala Zignago, Splendid, Meseta, Ponti. Gianni Arduini, Franco Butti, Tullio Merlini, Luigia Micciantuono, Maria Gemma Piva, Paolo Rognoni, Franco Salvemini, and Ennio Saska were members.
▶ Received the 1979 Premio Compasso d'Oro (pencil holder).
▶ Alfonso Grassi and Anty Pansera, *Atlante del Design Italiano 1940/80*, Milan: Fabbri 1980:298. Hans Wichmann, *Italien Design 1945 bis heute*, Munich: Sammlung, 1988. *Modo*, No. 148, March–April 1993:119.

Design Logic
▶ American design consultancy.
▶ After graduating from Cranbrook Academy of Art, David Gresham worked for IBM; while at Cranbrook, designed a video camera for RCA. After graduating from the Royal College of Art and Design, London, Martin Thaler worked at Siemens, Munich. They both taught in the department of design, ITT, Chicago, and founded the design consultancy Design Logic. The firm restyled the 3-D Viewer; designed toys for View-Master Ideal Group, and answering machines for Dictaphone; conducted design studies for RC computer company and Bang and Olufsen, both Denmark.

Deskey, Donald   (1894–1989)
▶ American industrial, furniture, and interior designer; born Blue Earth, Minnesota; active New York.
▶ Studied architecture, University of California at Berkeley; painting, Arts Students' League, New York, and School of the Art Institute of Chicago, Illinois; École de la Grande Chaumière, Paris.
▶ Deskey (with Raymond Loewy, Norman Bel Geddes, and Henry Dreyfuss) was an early consultant designer in the USA; in 1920, began his career as a graphic designer at an advertising agency in Chicago; was greatly influenced by his visit to the 1925 Paris 'Exposition Internationale des Arts Décoratifs et Industriels Modernes'; in 1926, became active as an interior designer in New York. His first commissions were Modern display windows for Saks Fifth Avenue and Franklin Simon department stores. He produced hand-painted screens for Paul Frankl's gallery; designed the interiors of apartments for prominent clients, including Adam Gimbel; in 1927, became an associate of Phillip Vollmer, setting up Deskey-Vollmer, a firm specializing in lighting and furnishings that lasted until the early 1930s; in 1932–33, came to prominence as the competition-winning creator of the furniture and furnishing for Radio City Music Hall, a *tour de force* of glamorous American Modernism with murals by Witold Gordon, paintings by Stuart Davis, and fabrics by Ruth Reeves. In the late 1920s, all of Deskey's designs were custom-made for wealthy clients; however,

in the 1930s, he collaborated with mass manufacturers such as Widdicomb Furniture Company. One of the great Modernist figures of the 1930s, his work was characterized by experimentation with new materials, including aluminum, cork, and linoleum. His furniture of this time used bakelite and aluminum in the dashing new style. Deskey designed not only furniture but interiors, lighting, exhibitions, products, and packaging; in the late 1920s, invented a stained-wood laminate called Weldtex; to c1970, was active in his own industrial design firm; designed a lighting fixture reproduced today by Ecart International.

▶ Work shown (with Walter von Nessen, sculptor William Zorach, Paul Frankl, and others) at John Cotton Dana's 1929 'Modern American Design in Metal' exhibition, Newark Museum, Newark, New Jersey. Dining room installed in West Gallery (Ely Jacques Kahn, director), 1935 'Contemporary American Industrial Art' exhibition, New York Metropolitan Museum of Art.

▶ Karen Davies, *At Home in Manhattan: Modern Decorative Arts, 1925 to the Depression*, New Haven: Yale, 1983:50. David A. Hanks and Jennifer Toher, *Donald Deskey*, New York: Dutton, 1987. Gail Davidson, 'Donald Deskey' in Mel Byars and Russell Flinchum (eds.), *50 American Designers, 1918–1968*, Washington: Preservation, 1994.

Desny

▶ French design firm; located Paris.

▶ Desny was active 1927–33 at 122 avenue des Champs-Elysées, Paris. The principals of the firm were the designers Desnet and René Mauny (or Nauny), and financial backer Tricot. There was a staff designer, Louis Poulain. The firm became known for its innovative Modern lighting fixtures incorporating glass and chrome-plated metal; also produced silverware, bath accessories, silverwares, carpets, and murals. Its work was characterized by severe geometrical forms and plain surfaces and influenced by Cubism. Rugs showed abstract geometric motifs. Its work, though of a distinctly Modern spirit, often included the use of exotic woods and other expensive materials. Its furniture sometimes included aluminum features. In 1931, it received commissions to design the interiors of the apartments of Georges-Henri Rivière and Pierre David-Weill and the highly sophisticated, elegant quarters of Mlle. Thurnauer. For ambient lighting, its chromium-plated sconces, chandeliers, and floor lamps had their bulbs concealed. For task lighting, the firm offered 'genre spot lights'; produced a range of illuminated bibelots in clear glass and in metal; commissioned designers André Masson (painted panels), Alberto and Diego Giacometti (fire dogs and crystal lamp bases in the apartment of David-Weill), Jean-Michel Frank (parchment walls of Thurnauer's apartment), Djo-Bourgeois, and Robert Mallet-Stevens, with whom Desny was associated on several decorating projects. When Desnet died in 1933, the business closed. Nauny later opened a small chain of costume jewelry shops called Hippocampe, Paris and Lyons, and designed some of the jewelry.

▶ Alastair Duncan, *Art Nouveau and Art Déco Lighting*, New York: Simon and Schuster, 1978:166–67. Cat., Aaron Lederfajn and Xavier Lenormand, *Le Louvre des Antiquaires présente: 1930 quand le meuble devient sculpture*, Paris, 1986. Pierre Kjellberg, *Art Déco: les maîtres du Mobilier, le décor des Paquebots*, Paris: Amateur, 1986:49. Alastair Duncan and Audrey Friedman, 'La Maison Desny,' *Journal of Decorative and Propaganda Arts*, Summer 1988:86–93.

Desprès, Jean (1889–1980)

▶ French silversmith and jeweler; born Souvigny; active Paris.

▶ Trained in jewelry at Avallon; apprenticed to a silver- and goldsmith, Paris, and studied painting.

▶ An airplane pilot and aeronautical draftsman, he acquired a fascination for machinery and geometrical forms. Desprès established his own workshop, making and selling silver, gold, pewter objects, and jewelry in severe geometric shapes. His work looked as if it were produced by machine rather than by hand, with quasi-technical ornamentation applied to smooth, shiny surfaces. Unlike other designers working in leading ateliers or freelance

designers, Desprès himself produced his own designs for jewelry and silver; in c1930, (with Etienne Cournault) collaborated on Surrealist jewelry forms; in 1934, became director of Galerie de l'Art et de la Mode, Paris; was often associated with the jewelry activities of UAM (Union des Artistes Modernes).

▶ From 1929, pewter work shown at Salons of Société des Artistes Décorateurs and, from 1930, at UAM exhibitions. Dressing table set shown at 1925 'Exposition Internationale des Arts Décoratifs et Industriels Modernes.' Work shown at various international exhibitions, including sessions of Salon des Indépendants and 1937 Paris 'Exposition Internationale des Arts et Techniques dans la Vie Moderne.'

▶ Victor Arwas, *Art Déco*, New York: Abrams, 1980. Pierre Cabanne, *Encyclopédie Art Déco*, Paris: Somogy, 1986:186. Annelies Krekel-Aalberse, *Art Nouveau and Art Déco Silver*, New York: Abrams, 1989:70,253.

Despret, Georges (1862–1952)

▶ French glass designer.

▶ Studied Université de Liège.

▶ In 1884, Despret became director of Glacerie de Jeumont, mass producers of window glass and mirrors; working in a research studio at the Jeumont factory, rediscovered the secret of polychrome *pâte-de-verre*; reinterpreted Japanese themes freely in his work, often applying them to cups, vases, and small sculptures made in thick-walled and lumpy *pâte-de-verre* designed for mass production; used *pâte-de-verre* to imitate marble, onyx, agate, and even stoneware; in 1908, founded Compagnie Réunie des Glaces et Verres Spéciaux du Nord de la France.

▶ After several exhibitions, work shown (with Géo Nicolet) at Paris 1900 'Exposition Universelle.'

▶ Yvonne Brunhammer et al., *Art Nouveau Belgium, France*, Houston: Rice University, 1976. Cat., *Verriers français contemporains: Art et industrie*, Paris: Musée des Arts Décoratifs, 1982.

Desrosiers, Charles (1865–1927)

▶ French jeweler.

▶ Desrosiers designed some of Georges Fouquet's best-known and most copied jewelry pieces, including the *Châtaigne* ('chestnut') pendant and the *Murier* ('mulberry') necklace.

▶ Yvonne Brunhammer et al., *Art Nouveau Belgium, France*, Houston: Rice University, 1976.

Dessau, Ingrid (1923–)

▶ Swedish fabric designer.

▶ 1939–35, studied at Konstfackskolan, Stockholm.

▶ From 1945–49, she worked for the Kristianstads läns hemslöjdsförening (Hand Craft Society of Kristianstad County); from 1954–57, was designer for Kasthalls Mattfabrik; from 1970–84, designer for Kinnasand; from 1953, freelance designer for hand-knotted and hand-tufted carpets; produced *rya* and knotted pile weaving and was perhaps more interested in the *rölakan* and basket weave or double weave.

Dessecker, Berhard (1961–)

▶ German designer; born Munich.

▶ Studied interior design.

▶ 1983–84, he worked at Studio Morsa, New York; from 1984, was a freelance designer and collaborator in the design team of Ingo Maurer.

▶ Albrecht Bangert and Karl Michael Armer, *80s Style: Designs of the Decade*, New York: Abbeville, 1990:229.

Dessonnaz, Georges

▶ Swiss inventor.

▶ Dessonnaz designed the 1940 *Gedess Minenschärfer* pencil sharpener, still in production today, in only four parts with a single screw and a rotating ball-bearing finial.

▶ Shown at 'Schweizer Erfindungen' exhibition, Globus department store, Basel, 1991.

DESTA

▶See Deutsche Stahlmöbel

Desvallières, Richard (1893–)

▶ French metalworker; born and active Paris.

▶ Desvallieres used medieval forging techniques; rejecting industrial methods, produced wrought-iron work for interiors of the 1920s and 1930s, including those designed by Suë et Mare at Compagnie des Arts français for their various commissions, including the banister in the reception hall of the 1924–25 villa of actress Jane Renouardt, 2 avenue Buzenval, St. Cloud. In his workshop, he produced grilles, fire dogs, fire screens, tables, consoles, and étagères; produced the choir stall and other ironwork for the Church of Sainte-Agnès in Maison-Alfort.

▶ Ironwork for the Cubist house of Raymond Duchamp-Villon shown at 1912 Salon d'Automne. Cockerel weather vane shown at 1920 Salon d'Automne and numerous grilles at 1925 Paris 'Exposition Internationale des Arts Décoratifs et Industriels Modernes.'

▶ Léon Deshairs, *Modern French Decorative Art*, Paris: Albert Lévy. Pierre Kjellberg, *Art Déco: les maîtres du Mobilier, le décor des Paquebots*, Paris: Amateur, 1986:50–51.

Deutsche Stahlmöbel (DESTA)

▶ Hungarian businessman Anton Lorenz established the firm Deutsche Stahlmöbel (DESTA) in 1929 to manufacture bent tubular steel furniture. It was set up in the workshop formerly occupied by Standardmöbel, Teltowerstrasse 47–48, Berlin, which had been bought by Thonet. Lorenz won the 1929 suit filed against him by Thonet, giving DESTA sole rights to the cantilever chair design principle; Lorenz then sold Thonet rights for resilient tubular steel furniture. DESTA closed in 1933, although Lorenz continued using its name until 1935.

▶ Otakar Mécel, 'Avant-garde Design and the Law: Litigation over the Cantilever Chair,' *Journal of Design History*, Vol. 3, Nos. 2 and 3, 1990:125–35.

Deutsche Werkstätten

▶ German arts and crafts group.

▶ The Deutsche Werkstätten was formed as an amalgamation of the Dresdner Werkstätten and the Werkstätten für Wohnungs-Einrichtung.

Deutscher Werkbund

▶ German artistic and production association.

▶ The Deutscher Werkbund was founded in 1907 by Peter Bruckmann (its first president), Peter Behrens, Hermann Muthesius, Josef Maria Olbrich, Fritz Schumacher, and Richard Riemerschmid. By 1909, membership had increased to 700, including Henry van de Velde, Mies van der Rohe, Walter Gropius, Marcel Breuer, and Frederich Naumann. Members, who included architects, industrialists, craftspeople, teachers, and publicists, argued that German products must be improved technically and aesthetically in order to compete abroad. Sharing the ideals of the Arts and Crafts movement in Britain, the Werkbund sought to revive the prestige of craft skills through a collaborative effort of art and industry, and a campaign of propaganda and education. Karl Scheffer made no secret of the fact that the Germans wished to capture the clientele of the Paris furniture makers: 'German industrial artists understand that it is not simply a question of aesthetics, but a question of life and death. ... We have to create an art industry that is capable of becoming a world-wide industry' (Catalog of the Exposition Internationale, 1910). Some industrialists recognized the commercial advantages of producing tasteful Modern goods: AEG founder Emil Rathenau hired Peter Behrens in 1907 as designer of the firm's factories, corporate graphics, products (including lighting), and workers' estates. New developments illustrated in the 1907–14 Yearbooks of the Deutscher Werkbund included automobiles by Ernst Naumann; factories by Hans Poelzig, Behrens, and Walter Gropius; steamship interiors by Bruno Paul; railway coaches by Gropius; and furniture produced by the Deutsche Werkstätten für Handwerkkunst, Hellerau, near Dresden. In 1914, the Deutscher Werkbund organized one of the most important exhibitions of industrial design of the 20th cen-

tury, the 1914 Cologne 'Deutscher Werkbund-Ausstellung.' It was an impressive manifestation of the Modern movement in Germany, where Bruno Taut's Glass Pavilion, Gropius's model factory building, and Henry van de Velde's Werkbund Theater were constructed. A vigorous debate ensued among members on the relative importance of individual design and industrial standardization. Against Muthesius's attempt to reconcile the two opposing principles, van de Velde, supported by Taut and Gropius, resisted any suggestion of canon or standardization. In 1919, Poelzig delivered a speech in Stuttgart opposing the mass-production approach advocated by Muthesius and Naumann and reaffirming handicraft as the standard for the Werkbund; meanwhile, Gropius, as head of the newly formed Bauhaus, suggested that humanity's needs could be best served by the machine. The Werkbund undertook a bold and unique project, the 1927 Stuttgart 'Weissenhofsiedlung' (Werkbund housing estate) exhibition, under the supervision of Ludwig Mies van der Rohe. Modernist architects and practitioners throughout Europe were invited to have their ideas realized. Mart Stam's 1925 cantilever tubular steel chair with leather seat and back-rest was shown; Mies's own cantilever steel chair, the *Weissenhof* in wicker and tubular steel, was shown for the first time. In the house designed by Gropius at the 'Die Wohnung' exhibition at Weissenhof, there were beds made from metal tubes by Le Corbusier and Alfred Roth that could be folded away during the day. Most of the furniture at 'Die Wohnung' was by Marcel Breuer. Similar exhibitions followed in Breslau (now Wrocław, Poland) in 1929 and Vienna in 1932. The Werkbund exhibition at the 1930 (XX) Salon of the Société des Artistes Décorateurs, Paris, was less than successful and, designed by Gropius with interiors and furniture by Marcel Breuer, focused on the efforts of the Bauhaus rather than the Werkbund, though the tubular-steel furniture shown created a sensation. Broken into factions with the advent of the Third Reich, the Werkbund's conservative members, including Mies and Winfried Wendland, sought an accommodation with the Nazis; in 1934, the organization was dissolved, although the Nazis attempted to co-opt the Werkbund's principles through the Amt Schönheit der Arbeit (Office for the Beauty of Work). Revived in 1947, the Werkbund designed the German Pavilion, 1958 'Exposition Universelle et Internationale de Bruxelles (Expo '58).' The buildings by Egon Eiermann and Sep Ruf, objects, and gardens by Walter Rassow demonstrated that Germany had returned to high quality in design. Never interested in the superficial aspects of mere 'good form,' the Werkbund was nevertheless dubbed by critics the Tassenwerkbund (Coffee-Cup Werkbund), implying that it was merely concerned with the design of trivial objects rather than with all aspects of the environment beyond the narrow parameters of industrial culture. Its early journals included *Jahrbücher des Deutschen Werkbundes* of 1912, 1913, 1914, 1915, 1917, and 1920, and *Die Form* of 1922, 1925–34. Later efforts were documented in the journal *Werk und Zeit* from 1952.

▶ Karl Scheffer, official catalog for the German pavilion, Brussels 'Exposition Internationale,' 1910. Gordon Logie, *Furniture from Machines*, London, 1933. Siegfried Giedion, *Mechanization Takes Command*, Oxford: Oxford University Press, 1948:493–94. Cat., *Zwischen Kunst und Industrie: Der Deutscher Werkbund*, Munich, 1975. Joan Campbell, *The German Werkbund, The Polity of Reform in the Applied Arts*, Princeton, NY: 1978. Lucius Burckhardt (ed.), *The Werkbund: Studies in the History and Ideology of the Deutscher Werkbund 1907–1933*, London: The Design Council, 1980. Kurt Junghanns, *Der Deutscher Werkbund: Sein erstes Jahrzehnt*, Berlin: 1982. Julius Posener in Vittorio Magnago Lampugnai, *Encyclopedia of 20th-Century Design*, New York: Abrams, 1986:80–83. Ot Hoffmann (ed.), *Der Deutscher Werkbund–1907, 1947, 1987*, Berlin, 1987. Cat., *Franz Singer/Friedl Dicker: 2X Bauhaus in Wein*, Vienna: Hochschule für angewandte Kunst, 1988. Sonja Günther (introduction), *Thonet Tubular Steel Furniture Card Catalogue*, Weil am Rhein: Vitra Design Publications, 1989. 'Documents,' *Journal of Design History*, Vol. 3, Nos. 2 and 3, 1990:167–68. Karin Kirsch, *The Weissenhofseidlung*, New York: Rizzoli, 1992.

Devesa, Sergi (1961–)
▶ Spanish designer.
▶ He designed lighting for Metalarte, Barcelona, including the all-metal *Zen* table light (with O. Devesa), and furniture for others.
▶ Albrecht Bangert and Karl Michael Armer, *80's Style: Designs of the Decade*, New York: Abbeville, 1990:229.

Devětsil
▶ Czech artists' and writers' group; active Prague.
▶ The association was founded in 1920 by Karel Teige; proclaimed a program of Czech Purism and Poetism; members included Josef Chochol and Bědrich Rozehnal, a collaborator of architect Auguste Perret in Paris. Devětsil's most active members were 'The Four Purists': Jaroslav Fragner, Karel Honzík, Eugen Linhart, and Vít Obrtel; included Josef Havlícek and Jaromír Krejcar. Krejcar published his almanac of new aesthetics *Život II* (1922–23) which encouraged Czech artists to develop contacts in international centers of architecture, art, theater, film, music, and literature. Its poets and writers, including Větězslav Nezval, Vladimír Vanícura, and Jaroslav Seifert, stressed the poetic aspects of architecture. Devětsil's journals were *DISK, Pásmo,* and *ReD*.
▶ Vladimír Šlapeta, *Czech Functionalism*, London: Architectural Association, 1987:9. Cat., *Devětsil: The Czech Avant-Garde of the 1920s and 30s*, Oxford: Museum of Modern Art, London: Design Museum, 1990.

Deyhle, Gebrüder
▶ German silversmiths; located in Schwäbisch-Gmünd.
▶ Gebrüder Deyhle was founded in 1820; produced flat- and hollow-ware.
▶ Annelies Krekel-Aalberse, *Art Nouveau and Art Déco Silver*, New York: Abrams, 1989:253.

Di Giuli, Peppe (1947–)
▶ Italian industrial designer; born Terni; active Terni and Milan.
▶ Studied Corso Superiore Disegno Industriale e Comunicazioni Visive, Rome, to 1971.
▶ He began his professional career in 1972; was a visual designer for Alfa Romeo and Pomigliano d'Arco; collaborated with architect Andries van Onck in Studio Pro and with Milano Studio Mari; became a member of ADI (Associazione per il Disegno Industriale).
▶ *ADI Annual 1976*, Milan: Associazione per il Disegno Industriale, 1976.

Diaghilev, Sergei Pavlovich (1872–1929)
▶ Russian theatrical impresario; born Novgrod.
▶ Diaghilev was the impresario of the Ballets Russes de Monte Carlo, which arrived in Paris in 1909 and in London in 1911. Diaghilev had already presented Russian bass singer Feodor Chaliapin in a season of Russian opera in Paris in 1908. The work of his set and costume designers, particularly Léon Bakst, were influential in their use of bright colors, which were used in interiors of the 1920s. Other set and costume designers included Alexandre Benois, Henri Matisse, Pablo Picasso, Marie Laurencin, Natalie Goncharova, and Georges Braque. Diaghilev's troupe included dancers Anna Pavlova, Vaslav Nijinsky, Lev Platonovich Karsavina, and Lydia Lopokova; choreographers Michel Fokine and Léonide Massine; and composers Claude Debussy, Maurice Ravel, Igor Stravinsky, and Sergei Prokofiev. Breaking with Russia, its home base became Paris.
▶ Lynn Garafola, *Diaghilev's Ballets Russes*, New York: Oxford, 1989. Mílitsa Pozharskaya and Tatiana Volodina, *The Art of the Ballet Russes: The Russian Seasons in Paris 1908–1929*, London: Arum, 1990.

Diamond, Freda (1905–)
▶ American glassware designer.
▶ Studied Cooper Union, New York.
▶ A consultant designer, Diamond was hired in 1942 by Libbey Glass to do market research; in the 1950s, became known for her inexpensive, tasteful tableware and furniture. One of Diamond's suggestions for production was 'theme' glassware in packaged sets supported by extensive advertising, some of which featured Diamond herself. She designed the 1950 *Classic Crystal* tumbler set and later more ornamental glassware, though she advocated unadorned wares; was an advisor on design and marketing to other manufacturers and retailers.
▶ *Classic Crystal* range shown at 1950 'Good Design' exhibition, New York Museum of Modern of Modern Art and Chicago Merchandise Mart.
▶ Freda Diamond, *The Story of Glass*, New York, 1953. 'Designer for Everybody,' *Life*, Vol. 36, April 5, 1954:69–70. Carl U. Fauster, *Libbey Glass since 1918*, Toledo, Ohio, 1979:100,133,140–41,161,186. Cat., Kathryn B. Hiesinger and George H. Marcus III (eds.), *Design Since 1945*, Philadelphia: Philadelphia Museum of Art, 1983. Cherie Fehrman and Kenneth Fehrman, *Postwar Interior Design, 1945–1960*, New York: Van Nostrand Reinhold, 1987.

Dichiara, André (1950–)
▶ Italian designer; born and active Ancona.
▶ Dichiara began his professional career in 1973; became a member of ADI (Associazione per il Disegno Industriale); had clients in Italy for furniture and furnishings for adults and children and kitchen systems including Mobilfer, Giancarlo Babini, Gieffe Cucine, Poltrone Babini, and Zuccari P.
▶ *ADI Annual 1976*, Milan: Associazione per il Disegno Industriale, 1976.

Dicker, Friedl (1899–1944)
▶ Austrian architect and furniture, interior, and textile designer; born Vienna.
▶ Studied photography; 1912–14, fabric design, Kunstgewerbeschule, Vienna; 1916–19, with Johannes Itten, Vienna; 1919–23, Bauhaus, Weimar, under Itten.
▶ 1923–26, Dicker was active with Franz Singer in their Werkstätten bildender Kunst, Berlin; in 1923, she settled in Vienna and set up a first studio with Anny Moller-Wottitz and, in 1924, a second studio with Martha Döberl; in 1926, amalgamated her studio with Singer's, Vienna, designing houses, apartments, kindergartens, offices, textiles, interiors, and furniture; in 1927, (with Singer) also worked in Stuttgart for a textile firm. When the Dicker-Singer studio closed, Dicker set up her own, Vienna, 1930–31; in 1934, was arrested during the Starhemberg Putsch in Vienna; 1934–38, in Prague, practiced interior architecture with Grete Bauer-Fröhlich, taught drawing, and was active as an artist and anti-fascist; in 1938, turned down a visa to settle in Palestine; in 1938–42, lived in Mettau (now Hronov, Czech Republic), teaching drawing and being active as an architect, artist, and, for B. Spiegler and Söhne, textile designer; 1942–44, was imprisoned in the Theresienstadt concentration camp near Prague, where she taught children's drawing courses; in 1944, was killed at Auschwitz-Birkenau Extermination camp.
▶ Received an award at 1924 Deutscher Spitzenmesse, Berlin, for efforts in the Werkstätten with Singer. Work shown at 1927 Kunstschau, Vienna; 1929 'Ausstellung Moderner Inneneinrichtungen' exhibition, Österreichisches Museum, Vienna; 1938 exhibition (gold medal and award for textiles for Spiegler) on the 20th anniversary of Czechoslovakia. Work subject of 1940 exhibition, Royal Academy, London, and (with Singer) of the exhibition, Hochschule für angewandte Kunst, Vienna, 1988–89.
▶ Cat., *Franz Singer/Friedl Dicker: 2X Bauhaus in Wein*, Vienna: Hochschule für angewandte Kunst, 1988. Sigrid Wortmann Weltge, *Women's Work: Textile Art from the Bauhaus*, London: Thames and Hudson, 1993.

Dieckmann, Erich (1896–1944)
▶ German designer and teacher.
▶ 1921–25, studied Bauhaus, Weimar.
▶ He designed a 1925 cherrywood and cane armchair and side chair while at the Bauhaus; after Marcel Breuer, was the most important furniture designer trained at the Bauhaus; 1925–30, was head of the joiners' workshop, Staatliche Bauhochschule, Weimar, under Otto Bartning; produced handcrafted furniture

designs for Haus am Horn; remained in Weimar when the Bauhaus moved to Dessau. The experience he acquired at the Bauhaus was later put to use on many chairs in wood and steel for Thonet and other firms. 1931–33, he was a master, Kunstgewerbeschule Burg Giebichenstein, Halle.

▶ Cat., *The Bauhaus: Masters and Students*, New York: Barry Friedman, 1988. Cat., *Erich Dieckmann, Praktiker der Avantgarde*, Weil am Rheim, Vitra Design Musuem, 1990.

Diederich, Wilhelm Hunt   (1884–)

▶ German metalworker; born Hungary; active New York.
▶ Studied Pennsylvania Academy of Fine Arts.
▶ Diederich settled in c1900 with his mother in the Boston house of his grandfather painter William Morris Hunt; in 1907, (with sculptor Paul Manship) traveled in Spain and alone to Africa, Rome, Berlin, and Paris; in Paris for the next ten years, studied with *animalier* Emmanuel Fremiet; by 1910, had become known as a sculptor of animals; met Polish sculptor Elie Nadelman and Russian sculptor Alekandr Archipenko, later renewing the friendships in New York. Diederich worked in cast bronze, sheet metal, and glazed ceramics, producing sculptures, weather vanes, metal wall reliefs, crayon drawings, paper silhouettes, and wood-cut prints. His furnishings included wrought-iron torchères, candlestands, and firescreens. His stylish and lighthearted objects interpreted images of cats, dogs, roosters, stags, and horses, many produced to his designs by blacksmiths in Greenwich Village, New York. His work was characterized by elegant, thin, curvaceous lines. He also produced bronze sculptures of romping and prancing animals frozen in a moment of action, including the 1913–16 *Playing Greyhounds* and 1916 *Antelope and Hound*, the former included in his first (1920) exhibition; in 1923 in Morocco, developed an interest in pottery, collected native examples, and began painting and glazing his own plates and bowls; in the 1930s, was a Nazi sympathizer; in 1937, moved to Mexico, where he remained during World War II in the company of other American sculptors; became well known both for his silhouettes and sculpture; in 1947, expelled from the National Institute of Arts and Letters for using its mailing envelopes to send anti-Semitic material.

▶ In the 1910s and 1920s, work shown regularly at Salon d'Automne, Paris. Received gold medal (pottery) at 1927 exhibition, Architecture League of New York. In the 1920s, work shown at Whitney Studio Club (precursor of the Whitney Museum of American Art). Work subject of 1917 exhibition, interior decorator's apartment, New York; 1920 'First American Exhibition of Sculpture of Hunt Diederich,' Kingore Galleries, New York; 1991 exhibition, Whitney Museum of American Art, New York.

▶ Cat., *Catalogue of the First American Exhibition of Sculpture by Hunt Diederich*, New York: Kingore Galleries, 1920. 'Diederich, W. Hunt,' *Who's Who in American Art*, 1936–37. Cat., Susan E. Menconi, *Uncommon Spirit: Sculpture in America 1800–1940*, New York: Hirschl and Adler Galleries, 1989:72–73. Jonathan M. Woodham, *Twentieth-Century Ornament*, New York: Rizzoli, 1990:107. Marvin D. Schwartz, 'Hunt Diederich,' *Antiques and Arts Weekly*, 9 Aug. 1991:1,36. Richard Armstrong, Whitney exhibition flyer, 1991.

Dietrich, Oscar   (1853–1940)

▶ Austrian silversmith; active Vienna.
▶ He took over the directorship of his father's silversmithy; in 1881, was admitted to the goldsmith's trade; produced designs by leading artists including Emanuel Josef Margold, Dogobert Peche, Franz Delavilla, Milla Weltmann, and architects A.O. Holub and Hans Bolek. The firm was closed in 1931 and for a short time subsequently was taken over by Carius.

▶ From 1909, firm's work shown at Österreichisches Museum für Kunst und Industrie, Vienna; 1900 Paris 'Exposition Universelle'; from 1924 and Jubilee exhibition, Wiener Kunstgewerbeverein; 1925 Paris 'Exhibition Internationale des Arts Décoratifs et Industriels Modernes.' Firm received awards in Vienna, 1873

and 1931; Paris, 1879; Wels, 1884; Linz, 1885; and 1914 Darmstadt Artists' Colony exhibition, Vienna.

▶ Annelies Krekel-Aalberse, *Art Nouveau and Art Déco Silver*, New York: Abrams, 1989:253. Deanna F. Cera (ed.), *Jewels of Fantasy: Costume Jewelry of the 20th Century*, New York: Abrams, 1992:104.

Dietz, Matthias   (1957–)

▶ German designer; born and active Frankfurt am Main.
▶ 1977–80, studied ecology, Freie Universität, Berlin; 1980, Hochschule der Künste, Berlin; 1984, Hochschule für bildende Künste, Hamburg.
▶ Became known for lighting design.
▶ Participated in exhibitions 1983–84 'Bettens,' Gutterbahnhof Halensee, Berlin, and at Galerie Strand, Munich; 1984 'Kaufhaus des Ostens,' Berlin, Munich, and Hamburg; 1986 'Keine Ausstellung,' Galerie Strand, Munich; 1985 'Plastikwelten,' Elefantengalerie, Berlin.
▶ Christian Borngraeber, *Prototypen: Avantgarde Design uit/aus Berlin*, Rotterdam: Uitgeverij 010, 1986.

Diffloth, Émile   (1856–)

▶ French ceramicist; born Couleuvre.
▶ Studied École des Arts Décoratifs, Paris.
▶ In c1899, he worked at Kéramis, the Belgian pottery of Boch Frères, La Louvière, where he became artistic director; departing c1910, joined Taxile Doat in University City, Missouri, where he became a ceramics instructor at the School of Ceramic Art; returned to France; was a member of the Société des Artistes français.
▶ Received a gold medal at 1929 Salon of Société des Artistes français. Work shown at the Musée Galliéra, Paris.
▶ Yvonne Brunhammer et al., *Art Nouveau Belgium, France*, Houston: Rice University, 1976.

Diffrient, Niels   (1928–)

▶ American industrial designer; born Star, Mississippi; husband of textile designer Helena Hernmarck.
▶ Studied aeronautical engineering, Cass Technical High School, Detroit, Michigan, and Cranbrook Academy of Art, Bloomfield Hills, Michigan.
▶ He worked in the office of Marco Zanuso, Milan; worked on 1949 General Motors car; 1946–51, worked in the office of architect Eero Saarinen, Bloomfield Hills, Michigan; 1951–52, in the office of Walter B. Ford; and, 1952–81, in the office of Henry Dreyfuss where, in 1956, he became partner; in 1981, set up his own studio and designed chairs and office systems for Knoll and others. His 1984 *Helena* steel and leather office chair by Sunar-Hauserman exemplifies his interest in ergonomics. He designed the *Jefferson* chair for Sunar-Hauserman; (with Alvin R. Tilley) published books *Humanscale 1-2-3* (1974), *Humanscale 4-5-6* (1981), and *Humanscale 7-8-9* (1981).
▶ Eric Larrabee and Massimo Vignelli, *Knoll Design*, New York: Abrams 1981:56. Ann Lee Morgan, *Contemporary Designers*, London: Macmillan, 1984. Michael Kimmelman, 'Last of the Heroes: This Man should Redesign American Industry,' *Connoisseur*, Vol. 216, Aug. 1986:36–41.

Dillon, Jane   (1943–)

▶ British furniture and lighting designer; born Manchester.
▶ Studied interior design, Manchester Polytechnic, 1965, and Royal College of Art, London, 1968.
▶ 1968–69, she worked at Knoll International UK and under Ettore Sottsass at Olivetti on the *Synthesi 45* furniture system as a color consultant and graphic designer; 1971–72, worked at Conran; (with Charles Dillon) was consultant to Casas for office and domestic seating. From 1973, Jane and Charles Dillon were agents in Britain for Casas and ICF. From 1972–73, she designed lighting for Disform, Spain, including *Cometa* hanging lamp, and, 1977–78, for Habitat; from 1978–79, was consultant to Wolff Olins and, 1982–85, to Habitat/Mothercare; in the mid-1980s, (with Peter Wheeler and her studio partner Floris van den

Broecke) produced one-off furniture commissions for architects; from 1968, taught at Royal College of Art, London; 1971–73, at Middlesex Polytechnic; 1973–79, at Kingston Polytechnic; from 1985, at Glasgow School of Art and Parnham Trust, Dorset.
▶ From 1968, member, exhibition juror, and award recipient of Design Council, London.
▶ Liz McQuiston, *Women in Design: A Contemporary View*, New York: Rizzoli, 1988:36.

DIM   (Décoration Intérieure Moderne)
▶ French interior design firm; located Paris.
▶ DIM was established in 1914 by René Joubert and Georges Mouveau, rue Royale, Paris. Joubert had earlier worked for decorating firm Jansen and was the prime mover in DIM. Having previously been involved with stage design (particularly for the Paris Opéra), Mouveau left DIM in 1922 to return to this specialty. In 1923 (after a brief period in 1922 when Viénot was co-director), Pierre Petit joined the firm as a partner. Joubert and Petit, as the firm is sometimes referred to, carried out a wide range of commissions; designed furniture of the finest quality in the firm's workshop. Production included lighting, mirrors, furnishings, fabrics, carpeting and rugs, and they designed the interiors of airplanes. Their metal and wood furniture was installed on 1930 oceanliner *Atlantique*. Later located at 19 place de la Madeleine, the firm moved to 40 rue du Colisée in 1925; by 1930, had become one of the largest studio-galleries in Paris. In addition to Joubert's and Petit's own designs, a number of artists designed the firm's lamps, including Jacques Le Chevallier, Gabriel Guévrékian, Jean Prouvé, Leroy, Jean Lesage, Daniel Stéphan, and, in Murano, Venini. In 1931, when Joubert died, Petit left the firm; its activities continued through the 1940s.
▶ Boutique located on Alexandre III Bridge at 1925 Paris 'Exhibition Internationale des Arts Décoratifs et Industriels Modernes' where Joubert and Petit also designed the dining room in 'Une Ambassade française,' pavilion of Société des Artistes Décorateurs. 'Cafeteria in New York' shown at 1928 Salon d'Automne.
▶ Victor Arwas, *Art Déco*, Abrams, 1980. Pierre Kjellberg, *Art Déco: les maîtres du Mobilier, le décor des Paquebots*, Paris: Amateur, 1986:51–52.
▶ See Joubert, René and Petit, Philippe

DIMEA
▶ French decorating studio; located Paris.
▶ Active in the early 1920s, Pierre and Max Bloch established the decorating firm of both Modern and period interiors at 14 avenue Victor-Emmanuel-III, Paris. The firm designed soberly classical furniture.
▶ Work shown at 1925 Paris 'Exposition Internationale des Arts Décoratifs et Industriels Modernes.'
▶ Pierre Kjellberg, *Art Déco: les maîtres du Mobilier, le décor des Paquebots*, Paris: Amateur, 1986:52.

Dinand, Pierre-François   (1931–)
▶ French designer; active Paris.
▶ Studied architecture, École Nationale des Beaux-Arts, Paris.
▶ He designed over 150 perfume bottle ranges, beginning with his first 1961 *Madame Rochas* container and including 1968 *Calandre* for Paco Rabanne; 1970 *Givenchy III*, *Eau Sauvage* for Christian Dior, *Opium* for Yves Saint Laurent; 1984 *Obsession* for Calvin Klein; in 1987–88, was commissioned to design a bottle for *Tiffany* by Francesco Smalto to celebrate Tiffany's 50th anniversary; has workshops in Paris, New York, and Tokyo.

Dinh Van, Jean   (1927–)
▶ French jewelry designer.
▶ 1945–58, Dinh was an apprentice at Cartier, Paris; in 1965, set up his own workshop; in 1976 opened his own boutique on rue de la Paix, Paris; working in gold and silver, one of his first pieces was a ring made of extruded square gold mounted with an iron pearl; became known for his innovative, simple shapes.
▶ François Mathey, *Au bonheur des formes, design français 1945–1992*, Paris: Regard, 1992.

Dioptaz, Laurent   (1948–)
▶ French designer, sculptor, and film animator.
▶ Trained École Supérieure des Arts Appliqués, Paris.
▶ In 1970, he set up his own office, Paris; designed 1969 *Isotope Chair* produced and marketed by Zol, Paris, from 1970, in polyurethane foam covered in nylon jersey.
▶ Work shown at 1969 Salon of Société des Artistes Décorateurs and 1970 Terres des Hommes, Montreal. *Isotope Chair* introduced at 1970 'Sitzen '70,' Vienna, and shown at 1970 'Modern Chairs 1918–1970,' Whitechapel Gallery, London.
▶ Cat., *Modern Chairs 1918–1970*, London: Lund Humphries, 1971.

Dirks-Preiswerk, Gertrud   (1902–)
▶ Swiss textile designer; born Basel.
▶ 1926–30, trained in the weaving workshop, Bauhaus, Dessau, under Gunta Stölzl; 1929, summer course, Johanna Brunsons's Weaving School, Stockholm; studied operation of silk power looms at Vereinigte Seiden Webereien.
▶ She settled in Hildesheim; in 1931, (with Heinrich Otto Hürlimann and Gunta Stölzl) founded the firm SPH Stoffe, Zürich. Until 1933, SPH Stoffe collaborated with the Wohnbedarf department store, Zürich.
▶ Cat., Gunta Stölzl, *Weberei am Bauhaus und ans eigener Werkstatt*, Berlin: Bauhaus-Archiv, 1987:148. Friederike Mehlau-Wiebking et al., *Schweizer Typenmöbel 1925–35, Sigfried Giedion und die Wohnbedarf AG*, Zürich: gta, 1989:226. Sigrid Wortmann Weltge, *Women's Work: Textile Art from The Bauhaus*, London: Thames and Hudson, 1993.

Disantavittoria, Alex   (1942–)
▶ Italian lighting designer; active Milan.
▶ Disantavittoria began his professional career in 1967; became a member of ADI (Associazione per il Disegno Industriale); had clients in Italy for lighting including Interni Luci, Areliano Tosso, Illum, and Fratelli Martini.
▶ *ADI Annual 1976*, Milan: Associazione per il Disegno Industriale, 1976.

Disform
▶ Spanish furniture manufacturer.
▶ In 1969, Carlos Riera, a member of the Riera family, proprietors of the Metalarte lighting firm, set up his own firm to produce domestic objects. 'Disform' represents 'Diseño y Forma' ('design and form'). Riera subcontracted component work to four metal workshops and two woodworking shops and assembled the final models in his own factory, St. Just Desvern. The Disform line was exclusively contemporary, even during the economic crisis of the 1970s when some Spanish manufacturers reverted to conservative models. The firm began with a table-calendar by Carlos Riart and Bigas Luna, waste-paper bin by Alberto Udaeta, and seat by Cristianni, and imported clocks by Joe Colombo, Pio Manzù, and Richard Sapper from Alessi in Italy, and Charles and Jane Dillon's 1972 *Cometa* hanging light from Britain. In 1977, Disform produced its first furniture. Most of its designs were by non-Spanish artists, including Philippe Starck, who designed the 1983 *Chincheta* coffee table in sheet aluminum and 1983 *Jon Lld* MDF shelving. Much of the collection was sold in kit form. Spanish designers included Sergi Devesa, who designed for Metalarte.
▶ Work shown (with B.d Ediciones de Diseño) at 1982 Salone del Mobile, Milan and 1984. Received 1990 European Community Design Prize.
▶ Guy Julier, *New Spanish Design*, London: Thames and Hudson, 1991.

Dittert, Karl   (1915–)
▶ Austrian industrial designer; active Schwäbisch-Gmünd (Germany).
▶ Trained as a silversmith.
▶ In 1950, he set up his own industrial design studio, Schwäbisch-Gmünd, where he produced designs for a number of products from office furniture systems to domestic goods;

designed stainless-steel and silver objects, including 1960 nesting cooking set and burner produced by Kühn, 1966 *Classica* cutlery range by Felix Gloria-Werk, and 1981 food slicer by Ritter.
► Graham Hughes, *Modern Silver Throughout the World*, New York, 1967: Nos. 83–101. *Industrial Design*, Vol. 28, Nov.–Dec. 1981:23. Cat., Kathryn B. Hiesinger and George H. Marcus III (eds.), *Design Since 1945*, Philadelphia: Philadelphia Museum of Art, 1984.

Ditzel, Jørgen (1931–61)
► Danish designer.
► 1944, graduated from the Kunsthåndvaerkerskolen, Copenhagen.
► In 1939, he completed furniture-upholsterer apprenticeship; from 1946–61, was active in his own studio with Nanna Ditzel.
► Cat., *The Lunning Prize*, Stockholm: Nationalmuseum, 1986: 76–79.
► See Ditzel, Nanna

Ditzel, Nanna (1923–)
► Danish architect and furniture, metalwork, ceramic, and textile designer; born Copenhagen; active Copenhagen and London.
► 1945, Studied furniture school of Det Kongelige Dansk Kunstakademi, Copenhagen; 1946, Kunsthåndvaerkerskolen, Copenhagen.
► In 1946, she married Jørgen Ditzel, and they set up their own design studio and collaborated together until his death in 1961. They produced jewelry designs for A. Michelsen and Georg Jensen. They created the 1952 experimental modular furniture system. In the 1950s and 1960s, Ditzel designed simple furniture including some cane and basketwork chairs produced by Wengler, wooden models (including the 1955 baby's high chair) by Poul Kold, and upholstered seating by LCP. Furniture (Britain) and Invincible Cane Furniture (Britain). In 1952, they began a cooperation with fabric firm Unikavaev and furniture firm Halling Koch; published the book *Danish Chairs* (1954); from 1954, began a lifelong cooperation with Georg Jensen's. Den Permanente commissioned them to design the 1961 'Deense Woonkunst' exhibition in Amsterdam. In 1967, she became associated with design magazine *Mobilia* with Poul Henningsen, Hans Bendix, Ågård, and others; in 1968, settled in Britain. From 1970, her clients included Domus Danica, Georg Jensen, Scandus, Dunflex form furniture, and Poul Kold. She produced a range of wooden tableware for Den Permanente; in 1980, began a cooperation with Brdr. Krüger Traedrejeri; in 1981, became chair, Design and Industries Association; in 1986, set up a studio, Copenhagen; in 1988, developed a color scheme for Danish State Railway's new IC3 train for textiles and other interior colors. Her 1989 *Bench for Two* and 1991 *Butterfly* chair were produced by Fredericia Stølefabrik and 1990 *Hallingdal* textile range in 15 colors by Kvadrat.
► Ditzels' jewelry designs for Michelsen and Jensen won numerous awards, including 1950 first prize, Goldsmiths' Joint Council competition; 1950 Cabinetmakers' Guild competition; silver medals, 1951 (IX), 1954 (X), and 1957 (XI) Triennali di Milano and gold medal at its 1960 (XII) session; 1953 Good Design Award New York Museum of Art; 1956 Lunning Prize; 1990 gold medal, International Furniture Design Competition, Asahikawa (Japan). Work subject of 1963 one-person exhibition, New York. Their work shown at 1944 Cabinetmakers' Guild exhibition. Nanna Ditzel's work alone shown at 1965 exhibition (with children's book authors Ågård Andersen and Egon Mathiesen), Museum of Decorative Art, Copenhagen; 1972 exhibition, Lerchenborg Castle; 1980 to 1984, 1986–91 Cabinetmakers' Autumn Exhibition, Copenhagen; 1991 exhibition, Østbanen, Århus.
► Bent Salicath and Arne Karlsen (eds.), *Modern Danish Textiles*, Copenhagen, 1959:28–29. 'Nanna Ditzel: An Exhibition,' *Interiors*, Vol. 123, Dec. 1963:102–03. 'Thirty-four Lunning Prize-Winners,' *Mobilia*, No. 146, Sept. 1967. Cat., *Georg Jensen—Silversmiths: 77 Artists, 75 Years*, 1980: Nos. 25–29. Frederik Sieck, *Nutidig Dansk Møbeldesign:—en kortfattet illustreret beskrivelse*, Copenhagen: Bondo Gravesen; 1990 Busck edition in English.

Cat., David Revere McFadden (ed.), *Scandinavian Modern Design 1880–1980*, New York: Abrams, 1982:263. Cat., Kathryn B. Hiesinger and George H. Marcus III (eds.), *Design Since 1945*, Philadelphia: Philadelphia Museum of Art, 1983. Cat., *The Lunning Prize*, Stockholm: Nationalmuseum, 1986:76–79. Film on Nanna Ditzel's designs and working methods, produced by the Danish Ministry of Education and National Center for Educational Materials, 1991. Henrik Sten Møller (ed.), *Nanna Ditzel*, Munkeruphus, 1992.

Diulgheroff, Nicolay (1901–1982)
► Bulgarian painter; born Kustendil.
► Diulgheroff settled in Italy in the early 1920s and designed ceramics and furniture; in 1926 in Turin, became a member of the Italian Futurist movement active in developing new Futurist theories, including Aeropainting.
► Work shown at several major Futurist exhibitions until 1938, including at 1928 Venice Biennale.
► Auction cat., Christie's New York, Lot No. 428, 26 May 1983. Pontus Hulton (organizer) *Futurismo & Futurismi*, New York: Abbeville, 1986.

Dixon and Sons, James
► British silversmiths; located in Sheffield.
► In 1806, the firm James Dixon and Sons was founded; from 1879, produced designs by Christopher Dresser; published catalogues illustrating numerous examples of his designs; produced silver in Art Déco and Art Nouveau styles.
► Annelies Krekel-Aalberse, *Art Nouveau and Art Déco Silver*, New York: Abrams, 1989:253.

Dixon, Arthur S. (1865–1940)
See Birmingham Guild of Handicraft

Dixon, Harry St. John (1890–1967)
► American metalsmith; active San Francisco.
► Studied California School of Arts and Crafts, Oakland, California.
► In 1908, Dixon became an apprentice to Dirk Van Erp, working concurrently in Van Erp's establishment and other craft shops, San Francisco Bay Area; trained in Lillian Palmer's shop for five years; subsequently, worked in the shipyards; in 1916 Van Erp left his shop in the care of his daughter and Dixon; opening his own shop *c*1921, Dixon began stamping his pieces with a punchmark in the image of a man forging a bowl that had been designed by his painter brother. Major commissions included elevator doors of San Francisco Stock Exchange Club in the 1920s and, his last, the 48-inch (1.2 m) sundial in the shape of a lotus blossom, Burbank Memorial Garden, Santa Rosa, California.
► Cat., Ann Yaffe Phillips, *From Architecture to Object*, New York: Hirschl and Adler, 1989. Bonnie Mattison in Timothy J. Andersen et al., *California Design 1910*, Salt Lake City: Peregrine Smith, 1980:86.

Dixon, Tom (1959–)
► British sculptor and designer; born and active London.
► Studied Chelsea School of Art, London, 1978.
► In 1983, he completed his first interior design project; from 1983, began designing furniture using scrap metal; in 1984, learned to weld to repair his motorcycle and, subsequently, welded scrap metal on stage as performance art at the Titanic Club, which he established, leading to an exhibition and commission; in 1985, (with André Dubreuil) decorated Rococo Chocolats boutique; designed one-off furniture pieces and fixtures, including chandeliers. Work included 1986–87 chair made from found cast-iron pieces, 1986 organ-pipe screen of galvanized steel, welded-steel and glass table, and 1988 *Rush S* chair made of wound rubber strips and versions in other material. In 1987, he set up the production workshop Dixon PID.
► Work (1988 rush-steel chair) shown at 1989 'British Design,' Museum Boymans-van Beuningen, Rotterdam.

▶ Frederique Huygen, *British Design: Image and Identity*, London: Thames and Hudson, 1989:133–36. Cat., *Tom Dixon*, Paris: Galerie Yves Gastou, 1989. 'Tom Dixon,' *Maison française*, July–Aug. 1989. 'Tom Dixon, l'enfant terrible de la ferraille coudée,' *Beaux-Arts Magazine*, No. 709, July–Aug. 1989. Albrecht Bangert and Karl Michael Armer, *80s Style: Designs of the Decade*, New York: Abbeville, 1990:71, 90–91,229. Cat., *Acquisitions 1982–1990 arts décoratifs*, Paris: Fonds National d'Art Contemporain, 1991.

Djo-Bourgeois, É.-B.
See Bourgeois, Édouard-Joseph

Djo-bourgeois, Elise
See Bourgeois, Elise

Doat, Taxile Maxmilien   (1851–1938)
▶ French ceramicist; born Albi; active University City, Missouri.
▶ Studied Dubouché school of sculpture; École des Beaux-Arts, Paris, under Dumont.
▶ In 1877, he joined the Sèvres factory; in *c*1892, installed a kiln in his home, rue Bagneaux, studying clays and glazes for porcelain until 1899; built a wood kiln at Sèvres a year later; combined stoneware and porcelain in the same piece. His crystalline and metallic glazes applied to gourd-shaped vases were made *c*1900. His technical study 'Grand Feu Ceramics' first appeared in the journal *Keramic Studio* and in a 1905 book by Keramic Studio Publishing Co, Syracuse, New York, with a condensation appearing in the 1906 and 1907 issues of the magazine *Art et Décoration*. In 1909, the American Women's League invited him to build an art pottery; Doat became director of the School of Ceramic Art, University City, Missouri, with the first kiln functioning by 1910. For a time, University City was one of the most successful potteries in America. In 1915, when the establishment closed, Doat returned to France.
▶ Work shown at 1900 Paris 'Exposition Universelle.'
▶ Yvonne Brunhammer et al., *Art Nouveau Belgium, France*, Houston: Rice University, 1976.

Doblin, Jay   (1920–)
▶ American industrial designer and teacher.
▶ 1939–42, studied Pratt Institute, Brooklyn, New York.
▶ In the early 1950s, he worked in the industrial design office of Raymond Loewy, New York; 1964–72, was co-founder of Unimark, Chicago; in 1972, founded Jay Doblin and Associates; 1948–52, director industrial-design evening, Pratt Institute; 1955–78, taught and co-directed School of Design, Chicago.
▶ Ann Lee Morgan (ed.), *Contemporary Designers*, London: Macmillan, 1984. Penny Sparke, *Introduction to Design and Culture in the Twentieth Century*, Allen and Unwin, 1986.

Dobson, Frank   (1888–1963)
▶ British sculptor.
▶ Studied painting, City and Guilds Schools, Kennington, London.
▶ In the 1910s, he met Percy Wyndham Lewis; in 1920, joined the artists' organization Group X, of which he was the only sculptor member; in 1922, joined the London Group, of which he was president 1924–28; in 1930, rendered ceramic reliefs for Hays Wharf building; in the 1920s, produced resist (or batik) printed fabrics; in the early 1930s, designed painted-composition fashion mannequins; throughout the 1930s, designed silk-screened fabrics, often in abstract vegetal motifs, produced by Allan Walton Textiles and lino-printed fabrics produced by himself; designed the 1935 *Calix Majestatis* silver-gilt cup commissioned by Llewelyn Amos, director of the National Jewellers' Association, presented to King George V; in 1940, became a Government war artist; in 1942, was appointed Associate, Royal Academy, and, in 1953, RA; was an early member, Society of Industrial Artists (formed in 1930); 1946–53, was professor of sculpture, Royal College of Art, London.

▶ In 1914, work shown at Chenil Galleries, London, and, in 1921, at Leicester Galleries. His fashion mannequin shown at 1933 'British Industrial Art in Relation to the Home,' Dorland Hall, London.
▶ Cat., *Thirties: British art and design before the war*, London: Arts Council of Great Britain, Hayward Gallery, 1979:91,138, 143,145,168,231,232,288. Valerie Mendes, *The Victoria and Albert Museum's Textile Collection, British Textiles from 1900 to 1937*, London: Victoria and Albert Museum, 1992.

Doesburg, Theo van   (b. Christiaan Emil Marie Küpper 1883–1931)
▶ Dutch poet, painter, and architect; born Utrecht.
▶ Beginning as a painter in 1908, he held his first exhibition, The Hague; adopted the principles of Vasalii Kandinskii in 1912; in 1915, planned a journal with fellow Dutch artist Piet Mondriaan to disseminate ideas of Neo-plasticism, which resulted in his first pictures in the Neo-plastic approach. In an effort to transfer his two-dimensional art into architecture, he collaborated with J.J.P. Oud and Jan Wils; in 1916, (with Oud) founded the artists' group Sphinx, Leiden, shut down in 1917; in 1917, formed the magazine *De Stijl*, resulting in the formation of the group of artists and architects of the same name seeking a 'radical renewal of art'; became the group's spokesperson. He became known for the use of primary colors, geometric stained-glass windows, and tiled floors. A distinctive example of his stained glass was illustrated by his *Composition IV* triptych window (executed by Vennootschap Crabeth of The Hague) installed in the 1917 Jan Wils townhouse, Alkmaar. He designed the 1917 hallway of the Oud residence, Noordwijkerhout, near Leiden, where he used painting to emphasize the structural elements of the architecture; in 1922, traveled to Berlin and Weimar, expounding the ideas of De Stijl to students at the Bauhaus. The Bauhaus included his book on art principles in the sixth of its 'Bauhausbücher' series, entitled *Grundbegriffe der bildenden Kunst* (1924). He developed contacts with artists El Lissitzky and László Moholy-Nagy, resulting in issues of *De Stijl* in 1922 on Suprematism and Lissitzky. His emphasis on the importance of fine art over architecture was attacked in the 1920s, resulting in his alienation from Oud. In 1922, the first exhibition of architectural designs of the De Stijl group was shown, and, in 1923, van Doesburg collaborated with Cornelis van Eesteren and Geritt Rietveld on models and architectural drawings for the De Stijl architecture exhibition, Léonce Rosenberg's Galerie l'Effort Moderne, Paris; this was the beginning of the organization's 'international phase' and a pronounced change in its membership, which led to Mondrian's withdrawal in 1925. Van Doesburg designed 1926–28 interior renovation (with Hans Arp), Café l'Aubette, Strasbourg; as the antithesis of the ideas of De Stijl, designed his own 1929–30 residence, Meudon-Val-Fleury; moved to Paris, built his own 1930–31 studio; having worked with Cor van Eesteren since the 1920s, (with van Eesteren) became active in town planning, applying the principles of De Stijl; published *De Nieuwe Beweging in de Schilderkunst* (1917), *Drie voordrachten over de nieuwe bildende Kunst* (1919), *Grondbegrippen der beeldenden Kunt* (1919), *Klassiek, borok, modern* (1920). De Stijl ended with van Doesburg's death.
▶ Work subject of 1947 exhibition, New York; 1968 exhibition, Eindhoven; 1989 exhibition, Museum Boymans-van Beuningen, Rotterdam.
▶ James Johnson Sweeney (ed.), *Theo van Doesburg*, New York, 1947. H.L.C. Jaffé, *de Stijl—1917–1931: The Dutch Contribution to Modern Art*, Amsterdam, 1956. Cat., *Theo van Doesburg 1883–1931*, Eindhoven, 1968. Joost Balieu, *Theo van Doesburg*, London, 1974. Jacob Johannes Vriend in Vittorio Magnago Lampugnani (ed.), *Encyclopedia of 20th-Century Design*, New York: Abrams: 1986:83–84. Jonathan M. Woodham, *Twentieth-Century Ornament*, New York: Rizzoli, 1990:111,112,114,129,130.

Dohner, Donald R.   (1907–44)
▶ American industrial designer; born Indiana; active East Pittsburgh, Pennsylvania.

▶ Dohner was a teacher of design, Carnegie Institute of Technology; 1927–30, was consultant to Westinghouse, East Pittsburgh, Pennsylvania; turning down offers to work at Marshall Field and Carson Pirie Scott, was director of art, engineering department, Westinghouse 1930–34, designing 128 products ranging from micarta ashtrays and vacuum cleaners to mechanical water coolers, electric ranges, and diesel-electric locomotives, including a stubby-silhouette locomotive he had painted to appear longer and more elegant. Intended as a stand at an exposition, the locomotive sold right off the exhibit floor.
▶ *Fortune*, Feb. 1934:90.

Domin, André (1883–1962)
See Dominique

Domingo, Alain (1952–)
▶ French designer; active Paris.
▶ Studied architecture to 1979.
▶ Domingo collaborated with François Scali under the name of Nemo, the design firm they established in 1982; were best known for their furniture designs for Science Museum, Parc de la Villette, Paris; produced carpets for Géométrie Variable and Élisée Éditions, graphic design for MBK and Motobécane, pasta shapes for Panzani, and packaging for Lesieur; designed furniture and furnishings for their own firm Tébong, Paris; 1982 *Faizzz* chair by Nemo Édition; 1985 computer screen; 1984 *Mediabolo* chair by Nemo Édition; 1984 print lamp by Formica and 1983 *Marini* and *Moreno* chairs by Nemo Édition. In Paris, they won design competitions including those sponsored by VIA and Le Mobilier National in 1983, the French minister of culture for a lamp in 1984 produced by Mégalit, public furniture for the park of La Villette in 1985, the layout of and furniture for the entrance hall of the offices of the Casse Nationale des Monuments Historiques et des Sites in the Hôtel de Sully, Paris, in 1986, and, with François Scali, the *Génitron* clock (counting down seconds to year 2000) in front of Centre Georges Pompidou for its 10th anniversary.
▶ Juli Capella and Quim Larrea, *Designed by Architects in the 1980s*, New York: Rizzoli, 1988. Cat., *Design français, 1960–1990: Trois décennies*, Paris: Centre Georges Pompidou/APCI, 1988. Cat., Catherine Arminjon et al., *L'Art de Vivre: Decorative Arts and Design in France 1789–1989*, New York: Vendome, 1989:40. Cat., *Les années VIA, 1980–1990*, Paris: Musée des Arts Décoratifs, 1990. Cat., *Acquisitions 1982–1990 arts décoratifs*, Paris: Fonds National d'Art Contemporain, 1991. François Mathey, *Au bonheur des formes, design français 1945–1993*, Paris: Regard, 1992.

Dominick and Haff
▶ American silversmiths; located New York.
▶ The firm of William Gale and Son was established in New York in 1821, changing its name to Gale, North and Dominick in 1868, when Henry Blanchard Dominick joined the firm. In 1867, Leroy B. Haff began working in its retail department; in 1870, became a partner, when firm's name was changed to Gale, Dominick and Haff at 451 Broome Street. In 1871, it moved to Bond Street; 1893–1904, was located at 860 Broadway, moving to various other addresses in the 1920s. Its customers included Bailey, Banks and Biddle, the jewelry and silver store in Philadelphia. Dominick and Haff was known for its high standards of craftsmanship; in c1880, acquired the silverware tools and patterns of Adams and Shaw, silver and silverplate manufacturers, when it was bought by Tiffany; in c1926, bought the McChesney Company, Newark, New Jersey; when H.B. Dominick died in 1928, was purchased by Reed and Barton, Taunton, Massachusetts.
▶ 'H.B. Dominick,' *The New York Times*, Dec. 24, 1928:13. Doreen Bolger Burke et al., *In Pursuit of Beauty: Americans and the Aesthetic Movement*, New York: Metropolitan Museum of Art and Rizzoli, 1986:421.

Dominioni, Luigi Caccia
See Caccia Cominioni, Luigi

Dominique
▶ French interior designers; located Paris.
▶ In 1922, André Domin (1883–1962) and Marcel Geneviève (1885–1967) founded the decorating firm Dominique at 104 rue du Faubourg Saint-Honoré, Paris, whose slogan was 'Delivery from the nightmare of the ancient' (*Délivré du cauchemar de l'ancien*). (Domin had been a journalist and art critic for journals including *Comœdia, Gil Blas*, and *L'Intransigeant*.) Their furniture was moderately priced but nevertheless elegant in exotic woods, inlaid brass and mother-of-pearl, fitted with gilt bronze, and with applied carved relief motifs. c1925–35, they frequently incorporated shagreen into their pieces; used fabrics by Hélène Henry and Raoul Dufy produced by Bianchini-Férier. They designed and furnished Jean Puiforcat's villa, Biarritz, in the so-called Parisian style of Gothic-Renaissance, and offices of the Houbigant perfume factory, Neuilly. Their furniture was produced in luxurious materials: amaranth, ebony, palissandre, shagreen, and parchment. Their door handles and silvered bronze plaques were produced by Puiforcat. In 1926, they formed Groupe des Cinq with Pierre Chareau, Pierre Legrain, Jean Puiforcat, and Raymond Templier, exhibiting in 1926 at Galerie Barbazanges. In 1929, Domin and Geneviève moved the design office and store to 29 avenue Kléber, Paris; about this time, began incorporating metal into their work in a limited manner; in 1933, began collaborating with Compagnie Générale Transatlantique on its oceanliners, furnishing four apartments on the 1935 *Normandie*. Domin was also a graphic designer of advertisements, posters, brochures, books and periodicals. In c1926, they began to design in a more rigorous Cubist manner, yet producing robust forms in the tradition of Jacques-Émile Ruhlmann; in 1929, moved to 104 rue du Faubourg Saint-Honoré, Paris; after World War II, designed some furniture for the Palais de l'Élysée. Until 1970, Dominique operated under the management of Alain Domin, elder son of André Domin.
▶ Work shown at Salon d'Automne from 1922 and Salons of the Société des Artistes Décorateurs. Small salon of private apartments shown in 'Une Ambassade française' pavilion, Société des Artistes Décorateurs, 1925 Paris 'Exposition Internationale des Arts Décoratifs et Industriels Modernes' and collaborated in other sections: musical instruments, Arts de la Rue, boutique of Maneaux Salf, and at 1935 'Exposition Universelle et Internationale de Bruxelles.'
▶ *Ensembles Mobiliers*, Paris: Charles Moreau, No. 17, 1954. Alastair Duncan, *Art Nouveau and Art Déco Lighting*, New York: Simon and Schuster, 1978:168. Victor Arwas, *Art Déco*, Abrams, 1980. Pierre Kjellberg, *Art Déco: les maîtres du Mobilier, le décor des Paquebots*, Paris: Amateur, 1986:55–58,79. Patricia Bayer, *Art Deco Interiors: Decoration and Design Classics of the 1920s and 1930s*, London: Thames and Hudson, 1990.

Domus Academy
▶ Italian design institution; located Milan.
▶ The Domus Academy was founded in 1982 by Maria Grazia Mazzocchi, Valerio Castelli, and Alessandro Guerriero. With Andrea Branzi as its first director, it offered the first post-graduate course in so-called New Design. Covering a range of subjects from socio-economic forecasting to industrial technology, its instructors included Branzi, Carlo Alfonsi, Valerio Castelli, Michele de Lucchi, Gian Franco Ferrè, Enzio Manzini, Alberto Meda, Francesco Morace, Gianni Pettena, Daniela Puppa, and Pierre Restany.
▶ Andrea Branzi, *La Casa Calda: Esperienze del Nuovo Disegno Italiano*, Milan: Idea Books, 1982.

Donald Brothers
▶ British fabric manufacturer; located Dundee.
▶ In the 1930s, its designers included P.A. Staynes, Marion Dorn, and E. Dean. It was described as a manufacturer of 'Old Glamis Fabrics' and listed its specialties as art canvas, art linens, and decorative fabrics; became known for high-quality linen upholstery fabric, as well as cotton and jute in natural colors. Often seen on cube chairs by Arundell Clarke, its *Festoon* pattern was a best seller. The firm was able to screenprint fabrics in a quality equal to its woven goods.

▶ Cat., *Thirties: British art and design before the war*, London: Arts Council of Great Britain, Hayward Gallery, 1979:90,91,144,145. Valerie Mendes, *The Victoria and Albert Museum's Textile Collection, British Textiles from 1900 to 1937*, London: Victoria and Albert Museum, 1992.

Donaldson, Douglas   (1882–1972)
▶ American metalworker; born Detroit; active Los Angeles.
▶ Donaldson taught design, metalwork and jewelry at numerous schools in and near Los Angeles, including his first position, director of manual arts, Throop Polytechnic (succeeded by Rudolph Schaeffer); subsequently, was a teacher, new Chouinard School of Art, and head, art department, Los Angeles Manual Arts High School; after teaching at Otis Art Institute, established his own School of Decorative Design, Hollywood, California, in the 1920s; (with his wife) established a decorative arts guild, showing distinctive crafts gathered nationwide; in 1925, was elected first vice-president of the newly organized Arts and Crafts Society of Southern California; associated with Arts and Crafts movement artisans, including Ernest Batchelder, James Winn, Ralph Johonnot, and Rudolph Schaeffer; emphasized to his students that 'the conception of beautiful ideas must lead the way — the technical processes simply being the words which compose the language of art.'
▶ Bonnie Mattison in Timothy J. Andersen et al., *California Design 1910*, Salt Lake City: Peregrine Smith, 1980:86.

Donner, Marina   (1958–)
▶ Industrial designer; born and active Berlin.
▶ 1978–84, studied industrial design, Hochschule der Künste, Berlin.
▶ From 1984, she was an independent consultant designer; in 1986, (with Heidemarie Kunert) set up the Amazonas Design studio, Berlin; designed electronic and scientific equipment, toys, exhibitions, and corporate identity programs.
▶ Work included 1987 and 1988 traveling exhibition 'Berlin Ways — Products and Design from Berlin' in Berlin, Zürich, Stockholm, and Barcelona. Received 1988 Mia Seeger Preis, Stuttgart.
▶ Cat., Design Center Stuttgart, *Women in Design: Careers and Life Histories Since 1900*, Stuttgart: Haus der Wirtschaft, 1989:60–61.

Donzelli, Rinaldo   (1921–)
▶ Italian designer; born and active Mariano Comense.
▶ 1935–40, he carved furniture; 1946–50, was a painter, decorator, scenic designer, designer of advertising, and exhibition designer at RIMA Palazzo dell'Arte, Milan, including stands for tourism and manufacturers of furniture, toys, automobile-bodies, radios, bicycles, and motorcycles; 1950–64, was a graphic and industrial designer, Moto Gilera; 1957–66, was a staff member, Biennale dello Standard nell'Arredamento, Mariano Comense; 1965–72, was a graphic and industrial designer, Moto Guzzi; from 1972, pursued research; became a member of ADI (Associazione per il Disegno Industriale).
▶ *ADI Annual 1976*, Milan: Associazione per il Disegno Industriale, 1976.

Doolittle, Harold L.
▶ American mechanical engineer, designer, photographer, and artist; active Pasadena, California.
▶ Studied Throop Polytechnic, Pasadena, California.
▶ A mechanical engineer by profession, he experimented with color photography on imported French plates in the early 1920s; in the late 1910s and early 1920s, made movies; was later interested in printing, including lithographs, etchings, mezzotints, and aquatints; produced furniture in the Arts and Crafts aesthetic.
▶ Timothy J. Andersen et al., *California Design 1910*, Salt Lake City: Peregrine Smith, 1980:120–21.

Dordoni, Rudolfo   (1954–)
▶ Italian consultant designer; born and active Milan.
▶ Studied architecture, Politecnico di Milano, to 1979.

▶ Active for a time in architects' offices, he began working in industrial design; from 1979–89, he was artistic director of Cappellini International Interiors and in charge of corporate image and communications; from 1982, he was consultant designer for several firms on pavilions, shops, and exhibition stands; had clients for furniture and lighting including Moroso, Barovier & Toso, Bassani Ticino, Realizza, Capellini, Fontana Arte, and Vistosi.
▶ Fumio Shimizu and Matteo Thun (eds.), *The Descendants of Leonardo: The Italian Design*, Tokyo, 1987:325. *Modo*, No. 148, March–April 1993:119.

Dorfles, Gillo
▶ Italian teacher, design activist, and theorist; born Trieste; active Milan.
▶ In 1948, with Soldatai, Monnet, and Munari, he was a founder of MAC (Movimento Arte Concreta). In 1956, he became a member of ADI (Associazione per il Disegno Industriale), of which he was promotion committee member; was a professor of aesthetics, Università di Trieste; was on the committee of 1955 industrial design exhibition, London; was a member of the international industrial design stand, 1957 (XI) Triennale di Milano; of the jury at 'BIO' Industrial Design Biennale, Ljubljana; of the jury at the event in Jablonec (now Czech Republic); commissioner of the industrial stand at 1960 (XII) Triennale di Milano; delegate at 1957 'Journée de l'Ésthetique Industrielle,' Paris; speaker at ICSID (International Congress of Industrial Designers), London; speaker at industrial section, 1957 Congresso dell'Aica, Naples. Dorfles participated in the congress, 1954 (X) Triennale di Milano; 1957 meeting of CIAM (Congrès Internationaux d'Architecture Moderne) in Venice; and in 1961–62 events at Instituto Disegno Industriale, Florence; Italian Institute, London; in 1963, Kunstgewerbemuseum, Zürich. He published books *Il Disegno Industriale e la sua estetica* (1963) and *Introduzione al Disegno Industriale* (1971); was one of the first to observe the kitsch in decoration and design, publishing *Kitsch* (1968).
▶ *ADI Annual 1976*, Milan: Associazione per il Disegno Industriale, 1976.

Dorman, Nicholas   (1961–)
▶ British industrial designer.
▶ Studied Polytechnic of the South Bank, London.
▶ He was a designer at the industrial design firm Moggeridge Associates, London.
▶ Albrecht Bangert and Karl Michael Armer, *80s Style: Designs of the Decade*, New York: Abbeville, 1990:210,229.

Dorn, Marion Victoria   (1899–1964)
▶ American fabric and carpet designer; born San Francisco; active London; wife of E. McKnight Kauffer.
▶ 1914–16, studied Stanford University, California.
▶ She worked in Paris 1921–25 and in New York 1925–40; settled in London with her future husband E. McKnight Kauffer; began to design and produce a variety of resist (batik) printed textiles and was commissioned to design exclusive soft furnishings, including one-off batiks for interiors, such as Matisse-like patterns for curtains; influenced by Cubist painters in Paris, was a prolific designer of carpets and textiles in Modernist abstract motifs for public places, including hotels Savoy in 1933–35, Claridges in 1932, and Berkeley, all London, and oceanliners including *Orion*, *Orcades*, and 1934 *Queen Mary*. Illustrated William Beckford's *Vathek* (1929); (with Kauffer) designed carpets produced by Wilton Royal Carpet Factory; by the mid-1930s, was the best-known carpet designer in Britain and recognized as a leading textile designer, with clients including Warner; Donald Brothers, Dundee; Old Bleach Linen, Randalstown; Alastair Morton's Edinburgh Weavers, Carlisle. A white carpet by Dorn appeared in Syrie Maugham's all-white 1933 living room, London. In 1934, Dorn set up a shop at 10 Lancashire Court, New Bond Street, London, and diversified into weaving; continued her textile practice from 1940 in New York; commissioned to design carpets

for the diplomatic lounge, White House, Washington; 1962–64, was active in a studio in Tangier.

▶ Work included in major decorative and industrial art exhibitions in the 1930s, including 1931 rug exhibition, Curtis Moffat Gallery, London, organized by *Vogue* editor Mage Garland, and 1979–80 'Thirties' exhibition, Hayward Gallery, London.

▶ Cat., *Thirties: British art and design before the war*, London: Arts Council of Great Britain, Hayward Gallery, 1979:74,87, 88,90,91,145,146,222,288,296.

Dorner, Marie-Christine (1960–)
▶ French furniture and interior designer; born Strasbourg.
▶ 1979–84, studied École Camondo, Paris.
▶ From 1984, she worked in Paris for Patrick and Daniel Rubin at Atelier d'Architecture Intérieure Canal and, until 1985, for Jean-Michel Wilmotte; in 1986, settled in Tokyo, where she designed a 13-piece collection of furniture based on origami forms produced by Idée, and interiors for a Tokyo clothing boutique and a restaurant in Yokohama; in 1987, designed a coffee table and armchair produced by Cassina and two shops and a café for Komatsu in Tokyo; in 1987, returned to Paris where she set up her own design office with clients including Cassina, Scarabat, Baccarat, Bernardaud, Élisée Éditions, and Artelano; designed 1988 *Asap* television table by Artelano, 1988 *Dede* illuminated console by Scarabat, furniture for the Au Printemps department store, Paris, and tableware, graphics, and interiors for others. In 1988, she designed the hotel La Villa near St.-Germaine des Près; 1989 furniture for the Comédie française cafeteria commissioned by the French Ministry of Culture; and 1991 *Dorner* porcelain dinnerware produced by Bernardaud.
▶ She won first prize in the 1985 design competition sponsored by Fondation des Galeries Lafayette for her table design. Idée furniture range shown in 1987 and subsequently at Axis Gallery, Tokyo; Cassina, Paris; New York; 'The Most Contemporary French Furniture,' London.
▶ Cat. Margo Rouard Snowman, *The Most Contemporary French Furniture*, London: Victoria and Albert Museum, 1988. Cat., Design Center Stuttgart, *Women in Design: Careers and Life Histories Since 1900*, Stuttgart: Haus der Wirtschaft, 1989:244–47. Albrecht Bangert and Karl Michael Armer, *80s Style: Designs of the Decade*, New York: Abbeville, 1990:109,229. François Mathey, *Au bonheur des formes, design français 1945–1992*, Paris: Regard, 1992.

Dossena, Leonardo Mario (1945–)
▶ Italian ceramicist; born and active Milan.
▶ He began his professional career in 1969; was best known for his architectonic ceramics for clients in Italy including Ceramica Mauri, Lorioseta, and Curcio Ceramiche Moderne; studied residential building components in Studio Valenti G. Paolo; became a member of ADI (Associazione per il Disegno Industriale).
▶ *ADI Annual 1976*, Milan: Associazione per il Disegno Industriale, 1976.

Dottori, Arduino (1946–)
▶ Italian industrial and graphic designer; born Cupra Montana; active Milan.
▶ Studied Instituto Statale d'Arte, Ancona; 1966–70, Corso Superiore di Disegno Industriale, Florence.
▶ He settled in Milan where, in 1971, he began his professional career in his own studio, designing objects for industry, furniture, and interiors; at the same time, was graphic designer to a pharmaceutical firm; in 1973, (with industrial designers Enrico Picciani and Roberto Ingegnere) set up studio ERA. Clients included Feraboli (agricultural machinery and corporate identity), Ama (agricultural machinery), Elektrolume (electrical appliances), Torelli (corporate identity and packaging), Panunion (graphic design), Teomr (electronic control systems), and Evoluzione (an interior design program for small apartments worldwide). From 1973, he was primarily occupied with industrial design; became a member of ADI (Associazione per il Disegno Industriale).

▶ *ADI Annual 1976*, Milan: Associazione per il Disegno Industriale, 1976.

Doucet, Jacques (1853–1929)
▶ French couturier and art collector; active Paris.
▶ Doucet amassed an impressive collection of 18th-century art and furniture between 1896 and 1910; in 1912, auctioned the entire collection, raising a record $3 million, and turned to 19th- and 20th-century art, furniture, and furnishings; collected paintings by Cézanne, Van Gogh, Monet, Sisley, Degas, and Manet; owned Picasso's *Les Demoiselles d'Avignon* (purchased in 1920) and *La Charmeuse de serpents* by Henri Rousseau. He commissioned furniture and furnishings by Pierre Legrain, Eileen Gray, Rose Adler, Paul Iribe, Marcel Coard, Jean-Charles Moreux, and others. He bought Gustav Miklos sculpture, carpets, and door handles; René Lalique glass doors, Degaine lacquerwork and enamels, Jean Lurçat rugs, Joseph Hecht lacquered panels, and Étienne Cournault decorated mirrors; met Miklos at 1919 Salon des Indépendants, Adler at École des Arts Décoratifs in 1923, and Lurçat at 1925 Paris 'Exposition Internationale des Arts Décoratifs et Industriels Modernes.' On the advice of André Breton, he purchased works by Francis Picabia, Joan Miró, Max Ernst, and André Masson. Architect Paul Ruaud built the 1926 *studio-moderne* annex in the courtyard of the house, rue Saint-James, Neuilly, near Paris, that Doucet's wife owned. Doucet had an apartment at 43 avenue du Bois (today avenue Foch), Paris; founded the Doucet Bibliothèque and Institut d'Historie de l'Art et d'Archéologie. Doucet's Art Déco collection remained intact following his death in 1929 until 1972, when it was auctioned at another sensational sale at Galerie Drouot, Paris.
▶ François Chapon, *Mystère et splendeurs de Jacques Doucet 1853–1929*, Paris: Lattès, 1984. Pierre Cabanne, *Encyclopédie Art Déco*, Paris: Somogy, 1986:187–89.

Doumergue, Louis
▶ French decorator and furniture designer; born Montpellier.
▶ Doumergue's furniture was ornate and classical, rendered in exotic woods and ivory.
▶ 1921–28, work shown at Salons of Société des Artistes Décorateurs (including a dining-room suite with A. Bourgeaud at the 1921 session) and at several sessions of Salon d'Automne.
▶ Pierre Kjellberg, *Art Déco: les maîtres du Mobilier, le décor des Paquebots*, Paris: Amateur, 1986:58. Léon Deshairs, *Modern French Decorative Art*, Paris: Albert Lévy.

Dourgnon, Jean (1901–85)
▶ French lighting designer and engineer.
▶ Studied École Supérieure d'Électricité, Paris, to 1923.
▶ In 1928, he began extensive research into lighting; in 1930, founded the Association française de l'Éclairage, which participated with architects Robert Mallet-Stevens and Georges-Henri Pingusson, designers René Herbst and Pierre Chareau, and lighting engineer André Salomon; in 1947, became its president; in 1930, became a member of UAM (Union des Artistes Modernes).
▶ Participated with UAM group from its 1930 (I) exhibition and presented dramatic lighting effects in its 1932 and 1935 events; (with André Sive) in UAM pavilion, 1937 Paris 'Exposition Internationale des Arts et Techniques dans la Vie Moderne.' Designed the vast vertical illuminated area (with Mallet-Stevens, and Salomon) at 1935 Salon de la Lumière. Was in charge of lighting and photographic sections, 1949 (I) 'Formes Utiles' exhibition of UAM. Participated in the preparation of the lighting, 1953 'Formes Utiles.'
▶ Jean Dourgnon, 'Confort, Lumière et Architecture,' *Cahiers du CSTB*, No. 492. Bernard Barraqué, *L'Éclairagisme entre art et science, Jean Dourgnon (1901–1985)*, Institut d'Urbanisme de Paris, 1986. Arlette Barré-Despond, *UAM*, Paris: Regard, 1986. Cat., *Les années UAM 1929–1958*, Paris: Musée des Arts Décoratifs, 1988:174–75.

Dovecot Studios
See Edinburgh Tapestry Company (Dovecot Studios)

Dózsa-Farkas, Kinga (1943–)
▶ Hungarian industrial designer; born Budapest.
▶ 1964–68, studied product design, Hochschule für Gestaltung, Ulm.
▶ In 1964, she settled in Germany; in 1968, married Andreas Dózsa-Farkas and, from 1970, was a freelance designer in the dózsa-farkas (sic) design team, Munich. Work included 1974 *Zitrosine* citrus fruit press by Buchsteiner, 1976 storage shelf by Buchsteiner, 1987 *argoflex 44* office-chair range by Albert Stoll Argoflex, 1987 parking system by Skidata Computerhandelsgesellschaft, 1988 control console system for washing installations by H. Kleindienst, and 1988 *Gass-Center* stove by Wamsler Herd und Ofen.
▶ Traffic lights (designed as a student in Ulm) shown at 1967 Montreal 'Universal and International Exhibition (Expo '67).'
▶ Cat., Design Center Stuttgart, *Women in Design: Careers and Life Histories Since 1900*, Stuttgart: Haus der Wirtschaft, 1989:104–09.

Dragsted, A.
▶ Danish silversmiths; located Copenhagen (Denmark).
▶ The firm A. Dragsted was founded in 1854; in 1913, produced some of the silver designs of Johan Rohde.
▶ Work (silver in contemporary Danish motifs and Viking-revival style) shown at 1910 Brussels Exhibition.
▶ Annelies Krekel-Aalberse, *Art Nouveau and Art Déco Silver*, New York: Abrams, 1989:217,253.

Draper, Dorothy (b. Dorothy Tuckerman 1889–1969)
▶ American interior designer; born Tuxedo Park, New York.
▶ After World War I, she initially became known through the renovation of her own house, Upper East Side Manhattan; owned a house, Tuxedo Park, New York, where she designed numerous houses; in 1925, established Architectural Clearing House, matching architects to appropriate commissions; in 1929, designed Carlyle Hotel public areas, 35 East 76th Street, New York, in a so-called 'Roman Deco' style. Her oversized, loudly spoken décors appeared in commissions that followed, including apartment buildings, restaurants, hotels, and department stores; established a reputation for hotels and restaurants with her décor for the Greenbriar resort, White Sulphur Springs, West Virginia, and, in 1935–36, the Hampshire House, Central Park South, New York City, whose cabbage-rose chintz became a highly popular Schumacher fabric; the vibrant scarlet doors with white frames and black exterior walls became a fashionable design appurtenance. She designed 1935 interiors, the Mark Hopkins Hotel, San Francisco; 1940. The Camellia House in Drake Hotel, Chicago; 1944 interiors, Quitandinha resort, Petrópolis (near Rio de Janeiro), Brazil; public and private rooms, Statler Hotel chain in the late 1930s and 1940s; 1954 the Roman-inspired restaurant of the Metropolitan Museum of Art, New York. A well-known personality, she wrote books, appeared on her own radio program, and produced a regular column for *Good Housekeeping* magazine during World War II and was director of the magazine's Studio of Living. She pioneered the picture window, white organdy curtains, and chenille bedspreads; in her interior design, incorporated dark, bold colors; used outsized fabric motifs, wide moldings, and large black-and-white marble floor tiles. Much of the furniture and textiles in America of the 1940s and 1950s were designed or inspired by Dorothy Draper. Designs included 1947 *Brazilance* and *Scatter Floral* fabrics for Schumacher and 1940s *Stylized Scroll* for Waverly. In 1960, she sold her business.
▶ Carelton Varney, *The Draper Touch*, New York, 1988. John Esten and Rose Bennett Gilbert, *Manhattan Style*, Boston: Little, Brown, 1990:9. Mitchell Owens, 'Larger than Life,' *Elle Decor*, September 1990:54–56. Mark Hampton, *The Legendary Decorators of the Twentieth Century*, New York: Doubleday, 1992.

Draper, Elisabeth (b. Elisabeth Carrington Frank 1900–93)
▶ American interior designer; born and active New York.

▶ Attended Spence School, leaving in 1918 before graduation; self-taught designer.
▶ She trained as a radio operator in World War I; established (with sister Tiffany Taylor) decorating firm Taylor & Low, New York; in 1936, established her own decorating firm under her own name; became one of the *grandes dames* of decorating when the discipline was dominated by women; decorated numerous country houses, city apartments, houses, and executive suites in banks, including house in Gettysburg, Pennsylvania, and the New York home of US President Dwight D. and Mamie Eisenhower; 1832 Seabury Tredwell residence (today Old Merchant's House) restoration, New York; USA Embassy, Paris for Ambassador Amory Houghton.
▶ Suzanne Slesin, 'Elisabeth Draper, Grande Dame of Interior Design, Is Dead at 93,' *The New York Times*, 8 July 1993:D19.

Dreier, Hans (1885–1966)
▶ German film set designer; born Bremen; active Germany and USA.
▶ Trained as an architect, Dreier worked 1919–23 at the UFA/EFA film studio, Berlin. Settling in the USA in 1923 at the invitation of Ernst Lubitsch, was art director 1923–28 and head of the design department 1928–51 at Paramount, Hollywood; brought the Bauhaus approach of team effort to his work there, willingly sharing screen credits with the art directors under his supervision, particularly from 1932; was the first supervising art director regularly to visit and look for new talent at design and architecture schools; strongly influenced by Modernism, designed films for Lubitsch productions including *Monte Carlo* (1930), *One Hour with You* (1932), and *Trouble in Paradise* (1932). Bauhaus furniture from Dreier's own residence was included in *Trouble in Paradise*, a high point in 1930s film design; the nickel-plated casement clock and hanging light fixture over the dining table are noteworthy. Every element in a Dreier-supervised film was fastidiously planned and coordinated; the canal water in *Top Hat* (1935), with white marble Art Déco Venetian architecture above, was tinted black.
▶ Received Academy Awards for *Frenchman's Creek* (1944), *Samson and Delilah* (1949), and *Sunset Boulevard* (1950).
▶ Ann Lee Morgan (ed.) *Contemporary Designers*, London: Macmillan, 1984. Howard Mandelbaun and Eric Myers, *Screen Deco: A Celebration of High Style in Hollywood*, New York: St. Martin's, 1985.

Drésa (aka André Saglio)
▶ French painter and decorator.
▶ Drésa designed for the Paris Opéra and other theatres, and fabrics and wallpapers for André Groult, DIM (Décoration Intérieure Moderne), and others; wrote on the arts in a number of books.
▶ Victor Arwas, *Art Déco*, Abrams, 1980. Léon Deshairs, *Modern French Decorative Art*, Paris: Albert Lévy.

Dresser, Christopher (1834–1904)
▶ British botanist, metalworker, ceramicist, and glass and industrial designer; born Glasgow.
▶ 1847–53, studied School of Design of Somerset House, London, and under botanist John Lindley.
▶ In 1852 he attended Owen Jones's lectures 'On the True and False in the Decorative Arts,' a prelude to Jones's 1856 work *The Grammar of Ornament* for which Dresser illustrated ten plates that showed designs from nature; in c1854, began to lecture on botany, School of Design; in 1857, wrote the first of several articles on botany in the *Art Journal*; was appointed professor of Botany Applied to the Fine Arts, Department of Science and Art, School of Design, South Kensington; failing to get the chair of botany, University College, London, he turned to design, focusing on the artistic value of plant forms; elected fellow of the Linnaean Society in 1861; published *The Art of Decorative Design*, expanded from an 1857 article and inspired by Japanese objects at 1862 London Exhibition; from the mid-1860s, was an active industrial designer, assisted by J. Moyr Smith and others; became associated with Wedgwood and Minton; from c1871, designed for Wat-

combe Pottery Company, Devon; 1879–82, was artistic director of Linthorpe Pottery; in c1871, began designing cast-iron furniture for Coalbrookdale Ironworks, Shropshire; designed for most of the major British carpet and textile manufacturers; in c1875, created tile designs for Minton; in 1876, visited Philadelphia 'Centennial Exposition,' where he delivered three lectures recommending improvements in the American art industry; while in the USA, designed wallpaper patterns and lectured at the new School of Industrial Design, Pennsylvania Museum; went to Japan, acquiring a large number of objects for Tiffany, New York. He published *Japan: Its Architecture, Art, and Art Manufactures* (1882) and *Modern Ornamentation* (1886). In partnership with Charles Holme of Bradford from 1879, he set up the short-lived Oriental warehouse Dresser and Holme, London; 1879–85, produced designs for electroplated metalware. From 1878, Hukin and Heath, Birmingham, produced his innovative silver designs. He supplied silver designs to Thomas Johnson, London, in c1880; James Dixon, Sheffield; Elkington, Birmingham, from 1884, as well as to foreign firms, including Boin-Tabert, Paris; designed wallpaper for Jeffrey, textiles for Warner, and carpets for Brinton. In 1880, he established the Art Furnishers' Alliance to sell furniture and ceramics of his own design; it closed in 1883 despite financial backing from Arthur Lasenby Liberty; in 1883, became editor of *Furniture Gazette*, an influential periodical; created pottery for Linthorpe Pottery, Middlesbrough, in c1880; brassware for Perry, Wolverhampton; and glassware for James Cooper, Glasgow, in c1885. In 1889, he set up a studio in Barnes, near London, where he employed ten assistants; before closing in the 1890s, it made designs for textiles and other products. He was a prolific metalworker, known primarily for tea sets and table goods executed in proto-Modern geometric forms. His shapes were strikingly stark and rigorous, presaging Bauhaus silhouettes. In his metalware, he used thin sheets of silver strengthened by rims or angles. In contrast, his ceramics showed his mastery of ornament and his sense of humor. He designed fabrics, metalware other than silver, 'and novel things in the most perfect accord with the process that is destined to translate them into being' (*The Studio*, November 1898:113).

▶ Work subject of 1972 one-person exhibition, Fine Arts Society, London. In 1860, received honorary doctorate, University of Jena.

▶ Nikolaus Pevsner, 'Minor Masters of the Nineteenth Century, 9: Christopher Dresser, Industrial Designer,' *Architectural Review*, No. 81, March 1937:183–86. Shirley Bury, 'The Silver Designs of Dr. Christopher Dresser,' *Apollo*, No. 76, Dec. 1962:766–70. Gillian Naylor, *The Arts and Crafts Movement*, 1971. Cat., Stuart Durant et al., *Christopher Dresser, 1834–1904*, London: Fine Arts Society Limited, 1972. Stuart Durant, 'Aspects of the Work of Dr. Christopher Dresser (1834–1904), Botanist, Designer, and Writer' (thesis, Royal College of Art), 1973. Cat., Michael Collins, *Christopher Dresser, 1834–1904*, London: Camden Arts Centre, 1979. Cat., *Christopher Dresser: Ein Viktorianischer Designer, 1834–1904*, Cologne: Kunstgewerbe Museum, 1981. Annelies Krekel-Aalberse, *Art Nouveau and Art Déco Silver*, New York: Abrams, 1989:253. Widar Halen, *Christopher Dresser*, Oxford: Phaidon/Christie's, 1990. Stuart Dresser, *Christopher Dresser*, London: Academy Editions, Berlin: Ernst & Sohn, 1993.

Dreyfuss, Henry (1904–72)

▶ American industrial designer; born and active New York.

▶ Studied Ethical Culture School, New York.

▶ In 1923, he became active as a stage designer for the theatre productions on Broadway, working with Norman Bel Geddes on several hit shows; served an unsatisfactory stint as design consultant for Macy's, where he insisted on collaborating with the manufacturers; in 1929, opened his own office in New York, with a traditional kitchen storage-jar as one of his first commissions; subsequently, opened a second office in Pasadena, California. He was a founding member of the Society of Industrial Design and first president of the Industrial Designers Society of America. The vast number of objects Dreyfuss designed included aircraft interiors for

Lockheed, hearing aids, clocks, Bell telephones (1930–33 *Bell 300* and 1965 *Trimline* model), Hoover products (from 1934), RCA TV sets (from 1946), decanters for Thermos, farm vehicles for John Deere (including 1956 *720* tractor), oceanliners *Constitution* and 1951 *Independence*, and New York Central Railroad's 1941 *Twentieth Century Limited*, which was more extravagant than usual for Dreyfuss. He developed a system of anthropometrics to provide a basis for ergonomic design, the results of which were published in a series of volumes by MIT Press and discussed in his books *Designing for People* (1955) and *The Measure of Man* (1960). The latter included his 'Joe and Josephine' figures representing the average man and woman and manifesting his lifelong interest in people's relationship to functional design. Niels Difrient, the collaborator on Dreyfuss's books, was a member of his staff. In 1968, after retiring from his design firm, Dreyfuss remained consultant to Bell Laboratories, Polaroid, and others.

▶ First Dreyfuss telephone for Bell shown at 1983–84 'Design Since 1945' exhibition, Philadelphia Museum of Art.

▶ Henry Dreyfuss, *Designing for People*, New York: Simon and Schuster, 1955. Henry Dreyfuss, *Industrial Design: A Pictorial Accounting, 1929–57*, New York, 1957. Henry Dreyfuss, *The Measure of Man*, New York: Whitney Library of Ideas, 1960. 'Henry Dreyfuss 1904–1972,' *Industrial Design*, Vol. 20, March 1973:37–423. Jeffrey L. Meikle, *Twentieth Century Limited: Industrial Design in America, 1925–1939*, Philadelphia, 1979. Cat., Kathryn B. Hiesinger and George H. Marcus III (eds.), *Design Since 1945*, Philadelphia: Philadelphia Museum of Art, 1983. Russell Flinchum, 'Henry Dreyfuss' in Mel Byars and Russell Flinchum (eds.), *50 American Designers, 1918–1968*, Washington: Preservation, 1994.

Driade

▶ Italian furniture manufacturer; located Milan.

▶ Driade was founded in 1968 by Enrico Astori, his sister Antonia Astori, and his wife Adelaide Acerbi, when the Astoris took over soft furnishings firm Ideal, Piacenza. It produced a full range of furniture, furnishings, and ceramics designed by Antonia Astori, Gio Ponti, Rodolfo Bonetto, Alberto Dal Lago, Rocco Serini, De Pas-D'Urbino-Lomazzi, Franco Fraschini, Enzo Mari, Adelmo Rascaroli, Giotto Stoppino, Philippe Starck, and Nanda Vigo; from the outset, used plastics, primarily ABS molding and fiberglass. At first, other manufacturers were commissioned to produce wood-frame, steel, and polyurethane components. Driade designers rejected Bauhaus models in favor of Neo-Dada, Pop Art, Arte Povera, Conceptual Art, and Earth Art. The 1968 *Driade I*, produced 1968–78, consisted of three pieces: the *Cherea* easychair and *Maia* armchair by Fraschini, and *Cidonio* table by Astori. Its 1970 *Alessia* chair and *Febo* table by Stoppino were produced in fiberglass. Its Adeph line by Starck was named *Ubik* after the science-fiction novel by Philip K. Dick. The factory moved from Piacenza to Fossadello di Caorso in 1969, when it produced only one furniture item: the *Duecavalli* armchair by De Pas, D'Urbino and Lomazzi. From 1972, the firm began manufacturing the *Ipercubo* series of soft furnishings by De Pas, D'Urbino and Lomazzi.

▶ Products included 1970 *Melania* armchair by Bonetto, 1970 *Canopo*, 1973 *Oikos*, and 1980 *Oikosdue* systems by Astori, 1974 *Ara* series and *Gazebo* settle by the Vignellis, 1974 *Makeba* club chair by Dal Lago, 1981 *Demel* couch and 1981 *Sacher* chair by Sottsass Associati, 1982 *Sabrina* couch by Alessandro Mendini, 1982 *Backbottom* seat by Deganello, 1982 *Sancarlo* chair by Castiglioni, and 1978 'Bris' system by Astori and Mari. Mari designed 1972 *Sof Sof* chair, 1972 *Day-Night* convertible sofa, 1976 *Gambadilegno* club chair and ottoman, 1977 *Capitello* table series, 1981 *Vela* side chair, and 1974 *Fratello* table. The 1985 *Ubik* series by Starck comprised *Sarapis* stool, *Mickville* chair-stool, *Von Vogelsang* chair, *Titos Apostos* table, and *Tippy Jackson* table.

▶ Work first shown abroad at 1974 Cologne furniture fair and, subsequently, at 1975 Salon de Mobilier, Paris, and regularly at Salone del Mobile, Milan. *Melaina* and *Alessia* chairs shown at 1972 'Design a Plastické Hmoty,' Uměleckoprůmyslové Muzeum, Prague.

▶ Cat., Milena Lamarová, *Design a Plastické Hmoty, Uměleckopr*ů *myslové Muzeum*, 1972: 52;180. Renato De Fusco, *Il 'gioco' del design: vent'anni di attività della Driade*, Naples: Electa, 1988.

Drocco, Guido (1942–)
▶ Italian designer; born S. Benedetto B.; active Turin.
▶ He began his professional career in 1967; was best known for his furniture and furnishings in the Radical-Design aesthetic; became a member of ADI (Associazione per il Disegno Industriale); designed multi-use furniture (including the cabinet-table) and, produced by Gufram, (with Piero Gilardi and Franco Mello) 1970 foam matt, 1972 *Cactus* foam coat rack, and 1966 *Pratone* (meadow) seating that were widely published.
▶ Work shown at numerous exhibitions.
▶ *ADI Annual 1976*, Milan: Associazione per il Disegno Industriale, 1976. Albrecht Bangert, *Italienisches Möbeldesign*, Munich: Bangert, 1989.

Dryad
See Peach, Harry

du Pasquier, Nathalie (1957–)
▶ French artist and textile designer; born Bordeaux; active Milan; wife of George J. Sowden.
▶ She joined Studio Rainbow in 1980 as a textile designer; worked for Memphis 1981–88. She frequently collaborated with George Sowden, both for Memphis and others. They designed the 'Progetto Decorazione' silkscreen printed papers series of the 1980s. Much of the visual excitement of early Memphis designs was due to du Pasquier's busy, vividly colored overall patterns inspired by her earlier travels. She designed Memphis's first fabrics, used for upholstered furniture by Sowden; (with Sowden) set up own design office, Milan, and was active in architecture projects, ceramics research, and textile studies; in 1982, joined the creative staff of Fiorucci. In 1985, the Maison des Couteliers (a cooperative of French cutler artisans) commissioned du Pasquier and Sowden to design flatware and pocket knives. Her work included moquettes, ceramics, and clocks for Lorenz (with Sowden), and fashion textiles for Pink Dragon, Missoni Kids, Esprit, NAS Oleari. In 1989, she turned from design to painting; appointed curator, Musée des Arts Décoratifs, Bordeaux; turned back to design.
▶ Her Memphis work included 1983 *Royal* chaise longue, 1985 *Cauliflower* and *Onion* ceramic bowls, 1986 *Madras* table, 1986 *Bombay* side table, 1986 *Bordeaux* table lamp, 1987 *Denise* armchair. Her Memphis textiles included 1981 *Mali* and *Burundi*, 1982 *Zambia*, *Zaire*, and *Gabon* and 1983 *Cerchio* cotton prints, and 1983 *Arizona* and *California* rugs. Her 1988 tableware was produced by Algorithme, France.
▶ Work included in 1981 (I) exhibition of Memphis, Salone del Mobile, Milan, and subsequently. Showed her 20 patterns on paper (with Sowden), a collection of 'Objects for the Electronic Age,' and 'Ten Modern Carpets' for Palmisano.
▶ Andrea Branzi, *La Casa Calda: Esperienze del Nuovo Disegno Italiano*, Milan: Idea Books, 1982. Cat., Kathryn B. Hiesinger and George H. Marcus III (eds.), *Design Since 1945*, Philadelphia: Philadelphia Museum of Art, 1983. *Les Carnets du Design*, Paris: MadCap Productions et APCI, 1986:75. Liz McQuiston, *Women in Design: A Contemporary View*, New York: Rizzoli, 1988:80. . Barbara Radice, 'Mosaici Morbidi,' *Modo*, No. 54, Nov. 1982:68.

du Plantier, Marc
▶ French painter, decorator, and furniture designer.
▶ In the 1940s, du Plantier was active in Paris and became known for his elegant furniture produced in natural materials including oak, white marble, and parchment; showed a preference for patinated bronze and wrought iron; painted frescoes in his own house in Boulogne, near Paris.
▶ François Mathey, *Au bonheur des formes, design français 1945– 1992*, Paris: Regard, 1992:236.

Dubb, Vincent Carl (1852–1922)
▶ Austrian silversmith; active Vienna.
▶ Dubb and his firm manufactured and designed flat- and hollow-ware.
▶ Annelies Krekel-Aalberse, *Art Nouveau and Art Déco Silver*, New York: Abrams, 1989:253.

Dubois, Fernand (1861–1939)
▶ Belgian sculptor and metalworker; born Renaix; brother of Paul Dubois.
▶ 1877, studied natural sciences, University of Brussels, and sculpture under Charles van der Stappen.
▶ He was a medalist and modeler of silver and bronze objects and jewelry. His 1901–06 house, 80 avenue Brugmann, Brussels, was designed by his friend Victor Horta. Working in bronze, pewter, and enamels, he produced a wide range of ornaments, including fans, candelabra, medallions, plaques, bas-reliefs, bronze, and pewter; is known for the exuberant five-branched candelabra in the Horta Museum, Brussels; from 1896, taught metalworking, École Industrielle, Brussels.
▶ Medals, jewelry, chandeliers, candelabra, an inkwell, and ivory figurines set in silver shown at 1894, 1895, 1897, and 1899 Salons de la Libre Esthétique. 'Marriage casket' in ivory and silver-bronze shown at Congo Palace, 1879 Tervueren chryselephantine sculpture exposition.
▶ Yvonne Brunhammer et al., *Art Nouveau Belgium, France*, Houston: Rice University, 1976. Alastair Duncan, *Art Nouveau and Art Déco Lighting*, New York: Simon and Schuster, 1978:49. Annelies Krekel-Aalberse, *Art Nouveau and Art Déco Silver*, New York: Abrams, 1989:253.

Dubois, Paul (1859–)
▶ Belgian designer; brother of Fernand Dubois.
▶ Dubois was colleague of sculptors Constantin Meunier and Victor Rousseau; a creator of monumental sculpture, designed and produced *objets d'art* including vases, candelabra, plaqettes, jugs, belt clasps, and paperweights; one of the most successful of the Belgian sculptors who produced work in both monumental forms and in the applied arts.
▶ Small objects frequently shown at exhibitions of Les Vingt and, subsequently, at Salons of La Libre Esthétique.
▶ Alastair Duncan, *Art Nouveau and Art Déco Lighting*, New York: Simon and Schuster, 1978:49.

Dubreuil, André (1951–)
▶ French interior and furniture designer; born Lyons; active London.
▶ Studied architecture, Switzerland, and design, Inchbald School of Design, London.
▶ In 1977, he began working in the antiques trade in London and as a *trompe l'œil* muralist and interior designer; in 1985, collaborated with Tom Dixon on the decoration of the Rococo Chocolats boutique; subsequently, took up designing and producing wrought-iron furniture in 1986, including his widely published 1987–88 *Spine* chair in limited quantities by Personalities, Japan, and 1988 *Paris* chair; in 1990, produced his first glassware collection, inspired by a small Roman vase and including large glass floor lamps and wall models. His glassware was sold at Daum.
▶ Albrecht Bangert and Karl Michael Armer, *80s Style: Designs of the Decade*, New York: Abbeville, 1990:70,230. Cat., *Acquisitions 1982–1990 arts décoratifs*, Paris: Fonds National d'Art Contemporain, 1991.

Dubuisson, Sylvain (1946–)
▶ French architect-designer; born Bordeaux; active Paris.
▶ Studied architecture, École Supérieure d'Architecture de Saint-Luc, Tournai (Belgium).
▶ He designed interiors, furniture, exhibitions, and lighting; in 1973, worked in the architecture office of Ove Arup, London; from 1980, was an independent architect; designed the 'Espace du Livre' at 1985 'Art et Industrie' exhibition, Musée National

des Monuments français; in 1986, designed exhibitions, Cité des Sciences et de l'Industrie, Parc La Villette, Paris, and Centre Georges Pompidou, Paris; in 1986, furniture for Tour Nord, Notre-Dame cathedral, and Caisse Nationale des Monuments Historiques et des Sites; in 1988, designed furniture by Fourniture for the director's office, Musée Historique des Tissus, Lyons; in 1987, designed 'Équerre d'Argent' (the trophy for grand prize in architecture) and trophy for the 'Initiative Qualité 87' prize, Ministère de l'Industrie et de la Recherche; in 1988, designed for lighting firm Yamagiwa, Tokyo, and various lamp studies for Daum; designed 1989 extension to the exhibition, Notre-Dame cathedral, Paris, and 1993 'Miroir du Siècle' exhibition, Grand Palais, Paris.
▶ Work included 1982–83 *Quasi una fantasia* woman's desk, 1983 *Le Castelet* child's desk, 1983 *Beaucoup de bruit pour rien* table lamp, all produced by Écart for the Fonds National d'Art Contemporain in 1984, 1984 *Le cuer d'amour épris* table lamp (unique piece), 1984 *Lulita* desk lamp (with engineer Jean-Sébastien Dubuisson) produced by Mazda Éclairage Lita, 1985 *Tetractys* table lamp produced by Galerie Néotù for Fonds National d'Art Contemporain in Bordeaux, 1985 *Applique A4* signage/lighting unit (with Jean-Sébastien Dubuisson) produced by Écart and installed in 1989 Mobilier National for the Centre National des Arts Plastiques for the National French Bicentennial exhibition, 1986 *La Licorne* lamp (unique piece), 1986 *T2/A3* disk clock (unique piece), 1986 *73 secondes* candlesticks produced in 1989 by Creative Agent, 1987 *Table composite* in carbon-steel tubing and mono-composite-epoxy film, 1987 *L'Elliptique* hot plate and 1987 *Volcan—un mont* ashtray produced by Algorithme for Nestor Perkal's 'La Collection,' 1987 *L'Aube et le temp qu'elle dure* one-piece aluminum chair sponsored by VIA, 1987 *L'Inconscient* bed produced by Fourniture, 1988 *Lettera amorosa* vase in blown glass by Lino Tagliapietra and metal, 1988 *Étagère JNF* wall-shelf produced by Fourniture, 1989 *Héraclite* aluminum clock, and elliptical *Desk 1989* in mahogany veneer and grey calf for office of Jack Lang, minister of culture, 1990 *L'aiguillère retrouvée* by Algorithme.
▶ His work was included in the 1985 'Onze Lampes' at the Galerie Néotù, Paris; 1985 'Lumières, je pense à vous,' at Centre Georges Pompidou, Paris; 1985 'Art et Industrie' at Espace du Livre at the Musée des Monuments français, Paris; 1987 exhibition at the Galerie Desco, Bordeaux; 1988 exhibition at BDX and 'Arc-en-Rêve' exhibition, CAPC, Musée des Arts Contemporains, Bordeaux; 1988 'MDF—des créateurs pour un matériau' at the Fondation Cartier, Jouy-en-Josas; 1988 'Tandem' at Musée de Romans, Salone del Mobile in Milan from 1988; 1988 Centre Culturel de Ribérac; 1989 'Sylvain Dubuisson: Objets et Dessins' retrospective exhibition at the Musée des Arts Deecoratifs in Paris; 1990 'Les années VIA' at the Musée des Arts Décoratifs, Paris; 1992 'Sylvain Dubuisson: Design and Dessin,' The Israel Museum, Jerusalem. Won 1984 competition sponsored by the Agence pour la Promotion de la Création Industrielle (APCI). Received 1989 VIA 'Carte Blanche' award for his 1989 *Desk*.
▶ Sophie Anargyros, *Intérieurs—Le Mobilier Français*, Paris: Regard/VIA, 1980:57–64. Cat., *Lumières, je pense à vous*, Paris: Centre Georges Pompidou/Hermé, 1985. Sophie Anargyros, *Le Style des Années 80, architecture, décoration, design*, Paris: Rivages, 1986:106–10. Christine Colin, *Design aujourd'hui*, Paris: Flammarion, 1988. Cat., *MDF—Des créateurs pour un matériau*, Paris: Fondation Cartier, 1988. Cat., *In-Spiration: Éloge de la Lumière*, Tokyo: Parco, 1988. Cat., Yvonne Brunhammer, *Sylvain Dubuisson: Objets et Dessins,* Paris: Musée des Arts Décoratifs, 1989. Cat., *Les années VIA*, Paris: Musée des Arts Décoratifs, 1990. Cat., *Acquisitions 1982–1990 arts décoratifs*, Paris: Fonds National d'Art Contemporain, 1991. François Mathey, *Au bonheur des formes, design français 1945–1992*, Paris: Regard, 1992:98,144,147,224,253, 259,295,297,307–08.

Duc, Christian   (1949–)

▶ Vietnamese designer; active Paris.
▶ Studied English literature and fine art.

▶ He worked as a book illustrator for an American publisher in Amsterdam; 1973–77, designed cinema and cafe interiors, Berlin; in 1977, established Galerie DCA (Duc et Cameroux Associés), Paris, for the distribution of furniture, rugs, and interior accessories designed by himself. Clients included Toronto Museum of Modern Art (lighting with Bruynzeel), V'Soske rugs, Mobilier International, African Queen restaurant (1988 furniture) in Paris, Elisée Éditions rugs (from 1988), Toulemonde Bochart rugs (from 1987), Faïenceries de Gien (1988). A number of his pieces and collections were sponsored by VIA. His 1987 spherical *Archéologie Future* lamp was produced by Delisle (with glass by Patrick Desserme and Bernard Pictet).
▶ *Archéologie Future* lamp received a prize at 1987 Salon du Luminaire, Paris. Received interior-design prize at 1985 Salon of Société des Artistes Décorateurs. Work shown at 1989 'L'Art de Vivre' exhibition, Cooper-Hewitt Museum, New York, and 1990 'Les Anées VIA' exhibition, Paris Musée des Arts Décoratifs.
▶ Cat., *Les années VIA*, New York: Vendome, 1989. François Mathey, *Au bonheur des formes, design français 1945–1992*, Paris: Regard, 1992:196,246.

Ducrot, Vittorio   (1867–1942)

▶ Italian furniture manufacturer; located Palermo.
▶ Active in the first three decades of the 20th century, Ducrot produced furniture and interior designs to the specifications of Ernesto Basile.
▶ *Mobili e Arredi di Ernesto Basile: nella produzione Ducrot*, Palermo: Novecento, 1980. Cat., Gabriel P. Weisberg, *Stile Floreale: The Cult of Nature in Italian Design*, Miami: The Wolfsonian Foundation, 1988.

Dudas, Frank

▶ Canadian industrial designer; active Toronto.
▶ Dudas and Doug and Jan Kuypers worked separately and together as industrial designers; designed furniture including seating for IIL International.
▶ Cat., *Seduced and Abandoned: Modern Furniture designers in Canada, the First Fifty Years*, Toronto: The Art Gallery at Harbourfront, 1986:21.

Dufet, Michel   (1888–1985)

▶ French interior designer and writer; born Deville-les-Rouen; active Paris.
▶ Studied painting and architecture, École des Beaux-Arts, Paris.
▶ In 1913, he established the decorating studio MAM (Mobilier Artistique Moderne), 3 avenue de l'Opéra, Paris, to produce Modern furniture, wallpaper, fabrics, and lighting; in 1918, collaborating with Paul Claudel, André Gide, Marcel Proust, and Gabriel Fauré, staged the revue *Feuillets d'Art*, which ran for two years; in 1920, began a collaboration with Louis Bureau on design at MAM; in 1924, sold MAM to the firm P.-A. Dumas, but continued to make furniture; 1922–24, was head of the interior-decorating firm Red Star, Rio de Janeiro; designed interiors of stores, cinemas, bars, and offices; 1924–39, worked with art critic Léandre Vaillat at the newly formed Le Sylve design studio of Le Bûcheron store, where he designed furniture and furnishings including a desk in Canadian birch for the director of Agence Havas and 1929 ebony, zinc- and cellulose-veneered desk for Compagnie Asturienne des Mines; in c1924, designed the first Cubist wallpapers. His commissions included interiors of the oceanliner *Foch*, children's playroom of 1926 oceanliner *Île-de-France*, 40 first-class cabins of 1935 oceanliner *Normandie*, and a yacht for Marcel L'Herbier. He wanted to design for mass production but received little interest from manufacturers. Influenced by neo-Cubism, his furniture was produced in exotic woods in elegant, refined lines. He designed numerous shops, theaters, offices, public spaces, and yachts; in 1933, became editor-in-chief of the journal *Décor d'Aujourd'hui*; in 1947, designed the layout for Musée d'Antoine Bourdelle. From 1950, a great part of his time was occupied with the promotion of the work of his father-in-law, sculptor Antoine Bourdelle.

► Several furniture pieces shown at 1914 Salon of the Société des Artistes français. From 1919, MAM's work shown at Salons of Société des Artistes Décorateurs, and sessions of Salon d'Automne. Designed the reception salon of Maréchal Lyautey, the commissioner general of the 1931 Paris 'Exposition Coloniale.' Was architect of French pavilion, 1939 'New York World's Fair.' Participated (with René Gabriel) in wallpaper pavilion, 1937 Paris 'Exposition Internationale des Arts et Techniques dans la Vie Moderne.'
► Léon Deshairs, *Modern French Decorative Art*, Paris: Albert Lévy. Victor Arwas, *Art Déco*, New York: Abrams, 1980. Pierre Cabanne, *Encyclopédie Art Déco*, Paris: Somogy, 1986:189–90. Pierre Kjellberg, *Art Déco: les maîtres du Mobilier, le décor des Paquebots*, Paris: Amateur, 1986:58–61. Auction cat., Sotheby's New York, 16 June 1989, Lot Nos. 372–73.

Duffner and Kimberly
► American lighting manufacturer; located New York.
► Active *c*1906–11 at 11 West 32nd Street, New York, Duffner and Kimberly produced leaded glass table and floor lamps, chandeliers, wall brackets, electric candle sconces, and electric chandeliers. Before 1906, Duffner and Kimberly may have been employees at the Tiffany studios. In 1911, the firm became Kimberly and was located at 317 East 38th Street, where the *Ancient Texture* lamp range was made in English antique glass with painted scenes illustrating heraldry, the crusades, and the signing of the Magna Carta.
► Alastair Duncan, *Art Nouveau and Art Déco Lighting*, New York: Simon and Schuster, 1978:44–45.

Duffy, William N.   (?–1952)
► British industrial designer; active London.
► 1931–52, he was staff industrial artist at Ferranti, Hollinwood, Lancashire, where he designed radio cabinets, electric clocks, and electric fires; collaborated with S.Z. de Ferranti on some projects.
► Cat., *Thirties: British art and design before the war*, London: Arts Council of Great Britain, Hayward Gallery, 1979:140,232, 233, 288.

Dufrêne, Maurice   (1876–1955)
► French furniture, textile, glassware, ceramic, and silverware designer; born Paris.
► Studied École Nationale Supérieure des Arts Décoratifs, Paris.
► In 1899, he became director and manager of Julius Meier-Graefe's La Maison Moderne, Paris, designing small silver objects such as umbrella handles; in 1904, was a co-founder of the Société des Artistes Décorateurs as a reaction against the excesses of Art Nouveau, favoring the spare ornamentation of the *Style 1900*; by 1906, used plain, solid shapes with little ornament; designed stoneware and porcelain for Pierre-Adrien Dalpayrat and worked in wood, metal, glass, textiles, and leather; 1912–23, taught at École Boulle and, subsequently, École des Arts Appliqués, both Paris; in 1919 (with Claude Autant-Lara), designed the first Modernist sets for Marcel L'Herbier's film *Le Carnaval des vérités*. 1921–52, Dufrêne was creator and director La Maîtrise design studio of Galeries Lafayette department store, Paris, where he designed furniture, silverware, carpets, wallpaper, ceramics, glassware, and complete layouts. His furniture pieces in refined forms were soberly decorated and inspired by 18th- and early 19th-century models. Advocating mass-production and industrial techniques, his Modernism had traditional leanings yet ranged eclectically from the interiors of the townhouse of Pierre David-Weill to a brand of baroque Art Déco for the apartment of Pierre Benoit and the avant-garde design of the late 1920s in glass, metal, and mirrors for the casino, Challes-les-Eaux. In the late 1920s, he executed commissions from Mobilier National for embassies and for the Palais de l'Élysée, Paris.
► Work first shown at Salon of the Société des Artistes Décorateurs in 1902 and, from 1903, regularly at sessions of Salon d'Automne and Salons of Société Nationale des Beaux-Arts.

Designed luxury boutiques on Alexandre III Bridge, layout and furniture for small salon 'Une Ambassade française,' and interior of La Maîtrise pavilion at 1925 Paris 'Exposition Internationale des Arts Décoratifs et Industriels Modernes.'
► Yvonne Brunhammer et al., *Art Nouveau Belgium, France*, Houston: Rice University, 1976. Victor Arwas, *Art Déco*, Abrams, 1980. Yvonne Brunhammer, *Art Déco Style*, London: Academy, 1983. Florence Camard, *Ruhlmann*, Paris: Regard, 1983. Pierre Kjellberg, *Art Déco: les maîtres du Mobilier, le décor des Paquebots*, Paris: Amateur, 1986:61–63. Pierre Cabanne, *Encyclopédie Art Déco*, Paris: Somogy, 1986:190–91. *Restaurants, dancing, cafés, bars*, Paris: Charles Moreau, Nos. 32–34.

Dufresne, Charles-Georges   (1876–1938)
► French painter and designer.
► Studied sculpture and pastel, École des Beaux-Arts, Paris.
► In 1923, he was a co-founder of the Salon des Tuileries; designed a set of tapestries woven at Beauvais for a furniture suite commissioned by the Mobilier National based on the story of Paul and Virginie.
► 1924 tapestries for suite of furniture designed by Süe et Mare shown at 1925 Paris 'Exposition Internationale des Arts Décoratifs et Industriels Modernes.' Refused all honors and awards except Carnegie Prize, Pittsburgh, Pennsylvania.
► Victor Arwas, *Art Déco*, Abrams, 1980. Cat., Aaron Lederfajn and Xavier Lenormand, *Le Louvre des Antiquaires présente: 1930 quand le meuble devient sculpture*, Paris, 1986.

Dufy, Raoul   (1877–1953)
► French painter and decorative designer; born Le Havre.
► Dufy was associated for a time with the Fauve artists' group through Othon Friesz and Albert Marquet; designed letterheads for fashion designer Paul Poiret, who commissioned him in 1911 to design fabrics, and set him up in a studio; 1923–30, designed a tapestry screen and seat cover for Beauvais; 1912–30, designed dress textiles, upholstery fabrics, and printed panels for Bianchini-Férier, Lyons. His balanced, over-all patterns are comparable compositionally to those of William Morris. For Poiret's houseboats moored on the river Seine near the 1925 Paris 'Exposition Internationale des Arts Décoratifs et Industriels Modernes,' he designed 14 large textile hangings: *Orgues*; designed fabric by Bianchini-Férier used by architect-designer Francis Jourdain in his 1925 de Noailles villa, Hyères; 1930–33, designed printed silk motifs for Amalgamated Silk and Onandaga New York.
► Work subject of numerous exhibitions including 1983 exhibitions 'Raoul Dufy, 1877–1953' organized by Arts Council of Great Britain, London. Work shown at Salons of Société des Artistes français from 1901 and at Salons d'Automne from 1903. Painted the vast 200-by-30 foot (60m × 10m) *La Fée Électricité*, said to be the world's largest picture, for the Pavilion du Lumière, 1937 Paris 'Exposition Internationale des Arts et Techniques dans la Vie Moderne.'
► Paul Poiret, *En Habillant l'Époque*, Paris, 1930:120–22. Victor Arwas, *Art Déco*, Abrams, 1980. Stuart Durant, *Ornament from the Industrial Revolution to Today*, Woodstock, NY: Overlook, 1986:245,322, passim.

Duiker, Johannes   (1890–1935)
► Dutch architect and furniture designer; born The Hague.
► Studied Technical College, Delft.
► In 1916, he and Bernard Bijvoët became partners in their own architecture office in Amsterdam. 1932–35, Duiker was editor of the journal *De 8 en Opbouw*; was best known for 1926–28 Zonnestraal Sanatorium (with Bijvoët), Hilversum, with its extensive glazing and projecting roof terraces. Architecture included 1928–30 Open Air School, Cliostraat, Amsterdam, for which he designed metal-and-wood furniture, and the Constructivist-inspired 1934 Handelsblad-Cineac Cinema, Amsterdam.
► T. Boga (ed.), *B. Bijvoet & J. Duiker 1890–1935*, Zürich. Johannes Duiker, *Hoogbouw*, Rotterdam, 1930. F.R. Yerbury, *Modern Dutch Buildings*, New York: Charles Scribner's Sons, 1931.

'Zonnestraal,' *Forum*, Vol. 16, No. 1, Jan. 1962. 'Bijvoet & Duiker,' *AA Quarterly*, Vol. 2, No. 1, 1970: 4—10. 'Duiker 1' and 'Duiker 2,' *Forum*, Nov. 1971 and Jan. 1972. Vittorio Magnago Lampugnani (ed.), *Encyclopedia of 20th-Century Architecture*, New York: Abrams, 1986:85.

Dulac, Edmund   (1881–1953)
▶ French illustrator and designer; born Toulouse; active England.
▶ A naturalized British citizen from 1912, Dulac produced caricature wax figurines, including those of George Moore and Thomas Beecham; in 1930, designed the Cathay Lounge for the oceanliner *Empress of Britain*. Work included playing-card designs and Dutch banknotes for De la Rue, 1935 *Old Plantation Chocolates* package for Cadbury's, and specimens of Edward VIII coins. 1940—45, philatelic designs included 1937 stamp for George VI's coronation, Free French issues, commemorative stamps 1951 London 'Festival of Britain,' and 1953 coronation of Queen Elizabeth II. His illustrated books included *Hans Andersen* (1912), *Edmund Dulac's Book for the French Red Cross* (1915), *The Green Lacquer Pavilion* (1926), *Myths the Ancients Believed in* (1932), and *Rock Climbs around London* (1938).
▶ Cat., *Thirties: British art and design before the war*, London: Arts Council of Great Britain, Hayward Gallery, 1979:200,201, 203, 288.

Dumas, Hélène   (1896–)
▶ French designer and bookbinder; born Valence; active Paris.
▶ 1924—27, studied bookbinding, École Nationale Supérieure des Arts Décoratifs, Paris, under Henri Lapersonne.
▶ She became an active bookbinder in 1927. From 1931, she and Germain de Coster collaborated. De Coster executed the designs and Dumas produced the bindings, assisted by gilders André Jeanne and Raymond Mondage. Their complicated geometric and abstract motifs were executed with exotic materials including snake skins, ostrich skins, beryls, and tourmalines. From 1934, Dumas taught bookbinding, Technical College of Applied Arts, where de Coster had been an instructor from the early 1920s. They continued to collaborate after World War II, producing some of their most important work.
▶ Henri Nicolle, 'La Reliure moderne,' *Les Arts français: la reliure d'art*, No. 36, 1919:11—12. Cat., *Reliure française contemporaine*, New York: The Grolier Club, 1987—88:34—39. Alastair Duncan and Georges de Bartha, *Art Nouveau and Art Déco Bookbinding*, New York: Abrams, 1989:24,190.

Dumas, Rena   (1937–)
▶ Greek interior architect and furniture designer; active Paris.
▶ Studied École Nationale Supérieure des Métiers d'Art, Paris, to 1961.
▶ In 1962, Dumas became a designer for Hermès, which produced her leather goods; in 1971, set up her own office, designing interiors of private houses, offices, restaurants, and shops; in 1983, began designing furniture with Peter Coles (1954—85); (with Coles) designed 1986 *Pippa* folding furniture collection for Hermès. She designed furniture for Galerie Agora; interiors of branches for Hermès, including those in New York (1983), San Francisco (1987), Milan (1987), Madrid (1990), Paris (the extension of the Faubourg Saint-Honoré main store, 1992; Ateliers Hermès de Pantin, 1992); 1991 *Complice* teapot for Hermès; 1992 *Pippa II* folding chair, desk, stool, screen, and campaign bed by Hermès.
▶ Dumas won the 1988 VIA 'Carte Blanche' award for her mobile, multi-functional units.
▶ Suzanne Tise, 'Innovators at the Museum,' *Vogue Décoration*, No. 26, June/July 1990:48.

Dumond, Jacques   (1907–)
▶ French designer; active Paris.
▶ Studied École Boulle, Paris.
▶ 1929—34, Dumond worked with architect Pierre Patout; in 1947, joined UAM (Union des Artistes Modernes); co-founded (with Jacques Viénot) and became vice-president of Institut

d'Esthétique Industrielle; was director of the revue *Art Présent* and of 'Formes Utiles' with André Hermant; produced 1943 rattan chair design for Société Industrielle; from 1947, taught at École Nationale Supérieure des Arts Décoratifs and at École Camondo, Paris; worked in glass and bentwood; designed the 1958 chair in a single sheet of plywood considered his masterpiece. He espoused the maxim 'new material + new technique = new shape.'
▶ Participated in 1943 Salon of Société des Artistes Décorateurs and 1949—50 'Formes Utiles' exhibitions, Pavillon de Marsan, Paris, and in 1956 (I) Triennale d'Art français contemporain, where he showed the office with glass tables, bentwood seating, and Formica furnishings (designed with André Renou, Jean-Pierre Génisset, and André Sive).
▶ René Chavance, 'Confort et Plaisir de Yeux pour un Aménagement de Jacques Dumond,' *Mobilier et Décoration*, No. 6, 1953. Jacques Dumond, interview by Pascal Renous, *Portrait de Décorateurs*, Paris: Vial. Arlette Barré-Despond, *UAM*, Paris: Regard, 1986:394. Cat., *Les années UAM 1929–1958*, Paris: Musée des Arts Décoratifs, 1988:176—77.

Dumoulin, Georges   (1882–1959)
▶ French painter, ceramicist, and glass designer; born Villecreux.
▶ He was a ceramicist at Manufacture de Sèvres for nine years.
▶ Glassware first shown before 1925. Enamel on metal and a number of elegant glass pieces shown at 1937 Paris 'Exposition Internationale des Arts et Techniques dans la Vie Moderne.'
▶ Cat., *Verriers français contemporains: Art et industrie*, Paris: Musée des Arts Décoratifs, 1982.

Dunaime, Georges
▶ French designer.
▶ 1921—27, Dunaime's work was marketed by five agents. He designed lighting for E. Etling. Most of his work was produced by founder and engraver Gagnon, including table lamps, *torchères*, and chandeliers in silver, gilt, and patinated bronze with cloth, cut glass, quartz, marble, and alabaster shades. He designed varied lighting for the 1921 oceanliner *Paris*.
▶ In 1922, lighting shown at Gagneau. Received first prize in 1922 competition of Union of Bronze Manufacturers and first prize (table lamp) and honorable mention (piano lamp) at 1924 Great Lighting Competition, Paris. Work shown at the stands of Gagnon, Gagneau, Bézault, and Christofle, 1925 Paris 'Exposition Internationale des Arts Décoratifs et Industriels Modernes.'
▶ Alastair Duncan, *Art Nouveau and Art Déco Lighting*, New York: Simon and Schuster, 1978:169.

Dunand, Bernard   (1908–)
▶ French artisan and painter; son of Jean Dunand.
▶ 1925—39, Dunand worked with his father, producing sketches and decorations and working with him in lacquer; without separate recognition, worked on the decorations for the 1931 oceanliner *Atlantique* and 1935 oceanliner *Normandie*.
▶ Lacquer paintings shown at Galerie Charpentier, Paris, in 1933. Received grand prize at 1937 Paris 'Exposition Internationale des Arts et Techniques dans la Vie Moderne.'
▶ Cat., *Decorative Arts 1925 Style*, New York: Didier Aaron, 1979.

Dunand, Jean   (b. Jules-John Dunand   1877–1942)
▶ Swiss sculptor, cabinetmaker, metalworker, and artisan; born Lancy, near Geneva.
▶ Studied École des Arts Industriels, Geneva.
▶ He settled in Paris in 1896; began working with sculptor Jean Dampt, an admirer of John Ruskin and the Arts and Crafts movement; worked as a sculptor 1896—1902; studied coppersmithing in Geneva and turned to metalworking; in 1903, set up a studio in Paris; in 1905, exhibited his first vases in the Art Nouveau style in hammered copper, steel, tin, lead, and silver. In 1909, seeing the work of Paris-based Japanese craftsmen, he turned to lacquer and changed his name to Jean Dunand; in *c*1913, moved from Art Nouveau to geometric forms; from 1912, learned lacquering from Japanese artist Seizo Sugawara, who had taught Eileen Gray;

in 1919, began producing lacquer panels, tables, chairs, and other piece work for Pierre Legrain, Eugène Printz, Jean Goulden, and Jacques-Émile Ruhlmann to incorporate into their works. His furniture designs after the war, in straight lines and planes, ideally suited lacquer decorations in near natural colors or tinted with black and red and in tortoiseshell effects. Dunand is credited with inventing the use of crushed eggshell in lacquer, known as *coquille d'oeuf*. In 1919, he opened a workshop, 70 rue Hallé, Paris, to meet the rapidly growing demand for his goods that included lacquer, metal, and cabinetry. His infrequent collaborators included Serge Rovinski, Georges Dorinac, Henri de Varoquier, and Bieler. He created monumental screens from his own designs and those by Paul Jouve, François-Louis Schmied, Ruhlmann, Printz, Gustav Miklos, and Jean Lambert-Rucki. His clients included clothing designers Madeleine Vionnet and Jeanne Lanvin, Ambassador Bertholet, Mme. Yakoupovitch, and Mme. Labourdette. For Mme. Labourdette's smoking salon, he produced four large decorative murals in lacquer with sculptured relief. Other commissions included lacquered panels for the 1927 *Île-de-France*, 1931 *Atlantique*, and 1935 *Normandie* oceanliners. Dunand and Lambert-Rucki collaborated on widely published lacquer screens and decorative pieces. Dunand diluted lacquer to paint fabrics for scarves and dresses for Agnès; designed handbags and belt buckles for Madeleine Vionnet.

▶ Work first shown (as sculptor-metalworker) at 1904 Salon of Société Nationale des Beaux-Arts in Paris. Work shown regularly at Salons of Société des Artistes Décorateurs and at 1910 Brussels 'Exposition Universelle et Industrielle.' In 1921 in group exhibition with Paul Jouve, François-Louis Schmied, and Jean Goulden, first pieces of lacquered furniture, screens, and panels shown at Galerie Georges Petit, Paris. Lacquer work in smoking room of 'Une Ambassade française' and (with Ruhlmann) Hôtel du Collectionneur at 1925 Paris 'Exposition Internationale des Arts Décoratifs et Industriels Modernes' and in 1931 Paris 'Exposition Coloniale.' Work subject of exhibition 1973 'Jean Dunand—Jean Gouden,' Galerie du Luxembourg, Paris.

▶ Yvonne Brunhammer, *Jean Dunand, Jean Goulden*, Galerie du Luxembourg, Paris, 1973: biblio. Philippe Garner, 'The Lacquer Work of Eileen Gray and Jean Dunand,' *Connoisseur*, Mar. 1973:3–11. Yvonne Brunhammer et al., *Art Nouveau Belgium, France*, Houston: Rice University, 1976. Katherine Morrison McClinton, 'Jean Dunand, Art Déco Craftsman,' *Apollo*, Sept. 1982:177–80. Pierre Cabanne, *Encyclopédie Art Déco*, Paris: Somogy, 1986:191–92. Alastair Duncan and Georges de Bartha, *Art Nouveau and Art Déco Bookbinding*, New York: Abrams, 1989:7,8, 21, 62, 68–71, 73, 75, 76, 88–89, 93, 95, 160, 162–64, 168–70, 172, 173, 190. Félix Marcilhac, *Jean Dunand: His Life and Work*, London: Thames and Hudson, 1991.

Dunn, Geoffrey   (1909–)

▶ British furniture retailer, manufacturer, and designer; active Bromley.

▶ Working in the family retail store in Bromley, he encouraged and supported contemporary design and young designers. Dunn's sold furniture by Marcel Breuer, Serge Chermayeff, and Alvar Aalto; fabric by Donald Bros., Edinburgh Weavers, and Warners; ceramics by Wedgwood and Michael Cardew. Geoffrey Dunn's own simple furniture was produced by Goodearl Brothers, William Barlett, Keen of High Wycombe, Stones of Banbury, and in Dunn's own workshops. In 1936, he became a member of the Council of Industrial Design; was chair of the design committee and independent member of the Domestic Handblown Glassware Working Party; in 1938, (with Crofton Gane, a retailer in Bristol known for subdued Modernism, and manufacturer Gordon Russell) established the Good Furnishing Group to select good Modern designs available at reasonable prices, and became its chair in 1953. In 1952, he was appointed managing director of the Council of Industrial Design. Dunn's of Bromley became part of the Heal's Group.

▶ In 1974, appointed Fellow of the Society of Industrial Artists and, in 1976, Commander of the British Empire. Received 1975 bi-centenary medal, Royal Society of Art.

▶ Michael Farr, *Design in British Industry: A Mid-Century Survey*, London: Cambridge, 1955:8ff,17,109. Cat., *Thirties: British art and design before the war*, London: Arts Council of Great Britain, Hayward Gallery, 1979:26,73,151,288.

Dupas, Jean   (1882–1964)

▶ French artist; active Paris.

▶ Studied École des Beaux-Art, Bordeaux, under Albert Besnard.

▶ Though awarded prizes at the Paris Salons, he did not receive international fame until the 1925 Paris Exposition; decorated the Church of Saint-Esprit, Paris; the silver-display room of the royal palace, Bucharest; reception rooms of the Bourse du Travail, Bordeaux, and various oceanliners, including painted-glass panels for 1935 *Normandie*. In 1941, he taught at Académie des Beaux-Arts and, in 1942, became a professor, École des Beaux-Arts.

▶ He received the first Grand Prix de Rome, 1910, and a gold medal at the 1921 or 1922 Salon of Société des Artistes français. Panels *Les Perruches* mounted in the grand salon of Jacques-Émile Ruhlmann's Hôtel du Collectionneur and *Le Vin* in the Tour de Bordeaux on the Esplanade des Invalides, 1925 Paris 'Exposition Internationale des Arts Décoratifs et Industriels Modernes.' In 1926, awarded Légion d'honneur.

▶ Yvonne Brunhammer, *Le Cinquantenaire de l'Exposition de 1925*, Paris: Musée des Arts Décoratifs, 1976:127. Pierre Cabanne, *Encyclopédie Art Déco*, Paris: Somogy, 1986:193.

Dupeux, Geneviève

▶ French textile designer; active Paris.

▶ In 1958, Dupeux open her own *atelier de recherches textiles*; was associated for a short time with Olivier Mourgue and Jean-Philippe Lenclos; 1971–85, taught at École Nationale Supérieure des Arts Décoratifs; in 1976, established Atelier National d'art textile, Gobelins; from 1980, was a textile advisor to Renault.

▶ Participated in numerous exhibitions including Tapestry Biennial, Lausanne. Work subject of exhibition, Centre Georges Pompidou, Paris, designed by Pierre Paulin.

Dupont, S.T.   (aka Tissot-Dupont)

▶ French accessories manufacturer; located Paris.

▶ The firm was founded in 1872, by Simon Tissot-Dupont; until World War II, produced expensive luggage; in 1940, introduced a lighter made of aluminum alloy. It was inspired by an earlier solid gold accessory designed for inclusion in an overnight bag for the Maharaja of Patiala, and became the model for the famous 1953 *Briquet* lighter. In 1973, Dupont began producing the *Montparnasse* line of writing instruments; in 1978, returned to luxury leather articles; from 1981, issued a line of timepieces including pocket alarm clocks and dress and sports (1984) wrist watches; in 1983, produced gold and silver jewelry created by Boucheron. Dupont was family-owned until 1973, when it was sold to Gillette group.

Dupraz, Claude   (1933–)

▶ Swiss industrial designer; born and active Geneva.

▶ His clients included Italian and Swiss firms. He was head of the industrial design department, École Cantonale des Beaux-Arts, Lausanne; was technical and artistic director, Pakistan Design Institute, Karachi; was vice-president of SID (the Swiss industrial designers' organization) and member of ADI (Associazione per il Disegno Industriale).

▶ *ADI Annual 1976*, Milan: Associazione per il Disegno Industriale, 1976.

Dupré-Lafon, Paul   (1900–71)

▶ French interior architect; born Marseilles; active Paris.

▶ Studied École des Beaux-Arts.

▶ In 1923, he settled in Paris, where he practiced as an interior architect, working on commissions in a variety of styles. Clients included the Dreyfus family, other rich collectors, and the firm

Hermès. He designed apartments, townhouses, and villas, as well as furniture and furnishings produced in luxurious materials.

▶ *Ensembles Mobiliers*, Paris: Charles Moreau, Vol. 5, Nos. 40–41; Vol. 6, Nos. 12–18, 1945. Cat., Aaron Lederfajn and Xavier Lenormand, *Le Louvre des Antiquaires présente: 1930 quand le meuble devient sculpture*, Paris, 1986. Pierre Kjellberg, *Art Déco: les maîtres du Mobilier, le décor des Paquebots*, Paris: Amateur, 1989:66. Thierry Couvrat Desvergnes, *Dupré-Lafon: décorateur des millionaires*, Paris: Amateur, 1990. François Mathey, *Au bonheur des formes, design français 1945–1992*, Paris: Regard, 1992:153.

Durbin, Leslie (1913–)

▶ British silversmith and designer; active London.

▶ Studied Central School of Arts and Crafts, London.

▶ As liveryman of the Goldsmiths' Company, his commissions included those for the Grocers' and Goldsmiths' companies and for Guildford Cathedral. He designed maces and badges of office for the Smithsonian Institution, Washington, and other bodies in the USA; taught at Central School of Arts and Crafts and Royal College of Art, both London.

▶Cat., *Thirties: British art and design before the war*, London: Arts Council of Great Britain, Hayward Gallery, 1979:138,288.

D'Urbino, Donato (1935–)

▶ Italian designer; born and active Milan.

▶ D'Urbino, Gionatan De Pas, and Paolo Lomazzi set up a design studio in Milan in 1961 (known as De Pas, D'Urbino & Lomazzi), working on architecture, design, and town-planning projects. 1968–70, it was known as Decursu, De Pas, D'Urbino & Lomazzi, with Giorgio Decursu active in the studio. D'Urbino was best known for his own furniture designs and those in collaboration with the group, including 1967 *Blow* clear PVC inflatable seating. The group's 1970 *Joe* chair in the shape of a baseball glove was an example of Italian Anti-Design. From the 1970s, the group focused on interchangeable and flexible units for modular seating, storage systems, shelving, and plastic and plywood furniture for BBB Bonacina, Driade, and Palina. More mainstream and fashionable furniture and furnishings designs were produced for Zanotta, Poltronova, Forges, Gabbianelli, Marcatré, Hamano, Ligne Roset, Stilnovo, and Sirrah. D'Urbino became a member of ADI (Associazione per il Disegno Industriale). The group made the TV program *Dal cucchiaio alla città; il design italiano dal 1950 al 1980*.

▶ See De Pas, Gionatan

D'Urso, Joseph Paul (1943–)

▶ American interior designer; born Newark, New Jersey.

▶ 1961–65, studied interior design, Pratt Institute, Brooklyn, New York; 1965–66, Pratt Institute School of Architecture; 1966–67, Royal College of Art, London; 1968, Manchester College of Art and Design.

▶ In 1968, he became a freelance designer, New York; from 1968, was founder and president, D'Urso Design, New York; designed private residences; 'I'-complex (restaurants, art gallery, library, media room, and discotheque), Hong Kong; Calvin Klein Menswear showrooms and offices, New York; 1980 range of seating and tables, Knoll International; showrooms, Esprit, Los Angeles;

in the 1970s, became known for his widely published minimalist, monochrome interiors. He was the innovator of the 'high-tech' style in interior design of the 1970s in USA.

▶ Received 1965 Cash Award for European travel; 1973 Burlington Industries Designer of the Year; best in show (Knoll table collection), 1982 Stuttgarter Messe; 1983 Bundespreis 'Die gute Industrieform' (Knoll table collection). Work subject of exhibitions at New York Museum of Modern Art (Manchester school studies and projects), 1968; Pratt Institute, 1968.

▶ 'The New Romantic Movement,' *The New York Times Magazine*, 28 Sept. 1980. 'A Los Angeles Apartment,' *Casa Vogue*, Jan. 1981. 'Designing the Post Industrial World,' *Art News*, Feb. 1981. 'Joe D'Urso: The Mastermind of Minimalism,' *Metropolitan Home*, June 1981. *Joe D'Urso/Designer*, Minneapolis, 1983. Anne Lee Morgan (ed.), *Contemporary Designers*, London: Macmillan, 1984:165–66.

Dwan, Terry (1957–)

▶ American architect and designer; active Milan.

▶ Studied Yale University. Collaborator-wife of Antonio Citterio.

▶ Chantal Granier, 'Présence d'Esprit,' *Maison et Jardin*, April 1992:22.

▶ See Citterio, Antonio

Dyson, James

▶ British industrial designer.

▶ Dyson designed the 1979 *G-Force Cyclonic* vacuum cleaner in pink and mauve produced by Apex, Tokyo, from 1986.

▶ Jonathan M. Woodham, *Twentieth-Century Ornament*, New York: Rizzoli, 1990:296.

Dysthe, Sven Ivar (1931–)

▶ Norwegian furniture and interior designer.

▶ Studied cabinetmaking, Royal College of Art, London.

▶ 1944–60, he was chief designer, Sønnico Fabrikker, Oslo; designed 1960 *System Dysthe* shelving for the store Egil Rygh, 1964 bentwood chairs, and 1986 bent-metal furniture by Møremøbler.

▶ He received the International Design Award, American Institute of Designers.

▶ Fredrik Wildhagen, *Norge i Form*, Oslo: Stenersen, 1988:153. Cat., David Revere McFadden (ed.), *Scandinavian Modern Design 1880–1980*, New York: Abrams, 1982:263.

Dziekiewicz, Victor I. (1951–)

▶ Argentine designer; active Chicago.

▶ Studied design, University of Detroit; architecture, Virginia Polytechnic Institute and State University, Blacksburg, Virginia.

▶ In 1980, Dziekiewicz set up DesignBridge, Chicago, to combine synergistic architecture, interior design, visual communications and product design; designed the corporate image of Brueton Industries, its *Tango* seating series, and *Concerto* series low tables; was associate professor, School of Art, Northern Illinois, University, De Kalb, Illinois.

▶ Received Outstanding Building Award, Association of American Architects; Citation of Merit, Interior Architecture Award, AIA; Silver Product Design Award, IBD; Merchandising Award, Sales and Marketing Council of Greater Chicago; Design Excellence Citation, *ID* magazine.

E

Eames Jr., Charles Ormond (1907–78)

▶ American architect-designer; born St. Louis, Missouri; active Bloomfield Hills, Michigan, and Venice, California; husband of Ray Kaiser Eames.

▶ 1924–26, Studied architecture, Washington University, St. Louis; 1936, Cranbrook Academy of Art, Bloomfield Hills, Michigan.

▶ Eames was one of the most influential furniture designers of the 20th century. He was a steel-mill worker before becoming a technical draftsman; 1925–27, worked for the architecture firm Trueblood and Graf, St. Louis; in 1930, was in private practice at Gray and Eames, St. Louis. In 1934, he traveled and worked in Mexico; in 1935, returned to private practice at Eames and Walsh, St. Louis; in 1936, received a fellowship to study at Cranbrook Academy of Art, Bloomfield Hills, Michigan, where he met his future second wife Ray Kaiser and friend Eero Saarinen; 1937–40, was head of the department of experimental design under the school's director Eliel Saarinen. 1939–40, Eames worked in Eero Saarinen's office. Together they came to prominence by winning the 1940 'Organic Design in Home Furnishings' competition, New York Museum of Modern Art. Their most notable design for the competition was a molded plywood seat with aluminum legs; the plywood was formed into a multi-curved shell that presaged forms taken by plastics after World War II. A chair of theirs was awarded a prize, but, due to wartime shortages, could not be produced. With Saarinen, he designed innovative seating for the Mary Seaton Room of the Streamline-Modern 1940 Kleinhans Music Hall, Buffalo, New York. In 1941, he moved to California, where he worked in the art department of Metro-Goldwyn-Mayer and experimented with molded plywood. His furniture combined steel rods with two-way bent plywood; the wood technique was developed from his and Saarinen's work for the US Navy in 1942 designing a leg splint. 1942–45, Eames operated a development laboratory with John Entenza, Gregory Ain, Margaret Harris, Griswald Raetze (joined in 1943 by Herbert Matter and Harry Bertoia) and, from 1944, was in partnership with his wife Ray Eames, first in Los Angeles, then in nearby Venice, California. In 1944, he founded the firm Evans Manufacturing. Eames's mass-produced designs were made by Herman Miller, where he became consultant designer in 1946. Eames's use of wood with bent metal greatly influenced Italian design in the late 1940s. In 1948, he designed his now classic fiberglass-shell chair with thin multiple metal rod leg supports, subsequently dubbed the 'Eiffel tower' base. (His designs attracted nicknames: a low elliptical coffee table became the 'surfboard', and a plywood chair, the 'potato chip'.) His fiberglass technology came from its use in wartime radar disks manufactured in a plant near his studio. The fiberglass was tinted in the grey, orange, and red colors popular in the 1950s. His influential chair designs included the 1951 wire-based group, 1956 black leather and rosewood-veneer lounge model and ottoman, and 1958 aluminum table and seating group. Eames's interest in exhibition design and film-making made him a more formidable and celebrated spokesman for American design than his relatively modest portfolio of mass-produced furniture would warrant. His accomplishments included the innovative 1959 US exhibition,

Moscow (employing a multi-screen audio-visual presentation), and his film *Powers of Ten* (1968). Eames made dozens of sophisticated short films, often with Elmer Bern-stein's background music. In 1949 in Pacific Palisades, California, Eames built his own house, a steel-frame building made with standard prefabricated parts and suggesting Japanese influence with its open plan, lightness, and obvious geometric articulation; it became a shrine for student designers from all over the world. 1953–56, he taught, lectured, and served as consultant, University of California, Los Angeles and Berkeley; Los Angeles public schools; University of Georgia, Athens; Yale University; and California Institute of Technology, Pasadena. For a time from 1943, Harry Bertoia, having met Eames at the Cranbrook Academy, worked with him in California; Eames's wire-grid chair seats were probably a Bertoia invention, though not acknowledged as such. In 1989, Eames's daughter Lucia sold her father's archive of furniture, prototypes and maquettes to Rolf Fehlbaum, founder of Vitra Design Museum near Basel, where the studio was recreated in c1994.

▶ Furniture and projects included: 1941 first molded plywood seat, 1942 molded plywood experiments and molded plywood prototypes for Navy Department splint, 1943 production of molded plywood splints and molded plywood glider, 1945 Case Study houses #8 and #9, 1945 experimental chairs and children's plywood furniture, 1945 first production-model plywood ('potato chip') chair with plywood legs, 1945 plywood tables, 1946 case goods, 1946 plywood ('potato chip') chair with metal legs, 1946 plywood folding screen, 1945 plywood tables (other models), 1947 plywood folding tables, 1947 Jefferson Memorial competition, 1948 first Herman Miller graphics, 1949 first Herman Miller showroom, 1949 'An Exhibition for Modern Living,' 1950 Eames Storage Units, 1950 'Good Design' exhibition, 1950 plastic armchairs and side chair, 1950 low table rod base, 1951 elliptical ('surfboard') table, 1952 wire chair, 1951 wire sofa, 1952 House of Cards game, 1953 Hang-It-All clothes rack, 1954 Sears compact storage, 1954 sofa compact, 1954 stadium seating, 1955 stacking chair, 1956 Eames lounge chair and ottoman, 1958 Aluminum Group chairs and tables, 1959 Revell toy house, 1960 Time-Life chair and stool, 1961 La Fonda chair, 1961 Eames contract storage, 1962 tandem seating, 1963 tandem shell seating, 1964 *#3473* sofa, 1964 segmented-base table, 1968 intermediate desk chair, 1968 metal-frame leather chaise, 1970 drafting chair, 1971 molded plastic chair, 1971 two-piece secretary's chair, 1971 loose-cushion chair, 1974 IBM Newton cards, and 1984 leather-and-teak sofa.

▶ Work shown widely, including 1940 'Organic Designs in Home Furnishings' (first prize award), New York Museum of Modern Art; 1946 and 1973 one-person exhibition, New York Museum of Modern Art; 1948 'International Competition for Low-Cost Furniture Design' exhibition (second prize), New York Museum of Modern Art; 1970 'Modern Chairs 1918–1970' exhibition, Whitechapel Gallery, London; 1977 'The Work of Charles and Ray Eames' exhibition, Frederick S. Wight Art Gallery (University of California, Los Angeles); 1982 'Shape and Environment: Furniture by American Architects,' Whitney Museum of

American Art, Fairfield County, Connecticut; 1983–84 'Design Since 1945' exhibition, Philadelphia Museum of Art. In 1960, elected Honorary Royal Designer for Industry, London.

▶ Don Wallance, *Shaping America's Products*, New York, 1956:177–81. 'Eames Celebration,' *Architectural Design*, Vol. 36, Sept. 1966. Cat., *Modern Chairs 1918–1970*, London: Lund Humphries, 1971. Charles Eames, 'General Motors Revisited,' *Architectural Forum*, Vol. 134, June 1971:21–27. Charles Eames, *A Computer Perspective*, Cambridge, Mass.: MIT Press, 1973. Arthur Drexler, *Charles Eames: Furniture from the Design Collection*, New York: Museum of Modern Art, 1973. 'Nelson, Eames, Girard, Probst: The Design Process at Herman Miller,' *Design Quarterly 98/99*, 1975. Cat., Philip Morrison, *Connections: The Work of Charles and Ray Eames*, Los Angeles: Frederick S. Wight Art Gallery (University of California, Los Angeles), 1976. Cat., Lisa Phillips (intro- duction), *Shape and Environment: Furniture by American Architects*, New York: Whitney Museum of American Art, 1982:24–25. Cat., Kathryn B. Hiesinger and George H. Marcus III (eds.), *Design Since 1945*, Philadelphia: Philadelphia Museum of Art, 1983. John Neuhart, Marilyn Neuhart, and Ray Eames, *Eames Design*, New York: Abrams, 1989. Mathew Ginal, *Progressive Architecture*, June 1990:28. Pat Kirkham, 'Charles Eames' in Mel Byars and Russell Flinchum (eds.), *50 American Designers, 1918–1968*, Washington: Preservation, 1994.

▶ See **Eames, Ray**

Eames, Ray   (b. Bernice Alexandra Kaiser   1912–88)

▶ American designer; born Sacramento, California; wife of Charles Eames.

▶ 1933–39, studied with Hans Hofmann, New York, Gloucester, and Provincetown, Massachusetts; and weaving, Cranbrook Academy of Art, Bloomingfield Hills, Michigan, under Marianne Strengel.

▶ She changed her name in 1954 to Ray Bernice Alexandra Kaiser. In 1936, became a founding member of the group American Abstract Artists. In 1941, she married Charles Eames; her gold wedding ring was designed and made by Harry Bertoia. In 1941, they settled in Southern California. In 1942, she produced her first plywood sculpture; 1942–48, designed covers for the journals *Arts* and *Architecture* and, 1948–53, magazine advertisements for her and her husband's furniture for Herman Miller. From the late 1940s, she and Charles Eames worked collaboratively, and all of his work should be attributed mutually.

▶ Work first shown at 1937 (I) American Abstract Artists exhibition, Riverside Museum, New York, and paintings in a 1944 group show, Los Angeles County Museum of Art.

▶ 'Nelson, Eames, Girard, Probst: The Design Process at Herman Miller,' *Design Quarterly 98/99*, 1975. John Neuhart, Marilyn Neuhart, and Ray Eames, *Eames Design*, New York Abrams, 1989. Martin Eidelberg (ed.), *What Modern Was*, New York: Le Musée des Arts Décoratifs and Abrams, 1991.

▶ See **Eames, Charles**

Eastlake, Charles   (1836–1906)

▶ British designer and writer; born Plymouth; active London.

▶ Apprenticed under architect Philip Hardwick and studied Royal Academy Schools.

▶ During the 1860s, he was a journalist, writing on furniture and decorations beginning with 1864 article 'The Fashion of Furniture' in *Cornhill Magazine*; 1866–71, was assistant secretary, Royal Institute of British Architects, becoming its first permanent paid secretary 1871–78. Eastlake's *Hints on Household Taste in Furniture, Upholstery, and Other Details* (1868) was greatly influential in the USA on the Aesthetic movement. The book was the first and most influential British publication on household art. The quotation from Viollet-le-Duc on its title page suggests the French theorist's influence on Eastlake. Eastlake included illustrations of furniture, wallpapers, tiles, and artifacts, influenced by medieval and early-English sources. His solid and undecorated furniture was markedly similar to the work of Bruce J. Talbert's

shown in *Gothic Forms Applied to Furniture, Metal Work, and Decoration for Domestic Purposes* (1867). Few examples exist of Eastlake's furniture for Jackson and Graham and wallpapers for Jeffrey. More effective as a tastemaker than a designer, he discuss- ed principles of good taste in everyday articles and was a prolific writer. In 1872, he published *A History of the Gothic Revival*. He influenced American cabinetmakers, including Herter Brothers, Daniel Pabst, and A. Kimbel and J. Cabus.

▶ In 1854, received a prize (architectural drawings) at the Royal Academy and, in 1855–56, showed architectural drawings.

▶ Elizabeth Aslin, *Nineteenth Century English Furniture*, New York, 1962:61. J. Mordaunt Crook (Introduction), Charles Locke Eastlake, *A History of the Gothic Revival*, reprint ed., Leicester and New York: 1970. Cat., *Eastlake-Influenced American Furniture, 1870–1890*, Yonkers, NY: Hudson River Museum, 1973. Doreen Bolger Burke et al., *In Pursuit of Beauty: Americans and the Aesthetic Movement*, New York: Metropolitan Museum of Art and Rizzoli, 1986:423–24.

Easton, Louis B.   (1864–1921)

▶ American architect and furniture designer, born Half Day, Illinois; active near Chicago, Illinois, and Pasadena, California; brother-in-law of Elbert Hubbard.

▶ Trained as a teacher, Bloomington Normal School, Bloomington, Illinois.

▶ He was vice-principal and taught manual arts, Lemont High School; as hobby, built furniture in oak and leather; in 1902, moved to Pasadena, California; in 1904, designed and built a house for his family and hung a sign outside reading 'Bungalows and Furniture'; with a few tradespeople, designed about 25 houses in the Pasadena area. The 1906 Carl Curtis ranch in redwood-and-batten construction was Easton's most notable building. The structure, with its deeply overhung roof, illustrated his belief that construction materials should serve the dual purpose of creating a finished surface and structural support. The furniture was designed for the house. Easton was said to have designed the house on the back of an envelope on receiving the commission; he worked on its details during construction while sitting on the floor of the unfinished dwelling. Some of the furniture, and the exterior of the house, were finished with a wire brush. In an Arts and Crafts aesthetic, the furniture could be easily disassembled due to its post-and-peg construction. Easton's typical buildings had wire-brushed redwood board-and-batten wainscoting, upper walls covered in undyed burlap or monk's cloth, low partitions, mortise-and-tenon joints with raised pegs, flat ceilings with redwood joists and exposed decking, exposed exterior redwood structural members, and untreated shingles or clapboards as infill panels. Easton designed the 1911 weekend beach house, near Palos Verdes, California, of architect Myron Hunt, using redwood inside and out and equipping it with custom furniture, integrated fixtures, and an elaborate fireplace. In 1914, Easton moved to rural Anaheim, California, where he remodeled an adobe house and farmed.

▶ Furniture shown at 1903 'Handicraft Exhibition,' Chicago Art Institute. House designs shown at 1913 Los Angeles Architectural Club exhibition.

▶ Timothy J. Andersen et al., *California Design 1910*, Salt Lake City: Peregrine Smith, 1980:122–23,127.

Ebendorf, Robert   (1939–)

▶ American artist and jeweler.

▶ His early designs included coffee-pots, tea-infuser, and umbrella handles in precious and semi-precious materials, including silver, walnut, ebony, moonstone; showing both American and Scandinavian influences, his 1965 silver coffee-pot had an ebony handle. In the 1970s, his work was primarily non-figurative. His jewelry of the 1980s was produced in non-precious materials, including paper and Formica; and in combinations of photographs, wood, and paper.

Eberson, John
► American designer.
► Eberson was known for his cinema décors. One of his earliest, the 1923 Majestic Theater in Houston, Texas, was a loosely recreated garden of a late-Renaissance palazzo in Italy. Through his workshop Michelangelo Studios, he was successful at producing elaborate plasterwork for his theater décors in Spanish, Moorish, Dutch, Chinese and other styles.
► Jonathan M. Woodham, *Twentieth-Century Ornament*, New York: Rizzoli, 1990:53–54.

Ebner, Eduard (1933–)
► Austrian furniture designer; born Eisenstadt.
► Ebner designed chairs and interiors, including a 1975–76 single-unit living-room system.
► Günther Feuerstein, *Vienna—Present and Past: Arts and Crafts—Applied Art—Design*, Vienna: Jugend und Volk, 1976: 61,63,80.

Écart International
See Putman, Andrée

Echerer, Bruno (1926–)
► Austrian designer; born Wels.
► Echerer designed office and domestic interiors that included High-Tech, Pop-Art, and Futurist elements.
► Günther Feuerstein, *Vienna—Present and Past: Arts and Crafts—Applied Art—Design*, Vienna: Jugend und Volk, 1976: 61,63,80.

Eckhoff, Tias (1926–)
► Norwegian metalworker, glass designer, and ceramicist.
► 1947–48, trained in ceramics, Saxbo, Copenhagen, under Nathalie Krebs; 1949, graduated Statens Håndverks -og Kunstindustriskole, Oslo.
► In 1949, he became designer at Porsgrunns Porselaensfabrik (Norway), and from 1953–60, was its artistic director. From *c*1950, designed for Georg Jensen (silver), Dansk Knivfabrik (cutlery), Halden Aluminumvarefabrik and Norsk Stålpress (metalware). His Triennale di Milano awards brought great success to Porsgrunns. Remaining a consultant designer to the firm, he set up his own design studio in 1957; consultant designer to Trio-Ving, Oslo; Ludtofte Design, Copenhagen; Norsk Stålpress, Bergen. He is known for the popular 1953 *Cypress* flatware pattern produced by Georg Jensen. His career in metalsmithing began with the Jensen's award for his *Cypress* pattern; he subsequently designed stainless-steel flatware *Fuga* and *Opus* produced by Dansk and 1961 *Maya* by Norsk.
► *Cypress* flatware won 1953 inter-Scandinavian design competition sponsored by Georg Jensen celebrating its 50th anniversary. Received prizes at 1954 (X) (two gold medals), 1957 (XI) (two gold medals), and 1960 (XII) (gold medal) Triennali di Milano; 1962, 1965, and 1966 emblems for good Norwegian design, Norwegian Design Centre; (with Henning Koppel) 1953 Lunning Prize.
► Tias Eckhoff, 'Keramiske materialer i husholdningen,' *Bonytt*, Vol. 15, 1955:183–85. Alf Bøe, *Industridesigneren Tias Eckhoff*, Oslo, 1965. Alf Bøe, *Porsgrunds porselaensfabrik: 1885–1965*, Oslo, 1965. Cat., *Georg Jensen Silversmithy: 77 Artists, 75 Years*, Washington: Smithsonian Institution Press, 1980. Cat., David Revere McFadden (ed.), *Scandinavian Modern Design 1880–1980*, New York: Abrams, 1982:263. Cat., Kathryn B. Hiesinger and George H. Marcus III (eds.), *Design Since 1945*, Philadelphia: Philadelphia Museum of Art, 1983. Cat., *The Lunning Prize*, Stockholm: Nationalmuseum, 1986:50–53. Jennifer Hawkins Opie, *Scandinavia: Ceramics and Glass in the Twentieth Century*, New York: Rizzoli, 1989.

Eckmann, Otto (1865–1902)
► German designer, printer, and painter; born Hamburg.
► Studied graphics, painting, and the applied arts, Kunstgewerbeschule, Hamburg and Nuremberg, and Munich academy.

► After beginning as a painter, he pursued the decorative arts, influenced by the techniques and art of Japanese printmaking. In 1896 and 1897, the journals *Pan* and *Die Jugend* printed his ornaments and illustration. He was professor at Kunstgewerbeschule, Berlin, where he specialized in the applied arts; designed furniture, rugs, and textiles; rendered ceramic tiles for Villeroy et Boch and interiors for the Grand Duke Louis IV of Hesse-Darmstadt, among others; was one of the major proponents of Jugendstil.
► Yvonne Brunhammer et al., *Art Nouveau Belgium, France*, Houston: Rice University, 1976. Kathryn Bloom Hiesinger (ed.), *Art Nouveau in Munich: Masters of Jugenstil*, Munich: Prestel, 1988.

École Boulle
► French learning institution; located Paris.
► The École Supérieure des Arts Appliqués aux Industries de l'Ameublement was founded in 1886, in the 12th arrondissement of Paris, near the furniture-making area of Faubourg Saint-Antoine. In 1891, its name was changed to honor André-Charles Boulle, Louis XIV's cabinetmaker, and acquired the nickname *la fille du Faubourg*. 1918–35, its director was André Fréchet, followed by Paul Beucher 1947–1972. Notable students included Armand-Albert Rateau, Raymond Subes, Maurice Jallot, Clément Rousseau, and Etienne Kohlmann; teachers included Louis Sognot, Maurice Pré, and Maxine Old.
► Student work shown at Salons of Société des Artistes Décorateurs; with Fréchet in both pavilions of the City of Paris, the décor and furniture of the Salon d'Honneur, 1925 Paris 'Exposition Internationale des Arts Décoratifs et Industriels Modernes'; 1935 'Exposition Universelle et Internationale de Bruxelles.'
► Pierre Kjellberg, *Art Déco: les maîtres du Mobilier, le décor des Paquebots*, Paris: Amateur, 1986:69. *100 années de création 1886–1986, L'École Boulle*, Paris: Syros Alternatives, 1986.

École de Nancy
► French artists' group; active Nancy.
► In 1901 under the leadership of Émile Gallé, the Alliance Provinciale des Industries d'Art (aka École de Nancy) was founded in Nancy. The artists included the Daum brothers, August Legras, Louis Majorelle, Victor Prouvé, Eugène Vallin, and d'Argental. When Gallé died, the Daum brothers headed the group.
► First exhibition of the group shown at 1903 Salon of Union Centrale des Arts Décoratifs, Paris.
► Jessica Rutherford, *Art Nouveau, Art Deco and the Thirties: The Furniture Collections at Brighton Museum*, Brighton: The Royal Pavilion, Art Gallery and Museums, 1983:14,18. Frederick Cooke, *Glass: Twentieth-Century Design*, New York: Dutton, 1986.

Eda Glasbruk
► Swedish glassworks.
► A glassworks was established at Eda in 1835 by two Norwegians; in 1838, went out of business; in 1842, was taken over and resumed by Eda Bruksbolag under Gustaf S. Santesson's management; began to produce bottles and tableware; became one of the first Swedish firms to produced molded glass; by *c*1900, began to hire glass cutters and produced decorative wares; in 1903, (with other firms) formed A.B. De Svenska Kristallglasbruken to foster good design; 1927–33, was managed by Edward Strömberg with designs by Gerda Strömberg; closed in 1953.
► Work shown at 1930 'Stockholmsutstäliningen.'
► Jennifer Hawkins Opie, *Scandinavian: Ceramics and Glass in the Twentieth Century*, New York: Rizzoli, 1989.

Edenfalk, Bengt (1924–)
► Swedish glassware designer.
► 1947–52, studied Konstfackskolan and Tekniska Skolan, Stockholm.
► From 1953–78, he was artistic director at Skruf; from 1978, he was a designer at the Kosta Boda glassworks, Kosta.
► Sales catalog, *The Kosta Boda Book of Glass*, 1986:5. Jennifer Hawkins Opie, *Scandinavia: Ceramics and Glass in the Twentieth Century*, New York: Rizzoli, 1989.

Edinburgh Tapestry Company (Dovecot Studios)
► British textile firm.
► The firm started as a company set up in 1912 by the 4th Marquess of Bute. The first two master craftsmen at Dovecot Studios came from William Morris's Merton Abbey workshops. One of the few tapestry manufacturers today, Edinburgh Tapestry commissioned famous artists, including David Hockney. Pepsi-Cola ordered a group of 11 tapestries illustrated by American painter Frank Stella. The firm stocked yarn in more than 1,500 hues.

Edinburgh Weavers
► British fabric and carpet manufacturers; located Carlisle.
► As the experimental unit of Sundour Fabrics, Edinburgh Weavers was known, like Wilton Royal Carpets, as a firm that took risks and produced knotted carpets in Modern avant-garde motifs; originally in Edinburgh, was established 1929 and merged with the main weaving factory in 1930. Alec Hunter and Theo Moorman were responsible for hand-woven prototypes. Hunter provided the groundwork for Edinburgh Weavers, which was later managed by Alastair Morton; he commissioned some of the most accomplished designers and artists of the 1930s. Hans Tisdall designed intriguing abstracts; Ashley Havinden, elegant curls, birds in flight, and ribbon motifs; and Marion Dorn, swirling abstractions. Artists Ben Nicholson and Barbara Hepworth designed the 1937 *Constructivist Fabrics* range. Edinburgh was taken over by Courtaulds in 1963.
► Cat., *Thirties: British art and design before the war*, London: Arts Council of Great Britain, Hayward Gallery, 1979:87,88,89, 144,145,147,187,188. Valerie Mendes, *The Victoria and Albert Museum's Textile Collection, British Textiles from 1900 to 1937*, London: Victoria and Albert Museum, 1992.

Eerste Nederlandse Mechanische Apparantenfabriek Ph. Dekker
► Dutch furniture manufacturer.
► From the 1930s, the firm produced domestic tubular-steel furniture designed by Paul Schuitema and Arie Verbeek.
► Barbie Campbell-Cole and Tim Benton (eds.), *Tubular Steel Furniture*, London: The Art Book Company, 1979:31.

Egender, Karl (1897–1969)
► Swiss architect and interior designer; born Burzwiller, Alsace (now France).
► 1912–1915, apprenticed as technical draftsman with Gebrüder Wasmer, Zürich.
► 1921–29, Egender and Adolf Steger were partners in an architecture practice, Zürich. 1930–39, Egender and Wilhem Müller were partners with co-worker Bruno Giacometti. As well as architecture, Egender was interested in fine art; in 1927, began his career as an interior decorator and was a member of the Schweizer Kollektivgruppe that furnished six apartments in Ludwig Mies van der Rohe's building at 'Die Wohnung' exhibition, 1927 'Weissenhofsiedlung,' Stuttgart; in 1930, designed furniture for his own apartment. In the mid-1930s, his designs for a tubular steel chair were put into production. In 1938, he designed chairs for Gübelin jewelers, Geneva and, in 1940, a garden chair.
► Architecture included 1927–30 Limmathaus, Zürich; 1927–33 Gewerbeschule, Kunstgewerbemuseum, Zürich; 1928–31 planning for the zoological garden, Zürich; 1936–38 stadium, Zürich-Oerlikon; 1937–41 Baur's Building, Colombo, Ceylon (now Sri Lanka); terrace restaurant and the fashion division, 1939 Zürich 'Landesausstellung' ('Swiss National Exposition').
► *Künstler-Lexikon der Schweiz, XX. Jahrhundert*, Frauenfeld 1963–1967, Vol. 1. Friederike Mehlau-Wiebking et al., *Schweizer Typenmöbel 1925–35, Sigfried Giedion und die Wohnbedarf AG*, Zürich: gta, 1989:226–27.

Ehrenlechner, Hermann
► German silversmith; active Dresden.
► Trained as a silversmith in workshops in Pforzheim, Munich, and Berlin.

► In 1904, he began working in Dresden; applied elaborate ornament to most of his designs, often incorporating precious stones and enameling; produced several silver pieces designed by Karl Gross.
► Annelies Krekel-Aalberse, *Art Nouveau and Art Déco Silver*, New York: Abrams, 1989:253.

Ehrlich, Christa (1903–)
► Austrian silversmith; active Vienna and The Hague.
► Studied Kunstgewerbeschule, Vienna.
► She was an assistant to Josef Hoffmann in his architecture practice; in 1927, moved to the Netherlands and produced some graphic-arts designs; designed Modern silver for Zilverfabriek Voorschoten, managed by Carel J.A. Begeer. She became one of the silver designers in the Netherlands producing severe, Modernist designs, although she introduced some playful minor decoration.
► Painted ceiling-height showcases in a leaf pattern, Austrian pavilion designed by Hoffmann and Haedtl, 1925 Paris 'Exposition Internationale des Arts Décoratifs et Industriels Modernes.' In charge of the construction and installation, Austrian section, 1927 Leipzig 'Europäisches Kunstgewerbe' exhibition, Grassi Museum.
► *Industry and Design in the Netherlands, 1850/1950*, Amsterdam: Stedelijk Museum, 1985:221. Annelies Krekel-Aalberse, *Art Nouveau and Art Déco Silver*, New York: Abrams, 1989: 149, 180,189,190,201,203,253.

Ehrlich, Franz (1907–1983)
► German designer.
► 1927–30, studied Bauhaus, Dessau, under Josef Albers, Paul Klee, Vasilii Kandinskii, and Joost Schmidt.
► He became involved in the Constructivist stage productions of Oskar Schlemmer, a master at the Bauhaus; worked in the architecture office of Walter Gropius; Berlin; was active in decoration, advertising, printing before being arrested by the Nazis for anti-Fascist activities; 1936–39, he was imprisoned in the concentration camp at Buchenwald, near Weimar; after the war, was active in Leipzig, designing numerous exhibitions.
► Lionel Richard, *Encyclopédie du Bauhaus*, Paris: Somogy, 1985: 185. Cat., *The Bauhaus: Masters and Students*, New York: Barry Friedman, 1988.

Ehrmann, Marli (b. Marie Helene Heimann 1904–82)
► German textile designer and teacher.
► 1923, studied Kunstgewerbeschule, Berlin; 1923–27, studied Bauhaus, Weimar and Dessau, and fabric design, Hamburg.
► 1926–27, she was an independent weaver, Bauhaus; became a teacher, Hamburg; 1932–33, Herzl School, Berlin; settled in the USA in 1937, where, 1939–47, she taught fabric design at the School of Design (later Institute of Design), and taught at Hall House, both Chicago; 1947–56, was a freelance designer; work included the curtains of Ludwig Mies van der Rohe's Lake Shore Apartments, Chicago; 1956, opened Elm Shop, Oak Park, Illinois.
► Lionel Richard, *Encyclopédie du Bauhaus*, Paris: Somogy, 1985: 185. Cat., Gunta Stölzl, *Weberei am Bauhaus und ams eigener Werkstatt*, Berlin: Bauhaus-Archiv, 1987:148.

Ehrner, Anna (1948–)
► Swedish glassware designer; born Stockholm.
► Ehrner was a designer at the Kosta Boda glassworks.
► Her work was shown in Stockholm, Japan, Germany, and Copenhagen.

Ehrström, Eric O.W.
► Finnish metalworker.
► Ehrström designed and executed the metalwork for some of the buildings of the Finnish architecture firm Gesellius, Lindgren & Saarinen, including the 1898–1900 Pohjola fire insurance company at Aleksanterinkatu and Mikonkatu, Helsinki; 1901–03 'Hvitträsk' house, Lake Hvitträsk; 1901–04 'Hvittorp' house; Remer house; 1902–12 Finnish National Museum; 1903–04 Pohjoismaiden Osakepankki bank, Helsinki.

► Marika Mausen et al., *Eliel Saarinen: Projects 1896–1923*, Cambridge: MIT Press, 1990.

Eichenberger, Walter (1936–)
► Italian industrial designer; born Milan; active Zug (Switzerland).
► He began his professional career in 1961; from 1967, was a partner at M + E Design, Zug; was a consultant designer of utensils, textile machinery and apparatus, and precision instruments, and to manufacturers of domestic electronics; designed kitchen components for Franke; became a member of ADI (Associazione per il Disegno Industriale).
► *ADI Annual 1976*, Milan: Associazione per il Disegno Industriale, 1976.

Eichler, Fritz (1911–91)
► German teacher and designer; active Ulm and Frankfurt.
► 1931–35, studied art history and drama, Berlin and Munich.
► 1945–63, he worked in theater-set design; became professor, Hochschule für Gestaltung; Ulm; hired by Artur Braun in 1954, was program director and became a Braun director; was responsible with the Braun brothers for commissioning a series of radios and phonographs from the Hochschule für Gestaltung, Ulm, establishing the stark Functionalist forms of the shavers, sound-equipment, and household wares that followed. Ulm teacher Hans Gugelot and student Dieter Rams later joined the design staff of Braun in Frankfurt.
► Early radios shown at 1955 'Radio Exhibition,' Düsseldorf, and at 1969 'Qu'est-ce que le design?' exhibition, Centre Georges Pompidou, Paris, and 1983–84 'Design Since 1945' exhibition, Philadelphia Museum of Art.
► 'Braun's Guiding Light,' *Design*, No. 180, Dec. 1963:61. Cat., *Qu'est-ce que le design?*, Paris: Centre Georges Pompidou, 1969. Jocelyn de Noblet, *Design*, Paris, 1974:265–66. François Burkhardt and Inez Franksen (eds.), *Dieter Rams*, Berlin, 1980–81:11–16. Cat., Kathryn B. Hiesinger and George H. Marcus III (eds.), *Design Since 1945*, Philadelphia: Philadelphia Museum of Art, 1983.

Eiermann, Charlotte (1912–)
► German interior designer; born Potsdam.
► 1938–42, Eiermann worked in the office of architect Egon Eiermann, Berlin, whom she married; 1959–69, led housing council of the Deutscher Werkbund, Berlin; designed the permanent exhibition 'Living'; 1970–80, worked at Internationalen Design Zentrum, Berlin; 1982–84, worked in the department of construction art, Hochschule der Künste, Berlin; in 1979, became a member of the board of directors, Bauhaus-Archivs, Berlin.
► Furnished model apartments at 1956–57 'Interbau' international construction fair, Berlin.
► Cat., Design Center Stuttgart, *Women in Design: Careers and Life Histories Since 1900*, Stuttgart: Haus der Wirtschaft, 1989:348–49.

Eikerman, Alma
► American jewelry designer and metalsmith; born Kansas.
► Studied liberal arts, Kansas State University, Emporia, Kansas, design, painting, and metalsmithing, University of Kansas, Lawrence, Kansas, and Columbia University, New York, to 1942.
► In 1945, she began to teach general design courses and jewelry design in Wichita; became a jewelry designer and metalsmith; from 1947, taught at Indiana University, where she developed one of the best schools for metalworking in the USA and became a key figure in the resurgence of metalsmithing in the postwar period. Her mentor in metalsmithing was goldsmith Karl Gustav Hansen, designer director at Hans Hansen Sølvmedie, Kolding (Sweden); she also studied with Baron Fleming in his Stockholm workshop; received 1968 Carnegie Foundation grant that funded her renowned workshop and resulted in the film *Creative Silversmithing*. Her work was influenced by artists Vasilii Kandinskii, Claude Cézanne, Henri Matisse, Arthur Dove, Georgia O'Keefe,

Stuart Davis, Charles Burchfield, Charles R. Sheeler, and Hans Hofmann.
► Received 1948 Handy and Harmon Silversmithing Award for study at Rhode Island School of Design under Baron Erik Fleming of Sweden. Work subject of 1985 exhibition, Indiana University Art Museum. Work included in a large number of exhibitions.
► Alma Eikerman, 'Creative Designing in Metal,' *Craft News* (Handy and Harmon), May 1952:4–9. 'Eikerman-Wilson-Martz Exhibition Review,' *Creative Horizons*, No. 18, July–Aug 1958:44. Cat., Constance L. Bowen, *A Tribute to Alma Eikerman: Master Craftsman*, Indiana University Art Museum, 1985.

Einarsdottir, Sigrun (1951–)
► Icelandic glassware designer.
► Studied in Denmark.
► In the late 1970s, she set up the first hot-glass workshop in Iceland; designed both unique works and production glassware decorated with fluidly rendered human figures.
► Cat., David Revere McFadden (ed.), *Scandinavian Modern Design 1880–1980*, New York: Abrams, 1982:263, No. 303.

Einarsson, Gudmundur (1895–1963)
► Icelandic ceramicist.
► 1921–26, studied in Munich.
► His double-walled ceramic pieces included pierced strapwork and animal figures. A leading figure in the development of the Icelandic ceramics tradition, he set up the first ceramics workshop in Iceland in 1927.
► Cat., David Revere McFadden (ed.), *Scandinavian Modern Design 1880–1980*, New York: Abrams, 1982:263, No. 106.

Eisch, Erwin (1927–)
► German glassware designer and craftsperson; active Bavaria.
► Trained in glass blowing under his father; studied engraving, Glasfachschule, Weissel, and Academy of Art, Munich, under Heinrich Kirchner.
► Eisch worked in hot glass; from 1960, experimented with glass as a sculptural medium; delivered an influential lecture to the Deutsche Glastechnische Gesellschaft in 1975; was a leading member of the New Wave Studio movement of the 1960s.
► Work subject of 1960 exhibition, Stuttgart.
► Frederick Cooke, *Glass: Twentieth-Century Design*, New York: Dutton, 1986:105. *Die Sammlung Wolfgang Kermer, Glasmuseum Frauenau*, Munich/Zürich: Schnell und Steiner, 1989:19–27.

Eisenberg
► American costume jeweler; located Chicago.
► The firm was established in 1914 by Jonas Eisenberg and became known for its high-quality women's clothing; in the 1930s managed by sons Harold and Sam Eisenberg, produced clothing under the name 'Eisenberg Originals'; began producing costume jewelry in gold and dramatic designs incorporating stones from Swarovski, Austria, into pewter-like metal. In 1935, the jewelry design services of Fallon and Kappel, New York, were commissioned. 1940–72, Eisenberg's jewelry was designed by Ruth M. Kamke, who produced figural pieces, sterling silver items, and the Swarovski crystal range. Using the lost-wax casting technique, white metal alloys were used until 1941 and silver 1941–45, when alloy was used again. In 1958, the firm stopped making clothing and began specializing in costume jewelry; in 1977, became a division of Berns-Friedman.
► Deanna F. Cera (ed.), *Jewels of Fantasy: Costume Jewelry of the 20th Century*, New York: Abrams, 1992.

Eisenloeffel, Jan W. (1876–1957)
► Dutch silversmith, metalworker, glass designer, and ceramicist; active Laren.
► Trained with the firm Hoeker en Zoon; in 1898, studied in Russia.
► He designed silver for a metal workshop in Amstelhoek. His wares at Hoeker en Zoon were not identified as his when shown in international exhibitions. In 1902, he set up his own company

with J.C. Stoffels; 1903–04, worked for De Woning, Amsterdam; until 1907, for Fabriek van Zilverwerk, Utrecht; in 1908, for Vereinigte Werkstätten in Munich. Begeer, director of Fabriek van Zilverwerk, credited his designers, including Eisenloeffel. Riemerschmid liked Eisenloeffel's work, and his copper sets appeared in Riemerschmid's interiors.

▶ Work in the geometrical style shown at Hoeker en Zoon stand, 1900 Paris 'Exposition Universelle,' where some of his (uncredited) wares won awards and were bought by Tiffany. Received medals for his own separately shown work and (uncredited) at Hoeker stand at 1902 Turin 'Esposizione Internazionale d'Arte Decorativa Moderna.' Silver objects shown at 1904 exhibition. Hermann Hirschwald's Hohenzollern Kunstgewerbehaus, Berlin.

▶ Annelies Krekel-Aalberse, *Art Nouveau and Art Déco Silver*, New York: Abrams, 1989:16,100,129,130,176,249,253. Cat., *Metallkunst*, Berlin: Bröhan Museum, 1990:142–53.

Eisenman, Peter (1932–)

▶ American architect and teacher; born Newark, New Jersey.

▶ Studied Cornell University, Ithaca, New York, Columbia University, New York, and Cambridge University.

▶ 1957–58, he collaborated with TAC (The Architects' Collaborative), Cambridge, Massachusetts; taught at Harvard University, Syracuse University, and Princeton University. From 1967, he taught at Cooper Union, New York; in 1967, founded the Institute for Architecture and Urban Studies, New York, of which he was director until 1982; was co-editor of the architecture journal *Oppositions*; was a member of the ad-hoc New York Five, along with John Hejduk, Richard Meier, Robert Graves, and Charles Gwathmey. His work was associated with Italian Rationalism; the red staircase in his House VI could not be climbed and did not lead anywhere. Known as a Deconstructivist, he designed eccentric non-site-specific buildings until the early 1980s, ceramic dinnerware in the 1980s produced by Swid Powell, and a 1991 34-fabric range by Knoll.

▶ Architecture included 1967–68 House I (Barenholtz Pavilion), Princeton, New Jersey; 1969–70 House II (Falk House), Hardwick, Connecticut; 1969–70 House III (Miller House), Lakeville, Connecticut; 1970 House VI (Frank House), Cornwall, Connecticut; 1978 E1 Even Odd House; 1990 Wexner Center for the Visual Arts, Ohio State University, Columbus, Ohio.

▶ Participated in various exhibitions at the New York Museum of Modern Art: 1967 'The New City: Architecture and Urban Renewal,' 1968 'Architecture of Museums,' and 1973 'Another Chance for Housing.' Work shown at 1970 (XV) Triennale di Milan, 1976 Biennale di Venezia, and 1978 'Assenza-Prensenza' in Bologna. His production in 'Cite Un Seen II' was included in 'Le Affinità Elettive,' Palazzo della Triennale, 1985 Triennale di Milano.

▶ Kenneth Frampton and Colin Rowe, *Five Architects: Eisenman, Graves, and Gwathmey, Hejduk, Meier*, New York: Wittenborn, 1972. Peter Eisenman, *House of Cards*, New York, 1978. *Le Affinità Elettive*, Milan: Electa, 1985. Auction cat., *Asta di Modernariato 1900–1986, Auction 'Modernariato,'* Milan: Semenzato Nuova Geri, 8 Oct. 1986.

Eisi, Thomas   (1947–)

▶ Austrian lighting designer; active Britain.

▶ Studied fine art, Central School of Arts and Crafts, London, to 1977.

▶ From 1981, and prolifically in the late 1980s, he designed mainly one-off lighting, sometimes as part of furniture units.

▶ Albrecht Bangert and Karl Michael Armer, *80s Style: Designs of the Decade*, New York: Abbeville, 1990:111,118,230.

Eitelberger, Rudolf von   (1817–1885)

▶ Austrian designer and theoretician; born Olmütz.

▶ A pioneer in Viennese applied art, Eitelberger was director, Österreichisches Museum für Kunst und Industrie, Vienna, supporting reform movements.

▶ Günther Feuerstein, *Vienna—Present and Past: Arts and Crafts—Applied Art—Design*, Vienna: Jugend und Volk, 1976: 23,80.

Ekberg, Joseph   (1877–1945)

▶ Swedish ceramicist.

▶ 1897–1945, Ekberg designed for the Gustavsberg factory, where he incorporated Art Nouveau plant forms into his motifs.

Ekco Products

▶ American manufacturer; located Chicago.

▶ Ekco Products was established in Chicago in 1888, as a producer of undistinguished kitchen tools; at the end of World War II, upgraded the design and quality of its merchandise, its own employees acting as designers. Its 1946 *Flint* kitchen tools were designed by manager Arthur Keating, industrial designer James Hvale (hired in 1944), and engineers Myron J. Zimmer and James Chandler. The tools were sold as a set with a metal holder in packaging designed by Richard Latham of Raymond Loewy Associates, Chicago. In the 1950s, Latham worked on marketing and product planning for Ekco's kitchen products.

▶ Eliot Noyes, 'The Shape of the Thing: Good Design in Everyday Objects,' *Consumer Reports*, Jan. 1949:27. 'The Change at Ekco: Merchandising Bows to a Unique Planning Group,' *Industrial Design*, Vol. 3, Oct. 1956:103–05. Don Wallance, *Shaping America's Products*, New York, 1956:129–31. Jay Doblin, *One Hundred Great Product Designs*, New York, 1970:46. Cat., Kathryn B. Hiesinger and George H. Marcus III (eds.), *Design Since 1945*, Philadelphia: Philadelphia Museum of Art, 1983.

Ekco Radio Company
See Cole, Eric Kirkham

Ekholm, Kurt   (1907–75)

▶ Finnish ceramicist.

▶ 1932–48, he was artistic director, Arabia pottery, Helsinki, where he contributed new designs. His everyday earthenware dinnerware was easy to produce and decorate. In 1943, he set up the Arabia Museum; 1949–50, worked for Rörstrand, Lidköping (Sweden).

▶ Cat., David Revere McFadden (ed.), *Scandinavian Modern Design 1880–1980,* New York: Abrams, 1982:263, No. 105.

Ekstrøm, Terje   (1944–)

▶ Norwegian furniture designer.

▶ In the 1980s, Ekstrøm designed furniture for Stokke Fabrikker.

▶ Fredrik Wildhagen, *Norge i Form*, Oslo: Stenersen, 1988:203.

Elam

▶ Italian furniture manufacturer; located Meda.

▶ Elam produced small tables and furniture pieces by designers Marco Zanuso and Lorenzo Forgez Davazati; in 1968, began using plastics, primarily fiberglass, ABS, and metacrylate; produced 1970 *Minisit* chair in ABS and metal tubing by Zanuso.

▶ Cat., Milena Lamarová, *Design a Plastické Hmoty*, Prague: Uměleckoprůmyslové Muzeum, 1972:52,180.

Electrolux

▶ Swedish domestic appliance firm.

▶ AB Lux was founded in 1901, in Stockholm; it was the first electrical appliance manufacturer to produce a horizontal-cylinder vacuum cleaner, including the 1915 '*Model 111.*' Its flexible hose made it possible to clean in places other floor models could not reach. In 1919, the firm was renamed Electrolux and became committed to good design. In 1924, the Electrolux vacuum cleaner was successfully introduced in the USA. In the 1930s, the firm, which produced other appliances including refrigerators, began hiring consultant designers, including Raymond Loewy, Carl Otto, and Lurelle Guild of the USA, and Sixten Sason of Sweden. Its distinctive shop on boulevard des Malesherbes, Paris, of the late 1920s was designed by architect Germain Debré.

Elixir
See Blet, Thierry

Elkington
▶ British silversmiths; located Birmingham (England).
▶ In 1829, George Richard Elkington became director of a family firm that produced gilt objects, gold spectacle cases, and small domestic accessories including silver-mounted scent bottles; during the 1830s, (with cousin Henry Elkington) patented various refinements of the electrogilding process; experimented with electroplating and, in 1840, patented the first commercially successful process for electroplating silver and gold. In 1841, Elkington's chief metallurgist Alexander Parkes filed for a patent for electrotyping. These patents advanced metallurgy at Elkington and had far-reaching effects in Britain and the USA. Having bought up other electroplating patents, the firm had control of the industry in Britain until c1875. Since electroplating was inexpensive, Sheffield plating became obsolete. With silverplated objects as popular as sterling silver by the 1860s, Elkington hired Danish consultant designer Benjamin Schlick, who designed historicist models in Greek and Roman styles, produced from 1845. In c1850, the South Kensington Museum (later Victoria and Albert Museum), London, had Elkington reproduce some of the objects in its collection. George Elkington's son Frederick joined the firm in the 1850s and, after 1865, was its director. As well as silverplated pieces, Elkington produced sterling silver and *champlevé-* and *cloisonné-* enameled objects. Its Renaissance and classical motifs were the result of the influence of French designers Émile Jeannest, who joined the firm c1848, Leonard Morel-Ladeuil, who joined in 1859, and Albert Willms, head of the design department from the 1860s to c1900. From 1865, Willms was instrumental in Elkington's introduction of Japanese forms and techniques. The firm produced objects designed by Christopher Dresser 1875–85 and, from 1935, Modern designs by John Walker, Bernard Cuzner, Reginald Hill, and Frank Nevile. Its 20th-century production was mostly domestic plate along with hot-brass stamping and copper refining. In 1954, Elkington moved to Goscote Lane, Walsall, near Birmingham; in 1956, became part of the Delta Group of Companies and is today part of Delta's metal products division Elkington Mansill Booth, producing industrial stampings in non-ferrous alloys.
▶ Represented Britain in silver presentation pieces at 1876 Philadelphia 'Centennial Exposition' and 1878 Paris 'Exposition Universelle.'
▶ Shirley Bury, 'Elkington's and the Japanese Style,' *Worshipful Company of Goldsmiths' Review*, 1874–75:27–28. Shirley Bury, 'The Silver Designs of Dr. Christopher Dresser,' *Apollo*, No. 76, Dec. 1962:766–70. Doreen Bolger Burke et al., *In Pursuit of Beauty: Americans and the Aesthetic Movement*, New York: Metropolitan Museum of Art and Rizzoli, 1986:424. Annelies Krekel-Aalberse, *Art Nouveau and Art Déco Silver*, New York: Abrams, 1989:253.

Ellens, Harm (1871–1939)
▶ Dutch silversmith; active Groningen and Amsterdam.
▶ Studied Academy, Groningen, and Rijksschool voor Kunstnijverheid, Amsterdam.
▶ He was the first director of the Varkschool voor Goud- en Zilversmeden in Schoonhoven in the 1920s. Ellens's silverwares were produced by the school and by E. Voet in Haarlem and H. Hooykaas in Schoonhoven.
▶ Annelies Krekel-Aalberse, *Art Nouveau and Art Déco Silver*, New York: Abrams, 1989:253.

Ellin and Kitson
▶ American architectural sculptors; located New York.
▶ Active from c1867, Ellin and Kitson produced architectural sculpture in carved wood and stone, modeled plaster, and *papiermâché*; specialists in church decoration, located 1887–89 at 513–519 West 21st Street, New York, with the building at no. 511 being occupied subsequently; 1891–1900, was located at the end of West 25th Street on the Hudson River. Its principals were Britons Robert Ellin and John W. Kitson. In the late 1860s, they hired architect P.B. Wight to carve capitals for the National Academy of Design; Wight was the architect of the building, completed in 1865. c1880–84, the firm furnished satinwood panels for the dining room of the Samuel J. Tilden House (the National Arts Club from 1906), Gramercy Park, New York, when Calvert Vaux supervised the remodeling of the building.
▶ Work (Jacobean-style oak sideboard) shown at 1876 Philadelphia 'Centennial Exposition.'
▶ 'Work on Mr. Tilden's House,' *New York Daily Tribune*, Jan. 29, 1882:12. Charles Rollinson Lamb, *The Tilden Mansion—Home of the National Arts Club*, New York, 1932:9. Doreen Bolger Burke et al., *In Pursuit of Beauty: Americans and the Aesthetic Movement*, New York: Metropolitan Museum of Art and Rizzoli, 1986:425–26.

Ellis, Eileen (1933–)
▶ British textile designer.
▶ 1950–52, studied Leicester College of Art; 1952–54, Central School of Arts and Crafts, London; 1954–57, Royal College of Art, London.
▶ 1957–59, she worked for Ascher, designing printed and woven fabrics for the garment trade and Marks and Spencer; in 1960, formed Orbit Design Group; designed fabrics for BEA's *Trident* airliner and others in the fleet, and proscenium curtains for a Birmingham theater; designed fabrics for Alastair Morton's Edinburgh Weavers, John Lewis, Morton Sundour, and others. In 1970, (with Ann Bristow) formed Weaveplan, becoming its sole partner in 1975 with five designers in her stable; worked for Irish Ropes, overseeing all carpet design; C. and J. Hirst furnishing fabrics; Vescom, Deurne, Holland wallcoverings; Abbotsford Fabrics; John Orr Eire upholstery fabrics; Jamasque fabric.

Ellis, Harvey (1852–1904)
▶ American architect and designer; born Rochester, New York.
▶ Attended West Point Military Academy.
▶ He began his career as a draftsperson in Albany, New York, with architect H.H. Richardson; 1879–84, practiced as an architect with brother Charles Ellis in Rochester; subsequently, worked as a journeyman draftsman in the Midwest; in the mid-1890s, returned to Rochester and designed in the manner of the British Arts and Crafts movement; from 1903, designed furniture for Gustav Stickley's United Crafts Workshop, Eastwood, New York, and wrote for Stickley's magazine *The Craftsman*. Ellis's furniture was influenced by H.H. Richardson. During the last months of his life, he designed the houses, furniture, and wall decorations at Stickley's workshop. Expensive to produce, his inlaid furniture, discontinued after 1904, was used mostly for display and speciality purposes. His late work was strongly influenced by British designers C.F.A. Voysey, Charles Rennie Mackintosh, and Hugh Baillie Scott. Ellis's wide table-top overhangs, arched skirts, inlaid elements, native-American, and Art Nouveau motifs departed from the sober lines of typical Stickley furniture. Mackintosh's influence appeared in his use of inlays in pewter, copper, and wood. Whether Ellis designed furniture for his own buildings is not clear, although his drawings reveal an interest in the relationship between furniture design and architecture.
▶ Inlaid furniture shown at 1904 St. Louis 'Louisiana Purchase Exposition.'
▶ Hugh M.G. Garden, 'Harvey Ellis, Designer and Draftsman,' *The Prairie School Review 5,* First/Second Quarter, 1968:36–39. Roger G. Kennedy, 'Long Dark Corridors: Harvey Ellis,' *The Prairie School Review 5,* First/Second Quarter, 1968:5–18. Cat., David Cathers, *Genius in the Shadows: The Furniture Designs of Harvey Ellis*, New York: Jordan-Volpe Gallery, 1981. Cat., Lisa Phillips (Introduction), *Shape and Environment: Furniture by American Architects*, New York: Whitney Museum of American Art, 1982: 26. Cat., Anne Yaffe Phillips, *From Architecture to Object*, New York: Hirschl and Adler, 1989:40–41.

Ellwood, G. Montague (1875–)

▶ British furniture designer.
▶ Ellwood designed for J.S. Henry, Old Street, London, a manufacturer of an extensive range of furniture in the early years of the 20th century. Ellwood's work was widely published, including in *The Studio*. He worked in a style close to continental Art Nouveau.
▶ *British Art & Design, 1900–1963*, 1983.

Elmslie, George Grant (1871–1952)

▶ British architect; born Aberdeenshire; active USA.
▶ Elmslie's family settled in Chicago in 1880; in 1885, he entered the office of architect Lyman Silsbee, first as an errand boy and subsequently as an apprentice; in 1890, joined the staff of architects Dankmar Adler and Louis Sullivan; worked alongside Frank Lloyd Wright in Silsbee's and Sullivan's offices; in the latter's office for 20 years, executed many of Sullivan's detailed designs for organic ornamentation and may have been the author of the ornamentation often credited solely to Sullivan; designed the interiors, furnishings, and ornamental windows of Sullivan's 1907–09 Henry B. Babson house, Riverside, Illinois, his last project for Sullivan. 1912–13, Elmslie made revisions on the Babson house and, in c1924, produced designs for some notable stained-glass windows that incorporated Modern geometric motifs; in 1910, joined William Gray Purcell and George Feick Jr. in their archicture office in Minnesota. 1910–13, the firm was known as Purcell, Feick and Elmslie and, 1913–22, as Purcell and Elmslie. Its commissions included numerous banks in small Midwestern towns. Like Wright and Sullivan, Elmslie and Purcell avoided obvious Beaux-Arts forms and neoclassical detailing, producing an indigenous American style; were known for their attention to integrated site-specific interiors. In a style of his own, though influenced by Sullivan, Elmslie designed furniture, stained glass, embroidery, carpets, and metalwork. A Prairie school architect, he was primarily interested in private houses; considered the house and its furnishings to be a unified entity. His use of ornamentation on furniture showed Sullivan's influence and was uncommon among Prairie school practitioners. Elmslie's furniture dates mainly from the time of his Purcell partnership.
▶ Work (with Purcell) subject of 1953 'Purcell and Elmslie: Architects, 1910–1922,' Walker Art Center, Minneapolis, Minnesota.
▶ Cat., David Gebhard, *Purcell and Elmslie: Architects, 1910–22*, Minneapolis: Walker Art Center, 1953. David Gebhard, *Drawings for Architectural Ornament, 1902–1936*, Santa Barbara, California: University Art Galleries, University of California, 1968. Cat., Lisa Phillips (introduction), *Shape and Environment: Furniture by American Architects*, New York: Whitney Museum of American Art, 1982:28. Cat., Anne Yaffe Phillips, *From Architecture to Object*, New York: Hirschl and Adler, 1989:72.

EMBRU-Werke (aka Eisen- und Metallbettenfabrik)

▶ Swiss furniture manufacturer; located Rüti.
▶ EMBRU manufactured tubular steel furniture designed by Swiss architects including Werner M. Moser, Max E. Haefeli, Alfred Roth, and Flora Steiger-Crawford, as well as Alvar Aalto and Marcel Breuer; from 1931, had rights to produce Thonet models. Its furniture was sold through Wohnbedarf. In the first half of the 1930s, Sigfried Giedion designed the factory building; in 1934, worked as a designer at EMBRU of garden, cinema, school, and hospital furniture.
▶ Friederike Mehlau-Wiebking et al., *Schweizer Typenmöbel 1925–35, Sigfried Giedion und die Wohbedarf AG*, Zürich: gta, 1989:83–84.

Emerson, A.R. (1906–)

▶ British designer; active London.
▶ Emerson taught at Central School of Arts and Crafts, where he became head of the metalwork department.
▶ Annelies Krekel-Aalberse, *Art Nouveau and Art Déco Silver*, New York: Abrams, 1989:253.

Emmert, Christine (1962–)

▶ German industrial designer; born Fulda.
▶ 1980–87, studied product design, Gesamthochschule Kassel-Universität.
▶ From 1987, she was an industrial designer at Ascom Autophon, Solothurn (Switzerland).
▶ Cat., Design Center Stuttgart, *Women in Design: Careers and Life Histories Since 1900*, Stuttgart: Haus der Wirtschaft, 1989:110–11.

Emoto, Masami (1950–)

▶ Japanese glass designer.
▶ Studied painting, Musashino Art University, Tokyo, to 1975, and stained glass, Sante Pittol Studio, Italy, 1977.
▶ Work shown at 1984 (III) 'Japan Stained Glass Association' exhibition; 1985 'Stained Glass Exhibition,' Kyoto National Museum, Kyoto; 1986 'International Exhibition of Glass Craft,' Industrial Gallery of Ishikawa; 1987 'Glass '87 in Japan,' Tokyo; 1988 'International Exhibition of Glass Craft,' Industrial Gallery of Ishikawa Prefecture, Kanazawa; 1989 'Encounter of Glass Crafts,' Kyoto City Artcrafts Gallery; 1990 'Glass '90 in Japan,' Tokyo; 1991 (V) Triennale of Japan Glass Art Crafts Association.
▶ Cat., *Glass Japan*, New York: Heller Gallery and Japan Glass Art Crafts Association, 1991: No. 1.

En Attendant les Barbares

▶ French design collaboration and gallery.
▶ Members of En Attendant les Barbares ('waiting for the barbarians') included Elisabeth Garouste and Mattia Bonetti, Jean-Philippe Gleizes, jewelry designers Patrick Retif and Christian and Marie-Thérèse Migeon, fashion designer Catherine Grimaldi, interior designer Jean Neuville, and musician Eric Schmitt. Part of the Barbarist movement of the 1980s in France and Britain, their designs eschewed the finesse and refinement of prevailing French design of the period. The Gallery was located in rue Étienne-Marcel, Paris.

Endell, August (1871–1925)

▶ German architect, sculptor, and designer; born Berlin; active Munich and Breslau (now Wroclaw, Poland).
▶ Studied philosophy, psychology, and aesthetics in Tübingen, and in Munich under philosopher Theodor Lipps.
▶ He was a member of the Munich group associated with Hermann Obrist, Richard Riemerschmid, Bernard Pankok, and the art journal *Jugend*; was acquainted with Lipps's ideas on empathy; in his architecture and interiors, applied restrained ornamentation to flat surfaces; combined the roles of theorist and architect. The 1898 essay *Um die Schönheit* began his writings on aesthetics. 1918–25, he was director of the academy in Breslau. Work included 1897–98 Photoatelier Elvira (Elvira Photographic Studio), Munich, reminiscent of Obrist's work; decoration of 1901 Buntes Theater (known as the Multi-Colored Theater), Berlin; 1912 Trabrennbahn, Berlin-Mariendorf; department stores in Berlin and Breslau.
▶ Elvira Photographic Studio subject of 1977 exhibition, Museum Villa Stuck, Munich, and 1986 exhibition, Stadtmuseum, Munich.
▶ August Endell, *Um die Schönheit: Eine Paraphrase über die Münchner Kunstausstellung 1896*, Munich, 1896. August Endell, 'Möglichkeiten und Ziele einer neuen Architektur,' *Deutsche Kunst und Dekoration*, Vol. 1, Darmstadt, 1897–98:141–53. August Endell, 'Formenschönheit und dekorative Kunst,' *Dekorative Kunst*, Vol. 1, Munich, 1898:75–77,119. Karl Scheffler, 'August Endell,' *Kunst und Künstler*, No. 5, 1907:314–24. August Endell, *Die Schönheit der grossen Stadt*, Stuttgart, 1908. Karl Scheffler, 'Neue Arbeiten von August Endell,' *Kunst und Künstler*, No. 11, 1913:350–59. Karl-Jürgen Sembach, *August Endell: Der Architekt des Photoateliers Elvira 1871–1925*, Munich, 1977. Peg Weiss (ed.), *Kandinsky in Munich: The Formative Years*, Princeton, 1979. Cat., H.E. Killy et al., *Poelzig-Endell-Moll und die Breslauer Kunstakademie: 1911–32*, Berlin, 1965. Vittorio Magnago Lampug-

nani (ed.), *Encyclopedia of 20th-Century Architecture*, New York: Abrams, 1986. Kathryn Bloom Hiesinger (ed.), *Art Nouveau in Munich: Masters of Jugendstil*, Munich: Prestel, 1988.

Endt, Evert

▶ Dutch industrial designer; active Paris.

▶ Studied in Zürich, 1950.

▶ He became artistic director of Raymond Loewy's CEI in 1958 and director in 1970; in 1975, established Endt Fulton Partners, Paris, associated with Fulton Partners, New York; specialized in industrial design, communication, and transportation; director of ENSCI (École Nationale Supérieure de la Création Industrielle), Paris.

ENFI Design
(Esthétique Nouvelle de la Forme Industrielle)

▶ French design agency; located Paris.

▶ ENFI Design was established in 1961 by Jacques Inguenaud; was active in product, graphic, and interior design for stores, transportation, and industries; by 1987, had become a leading French group for the design of public office spaces and corporate identity programs, including those for banks; designed the *Aramis* transportation system for Matra, 1977 Ecureuil public helicopter for Aérospatiale, and 1984 *Minitel* terminal for Alcatel.

Engø, Bjørn (1920–1981)

▶ Norwegian interior, furniture, and textile designer and enamelist.

▶ He set up a workshop in 1948; as a freelancer, designed for production; in 1955, (with Karl-Edvard Korseth) collaborated on furniture designs for Helsingborn on the *H-55* range. Design work included furniture, lighting, textiles, and the domestic wares in aluminum and enameled copper, for which he is best known.

▶ Fredrik Wildhagen, *Norge i Form*, Oslo: Stenersen, 1988:137. Cat., David Revere McFadden (ed.), *Scandinavian Modern Design 1880–1980*, New York: Abrams, 1982:263, No. 247.

Engberg, Gabriel (1872–1953)

▶ Finnish textile designer.

▶ Studied under Akseli Gallen-Kallela.

▶ Work (textiles for the Friends of Finnish Handicraft) shown at 1900 Paris 'Exposition Universelle.'

▶ Cat., David Revere McFadden (ed.), *Scandinavian Modern Design 1880–1980*, New York: Abrams, 1982:263.

Englehardt, Valdemar (1869–1915)

▶ Danish ceramicist.

▶ Trained as a chemical engineer.

▶ He succeeded Adolphe Clément in 1891 as technical manager, Royal Copenhagen Porcelain Manufactory; influenced by production at the Sèvres factory, he designed a series of crystalline glazes for Royal Copenhagen's ceramic artwares. His glazes moved away from the factory's late 19th-century naturalistic painted decorations.

▶ Cat., David Revere McFadden (ed.), *Scandinavian Modern Design 1880–1980*, New York: Abrams, 1982:263, No. 45.

Englinger, Gabriel (1898–)

▶ French artist, decorator, and furniture designer; born Paris.

▶ Studied École Boulle, Paris.

▶ 1922–28, he worked in La Maîtrise design workshop of Galeries Lafayette department store, Paris; concurrently, was a designer and furniture maker at the firm of Cornille. Various ensembles, including a 1928 boudoir and 1929 work cabinet and smoking stand, were produced by Studio Abran. He taught decoration in Grenoble and drawing in Voiron, where he settled after World War II; 1949–63, abandoning his other activities, taught decoration, École Régionale des Beaux-Arts, Rennes.

▶ From 1921, interiors shown (with student designers of École Boulle) at Cercle Volney. In 1923, dining room shown (with student designers of École Boulle) at Musée Galliéra, Paris. Small room (with Suzanne Guiguichon) for La Maîtrise and his design for Salon d'Honneur for Cornille in City of Paris Pavilion at 1925

Paris 'Exposition Internationale des Arts Décoratifs et Industriels Modernes.' Work shown regularly at 1926–29 Salons of Société des Artistes Décorateurs. A room shown in regional industries stand of Dauphiné pavilion at 1937 Paris 'Exposition Internationale des Arts et Techniques dans la Vie Moderne.' Work shown at 1946 and 1947 Salons d'Automne. Dining room (produced by La Maîtrise) shown at 1948 Salon of Société des Artistes Décorateurs.

▶ Pierre Kjellberg, *Art Déco: les maîtres du Mobilier, le décor des Paquebots*, Paris: Amateur, 1986:69–71.

Englund, Eva (1937–)

▶ Swedish glassware designer and ceramicist.

▶ Englund became active as a glassware designer in 1964; worked for a time for Pukeberg; from 1974, worked for Orrefors and became known for her revival of the *graal* technique (ornamentation within the glass) developed by Edward Hald and others at Orrefors; was also a ceramicist.

▶ Cat., David Revere McFadden (ed.), *Scandinavian Modern Design 1880–1980*, New York: Abrams, 1982:263, No. 311.

Ennis, Sandie (1962–)

▶ British textile designer.

▶ Studied textiles, Camberwell School of Art, to 1986.

▶ Work shown at 1990 'Diverse Cultures,' London and touring; 1991 'Chelsea Crafts Fair,' London; 1991–92 'Six Chairs and Six Rugs,' touring exhibition organized by Southern Arts.

▶ *Decorative Arts Today*, London: Bonhams, 1992: No. 11a.

ENSCI (École Nationale Supérieure de la Création Industrielle) (aka Les Ateliers)

▶ French industrial design school; located Paris.

▶ ENSCI was established in 1982 under the supervision of the French ministries of industry and culture.

Épinard Bleu

▶ French architecture-design collaboration; active Bordeaux.

▶ Épinard Bleu ('blue spinach') was founded in c1984 by architects Frédéric Druot, Jean-Luc Goulesque, Patrick Jean, Luis Felipe Pais de Figueredo, Jacques Robert, Hubert Saladin, and Jean-Charles Zebo. In 1985, work shown in the center of Lormont, France; two stands were designed for the Vinexpo, Bordeaux; 1988 vestibule of the Château Troplong Mondot, Saint-Émilion.

▶ Work first shown at 1984 exhibition of its work, Chantier du Chai, Bordeaux; 1985 FRAC Aquitaine-Maubuisson exhibition; 1985 'Ils créent pour demain,' Nantes; 1985 'Semaine des Jeunes Créateurs' of Éditions Autrement, Paris; 1985 'Architecture et Maîtres d'Oeuvre,' Bordeaux; 1985 Salon of the Société des Artistes Décorateurs, Grand Palais, Paris; 1985 exhibition, Galerie du Centre National des Arts Plastiques, Paris; 1986 exhibition of its work, Galerie Néotù, Paris.

▶ J. Hondelatte, 'Projets récents,' *Architecture d'aujourd'hui*, No. 236, 1984. 'Recherche sur les nouveaux territoires du logement,' *Architecture d'aujourd'hui*, No. 239. 'Special Design français,' *Architecture Crée*, June 1985. *Intramuros*, September 1985.

Epply, Lorinda (1874–1951)

▶ American ceramicist; active Cincinnati, Ohio.

▶ Studied Cincinnati Art Academy, and ceramics, Columbia University, New York.

▶ 1904–48, she worked at Rookwood Pottery, Cincinnati; during the late 1920s, (with William Hentschel) produced some of Rookwood's most individual work; (with others at the pottery) developed new glazes and forms of ornamentation.

▶ Represented Rookwood (with Hentschel) at 1926–27 'American Industrial Art, Tenth Annual Exhibition of Current Manufactures Designed and Made in the United States,' New York Metropolitan Museum of Art.

▶ Herbert Peck, *The Book of Rookwood Pottery*, New York: Crown, 1968. Virginia Raymond Cummins, *Rookwood Pottery Potpourri*, Silver Spring, Md.: Cliff R. Leonard and Duke Coleman, 1980. Karen Davies, *At Home in Manhattan: Modern Decorative Arts, 1925 to the Depression*, New Haven: Yale, 1983:40.

Ercole Moretti

▶ Italian jeweler; located Venice.

▶ Ercole Moretti was founded in 1911 by brothers Ercole, Norberto, and Iginio Moretti; was first located in the bead-stringing district at Cannaregio, Fondamenta della Misericordia, Venice; in the 1940s, moved to its present location, Fondamenta Navagero 42, Murano. Its production began with rosette and *al lume* beads and small Venetian glass pieces. In 1969, it began producing plates and bibelots; is managed by Gianni, Luciano, and Giuliano Moretti.

▶ Deanna F. Cera (ed.), *Jewels of Fantasy: Costume Jewelry of the 20th Century*, New York: Abrams, 1992:307.

Ergonomi Design Gruppen

▶ Swedish design research and development group.

▶ Designgruppen and Ergonomi Design were amalgamated in the late 1960s; based on ergonometric principles, pursued design research and development financed by the Swedish Work Environment Fund of the National Board for Occupational Health and Safety; undertook commissions for engineering, heavy equipment, plastics, and mechanical-technology firms. Its 14-member team executed designs, including cutlery, for the handicapped and elderly, and for printing and welding machinery. Two members of the group, Maria Benktzon and Sven-Eric Juhlin, specialized in products for handicapped people.

▶ Cat., *Gustavsberg 150 ar*, Stockholm: Nationalmuseum, 1975: Nos. 302,313–16,318–20,322–24,332–34,336,338–39. Cat., *Aktuell Svensk Form*, Skien, Sweden: Ibsenhuset, 1982:52–55. Cat., Kathryn B. Hiesinger and George H. Marcus III (eds.), *Design Since 1945*, Philadelphia: Philadelphia Museum of Art, 1983.

Ericsson, Henry   (1898–1933)

▶ Finnish painter, graphic artist, and designer; active Helsinki.

▶ Studied Taideteollinen Korkeakoulu, Helsinki, to 1915.

▶ His earliest silver designs were for Taito, including a plain oval tea set resembling designs by Jacob Angman of Sweden. He produced designs for textiles and glassware; a friend of Alvar Aalto, shared a studio with him for a while.

▶ Annelies Krekel-Aalberse, *Art Nouveau and Art Déco Silver*, New York: Abrams, 1989:241,253.

Ericsson, L.M.

▶ Swedish manufacturer.

▶ The L.M. Ericsson firm was Sweden's first and largest manufacturer of telephones. Employees Hugo Blomberg, Ralph Lysell, and Gösta Thames designed the widely published 1940 *Ericofon* one-piece telephone set as a smaller and lighter version of the standard model. The unit was further designed, engineered, and developed 1940–54. The idea was initially conceived by Blomberg, assisted by Lysell. From 1949, Thames was in charge of the telephone's design and mechanics.

▶ Hugo Blomberg, 'The Ericofon—The New Telephone Set,' *Ericsson Review*, Vol. 33, No. 4, 1956:99–109. Cat., Kathryn B. Hiesinger and George H. Marcus III (eds.), *Design Since 1945*, Philadelphia: Philadelphia Museum of Art, 1983.

Eriksen, Sigurd Alf   (1899–)

▶ Norwegian jewelry designer.

▶ Eriksen set up his own workshop in 1929; produced designs for Tostrup that showed a single-minded pursuit of elegant form.

▶ Fredrik Wildhagen, *Norge i Form*, Oslo: Stenersen, 1988:139.

Eriksson, Algot   (1868–1930)

▶ Swedish ceramicist.

▶ 1882–89, studied technical school, Stockholm, and in Denmark, Germany, and France.

▶ From the 1880s to 1920, he worked at Rörstrand pottery, Lidköping, along with other ceramicists known for sumptuous wares in the Natural style popular in the late 19th and early 20th centuries; was known for his ceramics with underglaze painting and relief decoration.

▶ Cat., David Revere McFadden (ed.), *Scandinavian Modern Design 1880–1980*, New York: Abrams, 1982:263, No. 13.

Erkins, Henry

▶ American designer.

▶ Erkins designed 1907 Murray's Roman Gardens, 228–232 West 42nd Street, New York. Its Egyptian dining room had mock-Egyptian motifs and ornamentation. Its illuminated atrium, with its mixture of classical motifs, was intended to represent a garden in ancient Pompeii. The building's entrance was redone in a design from the 18th-century Paris residence of Cardinal Rohan.

▶ Jonathan M. Woodham, *Twentieth-Century Ornament*, New York: Rizzoli, 1990:50.

Ermilov, Vasilii Dmitrievich   (1884–1968)

▶ Russian architect, book and set designer, interior designer, and illustrator; born Kharkov (now Ukraine).

▶ 1905–09, studied School of Decorative Arts, Kharkov; 1910–11, Kharkov Art School and private studios; from 1913, Moscow Institute of Painting, Sculpture, and Architecture under Petr Konchalovski and Il'ia Mashkov.

▶ After early contact with Cubists and Futurists, including David Burliuk and Vladimir Maiakovskii, from *c*1913, he explored Neo-Primitivism, Cubism, Futurism, and Suprematism. His decorations appeared in the Kharkov Futurist album *7 + 3*. His work for the album was influential on his later book designs and illustrations, including the first edition of Velimir Khlebnikov's *Ladomir* (1920) and the journal *Avangard* (1923–30); in 1918, he joined the Union 7 monumental artists' group; in 1919–20, was involved in the design of various agitprop projects including agit-posters, interiors of clubs, and agit-trains; in 1922, was a co-founder of Kharkov Art Technicum and was lecturer at Kharkov Art Institute; pursued architectural and theatrical design projects in the late 1920s and 1930s. Valerian Polishchuk published his 1931 monograph on Ermliov at Kharkov.

▶ Designed interior (with Anatolii Petritskii) of Ukrainian pavilion at 1937–38 Moscow 'All-Union Agricultural Exhibition.'

▶ V. Polishchuk, *Vasilii Ermilov: Ukrainske maliarstvo*, Kharkov, 1931. L. Zhadova, 'Prokty V. Ermilova,' *Dekorativnoe iskusstvo*, Moscow, no. 9, 1972:30–32. Z. Fogel, *Vasilii Ermilov*, Moscow, 1975. Stephanie Barron and Maurice Tuchman, *Avant-Garde Russia, 1919–1930*, New Perspectives, MIT, 1980. Cat., *The Great Utopia: The Russian and Soviet Avant-Garde, 1915–1932*, New York: Guggenheim Musem, 1992.

Ermolaeva, Vera Mikhailovna   (1893–1938)

▶ Russian writer, teacher, and illustrator; born Petrovsk.

▶ Studied from 1912 in the art school of Mikhail Bernstein, St. Petersburg, and Archeological Institute, Petrograd, from 1917.

▶ Her artistic development was marked from the beginning by contact with leading artistic figures of the time: Vladimir Tatlin, Larionov, and Union of Youth members including Pavel Filonov, Kazimir Malevich, and Mikhail Matiushin. In 1918, she became a member of Izo NKO; 1918–19, worked for the City Museum, Petrograd; interested in folk art, she wrote a paper on old shop signboards for the 1919 issue of *Iskusstvo kommuny* (*Art of the Commune*); illustrated children's books and met Annenkov, Lebedev, and others; up to the 1920s, was influenced by the ideas of Malevich through Suprematism and joined his group of followers; designed sets for the 1923 Kruchenykh/Matiushin opera *Victory Over the Sun*; in 1923, accompanying Malevich and his students, moved to Petrograd where she was head until 1926 of the color laboratory of the Petrograd branch of Inkhuk (Institute of Artistic Culture); from the mid-1920s, illustrated children's books by Aseev, Kharms, Vvedenskii, Zabolotskii, and others, including editions of Krylov's fables; because of her brother's involvement with the Mensheviks, was arrested and exiled to Siberia in 1934.

▶ Work shown at several exhibitions of the Suprematists.

▶ E. Kovtun 'Khudozhnitsa knigi Vera Mikhailovna Ermolaeva,' in D. Shmarinov (ed.), *Iskusstvo knigi*, Moscow, 1975:68–81. John

E. Bowlt, 'Malevich and His Students,' *Soviet Union*, Arizona State University, vol. 5, part 2, 1979:256–86. Cat., E. Kovtun, 'Vera Mikhailovna Ermolaeva,' *Women Artists of the Russian Avant-Garde 1910–1930*, Galerie Gmurzynska, Cologne, 1979:102–10. Stephanie Barron and Maurice Tuchman, *Avant-Garde Russia, 1919–1930*, New Perspectives, MIT, 1980:146. Cat., *The Great Utopia: The Russian and Soviet Avant-Garde, 1915–1932*, New York: Guggenheim Musem, 1992.

Ernst, Christoph (1958–)
▶ German designer; born Bielefeld; active Berlin.
▶ 1981–84, studied ethnology, Freie Universität, Berlin.
▶ In 1980, settled in Berlin; from 1983, designed and produced metal furniture.
▶ Work shown at 1988 'Berlin: Les Avant-Gardes du Mobilier,' at Centre Georges Pompidou, VIA, and Galerie Néotù, all Paris.
▶ Cat., *Berlin: Les Avant-Gardes du Mobilier*, Berlin: Design Zentrum, 1988.

Errazuriz, Eugenia (b. Eugenia Huici 1861–1954)
▶ Chilean society hostess; born Huici (Chile); active Paris and London.
▶ In 1880, she married the wealthy landscape painter José Thomas Errazuriz and settled in Paris. She furnished her homes sparsely, shunning suites of furniture, potted palms, and other clutter, and commanding: 'Throw out, and keep throwing out. Elegance means elimination.' She spent freely but lived simply, blending patrician and peasant tastes. In her main room, she preferred interesting chairs, flowers, a desk, plain inexpensive fabrics simply hung, and a bare scrubbed floor. Her affection for what she called 'Inca pink' was adopted by Elsa Schiaparelli as 'shocking pink.' Her friends included Madrazos, Bibescos, and Helleus. Around 1900, the Errazurizes moved to Cheyne Walk, London, where Eugenia's associates included the unconventional photographer Baron de Meyer, her nephew Tony de Gandarillas (an intimate of Cecil Beaton) and James Abbott McNeill Whistler. After her husband's death in 1913, she returned to Paris; was a friend of Igor Stravinsky; through Jean Cocteau, met Pablo Picasso, who drew her often; 1915–25, she and Picasso were close friends. When Picasso married Olga Koklova in 1918, they honeymooned at Errazuriz's Biarritz villa, 'La Mimoseraie.' Before 1914, the villa had while walls and terracotta tiles, although she used 18th-century French silver flatware. She was fond of jasmine, lavender, rose geranium, lemon verbena, and other aromatic plants in plain flowerpots. Her Paris home was in the 18th-century townhouse of Étienne de Beaumont; using primarily white and indigo, she was fastidious about her slipcovers made by Leitz. Wearing a simple black shift designed by Coco Chanel, she would entertain guests including Jean Hugo, Emilio Terry, Raymond Radiguet, and Georges Braque; was very influential on the tastes of Cocteau and Jean-Michel Frank. Le Corbusier designed the 1930 Errazuriz House (unrealized) for Vino del Mar (Chile) with a pitched roof and in timber and stone; it was his first essay incorporating primitive technical elements. (The house was built with a thatched roof for another client in Japan by a Le Corbusier pupil). In 1950, she sold up and returned to Chile. The influence of her aesthetic, with its carefully contrived Mediterranean simplicity as a setting for a few well-chosen pieces, was profound.
▶ Kenneth Frampton, *Modern Architecture: A Critical History*, New York: Oxford, 1980:184. John Richardson, 'Eugenia Errazuriz,' *House & Garden*, April 1987:76–84. Stephen Calloway, 'Perfectly Frank,' *House and Garden*, Feb. 1990; 180ff.

Erté (b. Romain de Tirtoff 1892–1990)
▶ Russian designer.
▶ Studied in St. Petersburg under Il'ia Repine; architecture in Kronstadt; in 1912, painting, Académie Julian, Paris.
▶ 'Erté' was derived from the French pronunciation of his initials. In 1913, he worked for Paul Poiret in Paris as a fashion designer alongside José de Zamora; 1914–22, he lived in Monte Carlo, where he executed cover designs and fashion illustrations. He

designed costumes and sets for music-hall personalities, including Mata Hari and Zizi Jeanmaire, and for other theatrical productions, including the Ziegfeld Follies and George White's *Scandals*, New York. His stage designs appeared in productions in Paris, London, Milan, Blackpool, Berlin, Naples, and New York. He designed clothing collections for the Henri Bendel and B. Altman stores, both New York; produced drawings for *Harper's Bazaar*; in 1920, created sets and costumes for the film *Restless Sex*; in 1925, signed a contract with MGM, moved to Hollywood, and designed costumes and sets for Louis B. Mayer and Cecil B. de Mille. He was known for an ostentatious style inspired by the Orient and using spangles, sequins, and *lamé* fabric on gowns with long trains; after the 1929 stock market crash, worked for Pierre Sandini on the Bal Tabarin and Folies Bergères, Paris, designing sets and costumes, and, concurrently, for Châtelet, Marigny, and ABC. From the 1960s, his small sculptures and graphics produced in multiple editions were successfully sold through a New York agent, bringing him unexpected renown in extreme old age.
▶ Work first shown in France at 1926 exhibition, Hôtel Charpentier, Paris. Work subject of 1966 and 1967 exhibitions, Paris, Milan, New York, and London.
▶ Charles Spencer, *Erté*, New York: Potter, 1970. Yvonne Brunhammer, *Le Cinquantenaire de l'Exposition de 1925*, Paris: Musée des Arts Décoratifs, 1976:1927–28. Victor Arwas, *Art Déco*, New York: Abrams, 1980. Pierre Cabanne, *Encylopédie Art Déco*, Paris: Somogy, 1986:194.

Esherick, Wharton (1887–1970)
▶ American sculptor and furniture designer.
▶ 1907–08, studied Philadelphia School of Industrial Arts; 1909–10, Pennsylvania Academy of the Fine Arts, Philadelphia.
▶ Living in Paoli, Pennsylvania, he began in 1919 to produce carved wood sculpture and furniture; familiar with the work of the German Expressionists, he became active in avant-garde theatre design. The oblique angles and triangular forms in his furniture were derived from the furniture of Frank Lloyd Wright and Cubism.
▶ He showed his work in a 1929 exhibition at the American Designers' Gallery in New York.
▶ *The Wharton Esherick Museum: Studio and Collection*, Paoli, Pa.: Wharton Esherick Museum, 1977. Karen Davies, *At Home in Manhattan: Modern Decorative Arts, 1925 to the Depression*, New Haven: Yale, 1983:100. Auction cat., 'Contemporary Works of Art,' Sotheby's New York, 14 March 1992. Mark Rabun, 'Wharton Esherick' in Mel Byars and Russell Flinchum (eds.), *50 American Designers, 1918–1968*, Washington: Preservation, 1994.

ESKAF
▶ Dutch ceramics firm; initially located Steenwijk.
▶ ESKAF was formed in 1919 by a group of wealthy Steenwijk residents organized by Hillebrand Ras. The plan was to employ local people to produce attractive wares. German émigré A.A. Schröder was technical director. The factory, opened in 1920, was designed by Amsterdam architect G.F. la Croix. German porcelain painters and faïence painters from Gouda were hired. A large number of ceramic wares were designed by Hildo Krop, whose father, Hendrik Krop, was a co-founder and chair; they were of the Amsterdam school, having an unusual plastic structure. Other designers included W.H. van Norden, J.H. de Groot and C. van der Sluys; J. Jongert and W. Bogtman also contributed. Van der Sluys's designs were severe and geometric. Some of ESKAF's wares were lightly decorated, others were undecorated. Decorations included multi-colored motifs by van Norden and the popular butterfly and *Sonja* and *Fuga* motifs. In 1927, the firm was bought by P. van Stam and H. Hamming; production continued in Huizen on a cooperative basis. Only van der Sluys was retained. ESKAF customers were mostly well-to-do with a taste for the Modern. Briefly successful, for the firm became bankrupt in 1934. For a time, CV Kunstaardewerkfabriek HAHO produced ESKAF models with the cold varnish pottery method. In 1935, CV HAHO was amalgamated with Potterie De Driehoek to sell new glazed goods.

After World War II, the pottery was prosperous for a time and, from 1951 when the factory was modernized, machine-made dinner sets were produced for the first time. Potterie De Driehoek is now the only firm manufacturing dinnerware in the Netherlands.
▶ *Industry and Design in the Netherlands 1850/1950*, Amsterdam: Stedlijk Museum, 1985.

Eskildsen, Flemming (1930–)
▶ Danish designer.
▶ Eskildsen was an apprentice silversmith at the Georg Jensen Sølvsmedie before joining the firm in 1958.

Eskolin-Nurmesniemi, Vuokko (b. Vuokko Eskolin 1930–)
▶ Finnish designer; wife of Antti Nurmesniemi.
▶ 1948–52, studied ceramics, Taideteollinen Korkeakoulu, Helsinki.
▶ 1952–53, designed ceramics and glassware for Wärtsilä-Arabia; in 1953, turned to textile design and began working for Marimekko; 1953–60, was Marimekko's chief designer, responsible for fabrics and clothing. Her color range for Marimekko was warmer than that of its earlier vivid geometric prints. She produced large graphic images often called panels because used flat; while at Marimekko, was consultant designer to Borås, Sweden, and Pausa, Germany; in 1964, set up her own design firm Vuokko, Helsinki, producing clothing, fashion accessories, and fabrics. Her husband Antti Nurmesniemi's furniture designs were executed in collaboration with Vuokko.
▶ Received a gold medal at the 1957 (XI) and grand prize at (with Antti Nurmesniemi) the 1964 (XIII) Triennale di Milano. Received 1964 Lunning Prize and 1968 Pro-Finlandia medal.
▶ 'Thirty-four Lunning Prize-Winners,' *Mobilia*, No. 146, Sept. 1967. Marja Kaipainen, 'Some Call Them Purists,' *Form Function Finland*, No. 2, 1981:13–16. Charles S. Talley, *Contemporary Textile Art: Scandinavia*, Stockholm, 1982:136–38. Cat., David Revere McFadden (ed.), *Scandinavian Modern Design 1880–1980*, New York: Abrams, 1982:263, No. 252. Cat., Kathryn B. Hiesinger and George H. Marcus III (eds.), *Design Since 1945*, Philadelphia: Philadelphia Museum of Art, 1983. Cat., *The Lunning Prize*, Stockholm: Nationalmuseum, 1986:148–51. Jeremy Myerson and Sylvia Katz, *Conran Design Guides: Kitchenware*, London: Conran Octopus, 1990:76.

Esslinger, Hartmut (1945–)
▶ German industrial designer.
▶ Studied electrical engineering, University of Stuttgart, and industrial design, College of Design, Schwäbisch Gmünd.
▶ In 1969, Esslinger established frogdesign in Altensteig, an industrial design consultancy whose first client was Wega Radio; became involved in the Japanese market when Wega was bought by Sony. Wega Radio's 1978 *Concept 51K* hi-fi was notable for its sleekness. In 1982, frogdesign opened a branch in California, with clients including Apple Computer, NeXT, Olympus, AT&T, AEG, and other Silicon Valley firms; subsequently, established an office in Taiwan. Clients in Europe included König und Neurath (office furniture), Villeroy et Boch, Rosenthal, and Erco. Esslinger's design work incorporated Functionalist forms with colorful Post-Modern influences, and was a mixture of the approaches of Dieter Rams and Ettore Sottsass, with an emphasis on the former. The studio established its own design award, the 'frogjunior.'
▶ Jeremy Myerson and Sylvia Katz, *Conran Design Guides: Home Office*, London: Conran Octopus, 1990:74. Uta Brandes, *Hartmut Esslinger & frogdesign*, Göttingen: Steidl, 1992.

Estlander, Oliver (1834–1910)
▶ Finnish art and design educator.
▶ At the end of the 19th century, Estlander reorganized the Finnish Society of Arts and Crafts, Helsinki.
▶ Penny Sparke, *Introduction to Design and Culture in the Twentieth Century*, London: Allen and Unwin, 1986.

Etamine
▶ French fabric and wallpaper firm.
▶ Etamine was established in 1974 by Françoise Royneau, Françoise Dorget, and Marilyn Gaucher. Dorget was its designer.

Etling, Edmond
▶ French metalware and glassware merchant; located Paris.
▶ Edmond Etling established his firm in Paris, where he sold small metal and glass *objets d'art*, including table lamps and lighted bibelots. His designers included Bonnet, Laplanche, Guillard, and Georges Dunaime. Though concealed lighting was popular, Etling met a demand for visible fixtures similar to Lalique's. His range included small chromium-plated metal and crystal lamps and lighted *bouts de table*.
▶ Illuminated *bouts de table* shown at 1934 (II) Salon of Light and 1937 Paris 'Exposition Internationale des Arts et Techniques dans la Vie Moderne.'
▶ Alastair Duncan, *Art Nouveau and Art Déco Lighting*, New York: Simon and Schuster, 1978:171. G. Henriot, *Luminaire*, 1937: plates 39–40.

Eureka Company, The
▶ American manufacturer; initially located Detroit.
▶ The Eureka Company was founded in Detroit in 1909; is located today in Bloomington, Illinois; by 1927, sold its vacuum cleaners through door-to-door salespeople; accounted for one-third of domestic sales of vacuum cleaners; established a large research and design department; by the mid 1980s, had more than 40 models. Chief industrial designer Samuel Hohulin, with Kenneth Parker, designed Eureka's 1982 *Mighty Mite* compact model in a colorful plastic casing.
▶ Cat., Kathryn B. Hiesinger and George H. Marcus III (eds.), *Design Since 1945*, Philadelphia: Philadelphia Museum of Art, 1983. Wolf von Eckardt, 'Fashionable Is Not Enough,' *Time*, Vol. 121, Jan. 3, 1983:76–77.

Eureka Pottery
▶ American ceramics manufacturer; located Trenton, New Jersey.
▶ The Eureka Pottery Company was established in Trenton, New Jersey, in 1883; influenced by the growing popularity of British brightly colored majolica shown at the 1876 Philadelphia 'Centennial Exposition,' it produced two successful lines called *Bird and Fan* and *Prunus and Fan*; 1883–85, was located on Mead Avenue, Trenton, New Jersey. In the first year, Leon Weil and R. Weil were known to have been associated with Eureka. 1885–86, Noah W. Boch was the proprietor, and Charles Boch was a potter there. 1886–87, Charles Boch was proprietor at the firm that became known at this time as the Eureka Porcelain Works, while Noah Boch became 'pottery superintendent.'
▶ M. Charles Rebert, *American Majolica, 1850–1900*, Des Moines, Iowa, 1981:63,69,82. Doreen Bolger Burke et al., *In Pursuit of Beauty: Americans and the Aesthetic Movement*, New York: Metropolitan Museum of Art and Rizzoli, 1986:426.

European Community Design Prize (ECDP)
▶ European design award.
▶ The ECDP arose in 1985 from a committee established by the Commission of the European Community. Members nominated by member countries come from design institutions including national ministries, public bodies, and professional design organizations. In 1988, the first ECDP was sponsored by the Danish Design Centre.

Evanson, James (1946–)
▶ American lighting designer.
▶ Studied architecture, Pratt Institute, Brooklyn, New York, and Art Center College of Design, New York.
▶ He is best known for his large lighting constructions that emulated buildings and entire skylines when amassed, including 1985–86, *Lightstruck* table lamp, *Hi-beam* floor lamp, and *Light Collection* produced by Art et Industrie.

▶ Albrecht Bangert and Karl Michael Armer, *80s Style: Designs of the Decade*, New York: Abbeville, 1990:230.

Exner, Bent (1932–)
▶ Danish jewelry designer and sculptor.
▶ Studied theology; in 1954, completed goldsmith apprenticeship with silver medal.
▶ From 1961, he was active (with Helga Exner from 1961–83) in a workshop in Northern Jutland; from 1969, was a member of the Curriculum Committee, Guldsmedehøjskolen, Copenhagen, and, in 1969, 1970 and 1972, was guest lecturer there.
▶ Received (with Helga Exner) 1969 Lunning Prize.
▶ Cat., *The Lunning Prize*, Stockholm: Nationalmuseum, 1986:194–97.

Exner, Helga (1939–)
▶ Czech jewelry designer and sculptor; born Jablonec nad Nisou (today Czech Republic).
▶ In 1960, she completed goldsmith apprenticeship in Bad Godesberg (Germany).
▶ 1961–83, was active (with Bent Exner) in a workshop in Northern Jutland; taught at Rudolf Steiner School, Århus.
▶ Received (with Bent Exner) 1969 Lunning Prize.
▶ Cat., *The Lunning Prize*, Stockholm: Nationalmuseum, 1986:194–97.

Exter, Alekandra Alexandrovna (1882–1949)
▶ Russian artist and textile, set, fashion, interior, and book designer; born Belestok (now Bialystok, Poland).
▶ Studied Kiev Art School to 1907.
▶ She traveled regularly to Paris and other Western European cities; in 1912, moved to St. Petersburg and continued to travel and met Russian and Western avant-garde figures; became close to poet Benedikt Livshits, to whom she gave some of her artworks; was associated with the Union of Youth. Her career in the theater began with design work for Innokentii Annenskii's *Thamira Khytharedes* (the first of several commissions with producer Alexandr Tairov) at the Chamber Theater, Moscow. In 1918, she set up her own studio where Ignatii Nivinskii, Anatolii Petritskii, Isaak Rabinovich, Nisson Shifrin, Pavel Tchelitchew, and Alexandr Tyshler participated. Exter and her group designed the Suprematist steamers for display on the Dnepr River. In 1923, she began working on sets and costumes for the film *Aelita* (1924); in 1924, moved to Paris, where she produced designs for the theater, fashion, interiors, and books.
▶ Participated in several Kiev exhibitions, including David Burliuk's 'Link,' and journal *V mire iskusstv (In the World of Art)*. Work shown at 1908 and 1909 exhibitions of St. Petersburg New Society of Artists, 1909–10 and 1911 Izdebskii Salons, 1911–12 Moscow Salon, first and last shows of the Union of Youth, 1915–16 'Tramway V' and 'The Store.' In c1924, designed decorations (with Nivinskii) for the Moscow 'First Agricultural and Handicraft-Industrial Exhibition.'
▶ Stephanie Barron and Maurice Tuchman, *Avant-Garde Russia, 1919–1930*, New Perspectives, MIT, 1980. Selim O. Khan-Magomedov, *Les Vhutemas*, Paris: Regard, 1990.

Eysselinck, Gaston (1907–53)
▶ Architect and furniture maker.
▶ Eysselinck designed the 1931 one-legged cantilever chair produced in bent steel with wooden seat and back rest.
▶ Cat., *Der Kragstuhl*, Stuhlmuseum Burg Beverungen, Berlin: Alexander, 1986:35,132.

F

Fabergé, Gustav (1814–81)

▶ Russian goldsmith and jeweler; born Pernay (now Latvia); father of Peter Carl Fabergé.

▶ Apprenticed to a St. Petersburg jeweler.

▶ Fabergé was descended from a Huguenot family. In 1842, he opened a jewelry shop in fashionable Bolshaia Morskaia Street, St. Petersburg; in 1860, left the business in the hands of his chief silversmith Zaiontchkovskii until 1870, when his son Peter Carl Fabergé became old enough to manage the firm.

▶ Charlotte Gere, *American and European Jewelry 1830–1914*, New York: Crown, 1975:175. A. Kenneth Snowman, *Fabergé: Jeweler to Royalty*, New York: Cooper-Hewitt Museum, 1983, biblio.

Fabergé, Peter Carl (1846–1920)

▶ Russian goldsmith and jeweler; born St. Petersburg; active St. Petersburg and Moscow; son of Gustav Fabergé.

▶ Trained in Frankfurt, and in St. Petersburg under Peter Heskias Pendin, goldsmith and chief assistant to his father.

▶ In 1870, he took over the firm his father had founded in 1842. Not a silversmith himself, Fabergé managed the activities of more than 500 assistants, designers, modelers, gem-cutters, enamelers, and metalsmiths at the peak of the firm's success. Its St. Petersburg silversmiths included S. Wäakewä, Jan Lieberg-Nyberg, J. Nevalainen, and J.A. Rappoport. Dutch metalsmith Jan Eisenloeffel worked for a time in the workshop, where he became interested in the *champlevé*-enamel technique. A Moscow branch was opened in 1887 and many more silver pieces were produced there; manager Michel Tchepournoff oversaw production in simple styles as well the Old Russian style popular in the second half of the 19th century. Fabergé produced pieces for Tiffany and Daum glass. The most famous products of the workshop were the 56 Imperial Easter eggs made from 1884. Having specialized in fashionable jewelry 1870–81, the firm received the Imperial warrant in 1881 from Czar Aleksandr and son Nicholas II for eggs for their wives and the Czar's mother each year thereafter. Each of these costly playthings contained a miniature ship, palace, coach, or the like. In 1883, Fabergé's younger brother Agathon joined the firm and thenceforth the firm became known for his cigarette cases, boxes, electric bells, photograph frames, desk accessories, and other bibelots in enamel, gold, semi-precious stones, and other luxury materials. In 1884, Fabergé goldsmith Edward Kollin produced copies of 4th-century BC ornaments found in the Crimea on the suggestion of Count Stroganoff. Working in minute detail and imbuing his jeweled *objets de fantaisie* with a certain preciousness, Fabergé was no innovator; his enameling was done in the *guilloché* or *skan* technique. The firm's *cloisonné* enamel work came from the workshops of Fedor Rückert. In 1890, the St. Petersburg branch moved to larger quarters. In 1905, branches were opened in Odessa and Kiev and, in 1906, in London. Workmasters operated separate workshops that Fabergé provided rent free; while Fabergé himself oversaw the production of each piece and supplied the designs and materials, the workmasters hired assistants and paid their wages. A.W. Holmström and A. Thielemann were his two chief workmasters. With jeweler Oskar Piehl as manager, the Moscow branch did not operate this system. In 1898, the St. Petersburg branch moved into even larger quarters where the workshops were all located. As jeweler to the Russian Imperial court, the firm closed after the 1917 Revolution; the Bolsheviks seized its remaining stock. Fabergé fled to Lausanne; in 1921, his sons Eugène and Alexandre founded the house in Paris under the name Fabergé et Cie.

▶ Received a gold medal at 1882 Moscow 'Pan-Russian Exhibition' and a gold medal at 1896 Nijny Novgorod 'Pan-Russian Exhibition.' Showed copies of 4th-century BC Crimean gold ornaments at 1885 Nuremberg 'International Goldsmiths' Exhibition.' At 1900 Paris 'Exposition Universelle' Fabergé was a juror and received the Légion d'honneur.

▶ Charlotte Gere, *American and European Jewelry 1830–1914*, New York: Crown, 1975:175–76. A. Kenneth Snowman, *Fabergé: Jeweler to Royalty*, New York: Cooper-Hewitt Museum, 1983, biblio. Annelies Krekel-Aalberse, *Art Nouveau and Art Déco Silver*, New York: Abrams, 1989:241,58,100,247–249,254.

Fabiani, Max (1865–1962)

▶ Slovenian architect; born Kobdil (now Slovenia).

▶ In 1894, Fabiani worked in the Vienna railway team office of Otto Wagner with Josef Hoffmann, Jožef Plečník, Josef Maria Olbrich, and Leopold Bauer. He was versatile and found employment in many fields, particularly in town planning throughout the Austro-Hungarian Empire. Like Adolf Loos and Wagner, certain aspects of his architecture were too far advanced for contemporary taste. His work anticipated Loos's Michaeler House. Two of his Vienna buildings included elements of Functionalism. The first was 1898–1900 shop, Ungarngasse, for furniture manufacturer Portois und Fix. His interior and exterior for the shop achieved a formal severity that presaged Wagner himself. The second was 1901 Artaria publishing house building, Kohlmarkt. Its simplicity was not appreciated in Vienna, where ornamentation was still very popular.

▶ Günther Feuerstein, *Vienna—Present and Past: Arts and Crafts—Applied Art—Design*, Vienna: Jugend und Volk, 1976:80. Robert Waissenberger, *Vienna 1890–1920*, Secaucus, NJ: Wellfleet, 1984:172,186.

Fabiano, Fabio (1939–)

▶ Italian designer; born Castello; active Sousse (Tunisia), Montreal, USA, and Saronno (Italy).

▶ Studied architecture, Florence, to 1964, and industrial design, Syracuse University, Syracuse, New York, to 1971.

▶ He began his professional career in 1971 in Montreal. In 1971, became a member of ADI (Associazione per il Disegno Industriale) and of ACID (Association of Canadian Industrial Designers); 1965–74, practiced town planning, architecture, and industrial design in Tunisia, Canada, and USA; was deputy director of Bureau d'Urbanisme, Sousse (Tunisia), developing tourism and residential housing; was a consultant to the city of Montreal at 1967 'Universal and International Exhibition (Expo '67)' on pavilion 'Man and His World'; was interior architect to Bank of Montreal, Royal Bank of Canada, consultant on systems and tools to

IPL Industries and Bombardier Ltée in Quebec; 1971–72, was assistant, Faculté de l'Aménagement, Université de Montréal; designed agricultural equipment, office accessories, and electronic apparatus. Clients included Guzzini (plastic kitchenware and domestic goods), Zevi, and Euroway.
▶ *ADI Annual 1976*, Milan: Associazione per il Disegno Industriale, 1976.

Fabiansen, Ib   (1927–)
▶ Danish industrial designer.
▶ Studied architecture, Det Kongelige Danske Kunstackademi, Copenhagen, to 1957.
▶ He designed Illum's Bolighus store, Copenhagen; in 1958, set up his own studio, becoming a consultant designer at Bang & Olufsen and designing 1962 *Horizon* TV set; designed commercial and domestic architecture and interiors and garden furniture and lighting for Fog & Morup.
▶ Cat., Chantal Bizot, *Bang & Olufsen: Design et Technologie*, Paris: Musée des Arts Décoratifs, 1990:8.

Fabricius, Preben   (1931–)
▶ Danish furniture and interior designer.
▶ Studied Skolen for Boligindretning, Copenhagen, to 1957.
▶ In 1952, he worked under Finn Juhl as a cabinetmaker and designed seating for the United Nations building, New York; 1962–70, was a partner with Jørgen Kastholm; from 1967, taught furniture design, Skolen for Boligindretning; in 1968, set up his own office, Holte, where Kastholm had an office. Reminiscent of a tractor seat, his 1962 *Scimitar Chair 63* (designed with Kastholm) was produced by Ivan Schlechter, Copenhagen. Other furniture designs were produced by Kill and by Arnold Exclusiv.
▶ In 1969, received Illum Prize, Bundespreis 'Die gute Industrieform,' and Erster Prize. *Scimitar Chair 63* first shown at 1963 'New Forms' exhibition, Charlottenborg Museum, Copenhagen, and included in 1966 'Vijftig Jaar Zitten' exhibition, Stedelijk Museum, Amsterdam, and 1968 'Les Assises du siège contemporain' exhibition, Paris Musée des Arts Décoratifs.
▶ Cat., *Modern Chairs 1918–1970*, London: Lund Humphries, 1971. Frederik Sieck, *Nutidig Dansk Møbeldesign:—en kortfattet illustreret beskrivelse*, Copenhagen: Bondo Gravesen; 1990 Busck edition in English.

Facchini, Umberto   (1935–)
▶ Italian industrial designer; born Villafranca, Verona; active Treviso.
▶ He began his professional career in 1962; designed domestic and office storage and shelving systems; collaborated on some projects with architect Paolo Bandiera; became a member of ADI (Associazione per il Disegno Industriale). Clients included Faram and Vidal Hermanos.
▶ *ADI Annual 1976*, Milan: Associazione per il Disegno Industriale, 1976.

Fahrner Sr., Theodor   (?–1919) and **Theodor Fahrner Jr.**   (1868–1928)
▶ German jewelry manufacturer; located Pforzheim.
▶ Seeger und Fahrner was founded in 1855 as a costume jewelry factory. When Seeger died, Theodor Fahrner continued as manager of the firm. By 1891 or earlier, the firm became known as Theodor Fahrner; from c1900, expanded its operations and employed numerous artists. Some of the consultant designers were from the artists' colony in Darmstadt, including Patriz Huber and Josef Maria Olbrich. Fahrner was known for his inexpensive jewelry produced largely for export. The firm mass produced Jugendstil designs in low-grade gold and silver, semi-precious stones, opaque hard stones, and *perles de coq*. In c1900, Henry van de Velde designed pieces for the firm. In 1914, Fahrner joined the Deutscher Werkbund. Gustav Braendle, a jeweler from Esslingen, bought the firm from Martha Fahrner; the firm became 'Gustav Braendle, Theodor Fahrner, Succ.' Joining the firm in 1900 as mounter and modeler, Fritz Katz was its master craftsperson up to 1934. The firm continued production during World War II

until bombed in 1945. In 1952, it resumed production under the management of Herbert Braendle, Gustav's son. During the 1960s and 1970s, it produced 'antique' jewelry as well as gold and silver models in Roman and Egyptian motifs. The firm closed in 1979.
▶ Received a silver medal (as a single firm and jointly with the Pforzheim Industrial Association) at its first international presentation at 1900 Paris 'Exposition Universelle.' Work shown at 1901 exhibition at Artists' Colony at Darmstadt and 1904 St. Louis 'Louisiana Purchase Exposition.'
▶ Charlotte Gere, *American and European Jewelry 1830–1914*, New York: Crown, 1975:176. Deanna F. Cera (ed.), *Jewels of Fantasy: Costume Jewelry of the 20th Century*, New York: Abrams, 1992.

Fährngen, John
▶ Swedish silversmith; active Stockholm.
▶ Fährngen taught in the 1920s at Konstfackskolan and Tekniska Skolan, Stockholm.
▶ Received a prize for his silver hollow-ware (later proving successful for serial production) at 1909 Stockholm decorative arts exhibition.
▶ Annelies Krekel-Aalberse, *Art Nouveau and Art Déco Silver*, New York: Abrams, 1989:244,254.

Faience Manufacturing Company
▶ American ceramics firm; located Brooklyn, New York.
▶ The Faience Manufacturing Company operated 1880–92 in the Greenpoint area, Brooklyn, New York; manufactured earthenware vases, *jardinières*, and baskets at first. 1884–90, British émigré Edward Lycett was artistic director and supervised at least 25 decorators; experimented with a fine grade of white porcelain; produced the metallic glazes of Persian lusterware; in 1890, retired to Atlanta, Georgia, to assist son William who had established a china-painting business there.
▶ Edwin AtLee Barber, *The Pottery and Porcelain of the United States*, New York, 1893:313–19,414. Cat., Doreen Bolger Burke et al., *In Pursuit of Beauty: Americans and the Aesthetic Movement*, New York: Metropolitan Museum of Art and Rizzoli, 1987:426–27.
▶ See Lycette, Edward

Falize, Alexis   (1811–98)
▶ French goldsmith and jeweler; active Paris; father of Lucien Falize.
▶ In 1833, apprenticed at Maison Mellerio.
▶ 1835–38, he was workshop manager at Maison Janisset; in 1838, set up his own business in Galerie des Valois, Palais Royale, Paris, while continuing to produce wares for Mellerio and Janisset; working for a time for Maison Carré, took over the business in c1850; in the mid-1860s, revived *cloisonné* enamel work on jewelry; in the manner of Alphonse Fouquet, produced pieces in a complicated neo-Renaissance style; retiring in 1876, turned over management of the firm to his son Lucien Falize.
▶ He showed *japoniste cloisonné*-enameled jewelry at the 1867 Paris 'Exposition Universelle.'
▶ Charlotte Gere, *American and European Jewelry 1830–1914*, New York: Crown, 1975:17–77.

Falize, André   (1872–1936)
▶ French goldsmith and jeweler; active Paris; son of Lucien Falize.
▶ From 1894, André worked with his father Lucien in the family jewelry business, Paris; when Lucien died in 1897, took over directorship of the firm; worked in the Art Nouveau style, directing the firm with the assistance of brothers Jean and Pierre under the name Falize frères.
▶ Charlotte Gere, *American and European Jewelry 1830–1914*, New York: Crown, 1975:177.

Falize, Lucien (1838–97)

▶ French goldsmith and jeweler; active Paris; son of Alexis Falize; father of André Falize.

▶ When his father retired in 1876, Lucien assumed directorship of the family business. He attempted to expand the business by showing at 1878 Paris 'Exposition Universelle' and becoming partners with Germain Bapst. In 1892, the partnership was dissolved. Reviving the *basse-taille* (painting on translucent enamels over engraved decoration) technique, Lucien experimented with enamels and used *cloisonné*. From c1880 until the turn of the century, distinctive pieces with fine goldwork and enameling in the *japoniste* manner were produced by the firm known at the time as Bapst et Falize. In the 1890s, Lucien Hirtz (formerly with Bucheron) became an associate of Lucien Falize.

▶ The firm's wares were shown at the 1878 Paris 'Exposition Universelle.' Neo-Renaissance jewelry in the manner of Hans Collaert was shown at the 1889 Paris 'Exposition Universelle.'

▶ Charlotte Gere, *American and European Jewelry 1830–1914*, New York: Crown, 1975:177.

Faniel, Stéphane (1909–78)

▶ French designer.

▶ In charge of design at Christofle in the 1950s, Faniel designed its 1951 tea service in silver and ebony.

Faraone, Raffaele (?–1961)

▶ Italian jewelry designer; born Naples.

▶ Faraone established himself as a jeweler in Milan in the late 1940s; his work typified the postwar revival of Milanese design. When Faraone died in 1961, his firm in via Montenapoleone was taken over by his friend Guido Settepassi, who had a jewelry store of his own, Ponte Vecchio, Florence. Both the Faraone and Settepassi firms are managed today by Guido's son Cesare Settepassi.

▶ Melissa Gabardi, *Les Bijoux des Années 50*, Paris: Amateur, 1987.

Farina, Roberto (1949–)

▶ Italian designer; born and active Milan.

▶ Studied Liceo Artistico, Brera, to 1970, and architecture, Politecnico di Milano.

▶ From 1971, he collaborated on a number of architecture and design studies, working in the studio of Giorgio Decursu, Milan, and, subsequently, in the studio of Alberto Meda on industrial and furniture design; designed furniture in the studios of Venosta and Serini; from 1974, worked on furniture and interior design independently and with Alina Vianini; became a member of ADI (Associazione per il Disegno Industriale).

▶ *ADI Annual 1976*, Milan: Associazione per il Disegno Industriale, 1976.

Farquharson, Clyne

▶ British glassware designer.

▶ In the 1930s, Farquharson was a major contributor to the design of British glassware. His documented career in glass began in 1935 with *Arches*, an engraved design on glass produced by John Walsh Walsh, where he produced other cut-crystal glassware as its head designer 1935–51. Moving to Stevens and Williams, Farquharson was its chief designer 1951–56, when he was replaced by Tom Jones.

▶ Work shown at 1937 Paris 'Exposition Internationale des Arts et Techniques dans la Vie Moderne' and at British Industries Fairs.

▶ Kenneth Farr, *Design in British Industry: A Mid-Century Survey*, London: Cambridge, 1955. Frederick Cooke, *Glass: Twentieth-Century Design*, New York: Dutton, 1986:69.

Fasano

▶ Italian jewelry firm; located Turin.

▶ In 1932, Mario and Stella Fasano founded their jewelry establishment in Turin. In 1952, the flagship store moved to the arcades, via Roma, where the business is managed today by Stella and her son Dario. In the 1950s, Fasano was known for its jewelry in animal forms with precious stones.

▶ Melissa Gabardi, *Les Bijoux des Années 50*, Paris: Amateur, 1987.

Fatra

▶ Czech furniture manufacturer; located Napajedla.

▶ The state enterprise Fatra Napajedla produced articles exclusively in plastic, including its 1969 children's toys designed by L. Niklová in PVC in various sizes.

▶ Cat., Milena Lamarová, *Design a Plastické Hmoty*, Prague: Uměleckoprůmyslové Muzeum, 1972:54,184.

Faubourg Saint-Antoine

▶ Street and neighborhood in Paris.

▶ Parisian furniture manufacturers in and around the Faubourg Saint-Antoine produced pastiches and copies of classical designs from the early 19th century. At the beginning of the 20th century, production became more original, first with the Art Nouveau style, and subsequently Art Déco in both the baroque, classically oriented forms and the unornamented Modern forms. Important furniture makers active in the 1920s included Gouffé, Speich frères, Soubrier, Beligant et Fesneau, Haentgè frères, Marquis et Krast, Meyniel frères, Schugt et Beaudoin, and Krieger. The studio Gué of Georges and Gaston Guérin was directed by Georges Champion. Mercier frères opened the shop Palais du Marbre, 77 avenue des Champs-Élysées, directed by Eric Bagge. Fernand and Gaston Saddier were active in the quarter.

▶ Pierre Kjellberg, *Art Déco: les maîtres du Mobilier, le décor des Paquebots*, Paris: Amateur, 1986:71.

Faure, Camille (1874–1956)

▶ French enameler and painter.

▶ Faure began working as a fabricator of enamel street signs; collaborating with daughter Andrée Faure, produced vases in geometric designs on enameled copper; about 1930, created a technique for applying enamel thickly with a spatula.

▶ Cat., Aaron Lederfajn and Xavier Lenormand, *Le Louvre des Antiquaires présente: 1930 quand le meuble devient sculpture*, Paris, 1986.

Faux, Alfred

▶ Canadian furniture designer.

▶ Studied Ryerson Polytechnic Institute to 1957.

▶ He designed a number of chairs sold by the firm L'Enfant and installed at the Ryerson Polytechnic Institute and Guelph University, and a 1967 bent chromium-plated tubular-steel chair; was best known for his drafting table (with Thomas Lamb) produced by Norman Wade.

▶ Cat., *Seduced and Abandoned: Modern Furniture designers in Canada, the First Fifty Years*, Toronto: The Art Gallery at Harbourfront, 1986:23.

Favre-Pinsard, Giséle (b. Giséle Favre)

▶ French ceramicist and designer.

▶ In 1935, with her father, mother, and sister, she founded Les quatre Potiers, where tableware and fixtures for the bath and kitchen were produced; laid out the interior of the house of couturier André Courrèges in the Netherlands; from 1937 with husband Pierre Pinsard, was a member of UAM (Union des Artistes Modernes).

▶ Arlette Barré-Despond, *UAM*, Paris: Regard, 1986:522.

Fayolle, Denise (1923–)

▶ French design theorist, advertising executive, and entrepreneur.

▶ Studied philosophy.

▶ 1950–52, worked as a journalist; 1953–57, was style and advertising manager for the Prisunic store chain; in 1966, produced the first catalog of contemporary furniture produced by Prisunic; 1968–86, was general manager and partner, Agence MAFIA (Maïmé Arnodin, Fayolle International Associées), the advertising and product design office; was consultant to Trois

Suisses, the mail-order firm where she promoted young designers including Philippe Starck, Gae Aulenti, and Sonia Rykiel; with Arnodin, established NOMAD (Nouvelle Organisation Maïmé and Denise).

Fazioli, Domenico (1937–)
▶ Italian designer; active Milan.
▶ Studied architecture, Rome, to 1971.
▶ 1960–64, he was responsible for interior design projects for MIM, Rome; designed the *Executive* range of office furniture, *Galileo* range of tables and desks, *Pascal* shelving and storage system in wood and plastic laminate, and *Compact* range of chairs for auditoria and meeting rooms; 1973–76, was in charge of the corporate image of Geres in Milan, the group of companies of MIM, Siam, and Viotto, and designed new showrooms for Siam in Milan, Paris, Brussels, and Turin; became a member of ADI (Associazione per il Disegno Industriale).
▶ *ADI Annual 1976*, Milan: Associazione per il Disegno Industriale, 1976.

Fear, Jeffrey (1945–)
▶ Canadian industrial designer; born Toronto.
▶ Studied Ryerson Polytechnic Institute.
▶ He worked for Salmon-Hamilton Design Consultants and subsequently for a contract-furniture manufacturer in California. His 1971 upholstered tubular-steel chair and ottoman were produced by Kinetics Furniture, Toronto.
▶ Cat., *Seduced and Abandoned: Modern Furniture designers in Canada, the First Fifty Years*, Toronto: The Art Gallery at Harbourfront, 1986:25.

Featherston, Grant (1922–)
▶ Australian designer.
▶ 1938–39, Featherston designed decorative-glass panels for Oliver-Davey Glass, Melbourne, and 1939–40 lighting for Newton and Gray, Melbourne; designed and made jewelry and invented manufacturing equipment 1946–52; 1947–50, designed and made webbing and the fabric-upholstered *Relaxation Chair*. His *Contour Chairs* were designed, patented, and manufactured 1950–52, followed by numerous other accompanying models and tables. He designed street decorations for the 1955 City of Melbourne Olympic Civic Committee; in 1956, moved to 7 Davidsons Place, Melbourne and, in 1957, to 131 Latrobe Street, Melbourne; was a consultant designer to numerous architects; in 1963, sold his firm Featherston Interiors to Aristoc Industries; formed a partnership with his wife, resulting in a collaboration on all their work from 1966 onwards; is Australia's best known furniture designer. Featherston expounded the virtues of good design; though he designed hundreds of chairs, did not consider himself to be essentially a designer of seat furniture; worked as a graphic and interior designer; designed textiles, ceramics, jewelry, toys, and trophies.
▶ *Talking Chair* shown at 1967 Montreal 'Universal and International Exhibition (Expo '67).' Produced furniture for Robin Boyd's model home shown at 1949 'Modern Home Exhibition,' Exhibition Buildings, Melbourne. Furniture shown at 1952 exhibition, Stanley Coe Gallery, Melbourne. Floating chairs, storage, and work stations subject of 1960 exhibition, Argus Gallery, Melbourne.
▶ Cat., *Featherston Chairs*, Victoria, Australia: National Gallery of Victoria, 1988.

Featherston, Mary (1943–)
▶ Australian designer.
▶ 1964–66, Featherston was an interior designer at Mockridge, Stahle and Mitchell, Carlton, architects; in 1966, (with husband) formed the Grant and Mary Featherston partnership; from 1966, was consultant to numerous furniture manufacturers and, from 1973, research consultant to the Melbourne government on children's playgrounds.
▶ Cat., *Featherston Chairs*, Victoria, Australia: National Gallery of Victoria, 1988.
▶ See Featherston, Grant

Fecarotta
▶ Italian jewelry firm.
▶ Giovanni Fecarotta was a goldsmith and precious stonecutter active around Naples and Palermo at the end of the 19th century. His sons established a jewelry store in Palermo; had goldsmith workshops elsewhere; produced jewelry for rich Sicilian families; sold their wares to some of the most prestigious jewelers in Europe. In 1899, Ernesto Fecarotta moved the business to via Etnea 170, Catania. Taking over from Ernesto, his sons Roberto and Vittorio co-managed the firm. Giuseppe Robotti was a designer at Fecarotta in the 1950s, when its production included a modest use of precious materials in exciting designs. Ernesto Fecarotta and his cousin Giuliana manage the firm today.

Federspiel, Carla (1934–)
▶ Italian designer; born and active Milan.
▶ Studied architecture, Milan, to 1959.
▶ From 1961, she collaborated with Adelaide Bonati, Silvio Bonatti, and Enrico De Munari in the studio Tetrarch, Milan; was active in architecture, town planning, interiors, and industrial design, designing storage systems, lighting, and sanitary fittings; designed *Pistolo* lamp produced by Valenti; became a member of ADI (Associazione per il Disegno Industriale).
▶ *ADI Annual 1976*, Milan: Associazione per il Disegno Industriale, 1976.

Fehling, Ilse (1896–1982)
▶ Polish theater designer; born Danzig (now Gdańsk, Poland).
▶ Studied theater school, Berlin; Kunstgewerbeschule, Berlin; 1920–23, Bauhaus, Weimar.
▶ For several years, she was a theater designer; from 1945, designed for publications, worked in the theater, and taught drawing; in 1947, settled in Munich.
▶ Lionel Richard, *Encyclopédie du Bauhaus*, Paris: Somogy, 1985: 185. Cat., *Experiment Bauhaus*, Berlin: Bauhaus-Archiv, 1988: 418.

Feick Jr., George (1881–1945)
▶ American architect and designer.
▶ Studied Cornell University, Ithaca, New York.
▶ At Cornell, he met William Gray Purcell, who later worked for five months in the architecture office Adler and Sullivan, Chicago; in 1907, (with Purcell) set up the architectural firm Purcell and Feick; in 1910, George Grant Elmslie joined the firm, which became known as Purcell, Feick and Elmslie. Feick left in 1913 and the firm became Purcell and Elmslie until 1922. The firm's commissions included numerous banks in small Midwestern towns. Like Frank Lloyd Wright, whom they met in the Sullivan office, and Sullivan himself, they avoided obvious Beaux-Arts forms and neoclassical detailing to produce an indigenous American style. They were known for their attention to integrated site-specific interiors, furniture, and fittings.
▶ Anne Yaffe Phillips, *From Architecture to Object*, New York: Hirschl and Adler, 1989:72.

Feildel, Jean
▶ French decorator and furniture designer.
▶ Active from 1928, Feildel designed furniture for 1932 Pavillon de la Chasse, Paris.
▶ Work first shown at 1927 Salon of Société des Artistes Décorateurs and 'Exposition Générale d'Art appliqué,' Palais Galliéra, Paris.
▶ Pierre Kjellberg, *Art Déco: les maîtres du Mobilier, le décor des Paquebots*, Paris: Amateur, 1986:71.

Feinauer, Albert
▶ German silversmith; active Weimar.
▶ Feinauer was an instructor in the silversmithing workshop, Institut für Kunstgewerbe und Kunstindustrie, Weimar, founded by Henry van de Velde in 1906; produced a number of tea sets designed by van de Velde and described by him as 'incomparable

in their craftsmanship and among the best things I have designed in my life.'

▶ Henry van de Velde, *Geschichte meines Lebens*, Munich 1962: 295. Annelies Krekel-Aalberse, *Art Nouveau and Art Déco Silver*, New York: Abrams, 1989:241,151,254.

Fellerer, Max (1889–1957)
▶ Austrian interior designer; born Linz.
▶ Although there was no distinctly Viennese approach to interior design after World War II, Fellerer offered some of the substance of a style, along with Otto Niedermoser, Erich Boltenstern, and Franz Schuster.
▶ Günther Feuerstein, *Vienna—Present and Past: Arts and Crafts—Applied Art—Design*, Vienna: Jugend und Volk, 1976: 61,80.

Fels, Jerry (b. Jerry Felsentein 1917–)
▶ American costume jewelry designer; born Brooklyn, New York.
▶ Studied fine art, Arts Students' League, and National Academy of Design, both New York.
▶ He was a freelance designer for department stores in New York and an executive at Gertz's department store; moved to California where, in 1946, he established firm Renoir of Hollywood, Boudrie Street, Los Angeles, with brother-in-law Curt Freiler and Nat Zausner; moved to a converted movie studio, Santa Monica Boulevard. In 1948, the firm moved to Hollywood Boulevard with its name changed to Renoir of California; then relocated to 1755 Glendale Boulevard, Los Angeles. Influenced by pop architecture, Fels designed high-quality jewelry that brought new respect for jewelry in copper. The firm's jewelry of the 1940s reflected crafts traditions and primitive art. Its work resembled that of Rebajes, New York. Artisan Freiler sheared, soldered, eyeletted, hammered, and polished all items by hand. Serially produced items were executed by Mexican metalsmiths with stamping, die cutting, punching, and bending machines, and finished by hand. A short-age of copper during the Korean War eliminated the production of belts and large bracelets and resulted in the bonding of copper with aluminum. Renoir's wares were sold in department stores, boutiques, and Indian trading posts, specializing in handmade silver and turquoise jewelry. In 1952, the 'Matisse, Ltd' line was introduced with enameled color inserts; Curtis Tann was hired for his training as a classical enamelist.
▶ Matthew L. Burkholz and Linda Lichtenberg Kaplan, *Copper Art Jewelry: A Different Lustre*, West Chester, Pennsylvania: Schiffer, 1992:72–79.

Fenand, Roger (aka Géo 1890–)
See Géo

Fendi
▶ Italian fashion house.
▶ Fendi was established in 1925 in Rome by Adele Fendi, whose five daughters (Alda, Anna, Carla, Franca, and Paola) subsequently took over its management, handling various aspects of the firm today. Fendi was best known for its clothing and accessories, often in leather and fur, the latter designed by Karl Lagerfeld; from 1989, produced furniture and, from 1993, linens.
▶ Showed leather-piped cushions, tapestry furnishings, and furniture models designed by Matteas Buser at 1989 Salone del Mobile, Milan, including the *Paolina* daybed, *Farnese* three-seat sofa, and *Augusto* two-seat sofa. *Augusto* sofa shown at 1991 'Mobili Italiani 1961–1991: Le Varie Età dei linguaggi' exhibition, Salone del Mobile, Milan.
▶ Mary Beth Jordan, *Metropolitan Home*, April 1990:132.

Fennemore, Thomas Acland (1902–55)
▶ British pottery, wallpaper, and textile designer.
▶ 1919–26, he worked in advertising for Samson Clarke; Peter Jones, London; Edgar Lawley (China and Glass), Stoke-on-Trent. 1927–29, (with others) he set up a business known as Fennemore, Haydon; 1929–31, was general manager of Paragon China; from 1932, director of pottery at Brain and Co, Fenton, where he

painted and designed china and hired artists, including Albert Rutherston, Vanessa Bell, and Duncan Grant to paint china; in 1936, became registrar of the National Register of Industrial Art Designers and founded the Central Institute of Art and Design to promote the activities of British designers during World War II; in 1947, became director of exhibitions, Odhams Press; 1947–53, was consultant designer to Sanderson, J.B. Brooks, Odhams Press, Antler Luggage, Lawley Group potteries, Bolton Leathers, and A.J. Wilkinson pottery; sold designs to Wilton Royal Carpet Factory, Heals, John Lewis, Bradford Fabrics, and Horrockses; founded and was vice-president of the Society of Mural Painters.
▶ Organized 1934 'Modern Art for the Table,' Harrods department store, London, where Brain and Co, A.J. Wilkinson, and Royal Staffordshire Pottery displayed the painted ceramics of artists including Bell, Sutherland, Grant, Rutherston, Laura Knight, and Paul Nash. Work shown at 1979–80 'Thirties' exhibition, Hayward Gallery, London.
▶ Cat., *Thirties: British art and design before the war*, London: Arts Council of Great Britain, Hayward Gallery, 1979:71,95,96,133, 151,154,155,289.

Fermigier, Étienne (1937–)
▶ French industrial designer, active Paris.
▶ Studied École Boulle, and École Nationale Supérieure des Arts Décoratifs, Paris, to 1954.
▶ He set up his own design office; was active in interior architecture and industrial design; in 1959 with Pierre Perrigault, established Meubles et Fonctions, the showroom and manufacturer of work by young designers Jean-Paul Barray, Michel Mortier, and Daniel Pigeon; designed furniture for Meubles et Fonctions and Mobilier de France and seating by Airborne, Arflex, and Sentou, lighting by Disderot and Verre et Lumière; taught at École Camondo, Paris.
▶ Received the 1967 René Gabriel Prize.
▶ François Mathey, *Au bonheur des formes, design français 1945–1992*, Paris: Regard, 1992:241,303–18.

Ferrara, Gianni (1928–)
▶ Italian designer; born and active Florence.
▶ In 1970, Ferrara, Carlo Bimbi, and Nilo Gioacchini set up the industrial design studio Gruppo Internotredici, Florence. Ferrara was a teacher at Istituto Superiore per l'Industria Artistica in Florence; at the 1975 Interdesign meeting of the ICSID in Bruges, participated in the 'Urban Traffic on a Human Scale' committee sponsored by ADI (Associazione per il Disegno Industriale), of which he was a member.
▶ Received Bayer special prize (furniture design) at 1970 (X) Concorso Internazionale del Mobile, Trieste, first and second prizes (laminated-plastic furniture by Abet-Print) at 1971 Concorso Nazionale, and first prize (alabaster accesories by Volterra) at the 1972 Concorso Nazionale, where he was a juror. Participated in Scuole di Disegno Industriale pavilion, 1967 Montreal 'Universal and International Exhibition (Expo '67)'; contributed furniture to 100m² apartment, 1971 'Mostra Selettiva del Mobile,' Cantù; 1972 'Italy: The New Domestic Landscape,' New York Museum of Modern Art; Italian section, 1973 (V) Biennale of Industrial Design, Ljubljana; 'Italia Oggi,' Gimbel's department store, Pittsburgh, Pennsylvania; furniture, sculpture, visuals, and an alabaster project, 'Volterra '73,' Italian-design pavilion, 1975 'Salon d'Ameublement,' Lausanne.
▶ *ADI Annual 1976*, Milan: Associazione per il Disegno Industriale, 1976.

Ferrari, Alberto
▶ Italian architect and designer; active Milan.
▶ Studied architecture to 1970.
▶ Ferrari collaborated with architects, engineers, and various firms on projects including industrial buildings, lighting, and fabrics; from 1971, (with Dante Benini) collaborated in own studio, Milan; became a member of ADI (Associazione per il Disegno Industriale).

▶ *ADI Annual 1976*, Milan: Associazione per il Disegno Industriale, 1976.

Ferrari-Hardoy, Jorge (1914–77); Juan Kurchan (1913–75); Antonio Bonet (1913–75)

▶ Architects Ferrari-Hardoy and Kurchan born Argentina. Architect Bonet born Barcelona.

▶ In 1937, Ferrari-Hardoy, Kurchan, and Bonet worked in the architecture office of Le Corbusier, Paris. They settled in Argentina, where they designed the *Butterfly* chair produced at different times under various names and manufacturers; more than 5 million were sold in the USA in the 1950s, produced by Knoll in USA and Airborne in France for a time from 1947. It was also known as the *AA* chair because of the welded-rod triangles that produced two points at the back and two at the seat, over which a canvas or leather cover was thrown. Bonet's, Ferrari's,and Kurchan's version was produced 1939–40 and known as the *BKF* chair. Another model had articulated points providing a folding capability and was probably adapted from a much earlier model intended for military or safari use.

▶ Guy Julier, *New Spanish Design*, New York: Rizzoli, 1991:23.

Ferreri, Marco (1958–)

▶ Italian architect and designer.

▶ Studied Politecnico di Milano.

▶ He worked as an architect for Manfiaroti, Zanuso e Munari until 1984, when he set up his own independent office with clients including Milan City Council, Olivetti, IBM, McCann Erikson, and others; (with Carlo Bellini) designed 1986–87 *Eddy* lamp produced by Luxo Italiana.

▶ Albrecht Bangert and Karl Michael Armer, *80s Style: Designs of the Decade*, New York: Abbeville, 1990:94,230.

Ferretti, Giulio (1943–)

▶ Italian designer; born and active Pordenone.

▶ Studied architecture.

▶ He began his professional career in 1970; a member of ADI (Associazione per il Disegno Industriale). Clients in Italy included Tatabi, Icar Sutrio, and Nusiam Follina.

▶ Received first prize at 1970 Concorso Print, Pordenone, and third prize at its 1971 session. Participated in Met-Ar-Plastic, Musile di Piave, Venice.

▶ *ADI Annual 1976*, Milan: Associazione per il Disegno Industriale, 1976.

Ferrieri, Anna Castelli

See Castelli Ferrieri, Anna

Festival of Britain

▶ British exposition.

▶ The 1951 'Festival of Britain' on the South Bank of the river Thames, London, was originally suggested by Gerald Barry to commemorate the 1851 London 'Great Exhibition of the Works of Industry of all Nations' (aka 'Crystal Palace Exhibition'). The director of architecture was Hugh Casson, and the newly formed Council of Industrial Design was responsible for the selection of industrially produced exhibits. Its uniformly high standard of Modern architecture, design, and town planning made it a landmark event; millions of Britons came to have their spirits lifted during difficult postwar times. The setting in central London offered a layout of buildings on various levels, the format recalling the 1930 'Stockholmsutstälininge.' The most notable piece of furniture was Ernest Race's *Antelope* chair. Other exhibits and events were concurrently organized throughout Britain. All the structures apart from the Festival Hall were destroyed at the end of the exhibition.

▶ Pavilions included Leslie Martin's Royal Festival Hall; the Architects' Co-Partnership's Minerals of the Land; Arcon's Transport; H.T. Cadbury-Brown's Land of Britain; Maxwell Fry's, Jane Drew's, and Edward Mills's administration building; R.Y. Goodden's and R.D. Russell's Lion and Unicorn; F.H.K. Henrion's and Brian O'Rorke's The Natural Scene and the Country; H.J. Reifenberg's and Grenfell Baines's Power and Production; Basil Spence's Sea and Ships; and Ralph Tubbs's Dome of Discovery.

▶ H. Casson, 'The 1951 Exhibition,' *Journal of the Royal Institute of British Architecture*, April 1950. Mary Banham and Bevis Hillier (eds.), *A Tonic for the Nation*, London, 1976. Vittorio Magnago Lampugnani (ed.), *Encyclopedia of 20th-Century Architecture*, New York: Abrams, 1986:96–97.

Festival Pattern Group

▶ British design project.

▶ In 1951, the Festival Pattern Group was established as a project by the British Council of Industrial Design to encourage manufacturers to produce decorative wares based on crystallographic structures shown at the 'Festival of Britain.' In the 1940s, Britain was a leader in crystallography. Brociacid, aluminum hydroxide, hemoglobin, and insulin were among the chemicals whose crystal structures influenced design attempts to unite science, industry, and art. Twenty-six diverse manufacturers participated, including Wedgwood, who produced a commemorative bone china plate. Other manufacturers included Goodearl Brothers, Chance Brothers, London Typographical Designer, Warerite, and Spicers. Many of these products were displayed at the exhibition. Plates by Wedgwood in the restaurant, decorative motifs in the Dome of Discovery in snowflake and atomic patterns, and Ernest Race's *Antelope* chair with its 'molecular' feet reflected the influence of the project.

▶ Jonathan M. Woodham, *Twentieth-Century Ornament*, New York: Rizzoli, 1990:204,206.

Feuerstein, Bedřich (1892–1936)

▶ Czech architect, set designer, and essayist; born Dobrovice.

▶ 1911–17, studied Czech University of Technology, and College of Arts and Crafts, Prague, under Jožef Plečník.

▶ He was introduced to Cubism and Purism in France where, 1920–21, he stayed with Josef Šíma; 1924–26, worked in Auguste Perret's studio, Paris, and, 1926–30, in Antonin Raymond's studio, Tokyo. 1913–22, his painting and architecture had both Cubist and classical elements. He designed the classical 1922–25 Zeměpisný ústav building, Prague; 1922–24 crematorium, Nymburk, in the Purist style and influenced by the Pantheon, Rome; 1921–22 sets in a 'structural logic' style in bright colors and Purist forms for National Theater, Prague. In 1925, he became opposed to Karel Teige's Constructivist 'elimination of art'; Teige was the Devětsil founder. From 1922 to its end in 1931, Feuerstein was a member of Devětsil; returning to Czechoslovakia in 1930, was active as a set designer until his suicide.

▶ Work shown in Prague (with Tvrdošíjní group) and at 1923 Bauhaus exhibition, Weimar.

▶ Cat., *Devětsil: Czech Avant-Garde Art, Architecture, and Design of the 1920s and 30s*, Oxford Museum of Modern Art Oxford and London Design Museum, 1990.

Feuillâtre, Eugène (1870–1916)

▶ French artist, sculptor, and metalworker; born Dunkerque; active Paris.

▶ Feuillâtre began experimenting in 1893 with complex enameling techniques on silver and platinum, becoming known as a remarkable enamelist and perfecting a technique for enameling on platinum; working with Lalique originally, set up his own workshop in 1899. Specializing in *plique-à-jour* enameling, his pieces were some of the most advanced examples of Art Nouveau metalwork. Feuillâtre began specializing in *cloisonné* and producing outstanding intricate Art Nouveau-style metalwork. His objects in translucent enamel with colors overlapping on engraved grounds were particularly attractive and incorporated natural motifs, including blackberries and fish, in *plique-à-jour* enamel on bowls and boxes. He also experimented with glass combined with enameled silver.

▶ Work (enameled silver objects) first shown under his own name at 1898 Salon of Société des Artistes français and in its 1910 Salon. Work shown at 1899 La Libre Esthétique exhibition, Brussels; New Gallery, London; 1900 Paris 'Exposition Universelle,' and 1902 'Esposizione Internazionale d'Arte Decorativa Moderna,' Turin.

▶ Charlotte Gere, *American and European Jewelry 1830–1914*, New York: Crown, 1975:178. Yvonne Brunhammer et al., *Art Nouveau Belgium, France*, Houston: Rice University, 1976. Annelies Krekel-Aalberse, *Art Nouveau and Art Déco Silver*, New York: Abrams, 1989:259–260,254.

Fiam

▶ Italian furniture manufacturer; located Tavullia.

▶ Fiam was founded in 1972 by Antonio Livi to produce furniture and furnishings, incorporating innovative bent glass and hardware; became known for its intricate one-piece glass furniture. Its art director was Angelo Cortesi and graphic designers Patrizia Pataccini and Carla Caccia. Rocco Serini was a consultant designer; Danny Lane's work for Fiam included 1988 *Shell* and *Atlas* tables. It produced Livi's 1984 *Ragno* table, Cini Boeri's 1987 *Ghost* one-piece glass chair (with Tomu Katyanagi), and Philippe Starck's 1992 glass-topped table *Illusion*, Enzo Mari's 1992 table *Montefeltro*, and designs by Massimo Iosa Ghini, Hans von Klier, Massimo Morazzi, and Makio Hasuike.

▶ *ADI Annual 1976*, Milan: Associazione per il Disegno Industriale, 1976. 'Milan à l'Heure du Design,' *Maison et Jardin*, April 1992:128.

fiberglass

▶ Fiberglass (or fiberglas) contains glass spun in a fibrous form. An early example of the use of fiberglass, formed as a solid by being mixed with polymers, was the dish for radar detection during World War II. Immediately after the war, Charles Eames had the Herman Miller Furniture Company, Zeeland, Michigan commission the production of the shells for his c1950 bucket-shaped chairs from radar-dish manufacturer Zenith Plastics, Gardena, California. Herman Miller later produced the seats independently. From the early 1950s, particularly in the USA, fiberglass became popular in the manufacture of furniture, automobile bodies, and a vast number of other products.

Figini, Luigi (1903–)

▶ Italian architect-designer; born Milan.

▶ Studied Politecnico di Milano to 1926.

▶ In 1926, he became a founding member of Gruppo Sette (Group Seven), the group of Italian architects who initiated the Rationalist movement. Figini was a member of MIAR (Movimento Italiano per l'Architettura Razionale); from 1929, collaborated with Gino Pollini; (with Pollini, Adalberto Libera, Guido Fretti, and Piero Bottoni) designed the 'Casa Elettrica' pavilion for Montedison Company at 1930 (IV) 'Esposizione Biennale delle Arti Decorative e Industriali Moderne,' Monza, with its prominently featured all-electric kitchen based on German and American models. It was the first public expression of Modern architecture in Italy. In 1930–33, Figini and Pollini designed the Craja Bar, Milan, and the offices of De Angeli Frua (with Luciano Baldesari). They are best known for the radio-gramophone that won the 1933 design competition sponsored by the National Gramophone Co and subsequently put into limited production. They designed an artist's studio at 1933 (V) Triennale di Milano; worked in the Rationalist style through the 1930s, designing 1934–35 Olivetti building, Ivrea, built in 1939–41; designed the 1935 *Studio 42* typewriter (with Xanti Schawinsky) for Olivetti. The New Brutalism was illustrated by their 1952–56 Church of the Madonna dei Poveri, Milan. After the deaths of Giuseppe Pagano and Giuseppe Terragni, Figini and Pollini became the standard-bearers of the Rationalist tradition.

▶ Work (with Pollini) shown at 1926 (II) Biennale di Monza. Designed (with Pollini and others) 'Casa Elettrica,' 1930 Biennale di Monza. Designed (with Pollini) villa-studio for an artist (in a park), 1933 (V) Triennale di Milano, with steel-and-wood furniture. Won (with Pollini) design competition for a writing desk sponsored by 1936 (VI) Triennale di Milano and designed the terrace setting there.

▶ Luigi Figini and Gino Pollini, 'Origines de l'architecture moderne en Italie,' *L'Architecture d'aujourd'hui*, Vol. 22, No. 41, June 1952:5–9. Eugenio Gentili Tedeschi, *Figini e Pollini*, Milan: Il Balcone, 1959. Cesare Blasi, *Figini e Pollini*, Milano: Ed. di Monumità, 1963. Luigi Figini, 'Architettura Italiana 1963,' special issue, *Edilizia Moderna*, No. 82–83, 1964. J. Rykwert, 'Figini & Pollini,' *Architectural Design*, Aug. 1967:369–78. Barbie Campbell-Cole and Tim Benton (eds.), *Tubular Steel Furniture*, London: The Art Book Company, 1979:47. Penny Sparke, *Design in Italy, 1870 to the Present*, New York: Abbeville, 1988. Richard A. Etlin, *Modernism in Italian Architecture, 1890–1940*, Cambridge: MIT, 1991.

Finch, Alfred William (1854–1930)

▶ Belgian ceramicist; born Brussels; active Finland.

▶ 1878–80, studied painting, École des Beaux-Arts, Brussels; ceramics at Boch frères, La Louvière.

▶ An Impressionist, he became a founding member of artists' group Les Vingt in 1884; in 1886, met James Whistler in London and tried unsuccessfully to get him to join Les Vingt. Finch became familiar with the Arts and Crafts movement, sharing a knowledge of it with Henry van de Velde and Les Vingt members. In 1888, Finch became interested in Pointillism through Georges Seurat. Les Vingt member Ann Boch introduced him to Kéramis, the Boch ceramics factory at La Louvière where he worked 1890–93. In 1896, he experimented with glazed pottery in his own studio, Forges-Chimay; from 1897–1902, was head of the ceramics department, Iris Factory, Porvoo (Finland); after the Iris factory closed, was head of the ceramics department, Taideteollinen Korkeakoulu, Helsinki until 1930.

▶ Yvonne Brunhammer et al., *Art Nouveau Belgium, France*, Houston: Rice University, 1976. Cat., David Revere McFadden (ed.), *Scandinavian Modern Design 1880–1980*, New York: Abrams, 1982:263, No. 40. Jennifer Hawkins Opie, *Scandinavia: Ceramics and Glass in the Twentieth Century*, New York: Rizzoli, 1989.

Fini, Gianfranco (1942–)

▶ Italian designer; born S. Benedetto; active Rome.

▶ He began his professional career in 1965; was known for his furniture and electronic appliances, including television sets; a member of ADI (Associazione per il Disegno Industriale). Clients included Triplex, Autovox, Poltronova, and Pentastudio.

▶ *ADI Annual 1976*, Milan: Associazione per il Disegno Industriale, 1976.

Finmar

See Aalto, Hugo Alvar Henrik

Finsterlin, Hermann (1887–1973)

▶ German theorist and architect; born Munich.

▶ Studied philosophy, biology, chemistry, physics, and other subjects; in 1913, painting in Munich under Franz von Stuck.

▶ An architectural designer rather than a practitioner, he never built a building. A participant in Bruno Taut's Utopian Correspondence (aka Prometh), he became a member of the Glass Chain; in c1930, was hired by Hannes Meyer to work briefly at the Bauhaus, Dessau; is today known as the author of abstruse writings published in reviews *Frühlicht*, *Wendingen*, and others.

▶ On Walter Gropius's invitation, work shown at April 1919 Berlin 'Ausstellung für unbekannte Architekten' ('Exhibition of Unknown Architects') sponsored by the Arbeitstrat für Kunst. Finsterlin's paintings and drawings were shown in numerous European cities. Work (erotic paintings and models) first shown in 1916. Work subject of 1973 exhibition, Stuttgart, and 1976 exhibition, Krefeld.

▶ Nikolas Pevsner, 'Finsterlin and Some Others,' *Architectural Review*, Nov. 1962:353–57. D. Sharp, 'Hermann Finsterlin and Formspiel' in *Modern Architecture and Expressionism*, London, 1966:97–108. F. Borsi (ed.), *Hermann Finsterlin: Idea dell'architettura*, Florence, 1969. D. Sharp, 'Hermann Finsterlin: Prometheus Unbound,' *Building Design*, 15 Sept. 1972. D. Sharp, 'The Last of the German Fantasts,' *Building Design*, 12 Oct. 1973. Cat.,

U.M. Schneede (ed.), *Hermann Finsterlin*, Stuttgart, 1973. Cat., *Hermann Finsterlin (1887–1973)*, Krefeld, 1976.

Fiorentino, Antonio (1953–)
▶ Italian designer; born Catanzaro; active Milan.
▶ Studied architecture.
▶ He began his professional career in 1971. He was a sculptor, painter, interior architect, designer, and a member of ADI (Associazione per il Disegno Industriale).
▶ *ADI Annual 1976*, Milan: Associazione per il Disegno Industriale, 1976.

Fiřt, Vladimír (1932–)
▶ Czech industrial designer.
▶ 1952–57, studied engineering construction, Technical University, Prague, and technical sciences to 1963.
▶ He published more than 40 works on the science of applied mathematics, stability, and dynamics of building structures, rheology and plasticity, soil mechanics, and membrane structures, 20 of which were presented at various meetings held in Czechoslovakia and abroad. In 1966, he began work on plastics for building purposes; applied for six Czech patents; for one of his three books, received a literary prize; was a senior scientific worker at Institute of Theoretical and Applied Mechanics, member of Czechoslovak Scientific and Technological Society for Mechanics and of the Academy of Sciences, and member of and instructor at Examination Board for practitioners in science; from 1963, was a member of Association Internationale des Ponts et Charpentes; in 1972, achieved status as a master mathematician.
▶ Cat., Milena Lamarová, *Design a Plastické Hmoty*, Prague: Uměleckoprůmyslové Muzeum, 1972:110.

Firth, T. F., and Sons
▶ British textile firm; located Brighouse and Heckmondwike.
▶ Edwin Firth founded the firm in 1822. It was incorporated 1889; 1936, produced Axminster, Wilton, Brussels, Velvet, and tapestry carpets at Brighouse, and seamless Axminster squares, a range of rugs, mantle cloths, and upholstery velvets at Heckmondwike.
▶ Valerie Mendes, *The Victoria and Albert Museum's Textile Collection, British Textiles from 1900 to 1937*, London: Victoria and Albert Museum, 1992.

Fischer, Christa (1957–)
▶ German industrial designer; born Würzburg; active Berlin.
▶ 1977–81, studied interior design, Fachhochschule, Rosenheim.
▶ In 1981, she settled in Berlin; 1981–86, worked in an architecture office; from 1986, set up her own interior-architecture office, began work as a freelance interior and exhibition designer in the Berliner Zimmer design group, designing under the pseudonym Craftcow.
▶ Work shown at the Berliner Zimmer stand, 1986 Cologne Fair; 1986 'Transit Berlin West,' Berlin; 1988 Cologne Fair; 1988 'Berlin: Les Avant-Gardes du Mobilier,' at Centre Georges Pompidou, VIA, and Galerie Néotù, all Paris.
▶ Cat., Berlin: *Les Avant-Gardes du Mobilier*, Berlin: Design Zentrum, 1988. Cat., Design Center Stuttgart, *Women in Design: Careers and Life Histories Since 1900*, Stuttgart: Haus der Wirtschaft, 1989:112–13.

Fischer, Richard (1935–)
▶ German industrial designer.
▶ Fisher designed products for Braun, Frankfurt.

Fischer, Robert (1906–41)
▶ German silversmith; active Schwäbisch-Gmünd.
▶ Trained with Wilhelm Binder; studied Staatliche höhere Edelmetallfachschule, Schwäbisch-Gmünd.
▶ Working in Berlin and Leipzig as an independent silversmith, he settled in Schwäbisch-Gmünd in 1932 and, from 1934, taught metalwork at Edelmetallfachschule.

▶ Received numerous awards. Work shown at exhibitions of 1930s and at 1937 Paris 'Exposition Internationale des Arts et Techniques dans la Vie Moderne.'
▶ Annelies Krekel-Aalberse, *Art Nouveau and Art Déco Silver*, New York: Abrams, 1989:146,254.

Fischer, Tuk (1939–)
▶ Danish metalworker.
▶ Studied Kunsthåndvaerkerskolen, Copenhagen, 1964.
▶ Trained as a goldsmith, she began working for Georg Jensen Sølvsmedie in 1962.
▶ Cat., *Georg Jensen Silversmithy: 77 Artists, 75 Years*, Washington: Smithsonian Institution Press, 1980.

Fischer, Uwe (1958–)
▶ German designer.
▶ In 1985 with Klaus Achim Heine, he founded the Ginbande design studio, Frankfurt, where highly articulated furniture for Vitra Edition and Sawaya & Moroni was designed. The studio's widely published 1988 *Tabula Rasa* table-bench combination for Vitra extended from 20 in (50 cm) to 197 in (500 cm).
▶ Albrecht Bangert and Karl Michael Armer, *80s Style: Designs of the Decade*, New York: Abbeville, 1990:87,230.

Fischer-Treyden, Elsa (1901–)
▶ Russian textile, glassware, and ceramics designer; active Berlin.
▶ 1925–32, studied Hochschule für bildende Künste, Berlin, under Wilhelm Wagenfeld.
▶ In the mid-1920s, Fischer-Treyden moved from Russia to Berlin, working as an independent designer while studying in Berlin; from 1953, worked for Rosenthal, designing glassware, porcelain, and stoneware, including the widely published 1965 *Fuga* glassware range.
▶ Received medals at 1951 (IX) and 1954 (X) Triennali di Milano and 1968 Bundespreis 'Die gute Industrieform' (*Fuga* glassware range).
▶ Cat., *Rosenthal: Hundert Jahre Porzellan*, Hanover: Kestner-Museum, 1982:174–75, Nos. 90,103,111–12. Cat., Kathryn B. Hiesinger and George H. Marcus III (eds.), *Design Since 1945*, Philadelphia: Philadelphia Museum of Art, 1983.

Fischl, Hans
▶ Swiss architect, painter, and sculptor.
▶ Studied Bauhaus, Dessau, 1928.
▶ He taught at the Kunstgewerbeschule, Zürich.
▶ Lionel Richard, *Encyclopédie du Bauhaus*, Paris: Somogy, 1985:187.

Fisher, Alexander (1864–1936)
▶ British painter, sculptor, and silversmith; active London.
▶ 1884–86, studied South Kensington Schools, London, and enameling, Paris and Sèvres.
▶ In Paris, he experimented with layering translucent enamels, sometimes including metal or foil similar to 18th-century *paillons*. This work was widely influential when shown later in Britain. He set up his own workshop in 1896; 1896–98, taught at Central School of Arts and Crafts, London; in 1904, established his own school in Kensington and taught enameling to Nelson Dawson, Boston-born Elizabeth Copeland, and many silversmiths. He wrote a number of papers on enameling, some published in *The Studio*. One of his most impressive pieces was the 1893–96 girdle with a buckle over four inches (10 cm) high and enameled plaques depicting Wagnerian scenes.
▶ Work shown regularly at Arts and Crafts Exhibition Society, London. Unfinished Wagner-opera enameled girdle shown at 1895 exhibition of the Royal Academy, London, and at 1896 exhibition of Arts and Crafts Exhibition Society.
▶ Charlotte Gere, *American and European Jewelry 1830–1914*, New York: Crown, 1975:178–79. Annelies Krekel-Aalberse, *Art Nouveau and Art Déco Silver*, New York: Abrams, 1989:22, 24,25,98,254.

Fisker, Kay (1893–1965)
▶ Danish architect, furniture designer, and metalworker; active Copenhagen.
▶ Studied Kunstakademiets Arkitektskole, Copenhagen, to 1920.
▶ The first of a new generation of architect-designers who produced historicist silver patterns with Modern leanings, he designed silver for A. Michelsen in Copenhagen in c1925 and furniture and book covers for others; 1936–63, he was professor, Kunstakademiets Arkitektskole.
▶ In 1921, received a gold medal in Ghent. Work subject of exhibitions in Berlin-Charlottenburg in 1934 and 1953, Paris in 1939, London in 1950, and Århus in 1953. Work shown at 1925 Paris 'Exposition Internationale des Arts Décoratifs et Industriels Modernes.'
▶ Annelies Krekel-Aalberse, *Art Nouveau and Art Déco Silver*, New York: Abrams, 1989:220,254. Cat., David Revere McFadden (ed.), *Scandinavian Modern Design 1880–1980*, New York: Abrams, 1982:263, No. 89.

Fjerdingstad, Carl Christian (1891–1968)
▶ Norwegian designer; born Kristiansand; active Blaricum (Norway), Netherlands, and Paris.
▶ He worked as a designer for Orfèvrerie Christofle, Paris, in 1921, and as an independent silversmith. Henry van de Velde regarded him as one of the best silversmiths of the time; he executed a 1922 tea set for van de Velde's new house, Wassenaar (Netherlands); sometimes executed his own designs. His work combined French ornamentation with the hammered surfaces and round forms of Danish silverwares. He designed Christofle's famous 1933 *Cygne* silver-plated gravy boat and its 1933 *Art Déco* tea set based on the circle, and reissued in 1983.
▶ Work (Christofle wares) shown at 1925 Paris 'Exposition Internationale des Arts Décoratifs et Industriels Modernes', where Christofle's display was entirely devoted to tableware.
▶ *Les Carnets du Design*, Paris: Mad-Cap Productions et APCI, 1986:62. Annelies Krekel-Aalberse, *Art Nouveau and Art Déco Silver*, New York: Abrams, 1989:67,137,221,222,254. Cat., *Metallkunst*, Berlin: Bröhan Museum, 1990:178–80.

Flamand, G.
▶ French metalworker; active near Paris.
▶ Flamand was active c1900; did not show his work at the Paris salons; executed small gilt-bronze vases, silvered bronze night lights, table lamps, and sconces. His output appears to have been small.
▶ Cat., *Europa 1900*, Ostend: Musée des Beaux-Arts, 1968:39. Alastair Duncan, *Art Nouveau and Art Déco Lighting*, New York: Simon and Schuster, 1978:76–77.

Flatøy, Torstein (1956–)
▶ Norwegian furniture designer.
▶ Torstein designed furniture produced by Bahus and 1984 *Totem* and 1986 *Concorde* chairs by Møre Lenostolfabrikk.
▶ Fredrik Wildhagen, *Norge i Form*, Oslo: Stenersen, 1988:203.

Flécheux, Luc (1966–)
▶ French designer.
▶ Flécheux designed furniture and tableware. His 1986 geometric exercise for earthenware dinner plates for Siècle was based on an amphitheatre. His work included set design.
▶ *Les Carnets du Design*, Paris: Mad-Cap Productions et APCI, 1986:34.

Fleming, Erik (1894–1954)
▶ Swedish designer and silversmith; active Stockholm.
▶ Studied in Berlin and Munich.
▶ In 1919 or 1920, Baron Erik Fleming founded Atelier Borgila, which became one of Sweden's leading Modern silver workshops and specialized in handmade silverwares. His designs of the 1920s were classical in form; those from the 1930s showed angular forms and stepped edges typical of Art Déco. In the 1930s, Fleming and Wiwen Nilsson were pre-eminent in Swedish silver. In 1932, the Swedish government commissioned him to produce an 800-piece silver set as a wedding present for Prince Gustaf Adolf and Princess Sybilla. Margaret Craver trained and worked for some years with Fleming. 1938–39, he was a teacher in the USA.
▶ Annelies Krekel-Aalberse, *Art Nouveau and Art Déco Silver*, New York: Abrams, 1989:67,124,245,246,254.

Fliege, Paul
▶ German silversmith; active Danzig (now Gdańsk, Poland).
▶ Fliege produced Modern silver designs in Danzig in the 1930s.
▶ Annelies Krekel-Aalberse, *Art Nouveau and Art Déco Silver*, New York: Abrams, 1989:254.

Flight, Claude
▶ British artist and decorator.
▶ Flight is best known for establishing the linocut method of printmaking; was a central figure in Grosvenor School of Modern Art (founded 1925) where he and Edith Lawrence taught; (with Lawrence) set up a small interior design and decoration firm; receiving modest commissions, (with Lawrence) applied their somewhat daring taste reminiscent of the colorful designs of the Omega workshop.
▶ Stephen Calloway, *Twentieth-Century Decoration*, New York: Rizzoli, 1988:163.

Flöckinger, Gerda (1927–)
▶ Austrian jewelry designer.
▶ Studied fine art; subsequently, design, jewelry, and enameling, Central School of Arts and Crafts, London.
▶ She settled in Britain in 1938. In the 1960s, her expressive precious and semi-precious bracelets, brooches, necklaces, and rings received favorable attention. A central figure in Modern British jewelry, she conducted an experimental jewelry course, Hornsey College of Art, London, in the 1960s.

Flögl, Mathilde (1893–c1950)
▶ Moravian textile designer; born Brno (now Czech Republic).
▶ 1909–16, studied Kunstgewerbeschule, Vienna, under Oskar Strnad, A. Böhm, A. von Kenner, and Josef Hoffmann.
▶ 1916–31, she was on the staff of the Wiener Werkstätte, designing textiles, clothing, fashion accessories, and lace, and contributing to the 1914–15 fashion folder *Die Mode*; produced jewelry in ivory and enamel.
▶ Günther Feuerstein, *Vienna—Present and Past: Arts and Crafts —Applied Art—Design*, Vienna: Jugend und Volk, 1976:35,80. Deanna F. Cera (ed.), *Jewels of Fantasy: Costume Jewelry of the 20th Century*, New York: Abrams, 1992.

Flos
▶ Italian lighting manufacturer.
▶ Dino Gavina established the lighting firm Flos in 1962 to complement his furniture manufacturing at Gavina. In Merano at first, it moved to the Brescia area. Maria Sinoncini and Cesare Cassina were directors, followed by Sergio Gandini. Pier Giacomo Castiglioni was put in charge of design, followed by his brother Achille Castiglioni and Tobia Scarpa. Flos's earliest models by the Castiglionis were the 1959 *Teli* synthetic-fabric and 1960 *Viscontea* and *Taraxacum* stretched-plastic-skin hanging lights. Other designers included Kazuhide Takahama, Mariyo Tagi with the Studio Simon, and Valerio Sacchetti.
▶ Viirgilio Vercelloni, *The Adventure of Design: Gavina*, New York: Rizzoli, 1987.

Flou
▶ Italian furniture firm.
▶ Rosario Messina established the firm Flou in 1970; began production with Lodovico Magistretti's so-called textile bed in numerous configurations, still in production today. The firm commissioned numerous designs from Magistretti, including the 1984 *Ermellino* bed.
▶ 'Milan à l'Heure du Design,' *Maison et Jardin*, April 1992:127.

Flygenring, Hans   (1881–1958)
▶ Danish ceramicist.
▶ 1907–22, studied Det Kongelige Danske Kunstakademi, Copenhagen under Johan Rohde.
▶ Flygenring worked from 1920–27 at Porsgrunds Porselaensfabrik, Porsgrunn, as artistic director.
▶ Fredrik Wildhagen, *Norge i Form*, Oslo: Stenersen, 1988:85. Jennifer Hawkins Opie, *Scandinavia: Ceramics and Glass in the Twentieth Century*, New York: Rizzoli, 1989.

Fog, Astrid   (1911–)
▶ Danish designer.
▶ Fog designed her first jewelry collection for Georg Jensen Sølvsmedie in 1969; designed clothing and lamps; was affiliated with Royal Copenhagen Porcelain Manufactory and Georg Jensen's.
▶ Cat., *Georg Jensen Silversmithy: 77 Artists, 75 Years*, Washington: Smithsonian Institution Press, 1980.

Follot, Paul   (1877–1941)
▶ French decorative artist and sculptor; born Paris.
▶ Studied École normale d'Enseignment du dessin, Paris, under Eugène Grasset.
▶ His early graphic design showed an interest in medieval and Pre-Raphaelite art. In 1901, he joined Julius Meier-Graefe's shop La Maison Moderne, Paris, where he met Maurice Dufrêne and for which he designed bronzes, jewelry, and fabrics; was a founding member of artists' group L'Art dans Tout; in 1904, began as an independent artist. Moving from abundant carved decoration influenced by English styles and the 18th-century *style tapissier*, in c1909–10 Follot began to seek *des architectures calmes* ('tranquil architecture') through the use of beautiful and rare materials, refined techniques, and harmonious and balanced forms in the emerging Art Déco style. Wedgwood commissioned him in 1911 to design a range of ceramics, its production delayed by World War I until 1919. He contributed to the decoration of oceanliners, including 1921 *Paris* and the *appartement de luxe* for 1935 *Normandie*; succeeded Grasset as professor of an advanced course on Parisian decorative arts; in 1923, became artistic director of interior-decoration studio Pomone of Au Bon Marché department store, Paris. His rugs were produced by Schenck. In the early 1920s, he designed silver for Orfèvrerie Christofle and, in 1925, for Lapparra. The wood carving on his furniture was produced by Laurent Malclès and by Harribey; painted wall panels and pictures by his wife Hélène Follot. Work included furniture, fabrics, wallpaper, carpets, and ceramics. In 1928, he was made co-director with Serge Chermayeff of the Modern Art Department of Waring and Gillow, a British firm with a branch in Paris; in 1928, it opened with an exhibition of about 60 furnished Modern interiors. He was also a teacher and theoretician; considered ornamentation an essential element of design and had no interest in the minimalism of *le style 25*; rejected 'mass-production art' in favor of the aristocratic tradition of luxury.
▶ Work first shown at 1901 Salon of Société des Artistes français; showed at Salons of Société des Artistes Décorateurs 1919–35, Société Nationale des Beaux-Arts, and Salon d'Automne 1920–32. Designed a display for Pomone at Au Bon Marché exhibit, antechamber of 'Une Ambassade française,' and motifs for Maison Pleyel (including three Pleyel pianos in various pavilions), and Pavillon de Roubaix-Tourcoing, all at 1925 Paris 'Exposition Internationale des Arts Décoratifs et Industriels Modernes.'
▶ *Deutsche Kunst und Dekoration*, 1902–03:552. Guillaume Janneau, 'Notre enquête sur le mobilier moderne: Paul Follot,' *Art et Décoration*, No. 40, Nov. 1921:141–48. Léon Riotor, *Paul Follot*, Paris: La Connaissance, 1923. G. Janneau, *Le Luminaire et les Moyens d'éclairage Nouveaux*, 1st series: plates 17–18,21,23,32, 44. Léon Deshairs, *Modern French Decorative Art*, Paris: Albert Lévy. *Ensembles Mobiliers*, Vol. II, Paris: Charles Moreau, 1937. E. Mannoni, *Meubles et Ensembles: Style 1900*, Paris: C. Massin, 1968:39. Yvonne Brunhammer et al., *Art Nouveau Belgium, France*, Houston: Rice University, 1976. Alastair Duncan, *Art Nouveau and Art Déco Lighting*, New York: Simon and Schuster, 1978:

170. Jessica Rutherford, 'Paul Follot,' *Connoisseur*, Vol. 204, June 1980:86–91. Victor Arwas, *Art Déco*, Abrams, 1980. Jessica Rutherford, *Art Nouveau, Art Deco and the Thirties: The Furniture Collections at Brighton Museum*, Brighton: The Royal Pavilion, Art Gallery and Museums, 1983:33. Yvonne Brunhammer, *Art Déco Style*, London: Academy, 1983. Annelies Krekel-Aalberse, *Art Nouveau and Art Déco Silver*, New York: Abrams, 1989:254. Maurice Dufrêne, *Ensembles Mobiliers, Exposition Internationale 1925*, Paris: Charles Moreau, 1925, Antique Collectors' Club edition, 1989:40.

Fong, Danny Ho
▶ Chinese furniture manufacturer; born Canton; active San Francisco.
▶ Fong settled in California in the 1930s; subsequently, founded Tropi-Cal, which became a leading producer of contemporary rattan furniture. Today most of the furniture is made in factories in the Philippines and Indonesia.
▶ Steve Holley, 'Tracy Fong's California Spin on Wicker,' *Elle Decor*, Aug. 1991:24.

Fong, Tracy   (1975–)
▶ American furniture designer; active San Francisco; granddaughter of Danny Ho Fong.
▶ Studied Art Center College of Design, Pasadena, California.
▶ In 1988, her first furniture line, a wicker collection named SOFA (Studio of Furniture Art), was shown at an international merchandise event, Tokyo. Her next collection of chairs and occasional pieces was shown at an international furniture event, Manila. She designed a special Southeast Asian promotion for Seibu department store, Tokyo. Her furniture designs included the three-drawer *Three-D* side chair and other seating for T-Style of Fong Brothers, where she was head designer.
▶ Her furniture for T-Style was shown at the 1991 New York 'International Contemporary Furniture Fair.'
▶ Steve Holley, 'Tracy Fong's California Spin on Wicker,' *Elle Decor*, Aug. 1991:24.

Fonsèque, Max   (1891–1965)
▶ French bookbinder; active Monte Carlo and Paris.
▶ Studied École Estienne, Paris.
▶ He worked for his bookbinder father, Georges Canape, Marcellin Lortic, and, 1920–25, in Monaco. By 1930, he had become a Modern designer, with linear forms and playful calligraphic motifs on his covers.
▶ Ernest de Crauzat, *La Reliure française de 1900 à 1925*, Vol. 2, Paris, 1932:57–58. Roger Devauchelle, *La Reliure en France de ses origines à nos jours*, Vol. 3, Paris, 1961:259. John F. Fleming and Priscilla Juvelis, *The Book Beautiful and the Binding as Art*, Vol. 1, New York, 1983:13. Alastair Duncan and Georges de Bartha, *Art Nouveau and Art Déco Bookbinding*, New York: Abrams, 1989:90,191.

Fontaine
▶ French interior designers; located Paris.
▶ 1920–40, Fontaine regularly commissioned consultant decorators, including Maurice Dufrêne, René Prou, André Groult, Louis Süe and André Mare, and Pierre-Paul Montagnac.
▶ Fontaine pavilion (designed by Süe and Mare) at 1925 Paris 'Exposition Internationale des Arts Décoratifs et Industriels Modernes.'
▶ Pierre Kjellberg, *Art Déco: les maîtres du Mobilier, le décor des Paquebots*, Paris: Amateur, 1986:75.

Fontana
▶ French goldsmiths and jewelers; located Paris.
▶ Thomas Fontana established Fontana et Cie in 1840. When he died in 1861, his two nephews Joseph Fontana and Auguste Templier assumed the management of the firm. From 1871, Fontana's son Charles directed the business; in 1881, Joseph Fontana formed a separate jewelry house with his brother Giacomo Fontana, already established in the Galerie des Valois. 1840–93, Fontana was located in the Galerie Beaujolais, Palais Royal, Paris, and,

from 1893, at 6 rue de la Paix. Joseph's son Pierre Fontana managed the firm after his father's death in 1897 and Auguste Templier's in 1899.

▶ Charlotte Gere, *American and European Jewelry 1830–1914*, New York: Crown, 1975:179.

Fontana Arte
See Chiesa, Pietro

Fontana, Carlo (1947–)
▶ Italian industrial designer; born Pietrasanta; active Florence.
▶ Studied architecture, Florence, to 1973.
▶ He began his professional career as a designer in 1974; in 1974, worked in the Assessorato Servizi Sociali of the provincial administration of Pavia; collaborated with Allessandra Giorgetti and Carlo Guenzi on research on kindergarten furniture, and furniture for J.A. Arredi Servizi Sociali in Milan; in 1975, began designing domestic sound systems for Milanielektro, produced from 1976; became a member of ADI (Associazione per il Disegno Industriale).
▶ *ADI Annual 1976*, Milan: Associazione per il Disegno Industriale, 1976.

Fontani, A.C. (1895–)
▶ Dutch silversmith; active Amsterdam.
▶ Fontani trained in his father's workshop and with Frans Zwollo Sr. Though not particularly original, his work showed sound craftsmanship.
▶ Annelies Krekel-Aalberse, *Art Nouveau and Art Déco Silver*, New York: Abrams, 1989:175,254.

Fontenay, Eugène (1823–87)
▶ French goldsmith, jeweler, and antiquarian; active Paris.
▶ Apprenticed to jeweler Édouard Marchand.
▶ He worked for a time with goldsmith-jeweler Dutreih; in 1847, set up his own workshop, 2 rue Favart, Paris; designed the 1858 diadem in diamonds, emeralds, and pearls for the Empress Eugénie; was best known for his fantastic and delicate trinkets in an ancient Etruscan style (*bijoux étrusques*) decorated with minute grains of gold and inspired by the Cavaliere-Campana cache confiscated by Napoleon III for the Louvre in 1860. Fontenay's book *Les bijoux anciens et modernes* (1887) on antique and Modern jewelry (in which he effusively praised Dutreih's work) was written after his retirement in 1882.
▶ Work (jewelry made from jade seized from the Peking Summer Palace and his *bijoux étrusques*) shown at 1867 Paris 'Exposition Universelle.'
▶ Charlotte Gere, *American and European Jewelry 1830–1914*, New York: Crown, 1975:179.

Forbicini, Fulvio (1952–)
▶ Italian industrial designer; born Ravenna.
▶ Studied industrial design, Florence, to 1975.
▶ For a time, he worked for furniture manufacturer Roche Bobois; subsequently, (with Fabrizio Ballardini) opened own studio; (with Ballardini) designed the widely published 1988–89 *Ribalta* sofa produced by Arflex. *Ribalta* was a kind of day bed, its corners turned up to form six different positions.
▶ *Ribalta* sofa shown at 1991 'Mobili Italiani 1961–1991: Le Varie Età dei linguaggi' exhibition, Salone del Mobile, Milan.
▶ Albrecht Bangert and Karl Michael Armer, *80s Style: Designs of the Decade*, New York: Abbeville, 1990:38,230. *Mobili Italiani 1961–1991: Le Varie Età dei linguaggi*, Milan: Cosmit, 1992.

Forcolini, Carlo (1947–)
▶ Italian designer; born Como; active Milan.
▶ Studied Liceo Artistico di Brera and Accademia di Belle Arti in Brera, both Milan.
▶ In 1965, Forcolini, Frederico Pedrocchi, and Maurizio Bertoni experimented with kinetic art. 1970–74, (with Roberto Coizet and Piergiorgio Vianello) designed first products (produced by Amar Collezioni, Milan). In 1975, his encounter with Vico Magistretti was influential on Forcolini's future work as a designer. In 1978,

he settled in London; in 1980 with partners, founded furniture manufacturer Alias UK to produce furniture and furnishings designed by Forcolini, Mario Botta, Giandomenico Belotti, Vico Magistretti, and Alberto Meda; in 1980, began designing lighting for Artemide, including *Polifemo* lamp of the mid-1980s and 1985 *Icaro* wall light; in 1981, founded Artemide GB as a subsidiary of Artemide Italy; in 1989, became artistic director of a new firm in the Artemide Group; returned to Italy; was artistic director for Sidecar. Alias furniture and furnishings included 1979 *Alien* side chair, 1982 *Aleph* mirror, 1983 *Buñel* dressing table, 1983 *Onlyou* plant stand, 1984 *Apocalypse Now* coffee table in rustable steel with a lighting fixture in the center, 1985 *Karaté* small table, 1985 *Bukowsky's Holiday* coat rack, 1986 *Signorina Chan* chair, 1987 *Ran* bookshelves, and 1987 *Le Voyeur* clock.
▶ From 1983, work shown worldwide. Participated (with Melotti, Botta, and Meda) in 1987 'Ways of Planning,' Villa Pignatelli Museum, Naples. Work shown at 1990 Tokyo 'Creativitalia' exhibition on Italian design.
▶ Fumio Shimizu and Matteo Thun (eds.), *The Descendants of Leonardo: The Italian Design*, Tokyo, 1987:325. Sales cat., *Alias*, 1988. *Carlo Forcolini: Immaginare le Cose*, Milan: Electa, 1990.

Forlani, M.
▶ Italian designer.
▶ 1955–60, Forlani collaborated with S. Conti and L. Grassi on seating furniture in bent-steel rods and upholstery constructed from loosely woven nylon threads.
▶ *Il design italiano degli anni '50*, Milan: Richerche Design Editrice. *Design degli anni '50*, Igis, 1981. *Arte Figurative*, 1962.

Formes Utiles
▶ French organization and exhibitions; located Paris.
▶ In 1949, Formes Utiles became an independent association of UAM (Union des Artistes Modernes) through the influence of René Herbst and Charlotte Perriand and its first exhibition held at Musée des Arts Décoratifs, Paris. Its theoretician was architect André Hermant. It opened its exhibitions to foreigners; from 1951, held exhibitions organized by Salon des Ménagers to present furniture, furnishings, and equipment designed for mass production; organized exhibitions based on subjects including sanitation in 1951; sanitary seating in 1952; portable and small lighting fixtures and drinking glasses in 1953; rattan chairs, cutlery, and door knobs in 1954; casseroles, children's furniture, and the first exhibition of plastic furniture in 1956; and table settings, tableware, and table cloths. Painters and sculptors were invited to all exhibitions; Le Corbusier, Fernand Léger, Joan Miró, and Alexander Calder were among those who participated.
▶ Arlette Barré-Despond, *UAM*, Paris: Regard, 1986:105–07. Cat., *Les années UAM 1929–1958*, Paris: Musée des Arts Décoratifs, 1988:178–79.

Formica
▶ Proprietary plastic laminate.
▶ Formica was first manufactured in 1913. Herbert A. Faber and Daniel J. O'Conor met in 1907 in their first year at Westinghouse in Pittsburgh. In 1911, O'Conor became head of process section, research engineering department. Bakelite was used at Westinghouse to impregnate heavy canvas in 1910. O'Conor produced his first laminated sheet by winding and coating paper on a mandrel. The resulting uncured tube was slit and then flatted in a press. The patent for the process was assigned to Westinghouse in 1918. Because Westinghouse did not make use of the product, Faber and O'Conor left Westinghouse in 1913 and settled in Cincinnati. Lawyer and banker, J.G. Tomlin bought a one-third share in their newly formed Formica Company of Cincinnati for $7,500. The product name, based on mica, the expensive mineral used for insulation, was coined by Faber. After a poor first year, Tomlin brought in two other partners, lawyer John L. Vest and banker David Wallace. The firm was incorporated as The Formica Insulation Company, producing only rings and tubes initially. By 1921, Formica laminate had begun to be used in the production of radio

cabinets. By 1923, the firm was financially sound and began the successful production of gears for automobile engines. In 1927, the addition of 'lithographed wood grain' marked the beginning of the modern Formica period and its decorative sheets. By 1930, Formica was both a consumer and an industrial product. Industrial designer Brooks Stevens worked with Formica in the late 1940s to create 'Luxwood,' the wood-grain laminate used on much of the furniture of the time and the replacement for its earlier unsatisfactory 'Realwood' pattern. The 1947 license agreement with De La Rue, London, opened the door for production in Europe until 1977. In 1956, the firm was purchased by American Cyanamid and became its subsidiary The Formica Company. In the 1950s, Raymond Loewy Associates designed patterns as well as the Formica logo; serif typeface was replaced by designer Michael Abramson in 1980 with sans-serif Helvetica. In 1982, solid laminate 'ColorCore' was introduced. In 1985, Formica senior managers and private investors bought the firm from American Cyanamid.
▶ The Formica House was built at 1939 'New York World's Fair,' the kitchen of which was rebuilt for 1989 'Remembering the Future: The New York World's Fairs from 1939 to 1964,' Queens Museum, New York. ColorCore was subject of Formica-sponsored exhibitions, including 'Surface and Ornament' and 'Material Evidence: New Color Techniques in Handmade Furniture,' that included the work of established designers, artists, and architects, and toured the USA. Formica subject of 1987 'A Material World' exhibition, National Museum of American History, Washington.
▶ Susan Grant Lewin (ed.), *Formica and Design: From the Counter Top to High Art*, New York: Rizzoli, 1991:91–97.

Formica, Giovannella
▶ Italian designer; born Florence.
▶ Studied architecture, Università di Firenze, to 1982.
▶ She taught architecture, Università di Firenze; subsequently, worked at Sottsass Associati primarily on architecture and interior and industrial design; collaborated with Beppe Caturegli.
▶ Participated in numerous exhibitions.
▶ Fumio Shimizu and Matteo Thun (eds.), *The Descendants of Leonardo: The Italian Design*, Tokyo, 1987:325.

Formosa, Daniel   (1953–)
▶ American industrial designer.
▶ Studied industrial design, Syracuse University, Syracuse, New York, and ergonomics and biomechanics, New York University.
▶ Holding several patents in consumer products and equipment design, he was a consultant at Smart Design, New York, from 1981. Clients included Atomic Energy of Canada, Raytheon Nuclear Diagnostics, Corning Glass sunglass products, Esselté Letraset, IBM, International Playtex infant care, Kepner-Tregoe, Merck Sharp & Dohme, Pfizer Medical, and Singer.
▶ Received three Designer's Choice Awards from *ID* magazine.

Fornasetti, Piero   (1913–88)
▶ Italian artist-designer; born Milan.
▶ 1930–32, studied Accademia di Belle Arti di Brera, Milan.
▶ After Gio Ponti saw his work at 1940 (VII) Triennale di Milano, he became a student of Ponti and subsequently his protégé and assistant, designing the Lunari commissioned by Ponti; in 1942, executed frescoes for Palazzo Bo, Padua; 1943–46, was exiled in Switzerland; (with Ponti) collaborated on a number of projects replicating the 17th-century technique of applying two-dimensional images to furniture for a three-dimensional effect. The models were designed by Gio Ponti and decorated by Fornasetti. Fornasetti's appliqués appeared on blanks produced by Eschenbach Arzberg, and· Richard Ginori. Fornasetti designed 1950 interiors of the Casino, San Remo, and 1952 oceanliner *Andrea Doria*; was a designer, artist, illustrator, printer, graphic designer, craftsperson, manufacturer, and business entrepreneur whose products were sold in shops including his own Galeria dei Bibliofili, established with associates in 1970, and in his shop Themes and Variations, London, established in 1980; received several major commissions, including

the ballroom in Time-Life building, New York. Working in a Surrealistic *trompe-l'oeil* black-and-white style applied to everything from cabinets and chairs to ceramics, slatted window blinds, and 1984 decorated bicycle, Fornasetti's career spanned three-quarters of a century. His work was widely published.
▶ Work included in numerous exhibitions including scarves at 1940 (VII) Triennale di Milano, ceramics commissioned by Ponti at 1947 (VIII) Triennale, 1948 Salon of Société des Artistes Décorateurs in Paris, 1950 'Italy at Work' traveling USA exhibition for a year. From 1944 in the Foyer des Étudiants, Geneva, work was subject of numerous exhibitions including 'Fornasetti: Designer of Dreams' exhibition, Victoria and Albert Museum, London, 1991–92.
▶ Patrick Mauriès, *Fornasetti: Designer of Dreams*, London: Thames and Hudson, 1991.

Forsell, Ulla   (1944–)
▶ Swedish glassware designer.
▶ 1966–71, studied Konstfackskolan and Tekniska Skolan, Stockholm; 1971–73, Orrefors Bruk glass school; 1972, Gerrit Rietveld Akademie, Amsterdam.
▶ Forsell worked at Orrefors; in 1974, set up her own workshop, Stockholm; (with Åsa Brandt, Eva Ullberg, and Anders Wingård) established the studio Freeblowers.
▶ Cat., David Revere McFadden (ed.), *Scandinavian Modern Design 1880–1980*, New York: Abrams, 1982:263, No. 270. Jennifer Hawkins Opie, *Scandinavia: Ceramics and Glass in the Twentieth Century*, New York: Rizzoli, 1989.

Forsmann, Ernst   (1910–)
▶ Danish goldsmith.
▶ 1953–75, Forsmann was associated with Georg Jensen Sølvsmedie, Copenhagen.
▶ Cat., *Georg Jensen Silversmithy: 77 Artists, 75 Years*, Washington: Smithsonian Institution Press, 1980.

Forster und Graf
▶ German silversmiths; located Schwäbisch-Gmünd.
▶ The firm Carl Forster und Graf was founded in 1884; produced small silver objects and silver-mounted leatherware.
▶ Annelies Krekel-Aalberse, *Art Nouveau and Art Déco Silver*, New York: Abrams, 1989:254.

Forstner, Leopold   (1878–1936)
▶ Austrian mosaic craftsperson; born Leonfelden.
▶ Known for his high level of craftsmanship, Forstner was active in his own mosaic workshop, Vienna.
▶ Günther Feuerstein, *Vienna—Present and Past: Arts and Crafts—Applied Art—Design*, Vienna: Jugend und Volk, 1976:28, 80.

Forsyth, Gordon Mitchell   (1879–1953)
▶ British artist, designer, decorator, ceramicist, calligrapher, teacher, and writer; father of Moira Forsyth.
▶ Studied Robert Gordon's College, Grays School of Art, Aberdeen.
▶ 1902–05, was artistic director, Minton, Hollins and Co; until 1915, artistic director at Pilkington's Royal Lancastrian Pottery, Manchester, where he specialized in lusterware, managing its pottery artists including Geuldys Rodgers, W.S. Mycock, and Richard Joyce; was a fellow, British Society of Master Glass Painters; principal, Stoke-on-Trent Schools of Art; superintendent, Art Institution of the City of Stoke-on-Trent; art advisor, British Pottery Manufacturers Federation. He published *Art and Craft of the Potter* (1934) and *Twentieth Century Ceramics* (1936).
▶ Received medals as a painter at exhibitions in Paris, Venice, Turin, Brussels, and Britain.
▶ *Europäisches Keramik des Jugenstils*, Düsseldorf, 1974, no. 158. Cat., *Thirties: British art and design before the war*, London: Arts Council of Great Britain, Hayward Gallery, 1979:133,287,289. *British Arts and Design, 1900–1960*, London: Victoria and Albert Museum, 1983.

Forsyth, Moira (1905–)

▶ British ceramicist and stained-glass artist; daughter of Gordon Mitchell Forsyth.

▶ Studied Burslem School of Art; 1926–30, stained glass, Royal College of Art, London, under Martin Travers.

▶ She set up her own workshop in Brickhouse Street, Burslem, using a local pottery for her firing; produced stained-glass commissions for buildings on which Edward Maufe was architect, including dome of St. Joseph's Church, Burslem, and windows in Guildford Cathedral and St. Columbia's Church, London; continued to produce earthenware figures; prepared 1942 report on the pottery industry for Nuffield College; 1943–46, was research officer, Ministry of Town and Country Planning, for southeast England; after World War II, rendered heraldic windows for chapel of Eton College, Benedictine window for Norwich Cathedral, and, in the 1970s, window for Benedictine Abbey, Fort Augustus; was a fellow and council member, Master Glass Painters.

▶ 1930–32 *Cello Player* earthenware figure shown at 1979–80 'Thirties' exhibition, Hayward Gallery, London.

▶ Cat., *Thirties: British art and design before the war*, London: Arts Council of Great Britain, Hayward Gallery, 1979:102,135,289.

Fortuny y Madrazo, Mariano (1871–1949)

▶ Spanish designer; born Granada.

▶ Studied in Paris.

▶ He was a painter, engraver, sculptor, interior designer, photographer, lighting and furniture designer, and theatrical-set and costume designer; collaborated with his wife Henriette on the design and printing of the famous Fortuny fabrics printed in metallic inks and made into narrow-pleated silks; created a secret method for printing and embossing fabric to replicate ancient silk brocades. His pleated textile technique was later replicated by Mary MacFadden for clothing and Gretchen Bellinger for interior design use. His garment designs, including Aesthetic-style Empire-line dresses, coats, and capes, changed little from the early 1900s to his death. His best known design was the 1909 *Delphos* dress with a hem weighted with beads, which he patented; warp-pleated and body-sheathing it was, according to Fortuny, properly worn with ancient Greek jewelry and sandals; it kept its pleats when tied in a knot and stored in a small box. After Fortuny's death, interior designer Elsie McNeil presided over the Fortuny estate, Palazzo Orfei, Venice, now the Fortuny Museum, where she attempted to guard the secrets of the fabric manufacture. His Paris shop was located at 67 rue Pierre-Charron. His large 1905 *Arc Lamp* was reissued from 1979 by Écart International. Work included 1909 *Knossos* scarves, and his first cyclorama, for the comtesse de Béarn's private theater, Paris, and its stage curtain. In the 1910s, AEG installed his dome and lighting system in a number of European theatres. His set designs at turn of the century included Wagner's opera *Tristan und Isolde*, La Scala, Milan, 1910.

▶ Work subject of numerous exhibitions including in 1934, Galerie Hector Brame, Paris; 1935, Galeria Dedalo, Milan; 1965, Ca Pesaro, Museo d'Arte Moderna, Venice; 1980, Biblioteca Nacional, Madrid.

▶ M. Zamacois, *Mariano Fortuny y Madrazo*, Milan: Galeria Dedalo, 1935. Elena Paez, *Exposición Fortuny y Marsal y Fortuny y Madrazo*, Madrid: Biblioteca Nacional, 1951. Anne-Marie Deschodt, *Mariano Fortuny: un magicien de Venise*, Paris: Regard, 1979. Guillermo de Osma et al., *Mariano Fortuny (1871–1949)*, Lyons: Musée Historique des Tissus, and Brighton: Brighton Museum, 1980.

Foster, Norman (1935–)

▶ British architect and designer; born Manchester; active London.

▶ Studied architecture and urbanism, Manchester University, to 1961, and architecture, Yale University.

▶ He began his architecture practice in 1963; in 1965, opened architecture office Team 4 with wife Wendy Foster, Su Rogers, and Richard Rogers; (with Richard Rogers) became a pioneer of High-Tech design based on the development of an architectural aesthetic determined by modern technological equipment and fittings. After 1967, the firm operated as Foster Associates with ten partners, Norman and Wendy Foster, Loren Butt, Chubby S. Chhabra, Spencer de Gray, Roy Fleetwood, Birkin Haward, James Meller, Graham Phillips, and Mark Robertson. 1968–83, Foster collaborated with Buckminster Fuller and lectured in the USA and Europe; was known for his neutral spaces that could be filled according to the occupant's requirements for differentiated functions; designed 1986–88 *Nomos* furniture system produced by Tecno, Italy. A configuration of workstations and tables, the Tecno system was made of aluminum, plastic, and steel with exposed construction showing the workings. His 1986 lighting system for Hongkong and Shanghai Bank was produced by Erco. In 1988, he designed carpets for the Dialog collection of Vorwerk, Germany; was vice-president of the Architectural Association, London; member of the council, Royal College of Art, London; honorary member, Bund Deutscher Architekten; member, International Academy of Architecture, Sofia. Buildings included 1971 passenger terminal and administration building, Fred Olsen Lines, London; 1975 Willis-Faber and Dumas building, Ipswich; 1978 Sainsbury Centre for the Visual Arts, University of East Anglia, near Norwich; 1979–86 Hammersmith Centre, London; 1981 Renault distribution center, Swindon; Hongkong and Shanghai Bank headquarters, Hong Kong; 1990 Stansted Airport, Essex; Century Tower, Hong Kong; Maison de la Culture, Nîmes.

▶ In 1983, received a gold medal from Royal Institute of British Architects. Work shown at New York Museum of Modern Art; Royal Academy, London; and exhibitions including 1979 'Transformations in Modern Architecture' and 1983 '3 Skyscrapers,' both New York Museum of Modern Art. *Nomos* furniture shown at 1991 'Mobili Italiani 1961–1991: Le Varie Età dei linguaggi' exhibition, Milan.

▶ 'Foster Associates,' *Architectural Design*, Vol. 47, Nos. 9–10, 1977:614–25. *Foster Associates*, London, 1979. 'Recent Works of Foster Associates,' *Architecture and Urbanism*, Feb. 1981:43–112. Vittorio Magnago Lampugnani (ed.), *Encyclopedia of 20th-Century Architecture*, New York: Abrams, 1986:103–04. *Norman Foster*, Milan/Paris: Electa Moniteur, 1986. *Foster Associates and Tecno: Nomos*, Milan: Tecno, 1986. Juli Capella and Quim Larrea, *Designed by Architects in the 1980s*, New York, Rizzoli, 1988. Volker Fischer, *Bodenreform: Teppichboden von Künstlern und Architekten*, Berlin: Ernst und Sohn, 1989. Albrecht Bangert and Karl Michael Armer, *80s Style: Designs of the Decade*, New York: Abbeville, 1990:50–51,191,230.

Fouquet, Alphonse (1828–1911)

▶ French goldsmith and jeweler; active Paris; father of Georges Fouquet.

▶ From 1839, Fouquet worked for various manufacturers of inexpensive jewelry in Paris; in 1854, began working as a designer with Jules Chaise; in 1855, joined Carre et Christofle working with Léon Rouvenat; in c1860, established his own jewelry business, 176 rue du Temple, Paris. His early jewelry was in neo-Greek and neo-Renaissance styles, indistinguishable from Vever, Fossin, Morel, and Mellerio. Fouquet produced heavy, complicated pieces with chimera and fantastic animals set with large diamonds and sapphires; in the 1870s, began to design the complicated neo-Renaissance pieces for which he became best known, heavily-worked gold items with painted enamels. On one bracelet alone, Carrier-Belleuse produced the sculpture, Honoré the engraving, and Grandhomme the enameling. In 1860, Fouquet moved the business and, in 1879, moved again to 35 avenue de l'Opéra, Paris. When he retired in 1895, his son Georges Fouquet, who with his brother-in-law had joined the firm in 1891, assumed the directorship.

▶ In 1888, received Légion d'honneur. Work shown and received gold medals at Paris 'Expositions Universelles' 1878–89. Fouquet family work subject of 1983 exhibition, Paris Musée des Arts Décoratifs.

▶ Cat., *Les Fouquet, Bijoutiers et Joailliers à Paris, 1860–1960*, Paris: Musée des Arts Décoratifs, 1983. Charlotte Gere, *American and European Jewelry 1830–1914*, New York: Crown, 1975:180–81.

Fouquet, Jean (1899–1984)

▶ French jewelry designer; active Paris; son of Georges Fouquet.

▶ In 1919, he joined as a designer in the family firm, 6 rue Royale, Paris; was a friend of Louis Aragon and Paul Eluard; 1920–25, collaborated on Le Corbusier's and Amédée Ozenfant's review *L'Esprit Nouveau: Revue International d'Esthétique*; in his jewelry, developed a liking for abstract compositions. From 1931, his jewelry designs were characterized by pure and simple geometry. In 1929, abandoning the Société des Artistes Décorateurs, he became a founding member of UAM (Union des Artistes Modernes); after the family business closed in 1936, worked on private, unique commissions; 1952–55 with enamelist Gaston Richet, produced a series of translucent enamel works; in 1952, organized a series of conferences, École Nationale des Arts Décoratifs, Paris; was active until 1960.

▶ Work first shown alongside other Fouquet designers at 1925 Paris 'Exposition Internationale des Arts Décoratifs et Industriels Modernes.' Work first shown under his own name at 1926 and 1928 Salons of the Société des Artistes Décorateurs. Work shown at all exhibitions of UAM, including the 1949–50 (I) 'Formes Utiles' exhibition, Pavillon de Marsan, Paris, where he was responsible for the silver-clock section; at 1937 Paris 'Exposition Internationale des Arts et Techniques dans la Vie Moderne'; from 1950, at 'Métiers d'Art: Le foyer d'aujourd'hui' section, Salon des Arts Ménagers; 1956 (I) Triennale d'Art français Contemporain, Pavillon de Marsan, Paris; 1958 'Exposition Universelle et Internationale de Bruxelles (Expo '58).' Organized 1951 'Prévues' exhibition, Galerie Bernheim-Jeune, Paris, aiming to show the finest jewelry that relied on high-quality materials. Fouquet family work subject of 1983 exhibition, Paris Musée des Arts Décoratifs.

▶ Cat., *Les Fouquet, Bijoutiers et Joailliers à Paris, 1860–1960*, Paris: Musée des Arts Décoratifs, 1983. Sylvie Raulet, *Bijoux Art Déco*, Paris: Regard, 1984. Melissa Gabardi, *Les Bijoux des Années 50*, Paris: Amateur, 1987. Arlette Barré-Despond, *UAM*, Paris: Regard, 1986:398–99.400–02. Cat., *Les années UAM 1929–1958*, Paris: Musée des Arts Décoratifs, 1988:182–83.

Fouquet, M. Georges (1862–1957)

▶ French goldsmith and jeweler; born and active Paris; son of Georges Fouquet; father of Jean Fouquet.

▶ In 1891, Fouquet began working for his father; in 1895, became head of the family's jewelry establishment and transformed the firm's production into more contemporary forms. The firm had become well known through its execution of jewelry designs for Sarah Bernhardt, on which father and son collaborated. In 1901, Alphonse Mucha designed the interior and exterior of Maison Fouquet, 6 rue Royale, Paris. In 1919, Fouquet's son Jean joined the family firm. Abandoning floral forms and enthusiastic about the Modern movement, Fouquet began producing jewelry in geometrical motifs and purchased the designs of architect Eric Bagge in the 1920s, artist Jean Lambert-Rucki in 1936, Charles Desrosiers, poster designer Cassandre, artist Mucha, painter André Léveillé, and enamelist Étienne Tourette. Fouquet's best-known pieces, including Desrosiers's *Chataigne* ('chestnut') pendant and the *Murier* ('mulberry') necklace, were widely copied by others. Fouquet's preference for baroque pearls introduced new motifs less delicate than those of Lalique and incorporated typical Art Nouveau patterns such as thistles, thorns, insects, and bats.

▶ Work shown at 1900 Paris 'Exposition Universelle.' Mucha's famous bracelet-ring for Sarah Bernhardt shown at 1906 Milan exposition. Participated in a number of international exhibitions. Member of the admissions committee and work (his own and that of chief manager Louis Fertey, Bagge, Léveillé, and Cassandre) shown at 1925 Paris 'Exposition Internationale des Arts Décoratifs et Industriels Modernes.' Work subject of 1983 exhibition, Paris Musée des Arts Décoratifs.

▶ Charlotte Gere, *American and European Jewelry 1830–1914*, New York: Crown, 1975:181–82. Yvonne Brunhammer et al., *Art Nouveau Belgium, France*, Houston: Rice University, 1976. Cat., *Les Fouquet, Bijoutiers et Joailliers à Paris, 1860–1960*, Paris: Musée des Arts Décoratifs, 1983. Sylvie Raulet, *Bijoux Art Déco*, Paris: Regard, 1984. *Die Fouquet, 1860–1960, Schmuckkünstler in Paris*, Zürich: Museum Bellrive, 1984. Pierre Cabanne, *Encyclopédie Art Déco*, Paris: Somogy, 1986:195.

Fouquet-Lapar

▶ French silversmiths; located Paris.

▶ Fouquet-Lapar manufactured Modern silver in the 1920s and 1930s.

▶ Annelies Krekel-Aalberse, *Art Nouveau and Art Déco Silver*, New York: Abrams, 1989:254.

Fournais, Kirsten (1933–)

▶ Danish jewelry designer.

▶ From 1978, Kirsten designed jewelry for Georg Jensen Sølvsmedie, Denmark.

▶ Work shown at 1980 'Georg Jensen Silversmithy: 77 Artists, 75 Years' exhibition, Smithsonian Institution, Washington.

▶ Cat., *Georg Jensen Silversmithy: 77 Artists, 75 Years*, Washington: Smithsonian Institution Press, 1980.

Fowler, John (1906–77)

▶ British interior decorator.

▶ Fowler worked first for a printer; subsequently, was a decorator-painter at Thorton Smith, London; worked for antiques dealer and decorator Margaret Kunzer and, from 1931, headed her painting studio in the Peter Jones home-furnishings store; in 1934, set up his own studio. In 1938, he went into partnership with Sybil Colefax; rarely inventing designs, he rather adopted them from 18th- and 19th-century fragments; studied draperies in decorative design books by French baroque designer Daniel Marot; during World War II, designed actor Michael Redgrave's house, in which he used parachute silk for curtains; Duchess of Hamilton's blue-and-white-chintz bedroom; Queen Elizabeth II's audience room, Buckingham Palace; rooms for Lord Rothermere, Daylesford; rooms for Evangeline Bruce, Albany; Mrs. James de Rothschild's Eythrope country house, Oxford. In 1946, American expatriot Mrs. Ronald Tree (later, Nancy Lancaster) bought Colefax and Fowler (Fowler himself never owned any part of the business). Fowler's most popular chintz design was, and remains, *Old Rose*. He used dyed tape borders as an edge to patterns such as *Berkeley Sprig*, now the logo of Colefax and Fowler. His chintz designs were influenced by Nancy Lancaster's fabric prints, which were deliberately faded by putting furniture in bright sunlight and dyeing them with tea. Another Fowler invention was silk bows attached to the tops of picture-hanging cords at the cornice.

▶ Elizabeth Dickson, 'English Elegance,' *Elle Decor*, Winter 1990:38. Mark Hampton, *The Legendary Decorators of the Twentieth Century*, New York: Doubleday, 1992.

Foxton, W.

▶ British textile manufacturer; located London.

▶ William Foxton (1861–1945) established the firm of W. Foxton in 1903; produced textiles designed by artists including Gregory Brown and Riette Sturge Moore. The firm's goods were innovative in the 1920s. Foxton intended to create a collaboration of artists with industry, an approach he promoted through the firm's advertising; was president of Wholesale Furnishing Textile Association; in 1915, became founding member, Design and Industries Association; was board member, BIIA.

▶ Brown's fabrics shown at 1925 Paris 'Exposition Internationale des Arts Décoratifs et Industriels Modernes,' and reproduced in Design and Industry Association's yearbook *Design in Modern Industry*. Brown's and Moore's fabrics shown at 1979–80 'Thirties' exhibition, Hayward Gallery, London.

▶ *British Arts and Design, 1900–1960*, London: Victoria and Albert Museum, 1983. Cat., *Thirties: British art and design before the war*, London: Arts Council of Great Britain, Hayward Gallery,

1979:144,289. Valerie Mendes, *The Victoria and Albert Textile Collection, British Textiles from 1900 to 1937*, London: Victoria and Albert Museum, 1992.

Fragner, Jaroslav   (1898–1967)
▶ Czech architect and interior and furniture designer; born Prague.
▶ 1917–22, studied Czech University of Technology, Prague.
▶ In 1922, he established his own architecture studio, Prague; from 1923 until its 1931 close, was a member of Devětsil group; 1921–23, was active in the Puristická čtyřka group with Evžen Linhart, Karel Honzík, and Vít Obrtel, who applied strong three-dimensional ornament to bare geometric structures and espoused Czech Cubist architecture; was the first Devětsil architect to turn to the International Style, illustrated by his 1924–28 children's ward in a hospital, Mukačevo (now Ukraine). He designed the 1927 apartment block, 30–32 Pod Kavalírkou St., Prague; apartment blocks, Chust (now Ukraine) in c1929; the important 1929–30 pharmaceutical factory, Dolní Měcholupy; 1928 Esso power station, Kolín; 1929–30 family house, 408 Bezručova St., Kolín, for Václav Budil. Budil commissioned Fragner in 1929–30 to design wooden furniture to accompany the Thonet bentwood chairs in the house. Fragner's Budil furniture was simpler than his earlier models. The most notable part of the house was the kitchen, completed in 1929, equipped with built-in cupboards and electric cooker, the first of its kind in Czechoslovakia.
▶ Participated in 1923 Bauhaus exhibition, Weimar.
▶ Cat., *Devětsil: Czech Avant-Garde Art, Architecture, and Design of the 1920s and 30s*, Oxford Museum of Modern Art, Oxford, and London Design Museum, London, 1990.

France & Son
▶ Danish furniture and industrial manufacturer; located Hillerød.
▶ France & Son was one of the factories of Royal System, founded by Poul Cadovius in 1945. Cadovius, originally working with six employees, successfully promoted himself as a Modern designer. The firm produced furniture, building systems, and boats. Its designers included Steen Østergaard, Leif Alring, and Sidse Werner. Its furniture was made mostly from wood products and upholstered.
▶ Cadovius received a silver medal at 1957 (XI) Triennale di Milano and a gold medal at 1961 (X) 'International Investors' Fair,' Brussels.
▶ Cat., Milena Lamarová, *Design a Plastické Hmoty*, Prague: Uměleckoprůmyslové Muzeum, 1972:54,56,186.

Francis, Sam   (1923–)
▶ American painter; born San Mateo, California.
▶ 1941–43, studied medicine; 1948–50, painting and art history under Mark Rothko; from 1950, painting in Atelier Fernand Léger, Paris.
▶ He took up painting in 1945; from 1950 in Paris, became acquainted with Jean-Paul Riopelle. His work was influenced by the group Art Informel in Paris and American artists including Jackson Pollock. In 1957, he visited Japan, where contemporary work influenced his own thinly textured canvases and his drip-and-splash style; he was particularly influenced by the exaggerated voids found in Japanese painting. In the mid-1960s, his work became more associated with the Minimalist style. He rendered painterly abstract canvases and prints in a colorful splattered technique; in 1988, designed a carpet for the Dialog collection of Vorwerk, Germany.
▶ Work subject of exhibitions including those at the Los Angeles County Museum of Art; Centre Georges Pompidou, Paris; Musée National d'Art Moderne, Paris; Louisiana Museum; Copenhagen/Humblebaek.
▶ Volker Fischer, *Bodenreform: Teppichboden von Künstlern und Architekten*, Berlin: Ernst und Sohn, 1989. Ian Chilvers et al., *The Oxford Dictionary of Art*, Oxford: Oxford, 1988:185. Albrecht Bangert and Karl Michael Armer, *80s Style: Designs of the Decade*, New York: Abbeville, 1990:194,230.

Franck, Kaj   (1911–)
▶ Finnish textile and glassware designer and ceramicist; born Viipuri.
▶ 1929–32, studied in the furniture department, Taideteollinen Korkeakoulu, Helsinki.
▶ He worked initially as a freelance designer; 1933–45, designed lighting and textiles. 1945–73, was a designer at Arabia pottery, Helsinki, becoming artistic director in 1950; from 1946–50, was a designer at Iittala glassworks, and from 1950–76 at Nuutajärvi-Notsjö glassworks; from 1945, was a teacher, Taideteollinen Korkeakoulu, and, 1960–68, its art director. In c1950, when Nuutajärvi-Notsjö merged with the Wärtsilä group, he produced his first glassware designs. His unbreakable 1952 *Kilta* was considered to be a revolution in everyday tableware and a classic Finnish design object. More than 25 million pieces of it were sold. Later reissued, it was chosen for the cafeteria of the Picasso Museum, Paris. In 1973, Franck left Arabia; in 1978, left the Wärtsilä group; from 1979, was a full-time designer, sometimes working for the Wärtsilä group (Arabia, Nuutajärvi, and sanitary porcelain and enamel); designed 1979 *Pitopöytäae* plastic plate and bowl range produced by Sarvis and 1981 *Theema* black or white stoneware.
▶ Received prizes at 1951 (IX) (gold medal), 1954 (X) (two diplomas of honor), and 1957 (XI) (grand prize) Triennali di Milano; 1955 Lunning Prize; 1957 Premio Compasso d'Oro; 1957 Pro Finlandia; 1965 Prince Eugen Medal; 1977 Finnish State Award for Industrial Arts; 1983 honorary doctorate, Royal College of Art, London. Work included in exhibitions in 1955, Gothenburg; in 1956, Copenhagen; 1954–57 USA 'Design in Scandinavia,' Hälsingborg (Sweden); 1956–59 West Germany 'Finnish Exhibition'; 1958 'Formes Scandinaves,' Paris Musée des Arts Décoratifs; 1961 'Finlandia,' Zürich, Amsterdam, and London.
▶ Kaj Franck, 'Finland,' *Craft Horizons*, Vol. 16, July 1956:24–25. Erik Zahle (ed.), *A Treasury of Scandinavian Design*, New York, 1961:273, nos. 207–09,232–35,325–28,343–46. Kaj Frank, 'Anonymity,' *Craft Horizons*, Vol. 27, March 1967:34–35. Kaj Franck, 'The Arabia Art Department,' *Ceramics and Glass*, Nos. 1–2, 1973:47–57. *Finland: Nature, Design, Architecture*, Helsinki: Finnish Society of Crafts and Design, 1980–81:60–66. Kaj Franck with Eeva Siltavuori, 'Constructive Thinking in Finnish Design: Our Organic Heritage,' *Form Function Finland*, No. 2, 1981:51–57. Cat., David Revere McFadden (ed.), *Scandinavian Modern Design 1880–1980*, New York: Abrams, 1982:263, nos. 166,171,196,236. Cat., Kathryn B. Hiesinger and George H. Marcus III (eds.), *Design Since 1945*, Philadelphia: Philadelphia Museum of Art, 1983. *Les Carnets du Design*, Paris: Mad-Cap Productions et APCI, 1986:17. Cat., *The Lunning Prize*, Stockholm: Nationalmuseum, 1986:70–75. Jennifer Hawkins Opie, *Scandinavia: Ceramics and Glass in the Twentieth Century*, New York: Rizzoli, 1989. Jeremy Myerson and Sylvia Katz, *Conran Design Guides: Tableware*, London: Conran Octopus, 1990:30,73.

Frank, Beat   (1949–)
▶ Swiss designer; active Berne.
▶ In 1986, Frank and Andreas Lehmann established the Atelier Vorsprung design office, Berne. Their limited-production 1989 *Sitzkreuz* furniture-sculpture was produced for a hotel lobby in the south of France and for an acting school. The Atelier's work occupied the area between art and utility, a popular orientation at the end of the 1980s.
▶ Albrecht Bangert and Karl Michael Armer, *80s Style: Designs of the Decade*, New York: Abbeville, 1990:80,230.

Frank, Jean-Michel   (1895–1941)
▶ French interior decorator and furniture designer; born Paris; active Paris and New York; great uncle of Anne Frank.
▶ Studied law.
▶ The approach he took to his design work was greatly influenced by Eugenia Errazuriz, whom he met in the 1920s. Impressed by Errazuriz's quest for simplicity and perfection, he mixed Modern

lighting fixtures with provincial Louis XVI furniture. After World War I, he worked as a cabinetmaker in Jacques-Émile Ruhlmann's workshop, Paris; while searching for furnishings for his own apartment on the rue de Verneuil, met decorator Adolphe Chanaux, who had worked with André Groult and Jacques-Émile Ruhlmann on the 1925 Paris 'Exposition Internationale des Arts Décoratifs et Industriels Modernes.' 1927–33, Frank probably produced designs for the Desny firm; (with his stable of designers) was the first to use white-leaded wood in the 1920s; in 1932, after a year of collaborating in a decorating business with workshops in La Ruche, (with Chanaux) opened the shop, 147 rue du Faubourg St.-Honoré, Paris, selling pieces designed by Frank and Chanaux and associates including Emilio Terry, Diego and Alberto Giacometti, Salvador Dalí, de Pisis, Rodocanachi, and painter Christian Bérard. At first Frank's designs were hard-edged and rectilinear, indebted to Le Corbusier and Robert Mallet-Stevens. It was through Mallet-Stevens that Frank acquired the commission to decorate the rooms of 1924–33 villa of vicomte and vicomtesse de Noailles, Hyères. One of the most important Modern interiors of the century was Frank's 1929 decorations and furnishings for rooms in the de Noailles's Hôtel Bischoffsheim residence, place des États-Unis, Paris. The walls were covered in beige vellum, in subtle contrast to the macassar ebony furniture and a Modernist carpet on an old parquet floor. The huge bronze door was trimmed in ivory. Sofas and chairs were upholstered in bleached leather and tables and screens covered in shagreen, leather, and lacquer. 'Pity the burglars got everything,' quipped Jean Cocteau, alluding to the sparseness of the furnishings. The 1930 salon in Frank's own residence showed straw applied to the ceiling and walls to suggest grained marquetry. Dark gypsum tables were placed among chairs, a 'tuxedo' sofa, and a screen covered in white leather. Frank shared with Emilio Terry an interest in the visionary 18th-century projects of Claude-Nicolas Ledoux and Étienne-Louis Boullée. Frank's work became more theatrical, and he introduced more complicated forms. By the mid-1930s, he collaborated more with the Giacomettis and commissioned their white plaster and patinated bronze decorative accessories. With them and others including Bérard, Frank created a dramatic setting for the Guérlain salon with trompe l'œil effects. Elsa Schiaparelli commissioned Frank to decorate her rooms, boulevard Saint-Germain. Bright chintz in the main room contrasted with black, including black porcelain plates in the dining room. Other clients included Baron de l'Epée, Lucien Lelong, and Philippe Berthelot. Frank's personality was reflected in his somber office, nicknamed 'the confessional.' He designed the so-called Parsons (or T-square) table, evolved from his lectures at Parsons School of Design, Paris. In 1940, he settled in New York with backing from interior design firm McMillen; he had earlier designed the 1937 interiors and furniture of Nelson A. Rockefeller's apartment, New York, and rooms for M. Templeton Crocker, San Francisco. Depressed and lovesick, he jumped to his death from a window of the Hotel St. Regis, after only one week in New York. His influence was wide, despite a career of a mere decade. Only one Frank project is intact today: Count Cecil and Countess Minie Pecci Blunt's 1930 three-room apartment, third floor of a 16th-century palace, near Rome. In 1986, Écart International, and later Palazzetti, began reproduction of Frank's canapé for Charles de Noailles's Paris house, the precursor of the 'tuxedo' sofa, as well as production of other models.
► Elsa Schiaparelli, Shocking Life, London, 1954:43. Van Day Truex, 'Jean-Michel Frank Remembered,' Architectural Digest, Sept.–Oct. 1976:71–75,170–71. Léopold Diego Sanchez, Jean-Michel Frank, Paris: Regard, 1980. Jessica Rutherford, Art Nouveau, Art Deco and the Thirties: The Furniture Collections at Brighton Museum, Brighton: The Royal Pavilion, Art Gallery and Museums, 1983:34. James Lord, Giacometti, New York: Farrar, Straus, Giroux, 1985:253. Pierre Cabanne, Encyclopédie Art Déco, Paris: Somogy, 1986:195. C. Ray Smith, Interior Design in Twentieth-Century America: A History, New York, Harper and Row, 1987. Stephen Calloway, 'Perfectly Frank,' House and Garden,

Feb. 1990:180ff. John Esten and Rose Bennett Gilbert, Manhattan Style, Boston: Little, Brown, 1990:7–8.

Frank, Josef   (1885–1967)
► Austrian architect, interior, furniture, and textile designer; born Baden; active Vienna and Stockholm.
► 1919–27, he was a professor, Kunstgewerbeschule, Vienna; 1925–34, (with Oskar Wlach) founded interior-design cooperative Haus und Garten, Vienna, which produced furniture, textiles, and utensils; in 1934, settled in Sweden; was a Modernist; in 1932, became chief designer at Svensk Tenn, where he worked until his death, designing furniture, printed fabrics, and interiors. His textile work included 1944 Vegetable Tree in bright, unusually combined colors. In his later furniture, he modified his earlier Purist ideas and included pattern and texture into his designs for furniture, lighting, and textiles; 1941–43, was a teacher, New School for Social Research, New York; published books including Architectur als Symbol (1930) and Accidentism (1958); was an early proponent of the Swedish Modern movement.
► Received Litteris et Artibus Medal. Work shown at 1925 Paris 'Exposition Internationale des Arts Décoratifs et Industriels Modernes,' 1928 Stuttgart 'Die Wohnung,' 1937 Paris 'Exposition Internationale des Arts et Techniques dans la Vie Moderne,' 1939 'New York World's Fair.'
► Günther Feuerstein, Vienna—Present and Past: Arts and Crafts—Applied Art—Design, Vienna: Jugend und Volk, 1976: 26,50–51,80. Cat., David Revere McFadden (ed.), Scandinavian Modern Design 1880–1980, New York; Abrams, 1982:263, No. 130. Jonathan M. Woodham, Twentieth-Century Ornament, New York: Rizzoli, 1990:226–27.

Frankl, Paul Theodore   (1887–1958)
► Austrian designer; born Vienna; active New York and California.
► Studied Vienna, Paris, Munich, and Berlin.
► Settling in the USA in 1914, he carried the custom-designed industrial-arts approach over into department-store exhibition of the late 1920s. His renowned 'skyscraper' bookcases were unique designs and never mass produced. He saw classic geometry as the key to good design. Many of Frankl's designs have little to do with the philosophy in his writings. His notable designs included large combined desk and bookcase of c1927, and a chrome, aluminum, and leather chair of c1929. In conjunction with the 1927 'Art in Trade' exhibition at Macy's department store, New York, he lectured on 'The Skyscraper in Decoration'; illustrated his and others' furniture and interior designs in his influential book Form and Re-Form (1930) in which he documented the best of American and European designers, and in his later books New Dimensions (1928) and Space for Living: Creative Interior Decoration and Design (1938); spent the early part of his career in New York and the latter part in California; in the late 1940s, specified cork veneer in furniture produced by Johnson Furniture Company. Frankl used materials lavishly and his work is comparable to that of the best French designers of the time, although the construction of Frankl's designs was inferior to French craftsmanship and materials. He was the main force behind the formation of the American Designers' Gallery in 1928 and AUDAC (American Union of Decorative Artists and Craftsmen) in 1930, both of which had memberships consisting of the best designers, architects, and photographers in America at the time.
► Work shown at 1927 'Exposition of Art in Trade at Macy's' at Macy's department store, New York, and (with that of Walter von Nessen, sculptor William Zorach, Donald Deskey, and others) at John Cotton Dana's 1929 'Modern American Design in Metal' exhibition, Newark Museum, Newark, New Jersey.
► 'American Modernist Furniture Inspired by Sky-scraper Architecture,' Good Furniture Magazine, Sept. 1927:119. Pierre Migennes, 'Un Artiste décorateur américain: Paul Th. Frankl,' Art et Décoration, Jan. 1928:49. 'Frankl, Paul T.,' Britannica Encyclopedia of American Art. Karen Davies, At Home in Manhattan: Modern Decorative Arts, 1925 to the Depression, New Haven: Yale, 1983.

Richard Guy Wilson et al., *The Machine Age in America 1918–1941*, New York: Abrams, 1986. Mel Byars (introduction), 'What Makes American Design American?' in R.L. Leonard and C.A. Glassgold (eds.), *Modern American Design, by the American Union of Decorative Artists and Craftsmen*, New York: Acanthus Press, 1992. Durwood Potter, 'Paul Frankl,' in Mel Byars and Russell Flinchum (eds.), *50th American Designers, 1918–1968*, Washington: Preservation, 1994.

Franzen, Ulrich (1921–)
▶ German architect and designer; born Düsseldorf.
▶ Studied Williams College, Williamstown, Massachusetts, to 1942; Graduate School of Design, Harvard University, under Walter Gropius and Marcel Breuer, to 1948.
▶ 1950–55, he worked for I.M. Pei and Partners, New York; from 1955, was principal, Ulrich Franzen and Associates, New York; was primarily influenced by Mies van der Rohe's International Style and shared Mies's sense of order and precision and admiration for precious materials. Franzen's few pieces of furniture included 1968 tractor-seat stool. (The tractor seat as stool was originally designed by the Castiglioni brothers in 1957 and put into production by Zanotta in 1971.) Buildings included 1981 Champion International headquarters and 1983 Philip Morris headquarters, both New York.
▶ Work shown at 1982 'Shape and Environment: Furniture by American Architects,' Whitney Museum of American Art, Fairfield County, Connecticut.
▶ Stanley Abercrombie, 'Ulrich Franzen: Architecture in Transition,' *Process Architecture*, No. 8, 1979:11–159. Ulrich Franzen, 'Changing Design Solutions for a Changing Era,' *Architectural Record*, No. 158, Sept. 1978:81–88. Cat., Lisa Phillips (introduction), *Shape and Environment: Furniture by American Architects*, New York: Whitney Museum of American Art, 1982:30–31.

Fraschini, Franco (1930–)
▶ Italian industrial designer; born and active Pavia.
▶ Fraschini began his professional career in 1958; designed irons, kitchenware, furniture, lighting, and the *Octans* table lamp produced by Zonca; became a member of ADI (Associazione per il Disegno Industriale). Clients in Italy included Indesit, Driade, Nuova Immi, Saima, Lai, and Roche.
▶ *ADI Annual 1976*, Milan: Associazione per il Disegno Industriale, 1976.

Fraser, Albert (1945–)
▶ British designer; born Glasgow; active USA and Milan.
▶ Studied Rhode Island School of Design, Providence, Rhode Island.
▶ He settled in Milan. Work included furniture, industrial design, and lighting for clients including Mont Blanc, Bausch & Lomb, B&B Italia, Wang Computer Laboratories, Artemide, and Arflex. His 1984–85 *Nastro* halogen table lamp with its electrical elements housed in a colorful, malleable arm was produced by Stilnova.
▶ Robert A. M. Stern (ed.), *The International Design Yearbook*, New York: Abbeville, 1985/1986: Nos. 202–04. Albrecht Bangert and Karl Michael Armer, *80s Style: Designs of the Decade*, New York: Abbeville, 1990:93,230.

Fraser, Claud Lovat (1890–1921)
▶ British textile designer, painter, illustrator and theater designer.
▶ Influenced by folk and traditional designs, Fraser was best known for his theatrical costumes and set designs, including most notably for the 1920 production of *The Beggar's Opera*; was successful as an illustrator; in the 1920s, executed patterns for fabrics produced by William Foxton.
▶ Stuart Durant, *Ornament from the Industrial Revolution to Today*, Woodstock, NY: Overlook, 1986:250,323. Valerie Mendes, *The Victoria and Albert Museum Textile Collection, British Textiles from 1900 to 1937*, London: Victoria and Albert Museum, 1992.

Fraser, June (1930–)
▶ British graphic and industrial designer.
▶ Studied Royal College of Art, London, to 1957.
▶ 1957–80, she worked at Design Research Unit; 1980–84, was head of graphic design, John Lewis; from 1984, was head of industrial design, The Design Council; became a member of The Design Council, DIA Board, Product Design Review Advisory Board, Court of the Royal College of Art, The London Institute, Bournemouth and Poole College of Art, and ICSID.
▶ Work shown internationally and widely published. Received numerous awards.
▶ Liz McQuiston, *Women in Design: A Contemporary View*, New York: Rizzoli, 1988:44.

Frateili, Enzo (1914–)
▶ Italian designer; born Rome; active Milan.
▶ Frateili began his professional career in 1955; 1955–60, worked at Stile Industria; in 1962, was the Italian correspondent to the journal *Form*. Books included *Architektur und Komfort* (1967) and *Design e Civiltà della Macchina* (1969) (received 1970 Premio Premio Compasso d'Oro). His paper on the theoretical and methodological aspects of problem-solving was published by the Instituto di Architettura e Urbanistica, Università di Trieste. In 1963, he led a seminar, Hochschule für Gestaltung, Ulm; 1963–65, taught a course, CSDI (now the ISIA), Venice; in 1968, led a lecture-conference, CSDI, Rome; 1962–64, was a member of the guidance committee, ADI (Associazione per il Disegno Industriale), Milan; in 1967, was a member of ADI's pre-selection committee, Premio Compasso d'Oro; in 1970, sat on ADI's awards preparation commission; in 1973, was coordinator of college direction, ADI. Work included furniture and shelving systems.
▶ *ADI Annual 1976*, Milan: Associazione per il Disegno Industriale, 1976.

Fratti
▶ Italian costume jeweler; located Milan.
▶ Established by Giuliano Fratti in the early 1930s, the studio produced mostly belts and buttons in via Manzoni 29, Milan. For a time, Fratti produced leather products with jewelry made by outside ateliers. Production consisted of primarily French prototypes specified by dressmakers. The firm closed in 1972.
▶ Deanna F. Cera (ed.), *Jewels of Fantasy: Costume Jewelry of the 20th Century*, New York: Abrams, 1992:307.

Frattini, Gianfranco (1926–)
▶ Italian architect and interior and industrial designer; born Padua; active Milan.
▶ Studied architecture, Politecnico di Milano, to 1953.
▶ Frattini began his professional career in 1948; 1952–54, collaborated in architecture with Gio Ponti; from 1954, worked for Cassina and, concurrently, collaborated with Gio Ponti on equipment for Triennale di Milano; set up his own studio for architecture and industrial and interior design; from 1956, was co-founder and member of ADI (Associazione per il Disegno Industriale). Work included upholstered furniture, lacquered wood, wicker, and plastics for clients Acerbis-Morphos, G.B. Bernini, Molteni, Ricci, Fratelli Faber, Lema, Gio Caroli, Profetti, Citterio, C&B Italia, and others. Designs included *Model 595 Sesann* armchair in leather and foam on a bent-wire frame produced by Cassina, (with Livio Castiglioni) lighting designs in the early 1970s for Artemide, including the snake-like 1971 *Boalum* lamp; produced designs for industrial plastics including hard hats for Montecatini in the late 1970s, and 1987 *Bull* sofa and chair range produced by Cassina; from 1983, was a board member, Triennale di Milano.
▶ Received gold medal and grand prize, Triennali di Milano; honorable mention (*Boalum* lamp), 1973, 'BIO 5' Industrial Design Biennale, Ljubljana; Oscar Plast; MACEF prize; Diamond International Award.
▶ *ADI Annual 1976*, Milan: Associazione per il Disegno Industriale, 1976. Alfonso Grassi and Anty Pansera, *Atlante del design*

italiano: 1940/1980: Milan: Fabbri, 1980:178,224,282. Cat., Kathryn B. Hiesinger and George H. Marcus III (eds.), *Design Since 1945*, Philadelphia: Philadelphia Museum of Art, 1983. Hans Wichmann, *Italien Design 1945 bis heute*, Munich: Die Neue Sammlung, 1988.

Frattini, Gigi
▶ Italian industrial designer; active Varese (Italy).
▶ Frattini designed refrigerators, calendars, and electronic devices for clients including Ignis; became a member of ADI (Associazione per il Disegno Industriale).
▶ *ADI Annual 1976*, Milan: Associazione per il Disegno Industriale, 1976.

Frau, Renzo (1880–)
▶ Italian designer; born Sardinia.
▶ At the beginning of the century, he worked as a joiner in the Italian royal household; in 1912, founded Poltrona Frau furniture company, designing the famous Poltrona armchair of same year; in 1926, was appointed supplier to the royal family; in the 1930s, was active as an interior designer to titled clients.

Fréchet, André (1875–1973) and Paul Fréchet
▶ French decorators and furniture designers; born Châlons-sur-Marne; active Paris.
▶ Working together and individually from 1906, the Fréchet brothers' furniture designs were produced by various firms including Jacquemin frères in Strasbourg, E. Verot, and Charles Jeanselme; 1909–11, André was professor, École des Beaux-Arts, Nantes; in 1911, settled in Paris and became director of studies, École Boulle and, 1919–34, was director; from 1923, was editor of magazine *Mobilier et Décoration*; designed for the Studium Louvre; 1935–39, taught at Académie Julian, Paris; executed numerous private commissions. Some of his students were recruited for Jacques-Émile Rhulmann's workshop. His tapestry designs were produced by Tapisserie de Beauvais for various rooms in the Palais de l'Élysée, Paris.
▶ Throughout the 1920s until the mid-1930s, work shown at Salons of Société des Artistes Décorateurs and sporadically at events of Salon d'Automne. With 72 of his students, designed pavilion of the city of Paris (with Pierre Lehalle and Georges Levard) and participated in pavilion of design atelier Studium of the Magasins du Louvre, both at 1925 Paris 'Exposition Internationale des Arts Décoratifs et Industriels Modernes.'
▶ *Ensembles Mobiliers*, Vol. II, Paris: Charles Moreau, 1937. Pierre Kjellberg, *Art Déco: les maîtres du Mobilier, le décor des Paquebots*, Paris: Amateur, 1986:76.

Frederick, William N. (1921–)
▶ American silversmith.
▶ In 1955, Frederick established his workshop, 1322 East 49th St., Chicago; from 1965, moved to 1858 North Sedgwick St., where he is still active today.
▶ Sharon S. Darling with Gail Farr Casterline, *Chicago Metalsmiths*, Chicago Historical Society, 1977.

Freij, Edler (1944–)
▶ Norwegian glassware designer and ceramicist.
▶ 1966–71, studied Statens Håndverks -og Kunstindustriskole, Oslo under Jens von de Lippe; 1970–73, studied Hochschule für angewandte Kunst, Vienna
▶ She designed glass with cut and sandblasted motifs. From 1968, she worked at Hadelands Glassverk, Jevnaker, from 1979 as head of product development; from 1973–c76, was active in own studio in Vienna.
▶ Cat., David Revere McFadden (ed.), *Scandinavian Modern Design 1880–1980*, New York: Abrams, 1982:263, No. 289. Jennifer Hawkins Opie, *Scandinavia: Ceramics and Glass in the Twentieth Century*, New York: Rizzoli, 1989.

Frémiet, Emmanuel (1824–1910)
▶ French sculptor and metalworker; active Paris; nephew of sculptor François Rude.
▶ Studied sculpture under Rude.
▶ In addition to sculptural lighting, he produced animal images including marabou storks, butterflies, pelicans, orangutans, and dragons that appeared on the friezes, column capitals, and antechamber floors of buildings; pioneered the use of lighting in his work where a combustion-type system would not have been possible; was one of the few Art Nouveau artists whose work expressed humor.
▶ Work (bronze animal group) first shown at 1843 Salon of Société des Artistes français.
▶ Cat., *Un Siècle de Bronzes Animaliers*, Paris: Galerie P. Ambroise, 1975:76–77. Alastair Duncan, *Art Nouveau and Art Déco Lighting*, New York: Simon and Schuster, 1978:77.

Frenning, Pelle (1943–)
▶ Swedish designer.
▶ Studied industrial arts at Gothenburg University.
▶ He worked for several interior architecture companies including Folke Sundberg and Lund Valentin before joining White Architects, Gothenburg; designed furniture.
▶ In 1980, received a first prize (lighting for the elderly) from Swedish Lighting Association. Work shown at several exhibitions.
▶ Robert A. M. Stern (ed.), *The International Design Yearbook*, New York: Abbeville, 1985/1986: No. 132.

Fretti, Guido
▶ Italian architect.
▶ Fretti and Adalberto Libera designed the furnishings for the living room, dining room, and master bedroom of Casa Elettrica (designed by fellow Gruppo Sette members Luigi Figini and Gino Pollini) for Montedison Company at 1930 (IV) 'International Exposition of Decorative Arts,' Monza. In its kitchen, features of German and American models were incorporated. Casa Elettrica was the first public expression of Modern architecture in Italy.
▶ Barbie Campbell-Cole and Tim Benton (eds.), *Tubular Steel Furniture*, London: The Art Book Company, 1979:47.

Frey, Albert (1903–)
▶ Swiss architect.
▶ Frey worked closely with Le Corbusier in Paris; in 1930, settled in New York; (with A. Lawrence Kocher) set up an architecture partnership; (with Kocher) designed subsistence farmsteads and the 1931 'Aluminaire House,' a prototype in aluminum for mass production. Originally built for an exhibition, the house was relocated on the property of architect Wallace K. Harrison, Syosset, New York; in c1991, it was relocated and rebuilt by architecture students on the grounds of New York Technical College, East Islip, New York. In 1935, Frey corresponded with Le Corbusier; moved to Palm Springs, California, where, until 1986 he designed numerous buildings suited to desert conditions with overhanging roofs and swimming pools in living rooms; designed his own house and the house of Raymond Loewy, both Palm Springs.
▶ 'Aluminaire' House shown at 1932 'The International Style: Architecture Since 1922' exhibition, New York Museum of Modern Art.
▶ Jeffrey Book, 'Statements of Style,' *Elle Decor*, Mar. 1991:20. Joseph Rosa, *Albert Frey, Architect*, New York: Rizzoli, 1990.

Frey, Patrick (1947–)
▶ French fabric designer.
▶ Studied in the USA.
▶ Pierre Frey established a firm in Paris in 1935 to produce decorative fabrics; in 1955, sister firm Patifet was set up to produce contemporary fabrics. In 1976, Frey's son Patrick became chair of the firm. From the late 1980s, the firm was prolific, producing 5,000 color ways and 30 designs each year. From 1983, Patrick Frey's own designs and those of freelance designers and illustrators were produced under the firm names of Patrick Frey, Natecru, and contract line Margueroy. The firm distributed the fabrics

of Valentino Piu, Warner Greef, and Yves Halard; from 1987, produced upholstered furniture, decorative accessories, household fragrances, and Frey's widely published 1991 teacup-motif print. In 1991, Pierre Frey took over Braquenie, manufacturers of fabrics and tapestries.
▶ 'Hot Property,' *House and Garden*, May 1991.

Frey, Paul (1855–)
▶ French jewelry designer.
▶ Frey worked for Antoine Touyon, a company in Paris that produced small luxury items including bracelets, buttons, medals, and assorted gold jewelry in the English style; in 1880, took over the firm and began collaborating with jewelers in Paris. Frey's son André assisted his father as a skilled jeweler.
▶ Won a silver medal at the 1900 Paris 'Exposition Universelle.'
▶ Yvonne Brunhammer et al., *Art Nouveau Belgium, France*, Houston: Rice University, 1976.

Freyrie, Leopoldo (1958–)
▶ Italian architect, designer, and teacher; born Milan.
▶ Studied Politecnico di Milano to 1983.
▶ From 1982, he collaborated with Guido Stefanoni; 1984–86, taught, European Design Institute, Milan; from 1987, was associated with design school Arte Design Tecnica.
▶ Participated in exhibitions 1983 'Light '83' and 1986 'Itinerari Manzoniani,' both Milan.
▶ Hans Wichmann, *Italien Design 1945 bis heute*, Munich: Die Neue Sammlung, 1988.

Friberg, Berndt (1899–1981)
▶ Swedish ceramicist.
▶ 1915–18, trained as a thrower at Höganäsbolaget stoneware factory, and Höganäs Technical School.
▶ From 1918–*c*34, he worked in workshops in Denmark and Sweden; from 1934–81, worked at Gustavsberg pottery, producing unique stoneware vessels in refined silhouettes and using Oriental-type glazes; from 1933–44, was a thrower for Wilhelm Kåge at Gustavsberg and was active in the studio there from 1944–81.
▶ Received gold medals at 1948 (VIII), 1951 (IX), and 1954 (VX) Triennali di Milano; 1965 first prize at Faenza; 1960 Gregor Paulsson trophy. Work subject of exhibitions, Nordiska Kompaniet, Stockholm, in 1954, 1956, 1959, and 1964. Work included in exhibitions at Nordiska Kompaniet, Stockholm, 1946; Nationalmuseum, Stockholm, 1949; 1954 Gothenburg and Karlstad 'Vi Tre'; 1956 Höganäs 'Stengods av Skånelera,' Malmö Museum, 1957; Smålands Museum, Växjö, 1958.
▶ Ulf Hård af Segerstad, *Berndt Friberg Keramiker*, Stockholm: Nordisk Rotogravyr, 1964. Cat., David Revere McFadden (ed.), *Scandinavian Modern Design 1880–1980*, New York: Abrams, 1982:263, No. 180. Jennifer Hawkins Opie, *Scandinavia: Ceramics and Glass in the Twentieth Century*, New York: Rizzoli, 1989.

Fric, Bernard
See Asymétrie

Fricker, Fritz (1928–)
▶ Italian architect and designer; born Genoa; active Milan.
▶ He practiced architecture in Switzerland. From 1959, was a member of ADI (Associazione per il Disegno Industriale); designed building components and interiors; was a consultant to Gulf, Swissair, and Swiss-government tourist office.
▶ *ADI Annual 1976*, Milan: Associazione per il Disegno Industriale, 1976.

Friedell, Clemens (1872–1963)
▶ American ceramicist; born New Orleans; active Vienna and California.
▶ He was an unpaid apprentice to a Vienna silversmith; in 1892, returned to USA, working for a silversmith in San Antonio, Texas; 1901–07, was employed by the Gorham company, America's largest silver factory, in Providence, Rhode Island; in 1908, settled in Los Angeles, producing silver ashtrays for Broadway Department

Store; in 1909, moved to Pasadena, California, and set up a workshop on the back porch of his own house; subsequently, had shops on North Lake Avenue and Colorado Boulevard and in the Huntington and Maryland hotels; was known for his fine craftsmanship, especially in his *repoussé* work. His most notable commission was a 107-piece dining set in hand-wrought and chased sterling silver; he spent more than 6,000 hours on it and applied over 10,000 orange-blossom images. For a number of years, Friedell designed the silver cups awarded to floats in the Tournament of Roses, Pasadena.
▶ Bonnie Mattison in Timothy J. Andersen et al., *California Design 1910*, Salt Lake City: Peregrine Smith, 1980:86–87.

Friedlander, Dan (1952–)
▶ American retailer and designer; active San Francisco.
▶ Collaborating with Kenneth Gilliam in the early 1990s, Friedlander designed furniture reflective of the 1960s and made by Design America.
▶ Arlene Hirst, 'Design Class at Last,' *American Home*, November 1990:101.

Friedländer, Gebrüder
▶ German silversmiths; located Berlin.
▶ Gebrüder Friedlander was founded in 1829; became court jeweler; produced some striking silver objects after designs of *c*1900 by painter Wilhelm Lucas von Cranach.
▶ Annelies Krekel-Aalberse, *Art Nouveau and Art Déco Silver*, New York: Abrams, 1989:139,254.

Friedländer-Wildenhain, Marguerite (b. Marguerite Friedländer 1896–1985)
▶ German ceramicist; active Germany, Netherlands, and USA.
▶ 1919–25, studied Bauhaus, Dessau.
▶ Like fellow Bauhaus student Trude Petri, she focused on non-ornamental objects; becoming successful in commercial ceramics, she worked for Staatliche Porzellan-Manufaktur, Berlin, 1925–33, and produced some designs there with Petri in 1930; designed 1927 *Halle* porcelain dinnerware by KMP, Berlin; 1925–33, taught at Keramische Werkstatt der Kunstgewerbeschule, Halle/Burg Giebichenstein, where she was director of the workshop from 1926; moved to the Netherlands and subsequently USA.
▶ Cat., *The Bauhaus: Masters and Students*, New York: Barry Friedman, 1988. Cat., *Keramik und Bauhaus*, Berlin: Berlin-Archiv, 1989:154–92,264.

Friedman, Dan
▶ American designer; active New York.
▶ Friedman began his career as a graphic designer for large corporations. He turned to furniture and environmental design and produced furniture collections by Galerie Néotù in Paris. His 1989 *Virgin Screen* and 1989 *Zoïd* sofa and chair were produced by Néotù.

Friedman, Stanley Jay (1938–)
▶ American designer.
▶ Studied Parsons School of Design, New York.
▶ He worked as an interior designer; in 1970, set up his own studio, New York, designing interiors and products including furniture and lighting; designs total environments from floor coverings to architectural elements; in 1971, began designing furniture for Brueton, including *Satellite Table*, *Jena Desk and Credenza*, and *Athens Table and Credenza*, and, subsequently, became design consultant to Brueton.
▶ Received five Roscoe Awards; two Product Design Awards; IBD; two Interior Design Awards, ASID; Du Pont Award; International Product Design Award, ASID.

Friedmann, Eduard
▶ Austrian silversmiths; located Vienna.
▶ The firm Eduard Friedmann was founded in 1877, closing in 1920; executed designs by Rudolf Karger, A.O. Holub, and Milla

Weltmann, and architects Hans Bolek, Philippe Häusler, Emanuel Josef Margold, and Otto Prutscher.
► Annelies Krekel-Aalberse, *Art Nouveau and Art Déco Silver*, New York: Abrams, 1989:200,254.

Friedrich, Kurrent (1931–)
► Austrian designer; born Hintersee/Feistenau.
► Active in Vienna from the late 1950s, Kurrent Friedrich, Wilhelm Holzbauer, and Spalt Johannes founded Arbeitsgruppe 4. Their furniture incorporated severe modular elements in bright colors.
► Günther Feuerstein, *Vienna—Present and Past: Arts and Crafts—Applied Art—Design*, Vienna: Jugend und Volk, 1976:61–62.

Friend, George T.
► British engraver; active London.
► Friend engraved the designs of R.M.Y. Gleadowe and Eric Gill. From 1929, he worked for the silversmithies Edward Barnard and Wakely and Sheeler in London. Friend taught engraving at Central School of Arts and Crafts, London.
► Annelies Krekel-Aalberse, *Art Nouveau and Art Déco Silver*, New York: Abrams, 1989:33–34,254.

Frink, I.P.
► American lighting manufacturer; located New York.
► Isaac P. Frink established the firm in 1857 in Newark, New Jersey, as the 'Original Inventor, Patentee, and Sole Manufacturer of the Silver-Plated and Crystal-Corrugated, Glass-Lined Reflectors.' His flat, rectangular reflector, working like a mirror, was attached to the outside of a building and directed sunlight into a room; light was reflected off a ceiling, creating ambient light. The invention was advantageous in dark Victorian interiors. The device was later attached to oil lamps and subsequently gaslights; in the 1880s, Frink's reflectors were widely used in public spaces and domestic interiors. In the late 1870s and 1880s, the firm added decorative lighting fixtures and chandeliers to its range; became known nationwide; 1863–1910, was located at 549–551 Pearl Street, Manhattan; in 1928, acquired the Sterling Bronze Company, manufacturers of ornamental fixtures and marine and custom lighting; moved to Long Island City, New York and, in the 1950s, to Brooklyn; known at this time as Frink Corporation, claimed to be the largest specialty-lighting company in the world; in 1960, was purchased by Westinghouse; produced lighting for the 1972–77 World Trade Center, New York; ceased trading in 1974.
► Denys Peter Myers, *Gaslighting in America: A Guide for Historic Preservation*, Washington, 1978:205, plate 98. Doreen Bolger Burke et al., *In Pursuit of Beauty: Americans and the Aesthetic Movement*, New York: Metropolitan Museum of Art and Rizzoli, 1987:427–28.

Fristedt, Sven (1940–)
► Swedish textile designer.
► From the 1960s, Fristedt designed textiles for Borås Wäfveri. His patterns were aligned with mid-1960s fine art, with sophisticated handling of repeats.
► Cat., David Revere McFadden (ed.), *Scandinavian Modern Design 1880–1980*, New York: Abrams, 1982:263, No. 257.

Fritsch, Antoine
► French industrial designer.
► Studied mechanical construction and École Nationale Supérieure de Création Industrielle, France.
► He designed picnic tableware that won recognition in a 1986 competition sponsored by APCI (Agence pour la Promotion de la Création Industrielle) and UGAP (Union des Groupements d'Achats Publics).
► *Les Carnets du Design*, Paris: Mad-Cap Productions et APCI, 1986:87.

frogdesign
See Esslinger, Hartmut

Froment-Meurice, François-Désiré (1805–55)
► French goldsmith and jeweler; located Paris.
► François Froment established a jewelry business in Paris in 1774. When his widow married master goldsmith Pierre Meurice, Froment's son François-Désiré took the name of his stepfather, becoming François-Désiré Froment-Meurice. In 1805, he was apprenticed to his brother-in-law Chalmette, who ran a jewelry workshop in Paris. Entering his stepfather's workshop as a boy, François-Désiré left in 1819 to study with a *ciseleur* and to enrol in sculpture and drawing classes; worked with silversmith Jacques-Henri Fauconnier and enamelist Karl Wagner. Froment-Meurice was immediately successful when he showed his work (some neo-Gothic pieces) for the first time in 1839; he was dubbed 'the Cellini of the 19th century.' The British admired his enameled neo-Renaissance jewelry, which influenced British work in the 1860s and 1870s. When he died in 1855, the management of the jewelry firm went to his wife. Their son Émile later became director of the business and continued working in the traditional style established at the firm. Practicing narrowly in the neo-Renaissance and Romantic taste popular at the turn of the century, he began experimenting with modified Art Nouveau forms, although traces of the former style lingered in the details of the settings.
► Exhibiting neo-Gothic pieces in 1839, Froment-Meurice showed work under his own name for the first time. Neo-Renaissance jewelry shown at 1851 London 'Great Exhibition of the Works of Industry of All Nations.'
► Hugh Honour, *Goldsmiths and Silversmiths*, London, 1971. Charlotte Gere, *American and European Jewelry 1830–1914*, New York: Crown, 1975:182–83.

Fronzini, A.G. (1923–)
► Italian architect and designer; born Pistoia.
► From 1945 Fronzini was an architect, industrial designer, and typographer; 1965–67, was an editor at the journal *Casabella*; designed 1963 attaché case for Valextra, 1964 *Serie 64* Rationalist furniture for Galli, 1966–67 reading room of Instituto di Storia dell'Arte, 1976 display design at Museo Walser, and 1979–80 display design at Palazzo Reale, Genoa; was consultant designer for much of Galli's production of furniture and furnishings.
► Alfonso Grassi and Anty Pansera, *Atlante del design italiano: 1940/1980*, Milan: Fabbri, 1980.

Frost, Derek (1952–)
► British interior designer; active London.
► Trained at Mary Fox Linton design firm, London.
► Frost set up his own design studio in London in 1984; designed both commercial and domestic interiors; produced one-off furniture designs, including 1987–88 stereo cabinet with silver doors painted by Yumi Katayama.
► Albrecht Bangert and Karl Michael Armer, *80s Style: Designs of the Decade*, New York: Abbeville, 1990:36,230.

Froussard, André
► French designer.
► Froussard designed occasional furniture and tableware. His place settings were manufactured by his own firm Plexinox, including 1972 *Rond* flatware in stainless steel with Plexiglas handles, and 1984 *Square* with parallel-piped collars.
► *Les Carnets du Design*, Paris: Mad-Cap Productions et APCI, 1986:67.

Fry, Henry Lindley (1807–95) and William Henry Fry (1830–1929)
► British woodcarvers; active Cincinnati, Ohio.
► Henry Fry was a wood carver and engraver in Bath (England). His important commissions included the screen designed by George Gilbert Scott for Westminster Abbey, and the decoration

of the chambers of the Houses of Parliament under architects Charles Henry and A.W.N. Pugin. In 1850, Fry joined his son William in New Orleans, Louisiana and, in 1851, moved to Cincinnati, Ohio, where, in 1853, he lived at 150 West Third Street. William Fry joined his father in Cincinnati in c1866. The Frys decorated several churches in Cincinnati, including the Church of New Jerusalem; decorated residences, including those of department store operators John Shillito and Henry Probasco, and the State House, Columbus, Ohio; produced a dining-room table for US President Rutherford B. Hayes; decorated the Joseph Longworth residence, Rookwood, during the late 1850s, and the Maria Longworth Nichols residence in 1868, both Cincinnati. Influenced by William Morris and John Ruskin, the Frys added ornamentation to every possible surface. Their style incorporated Aesthetic motifs of flowers and included medieval and Italianate elements, including images of the Pegasus, lions' heads, paws, scrolls, and acanthus leaves, and imported Italian mosaics. They taught wood carving privately. William taught at the Art Academy until 1926; his daughter Laura Fry was an accomplished ceramicist active at the Rookwood Pottery.
▶ Frys' work shown at 1876 Philadelphia 'Centennial Exposition.' William Fry received a prize for a carved Baldwin piano shown at 1900 Paris 'Exposition Universelle.' William Fry's work subject of 1910 exhibition, Saint Louis City Art Museum.
▶ Erwin O. Christensen, *Early American Wood Carving*, Cleveland and New York, 1952:91–92. Anita J. Ellis, 'Cincinnati Art Furniture,' *Antiques*, No. 121, April 1982:930–41. E. Jane Connell and Charles R. Muller, 'Ohio Furniture, 1788–1888,' *Antiques*, No. 125, Feb. 1984:468, plate 7. Doreen Bolger Burke et al., *In Pursuit of Beauty: Americans and the Aesthetic Movement*, New York: Metropolitan Museum of Art and Rizzoli, 1987:428.

Fry, Laura Anne   (1857–1943)
▶ American wood carver and ceramics decorator; born near Monticello, Indiana; active Cincinnati, Ohio; daughter of William Henry Fry.
▶ 1869–76 and 1886–88, studied drawing and sculpture, University of Cincinnati School of Design (later Art Academy of Cincinnati), under Benn Pitman, Maria Eggers, and Thomas Noble; 1886, Art Students' League, New York.
▶ In addition to the 1877–78 decoration of the Cincinnati Music Hall organ, she designed nine of its floral panels; working in the 'scratch-blue' technique, trained for a time in ceramics in Trenton, New Jersey; 1881–88, designed shapes and painted pieces at Maria Longworth Nichols's Rookwood Pottery; was an instructor at the short-lived Rookwood School of Pottery Decoration; in 1884, developed a technique of spraying colored slips through a mouth-blown apparatus onto moist clay that became a standard process for creating backgrounds at Rookwood. In 1889, she applied for a patent for a process that used a commercial atomizer, called the 'Fry method'; was briefly a freelancer for Rookwood; in 1891, became professor of industrial art, Purdue University, West Lafayette, Indiana, and founded the Lafayette Ceramic Club; 1892–94 in Steubenville, Ohio, worked for the Lonhuda Works, a Rookwood competitor, where she also used the atomizer technique; 1892–98, she was involved unsuccessfully in a lawsuit against Rookwood to bar its use of the 'Fry method'; in 1894, worked in her own studio, Cincinnati; was a founder of the Porcelain League of Cincinnati; returned in 1896 to Purdue University where she taught until her 1922 retirement.
▶ Received a prize (wood carving) at 1893 Chicago 'World's Columbian Exposition.'
▶ Herbert Peck, *The Book of Rookwood Pottery*, New York, 1968. Kenneth R. Trapp, ' "To Beautify the Useful": Benn Pitman and the Women's Woodcarving Movement in Cincinnati in the Late Nineteenth Century,' in Kenneth L. Ames, *Victorian Furniture: Essays from a Victorian Society Autumn Symposium*, Philadelphia, 1982:173–92. Chris Petteys, 'Laura Anne Fry' in *Dictionary of Women Artists: An International Dictionary of Women Artists Born Before 1900*, Boston, 1985:265. Doreen Bolger Burke et al., *In*

Pursuit of Beauty: Americans and the Aesthetic Movement, New York: Metropolitan Museum of Art and Rizzoli, 1987:429.

Fry, Roger   (1866–1934)
▶ British painter, writer, art critic, designer, and lecturer; born London.
▶ 1885–80, studied natural sciences, Cambridge University, and Académie Julian, Paris, 1892.
▶ He wrote articles for the *Athenaeum* and *Burlington Magazine*; published first book *Giovanni Bellini* (1899); 1906–10, was curator, New York Metropolitan Museum of Art, and in conflict with its chair J.P. Morgan; in 1910, met Clive and Vanessa Bell; became artistic leader of the Bloomsbury group; had affairs with Lady Ottoline Morrell and Vanessa Bell; c1911, produced paintings that showed Byzantine and Post-Impressionist influences; in 1913, opened the Omega Workshops in an attempt to apply Post-Impressionism to the decorative arts; 1913–19, was its co-director, designing textiles, pottery, and furnishings including painted furniture. The workshop was set up to provide income for Fry's young avant-garde artist friends, including Vanessa Bell and Duncan Grant. The printed and woven fabrics, carpets, and embroideries designed and sold by Omega Workshops artisans revolutionized textile design in Britain early in the 20th century. In 1919, Fry closed the workshop; in his last ten years, published eight more books on art; lectured on art at Queen's Hall, London; began to paint commissioned portraits; in 1933, became Slade professor, Cambridge University, espousing unorthodox views on Greek and ethnographic art. His ashes were interned in an urn decorated by Vanessa Bell.
▶ Paintings subject of 1912 exhibition, Grafton Galleries, London.
▶ D. Sutton (ed.), *Letters of Roger Fry*, London, 1972. F. Spalding, *Roger Fry*, London, 1980. *British Arts and Design, 1900–1960*, London: Victoria and Albert Museum, 1983. Alan and Veronica Palmer, *Who's Who in Bloomsbury*, New York: St. Martin's, 1987.

Frysia Workshops
▶ Norwegian ceramics, textile, glass firm.
▶ In c1970, Frysia set up a group of workshops and studios near Oslo. The facilities were later rented out to individual artisans including Lisbeth Daehlin, Ulla-Mari Brantenberg, Karen Klim, and Bent Saetrang.
▶ Jennifer Hawkins Opie, *Scandinavia: Ceramics and Glass in the Twentieth Century*, New York: Rizzoli, 1989.

Fujie, Kazuko   (1947–)
▶ Japanese designer; born Toyama Prefecture.
▶ 1967, graduated Junior College of Industrial Design, Musashino Fine Arts University.
▶ 1969, joined Miyawaki Architecture Office and Endo Planning; 1977, began as freelance designer and founded Field Shop Office; designed furniture for Maezawa Graden House in 1982, for Keio University New Library in 1982, for Toyama Airport in 1984; designed 1983 conference table for Dentsu, Osaka.
▶ Cat., *Kagu-Mobilier Japonais*, Shibaura Institute of Technology, 1985.

Fujita, Jun   (1951–)
▶ Japanese glass designer.
▶ Work subject of 1984 exhibition, Takashimaya department store, Tokyo. Work included in 1984 'Glass '84 in Japan,' Tokyo; 1985 'New Glass in Japan,' Badisches Landesmuseum, Karlsruhe; 1986 'International Exhibition of Glass Craft,' Industrial Gallery of Ishikawa Prefecture, Kanazawa; 1987 'Glass '87 in Japan,' Tokyo; 1988 'Arte en Vidro,' São Paulo Art Museum; 1990 'Glass '90 in Japan,' Tokyo; 1991 (V) Triennale of Japan Glass Art Crafts Association.
▶ Cat., *Glass Japan*, New York: Heller Gallery and Japan Glass Art Crafts Association, 1991: No. 2.

Fujita, Kyohei (1921–)
▶ Japanese glass designer.
▶ Studied Tokyo University of Arts, to 1944.
▶ Solo exhibitions included the 1977 Kunstsammlungen der Veste, Coburg (Germany), and 1988 and 1990 Heller Gallery, New York. Work included in the two-person 1989 exhibition with Harvey K. Littleton at the Glass Museum, Ebeltoft (Denmark); 1990 'Glass '90 in Japan,' Tokyo; and 1991 (V) Triennale of the Japan Glass Art Crafts Association. Honors included president of the Japan Glass Art Crafts Association Member of the Japan Art Academy; 1986 invited artist 'Japon des Avant Gardes,' Centre Georges Pompidou, Paris; 1986 prize of the Minister of Education, 'Japan Modern Decorative Arts,' Tokyo; invited artist and selection committee juror 1988 'World Glass Now '88,' Hokkaido Museum of Modern Art, Sapporo; 1989 Imperial Prize and Award, Japan Art Academy; and 1991 (V) Triennale of the Japan Glass Art Crafts Association.
▶ Cat., *Glass Japan*, New York: Heller Gallery and Japan Glass Art Crafts Association, 1991: No. 3.

Fujiwara, Makoto (1949–)
▶ Japanese glass designer.
▶ Studied Seikei University, Tokyo, to 1972; Kuwazawa Design Institute, Department of Industrial Design, Tokyo, to 1975; Pilchuck Glass School, Stanwood, Washington, 1985.
▶ Fujiwara worked in the department of development, Iwata Glass Company, Tokyo.
▶ Work shown at 1984 (XVI) 'Nitten' (Japan Fine Arts Exhibition), Tokyo; 1985 (XVII) 'Nitten,' Tokyo; 1990 'Glass '90 in Japan,' Tokyo; and 1991 (V) Triennale of Japan Glass Art Crafts Association.
▶ Cat., *Glass Japan*, New York: Heller Gallery and Japan Glass Artcrafts Association, 1991: No. 4.

Fuller, Richard Buckminster (1895–1983)
▶ American architect and inventor; born Milton, Massachusetts.
▶ 1913–15, studied Harvard University; US Naval Academy, Annapolis, Maryland.
▶ While at naval academy, he started his 'theoretical conceptioning' and worked on the 'flying jet-stilts porpoise' transport published in 1932; after World War I, developed a Modern movement principle based on getting more from less, calling it 'Dymaxion,' derived from 'dynamic' and 'maximum efficiency'; in 1927, designed the 'Dymaxion' house (unrealized until 1947); in 1932, established Dymaxion Corporation, Connecticut. His house design was a configuration of mechanical parts rather than a place for living. The 1933 'Dymaxion Three-Wheeled Auto' followed. His 1946 Wichita House in Kansas weighed only 6,000 lbs (2700kg) and was designed to collapse and fit into a steel cylinder for easy transport. In 1947, his study of structures led him to his highly publicized geodesic domes and his first major building, the 1958 Union Tank Car Repair shop, Baton Rouge, Louisiana, in which the spaces between struts were filled in with panels. At the time, the Baton Rouge dome, spanning 384 ft (117 m), was the world's largest clear-span enclosure. He designed the United States Pavilion, 1967 Montreal 'Universal and International Exhibition (Expo '67),' and several similar domes for the United States government that were used repeatedly at international exhibitions, including 1992 'Exposición universal de Sevilla (Expo '92).' He produced building systems that he called 'Tensegrity Structures,' derived from 'tension integrity'; popular with students and the press, he taught occasionally, Cornell University, Massachusetts Institute of Technology, Princeton University, and Yale University. 1949–75, he was professor, Southern Illinois Institute of Technology. A prolific writer and speaker, Fuller published numerous articles and books including *Ideas and Integrities: A Spontaneous Autobiographical Disclosure* (1963), *No More Secondhand God and Other Writings* (1963), *I Seem to Be a Verb* (1970), and *Critical Path* (1983).

▶ 'Dymaxion Car No. 3' shown at Keck's 'Crystal House,' 1933–34 Chicago 'A Century of Progress International Exposition.' In 1980, elected Honorary Royal Designer for Industry, London.
▶ J. Michale, 'Buckminster Fuller,' *Architectural Review*, July 1956:12–20. Robert W. Marks and Richard Buckminster Fuller, *The Dymaxion World of Buckminster Fuller*, Garden City, NY: Doubleday, 1960. J. Michale (ed.),'Richard Buckminster Fuller,' *Architectural Design*, special issue, July 1961. John McHale, *R. Buckminster Fuller*, New York, 1962. James Meller (ed.), *The Buckminster Fuller Reader*, London, 1970. Donald W. Robertson, *Mind's Eye of Buckminster Fuller*, New York, 1974. Martin Pawley, *Buckminster Fuller*, New York: Taplinger, 1990. Tony DeVarco, 'Richard Buckminster Fuller' in Mel Byars and Russell Flinchum (eds.), *50 American Designers, 1918–1968*, Washington: Preservation, 1994.

Fulper Pottery
▶ American pottery manufacturer; located Flemington and Trenton, New Jersey.
▶ The Samuel Hill Pottery was established in 1914 in Flemington, New Jersey; it ultimately became the oldest pottery manufacturer in the USA. In 1860, Abraham Fulper, a partner at Hill, acquired the firm, which produced drain tiles and utilitarian earthenware and stoneware. When Fulper died, his son William Hill Fulper turned the firm's production to high-quality pottery. After extensive experimentation, Fulper released its first art pottery in 1909 under the Vasekraft name. It was immediately successful. Other wares, such as *famille rose*, were prestigious and expensive. By the turn of the century, Fulper had become a supplier of relatively inexpensive, well-made art pottery. The rarest and most highly regarded of Fulper's wide range of glazes was the crystalline with 'Copper dust' with its unpredictable firing results. Successful through the 1920s, the Trenton plant expanded in 1928, was destroyed by fire in 1929. The second plant in Flemington continued, but the Vasekraft line was discontinued in 1929. In 1930, J. Martin Stangl acquired the firm, continuing the art pottery line until 1935. In 1955, the firm's name was changed to Stangl Pottery Company.
▶ Work (crystalline glazes) shown at 1915 San Francisco 'Panama-Pacific International Exposition.'
▶ 'The Oldest Pottery in America,' *Art World 3*, Dec. 1917:252–54. Robert W. Blasberg with Carol L. Bohdan, *Fulper Art Pottery: An Aesthetic Appreciation, 1909–1929*, New York: Jordan-Volpe Gallery, 1979. Cat., *American Art Pottery*, New York: Cooper-Hewitt Museum, 1987:116–17. Anne Yaffe Phillips, *From Architecture to Object*, New York: Hirschl and Adler, 1989:60.

Funakoshi, Saburo (1931–)
▶ Japanese glassware designer.
▶ Studied crafts, Tokyo University of Arts, to 1954.
▶ He was on the staff of the design department, Shizuoka Prefectural Industrial Institute; from 1957, worked as a glass designer, Hoya Crystal; became head of the Hoya design department, Musashi, where he produced designs for numerous crystal objects made both by machinery and by hand. Work included 1976 hand-pressed vessels with sand-blasted decorations and, for Hoya, 1978 soy-sauce bottle and 1981 *capsule* receptacles.
▶ Work subject of an exhibition, Matsuya department store, Tokyo. Work shown at 1979 'New Glass: A Worldwide Survey,' Corning Museum of Glass, Corning, New York; 1982 'Contemporary Vessels: How to Pour' exhibition, Tokyo National Museum of Modern Art; 1982 'World Glass Now '82,' Hokkaido Museum of Modern Art, Sapporo; 1982 'Design 19,' Matsuya Gallery, Ginza; 1983–84 'Design Since 1945' exhibition, Philadelphia Museum of Art; 1985 'World Glass Now '85,' Hokkaido Museum of Modern Art, Sapporo; 1985 'New Glass in Japan,' Badisches Landesmuseum, Karlsruhe; 1985 'Glass '84 in Japan,' Tokyo; 1986 'Japanese Glass—300 Years,' Suntory Museum of Art, Tokyo; 1987 'Glass '87 in Japan,' Tokyo; 1988 'Arte en Vidro,' São Paulo Museum; 1990 'Glass '90 in Japan,' Tokyo; 1991 (V) Triennale of Japan Glass Art Crafts Association. Received 1970 Osaka Design

House prize and 1979 and 1984 'Corning Glass Review' recognition in magazine *Neues Glas*.
▶ Cat., *New Glass: A Worldwide Survey*, Corning, NY: Corning Museum of Glass, 1979:255, no. 63. *Modern Japanese Glass*, Tokyo: Crafts Gallery (The National Museum of Modern Art), 1982, No. 142. Cat., *Contemporary Vessels: How to Pour*, Tokyo: Crafts Gallery, 1982: Nos. 189–90. Cat., Kathryn B. Hiesinger and George H. Marcus III (eds.), *Design Since 1945*, Philadelphia: Philadelphia Museum of Art, 1983. Cat., *Glass Japan*, New York: Heller Gallery and Japan Glass Art Crafts Association, 1991: No. 5.

Functionalism
▶ Architectural principle.
▶ Functionalism is a philosophical, symbolic, social, and economic approach to architecture and design whereby form is arrived at through its intended function. It is often thought to be one of the two approaches to architecture and design in the 20th century, historicism being the other. The roots of Functionalism can be traced back to the beginning of design theory, particularly to Vitruvius, the Roman architect and engineer of the 1st century BC who asserted that the design of a structure should be determined by its use or function. Prominent followers of Vitruvius included 18th-century Rationalists Fra Carlo Lodoli, Marc-Antoine Laugier, and Francesco Milizia, and in the 19th century, Eugène-Emmanuel Viollet-le-Duc, Henri Labrouste, and Gottfried Semper. With his motto 'form follows function,' American architect Louis Sullivan is considered the founder of 20th-century Functionalism. Functionalism became a label for an extremely wide variety of avant-garde architecture and design in the first half of the 20th century, including Ludwig Mies van der Rohe's classical Rationalism, Erich Mendelsohn's Expressionism, Giuseppe Terragni's unadorned, heroic structures, Frank Lloyd Wright's organic architecture, and Le Corbusier's Cubist solids. There is no clear distinction between Rationalism and Functionalism, despite much debate on the subject.
▶ E.R. de Zurko, *Origins of Functionalist Theory*, New York, 1957. Reyner Banham, *Theory and Design in the First Machine Age*, London, 1960. Julius Posener, *Anfänge des Funktionalismus: Von Arts and Crafts zum Deutscher Werkbund*, Berlin, Frankfurt, and Vienna, 1964. Peter Blake and Vittorio Magnago Lampugnani in Vittorio Magnago Lampugnani, *Encyclopedia of 20th-Century Architecture*, New York: Abrams, 1986:112–13. Martin Pawley, *Theory and Design in the Second Machine Age*, Oxford: Basil Blackwell, 1990.

Fundarò, Anna Maria (1936–)
▶ Italian industrial designer and architect; born Alcamo; active Palermo.
▶ Fundarò began her professional career in 1959; collaborated with Franco Santapà, Alfonso Porrello, and Antonio Martorana; taught architecture at the Università di Palermo; directed the Instituto di Disegno Industriale; headed the 'Annuario Design Sicilia'; became a member of ADI (Associazione per il Disegno Industriale).
▶ *ADI Annual 1976*, Milan: Associazione per il Disegno Industriale, 1976. *Modo*, No. 148, March–April 1993:120.

Furness, Frank (1839–1912)
▶ American architect; born Philadelphia.
▶ He learned drafting in the office of architect John Fraser; 1859–61, worked in the office of architect Richard Morris Hunt; 1867–71, worked with architect John Frazer; 1871–75, practiced architecture with anglophile George W. Hewitt; through Hewitt, was influenced by British botanical ornamentation, especially as executed by Owen Jones and Christopher Dresser; (with Hewitt) designed 1876 Pennsylvania Academy of Fine Arts, Philadelphia, although the Furness-Hewitt partnership was dissolved in 1875. Completed in time for 1876 Philadelphia 'Centennial Exhibition,' his designs for the Philadelphia Academy of Art showed metalwork influenced by Dresser and by French architecture. Louis H. Sullivan studied under Furness in 1873. A contemporary of H.H. Richardson, Furness designed churches, railroads, and libraries in the Gothic style; his buildings were heavily decorated. Highly architectonic, his earliest preserved pieces of furniture include the chairs for 1869–71 Rodef Shalom Synagogue, Philadelphia. The period 1881–95 included numerous railroad stations and suburban houses. His masterwork of this period was 1888–91 library of University of Pennsylvania (today called the Furness Building after his brother Horace Howard Furness). After 1895, he designed a number of large-scale commercial and small buildings. His posthumous reputation was low, until a revival of interest in his work in the 1970s.
▶ Work subject of 1973 'The Architecture of Frank Furness' exhibition, Philadelphia Museum of Art in Philadelphia, Pennsylvania. Furniture shown at 1982 'Shape and Environment: Furniture by American Architects,' Whitney Museum of American Art, Fairfield County, Connecticut.
▶ James C. Massey, 'Frank Furness in the 1870's: Some Less Known Buildings,' *Charette*, No. 43, Jan. 1963:13–16. Cat., James F. O'Gorman, *The Architecture of Frank Furness*, Philadelphia: Philadelphia Museum of Art, 1973. Cat., Lisa Phillips (introduction), *Shape and Environment: Furniture by American Architects*, New York: Whitney Museum of American Art, 1982:32–33. Doreen Bolger Burke et al., *In Pursuit of Beauty: Americans and the Aesthetic Movement*, New York: Metropolitan Museum of Art and Rizzoli, 1986:429–30. Cat., David A. Hanks and Donald C. Peirce, *The Virginia Carroll Crawford Collection: American Decorative Arts, 1825–1919*, Atlanta: High Museum of Art, 1983:78–19.

Furniture Shop, The
▶ American store and workshop; located San Francisco.
▶ By 1910, Arthur and Lucia Mathews were at the pinnacle of their success in representing the arts community in San Francisco and were identified with the California Decorative Style of the 1890s–1920s. They established The Furniture Shop, San Francisco, where they and their staff of craftspeople were prolific producers of frames, paintings, furniture, fixtures, and accessories in the Arts and Crafts tradition of integrating whole environments. 1906–20, The Furniture Shop benefited from the rebuilding of San Francisco after the 1906 earthquake and fire. John Zeile was a partner, financial backer, and business manager of the firm. Thomas McGlyn oversaw the execution of the shop's work from Arthur Mathews's sketches to the final pieces, managing 30 to 50 carpenters, cabinetmakers, wood carvers, and finishers, although fewer were there on a regular basis. They produced domestic and public pieces, including large suites of furniture and fixtures, and custom murals to the work intended for the Mathews's own use. The limited-production and contract furnishings were the more conservative in design. The Mathews's work is distinguishable from the plainer Craftsman-style furniture of the Stickleys and the furnishings of the Greenes. Lucia Mathews was fastidious in her decoration applied to smaller pieces; her picture frames were considered works of art.
▶ Harvey L. Jones in Timothy J. Andersen et al., *California Design 1910*, Salt Lake City: Peregrine Smith, 1980:88–93.

Furuta, Toshikazu (1947–)
▶ Japanese glass designer.
▶ Work subject of 1990 exhibition, Kyoto. Work shown in 1988 'International Exhibition of Glass Craft,' Industrial Gallery of Ishikawa Prefecture, Kanazawa; 1990 'Glass '90 in Japan,' Tokyo; 1991 (V) Triennale of Japan Glass Art Crafts Association.
▶ Cat., *Glass Japan*, New York: Heller Gallery and Japan Glass Art Crafts Association, 1991: No. 6.

Fusco, Massimo (1945–)
▶ Italian designer.
▶ Studied architecture, Università di Firenze, to 1973.
▶ He established his own architecture office in 1973; collaborated with Marco Balzarotti and Roberto Gangemi for Numeri SRL. His work was widely published.
▶ He received numerous design and architecture awards.

▶ Robert A.M. Stern (ed.), *The International Design Yearbook*, New York: Abbeville, 1985/1986: Nos. 95 and 97.

Futurism

▶ Artistic movement.

▶ Futurism expressed a radical rejection of the past, glorification of the machine, pleasure in the transient, and enthusiasm for speed. This combination of ideas was first expressed in poet Filippo Tommaso Marinetti's *Futurist Manifesto* (1909), and in *Manifesto of Futurist Painting*, signed by Carlo Carrà, Luigi Russolo, Giacomo Balla, Gino Severini, and Umberto Boccioni in 1910. The Futurists used Neo-Impressionist color techniques that Severini and Boccioni had acquired from Balla. By the time of 1912 Paris Futurist exhibition, followers of the movement had adopted Cubist techniques for depicting speed; as Marinetti declared in 1909, 'The splendor of the world has been enriched with a new form of beauty—the beauty of speed.' The Paris exhibition was accompanied by a manifesto that set forth the theoretical basis of the movement. Influential written works by Antonio Sant'Elia followed in 1914 with his 'Manifesto of Futuristic Architecture' in the library journal *Lacerba* and in his catalog introduction that year for 'Group of New Trends' exhibition, Milan. Sant'Elia left no constructed architectural works. Virgilio Marchi contributed his *Manifesto of Futurist Architecture—dynamic, a State of Mind, Dramatic* (1920). As an effective movement, Futurism did not last much beyond Boccioni's death in 1916 or the end of World War I in 1918. It had considerable influence in Russia, where the movement included Mikhael Fedorovich Larionov, Natal'ia Goncharova, and Kazimir Malevich. It had some influence on the Dadaists in France and on Vorticism in Britain. Marcel Duchamp and Robert Delaunay were also, in their different ways, indebted to the movement.

▶ Subject of 1986 'Futurismo e Futurismi,' Palazzo Grassi, Venice, and 1992 'Futurism 1909—44,' Hokkaido Museum of Art, Sapporo.

▶ Antonio Sant'Elia, 'L'architettura futurista,' *Lacerba*, 1 Aug. 1914. D. Gambillo and T. Fiori, *Archivi del futurismo*, Rome, 1958. Rosa Clough, *Futurism: The Story of a Modern Art Movement*, New York, 1961. Alberto Galardi, *New Italian Architecture*, New York: Praeger, 1967:12—16. Umbro Apollonio (ed.), *Futurist Manifestos*, London and New York, 1973. Pontus Hulten (organizer), *Futurism and Futurisms*, New York: Abbeville, 1986.

G

GAB
See Guldsmedsaktiebolaget

Gabino, Amadeo
▶ Italian sculptor.
▶ Gabino was commissioned by Portaceli to design dinnerware; 1980–82 at Portaceli, produced matt black-and-white enameled stoneware in a highly geometric design reminiscent of the Bauhaus style.
▶ *Les Carnets du Design*, Paris: Mad-Cap Productions et APCI, 1986:32.

Gabo, Naum (1890–1977)
▶ Russian sculptor; born Briansk; brother of Antoine Pevsner.
▶ Studied art at Munich University.
▶ In 1914, he moved to Scandinavia and became a sculptor; in 1917, returned to Russia; (with Antoine Pevsner) published the *Realistic Manifesto* (1920); 1922–32, lived in Berlin and, from the mid-1930s to 1946, in Britain, where he issued important statements on Constructivist art and (with J.L. Martin and Ben Nicholson) edited *Circle*, the international survey of Constructivist art; in 1946, settled in the USA; 1953–55, was professor, Graduate School of Architecture, Harvard University.
▶ Dennis Sharp, *Sources of Modern Architecture: A Critical Bibliography*, Westfield, NJ: Eastview, 1981:45–46. Cat., *The Great Utopia: The Russian and Soviet Avant-Garde, 1915–1932*, New York: Guggenheim Museum, 1992.

Gabriel, René (1890–1950)
▶ French decorator and furniture designer; born Maisons-Alforts; active Paris.
▶ A follower of Francis Jourdain, Gabriel designed wallpaper, fabric, rugs, porcelain (particularly for the Manufacture de Sèvres), and theatre sets (including those in 1927 for Louis Jouvet and his *Léopold le Bien-Aimé*). Some of his furniture was produced by Kurtz. From 1923, his limited-production furniture became very simple, and, in *c*1935, was produced in modular combinations of various elements, known as Éléments RG. He subsequently designed bent-metal tubular seating and structures; in 1920, established the small wallpaper store Au Sansonnet, rue de Solférino, Paris, and designed papers printed by Papiers Peints de France et Nobilis; in 1934, established Ateliers d'Art, Neuilly. Active in architecture and interior design, in 1947, he became president, Société des Artistes Décorateurs; continued the limited production of furniture in the style of Francis Jourdain; was a teacher, École des Arts Appliqués, Paris; from 1946, was director, École Nationale Supérieure des Arts Décoratifs, Paris; participated in the establishment of René Gabriel Prize.
▶ From 1919, work shown at Salon d'Automne and at Salons of the Société des Artistes Décorateurs. His girl's bedroom with a rug by Gaudissart and lighting by Jean Perzel was installed at 1925 Paris 'Exposition Internationale des Arts Décoratifs et Industriels Modernes.' Participated in pavilion of Société des Artistes Décorateurs at 1937 Paris 'Exposition Internationale des Arts et Techniques dans la Vie Moderne.'

▶ *Ensembles Mobiliers*, Vol. 2, Paris: Charles Moreau, 1937; Vol. 6, Nos. 19–23, 1945. René Chavanie, 'René Gabriel ou la continuité dans la recherche,' *Mobilier et Décoration*, V, 1949:15–25. Yolande Amic, *Intérieurs: Le Mobilier français 1945–1954*, Paris: Regard/VIA, 1983:78. Pierre Kjellberg, *Art Déco: les maîtres du Mobilier, le décor des Paquebots*, Paris: Amateur, 1986:77–78.

Gabrielsen, Bent (1928–)
▶ Danish metalworker.
▶ 1950–53, studied Danish College of Jewelry, Silversmithing and Commercial Design.
▶ 1953–56, he designed for Hans Hansen, Kolding and subsequently for Georg Jensen in Copenhagen. Special work included the communion silver and altarpieces of Braendkjaer Church, Kolding. In 1969, he set up his own workshop.
▶ Received a gold medal at 1960 (XII) Triennale di Milano and 1964 Lunning Prize. Work shown at 1956–59 Germany 'Neue Form aus Dänemark'; 1960–61 USA 'The Arts of Denmark'; 1964 'Modern Scandinavian Jewelry', New York; 1967 'Lunning Prize Winners'; Den Permanente in Copenhagen; 1968 'Two Centuries of Danish Design'; London; 1969 Moscow 'Modern Danish Design'; 1973, 1976, and 1979 'Jewelry Arts Exhibition,' Tokyo.
▶ Cat., *Georg Jensen Silversmithy: 77 Artists, 75 Years*, Washington: Smithsonian Institution Press, 1980. Cat., David Revere McFadden (ed.), *Scandinavian Modern Design 1880–1980*, New York: Abrams, 1982:263, Nos. 181–82.

Gaetani, Luigi (1948–)
▶ Italian designer and technician.
▶ Studied industrial technology in Alessandria.
▶ At Olivetti, he worked first in the numerical control division and subsequently technical industrial-design service; was active in developing the engineering design of calculators and other office machines; in 1974, worked at Centro Design Montefibre on color studies; from 1978–84, worked in the studio of Makio Hasuike on the design of Ariston products and a wide range of others; in 1979 with Gianluigi Arnaldi, was active in the AD Agenzia di Design, becoming Arnaldi & Gaetani Associati in 1989.
▶ *Modo*, No. 148, March–April 1993:120.

Gafforio, Luca (1956–)
▶ Italian architect-designer.
▶ Studied architecture, Instituto Universitario di Architettura, Venice, and industrial design, Domus Academy, Milan.
▶ He worked at the industrial-design firm Nolan.
▶ Hans Wichmann, *Italien Design 1945 bis heute*, Munich: Die Neue Sammlung, 1988.

Gaggia, Achille (1895–1961)
▶ Italian inventor; active Milan.
▶ Gaggia worked originally as a bartender in Milan; dissatisfied with coffee made by steam-driven machines, experimented on new models in his attic; devised a piston to force water through coffee grounds at high pressure, producing a better-tasting coffee brew with a foamy head; 1937–38, installed his first machines in Milan coffee shops. A process to produce espresso without the use of steam was patented in 1944; in 1947, founded Brevetti Gaggia

to manufacture his machines. The first machine, *Classico*, was operated by gas or electricity. Gaggia produced the world's first domestic electric espresso coffeemaker, the 1952—54 *Gilda*, named after the 1946 Rita Hayworth film.
▶ Jeremy Myerson and Sylvia Katz, *Conran Design Guides: Kitchenware*, London: Conran Octopus, 1990:16,61,73—74.

Gagnère, Olivier   (1952–)
▶ French designer.
▶ Studied economics and law, Paris.
▶ In the 1980s, he worked with the Memphis group, Milan, and, subsequently, alone. His abstract-form 1984 *Verseuse* teapot using industrial materials was produced by Néotù, as was his letter-opener. His ceramic tea service was produced by Martine Haddad and other work by Écart International and by Galerie Adrien Maeght, who also produced his 1987 *Théière* teapot in silver and wood.
▶ Participated in numerous French and foreign exhibitions, including at VIA, Paris. Received 1989 VIA 'Carte Blanche' award for his table in roughened oak.
▶ *Les Carnets du Design*, Paris: Mad-Cap Productions et APCI, 1986:4. Suzanne Tise, 'Innovators at the Museum,' *Vogue Décoration*, No. 26, June/July 1990:48. François Mathey, *Au bonheur des formes, design français 1945—1992*, Paris: Regard, 1992:163,206—07.

Gahkn   (State Academy of Artistic Sciences)
▶ Russian learning institution.
▶ Active 1921—31, Gahkn was the successor to the Museums of Artistic Culture, Moscow and Petrograd/Leningrad.
▶ Cat., *Kunst und Revolution: Russische und Sowjetische Kunst 1910—1932*, Vienna: Österreichisches Museum für angewandte Kunst, 1988. Cat., *The Great Utopia: The Russian and Soviet Avant-Garde, 1915—1932*, New York: Guggenheim Museum, 1992.

Gaillard, Eugène   (1862–1933)
▶ French designer and writer; brother of jeweler Lucien Gaillard.
▶ Gaillard was associated with Siegfried Bing's shop Maison de l'Art Nouveau, Paris; (with Georges de Feure) participated in activities of the group L'Art Nouveau; is best known for his refined moldings. 1900—14, he designed simple, elegant furniture. He felt that decoration, even though inspired by nature, should be 'unreal . . . so that it might be completely natural without evoking any precise form from the animal or vegetable kingdoms.'
▶ Showed work at Salons of the Société des Artistes Décorateurs, of which was founding member. Created Bing's stand of six fully decorated rooms (with de Feure and Edward Colonna) and bedroom and dining room at 1900 Paris 'Exposition Universelle.'
▶ Yvonne Brunhammer et al., *Art Nouveau Belgium, France*, Houston: Rice University, 1976. Pierre Kjellberg, *Art Déco: les maîtres du Mobilier, le décor des Paquebots*, Paris: Amateur, 1986:78.

Gaillard, Lucien   (1861–)
▶ French silversmith and jeweler; active Paris; brother of furniture designer Eugène Gaillard.
▶ Studied sculpture under Henri L. Levasseur.
▶ In 1840, Amédée Gaillard established a jewelry business, Paris, succeeded in 1860 by his son Ernest Gaillard. In 1878, Ernest's son Lucien became an apprentice in the Gaillard workshop and trained in a number of other workshops; when Ernest retired in 1892, became director of the family firm, specializing in *dinanderie*; studied gilding, alloys, and patinated silver; was influenced by research in Japanese mixed-metal techniques; employed Japanese craftsmen *c*1900 when the firm moved to larger quarters; himself incorporated *japonisme* into French Art Nouveau. His use of bronze with silver was a product of the Japanese influence. He knew how to lend different colors to metals, a technique he used often in his silver work. His friend René Lalique persuaded him to turn from silverware to jewelry. Showing Lalique's influence, he began working in a larger studio, 107 rue de la Boëtie, Paris, and used enameling and exotic materials such as ivory and horn.

From 1904, his jewelry was noted for its originality and color in its use of floral and insect motifs.
▶ Received a gold medal (heliographically engraved gold and silver) at 1889 Paris 'Exposition Universelle' and first prize (jewelry) at 1904 Salon of Société des Artistes français. Work (silver pieces) shown at 1900 Paris 'Exposition Universelle.'
▶ Charlotte Gere, *American and European Jewelry 1830—1914*, New York: Crown, 1975:183—84. Yvonne Brunhammer et al., *Art Nouveau Belgium, France*, Houston: Rice University, 1976, biblio. Annelies Krekel-Aalberse, *Art Nouveau and Art Déco Silver*, New York: Abrams, 1989:58—59,254.

Galaaen, Konrad   (1923–)
▶ Norwegian ceramicist.
▶ 1943—47, studied painting and ceramics, Statens Håndverks -og Kunstindustriskole, Oslo.
▶ From 1947, Galaaen designed serially produced ceramics and art pieces for Porsgrund, and received numerous commissions from others for architectural ceramics and tiles.
▶ Fredrik Wildhagen, *Norge i Form*, Oslo: Stenersen, 1988:87. Jennifer Hawkins Opie, *Scandinavia: Ceramics and Glass in the Twentieth Century*, New York: Rizzoli, 1989.

Galimberti, Maria Grazia   (1947–)
▶ Italian designer; born and active Milan.
▶ Studied architecture, Politecnico di Milano, to 1971.
▶ She began her professional career in 1971; designed fabrics, furniture and furnishings in wood, lighting accessories in wood, plywood, metal, cork, ABS plastic, and alabaster; designed interiors of shops, residences, and offices; was active as an architect and graphic designer; became a member of ADI (Associazione per il Disegno Industriale).
▶ Her lighting (with S. D'Asta) won an award at 1975 'Concorso di Nuove Idee,' Modena.
▶ *ADI Annual 1976*, Milan: Associazione per il Disegno Industriale, 1976.

Gallé, Émile   (1846–1904)
▶ French designer and glassmaker; born Nancy.
▶ Studied painting and design under local artists; 1862, botany, University of Nancy, under Dominique-Alexandre Godron; 1865—66, philosophy and mineralogy, Weimar, and Atelier für Architektur und Kunstgewerbe, Weimar; 1866—67, apprenticed in glassmaking at Burgun, Schverer & Co, Meisenthal (Germany).
▶ He learned the ceramics and glass crafts in his father Charles's workshops, Saint-Clément. His father ran a store in Nancy, selling ceramics and glassware, some of which he designed, finished, and decorated, and acquired partial proprietorship of a pottery near Saint-Clément. Gallé cut and enameled glassware and painted faïence; 1862—72, traveled, worked with his father, studied, and served in the Franco-Prussian War, after which he assisted E. du Sommerard in organizing the 'Art de France' exhibition in London; studied art in the collections at Cluny and the Louvre and cameos and precious stones in Galerie d'Apollon that later influenced his own cameo and cut-glass work; in 1874, assumed the directorship of the family firm; appeared as a glass artist at the 1884 Paris 'Exposition Universelle,' showing 300 pieces there, some in Islamic and medieval styles. Other designs were cased with up to four layers of glass and included air bubbles, enamels, and gold and platinum *paillons*, illustrating flowers, insects, vegetation, and, rarely, the human form. Through a search for wood bases for his glassware, he became interested in the grains of exotic woods and, in 1884, began designing furniture. The first series of Gallé's furniture, reflecting 18th-century cabinet work with Renaissance-type carving, was shown at the 1889 Paris 'Exposition Universelle.' He showed pieces that could be inexpensively machine produced and waxed (never polished or varnished); in 1884, began using opaque glass influenced by the Brandt collection of Chinese glass at Kunstgewerbemuseum, Berlin; in 1889, beginning to reduce the number of layers in his acid-etched glasswork to three, called himself the 'vulgarizer of art'; produced notable unique

pieces as well as limited editions known as the *grand genre* and *demi riche*. By this time the Gallé workshop produced many pieces neither of his hand nor of his design. By 1884, his unique pieces and prototypes were produced in Nancy and his industrial glass by Burgun und Schverer, Meisenthal. In 1886, he established a fully equipped cabinetmaking facility with steam sheds, workshops, sawmills, stores, offices, and showrooms; amassed a large library of reference works; grew plants, grouped by species, which he used as models for his marquetry; for his complicated decorative inlays, kept a stock of over 600 veneers; in 1897, applied for patents for marquetry and texturing (*patinage*). His *verres sculptés* produced *c*1900 appeared to be more sculpture than vessels. At the 1900 Paris 'Exposition Universelle' he received top prizes for his glassware, furniture, and collaborative work; in 1901, as founder of Alliance Provinciale des Industries d'Art (aka École de Nancy), became its first president. His wife and daughters managed the firm from his death until 1905, when his two sons-in-law and manager Émile Lang took over, assisted by Victor Prouvé; it closed in 1931. Gallé's dissertations on the applied arts were published posthumously as *Les Écrits pour l'Art*.

▶ Work first noticed at 1878 Paris 'Exposition Universelle' and shown at 1884 Salon of Union Centrale des Arts Décoratifs, 1889 Paris 'Exposition Universelle' and, winning prizes, 1900 Paris 'Exposition Universelle,' and École de Nancy's 1904 exhibition, Pavillon de Marsan, Paris. In 1900, received Légion d'honneur.

▶ Émile Gallé, 'Le Mobilier Contemporain orné d'après la nature,' *Revue des Arts Décoratifs*, Vol. XX, 1900:333–41,365–77. Louis de Fourcaud, *Émile Gallé*, Paris, 1903. R. and L. Grover, *Carved and Decorated European Art Glass*, Rutland, Vermont: Tuttle, 1970:121–29. J. Bloch-Dermant, *L'Art du Verre en France: 1860–1914*, Paris: Edita Denöel, 1975:90. Philippe Garner, *Émile Gallé*, London: Academy, 1976. Yvonne Brunhammer et al., *Art Nouveau Belgium, France*, Houston: Rice University, 1976. Alastair Duncan, *Art Nouveau and Art Déco Lighting*, New York: Simon and Schuster, 1978:77–78. Jessica Rutherford, *Art Nouveau, Art Deco and the Thirties: The Furniture Collections at Brighton Museum*, Brighton: The Royal Pavilion, Art Gallery and Museums, 1983: 13–14.

Gallen-Kallela, Akseli (aka Alex Gallén 1865–1931)
▶ Finnish painter and designer.

▶ Studied painting, Taideyhdistyksen Piirustuskoulu, Helsinki; 1881–84, Académie Julian and Atelier Fernand Cormon, both Paris.

▶ He changed his name in 1905 to Axel Gallén; was a pioneer and the prime exponent of the Finnish National Romantic Movement. His work covered a wide range of crafts media. In 1928, he painted the ceiling frescoes, Suomen Kansallismuseo, Helsinki. His textiles, including *ryijy* rugs, were produced with flamelike motifs arranged asymmetrically; most were produced by Suomen Käsityön Ystävät (Friends of Finnish Handicraft).

▶ Received a gold medal (furnishings for the Iris room) at 1900 Paris 'Exposition Universelle' where he painted frescoes for the Finnish pavilion. Work subject of 1906–08 retrospective, Hungary. Had his own section at 1914 Biennale di Venezia and at 1915 San Francisco 'Panama-Pacific Exposition.'

▶ D. Okkonen, *Akseli Gallen-Kallela*, Helsinki, 1936. Cat., David Revere McFadden (ed.), *Scandinavian Modern Design 1880–1980*, New York: Abrams, 1982:263, No. 30. Penny Sparke, *Introduction to Design and Culture in the Twentieth Century*, Allen and Unwin, 1986.

Gallerey, Mathieu
▶ French decorator, furniture designer, and metalworker; born and active Paris.

▶ Active in a workshop, 2 rue de la Roquette, Paris, he produced furniture, lighting, rugs, and wallpaper. His designs reflected the rustic, provincial French style. His work at 1937 Paris Exposition was designed in the Art Déco style in a very simple dining-room suite. 1904–24, he was a member of the Société des Artistes Décorateurs; in 1942, designed and furnished his own villa in Mandé.

▶ Work first shown at 1900 Paris 'Exposition Universelle' where he received second prize in the furniture competition for a dining-room suite; 1908 Salon of Société Nationale des Beaux-Arts; 1912 Salon of Société des Artistes Décorateurs, Salons d'Automne, and 1937 Paris 'Exposition Internationale des Arts et Techniques dans la Vie Moderne.'

▶ Léon Deshairs, *Modern French Decorative Art*, Paris: Albert Lévy. Pierre Kjellberg, *Art Déco: les maîtres du Mobilier, le décor des Paquebots*, Paris: Amateur, 1986:78.

Galli
▶ Italian furniture manufacturer; located Macerata Feltria.

▶ Galli was established in 1966 to produce mirrors. In 1975, its production was greatly expanded, producing furniture, furnishings, and accessories. A.G. Fronzoni was its primary consultant designer; he designed 1964 *Serie 64* furniture in a Rationalist style.

▶ *ADI Annual 1976*, Milan: Associazione per il Disegno Industriale, 1976.

Galloway and Graff
▶ American terracotta manufacturers; located Philadelphia.

▶ William Galloway and John Graff set up a partnership in Philadelphia in 1868, continuing the activities of a previous business begun in 1810. On Market Street, the firm produced utilitarian and ornamental terracotta ware including urns, pedestals, sundials, benches, bird baths, flower boxes, fountains, and architectural ornamentation. Its objects were produced from clays found in Pennsylvania, Maryland, and New Jersey. In 1876, it began producing vases and plaques based on antique models, possibly inspired by ancient Greek vases seen at the Danish Pavilion at the 1876 Philadelphia Exposition; in 1889, moved its plant to Walnut Street. By 1893, it conducted business under the name William Galloway; in 1911, was incorporated as Galloway Terra-Cotta Company, when Galloway's son William B. Galloway was its president; closed *c*1941.

▶ Work (including vases copied from examples in the British Museum, London) shown at 1876 Philadelphia 'Centennial Exposition.' Received a first prize at 1893 Chicago 'World's Columbian Exposition' and a grand prize at 1904 St. Louis 'Louisiana Purchase Exposition.'

▶ Edwin AtLee Barber, *The Pottery and Porcelain of the United States*, New York, 1909. Doreen Bolger Burke et al., *In Pursuit of Beauty: Americans and the Aesthetic Movement*, New York: Metropolitan Museum of Art and Rizzoli, 1986:431.

galuchat
See shagreen

Games, Abram (1914–)
▶ British graphic artist and industrial designer.

▶ Games is known for his posters of the 1940s and 1950s for the British War Office, London Transport, Shell, British Petroleum, and Guinness, and his graphics for 1951 London 'Festival of Britain'; during World War II, was active designing printed propaganda for the Ministry of Information; was one of the last graphic artists to draw directly on a lithographic stone rather than reproducing his work in the new photographic technique; designed the widely published and highly sculptural 1947 coffee percolator produced in 1949 by Cona, reworked in 1959 and still in production. In the early 1960s, he redesigned the housing and workings of the Gestetner duplicating machine, although, due to Gestetner's death, this was not put into production.

▶ Michael Farr, *Design in British Industry: A Mid-Century Survey*, London: Cambridge, 1955:145. Jeremy Myerson and Sylvia Katz, *Conran Design Guides: Kitchenware*, London: Conran Octopus, 1990:63,74.

Gammelgaard, Jørgen (1938–)
▶ Danish designer.
▶ 1959–62, studied Kunsthåndvaerkskolen; 1962–64, Det-Kongelige Danske Kunstakademi, both Copenhagen.
▶ 1962–64, he was associated with architects Grete Jalk, Steen Eiler Rasmussen, and Mogens Koch; 1965–67, he was a UN and UNESCO consultant in Samoa, the Sudan, and Sri Lanka; 1968–69, was associated with architect Arne Jabocsen; in 1970, with Jørgen Bos; and 1970–71, with Bernts. 1971–73, Gammelgaard was a consultant, Teknologisk Institut, Copenhagen; was a lecturer, School of Arts and Crafts and Industrial Design; in 1973, set up his own design office; from 1982, he designed for Schiang Production.
▶ Received 1971 Møbelprisen (Danish Furniture award).
▶ Frederik Sieck, *Nutidig Dansk Møbeldesign: -en kortfattet illustreret beskrivelse*, Copenhagen: Bondo Gravesen; 1990 Busck edition in English.

Gammelgaard, Niels (1944–)
▶ Danish architect and designer.
▶ Gammelgaard with four other architects founded Box 25 Architects in 1969; in 1970, became a staff member, School of Industrial Design, Royal Academy of Fine Arts, Copenhagen; in 1978 (with Lars Mathiesen) established Pelikan Design; taught at the Royal Academy and School of Architecture in Århus.
▶ Received prizes in Scandinavia and Japan.
▶ Robert A.M. Stern (ed.), *The International Design Yearbook*, New York: Abbeville, 1985/1986: Nos. 57–58,72.

Gandini, Innocente (1941–)
▶ Italian designer; born Legnano; active Varese.
▶ Active from 1969, Gandini designed metal accessories, ceramics, furniture, lighting, meat slicers, and bar and hotel utensils, corporate-image programs, furnishing fabrics, and exhibitions; was artistic director at ICCO; became a member of ADI (Associazione per il Disegno Industriale).
▶ Participated in the 1973 (XV) Triennale di Milano.
▶ *ADI Annual 1976*, Milan: Associazione per il Disegno Industriale, 1976.

Gandolini, Jole (1927–)
▶ Italian fabric designer; born Bergamo; active Milan.
▶ Gandolini began her professional career in 1963; designed textiles for Texital in Bergamo and Rossi in Albizzate; became a member of ADI (Associazione per il Disegno Industriale).
▶ *ADI Annual 1976*, Milan: Associazione per il Disegno Industriale, 1976.

Gangemi, Roberto (1947–)
▶ Italian architect-designer.
▶ Studied Università di Firenzi to 1973.
▶ He worked as interior designer and architect; in 1979, began collaborating with Marco Balzarotti and Massimo Fusco for Numeri SRL.
▶ Robert A.M. Stern (ed.), *The International Design Yearbook*, New York: Abbeville, 1985/1986: Nos. 95,97.

Garbe, Richard (?–1957)
▶ British sculptor.
▶ Studied ivory, horn, and hardwood turning, Central School of Arts and Crafts, London.
▶ He taught at Central School of Arts and Crafts; 1929–46, was professor of sculpture, Royal College of Art, London; 1933–39, designed for Doulton, Burslem, where he produced numerous large figures and plain matt-glazed ceramic sculptures including *Spring, The Spirit of the Pines, West Wind, Beethoven, Lady of the Rose, Lady of the Snows*, and 1937 *The Spirit of the Wind* in earthenware editions of 50 to 100; designed wall masks and other figurines.
▶ From 1905, work shown at the Royal Academy, London.
▶ Cat., *Thirties: British art and design before the war*, London: Arts Council of Great Britain, Hayward Gallery, 1979:152,290.

Gardberg, Bertel (1916–)
▶ Finnish jeweler and metalworker.
▶ 1938–41, studied Taideteollinen Korkeakoulu, Helsinki.
▶ First working in Copenhagen, Gardberg moved to Helsinki, where he maintained a studio 1949–66; executed silver and stainless-steel tableware designs produced by the Georg Jensen Sølvsmedie; Galeries Lafayette department store, Paris; and Kilkenny Design Workshops, Dublin; although known for his metalwares, also worked in wood and stone; 1951–53, taught at Taideteollinen Korkeakoulu, Helsinki; attempting to revive Ireland's decorative arts and promote craftsmanship locally, was artistic director, Kilkenny Design Workshop, Dublin, 1966–68, and head of design and technical director of Rionor, Kilkenny, 1968–71. His cutlery and stainless-steel models were produced by Fiskars, Hackman, and Hopeatehdas. He designed wooden pieces and ecclesiastical and domestic silver produced by Noormarkun Kotiteollisuus; in 1973, set up a studio, Pohja (Finland), where he continued his activities in woodworking, metalwares, and silver jewelry, into which he incorporated, as previously developed in Ireland, precious and semi-precious stones.
▶ Received gold medals (metalworking) at 1954 (X) and 1957 (XI) and four silver medals at 1960 (XII) Triennali di Milano. Received 1961 Lunning Prize. Work shown at 1955 exhibition, Gothenburg; 1956 exhibition, Copenhagen. Elected member of Academy of Finland, 1982.
▶ Erik Zahle (ed.), *A Treasury of Scandinavian Design*, New York: 1961: 273, Nos. 327,343–44,368,374,400–01,405,108,410–11. John Haycraft, *Finnish Jewellery and Silverware*, Helsinki, 1962: 38–47. Cat., *Georg Jensen Silversmithy: 77 Artists, 75 Years*, Washington: Smithsonian Institution Press, 1980. Cat., David Revere McFadden (ed.), *Scandinavian Modern Design 1880–1980*, New York: Abrams, 1982:264. Barbro Kulvik, 'Craftsmanship Is a Way of Life,' *Form Function Finland*, No. 1, 1983:34–39. Cat., Kathryn B. Hiesinger and George H. Marcus III (eds.), *Design Since 1945*, Philadelphia: Philadelphia Museum of Art, 1983. Cat., *The Lunning Prize*, Stockholm: Nationalmuseum, 1986:120–25.

Gardella, Ignazio (1905–)
▶ Italian architect-designer; born and active Milan.
▶ Studied engineering, Politecnico di Milano to 1931, and architecture, Instituto Universitario di Architettura, Venice, to 1949.
▶ Gardella began his career as an architect and town planner with interior decoration and rebuilding schemes including 1934 theatre, Busto Arsizio; entered the competition for the tower in Piazza del Duomo, Milan, followed by his design for 1937 Dispensario Provinciale e Laboratorio di Igiene e Profilassi, Alessandria (Italy); became active in industrial design and designed 1940 folding butterfly chair by Vigano; with the intention of having a place to experiment, (with Caccia Dominioni) set up the Azucena shop in 1949 and produced high-quality furniture and furnishings. He wrote for the journal *Casabella* during Ernesto Roger's editorship (1954–65); was professor of architectural composition, Instituto Universitario di Architettura, Venice. In the 1950s, Anna Castelli Ferrieri joined Gardella, becoming the architect and designer who was to realize Gardella's designs; worked with Gardella for 15 years on public-housing and furniture projects. Gardella was among the first to break with Italian Rationalism, reviving the neoclassical architectural tradition. His classical façade for 1945 Villa Borletti and Olivetti headquarters building, Ivrea, placed him at the center of the 1950s controversies discussed in Rogers's *Casabella*. He designed the *Digamma* armchair for Favina; street lighting for the Piazza San Babilia, Milan; pioneering plastic furniture with Ferrieri for Kartell; furniture for Rima; and 1960 Olivetti showroom, Düsseldorf. His buildings included 1950–53 transformation of Terme Regina Isabella, Lacco Ameno d'Ischia; 1950–51 IACP 'Mangiagalli' quarter (with Franco Albini), Milan; 1955–59 Olivetti refectory building, Ivrea; 1954–58 apartment building, Zattere; 1963–66 Chiesa di Sant'Enrico, Metanopoli; 1968–71 building for the technical offices of Alfa Romeo (with Ferrieri and Jacopo Gardella), Arese; 1968 competition project for the new

theatre, Vicenza; 1981—82 project for the reconstruction of Teatro Carlo Felice (with Aldo Rossi and Fabio Reinhart), Genoa. He was a member, CIAM, INU, MSA, INARCH; from 1956, member, ADI (Associazione per il Disegno Industriale); executive committee member, 1960 (XII) Triennale di Milano; administrative counsellor of its 1964 (XIII) and 1968 (XIV) sessions; jury member, 1955—57 Formica Domes competition and 1957 Premio Compasso d'Oro.
▶ 1947 'House for Three People' shown at RIMA exhibition. Shelving and cabinets for Spezzo shown at 1948 (VII) Triennale di Milano where he received a gold medal. Designed 'Standard' pavilion for 1951 (IX) Triennale di Milano where he received a gold medal for furniture by Azucena and showed his work at the chair exhibition at its 1954 (X) session. Received first national 1955 Olivetti prize in architecture and 1972 MIA gold medal (oval polyester table for Kartell with Ferrieri).
▶ *ADI Annual*, Milan: Associazione per il Disegno Industriale, 1976. Andrea Branzi and Michele De Lucchi, *Design Italiano degli Anni '50*, Milan: Editoriale Domus, 1980. A. Samonà, *Ignazio Gardella e il professionismo italiano*, Rome, 1981. M. Porta (ed.), *L'architettura di Ignazio Gardella*, Milan, 1985. Paolo Zermani, *Ignazio Gardella*, Bari: Laterza, 1991.

Gardner, James   (1907–)
▶ British designer.
▶ 1924—31, Gardner was a jewelry designer for Cartier; was chief designer of a team of 75, 1946 London 'Britain Can Make It' exhibition, Victoria and Albert Museum, for which Basil Spence was consulting architect; designed Battersea Pleasure Garden at 1951 'Festival of Britain'; participated in United Kingdom pavilion, 1958 'Exposition Universelle et Internationale de Bruxelles (Expo '58)'; 1962 Commonwealth Institute.
▶ In 1947, elected Royal Designer for Industry.
▶ Michael Farr, *Design in British Industry: A Mid-Century Survey*, London: Cambridge, 1955:216. Fiona MacCarthy and Patrick Nuttgens, *An Eye for Industry*, London: Lund Humphries, 1986.

Garouste, Elizabeth (1949–) and **Mattia Bonetti** (1953–)
▶ French and Italian furniture designers. Garouste: born Paris; active Marcilly, Eure. Bonetti: born Lugano; active Paris.
▶ Garouste studied École Camondo, Paris; trained as a theater and costume designer. Bonetti studied Centro Scolastico per l'Industria Artistica, Italy.
▶ Garouste began collaborating on design with her husband, painter Gérard Garouste; designed stage sets and costumes for Fernando Arrabal; was a stylist for Marie Berani; collaborated with Andrée Putman. Bonetti was a photographer and had an interest in textiles. Garouste commissioned Bonetti to redesign the graphics and window displays for her parents' store. In the early 1980s, they had as their first commission the decoration (with Gérard Garouste) of Le Privilège restaurant in Le Palace nightclub, Paris; launched their collaboration with their first series of *objets primitifs* and *objets barbares* first shown in 1981 at the interior-design firm Jansen. The sobriquet 'New Barbarians' originated with their 1981 *Chaise Barbare* of iron and horsehide, 1981 *Cage Haute* étagère, 1981 *Table à Onze Pieds*, and 1983 *Lampadaire Tripode*, all produced by Néotù. In 1982, they designed sets and costumes for *On loge la nuit café à l'eau* at Théâtre National de Chaillot, Paris; participated in 1983 revue *L'Ennemie* at Centre Georges Pompidou, Paris. Their 1984 *Console Menhie*, 1985 *Lampe Napoli*, 1985 *Chaise Prince Impérial*, 1986 *Table Bronze* coffee table, 1988 *Armoire Cathédrale*, 1988 *Semainier Arc en Ciel* cabinet, and 1988 *Le Jour et La Nuit* armchair were all produced by Néotù. They designed 1987 furniture and interiors for Christian Lacroix's clothing salon, rue du Faubourg Saint-Honoré, where they combined primitive styles with the baroque; 1987 Restaurant Géopoly, rue du Faubourg Montmartre; Hachette offices, boulevard St. Michel, and offices of publishers J.C. Lattes. At Centre de Recherche sur le Verre (CIRVA), they studied the possibilities of using glassware

in their furniture models; were closely associated with La Manufacture Nationale de Sèvres, from which their 1988 *Cabinet de Sèvres* was inspired; in 1989, designed *Trapani Collection* glassware and a dinner service for Daum; in 1990, produced cosmetics packaging designs for Nina Ricci, bedroom and living room decor and furnishings in Princess Gloria von Thurn und Taxis's castle in Bavaria in a sunflower theme accented in violet, and the restaurant entry and bookstore at the castle. Anthologie Quartett marketed the restaurant furnishings. Garouste and Bonetti's 1991 case goods, chair, and table in bamboo and unfinished wood were produced in signed limited editions by Lou Fagotin. In 1991, Daum produced their crystal and ceramics.
▶ Work first shown at Jansen, Paris, in 1981, with subsequent two-person exhibitions in Paris at Galerie Claudine Bréguet in 1983 and VIA center in 1984. 1981 *Chaise barbare* sponsored by VIA and shown in its gallery in 1984. Work subject of exhibitions at Furniture of the 20th Century Gallery, New York, 1985 and 1988; Bordeaux Musée des Arts Décoratifs, 1985; Galerie Néotù in Paris, numerous exhibitions from 1985; Mairie de Villeurbanne, 1987; David Gill Gallery, London, 1988. Work shown at 1983 'La Table,' Loggione Archivolto, Milan; 1985 'Onze Lampes,' Galerie Néotù, Paris; 1985 'Vivre en couleurs,' Fondation Cartier, Jouy en Josas; 1985 'Suzanne est au Salon,' École des Beaux Arts, Dunkerque; 1985 Salon, Société des Artistes Décorateurs, Paris; 1986 'Design Beyond Senses,' Kunstmuseum, Düsseldorf; 1986 'Neo Primitivism,' Shiseido department store, Tokyo; 1986 Salone di Gioie, Milan; 1988 'The Most Contemporary French Design,' Victoria and Albert Museum, London; 1988 'VIA et la Révolution,' Grande Halle de la Villette, Paris; 1988 'Design français 1960—1990: Trois décennies,' Centre Georges Pompidou, Paris; gallery of art, Seibu store, Tokyo. Received 1989 Carte Blanche award from VIA for *Patchwork* collection. Designed 1987 'Vraiment Faux' exhibition, Fondation Cartier, reorganized as 1991 traveling exhibition of the same name. Work shown regularly at Néotù, Paris, and subject of the gallery's initial 1990 exhibition opening its New York branch. Twig furniture for Lou Fagotin introduced at 1990 Salon du Meuble, Paris.
▶ 'Prehistoric Furniture,' *The New York Times*, October 15, 1981. Sophie Anargyros, *Intérieurs 80*, Paris: Regard, 1983. François Baudot, 'Une soirée manifeste néo-moderne,' *Beaux Arts*, No. 4, 1983. Sophie Anargyros, *Le Style des Années 80*, Paris: Rivages, 1986. Cat., Margo Rouard Snowman, *The Most Contemporary French Furniture*, London: Victoria and Albert Museum, 1988. Arlene Hirst, *Metropolitan Home*, April 1990:119. Suzanne Tise, 'Innovators at the Museum,' *Vogue Décoration*, No. 26, June/July 1990:46. Heidi Ellison, *Elle Decor*, October 1990:156—161. Michel Avelin, *Elizabeth and Mattia Bonetti*, 1990. 'Hot Properties,' *House and Garden*, May 1991:28.

Garrard
▶ British goldsmiths and jewelers; located London.
▶ Garrard was founded in London in 1721 and later appointed as court jewelers. In 1753, jeweler-silversmith George Wickes received his first royal appointment from Frederick, Prince of Wales. In 1747, Wickes took on partner Edward Wakelin and the firm subsequently became Wakelin and Tayler. In 1792, Robert Garrard became a partner of Edward Wakelin's son John, who took control of the firm in 1802. When Robert Garrard died in 1818, his sons Robert, James, and Sebastian managed the family business. The son of J.B.C. Odiot, jeweler to Napoleon I, was sent to study English craftsmanship at Garrard's. Robert Garrard the younger directed the firm throughout Victorian period. In 1843, when Garrard replaced Rundell and Bridge as the crown jewelers, it produced a number of commissions for Queen Victoria and Prince Albert. Best known for its fine precious stones, Garrard continued to serve the royal family up to today. Its Florence Nightingale jewelry and the collar and badge of the Order of the Star of India, shown at the 1862 International Exhibition, were designed by Prince Albert. Despite avant-garde designs in the 1950s, Garrard is a conservative house, selling antique wares

alongside its own designs. The business was managed by the descendants of Robert Garrard until 1952, when it was consolidated with the Goldsmiths' and Silversmiths' Company.
▶ Work shown at 1851 London 'Great Exhibition of the Works of Industry of All Nations' and London 'International Exhibition of 1862.'
▶ *Garrards, 1721–1911*, London: 1911. Charlotte Gere, *American and European Jewelry 1830–1914*, New York: Crown, 1975:147,184–85. Melissa Gabardi, *Les Bijoux des Années 50*, Paris: Amateur, 1987.

Gascoin, Marcel   (1907–86)
▶ French furniture designer and decorator.
▶ Studied architecture, École Nationale Supérieure des Arts Décoratifs, Paris, under Henri Sauvage.
▶ From 1950, he designed furniture in wood; specialized in furniture arrangements; developed a theory of the organization of living-spaces; in 1931, became a member of UAM (Union des Artistes Modernes). Many young designers, including Pierre Guariche, Pierre Paulin, Michel Mortier, and René-Jean Caillette, worked in Gascoin's *bureau d'études* after World War II.
▶ Work shown at 1930 (I) exhibition of UAM where he met Robert Mallet-Stevens; 1934 competition designing cabins of steel oceanliners organized by OTUA (Office Technique pour l'Utilisation de l'Acier); 1936 competition of school furniture; 1949–50 (I) 'Formes Utiles' exhibition, Pavillon de Marsan, Paris; 1956 (I) Triennale d'Art français Contemporain, Paris; in 1947, in charge of presenting seven apartments, 'Urbanisme et Habitation' exhibition, Grand Palais, Paris.
▶ Renée Moutard-Uldry, 'Marcel Gascoin,' *Art et Décoration*, Vol. LXVI, 1937. Marie-Anne Febvre-Desportes, 'Rationalisme Pratique et Fantaisie Démonstrative, Marcel Gascoin,' *Art et Décoration*, No. 4, 1947. Yolande Amic, *Intérieurs: Le Mobilier français 1945–1964*, Paris: Regard, 1983. Arlette Barré-Despond, *UAM*, Paris: Regard, 1986:404–05. Cat., *Les années UAM 1929–1958*, Paris: Musée des Arts Décoratifs, 1988:129.

Gaskin, Arthur Joseph   (1862–1928) and Georgina Gaskin   (b. Georgina Evelyn Frances Cave   1868–1934)
▶ Gaskin: British painter, illustrator, silversmith, and jeweler. Cave: British illustrator, silversmith, jeweler, and enamelist. Both active Birmingham
▶ Both studied Birmingham School of Art.
▶ Gaskin was a member of the group of staff and students of Birmingham School of Art known as the Birmingham Group of Painters and Craftsmen; met the silversmith and illustrator Georgina Cave at the school. They married in 1894, and in 1899 set up a joint metalworking workshop. Arthur Gaskin's jewel design style was based on curled gold- and silver-wire tendrils decorated with leaves and flowers set with colored semi-precious stones. They were influenced by the Pre-Raphaelites, several of whom were their friends, and were influenced by Eastern jewelry forms; later on, absorbed the style of metalsmith John Paul Cooper, whose work amalgamated medieval, Indian and Japanese motifs. From c1910, Arthur Gaskin applied bird motifs; employed the same style for the *Cymric* range of jewelry he designed for Liberty; collaborated with W.R. Blackband in c1912 on spiral forms inspired by British Iron Age jewelry; 1902–24, was head, Vittoria Street School of Jewellers and Silversmiths, Birmingham, replacing R. Catterson-Smith. The Gaskins were members of Birmingham Guild of Handicrafters.
▶ Work (simple jewelry) shown at 1899 exhibition of Arts and Crafts Exhibition Society, London, and afterwards; 26 pieces shown at 1901 'International Studio Exhibition.' Participated in numerous exhibitions with the Birmingham Guild of Handicrafts.
▶ Charlotte Gere, *American and European Jewelry 1830–1914*, New York: Crown, 1975:185–86. Toni Lesser Wolf, 'Women Jewelers of the British Arts and Crafts Movement,' *Journal of Decorative and Propaganda Arts*, No. 14, Fall 1989:38.

Gate, Simon   (1883–1945)
▶ Swedish artist-craftsman; born S. Fågelås, Saragorg.
▶ 1902–09, studied Konstfackskolan and Tekniska Skolan, Stockholm; from c1909, Kungliga Konsthögskolan, Stockholm.
▶ In 1915, Gate and Edward Hald became the first artists appointed at the Orrefors Glasbruk. Gate was associated with the firm's inexpensive Modern designs, as well as collectors' items until his death; in the 1920s, (with Hald and glass-blower Knut Bergqvist) developed the *graal* technique (patterns within glass). *Graal* art glass was produced by covering a thick layer of clear glass with a thin colored layer cut away to reveal the clear background, then heated to lend a smooth appearance, and covered with another layer of clear glass before being blown into a final shape. In his three decades at Orrefors, Gate designed a wide variety of utilitarian and decorative glass.
▶ Work shown internationally including 1917 'Ideal Homes Exhibition,' Liljevach's Art Gallery, Stockholm (organized by the Svenskska Slöjdforeningen); 1925 Paris 'Exposition Internationale des Arts Décoratifs et Industriels Modernes.'
▶ Arthur Hald (ed.), *Simon Gate, Edward Hald en Skildring av människorna och konstnärliga*, Stockholm: Norstedt, 1948. Cat., David Revere McFadden (ed.), *Scandinavian Modern Design 1880–1980*, New York: Abrams, 1982:263, Nos. 78–80,82. Penny Sparke, *Introduction to Design and Culture in the Twentieth Century*, London: Allen and Unwin, 1986. Jennifer Hawkins Opie, *Scandinavia: Ceramics and Glass in the Twentieth Century*, New York: Rizzoli, 1989.

Gates Potteries, The
▶ American pottery manufacturer; located Terra Cotta, Illinois.
▶ The Gates Pottery, a subsidiary of the American Terra Cotta and Ceramic Company, was founded in 1881 by William Day Gates. The pottery produced plain, undecorated garden pottery which it continued to make throughout its history; in 1895, added green-glazed Teco (from *terracotta*) ware to its production of tiles and decorative architectural items. Frank Lloyd Wright, William LeBaron Jenney, Max Dunning, William B. Mundie, Howard Van Doren Shaw, and Hugh M.G. Gardner executed designs for Gates which they used in their Prairie School interiors. Teco was established to produce inexpensive art ware cast from molds. The shapes, styles, and motifs were influenced by aquatic plants and classical motifs and reflected the architectonic forms of the Prairie School. Chief chemist Elmer Groton developed a matt glaze with a lustrous, waxy texture varying from silvery pale green to deep moss green. Rose, gray, blue, gold, yellow, four brown, and several new green matt glazes were added in 1910. Sold through its own offices, showrooms, mail-order catalogs, and magazine advertisements, the line grew to over 500 shapes. After 1912, the pottery's activities were cut back due to falling sales, and, in 1922, art pottery production was discontinued. The plant closed in 1930 when the parent firm was sold.
▶ Teco first shown in 1900. Received highest honors at 1904 St. Louis 'Louisiana Purchase Exposition.'
▶ William D. Gates, 'The Revival of the Potter's Art,' *Clay-Worker*, No. 28, Oct. 1897:275–76. 'The Potter's Art: Teco Ware,' *Fine Arts Journal*, No. 14, Jan. 1902:8–11. Sharon S. Darling, *Chicago Ceramics and Glass: An Illustrated History from 1871 to 1933*, Chicago: Chicago Historical Society/University of Chicago, 1979. Cat., *American Art Pottery*, New York: Cooper-Hewitt Museum, 1987:90–91. Cat., Ann Yaffe Phillips, *From Architecture to Object*, New York: Hirschl and Adler, 1989:98.

Gatti, Paolini, Teodoro
▶ Italian graphic and industrial design collaboration.
▶ Piero Gatti (1940–), Cesare Paolini (1937–), and Franco Teodoro (1939–) set up a design studio in Turin in 1965. Their 1970 *Sacco* bean-bag seat filled with polyurethane pellets was an example of Anti-Design's rebellion against conventional furniture and furnishings. Produced by Zanotta, it was the ultimate in flexible form; its producer claimed that twelve million plastic granules

208

adapted instantly to the sitter's body, giving firm support. It was covered in vinyl or leather and weighed 13 lb (6 kg).
▶ Cat., *Modern Chairs 1918–1970*, London: Lund Humphries, 1971. Victor Papanek, *Design for the Real World*, New York: 1974:103–04. *Moderne Klassiker: Möbel, die Geschichte machen*, Hamburg, 1982:91. Casciani Stefano, *Mobili come Architetture: Il Disegno della Prudzione Zanotta*, Milan, 1984:160. Cat., Kathryn B. Hiesinger and George H. Marcus III (eds.), *Design Since 1945*, Philadelphia: Philadelphia Museum of Art, 1983.

Gauchat, Pierre (1902–56)
▶ Swiss graphic and theater designer; born Zürich.
▶ Studied Kunstgewerbeschule, Munich, under F. H. Ehmcke, 1921; graphic design, Kunstgewerbeschule, Zürich, under E. Keller, Otto Baumberger, and E. Würtenberger, 1922.
▶ He set up his own graphic design studio, Zürich in 1924; 1926–45, was teacher of drawing, Kunstgewerbeschule, Zürich; from 1930, was considered one of the best Swiss graphic artists of book covers and illustrations, typography, advertising brochures, programs, logos, posters, stamps, bank notes, and exhibitions, as well as carpet designs. He created stage sets and costumes for operas, operettas, and plays, and numerous marionettes for the Zürcher-Marionettentheater, of which he was co-founder and artistic director. For many years, Gauchat was responsible for all printed material at the furniture manufacturer Embru, Rüti; until 1935, designed posters, advertisements, and brochures for Wohnbedarf department store, Zürich.
▶ *Künstler-Lexikon der Schweiz, XX Jahrhundert*, Frauenfeld, 1963–1967, Vol. 1. Friederike Mehlau-Wiebking et al., *Schweizer Typenmöbel 1925–35, Sigfried Giedion und die Wohnbedarf AG*, Zürich: gta, 1989:227.

Gaudenzi, Marco (1949–)
▶ Italian industrial designer; born and active Pesaro.
▶ Gaudenzi began his professional career in 1971; established studio Tamino Gaudenzi e Associati, Pesaro; became a member of ADI (Associazione per il Disegno Industriale). Designing furniture and lighting, clients included Bellazecca, Canestrari, Consorzio Pesaro Mobili, Effebi, Fastigi, and Gruppo Misa.
▶ *ADI Annual 1976*, Milan: Associazione per il Disegno Industriale, 1976.

Gaudernack, Gustav (1865–1914)
▶ Bohemian silversmith; active Norway.
▶ 1880–81, studied industrial design, Vocational School for Glass and Metal Industry; 1885–87, Ceramics Vocational School, Tetschen (now Děčín, Czech Republic); 1888–91, Kunstgewerbeschule, Vienna.
▶ In 1891, Gaudernack settled in Norway; in 1891, designed glassware for Christiania Glasmagasin; 1892–10, was artistic director of metalwork, David-Andersen firm, Kristiania (now Oslo). Gaudernack arrived at a new technique, making it possible to produce large objects in *plique-à-jour* enamel on which finely detailed naturalistic motifs were produced; in 1910 in Kristiania, set up his workshop, producing silver, filigree, and enamel; from 1912, taught at Statens Håndverks -og Kunstindustriskole, Kristiania.
▶ Received a silver medal at 1900 Paris 'Exposition Universelle'; a grand prize (with David Andersen) at 1904 'Louisiana Purchase Exposition,' St. Louis, and gold medal at 1914 'Centenary Exhibition,' Frogner, Kristiania. Work shown at 1898 exhibition, Bergen, and 1907 Salon, Paris.
▶ Alf Bøe, 'Gustav Gaudernack, Tegninger og utførte arbeider,' in *Kunstindustrimuseet i Oslo Årbok*, 1959–62:41–72. *Gustav Gaudernack en europeer i norsk jugend*, Oslo: Utgitt av Kunstindustrimuseet Oslo, 1979. Cat., David Revere McFadden (ed.), *Scandinavian Modern Design 1880–1980*, New York: Abrams, 1982:263, Nos. 5,20,21,23. Annelies Krekel-Aalberse, *Art Nouveau and Art Déco Silver*, New York: Abrams, 1989:242–43.

Gaudí i Cornet, Antonio (1852–1926)
▶ Spanish architect and designer; born Reus.
▶ 1873–78, studied architecture, Escola Superior d'Arquitectura, Barcelona.
▶ At the Barcelona architecture school, he was influenced by the Gothic revival tradition; admired Eugène-Emmanuel Viollet-le-Duc's *Entretiens sur l'architecture*; like other Catalan architects of the last quarter of the 19th century, benefited from the lack of an architectural tradition in Barcelona (excluding the Catalonian Gothic style). His cast-iron lamp designs of 1879 showed an interest in metalwork; father was a metalworker. His idiosyncratic version of Art Nouveau evolved in 1878–85 Casa Vicens and 1885–89 Palau Güell, both in Barcelona and influenced by Arabian art. His 1900–02 crypt and transept of the cathedral of La Sagrada Familia, sculptural and unfinished, represents his most visionary work and shows the influence of medieval art. His fondness for *objets trouvés* can be seen in the stucco façades where he incorporated broken tiles and pot sherds. He brought to his architecture his talents for sculpture, painting, ironsmithing, ceramics, mosaics, and furniture making; reflecting the influence of the Art Nouveau movement, he had an interest in new materials; designing site-specific furniture and furnishings, considered every element of a building down to its most minute details, like Henry van de Velde in Bloemenwerf, and Hector Guimard in Castel Béranger; pursued this attention to detail in the partitions and furniture for the ground floor of 1898–1900 Casa Calvet, the bone-like asymmetrical forms of the furniture and furnishings for the first floor of Casa Battló of c1907, and the benches in the crypt of 1898–1914 Colonia Güell church, Santa Coloma de Cervelló, near Barcelona. Gaudí exerts a continuing influence on Barcelona's architects. The 1902–04 chair for the Calvet apartment house, reissued in limited production in the 1980s, is possibly his most recognizable piece of furniture design.
▶ Drawings subject of 1977 exhibition, New York.
▶ J.F. Ráfols and R. Folguera, *Gaudí: el gran arquitecto español*, Barcelona, 1928. J. Bergós, *Gaudí: l'home i l'obra*, Barcelona, 1954. J. Perucho, *Gaudí una Arquitectura de Anticipación*, Barcelona, 1967. G.R. Collins, *A Bibliography of Antonio Gaudí and the Catalan Movement 1870–1930*, Charlottesville, 1973. J.A. Wideman, *Gaudí: Inspiration in Architektur und Handwerk*, Munich, 1974. Yvonne Brunhammer et al., *Art Nouveau Belgium, France*, Houston: Rice University, 1976. Cat., G.R. Collins, *The Drawings of Antonio Gaudí*, New York, 1977.

Gauguin, Jean (1881–1961)
▶ French ceramicist.
▶ The son of Paul Gauguin, he worked for Bing & Grøndahl Porcelaensfabrik.

Gauguin, Paul (1848–1903)
▶ French painter, sculptor, and graphic and decorative designer; born Paris.
▶ Gauguin is best known for his paintings of women in the South Seas; was the leader of the Pont-Aven artists' group and one of the painters who became involved in the decorative arts at the end of the 19th century; designed a large number of ceramic pieces, carved furniture, and other decorative items, and produced a small group of wooden vessels. Gauguin's career can be divided into three periods. During the first and most prolific, covering 1886–87, he worked in the ceramics studio of Ernest Chaplet, rue Blomet, Paris. On cylindrical vases and cups, Gauguin's signature appeared with Chaplet's and Haviland's marks. He produced motifs in *cloisonné* with gold highlights. Other pieces were less successfully hand molded. Gauguin's second period was begun with his return to Paris from Martinique in 1887. At the rue Blomet studio, he worked with Auguste Delaherche, who had taken over the premises from Chaplet. Departing further and further from traditional ceramics in his forms, Gauguin now spent more time on technique, clay composition, and glazes. With most of his completed pieces given to his family in Copenhagen and friends, he had little success with sales. In his third period, 1889–90, he

was attracted to sculpture and, except for stoneware executed *c*1893–95, abandoned ceramics altogether.

▶ Yvonne Brunhammer et al., *Art Nouveau Belgium, France*, Houston: Rice University, 1976, biblio.

Gautier, Gustave

▶ French decorator and furniture designer.

▶ Active around the 1950s, Gautier's workshop was located at 42 rue Rouelle, Paris, by 1954. His interiors included a country house in Britain.

▶ *Ensembles Mobiliers*, Paris: Charles Moreau, No. 48, 1954.

Gautier-Delaye, Pierre   (1923–)

▶ French industrial designer and decorator; active Paris.

▶ 1947–51, studied École Nationale Supérieure des Arts Décoratifs, Paris.

▶ 1951–58, he was director of the interior design department, CEI Raymond Loewy, Paris; in 1958, set up his own design office at 99 rue Saint-Honoré, Paris and was active in interior, product, and graphic design; designed furniture produced by Vergnières, sanitary fixtures by Jacob Delafon, Air France offices worldwide, and packaging for Formica.

▶ Received 1956 René Gabriel Prize.

▶ *Ensembles Mobiliers*, Paris: Charles Moreau, No. 33, 1954.

Gautrait, Lucien

▶ French jewelry designer and maker.

▶ Gautrait was active during the Art Nouveau period at the turn of the 20th century; is attributed with having worked for Maison Vever, Paris; is better known for being the chief engraver at Gariod's, where he made pendants and brooches.

▶ Yvonne Brunhammer et al., *Art Nouveau Belgium, France*, Houston: Rice University, 1976, biblio.

Gavina, Dino   (1932–)

▶ Italian furniture entrepreneur.

▶ Dino Gavina founded the firm Gavina in Foligno in 1960 as a subsidiary of his Dino Gavina company. Architect-designer Carlo Scarpa was appointed its titular president. The designs of Franco Albini and the earlier 1920s models of Marcel Breuer were reproduced. Breuer's 1928 *B32* chair, renamed *Cesca* (after Breuer's daughter Francesca), became highly successful in mass production and was followed by the reissue of the 1925 *Wassily* chair, 1924 *Laccio* tables, 1935 bentwood chaise, and 1955 *Canaan* desk. Its most distinguished Neo-Liberty design was the 1959 *Sanluca* armchair by the Castiglioni brothers with its curvaceous form. Gavina produced the *Tomasa* folding chair, taken from a 15th-century painting by Paolo Uccello. Having met Kazuhide Takahama at 1954 (X) Triennale di Milano, Gavina commissioned him to design furniture for the firm, starting with 1965 *Marcel*, *Raymond*, and *Suzanne* sofas. The firm produced the 1966 *Malitte* seating configuration designed by Sebastian Matta. Designers included Ignazio Gardella, Tobia Scarpa, Renzo Masetti, Vico Magistretti, and Marco Zanuso with Richard Sapper. In 1962, Gavina formed Flos for lighting manufacture with board members Maria Simoncini and Cesare Cassina. In 1968, Gavina was bought by Knoll International, and Gavina established Simón International to produce furniture.

▶ Virgilio Vercelloni, *The Adventure of Design: Gavina*, New York: Rizzoli, 1987. Cat., Leslie Jackson, *The New Look: Design in the Fifties*, New York: Thames and Hudson, 1991:127.

Gavoille, Kristian   (1956–)

▶ French architect and furniture designer; born Brazzaville (now Republic of the Congo); active Paris.

▶ Studied architecture, Toulouse.

▶ He settled in Paris in 1984; 1984–86, collaborated with several architecture firms in Toulouse and Paris and worked at Services d'Architecture de la Ville de Paris (government architecture office), Paris; from 1986, collaborated with Philippe Starck on numerous projects; designed 1986 group of table-service objects for Château de Belle Fontaine, Paris. In 1987, a prototype project was sup-

ported by VIA. From 1988, he produced furniture designs for Disform and Néotù, and theater sets in 1988 and 1989. His 1988 *Table Divine*, 1988 *Guéridon Divine*, and 1989 *Athéo* armchair were produced by Néotù.

▶ Work first shown at Disform and Néotù stands, 1988 Salone del Mobile Italiano.

▶ Odile Filion, *Archi Crée*, May 1988. *Design Français*, Paris: Flammarion, 1988. *Intramuros*, February and July 1988.

GDA

▶ French design studio.

▶ GDA was a collaboration around the turn of the century of Gérard, Dufraisseix, and Abbot in Limoges, and one of the oldest ceramics houses there; successor to a firm founded in 1797 by François Alluaud, it was directed 1877–81 by Charles Field Haviland, a cousin of Charles and Théodore Haviland of Haviland & Co who married into the Alluaud family; was taken over by Gérard, Dufraisseix, and Morel in 1882. Morel withdrew in 1890 to experiment with high-fired decoration. The studio operated under the name Gérard, Dufraisseix & Co until it assumed the name GDA in 1900, when Abbot, an American, became a director managing its activities in USA. From 1901, GDA produced ceramics for Siegfried Bing's L'Art Nouveau, Paris.

▶ Yvonne Brunhammer et al., *Art Nouveau Belgium, France*, Houston: Rice University, 1976, biblio.

GDV (Girault, Demay et Vignolet)

▶ French ceramics firm; located Bruère.

▶ GDV was founded in 1877, by merchant Louis Girault, ceramicist Claude Demay, and merchant Jean Vignolet.

▶ Work shown at 1889 Paris 'Exposition Universelle.' Received a gold medal at 1900 Paris 'Exposition Universelle.'

▶ *Europäische Keramik, 1880–1930*, Darmstadt: Hessisches Landesmuseum, 1986:101.

Gecchelin, Bruno   (1939–)

▶ Italian architect-designer; born Milan.

▶ Studied architecture, Politecnico di Milano.

▶ Beginning his professional career in 1962, he worked for many major firms; designed lighting for O-Luce, furniture for Busnelli and Frau, refrigerators and gas stoves for Indesit, glassware for Venini, items for Skipper and Fratelli Guzzini, 1989 *Atelier 75* range of four kitchen utensils, and 1987–88 *Shuttle* range of track lighting. The *Atelier 75* range was designed to commemorate the 75th anniversary of the founding of Guzzini. With Ettore Sottsass, he designed the Fiat *Coima* camper, Fiat *Panda* automobile, and Olivetti typewriters, calculators and computer terminals. Clients included Bazzani, Arteluce, Fiat, and Venini.

▶ The 1970 Olivetti *MC27* calculator, on which Gecchelin worked, received Premio Compasso d'Oro.

▶ Robert A.M. Stern (ed.), *The International Design Yearbook*, New York: Abbeville, 1985/1986: Nos. 194, 235. Albrecht Bangert and Karl Michael Armer, *80s Style: Designs of the Decade*, New York: Abbeville, 1990:97,230. Jeremy Myerson and Sylvia Katz, *Conran Design Guides: Kitchenware*, London: Conran Octopus, 1990:44,74.

Geddes, Norman Bel   (b. Norman Melancton Geddes 1893–1958)

▶ American industrial and theatrical designer; born Adrian, Michigan; active New York.

▶ Studied Art Institute of Chicago and in Cleveland, *c*1908.

▶ He worked first as an advertising draftsman, Detroit, in 1913, and, after six months, became an art director; in 1916, wrote a play, following which he designed six theatrical productions in Los Angeles, the first being Zoe Akins's *Papa*; designed over 200 plays and operas, including the renowned setting for Max Reinhardt's *The Miracle*; in 1918, was stage designer for the Metropolitan Opera Company, New York; in 1925, went to Hollywood and designed film sets for Cecil B. De Mille and D.W. Griffith; produced, directed and designed plays including *Jeanne D'Arc* with Eva Le Gallienne, Paris, and *Lysistrata* with Miriam Hopkins and

Fay Bainter, Hollywood; in 1927, became an 'industrial designer.' His technologically-orientated outlook was expressed in his book *Horizon* (1932), stylishly bound in blue and silver cloth, and in his and Otto Koller's model for 1929 *Super Airliner 4*; he designed 1932 interiors for J. Walter Thompson, 1929 stoves for SGE, scales for Toledo, 1931 radios for Philco, an automobile for Graham Page, radio cabinets for RCA, 1929 metal bedroom furniture for Simmons, and innovative 1928–30 windows for Franklin Simon department store, New York; became an influential prophet predicting, for example, the automobile freeway system, and the popularity of air conditioning. His work in standardization for home furnishing equipment, especially in the kitchen, was pioneering. In the 1930s, Eero Saarinen was his pupil, and he employed Eliot Noyes, who worked on the early IBM electric typewriter design. An exponent of Streamline styling, Geddes was the first of the consultant designers to gain public recognition when a profile of him appeared in a 1930 issue of magazine *Fortune*. Geddes's autobiography *Miracle in the Evening* (with William Kelley) (1960) was published posthumously.

▶ Designed General Motors' 'Futurama' building and interior display, 1939 'New York World's Fair,' resulting in his book *Magic Motorways* (1940).

▶ Lewis Mumford (obituary), *The New York Times*, 28 Jan. 1990:30. Arthur Pulos, 'Norman Bel Geddes' in Mel Byars and Russell Flinchum (eds.), *50 American Designers, 1918–1968*, Washington: Preservation, 1994.

Gefle Porslinsfabrik

▶ Swedish porcelain factory.

▶ Gefle was established in 1910 at Gävle on the same site as earlier tileworks O. Forsell Kakel-och Fajansfabrik; in 1913, was reorganized, with designer Arthur Percy working there; became known for its well-designed table and decorative wares; in 1936, was bought by Upsala-Ekeby group; closed in 1979.

▶ Jennifer Hawkins Opie, *Scandinavia: Ceramics and Glass in the Twentieth Century*, New York: Rizzoli, 1989.

Gehl, Ebbe (1942–)

▶ Danish furniture designer.

▶ 1963–66, studied Kunsthåndvaerkskolen, Copenhagen.

▶ 1959–63, Gehl worked for Rud. Rasmussen; 1966–67, collaborated with Nanna Ditzel; 1967–69, taught at Edinburgh College of Art; in 1970, set up an architecture office with Søren Nissen. Furniture designs were produced by Carl Hansen & Søn, Sannemanns Møbelfabrik, A. Mikael Laursen, and Jeki.

▶ Work shown at 1975 Danish furniture exhibition, Berlin, and 1976 'SCAN' exhibition, Washington.

▶ Frederik Sieck, *Nutidig Dansk Møbeldesign: -en kortfattet illustreret beskrivelse*, Copenhagen: Bondo Gravesen; 1990 Busck edition in English.

Gehle, Carl (1884–1951)

▶ German silversmith; active Hagen.

▶ Gehle produced Modern silver designs in the 1920s and 1930s.

▶ Annelies Krekel-Aalberse, *Art Nouveau and Art Déco Silver*, New York: Abrams, 1989:254.

Gehry, Frank O. (b. Frank Goldberg 1930–)

▶ Canadian architect, designer, and artist; born Toronto; active Los Angeles.

▶ 1949–51 and 1954, studied architecture, University of California in Los Angeles; 1956–57, Graduate School of Design, Harvard University.

▶ For a time, he was professor of design at Yale and Harvard universities; was influenced by Richard Neutra, Rudolf Schindler, and the Case Study Program sponsored by journal *Arts + Architecture*, which included Charles Eames's own 1949 house, Santa Monica, California; early on, produced commercial drawings for developer John Postman. His architectural drawings were rendered in a deliberately crude style. In 1954, he designed Wright-like furniture for dayrooms, Fort Benning, Georgia. 1953–54, he was architectural designer, Victor Gruen Associates; 1955–56, planner and designer, Robert and Company Architects, Atlanta; in 1957, architectural designer and planner, Hideo Sasaki Associates, Boston; 1957–58, architectural designer, Pereira and Luckman, Los Angeles; 1958–61, planner, designer, and project director, Victor Gruen Associates; and, in 1961, project designer and planner, André Remondet, Paris. In 1961, Gehry set up Frank O. Gehry Associates, Los Angeles, where, from the beginning, he was assisted by Greg Walsh; in the mid-1970s, came to public notice with the design of his own Santa Monica home; collaborated with artists Claes Oldenburg and Richard Serra and designed stage sets for choreographer Lucinda Childs. Widely published, his furniture and architecture attempted to be sculptural in form with minimal construction and inexpensive industrial materials. 1969–73, he produced corrugated cardboard furniture. His best known furniture designs included *Easy Edges* corrugated paper chairs, designed and produced from 1972, and reissued in 1982 as *Rough Edges* in a less rigid and more plastic interpretation. In 1987, models of the paper chairs were produced in limited quantities by Vitra. He designed the 1987 *Bubbles* lounge chair. In the mid-1970s, real-estate firm Rouse Company was his main client, for which he executed designs for housing, shopping malls, and its corporate headquarters, Columbia, Maryland. In 1976, he became a proponent of Deconstructivist architecture; in 1983, created his first 'fish-light,' commissioned by Formica in ColorCore plastic laminate. In 1984, Formica produced his *Ryba* fish lamps as well as his *Snake* lamps. The fish was a recurring theme since childhood and his astrological sign. Gehry was snubbed when the addition to Los Angeles County Museum of Art was commissioned from Hardy Holzman Pfeiffer Associates, and the Museum of Contemporary Art from Arata Isozaki; in 1991, he created a collection of furniture in woven wooden strips for Knoll and designed the limited-edition fish-form hand-blown goblet produced by Swid-Powell. Architects who worked in his office included Thom Mayne and Michael Rotundi of Morphosis, and Frank Israel. His exhibition designs included 1968 exhibition of the work of Billy Al Bengston, Los Angeles County Museum of Art; 1980 'The Avant-Garde in Russia, 1910–1930,' Los Angeles County Museum of Art; and 1986 Pitti Uomo menswear collection, Florence and Turin. Buildings included 1962 studio and house of graphic designer Lou Danziger; 1972 corrugated-metal house and studio of artist Ron Davis, Malibu, California; building for his own office and for artist Chuck Arnoldi, Venice, California; 1976–79 studio and gallery for print publisher Gemini Graphic Editions, Los Angeles; 1978 Wagner house (unrealized), Malibu; 1978 Familian house (unrealized), Santa Monica; his own 1978–79 house alteration, Santa Monica; 1983 Norton house, Venice, California; 1983 'Temporary Contemporary' building, Museum of Contemporary Art, Los Angeles; 1983–84 California Aerospace Museum, Exposition Park, Los Angeles; 1986 Sirmai-Peterson house, Thousand Oaks, California; 1986 Information and Computer Sciences (Engineering Research Lab), University of California in Irvine, California; 1987 Fish Dance Restaurant, Kobe (Japan); 1989 Vitra Design Museum and Vitra factory, Weil am Rhein (Germany); Walt Disney Concert Hall of c1989, Los Angeles; 1991 Chiat/Day/Mojo building, Venice, California; 1991 Vitra building, Basel; 1991 retail center, Vila Olimpica, Barcelona; 1992 American Center, Paris; 1992–93 Entertainment Center, Euro Disneyland, Marne-la-Vallée.

▶ Received numerous awards including 1989 Pritzker Prize. Was a fellow, American Institute of Architects. Work subject of 1986 'The Architecture of Frank Gehry' traveling exhibition in USA and 1991 'Projets en Europe,' Centre Georges Pompidou, Paris. Chairs shown at 1972 (*Easy Edges* chairs) and 1982 (*Rough Edges* chairs) exhibitions, Max Protetch Gallery, New York; 1983–84 'Design Since 1945' exhibition, Philadelphia Museum of Art. Work shown at 1974 'Contemporary Home Environs' exhibition, La Jolla Museum of Contemporary Art, California; 1982 'Shape and Environment: Furniture by American Architects,' Whitney Museum of

American Art, Fairfield County, Connecticut; 1981 'Collaboration' exhibition with Serra; 1984–85 exhibition of Formica ColorCore fish lighting, Metro Pictures, New York; 1985 performance, Venice, California, with Oldenburg; 1988 'Deconstruction Architecture' exhibition, New York Museum of Modern Art.
▶ 'Innovations: Easy Edges Does It,' *Architectural Forum*, No. 137, April 1972:69. 'Paper Currency,' *Industrial Design*, Vol. 19, May 1972:53. Cat., Jay Belloli, *Innovations: Contemporary Home Environs*, La Jolla, California: La Jolla Museum of Contemporary Art, 1974. Janet Nairn, 'Frank Gehry: the search for a "no rules" architecture,' *Architectural Record*, June 1976:95–102. Olivier Boissière, *Gehry, Site, Tigerman: Trois Portraits d'artiste en architecte*, Paris: Moniteur, 1981. Cat., Lisa Phillips (introduction), *Shape and Environment: Furniture by American Architects*, New York: Whitney Museum of American Art, 1982:34–35, fig. 23. Cat., Kathryn B. Hiesinger and George H. Marcus III (eds.), *Design Since 1945*, Philadelphia: Philadelphia Museum of Art, 1983. Peter Arnell and Ted Bickford, *Frank Gehry: Buildings and Projects*, New York: Rizzoli, 1985. Robert A.M. Stern (ed.), *The International Design Yearbook*, New York: Abbeville, 1985/1986: Nos. 154–55. Martin Filler, 'Maverick Master,' *House and Garden*, Nov. 1986: 208ff. John Howell, 'America in Paris,' *Elle Decor*, May 1990:50. Albrecht Bangert and Karl Michael Armer, *80s Style: Designs of the Decade*, New York: Abbeville, 1990:68–69,120,230. *Metropolitan Home*, September 1990:64. Paul Goldberger, 'Beyond the Master's Voice, Home Design,' *The New York Times Magazine*, 13 Oct. 1991:34.

Genêt et Michon
▶ French lighting manufacturers; located Paris.
▶ Philippe Genêt and Lucien Michon founded Genêt et Michon, the lighting, furniture, and chair manufacturer, in Paris in 1911. In 1919, the firm began to specialize in lighting, and produced fixtures for the Palais de l'Élysée, Paris, and for consulates and ministries. After extensive experiments, Genêt and Michon discovered that thick pressed glass multiplied reflections and increased the intensity of illumination more than thin glass of other forms. A mixture of silica, soda, and lime were melted at 1,300°F (700°C) and poured into a steel mold. The highly secret formula, unchanged until 1938, had no pigments added in order not to diminish brightness and glow. They sometimes etched press glass and combined it with crystal; sometimes incorporated glass beads into fixtures in the 19th-century manner; are credited with having introduced the illuminated ramps that bordered a room at 1925 Paris Exhibition; in the 1920s, were pioneers (with René Lalique and Jean Perzel) of the suspended illuminated sphere; produced ceiling *dalles*, lamps, lusters, wall brackets, epergnes, and illuminated friezes, tables, door architraves, cornices, vases, pilasters, and columns. By 1930, their complex designs incorporating bunches of grapes had given way to simpler forms with a more refined finish on their press glass. They designed lighting for the 1935 oceanliner *Normandie*, collaborated with decorators including Jacques-Émile Ruhlmann, Paul Follot, and Michel Dufrêne on lighting and glass, and produced numerous small Art Déco furniture pieces.
▶ Work (lighting fixtures and interiors) shown at 1922–38 Salons of Société des Artistes Décorateurs, 1922–24 sessions of Salon d'Automne, and others. Work shown at 1924 Grand Lighting Competition; 1923 (I) or 1925 (II) 'Esposizione Biennale delle Arti Decorative e Industriali Moderne'; 1934 (II) and 1935 (III) Salons of Light; Pavilion of Light, 1937 Paris 'Exposition Internationale des Arts et Techniques dans la Vie Moderne.'
▶ G. Henriot, *Luminaire Moderne*, 1937: Plates 20–23. Alastair Duncan, *Art Nouveau and Art Déco Lighting*, New York: Simon and Schuster, 1978:170–71. Pierre Kjellberg, *Art Déco: les maîtres du Mobilier, le décor des Paquebots*, Paris: Amateur, 1986:78–79.

Genevrière, Marcel   (1885–1967)
See Dominique

Génisset, Jean-Pierre   (1911–)
▶ French furniture designer; active Paris.
▶ Studied École des Arts Appliqués and École Nationale Supérieure des Arts Décoratifs, both Paris.
▶ In 1936, he joined La Crémaillère; from 1941, worked with friend André Renou.

Gensoli, Maurice   (1892–)
▶ Algerian ceramicist; born Oran.
▶ Trained under a master glassmaker in Oran.
▶ From 1921, Gensoli was a freelance designer, Manufacture Nationale de Sèvres; after the 1925 Paris 'Exposition Internationale des Arts Décoratifs et Industriels Modernes,' became chief of the decorating department, Sèvres.
▶ Work shown regularly at Salons of Société des Artistes Décorateurs and sessions of Salon d'Autmone. Received a number of prizes and diplomas.
▶ Yvonne Brunhammer, *Le Cinquantenaire de l'Exposition de 1925*, Paris: Musée des Arts Décoratifs, 1976:129, biblio.

Gentile, Thomas   (1936–)
▶ American jewelry designer; born Mansfield, Ohio.
▶ Work shown at 1981–82 'Good as Gold: Alternative Materials in American Jewelry,' Renwick Gallery, Washington; 1983 solo exhibition, The Gulbenkian Museum, Lisbon; 1985 Norton Art Gallery, West Palm Beach, Florida; 1986 Lowe Art Museum, University of Miami, Florida; 1986 Louisiana State Museum, New Orleans; 1986 Vancouver Museum, Vancouver; 1987 'Wally Gilbert/Thomas Gentile,' Victoria and Albert Museum, London; 1989 'Infinite Riches,' Museum of Fine Arts, St. Petersburg, Florida; 1989 'Ornamenta I,' Schmuckmuseum, Pforzheim (Germany); 1990 'American Dreams, American Extremes,' Museum Het Kruithuis, s'Hertogenbosch, and The Princinciaal Museum voor Moderne Kunst, Oostende. Received first prize (ornament) at 1984 International Jewelry Exhibition.

Gentleman, David   (1930–)
▶ British painter, graphic artist, and designer.
▶ 1947–48, studied St. Albans School of Art; 1950–53. Royal College of Art, London.
▶ He was active as a designer of wallpaper, postage stamps, and book illustrations, and known for his 1980s murals in the stations of the London Underground.
▶ Jonathan M. Woodham, *Twentieth-Century Ornament*, New York: Rizzoli, 1990:322.

Géo   (aka Roger Fenand   1890–)
▶ French decorator and furnituremaker; born La Ciotat.
▶ Active from the 1920s in Neuilly, near Paris, he designed furniture and suites in lacquer, his specialty; lighting; rugs in geometric motifs; and bent tubular-metal seating. From 1928, he designed swiveling chairs; designed furniture produced by various firms, including Cromos.
▶ 1933–61, work shown at Salons of Société des Artistes Décorateurs.
▶ Pierre Kjellberg, *Art Déco: les maîtres du Mobilier, le décor des Paquebots*, Paris: Amateur, 1986:79.

Geranzani, Piero   (1928–)
▶ Italian industrial designer; born Monza.
▶ Geranzani designed the 1959 *Candy* washing machine produced by Eden Tumagalli.
▶ *Candy* received 1960 Premio Compasso d'Oro.
▶ Penny Sparke, *Design in Italy, 1870 to the Present*, New York: Abbeville, 1988.

Gerlach, Ernest   (1890–)
▶ American silversmith.
▶ In 1914, Gerlach established The Cellini Shop, Chicago Ave. and Davis St., Evanston, Illinois, and, in 1934, (with Hans Gregg) established Cellini Crafts at the same locations. In 1969 and 1957, respectively, the firms were purchased by Randahl.

▶ Sharon S. Darling with Gail Farr Casterline, *Chicago Metalsmiths*, Chicago Historical Society, 1977.

Germain, Louise-Denise (1870–1936)
▶ French bookbinder and leatherworker.
▶ Germain began her career by producing small leather items, including boxes, cushions, and bags. Her book bindings included *Livre d'or* in parchment, *La Jeune Parque* and *Lettre à un ami* in lizard skin, and, for Louis Barthou, *Vie de Saint Dominique, Les Climats*, and *Les Chansons de Bilitis*.
▶ Work (including two volumes of *Pensées* in beige leather with silver metal bands) first shown at 1904 Salon of Société des Artistes Décorateurs. Received diploma of honor (bindings in Class XV) and was a judge (Class IX) at 1925 Paris 'Exposition Internationale des Arts Décoratifs et Industriels Modernes.'
▶ Louis Barthou, 'L'Évolution artistique de la reliure,' *L'Illustration*, Christmas 1930. Ernest de Crauzat, *La Reliure française de 1900 à 1925*, Vol. 2, Paris, 1932:135–37. Alastair Duncan and Georges de Bartha, *Art Nouveau and Art Déco Bookbinding*, New York: Abrams, 1989:20,91,191.

Germanaz, Christian (1940–)
▶ French industrial and furniture designer; active Paris.
▶ Studied École Boulle and École Nationale Supérieure des Arts Décoratifs, both Paris.
▶ In 1966, he designed a range of office furniture and his famous *Half and Half* seat produced by Airborne; in 1970, set up his own design office and designed many public interiors, including those for hotels, restaurants, and hospitals; as an interior architect, designed art galleries, museums, and Manufacture Nationale de Sèvres. He designed exhibition sets for the Paris Grand Palais, in Caen, and at École des Beaux-Arts; stage sets for dancer Maurice Béjart; seating, including *Comedia* produced through VIA Carte Blanche support and shown at VIA exhibition at Bloomingdale's, New York. He taught at École Nationale Supérieure des Arts Décoratifs.
▶ Cat., *Les années VIA 1980–1990*, Paris: Musée des Arts Décoratifs, 1990. François Mathey, *Au bonheur des formes, design français 1945–1992*, Paris: Regard, 1992.

Germer, George E. (1868–1936)
▶ German silversmith and jeweler; active Berlin.
▶ Studied in Berlin under Otto Gericke.
▶ He settled in the USA in 1893 and began working for various firms in New York, Boston, and Providence, Rhode Island. In 1912, he set up his own business in Boston, where he specialized in ecclesiastical silver; later, settled in Mason, New Hampshire, continuing to work on ecclesiastical models.
▶ Charlotte Gere, *American and European Jewelry 1830–1914*, New York: Crown, 1975:186.

Gero
▶ Dutch metalworking factory; located Zeist.
▶ 1909–13, a factory was formed from the foundations of M.J. Gerritsen with production only in spoons and forks in three patterns. Its production was drastically limited during World War I, when it produced buttons, waistband hooks, emblems and soldier uniform numbers. The Gero brand name was registered in 1917 and became the official name of the factory in 1925. An apprenticeship program was set up in 1918, when R. Lubach became head engraver. The firm began to produce pewterware. Spurred by orders from Dutch colonies, its success increased. In 1921, Gerritsen left the firm and set up competing manufacturer Sola. In 1923, a number of objects were designed by C.J. van der Hoef. From the early 1920s until after 1950, Gero's most important designer was Georg Nilsson, the Dane trained by Georg Jensen in Copenhagen who initially worked at Gero's branch in Denmark. The management, dissatisfied with van der Hoef, placed Thomas Hooft in charge of pewter design. Having worked at the firm from 1918, Hooft was more familiar with the technical demands of production. Jan Eisenloeffel executed only one design for Gero, 1929 *Model 70* cutlery. In 1930, 1931, and 1933, A.D. Copier

designed a set of bowls and vases. R. Hamstra designed its emblem and catalogues. 1929–33, Gero experienced financial difficulties due to the Great Depression and, in 1931, began producing *Zilmeta* stainless steel. In 1945, the factory was severely damaged by bombing. Becoming successful after World War II, the subsidiary Nieuw-Weerdinge near Emmen was set up in 1947.
▶ *Industry and Design in the Netherlands, 1850/1950*, Amsterdam: Stedelijk Museum, 1985:223–29.

Gérôme, Jean-Léon (1824–1904)
▶ French painter; born Vesoul.
▶ 1944–45, studied in Italy under Hippolyte-Paul Delaroche.
▶ From 1863, he was professor, École des Beaux-Arts. At the 1900 Paris 'Exposition Universelle,' he said to French President Émile Loubet upon entering the Impressionist salon, 'Stop, Mr. President, this room is the shame of French art.'
▶ *Webster's Biographic Dictionary*, Springfield: Merriam, 1976: 589. Pierre Kjellberg, *Art Déco: les maîtres du Mobilier, le décor des Paquebots*, Paris: Amateur, 1986:147.

Gerra, Pierluigi (1939–)
▶ Italian designer; born Vipiteno; active Milan.
▶ Gerra began his professional career in 1966; was a member of ADI (Associazione per il Disegno Industriale); became known for his metal accessories for clients in Italy, including Fede Cheti Milan, Gallotti e Radice, and the Riva foundry.
▶ *ADI Annual 1976*, Milan: Associazione per il Disegno Industriale, 1976.

Gerritsen (Koninklijke) & Van Kempen
▶ Dutch silver manufacturer; located Zeist.
▶ Koninklijke Gerritsen & Van Kempen was founded in 1924. 1934–77, Gustav Beran, a native of Vienna and pupil of Josef Hoffmann, was the head designer at the firm, which merged with Van Kempen & Begeer in Voorschoten in 1960.
▶ Beran's work shown at Gerritsen & Van Kempen's stand, 1937 Paris 'Exposition Internationale des Arts et Techniques dans la Vie Moderne.'
▶ Annelies Krekel-Aalberse, *Art Nouveau and Art Déco Silver*, New York: Abrams, 1989:190,254.

Gerth, Ruth
▶ American designer.
▶ Calling themselves Gerth and Gerth, Ruth Gerth and another party (possibly her brother) were metalworkers originally in the Arts and Crafts mode, later turning to Modernism. They may have been active in New York State before settling in Chicago. The Gerths designed a number of pieces in brass and chromium-plate for Chase Brass and Copper, Waterbury, Connecticut, including a watering can and small table lamp produced from plumbing floats. Their double candlestick for Chase was a notable, simple Modern statement.
▶ R.S. McFadden, 'Designers' Ability Salvages Waste,' *Design*, Vol. 35, No. 3, Sept. 1933:20–24.

Gesamtkunstwerk
▶ Artistic term; literally, 'complete-art-work.'
▶ A concept formed in the 19th century in Germany indicating an amalgamation of all the arts, originally and most famously associated with the operas of Richard Wagner. Its most prominent exponents in design were Josef Hoffmann in Austria and Frank Lloyd Wright in the USA. Complete design concepts were achieved in which the design of the architecture and its interiors were of one aesthetic theme with every element, including textiles, furniture, and objects, designed for the building.

Geyling, Remigius (1878–1974)
▶ Austrian stage designer, painter, and craftsperson; born Vienna.
▶ On the occasion of the 1908 (XVI) anniversary of Emperor Francis Joseph's accession to the throne of Austria, Geyling (with Heinrich Lefler, Berthold Löffler, and Oskar Kokoschka) designed the costumes for historical and folklore tableaux.

► Robert Waissenberger, *Vienna 1890–1920*, Secaucus, NJ: Wellfleet 1984:136,266.

Giacometti, Alberto (1901–66) and Diego Giacometti (1902–85)
► Swiss artist-designers; both active Paris.
► Alberto Giacometti studied in Geneva and Rome.
► In 1922, Alberto Giacometti moved to Paris, where he was joined a few years later by his brother. At first they shared a studio space, rue Froidevaux; in 1927, moved into the adjacent workroom, 48 rue Hippolyte-Maindron; 1927–33, designed accessories for the firm Desny; in 1933, began to design and produce lighting, bronze vases, candlesticks, medallions, mantelpieces, andirons, and other accessories for the clients of Paris decorator Jean-Michel Frank. At this time, Alberto was making little money on his fine art activities; commented, 'I attempted to make vases, for example, as well as I could, and I realized that I was working on a vase exactly as I did on sculpture.' The specific role of each brother in the production of their wares for Frank is not clear. Alberto probably designed the pieces while Diego oversaw their casting. Alberto designed the large stone sculpture *Figure* (1932) for the garden of vicomte and vicomtesse de Noailles's villa, Hyères. After Frank's business diminished, Diego found work designing perfume bottles and fashion accessories. From the early 1950s, he began making bronze furniture. Alberto insisted that Diego sign his work with his first name to avoid confusion and made sure that Diego was recognized in his own right. In 1966, after Alberto's death, Diego continued to cast pieces of his early tables and floor lamps. From this time on, Diego's furniture and furnishings reflected an interest in nature, particularly animals. An example of his later work can be seen in the group of objects produced for Musée Picasso, Hôtel Salé, Paris. In 1992, a group of vendors and manufacturers were charged with counterfeiting Diego's bronze furniture.
► James Lord, *Giacometti*, New York: Farrar, Straus, Giroux, 1985:122,210–11,212,214,253,331. Daniel Marchesseau, *Diego Giacometti*, New York: Abrams and Paris: Hermann, 1986.

Giannetti, Mario (1942–)
► Italian designer; born Trento; active Milan.
► Giannetti began his professional career in 1971; became a member of ADI (Associazione per il Disegno Industriale); designed exhibition stands for Oscam and Fratelli Tagliabue, and interior schemes. Clients included Elco, ICF, De Padova, Bernini, Confalonieri, Con & Con, Pozzi & Verga, Ebrille, Acerbis, and Scaltrini.
► *ADI Annual 1976*, Milan: Associazione per il Disegno Industriale, 1976.

Gibbons, Cedric (1893–1960)
► American film set designer; born Dublin.
► Gibbons became a set dresser for films, assisting art director Hugo Ballin at Edison Studios, New York, in 1914; soon accompanied Ballin to Hollywood, where he was hired by Samuel Goldwyn. Ballin resigned as art director to direct and produce, and Gibbons replaced him, assuming the novel title 'supervising art director.' Gibbons replaced painted backdrops with three-dimensional sets, and was dubbed the person who 'put the glove on the mantelpiece.' He managed a staff of talented unit art directors, not always recognized in screen credits, including Ben Carré, Merrill Pye, Richard Day, and Arnold Gillespie; signed a contract with MGM that gave him sole credit for every film the studio made in the USA; controlled the wardrobe, set-dressing, matte-painting, special-effects, and photography sections of the studio. The 1925 Paris 'Exposition Internationale des Arts Décoratifs et Industrials Modernes' profoundly influenced his approach, as seen in sets for *Our Dancing Daughters* (1928), with its expansive Art Déco interiors. Other glamorous films popularizing Art Déco followed, including *Our Modern Maidens* (1929) and *Our Blushing Brides* (1930), creating a craze for affectations that included venetian blinds, dancing figurines, and indirect lighting in middle-class décors of the time. Gibbons designed the Oscar

statuette in *c*1928 for the Academy of Motion Picture Arts and Sciences. His Streamlined showcase office on the MGM lot was designed by Merrill Pye, one of his set-design assistants, who worked with him on *Our Blushing Brides*. Hobart Erwin and Frederick Hope (under Gibbons) designed *Dinner at Eight* (1933), the set that incorporated the 'white telephone' look. Gibbons was congratulated by architects for his French Renaissance sets for *Marie Antoinette* (1938), although his designs were highly exaggerated. 1917–55, Gibbons had screen credits in more than 1,500 films and won 11 Academy Awards.
► John Hambley and Patrick Downing, *The Art of Hollywood*, London: Thames Television, 1979. Howard Mandelbaum and Eric Myers, *Screen Deco: A Celebration of High Style in Hollywood*, New York: St. Martin's, 1985.

Gibbons, Keith (1946–)
► British designer; born London.
► Studied Royal College of Art, London.
► He set up his own workshop in 1972; in 1974, opened a shop selling one-off and small-production furniture; in 1973, established Products, a company to manufacture his own work.
► Robert A.M. Stern (ed.), *The International Design Yearbook*, New York: Abbeville, 1985/1986: Nos. 105–06.

Gibson, Natalie
► British textile designer.
► 1956–58, studied painting, Chelsea School of Art, London.
► 1958–61, she printed textiles at Royal College of Art, London; designed for numerous firms including Heal's, Habitat, Fieldcrest, and Connaissance; became primarily active in fashion; designed fabrics for Mantero and Bini & Stehli and clothing for Cacharel, Chloë, Galeries Lafayette, Mafia, and Liberty; was senior lecturer, St. Martins School of Art, London. Her fabrics were published widely and shown in numerous exhibitions.
► Robert A.M. Stern (ed.), *The International Design Yearbook*, New York: Abbeville, 1985/1986: Nos. 355–60.

Giedion, Sigfried (1888–1968)
► Swiss art historian and designer; born Prague.
► Studied engineering, Technische Hochschule, Vienna; 1916–22, art history, Zürich, Berlin, and Munich, under Heinrich Wölfflin.
► In 1923, he met Walter Gropius at the Bauhaus, Dessau, and, in 1925, Le Corbusier in Paris; 1928–56, was general secretary, CIAM (Congrès Internationaux d'Architecture Moderne), of which he was a founder; published books *Bauen in Frankreich, Eisen, Eisenbeton* (*Building in France, Iron and Reinforced Concrete*) (1928) and *Befreites Wohnen* (1929); in 1931 (with Werner M. Moser and Rudolf Graber), founded the Wohnbedarf department store, Zürich, specializing in home furnishings; in 1932, designed bronzeware in the BAG factory, Türgi (Switzerland), a firm that he helped to reorganize, and designed its *indi* lamp series with Hin Bredendieck; designed the tubular-steel furniture factory of Embru, Rüti (Switzerland); 1934–35, was head of the technical division, Wohnbedarf department store. His international contacts with designers, including Alvar Aalto, Le Corbusier, Marcel Breuer, Lázsló Moholy-Nagy, and Herbert Bayer, proved decisive in Wohnbedarf's growth. In 1938, Giedion delivered a paper in the Charles Eliot Norton Lectures, Harvard University. From the early 1940s, he published books in English, beginning with *Space, Time and Architecture* (1941); under the tutelage of Heinrich Wölfflin, developed a theory of 'anonymous' history in his writings, best revealed in his speculative book *Mechanization Takes Command* (1948). Other books followed, including *Walter Gropius, Work and Teamwork* (1954), *Architecture You and Me* (1956), *The Eternal Present: The Beginnings of Art* (1962), and *The Beginnings of Architecture* (1964). His last book *Architecture and the Phenomena of Transition* was sent to his publisher on the day of his death.
► Stanislaus von Moos, 'Sigfried Giedion zum Gedenken' in *Schweizerische Bauzeitung*, 1968, No. 26, 467–68. Friederike

Mehlau-Wiebking et al., *Schweizer Typenmöbel 1925–35, Sigfried Giedion und die Wohnbedarf AG*, Zürich: gta, 1989:228.

Gien, Société Nouvelle des Faïenceries de
▶ French ceramics manufacturer; located Gien.
▶ The faïence factory was purchased in 1821 by Thomas Hulm, an Englishman known as 'Hall'; is still located today on its original site, the 15th-century convent of Minime, Gien, on the river Loire. A landmark in its production was its 1875 *Renaissance Fond Bleu* faïence. The factory was commissioned by European royal families to produce dinner services; made tiles for the interior walls of the stations of the Paris Métro; became known for its inexpensive faïence ware. Its freelance designers from the 1970s included Isabelle de Borchgrave, Jacqueline Deyme, Eliakim, Paco Rabanne, Jean-Pierre Caillères, Christian Duc, Pascal Mourgue, Martin Szekely, Jean-Michel Wilmotte, and Garouste et Bonetti.
▶ Received medals at exhibitions including 1839 (bronze), 1844 (bronze), 1855 (bronze), 1867 (silver), 1878 (gold), 1889 (grand prize), and 1900 Paris 'Expositions Universelles' and at 1876 Philadelphia 'Centennial Exposition' (gold), 1879–80 'Sydney International Exhibition' (gold), 1873 London 'Third Annual International Exhibition' (bronze), 1873 Vienna 'Welt-Ausstellung' (bronze), and 1878 exhibition (bronze) in Amsterdam.
▶ Roger Bernard and Jean-Claude Ronard, *La Faïence de Gien*, Paris: Sous le vent, 1981. Michèle-Cécile Gillard, *Faïence de Gien: formes et décors*, Paris: Massin, 1988. Cat., *L'Art de Vivre: Decorative Art and Design in France, 1789–1989*, New York: Vendome, 1989.

Gigante, Gian Nicola   (1934–)
▶ Italian industrial designer; born Spresiano; active Padua.
▶ Gigante began his professional career in 1962; collaborated with architects Marilena Boccato and Antonio Zambusi; became a member of ADI (Associazione per il Disegno Industriale).
▶ *ADI Annual 1976*, Milan: Associazione per il Disegno Industriale, 1976.

Gignoux, Michèle   (1944–)
▶ French designer, painter, and fashion designer.
▶ Studied Charpentier workshop, Paris.
▶ Calling herself a 'Pop romantic' artist, she invented the 1967 *Cube photo* frame in Plexiglas produced by Bac Design; designed 1989 *Vertige* chair in fluorescent colors and Formica, shown in various galleries including VIA; became known for her 'illuminated jacket' and 'photomontages.'
▶ Cat., *Michèle Gignoux*, Paris: Galerie Franka Berndt Bastille/ VIA/Différence, 1989.

Gigou, Louis
▶ French locksmith and lighting designer.
▶ He designed door handles, finger plates, escutcheons, and keys, together with a variety of lighting forms in bronze, wrought iron, and steel with ornamental copper overlays. Produced chiefly 1919–25, his distinctive lighting included table lamps, sconces, and floor lamps. After this time, he specialized in locksmithing.
▶ He showed his metalwork at the annual Salons of the Société des Artistes Décorateurs.
▶ G. Janneau, *Le Luminaire et les Moyens d'éclairage Nouveaux*, first series: plates 26, 43. Léon Deshairs, *Modern French Decorative Art*, Paris: Albert Lévy. Alastair Duncan, *Art Nouveau and Art Déco Lighting*, New York: Simon and Schuster, 1978:171.

Gilardi, Piero
See Drocco, Guido

Gilbert, Alfred   (1854–1934)
▶ British sculptor and metalworker.
▶ Gilbert produced the 1893 *Eros* memorial to Lord Shaftesbury in Piccadilly Circus, London, cast in aluminum; designed two notable official jewelry pieces which marked a peak of English Art Nouveau (though he disliked the style): the 1888 badge and chain of the Mayor and Corporation of Preston, and the 1891–96 presidential badge of the Royal Institute of Painters in Watercolour.

Gilbert drew a number of jewelry pieces in the neo-Renaissance style popular at the end of the 19th century; produced experimental pieces in silver and iron wire with glass and beads; worked in a manner that had affinities with René Lalique and Philippe Wolfers.

Gilbert, Odile   (1929–)
▶ French designer.
▶ Studied Union Centrale des Arts Décoratifs, Paris.
▶ Her first designs were a collection of matt opaline glassware, and a series of cast-glass vessels called *Zen*, produced by Quartz in 1985. She collaborated with Bernard Gilbert.
▶ *Les Carnets du Design*, Paris: Mad-Cap Productions et APCI, 1986:13.

Gili, Anna   (1960–)
▶ Italian designer; born Orvieto; active Milan.
▶ 1984, graduated ISIA, Florence; her project 'Vestito sonoro' was shown at the Padiglione d'Arte Contemporanea in Milan, at Seibu in Tokyo, and the Kunstmuseum in Düsseldorf.
▶ She designed ceramics for Tendentse, lighting and fabrics for Francis Cot, furniture for Tribu and Cappellini, jewelry for Cleto Munari; has contributed to the design journal *Ollo*.
▶ Gili's *Gin* vase by Porcellane Richard Ginori, *Cielo* and *Nuvola* laminates by Abet Laminati, and *Razio* armchair by Poltrona Frau were shown at 'Nuovo Bel Design: 200 Nuovi Oggetti per la Casa' Fiera di Milano, 1992.
▶ *Modo*, No. 148, March–April 1993:120.

Gill, Arthur Eric Rowton   (1882–1940)
▶ British sculptor, graphic artist, engraver and typographer.
▶ 1900–03, studied Chichester Art School; Central School of Arts and Crafts, London, under Edward Johnston.
▶ 1900–03, he was apprentice to an architect; in 1913, converted to Roman Catholicism; 1913–18, carved the *Stations of the Cross* for Westminster Cathedral, London; in c1918, became one of the founders of a semi-religious crafts community, the Guild of St. Joseph and St. Dominic, in Ditchling, Sussex; in 1920, became a founding member of the Society of Wood Engravers; in 1924, settled in Capel-y-ffin, Wales and began a collaboration with the Golden Cockerel Press; designed numerous typefaces, including 1927 *Perpetua* and 1928 *Gill Sans*, for Monotype; in 1928, settled in and set up a printing press at Pigotts, Buckinghamshire. His graphic design commissions came from various publishers including Faber and Faber, Limited Editions Club (New York), Dent, Cloverhill Press, Cranach Press, and Clarendon Press. In 1929–31, he produced sculpture for BBC Broadcasting House, London, and, in 1936, for the League of Nations building, Geneva. Gill's silver designs of c1930 were produced by H.G. Murphy of The Worshipful Company of Goldsmiths. In 1930, Gill designed a casement clock for Edward W. Hunter of the Sun Engraving Co, and the typography and embellishments of 1937 postage stamps (with the king's image by Edmund Dulac) for King George VI's coronation.
▶ Received 1935 honorary-associate award of Royal Institute of British Architects. In 1936, elected Royal Designer for Industry. In 1937, became associate of the Royal Academy and, in 1937, honorary associate of Royal Society of British Sculptors.
▶ Eric Gill, 'Paintings and Criticism,' *The Architecture Review*, March 1930. Eric Gill, *Autobiography*, London: Jonathan Cape, 1940. Robert Speaight, *The Life of Eric Gill*, London: Methuen, 1966. Cat., *Thirties: British art and design before the war*, London: Arts Council of Great Britain, Hayward Gallery, 1979:23,34,72, 77,100,124,129,139,176,177,201,203,206,290,291. Annelies Krekel-Aalberse, *Art Nouveau and Art Déco Silver*, New York: Abrams, 1989:27,254.

Gillgren, Sven Arne   (1913–)
▶ Swedish metalworker.
▶ 1933, trained as an engraver under C.F. Hallberg; 1936, studied Konstfackskolan and Tekniska Skolan, Stockholm.

▶ From 1937, he was a designer at Guldsmedsaktiebolaget, Stockholm, and, 1942–75, its artistic director; from 1944, designed for goldsmithy G. Dahlgren, Malmö. Sweden's neutrality during World War II permitted artisans like Gillgren to produce luxury crafts. His designs showed an interest in folk motifs. 1955–70, he was principal teacher in the department of metalworking and industrial design, Konstfackskolan and Tekniska Skolan; in 1975, set up his own studio.
▶ Received first prize at 1958 Stockholm Handicraft Society competition; first prize at 1960 'International Design Competition for Sterling Silver Flatware,' Museum of Contemporary Crafts, New York; 1963 prize of honor from Swedish Design Center, 1964 Prince Eugen Medal, and 1966 Eligius Prize.
▶ Cat., David Revere McFadden (ed.), *Scandinavian Modern Design 1880–1980*, New York: Abrams, 1982:263, No. 147.

Gilliam, Kenneth (1952–)
▶ American retailer and designer; active San Francisco.
▶ Collaborating in the early 1990s with retailer and designer Dan Friedlander, Gilliam designed furniture in a 1960s style, produced by Design America.
▶ Arlene Hirst, 'Design Class at Last,' *American Home*, November 1990:101.

Gimson, Ernest (1864–1919)
▶ British architect and designer; born Leicester.
▶ In 1881, he was an apprentice to an architect in Leicester; on William Morris's recommendation, joined the architecture office of J.D. Sedding in 1886; met Ernest and Sidney Barnsley; learned chair turning under Herefordshire craftsman Philip Clisrett and studied plaster work; in 1895, established his own workshop in the Cotswolds with Ernest and Sidney Barnsley. The Daneway Workshops were set up by Gimson and the Barnsley brothers in 1902 at Daneway House, Glouchestershire. In 1901, they were joined by Peter Waals, a Dutch cabinetmaker then living in London. The partnership broke up c1905, and Gimson continued on his own. Gimson's furniture ranged from simple, vernacular rush-seated chairs to elaborate cabinets with rich inlays and veneers. He refused to join the Design and Industries Association because he did not want his work to be produced by machine.
▶ Work shown at Arts and Crafts Exhibition Society events.
▶ W. R. Lethaby et al., *Ernest Gimson, His Life and Work*, Stratford-upon-Avon: Shakespeare Head, 1924. Cat., *Ernest Gimson*, Leicester: Leicester Museums and Art Gallery, 1969. Cat., *Ernest Gimson and The Cotswold Group of Craftsmen*, Leicester: Leicester Museums, 1969. *British Arts and Design*, 1900–1960, London: Victoria and Albert Museum, 1983.

Ginchuk
▶ Russian Institute of Artistic Culture; located Petrograd/Leningrad.
▶ See Inkhuk

Gioacchini, Nilo (1946–)
▶ Italian industrial designer; born Osimo; active Florence.
▶ 1968–69, he worked in the industrial design studio Nizzoli Associati, Milan; in 1970, (with Gianni Ferrara and Carlo Bimbi) established the industrial design studio Gruppo Internotredici, Florence, designing furniture, sanitary fittings, and table accessories; became a member of ADI (Associazione per il Disegno Industriale).
▶ Gruppo Internotredici received first prize at 1968 (VIII) 'Ottavo Concorso Internationale del Mobile,' Trieste; first prize at its 1969 (IX) session; the Bayer prize at its 1970 (IX) session; first and second prizes at 1971 'Concorso Nazionale' for plastic-laminated furniture sponsored by Abet-Print; 1972 first prize at competition for alabaster objects by Volterra. Their work shown at 1967 Montreal 'Universal and International Exhibition (Expo '67)'; 1971 (IX) 'Mostra Seletivva del Mobile,' Cantù, sponsored by Rassegna (where their 100m² apartment was shown); 1972 'Italy: The New Domestic Landscape,' New York Museum of Modern Art; 1973 'BIO 5' International Biennial of Industrial Design, Ljubljana;

'Italia Oggi' exhibition, Gimbel's department store, Pittsburgh; pavilion of Italian design, 1975 'Salon d'Ameublement,' Lausanne.
▶ *ADI Annual 1976*, Milan: Associazione per il Disegno Industriale, 1976.

Giot, Maurice
▶ French painter and silversmith; active Paris.
▶ Giot's silver designs for hollow-ware were produced c1900 by A. Debain, a Paris silversmith.
▶ Annelies Krekel-Aalberse, *Art Nouveau and Art Déco Silver*, New York: Abrams, 1989:63,254.

Gips, A.F. (1861–1943)
▶ Dutch metalworker and teacher; active Delft.
▶ In c1900, Gips designed silver for the Koninklijke Utrechtsche Fabriek van Zilverwerk C.J. Begeer, Utrecht.
▶ Gips's silverwork by Begeer, including a tea set, shown at 1900 Paris 'Exposition Universelle'.
▶ Annelies Krekel-Aalberse, *Art Nouveau and Art Déco Silver*, New York: Abrams, 1989:179,254.

Girard, Alexander Hayden (1907–93)
▶ American textile, wallpaper, furniture, and exhibition designer; born New York.
▶ Studied Architectural Association, London, to 1929, Royal School of Architecture, Rome, to 1931, and New York University, 1935.
▶ He worked in architecture offices in Florence, Rome, London, Paris, and New York; in 1930, opened an office in Florence; in 1937, opened an office in Detroit; designed interiors for 1943 Ford and 1946 Lincoln automobiles; 1951–52, was a color consultant on 1948–56 General Motors Research Center (architect Eero Saarinen), Michigan; in 1952, began designing textiles for Herman Miller, Zeeland, Michigan; in 1952, became director of Herman Miller's fabric division under design director George Nelson; designed upholstery fabrics and casement goods as well as exuberant, colorful, large-patterned prints for Herman Miller; in 1953, opened an office, Santa Fe, New Mexico; executed 1965 corporate-identity graphics program for Braniff Airlines, 1957 interior of film director Billy Wilder's home, Los Angeles; 1960 interiors for La Fonda del Sol restaurant in New York, and 1966 interior and furniture (produced by Knoll) of L'Étoile restaurant in New York. His work, particularly in the field of textile design, was influenced by his large collection of folk art. In 1961, he established the Girard Foundation, Santa Fe, an international collection of toys and related objects.
▶ Exhibition designs included Italian Pavilion and interior-design model rooms of Florentine Artisans Guild at 1929 'Exposición Internacional de Barcelona'; 1950 'Design for Modern Use, made in the USA' traveling exhibition to Europe organized by New York Museum of Modern Art; 1968 'El Encanto de un Pueblo' exhibition at 1968 'Hemisfair '68,' San Antonio, Texas. In 1965, elected Honorary Royal Designer for Industry, London.
▶ 'Out-Maneuvering the Plain Plane,' *Interiors*, Vol. 125, Feb. 1966:99–105. Alexander H. Girard, *The Magic of People*, 1968. Jack Lenor Larsen, 'Nelson, Eames, Girard, Propst: The Design Process at Herman Miller,' *Design Quarterly 98–99*, 1975. Ralph Caplan, *The Making of Herman Miller*, New York, 1976. Charles Lockwood, 'A Perfectionist at Play,' *Connoisseur*, Vol. 212, Jan. 1983:92–98. Cat., Kathryn B. Hiesinger and George H. Marcus III (eds.), *Design Since 1945*, Philadelphia: Philadelphia Museum of Art, 1983. Cherie Fehrman and Kenneth Fehrman, *Postwar Interior Design, 1945–1960*, New York: Van Nostrand Reinhold, 1987.

Gismondi, Ernesto (1931–)
▶ Italian lighting designer, entrepreneur, and teacher; born San Remo; active Milan.
▶ Studied aeronautical engineering, Politecnico di Milano, and Scuola Superiore di Ingeneria, Rome.
▶ In 1959, he founded the Artemide lighting company, which became a leader in lighting design and manufacture; invested in

other firms in Milan, including Alias and several Memphis collections; known for his ability to identify new trends, he provided showroom space for the Memphis collection from its beginning in 1981; in 1988, when Memphis's efforts were discontinued by Ettore Sottsass, established Meta-Memphis to produce the designs of fine artists rather than designers at high prices, but with little of Memphis's early success. A designer (alone and with others) at Artemide himself, he also employed numerous consultant designers. His own design work at Artemide included the 1975 *Sintesi* lamp. From 1984, he taught rocket technology, Politecnico di Milano, and at institutions, New York, Los Angeles, and Milan.
▶ Giancarlo Iliprandi and Pierluigi Molinari (eds.), *Industrial Designers Italiani*, Fagagna, 1985:110. Hans Wichmann, *Italien Design 1945 bis heute*, Munich: Die Neue Sammlung, 1988. Jeremy Myerson and Sylvia Katz, *Conran Design Guides: Lamps and Lighting*, London: Conran Octopus, 1990:75.

Gispen, Willem H.   (1890–1981)
▶ Dutch metalworker and lighting and furniture designer; active Rotterdam.
▶ Studied architecture, Koninklinke Academie voor Beeldende Kundsten en Technische Wetenschappen, Rotterdam, under Willem Kromhout.
▶ He became an architect's draftsman; worked briefly as designer in an artistic wrought-iron factory; 1911–12, traveled in England, coming into contact with Arts and Crafts ideas and works; was a member of the Nederlands Vereening voor in Ambachts-en-Nijverheidskunst (Netherlands Union for Handicraft and Industrial Art), founded in 1904; in 1915, opened a factory in the Netherlands; made wooden furniture before he began working with steel; in 1916, established the Gispen Fabriek voor Metaalbewerking (Gispen Metalwork Factory), Voorhaven 101, Rotterdam, where he designed and produced outdoor public and domestic furniture. In 1916–24, Gispen designed domestic and public metalwork; his stair railings were used in the 1911–16 Sheepvaarthuis, Amsterdam. His steel-tube bending was accomplished by filling the cores with sand, heating, and bending by hand. Soon after, he used machines for bending; in 1924, turned from handicraft to mechanization; in 1922, received the first of several commissions from architect L.C. Van der Vlught, for stairway and balcony railings for the Scala theatre, Rotterdam; in 1920, (with Kromhout, J.J.P. Oud, Granprè Moliere, and Van de Vlught) founded the architects' circle de Opbouw ('Construction'), Rotterdam; in 1920, joined VANK; in 1925, when Mart Stam returned to the Netherlands, became involved in the debate between Functionalism and formalism; in 1926, put *Giso* lighting range on the market; in 1929, set up a factory, Culemborg, encouraged by commissions for the 1927 Stuttgart 'Weissenhof-Siedlung' and the growth of sales in Europe. His designs were produced by 100 employees; C.J. Hoffman was his chief assistant. The 1924–29 Van Nelle Tobacco, Coffee and Tea Factory, Rotterdam, by Van de Vlught and J.A. Brinkmann (begun by Brinkmann's father) was furnished in 1929 with bent tubular-steel furniture and lighting by Gispen, including hanging lamps, small wall and desk lamps, writing desks and chairs for the main offices and small round tables (*No. 501* and *No. 1053*) in tubular steel with blue glass tops. By 1929, Gispen had a showroom in Amsterdam, where he sold lighting and furniture; in 1932, opened showrooms in The Hague, Paris at 212 rue La Fayette, London at 190 Kensington Church Street and High Holborn, and Nottingham at 8 East Circus Street. In the 1930s, Gispen and Jan Schröfer designed furniture independently of each other for the De Cirkel factory. For Hilversum town hall, the architect Willem Dudok used an array of Gispen furniture including the Van Nelle chair *No. 103* in leather upholstery, chromed-framed desk *No. 602* with a black top, glass-topped occasional tables, Van Nelle chair *No. 203* with 'Gisolite'-plastic arms in the canteen, armchair *No. 401* in the public waiting room, and a circular table. J.W. Buys used Gispen's chairs *No. 101* and *No. 201* in the offices of Volharding, The Hague. Brinkmann and Van der Vlught used Gispen's dining chair

No. 103 and easy chairs *No. 407* in the 1933 Sonneveld house, Rotterdam. All these commissions incorporated the Giso-lamps. Gispen furnished the 1933 AVRO radio buildings, Hilversum; fitted the liner *Dagenham* (the first vessel to use tubular-steel furniture), used by Ford Motor Company for transporting its employees; in 1928, designed his own flat incorporating his own furniture; was imprisoned in Scheveningen after co-signing a letter of protest against the Kulturkammer; when freed, moved to Gelderland and took up painting. After the war, the artistic line at the factory was reduced in favor of office furniture and Gispen resigned in 1949. From 1940–50, was chair of BKI (Bond voor Kunst in Industrie). From 1950–53, taught a weekend industrial-design course, Koninklijke Academie, The Hague. Designed wooden furniture and ran a ceramics factory. In 1951, turned away from his manufacturing business to paint and draw for pleasure. In 1953, founded the Kembo factory and designed furniture and lighting inspired by the Scandinavians and Italians. Other firms produced his work including Riemersma, Emmein Staal, and Polynorm. Stopped designing furniture in the early 1960s. Designed bungalows on the Costa Brava and a house in The Hague. In 1969, took etching lessons, Haagse Academie; from 1970, regularly showed graphic art.
▶ His lighting was included in the interiors of Oud at the 1927 Stuttgart 'Weissenhof-Siedlung.'
▶ W.H. Gispen, *Het Sirend Metaal in de Bouwkunst*, Rotterdam: R. Grusse, 1925. Barbie Campbell-Cole and Tim Benton (eds.), *Tubular Steel Furniture*, London: The Art Book Company, 1979:28–45. *Industry and Design in the Netherlands 1850/1950*, Amsterdam: Stedelijk Museum, 1985:268–71. André Koch, *Industrieel ontwerper Wh. Gispen een modern electicus (1890–1981)*, Rotterdam: de hef, 1988.

Giudici, Angelo   (1934–)
▶ Italian architect and designer; born and active Meda.
▶ Studied architecture.
▶ He began his professional career in 1964; designed furniture produced in Italy by Estasis Fabrica Salotti, Coima, and Cazzaniga, and kitchen systems by De Ponti Enrico; became a member of ADI (Associazione per il Disegno Industriale).
▶ *ADI Annual 1976*, Milan: Associazione per il Disegno Industriale, 1976.

Giudici, Battista   (1903–70) and Gino Giudici   (1914–)
▶ Swiss designers; born Locarno.
▶ The Giudici brothers collaborated on design in their workshop Fratelli Giudici, Locarno; developed a 1935–36 metal chaise longue which they patented in 1936; constructed a metal stool and table; in 1946, developed a prefabricated garage.
▶ Friederike Mehlau-Wiebking et al., *Schweizer Typenmöbel 1925–35, Sigfried Giedion und die Wohnbedarf AG*, Zürich: gta, 1989:228.

Giugiaro, Giorgio   (1938–)
▶ Italian industrial designer; born Garessio, Cuneo.
▶ Studied technical and graphic design, Accademia di Belle Arti, Turin.
▶ Giugiaro began his career in 1955 in the design department of Fiat; 1959–65, worked at Bertone Styling Center, Turin, with the sports-car designer Nuccio Bertone; 1965–68, was head of staff at Ghia, Turin; in 1968, (with Aldo Mantovani) founded ItalDesign to work on automobile styling; designed the last version of the 1978 *F3* and *F4* Nikon cameras, imbuing them with ergonometric attributes. Primarily a distinguished car designer, his work included Necchi sewing machines, including the 1982 *Logica* by his product-design firm Giugiaro Design, formed in 1981. ItalDesign employed some 200 designers, engineers, and computer specialists by the mid-1980s. Giugiaro designed 43 production-model automobiles, including the 1971 Alfa Romeo *Alfasud*, 1974 Volkswagen *Golf*, 1980 Fiat *Panda*, and 1983 Fiat *Uno*. Giugiaro's studio styled the Seiko *Chronograph* of the early 1980s, a design that exuded the trappings of high technology. ItalDesign's work

included sports equipment and street furniture for the city of Turin. Giugiaro produced the 1983 *Marielle* pasta design for Voiello, and men's clothing and accessories.

▶ Work (Giugiaro appliances) shown 1983–84 'Design Since 1945' exhibition, Philadelphia Museum of Art.

▶ G. Gardini and M. Bugli (eds.), *Design Giugiaro: la forma dell' automobile*, Milan: Automobilia, 1980. Alfonso Grassi and Anty Pansera, *Atlante del design italiano 1940/1980*, Milan, 1980:94, 243, 300. Steve Braidwood, 'Taxi to Turin,' *Design*, No. 386, Feb. 1981:27. Wolf von Eckardt, 'Creation, Italian-Style,' *Time*, Vol. 118: Feb. 22, 1982. Cat., Kathryn B. Hiesinger and George H. Marcus III (eds.), *Design Since 1945*, Philadelphia: Philadelphia Museum of Art, 1983.

Giuliano, Carlo   (?–1895)

▶ Italian goldsmith and jeweler; born Naples; active London.

▶ Giuliano settled in London in c1860; worked for Harry Emanuel; collaborated with Castellani on at least one piece of jewelry and was an adept jeweler in the archeological or Etruscan style; developed a recognizable style of his own that was much copied in the 1880s and 1890s. Giuliano's assistant, Italian-born Pasquale Novissimo, produced such delicate enamel decoration on Giuliano's pieces that they were difficult to copy. In 1861, Giuliano's jewelry manufacturing firm and goldsmithy was located at 13 Frith Street and, in 1875, at 115 Piccadilly, where he remained until retirement. Until 1877, the facilities at Frith Street were used as a workshop. In 1882, Frederico and Ferdinando Giuliano, probably his brothers, opened their own jewelry workshop at 24 Howland Street, moving in 1886–87 to 47 Howland Street. In 1896, Carlo Guliano left the business at 115 Piccadilly to his sons; it became known as Carlo and Arthur Giuliano. In 1903, Frederico and Ferdinando closed the business on Howland Street. In 1911–12, Carlo and Arthur Giuliano moved to 48 Knightsbridge and, by 1914–15, had closed.

▶ Charlotte Gere, *American and European Jewelry 1830–1914*, New York: Crown, 1975:187.

Gjerdrum, Reidun Sissel   (1954–)

▶ Norwegian ceramicist.

▶ Studied ceramics, art school, Trondheim.

▶ 1979–81, she worked at Municipal Workshop for Arts and Crafts, Trondheim; in 1981, set up her own workshop; on some wares, used Japanese *raku* firing, resulting in a crackle pattern in the glaze.

▶ Cat., David Revere McFadden (ed.), *Scandinavian Modern Design 1880–1980*, New York: Abrams, 1982:264, No. 278.

Gjerløv-Knudsen, Ole   (1930–)

▶ Danish furniture designer.

▶ Studied furniture design, Kunsthåndvaerkskolen, to 1955, and Det Kongelige Danske Kunstakademi, both Copenhagen.

▶ 1955–57 and 1960–62, he worked with architect Kay Korbing; 1957–60, with architect Vilhelm Lauritzen; and, from 1962, with architect Torben Lind. From 1962, he taught furniture design at Kunsthåndvaerkskolen; from 1967, was rector, Skolen for Brugskunst (formerly Det Tekniske Selskabs Skoler); from 1977, participated in Dansk Designråd and IDD (Industrielle Designere Danmark). Known for his demountable canvas-wood 'camp' furniture, his 1964 cot and 1966 lounge chair were produced by France & Søn and sold by Cato.

▶ His work was shown at the Museum of Contemporary Crafts, New York and the 1975–77 'Dansk Miljø' European traveling exhibition.

▶ Frederik Sieck, *Nutidig Dansk Møbeldesign: -en kortfattet illustreret beskrivelse*, Copenhagen: Bondo Gravesen; 1990 Busck edition in English.

Glaser, Milton   (1929–)

▶ American graphic designer; born and active New York.

▶ Studied Cooper Union, New York.

▶ In 1954, Glaser, Ed Sorel, Reynold Ruffins, and Seymour Chwast established the Push Pin Studios in New York, where

Glaser was president 1954–74. In 1974, he set up his own independent studio, New York; redesigned publications including *New York, Paris Match*, and *The Washington Post*; designed architectural interiors based on supergraphics for the Grand Union grocery-store chain and restaurants in the World Trade Center, New York; from 1961, designed more than 300 posters, the best known being the *Bob Dylan* poster for Columbia Records in the 1960s. His 'I ♥ NY' motif was subsequently much pirated. He designed the dinnerware for the Rainbow Room in Rockefeller Center, New York, and table/kitchenware in wood for the *Twergi* range produced Alessi.

▶ In the 1970s, work subject of exhibitions, New York Museum of Modern Art and Paris Musée des Arts Décoratifs. In 1979, elected Honorary Royal Designer for Industry, London.

▶ *Milton Glaser: Graphic Design*, New York: Overlook Press, 1973. *Issue 4*, London: Design Museum, Autumn 1990:6.

Glasgow School

▶ Scottish architecture-design group; active Glasgow.

▶ The Glasgow School was composed of a group of architect-designers associated with the Glasgow School of Art, including C.R. Mackintosh, Margaret and Frances Macdonald, George MacNair, and George Walton. Popular with the Secessionists in Vienna, the exponents of the Glasgow School expressed a conservative form of Art Nouveau, liberally incorporating Celtic motifs. Becoming internationally known at the turn of the 20th century, the group influenced industrial design in the first decades of the century, particularly in Austria and Germany.

▶ Showed work at 1895 Liège 'L'Oeuvre Artistique,' 1899 exhibition in Venice, 1900 (VII) Vienna Secession exhibition, 1902 Turin 'Esposizione Internazionale d'Arte Decorativa Moderna,' and 1911 Turin 'Esposizione Internazionale d'Arte Decorativa Moderna.'

▶ See Mackintosh, Charles Rennie

Glasshouse Gallery and Workshop, The

▶ British glassware workshop; located London.

▶ In the 1980s and 1990s, it was the only gallery in central London showing and producing contemporary glassware, both functional and non-functional. Sam Herman established The Glasshouse Gallery and Workshop in 1969 at 65 Long Acre, London. Artists included Annette Meech, David Taylor, Fleur Tookey, and Christopher Williams. The furnaces and ovens were on view at the gallery premises.

Gleadowe, Richard M. Yorke   (1888–1944)

▶ British silver designer; active London.

▶ Gleadowe taught art at Winchester College and was Slade Professor at Oxford University; from the late 1920s, was active as a silver designer for Edward Bernard and H.G. Murphy and, in the 1930s, for Wakely and Wheeler, London. At Barnard's, the chaser was B.J. Colson and engraver George Friend. Under the influence of Gleadowe, a growing interest in engraving developed. His work often showed detailed pictorial engraving. He produced a number of important commemorative pieces and presentation objects for The Worshipful Company of Goldsmiths and others; in 1934, gave a series of BBC radio talks on British Art.

▶ Received 1935 Freedom of the Company; from 1939, was a member of the Court of Assistants. In 1943, became a Commander of the Royal Victorian Order for his work on the Stalingrad Sword given by King George VI to the citizens of Stalingrad (now Volgograd). Work shown at 1979–80 'Thirties' exhibition, Hayward Gallery, London.

▶ Annelies Krekel-Aalberse, *Art Nouveau and Art Déco Silver*, New York: Abrams, 1989:27,33,254. Cat., *Thirties: British art and design before the war*, London: Arts Council of Great Britain, Hayward Gallery, 1979:139,206,290.

Glessner, Frances M.   (1848–1922)

▶ American amateur silversmith; active Chicago.

▶ Studied under Madeline Yale Wynne, also an amateur.

▶ A wealthy Chicago resident in the 1880s, Glessner was engaged in silversmithing as a hobby.

▶ Annelies Krekel-Aalberse, *Art Nouveau and Art Déco Silver*, New York: Abrams, 1989:104,254.

Global Tools
▶ Italian design group.
▶ Global Tools' members came from the studios of Archizoom, Superstudio, UFO, Gruppo 9999, and Zziggurat and included Remo Buti, Riccardo Dalisi, Gianni Pettena, and Ettore Sottsas, who convened in the Milan offices of the review *Casabella* to found the organization in 1973; proposed to set up 'a system of laboratories in Florence dedicated to prompting the study and use of natural technical materials and their relative behavioral characteristics. The object of Global Tools is to stimulate free development of individual creativity.' In fact, it served as a forum for radical architectural and design ideas in the 1980s.
▶ F. Raggi, 'Radical Story,' *Casabella*, No. 382, 1973:45.

Gočár, Josef (1880–1945)
▶ Czech architect; born in Semín, Pardubice.
▶ 1903–05, studied Baugewerbeschule (School of Industrial Design), Prague, under Jan Kotera.
▶ 1905–08, he worked in the office of Kotera; 1911–14, published an artistic review; became known for his furniture design; from 1929, taught at Academy of Fine Arts, Prague; in 1911, became a member of the Bohemian Artists' Group. His Functionalism could be seen in his 1935 filling station for Fanto, Prague. Buildings included the 1910 Wenke department store, Jaroměř; 1911 House of Flack Mother of God, Prague; and 1928–32 Wenceslas Church, Prague.
▶ Participated in the Czech interiors at 1914 Cologne 'Werkbund-Ausstellung.'
▶ Josef Gočár, P. Janák, and F. Kysela, *Tschechische Bestrebungen um ein Modernes Interieur*, Prague, 1915. Josef Gočár, *Hradec Králové*, Prague, 1930. M. Benešová, *Josef Gočár*, Prague, 1958. Z. Wirth, *Joseph Gočár*, Geneva, 1980. Vladimír Šlapeta, *Czech Functionalism*, London: Architectural Association, 1987:124.

Godelinais, Renan de la (1908–86)
▶ French decorator and furniture designer.
▶ Studied École des Beaux-Arts, Rennes.
▶ In 1948, he participated in the establishment of the Centre de Documentation de l'Habitation at the Pavillon de Marsan; in 1949, became a member of UAM (Union des Artistes Modernes); subsequently, participated in the selections of the 'Formes Utiles' exhibitions; 1949–50, worked with Charlotte Perriand, André Hermant, and René Herbst on its first exhibition, Pavillon de Marsan, Paris.
▶ His decorative door locks for Fontaine shown at 1956–57 (I) Triennale d'Art français Contemporain.
▶ Cat., *Les années UAM 1929–1958*, Paris: Musée des Arts Décoratifs, 1988:185.

Godley, Lyn
▶ American furniture designer; active New York; wife of Lloyd Schwan.
▶ In 1979, Godley and husband Lloyd Schwan set up the firm Godley-Schwan, New York, where they initially made jewelry, tabletop accessories, and other items; collaborated on the design of furniture sold through their firm. Their limited-production pieces were produced in a workshop, Brooklyn, New York. They were instrumental in setting up a New York- and New Jersey-state study of contemporary furniture making in the region.
▶ Work (sculptural seating and case goods) shown first internationally at 1989 Salone del Mobile, Milan.
▶ 'The New American Entrepreneurs,' *Metropolis*, May 1991:70.

Godwin, Edward William (1833–86)
▶ British architect; born Bristol; active Bristol and London.
▶ Trained in Bristol under William Armstrong.
▶ He worked for William Armstrong, city surveyor, architect, and civil engineer in Bristol, and soon took over projects from Armstrong; in 1854 in Bristol, set up his own practice; with no

significant commissions, lived in Ireland 1857–59, working with his engineer brother. His first commission of consequence was 1857 church, Saint Johnston, County Donegal (Ireland). Inspired by Ruskin's interpretation of the Gothic, he designed the town halls of Northampton in 1861 and Congleton in 1864; highly influenced by the London 'International Exhibition on Industry and Art of 1862,' experimented with interiors in his residence in Bristol, where he arranged Japanese prints on plain-colored walls, Persian rugs on bare floors, and 18th-century furniture; in 1862, began collecting Japanese artifacts at a time when few others were interested. In 1866, he worked with a fellow admirer of Gothic and Japanese design, William Burges, having moved to London in 1865. His partnership with Henry Crisp lasted 1864–71. In 1865, Godwin set up his own office in London; in 1866, began designing wallpaper for Jeffrey and Co, and furniture in various styles from c1867, the year his work on Dromore Castle, Ireland, was completed. His best known pieces were the stark Anglo-Japanese 'Art Furniture' made by William Wall. The Art Furniture Company manufactured his designs for a short time, with subsequent production by firms including Gillow, Green and King, Collingson and Lock, and W.A. Smee. The term 'Anglo-Japanese' was coined for the slender lines and geometric forms of Godwin's art furniture, often produced in ebonized wood without moldings, carving, or ornamentation. 1874–78, he collaborated with friend and painter James Whistler; designed 1876 houses in a vernacular style for Bedford Park Estate, Chiswick (Britain's first garden suburb), and was replaced on the project later by Richard Norman Shaw; named 'one of the most artistic spirits in England' by Oscar Wilde, he decorated Wilde's house, Tite Street, London, in 1884. A prolific writer, he became interested in costume and set designs towards the end of his life. His designs of the 1870s influenced subsequent industrial design and interiors and anticipated Modern design in Germany and France at the turn of the century.
▶ His first winning competition entry was the Italian-Gothic design for Northampton town hall. Suite of furniture (with Whistler's painted panels) produced by William Wall shown at 1878 Paris 'Exposition Universelle.'
▶ Elizabeth Aslin, *Nineteenth Century English Furniture*, New York, 1962:63–64. Elizabeth Aslin, 'The Furniture Designs of E. W. Godwin,' *Victoria and Albert Museum Bulletin 3*, Oct. 1967:145–54. Cat., Cleo Witt and Karin Walton, *Furniture by Godwin and Breuer*, Bristol: Bristol City Art Gallery, 1976. E.W. Godwin, *Art Furniture and Artistic Conservatories*, New York and London, 1978. Clive Wainright and Charlotte Gere, *Architect-Designers: Pugin to Mackintosh*, London: Fine Art Society Limited, 1981:32, Elizabeth Aslin, *E.W. Godwin: Furniture and Interior Decoration*, London, 1986. Doreen Bolger Burke et al., *In Pursuit of Beauty: Americans and the Aesthetic Movement*, New York: Metropolitan Museum of Art and Rizzoli, 1986:431–32.

Goffi, Fernando (1936–)
▶ Italian designer; born in and active Bergamo.
▶ Studied Università di Pavia.
▶ Goffi was at first interested in advertising design before he turned to furniture, lighting, and table accessories; became a member of ADI (Associazione per il Disegno Industriale).
▶ *ADI Annual 1976*, Milan: Associazione per il Disegno Industriale, 1976.

Goldfinger, Ernö (1902–87)
▶ Hungarian architect and designer; born Budapest; active Paris and London.
▶ Studied 1922–23 Atelier Jaussely; 1923, École des Beaux-Arts; 1924, Atelier Perret; 1926–28, École d'Urbanisme at Sorbonne University, all Paris.
▶ In 1925, he set up with others the Atelier Perret in a wing of the Palais de Bois, designed by Auguste Perret, at the Porte Maillot, near the Bois de Boulogne, Paris; 1925–29, (with fellow Hungarian architect A. Szivessy, aka André Sive) he set up a partnership; in 1926, he left the Atelier Perret and joined the Atelier Defrasse; in 1927, attended the Stuttgart 'Weissenhof-Siedlung' with Pierre

Chareau, and designed a cover for the magazine *L'Organisation Ménagère*; in 1929, attended the CIAM conference, Frankfurt, and designed the first version of the *Safari* chair, later produced for photographer Lee Miller; designed the 1931 *Entas* stacking metal chair and devised the 1932 (final version) Heliometer machine to measure an installation; designed 1933 'The Outlook' house conversion and new studio block for M. Lahousse, Cucq, et Le Touquet (his first complete building); in 1933, sailed to Athens as secretary of the French delegation to the CIAM, the floating congress that produced the Athens Charter; in 1934, settled in St. John's Wood, London, with an office at 7 Bedford Square; in 1935, moved to a flat, Highpoint, Highgate, designed by Tecton; in 1936, (with Gerald Flower) set up an architecture partnership. In 1937, Goldfinger's proposal to build on the site of four 19th-century cottages, Willow Road, Hampstead, provoked opposition from the local area protection society. Goldfinger was supported by Flora Robson, Roland Penrose, and Julian Huxley; became a member of MARS (Modern Architecture Research Group); in 1939, moved to the house he designed at 2 Willow Road, Hampstead; in 1945, (with Colin Pen) set up a partnership; in 1946, opened an office, 69–70 Piccadilly, and (with fellow Hungarian Pierre Vago) founded UIA (Union Internationale des Architectes); in 1950, designed a house (unrealized) for his brother George Goldfinger, Buffalo, New York; in 1971, was elected associate of the Royal Academy; in 1972, set up an office in Trellick Tower, 19 Golborne Road; in 1975, was elected a Royal Academician. He was one of the most important Modernist architects of the 1930s and after World War II in Britain.

▶ Designed exhibitions in London including children's section of 1935 London 'Dorland Hall Exhibition,' Lower Regent Street; 1937 Frank Lloyd Wright exhibition, Building Centre; ICI stand, 1938 British Industries Fair, Olympia, London; children's section, 1938 MARS exhibition, Burlington Galleries, London; 1938 exhibition of MARS, New Burlington Galleries; 1942 'Eastern Front' exhibition, Rootes Showroom; 1942 'Twenty-Five Years of Soviet Press,' Wallace Collection; 1942 travel-poster exhibitions (with his wife) commissioned by ABCA (Army Bureau of Current Affairs), the Admiralty, and Air Force Education; 1943 'The Cinema' exhibition of ABCA; 1943 'Food' exhibition of ABCA; 1943 'London Women's Parliament Exhibition,' Piccadilly Circus; 1944 'The LCC Plan for London' exhibition of ABCA; 1944 'Traffic,' 'Planning Your Kitchen,' 'Health Centres,' and 1945 'Planning Your Neighbourhood' exhibitions of ABCA; 1945 'Wartime Production' (with Misha Black), Oxford Street; 1946 'A National Health Service' and 'Planning Your Home' exhibitions of ABCA; entertainment complex and 30 vending kiosks at 1951 London 'Festival of Britain'; and 1956 'This Is Tomorrow,' Whitechapel Gallery.

▶ Work in Paris (except where noted) included his own 1925 apartment interior, 29 rue Abel Hovelaque; 1926 apartment interior and furniture for paint manufacturer M. Coutrot; film sets (with Robert Delaunay) with 'H' chairs for *Le Petit Parigot* directed by Marcel L'Herbier; 1926 furniture for Thonet design competition; 1926 furniture for Lehmann family, Berlin; first (1926) apartment for Suzanne Blum; 1926 library, Aghion House (originally designed by Auguste Perret), Alexandria (Egypt); 1927 Central European Express travel bureau, rue Godot de Mauroy, for M. Grossmann, with the interior in metal-faced plywood; 1927 tailor M. Lidvall's fitting-room interior; 1927 own apartment of two flats joined together; 1927 apartment of M. Titus (Helena Rubinstein's husband), rue de l'Ambre; 1927 Helena Rubinstein's salon, Grafton Street, London; 1928 Vigneau apartment, 22 rue M. Le Prince; 1928 Gaut Blancan factory canteen for M. Coutrot; 1928 'Le Portique' picture gallery, 99 boulevard Raspail; 1928 Cheftel apartment interior and furniture, rue d'Astorg; 1928 Grossman apartment interior; 1928 Alpina (snakeskin goods) exhibition stand, Foire de Paris, and at British Industries Fair, London; 1928 Brindejont-Offenbach record shop, arcade des Champs-Élysées; 1928 hygiene exhibition, Vitry-sur-Seine, for Dr. Hazeman; 1928 glass showroom furniture for Helena Rubinstein;

1929 Myrbor shop-front project (realized design by André Lurçat) and furniture for Mme. Cuttoli; 1929 shop front for Mlle. Couteaur, 35 avenue Matignon; 1929 Bugatti showroom, avenue des Champs-Élysées; 1929 Rees radio shop; 1929 Cuteaux monument, Jardin d'Acclimation, Algiers; 1929 apartment for Mme. Belime-Laugier; 1929 Myrbor carpet factory, Marrakesh (Morocco); 1929 apartment and furniture, rue de Babylone, for interior decorator De Verac; 1930 apartment interior and furniture for Mr. Hollender; 1930 Heyliger apartment interior, Île St. Louis; 1930 (second) apartment and office of Suzanne Blum; 1930 Mme. Weill's couture-shop Magazin Janine, avenue de Sufren; 1930 studio interior for Richard Wyndham, rue Froidevaux; his own 1931 apartment and studio interior, rue de la Cité Universitaire; 1934 (third) apartment for Suzanne Blum, 53 rue de Varennes. Work in London (except where noted) included 1931 penthouse studio, 50 Grosvenor Street; 1934 showroom in Endsleigh Street for Paul and Marjorie Abbatt; 1935 S. Weiss Lingerie shopfront and interior, 2 Golders Green Road; 1935 toys, children's alphabet, and logo for Abbatt; 1936 Abbatt toy shop, 94 Wimpole Street; 1936 apartment for P. and M. Abbatt, Tavistock Square; 1937 *Esiwork* furniture and fittings for Esiwork; 1937 Anglo-Continental Express office interior, 144 Regent Street; 1938 stage set for *Stay Down Miner*; 1938 Jacques Heim salon, interior, and furniture, Grafton Street; 1938 three-house complex, 1–3 Willow Road; 1938 flat and interior for John Vago, 29 Maddox Street; 1939 furniture and interiors for Mr. Benroy, Hendon, London; 1940 air raid shelter (with Mary Crowley), Bedales School, Sussex; 1946 *Daily Worker* building, 73 Farringdon Road; 1946 Communist Party headquarters, King Street, Covent Garden; 1946 house, Henley-in-Arden, Warwickshire, for Col. W.B. Fletcher; 1949 Fletcher Hardware warehouse and office, Pershore Street, Birmingham; 1950 primary school, Brandlehow Road, Wandsworth; 1950 primary school, Westville Road, Hammersmith; 1950 house, 74 avenue des Chênes, Brussels, for brother Oscar Goldfinger and father Paul Goldfinger; 1950 dairy farm and bungalow, Turville, Buckinghamshire, for P. and M. Abbatt; 1951 S. Weiss shopfront and interior (with Lillian Ladlow), 59–63 Shaftesbury Avenue; 1954 block of flats, 10 Regent's Park Road; 1956 office building, 45–46 Albemarle Street; 1956 Taylor-Woods showrooms, 45 Albemarle Street; 1956 house, Cherry Lane, Amersham, Buckinghamshire, for John Wallis; 1956 Hille factory, St. Albans Road, Watford, Hertfordshire; 1958 terrace housing, Abbotts Langley, Hertfordshire; 1959 French government tourist office (with Charlotte Perriand), Haymarket; 1959 Alexander Fleming House for the Ministry of Health, Phase I, Elephant and Castle; 1959 Hille House offices and showroom, St. Albans Road, Watford, Hertfordshire; 1961 house, Coombe Hill, Surrey, for Mr. & Mrs. Player; 1962 Hille Factory, Phase II, St. Albans Road, Watford, Hertfordshire; 1963 French government tourist office (with Charlotte Perriand; later altered) and SNCF tourist office, Piccadilly; 1963 Westminster Bank, Alexander Fleming House, Elephant and Castle; 1963 Odeon Cinema, Elephant and Castle; 1966 French government tourist office and SNCF office, 127 avenue des Champs-Élysées, Paris; 1967 housing, Edenham Street, North Kensington; 1968 wooden house 'Teesdale,' Westville Road, Windlesham, Surrey, for Mr. and Mrs. J. Perry; 1969 old peoples' home, Edenham Street; and 1972 housing, Rowlett Street, Poplar.

▶ Work subject of 1983 exhibition at Architectural Association, London. Work shown at 1979–80 'Thirties' exhibition, Hayward Gallery, London.

▶ Cat., *Thirties: British art and design before the war*, London: Arts Council of Great Britain, Hayward Gallery, 1979:191,193, 195,197,198,290. Cat., James Dunnett and Gavin Stamp (eds.), *Ernö Goldfinger*, London: Architectural Association, 1983.

Goldman, Jonathan (1959–)

▶ American artist, performer, and designer.
▶ Studied National Theater Institute, Eugene O'Neill Theater Center, Waterford, Connecticut, and Middlesex Polytechnic

School for the Performing Arts, 1979; 1981–82, Pennsylvania Academy of Arts; and Center for Advanced Visual Studies, Massachusetts Institute of Technology, Cambridge, Massachusetts, to 1985.

▶ Goldman established Goldman Arts, Boston, in 1986; designed 1990 300 ft (91m) ribbon for the opening of the Trump Taj Mahal Casino, Atlantic City, New Jersey, and numerous other installations from 1985. His wife Nicole Novick Goldman was president of the firm. Calling himself an environmental sculptor, Goldman designed in the 1980s the *Sawtooth* lamp, whose fan inflated the shade and cooled the bulb. His *Hairy Chair* in navy blue upholstery had inflatable yellow spikes. His *Venus Fly Trap* chair was 50 in (127cm) tall in forest green upholstery surrounded by bright blue cones. In 1980, he taught electronic imagery, Massachusetts Institute of Technology; 1985–86, art and dance, Brown University; 1987–90, fine art, Boston Architecture Center.

▶ Work shown in numerous group exhibitions from 1985 and subject of exhibitions at South Station, Boston, 1990; Joy Horwich Gallery, Chicago, 1989; Chapel Gallery, Newton, Massachusetts, 1988; Mills Gallery, Boston, 1986; List Art Center, Brown University, Providence, Rhode Island, 1986. Received awards including those from Industrial Fabrics Association International, 1991; International Festival Associations, 1990; National Endowment for the Arts/Rockefeller Foundation, 1987; WBZ Fund for the Arts-Visual Arts Grant, 1986; Cambridge Public Art Competition, 1983.

Goldschmidt, Denis   (1939–)

▶ French industrial designer.

▶ Studied architecture, École Nationale des Beaux-Arts, Paris.

▶ 1961–62, he collaborated with Harold Barnett and Georges Patrix; 1964–67 with Jean Guilleminot, set up the design office Atelier G, working on exhibitions, product design, and corporate identity programs.

▶ Won 1972 competition for urban furniture sponsored by CCI for his telephone booth produced by Mercelec.

▶ Gilles de Bure, *Le mobilier français 1965–1979*, Paris: Regard/VIA, 1983:74.

Goldsmiths' and Silversmiths' Company

▶ British silversmiths; located London.

▶ The retailer and manufacturer Goldsmiths' and Silversmiths' Company was founded in London in 1898; in the 1930s, it produced the designs of Harold Stabler, Bernard Cuzner, S.J. Day, Leslie Durbin, and A.E. Harvey.

▶ Annelies Krekel-Aalberse, *Art Nouveau and Art Déco Silver*, New York: Abrams, 1989:34,35,254.

Gomber, Henrike   (1955–)

▶ German ceramicist; born Dernbach.

▶ 1971–74, apprenticed to potter Rudi Stahl; 1975–76, studied materials engineering, Fachhochschule, Nuremberg; 1976–80, product design, Fachhochschule, Krefeld.

▶ 1981–84, she designed earthenware, decorative ceramics, and architectural ceramics at Ceramano; from 1985, was a product designer for Schuerich Keramik, Kleinheubach am Main, where she designed a 1988 casserole and soufflé dish.

▶ Cat., Design Center Stuttgart, *Women in Design: Careers and Life Histories Since 1900*, Stuttgart: Haus der Wirtschaft, 1989:114–15.

Gomperz, Lucie Marie   (1902–)
See Rie, Lucie

'Good Design'

▶ American design exhibitions held 1950–55.

▶ The 'Good Design' Exhibitions, first only at the New York Museum of Modern Art in 1950 and, 1951–55, also at the Merchandise Mart, Chicago (the largest commercial building in the world at the time), showed what Museum of Modern Art director René d'Harnoncourt and Mart general manager William O. Ollman called 'the best examples of Modern design in home fur-

nishings.' The exhibition was designed in 1950 by Charles and Ray Eames, by Finn Juhl in 1951, by Paul Rudolph in 1952, and by Alexander Girard in 1953. Pieces were selected from items submitted by manufacturers or requested by the jury, which consisted of one prominent retailer and one designer, in addition to Edgar Kaufmann Jr., the Museum of Modern Art curator who served as the permanent 'Good Design' chair. Selection committee members included Alexander Girard in 1952 and Serge Chermayeff. 'Good Design' was financially supported by and, from 1951, organized with the cooperation of the Merchandise Mart administration. Widely advertised and supported by retail stores, a 'Good Design' label was attached to selected designs for sale to the public. The exhibitions ran in parallel with design conferences in Aspen, Colorado, organized by Egbert Jacobsen, director of design at Container Corporation of America. The Canadian National Industrial Design Committee was similar to 'Good Design.'

▶ George Nelson (ed.), *Display*, New York: Whitney, 1953:128–43. Michael Farr, *Design in British Industry: A Mid-Century Survey*, London: Cambridge, 1955. Jonathan M. Woodham, *Twentieth-Century Ornament*, New York: Rizzoli, 1990:206,207. Esbjørn Hiort, *Finn Juhl: Furniture, Architecture, Applied Art*, Copenhagen: The Danish Architectural Press, 1990.

Goodden, Robert Yorke   (1909–)

▶ British architect and designer.

▶ 1926–31, studied Architectural Association, London.

▶ From 1932, he was in private practice. His varied output included wallpapers, domestic machine-pressed glassware for Chance Bros., 1953 coronation hangings for Westminster Abbey, gold and silverwares, ceremonial metalwork, glassware for King's College, Cambridge, 1961 metal-foil murals for the oceanliner *Canberra*, engraved and sandblasted glass murals for Pilkington, and (with R.D. Russell) the design of the Western sculpture and Oriental galleries and the print room of the British Museum, 1969–71. 1948–71, he was professor of jewelry, silversmithing, and industrial glass, Royal College of Art, London.

▶ In 1947, elected Royal Designer for Industry. Designed sports section of 1946 'Britain Can Make It' exhibition and sections of 1951 'Festival of Britain' exhibition, including the Lion and Unicorn Pavilion (with R.D. Russell).

▶ Fiona MacCarthy and Patrick Nuttgens, *An Eye for Industry*, London: Lund Humphries, 1986.

Gooson, Stephen

▶ American film set designer.

▶ Gooson designed sets for the film *Lost Horizon* (1937), directed by Frank Capra. Constructed on the Columbia Pictures lot in Hollywood, the set for the film *Shangri-La* was 90ft (27m) tall, taking 150 men two months to build. Its ostentatious architecture reflected contemporary neoclassical fascist German and Italian modes.

▶ Howard Mandelbaum and Eric Myers, *Screen Deco: A Celebration of High Style in Hollywood*, New York: St. Martin's, 1985.

Goossens, Robert   (1927–)

▶ French jewelry designer; active Paris.

▶ Goossens began as a goldsmith and worked in the atelier of Degorce, supplier to Coco Chanel from the 1930s; in the early 1950s, opened his own workshop and began to work for Chanel on his own, becoming her close collaborator; in the 1960s, produced the well-known pear/triple-ring-motif barrettes and earrings for Chanel through Degorce. The design alluded to Cartier's 1923 interlaced three-band ring by Santos-Dumond. In *c*1958, Goossens worked with Cristobal Balenciaga, who, unlike Chanel, wanted pieces that looked like fine jewelry; subsequently, with Yves Saint-Laurent. He was assisted by his son Patrick in the atelier and shop still located in Paris.

▶ Deanna F. Cera (ed.), *Jewels of Fantasy: Costume Jewelry of the 20th Century*, New York: Abrams, 1992:250.

Gorell Committee
▶ British government research committee on art and industry.
▶ In 1931, the Board of Trade under Lord Gorell set up a committee composed of artists, craftsmen, architects, critics, the director of the Victoria and Albert Museum, and the chair of the British Institute of Industrial Art. Initial members included Roger Fry, A.E. Gray, C.H. St. John Hornby, Sir Eric Maclagan, Howard Robertson, Sir Hubert Llewellyn Smith, Harry Trethowan, E.W. Tristram, and Clough Williams-Ellis. The group was asked to study the state of production and exhibition of everyday domestic goods. Published in 1932, the committee's report presented a survey of the collaboration of art and industry in Britain 1754–1914 and education requirements. It recommended further investigation into the relationship between art and industry, and a permanent exhibition on industrial art in London, travelling nationally.
▶ Cat., *Thirties: British art and design before the war*, London: Arts Council of Great Britain, Hayward Gallery, 1979:304.

Gorgoni de Mogar, Giovanni (1937–)
▶ Italian designer; born and active Milan.
▶ Gorgoni began his professional career in 1969; became a member of ADI (Associazione per il Disegno Industriale). Clients in Italy included Fratelli Turri (furniture), Leoni (furnishings), Arbazar (glassware and table accessories), Coin (furniture), Eurosalotto (fabric), Stilnova (lighting), and Greco (lighting), and, in Paris, Roche Bobois (furniture).
▶ *ADI Annual 1976*, Milan: Associazione per il Disegno Industriale, 1976.

Gorham
▶ American silversmiths; located Providence, Rhode Island.
▶ Gorham is one of the oldest silver factories in the USA. Jabez Gorham, after a seven-year apprenticeship with Nehemiah Dodge of Providence, Rhode Island, started a jewelry-making business with four other men in 1813. Making jewelry, the firm was known for its 'Gorham chain,' said to be of exceptional quality. The partnership was dissolved in 1818, and Gorham continued alone until 1831, when he took in Henry L. Webster, who made coin-silver spoons. In 1837, jeweler William G. Price joined the firm. Jabez Gorham took his son John Gorham into the firm, which became J. Gorham and Son, and retired in 1848. In partnership with his cousin Gorham Thurber for a short period during the 1850s, John Gorham was the titular director for 30 years, increasing mechanization and production and converting the plant to steam power. He installed a British stamping machine for the fast manufacture of flatware, began production of silver hollow-ware, and established a company sales program; Gorham was one of the first firms to produce silverware with the aid of machinery. In Britain in 1852, Gorham discovered the electroplating process at Elkington that, 11 years later, he introduced at the Providence plant. In 1863, the firm was named the Gorham Manufacturing Company. In 1868, the firm adopted the silver standard and greatly increased its production. In 1878, John Gorham declared bankruptcy and was replaced by William Crins, a Providence businessman. In 1894, Crins was succeeded by Edward Holbrook, who had joined the firm in 1870. As a wholesaler, Gorham supplied jewelers and small shops including Spaulding, Chicago; Black, Starr and Frost, New York; and Shreve, San Francisco. 1850–1915, the firm's workmen and most of its well-known designers came from Britain, including George Wilkinson of Birmingham, who came to Gorham in 1854 and was chief designer 1860–1891; Thomas J. Pairpoint, formerly with Lambert and Rawlings, responsible for Renaissance-revival and historicist designs, and at Gorham 1868–77; and A.J. Barrett, who came to Gorham in the late 1860s. Holbrook managed a small group of highly skilled silversmiths who produced the designs of a group of artists under the leadership of William Christmas Codman, who came to Providence from London in 1891. In *c*1900, the group's silverwork was sold under the trade name 'Martelé,' with most of the pieces in a hand-hammer finish. 1891–1914, Codman was the chief design director at Gorham, where he produced hand-made silver in the Art Nouveau style. In 1897, Codman's 'Martelé' range of hollow-ware was produced in 0.950 silver (Britannia Standard) rather than 0.925 sterling. Initially the 'Martelé' range included only vases, beakers, and bowls, followed by complete tea sets and dinner services. Hand-made 'Martelé' pieces in a watered-down Art Nouveau style, as well as Louis XV patterns, were produced and sold through Spaulding, Paris. Gorham's 'Athenic' range combined silver with other metals. Danish silversmith Erik Magnussen produced designs for the firm from 1925 in motifs characteristic of the Danish Modern style, although his triangular-faceted *Lights and Shadows of Manhattan* coffee service showed American influence. Julius Randahl was one of Gorham's silversmiths. In the 20th century, production expanded into bronze casting. By the 1920s, it had bought out several other East Coast silver manufacturers, including Whiting Manufacturing Company. In *c*1985, the firm moved its plant to Smithfield, Rhode Island.
▶ The *Century Vase* by Thomas J. Pairpoint and George Wilkinson shown at 1876 Philadelphia 'Centennial Exposition.'
▶ Larry Freeman, *Early American Plated Silver*, Watkins Glen, NY, 1973:46–48. Dorothy T. Rainwater, *Sterling Silver Holloware*, Princeton, NJ, 1973:7. Charlotte Gere, *American and European Jewelry 1830–1914*, New York: Crown, 1975:187–88. Charles H. Carpenter Jr., *Gorham Silver, 1831–1981*, New York, 1982. Cat., Doreen Bolger Burke et al., *In Pursuit of Beauty: Americans and the Aesthetic Movement*, New York: Metropolitan Museum of Art and Rizzoli, 1987:433–34. Annelies Krekel-Aalberse, *Art Nouveau and Art Déco Silver*, New York: Abrams, 1989:18, 98,100–01, 122,123,254.

Gori e Zucchi
See Uno A Erre

Gorska de Montaut, Adrienne (b. Adrienne Gorska 1899–1969)
▶ Polish architect, decorator, and furniture designer; born Moscow; active Paris.
▶ Studied École Spéciale d'Architecture, Paris, to 1924.
▶ She settled in Paris in 1919; collaborated in a design office with architect husband Pierre de Montaut; (with de Montaut) specialized in cinema design and, in *c*1930, met Reginald Ford, who commissioned them to design cinemas for the Cineac group; designed both interiors and furniture, especially models in chromium-plated metal, for offices, apartments, and cinemas; designed her painter sister Tamara de Lempicka's 1929 two-storey apartment and its furniture, rue Méchain, a building by architect Robert Mallet-Stevens. Clients of the 1920s and 1930s included the Marquis Somni Picenardi, Paris. She was a member of UAM (Union des Artistes Modernes); taught Eileen Gray architectural drawing; designed the Polish Pavilion, 1937 Paris 'Exposition Internationale des Arts et Techniques dans la Vie Moderne.'
▶ Pierre Kjellberg, *Art Déco: les maîtres du Mobilier, le décor des Paquebots*, Paris: Amateur, 1986:79. Arlette Barré-Despond, *UAM*, Paris: Regard, 1986:468–69. Baroness Kizette de Lempicka with Charles Phillips, *Passion by Design, The Art and Times of Tamara de Lempicka*, New York: Abbeville, 1987. Gilles Néret, *Tamara de Lempicka, 1898–1980*, Cologne: Benedikt Taschen, 1992.

Gough, Piers (1946–)
▶ British architect and designer; born Brighton.
▶ 1968–72, Gough was a partner in the architecture firm Wilkinson Calvert and Gough; 1972–75, practiced on his own; from 1975, in Campbell Zogolovitch Wilkinson and Gough. His 1987–88 bent-and-folded-metal chaise longue was produced by Aram Designs.
▶ Albrecht Bangert and Karl Michael Armer, *80s Style: Designs of the Decade*, New York: Abbeville, 1990:81,230.

Gould, Ernest (1884–1954)
▶ American metalworker; active Chicago.
▶ With Edmund Bocker, Gould established the Chicago Art Silver Shop in 1912 at 11 East Illinois Avenue, Chicago.

▶ Sharon S. Darling with Gail Farr Casterline, *Chicago Metalsmiths*, Chicago: Chicago Historical Society, 1977.

Goulden, Jean (1878–1946)
▶ French painter, musician, and craftsman; born Charpentry, Meuse; son-in-law of François-Louis Schmied.
▶ Studied medicine, École Alsacienne, Paris.
▶ In 1906, he published his thesis on the physiology of the heart; in 1908, became a consultant to hospital Laënnec, Paris; while near Mount Athos in Macedonia during the World War I, discovered Byzantine enamels; returning to Paris, persuaded Jean Dunand to teach him the art of *champlevé* enameling; through Dunand, became friendly with Jean Lambert-Rucki, Paul Jouve, and François-Louis Schmied; produced works in silver, polished or gilded copper or bronze with *champlevé* enamel highlights in the form of boxes, caskets, vases, flower stands, lamps, and candlesticks. His shapes were geometric with decorations composed like painting. His caskets were covered with overlapping and uneven block motifs, and his Cubist pendulum clocks were among his finest work. Goulden had a Paris studio up to 1928, when he moved to Rheims. His objects are rare, totaling only 180 known items including *coupés*, clocks, cigarette boxes, small boxes, and silver plaques for bindings by Georges Cretté and Schmied. His large book on his travels in Macedonia was bound by Schmied in crushed black morocco with silver-metal mounts and colored enameled *champs*.
▶ From 1924, work (with Dunand, Jouve, Lambert-Rucki, and Schmied) shown at Galerie Georges Petit and Galerie Charpentier, both Paris. Work shown independently and annually at Salons of Société des Artistes Décorateurs. Work (with Dunand) subject of 1973 commemorative exhibition, Galerie du Luxembourg, Paris.
▶ Jean Dunand, *Jean Goulden*, Paris: Galerie du Luxembourg, 1973. Victor Arwas, *Art Déco*, Abrams, 1980. Pierre Cabanne, *Encyclopédie Art Déco*, Paris: Somogy, 1986:196. Alastair Duncan and Georges de Bartha, *Art Nouveau and Art Déco Bookbinding*, New York: Abrams, 1989:92,93–95,191. Bernard Goulden, *Jean Goulden*, Paris: Regard, 1989.

Goupy, Marcel (1886–1980)
▶ French potter and glass artist; active Paris.
▶ Studied architecture, sculpture, and interior decoration, École Nationale Supérieure des Arts Décoratifs, Paris.
▶ He was a painter, silversmith, and jeweler until 1909, when he met Georges Rouard, who had recently opened Maison Geo. Rouard, avenue de l'Opéra, Paris; serving as Rouard's artistic director until 1954, designed a large amount of glassware, much of which was enameled inside and out, and porcelain and ceramic dinnerware. Most of Goupy's china was made by Théodore Haviland, Limoges. Goupy also designed silver and, for the La Sylve design studio of Le Bûcheron, ceramics; 1918–36 in his own atelier, produced noteworthy enameled and applied-gold glassware vases, bowls, and other vessels.
▶ Work shown at 1923 Exhibition of Contemporary Decorative Arts and in various pavilions including Rouard's at 1925 Paris 'Exposition Internationale des Arts Décoratifs et Industriels Modernes,' where he was vice-president of the glass jury.
▶ Yvonne Brunhammer et al, *Art Nouveau Belgium, France*, Houston: Rice University, 1976. Victor Arwas, *Art Déco*, Abrams, 1980. Cat., *Verriers français contemporains: Art et industrie*, Paris: Musée des Arts Décoratifs, 1982.

Govin, Bernard (1940–)
▶ French designer and interior architect; born Amiens; active Nice.
▶ Studied industrial design and interior architecture, École des Arts appliqués, Paris.
▶ He designed 1967 *Asmara* and 1975 *Satan* furniture ranges by Ligne Roset. Clients included Mobilier International (*Octa* chair), Saporiti Italia (*Eliptique* chair), Airborne, Allia Doulton (marble bathtubs), Dunlopillo (beds). In 1972, (with Christian Adam) designed the 'archi-meuble' environment and architectural inter-

iors for the mayor of Orléans, interior of SNIAS de l'Aérospatiale, and a hotel in Nice.
▶ From 1963, work shown regularly at Salons of the Société des Artistes Décorateurs.
▶ Bernard Govin and Christian Adam, 'Le nouvel habitat Archi-meuble, ou comment constituer son cadre de vie sur mesure,' *Architecture d'aujourd'hui*, June 1972. Bernard Govin, 'Lit et architecture,' *Hexaform*, No. 1, 1975. Cat., *Acquisitions 1982–1990 arts décoratifs*, Paris: Fonds National d'Art Contemporain, 1991.

Graber, Rudolf (1902–71)
▶ Swiss entrepreneur; born Basel.
▶ In the early 1920s, he settled in Munich, working as a volunteer in a bookstore; subsequently, worked in the typewriter office of Flachschreibmaschinen Karl Endrich, Zürich; 1927–30, was a salesperson for Elliott-Fischer und Sundstrand bookkeeping and adding machines, Cologne; returned to Switzerland and in 1931, (with Sigfried Giedion and Werner M. Moser) founded the Wohnbedarf department store, Zürich; investing all his capital in the store, was director of the sales division. In 1935, Wohnbedarf became the sole property of Graber and his mother; during an era of conservative taste, introduced antiques to the store, selling them alongside Modern furniture; in 1947, began to work with Hans Knoll, who had set up a furniture-design and manufacturing facility in the USA.
▶ Friederike Mehlau-Wiebking et al., *Schweizer Typenmöbel 1925–35, Sigfried Giedion und die Wohnbedarf AG*, Zürich: gta, 1989:228.

Grachev, Mikhail and Semen
▶ Russian silversmiths and enamelers; located St. Petersburg.
▶ The Grachev brothers established their firm in 1866; in 1896, were granted an Imperial warrant. Its aristocratic customers preferred *guilloché* enamel, and the Grachev firm provided them with *cloisonné-* and *champlevé*-enamel objects. It closed after the 1917 Revolution.
▶ Annelies Krekel-Aalberse, *Art Nouveau and Art Déco Silver*, New York: Abrams, 1989:18,98,100–01,122,123,254.

Gradl, Max Joseph (1873–1934)
▶ German architect, painter, graphic artist, and designer; born Dillingen an der Donau.
▶ 1888–92, studied Kunsgewerbeschule, Munich, under Theodor Spiess.
▶ He worked at the publishing house Alexander Koch, Darmstadt. His industrial designs and drawings appeared in *Decorative Models and The Modern Style*. C1899–1910, he was artistic advisor to Theodor Fahrner, although his work there was not marked to indicate his authorship.
▶ Work shown at 1903 'Fine Metals Exhibition,' Stuttgart.
▶ Deanna F. Cera (ed.), *Jewels of Fantasy: Costume Jewelry of the 20th Century*, New York: Abrams, 1992:110.

Grafton, F. W.
▶ British textile firm.
▶ In 1855, the founder, F. W. Grafton, took over Broad Oak printworks, Accrington. Grafton became part of Calico Printers' Association in 1899; in the 1920s, it specialized in printed voiles and printed dress and furnishings fabrics.
▶ Valerie Mendes, *The Victoria and Albert Museum's Textile Collection, British Textiles from 1900 to 1937*, London: Victoria and Albert Museum, 1992.

Gramigna, Giuliana (1929–)
▶ Italian architect and designer; born and active Milan.
▶ Gramigna began her professional career in 1956; was a member of ADI (Associazione per il Disegno Industriale); in 1961, became an associate of architect Sergio Mazza, collaborating on furniture for Poltrana Frau, Bacci, Cinova, and Full; lighting for Quattrofolio, Martinelli, and Artemide; interior architecture; appliances for Krupp Italia; and fabrics for Texital. She executed ceramics designs for Gabbianelli, including wall tiles and 1969 *Pomona* ceramic

dinnerware. From its founding in 1966 until 1988, she was editor of the journal *Ottagono*.

▶ Received first prize at 1961 competition Cedit-Piastrella; diplomas at 1964 (XIII) and 1968 (XIV) Triennali di Milano.

▶ Cat., *Italy: The New Domestic Landscape*, New York: Museum of Modern Art, 1972:35,77. *ADI Annual 1976*, Milan: Associazione per il Disegno Industriale, 1976. 'Sergio Mazza e Giuliana Gramigna,' *Interni*, No. 282, Sept. 1978:54–57. Alfonso Grassi and Anty Pansera, *Atlante del design italiano: 1940–1980*, Milan: Fabbri, 1980:168–290. Cat., Kathryn B. Hiesinger and George H. Marcus III (eds.), *Design Since 1945*, Philadelphia: Philadelphia Museum of Art, 1983. *Modo*, No. 148, March–April 1993:120.

Grand Feu Art Pottery

▶ American ceramics manufactory; located California.

▶ Active *c*1912–16, Grand Feu Art Pottery was founded in California by Cornelius Brauckman. Its output was of a high quality and aesthetically distinctive. Generically, *grand feu* is ceramic ware fired at 2500°F (1400°C), maturing its body and glaze simultaneously. *Grand feu* is both porcelain and gres, and Grand Feu Art Pottery specialized in the latter. Calling its wares 'Gres-Cerame,' Grand Feu produced a vitrified body that was neither pure nor translucent. Brauckman did not apply color, relying instead on the natural effects produced by an interaction of heat and glaze. His wares are considered to be on the highest level of those produced in the USA.

▶ Brauckman received a gold medal at 1915 San Diego 'Panama-California Exposition.' Work shown at 1916 (I) Los Angeles 'Annual Arts and Crafts Salon.'

▶ Paul Evans in Timothy J. Andersen et al., *California Design 1910*, Salt Lake City: Peregrine Smith, 1980.

Grand Rapids furniture

▶ Furniture produced in Grand Rapids, Michigan.

▶ The town of Grand Rapids, now located amid farms and corn fields, was settled in the 1830s by New Englanders sailing up the Grand River. The area is covered by hardwood forests appropriate to furniture manufacture. With the help of East Coast funding, the woodworkers made Grand Rapids into one of the largest furniture manufacturing centers in the USA, where the largest furniture company today is Steelcase. Other major firms are located nearby, including Herman Miller and Haworth.

▶ Margery B. Stein, 'Teaching Steelcase to Dance,' *The New York Times Magazine*, The Business World supplement, 1 April, 1990.

Grandhomme et Garnier

▶ French jewelers; located Paris.

▶ Paul Grandhomme met Alfred Garnier through mutual friend Raphaël Collin, when Garnier was seeking to learn enamel painting. Both partners had been inspired by reading Claudius Popelin's book *Émail des Peintres*. Grandhomme, who had a kiln in his home, taught Garnier enameling and encouraged him to learn further from more experienced enamelers. Garnier used an inheritance to set up a studio, which Grandhomme would supply commissions from jeweler Jules Brateau. Henceforth, they worked together, signing their pieces jointly. Their successful collaboration began with the showing at 1889 Paris Exhibition. In 1889, the Musée des Arts Décoratifs commissioned their version of the painting *Les Voix* by Gustave Moreau. In 1898, the partnership was discontinued, and Grandhomme showed his work alone.

▶ Work shown successfully together at 1889 Paris 'Exposition Universelle' and, 1891–98, at Salons of Société Nationale des Beaux-Arts in Paris.

▶ Yvonne Brunhammer et al., *Art Nouveau Belgium, France*, Houston: Rice University, 1976.

Grange, Jacques (1944–)

▶ French interior designer and entrepreneur.

▶ During the 1970s and 1980s, Grange worked for Yves Saint-Laurent, designing his private houses and offices; in 1990, designed Saint-Laurent's boutique for *haute-couture* accessories, Paris (including one-off historicist furniture); manufactured furniture and furnishings, selling through a worldwide chain of his own shops. From 1990, Andrée Putman produced rug designs for the Grange stores: Grange was commissioned as interior decorator by Ian Schrager to design the Barbizon Hotel, New York.

▶ Esther Henwood, 'Of Love and Accessories,' *Vogue Décoration*, No. 26, June/July 1990:61–63.

Grange, Kenneth Henry (1929–)

▶ British industrial designer; born London.

▶ 1944–47, studied Willesden School of Arts and Crafts, London.

▶ 1947–49, he trained as an illustrator; in 1948, was design assistant, Arcon Chartered Architects; 1949–50, was architectural assistant, Bronek Katz and Vaughn; 1950–52, designer with George Bower; and 1952–58, designer, Jack Howe and Partners, all in London; 1958–71, was active in his own design consultancy; in 1972, (with Theo Crosby, Ala Fletcher, Colin Forbes, and Mervyn Kurlansky) became a founding partner of Pentagram, London, which subsequently set up branch offices in New York and San Francisco. He was influenced by the sculptural simplicity of German postwar design, such as that of Braun; redesigned products for Kenwood, including their food mixer. 1987–88, he was president, Chartered Society of Designers. From the late 1980s an increasing number of his clients were Japanese, including Maruzen (sewing machines), Shiseido (toiletry bottles), and tile manufacturer Inax (bathroom fittings). His Industrial designs included 1959 *Brownie 44A* camera, 1964 *Brownie Vecta* camera, 1970 *Instamatic* camera, 1975 *Pocket Instamatic* camera, all for Kodak; 1960 parking meter for Venner; 1960 *Chef* food mixer, 1966 *Chefette* hand mixer, 1967 rechargeable electric knife, all for Kenwood; 1963 *Milward Courier* electric shaver for Needle Industries; 1972 *Safety* razor and 1977 *Royale* razor for Wilkinson Sword; 1965–67 hat-and-coat systems for A.J. Binns; 1968–72 corporate symbol, sewing machines, calculators, and typewriters for Maruzen, 1971–73 *125* high-speed train body for British Rail; and 1979 *Parker 25* fountain pen.

▶ In 1969, elected Royal Designer for Industry. Received 1963 Duke of Edinburgh's Prize for Elegant Design (*Courier* electric shaver), 1984 Commander of the British Empire, and 1959–81 Design Council Awards. Work subject of 1983 'Kenneth Grange at the Boilerhouse: An Exhibition of British Product Design,' Victoria and Albert Museum, London.

▶ Peter Grob (ed.), *Living by Design: Pentagram Design Partnership*, London, 1978:224–83. Cat., *Kenneth Grange at the Boilerhouse: An Exhibition of British Product Design*, London: The Conran Foundation, 1983. Fiona MacCarthy and Patrick Nuttgens, *An Eye for Industry*, London: Lund Humphries, 1986. 'The Camera,' London: Design Museum, 1989. Jeremy Myerson and Sylvia Katz, *Conran Design Guides: Kitchenware*, London: Conran Octopus, 1990:11,31,74–75.

Grant, Duncan (1885–1978)

▶ Scottish painter, muralist, and designer; born Rothiemerchus, Inverness.

▶ 1902–05, studied painting, Westminster School of Art, London; 1905–07, Slade School of Fine Art, London; 1906–07, Jacques-Émile Blanche's La Palette, Paris.

▶ From 1911, he was a member of the Camden Town group of painters; after meeting critic Roger Fry in 1912, joined the Omega Workshop in Fitzroy Square, London, the artists' community founded by Roger Fry; 1913–19, was co-director of Omega Workshops with Roger Fry and Vanessa Bell, living with Bell from 1916; at the workshops, designed textiles, pottery, and furnishings, including painted furniture with Bell, Wyndham Lewis, Henri Gaudier-Brzeska, and Nina Hamnett. A central figure of the Bloomsbury Group, he collaborated with Bell during the 1920s and 1930s on interiors, rugs, printed furnishings, embroideries, and tableware in a painterly style. His rugs illustrated a deliberate irregularity derived from folk art. He designed the décor and costumes for Jacques Copeau's productions of *Twelfth Night* in 1914 and *Pelléas et Mélisande* in 1917, both Paris, and continued to be active in theatre design throughout his life; in 1916, moved into the house 'Charleston,' Sussex, with Bell and David Garnett, living there for most of his life. The house was decorated and redecorated by Grant, Bell, and others of the Bell family for over six decades. Grant designed the 1926 décor (with Bell) of the Clive Bell house, 50 Gordon Square, and Mrs. St. John Hutchinson's house, 3 Albert Gate, Regent's Park, both in London; 1927–38, spent summers painting in the south of France; in interiors, created ornamentation applicable to almost any surface; in 1931, became a member of the London Artists' Association; in 1932, designed the ballet *The Enchanted Grove* produced by the Old Vic-Sadlers Wells; in 1932, was commissioned by Allan Walton to design printed fabrics on linen, cotton, cotton velvet, and cotton-rayon satin weave, including the famous *Daphne and Apollo* motif. His 1934 *Old English Rose* bone-china dinner service was produced by E. Brain, Fenton. In 1935, he produced three panels for the 1934 oceanliner *Queen Mary*, rejected by Cunard's chairman as 'too modern'; in the late 1930s, decorated ceramics produced by Phyllis Keyes.

▶ Work shown at 1915 London exhibition of Vorticist group. In 1934, work shown with the AIA. Ceramics shown at 1934 'Modern Art for the Table,' Harrods department store, London, organized by Thomas Acland Fennemore. Work subject of 1920 exhibition, Carfax Gallery; 1959 exhibition, Tate Gallery, London; 1975 exhibition, Scottish National Gallery of Modern Art; 1980 exhibition, Bluecoat Gallery, Liverpool.

▶ Richard Shone, *Bloomsbury Portraits*, London: Phaidon, 1976. Cat., *Thirties: British art and design before the war*, London: Arts Council of Great Britain, Hayward Gallery, 1979:43,46,70,84,91, 92,95,126,131,133,143,157,285,290. Cat., Richard Shone and Judith Collins, *Duncan Grant designer*, Liverpool: Bluecoat Gallery, 1980. Jessica Rutherford, *Art Nouveau, Art Deco and the Thirties: The Furniture Collections at Brighton Museum*, Brighton: The Royal Pavilion, Art Gallery and Museums, 1983:52–53. Fiona MacCarthy and Patrick Nuttgens. *An Eye for Industry*, London: Lund Humphries, 1986. Stephen Calloway, *Twentieth-Century Decoration*, New York: Rizzoli, 1988:153. Simon Watney, *The Art of Duncan Grant*, London, 1990.

Gras, Madeleine (1891–1958)
▶ French bookbinder; born and active Paris.
▶ Studied bookbinding, École des Arts Décoratifs, Paris, to 1922.
▶ From 1922 to c1930, worked with Henri Nouilhac, Paris; in c1930, set up her own workshop; in her Modern-style bindings, paid attention to the paper wrapping and the endpapers. Her spines lacked ribs, permitting uninterrupted titles. Volumes included *Carte blanche, Deux Contes, Pastiches et mélanges*, and *Carnets de voyage*. During the 1930s, she bound volumes in David David-Weill's library, destroyed during World War II.
▶ Work shown at Salons of Société des Artistes Décorateurs.
▶ Alastair Duncan, *Art Nouveau and Art Deco Lighting*, New York: Simon and Schuster, 1978:20,94,150,191.

Grasset, Eugène-Samuel (1845–1917)
▶ Swiss architect, writer, jeweler, and designer; born Lausanne.
▶ Studied architecture under Eugène-Emmanuel Viollet-le-Duc.
▶ An early admirer of Japanese art, particularly prints and paintings, he made decorative sculpture and worked as an architect in Lausanne. He settled in Paris in 1871. His first work to bring him general recognition was the *Les quatre fils Aymon* illustration, begun in 1881. From 1854, he designed a series of distinctive jewelry pieces for Vever; taught a course on Parisian decorative arts, École Normale d'Enseignement du Dessin, rue Vavin, Paris. His furniture commissions included a complete interior of c1880–85 for Louis Gillot's photographic studio, rue Madame, Paris. Gillot furniture showed influences of Renaissance architecture mixed with Art Nouveau's fauna-flora motifs stemming from the Middle Ages. Grasset designed mosaics, ceramics, and stained-glass windows and, 1905–07 with Frantz Jourdain, all the lettering for La Samaritaine department store, Paris. Windows, usually religious, were made by Félix Gaudin and included Grasset's famous Joan of Arc windows for the cathedral, Orléans. Grasset

was a prolific poster artist and had commissions from the USA; published books *La Plante et ses applications ornementales* (1897) and *La Méthode de composition ornementale* (1905) for and with the help of his students and very influential in the Art Nouveau movement.

▶ *Le Printemps* window and panels shown at 1900 Paris 'Exposition Universelle.' Work first shown at Salon de la Rose Croix and, subsequently, at sessions of Salon de la Libre Esthétique and Salon d'Automne.

▶ Yvonne Brunhammer et al., *Art Nouveau Belgium, France*, Houston: Rice University, 1976. Charlotte Gere, *American and European Jewelry 1830–1914*, New York: Crown, 1975:189. Anne Murray-Robertson, *Grasset: pionnier de l'art nouveau*, Lausanne: 24 heures, 1981. Yves Plauchaut and Françoise Blondel, *Eugène Grasset: Laussane 1841–Sceaux 1917*, Paris: Marchand, 1981. Arlette Barré-Despond and Suzanne Tise, *Jourdain*, Paris: Regard, 1988.

Grassi, Ezio (1942–)
▶ Italian architect and designer; born and active Milan.
▶ Studied architecture, Politecnico di Milano, to 1970; 1970–74, trained at Cassina's research and study center.
▶ He participated in furniture production at C&B Italia and Cassina in Meda; (with Sthorch van Besouw) designed the catalog cover for Cassina and was partially responsible for exhibitions of Cassina and of Muud; from 1975, was active in Milan in architecture and industrial and interior design; was a consultant to Cassina; became a member of ADI (Associazione per il Disegno Industriale).
▶ *ADI Annual 1976*, Milan: Associazione per il Disegno Industriale, 1976.

Grassini, Carlo (1931–)
▶ Italian industrial designer; born Pisa; active Pisa and Florence.
▶ Grassini began his professional career in 1962; became a member of ADI (Associazione per il Disegno Industriale). Clients included Lacs (crystal), Paoletti (linens), Bulleri (machinery), IMB Bacci, Solera, Lupi, Derbe, Ergee, Billi, CAS, Motofides, Rontani, and Superpila.
▶ *ADI Annual 1976*, Milan: Associazione per il Disegno Industriale, 1976.

Grasten, Viola (1910–)
▶ Finnish textile designer; active Sweden.
▶ Studied Taideteollisuuskeskuskoulu, Helsinki.
▶ Influential as a colorist and textile designer, Grasten's first work on *rya* rugs was inspired by Finnish folk art. 1945–56, she produced geometric and figurative patterns; from 1956 to the end of the 1960s, was artistic director of Mölnlycke textiles, Gothenburg: in the 1970s, was a freelance designer with clients including Kasthall and Borås.
▶ Erik Zahle (ed.), *A Treasury of Scandinavian Design*, New York, 1961:174, Nos. 143,149,302. *Design in Sweden*, Stockholm: The Swedish Institute, 1972:69. Cat., Kathryn B. Hiesinger and George H. Marcus III (eds.), *Design Since 1945*, Philadelphia: Philadelphia Museum of Art, 1983.

Graves, Michael (1934–)
▶ American architect; born Indianapolis, Indiana; active Princeton, New Jersey.
▶ Studied architecture, University of Cincinnati, to 1958; Graduate School of Design, Harvard University, to 1959; 1960–62, American Academy in Rome.
▶ In the late 1950s and early 1960s, he was an artist in a studio shared with Richard Meier, 10th Street, New York; from 1962 as Schirmer Professor of Architecture, taught architecture, Princeton University; in 1964, set up his own architecture practice, Princeton, New Jersey. His early work was inspired by classical art and Cubist painting; he used color on his structures to create metaphorical landscapes; one of the 'New York Five' group of architects during the early 1970s, was known only for his drawings until 1982, when his Post-Modern Public Services Building, Portland,

Oregon, was completed. (The other 'New York Five' architects were Richard Meier, John Hejduk, Peter Eisenman, and Charles Gwathmey.) At this stage, Graves was better known for his furniture and furnishings than for his architecture; in 1977, his first furniture collection was produced by Sunar Hauserman, and he produced widely published furniture designs for Memphis in the early 1980s, including 1981 *Plaza* dressing table. His 1985 stainless-steel teapot with its 'fledgling' whistle for Alessi became a popular icon of Post-Modern design, selling more than 500,000 pieces. The 1985 *MG2* armchair and *MG3* club chair were produced by Saways & Moroni. Graves's designs reflected the influences of mass-produced 1930s and 1940s goods, early 19th-century neoclassical designs, and the Wiener Werkstätte. He and 10 other architect/designers designed services for the Alessi's 1983 *Tea and Coffee Piazza* project. He designed 1988 carpet designs for the *Dialog* collection of Vorwerk and ceramics by Swid Powell, including 1985 *Big Dripper* coffee pot. His 1989 *Kyoto Collection* of furniture was produced by Kenneth Smith's Arkitektura firm. His furniture originally intended for the Disney corporate offices was produced by Dunbar in 1990 but designed earlier. He opened his own retail shop in 1993 in Princeton, New Jersey; designed 1993 *Mickey Mouse* teapot. Architecture in the USA included 1967 Hanselmann house, Fort Wayne, Indiana; 1972 Snyderman house, Fort Wayne, Indiana; 1977—78 Fargo-Moorhead Cultural Center; 1978 New Children's Museum; 1979—82 Public Services Building, Portland, Oregon; 1982—85 Humana building, Louisville, Kentucky; 1990 Newark Museum wing; 1989 Disney World Dolphin Hotel and 1990 Swan Hotel in Orlando, Florida; 1989—90 Whitney Museum of American Art addition; Museum of Art at Emory University, Atlanta, Georgia; library in San Juan Capistrano, California; and Pegase di Domaine Clos winery in the Napa valley of California. Graves and others developed the resort site plan, Euro Disneyland, Marne-la-Vallée, where he designed its New York Hotel. In his own residence, he mixed Biedermeier furniture with his own designs.

▶ Furniture shown at 1982 'Shape and Environment: Furniture by American Architects,' Whitney Museum of American Art, Fairfield County, Connecticut; and 1983—84 'Design Since 1945' exhibition, Philadelphia Museum of Art. Dining table and chairs shown at 1985 Triennale di Milano. Received *Progressive Architecture* award, National AIA award, and Arnold W. Brunner Prize in architecture.

▶ Kenneth Frampton and Colin Rowe, *Five Architects: Eisenman, Graves, Gwathmey, Hejduk, Meier*, New York: Wittenborn, 1972. Mario Gandelsonas and David Morton, 'On Reading Architecture: Eisenman and Graves—An Analysis,' *Progressive Architecture*, No. 53, March 1972:68—88. Allan Greenberg, 'The Lurking American Legacy,' *Architectural Forum*, No. 138, May 1973:54—55. Michael Graves, *Architectural Monographs 5*, New York, 1979. Cat., Lisa Phillips (introduction), *Shape and Environment: Furniture by American Architects*, New York: Whitney Museum of American Art, 1982:36—37. Marilyn Bethany, 'The Architect as Artist,' *The New York Times Magazine*, 25 April 1982:96. Paul Goldberger, 'Architecture of a Different Color,' *The New York Times Magazine*, 10 Oct. 1982:42—44,48—52,65—66. Officina Alessi, *Tea and Coffee Piazza . . .*, Milan: Crusinallo, 1983. Cat., Kathryn B. Hiesinger and George H. Marcus III (eds.), *Design Since 1945*, Philadelphia: Philadelphia Museum of Art, 1983. *Le Affinità Elettive*, Milan: Electa, 1985. Auction cat., *Asta di Modernariato 1900—1986*, Auction 'Modernariato,' Milan: Semenzato Nuova Geri, 8 Oct. 1986: lots 87—98. Volker Fischer, *Bodenreform: Teppichboden von Künstlern und Architekten*, Berlin: Ernst und Sohn, 1989. Arlene Hirst, 'World Class at Last,' *Metropolitan Home*, November 1990:100.

Gray, Eileen Moray (1878—1976)

▶ Irish architect and designer; born Enniscorthy, County Wexford.

▶ 1898—1902, studied painting and drawing, Slade School of Fine Art, London; 1900—02, lacquerwork at D. Charles furniture workshop, Dean Street, London; 1902—05, Atelier Colarossi, Paris; Académie Julian, Paris.

▶ She settled in Paris in 1907; from 1907, studied lacquerwork with Seizo Sugawara; in c1910, began to work on decorative panels and screens followed by furniture, desks, bookcases, and beds as one-off pieces for rich clients. Her first complete object, 1919—22 *Le Destin* folding screen, was produced for the residence of couturier Jacques Doucet, 43 avenue du Bois (now avenue Foch), Paris, along with some additional notable designs. She regretted the exclusivity of her work and devoted much thought from 1914 to a kind of furniture that could be batch-produced and more widely sold. During World War I, she worked in London in a studio near Cheyne Walk, Chelsea. In 1918, she returned to Paris, accompanied by Sugawara; 1919—22, her exotic first period, she designed the apartment of modiste Suzanne Talbot, rue de Lota, Paris, where the delicate setting showed luxury furniture alongside avant-garde work including mobile screens and the widely published 'gondola' daybed; 1922—30, Gray operated a shop, 217 rue du Faubourg Saint-Honoré, Paris, under the fictitious name 'Jean Désert,' where she sold unique pieces of furniture, furnishings, lighting, and carpets. In c1923, she was commissioned to produce rugs and furniture for the villa of vicomte and vicomtesse de Noailles, Hyères, through the intervention of its architect Robert Mallet-Stevens. Associating with the Parisian *beau monde*, her clients included architects Henri Pacon, Charles Siclis, Charles Moreux and collectors Jacques Doucet, Henri Laurens, Elsa Schiaparelli, the Maharaja of Indore, and the Countess of Oxford. In 1924, she designed furniture (produced in 1927) for the 1924 oceanliner *Transatlantique*; in c1925, designed her first pieces of furniture using metal; in 1926, designed a functional chair based on a desk-chair model. Prior to 1927, many of her designs were made in her studio under the direction of Evelyn Wyld, her companion as well as collaborator. Wyld left to set up a partnership with American painter and furniture designer Eyre de Lanux. Gray's geometric orientation began to appear as early as the 1923 Salon of Société des Artistes Décorateurs, where her work came to the attention of Dutch architect J.J.P. Oud, who had her work published for the first time internationally in the magazine *Wendingen*. In 1925, she was persuaded by architect Jean Badovici to pursue architecture; 1927—29, outfitted her own house 'E 1027,' Roquebrune-Cap-Martin, with Badovici's assistance. The interiors were clean, sparse, and comfortable. Every space was multifunctional, with collapsible furniture in tubular steel, glass, plate glass, and painted wood. Becoming more interested in architecture, she closed Galerie Jean Désert in 1930; in 1931, designed Badovici's apartment, 17 rue de Chateaubriand, Paris, where her furniture and rugs were installed; in 1932, turned over 'E 1027' to Badovici and built the house 'Tempe à Pailla,' near Castellar, also in the Alpes Maritimes, occupying it alone; in c1938, outfitted an apartment in Saint-Tropez. During World War II, she occupied a château restored by Henri Pacon and brothers Jan and Jöel Martel and harbored a number of artists; after the War, began to work on the reconstruction of the house 'Maubeuge' for Jean Badovici and returned to Castellar. Little known after World War II, she received some little notice with the publication of images of 'E 1027,' 'Tempe à Pailla,' and certain furniture in the 1956 exhibition catalog *25 années de l'UAM* and in a 1959 article in the journal *Architecture d'aujourd'hui*. Her furniture suitable for mass production was not made until the early 1970s, when she was in her 90s. Interest in her work revived in the 1970s.

▶ Work (Symbolist-inspired bas-relief) first shown at 1913 Salon of Société des Artistes Décorateurs (and at its 1923, 1924, and 1933 events) and, subsequently, at 1922 Salon d'Automne; 1930, 1932, and 1956 exhibitions of UAM (Union des Artistes Modernes); Pavilion des Temps Nouveaux, 1937 Paris 'Exposition Internationale des Arts et Techniques dans la Vie Moderne'; 1937 'Le Décor de la Vie de 1909 à 1925,' Pavilion Marsan in Paris; 1970 'Modern Chairs,' Whitechapel Gallery, London; 1976 'Cinquantenaire de l'Exposition de 1925,' Paris Musée des Arts Décoratifs; 1979 'Paris-Moscou,' Centre Georges Pompidou, Paris. In 1952, she participated in a project for an exhibition of UAM, Musée d'Art Moderne, Paris. Work subject of 1970 exhibitions, Graz and Vienna; 1972 exhibition sponsored by the Royal Institute of British Architects, Heinz Gallery, London; 1975 traveling American exhibition sponsored by the Architectural League of New York; 1979 exhibition sponsored by the Scottish Arts Council; 1980 'Eileen Gray and les Arts Décoratifs,' Rosa Esman Gallery, New York; 1970–80 traveling exhibition, New York Museum of Art and Victoria and Albert Museum, London; 1992 'Eileen Gray' exhibition, Design Museum, London. Some pieces shown at 1976 '1925' exhibition, Paris Musée des Arts Décoratifs. In 1972, admitted into Royal Society of Art, London; in 1972, elected Royal Designer for Industry, London; in 1973, became honorary fellow of the Institute of Architects, Ireland.

▶ 'L'appartement de Suzanne Talbot,' L'Illustration, No. 7, 1933:357. Joseph Rykwert, 'Eileen Gray: Pioneer of Design,' Architectural Review, 1972:357. Eveline Schlumberger, 'Eileen Gray (interview),' Connaissance des Arts, No. 258, 1973:72. Cat., Yvonne Brunhammer, Jean Dunnand—Jean Goulden, Paris: Galerie du Luxembourg, 1973:75. Stewart Johnson, Eileen Gray Designer, New York: Museum of Modern Art, 1979. Brigitte Loye, Eileen Gray 1879–1976, architecture design, Paris: Analeph/J.P. Viguier, 1984. Cat., Aaron Lederfajn and Xavier Lenormand, Le Louvre des Antiquaires présente: 1930 quand le meuble devient sculpture, Paris, 1986. Peter Adam, Eileen Gray: Architect-Designer, New York: Abrams, 1987. Stephen Calloway, Twentieth-Century Decoration, New York: Rizzoli, 1988:153. Cat., Les années UAM 1929–1958, Paris: Musée des Arts Décoratifs, 1988:186–87. Philippe Garner, Eileen Gray: Design and Architecture, 1878–1976, Cologne: Taschen, 1993.

Gray, George Edward Kruger

▶ British coin, medal, and stained-glass designer.
▶ Gray was one of the best known coin designers of the 1920s and 1930s; designed the Great Seal of George VI and plaques for the Greene King brewery made by Doulton and by Carter. His interest in heraldic motifs was shown in his stained-glass work and designs for coins. These heraldic devices appeared in his designs for the British silver coinage of 1927.
▶ Cat., Thirties: British art and design before the war, London: Arts Council of Great Britain, Hayward Gallery, 1979:200,291.

Gray, Milner Connorton (1899–)

▶ British industrial and graphic designer; born Blackheath, London.
▶ Studied painting and design, Goldsmiths' College School of Art, London University.
▶ 1917–19, he worked in the first war camouflage unit; in 1922, set up the design consultancy Bassett-Gray; in 1930, became one of the eight founding members of SIA (Society of Industrial Artists; later Society of Industrial Artists and Designers), of which he was honorary secretary 1932–40 and president 1943–48 and in 1968; in c1934, designed graphics for the packaging of 'Golden Mushrooms,' with air vents at the sides and clear film in a circular window on top. 1935–38, he was a council member of DIA (Design and Industries Association); 1932–40, was a senior partner of the design consultancy Industrial Design Partnership; was influenced by the work of Henry Dreyfuss and Raymond Loewy; 1937–40, was principal of Sir John Cass School and had numerous other teaching positions; from 1943, was a founding partner with Misha Black of DRU (Design Research Unit); played a leading role in the development of design consultancy in Britain; during World War II, worked with Black and others for the Ministry of Information designing propaganda exhibitions, including 'Dig for Victory.' He was a prominent member, chair, or president of almost every British and international body in graphic and industrial design. Best known as a graphic artist, he designed corporate identity programs for British Rail, Courage breweries, and Austin Reed;

(with William Vaugham) developed prototype domestic wares for the 'Ideal' fitted-kitchen installation at 1946 'Britain Can Make It' exhibition and was responsible for the overall design of the exhibition, and, jointly, for signage of 1951 London 'Festival of Britain'; in 1955, (with Kenneth Lamble) designed Pyrex glass kitchenware for James A. Jobling; designed the emblem for Queen Elizabeth II's 1977 Silver Jubilee.
▶ He was made a master in the Art-Workers' Guild; in 1937 elected Royal Designer for Industry; in 1963, Commander of the British Empire; received diploma 1957 (x) Triennale di Milano, and a large number of honors. Package designs shown 1979–80 'Thirties' exhibition, Hayward Gallery, London.
▶ Michael Farr, Design in British Industry: A Mid-Century Survey, London: Cambridge, 1955:145. Cat., Thirties: British art and design before the war, London: Arts Council of Great Britain, Hayward Gallery, 1979:26,76,78,231,232,233,291. Avril Blake, Milner Gray, London: Design Council, 1986. Jeremy Myerson and Sylvia Katz, Conran Design Guides: Kitchenware, London: Conran Octopus, 1990:11,51,75.

Graydon-Stannus, A.N.

▶ British glassmaker; active Battersea, London.
▶ Graydon-Stannus was an authority on English and Irish glass; in c1922, first made reproductions of early English and Irish glass from original recipes; in 1926, began her production of decorative and table glassware, later known as Gray-Stan, and mostly designed by A. Noel Billinghurst. Her factory was at 69 and 71 High Street, Battersea, and showrooms in London and the USA. In c1935–36 when James Manning, one of her chief foremen, left to set up his own small glass department at Bromley School of Art, Graydon-Stannus's factory closed. She was a fellow of Royal Society of Arts.
▶ Billinghurst Gray-Stan bowl of c1930 shown at 1979–80 'Thirties' exhibition, Hayward Gallery, London.
▶ Cat., Thirties: British art and design before the war, London: Arts Council of Great Britain, Hayward Gallery, 1979:152,285,291.

Graziani, Gianantonio (1938–)

▶ Italian industrial designer; born and active Milan.
▶ Graziani began his professional career in 1966; was artistic director at and designer of sanitary ceramics for Dozza; developed the graphic corporate image for Cava Ceramiche, Ceramiche Riunite, and Cava Inox (stainless-steel accessories) and corporate image and design for Idealceramiche; was a consultant on exhibition systems to Fratelli Baldi and designed silverwares for the Atelier des Orfèvres and public furniture for the cities of Rimini and Ferrara; became a member of ADI (Associazione per il Disegno Industriale).
▶ ADI Annual 1976, Milan: Associazione per il Disegno Industriale, 1976.

Green, A. Romney (1872–1945)

▶ British furniture maker, craftsperson, and sailor; brother of architect Curtis Green.
▶ He was influenced by Ernest Barnsley and Godfrey Blount early on; was a proponent of the Arts and Crafts movement in furniture. Eric Gill's woodcuts appeared in his book Woodwork in Principle and Practice (1918). His furniture showed influences of 19th-century styles. In the 1930s, Green and Stanley W. Davies of Windermere both worked in the same style.
▶ Cat., Thirties: British art and design before the war, London: Arts Council of Great Britain, Hayward Gallery, 1979:83,128, 291.

Green, Taylor (1914–)
See Van Keppel, Hendrik

Greene, Charles Sumner (1868–1957) and Henry Mather Greene (1870–1954)

▶ American architects, designers, and brothers; born Brighton, Ohio; active Pasadena, California.

► Charles studied architecture, Massachusetts Institute of Technology, Boston, to 1890; Henry to 1892.

► They attended Calvin Milton Woodward's Manual Training School, University of Washington, St. Louis, Missouri, an institution strongly influenced by John Ruskin and William Morris. In Boston, 1891–94, Charles worked for architects H. Lawford Warren and, subsequently, Winslow and Whetherall; 1891–94, Henry worked for architects Stickney and Austin, and, subsequently, Shepley, Rutan and Coolidge, and Chamberlin and Austin. The brothers visited the 1893 Chicago 'World's Columbian Exposition,' where they were greatly influenced by the Japanese section that included a structure known as Ho-o-den by Frank Lloyd Wright. Another influence may have come from Edward Morse's book *Japanese Homes and Their Surroundings* (1885). In 1893, they set up an architecture office, Pasadena, California. Their first furniture was influenced by Bradley's designs for the magazine *The Ladies' Home Journal* of 1901 and begun in that year. Bradley's style had in turn been influenced by British designers Hugh Baillie Scott, Charles Rennie Mackintosh, and C.F.A. Voysey. In 1903, the brothers set up an office, Los Angeles; from 1905, worked in a highly refined style. By 1906, their practice was flourishing, and most of the houses for which they are known today were produced in the next few years. Praised by Gustav Stickley in *The Craftsman* and Charles R. Ashbee in 1909, their lyrical work lacked the heaviness of some other Arts and Crafts pieces. They proceeded to build in and around Pasadena and Los Angeles a type of building known as the California Bungalow, of which the most impressive examples were 1907 Blacker and 1908 Gamble houses, Pasadena, and 1909 Pratt and Thorsen houses farther north. These blended an Arts and Crafts emphasis on materials with Chinese and Japanese approaches and the simplicity of local Franciscan missions of Spanish Colonial architecture. The Greenes' furniture and cabinetry incorporated intricate inlay and sensuous lines. Their first great patron was Adelaide Tichenor, for whom they built their first Craftsman Bungalow in Long Beach, California, in 1904. The Greenes, like Frank Lloyd Wright, included Stickley furniture in earlier residences, but increasingly designed their own furniture and furnishings from 1904. Their constructions took an exasperatingly long time to complete. The partnership began to founder when Charles moved to Carmel, California, in 1916; it broke up in 1922. From 1922, Charles designed some furniture on his own. From 1922, Henry continued to practice architecture.

► Buildings included 1896 Edward B. Hosmer House, 1902 James A. Culbertson House, 1903 Arturo Bandini House, 1904 Adelaide Tichenor House, 1904 Edgar W. Camp House, 1904 Jennie A. Reeve House, 1908 Gamble House, 1906 Robinson House, 1907 Freeman Ford House, 1909 Blacker House.

► Work shown at 1982 'Shape and Environment: Furniture by American Architects,' Whitney Museum of American Art, Fairfield County, Connecticut; 1989 'From Architecture to Object,' Hirschl and Adler gallery, New York; 1987–88 ' "The Art That Is Life": The Arts and Crafts Movement in America, 1875–1920' traveling exhibition organized by Boston Museum of Fine Arts.

► Esther McCoy, *Five California Architects*, New York: Reinhold, 1960. Karen Current, *Greene & Greene: Architects in the Residential Style*, Fort Worth, Texas: Amon Carter Museum of Western Art, 1974. William Current, *Greene and Greene: Architecture in the Residential Style*, Dobbs Ferry, New York, 1974. Janann Strand, *A Greene and Greene Guide*, Pasadena, 1974. Randell L. Makinson, *Greene & Greene*, Vol. 1, *Architecture as a Fine Art*; Vol. 2, *Furniture and Related Designs*, Salt Lake City, Utah: Peregrine Smith, 1977, 1979. Timothy J. Andersen et al., *California Design 1910*, Salt Lake City: Peregrine Smith, 1980:129. Cat., Lisa Phillips (introduction), *Shape and Environment: Furniture by American Architects*, New York: Whitney Museum of American Art, 1982:38–39. Cat., Wendy Kaplan (ed.), *'The Art That Is Life': The Arts and Crafts Movement in America, 1875–1920*, Boston: Museum of Fine Arts, 1987. Cat., *From Architecture to Object*, New York: Hirschl and Adler, 1989.

Greenwood Pottery

► American pottery; located Trenton, New Jersey.

► Trained as a 'dipper' and kiln stoker in Staffordshire (England), William Tams settled in the USA with his son James Tams (1845–1910). After working for a short time at Young's pottery in New Jersey, William opened a pottery with partner William Barnard. James joined his father's pottery, where James P. Stephens and Charles Brearly had become partners in the firm known as Brearly, Stephens and Tams, and succeeded him in 1866. In 1868, the firm was incorporated as Greenwood Pottery Company. James Tams was president, and James Stephens was secretary and treasurer. Until 1875, the pottery produced industrial white-granite and cream-colored tableware for restaurants, hotels, steamships, and railroads, and ceramic hardware including doorknobs and electrical insulations. In 1878, it began production of the *American China* range, whose success resulted in the acquisition of the older Eagle Pottery and Burroughs and Mountford Pottery. In the 1870s, some of its industrial ware was decorated. During the 1870s and 1880s, the firm began producing thin, translucent white porcelain. In 1882, when the plant was destroyed by fire and rebuilt, decorating departments and showrooms were added. In 1883, an English porcelain decorator called Jones, formerly at Royal Worcester Porcelain Company, joined Greenwood, and other artisans from Worcester followed. This hiring resulted in ware indistinguishable from English examples. Greenwood's deep blue glaze on vases imitated the King's Blue of Sèvres and was usually decorated in raised gold, silver, or bronze color. Its artistic ceramic production was short lived. After 1891, Greenwood returned to industrial whiteware.

► Jennie J. Young, *The Ceramic Art: A Compendium of the History and Manufacture of Pottery and Porcelain*, New York, 1879:462–63. Edwin AtLee Barber, *The Pottery and Porcelain of the United States*, New York, 1893:226–28. *The Work of the Potteries of New Jersey 1865 to 1876*, Newark: Newark Museum Association, 1914:22. *The Potter's Art*, Trenton: New Jersey State Museum, 1956:37. Doreen Bolger Burke et al., *In Pursuit of Beauty: Americans and the Aesthetic Movement*, New York: Metropolitan Museum of Art and Rizzoli, 1986:434–35.

Gregori, Bruno   (1954–)

► Italian designer; brother of architect Giorgio Gregori.

► Studied Accademia di Belle Arti, Brera, Milan.

► One of the founders of Alchimia in 1976, he was particularly active in its graphics program; in addition to graphic design for the journal *Domus*, he has worked on various furniture design projects.

► Furniture (with Alessandro Mendini) included 1984 *Tower Furniture* cabinet, 1984 *Atomaria* lamp, 1984 *Zabro* table-chair (hand-painted by Gregori), 1985 *Calamobio* cabinet, 1985 *Cerambrice* silkscreen desk, 1985 *Macaone* table.

► Participated in 1979 'Form Design' exhibition, Linz.

► Robert A.M. Stern (ed.), *The International Design Yearbook*, New York: Abbeville, 1985/1986: Nos. 122–26. Kazuko Sato, *Alchimia*, Berlin: Taco, 1988.

Gregori, Giorgio   (1957–)

► Italian architect and designer; born Rome; active Milan.

► Studied Facoltà di Architettura, Politecnico di Milano.

► From 1984, he was the architecture coordinator for Alchimia and, from 1980, for Studio Alchimia; participated in projects including 'Summer Architecture,' 'Unfinished Architecture,' and 'Black Out.'

► Work (*Ala* sofa by Arflex) shown at 1992 'Nuovo Bel Design: 200 Nuovi Oggetti per la Casa,' Fiera di Milano.

Gregorietti, Salvator   (1941–)

► Italian designer; born Palermo; active Milan.

► Gregorietti began his professional career in 1963; was an associate of the studio Unimark International; became a member of ADI (Associazione per il Disegno Industriale). Work included lighting and metal and glass table accessories. Clients included Rinascente,

Pirelli, Atkinsons, Motta, Standa, Brionvega, Molteni, and Sonzogno. His *Nalu* table lamp was produced by Sirrah and *Alice* hanging light by Valenti.

▶ *ADI Annual 1976*, Milan: Associazione per il Disegno Industriale, 1976.

Gregotti, Vittorio (1927–)

▶ Italian architect and designer; born Novara (Italy).

▶ 1948–1952, studied Politecnico di Milano.

▶ He was a partner with Ludovico Meneghetti and Giotto Stoppino in Architetti Associati in Navara 1952–64 and in Milan 1964–67; 1968–74, was in private practice in Milan; in 1974, (with Pierluigi Cerri and Hiromichi Matsui) established the architecture firm Gregotti Associati; 1964–78, taught at Politecnico di Milano and, from 1978, at Instituto Universitario di Architettura, Venice; was guest professor at universities in Tokyo, Buenos Aires, São Paulo, Berkeley (California), and Lausanne; was an editor on several journals including associate editor of *Cassabella-Continuità* 1952–60, *Edilizia Moderna* (responsible for monographs) 1962–64, and *Il Verri* (responsible for architecture section) 1963–65; from 1980, was director of *La Rassegna Italiana* and a member of the editorial board of the journal *Lotus*; published a number of books including *Il territorio dell' architittura* (1986) and *New Directions in Italian Architecture* (1969). Architecture included 1956–57 Italian Neo-Liberty block of flats for the Bossi company, Cameri, near Novara; 1962–67 town plan for Novara; 1969 project for the Quartiere Zen (with Francesco Amoroso, Salvatore Bisogni, Hiromichi Matsui, and Franco Purini), Palermo; building projects for Università di Palermo from 1970; 1975 competition project for new branch of Università di Calabria (with Emilio Battisti, Hiromichi Matsui, Pierluigi Nicolin, Franco Purini, Carlo Rusconi Clerici, and Bruno Viganò), near Cozenza; 1980 project for ACTV boatyards (with Augusto Cagnardi, Pierluigi Cerri, and Hiromichi Matsui), Guidecca (Venice); 1983–84 area of via Corassari (with members of his studio), Modena.

▶ Work shown at Triennale di Milano from 1951; 1979 'Architettura,' Palazzo delle Stelline, Milan; 1979 'Design and design,' Palazzo delle Stelline, Milan, and Palazzo Grassi, Venice; 1982 'Maquettes d'architectes,' Centre d'Art Contemporain, Geneva, and Le Nouveau Musée, Lyon-Villeurbanne. Received a first prize at 1964 (XIII) Triennale di Milano; 1968 Premio Compasso d'Oro, first prize at IACP Housing Development Competition, Parlero; first prize for 1971 University of Florence Competition entry; first prize for 1973 Università di Calabria competition entry. 1974–76, he was director of architecture and visual arts section, Biennale di Venezia.

▶ Vittorio Gregotti, *Il territorio dell'architettura*, Milan, 1966. Vittorio Gregotti, *New Directions in Italian Architecture*, New York, 1969. 'Vittorio Gregotti,' *Architecture and Urbanism*, July 1977. Manfredo Tafuri, *Vittorio Gregotti: Buildings and Projects*, New York, 1982. P. Lovero, 'La generazione dello Z.E.N. Evora, Vitoria, Palermo: tre quartieri a confronto,' *Lotus International*, No. 36, 1982:27–45. Manfredo Tafuri, *Vittorio Gregotti: Progetti e architetture*, Milan, 1982. S. Brandolini and P.-A. Croset, 'Gregotti associati, G 14 Progettazione—Studio GPI. Cadorna-Pagano: un progetto per il centro di Milano,' *Casabella* 48, No. 513, 1984:52–63. Vittorio Gregotti, 'La fabbrica universitaria: Dipartimenti dell'Università di Palermo di Vittorio Gregotti e Gino Pollini,' *Lotus International*, No. 45, 1985:41–53. Juli Capella and Quim Larrea, *Designed by Architects in the 1980s*, New York, Rizzoli, 1988.

Grenander, Alfred (1894–1956)

▶ German industrial designer.

▶ Grenander was an early member of the Deutscher Werkbund; designed many pieces of furniture along highly Functional lines produced by Berliner Möbelfabrik, and stations and passenger cars for the Berlin elevated tramway.

▶ Penny Sparke, *Introduction to Design and Culture in the Twentieth Century*, Allen and Unwin, 1986.

Gresham, David
See **Design Logic**

Gresley, Herbert Nigel (1897–)

▶ British engineer and designer.

▶ Trained under Francis Webb at Crew and John Aspinal, Horwich.

▶ In 1905, he became the carriage and wagon superintendent of the Great Northern Railway, succeeding H.A. Scott as locomotive superintendent in 1911; in 1923, became chief mechanical engineer of the London and North Eastern Railway; subsequently, developed new features of carriage and wagon designs; was best known for his designs of Britain's largest, most powerful, and fastest steam locomotives, particularly the streamline *Mallard* engine. Gresley designed a special carriage for the fast service between London and Edinburgh, commemorating the 1936 coronation of King George VI. In two shades of blue, the *Coronation* used Rexine on surfaces and uncut moquette for upholstery and carpets. Its exterior was trimmed in chrome-plated metal.

▶ Work (engine models) shown at 1979–80 'Thirties' exhibition, Hayward Gallery, London.

▶ Cat., *Thirties: British art and design before the war*, London: Arts Council of Great Britain, Hayward Gallery, 1979:104,218,291.

Gretsch, Hermann (1895–1950)

▶ German architect, engineer, and product designer.

▶ In the 1930s, Gretsch worked for the Porzellanfabrik Arzberg and others. His best known design was the 1931 *Form 1382* undecorated domestic white porcelain dinnerware, whose basic shape influenced the work of several designers. Like Wilhelm Wagenfeld, he worked in the Modern style in Germany during the Nazi period; when the Nazis closed the Deutscher Werkbund, he became head of its replacement, the Bund Deutscher Entwerfer (Association of German Designers); wrote and edited numerous publications on design for mass production. Considered a 20th-century classic, *Model 1382* was produced by Arzberg and was a synthesis of his design approach and theories. He designed the *2050*, *2200*, and 1954 *2000* ceramic ranges produced by Heinrich Löffelhardt, 1936 *Form 98* by Schönwald, and 1955 *Blattnetz* by KMP, Berlin.

▶ *Model 1382* received a gold medal at 1937 Paris 'Exposition Internationale des Arts et Techniques dans la Vie Moderne' and an award at 1936 (VI) Triennale di Milano.

▶ *Les Carnets du Design*, Paris: Mad-Cap Productions et APCI, 1986:13. Penny Sparke, *Introduction to Design and Culture in the Twentieth Century*, London: Allen and Unwin, 1986. Cat., *100 Jahre Porzellanfabrik Arzberg 1887–1987*, Hohengert: Museum der Deutschen Porzellanindustrie, 1987:66–71. Jeremy Myerson and Sylvia Katz, *Conran Design Guides: Tableware*, London: Conran Octopus, 1990:27,73–74.

Greubel, Jürgen

▶ German industrial designer.

▶ Greubel was employed by Braun to design its products; (with Dieter Rams) designed the 1986 range of furniture for Vitsœ, notably the 862 chair.

Grewenig, Leo (1898–)

▶ German ceramicist.

▶ Studied Bauhaus, Weimar.

▶ His work reflected the theory of simplicity of Otto Lindig, who was head of the Bauhaus production department from 1923. Grewenig's later work rejected the historicist forms that had influenced his earlier Bauhaus work. Handles added to his vessels of c1924 made the pieces easier to handle and lent distinction to the design.

▶ Cat., *The Bauhaus: Masters and Students*, New York: Barry Freidman, 1988.

Griegst, Arje (1938–)

▶ Danish designer.

▶ Studied in Rome and Paris.

33 *Studio 42* portable typewriter; crinkle-finish metal case, 1935. Designed by Luigi Figini and Gino Pollini with Alexander Schawinsky, produced by Olivetti, Ivrea, Italy. (Die Neue Sammlung, Staatliches Museum für angewandte Kunst, Munich)

34 *CLT1* telephone (no. 9330 2357); plastic housing, 1984. Designed by frogdesign, produced by AEG-Telefunken, Ulm, Germany. (Die Neue Sammlung, Staatliches Museum für angewandte Kunst, Munich)

35 Side chair; walnut, marquetry of various woods, fabric, c1900. Designed by Émile Gallé. (Cooper-Hewitt National Museum of Design, Smithsonian Institution/Art Resource, New York, gift of Mrs Jefferson Patterson, photography by John White)

36 Side chair; possibly cherrywood, nailed leather upholstery, 1908. Designed and produced by Hector Guimard. (Cooper-Hewitt National Museum of Design, Smithsonian Institution/Art Resource, New York, gift of Mme Hector Guimard, photography by John Parnell)

37 Music stand;
cherrywood, 1962.
Designed and produced
by Wharton Esherick.
(The Metropolitan Museum
of Art, New York, gift of
Dr Irwin R. Berman, in
memory of his father Allan
Lake Berman, 1979)

38 *Monroe* chair;
black-stained birch, vinyl,
1983. Designed by Arata
Isozaki, produced by
Tendo Mekko Company,
Japan. (The Brooklyn
Museum, Brooklyn, New
York, gift of the James
Corcoran Gallery)

59 *The Egg* chair; plastic,
oxhide, aluminium, 1959.
Designed by Arne Jacobsen,
produced by Fritz Hansen,
Allerød, Denmark.
(The Metropolitan Museum
of Art, New York, purchase,
Edward C. Moore Jr gift, 1961)

60 *How High the Moon* armchair; steel, 1986. Designed by Shiro Kuramata, produced by Vitra, Weil am Rhein, Germany. (Vitra)

61 *Numero Uno* armchair; chromed steel, ashwood, fabric, c1988. Designed by Massimo Iosa Ghini, produced by Moroso, Udine, Italy, from 1989. (The Brooklyn Museum, Brooklyn, New York, gift of Palazzetti)

62 Chandelier;
mahogany, leaded glass,
bronze, 1907. Designed by
Charles Sumner Greene
and Henry Mather Greene.
(The Metropolitan Museum
of Art, New York, gift of
Mr and Mrs Barton C.
English, 1986, from the
R. R. Blacker House,
Pasadena, California)

▶ 1963–65, he taught at Bezalet Academy of Arts and Design, Jerusalem; from 1965, designed silver for the Georg Jensen Sølvsmedie and ceramics for Royal Copenhagen Porcelain factory.
▶ Cat., *Georg Jensen Silversmithy: 77 Artists, 75 Years*, Washington: Smithsonian Institution Press, 1980.

Grierson, Martin
▶ British furniture and interior designer.
▶ Studied Central School of Arts and Crafts, London, to 1953.
▶ In 1960, he became an independent designer; in 1975, opened a workshop in London, where his own designs were made; lectured occasionally at Central School of Arts and Crafts.
▶ Furniture designs received numerous international awards including from 1959 Arflex-Domus competition.
▶ A. Best, 'Design Review: Martin Grierson: Cabinetmaker,' *Architectural Review*, Vol. CLXIII, No. 974, April 1978:229–31. Robert A.M. Stern (ed.), *The International Design Yearbook*, New York: Abbeville, 1985/1986: Nos. 185–86.

Grierson, Ronald   (1901–)
▶ British textile, carpet, and wallpaper designer.
▶ Studied Hammersmith School of Art and Grosvenor School of Modern Art.
▶ 1927–28, he designed posters and interiors; from the early 1930s, learned weaving. Jean Orage wove some of his rugs and tapestry designs; others were produced by craftspeople in India in knotted wool on cotton warps that produced a close pile. His motifs included elements of continental Modernism, with influences from Synthetic Cubism. His numerous clients for textile, carpet, and wallpaper designs included Old Bleach Linen, Campbell Fabrics, Wilton Royal Carpet Factory, Tomkinsons, and S.J. Stockwell. He and his wife produced embroideries. 1945–48, he taught at Camberwell School of Art and, until 1977, at the Hampstead Garden Suburb Institute; published the book *Woven Rugs* (1952).
▶ In the 1930s, work shown at most of the major decorative and industrial art exhibitions. Work subject of 1936 one-person exhibition, Redfern Gallery, London. Examples of his embroidery, rugs, and lino-prints included in the 1979–80 'Thirties' exhibition at the Hayward Gallery, London.
▶ Cat., *Thirties: British art and design before the war*, London: Arts Council of Great Britain, Hayward Gallery, 1980:88,127, 147,175,291. Jonathan M. Woodham, *Twentieth-Century Ornament*, New York: Rizzoli, 1990:158.

Griffen, Smith and Company
▶ American pottery; located Phoenixville, Pennsylvania.
▶ During the peak of its popularity in the 1880s, Griffen, Smith and Co was the most successful producer of majolica in the USA; in 1867, at Starr and Church Streets, Phoenixville, began as the Phoenix Pottery, Kaolin and Fire Brick Co; produced simple industrial wares and bricks for the furnaces of the Phoenix Iron Company (owned by John Griffen), located in an adjacent plant; by 1872, when the pottery was managed by W.A.H. Schreiber and J.F. Betz and Schreiber and Co, produced yellow, white, and Rockingham (manganese brown glaze) wares and terracotta animal heads used as decoration on tavern façades. In 1877, the premises were leased to Levi B. Beerbower and Henry Ramsay Griffen (son of John Griffen), who produced simple white ironstone china (aka graniteware). In 1879, it was reorganized as Griffen, Smith and Hill, whose partners were Henry R. Griffen, brother George S. Griffen, David Smith, and William Hill. The Griffens had graduated in civil engineering from Rensselaer Polytechnic Institute, Troy, New York. Smith was an Englishman who had worked at potteries in Stoke-on-Trent and Trenton, New Jersey. In 1880, Hill left, and the name became Griffen, Smith and Co. By 1879, the pottery was producing its 'Etruscan Majolica' from clays found in New Jersey, Pennsylvania, and Delaware. Some of its designs were based on English 18th-century models. Its begonia-leaf tableware and sunflower motif, developed in England in the 1870s, were extremely popular in the 1880s. In the 1880s, it produced

hard- and soft-paste porcelain and jetware in a black glaze with gold decoration. By 1886, it employed 50 decorators, including Susan Argue O'Neill and Susan Kelley Coyne. David Smith left in 1889. J. Stewart Love (Henry Griffen's father-in-law) assumed directorship of the firm, which became Griffen, Love and Co. Due to majolica's diminished popularity at the end of the 1880s and a fire that destroyed most of the plant in 1890, its majolica production ceased, and its name became Griffen China. For a time, Thomas Scott Callowhill (formerly of Worcester Royal Porcelain and Henry Doulton) was a decorator at Griffen. Out of business in 1892, the pottery continued from 1894–1902 as Chester Pottery of Pennsylvania, later as Penn China and finally as Tuxedo Pottery.
▶ It showed at the 1884–85 New Orleans 'World's Industrial and Cotton Centennial Exposition.'
▶ Edwin AtLee Barber, *The Pottery and Porcelain of the United States*, New York, 1893. Henry R. Griffen, *Clay Glazes and Enamels, with a Supplement on Crazing, Its Cause and Prevention*, Indianapolis, 1896. Anna M.P. Stern, 'Phoenixville Majolica,' *American Antiques Journal* 2, Aug. 1947:10–12. Charles Rebert, *American Majolica, 1850–1900*, Des Moines, Iowa, 1981. Doreen Bolger Burke et al., *In Pursuit of Beauty: Americans and the Aesthetic Movement*, New York: Metropolitan Museum of Art and Rizzoli, 1987:435–36.

Grimminger, Jakob
▶ German silversmiths; located Schwäbisch-Gmünd.
▶ The firm Jakob Grimminger was founded in 1893; in the 1930s, produced fine Modern silverwares.
▶ Annelies Krekel-Aalberse, *Art Nouveau and Art Déco Silver*, New York: Abrams, 1989:254.

Gripoix, Maison
▶ French costume jeweler; located Paris.
▶ Gripoix sold glass beads and buttons wholesale around 1890; subsequently, specialized in handmade imitations of precious and semi-precious jewels, including *parures* for Sarah Bernhardt; was associated with the couture houses Worth, Poiret, Piguet, Dior, and Fath, and produced costume jewelry for four generations. From the first half of the 1920s to 1969, Suzanne Gripoix worked with Coco Chanel. Josette Gripoix, who assisted her mother Suzanne, is assisted by son Thierry in the still-active family firm, 75 rue Turbigo, Paris.
▶ Deanna F. Cera (ed.), *Jewels of Fantasy: Costume Jewelry of the 20th Century*, New York: Abrams, 1992:250.

Gris
See **Riart, Carlos**

Grittel, Émile   (1870–1953)
▶ German ceramicist, painter, and sculptor; born Strasbourg (now France).
▶ Grittel was encouraged to pursue stoneware by Georges Hoentschel and Jean Carriès; in 1894, when Carriès died, Grittel made a portrait of him entitled *Carriès au chapeau*; worked both in Saint-Armand-en-Puisaye with Eugène Lion, and in his own Paris studio in Clichy, where he fired stoneware by Hoentschel. His own designs included pieces inspired by Japanese art with apples and pears and dark monochromatic glazes and gold, and vases with naturalistic reliefs.
▶ Yvonne Brunhammer et al., *Art Nouveau Belgium, France*, Houston: Rice University, 1976.

Griun, Oskar Petrovich   (1874–1931)
▶ Russian designer.
▶ Studied Central Art Institute of A. Stiglitz, St. Petersburg, to 1897.
▶ 1899–1919 and 1922–31, he worked as a textile designer in the textile combine known as Troikhgornaya Manufacture, Moscow; participated in several Soviet exhibitions abroad.

▶ Cat., *Kunst und Revolution: Russische und Sowjetische Kunst 1910–1932*, Vienna: Österreichisches Museum für angewandte Kunst, 1988.

Griziotti, Laura (1942–)

▶ Italian architect and designer; born Seregno; active Milan.

▶ Studied architecture, Politecnico di Milano, to 1966.

▶ She began her professional career in 1967; became a member of ADI (Associazione per il Disegno Industriale); 1967–74, collaborated with architect and designer Cini Boeri; in 1974, set up her own studio, Milan; participated in the planning of 1971 industrial design exhibition of ADI at the Design Centre, Brussels; (with Boeri) designed 1971 *Serpentone* seating and 1973 *Strips* upholstered furniture, both produced by Arflex; (with architect Pietro Salmoiraghi) designed 1975 seat for machine operators produced by Misal.

▶ *ADI Annual 1976*, Milan: Associazione per il Disegno Industriale, 1976.

Groag, Jacqueline (1903–86)

▶ Czech textile designer and ceramicist; born Prague; active Paris and London.

▶ Studied in Vienna.

▶ In 1937, she moved to Paris, where she designed dress prints for Jeanne Lanvin, Elsa Schiaparelli, and others; in 1939, settled in London and began designing textiles for clothing and furnishings; broke away from stereotyped floral prints of the time; in the early 1950s, designed silkscreen motifs for ceramic dinnerware produced by Johnson, Matthey, and colorful textile motifs in typical amorphic printed patterns for David Whitehead. Her designs appeared on wallpaper, laminates, carpets, greeting cards, and even Liberty book matches. She worked for Alastair Morton's Edinburgh Weavers, Bond-Worth carpets, de la Rue, British Rail, 1951 'Festival of Britain,' and others.

▶ In 1984, elected Royal Designer for Industry.

▶ Fiona MacCarthy and Patrick Nuttgens, *An Eye for Industry*, London: Lund Humphries, 1986. Michael Farr, *Design in British Industry: A Mid-Century Survey*, London: Cambridge, 1955:81, 145.

Gropius, Walter (1883–1969)

▶ German architect; born Berlin; active Germany, Britain, and USA.

▶ Studied architecture, Technische Hochschule, Munich, 1903–05, and Berlin, 1905–07.

▶ 1908–1910, he worked in the office of Peter Behrens in Berlin, where he designed office interiors and furnishings for the Lehmann department store in Cologne; in 1910, began his own architecture practice with Adolf Meyer in Neubabelsberg, near Berlin; became a member of the Deutscher Werkbund and, 1912–14, was editor of its *Jarhbücher*; (with Meyer) designed the 1911 Fagus factory, Alfeld; designed furniture for Karl Hertzfeld in 1913 in a neoclassical style reminiscent of Behrens, and a diesel locomotive for Königsberg; designed interiors at 1913 Ghent exhibition, furnishings and interiors for the 1913 Langerfeld and Mendel houses, and 1914 steel furniture (with Adolf Meyer) for the battleship *Von Hindenburg*; at the 1914 Cologne 'Deutscher Werkbund-Ausstellung,' showed a model factory, office building, and machinery hall and railway sleeping-car interior for the Deutsche Reichsbahn, and silver designed for Arthur Krupp of Berndorf. In 1915, Gropius was appointed director of the Grossherzoglich-Sachsen-Weimarische Hochschule für angewandte Kunst and of the Grossherzogliche Kunstakademie in Weimar; in 1919, merged the two into the Staatliches Bauhaus Weimar. Of note are his 1920 *Cube* armchair in wood and cloth and 1923 hanging tubular lamp for his own office, reminiscent of the 1920 lighting fixture by Gerrit Rietveld. In 1920, he and Meyer re-established their architecture practice, Berlin. In 1924, Gropius became a founder of the *Zehnerring* (Ring of Ten). His major early projects included 1921–22 house for the timber merchant Sommerfeld, 1921 abstract sculpture *Monument to the March Dead* in Weimar, and

entry in 1922 *Chicago Tribune* Building competition. In *c*1924–26, he and his assistants were commissioned by Karl Benscheidt Jr. to design his house and furnishing; with Ernst Neufert, Gropius produced some white-painted wood furniture. In 1925, the Bauhaus moved to Dessau and was renamed Bauhaus Dessau; Gropius resigned from it in 1928. 1925–34, Gropius was active in his own practice, working on the Siemenstadt housing estate; designed a prefabricated house for 1927 'Weissenhof-Siedlung,' Stuttgart; in 1925, he designed furniture for the Feder department store, Berlin; 1929–33, designed conventional automobile bodies for Adler; was assisted by Marcel Breuer, Herbert Bayer, and László Moholy-Nagy on 1930 'Deutscher Werkbund-Ausstellung,' Paris; in 1934, settled in Britain, where he worked in association with E. Maxwell Fry 1934–36; 1936–37, was a partner in an architecture practice with Fry; published *The New Architecture and the Bauhaus* (1935); 1936–37, designed furniture for Isokon, as did Breuer. His work for Isokon included a 1935 perforated-aluminum trash bin and 1936 plywood chair and table. In 1936, Gropius was made controller of design for Isokon; along with other refugees, lived in Jack Pritchard's 1934 Lawn Road flats, Hampstead, London; in 1937, left London and settled permanently in the USA; 1937–52, was professor of architecture, Graduate School of Design, Harvard University; built his own 1937–38 house, Lincoln, Massachusetts; 1937–42, was in partnership with Marcel Breuer; in 1945, founded The Architects' Collaborative (TAC), Cambridge, Massachusetts, and was devoted to group efforts. With Louis McMillen and Katherine de Souza, he designed 1968 *TAC 1* tea set and 1968 *TAC 2* coffee set produced by Rosenthal in Germany. A version of the tea set was produced with decoration known as *Bauhaus Homage II* by Herbert Bayer. In 1979, Tecta reissued the chair originally designed for the Fagus factory in 1910. Architecture included (with Breuer) housing in Chelsea, London; 1937 Woods House (for Jack Donaldson), Shipbourne, Kent; processing laboratories, Denham, Buckinghamshire; 1937–39 Impington Village College, Cambridgeshire, and numerous unrealized projects. His work in USA included 1957 Temple of Oheb Shalom, Baltimore, Maryland, and 1958 Pan Am Building, New York.

▶ Work shown at 1969 Bauhaus exhibition, Stuttgart. Subject of exhibition, Zürich; 1972 traveling exhibition sponsored by the International Exhibitions Foundation; 1974 traveling exhibition organized by the Bauhaus Archive; 1992 'Walter Gropius' Total Theatre Design,' Busch-Reisinger Museum, Cambridge, Massachusetts. *TAC 1* tea set received 1969 International Vicenza Prize. Received a gold medal (interiors) at 1913 Ghent 'Exposition Universelle et Industrielle;' 1954 Matarazzo International Grand Prize in Architecture, São Paulo; 1956 Royal Gold Medal, Royal Institute of British Architects; 1958 award, *Grosse Verdienst Kreuz mit Stern*; 1959 gold medal, American Institute of Architects; 1961 Gold Albert Medal, Royal Society of Arts; 1963 Gurlitt medal. In 1947, elected Honorary Royal Designer for Industry, London.

▶ Walter Gropius, *Idee und Aufbau des Staatlichen Bauhauses*, Munich and Weimar, 1923. James Marston Fitch, *Walter Gropius*, New York and London, 1960. Marcel Franciscono, *Walter Gropius and the Creation of the Bauhaus in Weimar*, Urbana, Illinois, 1971. Ise Gropius, *Walter Gropius: Buildings, Plans, Projects 1906–1969*, Lincoln, Massachusetts: International Exhibitions Foundation, 1972. Cat., *Thirties: British art and design before the war*, London: Arts Council of Great Britain, Hayward Gallery, 1979:19,20, 38,84,94,192,193,194,267,242,291. Reginald Isaacs, *Gropius: An Illustrated Biography of the Creator of the Bauhaus*, 1983, 1984, 1991. Lionel Richard, *Encyclopédie du Bauhaus*, Paris: Somogy, 1985:103. Cat., *Stuhlmuseum Burg Beverungen, Der Kragstuhl*, Berlin: Alexander, 1986:37,133. Cat., *The Bauhaus: Masters and Students*, New York: Barry Friedman, 1988.

Gross, Karl (1869–1934)

▶ German sculptor and silversmith; active Dresden and Munich.

▶ Trained with Fritz von Miller; studied Kunstgewerbeschule, Munich.

▶ In 1898, he became professor, Kunstgewerbeschule, Dresden. Theodor Heinze and Hermann Ehrenlechner of Dresden produced his silver designs. He designed furniture and porcelain. His flatware patterns were produced by Bruckmann und Söhne, Heilbronn. He worked for the Vereinigte Werkstätten für Kunst im Handwerk, Munich.
▶ Annelies Krekel-Aalberse, *Art Nouveau and Art Déco Silver*, New York: Abrams, 1989:254. Cat., *Metallkunst*, Berlin: Bröhan Museum, 1990:588.

Grot, Anton
▶ Film set designer; born Poland; active USA.
▶ Grot's earliest film designs were during the 1910s. His ink and charcoal sketches showed meticulous continuity from sequence to sequence, lighting positions, and camera angles. As Warner Brothers' supervision art director, he designed the precisely paced and organized films of Busby Berkeley. Grot's sense of space, starkness, and economy can be seen in Berkeley's *Gold Diggers of 1933* (1933), *Footlight Parade* (1933), and *Gold Diggers of 1935* (1935). Notable is Grot's gigantic setting for the 'mechanical ballet' in *Lilies of the Field* (1930), in which actress Corinne Griffith becomes the radiator mascot on a giant automobile. For the huge nightclub setting for Berkeley's 'Lullaby of Broadway' musical number in *Gold Diggers of 1935*, Grot went far beyond the Art Déco style and evoked German Expressionism.
▶ Howard Mandelbaun and Eric Myers, *Screen Deco: A Celebration of High Style in Hollywood*, New York: St. Martin's, 1985.

Grotell, Maija (b. Majlis Grotell 1899–1973)
▶ Finnish ceramicist; born Helsinki; active Finland and USA.
▶ Studied Taideteollinen Korkeakoulu, Helsinki, under Alfred William Finch, to c1920–21.
▶ 1938–66, was head of ceramics department, Cranbrook Academy of Art, Bloomfield Hills, Michigan, where students included Peter Voulkos, Carlton Ball, Harvey Littleton, and Charles Lakofsky.
▶ Ceramics shown at numerous exhibitions; produced a large body of one-off pottery.
▶ Robert Judson Clark et al, *Design in America: The Cranbrook Vision 1925–1950*, New York: Abrams, 1983. R. Craig Miller, *Modern Design, 1890–1990*, New York: Abrams, 1990. Auction cat., 'Contemporary Works of Art,' Sotheby's New York, 14 March 1992.

Groult, André (1884–1967)
▶ French furniture, textile, and wallpaper designer; born and active Paris.
▶ In the 1910s and 1920s, Groult worked in the traditional 18th- and early 19th-century style associated with Louis Süe and André Mare, with furniture that evoked a feeling of comfort and security. In 1912, he became interested in elegant wallpaper and *toile* (boldly printed, ornate fabric patterns). He published his own drawings as well as those of Marie Laurencin, d'Espagnat, Albert Laprade, Dresa (André Saglio), and Paul Iribe. His masterpiece was probably the anthropomorphic chest of drawers shown at the 1925 Paris Exposition. In 1925, he produced silver designs for Christofle. He was fond of furniture and walls in straw-yellow veneer.
▶ From 1910, work shown at sessions of Salon d'Automne and at Salons of Société des Artistes Décorateurs. Designed lady's bedroom in *Une Ambassade française* pavilion and parts of the Fontaine and Christofle/Baccarat pavilions, including the musical instrument and garden sections of the Grand Palais, at 1925 Paris 'Exposition Internationale des Arts Décoratifs et Industriels Modernes.'
▶ Léon Deshairs, *Modern French Decorative Art*, Paris: Albert Lévy. Victor Arwas, *Art Déco*, Abrams, 1980. Yvonne Brunhammer, *Art Déco Style*, London: Academy, 1983. Cat., Aaron Lederfajn and Xavier Lenormand, *Le Louvre des Antiquaires présente: 1930 quand le meuble devient sculpture*, Paris, 1986. Pierre

Kjellberg, *Art Déco: les maîtres du Mobilier, le décor des Paquebots*, Paris: Amateur, 1986:82–83.

Group Design MBD
▶ French design firm; located Paris.
▶ Group Design MBD was established in 1972 as a firm specializing in graphic, product, and environmental design.

Groupe 7
See Gruppo Sette

Groupe des Cinq
▶ French fraternity of designers; active Paris.
▶ Its members included Pierre Chareau, Raymond Templier, Dominique (André Domin and Marcel Genevrière), and Pierre Legrain. In 1926 and 1927, they showed their work as the Groupe des Cinq at Galerie Barbazanges, Paris. The gallery, at 109 rue du Faubourg St. Honoré, was designed by André Lurçat. The association is not to be confused with Les Cinq.

Gruber, Jacques (1870–1936)
▶ French stained-glass artist, designer, and teacher; born Sundhausen, Alsace.
▶ Studied École des Beaux-Arts, Paris, under Gustave Moreau.
▶ He was distinguished as a designer in the Art Nouveau idiom; 1894–97, worked for the Daum glassworks, designing complex figurative vases; learned the art of engraving, rendering decorations for Wagner's operas; taught and profoundly influenced painter and tapestry designer Jean Lurçat, poster designer Paul Colin, and architect André Lurçat at École des Beaux-Arts, Nancy; designed furniture for Majorelle, ceramics for the Mougin brothers, and bookbindings for René Wiener; was a founder of the School of Nancy; in 1900, set up his own practice to design and manufacture furniture, acid-etched cameo glass that was incorporated into his furniture pieces, wallpaper, and stained glass, closing in 1914. The glass for the tea room and cupola of Les Galeries Lafayette department store, Paris, were by Gruber. His interest in furniture gradually diminished, although he had previously designed models with Adolphe Chanaux. In 1914, he moved to a studio in the Villa d'Alésia, Paris, and concentrated on secular and religious stained glass in a full-blown geometric style retaining figuration. In 1936, his son took over the business. His commissions included the choir of the cathedral in Verdun, steel factory in Nancy, and French embassies.
▶ Work shown at Salons of Société des Artistes Décorateurs from 1908 and Société des Artistes français, Salon d'Automne, and at Museum Galliéra, Paris. Received numerous awards. Stained-glass panels were in a number of pavilions and shown at 1925 Paris 'Exposition Internationale des Arts Décoratifs et Industriels Modernes.'
▶ Yvonne Brunhammer et al., *Art Nouveau Belgium, France*, Houston: Rice University, 1976, biblio.

Grueby, William H. (1867–1925)
▶ American potter; active Boston.
▶ From 1882, he worked at the J. and J.G. Low Art Tile Works, Chelsea, Massachusetts, until about 1890, when he organized a short-lived company that produced architectural faïence in Revere, Massachusetts; in 1892, (with Eugene R. Atwood) established Atwood and Grueby, part of the larger Fiske, Coleman and Co, where architectural ceramics and glazed bricks for interior and exterior decoration were produced; supervised the Fiske, Coleman pavilion at 1893 Chicago 'World's Columbian Exposition,' where he became familiar with the *flambé* technique of French artist-potters Ernest Chaplet and Auguste Delaherche; after Atwood and Grueby was dissolved in 1893, established his own firm, Grueby Faïence, Boston, and produced architectural faïence and terracotta tiles inspired by 15th-century Italian ceramics by Luca della Robbia, Moorish designs, and Chinese ceramics; in 1897, discovered the matt glazes for which he became well known, and began to produce art pottery. The matt glaze was received with enthusiasm by the public and pottery manufacturers. Grueby produced

some surprisingly Modern forms in the Arts and Crafts idiom. His wares were admired by Gustav Stickley, in whose journal *The Craftsman*, Grueby's work was praised. 1897–1902, George Prentiss Kendrick was the designer at the pottery, followed by French architect Addison B. Le Boutiller. Grueby was responsible for the glazes. From 1899, the art pottery had the Grueby Pottery mark, the Grueby Faïence mark appearing only on architectural faïence. Siegfried Bing in Paris sold his works to prestigious collections including the Paris Musée des Arts Décoratifs. Decorations were drawn by women graduates of the School of the Museum of Fine Arts, Boston, and the Cowles Art School. Motifs were based on vegetal images suggested by Grueby's green glaze and its dense texture. The business was restructured as Grueby Pottery in 1907. Grueby incorporated another pottery whose production was limited to architectural faïence. After a fire in 1913, Grueby Faïence and Tile was rebuilt and production continued until 1919, when the firm was acquired by C. Pardee Works, Perth Amboy, New Jersey.

▶ Received numerous medals. Work shown at 1895 exhibition, Architectural League of New York, 1897 exhibition of Boston Society of Arts and Crafts, 1900 Paris 'Exposition Universelle' (gold medal for enamels and glazes, silver medal for pottery design, gold medal for matt enamels), 1901 Buffalo 'Pan-American Exposition' (jointly with Gustav Stickley), 1901 St. Petersburg exhibition, 1902 Turin 'Esposizione Internazionale d'Arte Decorativa Moderna.' Showed 40 objects (with French architect-designer Addison Le Boutillier) and received grand prize at 1904 St. Louis 'Louisiana Purchase Exposition.'

▶ Yvonne Brunhammer et al., *Art Nouveau Belgium, France*, Houston: Rice University, 1976. Robert W. Blasberg, *The Ceramics of William H. Grueby: Catalog of an Exhibition at the Everson Museum of Art*, Syracuse: Everson Museum of Art, 1981. Cat., *American Art Pottery*, New York: Cooper-Hewitt Museum, 1987:76–77. Richard Guy Wilson, *From Architecture to Object*, New York: Hirschl and Adler, 1989:61.

Gruel, Léon (1841–1923)

▶ French bookbinder and gilder; active Paris.

▶ In 1846, Léon Gruel's father took over a bindery established by Desforges in 1811 at 418 rue St.-Honoré, Paris. When Gruel père died in 1846, his widow managed the business until 1850, when she married printer-lithographer Jean Engelmann. In 1875, Engelmann died, and Mme. Engelmann turned the business over to her sons Léon Gruel and Edmond Engelmann. Léon Gruel published *Manuel historique et bibliographique de l'amateur de reliures* (1887); in the 1880s and 1890s, he argued with Henri Marius-Michel and other binders over the parameters of good taste in binding, and was accused of sacrificing good taste for dynamic design; in 1891, became sole owner of the bindery and manager of its large number of craftsmen. After 1900, his son Paul Gruel joined the firm. In 1923 when Léon died, Paul became the director. In 1923, Léon Gruel's library was sold, including a large number of volumes, bindings, reference materials, and tools.

▶ Octave Uzanne, *L'Art dans la décoration extérieure des livres en France et à l'étranger*, Paris, 1898:168,170,183,206–15. S.T. Prideaux, *Modern Bindings: Their Design and Decoration*, New York, 1906. Ernest de Crauzat, *La Reliure française de 1900 à 1925*, Paris, 1932, Vol. 1:27–32, Vol 2:44–45. Lucien Farnoux-Reynaud, 'La Reliure d'art: Triomphe du goût français,' *Mobilier et décoration*, Feb. 1938:58–78. Paul Elek, *The Art of the French Book*, Paris, 1947:146. Roger Devauchelle, *La Reliure en France de ses origines à nos jours*, Vol. 3, Paris, 1961:34–38,114–15, 119,124,127,144–45,172,261. Alastair Duncan and Georges de Bartha, *Art Nouveau and Art Déco Bookbinding*, New York: Abrams, 1989:13,15,17,24,94–95,191.

Gruppo 9999

▶ Italian architecture and design group; active Florence.

▶ The group was founded in 1967 by Giorgio Birelli, Carlo Caldini, Fabrizio Fiumi, and Paolo Galli in Florence to practice Radical architecture and art, espousing a kind of ecological utopia. In 1968, its members staged a 'design happening' on Ponte Vecchio, Florence. Another of its efforts included the interior environment for the 1969 Space Electronic discothèque, Florence. In 1972, at the large dance hall in Florence that the group managed, it organized the seminar 'S-S-Space World Festival no. 1' on conceptual and behavioral architecture, attended by Italian and foreign participants. It published the book *Memories of Architecture* (1973).

▶ Work (theoretical project) shown at 1972 'Italy: The New Domestic Landscape' exhibition, New York Museum of Modern Art.

▶ Andrea Branzi, *La Casa Calda: Esperienze del Nuovo Disegno Italiano*, Milan: Idea Books, 1982. Penny Sparke, *Introduction to Design and Culture in the Twentieth Century*, London: Allen and Unwin, 1986.

Gruppo Sette

▶ Italian architecture association.

▶ Gruppo Sette (Group [of] Seven) was organized in 1926 by the young Milanese architects Sebastiano Larco, Guido Frette, Carlo Enrico Rava, Luigi Figini, Gino Pollini, Giuseppe Terragni, and Adalberto Libera. They published a four-part manifesto in the journal *Rassegna*, launching the Italian Rationalist movement in architecture with an attempt to relate the European avant-garde movement in architecture with Italy's classical past. The Fascist regime opposed the group from its first exhibition of Rationalist architecture in 1927; they were accused of being 'fashionable Europeans' by Edoardo Persico. In 1928, the group MAR (Movimento Architettura Razionale) was started by the Gruppo Sette. The situation was complicated by the formation of MIAR (Movimento Italiano per l'Architettura Razionale), the publication of P.M. Bardi's *Rapporto sull Architettura (per Mussolini)*, the establishment of Bardi's journals *Quadrante* and *Casa-Bella* (with Giuseppe Pagano and Persico as editors of the latter), and Gruppo Sette's own exhibitions in New York and elsewhere abroad. The Italian avant-garde scene around this time included elements of the Futurists' second phase and the efforts of Gio Ponti and his journal *Domus*. The Fascist regime set up a rival to the MIAR.

▶ Work as a group first shown at 1927 (III) Monza 'Esposizione Biennale delle Arti Decorative e Industriali Moderne' and at its 1930 (IV) event, 1927 Stuttgart 'Werkbund-Ausstellung,' and elsewhere.

▶ Pietro Betta, 'Il "Gruppo 7" e l'architettura nuova' in *L'Architettura italiana*, anno XII, No. 2. Barbie Campbell-Cole and Tim Benton (eds.), *Tubular Steel Furniture*, London: The Art Book Company, 1979:46–47. Hanno-Walter Kruft, 'Rationalismus in der Architektur—eine Begriffsklärung,' *Architectura*, Vol. 9, 1979. Vittorio Magnago Lampugnani (ed.), *Encyclopedia of 20th-Century Architecture*, New York: Abrams, 1986:141. Penny Sparke, *Design in Italy, 1870 to the Present*, New York: Abbeville, 1988. Richard A. Etlin, *Modernism in Italian Architecture,1890–1940*, Cambridge, MA:MIT,1991.

Gruppo Strum

▶ Italian architecture and design organization.

▶ Based in Turin, Gruppo Strum was founded by Giorgio Geretti, Pietro Derossi, Carla Giammarco, Riccardo Rosso, and Maurizio Vogliazzo. It became an active participant in Italy's Radical Design movement of the late 1960s; used the technique of handing out picture stories to explain the socio-political background of the architectural culture of the time. Its members took an experimental approach, using architecture as an instrument for political propaganda. Its 1966–70 *Pratone* ('big meadow') furniture piece by Gufram was made of flexible polyurethane foam painted green, and was one of the few examples from an Anti-Design group actually to be produced. The group's name was derived from 'per una architettura strumentale' ('[the group] for instrumental architecture').

▶ Mounted 'Mediatory City' at 1972 'Italy: the new domestic landscape' exhibition, New York Museum of Modern Art.

▶ (Andrea Branzi, *La Casa Calda: Esperienze del Nuovo Disegno Italiano*, Milan: Idea Books, 1982. Penny Sparke, *Introduction to*

Design and Culture in the Twentieth Century, London: Allen and Unwin, 1986. Hans Wichmann, *Italien Design 1945 bis heute*, Munich: Die Neue Sammlung, 1988.

Guariche, Pierre (1926–)
▶ French furniture designer.
▶ Studied École Nationale Supérieure des Arts Décoratifs, Paris.
▶ c1949–52, he worked for Gascoin, where he met Michel Mortier; 1953–57, was associated with Mortier and Joseph A. Motte; they signed their designs 'A.R.P.' Guariche designed inexpensive serially-produced furniture models that were both practical and soberly elegant. In the 1950s, his furniture became known for its use of metal, including lacquered tubular steel, and modular elements. In his chairs, he pioneered the use of plastic foam and 'No-Sag' and 'Free-Span' springs. The 1954 *Tonneau* was the first molded-plywood chair commercially produced in France by Steiner, Paris. His work also included the *Catherine* hemispherical pivoting chair and the *Radar* foam-rubber chair. The 1960 *Vallée blanche* lounge chair was produced by Huchers Minvielle and compared to Le Corbusier's 1929 lounge chair. Other furniture was produced by Airborne and Steiner, and lighting by Disderot.
▶ Pascal Renous, *Portraits de créateurs*, Paris: H. Vial, 1969. Yolande Amic, *Intérieurs: Le Mobilier français, 1945–1964*, Paris: Regard/VIA, 1983:86–87.

Gübelin
▶ Swiss clockmakers; initially located Lucerne.
▶ Gübelin was established in the mid-19th century by clockmaker Maurice Breitschmid in the Pfistergasse district, Lucerne. Jacques-Édouard Gübelin joined the firm of his father-in-law Bretschmid. In 1905, Charles-Édouard Gübelin set up the firm's headquarters on quai Schweizerhof, Lucerne. Édouard Gübelin opened branches in 1919 in New York, Saint-Moritz, Zürich, and Geneva; his sons Édouard and Walter, themselves directors in their turn, were known as expert gemologists. After five generations of Gübelins, Marco and Thomas Gübelin manage the firm today.
▶ Melissa Gabardi, *Les Bijoux des Années 50*, Paris: Amateur, 1987.

Gudhjonsson, Jens (1920–)
▶ Icelandic metalworker; active Reykjavik.
▶ Gudhjonsson was the leading metalworker of his time in Iceland; produced mostly gold and silver jewelry and hollow-ware in his studio and showroom, Reykjavik. His pieces had highly textured surfaces.
▶ Work shown at 1980 'Scandinavian Modern Design 1880–1980' exhibition, Cooper-Hewitt Museum, New York.
▶ Cat., David Revere McFadden (ed.), *Scandinavian Modern Design 1880–1980*, New York: Abrams, 1982:264, Nos. 322,323.

Gudhnadottir, Jonina (1943–)
▶ Icelandic ceramicist; active Reykjavik.
▶ Studied Reykjavik School of Art; Myndlista -og Handidaskoli Islands (Icelandic College of Arts and Crafts), Reykjavik; and Konstfackskolan and Tekniska Skolan, Stockholm.
▶ She worked in her own studio.
▶ Work subject of exhibitions at Unuhus Gallery in 1977, Nordic House in 1975, and Solon Islandus Gallery in 1977, all Reykjavik. Work shown at exhibitions at Centre of Culture, Stockholm; Kjarvalsstadhir, Reykjavik, in 1980; 1981 traveling exhibition, Denmark.
▶ Cat., David Revere McFadden (ed.), *Scandinavian Modern Design 1880–1980*, New York: Abrams, 1982:264, No. 280.

Gudjonsdottir Runa, Sigrun (b. Sigrun
Gudjonsdottir 1926–)
▶ Icelandic ceramicist and illustrator; active Reykjavik.
▶ Trained as a painter.
▶ She taught at Myndlista -og Handidaskoli Islands (Icelandic College of Arts and Crafts), Reykjavik. Based on classical animal and figural subject matter, she painted some of the ceramic forms thrown by Gestur Thorgrimsson.

▶ Cat., David Revere McFadden (ed.), *Scandinavian Modern Design 1880–1980*, New York: Abrams, 1982:264, No. 308.

Gudme-Leth, Marie (1910–)
▶ Danish textile designer; active Copenhagen.
▶ Studied Industrial Art School for Women, Copenhagen; Det Kongelige Danske Kunstakademi, Copenhagen; and Kunstgewerbeschule, Frankfurt.
▶ 1931–48, Gudme-Leth was head of the textile department, Kunsthåndvaerkerskolen, Copenhagen; in 1935, co-founded Dansk Kattuntrykkeri, Copenhagen, where she was director until 1940; printed bold graphic patterns, some based on folk themes; in 1940, set up her own silkscreen workshop for printing textiles.
▶ Received gold medals at 1937 Paris 'Exposition Internationale des Arts et Techniques dans la Vie Moderne' and 1951 (IX) Triennale di Milano. Work shown at 1954–57 USA 'Design in Scandinavia' traveling exhibition, 1956–59 Germany 'Neue Form aus Dänemark' traveling exhibition, 1958 'Formes Scandinaves,' Paris Musée des Arts Décoratifs.
▶ Cat., David Revere McFadden (ed.), *Scandinavian Modern Design 1880–1980*, New York: Abrams, 1982:264, No. 119.

Gudmundsson, Annika (1951–)
▶ Swedish industrial designer; active Gothenburg and Stockholm.
▶ 1971–75, studied industrial design department, University of Gothenburg.
▶ In 1977, she joined the Industridesign Kunsult group, Gothenburg, where she executed designs for graphics and products, including objects rendered in metal and plastics for Guldsmeds; from 1981, was an industrial designer at Made Arkitektkontor, Stockholm.
▶ Cat., Kathryn B. Hiesinger and George H. Marcus III (eds.), *Design Since 1945*, Philadelphia: Philadelphia Museum of Art, 1983.

Gué
▶ French design workshop; located Paris.
▶ The studio Gué was established by brothers Georges and Gaston Guérin, rue du Faubourg Saint-Antoine, Paris. Its designer was Georges Champion.
▶ See Champion, Georges

Guéden, Colette (1905–)
▶ French decorator and furniture and jewelry designer.
▶ In 1931, when René Guilleré died, Guéden and Guilleré's widow Charlotte Chauchet-Guilleré became co-directors of Primavera, the decorating studio of the Au Printemps department store, Paris. In 1939, she took over as head of Primavera; in 1947, was commissioned by the wife of French President Vincent Auriol to design a child's room in the Palais de l'Élysée; in 1965, organized a large exhibition for the centenary of Au Printemps that influenced public taste in furniture design.
▶ Work shown at 1954 Salon of the Salon des Artistes Décorateurs.
▶ *Ensembles Mobiliers*, Paris: Charles Moreau, Vol. 6, Nos. 30–31, 1945.

Guénot, Albert-Lucien (1894–)
▶ French decorator and furniture designer; born Arcueil-Cachan.
▶ Studied École Boulle, Paris.
▶ He worked as a designer in the workshop of Maurice Dufrêne, where he became familiar with the Moderne style; 1914–18, worked in sculptured wood with Laurent Malclès; from 1920, in sculpture with Paul Follot; in 1922, for ironworker Edgar Brandt; and briefly for architect René Crevel. From 1923 and for the rest of his career he was at the Pomone design studio of Au Bon Marché department store, Paris; became the *chef d'atelier* under director Follot; in 1932 succeeded René Prou as its director, remaining there until 1955. Guénot designed the interiors of the hotels Château Frontenac (with decorative painting by Dumouchel), and George V, Paris, 1935 oceanliner *Normandie*, 1961 oceanliner *France*, and offices of Maison Militaire de l'Élysée.

▶ From 1920, work shown at Salons of Société des Artistes Décorateurs; from 1927, Salons d'Automne; 1925 Paris 'Exposition Internationale des Arts Décoratifs et Industriels Modernes'; 1931 Paris 'Exposition Coloniale'; 1937 Paris 'Exposition Internationale des Arts et Techniques dans la Vie Moderne'; Salons des Arts Ménagers; and numerous exhibitions abroad.

▶ *Restaurants, dancing, cafés, bars*, Paris: Charles Moreau, No. 38, *Ensembles Mobiliers*, Vol. II, Paris: Charles Moreau, 1937. R. Moutard-Uldry, *Dictionnaire des Artistes Décorateurs*, Paris: Mobilier et Décoration, 1953–57: Nov. 1953. *Ensembles Mobiliers*, Paris: Charles Moreau, Nos. 27–28, 1954. Pierre Kjellberg, *Art Déco: Les Maîtres du Mobilier, le décor des Paquebots*, Paris: Amateur, 1986:83–84. *Meubles, 1920–1937*, Paris: Musée d'Art Moderne de la Ville de Paris, 1986.

Guens, Van
▶ Dutch designer; active Paris.
▶ Collaborating with Clemens Rameckers, Guens produced handmade furniture, ceramics, blankets, bed linens, fabrics, and rugs in their Paris design studio, Ravage. They were previously fashion designers.
▶ Work subject of 1990 exhibition, Galerie Néotù, New York.

Guenzi, Carlo (1941–)
▶ Italian industrial designer; born Venice; active Milan.
▶ Studied Facoltà di Architettura, Politecnico di Milano, to 1966.
▶ 1965–76, he was editor of the journal *Casabella*; designed a system of institutional infant furniture produced by Jolli; became a member of ADI (Associazione per il Disegno Industriale). He organized round-table conferences in Rimini, San Marino, and Verrucchio; 1975 (VIII) and 1976 (IX) 'Biennali del Mobile,' Mariano Comese and Cantù; 1973 'Design als Postulat' and 1976 'Gestaltung von Kindertagesstatten,' IDZ, Berlin; 1974 'Contemporanea Incontri Internazionali d'Arte,' Rome; 1975 avant-garde and popular-culture exhibition, Bologna; 1976 conference on conditions in the workplace and ergonometrics, Pescara.
▶ *ADI Annual 1976*, Milan: Associazione per il Disegno Industriale, 1976.

Guerriero, Alessandro (1943–)
▶ Italian architect and designer; born Milan.
▶ Studied architecture, Politecnico di Milano.
▶ He was a founder of Studio Alchimia; produced the 1977 *Endless Furniture* concept, a mixture of design, fashion, and performance devised and directed by Alessandro Mendini with contributions by designers Andrea Branzi, Ugo La Pietra, Achille Castiglioni, Ettore Sottsass, and others, and painters Sandro Chia, Enzo Cucchi, Nicola de Maria, and Mimmo Paladino; in 1983, edited *Décoration*, Paris; in 1982, co-founded Domus Academy, Milan; from 1984, was artistic director at Zabro.
▶ Kazuko Sato, *Alchimia*, Berlin: Taco, 1988.

Guévrékian, Gabriel (1900–70)
▶ Turkish architect and furniture designer; born Constantinople (now Istanbul).
▶ From 1921, studied Kunstgewerbeschule, Vienna.
▶ 1919–21, he practiced architecture with Oskar Strnad and Josef Hoffmann in Vienna, executing small houses and interiors; in 1921, moved to Paris, where he worked with Henri Sauvage; 1922–26, collaborated with Robert Mallet-Stevens and designed five residences on rue Mallet-Stevens in Auteuil, near Paris, and residences of Jacques Doucet at Marley-sur-Seine and Paul Poiret at Melun-sur-Seine. Through Mallet-Stevens in 1923, Guévrékian designed the 'Cubist garden' of the villa of vicomte and vicomtesse de Noailles, Hyères; in the 1920s, designed furniture in a stark, somewhat quirky, Modern style, often incorporating plated bent-metal tubing; was a founding member of CIAM (Congrès Internationaux d'Architecture Moderne) and, in 1930, of UAM (Union des Artistes Modernes). The decorating firm DIM commissioned him to execute various lighting fixtures for its interiors. For the lighting requirements of his own interiors, he consulted with lighting engineer André Salomon. A 1929 Guévrékian-Salomon light-

ing fixture may have been inspired by the earlier 1928 *Couronne lumineuse* model by Eugène Printz. In 1927, he designed the renovated Paris apartment of photographer Thérèse Bonney. 1937–40, worked in the office of architecture firm Connell, Ward and Lucas, London; 1946–48, was instructor and head of the architecture department, French Academy, Saarbrücken (Germany); designed 1948–49 *brise-soleils* type office building, Casablanca; settling in the USA in 1948, taught architecture, Alabama Polytechnic Institute, Alburn, Alabama.

▶ Work ('water and light' garden next to Konstantin Melnikov's Russian pavilion) shown at 1925 Paris 'Exposition Internationale des Arts Décoratifs et Industriels Modernes' where he was a member of the architecture jury and vice-president of the musical instruments sections. As a member of UAM, showed his 1930 hotel project in Buenos Aires at its 1930 (I) exhibition. Showed a hammock and various architecture projects, 1931 exhibition, Galerie Georges Petit, Paris; a hotel project in Juan-les-Pins and metal window prototype at 1932 UAM exhibition; a service station model for the Société des Pétroles in Languedoc at 1933 UAM exhibition.

▶ Alastair Duncan, *Art Nouveau and Art Déco Lighting*, New York: Simon and Schuster, 1978:172. Arlette Barré-Despond, *UAM*, Paris: Regard, 1986:408–11. Elisabeth Vitou et al., *Gabriel Guévrékian une autre architecture moderne*, Paris: Connivences, 1987. Cat., *Les années UAM 1929–1958*, Paris: Musée des Arts Décoratifs, 1988:188–89.

Guffanti, Luigi Maria (1948–)
▶ Italian industrial designer; born and active Milan.
▶ Guffanti began his professional career in 1970; was active in public housing, tourism, and interior architecture; served as editor of journals *Milanocasa* and *Sinàat Italia*; became a member of ADI (Associazione per il Disegno Industriale). Clients included Elnagh (mobile homes and trailers), Bora (camping trailers), Candle-Riboli (lighting), and Cantieri Sciallino (motor yacht).
▶ *ADI Annual 1976*, Milan: Associazione per il Disegno Industriale, 1976.

Gugelot, Hans (1920–65)
▶ Dutch-Swiss architect and industrial designer; born Makassar (now Ujung Pandang, Indonesia); active Germany.
▶ 1940–42, studied architecture in Lausanne; 1942–46, Eidgenössische Technische Hochschule (Federal Technical College), Zürich.
▶ 1946–54, he worked with Max Bill and designed his first furniture, produced by Horgen-Glarus; in 1954, met Erwin Braun of the Braun electronic firm, where he was a designer until 1965; 1960–65, he was active in his own design studio Institut Gugelot, Ulm; from 1954, was head of the product design department, Hochschule für Gestaltung, Ulm, where, arguing that a product should function efficiently without disguise or decoration, he exerted a great influence on the forms adopted by postwar manufactured domestic goods. Dieter Rams was his pupil and later colleague in executing austere Functionalist forms for Braun. Gugelot's designs used muted grays, black, right angles, and no ornamentation. An expression of this approach can be seen in Braun's 1956 *Phonosuper* record player (with Rams), nicknamed *Schneewittchensarg* ('Snow White's Coffin') and illustrated the design principles for which its manufacturer became known. His 1962 *Sixtant* electric shaver for Braun set a new international standard. Gugelot designed a sewing machine produced by Pfaff and the *M125* storage unit by Bofinger furniture company; 1959–62, was a consultant to Hamburg U-bahn; continued to practice architecture.
▶ Work shown at 1963 'Ulm Hochschule für Gestaltung 1963' travelling exhibition and 1974 '5 Jahre Bundespreis "Gute Form"' exhibition, Rat für Formgebung, Munich. Work subject of 1984 'System-Design Bahnbrecher: Hans Gugelot 1920–1965,' Die Neue Sammlung, Munich.
▶ Alison and Peter Smithson, 'Concealment and Display: Meditations on Braun,' *Architectural Design*, July 1966:362–63. François

Burkhardt and Inez Franksen (ed.), *Dieter Rams*, Berlin, 1980–81. Cat. *System-Design Bahnbrecher: Hans Gugelot 1920–1965*, *Die Neue Sammlung*, Munich, 1984.

Guidastri, Edoardo (1930–)
▶ Italian designer; born Milan; active Parma.
▶ He was involved in the furniture industry in Brianza, Parma and Southern Italy; in 1971, turned to design and consultancy; became a member of ADI (Associazione per il Disegno Industriale). Clients in Italy included Mesaglio di Feletto Umberto, Salpol di Gallarate, and Arbor di Fontanellato. Others were in France and Germany, including Josef Rose.
▶ *ADI Annual 1976*, Milan: Associazione per il Disegno Industriale, 1976.

Guiguichon, Suzanne (1900–)
▶ French decorator and furniture designer; born and active Paris.
▶ From 1929, she was active as a designer with Maurice Dufrêne at La Maîtrise design atelier of Galeries Lafayette, Paris, designing, for the most part anonymously, furniture, clocks, lighting, fabrics, rugs, and accessories; in 1930, set up her own studio, 54 rue de Clichy, Paris, her furniture produced by various manufacturers in the Faubourg Saint-Antoine, particularly Speich frères. Clients included private and contract clients; she was commissioned to design an office for the mayor of the 6th arrondissement, Paris, and in 1947, bedrooms of French President Vincent Auriol in Château Rambouillet and the Palais de l'Élysée, Paris. She taught at École de l'Union Centrale des Arts Décoratifs, Paris.
▶ Work (a bedroom with Gabriel Englinger) shown in La Maîtrise pavilion at 1925 Paris 'Exposition Internationale des Arts Décoratifs et Industriels Modernes' receiving a gold medal. In the 1930s, work shown regularly at Salons of Société des Artistes Décorateurs and Salons d'Automne. Work shown at 1935 'Exposition Universelle et Internationale de Bruxelles' and 1937 Paris 'Exposition Internationale des Arts et Techniques dans la Vie Moderne.'
▶ *Ensembles Mobiliers*, Vol. II, Paris: Charles Moreau, 1937; Vol. V, No. 5, 1945; No. 2, 1954. Pierre Kjellberg, *Art Déco: les maîtres du Mobilier, le décor des Paquebots*, Paris: Amateur, 1986:85–86.

Guild, Lurelle Van Arsdale (1898–c1986)
▶ American industrial designer and writer; active Darien, Connecticut.
▶ Studied painting, Syracuse University, Syracuse, New York.
▶ Designing initially for the theater, Guild turned to industrial design in the 1920s; by 1920, was selling cover artwork to magazines *House and Garden* and *The Ladies' Home Journal*; subsequently, collaborated with wife Louise Eden Guild on drawings for *Women's Home Companion, McCall's, House Beautiful*, and other magazines; in 1927, became an industrial designer, executing 1,000 product designs or more a year. His drawings, based on a knowledge of mechanical engineering, could be used without alterations by his clients' engineers. He produced working models in his workshop and sometimes tested his designs by displaying them in department stores. His streamlined 1937 Electrolux *Model 30* vacuum cleaner with sleigh feet is among his best known designs. Guild redesigned the electric washing machine, reducing the controls from five to one. In aluminum and plastic, his 1934 compote for Alcoa's Kensington division was an elegant example of his work. A skilled metalworker, his work for Kensington was extensive. Guild's pots and pans for Wear-Ever were practical, innovative, and ubiquitous. His 1936 Alcoa showroom, New York, was a Streamline design with a model railroad car on view and lighting fixtures, furniture, and plinths all constructed of aluminum. He designed numerous domestic accessories and lights for Chase Brass and Copper, Waterbury, Connecticut; much of the lighting was historicist in nature, reflecting Guild's unashamed readiness to accommodate popular taste and his dictum, 'Beauty alone does not sell.' His Streamline designs ranged from table-top accessories such as ashtrays to heavy kitchen equipment, the 1934 May oil burner and a refrigerator for Norge. A prolific writer early in his career of articles on antique furniture for women's maga-

zines, Guild was interested in Early American crafts and moved an entire Early American village from New Hampshire to Darien, Connecticut, where he lived and worked.
▶ Work (Wear-Ever pots and pans) shown at 'Philadelphia Art Alliance Dynamic Design' exhibition.
▶ *Fortune*, Feb. 1934:90. Harry V. Anderson, 'Contemporary American Designers,' *Decorators Digest*, Feb. 1935:42–43,82,84. David Heskett, *Industrial Design*, London: Thames and Hudson, 1980. Martin Grief, *Depression Modern: The Thirties Style in America*, New York: Universe, 1975:60,174–79. Ralph Caplan, *By Design*, New York: McGraw-Hill, 1982:37. Anne-Marie Richard, 'Lurelle Van Arsdale Guild' in Mel Byars and Russell Flinchum (eds.), *50 American Designers, 1918–1968*, Washington: Preservation, 1994.

Guild of Handicraft
▶ British crafts group; located London and, subsequently, Chipping Campden, Gloucestershire.
▶ Charles Robert Ashbee founded the Guild of Handicraft, London, in 1888. Some of its early silversmiths in 1898 included David Cameron, J.K. Baily, William Hardiman, and W.A. White. Enamelers Fleetwood C. Varley and David Cameron used copious enamel and cabochon-cut semi-precious stones and mother-of-pearl, an approach soon copied by other English silversmiths. Ashbee translated Benvenuto Cellini's 16th-century manuals *Trattato del'Oreficeria* and *Trattato della Scultura* for his Guild metalworks. Ashbee's own work was separate from that of the Guild's collective talent. Its artisans in London produced furniture designed by H.M. Baillie Scott for the palace of the Grand Duke Louis IV of Hesse-Darmstadt. In 1902, Guild members moved to Chipping Campden. Their work was shown worldwide and became the source of inspiration to many. Unable to compete with firms that produced cheaper goods, the Guild closed in 1907. Ashbee noted, 'An artist under the conditions of Industrialism has no protection; any trades can steal his design.'
▶ C.R. Ashbee, *Modern English Silverwork*, 1909. Alec Miller, 'C. R. Ashbee and The Guild of Handicraft,' unpublished typescript in Victoria and Albert Museum MSS Collection, c1952. Alan Crawford, *C.R. Ashbee, Architect, Designer and Romantic Socialist*, New Haven: Yale, 1985. Annelies Krekel-Aalberse, *Art Nouveau and Art Déco Silver*, New York: Abrams, 1989:22,24,131,254.

Guillemard, Marcel (1886–1932)
▶ French decorator and furniture designer; born and active Paris.
▶ He trained as a furniture designer at Krieger, furniture makers in the Faubourg Saint-Antoine, Paris; became active also as an interior designer; from the late 1920s, worked with Louis Sognot for the Primavera workshop of the Au Printemps department store, Paris, where, 1918–29, he was chief of the office of design and decoration, sometimes collaborating with architect G. Wibo, including on the tearoom at Au Printemps; was the force behind the Au Printemps annual fairs and the new techniques of window display and merchandising. Guillemard's early work was reminiscent of 18th- and 19th-century French styles.
▶ Work shown at 1922 Salon of Société des Artistes Décorateurs (dining room with Charlotte Chauchet-Guilleré), Salons d'Automne. Designed dining room of Primavera pavilion at 1925 Paris 'Exposition Internationale des Arts Décoratifs et Industriels Modernes.'
▶ *Restaurants, dancing, cafés, bars*, Paris: Charles Moreau, No. 16, 1929. Alastair Duncan, *Art Nouveau and Art Déco Lighting*, New York: Simon and Schuster, 1978:185. Pierre Kjellberg, *Art Déco: les maîtres du Mobilier, le décor des Paquebots*, Paris: Amateur, 1986:87.

Guilleré, René (1878–1931)
▶ French entrepreneur, tastemaker, and lawyer; active Paris; husband of Charlotte Chauchet-Guilleré.
▶ In 1901, Guilleré was a founder of the Société des Artistes Décorateurs; in 1911, was its president; became legal advisor to the Société des Sculptures Modeleurs; was active in the manage-

ment of the Au Printemps department store, Paris, where, in 1913, he founded the Primavera decorating workshop, of which his wife Charlotte Chauchet-Guilleré was director initially.

▶ Pierre Kjellberg, *Art Déco: les maîtres du Mobilier, le décor des Paquebots*, Paris: Amateur, 1986:87−88.

Guillet, Serge
▶ French furniture and interior designer; active Paris.
▶ Studied mechanics.
▶ He collaborated with various architects; in 1983, set up his own design office, where he designed furniture.
▶ Won (with Norbert Scibbila) competition for office furniture sponsored by French Ministry of Culture and APCI (Agence pour la Promotion de la Création Industrielle).
▶ François Mathey, *Au bonheur des formes, design français 1945− 1992*, Paris: Regard, 1992.

Guillon, Jacques (1922−)
▶ Canadian furniture designer; born Paris; active Toronto.
▶ Studied architecture, McGill University, Toronto, and furniture design, Montreal.
▶ In the 1950s, he established his own industrial design firm Guillon, Smith, Marquart and Associates, which specialized in major transportation and product design projects; was best known for his lightweight 1952 laminated-wood and nylon-cord dining chair; in the mid-1960s, designed heavy-framed furniture produced by Paul Arno in Montreal.
▶ Cat., *Seduced and Abandoned: Modern Furniture Designers in Canada, the First Fifty Years*, Toronto: The Art Gallery at Harbourfront, 1986:14−15,20.

Guillot, Émile (aka E. Guyot; A. Guyot)
▶ French architect and furniture designer.
▶ Guillot worked for Thonet and also had an independent practice; some of his furniture was produced by Thonet-Czechoslovakia. He appears to have been associated with the UAM (Union des Artistes Modernes) around 1930 but little else is known about him.
▶ Work (produced by Thonet) shown at 1930 (I) UAM exhibition.
▶ René Chavance, 'Le meuble métallique en série,' *Mobilier et Décoration*, No. 12, Dec. 1929:221. Cat., *Les Années UAM 1929− 1958*, Paris: Musée des Arts Décoratifs, 1988:190−91.

Guimard, Hector (1867−1942)
▶ French architect and furniture designer; born Lyons.
▶ 1882−85, studied École Nationale des Arts Décoratifs, Paris, under architects Eugène Train and Charles Génuys; 1889, École des Beaux-Arts, Paris, under Gustave Gaulin.
▶ He designed the interior of the restaurant Grand Neptune (his first commission), quai d'Auteuil, Paris, and several houses in Paris and its environs; by the time of his 1893 villa for Charles Jassedé, avenue de Clamart (now avenue Charles de Gaulle), Paris, had already achieved an architectural maturity expressed by building's completely integrated exterior and interior. His unorthodox style was inspired by the Henri II style and Gothic revival through Eugène-Emmanuel Viollet-le-Duc's *Entretiens*. His 1894−97 Castel Béranger apartment house, Paris, typified his style: florid ornamentation and cast-iron stairways and balcony with asymmetrical, winding plant-like forms. In 1894, Guimard discovered English Domestic Revival architecture and saw Victor Horta's recently completed Hôtel Horta, Brussels. Guimard devoted much attention to public areas as well as private apartments, designing complete furnishings, ceiling ornaments, floor and wall coverings, fireplaces, and lighting fixtures. His most prolific period was 1899− 1901, when he constructed 1898−1900 Maison Coilliot, Lille; 1899−1900 Castel Henriette, Sèvres; and 1902 Humbert de Romans concert hall 1898−1900; Commissioned by the Compagnie générale du Métropolitain in 1903, he is best known for his rhythmical cast-iron Paris Métro subway station entrances, a design idiom that he pursued in the free form of his carved wooden furniture with bronzes executed in collaboration with chiseler M. Philippon. At his summit, Guimard's style was elegant, if severe,

and free of the mannerism that characterized his later works, such as 1902−05 Maison Nozal, 1910 Villa Flore, and 1911 Hôtel Mezzara. After World War I, Guimard's interest in materials and his innovative spirit appeared in his country home, Vaucresson, where he incorporated tubular asbestos elements designed by architect Henri Sauvage. In 1920, he issued his first serially produced standardized furniture; 1921 saw his first standardized apartment building and worker's house. As the Art Nouveau style fell into disrepute, his earlier successes were forgotten. In 1938, he settled in New York.

▶ Active in numerous exhibitions, he designed a small pavilion and 'Pavillon d'Électricité' at 1889 Paris 'Exposition Universelle' and won the 1899 façade competition for Castel Béranger, when he organized an exhibition of the building. Work shown at 1900 Paris 'Exposition Universelle,' 1925 Paris 'Exposition Internationale des Arts Décoratifs et Industriels Modernes,' Salons of Société des Artistes français from 1890, Salons of Société Nationale des Beaux-Arts from 1894, 1971 'Guimard, Horta, Van de Velde' exhibition, Paris. In 1902, became a member of Société des Artistes Décorateurs, showing at its Salons from 1904. Became a founding member of Société 'Le Nouveau-Paris.' Work subject of exhibitions at Galerie du Luxembourg, Paris, 1971; Musée Municipal, Saint-Dizier; Landesmuseum, Münster, 1975; New York Museum of Modern Art, 1980; Musée des Arts Décoratifs et des Tissus, Lyons, 1991.

▶ Hector Guimard, *Le Castel Béranger*, Paris, 1899. Hector Guimard, 'An Architect's Opinion of l'Art Nouveau,' *Architectural Record*, June 1902:130−33. Cat., *Europa 1900*, Ostend: Musée des Beaux-Arts, 1967: No. 220. F.L. Graham, *Hector Guimard*, New York, 1970. Cat., *Guimard, Horta, Van de Velde*, Paris, 1971. Yvonne Brunhammer et al., *Art Nouveau Belgium, France*, Houston: Rice University, 1976. Gillian Naylor and Yvonne Brunhammer, *Hector Guimard*, London, 1978. D. Dunster, *Hector Guimard*, London, 1978. Gillian Naylor, *Architectural Monographs, Guimard*, London, 1978. Alastair Duncan, *Art Nouveau and Art Deco Lighting*, New York: Simon and Schuster, 1978:78−79. Claude Frontisi, *Hector Guimard, Architectures*, Paris, 1985. Cat., Philippe Thiébaut (ed.), *Guimard*, Lyons: Musée des Arts Décoratifs et des Tissus, 1991.

Gulbrandsen, Nora (1894−1978)
▶ Norwegian designer; born Kristiania (now Oslo).
▶ Studied Statens Håndverks -og Kunstindustriskole, Oslo.
▶ Gulbrandsen was recommended by Landsforeningen Norsk Brukskunst (Association for Applied Arts) for employment at Porsgrund Porselaensfabrik, Porsgrunn, where she was artistic director 1928−45; in a program of renewel at Porselaensfabrik, introduced Modern designs and décor in a kind of Art Déco style. Her ceramic work in the 1920s showed Chinese influences, and her spirals and circles suggested speed and movement. She incorporated cubes, cylinders, and circles into her work. New and unusual color combinations of black, yellow, and red; black and gold; and blue and silver were frequent. She designed ceramics for mass-produced sets as well as unique pieces and glassware, textiles, book jackets, bookbinding, and wallpaper; leaving Porsgrund, set up her own pottery-design studio in 1946; from the 1960s, designed silver for David-Andersen.
▶ Work shown at 1927 exhibition, Bergen, sponsored by Norwegian Society of Arts and Crafts.
▶ Cat., David Revere McFadden (ed.), *Scandinavian Modern Design 1880−1980*, New York: Abrams, 1982:265, no. 75. Fredrik Wildhagen, *Norge i Form*, Oslo: Stenersen, 1988:87,510. Jennifer Hawkins Opie, *Scandinavia: Ceramics and Glass in the Twentieth Century*, New York: Rizzoli, 1989. Cat., Anne Wichstrøm, *Rooms with a View: Women's Art in Norway 1880−1990*, Oslo: The Royal Ministry of Foreign Affairs, 1990:24.

Guldsmedsaktiebolaget (aka GAB)
▶ Swedish silversmiths; located Stockholm.
▶ Guldsmedsaktiebolaget was founded in 1867; by the time Jacob Angman joined GAB in 1907 as artistic director, it was

Sweden's leading Modern silversmithy. Angman set the pattern for Modern Swedish silver design, and his 1916 *Three Holy Kings* jewel casket was notable. Together with Nils Fougstedt's work for Hallberg, Angman's silverwares were forerunners of the quality of design that established Sweden's high reputation in the 1930s. GAB's designers in the 1920s and 1930s included Just Andersen, Maja-Lisa Ohlsson, and Folke Arström. In 1961, GAB merged with C.G. Hallberg.
▶ Annelies Krekel-Aalberse, *Art Nouveau and Art Déco Silver*, New York: Abrams, 1989:237,244–45,254.

Gullaskruf Glasbruk
▶ Swedish glass factory.
▶ The factory was founded in Gullaskruf in 1895 for the production of window glass. Closed in 1920, it was reorganized in 1925 by engineer William Stenberg and his daughter. Stenberg designed molds for everyday glassware, the specialty of the firm that later included decorative wares designed by Hugo Gehlin and Arthur Percy. The firm began to include colored glass and experimented with various techniques including semi-opaque glass. In 1975, Gullaskruf was amalgamated with Royal Krona and subsequently with Orrefors.
▶ Jennifer Hawkins Opie, *Scandinavia: Ceramics and Glass in the Twentieth Century*, New York: Rizzoli, 1989.

Gulotta, Gerard
▶ American glassware designer, ceramicist, and teacher; active New York.
▶ An international designer, his work was produced in the USA, Europe, and the Far East for clients including Block, Dansk, Cristais de Alcobaca, Sociedad de Porcelanas, Ceramicas S. Bernardo, Porcelanas del Bidasoa, Ionia, and Tienshan; from the late 1960s, was a professor; organized and directed government-sponsored 1974 'Industrial Design Workshop 74,' Portugal; in 1976–77, designed the first foundation curriculum in industrial design for a new school of design at the University of Guadalajara, Mexico; in 1982, lectured on industrial design, Central School of Arts and Crafts, Beijing University of Hunan, Changsha, and College of Arts and Crafts, Jingdezhen.
▶ Received first prize at 1971 'Premio Internacional,' International Ceramic and Glass Competition, Valencia.

Gundlach-Pedersen, Oscar   (1886–1960)
▶ Danish designer and architect.
▶ Studied architecture, Det Kongelige Danske Kunstakademi, Copenhagen.
▶ He designed buildings in Denmark; 1927–31, served as manager of Georg Jensen Sølvsmedie. Designs included 1937 *Nordic* flatware patterns for Jensen.
▶ During the 1920s and 1930s, work shown at a number of exhibitions in Copenhagen.
▶ Cat., *Georg Jensen Silversmithy: 77 Artists, 75 Years*, Washington: Smithsonian Institution Press, 1980.

Gunnarsson, Hans   (1945–)
▶ Swedish architect and designer.
▶ Studied industrial design school, Gothenburg.
▶ He worked as a freelance interior designer of hotels, exhibitions, museums, and restaurants; in 1982, joined White Architects.
▶ Robert A.M. Stern (ed.), *The International Design Yearbook*, New York: Abbeville, 1985/1986: No. 130.

Günther, Kelp   (aka 'Zamp')
See Haus-Rucker-Co

Gurschner, Gustav   (1873–)
▶ German sculptor and designer; born Mühldorf, Bavaria.
▶ Studied art school, Bozen (now Bolzano, Italy) and Imperial Arts and Crafts School, Vienna.
▶ He settled in Vienna; produced monumental sculpture groups and portrait busts; turned to small domestic objects including door knockers, ashtrays, hand mirrors, inkwells, and dishes. Most of these items were sold by A. Forster, Vienna. He produced the

1909 memorial to the meeting between King Edward VII of Britain and Emperor Franz Josef of Austria-Hungary at Marienbad (now Mariánské Lázně, Czech Republic) in 1905, and medals for automobile races honoring Gordon Bennett and Herbert von Herkomer. In his lighting, Gurschner often incorporated the well-worn theme of naked women and sometimes sea shells. His small workshop staff produced metalwork and for a time ventured into jewelry and furniture production.
▶ Work shown at 1898 (I) Vienna Secession exhibition and, subsequently, at various exhibitions in Vienna, and in Munich, Monte Carlo, and Paris, including 1900 'Exposition Universelle.'
▶ Cat., *Jugendstil 20er Jahre*, Vienna: Künstlerhaus Galerie, plates 2–5. Hans Vollmer, *Allgemeines Lexikon der Bildenden Künstler des 20. Jahrhunderts*, Vol. II, Leipzig: Seemann, 1955:339. Alastair Duncan, *Art Nouveau and Art Déco Lighting*, New York: Simon and Schuster, 1978:122.

Gusrud, Svein   (1944–)
▶ Norwegian furniture designer.
▶ For Studio HÅG, Oslo, Gusrud designed the widely published 1982 *Balans Activ* ergonomic stool (with Hans Christian Mengshoel) and innovative 1983 prototype transportation seating; (with Oddvin Rykkens and Peter Opsvik) led the development of the ergonomic stool seating popular in the early 1980s.
▶ Cat., David Revere McFadden (ed.), *Scandinavian Modern Design 1880–1980*, New York: Abrams, 1982:265, No. 342. Fredrik Wildhagen, *Norge i Form*, Oslo: Stenersen, 1988:200–01.

Gustafson, Knut L.   (1885–1976)
▶ Swedish silversmith; born Stockholm; active Chicago.
▶ Apprenticed in Stockholm.
▶ He settled in Chicago in *c*1910; was associated with the Jarvie Shop, Lebolt, and the Randahl Shop; in 1932, founded the Chicago Silver Company. Although his firm produced most of its hollow-ware by spinning, some patterns bear noticeable hammer marks. He later concentrated on flatware, most of it decorated with a simple leaf pattern; during the 1940s, patented the hammered flatware patterns *Oak Leaf* and *Nordic*; in 1906, sold his dies for these two patterns to Spaulding, Chicago. His Chicago metalsmithies were located at 1741 W. Division St. 1923–30, 165 N. Wabash 1930–35, and 225 S. Wabash 1935–45.
▶ Sharon S. Darling in association with Gail Farr Casterline, *Chicago Metalsmiths*, Chicago Historical Society, 1977. Annelies Krekel-Aalberse, *Art Nouveau and Art Déco Silver*, New York: Abrams, 1989:123,254.

Gustavsberg
▶ Swedish ceramics factory.
▶ Gustavsberg was founded in 1640 as a brickworks on Värmdö island, 15 miles (25km) from Stockholm. It later produced practical and decorative ceramic ware; it made English china, Parian-ware figures, color-glaze majolica, and, later in the 19th century, *flambé*-glaze stoneware; 1869–1937, it expanded substantially; stocked imported patterns along with the designs by Gunnar Gunnarsson Wennerberg and August Malmström. 1897–1908, Wennerberg was artistic director, when imitation Wedgwood Jasperware was produced at Gustavsberg. He later designed dinnerware patterns, large vases, and urns in simple Art Nouveau motifs. Wennerberg's pupil Josef Ekberg designed for the factory 1897–1945, employing Art Nouveau plant forms. Beginning in 1917, Wilhelm Kåge became artistic director. One of the largest factories producing domestic tablewares in Sweden, Gustavsberg was sold to Kooperative Förbundet in 1937. In succession, Stig Lingberg and Karin Björquist were artistic directors. In 1987, the firm was bought by the Finnish firm Arabia and, in 1988, amalgamated with Rörstrand, becoming Rörstrand-Gustavsberg.
▶ *150 år Gustavsberg* Stockholm: Nationalmuseum, 1975–76. Jennifer Hawkins Opie, *Scandinavia: Ceramics and Glass in the Twentieth Century*, New York: Rizzoli, 1989.

Guyot, E. and A. Guyot
See Guillot, Émile

Guzzini (aka Fratelli Guzzini)

▶ Italian manufacturer.

▶ The firm was founded in 1914. Adolfo Guzzini was president and chief operating officer. It manufactured small domestic wares including kitchen utensils and lighting in metal and ABS plastic. Its Harveiluce division was set up to produce lighting for offices, homes, gardens, and industry. In 1989, Bruno Gecchelin designed a range of four kitchen utensils to commemorate the 75th anniversary of the founding of the firm, located today in Recanati. The firm had branches in Yugoslavia (now Croatia) and Canada. Adolfo Guzzini was a member of ADI (Associazione per il Disegno Industriale).

▶ Jeremy Myerson and Sylvia Katz, *Conran Design Guides: Kitchenware*, London: Conran Octopus, 1990:44,74. *ADI Annual 1976*, Milan: Associazione per il Disegno Industriale, 1976.

Gwathmey, Charles (1938–)

▶ American architect; born Charlotte, North Carolina; active New York.

▶ Studied University of Pennsylvania, Philadelphia, under Louis Kahn and Robert Venturi; and School of Architecture, Yale University, under Paul Rudolph, James Stirling, and Shadrach Woods.

▶ 1964–66, he was professor of design, Pratt Institute, Brooklyn, New York; subsequently, taught at Yale University, Princeton University, Harvard University, and University of California at Los Angeles; designed the widely published 1965–67 house and studio for his parents on Long Island, New York; was influenced by the work of Le Corbusier; in 1966, (with Richard Henderson) set up an architecture partnership, New York; in 1971, set up partnership with Robert Siegel; became one of the 'New York Five' group of architects. From the 1980s, Gwathmey's and Siegel's silver and ceramics echoing the Viennese Secession were produced by Swid Powell. Gwathmey designed 1969–71 Steel and Orly houses, Bridgehampton, New York; 1971–72 Cogan house (with Siegel), East Hampton, New York; de Menil house, East Hampton; 1981 East Campus Complex (with Emery Roth and Sons), Columbia University, New York; Busch-Reisinger Museum, Harvard University, Cambridge, Massachusetts. Gwathmey finished the ramp of Le Corbusier's Carpenter Center, Harvard University. Gwathmey and Siegel designed the controversial 1991–92 addition to Frank Lloyd Wright's Guggenheim Museum, New York. Architects working in the Gwathmey-Siegel office included Rank Lupo and Daniel Rowen.

▶ By 1990, the partnership had received over 50 design awards including 1982 Architecture Firm Award from American Institute of Architects and 1981 gold medal from New York American Institute of Architecture.

▶ Kenneth Frampton and Colin Rowe, *Five Architects: Eisenman, Graves, and Gwathmey, Hejduk, Meier*, New York: Wittenborn, 1972. Kay and Paul Breslow (eds.), *Charles Gwathmey and Robert Siegel: Wohnbauten 1966–1977*, Fribourg, 1979. Stanley Aberchrombie, *Gwathmey Siegel*, New York, 1981. Robert A.M. Stern (ed.) *The International Design Yearbook*, New York: Abbeville, 1985/1986: Nos. 81,277–278. Christine Pittel, 'The Hand of Geometry,' *Elle Decor*, Mar. 1991:44–55. Paul Goldberger, 'Beyond the Master's Voice,' *Home Design, The New York Times Magazine*, 13 Oct. 1991:34.

H

Haase, Lawrence H. (1908–)
▶ American metalworker; active Chicago.
▶ 1932–33, studied Design School, Chicago Art Institute; Bauhaus, Berlin; after 1933, Black Mountain College, North Carolina.
▶ He visited Walter Gropius several times in his architecture studio, Berlin; in his later work in the USA, was greatly influenced by the work of Josef Albers and Vasilii Kandinskii; was friends with Anni and Josef Albers, who were later teachers at Black Mountain College; worked at General Motors and the product development department of Sears Roebuck, Chicago; in Chicago, set up his own manufacturing business to produce innovative plastic products for the automotive, appliance, and packaging industries.
▶ Cat., *The Bauhaus: Masters and Students*, New York: Barry Friedman, 1988.

Haavardsholm, Frøydis (1896–1984)
▶ Norwegian furniture designer.
▶ Haavardsholm was active from the first quarter of the 20th century; designed early Modernist furniture that was typically Norwegian in that realistic images were incorporated into the designs.
▶ Fredrik Wildhagen, *Norge i Form*, Oslo: Stenersen, 1988:76.

Hablik, Wenzel (1881–1934)
▶ German architect, painter, designer, and interior decorator; active Itzehoe.
▶ Studied Kunstgewerbeschule, Vienna, and in Prague.
▶ He made silver flatware in the 1920s.
▶ Cat., *Hablik, designer, utopian, architect, expressionist, artist, 1881–1934*, London: The Architectural Association, 1980. Annelies Krekel-Aalberse, *Art Nouveau and Art Déco Silver*, New York: Abrams, 1989:255.

Hadaway, William S. (1872–1941)
▶ British silversmith, active London.
▶ Hadaway produced designs in silver and enamel; in 1908, traveled to India, where he worked as superintendent at Madras Government School of Arts.
▶ Annelies Krekel-Aalberse, *Art Nouveau and Art Déco Silver*, New York: Abrams, 1989:255.

Hadelands Glassverk
▶ Norwegian glassware manufacturer; located Jevnaker.
▶ On property owned by the Danish-Norwegian state under Christian VI, the factory was established in 1762 in Jevnaker; in 1765, started production of colored glass bottles, pharmaceutical glass, and fishing floats; in 1852, began to produce colorless glass, leading to tablewares; in 1898, became Christiana Glasmagasin with a shop Christiana square (now Oslo), and three factories: Hadeland (decorative and utility wares), Høvik Verk (lighting), and Drammens Glassverk (window glass). Hadelands continued production throughout World War II with designs by Sverre Pettersen, who was its first full-time designer, followed in the 1930s by Ståle Kylingstad. From 1947, Willy Johansson and his father were designers at Hadelands; they were instrumental in improving the quality and amount of its tablewares. Other designers included Herman Bongard until 1955, Arne Jon Jutrem from 1950, and Severin Brørby from 1956. Benny Motzfeldt was its chief designer in the 1960s and left in the 1970s to set up her own studio.
▶ Work (by W. Johansson) shown at 1933 (V) and subsequently, including 1954 (X) Triennale di Milano, where Johansson received the Diplome d'Honneur.
▶ Arne Jon Jutrem 'Glas og glassførmere på Hadeland,' in Nordenfjeldske Kunstindustriemuseum, Årbok, 1958. *Glas Er Vart Material*, Oslo: Hadelands, 1961. Frederick Cooke, *Glass: Twentieth-Century Design*, New York: Dutton, 1986:86. Jennifer Hawkins Opie, *Scandinavia: Ceramics and Glass in the Twentieth Century*, New York: Rizzoli, 1989.

Hadid, Zaha (1950–)
▶ Iraqi architect; born Bagdad; active London.
▶ Studied mathematics, American University of Beirut, to 1971; 1972–77, Architectural Association, London.
▶ In 1977, she joined the Office for Metropolitan Architecture, London; taught at the Architectural Association; in 1977, formed OMA with Rem Koolhaas and Elia Zenghelis; in 1980, set up a private practice in Clerkenwell, London, with designers, painters, and architects on the staff; became well known for her award-winning design for 1983 'The Peak' competition, Hong Kong, a private club and residential complex. Using radical methods of representation, she credited early Suprematist exercises as influences on her work. Work included furniture; 1985 apartments, London; 1986 Kurfürstendamm office building, Berlin; 1986 IBA Housing, Berlin; 1987 Tomigaya, Tokyo; and 1989–92 fire station, Vitra factory, Weil-am-Rhien. In 1986, she was visiting design critic at Harvard University School of Design, and, in 1987, Columbia University, New York; (with Michael Wolfson) designed 1987 *Wavy Back Sofa* produced by Edra.
▶ Work shown in galleries and museums worldwide. Received 1982 gold medal (apartment conversion, London) in *Architectural Digest* British Architecture Awards and 1983 first prize in 'The Peak' competition, Hong Kong. *Wavy Back Sofa* shown at 1991 'Mobili Italiani 1961–1991: Le Varie Età dei linguaggi' exhibition, Salone del Mobile, Milan.
▶ *Planetary Architecture* (folio of work), Z. Hadid and Architectural Association, London, 1983. Yukio Futagawa, (ed.), *GA Architecture: Zaha M. Hadid*, ADA Edita, Tokyo, 1986. Liz McQuiston, *Women in Design: A Contemporary View*, New York: Rizzoli, 1988:50. Albrecht Bangert and Karl Michael Armer, *80s Style: Designs of the Decade*, New York: Abbeville, 1990:63,231. *Mobili Italiani 1961–1991: Le Varie Età dei linguaggi*, Milan: Cosmit, 1992.

Hadley, Albert (1920–)
▶ American interior designer; born Nashville, Tennessee; active New York.
▶ Studied Parsons School of Design, New York.
▶ Hadley first worked for decorating firm A. Herbert Rogers, Nashville; c1949–54, he taught at Parsons School of Design; in 1954, he joined the interior design firm McMillen, New York, and his work included the restoration of Rosedown Plantation, Louisiana; in 1963, formed a partnership with Mrs. Henry 'Sister'

Parish; is known for his attention to architecture and the arrangement of art and furniture. Parish-Hadley Associates gained a worldwide reputation for its interiors for privileged and wealthy clients.

▶ Mark Hampton, *The Legendary Decorators of the Twentieth Century*, New York: Doubleday, 1992.

Haefeli, Max Ernst   (1901–76)

▶ Swiss architect and designer; born Zürich.

▶ 1919–23, studied architecture, Eidgenössische Technische Hochschule, Zürich, under Karl Moser.

▶ 1923–24, he worked in studio of Otto Bartning, Berlin; 1924–25, joined his father's architecture office Pfleghard und Haefeli; in 1925, set up an independent architecture practice; designed 1926 renovation design for Girsberger bookstore, Zürich, including chairs and tables for its interiors; in 1927, became head of Kollektivgruppe Schweizer Architekten; designed 1927–28 Rotachhäuser building, Wasserwerkstrasse, Zürich, an early example of the Modern 'Neues Bauen' style in Switzerland and a breakthrough in Zürich architecture. In the late 1920s, collaborated closely with Ernst Kadler-Vögeli and manufacturer Horgen-Glarus, Switzerland; 1928–31, was a member of the planning team for 1931 Siedlung Neubühl, Zürich; taught at Kunstgewerbeschule, Zürich, and Abendtechnikum Juventus; in 1937, became a cofounder of the architecture firm Haefeli, Moser und Steiger (HMS). HMS designed the Kongresshaus and 1942–51 cantonal hospital, both Zürich. Haefeli was responsible for the outer skin and interior spatial scheme of the hospital. His later work included the planning and building of swimming pools, cemeteries, zoos, and commercial buildings.

▶ Work (chair and table models for Girsberger bookstore) shown at 'Form ohne Ornament' exhibition of *c*1927; (furniture) at 'Das Neue Heim' exhibition of *c*1931, Wohnbedarf store, Zürich, put into production by the store; as head of Kollektivgruppe Schweizer Architekten, (furniture and accessories for several apartments by Ludwig Mies van der Rohe) at 1927 'Weissenhof-Siedlung,' Stuttgart.

▶ Friederike Mehlau-Wiebking et al., *Schweizer Typenmöbel 1925–35, Sigfried Giedion und die Wohnbedarf AG*, Zürich; gta, 1989:228.

Haerdtl, Oswald   (1899–1959)

▶ Austrian architect and designer; born Vienna.

▶ Studied Kunstgewerbeschule, Vienna, under Josef Hoffmann.

▶ In 1922, he became an assistant, and from *c*1928, a partner in the architecture firm of Josef Hoffmann; 1925–59, was professor, Kunstgewerbeschule, Vienna; became best known as a designer rather than an architect; designed graceful, delicate drinking sets, gift items, candlesticks, and crystal lighting produced by J. and L. Lobmeyr, including 1925 *Tableset 240* (aka *The Ambassadore*) and 1950 *Tableset No. 257* (aka *The Commodore*), and furniture, interiors, and domestic items. In *c*1930, Klinkosch produced a number of his silver objects.

▶ Assisted Hoffmann on Austrian pavilion at 1925 Paris 'Exposition Internationale des Arts Décoratifs et Industriels Modernes.' Designed a pavilion at 1934 Paris 'Exposition de l'Habitation.' *Tableset No. 257* was designed to be shown at 1951 (IX) Triennale di Milano.

▶ Günther Feuerstein, *Vienna–Present and Past: Arts and Crafts–Applied Art–Design*, Vienna: Jugend und Volk, 1976:49,50, 51,53,80. Cat., *Oswald Haerdtl 1899–1959*, Vienna: Hochschule für angewandte Kunst, 1978. Annelies Krekel-Aalberse, *Art Nouveau and Art Déco Silver*, New York: Abrams, 1989:245,255.

Hafner, Dorothy   (1952–)

▶ American ceramicist and metalworker; born Woodbridge, Connecticut.

▶ Studied art, Skidmore College, Saratoga Springs, New York, to 1974.

▶ Hafner at first produced her designs by hand in a Pop-art or comic-book style with flamboyant colors; in 1982, had her

domestic wares mass-produced by Rosenthal Studio Line, including ceramics, 1987 *Flash* tea set, and silver flatware; was the first woman among Rosenthal Studio Line's designers; was designer at Tiffany, lecturer, and panelist.

▶ Work subject of exhibitions in USA.

▶ Yvònne Joris (introduction), *Functional Glamour*, s'-Hertogenbosch: Museum Het Kruithuis, 1987:56–67. Albrecht Bangert and Karl Michael Armer, *80s Style: Designs of the Decade*, New York: Abbeville, 1990:138,231.

Hagenauer, Carl   (1872–1928)

▶ Austrian metalworker; active Vienna; father of Karl, Franz, and Grete Hagenauer.

▶ Hagenauer was an apprentice at goldsmiths Würbel und Czokally, Vienna; subsequently, was a journeyman goldsmith under Bernauer Samu, Pressburg (now Bratislava, Slovakia), becoming a gold chaser; in 1898, set up his own workshop, Werkstätten Hagenauer, Vienna, where he produced bronze ware designed by himself and others, and small sculptures by old masters in metal; produced metalwares designed by Josef Hoffmann, Otto Prutscher, E.J. Meckel, and others.

▶ Work shown in numerous exhibitions including those in Paris, London, and Berlin where he won prizes. Work subject of 1971 'Werkstätten Hagenauer 1898–1971 und Hochschule für angewandte Kunst, Meisterklasse für freies Gestalten in Metall' exhibition, Österreichisches Museum, Vienna.

▶ Cat., *Werkstätten Hagenauer, 1898–1971*, Vienna: Österreichisches Museum für angewandte Kunst, 1971. Cat., *Metallkunst*, Berlin: Bröhan Museum, 1990:105–589.

▶ See Hagenauer, Werkstätten

Hagenauer, Franz   (1906–86)

▶ Austrian sculptor and metalworker; born and active Vienna; son of Carl Hagenauer; brother of Karl and Grete Hagenauer.

▶ Studied in the children's course, Kunstgewerbeschule, Vienna, under Franz Cizek; from 1927, sculpture under Anton Hanak.

▶ From 1926, he worked in the family firm Werkstätten Hagenauer as a belt-buckle maker; became a member of the Kunstschau; produced mostly sculpture in copper and bronze, including the metal state coat-of-arms for the Austrian parliament building; subsequently, designed domestic objects in metal and wood, including those for the family firm; in 1962, chaired master class of non-molded sculpture, Hochschule für angewandte Kunst, Vienna.

▶ Participated in 1934 Biennale di Venezia. In the 1950s, received applied arts prize of the city of Vienna. Work included in 1971 'Werkstätten Hagenauer 1898–1971 und Hochschule für angewandte Kunst, Meisterklasse für freies Gestalten in Metall' exhibition, Österreichisches Museum, Vienna.

▶ Cat., *Werkstätten Hagenauer, 1898–1971*, Vienna: Österreichisches Museum für angewandte Kunst, 1971. Günther Feuerstein, *Vienna–Present and Past: Arts and Crafts–Applied Art–Design*, Vienna: Jugend und Volk, 1976:52,80. Cat., *Metallkunst*, Berlin: Bröhan Museum, 1990:105–589.

▶ See Hagenauer, Werkstätten

Hagenauer, Karl   (1898–1956)

▶ Austrian metalworker; born Pressburg (now Bratislava, Slovakia); active Vienna; son of Carl Hagenauer; brother of Franz and Grete Hagenauer.

▶ Studied Kunstgewerbeschule, Vienna, under Josef Hoffmann and Oskar Strnad; and architecture.

▶ From 1919, he worked in his father's workshop, designing and producing domestic wares in silver, bronze, copper, enamel, ivory, stone, and wood that showed influences of his former teacher Hoffmann and of the Wiener Werkstätte; when his father died in 1928, (with brother Franz and sister Grete Hagenauer) became director of the firm, which expanded to include a furniture workshop and sales shops in Vienna and Salzburg; showed his own work and interior design and domestic accessories from outside

Austria; was a member of the Österreichische Werkbund and the Österreichische Werkstätten.
▶ Work included in 1971 'Werkstätten Hagenauer 1898–1971 und Hochschule für angewandte Kunst, Meisterklasse für freies Gestalten in Metall' exhibition, Österreichisches Museum, Vienna.
▶ Cat., *Werkstätten Hagenauer, 1898–1971*, Vienna: Österreichisches Museum für angewandte Kunst, 1971. Günther Feuerstein, *Vienna–Present and Past: Arts and Crafts–Applied Art–Design*, Vienna: Jugend und Volk, 1976:52,80. Cat., *Metallkunst*, Berlin: Bröhan Museum, 1990:105–589.
▶ See Hagenauer, Werkstätten

Hagenauer, Werkstätten
▶ Austrian metalsmiths; located Vienna.
▶ In styles from Jungenstil, through Vienna Werkstätte, to Modernism, the Werkstätten Hagenauer greatly influenced the applied arts in Austria. 1870–1914, Viennese bronze work was particularly outstanding in the Austrian applied arts. In Vienna, the influence of the Ringstrasse construction and growing prosperity fostered the production of metalwork including candelabra, lamps, vases, watches, andirons, writing utensils, bookends, ashtrays, bar items, and other domestic accessories. In 1898, the Viennese metalworking industry included more than 230 factories and workshops. In this year, Carl Hagenauer established his Werkstätten Hagenauer, where he put to work his knowledge of gold, silver, and other metals in styles akin to the Jungenstil; he exported his wares worldwide. Joining the family firm in 1919, his son, Karl Hagenauer, was influenced by Josef Hoffmann and Oskar Strnad. Karl defied the Jungenstil of Strnad's generation and sought a contemporary foreign genre of the 1920s. The Hagenauer workshop expanded from metalworking into domestic accessories and furniture in an array of materials, particularly following Julius Jirisek's participation in the firm. The firm produced works by outside designers Otto Prutscher, E.J. Meckel, and Hoffmann. Its metalwork in plated silver and chromium incorporated carved woods and bronzes. In 1932, French designer René Coulon collaborated with Jacques Adnet on tempered-glass furniture produced by Hagenauer. The firm closed in 1956.
▶ Its work was the subject of the 1971 'Werkstätten Hagenauer 1898–1971 und Hochsule für angewandte Kunst, Meisterklasse für freies Gestalten in Metall' at the Österreichisches Museum für angewandte Kunst in Vienna.
▶ Cat., *Werkstätten Hagenauer, 1898–1971*, Vienna: Österreichisches Museum für angewandte Kunst, 1971. Annelies Krekel-Aalberse, *Art Nouveau and Art Déco Silver*, New York: Abrams, 1989:255. Cat., *Metallkunst*, Berlin: Bröhan Museum, 1990:105–589.

Hagenbund
▶ Austrian artisans' group.
▶ The Künstlerbund Hagen (better known as Hagenbund) was founded in Vienna in 1900 by Joseph Urban and Heinrich Lefler; unlike the Vienna Secession, it did not erect a new building for itself, but used the market-hall office known as the Zedlitzhalle, whose 1902 adaptation was designed by Urban and Lefler. In this renovation, a crafts background can be seen, though there were Secessionist motifs throughout.
▶ Robert Waissenberger, *Vienna 1890–1920*, Secaucus, NJ: Wellfleet 1984.

Hagener Silberschmiede
▶ German silversmiths; located Hagen.
▶ Karl Ernst Osthaus established Hagener Silberschmiede (Hagen Silver Workshop) in 1914. Its silverwares were designed by J.L.M. Lauweriks, Handfertigkeitsseminar director; F.H. Ehmcke; and E.H. Schneidler. On Lauweriks's recommendation, Frans Zwollo became its head designer. In a short-lived experiment, the silversmithy aimed to rival the Wiener Werkstätte; it closed within a year of the outbreak of World War I, when Zwollo returned to the Netherlands.

▶ Cat., *Franz Zwollo en zijn tijd*, Museum Boymans-van Beuningen, Rotterdam, 1982. Annelies Krekel-Aalberse, *Art Nouveau and Art Déco Silver*, New York: Abrams, 1989:8,142,255.

Hagler, and Stanley
▶ American costume jeweler.
▶ In 1953, Stanley Hagler and Edward Nakles founded Stanley Hagler and Co, Hollywood, Florida. Their jewelry designs reflected the flamboyant designs of the 1960s for women, although Hagler himself designed a range of necklaces and tie chains for men. Nakles left, and Hagler continued alone as director, designer, manufacturer, and salesperson; became known for designing jewelry with multiple functions: necklaces into bracelets, necklaces into brooches and hair ornaments, and add-on earrings.
▶ Deanna F. Cera (ed.), *Jewels of Fantasy: Costume Jewelry of the 20th Century*, New York: Abrams, 1992:215.

Haglund, Birger (1918–)
▶ Swedish metalworker.
▶ In 1964, he set up his own silversmithy; was known for juxtaposing materials, including silver with plastic.
▶ Cat., David Revere McFadden (ed.), *Scandinavian Modern Design 1880–1980*, New York: Abrams, 1982:265, No. 246.

Hahn, Karl Karlovitch
▶ Russian goldsmiths and jewelers; located St. Petersburg.
▶ The firm Karl Karlovitch Hahn held the royal warrant from Czar Nicholas II; it produced the diadem worn by Czarina Aleksandra (Princess Alix of Hesse-Darmstadt) at the 1896 coronation. The crown was marked by A. Tillander, one of Hahn's chief artisans whose specialty was *objets de fantaisie* in gold, silver, and enamel; 1860– *c*1917, he was active in his own St. Petersburg workshop.
▶ Annelies Krekel-Aalberse, *Art Nouveau and Art Déco Silver*, New York: Abrams, 1989:241,249,260. Charlotte Gere, *American and European Jewelry 1830–1914*, New York: Crown, 1975:189.

Hahn, Otto
▶ German silversmith; active Bielefeld and Berlin.
▶ Hahn produced hollow-ware in *c*1910 designed by sculptor Hans Parathoner. Charles Rennie Mackintosh's 1904 christening flatware for his godchild Friedrich Eckart Muthesius was marked 'C. Hahn, Berlin.'
▶ Annelies Krekel-Aalberse, *Art Nouveau and Art Déco Silver*, New York: Abrams, 1989:255.

Haile, Thomas Samuel (aka Sam Haile 1909–48)
▶ British painter and ceramicist; husband of ceramicist Marianne de Trey.
▶ 1931–34, studied pottery, Royal College of Art, London, under William Staite Murray.
▶ He designed Modern stoneware and slipware reminiscent of contemporary painting; in 1935, taught pottery, Leicester College of Art; in 1936, taught and worked in London; in 1939, (with Trey) traveled to USA and taught at New York State College of Ceramics, Alfred University, Alfred, New York, and College of Architecture, University of Michigan at Ann Arbor.
▶ Cat., *Thirties: British art and design before the war*, London: Arts Council of Great Britain, Hayward Gallery, 1979:98,131,169,291.

Haimi
▶ Finnish furniture manufacturer.
▶ Haimi was founded in Helsinki in 1943; in 1965, began using plastics, with the bulk of its products in fiberglass and acrylics. Yrjö Kukkapuro's designs for Haimi included 1965 *Karuselli 412* and 1969 *Haimi 415* fiberglass chairs.
▶ Work shown at 1966 Genoa 'Eurodomus I'; 1968 Turin 'Eurodomus II'; 1966 'Vijtig jaar zitten,' Stedelijk Museum, Amsterdam.
▶ Cat., Milena Lamarová, *Design a Plastické Hmoty*, Prague: Uměleckoprůmyslové Muzeum, 1972:56,58,188.

Haines, William (1900–73)

▶ American film actor and interior designer; born Virginia; active Los Angeles.

▶ Haines won a photo contest in New York sponsored by the Goldwyn film company and moved to Hollywood. In 1927, he was one of only ten Metro-Goldwyn-Mayer actors whose name was placed above the title; lived in a house on North Stanley Avenue, Hollywood, where he dabbled with interior design, critical of the hodge-podge of historical styles popular in the 1920s. He began decorating professionally before he left the movie business; was a partner with Mitchell Foster in an antiques shop; in 1930, left MGM and established an interior design firm on Sunset Strip called Haines Foster; using English antiques, decorated the Hyams and Berg house, Beverly Hills, designed by architect Paul R. Williams; decorated the Jack and Ann Warner house, designed by architect Roland E. Coate; collaborating with architect J.E. Dolena, designed the enlarged Beverly Hills house of George Cukor in a 'Regency Modern' style. The Cukor house was distinguished by its oval sitting room with copper cornice-lighting cover, copper fireplace, copper lampshades, suede walls, leather-laced curtains (a Haines trademark), and coral-colored leather and fabric side chairs. The Cukor design was an example of Haines's unexpected combinations of materials and textures. His taste was idiosyncratic yet rooted in traditionalism. During World War II, the Haines-Foster partnership was discontinued. After the war, he established the new decorating firm William Haines Designs, Beverly Hills. In 1946, Ted Graber (decorator of the family rooms of President Ronald Reagan in the White House) joined the firm. In the late 1940s, Haines worked in a Modern style akin to Richard Neutra, R.M. Schindler, and Charles Eames, illustrated by Haines's Sidney and Frances Brody house, Los Angeles, designed by architect A. Quincy Jones. The Haines-Jones collaboration resulted in six more houses, including another for Hyams and Berg, Walter Annenberg's 1966 desert house 'Sunnylands' and 1969 'Winfield House,' and the American ambassador's residence in Regent's Park, London.

▶ Pilar Viladas, 'Decorating's Leading Man,' *House and Garden*, August 1990:100ff.

Haipl, Wolfgang (1937–)

▶ Austrian furniture and interior designer; born St. Pölten.

▶ Active from the 1960s, Haipl designed 1969 *Kombination 500* seating modules and 1974 *Quarantine* room configuration (known as 'living landscape').

▶ Günther Feuerstein, *Vienna–Present and Past: Arts and Crafts–Applied Art–Design*, Vienna: Jugend und Volk, 1976:62–63,80.

Haité, George Charles (1855–1924)

▶ British textile designer.

▶ Prolific and successful, Haité was active in the late Victorian period; published *Plant Studies for Artists, Designers, and Art Students* (1886) and *How to Draw Floral and Vegetal Forms* (1870).

▶ Stuart Durant, *Ornament from the Industrial Revolution to Today*, Woodstock, NY: Overlook, 1896:42,323.

Hajdu, Etienne (1907–)

▶ Romanian sculptor; active Paris.

▶ Studied under Bourdelle.

▶ He designed 1976 *Diane* dinnerware which showed a dancing white abstract pattern on a deep blue background, and, for Sèvres, a 1970 dinner service.

▶ Received 1969 Grand Prix National des Arts. Work shown at numerous exhibitions.

▶ *Les Carnets du Design*, Paris: Mad-Cap Productions et APCI, 1986:21.

Halabala, Jindřich (1903–78)

▶ Moravian architect and furniture designer; born Koryčany (now Czech Republic).

▶ 1922–26, studied School of Applied Arts, Prague, under Pavel Janák.

▶ 1930–50, was head architect, Spojené UP závody, Brno; in the 1930s, collaborated on standard furniture systems; in 1931, designed two types of elastic tubular-steel chairs; was a consultant and publisher on Modern interior design.

▶ Jan van Geest and Otakar Máčel, *Stühle aus Stahl, Metallmöbel 1925–1940*, Cologne: König, 1980. A. Adlerová, *České užité umění 1918–1938*, Prague, 1983.

Halcyon Art Pottery

▶ American ceramics manufactory; located Halcyon, near San Luis Obispo, California.

▶ In 1904, a Theosophist group established a sanatorium in Halcyon, California, and the Temple Home Association in 1909; in 1910, it opened a school and art pottery with Alexander Robertson as instructor and director of pottery. Robertson had been active in his own Roblin Art Pottery, San Francisco, which closed after the 1906 earthquake. The decoration of Halcyon's pottery was frequently the responsibility of the students there. Its often unglazed forms, which lent themselves to modeling and carving, were frequently overwrought. The lizard was the most popular modeled decoration. Robertson's wares included incense burners, clay whistles, paperweights, vases, bowls, and pitchers. The pottery became successful and was the basis for the Industrial School of Arts and Crafts, Halcyon. The pottery closed in 1913 due to a revision of the Association's charter.

▶ Paul Evans in Timothy J. Andersen et al., *California Design 1910*, Salt Lake City: Peregrine Smith, 1980:65.

Hald, Dagny (1936–) and Finn Hald (1929–)

▶ Norwegian ceramicists; husband (Dagny) and wife (Finn).

▶ In 1951, Dagny Hald studied at the Academie delle Belle Arti, Faenza; 1952–54, Statens Håndverks -og Kunstindustriskole, Oslo; in 1955, trained in the workshops of Marianne and Iars Thiirsland, and Kaare B. Fjeldsaa, Blommenholm.

▶ Active in their own studio from 1956, the Halds were best known for their 1970 gnome-like ceramic figures; as clay artists, were unwilling to work for a ceramics factory.

▶ Fredrik Wildhagen, *Norge i Form*, Oslo: Stenersen, 1988:160. Jennifer Hawkins Opie, *Scandinavia: Ceramics and Glass in the Twentieth Century*, New York: Rizzoli, 1989.

Hald, Edward (1883–1980)

▶ Swedish glassware designer and ceramicist; born Stockholm.

▶ 1903–04, professional training in England and Germany; 1904–06, studied Technische Akademie, Dresden; 1907, studied painting, Artists' Studio School, Copenhagen; Artists' League School, Stockholm; 1908–12, in Paris under Henri Matisse.

▶ 1917–27, Hald worked as a freelance designer, Rörstrand porcelain factory, Lidköping; 1924–33, was designer and art director, Karlskrona porcelain factory. Concurrently, from 1917, his designs were produced by the Orrefors Glasbruk, where he was artistic director 1924–33 and managing director 1933–44 and developed the *graal* technique of blowing glass with colored decoration incorporated within the walls of his vessels. His association with Orrefors lasted until the late 1970s. He worked in ceramics in the 1920s.

▶ Received a grand prize at 1925 Paris 'Exposition Internationale des Arts Décoratifs et Industriels Modernes' and 1945 Prince Eugen Medal. In 1939, elected Honorary Royal Designer for Industry, London. Became member of Swedish Society of Industrial Design and elected honorary fellow of Society of Glass Technology, Sheffield.

▶ Cat., David Revere McFadden (ed.), *Scandinavian Modern Design 1880–1980*, New York: Abrams, 1982:265, Nos. 77,85, 86. Cat., *Edward Hall målare Konst industripianjär*, Stockholm: Nationalmuseum, 1983. Jennifer Hawkins Opie, *Scandinavia: Ceramics and Glass in the Twentieth Century*, New York: Rizzoli, 1989.

Haley, Reuben

See Consolidated Lamp and Glass

Hallbergs Guldsmeds
▶ Swedish silversmiths; located Stockholm.
▶ In 1900, Hallbergs Guldsmeds produced the silver work of designer Ferdinand Boberg, who worked in a naturalistic Art Nouveau style. In the 1920s, director C.G. Hallberg's designers included Edvin Ollers, Niels Fougstedt, Elis Bergh, and Hakon Ahlberg and, in the 1930s, Sylvia Stave. In 1961, it merged with Guldsmedsaktiebolaget (GAB).
▶ Annelies Krekel-Aalberse, *Art Nouveau and Art Déco Silver*, New York: Abrams, 1989:245,255.

Haller, Fritz (1924–)
▶ Swiss architect, designer, and town planner; born Solothurn.
▶ He was an apprentice to and collaborator with various architects in Switzerland, and Rotterdam, Willem van Tijen and H.A. Maaskant; in 1949, set up an architecture practice in Solothurn; 1966–71, was guest professor, University of Southern California, Los Angeles; concurrently, collaborated on movement studies with German architect Konrad Wachsmann; from 1977, taught at Technische Universität, Karlsruhe; became known for his structural steel industrial building systems. Resulting from the work on the building for USM (a metal construction firm), Karlsruhe, he developed the *Maxi* system for spanning extremely wide spaces. His *Mini* system was developed for smaller spans. Using the experiences of loftier building projects, Haller designed the widely published 1964–70 modular furniture system produced by jointventure firm USM Haller and, developed in the early 1970s, *Midi* building system for medium distance spans in industrial construction; was one of the best known members (with Franz Füeg) of the 'Solothurn School' of architecture in Switzerland; published two books on town planning: *Totale Stadt: Ein Modell* (1968) and *Totale Stadt: Ein globales Modell* (1975). Structures (all in Switzerland) included 1951–55 (1st phase) and 1958–62 (end phase) Wagsenring School, Basle; 1958–64 Canton School, Baden; 1960–64 buildings for USM, Münsingen; 1961–66 Höhere Technische Lehranstalt, Brugg-Windisch; and 1980–82 Railways Training Center (with Hans Zaugg and Alfons Barth), Morat, which first employed Haller's *Midi* system on a large scale.
▶ 'Die Solothurner Schule,' *Bauen + Wohnen*, Vol. 36, Nos. 7–8, 1981. Thomas Herzog in Vittorio Magnago Lampugnani (ed.), *Encyclopedia of 20th-Century Architecture*, New York: Abrams, 1986:142–43. Cat., Hans Wichmann, *System-Design: Fritz Haller, Bauten, Möbel, Forschung*, Munich: Die Neue Sammlung, 1989.

Halling-Koch, Annagrete (1947–)
▶ Danish designer; born Copenhagen.
▶ Trained as a ceramicist, Kunsthåndvaerkerskolen, Copenhagen.
▶ She worked at Bing & Grøndahl Porcelaensfabrik, where she designed and decorated ceramics; designed textiles for others.
▶ Work shown in Copenhagen and USA.
▶ Robert A.M. Stern (ed.), *The International Design Yearbook*, New York: Abbeville, 1985/1986: Nos. 353–54.

Hamada, Shoji (1894–1978)
▶ Japanese potter; born Tokyo.
▶ 1913–16, studied ceramics, Technical College, Tokyo, under Kanjiro Kawai; 1916–20, researched ceramics, Kyoto.
▶ A knowledgeable chemist, he became known for important experimentation, notably in ancient Korean and Chinese glazes; in 1919, met Bernard Leach in his workshop, Abiko, and decided to accompany him back to England, beginning a 60-year association; 1920–23, shared a studio with Leach, St. Ives, Cornwall; in 1924, returned to Japan and set up a studio in Mashiko, a traditional village of artisans north of Tokyo, where he specialized in simple plates; in the 1910s and 1920s, developed the idea of *Mingei* ('popular art') which had been created by philosopher Soetsu Yanagi, a friend of Leach; created simple forms, including unusual *sake* bottles inspired by models of Okinawa, teapots, vases and plates in the molded or turned greyware of Mashiko. Hamada's work was characterized by the great liberty he took with shapes and the spontaneity of his decorations.

▶ Work shown at 1962 'Grès d'aujourd'hui, d'ici et d'ailleurs' exhibition, Château de Ratilly (France), and 1962 'Maîtres potiers contemporains,' Paris Musée des Arts Décoratifs. In 1955, officially appointed a living national treasure in Japan.
▶ Cat., *Collection Fina Gomez: 30 ans de céramique contemporaine*, Paris: Musée des Arts Décoratifs, 1991:96.

Hamanaka, Katsu
▶ Japanese designer and artist.
▶ Studied painting and interior decoration, School of Kushiro, Hokkaido.
▶ In 1924, he settled in Paris; in 1935 under Jules Leleu's direction, decorated the 'Trouville' dining room of the 1935 oceanliner *Normandie*; was a technical collaborator with many of the prominent designers in Paris, including Jacques Adnet, Maurice Dufrêne, Jacques-Émile Ruhlmann, and Pierre-Paul Montagnac; was one of the rare specialists who worked with true lacquer (resin from a plant called 'Urushi no ki').
▶ 1926–38, work shown at Paris Salons and exhibitions organized by the Japanese Embassy.
▶ Cat., Aaron Lederfajn and Xavier Lenormand, *Le Louvre des Antiquaires présente: 1930 quand le meuble devient sculpture*, Paris, 1986.

Hamel, Maria Christina (1958–)
▶ British designer; born New Delhi; active Milan.
▶ Studied Scuola Politecnica di Design, Milan, to 1979.
▶ In 1972, she settled in Milan; collaborated on projects with Ugo La Pietra, Alchimia, Ambrogio Rossari, Alessandro Mendini; was an assistant instructor under Mendini at the Hochschule für angewandte Kunst, Vienna; taught at the National Institute of Design, Ahmedabad, Gujarat; has design clients including Alessi, Moretti, Lipparini, FGB, Sica, Tissot, Salviati, Kartell, Swarovski.
▶ Her *Devuja* ceramic dinner service by Mondo, *Pavone* glass vase, and *Ellis* vase by Richard Ginori shown at 'Nuovo Bel Design: 200 Nuovi Oggetti per la Casa,' Fiera di Milano, 1992.
▶ *Modo*, No. 148, March–April 1993:121.

Hamilton, Hugh
▶ Canadian furniture designer; active Toronto.
▶ Studied Ontario College of Art.
▶ In 1969, Hamilton and Philip Salmon set up Salmon-Hamilton Design Consultants, Toronto, becoming active as designers of tubular-steel and plywood furniture models. Their 1971 stool with one-piece bent tubular-steel base was widely published.
▶ Cat., *Seduced and Abandoned: Modern Furniture designers in Canada, the First Fifty Years*, Toronto: The Art Gallery at Harbourfront, 1986:25.

Hammel, Rudolf
▶ Austrian architect, designer, and teacher; active Vienna.
▶ In 1899, the same year as Josef Hoffmann's and Koloman Moser's appointments, Hammel became professor, Kunstgewerbeschule, Vienna; 1898–1903, designed silverware for the firm Josef Bannert and, in 1902, for A. Pollak.
▶ Work (silverwares by Bannert) shown at 1902 Turin 'Esposizione Internazionale d'Arte Decorativa Moderna.'
▶ Annelies Krekel-Aalberse, *Art Nouveau and Art Déco Silver*, New York: Abrams, 1989:193,255.

Hammer, Marius (1847–1927)
▶ Norwegian silversmith; active Bergen.
▶ Hammer was head one of Norway's largest silversmithies; was best known for his *plique à jour* enameled spoons, popular with tourists and exported in large quantities; produced the 'Norwegian brilliant enamel work' spoons offered in the 1896 and 1898 Christmas catalogues of Liberty, London. From 1905, one of Hammer's designers of Modern silver was Emil Hoye, a Dane who was artistic director 1910–16 and whose work was influenced by Mogens Ballin and later by Georg Jensen. Hoye continued to produce designs for Hammer even after he set up his own workshop.

▶ R.W. Lightbown, *Catalogue of Scandinavian and Baltic Silver*, London: Victoria and Albert Museum, 1975:147. Annelies Krekel-Aalberse, *Art Nouveau and Art Déco Silver*, New York: Abrams, 1989:142–43,255.

Hammond, Henry Fauchon (1914–)
▶ British ceramicist; active Farnham.
▶ 1934–38, studied pottery, Royal College of Art, London, under William Staite Murray, and mural painting.
▶ He produced mainly stoneware that showed fluent brushwork; from 1939, taught at Farnham School of Art; 1946, began producing stoneware pieces using local clays with slipware finishes; became head of the ceramics department, West Surrey College of Art and Design, Farnham.
▶ Work shown at 1937 Paris 'Exposition Internationale des Arts et Techniques dans la Vie Moderne.'
▶ Cat., *Thirties: British art and design before the war*, London: Arts Council of Great Britain, Hayward Gallery, 1979:98, 131,291.

Hanada, Yoshie (1954–)
▶ Japanese glass designer.
▶ Studied Musashino Art Junior College, Department of Fine Arts, Tokyo, to 1976; 1981–86, Academy of Fine Arts, Stuttgart.
▶ Work shown at 1985 'New Glass in Japan,' Badisches Landesmuseum, Karlsruhe; 1985 'Zweiter Coburger Glaspreis,' Kunstsammlungen der Weste, Coburg; 'Glass '87 in Japan' and 'Glass '90 in Japan,' Tokyo; 1991 (V) Triennale of Japan Glass Art Crafts Association, Heller Gallery, New York.
▶ Cat., *Glass Japan*, New York: Heller Gallery and Japan Glass Art Crafts Association, 1991: No. 7.

Hancocks
▶ British jewelry manufacturer and retailer.
▶ The firm of C.F. Hancock was established in 1848 by Charles Frederick Hancock at 29 Bruton Street, London. Hancock trained under Paul Storr and worked for a time for jewelers Storr and Mortimer. The firm was assigned the royal warrant in 1879. The royal family was regularly supplied plate and jewelry. Important commissions included 1855 mountings for part of the collection of antique cameos and jewelry of the Duke of Devonshire. In 1857, Hancocks were commissioned to produce the Victoria Cross, Britain's highest decoration for bravery in wartime, and made by the firm ever since. C.F. Hancock's sons Charles and Mortimer joined the firm, whose name was changed in 1870 to Hancocks and Co.
▶ Work shown at 1851 London 'Great Exhibition of Works of Industry of All Nations' and 1867 Paris 'Exposition Universelle' where Napoleon III bought Hancocks' gold collar bracelet, rings, and other items
▶ Charlotte Gere, *American and European Jewelry 1830–1914*, New York: Crown, 1975:189–90.

Handel, Philip
▶ American lighting manufacturer.
▶ Adolph Eyden and Philip Handel established a glass-decorating firm in 1885 in Meriden, Connecticut. In 1893, Handel bought out his partner, forming Handel and Co. In 1903, the name was changed to The Handel Co. Specializing in lampshades, the firm also made vases, tobacco jars, and *tazzas*. Handel's goods were produced by a large studio of artists and craftsmen. Its lampshades ranged from large ceiling- and floor-lamp fixtures to small night lights. The firm did not make its own glass but purchased machine-rolled glass blanks. Individually cut sheets were used for floral and geometric lampshades, and the blanks were reverse painted. Artists produced effects by enameling, etching, and filigreeing metal overlays, and by applying a chipped frosted finish to the outsides. The firm closed in 1941.
▶ Alastair Duncan, *Art Nouveau and Art Deco Lighting*, New York: Simon and Schuster, 1978:45–46.

Handler, Laura (1947–)
▶ American industrial designer; active Milan and New York.
▶ 1981–83, she worked with Sottsass Associati, Krizia, and Pomellato, and others in Milan; in 1983, set up her own design firm in New York and designed clocks, tabletop accessories, leather goods, and housewares; designed the atomizers for Prescriptives cosmetics and worked on projects for Pomellato and Alessi; developed the *Safari* cosmetics line for Ralph Lauren; taught at Parsons School of Design, Brooklyn, New York; had clients including Macy's, Williams-Sonoma, Fissler, Magniform, The May Company, Lenox China, Montgomery Ward, WMF, Dansk, Waechtersbach, Estée Lauder, Colgate-Palmolive, Calvin Klein, Fabergé, and Revlon.
▶ Received 1986 award (thermos and folding clock) and 1991 award (modular votive candle holder by Design Ideas) from *ID* magazine.

Hansen, Andreas (1936–)
▶ Danish furniture designer.
▶ Studied Kunsthåndvaerkerskolen, Copenhagen, to 1962, and Det Kongelige Danske Kunstakademiets Møbelskole, Copenhagen, to 1963.
▶ In 1957, he became a journeyman joiner; 1968–87, taught at Institute of Visual Communication, Det Kongelige Danske Kunstakademies Arkiteksskoles; in 1966, set up his own office; designed furniture produced by Hadsten Trœindustri, Form 75, and N. Eilersen.
▶ Frederik Sieck, *Nutidig Dansk Møbeldesign: -en kortfattet illustreret beskrivelse*, Copenhagen: Bondo Gravesen, 1981; 1990 Busck edition in English.

Hansen, Frida (1855–1931)
▶ Norwegian textile designer; born Hillevåg-by-Stavanger.
▶ In 1871, studied painting.
▶ She became active five years prior to Andreas Schneider; in 1882, set up an embroidery workshop, Stavanger; became familiar with the historic textile traditions of Norway, although she did not base her work on the designs of others; combining art and craft, she developed a distinctive style that included realistic images with abstract motifs; in 1889 completing her first tapestry, learned weaving on a standing loom at Kjerstina Hauglum, Sogn; in 1890, set up her own studio; in 1892, moved to Kristiania (now Oslo), where she became director of the weaving workshop DNB (Det Norske Billedvaeveri); was a pioneer in reviving old weaving techniques and in the use of natural plant dyes; known for her 'transparent weaving,' left open areas of the warp that contrasted with broad, richly colored expanses; collaborated with Gerhard Munthe on tapestries and, in the 1890s, became the most important practitioner of the weaving renaissance in Norway, though she was a maverick in her style and choices of subject-matter. She published the book *Husflid og Kunstindustri i Norge* (1899).
▶ Received gold medals (work for DNB) at 1900 Paris 'Exposition Universelle.' Work shown at 1893 Chicago 'World's Columbian Exposition.' Work subject of 1973 'Frida Hansen europeeren i Norsk Vevkunst' retrospective, Oslo.
▶ Cat., David Revere McFadden (ed.), *Scandinavian Modern Design 1880–1980*, New York: Abrams, 1982:265, No. 58. Fredrik Wildhagen, *Norge i Form*, Oslo: Stenersen, 1988:41–42. Cat., Anne Wichstrøm, *Rooms with a View: Women's Art in Norway 1880–1990*, Oslo: The Royal Ministry of Foreign Affairs, 1990:18.

Hansen, Fritz
▶ Danish furniture manufacturer; located Allerød.
▶ In 1872, Hansen founded a wood-turning business which introduced industrial processes into furniture making. The firm was involved in a legal dispute in 1933 with Lorenz-Thonet over cantilever chair design. In the 1930s, it produced the furniture designs of Mart Stam, Arne Jacobsen, Fritz Schlegel, and Magnus Stephensen and, subsequently, the works of Gunnar Andersen, Jens Ammundsen, Ebbe Clemmensen, Piet Hein, Peter Hvidt, Grete

Jalk, Arne Jacobsen, Jørgen Kastholm, Ib Kofod-Larsen, Orla Holgård-Nielsen, Berner Panton, Henrik Rolf, and Hans Wegner.
▶ Frederik Sieck, *Nutidig Dansk Møbeldesign: -en kortfattet illustreret beskrivelse*, Copenhagen: Bondo Gravesen, 1981; 1990 Busck edition in English. Cat., David Revere McFadden (ed.), *Scandinavian Modern Design 1880–1980*, New York: Abrams, 1982: nos. 209,215,217.

Hansen, Hans (1884–1940) and Karl Gustav Hansen (1914–)
▶ Danish silversmiths.
▶ In 1906, Hans Hansen established his silversmithy in Kolding; in the 1930s, produced Modern silverwares. Karl Gustav Hansen designed silverwares for his father's firm, where he was artistic director 1940–62 and artistic consultant and designer from 1962; concurrently, was a consultant designer to Rosenthal; known for his unblemished silver surfaces and precise planning and craftsmanship in geometric forms.
▶ Cat., David Revere McFadden (ed.), *Scandinavian Modern Design 1880–1980*, New York: Abrams, 1982:265, No. 332. Annelies Krekel-Aalberse, *Art Nouveau and Art Déco Silver*, New York: Abrams, 1989:255.

Hansen, Poul (1902–)
▶ Danish designer.
▶ From 1927, Hansen worked for Georg Jensen Sølvsmedie, where he was foreman of the goldsmith workshop from 1937.
▶ Cat., *Georg Jensen Silversmithy: 77 Artists, 75 Years*, Washington: Smithsonian Institution Press, 1980.

Hansen, Roald Steen (1942–)
▶ Danish architect and furniture designer.
▶ Studied Kunsthåndvaerkerskolen, Copenhagen, to 1967; architecture, Det Kongelige Danske Kunstakademiets Arkitektskole, Copenhagen, to 1972; Danish Academy of Science and Art, Rome.
▶ In 1962, he became a journeyman joiner; 1967–70, worked in the office of Arne Jacobsen; 1972–74, in the office of Knud Peter Harboe; 1980–81, in the office of Henning Larsen; designed furniture produced by Bjarne Bo Andersen, Søren Horns, and by Brdr. Sondt.
▶ Work shown at 1971 'Exempla,' Munich; 1972 Danish art and design exhibition, Viborg. Work subject of 1975 'Børn og møbler,' Kunstindustrimuseet, Copenhagen. Received 1971 Johns. Krøiers prize; 1976 Danish furniture prize; and 1984 ASID Design Award.
▶ Frederik Sieck, *Nutidig Dansk Møbeldesign:–en kortfattet illustreret beskrivelse*, Copenhagen: Bondo Gravesen, 1981:54; 1990 Busck edition in English.

Hansen, Rolf (1922–)
▶ Norwegian ceramicist.
▶ 1942, studied Statens Håndverks -og Kunstindustriskole, Oslo; 1943, studied advertising at a commercial school, Oslo; 1944, studied under Trygve Mosebekk; 1944–46, was an apprentice at Åros Keramikkfabrik, Royken.
▶ 1947–c57, worked in shape design at Kongsberg Keramikk Arnold Wiigs Fabrikker, Halden; in 1958, worked at Plus; became a consultant.
▶ Fredrik Wildhagen, *Norge i Form*, Oslo: Stenersen, 1988:122. Jennifer Hawkins Opie, *Scandinavia: Ceramics and Glass in the Twentieth Century*, New York: Rizzoli, 1989.

Hansen, Theopil von (1813–1891)
▶ Danish architect; born Copenhagen; active Vienna.
▶ Hansen was one of the designers in the 1890s of the Vienna Ringstrasse; became one of the historicists to give the *Gründerzeit* style its particular Viennese flavor in architecture, painting, sculpture, and the applied arts; designed 1864 *Déjeuner* porcelain dinner service and 1866 *Service No. 103* engraved crystal range.
▶ Günther Feuerstein, *Vienna–Present and Past: Arts and Crafts–Applied Art–Design*, Vienna: Jugend und Volk, 1976:20–21,25, 80. Robert Waissenberger, *Vienna 1890–1920*, Secaucus, NJ: Wellfleet 1984:171,267.

Haraszty, Eszter (1910–)
▶ Hungarian textile, interior, and clothing designer; active Budapest and New York.
▶ She set up a Budapest screen-printing studio in the 1930s; after World War II, resorted to printing on bed sheets, window shades, and other salvaged woven goods; in 1947, settled in the USA and became a consultant designer to Knoll; 1949–55, was director of Knoll Textiles during the revolutionary period in commercial upholstery fabrics; designed Knoll's *Transportation Cloth*; at Knoll, hired Marianne Strengell and Evelyn Hill to produce handwoven designs, and Angelo Testa to design prints; encouraged print designers Stig Lindberg, Sven Markelius, and Astrid Sampe to travel to the USA. Her mixing of oranges and pinks was audacious even for the colorful 1950s. Designs included 1951 *Knoll Stripes* and 1953 *Fibra*, and 1956 *Triad*. In 1958, she opened her own design studio, New York.
▶ Work (*Fibra* fabric and others) shown at 'Good Design' exhibitions of the 1950s, New York Museum of Modern Art and Chicago Merchandise Mart. Received AID International Design Award (*Triad* fabric).
▶ 'The Exhilarated World of Eszter Haraszty,' *Interiors*, Vol. 114, May 1955:92–99. Eric Larrabee and Massimo Vignelli, *Knoll Design*, New York: Abrams, 1981:92–93. Cat., Kathryn B. Hiesinger and George H. Marcus III (eds.), *Design Since 1945*, Philadelphia: Philadelphia Museum of Art, 1984. Cherie Fehrman and Kenneth Fehrman, *Postwar Interior Design, 1945–1960*, New York: Van Nostrand Reinhold, 1987.

Harcourt, Geoffrey (1935–)
▶ British furniture designer; born London.
▶ 1957–60, studied High Wycombe School of Art, and Royal College of Art, London.
▶ 1960–61, he worked at Latham, Tyler and Jensen, Chicago, and with Jacob Jensen in Copenhagen; in 1961, opened his own studio in London, specializing in furniture design; from 1962; began designing seating for Artifort, the Netherlands, who produced more than 20 models of his furniture designs; designed for other furniture companies, including in Japan. His chairs were popular with airport designers.
▶ Michael Farr, *Design in British Industry: A Mid-Century Survey*, London: Cambridge, 1955.

Hardman, John
▶ British ecclesiastical metalworkers.
▶ Hardman and Iliffe was originally a buttonmaker in Birmingham. John Hardman was a partner in Elkington, the large Birmingham manufacturer and electroplating firm; in 1838, he set up his own business, John Hardman and Co, with A.W.N. Pugin as chief designer, to manufacture church furnishings in the Gothic style. Describing themselves as 'mediaeval metalworkers,' the firm executed metalwork designed by Pugin for the Houses of Parliament, London; ecclesiastical designs; and Pugin's famous marriage jewelry. Hardman continued to produce jewelry in the same style as Pugin's marriage jewelry adapted from his own designs or those of William Burges. Some of Hardman's jewelry was even marked 'AP' in imitation of Pugin's own monogram 'AWP,' which appeared exclusively on metalwork.
▶ Work (jewelry in the Pugin manner) shown at London 'International Exhibition of 1862.'
▶ Charlotte Gere, *American and European Jewelry 1830–1914*, New York: Crown, 1975:191.

Härdtl, Oswald
See Haerdtl, Oswald

Hardy, Patrice
▶ French architect and furniture designer.
▶ For ten years, he worked with Pascal Morgue in Paris; subsequently designed furniture and boats, including the *Hop* trimaran (with the French Institute for Naval Studies and Research).
▶ Agnès Lévitte and Margo Rouard, *100 quotidiens objets made in France*, Paris: APCI/Syros-Alternatives, 1987:61.

Harild, Per (1934–)
▶ Danish designer.
▶ Trained as a silversmith; from 1955, studied in Germany.
▶ In the mid-1960s he designed gold jewelry for Georg Jensen Sølvsmedie; opened his own workshop.
▶ Cat., *Georg Jensen Silversmithy: 77 Artists, 75 Years*, Washington: Smithsonian Institution Press, 1980.

Häring, Hugo (1882–1958)
▶ German architect and designer; born Biberach.
▶ Studied Technische Hochschule, Stuttgart, under Theodor Fischer, and Technische Hochschule, Dresden, under Gurlitt, Schumacher, and Wallot.
▶ 1903–04, he practiced architecture in Ulm, and, 1904–14, in Hamburg; 1915–16, worked as an architect in Allenburg on projects in East Prussia (now Poland); after World War I, became a member of the Novembergruppe; in *c*1921, set up his own architecture practice and workshop, Berlin; in 1924, was active in the founding of the avant-garde architecture association Zehnerring ('Circle of Ten'), the group that opposed Berlin city architect Ludwig Hoffmann; in 1926, became secretary of Zehnerring, when it was enlarged to become Der Ring; in 1928, attended the first CIAM (Congrès Internationaux d'Architecture Moderne) conference, La Sarraz (Switzerland); lectured on and published books and essays concerning organic building. His ideas, localized at first, became popular in *c*1930. He was empathetic with the work of Hans Scharoun, Alvar Aalto, and Louis Kahn; was best known for farm complex Gut Garkau, near Lübeck; 1935–43, was director of the private art school Kunst und Werk, Berlin, which specialized in Beaux-Arts design; was a pioneer in furniture design, particularly the cantilever chair.
▶ Participated in 1924 'Berliner Architekturausstellung.' Work shown at 1932 Vienna 'Werkbund-Ausstellung' and (chair design) at 1986 'Der Kragstuhl' exhibition, Stuhlmuseum Burg Beverungen.
▶ Hugo Häring, 'Wege zur Form,' *Die Form*, Vol. 1, 1925. Hugo Häring, 'Geometrie und Organik,' *Baukunst und Werkform*, Vol. 9, 1951. Heinrich Lauterbach and Jürgen Joedicke (eds.), *Hugo Häring: Schriften, Entwürfe, Bauten*, Stuttgart, 1965. Hugo Häring, *Die Ausbildung des Geistes zur Arbeit an der Gestalt*, Berlin, 1968. Jürgen Joedicke (ed.), *Das andere Bauen–Gedanken und Zeichnungen von Hugo Häring*, Stuttgart, 1982. Cat., *Der Kragstuhl*, Berlin: Alexander, 1986:133. Jürgen Joedicke in Vittorio Magnago Lampugnani (ed.), *Encyclopedia of 20th-Century Architecture*, New York: Abrams, 1986:143–44.

Haring, Keith (1958–90)
▶ American artist; active New York.
▶ Haring was best known for his graffiti-like paintings, initially on the black paper used to cover discontinued billboard advertisements in the New York subway; designed 1989 nine-piece bronze furniture set (with art dealer Sam Havadtoy) including a writing table, three-panel screen, and coffee table; designed 1988 *On Taro* and *On Giro* tables (with artist Toshiyuki Kita) produced by Kreon and ceramics dinnerware by Villeroy et Boch in the early 1990s; set up a trust to fund research into Aids, the disease from which he died. The trust promotes the use of his images on toys, T-shirts, and other items.
▶ *New York Magazine*, February 25, 1991:18. Germano Celant (ed.), *Keith Haring*, Munich: Prestel, 1992.

Harkrider, John
▶ American theater and film set designer.
▶ Harkrider designed costumes in the 1920s for the Ziegfeld Follies, New York; settling in Hollywood, he became supervising art director at Universal; designed the interior of the Club Raymond and redecorated the Silver Sandal for the 1936 film *Swing Time*. Club Raymond (inspired by the Rainbow Room, New York, and Clover Club, Hollywood) had a quilted ceiling, seating for 300, a glass elevator, and a simulated view of New York at night. The Silver Sandal nightclub décor was redesigned by Harkrider into a glittering fantasy of black and silver, and was the setting for the Fred Astaire and Ginger Rogers 'Never Gonna Dance' sequence in the same film. The set was equipped with silver tablecloths and 'Saturn' lamps, a dance floor with a black and grey concentric diamond motif, and a curving staircase that rose up to huge windows revealing a starry night behind the musicians. He designed other film sets, including for *My Man Godfrey* (1936), the floating penthouse nightclub in *Top of the Town* (1937), and the 'jungle moderne' cabaret in *Three Smart Girls* (1937).
▶ Howard Mandelbaun and Eric Myers, *Screen Deco: A Celebration of High Style in Hollywood*, New York: St. Martin's, 1985.

Harmon Powell, David
See Powell, David Harmon

Harrison, Marc (1936–)
▶ American industrial designer.
▶ Studied Pratt Institute, Brooklyn, New York, and Cranbrook Academy of Art, Bloomfield Hills, Michigan.
▶ From 1959, he taught at Rhode Island School of Design, Providence; in his design work, focused on ergonomic and human-factor concerns; in his design studio, specialized in the design of industrial and medical equipment, including the patented 1972 Red Cross blood-collecting process used in the USA, and subway equipment for Massachusetts Bay Transit Authority; from 1978, was principal designer for Cuisinart's products and redesigned its food-processing range.
▶ Marc Harrison, 'Design for the Donor,' *Industrial Design*, Vol. 20, Nov. 1973:20–29. 'Product Portfolio,' *Industrial Design*, Vol. 28, July–Aug. 1981:20. Cat., Kathryn B. Hiesinger and George H. Marcus III (eds.), *Design Since 1945*, Philadelphia: Philadelphia Museum of Art, 1983.

Hart, George H. (1882–)
▶ British silversmith and designer.
▶ Hart was a member of C.R. Ashbee's Guild of Handicraft, Chipping Campden; after the Guild closed in 1907, he worked as a silversmith and designer at Huyshe and Warmington, Chipping Campden.
▶ Annelies Krekel-Aalberse, *Art Nouveau and Art Déco Silver*, New York: Abrams, 1989:23,255.

Hartman, Cedric (1929–)
▶ American lighting and furniture designer.
▶ Hartman executed designs for lighting and furniture produced in his own factory, Omaha, Nebraska; designed the widely published, award-winning 1966 *Pharmacy* floor lamp, which was subsequently much imitated.
▶ Work (*Pharmacy* lamp) shown at 1984 'Design Since 1945' exhibition, Philadelphia Museum of Art.
▶ Cat., Kathryn B. Hiesinger and George H. Marcus III (eds.), *Design Since 1945*, Philadelphia: Philadelphia Museum of Art, 1983. 'The 25 Best-Designed Products,' *Fortune*, Vol. 95, May 1977:271.

Hartwein, Peter (1942–)
▶ German industrial designer.
▶ 1960–62, trained as a joiner; 1962–65, Werkkunstschule, Kaiserslautern.
▶ 1965–70, he worked in several architecture studios in Munich and, from 1970, at Braun, designing its electronic products.

Hartwig, Josef (1880–1956)
▶ German sculptor; born Munich.
▶ 1904–08, studied art in Munich.
▶ In 1893, he became a master stone cutter and, subsequently, a sculptor; 1921–25, was at the Bauhaus, Weimar, as a workmaster in the stone and wood-carving workshops; designed the widely published 1923 chess set that illustrated Bauhaus machine aesthetics; 1925–45, taught in Frankfurt; from 1945, worked on the restoration of public sculptures for the city of Frankfurt.

▶ Lionel Richard, *Encyclopédie du Bauhaus*, Paris: Somogy, 1985: 153. Christie's Bauhaus catalog, 1989. Jonathan M. Woodham, *Twentieth-Century Ornament*, New York: Rizzoli, 1990:130.

Harvey, Arthur Edward

▶ British architect and silversmith; active Birmingham.
▶ Harvey was head of Department of Industrial Design, Birmingham Central School. In the 1930s, Harvey was one of several designers, artists, and architects designing mass-produced silver and electroplate wares for Mappin and Webb, Sheffield; Goldsmiths' and Silversmiths' Company, London; Hukin and Heath, Birmingham; and Deakin and Francis, Birmingham.
▶ Annelies Krekel-Aalberse, *Art Nouveau and Art Déco Silver*, New York: Abrams, 1989:33,34,255.

Haseler, W.H.

▶ British silversmiths; located Birmingham.
▶ William Hair Haseler founded the silversmithy in 1870; from 1901, was in partnership with Liberty, London; 1899–27, produced the successful *Cymric* range of silver in the Arts and Crafts style sold at Liberty. Other Liberty jewelry may have been manufactured at Haseler's premises at 34 Hatton Garden, London. In 1900, Haseler moved to Hylton Street, Birmingham; 1901–04, was known as Haseler Bros. Silversmiths, 89 Hatton Gardens. Although the firm was dissolved in 1927, it continued to provide Liberty with silver. Design attribution of the *Cymric* line is uncertain because designs were often altered for production, and because Liberty required its designers to be anonymous until the journal *The Studio* published *Cymric* designs by Oliver Baker and Bernard Cuzner, Birmingham silversmiths, Maud Coggin, and enameler Cecil Aldin. Talented chaser Harry Craythorn was head of Haseler's design department. Other early designers included Jessie Jones, Thomas Hodgetts, and Charles Povey.
▶ Charlotte Gere, *American and European Jewelry 1830–1914*, New York: Crown, 1975:203. Renate Wagner-Rieger (ed.), *Die Wiener Ringstrasse*, Vol. 8, Wiesbaden: Steiner, 1978:216. Annelies Krekel-Aalberse, *Art Nouveau and Art Déco Silver*, New York: Abrams, 1989:33–34,255.

Hasenauer, Karl von   (1833–94)

▶ Austrian architect; born and active Vienna.
▶ Hasenauer was one of the designers in the 1890s of the Vienna Ringstrasse, the circular boulevard lined with monumental buildings developed after a proclamation of 1857 to enlarge the city. He was one of the historicists who gave the *Gründerzeit* style its particular Viennese flavor in architecture, painting, sculpture, and the applied arts; became professor and head of the Special School of Architecture, Akademie der bildenden Künste, Vienna, where he was succeeded in 1894 by Otto Wagner.
▶ Robert Waissenberger, *Vienna 1890–1920*, Secaucus, NJ: Wellfleet. 1984:171,172,267.

Hashimoto, Kazuyo   (1941–)

▶ Studied sculpture, Kyoto City College of Art, to 1963.
▶ In 1963, Hashimoto joined Kamei Glass, Osaka.
▶ Work shown at 1986 'Japan Ebna Art Contest;' 'Glass '87 in Japan' and 'Glass '90 in Japan,' Tokyo; and 1991 (V) Triennale of Japan Glass Art Crafts Association, Heller Gallery, New York. Work subject of 1983 and 1984 exhibitions, Gallery Marronnier, Kyoto.
▶ Cat., *Glass Japan*, New York: Heller Gallery and Japan Glass Art Crafts Association, 1991: No. 8.

Haskell, Miriam

▶ American jeweler; located New York.
▶ Haskell set up a small gift shop in 1924 in the McAlpin Hotel, West 34th Street, New York, where she sold her jewelry. Frank Hess, a display artist at the nearby Macy's department store, became her principal designer. They collaborated on glass-bead and simulated-pearl jewelry that had an antique quality. By the 1930s, their business had grown to include separate manufacturing facilities. Some goods were sold through other retail outlets,

including Saks Fifth Avenue. Much of their jewelry had floral motifs that became more elaborate in the 1940s. Haskell incorporated leather, wood, and seashells into naturalistic intrepretations. They imported glass beads from Austria, Czechoslovakia, and Venice. During World War II, their jewelry was made exclusively of wood and plastic. They continued to work together until 1952, when Haskell's brother took over the business. In 1954, Hess retired and the firm was sold to Morris Kinsler, who, in turn, sold it to Stanford Moss in 1983. In 1989, Moss sold Haskell Jewels to Frank Failkoff, president of Victoria International, costume jewelers in Rhode Island.
▶ Deanna F. Cera (ed.), *Jewels of Fantasy: Costume Jewelry of the 20th Century*, New York: Abrams, 1992.

Haskins, Michael   (1944–91)

▶ American interior and product designer; active New York.
▶ Studied Bowling Green State University, Bowling Green, Ohio, to 1973.
▶ He first worked with Benjamin Thompson on the design of Faneuil Hall Marketplace, Boston; was associated with design development for Design Research stores headquarters, Boston; designed interiors for the Hay-Adams Hotel, Washington; E. Braun linen shop, Madison Avenue, New York; Bullocks Pavilion store, San Mateo, California; Scarborough soap and perfume flagship store, Los Angeles; offices (with Charles Pfister) for architects Skidmore Owings and Merrill; offices for Cannon Mills, New York; designed products for Gear home furnishings chain and for Marimekko.
▶ 'Michael Haskins, 44, Interior Designer, Dies,' *The New York Times*, April 1991.

Hassall, Thomas   (1878–1940)

▶ British ceramics designer.
▶ Studied Burslem School of Art.
▶ 1892–1940, he worked for Spode, where he was artistic director 1910–40 and where his brother Joe Hassall was chief engraver; designed decoration on ceramics by W.T. Copeland, Stoke-on-Trent, including *Ming* pattern stoneware of *c*1935.
▶ Cat., *Thirties: British art and design before the war*, London: Arts Council of Great Britain, Hayward Gallery, 1979:135,291.

Hassenpflug, Gustav   (1907–77)

▶ German architect, furniture designer, and writer; born Düsseldorf.
▶ 1926–28, studied painting, and furniture and industrial design, Bauhaus, Dessau, under Hannes Meyer and Mart Stam.
▶ 1929–31, he worked with Marcel Breuer, Berlin; 1931–34, was active as architect and city planner in Russia with Ernst May and Mosei Ginzburg; in 1934, returned to Germany and worked for L. + C. Arnold, Stendal, as a designer of school furniture; in 1934, worked as designer for Embru tubular-steel furniture company, Rüti (Switzerland), where his activities included the development of garden, cinema, school, and hospital furniture; published books *Möbel aus Stahlrohr und Stahlblech (Tubular Steel and Sheet Steel Furniture)* (1935), *Stahlmöbel (Steel Furniture)* (1960), and *Stahlmöbel für Krankenhaus und ärztliche Praxis (Steel Furniture for the Hospital and Medical Practice)* (1963); 1934–1936, collaborated with Ernst Neufurt on the book *Bauentwurfslehre (Building Design)*. 1940–45, he worked with Egon Eiermann; subsequently, became an independent architect; in 1945, received commissions to rebuild Berlin hospitals; in 1946, was appointed to the chair of urban and regional planning, Hochschule für Architektur, Weimar; 1950–56, was director of Landeskunstschule, Hamburg; in 1956, became professor of building design, Technische Hochschule, Munich.
▶ Work (high-rise building) shown at 1957 'Interbau' exhibition, Berlin.
▶ Friederike Mehlau-Wiebking et al., *Schweizer Typenmöbel 1925–35, Sigfried Giedion und die Wohnbedarf AG*, Zürich: gta, 1989:228–29.

Hassenpflug, Marie (1933–)

▶ German metalworker.

▶ Studied Werkkunstschule, Krefeld, and enameling, Werkkunstschule, Düsseldorf.

▶ In 1961, she set up her own workshop, Düsseldorf; from 1971, designed for the Georg Jensen Sølvsmedie, Copenhagen.

Cat., *Georg Jensen Silversmithy: 77 Artists, 75 Years*, Washington: Smithsonian Institution Press, 1980.

Hasuike, Makio (1938–)

▶ Japanese industrial designer; born Tokyo; active Milan.

▶ Graduated in architecture, 1962.

▶ Hasuike began his professional career in Tokyo in 1962; worked for Seiko, designing more than 20 timepieces, and for the Osaka Olympiad; in 1964, settled in Milan and worked in the studio of Rudolfo Bonetto; became a member of ADI (Associazione per il Disegno Industriale); in 1968, set up his own design studio, Milan; had clients including Gaggia, Frau, Gruppo Merloni (domestic electrical appliances), Cantieri Posillipo (nautical goods), Gela (domestic electrical appliances), Molveno-Cometti (electrical accessories), Cedit (ceramic tiles), Montedil (industrial buildings), and Italora (clocks); designed a television set produced by Seimart Elettronica, bathroom accessories by Gedy, the all-glass *Dama* console by Fiam, and a dinner service by Società Ceramiche Revelli.

▶ Participated in 1973 (XV) Triennale di Milano. Received 1979 and 1984 Premio Compasso d'Oro.

▶ *ADI Annual 1976*, Milan: Associazione per il Disegno Industriale, 1976. Giancarlo Iliprandi and Pierluigi Molinari (eds.), *Industrial Designers Italiani*, Fagagna, 1985:116. *Modo*, No. 148, March–April 1993:123.

Haugesen, Niels Jørgen (1936–)

▶ Danish architect and furniture designer.

▶ Studied Kunsthåndvaerkerskolen, Copenhagen, to 1961.

▶ In 1956, he became a journeyman joiner; 1962–64, worked with architects Sven Kaj-Larsen, Stockholm; 1964–66, with Orla Mølgård-Nielsen; and, 1966–71, with Arne Jacobsen. From 1971, he taught furniture design, Skolen for Brugskunst; in 1972, set up his own design studio; from 1980, collaborated with textile designer Gunvor Haugesen; in addition to OD-Møbler, designed furniture including the widely published 1977 wire and sheet-metal stacking chair produced by Hybodon.

▶ Work shown at 1960, 1961, and 1964 Cabinetmakers' Guild exhibition, Kunstindustrimuseet, Copenhagen; 1964 'Form i Malmö'; 1966 'Vijftig Jaar Zitten,' Stedelijk Museum, Amsterdam. Received first prize, 1963 Swedish Forestry Society competition; 1965 second prize and 1989 first prize, Danish Forestry Society competition; 1965 second prize, Swedish furniture industry, Nordic competition; 1968, 1969, and 1987 awards, Dansmarks Nationalbank Anniversary Foundation; 1982 and 1987 awards, Danish State Art Foundation.

▶ Frederik Sieck, *Nutidig Dansk Møbeldesign:–en kortfattet illustreret beskrivelse*, Copenhagen: Bondo Gravesen, 1981:55; 1990 Busck edition in English.

Haupt, Karl Hermann (1904–1983)

▶ German designer.

▶ 1920–23, studied painting, Kunstgewerbeschule, Burg Giebichenstein; 1925, Bauhaus, Dessau.

▶ A 1925 pencil drawing exists of a chair which may have been produced; 1926–31, he worked in a textile factory; became a pupil of Johannes Itten at Textilfachschule, Krefeld; worked as a pattern-drawer in a weaving factory; 1951–53, was a teacher, Hochschule für angewandte Kunst; subsequently, became a scientific designer and photographer, Akademie der Wissenschaften, Berlin.

▶ Cat., *The Bauhaus: Masters and Students*, New York: Barry Friedman, 1988.

Haus-Rucker-Co

▶ Austrian furniture group.

▶ Haus-Rucker-Co was founded in 1967 as an experimental and design group by Laurids Ortner, Günther Kelp, and Klaus Pinter,

who designed the 1975 *Quart* modular range of storage furniture produced by Elst.

▶ Günther Feuerstein, *Vienna–Present and Past: Arts and Crafts–Applied Art–Design*, Vienna: Jugend und Volk, 1976:62,64,80. Cat, *Haus-Rucker-Co*, Vienna: Kunsthalle, 1992.

Haussmann, Trix and Robert

▶ Architects and industrial designers; active Zürich.

▶ Robert Haussmann was a lecturer, Zürich Polytechnic. They participated with Alchimia, Milan, which produced their objects.

▶ Work shown at 1989 'Mobilier suisse,' Galerie des brèves du CCI, Centre Georges Pompidou, Paris.

▶ Kazuko Sato, *Alchimia*, Berlin: Taco, 1988.

Haustein, Paul (1880–1944)

▶ German enamelist, metalworker, ceramicist, and furniture and graphic designer; active Darmstadt and Stuttgart.

▶ Studied Kunstgewerbeschule, Dresden and Munich.

▶ He experimented with enamelwork and produced some designs in metal for Vereinigte Werkstätten für Kunst im Handwerk, Munich, and, from 1906, simple designs with rich abstract foliate scroll ornamentation for Bruckmann und Söhne, Heilbronn; in 1903, was one of the artists at the Darmstadt colony of the Grand Duke Louis IV of Hesse-Darmstadt; was interested in silver and copper, which he combined in highly original ways and in one early example applied enamel to copper. In 1903–05, his silver designs, like those of Hans Christiansen, were produced by E.L. Viëtor, the court silversmith at Darmstadt. Haustein taught the 'Applied Art Master Course' in Nuremberg established by Peter Behrens in 1901–02; from 1905, taught metalworking at Kunstgewerbeschule, Stuttgart, of which Bernhard Pankok was director. Haustein's tureen shown at the 1910 Brussels Exposition was one of the first examples of Art Déco style and a reaction against Henry van de Velde's plain Functional forms.

▶ Work shown at exhibitions in Darmstadt; 1904 St. Louis 'Louisiana Purchase Exposition' where he won a prize; Bruckman stand at 1910 Brussels 'Exposition Universelle et Internationale.'

▶ Cat., *Ein Document Deutscher Kunst*, Vol. 4, Mathildenhöhe: Die Künstler der Mathildenhöhe, 1976:85–91. Annelies Krekel-Aalberse, *Art Nouveau and Art Déco Silver*, New York: Abrams, 1989:132,133,134,140,255.

Haviland

▶ French porcelain factory.

▶ David Haviland, an American, established Haviland pottery in 1843 in Limoges. 1866–1921, his son Charles Haviland was director. In 1873, Félix Bracquemond opened a research studio at Auteuil, near Paris, where designs were created for the Limoges factory, where soft-paste porcelain and *faïence fine* was made. In 1875 at Auteuil, Ernest Chaplet began producing barbotine decorations whose designs were painted by the studio's own artists or freelance painters and sculptors. These vases did not sell well and were discontinued. In 1881, Bracquemond left Auteuil, and Chaplet departed soon after. Chaplet opened a Haviland studio, rue Blomet, Vaugirard. Until 1914, the Auteuil studio continued under Jochum producing decorations for porcelain made in Limoges.

▶ Yvonne Brunhammer, *Art Nouveau Belgium, France*, Houston: Rice University, 1976.

Havinden, Ashley Eldrid (1903–73)

▶ British painter and graphic and textile designer.

▶ Studied drawing and design, Central School of Arts and Crafts, London.

▶ In 1922, he became a trainee in the advertising agency W.S. Crawford, London, where, in 1929, he became a board member and director of art and design and, in 1960, vice-chairman; had clients including Milk Marketing Board, General Post Office, Brewers' Society, and Simpson's department store, London; published the book *Line Drawing for Reproduction* (1933); from 1933, designed rugs and textiles for the interior decorating firm J. Duncan Miller; through Wells Coates, met Walter Gropius,

Marcel Breuer, László Moholy-Nagy, and Herbert Bayer; in 1935, produced advertising for Morton Sundour Fabrics. In the 1930s, his rug and printed and woven designs were produced by Campbell Fabrics, London, and Wilton Royal Carpet Factory. His scroll motifs, birds in flight, and ribbon patterns were produced on fabrics by Alastair Morton's Edinburgh Weavers, Carlisle. He designed the book pavilion of the 1957 exhibition, Paris; in 1953, was president of the Society of Industrial Artists; published the book *Advertising and the Artist* (1956); in addition to being an abstract painter, was known for his poster designs.

▶ Work (rugs and fabrics) subject of exhibitions at Duncan Miller Gallery in 1937, (paintings) at London Gallery, and (advertising work) at Lund Humphries Gallery, all London. Work (fabrics) shown at 1939 San Francisco 'Golden Gate International Exposition'; (paintings) at 'Abstract Paintings by Nine British Artists,' Lefevre Gallery, London; (fabrics, rugs, and graphics) at 1979–80 'Thirties' exhibition, Hayward Gallery, London.

▶ Cat., *Thirties: British art and design before the war*, London: Arts Council of Great Britain, Hayward Gallery, 1979:38,77,89, 90,144,145,147,218,231,234,281,292. Stuart Durant, *Ornament from the Industrial Revolution to Today*, Woodstock, NY, 1986:275,286–87,324.

Havlíček, Josef (1899–1961)
▶ Czech architect, sculptor, painter, furniture designer, and theoretician; born Prague.
▶ 1916–24, studied Czech University of Technology, Prague; 1923–26, Academy of Fine Arts, Prague, under Professor Gočár.
▶ 1925–26, he worked in Gočár's studio and, 1927–28, in Polívka's studio; in 1922 with Karel Honzík, set up his own studio known as H&H. His first artworks and architecture were influenced by Cubism, and his architecture adhered to the 'tectonic organism.' In the 1920s, he became one of the leading proponents of Modernism in Czechoslovakia; was a member of the Devětsil group from 1923 until its close in 1931; designed for Polívka in the International Style, influenced by Le Corbusier. H&H studio produced 1929–30 Koldom community house and first phases of the 1932–34 Všeobecný penzijní ústav building, Prague, one of the most important International Style structures in Europe.
▶ Josef Havlíček, *Návrhy a stavby: 1925–60*, Prague, 1964. Cat., *Devětsil: Czech Avant-Garde Art, Architecture, and Design of the 1920s and 30s*, Oxford Museum of Modern Art and London Design Museum, 1990.

Haynes, D.F.
▶ American ceramics manufacturer.
▶ A pottery was established in 1880 by Henry and Isaac Brougham and John Tunstall at Nicholsen and Decatur Streets, Baltimore, Maryland. In 1882, David Francis Haynes, who had previously been a crockery jobber in Baltimore, bought the firm, expanding it from an operation with one kiln into one of the most successful art potteries in the USA. Haynes had sold ceramics in Lowell, Massachusetts; he traveled in England in 1856, visiting the Staffordshire potteries; worked for Abbott Rolling Iron Works, Baltimore, and, in 1858, for the oil and lamp merchant Ammidon, which had begun producing crockery; in 1872, became a partner in Ammidon; in 1877, became sole owner, renaming the firm D.F. Haynes and Co; in 1882, bought the Chesapeake Pottery; from 1879, was closely associated with Maryland Queensware, through which he sold the entire production of wares; designed some ceramics and, more successfully, sold and marketed his wares; in 1877–78, hired Englishmen Lewis Taft to handle supervision of the bodies, glazes, and kilns, and Frederick Hackney to handle artistic production, including mold making. Hackney probably developed *Clifton* ware (similar to majolica) and *Avalon* ware (ivory bodies). 1890–1910, the firm's highly successful production was in Parian tea roses mounted on velvet, portrait medallions of bulls, and a historicist porcelain clock case. In 1882, Chesapeake Pottery was enlarged; financially overstretched, Haynes sold the pottery in 1887 to Edwin Bennett of Baltimore. In 1890, Haynes, with partner E. Houston Bennett (Edwin Bennett's son),

bought back the firm, renamed Haynes, Bennett and Co. In 1895, Bennett retired, and Frank R. Haynes became a partner. In 1896, the name became D.F. Haynes and Son. The firm closed in 1914.
▶ Received prizes at 1901 Buffalo 'Pan-American Exposition' and 1904 St. Louis 'Louisiana Purchase Exposition.'
▶ 'David F. Haynes', *Baltimore American*, Aug. 28, 1908:14. Ulrich Thieme and Felix Becker (eds.), *Allgemeines Lexikon der Bildenden Künstler*, Vol. 16, Leipzig, 1923:182. Cat., *The Potter's Craft in Maryland: An Exhibition of Nearly Two Hundred Examples of Pottery Manufactured 1793 to 1890*, 1955. Paul J. FitzPatrick, 'Chesapeake Pottery,' *Antiques Journal* 33, Dec. 1978:16–19,48. Doreen Bolger Burke et al., *In Pursuit of Beauty: Americans and the Aesthetic Movement*, New York: Metropolitan Museum of Art and Rizzoli, 1986:436–37.

Heal, Ambrose (1872–1959)
▶ British furniture designer; born and active London.
▶ Studied Slade School of Fine Art, London.
▶ Heal served as an apprentice cabinetmaker at Plucknett, Warwick; in 1893, joined the family firm (established in 1810); in 1896, began to show his furniture designs; was a fine craftsman and began to design furniture in the Arts and Crafts idiom with a predilection for solid oak, sturdy craftsmanship, and simple, stark lines; was a member of the Art-Workers' Guild and, in 1915, played a role in the formation of the DIA (Design and Industries Association); from the early 1930s, adopted the more fashionable Modern approach to furniture, following the style of his designers J.F. Johnson and Arthur Greenwood. C.F.A. Voysey also designed for him. Heal was committed to good design, particularly throughout the 1920s and 1930s, and brought Modernism to the mass trade in Britain; after visiting the 1923 Gothenburg Exhibition, introduced Swedish glassware to Britain and sold Swedish furniture. In the 1950s, the firm employed many young British designers, especially of textiles. In 1983, Heal's was acquired by the Storehouse Group under Terence Conran, which included Habitat.
▶ In 1933, Ambrose Heal was knighted and, in 1939, elected Royal Designer for Industry.
▶ Kenneth Farr, *Design in British Industry: A Mid-Century Survey*, London: Cambridge, 1955. Cat., *Thirties: British art and design before the war*, London: Arts Council of Great Britain, Hayward Gallery, 1979:83,128,129,149,150,292. Pat Garratt, 'The Stuff of Dreams,' *The World of Interiors*, May 1990:47–54. Cat., Leslie Jackson, *The New Look: Design in the Fifties*, New York: Thames and Hudson, 1991:125.

Hearthshorne, Sally Ann
▶ British textile designer.
▶ Studied Leicester Polytechnic.
▶ In 1984, she established Waterside Studio, London; designed, printed, and hand-painted fabric for furnishings and clothing.
▶ Work shown at 1986 exhibition sponsored by the Design Council of Great Britain, and at an exhibition by the Whitworth Gallery, University of Manchester.
▶ Albrecht Bangert and Karl Michael Armer, *80s Style: Designs of the Decade*, New York: Abbeville, 1990:184,231.

Heath, Adrian (1923–)
▶ British industrial designer; active Denmark; husband of Ditte Heath.
▶ Studied Architectural Association, London, to 1951.
▶ He worked for Jacob Kjaer, Copenhagen; Ernest Race, London; and Peter Hvidt and Orla Mølgård-Nielsen, Copenhagen; opened his own office with wife Ditte Heath in Hadsten (Denmark); 1963–68, lectured on furniture design, Edinburgh College of Art; from 1969, taught industrial design history, Arkitekskolen, Århus; had clients including Søren Horn, Gimson and Slater, F.D.B. Denmark, and France and Son. Work included furniture, exhibition design, and lighting. He collaborated with his wife on designs including 1968 *Chair 194* in laminated wood and canvas produced by France and Son, Hillerod (Denmark).

▶ Work shown at 1963–69 annual exhibitions, Copenhagen Cabinetmakers' Guild; (*Chair 194*) at 1970 'Modern Chairs 1918–1970' exhibition, Whitechapel Gallery, London. Received 1961 Timber Development Association design award (office furniture), London; 1961 award, Danish Furniture Manufacturers' Association competition; 1963 award, international furniture competition sponsored by *Daily Mirror* newspaper, London.
▶ *Designers in Britain 6*, London, 1964. Cat., *Modern Chairs 1918–1970*, London: Lund Humphries, 1971.

Heath, Ditte (1923–)
▶ Danish interior, furniture, and furnishings designer; active Denmark; wife of Adrian Heath.
▶ Studied Det Kongelige Danske Kunstakademiets Bygningsskole, Copenhagen, to 1948.
▶ She worked for the Architects' Co-operative Partnership, London County Council Architects Department, architect Ole Buhl, architect Peter Hvidt, and architect Orla Mølgård-Nielsen; was a librarian at Århus School of Architecture; (with Adrian Heath) opened an office in Hadsten, Denmark. Their clients included Søren Horn, Gimson and Slater, F.D.B. Denmark, and France and Son. Her range of objects included furniture and lighting.
▶ Work shown with Adrian Heath.
▶ Cat., *Modern Chairs 1918–1970*, London: Lund Humphries, 1971. Frederik Sieck, *Nutidig Dansk Møbeldesign:–en kortfattet illustreret beskrivelse*, Copenhagen: Bondo Gravesen, 1981; 1990 Busck edition in English.

Heath, Edith (1911–)
▶ American painter, sculptor, and ceramicist.
▶ 1934–40, studied painting and sculpture, Art Institute of Chicago; ceramic chemistry, University of California.
▶ She opened a pottery workshop at her residence in California; with the help of numerous assistants, produced a range of hand-thrown dinnerware that sold in a San Francisco department store; abandoning hand-throwing for mass production, (with her husband) established a small factory in 1947 which produced the 1947 *Coupe* ovenproof range of stoneware (produced from 1949). Even though most of *Coupe* pieces were mass produced, some parts were handmade to lend a crafts flavor. In 1960, Heath Ceramics began producing tiles that were used for the sheathing of Pasadena Art Museum, Pasadena, California.
▶ Edith Heath, 'Pottery and Dinnerware,' *Arts and Architecture*, Vol. 66, Sept. 1949:38–39. Don Wallance, *Shaping America's Products*, New York, 1956:93–96. Cat., Kathryn B. Hiesinger and George H. Marcus III (eds.), *Design Since 1945*, Philadelphia: Philadelphia Museum of Art, 1983.

Heaton, Maurice (1900–)
▶ Swiss glassware designer; born Neuchatel; active New York
▶ 1920–21, studied Stevens Institute of Technology, Hoboken, New Jersey.
▶ His family settled in New York in 1910; he was introduced to glassmaking by his father, stained-glass designer Clement J. Heaton; from the late 1920s, pursued new methods for producing innovative glass designs; experimented with translucent white enamel glazes on handcut, bubbly glass sheets; working on a potter's wheel, was able to produce enamel spirals. Through the Architectural League of New York, his work became well known and was sold through the galleries of Eugene Schoen and Rena Rosenthal. For several interior schemes, Heaton was commissioned by Schoen to execute large glass murals, the most impressive of which was *The Flight of Amelia Earhart Across the Atlantic* for the 1932 interior of the RKO theater, Rockefeller Center, New York. Interested in producing affordable art glass, he was still active in the 1980s in his studio in Rockland County, New York.
▶ Eugene Clute, 'Craftsmanship in Decorated Glass,' *Architecture*, July 1931:11. 'An Illuminated Glass Mural,' *Architecture*, Dec. 1932:351. Eleanor Bitterman, 'Heaton's Wizardry with Glass,' *Craft Horizons*, June 1954:13. 'Heaton, Maurice,' *Who's*

Who in American Art, 1980. Karen Davies, *At Home in Manhattan: Modern Decorative Arts, 1925 to the Depression*, New Haven: Yale, 1983:61.

Hebert, Julien (1917–)
▶ Canadian artist and industrial designer; active Montreal.
▶ Studied École des Beaux-Arts, Montreal, and University of Montreal.
▶ He designed a 1954 aluminum-tube garden chair with canvas cover produced by Siegmund Werner, Montreal, and 1955 biomorphic 'ribbon'-edge coffee table produced by Snyder's, Waterloo, Ontario; 1981–85, was a member of the Canada Council.
▶ Received award in 1951 (I) industrial-design competition in Canada; subsequently, other awards.
▶ Cat., *Seduced and Abandoned: Modern Furniture designers in Canada, the First Fifty Years*, Toronto: The Art Gallery at Harbourfront, 1986:16.

Hebey, Isabelle (1935–)
▶ French industrial and furniture designer; active Paris.
▶ Studied psychology and sociology, École du Louvre, Paris.
▶ 1966–90, she designed all of Yves Saint-Laurent's Rive Gauche boutiques worldwide. Design work included 1972 interior (with Aérospatiale) of the *Concorde* airliner, 1979–82 interiors of the Honda *Accord* automobile, 1988–90 furniture and interiors of the new French ministry of finance, and personal desk of Danielle Mitterand, wife of the French President. She designed furniture for and the interior of the South Arch of the Arche de la Défense building complex (Otto von Sprekelsen, architect).
▶ Gilles de Bure, *Le mobilier français 1965–1979*, Paris: Regard, 1983. François Mathey, *Au bonheur des formes, design français 1945–1992*, Paris: Regard, 1992:151,282–83,308,320–33.

Hechter, Daniel (1939–)
▶ French housewares and clothing designer.
▶ Hechter was best known for his sportswear for men and women; in the mid-1980s, began working in interior design. In 1985, he designed and distributed glass and silver-mesh dinnerware produced by Gelb.
▶ *Les Carnets du Design*, Paris: Mad-Cap Productions et APCI, 1986:36.

Heerup, Henry (1907–)
▶ Danish painter, sculptor, and graphic designer.
▶ Heerup produced jewelry designs for Georg Jensen Sølvsmedie.
▶ Work shown at 1980 'Georg Jensen Silversmithy: 77 Artists, 75 Years' exhibition, Smithsonian Institution, Washington.
▶ Cat., *Georg Jensen Silversmithy: 77 Artists, 75 Years*, Washington: Smithsonian Institution Press, 1980.

Heetman, Joris
See Liberati, Anne

Hegermann-Lindencrone, Effie (1860–1945)
▶ Danish ceramicist.
▶ 1880–85, studied Tegneskolen for Kvinder under Pietro Krohn and others.
▶ 1885–86, worked at Københavns Lervarefabrik, Valby; 1886–1945, was a designer at Bing & Grøndahl Porcelaensfabrik, Copenhagen; was known for her pierced ceramic vessels; designed ceramics in the first quarter of the 20th century that were a continuation of the late 19th-century naturalistic style.
▶ Received diplôme d'honneur at 1925 Paris 'Exposition Internationale des Arts Décoratifs et Industriels Modernes.'
▶ Cat., David Revere McFadden (ed.), *Scandinavian Modern Design 1880–1980*, New York: Abrams, 1982:265, No. 22. Jennifer Hawkins Opie, *Scandinavia: Ceramics and Glass in the Twentieth Century*, New York: Rizzoli, 1989.

Heiberg, Jean (1884–1976)
► Norwegian sculptor, painter, and industrial designer.
► Studied painting, Munich and Paris.
► Heiberg was a follower of Henri Matisse and other Fauvists. In the early 1930s, Alf Rolfson rejected the commission to add visual appeal to the bakelite telephone model designed by engineer Johan Christian Bjerknes for Norsk Elektrisk Bureau. Rolfson turned over the assignment to Heiberg, who had just returned to Oslo and become professor, Statens Håndverks -og Kunstindustriskole. Heiberg designed the 1932 bakelite *EB-32* model telephone, which was distributed in Turkey, Greece, and Italy, and made under license in France and the USA.
► Jesper Engelstoft (ed.), *Lexikon över Modern Skandinavisk Konst*, Copenhagen: Raben & Sjögren, 1958. Cat., *Art and Industry*, London: Boilerhouse Project, Victoria and Albert Museum, 1982. Fredrik Wildhagen, *Norge i Form*, Oslo: Stenersen, 1988:108.

Heikkilä, Simo (1943–)
► Finnish furniture, exhibition, and interior designer; born Helsinki
► Studied Taideteollinen Korkeakoulu, Helsinki, to 1967.
► He was an assistant and collaborator at Marimekko fabrics; in the 1970s and 1980s, collaborated with Yrjö Kukkapuro on furniture and on the design of the subway stations in Helsinki, and with Yrjö Wiherheimo on accessories and furniture for Vivero, Helsinki. Their furniture was starkly industrial in appearance yet comfortable in use. 1979–83, Heikkilä pursued research and experimentation in interior furnishings; 1970–7, taught architecture and interior design at Helsingin Teknillinen Korkeakoulu, Helsinki, and at Teknillinen Korkeakoulu, Tampere; from 1975, taught at Taideteollinen Korkeakoulu, Helsinki.
► Work (*Palus Fini Articus* glass-and-wood chair and table) shown at 1985 (XVII) Triennale di Milano.
► Cat., David Revere McFadden (ed.), *Scandinavian Modern Design 1880–1980*, New York: Abrams, 1982:265, No. 339. *Le Affinità Elettive*, Milan: Electa, 1985. Auction cat., *Asta di Modernariato 1900–1986, Auction 'Modernariato,'* Milan: Semenzato Nuova Geri, 8 Oct. 1986: lots 99–100.

Heiligenstein, Auguste (1891–1976)
► French glass and ceramics designer; born Saint-Denis.
► Apprenticed at Legras glassworks.
► He worked at Prestat and at Baccarat as a glass painter, specializing in gold relief decoration; from 1910, worked as a commercial artist; in 1919, was hired by Marcel Goupy to produce enameled glass to Goupy's specifications for Maison Geo. Rouard on pieces signed by Goupy only; showed his work at Rouard's until 1926, when he switched to Edgar Brandt's gallery and worked as ceramicist and glass designer; for Florence Blumenthal, designed glass with enameling in an image by Léon Bakst; 1931–35, designed for Pantin; in c1933, created Syndicat des Artisans d'Art.
► In 1923, work (glassware) first shown at Musée Gallieria, Paris; subsequently, at Salon of Société des Artistes français where he received awards including 1947 medal of honor. In 1960, appointed Officier of Légion d'honneur.
► Félix Marcilhac, 'Auguste Heiligenstein,' *Encyclopédie Connaissance des Arts*, No. 295, Sept. 1976. Victor Arwas, *Art Déco*, Abrams, 1980. Cat., *Verriers français contemporains: Art et industrie*, Paris: Musée des Arts Décoratifs, 1982.

Hein, Piet (aka Kumbel 1905–)
► Danish author, inventor, mathematician, artist, and metalworker.
► Studied Kobenhavns Universitet and Kungliga Kunsthögskolan, Stockholm.
► He was known throughout Scandinavia as Kumbel, the author of thousands of popular poems which he named 'grooks'; in the 1960s, was a town planning consultant on the Sergels Square project, Stockholm; in an attempt to solve traffic problems, produced the concept of the 'superellipse,' a shape halfway between

an oval and a rectangle; developed the superellipse shape for tables and chairs, working with Bruno Mathsson, and for lighting, metalwork, china, glass, and textiles; designed furniture produced by Fritz Hansen and *Superegg* sterling-silver box in the 1960s by Georg Jensen Sølvsmedie; wrote on the relationship between art and science.
► Work shown at 1974 'I ord og rum' exhibition, Kunstindustrimuseet; 1980 'Georg Jensen Silversmithy: 77 Artists, 75 Years' exhibition, Smithsonian Institution; 1983–84 'Design Since 1945' exhibition, Philadelphia Museum of Art. In 1972, received honorary doctorate degree, Yale University, 1968 Alexander Graham Bell Silver Bell award, 1971 ID prize of Society of International Design, and 1971 Bundespreis 'Die gute Industrieform.'
► Carl E. Christiansson, 'Bruno Mathsson: Furniture Structures Ideas,' *Design Quarterly*, No. 65, 1966:5–9. Cat., *Georg Jensen Silversmithy: 77 Artists, 75 Years*, Washington: Smithsonian Institution Press, 1980. Frederik Sieck, *Nutidig Dansk Møbeldesign: - en kortfattet illustreret beskrivelse*, Copenhagen: Bondo Gravesen, 1981:57. Cat., Kathryn B. Hiesinger and George H. Marcus III (eds.), *Design Since 1945*, Philadelphia: Philadelphia Museum of Art, 1983.

Heine, Klaus Achim (1955–)
See Fischer, Uwe

Held, Marc (1932–)
► French designer; born and active near Paris.
► Studied kinesitherapy and dramatic arts.
► Held was a professor of physical education; in 1960, became founder-director of Archiform, the study center for industrial and interior design and architecture where designers, architects, and former students of the École Boulle, Paris, pursued research; in 1965, established the magazine *Échoppe*; 1966–68, was active as an interior architect with assignments including Hôtel Les Dromonts, Avoriaz; designed three chairs for Knoll, including the widely published 1967 *Culbuto* chair (produced in 1970); up to 1966, designed numerous private apartment interiors; designed 1969 plastic molded furniture for the houses of architect Georges Candilis, 1973 Limoges porcelain dinner service by Coquet and, in 1971, numerous pieces of plastic furniture (sold in Held's own boutique L'Échoppe) produced by Créateurs et Industrielles (distributed by Prisunic), including a tea-cart, writing desk, and bed, and 1974 Lip wrist watch collection; became active as an independent architect for clients including IBS; laid out the interior of the 1987 oceanliner *Wind Star*. Archiform designed the Grand Drawing Room of the Élysée Palace for François Mitterrand, interior of the Lintas advertising agency, and the interior of the oceanliner *Mermoz*.
► Participated in 1968 (XIV) Triennale di Milano. Work (molded plastic furniture) shown in architecture section, French pavilion, 1970 (III) Eurodomus, Palazzo dell'Arte, Milan; 1990 'Design français: 1960–1990: Trois décennies' exhibition, Centre Georges Pompidou, Paris. Designed 1969 'Construction et Humanisme' exhibition, Cannes.
► Cat., Milena Lamarová, *Design a Plastické Hmoty*, Prague: Uměleckoprůmyslové Muzeum, 1972:112, Nos. 56,57,58. Cat., *Marc Held: 10 ans de recherches*, Nantes: Musée des Arts Décoratifs, 1973. Cat., *Design français 1960–1990: Trois décennies*, Paris: APCI/Centre Georges Pompidou, 1988. 'Albert Memmi raconte Marc Held,' *Jardin des Modes*, March 1989. François Mathey, *Au bonheur des formes, design français 1945–1992*, Paris: Regard, 1992:191,251.

Helg, Franca (1920–)
► Italian architect and designer.
► Studied architecture, Politecnico di Milano, to 1943.
► She was a member of INU and Accademia di S. Luca; taught at the Politecnico di Milano; in 1951, joined Franco Albini's studio, Milan, renamed Studio di Architettura Franco Albini e Franca Helg; was active in the studio with Albini, from 1962 with Antonio Piva, and from 1965 with Marco Albini; (with Albini

and alone) taught at Technische Hochschule, Munich; Cordova Catholic University, Argentina; Peru; and Ecuador; (with Albini) designed sound equipment for Brionvega in the 1960s, 1950 wicker chair for Bonacina; 1955 club chair for Arflex; 1974 exhibition at the Basilica, Venice; Milan subway stations (with Antonio Piva and Bob Noorda) in 1963; 1982 government museum, Varese; 1984 post office, Gorizia; 1979 restaurant at Palazzo Lascari, Turin. Much of the furniture designed in the Albini studio may have been from Helg's hand alone

▶ Alfonso Grassi and Anty Pansera, *Atlante del Design Italiano 1940–80*, Milan: Fabbri, 1980. Andrea Branzi and Michelle De Lucchi, *Design italiano degli Anni '50*, Milan: Editoriale Domus, 1980. Fumio Shimizu and Matteo Thun (eds.), *The Descendants of Leonardo: The Italian Design*, Tokyo, 1987:330. Hans Wichmann, *Italien Design 1945 bis heute*, Munich: Die Neue Sammlung, 1988.

Helios
▶ British textile manufacturer; located Bolton.
▶ Helios was established in 1937 by Thomas Barlow of Barlow and Jones, the furnishings and dress fabrics firm in Lancashire. From the mid-1930s, Marianne Straub, an important contributor to the design and manufacture of British woven textiles, designed contemporary fabrics for the power looms at Helios, including her *Pony* dobby cotton of *c*1940.
▶ Cat., *Thirties: British art and design before the war*, London: Arts Council of Great Britain, Hayward Gallery, 1979:90,144.

Hellsten, Lars   (1933–)
▶ Swedish glassware designer.
▶ 1957–63, studied Konstfackskolan and Tekniska Skolan, Stockholm; 1954, sculpture and ceramics, Konstindustrieskolan, Gothenburg.
▶ 1964–72, Hellsten worked at the glassworks in Skruf and, from 1972, at Orrefors Glasbruk; exploiting the transparency of glass and incorporating globular architectonic forms, produced hot-worked, non-functional glass sculptures as well as utilitarian glassware; taught, Konstfackskolan and Tekniska Skolan.
▶ Work (*The Red Square* glass sculpture) shown at 1980 'Scandinavian Modern Design 1880–1980,' Cooper-Hewitt Museum, New York.
▶ Cat., David Revere McFadden (ed.), *Scandinavian Modern Design 1880–1980*, New York: Abrams, 1982:265, No. 233. Jennifer Hawkins Opie, *Scandinavia: Ceramics and Glass in the Twentieth Century*, New York: Rizzoli, 1989.

Hennell
▶ British goldsmiths, silversmiths, and jewelers; located London.
▶ The firm was established in 1735 by David Hennell. In 1766, his son Robert Hennell became a partner and was subsequently joined by his brother Samuel Hennell. In 1802, Samuel and his uncle Robert entered their marks at Goldsmiths' Hall. In 1839, another son, Robert George Hennell, set up his own business, supported by wealthy sponsors, and introduced jewelry manufacture into the business that he conducted with sons Edward and Montague in the firm known as R.G. Hennell and Sons. Their 1887 jewelry designs were similar to Chaumet's and Garrard's. The firm is still active today.
▶ Work shown at 1873 'Third Annual International Exhibition,' London.
▶ 'The Hennells, a Continuity of Craftsmanship,' *The Connoisseur*, February 1973. Charlotte Gere, *American and European Jewelry 1830–1914*, New York: Crown, 1975:192.

Henning, Gerhard   (1880–1967)
▶ Swedish ceramicist and textile designer; active Denmark.
▶ Studied sculpture.
▶ 1908–25 at Royal Copenhagen Porcelain Manufactory, he designed figurines in exotic costume and combined traditional elements of both the 18th and 20th centuries; designed patterns for textiles produced by his wife Gerda.
▶ Cat., David Revere McFadden (ed.), *Scandinavian Modern Design 1880–1980*, New York: Abrams, 1982:265, No. 72.

Henningsen, Poul   (1894–1967)
▶ Danish architect, writer, and designer.
▶ Studied Danmarks Tekniske Højskole, Copenhagen.
▶ Henningsen is best known for 1924 *PH* ceiling and table lamp range by Louis Poulsen, Copenhagen, still in production and used in the 1929–30 Tugendhat house, Brno, by Ludwig Mies van der Rhode; designed lighting with three or more diffusing saucers, like the *PH*; 1926–28, (with Kaare Klint) edited the journal *Kritisk Revy*, which was influential in spreading the Functionalist gospel in Denmark. He designed houses, theater interiors, and part of the Tivoli gardens, Copenhagen; he kept traditional forms wherever possible.
▶ Work shown at 1925 Paris 'Exposition Internationale des Arts Décoratifs et Industriels Modernes.'
▶ Erik Zahle (ed.), *A Treasury of Scandinavian Design*, New York: 1961:276, Nos. 49–50. *Mobilia*, No. 295, 1980:14–17. Cat., David Revere McFadden (ed.), *Scandinavian Modern Design 1880–1980*, New York: Abrams, 1982:265, Nos. 100,202–04. Cat., Kathryn B. Hiesinger and George H. Marcus III (eds.), *Design Since 1945*, Philadelphia: Philadelphia Museum of Art, 1983. Stephen Bayley (ed.), *The Conran Directory of Design*, New York: Villard, 1985:151.

Henri, Florence   (1893–1982)
▶ American dilettante; born New York.
▶ Studied music in Berlin; Académie Moderne, Paris; 1927–28, Bauhaus, Dessau.
▶ She moved to Rome in 1909 and, subsequently, to London; settling in Paris in 1930, set up a photographic studio and was associated with Fernand Léger, Amédée Ozenfant, and others; after World War II, returned to painting.
▶ Lionel Richard, *Encyclopédie du Bauhaus*, Paris: Somogy, 1985: 193. Cat., Aaron Lederfajn and Xavier Lenormand, *Le Louvre des Antiquaires présente: 1930 quand le meuble devient sculpture*, Paris, 1986.

Henriksen, Hans   (1921–)
▶ Danish designer.
▶ Studied Det Kongelige Danske Kunstakademie, Copenhagen.
▶ 1958–68, he was active in his own workshop, working for the Danish Broadcasting and Television Corporation from 1963.
▶ Work (1954 salt and pepper shakers) received 1955 prize in Georg Jensen Sølvsmedie's 50th anniversary competition.
▶ Cat., *Georg Jensen Silversmithy: 77 Artists, 75 Years*, Washington: Smithsonian Institution Press, 1980.

Henriksen, Niels Georg   (1855–1922)
▶ Danish sculptor and silversmith.
▶ Henriksen was artistic director at the firm A. Michelsen, which produced his work, with chased and embossed naturalistic flower, thistle, iris, and poppy motifs.
▶ Work (silverware) by A. Michelsen shown at 1900 Paris 'Exposition Universelle.'
▶ Annelies Krekel-Aalberse, *Art Nouveau and Art Déco Silver*, New York: Abrams, 1989:216,255.

Henrion, Frederick Henri Kay   (1914–)
▶ French exhibition and graphic designer; born Nuremberg; active Paris and London.
▶ 1932–33, studied graphic design at École Paul Colin, Paris.
▶ 1936–39, he was active in Paris and London; in 1936, settled in London; 1943–45, designed all the exhibitions of the British Ministry of Agriculture; in 1945, was consultant to the US Office of War Information. His poster work included those for the British General Post Office, BOAC, London Transport and CoID, and he designed the corporate identity for KLM (Royal Dutch Airlines). 1951–82, he was a principal of Henrion Design Associates, which became Henrion Design International in 1971 and Henrion, Ludlow and Schmidt in 1981. He became a consultant in 1982. 1961–63, he was president of the Society of Industrial Artists. His numerous books included *Design Coordination and Corporate*

Image (with Alan Parkin) (1969), *Top Graphic Design* (1983), and *AGI Annals* (1989).
► Participated in 1938 Glasgow 'British Empire Exhibition'; 1939 'New York World's Fair'; Agriculture and Natural Scene and the Country (natural-history) (with Brian O'Rorke) pavilions at 1951 London 'Festival of Britain'; 1967 Montreal 'Universal and International Exhibition (Expo '67).' In 1959, elected Royal Designer for Industry. Work (1939 poster for the General Post Office) shown at 1979–80 'Thirties' exhibition, Hayward Gallery, London.
► Cat., *Thirties: British art and design before the war*, London: Arts Council of Great Britain, Hayward Gallery, 1979:204,292. Fiona MacCarthy and Patrick Nuttgens, *An Eye for Industry*, London: Lund Humphries, 1986.

Henry, Hélène   (1891–1965)

► French textile designer; born Champagney; active Paris.
► In 1918, she set up hand looms in Paris to weave Modern fabrics in her own patterns using abstract printed motifs and textures; wove for designer friends including Jacques-Émile Ruhlmann, Pierre Chareau, Maurice Dufrêne, Francis Jourdain, René Herbst, and Robert Mallet-Stevens; was one of the first fabric designers to use artificial yarns combined with wool and cotton; participated in the decoration of numerous houses, cinemas, and oceanliners; decorated the reception area of the League of Nations; in 1929, became a founding member of UAM (Union des Artistes Modernes) and a member of its first executive committee.
► Work shown at many exhibitions including 1920 session of Salon d'Automne, (in the library of the Ambassade française) 1925 Paris 'Exposition Internationale des Arts Décoratifs et Industriels Modernes'; from 1930, UAM expositions; 'Formes Utiles' exhibitions at the Salon des Arts Ménagers; 1956 (I) Triennale d'Art français Contemporain, Paris.
► Jean Fuller, 'L'Œuvre d'Hélène Henry,' *Art et Industrie*, Sept.–Oct. 1933. Léandre Vaillat, 'Le Décor de la Vie,' *Le Temps*, 28 June 1933. Pierre Migennes, 'Hélène Henry et les Tissus de ce Temps,' *Art et Décoration*, Vol. LXV, 1936. Yvonne Brunhammer, *Le Cinquantenaire de l'Exposition de 1925*, Paris: Musée des Arts Décoratifs, 1976:131. Victor Arwas, *Art Déco*, Abrams, 1980. Arlette Barré-Despond, *UAM*, Paris: Regard, 1986:412–13. Cat., *Les années UAM 1929–1958*, Paris: Musée des Arts Décoratifs, 1988:192–93.

Henschel, Erich,   (1907–)   and Ruth Henschel-Josefek (b. Ruth Josefek 1904–82)

► Husband and wife. Henschel: German painter and decorator; born Görlitz. Josefek: German fabric designer; born Gleiwitz (now Gliwice, Poland).
► 1930–33, Henschel studied Bauhaus, Berlin.
► The Henschels met at the Bauhaus. In 1947, they set up their own studio in Löwenstein-Hirrweiler.
► Lionel Richard, *Encyclopédie du Bauhaus*, Paris: Somogy, 1985: 192. Cat., Gunta Stölzl, *Weberei am Bauhaus und aus eigener Werkstatt*, Berlin: Bauhaus-Archiv, 1987:152.

Hentschel, William   (1882–1962)

► American ceramicist; active Cincinnati, Ohio.
► Studied Art Students' League and ceramics, Columbia University, both New York.
► 1907–39. he was ceramics decorator at Rookwood Pottery, Cincinnati; in the late 1920s, (with Lorinda Epply) produced some of Rookwood's most individual work.
► Work (ceramics with Epply by Rookwood) shown at 1926–27 'American Industrial Art, Tenth Annual Exhibition of Current Manufacturers Designed and Made in the United States,' New York Metropolitan Museum of Art.
► Hentschel, William, *Who's Who in American Art*, 1940–41. Virginia Raymond Cummins, *Rookwood Pottery Potpourri*, Silver Spring, Md.: Cliff R. Leonard and Duke Coleman, 1980. Karen Davies, *At Home in Manhattan: Modern Decorative Arts, 1925 to the Depression*, New Haven: Yale, 1983:40.

Hepworth, Barbara   (1903–75)

► British sculptor and designer; born Wakefield, Yorkshire; wife first of artist John Skeaping and second of artist Ben Nicholson.
► 1919–20, studied Leeds College of Art; 1920–23, sculpture, Royal College of Art, London; 1924–26, British School in Italy; carving under Ardini.
► In 1926, she settled in London; 1929–39, lived in Hampstead; from 1931, worked with Ben Nicholson; 1931–35, was a member of the Seven by Five Society, London; in 1933, became a member of Abstraction-Création, Paris; 1933–35, was a member of Unit One. In 1937, Hepworth and Nicholson were commissioned by Alastair Morton to design fabric patterns for his Edinburgh Weavers's Constructive Art range. Edinburgh produced Hepworth's *Pillar* fabric with highly textured yarns which were weft inlaid and cropped on the surface around the motifs. 1939–45, she owned and operated a nursery and market garden in St Ives, Cornwall; designed sets and costumes for a 1951 production of *Electra* at the Old Vic Theatre and 1954 Michael Tippet's opera *The Midsummer Marriage* at the Royal Opera House, both London; from 1939 until her death, lived at St Ives.
► In 1928, work (sculpture with John Skeaping and William Norman) first shown at Beaux Arts Gallery, London. From 1933, began showing textiles at Lefevre Gallery, London. Work subject of more than 60 exhibitions including at 1950 Biennale di Venezia and 1930 exhibition, Arthur Tooth and Sons, London; 1932 and 1933 exhibitions (with Nicholson; including eight hand-printed textiles), Lefevre Gallery; 1969 retrospective exhibition at the Tate Gallery, London. Work shown at 1935 Abstraction-Création exhibition, 1934 Unit One exhibition, Mayor Gallery, and traveling; 1936 'Art Non-Figuratif'; 'Abstract and Concrete,' Oxford; 1937 'Abstract Art,' AIA; 'Constructive Art,' London Gallery; (*Pillar* fabric and sculpture pieces) at 1979–80 'Thirties' exhibition, Hayward Gallery, London. In 1958, appointed Commander of the British Empire.
► Alan Bowness, *Barbara Hepworth*, London, 1971. Cat., *Thirties: British art and design before the war*, London: Arts Council of Great Britain, Hayward Gallery, 1979:35,36,45,90,170,187,292. Muriel Emanuel *et al.* (eds.), *Contemporary Artists*, New York: St Martin's, 1983:402–03.

Herbst, René   (1891–1982)

► Architect and designer; active London, Frankfurt, and Paris.
► From 1908, Herbst had architectural practices in London and Frankfurt, before settling in Paris; became a leader in the Functionalist movement, shunning ornament. Herbst's work incorporated polished and plated metal, and what is called today 'bungee cord' (a type of rubber tube wrapped in cloth thread with hooks on the ends for creating a seating surface when used in multiples). On his furniture he used leather and frequently fabric designed by Hélène Henry. He was artistic advisor (with André Vigneau as artistic director) of the Siégel window display firm, Paris, and exerted an appreciable influence on the work of the firm principally known for its mannequins. 1929–32, he published four articles on lighting in the journal *Lux*, advising readers to consult a lighting engineer, an approach compatible with the ideas of Robert Mallet-Stevens. Some of his lighting was sold by Cottin. André Salomon, lighting engineer at the small firm Perfécla, advised Herbst on lighting, including the double-winged ceiling fixture shown at the 1928 Salon d'Automne. Herbst's lighting fixtures were not of a consistently high quality of manufacture. In 1930, Herbst designed the Prince Aga Khan apartment, Paris; furniture in chromium-plated tubular steel of *c*1932 for the Maharajah of Indore in India; numerous boutiques, stores, and houses of commerce, including the shop of Jean Puiforcat, boulevard Haussmann, Paris. One of the group which left the Salon of the Société des Artistes Décorateurs, he became a founding member in 1929 of UAM (Union des Artistes Modernes); a member of its executive committee with Hélène Henry, Francis Jourdain, Raymond Templier, and Robert Mallet-Stevens; in charge of its 1930 (I) exhibition with Jourdain; in 1945 on the death of Mallet-

Stevens, served as president; represented UAM at the committee organized by Office Technique pour l'Utilisation de l'Acier pour Étudier l'Aménagement Métallique des Paquebots (Technical Office for Steel Production in Oceanliner Design); until 1961, designed all UAM exhibitions on the French iron and steel industry; in 1950, was president of UAM's 'Formes Utiles.' He described himself and other UAM members as 'the puritans of art.' In 1942, he was vice-president, Société des Artistes Décorateurs; served as chief architect of 1953 'Exposition française.'

▶ Work shown regularly at sessions of Salon d'Automne from 1921 and at Salons of Société des Artistes Décorateurs from 1924, and furniture designs at all the international expositions of the time. Was a jury member of 1925 Paris 'Exposition Internationale des Arts Décoratifs et Industriels Modernes' where he designed stands for himself on Pont d'Alexandre-III, for Siégel, and couturière Lina Mouton. Work shown at exhibitions of UAM. Lighting shown at 1934 (II) Salon de la Lumière; French section (with Charlotte Perriand, Le Corbusier, Pierre Jeanneret, Louis Sognot, Fernand Léger) at 1935 'Exposition Universelle et Internationale de Bruxelles'; (furniture for multiple usage and other models) UAM pavilion and (architect-designer) 'Pavillon de la Publicité' at 1937 Paris. Exposition Internationale des Arts et Techniques dans la Vie Moderne.' Was architect of French section, 1954 (X), 1957 (XII), and 1960 (XII) Triennali di Milano; architect of 'Pavillon de la Sidérurgie française' at 1961 Moscow 'International Exposition.' A chair shown at 1968 'Les Assises du siège contemporain' at the Paris Musée des Arts Décoratifs. Received the 1935 Blumenthal Prize. Appointed Chevalier of the Légion d'honneur.

▶ André Boll, 'René Herbst,' Art et Décoration, Vol. LXII, 1933. 'René Herbst, Promoteur de Séries Métalliques,' Le Décor d'aujourd'hui, No. 35, 1946. Alastair Duncan, Art Nouveau and Art Déco Lighting, New York: Simon and Schuster, 1978:153,172. Victor Arwas, Art Déco, Abrams, 1980. Odile Fillion, 'René Herbst, l'Homme d'Acier,' Architecture Intérieure Crée, No. 194, 1983. Aaron Lederfajn and Xavier Lenormand, Le Louvre des Antiquaires présente: 1930 quand le meuble devient sculpture, Paris, 1986. Pierre Kjellberg, Art Déco: les maîtres du Mobilier, le décor des Paquebots, Paris: Amateur, 1986:89–91. Arlette Barré-Despond, UAM, Paris: Regard, 1986:414–21. Cat., Les années UAM 1929–1958, Paris: Musée des Arts Décoratifs, 1988:194–95. Solange Goguel, René Herbst: iconographie réunie et établie, Paris: Regard, 1990.

Heritage, Rachel (1958–)

▶ British industrial designer; born London; daughter of Robert Heritage.

▶ 1978–85, studied furniture design, Kingston Polytechnic, Kingston-upon-Thames; 1982–85, furniture design, Royal College of Art, London.

▶ 1981–82, she worked at the design and architecture studio Cini Boeri Associati, Milan, for clients including Fusital (door hardware), Tronconi (lighting), and Knoll (contract furniture); in 1985, (with brother Paul Heritage) set up Heritage Design, London, active in furniture and lighting design.

▶ Work shown at 1985 exhibition, ASB Gallery, London; 1986 'Style '86,' Olympia, London; 1988 'Design it Again,' Design Centre, London. Received 1981 Ambrose Heal Award, 1982 Antocks Lairn Bursary, and 1985 Concord Lighting Award.

▶ Cat., Design Center Stuttgart, Women in Design: Careers and Life Histories Since 1900, Stuttgart: Haus der Wirtschaft, 1989:268–71.

Heritage, Robert (1927–)

▶ British furniture and product designer; born Birmingham; father of Rachel and Paul Heritage.

▶ 1942–46, studied Birmingham College of Art; 1948–52, Royal College of Art, London, under R.D. Russell.

▶ 1951–53, he was a staff designer for G.W. Evans furniture manufacturer; in 1953, set up his own studio, designing furniture and lighting for British and foreign firms. His early furniture for Archie Shine illustrated the influence of R.D. Russell's simple and

understated approach on Heritage's own work. He was a consultant designer to Rotaflex, Race Furniture, and Beaver and Tapley; 1974–85, he was professor of furniture design, Royal College of Art, while maintaining an active design studio with his wife Dorothy. His lighting for Concord/Rotaflex was widely published. He designed the technically innovative 1968–69 QE2 cast-aluminum chair produced by Race Furniture, Sheerness, in aluminum alloy, with a special adhesive for the leg connection; cutlery for Yote; high-tech lighting, including 1973 Pan Parabolic track lamp for Concord; and household appliances.

▶ Work shown at 'British Week' exhibitions in Copenhagen, Milan, Lyons, Brussels, and Gothenburg. In 1969, QE2 chair first shown at the Design Centre, London. QE2 chair received 1969 Council of Industrial Design annual award and shown at 1970 'Modern Chairs 1918–1970' exhibition, Whitechapel Gallery, London. Work (high-tech lighting) shown at 1983–84 'Design Since 1945' exhibition, Philadelphia Museum of Art. Received more Design Council awards than any other person; from 1958, eight design awards (including four for furniture) from Council of Industrial Design; 1966 British Aluminium award; 1973 Design Council Award (Pan Parabolic track lamp). In 1963, elected Royal Designer for Industry.

▶ Michael Farr, Design in British Industry: A Mid-Century Survey, London: Cambridge, 1955:8ff. 'Race: Case Histories,' London: Race Furniture, 1969:19–25. Cat., Modern Chairs 1918–1970, London: Lund Humphries, 1971. Fiona MacCarthy, British Design since 1880, London, 1982: figs. 198,199,208,221. Cat., Kathryn B. Hiesinger and George H. Marcus III (eds.), Design Since 1945, Philadelphia: Philadelphia Museum of Art, 1983. Fiona MacCarthy and Patrick Nuttgens, An Eye for Industry, London: Lund Humphries, 1986.

Herløw, Erik (1913–)

▶ Danish architect and designer.

▶ Studied architecture, Det Kongelige Danske Kunstakademie, Copenhagen, to 1941.

▶ In 1945, he set up his own design studio in Copenhagen; became head of Det Kongelige Danske Kunstakademie; working primarily in metal, designed stainless steel and sterling silver wares for A. Michelsen, aluminum cooking wares for Dansk, and 1954 Obelisk cutlery for Universal Steel; from 1955, was artistic director, Royal Copenhagen Porcelain Manufactory; from 1959, designed jewelry for Georg Jensen Sølvsmedie.

▶ Arne Karlsen, Made in Denmark, New York, 1960:13,86–93,114–115. Contemporary Danish Design, Copenhagen: The Danish Society of Arts and Crafts and Industrial Design, 1960:17,58,87,90–91,94. Cat., Kathryn B. Hiesinger and George H. Marcus III (eds.), Design Since 1945, Philadelphia: Philadelphia Museum of Art, 1983.

Herman Miller

▶ American furniture manufacturer; located Zeeland, Michigan.

▶ Herman Miller was founded in 1923 in Zeeland, Michigan. With D.J. DePree as head of the company, it manufactured furniture in various classical styles. DePree reluctantly and gradually converted the firm to the Modern style in the 1930s through the design efforts of Gilbert Rohde, who was hired in 1932 as design director. When Rohde died in 1944, New York architect George Nelson took over, bringing in a stable of designers including Charles and Ray Eames and Isamu Noguchi. Herman Miller was the mass producer of the Eames classic molded-plywood chair that the company began making in the late 1940s. Nelson's 1959 CSS Storage System was produced until 1973. Architect Gordon Bunshaft's 1960 Union Carbide building, New York, furnished by Herman Miller, was an example of fully formed Functional planning, with interiors which were integrated with the external design. The landscape-office layout demanded furniture flexible enough to provide different design solutions for every office use, while being mass-produced. Herman Miller responded with system furniture based on a number of interchangeable panels from which desk tops, shelves, and storage units were hung. The

1962 *Action Office 2* system by Robert Probst revolutionized office design and became the first commercially successful furniture system. Many of Herman Miller's designs were executed in the Nelson design office in New York in collaboration with the staff of the Miller firm in Zeeland. Various Herman Miller products were designed by people other than Nelson: *Steelframe* storage and seating systems by John Pile, *Sling Sofa* by John Svezia, and *EOG* office system by Ernest Farmer. A new system named *Ethospace* was launched in 1986 and designed by Bill Stumpf, a vice-president of Herman Miller 1970–73.

▶ George Nelson, *Storage*, New York: Whitney Library of Ideas, 1954. Ralph Caplan, *The Design of Herman Miller*, New York, 1976. George Nelson, *George Nelson on Design*, New York, 1979. David Hanks, *Innovative Furniture in America*, New York, 1981. *The New York Times Magazine Business World*, Margery B. Stein, 'Teaching Steelcase to Dance,' April 1, 1990.

Herman, Sam (1936–)

▶ American glass designer and teacher, born Mexico.

▶ Studied sculpture, University of Wisconsin at Madison, under Leo Steppern; in 1966, glass making with Harvey Littleton and Dominick Labino; in 1966, Edinburgh College of Art; in 1967, Royal College of Art, London.

▶ 1969–74, he was an influential teacher at the Royal College of Art, where he became a tutor in glass. His work was close to that of mentors Labino and Littleton. In 1969, Herman and Graham Hughes (chair of the British Crafts Centre) founded The Glasshouse Gallery and Workshop, Neal Street, London, and moved shortly thereafter to nearby Long Acre. He founded the New Wave Movement in Australia, living there 1974–80 and establishing the Jam Factory glass workshop, Adelaide. In the 1970s in Belgium, he collaborated with Louis Leloup (the chief designer at Val-Saint-Lambert) on glass objects. Herman delivered a 1984 lecture at the Brighton conference of the Decorative Arts Society, where he restated the principles of the Studio Glass movement.

▶ Frederick Cooke, *Glass: Twentieth-Century Design*, New York: Dutton, 1986:105–06.

Hermant, André (1908–78)

▶ French architect and furniture designer.

▶ Studied École Spéciale d'Architecture, Paris.

▶ In 1936, he became a member of UAM (Union des Artistes Modernes); after World War II, participated in the reconstruction of the port of Le Havre under the direction of architect Auguste Perret; 1948–52, was vice-president of UAM and originated the idea of its 'Formes Utiles' manifested through the 1949–50 (I) exhibition, Pavillon de Marsan, Paris; published the book *Formes Utiles* (1959) under the sponsorship of Salon des Arts Ménagers; from the mid-1930s, designed sheet-metal and glass furniture; in 1969, was architect of Musée Marc Chagall, Nice.

▶ Designed the gallery of the architecture in the UAM pavilion and the Pavilion of Rubber at 1937 Paris 'Exposition Internationale des Arts et Techniques dans la Vie Moderne.' 'Economical' prefabricated house shown at 1954 (XI) Salon de l'Habitation sponsored by Salon des Arts Ménagers and later built for Dr. Faure as the 'Formes Utiles' house, Port-Marly.

▶ André Hermant, 'Questions Techniques dans la Construction des H.B.M.,' *L'Architecture d'aujourd'hui*, No. 7, July 1935. André Hermant, *Formes Utiles*, Paris: Salon des Arts Ménagers, 1959. Arlétte Barré-Despond, *UAM*, Paris, 1986:422–25. Cat., *Les années UAM 1929–1958*, Paris: Musée des Arts Décoratifs, 1988:196–97.

Hermès

▶ French leather-goods manufacturer and retailer; located Paris.

▶ In 1837, Thierry Hermès founded the firm in Paris as a harness-maker. From 1880, it manufactured saddles; in the 1920s, expanded its operation greatly, when handbags, traveling bags, couture, men's and women's sportswear, jewelry, watches,

perfume, and scarves were added to its range; after World War II, established new branches worldwide. Jean-Michel Frank designed its 1929 white-leather hand-sewn desk and, in the 1930s, the monumental double doors in leather with gilded bronze handles by Alberto Giacometti, and oak and leather 'movie director's' armchair. In the 1930–40s, Paul Dupré-Lafon designed desks and armchairs. Well known products include 1930s *à coins rapportés* suitcase, 1930s *sac à dépêches*, 1938 *chaîne d'ancre* bracelet, 1956 *brides de gala* scarf, and 1958 *Kelly bag* (named after Grace Kelly). Its notable work included the trunk for the 1929 Bugatti *Royal* automobile, 1976 interior of the *Corvette* twin-engine jet airplane, 1987 *Espace* carbon fiber suitcase. From 1983, Rena Dumas designed Hermès branch interiors worldwide as well as 1986 *Pippa* portable folding writing desk, folding stool, and folding chaise longue. 1988–92, Hilton McConnico designed its exhibitions in Paris, Tokyo, and Milan and 1989 new packaging for the perfume *Amazone*. Its designers of leather goods included Robert Dumas (1962), Catherine de Karolyi (1986), and Jean-Louis Dumas (1989); of couture, Victor Vasarely (1960s), Catherine de Karoli (from 1966), Bernard Sanz (1978–88), and Eric Bergère (1981–88); of watches, Jean-Louis Dumas (1978) and Henri d'Origny. Christiane Vauzelles designed 1984 *Les Pivoines* china dinnerware, Laurence Thioune 1986 *Toucans* china dinnerware, Zoe Pauwels 1988 *Marqueterie de Pierres d'Orient et d'Occident*, Philippe Mouquet 1992 *Moisson* crystal and flatware, and Rena Dumas 1991 *Complice* silverplated teapot. 1926–78, Annie Beaumel decorated the Hermès shop windows. From 1961, Leila Menchart worked with Beaumel and decorated the windows only from 1978. Hermès is a member of the Comité Colbert.

▶ Received a silver medal at Paris 'Exposition Universelle de 1867,' a gold medal at Paris 'Exposition Universelle de 1878,' a grand prize at 1889 and 1900 Paris 'Expositions Universelles,' and numerous other prizes and exhibitions.

Hermes, Gertrude (1902–)

▶ British illustrator, sculptor, and designer.

▶ 1919–20, studied Beckenham School of Art; 1922–25, wood-engraving and sculpture, Brook Green School, London.

▶ From 1926, (with husband Blair Hughes-Stanton) collaborated on wood-engraved illustrations in *The Pilgrim's Progress*; produced sculptures (including portrait busts) and decorative furnishings; was a member of Gregynog Press. Her best known work may be illustrations for books *The Story of My Heart* by Richard Jeffries (1938) and *The Compleat Angler* (1939). In 1932, she produced the mosaic floor and carved center stone of the fountain and door furniture for the Shakespeare Memorial Theatre, Stratford-upon-Avon; in 1935, became a member of the London Group; in 1938, was admitted to National Register of Industrial Designers.

▶ Thirty-foot (9m) glass window shown in British Pavilion at 1937 Paris 'Exposition Internationale des Arts et Techniques dans la Vie Moderne'; three glass panels in British Pavilion at 1939 New York 'World's Fair'; engravings (with six other engravers from Britain) at 1939 Venice international exhibition; 1930 *Willows and Water Lilies* wood engraving at 1979–80 'Thirties' exhibition, Hayward Gallery, London.

▶ Cat., *Thirties: British art and design before the war*, London: Arts Council of Great Britain, Hayward Gallery, 1979:175,292.

Hernmarck, Helena (1941–)

▶ Swedish textile designer; active Connecticut; wife of Niels Diffrient.

▶ Hernmarck worked as an independent textile designer, producing large tapestries for public spaces including Sweden House, Stockholm, and Federal Reserve Bank, Boston. Her images amalgamated the traditional with the Modern and old techniques with new. In the mid-1960s, she moved to Montreal, subsequently, to London, and thence to New York, where she set up her own studio.

▶ Cat., David Revere McFadden (ed.), *Scandinavian Modern Design 1880–1980*, New York: Abrams, 1982:265, No. 251.

Herter Brothers

▶ American furniture manufacturer and interior design firm; located New York.

▶ Gustave Herter (1830–1898), born in Stuttgart, worked for the architect Leins, designing the interior woodwork for the royal palace in Berg (Germany); in 1848, settled in New York, where he worked for Tiffany, Young and Ellis until 1851, when he became a cabinetmaker in his own workshop, 48 Mercer Street; associated with cabinetmaker Edward W. Hutchings, through whom Herter may have met Auguste Pottier. 1852–54, Herter's workshop was at 56 Beekman Street. In 1853, Herter operated a brief partnership with Pottier; in c1856, moved to 547 Broadway. In 1860, his half-brother Christian Herter settled in New York. He had previously studied in Stuttgart and at the École des Beaux-Arts, Paris; after a short time working for Tiffany, joined Gustave's firm in 1865, renamed Herter Brothers; encouraged by Gustave, returned to Paris and studied there 1868–1870 under Pierre-Victor Galland. Herter later commissioned murals from Galland for inclusion in the commissions of various clients including William H. Vanderbilt. In 1870, Christian returned to the USA and bought out his brother's interest in the firm. 1870–83, Christian achieved international stature through his progressive American furniture company. The firm's designs were influenced by the art furniture of E.W. Godwin of England. In c1876, the time of the Philadelphia exposition, the firm began producing finely crafted furniture in the new Anglo-Japanese style in light and ebony woods with asymmetrical patterns. After 1876, Christian Herter began to import embroideries, wallpaper, Chinese porcelain, Persian pottery, and Japanese *objets d'art* to complement his furniture. In 1870, William Baumgarten became a designer at Herter and, 1881–91, director. Frenchman Alexandre Sandier worked for the firm in the 1870s and, subsequently, was in charge of the art department at Sèvres. Sandier's designs were similar to Godwin's. William B. Bigelow and Francis H. Bacon were designers there, the latter leaving in 1881 and later joining A.H. Davenport. Architect-designer Wilhelm Kimbel worked for the firm in c1890. Throughout the 1870s Herter Brothers produced respectable historicist models in 18th- and early 19th-century English styles. It furnished its clients with textiles, mosaics, stained glass, plasterwork, carpets, and lighting to its own designs. Its 1879 commission for the decoration of the William H. Vanderbilt house (completed in 1882) at Fifth Avenue and 51st Street, New York, was its most prestigious commission and was widely published. The building was designed by Herter employees John B. Snook with Charles B. Atwood. 1883–91, Herter Brothers was managed by William Baumgarten and, 1891–1906, by William Nichols. Its lavish commissions continued, including the Oliver Ames Jr. house of c1883, Boston; 1884 W.D. Washburn house, Minneapolis; 1889 St. Elizabeth's Roman Catholic Church, Philadelphia. In the 1880s, Herter supplied paintings of the Barbizon School in France. Much of the contents of the firm's showrooms and gallery were sold in 1905, followed by the firm's formal dissolution in 1906.

▶ Gustave Herter showed work (Renaissance buffet produced with Erastus Bulkley and rosewood étagère for T. Brooks, Brooklyn) at 1953–54 New York Crystal Palace exhibition; work at 1876 Philadelphia 'Centennial Exposition'; Pompeian-theme vestibule with murals by Charles Caryl Coleman in New York State building at 1893 Chicago 'World's Columbia Exposition.'

▶ Cat. Mary Jean Smith Madigan, *Eastlake-Influenced American Furniture, 1870–1890*, Yonkers, New York: Hudson River Museum, 1973. William Sale, *The Tasteful Interlude*, New York, 1975:74–75. Cat., David Hanks, *Christian Herter and the Aesthetic Movement in America*, New York: Washburn Gallery, 1980. 'The Herter Brothers,' *House and Garden*, May 1985:17,20,24,28. Doreen Bolger Burke et al., *In Pursuit of Beauty: Americans and the Aesthetic Movement*, New York: Metropolitan Museum of Art and Rizzoli, 1986:439.

Hertz, Peter   (aka Peter Herz)

▶ Danish silversmiths; active Copenhagen.

▶ The Peter Hertz firm, the oldest silver factory in Denmark, was founded in Copenhagen in 1834; produced designs by Thorvald Bindesbøll, Just Andersen, and Johan Rohde. As seen in their wares for Hertz, Ballin and Bindesbøll anticipated Cubist forms of the 1920s. In 1914, Peter Hertz took over the workshop of Mogens Ballin.

▶ Annelies Krekel-Aalberse, *Art Nouveau and Art Déco Silver*, New York: Abrams, 1989:217.

Hesse, Kurt

▶ German designer.

▶ Studied architecture and design in Germany.

▶ In the beginning of his career, he designed domestic furnishings; in 1952, began designing lighting, working for a German lighting firm; in 1978, set up his own independent studio, with clients including PAF, in Milan.

Heymann-Marks, Margarete   (1899–)

See Marks, Margarete

Heythum, Antonín   (1901–54)

▶ Czech architect, set and furniture designer; born Brüx Most (now Czech Republic).

▶ Heythum was a member of the Devětsil group from 1924 and author of *Pictorial Poems*; designed stage sets in a Constructivist style; in 1926, became one of the founders of Osvobozené Divadlo (The Liberated Theater) where he became an influence on the early stage style of the theatre group; 1927–29, was chief set designer of the České Divadlo (Czech Theater), Olomouc; pursued experiments in using standard parts in mass-produced furniture. He moved to the USA before the outbreak of World War II. His teaching at the University of Syracuse, Syracuse, New York, and his practical knowledge went into his book *Design for Use: A Study of Relationships between Things and Men* (1944) in which he espoused a Functionalist approach to interior design. He produced a design for a collapsible couch in 1929, a proposed solution for small flats; designed two variants of a cantilever tubular-metal chair design in 1930; wrote on the design and production of such chairs (*Stavba*, No. 8, 1932:131–32). His economical use of space was illustrated in his design for a one-room flat in 1903.

▶ In the 1930s, designed a number of exhibition pavilions including Czechoslovak pavilions at 1939 'New York World's Fair,' 1935 'Exposition Universelle et Internationale de Bruxelles,' and San Francisco (unrealized). Designed several exhibitions at the Uměleckoprůmyslové Muzeum (Museum of Decorative Arts), Prague.

▶ Milena Lamarová, 'Antonín Heythum a interiér,' *Umění*, ročník XXXV, 1987:139–144, Academia Praha. Cat., *Devětsil: Czech Avant-Garde Art, Architecture, and Design of the 1920s and 30s*, Oxford Museum of Modern Art and London Design Museum, 1990.

Heywood Brothers   (aka Heywood Wakefield)

▶ American furniture manufacturer; located Gardner, Massachusetts.

▶ Levi Heywood founded Heywood Brothers and Co in Gardner, Massachusetts in 1826. It became one of the largest American producers of chairs including Windsor and bentwood models; in the 1870s, developed new methods for bending rattan and experimented with wrapped cane and reed. In 1897, Heywood bought Wakefield Rattan and became Heywood Brothers and Wakefield. Henry Heywood, nephew of founder Levi Heywood, took over management of the firm, and factories were set up in Wakefield and Gardner, Massachusetts; Chicago; and San Francisco. Selling to an international market, Heywood Wakefield produced wicker wares including chairs, cradles, baby carriages, tête-à-têtes, sofas, screens, window shades, and umbrella stands until the 1930s, when it began producion of imaginative furniture in light-colored woods. It closed in 1979.

▶ Andrea Di Noto, 'The Presence of Wicker,' *Connoisseur*, Vol. 214, June 1984:78–84. Doreen Bolger Burke et al., *In Pursuit of Beauty: Americans and the Aesthetic Movement*, New York: Metropolitan Museum of Art and Rizzoli, 1986:478–79.

Hicks, David Nightingale (1929–)

▶ British interior, furniture, and furnishings designer; born Coggeshall, Essex; active London.

▶ Studied Central School of Arts and Crafts, London.

▶ In 1953, he became an independent designer, designing the widely published interiors of his mother's house in South Eaton Place, London; 1956–59 with Tom Parr, was active in the decorating firm Hicks and Parr; 1960–70, in David Hicks Ltd; from 1970, in David Hicks International Marketing Ltd with offices in Australia, Belgium, France, Germany, Pakistan, and Switzerland. In 1960, he began to design textiles and carpets; from 1982, womenswear; from 1977, costume jewelry, eyeglasses, shoes, and menswear through the David Hicks Association of Japanese Manufacturers. He was a member and master of the Worshipful Company of Salters, and fellow of Royal Society of Arts, London. Hicks became known for his luxurious English interiors and eclectic mixture of styles and materials. He published *David Hicks on Decoration* (1966), the first of many books; designed interiors for royalty and wealthy private clients, and public interiors including the original nightclub on the 1969 oceanliner *Queen Elizabeth II*, Raffles nightclub, Chelsea, and ten Peter Evans Eating Houses, and numerous offices.

▶ S. Patterson, 'The Bigger the Challenge the Better I Like it,' *Réalités*, March 1970. R.J. Vinson, 'La salle de bains de David Hicks,' *Connaisance des Arts*, Nov. 1972. Ann Lee Morgan, *Contemporary Designers*, London: Macmillan, 1984:282. Mark Hampton, *The Legendary Decorators of the Twentieth Century*, New York: Doubleday, 1992.

Hicks, Sheila (1934–)

▶ American textile designer; active France.

▶ 1954–58, studied painting, Yale University, under Josef Albers and Rico Legrun.

▶ In Central and South America in the early 1960s, she began weaving and producing fabrications influenced by traditional methods and by Albers's Constructivist approach; in India, worked in a handloom factory producing commercial textiles, including her 1968 *Badagara* heavy double-sided cloth with a deep relief woven by the Commonwealth Trust in Kerala. Still in production in the 1980s, *Badagara* was used as a wall hanging. In 1967, Hicks set up her own studio, Paris, named Ateliers des Grands Augustins, while teaching and working worldwide including in Chile, Morocco, and Israel. In these places, she encouraged large-scale local production using traditional methods; in Paris, produced numerous large hangings and wallcoverings for various installations, including the conference room (with Warren Platner), Ford Foundation Building, New York; 1969 conference center, United Arab League, Mecca; and entrance, 1972 CB 12 tower, IBM, La Défence, Paris.

▶ *Badagara* weaving shown at 1983–84 'Design Since 1945' exhibition, Philadelphia Museum of Art.

▶ Cat., Kathryn B. Hiesinger and George H. Marcus III (eds.), *Design Since 1945*, Philadelphia: Philadelphia Museum of Art, 1983. Monique Lévi-Strauss, *Sheila Hicks*, New York, 1974. Mildred Constantine and Jack Lenor Larsen, *Beyond Craft: The Art Fabric*, New York, 1973:172–93.

Hielle-Vatter, Marga (1913–)

▶ German fabric designer.

▶ Studied in Dresden and Vienna.

▶ From 1933, she designed fabrics woven at her own mill; became known for her complex geometric patterns with long repeats, including 1981 *Alcudia* fabric by her own factory Rohi Stoffe, Geretsried (Germany).

▶ Received a silver medal 1957 (XI) Triennale di Milano. *Alcudia* pattern shown at 1983–84 'Design Since 1945' exhibition, Philadelphia Museum of Art.

▶ Jack Lenor Larsen and Jeanne Weeks, *Fabrics for Interiors*, New York, 1975:72–73. Cat., Kathryn B. Hiesinger and George H. Marcus III (eds.), *Design Since 1945*, Philadelphia: Philadelphia Museum of Art, 1983. Hans Wichmann, *Von Morris bis Memphis*,

Textilien der Neuen Sammlung, Ende 19. bis Ende 20. Jahrhundert, Basel: Birkhauser, 1990:224,226,228,268,284,304–05,312,333, 443.

Hiemstra, Chris (1942–)

▶ Dutch industrial designer and administrator; born Voorburg.

▶ Studied Rietveld Academy, Amsterdam, and Academie van Beeldende Kunsten, The Hague; 1965–68, industrial design, Koninlelijie Academie voor Geeldende Kunsten, The Hague.

▶ For three years he was an assistant in the office of Kho Liang Ie; 1967, was active as a freelance designer; from 1968, became associated with Harry J. Swaak's industrial-design office; from 1971, was a designer at Lumiance (formerly Hiemstra & Evolus), responsible for product development and presentation from 1976.

▶ Robert A.M. Stern (ed.), *The International Design Yearbook*, New York: Abbeville, 1985/1986: No. 236.

Higgins, David Lawrence (1936–)

▶ British industrial designer; born and active Stratford-upon-Avon.

▶ 1959–69, he was active in various large firms; worked in the studio of consultants Wilkes and Ashmore, England, for three years; at Philips, Eindhoven, for two years; on Olivetti projects in the studio of Ettore Sottsass for four years; and in the Information System Group, General Electric, Schenectady, New York. In 1969, he set up his own studio David Higgins Associates, Stratford-upon-Avon, specializing in graphic and industrial design and electronic machinery for industry and domestic electrical appliances. In 1970, (with other industrial designers) formed design-group Incateam with associates in Germany, the Netherlands, Switzerland, Norway, and Italy; became a member of ADI (Associazione per il Disegno Industriale).

▶ *ADI Annual 1976*, Milan: Associazione per il Disegno Industriale, 1976.

High-Tech

▶ Architectural and decorating style of the 1970s and 1980s.

▶ 'High Tech' was developed by Richard Rogers, Norman Foster, and others in the early 1970s. In domestic interiors, designers rejected elegant materials and furnishings and used industrial products and equipment, such as tables intended for restaurants and garage tool cabinets used as bedroom chests of drawers. The originator of the style in interior design in the USA was Joseph Paul D'Urso, who used flat industrial carpet, polished-metal swinging doors, and, on several occasions, the chaise by Le Corbusier, Jeanneret, and Perriand with its cover removed to expose the metal-slat supports.

Hildebrand, Margret (1917–)

▶ German fabric designer.

▶ Studied Staatliche Kunstgewerbeschule, Stuttgart, and Kunstschule für Textilindustrie, Plauen.

▶ From 1936, she worked at Stuttgarter Gardinenfabrik, where she was director 1956–66; attempted to amalgamate the Functional approach of design integrity with mass production; became Germany's best known fabric designer in the years immediately following World War II; from 1956, taught textile design, Hochschule für Bildende Künste, Hamburg.

▶ Received a gold medal at 1954 (X) Triennale di Milano.

▶ Otto Haupt, *Margret Hildebrand*, Stuttgart, 1952. Margret Hildebrand, 'Der tapfere Käufer,' in *Zeitgemässe Form: Industrial Design International*, Munich, 1967:109–11. Cat., Kathryn B. Hiesinger and George H. Marcus III (eds.), *Design Since 1945*, Philadelphia: Philadelphia Museum of Art, 1983. Hans Wichmann, *Von Morris bis Memphis, Textilien der Neuen Sammlung, Ende 19. bis Ende 20. Jahrhundert*, Basel: Birkhauser, 1990:223,228–29,232–33,238,248,443.

Hill, Evelyn (aka Evelyn Anselevicius 1925–)

▶ American textile designer.

▶ Studied Black Mountain College, North Carolina, under Josef Albers, and Institute of Design, Chicago.

▶ In the 1950s, she designed fabrics for Knoll and Cohama, introducing bright color combinations and fabrications in wool and monofilament for commercial interiors; from the 1960s under the name Evelyn Anselevicius, was an independent weaver in San Miguel de Allende (Mexico); in the early 1980s, settled in Albuquerque, New Mexico.
▶ Work (textiles for commercial interiors) shown at 1983–84 'Design Since 1945' exhibition, Philadelphia Museum of Art.
▶ 'Evelyn Hill,' *Everyday Art Quarterly*, No. 25, 1953:181–89. Mildred Constantine and Jack Lenor Larsen, *Beyond Craft: The Art Fabric*, New York, 1973:108–11. Cat., Kathryn B. Hiesinger and George H. Marcus III (eds.), *Design Since 1945*, Philadelphia: Philadelphia Museum of Art, 1983.

Hill, Oliver (1887–1968)
▶ British architect and designer.
▶ Studied Architectural Association, London.
▶ Edwin Lutyens, a friend of Hill's father, encouraged Hill to become an apprentice to a firm of builders. In 1909, he was an apprentice to the architect William Flockhart; in 1912, set up his own architecture practice; from 1918, was successful as a designer of country and town houses and an interior designer; in the early 1930s, designed furniture produced by Heal's. His interior design work included a house in Maryland, Hurtwood; North House, Westminster; and art historian Kenneth Clark's house in Hampstead. Architecture included 1931–33 Midland Hotel for the LMS Railway in Morecambe, Lancashire; 1933 'British Industrial Art in Relation to the Home' exhibition as coordinating architect and designer, Dorland Hall, London; 1930–32 Gayfere House, London; 1933–35 Miss Newton house, Holthanger, Wentworth; house in Virginia Water, Surrey; 1934–35 scheme for Frinton-on-Sea, Essex; British Pavilion at 1937 Paris 'Exposition Internationale des Arts et Techniques dans la Vie Moderne'; unrealized projects including primary school, London.
▶ Work (furniture, lighting, and images of his architecture) shown at 1979–80 'Thirties' exhibition, Hayward Gallery, London.
▶ Cat., *Thirties: British art and design before the war*, London: Arts Council of Great Britain, Hayward Gallery, 1979:24,86, 124,129,149,182,231,232,270,271,292.

Hill, Reginald Henry (1914–75)
▶ British silversmith; active London.
▶ Studied Central School of Arts and Crafts, London.
▶ In 1930, he was an apprentice to a silversmith; became a prolific silver designer to Elkington, Birmingham; Wakely and Wheeler, London; and later C.J. Vander, London; taught silversmithing at Central School of Arts and Crafts.
▶ Cat., *Thirties: British art and design before the war*, London: Arts Council of Great Britain, Hayward Gallery, 1979:140,292. Annelies Krekel-Aalberse, *Art Nouveau and Art Déco Silver*, New York: Abrams, 1989:255.

Hille
▶ British furniture manufacturer; located London.
▶ The firm was established in London in 1906 by the Russian émigré Salamon Hille, who was originally a restorer of 18th-century furniture in London's Whitechapel. After World War II, Leslie Julius, Hille's grandson, was successful in selling Modern furniture. Designers included Robin Day, Roger Dean, and Fred Scott. Day's polypropylene chair of the 1960s was Hille's most successful product, selling more than 12 million pieces. In 1983, Hille merged with Ergonom and was later resold.
▶ Robin Day's furniture for Hille received a gold medal at 1951 (IX) Triennale di Milano.
▶ Penny Sparke, *Introduction to Design and Culture in the Twentieth Century*, London: Allen and Unwin, 1986. Cat., Leslie Jackson, *The New Look: Design in the Fifties*, New York: Thames and Hudson, 1991:125.

Hiller, Dorothee (1945–)
▶ German industrial designer; born Schorndorf, Württemberg.
▶ 1966–67, trained as a joiner; 1967–71, studied interior and furniture design, Staatlichen Akademie der bildenden Künste, Stuttgart.
▶ In 1971, she joined the firm D-Team-Design, Stuttgart, where she was manager from 1972. Her work (with Rainer Bohl) included the 1978 *Bima Profi* industrial chair range by Biedermann, 1986 *FD 90* kitchenware range by Fissler, 1985 *Multibox* sink unit by Blanc, and 1988 *Tringle* chair (with Heike Salomon and Rainer Bohl) by Drabert Söhne.
▶ Cat., Design Center Stuttgart, *Women in Design: Careers and Life Histories Since 1900*, Stuttgart: Haus der Wirtschaft, 1989:98–101.

Hillfon, Hertha (1921–)
▶ Swedish ceramicist.
▶ 1953–57, studied Konstfackskolan and Tekniska Skolan, Stockholm.
▶ In 1959, Hillfon set up her own ceramics workshop. She was one of the artisans who extended the range of ceramics in the 1960s, with non-functional ceramics as art. Her images often included depictions of everyday objects, including clothing.
▶ Participated in 1960 (XII) Triennale di Milano. Received 1957 Medal for Proficiency and Industry of the Society for Industrial Design and 1962 Lunning Prize.
▶ Cat., David Revere McFadden (ed.), *Scandinavian Modern Design 1880–1980*, New York: Abrams, 1982:265, No. 273. Jennifer Hawkins Opie, *Scandinavia: Ceramics and Glass in the Twentieth Century*, New York: Rizzoli, 1989.

Hills, David (1923–)
▶ American glassware designer.
▶ Studied Pratt Institute of Arts, Brooklyn, New York.
▶ 1948–52, he was a glassware designer at Steuben, designing more than 20 production vessels including pitchers, candlesticks, urns, vases, and tumblers; designed some exhibition pieces for Steuben and the 1949 bud vase—one of Steuben's most popular items of the 1950s and still in production today.
▶ Cat., Kathryn B. Hiesinger and George H. Marcus III (eds.), *Design Since 1945*, Philadelphia: Philadelphia Museum of Art, 1983. Mary Jean Madigan, *Steuben Glass: An American Tradition in Crystal*, New York, 1982:98,101,103,196,227–28,262,265,267, 270,274,278,279–80.

Hilton, Matthew (1957–)
▶ British furniture, product, and interior designer; active London.
▶ Studied furniture design, Kingston Polytechnic, Kingston-upon-Thames.
▶ For five years, he worked with the product design consultancy CAPA on high-tech products; in his own studio from 1984, designed furniture, lighting, and interiors and a 1986 range of furniture produced by Sheridan Coakley; is best known for his 1987 *Antelope* aluminum and wood side table with its animal-like legs, and 1988 *Flipper* aluminum and glass low table with rotating fin-shaped legs. Clients include XO, France.
▶ Work (furniture for Sheridan Coakley) shown at 1986 and 1988 Salone del Mobile Italiano and 1988 (I) International Contemporary Furniture Fair, New York. Work subject of 1992 exhibition, Ferens Art Gallery, Hull.
▶ Albrecht Bangert and Karl Michael Armer, *80s Style: Designs of the Decade*, New York: Abbeville, 1990:60–61,231. *Contract*, July 1990:26.

Himsworth, Joyce (1905–)
▶ British silversmith and jeweler; born and active Sheffield.
▶ Trained by her father in Sheffield; studied School of Art, Sheffield.
▶ In the early 1930s, she set up her own workshop in her home in Sheffield; produced silver work and jewelry that included niello and enamel decorations.

▶ Work subject of 1978 retrospective, Weston Park Museum, Sheffield.
▶ Annelies Krekel-Aalberse, *Art Nouveau and Art Déco Silver*, New York: Abrams, 1989:225. Cat., *Thirties: British art and design before the war*, London: Arts Council of Great Britain, Hayward Gallery, 1979:137,292.

Hingelberg, Frantz
▶ Danish silversmiths; located Århus.
▶ The firm Frantz Hingelberg firm was founded in 1897. Its stable of craftspeople included Svend Weihrauch, who worked as a silversmith and designer from 1928. For silver drinking vessels for hot liquids, Weihrauch added strips of wood to handles and under bases.
▶ Work (silver by Weihrauch) first shown outside Denmark at 1935 'Exposition Universelle et Internationale de Bruxelles.'
▶ Annelies Krekel-Aalberse, *Art Nouveau and Art Déco Silver*, New York: Abrams, 1989:65,255.

Hirche, Herbert (1910–)
▶ German industrial designer.
▶ 1930–33, studied Bauhaus, Dessau and Berlin.
▶ 1934–38, Hirche collaborated with Ludwig Mies van der Rohe, Berlin; 1940–45, with Egon Eiermann; 1945–48, with Hans Scharoun. From 1948, he was a teacher, Hochschule für angewandte Kunst, Berlin-Weissensee, and, from 1952, professor, academy in Stuttgart. His furniture designs were produced by Deutsche Werkstätten and by WK-Verband. He worked at Braun designing its electronic products.
▶ Work subject of exhibition in Stuttgart.
▶ Cat., *Herbert Hirche, Architektur, Innenraum, Design, 1945–1978*, Stuttgart, 1978. Hans Wichmann, *Deutsche Werkstätten und WK-Verband, 1898–1990*, Munich: Prestel, 1992:327.

Hirtz, Lucien (1864–1928)
▶ French jewelry designer; born Alsace; active Paris.
▶ From 1893, Hirtz designed jewelry produced by Béthiot et Bisson for Boucheron; designed *objets d'art* often decorated with enamel; was known for his highly chased gold jewelry.
▶ Work (Boucheron pieces) shown at 1925 Paris 'Exposition Internationale des Arts Décoratifs et Industriels Modernes.'
▶ Annelies Krekel-Aalberse, *Art Nouveau and Art Déco Silver*, New York: Abrams, 1989:65,255. Charlotte Gere, *American and European Jewelry 1830–1914*, New York: Crown, 1975:155.

Hirzel, Hermann Robert Catumby (1864–)
▶ Argentine painter, graphic designer, commercial artist, and jewelry designer; born Buenos Aires.
▶ Studied at the academy in Berlin, 1893.
▶ From c1897, he designed jewelry for the manufacturer Louis Werner, Berlin; at about the same time, was one of the designers of the *Cymric* range of jewelry and silverwares produced by Liberty, London, who published a Hirzel design in its 1902 catalog. After a trip to Italy, he began using dull gold and mosaic in insect and flower settings, attempting to revive a waning technique; worked for Vereinigte Werkstätten, Munich.
▶ Charlotte Gere, *American and European Jewelry 1830–1914*, New York: Crown, 1975:193.

Hishinuma, Yoshiki (1958–)
▶ Japanese textile designer; born Sendai Prefecture.
▶ Hishinuma worked in the design studio of Issey Miyake in 1978; in 1984, founded the Hishinuma Institute, designing fashion, textiles, and handbags.
▶ Albrecht Bangert and Karl Michael Armer, *80s Style: Designs of the Decade*, New York: Abbeville, 1990:184,231.

Hislop, David
▶ British watchmaker, jeweler, and silversmith; active Glasgow.
▶ 1904–05, a watchmaker and jeweler in Glasgow, he was a dealer of silver and electroplated wares designed by Charles Rennie Mackintosh; was the vendor for the christening set made by C. Hahn of Berlin designed by Mackintosh for his god-child Friedrich

Eckart Muthesius, son of the German architect; sold Mackintosh-designed flatware (probably produced by Elkington) used at the Cranston tearooms, Glasgow.
▶ Annelies Krekel-Aalberse, *Art Nouveau and Art Déco Silver*, New York: Abrams, 1989:29,30,255.

Hitchcock, Henry-Russell (1903–1987)
▶ American historian.
▶ Studied Harvard University.
▶ He was one of the earliest historians of Modern architecture; was director for a time of the Museum of Art, Smith College, Northampton, Massachusetts. His only architectural commission was the James Thrall Soby house, Farmington, Connecticut, of c1937. Hitchcock and Philip Johnson were curators of the 1932 'Modern Architecture—International Exhibition' exhibition, New York Museum of Modern Art. He published more than 20 books, including *In the Nature of Materials* (1942) on Frank Lloyd Wright's work. He was a founding member and chair of the Victorian Society America; taught at Vassar College, Poughkeepsie, New York; Smith College; Wesleyan University, Middletown, Connecticut; Yale University; Harvard University; and Institute of Fine Arts, New York University.
▶ Helen Searing (ed.), *In Search of Modern Architecture: A Tribute to Henry-Russell Hitchcock*, Cambridge: MIT, 1982. Brendan Gill, 'The Singular Henry-Russell Hitchcock,' *Architectural Digest*, July 1990:33,36.

Hitier, Jacques
▶ French decorator and furniture designer.
▶ Studied École Boulle, Paris.
▶ 1930–34, he worked at the Primavera decorating department of Au Printemps department store, Paris; was a specialist in tubular metal furniture for schools; from 1946, taught at École Boulle and designed furniture; in 1960, decorated and furnished the officers' dining room of the 1961 oceanliner *France*.
▶ Work shown at Salons of Société des Artistes Décorateurs from 1948 and Salon des Arts Ménagers from 1950.
▶ Pascal Renous, *Portraits de créateurs*, Paris: H. Vial, 1969.

Hjelle, Lars
▶ Norwegian industrial designer.
▶ Hjelle designed the widely published and copied 1973 *T-4* toothbrush produced by Jordan.
▶ Fredrik Wildhagen, *Norge i Form*, Oslo: Stenersen, 1988:190.

Hjelm, Monica (1945–)
▶ Swedish textile designer.
▶ 1965–69, studied arts, crafts and design high school, Gothenburg.
▶ She worked as a designer for Mark Pelle Vävare, where she was in charge of curtain and cotton fabrics; designed domestic textiles including upholstery.
▶ Robert A.M. Stern (ed.), *The International Design Yearbook*, New York: Abbeville, 1985/1986: Nos. 315,316,318,319.

Hlava, Pavel (1924–)
▶ Czech artist and glassware designer.
▶ 1939–42, studied School of Glassmaking, Železný Brod; 1943–48, College of Applied Arts, Prague.
▶ He designed numerous glass tableware items and a range of domestic cut and engraved glass items in which he employed a wide range of color; 1952–58, was associated with Art Center for Glass Industry, Prague; from 1958, was associated with Institute for Interior and Fashion Design; from 1969, designed glass tableware for the Rosenthal Studio Line; in the 1980s, was active in the design of large-scale abstract decorative glass objects.
▶ Cat., *Modernes Glas*, Frankfurt: Museum für Kunsthandwerk, 1976:181, Nos. 191–95. *Czechoslovakian Glass: 1350–1980*, Corning, NY: The Corning Museum of Glass, 1981:167, Nos. 106,120–21. Cat., Kathryn B. Hiesinger and George H. Marcus III (eds.), *Design Since 1945*, Philadelphia: Philadelphia Museum of Art, 1983.

Hobbs, Brockunier and Co
▶ American glassware manufacturers; located Wheeling, West Virginia.
▶ John L. Hobbs (1804–1881), a superintendent of the cutting department and salesman at the New England Glass Company, and James B. Barnes, the engineer who designed and constructed its first furnace, bought the Plunkett and Miller Glasshouse, Wheeling, West Virginia, and began to produce lead-glass for solar chimneys, jars, vials, tumblers, and scent bottles. In 1849 Barnes was succeeded by his son James F. Barnes and the firm was renamed Hobbs, Barnes and Co. When James F. Barnes died, the firm was reorganized with Hobbs and his son, Charles W. Brockunier, and silent partner William Leighton as directors. Experienced in glassmaking, Leighton, son of Thomas Leighton of New England Glass, served as scientist and superintendent. His son William Leighton Jr. succeeded him in 1867. In 1864, the factory successfully produced a cheaper substitute for flint glass, called lime glass, a discovery which affected the entire glass industry. In colorless opal and lime glass, the firm produced cut and engraved flintware and pressedware in numerous patterns. By 1879, the firm had become one of the largest American glass factories. In the early 1880s, its reputation was established by its 'fancy glass,' including crackle or frosted glass called *Craquelle*, with spangled glass added to its line in 1883. In 1886, it began producing its art glass, *Peachblow*, produced from white opal glass coated with an amber-to-ruby shaded layer and resembling porcelain. Through an agreement in 1886 by Brockunier, Hobbs and New England Glass began producing pressed amberina glass. Its success in art glass waned c1887 when William Leighton Jr. and Charles Brockunier retired. John H. Hobbs remained as president of the firm, renamed J.H. Hobbs Glass. The firm closed in 1891 and was bought along with 17 other glass factories in the area by United States Glass.
▶ Josephine Jefferson, *Wheeling Glass*, Mount Vernon, Ohio, 1947. Albert Christian Revi, *American Pressed Glass and Figure Bottles*, New York, 1964:182–92. Cat., Eason Eige, *A Century of Glassmaking in West Virginia*, Huntington, W. Va: Huntington Galleries, 1980:4–15. Cat., T. Patrick Brennan, *The Wheeling Glasshouses*, Wheeling, W. Va: Oglebay Institute, Mansion Museum. Doreen Bolger Burke et al., *In Pursuit of Beauty: Americans and the Aesthetic Movement*, New York: Metropolitan Museum of Art and Rizzoli, 1986:440–41.

Hobé
▶ French jewelers; located Paris and Mt. Vernon, New York.
▶ Jacques Hobé began as a fine jeweler in Paris in 1848; after more than 15 years, was assigned the title of master goldsmith; became interested in new industrial methods and in developing a larger market without compromising quality. His sons Jacques, Maurice, and William managed the firm after their father. William Hobé traveled to New York to meet Florenz Ziegfeld, *Follies* producer, and secured a large order for costumes (as agent for a German firm) and inexpensive jewelry; Hobé set up a firm to produce costume jewelry in the USA. His sons Donald and Robert manage the firm today.
▶ Deanna F. Cera (ed.), *Jewels of Fantasy: Costume Jewelry of the 20th Century*, New York: Abrams, 1992:216.

Hobson, Stephen (1942–)
▶ American industrial designer, active Palo Alto, California.
▶ Studied Stanford University, California.
▶ He worked for Norse Micrographics, Coates and Welter, and Hewlett-Packard; in 1980, became a principal in ID Two, the American industrial design studio of Design Developments, London; was a project coordinator of the team who designed the *Compass*, one of the first portable computers.
▶ 'The Compass Computer: The Design Challenges Behind the Innovation,' *Innovation*, Winter 1983:4–8. Cat., Kathryn B. Hiesinger and George H. Marcus III (eds.), *Design Since 1945*, Philadelphia: Philadelphia Museum of Art, 1983.

Hochschule für Gestaltung
▶ German educational institution.
▶ A latter-day Bauhaus established in Ulm in 1951, its first director was Max Bill, who was succeeded by Argentine theoretician Tomás Maldonado. In 1968, when the institution closed, Maldonado became professor of design at University of Bologna. 1955–65, Hans Gugelot was head of the school's product design department. The institution was a major influence on the work of Hans Gugelot, teacher, and Dieter Rams, student, at the Braun appliance company, and contributed to the firm's success and to the high reputation of postwar German design.
▶ Tomás Maldonado and Gui Bonsiepe, 'Science and Design,' *Ulm*, Vols. 10–11, May 1964:16–18. Cat., *Hochscule für Gestaltung Ulm . . . Die Moral der Gegenstände*, Berlin: Ernst, 1987. Cat., *L'École d'Ulm: testes et manifestes*, Paris: Centre Georges Pompidou, 1988.

Hockney, David (1937–)
▶ British artist, photographer, and designer; born Bradford; active Los Angeles.
▶ 1953–57, studied Bradford College; 1959–62, Royal College of Art, London.
▶ He taught at various institutions in the USA; was a pioneer of British Pop Art at Royal College of Art; was a highly successful fine artist, stage designer, and photographer by his mid-20s; was the subject of a 1974 film *A Bigger Splash*; was known for the homo-erotic content of his work; illustrated numerous books including his 1967 version of *Poems* (1935) by Constantin Cavafis; in the mid-1970s, became active as a stage and costume designer, including Mozart's *The Magic Flute* and Stravinsky's *The Rake's Progress*; designed 1988 carpets produced by Vorwerk as part of its *Dialog* range.
▶ Work subject of 1988 retrospective, Los Angeles County Museum of Art, New York Metropolitan Museum of Art, and Tate Gallery, London.
▶ Cat., Mario Amaya, *Paintings and Prints by David Hockney*, Manchester, 1969. Cat., Günther Gercken, *David Hockney: Zeichnungen, Grafik, Gemälde*, Bielefeld, 1971. Nikos Stangos (ed.), *David Hockney by David Hockney*, London: 1976. Albrecht Bangert and Karl Michael Armer, *80s Style: Designs of the Decade*, New York: Abbeville, 1990:192,231.

Hödl, Linda (1922–)
▶ Austrian jewelry designer; born Klagenfurt.
▶ Hödl was interested in the nature and the aesthetics of materials; designed necklaces, pendants, and rings, combining semi-precious stones with gold or silver.
▶ Günther Feuerstein, *Vienna—Present and Past: Arts and Crafts—Applied Art—Design*, Vienna: Jugend und Volk, 1976:66,69,80.

Hoeker en Zoon
▶ Dutch jeweler; located Amsterdam.
▶ Hoeker en Zoon was founded in 1854. Before leaving for St. Petersburg and Moscow, Jan Eisenloeffel trained at the firm, working as a draftsman from 1896.
▶ Work (Eisenloeffel's geometrical-motif silver pieces by Hoeker) shown at 1900 Paris 'Exposition Universelle.'
▶ Annelies Krekel-Aalberse, *Art Nouveau and Art Déco Silver*, New York: Abrams, 1989:16,100,176,255.

Hoentschel, Georges (1855–1915)
▶ French decorator, ceramicist, and collector.
▶ Hoentschel was strongly influenced by *japoniste* decoration, like that of Jean Carriès, with whom he pursued research on stoneware; in the Japanese manner, decorated his pieces with gold-overflow glazes and metal mountings; after Carriès died, Hoentschel acquired a house in Montriveau where he worked with Émile Grittel; was active as interior decorator and furnishings designer; towards the end of his life, moved to Paris, where he worked in Grittel's studio. Armand-Albert Rateau worked for Hoentschel in 1898, aged 16.

► Work shown at salons of the Société Nationale des Beaux-Arts. Decorated and furnished Salon du Bois in the pavilion of Union Centrale des Arts Décoratifs at 1900 Paris 'Exposition Universelle.'
► Yvonne Brunhammer, *Art Nouveau Belgium, France*, Houston: Institute for the Arts, Rice University, 1976.

Hoff, Paul   (1945–)
► Swedish ceramicist and glassware designer; born Stockholm.
► 1963–68, attended postgraduate courses, Konstfackskolan and Tekniska Skolan, Stockholm.
► From 1969–74 and 1982–87, Hoff worked at Gustavsberg; 1972–82, was a designer at the Kosta Boda glassworks; from 1988, worked at Rörstrand-Gustavsberg; in 1982, set up own design company; c1987, was artistic advisor, Studioglas, Strömbergstyttan,
► His work was shown in Europe, Japan, Australia, and the USA.
► Jennifer Hawkins Opie, *Scandinavia: Ceramics and Glass in the Twentieth Century*, New York: Rizzoli, 1989.

Hoffer, Hans   (1948–)
► Austrian theater set designer; born Kollmitzberg/Amstetten.
► Hoffer designed stage sets at the Theater am Kärntnertor, Vienna, for productions of plays by Brecht, Ibsen, and others. His realistic and illusionistic set designs were directly related to Viennese object art.
► Günther Feuerstein, *Vienna—Present and Past: Arts and Crafts—Applied Art—Design*, Vienna: Jugend und Volk, 1976:70,75,80.

Hoffmann, Jochen   (1940–)
► German industrial designer; active Bielefeld.
► Studied Hochschule für bildende Künste, Brunswick.
► In 1970, he set up his own design studio; designed the 1985 *Trio* articulated sofa produced by Franz Fertig.
► Albrecht Bangert and Karl Michael Armer, *80s Style: Designs of the Decade*, New York: Abbeville, 1990:42–43,231.

Hoffmann, Josef Franz Maria   (1870–1956)
► Moravian architect and designer; born Pirnitz (now Brtnice, Czech Republic); father of Wolfgang Hoffmann.
► 1887–91, studied architecture, Höhere Staatsgewerbeschule, Brno (now Czech Republic); 1892–95, Akademie der bildenden Künste, Vienna, under Karl von Hasenauer and Otto Wagner.
► He entered the studio of Otto Wagner in 1896; in 1897, became a founding member of the Vienna Secession; was responsible for organizing an early Secession exhibition; from 1899, taught at Kunstgewerbeschule, Vienna, as part of the reforms begun by Arthur von Scala; in 1900, designed a suburb in Vienna where he built four villas 1901–05; in 1903, (with Koloman Moser and banker and arts patron Fritz Wärndorfer) established the Wiener Werkstätte Productiv-Gemeinschaft von Kunsthandwerkern, a group of workshops and crafts studios in Vienna inspired by C.R. Ashbee's Guild of Handicrafts and which helped to pioneer the style of the 1920s. Hoffmann, Moser, and Wärndorfer were later joined by C.O. Czeschka. Hoffmann kept in close contact with Mackintosh and the Glasgow School of Art; was a follower of the Modern movement in Belgium and France; worked in metal, designing accessories and lighting. Some of Hoffmann's furniture designs were produced by J. und J. Kohn. He is known for his *Gesamtkunstwerk* (total design) of the Fledermaus Café and other commissions. For Lobmeyr, he designed numerous drinking sets, flower bowls, and glasses in clear, cut enamel-painted crystal. His major work as an architect includes the 1904–05 Purkersdorf sanatorium, and 1905–24 Palais Stoclet in Brussels, for which he created in collaboration with Klimt a complex design of exterior architecture, interiors, furnishings, and decorations. In 1912, he founded the Österreichische Werkbund. At the 1914 Cologne 'Werkbund-Ausstellung,' Hoffman came into contact with the work of Gropius and the new forms of contemporary art and architecture. From 1922, his Kunstgewerbeschule student Oswald Härdtl worked in Hoffmann's architecture office and became a partner in c1928. Biffeplast reproduced early Hoffmann

metal grid-design accessories in the 1980s. Other firms have been active in reissuing his furniture.
► Designed rooms for the Kunstgewerbeschule and the Vienna Secession at 1900 Paris 'Exposition Universelle.' Participated in 1902 Turin 'Esposizione Internazionale d'Arte Decorativa Moderna,' 1902 Vienna 'Österreichisches Museum für Kunst und Industrie' exhibition, 1914 Cologne 'Werkbund-Ausstellung.' Designed a room setting at 1928 'Exposition of Art in Industry at Macy's,' New York; terraced houses for 1932 'Internationale Werkbundsiedlung'; Austrian Pavilion at 1934 Biennale di Venezia. Work subject of 1987–93 'Josef Hoffmann—Ornament zwischen Hoffnung und Verbrechen' traveling exhibition, Österreichisches Museum für angewandte Kunst, at Hoffmann's birthplace in the Czech Republic, and at IBM Gallery in New York.
► Leopold Kleiner, *Josef Hoffmann*, Berlin, Leipzig, and Vienna, 1927. Armand Weiser, *Josef Hoffmann*, Geneva, 1930. L.W. Rochowanski, *Josef Hoffmann*, Vienna, 1950. Giulia Veronesi, *Josef Hoffmann*, Milan, 1956. Eduard F. Sekler, 'The Stoclet House by Josef Hoffmann,' *Essays in the History of Architecture Presented to Rudolf Wittkower*, London: Phaidon, 1967:228–44. Peter Vergo, *Art in Vienna 1898–1918*, London: Phaidon, 1975. Yvonne Brunhammer et al., *Art Nouveau Belgium, France*, Houston: Institute for the Arts, Rice University, 1976. Eduard F. Sekler, *Josef Hoffmann*, Salzburg, 1982. Peter Vergo, 'Fritz Warndorfer and Josef Hoffmann,' *Burlington Magazine*, CXXV, 1983:402–10. Cat., *Josef Hoffmann, Ornament zwischen Hoffnung und Verbrechen*, Vienna: Österreichisches Museum für angewandte Kunst und Hochschule für angewandte Kunst, 1987.

Hoffmann, Pola   (1902–)
► Polish designer; wife of Wolfgang Hoffmann.
► Studied Kunstgewerbeschule, Vienna, under Oskar Strnad and Frank.
► See Hoffmann, Wolfgang.

Hoffmann, Wolfgang   (1900–69)
► Austrian designer; born Vienna; son of Josef Hoffmann; husband of Pola Hoffmann.
► Studied architecture, Kunstgewerbeschule, Vienna, under Oskar Strnad and Frank.
► For two years, he worked in the office of his father Josef Hoffmann, Vienna. In 1925, he and Pola Hoffmann moved to the USA. Hoffmann worked briefly for Joself Urban and Elly Jacques Kahn. His early work included the Little Carnegie Playhouse and other theaters, stores, and apartments, most in New York. By 1932, he had become interested in pewter accessories, lighting, and furniture; in 1933, was commissioned to design interiors of the Lumber Industry House at 'A Century of Progress,' Chicago; in 1934, redesigned the reception area of the Howell Furniture administration building. Wolfgang became active as a designer of furniture and furnishings, including numerous models of bent tubular-steel furniture, in the style of Marcel Breuer, for Howell Furniture, Chicago, where he moved to supervise the manufacture of his designs. Pola Hoffmann became known primarily as a textile designer, although she collaborated with her husband on metal tabletop accessories. In the 1930s, the Hoffmanns divorced and dissolved their business partnership. In 1936, he patented several tubular-metal chair designs, including an outdoor chair, open-arm lounge chair, club chair, and chaise longue; 1935–36, designed numerous smoking stands. From c1942–60, Hoffmann had turned from design, becoming active as a professional photographer.
► Work (pewterware by the Hoffmanns for Early American Pewter Company, Boston) shown at 1930–31 'Decorative Metalwork and Cotton Textiles,' American Federation of Arts in Washington, and included in 1983 'At Home in Manhattan' exhibition, Yale University. Designed rooms in the Lumber Industries house and worked with Joself Urban on the fair's general color system for 1933–34 Chicago 'International Exposition (A Century of Progress).'

▶ Harry V. Anderson, 'Contemporary American Designers,' *Decorators Digest*, May 1936:38–41,78. 'Pola Hoffmann,' *International Dictionary of Women Workers*. Marta K. Sironen, *A History of American Furniture*, East Stroudsburg, Pa: Towse, 1936:140–41. Karen Davies, *At Home in Manhattan: Modern Decorative Arts, 1925 to the Depression*, New Haven: Yale, 1983:77. Eric Baker, *Great Inventions, Good Intentions*, San Francisco: Chronicle, 1990:84–85. Ric Emmett, 'Wolfgang Hoffmann' in Mel Byars and Russell Flinchum (eds.), *50 American Designers*, Washington: Preservation Press, 1994.

Hofman, Jiří (1935–)
▶ Czech industrial designer.
▶ Studied School of Decorative Arts and Design, Liberec.
▶ He was head of the government department that managed Plastimat Liberec, for which he produced his first design in plastics in 1956 and 1970 disposable ice-cream cup and food containers; collaborated with I. Jakeš.
▶ Cat., Milena Lamarová, *Design a Plastické Hmoty*, Prague: Uměleckoprůmyslové Muzeum, 1972:114, Nos. 106,107.

Hofman, Vlastislav (1884–1964)
▶ Czech architect, designer, and painter; born Jitschia (now Jičín, Czech Republic).
▶ 1902–07, studied Czech Technical University under J. Fanta, J.E. Koula, and J. Schulz.
▶ He worked in the building department of the Prague magistrate; was a member of the Artěl Cooperative and Mánes Association of Plastic Artists; in 1911, left Mánes and joined the Group of Plastic Artists; wrote a number of theoretical essays for magazines; in 1912, left the Group and returned to Mánes. He was a founder of the Czech Modern movement, with a range of activities including architecture, applied arts, painting, and, from 1919, theater set design, primarily collaborating with Karel Hilar; contributed to the development of Czech Cubism through theoretical treatises.
▶ Received a gold medal at 1925 Paris 'Exposition Internationale des Arts Décoratifs et Industriels Modernes,' grand prize at 1937 Paris 'Exposition Internationale des Arts et Techniques dans la Vie Moderne,' and grand prize at 1940 (VII) Triennale di Milano.
▶ Alexander von Vegesack et al., *Czech Cubism: Architecture, Furniture, and Decorative Arts, 1910–1925*, New York: Princeton Architectural Press, 1992.

Hogan, James (1883–1948)
▶ British glass craftsman.
▶ Studied Central School of Arts and Crafts and Camberwell School of Art, both London.
▶ He was a member of the Art-Workers' Guild; became art director of James Powell, makers of Whitefriars glass; designed glass for quality production as well as handmade pieces; designed stained glass for American churches, and for his most important commission, two 100 ft (30m) windows of Gilbert Scott's Liverpool Cathedral.
▶ In 1936, elected Royal Designer for Industry.
▶ Fiona MacCarthy and Patrick Nuttgens, *Eye for Design*, London: Lund Humphries, 1986.

Höganäs-Billesholms
▶ Swedish ceramics factory.
▶ The pottery was established in 1797; during the 19th century, it produced a wide range of ceramic table and decorative wares, including some in the Art Nouveau style *c*1900; in 1903, changed its name to Höganäs-Billesholms. Berndt Friberg worked as a thrower 1915–18. In 1916, Edgar Böckman became artistic director. The firm closed in 1926.
▶ Jennifer Hawkins Opie, *Scandinavia: Ceramics and Glass in the Twentieth Century*, New York: Rizzoli, 1989.

Höglund, Erik (1932–)
▶ Swedish glassware and metalworker.
▶ Studied sculpture, Konstfackskolan and Tekniska Skolan, Stockholm.
▶ 1953–73, he was a glass designer at Boda; in the 1950s, became known for the inclusion of metallic particles, producing fine or uneven bubbles in vessel walls. His glass contrasted with the elegant, sophisticated ware of the 1950s. From 1973, visiting professor, Pitchuck Glass Center, Washington; from 1978–81, freelance designer, Pukeberg and Lindshammer; in 1986, freelance designer, Urigstads Kristalihytta; in *c*1987, freelance designer, Studioglas, Strömbergshyttan.
▶ Received 1957 Lunning Prize. Work shown in numerous exhibitions in Sweden and abroad, including 1980 'Scandinavian Modern Design 1880–1980' exhibition, Cooper-Hewitt Museum, New York.
▶ Cat., David Revere McFadden (ed.), *Scandinavian Modern Design 1880–1980*, New York: Abrams, 1982:265, Nos. 176,177. Jennifer Hawkins Opie, *Scandinavia: Ceramics and Glass in the Twentieth Century*, New York: Rizzoli, 1989.

Hohulin, Samuel (1936–)
▶ American industrial designer.
▶ From 1964, Hohulin was chief industrial designer, The Eureka Company, Bloomington, Illinois; assisted by Kenneth Parker, designed its 1982 *Mighty Mite* vacuum cleaner, known for its brightly colored plastic housing and compact size.
▶ *Mighty Mite* shown at 1983–84 'Design Since 1945' exhibition, Philadelphia Museum of Art.
▶ Cat., Kathryn B. Hiesinger and George H. Marcus III (eds.), *Design Since 1945*, Philadelphia: Philadelphia Museum of Art, 1983. Wolf von Eckardt, 'Fashionable Is Not Enough,' *Time*, Vol. 121: Jan. 3, 1983:76–77.

Holbein, Albert (1869–1934)
▶ German goldsmith, engraver, and chaser.
▶ Apprenticed as an engraver at Deyhle silverware factory and others in Berlin; studied Kunstwerbeschule, Frankfurt and Munich, under Professor Gysis.
▶ From the turn of the century to 1902, he collaborated with Georg Binhardt at the Work Cooperative for Artistic Jewelry, Schwäbisch Gmünd, where jewelry was produced industrially. 1910–20, Holbein taught part-time at the Polytechnic, Schwäbisch Gmünd; subsequently, worked in his own workshop; after World War I, produced plain and classical forms that became more geometrical and abstract.
▶ Deanna F. Cera (ed.), *Jewels of Fantasy: Costume Jewelry of the 20th Century*, New York: Abrams, 1992:107–08.

Holbek, Jørgen (1930–)
▶ Danish designer and inventor.
▶ Holbek designed the 1969 *Prism* flatware pattern (with Jørgen Dahlerup) produced by Georg Jensen Sølvsmedie; is known for making smoker's pipes.
▶ Cat., *Georg Jensen Silversmithy: 77 Artists, 75 Years*, Washington: Smithsonian Institution Press, 1980.

Holdaway, Bernard
▶ British furniture designer.
▶ He designed the 1966 *Tomotom* furniture range based on the tube and the spindle in conjunction with Peter Neubart of Hull Traders, Lancashire.
▶ Jonathan M. Woodham, *Twentieth-Century Ornament*, New York: Rizzoli, 1990:246–47.

Holiday, Henry George Alexander (1839–1927)
▶ British artist and designer.
▶ Studied Royal Academy Schools, London, from 1854.
▶ Through fellow students Simeon Solomon, William De Morgan, and W. Richmond, Holiday became associated with the Pre-Raphaelites; worked as a stained glass cartoonist and succeeded Edward Burne-Jones at James Powell, manufacturers of White-

friars glass, where he designed some of its best work. His glass windows were known for his freer hand and better organization of images than the confined perspectives and narrow framework of Morris and Co's early glass designs. His work included embroideries (often with his wife Catherine, who produced a number of embroidered panels for Morris), mosaics, enamels, and murals.

▶ In 1857, work first shown at the Royal Academy, London.

▶ Isabelle Anscombe and Charlotte Gere, *Arts and Crafts in Britain and America*, New York: Rizzoli, 1978.

Holland, Nick (1946–)

▶ British industrial designer and teacher.

▶ Holland became known for his teaching at Royal College of Art, London, before he set up an industrial design practice; designing hydraulic equipment at first, in 1973, became general manager of Design Objectives, a small home-accessories manufacturer, where the design of housewares became his specialty; 1976–82, was head of design development for Staffordshire Potteries; in 1982, established his own manufacturing company Nicholas John; in 1983, set up the design consultancy Nick Holland Design Group, Cardiff, where a wide range of products were designed, including kitchenware; designed 1988 electronic scale with ABS housing incorporating a new weighing mechanism for Waymaster.

▶ Jeremy Myerson and Sylvia Katz, *Conran Design Guides: Kitchenware*, London: Conran Octopus, 1990:43,75–76.

Hollein, Hans (1934–)

▶ Austrian architect and designer; born Vienna; active Vienna and Düsseldorf.

▶ Studied engineering and architecture, Bundesgewerbeschule, Akademie der bildenden Künste, Vienna, to 1956; 1958–60, Illinois Institute of Technology, Chicago; with Frank Lloyd Wright and Ludwig Mies van der Rohe; College of Environmental Design, University of California at Berkeley, to 1960.

▶ He set up an office in Vienna in 1964 becoming active as architect, urban planner, and designer; early in his career, became the most prominent figure in progressive exhibition design in Austria. His 1964–65 Retti candleshop, Kohlmarkt, Vienna, synthesized illusionist dream architecture and the machine aesthetic of the airplane. Because the street on which his Metek boutique was located was dark, he solved the problem with a striking décor. His 1973–74 Schullin jewelry store, Graben, Vienna, was presented as a deconstructed jewel. In shop after shop, he linked the street environment to the interior and, because of this approach, has been identified as the successor of fellow Austrians Otto Wagner, Adolf Loos, Josef Hoffmann, and Oswald Haerdtl. 1965–70, he was editor of the journal *Bau*, Vienna; from 1967, taught at Staatlichen Kunstakademie, Düsseldorf; in 1976, became professor, Akademie der bildenden Künste, Vienna. His architecture incorporated details in expensive materials, primarily marble, brass, and chrome. His 1981 *Marilyn* sofa produced by Poltronova and 1983 teaset by Alessi contributed to his popularity. He designed the 1981 *Schwarzenberg* briar wood table produced by Memphis; became known for combining traditional and industrial materials with a kitsch/Pop sensibility; from 1978, was the Austrian commissioner to Biennale di Venezia. Clients included Herman Miller, Knoll, Yamagiwa, Poltronova, Wittmann, American Optical Corporation, Cleto Munari, Swid Powell, and Baleri; design work included 1980 candelabrum produced by Rossi & Arcandi, 1980 metalware accessories by Rossi & Arcandi, 1984 *Mitzi* sofa by Poltronova, and a sofa at the 1984 Triennale di Milano. Architecture and interior-architecture work included 1963 Aircraft-Carrier City project; 1967–69 Richard Feigen Gallery, East 79th Street, New York; 1966 'Selection 66' and 'Austriennale' exhibitions, 1968 (XIV) Triennale di Milano; 1970 'Tod' ('Death') exhibition, Städtisches Museum, Mönchengladbach; 1970–75 Siemens central office, Munich; 1970–72 Carl Friedrich von Siemens Foundation, Monaco; 1971–72 Media-Linien (Media-Lines), Olympic Village, Munich; 1972–82 Abteiberg municipal museum, Mönchengladbach; 1976–78 Österreichisches Verkehrsbüro, Vienna;

1976–78 Museum of Glass and Ceramics, Tehran, in an old Qajar mansion; 1979 public school, Vienna; 1981–82 Schullin II jewelry store, Vienna; 1981 museum of applied art, Vienna; 1982–83 Frankfurt Museum of Modern Art; 1983 condominium IBA, Berlin; 1983 Kulturforum (cultural center), Berlin; 1981–83 Ludwig Beck shop, Trump Tower, New York; 1984–85 'Dream and Reality, Vienna 1870–1930' exhibition, Vienna.

▶ Received numerous prizes and honors including 1966 Reynolds Memorial Award, Austrian State Award for Art, German Architecture Award, and 1985 Pritzker Architecture Prize. Work shown widely including his divan *Berggasse 19* at 1985 Triennale di Milano.

▶ Cat., *Hans Hollein/Walter Pichlet, Architektur*, Vienna, 1963. Cat., *Dortmunder Architekturausstellung*, Dortmund, 1976. Günther Feuerstein, *Vienna—Present and Past: Arts and Crafts—Applied Art—Design*, Vienna: Jugend und Volk, 1976:61,65,80. Robert A.M. Stern (ed.), *The International Design Yearbook*, New York: Abbeville, 1985/1986: nos. 29,32,394. Officina Alessi, *Tea and Coffee Piazza: 11 Servizi da tè e caffè . . .*, Milan: Crusinallo, 1983. *Le Affinità Elettive*, Milan: Electa, 1985. *Les Carnets du Design*, Paris: Mad-Cap Productions et APCI, 1986:72. Auction cat., *Asta di Modernariato 1900–1986, Auction 'Modernariato,'* Milan: Semenzato Nuova Geri, 8 Oct. 1986: lot 102. *Nouvelles Tendances: les avant-gardes de la fin du XXe siècle*, Paris: Centre Georges Pompidou, 1986. Juli Capella and Quim Larrea, *Designed by Architects in the 1980s*, New York, Rizzoli, 1988. Cat., *Hans Hollein, opere 1960–1988*, Florence: Academia delle arti del disegno, 1988. Albrecht Bangert and Karl Michael Armer, *80s Style: Designs of the Decade*, New York: Abbeville, 1990:28–29,32–33,231. Jonathan M. Woodham, *Twentieth-Century Ornament*, New York: Rizzoli, 1990:284–85.

Holmboe, Thorolf (1866–1935)

▶ Norwegian ceramicist and textile designer.

▶ 1889–90, studied painting in Berlin and at Atelier Fernand Cormon, Paris; sculpture, Statens Håndverks -og Kunstindustriskole, Oslo.

▶ From c1895, he was a member of the late 19th-century Symbolist artists' group in Scandinavia; 1908–11, designed underglaze porcelain decoration at Porsgrunds Porselaensfabrik, in a more restrained manner than that practiced at Royal Copenhagen Porcelain Manufactory; illustrated and designed books.

▶ Work shown at 1900 Paris 'Exposition Universelle'; in Venice, Rome, and Vienna in 1909; Vienna in 1912; and 1915 San Francisco 'Panama Pacific Exposition.'

▶ Cat., David Revere McFadden (ed.), *Scandinavian Modern Design 1880–1980*, New York: Abrams, 1982:265, No. 17. Jennifer Hawkins Opie, *Scandinavia: Ceramics and Glass in the Twentieth Century*, New York: Rizzoli, 1989.

Holmegård Glasvaerk

▶ Danish glassware manufacturer.

▶ A glassworks using peat fuel was planned by Count C.C.S. Danneskiold-Samsø, owner of Holmegård Marsh, South Zealand. In 1825, a glassworks was founded there by his widow Countess Henriette Danneskiold-Samsø. The first furnaces was set up by Christian Wendt, the Norwegian glassmaker. From 1835, glassworkers from Bohemia and Germany produced traditional European models. *Margarethe* of c1905 by Svend Hammershøi was the first designed ware. From 1923, there was a commitment to employ designers, of whom the first was Oria Juul Nielsen followed by architect Jacob Bang in 1925. The *Primula* and *Viola* patterns were designed by Bang. Under Arne Bang, the firm produced stoneware figurines, decorative wares, and lighting. In 1941, Bang was succeeded by Per Lutken, who continued the production of Modern forms. Inspired by a study tour of Italy during the Triennale di Milano in the 1950s, Lutken introduced major changes in production and style. His style incorporated fluid forms in slightly colored glass with etching in some examples, and hot metal applied to formed shapes in others. In 1965, Holmegård merged with Kastrup, with Lutken as chief designer in charge of

a large team which produced free-blown glass objects. In 1975, the firm was acquired by Royal Copenhagen.
► Work shown at 1937 'Ten Years of Danish Art Glassware.'
► Robert A.M Stern (ed.), *The International Design Yearbook*, New York: Abbeville, 1985/1986. Frederick Cooke, *Glass: Twentieth-Century Design*, New York: Dutton, 1986:86. Jennifer Hawkins Opie, *Scandinavia: Ceramics and Glass in the Twentieth Century*, New York: Rizzoli, 1989.

Holmes, Kenneth
► British industrial designer.
► With N.R.P. Poynton and students of Leicester College of Art in the early 1950s, Holmes designed a stainless steel cruet set for the airline BOAC, flatware for Mitchells and Butler, and an electroplated coffee/tea set for Gladwin. With other students, he designed a coffee/tea service in plastic and stainless steel for Andrew Brothers.
► Michael Farr, *Design in British Industry: A Mid-Century Survey*, London: Cambridge, 1955:163–64.

Holmström, August Wilhelm   (1829–1903)
► Finnish goldsmith and jeweler; born Helsinki; active St. Petersburg.
► Holmström became the principal jeweler at Fabergé's St. Petersburg branch. Albert Holmström succeeded his father in 1903.
► Charlotte Gere, *American and European Jewelry 1830–1914*, New York: Crown, 1975:195.

Holscher, Knud   (1930–)
► Danish designer.
► Studied architecture, Det Kongelige Danske Kunstakademi, Copenhagen.
► The winner of many architectural competitions and design awards, Holscher doubled as an industrial designer and architect on commissions including Copenhagen airport and Bahrain Museum; in 1967, became a partner in the design firm Krohn & Hartvig Rasmussen; from 1968, taught at Det Kongelige Danske Kunstakademi; 1960–64, was associated with Arne Jacobsen, serving as supervising architect for his 1960–64 St. Catherine's College, Oxford. His work was widely published, including sanitary fittings, hardware (including *Modric* with Alan Tye) and, from 1974, metalwork for Georg Jensen and its 1975 stainless steel wire serving pieces.
► *Modric* hardware received several British design awards in 1966. Received 1970 Eckersberg Medal, ID Prize of Society of International Design, and numerous architecture competitions for schools, sports pavilions, town centers, and universities throughout Scandinavia and abroad.
► ' "Modric" Architectural Ironmongery,' *Design*, No. 209, May 1966:36–37. Cat., *Georg Jensen Silversmithy: 77 Artists, 75 Years*, Washington: Smithsonian Institution Press, 1980. Cat., Kathryn B. Hiesinger and George H. Marcus III (eds.), *Design Since 1945*, Philadelphia: Philadelphia Museum of Art, 1983.

Holt Le Son, Lucie   (b. Lucie Holt   1899–)
► American painter, sculptor, decorator, and designer; born Philadelphia; active USA and Paris.
► Active during the 1920s and 1930s, Le Son designed nickel-plated furniture and interiors; from 1927, designed wood-carved mannequins and screens for Siégel, the store-vitrine design manufacturer. In 1928, she began designing furniture that incorporated chromium-plated metal and frequently used the fabrics of Hélène Henry.
► Was the first American to show at annual sessions of Salon d'Automne (from 1926) and at Salons of Société des Artistes Décorateurs (SAD) (from 1927). Work (mannequins and screens) shown at 1927 Salon of the Société des Artistes Décorateurs and Salon d'Automne; (travel-agency décor with partly lacquered fibrous-cement panels) 1928 SAD Salon; (central salon of a ship produced by Art du Bois) 1929 SAD Salon; (hotel room and bath produced by Labor Métal) 1930 (I) Salon of Société des Artistes

Modernes; (furniture in different-colored woods) 1931 Paris 'Exposition Coloniale.'
► Pierre Kjellberg, *Art Déco: les maîtres du Mobilier, le décor des Paquebots*, Paris: Amateur, 1986:91–92.

Holub, Adolf O.   (1882–)
► Austrian architect and designer; active Vienna.
► Studied Kunstgewerbeschule, Vienna.
► 1911–12, he designed silver produced by Oscar Dietrich; was associated with forms and ornamentation of the Wiener Werkstätte; also designed furniture.
► Astrid Gmeiner and Gottfried Pirhofer, *Der Österreichische Werkbund*, Salzburg/Vienna: Residenz, 1985:231. Annelies Krekel-Aalberse, *Art Nouveau and Art Déco Silver*, New York: Abrams, 1989:200,255.

Holzbauer, Wilhelm   (1931–)
See Arbeitsgruppe 4

Holzer-Kjellberg, Friedl   (1905–)
► Austrian ceramicist; active Helsinki.
► 1924–70, she was a designer for Arabia, Helsinki; from 1948, its artistic director; was known for her one-off stoneware vessels and Chinese 'rice' pattern porcelain bowls whose effect was created by cutting a pattern into very thin porcelain, with the opening covered by the translucent glaze.
► Cat., David Revere McFadden (ed.), *Scandinavian Modern Design 1880–1980*, New York: Abrams, 1982:265, No. 131.

Hongell, Göran   (1902–73)
► Finnish glassware designer.
► Studied decorative art, Taideteollinen Korkeakoulu, Helsinki.
► Hongel taught decorative painting, Taideteollinen Korkeakoulu; in 1932, began working at Iittala and, from 1940, at Karhula glassworks; was best known for his mass-production glassware; after World War II, began designing Functional glassware without decoration.
► Cat., David Revere McFadden (ed.), *Scandinavian Modern Design 1880–1980*, New York: Abrams, 1982:265, No. 246.

Honzík, Karel   (1900–66)
► Czech architect, furniture designer, graphic artist, set designer, architectural theoretician, and writer; born Le Croisic.
► 1918–25, studied Czech University of Technology, Prague.
► He was a member of the Devětsil group from 1923 until its close in 1931, and chair of its architecture section ARDEV from 1926. His early designs were in the style of the Puristická čtyřka group, close to Linhart's contemporary works, and manifested in his Purist design for 1925–26 suburban house, Za Strahovem, Prague (a project taken over from Krejcar) and 1926–28 apartment block, Starokošířská St., Prague. In 1928 with Josef Havlíček, he set up the studio H&H. The International Style, to which he turned, is illustrated by his 1929–30 suburban house, Nad cementárnou St., as well as collaborative projects with Havlíček. From 1924, Honzík was known as an architecture theoretician; in 1926, began his polemic with Teige on the Constructivist 'elimination of art'; believed that, when there was an emphasis on art, the utilitarian character of architecture was enhanced.
► Participated in the 1923 Bauhaus exhibition, Weimar.
► Cat., *Devětsil: Czech Avant-Garde Art, Architecture, and Design of the 1920s and 30s*, Oxford Museum of Modern Art and London Design Museum, 1990.

Hood, Raymond Mathewson   (1881–1934)
► American architect; born Pawtucket, Rhode Island.
► Studied Massachusetts Institute of Technology, Cambridge, Massachusetts; from 1905, École des Beaux-Arts, Paris.
► He began working for Goodhue in 1907 and soon after left for Pittsburgh to work for Henry Hornsbostel, becoming his chief designer; 1924–31, collaborated with architects Jacques André Fouilhoux and Frederick A. Godley in the partnership Raymond, Fouilhoux and Godley, New York; in 1931, he practiced architecture alone; in 1922, (with John Mead Howells) won the *Chicago*

Tribune Tower competition (built 1925), being selected from 260 entries including those of Walter Gropius, Eero Saarinen, and Adolph Loos. He turned from historicism to a Modernism influenced by Art Déco, using almost no external ornamentation by 1930. As one of three architecture teams, Hood and Fouilhoux participated in the design of 1932–33 Rockefeller Center, New York, where the curtain-wall façade was introduced into what became known as the International Style. Hood's buildings included 1924 American Radiator building, 1929–30 *Daily News* building, and 1930 McGraw-Hill building, all New York. His work included furniture design.
▶ Work (apartment house loggia and business executive's office) installed at 1929 (XI) 'The Architect and the Industrial Arts: An Exhibition of Contemporary American Design,' New York Metropolitan Museum of Art.
▶ Arthur Rappan North, *Raymond M. Hood*, New York: Whittlesey House, 1931. Walter H. Kilham, *Raymond Hood, Architect*, New York, 1973. John B. Schwartzman, *Raymond Hood: The Unheralded Architect*, Charlottesville, Virginia, 1962. Cat., *Raymond M. Hood*, New York, 1982. Gerd Hatje in Vittorio Magnago Lampugnani (ed.), *Encyclopedia of 20th-Century Architecture*, New York, Abrams, 1986:153–54. R. Craig Miller, *Modern Design 1890–1990*, New York: Abrams, 1990.

Hoosemans, François (aka Franz Hoosemans)
▶ Belgian jeweler and silversmith; active Brussels.
▶ With Égide Rombaux, he produced works of distinction, including a range of candelabra and table lamps.
▶ Work (silver candelabra with nude female ivory figures by Rombaux) shown at 1897 exhibition, Musée Royal de l'Afrique Centrale, Tervuren (Belgium), and Belgian pavilion at 1900 Paris 'Exposition Universelle.'
▶ Cat., *Werke Um 1900*, Kunstgewerbe Museum, Berlin, 1966: Nos. 14,15. R. Barilli, *Art Nouveau*, London, 1966:45. M. Rheims, *L'Objet 1900*, Paris, 1964. Annelies Krekel-Aalberse, *Art Nouveau and Art Déco Silver*, New York: Abrams, 1989:94,255.

Hooykaas, H.
▶ Dutch silversmiths; located Schoonhoven.
▶ The firm was founded in 1875; in the 1920s, it produced the Modern silver designs of Harm Ellens.
▶ Annelies Krekel-Aalberse, *Art Nouveau and Art Déco Silver*, New York: Abrams, 1989:255.

Hope, Terje (1956–)
▶ Norwegian furniture designer.
▶ Hope designed the 1986 *Spring* chair with table for Møre Lenestolfabrikk.
▶ Fredrik Wildhagen, *Norge i Form*, Oslo: Stenersen, 1988:203.

Hopea-Untracht, Saara (1925–84)
▶ Finnish interior, furniture, glassware, and lighting designer, metalworker, and ceramicist; born Porvoo; active Helsinki and Porvoo.
▶ Studied interior design, Taideteollinen Korkeakoulu, Helsinki.
▶ 1946–52, she was an independent interior designer, executing furniture designs for Mobilia 1946–48 and lighting for Taito 1948–52; from 1951–80 off and on, constructed *himmelis* (traditional Finnish straw or stalk hangings). 1952–59, she worked at Nuutjärvi as assistant to Kaj Franck. She executed utility and decorative glassware designs, including the first (1951) Finnish nesting range in molded-blown colored glass. Also under Franck, she worked at Arabia. After working as a freelance enamelist from 1960–67, she began specializing in silver jewelry and enameling and was artistic director at her family's firm Ossian Hopea in Porvoo.
▶ She won silver medals for her glassware at the 1954 (X) and 1957 (XI) Triennali di Milano and for her jewelry design at the 1960 (XII) event. Her work was shown in Helsinki in 1953 and in Brussels in 1954 and included in the 1954–57 USA 'Design in Scandinavia' traveling exhibition, 1955 'H 55' exhibition in Hälsingborg (Sweden), 1956–57 West Germany 'Finnish Exhibi-

tion,' 1961 'Finlandia' traveling exhibition in Zürich, Amsterdam, and London.
▶ '15 Contemporary Finnish Designers,' *Design Quarterly*, No. 37, 1957:12–13. Tuula Koli, 'Saara Hopea-Untracht—Tapio Yli-Viikäri,' *Form Function Finland*, No. 3, 1982:12–13. Cat., Kathryn B. Hiesinger and George H. Marcus III (eds.), *Design Since 1945*, Philadelphia: Philadelphia Museum of Art, 1983. Cat., David Revere McFadden (ed.), *Scandinavian Modern Design: 1880–1980*, New York: Cooper-Hewitt Museum, 1982:266, Nos. 173,329. Jennifer Hawkins Opie, *Scandinavia: Ceramics and Glass in the Twentieth Century*, New York: Rizzoli, 1989.

Horák, Bohuslav (1954–)
▶ Czech sculptor and designer.
▶ In 1988, Horák joined design group Atika, established in 1987 and based in Prague. Atika produced his 1988 *A Rotten Luck Easy Chair* in welded iron wire and leather and 1988 *Flammenschrank* cupboard in stained wood and metal. His designs emphasized non-industrial production methods, incorporated traditional materials, including leather and wood, and exhibited a high regard for nature.
▶ Albrecht Bangert and Karl Michael Armer, *80s Style: Designs of the Decade*, New York: Abbeville, 1990:76–77,231.

Horejc, Jaroslav (1886–1983)
▶ Czech sculptor and designer; born Prague.
▶ Studied Specialized School of Jewelry and, 1906–10, School of Applied Arts, both Prague.
▶ From 1912, he collaborated with the cooperative Artěl and designed Cubist ceramic vases; 1918–48, was professor of metalwork, School of Applied Arts, Prague; designed metal latticework and screens with architect Jan Kotěra and others; designed important work in glass, including the four famous cut and engraved pieces, 1921 *Bacchus*, 1922–23 *Canaan*, 1923 *Dance*, and 1924 *Three Goddesses*. He designed noteworthy jewelry in the Art Déco style and a 1937 cut-glass monumental relief *The Earth and the Men* for the Palace of Nations, Geneva.
▶ Received grand prize (for cut glass collection) at 1925 Paris 'Exposition International des Arts Décoratifs et Industriels Modernes.'
▶ A. Adlerová, *České užité umění 1918–1938*, Prague, 1983. Cat., J. Horneková, *Jaroslav Horejc: Výběr z díla, Výstava k 85*, Prague: Uměleckoprůmyslové Muzeum, 1971.

Horgen-Glarus
▶ Swiss furniture manufacturer.
▶ From 1926, the firm produced wood furniture designed by Swiss architects Max. E. Haefeli, Arnold Itlen, Werner M. Moser, Flora and Rudolf Steiger, and sold by Wohnbedarf; furnished the Swiss Pavilion, 1929–30 'Exposición Internacional de Barcelona,' with chairs by Swiss architect Hans Hofmann. Wilhelm Kienzle designed trapezoid kindergarten tables.
▶ Friederike Mehlau-Wiebking et al., *Schweizer Typenmöbel 1925–35, Sigfried Giedion und die Wohnbedarf AG*, Zürich: gta, 1989.

Horta, Victor (1861–1947)
▶ Belgian architect and designer; born Ghent; active Brussels.
▶ 1876, studied architecture at the academy in Ghent, and at the académie des Beaux-Arts, Brussels, to 1881.
▶ An enthusiastic disciple of Eugène-Emmanuel Viollet-le-Duc, Horta took on the design of the building and its entire contents, including chandeliers, furniture, door handles, and key escutcheons. He was sympathetic with Viollet-le-Duc's view that structure was in itself an architectural expression. Horta worked for some time in the office of the neoclassical architect Balat. From 1892, rejecting historicism, he developed his own style, in which he exposed the framework of the building, including its iron pillars, balustrades, and window frames; this exercise created an association between the framework and the interior furnishings. The

iron supports as a decorative element became known as the 'Horta line.' He is best known for his own house, now a museum, on the rue Américaine in Brussels. He became the leading practitioner of the Belgian Art Nouveau idiom in architecture. His design of the Hôtel Tassel in Brussels was outstanding for its combination of craft and industrial techniques; it was the first house in which iron was used extensively. In 1912, he became professor at the Académie des Beaux-Arts, serving as the school's head 1927–31. His later architecture was classical and austere, with Art Nouveau waves replaced by straight lines, of which his concrete 1922–28 Palais des Beaux-Arts in Brussels was the principal example. His buildings in Brussels included the 1892–93 Hôtel Tassel, 1893 Autrique House, 1895–96 Winssinger house, 1895–1900 Hôtel Solvay, 1900 Hôtel Aubecq, Château de la Hulpe, Frison house, 1897–1900 Baron van Eetvelde house, 1901 'À l'Innovation' department store, and 1922–28 Palais des Beaux-Arts. Horta's 1896–99 Maison du Peuple for the Socialist Party in Brussels had the first iron-and-glass façade in Belgium.

▶ His work was included in the 1971 'Guimard, Horta, Van de Velde' exhibition in Paris.

▶ Victor Horta, *Considérations sur l'art moderne*, Brussels, 1925. Victor Horta, *L'Enseignement architectural et l'architecture moderne*, Brussels, 1926. Robert L. Delevoy, *Victor Horta*, Brussels, 1958. R. Puttemans et al., *Victor Horta*, Brussels, 1964. Paolo Portoghesi, *Victor Horta*, Rome, 1969. Cat., *Guimard, Horta, Van de Velde*, Paris, 1971. A. Hoppenbrouwers et al., *Victor Horta architectonographie*, Brussels, 1975. Alastair Duncan, *Art Nouveau and Art Deco Lighting*, New York: Simon and Schuster, 1978:50–51.

Horwitt, Nathan (1889–1990)
▶ Romanian industrial designer; active New York.
▶ Studied City University of New York, New York University, and Art Students' League, New York.
▶ In the late 1920s, he formed Design Engineers in Manhattan, a company that lasted three years, patenting ideas and trying to sell them to manufacturers. After World War II, he was hired by the pharmaceutical firm E.R. Squibb as an advertising copywriter, later becoming director of advertising. He designed the 1930 *Beta* chair, the 'frameless' picture frame (marketed as the *Bruquette* system), and a numberless black clock face produced by Movado Watch and later widely copied. As a publicity ploy and contrary to Horwitt's wishes, Movado named the design the 'museum watch' because of its inclusion in the collection of the New York Museum of Modern Art. Movado parlayed the basic design with a dot at the top of a circle into a range of fashion goods sold in its own boutiques. The design was altered from Horwitt's original and became a subject of litigation between the designer and the manufacturer. Horwitt's original 1947 watch was produced by Vacheron-Constantin-Le Coultre, Switzerland.
▶ The *Beta* chair was shown at the 1934 'Machine Art' exhibition at the New York Museum of Modern Art.
▶ Joan Cook, *The New York Times*, 'Nathan Horwitt, 92; His Designs Included The Movado Watch,' June 20, 1990:B8. Cat., Riva Castleman (ed.), *Art of the Forties*, New York: Museum of Modern Art, 1991:133.

Hosak-Robb, Bibs (1955–)
▶ German industrial designer; born in Neu-Ulm.
▶ 1975–80, studied industrial design, Fachhochschule, Munich; 1981–84, Royal College of Art, London.
▶ 1980–81, she worked for Bosch-Siemens Hausgeräte in Munich. From 1981, she was consultant designer for clients including BMW, WMF, Schlagheck Schultes Design, Trak Sport Articles, and Tristar Sports. Her work included the 1983 *Edo* silver flatware by Robbe & Berking, and 1988 *KunstDisco Seoul* dining-eating concept including the *Göffel* ('fork-spoon') eating utensil by Carl Mertens.
▶ Cat., Design Center Stuttgart, *Women in Design: Careers and Life Histories Since 1900*, Stuttgart: Haus der Wirtschaft, 1989:116–19.

Hose, Robert H. (1915–77)
▶ American industrial designer.
▶ Studied architecture, University of Minnesota, Minneapolis, to 1937, and Massachusetts Institute of Technology, Cambridge, Massachusetts.
▶ In 1939, he began working at Bell Telephone Laboratories, New Jersey, in the small industrial design laboratory where Henry Dreyfuss became a consultant in 1930. Until the 1920s, there was no distinction between technical design and styling in the telephone. During World War II, Hose and Dreyfuss collaborated on over 100 communications projects. In 1946, Hose became an associate in the industrial design office of Dreyfuss in New York, working on the *Model 500* desk-telephone project, and was subsequently a partner. In 1961, Hose left Dreyfuss and set up his own studio. 1953–54, he was president of the Society of Industrial Designers.
▶ Arthur Pulos, *The American Design Adventure 1940–1975*, Cambridge: MIT, 1988: 23.

Hosoe, Isao (1942–)
▶ Japanese designer; born Tokyo; active Milan.
▶ Studied mechanical engineering and aerospace technology, Hihon University, Tokyo, to 1967.
▶ In 1965, he settled in Italy; until 1974, he collaborated with Alberto Rosselli in Milan. Working in the studio Gruppo Professionale Pro, he designed furniture, furnishings, and lighting produced by Bilumen, Cesame, Elle, Flores, Kartell, Omfa, Reguitti, Rima, Saporiti Italia, and Valenti. His lighting was produced by Yamagiwa, Tokyo. He designed office furniture and furnishings produced by Arflex, Facomet Italia, HC 2001, Martini, and Sasea. He was a consultant designer to ICA, Camera di Commercio di Pesaro, and Fiat. He designed automobile bodies for Carrozzeria Boneschi, Carrozzeria Orlandi, and Fiat. In 1981, he established the Design Research Center in Milan. Working in plastics in the early 1980s, he designed the *Picchio* cantilever ABS table lamp for Luxo Italiana and, with Ann Marinelli, the *Snake* free-standing articulated wall system for Sacea. Work included 1991 *Oskar* table and chair by Cassina. He taught at the Scuola Politecnica del Design in Milan. He was a member of ADI (Associazione per il Disegno Industriale). In 1986, he established Hosoe Design in Milan.
▶ He received major prizes, showed his work worldwide, and wrote widely. He won the 1970 Premio Compasso d'Oro (project for Pullmann Fiat), 1973 gold medal at the 1973 (XV) Triennale di Milano, honorable mention at the 1973 'BIO 5' Industrial Design Biennale of Industrial Design at Ljubljana, and the 1974 Smau prize. He participated in the 1972 'Italy: The New Domestic Landscape' at the New York Museum of Modern Art.
▶ *ADI Annual 1976*, Milan: Associazione per il Disegno Industriale, 1976. Alfonso Grassi and Anty Pansera, *Atlante del Design Italiano 1940–80*, Milan: Fabbri, 1980:303. Robert A.M. Stern (ed.), *The International Design Yearbook*, New York: Abbeville, 1985/1986: Nos. 73,201. Hans Wichmann, *Italien Design 1945 bis heute*, Munich: Die Neue Sammlung, 1988. *Modo*, No. 148, March–April 1993:121.

Houillon, Louis
▶ French silversmith; active Paris.
▶ Houillon was considered the best enameler of his day. Étienne Tourette and Philippe Wolfers were pupils in his workshop in Paris.
▶ From 1878, Houillon and Tourette exhibited jointly. After 1893, he showed his work under his own name.
▶ Cat. *Die Fouquet, 1960–1960, Schmuckkünstler in Paris*, Museum Bellerive, Zürich, 1984:64. Annelies Krekel-Aalberse, *Art Nouveau and Art Déco Silver*, New York: Abrams, 1989:60,91.

Houtzager, Cees
See Studio Pro

Howdle, Annette (1938–)

▶ Danish jewelry designer; active London.

▶ Studied at the Jensen silverworks and Danish College of Jewelry, Silversmithing and Commercial Design.

▶ She worked at the Georg Jensen Sølvsmedie 1962–68.

▶ Cat., *Georg Jensen Silversmithy: 77 Artists, 75 Years*, Washington: Smithsonian Institution Press, 1980.

Høye, Emil (1875–1958)

▶ Danish silversmith; active Bergen and Christiania (now Oslo).

▶ Høye settled in Bergen in 1905. 1910–16, he was artistic director of Marius Hammer, one of Norway's largest silversmithies, which produced large quantities of souvenir silver spoons for tourists and export. After setting up his own workshop, he continued to produce silver designs for the firm. His work was influenced by Ballin and later by Georg Jensen.

▶ Annelies Krekel-Aalberse, *Art Nouveau and Art Déco Silver*, New York: Abrams, 1989:243,255.

Hubbard, Elbert Green (1856–1915)

▶ American furniture designer.

▶ Hubbard met William Morris in 1894 and the following year, inspired by Morris's Kelmscott Press, founded the Roycroft Press, East Aurora, near Buffalo, New York. Founder of the Roycrofters, an Arts and Crafts community, he organized workshops, lectured, and wrote as a highly effective champion of the Arts and Crafts philosophy. He established a group of enterprises, including book publishing and binding, furniture production, leatherwork, and metalware. There were more than 400 people in the utopian Roycroft community, based on the British Arts and Crafts movement, but with a commercial slant of its own. The Roycrofters operated a restaurant which served the many tourists who discovered its activities through its publications (*Little Journeys* pamphlets, *The Philistine* monthly journal, and mail-order catalogs advertising gift items and souvenirs). Hubbard was co-founder of the Larkin Company in Buffalo. He and his wife died aboard the oceanliner *Lusitania* in 1915. His son Elbert Hubbard Jr. became director of the Roycrofters until the community closed in 1938.

▶ Freeman Champney, *Art and Glory: The Story of Elbert Hubbard*, New York: Crown, 1968. Anne Yaffe Phillips, *From Architecture to Object*, New York: Hirschl and Adler, 1989:24. Leslie Greene Bowman, *American Arts and Crafts: Virtue in Design*, Los Angeles: Los Angeles County Museum, Boston: Bulfinch, 1990.

Huber, Patriz (1878–1902)

▶ German architect and interior, furniture, and silver designer; born Stuttgart; active Darmstadt and Berlin.

▶ Studied Kunstgewerbeschule, Mainz, under his father Anton Huber, and in Munich under painter L. von Langenmantel.

▶ He became interested in architecture, interior decoration, and design and, 1899–1902, was a member of the Darmstadt Artists' Colony of the Grand Duke Louis IV of Hesse-Darmstadt. 1901–02, he collaborated with Theodor Fahrner, who made his jewelry designs in his workshop in Pforzheim. In 1902, he set up his own studio. Martin Mayer in Mainz was the primary producer of thousands of pieces of his silver designs. Huber's simple geometrical ornamentation with angular spirals influenced the work of Munich court silversmith Carl Weishaupt, who borrowed his designs. He committed suicide in Berlin at the age of 24.

▶ Installations of his houses in Glückert and Habich and his furniture, umbrella handles, stoppers, and boxes were included in the 1901 exhibition at the Darmstadt Artists' Colony. A 1903 commemorative exhibition of his work was shown in Darmstadt.

▶ Charlotte Gere, *American and European Jewelry 1830–1914*, New York: Crown, 1975:196. Annelies Krekel-Aalberse, *Art Nouveau and Art Déco Silver*, New York: Abrams, 1989:131,132, 133,255. Deanna F. Cera (ed.), *Jewels of Fantasy: Costume Jewelry of the 20th Century*, New York: Abrams, 1992:110.

▶ Cat., *Patriz Huber, Ein Mitglied der Darmstädter Künstlerkolonie*, Darmstadt: Museum Künstlerkolonie, 1992.

Hucker, Thomas

▶ American furniture designer.

▶ Studied 1973 under Daniel Jackson, and 1974–76, under Leonoro Hilgner, both in Philadelphia; 1976–80, furniture design and fabrication, Boston University; 1989, industrial design, Domus Academy, Milan.

▶ In 1982, he was artist in residence in the architecture department of Tokyo University of Fine Arts and set up his own design studio for one-off and limited production furniture and lighting. His clients included Dansk (1986–90 table-top designs and crystal stemware) and Bernini (1990 wooden furniture). Hucker's 1991 furniture range was produced by Palazzetti.

▶ His work was included in the 1989 'New American Furniture' exhibition at the Boston Museum of Fine Arts, and traveling.

Huggins, Vera (?–1975)

▶ British ceramics designer and decorator.

▶ In 1923, she began working as a designer in the painting studios at Doulton, Lambeth. *c*1940–50, she produced a small amount of export stonewares.

▶ She showed original signed ceramic pieces at the 1935 exhibition at the Royal Academy in London, 1937 Paris 'Exposition Internationale des Arts et Techniques dans la Vie Moderne,' and other international events in Johannesburg, Sydney, and New York.

▶ Cat., *Thirties: British art and design before the war*, London: Arts Council of Great Britain, Hayward Gallery, 1979:94, 154,293.

Hugill, Lynne

▶ British textile designer.

▶ Studied fashion and textiles, Leicester Polytechnic.

▶ She was a consultant designer to various firms, including Habitat, Mothercare and Marks and Spencer.

▶ Albrecht Bangert and Karl Michael Armer, *80s Style: Designs of the Decade*, New York: Abbeville, 1990:184,231.

Hugo, François (1899–)

▶ French jeweler and metalworker; father of Pierre Hugo.

▶ At an early age, he met and befriended Jean Cocteau, Max Ernst, André Derain, Jean Arp, and Pablo Picasso. He developed a process of hammering precious metals on a bronze mold, resulting in an accurate and light reproduction of an original. He produced Picasso's first designs in silver in 1956. Other metal works of artists soon followed. Hugo produced Salvador Dalí's widely published 1957 *Mollusc* flatware in silver-gilt with glass.

▶ *Applied Arts by 20th Century Artists*, Christie's Geneva, 1991.

Hugo, Pierre (1947–)

▶ French jeweler and metalworker; son of François Hugo.

▶ 1968–75, he worked with his father on artists' jewelry; in 1975, set up his own workshop; organized artists' jewelry exhibitions worldwide; is still a noteworthy artist-jewelry editor.

▶ *Applied Arts by 20th Century Artists*, Christie's Geneva, 1991.

Huguenin, Suzanne

▶ Swiss textile designer, active New York and Mesingen (Switzerland).

▶ 1952–55, she was apprentice-assistant to Eszter Haraszty, who headed Knoll Textiles; 1955–63, succeeded Haraszty as head of the operation that produced textiles for the commercial market; developed the *Nylon Homespun* upholstery-fabric range produced with nylon carpet yarns (previously only available in filament form with an unpleasant glossy appearance); from 1964, was a consultant textile designer in New York and Switzerland.

▶ Eric Larrabee and Massimo Vignelli, *Knoll Design*, New York: Abrams, 1981:93. Cat., Kathryn B. Hiesinger and George H. Marcus III (eds.), *Design Since 1945*, Philadelphia: Philadelphia Museum of Art, 1983.

Hukin and Heath

▶ British crystal and silver firm.

▶ Hukin and Heath was founded in 1855, by J.W. Hukin and J.T. Heath in Birmingham. As a freelance designer closely associ-

ated with the firm, Christopher Dresser executed his first silver pieces for the firm in 1878. A.E. Harvey designed for the firm in the 1930s.
▶ Annelies Krekel-Aalberse, *Art Nouveau and Art Déco Silver*, New York: Abrams, 1989:14,21,34,256. Stuart Durant, *Christopher Dresser*, London: Academy Editions; Berlin: Ernst & Sohn, 1993.

Huldt, Johan (1942–)
▶ Swedish designer; born Stockholm.
▶ Studied Konstfackskolan and Tekniska Skolan, Stockholm, to 1968.
▶ He founded Innovator Design: 1974–76, was director of the Swedish Furniture Research Institute; in 1983, became chairman of the National Association of Swedish Interior Architects.
▶ Robert A.M. Stern (ed.), *The International Design Yearbook*, New York: Abbeville, 1985/1986: No. 35.

Hull-House Shops
▶ American vendor.
▶ Hull-House Shops was located at 800 S. Halstead, Chicago, 1898–c1940; producing wares in an Arts and Crafts style, was active through the late 1930s.
▶ Sharon S. Darling in association with Gail Farr Casterline, *Chicago Metalsmiths*, Chicago Historical Society, 1977.

Hummel, Richard O. (c1899–c1976)
See Cowan Pottery Studio.

Hunebelle, André (1896–1985)
▶ French designer, producer of glassware, lighting, metalwork, accessories, and film maker; born Meudon.
▶ Studied mathematics, École Polytechnique, Paris.
▶ 1922–39, he was a designer and decorator at 2 avenue Victor-Emmanuel-III, Paris; in addition to bibelots, produced small furniture pieces in glass and metal; 1937–39, was an administrator at a newspaper; in 1941, became a film producer and director for films including *Feu Sacré* (1941–42), *L'Inévitable Monsieur Dubois* (1943), *Florence est folle* (1944), *Leçon de Conduite* (1945), *Rendez-Vous à Paris* (1946), *Carrefour du Crime* (1947), *Métier de Fous* (1948), *Mission à Tanger, Millionaire d'un Jour* (1949), *Méfiez-Vous des Blondes* (1950), *Ma Femme est Formidable, Massacre en Dentelles* (winner of the Prix du Meill) (1951), *Monsieur Taxi, Mon Mari est Merveilleux* (winner of the Prix du Meill) (1952). He was a member of the Comité Directeur du Syndicat français des Production et Exportation des Films.
▶ Claude Morava, *L'Art Moderne dans la Verrerie: illustré par quelques oeuvres du maître verrier André Hunebelle*, Paris: Hunebelle, c1937.

Hunt, Martin (1942–)
▶ British ceramicist and glass designer.
▶ 1960–63, studied Gloucestershire College of Art; 1963–66, Royal College of Art, London.
▶ In 1966, he and ceramics designer David Queensberry established the Queensberry Hunt design group. He worked for Hornsea Pottery, Bing & Grøndahl Porcelaensfabrik, Wedgwood, Rosenthal, Thomas Glass, Watson's Potteries, Doulton, Ravenshead, Judge International, and Pilkington Glass. With Colin Rawson, he designed the 1977 *Concept* vitrified-clay dinnerware by Hornsea Potteries. He designed the *Tournée* porcelain range produced by Thomas. 1976–86, he was head of the department of glass of the Royal College of Art.
▶ He won four Design Council awards, including one jointly with James Kirkwood for ceramic lamps and three for Hornsea Pottery dinnerware sets. Work (*Concept* dinnerware) received Design Council Award. In 1981, elected Royal Designer for Industry.
▶ Fiona MacCarthy and Patrick Nuttgens, *An Eye for Industry*, London: Lund Humphries, 1986. Jeremy Myerson and Sylvia Katz, *Conran Design Guides: Tableware*, London: Conran Octopus, 1990:33,75.

Hunter, Alec (1899–1958)
▶ British textile designer and weaver; father of Eileen Hunter.
▶ Studied drawing and design, Byam Shaw School of Art, London.
▶ Hunter's father, Edmund Hunter, was owner of St. Edmundsbury Weaving Works, Haslemere, and, subsequently, of a Letchworth hand-weaving mill producing fine dress and furnishing fabrics for domestic and ecclesiastical use. Hunter became a partner. In 1928, the firm was bought by Morton Sundour Fabrics and became the basis for the establishment of Edinburgh Weavers, Carlisle. Hunter settled in Carlisle; oversaw Edinburgh Weavers' production prior to Alastair Morton's direction; in 1932–58, became production manager at both Edinburgh Weavers and Warner and Sons, Braintree, where he and Theo Moorman controlled the style and design of its production; was an advisor to freelance designers concerning cloth construction and yarns and fostered experimentation with power-loom production.
▶ Cat., *Thirties: British art and design before the war*, London: Arts Council of Great Britain, Hayward Gallery, 1979:88,127, 144, 293.

Hunter, Eileen
▶ British textile designer and writer; daughter of Alec Hunter.
▶ She founded Sun Engraving, engravers and process printers; 1933–39, was active in her own firm Eileen Hunter Fabrics in Grafton Street and Bond Street, both London, where she designed fabrics which were block printed by Warner and Sons, Braintree; had offices in Paris, New York, Canada, and the Netherlands. She disliked the popular pallid, washed-out colors in the textile patterns of the 1930s; wrote numerous articles on design and textiles for publications including *Vogue* and *Decoration*; under the nom-de-plume Laura Hunter, published books including *Vanished with the Rose* (1964), *The Profound Attachment* (1969), *Christabel, the Russell Case* (1973), and *Tales of Waybeyond* (1979).
▶ Participated in most of the major decorative arts exhibitions of her time including 1935 'British Art in Industry,' Royal Academy, London; 1937 Paris 'Exposition Internationale des Arts et Techniques dans la Vie Moderne'; (Modern nursery) at 1934 'Children's Exhibition,' Chesterfield House, London.
▶ Cat., *Thirties: British art and design before the war*, London: Arts Council of Great Britain, Hayward Gallery, 1979:91,92,144,293.

Hunzinger, George (1835–98)
▶ American furniture maker; active Brooklyn, New York.
▶ Hunzinger was best known for his high-quality furniture produced in imitation bamboo, which he made from wood turned on a lathe.
▶ Doreen Bolger Burke et al., *In Pursuit of Beauty: Americans and the Aesthetic Movement*, New York: Metropolitan Museum of Art and Rizzoli, 1986:479.

Hürlimann, Heinrich Otto (1900–1963)
▶ Swiss textile designer.
▶ Studied weaving, Bauhaus, Weimar, in 1924.
▶ He was active in Herrliberg (Switzerland) as a co-worker of Johannes Itten; (with colleague Gertrud Dirks-Preiswerk and former teacher Gunta Stölzl) founded the firm SPH to produce furniture, textiles and carpets. The firm was renamed S+H Stoffe when Dirks-Presiwerk left. In 1937, Hürlimann left the company; 1926–1962, taught textile design, Kunstgewerbeschule, Zürich.
▶ Friederike Mehlau-Wiebking et al., *Schweizer Typenmöbel 1925–35, Sigfried Giedion und die Wohnbedarf AG*, Zürich: gta, 1989:229.

Husson, Henri (1852–1914)
▶ French designer, born Les Vosges; active Paris.
▶ He experimented in silver and gold incrustations with painterly effects. In c1900, his work was discovered and sold by gallery owner H. Heibrand. Achieving great success from 1902, Husson designed vases, boxes, and jewelry that incorporated plant and animal ornamentation.

▶ Annelies Krekel-Aalberse, *Art Nouveau and Art Déco Silver*, New York: Abrams, 1989:65,256.

Husson, Thierry (1951–)
▶ French architect and designer.
▶ In 1986, he began collaborating with Fabienne Arietti in Paris. They designed the 1986 *Babylone Chair* sponsored by VIA and produced by Édition AH! A suite of *Babylone* furniture was installed in the offices of French minister of culture Jack Lang and in the National Assembly.
▶ Work shown at 1987 Salon du Meuble, Paris, receiving the young creator's prize for contemporary furniture.

Huszár, Vilmos (1884–1960)
▶ Hungarian architect and designer; born Budapest; active Netherlands.
▶ In 1905, Huszár settled in Voorburg (Netherlands); in 1917, co-founded the De Stijl group and designed its journal cover; in 1918, designed color applications for the bedroom of Bruynzeel house, Voorburg; 1920–21, (with Piet Zwart) collaborated on furniture designs; in 1923; left De Stijl and (with Gerrit Rietveld) designed the exhibition interior, 'Greater Berlin Art Exhibition'; from 1925, pursued painting and graphic design.
▶ Jean Badovici, 'Entretiens sur l'Architecture vivante: Intérieur par V. Huszar,' *L'Architecture vivante*, Fall–Winter 1924:14–15. Hans L.C. Jaffé et al., *De Stijl: 1917–31, Visions of Utopia*, Abbeville, 1982:237, passim.

Hutton, John
▶ New Zealand glassware designer; active Britain.
▶ Hutton became known as one of the most accomplished engravers and etchers of contemporary glass after World War II; was hired by Whitefriars Glass in the 1960s; designed a series of vases with acid-etched motifs taken from his own designs for the west window of Coventry cathedral; associated with Laurence Whistler, another reviver of stipple engraving, whose forms Whitefriars produced to his specifications.
▶ Frederick Cooke, *Glass: Twentieth-Century Design*, New York: Dutton, 1986:75.

Hutton, John (1947–)
▶ American furniture, fabric, and wallpaper designer; active New York.
▶ In 1978, Hutton succeeded Angelo Donghia as design director at Donghia Furniture and Textiles; designed in a quasi-Modern style with a traditional flavor similar to French designs of the 1980s and reminiscent of the voluptuous motifs of the 1950s; produced designs for furnishings, fabrics, wallpaper, and furniture including 1988 *San Marco* sofa and 1988 *Luciano* club chair produced by Donghia.
▶ *Metropolitan Home*, April 1990:80. Arlene Hirst, 'World Class at Last,' *Metropolitan Home*, November 1990:102. Albrecht Bangert and Karl Michael Armer, *80s Style: Designs of the Decade*, New York: Abbeville, 1990:37,231.

Hutton, William
▶ British silversmiths.
▶ William Hutton and Sons was founded in 1800 in Sheffield; sold some of its wares through various London retail vendors, including the Goldsmiths' and Silversmiths' Co. From 1901, Kate Harris designed Art Nouveau silver for the firm.
▶ Annelies Krekel-Aalberse, *Art Nouveau and Art Déco Silver*, New York: Abrams, 1989:32,255.

Hvidt, Flemming (1944–)
▶ Danish furniture designer.
▶ Studied Kunsthåndvaerkerskolen, Copenhagen, to 1970.
▶ From 1973, he collaborated with Jøorgen Bo, Peter Hvidt, and Orla Mølgård-Nielsen; 1974–78, was a consultant at the Teknologisk Institut.
▶ From 1966, received prizes in furniture and industrial design competitions including 1979 Danish furniture prize.

▶ Frederik Sieck, *Nutidig Dansk Møbeldesign: – en kortfattet illustreret beskrivelse*, Copenhagen: Bondo Gravesen, 1981; 1990 Busck edition in English.

Hvidt, Peter (1916–)
▶ Danish architect and cabinetmaker.
▶ Studied cabinetmaking, Kunsthåndvaerkerskolen, Copenhagen.
▶ In 1942, he opened an office where various designers worked: Orla Mølgård-Nielsen 1944–75, Hans Kristensen from 1970, and British designer Adrian Heath; had clients including Fritz Hansen, France and Son, Allerød, Møbelexport, and Søborg Møbelfabrik. The 1950 *AX* range of chairs and tables (with Mølgård-Nielsen), produced by Fritz Hansen from 1960, marked the introduction of the laminate-glueing process (originally used in tennis-racket man-ufacture) in furniture making, while the design fostered interest in Danish furniture. One sheet of laminated wood formed the chair's arms and seat frame. He also pioneered knock-down furniture.
▶ Work (with Mølgård-Nielsen) shown at 1956–57 German 'Neue Form aus Dänemark' traveling exhibition; 1958 'Formes Scandinaves' at the Paris Musée des Arts Décoratifs. Mølgård-Nielsen and Hvidt received diplomas of honor at 1951 (IX) and 1954 (X) Triennali di Milano and the 'Good Design' award in the USA in the 1950s for the *AX 6003* chair. *AX* chair shown at 1951 'Good Design' exhibition, New York Museum of Modern Art; 1966 'Vijftig Jaar Zitten,' Stedelijk Museum; 1970 'Modern Chairs 1918–1970' exhibition, Whitechapel Gallery, London; 1980 'Scandinavian Modern Design 1880–1980' exhibition, Cooper-Hewitt Museum, New York.
▶ Esbjørn Hiort, *Danish Furniture*, New York, 1956:11–12,86–93. Erik Zahle (ed.), *A Treasury of Scandinavian Design*, New York, 1961:277, Nos. 40–41. Gunnar Bratvold, *Mobilia*, July 1960:21. Cat., *Modern Chairs 1918–1970*, London: Lund Humphries, 1971. Frederik Sieck, *Nutidig Dansk Møbeldesign: – en kortfattet illustreret beskrivelse*, Copenhagen: Bondo Gravesen, 1981; 1990 Busck edition in English. Cat., David Revere McFadden (ed.), *Scandinavian Modern Design 1880–1980*, New York: Abrams, 1982:265, No. 217. Cat., Kathryn B. Hiesinger and George H. Marcus III (eds.), *Design Since 1945*, Philadelphia: Philadelphia Museum of Art, 1983.

Hvorslev, Theresia (1935–)
▶ Swedish silver designer.
▶ 1956–58, studied Staatliche Höhere Fachschule für das Edelmetallgewerbe, Schwäbisch Gmünd; 1960, Konstfackskolan, Stockholm.
▶ 1960–64, she trained as a silversmith at Georg Jensen Sølvsmedie and Bernadotte & Björn, both in Copenhagen; working in her preferred medium, designed silver hollow-ware, tableware, cutlery, and jewelry.
▶ From 1964, her work was included in numerous exhibitions worldwide. Received several international design awards including 1967, 1971, and 1974 Diamonds International Award.
▶ *Svenskt Silver Inför Åttiotalet*, Stockholm, 1979. Cat., *Georg Jensen Silversmithy: 77 Artists, 75 Years*, Washington: Smithsonian Institution Press, 1980.

Hydman-Vallien, Ulrica (1938–)
▶ Swedish glassware designer and ceramicist; born and active Stockholm.
▶ 1958–61, studied Konstfackskolan and Tekniska Skolan, Stockholm.
▶ In 1963, she set up her own workshop in Åfors; from 1972, designed for Kosta Boda glassworks; is best known for her vividly colored ceramic sculpture; from 1979, worked for Rörstrand; from 1981–88, taught at Pilchuck Glass Center, Washington State.
▶ Works shown in New York, Tokyo, London, Paris, Tel Aviv, Stockholm, and at 1975 'Adventures in Swedish Glass,' Australia.
▶ Cat., David Revere McFadden (ed.), *Scandinavian Modern Design 1880–1980*, New York: Abrams, 1982:265, No. 306. Jennifer Hawkins Opie, *Scandinavia: Ceramics and Glass in the Twentieth Century*, New York: Rizzoli, 1989.

Høye, Emil   1875–1958)

▶ Danish silversmith; active Bergen and Christiania (now Oslo).

▶ Høye settled in Bergen in 1905. 1910–16, he was artistic director of Marius Hammer, one of Norway's largest silversmithies, which produced large quantities of souvenir silver spoons for tourists and export. After setting up his own workshop, he continued to produce silver designs for the firm. His work was influenced by Ballin and later by Georg Jensen.

▶ Annelies Krekel-Aalberse, *Art Nouveau and Art Déco Silver*, New York: Abrams, 1989:243,255.

I

Iacci, Fabrizia (1949–)
▶ Italian architect and designer; born and active Milan.
▶ Studied architecture and industrial design, Politecnico di Milano, to 1973.
▶ She taught industrial planning and technology, IPSIA, Lissone, and at Instituto Statale d'Arte, Monza; became a member of ADI (Associazione per il Disegno Industriale).
▶ *ADI Annual 1976*, Milan: Associazione per il Disegno Industriale, 1976.

IBM
▶ American computer manufacturer.
▶ A former executive at the National Cash Register Company, Thomas J. Watson Sr. amalgamated several small firms to form the Computing-Tabulating-Recording Company in 1914. The firm produced scales and time clocks and gradually added other products; in 1924, changed its name to International Business Machines. Watson was renowned for his encouragement of aggressive salesmanship. Having joined his father's firm in 1945 and recognizing the value of good design, Thomas J. Watson Jr. hired Eliot Noyes as head design consultant. Noyes had earlier become associated with the firm while he was designing one of its first typewriters in the office of Norman Bel Geddes. Noyes hired the foremost architects of the day to design IBM's buildings, including Ludwig Mies van der Rohe, Edward Larabee Barnes, Marcel Breuer, and Eero Saarinen. Charles Eames made company presentations, including a number of international exhibitions and films. Noyes, who hired Paul Rand to design the graphics, himself designed the 1959 *Executive* and 1961 *Selectric* electric typewriters and the 1961 *Executary* dictating machine. When Noyes died, German industrial designer Richard Sapper became its industrial design consultant in 1980. By the 1980s, the design program was managed in IBM's corporate communications department, Stamford, Connecticut. In the late 1980s, Edward Tufte became a consultant on interface graphics; published the book *The Visual Display of Quantitative Information*.
▶ John Drexel (ed.), *The Facts on File Encyclopedia of the 20th Century*, New York: Facts on File, 1991:458. Peter Dormer (intro.), *The Illustrated Dictionary of 20th-Century Designers: The Key Personalities in Design and the Applied Arts*, New York: Mallard, 1991.

Ibuka, Masaru
See Sony

ICSID (International Council of Societies of Industrial Designers)
▶ International professional organization; located Paris.
▶ Founded in Paris in 1953, it is associated with UNESCO. The organization brings together designers worldwide and is associated with more than 50 design societies from 40 countries. Its concerns include professional practice standards, the promotion of design in developing countries, design education, and design-related terminology. Its congresses are held biannually.

ID Two
▶ American industrial design studio.
▶ ID Two was established in 1979 in Palo Alto, California, as an American branch of Design Developments, the London industrial design firm headed by Bill Moggeridge; specializing in computer design, had clients including Conversion Technologies and Decision Data; designed the 1982 *Compass* computer, a high-density unit in a magnesium case produced by Grid Systems, and one of the first portable computers. Stephen Hobson was a principal in the firm.
▶ Work (*Compass* computer) shown at 1983–84 'Design Since 1945' exhibition, Philadelphia Museum of Art.
▶ Cat., Kathryn B. Hiesinger and George H. Marcus III (eds.), *Design Since 1945*, Philadelphia: Philadelphia Museum of Art, 1983. *Central to Design, Central Industry*, London: Central School of Art and Design, 1983:95–96. 'The Compass Computer: The Design Challenges Behind the Innovation,' *Innovation*, Winter 1983:4–8.

Idée
▶ Japanese furniture manufacturer; located Tokyo.
▶ In 1984, Tentuo Kurosaki established Idée, producing furniture by Philippe Starck, Marie-Christine Dorner, Shiro Kuramata, and others; introduced the first designs of Marc Newson.

Idée, Rose
▶ French costume jewelry designer.
▶ Rose Idée, her husband, and goldsmith Joseph Woloch set up a costume jewelry workshop in 1939 in Paris that became known for its chiseled and hammered works; worked with couturiers in Paris and for retail stores including Galeries Lafayette. The atelier was moved to 14 rue Caffarelli. In 1966, Woloch's son Serge Eric Woloch took over management of the firm, when the name was changed from Rose Woloch to Rose Idée.
▶ Joseph Woloch was awarded (*Chien* brooch) Prix des Drags.
▶ Deanna F. Cera (ed.), *Jewels of Fantasy: Costume Jewelry of the 20th Century*, New York: Abrams, 1992:250.

Iittala (Iittalan Lasitehdas; Karhula-Iittala)
▶ Finnish glass factory.
▶ Iittala was founded in 1881 by Swedish glass blower Petter Magnus Abrahamsson; was initially staffed by Swedish workers who produced high-quality glassware; in 1917, was bought by Ahlström, which had already bought Karhula glassworks in 1915, and became known as Karhula-Iittala; in the 1930s, sponsored several design competitions (second prize to Aino Aalto at 1932 event and first prize to Alvar Aalto at 1936 event); from 1945 for a time, produced only container glass by Karhula. After Tapio Wirkkala received first prize in its 1946 competition, he was appointed chief designer at Iittala. From 1950, Timo Sarpaneva designed for the firm. Other designers included Jorma Vennola. Iittala became the largest utility and art glass producer in Finland; in 1987, was amalgamated into Nuutajärvi.
▶ Jennifer Hawkins Opie, *Scandinavia: Ceramics and Glass in the Twentieth Century*, New York: Rizzoli, 1989.

Ikuta, Niyoko (1953–)
▶ Japanese glass designer.
▶ Work shown at 1983 'Lighting Graffiti '83 by Matsushita Denko,' Japan; 1984 'Selected Exhibition,' Kyoto City Art Museum; 1985 'New Glass in Japan,' Badisches Landesmuseum, Karlsruhe; 1985 'Art Now '85,' Kyogo Prefecture Museum of Modern Art, Kobe, Japan; 1990 'Glass '90 in Japan,' Tokyo; and 1991 (V) Triennale of the Japan Glass Art Crafts Association. Niyoko was a 1987 participant 'Second Interglas Symposium,' Crystalex, Nový Bor (now Czech Republic), and won the 1987 Japan Glass Art Crafts Association prize, 'Glass in Japan '87,' Tokyo, and 1990 New Artist Prize in Kyoto City, Japan. Work subject of exhibitions at Branggiotti Gallery, Rotterdam, in 1989, and Lausanne Musée des Arts Décoratifs in 1987.
▶ Cat., *Glass Japan*, New York: Heller Gallery and Japan Glass Art Crafts Association, 1991: No. 9.

Ikuta, Susumu
▶ Japanese ceramicist; active Tokyo, New York, and North Carolina.
▶ Studied traditional ceramics techniques in Japan under Katoh Kohbei from 1973.
▶ He worked as a fashion designer in Tokyo; in 1958, moved to New York on the invitation of hatter Lilly Daché; studied ceramics in night classes in New York; in 1973, returned to Japan, where he studied with Kohbei and painted on unfired porcelain; in 1978, returned to the USA; working with only blue pigment initially, began adding polychrome overglazes; decorated classical Japanese porcelain forms in realistic flower, dragonfly, and spider's web motifs.
▶ Mary Frakes, 'Summery Abundance,' *Elle Decor*, November 1990:60.

Île-de-France
▶ French oceanliner.
▶ The *Île-de-France* was launched at Le Havre in 1926. It was the largest oceanliner of the time. The ship was owned and operated by the Compagnie Générale Transatlantique (founded in 1864). Its ironwork was designed by Raymond Subes; large tea room, corridors between the first salons, main stairway, and the great hall by Jacques-Émile Ruhlmann; main dining room by Pierre Patout; glass decorations by René Lalique; main salon by collaborators Louis Süe and André Mare; reading and writing room by Jules-Émile Leleu; and stone sculpture by Alfred-Auguste Janniot. Other designers included Maurice Dufrène and Michel Dufet. A floating ambassador of the French decorative arts, it was second in grandeur and expense only to the 1935 oceanliner *Normandie*.
▶ William H. Miller Jr., *The Fabulous Interiors of the Great Ocean Liners in Historic Photographs*, New York: Dover. William H. Miller Jr., *The First Great Oceanliners in Photographs, 1897–27*, New York: Dover. Howard Mandelbaum and Eric Myers, *Screen Deco: A Celebration of High Style in Hollywood*, New York: St. Martin's, 1985. Pierre Kjellberg, *Art Déco: les maîtres du Mobilier, le décor des Paquebots*, Paris: Amateur, 1986.

Illario
▶ Italian jewelers.
▶ Brothers Carlo and Vincenzo Illario established a jewelry store in 1920 in Valenza Po that specialized in Parisian goldsmithing techniques; from the beginning, were known for their large production of high-quality wares. Today the firm employs more than 100 people, managed by brothers Giovanni and Vittorio Illario.
▶ Melissa Gabardi, *Les Bijoux des Années 50*, Paris: Amateur, 1987.

Ilvessalo, Kirsti (1920–)
▶ Finnish textile designer.
▶ Studied Taideteollinen Korkeakoulu, Helsinki.
▶ From the 1950s, she was a designer for Marimekko, Helsinki, and active in rugmaking in the *ryijy* technique.
▶ Work shown at 1954–57 USA 'Design in Scandinavia' traveling exhibition; 1958 'Formes Scandinaves,' Paris Musée des Arts Décoratifs; 1961 'Finlandia' exhibition, Zürich, Amsterdam, and London.
▶ Cat., David Revere McFadden (ed.), *Scandinavian Modern Design 1880–1980*, New York: Abrams, 1982:265, No. 250.

Image, Selwyn (1849–1930)
▶ British priest, artist, and designer; born Bodiam, Sussex.
▶ Studied Oxford University and drawing at Oxford under John Ruskin.
▶ In 1873, Image was ordained a priest in the Church of England; in 1883, resigned his orders and turned to art; from 1882, was associated with A.H. Mackmurdo in forming the Century Guild and designed the first issue (1884) of the Guild's publication *The Hobby Horse*; produced designs for embroidery and stained glass; was a follower of John Ruskin and admirer of William Morris; became a master of the Art-Workers' Guild in 1900; 1910–16, was Slade Professor of Art, Oxford University.
▶ Stuart Durant, *Ornament from the Industrial Revolution to Today*, Woodstock, NY: Overlook, 1986:219,226. Cat., *A.H. Mackmurdo and the Century Guild Collection*, William Gallery.

Imans, Pierre
▶ Dutch mannequin designer and manufacturer; active Paris.
▶ From before 1900, Imans was active in a mannequin factory in Paris where, by the 1920s, his establishment was located at 10 rue de Crussol; became known for his faultlessly finished imitation human skin in wax; in 1922, developed 'carnesine' or 'carnisine' to simulate skin; developed a secret formula that was mainly plaster with gelatin; subsequently, produced models in various synthetic materials and wood mounted in store vitrines worldwide; produced figures in the images of well-known actresses and politicians.
▶ Work (anatomical wax busts) shown at 1900 Paris 'Exposition Universelle'; Salons of Société des Artistes Décorateurs and sessions of Salon d'Automne; 1915 San Francisco 'Panama-Pacific International Exposition'; 1925 Paris 'Exposition Internationale des Arts Décoratifs et Industriels Modernes' (in charge of 'street art' and own pavilion on Pont Alexandre-III). Received first prize at 1911 Turin 'Esposizone Internazionale dell'Industria e del Lavoro.'
▶ Nicole Parrot, *Mannequins*, Paris: Colona, 1981; London: Academy Editions, 1982.

Ingrand, Max (1908–69)
▶ French glass designer.
▶ Studied École Nationale Supérieure des Arts Décoratifs and École des Beaux-Arts, both Paris.
▶ He became involved in glass design, active in France, Europe, and the Americas; designed the illuminated glass fountain in Rond-Point of avenue des Champs-Élysées, Paris; decorated the residence of President Bourguiba, Skanes; worked for Saint-Gobain glass-works, Fontana Arte in Italy, Verre et Lumière in France; designed the wavy, thin-walled 1957 *Mouchoir* (handkerchief) vase by Fontana Arte and 1953 stained-glass windows in the church of Saint-Pierre de Montmartre, Paris; was counsellor of Commerce of Trade, vice-president of Société des Artistes Décorateurs, president of Association française de l'éclairage, Officier of the Légion d'honneur.
▶ Patrick Favardin, *Le Style 50: Un moment de l'art français*, Paris: Sous Le Vent–Vilo, 1987:74–80.

Inkhuk (Inchuk) (Institute of Artistic Culture)
▶ Russian specialized learning institution.
▶ Inkhuk was founded in Moscow in 1921 under the auspices of Izo (Department of Fine Arts) of Narkompros The People's Commissariat for Enlightenment; formed in 1917; headed by Vasilii Kandinskii; active 1921–24, its members included artists, architects, theoreticians, and art historians who attempted to associate the production of a work of art with its interpretation; was responsible for the theory and methodology of art and education. Kandinskii attempted to organize its research program according to principles he had set out before the 1917 Revolution in his essay *On the spiritual in art*. His approach was counter to the

politicized avant-garde, and he attempted to synthesize three-dimensional representation with other art forms. Constructivist (in the works of Leonid Vesnin) and Rational architecture (in the works of Nikolai Ladovskii and others) developed primarily within the Inkhuk group, and Constructivist tendencies appeared in painting and design (in the works of Aleksandr Rodchenko, Liubov' Popova, brothers Georgii and Vladimir Stenberg, Varvara Stepanova, and others). In 1921, Kandinskii was dismissed. The new head was Ossip Brik, a friend of poet Vladimir Maiakovskii and his closest collaborator on the journals *LEF* (active 1923–25) and *Novy LEF* (active 1927–28). Maiakovskii celebrated Brik's appointment with a lecture in which he encouraged artists to abandon art in favor of production. From 1923, Malevich was director of the Inkhuk in Leningrad (now St. Petersburg), known as Ginchuk (active 1923–27). Formerly the Museum of Artistic Culture, it had affiliations in Vitebsk and other Soviet cities.
▶ Igor Golomstock, *Totalitarian Art in the Soviet Union, The Third Reich, Fascist Italy and the People's Republic of China*, New York: Icon, 1990:66. Selim Om Magomedov, *Les Vkhutemas*, Paris: Regard, 1990. Cat., *The Great Utopia: The Russian and Soviet Avant-Garde, 1915–1932*, New York: Guggenheim Museum, 1992.

Institut d'Esthétique Industrielle
▶ French promotional organization.
▶ The Institut d'Esthétique Industrielle was established in 1949 in Paris to encourage good design in industry.

Institute of Design (School of Design)
▶ American school.
▶ At Walter Gropius's recommendation, László Moholy-Nagy left London in 1937 and became director of the New Bauhaus, Chicago, which failed; in 1939, he joined the independent School of Design, Chicago, (renamed Institute of Design in 1944) funded by Walter Papecke, head of Container Corporation of America. On Moholy-Nagy's death in 1946, the School of Design became a department under Serge Chermayeff (until 1951) at Armour Institute (renamed Illinois Institute of Technology). The original curriculum included design and literature and psychology studies. There was little pursuit of design for industry, and many students went on to become well known craftspeople.
▶ Karisztina Passuth, *László Moholy-Nagy*, Weingarten, 1986.

Instone, Bernard (1891–)
▶ British silversmith; active Birmingham.
▶ Studied Vittoria Street School, Birmingham.
▶ He was trained by Emil Lettré in Berlin and by J.P. Cooper; became known for his enameled silver.
▶ Annelies Krekel-Aalberse, *Art Nouveau and Art Déco Silver*, New York: Abrams, 1989:256.

International Silver Company
▶ American silversmiths; located Meriden, Connecticut.
▶ The International Silver Company was founded in 1898 by independent New England silversmiths; between the wars, produced noteworthy sterling and silverplate designs. Some pieces were designed by its in-house artists (including Ernest R. Beck, Edward J. Conroy, Jean G. Theobald, Alfred G. Kintz, Leslie A. Brown, and Frederick W. Stark), while the talents of leading industrial designers, architects, and artists (Eliel Saarinen, Alfons Bach, Donald Deskey, Paul Lobel, and Lurelle Guild) were employed. Guild designed the 1934–35 line of silverplate tableware. Other wares from International combined silver with semi-precious stones or new plastics. Some of its designs were less original, such as its pirated Georg Jensen *Acorn* flatware of 1915 by Johan Rohde and Jensen's *Blossom* pattern. International Silver is today the world's largest manufacturer of silverware.
▶ W. Scott Braznell, *American Silver Museum Newsletter*, Meriden, Connecticut, 1989. Annelies Krekel-Aalberse, *Art Nouveau and Art Déco Silver*, New York: Abrams, 1989:256.

International Style
▶ Style associated with the architecture of the Modern movement.
▶ The term was coined by Alfred H. Barr Jr. in 1931 in connection with Philip Johnson's and Henry-Russell Hitchcock's 1932 'Modern Architecture: International Exhibition' (with the accompanying book *International Style: Architecture Since 1922*) at the New York Museum of Modern Art, of which Barr was director. Barr saw in the designs of Le Corbusier, Ludwig Mies van der Rohe, J.J.P. Oud, Walter Gropius, and others the first new mode of Western architecture since the 13th century. The name was drawn from the 15th-century international style of painting in Europe. The exhibition introduced the work of Mies van der Rohe to Americans and traveled for seven years around the USA, including to such unlikely places as the Sears, Roebuck store in Chicago, and Bullock's Wilshire department store in Los Angeles. Barr wrote the foreword to the catalog and persuaded publicist Edward Bernays to spread news of the event, with front-page coverage in *The New York Times*. American architects included Frank Lloyd Wright, Claus and Daub, Raymond and Fouhilhoux, Howe and Lescasze, and Tucker and Howell. Other architects included Alvar Aalto, Josef Albers, Gunnar Asplund, Hans Borkowsky, Marcel Breuer, Brinkman and Van Der Vlugt, Erik Bryggman, Le Corbusier and Pierre Jeanneret, Eixenlohr and Pfennig, Otto Eisler, Joseph Emberton, Figini and Pollini, Brohuslav Fuchs, Walter Gropius, Haefeli, Haesler and Völker, Kellermüller and Hofmann, A. Lawrence Kocher and Albert Frey, H.L. de Koninck, Josef Kranz, Ludvik Kysela, Labayen and Aizpurua, J.W. Lehr, André Lurçat, Markelius and Ahren, Erich Mendelsohn and R.W. Reichel, Theodor Merrill, Ludwig Mies van der Rohe, Richard Neutra, J.J.P. Oud, Lilly Reich, Jan Ruhtenberg, Hans Scharoun, Hans Schmidt, Karl Schneider, Stam and Moser, Steger and Egender, Eskil Sundahl, Lois Welzenbacher, Mamoru Yamada, Nicolaiev and Fissenko, and various government architecture agencies.
▶ Subject of 1992 'International Style Exhibition 15 and MoMA' exhibition, Arthur Ross Architecture Gallery, Buell Hall, Columbia University, New York.
▶ Henry-Russell Hitchcock, *Modern Architecture: Romanticism and Reintegration*, New York: Payson and Clark, 1929. Theo van Doesburg, 'Obnova umjetnost i architekture u Evropi' ('The rebirth of art and architecture in Europe'), *Hrvatska Revija*, 4, 1931, 8:419–32. Alfred H. Barr, Jr., foreword to *Modern Architecture: International Exhibition*, New York: Museum of Modern Art, 1932. Sigfried Giedion, *Space, Time and Architecture: The Growth of a New Tradition*, Cambridge, Mass.: Harvard, 1941. Henry-Russell Hitchcock, 'The International Style Twenty Years After,' *Architectural Record*, 1951. *Alfred H. Barr, Jr.: A Memorial Tribute*, New York: Museum of Modern Art, 1981. Richard Power (ed.), 'Revising Modernist History,' *Art Journal*, Summer 1983 (special issue). Alice Goldfarb Marquis, *Alfred H. Barr, Jr., Missionary for the Modern*, Chicago: Contemporary Books, 1989:85,169–70,261,363. Cat., The International Style: Exhibition 15 and The Museum of Modern Art, New York: Rizzoli/cba, 1992.

International Tile and Trim
▶ American ceramics manufacturer.
▶ John Ivory founded the firm International Tile and Trim in 1882 at 92 Third Street, Brooklyn, New York. The funding and machinery to start the firm came from Britain, as did many artisans, including printers and engravers. Fred H. Wilde, who later wrote a history of the firm, worked for Haw, one of the largest tile manufacturers in Britain, before settling in the USA in 1885 when he began working for International Tile and Trim. The firm's work was similar to British tiles of the 1875–85 period, with draped female allegorical figures from classical literature. In 1884, a branch of the firm was established in Britain. In 1888, the firm was purchased by the New York Vitrified Tile Co.
▶ Thomas P. Bruhn, *American Decorative Tiles, 1870–1930*, Storrs, Connecticut: William Benton Museum of Art, 1979:19,30. Jill Austwick and Brian Austwick, *The Decorated Tile: An Illustrated*

History of English Tile-Making and Design, London, 1980:43–45, 59–63. Doreen Bolger Burke et al., *In Pursuit of Beauty: Americans and the Aesthetic Movement*, New York: Metropolitan Museum of Art and Rizzoli, 1986:442.

Introini, Vittorio (1935–)
► Italian architect, town planner, industrial designer, and teacher.
► Studied architecture, Politecnico di Milano, to 1961.
► From 1963, he worked as a consultant designer at Saporiti and later for its affiliate Proposals; designed Saporiti furnishings including a 1969 library system and its New York showroom in 1975; taught at Politecnico di Milano.
► Enrichetta Ritter, *Design italiano mobili*, Milan, 1968:175. 'Saporiti Italia on Fifth Avenue,' *Interior Design*, Vol. 47, Feb. 1976:142–43. Cat., Kathryn B. Hiesinger and George H. Marcus III (eds.), *Design Since 1945*, Philadelphia: Philadelphia Museum of Art, 1983. Hans Wichmann, *Italien Design 1945 bis heute*, Munich: Die Neue Sammlung, 1988.

Inventum
► Dutch appliance manufacturer; located in De Bilt/Bilthoven.
► The firm was established in 1908; in 1915, was named Inventum; produced electrical teamakers and toasters from the beginning of its activities and radios from the late 1940s. Its only artist appears to have been A.W. Verbeek in 1928. The firm is active today.
► *Industry and Design in the Netherlands 1850/1950*, Amsterdam: Stedelijk Museum, 1985.

Iosa Ghini, Massimo (1959–)
► Italian designer and artist; born Borgo Tossignano; active Bologna and Milan.
► Studied Florence and architecture, Milan.
► In 1981, he became a member of group Zak-Ark; early on, supplied comic-book-type illustrations to the magazine *Per lui* and rock magazines in the USA; worked on projects with Swatch, Solvay, and Centro Moda Firenze; was best known for illustrating children's comic books; from 1984, designed for the firm AGO; from 1982, designed discotheques, video projects, and magazines; from 1985, was consultant to RAI television network, designing sets, art movies, and graphics; in 1986, designed furniture, including for Memphis's 1986 *12 New Collection*, the *Roy* wood and metal table for its 1987 collection, the widely published 1987 *Bertrand* sideboard in wood and metal, and the *Juliette* armchair in metal with plastic and straw webbing; designed 1987 first furniture collection *Dynamic* for Moroso; designed 1988 Bolidio discotheque, New York; 1988 installation for the square at Centre Georges Pompidou, Paris. His furniture and furnishings were produced in amorphic forms in a neo-1950s Streamline style. The style is a manifestation of the Bolidismo movement which Iosa Ghini established in 1983 with Pierangelo Caramia and others. His clients included Fiam, for whom he designed the all-glass *Volgente* étagère and *Genio* and *Incontro* tables, Bieffeplast and Stildomus.
► Work shown widely and (1988 *Disco* stool by Moroso) at 1991 'Mobili Italiani 1961–1991: Le Varie Età dei linguaggi' exhibition, Salone del Mobile, Milan; 1989 first one-person exhibition of graphics and objects, Inspiration Gallery, Axis Centre, Tokyo. Received Roscoe award, USA.
► Fumio Shimizu and Matteo Thun (eds.), *The Descendants of Leonardo: The Italian Design*, Tokyo, 1987:325. Albrecht Bangert and Karl Michael Armer, *80s Style: Designs of the Decade*, New York: Abbeville, 1990:62–63,230. *Modo*, No. 148, March–April 1993:121.

Iribe, Paul (b. Paul Iribarne Garay 1883–1935)
► French designer and illustrator; born Angoulême; active Paris and Hollywood, California.
► He worked as a talented caricaturist for the journals *Le Rire, L'Assiette au beurre, Le Cri de Paris*, and others; in 1908, founded *Le Témoin*. Belonging to the world of high fashion, he influenced taste by illustrating a fashion portfolio for Paul Poiret; sub-

sequently, set up a decorating studio where he designed furniture, fabrics, wallpaper, and *objets d'art*, after collaborating with Pierre Legrain. At first finely carved, then more simple, his furniture was veneered with amaranth, ebony, Brazilian rosewood, and colored shagreen with inlays in contrasting color. After selling his outstanding collection of 18th-century furniture, couturier Jacques Doucet commissioned Iribe to furnish his entire apartment at 46 avenue du Bois (today avenue Foch), Paris. For the Doucet assignment, Iribe hired Pierre Legrain as assistant. Iribe's Modernism always tended to the baroque; he inclined towards a 19th-century sense of luxury, with chairs that virtually engulfed the sitter. In 1914, Iribe traveled to Hollywood and worked as a theatrical designer for various film producers including Cecil B. De Mille. The lush sets for De Mille's 1921 *The Affairs of Anatol* and 1934 *Cleopatra* were among Iribe's better known accomplishments. With architects Umbdenstock and Hourtieg, he wrote a 1926 manifesto against Modern art; as a 'traditionalist' he was opposed to the UAM (Union des Artistes Modernes). In 1930 he returned to France and illustrated periodicals and books, including a trilogy for Nicolas wines; designed the Lanvin emblem representing Jeanne Lanvin dressed for a ball with her daughter Marie-Blanche at her knee, and costume jewelry for Coco Chanel, who became a close friend; in 1935, founded magazine *Le Mot*.
► Victor Arwas, *Art Déco*, New York: Abrams, 1980. Raymond Bacholet et al., *Paul Iribe*, Paris: Denoël, 1982. Cat., Aaron Lederfajn and Xavier Lenormand, *Le Louvre des Antiquaires présente: 1930 quand le meuble devient sculpture*, Paris, 1986. Pierre Kjellberg, *Art Déco: les maîtres du Mobilier, le décor des Paquebots*, Paris: Amateur, 1986:93–94.

Iris
► Finnish domestic goods manufacturer.
► The Iris workshops were established in 1899 by Louis Sparre of Sweden and Finnish painter Akesli Gallen-Kallela; produced ceramics, textiles, metalwork, and furniture; sold to retailers in Paris and St. Petersburg. Alfred W. Finch was director of the ceramics section. In 1902, the operation closed.
► Work shown at 1900 Paris 'Exposition Universelle.'
► Jennifer Hawkins Opie, *Scandinavia Ceramics and Glass in the Twentieth Century*, New York: Rizzoli, 1989.

Isbrand, Hans (1941–) and **Lise Isbrand** (1942–)
► Danish furniture designers, active Albertslund.
► Studied cabinetmaking, Skolen for Brugskunst, Copenhagen.
► In 1965, they opened an office in Albertslund; became consultants to architects M. Hammer, H. Moldenhawer, Herman Olsen, Ole Hagen, and Arne Jacobsen; designed a range of objects including furniture, radio and TV sets, shop display units, and 1966 *PJ 35* chair produced by P. Jeppesen, Copenhagen, in laminated wicker cane and chromium.
► Work shown at 1966 'Formes Danoises,' Monaco; 1967 'Danish Arts and Crafts and Industrial Design' exhibition, Copenhagen; 1968 'Two Centuries of Danish Design' exhibition, Victoria and Albert Museum, London. *PJ35* chair shown at 1970 'Modern Chairs 1918–1970' exhibition, Whitechapel Gallery, London.
► Cat., *Modern Chairs 1918–1970*, London: Lund Humphries, 1971. Frederik Sieck, *Nutidig Dansk Møbeldesign:–en kortfattet illustreret beskrivelse*, Copenhagen: Bondo Gravesen, 1981; 1990 Busck edition in English.

Ishibashi, Chuzaburo (1948–)
► Japanese glass designer.
► Studied Tama Art University, Tokyo, to 1972, and Stourbridge School of Art, Stourbridge (England), to 1980.
► 1972–76, Ishibashi worked as designer at Joetsu Crystal, Gumma (Japan).
► Work included in 1985 'New Glass in Japan,' Badisches Landesmuseum, Karlsruhe; 1986 'Expression en Verre,' Musée des Arts Décoratifs, Lausanne; 1987 'Glass from Stourbridge,' Birmingham Museum of Art; 1988 'Arte en Vidro,' São Paulo Art Museum;

1990 'Glass '90 in Japan,' Tokyo; and 1991 (V) Triennale of Japan Glass Art Crafts Association, Heller Gallery, New York.
▶ Cat., *Glass Japan*, New York: Heller Gallery and Japan Glass Art Crafts Association, 1991: No. 10.

Ishii, Koji   (1946–)
▶ Japanese glass designer.
▶ Studied Tokyo University of Arts to 1971.
▶ 1971–77, Ishii worked for Hoya Crystal, Tokyo; in 1977, set up his own glass studio.
▶ Work shown at 1990 'Glass '90 in Japan,' Tokyo, and 1991 (V) Triennale of the Japan Glass Art Crafts Association, Heller Gallery, New York. Work subject of exhibitions at Seibu department store, Tokyo, 1979; Takashimaya department store, Yokohama, 1981; Tokyo Central Arts Gallery, 1982. Featured in 1988 'World of Art,' NTB-TV, Japan, and participated in 1976 'Hot Glass Seminar,' London.
▶ Cat., *Glass Japan*, New York: Heller Gallery and Japan Glass Art Crafts Association, 1991: No. 11.

Ishimoto, Fujiwo   (1941–)
▶ Japanese textile designer; born Ehime; active Finland.
▶ Studied design and graphic art, National University of Art, Tokyo.
▶ 1964–70, he worked for Ichida; in 1971, settled in Finland; 1970–74, was a designer for Decembre, Finland; in 1974, joined Marimekko, where he worked as a designer of printed fabrics; became known for his black-and-white palette and use of nature themes; incorporated geometric patterns reflective of the work of Maija Isola; in the early 1980s, produced prints more colorful and Japanese in effect; designed 1984 *Taival* fabric, 1987 *Uoma* tablecloth, and 1988 *Lainehtiva* fabric, all produced by Marimekko.
▶ Fabrics shown in Scandinavia, Central Europe, Japan, and USA. Received 1983 Roscoe Prize, USA, and honorable mention award at Finland Design Exhibition.
▶ 'Marimekko Oy,' *Domus*, No. 599, Oct. 1979:76–77. Bella Obermaier, 'Castle of the Winds,' *Mobilia*, No. 298, 1981:25–33. Cat., Kathryn B. Hiesinger and George H. Marcus III (eds.), *Design Since 1945*, Philadelphia: Philadelphia Museum of Art, 1983. Marja-Terttu Vuorimaa, 'Marimekko Exports Know-How,' *Form Function Finland*, No. 2, 1983:10–11. Albrecht Bangert and Karl Michael Armer, *80s Style: Designs of the Decade*, New York: Abbeville, 1990:163,178–79,231.

Ishøj, Ole   (1942–)
▶ Danish designer.
▶ Trained at Georg Jensen Sølvsmedie, Copenhagen.
▶ For a time he worked at Georg Jensen Sølvsmedie; 1972–78, at Andreas Mikkelsen; from 1978, designed jewelry for Jensen's.
▶ Work shown at 1980 'Georg Jensen Silversmithy: 77 Artists, 75 Years' exhibition, Smithsonian Institution, Washington.
▶ Cat., *Georg Jensen Silversmithy: 77 Artists, 75 Years*, Washington, DC.: Smithsonian Institution Press, 1980.

Isokon
See Pritchard, Jack

Isola, Maija   (1927–)
▶ Finnish painter and fabric designer.
▶ Studied Taideteollinen Korkeakoulu, Helsinki.
▶ In 1949, she joined Printex, where her colorful and bold patterns on printed textiles brought the firm renown in the 1950s and 1960s; used bed sheeting as material on which to silkscreen her huge geometric designs for Printex; from 1951, used the same method for producing clothing fabrics for Marimekko. Her early work was abstract; later she introduced patterns influenced by Byzantine decorations and eastern Finnish folk motifs of Karelia.
▶ Erik Zahle (ed.), *A Treasury of Scandinavian Design*, New York, 1961:277, Nos. 193,197–99. David Davies, 'Fabrics by Marimekko,' *Design*, No. 236, Aug. 1968:28–31. 'Marimekko Oy,' *Domus*, No. 599, Oct. 1979:76–77. Charles S. Talley, 'Contempor-

ary Textile Art,' *Scandinavia*, Stockholm, 1982:130–31. Cat., David Revere McFadden (ed.), *Scandinavian Modern Design 1880–1980*, New York: Abrams, 1982. Cat., Kathryn B. Hiesinger and George H. Marcus III (eds.), *Design Since 1945*, Philadelphia: Philadelphia Museum of Art, 1983.

Isozaki, Arata   (1931–)
▶ Japanese architect and designer; born Oita, Kyushu.
▶ Studied University of Tokyo under Kenzo Tange to 1954.
▶ Isozaki became one of Japan's best known architects of the last quarter of the 20th century. His work was direct, sometimes humorous, with geometric, solid forms. 1954–63, he worked in the office of architect Kenzo Tange; in 1963, set up his own architecture practice, while collaborating with other architects and studios; was visiting professor at University of California in Los Angeles; University of Hawaii; Rhode Island School of Design; Columbia University, New York; Yale University, and lectured at numerous institutions including universities in Cambridge, Massachusetts, Toronto, Houston, Sydney, Pennsylvania, and Cambridge. 1979–84, he was a jury member of the Pritzker Prize; in 1982, international competition for Parc de la Villette, Paris; in 1983, international competition for Hong Kong; and others. He published the book *The Dismantling of Architecture*; designed dinnerware for Swid Powell, rugs included in the 1988 Dialog range produced by Vorwerk, 1973–83 *Monroe* chair and table by ICF, 1981 *Fuji* cabinets by Memphis, bed at the Affinità Elettiva of 1985 Triennale di Milano, 1986 jewelry by Cleto Munari. With Tange, he was chief architect for 1970 'Japan World Exposition (Expo '70),' Osaka, and 1965–66 reconstruction plan (international competition winner; with Kenzo Tange) for Skopje (now Macedonia). Isozaki designed 1955–58 Kagawa prefectural offices, Takamatsu; 1957–58 city hall, Imabari; 1959–60 town plan for Tokyo; 1971–74 Gumma Prefecture Museum of Fine Arts, Takasaki; 1972–74 Kitakyushu City Museum of Art; 1972–74 Fujimi country club house, Oita; 1972–75 Kitakyushu central library; 1975 Shukosha building, Fukoka; 1976–78 Kamioka town hall, Gifu; 1977–78 audio-visual center, Oita; 1979–82 Tsukuba civic center; 1981 Museum of Contemporary Art, Los Angeles; 1983 Palladium discotheque, New York; 1986 new city hall, Tokyo; 1986 Los Angeles Museum of Modern Art; 1986–90 Art Tower Mito, Ibaragi (Japan); 1992 Guggenheim Museum Soho, New York.
▶ Work shown at 1968 (XIV) Triennale di Milano; 1976 and 1980 Biennali di Venezia; 1976–77 'Man-trans-Forms,' Cooper-Hewitt Museum, New York; 1977 Biennale di São Paulo; 'Dal Cucchiaio alla città 1983,' Triennale di Milano; (*Floor = Furniture* bed) Affinità Elettiva at 1985 Triennale di Milano. He received a special prize for his work on 'Expo '70'; 1967 and 1975 annual prizes of Architectural Institute of Japan; 1983 *Interiors* magazine award; 1986 gold medal, Royal Institute of British Architects; and others. In 1978, elected an honorary member of Accademia Tiberina, Roma; American Institute of Architects; Bund Deutscher Architekten in 1983.
▶ Philip Drew, *The Architecture of Arata Isozaki*, London and New York, 1982. *Le Affinità Elettive*, Milan: Electa, 1985. Auction cat., *Asta di Modernariato 1900–1986, Auction 'Modernariato,'* Milan: Semenzato Nuova Geri, 8 Oct. 1986: lots 99–100. Juli Capella and Quim Larrea, *Designed by Architects in the 1980s*, New York, Rizzoli, 1988. Volker Fischer, *Bodenreform: Teppichboden von Künstlern und Architekten*, Berlin: Ernst und Sohn, 1989. Carol Lufy, 'Isozaki's Architecture Bridges East and West,' *The World of Art*, Sept. 1991:17. Auction cat., *Memphis: La Collection Karl Lagerfeld*, Monaco: Sotheby's, 13 Oct. 1991.

Issel, Alberto   (1848–1926)
▶ Italian furniture designer; active Turin.
▶ By the time of the 1902 Turin Exposition, he was already well known and active in his own substantial workshop that employed more than 70 craftspeople; designed in the prevailing Stile Floreale with carved, lyrical floral decorative features.

▶ Work shown at 1898 Turin exhibition and 1902 Turin 'Esposizione Internazionale d'Arte Decorativa Moderna.'
▶ Cat., Gabriel P. Weisberg, *Stile Floreale: The Cult of Nature in Italian Design*, Miami: The Wolfsonian Foundation, 1988.

Ito, Kenji   (1960–)
▶ Japanese glass designer.
▶ In 1987, Kenji set up his own glass studio, Kawasaki.
▶ Work subject of 1990 'Glass '90 in Japan,' Tokyo, and 1991 (V) Triennale of the Japan Glass Art Crafts. Won the 1990 grand prize at the 'Young Glass Art '90' exhibition. Work subject of exhibition at Matsuya department store, Tokyo, 1988; Toyama Museum of Art, 1989; and Glass Gallery Yua, Osaka, 1990.
▶ Cat., *Glass Japan*, New York: Heller Gallery and Japan Glass Art Crafts Association, 1991: No. 12.

Itten, Johannes   (1888–1967)
▶ German theoretician and teacher.
▶ 1913–16, studied painting, Stuttgarter Akademie, under Adolf Hölzl.
▶ In 1916, he founded his own art school in Vienna; 1919–23, was a master at the Bauhaus, Weimar; was a central person at the Bauhaus, devising the preliminary course that became a new pedagogic concept for training artists. His approach was too mystical for the pragmatic Bauhaus director Walter Gropius, who dismissed him in 1923; 1926–34, managed his own Itten-Schule, Berlin; 1932–38, was director of Textilfachschule, Krefeld, and director of Kunstgewerbeschule, Zürich; 1949–56, was director of Museum Rietberg für aussereuropäische Kunst, Zürich.
▶ Willy Rotzler (ed.), *Johannes Itten, Werke und Schriften*, Zürich, 1978. Cat., *Johannes Itten, Künstler und Lehrer*, Bern: Kunstmuseum, 1984. Cat., *Johannes Itten und die Höhere Fachschule für Textile Flächenkunst in Krefeld*, Krefeld: Deutsches Textilmuseum, 1992.

Iwata, Hisatoshi   (1925–)
▶ Japanese glass designer.
▶ Studied crafts Tokyo University of Arts, to 1950.
▶ Iwata was on the board of trustees of 'Nitten' (Japan Fine Arts Exhibition), Kofukai, lifetime member and founder in 1972 of the Japan Glass Art Crafts Association.
▶ Work shown at 1945 'Nitten'; 1978, 1981, 1984, 1987, and 1990 'Glass in Japan' exhibitions; 1991 (V) Triennale of Japan Glass Art Crafts Association, Heller Gallery, New York. Received 1976 prize of Minister of Education at 1976 (VIII) annual 'Nitten,' Tokyo; 1981 (XXIII) Mainichi Art Prize; 1982 (XXXVIII) Prize of Japan Art Academy.
▶ Cat., *Glass Japan*, New York: Heller Gallery and Japan Glass Art Crafts Association, 1991: No. 11.

Iwata, Itoko   (1922–)
▶ Japanese glass designer.
▶ Iwata was president of Iwata Glass, Tokyo, and, in 1984, a member of the International Council of Pilchuck Glass School, Stanwood, Washington; was a trustee of The Corning Museum

of Glass, Corning, New York, and co-founder and secretary general of Japan Glass Art Crafts Association.
▶ Work shown at 1978, 1981, 1984, 1987, and 1990 'Glass in Japan' exhibition, Tokyo; 1991 (V) Triennale of Japan Glass Art Crafts Association, Heller Gallery, New York.
▶ Cat., *Glass Japan*, New York: Heller Gallery and Japan Glass Art Crafts Association, 1991: No. 14.

Iwata, Ruri   (1951–)
▶ Japanese glass designer.
▶ Studied Tokyo University of Arts, to 1977.
▶ Iwata was director of Iwata Glass, Tokyo.
▶ Work shown at 1990 'Glass '90 in Japan,' Tokyo; 1991 (V) Triennale of the Japan Glass Art Crafts Association, Heller Gallery, New York. Received 1989 (XIV) Yoshidaisoya Architecture Art Prize. Participated in 1988 (III) 'Interglas Symposium,' Crystalex Nový Bor (now Czech Republic).
▶ Cat., *Glass Japan*, New York: Heller Gallery and Japan Glass Art Crafts Association, 1991: No. 15.

Izo (Department of Fine Arts)
▶ Russian educational institution.
▶ Izo (Department of Fine Arts) was set up in 1918 as the Fine Arts Department of Narkompros (The People's Commissariat for Enlightenment). Its wide-ranging brief covered painting, graphics, sculpture, and architecture. Izo's head was artist David Shterenberg, and the majority of the members of Izo's artistic board were Futurists and Constructivists, including Natan Al'tman, Vladimir Baranov-Rossiné, Nikolai Punin, Maiakovskii, and Osip Brik. Vladimir Tatlin was appointed head of the artistic board of Moscow. Its early activities were considered by the Party leadership to be ineffective and even sometimes harmful; Narkompros's head was Anatolii Lunacharskii, whom Lenin thought 'sympathetic to the Futurists.' Lenin ordered the reorganization of Narkompros in 1920 and became personally involved; Inkhuk (Institute of Artistic Culture) was formed under Izo to handle art and artistic education. Inkhuk's first president was Vasilii Kandinskii, followed by Osip Brik. In 1922, the then head of Izo, David Shterenberg, was dismissed from his position. Up to this time Izo had been the only buyer of art and the distributor of State orders, subsidies, rations, advances, and other material goods. The theories of Constructivism and production continued to inspire the German Bauhaus, Dutch De Stijl, British Tekton, and other movements in Europe and the USA, but, within the Soviet Union, the last major avant-garde exhibition was the 1923 'Artists of all tendencies 1919–23' event, Petrograd. The avant-garde, which had been such an enthusiastic supporter of the Bolshevik takeover, became one of its victims.
▶ S. Fitzpatrick, *The Commissariat of Enlightenment*, Cambridge: Cambridge University Press, 1970. Igor Golomstock, *Totalitarian Art in the Soviet Union, The Third Reich, Fascist Italy and the People's Republic of China*, New York: Icon, 1990:14,36. Cat., *The Great Utopia: The Russian and Soviet Avant-Garde, 1915–1932*, New York: Guggenheim Museum, 1992.

J

Jack, George (1855–1932)

▶ British architect; born Long Island, New York; active Britain.

▶ From c1890, Jack was chief furniture designer for Morris and Co, London; in 1880, began working in the architecture office of Philip Webb; in 1900, took over Webb's practice but built nothing of consequence; published *Wood Carving: Design and Workmanship* (1903), included in John Jogg's 'The Artistic Crafts' series of technical handbooks.

▶ Stuart Durant, *Ornament from the Industrial Revolution to Today*, Woodstock, NY: Overlook, 1986:214–16,233–34.

Jackson, Dakota (1949–)

▶ American furniture designer; active New York.

▶ Jackson began his career as a consultant to stage magicians and to rock-music acts that wanted illusion incorporated into their performances; in c1970, produced his first furniture design (commissioned by Yoko Ono for John Lennon); manufactured his own furniture; in 1991, introduced his 'Vik-ter' range of furniture including the *Stacking Chair*; designs furniture that sometimes makes imaginative use of new materials; gave his pieces curious and sometimes unpronounceable titles.

▶ Work (*Saturn Stool*) shown at 'High Styles: Twentieth Century American Design' exhibition, Whitney Museum of American Art, New York; (other designs) at 1991 'Explorations: The New Furniture,' American Crafts Museum, New York; 1992 focus installation documenting the creation and development of 'Vik-ter' chair, Cooper-Hewitt Museum, New York.

▶ 'The New American Entrepreneurs,' *Metropolis*, May 1991: 69.

Jacob, Carl (c1925–)

▶ Danish furniture designer.

▶ 1950–51, he worked for Kandya, London; is best known for his 1950 *Jason* stacking chairs produced by Kandya in a bent beech shell and with turned wooden legs for use in restaurants, offices, schools, and homes. Its plywood shell, bent without the use of steam heat, was pulled into shape by a pneumatic jig and glued in place with synthetic resin. Jacob made some 27 prototypes before reaching the desired shape. One large man on the shoulders of another tested the immensely strong construction. The chair was used in the South Bank Restaurant and other sites at 1951 London 'Festival of Britain.' Production ceased c1970.

▶ Michael Farr, *Design in British Industry: A Mid-Century Survey*, London: Cambridge, 1955:8ff. Cat., *Modern Chairs 1918–1970*, London: Lund Humphries, 1971.

Jacober, Aldo (1939–)

▶ Italian architect and designer.

▶ Studied Politecnico di Milano.

▶ He set up his own office in Milan in 1964.

▶ Work shown at 1967 International Furniture Exhibition, Cantù; 1966–69 Furniture Exhibitions in Milan. Received first prize (*Trieste* folding chair, with Pierangela D'Aniello) at 1966 Fiera di Trieste; first prize at 1966 MIA Exhibition, Monza.

Jacobs, J.A. (1885–1968)

▶ Dutch silversmith; active Amsterdam.

▶ In 1917, Jacobs was a teacher in the silver department, Kunstnijverheidschool Quellinus (after 1924 renamed Instituut voor de Kunstnijverheid), Amsterdam; produced a 1922 bonbonnière with ornamentation typical of the Amsterdam School of Expressionist Dutch architecture.

▶ Annelies Krekel-Aalberse, *Art Nouveau and Art Déco Silver*, New York: Abrams, 1989:145,256.

Jacobsen, Arne (1902–71)

▶ Danish designer; born Copenhagen.

▶ Studied Det Tekniske Selskabs Skoler, Copenhagen, and architecture, Det Kongelige Danske Kunstakademi, Copenhagen, under Kay Fisker, to 1927.

▶ Jacobsen opened his own office in Hellerup in 1927. Influenced by Modern architecture of the 1930s, including that of Le Corbusier, Gunnar Asplund, and Ludwig Mies van der Rohe, he was Denmark's first exponent of Functionalism; his first major commission was the 1930–34 Bellavista housing project, Copenhagen. In 1950, he began to design furnishings for mass production. His most recognizable designs were produced by Fritz Hansen, a relationship which began in 1932. He designed the 1951–52 *Ant*, 1958 *Swan* chairs, 1955 *Series 7* group, and others. Among his earliest production, the 1951 three-legged stacking chair in plywood and steel was conceived for factory production by manufacturer Fritz Hansen. *Swan* first appeared in the glass-sheathed 1958–60 SAS Hotel, Copenhagen. The *3107* office chair of the 1950s produced by Fritz Hansen was adapted from the *Ant* chair, having casters and arms added. Flatware of 1957 for A. Michelsen appeared in the film *2001: A Space Odyssey* (1969). His 1967 *Cylinda Line* stainless-steel tableware range for Stelton proved highly popular. Clients included Allerød (furniture from 1932), Louis Poulsen (lighting), Stelton and Michelsen (silver and stainless steel), I.P. Lunds (bathroom fixtures), Grautex, Aug. Millech, and C. Olesen (textiles). His 1960–64 St. Catherine's College building, Oxford, for which he paid attention to every detail including lighting, textiles, cutlery, and tableware, is a manifestation of his interest in controlling all the elements of the physical environment, integrating architecture, interior furnishings, and utilitarian objects. Other architecture included 1937 Sterling House, Copenhagen; 1939–40 town hall (with Erik Møller), Århus; 1942 town hall (with Flemming Lassen), Søllerød; 1952 Massey-Harris exhibition and factory building, Glostrup; 1952–56 Munkegård School, Gentofte; 1955 Jespersen office building, Copenhagen; 1955 housing scheme, Søholm; 1955 town hall, Rødovre; 1956 Carl Christensen factory, Ålborg; 1961–67 Danish National Bank, Copenhagen; 1962–70 main administration building of Hamburgische Elektrizitäts-Werke, Hamburg; 1970–73 city hall building (completed by Hans Dissing and Otto Weitling), Mainz. 1956–65, he was professor emeritus, Skolen for Brugskunst (formerly Det Tekniske Selskabs Skoler), Copenhagen.

▶ Work (circular 'house of the future' [with Flemming Lassen] with a roof-top helicopter landing pad) shown at 1929 exhibition and at 1954–57 'Design in Scandinavia,' USA; 1968 'Formes Scandinaves,' Paris; 1960–61 'Arts of Denmark,' USA; 1968 'Two

Centuries of Danish Design,' London; 1966 'Vijftig Jaar Zitten' exhibition, Stedelijk Museum; 1968 'Les Assises du siège contemporain' exhibition, Paris Musée des Arts Décoratifs. Work subject of 1959 exhibition, Royal Institute of British Architects, London; 1968 exhibition, Glasgow. Received a silver medal at 1925 Paris 'Exposition Internationale des Arts Décoratifs et Industriels Modernes'; 1928 gold medal from Det Kongelige Danske Kunstakademi; 1936 Eckersberg Medal; 1954 Prize of Honor, Biennale of São Paulo; 1956 C.F. Hansen Medal; grand prize and silver medal at 1957 (XI) Triennale di Milano; 1960 Grand Prix Internationale, magazine *L'Architecture d'aujourd'hui*; 1962 medal of honor, Danish Architectural Association; 1962 Prince Eugen Medal; 1963 Fritz-Schumacher-Preis, Hamburg; 1963 bronze medal, Royal Institute of British Architects; 1967 and 1969 ID prize; 1967 Industrial Design Prize (*Cylinda Line*), Denmark; International Design Award (*Cylinda Line*), USA; 1969 Industrial Design Prize (*Vola* bathroom fixtures), Denmark; 1969 gold medal 'Pio Manzu,' San Marino; 1969 Die Plakette, Akademie der Künste, Hamburg; 1970 Wood Prize, Denmark; 1971 gold medal, Academie d'Architecture de France.

▶ J. Pedersen, *Arkitekten Arne Jacobsen*, Copenhagen 1954. Cat., *Arne Jacobsen: Architecture, Applied Art*, London: Royal Institute of British Architects, 1959. Arne Karlsen, *Made in Denmark*, New York, 1960:94–103,147. 'Arne Jacobsen: Immeuble de la SAS à Copenhague,' *L'Architecture d'aujourd'hui*, Nos. 91–92, 1960:56–62. Rebecca Tarschys and Henry End, 'Arne Jacobsen: From Stainless Flatware to the Royal Hotel in Copenhagen,' *Interiors*, Vol. 122, Oct. 1962:112–21. Tobias Faber, *Arne Jacobsen*, London, 1964. Cat., *Les Assises du siège contemporain*, Paris: Musée des Arts Décoratifs, 1968. *ID Prizes 1965–69*, Copenhagen: The Danish Society of Industrial Design, 1970:38–39,42–43. Cat., *Modern Chairs 1918–1970*, London: Lund Humphries, 1971. Poul Erik Shriver and E. Waade, *Arne Jacobsen*, Copenhagen, 1976. Cat., David Revere McFadden (ed.), *Scandinavian Modern Design 1880–1980*, New York: Abrams, 1982:265, Nos. 191,209,215,248. Cat., Kathryn B. Hiesinger and George H. Marcus III (eds.), *Design Since 1945*, Philadelphia: Philadelphia Museum of Art, 1983. Jeremy Myerson and Sylvia Katz, *Conran Design Guides: Tableware*, London: Conran Octopus, 1990:75–76. Cat., Leslie Jackson, *The New Look: Design in the Fifties*, New York: Thames and Hudson, 1991:40,41,47,50,51,60,127,138,141.

Jacobsen, Jacob (1901–)

▶ Norwegian industrial designer.

▶ Jacobsen was director of Jac. Jacobsen, Oslo; adapted the 1937 *Luxo 1001* lamp from the British *Anglepoise* prototype and bought rights to produce it in Norway; by the 1940s, had a monopoly on the product, which is produced today by the firm Luxo; (with Poul Henningsen) was a major innovator in lighting design in the early part of the 20th century.

▶ Cat., David Revere McFadden (ed.), *Scandinavian Modern Design 1880–1980*, New York: Abrams, 1982:105,265, No. 111. Fredrik Wildhagen, *Norge i Form*, Oslo: Stenersen, 1988:114.

Jalk, Grete (1920–)

▶ Danish furniture designer.

▶ Studied Kunsthåedvaerkerskolen to 1946, and Det Kongelige Danske Kunstakademi, Copenhagen, under Kaare Klint.

▶ 1940–43, Jalk served as an apprentice; in 1954, set up her own design studio; designed widely published 1963 two-piece multiple-fold plywood chair produced by P. Jeppesens Møbelfabrik and other models by Fritz Hansen.

▶ Work shown at 1951 (IX) Triennale di Milano; from 1956, at furniture fairs in Europe; 1968 'Two Centuries of Danish Design,' Victoria and Albert Museum, London; 1968 'Les assises du siège contemporain,' Paris Musée des Arts Décoratifs. Received 1963 (II) *Daily Mirror* International Furniture Competition award (one-piece circular plywood chair).

▶ Cat., *Les Assises du siège contemporain*, Paris: Musée des Arts Décoratifs, 1968. Frederik Sieck, *Nutidig Dansk Møbeldesign:—*

en kortfattet illustreret beskrivelse, Copenhagen: Bondo Gravesen, 1981; 1990 Busck edition in English.

Jallot, Léon (1874–1967)

▶ French artisan and designer; born Nantes; active Paris; father of Maurice Jallot.

▶ He began to make furniture in 1880; 1898–1901, was manager of the furniture workshop of Siegfried Bing's shop La Maison de l'Art Nouveau, Paris; in 1901, became a founding member of the first Salon of Société des Artistes Décorateurs; in 1903, established his own decorating workshop, where he designed and made furniture, fabrics, carpets, tapestries, glassware, lacquer, and screens; was skillful in the use of rabbeted woods; drew plans for his own house and for that of painter André Derain, rue du Douanier, Paris; was the first to turn away from the excessively floral ornamentation of Art Nouveau and to advocate the pursuit of linearism; as early as 1904, when his only decoration was the grain of the wood, championed rich materials rather than over-wrought forms to suggest luxury; from 1921 in partnership with his son Maurice, designed a wide variety of furniture and furnishings. His furniture had simple lines and flat surfaces which were lacquered, painted, or shagreen or leather covered. In the 1920s, the Jallots began to use synthetic materials and metal in their work. Léon's standard light fixtures were sold by Favre. After *c*1927, when he and Maurice began to design rooms with almost entirely indirect lighting, fixtures for their interiors were designed by Jean Perzel, G. Fabre, and Eugène Capon. The Jallots produced fluted columns lit from within for 1920 Salon of the Société des Artistes Décorateurs and a peripherally illuminated pelmet for 1928 Hôtel Radio (including interiors and restaurant by Maurice), boulevard de Clichy, Paris.

▶ Work shown at Salons of Société Nationale des Beaux-Arts from 1908, Société des Artistes Décorateurs, Salon d'Automne from 1919, (man's bedroom with Georges Chevalier and produced the furniture designed by Henri Rapin and Pierre Selmersheim) in Grand Salon of 'Une Ambassade française' and 'Hôtel du Collectionneur' at 1925 Paris 'Exposition Internationale des Arts Décoratifs et Industriels Modernes.'

▶ Alastair Duncan, *Art Nouveau and Art Déco Lighting*, New York: Simon and Schuster, 1978:173. *Restaurants, dancing, cafés, bars*, Paris: Charles Moreau, Nos. 39–44. *Ensembles Mobiliers*, Paris: Charles Moreau, 1945, Vol. 5, Nos. 6–7. Victor Arwas, *Art Déco*, Abrams, 1980. Cat., Aaron Lederfajn and Xavier Lenormand, *Le Louvre des Antiquaires présente: 1930 quand le meuble devient sculpture*, Paris, 1986. Pierre Kjellberg, *Art Déco: les maîtres du Mobilier, le décor des Paquebots*, Paris: Amateur, 1986:94,97.

Jallot, Maurice (1900–)

▶ French furniture designer and decorator; active Paris; son of Léon Jallot.

▶ Studied École Boulle, Paris, to 1921.

▶ In 1921, he began collaborating with father Léon Jallot, but was more of a Modernist; until 1950, was active as a decorator and designed schemes of stores and apartments including a stair railing produced by Raymond Subes, rugs, stained glass, and geometric-motif furniture panels.

▶ Work first shown under his own name alone at 1927 (XVIII) Salon of Société des Artistes Décorateurs; (furniture suite for the reception salon) in 'Une Ambassade française' at 1925 Paris 'Exposition Internationale des Arts Décoratifs et Industriels Modernes.'

▶ Pierre Kjellberg, *Art Déco: les maîtres du Mobilier, le décor des Paquebots*, Paris: Amateur, 1986:97.

Janák, Pavel (1882–1956)

▶ Czech architect, designer, and teacher, born Prague.

▶ Studied Czech Technical University under J. Schulz, German Technical University, Prague, under J. Zitek; 1906–08, Akademie der bildenden Künste, Vienna, under Otto Wagner.

▶ 1908–09, he worked in Jan Kotěra's studio in Prague; in 1908, became a member of the Union of Architects of the Mánes Association of Plastic Artists, and participated in the founding of the Artěl cooperative; in 1911, resigned from Mánes and joined the executive of the Group of Plastic Artists, serving as architect of its 1912 first exhibition; in 1912, was co-founder of Prague Artistic Workshops; in 1914, was founding member of Association of Czech Accomplishment; from 1924, was chair of SČSD (Czechoslovak Werkbund); in 1917, returned to Mánes; 1921–25, was editor of the magazine *Výtvarná práce*; 1921–42, was professor of architecture, School of Decorative Arts, Prague; in 1936, assumed the position as chief architect of Prague Castle. He was an important urbanist.

▶ Alexander von Vegesack et al., *Czech Cubism: Architecture, Furniture, and Decorative Arts, 1910–1925*, New York; Princeton Architectural Press, 1992.

japonisme
▶ Style in the decorative arts.
▶ With the opening up of trade with Japan following American Commodore Matthew Perry's 1853 expedition, interest in Japanese art in the West began to grow, particularly in France. One of the first interpreters of the style was artist Félix Bracquemond, a friend of the Goncourt brothers. His 1866 table service for the comte de Rousseau was produced by Lebœuf et Millet, Creil. Enthusiasm for the style was heightened by the profusion of Japanese prints and wares at the 1867 Paris 'Exposition Universelle.' Exponents of *japonisme* adopted Japanese motifs and images and imitated its ceramics techniques. In 1874, when Théodore Deck developed the *émaux-en-relief* process of enamel glazing in deep, saturated colors, the process was adopted by porcelain factories including the large facility in Bordeaux managed by Albert and Charles Vieillard. The Vieillards produced ironstone, stoneware, earthenware, and hard- and soft-paste porcelain. *Japonisme* became an integral aspect of the Art Nouveau 1880–1910. More sensitive than anyone else to the pulse of Art Nouveau, Siegfried Bing published *Le Japon Artistic* (1888–91) and *Le Americain Artistic* (1895). Christopher Dresser visited the 1876 Philadelphia 'Centenary Exposition,' went to Japan, acquired a large number of objects for Tiffany, New York, and published *Japan: Its Architecture, Art, and Art Manufactures* (1882). Japanese influences were seen in the USA in the work of, among others, Louis Comfort Tiffany, who had close ties with Bing in Paris, and, in Britain, through the enterprise of Arthur Lasenby Liberty as early as 1862.

▶ Cat., Gabriel P. Weisberg, *Art Nouveau Bing*, New York: Abrams, 1986. Cat., L. d'Albis, *Japonisme à la Manufacture Vieillard 1875–1890, projets de céramiques*, Paris: Galerie Fischer-Kiener, 1986. Mary L. Myers, Amédée de Caranza entry, *Recent Acquisitions: A Selection 1986–1987*, New York: Metropolitan Museum of Art, 1987.
▶ See Art Nouveau

Jarvie, Robert Riddle (1865–1941)
▶ American metalworker; born New York; active Chicago.
▶ He was employed by the Chicago Department of Transportation at the turn of the century; registered as a silversmith in Chicago 1893–1917; showed his work for the first time in 1900; by 1905, had opened The Jarvie Shop; advertised himself as 'the candlestick maker' 1901–04 in the magazine *House Beautiful* and was indeed largely supported by the success of his candlesticks, worked in Art Nouveau and Arts and Crafts styles, produced in intriguing forms. Émigrés J.P. Petterson from Norway and Knut L. Gustafson from Sweden worked for Jarvie. From c1912, he produced noteworthy gold and silver trophies including 1912 Aero Club trophy, 1917 trophy for a University of Illinois dairy exposition, and annual trophies for the Union Stock Yard Company and International Live Stock Exposition. Other designs included hand-beaten copper bowls, sconces, vases, trays, and bookends. He used geometric patterns derived from native-American motifs. He went out of business in 1920.
▶ Work first shown at 1900 'Arts and Crafts Society Exhibition,' Chicago; (candlesticks) at 1902 exhibition, Chicago Art Institute.

▶ Sharon S. Darling with Gail Farr Casterline, *Chicago Metalsmiths*, Chicago Historical Society, 1977. Cat., Anne Yaffe Phillips, *From Architecture to Object*, New York: Hirschl and Adler, 1989:100. Annelies Krekel-Aalberse, *Art Nouveau and Art Déco Silver*, New York: Abrams, 1989:102,123,256. *Metropolitan Home*, November 1990:54.

Jarvisalo, Jouko (1950–)
▶ Finnish designer; born Varkaus.
▶ Jarvisalo was active as an interior architect and freelance designer; practicing from 1983 in an interior-design studio, designed home and office furniture for clients including Artek, Asko, Arsel, and Laukaan Puu, and *Flap* wood and metal chair of c1986 by Inno-tuote.
▶ Robert A.M. Stern (ed.), *The International Design Yearbook*, New York: Abbeville, 1985/1986: No. 14.

Jastrzebowski, Adalbert (1885–)
▶ Polish designer.
▶ Studied School of Fine Art, Cracow.
▶ He designed the dining room at the Polish pavilion (with architect Josef Czajkowski) and murals for the pavilion courtyard, and organized Polish exhibitions in Grand Palais at 1925 Paris 'Exposition Internationale des Arts Décoratifs et Industriels Modernes.' He taught at School of Fine Art, Cracow.
▶ Maurice Dufrêne, *Ensembles Mobiliers, Exposition Internationale 1925*, Paris: Charles Moreau, 1925, Antique Collectors' Club edition 1989:160.

Jaulmes, Gustave-Louis (1873–1959)
▶ Swiss architect and designer; born Lausanne; active Paris.
▶ Studied architecture.
▶ An architect at first, he turned to decorative painting in 1901, to furniture design in 1910, and tapestry design in 1915; received important commissions including the Musée Rodin, Paris; designed tapestries and upholstery fabrics for Compagnie des Arts français; joined CAF when it was established by Louis Süe and André Mare; while there, executed several notable tapestries including *Le Départ des troupes américaines de Philadelphie pour la France*, and murals inspired by Berain and Du Cerceau depicting garlands, gathered fabric, and draperies in a lush 18th-century style. His upholstery fabrics were usually woven by his wife. He designed furniture for the decorating firm Damon; (with Süe and Mare) was commissioned to decorate the avenue des Champs-Élysées and designed the cenotaph commemorating World War I; decorated Salle des Fêtes in Grand Palais, on which Süe was the architect; painted murals for Théâtre de Chaillot and Paris Musée des Arts Décoratifs, including the curtain for Grand-Théâtre, Lyons, along with tapestries and paintings for numerous other theaters, monuments, casinos, and hotels; in 1944, was elected a member of Académie des Beaux-Arts.
▶ Work shown at Salons of the Société Nationale des Beaux-Arts from 1902, Salon d'Automne from 1908, and Salon des Artistes Indépendants from 1909. In 1910, began to show furniture. Painted areas of Hôtel du Collectionneur and 'Une Ambassade française,' six paintings illustrating *Les Mois en fête* in Salle des Fêtes of Grand Palais, and participated in Musée d'Art Contemporain organized by Compagnie des Arts français, all at 1925 Paris 'Exposition Internationale des Arts Décoratifs et Industriels Modernes.'
▶ Léon Deshairs, *Modern French Decorative Art*, Paris: Albert Lévy. Yvonne Brunhammer, *Le Cinquantenaire de l'Exposition de 1925*, Paris: Musée des Arts Décoratifs, 1976:132. Victor Arwas, *Art Déco*, New York: Abrams, 1980. Pierre Cabanne, *Encyclopédie Art Déco*, Paris: Somogy, 1986:201–02.

Jeanneney, Paul (1861–1920)
▶ French ceramicist; born Strasbourg.
▶ Jeanneney was a collector of Far Eastern ceramics; after the death of Carriès, whom he admired, Jeanneney learned stoneware techniques based on Carriès; in 1902, moved from Strasbourg to Saint-Amand-en-Puisaye. Jeanneney's work was influenced by

Chinese stoneware with *flambé* glazes and Japanese *trompe-l'oeil* stoneware, similar to that of Carriès. Inspired by Korean *chawans*, Jeanneney made gourd vases, bowls, bottles, and round vases; created the *champignon* vase decorated with bracket fungus, with a wooden lid; produced stoneware versions of a head of Balzac and heads of the Burghers of Calais, both by Auguste Rodin.

▶ Yvonne Brunhammer et al., *Art Nouveau Belgium, France*, Houston: Institute for the Arts, Rice University, 1976.

Jeanneret, Pierre   (1896–1967)

▶ Swiss architect and designer; cousin of Le Corbusier.

▶ Studied architecture in Geneva.

▶ In 1920, he settled in Paris, where he first worked in the architecture office of the Perret brothers; in 1922, began working as an architect in the office of Le Corbusier; collaborated with Le Corbusier and Charlotte Perriand on seminal furniture designs, although his specific contribution is not known; in 1923, met Purist painter Amédée Ozenfant, who had a strong influence on Jeanneret's own painting; in 1930, became a member of UAM (Union des Artistes Modernes). He designed the patented *Scissor Chair* of c1947 produced by Knoll and other furniture of his own. Introduced as the *No. 92*, the *Scissor* chair was constructed of birchwood with a chromium-plated steel bolt, and had foam rubber cushions upholstered in a linen-and-jute fabric. After World War II, Jeanneret pursued experiments with prefabrication and collaborated with Jean Prouvé on prefabricated housing and with Georges Blanchon on the town planning of Puteaux (France); from 1952, assisted Le Corbusier on the government buildings of Chandigarh (India); designed a number of public buildings, although his name was and remains in the shadow of Le Corbusier.

▶ Work (furniture with Le Corbusier and Perriand) shown at 1930 (I) UAM exhibition; in subsequent UAM exhibitions, (with Le Corbusier) showed architectural projects and models including photographs of 1931 Villa Savoye in Poissy, maquette of 1932 Palace of the Soviets, Moscow, and urban planning for Algiers.

▶ S. Randhawa, *L'Architecture d'aujourd'hui*, No. 136, Feb–March 1968:VI. Arlette Barré-Despond, *UAM*, Paris: Regard, 1986:426–27. *Dictionnaire encyclopédique de l'architecture moderne et contemporaine*, Paris: Vilo, 1987:182. Catherine Courtiau, 'Pierre Jeanneret,' in *Le Corbusier, Une Encyclopédie*, Paris: Centre Georges Pompidou/CCI, 1987. Cat., *Les années UAM 1929–1958*, Paris: Musée des Arts Décoratifs, 1988:198–99.

▶ See Le Corbusier

Jeanpierre, Roger

▶ French jewelry designer; active Paris.

▶ Jeanpierre became active as a jewelry designer c1934, when he began to collaborate with Jean Clément for Elsa Schiaparelli. He was in a management position for twelve years at Maison Winter. In c1960, he set up his own workshop at 11 place des Vosges, Paris. By the time his workshop closed in 1976, he had worked with most of the couture houses including Dior, Balenciaga, Lanvin, Givency, and Saint-Laurent.

▶ Deanna F. Cera (ed.), *Jewels of Fantasy: Costume Jewelry of the 20th Century*, New York: Abrams, 1992.

Jeffrey

▶ British wallpaper manufacturer.

▶ The firm was founded in 1836 as Jeffrey and Wise, Saint Helen's Place, London; in 1838, moved to Kent and Essex Yard, Whitechapel, London; by 1840, had begun using cylinders to print some of its designs, a technology derived from calico printing; produced the washable wallpaper invented by Crease, a paper stainer. In 1842, Robert Horne became a partner, and the name became Jeffrey, Wise and Horne, changed again in 1843 to Horne and Allen. A wallpaper shown at the 1851 London Exhibition, admired for the flatness of its design, was one of the first of its production of the 1870s and 1880s. By 1862, its name was Jeffrey and Co, Whitechapel, with partners including William Allen, Alfred Brown, and Edward Hamilton. In 1864, the firm merged with Holmes and Aubert, producer of hand-printed, flocked, and leaf-metal papers located at 64 Essex Street, Islington, London, where Jeffrey's headquarters then moved; Jeffrey became known for its high-quality papers following the merger. William Morris was not satisfied with his own production of papers and, in 1864, commissioned Jeffrey to print his 1862 *Daisy* pattern, the first Morris paper to be widely available. The firm continued to print Morris papers until 1930, using the same pearwood blocks; was assigned the printing by Jackson and Graham of Owen Jones's complicated papers for the Viceroy's Place, Cairo, requiring 58 separate wood blocks. When William Allen retired, Metford Warner became a junior partner in 1866. After partners Edward Hamilton and Alfred Brown died, Warner became sole proprietor in 1871 and elevated Jeffrey's production to an art, as shown in the Royal Albert Hall in 1873. Warner commissioned designs from leading British designers and architects, including Lewis F. Day, J.D. Sedding, C.F.A. Voysey, William Burges, Walter Crane, E.W. Godwin, Christopher Dresser, and Bruce J. Talbert; Charles Locke Eastlake designed the popular 1869 *Solanum* pattern. Godwin's work was first printed in 1872, becoming popular in the 1880s in the USA. From 1875, Ipswich architect Brightwen Binyon's idea of a combination of papers for the dado, filling, and frieze became popular. Metford Warner managed the firm until the 1920s with sons Albert, Marcus, and Horace. Sanderson bought the firm in 1930, the year Warner died, and in 1940, acquired Morris's printing blocks, still in use today.

▶ Wallpapers shown at 1851 London 'Great Exhibition of the Works of Industry of All Nations'; as fine art, first shown at 1873 London 'Annual Exhibition of All Fine Arts,' Royal Albert Hall. Design for three-part paper based on Chaucer's *Legend of Good Women* (by Crane) shown at 1876 Philadelphia 'Centennial Exposition,' receiving two gold medals. Received gold medals, 1878, 1889, and 1900 Paris 'Expositions Universelles' and 1893 Chicago 'World's Columbian Exposition'; international prizes throughout the late 19th century; grand prize, 1908 London 'Franco-British Exhibition.'

▶ Alan Victor Sugden and John Ludlam Edmondson, *A History of English Wallpaper, 1509–1914*, London and New York, 1926:209–12. E.A. Entwisle, *A Literary History of Wallpaper*, London, 1960:41–45. Catherine Lynn, *Wallpaper in America: From the Seventeenth Century to World War I*, New York, 1980:445–46. Doreen Bolger Burke et al., *In Pursuit of Beauty: Americans and the Aesthetic Movement*, New York: Metropolitan Museum of Art and Rizzoli, 1986:443–44.

Jenaer Glaswerke
See Schott und Genossen Glaswerke

Jencks, Charles A.   (1939–)

▶ American architect, designer, and critic; born Baltimore, Maryland; active London.

▶ Studied literature and architecture, Harvard University, and architecture, London University.

▶ From 1968, he taught at the Architectural Association, London; from 1974, at California University, Los Angeles. His writings on Post-Modern architecture were widely known. He designed influential and widely publicized buildings and furniture, some of which, with symbolic ornaments, was executed for the 'Summer Room' of a London house; pieces which had limited manufacture included 1984 *Sun* table with the image of a *trompe-l'oeil* solar disk, and *Sun* chair produced by Sawaya and Moroni. He was one of 11 architect designers commissioned for the 1983 *Tea and Coffee Piazza* project by Alessi; his designs were based on classical columnar shapes. His numerous books included *Meaning in Architecture* (1969), *Architecture 2000: Predictions and Methods* (1971), *Adhocism* (1972), *Modern Movements in Architecture* (1973), *The Language of Post-Modern Architecture* (1980), *Signs, Symbols and Architecture* (1980), *Skyscrapers–Skycities* (1981), *Post-Modern Classicism* (1982), *Architecture Today* (1982), *Current Architecture* (1983), *Towards a Symbolic Architecture* (1985), and *Post-Modernism: The New Classicism in Art and Architecture* (1987).

► Officina Alessi, *Tea and Coffee Piazza*, Milan: Crusinallo, 1983. Robert A.M. Stern (ed.), *The International Design Yearbook*, New York: Abbeville, 1985/1986: Nos. 140–43,398. *Les Carnets du Design*, Paris: Mad-Cap Productions et APCI, 1986:71. Juli Capella and Quim Larrea, *Designed by Architects in the 1980s*, New York, Rizzoli, 1988.

Jensen, Arthur Georg   (1866–1935)
► Danish metalworker; born Faavad.
► Apprenticed as a goldsmith; c1895–1901, studied sculpture, Det Kongelige Danske Kunstakademi, Copenhagen.
► He served his apprenticeship in Copenhagen for a time under Holm, becoming a journeyman in 1884; (with Christian Joachim) made ceramics c1898 in the workshop of painter and designer Mogens Ballin, near Copenhagen. Jensen worked in the potteries Aluminia and Bing & Grøndahl Porcelaensfabrik, Copenhagen; in 1904, began designing jewelry and silverwares and, in the same year with one assistant, opened his own small silversmithy. He disliked classical reproductions and wanted to make Modern designs a commercial success; his own designs were influenced by nature. Jensen's success was attributed to his ability to attract and foster the talents of Johan Rohde, Gundorph Albertus, Harald Nielsen, and Sigvard Bernadotte, and others. Two post World War II designers, Henning Koppel and Tias Eckhoff, continued the high level of innovation. Almost all of the original designs continue to be made by hand. Jensen also used stainless steel, originally a wartime substitute for silver. It gained popularity after the war and Jensen's postwar stainless-steel pieces were noteworthy. A showroom opened on New York's Fifth Avenue by 1920, its success assured when William Randolph Hearst bought the entire inventory at the 1915 San Francisco 'Panama-Pacific International Exposition.' The 1915 *Acorn* pattern by Rohde and *Blossom* motifs by Jensen himself were copied by International Silver in the USA. Finn Juhl executed glassware designs for the firm. After Jensen died, management of the firm passed to his son Jørgen Jensen.
► Work shown to acclaim in every major international exhibition of the applied arts in the first three decades of the 20th century, including 1900 Paris 'Exposition Universelle' (honorable mention with Petersen for ceramics); 1910 Brussels 'Exposition Universelle et Internationale' (gold medal); 1905 The Hague 'Exposition Internationale'; 1909 exhibition, Århus (Denmark); 1909 exhibition, Paris Musée des Arts Décoratifs; 1913 session of Salon d'Automne; 1915 San Francisco 'Panama-Pacific International Exposition' (first prize); 1925 Paris 'Exposition Internationale des Arts Décoratifs et Industriels Modernes' (grand prize); 1929 'Exposición Internacional de Barcelona' (grand prize). Work subject of 1966 exhibition, Goldsmiths' Hall, London; 1980 'Georg Jensen Silversmithy: 77 Artists, 75 Years' exhibition, Smithsonian Institution, Washington.
► Cat., *Georg Jensen Silversmithy: 77 Artists, 75 Years*, Washington: Smithsonian Institution Press, 1980. Cat., David Revere McFadden (ed.), *Scandinavian Modern Design 1880–1980*, New York: Abrams, 1982:265–66. Melissa Gabardi, *Les Bijoux des Années 50*, Paris: Amateur, 1987.

Jensen, Helge Vestergård   (1917–)
► Danish furniture designer.
► Studied furniture design, Kunsthåndvaerkerskolen, to 1942, and Det Kongelige Danske Kunstakademi, both Copenhagen.
► In 1937, Jesen served as an apprentice; in 1942, worked with architect Kaare Klint; 1944–46, with architect Mølgård Nielsen; 1946–48, with architect Palle Suenson; from 1950, with architect Vilhelm Lauritzen; in 1950, set up his own design practice; designed furniture produced by Søren Horn.
► 1954–58 and 1960–63, received Danish furniture prizes.
► Frederik Sieck, *Nutidig Dansk Møbeldesign:—en kortfattet illustreret beskrivelse*, Copenhagen: Bondo Gravesen, 1981:70.

Jensen, Henning   (1924–)
► Danish architect and furniture designer.
► Studied architecture, Det Kongelige Danske Kunstakademi, Copenhagen, to 1948.
► 1948–58, he worked for Palle Suenson; 1958–61, was chief architect, Federation of Retail Grocers; 1951–64, taught in the architecture school, Det Kongelige Danske Kunstakademi; designed furniture produced by Munch Møbler, Christensen og Larsen, and others.
► Work shown at 1962 and 1965 Cabinetmakers' Guild exhibitions (with Hanne and Torben Valeur); 1965 Danish Society of Arts and Crafts (with the Valeurs), Charlottenborg; 1960, 1963, 1972, and 1976 Spring Exhibition (with Torben Valeur), 1962 'Young Nordic Designers,' Röhsska Konstslöjdmusseet, Gothenburg; 1962 'Moderne Dänische Wohnkultur,' Vienna.
► Frederik Sieck, *Nutidig Dansk Møbeldesign:—en kortfattet illustreret beskrivelse*, Copenhagen: Bondo Gravesen, 1981; 1990 Busck edition in English.

Jensen, Jakob   (1926–)
► Danish industrial designer.
► Studied industrial design, Kunsthåndvaerkerskolen, Copenhagen, to 1952.
► 1952–59, he was chief designer at Kunsthåndvaerkerskolen under Sigvard Bernadotte; in 1961, formed a Copenhagen design consultancy with Richard Latham and others; from the late 1960s, was a designer of audio equipment for Bang & Olufsen, creating its distinctive, successful image of highly refined products, including 1960 *Beolit 600* radio with ergonomic controls, 1976 *Beogram 4000* record player with tangential-tracking pick-up arm, *Beosystem 5500* four-unit music system with remote control, and *Beocenter 9000* music system with touch-sensitive illuminated controls.
► Work subject of 1990 Bang & Olufsen exhibition, Paris Musée des Arts Décoratifs.
► Svend Erik Moller, 'A Non-Specializing Specialist,' *Danish Journal*, Vol. 76, 1973:30–32. Jens Bernsen, *Design: The Problem Comes First*, Copenhagen, 1982:90–95. Cat., Kathryn B. Hiesinger and George H. Marcus III (eds.), *Design Since 1945*, Philadelphia: Philadelphia Museum of Art, 1983. Cat., Chantal Bizot, *Bang & Olufsen, Design et Technologie*, Paris: Musée des Arts Décoratifs, 1990.
► See **Bang and Olufsen**

Jensen, Jens Jacob Herring Krog   (1895–1978)
► Danish ceramicist; active Cincinnati, Ohio.
► Studied Ryslinge and Askov Academy, Jutland.
► In 1927, he moved to the USA, working for Rookwood Pottery, Cincinnati; decorated pottery, sometimes inspired by contemporary painters in Europe; introduced glazes that produced floating images and curdled color areas.
► Work (with wares by William Hentschel and Wilhelmine Rehm) shown at Rookwood stand, 1931 (XII) 'Exhibition of Contemporary American Industrial Art', New York Metropolitan Museum of Art.
► Karen Davies, *At Home in Manhattan: Modern Decorative Arts, 1925 to the Depression*, New Haven: Yale, 1983:56.

Jensen, Jørgen   (1895–1966)
► Danish designer; son of Georg Jensen.
► In 1914, studied silversmithing in Munich under Leonhard Ebert.
► 1923–36, he ran a silversmithing workshop in Stockholm; designed silver flatware and jewelry while, 1936–62, working for the design department of Georg Jensen Sølvsmedie where he contributed mainly larger silverworks, including bowls, jugs, and tea sets.
► Michael Farr, *Design in British Industry: A Mid-Century Survey*, London: Cambridge, 1955:41.

Jensen, Søren Georg (1917–)
▶ Danish designer; son of Georg Jensen.
▶ From 1936, apprenticed in the family silversmithy; in 1945, studied silversmithing and sculpture, Kongelige Danske Kunstakademi, Copenhagen.
▶ 1962–74, he was head of the design department, Georg Jensen Sølvsmedie; in 1974, turned to sculpture.
▶ Work shown at 'Georg Jensen Silversmithy: 77 Artists, 75 Years,' Washington. Received a gold medal at 1960 (XII) Triennale di Milano; 1974 Thorvaldsen Medal.
▶ Graham Hughes, *Modern Silver throughout the World*, New York, 1967: No. 19. Cat., *Georg Jensen Silversmithy: 77 Artists, 75 Years*, Washington: Smithsonian Institution, 1980. Cat., Kathryn B. Hiesinger and George H. Marcus III (eds.), *Design Since 1945*, Philadelphia: Philadelphia Museum of Art, 1983.

Jess, Marga
▶ German silversmith; active Lüneburg.
▶ Studied Lehr- und Versuchs-Ateliers für angewandte und freie Kunst (Debschitz-Schule) Munich, under Karl Johann Bauer.
▶ Active from 1912, she was the first fully qualified woman silversmith in Germany. Compared to Emmy Roth's work in Berlin, Jess's silver designs showed a tentative Modernism; her designs included raised ornamentation and spirals.
▶ Annelies Krekel-Aalberse, *Art Nouveau and Art Déco Silver*, New York: Abrams, 1989:130,145,256.

Jirasek, Julius (1896–1966)
▶ Architect and designer; active Vienna.
▶ Studied architecture, Kunstgewerbeschule, Vienna, under Oskar Strnad.
▶ While a prisoner-of-war in Russia, he became interested in the ethnographic art of the Urals; when he returned in 1923, re-enrolled in the Kunstgewerbeschule, Vienna; became an independent architect in Vienna, where he designed residential and shop interiors; by 1930, worked at Werkstätten Hagenauer, which produced his designs for silver jewelry, ceramics, lighting, glassware, and furniture, and where he was a major contributor to the firm's success.
▶ Work shown at 1971 'Werkstätten Hagenauer 1898–1971 und Hochschule für angewandte Kunst, Meisterklasse für freies Gestalten in Metall' exhibition, Österreichisches Museum für angewandte Kunst, Vienna. Received 1951 prize for applied arts, Vienna.
▶ Cat., *Werkstätten Hagenauer, 1898–1971*, Vienna: Österreichisches Museum für angewandte Kunst, 1971.

Jiřičná, Eva (1938–)
▶ Czech interior designer; born Prague; active London.
▶ Studied Czech University of Technology, Prague, to 1963, and Academy of Fine Arts, Prague.
▶ She settled in London in 1968, working for a year as an architect with the Greater London Council schools division; for eight years, was an associate at Louis de Soissons Partnership, working principally on the Brighton Marina development; in 1979, (with David Hodges) set up an independent interior design practice; from 1980, designed interiors for fashion retailer Joseph Ettedgui, including Le Caprice restaurant, London, of c1982. 1981–82 in London, she designed her own residence, the Kenzo shop, and Joseph Tricot on Sloane Street and, 1985–87, a second residence for Ettedgui, L'Express café, Pour La Maison, and Joseph Tricot in Paris. In 1985, she formed Jiricna Kerr Associates and designed Joseph Bis on Draycott Avenue, Joe's Café, Joseph Pour la Ville, Legends nightclub and restaurant, The Sanctuary, Vidal Sassoon hair salon in Frankfurt, Thompson Twins apartment refurbishment, and a recording studio. In 1987, her design firm became Eva Jiricna Architects. She designed a folding table and chair manufactured by TAG Design Partnership for Formica. Jiřičná's studio collaborated with Richard Rogers on the interiors of the Lloyds building and with Czech-designer Jan Kaplicky on Harrods depart-

ment store's 'Way In' department. In 1988, she designed the entrance to the Vitra building in Weil am Rhein (Germany).
▶ Work (folding table and chair by TAG for Formica) shown at New British and French Colorcore Exhibition. 1980–82, received AD awards for her own residence, Joseph Ettedgui's first residence, the Kenzo Shop, and numerous others.
▶ Robert A.M. Stern (ed.), *The International Design Yearbook*, New York: Abbeville, 1985/1986: No. 181. Liz McQuiston, *Women in Design: A Contemporary View*, New York: Rizzoli, 1988:62.

Joachim, Christian (1870–1943)
▶ Danish ceramicist.
▶ 1889–92 and 1895, studied Det Kongelige Danske Kunstakademi, Copenhagen.
▶ From 1897–1900, Joachim made ceramics (with Georg Jensen) in a workshop outside Copenhagen; from 1901–33, worked for Royal Copenhagen Porcelain Manufactory, where his restrained neoclassical forms were sometimes decorated by Arno Malinowski; in 1904, became director of the pottery Aluminia, Copenhagen; from 1922–33, was artistic director of Royal Copenhagen Porcelain and Aluminia.
▶ Received a grand prize at the 1925 Paris 'Exposition Internationale des Arts Décoratifs et Industriels Modernes.' In 1939, elected Honorary Royal Designer for Industry, London.
▶ Cat., David Revere McFadden (ed.), *Scandinavian Modern Design 1880–1980*, New York: Abrams, 1982:266, No. 76. Jennifer Hawkins Opie, *Scandinavia: Ceramics and Glass in the Twentieth Century*, New York: Rizzoli, 1989.

Jobling, James A.
▶ British glassware manufacturer; located Sunderland.
▶ In 1921, James A. Jobling, a division of the Wear Flint Glass Works, purchased from Corning Glasswork the rights to manufacture Pyrex; originally produced Pyrex in forms developed by Corning, but soon designed new items to satisfy British taste; by the mid-1920s, manufactured oven-to-table glass which, according to its advertisements, added 'charm to your table with its glistening transparency amid your silver and glass ... Your dishes will keep hotter than they did in those unsightly obsolete metal and earthenware dishes.' In 1934, Harold Stabler redesigned Jobling's 1931 *Streamline* range. Jobling's Wearside factory produced Stabler's 1939 range of oven-to-table ware with spray-on colors in green, yellow, and blue, later withdrawn due to wartime shortages.
▶ Work shown at 1929 'Industrial Art for the Slender Purse' sponsored by British Institute for Industrial Art, Victoria and Albert Museum, London.
▶ Frederick Cooke, *Glass: Twentieth-Century Design*, New York: Dutton, 1986:60–62.

Jobs, Gocken (1914–)
▶ Swedish textile designer and ceramicist.
▶ Jobs worked in her family's studio, a business active from the 1940s in Leksand, where she handprinted fabrics and produced ceramics; worked alongside her sister Lisbet Jobs-Söderlung (1909–61) in the Leksand workshop. The firm was known for its meticulous work.
▶ Cat., David Revere McFadden (ed.), *Scandinavian Modern Design 1880–1980*, New York: Abrams, 1982:266, Nos. 145–46.

Joel, Betty (1896–)
▶ British furniture, textile, and interior designer.
▶ In c1919, she and husband David Joel established the firm Betty Joel with a showroom at 177 Sloane Street, London, and workshops at Hayling Island. In c1935, she opened a new workshop designed by H.S. Goodhart-Rendel in Kingston-upon-Thames. In 1937, Goodhart-Rendel redesigned the façade of her showroom. She was best known for her luxurious furniture designs in satin and frills (belated versions of 1920s Parisian models) and geometric-motif carpets. Her carpets, finer and denser than others of the time, were hand-knotted in Tientsin (China)

on a cotton warp and clipped into grooves around the edges of motifs. In the late 1930s, she designed case-goods furniture produced by G. Ashley and W.R. Irwin at the Token Works, Portsmouth.
► Work (bedroom) shown at 1935 'British Art in Industry,' Royal Academy, London.
► Cat., *Thirties: British art and design before the war*, London: Arts Council of Great Britain, Hayward Gallery, 1979:75,86, 87,88,147,148,293.

Johansfors Glasbruk
► Swedish glass factory.
► The factory was founded in 1891 in Broakulla, Småland; until *c*1900, specialized in painting on glass produced elsewhere; began to produce utility and table glass; hired Bengt Orup, who was artistic director 1951–73; in 1972, was bought by Kosta Boda.
► Jennifer Hawkins Opie, *Scandinavia: Ceramics and Glass in the Twentieth Century*, New York: Rizzoli, 1989.

Johanssdottir, Sigridur   (1948-)
► Icelandic textile designer.
► Johanssdottir was an independent textile designer in her own studio in Reykjavik, often producing weavings from the designs of husband Leifur Breidfjord.
► Cat., David Revere McFadden (ed.), *Scandinavian Modern Design 1880–1980*, New York: Abrams, 1982:266, No. 334.

Johansson, Willy   (1921–)
► Norwegian glassware designer.
► 1939–42, studied Statens Håndvaerks -og Kunstindustriskole, Oslo.
► His father was at the Hadelands Glassverk, Jevnaker, where Johansson joined the glassmaking workshop in 1936. He was best known for the white rim on his clear or smoked glasswares. The Johanssons contributed greatly to the expansion of the range and improvement of the quality of Hadelands's tablewares. He designed mass-production as well as one-off wares. From 1942–45, he worked in the sandblowing section at Hadelands under sculptor Staale Kyllingstad; from 1945–47, in the engraving workshop of Christiania Glasmagasin and at the night school of Statens Håndvaerks -og Kunstindustriskole; from 1947, was head of the design team, production, and art wares at Hadelands.
► Received the diploma of honor at 1954 (X), gold medal at 1957 (XI), and silver medal at 1960 (XII) Triennale di Milano.
► Cat., Kathryn B. Hiesinger and George H. Marcus III (eds.), *Design Since 1945*, Philadelphia: Philadelphia Museum of Art, 1983. 'Revolution in Scandinavian Design: Willy Johansson,' *Crafts Horizons*, Vol. 18, March 1958:32. Eileene Harrison Beer, *Scandinavian Design: Objects of a Life*, New York, 1975:116–18,120. Cat., David Revere McFadden (ed.), *Scandinavian Modern Design 1880–1980*, New York: Abrams, 1982:266, No. 175. Frederick Cooke, *Glass: Twentieth-Century Design*, New York: Dutton, 1986:86. Jennifer Hawkins Opie, *Scandinavia: Ceramics and Glass in the Twentieth Century*, New York: Rizzoli, 1989.

Johansson-Pape, Lisa   (1907–)
► Finnish exhibition architect and interior, textile, and lighting designer.
► 1927, studied Taideteollinen Korkeakoulu, Helsinki.
► 1928–30, she designed furniture for Kylmäkoski; 1928–37, was a textile designer for Friends of Finnish Handicraft and, from 1952, its artistic director; 1937–49, was a furniture, textile, and interior designer for Stockmann, Helsinki. From 1949, designed Rational and practical models for Stockmann-Orno lamp company. Work included ceramics, glass, and textiles.
► Received first and second prizes and diploma of honor at 1937 Paris 'Exposition Internationale des Arts et Techniques dans la Vie Moderne' and 1951 (IX) (silver medal), 1954 (X) (gold medal), and 1960 (XII) (silver medal) Triennali di Milano.
► Erik Zahle (ed.), *A Treasury of Scandinavian Design*, New York, 1962:278, Nos. 99,101. Marja Kaipainen, 'Lisa Johansson-Pape—Lauri Anttila,' *Form Function Finland*, No. 3, 1982:6–11. Cat.,

David Revere McFadden (ed.), *Scandinavian Modern Design 1880–1980*, New York: Abrams, 1982:266, No. 129. Cat., Kathryn B. Hiesinger and George H. Marcus III (eds.), *Design Since 1945*, Philadelphia: Philadelphia Museum of Art, 1983.

Johnová, Helena   (1884–1962)
► Czech sculptor and ceramicist; born Soběslav.
► Studied School of Applied Arts, Prague; 1909–11, Kunstgewerbeschule, Vienna, under Michael Powolny.
► In Vienna, she founded a ceramics firm that closed in 1920, and created a number of figurines and vessels in small series; 1919–42, was professor, School of Applied Arts, Prague; for the competition of SČSD (Czech Werkbund), designed a ceramic tea-coffee set that showed Modern influence; in the 1930s, created a number of monumental objects on floral themes.
► A. Adlerová, *České užité umění 1918–1938*, Prague, 1983.

Johnson, Philip   (1906–)
► American architect; born Cleveland, Ohio; active New York.
► 1923–30, studied philosophy, Harvard University; 1940–43, architecture, Harvard University, under Walter Gropius and Marcel Breuer.
► While at Harvard, Johnson worked in his own architecture office in Cambridge, Massachusetts. He was curator and wrote the book for the 1936 exhibition 'Mies van der Rohe' at the New York Museum of Modern Art, and arranged Mies's first trip to New York. From 1954, he worked as an architect in New York; 1964–67, collaborated with partner Richard Foster and, from 1967, with partner John Burgee; (with Phyllis Lambert) was effective in promoting the International Style through gifts and loans to museums, particularly the New York Museum of Modern Art; later rebelling against the International Style in architecture, (with Burgee) designed the pedimented AT&T building, New York, conceived in the 1970s and completed in 1984. Architecture in the USA included 1949 house, New Canaan, Connecticut; 1949–50 Mrs. John D. Rockefeller townhouse, 252 East 52nd Street, New York; 1951 Hodgson house (with Landes Gores), New Canaan; 1951 Oneto house (with Landes Gores), Irvington, New York; 1953 garden and subsequent addition to the building of New York Museum of Modern Art; 1954–56 Tifereth Israel Synagogue, Port Chester, New York; 1960 Roofless Church, New Harmony, Indiana; 1963 Sheldon Memorial Art Gallery, University of Nebraska, Lincoln; 1960–64 New York State Theater, Lincoln Center, New York; 1954–58 Seagram Building (assisting Mies van der Rohe), New York; 1962–64 Kline Geology Laboratory Tower, Yale University, New Haven, Connecticut; 1972 Art Museum of South Texas, Corpus Christi, Texas; 1973 Investors Diversified Services Center, Minneapolis, Minnesota; 1970–76 Pennzoil Place buildings, Houston, Texas; 1980 Crystal Cathedral, Garden Grove, California; 1986 Pittsburgh Plate Glass building, Pittsburgh, Pennsylvania.
► He was curator of numerous exhibitions at New York Museum of Modern Art, including 1932 'Modern Architecture—International Exhibition'; 1934 'Machine Art'; 1936 'Mies van der Rohe'; 1988 'Deconstruction Architecture.'
► Henry-Russell Hitchcock and Philip Johnson, *The International Style: Architecture Since 1922*, New York: Museum of Modern Art, 1932. Philip Johnson, *Machine Art*, New York: Museum of Modern Art, 1934. Philip Johnson, *Mies van der Rohe*, New York: Museum of Modern Art, 1947. John Jacobus Jr., *Philip Johnson*, New York, 1962. Henry-Russell Hitchcock, *Philip Johnson: Architecture 1949–1965*, New York and London, 1966. Charles Noble, *Philip Johnson*, London: Thames and Hudson, 1972. Robert A.M. Stern (ed.), *Philip Johnson, Writings*, New York, Oxford: 1979. Nory Miller, *Johnson/Burgee: Architecture*, New York, 1979. Alice Goldfarb Marquis, *Alfred H. Barr Jr.: Missionary for the Modern*, Chicago: Contemporary Book, 1989. Cat., Philip Johnson and Mark Wigley, *Deconstructivist Architecture*, New York: Museum of Modern Art, 1988. David Whitney and Jeffrey Kipnir (eds), *Philip Johnson, The Glasshouse*, New York, Pantheon, 1993.

Johnson, Rob (1965–)
▶ American furniture, lighting, and vehicle designer; born Spokane, Washington.
▶ In 1979, he moved to New York; studied welding and other industrial techniques that he used in the production of matt-black wrought-iron and welded furniture. In the early 1990s, collaborating with Jerry Morrell on glass-topped tables, Johnson's designs included mismatched legs and pseudo-flawed tops. Collaborating with leather designer Toshiki, Johnson produced steel-rod chairs with leather seat covers incorporating foam-filled domes and pyramids. His furniture and lighting in distinctive 'calligraphic' profiles incorporated rubber and found industrial parts. His *Curl* chair was widely published.
▶ Stephen Perrine, 'Furniture at 50 Miles an Hour,' *Elle Decor*, November 1990:52.

Joindy, F.J. (1832–1906)
▶ French sculptor and silversmith; active Paris.
▶ Joindy worked for Christofle, Falize, and Harleux; designed silver mounts for Gallé's vases.
▶ Annelies Krekel-Aalberse, *Art Nouveau and Art Déco Silver*, New York: Abrams, 1989:256.

Joly, Antoine (1838–1917)
▶ French bookbinder and gilder; born Lamarche; active Paris.
▶ Joly settled in Paris, where he worked for Léon Gruel and, in 1874, for Thibaron; in 1885, took over Thibaron's firm. In 1892, his son Robert Joly (c1870–1924) became director of the business. Known for the same high quality of his gilding as his father, Robert produced classically oriented covers; 1914–18, produced bindings commissioned by Henri Vever and designed by Jules Chadel and Adolphe Giraldon.
▶ Ernest de Crauzat, *La Reliure française de 1900 à 1925*, Vol. 1, Paris, 1932:76. Roger Devauchelle, *La Reliure en France de ses origines à nos jours*, Vol. 3, Paris, 1961:62,127,141,144,264. Alastair Duncan and Georges de Bartha, *Art Nouveau and Art Déco Bookbinding*, New York: Abrams, 1989:15,191.

Jonchery, Charles-Émile
▶ French designer; active Paris.
▶ Studied under Aimé Miller and Antoine Gauthier.
▶ His work included portrait medallions, busts, garniture clocks, candelabra, and table-lamps in plaster, bronze, and marble.
▶ 1883–1922, he showed his sculpture at the Salons of the Société des Artistes français. In 1903, he showed his lamp *The Wave*.
▶ *Revue des Arts Décoratifs*, 1901:262. Salon catalog, Société des Artistes français, 1903. *Allgemeines Lexikon der Bildenden Künstler*, 1955. Auction catalog, Hôtel Drouot, 20 June 1975, Lot 92. Alastair Duncan, *Art Nouveau and Art Déco Lighting*, New York: Simon and Schuster, 1978:79.

Jones, A.E. (1879–1954)
▶ British silversmith; active Birmingham.
▶ Studied Birmingham Central School of Art.
▶ He worked in the Birmingham Guild of Handicraft; in 1902, set up a silver department at his father's firm; like other Arts and Crafts metalsmiths, he produced hammered surfaces that he combined with pierced or interlaced rims.
▶ Annelies Krekel-Aalberse, *Art Nouveau and Art Déco Silver*, New York: Abrams, 1989:28,256.

Jørgensen, Erik-Ole (1925–)
▶ Danish furniture designer.
▶ 1946–48, studied Det Kongelige Danske Kunstakademi, Copenhagen, under Kaare Klint; Kunsthåndvaerkerskolen, Copenhagen, to 1948.
▶ 1941–44, he was active in furniture design; was associated with furniture manufacturers L.F. Foght 1953–64, Dux and Sverige 1958–64, and Halling-Koch Designcenter 1971.
▶ Work shown at 1954 (X), 1957 (XI), and 1960 (XII) Triennali di Milano. Received 1977 Award of the Year, Earls Court Fair, London.

▶ Frederik Sieck, *Nutidig Dansk Møbeldesign:—en kortfattet illustreret beskrivelse*, Copenhagen: Bondo Gravesen: 1990 Busck edition in English.

Jorio, Piercarlo (1927–)
▶ Italian industrial designer; born and active Turin.
▶ He began his professional career in 1955; 1956–62, worked in the styling department of Fiat; designed heavy equipment and boats; had clients in Italy including Climat, Telmi, Poltrona Frau, Filma, SIC Ceramica, Fratelli Sandretto, Invet, Microtecnica, Cirse, Linea T, Fratelli Pagliero, Mazzucchelli, OPL, and Frigat; became a member of ADI (Associazione per il Disegno Industriale).
▶ *ADI Annual 1976*, Milan: Associazione per il Disegno Industriale, 1976.

Joseff of Hollywood
▶ American costume jeweler; located Burbank, California.
▶ Eugene Joseff moved to Hollywood in 1929 and became a designer of costume jewelry for the cinema, which he made and rented for films including *Suez* (1938), *Algiers* (1938), *Gone with the Wind* (1939), and *The Thief of Bagdad* (1940). His private clients included Virginia Bruce and Vivian Leigh. Extant today, the firm is directed by his widow Joan Castle Joseff.
▶ Deanna F. Cera (ed.), *Jewels of Fantasy: Costume Jewelry of the 20th Century*, New York: Abrams, 1992:216.

Joubert, René (1931–)
▶ French decorator and furniture designer.
▶ Joubert worked in the workshop of the decorating firm Jansen and subsequently for Diot et Bouché; from 1912, was active as a furniture designer; in 1914, (with Georges Mouveau) established the decorating firm DIM (Décoration Intérieure Moderne), Paris.
▶ *Encyclopédie des Métiers d'Art*, Vol. I, p. 34, Paris: Albert Morancé. Pierre Kjellberg, *Art Déco: les maîtres du Mobilier, le décor des Paquebots*, Paris: Amateur, 1986:97.
▶ See DIM

Jourdain, Francis (1876–1958)
▶ French painter, graphic artist, and designer; born and active Paris; son of Frantz Jourdain; father of Frantz-Philippe Jourdain.
▶ Studied drawing under Joseph Chéret, 1894; Atelier Gervex, under Eugène Carrière and Paul-Albert Besnard.
▶ He began his career as a painter in 1912, showing his canvases with Paul Cézanne, Henri Matisse, Henri de Toulouse-Lautrec, Vassilii Kandinskii, and Maurice Denis at the Salons des Indépendants. Encouraged by Adolph Loos's famous 1908 pamphlet *Ornament und Verbrechen* ('Ornament and Crime'), in 1912 Jourdain set up his own workshop, Ateliers Modernes, where he designed and made furniture for mass production in cheap materials as well as unique pieces; opposed to Paul Follot's voluptuous *style tapissier*, preferring balanced proportions and harmonious and simple colors. By the end of World War I, he had set up a factory separate from his showroom and retail shop, Chez Francis Jourdain, rue de Sèze, Paris; designed furniture, fabrics, wallpaper, and ceramics and decorated apartments, offices, airplanes, and railway cars; designed the tea room, restaurant, wooden garden chairs, and smoking car for the Compagnie Paris-Orléans railway company. Jourdain designed some furniture for and decorated some of the rooms of the 1923–33 villa of the vicomte and vicomtesse de Noailles in Hyères (architect Robert Mallet-Stevens, with whom Jourdain had worked from 1922); interior of 1928 Mallet-Stevens Bally shoe showroom, boulevard des Capucines, Paris, including its metal furniture, showcases, and display units; interiors and innovative lighting (including a distinguished four-armed ceiling fixture) for Mallet-Stevens's own 1927–28 house, 12 rue Mallet-Stevens, Auteuil; fresco of Les Grand Magasins de la Samaritaine (with father Frantz Jourdain, architect), Paris. Jourdain published *Intérieurs* (1929), which illustrated his work and that of Mallet-Stevens, Le Corbusier, Pierre Chareau, and Gerrit Rietveld. He became a friend of Jean Renoir, Jules Vallès, Octave Mirbeau, and Émile Zola; was an active journalist; associated with Elie Faure, Fernand Léger, Léon-Paul Fargue, Léon Moussinac, and Aragon.

For Jean Vigo, he designed the barge in the film *L'Atalante*; published articles, books, and monographs, militantly supporting Rationalism; in 1929, became a founding member of UAM (Union des Artistes Modernes); in 1938, (with Chareau, Louis Sognot, and Jacques Adnet) designed the reception area and administration offices of Collège de France; was known for incorporating clocks into walls where only numerals and hands showed. He was one of the true originals of the 1920s and 1930s. He spent much of World War II in hiding or with the Resistance; after the war, wrote monographs on Pierre Bonnard, Henri de Toulouse-Lautrec, Albert Marquet, and Félix Valloton; was a novelist and published *Sans remords ni rancune* (1953) and the memoir *De mon temps* (1963); in 1946, was president of the committee of honor of the Mallet-Stevens Club; in 1948, honorary president of UAM; and, in 1949, principal director of 'Formes Utiles' exhibitions.

▶ Before 1912, work (paintings) first shown at Salon of Société Nationale des Beaux-Arts. Until 1938, work shown at Salon d'Automne (founded by his father Frantz Jourdain), beginning with the dining room and bedroom at its 1913 event. Received grand prize at 1911 Turin 'Esposizione Internazionale dell'Industria e del Lavoro.' Designed the smoking room and gymnasium of 'Une Ambassade française' and the Compagnie Paris-Orléans railway smoking car at 1925 Paris 'Exposition Internationale des Arts Décoratifs et Industriels Modernes.' From 1930, work shown at UAM exhibitions. Designed a modest ensemble composed of interchangeable and variously arranged furniture called *Essai de désencombrement pour jeune travailleuse intellectuelle et manuelle* at 1937 Paris 'Exposition Internationale des Arts et Techniques dans la Vie Moderne' and, in the Pavilion of Light there, his illuminated tables appeared, designed with lighting engineer André Salomon. Work subject of 1976 'Francis Jourdain (1876–1958)' exhibition, Musée d'Art et d'Histoire, Saint-Denis.

▶ Francis Jourdain, 'Les Besoins Individuels et l'Art Décoratif,' *Art et Décoration*, Vol. LXV, 1936. G. Henriot, *Luminaire Moderne*, 1937: plate 19. Léon Moussinac, *Francis Jourdain*, Paris: Pierre Cailler, 1955. Cat., *Francis Jourdain (1876–1958)*, Saint-Denis: Musée d'Art et d'Histoire, 1976. Alastair Duncan, *Art Nouveau and Art Déco Lighting*, New York: Simon and Schuster, 1978: 153,174. Pierre Cabanne, *Encyclopédie Art Déco*, Paris: Somogy, 1986:202–04. Arlette Barré-Despond, *UAM*, Paris: Regard, 1986:428–33. Cat., *Les années UAM 1929–1958*, Paris: Musée des Arts Décoratifs, 1988:200–02. Arlette Barré-Despond and Suzanne Tise, *Jourdain*, Paris: Regard, 1988.

Jourdain, Frantz-Calixte-Raphaël-Ferdinand-Marie (1847–1935)

▶ French architect, writer, and critic; born Antwerp; active Paris; father of Francis Jourdain.

▶ Studied École des Beaux-Arts, Paris, from 1867.

▶ He created the Salon d'Automne in 1903 in response to the spring Salons of groups such as Société Nationale des Beaux-Arts and Société des Artistes français, which he considered too academic. The work of architects, decorative artists, furniture and jewelry designers, and binders was shown, in an attempt to end the schism between the fine and applied arts. He encouraged his friend Émile Zola to write the editorial 'J'accuse' in defence of Captain Dreyfus; in 1898, became a founding member of the Ligue des Droits de l'Homme (Human Rights Association); was a prolific journalist, novelist, and playwright. His major work and masterpiece was the 1905–07 Samaritaine department store, Paris, one of the best examples of steel, glass, and concrete architecture in Paris. Its Art Nouveau design was influenced by Victor Horta's 1901 L'Innovation store, Brussels, and Louis Sullivan's 1899–1906 Carson Pirie Scott store, Chicago. His other architecture included 1892 villa, Saint-Leu and, in Paris, 1894 Edouard Schenck house (one of first Paris houses in concrete), 9 rue Vergniaud, Paris; perfumery pavilion, 1900 Paris 'Exposition Universelle'; 1907 Magasin 2, Samaritaine; 1926 Pont-Neuf extension (with Henri Sauvage), Samaritaine; 1912 building, 16 rue du Louvre; 1914 Samaritaine de Luxe.

▶ In 1894, appointed Chevalier of the Légion d'honneur.

▶ Victor Arwas, *Art Déco*, Abrams, 1980. Pierre Cabanne, *Encyclopédie Art Déco*, Paris: Somogy, 1986:202–04. Meredith L. Clausen, *Frantz Jourdain and the Samaritaine: Art Nouveau Theory and Criticism*, Leiden: Brill, 1987. Arlette Barré-Despond, *Jourdain*, Paris: Regard, 1988. Arlette Barré-Despond and Suzanne Tise, *Jourdain*, New York: Rizzoli, 1990.

Jourdain, Frantz-Philippe (1906–)

▶ French architect; son of Francis Jourdain active Paris.

▶ Studied École Spéciale d'Architecture, Paris.

▶ His first important commission was 1928 villa, Grandchamps; in 1934, became a member of UAM (Union des Artistes Modernes); designed several low-cost Modern buildings with André-L. Louis, including two 1934–36 villas, Grandchamps.

▶ Work (milliner's atelier) shown at 1931 UAM exhibition and (project for the design of an oceanliner cabin [with Louis] at 1934 session of Salon d'Automne in the competition organized by the OTUA (Office Technique pour l'Utilisation de l'Acier); (with Louis) at 'III Exposition de l'Habitation' sponsored by journal *Architecture aujourd'hui* and Groupe des Cinq; (furniture, ensembles, and models) at 1935 'Salon de la Lumière,' Paris. Collaborated with Georges-Henri Pingusson on the design of UAM pavilion at 1937 Paris 'Exposition Internationale des Arts et Techniques dans la Vie Moderne,' where he showed furniture designs.

▶ Jean Porcher, 'Une Villa par Frantz Philippe Jourdain,' *Art et Décoration*, Vol. LIX, Dec. 1930. Cat., *Les années UAM 1929–1958*, Paris: Musée des Arts Décoratifs, 1988:203. Arlette Barré-Despond, *Jourdain*, Paris: Regard, 1988. Arlette Barré-Despond and Suzanne Tise, *Jourdain*, New York: Rizzoli, 1990.

Jourdan, Eric (1966–)

▶ French furniture designer; born and active Paris.

▶ Studied École des Beaux Arts, Saint-Étienne, under François Bauchet; École des Arts Décoratifs, Paris; and with Luigi Colani.

▶ His 1988 *Chaise Ker* was produced by Néotù.

▶ Work included in 1987 exhibition of young designers, Galerie Néotù, Paris; 1987 'Exposition Desco' at Zeus, Milan; 1987 exhibition, VIA; Zeus stand, 1988 Salone del Mobile, Milan; VIA stand, 1988 Paris Salon du Meuble; 1980 'Nos Années 80,' Fondation Cartier, Jouy en Josas.

▶ *Casa Vogue*, December 1987. Christine Colin, *Design Français*, Paris: Flammarion. Cat., *Desco*, Milan: Zeus, 1987.

Jouve, Georges (1910–64)

▶ French ceramicist; active Paris.

▶ Studied École Boulle, Académie de la Grande Chaumière, and Académie Julian, all Paris.

▶ He became known for his exuberant ceramic work, particularly in the 1950s.

Jouve, Paul (1880–1973)

▶ French painter, sculptor, illustrator, ceramicist, engraver, and designer; born Marlotte.

▶ Studied École des Beaux-Arts, Paris.

▶ He was fascinated by wildlife, and conceived of illustrating *The Jungle Book* by Rudyard Kipling. The project begun in 1909 took more than ten years; 15 of his 90 woodcuts were cut by F.L. Schmied. Jouve illustrated *Un pèlerin d'Ankor* by Pierre Loti and *Poèmes barbares* by Leconte de l'Isle. He traveled in Cambodia, where he developed a new style; participated in the decoration of oceanliners including 1935 *Normandie*.

▶ In 1895 at the age of 15, he showed work (painting of Ethiopian lions) at Salon of Société Nationale des Beaux-Arts; with Schmied, Dunand, and Goulden, at Galerie Georges Petit, Paris, for ten years from 1921. Designed the great ceramic frieze of animals for the gate by René Binet at 1900 Paris Exposition Universelle. Work (panels) at 1931 'Exposition Coloniale'; (panels) at 1937 Paris 'Exposition Internationale des Arts et Techniques dans la Vie Moderne.'

▶ Cat., *Decorative Arts 1925 Style*, New York: Didier Aaron, 1979. Victor Arwas, *Art Déco*, Abrams, 1980. Cat., Aaron Lederfajn and Xavier Lenormand, *Le Louvre des Antiquaires présente: 1930 quand le meuble devient sculpture*, Paris, 1986. Pierre Cabanne, *Encyclopédie Art Déco*, Paris: Somogy, 1986:204–05.

Jozancy, Luc
See Rhinn, Eric

Jucker, Carl J.   (1902–)
▶ Swiss metalworker; born Zürich.
▶ 1918–1922, studied Kunstgewerbeschule, Zürich; 1922–23, under Muche; Bauhaus, Weimar, under Christian Dell, Paul Klee, and László Moholy-Nagy.
▶ Many of his lamp models were made for the interior of 1923 Haus am Horn, the most well known of which was the *Glaslampe*. This model was perfected by Jucker for serial production at the Bauhaus by Wilhelm Wagenfeld. Jucker worked with Marcel Breuer on the development of tubular steel furniture. In 1923, he returned to Switzerland and became designer at the silverware factory Jetzler, Schaffhausen; taught in Zürich and Schaffhausen and was a member of the design team for the yacht *Lacustre*.
▶ Friederike Mehlau-Wiebking et al., *Schweizer Typenmöbel 1925–35, Sigfried Giedion und die Wohnbedarf AG*, Zürich: gta, 1989:229. Cat., *Die Metallwerkstatt am Bauhaus*, Berlin: Bauhaus-Archiv, 1992:216–19,317.

Jugendstil
See Art Nouveau

Juhl, Finn   (1912–)
▶ Danish industrial designer and decorator.
▶ Studied architecture, Kongelige Danske Kunstakademi, Copenhagen, under Kaare Klint.
▶ In 1937, Juhl began a longstanding collaboration with Niels Vodder, who at first made furniture by hand. Their work consistently won awards at the Danish Cabinetmakers' Guild over the next decade. Executing restrained designs in furniture, Juhl broke with the Functional style; in 1939, designed a soft-edged sofa for Niels Vodder which offered a new approach in Danish design while reflecting the forms of Jean Arp; received many awards for the 1942 house he built for himself. It was to a large extent due to Juhl that Danish design came to international attention in the late 1940s. He was influenced by primitive, especially African, sculptural forms; 1944–55, was director of School of Interior Design at Fredericksberg Technical School; had clients including Niels Vodder, Allerød, France and Søn, Baker (furniture), Georg Jensen (glassware), Kay Bojesen (turned teak bowls), General Electric (refrigerators), Bing & Grøndahl Porcelaensfabrik (dinnerware), and Unika-Vaev (carpets). The 1945 sculptural lounge chair and 1949 plain *Chieftain* chair are notable examples of Juhl's work. In 1951 for Bakers Brothers Furniture of Grand Rapids, Michigan, he designed an extensive furniture line which introduced his designs to America. Other lines were later produced by Bovirke in Europe. Juhl was known for his 'floating seat,' as seen in the Baker group, which rested on crossbars rather than on the chair frame. In 1951, Juhl designed the Trusteeship Council Chamber, United Nations headquarters, New York. His first major exhibition-design commision, coming from Edgar Kaufmann Jr., was the 1951 (second) 'Good Design' exhibition at Merchandise Mart, Chicago, and New York Museum of Modern Art. In 1952, he designed a room in Trondheim Kunstindustrimuseum. His sculptural use of wood and elaboration of structural forms were notable. Juhl designed the 1960 trophy of the Kaufmann International Design Award, first won by Charles and Ray Eames in 1960, and the 1966 'Export Oscar' trophy of National Association for Danish Enterprise.
▶ Work shown at 1950 and 1955 'Good Design' exhibitions, New York and Chicago; 1951 (IX) (diploma of honor), 1954 (X), and 1957 (XI) (gold medal) Triennali di Milano; (1945 easy chair) 1945 Copenhagen 'Cabinetmakers' Guild Exhibition'; 1954–57 'Design in Scandinavia' traveling exhibition, USA; 1956–59 'Neue

Form aus Dänemark' traveling exhibition, Germany; 1958 'Formes Scandinaves,' Paris Musée des Arts Décoratifs; 1960–61 'The Arts of Denmark' traveling exhibition, USA; 1966 'Vijftig Jaar Zitten,' Stedelijk Museum, Amsterdam; 1968 'Two Centuries of Danish Design,' Glasgow, London, and Manchester; 1968 'Les Assises du siège contemporain' exhibition, Paris Musée des Arts Décoratifs; 1970 'Modern Chairs 1918–1970' exhibition, Whitechapel Gallery, London. Work subject of 1970 Charlottenborg Autumn Exhibition; 1973 exhibition, Cantù (Italy); 1982 exhibition, Museum of Decorative Art, Copenhagen. Received 1944 C.F. Hansen prize, 1947 Eckersberg Medal, diploma from Gentofte Municipality for 1955 Villabyernes Bio cinema, Vangede; 1964 AID prize for design in Chicago. In 1978, elected Honorary Royal Designer for Industry, London; in 1984, Knight of the Order of the Dannebrog.
▶ Cat., *Les Assises du siège contemporain*, Paris: Musée des Arts Décoratifs, 1968. Frederik Sieck, *Nutidig Dansk Møbeldesign:— en kortfattet illustreret beskrivelse*, Copenhagen: Bondo Gravesen, 1981; 1990 Busck edition in English. Cat., David Revere McFadden (ed.), *Scandinavian Modern Design 1880–1980*, New York: Abrams, 1982:265, Nos. 152,158. Esbjørn Hiort, *Finn Juhl: Furniture, Architecture, Applied Art*, Copenhagen: The Danish Architectural Press, 1990.

Juhlen, Sven-Eric   (1940–)
▶ Swedish ceramicist and industrial designer.
▶ In the 1960s, Juhlen worked for the Gustavsberg factory; in 1970, became a designer at Ergonomi Design Group, Stockholm, designing products for children and the physically disadvantaged; collaborated with Maria Benktzon on industrial design projects at Ergonomi.
▶ Cat., David Revere McFadden (ed.), *Scandinavian Modern Design 1880–1980*, New York: Abrams, 1982:266, No. 345.

Jujol, Josep Maria   (1879–1949)
▶ Spanish architect; born Tarragona, Catalonia; active Barcelona.
▶ Studied Escola Superior d'Arquitectura, Barcelona, directed by Lluís Domènech i Montaner.
▶ He was a member of the younger generation of Catalan *modernista* architects; apprenticed with Antoni Gaudí, which has, perhaps unfairly, labeled him as being nothing more than a simple follower. He may have indeed been a Gaudí collaborator, as seen in his work on Gaudí's buildings; iron railings for 1906–10 Casa Milà, and mosaic decorations for Park Güell and Battló apartment building, all in Barcelona. His decorative work presaged the Surrealists and Expressionists, and his own architecture — churches, shops, a theater, and other public buildings — including the remodeling of 1914–31 Casa Bofarull, near Tarragona. Residences included 1913–16 Torre de la Creu, Sant Joan Despí; 1923–24 Casa Planells, Barcelona; and Casa Dels Ous (House of Eggs), because of its curvaceous lines).
▶ Ignasi de Solà-Morales, *Jujol*, Cologne: Taschen, 1990. Thomas S. Hines, 'Brilliant Career of the Little-Known Catalan Modernist,' *Architectural Digest*, Nov. 1993:74–86.

Julmat, The
▶ American metalsmiths.
▶ The Julmat, producing works in the Arts and Crafts style, was founded in 1910 by Julius O. Randahl and Matthias William Hanck in Park Ridge, Illinois. The designers followed the early style of their mentor, Clara Welles, creating hammered-surface pieces in austere forms.
▶ Sharon S. Darling with Gail Farr Casterline, *Chicago Metalsmiths*, Chicago Historical Society, 1977.

Jung, Dora   (1906–80)
▶ Finnish textile designer.
▶ Studied Taideteollinen Korkeakoulu, Helsinki.
▶ She was a designer of fabrics at Tampella linen works,

Tampere; in 1932, set up her own studio in Helsinki; became known for her high standards; was a prominent weaver in Finland for more than 50 years of both mass-production and unique pieces.

▶ Work shown independently and in group exhibitions including in Gothenburg, 1955, and Copenhagen, 1956. Received a gold medal at 1937 Paris 'Exposition Internationale des Arts et Techniques dans la Vie Moderne' and grand prizes at 1951 (IX), 1954 (X), and 1957 (XI) Triennali di Milano. In 1979, elected Honorary Royal Designer for Industry, London.

▶ Cat., David Revere McFadden (ed.), *Scandinavian Modern Design 1880–1980*, New York: Abrams, 1982:266, Nos. 213,214.

Jung, Gunilla (1905–39)
▶ Finnish designer.

▶ Studied Taideteollisuuskeskuskoulu, Helsinki; in 1936 Institut Supérieur des Arts Décoratifs, Brussels.

▶ She designed lamps, silver, textiles, and enamel; in 1932, set up her own studio in Helsinki; specialized in damask weaving, both mass produced by Tampella and individually commissioned from clients including National Bank of Finland, Finnish National Theatre, and Finlandia Hall, Helsinki. Her first silver designs were produced by Taito and, later in the 1930s, others by Viri and Kultaseppät. She worked with Frans Nykänen, who was director at both silversmithies at different times. The dinner service she designed for Finnish silversmiths Lennart Baugartner was her largest commission.

▶ Work (1957 *Linenplay* machine-woven damask) shown at 1983–84 'Design Since 1945' exhibition at the Philadelphia Museum of Art. Received a gold medal at 1937 Paris 'Exposition Internationale des Arts et Techniques dans la Vie Moderne'; grand prizes at 1951 (IX), 1954 (X), and 1957 (XI) Triennali di Milano.

▶ Benedict Zilliacus, *Finnish Designers*, Helsinki, 1954. Erik Zahle (ed.), *A Treasury of Scandinavian Design*, New York, 1961:279, Nos. 123–25,127,181–82,344,408. Eeva Siltvuori, 'I Never Tire of Watching a Gull's Glide,' *Form Function Finland*, No. 2, 1981:58–63. Enid Marx, *Journal of the Royal Society of Arts*, March 1981:264. Charles S. Talley, *Contemporary Textile Art: Scandinavia*, Stockholm, 1982:107–13. Cat., Kathryn B. Hiesinger and George H. Marcus III (eds.), *Design Since 1945*, Philadelphia: Philadelphia Museum of Art, 1983. Annelies Krekel-Aalberse, *Art Nouveau and Art Déco Silver*, New York: Abrams, 1989:241,257.

Junger, Hermann (1928–)
▶ German jewelry designer.

▶ Studied Staatliche Zeichenakademie, Hanau.

▶ He began his jewelry designs through noteworthy watercolor renderings. His work appeared influenced by the work of German painter Julius Bissier. He was professor of goldsmithing, Akademie der bildenden Künste, Munich.

▶ Peter Dormer (intro.), *The Illustrated Dictionary of 20th-Century Designers: The Key Personalities in Design and the Applied Arts*, New York: Mallard, 1991.

Junkers, Hugo (1859–1935)
▶ German airplane designer and manufacturer.

▶ He founded Junkers Fabrik in 1895 for the production of water heaters and other apparatus; in 1907, patented a twin piston engine adapted in 1910 for aircraft; in 1919, he founded Junkers Flugzeugwerk, Dessau, and, in 1924, Junkers-Motorenbau; designed and produced the first all-metal airplane; in 1929, designed the first purpose-built airplane passenger cabin.

Jutrem, Arne Jon (1929–)
▶ Norwegian glassware and textile designer and metalworker.

▶ 1946–50, studied lithography, Statens Håndvaerks -og Kunstindustriskole, Oslo; in 1952, painting, Académie Léger, Paris, under Fernand Léger.

▶ From the 1940s, Jutrem designed graphics, furniture, textiles, carpets, ceramics, metalwork, and, principally, glassware, particularly, 1950–62, for Hadelands Glassverk, Jevnaker. His liquid forms were full of movement, with undulating surfaces. Some pieces incorporated bursts of bubbles; others were more sculptural with grotesque additions. In the 1960s, he designed heavy kitchen appliances; 1962–64, was consultant designer, Holmegård Glasvaerk, Copenhagen, where he designed a range of decorative and utilitarian glassware, including vases, bowls, plates, pitchers, and stemware with engraved decoration, strong colors, and matt finishes. In 1963, he became a founding member of the new Landsforbundet Norske Brukskunst and, from 1965–66, its chair; from 1964–72, was board member, Norsk Designcentrum; from 1965–70, was chair and board member of Statens Håndvaerks -og Kunstindustrieskole; in 1967, worked at Plus Glasshytte; from 1967, executed public commissions in glass, enamel, and metal.

▶ Work shown at 1967 Montreal 'Universal and International Exhibition (Expo '67).' Work subject of 1979 exhibition, Kunstindustrimuseum, Oslo. Received 1959 Lunning Prize and a gold medal (glassware) at 1954 (X) Triennale di Milano.

▶ 'Thirty-four Lunning Prize-Winners,' *Mobilia*, No. 146, Sept. 1967. Cat., *Arne Jon Jutrem*, Oslo: Kunstindustrimuseum, 1979. Cat., David Revere McFadden (ed.), *Scandinavian Modern Design 1880–1980*, New York: Abrams, 1982:266, No. 174. Kathryn B. Hiesinger and George H. Marcus III (eds.), *Design Since 1945*, Philadelphia: Philadelphia Museum of Art, 1983. Frederick Cooke, *Glass: Twentieth-Century Design*, New York: Dutton, 1986:86. Cat., *The Lunning Prize*, Stockholm: Nationalmuseum, 1986:102–05. Fredrik Wildhagen, *Norge i Form*, Oslo: Stenersen, 1988:127. Jennifer Hawkins Opie, *Scandinavia: Ceramics and Glass in the Twentieth Century*, New York: Rizzoli, 1989.

Južnič, Bohuml (1895–1963)
▶ Slovakian designer; born Požege (today Slovenia).

▶ Južnič was self-taught.

▶ He was originally an army officer; from 1931, worked at Krásná jizba (The Beautiful Room) which, together with the SČSD (Czechoslovak Werkbund), was instrumental in spreading Functionalist design in pre-war Czechoslovakia; designed mainly metal tableware and, by the end of the 1930s, ceramics, glass, and wood.

K

Kadlec, Zdeněk
▶ Czech industrial designer.
▶ Kadlec was head of the department of plastics at the School of Design in Uherské Hradiště; began producing designs in plastics in collaboration with the Tesla factory, Liptovský Hrádek on the occasion of a 1962 telephone design competition sponsored by the Union of Plastic Artists, in which he received second place. His first design alone was a vacuum-molded bar unit for Frigera Beroun.
▶ Cat., Milena Lamarová, *Design a Plastické Hmoty*, Prague: Uměleckoprůkamyslové Muzeum, 1972:116.

Kähler Keramik
▶ Danish ceramics factory.
▶ The factory was established in 1839 by Christian Herman Kähler at Naestved, South Zealand; until 1888, it specialized in the production of earthenware stoves; in 1872, Kaehler's son Herman August Kähler took over as director and introduced redware to the line that he had shown with some success in the 1880s; produced architectural ceramics including those by sculptor K.F.C. Hansen-Reistrup; into the 1920s, continued to produce lusterware designed by Herman Kähler and his brother Nils A. Kähler. In 1913 and 1917–41, Jens Thirslund was chief designer and introduced painted lusters in 1919.
▶ Jennifer Hawkins Opie, *Scandinavia: Ceramics and Glass in the Twentieth Century*, New York: Rizzoli, 1989.

Kagan, Vladimir   (1927–)
▶ German furniture designer; born Worms am Rhein; active New York.
▶ Studied architecture, Columbia University, New York.
▶ He settled in the USA in 1938; in 1947, joined his father's woodworking shop; in the late 1940s, began designing furniture; designed 1947–48 Delegates' Cocktail Lounge in the first United Nations headquarters, Lake Success, New York; in 1950, opened a showroom, 57th Street, New York. His corporate clients included General Electric, Monsanto, Prudential Insurance, Pioneer Industries, Warner Communications, American Express, Kenyon and Eckhart advertising, Walt Disney Enterprises, and A&P. Furniture clients included Marilyn Monroe, Xavier Cougard, Lily Pons, and Sherman Fairchilds. He set up Vladimir Kagan Design Group and became active as an interior design consultant to the home furnishings and contract industry; closed his factory and showroom and continued to design for manufacturers Directional, Giorgio Collection, The Lane Company, Alpha Metallix, Preview Furniture, and David Lynch; had interior design clients including Du Pont family, Wilmington, Delaware; and Black Clawson headquarters, New York. In New York, he was president, American Society of Interior Designers; president, ASID New York Chapter; chair, Advisory Commission of the School of Art and Design; member, Architectural League and American Society of Furniture Designers; taught at Parsons School of Design; lectured widely on Modern architecture and furniture design.
▶ Work shown at 1958 'Good Design' exhibition, New York Museum of Modern Art and Chicago Merchandise Mart, and 1991

'Organic Design' exhibition, Design Museum, London. Work subject of 1980 'Three Decades of Design,' Fashion Institute of Technology, New York.

Kåge, Algot Wilhelm   (1889–1960)
▶ Swedish ceramicist.
▶ 1908–09, studied painting, Valand Art School, Gothenburg; under Carl Wilhelmsson, Stockholm; 1911–12, Artists' Studio School under Johan Rohde, Copenhagen; Plakatschule, Munich.
▶ He was known initially as a poster designer; joined the Swedish Ceramic Company in Gustavsberg; 1917–60, designed ceramics there and was artistic director until 1949; encouraged the use of Modern designs and introduced stacking designs, simple forms, and heat-resistant dinnerware. His 1917 *Liljebala* (*Blue Lily*) dinnerware exemplified the attempt to raise the standards of taste in everyday wares accessible to the working class. His designs included 1933 *Praktika*, *Marina*, and *Pyro*. His molded stoneware of the 1950s, named *Farsta* after the island on which Gustavsberg is located, was influenced by Mexican and Chinese forms.
▶ Received a grand prize at 1925 Paris 'Exposition Internationale des Arts Décoratifs et Industriels Modernes.' Work shown at 1959 (XX) 'Ceramic International Exhibition,' Metropolitan Museum of Art, New York; 1975 'Gustavsberg 150 ar' exhibition, Nationalmuseum, Stockholm. Work subject of exhibitions at Liljevalchs Art Gallery, Stockholm, 1917; Nationalmuseum, Stockholm, 1953.
▶ Nils Palmgren, *Wilhelm Kåge: Konstnär och Hantverkare*, Stockholm, 1953. Cat., *Wilhelm Kåge, Gustavsberg*, Stockholm: Nationalmuseum, 1953. Cat., *Gustavsberg 150 ar*, Stockholm: Nationalmuseum, 1975. Cat., David Revere McFadden (ed.), *Scandinavian Modern Design 1880–1980*, New York: Abrams, 1982: 266, Nos. 73,74,102–04,132,134,161. Cat., Kathryn B. Hiesinger and George H. Marcus III (eds.), *Design Since 1945*, Philadelphia: Philadelphia Museum of Art, 1983. Jennifer Hawkins Opie, *Scandinavia: Ceramics and Glass in the Twentieth Century*, New York: Rizzoli, 1989.

Kähler, Herman August   (1846–1917)
▶ Danish ceramicist.
▶ Trained under sculptor H.V. Biesen, and in ceramics factories in Berlin and Zürich.
▶ In 1872, he took charge of his father's pottery workshop in Naestved, where the designs of Thorvald Bindesbøll, Karl Hansen-Reistrup, and O. Eckmann were produced.
▶ He exhibited at 1889 Paris 'Exposition Universelle,' 1893 Chicago 'World's Columbian Exposition,' 1899 exhibition of the Munich Secession, and 1900 Paris 'Exposition Universelle.'
▶ Cat., David Revere McFadden (ed.), *Scandinavian Modern Design 1880–1980*, New York: Abrams, 1982:68,266, No. 39.
▶ See Kähler Keramik

Kahn, Ely Jacques   (1884–1972)
▶ American architect and designer; born New York.
▶ Studied architecture, Columbia University, New York, to 1903, and École des Beaux-Arts, Paris, to 1911.

▶ In 1915, he taught design at Cornell University; in 1917, joined architects Buchman & Fox, New York; visited 1925 Paris 'Exposition Internationale des Arts Décoratifs et Industriels Modernes' which resulted in his shift to Modernism; 1925–31, designed 30 buildings in New York and interiors, furniture, and furnishings, including for the Frederick Rose apartment on Park Avenue, 1929, for Mrs. Maurice Benjamin's apartment, and a number of shops; collaborated with English émigré colorist Leon Solon, and became known for his use of vivid colors in his architecture; published *Design in Art and Industry* (New York: Whittlesey, 1935).

▶ Designed 1928 'Exposition of Modern French Decorative Art,' Lord & Taylor department store, New York. Was in charge of Industrial Design Section, 1932–33 Chicago 'Century of Progress' exposition. Work (textiles) shown at 1935 'Contemporary American Industrial Art, 1934' at the New York Metropolitan Museum of Art. Directed (with Paul-Philippe Cret) young industrial designers' section, 'Contemporary American Industrial Art, 1934' and 'Contempoary American Industrial Art: 1940, Fifteenth Exhibition,' both New York Metropolitan Museum of Art.

▶ Arthur Tappan North, *Ely Jacques Kahn*, New York: Whittlesey House, 1931. Karen Davies, *At Home in Manhattan: Modern Decorative Arts, 1925 to the Present*, New Haven: Yale, 1983. Mary Beth Betts, 'Ely Jacques Kahn' in Mel Byars and Russell Flinchum (eds.), *50 American Designers, 1918–1968*, Washington: Preservation, 1994.

Kaipiainen, Birger   (1915–88)
▶ Finnish ceramicist.
▶ 1933–37, studied Taideteollinen Korkeakoulu, Helsinki.
▶ 1937–54, he was a designer at Arabia, Helsinki, where he decorated Olga Osol's 1953 *Tapetti* dinnerware, produced until 1964; 1948–50, worked for Richard Ginori, Florence and Milan; 1954–58, worked at Rörstrand, Lidköping; in 1958, returned to Arabia; used a painter's technique on ceramic forms.
▶ Received awards including those at 1951 (IX) (diploma of honor) and 1960 (XII) (grand prize) Triennali di Milano, 1960 Pro Finlandia, 1982 Prince Eugen Medal of Sweden. Work shown at 1954–57 USA 'Design in Scandinavia' traveling exhibition, 1961 'Finlandia' exhibition in Zürich, Amsterdam, and London. Work subject of exhibitions in Helsinki, Malmö, Gothenburg, Milan, and New York.
▶ Cat., David Revere McFadden (ed.), *Scandinavian Modern Design 1880–1980*, New York: Abrams, 1982:266, No. 240. Jennifer Hawkins Opie, *Scandinavia: Ceramics and Glass in the Twentieth Century*, New York: Rizzoli, 1989.

Kaiser, Robert
▶ American furniture designer; born Detroit; active Toronto.
▶ Studied Institute of Design, Chicago.
▶ He designed a wide range of residential and contract furniture for manufacturers in Ontario, including Primavera; taught at Ontario College of Art and Ryerson Polytechnical Institute.
▶ Cat., *Seduced and Abandoned: Modern Furniture designers in Canada, the First Fifty Years*, Toronto: The Art Gallery at Harbourfront, 1986:18.

Kalinsky, Stuart Alan   (1951–)
▶ American product designer; active New York.
▶ Kalinsky set up a toothbrush manufacturing business in 1982 and designed molded Lucite-handled toothbrushes with embedded lace, gingham, chintz, leopard pattern, sequins, confetti, glitter, paisley, stripes, and other materials, including objects floating in water. He produced toilet accessories and fulfilled commissions for toothbrushes from corporate clients; patented a process for sealing materials in thick acetate sheets, which were then turned on a lathe and buffed.
▶ Work (toothbrushes) shown at 1990 'The Plastics Age,' Victoria and Albert Museum, London.
▶ Deborah Hofmann, 'Stylemakers,' *The New York Times*, 23 December 1990: Sec.1:26.

Kalo Shops
See Welles, Clara Barck

Kamiyama, Shunichi   (1947–)
▶ Japanese glass designer.
▶ Studied Tokyo University of Arts to 1970.
▶ In 1970, Kamiyama became a designer at Hoya Crystal, Tokyo.
▶ Work shown at 1978, 1981, 1984, 1987, 1990 'Glass in Japan,' Tokyo; 1983 'Little Objects,' Japan Glass Art Crafts Association; and 1991 (V) Triennale of Japan Glass Art Crafts Association, Heller Gallery, New York.
▶ Cat., *Glass Japan*, New York: Heller Gallery and Japan Glass Art Crafts Association, 1991: No. 16.

Kan, Shiu-Kay   (1949–)
▶ British lighting designer; born Hong Kong; active London.
▶ Studied Central London Polytechnic and Architectural Association, London.
▶ He worked for Foster Associates and Fiorucci, both London; in the mid-1970s, established SKK Lighting, London. His first lighting model was the *Kite Light*. Interested in new technologies, he produced low-voltage lighting and motorized models. His 1988 *Motorized Robotic Light* moved across the ceiling on horizontal conductive cables by programmable remote control; it was installed in the London Design Museum. He expanded his business to include a consultancy for contract lighting, a production subsidiary for developing new fittings, and a retail store.
▶ Jeremy Myerson and Sylvia Katz, *Conran Design Guides: Lamps and Lighting*, London: Conran Octopus, 1990:21,45,76.

Kandinskii, Vasilii   (1866–1944)
▶ Russian artist, writer, and teacher; born Moscow.
▶ Studied law and economics, University of Moscow, 1886; Anton Azbè's school, Munich, 1897, and Munich Academy, under Franz Stuck, 1900.
▶ He moved to Munich and turned from a career in law and economics to painting, playing an active role in the city's art world; was a visiting lecturer at the University of Dorpat in 1896; was in contact with V mire iskusstv (World of Art) members in St. Petersburg; in 1901, founded the Phalanx group and taught at a private art school in Munich. During the late 1900s, he became interested in Bavarian glass painting, icons, and primitive art; in 1909, began his *Improvisations* series of paintings and was a founding member of Neue Künstlervereinigung group; was the Munich correspondent for the St. Petersburg magazine *Apollon*; in 1910, joined the Jack of Diamonds group. His article 'Content and Form' appeared in the 1911 exhibition catalog of Vladimir Izdebskii's exhibition, Odessa; in 1911, (with Franz Marc, Gabriele Münter, and Kulbin) became a founding member of the Blaue Reiter group and, from 1912, contributed to its *Almanach*. In 1912 in Munich, he published *Über das Geistige in der Kunst (Concerning the Spiritual in Art)*; at the outbreak of World War I, returned to Moscow. When the Bolsheviks came to power, he became involved in various aspects of Izo NKP (The Institute of Artistic Culture), including teaching, writing, lecturing, exhibiting, and conference participation; in 1920, compiled the Inkhuk program, which embraced Suprematism, Tatlin's concept of the 'culture of materials,' and Kandinskii's own theories, and was opposed by the Constructivists; when Kandinskii moved in 1921 to the Bauhaus, Weimar, it formed the basis for the courses he taught there 1922–33 on Gropius's invitation. His experiments in industrial design led to porcelain designs for the Imperial/State/Lomonosov factory in Petrograd in 1922 (cups and saucers reproduced in 1972 by Haviland, Limoges). In 1933, he moved to Paris and joined the Abstraction-Création group. He pioneered an expressive form of abstraction in paintings that sought to portray spiritual values; he believed that all the arts had an underlying connection and that they could be synthesized. His teaching approach is reflected in his second major book *From Point and Line to Plane* (1926).

▶ Work shown at 1900–08 exhibitions of Moscow Association of Artists; 1904 New Society of Artists' exhibition, St. Petersburg; Vladimir Izdebskii's first 1909–10 Salon, Odessa, and other cities and his second (1911) in Odessa; from 1910, 'Jack of Diamonds' group's exhibitions; 1911–12 exhibitions, Blaue Reiter group; 1922 'Erste Russische Kunstausstellung,' Berlin. Work subject of 1929 exhibition, Galerie Zak, Paris.

▶ W. Grohmann, *Wassily Kandinsky*, New York, 1958. E. Hanfstaengl, *Kandinsky: Zeichnungen und Aquarelle im Lenbachhaus München*, Munich, 1974. R. Gollek, *Der Blaue Reiter im Lenbachhaus München*, Munich, 1974. Cat., *Wassily Kandinsky 1866–1944*, Munich: Haus der Kunst, 1976–77. John E. Bowlt and Rose-Carol Washton Long, *Vasilii Kandinsky: 'On the Spiritual in Art,'* Newtonville, Massachusetts, 1979. Cat., *Kandinsky*, Paris, Musée National d'Art Moderne, Centre Georges Pompidou, 1979. Peg Weiss, *Kandinsky in Munich—The Formative Jungendstil Years*, Princeton, 1979. Cat., Stephanie Barron and Maurice Tuchman, *The Avant-Garde in Russia, 1910–1930*, Cambridge, MA: MIT Press, 1980:162–64. Cat., *The Great Utopia: The Russian and Soviet Avant-Garde, 1915–1932*, New York: Guggenheim Museum, 1992.

Kantack, Walter

▶ American lighting designer; born Meriden, Connecticut.
▶ Studied Pratt Institute, Brooklyn, New York.
▶ Kantack worked in the drafting room of the Edward F. Caldwell decorating firm, New York; in 1915, began working at Sterling Bronze as a designer; in 1917, set up his own design firm and became a specialist in custom lighting until 1932; was vice-president of Architectural League of New York, honorary member of American Institute of Decorators, and member of Hoover Delegation to the 1925 Paris 'Exposition International des Arts Décoratifs et Industriels Modernes.'
▶ In the late 1920s and early 1930s, work shown in exhibitions of industrial design, New York Metropolitan Museum of Art. Received 1934 gold medal from American Institute of Architects.
▶ Harry V. Anderson, 'Contemporary American Designers,' *Decorators Digest*, Aug. 1935:45–49.

Karasz, Ilonka (1896–1981) and **Mariska Karasz** (1898–1960)

▶ Hungarian designers; sisters; born Budapest.
▶ Ilonka Karasz studied Royal School of Arts and Crafts, Budapest; Mariska Karasz studied The Cooper Union, New York, under Ethel Traphagen.
▶ Ilonka emigrated to the USA in 1913; became active first as a graphic artist; designed fabrics for Lesher-Whitman, Cheney, Susequehanna Silk Mills, Belding, Standard Textile, Mallinson, Du Pont Rayon, and Schwarzenbach-Huber; taught at Modern Art School, New York, and sold her work at the bookshop gallery The Sunwise Turn, which specialized in hand-dyed textiles and embroideries; 1930–c33, was a member of Designers' Gallery and AUDAC (American Union of Decorative Artists and Craftsmen). Her work showed an Eastern European crafts approach. She was active as a designer of ceramics, silver, wallpaper, and furniture and illustrator of books and covers for *The New Yorker* magazine. Mariska Karasz emigrated to the USA in 1914; specialized in handworked textiles; in the 1920s, designed women's and children's clothing; in 1939, designed clothing patterns published in women's magazines; designed embroideries and metalware.
▶ Ilonka Karasz showed work at 1928 and 1929 American Designers' Gallery and an executive committee member. Mariska Karasz showed work at 1930 and 1931 exhibition of AUDAC (American Union of Decorative Artists and Craftsmen; (child's rug) at 1928 'International Exposition of Art in Industry,' Macy's department store, New York, and traveling to ten American cities.
▶ Harry V. Anderson, 'Contemporary American Designers,' *Decorators Digest*, Dec. 1935:46–53. Karen Davies, *At Home in Manhattan: Modern Decorative Arts, 1925 to the Depression*, New Haven: Yale, 1983:43. Jonathan M. Woodham, *Twentieth-Century*

Ornament, New York: Rizzoli, 1990:101. Gillian Moss, 'Ilonka Karasz and Mariska Karasz' in Mel Byars and Russell Flinchum (eds.), *50 American Designers*, Washington: Preservation Press, 1994.

Karlsen, Arne (1927–)

▶ Danish architect and furniture designer.
▶ Studied architecture, Det Kongelige Danske Kunstakademi, Copenhagen, to 1950.
▶ 1950–56 and 1964–65, he taught in the architecture school, Det Kongelige Danske Kunstakademi, and, in 1965, furniture and design at the Arkitektskolen, Århus, where he was rector 1968–72.
▶ Frederik Sieck, *Nutidig Dansk Møbeldesign:—en kortfattet illustreret beskrivelse*, Copenhagen: Bondo Gravesen, 1981; 1990 Busck edition in English.

Karlskrona Porslinsfabrik

▶ Swedish ceramics factory.
▶ The factory was established in 1918 for the production of art- and tablewares. Edvard Hald served as artistic director 1924–33, and was succeeded by Sven-Erik Skawonius 1933–39. In 1942, the firm was amalgamated into Upsala-Ekeby; it closed in 1968.
▶ Jennifer Hawkins Opie, *Scandinavia: Ceramics and Glass in the Twentieth Century*, New York: Rizzoli, 1989.

Karnagel, Wolf (1940–)

▶ German designer and teacher; born Leipzig.
▶ Studied Hochscule der Kunst, Brunswick, under Bodo Kapmann.
▶ He worked as an associate designer at Staatliche Porzellan-Manufaktur, Berlin. He designed two ranges of glass: 1969 *Joy* and *Pandio* in the 1980s by Rosenthal Studio Line; also the 1986 *Epoca* flatware range by Wilkens, Bremen, and 1967 *Stambul* mocha service by KPM, Berlin. He had clients including Lufthansa and Hutschenreuther; was professor of design, Hochschule der Kunst, Berlin.
▶ Frederick Cooke, *Glass: Twentieth-Century Design*, New York: Dutton, 1986:96. Albrecht Bangert and Karl Michael Armer, *80s Style: Designs of the Decade*, New York: Abbeville, 1990:134,232.

Karppanen, Mikko (1955–)

▶ Finnish glassware designer.
▶ From 1983, Karppanen designed glassware at Iittala, Finland, and became its youngest designer. Designs included glassware with new watercolor-like decoration.

Karra, Alexandra (1962–)

▶ Greek industrial designer; born Katerini.
▶ 1980–85, studied architecture, Aristotelian University of Thessaloniki; 1987–88, industrial design, Domus Academy, Milan.
▶ Received prize for a series of objects in 'Pyramid' section, 1986 'Panhellenic Competition of Furniture Design—Furnidec,' Thessaloniki. Her work was included in the 1986 (VIII) Biennale of young artists from the Mediterranean in Thessaloniki; 1987 (III) 'European Exhibition of Creation SAD '87,' Grand Palais, Paris; 1988 'Bagno extra: a bath of sense and sensuality,' 'Cersale '88,' Bologna.
▶ Cat., Design Center Stuttgart, *Women in Design: Careers and Life Histories Since 1900*, Stuttgart: Haus der Wirtschaft, 1989:256–57.

Kartell

▶ Italian domestic goods manufacturer; located Binasco.
▶ Kartell was founded in 1949 by chemical engineer Giulio Castelli; specialized in and was an innovator of plastics; began producing household articles, adding lamps in 1958 and furniture in 1967. Its designers included Anna Castelli Ferrieri, Ignazio Gardella, Olaf von Bohr, Giotto Stoppino, Joe Colombo, Gae Aulenti, Anig Sarian, Marco Zanuso, Sergio Asti, Pierluigi Spadolini, and Pietro Felli. Its range stretched from the celebrated 1968 chair by Colombo to Philippe Starck's 1989 *Dr. Glob* chair. The 1991 collapsible table series by Antonio Citterio was widely published.

Designs included von Bohr's 1970 *Modular Bookshelves 4930–7*, Stoppino's *Stackable Tables 4905–7*, Columbo's *Table Lamps 4008, 4088, and 4029*, Asti's *Writing Tray 4640*, and a large number of works by Ferrieri.
► Received awards including gold and silver medals at numerous Triennali di Milano; 1955, 1957, 1959, 1960, and 1964 Premio Compasso d'Oro, 1965 Interplast award; 1968 Oscar Plast award; first prize, 1968 Fiera del Mobile, Trieste; 1967, 1968, and 1972 Macef prize; silver medal, 1972 Bauzentrum Wien; 1973 Bundespreis 'Die gute Industrieform'; 1974 Casa Amica prize. Numerous products selected at 1968 'BIO 3' and 1973 'BIO 5' Industrial Design Biennials in Ljubljana. Work shown at 1972 'Italy: The New Domestic Landscape,' New York Museum of Modern Art.
► Cat., Milena Lamarová, *Design a Plastické Hmoty*, Prague: Uměleckoprůmyslové Muzeum, 1972:60,62,192. *ADI Annual 1976*, Milan: Associazione per il Disegno Industriale, 1976. 'Milan à l'Heure du Design,' *Maison et Jardin*, April 1992:126.

Kashiwabara, Hiroyuki   (1942–)
► Japanese glass designer.
► Studied Nihon University, Tokyo, to 1968.
► In 1968, he began to work at Sasaki Glass, Tokyo, where he became chief designer.
► Received Prize for Excellence, 1978 'Japan Crafts' exhibition; Functional Design Prize, 1986 (XXX) 'Anniversary Exhibition of Crafts Design Association'; Achievement Award, 1988 'International Exhibition of Glass Craft,' Industrial Gallery of Ishikawa Prefecture, Kanazawa. Work shown at 1982 'Modern Japanese Crafts,' traveling Southeast Asia; 1987 and 1990 'Glass in Japan,' Tokyo; 1991 (V) Triennale of Japan Glass Art Crafts Association, Heller Gallery, New York.
► Cat., *Glass Japan*, New York: Heller Gallery and Japan Glass Art Crafts Association, 1991: No. 17.

Kastholm, Jørgen   (1931–)
► Danish architect and furniture designer; born Roskilde.
► 1954–58, studied Bygningsteknisk Skole, Fredericksberg, under Arne Jacobsen; 1959, Grafisk Højskole.
► He worked for furniture makers Fritz Hansen and Ole Hagen; in 1960, set up his own studio in Holte; 1962–70, was a partner of Preben Fabricius; in 1972, moved to Düsseldorf. Designs included furniture for Kill International and Ivan Schlechter, and cutlery, textiles, lighting, and books. From 1975, he taught furniture design, Gesamthochschule, Wuppertal University; designed 1962 tractor-seat-like *Scimitar Chair 63* produced by Ivan Schlechter, Copenhagen, and 1985 *Geo-Line* armchair, echoing 1930s models, by Franz Wittman, Austria.
► Work shown at 1966 'Vijftig Jaar Zitten,' Stedelijk Museum, Amsterdam; 1968 'Les Assises du siège contemporain,' Paris Musée des Arts Décoratifs; Museo de Arte, Portugal; Ringling Museum, USA, 1969; Royal Albert Hall, London. Work (furniture) received 1968 Illum Award; 1969 Ringling Museum Award; Bundes Award, Design Center Essen; Design Center Stuttgart 1972–77; Design Center Munich; 1972, 1974, and 1976 Bundespreis 'Die gute Industrieform'; 1973 grand prize, Museo des Arte Moderne, Brazil. 1962 *Scimitar Chair 63* shown first time at 'New Forms' exhibition, Charlottenborg Museum, Copenhagen.
► Cat., *Les Assises du siège contemporain*, Paris: Musée des Arts Décoratifs, 1968. Cat., *Modern Chairs 1918–1970*, London: Lund Humphries, 1971. Robert A.M. Stern (ed.), *The International Design Yearbook*, New York: Abbeville, 1985/1986: No. 25. Frederik Sieck, *Nutidig Dansk Møbeldesign:—en kortfattet illustreret beskrivelse*, Copenhagen: Bondo Gravesen; 1990 Busck edition in English.

Katavolos, William   (1924–)
► American designer; active New York and Cold Spring, New York.
► Studied industrial design, Pratt Institute, Brooklyn, New York to 1949; 1964, physics, New York University.

► 1949–55, he was a partner with Ross Littell and Douglas Kelley on furniture, textile, and dinnerware designs for Laverne Originals. Commissioned by Erwine and Estelle Laverne, they executed their first furniture collection, Laverne's 1949 *New Furniture Group* of chairs and tables in leather, chrome, glass, and marble. The 1952 *T Chair* was executed initially in wooden dowels, with production in chromium-plated steel. 1955–57, Katavolos worked at George Nelson, designing 1956–57 *Omni Pole* shelving system, Williamsburgh Restoration exhibit systems and Smithsonian Museum exhibition system, and collaborating on the Experimental House. In 1957, he was a freelance designer for the Agricultural Pavilion and Solar Energy Pavilion, USA exhibition, Salonika Fair, Greece; in 1958, designed the ceiling tension-ring structure for the interior dome of USA-Moscow Fair; 1959–63, taught design, Sarah Lawrence College, Bronxville, New York; in 1965, designed the experimental school building Education Tower; in 1965, (with J. Luss) designed the partition systems for offices of Time-Life, New York; in 1969, designed hospital and surgical products for Johnson and Johnson; in 1973, was chair of the curriculum of School of Architecture, Pratt Institute, and, from 1975, professor; in 1979, was invited by Technicon University, Haifa, to participate in the town planning of North Jerusaleum; in 1985, became a partner in Ergo Design, Boulder, Colorado; 1990–91, was consulting designer to Marai International, New York and Tokyo; published the book *Organics* and produced the film *Correlations* (1968).
► Work (*T Chair*) received 1952 AID award for best USA furniture design. Laverne work and Katavolos's textile designs shown at 1953 and 1955 'Good Design' exhibitions, New York Museum of Modern Art. From 1958, work shown in worldwide traveling exhibition sponsored by the US government. 'The Chemical City' shown at 1961 'Visionary Architecture' exhibition, New York Museum of Modern Art. In 1975, received George Becker grant for production of Hydronic Energy House, Higgins Hall, Pratt Institute.
► 'Good Design,' *Interiors*, Vol. 113, Aug. 1953:88–89,146–48. Roberto Aloi, *Mobili tipo*, Milan: 1956:97,121,187,216. Clement Meadmore, *The Modern Chair*, New York: 1975:98–101. Cat., Kathryn B. Hiesinger and George H. Marcus III (eds.), *Design Since 1945*, Philadelphia: Philadelphia Museum of Art, 1983.

Kauffer, Edward McKnight   (b. Edward Kauffer 1890–1954)
► American graphic artist and designer; active London; husband of Marion Dorn.
► Studied painting, USA.
► He adopted the name McKnight in honor of Joseph E. McKnight, who funded his 1913 study trip to Paris. He settled in Britain in 1914; in 1915, received his first important commission, a poster design for the London Underground, from its publicity manager Frank Pick, one of Kauffer's major clients for the next quarter century. He gave up painting in 1921 to concentrate on commercial art and design, becoming best known for his lively posters; had clients including Eastman, J.C. Eno, The Gas, Light and Coke Co, General Post Office, Orient Line steamships, Empire Marketing Board, Great Western Railway, Shell Mex, and British Petroleum. He illustrated books including *Don Quixote* (1930), *Triumphal March* (1931) by T.S. Eliot, and *Venus Rising from the Sea* by Arnold Bennett, numerous book jackets, and a cover for *The Studio*. He designed theatre costumes and sets including those for ballet *Checkmate* (1937). From the 1920s, he designed rugs with Modernist motifs for Wilton Royal Carpet Factory, as did his wife Marion Dorn; they were among the first British designers to match the standards of the carpet designs of the French *artistes-décorateurs*. In 1940, he moved to New York.
► Work (Wilton rugs with Dorn) at 1929 exhibition, decorators Arthur Tooth, London. In 1936, elected Honorary Designer for Industry. Work (graphics and rugs) shown at 1979–80 'Thirties' exhibition, Hayward Gallery, London. Work subject of 1989–90 exhibition, Cooper-Hewitt Museum, New York.

▶ Michael Farr, *Design in British Industry: A Mid-Century Survey*, London: Cambridge, 1955:192. Cat., *Thirties: British art and design before the war*, London: Arts Council of Great Britain, Hayward gallery, 1979:77,82,87,115,146,188,198,202,211,212, 213, 215,219,230,294. Mark Haworth–Booth, *E. McKnight Kauffer: A Designer and His Public*, London: Gordon Fraser, 1979.

Kauffer, Elizabeth
▶ American designer; active New York.
▶ Kauffer was originally associated with Gilbert Rohde; later became color coordinator for Herman Miller; designed a group of table lamps for Nessen Studio, Yonkers, New York, that featured bases in Italian marble.
▶ *Home Lighting and Accessories*, April 1985:22–26.

Kaufmann, Eugen (1892–)
▶ German architect; born Frankfurt-am-Main; active Germany and Britain.
▶ 1910–14, studied architecture, Charlottenburg technical university, Berlin; 1912, Technische Hochschule, Munich.
▶ 1919–21, he worked for architect Gustav Wolff, Halle; 1922–23, for architect Bruno Taut, Magdeburg; and, 1923–25, for architect Walter Norden, northern Italy. 1925–31, he was a city planning officer in Frankfurt under Ernst May; was responsible for Frankfurt's ambitious housing program; 1931–33, worked mainly on the Donbas development scheme in the USSR; in 1933, settled in Britain, where he set up an architecture partnership with Frederick Towndrow; was a member of MARS (Modern Architectural Research Group); from c1945, was active in his own independent architecture practice. His work in Britain included storefronts and interiors for Rothmans and Moss Bros., extensions to King Alfred's school in London, houses at Welwyn and Angmering-on-Sea, and some unrealized projects.
▶ Cat., *Thirties: British art and design before the war*, London: Arts Council of Great Britain, Hayward Gallery, 1979:193,194,294.

Kaufmann Jr., Edgar (1917–89)
▶ American museum curator, historian, and philanthropist; born Pittsburgh, active New York.
▶ Studied painting, New York, Vienna, Florence, and London; 1934–35, Frank Lloyd Wright's Taliesen Foundation, Scottsdale, Arizona.
▶ In 1935, he joined the family Kaufmann department store, Pittsburgh, and became merchandise manager for home furnishings. Wright designed the 1935–37 office of Kaufmann's father in the department store, and 1936 Kaufmann country home 'Fallingwater,' Bear Run, Pennsylvania. In 1940, Kaufmann became head of the design department, New York Museum of Modern Art, succeeding Eliot Noyes after the brief tenure of Suzanne Wasson-Tucker; focused the museum's permanent design collection on products and objects from Europe, particularly Italy and Scandinavia. His publications while at the Museum attempted to educate the public in good design. From 1950, he managed the first series of 'Good Design' exhibitions designed by Finn Juhl and others and shown at the Museum and at the Merchandise Mart, Chicago. In 1963, having inherited Fallingwater, he donated the house to the Western Pennsylvania Conservancy with a $500,000 endowment. In 1979, a pavilion on the property was designed by Kaufmann's companion Paul Mayen. He was for many years adjunct professor of architecture and art history, Columbia University, New York; published numerous essays and books on architecture and design, including *Fallingwater: A Frank Lloyd Wright Country House* (1986); in 1978, became a founding director, Architectural History Foundation.
▶ Organized numerous exhibitions at New York Museum of Modern Art and 1970 'The Rise of American Architecture 1815–1915,' Metropolitan Museum of Art, New York.
▶ Penny Sparke, *Introduction to Design and Culture in the Twentieth Century*, London: Allen and Unwin, 1986. Paul Goldberger, 'Edgar Kaufmann Jr., 79, Architecture Historian,' *The New York Times*, 1 August 1989.

Kawabe, Sachiko (1958–)
▶ Japanese designer; born Tokyo.
▶ Studied Women's Art University, Tokyo.
▶ She set up her own design office; executed 1988 *Kan Kan* lacquered wood tableware range produced by Yamada-Heiando.
▶ Albrecht Bangert and Karl Michael Armer, *80s Style: Designs of the Decade*, New York: Abbeville, 1990:142,151,232.

Kawakami, Motomi (1940–)
▶ Japanese furniture designer, active Hyogo-Ken.
▶ Studied architecture in Japan.
▶ He collaborated with architect and designer Angelo Mangiarotti, Milan; designed 1968 *Fiorenza Chair*, a design in a continuous band with slits for flexibility and drainage when used outdoors, produced by Alberto Bazzani, Milan.
▶ Work shown in international furniture exhibitions in Cologne, Paris, and Milan. Received 1967 Concorso MIA. *Fiorenza Chair* was shown at 1968 Cologne, Paris, and Milan international furniture fairs; 1966 Genoa 'Eurodomus I'; 1968 Turin 'Eurodomus II'; 1970 'Modern Chairs 1918–1970' exhibition, Whitechapel Gallery, London.
▶ Cat., *Modern Chairs 1918–1970*, London: Lund Humphries, 1971.

Kawasaki, Kazuo (1949–)
▶ Japanese designer, born Fukui City.
▶ Studied Kanazawa University of Arts to 1972.
▶ Until 1979, he was creative director of the product design department, Toshiba; 1979–80, was a freelance consultant designer; from 1980, was president of Ex-Design; designed 1987 *X* and *I* scissors produced by Takefu Knife Village; became a lecturer, Fukui University; instructor, Kanazawa University of Arts; and technical advisor to Fukui Prefecture.
▶ Albrecht Bangert and Karl Michael Armer, *80s Style: Designs of the Decade*, New York: Abbeville, 1990:220,232.

Kay, John Illingworth (1870–1950)
▶ British designer and teacher; born Kirkcaldy; active London.
▶ From the early 1890s to 1900, Kay began as a designer in Silver Studio; 1900–22, worked at Essex Wallpaper Co; was a teacher at London Central School of Arts and Crafts.
▶ Stuart Durant, *Ornament from the Industrial Revolution to Today*, Woodstock, NY: Overlook, 1896:46,325.

Kayser, Fredrik A. (1924–68)
▶ Norwegian furniture designer.
▶ Studied Statens Håndverks -og Kunstindustriskole, Oslo.
▶ He designed furniture for Rastad & Relling and Vatne Lenestolfabrikk; from 1956, was an independent designer.
▶ Cat., David Revere McFadden (ed.), *Scandinavian Modern Design 1880–1980*, New York: Abrams, 1982:266, No. 267. Fredrik Wildhagen, *Norge i Form*, Oslo: Stenersen, 1988:152–153.

Kayser, J.P.
▶ German pewter foundry; located Krefeld-Bochum.
▶ J.P. Kayser established a pewter foundry in 1862 in Krefeld-Bochum; in 1885, it was enlarged and modernized. In 1900, Kayser's son Engelberg Kayser set up his own studio in Cologne and designed pewterware for the firm. Kayser introduced copper and antimony for brightness and durability. The firm produced salvers, jardinières, candlesticks, and candelabra in the Art Nouveau style, sold through Liberty, London.
▶ Cat., *Jugendstil*, Darmstadt: Hessisches Landesmuseum, 1965. Cat., G. Woeckel, *Jugendstilsammlung*, Kassel: Staatliche Kunstsammlungen, 1968. Cat., *Liberty's 1875–1975*, London: Victoria and Albert Museum, 1975. Alastair Duncan, *Art Nouveau and Art Déco Lighting*, New York: Simon and Schuster, 1978:122–23. Cat., *Metallkunst*, Berlin: Bröhan Museum, 1990:284–343.

Keith, Howard
▶ British furniture designer.
▶ Keith produced furniture designs for his own company, HK Furniture, founded in 1933.

▶ Michael Farr, *Design in British Industry: A Mid-Century Survey*, London: Cambridge, 1955:8ff. Cat., Leslie Jackson, *The New Look: Design in the Fifties*, New York: Thames and Hudson, 1991:125.

Keler, Peter (1898–1982)
▶ German architect, graphic designer, and painter.
▶ 1920–25, studied Bauhaus, Weimar.
▶ He is best known for his brightly painted 1922 cradle that reduced the design to a blue circle, a yellow triangle, and a red square. His work was influenced by the theories of Bauhaus teacher Vasilii Kandinskii. He designed other furniture that was more mundane, including a 1925 armchair based on the campaign chair with a swivel back; was labeled a 'degenerate artist' by the Nazis; after World War II, taught in Weimar.
▶ Work (cradle) shown at 1923 exhibition, Bauhaus, Weimar. Work subject of 1978 exhibition, Halle.
▶ Lionel Richard, *Encyclopédie du Bauhaus*, Paris: Somogy, 1985: 196. Cat., *The Bauhaus: Masters and Students*, New York: Barry Friedman,1988.

Keller frères, Gustave
▶ French leatherworkers and silversmiths; located Paris.
▶ Gustave Keller frères was founded in 1857 as a producer of leather dressing cases; in *c*1880, began producing matching silver toilet articles and hollow-ware, arriving at new forms by way of the traditional chasing technique; by *c*1900, was one of the important Paris factories producing Modern silver and was known for its smooth, undecorated forms, highly unusual in France at this time.
▶ Wares shown at most major exhibitions in France and abroad, including 1900 Paris 'Exposition Universelle,' 1902 St. Petersburg 'Comité français des Expositions à l'Étranger,' and 1937 Paris 'Exposition Internationale des Arts et Techniques dans la Vie Moderne.'
▶ Annelies Krekel-Aalberse, *Art Nouveau and Art Déco Silver*, New York: Abrams, 1989:57,59,63,64,65,247,256.

Kelley, Douglas (c1924–)
▶ American designer.
▶ Studied Pratt Institute, Brooklyn, New York.
▶ 1949–55, he collaborated with Ross Littell and William Katavolos on furniture, textile, and dinnerware designs for Laverne Originals. Erwine and Estelle Laverne commissioned them to design Laverne's 1949 *New Furniture Group* of chairs and tables in leather, chrome, glass, and marble. The 1952 *T Chair* was executed initially with wooden dowels and ultimately manufactured in chromium-plated steel and leather.
▶ Received (for *T Chair* with others) 1952 AID award for the best USA furniture. Their work shown at 1953 and 1955 'Good Design' exhibition, New York Museum of Modern Art.
▶ 'Good Design,' *Interiors*, Vol. 113, Aug. 1953:88–89, 146–48. Roberto Aloi, *Mobili tipo*, Milan: 1956:97,121,187,216. Clement Meadmore, *The Modern Chair*, New York: 1975:98–101. Cat., Kathryn B. Hiesinger and George H. Marcus III (eds.), *Design Since 1945*, Philadelphia: Philadelphia Museum of Art, 1983.

Kelp, Günther
See Haus-Rucker-Co

Kenwood
▶ British domestic kitchen wares manufacturer.
▶ Kenwood was founded in 1947 by Kenneth Wood in a garage in Woking; when Kenneth Grange became consultant designer, it became one of the British companies in the vanguard of good design; had as its first product the 1947 *A100 Turn-Over* toaster, followed a year later by the first all-British food mixer, the 1950 *Chef*, which provided numerous functions in one machine: grinding coffee, peeling potatoes, opening cans, pulverizing, liquefying, extracting juice, sieving, and mincing. It was redesigned in 1960 by Kenneth Grange in a silhouette influenced by Braun.

▶ Jeremy Myerson and Sylvia Katz, *Conran Design Guides: Kitchenware*, London: Conran Octopus, 1990:11.

Kéramis
▶ Belgian ceramics factory.
▶ The Boch ceramics factory located at La Louvière, called Kéramis, was founded in 1841 by a family of metallurgists from Lorraine. They had already set up two ceramics factories elsewhere: in 1767 at Sept-Fontaines (Luxembourg) under the name Villeroy et Boch, and in 1809 in the former abbey of Metlach, Saarland (Germany). The factory made earthenware and stoneware, and in 1847, began to decorate earthenware.
▶ Work (imitation Delft china) shown at 1880 Brussels exposition; (imitation Rouen and Sèvres ware) at 1889 Paris 'Exposition Universelle.'
▶ Yvonne Brunhammer et al., *Art Nouveau Belgium, France*, Houston: Institute for the Arts, Rice University, 1976.

Kerr, William B.
▶ American silversmiths.
▶ Kerr and Thiery was founded in Newark, New Jersey, in 1855; in 1906, was purchased by Gorham Manufacturing and relocated in Rhode Island; became one of the oldest silverware factories in the USA.
▶ Annelies Krekel-Aalberse, *Art Nouveau and Art Déco Silver*, New York: Abrams, 1989:98,256.

Keswick School of Industrial Art
▶ British vocational institution; located Keswick.
▶ Evening classes at Keswick School of Industrial Art began in 1884. The school was directed by Canon and Mrs. Rawnsley. Daytime classes began in 1898. It produced small objects in an extremely simple and unsophisticated Arts and Crafts style, often with clasps and buckles in silver set with turquoises. Jeweler Herbert J. Maryon and metalworker Harold Stabler were both full-time directors and designers associated with the school.
▶ Charlotte Gere, *American and European Jewelry 1930–1914*, New York: Crown, 1975:197. Annelies Krekel-Aalberse, *Art Nouveau and Art Déco Silver*, New York: Abrams, 1989:256.

Ketoff, Sacha (1949–)
▶ French sculptor and designer.
▶ Studied Accademia di Belle Arti di Brera, Milan, and architecture, École des Beaux-Arts, Paris, in 1971.
▶ He was a sculptor in the early 1970s and produced 1977 'Aircrash' sculpture; subsequently, designed furniture, books, and film sets. His first furniture was manufactured from 1980, including the 1983 table and chairs produced by Ecart International. He published extensively; is best known for his 1985 Aluminor *WEO* desk lamp (with André Livigne) ('WEO' standing for the first names of aviators Wilbur and Orville Wright) produced by Aluminor Luminaires. *WEO* won 1985 competition 'Lampes de bureaux' sponsored by the French Ministry of Culture and APCI (Agence pour la Promotion de la Création Industrielle).
▶ Work shown in numerous exhibitions including 1989 'L'Art de Vivre' exhibition, Cooper-Hewitt Museum, New York. Work subject of 1975 exhibition, Galerie Space, Paris.
▶ Gilles de Bure, *Le mobilier français 1965–1979*, Paris: Regard/VIA, 1983:115,134. Robert A.M. Stern (ed.), *The International Design Yearbook*, New York: Abbeville, 1985/1986: No. 190. Auction cat., *Memphis: La Collection Karl Lagerfeld*, Monaco: Sotheby's, 13 Oct. 1991.

Khoury, Georges (1958–)
▶ French designer and interior architect.
▶ Khoury designed the 1987 silver-crystal *Agathe* oil-and-vinegar set by Puiforcat in the tradition of the 1920s and 1930s designs of René Puiforcat; designed other items for the firm. He was active in various industrial design projects, including marine design.

▶ *Les Carnets du Design*, Paris: Mad-Cap Productions et APCI, 1986:76.

Kieffer, Michel (1916–)
▶ French bookbinder; born and active Paris; son of René Kieffer.
▶ Studied École Estienne and École Nationale des Arts Décoratifs, both Paris.
▶ He began working in his father's bindery in 1935; over the next two years, developed a style of his own and became known for his *décor cloisonné* (jewels and glass cabochons surrounded by gold fillets and set into morocco-leather covers). The motifs for the *décor cloisonné* were reminiscent of the classical motifs of Henri Creuzevault and Georges Cretté of a quarter of a century earlier. He was known for his highly encrusted and three-dimensional work; remained active at least up to the late 1980s in the workshop in rue St.-André-des-Arts, Paris.
▶ Work shown independently and with his father at 1937 Paris 'Exposition Internationale des Arts et Techniques dans la Vie Moderne.'
▶ Lucien Farnoux-Reynaud, 'La Reliure d'art: Triomphe du goût français,' *Mobilier et décoration*, Feb. 1938:61,64,73. Roger Devauchelle, *La Reliure en France de ses origines à nos jours*, Vol. 3, Paris, 1961:264–66. Alastair Duncan and Georges de Bartha, *Art Nouveau and Art Déco Bookbinding*, New York: Abrams, 1989:23,191–92.

Kieffer, René (1875–1964)
▶ French bookbinder and publisher; active Paris.
▶ Studied École Estienne, Paris, in 1889.
▶ He was a gilder at the Chambolle-Duru bindery for ten years; in 1903, set up his own workshop at 99 boulevard St.-Germain, Paris; subsequently moved to 41 rue St.-André-des-Arts and finally, in 1910, to 18 rue Séguier. A disciple of Henri Marius-Michel, his work shifted from classical forms to motifs in the Art Nouveau idiom. He was known for his use of bright colors in careful designs; 1917–23, produced the designs of Pierre Legrain for Jacques Doucet's library; had clients including Franchetti, Freund-Deschamps, Dr. Henri Voisin, Count de Verlet, R. Marty, A. Ramuz, and Henri Vever; in the 1920s, began to publish books, some with George Blaizot. In the 1930s, his covers incorporated metal disks encrusted with cabochons of iridescent glass and red glass beads, seen in *Luxures* by Maurice Rollinat and *Roman de Renart* shown at 1937 Paris 'Exposition Internationale des Arts et Technique dans la Vie Moderne.' Others included *Pétrone et Anacréon* and *Le crépuscule des Dieux*, which showed metal panels and portrait medallions.
▶ Work first shown at 1903 Salon of the Société des Artistes Décorateurs. As a binder and publisher, he was vice-president of the book division of 1925 Paris 'Exposition Internationale des Arts Décoratifs et Industriels Modernes.' Work shown at 1937 Paris 'Exposition Internationale des Arts et Techniques dans la Vie Moderne.'
▶ S.T. Prideaux, *Modern Bindings: Their Design and Decoration*, New York, 1906. Gaston Quénioux, *Les Arts décoratifs modernes 1918–1925*, Paris, 1925:336,341. Louis Barthou, 'L'Evolution artistique de la reliure,' *L'Illustration*, Christmas 1930. Henri Clouzot, 'René Kieffer,' *Mobilier et décoration*, No. 11, 1931:195–200. Ernest de Crauzat, *La Reliure française de 1900 à 1925*, Vol. 1, Paris, 1932:44–48; Vol. 2:46–48. Gaston Derys, 'Le Vingt-Troisième Salon des artistes décorateurs,' *Mobilier et décoration*, June 1933:232. Magdeleine A-Dayot, 'De la Reliure: Une visite à René Kieffer,' *L'Art et les artistes*, March 1935:204–08. '5 Reliures,' *Mobilier et décoration*, April 1935:145. Georges Lecomte, 'Reliures modernes,' *Plaisir de France*, Dec. 1937:67,71. Lucien Farnoux-Reynaud, 'La Reliure d'art,' *Mobilier et décoration*, Feb. 1938:58–78. Roger Devauchelle, *La Reliure en France de ses origines à nos jours*, Vol. 3, Paris, 1961:127,129,135,141,144,153,155–57,165,171. John F. Fleming and Priscilla Juvelis, *The Book Beautiful and the Binding as Art*, Vol. 1, New York, 1983:23,42,65,66, 81,82,85,143,169,201,202. Alastair Duncan and Georges de Bartha,

Art Nouveau and Art Déco Bookbinding, New York: Abrams, 1989: 16,17,19,21,23,97–100,192.

Kielland, Gabriel (1871–1960)
▶ Norwegian architect and glassware and furniture designer.
▶ 1891–92, studied painting, Munich; 1892–94, Weimar; 1894, Paris.
▶ From the 1890s, he was active in Trondheim, where he was a painter, director of a private art school, and designer of posters and furniture for Nordenfjeldske Kunstindustrimuseum, which he furnished in an English version of Art Nouveau. His proto-Modern furniture in undecorated wood was known for its simplicity, straightforwardness, and power.
▶ Cat., David Revere McFadden (ed.), *Scandinavian Modern Design 1880–1980*, New York: Abrams, 1982:266, No. 64.

Kienzle, Wilhelm (1886–1958)
▶ Swiss furniture designer and metalworker; born Basel.
▶ 1901–02, apprentice carpenter, Zehnle und Bussinger, Basel; 1903–05, a furniture draftsman there, while studying Gewerbeschule, Basel.
▶ In 1908, he worked as a metalworker, chaser, and belt-buckle maker for Riggenbach, Basel; in 1909, was a designer in a furniture factory in Freiburg (Germany) and opened his own studio in Munich, where until 1911 he executed furniture designs for crafts and industries as well as interior decoration; achieved recognition for his poster designs; subsequently, worked in the architecture office of Ino A. Campbell, Munich, and, in 1914, in the architecture office of Peter Behrens, Neu-Babelsberg, near Berlin; 1914–16, worked at the K.B. Hofmöbelfabrik, Munich, under Valentin Witt; 1918–51, was teaching assistant and then director of the class for interior carpentry, Kunstgewerbeschule, Zürich. Work included the *Kienzle* bookshelf, a telephone table for Wohnbedarf furniture store, trapezoid kindergarten tables produced by Horgen-Glarus, the shoe rack for Wohnhilfe, and household utensils for the firm Therma, Schwanden (Switzerland).
▶ Participated in 1926 and 1928 'Das Neue Heim' (The New Home) exhibitions. Decorated 'Apartment for the First Five Years of Marriage' at 1931 'Wohnausstellung,' Neubühl settlement, Zürich.
▶ Friederike Mehlau-Wiebking et al., *Schweizer Typenmöbel 1925–35, Sigfried Giedion und die Wohnbedarf AG*, Zürich: gta, 1989:229.

Kiesler, Frederick (c1890–1965)
▶ Romanian or Austrian architect and industrial and furniture designer; active Vienna and New York.
▶ 1910–12, studied Akademie der bildenden Künste; 1912–14, Technische Hochschule, both Vienna.
▶ From 1920, he collaborated briefly with Adolf Loos; in the 1920s, designed theater sets and interiors; in 1923, joined the group De Stijl and, in the same year, developed the design of his 'Endless' house and theater. The concept was based on an egg shape and featured a flexible interior, inexpensive heating, and reduction in the number of joints. He was closely associated with the group G, founded by Werner Graeff, Hans Richter, and Ludwig Mies van der Rohe. He created the 1924 *L+T* (Leger und Trager) hanging system for galleries and museums; was artistic director and architect of 1924 'International Exhibition of New Theater Technique,' Konzerthaus, Vienna; was architect and director of the Austrian pavilion, designing its theater and architecture sections, at 1925 Paris 'Exposition Internationale des Arts Décoratifs et Industriels Modernes'; in 1926, moved to the USA; 1926–28, was in partnership with Harvey Wiley Corbett in New York; 1930–c1933, member of AUDAC (American Union of Decorative Artists and Craftsmen); 1934–37, director of scenic design, Julliard School of Music, New York; 1936–42, director of Laboratory for Design Correlation, School of Architecture, Columbia University, New York; directed the installation of 1947 'Exposition Internationale de Surréalisme,' Paris; from 1956–62, was in partnership with Armand Bartos in New York. Although he built

few buildings, his inventions influenced architects and artists. From 1936, he concentrated on interior and furniture design; in 1937, designed his space house; designed furniture which included the biomorphic 1935–38 *Two-Part Nesting Tables* in cast aluminum and 1942 *Multi-Use Rocker* and *Multi-Use Chair* for Peggy Guggenheim's 1942 Art of This Century gallery, New York, in which Kiesler put Surrealist canvases to spatial use. Originally intended for mass production, the *Two-Part Nesting Tables* were put into production by New York gallery Jason McCoy in 1990 and subsequently produced in Italy.

▶ Work subject of 1975 exhibition, Vienna; and 1990 and 1992 exhibitions, Jason McCoy gallery, New York; 1988 'Friedrich Kiesler—Visionär, 1890–1965' exhibition, Museum moderner Kunst, Vienna, and traveling. Work (drawings) shown at 1982 'Shape and Environment: Furniture by American Architects,' Whitney Museum of American Art, Fairfield County, Connecticut.

▶ Frederick Kiesler, *Inside the Endless House*, New York: Simon and Schuster, 1964. Cat., *Frederick Kiesler: Environmental Sculpture*, New York, 1964. 'Kiesler by Kiesler,' *Architectural Forum*, Sept. 1965. 'Frederick Kiesler 1923–1964,' *Zodiac*, No. 19, 1969:18–49. Cat., *Frederick Kiesler*, Vienna, 1975. Roger L. Held, *Endless Innovations: The Theories and Scenic Design of Frederick Kiesler*, Ph.D. dissertation, Bowling Green State University, Ohio, 1977. Cat., Lisa Phillips (introduction), *Shape and Environment: Furniture by American Architects*, New York: Whitney Museum of American Art, 1982:40–41. Dieter Bogner (ed.), *Friedrich Kiesler*, Vienna: Löcker, 1988. *Blueprint 57*, May 1989. 'Fitting Together 30s Design,' *The New York Times*, December 20, 1990:C3. Deborah Lewittes, 'Frederick Kiesler' in Mel Byars and Russell Flinchum (eds.), *50 American Designers, 1918–1968*, Washington: Preservation Press, 1994.

Kiga

▶ Italian furniture manufacturing holding company; located Foligno.

▶ Kiga was established in 1968 following the merger of the furniture manufacturing firms Knoll International and Gavina.

▶ *ADI Annual 1976*, Milan: Associazione per il Disegno Industriale, 1976.

▶ See Gavina, Dino

Kindt-Larsen, Edvard (1901–)

▶ Danish architect and furniture designer; husband of Tove Kindt-Larsen.

▶ Studied Bygningsteknisk Skole, Friedersberg, to 1922; architecture, Det Kongelige Danske Kunstakademi, Copenhagen, to 1927.

▶ Kindt-Larsen worked mainly on exhibitions and industrial design; 1945–53, was principal of Danish School of Arts, Crafts, and Design, Copenhagen; designed jewelry for Georg Jensen Sølvsmedie.

▶ Received (most jointly with Tove Kindt-Larsen) 1931 gold medal at Det Kongelige Danske Kunstakademi; 1938, 1940, 1941, and 1943 first prizes, Danish Cabinetmakers' Guild; 1949 Eckersberg Medal; second prize, A. Michelsen's 1940 jubilee competition; second prize, Holmegård's 1946 glass competition; 1946 prize, Danish Cabinetmakers' Guild; 1957 first prize, Riihimäen Lasi (Finland) Nordic glass competition; first prize, Georg Jensen Sølvsmedie's 1965 competition for flatware.

▶ Frederik Sieck, *Nutidig Dansk Møbeldesign:—en kortfattet illustreret beskrivelse*, Copenhagen: Bondo Gravesen, 1981; 1990 Busck edition in English.

Kindt-Larsen, Tove (1906–)

▶ Danish architect and designer; wife of Edvard Kindt-Larsen.

▶ Studied Det Kongelige Danske Kunstakademi, Copenhagen.

▶ Received awards at 1956, 1958, 1959, 1960, and 1961 California State Fairs and expositions, and numerous awards with Edvard Kindt-Larsen.

▶ Frederik Sieck, *Nutidig Dansk Møbeldesign:—en kortfattet illustreret beskrivelse*, Copenhagen: Bondo Gravesen; 1990 Busck edition in English.

▶ See Kindt-Larsen, Edvard.

King, Jesse Marion (1875–1949)

▶ British designer and illustrator.

▶ Studied Glasgow School of Art, and South Kensington.

▶ She was known primarily as a book illustrator; taught at Glasgow School of Art; became a prominent member of the ad-hoc Glasgow School of artists and designers with Charles Rennie Mackintosh and his wife Margaret Macdonald Mackintosh; was a participant in the Arts and Crafts movement; produced designs for fabrics and wallpaper and, for Liberty, the *Cymric* range of jewelry and silverwork, and other jewelry designs for Murrle, Bennett and Co. She was influenced by the elongated figural forms of Aubrey Beardsley; designed bookcovers, jewelry, murals, and mosaics and illustrated numerous books including *The Jungle Book* by Rudyard Kipling, *The Defence of Guenevere and Other Poems* (1904) by William Morris, *Comus* by John Milton, and *A House of Pomegranates* by Oscar Wilde. Her colors, childlike at first, became more intense, though with delicate touches of color after 1911, when she saw Léon Bakst's exotic costumes and sets for the Ballets Russes de Monte Carlo in Paris.

▶ With the Mackintoshes and MacNairs, exhibited at 1902 Turin 'Esposizione Internazionale d'Arte Decorativa Moderna' where she received a gold medal for her drawings and watercolors.

▶ Charlotte Gere, *American and European Jewelry 1830–1914*, New York: Crown, 1975:198. Diana L. Johnson, *Fantastic Illustration and Design in Britain, 1850–1930*, Providence: Rhode Island School of Design and New York: Cooper-Hewitt Museum, 1979. Toni Lesser Wolf, 'Women Jewelers of the British Arts and Crafts Movement,' *The Journal of Decorative and Propaganda Arts*, No. 14, Fall 1989:32–33:43.

King, Perry A. (1938–)

▶ British designer; born London; active Milan.

▶ Studied Birmingham College of Art to 1965.

▶ From 1956, he worked at Olivetti, where he designed office machinery; worked on the corporate design program (with Hans Von Klier) of C. Castelli; on the design of dictating machines for Süd-Atlas Werke, Monaco, and on the design of electronic apparatus and control systems for Praxis, Milan. He designed furniture and the catalogue produced by Planula, Agliana (Italy); designed the 1969 *Valentine* typewriter (with Ettore Sottsass); from 1972, was design coordinator for the corporate identity program of Olivetti. He also designed a typeface for Olivetti. From 1975 collaborating with Santiago Miranda in Milan on the project Limited Horizons, King-Miranda Associati executed environmental design, industrial design, furniture, interior designs, and graphics. King and Miranda designed posters and catalogs for Olivetti and corporate identity programs for others; executed designs for lighting for Arteluce (including the early 1970s *Donald* table lamp), Flos (many examples with Giancarlo Arnaldi), *Cable* office system and *Air Mail* chair by Marcatré, and power tools by Black and Decker. Their 1985 *Aurora* glass pendant lamp by Arteluce presaged designs by others. Their 1988 *Bloom* bookshelf system was produced by Tisettanta and 1987 *Bergamo* Murano glass bowl by Veart. They designed the 1991 *Lucerno* lighting range for public areas of 1992 Seville 'Expo '92.' King was a member of ADI (Associazione per il Disegno Industriale) and SIAD (Society of Industrial Artists and Designers).

▶ Work shown at 1979 'Design Process Olivetti 1908–1978' exhibition, Frederick S. Wight Art Gallery, University of California, Los Angeles.

▶ 'When Is a Dot not a Dot?,' *Design*, No. 317, May 1975:22. *ADI Annual 1976*, Milan: Associazione per il Disegno Industriale, 1976. Cat., *Design Process Olivetti 1908–1978*, Los Angeles: Frederick S. Wight Art Gallery, 1979:260. James Woudhuysen, 'Priests at Technology's Altar,' *Design*, No. 410, Feb. 1983:40–42. Cat., Kathryn B. Hiesinger and George H. Marcus III (eds.), *Design Since 1945*, Philadelphia: Philadelphia Museum of Art, 1983. Robert A.M. Stern (ed.), *The International Design Yearbook*, New York: Abbeville, 1985/1986: No. 244. Albrecht Bangert and

Karl Michael Armer, *80s Style: Designs of the Decade*, New York: Abbeville, 1990:59,150,232. Hugh Aldersey-Williams, *King and Miranda: The Poetry of the Machine*, New York: Rizzoli, 1991.

King, Robert   (1917–)
▶ American silversmith.
▶ 1947–49, studied silversmithing and enameling, School for American Craftsmen, Rochester Institute of Technology, Rochester, New York.
▶ 1949–62, he worked at Towle silversmiths as a designer; designed its 1951 *Contour* pattern and other cutlery and hollowware; 1962–77, worked for International Silver and, concurrently, produced handcrafted jewelry, enamels, and silver table pieces.
▶ Cat., Kathryn B. Hiesinger and George H. Marcus III (eds.), *Design Since 1945*, Philadelphia: Philadelphia Museum of Art, 1983. Lee Nordness, *Objects: U.S.A.*, New York: 1970:178.

Kinsbourg, Renée
▶ French decorator and furniture designer; born Rouen; active Paris.
▶ Kinsbourg designed furniture in a baroque Art Déco manner, produced by Les Arts de France; designed rugs, wallpaper, and numerous interiors, including the residence of Van Cleef of c1928.
▶ Work shown at Salons d'Automne from 1924 and at the 1928 Exposition Générale d'Art Appliqué at the Palais Galliéra, Paris.
▶ Pierre Kjellberg, *Art Déco: les maîtres du Mobilier, le décor des Paquebots*, Paris: Amateur, 1986:101.

Kinsman, Rodney   (1943–)
▶ British industrial designer.
▶ Studied Central School of Arts and Crafts, London.
▶ He established OMK Design in 1966 as a design group serving furniture manufacturers. In 1967, OMK began limited production of its own designs. Kinsman's designs were conservatively Modern. He designed the *Omstack* chair; designed furniture for Bieffeplast, including 1984 *Graffiti* shelving system and 1985 models in bent tubular metal in a style reminiscent of British designs of the 1930s, and 1990 multiple-module outdoor public seating for British Rail (produced by Trax, London) with optional upholstery, arms, and alternate underframes.
▶ OMK won several awards. Kinsman's work was widely shown and published.
▶ Robert A.M. Stern (ed.), *The International Design Yearbook*, New York: Abbeville, 1985/1986: No. 24. *Design 5*, London: Design Museum, Winter 1990.

Kirk, Arthur Nevill   (1881–1958)
▶ British metalworker; born Lewes, Sussex; active England and USA.
▶ 1916–20, studied Brighton School and Central School of Arts and Crafts, London.
▶ From 1920–27, he taught metalworking and miniature painting at Central School of Arts and Crafts; 1924–27, director, Chalice Well Crafts School, Glastonbury; in 1927, emigrated to the USA on the invitation of George G. Booth to instruct at Art School of the Detroit Society of Arts and Crafts; in 1929, became director of the metal workshop (with Charles Price and Margaret Biggar as assistants), Cranbrook Academy of Art, Bloomfield, Michigan. His work there consisted of expensive objects set with precious stones and applied enamel and showed influences of Omar Ramsden and Alexander Fisher. Some pieces were in the geometrical version of the Art Déco style. The Cranbrook workshop closed in 1933; Kirk later became an ecclesiastical metalworker in Detroit.
▶ Robert Judson Clark et al., *The Cranbrook Vision*, New York: Abrams and Metropolitan Museum of Art, 1983. Annelies Krekel-Aalberse, *Art Nouveau and 'MFS Boston Acquires Craver Silver Teapot'*, *Art Déco Silver*, New York: Abrams, 1989: 123,124,125,256. Jeanine Falino, 'MFS Boston Acquires Craver Silver Teapot,' *Arts and Antiques Weekly*, February 16, 1990:50.

Kiss, Paul   (1885–1962)
▶ Hungarian metalworker; born Bélabalva (now Romania); active Paris.
▶ He settled in Paris in 1907, where he worked for metalworkers Edgar Brandt and Raymond Subes; after World War I, set up his own workshop and showroom in rue Delhomme, Paris; designed and produced (sometimes with Paul Fehér) domestic ironwork and public monuments, and restored historic monuments; had clients including the Kings of Egypt and Siam (now Thailand); designed and forged Porte du Monument aux Morts de la Guerre, Levallois-Perret. Motifs of birds and plants, some figures, and geometric forms were incorporated into his wrought-iron lighting, stands, consoles, doors, grilles, and railings. Sometimes resembling Michel and Jules Nics's lighting, Kiss's fixtures were old-fashioned and of high technical quality, with the slenderest attenuations and mounts holding alabaster, engraved glass, and marble shades and panels.
▶ Received a silver medal for the monument at Levallois-Perret, shown at 1924 Salon of Société des Artistes français. Work shown at Salons of the Société des Artistes français, Société des Artistes Décorateurs, and (including a pair of wrought-iron doors for Pavillon Savary) 1925 Paris 'Exposition Internationale des Arts Décoratifs et Industriels Modernes.'
▶ G. Janneau, *Le Luminaire et les Moyens d'éclairage*, first series: plates 30, 43. George Denoinville, 'Paul Kiss Ferronier d'art,' *Mobilier et Décoration*, Dec. 1925:21–27. *Le Demeure français*, No. 2, 1925–26:32. Pierre Lahalle, 'Les Ferronneries de Paul Kiss,' *Mobilier et Décoration*, Jan.–June 1929:35–40. Alastair Duncan, *Art Nouveau and Art Déco Lighting*, New York: Simon and Schuster, 1978:175. Jessica Rutherford, *Art Nouveau, Art Deco and the Thirties: The Furniture Collections at Brighton Museum*, Brighton: The Royal Pavilion, Art Gallery and Museums, 1983:35. Pierre Kjellberg, *Art Déco: les maîtres du Mobilier, le décor des Paquebots*, Paris: Amateur, 1986:101–02.

Kita, Toshiyuki   (1942–)
▶ Japanese furniture and interior designer; born Osaka.
▶ Studied industrial design, University for Design, Osaka, to 1964.
▶ He set up his own design office in Osaka in 1964; in 1969, began designing furniture for Italian and Japanese firms; collaborated with Silvio Coppola, Giotto Stoppino, and Bepi Fiori for Bernini. He is best known for the 1980 *Wink* articulated armchair produced by Cassina, which took four years to design; had clients including Tribu, Interflex, and Sharp. Other work included 1983 *Kick* table by Cassina, 1983 *Tomo* lamp by Lucci, 1983 *Tabola Altabasso* table by Casadue; 1983 *Icchio* lamp by Yamagiwa, 1983 *Bone-Rest* chair by Johoku Mokko, 1986 *Urushi* dinnerware range by Koshudo, and 1989 *Always* table. Designed (with Keith Haring) 1988 *On Taro* and *On Giro* tables produced by Kreon. His designs are known for combining humor, technology, and comfort.
▶ *Wink* chair shown at 1981 Milan Furniture Fair, 1983–84 'Design Since 1945' exhibition, Philadelphia Museum of Art, and 1991 'Mobili Italiani 1961–1991: Le Varie Età dei linguaggi' exhibition, Milan. Received 1975 Japan Interior Design Award for his furniture designs, Mainichi Design Award and 1981 Kitaro Kuni Industrial Arts Prize. In 1987, participated in the tenth anniversary celebration of Centre Georges Pompidou, Paris.
▶ 'Arredi su dimensioni modulari,' *Ottagono*, No. 38, Sept. 1975:110–15. Cat., Kathryn B. Hiesinger and George H. Marcus III (eds.), *Design Since 1945*, Philadelphia: Philadelphia Museum of Art, 1983. Cat., *Kagu-Mobilier Japonais*, Shibaura Institute of Technology, 1985. *Nouvelles Tendances: les avant-gardes de la fin du XXe siècle*, Paris: Centre Georges Pompidou, 1986. *Toshiyuki Kita: Movement as Concept*, Tokyo: Rikuyo-Sha, 1990. Albrecht Bangert and Karl Michael Armer, *80s Style: Designs of the Decade*, New York: Abbeville, 1990:39,125,134,232.

Kitaoka, Setsuo   (1946–)
▶ Japanese designer; born Kouchi Shikoku.
▶ Studied Kuwazawa Design Institute to 1974.

▶ He began working for the lighting firm Yamaguchi in 1974; in 1977, set up his own studio, Kitaoka Design Office, Tokyo.
▶ Albrecht Bangert and Karl Michael Armer, *80s Style: Designs of the Decade*, New York: Abbeville, 1990:69,232.

Kittelsen, Grete Prytz (1917–)
▶ Norwegian jewelry designer and metalworker.
▶ Studied Statens Håndverks -og Kunstindustriskole, Oslo; in France; and School of the Art Institute, Chicago.
▶ In the 1950s, Kittelsen designed enamel and silver jewelry for J. Tostrup, Oslo; produced vessels alone and with Gunnar S. Gundersen. Her work included enameled stainless steel. She designed the stand for Tostrup in the Norwegian pavilion at 1954 (X) Triennale di Milano.
▶ Received 1952 Lunning Prize and awards 1954 (X) (grand prize), 1957 (XI) (gold medal), and 1960 (XII) (gold medal) Triennali di Milano.
▶ Cat., David Revere McFadden (ed.), *Scandinavian Modern Design 1880–1980*, New York: Abrams, 1982:266, No. 205. Fredrik Wildhagen, *Norge i Form*, Oslo: Stenersen, 1988:135,145.

Kittelsen, Theodor (1857–1914)
▶ Norwegian ceramicist and book illustrator.
▶ 1884–87, studied painting in Munich.
▶ In the early 1900s, he was a designer for Porsgrunds Porselaensfabrik, Porsgrunn; was known for his illustrated books of folk tales, particularly those including trolls and fairies, and for his children's books.
▶ Cat., David Revere McFadden (ed.), *Scandinavian Modern Design 1880–1980*, New York: Abrams, 1982:266, No. 46.

Kjaer, Jacob (1896–1957)
▶ Danish designer.
▶ Kjaer became a journeyman silversmith in 1915; 1918–20, was a joiner in Copenhagen; 1921–22, was at Kunstgewerbemuseum, Berlin; 1922–24, was an apprentice joiner in Paris; in 1926, became a journeyman in Copenhagen. He was active as a furniture designer.
▶ Work shown at 1929–30 'Exposición Internacional de Barcelona,' 1935 Brussels 'Exposition Universelle et Internationale de Bruxelles,' 1937 Paris 'Exposition Internationale des Arts et Techniques dans la Vie Moderne,' 1939–40 'New York World's Fair,' 1951 (IX) Triennale di Milano.
▶ Frederik Sieck, *Nutidig Dansk Møbeldesign:—en kortfattet illustreret beskrivelse*, Copenhagen: Bondo Gravesen, 1981.

Kjaerholm, Poul (1929–80)
▶ Danish furniture designer.
▶ Studied cabinetmaking and furniture design, Kunsthåndvaerkerskolen, to 1952; from 1955, studied at furniture school, Det Kongelige Dansk Kunstakademi, both Copenhagen.
▶ 1952–56, he taught at Kunsthåndvaerkerskolen; from 1955 at Det Kongelige Dansk Kunstakademi. Though trained as a cabinetmaker, he designed furniture exclusively for mass production; from 1955, was a designer to manufacturer Ejvind Kold Christensen, Copenhagen, and to Hellerup; was best known for his chromium, wood, wicker, and leather furniture produced by Christensen, including the widely published 1957 *Armchair II*; designed 1977 dining room of Royal Porcelain concert hall and 1978 restaurant Kanalen. Like the Bauhaus designers, he insisted on simple, high-quality construction in his austerely Functional but comfortable furniture.
▶ Work shown at 1956–59 'Neue Form aus Dänemark,' Germany; 1958 'Formes Scandinaves,' Paris Musée des Arts Décoratifs; 1960–61 'The Arts of Denmark' traveling USA exhibition; 1964 'Formes Danoises,' Paris; 1966 'Vijtig Jaar Zitten,' Stedelijk Museum, Amsterdam; 1968 'Two Centuries of Danish Design,' London, Manchester and Glasgow; 1970 'Modern Chairs 1918–1970,' Whitechapel Gallery, London; 1977 'Dänische Formgestaltung,' Berlin; 1978 'Danish Design,' Dublin. Received awards including 1957 (XII) (grand prize) and 1960 (XIII) (gold medal and designed the Danish industrial-design stand), 1958 Lunning

Prize, 1960 Eckersberg Medal, 1965 Engelhardt Legacy, 1968 Prix de la Critique III Biennale des Arts Graphiques Appliqués, Brno, 1973 ID prize. From 1962–72, was fellow of Akademirådet (Royal Academy).
▶ Cat., *Les Assises du siège contemporain*, Paris: Musée des Arts Décoratifs, 1968. Cat., *Modern Chairs 1918–1970*, London: Lund Humphries, 1971: Nos. 34,38,88,118. 'One Hundred Great Danish Designs,' *Mobilia*, Nos. 230–33, Dec. 1974: Nos. 12–14. Frederik Sieck, *Nutidig Dansk Møbeldesign:—en kortfattet illustreret beskrivelse*, Copenhagen: Bondo Gravesen, 1981; 1990 Busck edition in English. Per Møllerup, 'Poul Kjaerholm's Furniture,' *Mobilia*, Nos. 304–05, 1982:1–24. Cat., David Revere McFadden (ed.), *Scandinavian Modern Design 1880–1980*, New York: Abrams, 1982:266, Nos. 206,265. Cat., Kathryn B. Hiesinger and George H. Marcus III (eds.), *Design Since 1945*, Philadelphia: Philadelphia Museum of Art, 1983. Cat., *The Lunning Prize*, Stockholm: Nationalmuseum, 1986: 120–25.

Kjarval, Sveinn (1919–81)
▶ Icelandic furniture and interior designer.
▶ Studied Kunsthåndvaerkskolen, Copenhagen.
▶ With an interest in Icelandic traditions, he designed furniture in the 1950s and 1960s based on Danish forms that was influential on other Icelandic designers. He used natural native materials.
▶ Cat., David Revere McFadden (ed.), *Scandinavian Modern Design 1880–1980*, New York: Abrams, 1982:266, No. 220.

Kleemann, Georg (1863–1932)
▶ German jewelry, wallpaper, and ceramics designer and illustrator; born Oberwurmbach.
▶ Studied Kunstgewerbeschule, Munich.
▶ He was an apprentice in the workshop of Theodor Spiess, under whom he designed wallpaper and ceramics and illustrated books; from c1901, collaborated with him; in 1887, became professor of design, Kunstgewerbeschule, Pforzheim; published *Moderner Schmuck* (1900); supplied jewelry designs to Carl Herrmann, Lauer und Wiedmann, Victor Mayer, Rodi und Wienenberger, Söllner, and Zerenner in Pforzheim.
▶ A number of works shown at 1903 'Fine Metals Exhibition,' Stuttgart.

Klein, Jaque (1899–1963)
▶ French decorator and furniture designer; active Paris.
▶ He designed wallpaper and rugs for the Galeries Lafayette department store, Paris; in 1942, established his own firm, 31 rue de Miromesnil, Paris. Some of his furniture was produced by Delepoulle and by Gouffé.
▶ From 1920, work shown at Salons d'Automne. Dining-room suite (with Laurent Malclès) was installed at 1922 Salon of Société des Artistes Décorateurs and bedroom produced by Delepoulle at 1922 Salon d'Automne. In 1928, he discontinued his participation in Salon d'Automne but, after World War II, continued with Société des Artistes Décorateurs.
▶ *Ensembles Mobiliers*, Paris: Charles Moreau, Vol. 5, No. 28, 1945; Nos. 35–36, 1954. Pierre Kjellberg, *Art Déco: les maîtres du Mobilier, le décor des Paquebots*, Paris: Amateur, 1986:102.

Kleinhempel, Gertrud (1875–1948)
▶ German designer and teacher.
▶ Studied drawing in Dresden and Munich.
▶ She directed a private applied-arts school in Dresden with her brothers Fritz and Erich; at the turn of the century, was a designer at the Dresdner Werkstätten für Handwerkunst; from 1907, was a teacher of textile design, Handwerker- und Kunstgewerbeschule, Bielefeld, and, from 1921, professor; was one of the women designers to receive recognition at this time. Her restrained interiors emphasized utility and a crafts-oriented simplicity.
▶ Hans Wichmann, *Deutsche Werkstätten und WK-Verband, 1878–1990*, Munich: Prestel, 1992:330.

Klemm, Walter (1883–1957)
▶ German woodcarver, illustrator, and teacher.
▶ Studied Grand Ducal College of Fine Arts, Weimar; in Vienna; in 1913, Kunstgewerbeschule, Weimar, under Henry van de Velde.
▶ He joined an artists' colony in Dachau, Bavaria; taught at the College of Fine Arts, Weimar, where his students included Karl Peter Röhl, Johannes Malzahn, Robert Michel and Ella Bergman-Michel. Towards the end of the 1910s, some students, including the Michels, rebelled against the school's 'antiquated' drawing methods. 1919–21, he was one of the masters at the Bauhaus, Weimar, where Röhl, Malzahn, and the Michels had become students; became known as an illustrator and was considered an outstanding woodcarver.
▶ Lionel Richard, *Encyclopédie du Bauhaus*, Paris: Somogy, 1985:1957.

Klerk, Michel de
See de Klerk, Michel

Klinkosch, J.C.
▶ Austrian silversmiths; located Vienna.
▶ J.C. Klinkosch was founded in 1797; in 1902, produced the silver designs of Otto Wagner and, in the 1920s, a number of pieces by Otto Prutscher and Osvald Härdtl.
▶ Wares (Wagner silver) shown at Austrian stand at 1902 Turin 'Esposizione Internazionale d'Arte Decorativa Moderna' and 1902 winter exhibition, 'Österreichisches Museum für Kunst und Industrie,' Vienna.
▶ Annelies Krekel-Aalberse, *Art Nouveau and Art Déco Silver*, New York: Abrams, 1989:191,200,202,256.

Klint, Ebsen (1915–69)
▶ Danish industrial designer; son of Kaare Klint.
▶ Studied Royal Academy of Architecture, Copenhagen.
▶ 1938–39, he was an industrial designer for Philips; 1959–62, designed school furniture with Børge Mogensen and physiotherapist Eigil Snorrason, produced in four different sizes. Klint is best known for his 1947 folded-paper lighting fixtures produced by Le Klint and influenced by origami. (Le Klint was run by Tage Klint, who was not related to Kaare or Ebsen Klint.)
▶ Arne Karlsen, *Furniture Designed by Børge Mogensen*, Copenhagen, 1968:116–19. Svend Hansen, 'Le Klint,' *Mobilia*, No. 206, 1972. Cat., Kathryn B. Hiesinger and George H. Marcus III (eds.), *Design Since 1945*, Philadelphia: Philadelphia Museum of Art, 1983. Cherie Fehrman and Kenneth Fehrman, *Postwar Interior Design, 1945–1960*, New York: Van Nostrand Reinhold, 1987.

Klint, Kaare (1888–1954)
▶ Danish architect, furniture designer, and theorist.
▶ Studied painting, architecture and design, Teknisk Skole, Copenhagen, under his architect father P.V Jensen Klint and Carl Petersen.
▶ He set up his own office in Copenhagen in 1920. In 1924, he founded the department of furniture; in 1944, became professor of architecture, School of Cabinetmaking, Det Kongelige Danske Kunstakademi, Copenhagen, where Finn Juhl was one of his pupils; early on, designed furniture for N.M. Rasmussen of Holbaek and N.C. Jensen Kjaer; later on, designed chiefly for Rud Rasmussen, the producer of his 1933 deck chair. Rasmussen still produces his designs. He designed a collection of furniture and furnishings for the Fåborg Museum 1914–15; Thorvaldsens Museum, Copenhagen, 1922–25; and Det Danske Kunstindustrimuseum, Copenhagen, 1924–54; (with son Ebsen) designed plastic-coated folded-paper lighting for Le Klint, a business of Tage Klint, who was not a relative.
▶ Designed 1948 'Danish Art Treasures' exhibition, Victoria and Albert Museum, London. Work shown at 1937 Paris 'Exposition Internationale des Arts et Techniques dans la Vie Moderne'; 1939 'New York World's Fair'; 1968 'Les Assises du siège contemporain,' Paris Musée des Arts Décoratifs; 1970 'Modern Chairs 1918–1970,' Whitechapel Gallery, London; 1980 'Scandinavian

Modern Design 1880–1980,' Cooper-Hewitt Museum, New York. Work subject of 1956 memorial exhibition, Det Danske Kunstindustrimuseum. Received grand prize at 1929 'Exposición Internacional de Barcelona,' grand prize at 1935 'Exposition Universelle et Internationale de Bruxelles,' 1954 Eckersberg Medal, 1954 C.F. Hansen Medal. In 1949, elected Honorary Royal Designer for Industry, London.
▶ Erik Zahle, *Scandinavian Domestic Design*, London 1963. Cat., *Les Assises du siège contemporain*, Paris: Musée des Arts Décoratifs, 1968. Cat., *Modern Chairs 1918–1970*, London: Lund Humphries, 1971. Cat., David Revere McFadden (ed.), *Scandinavian Modern Design 1880–1980*, New York: Abrams, 1982:266, Nos. 93,94,98,122,154. Jeremy Myerson and Sylvia Katz, *Conran Design Guides: Lamps and Lighting*, London: Conran Octopus, 1990:38.

Klint, Vibeke (1927–)
▶ Danish textile designer.
▶ 1949–50, studied Kunsthåndvaerkskolen, Copenhagen, under Gerda Henning; in 1951, at Aubusson (France), under Jean Lurçat, and at St. Céré and in Brittany under Pierre Wemaère.
▶ She set up her own studio in 1951; from 1956, was an industrial fabric designer for C. Olesen (Cotil) and others.
▶ Received 1960 Lunning Prize. Work shown at 1956–57 Germany 'Neue Form aus Dänemark' traveling exhibition; 1958 'Formes Scandinaves,' Paris Musée des Arts Décoratifs; 1960–61 'The Arts of Denmark' traveling USA exhibition; 1980 'Scandinavian Modern Design 1880–1980' exhibition, Cooper-Hewitt Museum, New York.
▶ Cat., David Revere McFadden (ed.), *Scandinavian Modern Design 1880–1980*, New York: Abrams, 1982:266, Nos. 152,207. Cat., *The Lunning Prize*, Stockholm: Nationalmuseum, 1986:116–19.

Kliun, Ivan Vasil'evich (b. Ivan Vasil'evich Kliunkov 1873–1943)
▶ Russian sculptor and interior designer.
▶ Studied Drawing School, Association for the Encouragement of the Arts, Warsaw, in 1890; F. Rerberg's and L. Mashkov's private studio, Moscow, in 1900.
▶ From 1907, he was a follower of Kasimir Malevich; 1917–21, headed the exhibitions bureau of Izo; 1918–21, was a member of Inkhuk and taught at Vkhutemas; in 1925, became a member of the 4 Arts group.
▶ Work shown at 1922 Berlin 'Erste Russische Kunstausstellung'; 1913 exhibitions, Union of Youth; 1916 'Magazin'; 1916–17 'Jack of Diamonds.'
▶ Cat., *Kunst und Revolution: Russische und Sowjetische Kunst 1910–1932*, Vienna: Österreichisches Museum für angewandte Kunst, 1988.

Klode, Kurt (1904–)
▶ German graphic artist and industrial designer; born Veelbert.
▶ 1930–32, studied Bauhaus, Dessau.
▶ He worked as a designer of advertising, and in industrial design; from 1945, taught painting and was active as a painter.
▶ Lionel Richard, *Encyclopédie du Bauhaus*, Paris: Somogy, 1985.

Klotz, Blanche-Jeanne
▶ French decorator and furniture designer.
▶ From c1925, she was active as a designer of interior schemes; designed furniture influenced by rustic early 19th-century forms; 1927–28, worked in a more refined Rationalist style, shown in the 1928 dining room of M.E. Fould and 1929 décor of a Parisian banker; designed a cabin with lacquered aluminum furniture, stainless-steel lighting, and fabrics by Hélène Henry for the 1935 oceanliner *Normandie*; in 1930, became a member of UAM (Union des Artistes Modernes); in 1935, began a collaboration with cabinetmaker Schmit in rue de Charonne, Paris, producing furniture in limited editions; in 1938, became director of the artists' group Mai 36, and designed the office of the Pen Club, rue Pierre-Charron, Paris; designed several villas in Provence, including furni-

ture and décor for the villa (by architect Robert Mallet-Stevens) of the vicomte and vicomtesse de Noailles, Hyères; by 1954, was active in an atelier at 25 rue Henri-Rochefort in Paris.

▶ Into the 1950s, work shown at Salons of Société des Artistes Décorateurs. She designed studio-hall for a mountain chalet at 1925 Paris 'Exposition Internationale des Arts Décoratifs et Industriel Modernes'; office at 1930 (I) UAM exhibition; interior decoration of pavilion of Togo, 1931 Paris 'Exposition Coloniale.'

▶ *Ensembles Mobiliers*, Paris: Charles Moreau, No. 40/1, 1954. Pierre Kjellberg, *Art Déco: les maîtres du Mobilier, le décor des Paquebots*, Paris: Amateur, 1986:102. Arlette Barré-Despond, *UAM*, Paris: Regard, 1986:226,523.

Klug, Ubald (1932–)

▶ Swiss designer and interior architect; active Paris.

▶ 1952–55, studied Kunstgewerbeschule, Zürich.

▶ 1949–52, Klug was an apprentice in tapestry and interior decoration; 1965–68, was active in her own design office working on various industrial design projects; from 1968, worked with the design agency MAFIA.

Klutcis, Gustav Gustavovich (aka Klutsis; Klucis 1895–1944)

▶ Latvian artist and graphic, poster, and applied arts designer; born near Riga.

▶ 1913–15, studied City Art School, Riga; 1915–17, Drawing School, Association for the Encouragement of the Arts; 1918, private studio of I. Mashkov, Moscow; 1919–20, K. Korovin's and A. Pevsner's studio; 1921, Faculty of Painting, Vkhutemas.

▶ Klutcis participated in 1918 in the Moscow art workshop organized by the infantry regiment in which he was serving, led by Voldemar Andersen; painted scenes of army activities; in c1918, enrolled in Svomas/Vkhutemas and, by 1919–20, was producing posters and pursuing his interest in typography and architecture; in 1920–22, was influenced by El Lissitzky, particularly in his approach to spatial relations and color in graphics and photomontages; became a member of Inkhuk (Institute of Artistic Culture); in 1924, began teaching at Vkhutemas; in 1925, produced photomontages for Vladimir Maiakovskii's poem 'V.I. Lenin,' and similar work for the theater; in 1927, co-designed *Chetryre fonetiches-kikh romana (Four Phonetic Novels)* by Kruchenykh; in 1928, was co-founder of the October group, serving in its photo section until the group disbanded in 1932; until the late 1930s, produced posters and typographic designs; was one of the interior designers and director of the Soviet pavilion, 1937 Paris 'Exposition Internationale des Arts et Techniques dans la Vie Moderne', and, in 1932 and 1933, interior and graphic designer for Soviet exhibitions in the USA, France, Spain, and Brazil.

▶ Work shown at 1922 Berlin 'Erste Russische Kunstausstellung'; 1925 Paris 'Exposition Internationale des Arts Décoratifs et Industriels Modernes'; 1927 Moscow 'Lissitzky's All-Union Polygraphical' exhibition; 1928 'Pressa' international press exhibition, Cologne; 1933 and 1934 poster exhibitions, Belgium, Italy, and Britain; 1930 October group exhibition. In 1938, stopped showing his work. Work subject of 1959 and 1970 exhibitions, Riga.

▶ N. Shantyko, 'Klutsis-illustrator Maiakovskogo,' *Khudozhnik*, Moscow, 1970: No. 2. L. Oginskaia, 'Khudozhnik-agitator,' *Dekorativnoe iskusstvo*, Moscow, 1971, No. 5:34–37. M. Ostrovskii (ed.), *Sto pamiatnykh dat. Khdozhestvennyi kalendar*, Moscow, 1974:17–20. Cat., Stephanie Barron and Maurice Tuchman, *The Avant-Garde in Russia, 1910–1930*, Cambridge, MA: MIT Press, 1980:172. Cat., *Kunst und Revolution: Russische und Sowhjetische Kunst 1910–1932*, Vienna: Österreichisches Museum für angewandte Kunst, 1988. Selim Om Magomedov, *Les Vhutemas*, Paris: Regard, 1990.

Knag, Christian Christopher (1855–1942)

▶ Norwegian cabinetmaker and furniture designer.

▶ In 1878, he set up his own workshop and salesroom, Bergen, where he specialized in inlaid goods, with landscape motifs in Art Nouveau forms.

▶ Received a gold medal at 1900 Paris 'Exposition Universelle' and grand prize at St. Louis 'Louisiana Purchase Exposition.' Work subject of 1909 exhibition, Kunstindustrimuseet, Oslo.

▶ Cat., David Revere McFadden (ed.), *Scandinavian Modern Design 1880–1980*, New York: Abrams, 1982:266–67, No. 63.

Knight, Laura (1877–1970)

▶ British painter and ceramics decorator; born Long Eaton, Derbyshire; active Newlyn, Cornwall.

▶ 1892, studied Nottingham School of Art.

▶ She was a juror of the 1922 Carnegie International competition, Pittsburgh; designed both the shapes and the decorations for the 1933–34 *Circus* range of tableware produced by Arthur J. Wilkinson, Burslem, under Clarice Cliff's supervision. Further important work included 1937 coronation ceramics by Wedgwood and glassware by Stuart Crystal. 1939–40, she was an official war artist; in 1946, was an official artist at the Nuremberg Trials.

▶ From 1903, work (paintings) shown at Royal Academy, London, and (glassware) at 1934 'Modern Art for the Table,' Harrods department store, London. Work subject of 1936 'Oil Paint and Grease Paint' and 1965 'The Magic of a Line' exhibitions.

▶ Cat., *Thirties: British art and design before the war*, London: Arts Council of Great Britian, Hayward Gallery, 1979: 31, 35,95,96,153,159,174,280,294.

Knoll

▶ American and international furniture manufacturer.

▶ Established by Hans Knoll in 1938, initially the firm was called HG Knoll, on East 72nd Street, New York. In 1955, his wife Florence Knoll assumed directorship. In 1959, the firm was sold to Art Metal Inc, with W. Cornell Dechert as president and Florence Knoll as design consultant to both firms. By the 1960s, Knoll had 20 showrooms in the USA and 30 around the world. Robert Cadwallader replaced Florence Knoll as president in 1965. Graphic design and advertising had been executed by Herbert Matter, who also left in 1965, and one of Cadwallader's first moves was to appoint Massimo Vignelli in his place. In 1971, Knoll Planning Unit was dissolved. Furniture designers added to the stable included Gae Aulenti, Cini Boeri, Joe d'Urso, Hanna and Morrison, Carlos Riart, and Vignelli. Other designers' work included Charles Pfister's 1975 table, Robert Venturi's 1984 chairs, table, and sofa, Andrew Morrison's 1974 office furniture, Richard Meier's 1982 tables and chairs, Ettore Sottsass's 1983 and 1986 chairs and sofas, and Frank Ghery's 1991 bentwood collection. Knoll always used the finest materials and craftsmanship. In its Mies line, stainless steel (not chromium plating) was used. Undergoing many changes of ownership, Knoll attempted to maintain its status while adding cheaper lines of systems, furniture, and furnishings. In a successful effort to enliven its textile line, fashion fabric designer Jhane Barnes was selected in the late 1980s. Knoll did not sell through its own retail outlets; both the 1969 showroom at Georg Jensen's, Madison Avenue, New York, and the 1974 Bloomingdale's plan failed. In 1993, under current management, began selling directly to the general public.

▶ 'To the Trade and Beyond,' *Industrial Design*, October 1974:44–55. Edward Larrabee and Massimo Vignelli, *Knoll Design*, New York, 1981. *Contemporary Designer*, London: Macmillan, 1984:332–33. Margery B. Stein, 'Teaching Steelcase to Dance,' *The New York Times Magazine, The Business World*, April 1, 1990.

▶ See Knoll Bassett, Florence 'Shu' and Knoll, Hans

Knoll Bassett, Florence 'Shu' (b. Florence Schust 1917–)

▶ American interior, furniture, and textile designer, architect, and entrepreneur; active USA.

▶ 1932–34, studied architecture, Kingswood School, Bloomfield Hills, Michigan, under Eliel and Eero Saarinen and, intermittently 1934–39, Cranbrook Academy of Art, Bloomfield Hills, under the same and other teachers; 1937–38, Architectural Association,

London; 1940–41, Illinois Institute of Technology, Chicago, under Mies van der Rohe.

▶ She was profoundly influenced by her distinguished teachers. She worked for architects Wallace K. Harrison, New York, from 1941, and for Walter Gropius and Marcel Breuer, Cambridge, Massachusetts; in 1943, joined furniture manufacturer Hans Knoll, forming the Knoll Planning Unit in New York out of his extant furniture business with manufacturing facilities in Greenville, Pennsylvania; 1943–65, was director of Knoll's Planning Unit and of furniture and textile design development, the interior-planning service for the fledgling company. In 1946, she married Hans Knoll. She exerted a profound influence on Modern furniture and interiors after World War II; drawing on her many contacts, began reproduction in c1948 of Mies van der Rohe's 1929 *Barcelona Chair* and 1930 low glass and steel *Dessau* table (originally for the Tugendhat House in Brno). In 1948, Eero Saarinen designed the fiberglass-shell *Womb chair*, a design that evolved from molded plastic experiments conducted with Charles Eames in the early 1940s. Another Cranbrook colleague, Harry Bertoia, produced the Knoll's 1952 wire-grid chair. The woven fabrics designed by Anni Albers, Evelyn Hill, Eszter Haraszty, and Suzanne Huguenin were innovatory in their specificity to the office environment. Florence Knoll herself designed many of the firm's more functional pieces, including desks with modular storage, much-imitated cabinets in 1950s, and lounge chairs and sofas in 1954. Her 1961 oval desk/table on a plated-metal central column was notable. Her interior designs of the time established a standard for corporate headquarters. Saarinen's 1957 standard office chairs became ubiquitous. In 1960, Knoll added Mies's 1930 *Brno* chair, initially produced for Philip Johnson's Four Seasons restaurant in the Seagram Building, New York. In 1964 Mies's 1927 leather sling chairs, and 1929 chaise-couch were added to the Knoll collection. When Gavina was acquired in 1968, the license was obtained to manufacture Breuer and Scarpa designs. In 1969, Franco Albini's 1958 *Floating Mini-Desk* and Breuer's 1925 *Wassily* chair, 1925 *Laccio* table, and 1927 *Cesca* chair were added to the Knoll line. 1968–91, Knoll sold 250,000 copies of the *Cesca* chair. In 1970, Knoll acquired rights to Mies's sofa design of the early 1930s (originally for European projects and revised in 1967 for the Toronto Dominion Bank building). Others designing for Knoll included George Nakashima and Isamu Noguchi. In 1951, the first Knoll subsidiary was set up in Germany. All of Knoll's foreign subsidiaries were also manufacturers. Florence Knoll executed highly influential interior designs that included the 1948 and 1957 Rockefeller family installation, 1957 Connecticut General Life Insurance building, 1958 H.J. Heinz, 1962 Cowles Publications, 1964 CBS building, and Knoll showrooms worldwide. Her interior design projects conveyed the self-assurance and sophistication for which she became known, although she regarded of her own designs as relatively insignificant at the time. Her Rationalist and architecturally integrated interiors were based on the concept of an open-plan layout where junior and secretarial staff sat together in a central area, with executives' offices located along the window walls. With architects Skidmore Owings and Merrill, she further refined her ideas in the 1957 Connecticut General headquarters, Hartford, Connecticut. She was president of Knoll 1955–65. In 1959 she sold the firm to Art Metal Inc, serving as design consultant to both firms until her retirement in 1965.

▶ In the 1950s, Knoll work shown at 'Good Design' exhibitions, New York Museum of Modern Art and Merchandise Mart, Chicago; 1972 'Knoll au Louvre' exhibition, Paris Musée des Arts Décoratifs; 1975 'A Modern Consciousness: D.J. DePree, Florence Knoll' exhibition, Rewick Gallery, Washington. Florence Knoll received 1954 (I) AID International Design Award and 1961 gold medal for industrial design, American Institute of Architects.

▶ Cat., *Knoll au Louvre*, Paris: Musée des Arts Décoratifs, 1972. Cat., *A Modern Consciousness: D.J. DePree, Florence Knoll*, Washington, DC: Renwick Gallery, 1975. Eric Larrabee and Massimo Vignelli, *Knoll Design*, New York: Abrams, 1981:76–89. *Contemporary Designer*, London: Macmillan. Elaine Louie, *The New York*

Times, 'The Many Lives of a Very Common Chairs,' 7 Feb. 1991: C10. Mel Byars, 'Florence Knoll' in Mel Byars and Russell Flinchum (eds.), *50 American Designers, 1918–1968*, Washington: Preservation, 1994.

Knoll, Hans (1914–55)

▶ German furniture manufacturer; son of furniture manufacturer Walter Knoll.

▶ Knoll was sent by his father to Britain in 1938 to help promote the new line of *Elbo* easy chairs made in Borghams and at Russell of High Wycombe and sold under the Knoll name in the showroom of Plan, the British furniture firm of Serge Chermeyeff. He moved to the USA to work as a designer; unsuccessful at this, he set up his own workshop in Pennsylvania, later moving to another factory in Greenville, Pennsylvania, near where the Knoll factory is located today; in 1938, opened a showroom on East 72nd Street, New York; He established HG Knoll, a one-man operation, in 1939. The early 1940s chairs of Jens Risom, Knoll's first designer reflect the scarcity of materials in the immediate postwar period. In 1946, Knoll married Florence Schust and formed Knoll Associates, with showroom-offices on Madison Avenue with her financial support. In 1947, he began working with Rudolf Graber of the Wohnbedarf department store, Switzerland. Florence Knoll managed the firm from Knoll's death until 1959.

▶ Edward Larrabee and Massimo Vignelli, *Knoll Design*, New York, 1981. Akio Izutsu, *The Bauhaus: A Japanese Perspective and A Profile of Hans and Florence Schust Knoll*, Tokyo, 1992.

Knoll, Wilhelm (1839–1907),   Walter Knoll (1876–1971), and Willy Knoll (1878–1954)

▶ German furniture manufacturers; active Stuttgart.

▶ In 1898, Willy Knoll, the son of Wilhelm Knoll, was a leatherworker in his father's factory in Stuttgart. In 1906, the firm became known as Ledersitzmöbelfabrik Wilhelm Knoll. In 1907, Willy took over management from his father; moved the business to Forststrasse 71, Stuttgart, where he developed technical and aesthetic innovations; based on the success of his models, established a reputation worldwide and became an important European manufacturer. Knoll emphasized the comfort of its chairs, particularly its first *Klubfauteuil* (club chair) created by Willy Knoll. The firm produced chairs with wood frames and tied-on upholstery. Its *Derby* armchair was published in *Innen-Dekoration*, 1908. Shifting from historicist to Modern styles, the firm's new range was sold through outlets in Vienna and St. Petersburg. Knoll patented springs, new materials, and new techniques for upholstery; it constructed resilient and self-supporting loose cushions. In 1912, the firm Nestra was set up with improved manufacturing techniques; its furniture was made with leather upholstery free from the frame. A new factory in Stuttgart was set up to produce chairs. Knoll began making sofas in the same techniques as its chairs; in the 1930s, produced tubular-steel furniture with thick, loose cushions. In 1925, the Walter Knoll firm was founded; produced the 1928 *Prodomo* range; in 1937, established Herrenberge Sitzmöbel, Herrenberg; by 1954, had an outlet in Paris. In 1985, it took over the Wilhelm Knoll firm.

▶ Adolf Schneck, *Das Polstermöbel*, Julius Hoffmann, 1933. *Ensembles Mobiliers*, Paris: Charles Moreau, No. 32, 1954. Barbie Campbell-Cole and Tim Benton (eds.), *Tubular Steel Furniture*, London: The Art Book Company, 1979:13,24. Arno Votteler and Herbert Eilmann, *125 Jahre Knoll: Vier Generationen Sitzmöbel-Design*, Stuttgart: Karl Krämer, 1990.

Knox, Archibald (1864–1933)

▶ British silver designer; born Isle of Man.

▶ 1878–84, studied Douglas School of Art, Isle of Man.

▶ Until 1899, he taught at Douglas School of Art; in 1897, moved to London, first teaching at Redhill School of Art; was assisted in his metalwork by Christopher Dresser; from 1898, designed for Liberty; was the inspiration behind Liberty's *Cymric* and *Tudric* patterns that were influential in the Celtic revival of the 1890s; designed silver that was among the most refined of

the Edwardian era. From 1899 at Liberty, he designed interlace decoration, enamel work, Donegal carpets (produced c1902), pottery, and textiles; in 1898, designed textiles for Silver Studio, which he also used as an agency for his designs; in 1899, became design master at the Art School, Kingston-upon-Thames; designed 1917 gravestone of Arthur Lasenby Liberty; 1900–04, lived on the Isle of Man, sending his designs to Liberty. His work was sold at Liberty until the 1930s, although Knox stopped designing for the firm before World War I. He taught 1906–07 at Wimbledon Art School. In 1912, he visited the USA, where he designed carpets for Bromley, Philadelphia, and lectured at Pennsylvania School of Industrial Art. In 1911, he founded the Knox Guild of Craft and Design, which lasted until 1939. In 1913, he returned to the Isle of Man, where he painted and taught.
▶ Charlotte Gere, *American and European Jewelry 1830–1914*, New York: Crown, 1975:32,98,256. Peter Dormer (intro.), *The Illustrated Dictionary of 20th-Century Designers: The Key Personalities in Design and the Applied Arts*, New York: Mallard, 1991.

Kobayashi, Masakazu (1944–)
▶ Japanese textile designer.
▶ Studied University of Arts, Kyoto.
▶ 1966–75, he worked as a textile designer for Kawashima; manifested traditional textile techniques and aesthetics in his work; executed both production fabrics and large-scale fiber works. The repeated lines and stripes of his 1982 *Space Age* fabric by Sangetsu evoked *komon*, a textile-dyeing technique which uses paper patterns with small motifs. Other works suggestive of traditional weavings included 1977 *W to the Third Power* and, with threads suspended in frame, 1979 *Meditation*.
▶ Mildred Constantine and Jack Lenor Larsen, *Beyond Craft: The Art Fabric*, New York, 1973:20–21,42–43,190,197,263. Cat., Kathryn B. Hiesinger and George H. Marcus III (eds.), *Design Since 1945*, Philadelphia: Philadelphia Museum of Art, 1983.

Kobayashi, Mitsugi (1932–)
▶ Japanese glass designer.
▶ Studied Tokyo University of Arts to 1957.
▶ Kobayashi was a trustee, Japan Glass Art Crafts Association; associate member, 'Nitten' (Japan Fine Arts Exhibition), Tokyo; member, Japan Modern Decorative Arts Association; and juror of 1989 'Japan Modern Decorative Arts,' Tokyo.
▶ Received Governor's Prize at 1980 'Japan Modern Decorative Arts,' Tokyo, and Prize of Modern Decorative Arts at 1973 'Japan Modern Decorative Arts.' Work shown at 1978 'Modern Decorative Arts in Japan,' National Museum of Modern Art, Tokyo; 1982 'World Glass Now '82,' Hokkaido Museum of Modern Art, Sapporo; 1985 'New Glass in Japan,' Badisches Landesmuseum, Karlsruhe; 1990 'Glass '90 in Japan,' Tokyo; 1991 (V) Triennale of Japan Glass Art Crafts Association, Heller Gallery, New York. Work subject of 1986 exhibition at Nogoya, Tokyo.
▶ Cat., *Glass Japan*, New York: Heller Gallery and Japan Glass Art Crafts Association, 1991: No. 17.

Københavns Lervarefabrik
▶ Danish ceramics factory.
▶ The factory was managed by G. Eifrig, former head potter at J. Walmann's pottery, Utterslev Mark (Denmark). At both Købehavens Lervarefabrik and Walmann, painters experimented with ceramics as part of the Danish Skønvirke arts movement. 1883–90, Thorvald Bindesbøll, a Skønvirke proponent, worked at Walmann, and 1891–1901, at Københavns Lervarefabrik.
▶ Jennifer Hawkins Opie, *Scandinavia: Ceramics and Glass in the Twentieth Century*, New York: Rizzoli, 1989.

Koch, Mogens (1898–)
▶ Danish architect and designer.
▶ Studied architecture, Det Kongelige Danske Kunstakademi, Copenhagen, to 1925.
▶ 1950–68, he was professor, Det Kongelige Danske Kunstakademi, in 1956, visiting lecturer, Massachusetts Institute of Technology, Cambridge, Massachusetts, and, in 1962, at Industrial Art

Institute, Tokyo. In 1934, he set up his own design office; designed the 1932 *Safari* chair, still in production today by Interna in Frederikssund (Denmark); designed a range of objects, including furniture for Rasmussens Snedkerier, Ivan Schlechter, Cado, Danish CWS, and Interna; carpets; fittings; silver; and fabrics for use in the restoration of Danish churches. He published the book *Modern Danish Arts — Craftsmanship* (1948).
▶ His work was regularly shown at the Triennali di Milano and included in the 1925 Paris 'Exposition Internationale des Arts Décoratifs et Industriels Modernes,' 1937 Paris 'Exposition Internationale des Arts Décoratifs et Techniques dans la Vie Moderne,' 1958 'Formes Scandinaves' at the Paris Musée des Arts Décoratifs, 1960–61 USA 'The Arts of Denmark' traveling exhibition, 1968 'Two Centuries of Danish Design' at the Victoria and Albert Museum, London. He received the 1938 Eckersberg Medal and 1963 C.F. Hansen Medal.
▶ Arne Karlsen, Axel Thygesen, *Om Mogens Koch Arbejder*, Copenhagen 1965. Erik Zahle, *Scandinavian Domestic Design*, London, 1968. Axel Thygesen, *Tilegnet Mogens Koch . . .*, Copenhagen, 1968. Cat., *Les Assises du siège contemporain*, Paris: Musée des Arts Décoratifs, 1968. Cat., *Modern Chairs 1918–1970*, London: Lund Humphries, 1971. Frederik Sieck, *Nutidig Dansk Møbeldesign:—en kortfattet illustreret beskrivelse*, Copenhagen: Bondo Gravesen, 1881; 1990 Busck edition in English. Cat., David Revere McFadden (ed.), *Scandinavian Modern Design 1880–1980*, New York: Abrams, 1982:267, No. 126.

Koch und Bergfeld
▶ German silversmithy.
▶ Koch und Bergfeld was founded in 1829 in Bremen. Before 1910, Christoph Kay trained there. 1900–10, it produced the designs of Hugo Leven, Albin Müller, and Henry van de Velde and, in the 1920s and 1930s, the designs of Gustav Elsass and Bernhard Hötger, although it attached less importance than other smithies to working with renowned independent artists. Court jeweler Theodor Müller designed the 335-piece dinner service for the marriage of Grand Duke Louis IV of Hesse-Darmstadt; the commission was given to Koch und Bergfeld. The head of the firm's design studio was Heinrich von der Cammer who, in 1904, was succeeded by sculptor Hugo Leven. In 1909, Leven left for the directorship of the Königliche Preussische Zeichenakademie, Hanau, and was succeeded by Gustav Elsass. Leven was kept on as an artistic advisor. Wilhelm Wagenfeld first trained as a silversmith in the Koch und Bergfeld factory. In 1989, Koch und Bergfeld was bought by Villeroy et Boch.
▶ Work (Müller's centerpieces for Hesse-Darmstadt and two other services, including the silver designs of Albin Müller) shown at 1910 Brussels 'Exposition Universelle et Internationale.'
▶ Annelies Krekel-Aalberse, *Art Nouveau and Art Déco Silver*, New York: Abrams, 1989:134,136,140,141,150,256. Cat., *Metallkunst*, Berlin: Bröhan Museum, 1990:346–55.

Koehler, Florence (1861–1944)
▶ American artist, craftsperson, designer, and jeweler, active Chicago.
▶ After the turn of the century in Chicago, Koehler's jewelry in a crafts style was fashionable in artistic circles. Koehler became one of the leaders of the American crafts-revival in jewelry, related more to French than English styles.
▶ Charlotte Gere, *American and European Jewelry 1830–1914*, New York: Crown, 1975:200.

Koenig, Giovanni Klaus (1924–)
▶ Italian architect, designer, and teacher; born Turin.
▶ Koenig collaborated with Roberto Segoni; designed 1970 *Jumbo Tram* (produced from 1975), Milan; 1977 underground train, Rome; *Ale 804* and *Ale 884* express trains; wrote on Modern architecture and design; taught architecture, Università di Firenze.
▶ Paolo Portoghesi (ed.), *Dizionario Enciclopedico di Architettura e Urbanistica*, Vol. III, Rome, 1968:301. Vittorio Gregotti, *Il disegno del prodotto industriale: Italia 1860–1980*, Milan, 1982:

300,367—368. Hans Wichmann, *Italien Design 1945 bis heute*, Munich: Die Neue Sammlung, 1988.

Kofod-Larsen, Ib (1921–)
▶ Danish architect and designer.
▶ Studied architecture, Det Kongelige Danske Kunstakademi, Copenhagen.
▶ His furniture designs were produced in the 1950s by Fritz Hansen.
▶ Received annual prize, Danish Cabinetmakers' Guild; first prize, 1948 Holmegårds Glasvaerks competition.
▶ Frederik Sieck, *Nutidig Dansk Møbeldesign: - en kortfattet illustreret beskrivelse*, Copenhagen: Bondo Gravesen; 1990 Busck edition in English.

Kogoj, Oskar (1942–)
▶ Yugoslav industrial designer.
▶ Studied industrial design, Instituto Statale d'Arte, Venice to 1966.
▶ He first became known for his 1968 *Red Object* plastic wagon; focusing on organic forms primarily in plastic, designed cutlery, kitchenware, furniture, and children's toys. His ergonomic approach was manifested in his *Gondola* range of easy chairs, for which he developed a pattern from impressions of the seated human body, and in his plastic cutlery.
▶ Work (cutlery) shown at 1983–84 'Design Since 1945' exhibition, Philadelphia Museum of Art.
▶ 'Design in Action: Prototype Plastic Flatware,' *Industrial Design*, Vol. 19, Oct. 1972:60—61. 'Child Care,' *Industrial Design*, Vol. 24, May 1977:49—51. Cat., Kathryn B. Hiesinger and George H. Marcus III (eds.), *Design Since 1945*, Philadelphia: Philadelphia Museum of Art, 1983.

Kohlmann, Étienne (1903–)
▶ French designer and interior decorator; born and active Paris.
▶ Studied École Boulle, Paris to 1922.
▶ He was an accomplished cabinetmaker from an early age; in 1922, worked for a furniture manufacturer in the Faubourg Saint-Antoine, Paris; 1924—38, (with Maurice Matet) was director of the Studium decorating department of Grands Magasins du Louvre, Paris; at the Studium-Louvre, sometimes collaborated on designs with Maurice Matet and Dubard, and became artistic director. His work included deluxe interiors and the lounge of the 1926 oceanliner *Île-de-France* a number of Paris shop interiors for Mobilier National, and (often with architect Barrot) numerous private commissions. From 1928, he included metal in his furniture designs. The rugs, upholstery fabrics, and murals for his interior décors were produced by Mlle. Max Vibert. In 1934, he designed the offices of the laboratories of Dr. Debat, Garches, and commissions including stores, hotels, restaurants and numerous residences. On his less-than-successful lighting for the Studium-Louvre, he received occasional technical assistance from Jean Lévy and from lighting engineer P. Juget. Kohlmann designed lighting produced by Holophane. By 1954, his workshop was located at 22 quai du Louvre, Paris.
▶ Work shown at Salons of Société des Artistes Décorateurs from 1924 until the late 1930s, sessions of Salon d'Automne from 1923, and 1947 session of Salon des Tuileries. Participated in the Studium-Louvre pavilion at 1925 Paris 'Exposition Internationale des Arts Décoratifs et Industriels Modernes' and at 1931 Paris 'Exposition Coloniale'; 1934 (II) and 1935 (III) (Holophane fixtures) Salon of Light; 1939 'New York World's Fair'; 1937 Paris 'Exposition Internationale des Arts et Techniques dans la Vie Moderne.' Work (a lacquered metal chandelier and wall brackets by F. Gagneau) shown at 1937 Paris Exposition, where Kohlmann and Eugène Printz designed the general illumination of the corridors and vestibules of the Pavilion of Light.
▶ Léon Deshairs, *Modern French Decorative Art*, Paris: Albert Lévy. F. Henriot, *Luminaire*, 1937: plate 42. G. Janneau, *Le Luminaire et les Moyens d'éclairage Nouveaux*, first series: plates 32,36. *Ensembles Mobiliers*, Paris: Charles Moreau, Vol. 6, Nos.

44—48; Nos. 35—36, 1954. Alastair Duncan, *Art Nouveau and Art Déco Lighting*, New York: Simon and Schuster, 1978:175,181. Pierre Kjellberg, *Art Déco: les maîtres du Mobilier, le décor des Paquebots*, Paris: Amateur, 1986:103—06.

Kohn, J. und J.
▶ Moravian furniture manufacturer.
▶ Michael Thonet lost his monopoly for producing bentwood furniture in 1869 due to the expiry of his patent. In 1850, the Kohn family founded a lumber-producing firm in Holleschau, Moravia (now Holešov, Czech Republic) where local craftspeople were hired. In 1867, Jacob Kohn went into partnership with son Josef, forming Jacob und Josef Kohn. In 1869, the firm built its first factories in Wsetin and Litsch; in 1870, began production; with its business growing rapidly, established a manufacturing facility in Teschen, Austrian Silesia (now Těšin, Czech Republic/ Cieszyn, Poland) in 1871 and in Crakow (now Poland) and Gross-Poremba, with smaller facilities in Ratibor and Keltsch in Moravia and Wagstadt (now Bilovec), Skotschau, and Jablunkau (now Jablonka, Poland) in Silesia; became Thonet's major competitor, although by 1893 there were more than 50 bentwood-furniture firms; by 1882, had important branches in Berlin, Hamburg, London, and Paris. Large factories were constructed in Nowo-Radomsko (Poland) in 1884 and Holleschau in 1890. Copying Thonet's styles at first, by 1900, Kohn had begun manufacturing bentwood pieces designed by architects including Gustav Siegel, a pupil of Josef Hoffmann. In 1899, Siegel was appointed head of the design department. He and Wagner were probably responsible for the early Art Nouveau models by Kohn. Kohn played an important role in architect-designed bentwood furniture and produced the first architect-designed bentwood chair by Adolf Loos for the billiard room of 1899 Café Museum, Vienna. Kohn's success at the 1900 Paris 'Exposition Universelle' ushered in the production of furniture by eminent architects including Josef Hoffmann, Koloman Moser, and Otto Wagner. Other designers included Marcel Kammerer, Josef Urban, and Leopold Bauer. By 1904, Kohn's 6,300 employees produced 5,500 pieces of furniture daily in 407 different models in four facilities. In 1914, the firm merged with Mundus and, in 1918, moved to Zürich. Thonet merged with Kohn in 1922 and operated under the name Mundus-Commerce and Industrial Society in 1923, with 20 factories and 10,000 workers. In 1932, 'Kohn' disappeared from the firm's name in Germany.
▶ Work shown at 1876 Philadelphia 'Centennial Exhibition.' Received a grand prize (rooms by Siegel including furniture by Moser) at 1900 Paris 'Exposition Universelle.'
▶ Giovanna Massobrio and Paolo Portoghesi, *La Seggiola di Vienna*, Turin, 1976. *Jacob und Josef Kohn: Der Katalog von 1916*, Munich: Graham Day, 1980. Jessica Rutherford, *Art Nouveau, Art Deco and the Thirties: The Furniture Collections at Brighton Museum*, Brighton: The Royal Pavilion, Art Gallery and Museums, 1983:8. Graham Day, 'The Development of the Bent-Wood Furniture Industry, 1869–1914,' in Derek E. Ostergard (ed.), *Bent Wood and Metal Furniture 1850–1946*, New York: The American Federation of Arts, 1987.

Kokko, Valto (1933–)
▶ Finnish designer.
▶ In 1963, Kokko began working at the Iittala glassworks as a designer of lighting fixtures; subsequently, as head of the visual department, designed packaging, exhibitions, and promotional literature and supervised photography and industrial films; from the late 1970s, became active in the design of domestic utilitarian glassware, including the 1979 *Otso* drinking glass pattern.

Kollmar und Jourdan
▶ German jeweler; located Pforzheim.
▶ The firm was founded in 1885 by Emil Kollmar (1860–1939) and Wilhelm Jourdan to produce gold-plated (*or doublé*) chains; later added a range of gold-plated jewelry including pendants, brooches and black-and-white geometrically styled clips. Its pieces

were designed in Egyptian, Persian, and Japanese styles. In 1902, the firm built a new factory; by 1925, employed more than 1,800 workers. The factory was destroyed during World War II and subsequently rebuilt by Kollmar's son Max. The firm went out of business in 1977.

▶ Deanna F. Cera (ed.), *Jewels of Fantasy: Costume Jewelry of the 20th Century*, New York: Abrams, 1992:108.

Komai, Ray (1918–)
▶ American graphic, industrial, and interior designer.
▶ Studied interior, industrial, and graphic design, Art Center College, Los Angeles.
▶ He settled in New York in 1944 where he worked in advertising; in 1948, (with Carter Winter) set up a graphic-design and advertising office. Komai's 1949 molded plywood chair with a split seat and bent-metal legs was produced by J.G. Furniture, which also produced his other chairs, tables, and upholstered seating designs. From c1945, he designed wallpaper and textiles in figurative and abstract motifs (inspired by paintings by Pablo Picasso, Paul Klee, and Cubist painters) for Laverne International, New York. From 1952–60, he was associate art director for Advertising Forum; from 1963–76, designer at United States Information Agency and produced cultural exhibitions in Germany, Austria, India, and Japan.
▶ Received 1950 'Good Design' award (1949 split-seat chair) at New York Museum of Art. Work (plywood chair and textiles by Laverne) shown at 1983–84 'Design Since 1945' exhibition, Philadelphia Museum of Art.
▶ W.J. Hennessey, *Modern Furnishings for the Home*, New York, Vol. 1, 1952:115,272,278. George Nelson (ed.), *Chairs*, New York: Whitney Library of Ideas, 1953:59,92,155. Cat., Kathryn B. Hiesinger and George H. Marcus III (eds.), *Design Since 1945*, Philadelphia: Philadelphia Museum of Art, 1983. Cherie Fehrman and Kenneth Fehrman, *Postwar Interior Design, 1945–1960*, New York: Van Nostrand Reinhold, 1987. Martin Eidelberg (ed.), *Design 1935–65, What Modern Was*, New York: Le Musée des Arts Décoratifs de Montréal and Abrams, 1991.

Kongsberg
▶ Norwegian ceramics factory.
▶ The Kongsberg workshop was established in 1947 by potter Rolf Hansen. In the beginning, some of Hansen's students and various potters participated with him at the workshop, where he later worked alone.
▶ Jennifer Hawkins Opie, *Scandinavia: Ceramics and Glass in the Twentieth Century*, New York: Rizzoli, 1989.

König, Friedrich (1857–1941)
▶ Austrian painter, graphic artist, and designer; born and active Vienna.
▶ König was a founding member of the Vienna Sezession.
▶ Robert Waissenberger, *Vienna 1890–1920*, Secaucus, NJ: Wellfleet 1984:267.

Koolhaas, Rem (1944–)
▶ Dutch architect; born Rotterdam.
▶ From 1965, studied Architectural Association, London.
▶ After working as a copywriter in the Netherlands, he studied architecture in London and worked with Elia Zenghelis. In 1965, they became partners in OMA (Office for Metropolitan Architecture) and were joined by artists Zoe Zenghelis and Modelon Vriesendorp. The group was influenced by disparate disciplines and forms including the work of neo-Suprematist Ivan Leonidov and the Continuous Monument of the 1960s of Aldolfo Natalini and Superstudio. Koolhaas and Zenghelis entered the 1975 competition for the housing complex on Roosevelt Island in New York. In the mid-1970s, Koolhaas collaborated with Laurinda Spear on 1979 Spear house, Miami Beach, Florida, completed by Spear's firm Arquitectonica. Koolhaas published *Delirious New York: A Retroactive Manifesto for Manhattan* (1978), which presented fantasy projects reflecting OMA's philosophy. OMA's work included 1978 Parliament extension (with Zaha Hadid), The Hague, and 1981 design submitted for 1984 'Internationale Bauausstellung,' Berlin.
▶ 'OMA,' *Architectural Design*, Vol. 47, No. 5, 1977. Cat., *OMA Projects 1978–1981*, London, 1981. Kenneth Frampton in Vittorio Magnago Lampugnani (ed.), *Encyclopedia of 20th-Century Architecture*, New York: Abrams, 1986:190–91.

Kopka, Alfred (1894–1987)
▶ German metalworker.
▶ Studied Kunstgewerbeschule, Berlin, under Josef Wilm.
▶ Kopka became director in 1921 of the metal workshop, the Bauhaus, Dessau; taught metalwork at Vereinigte Staatsschulen für freie und angewandte Kunst (formerly the Kunstgewerbeschule), Berlin, and, 1923–31, in Breslau (now Wroclaw, Poland).
▶ Work (chased service) shown at 1922 'Deutsche Gewerbeschau,' Berlin.
▶ Annelies Krekel-Aalberse, *Art Nouveau and Art Déco Silver*, New York: Abrams, 1989:144,256. Cat., *Die Metallwerkstatt am Bauhaus*, Berlin: Bauhaus-Archiv, 1992:317.

Koppel, Henning (1918–81)
▶ Danish designer.
▶ 1936–37, studied at the sculptors' school of Det Kongelige Danske Kunstakademi, Copenhagen; 1938–39, Académie Ranson, Paris, under Malfrey.
▶ He was a refugee in Stockholm 1940–45, when he designed silver and gold jewelry for the first time and worked for both Svenski Tenn and Orrefors. He became associated with Georg Jensen Sølvesmedie from 1945–81, Bing & Grøndahl Porcelaensfabrik 1961–81, freelance at Louis Poulsen (lighting and clocks) from 1967, and freelance at Orrefors Glasbruk from 1971. He designed the 1962 *Form 24* tea set by Bing & Grøndahl; was best known for his sleek sculptural designs, particularly the silver items produced for Jensen over a 35-year period. In the 1950s, his style came to fruition in his expressive and languorous silver work. His innovative designs varied from abstract and glamorous tea-coffee sets with limpid handles and sensuous spouts in silver to inexpensive amorphic pieces in stainless steel. His 1954 silver fish dish with a cover for Jensen was widely published and exhibited.
▶ Received numerous awards including 1953 Lunning Prize (with Tias Eckhoff); gold medals at 1951 (IX), 1954 (X), and 1957 (XI) Triennali di Milano; and 1963 International Design Award (Jensen tableware), American Institute of Designers. He was a featured designer at 1966 'Centenary Exhibition,' Goldsmiths' Hall, London. Work (silver) shown at 1954–57 USA 'Design in Scandinavia' traveling exhibition; 1956–59 'Neue Form aus Dänemark' traveling German exhibition; 1958 'Formes Scandinaves,' Paris Musée des Arts Décoratifs; 1960–61 'The Arts of Denmark' traveling USA exhibition; 1975 'Adventures in Swedish Glass,' Australia.
▶ Arne Karlsen, *Made in Denmark*, New York, 1960:38–43,141,150,152. Viggo Sten Møller, *Henning Koppel*, Copenhagen, 1965. Graham Hughes, *Modern Silver throughout the World*, New York, 1967:237, plates 22–31. *Henning Koppel in D B & D*, Copenhagen: Danish Society of Arts and Crafts and Industrial Design, 1972:7–10. Cat., *Georg Jensen Silversmithy: 77 Artists, 75 Years*, Washington: Renwick Gallery, 1980. Cat., David Revere McFadden (ed.), *Scandinavian Modern Design 1880–1980*, New York: Abrams, 1982:267, Nos. 185,192. Cat., Kathryn B. Hiesinger and George H. Marcus III (eds.), *Design Since 1945*, Philadelphia: Philadelphia Museum of Art, 1983. Cat., *The Lunning Prize*, Stockholm: Nationalmuseum, 1986:54–57. Jennifer Hawkins Opie, *Scandinavia: Ceramics and Glass in the Twentieth Century*, New York: Rizzoli, 1989.

Köpping, Karl (1848–1914)
▶ German painter, graphic designer, and chemist.
▶ Studied chemistry, Akademie der bildenden Künste, Munich.

▶ His first work involved reproductive engraving in Berlin. In 1890, he returned to etching; in 1890, became head of Meisterateliers für Kupferstich und Radierung (Master Studios for Engraving and Etching) at the Akademie, Berlin; from the end of the 1890s, executed fragile, iridescent flower-form glass in the Art Nouveau style. Much of his work was made by Friedrich Zitzmann, Wiesbaden. Beginning in 1896, Köpping became editor of *Pan*, which was devoted to Art Nouveau and reproduced images of his own glass and etchings; from 1896, first began to design glass objects in vegetal forms with high stems; also in 1896, worked for a short time with Friedrich Zitzmann; from 1898, designed unusual glass objects, including drinking glasses.

▶ Cat., Helmut Ricke, *Reflex der Jahrhunderte: Die Glassammlung des Kunstmuseums Düsseldorf*, Leipzig: Museum des Kunsthandwerks Grassimuseum, 1989:213.

Kopriva, Erna (b. Ernestine Kopriva 1894–1984)

▶ Austrian ceramicist; born Vienna.
▶ 1914–19, studied Kunstgewerbeschule, Vienna, under A. Hanak, Josef Hoffmann, and Oskar Strnad.
▶ In 1919–28, Kopriva was among the women ceramicists who gained importance in the the Wiener Werkstätte; from 1928, was an assistant of Josef Hoffmann at Kunstgewerbeschule in textile design; from 1944, was a teacher at Werkstätte für Stoffdruck und Tapeten at Kunstgewerbeschule and, from 1953, a professor there.
▶ Günther Feuerstein, Vienna—Present and Past: Arts and Crafts—Applied Art—Design, Vienna: Jugend und Volk, 1976. Cat., *Expressive Keramik der Wiener Werkstätte 1917–1930*, Munich: Bayerische Vereinsbank, 1992:1130–31.

Kørbing, Kay (1915–)

▶ Danish furniture designer.
▶ Studied Teknisk Skole, Copenhagen to 1938; architecture, Det Kongelige Danske Akademi, Copenhagen, to 1942.
▶ Some of his furniture designs were produced by Gotfred H. Pedersen, including a 1955 fiberglass side chair with bent tubular metal legs.
▶ Frederik Sieck, *Nutidig Dansk Møbeldesign:—en kortfattet illustreret beskrivelse*, Copenhagen: Bondo Gravesen, 1981.

Korhonen, Harri (1946–)

▶ Finnish designer; born Helsinki.
▶ Korhonen designed furniture and lighting; ran Inno-tuote Oy; like manufacturers Vivero and Avarte, produced furniture in Minimalist forms in the style of Charles Eames's early work and that of Gerrit Rietveld; pursued a witty approach manifested in his 1985 couch-chair-lamp combination produced by Inno.
▶ Robert A.M. Stern (ed.), *The International Design Yearbook*, New York: Abbeville, 1985/1986: Nos. 133,135.

Korschann, Charles (1872–)

▶ Moravian sculptor, decorator, and medalist; born Brün (now Brno, Czech Republic).
▶ Studied schools of fine art in Vienna, Berlin, and Copenhagen.
▶ He lived in Paris 1894–1906, Berlin and Frankfurt 1906–14, and Crakow 1914–19; returning to Brno, became a professor. In Paris, he executed a series of small Art Nouveau bronzes, many cast by the foundry Lochet. His wares included objects in bronze and plaster, including clocks, inkwells, centerpieces, and lighting. He was known for his portrait busts of famous people, including one of Alphonse Mucha in 1904 for the Moravian Museum in Brno.
▶ Work shown at various exhibitions including Salons of Société des Artistes français 1894–1905.
▶ *Allgemeines Lexikon der Bildenden Künstler*, 1955. Cat., G. Woeckel, *Jugendstilsammlung*, Kassel: Staatliche Kunstsammlungen, 1968. Yvonne Brunhammer et al., *Art Nouveau Belgium*,

France, Houston: Institute for the Arts, Rice University, 1976. Alastair Duncan, *Art Nouveau and Art Déco Lighting*, New York: Simon and Schuster, 1978:123.

Korsmo, Arne (1990–68)

▶ Norwegian interior, furniture, and exhibition designer, and teacher.
▶ Studied Norges Tekniskne Högskole, Trondheim.
▶ He set up his own design office in 1929; 1936–56, was director of Statens Håndverks -og Kunstindustriskole, Oslo; from 1956, was a professor at the Norges Tekniskne Högskole; in 1953, designed wood and bent metal tubular furniture and flatware for J. Tostrup, Oslo.
▶ Received a grand prize and gold medal at 1954 (X) Triennale di Milano. Designed Norwegian section at 1937 Paris 'Exposition Internationale des Arts et Techniques dans la Vie Moderne' and at 1954 (X) Triennale di Milano.
▶ Cat., David Revere McFadden (ed.), *Scandinavian Modern Design 1880–1980*, New York: Abrams, 1982:267, No. 144. Fredrik Wildhagen, *Norge i Form*, Oslo: Stenersen, 1988:102.

Kortzau, Ole (1939–)

▶ Danish designer.
▶ Kortzau studied architecture.
▶ He worked with textiles, graphics, porcelain, and silver; from 1971, was active in his own design studio; in 1978, designed for the Royal Copenhagen Porcelain manufactory; in 1978, began designing silver hollow-ware for the Georg Jensen Sølvsmedie; from c1978, worked for Holmegård Glasvaerk.
▶ Cat., *Georg Jensen Silversmithy: 77 Artists, 75 Years*, Washington: Smithsonian Institution Press, 1980. Jennifer Hawkins Opie, *Scandinavia: Ceramics and Glass in the Twentieth Century*, New York: Rizzoli, 1989.

Kosta Boda

▶ Swedish glass manufacturer.
▶ The forests of fir and birch trees used in glass-furnaces attracted glassmakers to the Swedish villages of Boda, Johansfors, and Åfors in the early 18th century. In 1742, a glass factory was established and named for county governors A. Koskull and Bogislaus Stål von Holstein. At first, the main product was window glass made by German craftsmen. It soon became Sweden's leading producer of household glass. Boda was founded in 1864, Åfors in 1876, both by glassblowers from Kosta. The three merged in 1946. From the turn of the century, designers included Gunnar Wennerberg, Alf Wallander, Edvin Ollers, Elis Bergh. Kosta commissioned Wennerberg to design carved cameo-glass vessels in c1900. Kosta Boda produced a much-copied design for a drinking glass with a bubble incorporated into its thick base, produced in 1938 as the *Pippi* glass. In 1950, Vicke Lindstrand (formerly of Orrefors) became artistic director. From 1953, notable artwares were designed by Lindstrand, Erik Hoglund, Ulrica Hydma-Vallien, Bertil Vallien, Ann Wärff (later Ann Worff), Goran Wärff, and Signe Persson-Merlin. Goran Wärff designed the early-1970s range of flashed glass bowls with transparent layers peeled back by means of an etching process which exposed color layers beneath. Boda Nova was established in 1970 to produce ceramics, textiles, cork, fire-proof glass, and stainless steel goods. In 1970, Kosta Boda was renamed Åforsgruppen; in 1972, acquired by Johansfors; in 1975, amalgamated into Upsala-Ekeby and renamed Kosta Boda; in 1977, it acquired Skruf and Målerås Glasbruk from Royal Krona; in 1981, established the Boda Smide forging department; in 1983 was acquired by Proventus.
▶ Work shown internationally, beginning with 1900 Paris 'Exposition Universelle.'
▶ Frederick Cooke, *Glass: Twentieth-Century Design*, New York: Dutton: 1986:50. Jennifer Hawkins Opie, *Scandinavia: Ceramics and Glass in the Twentieth Century*, New York: Rizzoli, 1989. Peter Dormer (intro.), *The Illustrated Dictionary of 20th-Century Designers: The Key Personalities in Design and the Applied Arts*, New York: Mallard, 1991.

Kotal, Karl (1920–) and **Herma Kotal** (1925–)
▶ Austrian furniture designers; born Vienna; husband and wife.
▶ Along with Peter and Maria Tölzer and Oskar Payer, the Kotals were known for their affordable furniture in the postwar period in Vienna.
▶ Günther Feuerstein, *Vienna—Present and Past: Arts and Crafts—Applied Art—Design*, Vienna: Jugend und Volk, 1976:61,80.

Kotarbinski, Mieczylas (1890–1943)
▶ Polish painter and graphic artist.
▶ Studied schools of fine art, Warsaw and Cracow.
▶ In the 1920s, he taught at School of Applied Arts, Warsaw.
▶ He designed the study-office (produced by Michel Herodeck, Warsaw) in a kind of Cubist style using rare Polish woods at 1925 Paris 'Exposition Internationale des Arts Décoratifs et Industriels Modernes.'
▶ Maurice Dufrêne, *Ensembles Mobiliers*, Paris: Charles Moreau, 1925, Woodbridge: Antique Collectors' Club edition 1989:160.

Kotěra, Jan (1871–1923)
▶ Moravian architect; born Brünn (now Brno, Czech Republic).
▶ Studied Baugewerbeschule, Pilsen (now Plzeň, Czech Republic), and, 1894–97, Akademie der bildenden Künste, Vienna, under Otto Wagner.
▶ His 1906–12 municipal museum, Königgrätz (now Hradec Králové, Czech Republic), was the first structure in Europe to apply the ideas of Frank Lloyd Wright. 1900–10, Kotěra exerted a major influence on Modern architecture in Czechoslovakia; became a member of the Siebener Club, Vienna; 1898–10, was a professor, Academy of Applied Arts, Prague; 1910–23, professor, School of Fine Arts, Prague. 1898–1903, students in his studio pursued glass design. His 1903 punchbowl, refined in 1910, was a milestone in Modern glass design. In 1898, Kotěra designed railway carriage interiors for Ringhoffer and, subsequently, a number of private and public interiors including restaurants and banks. His furniture designs combined a Modernist attitude with a master's conception of detail. His buildings included 1905–16 water tower, Prague; 1905–07 National House, Prossnitz (now Prostějov); 1913 Lemberger Palais, Lwów (now Poland).
▶ Jan Kotěra, *Práce má a mých žáků 1898–1901* (*My and my pupils' work 1898–1901*), Vienna, 1901:168. Cat., *Czechoslovakia Glass 1350–1980*, New York: Dover, 1981. Vladimír Šlapeta, *Czech Functionalism*, London: Architectural Association, 1987:8.

Kotík, Jan (1916–)
▶ Czech glassware designer; born Turnau (now Turnov).
▶ 1935–41, studied Academy of Applied Arts, Prague, under Benda.
▶ Kotík produced free-blown forms made at the Plastic Art Center of the Glassworks at Nový Bor. 1949–64, his work, sometimes engraved by Čestmír Čejnar, showed an advanced sense of the possibilities of glass. He was active at Nový Bor at the same time as René Roubíček in off-hand shaped glass, engraved glass, and glass panels in dramatic three-dimensional forms.
▶ Work shown at 1958 Brussels World's Fair; 1957 (XI) and 1960 (XII) Triennali di Milano.
▶ Cat., *Czechoslovakia Glass 1350–1980*, New York: Dover, 1981:168. Frederick Cooke, *Glass: Twentieth-Century Design*, New York: Dutton, 1986:90.

Kræn, Anette (1945–)
▶ Danish designer.
▶ 1967–69, studied Danish College of Jewelry, Silversmithing and Commercial Design; in Germany and Switzerland to 1974.
▶ In 1978, she began working for the Georg Jensen Sølvsmedie.
▶ Work shown at several exhibitions and received awards.
▶ Cat., *Georg Jensen Silversmithy: 77 Artists, 75 Years*, Washington: Smithsonian Institution Press, 1980.

Krajevski, Max (1901–71)
▶ Polish metalworker and architect.
▶ Studied Bauhaus, Dessau, to 1927.

▶ He left Poland for Germany in 1919; worked as a metalworker in the Ruhr until 1923, when he became active as a watercolorist; for a time, was a mining-engineer trainee; while at the Bauhaus, designed lighting, tables, tea services, marionettes, and other small objects; worked in the office of architect Walter Gropius, Berlin; subsequently, was responsible for the construction of housing in Törten; in 1929, became chief of the lumberyard in Karsruhe on the construction of the city of Dammerstock; in 1931, settled in Moscow and worked as an architect.
▶ Lionel Richard, *Encyclopédie du Bauhaus*, Paris: Somogy, 1985:198–99.

Kramer, Ferdinand (1898–1985)
▶ German architect and furniture designer; active Frankfurt.
▶ Studied Bauhaus, Weimar, 1919; 1919–22, architecture in Munich.
▶ In 1920, he became a member of the Deutscher Werkbund; worked at the Hochbauamt, Frankfurt, under Ernst May, and was subsequently made artistic director. The 1925–26 *Kramer-Ofen* ('Kramer-Stove') was produced by Buderus. He managed the municipal architecture department of Frankfurt; designed 'type' furniture (*typenmöbel*) produced by Hausrat for new housing developments. A smaller version of his 1927 black-lacquered bentwood side chair for Thonet was used in Frankfurt elementary schools. In 1938, he moved to the USA and worked in the studios of Norman Bel Geddes and of Kahn and Jacobs, New York; in 1946, became a member of the American Institute of Architects; designed the *Rainbelle* furniture range produced 1948–51; in 1952, returned to Germany and became director of the architecture department, Frankfurt University.
▶ Ferdinand Kramer, 'Die Thonet Industrie,' *Die Form*, No. IV, 1929. Barbie Campbell-Cole and Tim Benton (eds.), *Tubular Steel Furniture*, London: The Art Book Company, 1979:12. Cat., *The Bauhaus: Masters and Students*, New York: Barry Friedman, 1988. Cat., *Ferdinand Kramer*, Der Charme des Systematischen, Zürich: Museum für Gestaltung, 1991.

Krásná jizba družstevní práce (aka KJ)
(Cooperative Work's The Beautiful Room)
▶ Czech design studio.
▶ Active 1927–48, KJ was established by the publishing house Družstevní práce to sell arts and crafts, decorative arts, graphic design, and objects for the home. Its first director was painter Emanuel Frinta. From 1929, Ladislav Sutnar was its artistic director. KJ was influential in encouraging the acceptance of Modern design, partly through the magazine *Panorama*, co-edited by Sutnar and with Josef Sudek as publicity photographer. In the late 1920s, KJ began a successful collaboration with a group of young designers and artists. Similar to the 1927 'Weissenhof-Siedlung' exhibition, Stuttgart, the 1928 'Výstava soudobé kultury' (Exhibition of Contemporary Culture) in Brno was an important turning-point. KJ sold designs by Sutnar, Ludvika Smrčková, Bohumil Južnič, Ladislav Žák, Antonín Kybal, Jan Vaněk, Jan Emil Koula, and others; lighting fixtures produced by the firm Inwald; tubular-steel furniture from Thonet-Mundus designed by Marcel Breuer; and textiles, ceramics, and lighting from the Bauhaus. From 1936, KJ was located in the center of Prague in a Functionalist building at Národní třída 36. In 1948, it was amalgamated with the Center for Art and Folk Crafts and lost its commitment to Modern design.
▶ A. Adlerová, *České užité umění 1918–1938*, Prague, 1983.

Krasnik, Antoinette
▶ Austrian painter and designer; active Vienna.
▶ Studied Kunstgewerbeschule, Vienna, under Koloman Moser.
▶ While at the Kunstgewerbeschule, she designed glass, porcelain, silver, and jewelry; designed silver for Alexander Sturm, including a 1902 cigarette case with a stylized dragonfly in blue *pique-à-jour* enamel.
▶ Work (Sturm cigarette case) shown at 1902–03 winter exhibition, Museum für Kunst und Industrie, Vienna.

▶ Annelies Krekel-Aalberse, *Art Nouveau and Art Déco Silver*, New York: Abrams, 1989:194,205,256.

Krebs, Nathalie (1895–1978)
▶ Danish ceramicist.
▶ Studied civil engineering, Danmarks Tekniske Højskole, Copenhagen.
▶ In 1929, Krebs and Gunnar Nylund set up their own stoneware pottery studio, Copenhagen. In 1930, Krebs and Eva Staehr-Nielsen took over the works, naming it Saxbo.
▶ Received a gold medal at 1957 (XI) Triennale di Milano. Work shown at 1954–57 'Design in Scandinavia' traveling USA exhibition; 1956–59 'Neue Form aus Dänemark' traveling German exhibition; 1958 'Formes Scandinaves,' Paris Musée des Arts Décoratifs; 1960–61 'The Arts of Denmark' traveling USA exhibition.
▶ Cat., David Revere McFadden (ed.), *Scandinavian Modern Design 1880–1980*, New York: Abrams, 1982:267, No. 162.

Krehan, Max (1875–1925)
▶ German ceramicist; born Thuringia.
▶ In April 1920, he met Walter Gropius; 1920–25, taught pottery at the ceramics annex of the Bauhaus in Dornburg.
▶ Lionel Richard, *Encyclopédie du Bauhaus*, Paris: Somogy, 1985: 157. Cat., *Keramik am Bauhaus*, Berlin: Bauhaus-Archiv, 1989: 265.

Krejcar, Jaromir (1895–1949)
▶ Czech architect, furniture designer, graphic artist, and architectural theoretician; born Hundsheim (Austria).
▶ 1917–21, studied Academy of Fine Arts, Prague, under Jan Kotěra.
▶ From 1922 to its close in 1931, he was a member of the Devětsil group and editor of the compendium *Život II* and journal *Disk*; in 1922, worked in the office of architect Josef Gočár; in 1923, set up his own office in Prague; was the Bauhaus representative in Czechoslovakia; was a friend of Teige and the leading architect of the Devětsil group; designed the 1924 and 1926 suburban house of Devětsil chairman Vladislav Vančura, Prague-Zbraslav. He designed the 1927 reconstruction of Fromek's *Odeon* publishing house, Prague, and 1927–28 reconstruction of Teige's flat with interiors, 14 Černá St., Prague. He designed 1926–27 building (with his wife Milena Jesenská) at 35 Spálené St., Prague. Krejcar designed the family house for the German writer Brete Reiner, who lived in Prague. The house was noteworthy for its many Modern innovations, including built-in bookcases and cupboards, a three-part couch with drawers for bedding, colored carpets, and upholstery in a simple geometrical motif. The house featured Krejcar's tables, armchairs, and swivelling chairs made by the Czach furniture company in Sudoměřice. An example of Devětsil's industrial-nautical style can be seen in Krejcar's 1925 street wing of the Olympic store. He pursued Constructivist and Bauhaus approaches after 1925. 1933–35, he was active in the USSR; 1946–48, was professor of architecture, Technical University, Brno; in 1948, settled in London, where he lectured at the Architectural Association.
▶ Work shown at 1923 Bauhaus exhibition, Weimar; 1927 exhibition of the OSA group, Moscow. Designed Czech pavilion at 1937 Paris 'Exposition Internationale des Arts et Techniques dans la Vie Moderne.'
▶ Karel Teige, *Práce Jaromíra Krejcara, Václav Petr*, Prague, 1933. Jaromír Krejcar, *Lázeňský dům/Spa House*, Prague: Knihovna lazreňské techniky, 1933. Cat., *Devětsil: Czech Avant-Garde Art, Architecture, and Design of the 1920s and 30s*, Oxford Museum of Modern Art and London Design Museum, 1990.

Kreuter
▶ German silversmiths.
▶ The firm was established in 1842 in Hanau; in the 1930s, produced Modern silver hollow-ware.
▶ Annelies Krekel-Aalberse, *Art Nouveau and Art Déco Silver*, New York: Abrams, 1989:256.

Kriege, Jan (1884–1944)
▶ Dutch sculptor and silversmith; active Woerden.
▶ Trained in the workshop of C.J. Begeer, Utrecht.
▶ He set up his own workshop in 1919; from 1932, taught metalwork at Instituut voor de Kunstnijverheid, Amsterdam.
▶ Annelies Krekel-Aalberse, *Art Nouveau and Art Déco Silver*, New York: Abrams, 1989:256.

Kristalunie
▶ Dutch glass firm; located Maastricht.
▶ Petrus L. Regout set up a glass cutting works in Maastricht in 1827; The firm started manufacturing its own glass, mainly tableware, in 1838. Its wares around 1850 were angular, decorated with vertical faceting. More elaborate after 1890, its services included the *Model 22*. Regout and his son's firm Stella merged in 1925 to form Kristalunie. Artists commissioned to design for the firm included architect Ed. Cuypers in c1927, architect J. de Meijer in c1927, Jan Eisenloeffel in c1928, P. Zwart 1927–29, and G.M.E. Bellefroid for the *Stramino* drinking glass set in c1939. The first full-time designer was graphic artist W.J. Rozendaal (at sister company De Sphinx 1924–28) 1928–33 and, part-time, 1933–37; he produced some designs 1937–38. The firm experienced growth after World War II, and became part of the Vereenigde Glasfabrieken; from 1978, it produced only packaging glass.
▶ *Industry and Design in the Netherlands, 1850/1950*, Amsterdam: Stedelijk Museum, 1985:190–95.

Kristiansen, Bo (1944–)
▶ Danish ceramicist.
▶ Studied Kunsthåndvaerkerskolen, Copenhagen.
▶ Kristiansen set up a studio in 1968 in Gudhjem, relocating to Copenhagen in 1979.
▶ Work shown at 1969, 1973, and 1980 exhibitions, Bornholms Museum, Copenhagen; 1973 exhibition, Det Danske Kunstindustrimuseum, Copenhagen; 1971 'International Ceramics' exhibition, London; 1975–77 'Dansk Miljø' traveling Eastern Europe exhibition; 1981 'Danish Ceramic Design,' University Park, Pennsylvania; 'Scandinavian Modern Design 1880–1980' exhibition, Cooper-Hewitt Museum, New York. Work subject of exhibitions at Galerie Inart, Amsterdam, 1980; Galerie der Kunsthandverk, Hamburg, 1981.
▶ Cat., David Revere McFadden (ed.), *Scandinavian Modern Design 1880–1980*, New York: Abrams, 1982:267, No. 315.

Kristiansen, Kai (1929–)
▶ Danish furniture designer.
▶ Studied Det Kongelige Danske Kunstakademi, Copenhagen, under Kaare Klint, to 1950.
▶ From 1949, Kristiansen was a journeyman cabinetmaker; in 1955, set up his own design workshop.
▶ Frederik Sieck, *Nutidig Dansk Møbeldesign:-en kortfattet illustreret beskrivelse*, Copenhagen: Bondo Gravesen, 1981.

Krog, Arnold (1856–1931)
▶ Danish architect and ceramicist.
▶ 1874–80, studied architecture, Det Kongelige Danske Kunstakademi, Copenhagen.
▶ While a student, he worked on the interior decoration and interior repairs of the Frederiksborg Palace from 1878–81; in 1883, worked in the design office of architect Henrik Hagemann; from 1884, worked at Royal Copenhagen Porcelain Factory, where he was artistic director 1885–1916 and developed a particular style of underglaze decoration.
▶ Work shown at 1888 'Scandinavian Exhibition of Industry, Agriculture and Art,' Copenhagen; 1889 and 1900 Paris 'Expositions Universelles.'
▶ Cat., David Revere McFadden (ed.), *Scandinavian Modern Design 1880–1980*, New York: Abrams, 1982:267, Nos. 18,37,45. Jennifer Hawkins Opie, *Scandinavia: Ceramics and Glass in the Twentieth Century*, New York: Rizzoli, 1989.

Krogh, Henrik (1886–1927)
► Swedish textile designer, metalworker, and ceramicist.
► He was active as a designer of ceramics, metalwork, and woven tapestries. Some of his tapestries were woven by Märta Måås-Fjetterström, Båstad.
► Work shown at 1888 'Scandinavian Exhibition of Industry, Agriculture and Art,' Copenhagen.
► Cat., David Revere McFadden (ed.), *Scandinavian Modern Design 1880–1980*, New York: Abrams, 1982:267, No. 56.

Krohn, Lisa (1963–)
► American industrial designer; born and active New York.
► Studied art history and fine arts, Brown University, Providence, Rhode Island, to 1985; 1985–86, three-dimensional form with Rowena Reed Kostello, New York; design, Cranbrook Academy of Art, Bloomfield Hills, Michigan to 1988.
► 1985–87, she was an editor at the Industrial Designers' Society of America, New York; 1986–87, designer and copywriter at Smart Design, New York; 1987–88, designer and research consultant at Johnson and Johnson; in 1988, designer and research consultant at Herman Miller Research, Ann Arbor, Michigan; 1988–89, designer in the studio of Mario Bellini, Milan. In 1989, she became a founding partner of the design collaborative Abel Industrial, New York, which produced products, graphics, furniture, lighting, and interior and stage set designs for clients including NYNEX, Estée Lauder, George Kovacs Lighting, Alessi, the Steelcase Design Partnership, and Ultradata; in 1988, was visiting lecturer, University of Monterrey (Mexico); from 1989, was visiting critic, industrial design department, Parson's School of Design, New York. Her best-known products include the *Manual Fax* and *Phonebook* machines.
► Received grand prize at 1987 Forma Finlandia competition 'Plastics for Tomorrow.'

Krohn, Pietro (1840–1905)
► Danish ceramicist.
► 1885–97, Krohn was artistic director, Bing & Grøndahl Porcelaensfabrik, Copenhagen; was active as a painter, costume designer, and illustrator; became the first director of Det Danske Kunstindustrimuseum, Copenhagen.
► Cat., David Revere McFadden (ed.), *Scandinavian Modern Design 1880–1980*, New York: Abrams, 1982:267, No. 14.

Krol, Leo (1955–)
► Dutch industrial designer.
► Studied Koninklijke Academie voor Beeldende Kunsten, The Hague.
► He worked for Frans de la Haye and Philips until 1989, when he joined the Lumiance Design Team.

Kroll, Boris (1913–91)
► American textile designer; born Buffalo, New York.
► He was apprenticed to furniture designer and brother Hammond Kroll; in 1938, set up his own firm Cromwell Designs, which at first produced Modern furnishings fabrics on a hand loom, with a bathtub for dyeing yarns; from 1939, began using power looms; in 1946, set up Boris Kroll Fabrics, New York; used cotton and novelty spun rayon; in 1956, was invited by the government of India to advise on updating hand-loom production. The firm expanded its original specialization to fabrics woven on a jacquard loom, where complex patterns were produced for the mass market. By 1991, the firm had 16 showrooms in the USA and a large manufacturing plant in Paterson, New Jersey.
► Received 13 awards at 1953 'Good Design' exhibition, Museum of Modern Art, New York, and Merchandise Mark, Chicago. Received 1971 honorary degree in textiles, Philadelphia College of Textiles and Science. Work shown at 1983–84 'Design Since 1945' exhibition at Philadelphia Museum of Art. Work subject of 1981 'Boris Kroll–Tapestries and Textiles' exhibition, Fashion Institute of Technology, New York.
► 'A New Home for the House of Boris Kroll,' *Interiors*, Vol. 111, Dec. 1951:115–18,180–81. Cat., *Boris Kroll–Tapestries and*

Textiles, 1980. Cat., Kathryn B. Hiesinger and George H. Marcus III (eds.), *Design Since 1945*, Philadelphia: Philadelphia Museum of Art, 1983. 'Celebrating Design Innovation,' *Designers West*, April 1991:32. 'Boris Kroll, 77, Owner of a Fabrics Company,' *The New York Times*, 9 June 1991.

Krondahl, Hans (1929–)
► Swedish textile designer.
► 1955–60, studied Konstfackskolan and Konsthögskolan, Stockholm.
► In 1960, he set up his own studio in Brösarp; 1959–75, was a consultant designer to Nordiska Kompaniet, where he produced designs for pictorial weavings and tapestries and printed furnishing fabrics in cotton, velvet, and fiberglass. His motifs were produced in large geometric and stylized figurative patterns and bright colors. 1974–75, he taught and worked in Scandinavia and the USA; from 1975–77, was a designer for Argos, Oak Grove Village, Illinois; from 1979–80, was UNIDO expert in textile design and product development in Indonesia. From 1981, he taught at Konstfackskolan, Stockholm; Kunstindustriskole, Oslo; Konstindustriskolan at Gothenburg University.
► Received 1965 Lunning Prize (fabric designs for Nordiska Kompaniet). Work subject of 1982 exhibition, Museet Kulturhuset, Borås.
► Cat., *Hans Krondahl*, Borås, Sweden: Musett Kulturhuset, 1982. 'Thirty-four Lunning Prize-Winners,' *Mobilia*, No. 146, Sept. 1967. Charles S. Talley, *Contemporary Textile Art: Scandinavia*, Stockholm, 1982:73–76. Hans Krondahl, 'Swedish Design,' *Handwoven*, March–April 1983:29–33. Cat., Kathryn B. Hiesinger and George H. Marcus III (eds.), *Design Since 1945*, Philadelphia: Philadelphia Museum of Art, 1983. Cat., *The Lunning Prize*, Stockholm: Nationalmuseum, 1986: 162–65.

Krupp, Arthur (1856–1938)
► Austrian designer.
► From 1879, he was director of Berndorfer Metallwarenfabrik, Berndorf (Austria), where he produced the silver designs of Walter Gropius, including bowls, compotes, and candlesticks.
► Work (Gropius designs) shown at 1914 Cologne 'Deutscher Werkbund-Ausstellung.'
► Annelies Krekel-Aalberse, *Art Nouveau and Art Déco Silver*, New York: Abrams, 1989:1942,166,256. Cat., *Metallkunst*, Berlin: Bröhan-Museum, 1992:20.

Kudriashev, Ivan Alexeevich (1896–1970)
► Russian artist and designer; born Moscow.
► From 1913, studied Moscow Institute of Painting, Sculpture, and Architecture.
► For the first anniversary celebration of the Revolution in Moscow in 1918, Kudriashev produced agitprop designs for automobiles; in 1920, participated on interior designs for the Summer Red Army Theater and First Soviet Theater, Orenburg; in the 1920s, investigated luminosity and refractivity in painting and produced paintings in the 'engineerist' style associated with Kliment Redko.
► Work shown at 1922 'Erste Russische Kunstausstellung,' Berlin; 1925 'First State Traveling Exhibition of Paintings,' Moscow; 1925 (I), 1926 (II), and 1928 (IV) OST exhibitions, Moscow. In 1928, stopped showing his work.
► Cat., Stephanie Barron and Maurice Tuchman, *The Avant-Garde in Russia, 1910–1930*, Cambridge, MA: MIT Press, 1980: 176. Cat., *The Great Utopia: The Russian and Soviet Avant-Garde, 1915–1932*, New York: Guggenheim Museum, 1992.

Kukkapuro, Yrjö (1933–)
► Finnish designer; born Yiipuri.
► Studied Helsinki University and Helsinki Institute of Crafts and Design.
► In 1959, he opened his own office in Kauniainen; was a teacher in the architecture department, Helsinki Institute of Technology; 1974–80, was professor, Taideteollinen Korkeakoulu, Helsinki, and rector 1978–80; designed furniture for Avarte and began

designing in plastics in 1965 (work produced by Haimi, Helsinki). His best known design is the 1966 *Chair 414 k*, produced by Haimi, in fiberglass on a pedestal base (with four options) in leather upholstery.

▶ Work (*Chair 414 k*) shown at 1967 Scandinavian Furniture Fair, Copenhagen; 1968 Turin 'Eurodomus II'. Work shown at numerous exhibitions including 1959, 1964, and 1968 Finnish Society of Crafts and Design Annual; 1960 (XII) and 1968 (XIV) Triennali di Milano; 1962 Ornamo '50th Anniversary Gala'; 1963 '60 Years of Finnish Industrial Design,' Stockholm; 1964 and 1967 'Finlandia Industrial Design,' Europe and USA; 1966 'Modern Chairs,' Stedelijk Museum, Amsterdam; 1966 Genoa 'Eurodomus I'; 1967 'Art of Living,' Salon of the Société des Artistes Décorateurs, Paris. Work subject of 1962 exhibition, Finnish Design Center. Received 1966 Lunning Prize; 1970 Design Award, Finland; 1982 Artek Prize; 1983 Pro Finlandia Award; 1984 IBD award (*Experimental Chair*), Institute of Business Design, USA.

▶ Cat., Milena Lamarová, *Design a Plastické Hmoty*, Prague: Uměleckoprůmyslové Muzeum, 1972:120. Cat., *Les Assises du siège contemporain*, Paris: Musée des Arts Décoratifs, 1968. Robert A.M. Stern (ed.), *The International Design Yearbook*, New York: Abbeville, 1985/1986: No. 134.

Kunert, Heidemarie (1958–)

▶ German industrial designer; born and active Berlin.

▶ 1977–83, studied industrial design, Hochschule der Künste, Berlin.

▶ From 1983, he was an independent consultant designer; 1984–85, designed exhibitions, including stand and corporate identity program for the 'Big Tech' and Kaufhold; coordinated workshops on corporate design; in 1986, (with Marina Donner) set up her own design office, Amazonas Design, Berlin.

▶ Work shown at 1987–88 traveling 'Berlin Ways—Products and Design from Berlin' exhibition in Berlin, Stuttgart, Stockholm, and Barcelona. Received 1988 Mia Seeger Preis, Stuttgart.

▶ Cat., Design Center Stuttgart, *Women in Design: Careers and Life Histories Since 1900*, Stuttgart: Haus der Wirtschaft, 1989:62–63.

Kunzli, Oto (1950–)

▶ German jewelry designer.

▶ Studied metalwork in Zürich and jewelry, Akademie der bildenden Künste, Munich, under Hermann Junger.

▶ His designs were unconventional, using foam and wallpaper to produce wearable ornaments; designed in a manner based on the forms of the block, cube, and stick.

▶ Peter Dormer (intro.), *The Illustrated Dictionary of 20th-Century Designers: The Key Personalities in Design and the Applied Arts*, New York: Mallard, 1991.

Kupittaan Savi

▶ Finnish ceramics factory.

▶ Kupittaan, Finland's oldest pottery, was founded as a brickworks in 1712; in 1915, began production of domestic ceramics used primarily for experimentation of acid-resistant ceramics and fire-resistant bricks; when designer Kerttu Suvanto-Vaajakallion was hired, the firm increased its production of table and kitchenwares and began exporting to the USA and Germany; closed in 1969.

▶ Received a silver medal (works by Laine Taitto, Linnea Lehtonen, and Marjukka Paasivirta) at 1954 (X) Triennale di Milano.

▶ Jennifer Hawkins Opie, *Scandinavia: Ceramics and Glass in the Twentieth Century*, New York: Rizzoli, 1989.

Kuppenheim, Louis

▶ German enamel manufacturers; located Pforzheim.

▶ In the early part of the 20th century, Louis Kuppenheim was the leading firm of enamelers in Germany; in *c*1990, produced the enameled pieces designed by Hans Christiansen of Darmstadt. Christiansen's objects included cigarette boxes and cases with enameled lids, showing a preference for colorful naturalistic motifs.

▶ Annelies Krekel-Aalberse, *Art Nouveau and Art Déco Silver*, New York: Abrams, 1989:133,256.

Kuramata, Shiro (1934–91)

▶ Japanese furniture and interior designer; born and active Tokyo.

▶ Studied woodworking, Tokyo Municipal Polytechnic High School to 1953, and in the Department of Living Design, Kuwazawa Institute of Design to 1956.

▶ He joined the Teikokukizai furniture factory in 1953; worked in the interior design departments of major Japanese department stores, including the San-Ai Co design atelier of the Matsuya department store, Tokyo, in 1957; in 1965, opened his own design office, Tokyo; took a minimalist approach to his furniture and interiors, reflecting the influence of traditional Japanese austerity, although the results combined Eastern and Western sensibilities. His first noteworthy furniture piece was the 1970 *Revolving Cabinet*. His commissions included interiors for Issey Miyake's clothing boutiques (1984 in Paris, 1986 in Tokyo, and 1987 worldwide), and, for the Seibu store (1987 in Tokyo), the Lucchino Bar and Caffe Oyx. From 1965, he designed more than 300 boutiques and restaurants. The 1970 wavy 18-drawer chests produced by Cappellini International Interiors won him acclaim, while illustrating his quirky and surrealistic sense of humor. Though he designed furniture for Aoshima and Ishimaru, his recognition came about through his pieces of 1970 *Furniture in Irregular Forms* range for Fijiko. His ultimate statement in high-tech romanticism, his *Blues in the Night* table had dozens of red diode tubes which glowed inside transparent acrylic. His large 1972 lamps used milk-white plastic sheets which were heated and hung over poles, creating naturally formed curves. From 1975, he was a consultant to Mainichi Design Awards. In 1988, he bought the 1927 house designed by Robert Mallet-Stevens for Joël and Jan Martell in rue Mallet-Stevens, Paris; set up an office in the rue Royale, Paris; designed the woman's handbag *Copacabana*. Working with the Memphis group and its leader Ettore Sottsass from 1981–83, designs included 1972 lamp *Fantôme*, 1978 *Marilyn Monroe* chest of drawers by Lappelini, 1981 *Imperial* three-part cabinets, 1982 *Kyoto* cement and glass side table, and 1987 *Sally* side table with a broken-glass top. Other work included 1964 *49 Drawers* by Aoshima Shoten, 1968 *Pyramid* furniture by Ishimaru, 1970 revolving cabinet by Ishimaru, 1976 glass chair for Mhoya Glass Shop, 1977 *Solaris* by Aoshima Shoten, 1983 *Star Peace* table by Ishimaru, 1985 *Begin the Beguine* chair homage to Josef Hoffmann, 1986 *How High the Moon* metal-mesh chair by Kurosaki (later, by Vitra), 1986 *Sing Sing Sing* armchair by XO, and 1986 *Drawers in Irregular Form* by Cappellini International Interiors, 1988 *BK 86000* bar stool by Pastoe, and 1989 *Miss Blanche* plexiglass chair.

▶ Work shown in numerous exhibitions including 1978 'MA Espace/temps au Japon' exhibition, Paris Musée des Arts Décoratifs, and various Memphis exhibitions. Received 1972 Mainichi Design Award and 1981 Japan Culture Design Award.

▶ *Memphis, the New International Style*, Milan: Electa, 1981. Cat., *The Works of Shiro Kuramata 1967–1981*, London: Aram Designs, 1981; Tokyo: Parco, 1981. Cat., *Kagu-Mobilier Japonais*, Shibaura Institute of Technology, 1985. 'Kuramata,' *City*, Sept. 1986. 'Les Scènes des années 80,' *Beaux-Arts Magazine*, April 1989. *Acquisitions arts décoratifs 1982–1990*, Paris: Fonds National d'Art Contemporain, 1991.

Kuramoto, Yoko (1950–)

▶ Japanese glass designer.

▶ Studied Musashino Art University, Department of Crafts and Industrial Design, Tokyo, to 1972.

▶ From 1982, Kuramoto worked at Ito Glass Studio.

▶ Work included in 1984, 1987, and 1990 'Glass in Japan,' Tokyo; 1985 'New Glass in Japan,' Badisches Landesmuseum, Karlsruhe; 1988 'International Exhibition of Glass Craft,' Industrial Gallery of Ishikawa Prefecture, Kanazawa; 1988 'Work Glass

Now '88,' Hokkaido Museum of Modern Art, Sapporo; 1989 'Arte en Vidro,' São Paulo Art Museum; 1991 (V) Triennale of Japan Glass Art Crafts Association, Heller Gallery, New York. Work subject of exhibitions at Takashimaya Gallery, Yokohama, 1981, and Isetan Fine Arts Salon, Tokyo, 1985.

▶ Cat., *Glass Japan*, New York: Heller Gallery and Japan Glass Art Crafts Association, 1991: No. 19.

Kurchan, Juan
See Ferrari-Hardoy, Jorge

Kurita, Yasuhisa   (1945–)
▶ Japanese glass designer; active Tokyo.
▶ Studied sculpture, Tokyo University of Education, Faculty of Fine Arts, Tokyo, to 1969; 1974–75, Konstfackskolan and Tekniska Skolan, Stockholm, under Bertil Vallien.
▶ Kurita was a designer at Hoya Crystal in Tokyo.
▶ Work included in 1981, 1984, 1987, and 1990 'Glass in Japan,' Tokyo; 1982 'New Glass Review 3,' The Corning Museum of Glass, Corning, New York; 1983 'Little Objects,' Japan Glass Art Crafts Association; and 1991 (V) Triennale of the Japan Glass Art Crafts Association, Heller Gallery, New York.
▶ Cat., *Glass Japan*, New York: Heller Gallery and Japan Glass Art Crafts Association, 1991: No. 20.

Kurokawa, Kisho   (1938–)
▶ Japanese architect and furniture designer.
▶ Studied architecture, Tokyo University, to 1964.
▶ He designed the 1984 Roppongi Prince Hotel, Tokyo; 1984 Wacoal Kojimachi Building, Tokyo; 1983 Japanese Studies Center, Bangkok; 1983 Japanese-German Culture Center, Berlin; 1983 National Bunraku Theatre, Osaka. His books included *Architecture of the Street* (1983), *A Cross Selection of Japan* (1983), and *Thesis on Architecture* (1982). He has designed distinctive furniture for Tendo and Kosuga.
▶ Work shown in numerous exhibitions in New York, Paris, London, Dublin, Moscow, Milan, Florence, Rome, Budapest, and Sofia.
▶ Robert A.M. Stern (ed.), *The International Design Yearbook*, New York: Abbeville, 1985/1986: Nos. 79,87.

Kurokawa, Masayuki   (1937–)
▶ Japanese furniture and lighting designer, born Nagoya.
▶ Studied architecture, Institute of Technology, Nagoya, to 1961; Graduate School of Architecture, Waseda University, to 1967.
▶ In 1967, he set up Masayuki Kurokawa Architect and Associates. His lighting designs were diverse, with some fixtures produced by Matsushita, including the 1984 *Angolo Slit T Bar* wall light. Designs included a 1986 flat-wave speaker produced by Seidenko, 1987 *Archi Version K* pencils by Sakura Color Products, and 1987 *Kite* ceiling light by Yamagiwa.
▶ Received numerous prizes including 1970 International Design Competition (mass-production house); 1973 competition for 'Interior Vertical Element of a House'; 1976 annual prize, Japan Interior Designers' Association; six IF awards for tables and lighting.
▶ Robert A.M. Stern (ed.), *The International Design Yearbook*, New York: Abbeville, 1985/1986: Nos. 253–62,376–81. Albrecht Bangert and Karl Michael Armer, *80s Style: Designs of the Decade*, New York: Abbeville, 1990:104,210,221,232.

Kurrer, Angela   (1945–)
▶ German designer; born Göttingen.
▶ Studied French, Sorbonne University, Paris; art; from 1969, industrial design, Hochschule für bildendeu Künste, Hamburg.
▶ In Hamburg, she was a freelance graphic designer and editor of design, architecture, and fashion at *Stern* magazine; from 1978, was an independent designer of furniture, accessories, wrapping papers, bags, and jewelry. Work included a 1988–89 screen of her own production, and 1981 *Chrom* and *Plyx* writing desk accessories by Waltraud Bethge Papiere, Hamburg.

▶ Cat., Design Center Stuttgart, *Women in Design: Careers and Life Histories Since 1990*, Stuttgart: Haus der Wirtschaft, 1989:126–29.

Kurz, Petra   (1962–)
▶ German product designer; born Schwäbisch Hall.
▶ 1979–82, studied Unterricht für Freie Kunst under Susanne Lüftner; design, Fachhochschule für Gestaltung, Schwäbisch Gmünd, to 1983.
▶ In 1988, she was a freelance designer of textiles, color, and lighting; in 1989, worked at the Design Center, Stuttgart, organizing and designing the exhibition and catalog '2. Design-Börse,' and the catalog for 'Women in Design' exhibition; in 1989, (with two partners) set up her own design office in Schwäbisch Gmünd.
▶ Received honorable mention award at 1988 '1. Design-Börse' and Mia Seeger Preis.
▶ Cat., Design Center Stuttgart, *Women in Design: Careers and Life Histories Since 1990*, Stuttgart: Haus der Wirtschaft, 1989:354–55.

Kutzner, Ingrid   (1949–)
▶ German industrial designer; born Börssum.
▶ 1965–68, apprentice draftsperson in an architecture office; 1969–76, studied industrial design, Hochschule der bildenden Künste, Brunswick.
▶ In 1976, she worked as an industrial designer at Richardson and Smith, Columbus, Ohio, and, in 1977, at AEG at the Institut für Produktgestaltung, Frankfurt; from 1983, set up the firm design linea, Frankfurt; in 1984, was a guest professor of product design, Ohio State University. Designs included 1980 *Aqualux* mouthspray, 1981 *Rotofix* universal cutter, and 1982 modular desk system, all by AEG.
▶ Cat., Design Center Stuttgart, *Women in Design: Careers and Life Histories Since 1900*, Stuttgart: Haus der Wirtschaft, 1989:130–31.

Kuypers, Jan
▶ Canadian industrial designer; active Toronto.
▶ In the 1950s, Kuypers was one of the best known furniture designers in Canada; designed furniture produced by Imperial Furniture, Stratford; (with Doug Rowan and Frank Dudas) worked separately and together as industrial designers. The group's furniture designs included seating for IIL International.
▶ Cat., *Seduced and Abandoned: Modern Furniture designers in Canada, the First Fifty Years*, Toronto: The Art Gallery at Harbourfront, 1986:21.

KVT (Koninklijke Vereenigde Tapijtenfabrieken)
▶ Dutch rug factory; located Rotterdam and Moordrecht.
▶ Deventer Tapijtfabriek was founded in 1797 in Rotterdam; in 1819, became the best known of three merged factories which formed the Koninklijke Vereenigde Tapijtenfabrieken. King Willem III was a shareholder and client, and encouraged its historicist styles with gifts of expensive illustrated books to the firm's design department. Its workers wove cowhair and other simple carpets and rugs and, from c1820, hand-knotted 'Smyrna' carpets. Sons of one of the company founders, G. Birnie, (including Johan Willem Birnie, manager 1820–48) were the designers. Much of the work at this time was imitation Turkish, Persian, other Oriental carpet adaptations, and European Renaissance, French, and Empire styles. The model that became known as *Deventer* was highly successful from the 1850s. The rugs and carpets were made to measure. From the turn of the century, both historicist and Modern styles were made. Founded in 1901 in The Hague, the 's-Gravenhaagsche Smyrnatapijtfabrike organized design competitions, one of which in 1901 had the theme 'Modern Style'; its winner was Chris Lebeau. In 1895, the factory was to be closed, but friends of artist Thomas A.C. Colenbrander, who designed for the company, took over the firm. In 1896, Amersfoortsche Tapijtfabriek was founded with J.G. Mouton as a new stockholder, W.P.A. Garjeanne as a director, and Colenbrander as 'aesthetic advisor.' The Amersfoot company became successful and Colen-

brander's carpets became widely known. In 1919 Amersfoot became a part of the Deventer Tapijtfabriek. Artists for the two companies included H.P. Berlage, Th. W. Nieuwenhuis, J.W. Gidding, C.A. Lion Cachet, W. Penaat, J.J. Gompertz, J. van den Boch, and C. van der Sluys. After the merger, more machine-made rugs were produced. After 1930, its only freelance designer was Jaap Gidding. New designs began to be made in the 1950s.

▶ Deventer received prizes at 1851 London 'Great Exhibition of the Works of Industry of All Nations' and 1878 Paris 'Exposition Universelle.' Koninklijke Tapijtfabriek Werklust (one of the firms founded in 1854 in Rotterdam) showed work at 1900 Paris 'Exposition Universelle' and 1902 Turin 'Esposizione Internazionale d'Arte Decorativa Moderna.'

▶ *Industry and Design in the Netherlands, 1850/1950*, Amsterdam: Stedelijk Museum, 1985.

Kybal, Antonin (1901–71)

▶ Czech painter, textile artist, and textile producer; born Nové Město nad Metují.

▶ Studied School of Applied Arts, and philosophy, Charles University, both Prague.

▶ In 1928, he set up his own textile studio in Prague; became a member of SČSD (Czech Werkbund); collaborated at Krásná jizba (The Beautiful Room); 1948–71, was professor, College of Applied Arts, Prague; in the 1920s–30s, was the leading influence in the Modern style of textiles for domestic use and became important in the production of handmade prints; designed a large number of hand-woven and machine-made carpets; collaborated with leading Czech architects; designed furnishing fabrics for family houses, in-

teriors of the Prague castle in 1936, and League of Nations Geneva, in 1937; published articles in magazines Žijeme in 1931, *Panorama* in 1935, *Architektura* in 1942, and others; created hand-woven tapestries and influenced the Modern Czech tapestry.

▶ Received gold medal at 1958 Brussels 'Exposition Universelle et Internationale de Bruxelles (Expo '58).'

▶ A. Adlerová, *České užité umění 1918–1938*, Prague, 1983.

Kysela, František (1881–1941)

▶ Czech designer and teacher; born Kouřim.

▶ 1900–04 and 1905–08, studied School of Decorative Arts, Prague, under K. Mašek; 1904–05, Academy of Fine Arts, Prague, under H. Schwaigr.

▶ In 1913, he became a professor, School of Decorative Arts, Prague; from 1921, taught a class in applied graphics; in 1908, joined Mánes Association of Plastic Artists and, in 1909, was elected to its executive; was a member of Artěl Cooperative; in 1911, left Mánes and joined the Group of Plastic Artists; worked in the editorial offices of Umělecký měsíčník; in 1917, rejoined Mánes; was active in various media, especially the applied arts; created frescoes, paintings on glass windows, textile designs for clothing and upholstery, jewelry, tapestries, postage stamps, banknotes, book illustrations, stage sets, and theatre costumes, including those for Smetana's operas at the National Theater, Prague.

▶ Received grand prize and gold medal at 1925 Paris 'Exposition Internationale des Arts Décoratifs et Industriels Modernes.'

▶ Alexander von Vegesack et al., *Czech Cubism: Architecture, Furniture, and Decorative Arts, 1910–1925*, New York: Princeton Architectural Press, 1992.

L

La Falaise, Alexis de (c1948–)
▶ French furniture designer; active Fontainebleau.
▶ Formerly a farmer, La Falaise founded a craftsmen's cooperative in Wales before moving to Fontainebleau; in the late 1980s, designed furniture designs in oak, sycamore, and mahogany, including the *Opera* TV cabinet, *Travail* work table, and *Obelisk* bookcase; in c1989, produced furniture for the winery at Château Bellevue Laforêt.
▶ Claire Wilson, 'Late Bloomer,' *Elle Decor*, November 1990:40.

La Farge, John Frederick Lewis Joseph (1835–1910)
▶ American artist, stained glass designer, and decorator; born and active New York.
▶ Leaving employment in a law firm in New York in 1856, he traveled to France and met author Théophile Gautier and poet Charles-Pierre Baudelaire through his cousin, journalist-critic Paul de Saint-Victor; during this time, copied and studied old masters' art works at the Louvre; studied for a few weeks in the studio of Théodore Chassériau; in 1857 returned to the USA via England, where he visited the Manchester Art Treasures Exhibition with its works by the Pre-Raphaelites; in 1858, set up his own studio in 10th Street Studio Building, New York; met architect Richard Morris Hunt, who encouraged La Farge to pursue painting and to study under his brother William Morris Hunt in Newport, Rhode Island. His work of the 1860s bore a similarity to that of Claude Monet. In c1865, he began to produce decorative painting, receiving a commission from architect Henry Van Brunt for the 1865 dining room of Boston builder Charles Freeland but, due to illness, was replaced by Albion Bicknell; in 1875, began working in stained glass, influenced by Edward Burne-Jones, Ford Madox Brown, and Dante Gabriel Rossetti, all of whom he had visited in England in 1873. La Farge's stained glass methods revolutionized the craft in America. He introduced opalescent glass to the USA, which offered tonality and eliminated traditional painting details, used first on a window in the Henry G. Marquand residence, Newport, Rhode Island, c1880; produced several thousand stained-glass windows. Commissioned by architect H.H. Richardson, from 1876 La Farge produced notable murals and architectural details, most of which he directed personally, for Trinity Church, Boston, Massachusetts. Other murals included those for St. Thomas Church in 1877, Church of the Incarnation in 1885, and Church of the Ascension in 1886–88, all New York. 1880–85, he directed the La Farge Decorative Art Company for interior decoration; in the early 1880s in New York, participated in the decoration of the Japanese Parlor of the William H. Vanderbilt residence and dining room and watercolor room of the residence of his son, Cornelius Vanderbilt II, both completed in cooperation with August Saint-Gaudens. In the 1880s and 1890s, La Farge traveled to Japan and the South Pacific, where he painted watercolors that illustrated his memoirs; published books including *Considerations on Painting* (1895), *Great Masters* (1903), and *The Higher Life in Art* (1908).
▶ In 1862, work (his first still-life paintings and figurative art) shown at National Academy of Design, New York. Work subject of 1936 exhibition, New York Metropolitan Museum of Art.

▶ James L. Sturm, *Stained Glass from Medieval Times to the Present: Treasures to Be Seen in New York*, New York, 1982:34–46. Doreen Bolger Burke et al., *In Pursuit of Beauty: Americans and the Aesthetic Movement*, New York: Metropolitan Museum of Art and Rizzoli, 1986:47–48. Cat., Henry Adams et al., *The Art of John La Farge*, Washington: National Museum of American Art, 1987.

La Mache, Didier (1945–)
▶ French designer and manufacturer.
▶ Studied art and industrial design, École Nationale Supérieure des Arts Décoratifs, Paris, and Royal College of Art, London.
▶ He produced and sold his own lighting, furniture, and accessories, including the 1987 *Ciel Bauhaus!* table lamp; designed 1987 *Bleu Electre* table lamp commissioned by VIA.
▶ François Mathey, *Au bonheur des formes, design français 1945–1992*, Paris: Regard, 1992:307–08,376.

La Nave
▶ Spanish design consultancy; located Valencia.
▶ In 1984, the design studios Caps i Mans and Enebecé merged to form the multi-disciplinary design consultancy La Nave, which received numerous public commissions in Valencia, including those from the Valencia regional government. Composed of 11 core members from various backgrounds, its staff included Sandra Figuerola, Marisa Gallén, and Luis Gonzáles (from fine art); Paco Bascuñán and Lorenzo Company (from graphic design); and Carlos Bento (from architecture). Gallén and Figuerola designed the 1987 *Fried-Eggs* inflatable for pools, produced by Torrente Industrial (TOI), 1989 linens by Castilla Textil, 1989 inflatable pool by TOI, and 1988 writing pad by Don Antonio. Daniel Nabot and Nacho Lavernia designed 1986 automobile ski racks and 1986 water fountain, produced by Indústrias Saludes.
▶ Guy Julier, *New Spanish Design*, London: Thames and Hudson, 1991.

La Pietra, Ugo (1938–)
▶ Italian designer; born Bussi, Pescara; active Milan.
▶ Studied architecture, Politecnico di Milano, to 1964.
▶ In 1964, he set up his own studio and became a design consultant to furniture, accessories, and lighting manufacturers; had clients including Busnelli, Zama, Sima, Poggi, Moro, Jabik & Colophon, Elam, Arosio, and Vecchione. From 1965, his numerous books included *Autoarchiterapia*, *L'Uso della città*, *Promemoria*, and *Abitare la città*. 1971–73, he was editor of the journal *IN*; 1973–75, *Progettare in Più and Fascicolo*; 1977–81, *Brera Flash* and *Fascicolo* and, 1978–86, editor of the design section of *Domus*. In 1973 with others, La Pietra founded the Radical Design group Global Tools; in c1984, became artistic director, Busnelli Industrial Group; until 1974, was assistant lecturer, Facoltà di Architettura, Politecnico di Milano and, 1967–79, at Facoltà di Architettura, Pescara; from 1977, was an instructor of industrial and environmental design, Instituto Statale d'Arte, Monza, and architecture professor, schools of architecture, Palermo and Turin. His metalwork for Alessi included anthropomorphic coffee pots. In 1990, he opened his own gallery 'Studio in Più,' Milan, where he showed

his own work; became a member of ADI (Associazione per il Disegno Industriale). Designs for Busnelli included 1984 *Pretenziosa* armchair, 1984 *Agevole* sofa, 1984 *Flessuosa* sofa, 1985 *Autorevole* armchair, 1985 *At-Tese* chair and table, 1985 *Incrocio* table and chair, and 1986 *Articolata* chair.

▶ He participated in the 1968 (XIV) (experimental environment) Triennale di Milano; exhibition designs included 1980 '50 Years of Architecture' exhibition, Milan; 'Cronografie' exhibition, 1982 Biennale di Venezia; audio-visual section, 1979 (XVI) Triennale di Milano; 'La Casa Telemática' exhibition, 1983 (LXI) Fiera Campionaria Internazionale, Milan; 1972 'Italy: The New Domestic Landscape' (1971 'Uno sull'altro' bookcase by Poggi), New York Museum of Modern Art. Received first prize at 1975 (I) architecture-film festival, Nancy; 1979 Premio Compasso d'Oro. Participated in over 300 exhibitions in Italy and abroad; exhibitions at New York Museum of Contemporary Crafts; IDZ Berlin; Architectural Association, London; Institut de l'Environnement, Paris; Museum Joanneum, Graz; Museum am Ostwall, Dortmund.

▶ Emilio Ambasz (ed.), Italy: *The New Domestic Landscape*, New York: Museum of Modern Art, 1972:55. *ADI Annual 1976*, Milan: Associazione per il Disegno Industriale, 1976. Alfonso Grassi and Anty Pansera, *Atlante del Design Italiano 1940–80*, Milan: Fabbri 1980:303. Helmuth Gsöllpointner et al. (eds.) *Design is unsichtbar*. Andrea Branzi, *La Casa Calda: Esperienze del Nuovo Disegno Italiano*, Milan: Idea Books, 1982. Robert A.M. Stern (ed.), *The International Design Yearbook*, New York: Abbeville, 1985/1986: Nos. 51,54. Mario Mastropietro et al., *Un'Industria per il Design: La ricerca, i designers, l'immagine B&B Italia*, Milan: Lybra Immagine, 1986. Juli Capella and Quim Larrea, *Designed by Architects in the 1980s*, New York, Rizzoli, 1988. *Modo*, No. 148, March–April 1993:121.

La Trobe-Bateman (1938–)
▶ British designer.
▶ Studied design, Royal College of Art, London, to 1968.
▶ Work shown at 1982 'Maker's Eye'; 1987 'Contemporary Applied Arts'; 1991 'Beyond the Dovetail,' Crafts Council, London.
▶ *Decorative Arts Today*, London: Bonhams, 1992: No. 41a.

Laba (formerly Nino Lembo)
▶ Italian costume jeweler; located Rome.
▶ In the mid-1960s, Nino Lembo began to produce costume jewelry for movies, television and the theater. Eva Serrao had worked for the variety-show companies directed by her husband and, at the end of the 1950s, established her own fashion accessory firm known as Eva Mode to furnish costume accessories to theatre companies. By the mid-1960s, the firm's production was devoted primarily to movie and television companies in Italy. When Lembo died, his wife took over management of the firm, changing the name to Laba (anacronym for Lembo Antonio Bigiotteria Artistica).
▶ Deanna F. Cera (ed.), *Jewels of Fantasy: Costume Jewelry of the 20th Century*, New York: Abrams, 1992:307–08.

Labino, Dominick
▶ American ceramicist and glassware designer.
▶ From 1953, studied glassmaking, University of Wisconsin.
▶ In the mid-1960s, he was the most productive of the first group in the studio-glass program, University of Wisconsin; was involved in glass technology; became a member of New Wave Studio-Glass Movement; developed two free-form techniques: immersion pieces made from many layers, and large off-hand forms produced by opening up asymmetrical bubbles and stretching with pincers. Sam Herman was a student of Labino's in 1966.
▶ Frederick Cooke, *Glass: Twentieth-Century Design*, New York: Dutton, 1986:105.

Lachenal, Edmond (1855–1948)
▶ French sculptor and ceramicist; born Paris; father of Raoul Lachenal.

▶ Lachenal joined the studio of Théodore Deck in 1870, later becoming director; in 1880, established his own studio at Malakoff, near Paris, and, in 1887, at Châtillon-sous-Bagneux; made pottery in the 'Persian style' influenced by Deck and decorated with stylized figures, landscapes, greenery, and flowers; in 1890, perfected a finish where the glaze surface was partially dulled with hydrofluoric acid; experimented with metallic luster glazes with Keller of Guérin; showed the results of these experimentations along with ceramic sculptures after works by Rodin, Fix-Masseau, Epinay, Madrassi, and Sarah Bernhardt at Galerie Georges Petit, Paris; developed an interest in enameled glass and began to work at Daum, Nancy. His vase forms at this time were inspired by fashionable plant motifs. He produced small figurines and animal forms; at the beginning of the 20th century, left ceramics and turned over his studio to his son Raoul Lachenel and his wife.
▶ From 1884, work shown annually at Galerie Georges Petit, and at 1900 Paris 'Exposition Universelle' (suite of stoneware furniture).
▶ Yvonne Brunhammer et al., *Art Nouveau Belgium, France*, Houston: Institute for the Arts, Rice University, 1976. *Europäische Keramik 1880–1930: Sammlung Silzer*, Darmstadt: Hessisches Landesmuseum, 1986. Elisabeth Cameron, *Encyclopedia of Pottery and Porcelain*, London: Faber and Faber, 1986:192.

Lachenal, Raoul (1885–1956)
▶ French ceramist; son of Edmond Lachenal.
▶ He succeeded his father in his studio, Châtillon-sous-Bagneux; from 1904, exhibited incised-relief and geometric-motif stoneware or colored glazes within *cloisonné*, outlined in deep orange; used matt and gray *flambé* effects in rare colors; in 1911, moved to Boulogne-sur-Seine; later on, produced porcelain and serial and one-off pieces; was fond of ovoid shapes, simple decoration, and black-and-white contrasts.
▶ Yvonne Bruhammer, *Les années '25,'* Paris: Musée des Arts Décoratifs, 1966:108. Yvonne Brunhammer, *Le Cinquantenaire de l'Exposition de 1925*, Paris: Musée des Arts Décoratifs, 1976:133. Elisabeth Cameron, *Encyclopedia of Pottery and Porcelain*, London: Faber and Faber, 1986:192.

Lacloche
▶ International jewelry firm; originally located Madrid.
▶ Lacloche was founded in 1875 in Madrid; set up branches in San Sebastian, Biarritz, and Paris. In 1920, the Lacloche brothers took over the Fabergé shop in London (closed after the 1917 Revolution) and its inventory; became successful in the next decade selling Fabergé clocks, accessories, and bibelots; had clients including the exiled duc d'Orléans; hired fabricators to produce its pendants and boxes, including Strauss, Allard, Meyer, brothers Verger, and various workshops for jewelry production. In 1931, it closed. 1933–35, Jacques Lacloche opened in Cannes and, in 1937, in Paris.
▶ Yvonne Brunhammer, *Le Cinquantenaire de l'Exposition de 1925*, Paris: Musée des Arts Décoratifs, 1976:133. Sylvie Raulet, *Bijoux Art Déco*, Paris: Regard, 1984. Melissa Gabardi, *Les Bijoux des Années 50*, Paris: Amateur, 1987.

Lacloche, Galerie
▶ French exhibition space and furniture producer.
▶ Until the 1970s in Paris, Galerie Lacloche produced widely published designs, including Roger Tallon's large 1965 chair in polished aluminum with polyester foam, and Bernard Rancillac's 1967 *Elephant Chair*.
▶ Gilles de Bure, *Le mobilier français 1965–1979*, Paris: Regard, 1983:51,65.

Lacombe, Georges (1868–1916)
▶ French carver; born Versailles.
▶ Studied painting under Roll; Académie Julian, Paris.
▶ In 1892, he became a member of the Nabis artists' group and, in 1893, showed his paintings with the group; in 1893–94, took up wood carving; produced furniture and panels carved in a style

relating to Gauguin's. He never sold his work, which was given to friends and neighbors.

▶ Yvonne Brunhammer et al., *Art Nouveau Belgium, France*, Houston: Institute for the Arts, Rice University, 1976.

Lacoste, Gerald (1909–)

▶ British architect, designer, and painter.

▶ In 1933, he designed the decorative glass for Casani's Club and the music room in glass for 1934 Queen's Gate Place, both London; best known for his 1934 silvery-gray-green glass fireplace with a glass-tile hearth produced by Pilkington and surrounding mirrored wall for Norman Hartnell's showroom, Bruton Street, London. In 1938, Lacoste designed the flat of Lord Mountbatten; after 1945, designed schools and residences, mostly in Essex.

▶ Cat., *Thirties: British art and design before the war*, London: Arts Council of Great Britain, Hayward Gallery, 1979:101,143,294.

Lacroix, Boris-Jean (1902–84)

▶ French designer; born Paris.

▶ Lacroix was a prolific designer of lighting, wallpaper, bookbinding, furniture, and interiors; in 1924, began working for couturier Madeleine Vionnet as a designer of dresses, handbags, and costume jewelry; soon after, decorated and designed her private residence. His designs were commissioned by Jean-Michel Frank and Jean Dunand. He designed furniture and chairs in Cubist forms for himself, produced by cabinetmaker Régamey; had clients including Damon, for whom he created a great many Modern lamps in engraved mirror and frosted glass tubes. He suggested that his lighting had no purpose other than to be harmonious with Modern interiors and predicted that lighting fixtures would become obsolete; executed practically every model of domestic lighting, including table lamps, illuminated ceilings, and pictures frames. Most of his polished and matt-finished nickel-plated copper lamps incorporated glass; some were produced only in metal. Damon used its special enamel-diffusing glass or the plain frosted variety. His articles were published in *Lux* in the late 1920s. In 1945, he became a member of UAM (Union des Artistes Modernes); pursued lighting and interior design independently.

▶ From 1927, work shown at sessions of Salon d'Automne and Salons of Société des Artistes Décorateurs.

▶ Janneau, *Le Luminaire et les Moyens d'éclairage Nouveaux*, second series: plates 22–24, third series: plates 27–33. *The Studio*, July–Dec. 1929:643. *Lux*, Jan. 1929:15, Dec. 1929:170, Dec. 1934:150. Alastair Duncan, *Art Nouveau and Art Déco Lighting*, New York: Simon and Schuster, 1978:154,175–76. Cat., Aaron Lederfajn and Xavier Lenormand, *Le Louvre des Antiquaires présente: 1930 quand le meuble devient sculpture*, Paris, 1986. Pierre Kjellberg, *Art Déco: les maîtres du Mobilier, le décor des Paquebots*, Paris: Amateur, 1986:185–86. Arlette Barré-Despond, *UAM*, Paris: Regard, 1986:523.

Lade, Jan (1944–)

▶ Danish interior architect and furniture designer.

▶ Studied College of Applied Arts, Copenhagen, to 1969.

▶ Lade and Svein Asbjørsen founded Møre Designteam in 1970; produced the *Split* concept; designed 1970 *Ecco* chairs produced by L.K. Hjelle Møbelfabrikk and 1985 ergonomic seat/bed/lounge unit designed to place the sitter's legs higher than his heart for supposed beneficial effects on circulation.

▶ Robert A.M. Stern (ed.), *The International Design Yearbook*, New York: Abbeville, 1985/1986: nos. 138,139. Fredrik Wildhagen, *Norge i Form*, Oslo: Stenersen, 1988:171–72.

Laeuger, Max (1864–1952)

▶ German architect, potter, painter, sculptor, and designer; born Lörrach.

▶ 1880–84, studied painting and interior design, Kunstgewerbeschule, Karlsruhe; 1892–93, Académie Julian, Paris.

▶ 1885–90, he was a teacher, Kunstgewerbeschule, Karlsruhe, working at potteries in Kandern during his holidays; from 1893, began to make lead-glazed slipware, some models of which were made in the J. Armbruster workshop, Kandern; was founder-

director of a craft pottery in Kandern, where plates were painted with metal oxides over white slip. Some models were crackled and bubbled, while others were faint and smoky due to reduction firing. From 1898, Laeuger was a professor, Universtät Karlsruhe; in 1907, became a founding member, Deutscher Werkbund; designed in a proto-Art Déco style; in 1916, founded a studio at Karlsruhe Majolikamanufaktur; concurrently, taught at institutions including the state art school in Baden 1920–22; in the 1920s, turned from painted decoration to techniques on glazes and slips fired to create subtle effects. Work included vases, bowls, plaques and experimentation with ceramic sculpture in animal forms (particularly elephants) and female figures. His turquoise glaze became known as Laeuger blue.

▶ Stuart Durant, *Ornament from the Industrial Revolution to Today*, Woodstock, NY: Overlook, 1986:249. Elisabeth Cameron, *Encyclopedia of Pottery and Porcelain*, London: Faber and Faber, 1986:192.

Lafaille, Maurice (1902–)

▶ French painter and furniture designer; born and active Paris.

▶ Studied cabinetmaking, École Boulle, Paris.

▶ He worked as a cabinetmaker for a manufacturer in the Faubourg Saint-Antoine, Paris; in 1928, assumed directorship of the shop L'Intérieur Moderne, Paris, and designed a luxurious bedroom (with Fraysse) for Mme. Francis Carco.

▶ 1925–26, work (as painter) shown at Salon d'Automne and, from 1927, (as decorator, with furniture produced by Atelier français) at Salons of Société des Artistes Décorateurs.

▶ Pierre Kjellberg, *Art Déco: les maîtres du Mobilier, le décor des Paquebots*, Paris: Amateur, 1986:107.

Lagares, Marcelo Joulia

See Naço, Studio

Laguiole

▶ French cutler; located plateau de l'Aubrac, Auvergne.

▶ Laguiole commissioned Philippe Starck to design its new building, a curved parallel ellipsoid; produced Yan Pennor's 1990 knife with its stylized Aubrac fly motif; in 1993, commissioned architect and designer Eric Ratty to design a knife.

▶ Starck's 1988 knife chosen by Comité Colbert for 1989 'L'Art de Vivre,' Cooper-Hewitt Museum, New York, and another knife at French Pavillion, 1992 'Exposición universal de Sevilla (Expo '92).' Received 1992 European Community Design Prize (renewal of corporate identity and use of contemporary designers).

▶ *European Community Design Prize*, Paris: Commission of the European Community, 1992.

Lahalle, Pierre (1877–1956)

▶ French architect, furniture designer, and interior decorator; born Orléans.

▶ Studied École des Arts Décoratifs, Paris.

▶ In *c*1902, Lahalle began designing furniture with Maurice Lucet (1877–1941), later joined in 1907 by Georges Levard. They moved from Art Nouveau to Art Déco styles based on 18th-century designs that they simplified and stylized. They used fine woods with ivory and mother-of-pearl inlays. Their color combinations of wood and lacquer, polychrome, and gilding were dramatic. The three worked together and apart. With Levard, Lahalle designed furniture for various firms including the Studium decorating atelier of Les Grands Magasins du Louvre, and occasionally worked for Primavera.

▶ Work (often with Levard) at Salons d'Automne and Salons of Société des Artistes Décorateurs. Designed (with Levard and André Fréchet) salon and boudoir in pavilion of Studium at 1925 Paris 'Exposition Internationale des Arts Décoratifs et Industriels Modernes.'

▶ Victor Arwas, *Art Déco*, Abrams, 1980. Pierre Kjellberg, *Art Déco: les maîtres du Mobilier, le décor des Paquebots*, Paris: Amateur, 1986:107–08.

Lalanne, Claude (1927–) and François-Xavier Lalanne

▶ French artists and designers; Claude Lalanne born Paris; François-Xavier Lalanne born Agen; wife and husband.

▶ Claude Lalanne studied architecture, École des Beaux-Arts and École des Arts Décoratifs, both Paris. François-Xavier Lalanne studied Académie Julian, Paris.

▶ The Lalannes began collaborating in 1956, although they mainly work separately. They became best known for their animal-shaped furniture and accessories in various media. Claude Lalanne's work included 1966 *Les Couverts* silver flatware and 1987 *Crocodile II* copper, bronze, and leather armchairs. François-Xavier Lalanne's work included 1976 *Rhino Ouvrant* copper container, 1977 *Hippopotame* bronze, wood, and silver cabinet, 1984 *Gorille de Surete* bronze-and-steel cabinet, 1985 *Grand Ane Bate* bronze container, 1987 *Le Poisson Boite* bronze book holder, and 1987 *Le Taureau* copper, wood and leather cabinet.

▶ François-Xavier Lalanne first showed paintings in 1952. In 1964, they had their first joint exhibition at Gallery J, Paris, followed by Galerie Alexander Iolas, Paris, in 1966, and Art Institute of Chicago, in 1967. Their early works were included in group exhibitions 1977 'Artiste/Artisan?,' Paris Musée des Arts Décoratifs; 1978 'L'Art et la Ville—Art dans la Vie,' Fondation Nationale des Arts Graphiques et Plastiques, Paris; 1979 'Weich und Plastisch,' Kunsthaus, Zürich. 1967–75, their work was shown at Alexander Iolas Galleries in Paris, New York, Milan, Geneva, Athens, and Madrid, and subsequently at Marisa Del Re Gallery, New York and Paris. Work on permanent display, Galerie Arteurial, Paris.

▶ Gilles de Bure, *Le mobilier français 1965–1979*, Paris: Regard, 1983:53–54. Cat., John Russell, *Les Lalannes—Claude and François-Xavier Lalanne*, New York: Marisa Del Re Gallery, 1988.

Lalique, Marc (1900–77)

▶ French glassmaker; active Paris; son of René-Jules Lalique.

▶ When Marc Lalique succeeded his father in 1945, he discontinued the production of glass in favor of crystal; is best known for his 1951 eight-leaf circular table.

▶ Marc and Marie-Claude Lalique, *Lalique par Lalique*, Lausanne: Edipop, 1977.

Lalique, Marie-Claude

▶ French glassware designer; daughter of Marc Lalique.

▶ Studied École des Arts Décoratifs, Paris.

▶ In 1977, she became chair of the Lalique firm and its sole designer.

▶ *Les Carnets du Design*, Paris: Mad-Cap Productions et APCI, 1986:39.

Lalique, René Jules (1860–1945)

▶ French glass designer, jeweler, furniture designer, painter, and sculptor; born Ay, Marne; active Paris.

▶ Apprenticed to goldsmith Louis Aucoc, Paris; 1878–80, studied in London; École des Arts Décoratifs, Paris.

▶ His early jewelry designs, stylistically conventional and technically unsophisticated, were sold to various jewelry manufacturers and published in the trade journal *Le Bijou*. In 1884, he met Jules Destape, who had a successful small jewelry workshop in Paris, which Lalique bought in 1885; continued to furnish a number of Parisian jewelers with designs, including Cartier, Boucheron, and his former master Aucoc; in 1887, moved to a larger space and, in 1890, moved once again to a new studio at 20 rue Thérèse and avenue de l'Opera, where he designed and made jewelry in gold decorated with precious stones, creating increasingly original designs. 1890–92, he studied enameling and experimented with new processes, creating a range of the soft colors characteristic of Art Nouveau. In 1902, he created a new process for molding glass; 1891–94, made much of the stage jewelry for Sarah Bernhardt and an Egyptian-style tiara in aluminum and glass for Mme. Barthet, started to assemble a spectacular jewelry series in 1896,

showing it at the 1900 Paris exposition; his reputation grew when museums bought his work. 1895–1912, he assembled a great series of 145 pieces for Calouste Gulbenkian. Lalique created a new style of jewelry influenced by Renaissance and Japanese art; in 1894, began to incorporate figurative designs (flowers, animals, insects, female figures, landscapes) into his work. His interest in glass led him to include pieces of crystal, carved into figurative forms, in his jewelry c1905. His sculpture was executed in bronze, ivory, and silver. He began experimentations in glass with the large 1904 molded-glass panel for the front door of his house in cours de la Reine, some scent bottles, and sculpture. In 1906–07, Lalique's career went into its second phase, when François Coty commissioned him to design scent bottles in pressed glass. Lalique followed with flacon designs for Marcel Rochas's *Femme* and the famous double-dove motif for Nina Ricci's *L'Air du Temps*. Establishing his own workshop in 1908 in Combs-la-Ville, he used both *cire perdue* (lost wax) and other molding methods. From c1910, his interest in glasswork was reflected in his late jewelry pieces in simple glass plauettes. Anticipating the importance of glass in 20th-century architecture, he designed and furnished in 1913 over 200 window panes for the Coty building, Fifth Avenue, New York. He established another workshop at Wingen-sur-Moder, Alsace, where it is located today. He abandoned jewelry in favor of pressed glass; although he finished pieces with hand-polishing and cutting, he used semi-industrial techniques to blow-mold and stamp. Lalique's production 1920–30 was prolific; he designed some 350 vases and bowls in molded clear, colored, or opalescent glass, along with a range of tableware, car mascots, jewelry, lighting, and scent bottles. He rediscovered the highly stable 'demi-crystal' and created one-off pieces by the *cire perdue* process; exploited the use of glass in indirect interior lighting; in 1932, produced a wide range of glass designs for the 1935 oceanliner *Normandie*. His work was widely copied by others including Sabino, Hunebelle, and Etling in France, and glassmakers worldwide. From 1945, the business was supervised by his son Marc Lalique. The firm is a member of Comité Colbert.

▶ Work (jewelry and silver incorporating enamel and glass) first shown at 1894 Paris Salon of the Société des Artistes français, and at 1900 Paris 'Exposition Universelle.' Work shown at 1902 Turin 'Esposizione Internazionale d'Arte Decorativa Moderna'; 1903 at Grafton Galleries, London; 1905 at Agnew's, London. First exhibition showing his glassware in 1912. His work was on display throughout 1925 Paris 'Exposition Internationale des Arts Décoratifs et Industriels Modernes', including at his own pavilion. Work shown at 1934 (II) Salon de la Lumière, Paris. In 1897, appointed Chevalier of the Légion d'Honneur.

▶ Katherine Morrison McClinton, *Lalique for Collectors*, Guildford: Lutterworth, 1975. Charlotte Gere, *American and European Jewelry 1830–1914*, New York: Crown, 1975:201. Yvonne Brunhammer et al., *Art Nouveau Belgium, France*, Houston: Institute for the Arts, Rice University, 1976. Christopher Vane Percy, *The Glass of René Lalique*, London: Studio Vista, 1977. Marc and Marie-Claude Lalique, *Lalique par Lalique*, Lausanne: Edipop, 1977. Victor Arwas, *The Glass of René Lalique*, London: Academy, 1980. Victor Arwas, *Art Déco*, Abrams, 1980. Jessica Rutherford, *Art Nouveau, Art Deco and the Thirties: The Furniture Collections at Brighton Museum*, Brighton: The Royal Pavilion, Art Gallery and Museums, 1983:36–37. Félix Marcilhac, *René Lalique 1860–1945, maître verrier*, Paris: Amateur, 1989. *Les bijoux de René Lalique*, Paris: Musée des Arts Décoratifs, 1991.

Lalique, Suzanne (1899–)

▶ French painter and decorator; daughter of René Lalique.

▶ Studied under Eugène Morand.

▶ She designed porcelain for Sèvres and Limoges, and fabrics and wallpaper; sold a painted screen to Jacques Doucet.

▶ She showed her work at the 1915 Salon d'Automne and later at Salons des Tuileries, Salons of Société Nationale des Beaux-Arts, and Société des Artistes Décorateurs.

Lallemant, Robert   (1902–54)
▶ French ceramicist and decorator.
▶ Studied ceramics, École des Beaux-Arts, Dijon; trained under Raoul Lachenal.
▶ Lallemant set up his own workshop in 1928, producing limited-production ceramic items and designing furniture; was active as an interior decorator; in 1929, became a member of UAM (Union des Artistes Modernes) and was its only ceramicist member; after 1930, turned to industrial architecture and furniture design.
▶ From 1926, work shown at Salons of the Société des Artistes Décorateurs. Work (ceramics and metal, wood, and glass furniture) shown at the events of UAM from its first exhibition in 1930 to 1937.
▶ Lucie Delarue-Mardrus, 'Les céramiques de Lallemant,' *abc antiquités, beaux-arts, curiosités*, No. 219, April 1983:37. Cat., *Robert Lallemant ou la céramique mécanisée*, Paris: Galerie Jacques de Voo, 1984. Pierre Kjellberg, *Art Déco: les maîtres du Mobilier, le décor des Paquebots*, Paris: Amateur, 1986:108. Arlette Barré-Despond, *UAM*, Paris: Regard, 1986:434–53. Cat., *Les années UAM 1929–1958*, Paris: Musée des Arts Décoratifs, 1988:204–05.

Lam, Izabel   (1948–)
▶ American fashion designer and sculptor.
▶ In 1988, Lam turned from fashion to industrial design; designed housewares in a neo-baroque idiom, including flatware, picture frames, candlesticks, vases, and letter openers. Her 15-piece lighting collection was made of curvaceous oxidized steel with metal-mesh shades. As Geoffrey Beene's former design assistant, Lam's work includes jewelry and sculpture.
▶ Arlene Hirst, *Metropolitan Home*, June 1990:31.

Lamb, Thomas
▶ Canadian furniture designer; born Orillia, Ontario.
▶ Lamb began designing furniture while at Robin Bush Associates, where he was active on furniture for the 1967 Montreal 'Universal and International Exhibition (Expo '67).' He assisted Alfred Faux on the design of the widely published drafting table produced by Norman Wade. Designing for both residential and contract furniture manufacturers, his work included the 1978 *Steamer* chair produced by Ambient Systems, Toronto.
▶ Cat., *Seduced and Abandoned: Modern Furniture designers in Canada, the First Fifty Years*, Toronto: The Art Gallery at Harbourfront, 1986:27.

Lambert, Théodore
▶ French architect, decorator, and furniture designer; born Besançon.
▶ Some of Lambert's furniture was produced by Decaux. For his décors, Théodore Lambert produced locks, lighting, *passementerie*, and other fittings.
▶ From 1907, work shown at Salons of Société Nationale des Beaux-Arts and, from its founding in 1904 to 1927, at Salons of Société des Artistes Décorateurs.
▶ *Ensembles Mobiliers*, Vol. II, Paris: Charles Moreau, 1937. Pierre Kjellberg, *Art Déco: les maîtres du Mobilier, le décor des Paquebots*, Paris: Amateur, 1986:108.

Lambert-Rucki, Jean   (1888–1967)
▶ Polish painter and sculptor; born Crakow.
▶ Studied Crakow School of Fine Arts.
▶ He moved to Paris in 1911 and shared a room with Amedeo Modigliani. Influenced by Cubism, Lambert-Rucki's most notable achievements were his collaborations with Jean Dunand, including lacquered panels and decorative pieces designed by him and executed by Dunand in whimsical animal motifs in the 1920s–30s. For Georges Fouquet 1936–37, he created jewelry designs inspired by West African art and machine aesthetics. He was friendly with architects Robert Mallet-Stevens and Georges-Henri Pingusson; in 1930, became a member of UAM (Union des

Artistes Modernes); from 1930, devoted his efforts to religious art; in 1936, furnished jewelry designs to Georges Fouquet.
▶ Work shown at Salon des Indépendants from 1920, Section d'Or group from 1922–24, Salon d'Automne, Galerie Léonce Rosenberg, Paris, in 1924, and Salon des Tuileries from 1933. Work (smoking room of French Embassy with Dunand) at 1925 Paris 'Exposition Internationale des Arts Décoratifs et Industriels Modernes'; at Union des Artistes Modernes exhibitions of the 1930s and at 1930 UAM exhibition (four sculptures). Contributed to design of 1936 (III) Salon de la Lumière, Paris. Designed a monumental bas-relief for UAM pavilion at 1937 Paris 'Exposition Internationale des Arts et Techniques dans la Vie Moderne.'
▶ Sylvie Raulet, *Bijoux Art Déco*, Paris: Regard, 1984. 'Lambert-Rucki,' in Sammlung Brohan, *Kunst der 20e und 30e Jahre*, Berlin: Karl Brohan, 1985. Cat., Aaron Lederfajn and Xavier Lenormand, *Le Louvre des Antiquaires présente: 1930 quand le meuble devient sculpture*, Paris, 1986. Arlette Barré-Despond, *UAM*, Paris: Regard, 1986:436–37. Cat., *Les années UAM 1929–1958*, Paris: Musée des Arts Décoratifs, 1988:206–07.

Lancel, Henri
▶ French decorator and furniture designer; active Paris.
▶ Studied drawing and painting, École Bernard Palissy, and École Nationale Supérieure des Arts Décoratifs, both Paris.
▶ He was friendly with Jean Dunand, Jacques-Émile Ruhlmann, and Pierre Legrain of Groupe des Cinq; 1928–30, traveled in South America and Cuba and worked in exotic woods; 1930–40, lived in Belgium; in 1945, returned to France; designed furniture, most of which was produced by MAF (Mobiliers et Ameublement français), and the chest of drawers and articulated mirror for the 1961 oceanliner *France*.
▶ Pascal Renou, *Portraits de Créateurs*, Paris: H. Vial, 1969.

Landault, Robert   (1919–)
▶ French ceramicist and furniture designer.
▶ 1933–37, studied École des Arts Appliqués, Paris.
▶ He produced ceramics for La Crémaillère, Paris; subsequently, worked at the Studium decorating department of Les Grands Magasins du Louvre, where he was artistic director 1945–55; had clients including individuals, hotels, and offices.
▶ Received 1955 René Gabriel Prize.
▶ Pascal Renous, *Portraits de Créateurs*, Paris: H. Vial, 1969.

Landberg, Nils   (1907–)
▶ Swedish engraver and glassware designer.
▶ 1925–27, trained at the School of Arts and Crafts, Gothenburg, and the school of glass engraving, Orrefors Glasbruk.
▶ 1927–72, Landberg was a designer at Orrefors Glasbruk, where he was first an engraver and became a designer of glass, including tableware, art pieces, and architectural decorations; had a preference for freely blown thin and delicate glass; in the 1960s, produced tall glasses with delicate bowls and slender stems; also produced studio glass.
▶ Received a gold medal at 1954 (X) Triennale di Milano. Work shown at 1937 Paris 'Exposition Internationale des Arts et Techniques dans la Vie Moderne'; 1939 'New York World's Fair'; 1948 and 1957 in Zürich; 1954–57 USA 'Design in Scandinavia' traveling exhibition; 1958 'Formes Scandinaves'; Paris Musée des Arts Décoratifs; 1959 in Amsterdam; 1980 'Scandinavian Modern Design 1880–1980' exhibition, Cooper-Hewitt Museum, New York; 1983–84 'Design since 1945' exhibition, Philadelphia Museum of Art.
▶ Cat., 'Nils Landberg,' *Design Quarterly*, No. 34, 1956:16–17. Erik Zahle (ed.), *A Treasury of Scandinavian Design*, New York, 1961:281, nos. 220,228. Eileene Harrison Beer, *Scandinavian Design: Objects of a Life Style*, New York, 1975:90,93,96. Cat., David Revere McFadden (ed.), *Scandinavian Modern Design 1880–1980*, New York: Abrams, 1982:267, No. 169. Kathryn B. Hiesinger and George H. Marcus III (ed.), *Design Since 1945*, Philadelphia: Philadelphia Museum of Art, 1983. Frederick Cooke, *Glass: Twentieth-Century Design*, New York: Dutton, 1986:85. Jennifer

Hawkins Opie, *Scandinavia: Ceramics and Glass in the Twentieth Century*, New York: Rizzoli, 1989.

Landes, Michael (1948–)
▶ German architect and designer; born Frankfurt.
▶ Studied architecture, Technische Hochschule, Darmstadt.
▶ 1980–86, he lectured in architecture, Technische Hochschule, Darmstadt; in 1981, set up an architecture partnership with Norbert Berghof and Wolfgang Rang. In a Biedermeieresque style, the team designed the 1985 *F1 Frankfurter Schrank* secretary desk and the 1986 *Frankfurter Stuhl III* armchair, both produced by Draenert Studio.
▶ Albrecht Bangert and Karl Michael Armer, *80s Style: Designs of the Decade*, New York: Abbeville, 1990:32–33,232.

Landesausstellung
See Schweizerische Landesausstellung

Landry, Abel (1871–1923)
▶ French architect and designer; born Limoges; active Paris.
▶ Studied École des Arts Décoratifs, Limoges; École des Beaux-Arts, Paris; and under William Morris in London.
▶ He became associated with Julius Meier-Graefe's shop La Maison Moderne, which made the majority of his objects, mostly in porcelain and metal. He preferred to create total interiors, including wallpaper, curtains, carved paneling, and artwork for the walls; was a member of La Poignée with Victor Prouvé and Jules Brateau; used stone and ceramics for exterior ornamentation in the private homes and villas he designed in Paris, Bordeaux, and Coteaux, and apartment buildings in Lyons and Marseilles. His style was similar to that of Georges de Feure, contained no superfluous ornamentation, and was easily adapted for mass production. After Meier-Graefe's shop closed, his work was sold at Déroullia et Petit, at Grands Magasins de Printemps, and at Maison Ballauf et Petitpoint.
▶ Work shown with La Poignée from 1904. Work (wrought-iron chandeliers, gilt and silvered bronze ceiling lamps, table lamps, and *flambeaux*) shown at Salons of Société des Artistes Décorateurs from 1904 and sessions of Salon d'Automne 1906–13.
▶ *Deutsche Kunst und Dekoration*, 1902–03:179,551,555. Yvonne Brunhammer et al., *Art Nouveau Belgium, France*, Houston: Institute for the Arts, Rice University, 1976. Alastair Duncan, *Art Nouveau and Art Déco Lighting*, New York: Simon and Schuster, 1978:79–80.

Lane, Danny (1955–)
▶ American painter and furniture designer; born USA; active London.
▶ Studied painting, Central School of Arts and Crafts, London to 1980.
▶ He moved to London in 1975 to work with stained glass designer Patrick Reyntiens; in 1981, set up his own studio in London's East End; in 1983, established the Glassworks cooperative in Hackney, where he and his workers used glass inventively to create one-off furniture and furnishings. By 1986, his studio was handling large-scale architectural works. In c1986, he collaborated with Ron Arad's One-Off workshop on commissions, including the executive offices of Bureaux, a clothing company, for which Lane designed dramatic glass screens; at Glassworks, designed 1986 stacked chair and table, using layered clear glass unevenly cut; created his shapes by hammering armor-plate glass. Fiam produced his 1988 *Shell* and *Atlas* tables.
▶ Albrecht Bangert and Karl Michael Armer, *80s Style: Designs of the Decade*, New York: Abbeville, 1990:74–75,232. *Acquisitions 1982–1990 arts décoratifs*, Paris: Fonds National d'Art Contemporain, 1991.

Lanel, Luc (1894–1966)
▶ French designer.
▶ Lanel designed a silver service in c1935 for the oceanliner *Normandie*, and other silverwares produced by Orfèvrerie Christofle.

▶ Léon Deshairs, *Modern French Decorative Art*, Paris: Albert Lévy.

Lang, Annette (1960–)
▶ German industrial designer; born Hamburg.
▶ 1980–85, studied Staatlichen Akademie der bildenden Künste, Stuttgart.
▶ From 1986–87, she worked at Studio Matteo Thun, Milan; 1986–87, at Studio Antonio Citterio, Milan; and, 1987–88, as a freelance designer at Sottsass Associati, Milan. She was active as a designer of household articles, furniture, lighting, mobile telephones, personal computers, office furniture, and exhibition systems; designed 1988 *Fantasy* flatware by ICM and 1988 *Chaiseletto* chaise longue in tubular steel with bicycle wheels by Valsazino; with Richard Sapper, taught at Staatlichen Akademie der bildenden Künste, Stuttgart.
▶ Cat., Design Center Stuttgart, *Women in Design: Careers and Life Histories Since 1900*, Stuttgart: Haus der Wirtschaft, 1989:132–35.

Lange, Gerd (1931–)
▶ German designer; born Wuppertal.
▶ Studied Werkkunstschule, Offenbach-am-Main, to 1956.
▶ 1956–61, he executed interior, industrial, and exhibition designs; from 1964 in his Kapsweyer studio, specialized in furniture and lighting mainly for contract manufacturers; from 1962, designed furniture for Thonet (including 1985 *Thonet-Cut* stacking chair), Wilhelm Bofinger (including knock-down 1966 *Farmer* chair), and Drabert, and lighting for Staff and Kartell.
▶ From 1964, work shown annually at 'Die gute Industrieform' exhibitions, Hanover, and at 1964 'Student Rooms Exhibition', Hanover; 1965 'Die gute Industrieform' exhibition, Design Center, London; 1966 'Vijftig Jaar Zitten' exhibition, Stedelijk Museum; 1968 'Contemporary Furniture' exhibition, Munich; 1970 'Rat für Formgebung,' Darmstadt. Received two first prizes in 1969 Bundespreis 'Die gute Industrieform' (chair designs).
▶ Cat., *Modern Chairs 1918–1970*, London: Lund Humphries, 1971: No. 70. 'A Chair for All Seasons from Thonet,' *Contract Interiors*, Vol. 136, July 1977: 20. Cat., Kathryn B. Hiesinger and George H. Marcus III (eds.), *Design Since 1945*, Philadelphia: Philadelphia Museum of Art, 1983.

Langenbeck, Karl (1861–1938)
▶ Ceramics designer; active USA.
▶ Langenbeck joined American Encaustic Tiling, Zanesville, Ohio, where he experimented with new glazes and Parian wares; in 1894, with Herman Mueller (also of American Encaustic), founded Mosaic Tile, Zanesville; departing in 1908, formed Mueller Mosaic, Trenton, New Jersey.
▶ Doreen Bolger Burke et al., *In Pursuit of Beauty*, New York: Metropolitan Museum of Art and Abrams, 1986.

Langenmayr, Albert (1951–)
▶ German furniture designer; born Lauingen; active Berlin.
▶ 1980–86, studied Hochschule der Künste, Berlin; 1980–86, studied cabinetmaking, becoming a master in 1986.
▶ In 1980, he was an apprentice cabinetmaker; from 1982, designed the interiors of houses in Berlin and USA; became known for his artful and technically sophisticated furniture designs. His 1990 *Tension* table incorporated suspension-bridge engineering, and his *Storch I* armchair and *Storch II* side chair were each held together by a single screw.
▶ Work shown at 1984 'IBA - Idee, Prozess und Ergebnis,' Martin-Gropius-Bau, Berlin; 1986 'Transit Berlin-West: Möbel und Mode,' IDZ Berlin, Hochschule der Künste, Berlin; 1988 'Berlin: Les avant-gardes du mobilier,' Galerie Néotù, Paris.
▶ Christian Borngräber, *Prototypen der Designwerkstätt*, Berlin: Ernst und Sohn, 1988. Cat., Angela Schönberger et al., *Berlin: Les Avant-Gardes du Mobilier*, Paris: Néotù, 1988.

Langrand, Jeanne

▶ French bookbinder and gilder; active Paris.

▶ 1909–13, studied École des Arts Décoratifs, Paris.

▶ Her sister Andrée Langrand was director of École des Arts Décoratifs, at which Jeanne became an instructor c1918. In 1934, she set up her own bindery and gilding workshop on pont de Champerret, Paris; had clients including Paul Hébert and Jacques Doucet; for Doucet, bound *La Belle Journée* and *Ubu Roi* with blind tooling and gold fillets in the geometric style for which she became known.

▶ Work shown at 1925 Paris 'Exposition Internationale des Arts Décoratifs et Industriels Modernes.'

▶ Gaston Quénioux, *Les Arts décoratifs modernes 1918–1925*, Paris, 1925: 343. Rose Adler, *Reliures, présenté par Rose Adler*, Paris, 1929: plate 28. Ph. Dally, 'Les Techniques modernes de la reliure,' *Art et décoration*, Jan. 1927: 20–22. Ernest de Crauzat, *La Reliure française de 1900 à 1925*, Vol. 2, Paris, 1932. Marie Michon, *La Reliure française*, Paris, 1951:134. Roger Devauchelle, *La Reliure en France de ses origines à nos jours*, Vol. 3, Paris, 1961:167,267. Alastair Duncan and Georges de Bartha, *Art Nouveau and Art Déco Bookbinding*, New York: Abrams, 1989:19,192.

Lanux, Eyre de

See de Lanux, Eyre 'Lise'

Lanvin, Jeanne   (1867–1946)

▶ French fashion designer; active Paris.

▶ Lanvin opened her fashion house in 1885 in rue du Marché Saint-Honoré, Paris; her clients included actresses, notably Yvonne Printemps. The emblem designed by Paul Iribe for the firm depicted Lanvin dressed for a ball with her daughter Marguerite (later renamed Marie-Blanche) at her feet. Armand-Albert Rateau designed Lanvin's fashion house and managed the Lanvin-Décoration department of interior design in the rue du Faubourg Saint-Honoré. Lanvin's apartment in the 1920–22 townhouse, rue Barbet-de-Jouy, that she had built next to that of her daughter was also designed by Rateau and partially reconstructed in the Paris Musée des Arts Décoratifs in 1965. In 1950, Marie-Blanche Lanvin hired designer Antonio Canovas del Castillo; 1963–84, Jules-François Crahay was stylist at Lanvin. From 1985, Maryll Lanvin was a designer. In 1989, the firm was purchased by Midland Bank and, in 1990, became part of Orcofi. In 1990, Claude Montana became director of *haute couture*.

▶ Participated in 1925 Paris 'Exposition Internationale des Arts Décoratifs et Industriels Modernes,' 1927 exhibitions in Prague and Athens, 1931 Paris 'Exposition Coloniale,' 1935 Brussels 'Exposition Universelle et Internationale de Bruxelles,' 1937 Paris 'Exposition Internationale des Arts et Techniques dans la Vie Moderne.' Lanvin's fashion show was held on the 1935 oceanliner *Normandie* during its maiden voyage from Paris to New York. In 1938, appointed Chevalier of the Légion d'honneur.

▶ Éveline Schumberger, 'Au 16 rue Barbet-de-Jouy avec Jeanne Lanvin,' *Connaissance des Arts*, No. 138, Aug. 1963:62–71. Yvonne Brunhammer, *Le Cinquantenaire de l'Exposition de 1925*, Paris: Musée des Arts Décoratifs, 1976:134.

Lanza, Aldo   (1942–)

▶ Italian designer; born Turin; active Brescia.

▶ Studied architecture, Politecnico di Milano, to 1969.

▶ He began his professional career in 1968; had clients in Italy including Alexia and Gufran; designed plastic furniture by Kartell and Valenti, and bath accessories by Bilumen; became a member of ADI (Associazione per il Disegno Industriale).

▶ *ADI Annual 1976*, Milan: Associazione per il Disegno Industriale, 1976.

Lanzani, Paola   (1933–)

▶ Italian architect and designer; born Nerviano; active Milan.

▶ She joined Ordine degli Architetti in Milan and Gescal; in 1972, became a member of ADI (Associazione per il Disegno Industriale); 1960–65, worked in a studio in Bogotà (Colombia), where she designed residences, buildings, and furnishings; was consultant designer to Shell Colombia, Ervico, and Olivetti; taught technical design, American University, Bogotà; in 1966, returned to Italy and worked on the renovation and architectural interiors of the Rinascente department store in Milan and Turin, and as consultant designer to the Richard-Ginori store, and to Lanerossi in Lecce and Mestre. In 1971, Lanzani and Franco Menna set up their own studio in Milan, designing the stores of Croff Centro Casa, industrial design, and interior architecture.

▶ Work shown at 1968 (XIV) and 1973 (XV) Triennali di Milano and in various Eurodomus sessions, Ljubljana.

▶ *ADI Annual 1976*, Milan: Associazione per il Disegno Industriale, 1976.

Lapidouse, Sylvie   (1954–)

▶ French furniture designer.

▶ Lapidouse became an interior designer in c1977; designed the 1986 *Epsilon* chair produced by Avant Scene, and the 1990 wood *Diver-desk* inspired by Oliver Sacks's book *The Man Who Mistook His Wife for a Hat*.

▶ *Vogue Décoration* No. 26: 21.

Laporte-Blairsy, Léo   (1865–1923)

▶ French sculptor and lighting designer; born Toulouse.

▶ Studied under Alexandre Falguière.

▶ He began as a sculptor and engraver of large monuments and busts; reduced the scale of his work in the late 1890s, becoming involved in lighting; became known for his Art Nouveau sculptural lighting with its high aesthetics and technical innovation; was one of the first to use incandescent bulbs in a manner impossible with combustion light; designed lamps, statuettes, vases, letter openers, and *épergnes* in bronze, marble, and plaster. His biscuit porcelain wares were produced by Sèvres. He executed objects in gold, silver, and translucent enamel, mostly sold by M. Houdebine. Other lighting was produced by the founders Susse frères. Some of his lighting or 'luminous fantasies' told a story (*La Fillette au Ballon* was about a young girl who bought a balloon from Les Grands Magasins du Louvre), while others were based on historical themes, and still others on pure decoration.

▶ Work shown at 1887 Salon of the Société des Artistes français, including smaller scaled works at the 1898 event.

▶ *Revue des Arts Décoratifs*, 1901:260. *L'Art*, 1902:40–47. *Éclairage de 1900 à nos jours*, Brussels: L'écuyer, Nos. 31,33,43. *Deutsche Kunst und Dekoration*, 1903–04:105. Alastair Duncan, *Art Nouveau and Art Déco Lighting*, New York: Simon and Schuster, 1978:80–81.

Lapparra

▶ French silversmiths; located Paris.

▶ Lapparra originally specialized in the production of flatware; from the 1920s, manufactured hollow-ware. The firm's designers included Paul Follot.

▶ Showed wares at 1925 Paris 'Exposition Internationale des Arts Décoratifs et Industriels Modernes' and 1930 Paris 'Décor de la Table' (including Follot's designs), Musée Galliéra, Paris.

▶ Annelies Krekel-Aalberse, *Art Nouveau and Art Déco Silver*, New York: Abrams, 1989:66,69,70,256.

Larche, François-Raoul   (1860–1912)

▶ French sculptor; born Saint-André-de-Cubzac.

▶ From 1878, studied École Nationale des Beaux-Arts, Paris, under François Jouffroy, Alexandre Falguière, and Eugène Delaplanche.

▶ He was known for his monumental sculptures, although after the turn of the century he turned to mass-produced castings of smaller pieces; produced designs for objects such as goblets, ashtrays, vases, and centerpieces made by Siot-Décauville; was best known for his table lamps in the swirling form of Loïe Fuller and her famous flowing costume; executed the group *La Loire et ses affluents*, commissioned in 1910 for place du Carrousel, Paris.

▶ Work first shown at 1881 Salon of the Société des Artistes français and, from 1884, regularly at École Nationale des Beaux-Arts, where in 1886 he won the second grand prize of the Prix de Rome. Received a gold medal at 1900 Paris 'Exposition Universelle.'

▶ Cat., *Exposition des Oeuvres de Raoul Larche, statuaire et peintre, et de Raymond Sudre, statuaire et peintre*, Paris: 57 rue Chardon-Lagarche. *Le Modern Style*, Paris: Baschet, 1974:172. Yvonne Brunhammer et al., *Art Nouveau Belgium, France*, Houston: Institute for the Arts, Rice University, 1976.

Larcher, Dorothy (1884–1952)

▶ British textile designer; active Painswick, Gloucestershire.

▶ Studied Hornsey School of Art, London.

▶ From the early 1920s, she and Phyllis Barron collaborated on textile production and design. In 1930, production was moved to Painswick, Gloucestershire, where they produced dressmaking and furnishing textiles using new and historic French blocks. In 1939, their fabrics were sold at Little Gallery, Ellis Street. Commissions included soft furnishings for the Duke of Westminster's yacht *The Flying Cloud* and the Senior Common Room of Girton College, Cambridge. With Enid Marx, they were the foremost exponents of hand-block-printed fabrics in the first half of the 20th century in Britain. They rejected aniline dyes in favor of vegetable dyes; revived the discharge-printing method; were best known for their bold monochromatic prints on unbleached cottons and linens.

▶ Cat., *Thirties: British art and design before the war*, London: Arts Council of Great Britain, Hayward Gallery, 1979: 92, 125,126,285,296.

Larsen, Ejner (1917–)

▶ Danish furniture designer.

▶ Studied cabinetmaking, Det Kongelige Danske Akademi, Copenhagen, to 1940.

▶ 1942–57, he was an instructor at Det Kongelige Danske Akademi; worked with Jacob Kjær and architects Mogens Koch, Peter Koch, and Palle Suenson; in 1947 with Askel Bender Madsen, set up his own design studio.

▶ Work shown at Triennali di Milano, 1954–57 USA 'Design in Scandinavia,' 1960–61 USA 'The Arts of Denmark,' 1965 exhibition of Danish arts and crafts at Das Kantonale Gewerbemuseum, Berne.

▶ Frederik Sieck, *Nutidig Dansk Møbeldesign: — en kortfattet illustreret beskrivelse*, Copenhagen: Bondo Gravesen; 1990 Busck edition in English.

Larsen, Jack Lenor (1927–)

▶ American textile designer; born Seattle.

▶ 1945–50, studied Washington University, Seattle; 1951–52, Cranbrook Academy of Art, Bloomfield Hills, Michigan.

▶ He opened his own workshop in New York in 1952 and received his first commission, from the architecture firm Skidmore, Owings and Merrill, for draperies for 1952 Lever House, New York. At this time, he began machine-weaving fabrics that had the appearance of handweaving; they were subsequently much imitated. In 1958, he set up Larsen Design Studio for experimentation, consultation, and fabrication for large architecture projects; designed fabrics for the decorating trade and institutional and airline use; lectured and traveled widely, studying textile design. Larsen's textile innovations included the first printed-velvet upholstery fabrics, the first stretch upholstery fabric in 1961, and the warp-knit Saran-monofilament casement fabric (including the 1960 *Interplay*). He created cabin upholstery fabrics for Pan Am in 1969 and Braniff 1972–78; the theater curtain for Filene Center for Performing Arts at Wolf Trap, Virginia, in 1971; quilted banners for Sears Tower, Chicago, 1974; upholstery fabric for Cassina (1967) in 1981, and for Vescom. He wrote numerous books, including *Elements of Weaving* with Azalea Thorpe and *Beyond Craft: The Art Fabric* (1973) with Mildred Constantine.

▶ Work subject of 1980 'Jack Lenor Larsen: 30 Years of Creative Textiles' exhibition, Paris Musée des Arts Décoratifs. Received a gold medal at 1964 (XIII) Triennale di Milano and 1964 Premio

Compasso d'Oro. In 1983, elected Honorary Royal Designer for Industry.

▶ Jack Lenor Larsen and Azalea Thorpe, *Elements of Weaving*, New York, 1967. Larry Salmon, 'Jack Lenor Larsen in Boston,' *Craft Horizons*, Vol. 23, April 1971:14–23. Mildred Constantine and Jack Lenor Larsen, *Beyond Craft: The Art Fabric*, New York, 1973. Jack Lenor Larsen et al., *The Dyer's Art: Ikat, Batik, Plangi*, New York, 1976. Mildred Constantine, 'Jack Lenor Larsen: The First 25 Years,' *American Fabrics and Fashions*, No. 113, Summer 1978. Jack Lenor Larsen and Mildred Constantine, *The Art Fabric: Mainstream*, New York, 1981. Cat., *Jack Lenor Larsen: 30 Years of Creative Textiles*, Paris: Musée des Arts Décoratifs, 1981. Cat., Kathryn B. Hiesinger and George H. Marcus III (eds.), *Design Since 1945*, Philadelphia: Philadelphia Museum of Art, 1983. Robert A.M. Stern (ed.), *The International Design Yearbook*, New York: Abbeville, 1985/1986: Nos. 311,313. Cherie Fehrman and Kenneth Fehrman, *Postwar Interior Design, 1945–1960*, New York: Van Nostrand Reinhold, 1987.

Larsen, Johannes (1912–)

▶ Danish engineer.

▶ Trained as a civil engineer in Copenhagen.

▶ In 1967, he opened his own office in Vanlose; designed a range of objects including furniture and milking machines, and the 1967–68 *Cylinder Cushion 272* floor seat produced by France & Søn.

▶ *Cylinder Cushion 181* lounger first shown at 1968 Annual Furniture Fair at Christianhus, Horsholm.

▶ Cat., *Modern Chairs 1918–1970*, London: Lund Humphries, 1971.

Larsen, Tove Kindt (1906–)

▶ Danish architect; born Copenhagen.

▶ Studied architecture, Royal Academy, Copenhagen.

▶ She worked with Danish architect Tude Svrss; after World War II, with Edward Kindt Larsen, opened her own studio, designing furniture, silver, and glassware; from 1960, worked with textiles and designed furniture.

▶ Robert A.M. Stern (ed.), *The International Design Yearbook*, New York: Abbeville, 1985/1986: No. 310.

Larsens, Bjørn A. (1926–)

▶ Norwegian furniture designer.

▶ Active from the 1950s, Larsens worked for Trio Fabrikker in 1952 and the Postverket in 1957.

▶ Received (with Terje Meyer and Jan Sverre Christiansen) 1973 Japanese design prize (for a bicycle model).

▶ Fredrik Wildhagen, *Norge i Form*, Oslo: Stenersen, 1988:153.

Larsson-Kjelin, Ann (1953–)

▶ Swedish textile designer.

▶ Studied Textile Institute, Stockholm, to 1974.

▶ From 1977, she was associated with the firm Marks Pelle Vävare; in addition to domestic textiles, contributed to a number of public works.

▶ Robert A.M. Stern (ed.), *The International Design Yearbook*, New York: Abbeville, 1985/1986: No. 314.

László, Paul (1900–93)

▶ Hungarian architect, decorator, and designer.

▶ László moved to Vienna in 1923 and set up a decorating firm; within a short time, worked on decorating commissions throughout Europe; in 1927, settled in Stuttgart; in 1936, moved to Los Angeles; designed furniture that was mass produced; decorated interiors for clients including Cary Grant, Elizabeth Taylor, Barbara Stanwyck, Robert Taylor and Barbara Hutton; in Los Angeles, designed stores for Bullock's Wilshire, Goldwater's, Robinson's, and Orbach's, and most of the casinos and showrooms of Howard Hughes's hotels in Las Vegas; became known for an exuberant style associated with the 1950s on the West Coast. His work included textiles and lighting, some furniture designed for Saltman

California, and, produced for a time in the 1940s, upholstery and furniture for Herman Miller.

▶ 'Paul Laszlo, 93, Dies; Architect to Celebrities,' *The New York Times*, 9 April 1993:D21.

Latham, Richard S.   (1920–)

▶ American industrial designer.

▶ Studied engineering and design, Illinois Institute of Technology, Chicago, under Mies van der Rohe.

▶ 1940–55, he was a product designer for Raymond Loewy; headed Loewy's Chicago office for most of this period, producing work including housings for Hallicrafters radios and televisions; with Loewy, designed and planned the marketing for a range of ceramic dinnerware produced by Rosenthal and, under his own name, designed glassware for Rosenthal Studio Line; in 1955 with Jakob Jensen and others, set up the design office of Latham Tyler Jensen in Chicago; Long Beach, California; and Copenhagen, and had clients including Xerox, Argus cameras, Ampex electronics, and Bang & Olufsen.

▶ Work shown at 1983–84 'Design Since 1945' exhibition, Philadelphia Museum of Art.

▶ Richard S. Latham, 'Is This Change Necessary?,' *Industrial Design*, Vol. 5, Feb. 1958:66–70. Richard S. Latham, 'The Artifacts as a Cultural Cipher,' in Laurence B. Holland (ed.), *Who Designs America?*, New York, 1966:257–80. Richard S. Latham, 'Der Designer in USA: Stilist, Künstler, Produkplaner?' *Form*, No. 34, 1966:28–31. Cat., Kathryn B. Hiesinger and George H. Marcus III (eds.), *Design Since 1945*, Philadelphia: Philadelphia Museum of Art, 1983.

Laughlin Pottery

▶ American ceramics manufacturer; located East Liverpool, Ohio.

▶ Brothers Shakespear and Homer Laughlin founded the Laughlin Pottery, East Liverpool, Ohio, in 1871. It was one of the first potteries in the USA to produce whitewares. Starting with 60 employees, it produced about 6,000 pieces of dinnerware per day. In 1879, Shakespear Laughlin left the firm; 1879–81, it was managed by Homer Laughlin. In 1889, William Edwin Wells joined the firm; Homer Laughlin sold his interest in the firm to Wells, Marcus Aaron, and others. The firm moved to nearby Laughlin Station where, by 1903, it began full production in two new buildings and a third purchased from another company. In 1906, a fourth plant was built in Newell, West Virginia, which began full production in 1907. In 1913, a fifth plant was added; in 1923, a sixth with a continuous tunnel kiln. The new production technique proved so successful that further plants were added in 1927 and 1929. At its peak, 2,500 workers produced 360,000 pieces of dinnerware per day in 1,500,000 square feet (140,000 m²) of production space. In 1929, all the East Liverpool factories were closed; the Newell site remained. In 1930, Wells was succeeded by his son Joseph Mahan Wells. Under the Aarons' management, the production included oven-to-table wares *Oven Serve* and *Kitchen Kraft*. In 1936, *Fiesta* dinnerware in the brightly colored glazes associated with Homer Laughlin was added to the firm's range, followed by *Harlequin* and *Rivera*. In 1936, a colorful decal pattern was applied to the *Nautilus* range, creating the *Harmony* line. In 1960, Joseph M. Wells became chair and son Joseph M. Wells Jr. executive vice-president. Homer Laughlin's 1,600 workers today produce over one million pieces of dinnerware per week.

▶ Received grand prize at 1876 Philadelphia 'Centennial Exposition.'

▶ Sharon and Bob Huxford, *The Collector's Encyclopedia of Fiesta*, Paducah, Kentucky: Collector Books, 1984.

Laurent, Micheline

▶ French fabric designer, wife of architect Georges Henri Pingusson.

▶ In 1932, Laurent and Pingusson became members of UAM (Union des Artistes Modernes). She worked on her husband's design of the Hôtel Latitude; specialized in curtains, pillows, and linen for the table.

▶ Work shown at UAM pavilion at 1937 Paris 'Exposition Internationale des Arts et Techniques dans la Vie Moderne.'

▶ Arlette Barré-Despond, *UAM*, Paris: Regard, 1986:523.

Lauro, Agostino   (1861–1924)

▶ Italian designer and entrepreneur; active Turin.

▶ By the 1890s, Lauro had a reputation as entrepreneur and designer with numerous private commissions, including the villa at Sordevolo of *c*1900, and assignments for the decoration of public buildings in Turin; operated a furniture gallery patronized by distinguished clients in the via Genoa, Turin; designed furniture in the prevailing Stile Liberty or Stile Floreale.

▶ The Palazzina Lauro, designed by architect Giuseppe Velati-Bellini, was built for the 1902 'Esposizione Internazionale d'Arte Decorativa Moderna,' Turin. Exhibited in numerous international expositions.

▶ Cat., Gabriel P. Weisberg, *Stile Floreale: The Cult of Nature in Italian Design*, Miami: The Wolfsonian Foundation, 1988.

Lauro, Mario Rosario   (1940–)

▶ Italian industrial and graphic designer; born and active Naples.

▶ 1963–65, he was active in research, analysis, and project design on the reconstruction of the northern section of Naples; was an architect in the partnership Lauro, Palomba, Pasca in Naples; from 1966, was involved in publishing and designed public furniture at 'Sudesign 75' pavilion of 1975 (I) Naples 'Festival Provinciale de L'Unità'; in 1975 with Palomba and Pasca, designed the publication *I legni* for Centro Ricerche Artigianato e Design of the cities of Campagna and Ellisse; became a member of ADI (Associazione per il Disegno Industriale).

▶ Received an honorable mention at Internazionale A. Olivetti prize (for his project 'La Nuova Città' on the restoration of Naples).

▶ *ADI Annual 1976*, Milan: Associazione per il Disegno Industriale, 1976.

Lausitzer Glaswerke
See Vereinigte Lausitzer Glaswerke

Lauweriks, J.L. Mathieu   (1864–1932)

▶ Dutch architect and designer; active Amsterdam, Düsseldorf, and Hagen (Germany).

▶ 1894–1903, Lauweriks taught at Haarlemsche School voor Kunstnijverheid; 1904–09, at the Kunstgewerbeschule, Düsseldorf, where the director was Peter Behrens. 1909–16, he was director of Handfertigkeitsseminar, Hagen, instructing crafts teachers, and worked for banker and art patron K.E. Osthaus; 1908–09, published the journal *Ring*, after which *Wendingen*, to which he also contributed, was modeled; under Zwollo at the Hagener Silberschmiede, designed most of its silver. On Lauweriks's recommendation, Zwollo was appointed the first metalwork teacher at Haarlemsche School voor Kunstnijverheid (1897–1907) and director of Hagener Silberschmiede where the aim was to rival the Wiener Werkstätte. Lauweriks believed that the mathematical proportions of an object's form determined its expressivity; used spirals because they produced undulating contours. In 1916, he became director of Kunstnijverheidsschool Quellinus, Amsterdam; subsequently, played an important role in the formation of the Amsterdam School.

▶ Cat., *Franz Zwollo en zihn tijd*, Museum Boymans-van Beuningen, Rotterdam, 1982. Wim de Wit (ed.), *The Amsterdam School: Dutch Expressionist Architecture, 1915–1930*, Cambridge, MIT, 1983. Annelies Krekel-Aalberse, *Art Nouveau and Art Déco Silver*, New York: Abrams, 1989:137–38,175,256.

Lavarello, Marcello   (1921–)

▶ Italian architect and designer; born and active Genoa.

▶ He began his professional career in 1954; designed the interiors of oceanliners *Leonardo*, *Michelangelo*, *Giulio Cesare*, and *Cristoforo Colombo*, and exhibitions including 'Ente Fiera' in Genoa,

'Industria Italiana' in Moscow, and 1971 and 1976 'Euroflora,' He designed hotels including Bellevue Cogne, Orizzonte Varazze, Sestriere, Madonna di Campiglio, and Desenzano, and numerous houses in Italy; offices in Genoa, Milan, Brescia, Rome, Vienna, and Paris; churches, chapels, gardens, and aircraft. He became a member of ADI (Associazione per il Disegno Industriale).
▶ *ADI Annual 1976*, Milan: Associazione per il Disegno Industriale, 1976.

Laverne, Erwine (1909–) and Estelle Laverne (1915–)
▶ American artists, designers, and entrepreneurs; active New York.
▶ Studied painting, Art Students' League, New York, under Hans Hofmann.
▶ They established Laverne Originals in c1938 with design studios on the old estate of L.C. Tiffany in Oyster Bay, New York. They initially produced fabrics and wallcoverings, including the popular *Marbalia* range of marbled murals. From c1945, Ray Komai designed some of their printed cotton and linen fabrics. 1949–55, the Lavernes commissioned William Katavolos, Ross Littell, and Douglas Kelley to design furniture, textiles, and dinnerware, including the *New Furniture Group* of chairs and tables. Laverne produced Katavolos's, Littell's, and Kelley's 1952 T chair. The 1957 *Invisible* group of see-through plastic furniture designed by the Lavernes was produced through techniques developed by the Lavernes and later licensed to others.
▶ T chair received 1952 AID award for the best USA furniture. Work (of Katavolos, Littell, and Kelley for Laverne, includes textiles) shown at 1953 and 1955 'Good Design' exhibitions; (clear plexiglass chair) at 1968 'Please Be Seated' exhibition, The American Federation of Arts; (T chair, fabric by Komai, and 1957 *Champagne* clear plexiglass chair) at 1984 'Design Since 1945' exhibition, Philadelphia Museum of Art.
▶ 'Good Design,' *Interiors*, Vol. 113, Aug. 1953:88–89,146–48. Roberto Aloi, *Mobili tipo*, Milan: 1956:97,121,187,216. Cat., *Please Be Seated*, New York: The American Federation of Arts, 1968: No. 68. Clement Meadmore, *The Modern Chair*, New York: 1975:98–101. Cat., Kathryn B. Hiesinger and George H. Marcus III (eds.), *Design Since 1945*, Philadelphia Museum of Art, 1983.

Lavonen, Maija (1931–)
▶ Finnish textile designer.
▶ Her work including designs for mass-produced and one-off pieces in techniques including *ryijy* and double weaves.
▶ Work (1977 *ryijy* rug) shown at 1980 'Scandinavian Modern Design 1880–1980' exhibition, Cooper-Hewitt Museum, New York.
▶ Cat., David Revere McFadden (ed.), *Scandinavian Modern Design 1880–1980*, New York: Abrams, 1982:267, No. 326.

Law, David (1937–)
▶ American designer; born Pittsburgh.
▶ Studied Art Center College of Design, Los Angeles.
▶ In 1967, he began as executive designer for the Detroit and Chicago branches of Unimark International; in 1972, co-founded Design Planning Group, Chicago; in 1985, became manager of packaging design at JCPenney, New York; in 1978, joined Vignelli Associates; designed graphics, packaging, exhibitions, furniture, products, environments, and interiors; collaborated with Lella and Massimo Vignelli on 1986 *Bordin* and *Aneic* flatware produced by Sasaki Crystal, and on *Handerkerchief* chair by Knoll and Serenissimo table by Acerbis International.
▶ Albrecht Bangert and Karl Michael Armer, *80s Style: Designs of the Decade*, New York: Abbeville, 1990:30,143,232.

Lax, Michael (1929–)
▶ American designer.
▶ Studied New York State College of Ceramics, Alfred University, Alfred, New York; in Finland; and in Rome.
▶ He set up his own design office in New York; executed designs for exhibitions, environments, graphic-information systems, furnishings, wallcoverings and lighting; had clients including Copco, Corning, Dunbar, Formica, Kimberley-Clark, Lightolier, and Salton.
▶ Work (glass bowls for Dunbar) shown at 1952 'Good Design' exhibition, New York Museum of Modern Art and Merchandise Mart, Chicago, and work at 1983–84 'Design Since 1945,' Philadelphia Museum of Art.
▶ Cat., Kathryn B. Hiesinger and George H. Marcus III (eds.), *Design Since 1945*, Philadelphia: Philadelphia Museum of Art, 1983. Jay Doblin, *One Hundred Great Product Designs*, New York, 1970: No. 99.

Lazzotti, Giulio (1943–)
▶ Italian designer, born Pietrasanta.
▶ Studied construction engineering, Università di Firenze.
▶ He was consultant designer to clients including Artipresent, Bernini, Camp, Casigliani, Gaiac, Mageia, and Up & Up.
▶ Robert A.M. Stern (ed.), *The International Design Yearbook*, New York: Abbeville, 1985/1986: No. 84.

Le Chevallier, Jacques (1896–1987)
▶ French lighting and furniture designer; born Paris.
▶ Studied École Nationale des Arts Décoratifs, Paris.
▶ 1920–45 in partnership with Louis Barillet, he established a stained glass workshop in rue Alain-Chartier, Paris. Work included painting, tapestries, engraving on wood, lighting, and secular and religious items. He designed a variety of quirky lamps evoking the machine age; used metal, exposed rivets and screws, hinges, and counterweights; often collaborated with Raymond Koechlin; designed lighting for Pierre Chareau's office, designed by Rob Mallet-Stevens. Other designs, similar to Boris Lacroix's, were more refined. He was commissioned by the interior design group DIM (Décoration Intérieur Moderne) to produce various components in their ensembles; in 1929, became a member of UAM (Union des Artistes Modernes); in 1945, established his own workshop at Fontenay-aux-Roses, where he produced stained glass with Barillet and drawings for mosaics and tapestries; in 1948, founded Centre d'Art Sacré and participated in the renovation of cathedrals in Besançon, Toulouse, and Angers.
▶ Work shown at Salons of Société des Artistes Décorateurs, sessions of Salon d'Automne, Salon des Indépendants, UAM exhibitions from 1930, and 1937 Paris 'Exposition Internationale des Arts et Techniques dans la Vie Moderne' (stained glass later installed in Notre-Dame Cathedral, Paris).
▶ *The Studio*, Jan.–June 1929:89. René Drouin, 'Au quatrième salon de l'UAM,' *L'Architecture d'Aujourd'hui*, No. 5, June 1933. *Jacques Le Chevallier*, Les Cahiers d'Art-Documents, No. 110, Geneva: Pierre Cailles, 1959. Alastair Duncan, *Art Nouveau and Art Déco Lighting*, New York: Simon and Schuster, 1978:177. Victor Arwas, *Art Déco*, Abrams, 1980. Cat., Aaron Lederfajn and Xavier Lenormand, *Le Louvre des Antiquaires présente: 1930 quand le meuble devient sculpture*, Paris, 1986. Cat., *Les années UAM 1929–1958*, Paris: Musée des Arts Décoratifs, 1988:208–09.

Le Corbusier (b. Charles-Édouard Jeanneret 1887–1965)
▶ Swiss architect; born La Chaux-de-Fonds; active Paris.
▶ Studied metal engraving, arts and crafts school, La Chaux-de-Fonds, under Charles L'Eplattenier.
▶ Le Corbusier worked in 1908 with Josef Hoffmann at the Wiener Werkstätte, refusing a permanent job; in 1908, with Tony Garnier in Lyons and Henri Sauvage in Paris. 1908–09 in Paris, he was an apprentice in the Perret brothers' architecture office, becoming familiar with reinforced-concrete methods before, 1910–11, joining the staff of Peter Behrens's office in Berlin, where he became interested in mass-produced furniture and came into contact with Mies van der Rohe and Walter Gropius. In 1918, he returned to Paris and met Amédée Ozenfant, with whom he developed a style of painting called Purism, and wrote the manifesto *Après le cubisme, le purisme* (1918), followed by *La Peinture*

moderne (1925). He used the pseudonym Le Corbusier (from *corbusier*, a type of bird) as an author from 1920, as an architect from 1922, and as a painter from 1928. His interest in Greek architecture and the machine was discussed in *Vers une Architecture* (1923), a collection of articles from *L'Esprit Nouveau: revue international d'esthétique*, which he, Ozenfant, and poet Paul Dermée produced 1920–25. By-lined 'Corbusier-Saugnier' (the latter being Ozenfant's pseudonym), the articles created a sensation. From 1921, Le Corbusier and his cousin Pierre Jeanneret worked in the architecture office at 35 rue de Sèvres, Paris. 1924–38, Jean Badovici documented their projects in the journal *L'Architecture vivante*. Le Corbusier's and Jeanneret's pavilion 'L'Esprit nouveau' at the 1925 Paris Exhibition, and his white concrete houses of the period, manifested what was later dubbed the International Style of architecture, of which Le Corbusier's 1919 Villa Savoye at Poissy is a prime example. The 1925 pavilion created a scandal that precipitated Le Corbusier's and others' departure in 1929 from the Société des Artistes Décorateurs to form UAM (Union des Artistes Modernes). Even at the 1937 Paris 'Exposition Internationale des Arts et Techniques dans la Vie Moderne,' his 'Temps Nouveau' pavilion was relegated to Porte Maillot, far from the fair grounds. In 1927, he began to design tubular steel furniture in association with Jeanneret and Charlotte Perriand, who, as a student of architecture, joined the Le Corbusier-Jeanneret workshop in 1927; she became responsible for most of the furniture designs. Not interested in originality, the team based the design of their best known metal models on mass-produced wooden furniture, as in the 1928 *Siège à dossier basculant* (swivel-back chair). In 1930, they designed the scheme for the office of the administrator of the review *La Semaine à Paris* (Robert Mallet-Stevens, architect). Some of the furniture pieces have become icons of 20th-century design, partly through their availability as reproductions. From the 1930s, Le Corbusier concentrated on architecture and planning, and his work in the 1950s made a distinct break with the Formalism of his earlier International Style and turned towards freer expression. His much-quoted term 'machine for living' is often wrongly interpreted as expressing a cold indifference to the provision of human shelter.

▶ Furniture credited to Le Corbusier, Jeanneret, and Perriand included 1927 *Siège à dossier basculant* appearing initially at Villa Church, Ville-d'Avray (the current version not produced until 1959); 1927 *Chaise longue à reglage continu* appearing initially at Villa Church, shown to the public at 1929 Salon d'Automne in Paris (called the 'real machine for rest' by Le Corbusier; after Thonet France, it was produced in the 1930s by Embru of Switzerland); 1927 *Grand Confort* (club chair) in various models, with and without the ball foot, including the wider 'female chair' version to allow legs to be crossed, 1927 *Siège tournant* (swivel chair) shown first at 1928 Salon des Artistes Décorateurs, 1928 table, and 1929 *Table en tube d'avion* shown first at 1929 Salon d'Automne. All the furniture of the Le Corbusier, Jeanneret, and Perriand team was first produced by Thonet France.

▶ Architecture included 1920–22 Citrohan house (shown at 1922 Salon d'Automne); 1922 Ville-contemporaine project; 1922 Ozenfant house, Paris; 1922 three-million-person city project; 1922 Villa Besnos, Vaucresson; 1923 Lipchitz house, Boulogne-sur-Seine; 1923 La Roche and Jeanneret houses, Auteuil, Paris; 1925 city-garden, Pessac, near Bordeaux; 'L'Esprit Nouveau' pavilion, 1925 Paris 'Exposition International des Arts Décoratifs et Industriels Modernes'; 1925 Plain-Voisin project for Paris; 1926 Cook house, Boulogne-sur-Seine; Cité Frugès and Armée du Salut, Paris; 1927 competition for the Palace of the League of Nations, Geneva; 1927 Villa Stein, Garches; two houses at 1927 Stuttgart 'Weissenhof-Siedlung'; 1929–31 Villa Savoye, Poissy; 1929–31 Centrosoyus building, Moscow; 1930–32 Clarté apartment house, Geneva; 1930–32 Pavillon Suisse, Cité Universitaire, Paris; 1931 competition for Palace of the Soviets, Moscow; 1932–33 Cité de Réfuge, Paris, 1932 Raoul La Roche house, Paris; 1932 Pierre Jeanneret house, Paris; 1936–43 Ministry of Health and

Education (executed by Lúcio Costa, Oscar Niemeyer, and Affonso Eduardo Reidy), Rio de Janeiro; 1947–50 United Nations building (executed by Wallace K. Harrison and Max Abramovitz), New York; 1947–52 Unité d'Habitation, Marseilles; housing at Nantes-Rezé (1952–57), Berlin (1956–58), Meaux (1957–59), Briey-en-Forêt (1957–60), and Firminy-Vert (1962–68); 1950–54 church of Notre Dame-du-Haut, Ronchamp; 1950–51 general plan (with Maxwell Fry and Jane Drew) and capitol area with government buildings, Chandigarh (India); 1952–56 Maison Jaoul, Neuilly-sur-Seine; 1957–60 Monastery of Ste. Marie-de-la-Tourette, Eveux-sur-l'Arbresle; four buildings in India 1955–56; 1961–64 Carpenter Center for the Visual Arts (his only North American building), Harvard University, Cambridge, Massachusetts; 1965 Maison de la Culture, stadium, and Unité d'Habitation, Firminy.

▶ In 1921, work (group of paintings) shown at Galerie Druet, Paris. Built pavilion 'L'Esprit nouveau' at 1925 Paris 'Exposition Internationale des Arts Décoratifs et Industriels Modernes'. 'Equipement intérieur d'une habitation' installed at 1929 Salon d'Automne. Furniture (extension table, pivoting and lounge chair by Thonet, and six chairs in the hall designed by Robert Mallet-Stevens) shown at 1930 (I) UAM exhibition; model of 'Ville Radieuse' and photographs of 'Villa Savoye' at UAM 1931 event; the project for the Centrosoyuz in Moscow at UAM 1932 event; and the town plan for Obus d'Alger at UAM 1933 event. For his last project associated with UAM, Le Corbusier with Perriand and Jeanneret designed the toilet prototype shown at UAM pavilion at 1937 Paris 'Exposition Internationale des Arts et Techniques dans la Vie Moderne.' The three architects designed 'Salle d'étude pour l'appartement d'un jeune homme' (reading room in the apartment of a young man) in the fine arts section of French pavilion at 1935 'Exposition Universelle et Internationale de Bruxelles.' Le Corbusier's Philips pavilion at 1958 Brussels exposition featured *poème électronique* multi-media presentation with other artists. Work subject of 1987 centenary exhibition, Centre Georges Pompidou, Paris, and 1992 'Le Corbusier Domestique: Furniture/ Tapestries 1927–67,' Carpenter Center for the Visual Arts, Cambridge, Massachusetts.

▶ Willy Boesiger (ed.) *Le Corbusier: Oeuvre complète*, Zurich, 1930 and onwards. S. Papadaki, *Le Corbusier: Architect, Painter, Writer*, New York, 1948. Françoise Choay, *Le Corbusier*, New York, 1960. Stanislav von Moos, *Le Corbusier: Elemente einer Synthese*, Freunenfeld, 1968. Charles Jencks, *Le Corbusier and the Tragic View of Architecture*, London, 1973. Renato De Fusco, *Le Corbusier designer i mobili del 1929*, Milan: Casabella, 1976. Cat., Kathryn B. Hiesinger and George H. Marcus III (eds.), *Design Since 1945*, Philadelphia: Philadelphia Museum of Art, 1983. Pierre Cabanne, *Encyclopédie Art Déco*, Paris: Somogy, 1986:208–09. Cat., Aaron Lederfajn and Xavier Lenormand, *Le Louvre des Antiquaires présente: 1930 quand le meuble devient sculpture*, Paris, 1986. Arlette Barré-Despond, *UAM*, Paris: Regard, 1986:438–43. *Le Corbusier, une Encyclopédie*, Paris: Centre Georges Pompidou/CCI, 1987. Gilles Ragot and Dion Mathilde, *Le Corbusier en France, Réalisations et Projets*, Paris: Electa Moniteur, 1987. Cat., *Les années UAM 1929–1958*, Paris: Musée des Arts Décoratifs, 1988:210–14.

Le Son, Lucie Holt
See Holt Le Son, Lucie

Le Teo, Catherine
▶ French industrial designer.
▶ Studied École Camondo, Paris.
▶ With Thierry Blet she formed the Elixir design team. They designed a picnic-tableware set that received recognition in the 1986 competition sponsored by APCI (Agence pour la Promotion de la Création Industrielle) and UGAP (Union des Groupements d'Achats Publics).
▶ *Les Carnets du Design*, Paris: Mad-Cap Productions et APCI, 1986: 87.

Leach, Bernard Howell (1887–1979)

▶ British ceramicist; born Hong Kong; active St. Ives, Cornwall, and Devon.

▶ From 1897, studied Slade School of Fine Art, London; London School of Art; engraving under Frank Brangwyn; from 1911, pottery under Ogata Kenzan in Japan.

▶ From 1909, he lived in Japan, where he taught design and engraving and studied and where, in 1911, he discovered pottery and met potter Ogata Kenzan VI, master of a long line of Japanese potters. He traveled to China 1916–18, and subsequently Korea. In 1920, after helping Kenzan build a new stoneware kiln near Tokyo, he established a pottery at St. Ives with associate Shoji Hamada; investigated the techniques and styles of early English pottery including the traditions of country slipware; developed slipware pieces and original ideas, both influenced by his earlier Japanese training; introduced to Britain the Japanese concept of a potter's complete responsibility for all stages of creative activity and the unity of the results; in the 1920s, shared his ideas and facilities with many potters who became well known in the 1930s. During the 1930s, when his son David joined the pottery, Leach became freer to travel and teach; from 1932, taught at Dartington Hall, Devon; in 1934, accepted the invitation of the National Craft Society to visit Japan, where he traveled for a year with Soetsu Yanagi and Shoji Hamada and worked in various potteries; in 1935, visited Korea; in 1936, set up a pottery at Dartington Hall. Gathering material while at the school, he published the book *A Potter's Book* (1940) with introductions by Soetsu Yanagi and Michael Cardew. (Cardew first met Leach and Hamada at St. Ives in 1923.) Leach was the leading exponent of studio pottery in Britain, and, through his writing and teaching, hugely influential.

▶ In 1932, appointed CBE (Commander of the Order of the British Empire), received 1966 Order of the Sacred Treasure (second class) in Japan, and, in 1973, made CH (Companion of Honour). Work shown at numerous exhibitions.

▶ Bernard Leach, *A Potter's Outlook*, London, 1928. Bernard Leach, *Kenzan and His Tradition*, 1966. Bernard Leach, *A Potter's Book*, London: Evelyn, Adams & Mackay, 1967. Carol Hogben, *The Art of Bernard Leach*, London: Faber, 1978. Cat., *Thirties: British art and design before the war*, London: Arts Council of Great Britain, Hayward Gallery, 1979:97–98,131,286,294.

Lebeau, Chris (b. Joris Johannes Christiaan Lebeau 1878–1945)

▶ Dutch decorator and designer; born Amsterdam.

▶ 1895–99, studied Kunstnijverheidsschool (Arts and Crafts School) and Rijksacademie voor Beeldende Kunsten, both Amsterdam.

▶ By 1899, he taught art at the Burgeravondsschool in Amsterdam. Shortly after, he began as a professional designer with wall decorations commissioned for the Netherlands Pavilion at the 1900 Paris 'Exposition Universelle' and at the same time began working in batik in the workshop of Agathe Wegerif-Gravenstein in Appeldoorn. Lebeau executed numerous folding screens in batik, some double-sided.

▶ His work was the subject of an exhibition at the Gemeentemuseum in The Hague, 1966. The Hague carpet firm 's-Gravenhaagsche Smyrnatapijtfabriek's 1901 design competition on the theme 'Modern Style' was won by Lebeau.

▶ Cat., *Chris Lebeau*, The Hague: Gemeentemuseum, 1966. M. Komaneck and V.F. Butera, *The Folding Image Screens by Western Artists of the Nineteenth and Twentieth Centuries*, New Haven: Yale University Art Gallery, 1984. Cat., *Chris Lebeau*, The Hague: Gemeentemuseum, 1966.

Lebedeva, Mariia Vasil'evna (1895–1942)

▶ Russian painter, graphic artist, book designer, decorative artist, and ceramics designer.

▶ Studied Drawing School of the Friends of Art, Petrograd, under I. Bilibin, to 1917.

▶ 1919–23, she produced designs on porcelain wares, portraying symbolic and fantastic themes for the Porcelain Factory, Petro-

grad; 1924–27, taught decorative arts at Vitebsk Technical School of Art and, 1924–27, at Minsk College of Fine Arts; 1934–40, worked at the Porcelain Factory, Leningrad (now St. Petersburg).

▶ Cat., *Kunst und Revolution: Russische und Sowjetische Kunst 1910–1932*, Vienna: Österreichisches Museum für angewandte Kunst, 1988. Nina Lobanov-Rostovsky, *Revolutionary Ceramics*, London: Studio Vista, 1990.

Lebolt, J. Meyer H. (1868–1944)

▶ American silversmith

▶ Lebolt established a silversmithy in 1899 at 167 S. State, Chicago. He opened branches in New York and Paris. The company ceased operation in 1960.

Lebovici, Yonel (1937–)

▶ Designer.

▶ In his own workshop, he designed a wide range of products including furniture, lighting, and glassware for clients Jansen, Cardin, Club Med and Lancel.

▶ Robert A.M. Stern (ed.), *The International Design Yearbook*, New York: Abbeville, 1985/1986: No. 180.

Lecoq, Jacqueline

See Philippon, Antoine

Ledru, Auguste (1860–1902)

▶ French glassmaker.

▶ Studied sculpture under Augustin Dumont and Jean Bannassieux.

▶ He, Joseph Chéret, and Raoul Larche were among the first designers to concentrate on the female form in the Art Nouveau style.

▶ Salon catalog, Société des Artistes français, 1901. *Éclairage de 1900 à nos jours*, Brussels: L'écuyer, No. 29. *Allgemeines Lexikon der Bildenden Künstler*, 1955. Alastair Duncan, *Art Nouveau and Art Déco Lighting*, New York: Simon and Schuster, 1978:82.

Ledru, Léon (1855–1926)

▶ French glassmaker.

▶ Ledru was manager of the design department of the Cristalleries du Val-Saint-Lambert in Belgium for 38 years. Through the work the firm showed at the 1897 Brussels 'Exposition Internationale,' he stimulated interest in avant-garde design. Reflecting the influence of Henry van de Velde, the crystal factory's vases, also shown at the 1901 exhibition of La Libre Esthétique, Brussels, were distinctly Modern. Pieces shown at the 1900 Paris 'Exposition Universelle' had floral decoration in a more naturalistic style, much like the work of the École de Nancy and Émile Gallé. Though he designed traditional pieces, Ledru is known for his innovations in technique, color, and decoration, brought about by his long association with Val-Saint-Lambert chemist Aldolphe Lecrenier.

▶ Yvonne Brunhammer et al., *Art Nouveau Belgium, France*, Houston: Institute for the Arts, Rice University, 1976. Alastair Duncan, *Art Nouveau and Art Déco Lighting*, New York: Simon and Schuster, 1978:82.

Lee, Arthur & Sons

▶ British textile firm; located Birkenhead, Lancashire.

▶ Arthur H. Lee founded the firm in 1888 as weavers, printers and embroiderers in Warrington, moving in 1908 to Birkenhead; produced some important Art Nouveau textiles by leading designers in the 1890s and early 1900s; subsequently, specialized in reproduction woven fabrics and embroidery for furnishings and upholstery; was an agent for Mariano Fortuny's printed textiles; closed 1972.

▶ Valerie Mendes, *The Victoria and Albert Museum's Textile Collection; British Textiles from 1900 to 1937*, London: Victoria and Albert Museum, 1992.

Leerdam Glasfabriek

▶ Dutch glassware manufacturer; located Leerdam.

▶ C.A. Jeekel set up the glass factory Hardglasfabriek Jeekel in Leerdam in 1875; in 1877, Jeekel, J.J. Mijnssen, and O.H.L.

Nieuwenhuyzen established Glasfabriek Jeekel, Mijnssen & Co to produce crystal and half-crystal wares. In 1915, the first consultant designer was architect K.P.C. de Bazel. 1919–23, he was primarily concerned with the design of a pressed-glass service. 1917–26, C. de Lorm designed for Leerdam; one of his first designs was a drop-shaped carafe with barrel-shaped drinking glasses. 1919–26, C.J. Lanooy designed domestic glassware. In 1923, architect H.P. Berlage came to Leerdam and designed a glass breakfast and dinner service. P. Zwart, Berlage's associate, designed a bright yellow pressed-glass breakfast set in a hexagonal shape. Painter and graphic artist J.J.C. Lebeau designed a carafe, water glasses (he was a teetotaller), a finger bowl, and a fruit plate while at Leerdam 1923–26. A new management-worker arrangement (the first in the Netherlands) was created and the plant was reorganized by P.S. Gerbrandy. A.D. Copier's *Unica* series of glassware designed *c*1925 remained in production until after World War II. 1920–30, numerous designers, including Frank Lloyd Wright, produced decorative glassware motifs; although Wright designed 16 pieces, including a full dinner service and glassware, only his tall green cut-glass vase was produced. From 1914, Copier was the only full-time designer; he worked under J. Jongert 1918–23. Copier supervised the work of de Bazel and de Lorm and, in 1920, began designing himself. At the firm from 1904, P.M. Cochius was put in charge of the general artistic management of the factory. In *c*1937, I. Falkenberg-Liefrinck, J.A.H.F. Nicolas, and W. Stuurman designed tableware and ornamental glass objects. In 1938, Leerdam was amalgamated into Vereenigde Glasfabrieken at Schiedam to form Vereenigde Leerdam Glasfabriek. 1946–50, Copier was its leading designer. In *c*1950, Leerdam's staff designers included teachers and former students of the Glass School, including Floris Meydam 1949–85, Sybren Valkema 1948–66, Willem Heesen 1950–70, and G.J. Thomassen from 1951. The firm became Koninklijke Nederlandsche Glasfabriek Leerdam in 1953. Copier left in 1971.

▶ It showed its *Unica* series at the 1925 Paris 'Exposition Internationale des Arts Décoratifs et Industriels Modernes,' where Copier was awarded a silver medal, and at the 1927 Stuttgart exhibition.

▶ *Industry and Design in the Netherlands, 1850/1950*, Amsterdam: Stedelijk Museum, 1985. Frederick Cooke, *Glass: Twentieth-Century Design*, New York: Dutton, 1986:96.

Lefèbvre, Eugène

▶ French silversmith; active Paris.

▶ Lefèbvre established the firm E. Lefèbvre in 1895. It manufactured silverwares and silver jewelry in traditional forms with Modern floral ornamentation. Lefèbvre was one of the smaller silver factories that could not take financial risks in producing large silver pieces in the new Modern mode as long as there was a preference for historicist styles.

▶ Annelies Krekel-Aalberse, *Art Nouveau and Art Déco Silver*, New York: Abrams, 1989:57,65,256.

Lefler, Heinrich   (1863–1919)

▶ Austrian designer; born Vienna.

▶ Lefler and brother-in-law Joseph Urban, with whom he often collaborated, designed a room at the 1897 winter exhibition at the Österreichisches Museum für Kunst und Industrie. In 1900, they founded the Künstlerbund Hagen (better known as the Hagenbund). Unlike the Sezession, the Hagenbund did not erect a new building for its own use but had a market-hall office (known as the Zedlitzhalle); the 1902 adaptation was assigned to Lefler and Urban. Their conversion hints at their crafts background though they incorporated Sezessionist ornamentation throughout.

▶ Günther Feuerstein, *Vienna—Present and Past: Arts and Crafts—Applied Art—Design*, Vienna: Jugend und Volk, 1976:23, 35,80. Robert Waissenberger, *Vienna 1890–1920*, Secaucus, NJ: Wellfleet, 1984.

Legrain, Jacques
See Anthoine-Legrain, Jacques

Legrain, Pierre-Émile   (1889–1929)

▶ French designer of furniture, furnishings, and bookbindings; born Levallois-Perret; active Paris.

▶ From 1904, studied sculpture, painting, and theater design, École des Arts Appliqués Germain-Croix, Paris.

▶ He submitted cartoons in 1908 for Paul Iribe's satirical reviews *Le Témoin, L'Assiette au beurre, Le Mot,* and *La Baïonnette.* Iribe invited Legrain to collaborate with him on projects including furniture and interior design, jewelry for Robert Linzeler, and dress designs for Paquin. A designer of geometric bookbindings for couturier Jacques Doucet from 1912, Legrain was put in charge of decoration and furniture for the couturier's studio in the rue Saint-Jacques in Neuilly; he quickly became one of the most creative designers of bookbinding in the world. He used a number of professional binders to execute his designs, particularly René Kieffer for his commissions; for a period from 1919, he worked exclusively with Kieffer on bookbindings. Doucet commissioned Legrain to design the bindings for his recently acquired collection of books by contemporary authors, including André Gide, André Suarès, Paul Claudel, and Francis Jammes. Legrain worked on the binding designs in Doucet's dining room, sometimes assisted by Doucet himself. The exhibition at the 1919 Salon proved a tremendous success, encouraging book collectors to embrace Modernism enthusiastically. His newly acquired clients included Louis Barthou, Baron R. Gourgaud, Georges and Auguste Blaizot, and Baron Robert de Rothschild in Paris and Florence Blumenthal and Daniel Sickles in the USA. He was invited in 1923 by decorators Briant et Robert to set up his workshop in their establishment at 7 rue d'Argenteuil. In *c*1925, Doucet commissioned him to decorate his Neuilly studio, whose architect was Paul Ruau. Alongside Kieffer, Legrain used binders Salvadore David, Georges Canape, George Huser, Georges Levitsky, Henri Nouilhac, Germaine Schroeder, Stroobants, Jeanne, Collet, Desmoules, Aufschneider, Dress, Vincent, and Lordereau. His work's success at the 1925 Paris Exposition encouraging him to set up his own bindery in 1926 in avenue Percier and soon after in rue Saint-Jacques. His bindings are known for their high level of craftsmanship, originality, and use of exotic materials. Legrain understood Cubism and African art, and the furniture he designed for Doucet shows both influences. One of his best known pieces was the Pleyel piano in plate glass and copper, with its works visible, designed for house of Pierre Meyer in the avenue Montaigne in Paris. He designed for friends of Doucet, including two apartments for milliner Jeanne Tachard, a suite of rooms for Maurice Martin du Gard, a bedroom for the vicomte and vicomtesse de Noailles, a house in the rue Villejust in Paris and at La Celle-St.-Cloud, and commissions from Suzanne Talbot, and Mme. Louis Boulanger. He designed a leather camera case for Kodak, a desk set for the Palais de l'Élysée, and cigarette boxes for Lucky Strike and Camel. He was a member of Groupe des Cinq with Pierre Chareau, Dominique, Jean Puiforcat, and Raymond Templier. In 1929, Legrain joined UAM (Union des Artistes Modernes); designing the logotype for the group, he died in 1929 shortly before its first exhibition, 'Hommage à Pierre Legrain.' In barely 12 years, he produced some 1,300 designs for book covers and revolutionized an ancient craft. 1931–32, Legrain's widow produced certain of his bindings.

▶ Doucet exhibited 20 of Legrain's binding designs at the 1919 Salon of the Société des Artistes français. Legrain, Robert Mallet-Stevens, Chareau, Ruhlmann, and Paul Poiret collectively designed the pavilion 'La réception et l'intimité d'un appartement moderne' at the 1924 Salon d'Automne. He participated in the 1925 Paris 'Exposition Internationale des Arts Décoratifs et Industriels Modernes' and, from 1926, in the exhibitions of Groupe des Cinq; the plate-glass piano was shown at the 1929 exhibition of Group des Cinq at the Galerie de la Renaissance in Paris.

▶ Pierre Legrain (presenter), 'Objet d'Art,' Paris: Charles Moreau. Victor Arwas, *Art Déco*, New York: Abrams, 1980. Pierre Cabanne, *Encyclopédie Art Déco*, Paris: Somogy, 1986:211. Alastair Duncan and Georges de Bartha, *Art Nouveau and Art Déco Bookbinding*, New York: Abrams, 1989:7,8,17,18–20,21,22,24,

26,37,61,94,97,106–17,192–93. Louis Barthou, 'L'Évolution art-istique de la reliure,' *L'Illustration*, Christmas 1930. Georges Blai-zot, *Masterpieces of French Bindings*, New York, 1947:14–66. Joseph Breck, 'Bookbindings by Legrain,' *Bulletin of the Metropol-itan Museum of Art*, No. 11, New York, Nov. 1932:235–36. Yvonne Brunhammer, *The Nineteen Twenties Style*, London, 1966. Ph. Dally, 'Les Techniques modernes de la reliure,' *Art et décora-tion*, Jan.–June 1927:15–17. Ernest de Crauzat, *La Reliure França-ise de 1900 à 1925*, Paris, 1932, Vol. 1:180–87, Vol. 2:15–31. Léon Deshairs, *Les Arts décoratifs modernes 1918–1925*, Paris, 1925:185–88. Roger Devauchelle, *La Reliure en France de ses ori-gines à nos jours*, Paris, 1961:149–64,166,168,170–71,175,200, 212,228–29. Edith Diehl, *Bookbinding, Its Background and Tech-nique*, Vols. 1 and 2, New York, 1946. Alastair Duncan, *Art Déco Furniture*, London and York, 1984:117–18. Jacques Guignard, *Pierre Legrain et la reliure: Évolution d'un style*, Paris. Léon Rosen-thal, 'Pierre Legrain, relieur,' *Art et décoration*, March 1923:65–70. Pierre Kjellberg, *Art Déco: les maîtres du Mobilier, le décor des Paquebots*, Paris: Amateur, 1986:111–12,115. Arlette Barré-Despond, *UAM*. Paris: Regard, 1986:448–49. Cat., *Les années UAM 1929–1958*, Paris: Musée des Arts Décoratifs, 1988:230.

Legrand, Roger

▶ French furniture designer; active Paris.
▶ In the 1960s, Legrand was well known for his 1964 *Pan U* elements in bentwood produced by Steph Simon.
▶ Participated (with Pierre Faucheux and Jean-Marie Serreau) in French section, 1964 (XIII) Triennale di Milano.
▶ Gilles de Bure, *Le mobilier français 1965–1979*, Paris: Regard/VIA, 1983:6–7.

Legras

▶ French glass factory; located Saint-Denis, near Paris.
▶ Verreries et Cristalleries de Saint-Denis et des Quatre-Chemins, of which Auguste J.F. Legras became manager in 1864, was renamed Legras et Cie. and became one of France's principal glass-works before 1914. By 1900 (under the management of François-Théodore Legras, succeeded by Charles Legras in 1909) it pro-duced a wide range of tableware, mainly vases and some table lamps in cameo, enameled, and intaglio-carved glass. Its ware depicted pastoral scenes and seascapes. It took over Vidié glass-works in Pantin in 1897 and by 1908 employed over 1,500 workers. Charles Legras admired Gallé and attempted to imitate his work, but the glasswork's products were not exceptional. Legras showed its pieces at the 1888 Barcelona exposition, win-ning a gold medal, and at the 1889 and 1900 Paris 'Expositions Universelles' winning grand prizes. The firm was reorganized after World War I as Verreries et Cristalleries de Saint-Denis et de Pantin Réunies.
▶ R. and L. Grover, *Carved and Decorated European Art Glass*, Rutledge, Vermont: Tuttle, 1970:130–31. H. Hilschenz, *Das Glas des Jugendstils*, Munich, 1973:317–24. Yvonne Brunhammer et al., *Art Nouveau Belgium, France*, Houston: Institute for the Arts, Rice University, 1976. Alastair Duncan, *Art Nouveau and Art Déco Lighting*, New York: Simon and Schuster, 1978:82–83.

Legrottaglie, Pietro (1941–)

▶ Italian designer; born Fasano; active Milan.
▶ Legrottaglie began his professional career in 1970. 1958–64, he worked for La Rinascente and, 1965–70, for Cini & Nils. Best known for table top accessories, lighting, and his use of plas-tics, his clients in Italy included, Garavaglia, Silga (lighting), Du Pont, Sorel (domestic electrical appliances), Rampinelli (motorcycle and bicycle accessories), Curta-Exiria-Reggiani-Fila (cosmetics), and Rima-Bianchi (furnishings). He was a member of ADI (Associazione per il Disegno Industriale).
▶ *ADI Annual 1976*, Milan: Associazione per il Disegno Industri-ale, 1976.

Lehmann, Andreas (1948–)

▶ Swiss designer.
▶ With Beat Frank in 1986, he established the Atelier Vorsprung design studio in Berne, Switzerland. Lehmann and Frank special-ized in abstract sculpture intended for seating. Their 1989 *Sitz-kreuz* furniture sculpture was installed in a hotel foyer in France, at a school for actors, and shown in a traveling exhibition.
▶ Albrecht Bangert and Karl Michael Armer, *80s Style: Designs of the Decade*, New York: Abbeville, 1990:80,232.

Leighton, Clare Veronica (1900–)

▶ British wood engraver, stained glass designer, and writer.
▶ Studied Brighton School of Art, Slade School of Fine Art, and wood engraving, Central School of Arts and Crafts, London, under Noel Rooke.
▶ Mainly figurative, her wood engravings were rendered both as fine art and as illustrations for mass reproduction. In 1930, a book of her art work was published with an introduction by Hilaire Belloc. She illustrated books including *Wuthering Heights* by Emily Brönte, *The Farmer's Years: a Calendar of English Husbandry* (with her text and decorations), *Four Hedges: a Gardener's Chronicle* (1935), and *Country Matters* (1937). She wrote 'Wood Engravings of the 1930s' for *The Studio* in 1936, and the book *Wood-engravings and Woodcuts* (1932). In 1939, she settled in the USA, where she designed a number of stained-glass windows and the 1951 set of twelve engravings for Wedgwood plates.
▶ She represented British wood engravers at the 1939 Biennale di Venezia. Her 1938 *Picking Primroses* wood engraving was included in the 1979–80 'Thirties' exhibition at the Hayward Gallery, London.
▶ Cat., *Thirties: British art and design before the war*, London: Arts Council of Great Britain, Hayward Gallery, 1979:175,294.

Leinonen, Karl F. (1866–)

▶ Finnish silversmith; active Turku (Finland) and Boston, Massachusetts.
▶ Leinonen settled in Boston in 1893. He became director of the Handicraft Shop in Boston, founded in 1901, which sold the work of various silversmiths who had workshop space there.
▶ Annelies Krekel-Aalberse, *Art Nouveau and Art Déco Silver*, New York: Abrams, 1989:98,256.

Leischner, Margaret (1908–70)

▶ German textile designer; born Dresden; active London.
▶ Studied in Dresden and, 1927–30, Bauhaus, Dessau.
▶ In 1931, she taught weaving at the Bauhaus. In 1931, she designed woven textiles at the Dresdener Deutsche Werkstätten and, 1932–36, was head of the weaving department at the Modes-chule, Berlin. She was head designer at Gateshead, a British fur-nishing fabric manufacturer, 1938–44. 1944–50, she was consult-ant designer to R. Grey and, for a time, to Fothergill and Harvey for car upholstery and radio baffle cloth. 1948–63, she headed the weaving department at the Royal College of Art, London. She designed Tintawn sisal carpeting in 1959 and was a consultant to Chemstrand for their Acrilan fiber. 1969, elected Royal Designer for Industry.
▶ Fiona MacCarthy and Patrick Nuttgens, *An Eye for Industry*, London: Lund Humphries, 1986. Cat., *Gunta Stölzl, Weberei am Bauhaus und aus eigener Werkstatt*, Berlin: Bauhaus-Archiv, 1987:158. Cat., *The Bauhaus: Masters and Students*, New York: Barry Friedman, 1988.

Lejambre, A. and H.

▶ American furniture manufacturer; located Philadelphia.
▶ Jean-Pierre Alphonse Lejambre emigrated to the USA during the second decade of the 19th century. He established an uphol-stery shop in Philadelphia. After Lejambre's death in 1843, his wife Anna managed the firm with son Alexis, who became a part-ner c1853. By 1853, they produced and imported French furni-ture, curtains, trimming, and cornices. Alexis died young in 1862, and, in 1865, Anna Lejambre became a partner with cousin Henri Lejambre, who had worked with the firm since the 1850s. In

1867, the name became A. and H. Lejambre. In the 1860s and 1870s, it produced massive pieces of furniture in the French Renaissance style then popular in Philadelphia, and some English style pieces. When Anna Lejambre died in 1878, the firm was managed by Henri Lejambre, son Eugène, and various nephews, with meager success until c1907.

▶ Doreen Bolger Burke et al., *In Pursuit of Beauty: Americans and the Aesthetic Movement*, New York: Metropolitan Museum of Art and Rizzoli, 1986:449. Peter L.L. Strickland, 'Furniture by the Lejambre Family of Philadelphia,' *Antiques*, Vol. 113, March 1978:600–13.

Leleu, Jules-Émile   (1883–1961)
▶ French sculptor and designer; born Boulogne-sur-Mer.
▶ Studied Académie des Beaux-Arts, Boulogne-sur-Mer, under Théophile Deman; private academy, Brussels; École Jean Goujon, Paris, under Secame; École des Arts Appliqués, Paris.
▶ In 1901, Leleu, with brother Marcel, took on their father's painting business, and began working as an interior designer. After World War I, he established his own interior design studio and furniture workshop in Paris. His furniture designs of the 1920s and 1930s were produced in his cabinetmaking workshops in Boulogne. He followed a pattern set by Süe et Mare and Jacques-Émile Ruhlmann in a classical, bulky, and lavish baroque Art Déco form. In the 1920s, his furniture designs were more delicate, with extensive use of exotic woods. In the 1930s, his lines and techniques became more simple, and he developed a Modern style of his own. In 1924, he set up showrooms at 65 avenue Victor-Emmanuel-III (today avenue-Franklin-Roosevelt), Paris. His monumental style was particularly appropriate to commissions for official and semi-official décors, including numerous French embassies and civic and royal residences. He designed the décors of and supplied furniture for more than 20 oceanliners, including the lecture room on the 1926 *Île-de-France*, interiors (with rugs by Ivan Da Silva Bruhns) on the 1931 *Atlantique*, first-class cabins on the 1935 *Normandie*, and used metal for the first time on the 1961 *France*; designed the dining room of the Palais de l'Élysée in Paris in 1937, where his Modern furniture first appeared. He executed décors in the League of Nations in Geneva and embassies in Japan, Brazil, Turkey, Poland, and the Netherlands. He often collaborated with artists and friends, including metalworker Edgar Brandt, architect André Lurçat, and lacquerist Jean Dunand. After World War II, he continued the family business, designing interiors, furniture, carpets, fabrics, and lighting with son André and daughter Paule.
▶ From 1905, he showed sculpture at Salons of the Société des Artistes français. In 1922, for the first time, showed design work at Salon of the Société des Artistes français and subsequently at the Salons of the Société des Artistes Décorateurs and the annual events of the Salon d'Automne and Salon des Tuileries. For the 1925 Paris 'Exposition Internationale des Arts Décoratifs et Industriels Modernes,' he made the chairs for the Grand Salon designed by Henri Rapin and Pierre Selmersheim and the music room by Sèzille; he designed and made a suite of living room furniture for his own stand on the Esplanade des Invalides. His 1931 Hôtel Nord-Sud in Calvi, Corsica, was shown at 1932 'The International Style: Architecture Since 1922' exhibition, New York Museum of Modern Art.
▶ *Ensembles Mobiliers*, Paris: Charles Moreau, No. 20, 1954. Cat., *Decorative Arts 1925 Style*, New York: Didier Aaron, 1979. Victor Arwas, *Art Déco*, Abrams, 1980. Jessica Rutherford, *Art Nouveau, Art Deco and the Thirties: The Furniture Collections at Brighton Museum*, Brighton: The Royal Pavilion, Art Gallery and Museums, 1983:37. Pierre Cabanne, *Encyclopédie Art Déco*, Paris: Somogy, 1986:211. Pierre Kjellberg, *Art Déco: les maîtres du Mobilier, le décor des Paquebots*, Paris: Amateur, 1986:115–16.

Lemmen, Georges   (1865–1916)
▶ Belgian painter; born Schaerbeek.
▶ He was an active member of Belgium's avant-garde movement and in contact with the pioneers of Art Nouveau in Belgium and

with Toulouse-Lautrec in France. Lemmen's work was initially in the Impressionist style. Like other members of the artists' group Les Vingt, Lemmen was active in reviving interest in the decorative arts. He designed rugs, tapestries, ceramics, jewelry, and mosaics, and illustrated books and rendered poster designs. Some of his jewelry was designed for jeweler Philippe Wolfers; Toulouse-Lautrec purchased a tapestry for which Lemmen designed the cartoon. Lemmen designed the typeface for Henry van de Velde's 1908 edition of Nietzsche's *Also Sprach Zarathustra*. Considering him 'pessimistic,' van de Velde thought his later work akin to that of Hermann Obrist and Otto Eckmann.
▶ From 1899, he showed his work annually at the salons of Les Vingt, and later of La Libre Esthétique.
▶ Yvonne Brunhammer et al., *Art Nouveau Belgium, France*, Houston: Institute for the Arts, Rice University, 1976. Stuart Durant, *Ornament from the Industrial Revolution to Today*, Woodstock, NY: Overlook, 1986:52,325.

Lenci, Fabio   (1935–)
▶ Italian designer; born and active Rome.
▶ Studied in Rome.
▶ He began his professional career in 1966. He set up a shop for contemporary furniture in Rome and began to explore the use of new plastics and manufacturing techniques in the production of his own furniture designs, including his *Chain* armchair with suspended upholstered rolls between plate-glass sides. From 1975 with Giovanna Talocci's established Studio Lenci Talocci; for a time, collaborated with Carlo Urbanati and Patrizia Lalle. His clients in Italy included Bonacina, Poltrona Frau, Ellisse, G.B. Bernini, Ilform, Incom, Sleeping International System Italia, and Tenco. He designed furniture, interiors, textiles, lighting and sanitary fixtures, including the 1974 *Aquarius* bath-shower unit produced (from 1975) by Teuco-Guzzini; became a member of ADI (Associazione per il Disegno Industriale).
▶ Work (1970 polyurethane table-chair set and table by Bernini) shown at 1972 'Italy: The New Domestic Landscape' at New York Museum of Modern Art.
▶ Emilio Ambasz (ed.), *Italy: The New Domestic Landscape*, New York: Museum of Modern Art, 1972:122. *ADI Annual 1976*, Milan: Associazione per il Disegno Industriale, 1976. Sylvia Katz, *Plastics: Designs and Materials*, London, 1978:96. Cat., Kathryn B. Hiesinger and George H. Marcus III (eds.), *Design Since 1945*, Philadelphia: Philadelphia Museum of Art, 1983. *Modo*, No. 148, March–April 1993:121.

Lendecke, Otto   (1886–1918)
▶ German draftsman, graphic artist, fashion and book designer; born Lemberg (now Lvov, Ukraine).
▶ Living in Paris for a time, he worked briefly with Paul Poiret. From 1911, he was associated with the Wiener Werkstätte and, in 1915, settled in Vienna. He designed theater sets and costumes for the Werkstätte. From 1917, he published the fashion magazine *Die Damenwelt (Ladies' World)* and was a contributor to others including *Wiener Mode, Die Dame* and the 1914–15 fashion folder *Die Mode*.
▶ Deanna F. Cera (ed.), *Jewels of Fantasy: Costume Jewelry of the 20th Century*, New York: Abrams, 1992.

Lenief, Alfred
▶ French dressmaker and decorator; active Paris.
▶ Lenief established a couture shop in Paris c1925, which he decorated himself in an austere style.

Lenoble, Émile   (1875–1940)
▶ French ceramicist.
▶ Studied École des Arts Décoratifs, Paris.
▶ After a seven-year apprenticeship, Lenoble turned in 1904 from earthenware to stoneware and high-temperature firing. Henry Rivière, his mentor and a connoisseur of Middle Eastern and Oriental art, introduced Lenoble to Korean pottery and Sung ceramics, which became a major influence on his work. In c1910, he began producing gray enamelwork. In his studio, in Choisy-le-Roy, near

Paris, Lenoble's hand-thrown pots, cylindrical vases, bottles, and bowls were made from kaolin mixed with stoneware for delicacy and lightness. His motifs were simple, geometric (chevrons and spirals), and floral (flowers and stylized leaves). 1920–30, his work showed Chinese influence and was rendered in a variety of colors, including turquoise, lapis-lazuli, yellows, browns, and celadon.

▶ Pierre Cabanne, *Encyclopédie Art Déco*, Paris: Somogy, 1986:213.

Lenox

▶ American ceramics factory; located Trenton, New Jersey.
▶ Walter Scott Lenox began producing high-quality porcelain wares in 1889 in an area known for ceramics production. The Lenox firm gained a reputation for its fine American tableware and provided the china for the White House in Washington from the 19th century to today. Its specialty is ivory-colored porcelain.
▶ Work shown at 1926–27 'American Industrial Art, Tenth Annual Exhibition of Current Manufactures Designed and Made in the United States' at the New York Metropolitan Museum of Art.
▶ *Lenox China: The Story of Walter Scott Lenox*, Trenton: Lenox. Karen Davies, *At Home in Manhattan: Modern Decorative Arts, 1925 to the Depression*, New Haven: Yale, 1983.

Léonard, Agathon (aka Léonard-Agathon van Weydeveldt 1841–)

▶ French designer; born Lille.
▶ Studied École des Beaux-Arts, Lille.
▶ He settled in Paris, becoming a member of the Société des Artistes français in 1887 and Société Nationale des Beaux-Arts in 1897. He executed portrait medallions, rose-quartz and green Egyptian marble statuettes and groups, bronze, ivory, plaster, and *flambé* earthenware. He is primarily known for his female figurine group *Jeu de l'écharpe* ('game with a scarf') commissioned by Sèvres in white bisque and subsequently produced by Susse fréres in bronze.
▶ *Jeu de l'écharpe* figurines first shown at 1897 Salon of the Société Nationale des Beaux-Arts in Paris and subsequently produced in white porcelain by Sèvres to be shown in its pavilion at the 1900 Paris 'Exposition Universelle.'
▶ Alastair Duncan, *Art Nouveau and Art Déco Lighting*, New York: Simon and Schuster, 1978:83. Martin Battersby, *Art Nouveau*, London, 1969:34. *Deutsche Kunst und Dekoration*, 1900–01:177.

Leonardi, Cesare (1935–)

▶ Italian industrial designer and architect; active Modena.
▶ Studied architecture, Università di Firenze, to 1970.
▶ Leonardi opened his own office in Modena in 1961. In 1962, Franca Stagi became a partner in the firm. They specialized in architecture, urban planning, and industrial design. They designed furniture for Bernini, Fiam, and Peguri; plastics for Elco; and lighting for Lumenform. Their best known design, the sculptural 1967 *Dondolo* rocking chair produced by Elco of Venice, became a classic.
▶ He showed furniture at 1968–69 'International Furniture Exhibitions,' Milan and Cologne, and 1970 'Design for Living, Italian Style' exhibition, London. *Dondolo* rocking chair first shown at 1968 Milan 'International Furniture Exhibition' and later at 1970 'Modern Chairs 1918–1970' exhibition at Whitechapel Gallery, London, and 1983–84 'Design Since 1945' exhibition, Philadelphia Museum of Art.
▶ 'Tavolini da Soggiorno in Vetroresina, Impignabili,' *Domus*, No. 483, Feb. 1970:43–44. Cat., *Modern Chairs 1918–1970*, London: Lund Humphries, 1971: no. 119. Cat., Kathryn B. Hiesinger and George H. Marcus III (eds.), *Design Since 1945*, Philadelphia: Philadelphia Museum of Art, 1983. *Casa Arredamento Giardino*, No. 19.

Leonidov, Ivan Ilich (1902–59)

▶ Russian architect; born Vlasikh, near Kalinin.
▶ From 1919, studied Tver' art school; from 1921, fine art, Vkhutemas, Moscow; Lenin Institute, Moscow, to 1928.
▶ He settled in Moscow in 1921, becoming a painter and studying in the Vkhutemas, where, under the influence of Aleksandr Vesnin, he turned from painting to architecture. In 1926, his school project for the *Izvestia* newspaper printing plant showed a full-blown Constructivist approach. In 1928, he became a lecturer at the Lenin Institute. As a Constructivist-Suprematist architect affected by Russian traditionalism, his style changed from dynamic, glass-walled structures to somewhat baroque structures, illustrated by his 1933 Narkomtiazprom-competition entry. Leonidov was able to produced only one notable building, the 1932 amphitheater and stairway for the Ordjohikedze Sanatorium in Kislovodsk. After World War II, he worked exclusively as an exhibition designer.
▶ In 1921, he entered a number of architecture competitions, receiving several prizes. His school project for the Lenin Institute of Moscow was shown at the 1927 (I) OSA (Union of Contemporary Artists) exhibition, Moscow.
▶ Selim O. Khan-Magomedov, 'Ivan Leonidov,' *Sovietskaia Architektura*, 16, 1964:103–116. S.O. Khan-Magomedov, 'I.I. Leonidov 1902–1959,' in O.A. Shvidovsky (ed.), *Building in the USSR, 1917–1932*, London and New York, 1971. Selim O. Khan-Magomedov, *Ivan Leonidov*, Moscow: Stroi-izdat, 1971. S.O. Khan-Magomedov, *I. Leonidov*, Moscow, 1973. V. Quilici and M. Scolari (eds.), *Ivan Leonidov*, Milan, 1975. R. Koolhaas and G. Oorthuys, *Ivan Leonidov*, New York, 1981. Andrei Gozak and Andrei Leonidov, *Ivan Leonidov*, London: Academy, 1988. Selim O. Khan-Magomedov, *Les Vhutemas*, Paris: Regard, 1990. Cat., *The Great Utopia: The Russian and Soviet Avant-Garde, 1915–1932*, New York: Guggenheim Musem, 1992.

Leonori, Luca (1951–)

▶ Italian designer; born and active Rome.
▶ Studied design, Università Internazionale dell'Arte, Florence, to 1973; architecture, Università di Roma, to 1976.
▶ From 1978, he worked as a designer, Pallucco, Rome; concurrently from 1976, with studio Passarelli, Rome, on architectural projects; from 1985, with architects L. De Lorenzo, F. Piferi, and S. Stefani in the graphic and design group Grafite.
▶ Fumio Shimizu and Matteo Thun (eds.), *The Descendants of Leonardo: The Italian Design*, Tokyo, 1987:326.

Lepape, Georges (1887–1971)

▶ French painter, illustrator, and designer.
▶ Studied École des Beaux-Arts, Paris under Cormon Atelier Humbert, Paris.
▶ At École des Beaux-Arts, he met André Marty, Pierre Brissaud, and Charles Martin; they were all known for their illustrations in fashion magazines and books; met Georges Braque, Francis Picabia, and Marie Laurencin at Atelier Humbert. In 1909, he was discovered by couturier Paul Poiret. Lepape translated Poiret's revolutionary ideas and creations in drawings and watercolors. In 1911, Lepape illustrated the portfolio *Les Choses de Paul Poiret vues par Georges Lepape*. In 1912, Jean-Louis Vaudoyer commissioned him to design the sets for *La Nuit persane* at the Théâtre des Arts in Paris. 1912–25, he rendered illustrations for the fashion magazine *Gazette du Bon Ton*. In 1915, he designed for the ballet-pantomime *Le Coup manqué* for the revue Rip at the Théâtre de l'Athénée and, in 1916, another set for a ballet for Rip at Théâtre de Marigny. In 1923, he designed the set for Maurice Maeterlinck's *L'Oiseau bleu*. Before World War I, he supplied Poiret with original couture models as well as some fabric designs. He went on to design film sets. 1924–38, he taught at New York School of Fine and Applied Arts.
▶ Cat., *Decorative Arts 1925 Style*, New York: Didier Aaron, 1979. Victor Arwas, *Art Déco*, Abrams, 1980. Claude Lepape and Thierry Defert, *Georges Lepape ou l'élégance illustrée*, Paris:

Herscher, 1983. Pierre Cabanne, *Encyclopédie Art Déco*, Paris: Somogy, 1986:213.

Leporskaia, Anna Alexandrovna   (1900–82)
▶ Russian painter, interior designer, decorative artist, and porcelain painter; wife of Nikolai Suetin.
▶ 1918, studied Pskov School of Decorative Arts under A. Radakov; from 1922, Academy of Arts, Petrograd, under K. Petrov-Vodkin, A. Savivov, and V. Sinaiskii.
▶ In 1925, she was an associate of Inkhuk in the department of Kasimir Malevich and active in interior decoration and book illustration. 1930–31, she was involved with design at the Krasny Theater and at the Muzikalnaya Komedia Theater, Leningrad (now St. Petersburg); in 1934, designed the interior of the Cultural Center of the Industrial Cooperative with husband Suetin; from 1945, designed porcelain forms; and, from 1948, was a designer at the Lomonosov Porcelain Factory, Leningrad. From 1952, she was a member of the examining committee of the College of Decorative Arts, Leningrad.
▶ She participated in the 1937 Paris 'Exposition Internationale des Arts et Techniques dans la Vie Moderne,' the installation of the 1939 'New York World's Fair' and, with Suetin, 1940 'National Agricultural Exhibition,' and Leningrad stand at the 'Great War of Defence' exhibition. She was winner of the Repin State Prize.
▶ Cat., *Kunst und Revolution: Russische und Sowjetische Kunst 1910–1932*, Vienna: Österreichisches Museum für angewandte Kunst, 1988. Cat., *The Great Utopia: The Russian and Soviet Avant-Garde, 1915–1932*, New York: Guggenheim Musem, 1992.

Lera, Roberto   (1945–)
▶ Italian architect and designer.
▶ His first work in plastics was the 1969 table for Fratelli Merati. He worked for Sormani, and was involved with the journal *La Stampa Sera* in Turin.
▶ Cat., Milena Lamarová, *Design a Plastické Hmoty*, Prague: Uměleckoprůmyslové Muzeum, 1972:120.

Lesage
▶ French embroidery house; located Paris.
▶ The original embroidery house was founded in 1858 by Michonet in Paris. In 1924, the firm was purchased by Albert Lesage. Its artisans produced cages of mother-of-pearl, flowers woven of straw, and blouses of ruched silk ribbons. For the Empress Eugénie, it produced embroidery on her clothing designed by Worth in 1898. Its clients included Guy Laroche, Yves Saint-Laurent, Claude Montana, and Christian Lacroix.
▶ Elaine Louie, 'Style Makers,' *The New York Times*, 9 June 1991:42.

Lesage, Jean
▶ French decorator and furniture designer; active Paris.
▶ In the 1920s, Lesage designed lighting for Damon, Paris, and subsequently furniture produced by VLG. By the 1950s, his studio was located at 15 rue d'Alésia.
▶ *Ensembles Mobiliers*, Paris: Charles Moreau, No. 21, 1954.

Lescaze, William   (1896–1969)
▶ Swiss architect and designer; born Onex, near Geneva; active Paris and the USA.
▶ Studied Collège de Genève to 1914; in 1915, École des Beaux-Arts, Geneva; architecture, École Polytechnique Fédérale, Zürich, under Karl Moser, to 1919.
▶ 1919–20, he worked on projects for the Committee for the Reconstruction of Devastated France and, for a time in Paris, in the architecture office of Henri Sauvage. In 1920, he emigrated to the USA and worked as a draftsman for architects Hubbell and Benes in Cleveland, Ohio. In 1921, he worked for Walter R. MacCornack, chief of the Bureau of Design of the Cleveland Board of Education, as a draftsman of schools and a planner and designed a 1922 warehouse. In 1923, he set up his own practice in New York with a commission for the townhouse of Simeon Ford at Sutton Place and Sutton Square in New York. 1929–35, he collab-

orated with George Howe in New York and Philadelphia. Lescaze and Howe are best known for the 1929–32 Philadelphia Savings Fund Society (PSFS) building, one of the most distinguished skyscrapers of all time and a notable early International Style structure. He designed 1931–36 buildings at Dartington Hall, Devon. Other architecture included Edgewood School (in collegiate Gothic style) in Greenwich, Connecticut; interiors (in Paris Modern) at the 1928 Macy's Exposition in New York; progressive schools (with Howe) in Philadelphia in 1929 and New York in 1931; 1930–31 Frederick Vanderbilt House, New Hartford, Connecticut, one of the first International Style residences in the USA; 1938 studios for Columbia Broadcasting System, Hollywood; 1942 Longfellow Building, Washington; 1950 100-unit residential complex Spinney Hill, Manhasset, New York; 1955 Borg-Warner Building, Chicago; and 1962 Church Peace Center Building, New York. After the dissolution of the partnership with Howe, Lescaze designed the Unity house in the Pocono Mountains of Pennsylvania, and Williamsbridge Housing in Brooklyn, New York. Active after World War II in the decorative arts and metalwork, he designed office spaces, including the building at 711 Third Avenue, New York. His most notable product designs and furniture were for the PSFS building and the CBS building in Los Angeles, including metal cantilever chairs, and upholstered seating. He designed furniture and lighting for Maison Bertel, 1928 de Sièyes house, his own 1933–34 house at 211 East 48th Street in New York, and 1928 Andrew Geller Shoes stores. He designed a 1932 clock, desk set, coat rack, desks, chairs and ceiling lighting fixture for the PSFS building and 1936 microphone and 1945 mobile truck unit for CBS.
▶ His paintings, furniture, fabrics, and accessories were included in the 1927 'Art in Industry' exhibition at Halle Brothers department store in Cleveland. He designed a room setting at 1928 'Exposition of Art in Industry at Macy's', New York. He designed a living room, Central Gallery of 1935 'Contemporary American Industrial Art, 1934' exhibition and a four-year-old's room in 1940 at the 'Contemporary American Industrial Art' exhibition, both Metropolitan Museum of Art. Work subject of 1992 'William Lescaze' exhibition, Institute for Architecture and Urban Studies, New York. Lescaze's and Howe's work shown in the 1931 European traveling exhibition and included in 1932 'International Exhibition of Modern Architecture', New York Museum of Modern Art.
▶ William Lescaze, *On Being an Architect*, New York, 1942. L. Wodehouse, 'Lescaze and Dartington Hall,' *Architectural Association Quarterly*, Vol. 8, No. 2, 1976. Cat., *Thirties: British art and design before the war*, London: Arts Council of Great Britain, Hayward Gallery, 1979:191,294. L. Cat., *William Lescaze*, New York: Institute for Architecture and Urban Studies. Vittorio Magnago Lampugnani (ed.), *Encyclopedia of 20th-Century Architecture*, New York: Abrams, 1986:200. Welling Lanmon Lorraine, *William Lescaze, Architect*, Philadelphia: The Art Alliance Press, 1987. R. Craig Miller, *Modern Design in Metropolitan Museum of Art 1880–1990*, New York: Metropolitan Museum of Art and Abrams, 1990. Cat., Lindsay Stamm Shapiro, *William Lescaze*, Basel: Wiese, 1993.

Lethaby, William Richard   (1857–1931)
▶ British architect, draftsman, and theorist; born Barnstaple, Devon.
▶ Studied Royal Academy Schools, London.
▶ He worked as an apprentice in the offices of Alexander Lauder at Barnstaple. From 1877, he worked under the architect Norman Shaw in London and, in 1881, became his principal assistant. Strongly influenced by William Morris and Philip Webb, he admired medieval art. Lethaby was one of the founders of the Art-Workers' Guild and created some of the most original buildings of the Arts and Crafts movement. In 1896, he and George Frampton were appointed joint advisors of the newly organized London Central School of Arts and Crafts, the first school of arts and crafts with workshops in various crafts and a prototype for the Bauhaus. Becoming joint principal with Frampton, Lethaby

remained until 1911. In 1900, he became the first professor of art at the Royal College of Art. He set out to break down the barriers between high and popular art, using the commonplace and the familiar to inspire the craftsperson and designer. He was a founding member of the Design and Industries Association in 1915; he published important theoretical books on art, craft, and design, and was editor of John Hogg's influential *The Artistic Crafts* series of technical handbooks. His notable buildings included the 1891 house 'Avon Tyrell' in Hampshire, 1899 Eagle Insurance building in Birmingham, and 1900–02 church in Brockhampton, Herefordshire.

▶ W.R. Lethaby, *Architecture, Mysticism and Myth*, London, 1892. W.R. Lethaby, *Leadwork, Old and Ornamental and for the Most Part English*, London, 1893. W.R. Lethaby, *Architecture*, London, 1911. W.R. Lethaby, *Designing Games*, Leicester, 1929. W.R. Lethaby, *Form in Civilization*, Oxford, 1922. W.R. Lethaby, *Philip Webb and His Work*, Oxford, 1935. H. Molesworth Roberts, *William Richard Lethaby, 1857–1931*, London, 1957. A.R.N. Roberts et al., *William Richard Lethaby, 1857–1931*, London, 1957. G. Rubens, *William Richard Lethaby and His Work*, London, 1983. Sylvia Backemeyer and Theresa Gronberg (eds.), *W.R. Lethaby, 1857–1931: Architecture, Design and Education*, London, 1984. Stuart Durant, *Ornament from the Industrial Revolution to Today*, Woodstock, NY: Overlook, 1986:220,325. Vittorio Magnago Lampugnani (ed.), *Encyclopedia of 20th-Century Architecture*, New York: Abrams, 1986:200–01.

Lettré, Emil (1876–1954)

▶ German silversmith; born Hanau; active Vienna, Budapest, Paris, and Berlin.

▶ Studied Königliche Preussische Zeichenakademie, Hanau, and in Vienna.

▶ He worked under Fritz von Miller in Munich and in Vienna, Budapest, and Paris. From 1905, he had a silversmith workshop in Berlin, where British silversmith Henry Wilson practiced for some years and H.G. Murphy worked as an apprentice in 1912. The condensed, severe forms of his work with its stylized animals presaged later styles. His objects, mostly silver and with simple geometric designs, were produced in his workshop; they were always simple, with smooth forms and fine linear chasing. In the 1920s, Lettré's flatware designs were produced by Bruckmann und Söhne in Heilbronn. In 1933, he was appointed director of the Staatliche Zeichenakademie in Hanau.

▶ Work included in a 1906 exhibition in Dresden and the 1914 Cologne 'Deutscher Werkbund-Ausstellung.' His cocktail shaker was shown at the 1937 Paris 'Exposition Internationale des Arts et Techniques dans la Vie Moderne.'

▶ Charlotte Gere, *American and European Jewelry 1830–1914*, New York: Crown, 1975:201. Cat., *Emil Lettré/Andreas Moritz*, Kunstgewerbeschulemuseum, Cologne, 1976. Annelies Krekel-Aalberse, *Art Nouveau and Art Déco Silver*, New York: Abrams, 1989:27,139,142,256. Cat., *Metallkunst*, Berlin: Bröhan-Museum, 1990.

Levanti, Giovanni (1956–)

▶ Italian designer; born Palermo.

▶ Studied architecture, Università di Palermo, to 1983; received a master's degree from the Domus Academy, Milan, 1985.

▶ He participated in design and architecture projects; designed the 1987 *Nastassja* side chair and 1987 *Alfonso* leather and metal bench produced by Memphis; subsequently, was a tutor, Domus Academy; concurrently, worked with Andrea Branzi; collaborated with Francesco Biondo; designed furniture for Campeggi and Edra.

▶ Participated in 1986 '12 New' exhibition, Milan, organized by Memphis.

▶ Fumio Shimizu and Matteo Thun (eds.), *The Descendants of Leonardo: The Italian Design*, Tokyo, 1987:326. *Modo*, No. 148, March–April 1993:121.

Levard, Georges

▶ French decorator and furniture designer; born Lettry, Calvados; active Paris.

▶ Studied École des Arts Décoratifs, Paris.

▶ From 1907, he collaborated with Pierre Lahalle and Maurice Lucet.

▶ Pierre Kjellberg, *Art Déco: les maîtres du Mobilier, le décor des Paquebots*, Paris: Amateur, 1986:117.

Léveillé, André (1880–1962)

▶ French artist and textile and jewelry designer.

▶ Léveillé produced patterns and weaves for industrial textiles. His paintings in the 1920s were used by jeweler Georges Fouquet on jewelry.

▶ David McFadden (ed.), *L'Art de Vivre*, New York: Vendôme, 1989. Sylvie Raulet, *Bijoux Art Déco*, Paris: Regard, 1984.

Leven, Hugo (1874–1956)

▶ German sculptor, designer, and metalsmith; active Düsseldorf, Bremen, and Hanau.

▶ Leven is best known for his designs for the Kayserzinn pewter factory. In 1904, he succeeded Heinrich von der Cammer as head of the design studio of Koch und Bergfeld in Bremen, where, in 1909, he was succeeded by Gustav Elsass. Leven stayed on as artistic advisor. He designed silver for the silversmiths Conrad Anton Beumers in Düsseldorf. From 1909, he was director of the Königliche Preussische Zeichenakademie in Hanau.

▶ Annelies Krekel-Aalberse, *Art Nouveau and Art Déco Silver*, New York: Abrams, 1989:141,256. Cat., *Metallkunst*, Berlin: Bröhan-Museum, 1990:592.

Levi-Montalcini, Gino (1902–74)

▶ Italian architect and designer.

▶ He was known as a Rationalist architect; in the 1930s, worked in Milan; is best known for his tubular steel and leather furniture.

▶ Penny Sparke, *Introduction to Design and Culture in the Twentieth Century*, London: Allen and Unwin, 1986.

Levin, Moisei Zerlikovich (1896–1946)

▶ Russian stage designer.

▶ Studied Vilno Art School to 1915.

▶ In 1921, he produced his first stage designs and joined the Constructivists; in 1923, he began designing for film; designed the set of B. Lavrentiev's play *Razlom* (Collapse) (1927).

▶ Cat., *Kunst und Revolution: Russische und Sowjetische Kunst 1910–1932*, Vienna: Österreichisches Museum für angewandte Kunst, 1988.

Levin, Richard

▶ British exhibition, graphic, and television designer.

▶ He designed stands for the 1936 'Building Trades Exhibition,' 1951 London 'Festival of Britain,' and 1949 'Bakelite Exhibition.' He collaborated on graphic designs with László Moholy-Nagy.

▶ November 1935 and February 1936 covers of the magazine *Self Appeal* designed with Moholy-Nagy were included in the 1979–80 'Thirties' exhibition at the Hayward Gallery, London.

▶ Cat., *Thirties: British art and design before the war*, London: Arts Council of Great Britain, Hayward Gallery, 1979:232,295.

Levinger und Bissinger

▶ German costume jeweler; located Pforzheim.

▶ In c1901, Emil Levinger set up a firm to manufacture jewelry designed by Austrian architect Otto Prutscher and others. After 1930, the firm became Levinger und Bissinger. The firms later split into Heinrich Levinger, jewelry manufacturers, and Heinrich Levinger, costume jewelry wholesalers.

▶ Deanna F. Cera (ed.), *Jewels of Fantasy: Costume Jewelry of the 20th Century*, New York: Abrams, 1992:108.

Levitsky, Georges (1885–)

▶ Russian bookbinder; born Ukraine; active Paris.

▶ Studied bookbinding in Odessa.

▶ He moved to Paris in 1907. He worked for Proute until 1910, when he set up his own workshop at 22 rue de l'Odéon. At first conventional, he developed a dynamic style after World War I. His clients included the politician Louis Berhou, King Alexander of Serbia, and King Albert I of Belgium.

▶ He showed covers for *Un Pélérin d'Angkor* in ivory, mother-of-pearl, and ebony; *Marrakech* in morocco encrusted with mother-of-pearl; and *Le Paradis Musulman* in ivory and mother-of-pearl at the 1927 Paris 'Exposition Internationale des Arts et Techniques dans la Vie Moderne.'

▶ Roger Devauchelle, *La Reliure en France de ses origines à nos jours*, Vol. 3, Paris, 1961:268–69. John F. Fleming and Priscilla Juvelis, *The Book Beautiful and the Binding as Art*, Vol. 1, New York, 1983: 2,134. Alastair Duncan and Georges de Bartha, *Art Nouveau and Art Déco Bookbinding*, New York: Abrams, 1989:19,119–23,193.

Lévy, Alfred

▶ Furniture designer and publisher; active Paris.

▶ In 1919, Lévy succeeded Louis Majorelle as head of Majorelle; subsequently, became a publisher and author of numerous books on French design.

▶ He showed furniture and interior design at the Salons in Paris.

Lévy, Claude   (1895–1942)

▶ French painter, architect, and designer; born Nantes.

▶ Lévy worked for the Primavera decorating department of the Au Printemps department store in Paris under its director Charlotte Chauchet-Guilleré, where she designed furniture and ceramics. She was active as a decorator of shops and offices, including that of the journal *La Semaine à Paris* (designed by architect Robert Mallet-Stevens) of the late 1920s, and façade and interior of the Edouard Loewy bookstore of *c*1928; in 1930, became a member of the UAM (Union des Artistes Modernes). In 1930, she retired to Menton, where Henri Matisse was influential on her painting.

▶ From 1921, her work was shown at Salons of the Société des Artistes Décorateurs and at the Salons d'Automne and, in 1930, at UAM's first exhibition (*Coin fantasque* chrome tube armchair with leather cushions produced by Primavera).

▶ Pierre Kjellberg, *Art Déco: les maîtres du Mobilier, le décor des Paquebots*, Paris: Amateur, 1986:117. Arlette Barré-Despond, *UAM*, Paris: Regard, 1986:302,532.

Lévy-Dhurmer, Lucien   (1865–1953)

▶ French ceramicist; born Algiers.

▶ Studied painting, lithography, design, and ceramics, Paris municipal school of drawing and sculpture.

▶ He was a ceramicist 1887–95 while working at Clément Massier's factory at Golfe-Juan as its artistic director. At the 1882 salon in Paris, he showed his copy on porcelain of Cabanel's painting *La Naissance de Vénus*. Lévy-Dhurmer may have been responsible for the rediscovery of the metallic luster glaze technique used in Middle Eastern ceramics from the 9th century and in Hispano-Moresque pottery of the 15th century, although the sheen on pieces by Massier and Lévy-Dhurmer has not lasted. He used primarily light-colored earthenware with gold highlights, and somber-glazed stoneware. His forms were both simple, and elaborate in the Islamic style. The painted or modeled decorations usually depicted typical Art Nouveau images. His interest in painting was revived during a trip to Italy in 1895. After 1900 he traveled throughout Europe and North Africa, particularly the Mediterranean coast, painting landscapes and doing figure studies. For a private home on Champ de Mars 1910–14, he painted murals and designed furniture and paneling for the living room, dining room, and library.

▶ He showed his work at the Salons des Artistes français from 1882, Salons of the Société Nationale des Beaux-Arts from 1897, and Salons d'Automne from 1930. He was a member of the Société de Pastellistes français and the Société des Orientalistes.

▶ Yvonne Brunhammer et al., *Art Nouveau Belgium, France*, Houston: Institute for the Arts, Rice University, 1976.

Lewis, David   (1939–)

▶ British industrial designer; active Copenhagen.

▶ Studied Central School of Arts and Crafts, London.

▶ 1960–68, he collaborated with Jakob Jensen on the design of radios and TV sets for various Danish firms. From 1962, he was assistant designer at Bang & Olufsen. In 1965, he began work on the *Beolab 5000* and developed the 'slide rule' device for regulating volume and tone. In 1967, he set up his own workshop in Copenhagen. From 1968, he collaborated with Henning Moldenhawer on products for Bang & Olufsen and other industrial clients. He designed the 1979 *Gori* boat propeller for Gori marine, 1982 *Odontoson 3* and *Odontosyringe 2* dental instruments for Goof, and 1989 *Multimec* switch for Mec. Working primarily for Bang & Olufsen from 1980 and specializing in TV set design, he executed numerous products from the 1973 *Beovision 3500* TV set to the 1989 *Beolink 7000* remote control unit.

▶ He won the 1979, 1982, 1986, and 1990 ID Prizes and the 1988 Design Prize of the European Community. His work was included in the 1990 'Bang & Olufsen: Design et Technologie' at the Paris Musée des Arts Décoratifs.

▶ Cat., Chantal Bizot, *Bang & Olufsen: Design et Technologie*, Paris: Musée des Arts Décoratifs, 1990:8–9.

Lewis, E. Wamsley

▶ British architect.

▶ Lewis was best known for his blue-and-green Art Déco design of the 1930 New Victoria Cinema in Westminster, London, with its dramatic auditorium ceiling influenced by Hans Poelzig's Grosses Schauspielhus in Berlin.

▶ Jonathan M. Woodham, *Twentieth-Century Ornament*, New York: Rizzoli, 1990:66.

Lewis, Wyndham   (1884–1957)

▶ British painter, writer, and designer.

▶ Lewis was the founder of Vorticism, the abstract art movement of 1912–15 embracing Futurist and Cubist concepts. He was an artist-member of the Omega Workshops, which he left in 1914 to establish the short-lived Rebel Art Centre. He had a difficult relationship with Omega's head, Roger Fry, and felt that the work of the painters there was outmoded. He employed an abstract style as opposed to the nudes and flowers of most of the Omega painters. He was an official war artist in World War I and continued to paint after the war and to publish. His novels included *Tarr* (1918), *The Apes of God* (1930), and the autobiographical *Blasting and Bombardiering* (1937).

▶ *British Arts & Design, 1900–1960*, 1983. Alan and Veronia Palmer, *Who's Who in Bloomsbury*, New York: St Martin's, 1987.

L'Herbier, Marcel   (1888–1979)

▶ French film director; born and active Paris.

▶ L'Herbier was the first director to incorporate Modern motifs in film sets. Elements of the new style appeared in his *Le Carnaval des vérités* (1919), designed by Michel Dufet and Claude Autant-Lara. L'Herbier's most daring venture was *L'Inhumaine* (1923), with contributions by art directors Alberto Cavalcanti and Autant-Lara, artist Fernand Léger, jewelry designer Raymond Templier, designer Pierre Chareau, and architect Robert Mallet-Stevens. Paul Poiret designed the costumes, Pierre Chareau furniture, Jean Puiforcat, René Lalique, and Jean Luce glassware and carpets. Darius Milhaud wrote the music. The film was shocking to audiences of the time, accustomed to neoclassical settings. L'Herbier continued to use Modern sets for his films, including *Eldorado* (1921), *Le Vertige* (1926), *Feu Mathias Pascal* (1925), *L'Argent* (1927), *Le Parfum de la dame en noir* (1929), *Forfaiture* (1927), and *La Nuit fantastique* (1942). In 1943, he founded the film school IDHEC (Institut des Hautes Études Cinématographiques).

▶ Howard Mandelbaun and Eric Myers, *Screen Deco: A Celebration of High Style in Hollywood*, New York: St. Martin's, 1985.

Jonathan M. Woodham, *Twentieth-Century Ornament*, New York: Rizzoli, 1990:128–29. *Petit Robert: Dictionnaire universelle des noms propres*, Vol. 1, Paris, 1991.
See de Noailles, vicomte Charles

Lhote, André (1885–1962)

▶ French painter, illustrator, teacher, and art critic; born Bordeaux; active Paris.
▶ Studied decorative sculpture, École des Beaux-Arts, Bordeaux.
▶ He became familiar with the work of Paul Gauguin in 1906, with that of Paul Cézanne through a retrospective mounted at the 1910 Salon d'Automne. In 1912, he became associated with French Cubism, and his geometric and smooth images were fractured, with color playing a dominant role. In the same mode as Roger de la Fresnaye, he adopted Synthetic Cubism. His focus on geometric fragmentation did not obscure the realism of his images, as was illustrated by his painting with sports themes (*Rugby* of 1917 and *Football* of 1920). In 1922, founded his own art school, Montparnasse, Paris. His theoretical books included *Traité du Paysage* (1938) and *Traité de la Figure* (1950). Numerous notable artists were his students, including Tamara de Lempiscka. He wrote the preface for *Sonia Delaunay, ses peintures, ses objects, ses tissus simultanés, ses modes.*
▶ In 1910, the first exhibition of his work was mounted at the Galerie Druet. He decorated the Pavillon du Gaz at the 1937 Paris 'Exposition Internationale des Arts et Techniques dans la Vie Moderne.'
▶ Pierre Cabanne, *Encyclopédie Art Déco*, Paris: Somogy, 1986:186,213.

Liaigre, Christian (1943–)

▶ French interior designer; active Paris.
▶ Studied École des Beaux-Arts, Paris.
▶ As an interior designer, he furnished Lloyds in London; French embassies in New Delhi, Warsaw, and Ottawa; Kenzo in Paris, Hotel Guanahani in the West Indies, Société Générale de Belgique in Brussels; Julien Cornic art bookshop in Paris and Tokyo; and various private apartments. He designed 1988 travel furniture for Louis Vuitton. Distributing and marketing his own furniture, he designed some tables in a Brancusi rough-hewn manner as well as more highly finished models. His 1992 *Remember* lamp was produced by Manufactor.
▶ Cat., *Les années VIA*, Paris: Musée des Arts Décoratifs, 1990.

Libbey Glass

▶ American glassware manufacturer; located Toledo, Ohio.
▶ In 1878, William L. Libbey (1827–83) leased New England Glass Co; moved in 1888 to Toledo, Ohio, by Libbey's son Edward Drummond Libbey (1854–1925). The years 1890–1915 were known as the 'Brilliant Period,' when it became the largest cut-glass factory in the world. 1883–1940, it produced colored, ornamental glassware in new processes developed by Joseph Locke, including Amberina, Agata, Pomona, Maize, and Peach Blow. From 1925, the firm was controlled by J.D. Robinson and his sons. In 1931, they hired A. Douglas Nash who introduced the high-quality 1933 Libbey-Nash Glassware. Part of Owens-Illinois from 1936 and a major producer of domestic and utility glassware, Libbey Glass Division produced the designs of Freda Diamond, including the 1957 *Golden Foliage* table glass. 1940–45, the ornamental lead crystal glassware of Edwin W. Feurst was put into production. The Scandinavian-inspired and inexpensive *Accent Stemware* glass range in the 1960s in smoky gray and was one of its most successful products. For patterns on its party-style drinking glasses, an epoxy-resin printing process was employed. Today only machine-made tableware is produced by Libbey; its last hand-crafted glassware was the 1940 *Modern American* series.
▶ It operated the Glass Pavilion at the 1893 Chicago 'World's Columbian Exposition,' where 130 craftspeople cut and blew glass.

▶ Harold Newman, *An Illustrated Dictionary of Glass*, London: Thames and Hudson, 1977:183–84. Frederick Cooke, *Glass: Twentieth-Century Design*, New York: Dutton, 1986:101.

Libera, Adalberto (1903–63)

▶ Italian architect; born Villa Lagarina, Trento; active Rome.
▶ In 1921, studied architecture in Parma; from 1925, Regia Scuola di Architettura, Rome; Università di Roma to 1927.
▶ In Cologne Libera was invited in 1927 to become a member of Gruppo Sette (Group of 7), originally organized in 1926; he replaced Ubaldo Castagnoli. Libera and architecture critic Gaetano Minnucci organized the 1928 (I) 'Esposizione dell'architettura razionale' in Rome, which offered an opportunity for young Rationalists to compete with academic architects. He was secretary of MIAR (Movemento Italiano per l'Architettura Razionale), the group of architects active in Rome who attempted unsuccessfully to have the Fascist regime adopt Rationalist architecture; in 1937, Rationalism was officially condemned. Libera and Guido Frette, with Luigi Figini and Gino Pollini (Gruppo Sette members) and Piero Bottoni, designed the Casa Elettrica for Montedison at the 1930 (IV) Biennale di Monza, the first public expression of Modern architecture in Italy. His work included the 1930 'SAC' pavilion, Fiera di Milano; 1931–34 elementary school, piazza Raffaello Sanzio, Trento Concorso; 1932 'Mostra del decannale della rivoluzione fascista,' Rome; 1933–34 post office building (with C. Cirella, G. Corre, V. Di Berardino); 1935 Italian pavilion, International Exposition, Brussels; 1942 'E 42' (unrealized), Rome; 1937 exhibition, Circo Maximo, Rome; 1938–43 Villa Malaparte, Capri; 1949 housing block, Trento; 1951 tobacconist's interior, Milan; 1955 housing block, via Pessina, Cagliari; 1956–58 office building, via Torino, Rome; 1959 Pfizer laboratory, Latina, and 1959 Olympic Village (with others), Rome.
▶ His work was the subject of the 'Adalberto Libera' exhibitions at the Museo Provinciale d'Arte, Trento, and Palazzo della Triennale, Milan, 1989.
▶ A. Alieri et al., 'Adalberto Libera,' *L'architettura—cronache e storia*, Nos. 124–33, Rome, 1966. Giulio Aragon, *Adalberto Libera*, Rome 1976. Barbie Campbell-Cole and Tim Benton (eds.), *Tubular Steel Furniture*, London: The Art Book Company, 1979:47. Vittoro Gregotti in Vittorio Magnago Lampugnani (ed.), *Encyclopedia of 20th-Century Architecture*, New York: Abrams, 1986:169,201. Cat., *Adalberto Libera: Opera completa*, Milan: Electa, 1989.

Liberati, Anne (1961–) and **Joris Heetman** (1957–)

▶ French and Dutch furniture designers; active Paris.
▶ Liberati studied Met de Penninghen school, Paris; Heetman studied Design Academy, Eindhoven.
▶ They worked together for three years in the design office Endt Fulton Partners, Paris; in 1987, were freelance designers; in 1987, set up their own design office, Chaperon et Méchant Loup; designed furniture including *Pin Up* produced by Néotù.
▶ Work subject of 1990 exhibition, VIA gallery, Paris.
▶ Cat. *Les années VIA 1980–1990*, Paris: Musée des Arts Décoratifs, 1990:186.

Liberty, Arthur Lasenby (1843–1917)

▶ British entrepreneur.
▶ Liberty worked from 1862 for the Great Shawl and Cloak Emporium on Regent Street, London, whose sales had been spurred by a growing interest in Japanese goods. 1864–75, he was manager of their Oriental Emporium. Liberty established his own business on the same street, at about the same time as Siegfried Bing set up his shop L'Art Nouveau in Paris. The operation was successful; in 1883, he acquired additional quarters in Regent Street, named Chesham House, after his birthplace. In 1884, he established a costume shop, managed by E.W. Godwin, that sold progressive clothing influenced by Paris styles. He visited Japan in 1888–89 and later wrote a book on his trip. He sold Japanese metalwork and Indian enamels, which he had mounted in Britain. The furniture design studio was managed by Leonard F. Wyburd,

who designed its rustic *Althelstan* range of furniture. Liberty's furniture styles of the 1880s and 1890s covered a wide range from fashionable Moresque and Arabic to historicist and Modern. Popular throughout Europe, Liberty's furniture could be bought in Paris, Vienna, Berlin, and Brussels. Gustave Serrurier-Bovy set up a Liberty concession in his shop in Nancy. Liberty imported the work of continental designers including Richard Riemerschmid, a practice the firm continued up to the 1950s. His customers and Oriental-art enthusiasts included E.W. Godwin, William Burges, Dante Gabriel Rossetti, Edward Burne-Jones, and James Whistler. Realizing that crafts metalwork would become popular, Liberty began commissioning work from British designers and craftspeople. Liberty became involved with Christopher Dresser from the 1890s, Archibald Knox who designed the firm's 1899 silver *Cymric* and 1901 *Tudric* patterns, and with Reginald Silver. Later adopting Tudor revival designs, Liberty stopped production of these ranges at the end of the 1920s. Most of the *Cymric* range was made 1900–27 by W.H. Haseler of Birmingham. Identical pieces were also produced by the firms Murrle, Bennett, and the as yet unidentified L.C. and Co. Liberty had a policy of not revealing the names of its designers; they included Oliver Baker, A.E. Jones, Arthur Gaskin, Bernard Cuzner, Harry Craythorn, C. Carter, Rex and Harry Silver, Jessie M. King, Thomas Hodgetts, Charles Povey, Jessie Jones, and Maud Coggin. Patterns from designers were often not used in their original forms, making attribution difficult. The influence and popularity of Liberty's work was such that in Italy one of the contemporary names by which Art Nouveau became known was *Lo Stile Liberty*. The shop is still located in Regent Street, with branches worldwide; some of its textile and wallpaper designs are commissioned from freelance designers.

▶ The 1975 centenary exhibition 'Liberty's 1875–1975' was mounted at the Victoria and Albert Museum, London.

▶ Alison Adburgham, *Liberty's, a biography of a shop*, London: George Allen and Unwin, 1975. Charlotte Gere, *American and European Jewelry 1830–1914*, New York: Crown, 1975:202–03. Cat., *Liberty's 1875–1975*, London: Victoria and Albert Museum, 1975. Jessica Rutherford, *Art Nouveau, Art Deco and the Thirties: The Furniture Collections at Brighton Museum*, Brighton: The Royal Pavilion, Art Gallery and Museums, 1983:20. *British Arts and Design, 1900–1960*, London: Victoria and Albert Museum, 1983. Annelies Krekel-Aalberse, *Art Nouveau and Art Déco Silver*, New York: Abrams, 1989:30,32,256. Stephen Calloway, *Liberty of London, Masters of Style & Decoration*, London: Thames and Hudson, 1992.

Libidarch

▶ Italian radical architecture group.

▶ Libidarch was founded in 1971 in Turin by Edoardo Ceretto, Maria Grazia Daprà Conti, Vittorio Gallo, Andrea Mascardi, and Walter Mazzella. Active until 1975, the group was active in research on 'poor' and 'banal' urban projects. They produced the video *A proposal for the methodological definition of 'poor' architecture* (1972). Some of their furniture was produced by Busnelli. Certain members got together later to participate in exhibitions, including the 1983 event in the Parc de la Villette in Paris.

▶ They participated in the 1973 (XV) Triennale di Milano and biennale of architecture in São Paulo.

▶ Andrea Branzi, *La Casa Calda: Esperienze del Nuovo Disegno Italiano*, Milan: Idea Books, 1982.

Lichtblau, Ernst (1883–1963)

▶ Austrian architect and furniture and interior designer; born and active Vienna.

▶ Studied Akademie der bildenden Künste, Vienna, under Otto Wagner.

▶ In 1912, he designed silver with enamel for Alfred Pollak. Around the 1920s, he set up his own workshop in Vienna. He settled in the USA in 1939 and taught at Rhode Island School of Design, Providence, Rhode Island.

▶ Günther Feuerstein, *Vienna—Present and Past: Arts and Crafts—Applied Art—Design*, Vienna: Jugend und Volk, 1976:49,80. Astrod Gmeiner and Gottbried Pirhofer, *Der Österreichische Werkbund*, Saltzburg/Vienna: Residenz, 1985:235. Annelies Krekel-Aalberse, *Art Nouveau and Art Déco Silver*, New York: Abrams, 1989:256.

Lichtenstein, Roy (1923–)

▶ American artist and designer; active New York State.

▶ Studied Ohio State University, Columbus, Ohio.

▶ His Abstract Expressionism period preceded his Pop art style, for which he was best known. His large images were reproduced in primary colors revealing the Ben Day dots of the comic strips that inspired his work. Fond of kitsch, he showed a mastery of color and composition in his work. In the mid-1960s, he converted famous works of art into comic-strip interpretations. His 1966 dinner service in heavy institutional china was produced by Jackson China. His later work included sculpture, sometimes in brass, and three-dimensional adaptations of images. His furniture imitated the Art Déco style of the 1930s. His rug designs were included in two 1988 *Dialog* ranges produced by Vorwerk.

▶ His first one-person exhibition was in 1962 at the Leo Castelli Gallery, New York.

▶ Leo Castelli and The Mayor Gallery, *Roy Lichtenstein Sculpture*, London: 1977:4. Ian Chilvers et al., *The Oxford Dictionary of Art*, Oxford and New York: Oxford, 1988:289. Volker Fischer, *Bodenreform: Teppichboden von Künstlern und Architekten*, Berlin: Ernst und Sohn, 1989.

Lichtwark, Alfred (1852–1914)

▶ German art historian.

▶ Lichtwark was director of the Hamburg Gallery. His 1896–99 lectures on the English Art and Crafts movement were influential on German art education in the early 20th century.

▶ Penny Sparke, *Introduction to Design and Culture in the Twentieth Century*, London: Allen and Unwin, 1986.

Lidköpings Porslinsfabrik

▶ Swedish ceramics factory.

▶ Nymans Porslinsmaleri was established in 1900 at Lidköping to paint and decorate blank ware; in 1911, was renamed Lidköping and began its own porcelain production; by *c*1920, commissioned freelance designer Einar Forseth; in 1927, was bought by Arabia; in 1932, was bought by Rörstrand, which moved its production to Lidköping. In 1939, the name was absorbed into Rörstrand.

▶ Jennifer Hawkins Opie, *Scandinavia: Ceramics and Glass in the Twentieth Century*, New York: Rizzoli, 1989.

Liebes, Dorothy (1899–1972)

▶ American textile designer; active San Francisco and New York.

▶ Studied University of California at Berkeley, California, and Columbia University, New York.

▶ In 1930, she set up a design studio in San Francisco, where she specialized in custom handwoven goods for architects and decorators. In 1940, she received her first commission for large-scale production fabrics from Goodall Fabrics in Sanford, Maine. In 1948, she moved her design studio to New York and in *c*1958 abandoned her custom work in favor of industrial consulting and designing textiles for mass production. Her commissions included work for E.I. Du Pont de Nemours in 1955, Bigelow-Sanford in 1957, and Sears Roebuck in 1969. She became one of the first American textile designers to apply hand techniques for weaving to mass production, in fabrications noted for their unusually combined bright colors; she used unconventional yarns and materials, including sequins, leather strips, grass, plastics, ticker tape, and bamboo.

▶ Her work subject of 1970 'Dorothy Liebes' exhibition, Museum of Contemporary Crafts, New York.

▶ Cat., *Dorothy Liebes*, New York: Museum of Contemporary Crafts, 1970. Cat., Kathryn B. Hiesinger and George H. Marcus III (eds.), *Design Since 1945*, Philadelphia: Philadelphia Museum of Art, 1983:220,VII–37–40. Gillian Moss, 'Dorothy Liebes' in Mel Byars and Russell Flinchum (eds.), *50 American Designers, 1918–1968*, Washington: Preservation, 1994.

Lie-Jørgensen, Thorbjørn (1900–61)
▶ Norwegian metalworker.
▶ Apprenticed to silversmith Henrik Lundat Notodden; studied Statens Handverks -og Kunstindustriskole, Oslo, under Henrik Lund, and painting, Statens Kunstakademi, Oslo.
▶ 1939–61, he was department head at the Statens Håndverks -og Kunstindustriskole. In 1927, he joined the firm David-Andersen, Oslo.
▶ He won a gold medal at the 1954 (X) Triennale di Milano and in 1955 in Munich. He won the 1948 competition for table silver for the town hall in Oslo.
▶ Cat., David Revere McFadden (ed.), *Scandinavian Modern Design 1880–1980*, New York: Abrams, 1982:267, Nos. 120,142. Fredrik Wildhagen, *Norge i Form*, Oslo: Stenersen, 1988:88.

Liévore, Alberto (1948–)
▶ Argentine designer and architect.
▶ Studied architecture in Buenos Aires.
▶ He and Jorge Pensi established a design practice in 1977 in Barcelona, like other Argentines, including Carlos Rolando, América Sánchez, and J. García Garay. They designed many of the 1984 stands for SIDI and, for Perobell, the *Latina* range of furniture of the early 1980s. With critics and theorists Oriol Pibernat and Norberto Chaves, they set up the design consultancy Grupo Gerenguer. From 1984, Liévore and Pensi began to work separately; the latter pursued furniture and lighting. Liévore designed the widely published 1988 *Manolete* one-arm chair and, with Pensi, the 1987 *Helsinoor* armchair by Perobell.
▶ Guy Julier, *New Spanish Design*, London: Thames and Hudson, 1991.

Liisberg, Carl Frederick (1860–1909)
▶ Danish ceramicist.
▶ 1885–1909, Liisberg was a sculptor and underglaze painter at Royal Copenhagen Porcelain Manufactory. He was an innovator in the use of slip in porcelain painting, which lent relief to an image.
▶ Cat., David Revere McFadden (ed.), *Scandinavian Modern Design 1880–1980*, New York: Abrams, 1982:267, No. 32.

Liisberg, Hugo (1896–1958)
▶ Danish sculptor and jewelry designer.
▶ Liisberg apprenticed at the Royal Copenhagen Porcelain Manufactory from 1915. He designed jewelry for the Georg Jensen Sølvsmedie in the 1940s.
▶ He won a gold medal from Det Kongelige Danske Kunstakademi, Copenhagen, and the Eckersberg Medal in 1942.
▶ Cat., *Georg Jensen Silversmithy: 77 Artists, 75 Years*, Washington: Smithsonian Institution Press, 1980.

Likarz-Strauss, Maria (b. Maria Likarz)
▶ Austrian draftsperson, ceramics decorator, painter, and fashion and accessories designer; born Przemysl (now Poland).
▶ 1908–10, studied Art School for Women and Girls, Vienna, under O. Friedrich and, 1911–15, Kunstgewerbeschule under A. von Kenner and Josef Hoffmann.
▶ 1916–17 and in 1920, she taught at the Crafts School in the Giebichenstein Castle, Halle (Germany), and, 1912–14, was on the staff of Neue Werkbund Österreichs and Wiener Frauenkunst (Vienna Women's Art Group). Her jewelry incorporated pearls and enamel. She designed fashion postcards and designs, textiles and leather, lace, and pearl work for the Wiener Werkstätte and contributed to the 1914–15 fashion folder *Die Mode*.
▶ Deanna F. Cera (ed.), *Jewels of Fantasy: Costume Jewelry of the 20th Century*, New York: Abrams, 1992:106.

Liljedahl, Bengt (1932–)
▶ Swedish metalworker.
▶ Studied Konstfackskolan and Tekniska Skolan, Stockholm, to 1953; 1958, École Nationale Supérieure des Arts Décoratifs, Paris.
▶ He set up his own workshop in Stockholm in 1954; producing silver hollow-ware.
▶ *Svenskt Silver Inför Åttiotalet*, Stockholm, 1979. Cat., David Revere McFadden (ed.), *Scandinavian Modern Design 1880–1980*, New York: Abrams, 1982:267, No. 242.

Liljefors, Anders B. (1923–70)
▶ Swedish ceramicist.
▶ 1942–43, studied sculpture and painting, Grünewalds måiarskola, Stockholm; 1945–47, Det Kongelige Danske Kunstakademi, Copenhagen.
▶ 1947–53 and 1955–57, he worked for Gustavsberg. In c1947, he set up his own workshop in Karlskrona. In addition to functional objects, he produced a number of sculpture pieces. From the 1950s, Liljefors was one of the potters who redefined the role of the craft potter.
▶ His work was the subject of one-person exhibitions at the Nordiska Kompaniet in Stockholm in 1952, another in Stockholm, and in Gothenburg in 1957. His work was included in numerous group exhibitions.
▶ Cat., David Revere McFadden (ed.), *Scandinavian Modern Design 1880–1980*, New York: Abrams, 1982:267, No. 164. Jennifer Hawkins Opie, *Scandinavia: Ceramics and Glass in the Twentieth Century*, New York: Rizzoli, 1989.

Lillie, Jacqueline (1941–)
▶ French jewelry designer; born Marseilles.
▶ 1962–65, studied metalwork, Akademie der bildenden Künste, Vienna, under Hagenauer.
▶ Her one-person exhibition was mounted at the Galerie am Graben in Vienna.

Limbert, Charles P. (1854–1923)
▶ American furniture designer and maker.
▶ During the 1880s, Limbert worked for the furniture firm John A. Colby in Chicago. In 1889, he set up the Limbert and Klingman Chair Co in Grand Rapids, Michigan, with Phillip Klingman. The firm was closed in 1894, when C.P. Limbert and Co was formed. In 1902, he established the Holland Dutch Arts and Crafts furniture company in Grand Rapids and Holland, Michigan. He marketed eclectic designs based on Mission furniture models. 1904–06, Limbert produced his most imaginative work. Echoing some of C.R. Mackintosh's, C.F.A. Voysey's, and Hugh Baillie Scott's designs, Limbert's trademark was pierced rectangles with rounded corners; his tables had flaring bases and top with sides protruding beyond the legs of the table. Like other designers in the Grand Rapids area, he was sympathetic with the work of Josef Hoffmann in Austria and Mackintosh in Scotland. Though strongly influenced by others, Limbert synthesized the more lyrical European style with the American Arts and Crafts aesthetic. While his 1905 *Square-Cut Café Chair* and 1906 *Oval Center Table* were inspired by the chairs in Mackintosh's Willow Tea Rooms in Glasgow, Lambert's table was more graceful and dynamic.
▶ He showed his work at the 1904 St. Louis 'Louisiana Purchase Exposition.'
▶ *Limbert's Holland Dutch Arts and Crafts Furniture*, Charles P. Limbert Company Cabinetmakers, New York: Turn of the Century, 1981. Anne Yaffe Phillips, *From Architecture to Object*, New York: Hirschl and Adler, 1989:70,78.

Limoges
▶ French faïence factory; located Limoges.
▶ The Limoges factory was established in 1736, producing domestic ceramic ware for a number of years. Kaolin and petuntse were quarried from 1768 near Limoges and used at Sèvres. In 1771, hard-paste porcelain began to be produced under the patronage of the Comte d'Artois, brother of Louis XVI. André Massier was the first to produce all-French porcelain wares. In 1784, it

was taken over by Louis XVI himself and became the Manufacture Royale to produce plain white ware. After the 1789 Revolution, numerous factories were established in the area, including those of Pierre-Léon Sazerat and François Alluaud. By 1840, the area had more than 30 manufacturers; they were joined by New York merchant David Haviland, who took over the Alluaud factory. Still known for its ordinary tablewares, the area remains the center of porcelain production in France.
▶ J. d'Albis and C. Romanet, *La Porcelaine de Limoges*, Paris, 1980. Françoise Kostolany, 'Everlasting Porcelain: Its Bountiful Past and Dynamic Present,' *Vogue Décoration*, No. 26, June/July 1990:172.

Lin, Maya (1960–)
▶ American architect; born Ohio.
▶ Studied architecture, Yale University, to 1981.
▶ She won the 1981 competition to design the Vietnam Veterans' Memorial in Washington, for which she produced a black granite sculpture. The construction was widely opposed at the time of its installation in favor of a more traditional rendering. She designed the Civil Rights Memorial at the Southern Poverty Law Center in Montgomery, Alabama.
▶ Julie V. Iovine, *Metropolitan Home*, April 1990:108.

Lindau, Börge (1932–)
▶ Swedish furniture and interior designer.
▶ 1957–62, studied Slöjdföreningens Skola (today Kunstindustriskolan), Gothenburg.
▶ Lindau and Bo Lindekrantz met at the Arts and Crafts School, Gothenburg; from 1964, worked together after a brief interlude with an architecture firm in Hälsingborg; were active primarily for Lammhults Mekaniska, Lammhult, from 1965; developed a series of furniture designs using chromium-plated bent-metal tubing. Work included flexible display system for Form Design Center in Malmö, 1963 *Opalen* stackable armchair (still in production), 1968 *S–70–1* chromium tubular-steel stackable stool, furniture for a day nursery in Hälsingborg, furnishings for 1969 library in Norrköping, 1970 *Peking* stackable hook-on armchair in chromium tubular steel, 1982 *Duet 8* upholstered lounge chair in tubular steel and birch.
▶ Received (with Lindekrantz) 1969 Lunning Prize.
▶ Cat., David Revere McFadden (ed.), *Scandinavian Modern Design 1880–1980*, New York: Abrams, 1982:267, No. 262. Cat., *The Lunning Prize*, Stockholm: Nationalmuseum, 1986:198–201.

Lindberg, Stig (1916–82)
▶ Swedish ceramicist and textile designer; active Stockholm.
▶ 1935–37, studied Konstfackskolan and Tekniska Skolan, Stockholm; 1937–40, at Gustavsberg under Wilhelm Kåge; and in Paris.
▶ He was best known for his ceramics, although he also designed plastics, textiles, appliances, enamels, glassware, and graphics. 1957–72, he taught at Konstfackskolan and Tekniska Skolan. From 1937, he was employed by Gustavsberg and was influenced by its artistic director Wilhelm Kåge. 1949–57 succeeding Kåge and 1972–78, he was artistic director at Gustavsberg, for which he designed decorative and utilitarian ceramics and developed painted decorations for its enamelwares. 1945–47, he was a designer for Målerås glassworks. From 1947, he designed hand-printed textiles for Nordiska in Stockholm. 1957–70, he was senior lecturer at the Konstfackskolan and Tekniska Skolan. The influenced of Kåge can be seen in Lindberg's 1949 dinner service with its softly rounded silhouette. He produced large-scale murals and public works. From 1980, he was active in his own studio in Italy.
▶ He won gold medals at the 1948 (VIII) and 1957 (XI) Triennali di Milano and grand prizes at its 1951 (IX) and 1954 (X) sessions, gold medal in 1955 at Cannes, 1957 Gregor Paulsson trophy, and 1968 Prince Eugen Medal; 1973 gold medal at Faenza. His work was the subject of one-person exhibitions in Europe, Japan, and the USA, and was included in the 1939 'New York World's Fair,'

1954–57 USA 'Design in Scandinavia' traveling exhibition, 1955 'H 55' exhibition in Hälsingborg, 1958 'Formes Scandinaves' at the Paris Musée des Arts Décoratifs, and 1975 'Gustavsberg 150 ar' exhibition at the Nationalmuseum, Stockholm.
▶ 'Stig Lindberg,' *Everyday Art Quarterly*, No. 25, 1953:14–15. Berndt Klyvare and Dag Widman, Kim Taylor, 'Stig Lindberg,' *Graphis*, Vol. 15, July 1959:308–15. Berndt Klyvare and Dag Widman, *Stig Lindberg—Swedish Artist and Designer*, Stockholm: Rabén & Sjögren, 1963. Cat., *Gustavsberg 150 ar*, Stockholm: Nationalmuseum, 1975. Cat., David Revere McFadden (ed.), *Scandinavian Modern Design 1880–1980*, New York: Abrams, 1982: 267, Nos. 135,165,227. Cat., Kathryn B. Hiesinger and George H. Marcus III (eds.), *Design Since 1945*. Philadelphia: Philadelphia Museum of Art, 1983:220,II–N32,VII–41. Jennifer Hawkins Opie, *Scandinavia: Ceramics and Glass in the Twentieth Century*, New York: Rizzoli, 1989.

Lindblad, Gun (1954–)
▶ Swedish glassware designer; born Lapland.
▶ 1977–81, studied glass and ceramics, Konstfackskolan and Tekniska Skolan, Stockholm.
▶ 1982–87, designer at the Kosta Boda glassworks; from 1987, active in his own studio in Stockholm; from c1987, artist-in-residence, California College of Arts and Crafts, USA; from 1987, consultant, Studio Glas, Strömbergshyttan.
▶ Works shown in Norway, Finland, Sweden, and Switzerland.
▶ Jennifer Hawkins Opie, *Scandinavia: Ceramics and Glass in the Twentieth Century*, New York: Rizzoli, 1989.

Lindekrantz, Bo (1932–)
▶ Swedish furniture and interior designer.
▶ Lindekrantz and Börge Lindau collaborated on furniture designs produced by Lammhults Mekaniska. They designed furniture that often incorporated chromium-plated bent metal tubing.
▶ They won the 1969 Lunning Prize.
▶ Cat., David Revere McFadden (ed), *Scandinavian Modern Design 1880–1980*, New York: Abrams, 1982:267, No. 262.

Lindfors, Stefan (1962–)
▶ Finnish sculptor and interior and furniture designer; born Maarianhamina.
▶ 1982–88, studied interior and furniture design, University of Industrial Arts, Helsinki.
▶ In 1988, he designed the set for the evening news television program of the Finnish Broadcasting Company. His 1988 *Scaragoo* articulated table lamp, which lit up when touched, was designed with and produced by Design M (Ingo Maurer) of Germany. In 1989, Lindfors designed the interiors and furniture for the restaurant of the Museum of Industrial Arts in Helsinki.
▶ Among other awards, he received the silver medal at the 1986 Triennale di Milano. His sculpture was the subject of a 1988 exhibition at the Gallery Titanik in Turku.
▶ Albrecht Bangert and Karl Michael Armer, *80s Style: Designs of the Decade*, New York: Abbeville, 1990:120–21,232.

Lindgren, Amas Eliel (1874–1929)
▶ Finnish architect.
▶ Studied Helsinki Polytechnical Institute to 1897.
▶ He was a fellow student of Eliel Saarinen and Herman Gesellius, with whom he formed a partnership in 1896. Their offices were located, 1896–1905, in Helsinki; 1903–1905, in the 1902 house 'Hvitträsk' in Kirkkonummi, on Lake Vitträsk which was the joint studio and home of the Gesellius, Lindgren, and Saarinen families and employees; after 1916, Saarinen lived there alone. It became a mecca for artists. 1899–1900, Lindgren worked as a secretary at the Antiquities Board; 1899–1901, as a teacher of art history at the Polytechnical Institute; from 1902, as artistic director and teacher at the Central School of Applied Arts. Lindgren left the partnership in 1905. Metalwork on their buildings was designed and executed by Eric O.W. Ehrströn, including that for Pohjola fire insurance company, 'Hvitträsk' house, 'Hvittorp' house, Reimer house, Finnish National Museum, and Pohjois-

maiden Osakepankki bank (brass doors). Gesellius, Lindgren, and Saarinen work included the 1898–1900 Finnish pavilion at the 1900 Paris 'Exposition Universelle' and 1899–1901 Pohjola fire insurance company at Aleksanterinkatu and Mikankatu in Helsinki (with masks by Hilda Flodin); 1897–98 Talberg apartment building, Katajanokka; 1900–01 building in Fabrianinkatu 17, Katajanokka; 1900–02 Olofsborg apartment building; 1901–03 Eol apartment building; 1901–02 'Suur-Merijoki' house in Merijoki, west of Viipuri (now Russia); 1901–03 'Hvitträsk' house on Lake Vitträsk; 1901–04 'Hvittorp' house (residence of Robert Emil Westerlund; stone fireplace by Jarl Eklund) on Lake Vitträsk; 1903 Bobrinky house (unrealized); 1905–07 house for German poet Paul Remer, Mark Brandenburg (Germany); 1902–12 Finnish National Museum (copperwork by Ehrström, decorations by Armas Lindgren and Emil Wikström, and, in 1928, Akseli Gallen-Kallela fresco); 1903–04 Pohjoismaiden Osakepankki bank (decorations in copper by Lindgren produced by Alpo Sailo) in Helsinki.

▶ Marika Mausen et al., *Eliel Saarinen: Projects 1896–1923*, Cambridge: MIT Press, 1990.

Lindh, Richard (1929)

▶ Finnish ceramicist.

▶ 1952–53, studied Taideteollinen Korkeakoulu, Helsinki.

▶ 1953–55, shared a studio with his wife Francesca Lindh in Helsinki; from 1955, worked for Arabia in Helsinki, where he was head of the industrial art department from 1960 and artistic director from 1973–c1985.

▶ He received first prize in a competition at the Museum of Contemporary Crafts in New York. His work was included in the 1955 'H 55' exhibition in Hälsingborg (Sweden), 1961 'Finlandia' exhibition in Zürich, Amsterdam, and London, and 1957 (XI) and 1960 (XII) Triennali di Milano.

▶ Cat., David Revere McFadden (ed.), *Scandinavian Modern Design 1880–1980*, New York: Abrams, 1982:267, No. 231. Jennifer Hawkins Opie, *Scandinavia: Ceramics and Glass in the Twentieth Century*, New York: Rizzoli, 1990.

Lindig, Otto (1895–1966)

▶ German ceramicist.

▶ 1919–25, studied Bauhaus, Weimar.

▶ He was an enthusiastic supporter of the pottery workshop at the Bauhaus, contending that it should be included in the school's curriculum. When it was separated into design and production workshops, Lindig supervised the latter, combining hand work and mass production approaches. At the Bauhaus pottery department, Dornburg, his production was typically elegant in form, and he used semi-opaque glazes that resulted in a wide variety of finishes on individually unique pieces. His work signalled a break from historicist forms towards mass production. In 1923, pursuing the Bauhaus philosophy, he went on to teach. He designed ceramics in 1930 for the Staatliche Majolikamanufaktur Karlsruhe.

▶ Cat., *The Bauhaus: Masters and Students*, New York: Barry Friedman, 1988. Cat., *Otto Lindig–der Töpfer*, Museum der Stadt Gera/Badisches Landesmuseum, Karlsruhe, 1990.

Lindinger-Loewy, Lone (1956–)

▶ Danish industrial designer; active Copenhagen; wife of Gideon Loewy.

▶ Studied design, Det Kongelige Danske Kunstakademi, Copenhagen.

▶ She and husband Gideon Loewy set up their own studio. With Bang & Olufsen as their first client, they designed the *Beolab Penta 2* tall speaker system. In 1983, they researched lighting for Louis Poulsen. They designed the 1983 *Beocom 1000* and *Beocom 2000* telephones for Bang & Olufsen and 1984 plastic jewelry for Buch & Deichmann. 1985–90, they produced numerous products for Bang & Olufsen and ceramic ware for Bing & Grøndahl Porcelænsfabrik, including the 1987–88 *Stripes and Stars* dinnerware range.

▶ Cat., Chantal Bizot, *Bang & Olufsen: Design et Technologie*, Paris: Musée des Arts Décoratifs, 1990:10.

Lindstrand, Vicki (b. Victor Emmanuel Lindstrand 1904–1983)

▶ Swedish glassware designer.

▶ 1924–27, studied Konstindustriskolan, Gothenburg.

▶ 1928–40, Lindstrand was a glassware designer at Orrefors Glasbruk; 1935–36, at Kariskrona Porslinsfabrik; 1936–50, at Upsala-Ekeby (art director from 1943–50); worked at the Kosta Boda glassworks, where he was design director 1950–73, while active in his own studio in Århus. His free-form work was often engraved.

▶ Lindstrand's 22 ft (7m) high windows were installed in the Swedish pavilion at the 1937 Paris 'Exposition Internationale des Arts et Techniques dans la Vie Moderne', and his public glass fountain was mounted at the 1939 'New York World's Fair.' His work was shown at the Triennali di Milano from 1933 (V), 1930 'Stockholm Exhibition,' 1955 'H 55' exhibition at Hälsingborg, and in 1959 in Amsterdam.

▶ Cat., David Revere McFadden (ed.), *Scandinavian Modern Design 1880–1980*, New York: Abrams, 1982:267, No. 113. Jennifer Hawkins Opie, *Scandinavia: Ceramics and Glass in the Twentieth Century*, New York: Rizzoli, 1989.

Linea B

▶ Italian domestic goods manufacturer.

▶ Linea B first began production in plastics with the 1969 *Gabbiano Stool* designed by Roberto Lera. The firm produced small furniture pieces and accessories. Its witty designs began to draw attention at the furniture exhibitions of the early 1970s.

▶ Its 1972 *Tovaglia* fiberglass table designed by Studio Tetrach was included in the 1972 'Design a Plastické Hmoty' at the Uměleckoprůmyslové Muzeum, Prague.

▶ Cat., Milena Lamarová, *Design a Plastické Hmoty*, Prague: Uměleckoprůmyslové Muzeum, 1972:64,194.

Linhart, Evžen (1898–1949)

▶ Czech architect, interior designer, and painter; born Kouřim.

▶ 1918–24, studied Czech University of Technology, Prague.

▶ He worked at the city building department in Prague after graduating. 1922–26, distinguished by their subtle use of light and detailing, his designs followed the style of the Puristická čtyřka group. He was a member of the Devětsil group from 1923 until its close in 1931. His own house, where he lived 1927–29, showed three innovative examples of his design activity: a long, shallow sideboard with asymmetrical paneling and doors on rollers in a Constructivist style; three retractable pedestal tables; and a nickel-plated standard lamp. Accompanied by fellow Devětsil member Jan Rosůlek, he traveled to Paris and saw the 1927 'Die Wohnung' exhibition in Stuttgart. He was greatly influenced by Le Corbusier, as can be seen in his own 1927–29 family house at 46 Na viničních horách St. and in the 1931–32 family house at 50 Na ostrohu St. (designed with Antonin Heythum). Whereas his friend Jaroslav Fragner emphasized Functionality, Linhart expressed aesthetic ideas in the interior of his own house at Prague-Dejvice. The deep coloring of the internal walls, the numerous built-in elements in spray-coated concrete, and the impressive ramp with white banisters attested to Le Corbusier's profound influence. The wood and metal furniture pieces were production models from Thonet and included a Linhart-designed sideboard, metal lamp, and set of simple tables.

▶ He participated in the 1923 Bauhaus exhibition in Weimar.

▶ Cat., *Devětsil: Czech Avant-Garde Art, Architecture, and Design of the 1920s and 30s*, Oxford Museum of Modern Art Oxford and London Design Museum, London, 1990. Alexander von Vegesack (ed.), *Czech Cubism: Architecture, Furniture, and Decorative Arts 1910–1925*, New York: Princeton Architectural Press and Vitra, 1992.

Linke, Norbert (1939–)
▶ German industrial designer; born Stuttgart; active Milan.
▶ Linke began his professional career in 1962. His clients included Bosch (domestic electrical appliances), Brunell (silverwares), Concord (cutlery), St. Dupont, Hofman Rheem (irons), Sama (coffeemakers), Silma (film projectors), Vallecchi FPCT (technical publications), Walter Frank, and Weco (optical equipment). In the 1970s, he designed television sets for Philco. He was a member of VDID (Verband Deutscher Industrie Designer) and of ADI (Associazione per il Disegno Industriale). He was on the jury of the 1975 'Design Center Stuttgart' competition and 1975–76 'Industrieform' competition in Hanover.
▶ *ADI Annual 1976*, Milan: Associazione per il Disegno Industriale, 1976.

linoleum
▶ Floor covering.
▶ Linoleum was invented by Frederick Walton in 1860 in Britain. Searching for an inexpensive floor covering, Walton coated flax cloth with a mixture of gum, cork dust, resin, and linseed oil. The name linoleum is an amalgamation of the Latin *linum* ('flax') and *oleum* ('oil'); 'Floor cloth,' which preceded linoleum, was made by applying an oil-based paint to canvas. Since linoleum was springier, longer lasting, easy to clean, and waxable, it became popular with the Victorians. In 1908 in Pittsburgh, Thomas Armstrong created linoleum in a wide range of colors and patterns, including a simulation of wood, flowered chintz, and Cubist art. Linoleum simulating cobblestones was Armstrong's most popular pattern. Linoleum became popular for a time as a medium for art prints, either when lithographic stones were not available because of war shortages or when a special effect was desired. It was also used in the printing of posters. Because its applied surface design wears off through continued use, linoleum has come to be replaced by vinyl, a synthetic polymer which can take impregnated designs and is more durable, offering resistance to heavy abrasion and pointed heels. With the nostalgia movement of the 1980s, vinyl began to appear in motifs that had earlier been applied on linoleum.
▶ Diane di Costanzo, *Metropolitan Home*, October 1990:64.

Linossier, Claudius (1893–1953)
▶ French metalworker.
▶ He moved to Paris from Lyons and worked as a silversmith and goldsmith before joining Jean Dunand for three months to learn *dinanderie*. Like Dunand, he specialized in geometric and abstract forms. Though Linossier produced work of quality, it was lacking in innovation, with repeated use of the same techniques and motifs.
▶ He showed his work in several stands at the 1925 Paris 'Exposition Internationale des Arts Décoratifs et Industriels Modernes' and at the Salon of the Société des Artistes français, Salon d'Automne, and the Salon of the Société des Artistes Décorateurs. He received the Légion d'honneur in 1932.
▶ Victor Arwas, *Art Déco*, Abrams, 1980.

Lipofsky, Marvin
▶ American glassware and ceramics designer and teacher.
▶ Studied glassmaking, University of Wisconsin, to 1963.
▶ Lipofsky became head of ceramics at Berkeley, California. He was interested at first in asymmetrical, misshapen forms, and later in the 1970s produced work that was sometimes comic and often kitsch.
▶ Frederick Cooke, *Glass: Twentieth-Century Design*, New York: Dutton, 1986:105.

Lippe, Jens von der (1911–)
▶ Norwegian ceramicist.
▶ Studied Statens Håndverks -og Kunstindustriskole, Oslo, Staatliche Keramische Fachschule, Schlesien (now Silesia, Poland), and Instituto Statale d'Arte per la Ceramica, Faenza.
▶ In 1933, he and his wife Margrethe set up their own pottery workshop in Oslo. 1939–75, Lippe was a teacher at the Statens Handverks -og Kunstindustriskole and, from 1956, head of its ceramics department.
▶ Cat., David Revere McFadden (ed.), *Scandinavian Modern Design 1880–1980*, New York: Abrams, 1982:267, No. 226.

Lippincott, J. Gordon (1909–)
▶ American industrial designer.
▶ Studied engineering, Swarthmore College and Columbia University, New York.
▶ He set up his own design studio in 1935; clients included Waterman, Paramount Pictures, Republic Aircraft, Fuller Brush Co, Walgreen Drug Stores, RCA, General Electric, Macy's, Mead-Johnson drugs, Northwest Airlines, and Barbizon Plaza Hotel. He styled appliances such as vacuum cleaners, office duplicating equipment, fountain pens, and packaging for cosmetics and perfume, as well as heavy industrial equipment, including airplanes. He designed gasoline stations, stores, theaters, hotel interiors, and supermarkets. He wrote *Design for Business* (1947).
▶ J. Gordon Lippincott, *Design for Business*, Chicago: Paul Theobald, 1947.

Lippmann, Herbert (1889–1978)
▶ American architect and designer; active New York.
▶ Studied architecture, Columbia University, New York.
▶ For the Lowell apartment house on East 63rd Street in New York, Lippmann and partner Henry C. Churchill commissioned metalwork from Edgar Brandt and Walter von Nessen. Lippmann designed and furnished several suburban New York houses. Inspired by the 'skyscraper' furniture of Paul Frankl, he designed in the angular French Cubist style and used veneers in a Viennese manner.
▶ Cervin Robinson and Rosemarie Haag Bletter, *Skyscraper Style: Art Deco New York*, New York and Oxford, 1975:15–16. R.W. Sexton, *The Logic of Modern Architecture*, New York: Architectural Book Publishing, 1929:73–75. Karen Davies, *At Home in Manhattan: Modern Decorative Arts, 1925 to the Depression*, New Haven: Yale, 1983:74.

Lipska, Madame
▶ Russian dressmaker and interior designer; born Russia; active Paris.
▶ Studied under Léon Bakst.
▶ In the 1920s, she established a couture shop, avenue des Champs-Élysées, Paris. She designed the apartment of the Marquis Somni Picenardi, Paris; in c1930, the renovation of the house of Barbara Harrison, Château Rambouillet; and c1933, the duplex apartment of perfumer Antoine.

Lissitzky, El (b. Lazar Markovich Lissitzky 1890–1941)
▶ Russian artist and architect; born Polshinotz, near Smolenski.
▶ 1909–14, studied architecture, Technische Hochschule, Darmstadt; 1915–16, Riga Polytechnic.
▶ On the invitation of Marc Chagall, he taught graphics and architecture at Vitebsk 1917–19. In 1919, he joined Kazimir Malevich's Unovis group, where he transformed Suprematism into his own PROUN 'Project for the Affirmation of the New'), an approach synthethizing architecture and painting. He designed the 1920 sloping steel speaker's platform for Lenin. In 1921, he taught at Vhkutemas (the official Soviet design institute) and, 1922–25, in Germany and Switzerland. He designed the cover for the *Wendingen* monograph on Frank Lloyd Wright of 1921. Traveling often in the 1920s, he associated with Dada artists, Bauhaus designers, and De Stijl members. He and Mart Stam (whom he met in 1914) designed the 1924–25 'Wolkenbügel' ('Cloud Props') project, the cantilevered office block on large piers. In Germany, he designed 1923 Proun Room at the Greater Berlin Art Exhibition, and 1926 Exhibition Room (first), International Art Exhibition, Dresden. Returning to Vhkutemas in 1925, he began teaching furniture and interior design in the metalwork and woodworking department in 1926. He was associated with Theo van Doesburg and Ludwig Mies van der Rohe, and was a co-founder of Constructivism. Thereafter he was primarily an exhibi-

tion and typographical designer. In 1930, he designed an armchair (his only realized furniture design) that showed clear Bauhaus influence, and executed three examples for the Hygiene-Ausstellung in Dresden. Lissitzky experimented constantly with interior design, graphics, book design, typography, photography, and photograms. The 1941 *Provide More Tanks* propaganda poster was his last work. He was an important link between Russian Constructivism and the Western European avant-garde.

▶ He showed his decorative paintings under the titles of *The Leader* and *Jericho* at the 1917 'V mire iskusstv' ('World of Art') exhibition in Petrograd; contributed to many exhibitions in Russia and abroad; and, in 1922, participated in the 'Erste Russische Kunstausstellung,' Berlin. His work was the subject of exhibitions in Cologne in 1976, Galerie Gmurzynska in Cologne in 1976, and the Oxford Museum of Modern Art in 1977.

▶ H. Richter, *El Lissitzky: Sieg über die Sonne–Zur Kunst des Konstruktivismus*, Cologne, 1958. S. Lissitzky-Küppers, *El Lissitzky: Life, Letters, Texts*, London, 1968. Kenneth Frampton, 'The Work and Influence of El Lissitzky,' Architect's Year Book, No. 12, 1968:253–68. El Lissitzky, *Russia: An Architecture for World Revolution*, Cambridge, MA: 1970. J. Tschichold, *Werke und Aufsätze von El Lissitzky (1890–1941)*, Berlin, 1971. Cat. *El Lissitzky*, Galerie Gmurzynska, Cologne, 1976. Cat., *Lissitzky*, Museum of Modern Art, Oxford, 1977. Stephanie Barron and Maurice Tuchman, *The Avant-Garde in Russia, 1910–1930*, Cambridge, MA: MIT Press, 1980:184,192. Cat., *Der Kragstuhl*, Stuhlmuseum Burg Beverungen, Berlin: Alexander, 1986:134. Vittorio Magnago Lampugnani (ed.), *Encyclopedia of 20th-Century Architecture*, New York: Abrams, 1986:201–02. Selim Om Khan-Magomedov, *Les Vhkutemas*, Paris: Regard, 1991.

Lito
▶ French watchmakers.
▶ Lito was founded in 1988 by Françoise Adamsbaum and Bernard Tibi to produce high quality watches designed by contemporary artists including Arman, César, Ben, Keith Haring, Bernard Venet, Robert Combas, Hervé di Rosa, François Boisrond, Rémi Blanchard, and Daniel Spoerri.
▶ François Mathey, *Au bonheur des formes, design français 1945–1992*, Paris: Regard, 1992:100.

Littell, Ross (1924–)
▶ American designer, active New York.
▶ Studied Pratt Institute of Arts, Brooklyn, New York.
▶ 1949–55, he collaborated with William Katavolos and Douglas Kelley on furniture, textile, and dinnerware designs for Laverne Originals. Commissioned by Erwine and Estelle Laverne, they executed the 1949 *New Furniture Group* of chairs and tables in leather, chrome, glass, and marble. The team's three-legged 1952 *T Chair*, with a prototype in wooden dowels, was produced in chromium-plated steel and Littell designed the 1987 *RL 2* side chair for Atelier of Italy.
▶ The *T Chair* won the 1952 AID award for the best USA furniture. Their work was shown at the 1953 and 1955 'Good Design' exhibitions at the New York Museum of Modern Art, including Littell's textile designs, and 1983–84 'Design Since 1945' exhibition of the Philadelphia Museum of Art.
▶ 'Good Design,' Interiors, Vol. 113, Aug. 1953:88–89,146–48. Roberto Aloi, *Mobili tipo*, Milan: 1956:97,121,187,216. Clement Meadmore, *The Modern Chair*, New York: 1975:98–101. Cat., Kathryn B. Hiesinger and George H. Marcus III (eds.), *Design Since 1945*, Philadelphia: Philadelphia Museum of Art, 1983.

Little, Mary (1958–)
▶ British furniture designer; born Northern Ireland.
▶ Studied Ulster Polytechnic, Northern Ireland, to 1981 and Royal College of Art, London, to 1985.
▶ Her career began with an occasional table in 1981 and an armchair in 1985 for the degree shows at the Royal College of Art. She made and painted the *Davis Table* designed by Floris van den Broecke for the book *Master Pieces* (1983). She was design

assistant to architects Faulkner Brown Hendy Watkinson Stonor, working on furniture for leisure centers. She produced furniture for shops and restaurants for interior designers Maurice Broughton Associates. A 1985 armchair was widely published; it combined elements of Catalan, Scandinavian, and late punk styles into a functional piece of furniture. As a freelance designer in Milan from 1986, she worked for Daniela Puppa, Franco Raggi, Emilio Ambasz, Nanni Strada, and Massimo Morozzi. Her diverse work included bathroom accessories, chairs, belts, dining tables, tea sets, bags for schoolchildren, lamps, and sofas. She produced lighting for Memphis in 1988 and worked for Vitra. She taught at the Glasgow School of Art, Loughborough College of Art and Design, and Wimbledon School of Art.
▶ Her work was included in the 1986 'Les Assises du siège contemporain' exhibition at the Paris Musée des Arts Décoratifs, 1983 'Experimental Furniture' at the Octagon Gallery in Belfast, 1983 'Young Blood' at the Barbican in London, 1983 'Master Pieces' at the Hille showrooms in London and at the Oxford Museum of Modern Art, 1985 exhibition at ASB Marketing in London, 1985 'La Créativité Britannique' at Au Printemps department store in Paris, 1985 'Armchairs' at Néotù in Paris, 1986 Caravelles 'Enjeu de l'objet' at the Lyons Musée des Arts Décoratifs.
▶ Cat., *Les Assises du siège contemporain*, Paris: Musée des Arts Décoratifs, 1986. Liz McQuiston, *Women in Design: A Contemporary View*, New York: Rizzoli, 1988:66. *Acquisitions 1982–1990 arts décoratifs*, Paris: Fonds National d'Art Contemporain, 1991.

Littleton, Harvey K. (1922–)
▶ American glassware designer; born Corning, New York; active USA and Britain.
▶ 1939–42 and 1946–47, studied University of Michigan, Ann Arbor, Michigan, receiving a bachelor's degree in design; 1941 and 1949–51, studied Cranbrook Academy of Art, Bloomfield Hills, Michigan, receiving a master's degree in ceramics; 1945, Brighton School of Art, Brighton, under Nora Braden.
▶ He worked in the manufacturing section of Steuben Glassworks. He and a small group developed glass as an expression of abstract art intended for use in domestic interiors. Serving in Britain during World War II, he enrolled in Nora Braden's pottery classes near Brighton. In 1945, he joined Corning Glassworks in Corning, New York. From 1946, he taught part-time at the Toledo Museum of Art in Toledo, Ohio, and subsequently at the University of Wisconsin in Madison, Wisconsin. Littleton became a well-known teacher and member of the American Crafts Council. In 1957, he studied Hispano-Moresque pottery and was commissioned by the Corning Museum to do research on Spanish glass. He went to Venice to study Murano glassmakers' techniques and set up an artists' group in the USA based on their practices. He evolved glass as a sculptural medium with little reference to the methods typically used in vessel production.
▶ Robert Judson Clark et al., *The Cranbrook Vision*, New York: Abrams and Metropolitan Museum of Art, 1983. Frederick Cooke, *Glass: Twentieth-Century Design*, New York: Dutton, 1986:103–04.

Lloyd, Marshall Burns (1858–1927) and Lloyd Loom
▶ American furniture manufacturer; born Minneapolis, Minnesota; active Menominee, Michigan.
▶ He rented a blacksmithy in 1883 in St. Thomas, South Dakota, where he formed the Lloyd Scale Company to produce a combination sack-holder and scale device. In 1894, he became president of the firm C.O. White. He invented a method for manufacturing bedsprings and mattresses, bought out White, and, in 1900, changed the firm's name to Lloyd Manufacturing Co. In 1906, he moved his plant to Menominee, Michigan, where he became mayor 1913–17. In 1914, the firm began producing reed baby-carriage bodies as part of its range of prams and handcarts. In 1917, Lloyd patented a new system for producing wicker products. He used twisted kraft paper, developed as a substitute for wicker when supplies of rattan and cane were interrupted by World War I. The phrase 'woven fiber' was coined to replace

the humble term 'twisted paper.' Claiming that the material was impervious to damp and dirt, hygienic, and warp resistant, Lloyd produced over 100 furniture models; by 1940, over 10 million pieces had been sold. A sign in Lloyd's office, whose walls were covered in Lloyd Loom woven fiber, read 'I never do what anyone else can do.' In 1921, Lloyd Loom became part of the firm Heywood-Wakefield. After 1920, French rights were sold to René Duval and Pierre Mouronval, both in the wicker business. They furnished some Lloyd-type furniture to the 1926 oceanliners Île-de-France and Champlaine. In 1922, a German factory was set up, organized by Lloyd with German workers trained in Menominee, in Fulda. In the 1920s and 30s, Lloyd Loom furniture was also a household name in Britain. Lloyd initiated an ambitious program for improving the line; in 1924, he retired from the Menominee factory, remaining a director of Heywood-Wakefield and maintaining an independent experimental workshop near Menominee with a dozen assistants.
▶ Lee J. Curtis, *Lloyd Loom Woven Fiber Furniture*, New York: Rizzoli, 1991.

Lluscà, Josep (1948–)
▶ Spanish designer; born Barcelona.
▶ From 1968, studied design, Escuela de Diseño Eina, Barcelona, and École des Arts et Métiers, Montreal.
▶ In the 1970s, he pursued a wide range of design disciplines, later specializing in furniture and lighting. His clients included Norma Europa. Associating himself with sculptors, his work incorporated elements from Antonio Gaudí and 1950s Rationalism. He worked on the development of a mechanism for an office chair, resulting in the 1989 *Lola* range of chair by Oken. 1985–87, he was vice-president of the Adi-Fad, the industrial designers' association of Spain, and a member of the Design Council of the Catalonian government. He taught at the Escuela Eina. His 1986 *Andrea* chair (based on a 1944 three-legged chair by Charles Eames) was produced by Andreu World. His 1989 *Ketupa* lamp (with silversmith Joaquín Berao) and 1986 *Anade 4169* lamp were produced by Metalarte, and his 1988 *BCN* armchair by Enea.
▶ Albrecht Bangert and Karl Michael Armer, *80s Style: Designs of the Decade*, New York: Abbeville, 1990:108,232. Guy Julier, *New Spanish Design*, London: Thames and Hudson, 1991.

Lobmeyr
▶ Austrian glassware manufacturer.
▶ Joseph Lobmeyr (1792–1855) founded a glassworks in 1823 under his own name. From 1855, he produced about 100 different drinking glasses in clear, cut, engraved, and enamel-painted crystal, and subsequently lighting fixtures and mirrors in bronze and crystal, as well as the first electrified chandeliers in 1883. His sons Josef (1828–64) and Ludwig (1829–1917) succeeded him in managing the firm; Ludwig Lobmeyr appears to have designed as well as being principal director of the firm. He commissioned designs from Viennese artists including architect Theophil von Hansen, and was associated with the Österreichisches Museum für angewandte Kunst (founded in 1864). Known for its craftsmanship and design, the firm supplied the Austrian court and aristocracy with services, and began producing mousselin glass designed by Ludwig Lobmeyr in 1856. At this time, Lobmeyr's products were in historicist designs, although its drinking glasses were sometimes simple and austere. Ludwig Lobmeyr's nephew Joseph Rath (1876–1960) took over management of the firm in 1902 when production consisted of Art Nouveau and later Art Moderne styles. The designs of Vienna Sezession artists and co-director Josef Hoffmann were commissioned by Rath; some of Hoffmann's are still in production, including models *TS238* and *TS240* in glass chiffon (black lacquer on mouth-blown glass with two different etched motifs). Adolf Loos's unadorned *Service No. 248* drinking glasses (with Oskar Strnad) of 1931 were made by Lobmeyr.
▶ Stephan Rath, *Lobmeyr*, Vienna, 1963. Cat., *150 Jahre Österreichische Glaskunst: Lobmeyr 1923–1973*, Vienna, 1973. W. Neuwirth, *Orientalisierende Gläser von J. und L. Lobmeyr*, Vienna, 1981.

Locatelli, Antonio
See Studio Pro

Locher, Robert Evans (1888–1956)
▶ American silversmith.
▶ Locher designed simple Modern forms for Rogers, Lunt and Bowlen, Silversmiths, of Greenfield, Massachusetts, and lighting in the 1940s.
▶ 'Wide Range of Objects Sought,' American Silver Museum newsletter, 1989.

Lock, Josef Michael (1875–1964)
▶ German sculptor and designer.
▶ Lock's silver designs were produced by Bruckmann and Söhne in Heilbronn, where he was artistic director. He was a teacher at the Bruckmann School.
▶ Annelies Krekel-Aalberse, *Art Nouveau and Art Déco Silver*, New York: Abrams, 1989:137–38,175,257. Reinhard W. Sänger, *Das deutsche Silber-Besteck*, Stuttgart: Arnoldsche: 1991:156–57.

Loetz-Witwe
▶ Bohemian glassware factory; located Klostermühle.
▶ Johann Loetz founded a glassmaking facility in 1840 in Klostermühle, Bohemia. In 1844, his widow took over management of the firm, passing it in 1879 to grandson Max Ritter von Spaun. Under Ritter's management, Loetz produced *glaser à la Tiffany* (a kind of carnival glass), expanded and modernized the facilities and gained international recognition by winning world's fair prizes. It began to produce early imitations of semi-precious stones, including jasper, aventurine, and chalcedony. It produced Art Nouveau tableware based on the Tiffany iridescent-glass technique at the turn of the century, including vases, rosewater sprinklers, lamps, and candlesticks in a vivid range of colors. It made the glass shades for Gustav Gurschner's bronze-sculpture lamps.
▶ Loetz won grand prizes at the 1889 and 1900 Paris 'Expositions Universelles.' It first showed its *verres papillons* at the 1899 Paris 'Exposition Universelle.'
▶ Cat., Dr. G. Woeckel, *Jugendstilsammlung*, Kassel: Staatliche Kunstsammlungen, 1968. Cat., *Loetz Austria*, Munich: Stuck-Villa, 1972. R. and L. Grover, *Carved and Decorated European Art Glass*, Rutland, Vermont: Tuttle, n.d.:17. H. Hilschenz, *Das Glas des Jugendstils*, Munich, 1973:390–91. *L'Art Verrier à l'aube du XXe siècle*, Lausanne: Galerie des Arts Décoratifs, 1973:73–79. *Objekte des Jugendstils*, Bern: Benteli, 1975. Alastair Duncan, *Art Nouveau and Art Déco Lighting*, New York: Simon and Schuster, 1978:123–24. Frederick Cooke, *Glass: Twentieth-Century Design*, New York: Dutton, 1986. Waltrand Neuwirth, *Loetz Austria 1905–1918*, Vienna: 1986.

Loewy, Gideon (1952–)
▶ British industrial designer; active Copenhagen; husband of Lone Lindinger-Loewy.
▶ Studied design, Det Kongelige Danske Kunstakademi, Copenhagen.
▶ See Lindinger–Loewy, Lone

Loewy, Raymond Fernand (1893–1986)
▶ French designer; born Paris; active Paris and New York.
▶ Studied electrical engineering in Paris.
▶ In 1909, he designed, built, and sold a successful airplane model. Settling in New York in 1919, he was employed for a short time as a window dresser at Macy's department store. He became a fashion illustrator c1923–28; one of his main clients was *Harper's Bazaar*. In 1923, he designed a trademark for Neiman Marcus. He designed advertisements for Kayer hosiery and a fashion brochure of 1928 for the Bonwit Teller store. In 1929, he redesigned the housing for the duplicating machinery of Sigmund Gestetner, using modeling clay to give a sleek shape, a technique later employed in the design of automobile bodies. Loewy's interest in car design was shown in the 1934 Hupmobile, the 1947 Studebaker *Champion*, 1953 European-styled *Starline* coupe, and the 1962 Studebaker *Avanti*. His design in 1934 of the Sears

Coldspot refrigerator housing was his first major achievement. Loewy designed the first mass-produced American 35mm camera in 1936, the Argus A for International Research in Michigan. With Carl Otto, he designed for British manufacturers 1936–52 from a London office. In 1951, he established CEI (Compagnie de l'Esthétique Industrielle), Paris. His work included packaging, Coca-Cola dispensers, locomotive engines and passenger-car interiors, Greyhound coaches, and, 1967–72, interiors for NASA's Skylab. He and his staff designed Le Creuset cookware in the late 1950s and Elna appliances in the late 1960s. In 1986, they produced the dinner service and flatware for the *Concorde* airliner. Loewy designed the interior of President Kennedy's Boeing 707 'Air Force One' airplane. Other work included postage stamps, trademarks, radios, electric shavers, china, textiles, and furniture, including popular china for Rosenthal. His dinner sets for Rosenthal included the 1967 *Aries* and, with Richard Latham, the 1954 *Form 2000*. In 1937, Loewy's staff included 38 architects, technicians, and engineers; in 1939, 100; in 1951, over 140. He designed wallpaper patterns for the 1960 *Centenary Collection* produced by Sanderson. His books included *The Locomotive: Its Esthetics* (1937), *Industrial Design* (1978), and *Never Leave Well Enough Alone* (1951).

▶ His work was the subject of the 1976 'The Designs of Raymond Loewy' exhibition at the Renwick Gallery in Washington, and 1990–91 one-person traveling exhibition 'Raymond Loewy: Pioneer of American Industrial Design' organized by the Design Zentrum in Berlin. In 1939, elected Honorary Royal Designer for Industry, London.

▶ Raymond Loewy, *The Locomotive: Its Esthetics*, London: Studio, 1937. C.F.O. Clarke, 'Raymond Loewy Associates: Modern American Industrial Designing,' *Graphis*, Vol. 2, Jan.–Feb. 1946:94–97. Raymond Loewy, *Never Leave Well Enough Alone*, New York: Simon and Schuster, 1951. David Pleydell-Bouverie and Zlec Davis, 'Popular Art Organised: The Manner and Methods of Raymond Loewy Associates,' *Architectural Review*, Vol. 110, Nov. 1951:319–26. *Current Biography*, 1953. Cat., *The Designs of Raymond Loewy*, Washington, DC: Renwick Gallery, 1976. *Raymond Loewy, Industrial Design*, New York: Overlook, 1979. Ralph Caplan, *By Design*, New York: St. Martin's Press, 1982:41. Cat., Kathryn B. Hiesinger and George H. Marcus III (eds.), *Design Since 1945*, Philadelphia: Philadelphia Museum of Art, 1983:220,I–20–21,II–31. Cat., Angela Schönberger et al., *Raymond Loewy: Pioneer of American Industrial Design*, Munich: Prestel, 1990. Durwood Potter, 'Raymond Fernand Loewy' in Mel Byars and Russell Flinchum (eds.), *50 American Designers, 1918–1968*, Washington: Preservation, 1994.

Löffelhardt, Heinrich (1901–79)
▶ German ceramics and glassware designer.

▶ 1920–23, trained at silversmiths P. Bruckmann, Heilbronn; 1924–28, studied sculpture under Georg Kolbe in Berlin.

▶ 1929–36, he was a sculptor. 1937–41, he worked at the Vereinigte Lausitzer Glaswerke in Weisswasser under its artistic director Wilhelm Wagenfeld. After the war, Wagenfeld arranged for Löffelhardt's appointment as director of design at Landesgewerbeamt (District Trade and Craft Offices) in Stuttgart. Succeeding Hermann Gretsch, 1952–71, he was artistic director of the Arzberg and Schönwald porcelain factories, his work following closely Gretsch's prewar models, including the 1954 *Arzberg 2000*, 1953 *Schönwald 411*, 1957 *Arzberg 2025*, 1958 *Schönwald 511*, 1961 *Schönwald 498*, and 1963 *Arzberg 2075* dinnerwares. Succeeding Wilhelm Wagenfeld, 1954–77, he was design director of the Jenaer Glaswerk Schott und Genossen in Mainz and its affiliate in Zwiesel. At Lausitzer, he was responsible for a number of suites of glasses for domestic and utility use that were considered innovative in the 1950s and 1960s. He continued as a consultant designer with Schott und Genossen, working for its utility glass and lighting divisions. He produced designs for the 1957 range of heat-resistant borosilicate glass, including a tea set, cups and saucers, plates, and bowls. While mass production caused Löffelhardt's early glassware to be discontinued, his *Neckar* white wine glass for Vereinigte Farbenglaswerke sold 240 million copies by 1978.

▶ His 1959 *Arzberg 2050* dinnerware won a grand prize at the 1960 (XII) Triennale di Milano and prizes at the 1961 and 1962 Salone Internazionale della Ceramica in Vicenza. His 1959 redesign of Wagenfeld's heat-resistant dishes won a grand prize at the 1960 (XII) Triennale di Milano. His work was the subject the 1980 'In Memoriam Heinrich Löffelhardt, 1901–1979: Design für die Glas- und Porzellanindustrie' exhibition at the Badisches Landesmuseum in Karlsruhe. The dishes and *Arzberg 2050* dinner service were included in the 1983–84 'Design Since 1945' exhibition at the Philadelphia Museum of Art.

▶ Frederick Cooke, *Glass: Twentieth-Century Design*, New York: Dutton, 1986:92. Cat., Kathryn B. Hiesinger and George H. Marcus III (eds.), *Design Since 1945*, Philadelphia: Philadelphia Museum of Art, 1983:220,II–34–35. Cat., *In Memoriam Heinrich Löffelhardt, 1901–1979: Design für die Glas- und Porzellanindustrie*, Karlsruhe: Badisches Landesmuseum, 1980.

Löffler, Berthold (1874–1960)
▶ Austrian painter, designer, ceramicist, illustrator and graphic artist; born Nieder-Rosenthal (now Liberec, Czech Republic).

▶ Löffler taught at the Kunstgewerbeschule in Vienna. In 1903 or 1905, he and Michael Powolny founded Wiener Keramik, a high point in the decorative phase of late Art Nouveau. The factory worked for the Wiener Werkstätte, producing ceramics showing folklore influences, including some from Russia. Löffler was also known for his distinctive poster designs in the 1910s.

▶ Günther Feuerstein, *Vienna—Present and Past: Arts and Crafts—Applied Art—Design*, Vienna: Jugend und Volk, 1976:28,42,80. Cat., *Berthold Löffler*, Hochschule für angewandte Kunst, Vienna, 1978. Robert Waissenberger, *Vienna 1890–1920*, Secaucus, NJ: Wellfleet 1984:136,268.

Lohmann, Jan (1944–)
▶ Danish metalworker.

▶ 1966–68, studied in a workshop in Switzerland.

▶ In 1968, he set up his own workshop in Copenhagen. In 1976, he studied on tours to Peru, Mexico, Guatemala, Ecuador, and New York.

▶ He received the 1966 silver medal from Goldsmiths' Guild and 1972, 1976, and 1978 Goldsmiths' Guild Scandinavian Design Award. His work was included in the 1974 exhibition at Det Danske Kunstindustrimuseum in Copenhagen, 1975–77 Eastern Europe 'Danske Miljø,' and 1978 and 1980 exhibitions at the Gallery for Contemporary Silver and Goldsmith's Art in Copenhagen.

▶ Cat., David Revere McFadden (ed.), *Scandinavian Modern Design 1880–1980*, New York: Abrams, 1982:267, No. 318.

Lôlô (b. Laurent Bernard 1964)
▶ French designer.

▶ Studied advertising and marketing.

▶ He was assistant to industrial designer Gilles Derain, Paris; worked at Pierre Balmain; in 1992, set up his own design office, Lôlô, working on interior architecture and furniture; designed rugs and tableware by Axis and various objects by Ardi.

▶ His 1991 *Paris* lamp with polypropylene interchangeable shades in ten colors was produced by Absolu and shown at 1992 International du Luminaire.

Lomazzi, Paolo (1936–)
▶ Italian designer; born and active Milan.

▶ In 1961, Lomazzi, Gionatan De Pas, and Donato D'Urbino set up a design studio, working on architecture, design, and townplanning projects. They were best known for their innovative 1967 *Blow* clear plastic inflatable chair, and 1970 *Joe* seat in the form of a baseball glove, reminiscent of the soft sculptures of Claes Oldenburg. From the 1970s, they designed interchangeable and flexible units for modular seating, storage systems, and plastic and plywood furniture for BBB Bonacina, Driade, Levesta, and Palina. The *Dado e Vite* (Cube and Screw) range of knock-down plywood furniture and 1972 *Flap* modular range of quilted seating were produced for BBB Bonacina, Driade, and Palina. More mainstream furniture and furnishing designs were produced for Zanotta, Poltronova, Forges, Gabbianelli, Marcatré, Hamano, Ligne Roset, Stilnovo, and Sirrah. Lomazzi was a member of ADI (Associazione per il Disegno Industriale). They made the TV film *Dal cucchiaio alla città; il design italiano dal 1950 al 1980* on recent Italian design.

▶ See De Pas, Gionatan

Lomonosov Porcelain Factory

▶ Russian ceramics factory; located St. Petersburg.

▶ The Imperial Porcelain Factory, located on what is now the Obukhovskoy Oborony Prospekt in St. Petersburg, was established in the first half of the 18th century. Its early production was exclusively for the Imperial court, and the factory supplied dinner services, vases, figurines, presentation services, and furnishings for palaces and yachts. It also produced wares for the army and its hospitals. It was renamed the State Porcelain Factory 1917 and, in 1925, was Lomonosov Porcelain Factory after the scientist Mikhail Vasil'evich Lomonosov. After the Bolshevik Revolution, the factory's operation was briefly under the Commissariat of Agriculture and, in 1918, under the Narkompros institution. At this time, Sergei Chekhonin, a consultant to the Commissariat of Agriculture, organized a group to oversee the artistic industries in the country. Izo (Department of Fine Arts) of Narkompros (The People's Commissariat for Enlightenment) was involved in the factory's production, as Izo's head, David Shterenberg, along with energetic reformers Petr Vaulin and Chekhonin, were directors of the factory. There were 12 workers in the painting section and 100 factory workers. The artists in 1918 included Mikhail Adamovich, Vasilii Timorev, Varvara Freze, Yelizaveta Rozendorf, Elena Danko, Mariia Ivashintsova, Elizaveta Potapova, and Alexandra Shehekotikhina-Pototskaia. In 1919, Ekatrina Bolsheva, Liubov' Gaush, Alisa Golenkina, Mariia Kirilova, Mariia Lebedeva, Varvara Rukavishnikova, and others joined the staff. Zinaida Kobyletskaia rejoined in 1918, after working there 1912–14. Established artists created designs for the State Porcelain Factory, including Natan Al'tman, Veniamin Belkin, Mstislav Dobujinskii, Vladimir Lebedev, Vasilii Kandinskii, and Valentin Sherbakov. The factory produced agitprop designs using porcelain blanks of the pre-Revolutionary period onto which they affixed images and slogans in vivid colors.

▶ Nina Lobanov-Rostovsky, *Revolutionary Ceramics*, London: Studio Vista, 1990. Igor Golomstock, *Totalitarian Art in the Soviet Union, The Third Reich, Fascist Italy and the People's Republic of China*, New York: Icon, 1990:14. Cat., Ian Wardropper, *News from a Radiant Future: Soviet Porcelain from the Collection of Craig H. and Kay A. Tuber*, Art Institute of Chicago, 1992. Cat., Deborah Sampson Shinn, *Soviet Porcelains (1918–1985)*, New York: Cooper–Hewitt National Museum of Design, 1992.

Loos, Adolf (1870–1933)

▶ Moravian architect and designer; born Brünn (now Brno, Czech Republic); active Austria.

▶ Studied Reichenberg Polytechnik and Technische Hochschule, Dresden.

▶ 1893–96, he traveled in America and worked as a mason and floor layer; he saw the work of the Chicago School, including William Le Baron Jenny, Burnham and Root, and Louis Sullivan. He settled in Vienna in 1896 and began to write and work as a designer and architect, turning away from the Vienna Sezession style and abandoning all decoration and ornamentation. His first series of articles condemning the aesthetics of painter Gustav Klimt and the styles of Joseph Maria Olbrich and Josef Hoffmann appeared in the journal *Neue Freie Presse* (1897–98); he codified his thesis in the seminal essay 'Ornament und Verbrechen' (Ornament and Crime) (1908). Loos worked for a time with architect Otto Wagner and admired the Scottish architects Charles Rennie Mackintosh and Hugh Baillie Scott; his own architecture drew on neoclassicism and the work of Karl Friedrich Schinkel.

His 1910 Steiner House was one of the first domestic dwellings to be built in reinforced concrete and included many innovations, including a new use of internal space, pure straight lines, horizontal windows, and solids formed in a Cubist shape. 1920–22, he was in charge of municipal housing in Vienna and entered his visionary Doric-column project in the 1922 *Chicago Tribune* competition. 1923–28, he lived in Paris, where he designed the 1926–27 house and interior of Dadaist Tristan Tzara with African masks, tube lighting over the doors, and 17th-century chairs. His other buildings included the 1906 Villa Karma (renovation) in Clarens, near Montreux, 1907 Kärntner Bar in Vienna, 1910 commercial block on the Michaelerplatz in Vienna, 1922 Rufer House in Vienna, 1928 Möller house in Pötzleinsdorf, 1930 Kuhner House in Payerback, and 1930 Müller house in Prague. Apart from his architecture, he designed little; his starkly simple and almost imperceptibly tapered 1931 water pitcher and glasses (known as *Service No. 248*), originally for the Loos Bar in Vienna, are still manufactured by Lobmeyr in Austria. For his own use, he chose 18th-century furniture, although his peculiar chaise longue for the Knize haberdashery shop of the mid-1920s in Paris was an odd amalgamation of Modern and Art Nouveau. His 1930 Müller house in Prague influenced architects including André Lurçat, Richard Neutra, Rudolph Schindler, and Erich Mendelsohn.

▶ Adolf Loos, 'Ornament und Verbrechen,' Vienna, 1908. A. Marilaun, *Adolf Loos*, Vienna, 1922. Bruno Taut, J.J.P. Oud et al., *Adolf Loos, zum 60. Geburtstag, am 10. Dezember 1930*, Vienna, 1930. H. Kulka, *Adolf Loos, das Werk des Architekten*, Vienna, 1931. L. Münz and G. Künstler, *Adolf Loos: Pioneer of Modern Architecture*, London, 1966. L. Münz and G. Künstler, *Adolf Loos: Pioneer of Modern Architecture*, London and New York, 1966. Günther Feuerstein, *Vienna—Present and Past: Arts and Crafts—Applied Art—Design*, Vienna: Jugend und Volk, 1976:28, 35,40,49,53,80. Berkhard Rukschcio and Roland Schachel, *Adolf Loos—Leben und Werk*, Salzburg/Vienna: Residenz, 1982. Adolf Loos, *Spoken into the Void: Collected Essays*, Cambridge, Massachusetts, 1982. Robert L. Delevoy in Vittorio Magnago Lampugnani (ed.), *Encyclopedia of 20th-Century Architecture*, New York: Abrams, 1986:202–03. Stephen Calloway, *Twentieth-Century Decoration*, New York: Rizzoli, 1988:157.

Looze, Hervé de
See de Looze, Hervé

Lorenz, Anton (1891–1964)

▶ Hungarian furniture designer and manufacturer; active Berlin.

▶ In 1928, Anton Lorenz joined the firm Standardmöbel Lengyel shortly after its formation in Berlin by Marcel Breuer and Kálmán Lengyel. The venture was not successful, and Breuer sold his rights to Standardmöbel, although his designs of 1927–28 were not transferred to the firm. In 1928, Lorenz began to render studies of his own of upholstered steel armchairs, including his patent no. 348590, often mistakenly attributed to Breuer. Breuer's famous *B33* and *B34* chair with and without arms was produced by both Standardmöbel and Thonet, with which Breuer had entered into an agreement in 1928, in slightly different versions. In 1929, Thonet bought Standardmöbel. The 1929 suit between Lorenz and Thonet was based on Thonet's assertion that rights to Breuer's cantilever chair were to be transferred in the Standardmöbel sale. Lorenz's newly formed firm Deutsche Stahlmöbel (DESTA) was included in the dispute. Lorenz won the suit in 1930 and secured an injunction in 1932 to stop Thonet producing the cantilever chairs *L33* and *L34*; Thonet thereafter produced the chairs under a licence agreement with Lorenz. Lorenz discontinued his own production and concentrated on selling his rights to the chairs abroad, while Thonet was in charge of their production. In 1931, Lorenz lodged a complaint with the firm C. Beck und A. Schultze (CEBASCO) in Ohrdruf concerning chairs designed by Erich Dieckmann. CEBASCO signed a license agreement with Lorenz that lasted until 1934. Lorenz also claimed that the production of a chair designed by Heinz Rasch and produced by L. und C. Arnold infringed Lorenz's patent of 1929; since the chair was

proved to have been produced since 1928, the claim was dropped. In a 1933 court case between Fritz Hansen and the Lorenz-Thonet team, the latter's copyright was upheld. In 1934, Gispen won in a case brought against it by Thonet in Rotterdam; Lorenz-Thonet also lost a 1934 case against A.W. Nilsons Fabriker in Malmö. Because of the volume of production in foreign countries, it was not possible for Lorenz to keep his hold on the cantilever principle. Though DESTA was closed in 1933, Lorenz used the firm's name until 1935. In the late 1930s, he settled in the USA and, after World War II, introduced his highly popular *Barca Lounger*.
▶ Lorenz's 1928 model upholstered steel armchairs were shown at the 1931 'Berlin Bauhausstellung.'
▶ Barbie Campbell-Cole and Tim Benton, *Tubular Steel Furniture*, London: The Art Book Company, 1979:13,20. Otakar Máčel, 'Avant-Garde Design and the Law: Litigation over the Cantilever Chair,' *Journal of Design History*, Vol. 3, Nos. 2 and 3, 1990:125–32.

Lorenzi, Momi   (1940–)
▶ Italian designer; born Vicenza; active Milan.
▶ Lorenzi became a professional designer in 1970; designed metal tableware for Lagostina; was a member of ADI (Associazione per il Disegno Industriale).
▶ *ADI Annual 1976*, Milan: Associazione per il Disegno Industriale, 1976.

Lortic, Marcellin   (1852–1928)
▶ French bookbinder and gilder; active Paris.
▶ For a short time, he worked with his brother Paul before setting up his own workshop in 1884 on the premises of the family bindery in the rue de la Monnaie. His elaborate covers were traditional. In the 1890s, his designs became of the Art Nouveau mode, illustrated by his covers for *Tartarin de Tarascon*, *Zadig*, and *Le Roman de Tristan et Iseult*. For Henri Vever's library, he produced several covers decorated by Adolphe Giraldon. His clients included Hirsch, Meynial, Delacœur, and Saint-Chamant.
▶ Alastair Duncan and Georges de Bartha, *Art Nouveau and Art Déco Bookbinding*, New York: Abrams, 1989:13,193. Ernest de Crauzat, *La Reliure française de 1900 à 1925*, Vol. 1, Paris, 1932:58–59. Roger Devauchelle, *La Reliure en France de ses origines à nos jours*, Vol. 3, Paris, 1961:16,21,25,28,56–61,64, 127,141,269.

LOV
▶ Dutch furniture manufacturer; located Oosterbeek.
▶ Oosterbeeksche Meubelfabriek 'Labor Omnia Vincit' ('Work Conquers All') (LOV) was established in 1910 by G. Pelt, who wished to bring about social and political reform and based LOV's organization on 'co-partnership,' whereby the employees participated in the company management and worked in the factory under safe and hygienic conditions. An enthusiastic proponent of the machine, Pelt was not sympathetic with Morris's views on restoring and ennobling the art of craftsmanship. H.F. Mertens, who worked as factory manager from 1911, designed disassemblable bent tubular steel furniture for Loeb's UMS furniture factory. LOV products were largely handmade and thus quite expensive, with extensive use of mahogany and walnut. The firm used numerous consultant designers, including J. Crouwel, J.B. van Loghem, A.H. Jansen, and C. Alons. Though never avant-garde, LOV's furniture reflected current trends. The factory executed large orders for the Rotterdam City Hall and the Troelstra resort in Beekbergen. The 1925–30 model rooms in the factory were completely fitted with glass, ceramics, carpets, and curtains; goods from Leerdam (glassware), Weverij De Ploeg (ceramics), Potterij De Rijn (pottery), and KVT (rugs) could be purchased at LOV. The plant closed in 1935 and Pelt's original goal to make inexpensively constructed and reliable workers' furniture was never realized.
▶ *Industry and Design in the Netherlands, 1850/1950*, Amsterdam: Stedelijk Museum, 1985.

Lovegrove, Ross
▶ British designer.
▶ Studied Royal College of Art, London, to 1982.
▶ Lovegrove worked for Knoll, Paris, and frogdesign, Altensteig (Germany); he designed the 1991 one-piece fiberglass side chair on a tubular frame, known as the *FO8 Stacking* chair, produced by XO in France.
▶ His *FO8 Stacking* chair was shown at the 1991 Salone del Mobile in Milan.
▶ *Issue 5*, London: Design Museum, 1990.

Low Art Tile Works, J. and J.G.
▶ American ceramic tile manufacturer; located Chelsea, Massachusetts.
▶ John Gardner Low (1835–1907) worked at the Chelsea Keramic Art Works in the early 1870s and painted vases in a classical Greek style. Inspired by the 1876 Philadelphia Exposition, he and father John Low in 1877 founded the firm J. and J.G. Low. After 1883, it was named J.G. and J.F. Low, when John Farnsworth Low (1862–1939), son of John Gardner Low, replaced John Low. The firm was the first to combine art with mass production in its decorative tiles. In 1883, it began to produce vessels. In 1879, Low patented the 'natural process,' employed in England since 1840, of pressing leaves, fabrics, and flowers into clay tiles; he subsequently found that the same pattern could be pressed into a second clay tile, producing an intaglio version. During the 1880s, the firm's artists included British sculptor Arthur Osborne. In 1878, Low hired George W. Robertson, who had worked at the Chelsea Keramic Art Works. Low's wares were sold through more than 30 distributors throughout the USA. Its tiles were used for fireplace surrounds, wall decorations, and various ornamental uses, including clocks. Magee Art Castings of Chelsea, Massachusetts, produced its brass and metalwork, including umbrella stands and picture frames. Its tiles were used on the cast-iron stove under the name Art Westminster produced by Rathbone, Sard and Co of Albany, New York. Low produced elaborate ceramic soda fountains for drugstores. The firm stopped production in 1902.
▶ The firm won a silver medal at the 1879 Cincinnati 'Industrial Exposition' and a gold medal at an 1880 British competition. Its wares were shown at the 1882 exhibition of the Fine Art Society in London. A 1903 exhibition of the firm's works was mounted at the Worcester Art Museum in Worcester, Massachusetts.
▶ Everett Townsend, 'Development of the Tile Industry in the United States,' *Bulletin of the American Ceramic Society*, Vol. 22, May 15, 1943:129. Lura Woodside Watkins, 'Low's Art Tiles,' *Antiques*, Vol. 45, May 1944:250–52. Julian Barnard, *Victorian Ceramic Tiles*, Greenwich, Conn., 1972:36,86–88,109,166, figs. 31,70–71,77,79,81,95,97. Barbara White Morse, 'The Low Family of Chelsea, Massachusetts, and Their Pottery,' *Spinning Wheel*, Vol. 33, Sept. 1977:28–33. Doreen Bolger Burke et al., *In Pursuit of Beauty: Americans and the Aesthetic Movement*, New York: Metropolitan Museum of Art and Rizzoli, 1986:449–50.

Löw-Lazar, Fritzi   (b. Friederike Löw   1891–1975)
▶ Austrian book illustrator and graphic and fashion designer; born Vienna.
▶ 1907–10, studied Art School for Women and Girls, Vienna, under A. Böhm; 1910–18, Kunstgewerbeschule under Josef Hoffmann, Oskar Strnad, and Michael Powolny.
▶ She was a member of the Wiener Frauenkunst (Vienna Women's Art Group) and the Neue Werkbund Österreichs. She contributed to the 1914–15 fashion folder *Die Mode* and designed fashion accessories, textiles, jewelry, tulle embroidery, and lace.
▶ Deanna F. Cera, *Jewels of Fantasy: Costume Jewelry of the 20th Century*, New York: Abrams, 1991:106.

Loy, Mina   (1882–1966)
▶ American designer, actress, and model; active Paris and New York.

► Loy worked in shops financially supported by Peggy Guggenheim in the 1930s in Paris and New York. She produced hundreds of lamps and lampshades. A stage actress and model for Man Ray, she was the only woman member of the Futurist group.

Lubetkin, Berthold (1901–)

► Russian architect; born Tbilisi (now Georgia; active Paris and London.

► Studied architecture in Moscow and École des Beaux-Arts and Atelier Perret, Paris.

► He supervised the construction of the Soviet pavilion by Konstantin Mel'inkov at the 1925 Paris 'Exposition Internationale des Arts Décoratifs et Industriels Modernes.' 1927–30, he collaborated with Jean Ginsburg in Paris. In 1930, he settled in London. In 1932, Lubetkin, Anthony Chitty, Lindsey Drake, Michael Dugdale, Valentine Harding, Godfrey Samuel, and R.T.F. Skinner formed the Tecton architectural partnership. In 1934, Harding and Samuel departed, forming a partnership together; subsequently, Chitty and Dugdale left. After Tecton was dissolved, the partnership of Skinner, Bailey and Lubetkin was formed. At Tecton, Lubetkin was best known for his 1933–34 penguin pool at the Regent's Park Zoo, London, a celebrated example of 1930s Functionalist architecture in England. Tecton's other work included, at Regent's Park, the 1932 Gorilla House, 1935–37 Studio of Animal Art, and 1936–37 New Elephant House; at Whipsnade Zoo, the 1934–36 Giraffe House and Shelter and 1934–37 New Elephant House and Shelter; Dudley Zoo; 1938– 39 Finsbury Health Centre, London; 1933–35 Highpoint I and 1936–38 Highpoint II in Highgate, London; houses at Bognor Regis, Dulwich, Farnham, Gidea Park, and Haywards Heath; 1934–36 bungalows at Whipsnade; various projects including first-prize-winning design for the 1935 'Competition for working-class flats in reinforced concrete.' Lubetkin also worked on the planning of Peterlee New Town. He received the 1982 RIBA gold medal.

► Images of his work were included in the 1979–80 'Thirties' exhibition at the Hayward Gallery, London.

► R.F. Jordan, 'Lubetkin,' *Architectural Review*, July 1955:36–44. Cat., *Thirties: British art and design before the War*, London: Arts Council of Great Britain, Hayward Gallery, 1979:47–49,56, 59,189,190,241,269,295. Peter Coe and Malcolm Reading, *Lubetkin and Tecton: Architecture and Social Commitment*, London and Bristol, 1981. Vittorio Magnago Lampugnani (ed.), *Encyclopedia of 20th-Century Architecture*, New York: Abrams, 1986:203–04.

Lucchini, Alberto Valento (1947–)

► Italian designer; born Cuneo; active Milan.

► Lucchini began his professional career in 1972. His clients in Italy included Sormani (furniture, accessories, and lighting) from 1972, Brevetto (heavy industry) from 1972, the magazine *Nuovi Orizzonti* of the Italian tourist board (graphic design) from 1973, Mopoa (clocks) from 1974, Velca Legnano (furniture) from 1975, and Gabbianelli (tableware) from 1975. He designed furniture for the 1972 'Interieur 72' competition. He was a member of ADI (Associazione per il Disegno Industriale).

► He won honorable mention in the 1973 'International Pottery Design Competition.'

► *ADI Annual 1976*, Milan: Associazione per il Disegno Industriale, 1976.

Lucci, Roberto (1942–)

► Italian designer; born Milan.

► Studied Institute of Design, Chicago, and Corso Superiore di Design, Venice.

► He worked with Marco Zanuso for several years. In 1970, he and Paolo Orlandini collaborated independently for a number of clients, designing lamps and chairs produced by Artemide and Martinelli Luce; products by Antonelli and ArcLinea; television sets by Brionvega; refrigerators by Candy-Kelvinator; furniture by Magis; and office furniture by Velca. Other clients included Knoll and Tisettanta. Lucci and Orlandini collaborated with Marco

Zanuso and Richard Sapper for some years. From 1974, Lucci taught at the Instituto Europeo di Design, Milan and at universities in Australia and the USA.

► Robert A.M. Stern (ed.), *The International Design Yearbook*, New York: Abbeville, 1985/1986: Nos. 7–9. *Modo*, No. 148, March–April 1993:121.

Luce, Jean (1895–1964)

► French ceramicist and glassware designer; born Paris.

► Luce worked in his father's ceramics shop, which made table crockery. In 1923, he opened his own shop although he was not able to take over its direction until 1931. From 1931 onwards, specializing in ceramics and glass for the table, Luce concentrated on the double problem of shape and decoration. Painted by hand or from stencils, his motifs were linear and naturalistically styled in the Art Moderne manner, highlighted with gold for luxury pieces. His early work was in clear enameled decoration, and, from *c*1924, he used sandblasting. In 1935, he designed porcelain and glass for the oceanliner *Normandie* adopted by the Compagnie Générale Transatlantique for their other ships. In the early 1930s, he designed glassware produced by Cristal de Saint-Louis and, in the late 1950s, stainless-steel flatware for Sola France. In 1937, he became a member of UAM (Union des Artistes Modernes). He taught at the École des Arts Appliqués in Paris and was a technical advisor at Sèvres. In the mid-1980s, Les Verreries de la Rochere reproduced Luce's mouth-blown drinking glasses from original designs of *c*1925. A coffee-tea set was reissued by Lumen Center 1988–91.

► In 1921, he first showed his work at the Musée Galliéra, Paris, and subsequently at the Salons d'Automne and Salons of the Société des Artistes Décorateurs. He was a juror at the 1925 Paris 'Exposition Internationale des Arts Décoratifs et Industriels Modernes' and 1937 Paris 'Exposition Internationale des Arts et Techniques dans la Vie Moderne', and showed his work in the UAM pavilion there. He was responsible for the glassware-plate section of the 1949–50 (I) 'Formes Utiles' exhibition at the Pavillon de Marsan and exhibited in its 1953 and 1958 exhibitions.

► Victor Arwas, *Art Déco*, Abrams, 1980. *Les Carnets du Design*, Paris: Mad-Cap Productions et APCI, 1986:40. Arlette Barré-Despond, *UAM*, Paris: Regard, 1986:456–58, Cat., *Les années UAM 1929–1958*, Paris: Musée des Arts Décoratifs, 1988:220– 21.

Lucet, Maurice (1877–1941)

► French architect and designer; born Orléans.

► From 1902, he collaborated with Pierre Lahalle.

► Pierre Kjellberg, *Art Déco: les maîtres du Mobilier, le décor des Paquebots*, Paris: Amateur, 1986:117.

Lucini, Ennio (1934–)

► Italian packaging, product, and graphic designer; active Milan.

► He executed small objects for the home in ceramics and glass produced by Gabbianelli, and metalware by Barazzoni. He designed the hemispherical *Ponte di Brera* drinking glasses (from 1965 by Ponte di Brera, 1968–75 by Gabbianelli) and 1968 *Tummy* range of stainless-steel cookware by Barazoni. His clients included La Rinascente-Upim, Anonima Castelli, Bossi Tessuti, Christian Dior, De.Bi., Du Pont, Estée Lauder (Aramis and Clinique cosmetic ranges), Fanini Fain, Fiori, Fratelli Rossetti, Gabbianelli (ceramics and glass), Gavina, Fratelli Guzzini, Henraux Marmi, Instituto Commercio Estero, Instituto Franco Tosi, Lema Lidman, Ligure Lombarda, Malferrari, Midy, Mira Lanza, Pierrel, Pirelli, Poltrona Frau, Poggi, Richard Ginori, Prodotti Roche, Rootes Autos, Schiffini, Snia Viscosa, Stella Unitex, Sorgente dei Mobili, Vefer, Galeries Lafayette department store in Paris, Saifi, Central Adams, Mc. IN Comifan, Itres, Paolo Barazzoni, and P.A. Bonacina. He coordinated corporate image programs for Anonima Castelli, Barazzoni, Centro Duchamp, Ligure Lombarda, Fanini Fain, Falconi, Palazzo Durini, Ponte di Brera, Cafecrem, Mc. IN, Itres, Galeries Lafayette, and C. Broumand. He was a graphic designer for magazines *Pacco, Forme, Design Italia*, and *Stilitaria* and, 1975–80, art director of *Domus*. He was a member of ADI (Associazione per il Disegno Industriale) and founding member of ADCM (Art Directors Club Milano). In 1968, he taught graphic design at the Scuola Umanitaria in Milan.

▶ He participated in the 1968 (XIV) Triennale di Milano and the Eurodomus fairs. His *Tummy* range was awarded the 1979 Compasso d'Oro. The *Tummy* range and *Ponte di Brera* glasses were included in the 1984 *Design Since 1945* exhibition at the Philadelphia Museum of Art.

▶ *ADI Annual 1976*, Milan: Associazione per il Disegno Industriale, 1976. 'Designers d'oggi: Ennio Lucini,' *Interni*, April 1979:54–55. Cat., Kathryn B. Hiesinger and George H. Marcus III (eds.), *Design Since 1945*, Philadelphia: Philadelphia Museum of Art, 1983:II–37,V–25. Carla Caccia, 'Parliamo di design con . . . Ennio Lucini,' *Arredorama*, Jan. 1983:9–14.

Luckhardt, Wassili (1889–1972) and Hans Luckhardt (1890–1954)

▶ German architects and designers; brothers; born Berlin.

▶ Wassili Luckhardt studied Technische Hochschule, Berlin-Charlottenberg, and in Munich and Dresden; Hans Luckhardt, Technische Hochschule, Karlsruhe.

▶ The Luckhardts were signatories of the Architecture Program issued by the Arbeitsrat für Kunst in 1919 and contributed letters and drawings to the 'Utopian Correspondence' of Bruno Taut. 1921–54 in Berlin, they worked in partnership, for a time in association with Alfons Anker. Their first Expressionist structures were the 1921 Hygiene Museum in Dresden and 1922 office-tower project for the Friedrichstrasse station, Berlin. Their other buildings included 1927 experimental housing in the Schorlemer Allee, Berlin, 1928 houses on the Rupenhorn, Berlin, 1951 Berlin pavilion at the 'Constructa' exhibition in Hanover, 1929 Alexanderplatz rearrangement projects in Berlin, 1933 Medical College, Bratislava, and 1952 Freie Universität, Berlin-Dahlem. From the mid-1920s, they worked in the Rationalist mode. Their most accomplished work was not built due to the events of World War II. Continuing to work in Berlin after the war, their unornamental designs showed a certain elegance, with well-defined silhouettes. They produced notable bent plated-metal furniture designs.

▶ Work subject of 1990 exhibition, Akademie der Künste, Berlin.

▶ Udo Kultermann (ed.), *Wassili und Hans Luckhardt: Bauten und Entwürfe*, Tübingen, 1958. Hans Luckhardt, letters in *Die Gläserne Kette*, Berlin, 1963. H. Kliemann, *Wassili Luckhardt*, Tübingen, 1973. Vittorio Magnago Lampugnani (ed.), *Encyclopedia of 20th-Century Architecture*, New York: Abrams, 1986:204. Cat., *Brüder Luckhardt und Alfons Anker*, Berlin: Akademie der Künste, 1990.

Ludvika, Smrčková (1903–91)

▶ Czech glass artist, painter, and graphic designer.

▶ Studied School of Decorative Arts, Prague, under Emil Dítě, V.H. Brunner, František Kysela, and Charles University, Prague.

▶ She began her career in glass under Brunner, following the simple shapes of Constructivism shown in Paris at the 1925 Exposition; 1928–48, taught at Czech high schools in Příbor, Litomyšl, Kladno, and Prague; from 1928, was a member of SČSD (Czechoslovak Werkbund); 1930–48, worked mainly for the firm Ruckel, Nižbor; collaborated with the agency Krásná jizba (The Beautiful Room) and introduced simple, dynamic shapes (often formed by cut edges) into table glassware; in the 1930s, designed vases and bowls with geometric cut motifs; from 1948, designed for the firms Inwald and Skloexport and for Center of Glass Industry and Fine Ceramics, Prague; in the 1960s and 1970s, experimented with engraved and painted glass. She was also active as a painter and graphic artist, and interested in book design and bindings.

▶ Received a grand prize at 1935 'Exposition Universelle et Internationale de Bruxelles' and a grand prize and gold medal at 1937 Paris 'Exposition Internationale des Arts et Techniques dans la Vie Moderne.'

▶ A. Adlerová, *České užité umění 1918–1938*, Prague, 1983. Cat., *Tschechische Kunst der 20+30 Jahre, Avantgarde und Tradition*, Darmstadt: Mathildenhöhe, 1988–89.

Lukander, Minni (1930–)

▶ Finnish ceramicist.

▶ In 1950, Lukander became an independent ceramicist and was one of the founders of the studio Pot Viapori in Suomenlinna, near Helsinki.

▶ Cat., David Revere McFadden (ed.), *Scandinavian Modern Design 1880–1980*, New York: Abrams, 1982:268, No. 285.

Lund, Johan (1861–1939)

▶ Norwegian designer and silversmith; active Christiania (now Oslo) and Drammen.

▶ Lund designed and executed silver for David-Andersen around the time of that firm's shift from *champlevé* and *cloisonné* enamel to *plique à jour*, a technique in which Lund worked, at the turn of the century. 1894–98, he was director of the Norsk Filigransfabrik. He settled in Drammen in 1899.

▶ His oil lamp for David-Andersen with a large *plique-à-jour* shade was featured on the Norwegian stand at the 1893 Chicago 'World's Columbian Exposition.'

▶ Annelies Krekel-Aalberse, *Art Nouveau and Art Déco Silver*, New York: Abrams, 1989:242,257.

Lundin, Ingeborg (1921–)

▶ Swedish glassware designer.

▶ 1941–46, studied Konstfackskolan and Tekniska Skolan, Stockholm.

▶ 1947–71, Lundin worked at the Orrefors Glasbruk. Her 1955 *Äpplet* (Apple) vase characterized her dynamic blown-glass work. Other glass works included 1954 *Timglas* (Hour-glass) and 1954 *Bamby* vases. She produced subtle forms that expressed the plasticity and quality of crystal.

▶ She received the 1954 Lunning Prize. Her work was the subject of the 1959 one-person exhibition in Stockholm and was shown at the 1957 (XI) and 1960 (XII) Triennali di Milano, 1954–57 USA 'Design in Scandinavia' traveling exhibition, 1955 'H 55' exhibition in Hälsingborg, 1958 'Formes Scandinaves' at the Paris Musée des Arts Décoratifs, 1957 exhibition in Zürich, and 1959 exhibition in Amsterdam.

▶ Cat., David Revere McFadden (ed.), *Scandinavian Modern Design 1880–1980*, New York: Abrams, 1982:268, No. 170. Frederick Cooke, *Glass: Twentieth-Century Design*, New York: Dutton, 1986:85. Cat., *The Lunning Prize*, Stockholm, Nationalmuseum, 1986:58–61.

Lunning Prize

▶ Danish-American design award.

▶ Previously the head of the shop of Georg Jensen Sølvsmedie in Copenhagen, Frederik Lunning founded the New York branch of Georg Jensen in 1923. In 1951, based on an idea of Kaj Dessau and on the 70th birthday of Lunning, he established the Lunning Prize in his own name with the intention of stimulating design excellence in the decorative arts. Its recipients included Hans J. Wegner and Tapio Wirkkala, 1952; Carl-Axel Acking and Grete Prytz-Kittelsen, 1952; Tias Eckhoff and Henning Koppel, 1953; Ingeborg Lundin and Jens H. Quistgaard, 1954; Ingrid Dessau and Kaj Franck, 1955; Nanna and Jørgen Ditzel and Timo Sarpaneva, 1956; Hermann Bongard and Erik Höglung, 1957; Paul Kjærholm and Signe Persson-Melin, 1958; Arne Jon Jutrem and Antti Nurmesniemi, 1959; Torun Bülow-Hübe and Vibeke Klint, 1960; Bertel Gardberg and Erik Pøen, 1961; Hertha Hillfon and Kristian Vedel, 1962; Karin Björquist and Börje Rajalin, 1963; Vuokko Eskolin-Nurmesniemi and Bent Gabrielsen, 1964; Eli-Marie Johnsen and Hans Krondahl, 1965; Erik Magnussen and Kristi Skintveit, 1967; Björn Weckström and Ann and Göran Wärff, 1968; Helga and Bent Exner and Börje Lindau and Bo Lindekrantz, 1969; Kim Naver and Oiva Toikka, 1970. The prize was discontinued in 1970.

▶ Cat., *The Lumming Prize*, Stockholm, Nationalemuseum, 1986.

Lurçat, André (1894–1970)
▶ French architect and furniture designer; born Bruyères, Vosges; brother of Jean Lurçat.
▶ 1911–13, studied École Municipale des Beaux-Arts; 1918–23, École Nationale Supérieure des Beaux-Arts, Paris.
▶ In 1928, he became a founding member of the CIAM (Congrès Internationaux d'Architecture Moderne); Lurçat was head of the commission on urbanism. His furniture of the 1920s was in geometrical forms influenced by Cubism, as was his architecture; his furniture for the École Karl-Marx, produced by Thonet, resembled bent metal tubular furniture by Marcel Breuer. In France, he produced pioneering structures, including his 1925–26 Villa Seurat artists' studios in Paris, the 1925 Gromaire House in Versailles, 1926 Bomsel House in Versailles, 1926–27 painter Guggenbuhl's house in the rue Nansouty in Paris, and 1927 sculptor Froriep de Sallis's house in Boulogne. Many of his unrealized domestic buildings were radical. In 1930, he published the manifesto *Architecture*, built the Hôtel Nord-Sud in Calvi on the Mediterranean, and joined a Marxist group that focused on urbanism. He designed the 1931–33 École Karl-Marx primary school, Villejuif, near Paris, with frescoes by his brother Jean Lurçat. In 1932, he opened his own architecture office in Paris and became a member of UAM (Union des Artistes Modernes). A fervent admirer of and frequent visitor to the Soviet Union, he studied architecture there with others of the Villejuif group and was the only foreign architect allowed to compete for the USSR Sciences Academy Building. His interest in monumentality and axiality was reflected in his buildings for the reconstruction of Maubeuge and the renovation of Saint-Denis after World War II, and in his essay *Formes, composition et lois d'harmonie* (1953–57).
▶ He showed his first houses of the Villa Seurat at the Salons d'Automne and participated in the 1925 Paris 'Exposition Internationale des Arts Décoratifs et Industriels Modernes,' the opening of the Bauhaus, Dessau, and exhibition of Viennese plastic arts in France.
▶ André Lurçat, 'Urbanisme et architecture,' *L'Architecture d'aujourd'hui*, No. 1, May–June 1945. 'André Lurçat,' *Architecture, Mouvement, Continuité*, No. 40, 1976:5–38. Jean-Louis Cohen, *L'Architecture d'André Lurçat (1894–1970), Autocritique d'un Moderne*, doctoral thesis, Paris: École des Hautes Études en Sciences Sociales, 1985. Jean-Louis Cohen in Vittorio Magnago Lampugnani (ed.), *Encyclopedia of 20th-Century Architecture*, New York: Abrams, 1986:204. Cat., Aaron Lederfajn and Xavier Lenormand, *Le Louvre des Antiquaires présente: 1930 quand le meuble devient sculpture*, Paris, 1986. Pierre Cabanne, *Encyclopédie Art Déco*, Paris: Somogy, 1986:214–15. Arlette Barré-Despond, *UAM*, Paris: Regard, 1986:452–53. Cat., *Les années UAM 1929–1958*, Paris: Musée des Arts Décoratifs, 1988:222–23.

Lurçat, Jean (1892–1966)
▶ French painter and tapestry designer; brother of André Lurçat.
▶ He worked with Victor Prouvé in Nancy; in 1917, designed his first two tapestries *Filles Vertes* and *Soirée dans Grenade*, made by his mother; from 1920, lived in rue Nollet, Paris, where he met Pierre Chareau, for whom he later produced tapestries for the Bernheim family's Château de Villefix and for Maison de Verre, Paris; in 1940, met François Tabard; after seeing the 14th-century *Apocalypse* tapestry in Angers, became devoted to his textile work and known for the revival of medieval techniques and a nomenclature of colors and fringes; from 1957, produced a large number of hangings including *Le Chant du Monde*; was also active as a painter, lithographer, ceramicist, and wallpaper designer; in c1930, joined UAM (Union des Artistes Modernes).
▶ Work (rugs) shown in Myrbor stand at 1925 Paris 'Exposition Internationale des Arts Décoratifs et Industriels Modernes'.
▶ *Sammlung Bröhan: Kunst der 20er und 30er Jahre*, Vol. 3, Berlin: Karl H. Bröhan, 1985. Arlette Barré-Despond, *UAM*, Paris: Regard, 1986: 454–55.

Lurje, Viktor
▶ Austrian designer.
▶ Active with Josef Hoffmann and Otto Prutscher and working in their simple mode, Lurje designed very plain furniture and interiors.
▶ Günther Feuerstein, *Vienna—Present and Past: Arts and Crafts—Applied Art—Design*, Vienna: Jugend und Volk, 1976: 35,80.

Luthersson, Petur B. (1936–)
▶ Icelandic furniture, interior, and lighting designer.
▶ He designed domestic and public spaces and was Iceland's most important furniture designer. His domestic and office furniture was produced in wood and metal. His 1969 aluminum hanging light was produced by Amundi Sigurdhsson of Reykjavik. He designed a wide range of lighting in spun aluminum.
▶ Cat., David Revere McFadden (ed.), *Scandinavian Modern Design 1880–1980*, New York: Abrams, 1982:268, No. 263.

Lütken, Per (1916–)
▶ Danish glassware designer.
▶ 1937, studied painting and technical drawing, Kunsthåndværkerskolen, Copenhagen.
▶ From 1942, Lütken was chief designer at Kastrup & Holmegård Glasværk, where he continued the Modern forms established by his predecessor Jacob Bang. Inspired by the Triennali di Milano in the 1950s, he introduced major changes in production and style at Holmegård. His designs incorporated fluid forms in lightly colored glass, some with etching that produced a satin-finish. He applied hot metal to formed glass shapes.
▶ From its 1951 (IX) session, he participated in the Triennale di Milano. His work was included in the 1954–57 USA 'Design in Scandinavia' traveling exhibition, 1956–59 Germany 'Neue Form aus Dänemark' traveling exhibition, 1958 'Formes Scandinaves' exhibition at the Paris Musée des Arts Décoratifs, 1960–61 USA 'The Arts of Denmark' traveling exhibition, 1962 'Creative Craft in Denmark Today' in New York, 1980 'Scandinavian Modern Design 1880–1980' exhibition at the Cooper-Hewitt Museum, New York, and 1983–84 'Design Since 1945' exhibition at the Philadelphia Museum of Art.
▶ *150 Years of Danish Glass*, Copenhagen: Kastrup & Holmegård Glassworks, Nos. 209–37. Arne Karlsen, *Made in Denmark*, New York, 1960:50–55,119. Per Lütken, in *DB&D*, Copenhagen: Danish Society of Arts and Crafts and Industrial Design, 1972:21–22. Erik Lassen and Mogens Schlüter, *Dansk Glas: 1925–1975*, Copenhagen, 1975. Cat., David Revere McFadden (ed.), *Scandinavian Modern Design 1880–1980*, New York: Abrams, 1982:268, No. 172. Cat., Kathryn B. Hiesinger and George H. Marcus III (eds.), *Design Since 1945*, Philadelphia: Philadelphia Museum of Art, 1983:II–38. Frederick Cooke, *Glass: Twentieth-Century Design*, New York: Dutton, 1986:86. Jennifer Hawkins Opie, *Scandinavia: Ceramics and Glass in the Twentieth Century*, New York: Rizzoli, 1989.

Lutyens, Candia
▶ British entrepreneur; granddaughter of Edwin Lutyens.
▶ Lutyens set up a firm in 1990 to reproduce Edwin Lutyens's sofas, chairs, and tables. Production included his 1931 *Spiderback* chair and 1928 *Pall Mall* chair, both originally designed for a London plumbing company showroom; the so-called *Napoleon* chair used in his own house; and 1930 *New Delhi Circleback* chair for the Viceroy's house in India.
▶ Cat., *Lutyens: The Work of the English Architect Sir Edward Lutyens*, London: Arts Council, 1981. Suzanne Slesin, 'Lutyens's Furniture from the Originals,' *The New York Times*, 25 July 1991:C3.

Lutyens, Edwin Landseer (1869–1944)
▶ British architect and designer; born London.
▶ 1885–87, studied Kensington School of Art, London.
▶ In 1887, he worked under architect Ernest George in the firm George and Peto, where he met Herbert Baker, later a colleague

in New Delhi. He was influenced by Richard Norman Shaw and Philip Webb. Edward Hudson promoted the young Lutyens in *Country Life* magazine. His earliest designs were for garden furniture. For his first married home, Lutyens designed most of the sparse furnishings, and later returned repeatedly to these furniture themes. Historicist pieces for the house included an oak refectory table with heavy pillar supports, and a four-poster bed and dressing table. In 1889, he received his first assignment and set up his own architecture practice. His approach embraced the styles of the Arts and Crafts movement, Queen Anne style, English Regency, Mughal, and neoclassicism. Lutyens's 1906–12 Folly Farm in Sulhampstead, Berkshire, broke new ground in its architecture and interior design, incorporating crisp white painted woodwork and ceilings, glossy black walls, red fretwork and lacquered furniture. Among his extensive furniture designs was a wooden garden settee with the characteristics of padded upholstery, still in production and widely made and published. In 1905, he designed 21 chairs for the boardroom of *Country Life*. By the end of World War I, his furniture became bolder, and his ideas about decorating uncompromising. Lutyens's quirky taste was expressed in his residence in Mansfield Street in London, which included his eccentric chairs inspired by Napoleon's *meridiennes*, with one arm lower than the other to accommodate a draped leg. He was the architect of the 1919–20 Cenotaph in London, the 1926 Thiepval Arch war memorial on the Somme, many English country houses, and, in 1912–31, a large complex of government buildings in New Delhi, including the Viceroy's House. The New Delhi complex resulted in his best-known designs for massively scaled lighting, tables, and chairs. For smaller rooms in the viceroy's residence and minor offices he had a freer design hand: in the nursery, there were light-hearted chandeliers with animal cut-outs, and an amorphous clock. Another clock had hands that extended as they rounded the oval dial. Furniture and lighting for the 1928–31 offices of the sanitary fittings firm Crane Bennet on Pall Mall, London, were reworkings of some of the New Delhi designs. Furniture for the 1934–35 Reuters and Press Association building in London reflected designs for his own house in Bloomsbury almost 40 years earlier. In 1942, he conceived the 'RA Plan for London,' based on the 1938 Bressey-Lutyens Report. He was president of the Royal Academy from 1938; buried Westminster Abbey, London.

▶ Architecture included numerous Arts and Crafts-style country houses in England, including Deanery Garden in Sonning; the neo-Baroque houses 1906 Heathcote in Ilkley and 1905–08 Nashdom in Taplow; English Free Style work at Hampstead Garden Suburb in London; and neo-Georgian houses. After World War I, he designed commercial and government buildings, including 1924–39 Britannic House, the Midland Bank head office, and townhouses, all in London. In the 1930s, his major commission was the Metropolitan Cathedral of Christ the King in Liverpool, in a style, reminiscent of Christopher Wren, that Lutyens called 'Wrenaissance.' It was to be the world's second largest Christian church, and Lutyens was prepared for construction to take 100 years. The foundation stone was laid in 1933; most of the crypt work was completed by 1939; work was abandoned in 1941; costs after World War II prohibited completion of the Lutyens design. Other commissions included the 1933–36 Champion Hall in Oxford, and 1937–38 Middleton Park in Oxford (with Robert Lutyens).

▶ His 518-inch (13·2m) model for the 1929 Liverpool Cathedral was shown at the 1934 exhibition at the Royal Academy, at the 1979–80 'Thirties' exhibition, and (along with drawings and photographs of New Delhi) at the Hayward Gallery, both London. His work was the subject of the 1978 exhibition, Museum of Modern Art, New York, and 1981 'Lutyens: The Work of the English Architect Sir Edwin Lutyens (1869–1944)' exhibition in London. Knighted 1918; Order of Merit 1942; gold medal RIBA 1921; medal AIA 1924; master, Art-Workers' Guild from 1933.

▶ Edwin Lutyens, 'What I Think of Modern Architecture,' *Country Life*, Vol. 69, 1931:775–77. C. Reilly, *Representative British*

Architects, Batsford, 1931. A.S.G. Butler, with George Stewart and Christopher Hussey, *The Architecture of Sir Edwin Lutyens*, London, 1950. A.S.G. Butler, 'The Architecture of Sir Edwin Lutyens,' *Country Life*, 1950. C. Hussey 'The Life of Sir Edwin Lutyens,' *Country Life*, 1950. Alan Greenberg, 'Lutyens' Architecture Restudied,' *Prospecta*, No. 12, 1969:129–52. Peter Kinskip, *Edwin Lutyens*, London, 1979. Cat., *Thirties: British art and design before the war*, London: Arts Council of Great Britain, Hayward Gallery, 1979:18,54,63,122–23,179,295,302. Daniel O'Neill, *Edwin Lutyens: Country Houses*, London, 1980. R. Gradidge, *Edwin Lutyens: Architect Laureate*, London, 1981. *British Arts and Design, 1900–1960*, 1983. Stephen Calloway, 'Lutyens as Furniture Designer,' *Christie's International Magazine*, February 1991:6–10.

Lutz, Rudolf (1895–1966)

▶ German architect; born Heilbronn.

▶ 1914–16, studied Kunstgewerbeschule, Stuttgart; 1919–21, Bauhaus, Weimar.

▶ At the Bauhaus, he worked in the office of architecture. He settled in Stuttgart and worked as an architect.

▶ Lionel Richard, *Encyclopédie du Bauhaus*, Paris: Somogy, 1985: 201. Cat., *Bauhaus 1919–1933*, Museum für Gestaltung Zürich/Kunstgewerbemuseum, Zürich: 1988:138–39.

Luxton, John

▶ British glassware designer.

▶ 1936–39, Luxton studied Stourbridge School of Art; 1946–49, Royal College of Art, London.

▶ He designed glassware for Stuart and Sons, including drinking glasses in robust silhouettes.

▶ Frederick Cooke, *Glass: Twentieth-Century Design*, New York: Dutton, 1986:78.

Lycett, Edward (1833–1910)

▶ British ceramicist; born Newcastle under Lyme, active New York.

▶ He was apprenticed at an early age to Copeland and Garrett, Stoke-on-Trent, under Thomas Battam. In 1852, he worked in the London decorating shop of Thomas Battam, where he painted copies of Greek bases in the British Museum. In 1861, he settled in New York and opened a decorating workshop on Greene Street, where about 40 people eventually worked. At first he painted earthenware vases produced by Williamsburg Terra Cotta, Long Island, and painted imported blank Sèvres and Haviland china. Known for his raised goldwork and rich over- and underglazed dark blue, he was adept at rendering realistic images of fish, birds, fruits, and vegetables. In 1865, commissioned by John Vogt, he painted the monogrammed china service (of another designer) of Abraham Lincoln. His firm produced painted washbasins and porcelain panels incorporated into furniture. Architect Richard Morris Hunt commissioned Lycett to decorate large enameled-iron panels for the 1871–73 Van Rensselaer Building in New York. In the late 1860s, Lycett added classrooms to his workshop, offering women's pottery-painting lessons. Lycett left his son William in charge of the workshop while he taught china painting at the Saint Louis School of Design in 1877 and in Cincinnati. The studio at this time was called Warrin and Lycett. In 1879, with John Bennett, he set up a china-painting workshop at 4 Great Jones Street. The partnership was dissolved in 1882. 1884–90, Lycett was artistic director at the Faience Manufacturing Co, Brooklyn, experimenting with fine-grade white porcelain and producing iridescent metallic glazes on Persian lusterware. In 1890, he retired to Atlanta, Georgia, to assist his son William, who had set up a china-painting workshop there in 1883.

▶ His work for Copeland and Garrett was included in the 1851 London 'Great Exhibition of the Works of Industry of All Nations.' He showed several pieces in the 1878 Cincinnati Women's Art Museum Association exhibition.

▶ Edwin AtLee Barber, 'Recent Advances in the Pottery Industry,' *Popular Science Monthly*, No. 40, Jan. 1892:297–98. Edwin AtLee

Barber, *The Pottery and Porcelain of the United States*, New York, 1893:313–19,414. Doreen Bolger Burke et al., *In Pursuit of Beauty: Americans and the Aesthetic Movement*, New York: Metropolitan Museum of Art and Rizzoli, 1986:427.

Lynggaard, Finn (1930–)
▶ Danish ceramicist and glassware designer.
▶ Studied painting and ceramics, Kunsthåndværkskolen, Copenhagen.
▶ He set up his own workshop in 1958, becoming a pioneer in Danish studio glass. His glass work is known for deeply colored floral motifs on clear grounds.
▶ He participated in the 1960 (XII) Triennale di Milano. His work was included in the 1960–61 USA 'The Arts of Denmark' traveling exhibition.

▶ Cat., David Revere McFadden (ed.), *Scandinavian Modern Design 1880–1980*, New York: Abrams, 1982:268, No. 292.

Lysell, Ralph (1907–)
▶ Swedish industrial designer; active USA, Germany, and Sweden.
▶ After working in the USA and Germany, he returned to Sweden. 1939–45, he worked for Ericsson, where he assisted Hugo Blomberg on the initial concept of the *Ericofon* telephone. He, Blomberg, and Gösta Thames developed the design and engineering for the telephone 1940–54.
▶ Hugo Blomberg, 'The Ericofon—The New Telephone Set,' *Ericsson Review*, Vol. 33, No. 4, 1956:99–109. Cat., Kathryn B. Hiesinger and George H. Marcus III (eds.), *Design Since 1945*, Philadelphia: Philadelphia Museum of Art, 1983.

M

Måås-Fjetterström, Märta (1873–1941)
► Swedish textile designer.
► She set up a workshop in Båstad in 1919, becoming a leading textile artist. An influential weaver, she was responsible for the development of many important artists. She combined a painterly approach with traditional textile techniques in abstract motifs and strong colors. Barbro Nilsson succeeded her as director of the workshop, which is still in operation.
► Cat., David Revere McFadden (ed.), *Scandinavian Modern Design 1880–1980* New York: Abrams, 1982:268, No. 150.

Macchi Cassia, Antonio (1937–)
► Italian industrial designer; born and active Milan.
► In 1967, he became a member of ADI (Associazione per il Disegno Industriale) and committee director 1971–73; 1968–70, was active in Studio Bonfanti-Macchi Cassia-Porta; 1969–81, was industrial design consultant to Olivetti and worked for Steiner International; in 1971, (with R. Beretta) set up a studio in Milan. His clients included La Rinascente (graphics), Mellin d'Italia (graphics and package design), Ascensori Falconi (control devices), Arteluce (lighting), Stilnovo (lighting), Radiomarelli (television sets), Condor (television sets), Artemide (research on furniture components), Tosimobili (furniture systems), Focchi, Crouzet (measuring instruments), Burgo Scott, Steiner Co, Totalgas, and Condor. For Olivetti, he designed the *Divisumma 18* adding machine, *Copia 2000* copier, and *M20* personal computer.
► *ADI Annual 1976*, Milan: Associazione per il Disegno Industriale, 1976. Cat., *Design Process: Olivetti 1908–1983*, Milan, 1983:380–81. Cat., *Donation Olivetti: Die Neue Sammlung München*, Frankfurt: 1986:38.

Macdonald, Frances (1874–1921) and **Margaret Macdonald** (1865–1933)
► British artists and designers; sisters.
► Studied Glasgow School of Art.
► At the Glasgow School of Art they met their future husbands J. Herbert MacNair and Charles Rennie Mackintosh, with whom they were members of 'The Four.' Influenced by the Arts and Crafts movement, the Pre-Raphaelites, and the revival of Celtic and Japanese art, they developed an arch and elegant personal style of design and decoration. In 1894, The Four organized an exhibition of furniture, metalwork, and embroidery. Their work was published in the *Studio*. In *c*1894, the sisters opened their own studio on Hope Street, Glasgow. Their style rejected the medievalism of John Ruskin and William Morris and combined Katsushika Hokusai's mannerism with Aubrey Beardsley's elongated figures; this bizarre combination encouraged critics to label them the Spook School. Margaret Macdonald's influence can be seen in the work of husband Mackintosh from the time of their marriage, and her graphic design skills were put to use in the menus and other designs for Miss Cranston's Tea Rooms in Glasgow for which Mackintosh designed interiors; she was also known for her embroideries. Frances Macdonald taught enameling and gold- and silversmithing at the Glasgow School of Art; her few jewelry pieces, leaded glass, and plaster and wire-wall decorations influenced the jewelry work of the *fin-de-siècle* as well as her pupils, including Agnes B. Harvey.
► In 1895, The Four showed their work at 'L'Oeuvre Artistique' in Liège. They exhibited at the 1896 Arts and Crafts Exhibition in London, 1900 (VIII) Sezession Exhibition in Vienna, 1902 Turin 'Esposizione Internazionale d'Arte Decorativa Moderna' (including Frances's jewelry and *repoussé* silver panels), and in Budapest, Dresden, Munich, and Moscow. The MacNairs showed jewelry at the 1901 Education Exhibition at St. George's Hall, Liverpool.
► Charlotte Gere, *American and European Jewelry 1830–1914*, New York: Crown, 1975:204. Anthea Callen, *Women Artists of the Arts and Crafts Movement 1870–1914*, New York: Pantheon, 1979:159. David Brett, 'The Eroticization of Domestic Space: A Mirror by C.R. Mackintosh,' *The Journal of Decorative and Propaganda Art*, Fall 1988:6–13. Toni Lesser Wolf, 'Women Jewelers of the British Arts and Crafts Movement,' *The Journal of Decorative and Propaganda Arts*, No. 14, Fall 1989:40–41. David Brett, *C.R. Mackintosh: The Poetics of Workmanship*, London: Reaktion Books, 1992.

Mack, Daniel (1947–)
► American furniture designer; born Rochester, New York; active New York and Warwick, New York.
► Studied anthropology, University of Toronto, and media studies, The New School for Social Research, New York, to 1975.
► He pursued a career in radio and television journalism and teaching. In the 1970s, he worked for the Canadian Broadcasting Corporation, was an interviewer on the WRVR radio station in New York, and produced documentaries for the *Today* program on NBC. In 1979, he began to make twig furniture and eventually played a major role in the revival of 19th-century rustic furniture. Though made from natural and found forms, the rectilinearity of his chairs and their high backs suggest the work of Frank Lloyd Wright and Charles Rennie Mackintosh. He wrote *Making Rustic Furniture* (1991) and taught media studies at The New School for Social Research, and, 1986–90, furniture making at the Lake Placid, New York, Center for the Arts.

Mackay, David (1933–)
► British architect and industrial designer; born Eastbourne, Sussex.
► Studied architecture, North London Polytechnic, to 1958, and School of Architecture, Barcelona, to 1966.
► In 1959, he settled in Barcelona, where he became a partner in the architecture firm Martorell, Bohigas, Mackay.
► Mackay, Oriol Bohigas, and Josep Martorell won the 1959, 1962, 1966, and 1979 FAD awards for architecture; 1966 and 1976 Delta de Plata prize (for industrial design); first prize at the 1984 'Internationale Bauaussetellung' in Berlin; and two first prizes in the Prototype Schools Competition of the Ministry of Education in Madrid. Their work was included in the 1986 'Contemporary Spanish Architecture: An Eclectic Panorama' exhibition at the Architectural League in New York.
► Antón Capitel and Ignacio Solà-Morales in *Contemporary Spanish Architecture*, New York: Rizzoli, 1986:64–67.

Mackintosh, Charles Rennie   (1868–1928)

▶ British architect and designer; born and active Glasgow; husband of Margaret Macdonald.

▶ 1885–89, studied Glasgow School of Art.

▶ In 1884, he was apprenticed to the architect John Hutchinson. In 1889, he met J. Herbert MacNair in the office of architects J. Honeyman and Keppie, a major Glasgow partnership, where they worked as draftsmen. In the 1890s Mackintosh became a leading figure of 'The Four' of the Glasgow School of Art with MacNair and Margaret and Frances Macdonald, designing posters and metalwork that was published in the *Studio*. In 1894, Mackintosh with MacNair and the Macdonalds organized an exhibition of furniture, metalwork, and embroidery. Including leaded glass, furniture, book illustration, and jewelry, their work was influenced by the Arts and Crafts movement, the Pre-Raphaelites, and the revival of Celtic and Japanese art. Working in a Scottish idiom and the neo-Gothic style, the group became known as the 'Glasgow School' and throughout Europe as 'school of the Ghosts.' Mackintosh became a prolific designer of furniture, textiles, and graphics, and an accomplished watercolorist. As the leader of Art Nouveau in Britain, he made a contribution of great consequence and drew on ornamentation of the ancient Celts and the decorations of Japan. In 1900, Mackintosh married Margaret Macdonald, the same year as the invitation to the 8th Vienna Sezession exhibition, where the group exerted a great influence. The 1894 corner tower of the Glasgow Herald Building was Mackintosh's first executed work. While still working at Honeyman and Keppie, he won the 1896 competition to designed the new Glasgow School of Art building, designed in two stages, 1897–99 and 1907–09; he also designed Miss Cranston's two Tea Rooms in Glasgow. His Glasgow School of Art building and interiors, little publicized at the time, are now considered to be a brilliant example of proto-Modernism. He designed only two pieces of jewelry: a necklace with pendant in the form of a flight of birds (made by Margaret Macdonald), and a ring. The necklace has been frequently copied. In Scotland, he designed the 1897–98 Queen's Cross Church in Glasgow, 1899–1901 Windyhill at Kilmalcolm, 1902–04 publisher Walter Blackie's Hill House in Helensburgh. In 1913, he moved to London, where his design work included furniture and printed fabrics. His work was known throughout Europe but not widely recognized in Britain. He became a close friend and mentor of Josef Hoffmann. Mackintosh's reputation was enhanced by the publication of a portfolio of his competition designs for the 'House for an Art Lover' published by Hermann Muthesius. Mackintosh's work for the 1916–17 house for W.J. Bassett-Lowke at 78 Derngate, Northampton, included the use of plastics and other adventurous materials, influenced by Chinese design. In some cases, his designs for silver and electroplated flatware show the mark of David Hislop, possibly produced by Elkington, Birmingham. The extent of the collaboration of Margaret Macdonald and Mackintosh cannot now be determined, but it was obviously close and extensive, as evidenced in their apartment at 120 Main Street, Glasgow. Mackintosh designed a 1904 silver christening-set produced by Hahn in Berlin for Hermann Muthesius's son. From 1915 to the early 1920s, he completed numerous textile designs; in 1919, his fabric designs were produced by W. Foxton in London. He gave up architecture entirely in 1920 in favor of watercolor painting, later living in Port-Vendres in the Pyrenees 1923–27. From the 1984, his silver flatware patterns were reproduced by Sabattini Argenteria, including the *Black and White* vase, 1904 ewer and bowl shown in the bedroom for the 1903 Dresdner Werkstätten, 1903 *Willow* bowl, 1904 *Cranston* candlestick or flower holder, 1904 ewer and bowl for Catherine Cranston at Hous'hill, 1904 christening fork and spoon, 1902 cutlery for Jessie Newberry, and 1900–03 *MMM*, along with many of his furniture designs produced by Cassina and others.

▶ He won several architectural students' competitions, including the 1892 Alexander Thomson traveling scholarship. Mackintosh with the Macdonalds and MacNair organized the 1894 exhibition of their work at the Glasgow School of Art. In 1895, The Four

showed their work at the 1895 Liège 'L'Oeuvre Artistique.' He won second prize in the 1901 design competition of the Grand Duke Louis IV of Hesse-Darmstadt under the auspices of the journal *Zeitschrift für Innendekoration*. Mackintosh designed the Scottish section of the 1900 (VIII) Vienna Sezession exposition and of the 1911 Turin 'Esposizione Internazionale d'Arte Decorativa Moderna.' In addition to the 1900 Vienna Sezession exhibition and 1902 Turin exposition, Mackintosh, his wife, and the MacNairs showed their works in London in 1896, Moscow in 1903, Budapest, Dresden, and Munich. His work was the subject of the 1968 exhibition 'Charles Rennie Mackintosh, Architecture, Design and Painting' at the Scottish Arts Council in Glasgow.

▶ Hermann Muthesius, *Meister der Innen-Kunst*, Vol. II: 'Charles Rennie Mackintosh, Glasgow: Das Haus eines Kunstfreundes,' Darmstadt: Alexander Koch, 1901. Nikolaus Pevsner, *Charles Rennie Mackintosh*, Milan, 1950. Thomas Howarth, *Charles Rennie Mackintosh and the Modern Movement*, London, 1952. Robert Macleod, *Charles Rennie Mackintosh*, London, 1968. Cat., Andrew McLaren Young, *Charles Rennie Mackintosh, Architecture, Design and Painting*, Glasgow: Scottish Arts Council, 1968. Filippo Alison, *Charles Rennie Mackintosh as a Designer of Chairs*, London, 1974. Roger Billcliffe, *Architectural Sketches and Flower Drawings by Charles Rennie Mackintosh*, London, 1977. Roger Billcliffe and Peter Vergo, 'Charles Rennie Mackintosh and the Austrian Art Revival,' *Burlington Magazine*, Vol. CXIX, 1977:739–46. Roger Billcliffe, *Charles Rennie Mackintosh: The Complete Furniture Drawings and Interior Design*, Guildford and London: Lutterworth Press, 1979. Jackie Cooper (ed.), *Mackintosh Architecture: The Complete Buildings and Selected Projects*, London, 1978. *Les Carnets du Design*, Paris: Mad-Cap Productions et APCI, 1986:13. Yvonne Brunhammer et al., *Art Nouveau Belgium, France*, Houston: Institute for the Arts, Rice University, 1976. *British Arts and Design, 1900–1960*, 1983. David Brett, 'The Eroticization of Domestic Space: A Mirror by C.R. Mackintosh,' *The Journal of Decorative and Propaganda Art*, Fall 1988:6–13. Annelies Krekel-Aalberse, *Art Nouveau and Art Déco Silver*, New York: Abrams, 1989:29. Stephen Calloway, *Twentieth-Century Decoration*, New York: Rizzoli, 1988:59. Charlotte Gere, *American and European Jewelry 1830–1914*, New York: Crown, 1975:204–05. David Brett, *C.R. Mackintosh: The Poetics of Workmanship*, London: Reaktion Books, 1992.

Mackmurdo, Arthur Heygate   (1851–1942)

▶ British architect, designer, and economist.

▶ Apprenticed to Chatfield Brooks and James Brooks, the Gothic-revival architects, from 1869.

▶ About 1874 Mackmurdo was encouraged by John Ruskin to become an architect; he set up an office in the Strand in London in 1875 and met William Morris and James Abbott McNeill Whistler. Mackmurdo developed a style, singular in its striking simplicity, that brought him wide renown. He was influenced by a diverse group, including Victor Horta, Gustave Serrurier-Bovy, Charles Rennie Mackintosh, and C.F.A. Voysey. (Voysey later became a friend and pupil.) In 1882, Mackmurdo with Herbert, P. Horne, Selwyn Image, and Bernard Creswick founded The Century Guild, a cooperative organization of craftsmen and artists inspired by Morris and Ruskin. The group designed interiors and produced wallpaper, furniture, carpets, and metalwork, successfully shown at exhibitions in London, Manchester, and Liverpool. The principles of the Century Guild inspired C.R. Ashbee. Known as one of the originators of Art Nouveau, Mackmurdo was also involved in typography, textile design, and graphics. He was an author of books including *Wren's City Churches* (1883), whose cover design of flame-like curves is thought the earliest example of Art Nouveau. At the Century Guild he started a periodical called *The Hobby Horse* in 1884; it attempted to synthesize all the arts, including music and literature. Original in its design and typography, it was one of the most important and influential journals of the time. From 1886, he designed furniture that was simple, elegant, and original; these designs strongly influenced

Voysey. His architectural work included 1889 parts of the Savoy Hotel (with H. Horne) in London and the 1899 Mortimer Mempes house. Retiring in 1904 in Essex, he concentrated on social and economic issues and writing for the next four decades.

▶ Yvonne Brunhammer et al., *Art Nouveau Belgium, France*, Houston: Institute for the Arts, Rice University, 1976. Cat., *The Eccentric A.H. Mackmurdo, 1851–1942*, Colchester: The Minories, 1979. Cat., *A.H. Mackmurdo and the Century Guild Collection*, William Gallery.

Macleish, Minnie (1876–)

▶ British textile designer.

▶ She was associated with Charles Rennie Mackintosh and Constance Irving at Foxton textiles in London, and Metz store in Amsterdam. Active in the 1920s and 1930s, Macleish was a prolific designer producing patterns for fabrics produced by Morton Sundour.

▶ She participated in the British sections of the 1927 'Europäisches Kunstgewerbe,' Grassi Museum, Leipzig, and in textile exhibitions in Paris and Vienna.

▶ Giovanni and Rosalia Ranelli, *Il tessuto moderno*, Florence, 1976:181,217. *Journal of the Decorative Arts Society 1890–1940*, No. 4, 1979:26ff. Stuart Durant, *Ornament from the Industrial Revolution to Today*, Woodstock, NY: Overlook, 1986:252,255. Hans Wichmann, *Von Morris bis Memphis: Textilien der Neuen Sammlung, Ende 19. bis Ende 20. Jahrhundert*, Basel: Birkhäuser, 1990:445.

MacNair, J. Herbert (1870–1945)

▶ British architect, designer, and illustrator.

▶ Studied Glasgow School of Art.

▶ In 1889, while working for architects Honeyman and Keppie in Glasgow, he met Charles Rennie Mackintosh. They met sisters Margaret and Frances Macdonald at the Glasgow School of Art. MacNair was not happy as an architect and turned to the decorative arts. At the Glasgow School, MacNair, Mackintosh, and the Macdonalds formed The Four; influenced by the Arts and Crafts movement, the Pre-Raphaelites, and the revival of Celtic and Japanese art, they developed a personal style of design and decoration. In 1894, The Four organized an exhibition of furniture, metalwork, and embroidery. Their work was published in the *Studio*. MacNair married Frances Macdonald in 1899. His work was influenced by the same Celtic forms and mysticism as the Macdonalds'. Much of Frances and Herbert MacNair's work became indistinguishable after their marriage.

▶ They organized the 1894 exhibition of their work at the Glasgow School of Art. In 1895, The Four showed their work at 1895 'L'Oeuvre Artistique' in Liège. MacNair showed his jewelry at the 1896 Arts and Crafts Exhibition in London. The MacNairs and the Mackintoshes showed their work at the 1900 (VIII) Vienna Sezession exposition. At the 1902 Turin 'Esposizione Internazionale d'Arte Decorativa Moderna,' the MacNairs exhibited two show tables: one with jewelry made by themselves and the other with enamels by Lily Day, an enamelist and jeweler who taught in the architecture and applied arts department at Liverpool University. The Four also showed in Budapest, Dresden, Munich, and Moscow.

▶ Charlotte Gere, *American and European Jewelry 1830–1914*, New York: Crown, 1975:205. Toni Lesser Wolf, 'Women Jewelers of the British Arts and Crafts Movement,' *Journal of Decorative and Propaganda Arts*, No. 14, Fall 1989:40–41.

Madsen, Askel Bender (1916–)

▶ Danish furniture designer.

▶ Studied furniture design, Kunsthåndværkerskolen, Copenhagen, to 1940, and Det Kongelige Danske Kunstakademie.

▶ 1940–43, he worked for architects Kaare Klint and Arne Jacobsen and, from 1954, was active in decorating in Copenhagen. 1946–54, he taught furniture design at the Kunskhåndværkerskolen. In 1947, he set up his own studio with Ejner Larsen. Much of Madsen's furniture was produced by Willy Beck.

▶ Work first shown in 1943 and subsequently in the Triennali di Milano, 1954–57 USA 'Design in Scandinavia,' 1960–61 USA 'The Arts of Denmark,' and in 1965 at the Gewerbemuseum, Bern.

▶ Frederik Sieck, *Nutidig Dansk Mobeldesign: -en kortfattet illustreret beskrivelse*, Copenhagen: Bondo Gravesen; 1990 Busck edition in English.

Madsen, Eric (1915–)

▶ Danish industrial designer.

▶ Studied engineering.

▶ In 1937, he began working for Bang & Olufsen, where he became chief engineer specializing in acoustics. In 1958, he began development of the firm's first platinum stereo turntable and its tangential pick-up arm. He left Bang & Olufsen in 1975 for Spain, where he studied solar energy.

MAFIA
(Maïmé Arnodin Fayolle International Associées)

▶ French communications and design agency.

▶ MAFIA was founded in Paris in 1968; was active in fields including styling, design, products, packaging, production, public relations, promotion, and film and TV production; originally specialized in fashion and textiles; conceived as well as promoted its own products. Its first big success was Yves Saint-Laurent's *Opium* scent, for which it devised the slogan 'For the addict'; it promoted the fashion and furniture of young designers through mail order, including Issey Miyake, Azzedine Alaïa, and Philippe Starck, none well known at the time.

Maganan, Nicolas
See Naço, Studio.

Maggiori, Bepi (b. Giuseppe Maggiori)

▶ Italian designer and entrepreneur; born Rimini.

▶ Studied architecture in Florence to 1978.

▶ He collaborated with Marco Zanuso Jr designing for several furniture firms. Maggiori and Luigi and Pietro Greppi founded the lighting firm Oceano Oltreluce. From 1982, he wrote on design for *Casa Vogue*. He organized exhibitions including 1982 'Camera Design' in Milan, 1982 'For Sale' in Vienna, 1982–83 'Möbel Perdu' in Hamburg, 1982 'Conseguenze impreviste: art, fashion, design' in Prato, 1983 'Design Balneare' in Cattolica, 1982 'Mobili mobili' in Lerici, and 1983 'Light' in Milan.

▶ He participated in the 1979 (XVI) Triennale di Milano.

▶ Andrea Branzi, *La Casa Calda: Esperienze del Nuovo Disegno Italiano*, Milan: Idea Books, 1982.

Magistretti, Vico (1920–)

▶ Italian architect, furniture and interior designer, and urban planner; born and active Milan.

▶ Studied architecture, Politecnico di Milano, to 1945.

▶ In 1945, he joined his father's studio. Like many postwar designers, he pursued design as well as architecture during Italy's reconstruction period, although at first he was mainly concerned with architecture, town planning, and the interior layouts of buildings. He developed a practice in interior design, industrial design, and town planning, with architecture including the 1955 civic center for Campana (Argentina); 1956 Torre del Parco office building; and 1970 Hispano Olivetti training center in Barcelona. His 1946 bookcase had expanding tubes pressed to floor and ceiling. He designed numerous bookcases, including 1950 ladder-like shelving in 1950, which leaned against a wall. In c1960, he began independently to design consumer products. In c1960, his relationship with Cassina began. His 1963 *Chair 892* for Cassina was part traditional and part Modern, with its rush seat on a brightly stained wooden frame. He was one of the first Italian designers to work in plastics with the 1966 *Stadio* table; the 1969 *Selene* chair, and 1963 *Demetrio*, all for Artemide, followed. His best-known piece, the orange-dyed wood chair 1960 *Crimate*, for the Crimate country club, produced by Cassina, had a rush seat and was reminiscent of 19th-century Italian country chairs. The *Pan* chair and table produced by Cassina was whimsical and less accessible. His 1981 *Sinbad* chair for Cassina was derived from a horse blanket draped over a piece of furniture. Beginning in the 1960s, his clients included B&B Italia, Conran, Knoll, Stendig, Azucena, La Rinascente, De Padova, Montina Fratelli, Poggi, Oca, and Asko. A consultant designer, he worked with only one assistant and architect in his office. His work was widely published and included 1966 *Chimera* light by Artemide, 1967 *Eclisse* table lamp by Artemide, 1970 *Gaudi* and *Vicario* chairs by Artemide, 1973 *Maralunga* chair by Cassina, 1977 *Atollo* lamp by O-Luce, 1980 *Kuta* lamp by O-Luce, 1980 *Nara* lamp by O-Luce, 1980 cutlery by Rossi & Arcadi, 1977 *Nuvola Rossa* folding bookcase by Cassina, 1981 *Kalaari 440* lamp, 1983 *Veranda 3* sofa by Cassina, 1984 *Idomeneo* lamp by O-Luce, 1985 *Edison* table by Cassina, 1986 *Planet* lamp by Venini, 1986 *Cardigan* modular seating by Cassina, 1989 *Silver* aluminum desk chair by De Padova, and 1990 *Campiglia* kitchen system by Schiffini. He was honorary visiting professor, Royal College of Art in London; in 1961, guest professor, Universitario di Architettura, Venice; from 1967, Accademia di San Luca, Rome; in 1975, COAC, Barcelona; in 1986, School of Architecture, Tokyo; taught, Domus Academy, Milan; and other institutions in Brazil, England, and Germany. He was committee member of Edilizia Comune di Milano, competition board member of 1951 (IX) and 1954 (X) Triennali di Milano, member of the technical jury of the 1960 (XII) Triennale, and member of ADI (Associazione per il Disegno Industriale).

▶ From 1948, he participated in almost all the Triennali di Milano, where he received first prize awards at the 1948 (VIII) and 1954 (X) events and a gold medal at 1951 (IX) session. He won the 1957 silver medal at the Comune di Milano, and 1950 Vis prize. Received 1967 (*Eclisse* table lamp), 1973 (*Maralunga* chair), 1977 (*Atollo* lamp), and 1979 (*Gaudí* chair) Premio Compasso d'Oro; 1986 gold medal, Society of Industrial Artists and Designers. Appointed honorary member, Royal College of Art, London, in 1983, and of Royal Incorporation of Architects, Scotland. His work was included in the 1972 'Milano 70/70: Un secolo d'arte' exhibition at the Museo Poldi Pezzoli in Milan, 1972 'Design a Plastické Hmoty' exhibition at the Uměleckoprůmyslové Muzeum in Prague, 1979 'Design Process Olivetti: 1908–1978' exhibition at the Frederick S. Wight Art Gallery in Los Angeles, 1984 'Design Since 1945' exhibition at the Philadelphia Museum of Art, and 1991 'Mobili Italiani 1961–1991: Le Varie Età dei linguaggi' exhibition in Milan.

▶ Cat., Milena Lamarová, *Design a Plastické Hmoty*, Prague: Uměleckoprůmyslové Muzeum, 1972:124. Cat., *Milano 70/70: Un secolo d'arte, Dal 1946 al 1970*, Vol. 3, 1972:304–05. *ADI Annual 1976*, Milan: Associazione per il Disegno Industriale, 1976. Cat., *Design Process Olivetti: 1908–1978*, Los Angeles: Frederick S. Wight Art Gallery, 1979. Alfonso Grassi and Anty Pansera, *Atlante del design italiano: 1940–1980*, Milan, 1980:283. Cat., Kathryn B. Hiesinger and George H. Marcus III (eds.), *Design Since 1945*, Philadelphia: Philadelphia Museum of Art, 1983:220,III–46,IV–25. Robert A.M. Stern (ed.), *The International Design Yearbook*, New York: Abbeville, 1985/1986: Nos. 5,60,189,195. Juli Capella and Quim Larrea, *Designed by Architects in the 1980s*, New York: Rizzoli, 1988. Vanni Pasca, *Vico Magistretti Designer*, New York: Rizzoli, 1990.

Magnussen, Erik   (1884–1961)

▶ Danish metalworker; born and active Copenhagen, Chicago, and Los Angeles.

▶ Trained as a modeler and silversmith; 1907–09, studied Kunstgewerbeschule, Berlin.

▶ He set up his own workshop in Copenhagen in 1909, when his work was influenced, as so many others were in Denmark, by Thorwald Bindesbøll and Georg Jensen. In 1925, he settled in the USA on the invitation of Gorham Manufacturing which wanted a European artist to produce Modern forms. He was its art director until 1929. Magnussen's designs were produced with the soft curves, hammered surfaces, and restrained ornament characteristic of the Danish style. In 1929, he began working for the firm August Dingeldein, which had factories in Germany and a retail store in New York. In 1932 in Chicago, he opened his own workshop and, 1933–38, worked in Los Angeles. When AUDAC (American Union of Decorative Artists and Craftsmen) established a chapter in Chicago in 1932, Magnussen was its vice-president. 1938–39, he designed for the International Silver Company in Meriden, Connecticut. In the 1920s and 1930s, his output was primarily for useful objects, including tea and coffee sets, tazzas, bowls, and other pieces. Though untypical, his best known work was the 1927 *Lights and Shadows of Manhattan* silver coffee service for Gorham with a trapezoid tray and salad set; the silver facets of its Cubist forms were burnished, gilded, and oxidized. In 1939, he returned to Copenhagen and to a more conservative approach.

▶ His work was included in the 1901, 1904, and 1907 exhibitions at Det Kunstindustrimuseet, Copenhagen; 1930 Art Center, New York; 1931 Architectural League, New York; 1922 Salon d'Automne, Paris; 1926, 1927, and 1937 exhibitions at the New York Metropolitan Museum of Art; 1931 and 1937 exhibitions at the Brooklyn Museum, New York.

▶ Charles H. Carpenter Jr., *Gorham Silver: 1831–1981*, New York: Dodd, Mead, 1982. Annelies Krekel-Aalberse, *Art Nouveau and Art Déco Silver*, New York: Abrams, 1989:122,221,257.

Magnussen, Erik   (1940–)

▶ Danish designer; born Copenhagen.

▶ Studied ceramics, Kunsthåndværkerskolen, Copenhagen, to 1960.

▶ He set up his own workshop, where he designed stoneware, glassware, cutlery, tableware, lighting, and furniture for various clients. From 1962, he worked at the Bing & Grøndahl Porcelænsfabrik; in 1975, with Stelton; from c1976–77, with Kevi furniture; and from 1978, as a hollow-ware designer at the Georg Jensen Sølvsmedie in Copenhagen. His designs for Jensen were widely published. His 1968 steel and fabric *Z-stolen* (Z chair) was produced by Torben Ørskov. His 1977 line of water pitchers, teapots, and containers for Stelton were popular. He sought to reduce his designs to essentials, to make pieces interchangeable and stackable, and to lend them temperature-retaining forms. He taught at Det Kongelige Danske Kunstakademi, Copenhagen.

▶ His awards include the 1967 Lunning Prize; 1972 and 1978 ID prize in Denmark; elected 1983 Designer of the Year by Danish Design Council.

▶ Cat., *Georg Jensen Silversmithy: 77 Artists, 75 Years*, Washington: Smithsonian Institution Press, 1980. *Les Carnets du Design*, Paris: Mad-Cap Productions and APCI, 1986:65. Cat., Kathryn B. Hiesinger and George H. Marcus III (eds.), *Design Since 1945*, Philadelphia: Philadelphia Museum of Art, 1983:221,II–39,V–26. 'Thirty-four Lunning Prize-Winners,' *Mobilia*, No. 146, Sept. 1967. Cat., David Revere McFadden (ed.), *Scandinavian Modern Design 1880–1980*, New York: Abrams, 1982:268, Nos. 260,331. Cat., *The Lunning Prize*, Stockholm: Nationalmuseum, 1986:176–79. Jennifer Hawkins Opie, *Scandinavia: Ceramics and Glass in the Twentieth Century*, New York: Rizzoli, 1989.

Magnusson, Gunnar   (1933–)

▶ Icelandic furniture and interior designer.

▶ A foremost Icelandic designer, he furnished public spaces and taught; designed furniture known for exposed construction and overt simplicity.

▶ Cat., David Revere McFadden (ed.), *Scandinavian Modern Design 1880–1980*, New York: Abrams, 1982:268, No. 269.

Magris, Roberto   (1935–)

▶ Italian industrial designer; born and active Florence.

▶ Studied Instituto Universitario di Firenze.

▶ 1955–67, he worked as an industrial and graphic designer and illustrator. In 1967, Magris, Adolfo Natalini, Cristiano Toraldo di Francia, Piero Frassinelli, and brother Alessandro Magris set up Superstudio Design Architettura Ricerca in Florence. Magris designed heavy construction equipment, train cars, exhibition and interior design schemes, ceramics, glassware, and optical equipment. With gruppo 9999, he proposed the Scuola Separata per l'Architettura Concettuale Espansa (S-Space). 1973–75, he was active in Global Tools, an experimental creative collective. He produced a series of films on architecture. Magris was a member of ADI (Associazione per il Disegno Industriale).

▶ His work was included in the 1972 'Italy: The New Domestic Landscape' at the New York Museum of Art, and at the 1973 (XV) Triennale di Milano. 1973–75, an exhibition of Superstudio's work traveled in Europe and the USA.

▶ *ADI Annual 1976*, Milan: Associazione per il Disegno Industriale, 1976.

Maharaja of Indore (Prince Yeshwant Rao Holkar Bahadur) (1900–)

▶ Indian patron and ruler of Indore (now Madhya Pradesh).

▶ Studied Oxford University.

▶ He was introduced to European art at Oxford and, in 1929, befriended Friedrich Eckart Muthesius, son of Hermann Muthesius, founder of the Deutscher Werkbund. In 1925, he was invested as the Maharaja of Indore, where he planned a Modern palace known as Manik Bagh (Garden of Rubies). 1929–33, Muthesius collaborated with Klemens Weigel on the design of the décor, which included the private apartment of the Maharaja, banquet hall, ballroom, many guest suites, and music room. Much of the furniture and lighting was designed by Muthesius, with other furniture by Jacques-Émile Ruhlmann, Le Corbusier and his team, Louis Sognot, Charlotte Alix, and others; with carpets by Bruno Da Silva Bruhns, chandeliers by René Lalique, and silver by Jean Puiforcat. Eileen Gray furnished two *Transat* chairs (one of which sat beside the Maharaja's metal and mirrored bed by Sagnot) and the dramatic *Satellite* chandelier. Three ships filled with furniture, steel doors, and marble sailed from Hamburg for Indore. In 1970, the heirs of the Maharaja were unsuccessful in commissioning Gray to design more furniture for the pool area. Today, Manik Bagh (its contents sold in 1980) is the headquarters of the Ministry of Finance in Indore.

▶ Peter Adam, *Eileen Gray, Architect/Design*, New York: Abrams, 1987:143,187–89.

Maher, George Washington (1864–1926)

▶ American furniture designer.

▶ Apprenticed in the architecture office of Joseph Lyman Silsbee, alongside Frank Lloyd and George Grant Elmslie.

▶ Maher's early work was ornate and monumental; after 1905, he began to work in a less elaborate style, influenced by C.F.A. Voysey. A notable example of this later style was his design for the 1912 'Rockledge' house for E.L. King in Homer, Minnesota, where the principal architectural device was the segmented arch with its short flanges set on canted buttresses. His chairs featured such architectonic features as the arch, guttae, tapered stiles, and wide bases. He included certain architectural devices throughout his houses; his lamps, for example, featured segmented arches, guttae, and stained-glass motifs linking them with the exterior landscape. A Prairie-school architect, he collaborated with Claude & Starck architects in the Wisconsin area; showed awareness of Peter Behrens and others.

▶ Anne Yaffe Phillips, *From Architecture to Object*, New York: Hirschl and Adler, 1989:78.

Mahlau, Alfred (1894–1967)

▶ German painter, poster designer, and theater designer; born Berlin.

▶ Mahlau began working in Lübeck in 1919. In 1940, he returned to Berlin. From 1946, he was a teacher in Hamburg.

Mahler, Marion

▶ British fabrics designer.

▶ Mahler produced designs in the early 1950s for Edinburgh Weavers in Carlisle.

▶ Michael Farr, *Design in British Industry: A Mid-Century Survey*, London: Cambridge, 1955.

Maiakovskaia, Ludmilla Vladimirovna (1884–1963)

▶ Russian textile designer.

▶ 1904–10, studied textile printing, Stroganov School of Applied Art, Moscow.

▶ In 1909, she worked in the silk mill of Muss and was head of the painting workshop at the Manufacture of Prokhorovo under Oskar Griun. 1921–30, she taught at the Vkhutemas and Vkhutein and, from 1931, lectured at the Institute of Textiles in Moscow.

▶ She participated in the 1925 Paris 'Exposition Internationale des Arts Décoratifs et Industriels Modernes.'

▶ Cat., *Kunst und Revolution: Russische und Sowjetische Kunst 1910–1932*, Vienna: Österreichisches Museum für angewandte Kunst, 1988. Cat., *The Great Utopia: The Russian and Soviet Avant-Garde, 1915–1932*, New York: Guggenheim Museum, 1992.

Maierhofer, Fritz (1941–)

▶ Austrian jewelry designer; born Vienna.

▶ He used transparent color and High-Tech components.

▶ Günther Feuerstein, *Vienna–Present and Past: Arts and Crafts–Applied Art–Design*, Vienna: Jugend und Volk, 1976:57,66,80.

Maillol, Aristide (1861–1944)

▶ French sculptor, painter, and ceramicist; born Banyuls-sur-Mer.

▶ Studied painting under Cabanel and Gérôme, and École des Beaux-Arts, Paris.

▶ His painting in the 1880s and 1890s was greatly influenced by Paul Gauguin, Claude Monet, and Pierre Puvis de Chavannes. Associated with the Nabis from 1893, he shared their commitment to the decorative arts and abandoned painting in 1900 for sculpture and tapestry. He dyed his own wools. Maillol established a tapestry studio in Banyuls-sur-Mer; produced sculptures permanently installed in the Jardin des Tuileries, Paris, including *Pomone* (1907), *Île-de-France* (1910), and *Flore* (1911).

▶ Yvonne Brunhammer et al., *Art Nouveau Belgium, France*, Houston: Institute for the Arts, Rice University, 1976.

Mairet, Ethel (b. Ethel Partridge 1872–1952)

▶ British weaver; born Barnstaple, Devon; active Ceylon (now Sri Lanka) and Chipping Campden, Gloucestershire.

▶ 1903–06, she lived in Ceylon, and, 1906–10, in Chipping Campden, where she had close contact with C.R. Ashbee and his Guild of Handicraft. In 1911–12, she began weaving in Taunton. In 1918, she moved to Ditchling, Sussex, where she set up her workshop, Gospels. Eric Gill also worked in Ditchling at the time. Gospels became a meeting place for weavers including Marianne Straub, Margery Kendon, Valentine Kilbride, and, from 1917, Elizabeth Peacock. Mairet sought a fresh educational approach to hand-weaving and to its relationship to power looms. She was particularly knowledgeable about vegetable dyes. The acknowledged leader of the hand-weaving revival in England, she had a keen color sense. Gospels produced a wide range of hand-woven goods known for their excellent hang, drape, and harmonious colors. A prolific writer, her books included *The Dipavamsa and Mahavamsa and their Historical Development in Ceylon* (1908) by E.M. Coomaraswamy (afterwords by Ethel Mairet), *The Future of Dyeing, or, the Conflict Between Science and Art in the Making of Colour* (1915), *A Book on Vegetable Dyes* (1916), *An Essay on Crafts and Obedience* (1918) with husband Philip A. Mairet, *Vegetable Dyes* (1931), *Hand-Weaving To-day, Traditions and Changes* (1939), *Hand Weaving and Education* (1942), and *Handweaving notes for Teachers* (1949).

▶ In 1938, elected Royal Designer for Industry. Her weavings were included in the 1979–80 'Thirties' exhibition at the Hayward Gallery, London.

► Cat., *Thirties: British art and design before the war*, London: Arts Council of Great Britain, Hayward Gallery, 1979:26,92,295,298. Fiona MacCarthy and Patrick Nuttgens, *An Eye for Industry*, London: Lund Humphries, 1986.

Maîtrise, La

► French decorating studio; located Paris.
► La Maîtrise was established in 1922 as the decorating and design studio of the Galeries Lafayette department store in Paris. From its beginning to 1952, it was managed by Maurice Dufrêne. Commissions included apartments and townhouses. Dufrêne's regular collaborators included Suzanne Guiguichon, Gabriel Englinger, Eric Bagge, Fernand Nathan, Geneviève Pons, and Jacques Adnet. Édouard Bénédictus designed tapestries.
► An exhibition of its work was installed at the 1922 Salon d'Automne. Seven rooms were installed in its pavilion at 1925 Paris 'Exposition Internationale des Arts Décoratifs et Industriels Modernes.'
► Guillaume Janneau, 'La Maîtrise,' *La Renaissance de l'Art français et des Industries de luxe*, No. 8, May 1925:221–29. Michael B. Miller, *The Bon Marché: Bourgeois Culture and the Department Store, 1869–1920*, Princeton: Princeton University Press, 1981. Pierre Kjellberg, *Art Déco: les maîtres du Mobilier, le décor des Paquebots*, Paris: Amateur, 1986:119–20.

Majorelle, Louis (1859–1926)

► French designer and cabinetmaker; born Toul.
► From 1877, studied painting in Nancy and École des Beaux-Arts, Paris, under Jean Millet.
► Majorelle took over the family cabinetmaking and ceramics business in Nancy in 1879. In the late 1880s, he began designing Modern furniture. Working in the Art Nouveau style, Majorelle was the most dynamic practitioner of the School of Nancy. By mechanizing his factory, he produced great quantities of highly decorated commercial furniture and more elaborate pieces using expensive materials such as mahogany, burr walnut, and ormolu. The firm's catalog included a wide range of furniture models in both historicist and Art Nouveau styles. Known primarily for his unconventional furniture, he designed pianos, desks, armchairs, and, when his workshop included metalworking, wrought-iron banisters, ormolu, iron mounts, and lighting. He produced the metalwork for Daum, and it produced the glassware for Majorelle's lighting. Majorelle designed lamp bases with cloth shades similar to those of Louis Comfort Tiffany. In 1901, he became vice-president of École de Nancy. After World War I, he moved into the Art Déco idiom with more severe forms and restricted ornamentation. His residence in Nancy was designed by Henri Sauvage. The firm continued after Majorelle's death under the management of Alfred Lévy, its artistic and technical director. In the mid-1930s, Lévy was joined in the Atelier Majorelle by Paul Beucher. The firm had showrooms in Nancy, Paris, and Lyons.
► Work shown at 1903 École de Nancy exhibition, Paris. With Alfred Lévy, he designed the study for the Nancy pavilion at the 1925 Paris 'Exposition Internationale des Arts Décoratifs et Industriels Modernes.'
► Alastair Duncan, *Art Nouveau and Art Déco Lighting*, New York: Simon and Schuster, 1978:83–84. *Éclairage de 1900 à nos jours*, Brussels, L'écuyer, Nos. 42,74. *Le Modern Style*, Paris: Baschet, 1974:176,178. *Revue Lorraine Illustrée*, Vol. 3, 1908:33. J. Bloch-Dermant, *L'Art du Verre en France, 1860–1914*, Paris, 1975:138–43. Jessica Rutherford, *Art Nouveau, Art Deco and the Thirties: The Furniture Collections at Brighton Museum*, Brighton: The Royal Pavilion, Art Gallery and Museums, 1983:14–15. P. Juyot, *Louis Majorelle, Artiste décorateur maître ébéniste*, Nancy, 1927. Yvanhoé Rambosson, 'Majorelle,' *Mobilier et Décoration*, July 1933:284–93. Hugh Honour, *Cabinet Makers and Furniture Designers*, London: Weidenfeld and Nicolson, 1969:258–63. Pierre Kjellberg, *Art Déco: les maîtres du Mobilier, le décor des Paquebots*, Paris: Amateur, 1986:120.

Makepeace, John (1939–)

► British furniture designer.
► Studied Denstone College, Staffordshire, and under Keith Cooper.
► He started designing furniture in 1961. In 1964, he set up a workshop in Farnsborough Barn, Banbury, moving in 1976 to Parnham House in Dorset, where he established the Parnham Trust and School for Craftsmen in Wood in 1977. In 1989, he started training students in product design and development, and to use wood thinning, a waste product.
► Work shown at 1973 'Craftsman's Art,' London; 1982 'The Maker's Eye,' London; 1990 'New Art Forms Exposition,' Chicago; 1991 'Beyond the Dovetail,' London. Work subject exhibitions at New Art Centre, London, 1971, and Fine Art Society, London, 1977.
► Robert A.M. Stern (ed.), *The International Design Yearbook*, New York: Abbeville, 1985/1986: Nos. 182–83. *Decorative Arts Today*, London: Bonhams, 1992: No. 45a.

Maldonado, Tomás (1922–)

► Argentine teacher; born Buenos Aires.
► Maldonado was the design theoretician invited by Max Bill to assume the directorship in 1954 of the Hochschule für Gestaltung in Ulm; he was head of the institution until 1967. 1968–70, he was professor at the School of Architecture of Princeton University; 1971–83, at the University of Bologna; and professor of environmental design, architecture faculty, Milan. 1976–81, he was managing editor of the journal *Casabella*.
► Tomás Maldonado, *Max Bill*, Buenos Aires, 1955. Tomás Maldonado and Gui Bonsiepe, 'Science and Design,' *Ulm*, Vols. 10–11, May 1964:16–18. Tomás Maldonado, *La speranza progettuale*, Turin: Einaudi, 1970. Andrea Branzi, *La Casa Calda: Esperienze del Nuovo Disegno Italiano*, Milan: Idea Books, 1982. Cat., *Hochschule für Gestaltung Ulm . . . Die Moral Der Gegenstände*, Berlin: Bauhausarchiv, 1987:273.

Malevich, Kazimir Severinovich (1878–1935)

► Russian artist artist and designer; born near Kiev.
► 1895–96, studied Kiev Drawing School; 1903, Moscow Institute of Painting, Sculpture, and Architecture.
► 1910–12, he was influenced by Neo-Primitivism, then Cubism and Futurism. In 1913, he participated in the Futurist conference in Uusikirkko (Finland); designed the décor for the Kruchenykh/Matiushin opera *Victory Over the Sun*; and illustrated Futurist booklets, including *Troe (The Three)*, *Porosiata (Piglets)*, and *Vozropshchem (Let's G-r-r-rumble)*. In 1914, he met Marinetti on his arrival in Russia. In 1915, he formalized Suprematism, a version of abstract art where geometrical forms played on white backgrounds; he explained it as 'the supremacy of pure emotion,' and more the theoretical work *Ot kubizma i futurizma k suprematizmu: Novyi zhivopisnyi realizm (From Cubism and Futurism to Suprematism: The New Painterly Realism)*. In 1918, he was involved in Izo NKP (Fine Arts Department at Narkompros); published the tract *O novykh sistemakh v iskusstve (On New Systems in Art)* in Vitebsk, where he took over the directorship of the art school from Marc Chagall after the Revolution; and founded Posnovis/Unovis, around which talented students gathered, including Il'ia Chashnik, El Lissitzky, and Nikolai Suetin. In 1920, he designed covers for *Tsikl lektsii (Cycle of Lectures)* by Nikolai Punin. Moving to Petrograd with some of his students, in 1922 he set up a branch of Inkhuk. His ceramics were made by the Lomonosov factory, where Suetin worked. In the 1920s, he produced architectural models and textile and porcelain designs. In 1927, he visited Warsaw and Berlin, where his 1927 one-person exhibition was authorized by the Soviet government; anticipating the fate of the Soviet avant-garde, he entrusted his archives to his German friends, together with the approximately 70 works shown. The note accompanying the exhibition, known as Malevich's Testament read 'In case I die or am innocently imprisoned . . . .' Malevich visited the Bauhaus in 1927: the school subsequently published his book *The Non-Objective World*. His painting style

became more figurative from 1930, and in some cases portrayed political subjects such as Working Woman, The Smith, and Red Calvary. In 1930, his property was confiscated and he was held for a time as a German spy.

▶ He participated in Larionov's Jack of Diamonds exhibition of c1912. 1911–17, he contributed to numerous avant-garde exhibitions, including 'Donkey's Tail,' '0–10' (the first public showing of Suprematist works), and 'The Store.' In 1919, he contributed to the 'Tenth State Exhibition: Non-Objective Creation and Suprematism' and to numerous other exhibitions in the 1920s in Russia and abroad. His work was shown in a 1927 one-person exhibition in Warsaw and Berlin. His work was the subject of the 1990–91 traveling exhibition in the USA organized by the National Gallery of Art, Washington.

▶ Kasimir Malevich, *The Non-Objective World*, Chicago, 1959. Troels Andersen, *Malevich*, Amsterdam, 1970. Stephanie Barron and Maurice Tuchman, *The Avant-Garde in Russia, 1910–1930*, Cambridge, MA:MIT Press, 1980:194. Lorissa A. Zhadova, *Malevich: Suprematism and Revolution in Russian Art, 1910–1930*, London, 1982. Cat., John Bowlt, *Kazimir Malevich 1878–1935*, Washington: Smithsonian Institution, 1990. Igor Golomstock, *Totalitarian Art in the Soviet Union, The Third Reich, Fascist Italy and the People's Republic of China*, New York: Icon, 1990:66. Cat., *The Great Utopia: The Russian and Soviet Avant-Garde, 1915–1932*, New York: Guggenheim Museum, 1992.

Malimpensa, Giuliano (1949–)
▶ Italian designer; born Cadorago, Como.
▶ In 1980, he set up his own studio in Cadorago; had clients including Riedel and Kufstein & Mesa, both Cadorago.
▶ Hans Wichmann, *Italien Design 1945 bis heute*, Munich: Die Neue Sammlung, 1988.

Malinowski, Arno (1899–1976)
▶ Danish sculptor and metalworker.
▶ 1919–22, studied Det Kongelige Danske Kunstakademi, Copenhagen. From 1914–19, Malinowski was an apprentice under Danish Royal Court engraver S. Lindahl.
▶ From 1921–35, he executed figurines for the Royal Copenhagen Porcelain Manufactory and decorated others forms, including those of designer Christian Joachim. From 1934–39, he taught at the Kunsthåndværkerskolen, Copenhagen. 1936–65, he designed jewelry for the Georg Jensen Sølvsmedie in Copenhagen, including the medal produced by Jensen for the 70th birthday of King Christian X that was worn by thousands of Danes during World War II and became a patriotic symbol.
▶ He received a silver medal at the 1925 Paris 'Exposition Internationale des Arts Décoratifs et Industriels Modernes' and the 1933 Eckersberg Medal.
▶ Cat., *Georg Jensen Silversmithy: 77 Artists, 75 Years*, Washington: Smithsonian Institution Press, 1980. Cat., David Revere McFadden (ed.), *Scandinavian Modern Design 1880–1980*, New York: Abrams, 1982:268, No. 76. Jennifer Hawkins Opie, *Scandinavia: Ceramics and Glass in the Twentieth Century*, New York: Rizzoli, 1989.

Malinowski, Ruth (1928–)
▶ Austrian textile designer; active Denmark and Sweden.
▶ Studied Kunsthåndværkerskolen, Copenhagen.
▶ In 1958, she set up her own workshop in Reftele (Sweden). Her textiles were woven in simple, flat-woven geometric patterns in a painterly style.
▶ Her work was the subject of the one-person exhibitions at the Nationalmuseum in Stockholm in 1968, the Röhsska Konstslöjdmuseet in Gothenburg in 1969, and Det Danske Kunstindustrimuseum in Copenhagen in 1977.
▶ Cat., David Revere McFadden (ed.), *Scandinavian Modern Design 1880–1980*, New York: Abrams, 1982:268, No. 269.

Mallet-Stevens, Robert (1886–1945)
▶ French architect and designer; born and active Paris.
▶ 1905–10, studied École Spéciale d'Architecture, Paris.

▶ He made his name at the 1913 Salon d'Automne by designing a hall and music room notable for their vibrant color, purity, and clarity. He used geometric shapes for his furniture in painted metal and nickel-plated tubular steel, and was the first architect to introduce the new concepts of simplification and Functionalism to the rich tastes of France. He was influenced by Josef Hoffmann's crusade against the excesses of Art Nouveau, and wrote about his views in a series of articles in the 1911–12 issues of reviews *le Home, Tekné, Lux*, and *L'Art Ménager*. In 1922, he published the portfolio of architecture drawings *Une Cité Moderne* with preface by Frantz Jourdain; from 1923, with Ludwig Mies van der Rohe and Theo van Doesburg, was associated with the journal *L'Architecture moderne*; from 1924, he taught at the École Spéciale d'Architecture in Paris. Influenced by Cubism, Charles Rennie Mackintosh, and Hoffmann, his structures were severely geometrical with intricate planes, rectangular solids, and white stucco surfaces, he was rigorously opposed to all superfluous decorations. Mallet-Stevens's notable designs include the 1925 Alfa Romeo showroom in the rue Marbeuf, Paris. Film-maker Marcel L'Herbier hired Mallet-Stevens, Pierre Chareau, art directors Alberto Cavalcanti and Claude Autant-Lara, artist Fernand Léger, and furniture designer Pierre Chareau to participate in the film *L'Inhumaine* (1923–24); its ultra-Modern design was shocking to audiences accustomed to neoclassical settings. Mallet-Stevens went on to create sets for films *Le Vertige* (1926), *Jettatura, Le Secret de Rosette Lambert*, and *La Singulière aventure de Neil Hogan, jockey*. His maquettes and film sets offered a platform for experimentation. Mallet-Stevens designed the 1924–33 villa (and some of its furnishings) for the vicomte and vicomtesse de Noailles in Hyères, along with associates Francis Jourdain, Édouard-Joseph Bourgeois, Pierre Chareau, Blanche Klotz, and others as collaborators. Mallet-Stevens with Paul Ruaud designed the 1924 villa (unrealized) of Jacques Doucet at Marly. Mallet-Stevens took over the unfinished Château Yvelines (due to Paul Poiret's bankruptcy) in Mezy. He designed the 1926 Collinet townhouse in Boulogne and 1928 casino at St.-Jean-de-Luz. Other works included the late-1920s Café du Brésil in the avenue de Wagram in Paris, 1928–29 office of the periodical *Semaine à Paris* (with stained-glass windows by Louis Barillet), 1930 apartment house (where Tamara de Lempicka had a studio) in the rue Méchain in Paris, the 1935 firehouse-barracks in the rue Mesnil, and various stores and a distillery in Istanbul. His most complete complex is a group of white buildings along rue Mallet-Stevens, Paris, in 1927. The houses included one for himself (No. 12) and a studio for the Martel twins (No. 10), with whom he often worked. (The studio was occupied by Shiro Kuramata until his death.) He frequently used tubular steel in his furniture designs, which were painted bright colors as well as white and light green. His tubular steel side chair with a curved metal back and vertical flat stays, reproduced by Écart International, has become an icon of 20th-century design, appearing most often in dining rooms and restaurants. Others of his furniture models have only been reproduced from the 1980s. Only for the Villa Cavrois in Crois did he create all the furniture designs alone. His early lighting designs were produced by Baguès, Fabre, and Martine with subsequent work by André Salomon's firm Perfécla. With Salomon, he executed wall and ceiling lighting for Paul Poiret's shop and the entrance hall to the 1930 exhibition of the Union des Artistes Modernes. For his own Auteuil residence, he commissioned Chareau and Jourdain to execute various lighting models; two of Chareau's alabaster slab chandeliers hung from the living-room ceiling, and Jourdain's four-armed ceiling light was mounted in the vestibule. In 1946, UAM members established the Club Mallet-Stevens as an information center on art and Modern architecture.

▶ He showed his furniture at the 1912, 1913, and 1914 Paris Salons d'Automne, including projects, drawings and models, dining room, garden furniture, town houses, concert halls, boutiques, and villas. He organized an exhibition in 1924 that combined the works of the De Stijl designers, Chareau, and Jourdain. At the 1925 Paris 'Exposition Internationale des Arts Décoratifs et Industriels Modernes,' Mallet-Stevens designed the tourism pavilion for the garden of the Habitation Moderne, planted with Cubist trees in reinforced concrete designed by the Martel brothers and painted by Sonia Delaunay, and 'Une Ambassade française,' in the hall of which he hung paintings by Robert Delaunay and Fernand Léger. As a founding member of the Union des Artistes Modernes in 1929 and its first president, he showed at all its exhibitions from 1930. The apex of his career was the execution of five pavilions at the 1937 Paris 'Exposition Internationale des Arts et Techniques dans la Vie Moderne,' including the Pavillons d'Hygiène, Electricité, Solidarité nationale, and Tabac, and Café du Brésil pavilion. At the 1935 (III) Salon de la Lumière, he showed a series of illuminated balloons, hung axially above the river Seine at the 1937 Exposition.

▶ Léon Moussinac, *Mallet-Stevens*, Paris: G. Crès, 1931. 'Architecture Moderne,' *L'Architecture d'aujourd'hui*, No. 8, 1932. Victor Arwas, *Art Déco*, Abrams, 1980. Cat., *Rob Mallet-Stevens Architecte*, Brussels: Archives d'Architecture Moderne, 1980. Pierre Cabanne, *Encyclopédie Art Déco*, Paris: Somogy, 1986:215–17. Alastair Duncan, *Art Nouveau and Art Déco Lighting*, New York: Simon and Schuster, 1978:178. Jean Claude Delorme and Philippe Chair, *L'École de Paris: 10 architectes et leur immeubles, 1905–1937*, Paris, 1981:61–70. *Restaurants, dancing, cafés, bars*, Paris: Charles Moreau, Nos. 32–34, 1929. Arlette Barré-Despond, *UAM*, Paris: Regard, 1986:458–65. Cat., *Les années UAM 1929–1958*, Paris: Musée des Arts Décoratifs, 1988:224–25. Jean-François Pinchon (ed.), *Rob Mallet-Stevens, Architecture, Mobilier, Décoration*, Paris: Philippe Sers Editeur, 1986; English ed., Cambridge: MIT, 1990.

Malmsten, Carl   (b. Charley Per Hendrik Malmsten 1888–1972)

▶ Swedish furniture and textile designer and maker.
▶ Studied Pahlmanns Handelsinstitut and Hogskolan, Stockholm; in 1910, economics in Lund; 1910–12, trained under cabinetmaker Per Jönsson in Stockholm; 1912–15, handicrafts and architecture under Carl Bersten in Stockholm.
▶ He was a freelance furniture and interior designer in Stockholm and, 1916–19, was active in his own workshops at Tunnelgatan; 1919–22, at Arbertargatan; 1940–50, at Krukmakargatan; and, 1950–72, at Renstiernagatan. Malmsten used Gustavian forms in his chairs, wooden sofas and small tables, creating austere rooms anticipating the Swedish Modern style. He included elements of late 18th-century paintings, experimenting with paint finishes. Until 1923, he worked at Stockholm Town Hall. He designed the 1924–25 Stockholm Concert Hall. In 1928, he founded the Olof School in Stockholm, where he was director until 1941. In 1945, he founded the Nyckelvik School for handicrafts and folk art in Stockholm and subsequently the Capellagården School for creative work in Vickelby.
▶ He won first and second prizes for furniture design at the 1916 event at the Stockholm Town Hall, the 1926 Litteris et Artibus Medal, and 1945 Prince Eugen Medal. His work was shown at the 1917 Blanchs Konstsalon exhibition in Stockholm, 1923 and 1956 exhibitions in Gothenburg, Swedish pavilion at the 1925 Paris 'Exposition Internationale des Arts Décoratifs et Industriels Modernes,' and 1939 'New York World's Fair.' His work was the subject of the 1944 retrospective at the Nationalmuseum in Stockholm.
▶ Cat., David Revere McFadden (ed.), *Scandinavian Modern Design 1880–1980*, New York: Abrams, 1982:268, No. 95. Stephen Calloway, *Twentieth-Century Decoration*, New York: Rizzoli, 1988:131,144,286.

Malmström, August   (1829–1901)

▶ Swedish ceramicist.
▶ 1849–56, studied painting, Kungliga Konsthögskolan, Stockholm; 1857–58, in Paris; 1859–60, in Italy.
▶ From 1867, he taught at the Kungliga Konsthögskolan and subsequently became director. 1868–74, he was a designer at Gustavsberg, where he and Daniel J. Carlsson revived traditional

Viking designs. Carlsson rendered the decoration on Malmström's forms.
▶ Cat., David Revere McFadden (ed.), *Scandinavian Modern Design 1880–1980*, New York: Abrams, 1982:268, No. 2.

Maloof, Sam   (1916–)

▶ American furniture designer and maker; born Chino, California; active California.
▶ Self-taught.
▶ In 1934, Maloof began to work as a graphic artist, Padua Hills Theater; worked for industrial designer Harold Graham in Clermont, California, designing interior displays for Bullock's department store, Los Angeles; 1947, worked with Millard Sheets; in 1948, established independent furniture workshop; c1948, received first furniture commission, a suite for the home of industrial designer Henry Dreyfuss; from c1945–50, received furniture commissions from interior designer Kneedler-Fouchere; in 1953, settled in Alta Loma, California, where he built a workshop in 1954 and is still active today; in 1959, worked as designer, woodworker, and technician for Dave Chapman Inc, Chicago, Illinois, as a consultant on a USA State Department project in Lebanon and El Salvador.
▶ In 1948, work shown for the first time, Los Angeles County (California) Fair and subject of 1976 'Please Be Seated,' Museum of Fine Arts, Boston, Massachusetts. At American Crafts Council, was craftsman-trustee from 1973–76, named fellow in 1975, became a trustee in 1979.
▶ Film, William Kayden, *On the Go*, NBC, 1959. Film, *Sam Maloof, Woodworker*, Maynard Orme producer, 1973. Julie Hall, *Tradition and Change: The New American Craftsman*, New York: Dutton, 1977. Film, Barbaralee Diamondstein, *Handmade in America*, ABC, 1982. Film, *Sam Maloof: The Rocking Chair*, Bob Smith producer, 1983. *Sam Maloof, Woodworker*, Tokyo: Kodansha, 1983. Auction cat., 'Contemporary Works of Art,' Sotheby's New York, 14 March 1992.

Maly, Peter   (1936–)

▶ German designer.
▶ Clients included Cor, Germany, for whom he designed 1984 *Zyklus* chair, and Ligne Roset, France, for whom he designed numerous pieces of furniture, including 1983 *Maly* bed.

MAM
See Mobilier Artistique Moderne

Mamontov, Elizabeth   (1847–1909) and **Savva Mamontov**   (1841–1918)

▶ Russian industrialists and patrons of the arts.
▶ The Mamontovs originally attempted to form a private opera company with a group of artists, musicians, and critics that they persuaded to come to Abramtsevo. They expanded the concept into a center for the rejuvenation of Russian popular art, teaching crafts to Russian peasants. The participants included Korovin, Vrubel, and Vastnetsov, all contributors to Modernism in Russia. The writings of William Morris and John Ruskin were the basis of the approach.

Mandrot, Hélène de
See de Mandrot, Hélène

Mangiarotti, Angelo   (1921–)

▶ Italian designer; born and active Milan.
▶ Studied architecture, Politecnico di Milano, to 1948.
▶ He was guest professor, Institute of Design, Illinois Institute of Technology, Chicago, where Ludwig Mies van der Rohe was director; had a design office in Ohio; in 1955, returned to Italy, active as architect, designer, and teacher; was a member of ADI (Associazione per il Disegno Industriale); 1955–60, collaborated in a consultant design office in Milan with Bruno Morassutti and, from 1960, worked alone in the fields of architecture, design, and town planning, emphasizing industrial production solutions. His

buildings were in the International Style, with construction elements resembling those of Pier Luigi Nervi. Mangiarotti produced prefabricated structures, primarily in reinforced concrete. His design work included the 1962 *Secticon* clock for Portescap, an example of how, during this period, Italians combined sculpture with a rational approach to function. His 1963 chair produced by Cassina was an example of his concern for strong plastic silhouettes in everyday objects. He designed collapsible furniture, glassware, and metalware, including silverware for Cleto Munari and marble pieces for Knoll. His 1969 *IN* chair, produced by Zanotta, was self-surfaced in one-piece molded multi-density polyurethane. Other design work included faïence tableware by Danese, 1981 *Asolo* table by Skipper, 1982 *Estrual* bookcase by Skipper, 1983 vases by Cleto Munari, range of marble tables and 1984 *Terra Blanca* table by Skipper, 1984 tea-and-coffee service by Cleto Munari, 1985 *Ganci* lamp by Skipper, 1986 *La Badoera* table by Poltronova, 1986 *Pericle* lamp by Artemide, 1988 *First Glass* vase by Colle, and 1988 *More* table by Skipper. He collaborated with Matomi Kawakami and, in 1970, was a visiting instructor at the University of Hawaii. 1982–84, taught at the Facoltà di Architettura, Palermo and Florence. His buildings included the 1957 Mater Misericordiae church in Baranzate, near Milan; 1963 exhibition pavilion for the Fiera del Mare in Genoa; 1964 workshop hall of the Società Elmag in Lissone, near Monza; and 1968 administration and factory building in Cinisello Balsamo, near Milan.

▶ His work was shown at various Triennali di Milano and 1970 'Modern Chairs 1918–1970' exhibition, Whitechapel Gallery, London. His *Secticon* clock was included in the 1983–84 'Design Since 1945' exhibition at the Philadelphia Museum of Art, and *More* table in the 1991 'Mobili Italiani 1961–1991: Le Varie Età dei linguaggi' exhibition at the Salone del Mobile in Milan. He received a number of national awards for architectural work.

▶ *Angelo Mangiarotti*, Tokyo, 1965. 'Angelo Mangiarotti,' *Architecture and Urbanism*, Sept. 1974. Giulia Veronesi, *Mangiarotti (1962–1963): Profili*, Florence, 1969. D.E. Bona, *Angelo Mangiarotti*, Milan, 1979. Enrico D. Bona, *Angelo Mangiarotti: Il processo del costruire*, Milan, 1980. *Architectural Digest*, March 1964. Cat., *Modern Chairs 1918–1970*, London: Lund Humphries, 1971. Cat., Kathryn B. Hiesinger and George H. Marcus III (eds.), *Design Since 1945*, Philadelphia: Philadelphia Museum of Art, 1983:221, I–22. Gillo Dorfles, *Il disegno industriale e la sua estetica*, Bologna, 1963, figs. 67–71,68–81. Andrea Branzi and Michael De Lucchi (eds.), *Il design italiano degli anni '50*, Milan, 1981:72,104, 106,264,267,274. Axel Menges in Vittorio Magnago Lampugnani (ed.), *Encyclopedia of 20th-Century Architecture*, New York: Abrams, 1986:210–11. Juli Capella and Quim Larrea, *Designed by Architects in the 1980s*, New York, Rizzoli, 1988.

Manship, Paul Howard (1885–1966)

▶ American sculptor.

▶ Manship was influenced by Hindu and Buddhist Indian sculpture. Grace Rainey Rogers commissioned the artist to produce the 1934 Paul J. Rainey memorial gateway of the New York Zoological Park, Bronx Zoo, New York; to complete the assignment, he worked with five assistants in Paris and New York for five years; worked in a refined Streamline style; achieved great success in the creation of public monuments; best known for the gilded-bronze *Prometheus* (1933) at Rockefeller Center Plaza, New York; was an accomplished portraitist; basing his work on archaic sculpture, was known as an academic artist only after 1940.

▶ Albert E. Gallatin, *Paul Manship: A Critical Essay on his Sculpture and an Iconography*, 1917. Paul Vitry, *Paul Manship, Sculpteur Américain*, 1927. Edwin Murtha, *Paul Manship*, 1957. Cat., *Paul Howard Manship: An Intimate View*, St. Paul: Minnesota Museum of Art, 1972. Cat., *Paul Manship: Changing Taste in America*, St. Paul: Minnesota Museum of Art, 1985. Cat., *Modern Times: Aspect of American Art, 1907–1956*, New York: Hirschl and Adler Galleries, 1986. Susan E. Menconi, *Uncommon Spirit: Sculpture in America 1800–1940*, New York: Hirschl and Adler Galleries, 1989:76–85. John Manship, *Paul Manship*, New York: Abbeville, 1989.

Mantelet, Jean

▶ French industrial designer.

▶ Mantelet founded the Moulinex firm in 1937 and designed its *Moulin à légumes* (vegetable chopper). Moulinex continues to be innovative in the production of domestic appliances; Jean-Louis Barrault was head of its design department.

Manzali, Giorgio (1941–)

▶ Italian teacher, painter, sculptor, architect, and designer; born and active Ferrara.

▶ in 1961, he turned from teaching painting to work as a painter, sculptor, and architect. He worked on urban planning, interior architecture, and furniture projects in the studio Bichy in Vicenza, and designed furniture produced by Art & Form, tables by Amar, and a range of furniture by Junior Mobili. He was a member of ADI (Associazione per il Disegno Industriale).

▶ His *Saffo* living-room furniture range produced by Art & Form was shown at furniture fairs in Milan, Paris, and Cologne.

▶ *ADI Annual 1976*, Milan: Associazione per il Disegno Industriale, 1976.

Manzini, Ezio

▶ Italian teacher.

▶ Studied architecture and engineering.

▶ Manzini was associate professor of architecture at the Politecnico di Milano and director of design at the Domus Academy in Milan. He published the books *Materials of Invention* (1989) and *Artefatti* (1992).

Manzù, Pio (1939–69)

▶ Italian designer.

▶ Studied Hochschule für Gestaltung, Ulm.

▶ He designed automobiles, taxis, and tractors for Fiat; lighting and appliances; packaging for Olivetti; and wrote for *Form, Industrial Design, Style Auto*, and *Interiors*. He designed the *Parentesi* lamp, completed in the late 1970s by Achille Castiglioni.

▶ Work (*Parentesi* lamp) received 1979 Compasso d'Oro. Work (*Parentesi* lamp) shown at 1983–84 'Design Since 1945' exhibition, Philadelphia Museum of Art; (1968 battery plastic clock by Italora) at 'Italy: The New Domestic Landscape,' New York Museum of Modern Art.

▶ Cat., Kathryn B. Hiesinger and George H. Marcus III (eds.), *Design Since 1945*, Philadelphia: Philadelphia Museum of Art, 1983:221,IV-12. Alfonso Grassi and Anty Pansera, *Atlante del design italiano: 1940–1980*, Milan, 1980:91,177,244,305.

Mappin and Webb

▶ British silversmiths; located Sheffield.

▶ Mappin and Webb was founded in 1863. Until 1935, A. Hatfield was its chief designer. In the 1930s, the firm produced Modern silver designed by A.E. Harvey, Keith Murray, and James Warwick. Modern silver remained a sideline; the firm continued to produce Art Nouveau and Arts and Crafts style silver.

▶ Annelies Krekel-Aalberse, *Art Nouveau and Art Déco Silver*, New York: Abrams, 1989:18,32,34,35,257.

Marangoni, Alberto (1943–)

▶ Italian designer; active Milan.

▶ Studied Accademia di Belle Arti di Brera, Milan, to 1964.

▶ He began his professional career in 1964 working on graphic and industrial design in the studio MID in Milan. In 1967, he became a member of ADI (Associazione per il Disegno Industriale), participating in its guidance committee in 1973. 1971–73, he taught graphic design at the Società Umanitaria. His clients included Anic, Borsa Valori, Ciba Geigy, Falk, Fratelli Fabbri Editori, Ferrania, Honeywell, IBM Italia, Ideal Standard, Liquigas, Mondadori, 3M Italia, Pierrel, Profina, Rizzoli, Università di Pavia, and Citroën Italia. He designed museum exhibitions for clients including IBM Italia.

▶ He participated in the 1968 (XIV) Triennale di Milano, 1968 'BIO 3' Industrial Design Biennial in Ljubljana, 1968 'Maggio Mus-

icale Fiorentino' in Florence, and 1967 Biennial of International Graphics in Warsaw.
▶ *ADI Annual 1976*, Milan: Associazione per il Disegno Industriale, 1976.

Marblehead Pottery
▶ American pottery; located Marblehead, Massachusetts.
▶ Herbert J. Hall established the Marblehead Pottery in 1904 as one of several 'handcraft shops' providing occupational therapy for 'nervously worn out patients.' The shops produced handweaving, woodcarving, and metalwork, with pottery being the most successful. Hall hired Arthur Eugene Baggs, a student at Alfred University, New York State School of Clay-Working and Ceramics; by 1908, the Marblehead Pottery was producing almost 200 pieces a week, including vases, decorated tiles, and jardinières. Staff members were Arthur Irwin Hennessey, Maude Milner, and Hannah Tutt; the kiln person was E.J. Lewis and the thrower John Swallow. A combination of brick clay from Massachusetts and stoneware clay from New Jersey was used. The pottery moved from workrooms at the Devereux mansion of Dr. Hall to 111 Front Street, Marblehead. Baggs took over ownership of the pottery in 1916. From the 1920s, Baggs was there only in the summer and, 1925–28, was a glaze chemist at the Cowan Art Pottery Studio, near Cleveland, Ohio. 1928–47, he was a professor at Ohio State University. Marblehead Pottery closed in 1936.
▶ Arthur E. Baggs, 'The Story of a Potter,' *Handicrafter*, No. 1, April–May 1929:8–10. *Marblehead Pottery*, Marblehead: Marblehead Potteries, 1919. 'The Pottery at Marblehead: The exquisite Work Produced on the Massachusetts Coast,' *Arts and Decoration*, No. 1, Sept. 1911:448–49. Elizabeth Russell, 'The Pottery of Marblehead,' *House Beautiful*, No. 59, March 1926:362,364,366. *American Art Pottery*, New York: Cooper-Hewitt Museum, 1987:124.

Marcato, Stefano
▶ Italian designer.
▶ Studied Instituto Universitario di Architettura, Venice, to 1978
▶ In 1978, he began working in restoration and designing domestic furnishings. He collaborated with glassworks in Murano. In 1980, he began designing for PAF, which produced his 1984 *Maia* lamp.

Marchetti, Sergio   (1944–)
▶ Italian industrial and graphic designer; born Molini di Triora; active Milan.
▶ Marchetti began his professional career in 1971. His work included furniture and domestic electrical appliances. His clients in Italy included DCF, Mercury, Ready, Sabo, Vesta, Formapiù, Mobilsed, and Veneta Arredamenti. He was a member of ADI (Associazione per il Disegno Industriale).
▶ *ADI Annual 1976*, Milan: Associazione per il Disegno Industriale, 1976.

Marcks, Gerhard   (1889–1981)
▶ German sculptor and potter; born Berlin.
▶ Studied sculpture under Georg Kolbe and Richard Scheibe, and in Paris.
▶ He was a member of the November-Gruppe in Berlin. In 1918, with Walter Gropius, he became a member of the Arbeitsrat für Kunst. He taught at the Kunstgewerbeschule in Berlin. In 1919, Marcks was appointed by Gropius as *Formmeister* of the production workshop in the ceramics annex of the Bauhaus in Dornburg. Much of Marcks's design during the Dornburg period was ornate and archaic; it later became innovative. His *Kaffeemaschine* of 1925 produced by Schott & Gen. Jenaer Glaswerke illustrated an understanding of materials and mass production processes. After leaving the Bauhaus in 1925, he taught at the school of applied arts in Halle; when the Nazis took power, the school's activities were suspended. After World War II, he taught in Hamburg. The Gerhard Marcks Foundation was established in 1971 in Bremen.

▶ He created the sculpture for the main entrance of Walter Gropius's installation at the 1914 Cologne 'Deutscher Werkbund-Ausstellung.'
▶ Lionel Richard, *Encyclopédie du Bauhaus*, Paris: Somogy, 1985: 158. Cat., Marlina Rudloff (ed.), *Gerhard Marcks 1889–1981*, Cologne, Berlin, Bremen, 1987. Cat., *The Bauhaus: Masters and Students*, New York: Barry Friedman, 1988.

Marcot, Alain
▶ French interior architect.
▶ Studied École des Arts Décoratifs, Nice, and École Nationale Supérieure des Arts Décoratifs, Paris.
▶ He was an instructor and vice-president of the École Nationale Supérieure des Arts Décoratifs. A freelancer from 1977, he was an associate in the Cabinet Concepteurs Associés.
▶ He won several awards including the Formica prize in 1966 and the Prix Révélations CREAC UNIFA in 1969.
▶ Robert A.M. Stern (ed.), *The International Design Yearbook*, New York: Abbeville, 1985/1986: No. 173.

Marcoussis, Louis   (1883–1941)
▶ Polish painter and textile designer; born Warsaw; active Paris.
▶ In the 1920s, Marcoussis designed rugs for couturier Jacques Doucet, and painted in a Cubist style.

Mare, André   (1887–1932)
▶ French painter, decorator, and furniture designer; born Argentan; active Paris.
▶ Studied painting, Académie Julian, Paris.
▶ 1903–04, he shared a studio with Fernand Léger; from c1911, he worked closely with Roger de la Fresnaye. The decorative arts began showing up in his work submitted to the annual Salons in Paris, although he considered himself primarily a painter at the time. With architect Louis Süe, he began designing furniture in 1910 in the workshop Atelier français on the rue de Courcelles in Paris. He produced radical Cubist furniture designs for Raymond Duchamp-Villon's Maison Cubiste at the 1912 Salon d'Automne. Some time before 1914, he began bookbinding, preferring vellum and parchment and using a vivid palette akin to the Ballets Russes sets and costumes and German avant-garde painting, although his motifs were influenced by Louis-Philippe decoration. His bindings included covers for *Le Temple de Gnide*, *Les Fioretti*, *La Nuit Vénitienne*, *Les Jardins*, and *Des Voyages et des parfums*. During World War I, his wife Charlotte executed his furniture, rug, and fabric designs while he served in the armed forces. In 1919, with Louis Süe and Gustave Jaumes, he decorated the cenotaph beneath the Arc de Triomphe for the 'Fêtes de la Victoire.' By 1918, Mare and Süe had begun their association under the name Belle France in the avenue Friedland in Paris and, in 1919, set up as interior designers in the firm Compagnie des Arts Français (CAF) at 116 rue du Faubourg Saint-Honoré. They designed the costumes and sets for the 1921 production of Maurice Ravel's *L'Heure Espagnole* at the Opéra de Paris. At CAF, they drew on the talents of friends including Maurice Marinot and André Marty to take on any aspect of interior design. Other collaborators included Marie Laurencin, André Derain, and Raoul Dufy. Süe's and Mare's furniture was distinguished by deep curves, carved garlands, contrasting woods, and gilded bronze panels; its inspiration was derived from the style of the Louis Philippe period. They designed lighting and *objets d'art*. In 1921, a portfolio of their work and projects with text by Paul Valéry was published as *Architecture*. With Léandre Vaillat, Süe published *Rythme de l'Architecture* (1923), and Jean Badovici issued *Intérieurs de Süe et Mare* (1924). Mare managed the interior decoration activities of the firm and the execution in 1910–12 of several ensembles of furniture. In the 1920s, Süe and Mare designed silver for Orfèvrerie Christofle and Tétard Frères. The team designed interiors for several oceanliners and the shop in Paris in 1925 for d'Orsay perfume, including its flacon. Clients included Helena Rubinstein and Jean Patou. 1927–28, they constructed and furnished the villa of the actress Jane Renouard at Saint-Cloud. In 1928, Jacques Adnet took

over as director of design at CAF, Süe returned to architecture while continuing to decorate, and Mare returned to painting.

▶ 1903–04, he first exhibited his work in the Salons in Paris. Mare showed the decorations and furnishings of the Maison Cubiste conceived by Raymond Duchamp-Villon at the 1912 Salon d'Automne. Süe and Mare designed two pavilions for the 1925 Paris 'Exposition Internationale des Arts Décoratifs et Industriels Modernes,' one for CAF and the other for the Musée des Arts Contemporains, and had work included in the pavilions for Christofle and Baccarat. Work was subject of 'André Mare et la Compagnie des Arts français (Süe et Mare),' Ancienne Douane Strasbourg, 1971.

▶ Annelies Krekel-Aalberse, *Art Nouveau and Art Déco Silver*, New York: Abrams, 1989:15,67,257. Tony Bouilher, *L'Orfèvrerie français au 20ème siècle*, Paris, 1941. Victor Arwas, *Art Déco*, Abrams, 1980. Pierre Cabanne, *Encyclopédie Art Déco*, Paris: Somogy, 1986:235–39. Alastair Duncan and Georges de Bartha, *Art Nouveau and Art Déco Bookbinding*, New York: Abrams, 1989: 17,21,126–27,193–94. Ami Chantre, 'Les Reliures d'André Mare,' *L'Art Décoratif*, July–Dec. 1913:251–58. Cat., *Un Demi-Siècle de reliures d'art contemporain en France et dans le monde*, Paris: Bibliothèque Forney, 1984. Alastair Duncan, *Art Deco Furniture*, London and New York, 1984:166–68. Gaston Quénioux, *Les Arts Décoratifs modernes 1918–1925*, Paris, 1925:345–46. Raymond Foulk, *The Extraordinary Work of Süe and Mare*, London: The Foulk Lewis Collection, 1979. Margaret Mary Malone, 'André Mare and the 1912 Maison Cubiste,' MA thesis, University of Texas at Austin, 1980. Jessica Rutherford, *Art Nouveau, Art Deco and the Thirties: The Furniture Collections at Brighton Museum*, Brighton: The Royal Pavilion, Art Gallery and Museums, 1983:44–45. Pierre Kjellberg, *Art Déco: les maîtres du Mobilier, le décor des Paquebots*, Paris: Amateur, 1986:122.

Margold, Emanuel Josef   (1889–1962)

▶ Austrian architect, interior designer, ceramicist, and silversmith; born Vienna; active Vienna, Darmstadt, and Berlin.

▶ Studied Kunstgewerbeschule, Vienna, under Josef Hoffmann.

▶ He became an assistant of Hoffmann at the Wiener Werkstätte. In 1911, he went to the artists' colony in Darmstadt of the Grand Duke Louis IV of Hesse-Darmstadt; he and Theodor Wende were the last artists to settle there. At Darmstadt, he was a prolific producer of designs for furniture, glass, and porcelain. In 1913, Bruckmann und Söhne of Heilbronn commissioned him to execute silver designs. His umbrella handles were produced by K. Jordan in Darmstadt. His silverwork for Bruckmann showed fine beading, fluting, and heart-shaped leaves. He treated floral decoration with the same simple approach as Hoffmann. Margold designed packaging for the bakery Bahlens Keksfabrik, Hanover. In 1929, he settled in Berlin; was listed in the 1949 UAM (Union des Artistes Modernes) manifesto as a foreign contributor.

▶ His display won the grand prize at the 1910 Brussels 'Exposition Universelle et Internationale.'

▶ Günther Feuerstein, *Vienna–Present and Past: Arts and Crafts–Applied Art–Design*, Vienna: Jugend und Volk, 1976:35,80. Cat., *Ein Dokument Deutscher Kunst*, Vol. 4, Darmstadt: Die Kunstler der Mathildenhöhe, 1976:132–43. Annelies Krekel-Aalberse, *Art Nouveau and Art Déco Silver*, New York: Abrams, 1989: 135,140,257. Stuart Durant, *Ornament from the Industrial Revolution to Today*, Woodstock, NY: Overlook, 1986:59.

Mari, Enzio   (1921–)

▶ Italian technician; born Novara; active Milan.

▶ 1952–56, studied Accademia di Belle Arti di Brera, Milan.

▶ In the beginning of his career, he experimented in aeronautics. 1945–57, he worked for the clock manufacturer Italora, becoming director general. 1958–71, he was an executive at Rheem Safim. In 1958, he developed the Gardrail, a street-barricade system. In 1959, he reorganized the Filiale Italiana in Rome, where he acquired technical experience in metal furniture, water heaters, kitchen units, and shelving. In 1960, he became a member of the Ordine dei Giornalistic nell'Albo Speciale per Direttori Responsab-

ili di Periodici a carattere Tecnico, Professionale e Scientifico. In 1960, while serving as director of a new firm, he worked in the industrial design studio of Joe Colombo. In 1960, he supervised the construction of a new plant for Rheem Safim Tubi in Palermo. He studied production-line procedures and various aspects of transporting gas by pipelines and by other means. In 1965, he joined the studio of Enzo Mari and, in 1971, the technical studio G. Mari in Milan. In 1972, he became general secretary of ANGAISA (Italian association for water sanitation and heating equipment), coordinating the function of the regional department with the central association. He was a member of ADI (Associazione per il Disegno Industriale).

▶ *ADI Annual 1976*, Milan: Associazione per il Disegno Industriale, 1976.

Mari, Enzo   (1932–)

▶ Italian designer; born Novara; active Milan.

▶ 1952–56, studied Accademia di Belle Arti di Brera, Milan.

▶ He first became interested in design in 1956, especially of books and children's games and, in 1957, began working for Danese, for which some of his designs and ideas for games and puzzles were executed, including the 1957 wooden child's puzzle. His first experimental objects in plastics date from 1959, and the 1962 cylindrical umbrella stand in PVC and 1969 reversible *Vase 3087* in ABS plastic were produced by Danese. Most of his designs for Danese were in plastics and intended for the table. In 1963, he became a member of the movement Nuove Tendenze. 1963–66, he taught design methodology and graphics, Scuola Umanitaria, Milan; in 1970, taught at Centro Sperimentale di Cinematografia, Rome; in 1972, at Instituto di Storia dell'Arte, Università di Parma; at Accademia di Belle Arti, Carrara; and at Facoltà di Architettura, Politecnico di Milano. From 1965, he collaborated with Elio Mari. Enzo Mari's design and research theories were published in his *Funzione della ricerca estetica* in 1970. He designed the 1972 bookcase produced by Fabina with Elio Mari; 1974 grid-pattern *Quaderna* table and 1979 *Delfina* chair, both produced by Driade; 1973 *Day-Night*; 1979 *Elementare* wall tiles by Gabbianelli; and 1985 *Tonietta* chair by Zanotta. His clients included Anonima Castelli, Artemide, Driade, Editore Boringhieri, Gabbianelli, Gavina-Knoll, ICF, De Padova, La Rinascente-Upim, Olivetti, Simón International, and Le Creuset. 1976–79, he was the president of ADI (Associazione per il Disegno Industriale).

▶ Refusing to execute an environment for the 1972 'Italy: The New Domestic Landscape' exhibition at the New York Museum of Modern Art, he supplied an 'anti-design' statement instead. Received Premio Compasso d'Oro in 1967 for his design research, in 1979 for his *Delfina* chair by Driade, and in 1987. His work was included in the 1972 'Design a Plastické Hmoty' at the Uměleckoprůmyslové Muzeum in Prague, 1983–84 'Design Since 1945' at the Philadelphia Museum of Art, and 1991 'Mobili Italiani 1961–1991: Le Varie Età dei linguaggi' exhibition in Milan.

▶ Enzo Mari, *Funzione della ricerca estetica*, Milan: Comunità: 1970. Max Bill and Bruno Munari, *Enzo Mari*, Milan, 1959. Renato Pedio, *Enzo Mari designer*, Bari, 1980. Arturo Carlo Quintaballe, *Enzo Mari*, Parma, 1983. Paolo Fossati, *Il design in Italia*, Turin, 1972:141–46,243–49, plates 450–508. Cat., Emilio Ambasz, *Italy: The New Domestic Landscape*, 1972:54,76–77,83,89–91,262–65. 'Coloqui Di Modo: Artigianato non esiste,' *Modo*, No. 56, Jan.–Feb. 1983:22–25. Cat., Kathryn B. Hiesinger and George H. Marcus III (eds.), *Design Since 1945*, Philadelphia: Philadelphia Museum of Art, 1983:221,VI–11–14.

Mari, Gianantonio   (1946–)

▶ Italian industrial designer; born Varese; active Milan.

▶ Studied architecture to 1971.

▶ 1967–68, he worked in the office of architect Mozzani on surveys and building projects. 1968–71, he worked in the industrial design studio of Joe Colombo. In 1971, he set up his own technical studio G. Mari in Milan. In 1972, he was a consultant designer to Rheem-Siv in Milan on a projects concerning plastic containers for fuel, pharmaceutical, and automobile industries, and to Sitam in Modena on sanitary accessories and faucets. In 1973, he was a consultant to Ricagni Elettrodomestici in Milan, where he designed the air-conditioner *Easy Mounting*, and, in 1974, to Fatif on professional photographic equipment. In 1975, he joined the central study and research center ANGAISA (Italian association for water sanitation and heating equipment). He was a member of ADI (Associazione per il Disegno Industriale).

▶ He won an award for young designers for his modular environment at the 1972 'Italy: The New Domestic Landscape' exhibition at the New York Museum of Modern Art, and for a project in collaboration with Enzio Mari at the 1972 (I) Baderam competition.

▶ *ADI Annual 1976*, Milan: Associazione per il Disegno Industriale, 1976.

Mariani, Massimo (1951–)

▶ Italian designer; born Pistoia; active Florence and Montecatini Terme.

▶ In 1980 with Alberto Casciani, he established Stilema Studio to design and produce furnishings for public and private clients.

▶ Work shown at 'Wohnen von Sinnen' exhibition, Kunstmuseum, Düsseldorf.

▶ Fumio Shimizu and Matteo Thun (eds.), *The Descendants of Leonardo: The Italian Design*, Tokyo, 1987:326.

Marimekko

▶ Finnish fabric manufacturers and retail chain.

▶ Armi Ratia worked in her own weaving workshop in Vyborg until 1939, selling the *rya* rugs that she designed. In 1949, she joined her husband's firm Printex, which at the time produced oilcloth. Ratia reorganized the factory to accommodate silkscreen printing by hand on thin cotton sheeting. A number of designers began producing motifs for Ratia, including Maija Isola and Vuokko Eskolin-Nurmesniemi. In 1951, the first made-up dresses in Printex's new cotton fabric were presented under the name Marimekko, 'a little dress for Mary.' At a later date the entire operation took this name. The motifs became larger and bolder in the 1960s, particularly in the designs of Isola, and flower and bird silhouettes were introduced. In the 1960s and 1970s, the firm's products included cotton, jersey, and wool fabrications along with paper, laminated plastics, and table coverings. Through franchises worldwide today, the store also sells simple clothing for women and children along with some household accessories and furniture, including pieces by Alvar Aalto.

▶ *The Marimekko Story*, Helsinki: Marimekko Printex, 1964. Cat., Kathryn B. Hiesinger and George H. Marcus III (eds.), *Design Since 1945*, Philadelphia: Philadelphia Museum of Art, 1983:228, VII–51. David Davies, 'Fabrics by Marimekko,' *Design*, No. 236, Aug. 1968:28–31. 'The Finn-Tastics,' *Sphere*, March 1975. Ristomatti Ratia, 'The Legacy of Armi Ratia,' *Form Function Finland*, Nos. 1–2, 1980:10–11.

Marini, Marino (1939–)

▶ Italian design promoter; born Nettuno; active Rome.

▶ Studied economics to 1962.

▶ From 1963, he was active in the organization and promotion of Italian design in exhibitions worldwide. He was a member of ADI (Associazione per il Disegno Industriale).

▶ *ADI Annual 1976*, Milan: Associazione per il Disegno Industriale, 1976.

Marinot, Maurice (1882–1960)

▶ French painter and glassmaker; born Troyes.

▶ From 1889, studied painting and sculpture, École des Beaux Arts, Paris.

▶ In *c*1900, he became a member of artists' group Les Fauves. In 1911, Marinot's interest in glass was sparked when he visited the glasshouse of brothers Eugène and Gabriel Viard at Bar-sur-Seine. At the Viards at first, he designed decorations applied in

enamel by an artisan, and later applied by himself. He produced bold motifs in stark colors. From 1913, he learned to make glass, and abandoned enamel decoration by 1921 to produce thick-walled, internally decorated pieces. At first he incised them deeply; later he worked at the furnace. Marinot developed special glasses produced at lower temperatures, enabling him to construct massive, complex forms with very thick gathers laid one upon the other. His work became widely known through exhibitions and articles in journals; priced beyond the means of most people, his work was sought after by museums. After World War II, Marinot returned to painting.

▶ Until 1913 at the 'Armory Show' in New York, he exhibited paintings with Les Fauves at the 1905 Salon d'Automne. He first exhibited his glassware at the 1912 Salon d'Automne. In Paris, his work was on continuous display at Galerie Adrien Hebrand on rue Royale. His work was included in a 1925 exhibition at the New York Museum of Modern Art. He won first prize in the glass section at the 1937 Paris 'Exposition Internationale des Arts et Techniques dans la Vie Moderne.'

▶ Yvonne Brunhammer et al., *Art Nouveau Belgium, France*, Houston: Rice University, 1976. Frederick Cooke, *Glass: Twentieth-Century Design*, New York: Dutton, 1986:46,48.

Mariscal, Javier (1950–)

▶ Spanish designer; born Valencia; active Barcelona.

▶ Studied Escuela de Grafismo Elisava, Barcelona, to 1971.

▶ His poster designs of the 1970s included one for the city of Barcelona as a pictogram of the words *bar* ('bar')/*cel* ('sky')/*ona* ('wave'). In addition to Memphis furniture, Mariscal's work included neo-deco graphics, a 1950s pop-art canine-featured comic strip character called 'Garriris' (which made his name), quasi-ethnic carpets, neo-baroque ersatz bronze sculpture, pop-comic zig-zag lamps, bold primary-colored Klee/Morris-type textile patterns, grinning cats, Kandinskii-like ceramics, and objects of intentionally kitsch taste. Beginning as a cartoonist, he drew a series called 'Comix Underground' for *El Rollo Enmascarado* in 1973. In 1978, he began decorating houses in Barcelona and Valencia and created his first textile range for Marieta. His first piece of furniture was the brightly colored, asymmetrical 1980 *Duplex* bar stool. Mariscal came to the attention of Ettore Sottsass through Mariscal's work on a 1980 bar (with Fernando Salas) in Valencia and the subsequent 1980 'Meubles Amorales' (Amoral Furniture) exhibition (with Pepe Cortes) at the Sala Vinçon. He participated in Memphis's initial 1981 collection, designing the backwardly slanted 1981 *Hilton* tea cart in clear glass and metal tubing and rods, 1981 *Table à Café*, and 1981 *Luminaires Impossibles*. His 1985 ceramic range was produced by Vinçon, Barcelona, and 1986 ceramic range by Axis, Paris. His *Torero* and *Tio Pepe* chairs for the Centre Georges Pompidou exhibition in 1987 in Paris parodied Spanish culture. Active at Akaba, he designed the 1986 *MOR* sofa and 1986 *Trampolín* chair (with Cortes). He designed the 1986–87 fabric collection for Seibu, Japan; the *Cobi* mascot for the 1992 Olympic Games in Barcelona; and the mascot for the 1992 Seville 'Exposición universal de Sevilla (Expo '92).'

▶ The 1980 exhibition 'Meubles Amorales' included prototypes of his furniture produced by Vinçon; his 1982 fabric collection was in the exhibition 'Mariscal' in the Espace Actuel, Paris; he participated in the 1986 'Nouvelle Tendances' exhibition at CCI/Centre Georges Pompidou, Paris, and 1986 'Barcelona' exhibition in Espace MCC in Saint-Étienne. His printed textiles for Marieta and furniture were included in the 1983–84 'Design Since 1945' exhibition at the Philadelphia Museum of Art. A 1989 one-person exhibition of his work was mounted in London.

▶ Cat., *Nouvelle Tendances: les avant-gardes de la fin du XXe siècle*, Paris: Centre Georges Pompidou, 1986. Cat., Kathryn B. Hiesinger and George H. Marcus III (eds.), *Design Since 1945*, Philadelphia: Philadelphia Museum of Art, 1983:221,VI–42–43,III–47. *Graphic Design*, No. 76, Dec. 1979:52. Barbara Radice (ed.), *Memphis: The New International Style*, Milan, 1981:39–40. 'Mariscal,' *De Diseño*, No. 10, 1987. Guy Julier, *New Spanish Design*,

London: Thames and Hudson, 1991. Emma Dent Coad, *Javier Mariscal: Designing The New Spain*, New York: Rizzoli, 1991.

Marius-Michel (b. Henri-François-Victor Michel **1846– 1925**)

► French bookbinder and gilder; active Paris.

► He adopted his father's name when he joined the family bindery at 15 rue du Four, Paris, in 1876. He argued that binding needed a new and Modern approach in his book *La Reliure commerciale et industrielle depuis l'invention de l'imprimerie jusqu'à nos jours* (1881). By 1885, other binderies were imitating his plant and floral motifs. His incised and modeled panels were executed by Guétant, Lepère, and Steinlen, and his poster covers (or *reliures affiches*) were designed by artists including Ruban, Raparlier, Meunier, and Gruel. By the mid-1890s, Marius-Michel's leadership in the new movement was recognized. Collectors of his work included Descamps-Scrive, Quarré, Bénard, Béraldi, Barthou, Borderel, and de Piolenc. In 1925, management of the firm was turned over to Georges Cretté.

► He showed his binding based on nature (*La Flore Ornamentale*) at the 1878 Paris 'Exposition Universelle.' He was awarded the grand prize and appointed Chevalier de la Légion d'honneur at 1900 Paris 'Exposition Universelle.'

► Alastair Duncan and Georges de Bartha, *Art Nouveau and Art Déco Bookbinding*, New York: Abrams, 1989:11–13,12,15,16– 21,36,66,97,144–49,159,195. Georges Blaizot, *Masterpieces of French Modern Bookbindings*, Paris, 1947. Ernest de Crauzat, *La Reliure française de 1900 à 1925*, Vol. 1, Paris, 1932:23–27. Roger Devauchelle, *La Reliure en France de ses origines à nos jours*, Vol. 3, Paris, 1961:117,123,126,129,135–36,138,143–48,150– 51,160,166,168,172,175,212,269. Marius-Michel, *La Reliure française commerciale et industrielle depuis l'invention de l'imprimerie jusqu'à nos jours*, Paris, 1881. Octave Uzanne, *L'Art dans la décoration extérieure des livres en France et à l'étranger*, Paris, 1898:166, 184,195,197.

Markelius, Sven (1889–1972)

► Swedish architect, town planner, and textile designer; born Stockholm.

► Studied Kungliga Tekniska Högskolan and Kungliga Konsthögskolan, Stockholm.

► Markelius began his career in the office of Ragnar Östberg and participated in the Functionalist movement of the mid-1920s, influenced by Le Corbusier. He built apartments, offices, and the 1934 concert hall in Hälsingborg. He first won international recognition for his Swedish pavilion at the 1939 'New York World's Fair.' 1938–44, he was a building administration member of Stockholm; 1944–54, was head of the town-planning department and responsible for the 1953–59 satellite-town Vällingby, with a central pedestrian zone and a variety of architectural designs. The Vällingby model presaged subsequent approaches to town planning. Co-author of *Accept* (1931), he assisted with the 1930 'Stockholm Exhibition,' designed the Swedish pavilion at the 1939 'New York World's Fair,' and participated in the planning of the UN building in New York. His buildings included the 1935 'Collective house' in Stockholm. He taught in Stockholm and at Yale University. In the 1950s, Markelius designed simple wooden furniture and printed fabrics with Astrid Sampe, produced by Nordiska in Stockholm. His textiles were marketed by Knoll Textiles.

► Sven Markelius in C.E. Kidder Smith, *Sweden Builds*, London, 1957. 'Architecture in a Social Context: The Work of Sven Markelius,' *Architectural Record*, April 1964:153–64. Stefano Ray, *Il Contributo svedese all'architettura contemporanea e l'opera di Sven Markelius*, Rome, 1969. Cat., David Revere McFadden (ed.), *Scandinavian Modern Design 1880–1980*, New York: Abrams, 1982:268, No. 194. Vittorio Magnago Lampugnani (ed.), *Encyclopedia of 20th-Century Architecture*, New York: Abrams, 1986:211.

Markham, Herman C. (?–1922)

► American ceramicist; active Ann Arbor, Michigan, and National City, California.

► Markham, a traveling salesperson living in Ann Arbor, Michigan, was a rose enthusiast; dissatisfied with containers for displaying flowers, he began potting, at first with clays from his own yard. In 1905, he and son Kenneth Markham began producing pottery wares commercially. Using molds made after prototypes, their wares had the appearance of excavated relics. The forms were based on classical models. In 1913, they settled in National City, California, and set up a pottery where native clays were conveniently available. Its wares were of two types: 'Reseau' with fine texturing and delicate veins and 'arabesque' with a coarser rough texture. The operation continued until 1921.

► Paul Evans in Timothy J. Andersen et al., *California Design 1910*, Salt Lake City: Peregrine Smith, 1980:76.

Marks, Gilbert Leigh (1861–1905)

► British silversmith; active London.

► Apprenticed to silversmiths Johnson, Walker and Tolhurst.

► He set up a silversmithy in 1895. He was best known for his tazzas and dishes with embossed flower motifs. Some of his work was influenced by 17th-century silver; other work was in contemporary styles.

► Annelies Krekel-Aalberse, *Art Nouveau and Art Déco Silver*, New York: Abrams, 1989:22,257.

Marks, Margarete (aka Margarete Heymann-Marks 1899–c1988)

► German ceramicist; active Germany and London.

► Studied Kunstgewerbeschule, Cologne; Kunstakademie, Düsseldorf; 1920–21, Bauhaus, Weimar.

► She rendered free-form abstract pottery, greatly influenced by Vasilii Kandinskii. From 1922, she worked at the Steingutfabriken Velten-Vordamm. In 1923, she founded the Haël Werkstätten für Künstlerische Keramic in Marwitz; it closed in 1932. In 1935, she moved to Britain; from 1936, designed for the Minton factory, Stoke-on-Trent; and, until 1939, was active in her own workshop Greta Pottery. After World War II, she worked in her own studio pottery workshop.

► Cat., *The Bauhaus: Masters and Students*, New York: Barry Friedman, 1988. Cat., *Keramik und Bauhaus*, Berlin: Bauhaus-Archiv, 1989:264.

Maromme Printworks

► British textile firm with headquarters at 6 Snow Hill, London.

► Printed French cretonnes, delaine, silk and flannel at Rouen (France); was contracted by Roger Fry to print linens for the Omega Workshops using roller printing in a special manner.

► Valerie Mendes. *The Victoria & Albert Museum's Textile Collection, British Textiles from 1900 to 1937*, London: Victoria & Albert Museum, 1992.

Marot-Rodde, Mme. (?–1935)

► French bookbinder; active Paris.

► Studied École Estienne, Paris, under Charles Chanat.

► She set up her own workshop in the early 1920s at 86 boulevard Suchet in Paris. Petrus Ruban guided her in her technique. In a distinctive style using geometrics and florals, her covers included *La Leçon d'amour dans un parc* and *Scènes mythologiques* for P. Hébert, *L'Océan* and *L'Eventail* for P. Harth, and *Ballades françaises*, *L'Ame et la danse*, and *Marrakech* for politician Louis Barthou. By 1932, her daughter had joined the firm, where several binders and two gilders were employed.

► She showed her work at the 1924 event of the Salon d'Automne and 1925 Salon of the Société des Artistes Décorateurs. She received a silver medal at the 1925 Paris 'Exposition Internationale des Arts Décoratifs et Industriels Modernes.'

► Louis Barthou, 'L'Évolution artistique de la reliure,' *L'Illustration*, Christmas 1930. Ernest de Crauzat, *La Reliure française de 1900 à 1925*, Vol. 2, Paris, 1932:137–41. Roger Devauchelle, *La Reliure en France de ses origines à nos jours*, Vol. 3, Paris, 1961: 168,171,269. Alastair Duncan and Georges de Bartha, *Art Nouveau and Art Déco Bookbinding*, New York: Abrams, 1989: 20,130–33,194.

MARS (Modern Architectural Research Group)

▶ British architecture organization.

▶ The Modern Architectural Research Group (MARS) was founded in Britain in 1933 by architects Wells Coates, E. Maxwell Fry, and others, including architectural journalists, critics, and engineers. MARS was affiliated with the CIAM (Congrès Internationaux d'Architecture Moderne). Its purpose was to provide a forum for discussion and research into the social and technical aspects of Modern architecture and to contribute analyses and projects to the events of CIAM and CIRPAC (Comité Internationale pour la Réalisation des Problèmes Architecturaux Contemporains). MARS concerned itself with social needs relating to architecture, construction relating to industrial production, and various aspects of town planning. It produced the MARS Plan for London and the Analysis of Bethnal Green in London's East End. It contributed to exhibitions on housing and town planning, and mounted its own 1938 London 'New Architecture' exhibition of international Modern architecture. In 1938, MARS had 71 members. Its members were active in the 1951 London 'Festival of Britain,' new town development, and school building. The group disbanded in 1957.

▶ Cat., *Thirties: British art and design before the war*, London: Arts Council of Great Britain, Hayward Gallery, 1979:304.

Marteinsdottir, Steinunn   (1936–)

▶ Icelandic ceramicist.

▶ One of Iceland's best known ceramicists, Marteinsdottir worked in her own studio near Reykjavik.

▶ Cat., David Revere McFadden (ed.), *Scandinavian Modern Design 1880–1980*, New York: Abrams, 1982:268, No. 279.

Martel, Jan   (1896–1966) and Joël Martel   (1896–1966)

▶ French sculptors; brothers; born Nantes; active Paris.

▶ Studied École Nationale des Arts Décoratifs, Paris.

▶ They experimented with cement, glass, steel, mirrors, ceramics, lacquers, and synthetics. Their first work was the 1920–22 Vendée memorial monument. Influential on Cubists, they produced sculpture both small and monumental. They were best known for their 20m (6 ft) reinforced concrete trees in the tourism pavilion of the 1925 Paris exposition. Working in the Mallet-Stevens designed studio in rue Mallet-Stevens in Auteuil, they collaborated with the architect on a large number of projects. Their work was characterized by deformed figures and harmonious forms within simple volumes. Working in plaster, stone, cement, and metal, they produced sculptures *L'Accordéoniste*, *Le Joueur de polo*, and *L'Île d'Avalon*; they also worked in polished zinc and in modular units, including commissions for the Lion de l'Hôtel, Belfort Post Office, and pieces including *L'Homme à la scie musicale* and the portrait of Gaston Wiener. The 1929 *La Trinité* marked a transition towards more monumental works, which included the decoration for the pavilion of the Chemins de fer at the 1931 Exposition Coloniale. Their 1930 *La Locomotive en marche* in polished zinc expressed notions that grew out of Futurism. Their monument to Claude Debussy was constructed in 1932 in the Bois de Boulogne, Paris. They later designed the monument of Guy de Lubersac in Soissons. They produced the *Christ en croix* sculpture, candlesticks in the chapel of the 1935 oceanliner *Normandie*, and other works for churches including the Église de Saint-Esprit in Paris and the cathedral in Blois. Around 1937, their work became more abstract, illustrated by *Le Faucheur*, *La Danseuse*, and *Mélusine* produced for the dam at Mervent in Vendée. The brothers produced a number of monuments after World War II, including those to the war dead in Vendée, Haut-Rhin, Loiret, and Finistère, and to navigator Alain Gerbault, politician Pierre Laval, and painter Milcendeau. Their sculpture *Oiseaux de mer* for the church of Saint-Jean-de-Monts was notable; they produced decorations for the cathedral in Metz. The Martels and Henri Pacon restored the château in Lourmarin occupied by Eileen Gray during World War II.

▶ They showed their work at the 1921 Salon des Indépendants. For the 1925 Paris 'Exposition Internationale des Arts Décoratifs et Industriels Modernes,' they designed Mallet-Stevens's tourism pavilion, the reliefs and plinths for the Concorde gate (Pierre Patout, architect), the interior décor for the bathroom of the Sèvres pavilion, and the Cubist reinforced-concrete trees for Mallet-Stevens's garden. As members of the Union des Artistes Modernes from 1929, they showed at its exhibitions from 1930. They collaborated on several pavilions at the 1937 Paris 'Exposition Internationale des Arts et Techniques dans la Vie Moderne' and (with Jean Burkhalter) designed the fountain of the commissariat of tourism there. Work subject of 1977 retrospective, Saint-Jean-de-Monts.

▶ Joël Martel, *Cadre de la Vie Contemporaine*, No. 2, Feb.–April 1935:48. Paul Fiérens, 'Jan and Joël Martel,' *L'Art et les Artistes*, June 1936. Cat., *Rétrospective Jan et Joël Martel, Sculpteurs*, Saint-Jean-de-Monts, 1977. Victor Arwas, *Art Déco*, Abrams, 1980. Pierre Cabanne, *Encyclopédie Art Déco*, Paris: Somogy, 1986:291. Arlette Barré-Despond, *UAM*, Paris: Regard, 1986:466–67. Cat., *Les années UAM 1929–1958*, Paris: Musée des Arts Décoratifs, 1988:227.

Martin, Camille   (1861–98)

▶ French painter, decorative artist, and leatherworker.

▶ Martin's bookbindings were produced by himself, with Victor Prouvé, and by René Wiener for *L'Espagne* and *L'Argent*. Paintings were transferred directly onto the leatherwork. A proponent of the Nancy movement, his bindings included *La Mélancolie d'automne*, *Récits de guerre*, *L'Estampe originale*, *La Pensée dans l'espace*, *Les Aveugles*, and *Les Harmonies du soir*.

▶ Alastair Duncan and Georges de Bartha, *Art Nouveau and Art Déco Bookbinding*, New York: Abrams, 1989:13–14,156,179,194. Thérèse Charpentier, *L'École de Nancy et la reliure d'art*, Paris, 1960:26–29,47,49. Cat., *Le Cuir au Musée*, Nancy: Musée de l'École de Nancy, 1985. Cat., *Exposition Lorraine (École de Nancy)*, Paris: Musée de l'Union Centrale des Arts Décoratifs, Paris, 2nd series, 1903. 'Modern Bookbindings and Their Designers,' *The Studio*, Special Winter Issue 1899–1900:3–82. Octave Uzanne, *L'Art dans la décoration extérieure des livres en France et à l'étranger*, Paris, 1898:210.

Martin, Charles   (1848–1934)

▶ French graphic artist and designer.

▶ Studied Écoles des Beaux-Arts, Montpellier and Paris, and Académie Julian under Cormon.

▶ He was prolific as a graphic artist, including of book illustrations. He designed stage sets and costumes for plays, revues, and ballets, and for several decorators, including Groult, furniture, furnishings, fabrics, and wallpaper. For Groult, he painted panels and screens.

▶ He showed his work at the Salon d'Automne and the Salon des Humoristes.

▶ Victor Arwas, *Art Déco*, Abrams, 1980. Léon Deshairs, *Modern French Decorative Art*, Paris: Albert Lévy.

Martin, Étienne-Martin

▶ French decorator and furniture designer.

▶ Studied École Boulle, Paris.

▶ He met Gilbert Poillerat at the École Boulle; worked for Edgar Brandt for three years; 1938–45, was artistic director of Les Magasins du Louvre, Paris; subsequently, was artistic director of Bon Marché, Brussels. He was influenced by the work of Louis Sognot and René Guilleré; by 1954, had set up a workshop at 6 avenue de Clamart, Vanves, near Paris; designed furniture, some of which was produced by JER, Borgeaud, and Soubrier.

▶ *Ensembles Mobiliers*, Vol. 2, Paris: Charles Moreau, 1937. *Ensembles Mobiliers*, Vol. 5, Paris: Charles Moreau, 1954, Nos. 8–9. Pascal Renous, *Portraits de Décorateurs*, Paris: H. Vial, 1969.

Martine, Atelier

▶ French interior design studio; located Paris.

▶ Fashion designer Paul Poiret set up the design studio Martine in 1911 primarily to sell the designs of the working-class students of his École Martine. Classes for young women were at first run by Madame Sérusier, wife of the Symbolist artist Paul Sérusier; instruction was later altered to a more experimental approach through, among other activities, visits to zoos, botanical gardens, and the countryside. They designed fabrics, wallpapers, and murals. They also produced Cubist designs for wood furniture in bright colors or with busy-patterned veneers, recognizable for their colorful, flat, and often floral motifs. They produced rugs, fabrics, wallpapers, and interior design schemes. Their wares were much in demand; the furniture was produced by Pierre Fauconnet. Poiret opened an interior decoration business through which he sold a range of wares and offered decoration consultancy to hotels, restaurants, offices, and private clients. In 1924, a branch in London was opened; goods were exported widely, including to the USA. In 1910, Poiret met Josef Hoffmann in Vienna and was particularly attracted to the Wiener Werkstätte's folk-derived textiles in floral patterns. Raoul Dufy collaborated with the Martines and Poiret before he joined textile firm Bianchini et Férier in Lyons in 1912, although he continued to be associated with Poiret. The group designed the *Chantilly* deluxe suite on the 1926 oceanliner *Île-de-France*. At first set up at 83 rue du Faubourg Saint-Honoré, the shop was moved to the avenue Victor-Emmanuel-III and Rond-Point of avenue des Champs-Élysées in 1924, where it remained until closing in 1934.

▶ The Martine students first showed their work through sketches and patterns in two rooms at the 1912 Salon d'Automne. They designed Poiret's three houseboats (*Amour, Délice,* and *Orgues*), which docked near the 1925 Paris 'Exposition Internationale des Arts Décoratifs et Industriels Modernes.'

▶ Victor Arwas, *Art Déco*, Abrams, 1980. Pierre Kjellberg, *Art Déco: les maîtres du Mobilier, le décor des Paquebots*, Paris: Amateur, 1986:122—24. Jonathan M. Woodham, *Twentieth-Century Ornament*, New York: Rizzoli, 1990:19—21,61,316.

Martineau, Sarah Madeleine   (1872–)

▶ British goldsmith, silversmith, and jeweler.

▶ Studied Liverpool School of Art, and Sir John Cass Technical College, London.

▶ Though often published in *The Studio* during 1908—19, when she was active, Martineau produced only a small amount of jewelry and silverwork and did not work on a commercial basis. Her use of gold was unusual among Arts and Crafts exponents. The enamels that she used were vibrantly colored.

▶ She showed her work at the Liverpool School of Art and in Cambridge, and won first prize in the 1911 *Studio* competition.

▶ Charlotte Gere, *American and European Jewelry 1830–1914*, New York: Crown, 1975:205—06. Toni Lesser Wolf, 'Women Jewelers of the British Arts and Crafts Movement,' *The Journal of Decorative and Propaganda Arts*, No. 14, Fall 1989:37.

Martinelli, Elio   (1922–)

▶ Italian lighting designer; born Lucca.

▶ Studied painting and architecture, Accademia di Belle Arti, Florence.

▶ In 1942, he and others set up a lighting firm; in 1956, established the lighting firm Martinelli Luce in Lucca, designing in plastics and metal and producing a hanging lamp in perspex published in *La Rivista dell' Arredamento*. The firm's production included plastics from the beginning, with only acrylics at first. It followed with metacrylate, melamine, ABS, and Delrin. Its designs were based on the square, the sphere, and derived forms. Designers included Gae Aulenti, Sergio Asti, Studio DA, Giovanni Bassi, Sergio Martinelli, and director Elio Martinelli. Production was in small series.

▶ Work was included in the 1966 Genoa 'Eurodomus I,' 1967 Turin 'Eurodomus II,' 1968 (XIV) Triennale di Milano, and Domus Design in Switzerland and the Netherlands. Elio Martinelli's 1970 *Table Lamp 643* and 1967 *Flessibile* working lamp and Asti's *Profiterolles* table lamp were included in the 1972 'Design a Plastické Hmoty' exhibition at the Uměleckoprůmyslové Muzeum, Prague.

▶ Cat., Milena Lamarová, *Design a Plastické Hmoty*, Prague: Uměleckoprůmyslové Muzeum, 1972:66,130,196. *Moderne Klassiker:* *Möbel, die Geschichte machen*, Hamburg, 1982:61. Hans Wichmann, *Italien Design 1945 bis heute*, Munich: Die Neue Sammlung, 1988.

Martínez Lapeña, José Antonio   (1941–)

▶ Spanish designer; born Tarragona.

▶ Studied building to 1962 and architecture, Escuela Técnica Superior de Arquitectura, Barcelona, to 1968.

▶ Martínez and Elias Torres Tur set up an architecture practice in 1968. From 1984, Martínez was professor of design at the Escuela Técnica Superior de Arquitectura in Vallés and, from 1980, professor of design at the Escuela Técnica Superior de Arquitectura in Barcelona. He and Torres designed the 1986 *Lampelunas* street light by Cemusa, 1986 *Barcelona* and 1986 *Hollywood* rugs by BVD, and 1987 bus shelter (with José Luís Canosa) by Cemusa.

▶ He was awarded the 1986 Delta de Oro of ADI/FAD de Diseño Industrial.

▶ Juli Capella and Quim Larrea, *Designed by Architects in the 1980s*, New York: Rizzoli, 1988.

Martini, Alfredo   (1923–)

▶ Italian designer; born Cervia.

▶ Martini was best known for his work in plastics, including furniture and case goods; became a member of ADI (Associazione per il Disegno Industriale).

▶ *ADI Annual 1976*, Milan: Associazione per il Disegno Industriale, 1976.

Martorell, Josep   (1925–)

▶ Spanish architect and industrial designer; born Barcelona.

▶ Studied architecture and town planning, School of Architecture, Barcelona, to 1963.

▶ Mackay, Oriol Bohigas, and Josep Martorell won the 1959, 1962, 1966, and 1979 FAD Awards for Architecture; 1966 and 1976 Delta de Plata prize (for industrial design); first prize at the 1984 'Internationale Bauaussetelling' in Berlin; and two first prizes in the Prototype Schools Competition of the Ministry of Education in Madrid. Their work was included in the 1986 'Contemporary Spanish Architecture: An Eclectic Panorama' exhibition at the Architectural League in New York.

▶ Antón Capitel and Ignacio Solà-Morales in *Contemporary Spanish Architecture*, New York: Rizzoli, 1986:64—67.

Marty, André E.   (1882–1974)

▶ French illustrator, painter, and designer.

▶ His illustrations appeared in publications including *Comédia*, *La Gazette du Bon Bon*, *Vogue*, and *Fémina*. He illustrated more than fifty deluxe limited-edition books. He worked for the CAF (Compagnie des Arts français) of Louis Süe and André Mare.

▶ Collaborating with CAF, he designed the screen and wall hangings for the dining room at the Fontaine pavilion at the 1925 Paris 'Exposition Internationale des Arts Décoratifs et Industriales Modernes.'

▶ Pierre Cabanne, *Encyclopédie Art Déco*, Paris: Somogy, 1986:219—20.

Marucco, Pierangelo   (1953–)

▶ Italian textile and ceramics designer; born and active Milan.

▶ Studied Liceo Artistico di Brera, Milan, to 1970, and Facoltà di Architettura, Milan.

▶ He set up the studio Designers 6R5 in 1970, producing designs for textiles and ceramics. In 1975, Marucco, Maurizio Alberti, Giuseppe Bossi, Francesco Roggero, and Bruno Rossio set up the studio Original Designers 6R5 in Milan, designing textiles for clients in Italy including Lanerossi, Sasatex, Taif, and Bassetti, and in Spain including Griso and Jover. They designed tapestry murals for Printeco in Italy and Le Roi, Grifine Marechal in France, and wallpaper for firms in France. He was a member of ADI (Associazione per il Disegno Industriale).

▶ *ADI Annual 1976*, Milan: Associazione per il Disegno Industriale, 1976.

Marx, Enid Crystal Dorothy (1902–93)
▶ British textile and graphic designer, printmaker, and illustrator; born London.
▶ Studied Central School of Arts and Crafts, and painting and wood engraving, Royal College of Art, London.
▶ After working with Barron and Larcher 1925–27, she set up her own textile printing workshop. Her work brought her to the attention of Gordon Russell, who helped her career. A versatile and prolific designer of decorative items, she executed patterned papers for books and wrapping, book jackets for Chatto and Windus and Penguin, illustrations, trademarks, printed and woven fabrics, wallpapers, posters for London Transport, calendars for Shell, ceramics, plastics, and postage stamps. In 1937, she designed a range of Modern moquette fabrics for London Transport. She wrote the book *When Victoria Began to Reign* (1939) on British folk art with Margaret Lambert. 1944–47, she was a member of the Utility Furniture Advisory Panel, designing a series of upholstery fabrics and most of the Utility furniture, working with very limited materials. She designed fabrics for Edinburgh Weavers and some that she herself printed; her fabrics produced by Morton Sundour included a textile at the 1951 'Festival of Britain.' Her serviceable and richly textured textile designs were produced in muted abstract patterns of chevrons, stripes, stars and circles.
▶ In 1944, she was elected Royal Designer for Industry. She participated in the 1946 'Britain Can Make It' exhibition and 1951 'Festival of Britain.' Her work was the subject of an exhibition at the Camden Arts Centre in London, and included in the 'CC41: Utility Furniture and Fashion, 1941–1951' exhibition at the Geffrye Museum in London.
▶ Fiona MacCarthy and Patrick Nuttgens, *An Eye for Industry*, London: Lund Humphries, 1986. Cherie Fehrman and Kenneth Fehrman, *Postwar Interior Design, 1945–1960*, New York: Van Nostrand Reinhold, 1987. Cat., Kathryn B. Hiesinger and George H. Marcus III (eds.), *Design Since 1945*, Philadelphia: Philadelphia Museum of Art, 1983:221,VII–44. Cat., *Enid Marx*, London, Camden Arts Centre, 1969. Cat., *CC41: Utility Furniture and Fashion, 1941–1951*, 1974:30–31. Jacqueline Herald, 'A Portrait of Enid Marx,' *Crafts*, No. 40, Sept. 1979:17–21.

Marzano, Stefano (1950–)
▶ Italian industrial and graphic designer; born and active Varese.
▶ Marzano began his professional career in 1974; worked in the design studio of Makio Hasuike in Milan and the Studio Design Broletto in Varese; had clients including Siareti, IRE, and Philips; became a member of ADI (Associazione per il Disegno Industriale).
▶ *ADI Annual 1976*, Milan: Associazione per il Disegno Industriale, 1976.

Masaki, Yuri (1950–)
▶ Japanese glass designer.
▶ Masaki was president of the Masaki Glass and Art Studio.
▶ Work included in 1987 and 1990 'Glass in Japan,' Tokyo, and 1991 (V) Triennale of the Japan Glass Art Crafts Association, Heller Gallery, New York. Work subject of exhibitions at 1988 Senbikiya Gallery, Tokyo; 1987 Glass Plaza, Osaka; and 1986–88 'Art of the Environment,' touring Kyoto, Tokyo, and Osaka. Won the grand prize at the 1988 Suntory Museum of Art Competition, Tokyo.
▶ Cat., *Glass Japan*, New York: Heller Gallery and Japan Glass Art Crafts Association, 1991: No. 21.

Mascher-Elsässer, Eva (1908–)
▶ German silversmith; born Halle; active Halle, Göttingen, Brunswick, Berg, and Pfaltz.
▶ Studied Kunsthandwerkerschule Burg Giebichenstein, Halle, under Karl Müller, and Kunstschule, Cologne, under Richard Riemerschmid.
▶ 1929–35, she and former fellow student Hildegard Risch worked together in a workshop of their own. After 1935, she continued in her own workshop, turning to jewelry production.

In 1949 in Göttingen, she set up a new workshop and, in 1957, moved again to Brunswick.
▶ Mascher-Elsässer and Risch collaborated on their first exhibition, where they showed a tea-set purchased by the museum in Leipzig.
▶ Annelies Krekel-Aalberse, *Art Nouveau and Art Déco Silver*, New York: Abrams, 1989:147,257. Cat., *Goldschmiedearbeiten von Hildegard Risch und Eva Mascher-Elsässer*, Brunswick, 1979.

Mascheroni, John (1932–)
▶ American furniture and industrial designer; active New York.
▶ Studied Pratt Institute in Brooklyn, New York.
▶ He opened his own design office and furniture factory in New York. Mascheroni designed furniture for manufacturers in High Point, North Carolina. From 1990, his furniture designs were produced by Swaim and, from 1991, others by Jeffco.
▶ His work was shown at the 1969 'Plastic as Plastic' exhibition at the New York Museum of Contemporary Crafts and the 1969 Annual Design Review at the Museum of Science and Industry in Chicago. His *Chair 424* was shown at the 1970 'Modern Chairs 1918–1970' exhibition at the Whitechapel Gallery in London.
▶ Cat., *Modern Chairs 1918–1970*, London: Lund Humphries, 1971. Arlene Hirst, 'World Class at Last,' *American Home*, November 1990:102.

Masenza, Mario (1913–)
▶ Italian jeweler; born Rome.
▶ Masenza took over a jewelry business established at the turn of the century by his father in Rome. From 1946, Masenza's innovative designs, influenced by classical Roman jewelry, were produced from drawings by Italian artists with whom he collaborated, including Afro, Mirko, Birolli, Guttuso, Savinio, Manzullo, Greco, and Mafai.
▶ Melissa Gabardi, *Les Bijoux des Années 50*, Paris: Amateur, 1987.

Masi, Gianfranco (1931–)
▶ Italian designer; born and active Bologna.
▶ Studied architecture, Instituto Universitario di Firenze, to 1958.
▶ He began his career in 1968, designing furniture, interiors, and buildings; designed the *Ghiro* folding seat produced by Ny Form, Bologna; became a member of ADI (Associazione per il Disegno Industriale).
▶ *ADI Annual 1976*, Milan: Associazione per il Disegno Industriale, 1976.

Masina, Alessandro (1937–)
▶ Italian industrial designer; born and active Milan.
▶ Masina began his career as a designer in 1960. He was on the jury of the 1975 Smau industrial design competition and, in 1975 and 1976, a member of the guidance committee of ADI (Associazione per il Disegno Industriale).
▶ He participated in the Italian pavilion of the 1973 (XV) Triennale di Milano and 1965 (IV) and 1971 (VII) ICSID congress.
▶ *ADI Annual 1976*, Milan: Associazione per il Disegno Industriale, 1976.

Masriera, Luis (1872–1958)
▶ Spanish goldsmith, jeweler, and designer; active Barcelona.
▶ Studied School of Art, Geneva, under enamelist Lossier.
▶ Masriera and his brother inherited the family jewelry and goldsmith firm founded in Barcelona in 1839, known as Masriera y Hijos in 1872 and Masriera Hermanos from 1886. Inspired by a visit to the 1900 Paris 'Exposition Universelle,' Masriera is said to have melted down all the stock; six months later, he reopened with his designs in the Art Nouveau style. Though the firm continued to produce his original designs, the subsequent quality of production declined.
▶ He won the grand prize for jewelry at the 1908 Saragossa Exhibition and another prize at the 1913 Ghent 'Exposition Universelle et Industrielle.'

► Charlotte Gere, *American and European Jewelry 1830–1914*, New York: Crown, 1975:206–07.

Massari, Noti
See Toso, Aureliano

Massier, Clément (1844–1917)
► French ceramicist; born Vallauris.
► Massier learned pottery in his father's workshop; in 1864, set up his own workshop; from 1883, produced ceramics in *faïence vernisée* at Golfe-Juan, near Cannes, where numerous potters, including Jacques Sicard, were trained. He produced his first luster glaze in 1886. 1885–95, the young painter Lucien Lévy-Dhurmer managed Massier's enterprise. Manus Alexandre and Jean-Baptiste Barol often collaborated with Massier. His influence led to the establishment of new workshops for lusterware; many manufacturers and artists used his work as a model for lusterware production. The Massier factory continues as a family business.
► Work shown (with Optat Milet of Sèvres) at 1878 and 1889 Paris 'Expositions Universelles.'
► *Europäische Keramik 1880–1930, Sammlung Silzer*, Darmstadt: Hessisches Landesmuseum, 1986:128.

Massoni, Luigi (1930–)
► Italian industrial designer; born Milan; active Cermenate.
► Massoni began his professional career in 1954. From 1972, he was president and responsible for the architecture and industrial design department of A&D. His clients in Italy included Boffi (kitchen systems) from 1959, Poltrona Frau (furniture) from 1967, Fratelli Guzzini (plastic tableware and accessories) from 1964, Nazareno Gabrielli (leatherwork) from 1969, Gallotti & Radice (crystal) from 1969, and Palini (school furniture) from 1974. He was editor and designer of the journal *Forme* from 1962, editor of *Marmo Tecnica Architettura* from 1956–63, *Popular Photography* from 1963–66, *Design Italia* from 1968–72. He was artistic director at Centro Forms from 1973. He was a member of ADI (Associazione per il Disegno Industriale); founded studio Mabilia for industrial and furniture design.
► His *Nodi* and *Cerniere* containers were shown at the 1985 Triennale di Milano.
► *ADI Annual 1976*, Milan: Associazione per il Disegno Industriale, 1976. *Le Affinità Elettive*, Milan: Electa, 1985. Auction cat., *Asta di Modernariato 1900–1986*, Auction '*Modernariato*,' Milan: Semenzato Nuova Geri, 8 Oct. 1986: lot 102. *Modo*, No. 148, March–April 1993:122.

Massoul, Félix (1872–1942)
► French ceramicist; born Saint Germaine.
► Studied École des Arts Décoratifs, Paris.
► He was active in enameling with metallic flecks on faïence; frequently worked with his archeologist wife Madeleine and studied blue Egyptian faïence. He used ornate decoration in two blues; developed new glaze and stoneware *pâte-sableuse*; produced forms and designs in simple geometric patterns in blue, green, and burnished gold; with his wife, wrote and lectured on historic ceramics.
► In 1895, work first shown (with his wife) and, from 1903, at Salons of Société des Artistes français and Société des Artistes Décorateurs, and in exhibitions in France and abroad.
► Yvonne Brunhammer, *The Art Deco Style*, London: Academy, 1983:143. *Europäische Keramik 1880–1930, Sammlung Silzer*, Darmstadt: Hessisches Landesmuseum, 1986:137. Edgar Pelichet, *La Ceramic Art Déco*, Lausanne: Grand-Pont, 1988.

Masuda, Hideko (1947–)
► Japanese glass designer.
► Studied Tokyo Glass Crafts Institute to 1988
► Work included in 1987 'The Art of Contemporary Japanese Studio Glass,' Heller Gallery, New York; 1988 and 1989 'Japan Crafts,' Japan; 1988 'Japan Modern Decorative Arts,' Tokyo; 1989 'Arts in Hiroshima,' Hiroshima; 1990 'Glass '90 in Japan,' Tokyo; 1990 'Asahi Modern Crafts,' Tokyo; and 1991 (V) Triennale of the Japan Glass Art Crafts Association, Heller Gallery, New York. Included in 1987 'Corning Glass Review,' *Neues Glas* magazine.
► Cat., *Glass Japan*, New York: Heller Gallery and Japan Glass Art Crafts Association, 1991: No. 22.

Matégot, Mathieu (1910–)
► French decorator and furniture designer.
► Matégot's studio was at 49 rue d'Hautpoul, Paris, by 1954. He used metal as a basic component for his furniture, including steel rod and perforated-steel metal, and stressed function rather than decoration. His best-known design was the three-legged *Nagaski* chair of the 1950s with its perforated metal seat and tubular steel frame.
► Work (*Kioto* and *Panama* chairs) shown at 1955 Salon des Arts Ménagers.
► *Ensembles Mobiliers*, Paris: Charles Moreau, Nos. 13–14, 1954. Yolande Amic, *Intérieurs: Le Mobilier français 1945–1965*, Paris: Regard, 1983:54. Cat., Leslie Jackson, *The New Look: Design in the Fifties*, New York: Thames and Hudson, 1991:124.

Mategot, Xavier (1956–)
► French architect and furniture designer.
► Mategot collaborated with other architects in the design of office and domestic interiors in Paris. He was active in industrial design and, from 1983, in furniture design; in his furniture, blended 1930s Constructivism with 1950s eccentricity; was interior architect of the office furniture producer Christian Farjon; designed the stand of Institut français de restauration des oeuvres d'art at the 1990 Salon International des Musées.
► Received 1983 VIA Appel permanent award for *XM2* bookcase and *XM3* side chair (produced by Farjon). Participated in interior architecture competitions, including Counsel General's office at Belfort, Cogedim competition, Counsel General of Hauts-de-Seine and Cultural Center of Boulogne-Billancourt (*SM7* chair). Received 1987 Bourse Agora award.
► Suzanne Tise, 'Innovators at the Museum,' *Vogue Decoration*, No. 26, June/July 1990:48. Cat., *Les années VIA 1980–1990*, Paris: Musée des Arts Décoratifs, 1990:130–31.

Matet, Maurice (1903–)
► French decorator and furniture designer; born Colombes.
► Studied École des Arts Décoratifs, Paris.
► From 1923, Matet worked as a designer and decorator at the Studium decorating atelier of Grands Magasins du Louvre, where he sometimes collaborated with Étienne Kohlmann and Dubard. In *c*1930, he became professor at the École des Arts Appliqués in Paris; continuing to design furniture, particularly after World War II, he designed models in metal and glass and silver tableware along radically Modern lines.
► He designed the bedroom and office (with Étienne Kohlmann) installed in the 1923 Salon d'Automne and the dining room at the 1926 Salon of the Société des Artistes Décorateurs (SAD). Matet, Kohlmann, Édouard-Joseph Bourgeois, René Herbst, and Charlotte Perriand designed tubular-metal furniture with rubber and leather fittings shown at the 1928 Salon of SAD. Matet's more traditional Art Déco furniture (produced by Saddier) was shown at the 1929 event. He designed the dining room of Studium Louvre at 1925 Paris 'Exposition Internationale des Arts Décoratifs et Industriels Modernes.'
► Léon Deshairs, *Modern French Decorative Art*, Paris: Albert Lévy. Pierre Kjellberg, *Art Déco: les maîtres du Mobilier, le décor des Paquebots*, Paris: Amateur, 1986:124. Maurice Dufrêne, *Ensembles Mobiliers, Exposition Internationale 1925*, Paris: Charles Moreau, 1925, Antique Collectors' Club edition 1989:32.

Mathews, Arthur Frank (1860–1945) and Lucia Mathews (b. Lucia Kleinhans 1870–1955)
► American artists, muralists, and furniture designers; active San Francisco; husband and wife.
► Mathews studied painting, Académie Julian, Paris, under Boulanger and LeFebvre. Kleinhans studied Mark Hopkins Institute, under Arthur F. Mathews.

▶ While studying in Paris, Mathews was influenced by the new ideas current there in the 1880s and by Oriental art, especially Japanese woodcuts. 1890–1906, he was dean of the Mark Hopkins Institute in San Francisco, responsible for a faculty trained in the beaux-arts tradition in Paris. He established a regional figurative tradition in the arts. Lucia Kleinhans met Mathews at the Mark Hopkins Institute, where she was his prize student, and became his sometime collaborator on decorative projects. He approached his work from an architect's or muralist's perspective, while she had a more painterly style and produced watercolors and pastels of flowers, landscapes, and children. Together, they produced unique handmade pieces in a Beaux-Arts, rather than Arts and Crafts, style. By 1910, the Mathewses were at the peak of their success as leaders of the arts community in San Francisco and were identified with what came to be called the California Decorative Style of the 1890s–1920s. Through their business The Furniture Shop in San Francisco, they undertook the prolific execution of frames, paintings, furniture, fixtures, and accessories. 1906–20, the shop prospered during the rebuilding of San Francisco after the 1906 earthquake and fire. John Zeile was a partner, financial backer, and business manager. Thomas McGlynn oversaw 30 to 50 carpenters, cabinetmakers, woodcarvers, and finishers. Production consisted of domestic and public pieces, including large suites of furniture, and fixtures and custom murals. Lucia Mathews was fastidious in her application of decoration to smaller pieces and picture frames. Arthur's monthly magazine *Philopolis* debated the ethical and aesthetic aspects of art, town planning, and the reconstruction of San Francisco, to which the Mathewses were so committed that they shunned opportunities to expand their business nationally. Memory of their work having become obscure, they were rediscovered in the 1970s.
▶ Harvey L. Jones in Timothy J. Andersen et al., *California Design 1910*, Salt Lake City: Peregrine Smith, 1980:88–93.

Mathiesen, Lars (1950–)
▶ Danish architect and designer.
▶ Studied architecture.
▶ He collaborated with Box 25 Architects and Vast-Kyst Stugan. In 1978, he established Pelikan Design with Neils Gammelgaard. He taught at Det Kongelige Danske Kunstakademi, Copenhagen.

Mathieu, Paul (1950–)
▶ French designer.
▶ He collaborated with the American designer Michael Ray; their furniture designs, including club chair, sofa, and coffee table produced by Écart International, incorporated pale woods and fabrics in a style suggesting influences of Art Déco and Art Nouveau.
▶ Work (furniture by Écart) shown at 1991 Salon du Meuble, Paris.
▶ Ben Lloyd, *Metropolitan Home*, April 1990:180. 'Hot Properties,' *House and Garden*, May 1991:26. François Mathey, *Au bonheur des formes, design français 1945–1992*, Paris: Regard, 1992: 237,263.

Mathsson, Bruno (1907–)
▶ Swedish designer and architect; active Värnamo.
▶ Trained as a cabinetmaker and designer in Värnamo under his father.
▶ He opened an office in Värnamo. Specializing in natural wood, principally beech, and stemming from his research into the physiology of seating, he designed furniture with organic, flowing lines. Many of his designs were produced in the family furniture factory Karl Mathsson in Värnamo, with his later designs produced by Dux Möbel. His 1934 chair and compact 1946 extension table are still in production. He is best known for his 1934 *Eva* chair, produced from 1935 by Karl Mathsson; it was redesigned with arms in 1941. In the early 1960s, Mathsson collaborated with Piet Hein on adapting Hein's 'super-ellipse' ideas for furniture production and on developing a versatile self-clamping leg model. Pusuing tubular-steel construction, he designed the upholstered *Jetson* and leather-cushioned *Karin* chairs. As an architect and interior designer and influenced by a visit to the USA, he pioneered glass-wall construction in Sweden, and was one of the leading figures in the Modern movement in that country.
▶ Mathsson's work was shown at the 1937 Paris 'Exposition Internationale des Arts et Techniques dans la Vie Moderne,' 1939–40 San Francisco 'Golden Gate International Exposition,' 1939 New York 'World's Fair,' 1946 Copenhagen 'Svensk Form,' 1955 'H 55' Hälsingborg exhibition, 1954–57 USA 'Design in Scandinavia,' 1957 'Interbau' in Berlin, 1958 'Formes Scandinaves,' 1959 in Amsterdam, 1960 in Zürich and Munich, and 1980 'Scandinavian Modern Design 1880–1980' at the Cooper-Hewitt Museum in New York. His *T 102* chair was shown at the 1936 one-person exhibition at the Röhsska Konstslöjdmuseet in Gothenburg and at the 1937 Paris 'Exposition Internationale des Arts et Techniques dans la Vie Moderne.' He received the 1955 Gregor Paulsson trophy. In 1978, he was elected Honorary Royal Designer for Industry, London.
▶ Cat., Kathryn B. Hiesinger and George H. Marcus III (eds.), *Design Since 1945*, Philadelphia: Philadelphia Museum of Art, 1983:221,III–48. Cat., *Modern Chairs 1918–1970*, London: Lund Humphries, 1971: Nos. 20,111. *Design Quarterly*, Vol. 65, 1966. Erik Zahle (ed.), *A Treasury of Scandinavian Design*, New York, 1961:284, Nos. 3–4. Cat., *Les Assises du siège contemporain*, Paris: Musée des Arts Décoratifs, 1968. Cat., David Revere McFadden (ed.), *Scandinavian Modern Design 1880–1980*, New York: Abrams, 1982:268, No. 127.

Matsunaga, Naoki (1936–)
▶ Japanese designer; born Tokyo; active Milan.
▶ Studied University of Tokyo to 1961.
▶ With Rudolfo Bonetto, he designed tables, seating, case goods, and other domestic products for clients in Italy including Olivetti, Voxon, Sair Falconi, BCM, Candy, Cimbali, Simail, and Fratelli Guzzini and, in Brazil, Romi; became a member of ADI (Associazione per il Disegno Industriale).
▶ Received first prizes at 1960 Mainichi Industrial Design competition, 1965 (I) Japan Display Design competition, and 1966 (I) MIA competition, Monza.
▶ *ADI Annual 1976*, Milan: Associazione per il Disegno Industriale, 1976.

Matsushima, Iwao (1946–)
▶ Japanese glass designer.
▶ Studied Okayama University to 1970.
▶ In 1982, Matsushima lectured on ancient glass techniques at Okayama Municipal Museum of Oriental Art.
▶ Solo exhibition in 1984 at Keio department store, Tokyo. Work included in 1980 and 1982 Kokuten exhibitions; 1981 'Contemporary Glass,' National Museum of Art, Kyoto and Tokyo; 1990 'Glass '90 in Japan,' Tokyo; and 1991 (V) Triennale of the Japan Glass Art Crafts Association, Heller Gallery, New York. Invited artist at the 1986 Asahi Modern Crafts Exhibition, Japan.
▶ Cat., *Glass Japan*, New York: Heller Gallery and Japan Glass Art Crafts Association, 1991: No. 23.

Matsuura, Akane (1963–)
▶ Japanese glass designer.
▶ Studied Tama Art University, Tokyo, to 1987.
▶ Matsuura began working for Azumino Glass Studio in 1987. In 1987, he participated in the Society for the Study of Crafts Design at Tama Art University in Tokyo.
▶ Work included in 1988 'Arte en Vidro,' São Paulo Art Museum; 1989 Tamagawa Takashimaya department store, Tokyo; 1990 'Glass '90 in Japan,' Tokyo; and 1991 (V) Triennale of the Japan Glass Art Crafts Association, Heller Gallery, New York. Included in the 1988–89 'Corning Glass Review,' *Neues Glas* magazine.
▶ Cat., *Glass Japan*, New York: Heller Gallery and Japan Glass Art Crafts Association, 1991: No. 21.

Matta (aka Roberto Sebastian Matta Echaurren 1911–)
▶ Chilean designer; born Chile; active Paris.
▶ Trained as an architect in Santiago and, in the 1930s, in the office of Le Corbusier in Paris.
▶ In the mid-1960s, he executed designs produced by Gavina in Italy, including the 1966 *Malitte* component seating system (sold in the USA by Knoll). The widely published system was composed of puzzle-like forms that stacked into a square when not in use.
▶ Cat., Kathryn B. Hiesinger and George H. Marcus III (eds.), *Design Since 1945*, Philadelphia: Philadelphia Museum of Art, 1983:221,III–49. Eric Larrabee and Massimo Vignelli, *Knoll Design*, New York: Abrams, 1981:172,176,178–9. David McFadden (ed.) *L'Art de Vivre*, New York: Vendôme, 1989.

Mattu, Diego (1946–)
▶ Italian designer; born and active Rome.
▶ Studied Corso Superiore di Disegno Industriale e Communicazioni Visive, Rome, to 1970.
▶ In 1970, he was a research assistant at the Instituto di Psicologìa of CNR. In 1971, he was a designer for ICF/De Padova, worked in the design studio of Enzo Mari in Milan, and was a graphic artist in the studio Salaroli Piludu in Rome. From 1972, he was a designer and graphic artist in the CIFA group in Rome, working on designs for ItalBed and Uno Pi. 1968–72, he developed an exhibition system for a department store, designed machinery, rendered maps and graphics for IASM, and designed graphics for Italsonics. He was a consultant designer to Mautren-Mec in Aprilia. He was a designer and graphic artist to Drobeta in Pomezia, Tortora in Prato, and Betti and Pallucco in Rome. He was a graphic designer to journals including *Rassegna Artistica, Casabella, Esso Rivista, MD, Albergo Moderno*, and others. He designed furniture and case goods, often in plastics. He was a member of ADI (Associazione per il Disegno Industriale). 1968–74, he designed the signage of the Compasso d'Oro award events.
▶ *ADI Annual 1976*, Milan: Associazione per il Disegno Industriale, 1976.

Mauboussin
▶ French jewelry firm.
▶ The original firm was established in 1827 in rue Greneta in Paris, where it produced jewelry. From 1903, M.B. Noury was proprietor and nephew Georges Mauboussin, who had worked in the firm since 1877, director. In 1923, Mauboussin succeeded Noury, changed the name of the firm to Mauboussin, and purchased two connecting buildings at the intersection of the rue Saint-Augustin, rue de Choiseul, and rue Monsigny in Paris, with the address 3 rue de Choiseul. The firm set up branches in New York, Buenos Aires, and Rio de Janeiro. Moving to the place Vendôme, Mauboussin became known for its impeccable choice of precious materials and expert craftsmanship. The firm is a member of Comité Colbert.
▶ It successfully exhibited at the Pavilion of Marsan at the Louvre in the 1920s and participated in the 1924 New York 'French Exhibition,' 1923 and 1924 Milan exhibitions, and 1924 Strasbourg 'Exposition Coloniale.' At the 1925 Paris 'Exposition Internationale des Arts Décoratifs et Industriels Modernes,' it was awarded the grand prize.
▶ Sylvie Raulet, *Bijoux Art Déco*, Paris: Regard, 1984. Melissa Gabardi, *Les Bijoux des Années 50*, Paris: Amateur, 1987.

Maugham, Syrie (b. Gwendoline Maude Syrie Barnardo 1879–1955)
▶ British interior and furniture designer; born and active London; daughter of Dr. Barnardo, founder of the Barnardo Homes; wife of W. Somerset Maugham.
▶ After a scandal-filled youth, she began her decorating career on her own house in 1926 at 213 King's Road, Chelsea, London, which she painted almost entirely white as a successful publicity stunt. In 1922, her first shop opened at 85 Baker Street. Her customers included Noël Coward, Tallulah Bankhead, Clare Booth Luce, Ava and Paul Mellon, Mary Pickford, and the Duke and Duchess of Windsor. She designed a house for male-impersonator Vesta Tilley. Her trademark was the cala lily. Marion Dorn, Oliver Messel, and Christian Bérard designed rugs, furnishings, and murals for her clients. She sold furniture wiped with a white paint solution, creating a so-called 'pickled' finish, and was notorious for applying this treatment to fine 18th-century pieces. She was parodied in Evelyn Waugh's *A Handful of Dust* as Mrs. Beaver and in Beverly Nichols's *For Adults Only* as the Countess of Wesbourne. Success encouraged her to move in c1924 to headquarters in Grosvenor Square. By 1933, she had abandoned her all-white style for a blue one, followed by red one, then for a Victorian period, followed by what Cecil Beaton called 'the vivid colors of lobster salad.' Her rival in the 1930s was the decorator Lady Sybil Colefax. She became bankrupt; in the early 1950s, she executed a few commissions in the USA. Her 'white look' influenced Hollywood film sets and was emulated by American interior designer Michael Taylor with his 'California look' in the 1960s–70s.
▶ Her mirrored screen of c1934 was included in the 1979–80 'Thirties' exhibition at the Hayward Gallery in London.
▶ Richard B. Fisher, *Syrie Maugham*, London: Duckworth, 1978. Cat., *Thirties: British art and design before the war*, London: Arts Council of Great Britain, Hayward Gallery, 1979: 74,84,87, 130,296. Jessica Rutherford, *Art Nouveau, Art Deco and the Thirties: The Furniture Collections at Brighton Museum*, Brighton: The Royal Pavilion, Art Gallery and Museums, 1983:54. Mitchell Owens, 'White Magic,' *Elle Decor*, September 1990:92–96.

Maugirard, Charlotte (1968–)
▶ French designer; active Paris; daughter of Jean-Claude Maugirard.
▶ She designed a 1990 collection of lighting fixtures, candelabra, and vases constructed from bakery equipment.
▶ *Metropolitan Home*, Sept. 1990:42.

Maugirard, Jean-Claude (1939–)
▶ French industrial and furniture designer; active Paris; father of Charlotte Maugirard.
▶ 1955–60, studied École Boulle, Paris.
▶ In 1965, he invented the *MCS* (Mobile Cable System) for hanging paintings and objects in exhibitions; in 1967 with François Barré, designed the 'Sigma 3' exhibition, Bordeaux; in 1968, designed *Fosse de conversation* with modular elements in foam; in 1971, worked with injection-molded plastic and designed *CH 131* elements and *Kangourou* boxes produced by Formag; was artistic director, Rattan Design Group; invented a range of 'new rustic' furniture produced by Bruynzeel-France; taught furniture design, École Nationale Supérieure des Arts Décoratifs, Paris; from 1978, was head of VIA.
▶ Gilles de Bure, *Le mobilier français 1965–1979*, Paris: Regard/VIA, 1983:44,61–62,74,100,108–09.

Maurandy, Daniel (1922–)
▶ French industrial designer.
▶ Studied law and architecture.
▶ In 1960, he founded APES (Agence Parisienne d'Esthétique Industrielle); in the 1970s, carried out an urban design program for Vitry-sur-Seine, designing public furniture, signage, and transportation. He designed the corporate images of FNAC (hi-fi and domestic appliances), Merlin Gérin (electronics), and Nobel Bozel (chemistry), and often collaborated with Gérard Guerre. In 1975, APES was amalgamated into Technès, becoming Technès/Maurandy.
▶ François Mathey, *Au bonheur des formes, design français 1945–1992*, Paris: Regard, 1992:161,174,319,324. Cat., *Design français 1960–1990*, Paris: Centre Georges Pompidou/APCI, 1988.

Maurer, Ingo (1932–)
▶ German graphic and lighting designer; born Reichenau, Lake Constance.
▶ Trained as a typographer at Lake Constance and, 1954–58, as a graphic artist in Germany and Switzerland.

▶ He worked in the USA for Kayser Aluminum and IBM as a designer in 1960, returning to Europe in 1963, where he was active as a graphic designer. In 1966, he set up his own lighting design firm Design M and became known for his witty and innovatory ideas. His hanging cotton fabric, intriguing *Willydilly* fluorescent light fixture, and *Ilios* rocking lamp of the early 1980s were widely published. His 1980 *Bulb Bulb* fixture was a Pop Art statement in the form of a giant light bulb. His first halogen fixture was the 1983 *Ilios*. Maurer's *Baka Ru* and intricate 1984 *Ya Ya Ho* low-voltage ceiling system used a novel high-wire cable suspension system. Other designs included the 1982 *Bibibbibi* and 1986 *Fukusu*. Lindfors Stefan's 1988 *Scaragoo* articulated table lamp, which lit up when touched, was designed with and produced by Design M. In the late 1980s, he was an innovator of miniature low-voltage lights whose metal arms could be moved along uninsulated cables.
▶ 'Ingo Maurer, poète lumière,' *Intromuros*, Sept. 1985. Cat., *Luminaires*, Paris: CCI/Centre Georges Pompidou, 1985. Robert A.M. Stern (ed.), *The International Design Yearbook*, New York: Abbeville, 1985/1986: Nos. 216,231. 'Ingo Maurer, le phare de la lumière,' *Bureaux de France*, Dec. 1986. 'Jeux de reflets,' *Intramuros*, Dec. 1986. Jeremy Myerson and Sylvia Katz, *Conran Design Guides: Lamps and Lighting*, London: Conran Octopus, 1990:21,43,70,77. *Acquisitions arts décoratifs 1982–1990*, Paris: Fonds National d'Art Contemporain, 1991.

Mayer, Martin
▶ German silversmiths; located Mainz.
▶ The firm Martin Mayer was founded in 1888; it produced small silver objects, designs of the Wiener Werkstätte, and of Peter Behrens, Hans Christiansen, and Patriz Huber.
▶ Annelies Krekel-Aalberse, *Art Nouveau and Art Déco Silver*, New York: Abrams, 1989:196.

Maylander, Émile (1867–1959)
▶ French bookbinder and gilder; active Paris.
▶ Apprenticed in the workshop of Gustave Bénard and studied under Domont.
▶ In 1888, he began working with Francisque Cuzin as a gilder. In 1892, Cuzin died and was succeeded by Émile-Philippe Mercier, with whom Maylander became a principal collaborator. Maylander set up his own workshop in the rue de la Harpe when Mercier died in 1910. Maylander began bookbinding during World War I to supplement his gilding work. His bindings for Henri Vever were decorated by Jules Chadel; they included *Le Puits de Sainte-Claire, La Faune parisienne, Contes choisis*, and *Au Flanc du vase*. Maylander's sons took over management of the bindery in the 1920s.
▶ Ernest de Crauzat, *La Reliure française de 1900 à 1925*, Vol. 1, Paris, 1932:60. Roger Devauchelle, *La Reliure en France de ses origines à nos jours*, Paris, 1961:144,172,203,206–07,273. Alastair Duncan and Georges de Bartha, *Art Nouveau and Art Déco Bookbinding*, New York: Abrams, 1989:15,17,21,134–35,194.

Mayodon, Jean (1893–1967)
▶ French ceramicist.
▶ Mayodon began as a painter before his first ceramic pieces, strongly influenced by Persian pottery, were produced in 1912. His work was known for its rich colors. His pottery was made heat resistant by the addition of powdered clay. His decoration was painted with a brush or was in low relief highlighted with gold. He fired some pieces five or six times, creating colors with a metallic sheen. During World War II, Mayodon became director of the Manufacture Nationale de Sèvres.
▶ After World War I, he showed his work at the Musée Galliéra.
▶ Cat., *Decorative Arts 1925 Style*, New York: Didier Aaron, 1979.

Mayrhofer, Adolf von (1864–1929)
▶ German silversmith and enameler; active Munich.
▶ Apprenticed in the workshop of F. Harrach, Munich.

▶ For 12 years, he was an assistant to E. Wollenweber, silversmith to the Bavarian court. He set up his own silversmithy in 1903 and produced hand-raised beakers and slightly curved, somewhat foreshortened boxes with undecorated areas and carved ivory and ebony finials and handles. He produced *cloisonné* pieces, and on others incorporated spiral ornamentations. In the 1920s, he produced silver designs by Else Wenz-Viëtor and Hermann Haas. 1921–24, Franz Rickert and Dietrich Bruckmann, son of Peter Bruckmann, apprenticed in Mayrhofer's workshop. Mayrhofer's silver was sold in Carel Begeer's shops.
▶ His work was included in the Munich silversmiths' collective display at the 1910 Brussels 'Exposition Universelle et Internationale' and won a gold prize. He showed his work at the 1914 Cologne 'Deutscher Werkbund-Ausstellung.'
▶ Annelies Krekel-Aalberse, *Art Nouveau and Art Déco Silver*, New York: Abrams, 1989:131,142,144,150,179,257. Reinhard W. Sänger, *Das deutsche Silberbesteck 1805–1918*, Stuttgart: Arnoldsche, 1991:158–63.

Mazairac, Pierre (1943–)
▶ Dutch designer.
▶ Studied Academy of Modern Art, Utrecht.
▶ He worked for the Dutch furniture firm UMS-Pastoe; in 1979, set up his own design studio with Karel Boonzaauer.
▶ Robert A.M. Stern (ed.), *The International Design Yearbook*, New York: Abbeville, 1985/1986: No. 19.

Mazer
▶ American jewelry firm; located New York.
▶ The Franco-American Bead Co began producing jewelry in 1917 in Philadelphia, first with shoe buckles. In 1926, it moved to New York, and in 1939, established an office on 33rd Street to produce high-quality costume jewelry. The firm was managed by Joseph Mazer as treasurer and brothers Abe and Harry Mazer, and became known for its innovative production methods and experimentation with metal alloys and refinishing processes. Stones often came from Swarovski in Austria. Marcel Boucher was one of its designers, later setting up his own costume jewelry firm. From *c*1945, the chief designer at Mazer was André Fleurides, formerly of Van Cleef and Arpels. In 1946, Louis Mazer opened his own firm Jomaz. Louis Mazer (another brother) stayed at Mazer until 1951, when he designed his last collection.
▶ Deanna F. Cera (ed.), *Jewels of Fantasy: Costume Jewelry of the 20th Century*, New York: Abrams, 1992.

Mazer, Joseph A.
▶ American jewelry firm; located New York.
▶ In business by 1927, the firm's peak of business success was in the late 1950s, continuing to the beginning of the 1970s. Its wares were traditional, based on precious jewelry models, and included imported glass stones. In 1953, it was located on West 36th Street.
▶ Deanna F. Cera (ed.), *Jewels of Fantasy: Costume Jewelry of the 20th Century*, New York: Abrams, 1992.

Mazza, Sergio (1931–)
▶ Italian interior architect and designer; born and active Milan.
▶ Studied Institute of Architecture, Lausanne, to 1954.
▶ He began his professional career in 1955. In 1956, he opened his own office in Milan, collaborating with Giuliana Gramigna on domestic furnishings and industrial design. His clients included Artemide (furniture), Saporiti Italia (furniture), Cinova, Poltrona Frau (furniture), Cedit (ceramics), Formica, Full, Krupp (domestic electrical appliances), and Lema. His *Torlonia* hanging light was produced by Quattrifolio. Best known for his work in plastics, he designed shelving, mirrors, and lighting. His best known pieces are the 1968 *Toga* fiberglass chair and 1969 *Bacco* low, fitted mobile bar, both produced by Artemide. From 1961, he continued collaborating with Giuliana Gramigna on product design at their Studio SMC Architettura. In 1966, he founded the journal *Ottagono* which he directed until 1988. He was a member of ADI (Associazione per il Disegno Industriale).

▶ From 1954, he was a participant in the Triennali di Milano. He received the 1960 Compasso d'Oro for lighting. The *Toga* chair was shown at the 1969 International Furniture Exhibition in Milan and 1970 'Modern Chairs 1918–1970' exhibition at the Whitechapel Gallery in London. His work was included in the 1972 'Italy: The New Domestic Landscape' exhibition at the New York Museum of Modern Art. The *Bacco* mobile bar was shown at the 1983–84 'Design Since 1945' exhibition at the Philadelphia Museum of Art.

▶ Cat., *Modern Chairs 1918–1970*, London: Lund Humphries, 1971. Cat., Kathryn B. Hiesinger and George H. Marcus III (eds.), *Design Since 1945*, Philadelphia: Philadelphia Museum of Art, 1983:222,III–50. Cat., *Italy: The New Domestic Landscape*, New York: Museum of Modern Art, 1972:35,56. 'Sergio Mazza e Giuliana Gramigna,' *Interni*, No. 282, Sept. 1978:54–57. Alfonso Grassi and Anty Pansera, *Atlante del design Italiano: 1940–1980*, Milan, 1980:162,168,290. *ADI Annual 1976*, Milan: Associazione per il Disegno Industriale, 1976. *Modo*, No. 148, March–April 1993:122.

Mazzoni delle Stelle, Alessandro (1941–)
▶ Italian designer; born and active Florence.
▶ Studied industrial design at the ISIA in Florence.
▶ Mazzoni began his professional career in 1970, founding the group A.r.d.i.t.i. for industrial design. Designing furniture and accessories, he was best known for his loosely covered foam club chair of the 1970s. He was a member of ADI (Associazione per il Disegno Industriale); in 1977, he left A.r.d.i.t.i. and worked with other designers and technicians; in 1985, he began a collaboration with Gianfranco Gualtierotti.
▶ *ADI Annual 1976*, Milan: Associazione per il Disegno Industriale, 1976. *Modo*, No. 148, March–April 1993:122.

Mazzucchelli, Franco (1939–)
▶ Italian industrial designer; born and active Milan.
▶ Mazzucchelli began his professional career in 1968. He was best known for his inflatable plastic objects, sometimes as giant public monuments. His clients included Arflex, Anny di Gennaro, Forme & Superfici, Garavaglia, Habitat in Italy and Tokyo, Quirra, and Sir. He was a member of ADI (Associazione per il Disegno Industriale).
▶ *ADI Annual 1976*, Milan: Associazione per il Disegno Industriale, 1976.

Mazzucotelli, Alessandro (1865–1938)
▶ Italian metalsmith; born Lodi.
▶ Studied architecture.
▶ Leaving the family smithy in 1895, he set up his own workshop in Milan, producing wrought iron in the Art Nouveau style; in 1902, became one of the founders of the Instituto Superiore di Arti Decorative, Monza. His complex floral and insect designs included balconies, banisters, grilles, and lighting. Active on the buildings of Giuseppe Sommaruga, he designed architectural ironwork for the 1901–03 Palazzo Castiglioni in Milan, a major example of *stile liberty* that included furniture by Ernesto Quarti. After World War I, his style moved towards Art Déco.
▶ He won a diploma at the 1902 'Esposizione Internazionale d'Arte Decorativa Moderna' in Turin.
▶ R. Bussaglia, *Mazzucotelli: The Italian Art Nouveau Artist of Wrought Iron*, Milan, 1971.

McArthur, Warren (1885–1961)
▶ American industrial designer and manufacturer; active Los Angeles and New York.
▶ McArthur worked in aluminum from the late 1920s. Even though he patented the early use of aluminum in furniture in 1930, his lightweight furnishings, of which there were more than 600 designs, did not become popular until the late 1980s. In 1924, McArthur designed the recreational vehicle *Wonderrbus*; in 1930, established his own furniture manufacturing company in Los Angeles, where clients included movie stars and studios; in 1933, he moved his factory to Rome, New York, with offices in Manhattan; in 1937, he again moved factory to Bantam, Connecticut; in 1938, he accepted the prototype-furniture commission for Frank Lloyd Wright's Johnson Wax Building. He submitted a prototype desk, a secretary's chair, and a low half-round table, based on Wright's drawings for metal furniture designs, but Steelcase furniture company was awarded the contract. McArthur's version of Wright's chair was rendered in aluminum. During World War II, McArthur produced aluminum and magnesium seating for aircraft bombers. Some of his furniture models, although Modern in their use of aluminum, were oddly historicist in form and constructed of interchangeable standardized tubular metal parts fastened with interior screws concealed under aluminum bands. In 1947, McArthur founded Mayfair Industries in Yonkers, near New York. Even though interest in aluminum furniture faded after World War II, his models continued to be produced until the 1960s.
▶ 'Warren McArthur,' *The New York Times*, 18 Dec. 1961:35. Sale cat., *Frank Lloyd Wright*, Chicago: Kelmscott Gallery, 1981. Jonathan Lipman, *Frank Lloyd Wright and the Johnson Wax Building*, New York: Rizzoli: 1986:87–88,185. Suzanne Slesin, 'It's Back to the Futuristic Machine Age,' *The New York Times*, 17 Dec. 1992:C3. Avis Berman, 'Warren McArthur' in Mel Byars and Russell Flinchum (eds.), *50 American Designers*, Washington: Preservation, 1994. Mel Byars, *The Chairs of Frank Lloyd Wright: Seven Decades of Design*, Washington: Preservation, 1994.

McCarthy, Rory (1948–)
▶ American architect; born New York.
▶ McCarthy showed his work at the American Crafts Museum in New York; received the 1984 Furniture Design Competition prize of *Progressive Architecture* magazine.
▶ Robert A.M. Stern (ed.), *The International Design Yearbook*, New York: Abbeville, 1985/1986: No. 172.

McClelland, Nancy Vincent (1877–1959)
▶ American designer; born Poughkeepsie, New York; active Philadelphia, Pennsylvania, and New York.
▶ 1897, graduated Vassar College, Poughkeepsie.
▶ From 1897–1901, she worked for the newspaper *Philadelphia Press*; from 1901–07, worked in advertising department of Wanamaker's department store, Philadelphia; from 1907–13, sent by Wanamaker's to Paris; she studied, edited her own bulletin on fashion trends, collected documentary wallpapers, and traveled widely; in 1913 at Wanamaker's in New York, she founded the Au Quatrième decorating studio, said to be the first antique and decorating department established in a department store; in 1922, she set up her own interior-design business at 15 East 57th Street, New York, showing French furniture in paneled rooms and becoming known for her historic wallpaper reproductions made in France. She published numerous books on design and decoration, including *Historic Wallpapers* (Philadelphia: Lippincott, 1924), said to be the first complete history on the subject; had a great interest in the restoration of historic museums and buildings in USA; participated in the restoration of Roger Morris-Jumel Mansion, New York; Mount Vernon, Virginia; General Robert E. Lee's headquarters, Fredericksburg, Virginia; Henry Wadsworth Longfellow house, Portland, Main; and House of History, Kinderhoek, New York.
▶ Appointed Chevalier de la Légion d'honneur in 1930; fellow of Royal Society for the Encouragement of Arts, Manufactures and Commerce; for three years, national president, American Institute of Decorators, becoming fellowship member in 1948; received 1946 (I). F. Allman (wallpaper merchant) Award of the National Wallpaper Wholesaler's Association for contributing to the renewal of wallpaper's popularity.
▶ 'Nancy McClelland First to Win Justin Allman Wallpaper Award,' *The New York Times*, 11 Oct. 1946. 'Miss M'Clelland, Antiquary, Here,' *The New York Times*, 2 Oct. 1959. John Esten and Rose Bennett Gilbert, *Manhattan Style*, Boston: Little, Brown, 1990:4.

McCobb, Paul (1917–69)
▶ American furniture designer.
▶ McCobb set up his own studio in 1945, working as a painter, interior decorator, and display designer. In 1950, with distributor B.G. Mosberg, introduced his first low-cost furniture collection, the *Planner Group*. His higher-priced furniture ranges *Directional*, *Predictor Linear*, and *Perimeter* were produced by Winchendon Furniture in Massachusetts and marketed and distributed by McCobb himself. His designs of the 1950s were also produced by H. Sacks in Brookline, Massachusetts, and Calvin Furniture in Grand Rapids, Michigan. Similar in form to Charles Eames's and Eero Saarinen's designs, McCobb's interchangeable chests, cabinets, and bookcases had bench bases which also served as separate tables. His desk tops had bevelled edges to make them look thinner. McCobb popularized modular furniture and created 'living walls' with moveable room dividers and storage systems. He created an entirely new American style of décor and believed in giving the customer good value; his renown in the 1950s was considerable, though his name became little known from the 1960s.
▶ His work was shown at the 'Good Design' exhibitions of the New York Museum of Modern Art and Merchandise Mart in Chicago. In 1957, Bloomingdale's department store showed 348 pieces of his furniture in 15 room settings. Furniture from the *Planner Group* was included in the 1983–84 'Design Since 1945' exhibition at the Philadelphia Museum of Art.
▶ Cherie Fehrman and Kenneth Fehrman, *Postwar Interior Design, 1945–1960*, New York: Van Nostrand Reinhold, 1987. Roberto Alio, *Mobili Tipo*, Milan: Hoepli, 1956:109. Cat., Kathryn B. Hiesinger and George H. Marcus III (eds.), *Design Since 1945*, Philadelphia: Philadelphia Museum of Art, 1983:222. 'McCobb's Predictor Solves Many Problems Simultaneously,' *Interiors*, Vol. 111, Oct. 1951:126–29. 'An Interior View: Paul McCobb,' *Art Digest*, Vol. 26, 15 Sept. 1952:19. George Nelson (ed.), *Storage*, New York: Whitney Library of Ideas, 1954:32,48,60,62,67,76,92. *Current Biography*, 1958. Jay Doblin, *One Hundred Great Product Designs*, New York, 1970: No. 60.

McConnico, Hilton (1943–)
▶ American furniture designer; born Memphis, Tennessee; active Paris.
▶ He moved to Paris in 1965; became an assistant to Ted Lapidus, designing a collection of couture dresses, worked for Yves Saint-Laurent, designing the first ready-to-wear menswear collection, and Jacques Heim. He designed furs for Neiman Marcus. McConnico created his first film set for friend and director Bob Swaim and, from 1974, worked on 22 film set designs and created more than 30 television commercials in France. He executed designs for Jean-Jacques Beineix's films *Diva* (1981) and *La Lune dans le caniveau* (1983) and won a César French film award for the latter. Other film sets were designed for François Truffaut and Claude Chabrol. In 1985, he became active in the decorative arts and designed *pâte-de-verre* glassware for Daum in the late 1980s, incorporating a cactus motif. From the late 1980s, he designed rugs for Toulemonde Bochart, porcelain and a silk foulard for the 1989 French Revolution bicentennial for Hermès, and, under McConnico's own label, furnishing rugs and fabrics for Galeries Lafayette. In 1989, he designed a museum of horse racing at the Longchamps racecourse in the Bois de Boulogne, Paris, and a museum of costume history in Château Chinon. In 1989, he designed a limited-edition cactus-motif rug for Art Surface and, with partner Gilles Le Gall, refurbished the Paris métro station Chaussée-d'Antin.
▶ Peter S. Green, 'McConnico Unlimited,' *House and Garden*, July 1989. Suzanne Slesin, 'A Designer's Whimsical Essays in "Tex-Baroque," ' *The New York Times*, 15 June 1989:C12.

McCoy, Michael (1945–)
▶ Industrial designer and teacher.
▶ McCoy was head of the design department at the Cranbrook Academy in Michigan. A proponent of using design to humanize

technology, he created products for Philips and office furniture for Knoll and Brayton, collaborating with Dale Fahnstrom. He wrote a number of scholarly papers.
▶ Mary Beth Jordan, *Metropolitan Home*, April 1990:107.

McCulloch, Peter (1933–)
▶ British textile designer.
▶ Studied Glasgow School of Art.
▶ In the early 1960s, he taught at the Falmouth School of Art in Cornwall. Some of his textiles incorporated contrasting colors in small dots suggesting printed circuitry, as in his 1963 *Cruachan* fabric produced by Hull Traders.
▶ Cat., Kathryn B. Hiesinger and George H. Marcus III (eds.), *Design Since 1945*, Philadelphia: Philadelphia Museum of Art, 1983:222,VII–45. 'Design Centre Awards 1963,' *Design*, No. 174, June 1963:44–45.

McCurry, Margaret (1943–)
▶ American architect; husband of architect Stanley Tigerman.
▶ Studied art history, Vassar College, Poughkeepsie, New York, to 1964.
▶ She was a packaging designer at first; 1966–77, worked on interiors at architects Skidmore Owings and Merrill, Chicago, for the 1968 Container Corporation headquarters, 1968–77 National Life and Accident headquarters, 1972–74 St. Joseph Valley Bank, 1974–76 Baxter Laboratories headquarters, and 1975–77 Holiday Inn Mart Plaza. In 1977, she set up her own studio and designed the interior of Van Straatan Art Gallery, Chicago; from 1982, collaborated with husband Stanley Tigerman in Chicago; (with Tigerman) designed ceramics, including the *Heaven* range and *Teaside* coffee and tea set and metalware by Swid Powell from the 1980s, a tea set for Alessi's 1983 *Tea and Coffee Piazza* project, a showroom for American Standard in New York, and the *Heritage* faucet range by American Standard; (with Tigerman) was an outspoken voice on contemporary architecture. She designed the American Bar Association building; 'Wit's End' house in Sawyer, Michigan; and became the first woman to chair the National AIA Committee on Design.
▶ Herman Miller showroom design shown at 1984 Neocon, Chicago. Received Chicago AIA award. Appointed 1990 Hall of Fame member, *Interior Design* magazine.
▶ Robert A.M. Stern (ed.), *The International Design Yearbook*, New York: Abbeville, 1985/1986: No. 273. Beverly Russell, *Women of Design*, New York: Rizzoli, 1992:174–75,214–17.

McGrath, Raymond (1903–77)
▶ Australian architect and designer; active London.
▶ 1920–21, studied Sydney University; 1921–25, School of Architecture, Sydney University; 1926, Brixton School of Building and Westminster School of Art, London; 1927–30, Cambridge University.
▶ He settled in Britain in 1926. His first independent commission was the 1929 remodeling of the Mansfield Forbes residence 'Finella.' The Regency house was outfitted in colored glass and copper with walls in pink and green. Widely published, the assignment helped to promote McGrath as a leading designer and architect and resulted in his being appointed 'decoration consultant' for the 1930–32 interiors of BBC Broadcasting House, London, where he headed a design team that included Serge Chermayeff and Wells Coates. He was responsible for the 1935 Manchester studios of the BBC. In 1930, he set up a practice in London. From *c*1932, he was an industrial and interior designer. McGrath was a leading exponent of Modernism during the 1920s and 1930s. He used glass extensively, with natural colored materials and indoor plants. He wrote *Twentieth Century Homes* (1934). In 1940, he settled in Ireland, where he was architect to the Office of Public Works and principal architect 1948–68. His work included 1932 lighting and *Synchronome* wall clock by Abbey Electric Clock Works for the BBC studios; numerous exhibition stands and showrooms, including for GEC and Imperial Airways; radio cabinets for Ekco; unit furniture for Easiwork; interiors for Atlanta aircraft

for Imperial Airways; oil-dispensing equipment for Vacuum Oil; 1932 Fischers Long Bar and Restaurant in New Bond Street, London; 1932–33 Embassy Club; electrical section of the 1933 London 'Ideal Home' exhibition; the Kingstone store of c1935 in Leicester; 1935–37 houses in Chertsey, including 1936–37 house at St. Ann's Hill with its circular two-storey spaces; 1936–39 houses in Gaulby; numerous unrealized projects, including the 1938 Aspro Factory in Slough; 1934 *Six Ages of Architecture* panels (Greek, Roman, Chinese, Gothic, Florentine, and Modern) door panels for the Royal Institute of British Architects, London; 1935 plate-glass and metal sales trophy for Austin Reed; 1937 heat-resistant glassware (*Phoenix* ware) (with Elizabeth Craig) produced by British Heat Resisting Glass, Birmingham.

▶ Numerous examples of his work were included in the 1979–80 'Thirties' exhibition at the Hayward Gallery, London.

▶ Philippe Garner, *The Encyclopedia of Decorative Arts, 1890–1940*, Secaucus, N.J.: Chartwell, 1978. Cat., *Thirties: British art and design before the war*, London: Arts Council of Great Britain, Hayward Gallery, 1979:55,73,84,101–02,148,156,181,192–94,207–08,233,235–36,271,296.

McGugan, Steve   (1960–)

▶ Canadian industrial designer; born Vancouver; active Copenhagen.

▶ Studied Art Center College of Design, Pasadena, California.

▶ 1982–84, he worked for Bang & Olufsen in Struer, Denmark. 1985–87, he worked in the studio of David Lewis in Copenhagen. In 1988, he opened his own studio and designed electronic and medical products. He designed the widely published 1985 *Form 2* earphones for Bang & Olufsen, 1988 taxi-cab meter for F. Frogne, and 1989 *NovoLet* syringe for insulin injections for Novo Nordisk and Pharma-Plast.

▶ The *NovoLet* syringe won the 1990 ID Prize.

▶ Cat., Chantal Bizot, *Bang & Olufsen: Design et Technologie*, Paris: Musée des Arts Décoratifs, 1990:11.

McIntosh, Lawrie

▶ Canadian designer; born Ontario; active Toronto.

▶ Studied mechanical engineering, University of Toronto, to 1946, and product design, Illinois Institute of Technology, Chicago, to 1951.

▶ In the early 1950s, he set up McIntosh Design Associates, Toronto, becoming active in industrial design, furniture design, and research. He was an instructor at the Ontario College of Art.

▶ Cat., *Seduced and Abandoned: Modern Furniture designers in Canada, the First Fifty Years*, Toronto: The Art Gallery at Harbourfront, 1986:14.

McKim, Mead and White

▶ American architectural partnership; located New York.

▶ The principal partners of the large, prolific architecture firm at the turn of the century were Charles Follen McKim (1847–1909), William Rutherford Mead (1846–1928), and William Stanford White (1853–1906). By 1919, the firm had built over 1,000 structures. In historicist forms with some innovative structures, the firm's work included decorative and picturesque elements, largely by White. McKim produced studied, austere monumental designs. The office was organized by Mead. The partners' fame was established by Shingle-Style mansions and country clubs in the USA, including the 1886–87 William G. Low house in Bristol, Rhode Island, and 1879–80 Newport Casino in Newport. The group's work was influenced by H.H. Richardson, with whom McKim and White worked in the early 1870s. Their 1882–86 H.A.C. Taylor house in Newport marked the revival of interest in the USA in colonial architecture. White's own house at 121 East 21st Street exemplified the taste of a dilettante art collector. The décor of the 1882–85 Villard house at 455 Madison Avenue was an outstanding example of American neo-Renaissance design. McKim designed the 1887–98 Public Library in Boston, a reworking of the Bibliothèque Sainte-Geneviève, Paris, designed by Henri Labrouste. The firm produced a new interpretation of urban architecture.

Other work included the 1891–1903 State Capitol in Providence, Rhode Island, and, in New York, 1893–1902 Columbia University building, 1902–11 Pennsylvania Station, and 1893–1915 Brooklyn Museum. Architects Cass Gilbert, Henry Bacon, John Merven Carrière, and Thomas Hastings trained in the firm's office.

▶ *A Monograph of the Works of McKim, Mead and White, 1879–1915*, New York, 1915, reprinted 1973. Charles H. Reilly, *McKim, Mead, and White*, New York, 1924. Charles Baldwin, *Stanford White*, New York, 1931. Vincent Scully, *The Shingle Style*, New Haven: Yale University, 1955. Leland M. Roth, *The Architecture of McKim, Mead and White, 1870–1920: A Building List*, New York, 1978. William A. Cole, 'The genesis of a classic,' in Edith Wharton and Ogden Codman Jr., *The Decoration of Houses*, New York: Norton, 1978. Leland M. Roth, *McKim, Mead and White, Architects*, New York, 1983, and London, 1984. Barry Bergdoll in Vittorio Magnago Lampugnani (ed.), *Encyclopedia of 20th-Century Architecture*, New York: Abrams, 1986:206. Stephen Calloway, *Twentieth-Century Decoration*, New York: Rizzoli, 1988:56.

McKinney, Nanny
See **Still McKinney, Nanny**

McLaughlin, Mary Louise   (1847–1939)

▶ American pottery and porcelain decorator; active Cincinnati, Ohio.

▶ Studied art in Cincinnati and University of Cincinnati School of Design under Benn Pitman.

▶ She was a pioneer of china-painting in the USA, profoundly influencing contemporary and later ceramicists. Initially exposed to painting through Benn Pitman and German instructor Maria Eggers in Cincinnati, and influenced by the underglaze slip-decorated Haviland faïence made in Limoges, McLaughlin began to copy the technique. She published *China Painting: A Practical Manual for the Use of Amateurs in the Decoration of Hard Porcelain* (1877). In 1877, she successfully duplicated Limoges faïence at P.L. Coultry's pottery in Cincinnati. In 1879, she, Laura Fry, Agnes Pitman, and Elizabeth Nourse founded the Cincinnati Pottery Club (disbanded in 1890), of which McLaughlin was president. Members fired their pieces at the Frederick Dallas Pottery and later at Maria Longworth Nichols's Rookwood Pottery until 1883. In 1894, she began experimenting at the Brockman Pottery by painting decoration on the interior of molds with slip before casting. Calling this work 'American faience' (patented by her in 1894), she was dissatisfied with its results and soon abandoned it. In 1890, she founded the Associated Artists of Cincinnati, a group of metalworkers and ceramics decorators, and was its president. She published *Pottery Decoration under the Glaze* (1880). Her 40-inch (1m) *Ali Baba* vase was the largest made in the USA; three models were produced. Working in copper for a time, she returned to ceramics in 1895, producing carved ware known as *Losanti* that she made until 1904, the year she gave up pottery to write on history and politics. McLaughlin was assisted by Margaret Hickey, who cast the porcelain and tended the kiln. In 1914, McLaughlin became involved once more with metalwork, jewelry making, needlework, etching, painting, and sculpture, and was active until the age of 92.

▶ She showed her carved desk (under the direction of Henry Lindley Fry and William Henry Fry) at the 1876 Philadelphia 'Centennial Exposition.' In c1877, her Limoges-type faïence was shown in Cincinnati and New York, and, receiving an honorable mention, at the 1878 Paris 'Exposition Universelle.' She showed 20 pieces of her *Losanti* ware at the 1899 exhibition of the Cincinnati Art Museum. She received a bronze medal for her work at the 1901 Buffalo 'Pan-American Exposition' where she exhibited 27 pieces, and a silver medal for her metalwork at the 1900 Paris 'Exposition Universelle.'

▶ Edwin AtLee Barber, 'Recent Advances in the Pottery Industry,' *Popular Science Monthly*, Vol. 40, Jan. 1892:289–322. Edwin AtLee Barber, *The Pottery and Porcelain of the United States*, New York, 1893:275–84. 'Mary Louise McLaughlin,' *American Ceramic Society Bulletin*, No. 17, May 1938:217–25. Cat., *The Ladies, God*

Bless 'Em: The Women's Art Movement in Cincinnati in the Nineteenth Century, Cincinnati: Cincinnati Art Museum, 1976. Joan Siegfried, 'American Women in Art Pottery,' *Nineteenth Century*, Vol. 9, Spring 1984:12–18. Doreen Bolger Burke et al., *In Pursuit of Beauty: Americans and the Aesthetic Movement*, New York: Metropolitan Museum of Art and Rizzoli, 1986:451–52. *American Art Pottery*, New York: Cooper-Hewitt Museum, 1987:132.

McLauren, Denham (1903–)
▶ British painter and furniture designer; born Denham, Buckinghamshire.
▶ 1920–21, studied Académie Julian, Paris; 1922–24, Cambridge University; 1925, Slade School of Fine Art, London, and London University.
▶ *c*1927–30, he designed furniture for the exhibition stands produced by the Arundell Display firm. In 1930, he set up his own studio showrooms in London, first in Davies Street, then in Grosvenor Street. In 1930, he began incorporating glass into his furniture, as in the chromed-steel tables entered in Lord Benbow's competition by Paul Nash. In the late 1930s, he turned from furniture design to estate management.
▶ His 1930 coromandel, sycamore, glass, and chrome desk was included in the 1979–80 'Thirties' exhibition at the Hayward Gallery in London.
▶ Cat., *Thirties: British art and design before the war*, London: Arts Council of Great Britain, Hayward Gallery, 1979:84, 150,295.

McLeish, Minnie (1876–1957)
▶ British textile designer.
▶ In the 1920s, was a freelance textile designer, working for several firms, most notably W. Foxton; designed bold, colorful patterns for printed furnishing fabrics.
▶ Valerie Mendes, *The Victoria & Albert Museum's Textile Collection, British Textiles from 1900 to 1937*, London: Victoria & Albert Museum, 1992.

McMillen, Eleanor
See Brown, Eleanor McMillen

McVickers, Julia (1906–90)
▶ American textile designer; born Memphis, Tennessee.
▶ Studied Institute of Design, Chicago, under Marli Ehrman.
▶ 1945–80, with Else Regensteiner, founded Reg/Wick Handwoven Originals in Hyde Park, Illinois; designed custom handwoven fabrics for designers and architects and for industry; was a founding member of Midwest Designer Craftsmen.
▶ Sigrid Wortmann Weltge, *Women's Work: Textile Art from the Bauhaus*, London: Thames and Hudson, 1993.

Mead, William Rutherford (1846–1928)
See McKim, Mead and White

Meazza, Roberto (1934–)
▶ Italian exhibition and industrial designer; born and active Milan.
▶ Meazza began his professional career in 1965. His clients included 3M Italia (camera) and Hewlett Packard. He worked for Studio Ideogramma, designed the exhibition of the Samu Industrial Design competition, and was a member of ADI (Associazione per il Disegno Industriale).
▶ *ADI Annual 1976*, Milan: Associazione per il Disegno Industriale, 1976.

Med (1957–)
▶ Moroccan designer; born Casablanca.
▶ Studied medical science, École Polytechnique, Paris.
▶ He took up painting and subsequently sculpture and design. In his decorative work, he incorporated the traditional materials of his native North Africa—wood, hides, bladders, horn, and bone.
▶ 'Les Designers du soleil,' *Maison Française décoration internationale*, June 1992.

Meda, Alberto (1945–)
▶ Italian engineer and designer; born Lenno Tremezzina; active Milan.
▶ Studied mechanical engineering, Politecnico di Milano, to 1969.
▶ From 1970–75, he was assistant director of production at Magneti Marelli; in 1973, became technical director and controller of planning at Kartell in Binasco and initiated research into the use of polyurethane. In 1979, he began his independent professional career as engineer, designer, and consultant for product engineering; was a consultant to Alfa Romeo Auto and Italtel on new products. From 1983, he taught industrial technology at the Domus Academy in Milan. In 1986, he began to design furniture; other designs included the 1987 *LightLight* chair and *Dry* table produced by Alias in Milan. The *LightLight* was formed in an epoxy-resin matrix sandwiched in a beehive of Nomex and unidirectional carbon fiber. Meda and Paolo Rizzato designed the 1990 *Titania* hanging light produced by Luce Plan.
▶ *Modo*, No. 148, March–April 1993:122.

Medici, Roberto (1937–)
▶ Italian industrial designer; born Bologna; active Ponticella di S. Lazzaro di Savena.
▶ Medici began his professional career in 1965. He designed heavy machinery and medical measuring devices for MG2, Alsa, and General Data. He designed advertising for Battaglia-Rangoni engineering, ACMA, MG2, Data Logic, Lippo, ALSA, MAG, and General Data. He was a member of ADI (Associazione per il Disegno Industriale).
▶ *ADI Annual 1976*, Milan: Associazione per il Disegno Industriale, 1976.

Medjeber, Cherif
See Chérif

Medley, Robert (1905–)
▶ British painter and theater designer.
▶ 1921, studied Byam Shaw School and Royal Academy School, 1923–26, Slade School of Fine Art, London.
▶ He became a member in 1930 of the London Group and of the London Artists' Association. From 1933, he designed for the Group Theatre, founded by Rupert Doone. He designed costumes and sets for the plays *Dance of Death* (1933) by W.H. Auden, *Sweeney Agonistes* (1935–36) by T.S. Eliot, *The Dog Beneath the Skin* by Auden and Christopher Isherwood, and *The Ascent of F6* by Auden and Isherwood, at the Mercury Theatre in London. He contributed the article 'Hitler's Art in Munich' in the journal *Axis* 8 (1937).
▶ His work was the subject of a 1930 one-person exhibition at the Cooling Galleries. His work was included in the 1936 'International Surrealist Exhibition' and his gouache painting *Tenements* (1935) in the 1979–80 'Thirties' exhibition at the Hayward Gallery in London.
▶ Cat., *Thirties: British art and design before the war*, London: Arts Council of Great Britain, Hayward Gallery, 1979: 35,245,296.

Meier, Otto (1910–82)
▶ Swiss architect and furniture designer; born and active Basel.
▶ Served masonry and carpentry apprenticeships in Basel.
▶ In 1925, he and Ernst Mumenthaler established an architecture office and contracting firm in Basel. They developed the modular furniture system *3M-Möbel*, constructed by Meier himself. Their award-winning *c*1928 cabinets shown at the 'Das Neue Heim II' exhibition were further developed in lightweight plywood. In 1944, they and architect August Künzel designed the housing development Drei Linden in Basel. The office of Mumenthaler and Meier closed in 1972.
▶ Meier and Mumenthaler won first prize in a competition held at 1928 'Das Neue Heim II' (The New Home II) exhibition in the Kunstgewerbemuseum in Zürich.

▶ Friederike Mehlau-Wiebking et al., *Schweizer Typenmöbel 1925–35, Sigfried Giedion und die Wohnbedarf AG*, Zürich: gta, 1989:229.

Meier, Richard Alan (1934–)
▶ American architect; born Newark, New Jersey.
▶ Studied architecture, Cornell University, to 1957.
▶ 1958–59, he worked for architects Davis, Brody and Wisniewski in New York; 1959–60, for Skidmore, Owings and Merrill in New York; and, 1960–63, for Marcel Breuer and Associates. In the late 1950s and early 1960s, he was an artist in a studio he shared with Michael Graves on 10th Street. In 1963, he set up his own practice. 1964–73, he was professor of architecture at the Cooper Union in New York; 1975–77, at Yale University; and, in 1977, at Harvard University. In the 1970s, he was a member of the New York Five with Peter Eisenman, Michael Graves, Charles Gwathmey, and John Hejduk. Meier's architecture reflected the influence of Le Corbusier's Cubist designs of the 1920s, and for three decades he sought the Modernist ideal, as in his parents' Old Westbury, New York, house. His first furniture was produced in 1978, including the 1978–82 chairs, stool, telephone stand, and chaise produced by Knoll. His designs were often derivative of previous 20th-century designers' works, including the tea set (reflective of Malevich's work, for Alessi's 1983 *Tea and Coffee Piazza* project, and his metalwork and ceramics (quoting Josef Hoffmann's grid designs) for Swid Powell. He executed the ceramic designs *Joseph*, *Peachtree*, and *Anna*, and glassware *Spiral*, *Lattice*, and *Professor* for Swid Powell in the early 1980s. He designed a 1991 fabric collection for Design Tex. His work may be defined as neo-Modern rather than Post-Modern. His buildings included his own 1965 house in Essex Fells, New Jersey; 1965–67 Smith house in Darien, Connecticut; 1967–69 Saltzman house in East Hampton, New York; Westbeth artists' apartment conversions in New York; 1968–72 Physical Education Center for the New York State University in Fredonia, New York; 1969–74 Twin Parks housing in the Bronx, New York; 1970–71 Bronx Developmental Center in New York; 1971–73 Douglas house in Harbor Springs, Michigan; 1975–79 Atheneum in New Harmony, Indiana; 1980–84 Museum für Kunsthandwerk (1979 competition winner) in Frankfurt; 1983 High Museum, Atlanta, Georgia; 1985 Getty Museum in Los Angeles; and City Hall in The Hague.
▶ His work was shown in the 1969 'New York Five' exhibition in New York, and included in the 1966 '40 under 40' exhibition in New York; 1974 'Five Architects' exhibition at Princeton University; and 1982 'Shape and Environment: Furniture by American Architects' exhibition at the Whitney Museum of American Art in Fairfield County, Connecticut. Knoll range won the 1983 IBD Award and 1983 Roscoe Award, Arnold W. Brunner Memorial Prize, Reynolds Memorial Award, and 1984 Pritzker Architecture Prize.
▶ Kenneth Frampton and Colin Rowe, *Five Architects: Eisenman, Graves, Gwathmey, Hejduk, Meier*, New York: Wittenborn, 1972. Richard Meier, *Richard Meier, Architect: Buildings and Projects, 1966–76*, New York: Oxford, 1976. Cat., Lisa Phillips (introduction), *Shape and Environment: Furniture by American Architects*, New York: Whitney Museum of American Art, 1982:42–43. *Richard Meier: Buildings and Projects 1965–1981*, Zürich, 1982. Officina Alessi, *Tea and Coffee Piazza: 11 Servizi da tè e caffè . . .*, Milan: Crusinallo, 1983. *Richard Meier, Architect*, New York, 1984. Film by Michael Blackwood, *Richard Meier*, 1985. Robert A.M. Stern (ed.), *The International Design Yearbook*, New York: Abbeville, 1985/1986: Nos. 265–65,300–02,385–87. Juli Capella and Quim Larrea, *Designed by Architects in the 1980s*, New York, Rizzoli, 1988.

Meier-Graefe, Julius (1867–1935)
▶ Romanian writer, art critic, and entrepreneur; active Germany and France.
▶ In 1893, he met William Morris, Edward Burne-Jones, and Aubrey Beardsley; was a specialist in 19th-century French painting and a champion of Expressionism with Siegfried Bing in 1895,

traveled in Belgium, Britain, Holland, Denmark, Germany, Austria. He embraced the role of industry and the ending of the romantic notion of the artist's isolation from industrial culture. In 1897, he founded the journal *Dekorative Kunst* and, in 1899, gave up its editorship to open the shop La Maison Moderne, rue des Petits-Champs, Paris, commissioning Henry van de Velde to design its exterior and interior. He publicized the shop as an association of artists coming together for commercial purposes, and for the creation of designs appropriate for production in quantity, an idea drawn from the Vereinigten Werkstätten für Kunst im Handwerk and contrasting with contemporary French practice. He showed Louis Comfort Tiffany's stained-glass windows, enamels, glass mosaics, and lighting at the Maison d'Art in 1895. He became increasingly alienated from Bing's enterprise L'Art Nouveau. He was forced to close the shop in 1904 and liquidate at half price, including van de Velde's furniture and fittings, losing his investment and inheritance. He returned to Germany, where Hermann Muthesius designed his house in 1921; in 1934, he left Germany and settled in France.
▶ Julius Meire-Graefe, 'Einiges aus "La Maison Moderne,"' *Dekorative Kunst*, No. 5, Oct. 1899–March 1900:209–12. *Documents sur l'art industriel au vingtième siècle: Reproductions photographiques des principales œuvres des collaborateurs de La Maison Moderne*, Paris: La Maison Moderne, 1901. Maurcie Dufrêne, 'Notre Enquête sur Le Mobilier Moderne,' *Art et Décoration*, No. 39, 1921:129–43. Kenworth Moffett, *Meier-Graefe as Art Critic, Studien zur Kunst des neunzehnten Jahrhunderts*, No. 18, Munich: Prestel, 1973. Florence Camard, *Ruhlmann*, Paris: Regard, 1983. Simon Jervis, *Dictionary of Design and Designers*, London: Penguin, 1984. Nancy J. Troy, *Modernism and the Decorative Arts in France: Art Nouveau to Le Corbusier*, New Haven: Yale, 1991.

Meinzer, Manfred (1943–)
▶ German industrial designer; active Cologne and Berlin.
▶ Studied industrial design, Art Center College in Los Angeles.
▶ He worked for Ford in Cologne and Telefunken in Berlin. From 1965, he was chief designer of Studer Revox. He substituted transistors for vacuum tubes and incorporated modular components into the Functionalist sound equipment housing at Revox. His first important design essay was the 1967 Revox stereo tape recorder, produced 1967–80.
▶ The Revox tape recorder was included in the 1983–84 'Design Since 1945' exhibition at the Philadelphia Museum of Art.
▶ Cat., Kathryn B. Hiesinger and George H. Marcus III (eds.), *Design Since 1945*, Philadelphia: Philadelphia Museum of Art, 1983:222,I–23.

Mellerio
▶ French jewelers; active Paris.
▶ Jewelers from the 16th century, the Mellerio family was originally active in Lombardy. In 1515, they settled in France. In 1750, the family opened a boutique on the rue des Lombards in Paris and afterwards another in the rue Vivienne. They worked for the court at Versailles and were patronized by Marie-Antoinette. In 1796, Jean-Baptiste Mellerio returned to the rue Vivienne, where he re-established a shop with a crown of iron as its insignia. 1797–1836, Pierre-Louis Foullé worked exclusively for the firm. In 1815, Mellerio moved from rue du Coq St. Honoré to 22 rue de la Paix and in 1836 to 5 rue de la Paix, where it is located today. In 1830 and 1840, Mellerio received royal warrants. In 1836, Ramsden, the son-in-law of Pierre-Louis Foullé, became the firm's designer and, in 1859, was succeeded by Henri Foullé, who designed for Mellerio until 1882. Branches were opened in Baden-Baden and Madrid in 1848, and Biarritz in 1862. The Empress Eugénie and Napoleon III were among the best customers during the Second Empire (1852–70). From 1936, Mellerio created Academicians' Swords and sports trophies, including the cup of the Roland Garros Tennis Tournament. The firm is managed today by the 14th generation of the family; a member of La Haute Joaillerie de France, it is the oldest member of the Comité Colbert trade organization.

▶ The firm was awarded a gold medal at the 1855 Paris 'Exposition universelle des produits de l'agriculture, de l'industrie et des beaux-arts de Paris,' medal of excellence at the London 'International Exhibition on Industry and Art of 1862,' gold medal at the 1867 Paris 'Exposition Universelle de Paris,' *grand diplome d'honneur* at the 'Welt-Ausstellung 1873 in Wien,' gold medal at the Paris 'Exposition Universelle de 1878,' and grand prize at the 1931 Paris 'Exposition Coloniale.' In 1878, Jean-François Mellerio was awarded the cross of the Légion d'honneur.

▶ Melissa Gabardi, *Les Bijoux des Années 50*, Paris: Amateur, 1987. Charlotte Gere, *American and European Jewelry 1830–1914*, New York: Crown, 1975:207. Joseph Mellerio, *Les Mellerio, leur origine et leur histoire*, Paris, 1895.

Mello, Franco
See Drocco, Guido

Mellor, David (1930–)
▶ British metalworker, manufacturer, and retailer; born Sheffield.
▶ 1946–48, studied Sheffield College of Art; 1950–54, Royal College of Art, London; 1953–54, British School in Rome.
▶ While he was still at Sheffield College of Art, his silver coffee set received a national prize in 1950. His 1951 silver coffee set was widely published, and his 1951 *Pride* flatware was produced by Walker and Hall, Sheffield, from 1954. In 1954, he set up his own silversmithing and industrial design workshop in Sheffield, the center of the metal tableware industry in Britain. He designed the 1963 *Embassy* flatware and teapot for use in British embassies, and 1965 *Thrift* stainless-steel set for government canteens, prisons, and hospitals. He designed a 1957 bus shelter in galvanized steel and vitreous enamel for the Ministry of Transport. From 1969, he manufactured cookware, hardware, textiles, and woodenware, and established a retail outlet selling domestic kitchen supplies and tableware by himself and others in Sloane Square, London; in 1980, in Manchester; and in 1981, in James Street, Covent Garden, London. In the early 1970s, he began manufacturing his own flatware using innovative methods at Broom Hall, Sheffield, an historic building that he restored and converted into purpose-designed workshops where all design and development on his cutlery was executed. Mellor's clients included ITT, Abacus Municipal, Glacier Metal, the Post Office, British Rail, James Neill Tools, and the British Department of the Environment. He received silver commissions from The Worshipful Company of Goldsmiths, London; The Cutlers' Company, Sheffield; Essex University; Southwell Minster; and Darwin College, Cambridge. 1981–83, he was chair of the Design Council Committee of Enquiry on British consumer goods design standards; from 1982, member of the National Advisory Body, Art and Design Working Group; and, from 1982, chair of the Crafts Council.
▶ He won the 1950 National Design Competition of the Design and Research Centre for Gold, Silver and Jewellery for a silver coffee set; 1957 Design Council Award for his *Pride* flatware; 1953 silver medal from the Royal College of Art; 1957, 1959, 1962, 1965, 1974, 1977 and other Design Council Awards; 1975 Architectural Heritage Year Award for conversion of Broom Hall; 1981 Duke of Edinburgh's Royal Society of Arts Presidential Award for Design Management. In 1962, elected Royal Designer for Industry, in 1964, fellow of the Society of Industrial Artists and Designers; in 1979, honorary fellow of Sheffield Polytechnic; in 1981, liveryman of the Worshipful Company of Goldsmiths; in 1981, freeman of the Cutlers' Company; in 1981, OBE (Order of the British Empire). He was made a trustee of the Victoria and Albert Museum in 1984. His work was exhibited at the Stedelijk Museum, Amsterdam, in 1968 and National Museum, Cardiff, in 1972.
▶ Michael Farr, *Design in British Industry: A Mid-Century Survey*, London: Cambridge, 1955:175. Graham Hughes, *Modern Silver throughout the World*, New York, 1967: Nos. 122,384–89,424–25. *Design*, No. 342, June 1977:47. *Classics*, London: Heal & Sons, Spring 1981: Nos. 15–16,44. Fiona MacCarthy, *British Design Since 1880*, London, 1982: figs. 153,166,185–86,193,211.

Cat., Kathryn B. Hiesinger and George H. Marcus III (eds.), *Design Since 1945*, Philadelphia: Philadelphia Museum of Art, 1983:222,V–27. Fiona MacCarthy and Patrick Nuttgens, *An Eye for Industry*, London: Lund Humphries, 1986.

Memory Hotel Studio
▶ Italian design group; located Florence.
▶ In 1983, Fabrizio Galli and Anna Perico, who studied architecture in Florence, established Memory Hotel Studio, specializing in design and production of furniture and small products.
▶ From 1981, they participated in numerous national and international exhibitions.
▶ Fumino Shimizu and Matteo Thun (eds.), *The Descendants of Leonardo: The Italian Design*, Tokyo, 1987:326.

Memphis
▶ Design cooperative and firm.
▶ Memphis was the name given to the group of architect-designers designing furniture, fabric, glass, and ceramics led by Ettore Sottsass at the 1981 Milan Furniture Fair. Its début caused an international sensation. It was organized in opposition to the ideas of the earlier Studio Alchimia, the proto-Memphis group that examined the metaphysical rather than the technological aspects of design. Memphis became commercially successful by selling items in quantity. Artemide was supportive by offering display space in its showroom on Corso Europa in Milan. Memphis designs used a hodgepodge of styles from the brash tastes of the 1950s to ancient art. Originally stimulated by the kitsch taste of the Italian, bourgeoisie, Sottsass saw the designs as 'quoting from suburbia.' The Memphis name was derived both from the Tennessee city and the Egyptian site. Its numerous designers included Marco Zanini, Sottsass, Daniel Weil, Shiro Kuramata, George Sowden, Michele De Lucchi, Aldo Cibic, Nathalie du Pasquier, Andrea Branzi, and Javier Mariscal. Its art director was Barbara Radice. From being a purveyor of goods of dubious taste, Memphis came to be seen as a highly desirable expression of contemporary culture. A joke was developed into a profitable enterprise with its work shown worldwide, including the 1982 'Memphis Milano in London' at the Boilerhouse of the Victoria and Albert Museum. The widely published apartment in Monte Carlo of clothing designer Karl Lagerfeld, which was furnished exclusively in Memphis products, popularized the look; the high prices of Memphis items encouraged an elitist cult image.
▶ Cat., *Memphis Milano in London*, The Boilerhouse Project, London: Victoria and Albert Museum, 1982. Barbara Radice, *Memphis*, New York: Rizzoli, 1984. Paolo Martegani, Andrea Mazzoli, and Riccardo Montenegro, *Memphis una Questione di Stile*, Rome, 1987. Gilles de Bure, *Ettore Sottsass Jr.*, Paris, 1987. *Memphis 1981–1988*, Groninger. Auction cat., *Memphis: La Collection Karl Kagerfeld*, Monaco: Sotheby's, 13 Oct. 1991.

Mendelson, Shari M.
▶ American jeweler and metalsmith.
▶ Studied jewelry and metalsmithing, Arizona State University and State University of New York, New Paltz, New York.
▶ She produced one-off bowls and other vessels in a variety of materials, including copper and gold foil.
▶ Her bowls were shown throughout the USA. She received the Prize for Excellence at the 1986 Designer Craft Council Show at the Schenactady, New York, Museum.
▶ Albrecht Bangert and Karl Michael Armer, *80s Style: Designs of the Decade*, New York: Abbeville, 1990:148,233.

Mendini, Alessandro (1931–)
▶ Italian designer; born and active Milan.
▶ Studied architecture, Politecnico di Milano.
▶ He began his professional career in 1956. Until 1970, he was a partner in the industrial design studio Nizzoli Associati, Milan. In 1973, he and others founded the radical design group Global Tools, creating objects, architecture, and urban planning solutions. 1970–76, he was managing editor of *Casabella*; 1977–81,

founder and managing editor of *Mode*, and, 1980–85, managing editor of *Domus*; directed journal *Ollo*. Active as a design philosopher from 1978, Mendini organized exhibitions, primarily with Studio Alchimia, where he propagated the concept of Banal Design. He was an advocate of neo-Modern design, author of seminars, and curator of design exhibitions. He doggedly championed banal, inconsequential, and kitsch furniture and furnishings, questioning traditional attitudes towards value and function and encouraging individual thinking. His best known works were the redesign in 1978 of a sideboard with decoration inspired by Kandinskii of the 1940s, and his 1978 *Poltrona di Proust (Proust's Armchair)* painted in a divisionist technique for the Alchimia 'Bau.Haus' collection. He was involved in the Anti-Design movement in Italy from the 1960s to the 1980s. His *Kandissi* chair for Studio Alchimia, which was part of the 'Bau.Haus uno' collection of 1980, controversially turned fine art into kitsch. He participated in the Bracciodiferro project, a workshop for experimenting with furniture for Cassina in 1981, when he collaborated with Meuble Infini and executed designs for domestic metalware produced by Alessi, including a set included in Alessi's 1983 *Tea and Coffee Piazza* project, for which he was design and communications director. Having been responsible in part for Alessi's success, he designed pots and pans for the metalware firm. Clients included Zanotta, Fiat, Zabro, Driade, MIM, Poltronova, Elam, and Abet Laminati. In 1983, Mendini became a lecturer in design at the Vienna Design School. He was a member of the scientific committee of the Domus Academy. He established the Genetic Laboratory for Visual Surprises to question established values of taste and function. Mendini was a member of the CDM (Consulenti Design Milano) and of ADI (Associazione per il Disegno Industriale). He published *Paesaggio casalingo* (1978), *Architettura addio* (1981), and *Il progetto infelice* (1983). In the second half of the 1980s, his *œuvre* included painting. His other work included covers for *Modo*, *Casabella*, and *Domus* in the 1970s and 1980s, 1974 *Lassù (Up There)* burning chair (performance art), 1974 polyurethane *Armchair* by Piero Gilardi with Gufram, 1978 *Redesigned Chairs from the Modern Movement* (one-off furniture), 1981 *Modulando 1–4* cabinet by Alchimia, 1981 *Cipriani* liquor cabinet by Memphis, 1981 *Sedia Redesign Breuer Chair*, 1982 *Arredo vestitivo (Furniture Dress)* (performance art with Alchimia) for Fiorucci in Milan, 1982 *Galla Placidia* plastic-laminate design by Abet Laminati, 1983 tea-coffee set by Alessi, 1984 *Tower Furniture* cabinet (with Bruno Gregori), 1984 *Cristina* and *Riflesso* rugs by B.d Ediciones de Diseño, 1985 *San Leonardo Collection* seating by Matteo Grassi, 1985 *Karina* bench by Baleri Italia, 1985 ceramic panel by Tendentse, 1985 *Poko* steel shelf by Baleri Italia, 1985 *Laverda* motorcycle redesign, 1985–86 *Casa della Felicita* showcase residence (with Francesco Mendini and the studio Alchimia) of Alberto Alessi, 1986 *Homage to Gropius* aluminum door handle by FBS-Franz Schneider Brakel, 1986 small silver case (with Sinya Okayama) by Daichi, 1986 jewelry by Acme, 1986 *Velasca Series* glass and metal coffee table, stool, coat hanger, and table by Elam Uno, 1986 *Mobile metafisico (Metaphysical Furniture)* modular furniture (with M. Christina Hamel) by Mirabili, 1987 *Programma Tempietto (Small Temple Program)* tables and bookshelves by Up & Up, 1987 *Steel Sculptures* (with Sinya Okayama) by Daichi, 1988 *Lampada di Milo* floor lamp by Segno, 1988 first cover for journal *Ollo*, 1988 blown-glass vase by Venini, 1988 watch and jewelry collection (with M. Christina Hamel) by Türler, and 1988 *Sette + Sette (Seven + Seven)* silver jewelry (with Sinya Okayama) by Daichi. For Zabro, he designed the 1984 *Dorifora* armchair, 1984 *Simulia* coffee table, 1984 *Atomaria* lamp (with Bruno Gregori), 1984 *Zabro* table-chair (hand-painted by Bruno Gregori), 1985 *Calamobio* cabinet (with Bruno Gregori), 1985 *Atalia* folding chair, 1985 *Cerambrice* silkscreen desk (with Bruno Gregori), 1985 *Macaone* table (with Bruno Gregori), 1985 *Attelabo* cabinets, 1986 *Faggiolo* cabinet-shelves, 1986 *Archeto (Little Arch)* by Mobileffe, 1986 *Cantaride* bar-cabinet, 1986 *Papilia* table, 1986 *Agrilo* tables, 1986 *Meligete* console, 1986 *Dipluro* hand-painted cabinet, 1986 *Sirfo* duck table, 1986 *Deabata* ceramic vases, 1986 ceramic wall clock, and 1987 armoire.

▶ In the 1970s, Mendini organized exhibitions, mainly with Studio Alchimia. He was awarded the 1979 Compasso d'Oro (*San Leonardo* armchair). His interest in Anti-Design was displayed at his 'The Banal Object' exhibition at the 1980 Venice Biennale. His sculpture *Casa degli sposi (Matrimonial Suite)* by Alessandro Guerriero and Alchimia was in the 1983 exhibition 'Houses of the Triennale' in Milan. His *Black Out* range (mobile-bar, credenza, side chair, club chair, lamp, and rug with Alchimia, Giorgio Gregori, Reiner Haegele, M. Christina Hamel, and Jeremy King) was included in 'Le affinità elettive' exhibition at the 1985 Treinnale di Milano. *Design pittorico (Painting Design)* installation (with Alchimia) shown at the 'Caravelles' exhibition at the 1986 Quadriannale Internationale de Design, Musée Saint-Pierre, Lyons. In 1987, *6 mobiletti (Six Small Furniture Objects)* (with Sinya Okayama) in the Lunar Design Collection shown at the Museo Alchimia) Milan. Installation and 'Universal Museum' model (with Giorgio Gregori) shown at 'Documenta 8' in Kassel. His *Calamobio* furniture by Zanotta was introduced at the 1989 Salone del Mobile in Milan, and his work the subject of the 'Alessi/Mendini: Dix ans de collaboration' exhibition at Centre Georges Pompidou in Paris, 1989–90.

▶ Rosa Maria Rinaldi, *Mobile Infinito*, Milan: Alchimia Editore, 1981. Fulvio Raggi, *Stanze: un'idea per la casa*, Milan: Alchimia Editore, 1981. Kazuko Sato, *Alchimia*, Berlin: Taco, 1988. *Nouvelles Tendances: les avant-gardes de la fin du XXe siècle*, Paris: Centre Georges Pompidou, 1986. Albrecht Bangert and Karl Michael Armer, *80s Style: Designs of the Decade*, New York: Abbeville, 1990:46–47,52,216–17,233. Officina Alessi, *Tea and Coffee Piazza: 11 Servizi da tè e caffè ...* , Milan: Crusinallo, 1983. *ADI Annual 1976*, Milan: Associazione per il Disegno Industriale, 1976. Auction cat., *Asta di Modernariato 1900–1986, Auction 'Modernariato,'* Milan: Semenzato Nuova Geri, 8 Oct. 1986: lot 102. Juli Capella and Quim Larrea, *Designed by Architects in the 1980s*, New York, Rizzoli, 1988. Cat., *Le Affinità Elettive*, Milan: Electa, 1985. Vincent Lemarchand, *Caravelle*, Lyons: Quadriennale Internationale de design, 1986. Achille Bonito Oliva et al., *Alessandro Mendini*, Milan: Giancarlo Politi Editore, 1989.

Meneghetti, Renato   (1947–)

▶ Italian designer; born Rosà; active Padua, Italy.
▶ Meneghetti began his professional career in 1968. His clients included Felsina (watch bands), DD&D Design (domestic furnishings and accessories), Balestra (industrial goldsmithing), Caleppio (plastics), Vicentine (dinnerware), and Grundig Italiana (radio, television, record, hi-fi equipment). He was a member of ADI (Associazione per il Disegno Industriale).
▶ *ADI Annual 1976*, Milan: Associazione per il Disegno Industriale, 1976.

Menghi, Roberto   (1920–)

▶ Italian industrial designer; born and active Milan.
▶ Studied architecture, Politecnico di Milano, to 1944.
▶ He began his professional career in 1950; collaborated with Marco Zanuso and, in 1953, with Anna Castelli and Ignazio Gardella; 1953–54, assisted Franco Albini at Facoltà di Venezia; from 1955 specializing in plastics, designed furniture, industrial containers, electronic equipment, glassware, and housing. His clients included Arflex, Bormioli, Gulf, Fontana, IPI, Moneta, Merioni, Pirelli, Siemens, Velca, and Venini; was a member of ADI (Associazione per il Disegno Industriale); designed the 1964 house of Giovanni Pirelli, Varese. Designs included 1966 camping shelter produced by ICS, 1972 *Abitere* tent by Moretti, washing machine by Sub Matic, 1959 plastic kitchen accessories by Kartell, and 1963 modular kitchen by Ariston.
▶ *ADI Annual 1976*, Milan: Associazione per il Disegno Industriale, 1976.

Mengshoel, Hans Christian   (1946–)

▶ Norwegian furniture designer.
▶ He was a collaborator with Svein Gusrud and with Peter Opsvik on the design of the 1979 ergonomic chairs in the *Balans* series produced by Håg in Oslo.

▶ Cat., David Revere McFadden (ed.), *Scandinavian Modern Design 1880–1980*, New York: Abrams, 1982:268, Nos. 342,343.

Menna, Franco (1943–)
▶ Italian industrial and retail designer; born Cheti; active Milan.
▶ Studied geometry, interior architecture, and scenic design in Rome.
▶ In Rome 1963–74, he was a consultant designer at La Rinascente in the interior design department, and for the shop Croff Centro Casa. From 1974, he worked on the magazine *Amica*. From 1972, he was a member of ADI (Associazione per il Disegno Industriale) and, from 1972, the Ordine dei Gironalisti elenco Pubblicisti. In 1971, Menna and architect Paola Lanzani set up a studio working on industrial design and interior architecture.
▶ He participated in various Eurodomus events and the 1973 (XV) Triennale di Milano.
▶ *ADI Annual 1976*, Milan: Associazione per il Disegno Industriale, 1976.

Mentula, Perttu (1936–)
▶ Finnish architect and interior, exhibition, product, graphic, and furniture designer.
▶ 1958–60, studied Taideteollinen Korkeakoulu, Helsinki.
▶ 1958–60, he was active as an interior and product designer in the offices of Antti Nurmesniemi and Timo Sarpaneva, and of Toivo Korkonen and Reino Lamminsoila, all Helsinki; 1960–77, was active in his own design studio; 1964–77, was a designer for Wärtsilä Shipyards, Helsinki; from 1977, was director of Studio Perttu Mentula Oy. In 1970 and 1978–80, he was a board member, Ornamo (Federation of Industrial Arts), Helsinki; from 1974, member, Fine Art Commission, Helsinki Festival; 1978–80, chair, SIO (Interior Architects Society), Helsinki; 1978, member, Representational Arts Commission; 1978, member, Idea Group; 1981–83, vice-president, International Federation of Interior Designers; from 1981, executive committee and organizing committee, Design 81 Congress; 1981, coordinator, D'81 Creative Group; from 1982, design manager, Keriland Project, Kerimaki. Designs included 1971–74 *Ringside* hanging chairs, *Rs 656 R* by Avitom, and 1961 sauna stool.
▶ Received 1963 first and second prizes, Export Furniture Competition, Helsinki; silver medal, 1964 (XIII) Triennale di Milano; two awards, International Lighting Competition, Tokyo; first prize, Scandinavian Environment and Furniture Competition, Copenhagen; first prize, Community Development Competition, Kerimaki. Appointed honorary member, AIPI (Italian Interior Architects Assoc.). Work shown at 1966 'Total Environment,' Finnish Design Center, Helsinki; 1975 'Uniform-Project,' Milan; 1977 'Wood and Textile,' Savonlinna Opera Festival; 1980 'Finnish Design', Finlandia Hall, Helsinki.
▶ Ulf Hard af Segerstad, *Modern Finnish Design*, New York, 1969. Donald J. Willcox, *New Design in Wood*, New York, 1970. Ann Lee Morgan (ed.), *Contemporary Designers*, London: Macmillan, 1984:405–07.

Menzies, William Cameron (1896–1957)
▶ American film set designer; born New Haven, Connecticut; active Hollywood, California.
▶ Studied Yale University; University of Edinburgh; and Art Students' League, New York.
▶ 1920–22, he worked in special effects and design for Famous Players-Lasky in London and New York and, in 1923, settled in Hollywood. Menzies became the most respected and highest paid Hollywood designer of the 1920s. He designed the sets for *Serenade* (1921). He worked as art director for Pickford-Fairbanks, Alexander Korda, David O. Selznick, Sam Wood, and major studios. Working as a writer (with Norman Z. McLeod) on the *Alice in Wonderland* (1933), he invented the 'story board' technique. Drawing on his earlier career of designing children's books, Menzies combined baroque Art Déco with 1920s illustrations for juveniles for *The Thief of Bagdad* (1924). In 1929, he received the first Academy Award for art direction for both *The Tempest* (1928) and

The Dove (1928). For *Things to Come* (1936), filmed in Britain, Vincent Korda designed the sets, Ned Mann the special effects, and René Hubert, the Marchioness of Queensberry, and John Armstrong the costumes, but the spectacular production design was Menzies's. On a sound stage in Hollywood, he created the vast mythical ship *L'Amerique* for the landmark Art Déco film *Reaching for the Moon* (1931). He designed the speakeasy in *I Loved You Wednesday* (1933). As production designer, Menzies's work can be seen in *Gone With the Wind* (1939). From 1943, he was a director and producer.
▶ He received the Academy Awards for Art Direction for *The Dove* (1927), *The Tempest* (1927) and *Gone with the Wind* (1939).
▶ Howard Mandelbaum and Eric Myers, *Screen Deco: A Celebration of High Style in Hollywood*, New York: St. Martin's, 1985.

Mercatali, Davide (1948–)
▶ Italian designer; born and active Milan.
▶ Studied architecture, Politecnico di Milano, to 1973.
▶ He worked independently as a graphic and product designer and illustrator for advertising agencies, publishers, and his own clients; worked for the Società Donchi Formart, Milan; in 1978 with Paolo Pedrizzetti, set up an industrial design studio where he initially designed for materials and tiles; worked on promotional accessories and point-of-sale displays in retail stores, and designed fabrics and dinnerware; (with architect M. Dall'Asta) designed the *Nomade* seating systems with buckles and straps; (with Paolo Pedrizzetti) designed the 1978 *I Balocchi* collection of colored faucets and bathroom fixtures produced by Fantini and, in the 1980s, *Selz* flatware in stainless steel with nylon handles by Case Casa-Industrie Casalinghi Mari; in 1982, (with Pedrizzetti) formed the Associated Studio, which produced designs for domestic goods, electrical appliances, interior decoration, lighting, accessories, and building components and tools. He was a member of ADI (Associazione per il Disegno Industriale); in 1984, was a founder of the group Zeus (Noto) for the design of furniture and furnishings; in 1989, coordinated Metals, a group of jewelry designers for the production of objects and articles in metal.
▶ Received 1981 (*Calibro* with Pedrizzetti) Compasso d'Oro, and once subsequently.
▶ *ADI Annual 1976*, Milan: Associazione per il Disegno Industriale, 1976. Giancarlo Iliprandi and Pierluigi Molinari (eds.), *Industrial Designers Italiani*, Fagagna, 1985:143. Robert A.M. Stern (ed.), *The International Design Yearbook*, New York: Abbeville, 1985/1986: Nos. 207,408,422–425. Fumio Shimizu and Matteo Thun (eds.), *The Descendants of Leonardo: The Italian Design*, Tokyo, 1987:326. Hans Wichmann, *Italien Design 1945 bis heute*, Munich: Die Neue Sammlung, 1988. *Modo*, No. 148, March–April 1993:122.

Mercier, Émile-Philippe (1855–1910)
▶ French bookbinder and gilder; active Paris.
▶ Studied gilding under Francisque Cuzin.
▶ Mercier was an apprentice in the workshop of Charles Magnier père in the rue Séguier in Paris. In 1890, he took over the management of the workshop of gilder Francisque Cuzin. Mercier's bindings included *La Mort amoureuse* and *Crainqueville*; his clients included Miguet, Delafosse, and Descamps-Scrive. His son Georges joined the firm in 1898 and took over its management in 1910.
▶ Alastair Duncan and Georges de Bartha, *Art Nouveau and Art Déco Bookbinding*, New York: Abrams, 1989:8,13,14–15,16, 24,136,159,194. Émile Bosquet, 'La Reliure française à l'exposition,' *Art et décoration*, July–Dec. 1900:47–48. Ernest de Crauzat, *La Reliure française de 1900 à 1925*, Vol. 1, Paris, 1932:32–35. 'Modern Bookbindings and Their Designers,' *The Studio*, Special Winter Issue 1899–1900:64. Henri Nicolle, 'La Reliure moderne,' *Les Arts français: la reliure d'art*, No. 36, 1919:190,196. S.T. Prideaux, *Modern Bindings: Their Design and Decoration*, New York, 1906:62,72,80,82,84,89–91. Octave Uzanne, *L'Art dans la décoration extérieure des livres en France et à l'étranger*, Paris, 1898:177,180–82,184,194,204–06.

Mercier frères

▶ French decorators and furniture makers; located Paris.

▶ The brothers Mercier produced their furniture in a workshop in the Faubourg Saint-Antoine area; in 1925, opened Palais du Marbre decorating shop, 77 avenue des Champs-Elysées, whose artistic director 1925–29 was Eric Bagge.

▶ *Ensembles Mobiliers*, Vol. II, Paris: Charles Moreau, 1937. Pierre Kjellberg, *Art Déco: les maîtres du Mobilier, le décor des Paquebots*, Paris: Amateur, 1986:133.

Mère, Clément   (1870–)

▶ French painter, tabletier, designer, and furniture maker; born Bayonne, active Paris.

▶ Studied painting, École des Beaux-Arts, Paris, under Jean-Léon Gérôme.

▶ He designed bookbindings, embroideries, and objects in the Art Nouveau manner; *c*1900, joined Julius Meier-Graefe's stable at La Maison Moderne, Paris, where he met Franz Waldraff, with whom he designed and made intricate ivory panels and wood and ivory boxes, and supplied dress fabrics, buttons, and other dressmaker's materials. On his own Mère specialized in creating costly furniture in exotic woods and materials. His cabinets, cases, desks, and decorative work were influenced by his training as a painter and a craftsman of overlays. His shapes were classically geometric rather than Cubist.

▶ Work shown at the Salons d'Automne, Salons of the Société des Artistes Décorateurs (from 1910), and Salons of the Société Nationale des Beaux-Arts.

▶ Victor Arwas, *Art Déco*, Abrams, 1980:303.

Mergier, Paul   (1891–)

▶ French aeronautical engineer, painter, metalworker, enameler, furniture maker, and decorator; born Orthez.

▶ From 1920, studied engineering and enameling.

▶ Incorporating new methods and applications, he used pastes rather than powders to make both small and very large enamel plaques. He painted and drew still lifes. His metalwork had figurative scenes; his furniture was covered in leather and inlaid with mother-of-pearl, ivory, and other precious materials. He wrote a book on the association between the arts and the sciences, and another on enameling techniques.

▶ He showed his work at the Salon d'Automne, the Salon of the Société des Artistes Décorateurs (in 1928), the Salon of the Société des Artistes français, the Salon des Tuileries, the Salon des Indépendants, 1937 Paris 'Exposition Internationale des Arts et Techniques dans la Vie Moderne,' and 1939 'New York World's Fair.'

▶ Pierre Kjellberg, *Art Déco: les maîtres du Mobilier, le décor des Paquebots*, Paris: Amateur, 1986: 126,129.

Meriden Britannia

▶ American silverplate factory; located West Meriden, Connecticut.

▶ A group of Britannia-ware producers consolidated their efforts in 1852, forming Meriden Britannia. Britannia metal is a silver-white alloy largely of tin, antimony, and copper, similar to pewter. The group of seven directors included Isaac Chauncey Lewis (the firm's first president), Horace Cornwall Wilcox, and Samuel Simpson (founder of Simpson, Hall, Miller and Co in Wallingford, Connecticut). Using first Britannia metal and then nickel silver for its bases, Meriden Britannia began the production of silver-plated objects, including teapots, candlesticks, épergnes, punch bowls, flatware, and vessels. With sales offices in Chicago, San Francisco, New York, and London, it was the largest silver plate ware manufacturer in the world by 1870. In 1881, it opened a second factory in Hamilton, Ontario, and later a third. Its success was supported by the refinement of the electroplating process by Elkington in Britain and the 1859 discovery of silver in the Comstock Lode in Nevada. At the 1876 Philadelphia exhibition, it showed Theodore Bauer's silverplated centerpiece, based on his sculpture *The Buffalo Hunt*. In 1895, the firm purchased Wilcox and Evertson, silversmiths in New York, which resulted in its 1897 fine silver flatware

range. In 1898, the firm amalgamated with others to form International Silver.

▶ Showing at international exhibitions in the USA 1876–93, its most effective presentation was at the 1876 Philadelphia 'Centennial Exposition.'

▶ Earl Chapin May, *Century of Silver, 1847–1947: Connecticut Yankees and a Noble Metal*, New York, 1947. Dorothy T. Rainwater and H. Ivan Rainwater, *American Silverplate*, Nashville, Tenn., and Hanover, Pa., 1968:13–27,39–132,138–40. Doreen Bolger Burke et al., *In Pursuit of Beauty: Americans and the Aesthetic Movement*, New York: Metropolitan Museum of Art and Rizzoli, 1986:453.

Meroni, Gabriele   (1945–)

▶ Italian industrial designer; born Erba; active Milan.

▶ He began his professional career in 1970, designing accessories, lighting, and furniture. His clients in Italy included B. Communications, IAG, Studio Castello, Poretti, E.Ed. Edizioni Design, and Ceramica di Faetano. He was a member of ADI (Associazione per il Disegno Industriale).

▶ *ADI Annual 1976*, Milan: Associazione per il Disegno Industriale, 1976.

Meroni, Giampaolo   (1950–)

▶ Italian graphic and industrial designer; born and active Mariano Comense.

▶ He began his professional career in 1974, designing graphics and kitchen systems. His clients in Italy included Boffi kitchens, Spinelli, Gelosa, Noalex, Camar, and MG2. He was a member of ADI (Associazione per il Disegno Industriale).

▶ *ADI Annual 1976*, Milan: Associazione per il Disegno Industriale, 1976.

Mertens, H.F.

See LOV.

Merù Gioielli

▶ Italian costume jeweler; located Milan.

▶ Francesco Merù established a clock-repair shop in the via del Lauro in 1960. In 1967, he began to produce costume jewelry and gold 'mini jewelry.' Working alone, mainly on one-of-a-kind pieces, Merù used steel, plastics, and Plexiglas in novel forms. The 'mini jewelry' models brought Merù recognition from abroad, and he discontinued costume jewelry production in the mid-1970s.

▶ Deanna F. Cera (ed.), *Jewels of Fantasy: Costume Jewelry of the 20th Century*, New York: Abrams, 1992:308.

Messel, Oliver   (1904–78)

▶ British theater, film, and interior designer; active London and Barbados.

▶ Studied Slade School of Fine Art, London.

▶ While at the Slade, he met Rex Whistler, with whom he took up making *papier-mâché* masks. These interested Sergei Diaghilev, who commissioned Messel to produce masks for the 1925 Ballets Russes production *Zéphyre et Flore*. Nöel Coward commissioned sets and costumes for his 1928 play *This Year of Grace*. Messel designed sets and costumes for the 1935 film *The Scarlet Pimpernel*, and costumes for a production of Mozart's *The Magic Flute*. Messel's designs were historicist and included columns, entablatures, drapery swags, and baroque ornamentation. In 1952, he designed the commemorative silk scarf and the exterior decorations of the Dorchester hotel in London to celebrate the coronation of Queen Elizabeth II. In 1953 at the Dorchester, he completed the Oliver Messel Suite; in 1953, the Penthouse Suite; and, in 1956, the Pavilion Room. Messel's rugs for the hotel were woven in Bangkok. In 1991, the hotel's décor was restored under the direction of John Claridge, who had worked on the original project; the decoration was inspired by Messel's designs for the 1946 production of *The Sleeping Beauty* for Sadler's Wells. Through his social connections, he executed commissions for lavish parties and weddings, including the 1955 marriage of Princess Ira von Fürstenberg to Prince Alfonso von Hohenlohe-Langenburg. In 1966, he retired to Barbados, where he planned to paint and relax; instead, he began a second career designing gardens and houses, including the estate 'Prospero.' Princess Margaret lived in a Messel house in Barbados. He used non-traditional, improvisational procedures in building his houses, incorporating humble materials and simple building techniques. He was fond of lush garden effects. Messel was influential in establishing much of today's architectural tone on the islands. In 1959, Messel designed the houses on the 1,200-acre (500 ha) parcel on Mustique for Lord Glenconner. Messel died before the completion of Glenconner's 'Great House,' which he called an 'Indo-Asiatic ragbag.'

▶ John Claridge, 'Restoration Drama,' *House and Garden*, April 1991:50,51. John Mayfield, 'Sounds and Sweet Airs,' *Elle Decor*, June/July 1991:40,42.

metal furniture
See tubular steel furniture

Metalarte
▶ Spanish lighting firm.
▶ The Riera family are proprietors of Metalarte. The firm began to produce a Modern line of lighting in the 1960s along with its historicist turned-brass models. Enric Franch's 1975 *Calder* halogen swivel table lamp represented an exception to a return to conservative production. In the 1980s, it again produced avant-garde lighting, with its 1988 *Maja* standard lighting and other models by Sergi Devesa, and the 1989 *Ketupa* lamp by Josep Lluscá and Joaquin Berao.
▶ Guy Julier, *New Spanish Design*, London: Thames and Hudson, 1991.

Meta-Memphis
▶ Italian furniture manufacturing firm.
▶ Meta-Memphis was set up in 1988 when Ettore Sottsass, the original founder of Memphis (1981–88), decided to close shop, stating that an innovative idea has a life of five to seven years. Ernesto Gismondi, president of Artemide, which originally sold the Memphis line and gave it showroom space, retained ownership of the Memphis name. In 1989 in Venice, Gismondi unveiled what he called 'Meta-Memphis.' The initial collection consisted of 20 pieces by ten artist designers (in contrast to Sottsass's industrial designers), including Sandro Chia, Joseph Kossuth, Lawrence Weiner, and Michelangelo Pistoletto. Sottsass scornfully disapproved of 'art furniture' and likewise of Meta-Memphis. The firm's line was priced as if it were fine art and not limited-production furniture. The old designs from the Memphis collection continued to be produced.
▶ Arlene Hirst, *Metropolitan Home*, August 1989:22.

Metcalf, Helen Adelia Rowe (1831–95)
▶ American teacher; active Providence, Rhode Island.
▶ She established the Rhode Island School of Design in 1877. It was begun with seed funds from the Women's Centennial Commission of the Rhode Island delegation to Philadelphia, Pennsylvania. In the 1870s, opinion in the USA was sympathetic to education in the arts; the decade saw the establishment of the Metropolitan Museum of Art in New York, the University of Cincinnati School of Design, and the School of Practical Design in Lowell, Massachusetts. In 1854, the Rhode Island State government had expressed an interest in establishing an institution for industrial arts training by chartering the Rhode Island Art Association to present an annual exhibition and establish a school. Metcalf was active in the activities of the Rhode Island School of Design; her directorship was taken over by daughter Eliza Metcalf Radeke. Metcalf 's husband Jesse supported the school financially and donated the building at 11 Waterman Street when the school expanded in 1893, and three exhibition galleries named for his wife and completed in 1897. In 1885, son-in-law Gustav Radeke donated a collection of industrial materials, models, and casts collected in Europe. Annual exhibitions of student work began in 1879. In 1880, the industrial museum was established. In 1884, alumni exhibitions were begun. A museum building donated by

the Metcalfs was opened in 1893 to show painting, bronzes, pottery, metalwork, casts, and needlework, with a permanent display opening in 1894. In the 1890s, emphasis turned from industrial art to fine art training, with a more formal administrative framework.
▶ Doreen Bolger Burke et al., *In Pursuit of Beauty: Americans and the Aesthetic Movement*, New York: Metropolitan Museum of Art and Rizzoli, 1986:453–54. Carla Mathes Woodward, 'Acquisition, Preservation, and Education: a History of the Museum,' in *A Handbook of the Museum of Art, Rhode Island School of Design*, Providence, 1985:10–60.

Metelák, Alois (1897–1980)
▶ Czech architect and glass designer; born Martěnice.
▶ Studied School of Applied Arts, Prague, and decorative architecture under Jozef Plečnik.
▶ 1924–48, he was director, School of Glass, Železný Brod; 1948–52, director, School of Jewelry, Turnov; from 1920, was a member of SČSD (Czechoslovak Werkbund); specialized in cut, engraved, and etched glass. In the 1930s particularly, his architectural training showed in the rich plasticity of his glass vases and bowls. In the 1920s–30s, some of his table glass acknowledged Czech Modernism.
▶ A. Adlerová, *Alois Metelák: Sklo z let 1924–1963*, Prague, 1963. D. Šindelář, *Současné umělecké sklo v Československu*, Prague, 1970. A. Adlerová, *České užité umění 1918–1938*, Prague, 1983.

Metsovaara, Marjatta (1928–)
▶ Finnish textile artist and designer; active Helsinki.
▶ In 1949, studied Taideteollinen Korkeakoulu (Institute of Industrial Arts), Helsinki.
▶ She set up a workshop in 1954. She executed rich effects on a handicraft basis using both traditional and synthetic materials. For mass production, she designed woven and printed furnishing fabrics produced by Uniwool and Tampella. Her designs for dress fabrics were produced by Finn-Flare, the fashion house she established with Maj Kuhlefelt in 1963. In her studio, she made wool and mohair lap robes and stoles, *rya* rugs, and carpets.
▶ She won medals at the 1957 (XI) and 1960 (XII) Triennali di Milano.
▶ Erik Zahle (ed.), *A Treasury of Scandinavian Design*, New York: Golden, 1961:285. Eileene Harrison Beer, *Scandinavian Design: Objects of a Life Style*, New York, 1975:137,139,146–47,155. Cat., Kathryn B. Hiesinger and George H. Marcus III (eds.), *Design Since 1945*, Philadelphia: Philadelphia Museum of Art, 1983:222,VII–46.

Metthey, André (1871–1921)
▶ French ceramicist; born Laignes.
▶ Metthey apprenticed in decoration and sculpture, later becoming a potter. 1901–06, he made *flambé* stoneware in Japanese and Korean styles. After pursuing often fruitless research, he became interested in faïence in the French tradition, opening a studio in Asnières. Odilon Redon, Georges Rouault, Henri Matisse, Pierre Bonnard, Jean Édouard Vuillard, Valtat, André Derain, Maurice de Vlaminck, and Othon Friesz decorated Metthey's works. Metthey abandoned faïence for glazed earthenware. He returned to stoneware in 1912. Towards the end of his career, he experimented with *pâte-de-verre*.
▶ Yvonne Brunhammer et al., *Art Nouveau Belgium, France,* Houston: Institute for the Arts, Rice University, 1976.

Metz
▶ Dutch drapery and furniture store; located Amsterdam.
▶ Samuel Moses Metz established a fabric store in Amsterdam in *c*1740. It began selling products made by others and, from *c*1910 to the 1960s, made limited-production items for sale in its own stores. Most of its goods were produced by craftspeople. The firm was distinguished by its design policy and its association with a large number of freelance designers. Responsible for its enlightened approach to design was Joseph de Leeuw (1876–

1944), owner and director from c1900. Liberty goods were imported from Britain, and products from French, Viennese, and Dutch designers, Leerdam (glassware), De Distel (ceramics), and De Ploeg (fabrics) were sold. At the end of the 1910s, Metz began its own production. 1918–24, Paul Bromberg designed furniture and advised clients on interior furnishings. He was succeeded by interior architect W. Penaat. Moderately Functional furniture was designed by H.P. Berlage and K.P.C. de Bazel. De Leeuw had little regard for most Dutch designers and had the firm's Metzco clothing and upholstery fabrics design by foreigners, including Sonia Delaunay, who made bright geometric patterned fabrications. In c1930, a stylistic departure followed de Leeuw's meetings with architect Gerrit Rietveld and painter B. van der Leck. At this time, numerous other artists worked for the firm, including J.J.P. Oud, Mart Stam, and I. Falkenberg-Liefrinck of the Netherlands, and Jean Burkhalter and Édouard-Joseph Bourgeois of France. Others artists included A.M. Cassandre in 1930 and Jean Carlu in 1933. Gerrit Rietveld designed for Metz until the 1950s. Metz made its own wood furniture, whereas tubular steel models were contracted out. A supervisor of the Metz furniture workshop 1922–46, E. Berkovich designed furniture and lamps for the firm in the 1930s. Though he provided almost unbridled freedom to his consultant designers, de Leeuw did not pay them well.
▶ Barbie Campbell-Cole and Tim Benton (eds.), *Tubular Steel Furniture*, London: The Art Book Company, 1979:31. *Industry and Design in the Netherlands, 1850/1950*, Amsterdam: Stedelijk Museum, 1985.

Meubles et Fonctions International (MFI)
See Perrigault, Pierre

Meunier, Charles (1865–1940)
▶ French bookbinder, gilder, and publisher; born and active Paris.
▶ Meunier was apprenticed to Gustave Bénard. He worked for a short time for Jules Domont and Maillard. In 1881, he began working for Marius-Michel. Bored with traditional binding, in 1885, he set up his own workshop in the rue Mazarine, subsequently moving to 75 boulevard des Malesherbes in Paris. Prolific as it was, his work was not respected by contemporary critics. 1900–03, he published the quarterly journal *L'Oeuvre et l'image* on aspects of book production. He published other works, including the four-volume *Réflexion d'un praticien en marge de la reliure du XIXᵉ siècle de M. Henri Béraldi* (1908), *La Reliure du XIXᵉ siècle* (1818–20) and *Paroles d'un praticien pour l'art et la technique du relieur-doreur* (1918–20).
▶ Declining to show at the 1900 Paris 'Exposition Universelle,' he mounted an exhibition at his own studio, receiving much publicity.
▶ Alastair Duncan and Georges de Bartha, *Art Nouveau and Art Déco Bookbinding*, New York: Abrams, 1989:14,15,16,33,137–43,194–95. Émile Bosquet, 'La Reliure française à l'exposition,' *Art et décoration*, July–Dec. 1900:47,49,50,53,55. Cat., *Cent Ans de reliures d'art 1880–1980*, Toulouse: Bibliothèque Municipale de Toulouse, 1981. Ernest de Crauzat, *La Reliure française de 1900 à 1925*, Vol. 1, Paris, 1932:19,35–44. Roger Devauchelle, *La Reliure en France de ses origines à nos jours*, Vol. 3, Paris, 1961:85,98–104,118,126–27,134–35. Paul Elek, *The Art of the French Book*, Paris, 1947:141–45. Octave Uzanne, *L'Art dans la décoration extérieure des livres en France et à l'étranger*, Paris, 1898:161,169,172,174–75,186–90.

Meydam, Floris (1919–)
▶ Dutch glassware designer.
▶ Producing both freely formed unique pieces and tableware ranges at Vereenigde Leerdam Glasfabriek in the Netherlands, his work was spare and unadorned. In 1935, he became an assistant to Leerdam artistic director Andries Copier. In 1943, he became a trainee in the Leerdam glass school, where he began to teach in 1944. Returning to the factory, he was its chief designer from 1949.

▶ His work was included in the 1953 'Good Design' exhibition at the New York Museum of Modern Art and Merchandise Mart in Chicago.
▶ Frederick Cooke, *Glass: Twentieth-Century Design*, New York: Dutton: 1986:96. Cat., Kathryn B. Hiesinger and George H. Marcus III (eds.), *Design Since 1945*, Philadelphia: Philadelphia Museum of Art, 1983:222,II–40. Geoffrey Beard, *International Modern Glass*, London, 1976: plates 91,93,253.

Meyer, Grethe (1918–)
▶ Danish architect, ceramicist, and furniture and glassware designer; born Svendborg.
▶ Studied architecture, Det Kongelige Danske Kunstakademi, Copenhagen, to 1947.
▶ 1944–55, she was on the editorial staff of *The Building Manual*. Working frequently with Børge Mogensen, she was influential in his research in the standardization of sizes of consumer products. They designed the 1957 *Boligens Byggeskabe* (BB) and Øresund cabinet-storage systems. 1955–60, she worked at the State Institute for Building Research, collaborating with Paul Kjærgaard and Bent Salicath on research on housing and consumer products. In 1959, she and Ibi Trier Mørch designed glassware for Kastrup and Holmegård glassworks. In 1960, she set up her own drawing office. From 1960, she designed tableware for the Royal Copenhagen Porcelain Manufactory; (with Mørch) designed the 1972 *Weisstopf* dinnerware, 1976 *Feuerpott* oven-to-table range of kitchenware, 1964–65 *Blaukant* ceramic tableware, and 1989 *Ocean* vases produced by Royal Copenhagen. She was a member of the Association of Academic Architects and of the Danish Design Council.
▶ Her work won the 1965 Kay Bojesen Commemorative Prize, 1965 Danish ID prize, silver medal at the 1965 Vicenza 'International Exhibition of Ceramics,' 1965 silver medal at Faenza, 1973 Scandinavian Industrial Art and Design Award, and 1983 Bindesbøll Medal. In 1972, elected Honorary Royal Designer for Industry, London. Work shown at Triennali di Milano, 1960–61 USA 'The Arts of Denmark' traveling exhibition, 1980 'Scandinavian Modern Design 1880–1980' exhibition at the Cooper-Hewitt Museum in New York, and 1983–84 'Design Since 1945' exhibition at the Philadelphia Museum of Art.
▶ Cherie Fehrman and Kenneth Fehrman, *Postwar Interior Design, 1945–1960*, New York: Van Nostrand Reinhold, 1987. Cat., Kathryn B. Hiesinger and George H. Marcus III (eds.), *Design Since 1945*, Philadelphia: Philadelphia Museum of Art, 1983:222,II–42. Arne Karlsen, *Made in Denmark*, New York, 1960:118–19. Arne Karlsen, *Furniture Designed by Børge Mogensen*, Copenhagen, 1968. Jens Bersen, *Design, The Problem Comes First*, Copenhagen, 1982:64–67. Eileene Harrison Beer, *Scandinavian Design: Objects of a Life Style*, New York, 1975:137,139,146–47,155. Cat., David Revere McFadden (ed.), *Scandinavian Modern Design 1880–1980*, New York: Abrams, 1982:268, No. 225. Cat., Design Center Stuttgart, *Women in Design: Careers and Life Histories Since 1900*, Stuttgart: Haus der Wirtschaft, 1989:230–31. Jennifer Hawkins Opie, *Scandinavia: Ceramics and Glass in the Twentieth Century*, New York: Rizzoli, 1989.

Meyer, Hannes (1889–1954)
▶ Swiss teacher and designer; born Basel; husband of textile designer Léna Bergner.
▶ 1905–09, studied masonry and architectural drafting, Gewerbeschule, Basel, and subsequently Kunstgewerbeschule, Landwirtschaftsakademie, and Technische Hochschule, Berlin; 1912–13, studied in England.
▶ He was active in the land reform movement and designed the 1919–24 Freidorf estate in Muttenz, near Basel. 1916–19, he participated in housing projects in Munich, Essen, and Lausanne. From 1916 in Basel, he assisted Georg Wittwer in the design of workers' housing, and thereafter for Krupp. In 1919, he set up his own architecture practice in Basel and, in 1926, became a partner of Hans Wittwer. In 1926, he attended the Bauhaus; from 1927, was a teacher in its architectural department; and, in 1928,

succeeded Gropius as director. 1928–29, he published the eight issues of the journal *Bauhaus*. Because of his rigorously left-wing approach to architecture and design, his tenure was short. He designed the 1928–30 Gewerkschaftsschule (Trade Unions' School) in Bernau. In 1930, Ludwig Mies van der Rohe assumed the Banhaus directorship when Meyer decamped to the Soviet Union with a group of his students. He became a professor at the College of Architecture, Moscow. In 1930, he designed an inventive chair with an adjustable seat. 1930–36, he was active in the Soviet Union, and subsequently worked on town planning projects in Geneva, lived in Mexico 1939–49 and Lugano in 1949. He shunned architecture founded on aesthetic formalism, a position that created friction with Bauhaus teachers, including László Moholy-Nagy. His most important work was the 1926–27 League of Nations Palace project (with Hans Wittwer) in Geneva. Other structures included the 1928–30 Allgemeiner Deutscher Gewerkschaftsbund (United German Workers' Union) building in Bernau, near Berlin. He designed the 1932 housing plan for Sozgorod Gorki (Russia).
▶ Claude Schnaidt, *Hannes Meyer, Bauten, Projekte und Schriften*, Teufen, 1965; English-German edition, London, 1965. Cat., *Der Kragstuhl*, Stuhlmuseum Burg Beverungen, Berlin: Alexander, 1986:134. Cat., *The Bauhaus: Masters and Students*, New York: Barry Friedman, 1988. Igor Golomstock, *Totalitarian Art in the Soviet Union, the Third Reich, Fascist Italy and the People's Republic of China*, New York: Icon, 1990:67.

Meyer, Jenny (1866–1927)
▶ Danish ceramicist and painter.
▶ From 1892, Meyer worked at the Royal Copenhagen Porcelain Manufactory, where her pieces were produced with delicate and distinctive motifs in the Art Nouveau style.
▶ Cat., David Revere McFadden (ed.), *Scandinavian Modern Design 1880–1980*, New York:Abrams, 1982:268, No. 43.

Meyer, Terje (1942–)
▶ Norwegian furniture designer.
▶ Meyer is best known for his widely published 1968 plastic furniture for Strongpack and 1970 multi-media room. He collaborated with Mona Kinn on the 1968 *Uni-Line* furniture range for Dokka Møbler. With Jan Sverre Christiansen, he designed a 1976 low-cost house in plastics.
▶ Meyer won the 1973 Japanese design prize for a bicycle model designed with Bjørn A. Larsen and Christiansen.
▶ Fredrik Wildhagen, *Norge i Form*, Oslo: Stenersen, 1988:170.

Michel, Eugène (?–c1905)
▶ French glassmaker; born Lunéville, Meurthe-et-Moselle.
▶ In 1867, Michel worked as an engraver and decorator for Eugène Rousseau, and later for Rousseau's successor Eugène Léveillé. He became an independent glassmaker in Paris c1900. Like Rousseau, he worked primarily with crackled glass in several different colored layers, deeply engraved, creating a dramatic effect. His work was strongly influenced by 18th- and 19th-century Chinese glassware. Lelièvre, with whom Michel collaborated for a time, made metal mountings for Michel's cut and engraved crystal bottles.
▶ Yvonne Brunhammer et al., *Art Nouveau Belgium, France*, Houston: Institute for the Arts, Rice University, 1976.

Michelsen, A.
▶ Danish silversmiths; located Copenhagen.
▶ Founded by Anton Michelsen in 1841, the firm was the only Danish one to show silver at the 1900 Paris exhibition. In the early years of the 20th century, the firm executed the designs of Mogens Ballin and Thorvald Bindesbøll. Fr. Hegel began working for Michelsen in 1906; his work was influenced by Bindesbøll and Holger Kyster of Kolding. Niels Georg Henriksen was the firm's artistic director; his work showed chased and embossed naturalistic thistles, irises, and poppies. Harald Slott-Møller, another of the firm's designers influenced by Bindesbøll, produced designs of abstract, playful ornament. In the 1920s, the designs of Kay Fisker

were produced; in the 1930s, those of Palle Svenson and Kay Gottlob. Its stainless steel ware of the 1930s was widely published.
▶ The firm showed its silver at the 1900 Paris 'Exposition Universelle,' including the work of Henriksen and Slott-Møller.
▶ Annelies Krekel-Aalberse, *Art Nouveau and Art Déco Silver*, New York: Abrams, 1989:18,102,216–17,220,257.

Michon, Lucien
See **Genêt et Michon**

Midavaine, Louis (1888–1978)
▶ French accessories and furniture designer; born Roubaix.
▶ Studied École des Beaux-Arts, Roubaix.
▶ Before World War I, he worked for the family painting and decoration firm in the village of Grièvement. Injured and taken prisoner in Germany, he was introduced to the techniques of lacquer by the brother of his nurse. After the war, he moved to Issy-les-Moulineaux, where he decorated objects in lacquer that were sold to benefit the Red Cross, whose director, the duchesse de La Rochefoucauld, established Midavaine in a studio in Paris in 1917. He designed numerous Modern lacquer pieces that were principally in the form of animals. He participated in the decoration of oceanliners including the *Pasteur* and the 1935 *Normandie* and, in 1950, decorated the residence in the Côte d'Azur of Bao-Daï, emperor of Annam (Vietnam). After World War II, he decorated private residences as well as state interiors, including the dining room of the French President of the Senate.
▶ He showed his work at all the Salons of the Société Nationale des Beaux-Arts.
▶ *Meubles 1920–1937*, Paris: Musée d'Art Moderne de la Ville de Paris, 1986.

Middelboe, Rolf (1917–)
▶ Danish graphic and textile designer.
▶ Middleboe set up his own workshop in 1941, where he printed textiles and executed graphic designs. He furnished printed and woven fabric designs to Danish firms, including Spindegården and Unika-Vaev. He used various techniques in his regular, screen-printed geometric motifs and increased the variety of effects through the use of positive and negative alternations.
▶ Arne Karlsen, *Made in Denmark*, New York, 1960. Erik Zahle (ed.), *A Treasury of Scandinavian Design*, New York, 1961:285, No. 158. Cat., Kathryn B. Hiesinger and George H. Marcus III (eds.), *Design Since 1945*, Philadelphia: Philadelphia Museum of Art, 1983:222,VII–47.

Mies van der Rohe, Ludwig (b. Ludwig Mies 1886–1969)
▶ German architect and designer; born Aachen.
▶ 1900–02, worked as a stonemason in his family's business in Aachen and was a trainee on building sites; 1906–07, studied Staatliche Kunstschule des Kunstgewerbe Museums, Berlin.
▶ 1903–04, he was apprenticed to a group of architects in Aachen specializing in wooden structures, and was a draftsman in a stucco decorating studio in Aachen. In 1905, he moved to Berlin and worked for the Berlin borough of Rixdorf to furnish the council chamber. 1905–07, he was apprenticed to architect and furniture designer Bruno Paul in Berlin, and studied wooden furniture design. He designed furniture for all his early houses, including the Werner house; for the 1928–30 Tugendhat house, he designed everything with assistance from Lilly Reich. 1907–08, was in his own architecture practice in Berlin. He worked in the office of Peter Behrens in Neubabelsberg, Berlin, 1908–11; Le Corbusier, Walter Gropius, Hans Meyer, Jean Krämer, and Peter Grossman also worked in the Behrens office around this time on AEG projects and on the German embassy in St. Petersburg. In 1913, he changed his name from Mies to the more distinguished-sounding Mies van der Rohe by adding his mother's maiden name

Rohe. In 1913, he opened a practice in Berlin and, 1914—15, served in the military. With his earliest work inspired by Karl Friedrich Schinkel, he was interested in Expressionism in architecture, subsequently becoming a creator of the International Style. In 1921, he became a co-founder of the architects' organization Der Ring and joined the Deutscher Werkbund, of which he was vice-president 1926—32. 1921—25, he was director of architecture exhibitions for the Novembergruppe. 1923—24, he was joint editor of the journal G; 1923—25, chairman of the Zehnerring and, from 1926, director of the Werkbund exhibition 'Die Wohnung' in Stuttgart, heading the Weissenhof-Siedlung building project there, which opened in 1927. Mies began work on the 1927 MR cantilever curved-legged chair in the mid-1920s, introducing the finished product (with and without arms) at the Weissenhof exhibition (alongside Mart Stam's and Marcel Breuer's cantilever chairs), where models were fitted with iron-yarn belting fabric or special wickerwork by Lilly Reich; the chairs were included in Reich's installation at the 1927 Berlin 'Mode der Dame.' The originator of the cantilever design was Mart Stam; as Sergius Ruegenberg, an assistant of Mies, recalled, 'Mies came back from Stuttgart in November 1926 and told us about Mart Stam's idea for a chair. . . . Mies drew the chair . . . and he said, "Ugly, those fittings are really ugly [referring to the pipe joints]. If only he'd rounded them off—there, that looks better," and he drew a curve. A simple curve from his hand on the Stam sketch had made a new chair out of it!' Mies patented the cantilever tubular steel chair in 1927. The chairs were first produced by Berliner Metallgewerbe Joseph Müller, a locksmith in Neubabelsberg, by Bamberg Metallwerkstätten, and, after 1929, by Thonet. From the 1940s, Mies's furniture designs were licensed to Knoll, whose deft marketing turned his 1920s and 1930s furniture pieces into status symbols. As companion pieces, Mies designed a tubular stool with a leather sling and a low table with a round glass top. His chair for the 1929 Barcelona exhibition, known as the *Barcelona* chair, is still in production, as is all his furniture. Expensive to produce, it was first made by Joseph Müller. The early version was constructed from separate elements that were chromium plated and then assembled with lap joints and chrome-headed bolts. Leather straps were added for additional support. The commission of the 1929—30 Tugendhat house in Brno produced a variant of the *Barcelona* chair with arms, and several other pieces, including a rosewood desk on steel tubular legs and a low vitrine serving as a room divider. In 1927, Mies met Lilly Reich; she had a hand in the design of much of the furniture usually credited solely to Mies, including the 1930 chaise-sofa shown at the 1931 Berlin 'Deutsche Bauausstellung,' and reissued by Knoll in the early 1960s. Mies and Reich designed the 'Velvet and Silk Café' at the 1927 Weissenhof exhibition. 1928—29, he was director of the German contribution to the Barcelona exhibition, where he designed the German National Pavilion and the AEG pavilion. 1931—38, he was a member of the Prussian Academy of Arts. 1930—32, he was the last director of the Bauhaus at Dessau, and was director of the Bauhaus in Berlin until the Nazis closed it in 1932. In 1931, he and Lilly Reich were directors of the Deutscher Werkbund exhibition 'Der Wohnung' in Berlin. He designed the 1934 'Deutsches Volk, Deutsche Arbeit' exhibition and the German National Pavilion project (unrealized) for the 1935 'Exposition Universelle et Internationale de Bruxelles.' He visited New York in 1937, and was appointed director of the Armour Institute in Chicago. In 1938, he left Germany to settle permanently in Chicago. As head of architecture at the Illinois Institute of Technology (formerly the Armour Institute) 1939—59, he brought Bauhaus colleagues Ludwig Hilberseimer and Walter Peterhans to the USA. In 1939, Lilly Reich joined Mies in Chicago for a short time. After his association with Reich was severed, neither of them produced any more furniture. Mies's own residence in a neoclassical apartment house was sparsely furnished with his own pieces, Japanese *tatami* mats, and drawings by former Bauhaus colleague Vasilii Kandinskii.

▶ His buildings and unrealized structures included 1907 Villa Riehl in Neubabelsberg, 1911 Villa Perls in Zehlendorf, 1912 Kröller house (project), 1913 villa on the Heerstrasse, 1913 Villa Werner in Zehlendorf, 1921 glass skyscraper project, 1914 Villa Urbig in Neubabelsberg, 1922 Villa Eichstaedt in Wannsee, 1923 reinforced-concrete office building (project), 1923 brick country house project, 1923 concrete country house project, 1924—26 Villa Mosler in Neubabelsberg, 1925—26 Wolf house in Guben, 1926 Rosa Luxemburg and Karl Liebknecht memorial in Berlin, 1926 apartment on the Afrikanische Strasse in Berlin and at the Weissenhof in Stuttgart, 1928 Langein Krefeld house, 1928 Esters house in Krefeld, 1928—30 Tugendhat house in Brno, 1932 Lemcke house in Weissensee, 1932—33 chimney and factory building for the silk industry in Krefeld, 1934 country house projects, 1934 'Mountain House for the Architect' project, 1946—50 Farnsworth House in Plano, Illinois, 1953 Mannheim Opera House project, 1942—56 buildings at Illinois Institute of Technology in Chicago, 1953 Chicago convention hall project, 1954—58 Seagram building (with Philip Johnson) in New York, and 1962—68 New National Gallery in Berlin.

▶ The furniture credited to Mies, all completed by 1930 (with the exception of a tuxedo-type sofa for Knoll in the 1960s), included, with the original catalog numbers of Bamberg Metallwerkstätten in Berlin-Neukölln, chair (MR1), S chair (MR10), S chair with arms (MR20), S chair with upholstery cushions (MR30), S chair with upholstery cushions and arms, *Bruno* chair (MR50), *Tugendhat* chair (MR60), *Tugendhat* chair with arms (MR70), *Barcelona* stool with flat leather sling (MR80), *Barcelona* chair (MR90), tubular lounge chairs with cushions (MR100 and MR110), side chair (LR120), round side tables with notched-glass top (MR130, MR140), glass tables (MR150, LR500, LR510), coffee tables (LR520, LR530), and beds (LR600, LR610, LR620).

▶ He was in charge of the 1927 'Weissenhof-Siedlung' project exhibition in Stuttgart. He and Lilly Reich designed stands at the 1927 Berlin 'Exposition de la Mode,' 1931 Berlin 'Deutsche Bauausstellung,' and 1943 Berlin 'Deutsches Volk und Deutsche Arbeit' exhibition. He designed the German Pavilion and 'Sede' stand at the 1929 'Exposición Internacional de Barcelona,' where his designs included two chairs, situated at right angles to an onyx wall, for King Alfonso XIII and Queen Victoria Eugénie of Spain to use as Modern thrones. His work was the subject of one-person 1936, 1948, and 1960 'Mies van der Rohe' exhibitions at the New York Museum of Modern Art, and 1977 'Furniture and Furniture Drawings from the Design Collection and Mies van der Rohe Archive' at the New York Museum of Modern Art. Work included in the 1982 'Shape and Environment: Furniture by American Architects' at the Whitney Museum of American Art in Fairfield County, Connecticut.

▶ Philip Johnson, *Ludwig Mies van der Rohe*, New York: Museum of Modern Art, 1948, 2nd ed. 1953. Ludwig Hilberseimer, *Mies van der Rohe*, Chicago, 1956. Cat., *Der Kragstuhl*, Stuhlmuseum Burg Beverungen, Berlin: Alexander, 1986:135. Elaine S. Hochman, *Architects of Fortune*, New York: Wiedenfeld and Nicholson, 1989. Stephen Calloway, *Twentieth-Century Decoration*, New York: Rizzoli, 1988:158—59. Cat., Lisa Phillips (introduction), *Shape and Environment: Furniture by American Architects*, New York: Whitney Museum of American Art, 1982:44—45. Arthur Drexler, *Ludwig Mies van der Rohe*, New York: Braziller, 1960. Ludwig Glaeser, *Furniture and Furniture drawings from the Design Collection and Mies van der Rohe Archive*, New York: Museum of Modern Art, 1977. Henry-Russell Hitchcock, 'The Evolution of Wright, Mies and Le Corbusier,' *Perspecta, The Yale Architectural Journal*, No. 1, Summer 1952:8—15. *Mies van der Rohe: European Works*, London: Academy, 1986. 'Documents,' *Journal of Design History*, Vol. 3, Nos. 2 and 3, 1990:172—74. Otakar Máčel, 'Avant-garde Design and the Law-Litigation over the Cantilever Chair,' *Journal of Design History*, Vol. 3, Nos. 2 and 3, 1990:125.

Migeon et Migeon

▶ French designers.

▶ In the 1980s, they had a design practice in Paris; were part of the 'New Barbarian' group of designers in Paris; with Elizabeth

Garouste and Mattia Bonetti, employed unorthodox materials including brightly colored resins.

Mikkelsen, Andreas (1928–)
▶ Danish designer.
▶ Mikkelsen was associated with the Georg Jensen Sølvsmedie for many years; designed starkly simple silver jewelry, including the 1973 *Armring* with its handmade hinge and clasp.
▶ Cat., *Georg Jensen Silversmithy: 77 Artists, 75 Years*, Washington: Smithsonian Institution Press, 1980.

Miklós, Gustave (1888–1967)
▶ Hungarian sculptor, painter, and designer; born Budapest; active Paris.
▶ Studied School of Decorative Arts, Budapest, and various institutions in Paris, including École Spéciale d'Architecture.
▶ In the French army during World War I, he discovered the art of Greece and Byzantium. In Paris after the war, he met Jacques Doucet, for whom he designed silverware, enamels, tapestries and carpets for the residence on the avenue du Bois (today avenue Foch). In c1923 he turned to sculpture and completed commissions for Doucet and others in a Cubist style; befriended François-Louis Schmied; designed furniture, supplied painted panels and carvings for Jean Dunand and others; designed stained glass and jewelry; illustrated books; produced decorative sculpture that showed influences of Cubism and West African art; in 1930, became a member of UAM (Unions des Artistes Modernes); in 1940, left Paris and taught in Oyonnax.
▶ Work shown at sessions of Salon d'Automne; Salons of Société des Artistes Décorateurs; in 1922, at Léonce Rosenberg's L'Effort Moderne gallery, Paris; in 1928, at La Renaissance gallery, Paris. From 1930, work shown at UAM exhibitions. Work subject of 1983 exhibition, Centre Culturel Aragon, Oyonnax.
▶ Cat., *Gustave Miklos, Exposition Rétrospective*, Ville d'Oyonnax: Centre Culturel Aragon, 1983. Pierre Cabanne, *Encyclopédie Art Déco*, Paris: Somogy, 1986:223. Arlette Barré-Despond, *UAM*, Paris: Regard, 1986:470–71. Cat., *Les années UAM 1929–1958*, Paris: Musée des Arts Décoratifs, 1988:230.

Milà, Alfonso (1924–)
▶ Spanish architect; born Barcelona.
▶ Studied School of Architecture, Barcelona, to 1952.
▶ From 1952, he collaborated in an architecture office with Frederico Correa; 1971–73, he was a member of the Board of Architects' Association of Catalonia; and, from 1970, professor at the School of Architecture in Barcelona. Correa's and Milà's buildings included the 1962 Godó y Trias factory in Barcelona.
▶ He and Correa won the 1972 FAD Prize for Architecture for the Alalaya building in Barcelona, 1974 FAD Prize for Architecture for Il Giardinetto Restaurant, and 1984 first prize for the Olympic Ring Competition. His work was included in the 1986 'Contemporary Spanish Architecture: An Eclectic Panorama' exhibition at the Architectural League in New York.
▶ Antón Capitel and Ignacio Solà-Morales (essays), *Contemporary Spanish Architecture*, New York: Rizzoli, 1986:56–59.

Milà, Miguel (1931–)
▶ Spanish industrial designer; active Barcelona.
▶ Studied School of Architecture, Barcelona.
▶ He came to design via interior design and collaborating with architect brother Alfonso Milà and Frederico Correa. One of his first designs, the 1956 TMC lamp was produced by himself and others, including Polinax (1962), B.d Ediciones de Diseño, and Santa & Cole, with continuing modifications. Milà designed the 1967 BM street lamp (with Pep Bonet) by Diseño Ahorro Energetico for Polinax, and the 1977 *Ximenea* fireplace unit by Diseño Ahorro Energetico.
▶ He received the 1965 ADIFAD award for his ice tongs and the 1987 National Design Prize.
▶ Guy Julier, *New Spanish Design*, London: Thames and Hudson, 1991.

Milani, Marzio (1945–)
▶ Italian furniture designer; born Florence; active Verona.
▶ He began his professional career in 1973, designing furniture in plastics, metal, and glass. He was a member of ADI (Associazione per il Disegno Industriale).
▶ *ADI Annual 1976*, Milan: Associazione per il Disegno Industriale, 1976.

Miller, Elmer (1901–60)
▶ American glassware designer.
▶ In 1915, Miller began as a moldmaker, and later became superintendent, of the New Martinsville glass factory in Virginia (later named Viking Glass), where he designed elegant glassware including a pitcher with an exaggerated lip and a candleholder.
▶ *Glass 1959*, Corning, NY: The Corning Museum of Glass, 1959: No. 289. Cat., Kathryn B. Hiesinger and George H. Marcus III (eds.), *Design Since 1945*, Philadelphia: Philadelphia Museum of Art, 1983:222,II–43.

Mills, Ernestine Evans (b. Ernestine Evans Bell 1871–1959)
▶ British jewelry designer.
▶ Studied Royal College of Art, and Slade School of Art, both London.
▶ Her style as similar to that of Alexander Fisher, from whom she learned enameling.
▶ She won a silver medal at the 1955 Salon in Paris.
▶ Toni Lesser Wolf, 'Women Jewelers of the British Arts and Crafts Movement,' *The Journal of Decorative and Propaganda Arts*, No. 14, Fall 1989:34.

Milner, Alison (1958–)
▶ British designer; born Sevenoaks, Kent.
▶ Studied furniture design, Middlesex Polytechnic, to 1985, and Royal College of Art, London, to 1987.
▶ In freelance practice, she designed a chair in 1986 with textile designer Caroline McKintey that was widely published. She designed a collection of bedroom furniture for mass production by Indian craftsmen for India Works in Chelsea.
▶ She won the 1986 Prince of Wales award. Her 1987 *Mirror Lamp* won second prize in the 1987 Design Council competition 'British Design in Japan.'
▶ Liz McQuiston, *Women in Design: A Contemporary View*, New York: Rizzoli, 1988:74.

Májek, Miloš (1926–78)
▶ Czech designer; born Sázava nad Sázavou.
▶ Studied school of glassmaking, Železný Brod.
▶ In the 1950s, he was active as a designer of consumer products, including glass frames, mail boxes, irons, vacuum cleaners, and pumps. He introduced aerodynamic and organic forms into the design of everyday goods; had clients including Chirana (dentist lighting and pharmaceutical interiors in the late 1960s).
▶ Milena Lamarová, *Průmyslový design*, Prague: Odeon, 1984:28–30.

Minagawa, Masa (1917–)
▶ Japanese industrial designer; born Tokyo.
▶ Studied High Industrial Arts School, Tokyo, under Takao Miyashita, to 1940.
▶ He was a designer for Tokyo Electric Company; from 1954, founder-president of Masa Minagawa Design, Tokyo; specialized in the design of lighting and electrical appliances; 1957–63, lecturer, Chiba University, Tokyo; 1963–83, dean, Industrial Design Department, Tokyo University of Arts and Design; in 1963, became founder-member of Japan Industrial Designs Association.
▶ Received 1978 Blue Ribbon Medal from the Japanese government.
▶ 'Office Visit,' *Industrial Design*, Aug. 1983. Ann Lee Morgan (ed.), *Contemporary Designers*, London: Macmillan, 1984:415–16.

Minale, Marcello (1938–)
► Italian designer; born Tripoli.
► Studied technical school, Naples.
► He was designer at the Taucker advertising agency, Finland; art director at Mackkinointi Uiherjuuri, Finland; until 1964, was design director, Young and Rubicam advertising agency, London; in 1964 with Brian Tattersfield, set up a design firm; in 1982, became president of the Designers' and Art Directors' Association, London; designed graphics, furniture, interiors, and packaging (for Suchard, Boots, and Gilbey's); other clients included Cubic Metre Furniture, Zanotta, and Aqualisa Showers.
► Work shown at 1979 Design Centre exhibition, London, and 1983 exhibition, Museo d'Arte Contemporanea, Milan. Received 1977 gold medal, New York Art Directors' Club.
► Ann Lee Morgan (ed.), *Contemporary Designers*, London: Macmillan, 1984:417–18. Hans Wichmann, *Italien Design 1945 bis heute*, Munich: Die Neue Sammlung, 1988.

Minoletti, Giulio (1910–)
► Italian industrial designer; born Milan.
► Studied Scuola Superiore di Architettura, Politecnico di Milano, to 1931.
► He was president of Movimento Studi di Architettura; in 1947, founder-member of the INU, the city planning commission of Milan; a founder of the Compasso d'Oro. He collaborated with Albini, Palanti, Bottoni, Gardella, Gentili, and Tevarotto (architects) and with G. Chiodi and F. Clerici (engineers). Designs included 1949 *ETR 300 Settebello* high-speed electric train by Breda Ferroviaria, 1949 *Better Living* bathroom fixtures, and 1957 kitchen sinks.
► Received gold medal, first Triennale di Milano, and grand prize for architecture at its 1957 (XI) session.
► Alfonso Grassi and Anty Pansera, *Atlante del Design Italiano 1940–80*, Milan: Fabbri 1980:331,273. Hans Wichmann, *Italien Design 1945 bis heute*, Munich: Die Neue Sammlung, 1988.

Minton
► British ceramics firm; located Stoke-on-Trent.
► Thomas Minton bought a pottery in Stoke-on-Trent in 1793 and, in 1796, began production of inexpensive blue transfer-printed earthenware. His son Herbert Minton became director in 1836, expanded the range of wares, and hired artists. In the 1840s and 1850s, Henry Cole designed the shapes of tablewares with printed decorations by A.W.N. Pugin; both were friends of Herbert. In 1849, Léon Arnoux became artistic director and introduced majolica with bright glazes, naturalistic forms, and amusing shapes popular until the 1880s. From the early 1840s to the turn of the century, the firm produced vast amounts of decorative tiles, starting with encaustic examples for flooring. The firm produced printed tiles with designs by artists including J. Moyr Smith and Christopher Dresser. Its tiles were also used to decorate furniture. In 1858, Herbert Minton's nephew Colin Minton Campbell became director. Minton's domestic wares were for a mass market. Minton established the Art Pottery Studio in South Kensington, London, in 1871, where earthenware decoration was taught; it practiced china painting during the time of the Aesthetic movement. The studio was directed by William S. Coleman, who began employment at Minton in 1869. The studio closed when its building burned down in 1875. From the early 1860s, Minton's wares were influenced by Eastern and Middle-Eastern designs, motifs, and materials. In the 1870s, when large numbers of French artists came to Britain, Minton began production of *pâte-de-pâte* pieces with classical decoration. At the turn of the century, its wares began to show Art Nouveau and German Sezession influences. In 1968, Minton became a member of the Royal Tableware Group.
► Its majolica was shown at the 1851 London 'Great Exhibition of the Works of Industry of All Nations.'
► Geoffrey A. Godden, *Victorian Porcelain*, London, 1961. Geoffrey A. Godden, *Minton Pottery and Porcelain of the First Period, 1793–1850*, New York and Washington: 1968. Cat., Elizabeth Aslin and Paul Atterbury, *Minton, 1798–1910*, London: Victoria

and Albert Museum, 1976. Paul Atterbury, *The History of Porcelain*, New York, 1982:155–77. Doreen Bolger Burke et al., *In Pursuit of Beauty: Americans and the Aesthetic Movement*, New York: Metropolitan Museum of Art and Rizzoli, 1986:454–55.

Minton, (Francis) John (1917–57)
► British painter and designer.
► Studied St. John's Wood School of Art and Royal College of Art, London.
► He taught at the Royal College of Art. An accomplished portrait painter, he designed posters for the theater and, in the early 1950s, produced designs for wallpaper for John Line.
► Michael Farr, *Design in British Industry: A Mid-Century Survey*, London: Cambridge, 1955. Stuart Durant, *Ornament from the Industrial Revolution to Today*, Woodstock, NY: Overlook, 1986: 293,326.

Minuth, Fred G. (1884–1966)
► American silversmith; active Chicago.
► Minuth and Frank S. Boyden established the Frank S. Boyden Co at 42 Madison (later 29 E. Madison) in Chicago in 1903; it subsequently became the Boyden-Minuth Co. The firm produced heavily embellished objects for ecclesiastical use, and jewelry. Until the 1950s, the firm produced silver trophies. The company is still in operation.
► Sharon S. Darling with Gail Farr Casterline, *Chicago Metalsmiths*, Chicago Historical Society, 1977.

Mir Iskusstva
See World of Art, The

Miralles, Pedro (1955–)
► Spanish architect and designer; born Valencia; active Madrid and Valencia.
► Studied Escuela Técnica Superior de Arquitectura, Madrid, to 1980, and Domus Academy, Milan, to 1987.
► He worked in the office of fashion designer Jesús del Pozo and in theatrical archives. His industrial designs, with references to cinema, literature, and popular music, were produced by Luis Adelantado, NMF, B.d Ediciones de Diseño, Arflex & José Martinez Medina, and Artespaña. His work included the 1985 *Acuatica* chair by NMF, 1985 *Dry Martini* stool, 1986 *Armchair 115*, *Voyeur* folding screen, *Egyptian* lamp, and *Calzada* rug by NMF. His 1988 *Andrews Sisters* three-part interlocking tables in bubinga wood were produced by Punt Mobles, and 1987 *Egipcia* floor lamp by Santa & Cole. He designed the waste bins installed at the 1992 Seville 'Expo '92'; made of concrete and sheet iron with a built-in ashtray, their dodecahedron shape was inspired by the Torre del Oro, the 13th-century 12-sided tower overlooking the Guadalquivir.
► Juli Capella and Quim Larrea, *Designed by Architects in the 1980s*, New York, Rizzoli, 1988. Emma Dent Coat, *Seville Expo '92*, Metropolis, Oct. 1991:51. Guy Julier, *New Spanish Design*, London: Thames and Hudson, 1991.

Miranda, Santiago (1947–)
► Spanish designer; born Seville.
► Studied Escuela de Artes Aplicadas y Oficios Artisticos, Seville.
► Moving to Italy, he collaborated with Perry King from 1977 in Milan; their studio executed environmental design, industrial design, furniture, interior designs, and graphics. King and Miranda designed posters and catalogs for Olivetti and corporate identity programs for others. They executed designs for lighting for Arteluce (including the 1977–78 *Donald* table lamp) and Flos (many examples with Giancarlo Arnaldi), the 1983 and on-going *Cable* office system and 1981 *Air Mail* chair for Marcatré, and power tools for Black and Decker. Their 1985 *Aurora* glass pendant lamp produced by Arteluce presaged similar designs by others. Their 1988 *Bloom* bookshelf system was produced by Tisettanta, and 1987 *Bergamo* Murano-glass bowl by Veart. They designed the 1991 *Lucerno* lighting range for the public areas of the 1992 Seville 'Expo '92.'

▶ Work shown in numerous exhibitions including 1986 'Donation Olivetti' and 1988 'Italien Design 1945 bis heute,' Die Neue Sammlung, Munich; 'Design Process: Olivetti 1908–1983,' Frederick S. Wight Art Gallery, University of California, Los Angeles, 1979.

▶ 'When Is a Dot not a Dot?' *Design*, No. 317, May 1975:22. *Design Process Olivetti 1908–1978*, Los Angeles: Frederick S. Wight Art Gallery, University of California, 1979:260. James Woudhuysen, 'Priests at Technology's Altar,' *Design*, No. 410, Feb. 1983:40–42. Cat., Kathryn B. Hiesinger and George H. Marcus III (eds.), *Design Since 1945*, Philadelphia: Philadelphia Museum of Art, 1983. Robert A.M. Stern (ed.), *The International Design Yearbook*, New York: Abbeville, 1985/1986: Nos. 242–52. Hugh Aldersey-Williams, *King and Miranda: The Poetry of the Machine*, New York: Rizzoli, 1991.

Mirenzi, Franco   (1942–)
▶ Italian industrial designer; born Trieste; active Milan.
▶ He began his professional career in 1964. He worked in the office of Unimark International in Milan. Designing furniture, accessories, lighting, ceramics, hi-fi equipment, domestic electrical appliances, and exhibitions, his clients in Italy included Agip, Boston, Brionvega, Cedit, Citterio, Dreher, Fabbri, General Electric, Honeywell, Molteni, Norex, Sirrah, and Unifor. Widely published, his *Zeta* lamp was produced by Valenti. He was a member of ADI (Associazione per il Disegno Industriale).
▶ He won the 1970 Compasso d'Oro and first prize in the 1971 Smau Industrial Design competition.
▶ *ADI Annual 1976*, Milan: Associazione per il Disegno Industriale, 1976. Giancarlo Iliprandi and Pierluigi Molinari (eds.), *Industrial Designers Italiani*, Fagagna, 1984:144. Hans Wichmann, *Italien Design 1945 bis heute*, Munich: Die Neue Sammlung, 1988.

Missiaglia
▶ Italian jewelry firm; located Venice.
▶ The Missiaglia firm was founded in Venice in 1839 by Angelo Missiaglia. In 1870, the jewelry store was moved to the Piazza San Marco. In 1946, Ottavio Croze, a descendant of the Missiaglias through marriage, took over ownership of the firm. In the 1950s, its designs were characterized by jewelry in platinum, often incorporating diamonds.
▶ Melissa Gabardi, *Les Bijoux des Années 50*, Paris: Amateur, 1987.

Mission Inn
▶ American hostelry; located Riverside, California.
▶ Frank Miller established the Mission Inn for early tourists to California. In a Spanish-colonial style, it was constructed and altered over many years. Production for its construction, including balcony railings, lighting fixtures, and door hardware, was performed on the premises in its catacombs. Before being applied, its iron was laid out in the sun and sprinkled with water for weathering. The original furniture was supplied by Gustav Stickley, the Limberts, and other East Coast firms; when construction got underway, craftsmen working in situ included resident potters such as Cornelius Brauckman and Fred H. Robertson, who produced souvenirs. Influenced by Spanish-Mission styles, the Inn's Arts and Crafts furniture had exaggerated lines.
▶ Timothy J. Anderson et al., *California Design 1910*, Salt Lake City: Peregrine Smith, 1980 (reprint of 1974 ed.):125.

Missoni, Ottavio 'Tai'   (1921–)   and **Rosita Missoni** (b. Rosita Jelmini   1931–)
▶ Italian fabric and fashion designers; husband and wife; Missoni born Dubrovnik (Croatia); Jelmini born Italy.
▶ Missoni and Jelmini set up a small workshop and factory producing knitted ready-to-wear clothing at Gallarate, near Milan. They subsequently added the production of menswear, fragrances, linens, and home furnishings, particularly rugs. In the 1980s, the management of the firm included their two sons and a daughter. Refining their goods from 1953, they perfected certain machine-knitted fabrications, including 1961 patchwork knitwear and the

1962 flame stitch. In the mid-1950s, the Missonis were associated with Biki of Milan and Emmanuelle Khanh of Paris and, in the late 1960s, established their own label.
▶ Gloria Bianchino et al. (eds.) *Italian Fashion*, Vol. 1, Milan, 1987:294. Hans Wichmann, *Italien Design 1945 bis heute*, Munich: Die Neue Sammlung, 1988.

Miturich, Petr Vasil'evich   (1887–1956)
▶ Russian artist and industrial and graphic designer; born St. Petersburg.
▶ Studied 1906–09 Kiev Art Institute and, 1909–16, Academy of Arts, St. Petersburg, under Nikolai Samōkish.
▶ From 1914, he developed an interest in aviation, resulting in his designs for dirigibles in the late 1920s. In 1918, he became a member of the Left Association of Petrograd Artists. 1918–22, he worked on 'spatial graphics' and 'spatial paintings,' and, 1920–22, designed numerous covers for the music of Artur Lurie, including *Roial v detskoi (The Piano in the Nursery)* and the cover of *Zangezi* by Viktor Khlebnikov. He became a professor in the graphic and architectural departments at Vkhutemas. He was a member of the Four Arts group 1925–29, and designed children's books in 1928, including *Miau (Meow)* by Alexandr Vvedenskii. He painted chiefly landscapes and portraits from 1930.
▶ From 1915, he contributed to numerous exhibitions, including the 1915 Moscow 'Exhibition of Painting,' 1916 Petrograd 'Contemporary Russian Painting,' and 1915–18 Petrograd 'World of Art.' In 1924, he contributed to the 1924 Venice 'Esposizione Internazionale.'
▶ N. Rozanova, *Petr Vasilievich Miturich*, Moscow, 1973. Stephanie Barron and Maurice Tuchman, *The Avant-Garde in Russia, 1910–1930*, Cambridge, MA: MIT Press, 1980:212. Selim O. Khan-Magomedov, *Les Vhutemas*, Paris: Regard, 1990:401–03.

Miyamoto, Eiji   (1948–)
▶ Japanese textile designer; born Tokyo.
▶ Studied Hosei University to 1970.
▶ In 1975, Miyamoto began experimenting with and designing fabrics, later supplying goods to Issey Miyake and other Japanese fashion designers. Distinguished one-off fabrications were produced by Miyashin in 1987.
▶ Albrecht Bangert and Karl Michael Armer, *80s Style: Designs of the Decade*, New York: Abbeville, 1990:163,233.

Mobilier Artistique Moderne   (MAM)
▶ French interior decorating firm; located Paris.
▶ In 1913, Michel Dufet established the MAM (Mobilier Artistique Moderne) at 3 avenue de l'Opéra in Paris to produce Modern furniture, wallpaper, fabrics, and lighting, sometimes with Louis Bureau.
▶ Léon Deshairs, *Modern French Decorative Art*, Paris: Albert Lévy. *Ensembles Mobiliers*, Vol. II, Paris: Charles Moreau, 1937. Pierre Kjellberg, *Art Déco: les maîtres du Mobilier, le décor des Paquebots*, Paris: Amateur, 1986:122.

Mobilier National, Le
▶ French governmental institution.
▶ Le Mobilier National was founded in 1663 by Jean-Baptiste Colbert, Louis XIV's minister. It was the only State furniture depository until French minister of culture André Malraux commissioned Jean Coural to create the Atelier de Création in 1965 with the intention of promoting contemporary French furniture and funding prototypes that would encourage ultimate production. Its collection represents a complete history of French furniture from which ministers, public administrators, and embassy officials may choose pieces to furnish their offices, salons, and waiting rooms.

Mobles 114
▶ Spanish furniture manufacturer and design studio.
▶ In c1973, Josep M<u>a</u> Massana and Josep M<u>a</u> Tremoleda established the furniture shop and design studio Mobles 114. Massana, Tremoleda, and Mariano Ferrer designed the 1977 *Gira* lamp as

an alternative to the *Flexo* lamp by an unknown designer, an evolving model popular in Spain from the 1940s.

Modern Architectural Research Group
See MARS

Modernismo (aka Modernista; Catalan school)
See Art Nouveau

Moffat, E. Curtis (c.1888–1942)
▶ American photographer and interior designer; active London.
▶ Moffat worked in association with John Duncan Miller. In 1929, Moffat opened an avant-garde furniture gallery in London, designed by Frederick Etchells. The gallery's exhibitions showed the works of Marion Dorn, Eyre de Lanux, and others. In 1932, he opened a picture gallery. In 1932, both influential galleries closed, and he returned to photography.
▶ The 1934 poster 'Photographers Prefer Shell,' bearing his photograph, was included in the 1979–80 'Thirties' exhibition at the Hayward Gallery in London.
▶ Cat., *Thirties: British art and design before the war*, London: Arts Council of Great Britain, Hayward Gallery, 1979:212,296.

Mögelin, Else (1887–1982)
▶ German textile designer; born Berlin.
▶ Studied School of Arts and Crafts, Berlin–Charlottenburg, to 1919; 1919–21, Bauhaus Pottery workshop, Dornburg, under Gerhard Marcks; 1921–23, Bauhaus Weaving Workshop and in the Metal Workshop.
▶ 1923–27, was active in her own textile workshop; 1927–45, directed textile instruction, School of Arts and Crafts Stettin; in 1933, the Nazis confiscated her art supplies; 1945–52, was instructor and director of weaving, Hochschule für bildenden Künste; 1952, retired from teaching and continued weaving.
▶ Sigrid Wortmann Weltge. *Women's Work: Textile Art from the Bauhaus*, London: Thames and Hudson, 1993.

Mogensen, Børge (1914–72)
▶ Danish furniture designer.
▶ 1936–38, studied Kunsthåndværkerskolen, Copenhagen, and 1938–42, furniture, Det Kongelige Danske Kunstakademi, Copenhagen, under Kaare Klint.
▶ 1942–50, he was chair of the furniture design department of the Association of Danish Cooperative Wholesale Societies, designing simple utilitarian pieces. 1945–47, he was an assistant to Kaare Klint at Det Kongelige Danske Kunstakademi. 1945–46, he worked with Hans Wegner. In 1950, he opened his own office in Copenhagen. Mogensen worked for various architects, including Mogens Koch and Kaare Klint, 1938–42. In 1962 with Klint, he designed school furniture. He was a design consultant to Karl Andersson, Søborg Møbelfabrik, Fredericia Stolefabrik, Hüskvarna, P. Lauritsen, and Erhard Rasmussen. From 1953, he was artistic consultant to C. Olesen, for which he designed wooden furniture combined with leather and fabric; the fabric was designed with Lis Ahlmann. He designed traditional types of Chinese furniture, Windsor chairs, and Shaker models. They were practical and popular, and some are still in production today. Mogensen is best known for his 1964 *Asserbo Chair 504*, produced by Karl Andersson of Hüskvarna. After extensive research into the ideal proportions and standardized measurements for objects of daily use, he designed the *Øresund* system with Grethe Meyer.
▶ 1938–62, his work was shown at the 'Copenhagen Cabinetmakers' Guild' annual exhibitions and those of the Danish Society of Arts and Crafts and Industrial Design. His work was included in the 1968 'Two Centuries of Danish Design' at the Victoria and Albert Museum, London. He received awards including the 1945 Bissen Legacy, 1950 Eckersberg Medal, 1953 Dansk Købestaevne (Danish Trade Fair) Silver Medal, 1958 Copenhagen Cabinetmakers' Guild award of honor, and 1971 Danish furniture prize. In 1972, elected Honorary Royal Designer for Industry.
▶ Arne Karlsen, *Furniture Designed by Børge Mogensen*, Copenhagen, 1968. Erik Zahle, *Scandinavian Domestic Design*, London,

1963. Cat., *Modern Chairs 1918–1970*, London: Lund Humphries, 1971. Cat., Kathryn B. Hiesinger and George H. Marcus III (eds.), *Design Since 1945*, Philadelphia: Philadelphia Museum of Art, 1983:222–23,III–52. Arne Karlsen, *Furniture Designed by Børge Mogensen*, Copenhagen, 1968. Bent Salicath and Arne Karlsen (eds.), *Modern Danish Textiles*, Copenhagen, 1959:12–15. Arne Karlsen, *Made in Denmark*, New York, 1960:104–27. Cat., David Revere McFadden (ed.), *Scandinavian Modern Design 1880–1980*, New York: Abrams, 1982:268, No. 218. Frederik Sieck, *Nutidig Dansk Møbeldesign:-en kortfattet illustreret beskrivelse*, Copenhagen: Bondo Gravesen; 1990 Busck edition in English.

Moggeridge, Bill (1943–)
▶ British industrial designer; active London (England).
▶ 1965, studied Central School of Arts and Crafts, London.
▶ He set up his own industrial design studio in London in 1969, executing models for scientific and consumer products for American Sterilizer, Pitney Bowes, and Hoover. In 1977, Moggeridge moved to California and established Industrial Design Models in London as an entity under which he set up ID Two in Palo Alto, California, and Design Models in London. ID Two designed the first portable computer, the 1982 *Compass*, produced by Grid.
▶ The *Compass* computer was included in the 1983–84 'Design Since 1945' exhibition at the Philadelphia Museum of Art.
▶ Cat., Kathryn B. Hiesinger and George H. Marcus III (eds.), *Design Since 1945*, Philadelphia: Philadelphia Museum of Art, 1983. *Central to Design, Central to Industry*, London: Central School of Art and Design, 1983:95–96. 'The Compass Computer: The Design Challenges Behind the Innovation,' *Innovation*, Winter 1983:4–8.

Møhl-Hansen, Kristian (1876–1962)
▶ Danish designer and artist.
▶ Studied painting, Det Kongelige Danske Kunstakademi, Copenhagen, and Zahrtmann School.
▶ He worked for the Georg Jensen Sølvsmedie, where his 1916 silver and amber cup was produced until 1930.
▶ He was awarded the Eckersberg Medal in 1920 and a gold medal at the 1925 Paris 'Exposition Internationale des Arts Décoratifs et Industriels Modernes' for his embroidered textiles.
▶ Cat., *Georg Jensen Silversmithy: 77 Artists, 75 Years*, Washington: Smithsonian Institution Press, 1980.

Möhler, Fritz (1896–)
▶ German silversmith; active Schwäbisch-Gmünd.
▶ Trained as a steel engraver in his father's workshop; studied metalwork at technical school, Schwäbisch Gmünd, and Kunstgewerbeschule, Munich.
▶ He set up his own workshop in Schwäbisch Gmünd in 1923. He executed numerous commissions for ecclesiastical silverwork and secular pieces. He was a skilled enameler and produced pieces incorporating *cloisonné* and *champlevé* enamel decoration. In the period before World War I in Germany, Möhler was considered one of the most important silversmiths, and contributed to the resurgence of interest in the goldsmith's craft.
▶ Annelies Krekel-Aalberse, *Art Nouveau and Art Déco Silver*, New York: Abrams, 1989:146,257.

Moholy-Nagy, László (1895–1946)
▶ Hungarian painter, photographer, film maker, graphic designer, typographer, stage designer, and writer; born Bácsborsód.
▶ Studied law in Budapest and drawing and painting elsewhere.
▶ He started to draw during World War I, and became interested in Kasimir Malevich and El Lissitzky, and, in 1919, moved to Vienna and, in 1920, to Berlin. Reflecting an interest in both Dada and Constructivism, his work was produced in the avant-garde Hungarian magazine *Ma* and shown at Herwarth Walden's Der Sturm gallery. He was friendly with the Constructivists and participated in the 1922 Dadaist-Constructivist Congress in Weimar

organized by Theo van Doesburg. Walter Gropius was director of the Bauhaus; on his invitation, Moholy-Nagy was at the Bauhaus in Weimar and Dessau 1923–28, where he practiced book design, film making, photography, and typography. At the Bauhaus in Weimar, he succeeded Johannes Itten as director of the Vorkurs (preliminary course) and Paul Klee as director of the metal workshop; Christian Dell, Wilhelm Wagenfeld, and Marianne Brandt were among his pupils. Moholy-Nagy and Gropius edited the *Bauhausbücher* publication series. He developed the photogram. In 1928 he left the Bauhaus for Berlin, where, 1928–33, he was a stage designer, painter, photographer, and film maker, and was active at the Theater of Piscator. His widely published modular illuminated structure was shown at the 1930 Werkbund exhibition at the Salon in Paris. In 1934 he moved to Amsterdam and worked in London 1935–37; his graphic design work stimulated the poster scene there. He worked with Richard Levin on some graphic designs, including covers of the magazine *Shelf Appeal* in the mid-1930s. Moholy-Nagy contributed to the illustrated weekly magazines *Lilliput* and *Picture Post*. Along with other refugees, he resided in Jack Pritchard's Lawn Road flats (built in 1934) in Hampstead in London. His work in Britain included films, layout and poster designs for International Textiles, traveling exhibitions and publicity materials for Imperial Airways, posters for London Transport, publicity and display work for Simpson's store, special visual effects for Alexander Korda's 1936 film *Things to Come* (not in the final cut), publicity materials for the Isokon furniture firm, exhibition displays, and cover designs and photographs. At Gropius's recommendation, he left London in 1937 and became director of the short-lived New Bauhaus in Chicago. In 1939, Moholy-Nagy set up the independent School of Design, Chicago (renamed Institute of Design in 1944), which became a department under Serge Chermayeff at Armour Institute of Technology (renamed Illinois Institute of Technology on Moholy-Nagy's death. Moholy-Nagy's books were influential and included *The New Vision: From Material to Architecture* (1928) and *Vision in Motion* (1947).

▶ In the early 1920s, his Dada and Constructivist-influenced paintings were shown at Herwarth Walden's gallery Der Sturm in Berlin. His work was the subject of a 1936 one-person exhibition at the London Gallery and 1937 Royal Photographic Society in London. Examples of his work were included in the 1979–80 'Thirties' exhibition at the Hayward Gallery in London.

▶ Cat., *Thirties: British art and design before the war*, London: Arts Council of Great Britain, Hayward Gallery, 1979:20, 38,51,77,219,232,266–67,279,296. Karisztina Passuth, *Laszlo Moholy-Nagy*, Weingarten, 1986.

Moje, Klaus (1936–)

▶ German glass designer; born Hamburg.

▶ 1951–55, trained in his family's workshop in Hamburg; 1957–59, glass schools, Rheinbach and Hadamar.

▶ 1960–61, he worked in industry and crafts and, in 1961, set up a studio with Isbard Moje-Wohlgemuth. 1961–65, he was commissioned to design stained-glass windows for churches, public buildings, and restoration projects. 1969–73, he was a representative of the Arbeitsgemeinschaft des Deutschen Kunsthandwerks at the World Crafts Council and became a member of the board of directors. In 1976, he became a founding member of the Galerie der Kunsthandwerker (formerly Workshop Galerie), Hamburg. From 1979, he was a guest lecturer at the Pilchuck Glass School in Stanwood, Washington; Kunsthåndværkerskolen, Copenhagen; Middlesex Polytechnic, London; California College of Arts and Crafts; and Rietveld Academy, Amsterdam. In 1982, he set up the glass workshop, of which he was head, at the Canberra School of Art.

▶ He participated in numerous exhibitions from 1969, and his and Dale Chihuly's works were the subject of the 1992 exhibition at the Ebeltoff Museum, Denmark. Moje received the Dr. Maedebach memorial Prize at the 'Zweite Coburger Glaspreis für Moderne Glasgestaltung in Europa 1985.'

▶ Klaus Moje, 'Material and Medium Glass,' *Kunst und Handwerk*, Oct. 1976:364. Klaus Moje, 'Studio Glass USA,' *New Glass*, Jan. 1980:18–25.

Moleri, Armando (1928–)

▶ Italian industrial and graphic designer; born Pontirolo Nuovo; active Milan; husband of Carla Nencioni.

▶ 1943–51, studied Accademia di Belle Arti, Bergamo.

▶ Moleri settled in Milan in 1956, where, until 1965, he was art director in an advertising agency. Until 1968, he was on the magazine *Stile Casa*. Moleri and wife Carla Nencioni collaborated on stainless-steel tableware produced by Zani, including the 1971 *Uni* picnic flatware set, and on designs produced by Tecno Com Guastalla. He was a member of ADI (Associazione per il Disegno Industriale).

▶ *ADI Annual 1976*, Milan: Associazione per il Disegno Industriale, 1976.

Molesworth, Thomas (1890–1977)

▶ American furniture designer; born Kansas.

▶ Studied Art Institute of Chicago.

▶ Moving in 1931 from Billings, Montana, he soon after established Shoshone Furniture, named after the native-American tribe, in Cody, Wyoming, the town founded in 1901 by Col. William F. ('Buffalo Bill') Cody to market the 'Wild West' to tourists. Molesworth did not invent the Western look in the USA, but rather perfected it. Molesworth's furniture for the TE Ranch building, originally for Cody, was exemplified in an easy chair with Chimayo-weave cushions and moose-antler 'wings.' In 1930s–1950s America, his furniture flourished in hotel lobbies, dude ranches, and private houses, including a Wyoming ranch for Moses Annenberg and a den for President Dwight D. Eisenhower in Gettysburg, Pennsylvania. Although his designs were meant to suggest primitivism, they had Modern lines. Molesworth used honey-colored woods, fir and pine burls, and pastel leather upholstery trimmed in brass tacks, to reflect the romantic image of the American West purveyed by 1930s Hollywood movies. His most complete architectural unit showed bucking broncos in linoleum, a wrought-iron and steel ashtray in a burro design with removeable receptacles in its saddlebags, chairs with pierced bow-legged cowboy forms, and rope trim. He catered to a monied clientele; collecting the work of friends, he had an extensive art collection.

▶ The 1990 exhibition 'Interior West: The Craft and Style of Thomas Molesworth' was mounted at the Gene Autry Western Heritage Museum in Los Angeles.

▶ Patricia Leigh Brown, 'How the West Was Done,' *The New York Times*, April 5, 1990:C1ff. Elizabeth Clair Flood, *Cowboy High Style: Thomas Molesworth to the New West*, Layton, Utah: Gibbs Smith, 1992.

Molezùn, Ramón Vazquez (1922–)

▶ Spanish architect; born La Coruña.

▶ Studied School of Architecture, Madrid, to 1948.

▶ 1960–62, he was professor at the School of Architecture in Madrid; he collaborated with José Antonio Corrales on the 1954–56 high school and vocational training school in Herrera del Pisuerga.

▶ He was awarded the grand prize as a fellow of the Academia de España and 1952 fine arts medal in Madrid. His joint awards included the Kursaal building in San Sebastian and first prize for the residence for Banco Exterior de España in Cadiz. His work was included in the 1986 'Contemporary Spanish Architecture: An Eclectic Panorama' exhibition at the Architectural League in New York.

▶ Antón Capitel and Ignacio Solà-Morales (essays), *Contemporary Spanish Architecture*, New York: Rizzoli, 1986:48–51.

Mølgård-Nielsen, Orla (1907–)

▶ Danish architect, cabinetmaker, and furniture designer.

▶ Studied cabinetmaking and furniture design, Kunsthåndværkerskolen, Copenhagen, and Det Kongelige Danske Kunstakademie, Copenhagen, under Kaare Klint.

▶ He introduced laminates and plywood to the Danish furniture industry. 1936—45, he taught at the Kunsthåndværkerskolen. In 1944, he and architect-cabinetmaker Peter Hvidt opened their own office. After World War II, they created a sectional furniture group of seating that was easy to ship and assemble. Their clients included Fritz Hansen in Allerød, France & Søn, and Søborg Møbelfabrik. Introducing knock-down furniture principles, their 1950 *AX* range of chairs and table was put into production by Fritz Hansen in 1960. The *AX Chair 6003* marked the introduction of the lamella-gluing principle in furniture making, and fostered international interest in Danish furniture.

▶ Mølgård-Nielsen's and Hvidt's work was shown at the 1954—57 USA 'Design in Scandinavia' traveling exhibition, 1956—59 Germany 'Neue Form aus Dänemark' traveling exhibition, 1958 'Formes Scandinaves' at the Paris Musée des Arts Décoratifs, and 1960—61 USA 'The Arts of Denmark' traveling exhibition. The *AX Chair 6003* was awarded diplomas of honor at the 1951 (IX) and 1954 (X) Triennali di Milano and included in the 'Good Design' exhibitions of the 1950s at the New York Museum of Modern Art and Chicago Merchandise Mart, and 1966 'Vijftig Jaar Zitten' at the Stedelijk Museum in Amsterdam.

▶ Esbjørn Hiort, *Danish Furniture*, New York, 1956:11—12,86—93. Gunnar Bratvold, *Mobilia*, July 1960:21. Erik Zahle (ed.), *A Treasury of Scandinavian Design*, New York, 1961:277, Nos. 40—41. Cat., *Modern Chairs 1918—1970*, London: Lund Humphries, 1971: No. 50. Cat., David Revere McFadden (ed.) *Scandinavian Modern Design 1880—1980*, New York: Abrams, 1982:268—69, No. 217. Cat., Kathryn B. Hiesinger and George H. Marcus III (eds.), *Design Since 1945*, Philadelphia: Philadelphia Museum of Art, 1983:223,III—31. Frederik Sieck, *Nutidig Dansk Møbeldesign: -en kortfattet illustreret beskrivelse*, Copenhagen: Bondo Gravesen; 1990 Busck edition in English.

Molinari, Pierluigi   (1938—)

▶ Italian industrial designer; born and active Milan.

▶ Studied Liceo Artistico di Brera and Accademia di Belle Arti di Brera, Milan.

▶ He began his professional career in 1961; had clients including Ampaglas (plastics), Pozzi (seating), Aspaco (public furniture), Asnaghi (furniture), Farmitalia (industrial chemicals), Filab (lighting), Interzoom (furniture), Italora (clocks), Lisiline (sanitary fittings), Lineas (furniture), Merlett (plastics), Schiume (bathroom accessories), Salpol (upholstery fabrics), and Triplex (domestic electrical appliances); in 1971, became a member of ADI (Associazione per il Disegno Industriale), and was president from 1988—91; (with Carlo Antonio Cerbaro) designed 1975 ADI exhibition, Lausanne, and 1979 'Design & design' Palazzo delle Stelline, Milan, and Palazzo Grassi, Venice.

▶ He participated in numerous national and international exhibitions and won the 1973 gold metal at the MIA.

▶ *ADI Annual 1976*, Milan: Associazione per il Disegno Industriale, 1976. Alfonso Grassi and Anty Pansera, *Atlante del Design Italiano 1940—80*, Milan: Fabbri 1980:305. Hans Wichmann, *Italien Design 1945 bis heute*, Munich: Die Neue Sammlung, 1988. *Modo*, No. 148, March—April 1993:123.

Molinié et Nicod

▶ French architects and designers.

▶ In the late 1920s, Émile Molinié (1877—1964) and Charles Nicod (1878—1967) were best known for their designs for the Hôtel de Paris.

▶ *Restaurants, dancing, cafés, bars*, Paris: Charles Moreau, Nos. 28—31. Paul Chemetov et al., *Banlieue*, Paris: Bordas, 1989.

Molinis, Luigi   (1940—)

▶ Italian industrial designer; born Udine; active Pordenone.

▶ Molinis began his professional career in 1969. He worked for Zanussi, designing domestic electrical appliances, televisions, and hi-fi equipment. He was a member of ADI (Associazione per il Disegno Industriale).

▶ *ADI Annual 1976*, Milan: Associazione per il Disegno Industriale, 1976.

Møller, Inger   (1886—1966)

▶ Danish silversmith; active Copenhagen (Denmark); wife of Just Andersen.

▶ Trained under Georg Jensen.

▶ 1909—21, she worked for the Georg Jensen Sølvsmedie. In 1922, she set up her own workshop. Her work was rendered with simple motifs soldered onto smooth surfaces. Her austere 1937 silver vegetable dish could almost be mistaken for a cooking-pot.

▶ She showed her work abroad for the first time at the 1925 Paris 'Exposition Internationale des Arts Décoratifs et Industriels Modernes.'

▶ Annelies Krekel-Aalberse, *Art Nouveau and Art Déco Silver*, New York: Abrams, 1989:221,257.

Møller, Jørgen Henrik   (1948—)

▶ Danish furniture designer.

▶ 1971—74, studied Kunsthåndværkerskolen, Copenhagen.

▶ He was designer and director of his own firm J. L. Møllers Møbelfabrik, Højberg.

▶ Frederik Sieck, *Nutidig Dansk Møbeldesign: —en kortfattet illustreret beskrivelse*, Copenhagen: Bondo Gravesen; 1990 Busck edition in English.

Møller, Niels O.   (1920—)

▶ Danish cabinetmaker and furniture designer.

▶ 1939, apprenticed to a cabinetmaker; studied Konstruktørskolen, Århus.

▶ In 1944, he opened his own office and factory in Højberg. He won the Danish bronze medal for craftsmanship. Reminiscent of Gio Ponti's 1956 *Superleggera* chair, Møller's 1964 *Chair 79* with a strip-leather seat was produced by J.L. Møller Møbelfabrik of Højberg, where he was director.

▶ His *Chair 79* was first shown at the 1964 'Scandinavian Furniture Fair' in Copenhagen. Won the Danish bronze medal for craftsmanship.

▶ Cat., *Modern Chairs 1918—1970*, London: Lund Humphries, 1971.

Mollino, Carlo   (1905—73)

▶ Italian architect and designer; born Turin.

▶ Studied engineering; 1929, art history, Ghent art school; Royal School of Architecture, University of Turin, to 1931.

▶ He began his career as an architect in his father's office in Turin. Later he worked independently but stayed in his father's office. His 1944 residence of Ada and Cesare Minola in Turin illustrated his 'Streamline Surrealism' style. His 1947 'House of the Sun' was built in Cervinia. His work contrasted with the more Rationalistic designs emerging from Milan at this time. Influenced by the organic forms reproduced in issues of *Domus* in the late 1940s, such as Henry Moore's sculptures, his fantastic designs for furniture reflected these shapes. Most of his important furniture was made at the Apelli & Varesio joinery in Turin. He was also influenced by the works of Antonio Gaudí, Charles Rennie Mackintosh, Charles Eames, Le Corbusier, and Alvar Aalto. He executed a series of glass tables with one-piece bent-plywood bases, and chairs in organic forms. His wide-ranging work included aeronautics, art, photography, set design, town planning, teaching, automobile bodies, clothing, furniture, interior decoration, and architecture. Much of his furniture and furnishings was site-specific and one of a kind, executed in glass and bentwood (furniture), plastic rods (lamps), and industrial materials (shelving) in the late 1940s and early 1950s. A sense of decadent kitsch pervaded his work. He used natural and artificial light, mirrors, water, and giant images. He designed 1950—60 flats in Turin, 1950 house in San Remo, Teatro Regio in Turin, furnishings for a bachelor's apartment in Turin, furnishings for MUSA, housing and the Casa de Sole in Cervinia, the radio pavilion of the AGIP stand, and exhibitions for art, sports and cars. 1950—60, he produced prototypes, few of which were manufactured. He patented articulated lamps with Birri, cupboard-and-panel systems, and cold-bent plywood (used in his furniture). He designed three-legged stools, fold-up and transforming furniture, and the 1954 Osca automobile. He was a member of ADI (Associazione per il Designo Industriale).

▶ He showed his work at the 1954 (X) and 1957 (XI) Triennali di Milano. He won the Reed and Barton cutlery competition. A Mollino chair was included in the 1983–84 'Design Since 1945' exhibition at the Philadelphia Museum of Art. His work was the subject of the 1989–90 exhibition 'Carlo Mollino 1905–1973' at Galerie du CCI, Centre Georges Pompidou, Paris 1989–90.

▶ Roberto Aloi, *Esempi di Arredamento*, Milan, 1950, Vol. 105. 'Across the Seas Collaboration for the New Singer Collection,' *Interiors*, Vol. 111, Dec. 1951:120–29,150. L.L. Ponti and E. Ritter (eds.) *Mobili e interni di architetti italiani*, Milan, 1952:4,21,36–41,68,73,91. 'Nuovi Mobili di Mollino,' *Domus*, Vol. 270, 1952:50–53. Andrea Branzi and Michele De Lucchi, *Design Italiano Degli Anni '50*, Milan: Editoriale Domus, 1980. Cat., Kathryn B. Hiesinger and George H. Marcus III (eds.), *Design Since 1945*, Philadelphia: Philadelphia Museum of Art, 1983:223. *Casa F.G. Minola*, Turin, 1944. G. Brino, *Carlo Mollino, Architettura come autobiografia*, Milan, 1985. Penny Sparke, *Design in Italy, 1870 to the Present*, New York: Abbeville, 1988.

Molteni

▶ Italian furniture firm.

▶ Established in the 1930s, Molteni always operated contrary to fashion. In 1970, it established the firm Unifor as a specialized manufacturer of office furniture and, in 1980, Dada as a kitchen furniture firm. Unifor's designers included Luca Meda, Aldo Rossi, and Richard Sapper.

▶ 'Milan à l'Heure du Design,' *Maison et Jardin*, April 1992:123.

Moltzer, Kim

▶ Austrian artist and furniture designer; active Paris.

▶ Moltzer collaborated often with Jean-Paul Barray; designed furniture, lighting, and decorative objects; in the 1970s, showed work in numerous exhibitions.

▶ Gilles de Bure, *Le mobilier français 1965–1979*, Paris: Regard/VIA, 1983:37.

Moncur, Jennie (1961–)

▶ British textile designer.

▶ Studied textile design, Goldsmiths' College, London, to 1984, and tapestry, Royal College of Art, to 1986.

▶ Work shown at 1987–88 'Wall to Wall, textile for interiors' touring exhibition; 1988–89 'Choice Objects' touring exhibition; and 1990 'Contemporary British Weave,' Contemporary Textile Gallery, London.

▶ *Decorative Arts Today*, London: Bonhams, 1992: No. 13a.

Moneo, José Rafael (1937–)

▶ Spanish architect; born Tudela, Navarra.

▶ Studied architecture, Escuela Técnica Superior de Arquitectura, Madrid.

▶ 1958–61, he worked in the office of architect Francisco Javier Sáenz de Oiza and, 1961–62, in the office of Jørn Utzon in Hellebaek (Denmark). 1970–80, he was the chair of and taught at the Escuela Técnica Superior de Arquitectura in Barcelona. From 1980, he was professor at the Escuela Técnica Superior de Arquitectura in Madrid. In 1965, he set up his own practice in Madrid. He was an active architecture critic. He used brick to humanize his architecture and soften its extreme simplicity. In 1976, he was invited to work at the Institute for Architecture and Urban Studies in New York and was associated with the Irwin S. Chanin School of Architecture of the Cooper Union in New York. He was Ospite Professor of the Institute of Architecture in Lausanne and Princeton University. In 1985, he became chair of the Graduate School of Design at Harvard University and lectured worldwide. He was co-founder and on the editorial board of the journal *Arquitecturas Bis* and wrote numerous articles. His buildings included the 1963–67 Diestre factory in Saragossa, 1967 addition to the Plaza de

Toros in Pamplona, 1969–71 Urumea mansion in San Sebastian, 1973–81 town hall in Logroño, 1973–76 Bankinter (with R. Bescòs) in Madrid, and 1980–84 Museo de Arte Romana in Mérida (Mexico).

▶ He received the 1986 Delta de Plata of ADI/FAD de Diseño Industrial. His *El viaje paralelo del libro y de la vida* desk chair was included in the 'Affinità Elettive' exhibition at the 1985 Triennale di Milano.

▶ 'José Rafael Moneo,' *Nueva Forma*, Jan. 1975. *Le Affinità Elettive*, Milan: Electa, 1985. Auction cat., *Asta di Modernariato 1900–1986, Auction 'Modernariato,'* Milan: Semenzato Nuova Geri, 8 Oct. 1986: lot 114. Juli Capella and Quim Larrea, *Designed by Architects in the 1980s*, New York, Rizzoli, 1988.

Monet Jewelers

▶ American costume jewelry firm; located New York and Providence, Rhode Island.

▶ The firm was originally founded as Monocraft in 1929 by brothers Michael and Jay Chernow to produce monograms for purses and handbags. In 1937, they began producing costume jewelry signed 'Monet' in the Providence factory. 1940–60, they produced stoneless gold-plated ribbons and bows, geometric designs, and Roman- and Greek-related themes. In 1969, the firm became a subsidiary of General Mills and, in 1987, part of Crystal Brands of Southport, Connecticut.

▶ Deanna F. Cera (ed.) *Jewels of Fantasy: Costume Jewelry of the 20th Century*, New York: Abrams, 1992:218.

Monk, John Lawrence (1936–)

▶ American industrial designer; born Los Angeles; active Varese, Italy.

▶ Monk began his professional career in 1960. He worked for Sottsass in Milan on electronic equipment, Lesa (domestic electrical appliances and sound equipment), Duben Haskell Jacobson (industrial machinery), Oerre (vacuum cleaners and appliances), Artsana (small medical apparati), Cafèbar (beverage dispenser with David Lawrence Higgins) in Stratford (England), Forma & Funzione (lighting), and Caravans International in Varedo. Monk designed a calculator with Ettore Sottsass and Higgins produced by Olivetti, and a medical portable aerosol device for Artsana. He worked in the industrial design studio Incateam with offices in Norway, Germany, Britain, Switzerland, the Netherlands, and Italy. He was a member of ADI (Associazione per il Disegno Industriale).

▶ *ADI Annual 1976*, Milan: Associazione per il Disegno Industriale, 1976.

Monpoix, André (1925–76)

▶ French furniture designer; active Paris.

▶ From 1945, studied École Nationale Supérieure des Arts Décoratifs, Paris.

▶ He learned decoration while working for Maxime Old, René Gabriel, and Jacques Dumond; often collaborated with Alain Richard at Richard et Monpoix, designing furniture produced by Meubles TV.

▶ From 1953, work shown at Salons des Arts Ménagers and Salons of Société des Artistes Décorateurs.

▶ Pascal Renou, *Portraits de créateurs*, Paris: H. Vial, 1969. Gilles de Bure, *Le mobilier français 1965–1969*, Paris: Regard/VIA, 1983:75.

Montagnac, Pierre-Paul (1883–1962)

▶ French painter, architect, decorator, and furniture designer.

▶ Studied under Eugène Carrière and Grande Chaumière.

▶ From 1918, he worked for a time in the workshop of André Mare and subsequently pursued a career as architect and decorator, constructing housing, designing interiors, and rendering furniture. He worked equally in the fine and applied arts and designed furniture in solid classical forms, well constructed. Dissatisfied with the furniture manufacturers in the Faubourg Saint-Antoine area, he had Robert Sangouard in Saint-Ouen produce his work. From 1922, he collaborated with Maurice Dufrène at La Maîtrise and furnished the studio with furniture models. He was active as a designer of lighting, ceramics, and tapestries. His furniture in limited editions was produced by Fontaine. He designed a number of offices, stores, and apartments and a large number of tapestries for Gobelins and furniture for several firms, and designed suites on the 1931 oceanliner *Atlantique*, 1935 *Normandie*, and *Pasteur*. 1930–38, he was president of the Société des Artistes Décorateurs. 1940–45, he studied serial furniture production, shown at 1950s events of the Société des Artistes Décorateurs and the Salon d'Automne. In 1947, became president of the Salon d'Automne.

▶ He first showed his work in the Salons in 1912. His paintings were exhibited at the 1920 Paris Salon d'Automne, where he was awarded a traveling scholarship. He showed his applied art work at the Salon of the Société des Artistes-Décorateurs, the Salon des Architectes Modernes, and international exhibitions in Barcelona and Leipzig. At the 1925 Paris 'Exposition Internationale des Arts Décoratifs et Industriels Modernes,' he designed the reception room in the Esplanade des Invalides and supplied furniture for the Grand Salon by Rapin and Selmersheim for the French Embassy. He participated in and organized the pavilion of the Société des Artistes Décorateurs at the 1937 Paris 'Exposition Internationale des Arts et Techniques dans la Vie Moderne.'

▶ *Ensembles Mobiliers*, Vol. II, Paris: Charles Moreau, 1937. Pierre Kjellberg, *Art Déco: les maîtres du Mobilier, le décor des Paquebots*, Paris: Amateur, 1986:129–30.

Montanari, Pier Paolo (1953–)

▶ Italian industrial designer; born and active Reggio Emilia.

▶ Studied applied art and industrial design, Institute of Art, Reggio Emilia, industrial design, Università di Bologna, under Tomás Maldonado, and industrial design, Florence.

▶ He worked in various interior and industrial design studios. His modular exhibition system was produced by Ottavianelli. He worked with Gruppo S, where he designed furniture produced by Snaidero. He designed bathrooms for Supellex and a range of dining and game tables for Aluper Italia. Working at the cooperative IAB in Budrio, he designed a range of refrigerators for hotels, restaurants, and bars. Montanari was a member of the technical organization SGA and of ADI (Associazione per il Disegno Industriale).

▶ *ADI Annual 1976*, Milan: Associazione per il Disegno Industriale, 1976.

Montgomery, Paul

▶ American industrial designer.

▶ Studied North Carolina State University; University of Georgia in Cortona (Italy); and Cranbrook Academy of Art in Bloomfield Hills, Michigan, to 1987.

▶ He designed computer systems, TV sets, medical and office products, and luggage. He worked for Texas Instruments in Austin, Texas; PA Technology in Princeton, New Jersey; and frogdesign in California. His 1987 prototype for the *Picture Phone* was widely published.

▶ He received the 1987 award for his digital still camera from the Industrial Designers Society of America, frogdesign's 'frogjunior' award, and *ID* magazine's 'Designer's Choice.'

▶ Albrecht Bangert and Karl Michael Armer, *80s Style: Designs of the Decade*, New York: Abbeville, 1990:200,233.

Monti GPA, Studio

▶ Italian design studio; located Milan.

▶ In 1948, siblings Gianemilio Monti (1920–), Pietro Monti (1922–), and Anna Bertarini Monti (1923–) set up Studio Monti GPA in Milan. They designed the 1963 *Orsola* chest produced by Stildomus. Their work included the 1955 bed and hallstand for ICF, 1959–65 plastic lamps for Kartell, 1964 furniture for Stildomus, 1972–76 lamps for Fontana, and buildings and restaurants in Italy. The Montis were members of INU (Instituto Nazionale Urbanistica); ADI (Associazione per il Disegno Industriale); and, 1954–60, MSA (Movimento Studi Architettura).

▶ *ADI Annual 1976*, Milan: Associazione per il Disegno Industriale, 1976. Alfonso Grassi and Anty Pansera, *Atlante del design italiano: 1940–1980*, Milan: Fabbri, 1980. Giancarolo Iliprandi and Pierluigi Molinari (eds.), *Industrial Designers Italiani*, Fagagna, 1985:147. Christina Morozzi, *1956–1988 Trent'Anni e Più di Design*, Idea Books Italy, 1988. Hans Wichmann, *Italien Design 1945 bis heute*, Munich: Die Neue Sammlung, 1988.

Moorcroft

▶ British ceramics firm; located Burslem.

▶ Designer William Moorcroft founded the pottery works in *c*1925 in Burslem. All ware was hand-thrown and turned. Moorcroft prided himself on the correctness of the shapes he produced and on their high level of craftsmanship. The firm's potters were not expected to innovate; original designs from the 1920s continued to be produced into the 1950s.

▶ Michael Farr, *Design in British Industry: A Mid-Century Survey*, London: Cambridge, 1955. Paul Atterbury, *Moorcroft*, 1990.

Moore, Charles Willard (1925–)

▶ American architect; born Benton Harbor, Michigan; active Connecticut and California.

▶ Studied University of Michigan, Ann Arbor, and Princeton University.

▶ Moore was a partner in Moore, Grover, Harper, architects, in Connecticut and in Moore, Ruble, Yudell, architects, in California. Principal architect of the Urban Innovations Group, he was head of the architecture program at the University of California, Los Angeles. His work in a kind of super-graphics style, widely published in the 1970s, contributed to the development of Post-Modernism.

▶ His *Corner Cupboard* for Formica's 1983 promotion of its new material, Colorcore, received recognition. Received numerous architectural awards.

▶ Robert A.M. Stern (ed.), *The International Design Yearbook*, New York: Abbeville, 1985/1986: Nos. 158–59.

Moore, Edward Chandler (1827–91)

▶ American silversmith; active New York.

▶ Moore was an accomplished designer known for his fine craftsmanship. In 1852, Moore encouraged Tiffany to become the first American company to adopt the English sterling standard (92.5 per cent silver). In 1868, Tiffany bought Moore's workshop, and he became silver department director. In the late 1860s or early 1870s, there being no silver training schools in New York, he set up a program for silversmiths in the Tiffany workshops, then located on Prince Street. He was enthusiastic about the Japanese style, having seen pieces at the 1867 Paris 'Exposition Universelle.' By 1871, the firm produced Japanese-influenced flatware patterns and, from 1873, hollow-ware. In many of Moore's pieces, he combined Western and Eastern themes and motifs. Under Moore, Tiffany produced jewelry in the Japanese style for New York's socialites.

▶ In 1889, he was appointed Chevalier of the Légion d'honneur.

▶ 'The Edward C. Moore Collection,' *Bulletin of the Metropolitan Museum of Art*, Vol. 2, June 1902:105–06. Henry H. Hawley, 'Tiffany's Silver in the Japanese Taste,' *Bulletin of the Cleveland Museum of Art*, Oct. 1976:236–45. Bruce Kamerling, 'Edward C. Moore: The Genius Behind Tiffany Silver,' Parts 1 and 2, *Silver*, Vol. 10, Sept.–Oct. 1977:16–20. Charles H. Carpenter Jr., 'Tiffany Silver in the Japanese Style,' *Connoisseur*, Vol. 200, Jan. 1979:42–47. Doreen Bolger Burke et al., *In Pursuit of Beauty: Americans and the Aesthetic Movement*, New York: Metropolitan Museum of Art and Rizzoli, 1986:472–73.

Moore, Riette Sturge

▶ British textile designer.

▶ Studied interior decoration in Paris and London.

▶ She worked for interior designer E. Curtis Moffat, furniture designer Arundell Clarke, and furnisher Heal's. From the mid-1930s, she designed and printed textiles, including those produced by W. Foxton in London.

▶ Her work was the subject of the 1938 one-person exhibition at Heal's in London. Her work was included in most of the important exhibitions in the 1930s in London, and the 1935 *Ribbons* jacquard cotton fabric in the 1979—80 'Thirties' exhibition at the Hayward Gallery in London.
▶ Cat., *Thirties: British art and design before the war*, London: Arts Council of Great Britain, Hayward Gallery, 1979:91,144, 296.

Moorman, Theo (1907–90)
▶ British weaver and designer.
▶ 1925–8, studied Central School of Arts and Crafts, London.
▶ 1928–35, she was a freelance weaver and designer. 1935–39, she worked at the fabric-firm Warner in Braintree, where she designed and wove hand and power-loom fabrications. She was responsible for hand-woven models intended eventually for power-loom production. She experimented with unusual and new yarns to produce fabrics in Modern motifs and patterns, including the use of brocade techniques, weft inlays, and yarns such as natural fibers, trail rays, metallic strips, and cellophane. 1944–53, she was assistant regional director of the Arts Council of Great Britain and, from 1953, a freelance weaver, known for wall hangings and ecclesiastical fabrics. 1968–78, she lectured and taught in the USA.
▶ Some of Moorman's hand-woven fabrications were included in the 1979—80 'Thirties' exhibition at the Hayward Gallery in London.
▶ Cat., *Thirties: British art and design before the war*, London: Arts Council of Great Britain, Hayward Gallery, 1979:89, 126,144,296.

Moos, Peder (1906–)
▶ Danish furniture designer.
▶ 1925, apprenticed to a cabinetmaker; 1925–30, studied cabinetmaking in Switzerland and France; 1935–38, Det Kongelige Danske Akademi, Copenhagen, under Kaare Klint.
▶ 1941–43, he taught at the Teknologisk Institut and, 1950–53, at the Copenhagen Commune school.
▶ His work was included in the 1948 'Deense Kunsthandwerk' at the Gemeente Musem, The Hague, and 1960–61 USA 'The Arts of Denmark.'
▶ Frederik Sieck, *Nutidig Dansk Mobeldesign: – en kortfattet illustreret beskrivelse*, Copenhagen: Bondo Gravesen; 1990 Busck edition in English.

Morandini, Marcello (1940–)
▶ Italian designer; born Mantua; active Varese.
▶ Studied fine art, Accademia di Brera, Milan.
▶ He began as a designer in Milan in 1960; in 1963, opened his own studio. In 1979, he moved to Sydney, and subsequently worked in Singapore. For several years, he designed ceramics produced by Rosenthal, and designed the façade of its offices in Selb. With references to 1920s decoration and De Stijl forms, his *Corner* unit was produced by Rosenthal in the 1980s.
▶ In 1965, he showed his first three-dimensional structures in Genoa.
▶ Giancarlo Iliprandi and Pierluigi Molinari (eds.), *Industrial Designers Italiani*, Fagagna, 1985:148. Hans Wichmann, *Italien Design 1945 bis heute*, Munich: Die Neue Sammlung, 1988. Albrecht Bangert and Karl Michael Armer, *80s Style: Designs of the Decade*, New York: Abbeville, 1990:142,188–89,233.

Morassutti, Bruno (1920–)
▶ Italian industrial designer; born Padua; active Milan.
▶ Studied architecture in Venice to 1947.
▶ 1949–50, he worked in the Taliesin West studio of Frank Lloyd Wright, Scottsdale, Arizona; 1955–60, collaborated with Angelo Mangiarotti; in 1968, (with Mario Memoli, Giovanna Gussoni and M. Gabriella Benevento) set up a partnership in Milan; became a member of ADI (Associazione per il Disegno Industriale).

▶ His career began with participation in 1947 (VIII) Triennale di Milano. Work shown at 1972 'Milano 70/70,' Museo Polid Pezzoli, Milan.
▶ Cat., *Milano 70/70*, Milan, 1972. *ADI Annual 1976*, Milan: Associazione per il Disegno Industriale, 1976. Hans Wichmann, *Italien Design 1945 bis heute*, Munich: Die Neue Sammlung, 1988.

Mørch, Ibi Trier (1910–)
▶ Danish architect and industrial designer.
▶ Studied architecture, Det Kongelige Danske Kunstakademi, Copenhagen.
▶ Specializing in silver and glassware, she collaborated with Erik Herlow 1951–60. Morch and Grethe Meyer designed the 1958 *Stub* range of stacking glassware produced by Kastrup glassworks.
▶ Cat., Kathryn B. Hiesinger and George H. Marcus III (eds.), *Design Since 1945*, Philadelphia: Philadelphia Museum of Art, 1984:223,II–41. 'One Hundred Great Danish Designs,' *Mobilia*, Nos. 230–33, Dec. 1974: No. 47. Cat., *Danskt 50 Tal: Scandinavian Design*, Stockholm: Nationalmuseum, 1982:36, No. 126.

Moretti, Carlo (1934)   and Giovanni Moretti
▶ Italian glassmakers; active Murano.
▶ At the end of the 19th century, Vincenzo Moretti established a glass and bead factory near Venice. In 1958, his grandsons Carlo and Giovanni Moretti established the Carlo Moretti company, producing engraved glassware, colored liqueur glasses, and opaline goblets; in 1973, it began to make more technically sophisticated objects, most of them in Murano glass, produced by master glass blowers. Moretti designed hexagonal glasses with gold borders, and widely published octagonal glasses.
▶ *Les Carnets du Design*, Paris: Mad-Cap Productions et APCI, 1986:54. Robert A.M. Stern (ed.), *The International Design Yearbook*, New York: Abbeville, 1985/1986: Nos. 297–98.

Moreux, Jean-Charles (1889–1956)
▶ French architect, painter, and designer.
▶ Moreux began his career in 1924 with a commission from the vicomte Charles de Noailles; designed a number of townhouses, vacation houses, and studios (including those of Luc-Albert Moreau and de Jos Hessel). Some of his furniture was lacquered, some in metal; though sometimes massive, it was elegant in precious woods. His architecture and interiors included apartment of Robert de Rothschild; 1928 music pavilion of Wanda Landowska; house of A.D. Mouradian, St. Cloud, in *c*1926; 1943—44 apartment of Raphaël Lopez in avenue Pierre-ler-de-Serbie, Paris; and Château Maulny in Sarthe. He designed a table in ebony, crocodile, galuchat, crystal, and ivory (probably made by Jean Legrain) for couturier Jacques Doucet; in 1931, joined UAM (Union des Artistes Modernes); collaborated for a time with architect André Lurçat; participated in the 1938 design of the apartment of Helena Rubenstein, Paris, by Louis Süe; was Architecte des Palais Nationaux, including the Louvre; published *Carnet de Voyage* (1954) with his architectural sketches; designed 1952 garden and 1955 library of Henry Spitzmuller, Château de Henry, Yonne; and gardens of Shepheard's Hotel, Cairo.
▶ Participated in 1925 Paris 'Exposition Internationale des Arts Décoratifs et Industriels Modernes,' 1931 UAM exhibition, and 1939 Salon of Société des Artistes Décorateurs.
▶ Albert Laprade, 'L'œuvre de J-Ch Moreux,' *L'Architecture*, 1939. Pierre Kjellberg, *Art Déco: les maîtres du Mobilier, le décor des Paquebots*, Paris: Amateur, 1986:130–31. Arlette Barré-Despond, *UAM*, Paris: Regard, 1986:22–21,256,311. Patrick Mauries, 'Jean-Charles Moreux: Néoclassicisme Inspiré,' *Vogue Décoration*, No. 39, Aug–Sept. 1992:77–81.

Morgan, David (1951–)
▶ British industrial designer.
▶ Studied physics, London University, and industrial design, Royal College of Art, London.
▶ He joined the design department of Thorn Lighting. In 1981, he established David Morgan Associates in London, where he spe-

cialized in lighting products. He is best known for his 1986 *Burlington* desk lamp.

► His *Burlington* lamp won the 1987 British Design in Japan competition.

► Jeremy Myerson and Sylvia Katz, *Conran Design Guides: Lamps and Lighting*, London: Conran Octopus, 1990:77.

Morgan, William De (1839–1917)
See De Morgan, William Frend

Mori, Edoardo (1953–)
► Italian designer; born and active Camerano.
► Mori began his professional career in 1975. His clients included Babini (seating), Ferri Fratelli, and Zuccari. He was a member of ADI (Associazione per il Disegno Industriale).
► *ADI Annual 1976*, Milan: Associazione per il Disegno Industriale, 1976.

Morita, Akio
See Sony

Morita, Masaki (1950–)
► Japanese interior and furniture designer; active Paris.
► Studied Kuwazawa Design Institute.
► His *Planet* chair was made by Tribu.

Moroni, Donato (1941–)
► Italian designer; born Gravellona Toce; active Milan.
► Studied architecture, Politecnico di Milano, to 1967.
► Moroni began his professional career in 1968. He worked at Lagostina in Omegna, and at Maltignano designing metal tableware. He was a member of ADI (Associazione per il Disegno Industriale).
► *ADI Annual 1976*, Milan: Associazione per il Disegno Industriale, 1976.

Morozzi, Massimo (1941–)
► Italian architect and designer; born Florence; active Milan.
► Studied architecture in Florence to 1966.
► In 1968, (with Andrea Branzi, Gilberto Corretti, and Paolo Deganello) he founded Archizoom Associati, which produced industrial and architectural designs and town planning, and was a leading Italian architecture firm until 1972. 1972–77, he coordinated the efforts of Montedison's Centro Design Montefibre for the promotion of furnishing and textile products. He carried out research into color and interior decoration, and introduced a new 'soft' approach in furniture design. Morozzi collaborated at Archizoom on the 1974 *AEO* chair produced by Cassina. In 1976, (with Branzi, Gianni Cutolo, Alessandro Mendini, Clino Trini Castelli, and Ettore Sottsass) he founded the firm CDM (Consulenti Design Milano), which handled large-scale projects including the corporate image and landscaping of Leonardo da Vinci airport, Rome, an information system for the Italian post office, a center for creative colorimetrics for the 'Colorterminal,' the Piaggo color system, and some of the activities of the Montefibre Design Center. In 1982, he set up his own design firm, specializing in domestic products and industrial design for clients including Fiam, Edra, Mazzei, Giorgetti, Ideal Standard, Cassina, Alessi, and Driade; worked in Japan and Australia. His multi-colored, seven part 1983 *Tangram* table was produced by Cassina.
► Received 1979 Premio Compasso d'Oro (for *Colordinamo, Decorativo*, Fibermatching 25).
► Andrea Branzi, *La Casa Calda: Esperienze del Nuovo Disegno Italiano*, Milan: Idea Books, 1982. Fumio Shimizu and Matteo Thun (eds.), *The Descendants of Leonardo: The Italian Design*, Tokyo, 1987:338. Albrecht Bangert and Karl Michael Armer, *80s Style: Designs of the Decade*, New York: Abbeville, 1990:27,233. *Modo*, No. 148, March–April 1993:123.

Morris, May (1862–1938)
► British designer, needleworker, jeweler, and teacher; daughter of William and Jane Morris.

► Morris produced designs for fabrics, embroideries, and wallpaper for Morris and Co. Her work resembled that of her father. She designed and made many pieces of jewelry, including string necklaces in various color combinations and textures. She created the jewelry her mother wore in portraits by Dante Gabriel Rossetti at the age of 12, and the jewelry she herself wore in the Rossetti triple-portrait *Rosa Triplex* (1874). Her jewelry designs were based on floral and leaf forms, and included cabochon semi-precious stones. She incorporated glass into her jewelry including unusual beads of Venetian glass. From 1886, she managed the embroidery shop at Merton Abbey, the site of William Morris's design company, and taught at the Central School of Arts and Crafts in London. In 1907, she was a founding member of the Women's Guild of Arts, and subsequently chair. In 1910, she lectured in the USA on embroidery, costume and pattern design, and jewelry. She sold her jewelry at the Fordham Gallery in Maddox Street and at the Arts and Crafts Exhibition Society. She published *William Morris, Artist, Writer, Socialist* (1936) and *Decorative Needlework* (1910), and was the editor of her father's collected papers.

► May Morris (ed.), *The Collected Works of William Morris*, 24 vols., London, 1899. Charlotte Gere, *American and European Jewelry 1830–1914*, New York: Crown, 1975:208–09. Stuart Durant, *Ornament from the Industrial Revolution to Today*, Woodstock, NY: Overlook, 1986:219,326. Toni Lesser Wolf, 'Women Jewelers of the British Arts and Crafts Movement,' *The Journal of Decorative and Propaganda Arts*, No. 14, Fall 1989:32.

Morris, Neil (1918–)
► British furniture designer.
► Morris designed the cloud-shaped occasional table in the late 1940s for Morris of Glasgow.
► Cat., Leslie Jackson, *The New Look: Design in the Fifties*, New York: Thames and Hudson, 1991:125.

Morris, Robert Lee (1948–)
► American designer.
► Morris settled in New York in the early 1970s and gained a reputation for his sculptural gold jewelry in Minimalist styles. His work was first sold at Sculpture To Wear at the Plaza Hotel, New York. In 1977, he established the jewelry firm Artwear. He collaborated with Donna Karan on her costume jewelry line in the late 1980s, and with Calvin Klein, Geoffrey Beene, and Karl Lagerfeld. He designed over 10 collections each year. From 1983, he established a chain of retail outlets in Japan through Vendome Yamada. His handbag designs were sold through Mode et Jacomo. He designed a line of brass domestic products in 1990, including ritualistic forks and knives, candlesticks, boxes, and vessels. In 1992, he designed the *Camelot* dinnerware for Swid Powell, leather belts for Max Leather, *Rituals of Color* cosmetics range for Elizabeth Arden, and hardware for the Spanish leather goods firm Loewe.
► He received the 1981 Coty Award, 1985 Council of Fashion Designers of America Award, a special award from the International Gold Council for his influence on gold jewelry, and 1992 American Accessories Achievement Award of FABB for jewelry design.
► Brad Kessler, *Metropolitan Home*, July 1990:14.

Morris, Talwyn (1865–1911)
► British designer and metalworker; active Glasgow.
► Studied architecture.
► He became a member of the Glasgow School with Charles Rennie Mackintosh, Herbert MacNair, the Macdonald sisters and Jessie M. King. He produced beaten copper jewelry, and was one of the first craftsmen to use aluminum for jewelry.
► Charlotte Gere, *American and European Jewelry 1830–1914*, New York: Crown, 1975:209.

Morris, William (1834–96)
► British writer, poet, and designer; born Walthamstow, Essex.
► 1853–55, studied theology, Oxford University.

63 *Mirella* sewing machine; plastic, metal, 1957. Designed by Marcello Nizzoli, produced by Necchi, Pavia, Italy. (Die Neue Sammlung, Staatliches Museum für angewandte Kunst, Munich)

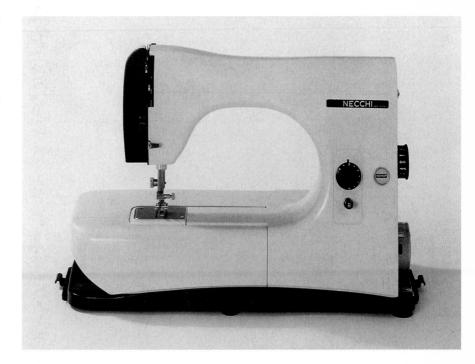

64 *686* table lamp; metal, c1976. Designed by Elio Martinelli, produced by Martinelli Luce, Italy. (Die Neue Sammlung, Staatliches Museum für angewandte Kunst, Munich)

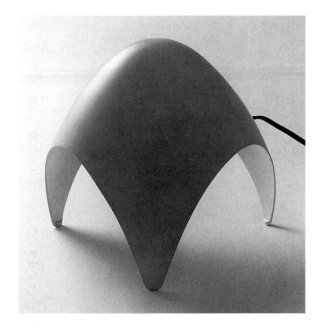

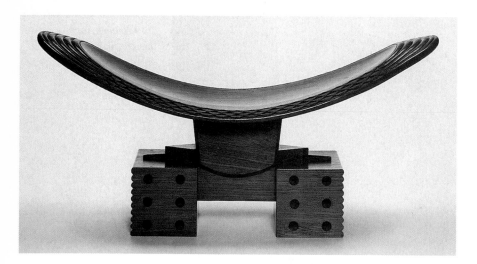

83 Stool; rosewood, 1922–9. Designed by Pierre-Émile Legrain. (The Metropolitan Museum of Art, New York, Fletcher Fund, 1972)

84 Swivel chair; chromed steel, foam rubber, red wool textile, 1958–9. Designed by Verner Panton, produced by Plus-linje, Copenhagen. (The Brooklyn Museum, Brooklyn, New York, gift of Barry Friedman)

85 *Möbelprotos* side chair; ashwood, 1982. Designed and produced by Albert Langenmayr. (Cooper-Hewitt National Museum of Design, Smithsonian Institution/Art Resource, New York, gift of Manfred Ludwig, photography by John Parnell)

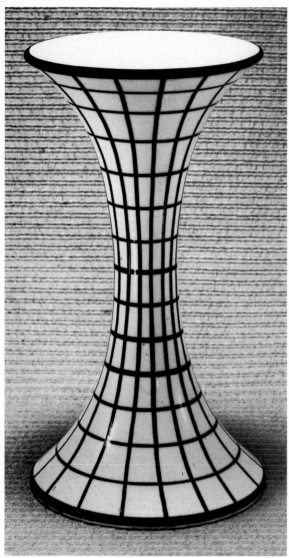

86 Vase; glazed
earthenware, 1906.
Designed by Michael
Powolny, produced in the
Wiener Keramik, Vienna.
(The Metropolitan Museum
of Art, New York,
purchase, Emilio Ambasz
gift, 1990)

87 Covered urn; white porcelain with overglaze
'Passeggiata archeologica' design in purple, grey, and
gold, 1924. Designed by Gio Ponti, produced by Richard
Ginori, Milan. (The Metropolitan Museum of Art, New
York, purchase, Edward C. Moore Jr gift, 1931)

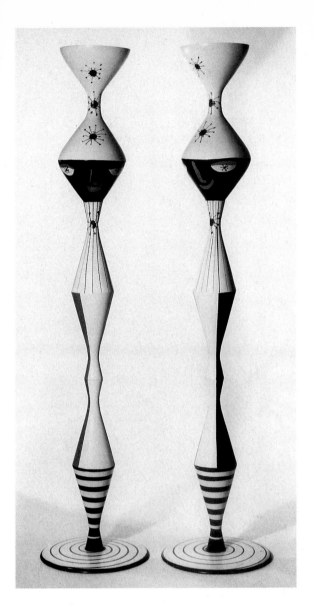

88 Planters; hand-painted wood, c1953. Designed by Estelle and Erwine Laverne, produced by Laverne International, New York. (Fifty-50, New York)

89 *Bambù* vases; unglazed porcelain, 1969. Designed by Enzo Mari, produced by Danese, Milan. (The Metropolitan Museum of Art, New York, gift of Jacqueline and Bruno Danese, 1988)

90 *Ball* clock (no. 4755);
birch, brass, steel, 1947.
Designed by Irving Harper
in the office of George
Nelson, New York,
produced by Howard
Miller Clock Company,
Zeeland, Michigan.
(Fifty-50, New York)

► While at Oxford, he met Edward Burne-Jones; they both read John Ruskin and Thomas Carlyle and planned careers in art and architecture. Morris joined the office of the Gothic Revival architect George Edmund Street in Oxford, where he met and befriended Philip Webb, Street's senior assistant. Morris followed Street's move to London, where he shared a house with Burne-Jones from 1856. He began to design large, heavy furniture pieces, painting their surfaces with medieval figures and inscriptions. Guided by Dante Gabriel Rossetti, he began to paint in 1857; they worked together on the 1857 frescoes at the Oxford Union debating hall, to which Morris contributed scenes from the 15th-century *Morte d'Arthur*. In 1859, he married Jane Burden, later the model for Rossetti's idealized Pre-Raphaelite woman. In 1858, Morris published his first volume of poetry, *The Defence of Guenevere and Other Poems*. Webb designed Morris's Red House in Bexleyheath in 1859, a domestic architecture landmark. Webb, Burne-Jones, and Morris collaborated on most of its furniture; Ford Madox Brown suggested they form a group to produce decorative works, and the firm of Morris, Marshall, and Faulkner was established in 1861 with Burne-Jones, Webb, Rossetti, and Ford Madox Brown. Early commissions were mostly for stained-glass windows designed by Marshall, Burne-Jones, Webb, Brown, Rossetti, and Morris. Its tiles and pottery were painted by Faulkner's sisters Lucy and Kate, many to designs by William De Morgan. Morris learned embroidery and trained his wife, sister-in-law Elizabeth Burden, and Georgiana Burne-Jones, who ran the firm's embroidery workshop. Morris began designing wallpaper in 1862; *Daisy*, *Fruit*, and *Trellis* were printed in 1864, with wider production beginning in the 1870s, by which time they were available in Boston. By the mid-1860s, the firm received major commissions, including the 1867 refreshment room at the South Kensington Museum (now Victoria and Albert Museum) and two rooms in St. James's Palace, both London. Morris's renown as a poet grew in the late 1860s and early 1870s; in 1869, his translations of Icelandic sagas were published. By the mid-1870s the firm was in financial trouble; Morris paid his partners off and launched Morris and Co in 1875. In 1877, he began lecturing and weaving in Hammersmith, and founded the Society for the Protection of Ancient Buildings. In 1881, he set up looms in Merton Abbey, near his friend De Morgan, the Arts and Crafts tilemaker. In 1883, he joined the Democratic Federation, Britain's first Socialist political organization, and lectured on social and economic issues. In 1890, he set up the Kelmscott Press; 1891–98, beautiful handmade books were produced there, one of the first being Ruskin's *The Nature of Gothic* (1892). It published 53 titles on handmade paper in limited editions, almost all designed by Morris himself in a style evoking medieval manuscripts and early printed books. Morris's Socialism directly influenced Walter Crane and C.R. Ashbee, and his championing of handicrafts and the decorative arts inspired guilds and groups throughout Britain, America, Germany, and Belgium. His passionate opposition to industrialism, which he held responsible for material and spiritual ugliness, and his belief that beautiful and well-made objects ought to be available to the masses, contained a contradiction only partially resolved when his successors embraced mass production.

► Morris, Marshall and Faulkner had two stalls at the London 'International Exhibition of 1862.' Work by Morris was included in the 1986–87 'In Pursuit of Beauty' exhibition at the Metropolitan Museum of Art in New York.

► May Morris (ed.), *The Collected Works of William Morris*, 24 vols., London, 1899. Cat., *Catalogue of an Exhibition in the Celebration of the Centenary of William Morris*, London: Victoria and Albert Museum, 1934. Asa Briggs and Graeme Shankland (eds.), *William Morris: Selected Writings and Designs*, Baltimore, 1962. Philip Henderson, *William Morris: His Life Work and Friends*, London, 1967. Ray Watkinson, *William Morris as Designer*, New York, 1967. Jack Lindsay, *William Morris: His Life and Work*, London, 1975. Paul Thompson, *The Works of William Morris*, London, 1977. Doreen Bolger Burke et al., *In Pursuit of Beauty: Americans and the Aesthetic Movement*, New York: Metropolitan Museum of Art and Rizzoli, 1986:456–57.

Morrison, Andrew Ivar (1939–)

► American designer; born Washington.

► Studied at the Pratt Institute, Brooklyn.

► He taught at the Pratt Institute, where he had met Bruce Hannah when they were students; from 1969, they designed furniture for Knoll, including a cast-aluminum and upholstered range.

► Received numerous awards. Work (with Hannah) shown at 1970 'Ventures in Design' exhibition, and (Morrison alone) at the Design Zentrum, Stuttgart.

► Hans Wichmann, *Industrial Design, Unikate und Serienerzeugnisse: Die Neue Sammlung. Ein neuer Museumstyp des 20. Jahrhunderts*, Munich: Prestel, 1985.

Morrison, Jasper (1959–)

► British designer; born and active London.

► 1979–82, studied Kingston School of Art and Design; 1982–85, Royal College of Art, London.

► Morrison produced, quirky, satiric, understated furniture. His 1986 South Kensington flat was widely published. He designed 1988 *Door handles I and II*, and a 1989 range of aluminum handles produced by FSB in Germany. He was a founding member of the NATO (Narrative Architecture Today) group of architects in London. Clients included Sheridan Coakley, Vitra, SCP, and Aram Designs. Mostly in small-batch production, his design work included the 1981 *Handlebar Table*, 1983 *Flower-Pot Table* produced by Cappellini, 1984 *Office System*, 1987 *Hat Stand* by Aram Designs, 1984 *Wing-Nut Chair*, 1982 stools by SCP, 1984 side table by SCP, 1986 console table by SCP, 1985 *A Rug of Many Blossoms*, 1985 *Rise Table*, 1986 dining chair, 1986 *Thinking Man's Chair* by Cappellini, 1988 *Chair 3* by Cappellini, 1984 *Ribbed Table* by Aram Designs, 1985 *Wingnut* chair, 1987 *One-Legged Table* by Cappellini, 1987 chaise longue, 1987 day bed by Cappellini, 1988 sofa by SCP, 1988 plywood desk by Galerie Néotù, benches for the 1989 Frankfurt Art Fair, 1988 *3 Green Bottles that Could also Be Clear*, 1988 plywood chair by Vitra, three carpets in 1988, 1989 low plywood table, and 1989 *Panton Project for Vitra*.

► In 1984, he won a Berlin scholarship. His work was included in the 1986 exhibition at the Shiseido department store in Tokyo, 1986 'British Design' exhibition in Vienna, 1986 'English Eccentrics' exhibition at Galerie Néotù in Paris, 1987 'Documenta 8' (Reuters News-Centre) in Kassel, 1988 'Documenta 9' in Berlin, and 1987 exhibition at Parco department store in Tokyo. In 1988, one-person exhibitions were mounted at the Galerie Pentagon in Cologne, Galerie Prodomo in Vienna, and his 1988 'Some new items for the house' exhibition at the DAAD gallery in Berlin. His *Thinking Man's Chair* was shown at the 1988 Salone del Mobile in Milan. His 1989 'A world slide show' exhibition was shown at the Leiptien 3 gallery in Frankfurt, 1989 'Some new items for the house, Part II' for Vitra at the Facsimilé gallery in Milan, and 1989 one-person exhibition at Galerie Néotù in Paris. Work for Sheridan Coakley was shown at the Salone del Mobile in Milan from 1986 and 1989 (I) International Contemporary Furniture Fair in New York. With Matthew Hilton's work, Morrison's was included in a 1987 exhibition in Tokyo.

► *Contract*, July 1990:26. Peter Dormer, *Jasper Morrison: Designs, Projects and Drawings, 1981–1989*, London: Architecture Design and Technology Press, 1990.

Mortier, Michel (1925–)

► French furniture designer.

► 1940–45, studied École des Arts Appliqués, Paris.

► From 1946 with teacher Étienne-Henri Martin, he worked in the interior design department, Bon Marché department store, Brussels; 1955–60, worked in Marcel Gascoin's workshop; subsequently, with Pierre Guariche and Joseph-André Motte, founded the group ARP; 1963–67, worked on 1967 'Exposition Universelle et Internationale Montréal (Universal and International Exposition) (Expo '67)' and taught at Institute of Applied Arts, Montreal; returning to Paris, worked for MFI (Meubles et Fonctions International) on office and other furniture, and for Renz, Germany; taught at École des Arts Appliqués, École Nationale Supérieure des Arts Décoratifs, École Camondo, and Met de Penningen, all Paris.

▶ Received René Gabriel Prize and numerous prizes at Triennali di Milano.

▶ Yolande Amic, *Intérieurs: Le Mobilier français 1945–1964*, Paris: Regard/VIA, 1983:90–91.

Morton, Alastair J.F. (1910–63)

▶ British textile manufacturer and painter.

▶ Studied Edinburgh University and Oxford University.

▶ In 1931, Morton joined his family firm Morton Sundour Fabrics and supervised its first screen-printed fabrics. From 1932, he was artistic director and principal designer of Edinburgh Weavers in Carlisle, formed in 1928 as Morton Sundour's creative design unit. A follower of the Modern movement from the 1930s, he commissioned designs from notable painters and designers. In 1937, he conceived the *Constructivist Fabrics* range with designs by Barbara Hepworth and Ben Nicholson. His 1937–38 Brackenfell house in Brampton was designed by J. Leslie Martin and Sadie Speight. A painter and textile designer himself, he designed dress prints for Horrockses and Edinburgh Fabrics, for which he designed the 1946 *Unit Prints* series. He studied hand spinning and weaving under Ethel Mairet in her Ditchling workshop. In 1962, he became chief executive director of Morton Sundour. He was a frequent lecturer. He became a member of the Council of Industrial Design and an assessor for the four central art schools in Scotland.

▶ His fabrics, fine art, and a photograph of his Brackenfell house were included in the 1979–80 'Thirties' exhibition at the Hayward Gallery in London.

▶ *The Mortons: Three Generations of Textile Creations*, London: Victoria and Albert Museum, 1973. Cat., *Thirties: British art and design before the war*, London: Arts Council of Great Britain, Hayward Gallery, 1979:89,171,193,292,296,297. Fiona MacCarthy and Patrick Nuttgens, *An Eye for Industry*, London: Lund Humphries, 1986.

Morton, Alexander, & Co

▶ British textile firm; located Darvel and Carlisle.

▶ The firm was established by Alexander Morton (1844–1921) as a madras-weaving factory; successfully introduced lace-making power machinery; 1890, began manufacturing carpets (with its Donegal hand-knotted carpets made in Ireland). Alexander's second son James commissioned imaginative designs by C.F.A. Voysey, L.P. Butterfield and others in the late 19th and 20th centuries. From 1900, the factory was located at Carlisle with madras and lace production remaining at Darvel. From 1912, it had its own hand-block printing unit. In 1921, Morton Sundour roller-printing began and screen printing in 1931. In 1914, almost all of Alexander Morton's production, except for carpets and lace, was taken over by Morton Sundour under James Morton's direction.

▶ Valerie Mendes, *The Victoria & Albert Museum's Textile Collection, British Textiles from 1900 to 1937* London: Victoria and Albert Museum, 1992.

Morton Sundour Fabrics

▶ British textile firm.

▶ The firm was founded in 1914, with James Morton (1867–1943) as governing director. It took over almost all of Alexander Morton's textile production, except for lace and carpets; produced 'Sundour' non-fading fabrics; from 1914, produced synthetic vat dyestuffs, and well-designed goods at reasonable cost.

▶ Valerie Mendes, *The Victoria & Albert Museum's Textile Collection British Textiles from 1900 to 1937*, London: Victoria and Albert Museum, 1992.

Moser, Henri

▶ French interior and furniture designer; active Paris.

▶ Moser worked in the 1920s as an interior designer for the Primavera decorating department of the Au Printemps department store, Paris.

▶ Alastair Duncan, *Art Nouveau and Art Déco Lighting*, New York: Simon and Schuster, 1978:185.

Moser, Koloman (1868–1918)

▶ Austrian painter, designer, metalworker, and graphic artist; born Vienna.

▶ 1889–92, studied painting and design, Akademie der bildenden Künste, Vienna; 1893–95, graphic design, Kunstgewerbeschule, Vienna.

▶ He designed for the *Wiener Mode* and, in 1895, with publisher Martin Gerlach and other artists in Vienna, producing the *Allegories* set of folio volumes. At this time he met Gustav Klimt. In 1895, a group of progressive artists, including Moser, Josef Hoffmann, and Joseph Maria Olbrich, formed the Siebener Club. In 1897, the Sezession was formally introduced in Vienna as an autonomous group of artists; it followed the example of the Munich Sezession. (Moser with the Klimt group left the Sezession in 1905.) Moser organized and designed Sezession exhibitions. In 1898, he contributed numerous illustrations to the first issue of the Sezessionist journal *Ver Sacrum*, and was involved with its launch. His decorative style in graphics at this time showed naturalistic ornamentation on a square grid. From 1901, he developed his characteristic checker pattern, derived from abstract floral patterns rather than black-and-white-square patterns, and based on Assyrian and Egyptian art. In his transitional period, naturalistic and abstract motifs of the Sezessionist style lingered alongside geometrical patterns. In 1899, he was appointed professor of painting at the Kunstgewerbeschule of the Österreichisches Museum für Kunst und Industrie in Vienna and became its director in 1900, coming in contact with Josef Hoffmann. Teaching students to work in a Sezession style, he designed graphics, glass, leather, book covers, metalwork, stained-glass windows, stage sets, ceramics, and toys. As a graphic designer, he produced banknotes, postage stamps, posters, and typography. In 1903, he founded the Wiener Werkstätte with Hoffmann and backer Fritz Wärndorfer; it was the Austrian equivalent of the Deutscher Werkbund. He was editor of the magazine *Hohe Warte*, published by the Werkstätte. His boxes were produced by Georg Adam Scheid and his jewelry by Rozet und Fischmeister of Vienna. He designed silver hollow-ware for the Wiener Werkstätte. Much of his furniture was made by commercial firms, including Caspar Hrazdil and Portois und Fix. His work illustrates the spread of the Mackintosh style in Germany c1910. In 1907, he left the Werkbund. His Werkstätte designs continued to be produced for some years, although he executed no silver designs after 1907. His theater design work started with sets (using drapes in place of convential décor) for the youth theater of Felix Salten. In 1907, he returned to painting, but continued with theater design.

▶ The glass he designed for the Sezession was shown at the 1900 (VIII) Vienna-Sezessionist exhibition. He first showed his work as an artist at a 1911 exhibition at the Miethke Gallery. His, Klimt's, and others' works were included in a 1920 exhibition organized by Hoffmann and others. Moser's work was the subject of the 1920 retrospective exhibition in Vienna organized by art-publisher Wolfrum, and of the 1979 exhibition at the Hochschule für angewandte Kunst in Vienna.

▶ Charlotte Gere, *American and European Jewelry 1830–1914*, New York: Crown, 1975:209. Peter Vergo, *Art in Vienna 1898–1918*, London: Phaidon, 1975. Fenz Werner, *Kolo Moser*, Salzburg, 1976. Cat., *Koloman Moser*, Vienna: Hochschule für angewandte Kunst, 1979. Stephen Calloway, *Twentieth-Century Decoration*, New York: Rizzoli, 1988:70. Annelies Krekel-Aalberse, *Art Nouveau and Art Déco Silver*, New York: Abrams, 1989:192, 194,195,197,199,200,257.

Moser, Werner Max (1896–1970)

▶ German architect, furniture designer, and writer; born Karlsruhe.

▶ 1916–21, studied Eidgenössische Technische Hochschule, Zürich, under his father Karl Moser.

▶ 1921–23, he worked in the office of M.H. Grandpré-Molière in the Netherlands. 1923–26, he worked in various architectural offices in the USA, including that of Frank Lloyd Wright. In 1927, he became a member of the Swiss group that designed furniture for several apartments in Mies van der Rohe's Weissenhof apartments in Stuttgart. Moser, Mart Stam, and Ferdinand Kramer designed the 1929–30 Budget Home in Frankfurt. In 1928, he was a founding member of CIAM (Congrès International d'Architecture Moderne) and was the Swiss delegate to the Congress in 1931. In 1931, Moser, Sigfried Giedion, and Rudolf Graber founded the Wohnbedarf department store in Zurich. In 1932, he applied for patents for furniture models known as 'wohnbedarf-typen.' Moser, future partners Max Ernst Haefeli and Rudolf Steiger, and others designed the building and interiors of the 1931–33 Neubühl settlement near Zürich. He became a specialist in school and church architecture. He published the book and organized the 1933 exhibition Das Kind und sein Schulhaus (The Child and His Schoolhouse), which influenced the design of subsequent school buildings. 1938–41, he designed a church in Zürich-Altstetten, finding a sensitive solution to Modern building in an historical context. In 1937, he formed the architecture partnership Haefeli Moser Steiger. In 1953, he was a guest professor at Harvard University. In 1958, he was appointed to the chair at Eidgenössische Technische Hochschule in Zürich, where he taught until 1963.

▶ He furnished the 'Working Apartment for a Journalist Couple' included in the opening exhibition at Neubühl. His competition project for the Kongresshaus in Zürich was a successful entry at the 1939 Schweizer Landesausstellung (Swiss National Exposition). In 1958, he received an honorary doctorate from University of Stuttgart.

▶ Friederike Mehlau-Wiebking et al., Schweizer Typenmöbel 1925–35, Sigfried Giedion und die Wohnbedarf AG, Zürich: gta, 1989:229–30.

Mosgau, Franz

▶ German silversmiths; located Berlin.
▶ The firm Franz Mosgau, founded in 1807, produced flatware designed by Peter Behrens.
▶ Annelies Krekel-Aalberse, Art Nouveau and Art Déco Silver, New York: Abrams, 1989:257.

Mossoul, Félix (1869–1942)

▶ French ceramicist; born Saint Germain.
▶ From 1903, he showed his work at the events of the Salon des Arts français and the Société des Arts Décoratifs.
▶ Europäische Keramik 1880–1930: Sammlung Silzer, Darmstadt: Hessisches Landesmuseum, 1986:137.

Mott, Joseph H.

▶ British ceramicist.
▶ Mott began working in 1880 at Doulton, Lambeth, where he was artistic director 1897–1935. Known as an authority on ceramic glazes, colors, and bodies, he worked on laboratory porcelains c1914–19. From the 1920s to 1935, he worked on the development of glazes, including flambé, matt, semi-matt, luster, and crystalline, and designed shapes. 1935–50, he was retained as a counsellor in ceramics.
▶ Cat., Thirties: British art and design before the war, London: Arts Council of Great Britain, Hayward Gallery, 1979:154,297.

Motte, Joseph-André (1925–)

▶ French furniture designer and painter.
▶ Studied painted and sculpture; in 1948, École des Arts Appliqués, Paris.
▶ He worked for the Au Bon Marché department store, Paris, with Albert Guenot; with Pierre Guariche and Michel Mortier, set up the design office ARP in 1948, becoming an independent designer in 1951; in 1954 and 1958–61, worked on interior design for Administration de Grands Travaux, and designed the chapel, transit hall, and bar at Orly airport, the maritime train station and central administration headquarters in Le Havre, and

Roissy airport. He participated in the renovation of the grand gallery of the Louvre Museum, Paris; was commissioned by the Mobilier National to design office furniture for use in prefecture buildings; furnished the offices of a number of firms; and designed furniture for serial production. His best known designs included chairs produced by Steiner in the late 1950s; 1950 Tripode chair in steel, beechwood, and rattan produced by Rousier, and stainless-steel chairs produced by Moebius, which inspired several prototypes in stainless steel produced by Ugine Gueugnon in 1963. He designed a number of wooden tables with bentwood bases; collaborated on the design of sea and river ports (Le Havre, 1962; Strasbourg and Dunkerque, 1965; Marseilles, 1968–69) and airports (Roissy-Charles de Gaulle, 1969 and 1976; Lyons Satolas, 1974); and was a teacher in charge of a workshop, École Nationale Supérieure des Arts Décoratifs, Paris.
▶ Received 1970 Premio Compasso d'Oro (Graphis chair produced by Tecno).
▶ Yolande Amic, Intérieurs: Le Mobilier français 1945–1964, Regard/VIA, 1983:92.

Motzfeldt, Benny (1909–)

▶ Norwegian glassware designer; born North-Trøndelag; active Fredrikstad.
▶ Studied graphic design, Statens Håndverks -og Kunstindustriskole, Oslo.
▶ She rendered decorations for sandblasting and engraving on crystal and glass windows. Becoming more interested in glass, she began working directly with glass blowers; together they experimented by adding metal dust, wire netting, and different colors. From 1955, she worked at Christiana Glasmagasin; from 1955–67, she was the chief designer at the Hadelands Glassverk and, 1967–70, at Randsfjords Glassverk. From 1970, she was director of the small glass studio for serial production Plus Centre in Fredrikstad.
▶ Received 1969 Jacob-prize. Work shown at a 1971 exhibition at the Danish Museum of Applied Arts in Copenhagen. Subsequent exhibitions included the 1977 one-person exhibition in Germany, and 1979–81 Smithsonian Institution Traveling Exhibition, USA.
▶ Cat., David Revere McFadden (ed.), Scandinavian Modern Design 1880–1980, New York: Abrams, 1982:268–69, No. 288. Frederick Cooke, Glass: Twentieth-Century Design, New York: Dutton, 1986:86. Cat., Anne Wichstrøm, Rooms with a View: Women's Art in Norway 1880–1990, Oslo: The Royal Ministry of Foreign Affairs, 1990:34. Jennifer Hawkins Opie, Scandinavia: Ceramics and Glass in the Twentieth Century, New York: Rizzoli, 1989.

Mougin, Joseph (1876–1961) and Pierre Mougin (1879–1955)

▶ French ceramicists; brothers; born Nancy.
▶ Joseph Mougin studied academy in Nancy and sculpture, École des Beaux-Arts, Paris, under Louis-Ernst Barrias.
▶ Joseph Mougin decided to become a ceramicist after seeing an exhibition of Jean Carriès's pottery in 1894. He set up a studio and kiln in Montrouge with the help of sculptor friend Lemarquier and brother Pierre Mougin. After two years, because the kiln was poorly constructed and would not fire properly, Lemarquier left. Mougin worked briefly at Sèvres. Returning from Paris, he and his brother set up a new kiln in Vaugirard; it too had problems, but they nevertheless produced some innovative ceramics. Encouraged by fellow Nancy artist Victor Prouvé, they showed their work at various Paris salons, gaining favorable notices and sales to museums, collectors, and the French government. In 1905, the brothers moved their operation to Nancy, where they became members of Émile Gallé's artists' group École de Nancy. They collaborated with Prouvé, Alfred Finot, and Ernest Bussière on pieces in an Art Nouveau style. After World War I, the brothers made volume production art pottery at the Faïencerie de Lunéville. In the early 1930s, Joseph Mougin left Paris for his old studio in

Nancy; 1936–60, he continued to make new forms and glazes with his daughter Odile and son François.

▶ Pieces designed with Prové, Finot, and Bussière were shown in Paris and included in the exhibitions of the École de Nancy up to 1914. Joseph Mougin was awarded the grand prize for ceramics at the 1925 Paris 'Exposition Internationale des Arts Décoratifs et Industriels Modernes.'

▶ Yvonne Brunhammer et al., *Art Nouveau Belgium, France*, Houston: Institute for the Arts, Rice University, 1976.

Mouille, Serge (1922–)

▶ French lighting designer; born and active Paris.

▶ Studied silversmithing, École des Arts Appliqués, Paris, to 1941.

▶ In 1937, he worked in silversmith and sculptor Gilbert Lacroix's studio; in 1945 set up a studio while teaching at École des Arts Appliqués, Paris; in 1953, was commissioned by Jacques Adnet, director of CAF, to design his first lighting fixtures; in 1955, became a member of the Société des Artistes Décorateurs and Société Nationale des Beaux-Arts; in the 1950s, was best known for his spindly black lighting fixtures, including 1953 Œil, 1954 *Flammes*, and 1958 *Saturn*. His lighting from the late 1950s was more solidly architectonic. He designed lighting for Université d'Antony, schools in Strasbourg and Marseilles, and Cathédrale de Bizerte; in 1961, established SCM (Société de Création de Modèles) to encourage young lighting designers.

▶ Work shown from 1956 at the gallery of Steph Simon, Paris. *Colonnes* lighting shown at the 1962 Salon des Arts ménagers et Batimat, lighting and jewelry at the 'Formes françaises' exhibition in Stockholm, sculpture and metalwork for silversmith Saglier at the Grand Palais, Paris. Received diploma of honor, 1958 'Exposition Universelle et Internationale de Bruxelles (Expo '58)'; 1963 gold medal, Société d'Encouragement à l'Art et à l'Industrie'; medal of the City of Paris from directors of Métiers d'Art; 1955 Charles Plumet prize. Work subject of 1983 exhibition, Galerie 1950, Paris.

▶ Cat., *Serge Mouille, luminaires, 1953–1963*, Paris: Galerie 1950, 1983. Anthony Delorenzo, *Two Master Metalworkers*, New York, 1983. Cat., *Jean Prouvé, Serge Mouille, deux maîtres du métal*, New York, 1985. Patrick Favardin, *Le Style 50: Un moment de l'art français*, Paris: Sous Le Vent–Vilo, 1987:58–65. Thierry de Beaumont, 'Serge Mouille,' *L'atelier*, No. 115, Feb. 1987. Jean-François Archieri, 'Serge Mouille: des lignes de lumière,' *Techniques et Architecture*, No. 383, April–May 1989. *Acquisitions arts décoratifs 1982–1990*, Paris: Fonds National d'Art Contemporain, 1991.

Mount Washington Glass

▶ American glassware manufacturer; located South Boston and New Bedford, Massachusetts.

▶ Founder of Boston and Sandwich Glass, Deming Jarves set up a factory in South Boston, Massachusetts. His son George Jarves was manager there, first with John D. Labree and subsequently with Henry Comerais. Jarves and Comerais, known as the Mount Washington Glass Works, was active until 1861, when its bookkeeper William L. Libbey and clerk Timothy Howe became directors of the firm. Libbey became sole director when Howe died. During this time, the firm produced kerosene lamps and blown, pressed, and cut glassware. In 1869, Libbey moved the factory from South Boston to the premises of the failed New Bedford Glass in New Bedford, Massachusetts, installing new equipment; W.L. Libbey and Co began to experiment with art glass in the 1870s and 1880s. In 1871, the Smith brothers were in charge of the decoration department. In 1872, Libbey left and became an agent for New England Glass. His brother Henry Libbey managed the firm, which closed in 1873. Reopened in 1874 under the management of Englishman Frederick Stacey Shirley, it was named Mount Washington Glass. From 1884, it produced rose-amber glassware, Shirley's imitation of the amberina ware invented in 1883 by Joseph Locke at New England Glass. In 1885, its Burmese glass was patented and made in more than 250 forms, several

examples of which were presented to Queen Victoria. In 1886, Thomas Webb was given a license to produce the 'Queen's Burmese.' In 1889, the firm began producing luxurious gilded and enameled opal wares; it also produced brilliant-cut and engraved crystal and acid-etched cameo glass. In 1880, when the Pairpoint Manufacturing Co opened an adjacent factory, Mount Washington Glass began to use silverplated mounts. In 1894, the glassworks were brought by Pairpoint. Mount Washington Glass, during Shirley's tenure 1874–94, produced a wide range of very high-quality glassware and, by 1890, was dubbed the 'headquarters of art glassware in America.' In 1895, Shirley and partner John P. Gregory reopened Boston and Sandwich Glass; it failed the next year.

▶ Showed cut-glass chandeliers and opal glass and won awards at the 1876 Philadelphia 'Centennial Exposition.' Its wares were included in the 1986–87 'In Pursuit of Beauty' exhibition at the Metropolitan Museum of Art in New York.

▶ Doreen Bolger Burke et al., *In Pursuit of Beauty: Americans and the Aesthetic Movement*, New York: Metropolitan Museum of Art and Rizzoli, 1986:457–58. Leonard E. Padgett, *Pairpoint Glass*, Des Moines, Iowa, 1979. George S. McKearin and Helen McKearin, *American Glass*, New York, 1941:207,411–12,420,602. Kenneth M. Wilson, *New England Glass and Glassmaking*, New York and Toronto, 1972:261–68,282–83,297–99,339–65,370–74.

Mourgue, Olivier (1939–)

▶ French designer; born Paris; active Brittany; brother of Pascal Mourgue.

▶ 1946–54, studied interior design, École Boulle, Paris; 1954–58, interior architecture; 1958–60, École Nationale Supérieure des Arts Décoratifs, Paris.

▶ He opened an office in Paris in 1960 and was consultant to Airborne, Prisunic, Mobilier National, Disderot, Air France, and Renault. He designed furniture, textiles, environments, and toys. His furniture in stretched red Latex fabric on steel and foam, including the 1965 *Djinn Chaise Longue* produced by Airborne, was noticeable in his interiors for the Stanley Kubrick film *2001: A Space Odyssey* (1968). Other Airborne furniture included *Tric-Trac* and *Whist*. The 1969 carpet-covered low seating was widely published. He designed 1969 furniture and seating range for Prisunic and the interiors of the Boeing 747 for Air France. With other units by Joe Colombo and Vernon Panton, he designed the 1971 *Visiona 3* domestic environment at Bayer, Germany. He developed a wheeled design studio in 1970, an open-plan domestic environment, a soft-surface bathroom suite for himself in 1970, and studies commissioned by Renault on automobile interior space and color in 1977. Concerned with space and mobility, Mourgue's supple, undulating forms typified French design to the world in the 1960s. In 1976, Mourgue moved to Brittany, where he taught at the École des Beaux-Arts in Brest.

▶ *Djinn Chaise Longue* first shown at the 1965 Salon de Meuble, Paris. He designed chairs for the reception area of the French pavilion at 1967 'Universal and International Exhibition (Expo '67)' in Montreal, and 1968 *Bouloum* lounge chair for French pavilion at 1970 Osaka 'Universal and International Japanese Exposition (Expo '70)'. He showed his work at 1964, 1966, and 1968 Cologne furniture fairs. Work subject of 1976 exhibition, Musée des Arts Décoratifs, Nantes. Received award (for 'Mobile Studio') at 1968 Turin 'Eurodomus II,' 1968 AID award (for *Djinn Chaise Longue*) in Chicago, and 1969 Gold Medal from Société d'Encouragement à l'Art et à l'Industrie.

▶ Cat., *Les Assises du siège contemporain*, Paris: Musée des Arts Décoratifs, 1968. Cat., *Modern Chairs 1918–1970*, London: Lund Humphries, 1971. Cat., *Design Français*, Paris: Centre de Création Industrielle, 1971: No. 138. 'Visiona 3,' *Industrial Design*, Vol. 19, May 1972:42–45. J. Roger Guilfoyle, 'An Atelier for Living,' *Industrial Design*, Vol. 20, Oct. 1973:28–32. Cat., *Olivier Mourgue*, Nantes: Musée des Arts décoratifs, 1976. Cat., Kathryn B. Hiesinger and George H. Marcus III (eds.), *Design Since 1945*, Philadelphia: Philadelphia Museum of Art, 1983:223,III–54. Cat.,

Mobilier national: 20 ans de création, Paris: CNACGP, CCI, CNAP, 1984. *Acquisitions arts décoratifs 1982–1990*, Paris: Fonds National d'Art Contemporain, 1991. François Mathey, *Au bonheur des formes, design français 1945–1992*, Paris: Regard, 1992: 257,264,338.

Mourgue, Pascal (1943–)

▶ French designer and artist; active Paris; brother of Olivier Mourgue.

▶ Studied École Boulle and École des Arts Décoratifs, both Paris.

▶ He began in 1960 as an interior designer, executing furniture designs produced by Vinco, Mobilier International, and Knoll. From 1982, he produced furniture, furnishings, and textiles' designs for Scarabat, Sopamco, Artelano, and Fermob. He designed the 1985 *Lune l'Argent* chair and stool produced by Fermob, 1988 *Ikmisou* sofa by Fermob, Motobécane mopeds, and, with Patrice Hardy, the *Yob* trimaran for Kental International. He designed the 1986 glass and metal three-legged café table and 1987 *Atlantique* furniture collection produced by Artelano, carpets for Toulemonde Bochart, a sofa for Guermonprez, and a desk for Mobilier International. Some of his projects were funded by VIA. His wife Marie Mourgue participated in the management of the studio business. In 1988, he established the Galerie Différences near the Musée Picasso in Paris to show his fine art; designed glass sculpture for the CIRVA, Marseilles.

▶ His *Arc* lounge-armchair won the 1983 VIA/Bloomingdale's first prize. He was named 1984 designer of the year in France and won grand prize in the 1986 Critique du Meuble Contemporain. His *Lune l'Argent* chair won the competition for contemporary art sponsored by the Fondation Cartier. His work was shown at the 1988 French contemporary furniture exhibition at the Victoria and Albert Museum, London, 1989 'L'Art de Vivre' exhibition at the Cooper-Hewitt Museum, New York, 1989 Salon du Meuble in Paris, and the 1990 'Les années VIA' exhibition at the Paris Musée des Arts Décoratifs. His work was the subject of a 1989 solo exhibition mounted by the Steelcase Design Partnership in New York.

▶ Cat. Margo Rouard Snowman, *The Most Contemporary French Furniture*, London: Victoria and Albert Museum, 1988. Cat. *Les années VIA, Paris*; Musée des Arts Décoratifs, 1990. Albrecht Bangert and Karl Michael Armer, *80s Style: Designs of the Decade*, New York: Abbeville, 1990:48,233. Suzanne Tise, 'Innovators at the Museum,' Vogue Décoration, No. 26, June/July 1990:46. François Mathey, *Au bonheur des formes, design français 1945–1992*, Paris: Regard, 1992:206,231,243–49,271.

Mouron, Adolphe
See Cassandre.

Mouveau, Georges
See DIM.

Mozer, Jordan

▶ American interior and furniture designer.

▶ Studied University of Wisconsin.

▶ He designed a number of Chicago restaurants, including the 1990 Viveré, and clubs. Shelby Williams produced Mozer's 1990 suite of hospitality seating. His *Cairo* bar stool was included in the range.

▶ His furniture was introduced in the Jordan Mozer Collection at the 1990 Neocon in Chicago.

▶ Laura E. Mayer, *Contract*, April 1990:66–67.

Mucchi, Gabriele (1899–)

▶ Italian artist, designer, and architect; active Milan.

▶ Studied Turin, Rome, Catania, Correggio, and Bologna.

▶ In 1934, he settled in a house in Milan that was the meeting point for anti-Fascists and artists who subsequently formed the group Corrente; in the 1930s, was active with Corrente and as

an architect; identified with the Rationalist architectural movement and executed some furniture designs in this idiom; designed the 1934–36 *Genni* armchair and wide chair in bent metal tubing and wicker produced by Crespi, Emilio Pino, and reissued by Zanotta from 1982.

▶ Participated in numerous exhibitions including 1926 'Italian 20th Century,' Milan; 1931–33 private show Galérie Bonaparte, 1949 Magneti Marelli and House of Culture, Milan; in 1955, exhibitions in Prague, Berlin, and Dresden; 1978 'Trend, art and society' and 'Literature, art and myths of the 20th century.' In 1984, received honorary doctorate, Humboldt-Universität, Leipzig.

▶ Fumio Shimizu and Matteo Thun (eds.), *The Descendants of Leonardo da Vinci: The Italian Design*, Tokyo, 1987:331. Hans Wichmann, *Italien Design 1945 bis heute*, Munich: Die Neue Sammlung, 1988.

Mucha, Alfons Maria (aka Alphonse Mucha 1860–1939)

▶ Moravian decorator, painter, and graphic artist.

▶ Mucha first designed stage sets in Vienna; moved to Munich in 1885 and Paris in 1887; produced wall decorations for the country estate Schloss Emmahof, near Grussbach (now Hrušovany, Czech Republic, of Count Khuen-Belasi; became involved in book and journal illustration and produced his first lithographs with Lemercier, Paris; with lithographer Champenois, combined his artistry with the printer's business expertise; experimented with screen designs *c*1885–88, when he made a three-panel painted screen for Count Khuen-Belasi; was best known for his poster designs for Sarah Bernhardt, of which the first example was printed in 1894. Georges Fouquet produced the jewelry Mucha designed for Bernhardt. He designed the interior of Fouquet's shop, 6 rue Royale, Paris. He designed furnishings, room settings, and objects that attempted to relate Art Nouveau motifs to the three-dimensionality of interior design; in 1904, collaborated on jewelry designs with Louis C. Tiffany making four trips 1903–22, was successful in the USA where industrialist Charles Richard Crane, a Slavophile resident of Chicago, sponsored the 20-painting series *Slav Epic*. Returning in 1922 to Czechoslovakia, his designs included postage stamps and banknotes. Designs, including jewelry, published in the 1902 pattern book *Documents Décoratifs*.

▶ Work subject of 1980 exhibition, Grand Palais, Paris.

▶ Jiri Mucha, *Alphonse Mucha: Posters and Photographs*, 1971. Charlotte Gere, *American and European Jewelry 1830–1914*, New York: Crown, 1975:209. Alastair Duncan, *Art Nouveau and Art Déco Lighting*, New York: Simon and Schuster, 1978:124. M. Komaneck and V.F. Butera, *The Folding Image Screens by Western Artists of the Nineteenth and Twentieth Century*, New Haven: Yale University Art Gallery, 1984:165–68. Stephen Calloway, *Twentieth-Century Decoration*, New York: Rizzoli, 1988:46.

Muehling, Ted (1953–)

▶ American designer.

▶ Studied industrial design, Pratt Institute, Brooklyn, New York, to 1971.

▶ He set up his own design studio in 1977. He designed limited production jewelry and home accessories.

▶ He received the 1977 Coty award.

▶ *Metropolitan Home*, September 1990:89–92.

Mueller, Herman (b. Hermann Müller)

▶ German artist and designer; active USA.

▶ Studied sculpture, Munich and Nuremberg.

▶ He settled in Cincinnati, Ohio. In *c*1887, he joined American Encaustic Tiling in Zanesville, Ohio, where he rendered images produced on tiles, including classically draped figures in pastoral settings. In 1894, Mueller and Karl Langenbeck founded Mosaic Tile in Zanesville. Leaving in 1908, he formed Mueller Mosaic in Trenton, New Jersey.

▶ Doreen Bolger Burke et al., *In Pursuit of Beauty*, New York: Metropolitan Museum of Art and Abrams, 1986.

Mühlhaus, Heike (1954–)
▶ German designer; born Wiesbaden.
▶ 1977–81, studied design and ceramics, Fachhochschule, Wiesbaden, under Margot Münster.
▶ In 1981, she began the Projekt Cocktail with Renate von Brevern. Their work included the 1988 mirror and 1986 Sisters vases, marketed by Herbert Jakob Weinand in limited editions.
▶ From 1984, they participated in numerous design exhibitions of their own, and with their work included in group shows.
▶ Cat., Design Center Stuttgart, Women in Design: Careers and Life Histories Since 1900, Stuttgart: Haus der Wirtschaft, 1989:94–95.

Mukaide, Keiko (1954–)
▶ Japanese glass designer.
▶ Studied commercial design, Musashino University of Art, Tokyo, to 1977; Penland School, Penland, North Carolina, to 1983; 1982–87, Pilchuck Glass School, Stanwood, Washington, and Royal College of Art, London.
▶ Mukaide began working for Miasa Glass Workshop in 1988.
▶ Solo exhibition 1987–88 at Gallery Koga, Tokyo. Work included in 1987 'The Art of Contemporary Japanese Studio Glass,' Heller Gallery, New York, 1990 'Glass '90 in Japan,' Tokyo; and 1991 (V) Triennale of the Japan Glass Art Crafts Association, Heller Gallery, New York.
▶ Cat., Glass Japan, New York: Heller Gallery and Japan Glass Art Crafts Association, 1991: No. 25.

Mulholland, Walter and David Edward Mulholland
▶ American silversmiths.
▶ The Mulholland brothers established a workshop in Park Ridge, Illinois, in 1912, which operated until 1934 as Mulholland Silver (Mulholland Brothers 1916–1924).

Müller, Albin (1871–1941)
▶ German architect and designer; active Magdeburg and Darmstadt.
▶ Studied Schools of Arts and Crafts in Mainz and Dresden.
▶ 1900–06, he taught at the School of Arts and Crafts in Magdeburg. From 1906, he worked at the Darmstadt artists' colony of the Grand Duke Louis IV of Hesse-Darmstadt, where he produced designs influenced by Peter Behrens and Josef Maria Olbrich. In 1908, after Olbrich's death, Müller became the leading architect at Darmstadt, although the fame of the colony had by that stage declined. He designed special exhibition products for Darmstadt manufacturers, including clocks and chairs. His silver designs were produced by Koch und Bergfeld of Bremen, Johann L. Brandner, and J. Götz in Regensburg. His pewterware was produced by E. Hueck, Lüdenscheid. He designed cutlery for M.H. Wilkens. While a professor at Darmstadt's Technical School, he designed buildings for the colony. Published in the review Alte und Neue Stadtbaukunst in 1920, his architecture was then showing the influence of Expressionism.
▶ He showed two centerpieces at the 1910 Brussels 'Exposition Universelle et Internationale.'
▶ Annelies Krekel-Aalberse, Art Nouveau and Art Déco Silver, New York: Abrams, 1989:132,134,257. Cat., Künstlerkolonie Darmstadt, Darmstadt, 1990:155.

Müller, Émile (?–1889)
▶ French engineer and ceramicist.
▶ Müller founded the tileworks Grande Tuilerie d'Ivry, in 1854, perfecting a high-fired glaze and a body resistant to abrupt temperature changes. His interest was in producing tiles for monumental decoration rather than the small, regular tiles then available, so that architects could execute their own designs. The Müller factory's numerous products included revetment tiles, decorative terracotta, stoneware, and glazed bricks. The firm became Émile Müller et Cie when his son Louis assumed directorship in 1889 and introduced flambé-glazed, high-fired stoneware copies of sculpture by Donatello, Verrocchio, Antoine Barye, Alexandre Charpentier, Eugène Grasset, and James Vibert. In 1893, the factory made the glazed ceramic panels and roof tiles designed by Hector Guimard for the 1895 Hôtel Jassedé, Paris, and executed a frieze for the monumental gateway by Anatole Guillot, named Frise du Travail, for the 1900 Paris 'Exposition Universelle.'
▶ Received a grand prize at the 1889 Paris 'Exposition Universelle' and work appeared on the Guillot gateway frieze at the 1900 Paris 'Exposition Universelle.'
▶ Yvonne Brunhammer et al., Art Nouveau Belgium, France, Houston: Institute for the Arts, Rice University, 1976.

Müller Frères
▶ French glass manufacturer; located Nancy.
▶ Brothers Désiré and Eugène Müller worked in the Gallé workshop in Nancy; three other Müller brothers, Henri, Victor, and Pierre, were later apprentices there. The family set up their own workshop in the rue Sainte-Anne in Lunéville; the glass was blown at the Hinzelin Gabeleterie in nearby Croismare under the Müllers' direction. The most common product was cameo glass, which had up to seven layers and was acid-etched or wheel-cut. The Müllers produced tableware including pitchers, vases, and bowls, table lamps, chandeliers, and night lights in Art Nouveau and Art Déco models. Production ceased during World War I, but the Müllers' arrangement with Hinzelin was re-established in 1919 and production resumed. Before the firm closed in 1936, its employees numbered 300.
▶ B. and H. Blount, French Cameo Glass, Des Moines, Iowa, 1968:134. L'Art Verrier à l'aube du XXe siècle, Lausanne: Galerie des Arts Décoratifs, 1973:58–59. J. Bloch-Dermant, L'Art du Verre en France, 1860–1914, Paris, 1975:163. Alastair Duncan, Art Nouveau and Art Déco Lighting, New York: Simon and Schuster, 1978:84–85.

Müller, Gerd Alfred (1932–)
▶ German industrial designer.
▶ In 1952, apprenticed as a joiner; studied interior design, Werkkunstschule, Wiesbaden.
▶ From 1955, he worked at Braun and in the Functionalist approach that the firm was then espousing. He executed designs for some of Braun's best known products, including electric razors, 1957 KM3 multi-purpose kitchen machine, and 1957 Multipress MP 32. He set up his own design studio in Eschborn in 1960.
▶ His kitchen machine for Braun was included in the 1983–84 'Design Since 1945' exhibition at the Philadelphia Museum of Art.
▶ Cat., Kathryn B. Hiesinger and George H. Marcus III (eds.), Design Since 1945, Philadelphia: Philadelphia Museum of Art, 1983:223,I–24. 75 Jahre Deutscher Werkbund, Frankfurt, 1983.

Müller, Hermann
See Mueller, Herman

Müller, Karl (1888–1972)
▶ German silversmith; active Halle.
▶ Studied Akadamie der Künste, Berlin.
▶ 1923–58, he taught metalwork at the Kunstgewerbeschule Burg Giebichenstein in Halle, which was more geared to commercial production than the Bauhaus. Eva Mascher-Elsässer and Hildegard Risch were students of Müller's. When the Bauhaus moved to Dessau in 1927, Wolfgang Tümpel moved to the Halle workshop under Müller. Müller designed sculptures, domestic objects, lighting, cutlery, and other items.
▶ He received a gold medal at the 1937 Paris 'Exposition Internationale des Arts et Techniques dans la Vie Moderne.'
▶ Cat., Karl Müller 1888–1972, 100 Arbeiten, Halle: Staatliche Galerie Moritzburg, 1988. Annelies Krekel-Aalberse, Art Nouveau and Art Déco Silver, New York: Abrams, 1989:147,149,257. Katja Schneider, Burg Giebichenstein, Weinheim: VCA, 1992:253–71,468–70.

Muller, Keith
▶ Canadian designer.
▶ Studied industrial design, Ontario College of Art.

▶ Active as a furniture, product, and hospital equipment designer from the 1960s, he designed office systems and was a space planner. Muller and Michael Stewart designed the popular *Image* sofa and chair in the late 1960s and the 1968 molded-plywood stacking chair produced by Ambiant Systems in Toronto.

▶ Cat., *Seduced and Abandoned: Modern Furniture designers in Canada, the First Fifty Years*, Toronto: The Art Gallery at Harbourfront, 1986:22.

Müller, Theodor

▶ German silversmith; active Weimar.

▶ Müller was court jeweler in Weimar and was put in charge of the Grand Duke of Saxe-Weimar's wedding present, a 335-piece silver dinner service designed by Henry van de Velde, who had been brought to Weimar in part to supervise the production of the dinner service. Müller could not cope with such an enormous commission; it went to Bremen silversmiths Koch und Bergfeld.

▶ Annelies Krekel-Aalberse, *Art Nouveau and Art Déco Silver*, New York: Abrams, 1989:136,245,257.

Müller-Hellwig, Alen   (b. Alen Müller, 1902–)

▶ German textile designer; born Lauenburg.

▶ 1920–23, studied Kungstgewerbeschule, Hamburg; 1923–24, Kunstgewerbeschule, Munich.

▶ From 1926, she was active in her own studio in Lübeck; in 1937, married violin maker G. Müller.

▶ Received a gold medal at 1937 Paris 'Exhibition Internationale des Arts et Techniques dans la Vie Moderne'; awards at 1940 (VII) and 1951 (IX) Triennali di Milano'; art award of Schleswig-Holstein, 1954; award from Kunstewerbeverein, Hamburg; honors from the city of Lübeck.

▶ Sigrid Wortmann Weltge, *Women's Work: Textile Art from the Bauhaus*, London: Thames and Hudson, 1993.

Müller-Munk, Peter   (1904–67)

▶ German designer: born Berlin; active Berlin and New York.

▶ Studied University of Berlin and Kunstgewerbeschule, Berlin (in 1924 renamed the Vereinigte Staatsschulen für freie und angewandte Kunst in Berlin-Charlottenburg), under Bruno Paul and Waldemar Rämisch.

▶ He settled in New York in 1926 and worked for Tiffany before, in 1927, he set up his own workshop. He became an associate professor at the Carnegie Institute in Pittsburgh, and moved into industrial design. At the Carnegie Institute 1934–45, he established the first degree-granting industrial design department in an institution of higher learning in the USA. His metalwork was angular with accentuated vertical and horizontal lines, revealing his German training; his candelabrum was published in *The Studio* in 1928. He was interested in reviving ancient silver production techniques, but is best known for his sleekly simple 1935 chromium-plated pitcher *Normandie*, based on the silhouette of the 1935 French oceanliner *Normandie*, mass produced by Revere in Rome, New York. He was a member of the American Society of Industrial Designers (president 1954–55) and International Council of Industrial Designers (president 1957–59).

▶ His first New York exhibition was held at the Chase Bank Building in 1928.

▶ Augusta Owen Patterson, 'The Decorative Arts,' *Town and Country*, 15 April 1928:71. Helen Appleton Read, 'The Modern Theme Finds a Distinctive Medium in American Silver,' *Vogue*, 1 July 1928:98. Peter Müller-Munk, 'Machine-Hand,' *The Studio*, October 1929:709ff. 'Müller-Munk, Peter,' *Who's Who in America*, 1947. Annelies Krekel-Aalberse, *Art Nouveau and Art Déco Silver*, New York: Abrams, 1989:121,256. Arthur Pulos, 'Peter Müller-Munk' in Mel Byars and Russell Flinchum (eds.), *50 American Designers*, Washington: Preservation, 1994.

Mumenthaler, Ernst   (1901–78)

▶ Swiss architect and furniture designer; active Basel.

▶ He and Otto Meier established an architecture office and contracting firm in Basel in 1925. The construction of their modular furniture system *3M-Möbel* was accomplished by Meier himself. Their award-winning 1928 cabinet designs shown at the 'Das Neue Heim II' exhibition were further developed in a lightweight plywood construction. In 1944, they and architect August Künzel designed the housing development Drei Linden in Basel.

▶ Mumenthaler and Meier won first prize in a competition held at the 1928 'Das Neue Heim II' exhibition in the Kunstgewerbemuseum in Zürich.

▶ Friederike Mehlau-Wiebking et al., *Schweizer Typenmöbel 1925–35, Sigfried Giedion und die Wohnbedarf AG*, Zürich: gta, 1989:229.

Mumford, Lewis   (1895–1990)

▶ American social philosopher and architecture and design critic; born Flushing, New York.

▶ Studied Columbia University and The New School for Social Research, New York.

▶ Mumford was most famous for his 'Sky Line' column for *The New Yorker* magazine. From the 1930s to the 1950s, he commented on skyscrapers, housing, urban renewal, and the general urban outlook for the magazine. He was an early opponent of congestion and over-building. He taught a course on American architecture at The New School, and at Columbia University on the machine age. The first book in his 'Renewal of Life' series was *Technics and Civilization* (1934), which challenged the theory that the Industrial Revolution started with the steam engine and suggested that medieval technology was less backward than generally supposed. The other titles in the series were *The Culture of Cities*, (1938), *The Condition of Man* (1944), and *The Conduct of Life* (1951). He was a prolific writer; his other work included *The City in History* (1961). Mumford's intellect and morality were steeped in 19th-century America, as exemplified in the works of Whitman, Emerson, Thoreau, Melville, and in the approach of the Scottish polymath and town planner Sir Patrick Geddes. Mumford believed that self-realization was only possible under conditions of humanism and in a personal society. Norman Bel Geddes and his writings had a profound effect on him. 'It is not the apparatus of the machine that's wrong, but the organized cult of machinery that is really evil. It is a monster that can transform man into a passive, purposeless animal,' wrote Mumford; he asserted that science without conscience 'is the ruin of the soul.'

▶ *The New York Times*, 28 Jan. 1990:30.

Munari, Bruno   (1907–)

▶ Italian artist and designer; born and active Milan.

▶ Munari began his career as a sculptor and painter, showing in Futurist exhibitions in Milan in the late 1920s and 1930s. In 1933 he produced his first suspended kinetic objects called 'Useless Machines,' exhibiting in 1933 and 1945. His first abstract-geometric picture was executed in 1935. In 1945, he designed a kinetic complex called *Hour X*, later made by Produzione Danese in Milan. In 1948 with Soldati, Dorfles, and Monnet, he was a founder of MAC (Movimento Arte Concreta). In 1950, he created positive and negative pictures as experimentations in color interaction. His earliest industrial designs appeared in the 1950s, including the 1954 toy monkey produced by Pigomma. The 1957 cubic ashtray in melamine, his first exercise in plastics, was the beginning of a long association with its producer, Danese. He designed a series of collapsible lamps and wooden puzzles in the late 1950s and early 1960s produced by Danese, including the 1963 *Calza* made from metal hoops and white stretched fabric. He divided his time between the fine and applied arts, pondering the relationship between aesthetics and function. The 1971 space-frame environment, 1972 hanging shelves produced by Robots, *Abitacola* bed-shelf living module, and designs for Zanotta reflected a high-tech approach. He was invited by Harvard University to teach a research and experimentation course on design and communication, and, from 1970, was a professor at the Scuola Politecnica in Milan; set up an educational laboratory for babies; published numerous books for Laterza, Einaudi, Zanichelli.

▶ In 1953, his color experiments were presented in Milan, New York, Stockholm, Paris, and others cities including Shuzo Takiguchi, Tokyo. Received 1954 (monkey toy), 1955 (ice bucket), 1971 (space-frame environment), and 1979 (hanging bookshelves) Premio Compasso d'Oro. In 1962, he organized the first exhibition of 'program art,' where the works of Group T, Group N, Enzo Mari, and Munari's own toured American museums and universities. Work shown in exhibitions in Tokyo in 1965; Rome in 1966; Stockholm, New York at the Howard Wise Gallery; Graz in 1970; and Basel at the Allgemeine Gewerbeschule. His work was the subject of a one-person exhibition at the Biennale di Venezia and 1988 'Bruno Munari' exhibition at the Israel Museum in Jerusalem.

▶ Max Bill and Bruno Munari, *Enzo Mari*, Milan, 1959. Bruno Munari, *Discovery of the Square*, Milan: Scheiwiller, 1960. Bruno Munari, *Discovery of the Circle*, Milan: Scheiwiller, 1964. Bruno Munari, *Art as a Craft*, Bari: Laterza, 1966. Bruno Munari, *Illegible Book N.Y. 1*, New York: Museum of Modern Art, 1967. Bruno Munari, *Design and Visual Communications.*, Bari: Laterza, 1968. Bruno Munari, *Obvious Code*, Turin: Einaudi, 1971. Bruno Munari, *Artist and Designer*, Bari: Laterza, 1971. Bruno Munari, *Design As Art*, Baltimore, 1971. Cat., Milena Lamarová, *Design a Plastické Hmoty*, Prague: Uměleckoprůmyslové Muzeum, 1972: 134. Paolo Fossati, *Il design in Italia*, Turin, 1972, plates 78–94, biblio. Alfonso Grassi and Anty Pansera, *Atlante del design italiano: 1940–1980*, Milan: Fabbri, 1980:274. Cat., Kathryn B. Heisinger and George H. Marcus III (eds.), *Design Since 1945*, Philadelphia: Philadelphia Museum of Art, 1983:223. A. Tachis, *Bruno Munari*, Milan, 1986.

Munari, Cleto (1930–)
▶ Italian jeweler; born Gorizia; active Vicenza.
▶ From 1960–70, Munari was an executive administrator at industrial firms; in the 1970s, he became associated with design, and, in 1973, had silver designed for his own use; met Carlo Scarpa and began a close association when the architect moved to Vicenza; in 1974, began the production of Scarpa's metalware; in 1977, he set up a firm in his own name to produce tabletop and household accessories in silver, gold, semi-precious stones, and glass; in 1985, set up a laboratory for the design of jewelry by established designers. As part of the trend to use architects as designers, some of his first wares were designed by Carlo Scarpa and Sami Wirkkala, and those following included Gae Aulenti, Mario Bellini, Robert A.M. Stern, Achille Castiglioni, Vittorio Gregotti, Hans Hollein, Vico Magistretti, and Robert Venturi.
▶ Cat., Alessandro Vezzosi, *Il Tesoro dell'Architettura: Gioielli, Argenti, Vetri, Orologi, 1980/1990*, Cleto Munari, Florence: EDIFIR, 1990.

Münchner Sezession (Munich Secession)
▶ German artists' exhibition group; located Munich.
▶ Rejecting the existing exhibition association Münchener Künstlergenossenschaft, over 100 local artist dissidents met in the Kunstgewerbehaus in 1892 and named the new association Verein Bildender Künstler Münchens (Munich Society of Visual Artists). In its first four months, the group grew tenfold and became popularly known by public and press as the Münchner Sezession, a title it officially adopted. Mounting its own show in 1893, the new group was the first art secession in the German-speaking countries; Vienna followed with its own group in 1897, and Berlin in 1898. Munich was at this time the capital of the visual arts in Central Europe. The Münchner Sezession was a progressive force in German art for nearly a decade.
▶ Maria Makela, *The Munich Secession: Art and Artists in Turn-of-the-Century Munich*, Princeton: Princeton University, 1990.

Münchner Vereinigte Werkstätte für Kunst im Handwerk
▶ German applied arts group.
▶ The success of the presentation of the works of Bruno Paul, Berhard Pankok, Hermann Olbrist, and others, in the small decorative arts section of the 1897 'Glaspalast' exhibition in Munich led to the formation of the Vereinigte Werkstätten für Kunst im Handwerk (United Workshops for Art in Handwork). Directed by painter Franz August Otto Krüger, the group, with its own workshop and showroom, was the first of its kind in Germany. In addition to Paul, Pankok, and Olbrist, designers included Peter Behrens and Richard Riemerschmid. Short-lived, the group achieved little success and soon disbanded, leaving Munich.
▶ The Vereinigte Werkstätte first showed its members' works at the 1898 Munich 'Glaspalast' exhibition. Pankok, Paul, and Riemerschmid showed at the 1900 Paris 'Exposition Universelle,' Paul at the 1904 St. Louis 'Louisiana Purchase Exposition,' and Troost, Schröder, and Paul at the 1910 'Exposition Universelle et Internationale de Bruxelles.'

Munthe, Gerhard (1855–1929)
▶ Norwegian textile, furniture, and interior designer.
▶ Studied painting in Oslo under J.F. Eckersberg, Knud Bergslien, and Julius Middletun and, in 1874, in Düsseldorf.
▶ 1877–82, he lived in Munich. Drawing on Norwegian folk art and poetry, he illustrated books and designed tapestries for firms including DNB (Det Norske Billedvæveri). He illustrated the deluxe edition of Snorr's *Saga of the Norwegian Kings* (1899). Munthe's 1892 dinner service, produced by Porsgrunds Porselænsfabrik, was based on a nature-oriented theme rather than an historical approach. As pictorial artist, he brought about the break with historicism in Norway. His 1895 furniture for the Holmenkollen Turisthotell had dragons in the pierced backs of wooden armchairs.
▶ He won a gold medal at the 1900 Paris 'Exposition Universelle.'
▶ Hilmar Bakken, *Gerhard Munthes dekorative kunst*, Oslo, 1946. Hilmar Bakken, *Gerhard Munthe: ein biografisk studie*, Oslo, 1952. 'Gerhard Munthe om inspirasjonen til "c'est ainsi,"' in Kunstindustrimuseet i Oslo Årbok, 1965:94–97. Cat., David Revere McFadden (ed.), *Scandinavian Modern Design 1880–1980*, New York: Abrams, 1982:269, Nos. 4,8. Frederik Wildhagen, *Norge i Form*, Oslo: Stenersen, 1988:37.

Munthe-Kaas, Herman (1890–1977)
▶ Norwegian architect and furniture designer.
▶ He set up an architecture office with Gudolf Blakstad in the 1920s. Munthe-Kaas produced designs in a Modern style. His Functionalist interpretation of the wing-back chair was published in the 1924 *Form og Farve*. As one of the early exponents of tubular steel furniture in Norway, he designed the 1929 cantilever, bent-metal, nickel-plated furniture for Christiania Jernsengfabrik in Oslo.
▶ Cat., David Revere McFadden (ed.), *Scandinavian Modern Design 1880–1980*, New York: Abrams, 1982:269, No. 99. Fredrik Wildhagen, *Norge i Form*, Oslo: Stenersen, 1988:82.

Muona, Toini (1904–87)
▶ Finnish ceramicist.
▶ 1927–33, studied Taideteollinen Korkeakoulu, Helsinki, and ceramics under Alfred William Finch.
▶ 1931–70, Muona worked at the pottery factory Arabia in Helsinki; from 1963–64, at Nuutjärri.
▶ Won awards at the 1929 'Exposición Internacional de Barcelona'; 1933 (V), 1951 (IX), 1954 (X), and 1957 (XI) Triennali di Milano; gold medal at 1935 'Exposition Universelle et Internationale de Bruxelles'; gold medal for ceramics and silver medal for glass at 1937 Paris 'Exposition Internationale des Arts et Techniques dans la Vie Moderne'; 1957 Pro Finlandia. Work subject of 1955 exhibition in Cannes. Work included in the 1954–57 USA 'Design in Scandinavia' traveling exhibition, 1955 'H 55' exhibition in Hälsingborg, 1956–57 West Germany 'Finnish Exhibition,' 1958 'Formes Scandinaves' at the Paris Musée des Arts Décoratifs, 1961 'Finlandia' exhibition in Zürich, Amsterdam, and London.

▶ Cat., David Revere McFadden (ed.), *Scandinavian Modern Design 1880–1980*, New York: Abrams, 1982:269, No. 159. Jennifer Hawkins Opie, *Scandinavia: Ceramics and Glass in the Twentieth Century*, New York: Rizzoli, 1989.

Murakami, Tatsuo (1950–)
▶ Japanese glass designer.
▶ In 1970, Murakami began working in the design department of Shibata Hario Glass in Tokyo, where he became director of marketing. He was a member of the Japan Crafts Design Association.
▶ Work included in 1984, 1987, and 1990 'Glass in Japan,' Tokyo; 1988 'International Exhibition of Glass Craft,' Industrial Gallery of Ishikawa Perfecture, Kanazawa; and 1991 (V) Triennale of the Japan Glass Art Crafts Association, Heller Gallery, New York. Received the 1975 Ministry of International Trade and Industry Design Award.
▶ Cat., *Glass Japan*, New York: Heller Gallery and Japan Glass Art Crafts Association, 1991: No. 26.

Muratore, Nicolas
▶ French furniture maker.
▶ In his workshop at 17 boulevard Victor-Hugo in Nice, Muratore produced furniture in Modern geometric forms during the 1920s.
▶ His furniture was installed in the pavilion of Art Colonial at the 1925 Paris 'Exposition Internationale des Arts Décoratifs et Industriels Modernes.' A white and blue enamel bedroom suite was shown at the 1927 Salon d'Automne.
▶ Pierre Kjellberg, *Art Déco: les maîtres du Mobilier, le décor des Paquebots*, Paris: Amateur, 1986:131.

Murdoch, Peter (1940–)
▶ British furniture, interior, graphic, and industrial designer.
▶ Studied Royal College of Art, London.
▶ He opened his own studio in London in 1969. His 1964 *Spotty* child's chair was widely published; its polyethene fiberboard was printed in a large polka-dot motif. A redesigned group of children's furniture in brightly colored plastic-coated cardboard was produced by Perspective Designs in 1967 and widely distributed in Britain and abroad. It earned Murdoch a reputation as a Pop designer. He was a consultant to Hille and Price. With Lance Wyman, he designed graphics for the 1968 Mexico City Olympic Games, and graphics and corporate identity programs for other clients.
▶ The *Spotty* child's chair was shown at the 1965 USA 'Industrial Design Exhibition' in the USSR, 1970 'Modern Chairs 1918–1970' exhibition at the Whitechapel Gallery in London, and 1983–84 'Design Since 1945' exhibition at the Philadelphia Museum of Art. The chair won the 1966 Gold Award from the National Fiber Box Manufacturers in the USA. The redesigned children's furniture range won the 1968 Council of Industrial Design Annual Award in Britain.
▶ 'Children's Table, Chair and Stool: Perspective Designs Those Things,' *Design*, No. 233, May 1968:33. Cat., *Modern Chairs 1918–1970*, London: Lund Humphries, 1971: No. 69. Cat., Kathryn B. Hiesinger and George H. Marcus III (eds.), *Design Since 1945*, Philadelphia: Philadelphia Museum of Art, 1983:223,II–56. Cat., Linda Brown and Deyan Sudjic, *The Modern Chair*, London, 1989.

Muro, Shinichi (1949–)
▶ Japanese glass designer.
▶ Studied craft design, Kanazawa College of Art.
▶ Muro began working at Joetsu Crystal, Gumma, in 1973; He was a part-time lecturer at Kanazawa College of Art.
▶ Solo exhibitions at 1986 and 1988 Seibu department store and 1989 Tomoe-do, Tokyo. Work included in 1984 and 1990 'Glass in Japan,' Tokyo, 1985 'New Glass in Japan,' Badisches Landesmuseum, Karlsruhe; 1986 'Japanese Glass—300 Years,' Suntory

Museum of Art, Tokyo; 1988 'World Glass Now '88,' Hokkaido Museum of Modern Art, Sapporo; and 1991 (V) Triennale of the Japan Glass Art Crafts Association, Heller Gallery, New York. Won 1987 Suntory Museum of Art Award, 'Glass '87 in Japan,' Tokyo.
▶ Cat., *Glass Japan*, New York: Heller Gallery and Japan Glass Art Crafts Association, 1991: No. 21.

Murphy, Henry George (1884–1939)
▶ British jeweler and silversmith; active London.
▶ Studied Central School of Arts and Crafts, London, under Henry Wilson.
▶ In 1898, Murphy was apprenticed to Henry Wilson (the architect turned sculptor, metalworker, and jeweler), later working with him on ecclesiastical commissions. From 1909, he taught at the Royal College of Art and then at the Central School of Arts and Crafts, both London. 1912–13, he worked in the Berlin workshop of Emil Lettré. In 1913, he set up his own workshop in London. He became head of the jewelry and silversmithing department at the Central School of Arts and Crafts and, in 1937, principal. His workshop at 'The Sign of the Falcon' was located in Weymouth Street, London. During the years after World War I, he moved away from the Arts and Crafts style towards the fashionable Art Déco style. He produced his own work as well as the designs of Eric Gill and designer R.M.Y. Gleadowe. Some of Murphy's designs reflected German and Austrian designs of the 1920s.
▶ In 1936, elected Royal Designer for Industry. In 1929, he received the Freedom of the Goldsmiths' Company and, in 1938, became a member of the Court of Assistant. Numerous examples of his silver work were included in the 1979–80 'Thirties' exhibition at the Hayward Gallery in London.
▶ H.G. Murphy, 'British Silver To-day,' *The Studio*, January 1936:36–42. Charlotte Gere, *American and European Jewelry 1830–1914*, New York: Crown, 1975:211. Cat., *Thirties: British art and design before the war*, London: Arts Council of Great Britain, Hayward Gallery, 1979:23,99,137,139,297. Annelies Krekel-Aalberse, *Art Nouveau and Art Déco Silver*, New York: Abrams, 1989:27,33,35,257.

Murphy Radio
▶ British domestic electronics manufacturer.
▶ Murphy Radio's founder Frank Murphy contracted Gordon Russell in the early 1930s to design radio cabinets; he in turn passed on the commission to his brother R.D. Russell, who produced an influential series of veneered plywood cabinets. R.D. Russell was staff designer at Murphy Radio 1934–36 and a consultant there in 1936. His innovative series of housings included the 1932 *AS* model. As a consultant designer, he continued to design Murphy's radio cases after the war, rendering bare Modern veneer essays. His 1936 square floor model and 1948 tapering concave-frame cabinet, with its central sound hole, have been widely published. In the early 1950s, he continued his work with Murphy on TV cabinets.
▶ Michael Farr, *Design in British Industry: A Mid-Century Survey*, London: Cambridge, 1955. *The Radio*, London: Design Museum, 1989.

Murray, Keith Day Pearce (1892–1981)
▶ New Zealand architect and designer; born Auckland; active Britain.
▶ 1915–18 studied Architectural Association, London.
▶ He first worked for the James Powell Whitefriars Glassworks. From 1932, he worked part-time as a ceramics and glass designer at Stevens and Williams's Brierley Hill Glassworks, followed, from 1933, at Wedgwood. He designed many successful shapes and decorations for both firms, some historicist, but most in the Functionalist Modern style. Influenced by the glassware at the 1925 Paris 'Exposition Internationale des Arts Décoratifs et Industriels

Modernes' and Swedish glassware at the 1931 London 'Swedish Exhibition,' he produced simple, geometric forms. In 1934, Mappin and Webb hired Murray for silver designs, including a covered silver-and-ivory cup and Modern silver-plated cocktail shaker. In 1936, he set up an architecture practice with C.S. White. He designed the Wedgwood factory at Barlaston, Staffordshire, opened in 1940. His celebrated matt-glazed pottery for Wedgwood, particularly his matt green and matt straw glazes of 1933–35, became a classic of 1930s Modernism in Britain. In 1946, he returned briefly to Wedgwood, designing sprigged ware not commercially sold, and the *Commonwealth Service*. He returned full time to architecture, practicing in the firm of Murray Ward in London.

▶ His work was included in the 1933 'British Industrial Art in Relation to the Home' exhibition at Dorland Hall in London, at the 1933 (V) Triennale di Milano where he won a gold medal, 1935 'British Art in Industry' at the Royal Academy in London, 1935 'English Pottery Old and New' at the Victoria and Albert Museum in London, and 1979–80 'Thirties' exhibition at the Hayward Gallery in London. His work was the subject of the 1935 one-person exhibition at the Medici Galleries in London. His *Commonwealth Service* by Wedgwood was shown in the 'Design at Work' exhibition of the Royal Society of Arts and the Council of Industrial Design. In 1936, he was named one of the first ten Designers for Industry.

▶ Cat., *Thirties: British art and design before the war*, London: Arts Council of Great Britain, Hayward Gallery, 1979:23,93, 95,134,140,155,156,188,297,303.

Murray, William Staite
See Staite Murray, William.

Murrle, Bennett and Co
▶ British jeweler and silverware importer; located London.

▶ German entrepreneur Ernst Mürrle settled in Britain early in his business life. In 1895, he joined the firm and, in 1896, became co-owner of Murrle Bennett at 13 Charterhouse Street, London. Most of its inventory was imported from Pforzheim, particularly from Theodor Fahrner (including pieces by M.J. Gradl and Patriz Huber) and Wilhelm Führner. Some of these imports may have been specifically designed for the British market. The firm produced jewelry in the Modern style, influenced by Liberty's *Cymric* range, in an extensive range of designs, many in gold. Much of the high quality work was designed by established artists in the Arts and Crafts movement. Alongside close imitations of Liberty pieces, it produced models in the designs of Darmstadt and Munich Jugendstil. The firm had representatives in Edinburgh and South Africa, and exported to France. Immanuel Saake, a partner, managed the export activities of the firm; he was managing director, and Carl Hirth business manager, of the subsidiary Artistic Rolled Gold which became Artistic Novelties in 1909. Murrle Bennett was closed at the outbreak of World War I. Mürrle was interned on the Isle of Man and, in 1916, exchanged for prisoners. In 1916, the firm's stock and premises became the property of the British employees and was renamed Whyte, Redgrove and Whyte. After the war, Mürrle and Saake set up a new export and wholesale operation.

▶ Charlotte Gere, *American and European Jewelry 1830–1914*, New York: Crown, 1975:211–12. Deanna F. Cera (ed.), *Jewels of Fantasy: Costume Jewelry of the 20th Century*, New York: Abrams, 1992:110.

Muthesius, Friedrich Eckart (1904–89)
▶ German designer and architect; born Berlin; son of Hermann Muthesius.

▶ Studied Vereinigte Staatsschule für angewandte Kunst, Berlin, and London Polytechnic.

▶ Charles Rennie Mackintosh designed the 1904 christening flatware set for his godchild Friedrich Muthesius. Muthesius worked for architects James and Yerbury, Raymond Unwin, and for his father Hermann Muthesius. With Klemens Weigel, Muthes-

ius supervised the 1929–33 decoration and furnishing of the palace Manik Bagh (Garden of Rubies) of the Maharaja of Indore, whom Muthesius met in 1929 at Oxford. He coordinated the contributions of Jacques-Émile Ruhlmann, Eileen Gray, Le Corbusier, René Herbst, Louis Sognot, Charlotte Alix, and others, although much of the furniture and lighting was designed by Muthesius. The writer Henri-Pierre Roché assembled the collection. 1936–39, Muthesius was consulting architect to the Board of Planning and Restoration of Indore in the state of Madhya Pradesh (India), returning at the onset of World War II to Berlin, where he worked as an architect.

▶ Peter Adams, *Eileen Gray, Architect/Designer*, New York: Abrams, 1987:187–88. Annelies Krekel-Aalberse, *Art Nouveau and Art Déco Silver*, New York: Abrams, 1989:29.

▶ See **Maharaja of Indore**

Muthesius, Hermann (1861–1927)
▶ German architect, designer, and theorist; born Gross-Neuhausen; father of Friedrich Muthesius.

▶ Studied Technische Hochschule, Berlin-Charlottenburg.

▶ He worked in the offices of Wallot, and of Ende und Böckmann in Tokyo. 1896–1903, he was 'attaché for architecture' at the Germany Embassy in London and reported on the British Arts and Crafts movement. In 1898, he wrote on C.R. Ashbee's Guild and School of Handicrafts in *Dekorative Kunst* magazine, and *Der Kunstgewerbliche Dilettantismus*, drawing attention to the London Home Arts and Industries Association, which held annual exhibitions at the Royal Albert Hall. He also published two books on contemporary British architecture, followed by another on British church architecture. The three-volume *Das englische Haus* (1904–05), publishing the work of C.F.A. Voysey and others, contributed to a renaissance in domestic architecture on the continent. Muthesius wrote the British section in *Die Krisis im Kunstgewerbe*, edited by R. Graul, which played a key role in introducing British Arts and Crafts doctrines to German industry and paved the way for the Modern movement. From 1904, he was important in the reform of German schools of design and actively promoted design in German industry. In 1904, he visited the 'Louisiana Purchase Exhibition' in St. Louis, Missouri. In 1907, as superintendent of the Prussian Board of Trade for Schools of Arts and Crafts, he became a founding member with Walter Gropius, Marcel Breuer, Peter Behrens, and others of the Deutscher Werkbund, and was a strong advocate of standardization through that organization. He was a friend of Charles Rennie Mackintosh, godfather of Muthesius's son Friedrich.

▶ The 'Hermann Muthesius, 1861–1927' exhibition was mounted in Berlin in 1978 and at the Architectural Association in London in 1979.

▶ J. Posener, 'Hermann Muthesius,' *Architects' Year Book*, No. 10, 1962:45–61. Cat., J. Posener and S. Günther (eds.), *Hermann Muthesius 1861–1927*, Berlin: Akademie der Künste, 1977. Dennis Sharp (ed.), *Hermann Muthesius 1861–1927*, London: Architectural Association, 1979. Hans-Joachim Hubrich, *Hermann Muthesius, Die Schriften*, Berlin: Gebrüder Mann, 1980.

MUZHYZ
See Vhutemas

Muzika, František (1900–74)
▶ Czech painter and book and set designer.

▶ He was linked to the Devětsil group. Muzika's early work showed a kind of poetic primitivism. He left Devětsil in 1922 and joined the Nová skupina group, whose members were followers of the original Devětsil plan. Turning to Cubism in 1926, he worked in the 1930s in a style close to Surrealism.

▶ A large collection of his works were shown at the 1922 First Sprint Exhibition.

▶ Cat., *Devětsil: Czech Avant-Garde Art, Architecture, and Design of the 1920s and 30s*, Oxford Museum of Modern Art and London Design Museum, 1990.

Muzio, Giovanni (1893–1982)
▶ Italian architect; born Milan.
▶ Studied Politecnico di Milano to 1915.
▶ Muzio, along with Marcello Piacentini, Piero Portaluppi, and Giò Ponti, was a leading figure in Italian neo-Monumentalism, which was influenced by classical Roman forms, opposed to Rationalism, and came to be the official architectural expression of Fascism. Muzio's 1923 Ca'brutta house (his best known early work) in Milan, Vittorio Colonnese's house in the Via Moscova in Milan, and Piacentini's group of buildings at the Piazza della Vittoria in Genoa and his Ambasciatori Hotel in Rome were typical examples of the official architectural vocabulary. Muzio's Ca'brutta formally paid homage to the paintings of Giorgio de Chirico. He designed the classical-Modern Palace of the Arts in the park near the Sforza castle in which the 1933 (V) Triennale di Milano was housed, exhibiting a series of shows of the works of Walter Gropius, Mies van der Rohe, Erich Mendelsohn, Adolf Loos, Le Corbusier, Frank Lloyd Wright, André Lurçat, and Antonio Sant'Elia and rooms devoted to CIAM. Muzio and Sironi also designed the graphic arts hall there. 1935–63, Muzio taught at the Politecnico di Milano. His work after World War II included urban projects in Bergamo, Milan, Portugal, and elsewhere, and numerous churches and apartment and office buildings in Lombardy.
▶ His work was included in the 1930 (IV) Monza 'Esposizione Triennale delle Arti Decorative e Industriali Moderne.'
▶ Alberto Galardi, *New Italian Architecture*, New York: Praeger, 1967:14. Barbie Campbell-Cole and Tim Benton (eds.), *Tubular Steel Furniture*, London: The Art Book Company, 1979:46. Richard Etlin, 'In Memoriam, Giovanni Muzio: 1893–1983,' *Skyline*, Nov. 1982:17. Vittorio Gregotti in Vittorio Magnago Lampugnani (ed.), *Encyclopedia of 20th-Century Architecture*, Abrams, 1986:169.

Myrbach, Felician von (1853–1940)
▶ Polish painter, designer, and graphic artist; born Zaleszczyki (now Ukraine).
▶ Myrbach became head of the Kunstgewerbeschule, Vienna, in 1899. Under him, Josef Hoffman was in charge of architecture and Koloman Moser of painting. In 1903, Myrbach became a founding member of the Wiener Werkstätte.
▶ Robert Waissenberger, *Vienna 1890–1920*, Secaucus, NJ: Wellfleet 1984:125,268.

Myrbor
▶ French collaborative and gallery; located Paris.
▶ The Myrbor workshop and gallery was established in the 1920s by Marie Cuttoli in Paris. In 1929, André Lurçat designed its store at 17 rue Vignon. In 1929, Ernö Goldfinger designed its Marrakesh carpet factory (unrealized). Primarily a gallery for paintings and *objets d'art*, Myrbor operated a small workshop for weaving rugs and was frequently commissioned to execute the decoration of interiors. Pablo Picasso, Jean Lurçat, Joan Miró, Marcel Dufy, and Fernand Léger designed rugs made in limited editions. During the 1920s and 1930s, the popularity of these weavings led to a revival not only of the French rug but also of tapestry.
▶ James Dunnett and Gavin Stamp (eds.), *Ernö Goldfinger*, London: Architectural Association, 1983:18.
▶ See Cuttoli, Marie

Myrdam, Leif Heiberg (1938–)
▶ Norwegian ceramicist.
▶ Studied Statens Håndverks -og Kunstindustriskole, Oslo.
▶ He was apprenticed under Erik Pløen and, in 1967, set up his own workshop.
▶ Fredrik Wildhagen, *Norge i Form*, Oslo: Stenersen, 1988:164.

N

Nabis

▶ French artists' group; active Paris.

▶ Paul Sérusier, Jean-Édouard Vuillard, Maurice Denis, H. G. Ibels, Paul Ranson, and Pierre Bonnard studied together at the Académie Julian in Paris in the late 1880s, regularly congregating in the nearby café Brady. Led by Sérusier and Paul Gauguin, the artists formed the Nabis group in 1888. Its name, coined by poet Henri Cazalis, was based on the Hebrew word for 'prophets,' and was an ironic allusion to the fact that their attitude towards Gauguin's work was based on a kind of religious enlightenment. Bonnard became known as the *Nabi japonard*; his early work incorporated flat silhouettes and arabesques that were greatly influenced by Japanese prints, Symbolists painters, and the canvases of Gauguin. Before he turned to sculpture, Aristide Maillol showed his work with the Nabis, whose members included musician Claude-Achille Debussy for a time. The group emphasized color and form, revolutionizing traditional aesthetics in painting, printmaking, posters, book illustration, theater design, and the design of textiles, furniture, graphics, and stained glass. Opposed to the naturalism of Impressionism and attracted to linear distortion, the group was influential among the Symbolists in literature, poetry, theater, journalism, as illustrated in *Revue Blanche*.

▶ The Nabis mounted their last exhibition in 1889 at Galerie Durand, Paris, in homage to Odilon Redon. The 1892 exhibition of Nabis works was mounted at the gallery of art dealer Le Barc de Boutteville, Paris.

▶ Yvonne Brunhammer et al., *Art Nouveau Belgium, France*, Houston: Rice University, 1976. Ian Chilvers and Harold Osborne (eds.), *The Oxford Dictionary of Art*, Oxford: Oxford University, 1988:349. Claire Frèsches-Thory and Antoine Terrasse, *The Nabis: Bonnard, Vuillard and Their Circle*, New York: Abrams, 1991. *Dictionnaire de l'art moderne et contemporain*, Paris: Hazan, 1992: 440.

Naço, Studio

▶ French group of architects and designers; active Paris.

▶ Architects Marcelo Joulia Lagares, Nicolas Maganan, and Alain Renk founded Studio Naço in Paris in 1986, becoming active in interior architecture, industrial design, and communication. They designed schemes for stores, including Kookaï, Bathroom Graffiti, and Michel Bachoz, and for offices and exhibitions. Their 1988 *Belfort* armchair in cast aluminum for the General Council of Belfort was sponsored by VIA and produced by Mobilier National. The group designed lighting fixtures for Luminance in the Netherlands and, in France, for Electrorama and Lucien Gau. Its electrical appliance line was produced by Dewoo in Korea, tea service and lighting by Hisense in Japan, and 1992 *Ondine* table lamp by Lucien Gau.

▶ The group won the 1988 prize for the design of the office of the General Council of Belfort and first prize for its furniture at the 1988 'Objet 2000' exhibition. In 1987, its work was shown at the VIA gallery in Paris and its *Ondine* lamp at the 1992 Salon du luminaire in Paris.

▶ Cat., *Les années VIA*, Paris: Musée des Arts Décoratifs, 1990. Suzanne Tise, 'Innovators at the Museum,' *Vogue Décoration*, No. 26, June/July 1990:48. François Mathey, *Au bonheur des formes, design français 1945–1992*, Paris: Regard, 1992:130,176, 212, 300.

Naggar, Patrick (1946–)

▶ French architect and designer.

▶ Studied École des Beaux-Arts, Paris, to 1972; 1977–82, philosophy under Michel Serres.

▶ From 1972, he collaborated with Dominique Lachevsky on architecture, interior design, furniture design, and packaging. They designed displays for Cacharel and Paloma Picasso perfumes and furniture produced by Arc International and Écart International. Their 1989 *Fauteuil Elytre* and 1989 *Miroir 1* and *Miroir 2* were produced by Néotù.

▶ His and Lachevsky's furniture was included in the 1985 exhibition at the Jensen showroom in Paris.

Nakao, Yuko (1956–)

▶ Japanese glass designer.

▶ 1987, studied Pilchuck Glass School, Stanwood, Washington; Tokyo University of Arts to 1983; and Tokyo Glass Crafts Institute to 1988.

▶ Work included in 1988 'International Exhibition of Glass Craft,' Industrial Gallery of Ishikawa Prefecture, Kanazawa; 1989 'Arte en Vidro,' São Paulo Art Museum; 1990 ' Glass '90 in Japan,' Tokyo; and 1991 (V) Triennale of the Japan Glass Art Crafts Association, Heller Gallery, New York. Included in 1988–89 'Corning Glass Review,' *Neues Glas* magazine. Received 1990 Section Prize, 'Asahi Modern Craft,' Japan.

▶ Cat., *Glass Japan*, New York: Heller Gallery and Japan Glass Art Crafts Association, 1991: No. 28.

Nakashima, George (1905–1990)

▶ American woodworker and designer; born Spokane, Washington.

▶ Studied architecture, University of Washington, Seattle, to 1929; 1929, École Americaine des Beaux-Arts, Fontainebleau; architecture, Massachusetts Institute of Technology, Cambridge, Massachusetts, to 1930.

▶ In 1934, he worked in the Indian office of American architect Antonin Raymond and, in 1937, in the Tokyo office, where he studied Japanese carpentry techniques. In 1941, he set up his first workshop in Seattle. Interned in 1942 in Idaho, Nakashima studied with an old Japanese carpenter until Antonin Raymond arranged his release; Raymond had a farm and office in New Hope, Pennsylvania, where Nakashima moved in 1943 and started a small furniture business. He regarded his work as fine art and seldom sold to manufacturers or retail clients. Most of his work was custom made and site specific. Nakashima worked with untrimmed slabs of wood, particularly black walnut and redwood, leaving rough edges and knot holes in the final piece; he did most of the shaping and finishing by hand. His designs showed the influences of the Windsor chair, Shaker craftsmanship, Japanese woodworking, and contemporary forms. He made furniture and furnishings for Nelson A. Rockefeller's Tarrytown, New York, home and designed interiors for International Paper and Columbia

University, both in New York. From a piece of English walnut weighing 1,500 lbs (700kg), he executed the 1968 heart-shaped *Altar for Peace* at the Cathedral of St. John the Divine in New York. At the time of his death, he was working to replace the 111-piece collection of furniture and furnishings in a Princeton, New Jersey, home destroyed by fire in 1989. His daughter Mira Yarnall-Nakashima became vice-president of George Nakashima Woodworker.

▶ He was awarded the 1952 gold medal for craftsmanship by the American Institute of Architects, made a fellow of the American Craft Council in 1979, and received the 1981 Hazlett Award. His work was shown at the New York Museum of Modern Art, Renwick Gallery in Washington, 1983–84 'Design Since 1945' exhibition at the Philadelphia Museum of Art, and 1989 one-person exhibition at the American Craft Museum in New York.

▶ Wolfgang Saxon, *The New York Times*, 17 June 1990: L30. Cat., Kathryn B. Hiesinger and George H. Marcus III (eds.), *Design Since 1945*, Philadelphia Museum of Art, 1983:223,III–57. George Nakashima, *The Soul of a Tree: A Woodworker's Reflections*, Tokyo, 1981. *The Torch*, No. 91, June 1991:8. Derek E. Ostergard, *George Nakashima: Full Circle*, New York: Weidenfeld and Nicholson, 1989. Whitney Blousen, 'George Nakashima' in Mel Byars and Russell Flinchum (eds.), *50 American Designers*, Washington: Preservation, 1994.

Nancy, École de
See École de Nancy

Nannipieri, Renzo (1934–)
▶ Italian designer; born Cascina; active Pisa.
▶ Nannipieri began his professional career in 1959. His clients in Italy included Pianca, Map, Battistelli, Cosmo, Roberti, Luxor, Tisa, LBA, and GBF. He was a member of ADI (Associazione per il Disegno Industriale).
▶ *ADI Annual 1976*, Milan: Associazione per il Disegno Industriale, 1976.

Napier
▶ American costume jewelry firm; located Meriden, Connecticut.
▶ Whitney and Rice was founded in 1875 in North Attleboro, Massachusetts. In 1882, the name was changed to Carpenter and Bliss, then E.A. Bliss. Producing personal objects and gift items, it moved to Meriden, Connecticut, in 1891. The factory produced war materials during both World Wars. Named for its president James H. Napier, the firm became Napier in 1922. Its designs were known for simple forms (circles, triangles, and squares) and clean lines. Still active today, the firm is the largest private producer of costume jewelry in the USA, with factories in Meriden and Providence, Rhode Island.
▶ Deanna F. Cera (ed.), *Jewels of Fantasy: Costume Jewelry of the 20th Century*, New York: Abrams, 1992:218.

Nardi, Claudio (1951–)
▶ Italian designer; born Parto, Firenze.
▶ 1971–78, Nardi was active in interior design, first with Design Center and subsequently with International Design. He designed homes and shops including Ferragamo, Capri; posters and publicity and (with Carlo Scarpa) a new shop for International Design; 1977–79, was active in interior design and (with the cooperative Cooplan) worked on town planning for Roccastrada; in 1980, when Cooplan was dissolved, he became an independent designer; designed part of 'GlasHominis' exhibition sponsored by Florence town council, and the 'Scenic Parks' exhibition; renovated apartments, offices and showrooms including Luisa Via Roma, Luisa il Corso, Studio Piccinini, Ausonia offices, and Touche showroom, Rome; designed jewelry, lighting, furniture, and ceramics.
▶ Fumio Shimizu and Matteo Thun (eds.), *The Descendants of Leonardo: The Italian Design*, Tokyo, 1987:327.

Narkompros
▶ Soviet government institution.
▶ Narkompros (The People's Commissariat for Enlightenment) was established in 1917 in Petrograd and Moscow under A. Lunacharsky, who recruited many artists, mainly in its Izo (Fine Arts Department). Futurist artist David Shterenberg was overall president and deputy head of the Moscow Izo, with Vladimir Tatlin. The department was in charge of all visual arts activities from exhibitions to art education, including the establishment of Svomas (The Moscow Free State Art Studios) in Petrograd and Moscow. Izo's board initially consisted of David Shterenberg (president), Nikolai Punin (deputy head, Petrograd), Petr Vaulin, Alexei Karev, Aleksandr Matveev, Natan Al'tman, Sergei Chekhonin, and Yatmonov. The Petrograd Izo was moderate and artistically eclectic. Vaulin, Chekhonin, and Shterenberg were in charge of the Lomonosov Porcelain Factory. The artists who held executive positions within the system were granted the power to 'construct everything anew.'
▶ Nina Lobanov-Rostovsky, *Revolutionary Ceramics*, London: Studio Vista, 1990. Igor Golomstock, *Totalitarian Art in the Soviet Union, The Third Reich, Fascist Italy and the People's Republic of China*, New York: Icon, 1990:14–15. Cat., *The Great Utopia: The Russian and Soviet Avant-Garde, 1915–1932*, New York: Guggenheim Museum, 1992.

Nash, Paul (1889–1946)
▶ British painter and designer; born London.
▶ 1906–08, studied Chelsea Polytechnic, London; from 1908, London County Council Art School; 1910–11, Slade School of Fine Art, London.
▶ He worked at the Omega workshops in 1914 and became a member of the London Group. In 1919, he became a member of the New English Art Club. 1917–19, he was an official war artist. 1924–25 and 1938–40, he was assistant instructor at the Royal College of Art in London. In 1927, he became a member of the London Artists' Association. In 1928, Curwen Press produced his patterned paper and, in the same year, the London Passenger Transport Board used his moquette fabric for seating in railway cars. Under the pseudonym Robert Derriman, he was art critic for the periodicals *New Witness*, 1919; *Weekend Review*, 1930–33; and *The Listener*, 1931–35. 1925–29, his first textiles were hand-printed by Mrs Eric Kennington at her workshop Footprints. He designed dress fabrics for Tom Heron's firm Cresta Silks Ltd; He executed watercolor illustrations with collotype bases, colored by stencil (the last to be reproduced this way) and printed in a 1930 edition of *Urne Buriall and the Gardens of Cyrus* by Thomas Browne. Nash was a juror for the Carnegie International Competition in Pittsburgh. His 1932 bathroom design for the dancer Tilly Losch incorporated glass in a dazzling manner; it was covered in silvered 'Stippled Cathedral' glass; the sanitary fittings were black-glazed earthenware. In 1933, he founded the artists' group Unit One, whose purpose was primarily promotional. 1933–36, he designed decorations for ceramic tableware produced by E. Brain of Fenton (where T.A. Fennemore was artistic director). In 1934, Nash designed crystal produced by Stuart of Stourbridge. He published the *Shell County Guide to Dorset* (1935) and *Shell County Guide to Buckinghamshire*. He contributed to the journal *Axis 1*. 1940–45, he was again an official war artist for the War Artists Committee chaired by Kenneth Clark. One of the eight founding members of the Society of Industrial Artists, Nash was the first practicing designer to be president, 1932–34.
▶ His work was the subject of the 1912 one-person exhibition at the Carfax Gallery. In 1914, he exhibited at the Friday Club. In 1917, his war drawings were shown at the Goupil Gallery and Leicester Gallery. His ceramics were included in the 1934 'Modern Art for the Table' exhibition at Harrods department store in London. His work was included in the 1934 exhibition of Unit One members at the Mayor Gallery and traveling elsewhere; 1936 London 'International Surrealist Exhibition'; 1937 exhibitions at the Redfern Gallery and London Gallery; 1937 Surrealist Section of

the American Institute of Architects; and 1939 New York 'World's Fair.'

▶ Cat., *Paul Nash as Designer*, London: Victoria and Albert Museum, 1975. Cat., *Thirties: British art and design before the war*, London: Arts Council of Great Britain, Hayward Gallery, 1979:35,36,81,95,133,155,168,177,185,220,231,280,286,289, 297. Muriel Emanuel et al. (eds.), *Contemporary Artists*, New York: St. Martin's, 1983:664. Valerie Mendes, *The Victoria & Albert Museum's Textiles from 1900 to 1937*, London: Victoria and Albert Museum, 1992.

Nason e Moretti
▶ Italian glassware manufacturer; located Venice.
▶ The firm was founded in Venice in 1923. Its directors, Umberto Nason and Carlo Moretti, executed glassware of their own designs. In 1955, Nason developed a technique whereby white glass was used on the insides of bowls and drinking glasses.
▶ The firm's 1955 white-glass-lined vessels won the 1955 Premio Compasso d'Oro and were included in the 1979 'Design & design' exhibition in Milan and Venice.
▶ Cat., Kathryn B. Hiesenger and George H. Marcus III (eds.), *Design Since 1945*, Philadelphia: Philadelphia Museum of Art, 1983:224,II—44. Cat., *Design & design*, Milan: Palazzo delle Stelline, 1979:42.

Natalini, Adolfo   (1941–)
▶ Italian designer; born Pistoia.
▶ Studied architecture, Università di Firenze, to 1966.
▶ In 1966 with Cristiano Toraldo di Francia, he established the Superstudio group, Florence, which took a more conceptual route to design than its sister group Archizoom. Superstudio's members included Natalini, Toraldo di Francia, Roberto Magris, Gian Piero Frassinelli, and Alessandro Magris. Natalini specialized in town planning and, along with Superstudio members, initiated Radical Architecture in the early 1970s; in 1979, participated in a number of projects for historical cities including Frankfurt, Jerusalem, Mannheim, Karlsruhe, Strasbourg, Parma, and Florence; from 1973, taught architecture, Università di Firenze; designed the 1987 *Volumina* secretaire (with Guglielmo Renzi) produced by Sawaya & Moroni. Design clients included Poltronova, Arflex, Driadle, Mirabili; was artistic director for numerous firms; published *Figure di Pietra* (1984) and *Architetture raccontate* (Electa, 1989).
▶ Received first prize in Internazionale Architetture di Pietra; 1988 Marble Architectural Award. His *Torri d'avorio su terremoti* study area was shown at the 1985 (XVIII) Triennale di Milano.
▶ *Le Affinità Elettive*, Milan: Electa, 1985. Auction cat., *Asta di Modernariato 1900–1986, Auction 'Modernariato,'* Milan: Semenzato Nuova Geri, 1986: Lot 115. Albrecht Bangert and Karl Michael Armer, *80s Style: Designs of the Decade*, New York: Abbeville, 1990:33,233. *Modo*, No. 148, March–April 1993:123.

Nathan, Fernand
▶ French painter, decorator, and furniture designer; born Marseilles.
▶ A painter before becoming active as an interior architect, he was a cabinetmaker and designer of lighting, printed fabrics, and furniture. His furniture reflected the influences of Chippendale, Louis XVI, Directoire, Restauration, and Louis Philippe styles. Some of Nathan's furniture was produced by Beyne. From 1922, he designed simple lacquered models for La Maîtrise decorating studio of the Galeries Lafayette department store in Paris. Some of his fabric designs were produced by Cornille.
▶ He first showed his work (a dining room) at the 1913 Salon of the Société des Artistes Décorateurs.
▶ *Ensembles Mobiliers*, Vol. II, Paris: Charles Moreau, 1937. Pierre Kjellberg, *Art Déco: les maîtres du Mobilier, le décor des Paquebots*, Paris: Amateur, 1986:131–32.

Natter, Alice
▶ French milliner; active Paris.
▶ After World War I, couturier and decorator Paul Poiret commissioned hats from his friend Madeleine Panizon. Alice Natter had been a student at Poiret's Martine School and worked with Poiret after World War I; he assigned her to work with Panizon to design hats and hairstyles appropriate for his dresses.
▶ Victor Arwas, *Art Déco*, Abrams, 1980. Cat., *Decorative Arts 1925 Style*, New York: Didier Aaron, 1979.

Natzler, Gertrude Amon   (1908–71) and Otto Natzler (1908–)
▶ Austrian ceramicists; born Vienna.
▶ 1926, Gertrude Natzler studied Handelsakademie, Vienna; Otto Natzler studied Lehranstadt für Textilindustrie, Vienna; 1934, both studied under Franz Iskra, Vienna.
▶ Until 1933, they worked as textile designers; in 1934, they set up their first studio and developed a purist style distinct from the ornate work of the Wiener Werkstätte. Gertrude threw the forms and Otto handled the glazes. In 1939, they settled in Los Angeles; 1939–42, taught ceramics; became known for their technical expertise, especially in their art pottery and glaze technology. In 1976, Otto Natzler began to produce slab work.
▶ They received numerous awards including a silver medal at 1937 Paris 'Exposition Internationale des Arts et Techniques dans la Vie Moderne'; first prize, Ceramic National, Syracuse, New York. Work shown at 1959 (XX) 'Ceramic International Exhibition' at the Metropolitan Museum of Art in New York. Otto Natzler's work (slab constructions) shown at 1977 exhibition, Craft and Folk Art Museum, Los Angeles, and other work elsewhere. Work was the subject of a 1993 exhibition at American Craft Museum, New York.
▶ Garth Clark, *American Ceramics: 1876 to the Present*, New York: Abbeville, 1987:285–86. R. Craig Miller, *Modern Design, 1890–1990*, New York: Abrams, 1990. Auction cat., 'Contemporary Works of Art,' Sotheby's New York, 14 March 1992.

Naumov, Aleksandr Il'ich   (1899–1928)
▶ Russian poster and interior designer.
▶ 1909–17, studied Stroganov School of Applied Art, Moscow; 1918–21, Vkhutemas, Moscow.
▶ From 1918, he participated in several exhibition, was a member of the Union of Youth of the October Group and of the Bmokhuo, designed sets for theaters in Moscow and film posters, and organized exhibitions. In 1928, he settled in Cologne.
▶ Cat., *Kunst und Revolution: Russische und Sowjetische Kunst 1910–1932*, Vienna: Österreichisches Museum für angewandte Kunst, 1988.

Nautilus-Technologia Creativa Associati
▶ Italian design group; located Milan.
▶ The cooperative was established in 1985 by a group of young designers in charge of various areas: Vincenzo Di Dato (industrial design), Ivano Boscardini (visual design), Giacomo Schieppati (electronic hardware engineering), and Morerio Manzini (electronic software engineering). (Di Dato and Boscardini had collaborated from 1982.) The firm specialized in industrial and visual design, electronic engineering, and the application of new technologies; had clients including Alacta, Ectasis, Axil.
▶ Received 1987 Premio Compasso d'Oro for a climbing boot for Asolo.
▶ Fumio Shimizu and Matteo Thun (eds.), *The Descendants of Leonardo: The Italian Design*, Tokyo, 1987:327. *Modo*, No. 148, March–April 1993:123.

Nava, Cesare Augusto   (1941–)
▶ Italian designer; active Desio.
▶ Nava began his professional career in 1970, designing furniture and furnishings for various clients. He was a member of ADI (Associazione per il Disegno Industriale).
▶ *ADI Annual 1976*, Milan: Associazione per il Disegno Industriale, 1976.

Nava, Riccardo (1942–)

▶ Italian industrial designer; born and active Milan.

▶ Nava, Giorgio Romani, Duccio Soffientini, and Alessandro Ubertazzi set up the interior design center DA in 1968. He was associated with the magazine *Interni* and the firm Faema, and in 1968 was on the committee of the Compasso d'Oro award of ADI. He designed technical instruments and clocks and, from 1970, was a consultant on the ergonomic aspects of precision instruments. From 1975, he designed a range of sailboat equipment (including block and tackle) for Nemo in Sarsina and the Comar shipyard in Forlì. His clients in Italy included Italora (domestic clocks and electronics), Superband (large thermoformed production), and Svaba. He was a member of ADI (Associazione per il Disegno Industriale).

▶ He participated in national and international competitions.

▶ *ADI Annual 1976*, Milan: Associazione per il Disegno Industriale, 1976.

Navarre, Henri (1885–1970)

▶ French sculptor, architect, silversmith, and glassmaker; born Paris.

▶ Served apprenticeships in architecture, goldsmithing, and silversmithing; studied wood carving, École Bernard Palissy, and stained glass and mosaics, Conservatoire des Arts et Métiers, both Paris.

▶ He executed a number of monumental sculptures and architectural carvings. Influenced by Maurice Marinot, in 1924, he began to make simply shaped thick-walled glass vessels with internal decoration. His work in glass was produced in collaboration with André Thuret. In 1927, he executed a gilded reredos for the chapel of the 1926 oceanliner *Île-de-France*.

▶ At the 1925 Paris 'Exposition Internationale des Arts Décoratifs et Industriels Modernes,' he executed the frieze on the Monumental Gate. He designed the Grille of Honor of the Colonial Museum at the 1931 Paris 'Exposition Coloniale.' Exhibiting in Brussels, Cairo, Stockholm, Oslo, Athens, and New York, he also showed his work at the Salons of the Société Nationale des Beaux-Arts, Salons d'Automne, and Salons of the Société des Artistes Décorateurs.

▶ Cat., *Verriers français contemporains: Art et industrie*, Paris: Musée des Arts Décoratifs, 1982.

Naver, Kim (1940–)

▶ Danish weaver and designer.

▶ In 1966, Naver completed weaving apprenticeship under Lis Ahlmann and Vibeke Klint.

▶ In 1966, she set up her own workshop; designed industrial and ecclesiastical textiles and wove tapestries and carpets; from 1971, designed jewelry for the Georg Jensen Damaskværveriet, Kolding. Her commissions included five 1978–79 tapestries for the reception hall of the National Bank of Denmark, Copenhagen, and, in 1978, designs for C. Olesen (Cotil); Paustian; C. Danel, and Finnlayson. In 1978, she became a member of the Sterling Committee of the Skolen for Brugskunst, Copenhagen; in 1982, chair of the Kunsthåndværkerrådet (Decorative Arts Council).

▶ Received 1970 Lunning Prize.

▶ Cat., *Georg Jensen Silversmithy: 77 Artists, 75 Years*, Washington: Smithsonian Institution Press, 1980. Cat., *The Lunning Prize*, Stockholm: Nationalmuseum, 1986:202–05.

Navone, Paola (1950–)

▶ Italian designer; active Milan.

▶ Studied architecture, University of Turin, to 1973.

▶ She collaborated with design magazines in Italy and, 1974–78, worked at the Kappa Center. She directed research at the Domus Study Center, and worked as a design consultant, including for Abet Laminati and lighting firms.

▶ Andrea Branzi, *La Casa Calda: Esperienze del Nuovo Disegno Italiano*, Milan: Idea Books, 1982.

Neagle, Richard (1922–)

▶ American industrial designer.

▶ Studied Pratt Institute, Brooklyn, New York.

▶ He joined a design partnership in 1949 and, in 1954, opened his own office in Westport, Connecticut. He was design director of Admiral Italiana and Pye Electronics in Italy, and design consultant to Armstrong Cork and Monsanto in the USA. His range of objects included furniture, radio and TV sets, refrigerators, washing machines, telephones, plastic housewares, and partition systems. Neagle's 1968 *Nike* chair, produced by Sormani, was among the first to be made in plastic by the process of vacuum forming.

▶ The *Nike* chair was first shown at the 1968 Salone del Mobile in Milan, and at the 1970 'Modern Chairs, 1918–1970' exhibition at the Whitechapel Gallery in London.

▶ Cat., *Modern Chairs, 1918–1970*, London: Lund Humphries, 1971.

Nechanski, Arnold (1888–1938)

▶ Austrian architect and silversmith; active Vienna and Berlin.

▶ 1909–13, studied Kunstgewerbeschule, Vienna, under Josef Hoffmann.

▶ He designed for the Wiener Werkstätte from 1912. In 1913, he designed silver for A. Pollak in Vienna. 1919–33, he was an instructor at the Kunstgewerbeschule in Berlin and, 1921–33, taught metalworking at the Meisterschule für Kunsthandwerk in Berlin.

▶ Annelies Krekel-Aalberse, *Art Nouveau and Art Déco Silver*, New York: Abrams, 1989:257.

Nelson, George (1907–1986)

▶ American industrial designer; born Hartford, Connecticut; active New York.

▶ 1928–31, studied architecture, Yale University; 1931, Catholic University of America, Washington; 1932–34, American Academy in Rome.

▶ 1936–37, he wrote about International Style architects in a series of articles in the journal *Pencil Points*. He promoted Modernism and was instrumental in introducing Mies van der Rohe to America; 1935–43, Nelson was associate editor of the journal *Architectural Forum* and, 1944–49, consultant editor. 1936–41, in partnership with William Hamby in New York, he worked on architecture and interior design projects. He pioneered pedestrian malls in his 1942 'Grass on Main Street' concept. 1942–45, he taught at Columbia University in New York. In 1947, he opened his own architecture and design office in New York. From 1953, he was a partner in New York with Gordon Chadwick on architecture and industrial design projects. Although an architect by training and profession, he designed few buildings; his interests lay with furniture, and industrial, exhibition, and urban design, although most of his firm's designs were done by others on his staff: Ernest Farmer executed many furniture designs for Herman Miller, including the *EOG* office system; John Pile, the *Steelframe* storage system, seating systems, and other Herman Miller products; William Renwick, the *Bubble* lamp and GE kitchen systems; John Svezia, the *Sling* sofa; and Don Ervin and George Tscherny, graphics. Conceived in Nelson's office, the *Storagewall* concept received wide public notice through its initial appearance in a 1945 issue of *LIFE* magazine and led to a collaboration with Herman Miller, for which he executed numerous furniture designs. 1946–65, he was design director at Herman Miller. Nelson was responsible for Herman Miller's distinguished rostrum of designers, including Charles Eames from 1946 and Alexander Girard from 1952. Though a productive designer, Nelson was best known during his lifetime for his writing and lectures. He repudiated, with others of the European School, the commercialism of Raymond Loewy and other purveyors of styling. He executed designs for thin-skinned *Bubble* lamps (with Renwick) of *c*1953 and for numerous clocks produced by Howard Miller and plastic dinnerware produced by Prolon. Nelson's office design credits for Herman Miller included the slat bench and accompanying 1946 modular system of cabinets, 1954 *Steelframe* group, 1956 *Coconut* chair and thin-edge case goods, 1959 *Catenary* furniture group, 1963 *Sling* sofa, *Marshmellow* sofa, 1964 *Action Office 1* (based on a Robert Probst concept), and 1971 *Executive Office* group. Nelson's office designed the 1968 *Editor 2* typewriter by Olivetti. Herman Miller interiors included the 1948 Chicago showroom; 1953 and 1956 New York showrooms; 1964 Washington showroom; and 1962 and 1966 factory building in Zeeland, Michigan. In the late 1950s, Nelson became interested in exhibition design and concentrated on urban design problems. He designed the 1959 US exhibition in Moscow with Charles Eames, the 1967 US Industrial Design pavilion in the USSR, the Chrysler and Irish pavilions at the 1964 'New York World's Fair,' and 1976 'USA '76: The First Two Hundred Years' exhibition.

▶ His chairs were shown at the 1966 'Vijftig Jaar Zitten' at the Stedelijk Museum in Amsterdam, 1968 'Les Assises du siège contemporain' exhibition, Paris Musée des Arts Décoratifs, and 1982 'Space and Environment: Furniture by Architects' at the Whitney Museum of American Art in Fairfield, Connecticut. He won the 1964 Industrial Arts Medal from the American Institute of Architects and the 1965 Alcoa Industrial Design Award. In 1973, elected Honorary Royal Designer for Industry, London.

▶ George Nelson, *Tomorrow's House*, New York, 1945. George Nelson, *Living Spaces*, New York: Whitney Library of Ideas, 1952. George Nelson, *Chairs*, New York: Whitney Library of Ideas, 1953. George Nelson, *Problems of Design*, New York: Whitney Library of Ideas, 1957. George Nelson, *On Design*, New York: Whitney Library of Ideas, 1979. George Nelson, 'Modern Furniture: An Attempt to Explore Its Nature, Its Sources, and Its Probable Future,' *Interiors*, No. 108, July 1949:76–117. Cat., *Modern Chairs 1918–1970*, London: Lund Humphries, 1971. Cat., Kathryn B. Hiesinger and George H. Marcus III (eds.), *Design Since 1945*, Philadelphia: Philadelphia Museum of Art, 1983: 224,IV–27,VI–16. Olga Gueft, 'George Nelson' in 'Nelson/Eames/Girard/Probst: The Design Process at Herman Miller,' *Design Quarterly*, Nos. 98–99, 1975:11–19. Cat., *Les Assises du siège contemporain*, Paris: Musée des Arts Décoratifs, 1968. Cat., Lisa Phillips (introduction), *Shape and Environment: Furniture by American Architects*, New York: Whitney Museum of American Art, 1982:46–47. John Pile, *Dictionary of 20th Century Design*, New York: Facts on File, 1990:184–85. Olga Gueft, 'George Nelson' in Mel Byars and Russell Flinchum (eds.), *50 American Designers*, Washington: Preservation, 1994.

Nemo
See Domingo, Alain

Nencioni Moleri, Carla
▶ Italian designer; born and active Milan; wife of Armando Moleri.
▶ 1943–51, studied Accademia di Belle Arti, Bergamo.
▶ She began her professional career in 1968. She and her husband Armando Moleri collaborated on stainless-steel tableware produced by Zani & Zani, including the 1971 *Uni* picnic-flatware set, and on designs produced by Tecno Com Guastalla. She was a member of ADI (Associazione per il Disegno Industriale).
▶ *ADI Annual 1976*, Milan: Associazione per il Disegno Industriale, 1976.

Neo-Liberty, Stile
▶ Italian design movement.
▶ The Stile Neo-Liberty (Neo-Liberty Style) was a late 1950s revival of Art Nouveau forms. Its name was derived from Stile Liberty, the Italian expression of European Art Nouveau that flourished at the turn of the century and was named after Liberty in London.
▶ Cat., Kathryn B. Hiesinger and George H. Marcus III (eds.), *Design Since 1945*, Philadelphia: Philadelphia Museum of Art, 1983.

Néotù
▶ French furniture and furnishings gallery; located Paris.
▶ Néotù was founded in 1984 by Pierre Staudenmeyer and Gérard Dalmon. It represented the limited-production designs of Martin Székely, Bořek Šípek, Pucci de Rossi, Dan Friedman, Sylvain Dubuisson, the team of Elisabeth Garouste and Mattia

Bonetti, and others. The gallery was instrumental in establishing new French design in the 1980s, and assisted with production. In 1990, its branch in New York was established and, in 1992, began representing VIA there.
▶ See Dalmon, Gérard

Nervi, Pier Luigi (1891–1979)
▶ Italian architect; born Sondrio, Lombardy.
▶ Studied engineering, University of Bologna, to 1913.
▶ After experience with a concrete contractor, he set up his own firm in Bologna in 1923. His first structure was a 1927 cinema in Naples. His first important work was the 1930–32 Communal Stadium in Florence, widely published as an early example of Modern architecture. As he frequently argued in his writings, he believed that the creation of form was an activity equivalent to that of the artist or technician. He became known as the artist of reinforced concrete. His 'strength through form' experiments were expressed in his 1948–49 Turin exhibition building, considered his masterpiece, in which biomorphic units were used in a peripherally supported ceiling of enormous span. He later designed buildings that were simpler and quicker to construct. 1946–61, he was professor of structural engineering in the architecture department of the University of Rome. His other buildings included airplane hangars in Orvieto of 1935–38 and in Orbetello and Torre del Lago of 1940–43, 1950 Casino at the Lido in Rome, 1953–57 conference hall of the UNESCO building (with Marcel Breuer and Bernard Zehrfuss) in Paris, 1955–58 Pirelli building (with Gio Ponti and others) in Milan, 1955 Centre National des Industries (with Jean Prouvé) in Paris, 1956 circular exhibition building in Caracas (Venezuela), 1956–57 Palazzetto dello Sport Lavoro in Turin, and 1971 Papal audience chamber in the Vatican in Rome.
▶ Giulio Carlo Argan, *Pier Luigi Nervi*, Milan: Ed. Il Balcone, 1954. Gerd Hatje, *The Works of Pier Luigi Nervi*, London: Architectural Press, 1957. Ada Louise Huxtable, *Pier Luigi Nervi*, London, New York, 1960. Pier Luigi Nervi, *Nuove strutture*, Milan: Ed. di Monunità, 1963. L. Ramazzotti (ed.), *Nervi Oggi* (proceedings of the convention in Ancona), Rome, 1983.

Nespolo, Ugo (1941–)
▶ Italian painter, film maker, and designer; born Mosso Santa Maria; active Turin.
▶ He designed the 1987 collection of seven handmade rugs in the style of quilts produced by Elio Palmisano's Edizioni Tessili. His designs were hand-knotted with 40,000 Ghordes knots per square meter (1550 sq ins).
▶ His work was shown in New York, Cologne, London, Tokyo, Helsinki, Paris, Venice, Milan, and Turin.
▶ Albrecht Bangert and Karl Michael Armer, *80s Style: Designs of the Decade*, New York: Abbeville, 1990:183,233.

Neter-Kähler, Greten (1906–86)
▶ German textile designer; born Schleswig.
▶ 1924–25, apprenticed in handweaving studio, Munich; 1926–27, Kunstgewerbeschule, Flensburg; 1929–32, Bauhaus weaving workshop, Dessau.
▶ In 1928, she worked in a fashion house in Hamburg; in 1932 settled in the Netherlands and collaborated with Kitty van der Mijll Dekker and Hermann Fischer in a handweaving studio; 1929–34, was wife of Herman Fischer and, from 1934, of Bob Neter; specialized in silk and linen fabrics and liturgical textiles; 1935–37, was director of 'De Kerkuil' weaving studio, Amsterdam; 1945–82, directed textile department, School of Applied Arts, Amsterdam, and worked as a freelance weaver and designer.
▶ Sigrid Wortmann Weltge, *Women's Work: Textile Art from the Bauhaus*, London: Thames and Hudson, 1993.

Neubohn, Susanne (1960–)
▶ Swedish designer; born Kiruna; active Berlin.
▶ 1978–80, studied industrial design, Hochschule der Künste, Berlin.

▶ Neubohn, Inge Sommer, John Hirschberg, and Christof Walther set up the design office Berlinetta in Berlin in 1984. In addition to furniture, they were involved with town planning and environmental protection. Neubohn's limited-production 1988 *Floh* stool was produced by Berliner Zimmer.

▶ Berlinetta's work was included in numerous exhibitions including the 1988 'Les Avantgardes du Mobilier: Berlin' at Centre Georges Pompidou and Galerie Néotù in Paris, and 1987 solo exhibition 'Berlinetta-Furniture 84–86' in Cologne.

▶ Cat., Design Center Stuttgart, *Women in Design: Careers and Life Histories Since 1900*, Stuttgart: Haus der Wirtschaft, 1989: 78–81. Albrecht Bangert and Karl Michael Armer, *80s Style: Designs of the Decade*, New York: Abbeville, 1990:73,233.

▶ See Berlinetta

Neue Sachlichkeit

▶ German artists' movement.

▶ The term (meaning 'New Objectivity') was coined in 1924 by G.F. Hartlaub. *c*1923–33, the movement emphasized a new, supposedly impersonal, manner in architecture, design, fine art, graphics, and photography. Neue Sachlichkeit rejected Impressionism and, in particular, Expressionism; it valued Functionalism and social engagement. The 1925 'Magic Realists' exhibition in Mannheim was identified as being of the Neue Sachlichkeit. The term came to be applied to architecture of the Rationalist school, particularly in Germany.

Neutra, Richard Josef (1892–1970)

▶ Austrian architect and designer; born Vienna; active Los Angeles.

▶ Studied Technische Hochschule, Vienna, to 1917.

▶ Neutra's work was initially influenced by the Viennese Modernists, including Otto Wagner and Adolf Loos. In 1911, Neutra discovered the work of Frank Lloyd Wright through the portfolio *Ausgeführte Bauten und Entwürfe von Frank Lloyd Wright* (1910). After World War I, he worked in Switzerland; in 1919, Neutra and Karl Moser conducted seminars at the Eidgenössische Technische Hochschule in Zürich. 1919–20, he worked with landscape architect Gustav Amann in Zürich; in 1921, Neutra met Erich Mendelsohn while employed in the Municipal Building Office in Luckenwalde (Germany) and began working in Mendelsohn's office in Berlin. In 1923, he settled in the USA and worked in various architecture offices. In 1924, he met Louis Sullivan in Chicago; in 1924, Frank Lloyd Wright; and, in 1924, worked alternately at Holabird and Roche in Chicago and for Wright in Spring Green, Wisconsin. In 1924, when Erich Mendelsohn visited Wright in Wisconsin, Neutra acted as translator. 1925–30, Neutra lived in the house of Austrian architect Rudolph Schindler in Los Angeles and worked on architecture with him. 1930–39, Neutra practiced alone in Los Angeles; 1949–58, in partnership with his son Dion. From 1949, Neutra began to collaborate with Robert Alexander on numerous large commissions. Neutra designed mostly houses in the International Style, along with simple, if quirky, site-specific furniture arranged in large open spaces, including chromium-plated tubular furniture. His simple, elegant structures revealed the influence of Wagner and Loos; they dissolved the separation between interior and exterior spaces with expansive fenestration. He frequently followed Wright in including built-in furniture units to create open interior spaces. Neutra was best known for the 1929 Lovell and 1942 Nesbitt houses, both Los Angeles. His other buildings included the 1927 competition entry (with Rudolph Schindler) for the League of Nations; 1932 VDL Research House in Los Angeles; 1935 Josef von Sternberg house in Northridge, California; 1937 Strathmore Apartments in Los Angeles; 1927 Landfair Apartments in Los Angeles; 1938 Schiff house in Los Angeles; 1942–44 Channel Heights Housing in San Pedro, California; 1947 Kauffmann house in Palm Springs, California; and 1947–48 Tremaine house in Santa Barbara, California. Reproduced in limited production from 1990 by Prospettive in Italy, his site-specific furniture included the 1929 *Cantilever Chair* in tubular steel for the Lovell house, a low-backed bentwood model for the 1942 Branch house, and a high-backed bentwood model for the 1947 Tremaine house; the 1940 *Camel Table* with wooden legs for the Sidney Kahn house and 1951 revised version with metal legs for the Logar house; the asymmetical *Alpha Sofa* of the early 1930s; and the 1942 *Boomering Chair* with and without arms for the Nesbitt house. A prolific writer, he was a foreign member of UAM (Union des Artistes Modernes).

▶ Work was the subject of the 1982 exhibition at the New York Museum of Modern Art and furniture in the 1982 'Space and Environment: Furniture Design by Architects' at the Whitney Museum of American Art in Fairfield County, Connecticut.

▶ Frank Lloyd Wright, *Ausgeführte Bauten und Entwürfe von Frank Lloyd Wright*, Berlin: Ernst Wasmuth, 1910. Richard Neutra, *Wie baut Amerika?*, Stuttgart, 1927. Willy Boesiger (ed.), *Richard Neutra: Buildings and Projects*, Zürich, 1951, 1959, 1966. Richard Neutra, *Survival Through Design*, New York, 1954. Esther McCoy, *Richard Neutra*, Ravensburg, 1960. Esther McCoy, *Vienna to Los Angeles: Two Journeys*, Santa Monica, California: Arts and Architecture Press, 1979. Thomas S. Hines, *Richard Neutra and the Search for Modern Architecture*, New York: Oxford, 1982. Cat., Arthur Drexler, *The Architecture of Richard Neutra*, New York, 1982. Cat., Lisa Phillips (introduction), *Shape and Environment: Furniture by American Architects*, New York: Whitney Museum of American Art, 1982:48–49. Manfred Sack and Dion Neutra, *Richard Neutra*, Zürich: Verlag für Architektur, 1992. David Gebhard, 'Richard Neutra' in Mel Byars and Russell Flinchum (eds.), *50 American Designers*, Washington: Preservation, 1994.

Newcomb Pottery

▶ American pottery; located New Orleans.

▶ William Woodward, who had trained at the Massachusetts Normal Art School and Rhode Island School of Design, was the first art instructor at Tulane University in New Orleans. He held evening and Saturday classes in the decorative arts and drawings. His brother Ellsworth Woodward formed the Tulane Decorative Arts League, a group of about 30 women who had an interest in handicrafts. In 1886, the H. Sophie Newcomb Memorial College for women was founded by Tulane University. In 1887, Ellsworth Woodward became head of its art program and was joined by William Woodward and Gertrude Roberts (later Smith). *c*1887–90, William Woodward and a small number of his evening-class students operated the New Orleans Art Pottery, joined briefly by George E. Ohr, already an established potter in Biloxi, Mississippi. Ellsworth Woodward set up a pottery on the college grounds in 1894, and Mary Given Sheerer, an accomplished china painter from Cincinnati, Ohio, became his assistant and began teaching china painting and pottery design; she remained at the pottery until 1931. Clays and glazes were tested during Newcomb College Pottery's first year. Most of the clays early on came from Bayou Bogufalaya; others, mixed at Newcomb, from elsewhere in the South. A two-year training program was put into place. Jules Gabry, from Clément Messier's Golfe Juan Pottery in France, taught at the school for a year, succeeded by George Wasmuth, who also stayed only briefly. 1896–1927, Joseph Fortune Meyer held the potter's job. As at Rookwood, Newcomb had women design and produce the decorations while men potted, fired and glazed. The Newcomb Pottery was intended to provide continuing education to graduates of the art school. Undergraduate decorators were used at first; later, some ten graduate women were hired. During the pottery's history, about 90 'art craftsmen' or decorators maintained a high quality.

▶ The first public exhibition and sale of Newcomb Pottery produce was held in 1896. Newcomb Pottery received a bronze medal at the 1900 Paris 'Exposition Universelle.'

▶ Kenneth E. Smith, 'The Origin, Development, and Present Status of Newcomb Pottery,' *American Ceramic Society Bulletin*, No. 17, June 1938:257–60. Robert W. Blasberg, 'Newcomb Pottery,' *Antiques*, No. 94, July 1968:73–77. Suzanne Ormond and Mary E. Irvine, *Louisiana's Art Nouveau: The Crafts of the Newcomb Style*, Gretna, Louisiana: Pelican, 1976. Jessie Poesch, *New-*

comb Pottery: An Enterprise for Southern Women, 1895–1940, Exton, Pennsylvania: Schiffer, 1984. *American Art Pottery*, New York: Cooper-Hewitt Museum, 1987.

Newman, Mrs. Philip

▶ British goldsmith and jewelry designer.

▶ She studied under John Brogden and was his assistant. Active 1870–1910, she specialized in gold and enamel in the 'archeological' jewelry and neo-Renaissance and Holbeinesque work for which Brogden was known. After Brogden died in 1885, she continued to work in his style, with some of his employees, on models and designs from his workshops and with a number of his recipes for enameling and metalworking. She subsequently set up her own business at 10 Savile Row in London. A number of her apprentices produced pieces to specific orders.

▶ She showed her work with Brogden at the 1867 and 1878 Paris 'Expositions Universelles'; at the latter, Brogden was awarded the Légion d'honneur and the Médaille d'honneur.

▶ Charlotte Gere, *American and European Jewelry 1830–1914*, New York: Crown, 1975:212.

Newson, Mark (1962–)

▶ Australian industrial designer; born Sydney.

▶ Studied jewelry design, College of Art, Sydney.

▶ Tentuo Kurosaki of the Idée furniture company invited Newson to Milan. Having worked with Ron Arad in London, Newson was best known for his 1985 *Lockheed Lounge* steel chaise, installed in the lobby of the 1990 Paramount Hotel, New York. He designed the 1990 black *Pod* clock, circular from the front and elliptical from the side. Its white rotating dots were inspired by turn-of-the-century Cartier models. His 1993 *TV Chair* and *TV Table* were produced by Moroso.

▶ Received Designer of the Year award, Salon du Meuble, Paris.

▶ Lucie Young, *American Home*, October 1990:19. 'Design Diplomats,' *Metropolitan Home*, March 1990:87. Andrée Putman (ed.), *International Design Yearbook*, New York: Abbeville, 1992.

Nicholls, David Shaw (1959–)

▶ British furniture designer; born Glasgow; active New York and Milan.

▶ Studied Edinburgh College of Art and Domus Academy, Milan, to 1984.

▶ 1980–82, He established Asflexi to design and produce metal furniture; 1984–85, worked in the design office Sottsass Associati, Milan, on projects including Snaporazz Restaurant, Los Angeles; the Academy Bridge, Venice; and Esprit showrooms in Europe. From 1985, he was active in his own studio and designed Bar Montmartre, Milan, and several fashion showrooms and residences in Italy; in 1987, settled in New York and pursued architecture and interior design. Sergio Palazzetti commissioned from him the 1991 *DSN* sofa and chair for Palazzetti's Maverick Collection, produced in High Point, North Carolina. He designed the *Arno* chair, *Aria* and *Arianne* tables, and *Aston* credenza by Beast; scent bottle and display systems for Elizabeth Arden; *Gardens*, *Pompeii*, *Piazza*, and *Chivalry* rugs by DSN; and *Mari*, *Bride n'Groom*, and *Seven Palaces* dinnerware and tabletop accessories by Swid Powell.

▶ Work shown at 1980 'British Designer Craftsmen,' Edinburgh International Festival; 1981 'Charles Rennie Mackintosh and International Furniture,' Fine Arts Society, London; 1985 (III) Biennale di Architettura, Venice; International Contemporary Furniture Fair, New York from 1990 (I).

▶ 'The New American Entrepreneurs,' *Metropolis*, May 1991: 66–67.

Nichols, Maria Longworth

See Rookwood Pottery

Nicholson, Ben (1894–1982)

▶ British painter, sculptor, and textile designer; husband of Barbara Hepworth.

▶ 1910–11, studied Slade School of Fine Art, London.

▶ 1924–36, he was a member of the artists' group Seven and Five Society. In 1924, he produced his first abstract painting. In 1932, he became a member of the Association Abstract-Création in Paris; in 1933, of the artists' group Unit One. In 1937, he was co-editor of the art journal *Circle*. With his second wife Barbara Hepworth, he produced fabric designs for the 1937 *Constructivist Fabrics* range produced by Edinburgh Weavers, under artistic director Alastair Morton. 1943–58, he lived in St. Ives, Cornwall. In 1948, he designed limited-edition screen-printed silk squares produced by Zika Ascher. He painted the mural at the Regatta Restaurant of the 1951 London 'Festival of Britain.' 1958–72, he lived near Ascona (Switzerland), working on a concrete relief for 'Documenta 3' at Kassel.

▶ His work was the subject of the 1922 one-person exhibition at the Adelphi Gallery and more than 95 exhibitions, including the 1922 'Modern British Art' exhibition at the Whitechapel Gallery in London. In 1932, 1933, 1935, 1937, and 1939, he showed his work at Lefevre Gallery in King Street, London. His work was included in the 1935 'All Abstract' exhibition of the Seven and Five Society; abstract section of the 1937 AIA exhibition; and 1939 'Living Art in England' exhibition at the London Gallery and in the British section of the 1939 'New York World's Fair.' He won the first prize in the 1952 Carnegie International Competition in Pittsburgh, and 1968 Order of Merit. His work was the subject of the 1969 retrospective at the Tate Gallery in London and 1978–79 retrospective at the Albright-Knox Art Gallery in Buffalo, New York.

▶ Herbert Read, *Ben Nicholson: Paintings, Reliefs, Drawings*, London, 1948. Herbert Read, *Ben Nicholson: Paintings*, London, 1962. Herbert Read, *Ben Nicholson: Architectural Suite*, London, 1966. Cat., Steven A. Nash, *Ben Nicholson: 50 Years of His Art*, Buffalo, New York, 1978. Muriel Emanuel et al. (eds.), *Contemporary Artists*, New York: St Martin's, 1983:675–76. Cat., *Thirties: British art and design before the war*, London: Arts Council of Great Britain, Hayward Gallery, 1979:31–46,90,170,171,187, 188,210,212,267,297. Valerie Mendes, *The Victoria & Albert Museum's Textile Collection, British Textiles from 1900 to 1937*, London: Victoria & Albert Museum, 1992.

Nicholson, Roger (1922–)

▶ British painter, muralist, and designer.

▶ Nicholson taught graphic design at St. Martin's School of Art, London, and, 1958–84, was professor of textile design at the Royal College of Art. He was a consultant designer to several major manufacturers. In the late 1950s and 1960s, he designed wallpaper patterns in the *Palladio Collections* produced by Sanderson.

▶ Stuart Durant, *Ornament from the Industrial Revolution to Today*, Woodstock, NY: Overlook, 1986:283,296,327.

Nics frères (Michel and Jules Nics)

▶ Hungarian metalworkers and furniture makers; brothers; active Paris.

▶ Active from *c*1907 at 98 avenue Félix-Faure in Paris, Michel and Jules Nics were known for their fine ironwork produced to the highest standards of 18th- and 19th-century French work. They made consoles, balustrades, dumb waiters, iron gates, balcony railings, and various models of lighting. Their chandeliers, *torchères*, and sconces constructed in wrought iron housed opalescent glass shades or panels. Their invariably applied *martelé* finish gained their work some distinction, though they were not innovators. In 1925, they were commissioned to render wrought-iron furnishings for a hairdressing salon by Jacques-Émile Ruhlmann.

▶ They participated in the 1914 Salon of the Société des Artistes français.

▶ Jean Lort, 'La Ferronnerie Moderne des frères Nics,' *Mobilier et Décoration d'Intérieur*, April–May 1923:27–31. Henri Clouzot, *La Ferronnerie Moderne* (2nd series), Paris: Charles Moreau, 1926: plate 31, fig. 5. Alastair Duncan, *Art Nouveau and Art Déco Lighting*, New York: Simon and Schuster, 1978:179. G. Janneau, *Le Luminaire et les Moyens d'éclairage Nouveaux*, 2nd series: plate

31, 3rd series: plates 34—36. Jessica Rutherford, *Art Nouveau, Art Deco and the Thirties: The Furniture Collections at Brighton Museum*, Brighton: The Royal Pavilion, Art Gallery and Museums, 1983:40. Pierre Kjellberg, *Art Déco: les maîtres du Mobilier, le décor des Paquebots*, Paris: Amateur, 1986:132.

Niedecken, George Mann   (1878–1945)

▶ American furniture designer and maker and interior designer; born Wisconsin; active Chicago.

▶ 1890, studied Wisconsin Art Institute; 1897—98, in Louis Millet's decorative-design class, School of the Art Institute of Chicago; 1899—1900, in Paris.

▶ He described himself as an interior architect, functioning successfully as the intermediary between client and architect. In some of his earliest drawings and watercolors produced 1896—97, he recorded the landscape around his native state of Wisconsin. He toured Europe, after which he returned home and began showing his work with the Society of Milwaukee Artists. c1904—20, he produced Prairie-style murals for a number of domestic interiors, many of which were designed by Frank Lloyd Wright. He was familiar with British Arts and Crafts, French Art Nouveau, Viennese Sezession, German Jugendstil, and the work of Wright, and his work was influenced by all of these. His business associate F.H. Bresler was a furniture maker, print dealer, and art importer, who specialized in American Arts and Crafts materials, Chinese ceramics, and Japanese prints. Bresler helped Niedecken realize his first interior design commissions and invested in the firm of Niedecken-Waldbridge, which, 1907—10, supervised the production of Wright furniture made by the F.H. Bresler Co, Milwaukee. With Frank Lloyd Wright in 1904, Niedecken designed the showroom of the Bresler Gallery and, alone, some interiors and furniture for Wright's structures.

▶ His work was included in the 1989 'From Architecture to Object' exhibition in the Hirschl and Adler Galleries in New York.

▶ George M. Niedecken, 'Relationship of Decorator, Architect and Clients,' *The Western Architect*, May 1913:42—44. David A. Hanks, *The Decorative Designs of Frank Lloyd Wright*, New York: Dutton, 1979:215—17 passim. Cat., *The Domestic Interior (1897–1927): George M. Niedecken, Interior Architect*, Milwaukee: Milwaukee Art Museum, 1981. Mel Byars, *The Chairs of Frank Lloyd Wright: Seven Decades of Design*, Washington, D.C., Preservation, 1994.

Nielsen, Erik   (1857–1947)

▶ Danish ceramicist.

▶ 1885—86, studied Det Kongelige Danske Kunstakademi, Copenhagen.

▶ Was an apprentice woodcarver; in c1886—87, worked at the Royal Copenhagen Porcelain Manufactory and collaborated with Arnold Krog on one-off ceramics. He was influenced by naturalism and Japanese designs. From 1887—1947, was a medal maker and signing artist at Royal Copenhagen and produced models for Kähler Keramik.

▶ Cat., David Revere McFadden (ed.), *Scandinavian Modern Design 1880–1980*, New York: Abrams, 1982:269, No. 37. Jennifer Hawkins Opie, *Scandinavia: Ceramics and Glass in the Twentieth Century*, New York: Rizzoli, 1989.

Nielsen, Evald Johannes   (1879–1958)

▶ Danish silversmith; active Copenhagen.

▶ Trained in the workshop of August Fleron, and in Berlin.

▶ He opened his own workshop in 1905. Influenced by Georg Jensen at first, his work in the 1920s became simpler, with subtle stylized ornamentation.

▶ He showed his silverwares and jewelry from 1911 at international exhibitions.

▶ Annelies Krekel-Aalberse, *Art Nouveau and Art Déco Silver*, New York: Abrams, 1989:220,257.

Nielsen, Harald   (1892–1977)

▶ Danish silver designer; active Copenhagen; brother-in-law of Georg Jensen.

▶ Nielsen became one of Jensen's closest colleagues, beginning in 1909 as an apprentice at the Georg Jensen Sølvsmedie. Jensen's comment on Nielsen's *Pyramid* flatware pattern is said to have been 'It's neat but it won't sell'; the geometric design went on to become one of the firm's top three best-selling patterns. Nielsen worked as a Jensen designer of tableware and jewelry and, after Jensen died in 1935, the firm's artistic director for almost 30 years. A prolific designer, his work covered the entire field of silver from jewelry and some famous designs in tableware to bowls, coffee and tea sets, jugs, and dishes. His designs were distinguished by smooth, undecorated forms with straight edges and sharp angles.

▶ 'The Artists of Georg Jensen Silver,' *Fifty Years of Danish Silver in the Georg Jensen Tradition*, Christian Ditlev Reventlow, New York: Georg Jensen. Michael Farr, *Design in British Industry: A Mid-Century Survey*, London: Cambridge, 1955: 8ff. Graham Hughes, *Modern Silver*, London 1957:94. Cat., *Georg Jensen Silversmithy: 77 Artists, 75 Years*, Washington: Smithsonian Institution Press, 1980. Annelies Krekel-Aalberse, *Art Nouveau and Art Déco Silver*, New York: Abrams, 1989:27,69,219,257.

Niemeyer, Oscar   (1907–)

▶ Brazilian architect and designer; born Rio de Janeiro.

▶ Studied architecture, National School of Fine Arts, Rio de Janeiro.

▶ He worked in the office of architect Lucio Costa and collaborated with Le Corbusier on the Ministry of Education building in Rio de Janeiro and on the United Nations building in New York. He was professor of architecture at the University of Brazilia. He won the 1947 competition for the Aeronautical Training Center, later cancelled, and, in 1947, was invited to participate in the building of the United Nations. Denied entry to the USA as a Communist sympathizer, he was unable to accept the invitation as guest professor at Yale University. Niemeyer is best known for his design of the major buildings of Brazilia. His 1985 furniture series was produced by Estel.

▶ He received the Medalla al Trabajo.

▶ S. Papadaki, *The Work of Oscar Niemeyer*, New York, 1950. S. Papadaki, *Oscar Niemeyer: Works in Progress*, New York, 1956. S. Papadaki, *Oscar Niemeyer*, Ravensburg, 1962. Juli Capella and Quim Larrea, *Designed by Architects in the 1980s*, New York: Rizzoli, 1988.

Nienhaus, Lambert   (1873–1960)

▶ Dutch ceramicist, enamelist, and jewelry designer.

▶ From 1905, Nienhaus taught enameling in Haarlem and subsequently in The Hague and at the School of Applied Arts in Amsterdam; 1905—18, designed some jewelry pieces for W. Hoeker of Amsterdam in a style akin to the Jugendstil. He produced some silver work.

▶ Charlotte Gere, *American and European Jewelry 1830–1914*, New York: Crown, 1975:212.

Nies-Friedlaender, Cordula Kianga   (1958–)

▶ German industrial designer; born Kassel.

▶ 1978—79, apprenticed at Daimler-Benz; 1979—84, studied product design, Staatlichen Akademie der bildenden Künste, Stuttgart; 1985—87, Royal College of Art, London.

▶ 1984—85, she was an independent designer with clients including FAG in Frankfurt and Schmidt Motor Sport in Nuremberg. In 1986, she worked at the industrial design studio Moggeridge Associates and, from 1987, as a designer in the architecture office Foster Associates, both in London. Her work included office furniture for Tecno, interior decoration, sale systems for Esprit London, and planning and detail studies in architecture.

▶ Cat., Design Center Stuttgart, *Women in Design: Careers and Life Histories Since 1900*, Stuttgart: Haus der Wirtschaft, 1989: 138—41.

Niklová, Libuše
▶ Czech industrial designer.
▶ Studied plastics design, College of Decorative Arts, Gottwaldov (now Zlín, Czech Republic).
▶ She designed for Fatra Napajedla. Her first designs in plastics were rubber toys for Gumotex Břeclav. In 1961, she began using PVC and polyethylene for inflatable toys, seating furniture, boats, and other items.
▶ Her toy designs received the 'Outstanding Product of the Year' awarded by the Czechoslovak ColD. Her work was shown in numerous exhibitions in Czechoslovakia and abroad, including the 1967 'Design in Czechoslovakia' exhibition in London.
▶ Cat., Milena Lamarová, *Design a Plastické Hmoty*, Prague: Uměleckoprůmyslové Muzeum, 1972:136.

Nilsson, Barbro (b. Barbro Lundberg 1899–)
▶ Swedish textile designer; born Malmö.
▶ 1913–17, studied weaving, Brunsson Vavskola, under Johanna Brunsson and Alma Jakobsson; 1917–20, Konstfackskolan and Tekniska Skolan, Stockholm; 1920–24, Hogre Konstindustrielle Skolan, Stockholm.
▶ 1919–41, she was instructor at Brunssons Vavskola; 1924–25, director and chief instructor (with Maria Nordenfelt) at the Crafts and Design Seminarium in Gothenburg, Sweden; 1924–25, instructor at the Kunstindustrie Skolan, Kunstindustrie Dagskolan, and Kunstindustrie Aftonskolan in Stockholm; and visiting instructor at the Konstfackskolan, Stockholm, and Kunsthandvaerkerskolen, Copenhagen. In 1927, she set up her own workshop in Stockholm. 1942–71, she was artistic director of the AB Märta Måås-Fjetterström in Båstad, the position she assumed after the death of Måås-Fjetterström.
▶ She received the 1948 Litteris et Artibus Medal and 1954 Prince Eugen Medal. Her work was included in the 1954–57 USA 'Design in Scandinavia' traveling exhibition, 1955 'H 55' exhibition in Hälsingborg, and 1958 'Formes Scandinaves' at the Paris Musée des Arts Décoratifs.
▶ Cat., David Revere McFadden (ed.), *Scandinavian Modern Design 1880–1980*, New York: Abrams, 1982:269, No. 150.

Nilsson, Wiwen (aka Edvin Wiwen-Nilsson 1897–1974)
▶ Swedish silver designer; born Lund.
▶ Trained in the workshop of his father Anders Nilsson; studied Königliche Preussische Zeichenakademie, Hanau (Germany), and in the Paris studio of Georg Jensen while at the Académie de la Grande Chaumière and Académie Colarossi.
▶ From 1923, Nilsson worked in his father's workshop in Lund, assuming its management in 1928. In the 1920s and 1930s, he worked in a geometrical style, incorporating cylinders, hemispheres, and sharp angles into his large vessels. Under Nilsson's leadership, and that of Erik Fleming, Swedish silver acquired a character uniquely its own.
▶ He received a gold medal at the 1925 Paris 'Exposition Internationale des Arts Décoratifs et Industriels Modernes,' 1955 Gregor Paulsson trophy,1956 Swedish Goldsmiths' and Jewellers' Guild gold medal, and 1958 Prince Eugen Medal. His work was shown at the 1939 'New York World's Fair,' 1955 'H 55' exhibition in Hälsingborg, 1954–57 USA 'Design in Scandinavia' traveling exhibition, and 1958 'Formes Scandinaves' at the Paris Musée des Arts Décoratifs.
▶ Cat., David Revere McFadden (ed.), *Scandinavian Modern Design 1880–1980*, New York: Abrams, 1982:269, Nos. 117–18. Sylvie Raulet, *Bijoux Art Déco*, Paris: Regard, 1984. Annelies Krekel-Aalberse, *Art Nouveau and Art Déco Silver*, New York: Abrams, 1989:245,246,257.

9999
See Gruppo 9999

Nisbel, Nils (1932–)
▶ Swedish metalworker.
▶ Studied Konstfackskolan, Stockholm, to 1956.

▶ 1956–68, he worked as a designer at the Guildsmedsaktiebolaget in Stockholm and, in 1968, set up his own design studio. From 1963, he was a teacher at the Konstfackskolan, Stockholm.
▶ *Svenskt Silver Inför Åttiotalet*, Stockholm, 1979.

Nishi, Etsuko (1955–)
▶ Japanese glass designer.
▶ Studied Canberra Institute of Arts to 1990.
▶ Work included in the 1986 'National Glass' exhibition at Downey Museum of Art in Downey, California; 1987 'Contemporary Glass' exhibition at D'Erlien Gallery in Milwaukee; 1987 'The Art of Contemporary Japanese Studio Glass' at Heller Gallery in New York; 1988 'International Exhibition of Glass Craft' at the Industrial Gallery of Ishikawa Prefecture, Kanazawa; 1990 'Glass '90 in Japan' in Tokyo; 1990 'Chicago International New Art Forms Exposition' in Chicago; and 1991 (V) Triennale of the Japan Glass Art Crafts Association at Heller Gallery. Work won the 1990 Prize of Australian National University and included in 1989 and 1990 'Corning Glass Review,' *Neues Glas* journal.
▶ Cat., *Glass Japan*, New York: Heller Gallery and Japan Glass Art Crafts Association, 1991: No. 29.

Nissen, Søren (1944–)
▶ Danish architect and furniture designer.
▶ Studied Kunsthåndværkerskolen, Copenhagen, to 1968.
▶ In 1965, he was apprenticed at furniture manufacturer Rud. Rasmussen; from 1970, worked with Ebbe Gehl. His furniture designs (with Gehl) were produced by Ry Møbler.
▶ His work was included in the 1975 'Danske Fyrretræsmøbler' exhibition, Berlin, and 1976 'SCAN' exhibition, Washington.
▶ Frederik Sieck, *Nutidig Dansk Møbeldesign:-en kortfattet illustreret beskrivelse*, Copenhagen: Bondo Gravesen; 1990 Busck edition in English.

Nixon, Harry
See Noke, Cecil Jack

Nizzoli, Marcello (1887–1969)
▶ Italian industrial designer; born Boretto.
▶ 1910, studied architecture, materials, and graphics, Scuola di Belle Arti, Parma.
▶ Initially a painter, he was later involved with the design of fabrics, exhibitions, and graphics, including posters for Campari in 1926; 1934–36, (with Edoardo Persico) became partners in a studio where they designed two 1934 Park Pen shops in Milan, the Hall of Gold Medals at the 1934 'Aeronautical Exhibition,' a tubular-steel advertising structure in the Galleria in Milan, and primary-exhibit 'Victory' salon at 1936 (VI) Triennale di Milano. In 1931, industrialist Adriano Olivetti set up an advertising department in Olivetti's corporate headquarters, where, in 1940, Nizzoli began work as the first and most influential product designer at Olivetti, designing machines that became classics, including the 1948 *Lexicon 80*, 1950 *Lettera 22*, 1959 *Diaspron 82* typewriters, and 1956 *Divisumma 24* and *Summa 40* adding machines; from 1950, was an architect to Olivetti; from 1948, collaborated with G.M. Oliveri; designed *Supernova* and 1956 *Mirella* sewing machines produced by Necchi, Milan. In all of Nizzoli's work, the machinery is housed in organically curved skins, with attention paid to outline and applied graphics.
▶ Work shown in numerous exhibitions and subject of 1968 exhibition, Milan. Received 1954 (*Lettera 22*) Premio Compasso d'Oro. In 1961, elected Honorary Royal Designer for Industry. In 1962, received honorary doctorate in architecture, Politecnico di Milano.
▶ L. Sinisgalli, *Biografia e bibliografia di Nizzoli: La botte e il violino*, No. 1, 1964. Germano Celant, *Marcello Nizzoli*, Milan: Comunità, 1968. Cat., *Marcello Nizzoli*, Milan, 1968. Barbie Campbell-Cole and Tim Benton (eds.), *Tubular Steel Furniture*, London: The Art Book Company, 1979:46. B. Gravagnuolo (ed.), *Gli studi Nizzoli, architettura e design*, 1948–1983, Milan, 1983. Cat., *Design Process: Olivetti 1908–1983*, Milan, 1983:381–82.

Fumio Shimizu and Matteo Thun (eds.), *The Descendants of Leonardo: The Italian Design*, Tokyo, 1987:331.

Noailles, de
See de Noailles, vicomte Charles and vicomtesse Marie-Laure

Nocq, Henri Eugène   (1868–)
▶ French sculptor and medalist; born Paris.
▶ An occasional illustrator and graphic designer, Nocq was best known for his metalwork, including lamps, mirrors, jewelry, and domestic accessories. As a critic and historian, he wrote numerous journal articles. His major work on silver marks is *L'Orfèvrerie civile française du XVIe au début XIXe siècle*.
▶ Yvonne Brunhammer et al., *Art Nouveau in Belgium, France*, Houston: Institute for the Arts, Rice University, 1976.

Nogard, Charlotte   (aka Charlotte Derain)
▶ French designer and graphic and fine artist; wife of Gilles Derain.
▶ Studied École des Arts Décoratifs, Paris, École de la Cambre, Brussels, École Rembrandt, Amsterdam, and École du Louvre, Paris.
▶ She designed fabrics for Teskid in Italy, graphic design and packaging for Herboristerie du Palais Royal, and film posters for Paramount-Gaumont. Her murals and decorations appeared in the Ragtime bar in Cannes. In 1989, she produced rugs for Géométrie Variable, including designs for children. In 1987, she was commissioned for package designs for toiletries for Prince Abdul Aziz Bin Khalifa Al Thani.

Noguchi, Isamu   (1904–1988)
▶ American sculptor and designer; born Los Angeles; active New York.
▶ 1921–22, studied Columbia University, New York.
▶ In 1917, he trained as a cabinetmaker in Japan and, in 1918, returned to the USA. In c1922, he assisted the director of the Leonardo da Vinci Art School in New York. During the 1920s and 1930s, Noguchi was a maker of portrait busts. 1927–1929, he was Constantin Brancusi's assistant in Paris, where he met Alberto Giacometti. From 1932, Noguchi lived mainly in New York, where he was a sculptor. He designed the 1937 helmet-like bakelite radio for Zenith of Chicago and executed 1940 designs for Steuben Glassworks. Noguchi designed a 1939 free-form glass-topped coffee table for the house of A. Congers Goodyear, president of the New York Museum of Modern Art. There were other variations of this table by Noguchi, including the version (*IN50*) mass produced from 1944 by Herman Miller, discontinued in 1973, and put back into production in the 1980s. Other Herman Miller furniture included the 1946 *IN70* sofa and matching *IN71* ottoman, 1949 *IN20* rudder dining table, *IN52* rudder coffee table, and *IN22* rudder stool. Noguchi designed ceramics produced in Japan. He married expressive biomorphic forms with Oriental elegance in his furniture designs. His sculpture gardens, including the example at the Bienecke Rare Book Library of Yale University, fused design, sculpture, and architecture. His line of chochin-type lighting fixtures made of mulberry paper and spirally woven bamboo (in 1944 and 1951–66), produced by Ozeki, Gifu, and called *Akari* ('light'), are still in production today. For mass production, he designed an amusing 1954 rocking stool-table and 1955 group of wire-and-Formica tables for Knoll, and biomorphic tables, a sofa, and an ottoman for Herman Miller. The stuffed sofa and ottoman of the late 1940s, originally produced in a limited edition by Herman Miller, were reproduced by an Italian manufacturer from the 1980s. In the 1980s, he established a museum in Long Island City, New York, to exhibit his work.
▶ The first design in the *Akari* light fixture range was shown at the 1983–84 'Design Since 1945' exhibition at the Philadelphia Museum of Art. Exhibitions of his sculpture included the Whitney Museum in New York in 1968 and 1978 'Noguchi's Imaginary Landscapes' at the Walker Art Center in Minneapolis.
▶ Isamu Noguchi, 'Japanese Akari Lamps,' *Craft Horizons*, Vol. 14, Sept. 1954:16–18. Isamu Noguchi, 'Akari,' *Arts and Architec-*

ture, Vol. 72, May 1955:14,31. *Isamu Noguchi*, New York: Whitney Museum of Art, 1968. *Noguchi's Imaginary Landscapes*, Minneapolis: Walker Art Center, 1978. Cat., Kathryn Hiesinger and George H. Marcus III (eds.), *Design Since 1945*, Philadelphia: Philadelphia Museum of Art, 1983:224, IV–29. Charlotte Fiell and Peter Fiell, *Modern Furniture Classics Since 1945*, London: Thames and Hudson, 1991. Bruce Altschuler, 'Isamu Noguchi' in Mel Byars and Russell Flinchum (eds.), *50 American Designers*, Washington: Preservation, 1994.

Noirot, Emmanuelle   (1961–)
See Torck, Emmanuelle

Noke, Charles John   (1858–)
▶ British ceramicist.
▶ Trained at Worcester Royal Porcelain under Charles Binns.
▶ In 1889, he became a modeler at Doulton in Burslem. 1893–98, he modeled vases (including *Columbis* and *Diana*) and figures (including *Holbein* and *Rembrandt* vases). From the late 1890s to the early 1900s, he began experimenting with the reproduction of Sung, Ming, and early Ch'ing dynasty blood-red *rouge flambé* and *sang-de-boeuf* glazes with Cuthbert Bailey and John Slater. In c1906, Noke and William Edmund Grace introduce 'series' wares. 1914–36, he was artistic director at Doulton; in c1914, introduced *Titania* ware; and, in c1915, *Sung* ware. Noke, with Harry Nixon and son Cecil Jack Noke, developed *flambé* glaze designs and introduced *Chang* ware, named after the southern Sung potter Chang the Elder. In 1936, Noke retired and was succeeded by his son. Until 1940, all the glazes were in production. By 1965, *Sung* and *rouge flambé* glazes were put back into production.
▶ Cat., *Thirties: British art and design before the war*, London: Arts Council of Great Britain, Hayward Gallery, 1979:298.

Nolan, Harry E.
▶ American furniture designer and inventor; active Des Moines, Iowa.
▶ Nolan patented an eccentric 'lawn chair' based on the cantilever principle in 1922; this was the basis of the legal action of 1931 in Berlin, in which Anton Lorenz sued Thonet over rights to his and other tubular-steel furniture. Nolan's design used solid steel rods rather than the tubular steel used by Lorenz, Ludwig Mies van der Rohe, Marcel Breuer, and Mart Stam.
▶ Barbie Campbell-Cole and Tim Benton (eds.), *Tubular Steel Furniture*, London: The Art Book Company, 1979:14. 'Documents,' *Journal of Design History*, Vol. 3, Nos. 2 and 3, 1990:171–72.

Noll, Alexandre   (1880–1970)
▶ French sculptor and furniture designer.
▶ Noll began working in wood in 1920. In 1925, he showed his work at the La Crémaillère shop in Paris. He explored the plastic nature of wood in furniture, furnishings, and vessels that hovered between fine art and utility. Like his sculpture, each piece was a one-off.
▶ Patrick Favardin, *Le Style 50: Un moment de l'art français*, Paris: Sous Le Vent–Vilo, 1987:66–73. François Mathey, *Au bonheur des formes, design français 1945–1992*, Paris: Regard, 1992:208–09.

Nonné-Schmidt, Helene   (1891–1976)
▶ German textile designer; born Magdeburg; wife of Joost Schmidt.
▶ Studied drawing pedagogy, Königliche Kunstgewerbeschule, Berlin; 1924–30, studied Bauhaus weaving workshop, Weimar and Dessau; 1930–33, continuing art instruction.
▶ In 1925, she married Schmidt; in 1933 moved to Berlin, where she was denounced to the Nazis, worked secretly and had her studio destroyed by bombs; 1945–48 was active with her husband towards the revival of the Bauhaus idea; 1953–54, was appointed by Max Bill as color-course instructor, Hochschule für Gestaltung, Ulm; 1961, moved to Darmstadt to document (unsuccessfully) her husband's career.

▶ Sigrid Wortmann Weltge, *Women's Work: Textile Art from the Bauhuas*, London: Thames and Hudson, 1993.

Noorda, Bob (1927–)

▶ Dutch designer and graphic artist; born Amsterdam; active Milan.

▶ Studied Institute of Design, Amsterdam, to 1950.

▶ In 1961, he became a member of ADI (Associazione per il Disegno Industriale) and, 1963–64 and 1964–65, was a member of its guidance committee. He was a member of the AGI (Alliance Graphique Internationale) and, 1969–70, its secretary general. From 1968, he was a member of the commission on research and visual communication of the ICSID and, from 1970, a member of the Comitato Scientifico Didattico of the Instituto Superiore per il Design grafico in Urbino. 1962–65, he taught graphic design at the Società Umanitaria in Milan and, 1964–65, graphics and industrial design in Venice. In 1961, he was art director at Pirelli; from 1962, artistic consultant to Vallecchi; and 1963–64, artistic consultant on packaging to Rinascente-Upim. In 1965, he co-founded and was senior vice-president at Unimark International, a design and marketing firm. He designed the environmental graphics for subways in New York, Milan, and São Paulo, and the IBM office in Milan. In 1962, the Milan subway commission was executed in collaboration with Franco Albini, Franca Helg, and Antonio Piva. Clients included Brionvega, Birra Dreher, Chiari & Forti, Olivetti, Zanussi, and Rhodiatoce in Italy, Stella Artois in France, and Boots cosmetics, Gilbey Vintners, Spear and Jackson, and Truman Beers in Britain.

▶ Alfonso Grassi and Anty Pansera, *Atlante del design italiano: 1940–1980*, Milan, 1980. *ADI Annual 1976*, Milan: Associazione per il Disegno Industriale, 1976.

Nordström, Patrick (1870–1929)

▶ Swedish ceramicist; active Denmark.

▶ 1889–90, studied Svenska Slöjdföreningens Skola, Gothenburg; 1894–95, Tekniska Yrkesskolan, Lund.

▶ 1902–07, he was active in his own workshop, at Bakkegårdsalle, Copenhagen; 1907–10, at Vanlose; 1911–23, he worked at the Royal Copenhagen Porcelain Factory and subsequently in his own workshop in Islev from 1923–29. A pioneer in Danish stoneware, he became known for his unusual glazes.

▶ His work was shown at the 1900 Paris 'Exposition Universelle' and 1914 'Baltic Exhibition' in Malmö, was the subject of the 1956 one-person exhibition at Det Danske Kunstindustrimuseum in Copenhagen, and was included in the 1982–83 'Scandinavian Modern Design 1880–1980' exhibition at the Cooper-Hewitt Museum in New York.

▶ Cat., David Revere McFadden (ed.), *Scandinavian Modern Design 1880–1980*, New York: Abrams, 1982:269, No. 71. Jennifer Hawkins Opie, *Scandinavia: Ceramics and Glass in the Twentieth Century*, New York: Rizzoli, 1989.

Normandie

▶ French oceanliner commissioned in 1935.

▶ A symbol of the machine age, the *Normandie* was under contract to the French Line and the French government. With tonnage almost twice that of the 1926 oceanliner *Île-de-France*, the ship was decorated in baroque Art Déco, with the exception of two suites in the French 18th-century style. The dining room was 305 ft (93m) long, 46 ft (14m) wide, and 25 ft (8m) high, seating 700 passengers. René Lalique executed 38 wall panels, two huge chandeliers, and 12 ornate decorative lighting fixtures. Four 24-ft (7.3m) panels depicted Normandy village scenes. A 12-ft (3.7m) statue by Louis Dejean was installed. The walls were hammered glass with a ceiling in a honeycomb pattern of recessed lighting. Jacques-Émile Ruhlmann, Jean Dunand, Charles Despiau, and Raymond Subes made decorative contributions. The ship was featured in films, including Sacha Guitry's *Les Perles de la couronne* (1937) with the climax photographed in the main dining room, Yves Mirande's *Paris-New York* (1940), and Alfred Hitchcock's *Saboteur*

(1942). In 1942, *Normandie* burned in New York harbor and sank during salvage operations; some fittings had been removed.

▶ William H. Miller Jr., *The Fabulous Interiors of the Great Ocean Liners in Historic Photographs*, New York: Dover. Howard Mandelbaum and Eric Myers, *Screen Deco: A Celebration of High Style in Hollywood*, New York: St. Martin's, 1985. Pierre Kjellberg, *Art Déco: les maîtres du Mobilier, le décor des Paquebots*, Paris: Amateur, 1986.

Northwood Glass

▶ American glassware manufacturer; located Whelling, West Virginia.

▶ Harry Northwood founded Northwood Glass in 1900; in 1908, the firm started production of glass similar to the pressed luster glass introduced by Fenton Art Glass.

▶ Frederick Cooke, *Glass: Twentieth-Century Design*, New York: Dutton, 1986:55.

Nouilhac, Henri (1866–1931)

▶ French bookbinder and gilder; born Chateauroux; active Paris.

▶ Nouilhac was an apprentice bookbinder in Chateauroux. In 1894, he settled in Paris and set up a workshop at 10 rue de Buci. He produced plain leather bindings and historicist 18th-century bindings at first. By 1900, his work included floral and dentiled-fillet-bordered motifs. He produced the bindings of painter Adolphe Giraldon, whose daughter began designing in the Nouilhac workshop c1914. Nouilhac's bindings included *Poèmes et proses* by Paul Verlaine, *Lysistrata* (1921) by Aristophanes, *Daphnis et Chloë*, and *Madame Bovary* (1922) by Gustave Flaubert. His main clients were H. Béraldi, de Piolenc, Renevey, Marcel Bernard, and Belinac. During World War I, Nouilhac produced the bindings designed for Henri Vever by Jules Chadel, including *Pastels, Causerie sur l'art dramatique, Ce Brigand d'armour*, and *Cyrano de Bergerac*. As an instructor in binding, his students included Madeleine Gras and Rose Adler.

▶ Ernest de Crauzat, *La Reliure française de 1900 à 1925*, Paris, 1932, Vol. 1:61; Vol. 2:49–52. Cat., *Le Décor de la vie de 1900 à 1925*, Paris: Pavillon de Marsan, Palais du Louvre, 1937:65–67. Roger Devauchelle, *La Reliure en France de ses origines à nos jours*, Paris, 1961:127,141,144,153,274–75. Alastair Duncan and Georges de Bartha, *Art Nouveau and Art Déco Bookbinding*, New York: Abrams, 1989:16,17,19,150–53,195.

Nouvel, Jean (1945–)

▶ French architect and designer; born Fumel.

▶ 1966–71, studied architecture, École Nationale Supérieure, Paris.

▶ He set up his first office in 1970 with architect and scenographer François Seigueur; in 1980, became a founding member and artistic director, Biennale di Architecture, Paris; in 1985, set up his own architecture practice; was active in numerous projects for the theater, working with scenographer Jacques Le Marquet on the Théâtre de Jean-Maire Serreau, the Cartoucherie de Vincennes, part of the Théâtre de Belfort, and the Opéra in Lyons; as an architect, was best known for the 1981–87 Institut du Monde Arabe (with its widely published sun-sensitive lenses on the south window wall), quai Saint-Bernard, Paris. Nouvel designed the Institute's interiors and reception room furnishings. Other architecture included 1977 renovation, Gaieté Lyrique, Paris; 1978 renovation and extension of clinic Centre Médico-Chirurgical, Bezons (with Gilbert Lézènes); 1979 college Anne Frank; 1981–83 municipal theater renovation, Belfort (with Lézènes and Dominique Lyon); 1982 competition, new Ministère des Finances building and Parc de la Villette, both Paris; 1983 competitions, Operations Center in Tête-Défense and Bibliothèque de France; 1984 competition, Centre d'Art Contemporain et la Médiathèque, Nîmes and Paris; 1985–89 Nemausus 1 public housing, Nîmes; 1985 competition, Opera House, Tokyo (Japan); 1988 competition, Kansaï Airport, Osaka; 1989 La Tour sans fin à la Défense, Paris; 1989 King's Cross (with Norman Foster), London; 1989 furniture and architecture, Alain-Dominique Perrin's office, Cartier headquarters, Paris;

1990 French Pavilion, Biennale di Venezia. His furniture in general was simplified to its barest form, and pieces of the late 1980s were reminiscent of Louis Cuny's designs of the 1920s. He designed the prototype 1987 *BAO* articulated aluminum chest, innovative cold-molded polyurethane 1989 divan as part of his *Profils* range produced by Ligne Roset, and installation of the 1988 'Les années 50' exhibition, Centre Georges Pompidou, Paris. His other furniture included 1987 *IAC* table and unnamed folding table (Carte Blanche award by VIA), 1987 extending bookshelves (Carte Blanche award by VIA), and a furniture range by Knoll.

▶ Received 1983 silver medal from Academy of Architecture and honorary doctorate from the University of Buenos Aires; 1987 Architecture Grand Prize, 'Équerre d'Argent' Aga Khan Prize for Institut du Monde Arabe, and Créateur de l'année at Salon du Meuble, Paris; 1990 *Architectural Record* Prize for hotel-restaurant 1987—89 Saint James, Bouliac. He was awarded the 1987 'Carte Blanche' by VIA to produce a range of aluminum furniture. Furniture shown at 1988 contemporary French furniture exhibition at Victoria and Albert Museum, London.

▶ Patrice Goulet, *Jean Nouvel*, Paris: Electa Moniteur, 1987. Cat., Garth Hall and Margo Rouard Snowman, *Avant Premiere: Contemporary French Furniture*, London: Éprouvé, 1988. Cat., *Les années VIA, 1980—1990*, Paris: Musée des Arts Décoratifs, 1990. Olivier Boissière, *Jean Nouvel*, Zürich: Artemis, 1992.

Novembergruppe

▶ German artists' and architects' group.

▶ The Novembergruppe was founded in Berlin in 1918 as an informal association of radical artists. Influenced by the abortive November 1918 revolution, its establishment was encouraged by painters César Klein and Max Pechstein. More artistic and less radical than the Arbeitsrat für Kunst group, they shared some members. The Novembergruppe's orientation was defined as 'radical in the rejection of previous forms of expression—radical in the use of new expressive techniques.' Members included avant-garde musicians and experimental film makers, composer Hans Eisler, and architects Otto Bartning, Alfred Gellhorn, Walter Gropius, Hugo Häring, Ludwig Hilberseimer, Hans and Wassili Luckhardt, Erich Mendelsohn, Ludwig Mies van der Rohe, and Bruno and Max Taut. Painters included Lyonel Feininger, Vassilii Kandinskii, Paul Klee, and Ludwig Meidner. In 1933, the Nazis officially banned the organization, which had in practice discontinued its activities in 1931.

▶ 1919—32, the group had 19 exhibitions in Berlin. The 1920 exhibition of graphics and watercolors was mounted in Rome in conjunction with Filippo Tommaso Marinetti, and its 1924 traveling exhibition went to Moscow and Japan. A 1977 retrospective was mounted in Berlin.

▶ Helga Kliemann, *Die Novembergruppe*, Berlin, 1964. Cat., *Die Novembergruppe*, Berlin, 1977. Iain Boyd Whyte in Vittorio Magnago Lampugnani (ed.), *Encyclopedia of 20th-Century Architecture*, New York: Abrams, 1986:251—52.

Novotný, Otakar   (1880—1959)

▶ Czech architect and designer; born Benešov.

▶ Studied School of Decorative Arts, Prague, under Jan Kotěra, to 1903.

▶ After 1903, he worked in Kotěra's studio; in 1902, became a member of Mánes Association of Plastic Artists and served as its chair 1913—15 and 1920—32; 1929—54, was professor, School of Decorative Arts, Prague; was commissioner of exhibitions in Paris, Rome, and Vienna; was influenced by Henrik Berlage's brick architecture in the Netherlands; was an important proponent of Cubism in architecture and design. Commissions included exhibition halls for the Association of Czech Accomplishment at the German Werkbund exhibition, Cologne, 1927—30 Mánes Association building, Prague.

▶ Received a grand prize at 1925 Paris 'Exposition Internationale des Arts Décoratifs et Industriels Modernes.'

▶ Alexander von Vegesack et al., *Czech Cubism: Architecture, Furniture, and Decorative Arts, 1910—1925*, New York: Princeton Architectural Press, 1992.

Noxon, Court

▶ Canadian industrial designer and manufacturing executive; active Toronto.

▶ Studied architecture, University of Toronto, to 1953.

▶ From the mid-1950s, he designed metal furniture and subsequently became active in contract furniture design and manufacturing through his own firm Metalsmiths in Toronto, of which he assumed the direction from his father Kenneth Noxon. Consultant designers to Metalsmiths included George Boake. For other firms in the USA, he designed furniture under license.

▶ He won a number of National Industrial Design Council (Canada) awards for his furniture and other metal products, including his coat and hat racks.

▶ Cat., *Seduced and Abandoned: Modern Furniture designers in Canada, the First Fifty Years*, Toronto: The Art Gallery at Harbourfront, 1986.

Noyes, Eliot Fette   (1910—77)

▶ American architect and industrial designer; born Boston; active New Canaan, Connecticut.

▶ 1928—32, studied architecture, Harvard University; 1932—35 and 1937—38, Harvard Graduate School of Design, under Walter Gropius and Marcel Breuer.

▶ Noyes became an advocate of the Modern European design ethic after reading Le Corbusier's book *Vers une architecture* (1925) and Gropius's published teachings. In 1938, Noyes worked in the office of architects Coolidge, Shepley, Bulfinch and Abbot in Boston and, 1939—40, in the office Gropius and Breuer in Cambridge. On Gropius's recommendation, he served as the first director of industrial design 1940—42 at the New York Museum of Modern Art, where he was curator of the 1940 'Organic Design in Home Furnishings' competition and exhibition. 1946—47 in the office of industrial designer Norman Bel Geddes, the IBM *Model A* electric typewriter design was assigned to Noyes. When the Bel Geddes design firm closed, Noyes was retained by IBM to set up a corporate program of design along the lines of Olivetti. From 1947, he was in private practice in New Canaan, Connecticut. 1956—77, Noyes was corporate design director of IBM, where he rejected annual model changes and concessions to marketing. He took the same approach for clients including Westinghouse 1960—76, Mobil 1964—77, Pan Am 1969—72, and as president of MIT 1972—77. Noyes appointed graphic designers sympathetic with his approach, such as Paul Rand for IBM, and Ivan Chermayeff for Mobil. Noyes was instrumental in shaping the image of the major companies for which he worked; he suggested Breuer and other prominent architects to design IBM buildings throughout the world. His product designs for IBM included the 1959 *Executive*, 1961 *Selectric* electric typewriters, 1961 *Executary* dictating machine (hardly distinguishable from a Braun product), 1961 *Golfball 72* electric typewriter, and 1440 Data Processing System. He designed many of IBM's corporate office buildings and interiors as well as those for others. His 1964 Mobil filling station was adopted as a model for the company's filling stations worldwide. His so-called balloon house at Hobe Sound, Florida, was constructed by spraying wet concrete onto a large inflated balloon to create a hemisphere. His houses incorporated open plans with spaces created by furniture or fireplaces and featured natural materials, including stone and wood, as in some houses by Breuer. Noyes's own house in New Canaan won *Progressive Architecture*'s 1954 design award as a distinguished example of American Modernism. 1947—54, he wrote a column on design for *Consumer Reports* magazine. 1965—70, he was president of the International Design Conference in Aspen, Colorado. In his office, Noyes displayed a child's version of Harley Earl's automobile fascia to illustrate to his staff and clients 'false principles' and vulgarity in design.

▶ His 1961 *Selectric* typewriter was included in the 1983–84 'Design Since 1945' exhibition at the Philadelphia Museum of Art.
▶ Eliot Noyes, *Organic Design and Home Furnishing*, New York: Museum of Modern Art, 1941. Walter McQuade, 'An Industrial Designer with a Conspicuous Conscience,' *Fortune*, Aug. 1963:135–38,183–88,190. 'The Work of Eliot Noyes and Associates,' *Industrial Design*, June 1966. 'Eliot F. Noyes (1910–1977),' *Industrial Design*, June 1966. Jay Doblin, *One Hundred Great Product Designs*, New York, 1970: No. 93. Cat., Kathryn B. Hiesinger and George H. Marcus III (eds.), *Design Since 1945*, Philadelphia: Philadelphia Museum of Art, 1983:225,I–30. Vittorio Magnago Lampugnai (ed.), *Encyclopedia of 20th-Century Architecture*, New York: Abrams, 1986:252. Gordon Bruce, 'Eliot Noyes' in Mel Byars and Russell Flinchum (eds.), *50 American Designers*, Washington: Preservation, 1994.

Nugent, Walter

▶ Canadian furniture designer; active Oakville, Ontario.
▶ Until the late 1950s, Nugent was an advertising executive in Toronto; interested in furniture, he studied design and manufacturing in Canada and Europe. He perfected a one-piece, tempered-steel-rod internal frame, which he employed in different ways. Through his firm in Oakville, Ontario, he designed and manufactured a wide range of residential and contract seating, including those for patient use in hospitals and healthcare facilities.
▶Cat., *Seduced and Abandoned: Modern Furniture designers in Canada, the First Fifty Years*, Toronto: The Art Gallery at Harbourfront, 1986:19.

Nummi, Yki   (1925–)

▶ Finnish lighting and interior designer and colorist; born China.
▶ 1945–47, studied mathematics and physics in Helsinki and Turku; 1946–50, painting, Taideteollinen Korkeakoulu, Helsinki.
▶ 1950–75, he designed lighting for Stockmann in Helsinki; his fixtures incorporated innovative materials, including colored and white acrylics, opaline glass, aluminum, and brass. From 1958, he was head of the color design department of paint manufacturer Schildt & Hallberg. In the early 1960s, he designed a color plan for the Helsinki cathedral. He executed lighting designs for numerous firms in Finland and collaborated with Lisa Johansson-Pape as color specialist at Stockman/Orno in Kerava. He became an independent designer of lighting, furniture, and furnishings. He wrote a number of essays on color, lighting, and design principles.
▶ For his lighting, he won gold medals at the 1954 (X) and 1957 (XI) Triennali di Milano. He received the 1971 Pro-Finlandia Medal. His work was shown at the 1954–57 USA 'Design in Scandinavia' traveling exhibition, 1955 'H 55' exhibition in Hälsingborg, 1958 'Formes Scandinaves' exhibition at the Paris Musée des Arts Décoratifs, 1956–57 West Germany traveling 'Finnish Exhibition,' and 1961 'Finlandia' exhibition in Zürich, Amsterdam, and London.
▶ Erik Zahle (ed.), *A Treasury of Scandinavian Design*, New York, 1961:287, No. 100. Cat., David Revere McFadden (ed.), *Scandinavian Modern Design 1880–1980*, New York: Abrams, 1982:269, No. 216.

Nurmesniemi, Antti Aarre   (1927–)

▶ Finnish interior and industrial designer; born Hämeenlinna; active Helsinki; husband of Vuokko Eskolin.
▶ Studied interior design, Taideteollinen oppilaitos, Helsinki, to 1950.
▶ 1949–50, he was a furniture designer at the Stockmann design office, Helsinki; 1951–56, was furniture and interior designer in the Viljo Revell architecture office, Helsinki; and 1954–55, was active in the office of the Giovanni Romano architecture office in Milan. He designed interiors for hotels, restaurants, and banks. Returning to Finland in 1956, he set up his own design studio. He produced popular designs for furniture (sometimes with his wife Vuokko Eskolin) for various firms and his own firm; lighting; glassware; wallpaper; textiles; transportation with Barge Rajalin; and metalwork, including the 1958 *Finel* coffee pot in two sizes

for Wärtsilä (a standard in Finnish homes). His numerous interior designs included public and corporate offices, restaurants, hotels, and banks. For the Palace Hotel in Helsinki, he designed a widely published 1953 sauna stool. He designed the 1974 railway carriages for the President of Finland and the Council of State. His clients included Artek (furniture and lighting) 1957–60, Merivaara (furniture) 1963–66, Vecta Möbel (furniture) in 1978, and Cassina (furniture) in 1985. He was active in restoration projects, lectured worldwide, and designed a large number of exhibitions. His work combined the bareness of Modernism with the traditions of Finnish design. He was president of Ornamo, an association of Finnish designers; from 1982, was a member of the European Council of Science, Art and Culture.
▶ He won the 1959 Lunning Prize and grand prizes at 1957 (XII) and 1964 (XIII) (sauna stool); Triennali di Milano and a grand prize at its 1960 (XII) session. Other awards included the first prize at the 1955 Finnish Society of Crafts and Design Competition for the 80th anniversary exhibition, 1975 Finnish State Design Award, 1981 Medal of the UK Society of Industrial Artists and Designers, 1986 Honorary Royal Designer for Industry, and 1991 Japan Design Foundation Award. His work was included in the 1954–57 USA 'Design in Scandinavia' traveling exhibition, 1956–57 West German traveling 'Finnish Exhibition', 1961 'Finlandia' exhibition in Zürich, Amsterdam, and London. His work was the subject of the 1992 exhibition in Helsinki.
▶ Erik Zahle (ed.), *A Treasury of Scandinavian Design*, New York, 1961:287,332, Nos. 19–20. 'Thirty-four Lunning Prize-Winners,' *Mobilia*, No. 146, Sept. 1967. Cat., *Modern Chairs 1918–70*, London: Lund Humphries, 1971, No. 35. Marja Kaipainen, 'Some Call Them Purists.' *Form Function Finland*, No. 2, 1981:12–16. Cat., David Revere McFadden (ed.), *Scandinavian Modern Design 1880–1980*, New York: Abrams, 1982:269, Nos. 193,261. Cat, Kathryn B. Hiesinger and George H. Marcus III (eds.), *Design Since 1945*, Philadelphia Museum of Art, 1983:225,II–60. Cat., *The Lunning Prize*, Stockholm: Nationalmuseum 1986:106–11. Jeremy Myerson and Sylvia Katz, *Conran Design Guides: Kitchenware*, London: Conran Octopus, 1990:64,76. Cat., *Antti Nurmesniemi: Ajatuksia Ja Suunnitelmia*, Helsinki, 1992.

Nuutajärvi Lasi

▶ Finnish glass factory.
▶ The Notsjö glass factory was established in 1793 at Nuutajärvi by Swedish owners. It produced mainly window panes and bottle glass; from 1851, began to produce pressed glass; in 1853, was bought by Adolf Törngren, who improved production methods and used higher quality raw materials; 1861–78, manufactured ceramics; in 1865, set up its own glass shop Stockmann, which evolved into the largest and best known department store in Helsinki; 1946–48, appointed Gunnel Nyman as designer, who created a close working relationship between designer and glassworker and set high standards in glass design; in 1950, was closed for a short time due to a fire; was bought by Wärtsilä. 1950–76, Kay Franck was artistic director of Nuutajärvi and Arabia (with Saara Hopea), both Wärtsilä companies. Bottle production was discontinued, and art and household glass was emphasized. In 1963, Oliva Toikka became artistic director. Designers included Kerttu Nurminen, Heikki Orvola, and Markku Salo. In 1987, the factory was amalgamated with Iittala, forming a new company.
▶ Jennifer Hawkins Opie, *Scandinavia: Ceramics and Glass in the Twentieth Century*, New York: Rizzoli, 1989.

Nykänen, Frans Evald   (1893–1951)

▶ Finnish silversmith; born St. Petersburg; active Helsinki.
▶ Trained in his father's workshop in Sortavala (Sweden, now Finland).
▶ He founded Viri, which produced silver items in small series and worked for others. From 1918, he was director of Taito silversmiths, where one of his consultant designers was Gunilla Jung. Nykänen was considered the best chaser in Finland at the time.
▶ Annelies Krekel-Aalberse, *Art Nouveau and Art Déco Silver*, New York: Abrams, 1989:241,257.

Nyman, Gunnel Gustafsson   (1909–48)
▶ Finnish glassware, furniture, and textile designer.
▶ 1928–32, studied Taideteollinen Korkeakoulu, Helsinki, under Arttu Brummer.
▶ Nyman worked for all the great Finnish glass manufacturers of the 20th century: Riihimäki from 1932–47, Nuutajärvi-Notsjö from 1946–48, and Karhula from 1935–37 (and at Iittala from 1946–47). She designed for both production and studio glass. Her style was characterized by a strong sense of form and the plastic quality of molten glass, along with a subtle articulation of surface and mass. She was also a designer of furniture at Taito Oy from 1935–37, textiles, and lighting fixtures.
▶ Received third prize in 1993 Riihimäki glass competition, second and third prizes in its 1936 competition, second and third prizes in 1936 Karhula glass competition, gold medal (glass) and silver medal (furniture) at 1937 Paris 'Exposition Internationale des Arts et Techniques dans la Vie Moderne,' gold medal (glass) at 1951 (IX) Triennale di Milano.

▶Cat., David Revere McFadden (ed.), *Scandinavian Modern Design 1880–1980*, New York: Abrams, 1982:269, No. 216. Frederick Cooke, *Glass: Twentieth-Century Design*, New York: Dutton, 1986:52,83. Jennifer Hawkins Opie, *Scandinavia: Ceramics and Glass in the Twentieth Century*, New York: Rizzoli, 1989.

Nymølle Fajansfabrik
▶ Danish ceramics factory.
▶ The pottery factory Fuurstrøm was established in *c*1937 at Kongens Lyngby by Schou Ravnholm, a retail firm that sold imported ceramics and inexpensive goods, to manufacture inexpensive earthenware. After World War II, it commissioned Jacob Bang to supervise more artistic wares made in the factory renamed Nymølle. In 1946, Bang invited Bjørn Wiinblad to design at the firm. 1946–56, most of the line was designed for copper-plate engraving of transfer prints by Wiinblad. The firm went into bankruptcy in 1974; in 1976 Nymølle was purchased by Wiinblad.
▶ Jennifer Hawkins Opie, *Scandinavia: Ceramics and Glass in the Twentieth Century*, New York: Rizzoli, 1989.

Oberheim, Robert (1938–)
▶ German industrial designer.
▶ Studied Werkkunstschule, Wiesbaden.
▶ From 1972, he was the second director of the design studio of Braun, the domestic electrical appliance manufacturer.

Oberle, Philippe (1877–1950)
▶ German metalsmith; active Strasbourg and Pforzheim.
▶ Studied Munich, Brussels, and Antwerp.
▶ From 1904, he was a teacher at the Kunstgewerbeschule in Strasbourg and, after 1920, at the Goldschmiedeschule in Pforzheim.
▶ Annelies Krekel-Aalberse, *Art Nouveau and Art Déco Silver*, New York: Abrams, 1989:257.

Obrist, Hermann (1862–1927)
▶ Swiss sculptor and designer; active Germany.
▶ Studied medicine and natural sciences; from 1888, ceramics; subsequently sculpture in Paris.
▶ In 1886, prompted by a vision of a radiant city, he turned to art. In 1892, he settled in Florence, concentrating on marble techniques. In 1895, he established a studio for embroidery in Munich. Following the lead of Koloman Moser's and Josef Hoffmann's Wiener Werkstätte, in 1897, Obrist, Peter Behrens, Bruno Paul, Bernhard Pankok, and Richard Riemerschmid founded the Münchner Vereinigte Werkstätten für Kunst im Handwerk (The Munich United Workshops for Art in Handwork), aiming to sell everyday objects designed by Modern artists. Obrist was one of the leading designers of the Jugendstil, and designed furniture and textiles.
▶ Frederick Cooke, *Glass: Twentieth-Century Design*, New York: Dutton, 1986:36–38. Stuart Durant, *Ornament from the Industrial Revolution to Today*, Woodstock, NY: Overlook, 1986:47,327. Cat., Kathryn Bloom Hiesinger (ed.), *Die Meister des Münchner Jugenstils*, Munich: Stadtmuseum, 1988:79–87.

Obrtel, Vit (1901–88)
▶ Czech architect, book, set and furniture designer, poet, and theoretician; born Olomouc.
▶ 1918–25, studied České vysoké učení technické, Prague.
▶ From 1923 until its close in 1931, he was a Devětsil group member. He worked in the Prague city construction department and at the ministry of posts and telegraphs. In 1925, he moved to Paris. His early architecture work hovered between Cubism and the style of the Puristická čtyřka group, while strongly influenced by neo-Classicism. In the mid-1920s, he began to produce designs in the International Style and, by the end of the 1920s, became interested in Hugo Häring's organic architecture. Obrtel designed the 1927–28 family house at 561 Nábřeží Dukelských Hrdinů in Rožnov pod Radhoštěm and the 1927–28 house with a bakery at 65 Husova St. in Jičín. By 1926, Obrtel began to be known as a book illustrator and for his Constructivist covers. He converted his typographic designs into three dimensions in his 1927 set for the Osvobozené Divadlo (The Liberated Theater). Essays on architecture were published in magazines *Tam-tam, ReD, Fronta,*

Plán, and *Kvart* and, from 1926, opposed architect Karel Teige's scientific-Constructivist theories.
▶ He participated in the 1923 Bauhaus exhibition in Weimar.
▶ Cat., *Devětsil: Czech Avant-Garde Art, Architecture, and Design of the 1920s and 30s*, Oxford Museum of Modern Art Oxford and London Design Museum, 1990.

Obsieger, Robert (1884–1958)
▶ Austrian designer and potter; born Lundenburg.
▶ 1909–14, studied Kunstgewerbeschule, Vienna.
▶ In the 1920s and 1930s, he carried on the ceramics tradition of the Jugendstil; 1939–45, was director of the Kunstgewerbeschule in Vienna; became a member of Österreichische Werkbund; after World War II, passed on his expertise through students including Kurt Ohnsorg.
▶ Günther Feuerstein, *Vienna—Present and Past: Arts and Crafts—Applied Art—Design*, Vienna: Jugend und Volk, 1976: 66,80. Astrid Gmeiner and Gottfried Pirhofer, *Der Österreichische Werkbund*, Salzburg/Vienna: Residenz, 1985:239.

Oceano Oltreluce
▶ Italian lighting manufacturer.
▶ Oceano Oltreluce was founded in 1981 by Marco Zanuso Jr., Luigi Greppi, Pietro Greppi, and Bepi Maggiori. It produced Denis Santachiara's 1985 *Sparta* lamp stanchions.
▶ Fumio Shimizu and Matteo Thun (eds.), *The Descendants of Leonardo: The Italian Design*, Tokyo, 1987:330.

Oddo, Adriano M. (1948–)
▶ Italian designer; born Cairo; active Milan.
▶ Studied architecture to 1973.
▶ He taught at the Facoltà Architettura in Milan and at the Liceo Artistico in Novara. His clients included Sormani (furniture, furnishings, and lighting), Mopoa (clocks) in 1974, Velca (furniture) in 1975, and Gabbianelli (tableware) in 1975. In 1972, he patented a mechanical knuckle joint; produced signage for the 1972 'Interieur 72' furniture competition; and, in 1973, designed the magazine *Nuovi Orizzonti* for the Italian tourist bureau. He was a member of ADI (Associazione per il Disegno Industriale).
▶ He received an honorable mention at the 1973 'International Pottery Design Competition.'
▶ *ADI Annual 1976*, Milan: Associazione per il Disegno Industriale, 1976.

Odom, William (–1942)
▶ American teacher; born Georgia; active New York and Paris.
▶ Studied New York School of Fine and Applied Art under William Merritt Chase to 1908; music under Leopold Stokowski; and design and architecture, École des Beaux-Arts, Paris.
▶ Dubbed 'Mr. Taste,' by 1920, he had persuaded Frank Parsons, under whom he taught at the New York School of Fine and Applied Art, to open a branch of the school in Paris. Odom lived on the place des Vosges in Paris in a 17th-century townhouse furnished in period French furniture and fitted with typical *boiserie* walls. He subsequently returned to New York. 1915–16, he and Frank Parsons led study trips abroad; through his social connec-

tions, students were able to visit public and private buildings of importance in France. In c1922, Odom became head of the department of interior architecture and decoration, where he emphasized architecture and exerted a lasting influence on interior design. 1930–42, he was president of the school, renamed Parsons School of Design in 1940. He never decorated professionally and could not tolerate working with clients. In the décors he rendered for himself, almost everything was arranged symmetrically and often fitted out in pairs of furniture pieces and objects. At his own request, he was buried in London, and part of his furnishings went to the Musée des Arts Décoratifs, Paris.
▶ 'The Influence of William Odam on American Taste,' *House and Garden*, July 1946. John Esten and Rose Bennett Gilbert, *Manhattan Style*, Boston: Little, Brown, 1990:vii,6–7.

Oerley, Robert   (1876–1945)
▶ Austrian architect, painter, and designer; born and active Vienna.
▶ Oerley was a founding member of the Hagenbund and, 1907–39, a member of the Vienna Secession. He designed furniture and was an architect. His motifs were produced on silk by Backhausen.
▶ Günther Feuerstein, *Vienna—Present and Past: Arts and Crafts—Applied Art—Design*, Vienna: Jugend und Volk, 1976: 42,81. Astrid Gmeiner and Gottfried Pirhofer, *Der Österreichische Werkbund*, Salzburg/Vienna:Residenz, 1985:239.

Oestreicher, Lisbeth   (b. Lisbeth Birman 1902–89)
▶ German textile designer; born Karlsbad, Bohemia.
▶ 1926–30, studied Bauhaus weaving workshop, Dessau.
▶ She produced prototypes for firms Polytex and Pausa and designed dress patterns for publishing firms Ullstein and Bayer while at the Bauhaus; in 1930, settled in the Netherlands and set up her own studio, working as a freelance designer to 1942; 1942–45, was interned in Westerbork concentration camp; in 1945, married Otto Birman and became a freelance designer.
▶ Sigrid Wortmann Weltge, *Women's Work: Textile Art from the Bauhaus*, London: Thames and Hudson, 1993.

Offredi, Giovanni   (1927–)
▶ Italian product designer; born and active Milan.
▶ He began his professional career in 1963; after a brief period working as an architect, he began to design products; clients in Italy included Saporiti Italia (furniture and kitchens), Crassevig (bentwood furnishings, including the *Johan* clothes rack), MC di Marco Contini, Bando Line, ITT, GiPi of G. Pizzitutti, GM Arradamenti, Tosi Mobili, Bazzani, Ultravox (sound equipment), Sirrah, Grappo Snaidero, Abaco & Mobiam, Face Alcatel, and Sintesi (kitchens). He was a member of ADI (Associazione per il Disegno Industriale).
▶ Received 1957 Plasti Riv, 1965–70 Mia Print, 1968 prize at Fiera di Trieste, 1984 Premio Compasso d'Oro, 1985 Smau prize, and prizes at the Biennale di Mariano and Monza fair.
▶ *ADI Annual 1976*, Milan: Associazione per il Disegno Industriale, 1976. Sergio Saporiti and Giorgio Saporiti, *Il nostro lavoro con Offredi*, Marnate, 1978. Giancarlo Iliprandi and Pierluigi Molinari (eds.), *Industrial Design Italiani*, Fagagma, 1985:155. Fumio Shimizu and Matteo Thun (eds.), *The Descendants of Leonardo: The Italian Design*, Tokyo, 1987:334. *Modo*, No. 148, March–April 1993:123.

Ofterdinger, August   (1855–1934)
▶ German silversmith; active Hanau.
▶ Trained in Hanau, Schwäbisch-Gmünd, Vienna, and Paris.
▶ From 1882, he taught chasing and embossing at the Königliche Preussische Zeichenakademie in Hanau.
▶ Annelies Krekel-Aalberse, *Art Nouveau and Art Déco Silver*, New York: Abrams, 1989:258.

Ogawa, Isao   (1944–)
▶ Japanese designer; born Tokyo; active Milan.
▶ Ogawa began his professional career in 1965. 1971–74, he worked in the Studio Ammannati e Vitelli and designed furniture,

furnishings, and lighting. He was a member of ADI (Associazione per il Disegno Industriale).
▶ Ogawa, Makoto Shimazaki, and Akiraka Takaghi won the 1966 'Good Design Japan' award. Ogawa won the 1968 'Good Design Japan' award. With a group of Japanese designers, he showed his work at the 1973 Triennale di Milano.
▶ *ADI Annual 1976*, Milan: Associazione per il Disegno Industriale, 1976.

Ohgida, Katsuya   (1957–)
▶ Japanese glass designer.
▶ Studied Kanazawa College of Art to 1980; 1983–85, Tokyo Glass Crafts Institute, Tokyo.
▶ Ohgida was a member of the Japan Crafts Design Association.
▶ Work shown at 1987 and 1990 'Glass in Japan,' Tokyo, and 1991 (V) Triennale of the Japan Glass Art Crafts Association, Heller Gallery, New York. Received grand prize and special prize by Asa Brandt in 'International Exhibition of Glass Craft,' Industrial Gallery of Ishikawa Prefecture, Kanazawa.
▶ Cat., *Glass Japan*, New York: Heller Gallery and Japan Glass Art Crafts Association, 1991: No. 30.

Ohlsson, Olle   (1927–)
▶ Swedish metalworker.
▶ 1954–59, studied Konstindustriskolan, Gothenburg.
▶ In 1949, he was apprenticed to Hallberg Jewelers and, 1954–59, worked in the Atelier Borgila with Erik Fleming. He was a designer at Gekå Jewels and, in 1963, set up his own workshop.
▶ He received a second prize and diploma at the 1974 'World Silver Fair' in Mexico City. His work was the subject of the 1966 one-person exhibition at Nordiska Kompaniet in Stockholm. His 1977 teapot was included in the 1980 'Scandinavian Modern Design 1880–1980' exhibition at the Cooper-Hewitt Museum in New York.
▶ Cat., David Revere McFadden (ed.), *Scandinavian Modern Design 1880–1980*, New York: Abrams, 1982:269, No. 305.

Ohnsorg, Kurt   (1927–70)
▶ Austrian ceramicist; born Siegmundsherberg.
▶ A pupil of ceramicist Robert Obsieger, Ohnsorg became a craftsperson of some note and ceramicist who transcended the utilitarian nature of pottery through his unusual imagination.
▶ Günther Feuerstein, *Vienna—Present and Past: Arts and Crafts—Applied Art—Design*, Vienna: Jugend und Volk, 1976:66,81.

Ohr, George Edgar   (1857–1918)
▶ American potter; active Biloxi, Mississippi.
▶ 1879–81, he was apprenticed as a potter under family friend Joseph Fortune Meyer. In c1882, he set up a pottery in Biloxi, Mississippi, where he produced earthenware characterized by boldly colored, bent, and twisted designs combining whimsy and art and resembling the later Modern works of others. Rarely recognized outside Mississippi, he was dubbed 'the mad potter of Biloxi.' He worked alone, though sometimes his son Leo helped him prepare the clay. He threw on a handmade wheel with clays from the Tchouticabouffe and Pascagoula Rivers. Ohr's forms are unlike those of any other American's work, but show a similarity to Christopher Dresser's ceramics from 1879 for Linthorpe, the English pottery in Middlesbrough. He stopped potting c1909 but kept his *œuvre* intact, hoping to sell it to a national collection; over 6,000 pieces of his work were kept in the attic of the Ohr Boys Auto Repair Shop in Biloxi until the early 1970s, when they were sold and dispersed.
▶ He showed over 600 uniquely shaped pieces at the 1884 New Orleans 'World's Industrial and Cotton Centennial Exhibition,' and won a prize for originality at the 1904 St. Louis 'Louisiana Purchase Exposition.' Work shown at 1900 'Arts and Crafts Exhibition' in Buffalo, New York. Work subject of 1983 'George E. Ohr: An Artworld Homage,' Garth Clark Gallery, New York, and included in images of Jasper Johns paintings shown at 1983 exhibition, Leo Castelli Gallery, New York.

▶ Robert W. Blasberg, *George E. Ohr and His Biloxi Art Pottery*, Port Jervis, NY: Carpenter, 1973. Garth Clark, *The Biloxi Art Pottery of George Ohr*, Jackson, Miss: Mississippi Department of Archives and History and the Mississippi State Historical Museum, 1978. Garth Clark, 'George E. Ohr,' *Antiques*, No. 128, September 1985:490–97. Robert W. Blasberg, *The Unknown Ohr: A Sequel to the 1973 Monograph*, Milford, Pa: Peaceable Press, 1986. Garth Clark, *American Ceramics: 1876 to the Present*, New York: Abbeville, 1987:288–89. *American Art Pottery*, New York: Cooper-Hewitt Museum, 1987.

Ohta, Ken (1934–)
▶ Japanese glass designer.
▶ Studied industrial design, Faculty of Fine Arts of Nihon University, Tokyo, to 1962.
▶ In 1962, Ohta joined Sasaki Glass, Tokyo, and later became its manager of marketing.
▶ Work shown at 1981, 1984, and 1990 'Glass in Japan,' Tokyo; 1986 (VII) 'Katsuragi Craft Arts,' Yamaha; 1988 'International Exhibition of Glass Craft,' Industrial Gallery of Ishikawa Prefecture, Kanazawa; and 1991 (V) Triennale of the Japan Glass Art Crafts Association, Heller Gallery, New York.
▶ Cat., *Glass Japan*, New York: Heller Gallery and Japan Glass Art Crafts Association, 1991: No. 31.

Olbrich, Josef Maria (1867–1908)
▶ Austrian artist, architect and designer; born Troppau (now Opava, Czech Republic); active Vienna and Darmstadt.
▶ From 1882, studied Staatsgewerbeschule, Vienna, under Camillo Sitte and others; 1890, Akademie der bildenden Künste, Vienna, under Carl von Hasenauer.
▶ From 1894, he worked for Otto Wagner and became friends with Josef Hoffmann. In 1897, Olbrich became a founding member of the Vienna Secession with Hoffmann and Koloman Moser, and designed with Gustav Klimt its 1897–98 Exhibition Hall. In 1899, he became a participant in the Darmstadt artists' colony of the Grand Duke Louis IV of Hesse-Darmstadt, where he was responsible for a portion of the Art Nouveau architecture and decoration at the Mathildenhöhe complex and the Grand Duke's house at the 1901 exhibition, and a number of houses for colleagues. In 1907, he became a founding member of the Deutscher Werkbund. In some ways anticipating Expressionism, Olbrich's buildings at Darmstadt exerted an influence on later architecture. His silver designs were not successful with only a handful surviving (candelabrum, tea-table pieces, tea caddy, sugar bowl, and biscuit barrel), all evidently produced by Bruckmann und Söhne in Heilbronn. He designed a number of pieces of jewelry (often set with mother-of-pearl and opaque stones) for D. und M. Loewenthal and Theodor Fahrner, and executed some electroplated flatware patterns. He designed numerous lighting fixtures, including pewter, brass, and silver candelabra, electric ceiling models, and gas wall sconces. His designs were clean and functional, reflecting Charles Rennie Mackinstosh's and Viennese school members' fondness for cubes and rectangles.
▶ In 1893, he received the Prix de Rome while in his third year at the Akademie in Vienna. At the 1901 'A Document of German Art' exhibition in Darmstadt, he designed one of the two domestic houses built for the occasion. His work was the subject of the 1967 'Joseph M. Olbrich, 1867–1908: Das Werk des Architekten' retrospective exhibition at the Hessisches Landesmuseum in Darmstadt.
▶ *J.M. Olbrich, Ideen*, Vienna, 1899. *Deutsche Kunst und Dekoration*, 1899–1900:478. *J.M. Olbrich, Architektur*, 30 portfolios, Berlin, 1901–14. Joseph August Lex, *Joseph M. Olbrich*, Berlin, 1919. Cat., *Joseph M. Olbrich, 1867–1908, Das Werk des Architekten*, Darmstadt: Hessisches Landesmuseum, 1967. Karl Heinz Schreyl, *Joseph Maria Olbrich: Die Zeichnungen in der Kunstbibliothek Berlin*, Berlin, 1972. Charlotte Gere, *American and European Jewelry 1830–1914*, New York: Crown, 1975:213. Alastair Duncan, *Art Nouveau and Art Déco Lighting*, New York: Simon and Schuster, 1978:125. Ian Latham, *Joseph Maria Olbrich*,

London, 1980. Robert Waissenberger, *Vienna 1890–1920*, Secaucus, NJ: Wellfleet 1984:268. Annelies Krekel-Aalberse, *Art Nouveau and Art Déco Silver*, New York: Abrams, 1989:132,133–34,142,258. Cat., *Museum Künstlerkolonie Darmstadt*, Darmstadt, 1990:183–215.

Old-Bleach Linen Company
▶ British textile manufacturer; located Randalstown, Northern Ireland.
▶ Founded in 1870 by C. J. Webb. The firm operated a weaving mill and printing shed, producing screen printing equal in quality to its woven goods; produced embroidery, dress and furnishing linens, damask table linens; published *The Embroideress* (with James Pearsall & Co, manufacturers of knitting wools and embroidery yarns). In the 1930s, it commissioned designers Marion Dorn, Norman Webb, J.L. Lindsay, Ronald Grierson, and Mansouroff.
▶ Cat., *Thirties: British art and design before the war*, London: Arts Council of Great Britain, Hayward Gallery, 1979:90,91,144,145. Valerie Mendes, *The Victoria & Albert Museum's Textile Collection, British Textiles from 1900 to 1937*, London: Victoria and Albert Museum, 1992.

Old, Maxime (1910–)
▶ French decorator and furniture designer.
▶ Studied École Boulle, Paris.
▶ Until 1934, he was an apprentice in Jacques-Émile Ruhlmann's workshop. He participated in the furnishing of oceanliners including the 1926 *Île-de-France, Liberté, Ville de Marseille*, and *Flandre*. After World War II, he was commissioned by the French government to produce furniture ensembles for the minister of finance and the legation in Helsinki. His designs and furniture were known for refinement and elegance. He designed all the furnishings (mahogany and woven-cane furniture) for Hôtel Marhaba, Casablanca, characteristic of his work in the 1950s; was active in a workshop at 37 rue de Chanzy, Paris; in 1960, began to use metal in his furniture.
▶ *Ensembles Mobiliers*, Paris: d'Art Charles Moreau, Vol. 6, No. 25, 1945; No. 19, 1954. Yolande Amic, *Intérieurs: Le Mobilier français, 1945–1964*, Paris: Regard/VIA, 1983:42–43.

Oliveri, G. Mario (1921–
▶ Italian industrial designer; born Palermo; active Milan.
▶ Studied architecture to 1952.
▶ 1952–53, he designed a gasoline pump for Agip and telephone for Safnat with Marco Nizzoli. 1965–71, he was active in the industrial design studio Nizzoli Associati in Milan. He designed covers for the magazine *L'Architettura*. His clients in Italy included Stilnovo (lighting and accessories), Zucchetti (*Z 80* faucet range), Ceccato (service-station equipment), Fidenza (glass lighting fixtures), Lombardini (spark plugs), Solari (heating appliances), and Fiamm (horns and batteries for automobiles). From 1972 at Nizzoli Sistemi, he worked on agricultural machinery for Laverda and Gallignani with R. Ingegnere, trailers and mobile homes for Laverda with G. Giuliani, R. Ingegnere, industrial sanitary fitting for Ideal Standard with Giuliani, Ingegnere, Picciani, and Matessi, and lighting and kitchenware in glass for Fidenza with Giuliani and Picciani. He was a member of ADI (Associazione per il Disegno Industriale).
▶ *ADI Annual 1976*, Milan: Associazione per il Disegno Industriale, 1976.

Olivetti
▶ Italian office machinery and furniture firm; located Ivrea.
▶ The Olivetti office machinery company was founded in 1908 by Camillo Olivetti, who designed its first typewriter, the *M1*, produced by assembly-line methods. Early on, its works were housed in fortress-like brick factory buildings. Olivetti commissioned Luigi Figini and Gino Pollini to design a complex including factory, workers' housing, and hospital. The housing was completed in 1939 and the factory in 1940. In 1940–41, its nursery school was replaced with a new building by Figini and Pollini. From 1938, Olivetti's son Adriano was president of the firm and

initiated the policy of using consultant designers. Hired in 1938 to work in the advertising office, Marcello Nizzoli produced some of its most recognizable products, including the 1948 *Lexicon 80* and 1950 *Lettera 22* typewriters, and 1956 *Divisumma 24* calculator. He designed its graphics in the 1940s and 1950s. In the 1950s, art director Giovanni Pintori designed displays for store windows as well as graphics, while Leo Lionni designed Olivetti's magazine advertising; prior to Lionni, Olivetti's artists included Xanti Schawinsky and Costantino Nivola. Hired in 1957, Ettore Sottsass produced designs for computers, typewriters and systems furniture, including his widely published 1968 *Valentine* portable typewriter and similar 1968 *Lettera 36*. His *Synthesis 45* system of furniture for Olivetti answered the need in the 1970s for new shapes, materials, and ergonomic considerations in office design. Sottsass's system was distinguished by bright colors and bold, witty plastic details characteristic of the 1970s, with its more relaxed attitude towards work. Sottsass was in charge of the design of systems and furniture, collaborating with Albert Leclerc, Bruno Gecchelin, George Sowden, and Masanori Umeda. Mario Bellini was in charge of consumer products, collaborating with Antonio Macchi Cassia, Gianni Pasquini, and Sandro Pasqui.
▶ The *M1* typewriter was introduced at the 1911 Turin 'Esposizione Internazionale dell'Industria e del Lavoro.' Olivetti's products were shown at all the international fairs and included in important exhibitions, and the subject of the 1952 'Olivetti: design in industry' exhibition at the New York Museum of Modern Art, and the 1979 'Design Process Olivetti 1908–1978' exhibition at the Frederick S. Wight Art Gallery, Los Angeles.
▶ *Olivetti: design in industry (Museum of Modern Art Bulletin)*, New York: Museum of Modern Art, 1952. Cat., Milena Lamarová, *Design a Plastické Hmoty*, Prague: Uměleckoprůmyslové Muzeum, 1972:66,68,198. *ADI Annual 1976*, Milan: Associazione per il Disegno Industriale, 1976. Cat., *Design Process Olivetti 1908–1978*, Los Angeles: Frederick S. Wight Art Gallery, 1979. Penny Sparke, *Design in Italy, 1870 to the Present*, New York: Abbeville, 1988.

Olivetti, Camillo   (1868–1943)
▶ Italian engineer and industrialist.
▶ He founded the Olivetti office machinery company in 1908. He designed the company's, and Italy's, first typewriter, the *M1*, manufacturing it on a moving assembly line similar to the one introduced by Henry Ford in 1913. The 1911 *M1* may have been based on an Underwood model. In the late 1920s, he visited the USA to observe new manufacturing techniques and to study new products.
▶ Cat., Milena Lamarová, *Design a Plastické Hmoty*, Prague: Uměleckoprůmyslové Muzeum, 1972:66,68,198. Penny Sparke, *Design in Italy, 1870 to the Present*, New York: Abbeville, 1988.

Ollers, Edvin   (1888–1959)
▶ Swedish glassware designer, metalworker and ceramicist.
▶ In 1917, Ollers worked for the Kosta Glasbruk and, 1918–20, for the Rejmyre Glasbruk in Rejmyra. 1931–32, he returned to Kosta. He designed glassware for mass production in inexpensive soda glass with its natural bubbles and blisters. He also designed in pewter, silver, and ceramics.
▶ Cat., David Revere McFadden (ed.), *Scandinavian Modern Design 1880–1980*, New York: Abrams, 1982:269, No. 84.

Ollestad, Andreas   (1857–1936)
▶ Norwegian ceramicist.
▶ From 1886, he worked at the Egersunds Fayancefabrik in Egersund, where he was production manager from 1905, and where he introduced the Art Nouveau style. His ceramic pieces integrated decoration and modeled relief.
▶ Cat., David Revere McFadden (ed.), *Scandinavian Modern Design 1880–1980*, New York: Abrams, 1982:269, No. 19.

Ollier, Bénédicte   (1963–)
▶ French furniture designer; active Paris.
▶ Studied École Nationale Supérieure des Arts Décoratifs, Paris.

▶ She designed the *Milou* stool produced by Artistes et Modèles under the sponsorship of VIA's Appel permanent grant, received in 1989.
▶ Work (*Milou*) shown at 1990 Salon du Meuble, Paris.
▶ Cat., *Les années VIA 1980–1990*, Paris: Musée des Arts Décoratifs, 1990:188.

Olofs, Max   (1889–1969)
▶ German sculptor and silversmith; active Munich.
▶ Trained with Fritz von Miller and studied at the Academy in Munich.
▶ In 1919, he set up a workshop in Munich with Johann Scheidacker and René Sammann; the latter two left in c1922.
▶ Annelies Krekel-Aalberse, *Art Nouveau and Art Déco Silver*, New York: Abrams, 1989:258. Cat., *Münchner Schmuck 1900–1940*, Munich: Bayerisches Nationalmuseum, 1990:90–92.

Olsen, Hans   (1919–)
▶ Danish furniture designer.
▶ Studied Kunsthåndværkerskolen, Copenhagen, to 1943.
▶ In 1941, he was an apprentice cabinetmaker. In 1953, he became an independent designer. His furniture designs were produced by Bondo Gravesen, Frem Røjle, and Schou Andersen Møbelfabrik.
▶ He received the 1965 International Design Award.
▶ Frederik Sieck, *Nutidig Dansk Møbeldesign:—en kortfattet illustreret beskrivelse*, Copenhagen: Bondo Gravesen; 1990 Busck edition in English.

Olsen, Harald   (1851–1910)
▶ Norwegian architect and furniture and glassware designer, metalworker, and enamelist.
▶ In the 1880s, Olson practiced architecture in Kristiania (now Oslo). He was a designer at Hadelands Glasverk in Jevnaker and designed silver and enamelwork for J. Tostrup and David-Andersen, both in Oslo. His curvaceous furniture designs showed influences from France and Belgium, and some of his furniture was produced for Christiania Haandværks og Industriforening and De Samvirkende Fagforeninger.
▶ Cat., David Revere McFadden (ed.), *Scandinavian Modern Design 1880–1980*, New York: Abrams, 1982:269.

Omega Workshops
▶ British cooperative producing furniture, furnishings, ceramics, and textiles.
▶ The Omega Workshops were set up in 1913 by painter, art critic, and lecturer Roger Fry to create employment for his young avant-garde artist friends. His aim being to unite art and design, he recruited artists rather than craftspeople. He used the Wiener Werkstätte and Paul Poiret's Studio Martine as models. A range of domestic furnishings and goods, including pottery, was designed in an attempt to escape the prevailing historism in Britain at the time. The group designed the 1914 interior of the Cadena Café at 49 Westbourne Grove in London, including waitresses' uniforms, murals, rugs, and lighting. Some of the Workshops' pottery was put into limited commercial production; it presaged the angular shapes of the British Modern movement of a decade later. Omega's linens were printed in France. With studios in Fitzroy Square in London, Omega's designers included Fry, Vanessa Bell, and Duncan Grant; Wyndham Lewis worked there briefly. The group's activities attracted the participation of leading artists of the day, including David Bomberg, Paul Nash, and graphic designer McKnight Kauffer. The Workshops' painted furniture was decorated in designs contrived to fit the geometry of a piece rather than arbitrarily applied. The main motifs were nudes and flowers, except for Lewis's abstract patterns. Lewis left in 1914 to establish The Rebel Art Centre; he felt that the work of the Omega painters was outmoded, and found few buyers for the Workshops' wares. The most successful work was from Fry himself, particularly pottery and the Cubist-inspired textile range called *Amenophis*. The activities of the workshop continued until 1919.

▶ Nikolaus Pevsner, 'Omega,' *Architectural Review*, Vol. 90, 1941. Cat., *Omega Workshops: Furniture, Textiles and Pottery 1913–1918*, London: Victoria and and Albert Museum, 1946. Francis Spalding, *Roger Fry*, London: Elek/Granada, 1980. Isabelle Anscombe, *Omega and After: Bloomsbury and the Decorative Arts*, Thames and Hudson, 1981. Cat., *British Arts and Design, 1900–1960*, London: Victoria and Albert Museum, 1983.

OMK Design
▶ British design group.
▶ OMK Design was established in 1966 by Jerzy Olejnik, Bryan Morrison, and Rodney Kinsman, all trained at the London Central School of Arts and Crafts. The group produced its own furniture, including its widely published 1969 *T5* chair.
▶ OMK Design's works were shown at the 1966 Redfern Gallery exhibition in London, 1970 'Ideal Home' in London, 1970 Expo '70, Osaka, and 1970 'International Airport Exhibition' in Amsterdam. Its *T5* chair was shown at the 1969 'Décor International' exhibition in London and 1970 'Modern Chairs 1918–1970' exhibition at the Whitechapel Gallery in London; it was awarded the 1969 Observer Design Award.
▶ Cat., *Modern Chairs 1918–1970*, London: Lund Humphries, 1971.

Onken, Oscar (1858–1948)
▶ American entrepreneur; active Ohio.
▶ Onken was a prominent businessman and philanthropist. Impressed with the Gustav Stickley and Austrian stands at the 1904 St. Louis 'Louisiana Purchase Exposition,' he founded The Shop of the Crafts in Cincinnati in 1904. He hired Hungarian designer Paul Horti, who had designed the Austrian stand at the fair; there was a distinctly European air to the Shop's furniture, with its inlays, applied carvings, and painted designs.
▶ Cat., Anne Yaffe Phillips, *From Architecture to Object*, New York: Hirschl and Adler, 1989:80. Cat., Wendy Kaplan (ed.), 'The Art That Is Life': The Arts and Crafts Movement in America, 1875–1930*, Boston: Museum of Fine Arts, 1987:248.

Opbouw, de
▶ Dutch architecture group.
▶ In 1920, Wilhelm Gispen, Willem Kromhout, J.J.P. Oud, Granprè Moliere, and Jan Van de Vlught founded the architecture club de Opbouw ('Construction'), which was particularly active in Rotterdam 'to promote more exclusively modern ideas about architecture and to keep the movement free from commercial influence' (Gispen). In the early 1920s, Oud was chair, a position assumed by Mart Stam in 1925. The group represented CIAM's Functionalism for three decades.
▶ Barbie Campbell-Cole and Tim Benton (eds.), *Tubular Steel Furniture*, London: The Art Book Company, 1979:29.

OPI, Studio
▶ Italian design cooperative.
▶ Studio OPI was established in the 1960s by Franco Bettonica and Mario Melocchi. They designed smoking, desk, and bar accessories in stainless steel and plastics produced by Melocchi's associated firm Cini e Nils.
▶ Studio OPI's work was shown at the 1972 'Italy: The New Domestic Landscape' exhibition at the New York Museum of Modern Art; its bar accessories were included in the 1984 'Design Since 1945' exhibition at the Philadelphia Museum of Art.
▶ Cat., Kathryn B. Hiesinger and George H. Marcus III (eds.), *Design Since 1945*, Philadelphia: Philadelphia Museum of Art, 1983:232,V–44. Emilio Ambasz (ed.), *Italy: The New Domestic Landscape*, New York: Museum of Modern Art, 1972:80–81,84.

Oppenheim, Meret (1936–72)
▶ German artist; born Berlin.
▶ 1918–30, studied at various German and Swiss schools; 1929–30 and 1938–40, Kunstgewerbeschule, Basel; 1932–33, Académie de la Grande Chaumière, Paris.

▶ From 1932 as an independent artist in Paris, she associated with surrealists Alberto Giacometti, Sophie Taeuber, and Hans Arp; from 1948, she lived in Bern. Her fur-wrapped cup, saucer, and spoon became one of the defining images of Surrealism. Her work included photography, sculpture, furniture, and performance. Her gilded side table with bronze bird's legs and feet was produced by Simón in Italy.
▶ Beginning in 1936 at the Galerie Schultess in Basel, her work was the subject of more than 25 exhibitions, including at the Institute of Contemporary Arts in London in 1989.
▶ Alfred H. Barr, *Fantastic Art, Dada and Surrealism*, New York: Museum of Modern Art, 1936. Cat., Hans Christoph von Tavel, *Meret Oppenheim*, Solothurn: 1974. Cat., Patrick Waldberg, *Meret Oppenheim et ses Jeux d'Été*, Paris, 1974. Cat., Jürgen Glaesemer, *Meret Oppenheim: Arbeiten von 1930–1978*, Hamburg, 1978. Muriel Emanuel et al (eds.) *Contemporary Artists*, New York: St Martin's, 1983:701–02. 'Briefing,' *Blueprint*, July/Aug. 1989:56.

Opsvik, Peter (1939–)
▶ Norwegian furniture designer.
▶ In the 1960s, studied ergonomics under Ulrich Burandt and in design schools in Bergen and Oslo; in the 1970s, in Britain and Volkwangschule für Kunstgewerbe, Essen.
▶ 1965–70, he was a designer at the Tandberg Radio Factory and subsequently collaborated with Hans Christian Mengshoel on the development of ergonomic seating. From 1972, he was a freelance designer. His 1972 *Tripp-trapp* stool-chair was produced by Stokke Fabrikker. Opsvik is best known for his widely published 1981 *Balans Variable* ergonomic stool for Stokke. Along with Oddvin Rykkens and Svein Gusrud, he was an innovator in the ergonomic stool seating popular in the early 1980s.
▶ Cat., David Revere McFadden (ed.), *Scandinavian Modern Design 1880–1980*, New York: Abrams, 1982:269, No. 343. Fredrik Wildhagen, *Norge i Form*, Oslo: Sternersen, 1988:187.

Orazi, Manuel
▶ Spanish lithographer; active Paris.
▶ In Paris during last quarter of the 19th century, Orazi created several of the most notable Art Nouveau posters of the period. He designed the 1884 Théodora poster for Sarah Bernhardt with Gorguet. Others of his posters were for Peugeot bicycles, the opera *Aben Hamet*, and, in the form of an old torn manuscript, for the opera *Thaïs* by Jules Massenet. Orazi's most notable posters were the Loïe Fuller image for the 1900 Paris 'Exposition Universelle,' illustrations of the inventory of Art Nouveau objects sold in Julius Meier-Graefe's La Maison Moderne shop in Paris, and the Vercingétorix for the opening of the Hippodrome in Paris. Orazi created several jewelry and table service designs for Meier-Graefe.
▶ Yvonne Brunhammer et al., *Art Nouveau Belgium, France*, Houston: Institute for the Arts, Rice University, 1976.

Origlia, Giorgio (1943–)
▶ Italian industrial designer; born Turin; active Milan.
▶ Studied architecture, Politecnico di Milano, to 1968.
▶ He began his professional career in 1973 as a designer in the studio of Mario Bellini, working on lighting for Artemide and the *Pianeta Ufficio* office furniture system for Marcatré.
▶ He participated in Bellini's 'Kar-a-sutra' prototype included in the 1972 'Italy: The New Domestic Landscape' exhibition at the New York Museum of Modern Art.

Orivit
▶ German silversmiths; located Cologne-Braunsfeld.
▶ Between 1896 and 1908, the firm, founded by Ferdinand Hubert Schmitz, produced nearly 2,800 models. Orivit was the name given to an alloy with a low silver content. For a short time, the firm made silver hollow-ware on the new 'Huberpresse' machine, which stamped out pieces with simple ornamentation under hydraulic pressure. In 1905, the firm was taken over by WMF (Württembergische Metallwaren Fabrik); Orivit's production stopped in 1928.

► It showed a silver service at the 1904 St. Louis 'Louisiana Purchase Exposition.'

► Annelies Krekel-Aalberse, *Art Nouveau and Art Déco Silver*, New York: Abrams, 1989:141,258. Cat., *Metallkunst*, Berlin: Bröhan-Museum, 1990:382–87.

Ornella

► Italian costume jeweler; located Milan.

► Piera Barni Albani reorganized the Visconti di Modrone company in 1946 to produce costume jewelry, overseen by the goldsmiths Calderoni. The Ornella headquarters was opened by Albani in piazza Piola 5 with three workers. In the mid-1950s, Albini's daughter Maria Vittoria joined the firm as the designer. The firm's production was noted for its hand-painted wooden beads, Venetian glass beads, shells, and hand-molded ceramics in an idiosyncratic style.

► Deanna F. Cera (ed.), *Jewels of Fantasy: Costume Jewelry of the 20th Century*, New York: Abrams, 1992:308.

O'Rorke, Brian   (1901–74)

► New Zealand architect and interior designer; active Britain.

► Studied architecture, Cambridge University and Architectural Association, London.

► His style was uncompromisingly Modern. The 1932 music room he designed for Mrs. Robert Solomon in London included a swirl-motif rug by Marion Dorn. O'Rorke established a small studio that specialized in interior design, particularly for ships, aircraft, and trains. In the 1930s, he designed interiors for oceanliners 1935 *Orion* (commissioned by Colin Anderson) and *Orcades*, which broke from traditional modes. He executed the interior for other ships of the Orient Line and, in 1946, the *Vickers Viking*. He was the architect for the 1947 Orient Steam Navigation building in Sydney. He designed a number of houses, including a semi-detached house complex and the 1933–36 Ashcombe Tower for Major Ralph Rayner. O'Rorke and F.H.K. Henrion designed The Natural Scene and the Country (natural history) pavilion at the 1951 London 'Festival of Britain.'

► Cat., *Thirties; British art and design before the war*, London: Arts Council of Great Britain, Hayward Gallery, 1979:88,122, 123,182,183,298.

Orrefors Glasbruk

► Swedish glassware manufacturer.

► An ironworks was established in 1726 on the property of Halleberg (the Orrefors estate), Socken, Småland; it started production of ink bottles in 1898. In 1913, Johan Ekman purchased the estate and placed forester Albert Ahlin in charge. Ekman produced art glass with little success at first, until he hired Simon Gate in 1916 and Edward Hald in 1917, members of the Slöjdföreningen (Swedish Crafts Society), as designers. The two artists had done no glass designing before. Gate and Hald collaborated with the glass blowers and former cutter Gustav Abels on reviving engraved glass. With master glass blower Knut Bergqvist, they developed the *graal* technique in 1916. In 1933, Gate became director of Orrefors. Orrefors also produced a full range of tableware. Designers Edvin Öhrström, Vicke Lindstrand and blower Gustav Bergqvist developed the *ariel* technique. In 1889, the Sandvik glassworks was leased and, in 1918, purchased by Orrefors; it specialized in plain, inexpensive table and household soda glass and expanded the Orrefors range. The firm today operates a school for glass blowers and engravers from among whom it draws its workforce. Designers included Nils Landberg, Gunnar Cyrén, Eva Englund, and Lars Hellsten. In 1975, Orrefors bought Strömbergshyttan; in 1984, the SEA and Alghuit glassworks.

► Received three grand prizes and three gold medals at 1925 Paris 'Exposition Internationale des Arts Décoratifs et Industriels Modernes.' Work (by Edvin Öhrström) shown at 1937 Paris 'Exposition Internationale des Arts et Techniques dans la Vie Moderne.'

► Jennifer Hawkins Opie, *Scandinavia: Ceramics and Glass in the Twentieth Century*, New York: Rizzoli, 1989.

Ortner, Laurids

See Haus-Rucker-Co

OSA (Union of Contemporary Artists)

► Soviet architects' association.

► Active 1925–32 OSA was an association of Constructivist architects, including Moisei Ginzburg and brothers Alekandr, Leonid, and Viktor Vesnin. Competition between the Asnova and OSA raised the standards of the new architecture.

► Cat., *Kunst und Revolution: Russische und Sowjetische Kunst 1910–1932*, Vienna: Österreichisches Museum für angewandte Kunst, 1988. Cat., *The Great Utopia: The Russian and Soviet Avant-Garde, 1915–1932*, New York: Guggenheim Museum, 1992.

Osipow, Anna Maria   (1935–)

► Finnish ceramicist.

► In her own workshop, she produced utility ceramics and was a sculptor.

► Cat., David Revere McFadden (ed.), *Scandinavian Modern Design 1880–1980*, New York: Abrams, 1982:269, No. 275.

Osslund, Helmer   (1866–1938)

► Swedish ceramicist.

► Studied painting.

► 1889–94, Osslund worked at Gustavsberg and, in 1897, at the Höganäs Stenkohlsverk.

► Cat., David Revere McFadden (ed.), *Scandinavian Modern Design 1880–1980*, New York: Abrams, 1982:269, No. 16.

Østergaard, Steen   (1935–)

► Danish designer.

► Studied Kunsthåndværkerskolen, Copenhagen to 1960.

► 1962–65, he worked with architect Finn Juhl and, in 1965, set up his own design studio. Østergaard's first plastic object, the 1970 *Chair 290* in polyamid, was produced by France & Son in Denmark. The chair was the first to be extruded as a single unit; its fiberglass reinforced-polyester molded shell was upholstered on the inside and supported by an underframe of chromium-plated metal. A stacking chair and other plastic models were produced by Cado.

► His work was shown at the Kunstindustrimuseet, Stockholm, in 1962 and 1964, Erikholm in 1965, London in 1970, Milan in 1971, and at the Boutique Danoise in Paris in 1972. He was awarded a first prize at the 1963 furniture fair in Cantù, 1966 Johannes Krøiers prize, and recognition in San Cataldo in 1966.

► Cat., Milena Lamarová, *Design a Plastické Hmoty*, Prague: Uměleckoprůmyslové Muzeum, 1972:138. Frederik Sieck, *Nutidig Dansk Møbeldesign:—en kortfattet illustreret beskrivelse*, Copenhagen: Bondo Gravesen; 1990 Busck edition in English.

Østern, Bjørn Sigurd   (1935–)

► Norwegian metalworker.

► 1955–56, studied Kunsthåndverksskole, Bergen; 1956–61, Statens Håndverks -og Kunstindustriskole, Oslo.

► From 1961, he was a designer at David-Andersen.

► Cat., David Revere McFadden (ed.), *Scandinavian Modern Design 1880–1980*, New York: Abrams, 1982:269, No. 249.

Otte-Koch, Benita   (1892–1976)

► German fabric designer; born Stuttgart.

► 1911–13, studied drawing in Düsseldorf, receiving a teacher's certificate; 1920–25, studied Bauhaus, Weimar.

► 1925–33, she was artistic director of handweaving at the Kunstgewerbeschule Burg Giebichenstein in Halle; 1929, married Heinrich Koch, interior designer and photographer; 1933–34, was freelance designer in Prague; 1934–57, director of weaving at the Bodelschwinghschen Anstalten in Bethel, near Bielefeld.

► Lionel Richard, *Encyclopédie du Bauhaus*, Paris: Somogy, 1985: 204. Katja Schneider, *Burg Giebichenstein*, Weinheim: VCH, Acta Humamiora, 1992:314–23,462–63. Sigrid Wortmann Weltge, *Women's Work: Textile Art from the Bauhaus*, London: Thames and Hudson, 1993.

Oud, Jacobus Johannes Pieter   (1890–1963)
▶ Dutch architect; born Purmerend.
▶ Studied Quellinus School of Arts and Crafts, State School of Draftsmanship, Amsterdam, Technical College, Delft.
▶ He worked for architects Jan Stuyt and for P.J.H. Cuypers, both in Amsterdam; for Theodor Fischer in Munich in 1911; and for Willem Dudok in Leiden in 1913. 1915–16, he met Theo Van Doesburg and Gerrit Rietveld; became an active member of the De Stijl group, formed in 1917; and came into contact with the Elementarists. Oud was surprisingly successful in translating De Stijl's difficult theories into practice. He admired Dutch architect H.R. Berlage and was an exponent of the Neue Sachlichkeit approach. Oud opened his own architecture offices in Purmerend and Leiden. 1918–33, he was the city architect of Rotterdam, responsible for the 1920 Tussendijken and Spangen housing estates. He designed and furnished houses at the 1927 Stuttgart 'Weissenhof-Siedlung' (installing W.H. Gispen's lighting fixtures). His work included the 1917 terraced housing (project) on the promenade at Scheveningen, 1919 factory at Purmerend, 1922–24 housing layouts in Oud-Mathenesse, 1924–25 Café de Unie at Rotterdam, 1925 housing layouts at Hook of Holland, 1928–29 Kiefhoek development at Rotterdam, 1938–42 Shell building in The Hague, and 1952–60 Cio-Children's Convalescent Home near Arnhem. His architecture and quirky furniture forms in bent metal and flat wood surfaces shared the De Stijl emphasis on cubic volumes. He attended the opening of the 1923 Bauhaus exhibition in Weimar and was instrumental in widening Eileen Gray's reputation after he saw her work at the 1923 Paris Salon of the Société des Artistes Décorateurs. In 1927, Oud designed tubular-steel chairs and tables for his modifications to the Villa Allegonda in Katwijk; the furniture pieces were produced by a local motorcycle manufacturer. The chairs were painted light blue with spring seats; some of his other furniture models were produced by Metz. From c1935, he took a Functionalist approach, for which he was severely criticized. 1933–54, he was an independent architect in Rotterdam; from 1954, his practice was located in Wassenaar. He was awarded an honorary doctorate by the Technical College in Delft.
▶ His work was included in the 1932 'Modern Architecture' exhibition at the New York Museum of Modern Art and was the subject of the 1965 'J.J.P. Oud: Bauten 1906–63' exhibition in Munich.
▶ J.J.P. Oud, Holländische Architektur (Bauhausbuch 10), Munich, 1926. Henry-Russell Hitchcock, J.J.P. Oud, Paris, 1931. Giulia Veronesi, J.J.P. Oud, Milan, 1953. J.J.P. Oud, Mijn Weg in 'De Stijl,' Rotterdam, 1961. Cat., Wend Fischer, J.J.P. Oud: Bauten 1906–63, Munich, 1965. Barbie Campbell-Cole and Tim Benton (eds.), Tubular Steel Furniture, London: The Art Book Company, 1979:38.

Ovchinnikov
▶ Russian silversmiths; located Moscow.
▶ Pavel Akimovich founded Ovchinnikov in Moscow in 1853. The firm championed traditional Russian silversmithing. The most important silver factory after Fabergé, Ovchinnikov was granted an Imperial Warrant in 1883. Typically, its pieces were covered with cloisonné enamel in overall patterns of multi-colored arabesques on silver-gilt grounds. Its champlevé wares frequently incorporated simpler, brightly colored geometric motifs based on folk-art themes. Pavel Akimovich's sons Mikhail, Aleksandr, Pavel, and Nikolai became directors of the firm, which closed after the Revolution of 1917.

▶ It won awards for its enamel wares at the 1893 Chicago 'World's Columbian Exhibition' and 1900 Paris 'Exposition Universelle.'
▶ Annelies Krekel-Aalberse, Art Nouveau and Art Déco Silver, New York: Abrams, 1989:248,258.

Overbeck Pottery
▶ American ceramics studio; located Cambridge City, Indiana.
▶ The Overbeck Pottery was set up in 1910 in the home of sisters Margaret, Mary Frances, Elizabeth, and Hannah Overbeck in Cambridge City, Indiana. Margaret Overbeck taught art at DePauw University, worked one summer at a pottery in Zanesville, Ohio, and became interested in setting up her own pottery studio; though she and her sisters achieved her ambition, she died in 1911. The three surviving sisters studied art, design, and ceramics and worked at their pottery: Mary Frances (a student at Columbia University of Arthur W. Dow) was in charge of glazing and did some designs; Hannah (with little formal training) became an accomplished designer and decorator; and Elizabeth (a student at Alfred University of Charles F. Binns) handled wheel-thrown shapes and the formulation of glazes. They contributed designs to and wrote criticism for Adelaide Alsop Robineau's journal Keramic Studio.
▶ Artists in Indiana Then and Now: The Overbeck Potters of Cambridge City, 1911–1955, Muncie, Indiana: Ball State University, 1975. American Art Pottery, New York: Cooper-Hewitt Museum, 1987:122.

Ozenfant, Amédée   (1886–1966)
▶ French painter and theoretician; born Saint-Quentin.
▶ 1904–05, studied drawing at École Municipale de Dessin, Saint-Quentin; in 1905, architecture in the studio of Guichard et Lesage, Paris; in 1905, painting, Académie de la Palette, Paris, under André Dunoyer de Segonzac, Roger de la Fresnaye, and Charles Cottet.
▶ In 1915, Ozenfant, Pablo Picasso, Max Jacob, and Guillaume Apollinaire founded the review L'Élan in Paris; Ozenfant was editor 1915–17. He used the pseudonym De Rayet in some writings. 1917–25, he worked with Le Corbusier; they developed ideas on painting and jointly published the Purist manifesto Après le cubisme (1918). 1920–25, Ozenfant with Le Corbusier and poet Paul Dermée edited the periodical L'Esprit Nouveau: Revue Internationale d'Esthétique, the source from which Le Corbusier culled his 1925 Vers une Architecture. In 1924 with Fernand Léger, Ozenfant opened a school of painting; worked with Le Corbusier on the Pavilion de l'Esprit Nouveau at the 1925 Paris 'Exposition Internationale des Arts Décoratifs et Industriels Modernes'; 1935–38, was a lecturer in art history at the French Institute in London. His book Art (1928) became a classic. In 1939, he settled in New York, opened the Ozenfant School of Fine Art, and 1942–54, had a weekly informal radio program as an artistic commentator for 'Voice of America.'
▶ He received the 1962 Medal of Honor from Lund (Sweden) University and 1949 Chevalier de la Légion d'honneur and, in 1962, became a member of the Ordre des Arts et des Lettres.
▶ Amédée Ozenfant and Le Corbusier, Après le cubisme, Paris: Galerie Thomas, 1918. K. Nierendorf, Amédée Ozenfant, Berlin, 1931. Raymond Cogniat et al., Ozenfant, Paris, 1963. Cat., John Golding, Ozenfant, New York, 1973. Suzan L. Ball, Ozenfant and Purism: The Evolution of a Style 1915–1930, Ann Arbor: UMI, 1981. Muriel Emanuel et al. (eds.), Contemporary Artists, New York: St. Martin's, 1983:664.

P

Pabst, Daniel (1826–1910)
▶ German furniture designer and cabinetmaker; born Langenstein, Hesse-Darmstadt; active Philadelphia.
▶ Studied technical high school, Hesse-Darmstadt.
▶ In 1849, he was one of the hundreds of German craftsmen and furniture workers who had settled in Philadelphia in the mid-19th century. For a short time, he was a journeyman furniture maker. In 1854, he opened his own workshop at 222 South Fourth Street in Philadelphia; 1860–70, his financial partner was Francis Krauss, a confectioner. From 1870, his workshop was located at 269 South Fifth Street. His Renaissance revival style, highly carved furniture of the 1860s was produced for clients including Bullitt, Disston, Furness, Ingersoll, Newbold, McKean, Parry, Wistar, and Wyeth. He made a furniture suite of c1868 for historian Henry Charles Lea. In the 1870s, he turned to the neo-Gothic style. His work appears to have been influenced by British designers Bruce J. Talbert and Christopher Dresser. Frank Furness may have designed cabinets produced by Pabst; Pabst may have collaborated with Henry Pratt McKean and son Thomas on the woodwork and furniture for the house of Theodore Roosevelt on Long Island, New York. In 1894, Pabst's son joined the workshop, which closed in 1896. From 1860, he carved centennial spoons for the University of Pennsylvania every year.
▶ He showed a walnut sideboard, which won an award, at the 1876 Philadelphia 'Centennial Exposition.' He made a desk shown at the 1904 St. Louis 'Louisiana Purchase Exposition.' In 1910, he was honored by the University of Philadelphia.
▶ Cat., James F. O'Gorman, *The Architecture of Frank Furness*, Philadelphia: Philadelphia Museum of Art, 1973: figs. 14–1,15–1. David A. Hanks and Page Talbott, 'Daniel Pabst, Philadelphia Cabinetmaker,' *Philadelphia Museum of Art Bulletin*, Vol. 73, April 1977:4–14. David Hanks, 'Daniel Pabst, Philadelphia Cabinetmaker,' *Art and Antiques*, Vol. 3, Jan.–Feb. 1980:94–101. Doreen Bolger Burke et al., *In Pursuit of Beauty: Americans and the Aesthetic Movement*, New York: Metropolitan Museum of Art and Rizzoli, 1987:460–61.

Paganini, Paolo (1960–)
▶ Italian designer; born and active Bologna.
▶ His *Suppergiù* desk accessory, *Puntuale* light fixture by Luceplan, and *Maria* glass chair by Fiam were shown at 'Nuovo Bel Design: 200 Nuovi Oggetti per la Casa' Fiera di Milano, 1992.

Pagano, Giuseppe (b. Giuseppe Pogatschnig; aka Giuseppe Pagano-Pogatschnig 1896–1945)
▶ Italian architect; born Parenzo.
▶ Studied architecture, Politecnico di Milano, to 1924.
▶ He changed his name to the Italian-sounding Pagano when he enlisted in the Italian army in 1915. Pagano and Gino Levi-Montalcini designed the 1928–30 Gualino Office Building and several exhibition buildings at the 1928 'Esposizione di Torino,' considered the earliest Rationalist structures in Italy. They were invited to design the Italian pavilion at the 1930 international industrial exposition in Liège. The 1928 Turin exhibition provided a platform for experimentation by young architects including Alberto Sartoris, Lavinia Perona, Montalcini and Pagano, they

formed the Group of Six, led by Edoardo Persico. From 1931, Pagano was one of the advisors of the revised review *Architettura e Arti Decorative*, renamed simply *Architettura*. 1930–43 with Persico, Pagano worked on the editorial staff of Pier Maria Bardi's *Casabella* magazine, later *La Casa Bella*, of which Pagano was editor from 1933. He designed the 1939–41 bentwood furniture produced by Maggioni for the Università Bocconi. Pagano was the second personality of Italian Rationalism along with Giuseppe Terragni, and played a significant part as its theoretician through his writings. He was known for his Rationalist buildings, condemned by contemporary critics as architecture reduced to engineering. Pagano, Bottoni, and Mario Pucci proposed a permanent 'experimental neighborhood' to be undertaken by the Triennale di Milano in 1934–36. Terragni, the BBPR team, and Pagano separately entered the 1936 competition for the Palazzo del Littorio on the via dell'Impero in Rome. In his article 'Discorso sull'architettura italiana di oggi' ('Italian architecture today'), read to architecture groups in Copenhagen, Stockholm, and Helsinki, and published in *La Tecnica Fascista* in 1939, he endorsed 'the triumph of modern life promoted by Fascism' and praised the 1932 'Mostra della Rivoluzione Fascista' ('Exhibition of the Fascist Revolution'). Pagano designed the 1932 Institute of Physics (part of the University Precinct in Rome designed by Massimo Piacentini) and the 1938–41 Università Bocconi (with Predaval) in Milan. A Fascist from 1920, Pagano left the Fascist Party in 1942, participated in the Resistance, and died in Mauthausen concentration camp.
▶ He was a member of the architecture jury of the 1942 'Esposizione Universale di Roma.' He and his team designed the steel high-rise at the 1933 (V) Triennale di Milano and participated in the 1937 Paris 'Exposition Internationale des Arts et Techniques dans la Vie Moderne.' He was director of the 1936 (VI) Triennale di Milano.
▶ Giuseppe Pagano-Pogatschnig, 'Dell'uso di certi aggettivi,' *La Casa Bella*, July 1930:9–10. Giuseppe Pagano, 'Mussolini salva l'architettura italiana,' *Casabella*, June 1934:2–3. Giuseppe Pagano, 'Discorso sull'architettura italiana di oggi,' *La Tecnica Fascista*, 25 Feb. 1939. Barbie Campbell-Cole and Tim Benton (eds.), *Tubular Steel Furniture*, London: The Art Book Company, 1979:47. Giuseppe Pagano, 'Edoardo Persico' in *Casabella*, No. 109. Giancarlo Palanti, *Giuseppe Pagano Pagatschnig: architetture e scritti*, Milan: Ed. Domus, 1947. Gino Levi-Montalcini, 'Giuseppe Pagano,' *Agorà*, Nov. 1945. Carlo Melograni, *Giuseppe Pagano*, Milan, 1955. Sam Polistina, 'Giuseppe Pagano,' *Avant!*, 29 Sept. 1945. Carlo Ludovico Ragghianti, 'Ricordo di Pagano,' *Metron*, Vol. 7. Richard A. Etlin, *Modernism in Italian Architecture, 1890–1940*, Cambridge: MIT, 1991:228,233,261,265,322,343,379, 389,487,494,498,514,522,580–81,589–95.

Pagella, Carlo (1938–)
▶ Italian designer; born Sesto S. Giovanni; active Milan.
▶ Pagella began his professional career in 1975. His clients in the Udine vicinity in Italy included Danielis, Germa and Mobilsed. His early seating and tables showed an extensive use of naturally finished wood. He was a member of ADI (Associazione per il Disegno Industriale).

▶ *ADI Annual 1976*, Milan: Associazione per il Disegno Industriale, 1976.

Pagnon, Patrick (1935–) and Claude Pelhaitre (1954–)

▶ French furniture designers; active Paris.
▶ Studied École Nationale Supérieure des Arts Décoratifs and École Boulle, Paris.
▶ They set up an office in 1981, specializing in furniture design produced by Artelano, Bauman, Habitat, Mobilier International, and others; in 1984, received VIA's Carte Blanche sponsorship for the *Straty* range of furniture, produced by Ligne Roset as the *Domus* range.
▶ Received 1985 SM d'Or (*Straty* range) and 1989 SM d'Or at the Salon du Meuble, 1989 Prix de l'Industrie, and 1989 Janus de l'Industrie.
▶ Cat., *Les années VIA 1980–1990*, Paris: Musée des Arts Décoratifs, 1990:140.

Pahlmann, William (1900–)

▶ American interior designer; born Illinois; active New York.
▶ From 1927, studied interior design, Parsons School of Design, New York, and in 1930, Parsons School of Design, Paris.
▶ Pahlmann worked as a traveling salesperson and actor before studying design, becoming active as an interior designer in 1933; in the 1930s, he became known for his colorful, eclectic rooms for the Lord and Taylor department store on Fifth Avenue in New York where he worked from 1936–42; in 1946, he opened his own design firm in New York; wrote a newspaper column 'A Matter of Taste'; was a member of the American Institute of Decorators; designed numerous houses in Texas and interiors of the 1959 restaurant Four Seasons (Philip Johnson, architect), Seagram Building, and restaurant Forum of the Twelve Caesars, both New York; had numerous clients including Abe Burrows, Walter Hoving Sr., and Billy Rose; published *The Pahlmann Book of Interior Design* (1955). Decorators in his office included Anne Winkler, Dorothy Tremble, A.J. Conner, Daren Pierce, Jack Hartrick, and George Thiele.
▶ John Esten and Rose Bennett Gilbert, *Manhattan Style*, Boston: Little Brown, 1990:10. Mark Hampton, *The Legendary Decorators of the Twentieth Century*, New York: Doubleday, 1992.

Pairpoint, Thomas J. (1847–1902)

▶ American metalworker.
▶ Formerly with Gorham Manufacturing, Pairpoint was the first superintendent of Pairpoint Manufacturing.
▶ Doreen Bolger Burke et al., *In Pursuit of Beauty: Americans and the Aesthetic Movement*, New York: Metropolitan Museum of Art and Rizzoli, 1986:457.

Palais du Marbre

▶ French decorating workshop.
▶ Palais du Marbre was established in 1925 as the Modern furniture and decorating store of the firm Mercier frères, 77 avenue des Champs-Élysées, Paris. In 1929, Eric Bagge became its artistic director.
▶ It participated in the 1925 Paris 'Exposition Internationale des Arts Décoratifs et Industriels Modernes.'
▶ Pierre Kjellberg, *Art Déco: les maîtres du Mobilier, le décor des Paquebots*, Paris: Amateur, 1986:133.

Palanti, Giancarlo

▶ Italian architect.
▶ Palanti, architect Edoardo Persico, and designer Marcello Nizzoli designed the exhibition 'Sala della Vittoria' ('Victory Salon') of the Palazzo dell'Arte for the 1936 (VI) Triennale di Milano; Lucio Fontana's classical allegorical statue was mounted at one end of the rather stark space.
▶ Richard A. Etlin, *Modernism in Italian Architecture, 1890–1940*, Cambridge: MIT, 1991:487,489,522–23.

Palazzetti, Sergio (1949–)

▶ Italian furniture dealer and manufacturer; active New York.
▶ Palazzetti set up a showroom in New York in 1981. It sold to both retail and wholesale customers, and, by 1991, had eight showrooms in the USA selling Modern classics and Palazzetti's own line of furniture manufactured in High Point, North Carolina. He began his own furniture production with the *Maverick Collection* with designers David Shaw Nicholls, Thomas Hucker, and Mark Zeff and followed with others.

Paley, Albert (1944–)

▶ American metalworker; born Philadelphia.
▶ Studied Tyler School of Art, Temple University, Philadelphia, to 1969.
▶ From 1968, he taught crafts at various institutions including Rochester Institute of Technology in Rochester, New York. Trained as a blacksmith, he became known for architectural metalwork made with traditional wrought-iron techniques and modern hydraulic presses. He designed metal furniture, gates, railings, and staircases. He was active in his own workshop with other artisans at Rochester, New York. Art Nouveau and simple Romanesque architectural forms can be seen in his work. He also produced jewelry in precious metals.
▶ His numerous awards included the 1982 Award of Excellence from the American Institute of Architects for the 1980 gates of the New York State Senate Chambers. One-person exhibitions included those at the Peter Joseph Gallery, New York, in 1992; University of the Arts, Philadelphia, in 1991; Renwick Gallery, Washington, in 1991; and Roanoke, Virginia, Museum of Fine Arts.
▶ Auction cat., 'Contemporary Works of Art,' Sotheby's New York, 14 March 1992.

Pallavicini, Gigi (1949–)

▶ Italian designer; born and active Lissone.
▶ Pallavicini began her professional career in 1969 in the studio PAD. In 1973, she worked in Protostudio and, in 1973, set up her own studio in Lissone. Her clients in Italy included Fratelli Resnati, Fratelli Piazza, Mariani Armadi, Cappillini, and Tagliabue. She was a member of ADI (Associazione per il Disegno Industriale).
▶ Collaborating with IACP, she participated in the 1971 'Ente Communale del Mobile' competition in Lissone.
▶ *ADI Annual 1976*, Milan: Associazione per il Disegno Industriale, 1976.

Pallucco, Paolo (1950–)

▶ Italian architect, furniture designer, and manufacturer; born Rome.
▶ Studied architecture in Rome.
▶ In 1980, he established Pallucco, which produced new designs of his own and of others (including Simón), and reissued Modern classics; in 1984, established Pallucco Design, where his own work was managed separately; designed the 1984 *Fra Dolcino* shelving; (with Mareille Rivier) collaborated on various furniture pieces, including the 1987 *Tankette* table, emulating the treads of a tank; produced 1984 *Lizie* armchair designed by Régis Protière.
▶ Albrecht Bangert and Karl Michael Armer, *80s Style: Designs of the Decade*, New York: Abbeville, 1990:82,234. Fumio Shimizu and Matteo Thun (eds.), *The Descendants of Leonardo: The Italian Design*, Tokyo, 1987:327.

Palmqvist, Sven Ernst Robert (1906–84)

▶ Swedish glassware designer.
▶ From 1928, trained in the engraving school of the Orrefors Glasbruk; 1931–33, studied Konstfackskolan and Tekniska Skolan, Stockholm; 1934–36, Kungliga Konsthögskolan, Stock-holm; and in Germany, Czechoslovakia, France (Académie Ranson, Paris, under Paul Cornet and Aristide Maillol), Italy, and the USA.
▶ 1930–72, Palmqvist was a designer at the Orrefors Glasbruk, where his work signaled the return to the graceful lines of pre-Functionalist glasswares. In 1954, he invented a new technique

of forming glass bowls by spinning molten glass in a centrifugal mold to eliminate hand finishing. He produced the delicately blown crystal forms of the boldly colored *Ravenna* series with simple non-figurative inlaid patterns, produced by Orrefors 1950–81. From 1972–84, he was a freelance designer at Orrefors.

▶ Received a gold medal and a grand prize at the 1957 (XI) Triennale di Milano for his spun-glass objects; grand prize at 1976 Biennale di Venezia; 1977 Prince Eugen Medal. His *Light and Dark* wall at the Geneva 'Union Internationale des Telecommunications' exhibition was constructed from blocks of *Ravenna* glass and gray and white crystal; the idea was repeated at the 1967 Montreal 'Universal and International Exposition (Expo 67).' His work was shown at the 1937 Paris 'Exposition Internationale des Arts et Techniques dans la Vie Moderne,' 1939 'New York World's Fair,' 1958 'Formes Scandinaves' exhibition at the Paris Musée des Arts Décoratifs, and 1958 Orrefors traveling exhibitions.

▶ 'Sven Palmqvist,' *Design Quarterly*, No. 34, 1956:21–23. Erik Zahle (ed.), *A Treasury of Scandinavian Design*, New York, 1961: 287, Nos. 217,219,231. Cat., David Revere McFadden (ed.), *Scandinavian Modern Design 1880–1980*, New York: Abrams, 1982: 269, Nos. 141,187. Cat., Kathryn B. Hiesinger and George H. Marcus III (eds.), *Design Since 1945*, Philadelphia: Philadelphia Museum of Art, 1983. Frederick Cooke, *Glass: Twentieth-Century Design*, New York: Dutton, 1986:83–85. Jennifer Hawkins Opie, *Scandinavia: Ceramics and Glass in the Twentieth Century*, New York: Rizzoli, 1989.

Palombi Sirani, Ettore   (1930–)
▶ Italian designer; born Rome; active Milan.
▶ He began his professional career in 1950. Specializing in plastics production, he worked with architect Fabio Mello and in the Studio Astarte in Rome, designing tables, chairs, and furnishings. He was a member of ADI (Associazione per il Disegno Industriale).
▶ *ADI Annual 1976*, Milan: Associazione per il Disegno Industriale, 1976.

Palterer, David   (1949–)
▶ Israeli designer; born Haifa; active Florence.
▶ Studied architecture, Università di Firenze, to 1979.
▶ He was an assistant lecturer to Adolfo Natalini at the Facoltà di Architettura in Florence and taught a design course at Syracuse University in Syracuse, New York, Werkbund in Stuttgart, and Bezalel School of Arts and Crafts, Jerusalem. In 1983, he established the design and manufacturing firm Alterego in Amsterdam with Bořek Šípek; designed the interior architecture (with Luigi Zangheri) of the San Casciano theater, Florence airport, and parks in Pesaro (Italy) and Tel Aviv; designed furniture, furnishings and products for Cleto Munari, Nuova Vilca, Artelano, Mancioli, and Zanotta.
▶ He organized and participated in numerous competitions in Italy and abroad including 'L'interno dopo la forma dell'utile' at 1979 (XVI) Triennale di Milano, Biennale in São Paulo, re-evaluation (with Adolfo Natalini's group) of the old city plan of Parma, and International Interior Design competition sponsored by journal *Architectural Design*.
▶ Andrea Branzi, *La Casa Calda: Esperienze del Nuovo Disegno Italiano*, Milan: Idea Books, 1982. Cat., Alessandro Vezzosi, *Il Tesoro dell'Architettura: Gioielli, Argenti, Vetri, Orologi, 1980/1990*, Cleto Munari, Florence: EDIFIR, 1990. *Modo*, No. 148, March–April 1993:124.

Palyart, Jacques   (?–1928)
▶ French decorator and furniture designer.
▶ Some of Palyart's furniture, particularly models inspired by the Directoire style, was produced by Atelier français and metalwork by Orfèverie Christofle.
▶ He showed his furniture (with Louis Süe) at the 1913 Salon d'Automne and participated in the 1923 (I) 'Exposition des Arts Décoratifs Contemporains' at the Pavillon Marsan.

▶ Léon Deshairs, *Modern French Decorative Art*, Paris: Albert Lévy. Pierre Kjellberg, *Art Déco: les maîtres du Mobilier, le décor des Paquebots*, Paris: Amateur, 1986:133.

Pamio, Roberto   (1937–)
▶ Italian architect and designer; born Mestre, Venice.
▶ Studied architecture, Università di Venezia, to 1968.
▶ He became active in 1961 as an architect and furniture and industrial designer; (with Renato Tosso) collaborated on furniture and lighting; had clients including Zanussi-Rex, Peguri, Stilwood, Arclinea, Cidue, FAI, Leucos, and Arflex.
▶ Received 1985 Product Design Award, Chicago; 1985 Roscoe Award, New York; 1987 Premio Compasso d'Oro.
▶ *Moderne Klassiker: Möbel, die Geschichte machen*, Hamburg, 1982:139. Giancarlo Iliprandi and Pierluigi Molinari (eds.), *Industrial Designers Italiani*, Fagagna, 1985:162. Hans Wichmann, *Italien Design 1945 bis heute*, Munich: Die Neue Sammlung, 1988. *Modo*, No. 148, March–April 1993:124.

Pander
▶ Dutch furniture manufacturer; located Gouda (1863–65), The Hague (1865–85), Amsterdam (1885–1915), Rotterdam (1915–85).
▶ In 1882, Hendrik Pander expanded his housewares mart and carpet business to include curtains, linoleum, blankets, and furniture and, in 1887, set up a furniture factory. Its products were designed in Louis XVI and 'Old Dutch' styles. Pander sold machine-made furniture wholesale and interior furnishings on special orders. 1914–34, Hendrik Wouda worked at the firm as interior architect and became head of the department of Modern Interior Art. 1914–16, F. Spanjaard was a designer at Pander; 1917–23, Cor Alons worked under Wouda. Interior architect Paul Bromberg, having previously worked for Metz, was a member of the Pander staff 1924–34. Through the efforts of Wouda and Bromberg, Pander clients were offered a choice of Modern types; Wouda's work was austere and cubical, while Bromberg's was more sculptural. In 1917, a large factory complex was built in The Hague; it produced furniture for domestic and foreign sales. In 1927, Pander acquired the airplane producer Maatschappij tot Vervaardiging van Vliegtuigen Pander. From 1930, furniture was produced both by traditional joinery techniques, and by volume production processes. 1933–41, tapestry artist and interior architect S.F. Semeij was a member of the Modern Interior Art department and, in 1934, Wouda and Bromberg departed. 1938–*c*41, French designer E.B. Dubourcq worked for Pander; during this time, contemporary designs were dropped. Consultant designers included architect L.C. van der Vlugt, J. H. van den Broek, J. Wils, F.A. Eschauzier, J. van Erven Dorens, and decorative artist C.A. Lion Cachet. In 1985, Pander went into liquidation.
▶ *Industry and Design in the Netherlands, 1850/1950*, Amsterdam: Stedelijk Museum, 1985:260–63.

Panelli, Roberto   (1930–)
▶ Italian industrial designer; born Pisa; active Udine.
▶ He began his professional career in 1957. His clients in Italy included Lorenzon (furnishings), Burelli (kitchens), Cosatto (baby furniture), Phillinini (furnishings), Moroso (chairs and divans), Cumini (kitchens), Moretuzzo (kitchens), and Mobian (furnishings). He was a member of ADI (Associazione per il Disegno Industriale).
▶ *ADI Annual 1976*, Milan: Associazione per il Disegno Industriale, 1976.

Panizon, Madeleine
▶ French milliner; active Paris.
▶ Before World War I, Panizon had a workshop at 8 rue de Ponthieu in Paris. After the war, decorator and couturier Paul Poiret commissioned Panizon to create hats appropriate to his dresses. To work with Panizon, Poiret assigned Alice Natter, a former student at his Martine School, who also produced designs and goods.

▶ Victor Arwas, *Art Déco*, Abrams, 1980. Cat., *Decorative Arts 1925 Style*, New York: Didier Aaron, 1979.

Pankok, Bernhard (1872–1943)

▶ German designer and graphic artist; born Münster.
▶ Apprenticed as a restorer and decorator in Münster; studied painting in Düsseldorf and Berlin, until 1892.
▶ 1892–1902, he worked in Munich, contributing to the journal *Jugend* and designing rather heavy-handed furniture in an Art Nouveau style. Following the lead of Koloman Moser's and Josef Hoffmann's Wiener Werkstätte, in 1897, Pankok, Hermann Obrist, Bruno Paul, Peter Behrens, and Richard Riemerschmid founded the Münchner Vereinigte Werkstätten für Kunst im Handwerk (The Munich United Workshops for Art in Handwork), aiming to sell everyday objects designed by Modern artists. In 1902, he settled in Stuttgart, where, 1913–17, he was director of the Staatliche Kunstgewerbeschule. He designed the 1900 Haus Lange and the airship *Friedrichshafen*. In 1911, he designed an aluminum-tube chair for the zeppelin.
▶ His work was the subject of the 1973 'Bernard Pankok 1872–1943' exhibition, Württembergisches Landesmuseum, Stuttgart. Work shown at 1970 'Pankok–Riemerschmid–Paul: Interieurs Münchner Architekten um 1900,' Museum Villa Stuck, Munich.
▶ S. Günther, *Interieurs um 1900: Bernhard Pankok, Bruno Paul, und Richard Riemerschmid als Mitarbeiter der Vereinigten Werkstätten für Kunst im Handwerk*, Munich, 1971. Cat., *Bernard Pankok 1972–1943*, Stuttgart, 1973. Cat., Kathryn B. Hiesinger and George H. Marcus III (eds.), *Design Since 1945*, Philadelphia: Philadelphia Museum of Art, 1983. Cat., *Bernhard Pankok: Malerei, Grafik, Design im Prisma des Jugendstils*, Munich: Westfälisches Landesmuseum, 1986. Cat., Kathryn Bloom Hiesinger, *Die Meister des Münchner Jugendstils*, Munich: Stadtmuseum, 1988:88–93.

Pantin, Cristallerie de

▶ French crystal factory; located Pantin.
▶ E.S. Monot founded the Cristallerie de La Villette in 1851, specializing in cut clear-glass production. In 1855, it was renamed Cristallerie de Pantin when it was moved to the town of the same name in the north-eastern suburb of Paris. Adding color techniques in the 1860s, Pantin was known for its opalescent and iridescent glass. The operation was reorganized as Stumpf, Touvier, et Viollet when Monot retired in *c*1886. From 1888, it produced glass in an Art Nouveau style. Along with iridescent, enameled, and frosted glass, it began producing imitations of semi-precious stones under its artistic director Touvier. In 1900, its director Stumpf was succeeded by Camille Turré de Varreux, under whom it expanded its production to include cased glass with finely detailed, etched, and wheel-cut decorations, and table services based on designs by Dutch architect Hendrik Berlage.
▶ Pantin showed its imitations of rock crystal and Venetian glass at the 1878 Paris 'Exposition Universelle.'
▶ Yvonne Brunhammer et al., *Art Nouveau in Belgium, France*, Houston: Institute for the Arts, Rice University, 1976.

Panton, Verner (1926–)

▶ Danish architect and designer; born Funen Island; active Binningen (Switzerland) and the USA.
▶ Studied Odense Tekniske Skole, and architecture, Det Kongelige Danske Kunstakademi, Copenhagen, to 1951.
▶ 1950–52, he collaborated with Arne Jacobsen on experimental furniture. In 1955, he set up an office in Binningen (Switzerland); Thonet produced his *Zig-Zag* chair in laminated wood. His reputation was established by his innovative 1957 Cardboard House and 1960 Plastic House. A prolific designer, his range of work included designs for furniture, lighting, carpets, textiles, and exhibitions, although he concentrated on chair design earlier in his career. He executed commissions for the offices of the magazine *Der Spiegel* in Hamburg and for the Bayer ships of 1968

and 1970. Panton pioneered the world's first one-piece, cantilever plastic chair in a fiberglass shell; his best known design, the 1960 *Stacking Chair*, was produced by Herman Miller from 1967. His cone-shaped chairs were produced from the late 1950s, including his 1959 *Heart Chair*, upholstered in stretch-knit fabric. Other chair designs included the 1965 *S-Chair* produced from a single sheet of plywood, and 1982 jigsaw plywood models. From 1969, he designed floor coverings and furnishing textiles for Mira-X in Suhr (Switzerland), including 1984 cotton chintz fabrics in the *Diamond Collection* and 1987 cotton fabric in the *Cubus Collection*. He designed exhibitions, including contributing to the 1971 'Visiona 2' for Bayer with Joe Colombo and Olivier Mourgue, and lighting for Louis Poulsen. In the late 1980s, he executed bizarre, organically shaped plastic chairs and Post-Modernist lighting fixtures.
▶ He received the 1963 and 1968 International Design Awards from the American Institute of Designers, 1967 Rosenthal Studio Prize, 1967 PH prize, an award at the 1968 (II) Eurodomus in Turin (Italy), a medal at the 1968 Österreichisches Bauzentrum (International Furniture Exhibition), 1969 diploma of honor, 1972 Bundespreis 'Die gute Industrieform,' and 1973 Knight of Mark Twain, USA.
▶ 'Experimentator in Design,' *Form*, May 1969:2–7. Cat., *Qu'est-ce que le design?*, Paris: Centre de Création Industrielle, 1969. Cat., *Modern Chairs 1918–1970*, London: Lund Humphries, 1971: No. 56. Sylvia Katz, *Plastics: Designs and Materials*, London, 1978:87,138,142–43,156,169. Frederik Sieck, *Nutidig Dansk Møbeldesign:—en kortfattet illustreret beskrivelse*, Copenhagen: Bondo Gravesen; 1990 Busck edition in English. Cat., David Revere McFadden (ed.), *Scandinavian Modern Design 1880–1980*, New York: Abrams, 1982:269, No. 266. Cat., Kathryn B. Hiesinger and George H. Marcus III (eds.), *Design Since 1945*, Philadelphia: Philadelphia Museum of Art, 1983:225,III–61,VII–48,49. Jeremy Myerson and Sylvia Katz, *Conran Design Guides: Lamps and Lighting*, London: Conran Octopus, 1990:77. Cat., *Acquisitions 1982–1990 arts décoratifs*, Paris: Fond National d'Art Contemporain, 1991.

Paolozzi, Eduardo Luigi (1924–)

▶ British sculptor, printmaker, and designer; born Leith (Scotland).
▶ 1943, studied Edinburgh College of Art; 1944, Slade School of Fine Art, London.
▶ 1947–50, he worked in Paris and, in 1950, returned to London. In the 1950s, he introduced the imagery of American mass consumerism into British art. He was a member of the Independent Group at the Institute of Contemporary Arts in London; at its meetings in the early 1950s, the group considered themes including automobile styling, popular culture, advertising, and science fiction. A leading British Pop artist, 1949–55, he taught in the textile department of the London Central School of Arts and Crafts. 1955–58, he taught sculpture at St. Martin's School of Art; 1960–62, was a visiting professor at the School of Fine Arts in Hamburg; from 1968, lectured in ceramics at the Royal College of Art in London; from 1978, was a professor of ceramics at the Fachhochschule in Cologne; and, from 1981, was a professor of sculpture at the Akademie der bildenden Künste in Munich. He designed ceramics for Rosenthal; his 1970 *Variations on a Geometric Theme* ceramic tableware for Wedgwood was issued in a limited edition of 200 sets. In 1984, he completed the mosaic decoration of Tottenham Court Road station on the London Underground.
▶ He showed his work at the 1956 'This Is Tomorrow' exhibition at the Whitechapel Gallery in London and many others. He won numerous awards; received honorary doctorates from numerous institutions; made honorary member Architectural Association, London, 1981, and Commander of the British Empire, 1968.
▶ Stuart Durant, *Ornament from the Industrial Revolution to Today*, Woodstock, NY: Overlook, 1986:295. Jonathan M. Woodham, *Twentieth-Century Ornament*, New York: Rizzoli, 1990:260, 302.

Pap, Gyula (1899–1983)
▶ Hungarian metalworker; born Budapest.
▶ After 1925, studied Bauhaus, Weimar.
▶ He was one of the best known of the Bauhaus metalsmiths. In 1934, he returned to Budapest.
▶ Annelies Krekel-Aalberse, *Art Nouveau and Art Déco Silver*, New York: Abrams, 1989:149,258.

Papenek, Victor (1925–)
▶ Austrian writer, teacher, and product designer; active USA.
▶ 1942–48, studied The Cooper Union, New York; 1949, under Frank Lloyd Wright; Massachusetts Institute of Technology, Cambridge, Massachusetts; 1956, Institute of General Semantics, Chicago.
▶ He set up his own design office in 1964; was a design consultant to Volvo, Dartington Industries, Planet Products, World Health Organization, Midwest Applied Science, and others; 1954–59, was instructor, Ontario College of Art, University of Toronto; in 1959, visiting professor, Rhode Island School of Design, Providence, Rhode Island; 1959–62, associate professor, State University of New York, Buffalo, and numerous other institutions subsequently; founding member of industrial design organizations including Industrial Designers' Society of America.
▶ Received numerous awards. Work shown in exhibitions and subject of 1974 exhibition, Gallery Grada, Zagreb.
▶ Ann Lee Morgan, *Contemporary Designers*, London: Macmillan, 1984.

Parent, Guillaume (1961–)
▶ French furniture designer; active Paris.
▶ Studied École Nationale Supérieure des Arts Décoratifs, Paris.
▶ He was first an apprentice cabinetmaker; from 1985, was an independent cabinetmaker; designed furniture for Musée Carnavalet, Paris, in 1989; for libraries of Réunion des Musées Nationaux in 1992, and signage for Châteaux de Versailles and de Trianon.

Pareschi, Gianni (1965–)
▶ Italian industrial designer; active Milan.
▶ Studied Politecnico di Milano to 1965.
▶ From 1975, he worked in the industrial design department of the G14 Progettazione. A specialist in ergonomics, he was a member of ADI (Associazione per il Disegno Industriale).
▶ *ADI Annual 1976*, Milan: Associazione per il Disegno Industriale, 1976.

Parigi, Paolo (1936–)
▶ Italian industrial designer; born Borgo San Lorenzo, Florence; active Borga S. Lorenzo.
▶ He began his design career in 1964; (with Heron Parigi) was active in his own firm Parigi Design; was best known for his office furniture, including a range of drawing boards; became a member of ADI (Associazione per il Disegno Industriale).
▶ Work shown in numerous exhibitions. Received 1975 Smau prize (*Polo* chair), 1979 Premio Compasso d'Oro, 1987 Goed Industrieel, Antwerp.
▶ *ADI Annual 1976*, Milan: Associazione per il Disegno Industriale, 1976. Giancarlo Iliprandi and Pierluigi Molinari (eds.), *Industrial Design Italiani*, Fagagma, 1985:164. Hans Wichmann, *Italien Design 1945 bis heute*, Munich: Die Neue Sammlung, 1988.

Parigi, Vittorio (1937–)
▶ Italian industrial designer; born Borgo San Lorenzo, Florence; active Milan.
▶ Studied architecture to 1964.
▶ He began his professional career in 1960. His range of plastic bedroom furniture was produced by Molteni and storage system by Citterio. Clients in Italy included Sormani, Sordelli, Lem Blu-Red and Zevi. He designed sailboats and mobile homes. He collaborated with architects Mezzedini in Ethiopia and Bazzoni in Milan. Parigi was a member of ADI (Associazione per il Disegno Industriale).

▶ *ADI Annual 1976*, Milan: Associazione per il Disegno Industriale, 1976.

Parish, Sister (aka Mrs. Henry Parish II; b. Dorothy May Kinnicutt 1910–)
▶ American interior decorator; active New York.
▶ Parish was known as 'Sister' by her four brothers, a name that was to stick. In 1930, she married banker Henry Parish II; while on honeymoon in Paris, she decided to become a decorator. The Parishes' house in Gracie Square in New York was decorated by Eleanor Brown of McMillen. When the Parishes took a small house in New Jersey, 'Sister' Parish designed the interiors herself. She was asked to design the time-worn interiors of the Essex Hunt Club, at the beginning of her professional design career. Other early work included the homes of friends in Far Hills, New Jersey. She opened a shop on Madison Avenue in New York. Her decorating style was layered with themes from the past. Parish became known in the early 1960s through her work on the redecoration of the White House in Washington for the Kennedys. She became partners with Albert Hadley in 1963 in the firm Parish-Hadley Associates in New York. Hadley brought a more contemporary approach to the firm's activities. Parish perfected the 'English manor-house look.' Though known for her décors of great richness, in her own house in Maine, patchwork quilts and rag rugs were combined with painted floors and stiff organdy curtains, creating a synthetic nostalgia.
▶ Mark Hampton, *House and Garden*, May 1990:145–49,214. John Esten and Rose Bennett Gilbert, *Manhattan Style*, Boston: Little, Brown, 1990:10. Mark Hampton, *The Legendary Decorators of the Twentieth Century*, New York: Doubleday, 1992.

Parisi, Ico (1916–)
▶ Italian artist and designer; born Palermo; active Como.
▶ 1931–35, studied building construction, Como; 1949–52, architecture, Institute Atheneum, Lausanne, under Alberto Sartoris.
▶ 1935–36, he worked in the office of architect Giuseppe Terragni, Como; 1937–38, was an independent film maker, Como; in 1939, freelance stage designer, Como; was a freelance designer and visual artist and, from 1945, was active with Luisa Parisi in his own Studio La Ruota; in the 1950s, designed some furniture in the Modern style; had clients in Italy including Spartaco Brugnoli, Fratelli Rizzi, Terraneo, and Zanolli e Sebellin; in 1956, became a member of ADI (Associazione per il Disegno Industriale) and, in 1952, of Art Club di Milano; 1935–40 with others, was active as founder member of the Como Group of architects and, in 1936 with others, of the Alto Quota group of architects, Como. His designs included 1968 Contenitoriumani, 1973 Impotesi per una casa esistenziale, 1977 Utopia realizzabile, 1979 Apocalaisse gentile, 1980 Crolli edificanti, 1982 Architetturadopo, and 1983 Liberta e uscire dalla scatola.
▶ Received 1937 film prize, Città di Como; diploma of honor, 1954 (X) Triennale di Milano; 1955 Premio Compasso d'Oro; gold and silver medals, 1957 'Colori e Forme' exhibition, Como; 1959 Lurago d'Erba Gold Medal; 1971 Knight of Mark Twain Award, Kirkwood, Missouri; 1974 Premio Marco Aurelio, Rome. Work shown in numerous exhibitions including 1951 (IX) and 1954 (X) Triennali di Milano; 1974 'IN-Arch,' Rome; 1976 Biennale di Venezia.
▶ *Ico e Luisa Parisi*, Chiasso, 1970. 'Recente Lavori di Ico e Luisa Parisi,' *Casa Vogue*, Jan.–Feb. 1973. *ADI Annual 1976*, Milan: Associazione per il Disegno Industriale, 1976. Cat., G. de Marchis, *Ico Parisi: Operazione Arcevia*, Rome 1979. Cat., F. Farini, *Ico Parisi*, Ferrara, 1981.

Parker, Kenneth (1957–)
▶ American industrial designer; active Detroit.
▶ Parker assisted Samuel Hohulin with the design of the 1982 *Mighty Mite* vacuum cleaner, known for its compactness and bright color.

▶ The *Mighty Mite* was shown at the 1983–84 'Design Since 1945' exhibition at the Philadelphia Museum of Art.
▶ Cat., Kathryn B. Hiesinger and George H. Marcus III (eds.), *Design Since 1945*, Philadelphia: Philadelphia Museum of Art, 1983. Wolf von Eckardt, 'Fashionable Is Not Enough,' *Time*, Vol. 121, Jan. 3, 1983:76–77.

Parsons, Frank Alvah   (?–1930)
▶ American teacher; active New York.
▶ In 1904, William Merritt Chase offered interior decoration courses at the New York School of Fine Art, which he founded in 1896 and where, at about this time, Parsons taught interior design; he was president from 1913. In 1940, the school was renamed Parsons School of Design. Students were taught drafting, color, elevation drawing, period design, and constructive and decorative architecture. Parsons wrote the book *Interior Decoration: Its Principles and Practice* (1916) and established courses focusing on materials (rugs, fabrics, and wallpapers) and cost accounting. The school sponsored student trips abroad to study historical styles 'in their natural environment.' 1915–16, Parsons and former student William Odom conducted study tours abroad. Odom persuaded Parsons to open a branch in Paris c1920. In the 1980s, Parsons' School of Design was taken over by the New School for Social Research, but retained its name. A master's degree program in the decorative arts was established in cooperation with the Cooper-Hewitt Museum and the Smithsonian Museum of Design. The school on lower Fifth Avenue offered a wide range of courses, including fashion, interior, furniture, and industrial design.
▶ Frank Alvah Parsons, *Interior Decoration, Its Principles and Practice*, New York: Doubleday, Page, 1916. John Esten and Rose Bennett Gilbert, *Manhattan Style*, Boston: Little, Brown, 1990:5–6.

Parthenay, Jean   (1919–)
▶ French industrial designer; active Paris.
▶ Studied École Nationale Supérieure des Arts Décoratifs, Paris.
▶ 1948–78, he worked at Agence Technès with Roger Talon, Daniel Maurandy, and Roger Riche, and supervised industrial design work for Poclain, Seb, Calor, Thomson, and others; from 1971, taught at École des Arts Appliqués, Paris; in 1980 with others, founded the firm Obectif Design, where the alphanumeric telephone *Alpha X* was designed.
▶ Received 1965, 1966, 1968, and 1976 industrial design awards for Poclain hydraulic shovels. Work (*Alpha X* telephone) shown at Consumer Electronic Show, Chicago.
▶ Cat., *Design français 1960–1990*, Paris: Centre Georges Pompidou/APCI, 1988. François Mathey, *Au bonheur des formes, design français 1945–1992*, Paris: Regard, 1992:322–25.

Partridge, Fred T.
▶ British metalworker and jeweler.
▶ Partridge went to Chipping Campden in the Cotswolds in 1902, when C.R. Ashbee moved the Guild of Handicraft there from Essex House in London. Partridge was a member of the Barnstaple Guild of Metalworkers, founded by G. Lloyd Morris in 1900; Partridge worked there and, concurrently, with Ashbee. Active c1900–08, he was among the few British craftspeople strongly influenced by French Art Nouveau, including the work of René Lalique and Charles Desrosiers. His wife Mary Hart Partridge was an enameler for some of Ashbee's jewelry and silverwares.
▶ With Ashbee and the Guild of Handicraft, Partridge showed his work at the 1902 exhibition of the Arts and Crafts Society.
▶ *Der moderne Stil*, Vol. V, plate 41. Charlotte Gere, *American and European Jewelry 1830–1914*, New York: Crown, 1975:213.

Pasanella, Marco   (1962–)
▶ American furniture designer; active New York.
▶ Studied Yale University to 1984.
▶ 1985–86, he was an associate in Pasanella + Klein Architects and, subsequently, Pasanella, Klein, Stolzman, Berg Architects; in

1986, established The Pasanella Company to design and manufacture furniture and furnishings. From 1987, he was also a freelance writer and photographer for magazines *Elle, Harper's Bazaar, International Design*, and *Casa Vogue* (Spain). 1987–90, he was a contributing editor of the magazine *Taxi*. One of his best known designs is the 1991 sideways rocking chair.
▶ He received the 1987 and 1988 Design Excellence award from *ID* magazine and won the 1991 competition '2001: How Will We Live?' sponsored by Sony, *Metropolis* magazine, and Parsons School of Design.

Pasca di Magliano, Emmanuele   (1941–)
▶ Italian industrial designer; born Homs, Tripolitania (Libya); active Naples.
▶ 1963–65, he was active in research, analysis, and project design on the reconstruction of the northern section of Naples through the partnership Studio Lauro, Palomba, Pasca in Naples. In 1975, Pasca, Palomba, and Lauro designed the publication *I legni* for the Centro Ricerche Artigianato e Design of the cities of Campagna and Ellisse. He was a member of ADI (Associazione per il Disegno Industriale).
▶ The partnership won an honorable mention at the Internazionale A. Olivetti prize for its project on the theme 'La Nuova Città' concerning the restoration of the northern section of Naples.
▶ *ADI Annual 1976*, Milan: Associazione per il Disegno Industriale, 1976.

Pascaud, Jean   (1903–)
▶ French decorator and furniture designer; born Rouen.
▶ Studied engineering, École Centrale des Arts et Manufactures, to 1924.
▶ After the 1925 Paris 'Exposition Internationale des Arts Décoratifs et Industriels Modernes,' he turned to the applied arts, in particular furniture. Around 1935, his furniture began to incorporate silvered glass. His commissions included ministry offices and embassies, the Mobilier National, the Château de Rambouillet, various public and private organizations, and oceanliners including 1935 *Normandie, Pasteur*, and *Laos*.
▶ From the early 1930s, he showed his work in Salons and expositions in France and abroad. Received a grand prize at 1937 Paris 'Exposition Internationale des Arts et Techniques dans la Vie Moderne.'
▶ *Ensembles Mobiliers*, Vol. II, Paris: Charles Moreau, 1937. *Ensembles Mobiliers*, Vol. V, No.13, Paris: Charles Moreau, 1945. Pierre Kjellberg, *Art Déco: les maîtres du Mobilier, le décor des Paquebots,*, Paris: Amateur, 1986:133.

Pasini, Gianni   (1941–)
▶ Italian designer; born Venice; active Milan.
▶ Pasini began his professional career in 1965; had clients including Olivetti, Fabbrica Italiana, Magneti Marelli, and Crinospital; became a member of ADI (Associazione per il Disegno Industriale). In the Olivetti information bureau, he designed electronic machinery including a text-editing system, minicomputer, and copier; from 1974 with Sandro Pasqui, was active in the design studio Pasqui e Pasini.
▶ Pasqui e Pasini received 1982 and 1984 Smau award.
▶ *ADI Annual 1976*, Milan: Associazione per il Disegno Industriale, 1976. Giancarlo Iliprandi and Pierluigi Molinari (eds.), *Industrial Design Italiani*, Fagagma, 1985:166. Hans Wichmann, *Italien Design 1945 bis heute*, Munich: Die Neue Sammlung, 1988.

Pasqui, Sandro   (1937–)
▶ Italian industrial designer; born Castello; active Milan.
▶ He began his professional career in 1963, working for Olivetti until 1967. From 1968, he was active in his own studio with clients including Magneti Marelli, Crinospital, and Olivetti; participated in congresses sponsored by ADI (Associazione per il Disegno Industriale) and Olivetti; became a member of ADI (Associazione per il Disegno Industriale); in 1974 with Gianni Pasini, set up the design studio Pasqui e Pasini.

▶ He participated in the 'Milano 70–70' exhibition. He won the 1970 Compasso d'Oro prize for his *Logos 270* office machine by Olivetti, designed with Mario Bellini. He won an honorable mention for the *Auditronic 770* office machine by Olivetti designed with Mario Bellini and Derkjan I. de Vries.

▶ *ADI Annual 1976*, Milan: Associazione per il Disegno Industriale, 1976. Giancarlo Iliprandi and Pierluigi Molinari (eds.), *Industrial Design Italiani*, Fagagma, 1985:166. Hans Wichmann, *Italien Design 1945 bis heute*, Munich: Die Neue Sammlung, 1988.

Pastoe
See UMS

Pastore, Gino (1950–)
▶ Italian designer.
▶ Pastore established industrial design school ISIA, Rome; from 1972, was active in interior and industrial design; collaborated with Ykiko Tanaka.
▶ Received an award at 1984 'Una sedia italiana per gli USA,' Udine.
▶ Giancarlo Iliprandi and Pierluigi Molinari (eds.), *Industrial Design Italiani*, Fagagma, 1985:168. Hans Wichmann, *Italien Design 1945 bis heute*, Munich: Die Neue Sammlung, 1988.

pâte-de-verre
▶ Glassmaking technique.
▶ First appearing in Egypt around 1570 BC, *pâte-de-verre* is produced by grinding down glass and refiring in a mold. Reintroduced by sculptor Henri Cros for large relief sculptures, the process was pursued and refined into vessels by Albert-Louis Dammouse from 1898 and by François-Émile Décorchement from 1900.

Patout, Pierre (1879–1965)
▶ French architect and designer.
▶ Studied École des Beaux-Arts, Paris, to 1903.
▶ He was one of the creators of the *style paquebot*, the luxurious style of interiors installed in oceanliners of the 1920s and 1930s. He designed interiors and furnishings for the oceanliners 1926 *Île-de-France* (including the first-class dining room with ceiling dalles of light by René Lalique), 1931 *Atlantique* with Jacques-Émile Ruhlmann, and 1935 *Normandie*. He designed the Robert Bély department store on the boulevard Haussmann in Paris in c1928. His rather ostentatious taste was illustrated in his own residence at 3–5 boulevard Victor in Paris in 1929, where the influence of Auguste Perret was obvious. As the architect of the Galeries Lafayette department store annex in Paris in 1932, he installed the same kind of opulence as in his oceanliner interiors, and produced a simple, if heavy, façade on the rue de la Chaussée-d'Antin in Paris, punctuated by grand columns sheathed in back-lit glass. He designed several townhouses in Paris; designed 1934 'Paquebot'—Immeuble, 1930 square Henri-Paté, 1928 Logements at 5 rue du Docteur-Blanche, Maison Lombard, 1929 Hôtel Mercédès, all Paris.
▶ At the 1925 Paris 'Exposition Internationale des Arts Décoratifs et Industriels Modernes,' he was architect of the grand gateway Porte de la Concorde (with René Binet) with its nine rectangular totems arranged in a circle and a gold female figure by Louis Dejean at its entry, pavilion of Manufacture Nationale de Sèvres, and Hôtel du Collectionneur. He designed the pavilion of Société des Artistes Décorateurs at 1937 Paris 'Exposition Internationale des Arts et Techniques dans la Vie Moderne' and, with Robert Expert, the French pavilion at the 1937 'New York World's Fair.'
▶ Pierre Cabanne, *Encyclopédie Art Déco*, Paris: Somogy, 1986: 224. *Restaurants, dancing, cafés, bars*, Paris: Charles Moreau, Nos. 8–9, 1929 Nancy J. Troy, *Modernism and the Decorative Arts in France*: Art Nouveau to Le Corbusier, New Haven: Yale, 1991.

Patrix, Georges (1920–92)
▶ French industrial designer; active Paris.
▶ Studied universities in Caen and Cologne, and École Nationale des Beaux-Arts, Paris.

▶ He began his career in 1947 as a consulting engineer; in 1950, set up his own office specializing in industrial design and architecture; from the 1960s, designed more than 2,200 factories throughout Europe and products for Air France, including a 1966 flight meal tray (still in use), machine tools, and packaging for Nescafé and Pernod; with Michel Ragon, Iona Friedman, Nicolas Schoffer, and Walter Jonas, became a founding member of Groupe International d'Architecture Prospectif; published the book *L'Esthétique Industrielle* (1961).
▶ Cat., *Design français 1960–1990*, Paris: Centre Georges Pompidou/APCI, 1988. François Mathey, *Au bonheur des formes, design français 1945–1992*, Paris: Regard, 1992:83,117.

Paul, Bruno (1874–1968)
▶ German architect, cabinetmaker, designer, and teacher: born Seifhennersdorf.
▶ Studied Kunstgewerbeschule, Dresden, from 1886; painting Akademie für Kunst, Munich, under Paul Höcker and Wilhelm von Diez, from 1894.
▶ In 1892, he settled in Munich; following the lead of Koloman Moser's and Josef Hoffmann's Wiener Werkstätte, with Peter Behrens, Hermann Obrist, Bernhard Pankok, and Richard Riemerschmid and others founded the Münchner Vereinigte Werkstätten für Kunst im Handwerk (The Munich United Workshops for Art in Handwork), aiming to sell everyday objects designed by Modern artists. Mies van der Rohe, who moved to Berlin in 1905, was an apprentice to Paul until 1907. In 1908, Paul designed simple, practical *Typenmöbel* (batch-production furniture) for the Deutsche Werkstätten, of which he was a founder; the furniture embodied the most elegant style achievable through machine production. Karl Schmidt's factory Dresdner Werkstätten für Handwerkkunst produced some of Paul's furniture designs. At this time, he contributed illustrations to the journal *Jugend*, which lent its name to Jugendstil, and to the Munich magazine *Simplicissimus*. In 1907, Paul became one of the founders of the Deutscher Werkbund and, in 1906, principal of the Kunstgewerbeschule in Berlin, where he was director 1924–33; it was renamed the Vereinigte Staatsschulen für freie und angewandte Künst in Berlin-Charlottenburg and had a great influence on the development of industrial design in Germany. He designed the interiors of the 1909 oceanliner *Kronprinzessin Cecelie*. He taught Walter von Nessen, Peter Müller-Munk, and Kem Weber the importance of careful workmanship in the tradition of the Werkbund and Vienna Secession aesthetics. Paul designed furniture in both neo-Biedermeier and Modern styles. His architecture developed from an amalgam of Italian Renaissance, Jugendstil, Art Déco, and the International Style. As a practicing architect and designer, he rendered interiors in c1910 that had the lyrical feel of watercolors of the 1820s and 1830s. His architecture included the Hainerberg House (before 1909), near Konigstein am Taunus; Pützsche Sanitorium (before 1909), near Bonn; 1914 Asiatische Museum, Dahlem, Berlin; 1914 'Deutscher Werkbund-Ausstellung' buildings, Cologne; 1925 Das Plattenhaus, Hellerau; 1929–30 Katehreinerhochhaus, Kleistpark, Berlin; and 1935 Traub House, near Prague.
▶ He designed the Jugendstil Hunting Room at the 1900 Paris 'Exposition Universelle.' His work was shown at the 1904 St. Louis 'Louisiana Purchase Exposition,' 1910 Brussels 'Exposition Universelle et Internationale.' He designed a room setting at the 1928 'Exposition of Art in Industry at Macy's' at Macy's department store in New York.
▶ Joseph Popp, *Bruno Paul*, Munich, 1916. S. Friedrich Ahlers-Hestermann, *Bruno Paul: oder die Wucht des Komischen*, Berlin, 1960. Sonja Günther, *Interieurs um 1900: Bernhard Pankok, Bruno Paul, und Richard Riemerschmid als Mitarbeiter der Vereinigten Werkstätten für Kunst im Handwerk*, Munich, 1971. Lothar Lang (ed.), *Bruno Paul*, Klassiker der Karikatur, No. 1, Munich, 1974. Cat., Kathryn B. Hiesinger and George H. Marcus III (eds.), *Design Since 1945*, Philadelphia: Philadelphia Museum of Art, 1983. Frederick Cooke, *Glass: Twentieth-Century Design*, New York: Dutton: 1986:39. Stephen Calloway, *Twentieth-Century Decoration*, New

York: Rizzoli, 1988:114,118,121. Cat., Alfred Ziffer (ed.), *Bruno Paul*, Munich: Stadtmuseum, 1992.

Paul, Francis

▶ French lighting designer.

▶ From the early 1930s until the beginning of World War II, Paul's lighting designs were advanced in their form and conception. Designed for mass production, his models included chromed chandeliers, standard lighting in various metals including copper, and vases for direct, indirect, and semi-indirect illumination. His early work was sold by Décor et Lumière; later models (including the stainless-steel ceiling light for 1935 oceanliner *Normandie*) were sold by René Pottier.

▶ His lighting was included in the Salons of the Société des Artistes Décorateurs, in the 1934 (II) and 1935 (III) Salons of Light in Paris and in the Pavilion of Light at the 1937 Paris 'Exposition Internationale des Arts et Techniques dans la Vie Moderne.'

▶ Alastair Duncan, *Art Nouveau and Art Déco Lighting*, New York: Simon and Schuster, 1978:156,179–80. G. Henriot, *Luminaire Moderne*, 1937: plates 31,32. G. Janneau, *Le Luminaire et les Moyens d'éclairage Nouveaux*, second series: plate 13.

Paul Revere Pottery

▶ American ceramics firm; located Boston.

▶ The Saturday Evening Girls' Club in Boston was a cultural and social organization for young women, mainly from poor Jewish and Italian immigrant families. Edith Brown and Edith Guerrier started a pottery as an addition to the club's activities in the hope of providing the girls with an income. Mrs. James J. Storrow provided the money to set up a small kiln in 1906; she supported the pottery for a number of years. Glazing and firing were handled by a hired ceramicist from the Merrimac Pottery, Newburyport, Massachusetts. By 1908, production had begun in the basement area of a settlement house in Brookline, Massachusetts, and subsequently moved to a larger space in the Library Club House, 18 Hull Street, Boston, with a small staff. The historical nature of the neighborhood suggested the name of Paul Revere Pottery in c1912, although it was also known as the Bowl Shop. Its wares were floral and figural in simple motifs outlined in black or incised. Its production included vases both plain and decorated, electric lamps, dinner services, bowls, candlesticks, and tea sets. The pottery became known for its breakfast sets for children, often with custom monograms. Its wares were almost all hand thrown by young women who had trained for one year. In 1915, Mrs. Storrow funded a new building at 80 Nottingham Road, Brighton, Massachusetts. The facilities housed four kilns and a staff of 20, although it was never profitable. In 1932 when Edith Brown died, the pottery began to have financial difficulties; with Mrs. Storrow's support it survived until 1942.

▶ Mira B. Edson, 'Paul Revere Pottery of Boston Town,' *Arts and Decoration*, No. 2, Oct. 1911:494–95. 'The Paul Revere Pottery: An American Craft Industry,' *House Beautiful*, No. 51, Jan. 1922:50,70. *American Art Pottery*, New York: Cooper-Hewitt Museum, 1987.

Paulin, Pierre (1927–)

▶ French designer; born and active Paris.

▶ From 1946, studied École Camondo, Paris.

▶ He was active in research for the government-sponsored Mobilier International. His first plastic object was the 1953 *Chair 157* in polyester, ABS, and elastomers produced by Artifort of Maastricht. Around 1955, he was one of the first to work in elasticized fabrics, first for Thonet and subsequently for Artifort. In the mid-1960s, he set up his own design studio in Paris, designing automobile interiors for Simca, telephones for Ericsson, and packaging for Christian Dior. 1958–59, he worked in the Netherlands, Belgium, Germany, the USA, and Japan. In the mid-1960s, he designed a succession of sculptural furniture forms composed of a tubular steel structure covered in foam and upholstered in elasticized fabric, produced by Artifort. These models departed dramatically from the upholstered seating on black tubular metal legs that he

designed for Thonet in the 1950s. At the design collaboration AS.DA, he worked with Roger Tallon on the 1980 *Dangari* plastic outdoor chair. His ribbon-like 1965 *Chair 582*, produced by Artifort, was widely published. 1967–78, Paulin participated in refurbishing the Louvre. In 1968, he collaborated with the Mobilier National, resulting in the 1971 'endless' sofa produced by Alpha. His other work for the Mobilier National included furniture and the decoration of President Georges Pompidou's private quarters in the Palais de l'Élysée in 1970; special seating for the French pavilion at 1970 Osaka 'Japan World Exposition (Expo 70)'; and public seating for the Louvre.

▶ His work was included in the Utrecht Furniture Fairs from 1962, where *Chair 582* was shown in 1965; Paris Salon du Meuble from 1963. He won gold medals at the 1958 Brussels 'Exposition Universelle et Internationale de Bruxelles (Expo 58),' 1968 (XIV) Triennale di Milano, and 1970 Osaka 'Japan World Exposition (Expo 70).' He received the 1969 USA Interior Design International Award for *Chair 582*. A 1983 retrospective of his work was mounted at the Paris Musée des Arts Décoratifs.

▶ Cat., *Modern Chairs 1918–1970*, London: Lund Humphries, 1971. Cat., Milena Lamarová, *Design a Plastické Hmoty*, Prague: Uměleckoprůmyslové Muzeum, 1972:136. Cat., *Les Assises du siège contemporain*, Paris: Musée des Arts Décoratifs, 1968. *Design Français*, Paris: Centre de Création Industrielle, 1971: Nos. 120–22,140. Cat., Kathryn B. Hiesinger and George H. Marcus III (eds.), *Design Since 1945*, Philadelphia: Philadelphia Museum of Art, 1983: 225,III–62. Cat., *Acquisitions 1982–1990 arts décoratifs*, Paris: Fonds National d'Art Contemporain, 1991. François Mathey, *Au bonheur des formes, design français 1945–1992*, Paris: Regard, 1992:167,179,243,248,256–57,260,364. Anne Chapoutot, *Pierre Paulin: Un univers de formes*, Paris, 1992.

Paulsson, Gregor (1889–1977)

▶ Swedish architect and theorist.

▶ From c1914, Paulsson was director of Svenska Slöjdforeningen (Swedish Design Society). He published the book *More Beautiful Everyday Things* (1919); highly influential in Sweden, it contributed extensively to the 1930 Stockholm Exhibition, of which he was co-director (with Gunner Asplund).

▶ Penny Sparke, *Introduction to Design and Culture in the Twentieth Century*, Allen and Unwin, 1986.

Pavesi, Giorgio (1931–)

▶ Italian industrial designer; born and active Varese.

▶ He began his professional career in 1954.

▶ He designed fabric for Isa, graphics and design for the furniture firm Saporiti Italiana, and a mobile bar and trolley for Longhi. From 1969, he was a consultant to Ignis Ire for the development and production of domestic electrical appliances. He designed luggage and ceramics and was a member of ADI (Associazione per il Disegno Industriale).

▶ He participated in the 1957 (XI) Triennale di Milano.

▶ *ADI Annual 1976*, Milan: Associazione per il Disegno Industriale, 1976.

Payer, Oskar (1903–73)

▶ Austrian furniture designer; born Vienna.

▶ In the period after World War II, under difficult circumstances for acquiring raw materials, Payer created affordable furniture.

▶ Günther Feuerstein, *Vienna—Present and Past: Arts and Crafts—Applied Art—Design*, Vienna: Jugend and Volk, 1976: 61,81.

Peach, Harry Hardy (1874–1936)

▶ British industrialist; born Toronto (Canada).

▶ In 1902, set up as a bookseller in Leicester; a member of the Fabian Society from 1918, his interest in politics eventually turned to a concern for design; in 1906, searching for a cane chair for his father-in-law, he began a lengthy discussion with teacher and designer Benjamin Fletcher on cane furniture production; with Fletcher's students at his art school in Leicester supplying designs, set up Dryad Handicrafts in 1907; based on Dryad's success, set up (with designer and metalworker William Pick) Dryad Metal Works in 1912, after an unsuccessful attempt at carpet manufacture. Later called Dryad Furniture Company, the firm furnished cane chairs for the 1919 Vickers Vimy Passenger Aeroplane; furniture for the 1934 oceanliner *Queen Mary*; cane-tubular-steel furniture designed by Oliver Bernard for the Cumberland Palace Hotel, Marble Arch, London. Its 1911 *Bachelor's Joy* armchair was probably designed by Albert Crampton. Fletcher designed the *Abundance* chair and settee of *c*1910 and 1907 *Alcover* high-back armchair. Furniture was exported to Japan, South America, and, from 1908, the USA. Peach was a founding member of the British Design and Industries Association.

▶ Dryad received gold medals at the 1910 'Japan-British Exhibition' and 1911 'Festival of Empire' and silver medal at 1910 'Exposition Universelle et Internationale de Bruxelles.' Exhibited at 1908 'Franco-British Exhibition,' 1910 'London Arts and Crafts Exhibition,' 1911 London 'House or Home' exhibition, 1911 Turin 'Esposizione Internazionale dell'Industria e del Lavoro,' and 1914 Paris 'British Arts and Crafts Exhibition.'

▶ Pat Kirkham, *Harry Peach: Dryad and the DIA*, London: Design Council, 1986.

Peacock, Elizabeth   (1880–1969)

▶ British textile designer and teacher.

▶ Peacock began to weave in 1917 with Ethel Mairet. In 1922, she set up her own workshop and, in 1931, co-founded the Guild of Weavers, Spinners and Dyers. She was known for producing the eight banners of 1934–38 commissioned by Leonard and Dorothy Elmhirst for the Great Hall in Dartington. She was a spinner, dyer, and weaver and, 1940–57, an influential teacher.

▶ Her work was the subject of the 1970 'Memorial Exhibition' at West Surrey College of Art and Design, and 1979 exhibition at the Crafts Study Centre in Bath. Two of her Dartington Hall banners were included in the 1979–80 'Thirties' exhibition at the Hayward Gallery in London.

▶ *Elizabeth Peacock*, Bath: Crafts Study Centre, 1978. Cat., *Thirties: British art and design before the war*, London: Arts Council of Great Britain, Hayward Gallery, 1979: 124,298.

Peche, Dagobert   (1887–1923)

▶ Austrian architect, painter, metalworker, glass and ceramics artist, and jewelry designer; born St. Michael, near Salzburg; active Vienna and Zürich.

▶ 1906–10, studied engineering; subsequently, architecture, Akademie der bildenden Künste, Vienna.

▶ He began designing for industry in 1912, specifically ceramics and carpets. Peche created a highly distinctive and unique idiom, amalgamating decorative elements from the Baroque and Rococo. In 1915, he joined the Wiener Werkstätte, becoming co-director 1917–23; it influenced the highly architectural style seen in his lamp designs of about 1920, more classically ornamented than his later, more abstract, work. 1917–19, he designed and directed the Wiener Werkstätte's shop in Zürich. Along with Hoffmann, Peche was the most important designer at the Werkstätte at this time. Peche's metalwork included dense ornamentation and rich decoration. He introduced completely new, playful forms, often in simple materials like tôle and cardboard; inexpensive raw materials were necessitated by the conditions created by World War I. After the war, he produced utilitarian silver objects as well as purely decorative silver ornaments, an example of which was the 1920 50th birthday gift presented to Josef Hoffmann by the Wiener Werkstätte; the articulated fruits in the piece represented sculpture, painting, and architecture.

▶ His work was the subject of the 1923 exhibition at the Hochschule für Angewandte Kunst in Vienna.

▶ Cat., Max Eisler, 'Dagobert Peche Gedächtnis Ausstellung,' plate. 25. Cat., H. Ankwicz-Kleehover, *Dagobert Peche*, Vienna, 1923. Sylvie Raulet, *Bijoux Art Déco*, Paris: Regard, 1984. Annelies Krekel-Aalberse, *Art Nouveau and Art Déco Silver*, New York: Abrams, 1989:200,258.

Pécs pottery

See Zsolnay

Peddemors, A.

▶ Dutch silversmith; active Haarlem.

▶ Studied Haarlemsche School voor Kunstnijverheid under Frans Zwollo Sr.

▶ 1907–17, he taught at the Haarlemsche School voor Kunstnijverheid, where he was in charge of instruction in enameling from 1912.

▶ Annelies Krekel-Aalberse, *Art Nouveau and Art Déco Silver*, New York: Abrams, 1989:175,258.

Pedersen, Gustav   (1895–1972)

▶ Danish metalworker.

▶ Pedersen began working in 1915 at the Georg Jensen Sølvsmedie, becoming foreman of the hollow-ware department in 1917. He designed Jensen's popular *Parallel* flatware pattern and 1938 gravy boat, and others.

▶ Cat., *Georg Jensen Silversmithy: 77 Artists, 75 Years*, Washington: Smithsonian Institution Press, 1980.

Pedrizetti, Paolo   (1947–)

▶ Italian architect and designer; active Milan.

▶ Studied architecture, Politecnico di Milano, to 1973.

▶ He was active in publishing and boating before setting up an industrial design studio in 1978 with Davide Mercatali; in 1982, opened his own independent design studio; in 1982, (with Mercatali) formed the Associated Studio to design furniture, furnishings, and bath accessories; in 1988, directed magazines *Blu & Rosso* and *Bagno & Bagni*.

▶ Received 1981 (*Calibro* with Mercatali) Premio Compasso d'Oro.

▶ Giancarlo Iliprandi and Pierluigi Molinari (eds.), *Industrial Design Italiani*, Fagagma, 1985:166. Hans Wichmann, *Italien Design 1945 bis heute*, Munich: Die Neue Sammlung, 1988. *Modo*, No. 148, March–April 1993:124.

▶ See Mercatali, Davide

Pedrotti, Vittorio   (1950–)

▶ Italian designer; born and active Milan.

▶ He began his professional career in 1974. He was probably best known for his wooden lighting fixtures for Arbazaar in Bologna. He was a member of ADI (Associazione per il Disegno Industriale).

▶ *ADI Annual 1976*, Milan: Associazione per il Disegno Industriale, 1976.

Peduzzi, Richard   (1943–)

▶ French painter and scenic and furniture designer; active Paris.

▶ Studied drawing and sculpture under Charles Auffret.

▶ He met theater director Patrice Chéreau in 1967 and, from 1969, designed all his productions; in 1979, was commissioned by Michel Laclotte, chief curator of Le Musée du Louvre, Paris, to work on interior architecture, museography, and new presentation of art works; in 1988, was commissioned by Jean Coural, ex-director of Mobilier National, to design a furniture collection; as an interior architect, restored the library and museum of Opéra Garnier, Paris, and designed the 1990 *Opéra* chair for its library, produced by Plan Venise; designed more than 20 plays including those of Shakespeare, Marivaux, Wedekind, Koltes, and Heiner Müller, and operas including those of Rossini, Wagner, Alban Berg, and Mozart; with Patrice Chéreau and Daniel Barenboim, worked on Mozart's *Don Giovanni* at the 1994 Salzburg Festival; from 1991, was principal of the École Nationale Supérieure des Arts Décoratifs, Paris.

▶ François Mathey, *Au bonheur des formes, design français 1945–1992*, Paris: Regard, 1992:236.

Pehrson, Anders   (1912–)

▶ Swedish lighting designer.

▶ Pehrson was director of Ateljér Luktan, Åhus, for which he designed lighting.

▶ Cat., David Revere McFadden (ed.), *Scandinavian Modern Design 1880–1980*, New York: Abrams, 1982:269.

Peiffer-Watenphul, Max   (1896–1976)

▶ German painter and metalworker.

▶ Studied medicine to 1919; from 1921, Bauhaus, Weimar.

▶ Settling in Salzburg, he set up a studio where he worked in enamel. Known primarily as a painter, he was a follower of Oskar Kokoschka at the Sommerakademie in Salzburg. 1921–44, he taught at the Kunsgewerbeschule, Vienna.

▶ Lionel Richard, *Encyclopédie du Bauhaus*, Paris: Somogy, 1985: 205. Bert Bilzer, *Peiffer-Watenphul*, Göttingen, 1974. Cat., *Experiment Bauhaus*, Berlin: Bauhaus-Archiv, 1988:422.

Pel

▶ British furniture manufacturer; located Oldbury, Birmingham.

▶ 1914–19, the tubular steel industry in Britain was stimulated by demand for materials during World War I. In 1919, a number of the manufacturers joined to form Tubular Investments, including the two major firms Accles and Pollock, and Tubes Ltd. The directors of Tubes Ltd were Arthur Chamberlain (cousin of politician Neville Chamberlain) and John Herbert Aston; of Accles and Pollock, Charlie Barlow and Job Baker and, from 1922, Walter Hackett. In 1927, Tube Investments formed Tube Products to exploit the new arc-welding process; it supplied most of the manufacturers of tubular steel furniture in England during the 1930s. 1927–30, Tube Investments absorbed ten small steel tube companies. In 1929, Accles and Pollock established a department at its Paddock Works in Oldbury, where tubular steel furniture frames were produced on a small scale to their own designs; upholstery was undertaken by other firms. Its 1930 *SP1* spring pattern chair with chromed frame, and a cane or seagrass back and seat woven by inmates at the Birmingham Institute for the Blind, was one of its first, and best, designs; this model was one of the four Accles and Pollock products to be included in Pel's initial range of 1932. In 1931, Practical Equipment Ltd was set up with P.G. Carew as managing director (also a director of Tube Investments, and son-in-law of Arthur Chamberlain), George Hackett as technical manager, and theatrical designer Oliver Bernard as consultant designer. Carew and Hackett had seen Bernard's 1930 Strand Palace Hotel in London, where he used two steel chairs (probably by Thonet); they became enthusiastic about the designer and the potential of steel tubes for domestic use. As a member of the Design and Industries Association, Carew was aware of design issues, although his lack of commercial experience showed in Pel's amateurish launch. A showroom was opened in 1932 at 15 Henrietta Street in London, where an array of tubular furniture was displayed. Starting with 18 employees, the firm occupied a corner of Accles and Pollock's Paddock factory. To avoid confusion with Practical Furniture Ltd, the firm was renamed Pel in 1932. In the 1930s, Pel produced domestic bent metal tubing for bedding, tables, seating, and case goods that were painted or nickel plated. Its first catalog was published to coincide with the 1932 'Ideal Home' exhibition in London. Riding the wave of popularity of chromed tubular steel, the firm produced versions of 1920s German models and versions designed by Bernard and Serge Chermayeff. Its products were fashionable and inexpensive. Its 1932 steel nesting chairs designed by Chermayeff for the BBC's 1928–32 Broadcasting House in Langham Place, London, were made with canvas seats; 100 chairs could be stowed in 20 square feet (2m²) of space. He designed other Pel models for the Broadcasting House commission. By 1936, there were *RP6* chairs in 11 broadcasting houses all over the world. The firm Joseph designed Pel's 1933–36 *HT21* steel, rubber, and wood table, and 1936 *SB9B* steel and rexine chairs for Prudential Assurance offices. Bernard left in 1933; Pel did not replace him with a full-time design consultant. Pel's customers included designers McKnight Kauffer, Marion Dorn, Arundel Clarke, Duncan Miller, and Betty Joel. Its bathroom stools were used by Claridges hotel, its steel furniture in tartan upholstery by the Metropole in Brighton, and other models by the Berkeley and Savoy hotels, London. Its range was retailed by Heal's, Harrods, and, in Camden Town, by Bowman's. In 1934, Pel won its largest order, to furnish bungalows, administrative buildings, and sports clubs for Iraq Petroleum. In 1934, Pel acquired rights to the *RP6* stacking chair from its designer Bruno Pollack; it had been producing the *RP6* since 1932 and had been sued by Pollack's agent in Britain. Pel was able until 1951 to collect royalties from other manufacturers, such as Cox and Kingfisher. Pel produced furniture to the specifications of Wells Coates for his 1935 Embassy Court in Brighton and for Erich Mendelsohn and Chermayeff for their 1935 De La Warr Pavilion in Bexhill-on-Sea. Later, Pel made up furniture for Coates's own flat in Yeoman's Row in Knightsbridge, London. The design and manufacture of Accles and Pollock's earlier furniture range had been supervised by Hackett, who, in 1936, left Pel to work in another section of Tube Investments. The success of Pel was probably due to the efforts of Oliver Bernard and its enlightened management; competitors such as Cox, Steelchrome, and Biddulph Industries never hired professional designers and had their wares designed by directors. Its growth was underwritten by the capital resources of Tube Investments, and its manufacturing expertise was enhanced by the facilities and personnel of Accles and Pollock. Competitors had to buy raw tubing from a sister firm of Pel's. In 1938, Pel's production was restricted to stretchers in green tubing and wire mesh; during World War II, Pel furnished naval vessels. After the war, Pel was set up in its own premises, though production was hampered by cumbersome postwar procedures for purchasing steel. A Pel 1993 chromed tubular steel bed was reissued by Alivar, Italy.

▶ Pel's steel furniture was first shown at the 1932 'Ideal Home' exhibition in London. Chermayeff included its furniture in his 'Weekend House' set of interiors at the 1933 'British Industrial Art in Relation to the Home' exhibition at Dorland Hall in London. Its furniture was the subject of the 1988 exhibition at the Architectural Association in London and was included in the 1979–80 'Thirties' exhibition at the Hayward Gallery in London.

▶ Cat., Dennis Sharp et al., *Pel and Tubular Steel Furniture of the Thirties*, London: Architectural Association, 1977. Cat., *Thirties: British art and design before the war*, London: Arts Council of Great Britain, Hayward Gallery, 1979:84,86,149,232.

Pelhaitre, Claude
See Pagnon, Patrick

Pellegrini, Silvano D.   (1939–)

▶ Italian designer; born Foggia; active Milan.

▶ He was active in Milan on various projects in reinforced concrete and worked for a time in Paris. Pellegrini began his professional career in design in 1969. His clients in Italy included MTZ Settore (design), DID Industrial Design, Maxform Collezioni (furnishings), and CAAI. His metal furniture models (including *Tuscania*, *Nubecula*, and *Denebola* chairs) were produced by Maxform and furnishings by Venia. He designed the *Cama* boat for LM Kado in Paris. He was a member of ADI (Associazione per il Disegno Industriale).

▶ 1966–67, he participated in exhibitions in Milan, Turin, Foggia, Rome, and Brescia.

▶ *ADI Annual 1976*, Milan: Associazione per il Disegno Industriale, 1976.

Pellini, Emma Caimi

▶ Italian costume jeweler; active Milan.

▶ Emma Caimi Pellini set up a studio after World War II in via Catalani 17 in Milan. Her designs were shown at the fashion presentations at the Palazzo Pitti in the 1950s. Her collaboration with Giorgini resulted in her wares being sold in the USA. She incorporated Venetian glass into her work; Lucchesi along with Le Perla was her principal source. In 1960, her daughter Carla took over management of the business, subsequently assumed by her granddaughter in 1976.

▶ Deanna F. Cera (ed.), *Jewels of Fantasy: Costume Jewelry of the 20th Century*, New York: Abrams, 1992:307.

Pennati, Luisella (1947–)
▶ Italian architect and designer; born and active Bovisio Masciago.
▶ Studied architecture, Bocconi School of Design, to 1973.
▶ She became an independent designer in 1975–76. Her clients in Italy included Poltronova-Design Center (office furniture) and Elleduemila (office furniture), where she was director with designers Becchi and Banci. She collaborated on the magazine *Abitare* in Milan with Anna Gualtieri, and was on the staff of Pencol Arredamenti in Venegono for interior design. Pennati collaborated on the design of buildings with architect Rosaldo Bonicalzi in Fagnano Olona. She was a member of ADI (Associazione per il Disegno Industriale).
▶ *ADI Annual 1976*, Milan: Associazione per il Disegno Industriale, 1976.

Pennino
▶ American costume jewelry firm; located New York.
▶ In 1928, Oreste Pennino registered a series of 12 trademarks used from 1926 and illustrating signs of the Zodiac. The firm produced bracelets, rings, clips, earrings, lockets, and brooches and, from 1947, watches and watchcases. Its wares were designed in the forms of flower bouquets, fruit, leaves, and trees in rose, pale and dark blue, and violet. The firm closed in 1961.
▶ Deanna F. Cera (ed.), *Jewels of Fantasy: Costume Jewelry of the 20th Century*, New York: Abrams, 1992:218.

Pensi, Jorge (1949–)
▶ Argentine designer; active Barcelona.
▶ Studied architecture in Buenos Aires.
▶ He and Alberto Liévore established a design practice in Barcelona in 1977. They designed 1984 exhibition stands for SIDI and, for Perobell, much of the furniture in the *Latina* range of the early 1980s and their corporate identity. With critics and theorists Oriol Pibernat and Norberto Chaves, they set up the design consultancy Grupo Berenguer. Working largely alone from 1984, Pensi designed furniture and lighting. With Liévore, he designed the 1987 *Helsinoor* armchair by Perobell. His 1988 *Toledo* aluminum chair and table by Amat was marketed by Knoll, and 1989 *Orfila* chair was produced by Thonet.
▶ Guy Julier, *New Spanish Design*, London: Thames and Hudson, 1991.

Pentagram
▶ British industrial and graphic design firm.
▶ Pentagram was established in 1971, growing out of the 1950s graphic design consultancy of the firm Forbes, Fletcher and Gill. Kenneth Grange, the industrial designer known for his work for Kenwood, joined the firm in the early 1970s. Subsequent members included Marvyn Kurlansky, John McConnell, and Daniel Weil.
▶ Penny Sparke, *Introduction to Design and Culture in the Twentieth Century*, Allen and Unwin, 1986.
▶ See **Grange, Kenneth Henry**

PER, Studio
▶ Spanish architecture and design partnership; active Barcelona.
▶ The umbrella partnership was formed in Barcelona in 1965 to include two separate architecture design workshops. In one section were Oscar Tusquets Blanca and Lluís Clotet, and in the other were Christian Cirici and Pep Bonet. All students of Federico Correa, they were meticulous in their detailing of furniture, interiors, and buildings. The partners resolutely opposed to orthodox architectural norms and expressed their views in critical texts and through their architecture. Tusquets and Clotet designed the 1968 Penina house in Cardedeu, 1972 Belvedere 'Georgina' weekend house in Llofriu, and 1974 Vittoria house in Pantelleria (Italy). Cirici's and Bonet's more conservative work included the 1973 Profitos furniture factory in Polinya, 1974 Tokyo housing block in Barcelona, and Bonet's own 1976 house in Vilamajor. Effective in gaining some international recognition for themselves and for contemporary Spanish design, the furniture of every member of the team was widely published.

▶ 'Studio PER,' *Architecture and Urbanism*, No. 4, 1977. David Mackay in Vittorio Magnago Lampugnani (ed.), *Encyclopedia of 20th-Century Architecture*, New York: Abrams, 1986:323.

Péral, Jeanne
▶ French costume jewelry designer; active Paris.
▶ During the 1960s and 1970s, Péral was known for her costume jewelry for couture houses. She produced her delicate designs at 21 rue d'Hauteville in Paris.
▶ Deanna F. Cera (ed.), *Jewels of Fantasy: Costume Jewelry of the 20th Century*, New York: Abrams, 1992.

Percy, Arthur Carlsson (b. Carl Arthur Percy Carlsson 1886–1976)
▶ Swedish ceramicist and glassware and textile designer.
▶ 1905–08, studied Konstnärsföbundets Skola (Artists' Union School), Stockholm, and, in 1908, under Henri Matisse in Paris.
▶ 1922–29, he was a designer at the Gefle porcelain works in Gävle and, from 1943–51, at the Karlskrona porcelain works. From 1936, he designed printed fabrics for Elsa Gullberg; from 1951–70 worked at the Gullaskruf glassworks.
▶ He received the diploma of honor at the 1925 Paris 'Exposition Internationale des Arts Décoratifs et Industriels Modernes' and 1957 Prince Eugen Medal. His work was the subject of one-person exhibitions in Stockholm in 1957 and in Gävle in 1971. His work was shown at the 1925 Paris exposition, 1929 'Exposición Internacional de Barcelona,' 1930 'Stockholm Exhibition,' 1937 Paris 'Exposition Internationale des Arts et Techniques dans la Vie Moderne,' 1939 'New York World's Fair,' 1955 'H 55' exhibition in Hälsingborg, and 1980 'Scandinavian Modern Design 1880–1980' exhibition at the Cooper-Hewitt Museum in New York.
▶ Cat., *Arthur Percy*, Nordiska Museet, 1980. Cat., David Revere McFadden (ed.), *Scandinavian Modern Design 1880–1980*, New York: Abrams, 1982:269–70, No. 108. Jennifer Hawkins Opie, *Scandinavia: Ceramics and Glass in the Twentieth Century*, New York: Rizzoli, 1989.

Peregalli, Maurizio (1951–)
▶ Italian designer; born Varese; active Milan.
▶ Studied in Milan.
▶ He started by working on fashion showrooms and designing shops for Giorgio Armani. In 1984 with five other designers, he established Zeus in Milan, a gallery selling furniture, ceramics, glass, and textiles. He was a partner in Noto, the interior design and manufacturing company established in 1984, which produced his 1982 *Poltrona* armchair (with Sergio Calatroni) and 1986 *Poltrocino Cromo* armchair (part of the Zeus collection); was artistic director and director of design collections and exhibitions at Zeus and in charge of the promotion of its international designers.
▶ Albrecht Bangert and Karl Michael Armer, *80s Style: Designs of the Decade*, New York: Abbeville, 1990:48,234. *Modo*, No. 148, March–April 1993:124.

Peressutti, Enrico (1908–76)
▶ Italian architect and designer; born Pinzana al Tagliamento, Udine.
▶ 1951–52, he taught at the Architectural Association, London; in 1952, at Massachusetts Institute of Technology, Cambridge, Massachusetts; 1953–59, at Princeton University; and, in 1957 and 1962, at Yale University.
▶ See **BBPR**

Peretti, Elsa (1940–)
▶ Italian jewelry designer; born Florence; active New York, Rome, and Sant Martí Vell (Spain).
▶ She settled in New York in 1968, becoming a fashion model and jewelry designer. Her first jewelry was a small teardrop and tiny silver bud vase, both worn as necklaces. The base holding a flower was first shown at the 1968 show of the clothing of Giorgio di Sant'Angelo. In the early 1970s, she worked closely with Halston (Ray Halston Frowick), as a model and designer of jewelry. In 1974, she began designing jewelry exclusively for Tiffany.

Though her designs were produced in materials ranging from diamonds and gold to bamboo and lacquer, she is best known for her work in sterling silver, a material she used from the late 1960s. Her work incorporated motifs based on heart shapes, bones, scorpions, beans, snakes, and other shapes. Halston also used Peretti for package designs for his Revlon cosmetics line, including a heart-shaped compact and lipstick cases. In addition to traditional silver and gold jewelry for Tiffany, her work included teapots, candlesticks, flatware, and leather goods. From c1982, she began rebuilding the village of Sant Martí Vell, near Barcelona, home of the craftspeople with whom she worked on her jewelry.

▶ A 1990 solo exhibition of her work was mounted at the Fashion Institute of Technology, New York.

▶ 'Show of Peretti Designs Celebrates Tiffany Era,' *The New York Times*, 26 April 1990. Anne-Marie Schiro, 'Classic Hearts and Imperishable Beans,' *The New York Times*, 23 June 1992:B8.

Perriand, Charlotte (1903–)

▶ French designer; born and active Paris.

▶ 1920–25, studied École de l'Union Centrale des Arts Décoratifs, Paris.

▶ 1927–37, she worked with Le Corbusier and his cousin Pierre Jeanneret. She was responsible for the furniture designs for their 'machines for living.' Perriand deserves credit for the design of most of the furniture rendered in the Le Corbusier office during this time, with the possible exception of case goods. This furniture work included 1928 *LC 1* sling chair (from 1965 by Cassina), 1928 *LC 4* chaise longue (from 1965 by Cassina), 1929 *LC 7* revolving small armchair (from 1978 by Cassina), and 1955 *Synthèse des Arts, Tokyo* chair. In 1929, became a founding member of UAM (Union des Artistes Modernes). In 1930, she met Fernand Léger, beginning a long-standing friendship. In 1940, Perriand, Jean Prouvé, Pierre Jeanneret, and Georges Blanchon set up an office in the rue La Cases in Paris to design temporary prefabricated housing in aluminum, including huts, dormitories, dining halls, art rooms, and factory extensions. In 1940, she was invited by the Japanese ministry of commerce and trade to become an advisor on arts and crafts, like Bruno Taut in 1933. She mounted two exhibitions on French design there. She published *Contact with Japan* (1942) (with Sakakura). In 1946, she returned to France and, 1946–49, designed furnishings for the holiday resorts in Méribel-les-Allues, Savoie. In 1950, she produced kitchen prototypes for the building Unité d'Habitation in Marseilles by Le Corbusier and, in 1953, furnishings for the Maison de l'Étudiant on the rue Saint-Jacques in Paris and in the Hôtel de France in Conakry. Her and Jean Prouvé's 1953 bookcases for the Maison de la Tunisie at the Cité Universitaire in the south of Paris were widely published, as were their 3m (118in.) long and low tables for the Maison de l'Étudiant. 1955–74, Galerie Steph Simon produced Perriand's and Jean Prouvé's furniture. In 1957, she designed furnishings for the Air France airline office in London and, in 1959, furnishings for the student and common rooms of the Brazilian House in the Cité Universitaire, built by Le Corbusier and Lucio Costa, and furnishings in the Air France offices (with Junzo Sakakura and Pen Suzuki) in Tokyo. 1959–70, she participated in the refurbishment of various conference rooms of the United Nations, Geneva. In 1960, she designed furnishings for the chalets in Méribel-les-Allues and, in 1962, for an apartment (with Maria Elisa Costa) in Rio de Janeiro. 1964–82, she designed the interiors and furnishings for hotels in Les Arcs, Savoie. She was president of the jury for the 1983–84 International Competition for New Office Furniture in Paris sponsored by the French ministry of culture. In the 1980s, she was a consultant to Cassina, the manufacturer of reproductions of Le Corbusier, Jeanneret, and Perriand furniture.

▶ Perriand's work was shown at the 1925 International Arts and Crafts Exhibition, Paris; 1926, 1927, and 1928 Salons of the Société des Artistes Décorateurs; 1927 Salon d'Automne ('Bar under the Roof'); 1929 Salon d'Automne (together with Le Corbusier's and Jeanneret's *Apartment Type* made by Thonet); 1930 first solo exhibition in the Musée des Arts Décoratifs in Paris; 1931 exhibition in Cologne with Le Corbusier and Jeanneret showing furniture, including *LC 4* chaise longue; 1935 'Exposition Universelle et Internationale de Bruxelles' with Le Corbusier and Jeanneret in their 'Study Room,' part of the French team project 'La Maison du Jeune Homme'; 1936 Salon des Arts Ménagers in Paris; in Pavillon des Temps Nouveaux (by Le Corbusier) at 1937 Paris 'Exposition Internationale des Arts et Techniques dans la Vie Moderne,' where she was in charge of communications; 1947 'International Exhibition of Town Planning and Residence' in the Grand Palais in Paris; 1949 solo exhibition at the Musée des Arts Décoratifs in Paris; 1951–52, and 1957 Salons des Arts Ménagers in Paris; 1951 (IX) Triennale di Milano, where the French participated under Perriand's direction; 1955 solo exhibition at the Takashimaya department store, Tokyo, where she showed her *Synthèse des Arts, Tokyo* chair; 1965 solo exhibition of furniture at the Musée National d'Art Moderne in Paris, and 1985 'Charlotte Perriand: Un Art de Vivre' retrospective at the Paris Musée des Arts Décoratifs. She designed the 1941 'Tradition, Selection, Creation' exhibition in Japan.

▶ Charlotte Perriand, 'Wood or Metal?,' *The Studio*, Vol. 97, 1929. Charlotte Perriand, 'L'Habitation Familiale: Son Développement Économique et Social,' *L'Architecture d'aujourd'hui*, No. 1, 1935. Cat., *Charlotte Perriand: Un Art de Vivre*, Paris: Flammarion, 1985. Cat., *Der Kragstuhl*, Stuhlmuseum Burg Beverungen, Berlin: Alexander, 1986:136. Arlette Barré-Despond, *UAM*, Paris: Regard, 1986:482–85. Cat., *Les années UAM 1929–1958*, Paris: Musée des Arts Décoratifs, 1988:232–33. Cat., Design Center Stuttgart, *Women in Design: Careers and Life Histories Since 1900*, Stuttgart: Haus der Wirtschaft, 1989:248–55.

Perrigault, Pierre (1931–)

▶ French furniture manufacturer; active Paris.

▶ 1947–51, studied École Boulle, Paris; 1951–52, management in Britain.

▶ In c1953, he was active in Lyons, managing the first Knoll showroom there; he subsequently established Galerie Lambert in Lyons, where he showed the work of young French designers including Pierre Paulin and Etienne Fermigier; in 1959, set up his own shop Meubles et Fonctions, boulevard Raspail, Paris, and produced and exhibited the work of French and foreign designers including Michel Mortier, Jean-Paul Barray, Daniel Pigeon, Arne Jacobsen, Verner Panton, Poul Kjaerholm, and Hans Guguelot; in 1980, organized (with Jean-Louis Berthet, president of Salon des Artistes Décorateurs) the '1930–1980, cinquante ans de créateurs SAD' exhibition, Grand Palais, Paris.

▶ François Mathey, *Au bonheur des formes, design français 1945–1992*, Paris: Regard, 1992:381–82.

Perry, Mary Chase (aka Mary Chase Stratton 1867–1961)

▶ American ceramicist.

▶ 1887–89, studied clay modeling and sculpture, Art Academy of Cincinnati, Ohio, and Detroit under painter Franz A. Bischoff.

▶ After teaching china painting in Asheville, North Carolina, she returned to Detroit in 1893 and opened a small studio. She initially applied overglaze porcelain decorations on vessels fired in kilns used for the production of false teeth. With kiln owner Horace James Caulkins, inventor of the 1892 gas-fired Revelation China Kiln for art potteries, Perry promoted the product demonstrating its features all round the country. She began experimenting on her own by 1898 and became known for her essays on watercolor design and china painting. After 1900, she began writing for Adelaide Alsop Robineau's journal *Keramic Studio*. In 1903, withdrawing from membership in the National League of Mineral Painters, she founded Revelation Pottery with Caulkins. It soon became known as Pewabic Pottery, after the upper Michigan state region where Perry was born. Perry's early Art Nouveau wares were influenced by Louis Comfort Tiffany, William Grueby, Auguste Delaherche, and early Chinese pottery, and produced in simple forms with iridescent glazes. In 1906, she constructed a

new pottery designed by the firm of William Buck Stratton, whom she married in 1918. Pewabic's work was encouraged by Charles Lang Freer, the Detroit art connoisseur. Architect Ralph Adams Cram used Pewabic tiles for the interior pavement of St. Paul's Cathedral in Detroit in 1908. Receiving numerous other architectural commissions, the pottery's activities concentrated on tile mosaics, tiles, and interior fittings. She perfected crystalline and volcanic glazes and, in 1909, introduced her famous *Persian* or *Egyptian* blue glaze. From 1924 to the later 1940s, Perry taught classes at the pottery. When her health began to fail, Ella J. Peters took over direction of the pottery. The pottery was in operation until 1965, when it was incorporated into Michigan State University. It was reopened in 1968 and is today a pottery studio and museum.
▶ She showed 23 pieces at the 1904 St. Louis 'Louisiana Purchase Exposition.'
▶ Marjorie Hegarty, 'Pewabic Pottery,' *Detroit Institute of Arts Bulletin 26*, No. 3, 1947:69–70. Thomas Brunk, 'Pewabic Pottery' in *Arts and Crafts in Detroit, 1906–1976: The Movement, The Society, The School*, Detroit: Detroit Institute of Arts, 1976. L.M. Pear, *The Pewabic Pottery: A History of its Products and its People*, Des Moines, 1976. Fred Bleicher et al., *Pewabic Pottery: An Official History*, Ann Arbor: Ars Ceramica, 1977. *American Art Pottery*, New York: Cooper-Hewitt Museum, 1987:112–13.

Persico, Edoardo (1900–36)
▶ Italian architect; born Naples.
▶ In 1928, an exhibition held in Turin provided a platform for experimentation by young architects, including Alberto Sartoris, Lavinia Perona, Giuseppe Pagano, and Gino Levi-Montalcini (architect of the 1929 Gualino office building with Pagano), who formed the Group of Six, led by Persico. Persico became involved in architecture after 1929 when he arrived in Milan, where he first worked at Pier Maria Bardi's art gallery and subsequently at the Galleria del Milione. He became a member of the editorial staff of the design journal *La Casa Bella* (later *Casabella*), for which he designed austere covers. From the early 1930s, he transformed the journal into an influential publication. He wrote important articles in Gio Ponti's journal *Domus*, and became known for his opposition to Italian Rationalist architecture. In the early 1930s, Persico set up a design partnership with Marcello Nizzoli. Persico's work included the two 1934 Parker Pen Shops (with Nizzoli), Largo Santa Margherita, Milan; 1934 tubular-steel advertising structure in the Galleria Vittorio Emanuele (with Nizzoli), Milan; 1935 Honor Court (with Nizzoli and Giancarlo Palanti); 1935 Parker Pen Shop (with Nizzoli), Corso Vittorio Emanuele, Milan; exhibition 'Sala della Vittoria' ('Victory Salon') at the 1936 (VI) Triennale di Milano.
▶ He won the 1934 gold medal (with Nizzoli) for the 'Sala delle Medaglie d'Oro' ('Hall of Gold Medals') at the 'Italian Aeronautical Exhibition,' Palazzo dell'Arte, Milan.
▶ Edoardo Persico, 'Gli architetti italiani,' *L'Italia Letteraria 9*, 6 Aug. 1933, and in Giulia Veronesi (ed.), *Scritti d'architettura (1927–1935)*, 1968:64–65. Edoardo Persico, *Profezia dell'architettura*, Milan: Muggiani, 1945. Edoardo Persico, *Scritti critici e polemici*, Milan: Alfonso Gatt, Rosa e Ballo, 1947. Giulia Veronesi, *Difficoltà politiche dell'architettura in Italia, 1920–1940*, Milan: Politecnica Tamburini, 1953. Giula Veronesi (ed.), *Tutte le opere: 1923–1935*, Milan: Comunità, 1964. Barbie Campbell-Cole and Tim Benton (eds.), *Tubular Steel Furniture*, London: The Art Book Company, 1979:46. Penny Sparke, *Design in Italy, 1870 to the Present*, New York: Abbeville, 1988. Edoardo Persico, 'L'esempio di Sant'Elia,' *Casabella*, No. 82. Richard A. Etlin, *Modernism in Italian Architecture, 1890–1940*, Cambridge: MIT, 1991:224,226, 490.

Persson, Inger (1936–)
▶ Swedish ceramicist.
▶ Studied Konstfackskolan and Tekniska Skolan, Stockholm.
▶ She began working in 1959 for Rörstrand in Lidköping as a designer of ceramic dinnerware and decorative objects. In 1971, she set up her own workshop, but subsequently returned to Rörstrand. Her 1972 *Pop* porcelain dinnerware illustrated new forms and colors more reflective of earthenware.
▶ She won a gold medal at the 1969 international ceramic exhibition in Faenza. Her *Pop* service was included in the 1983–84 'Design Since 1945' exhibition at the Philadelphia Museum of Art.
▶ Lennart Lindkvist (ed.), *Design in Sweden*, Stockholm, 1972:39. Cat., Kathryn B. Hiesinger and George H. Marcus III (eds.), *Design Since 1945*, Philadelphia: Philadelphia Museum of Art, 1983:225,II–47. Jennifer Hawkins Opie, *Scandinavia: Ceramics and Glass in the Twentieth Century*, New York: Rizzoli, 1989.

Persson, Sigurd (1914–)
▶ Swedish metalworker and glassware designer.
▶ Studied silversmithing in Hälsingborg under his father Fritiof Persson; 1937–39, Akademie für angewandte Kunst, Munich; 1942, Konstfackskolan, Stockholm.
▶ He set up his own silver workshop in 1941, and designed jewelry and cutlery. He executed the 1953 cutlery for the Kooperative Förbundet (Cooperative Society of Sweden). He designed in-flight tableware for various airlines and was a designer at the Kosta Boda glassworks. He published the book *Modern Swedish Smycken* (1950).
▶ He won medals at the 1951 (IX), 1954 (X), 1957 (XI) and 1960 (XII) Triennali di Milano, 1959 competition for cutlery sponsored by Scandinavian Airlines (included in the 1983–84 'Design Since 1945' exhibition at the Philadelphia Museum of Art), 1970 Prince Eugen Medal, 1967 Swedish Prize for Artists, and Gregor Paulsson Trophy. His work was the subject of the 1961 one-person exhibition at the Malmö Museum. Work shown at 1950 Swedish exhibition, 1954–57 USA 'Design in Scandinavia' traveling exhibition, 1954 Sydney exhibition, 1955 Pforzheim exhibition, 1955 "H 55" exhibition in Hälsingborg, and 1956 Havana exhibition.
▶ *Sigurd Persson Silver*, 1979. *Sigurd Persson Smycken*, 1980. Cat., David Revere McFadden (ed.), *Scandinavian Modern Design 1880–1980*, New York: Abrams, 1982:270, Nos. 188,301,310. Cat., Kathryn B. Hiesinger and George H. Marcus III (eds.), *Design Since 1945*, Philadelphia: Philadelphia Museum of Art, 1983: 225,V–29. Erik Zahle (ed.), *A Treasury of Scandinavian Design*, New York, 1961:287, Nos. 394,397,418. Graham Hughes, *Modern Silver throughout the World*, New York, 1967: Nos. 137,167–87. Sigurd Persson, *Modern Swedish Smycken*, Stockholm, 1950. *Sigurd Persson Design*, Malmö: Malmö Museum, 1961.

Persson-Melin, Signe (1925–)
▶ Swedish glassware designer and ceramicist.
▶ 1945–46 and 1948–50, studied ceramics and sculpture, Konstfackskolan, Stockholm, under Robert Nilsson; 1947–48, ceramics, Det Kongelige Danske Kunstakademi, Copenhagen, under Nathalie Krebs; from c1949–50, was an apprentice at Andersson & Johansson, Häganäs.
▶ From 1951–66, was active in her own studio in Malmö; from 1967–77 was a designer at the Kosta Boda glassworks; in 1970, was a founding member of the design group Boda Nova; from 1980–87, worked at Rörstrand in Lidköping; in 1985, was appointed first professorship, Konstfackskolan, Stockholm.
▶ She received the 1958 Lunning Prize. Her work was the subject of one-person exhibitions in Stockholm in 1953, Gothenburg in 1954, and Malmö in 1954. Her work was shown at the Triennali di Milano, 1954–57 USA 'Design in Scandinavia' traveling exhibition, 1959 Amsterdam exhibition, and 1975 'Adventures in Swedish Glass' in Australia.
▶ Cat., David Revere McFadden (ed.), *Scandinavian Modern Design 1880–1980*, New York: Abrams, 1982:270, Nos. 228,313. Cat., *The Lunning Prize*, Stockholm: Nationalmuseum, 1986:98–103. Jennifer Hawkins Opie, *Scandinavia: Ceramics and Glass in the Twentieth Century*, New York: Rizzoli, 1989.

Perusat, Pierre (1908–)

▶ French ironworker; born Bordeaux.

▶ Studied locksmithing under his father.

▶ He worked for ironworkers Édouard and Marcel Schenck and Adalbert Szabó in Paris. He opened an atelier in Bordeaux in which he was active from the early 1930s to 1962. Influenced by Edgar Brandt, his work included firedogs, tables, consoles, radiator covers, staircases, banisters, and grilles for clients in Bordeaux.

▶ Pierre Kjellberg, *Art Déco: les maîtres du Mobilier, le décor des Paquebots*, Paris: Amateur, 1986:186–88.

Perzel, Jean (1892–)

▶ Austrian designer; born Bruck (now Mostpri Bratislave, Slovakia); active Munich and Paris.

▶ At a young age, he painted on glass and was a stained glass artist in Munich. In Paris from 1919, he worked in several workshops including that of Jacques Gruber. He realized that the forms of electric lighting had been merely transformed from those of oil lamps and candlesticks. He first produced lamps in the technique of Romanesque church windows. In 1923, he set up his own workshop Jean Perzel Luminaires, 3 rue de la Cité Universitaire, Paris, where in his lighting he used metal supports and reflectors with clear, opaque, American, and tinted glass, sometimes with rough edges. He was one of the first to study the lighting of very large interior spaces, such as those found in the oceanliners of the time, the palace of the League of Nations in Geneva, the cathedral in Luxembourg, and the train station at Mulhouse. He designed lighting for the Henry Ford house in Detroit, the Savoy hotel in London, and residences in Bangkok and of the Maharaja of Indore. His aim in domestic lighting was to create surfaces that diffused both evenly and efficiently; he developed a frosted (or sandblasted) inner glass surface that was enameled to modify its opacity. He also used tinted enamels in beige and pink. His mountings were nickel-plated or lacquered. Though his range of lighting fixtures was limited, he concentrated his mass production on a few models, including table lamps, chandeliers, ceiling lights, columns, ceiling dalles, and illuminated tables. Decorators Maurice Jallot, Lucien Rollin, the Tétard brothers, architect Michel Roux-Spitz, and others commissioned Perzel to design lighting for their décors. The Perzel firm is still extant today.

▶ He showed his work at events of the Salon d'Automne 1929–39, the Salons of the Société des Artistes Décorateurs 1926–39, the Salons of the Société Nationale des Beaux-Arts, including a number of international exhibitions, receiving numerous awards. He showed his famous *Drops of Water* at the 1924 Salon des Artistes Décorateurs. His lighting was included in the Salons of Light in Paris in the 1930s and the 1925 Paris 'Exposition Internationale des Arts Décoratifs et Industriels Modernes.'

▶ *Lux*, Dec. 1928:174, Sept. 1929:119, June–Aug. 1930:108, Sept. 1931:101, Dec. 1934:150. Alastair Duncan, *Art Nouveau and Art Déco Lighting*, New York: Simon and Schuster, 1978:180–81. Cat., *Decorative Arts 1925 Style*, New York: Didier Aaron, 1979. Pierre Cabanne, *Encyclopédie Art Déco*, Paris: Somogy, 1986:226.

Pesce, Gaetano (1939–)

▶ Italian architect, designer, and sculptor; born La Spezia; active Padua, Venice, Paris, and New York.

▶ 1958, studied Instituto Universitario di Architettura, Venice, and, 1959–65, Design Institute in Venice.

▶ He opened an office in Padua where, in 1959, he became a founding member of Gruppo N; he experimented in programmed art and collaborated with Gruppo Zero in Germany, Groupe de Recherche d'Art Visuel in Paris (at this time known as Motus), and Gruppo T in Milan. He rejected the smooth contours of early 1960s Italian design in favor of Pop art and the kinetic and conceptual design movements. In 1961, he worked at the Hochschule für Gestaltung in Ulm; he began to design in 1962, to explore plastics in 1964, and to execute furniture in 1968. His work in plastics was first realized in his innovative 1969 *UP* series of inexpensive chairs produced by B&B Italia, including the doughnut-shaped *UP 5* armchair; the *UP 7* was a flesh-colored model in the form of a giant foot. Pesce rendered quilt-draped furniture pieces for Cassina. He was a participant in the Anti-Design movement with Ugo La Pietra, and was active in avant-garde groups, including Gruppo Strum and UFO. His work in the fields of art, audio-visual presentations, architecture, and design were realized through kinetic objects, multiples, and serigraphs. He published *Manifesto on Elastic Architecture* (1965). Pesce explored what he saw as the alienation between people and objects in consumer culture; he used distortion and exaggeration to draw attention to this. Among other objects, he produced nihilistic pieces of 'decaying' design. His design work included the 1971–72 *Reconstruction of an Underground City and a Habitat for Two People in An Age of Great Contaminations*, 1972–73 *Golgotha Suite*, 1975 *Sit Down* suite of armchairs, 1980 *Sansone* tables and *Dalila Uno, Due*, and *Tre* armchairs produced by Cassina, 1983 *Suite of Nine Pratt Chairs*, 1986–89 thermo-formed bottle for Vittel water, 1986–88 *Unequal Suite* of tables and felt armchairs, and 1986 *Airport, Square, and Bastone* lamps. His 1987 *Feltri* chair in thick felt and quilted fabric produced by Cassina brought him close to his goal of creating individualistic and expressive forms of architecture-furniture; he liked felt for its cheapness, recycleability, and suitability for the developing world. His approach remained unorthodox for his 1980 seating for Cassina, *Tramonto a New York (Manhattan Sunrise)*, in which a vinyl-upholstered 'sun' rose over foam-covered cushions in a weave suggesting buildings. His 1985–86 design of the interior of photographer and collector Marc-André Hubin on the avenue Foch in Paris was widely published. He taught architecture at the Instituto Universitario di Architettura, Venice, and Pratt Institute in Brooklyn, New York, and, in 1987, was visiting professor at the School of Architecture in São Paulo. From the late 1970s, he taught at École d'Architecture, Strasbourg, influencing a new generation of designers.

▶ He showed his art work in the late 1950s in galleries in various Italian cities. His design work was shown extensively worldwide and in one-person exhibitions in Bologna, Genoa, Milan, Naples, Rome, Turin, Venice, New York and at the Finnish Design Center in Helsinki. His work was included in the 1970 'New Spaces' exhibition at the Paris Musée des Arts Décoratifs, 1970 'Modern Chairs 1918–1970' at the Whitechapel Gallery in London, 1970 'Graphics I' exhibition, 1972 'Italy: The New Domestic Landscape' at the New York Museum of Modern Art, 'Urbanité?' at the 1980 Biennale de Paris, 1981 'Furniture by Architects' exhibition at the Massachusetts Institute of Technology, 1984 'Architecture et Industrie' at the Centre Georges Pompidou in Paris, and 1983–84 'Design Since 1945' at the Philadelphia Museum of Art. His work was the subject of the 1965 exhibition at the Hochschule für Gestaltung in Ulm, 1965 exhibition at the Finnish Design Center, 1975 'Le futur est peut-être passé' ('The Future May Be Past') solo exhibition at the Centre de Création Industrielle at the Paris Musée des Arts Décoratifs, 1984 'Architecture et Design de Gaetano Pesce' exhibition at the Montreal Musée des Arts Décoratifs, 1986 'Gaetano Pesce' at the Strasbourg Musée d'Art Moderne, 1991 'Mobili Italiani 1961–1991: Le Varie Età dei linguaggi' exhibition in Milan, 1991 'Les Annés VIA, 1980–1990' at the Paris Musée des Arts Décoratifs, and 1991 one-person exhibition at the Peter Joseph Gallery in New York.

▶ Cat., *Modern Chairs 1918–1970*, London: Lund Humphries, 1971. Cat., Milena Lamarová, *Design a Plastické Hmoty*, Prague: Uměleckoprůmyslové Muzeum, 1972:142. Emilio Ambasz (ed.), *Italy: The New Domestic Landscape*, New York: Museum of Modern Art, 1972:35,97–98,212–22. Cat., Gaetano Pesce, *Le futur est peut-être passé*, Paris: Musée des Arts Décoratifs, 1975. Gaetano Pesce, 'Der Kollektive Schiffbruch,' in *Design ist unsichtbar*, Vienna, 1981:299–304. 'Talking with Four Men Who Are Shaping Italian Design,' *Industrial Design*, Vol. 28, Sept.–Oct. 1981:30–35. Andrea Branzi, *La Casa Calda: Esperienze del Nuovo Disegno Italiano*, Milan: Idea Books, 1982. Cat., Kathryn B. Hiesinger and George H. Marcus III (eds.), *Design Since 1945*, Philadelphia: Philadelphia Museum of Art, 1983:226,III–64. France Vanlaethen, *Gaetano Pesce, Architecture Design Art*, Rizzoli, 1989. Albrecht Bangert and Karl Michael Armer, *80s Style: Designs of the Decade*, New York: Abbeville, 1990:66–67,125,234.

Peteranderl, Angelika   (1958–)
▶ German industrial designer; born Munich.
▶ 1979–83, studied industrial design, Fachhochschule, Munich, and at BMW and Siemens.
▶ 1983–84, she was an independent designer of medical and engineering apparatus and instruments. From 1985, she worked as a designer at Siemens in Munich in the communication and information systems group. Her work included the 1985 *Mobida 4* portable personal computer, 1985–86 *MX 500* and 1987 *MX 300* multi-user computer, and 1987 *7·500* department computer, all by Siemens.
▶ Cat., Design Center Stuttgart, *Women in Design: Careers and Life Histories Since 1900*, Stuttgart: Haus der Wirtschaft, 1989:142–45.

Petersdorf glassworks
▶ German glass factory.
▶ Fritz Heckert founded a factory in 1866 in Petersdorf, near Warmbrumm, in the Riesengebirge. The factory became active in the production of historicist glassware, including enameled *humpen* (a vessel for beer) and *jodhpur-gläser* influenced by Indian metalwork. In 1923, the Schreiberhau glasshouse bought Hecker's firm.
▶ Cat., B. Mundt, *Historismus*, Berlin: Kunstgewerbemuseum, 1973.

Petersen, Arne   (1922–)
▶ Danish metalworker.
▶ Petersen learned techniques of silver- and goldsmithing at the firm C.C. Herman in Copenhagen. In 1948, he joined the Georg Jensen Sølvsmedie, working in its hollow-ware department from 1976. His 1975 *Bottle Opener* in stainless steel soldered with brass was widely published.
▶ ▶ His work was included in the 1980 'Georg Jensen Silversmithy: 77 Artists, 75 Years' exhibition at the Smithsonian Institution, Washington. The *Bottle Opener* was included in the 1983–84 'Design Since 1945' at the Philadelphia Museum of Art.
Cat., *Georg Jensen Silversmithy: 77 Artists, 75 Years*, Washington: Smithsonian Institution Press, 1980. Cat., Kathryn B. Hiesinger and George H. Marcus III (eds.), *Design Since 1945*, Philadelphia: Philadelphia Museum of Art, 1983:226, V–30.

Petersen, Ole Bent   (1938–)
▶ Danish metalworker.
▶ 1957–59, studied at Kunsthåndværkerskolen and, 1959–60, Det Kongelige Danske Kunstakademi, both Copenhagen.
▶ In 1960, he set up his own workshop, where he produced simple, direct jewelry and small sculptures. From 1978, he worked for Georg Jensen in Copenhagen.
▶Cat., *Georg Jensen Silversmithy: 77 Artists, 75 Years*, Washington: Smithsonian Institution Press, 1980. Cat., David Revere McFadden (ed.), *Scandinavian Modern Design 1880–1980*, New York: Abrams, 1982:270, Nos. 297,298.

Petit, Philippe   (1900–45)
▶ French painter, decorator, and furniture designer; active Paris.
▶ Studied École Bernard Palissy, Paris.
▶ He worked first at the Primavera studio of the Au Printemps department store, Paris, with Louis Sognot and Marcel Guillemard. 1924–31, he worked at DIM (Décoration Intérieur Moderne), replacing partner Georges Mouveau and collaborating with the remaining partner René Joubert. Joubert et Petit executed numerous commissions for interior schemes and furniture models. Designing furniture both together and separately, their pieces were produced in the firm's own workshop.
▶ DIM's stand was on the Alexandre III Bridge at the 1925 Paris 'Exposition Internationale des Arts Décoratifs et Industriels Modernes'; Joubert and Petit also designed the dining room in the

French Embassy pavilion. He showed his work at the Salons d'Automne. Petit's and Joubert's furniture (produced by Degorre) was shown at the 1937 Paris 'Exposition Internationale des Arts et Techniques dans la Vie Moderne.'
▶ Cat., *Decorative Arts 1925 Style*, New York: Didier Aaron, 1979. Victor Arwas, *Art Déco*, New York: Abrams, 1980. Pierre Kjellberg, *Art Déco: les maîtres du Mobilier, le décor des Paquebots*, Paris: Amateur, 1986:135.

Petit, Pierre-Étienne   (1900–69)
▶ French painter, architect, decorator, and furniture designer.
▶ 1914–18, studied cabinetmaking, École Boulle, Paris.
▶ He worked initially at Siègel, the mannequin and store-design firm. 1924–27, he was a decorator and designer of furniture, lighting, and grillework. He set up his own workshop in 1928 and, from 1930, collaborated with prominent painters, sculptors, glassware designer, and ceramicists. From 1935, he was active as an architect of townhouses, vacation houses, and stores, including their furniture, décors, and rugs in geometric motifs.
▶ He showed a dining room based on Cubist forms at the 1928 Salon d'Automne. He showed furniture in clear glass, opaline glass, and marbrite produced by Saint-Gobain at the 1935 Salon of the Société des Artistes Décorateurs.
▶ *Ensembles Mobiliers*, Vol. II, Paris: Charles Moreau, 1937. Pierre Kjellberg, *Art Déco: les maîtres du Mobilier, le décor des Paquebots*, Paris: Amateur, 1986:135–37.

Petrini, Rinaldo   (1931–)
▶ Italian teacher and designer; born Pistoia; active Milan.
▶ Studied architecture to 1954; design to 1967; and sociology to 1973.
▶ He was coordinator in 1969 of the pedagogical group ICSID. In 1965, he taught architecture at the University of Tennessee and, in 1967, industrial design at the University of Montreal. In 1971, he was director of design research and industrial development at the University of Nairobi and, in 1972, taught conservation and restoration at the Institut d'Architecture et d'Urbanisme in Paris. He was a member of ADI (Associazione per il Disegno Industriale).
▶ *ADI Annual 1976*, Milan: Associazione per il Disegno Industriale, 1976.

Petri-Rabin, Trude   (b. Trude Petri   1906–89)
▶ German ceramicist; born Hamburg; active Germany and the USA.
▶ From 1927, studied porcelain, Vereinigten Staatsschulen für freie und angewandte Kunst, Berlin, and Staatliche Porzellan-Manufaktur, Berlin.
▶ Like Marguerite Friedländer-Wildenhain, Petri produced entirely unornamented objects. Her use of high-glaze on porcelain produced pieces suggesting industrial use. Friedländer-Wildenhain and Petri produced porcelain designs for the Staatliche Porzellan-Manufaktur in Berlin in 1930; Petri was employed there 1925–33. Her 1930–32 *Urbino* dinner service by KPM (Königliche Porzellan-Manufaktur), Berlin, showed Bauhaus and Deutscher Werkbund influences; the service included a 'coupe-plate' replacing the traditional flat-rimmed plate. Until 1938, she designed vases, ashtrays, and chandeliers for KPM. She designed the 1938 *Arkadische* service with unglazed medallions decorated by sculptor Sigmund Schütz. The *Arkadische* pattern was suggested by Werkbund member Günther von Pechmann, director of the Staatliche Porzellan-Manufaktur from 1929 and dismissed for political reasons in 1938. She designed the 1931 *Neu-Berlin* porcelain dinner service by KPM. She designed the 1947–48 *Urbino Oval* services by KPM and 1985 *City* service by Arzberg. In 1950, she moved to Chicago but continued to work for KPM, producing bar bottles in white and celadon porcelain; vases in 1953; vases, ashtrays, the *Igel* (hedgehog) salt and pepper cellars in 1950; 1953 *Urbino* salad service; and a porcelain chess set in 1966.
▶ A 1930 covered bowl from the *Urbino* service received a gold medal at the 1937 Paris 'Exposition Internationale des Arts et

Techniques dans la Vie Moderne'; the bar bottles in white and celadon received an award at the 1954 (X) Triennale di Milano.
▶ Erich Köllmann, *Berliner Porzellan*, Brunswick, 1966. Barbara Mundt, *40 Jahr Porzellan*, Berlin, 1986. Margarete Jarchow, *Berliner Porzellan im 20. Jahrhundert*, Berlin, 1988. Cat., *The Bauhaus: Masters and Students*, New York: Barry Friedman, 1988. Cat., Design Center Stuttgart, *Women in Design: Careers and Life Histories Since 1900*, Stuttgart: Haus der Wirtschaft, 1989.

Petroli Garati, Franca (1935–)
▶ Italian designer; born and active Milan.
▶ Studied architecture, Politecnico di Milano, to 1964.
▶ Designing ceramics, lighting, glassware, and storage systems, she was a consultant designer to V & P (interior design) in Vimercate. She was a member of ADI (Associazione per il Disegno Industriale).
▶ *ADI Annual 1976*, Milan: Associazione per il Disegno Industriale, 1976.

Pettersen, Sverre (1884–1959)
▶ Norwegian glassware and industrial designer.
▶ Studied Statens Håndverks -og Kunstindustriskole, Kristiania (now Oslo).
▶ Pettersen became chief designer of Glasmagasinet in 1928. In the late 1920s, he produced pressed glass for Høvik Glass and, 1928–49, was artistic director at Hadelands Glasverk where he had worked since 1926. From *c*1930, he was director of the Statens Håndverks -og Kunstindustriskole and was active in the design of ceramics, textiles, and books. From 1947, he was head of the design office of Christiana Glasmagazin.
▶ Cat., David Revere McFadden (ed.), *Scandinavian Modern Design 1880–1980*, New York: Abrams, 1982:270, Nos. 81,83. Fredrik Wildhagen, *Norge i Form*, Oslo: Stenersen, 1988:86. Jennifer Hawkins Opie, *Scandinavia: Ceramics and Glass in the Twentieth Century*, New York: Rizzoli, 1989:167.

Petterson, John Pontus (1884–1949)
▶ Norwegian metalworker; active New York and Chicago.
▶ Studied silversmithing, Statens Håndverks -og Kunstindustriskole, Kristiania (now Oslo).
▶ 1905–11, he worked for Tiffany in New York. In 1911, he settled in Chicago, where he worked for Robert Jarvie for some years. In *c*1912, he founded The Petterson Studio, a home workshop at 5618 S. Homan Ave., Chicago, producing only handraised silver, as in the Kalo and Jarvie Shops.
▶ Sharon S. Darling with Gail Farr Casterline, *Chicago Metalsmiths*, Chicago Historical Society, 1977. Annelies Krekel-Aalberse, *Art Nouveau and Art Déco Silver*, New York: Abrams, 1989:123,258.

Pevsner, Nikolaus Bernhard (1902–83)
▶ German art historian and critic; active Britain.
▶ Pevsner began his career at the University of Göttingen. In 1933 he settled in Britain, lecturing at the universities of Oxford, Cambridge, and London. In 1929, Gordon Russell opened a shop in Wigmore Street, London, where Pevsner was manager and, until 1939, buyer. He became an influential writer on modern architecture and design. His affection for the ideals of the European Modern movement colored his writings and ideas. In the 1960s, he was among the first to realize that an expressive, non-Rational, and non-autocratic type of architecture was emerging which consciously rejected the tenets of Modernism. He was best known for his books *Pioneers of the Modern Movement* (1936), reprinted as *Pioneers of Modern Design* (1960), and the 46-volume series *The Buildings of England* (1951–74).
▶ Nikolaus Pevsner, *Pioneers of the Modern Movement*, London: Faber, 1936. Nikolaus Pevsner, *An Enquiry into Industrial Art in England*, Cambridge: Cambridge University, 1937. Nikolaus Pevsner, *The Sources of Modern Design*, London: Thames and Hudson, 1968. Nikolaus Pevsner, *Studies in Art, Architecture and Design*, London: Thames and Hudson, 1968.

Pewabic Pottery
See Perry, Mary Chase

Pezetta, Roberto (1946–)
▶ Italian industrial designer; born Treviso.
▶ 1969–74, Pezetta worked in the industrial design department of Zoppas. Except for a short stint at Nordica from 1974, he worked at the household appliance firm Zanussi, becoming head of the industrial design department in 1984. He designed the *Wizard* collection refrigerator of the late 1980s; though inventive, widely published, and favorably received by the design world, the refrigerator was a sales flop.
▶ He received the 1981 Compasso d'Oro award and its 1987 special-mention recognition. He won gold medals at industrial design events in the Netherlands and in Ljubljana.
▶ *Issue 2*, London: Design Museum, 1989. Albrecht Bangert and Karl Michael Armer, *80s Style: Designs of the Decade*, New York: Abbeville, 1990:216–17,234.

Pfister, Charles (1939–90)
▶ American interior and furniture designer and architect; active San Francisco.
▶ Studied architecture and design, University of California at Berkeley.
▶ 1965–81, Pfister was a designer of corporate interiors in the San Francisco branch of architects Skidmore, Owings and Merrill, where he became active in mass production design and was associate partner and director of the interior design department. He was known for interiors of elegant simplicity. In 1981, Pfister, James Leal, and Pamela Babey established Charles Pfister Associates in San Francisco. His extensive list of clients included Deutsche Bank in Frankfurt, and Citicorp. He produced the interiors for the 21 Club restaurant, New York; Square One restaurant, San Francisco; Grand Hotel, Washington; Shell central headquarters, The Hague; United Overseas Bank, Singapore; and a hotel in a 13th-century monastery in Milan. He designed rugs for V'Soske, seating for Metropolitan and Bernhardt, and lighting for Boyd and Casella. His office furniture and accessories for Knoll included the 1975 range of clear glass ashtrays and bowls produced by Vistosi in Murano. His 40-piece 1990 *Premier Collection* of residential furniture produced by Baker was said by him to owe its design to a variety of sources, including the work of Terence Robsjohn-Gibbings (to whom the range was dedicated), 19th-century Russia, 18th-century Sweden, and 'steamship moderne.' He also designed case-goods, seating, and tables for Baker Executive Office. In 1988, Pfister's firm was renamed The Pfister Partnership, with offices in San Francisco and London.
▶ Carolyn Englefield (ed.), *House and Garden*, July 1990:124–31,136. Lois Wagner Green, *Elle Decor*, September 1990:172. 'Celebrating Design Innovation,' *Designers West*, April 1991:30.

Pfohl, Karl (1826–94)
▶ Bohemian glass engraver; active Steinschönau (now Kamenický Šenov, Czech Republic) and Haida (now Nový Bor, Czech Republic).
▶ Pfohl engraved red and blue cased-glass vessels. His later engravings were after images of Flemish Old Master paintings, including those of Rubens.
▶ John Fleming and Hugh Honor, *Dictionary of the Decorative Arts*, London: Penguin, 1989:629.

Philco
▶ American electronics firm; located Philadelphia.
▶ Philco was founded in Philadelphia in 1892. In 1929, using assembly-line techniques, the firm produced the first truly low-priced radios. The firm became a leading manufacturer of audio products, adding domestic stoves, refrigerators, air conditioners, and other appliances to its line. In the 1950s, it produced a series of television set housings in historicist cabinets with technologically advanced features and large screens. The 1958 *Predicta* line's floor and table models had screens that swivelled on blonde-wood

bases; the portable model's screen could be moved about a room, while the chassis remained stationary.

▶ Cat., Kathryn B. Hiesinger and George H. Marcus III (eds.), *Design Since 1945*, Philadelphia: Philadelphia Museum of Art, 1983:226,I–31. '15 Years of Industrial Design,' *Industrial Design*, Vol. 16, April 1969:50.

Philippon, Antoine (1930–)
and **Jacqueline Lecoq** (1932–)

▶ French designers.

▶ Philippon studied École Boulle; Lecoq, École Nationale Superieure des Arts Décoratifs, both Paris.

▶ Philippon worked for a time with Marcel Gascoin, who had a profound effect on his work. Lecoq spent several months there. In 1954, they set up their own studio, and designed furniture for offices and stores in France, Germany, and Austria. Their austere furniture in cubical volumes included a 1958 hanging cabinet by Bofinger, similar 1962 white lacquered credenza by Behr, and other furniture by Airborne. An example of their rigorously simple forms was the 1958 *60* chair. Their exhibition designs included those for Behr.

▶ Yolande Amic, *Intérieurs: Le Mobilier français, 1945–1964*, Paris: Regard/VIA, 1983:106–09.

Philips

▶ Dutch electrical appliance manufacturer; located Eindhoven.

▶ Gerard and Anton Philips founded the Philips appliance firm in 1891 in Eindhoven, where an initial staff of ten produced light bulbs. In 1919, its first subsidiary was established in Brussels. Radio valves were manufactured from 1918 and, by 1924, other radio components were added to its range, marking the beginning of the collaboration between NSF (Nederlandsche Seintoestellen Fabriek) and Philips; the former designed and made the rectifiers for Philips light bulbs. Philips-NSF's earliest designer was probably H.A. van Anrooy in the early 1920s. The 1925 *Queen's Set* radio cabinet which NSF presented to Princess Juliana was designed by architect W.M. Dudok. In 1930, W. Penaat was commissioned for design work while working for Metz. Advertising poster artists included Th. W. Nieuwenhuis in 1918 for light bulbs and A.M. Cassandre in the 1930s for radios. The firm's first appliance was a tea warmer; in 1927, its first radio sets appeared. Philips did not itself manufacture all of its products; at first, NSF designed and made radio cabinets with Philips components. In 1947, the firm was amalgated into Philips. Other sources made furniture cabinets for Philips. In 1926, Bakelite was first supplied by Ebena and was later replaced by Philips's own 'philite.' Its notable radio design included the 1931 *932-A* in Bakelite-impregnated paper printed in a wood pattern, 1932 *730-A* in wood with push buttons, 1937 *461A* (*Overture*) in all-black Bakelite, and 1938 *752-A* in wood and Bakelite.

▶ Barbie Campbell-Cole and Tim Benton (eds.), *Tubular Steel Furniture*, London: The Art Book Company, 1979:30. John Heskett, *Philips*, London: Trefoil, 1989.

Phillips, Robert (?–1881)

▶ British goldsmith and jeweler.

▶ Phillips was one of the first to produce so-called archeological jewelry in the fashionable Italian style. These wares and others were produced in his workrooms and sold in his shop. He employed Carlo Giuliano and Carlo Doria, and probably other Italian craftsmen.

▶ He showed a Greco-Etruscan style necklace at the London 'International Exhibition of 1862.'

▶ Charlotte Gere, *American and European Jewelry 1830–1914*, New York: Crown, 1975:213. Mrs. Haweis, *The Art of Beauty*, 1878.

Piacentini, Marcello (1881–1960)

▶ Italian architect; born and active Rome.

▶ Studied Accademia di San Luca, Rome.

▶ From 1906, he was active as an independent architect at the

Accademia di San Luca. He was professor at the Scuola Superiore di Architettura in Rome. 1910–20, his buildings embodied the academic eclecticism popular at the time. From the early 1920s, Piacentini was editor of the review *Architettura e Arti Decorative*, renamed *Architettura* in 1931. While traditional, his buildings illustrate involvement with Modern experimentation. He declared the death of Art Nouveau after he visited the 1913 Leipzig exhibition and recognized the birth of a new architecture through new construction methods. He was involved with the Fascists and their ill-defined architectural pursuits that combined the Novecento Italiano with neo-Classicism. His close alignment with the Fascists created numerous commissions. In Rome, he designed the buildings for the 1911 'Esposizione Nazionale per il Cinquantenario dell'Unità d'Italia', proposed a redesign (with Armando Brasini) of the curved side of the Piazza Navona, 1914–15 remodeling of the Quirino Theater, 1915–18 'Corso Cinema-Theater' (with Giorgio Wenter-Marini) in the Piazza San Lorenzo in Lucina, 1921 Villetta Novili (near Rome), 1921 prize-winning design of the Instituto Nazionale per Instruzione Professionale, 1922 apartment at 42 Viale Parioli (now Viale Liegi), 1924 apartment building in the via Flaminia, 1925 'Grande Roma' (utopian version of Rome) project, 1926 Hotel Ambasciatori, 1928 Casa Madre dei Mutilati, 1931 Theatro Barbarini, 1931–34 Church of Cristo Re, 1932 via Regina Elena, 1932 via della Conciliazione (with Attilio Spaccarelli), 1932–35 'Città Universitaria' (with Pietro Aschieri, Giuseppe Capponi, Arnaldo Foschini, Giovanni Michelucci, Gaetano Minnucci, Eugenio Montuori, Gio Ponti, and Faetano Rapisardi), Italian pavilion (with Cesare Valle) at the 1937 Paris 'Exposition Internationale des Arts et Techniques dans la Vie Moderne,' 1937–42 'Esposizione Universale di Roma' satellite town (with Giuseppe Pagano, Luigi Piccinato, Ettore Rossi, and Luigi Vietti) near Rome for the 'E42' exhibition (unrealized), 1942 site plan (with others) and architectural supervision of the 1942 'Esposizione Universale di Roma,' and 1959 Palazzo dello Sport (with Luigi Nervi). He designed the 1917 proposed project for the center of Bologna; 1923–28 Palazzo di Giustizia, Messina; 1925–28 'Monumento alla Vittoria,' Bolzano; 1927–32 'Torrioni' (12-storey tower), post office, and Tower of the Revolution in the Piazza della Vittoria, Brescia; 1938 via Roma, Turin; and 1942 Piazza della Vittoria, Genoa. Through his writings, buildings and teaching, Piacentini had a great influence on 20th-century Italian architecture.

▶ Marcello Piacentini, 'L'Esposizione d'architettura a Lipsia,' *Annuario d'Architettura Associazione Artistica fra i Cultori d'Architettura in Roma*, Milan, 1914:ix–xx. Antonio Muñoz, 'Marcello Piacentini,' *Architettura e Arti Decorative*, No. 5, Sept.–Oct. 1925:3–96. Marcello Piacentini, 'La mostra di Architettura nelle sale della ENAPI,' *La Tribune*, Rome: 22 June 1932. Agnoldomenico Pica, *Architettura moderna in Italia*, Milan, 1941. Marcello Piacentini, *Architettura d'oggi*, Rome, 1930. Marcello Piacentini, *Volto di Roma*, Rome, 1945. Marcello Piacentini, 'L'opera di Raimondo D'Aronco,' *Emporium*, Vol. 19, No. 220. Paolo Portoghesi, *L'eclettismo a Roma 1870–1922*, Rome, 1969. Richard A. Etlin, *Modernism in Italian Architecture 1890–1940*, Cambridge: MIT, 1991. Mario Lupano, *Marcello Piacentini*, Bari: Laterza, 1991.

Piazzesi, Adriano

▶ Italian designer; born and active Florence.

▶ Piazzesi began in industrial design in 1969. His upholstered *Premier* and *Spring* chairs and *Bikelio* and modular *Kontiki* divans were produced by Tre D. He was a member of ADI (Associazione per il Disegno Industriale).

▶ *ADI Annual 1976*, Milan: Associazione peril Disegno Industriale, 1976.

Picasso, Pablo Ruiz (1881–1973)

▶ Spanish painter, sculptor, graphic artist, ceramicist, and designer; born Málaga.

▶ Studied in Pontevedra, La Coruña, and Barcelona.

▶ In Barcelona, he published the review *El Renacimiento*. 1900–

04, he moved between Paris and Barcelona during the time of his Blue Period, when he painted the poor. He settled in Paris in 1904, associating with avant-garde artists and writers including Guillaume Apollinaire. He met influential connoisseurs, including Sergei Shchukin and Leo and Gertrude Stein. During his Rose Period of c1905–08, he depicted acrobats, dancers, and harlequins. During this time his sculptures were first produced. In 1906, he met Henri Matisse. His Negro Period of 1906–09, when he attempted to analyze and simplify form, was influenced by the work of Paul Cézanne and West African sculpture. He painted *Les Demoiselles d'Avignon* (1906–07), a landmark in 20th-century painting, a signal of the arrival of Cubism, a violent revolt against Impressionism, and a painting understood by few other than Matisse and André Derain. It was not shown to the public until 1937. From 1907 to the beginning of World War I, Picasso developed Cubism with Georges Braque and Juan Gris. In 1917, he and Jean Cocteau designed costumes and sets for the ballet *Parade in Rome* and subsequently for productions of Sergei Diaghilev's Ballets Russes de Monte Carlo in Paris. He worked in a style of monumental Classicism in the 1920s; from c1925, he produced works embodying anguish and emotional tension, leading to his painting *Guernica* (1937), originally produced for the Spanish Pavilion at the 1937 Paris 'Exposition Internationale des Arts et Techniques dans la Vie Moderne.' His sculpture was foreshadowed by the drama of his paintings. Picasso was one of the first to make sculpture from found objects, including his widely published *Head of a Bull, Metamorphosis* (1943), made from a bicycle handlebar and saddle. As a draftsman, etcher, lithographer, linocutter, and book illustrator, his graphics were of a quality and importance equal to his painting. In 1946, he moved to the south of France, where he visited a pottery exhibition in Vallauris and expressed an interest in the Madoura stall. Suzanne and Georges Ramié invited him to use the kilns there. In 1947, his pottery designs began to be produced; many are still in production. In 1956, his silver plates were the result of his, François Hugo's, and Douglas Cooper's association. Picasso was unquestionably the best known, most versatile, and most prolific artist of the 20th century, and was a key figure in developments in the visual arts during most of the first half of the 20th century, though the brilliance of his pre-World War II output overshadowed his subsequent work.
▶ *Webster's Biographical Dictionary*, Springfield, Massachusetts: Merrian, 1976:1182. Douglas Cooper, *Picasso 19 plats en argent par François et Pierre Hugo*, Paris, 1977. Ray Anne Kibbey, *Picasso: A Comprehensive Bibliography*, London: 1977. A. Ramié, *Picasso Catalogue de l'Oeuvre Céramique édité, 1947–1971*, Vallauris, 1988. Auction cat., *Applied Arts by Twentieth Century Artists*, Christie's, Geneva: 13 May 1991. Ian Chilvers et al., *The Oxford Dictionary of Art*, Oxford and New York: Oxford, 1988:383–84.

Picasso, Paloma (1949–)
▶ French fashion and furnishings designer; daughter of Pablo Picasso.
▶ Picasso began her design career in the 1980s; designed fashion accessories including handbags and jewelry for Tiffany, before her cosmetics line was launched in c1989; in the early 1990s, established a shop, rue de la Paix, Paris. Her range of glassware, ceramics, and flatware was produced by Villeroy et Boch from 1991, fabrics (*La Maison* range) by Motif Designs, and eyeware by Optyl.
▶ *Metropolitan Home*, September 1990:42.

Piccaluga, Aldo and Francesco Piccaluga
▶ Italian industrial designers.
▶ The Piccaluga brothers moved to Canada in the 1960s and were active in furniture, product, and architecture designs. Their 1970 *Sigma* range of spun steel tables and stools was produced by Synthesis in Toronto.
▶ Cat., *Seduced and Abandoned: Modern Furniture designers in Canada, the First Fifty Years*, Toronto: The Art Gallery at Harbourfront, 1986:24.

Picciani, Enrico (1945–)
▶ Italian industrial designer: born Chieti; active Milan.
▶ 1963–67, studied ISIA, Florence.
▶ He settled in Milan in 1969, where he began working in the studio of Marcello Nizzoli. In 1973, Picciani, Arduino Dottori, and Roberto Ingegnere founded the studio ERA in Milan, where he designed products, graphics, and packaging. His clients included Lombardini (agricultural machinery), Ceccato (car wash stations), Laverda Feraboli (agricultural machinery), Solar (heating devices), Fidenza Vetraria (glassware), Fiamm (automobile batteries and tires), Zucchetti (faucets), Ideal Standard (sanitary fittings), Evoluzione, Laverda (trailers and mobile homes), Pozzi-Ginori, and Pirelli. He was a member of ADI (Associazione per il Disegno Industriale).
▶ *ADI Annual 1976*, Milan: Associazione per il Disegno Industriale, 1976. *Modo*, No. 148, March–April 1993:124.

Pick, Frank (1878–1941)
▶ British theorist and administrator; active London.
▶ A founding member of the British Design and Industries Association, Pick was the mastermind behind the redesign of the London Underground in the 1920s and 1930s. He employed graphic designer Charles H. Holden, architect Edward Johnston, poster designer McKnight Kauffer, and Charles Paine to design the image of the newly unified public subway system. He managed the Ministry of Information set up in 1939.
▶ Penny Sparke, *Introduction to Design and Culture in the Twentieth Century*, London: Allen and Unwin, 1986. Frederique Huygen, *British Design: Image and Identity*, London: Thames and Hudson, 1989:19,65,74,94.

Pickard, Mitchell (1958–)
▶ American architect and designer.
▶ Studied School of Architecture, University of Texas.
▶ He worked for architecture and design firms; in 1990, set up his own design studio in Dallas, focusing on the study, design, and development of furnishings; designed the *Willow Chair* for Brueton Industries.

Piel frères
▶ French jewelry firm; located Paris.
▶ At 31 rue Meslay in Paris, Piel frères produced inexpensive art jewelry and was managed by Alexandre Piel. His artistic director was sculptor Gabriel Stalin who designed jewelry in plastic, celluloid, copper, and silver.
▶ Its pieces were shown at the 1900 Paris 'Exposition Universelle'.
▶ Deanna F. Cera (ed.), *Jewels of Fantasy: Costume Jewelry of the 20th Century*, New York: Abrams, 1992.

Piferi, Filippo (1950–)
▶ Italian designer; born Rome.
▶ Studied architecture.
▶ He was active in furniture and graphic design; from 1979, worked as a designer with Pallucco, Rome; in 1985, (with L. De Lorenzo, L. Leonori, and S. Stefani) founded the studio Grafite, Rome.
▶ Fumio Shimizu and Matteo Thun (eds.), *The Descendants of Leonardo: The Italian Design*, Tokyo, 1987:328.

Pigeon, Daniel (1934–)
▶ French interior and furniture designer; born and active Paris.
▶ Studied École Nationale Supérieure des Arts Décoratifs, Paris.
▶ He was a founding member of VIA (Valorisation de l'Innovation dans l'Ameublement); designed furniture produced by Prisunic, Habitat, and Seibu; taught at École des Arts Décoratifs, Paris.
▶ Won 1981 VIA/IPEA competition for kit furniture (*Sake* produced by Bruynzeel and by Ciolino) and 1983 prize for a rattan chair designed for the VIA exhibition, Bloomingdale's, New York.

► Cat., *Les années VIA 1980–1990*, Paris: Musée des Arts Décoratifs, 1990:146. François Mathey, *Au bonheur des formes, design français 1945–1992*, Paris: Regard, 1992:117,194,246.

Pikionis, Dimitris (1887–)
► Greek architect and painter.
► Studied painting in Paris and Athens under Giorgio de Chirico.
► Though a contemporary of Le Corbusier and Ludwig Mies van der Rohe, Pikionis worked counter to Modernism. Later in his career, his designs were reflective of the contemporary Greek vernacular style.
► His work was the subject of the 1989 exhibition at the Architectural Association in London.
► *Blueprint*, June 1989:68.

Pilati, Tiziano (1945–)
► Italian furniture designer; born Bologna.
► He began his professional career in 1970. He worked in collaboration with the studio Montini in Bologna, for clients including the department store La Rinascente in Milan and Coin.
► *ADI Annual 1976*, Milan: Associazione per il Disegno Industriale, 1976.

Pilkington's Royal Lancastrian Pottery and Tile Co
► British ceramics factory.
► In 1882, the Pilkington family, who owned glassworks and coalmines, and William Burton, previously a chemist at Wedgwood, founded a ceramics factory near Manchester; Burton's brother Joseph was director. The firm produced tiles, and, from 1897, vases were produced until 1903 by the Lancashire factory or acquired from other sources and glazed on the premises. The Burton brothers perfected a luster decorating process and a new hard transparent glaze, beginning large-scale production in 1903. The firm's consultant artists included C.F.A. Voysey, Louis Foreman Day, and Walter Crane. In 1937, the factory discontinued its domestic wares, while continuing to produce tiles. 1948–57, it once again produced ornamental ware.
► It showed its wares at the 1900 Paris 'Exposition Universelle.'
► A.J. Cross, *Pilkington's Royal Lancastrian Pottery and Tiles*, London, 1980.

Pillivuyt
► French porcelain factory.
► The firm was established in 1818 and, from c1904, produced cups and saucers in a design used in bars and restaurants throughout France, establishing a standard. In the late 1980s, it commissioned Jean-Pierre Caillères to design dishes for use in microwave ovens.

Pilstrup, Henry (1890–1967)
► Danish designer.
► Joining the Georg Jensen Sølvsmedie in 1904, Pilstrup became the first apprentice of Georg Jensen. 1918–57, he was foreman of the jewelry department, where he designed numerous pieces of gold and silver jewelry.

Pincombe, E. Helen (1908–)
► British ceramicist; born India.
► Studied pottery, Camberwell School of Art and Central School of Arts and Crafts, both London.
► In 1925, she became a teacher of pottery at the Royal College of Art in London. After World War II, she set up her own pottery workshop in Oxshott, Surrey.
► Cat., *Thirties: British art and design before the war*, London: Arts Council of Great Britain, Hayward Gallery, 1979:132,298.

Pinter, Klaus
See Haus-Rucker-Co

Piper, John (1903–92)
► British painter and designer.
► 1928–29, studied Royal College of Art, London.
► From 1927, he was art critic for the journal *The Nation*. In 1933, he became a member of the London Group and, 1934–

35, of the artists' group Seven and Five Society. 1935–37, he collaborated with his second wife Myfanwy Evans on the art journal *Axis*. For the Architectural Press and on the Shell Guides, he wrote with John Betjeman. He produced stage designs for *Trial of a Judge* (1938) by Stephen Spender. 1940–41, he was an official war artist, painting bomb-devastated buildings and landscapes in Britain. He designed sets and costumes for operas by Benjamin Britten, including *Rape of Lucretia* (1946), *Albert Herring* (1947), and *Billy Budd* (1951). In 1959, he designed stained glass for Coventry Cathedral and, in 1965, for Metropolitan Cathedral, 1979 memorial window for Benjamin Britten in Aldeburgh Parish Church, Suffolk, and a large 1965–66 tapestry for Chichester Cathedral, Sussex.
► His work was shown in the 1948 exhibition at the Curt Valentine Gallery in New York and in the 1942 'English Romantic Artists' exhibition. His work was the subject of the 1979 retrospective at the Museum of Modern Art in Oxford and 1983 retrospective at the Tate Gallery, London.
► Cat., *Thirties: British art and design before the war*, London: Arts Council of Great Britain, Hayward Gallery, 1979.

Pirali, Ezio (1921–)
► Italian engineer and industrial designer.
► Pirali was managing director of Zerowatt, the Italian manufacturer of domestic electrical appliances; he developed the firm's products and contributed to their styling.
► Received 1954 Premio Compasso d'Oro (1954 table-top fan). Work shown at 1979 'Design & design' at the Palazzo delle Stelline in Milan and 1983–84 'Design Since 1945' exhibition at the Philadelphia Museum of Art.
► Cat., Kathryn B. Hiesinger and George H. Marcus III (eds.), *Design Since 1945*, Philadelphia: Philadelphia Museum of Art, 1983:226,I–31. Cat., *Design & design*, Milan: Palazzo delle Stelline, 1979:29. Hans Wichmann, *Italien Design 1945 bis heute*, Munich: Die Neue Sammlung, 1988.

Piretti, Giancarlo (1940–)
► Italian designer; born Bologna.
► Studied art education, Instituto Statale d'Arte, Bologna, to 1960.
► 1963–70, he taught interior design, Instituto Statale d'Arte, Bologna; from 1960–72, worked as a designer on office and domestic furniture at Anonima Castelli, who produced his first plastic work, the 1969 *Plia* folding chair. He developed numerous innovative furniture designs, primarily seating that was prefabricated, modular, and suitable for the assembly-line production techniques at Castelli. His designs included the 1969 *Plana* folding armchair, 1971 *Platone* folding desk chair, and *Pluvium* umbrella stand. He collaborated with Emilio Ambasz on award-winning designs, including two ranges of ergonomic seating, and *Dorsal* and 1979 *Vertebra* seating systems produced by Open Ark. They designed the 1980 *Logotec* and 1984 *Oseris* low-voltage spotlight ranges for Erco Lighting. From 1984, he worked for Castilia. The 1988 Piretti Collection of 50 chairs was produced by Krueger of the USA.
► Received 1971 (*Plia* chair) Smau prize; 1971 'Bio 4' (*Plia*), Ljubljana; 1973 Bundespreis 'Die gute Industrieform'; 1977 gold medal (*Vertebra* seating system with Ambasz) Industrial Design Award, IBD; 1979 (*Vertebra*) Smau prize; 1980 Industrial Design Award (*Logotec* lighting), IBD; 1981 (*Vertebra*) Premio Compasso d'Oro. Work (*Plia* chair) shown at 1983–84 'Design Since 1945' exhibition, Philadelphia Museum of Art.
► Cat., Milena Lamarová, *Design a Plastické Hmoty*, Prague: Uměleckoprůmyslové Muzeum, 1972:144. Albrecht Bangert and Karl Michael Armer, *80s Style: Designs of the Decade*, New York: Abbeville, 1990:97,227,234. Cat., Kathryn B. Hiesinger and George H. Marcus III (eds.), *Design Since 1945*, Philadelphia: Philadelphia Museum of Art, 1983:226,III–66. Adalberto Dal Lago, *Italian Look*, Milan, 1972. *Classics*, London: Heal and Son, Spring 1981: No. 71. 'Vertebra Seating System,' *Domus*, No. 572, June 1977:

38–39. *Moderne Klassiker: Möbel, die Geschichte machen*, Hamburg, 1982:13–14. Fumio Shimizu and Matteo Thun (eds.), *The Descendants of Leonardo: The Italian Design*, Tokyo, 1987:338. Jeremy Myerson and Sylvia Katz, *Conran Design, Home Office*, London: Conran Octopus, 1990:78.

Pistoletto, Michelangelo   (1933–)
▶ Italian sculptor, painter, and designer.
▶ Pistoletto was a co-founder of the Italian *arte povera* movement in Berlin. He was best known for his super-realistic mirror paintings and produced sculptures and installations that were widely published. In 1989, he designed furniture for Meta-Memphis, including his 1989 *Tutti Designers* wall lamp in neon with its accompanying silkscreened aluminum briefcase to hold the transformer.
▶ Albrecht Bangert and Karl Michael Armer, *80s Style: Designs of the Decade*, New York: Abbeville, 1990:123,234.

Pistrucci, Elena   (1822–1886)
and   Eliza Maria Pistrucci   (1824–1881)
▶ Italian gem engravers and shell cameo cutters; born England.
▶ Their father Benedetto Pistrucci was well known as a cameo portraitist in his native Rome. He settled in Britain and became chief engraver at the Royal Mint. His sponsor and patron Sir Joseph Banks arranged several valuable commissions for portraits. His commissions included the 1819 Waterloo medal, 1821 coronation medal and cameo portrait of King George IV, 1838 coronation medal of Queen Victoria, and 1840 royal wedding medal. The 1821 and 1838 coronation medals were made by royal jewelers Rundell and Bridge. Pistrucci's daughters Elena and Eliza Maria returned to Italy as young girls with their mother. Accomplished as gem engravers, they produced shell cameos popular in the mid-19th century.
▶ Benedetto Pistrucci in A.W. Billing, *The Science of Gems*, 1867. Charlotte Gere, *American and European Jewelry 1830–1914*, New York: Crown, 1975:214.

Pitman, Agnes   (1850–1946)
▶ American wood carver and ceramics decorator; born Sheffield; daughter of Benn Pitman; active Cincinnati, Ohio.
▶ Studied wood carving under William Henry Frey; 1874, china painting under Maria Eggers; design, University of Cincinnati School of Design, to 1877.
▶ Her family settled in Cincinnati in 1853. In the 1870s, she and her mother Jane Bragg Pitman carved the furniture, doors, and woodwork that her father Benn Pitman designed. In 1873, she assisted her father in his wood carving classes at the University of Cincinnati School of Design. During the 1870s she taught wood carving at the Mercantile Library Building and at Woodward High School. She was a member of the Women's Art Museum Association and, in 1879, became a founding member of the Cincinnati Pottery Club. She active in wood, ceramics, and wall decoration.
▶ Furniture produced with her mother and designed by her father was shown at the 1872 (III) 'Annual Cincinnati Industrial Exhibition.' Her chest of drawers with carved floral motif was shown in the Cincinnati Room of the Women's Pavilion at the 1876 Philadelphia 'Centennial Exposition.' Her work was included in industrial exhibitions in Cincinnati of the 1870s and in the 1878 Cincinnati loan exhibition of the Women's Art Museum Association. She painted wall decorations in the interior of the Cincinnati Room in the Women's Pavilion at the 1893 Chicago 'World's Columbian Exposition.'
▶ Cat., *The Ladies, God Bless 'Em: The Women's Art Movement in Cincinnati in the Nineteenth Century*, 1976:68. Anthea Callen, *Women Artists of the Arts and Crafts Movement, 1870–1914*, New York, 1979:164,165,169–70,225. Doreen Bolger Burke et al., *In Pursuit of Beauty: Americans and the Aesthetic Movement*, New York: Metropolitan Museum of Art and Rizzoli, 1987:461–62.

Pitman, Benn   (1822–1910)
▶ British teacher and wood carver; born Trowbridge, Wiltshire; father of Agnes Pitman; active Cincinnati, Ohio.

▶ In the early 1830s, he moved to Bath, where he was apprenticed as an architect. His brother Isaac Pitman had a school in Bath and invented a system of phonetic shorthand. Benn Pitman taught the system throughout Britain for a decade until Isaac suggested that he promote the method in the USA. They moved to Philadelphia in 1852; in 1853, they settled in Cincinnati. Pitman set up the Phonography Institute and wrote, designed, and illustrated numerous textbooks on the shorthand method. In 1856, he invented relief engraving for printing. Through Henry Lindley Fry and his son William Henry Fry, who settled in Cincinnati and whom he probably met in Bath, Pitman developed an interest in wood carving. In 1873, Pitman set up the wood carving department of the University of Cincinnati School of Design, where he taught many women from wealthy Cincinnati families until 1893. He encouraged his students to use clay modeling as a preliminary to carving; they included Laura Fry, M. Louise McLaughlin, Adelaide Nourse, and his daughter Agnes. In 1874, he established china painting classes at the school. In 1877, Pitman, the Frys, and their students began the decoration of the organ of the Cincinnati Music Hall. A follower of John Ruskin, Pitman saw in nature an endless source of ornamental motifs and decoration as an integral part of useful objects. Pitman's highly ornamented house in Cincinnati is extant today. In the 1880s, he wrote widely on wood carving and decoration and, in 1889, became a lecturer in decorative design at the Art Academy of Cincinnati. He published books *American Art—Its Future Dependent on Improved Social Conditions* (1891) and *A Plea for American Decorative Art* (1895). In 1893, William Fry took Pitman's post at the Art Academy of Cincinnati, and Pitman resumed his work in phonography, publishing several books on the subject, including *A Plea for Alphabetic Reform* (1905).
▶ He, wife, and daughter showed wood carvings at the 1872 (III) 'Annual Cincinnati Industrial Exhibition.' The highly carved bed shown in the 1883 'Cincinnati Industrial Exhibition' was carved by wife Adelaide Nourse with painted panels by her sister Elizabeth Nourse.
▶ Kenneth R. Trapp, ' "To Beautify the Useful": Benn Pitman and the Women's Woodcarving Movement in Cincinnati in the Late Nineteenth Century,' in Kenneth R. Ames (ed.), *Victorian Furniture: Essays from a Victorian Society Autumn Symposium*, Philadelphia, 1872:173–92. Cat., *The Ladies, God Bless 'Em: The Women's Art Movement in Cincinnati in the Nineteenth Century*, 1976:65–66. Cat., Kenneth R. Trapp (ed.), *Celebrate Cincinnati Art*, Cincinnati: Cincinnati Art Museum, 1982:48–55,67–70. Doreen Bolger Burke et al., *In Pursuit of Beauty: Americans and the Aesthetic Movement*, New York: Metropolitan Museum of Art and Rizzoli, 1987:462–63.

Piva, Antonio   (1936–)
▶ Italian architect and designer; born Padua; active Milan.
▶ Studied Instituto Universitario di Architettura, Venice, to 1962.
▶ From 1962, he taught at Facoltà di Architettura, Politecnico di Milano. He began his professional career in 1962, working in the architecture partnership Franco Albini, Franca Helg, Antonio Piva, Marco Albini in Milan; collaborated on 1962 Metropolitana Milanese (Milan subway), 1982 government museum, Varese, 1984 post office, Gorizia, and 1985 restoration of Castello di Masnago. 1968–72, he taught design, Corso Superiore di Disegno Industriale, Venice; became a member of ADI (Associazione per il Designo Industriale); in 1975, advised on the founding of a museum in Venezuela for UNESCO; in 1983, taught at Salvador de Bahia University, Brazil; from 1985, wrote the column 'Museografia' in *Il Sole 24ore*; promoted and directed seminars, lectures, and post-graduate courses on museology and museography at Facoltà di Architettura, Politecnico di Milano; judged architectural competitions; was active in the organization of architecture and design at Contemporary Art Hall, Milan, and New York International Design Center, Long Island City; designed silver, glass, and a tea set for San Lorenzo, and lighting for Sirrah.

▶ *ADI Annual 1976*, Milan: Associazione per il Disegno Industriale, 1976. Andrea Branzi and Michele de Lucchi, *Design Italiano degli Anni '50*, Milan: Editoriale Domus, 1980. *Moderne Klassiker: Möbel, die Geschichte machen*, Hamburg, 1982:58. Giancarlo Iliprandi and Pierluigi Molinari (eds.), *Industrial Design Italiani*, Fagagna, 1985:19. Fumio Shimizu and Matteo Thun (eds.), *The Descendants of Leonardo: The Italian Design*, Tokyo, 1987:330.

Piva, Paolo   (1950–)
▶ Italian designer; born Adria; active Venice.
▶ Studied architecture in Venice to 1973.
▶ Piva began his professional career in 1970. Designing kitchen systems, seating, and case goods, his clients included Dada, Giovannetti, Poliform, B&B Italia, De Sede, Fama, Burelli Cucine, Mobel Italia, Saima, and Lumenform in Italy, and, in Austria, Wittmann, Thonet, and Team 7. His *Easy System* seating was produced by Open of S. Lucia di Piave. He was a member of ADI (Associazione per il Disegno Industriale); (with Manfredo Tafuri) organized and designed the 1980 exhibition 'Vienna Rossa' in Rome; in 1980, designed embassies in Kuwait and Qatar; in 1981, designed the interiors of a chain of dress shops.
▶ *ADI Annual 1976*, Milan: Associazione per il Disegno Industriale, 1976. *Modo*, No. 148, March–April 1993:124.

Plan
▶ British furniture dealer.
▶ Established in 1932, Plan became one of the more notable retailers of Modern furniture in Great Britain in the 1920s and 1930s. Tubular steel, plywood, and upholstery fabrics in geometrics and stripes were used in the construction of its furniture based on German models. F.H. Miles was Plan's first director; its founder was architect and designer Serge Chermayeff, who had discontinued his relationship with Waring and Gillow in 1931. Even before Plan was set up, its furniture, identical to that of Pel, appeared in the 1931–32 BBC studios designed by Chermayeff and was published in *Architectural Review*. All of Plan's furniture was produced by other firms. Its wooden models were manufactured by Henry Stone of Banbury, tubular steel furniture by Pel of Oldbury, hand-knotted rugs by Morton Sundour, upholstery fabrics by Donald Bros., and lighting by Best and Lloyd of Smethwick. Plan was located in the Chermayeff offices in the Pantheon building in Oxford Street, London. Early Plan models may have been assembled by Pel from parts supplied by Walter Knoll of Stuttgart and upholstered with material imitating Knoll's. In 1936, Plan was sold to German refugee Walter Trier and British designer F.J. Porter. In 1938, Walter Knoll sent his son Hans to Britain to promote their new line of *Elbo* easy chairs made in Borghams and by a firm in High Wycombe and sold under the Knoll name in the same showroom with Plan models. The Knoll-Plan venture failed and Plan closed in 1938.
▶ Plan furniture was first shown at the 1933 'British Industrial Art in Relationship to the Home' exhibition in Dorland Hall, London, where the 'Weekend House' of Chermayeff was mounted.
▶ Barbara Tilson, 'Plan Furniture 1932–38: The German Connection,' *Journal of Design History*, Vol. 3, Nos. 2 and 3, 1990: 145–55.

Plan Créatif
▶ French design firm; located Paris.
▶ Plan Créatif was established in 1985 by Claude Braunstein and Clément Rousseau in Paris with associates Gérard Lecœur and David McKay and offices in Geneva and London; it designed products including electric irons, 1986 mixer tap *Porphyre* produced by Porcher, 1991 pilot's station of Airbus *A330* airplane, Casino store concept, 1992 signage of Winter Olympic Games, Albertville (France), and 1993 telephone for France Telecom.
▶ Received 1986 Janus award from the Ministère de l'Industrie.
▶ François Mathey, *Au bonheur des formes, design français 1945– 1992*, Paris: Regard, 1992:346,362–64.

Plastimat   (aka Plastimat Jablonec and Nisou)
▶ Czech manufacturer specializing in plastics; located Liberec.
▶ A number of small prewar enterprises were expropriated and amalgamated in 1946 into Plastimat Jablonec nad Nisou. It produced small domestic products and toys, followed by household accessories. Using a range of plastics processes and materials, Plastimat produced industrial moldings and semi-manufactured goods. In 1957, a design studio was established. By 1972, its head was Jiří Hofman; its design consultants included architect Josef Saal and tutor Gustav Hlávka of the College of Decorative Arts, Prague. Plastimat's products included the 1965 tableware for Czechoslovakia Airlines by I. Jakeš, and a 1972 polysytrene decorative screen by Josef Saal. Hofman's work for Plastimat included the 1970 disposable ice-cream cup, 1970 food containers, 1966 coffee box, and 1968 beer jug and beaker. The factory and its designers consulted a small group of retailers to determine the nature of production, which largely failed to satisfy consumer demand.
▶ Cat., Milena Lamarová, *Design a Plastické Hmoty*, Prague: Uměleckoprůmyslové Muzeum, 1972:68,69,200.

Platner, Warren   (1919–)
▶ American architect and designer.
▶ Studied architecture, Cornell University, Ithaca, New York.
▶ He worked in the offices of Raymond Loewy, Eero Saarinen, I.M. Pei, and Kevin Roche and John Dinkeloo. 1953–57, he executed a range of vertical steel wire tables and chairs produced by Knoll. He devised the method and tooling for its production himself; more than 1,400 welds were required to produce the lounge chair in the line. The wires created a deliberate moiré effect. In 1967, he set up his own design studio in North Haven, Connecticut, where he executed office furniture for Knoll and Lehigh and worked on commissions including architecture, interiors, lighting, and furnishings. He designed the Georg Jensen Design Center, Windows on the World restaurant in the World Trade Center in New York, and Water Tower Place in Chicago.
▶ Warren Platner, 'Designing in Steel,' *Industrial Design*, Vol. 16, June 1969:62–66. 'Prototypes and Principles,' *Industrial Design*, Vol. 17, Sept. 1970:54–59. Barbaralee Diamonstein, *Interior Design: The New Freedom*, New York, 1982:238–43. Cat., Kathryn B. Hiesinger and George H. Marcus III (eds.), *Design Since 1945*, Philadelphia: Philadelphia Museum of Art, 1983:226, III–67.

Plečnik, Jože   (aka Josip Plečnik 1872–1957)
▶ Slovenian architect and designer; born Laibach (now Ljubljana); active Vienna, Laibach, and Prague.
▶ Studied Kunstgewerbeschule, Graz; 1895–97, Akademie der bildenden Künste, Vienna, under Otto Wagner.
▶ He worked for Otto Wagner in the office of the city railway project in Vienna, where staff designed more than 30 railway stations as well as bridges and viaducts. Plečnik's most notable work was the 1903–05 shop and apartment block near St. Stephen's Cathedral in Vienna for manufacturer J.E. Zacherl; the architect used iron construction and granite slabs held in place by vertical sections, both the latest techniques of the time. Also innovative were the undulating walls that terminated below the roof line in carved atlantes. (The sculpture of Archangel Michael by Ferdinand Andri was added in 1909.) Plečnik's second major Viennese work was the Church of the Holy Ghost on the Schmelz, where he again used new techniques, here in concrete construction. Plečnik was recommended by Wagner to succeed him at the Akademie der bildenden Künste in 1911, but rejected in favor of Leopold Bauer, another of Wagner's pupils; 1911–21, taught at School of Applied Arts, Prague; practiced architecture in the 1920s and 1930s in Prague and Ljubljana; with the restorative architecture, executed notable and unusual decorative art from the Prague Castle; from 1921 to his death, was head of architecture department, Technical Faculty, University of Ljubljana.
▶ Received gold medal for exhibition design 1904, St. Louis 'Louisiana Purchase Exposition.' His work was the subject of the 1989 'Jozef Plečnik architecte' traveling exhibition, originating at Centre Georges Pompidou, Paris.

▶ Jože Plečnik 1872–1957, *Architecture and the City*, Oxford: Urban Design, 1983. Cat, François Burkhardt et al. (eds.), *Jože Plečnik, Architecte: 1872–1957*, Paris: Centre Pompidou/CCI, 1986.

Pløen, Erik (1925–)
▶ Norwegian ceramicist.

Pleydell-Bouverie, Katherine (1895–)
▶ British ceramicist.
▶ 1921–23, studied pottery, Central School of Arts and Crafts, London; 1924, under Bernard Leach at St. Ives.
▶ Aided by Japanese potter Matsubayashi, she set up a pottery workshop in 1925 in Coleshill, Wiltshire, where she worked 1928–36 with Norah Braden. They experimented with wood and vegetable ash glazes. In 1946, she set up a pottery workshop in Kilmington Manor, Wiltshire, where she was active into the 1980s.
▶ Cat., *Thirties: British art and design before the war*, London: Arts Council of Great Britain, Hayward Gallery, 1979:132,299. *Katherine Pleydell-Bouverie*, Bath: Crafts Study Centre, 1980.

Pløen, Erik (1925–)
▶ Norwegian ceramicist.
▶ Pløen trained in ceramics at the Schneider & Knutzen workshop near Oslo.
▶ In 1946, he set up his own pottery workshop in Ljan and produced hand-thrown vessels. In 1957, he broke with established pottery traditions and explored self-expression, abandoning unity. 1963–64, he was visiting professor at the University of Chicago.
▶ He received the 1961 Lunning Prize. His work was included in numerous exhibitions.
▶ Cat., David Revere McFadden (ed.), *Scandinavian Modern Design 1880–1980*, New York: Abrams, 1982:270, No. 277. Cat, *The Lunning Prize*, Stockholm: Nationalmuseum, 1986:126–29. Frederik Wildhagen, *Norge i Form*, Oslo: Sternersen, 1988:159.

Plumelle, Georges (1902–)
▶ French bookbinder and gilder; active Paris.
▶ He was apprenticed to gilder Pagnier and subsequently binder-gilder Émile Maylander. Plumelle met Marcellin Semet in the workshop of Léon Gurel; in 1925, they bought the bindery Pinardon at 19 rue Guisarde in Paris, where they produced Modernist bindings including *A.O. Barnabooth*, *Le Siège de Jerusalem*, and *Les Fleurs du mal*. Plumelle was active to 1980.
▶ Alastair Duncan and Georges de Bartha, *Art Nouveau and Art Déco Bookbinding*, New York: Abrams, 1989:23,176–7,196–97. Roger Devauchelle, *La Reliure en France de ses origines à nos jours*, Vol. 3, Paris 1961:204,206–07, plate XCII. John F. Fleming and Priscilla Juvelis, *The Book Beautiful and the Binding as Art*, New York, Vol. 1, 1983:113; Vol. 2, 1985:21,24,30.

Plumet, Charles (1861–1928)
▶ French architect and designer; born Circy-sur-Verouze, Meurthe-et-Moselle; active Paris.
▶ Having practiced in the Art Nouveau style before World War I, Plumet was one of those who sought the Modern style through a synthesis of the arts; was a member of artists' group L'Art dans Tout and, in 1903 with Frantz Jourdain, became a founding member of the Salon d'Automne; designed furniture with Tony Selmershiem, shown in various salons in the 1920s, and built elegant townhouses in the 16th arrondissement and a rather sober structure at 50 avenue Victor-Hugo, both in Paris. Designer of masonry buildings and furniture, he was chief architect of the 1925 Paris 'Exposition Internationale des Arts Décoratifs et Industriels Modernes,' where he erected four massive towers in no identifiable style that flanked the four corners of the Esplanade des Invalides; the structures housed restaurants.
▶ Pierre Cabanne, *Encyclopédie Art Déco*, Paris: Somogy, 1986: 226. Pierre Kjellberg, *Art Déco: les maîtres du Mobilier, le décor des Paquebots*, Paris: Amateur, 1986:137. Arlette Barré-Despond and Suzanne Tise, *Jourdain*, Paris: Regard, 1988.

Plus Glasshytte
▶ Norwegian ceramics and glass factory; located Fredrikstad.
▶ The Plus workshop cooperative was founded in 1958 by Per Tannum. Originally intended to supply designers and models to industry, it became a place for craftspeople's workshops. From 1970, Plus Glasshytte was managed by Benny Motzfeldt.
▶ Jennifer Hawkins Opie, *Scandinavia: Ceramics and Glass in the Twentieth Century*, New York: Rizzoli, 1989.

Poelzig, Hans (1869–1936)
▶ German architect and designer; born Berlin.
▶ 1888–95, studied Technische Hochschule, Berlin-Charlottenburg and Technische Hocschule, Berlin, under Karl Schäffer.
▶ 1899–1916, he worked in his own office in Breslau (now Wroclaw, Poland) and, 1900–16, taught at the Kunst- und Kunstgewerbeschule (after 1911, called the Akademie für Kunst und Kunstgewerbe) in Breslau, where he was director from 1903. 1916–20, he was municipal architect of Dresden and taught at the Technische Hochschule there. From 1920, he was head of a studio at the Preussiche Akademie der Künste in Berlin and, in 1923, became professor at the Technische Hochschule in Berlin-Charlottenburg, where pupils included architects Konrad Wachsmann, Rudolf Schwartz, Julius Posener, and Egon Eiermann. He turned to monumental buildings with work including the *tour-de-force* of Expressionism, the reconstruction of Reinhardt's Schumann Circus as the 1918–19 Grosses Schauspielhaus in Berlin. The influence of the building could be seen in E. Walmsley Lewis's New Victoria Cinema interior in London. He set up an architectural practice in Berlin. His other work included the 1911 office building in Breslau, 1911 water tower at Posen (now Poznan, Poland), 1911–12 chemical factory at Luban (now Poland), 1913 Centenary Exhibition (with Max Berg) at Breslau, 1920–22 Salzburg Festival Theater, 1928–31 IG Farben administration complex in Frankfurt-am-Main, and Festival Hall project in Salzburg.
▶ Theodor Heuss, *Hans Poelzig, Lebensbild eines deutschen Baumeisters*, Tübingen, 1939 and 1955. Julius Posener, 'Poelzig,' *Architectural Review*, June 1963:401–05. Julius Posener (ed.), *Hans Poelzig: Gesammelte Schriften und Werke*, Berlin, 1970.

Poggi, Carlo
▶ Italian furniture manufacturer.
▶ Founded in 1949, Poggi hired Franco Albini as its design consultant; 1950–68, produced Albini's designs exclusively, including the 1950 *Luisa* chair. Subsequent designers included Mario Bellini, Achile Castiglioni, Ugo La Pietra, Ennio Lucini, and Vico Magistretti.
▶ Work (La Pietra's 1971 *Uno sull'altro* bookcase) shown at 1972 'Italy: The New Domestic Landscape,' New York Museum of Modern Art and other work in numerous exhibitions worldwide.
▶ Cat., Leslie Jackson, *The New Look: Design in the Fifties*, New York: Thames and Hudson, 1991:126.

Pohl, Josef (1894–1975)
▶ Czech lighting designer.
▶ 1929–33, studied Bauhaus.
▶ He designed the 1929 precursor of the adjustable architect's lamp. His model was produced by Gerd Balzer. A similar lamp was produced by Körting und Mathieson as part of its *Kamden* range. Pohl and others at the Bauhaus also executed the prototype adjustable wall lamp illustrated in *Staaliches Bauhaus, Weimar 1919–1923* and produced by K.J. Jucker. Balzer and Pohl were given the task in 1932 of organizing Bauhaus students' work, which resulted in a conference and furniture design competition.
▶ Cat., *The Bauhaus: Masters and Students*, New York: Barry Friedman, 1988. Cat., *Die Metallwerkstattam Bauhaus*, Berlin: Bauhaus-Archiv, 1992:319.

Pöhlmann, Josef (1882–1963)
▶ German silversmith; active Munich and Nuremberg.
▶ Pöhlmann set up his own workshop in 1908. He was a teacher at the metal workshop of the Gewerbliche Fortbildungsschule in

Nuremberg. 1919–45, he taught silversmithing at the Kunstgewerbeschule in Nuremberg, where one of his pupils was Ludwig Riffelmacher. Pöhlmann's designs of the early 1920s were frequently simple, incorporating enameled columbines and larkspur reminiscent of the work of 16th-century silversmith Wenzel Jamnitzer of Nuremberg.
▶ Annelies Krekel-Aalberse, *Art Nouveau and Art Déco Silver*, New York: Abrams, 1989:146,258.

Poillerat, Gilbert (1902–88)
▶ French designer.
▶ Studied engraving, École Boulle, Paris, to 1921.
▶ 1921–27, he worked for metalworker Edgar Brandt in the rue Marat in Paris as a designer and creator of wrought-iron furniture and furnishings. In 1927, he began working for Baudet, Donon et Roussel, the carpentry and metal construction workshop, in charge of its new wrought iron section. He designed and produced grillework, tables, chairs, consoles, screens, lighting, and firedogs. Working in a variety of media from jewelry to clothing, Poillerat's metalwork was rendered in characteristic winding calligraphic forms. He designed the 1934 ornamental door with folk scenes for a scholarly group in Maisons-Alfort, inexpensive jewelry for couturier Jacques Heim, and a bronze door for the 1935 oceanliner *Normandie*. Commissions included work for the Bibliothèque Nationale and the Palais de Chaillot. In 1946, he became a professor at the École Nationale des Arts Décoratifs and set up his own workshop. Abandoning furniture and furnishings, he turned to monumental wrought-iron work, filling a number of commissions, including those for public and governmental buildings and the Palais de l'Élysée. In 1957, he designed the façade ironwork of the new synagogue in Strasbourg. He often worked with Jacques Adnet.
▶ Showing his work for the first time, Poillerat's grille was seen at the 1928 Salon d'Automne.
▶ *Ferronnier d'aujourd'hui*, Paris: Charles Moreau, 1962. Pierre Kjellberg, *Art Déco: les maîtres du Mobilier, le décor des Paquebots*, Paris: Amateur, 1986:138. François Baudot, *Gilbert Poillerat, maître ferronnier*, Paris: Hazan, 1993.

Point, Armand (1861–1932)
▶ French artist; born Algiers.
▶ Point was a leader in the movement to purify Modern art by returning to an earlier tradition. Strongly influenced by John Ruskin and the Pre-Raphaelites, Point attempted to emulate 15th- and 16th-century styles, like those of Leonardo da Vinci and Sandro Botticelli. Point showed his work with the Salon de la Rose Croix group from its beginning in 1892 and designed its exhibition posters in 1895 and 1896. He founded Hauteclaire, a community of artists and craftspeople at Marlotte, where he oversaw the production of bronzes, embroideries, ceramics, enamels, and other decorative pieces.
▶ Yvonne Brunhammer et al., *Art Nouveau Belgium, France*, Houston: Institute for the Arts, Rice University, 1976.

Poiret, Paul (1879–1944)
▶ French couturier and entrepreneur; active Paris.
▶ Poiret's meeting couturier Jacques Doucet was a decisive point in his career. He began handling all of Doucet's graphic production and fashion designs. His costumes for famous personalities brought him fame, including a mauve and black coat for Réjane for the stage production *Zana*, and the costume for Sarah Bernhardt in *L'Aiglon*. The association ended after a dispute with Doucet. Poiret became a pattern maker at Worth. In 1904, he opened his own establishment at 5 rue Auber in Paris, where he achieved success with a new natural style which freed women from their corsets. Several years later he eliminated tight skirts. Poiret befriended avant-garde painters, particularly André Derain and Maurice de Vlaminck; Paul Iribe illustrated Poiret's 1908 portfolio *Les robes de Paul Poiret racontées par Paul Iribe* and Georges Lepape the 1911 *Les choses de Paul Poiret vues par Georges Lepape*. The 'new female,' as revealed in Iribe's and Lapape's drawings,

was born. They wore clothes influenced by the Orient and the fashions of the Directoire: high waist lines, *décolleté*, flowing fabrics, turbans, large embroidered coats, shimmering fabrics, and strong contrasting colors. Poiret's style rapidly became popular, though, after World War I, it was increasingly out of touch with the androgynous *garçonne* style popular in the 1920s. In 1911, Poiret founded the École Martine, a school for young women who were taught to paint freely from nature. He wanted to break with the fussy, timid styles of the time and employed gifted working-class girls to create fresh and naïve motifs. The results of Poiret's efforts through Martine were translated into textiles, wallpapers, and carpets, characterized by a colorful, loose graphic style drawn by the students and sold through Maison Martine. From 1909, Poiret's couture showroom was located in a townhouse that he restored at the intersection of faubourg Saint-Honoré and (now) avenue Franklin Roosevelt in which he gave dazzling parties attended by the *beau monde* of the day, including André Derain, André Dunoyer de Segonzac, Raoul Dufy, Jean-Louis Forain, Kees Van Dongen, and by dancers Isadora Duncan, Carlotta Zambelli, and Régina Badet. Poiret entertained principally at the Pavillon du Butard in the Bois de Fausses-Reposes, organized parties for the aristocracy, and designed theater sets. By 1919, the Martine school began producing bold and often painted furniture. On one project, a pair of shagreen and inlaid-ivory petite commodes, Poiret appears to have collaborated with Adolphe Chanaux in c1921. In 1925, Poiret sold part of his collection of paintings to save his business; his fortunes declined inexorably thereafter.
▶ At the Alexandre III Bridge during the 1925 Paris 'Exposition Internationale des Arts Décoratifs et Industriels Modernes,' Poiret conceived the idea of glamorously equipping three barges, named *Amours*, *Délices*, and *Orgues*, decorated with fabric-tufted ceilings and wall hanging designed by Dufy.
▶ Palmer White, *Poiret*, New York: Potter, 1973. Pierre Cabanne, *Encyclopédie Art Déco*, Paris: Somogy, 1986:226–27. Yvonne Deslandres with Dorothé Lalanne, *Poiret: Paul Poiret 1897–1944*, Paris: Regard, 1986; New York: Rizzoli, 1987.
▶ See Martine, Atelier

Polato, Piero (1936–)
▶ Italian industrial designer; born Noventa; active Milan.
▶ Polato taught metallurgy at ISIA, Urbano; published books on design education. His clients included Saiet, Avancart, La Rinascente department store, Pellizzari, RAI, Televisione Svizzera Italiana, Bayerischer Rundfunk, Franco Rosso International, Fratelli Coppola, Furla, Mursia Editore, Robots, Zucchi, Il Bustese, and Muncherner Rück. He was a member of ADI (Associazione per il Disegno Industriale); established a workshop at the Triennale di Milan, (with Bruno Munari) workshops 'Giocare con l'arte' and for UNESCO, and the commune of Milan; was involved in numerous television programs on design; designed more than 250 sets for RAI television and German and Swiss television.
▶ Received 1981 Premio Compasso d'Oro; prize at the Bio in Ljubljana.
▶ *ADI Annual 1976*, Milan: Associazione per il Disegno Industriale, 1976. *Modo*, No. 148, March–April 1993:124.

Polglase, Van Nest (1898–)
▶ American film set designer; born Brooklyn, New York; active Hollywood.
▶ As a designer for RKO motion picture studio, he became known for his 'Big White Set,' as seen in Fred Astaire and Ginger Rogers musical productions of the 1930s. From the 1920s, his sets could be designed in white as arc lamps (necessitating pink and green colors used in the sets) were replaced by incandescent bulbs. The change from orthochromatic to more sensitive panchromatic film stock made possible a crisp, glossy effect. Polglase and his assistants decorated Ginger Rogers's house in Hollywood. On *Top Hat* (1935), as supervising art director, he had five unit art directors, including Carroll Clark, and 110 people handing such particulars as carpets and furniture. Polgase's recreation of Venice for the film soared two storeys, occupied two adjoining sound stages, had

winding canals, three bridges, a piazza, dance floors, balconies, and terraced cafés. His first film was probably *A Kiss in the Dark* (1925) and his last *Slightly Scarlet* (1956).

▶ Howard Mandelbaum and Eric Myers, *Screen Deco: A Celebration of High Style in Hollywood*, New York: St. Martin's, 1985. Ephraim Katz, *The Film Encyclopedia*, New York: Harper & Row, 1990.

Poli, Flavio   (1900–)
▶ Italian glassware designer; born Chioggia; active Venice.
▶ Poli participated in 1936 in the formation of Seguso Vetri d'Arte, Murano, becoming artistic director in 1963 responsible for its high-quality glass production. After World War II, he designed a distinctive line of undecorated blown-glass vessels. In the later 1950s, he executed heavy vases, bowls, and drinking glasses in bold contrasting colors exemplary of innovatory Murano glass of the time.
▶ Received prizes at the Triennale di Milano and 1958 Brussels 'Exposition Universelle et Internationale de Bruxelles (Expo '58).'
▶ Hans Vollmer, *Allgemeines Lexikon der bildenden Künstler des 20. Jahrhunderts*, Vol. 6, Leipzig, 1962:354 passim. Cat., Kathryn B. Hiesinger and George H. Marcus III (eds.), *Design Since 1945*, Philadelphia: Philadelphia Museum of Art, 1983:226, II–48. *Glass 1959*, Corning, NY: The Corning Museum of Glass, 1959: Nos. 182–87. Gio Ponti, 'Alta Fedeltà: Vetro di Flavio Poli,' *Domus*, No. 410, 1964:50–52.

Polikoff, Leonard
▶ American interior designer and entrepreneur; active Los Angeles.
▶ Studied University of California at Los Angeles.
▶ He established California Drop Cloth in 1975, where craftspeople splattered cloth with ostensibly random pigments. More than 70 Jackson Pollock-like patterns were produced in both standard and custom colorations.
▶ Les Gilbert, 'Happenings West: Drop Cloths Turn to Fabric Art,' *Home Fashions Textiles*, Vol. 1, June 1980:63,65.

Polinsky, Glenn   (1963–)
▶ American designer; active San Francisco.
▶ Studied industrial design, University of Washington, St. Louis, Missouri.
▶ He worked at Friedman Design, San Francisco, designing products for public and domestic furniture manufacturers. He designed the *Balerafon Chair* produced by Brueton Industries.
▶ Received 1988 *ID* magazine Annual Award (paper cutter), 1988 IDEA competition (paper cutter), IDSA; 1988 Workspace Competition (computer desk), LIMN.

Pollack, Bruno
▶ Austrian furniture designer.
▶ 12 June 1930, Pollack patented a stacking chair in tubular steel produced from *c*1932 as model *RP7*, whose stacking principle facilitated mass production and revolutionized auditorium seating. British furniture manufacturer Cox was involved in 1934 in legal action with competitor Pel over its *RP6* stacking chair, the rights to which Pel had purchased from Pollack.
▶ *The Cabinet Maker*, July 1931. Cat., Dennis Sharp et al., *Pel and Tubular Steel Furniture of the Thirties*, London: Architectural Association, 1977. Barbie Campbell-Cole and Tim Benton (eds.), *Tubular Steel Furniture*, London: The Art Book Company, 1979:13.

Pollak, Alfred   (?–1909)
▶ Austrian silversmith; active Vienna.
▶ The firm of Alfred Pollak was founded in 1878. It produced designs by Arnold Nechanski, Ernst Lichtblau, Hans Bolek, and Rudolf Hammel, and students of the Kunstgewerbeschule in Vienna.
▶ Silverwork of Hammel and students of the Kunstgewerbeschule made by Alfred Pollak was shown at the 1902 Turin 'Esposizione Internazionale d'Arte Decorativa Moderna.'

▶ Annelies Krekel-Aalberse, *Art Nouveau and Art Déco Silver*, New York: Abrams, 1989:193,199,200,258. Waltrand Neuwirth, *Wiener Gold- und Silberschmiede und ihre Punzen 1867–1922*, Vienna, 1977:112–16.

Pollini, Gino   (1903–)
▶ Italian architect and designer; born Rovereto.
▶ From 1927, studied Politecnico di Milano.
▶ He often collaborated with Luigi Figini; in 1926, they were among the founding members of Gruppo Sette, the architectural fraternity that launched Italian Rationalist architecture with the 1926–27 publication of its four-part manifesto. Pollini joined the Fascist Party in 1928. In 1930, Bottoni and Pollini replaced Carlo Enrico Rava and Alberto Sartoris as delegates of CIAM (Congrès Internationaux d'Architecture Moderne); they participated until 1946. Pollini and Figini with Adalberto Libera and Guido Fretti (all Gruppo Sette members) and Piero Bottoni designed the Casa Elettrica for Montedison at the 1930 (IV) 'International Exposition of Decorative Arts' in Monza, where an all-electric kitchen was featured, based on German and American models. Pollini had earlier designed the 'Appartamento Elettrico' for the 1929 'Esposizione dell'Alto Adige' in Bolzano. Pollini and Bottoni organized the international exhibition Milan 'Lotizzamento razionale' in 1932. Through the 1930s, Pollini worked in the Italian Rationalist style. Figini and Pollini designed 1934–35 Olivetti building in Ivrea, built 1939–41. With Xanti Schawinsky, they designed the 1935 *Studio 42* typewriter for Olivetti.
▶ He designed the 'Villa-Studio per un artista' (with Figini) at the 1933 (V) Triennale di Milano, 1934 Palazzo del Littorio (competition project with Gian Luigi Banfi, Lodovico Belgiojoso, Arturo Danusso, Luigi Figini, Enrico Peressutti, and Ernesto Rogers) in Rome, and 1938 Malparte house on Capri, Piazza delle Forze Armate (with Mario De Renzi and Figini) at the 1942 'Esposizione Universale di Roma.'
▶ Eugenio Gentili Tedeschi, *Figini e Pollini*, Milan: Ed. Il Balcone, 1959. Cesare Blasi, *Figini e Pollini*, Milano: Ed. di Monumità, 1963. Luigi Figini and Gino Pollini, 'Origini dell'architettura italiana alla cultura internazionale,' *L'Architettura d'aujourd'hui*, Vol. 22, No. 41. Cat., *Design Process: Olivetti 1908–1983*, Milan, 1983:377. Richard A. Etlin, *Modernism in Italian Architecture, 1890–1940*, Cambridge: MIT, 1991:227,233,390,494,523–24,554,641n32.

Pollitzer, Sigmund   (1913–)
▶ British painter, decorative glass designer, and writer; born London.
▶ Studied in London, Switzerland, and Hanover.
▶ He worked on the commissions of architect and designer Oliver Bernard, including the 1930 Cumberland Hotel and 1932 Marble Arch Corner House, both in London. Pollitzer and Kenneth Cheesman were protégés of Bernard. 1933–38, Pollitzer was chief designer at Pilkington's glassmakers, for which he designed showrooms in Glasgow, Leeds, Nottingham, St. Helens, and Piccadilly in London and for the stand at the 1937 'Glass Train,' a publicity project fitted with a range of decorative glass and shown at railway stations throughout Britain. His decorative glass features were included in the interiors of Kenneth Cheesman, including those for British Vitrolite in 1934 and 1934 Kirk Sandall Hotel near Doncaster (T.H. Johnson, architect). Other commissions included accoutrements for the 1936 oceanliner *Queen Mary* and 1937 McVitties Guest Restaurant, 1938 oceanliner *Mauretania*, 1938 Gaumont theater in the Haymarket in London, and at the 1937 Paris 'Exposition Internationale des Arts et Techniques dans la Vie Moderne,' 1938 Glasgow 'British Empire Exhibition,' and 1939 New York City 'World's Fair.'
▶ He contributed to the bedroom designed by Oliver Hill for the 1933 London 'British Industrial Art in Relation to the Home' in Dorland Hall and 1935 'British Art in Industry' at the Royal Academy. His glassware designs were included in the 1979–80 'Thirties' exhibition at the Hayward Gallery in London.

▶ Cat., *Thirties: British art and design before the war*, London: Arts Council of Great Britain, Hayward Gallery, 1979:102,143, 156,271,299.

Pollock, Charles (1930–)
▶ American industrial designer.
▶ Pollock studied industrial design, Pratt Institute, Brooklyn, New York.
▶ He worked in the industrial design office of George Nelson, New York City, where he designed fiberglass furniture with tapering tubular metal legs; 1958, set up his own design office where he designed the 1960 657 sling chair in leather for the seat with a steel-frame support and the 1965 fiberglass-shell swivel office chair, both for Knoll; subsequently, designed chairs for Thonet and the 1981 *Penelope* metal-mesh chair for Castelli.
▶ *Dal cucchiaio alla città nell'itinerario di 100 designers*, Milan, 1983. John Pile, *Dictionary of 20th-century Design*, New York: Facts-On-File, 1990:206–07. Hans Wichmann, *Die Realisation eines neuen Museumtyps*, 1980–90, Munich: Die Neue Sammlung, 1990:104–05.

Poloni, Arnaldo (1931–)
▶ Italian industrial designer; born Bergamo; active Milan.
▶ Poloni designed television sets, sound systems, and electronic equipment for clients including CGE, SNT, Siemens, Minerva, Körting, and Grundig Italiana. He was a member of ADI (Associazione per il Disegno Industriale).
▶ *ADI Annual 1976*, Milan: Associazione per il Disegno Industriale, 1976.

Poltrona Frau
▶ Italian furniture manufacturer; located Angliana, Pistoia.
▶ Renzo Frau established the firm in 1919. Designers included Gae Aulenti, Marco Zanuso, F. A. Porsche and Tito Agnoli. The firm was known for its leather covered seating models, some available in 66 colors. Outfitting automobiles, airplanes, and other users of industrial leather seating, 'le Frau' set up a department for the production of office furniture, for which Pierluigi Frau designed its 1985 *Pausa* leather sofa.
▶ 'Milan à l'Heure du Design,' *Maison et Jardin*, April 1992:129.

Pomone
▶ French decorating studio.
▶ Pomone was established in 1922 at the Bon Marché department store in Paris. Paul Follot was artistic director from 1923 and director until 1928, when he was succeeded by René Prou, who became director in 1932. Albert Guénot was a designer, sometimes in collaboration with Prou, from 1923.
▶ *Les Grands Magasins du Bon Marché*, Paris, 1914.

Pompe, Antoine (1873–1980)
▶ Belgian architect and designer; active Brussels.
▶ Around 1903, Pompe designed silver flatware and hollow-ware in the style of Henry van de Velde. Pompe is the only turn-of-the-century Belgian architect whose silver designs have survived, although they may never have been produced.
▶ Annelies Krekel-Aalberse, *Art Nouveau and Art Déco Silver*, New York: Abrams, 1989:90,258.

Pond, Edward (1929–)
▶ British designer.
▶ From the 1950s, Pond designed textiles and wallpapers for manufacturers in Britain and abroad. In the 1960s, his designs embraced Pop art and Op art motifs, and some historicist patterns. In 1976, he set up Edward Pond Association, where many areas of design production were pursued.
▶ Jonathan M. Woodham, *Twentieth-Century Ornament*, New York: Rizzoli, 1990:324.

Pons, Geneviève
▶ French decorator and furniture designer; active Paris.
▶ Studied École Nationale Supérieure des Arts Décoratifs, Paris.

▶ She was an apprentice under René Prou; from the late 1920s, Pons worked at the Primavera decorating department, Au Printemps department store, Paris; subsequently at La Maîtrise decorating department, Galeries Lafayette department store, Paris.
▶ *Ensembles Mobiliers*, Paris: Charles Moreau, Nos. 3–4, 1954.

Pontabry, Robert
▶ French designer.
▶ Pontabry designed the kiosks at the 1925 Paris 'Exposition Internationale des Arts Décoratifs et Industriels Modernes,' and woman's desk for the 1927 competition organized by the Union Centrale des Arts Décoratifs.
▶ Pierre Kjellberg, *Art Déco: les maîtres du Mobilier, le décor des Paquebots*, Paris: Amateur, 1986:187.

Ponti, Gio (Giovanni Ponti 1891–1979)
▶ Italian architect and designer; born and active Milan.
▶ 1918–21, studied architecture, Politecnico di Milano.
▶ In 1921, he worked in an architectural office, Milan, with Mino Fiocchi and Emilio Lancia. 1923–30, he designed Wiener Werkstätte-inspired ceramics produced by Richard Ginori, where he worked 1923–28. He was director of the Biennale di Monza (later named Triennale di Milano) 1925–79, serving as head of the executive board 1924–39, and, in 1956, became a founding member of ADI (Associazione per il Disegno Industriale). From 1927, he worked with glassmaker Paolo Venini; 1923–36, (with Lancia) worked in a studio, Milan; in 1928, founded the journal *Domus*, serving as its first editor 1938–41, and 1948–79; 1933–45, worked in a studio, Milan, with Antonio Fornaroli and Eugenio Sohcini. Piero Fornasetti became a student of Ponti and, subsequently, protégé and assistant, designing the Lunari and collaborating with Ponti on a number of projects in their distinctive 17th-century image applying technique, designed by Ponti and decorated by Fornasetti. From the 1930s, Ponti designed enamels for Paolo di Poli, mosaics for Gabbianelli, printed fabrics, flatware, ceramics and ceramic tiles, automobile bodies, lighting, sewing machines, 1951 cutlery by Krupp of Essen, 1953 sanitary equipment by Ideal-Standard, and stage sets at La Scala in Milan. His work was Modern in essence but drew on traditional motifs and imagery, illustrating the eclecticism of the early years of Fascism. Before abandoning his neo-Classical orientation, he served on the executive committee of the 1933 (V) Triennale di Milano. 1936–61, he taught at the Politecnico di Milano. He became Italy's best known postwar architect. For his first (1936) Montecatini building in Milan, he designed everything down to door knobs and sanitary fittings. In 1945, he founded the journal *Stile*, of which he was director until 1947. His widely published 1948–49 espresso machine produced by La Pavoni owed a great deal to Streamline designs from America of this period. His best known building was the 1956 Pirelli office tower (with Alberto Rosselli, Antonio Fornaroli, and engineer Pier Luigi Nervi). 1952–76, Ponti was in partnership with Alberto Rosselli and Antonio Fornaroli; after Rosselli's death, he worked with Fornaroli. He was influential on a number of younger designers and employees, including Lino Sabatini and Richard Sapper, who worked in his office 1958–59. Ponti's best known furniture design was the 1952 *Superleggera 646* chair made by Cassina; it was a play on vernacular Italian forms. His clients for furniture included Arflex, Cassina, Singer, and the Nordiska Kompaniet. His toilet fixture for Ideal Standard was a classic in its field. He wrote nine books, edited eight books alone and with others, and produced a number of journal articles.
▶ He designed a room setting at the 1928 'Exposition of Art in Industry at Macy's' at Macy's department store in New York. He participated in first 1923 'Esposizione Biennale delle Arti Decorative e Industriali Moderne,' Monza. His cutlery for Krupp was shown at the 1951 (IX) Triennale di Milano. He was general supervisor of the 1961 Turin 'Italia 61,' 1966 Genoa 'Eurodomus I,' and 1968 Turin 'Eurodomus II.' His Venini-produced glassware was shown at the 1956 Biennale di Venezia. His *Superleggera* chair and toilet were included in the 1983–84 'Design Since 1945' exhibition at the Philadelphia Museum of Art. His work was the

subject of the 1965 'The Expression of Gio Ponti,' University of California, Los Angeles, and 1987 'Gio Ponti: ceramica et architettura' exhibition in Faenza. He received numerous awards including 1956 national grand prize of Premio Compasso d'Oro and honorary degree from Royal College of Art, London.

▶ Gio Ponti, *Amate l'architettura*, Milan, 1957 (Gio Ponti, *In Praise of Architecture*, New York 1960). Giulia Veronesi, *Difficolta Politiche dell'Architettura in Italia 1920–40*, Milan, 1953. James S. Plaut, *Espressione de Gio Ponti, Milan*, 1954. 'Espressione di Gio Ponti,' *Aria d'Italia*, Vol. 8, 1954. Nathan H. Shapira (ed.), *The Expression of Gio Ponti*, Minneapolis, 1967. Nathan H. Shapira, 'The Expression of Gio Ponti,' *Design Quarterly*, Nos. 69–70, 1967. Cat., *Modern Chairs 1918–1970*, London: Lund Humphries, 1971. Barbie Campbell-Cole and Tim Benton (eds.), *Tubular Steel Furniture*, London: The Art Book Company, 1979:46. Paolo Portoghesi and Anty Pansera, *Gio Ponti alla Manifattura di Coccia*, Milan, 1982. Penny Sparke, *Ettore Sottsass Jnr*, London: Design Council, 1982. Cat., Kathryn B. Hiesinger and George H. Marcus III (eds.), *Design Since 1945*, Philadelphia: Philadelphia Museum of Art, 1983:226,I–33,III–68. Cat. *Gio Ponti: Ceramica e Architettura*, Faenza, 1987. Lisa Licitra Ponti, *Gio Ponti: The Complete Work 1923–1978*, Cambridge: MIT Press, 1990.

Ponzio, Emanuele

▶ Italian designer.
▶ From 1965, Ponzio was active in Studios DA with Cesare Casati; designed interiors of hotels, banks, and government buildings; had clients including Phoebus, Nai Ponteure, and Autovox.
▶ Giancarlo Iliprandi and Pierluigi Molinari (eds.), *Industrial Design Italiani*, Fagamma, 1985:81. Hans Wichmann, *Italien Design 1945 bis heute*, Munich: Die Neue Sammlung, 1988.

Poor, Henry Varnum   (1888–1971)

▶ American ceramicist; born Chapman, Kansas; active New York.
▶ Studied painting, Stanford University, Stanford, California; 1910, Slade School of Art, London; 1911, Académie Julian, Paris.
▶ He taught art at Stanford and, in c1918, settled in New York. He turned to ceramics as a means of income, completely abandoning painting in the 1920s. In his ceramic work, he used the Persian technique of painting and etching on damp slip before applying the glaze. He built his studio Crowhouse in Rockland County, New York, subsequently selling his utilitarian pieces through art galleries in Manhattan. Not caring if a plate was warped, he sought spontaneity in decoration and form. Published *A Book of Pottery: From Mud to Immortality* (1958).
▶ Karen Davies, *At Home in Manhattan: Modern Decorative Arts, 1925 to the Depression*, New Haven: Yale, 1983:55. R. Craig Miller, *Modern Design 1890–1990*, New York: Abrams, 1990.

Popova, Liubov' Sergeevna   (1889–1924)

▶ Russian artist and designer; born near Moscow.
▶ Studied 1907–08 under Stanislav Zhukovsky and Konstantin Yuon in Moscow.
▶ Popova was originally a Constructivist, who abandoned the 'dead ends of representation' to become an 'artist-constructor.' In 1912, she worked in Moscow in the studio called The Tower with Viktor Bart, Vladimir Tatlin, and Kirill Zdanevich. 1912–13, she worked in Paris, visiting the studios of Henri Le Fauconnier and Jean Metzinger, where she met Vera Pestel and Nadezhda Udal'tsova. In 1913, she returned to Russia, working again with Tatlin and Udal'tsova and Alekandr Vesnin. 1916–18, she painted architectonic compositions; 1919–21, executed painterly constructions. In 1918, she taught at Svomas/Vkhutemas and, in 1920, became a member of Inkhuk. Rejecting studio painting, she experimented with designs for books, ceramics, textiles, and dresses. In 1922, she created the sets and costumes for Vsevolod Ermilievitch Meyerhold's production of Fernand Crommelynck's farce *The Magnanimous Cuckold*. In 1923, she designed dresses and textiles for the First State Textile Factory in Moscow.

▶ 1914–16, her work was shown at the 1914 and 1916 'Jack of Diamonds' exhibition in Moscow, 'Tramway V,' '0–10' and 'The Store.' She contributed to the 1918 5th State Exhibition 'From Impressionism to Non-Objective Art,' 1919 10th State Exhibition 'Non-Objective Creation and Suprematism,' 1921 '5×5=25' exhibition and 1922 'Erste Russische Kunstausstellung' in Berlin. A 1924 posthumous exhibition of her work was mounted in Moscow.
▶ Stephanie Barron and Maurice Tuchman, *The Avant-Garde in Russia, 1910–1930*, Cambridge, MA: MIT Press, 1980:218. Magdalena Dabrowski, *Liubov Popova*, New York, 1991. Dmitri Sarabianov and Natalia L. Adaskina, *Popova*, New York: Abrams, 1990. Cat., *The Great Utopia: The Russian and Soviet Avant-Garde, 1915–1932*, New York: Guggenheim Musem, 1992. Selim Om Khan-Magomedov, *Les Vhutemas*, Paris: Regard, 1990:420–23.

Porsche, Ferdinand Alexander 'Butzi'   (1935–)

▶ German designer; active Germany and Austria; son of Ferdinand 'Ferry' Porsche (1909), automobile designer, and grandson of Prof Dr Ferdinand Porsche (1875–1951), Porsche automobile founder.
▶ Studied Hochschule für Gestaltung, Ulm.
▶ He worked for an engineering company before joining the family automobile firm Porsche. Becoming the company's chief designer, he designed two cars, including the celebrated 911 still in production. In 1972, he set up his own design studio in Zell-am-See (Austria), where he designed various accessories including watches, pipes, sunglasses, and leather goods. In the 1980s as part of the trend towards the deluxe, his expensive wares were popular items. For other firms including Poltrona Frau, Artemide, and Inter Profil, he designed furniture, lighting, and electrical products. His 1985 lighting range for Luci included the *Platone* ceiling, *Parete PL* wall, *Lettura PL* floor, and *Soffitto* pendant lamps. His *Jazz* lamp was produced by PAF. All of his designs manifested his stark Ulm School training.
▶ His 1984 *Antropovarius* leather seating for Poltrona Frau was included in the 1991 'Mobili Italiani 1961–1991: Le Varie Età dei linguaggi' exhibition at the Salone del Mobile in Milan and work in numerous exhibitions worldwide.
▶ Albrecht Bangert and Karl Michael Armer, *80s Style: Designs of the Decade*, New York: Abbeville, 1990:98,99,234. *Mobili Italiani 1961–1991: Le Varie Età dei linguaggi*, Milan: Cosmit, 1992. *Ferdinand Alexander Porsche, Designer: Damit das Denken am Leben bleibt*, Hanover, 1992.

Porsgrunds Porselænsfabrik

▶ Norwegian ceramics factory; located Porsgrunn.
▶ The Porsgrunds Porselænsfabrik was founded in 1886 by John Jeremiassen; it hired Carl Maria Bauer as its technical manager. Its early production was in traditional underglaze painted and transfer-printed motifs, including those of Royal Copenhagen and Meissen. In c1900, the Nordic style was introduced in patterns by Gerhard Munthe, Henrik Bull, Thorolf Holmboe, and others. From 1889, when Jeremiassen died, the firm was managed by brother-in-law Gunnar Knudsen, member of the national assembly of Norway and subsequently prime minister. Successful Modern designs began to be produced with the hiring of designers Hans Flygenring in 1920 and Nora Gulbrandsen in 1927. In 1952, Tias Eckhoff became artistic director. Designers included Anne Marie Ødegaard, Konrad Galaaen, and Eystein Sandnes. Norway's largest porcelain factory by the 1980s, its manager was Stein Devik.
▶ Fredrik Wildhagen, *Norge i Form*, Oslo: Stenersen, 1988. Jennifer Hawkins Opie, *Scandinavia: Ceramics and Glass of the Twentieth Century*, New York: Rizzoli, 1989.

Porteneuve, Alfred   (1896–1949)

▶ French furniture designer; nephew of Jacques-Émile Ruhlmann.
▶ Studied architecture, École des Beaux-Arts, Paris, to 1928.
▶ He worked with Ruhlmann in Paris and participated in the design of the 'Hôtel du collectionneur' at the 1925 Paris 'Exposition Internationale des Arts Décoratifs et Industriels Modernes.'

When Ruhlmann died in 1933, he opened his own workshop at 47 rue de Lisbonne in Paris, designing furniture that abandoned Ruhlmann's use of exotic woods in favor of fruit woods, laminates, and metal. Porteneuve decorated and furnished numerous apartments, government and commercial offices, and interiors of the oceanliner *Pasteur*. He collaborated with Jean Dunand.
▶ *Ensembles Mobiliers*, Vol. II, Paris: Charles Moreau, 1937. Florence Camard, *Ruhlmann*, Paris: Regard, 1983. Pierre Kjellberg, *Art Déco: les maîtres du Mobilier, le décor des Paquebots*, Paris: Amateur, 1986:187.

Porter, Bruce (1865–1953)
▶ American designer, painter, poet, and critic; born and active San Francisco.
▶ He designed gardens, painted murals, and created numerous church windows in San Francisco, San Mateo, Stockton, and Pacific Grove, all California. He designed windows for the Christ Episcopal Church in Coronado, California, and the Children's Home in San Diego. He and Gelett Burgess edited the journal *The Lark*, producing some of its essays, poetry, cover designs, and illustrations. Porter wrote the preface to the book *Art in California* (1909). He was a member of Les Jeunes, a group of San Francisco bohemians, secretary of the San Francisco Guild of Arts and Crafts, and best known for his monument to Robert Louis Stevenson in Portsmouth Square in San Francisco.

Porthault, Madeleine (1905–79)
and Daniel Porthault (1901–74)
▶ French producers and vendors of household linens; active Paris.
▶ Madeleine Porthault began working for couturière Maggy Rouff in Paris and was sent to the USA, where she designed, sold, and took measurements for clothing orders made up in Paris. Returning to Paris, she married Daniel Porthault, owner of a lingerie firm that supplied Rouff. In 1924, the Porthaults started producing household linens. In 1935, a factory was established to weave linens for embroidery and printing. In 1950, the company purchased its first factory for printing linens. Prints on linen fabric were reproduced by hand with wooden blocks. Their first clients included the Ford and Mellon families in the USA. In 1955, Madeleine Porthault designed the carnation print for the Duchess of Windsor. In 1956, the firm was commissioned to make linens for Aristotle Onassis's yacht *Christina* in a goldfish motif. Other clients included the Rothschilds, the Shah of Iran, the Kennedys, and French presidents. Its first shop was located on rue de la Grange Batelière, Paris. In 1960, Porthault opened its first boutique in New York on East 57th Street and, in 1964, its boutique in Paris was on the avenue Montaigne; others followed. Today, the firm is managed by the Porthaults' son Marc and his wife Françoise. Their delicate screen-printed and hand-embroidered linens are considered to be some of the finest worldwide. Marc Porthault designed the 1986 tulip print, the 1965 four-leaf clover motif and matching Limoges porcelain for Louise de Vilmorin, and 1985 print of ducks, rabbits, and brass horns. In 1991, the firm reissued the satin sheets with images of Grecian maidens in antique lace, originally created for Barbara Hutton. It is a member of the Comité Colbert.
▶ Christopher Petkanas, 'Customs of the Country,' *House and Garden*, May 1991:146–53,192.

Portoghesi, Paolo (1931–)
▶ Italian architect, designer, and teacher; born Rome.
▶ Studied Università di Roma to 1957.
▶ He set up his own architectural office in Rome in 1958. 1962–66, he was professor of architecture at the Università di Roma, serving as president 1968–76. 1967–77, taught at Politecnico di Milano, and was its dean 1968–76; from 1980, taught at Università della Sapienza, Rome; from 1979, directed the architecture section, Biennale di Venezia, serving as president from 1983. 1969–83, he was editor of *Controspazio*; from 1977, of *taca*, the journal of the Institute for the History of Architecture; and, from 1983, of *Eupalino*. He designed silver flatware by Cleto Munari

in 1981, the 1985 *Rabirio* desk by Ceccotti, 1986 *Sesguialtera* lamp by Societa del Travertino Romano, *Liuto* seat by Poltronova, and 1986 *Aldebarhan* table by Officina Roman del Disegno. His books included *After Modern Architecture* (1982) and *Postmodern: The Architecture of the Post Industrial Society* (1983). His hexagonal tea set was one of 11 in Alessi's 1983 *Tea and Coffee Piazza* project. He was a member of organizations including the Accademico Nazionale di San Luca from 1984, Accademia della Arti e del Disegno of Florence from 1977, and Accademia Ligustica in Genoa from 1977. A leading Post-Modern architect and town planner, his architecture included 1959 Casa Baldi and Casa Papanice, both Rome; 1968 Institute for Technology and Industry, L'Aquila; 1973 International Airport, Khartoum; 1974 Royal Palace, Amman; 1976 Mosque and Center for Islamic Culture, Rome; 1977 Thermal Center, Musignano, Canino; 1978 headquarters of the Accademia di Belle Arti, L'Aquila; 1978 Mosque, Rome; 1981 ENEL residential complex at Tarquinia; and 1984 Popolare del Molise, Campobasso.
▶ His work was shown in numerous exhibitions and galleries in the USA and Europe and the subject of a 1985 exhibition in Modena. In 1984, he received an honorary degree from the University of Lausanne. He won the competition for the town of Salerno. His *Città del sogno* alcove bed was included in the 'Affinità Elettive' exhibition at the 1985 Triennale di Milano.
▶ Officina Alessi, *Tea and Coffee Piazza: 11 Servizi da tè e caffè . . .*, Milan: Crusinallo, 1983. G. Priori, *L'architettura ritrovata: Opere recenti di Paolo Portoghesi*, Rome, 1985. G. Priori, *Paolo Portoghesi*, Bologna, 1985. Cat., Claudio D'Amato, *Paolo Portoghesi: Opere*, Modena, 1985. *Les Carnets du Design*, Paris: MadCap Productions et APCI, 1986:71. Auction cat., *Asta di Modernariato 1900–1986, Auction 'Modernariato,'* Milan: Semenzato Nuova Geri, 8 Oct. 1986: lot 116. Paolo Portoghesi, 'Tendenze delle nuove generazioni di architetti,' *Comunità*, Vol. 17, No. 115, 1963:44–59. Juli Capella and Quim Larrea, *Designed by Architects in the 1980s*, New York, Rizzoli, 1988. *Le Affinità Elettive*, Milan: Electa, 1985.

Portzamparc, Christian de (1944–)
▶ French architect; born Casablanca; active Paris.
▶ 1962–69, studied École Nationale Supérieure des Beaux-Arts, Paris; under Eugène Beaudoin; and under Georges Candilis.
▶ He built his first work, a water tower, 1971–74. His first major building (1976–79, with Giorgia Benamo), was on rue des Hautes Formes, Paris. He designed furniture and the interior of Café Beaubourg, Paris, and chairs and tables produced by Le Tracé Intérieur.
▶ Participated in 1980 Biennale di Venezia, designing façades of Strada Novissima. Won 1984 competition for Opera Dance School, Nanterre (France), and 1985 competition for Cité de la Musique, Parc de la Villette, Paris.
▶ *Dictionnaire Encyclopédique de l'architecture moderne et contemporaine*, Paris; Sers/Vilo, 1987. François Mathey, *Au bonheur des formes, design français 1945–1992*, 1992:168.

Posnovis
See Unovis

Post-Modernism
▶ Critical term.
▶ The term was first used in the context of literary criticism by Jean Baudrillard and Jacques Derrida among others; it was first applied to architecture in the 1960s by British art historian Nikolaus Pevsner, who realized that an expressive, non-rational, and non-autocratic type of architecture was emerging that rejected many of Modernism's tenets. In the 1970s, American architecture historian and critic Charles Jencks extended Pevsner's ideas, defining as Post-Modernist a range of architecture that, moving beyond Modernism's constraints, included works by American architects Michael Graves and Robert Venturi and Luxembourgian architect Leon Krier, who practiced in London after 1974. Post-Modernism made references to mass culture and embodied pluralism, eclecticism, historicism, humor, the linguistic (or 'semiotic') meanings

of constructed forms, and emotionally satisfying solutions in design. Post-Modern became a term used to describe those products of the 1970s and 1980s which rejected the Functionalist Bauhaus-Ulm approach, using criteria for design which undermined, or at least mocked, Modernism. The work of Ettore Sottsass and his Memphis studio group, with its celebration of bad taste, vulgar color, ironic wit, dislocation, playful historical references, and eclecticism, characterized Post-Modern design. Post-Modern architects in Japan, the USA, and Spain contributed to the movement, as did a number of prominent manufacturers such as Alessi in Italy and Knoll in the USA. The movement ebbed somewhat in the 1990s, when its frivolity began to seem out of step with the mood of economic pessimism and environmental concern. Modernism looked likely to have more staying power than its supposed successor, which seemed stalled at the point of defining itself in terms of what it was not.

▶ Jean Baudrillard, *L'échange symbolique et la mort*, Paris: Gallimard, 1976. Paolo Portoghesi, *After Modern Architecture*, New York: Rizzoli, 1982. Charles Jencks, *The Language of Post-Modern Architecture*, London: Academy, 1984. Mark Poster (ed.), *Jean Baudrillard: Selected Writings*, Stanford: Stanford University Press, 1988. Jean Baudrillard, 'The End of Production,' *Polygram*, 1988:5−29. Michael Collins, *Post-Modern Design*, London: Academy, 1991.

Pott, Carl Hugo   (1906−85)

▶ German metalworker.

▶ Studied design and metallurgy, technical school, Solingen, and Forschungsinstitut und Profieramt für Edelmetalle, Schwäbisch-Gmünd.

▶ He joined the metalwares firm founded by his father. During the 1920s, he became interested in the ideas of the Deutscher Werkbund, the Bauhaus, and other advanced design movements in Germany. He completely changed the design of the firm's products into simple unadorned forms, abandoning the heavily ornamented work of the time. After World War II, his designs and those of others commissioned by him were widely published, repeatedly winning awards; the other designers included Josef Hoffman, Hermann Gretsch, Wilhelm Wagenfeld, Elisabeth Treskow, and Don Wallance.

▶ He won a diploma of honor at the 1937 Paris 'Exposition Internationale des Art et Techniques dans la Vie Moderne' (where his work was first shown), a silver medal at the 1940 (VII) Triennale di Milano, and repeated awards at the events in Milan, Düsseldorf, Brussels, and Ljubljana. Pott's flatware was included in the 1983−84 'Design Since 1945' exhibition at the Philadelphia Museum of Art.

▶ Heinz Georg Pfaender, 'Der Designer Carl Hugo Pott,' *Architektur und Wohnform*, Vol. 74, 1966:371−74. Graham Hughes, *Modern Silver throughout the World*, New York, 1967: plates 63−67. Cat., Kathryn B. Hiesinger and George H. Marcus III (eds.), *Design Since 1945*, Philadelphia: Philadelphia Museum of Art, 1983:226,V−31−32.

Poulsen, Louis

▶ Danish lighting manufacturer; located Copenhagen.

▶ The firm began production in the 1920s. Poul Henningsen's widely published ceiling lamp for Poulsen was installed in the 1929−39 Tugendhat house by Ludwig Mies van der Rohe in Brno. Lamps based on Henningsen's model (the *PH* series) as well as other early designs are still in production. In the later 1960s and early 1970s, Arne Jacobsen designed for Poulsen; Verner Panton produced numerous designs. The firm began using plastics in its production from 1950, using acrylics for shades, diffusers, and light-fittings.

▶ Henningsen won a 1924 competition for the design of lamps in the Danish pavilion at the 1925 Paris International Exposition and numerous other awards for his lighting designs for Poulsen.

▶ Cat., Milena Lamarová, *Design a Plastické Hmoty*, Prague: Uřeleckoprůmyslové Muzeum, 1972:202.

Poulsen, Tage   (1940−)

▶ Danish furniture designer.

▶ Studied Kunsthåndværkerskolen, Copenhagen, to 1964.

▶ In 1959, Poulsen was an apprentice cabinetmaker. He became a designer for Gramrode Møbelfabrik, Hirtshals Savværk, Eigil Rasmussen, and Goth. He set up his own design studio in 1965.

▶ He received the 1974 Danish furniture prize and 1975 Johannes Krøiers award.

▶ Frederik Sieck, *Nutidig Dansk Møbeldesign:−en kortfattet illustreret beskrivelse*, Copenhagen: Bondo Gravesen; 1990 Busck edition in English.

Povey, Albert John Stephen   (1951−)

▶ British furniture and interior designer; born London.

▶ 1976−79, studied furniture design, Royal College of Art, London, under Robert Heritage.

▶ He became a freelance designer in 1981 and, 1981−83, designed the British American Tobacco exhibition and worked for various clients. In 1983, he open a design studio in King's Cross, London, where he designed the 1985 Diametric range of furniture, including the *Curved-Rail Bed*, *Y Trestle Table*, and *Eclipse Sofa*, all in steel, and designed furniture for the Phoenix Café, Kensington. A specialist in metal furniture, his work included the 1986 *Macstack Table* for Macfarlanes Solicitors, *Akrosystem* modular shelving, *Utility Chair*, and *Tulip Lighting*. In 1988, he opened the Diametric retail shop in Covent Garden and designed furniture and lighting for the Tilby and Leeves advertising agency, and *Stacking Steel Filing Tray* for the BBC. Clients included Lincoln Hannah, Sloane Helicopters, TV Register Group, Quandrance Communications, and Relocation Project Management. Povey's factory in Cannock, Staffordshire, was opened in 1990. Povey was known for his clever interpretations in steel of classic British styles including Queen Anne and those of Charles Rennie Mackintosh.

Powell, Alfred Hoare   (1865−1960) and **Louise Powell**

▶ British potters; husband and wife.

▶ Alfred Powell studied Slade School of Fine Art, London.

▶ Until 1892, Alfred Powell worked for architect J.D. Sedding. The Powells were active in the Arts and Crafts movement. 1903−30, Alfred Powell was associated with Wedgwood; the Powells visited the plant regularly in the 1930s and bought blanks that they fired there. Millicent Taplin trained under the Powells.

▶ They regularly showed their work at the Arts and Crafts Exhibition Society in London.

▶ *British Arts and Design, 1900−1960*, London: Victoria and Albert Museum, 1983.

Powell, David Harmon   (1933−)

▶ British designer.

▶ 1954−60, he worked on the development of melamine tableware at British Industrial Plastics. 1960−68, he was chief designer at Ekco Plastics in Southend, where he executed innovatory designs for its industrial and domestic products. Ekco produced his 1968 *Nova* injection-molded plastic stacking tableware, *Ekcoware* kitchen storage containers, and 1970 semi-disposable cutlery. In 1968, he set up his own studio and became the first tutor in molded plastics in the School of Industrial Design at the Royal College of Art in London.

▶ The 1970 cutlery won the 1970 Council of Industrial Design Award and was included in the 1983−84 'Design Since 1945' exhibition at the Philadelphia Museum of Art.

▶ John Heyes, 'Getting It Right the First Time,' *Design*, No. 271, Jan. 1967:47−53. 'Disposable Plastics Cutlery,' *Design*, No. 258, June 1970:45. Cat., Kathryn B. Hiesinger and George H. Marcus III (eds.), *Design Since 1945*, Philadelphia: Philadelphia Museum of Art, 1983:227,VI−27.

Powell, Edmund Barnaby   (1891−1939)

▶ British glassware designer; son of James Crofts Powell.

▶ 1909−14, studied Architectural Association, London.

▶ In 1918, he joined the family firm of James Powell of the Whitefriars Glassworks in Wealdstone, where he subsequently

became director and designer of decorative and domestic glass-ware. He specialized in decorative glassware on a large scale, based on the malleable qualities of blown glass. Together with a few British contemporaries, Powell and colleague William Wilson at Whitefriars brought worldwide acclaim to British glasswork.
▶ Several examples of his glassware were included in the 1979–80 'Thirties' exhibition at the Hayward Gallery in London.
▶ Cat., *Thirties: British art and design before the war*, London: Arts Council of Great Britain, Hayward Gallery, 1979:94,95,134, 155,299.

Powell, James
▶ British glassware manufacturer.
▶ *c*1880–*c*1908, James and Harry Powell produced their own glass designs and those of freelance designers, executing Venetian styles in green soda glass. The firm's patterns were based on examples depicted in 16th- to 19th-century Italian and Dutch paintings. It reissued Philip Webb's and Thomas Jackson's glass designs. In 1928, following its move to Wealdstone, William Wilson joined the firm, which produced Modern forms in the 1930s.
▶ It showed its work at the 1900 Paris 'Exposition Universelle' and 1903 Arts and Crafts exhibition.
▶ Frederick Cooke, *Glass: Twentieth-Century Design*, New York: Dutton, 1986:74.

Powell, John Hardham   (1827–95)
▶ British jeweler and metalworker.
▶ From 1844, Powell was an apprentice and assistant to A.W.N. Pugin. In 1850, he married Pugin's daughter Anne and, when Pugin died in 1852, succeeded him as chief designer at John Hard-man, where his father was a partner. Powell's work there was similar to Pugin's.
▶ Charlotte Gere, *American and European Jewelry 1830–1914*, New York: Crown, 1975:214.

Powolny, Michael   (1871–1954)
▶ Austrian sculptor, ceramicist, and teacher; born Judenburg.
▶ In 1905, under the aegis of the Wiener Werkstätte, he and Berthold Löffler founded the Wiener Keramik, which represented a high point in the decorative phase of late Art Nouveau. The workshop produced ceramics showing folklore influence from as far afield as Russia. In *c*1910, he designed glassware produced by J. und L. Lobmeyr.
▶ Günther Feuerstein, *Vienna—Present and Past: Arts and Crafts—Applied Art—Design*, Vienna: Jugend und Volk, 1976:28, 34,49.81. Robert Waissenberger, *Vienna 1890–1920*, Secaucus, NJ: Wellfleet 1984:136,269. Elisabeth Frottier, *Michael Powolny*, Vienna/Cologne: Böhlau, 1990.

Pozzi, Ambrogio   (1931–)
▶ Italian industrial designer; born Varese; active Gallarate.
▶ He worked in the family firm Ceramica Franco Pozzi in Gallarate from 1951, and redesigned its traditional products in an award-winning Functional style. His widely published 1970 *Compact* stacking coffee service was designed for machine production in three sizes. He set up his own design practice, where clients included Riedel, Rossi, Guzzini, Pierre Cardin, Rosenthal, Norex, La Rinascente department store, and Alitalia. His 1968 *Duo* dinnerware and limited-edition 1987 cup and saucer included in the *Collector's Cup* range were produced by Rosenthal. He was a member of ADI (Associazione per il Disegno Industriale).
▶ 1954–73, he participated in all the Triennali di Milano. He won the 1958–64, 1966, and 1970 first prizes for industrial design in Vicenza. For the family firm, he won two 1970 Compasso d'Oro awards for the *Compact* coffee service and *TR 113* tableware range. His work was shown at the 1980 'Arte e design' exhibition at the Palazzo delle Esposizioni in Faenza. The *Duo* dinnerware was included in the 1983–84 'Design Since 1945' exhibition at the Philadelphia Museum of Art and won the 1968 gold medal at the Faenza International Porcelain and Ceramics Competition. His porcelain service for Alitalia won the 1973 gold

metal at the Faenza International. 1967–74, he received the Bundespreis 'Die gute Industrieform' in Hanover and was a member of its juries 1969–70, 1970 Concorso Internazionale della Ceramica in Faenza, and 1971–74 industrial design competition in Valencia.
▶ Albrecht Bangert and Karl Michael Armer, *80s Style: Designs of the Decade*, New York: Abbeville, 1990:139,234. Cat., Kathryn B. Hiesinger and George H. Marcus III (eds.), *Design Since 1945*, Philadelphia: Philadelphia Museum of Art, 1983:227,II–49. *Premio Compasso d'Oro*, 1971:122–25. Cat., *Arte e design*, Faenza: Palazzo delle Esposizioni, 1980. *ADI Annual 1976*, Milan: Associazione per il Disegno Industriale, 1976.

Pozzi, Giancarlo   (1924–)
▶ Italian industrial designer; born Turin; active Milan.
▶ Pozzi began his professional career in 1950. 1963–67, he collaborated with architect Alberto Rosselli; 1970–74, with Achile Castiglioni; and with the Studio Ponti/Fornaroli/Rosselli. His clients included Feal, Fiat, Moviter, Lancia, Omsa, Cassina, Montecatini, Vis-Securit, Malugani, and Arflex. He was a member of ADI (Associazione per il Disegno Industriale); edited *Domus* in mid-1960s with Franco Santi Gualtieri under Rosselli's directorship; was an organizer of the Premio Compasso d'Oro.
▶ *ADI Annual 1976*, Milan: Associazione per il Disegno Industriale, 1976.

Practical Equipment Ltd
See Pel

Pré, Maurice   (1908–)
▶ French decorator and furniture designer; active Paris.
▶ From 1921 studied École Boulle, Paris.
▶ He worked for eight years in the studio of Jacques-Émile Ruhlmann; in 1955, taught at École Boulle; was known for combining different materials (metal, wood, Formica) in furniture.
▶ Participated with Ruhlmann at 1925 Paris 'Exposition Internationale des Arts Décoratifs et Industriels Modernes.'
▶ Pascal Renous, *Portraits de créateurs*, Paris: H. Vial, 1969.

Pree, D.J. De
See DePree, Dirk Jan

Preiss, Johann Philipp Ferdinand   (aka Fritz Preiss 1882–1943)
▶ German designer.
▶ Studied in Paris.
▶ He began a successful collaboration with Otto Poertzel. Preiss worked in Berlin during the years that Demêtre Chiparus was active in Paris; though both are known for their chryselephantine statuettes of bronze and ivory, their style and appeal are very different. Working in a smaller scale, Preiss is known for the fine quality of his ivory carving and for the cold-painted clothing of his figures. His images of athletic children and youths represented contemporary German ideals of athletic prowess and perfection, including *The Archer*, *Posing*, and *Thoughts*. The association with Poertzel resulted in many of their figures being similar in form. In 1906, Preiss and his partner Walter Kassler opened a foundry in Berlin, active until Preiss's death. In 1929, they bought the rival workshop Rosenthal und Maeder. Preiss's bronzes were enormously popular in Germany and abroad, being sold by galleries such as Phillips and MacConnal in London.
▶ Auction cat., Christie's New York, 26 May 1983: Lots 448, 449,450.

Preiswerk, Gertrud   (aka Gertrud Dirks 1902–)
▶ Swiss textile designer.
▶ 1926–30, studied Bauhaus, Dessau; 1929, attended summer courses, Johanna Brunson's Weaving School, Stockholm; studied silk-power-loom operation, Vereinigte Seiden Webereien.
▶ 1931–33, she was active in S-P-H- Stoffe in Zürich, the firm for furniture and fabrics that she founded with Gunta Stölzl and Heinrich Otto Hürlimann.

▶ Cat., *The Bauhaus: Masters and Students*, New York: Barry Friedman, 1988. Cat., Gunta Stölzl, *Weberei am Bauhaus und ams eigener Werkstatt*, Berlin: Bauhaus-Archiv, 1987:148.

Premsela, Benno (1920–)
▶ Dutch textile and exhibition designer.
▶ Studied interior design, Nieuwe Kunstschool, Amsterdam.
▶ 1949–51, he worked in the furniture department of Bijenkorf, the largest department store in Amsterdam and, 1956–63, was head of display there. 1951–53, he worked in Italy, where he designed and printed textiles and, in 1963, set up a studio in partnership with architect Jan Vonk. From 1967, Premsela was responsible for product development and design for Van Besouw in Goirle; from 1972, wallcoverings for Vescom; and, from 1975, upholstery fabrics for Gerns & Gahler.
▶ His work was the subject the one-person 1981–2 'Benno Premsela onder anderen' exhibition at the Stedelijk Museum in Amsterdam.
▶ Cat., Kathryn B. Hiesinger and George H. Marcus III (eds.), *Design Since 1945*, Philadelphia: Philadelphia Museum of Art, 1983:227,VII–50. Cat., *Benno Premsela onder anderen*, Amsterdam: Stedelijk Museum, 1981.

Preobrazhenzkaia, Daria Nikolaevna (1908–1972)
▶ Russian textile designer.
▶ 1924–29, she studied at the textile factory of Vkhutemas/Vkhutein; 1929–31, was a textile designer at the textile mill in Ivanovo-Voznesensk and subsequently of the Trikhgornaya Manufacture in Moscow; participated in several Soviet exhibitions abroad.
▶ Cat., *Kunst und Revolution: Russische und Sowjetische Kunst 1910–1932*, Vienna: Österreichisches Museum für angewandte Kunst, 1988.

Pre-Raphaelites
▶ British artists' group.
▶ From 1848, the Pre-Raphaelite Brotherhood was led by Dante Gabriel Rossetti and Edward Burne-Jones. Their inspiration came from fairy-tale imagery and early Renaissance artists, and their ideal of the female figure and face was seen in William Morris's wife, Janey. They tended to emphasize the neck and head, and necklaces with pendants in the Renaissance manner were the jewelry most seen in their paintings. Burne-Jones and Rossetti influenced jewelry styles, and they both collected Oriental and North African jewelry, considered erotic.
▶ Toni Lesser Wolf, 'Women Jewelers of the British Arts and Crafts Movement,' *The Journal of Decorative and Propaganda Arts*, No. 14, Fall 1989.

Prestini, James L. (1908–93)
▶ American woodworker; born Waterford, Connecticut.
▶ Studied mechanical engineering, Yale University; 1938, University of Stockholm; 1939, Institute of Design, Illinois Institute of Technology, Chicago; 1943–53, Armour Research Foundation, Chicago 1953–56, sculpture in Italy.
▶ Trained first as a machinist's apprentice; in 1938, became an apprentice in furniture design to Carl Malmsten in Stockholm. In 1948, he submitted a one-piece plastic molded chair to the low-cost furniture competition at the New York Museum of Modern Art. Admired by Functionalist designers, his thin, symmetrical metalwork was produced by spinning. Though the objects had a handcrafted appearance, his turned wood vessels, for which he was best known, were produced through semi-mechanical techniques. He taught mathematics, design, and engineering in numerous institutions, including, 1939–46 and 1952–53, at the Institute of Design at the Illinois Institute of Technology in Chicago and, from 1956, at the University of California in Berkeley. In 1962, he was a design education consultant to the government in West Germany; 1962–63, in India; and, in 1964, in the USA. He also worked as a sculptor; retired in 1975.
▶ He receive first prizes in Contemporary Crafts at the 1952 Los Angeles County Fair, diploma d'onore for designs in wood and plywood at the 1954 (X) Triennale di Milano, 1972 R.S. Reynolds Memorial Sculpture Award of the American Institute of Architects, diploma de collaborazione of the 1973 (XV) Triennale di Milano, and 1975 Berkeley Award of the University of California. He was a 1962–63 Ford Foundation Fellow and 1972–73 Guggenheim Fellow.
▶ Edgar Kaufmann, Jr., *Prize Designs for Modern Furniture*, New York: Museum of Modern Art, 1950:44–47. Don Wallance, *Shaping America's Products*, New York, 1956:152. John Kelsey, 'The Turned Bowl,' *Fine Woodworking*, Jan.–Feb. 1982. Cat., Kathryn B. Hiesinger and George H. Marcus III (eds.), *Design Since 1945*, Philadelphia: Philadelphia Museum of Art, 1983:227, VIII–6–7. 'James L. Prestini, 85, Sculptor and Teacher,' *The New York Times*, 31 July, 1993:50.

Preston, Jessie M.
▶ American jeweler; active Chicago.
▶ She established herself as a jeweler in 1900 at 203 Michigan Avenue, Chicago. She was recognized nationally for her jewelry in the Arts and Crafts style. She settled in Paris in 1918.
▶ Sharon S. Darling with Gail Farr Casterline, *Chicago Metalsmiths*, Chicago Historical Society, 1977.

Price, Charles Douglas (1906–)
▶ American silversmith; active Bloomfield Hills, Michigan.
▶ In 1927, when Arthur Nevill Kirk became director of the metal workshop at the Cranbrook Academy of Art in Bloomfield Hills, Charles Price and Margaret Biggar became his assistants. 1935–37, Price taught silversmithing and metalworking at the Cranbrook, where he produced the designs of school director Eliel Saarinen.
▶ Annelies Krekel-Aalberse, *Art Nouveau and Art Déco Silver*, New York: Abrams, 1989:123,124,258.

Primavera
▶ French decorating studio; located Paris.
▶ In 1913, René Guilleré, a founder of the Sociéte des Artistes Décorateurs, established the Primavera decorating studio of the Au Printemps department store on the Boulevard Haussmann in Paris. In the 1920s and 1930s, the efforts of the studio were pace-setting. In 1931 when Guilleré died, his widow Charlotte Chauchet-Guilleré and Colette Guéden became co-directors. In 1939, Guéden took over as head of Primavera. Philippe Petit first worked at Primavera alongside Louis Sognot and Marcel Guillemard. René Buthaud organized its ceramics factory at Sainte-Radegonde.
▶ Primavera in its pavilion at the 1925 Paris 'Exposition Internationale des Arts Décoratifs et Industriels Modernes,' designed by architect Henri Sauvage, showed work by Chauchet-Guilleré, Jean Burkhalter, Marcel Guillemard, Henri Moser, Pierre Lahalle, Louis Sognot, Claude Lévy, Mlle. Tavernier, M.-M. R. Coquery, and Mme. Souguez.
▶ Pierre MacOrlan, *Le Printemps*, Paris: Gallimard, 1930. Pierre Kjellberg, *Art Déco: les maîtres du Mobilier, le décor des Paquebots*, Paris: Amateur, 1986:138–39.

Prina, Alberto (1941–)
▶ Italian industrial designer; born and active Milan.
▶ Studied Liceo Artistico di Brera, Milan.
▶ 1960–62, he worked on a project for machine tools; 1964–66, with plastic laminates for kitchen systems; 1966–68, for the magazine *Votre Beauté* as art director. He set up a studio for graphic and industrial design and publicity in 1968. His clients included Mobilificio Garavaglia (furniture and kitchen systems), Gruppo Emme (furniture and shelving systems), Metalpilter (silverplate tableware), Vetreria Pavese (glassware for the bath); MaxForm (accessories and furnishings), Ranco Controls (electronic equipment), Harvey Guzzini (lighting), Forme e Superfici, Lamter (lighting), Lamperti (lighting), Nenzi, DID (furniture and accessories), First (upholstered furniture), Volani, Fratelli Guzzini (metal tabletop accessories), Interspazio (furnishings), and Teuco (bathroom fixtures). In 1968, he founded the magazine *Formaluce*

and was director until 1971. 1972–74, he taught publication design at the Instituto Europeo di Design. He designed numerous exhibitions and was a member of ADI (Associazione per il Disegno Industriale).

▶ *ADI Annual 1976*, Milan: Associazione per il Disegno Industriale, 1976.

Prina, Nani (1938–)

▶ Italian architect and industrial and graphic designer; born and active Milan

▶ Studied Politecnico di Milano.

▶ He began his professional career in industrial design in 1968. Prina's writing and publishing activities were extensive. Active in research in plastics, Prina's first work was the 1968 one-piece bed produced by Moltani, Giussano. His clients in Italy included Sormani, Cassina, FEG, Aba Design, Roller, Bazzani, and Cazzaniga. Prina was a member of ADI (Associazione per il Disegno Industriale).

▶ His work was shown in the 1972 'Design a Plastické Hmoty' exhibition at the Uměleckoprůmyslové Muzeum in Prague.

▶ *ADI Annual 1976*, Milan: Associazione per il Disegno Industriale, 1976. Cat., Milena Lamarová, *Design a Plastické Hmoty*, Prague: Uměleckoprůmyslové Muzeum, 1972:146.

Printz, Eugène (1889–1948)

▶ French decorator and furniture designer; born Paris.

▶ Printz worked in the workshop of his father in the rue du Faubourg Saint-Antoine in Paris, where he formed a staff of experimental practitioners. He used materials from the past in his Modern furniture pieces, including forged iron, plated metals, and leather. He showed a preference for exotic woods, including sycamore, wild cherry, Rio rosewood, palissandre, and palm kekwood. He set up his own workshop at 12 rue Saint-Bernard in Paris, where he produced cabinets, rugs, drawings, and paintings. In 1930, he rendered the interior scheme of the boudoir of the Princesse de la Tour d'Auvergne in the Château de Grosbois, the private office of Jeanne Lanvin, the reception salon of Field Marshal Lyautey, and the arrangement of the Musée de la France d'Outre-Mer on the occasion of the 1931 Paris 'Exposition Coloniale.' He became interested in lighting and wrote on the subject for the journal *Lux* in the 1930s. He felt that lighting should be considered at the very beginning of an interior-design project. Shown at the 1928 Salon, his *couronne lumineuse* ('crown of light') was widely imitated, including by architect Gabriel Guévrékian and lighting engineer André Salomon in 1929. He opened his own gallery at 81 rue de Miromesnil in Paris. He designed offices, banks, press bureaux, and interior schemes in Britain, Belgium, the USA, and Mexico. Commissioned by Louis Jouvet, he designed sets for *Domino* and *Jean de la Lune* at Théâtre Athenée, Paris. On the eve of World War II, Printz, Dominique, Maurice Jallot, Jules Leleu, and René Prou formed the group Décor de France. After the war, his furniture was produced in limited editions.

▶ He first showed his work in 1924; then regularly in the annual events of the Salon d'Automne and subsequently at the Salons of the Société des Artistes Décorateurs. He made his international debut at the 1925 Paris 'Exposition Internationale des Arts Décoratifs et Industriels Modernes.' A chandelier shown at the 1928 Salon d'Automne in gray metal was widely published. He designed one of the salons (the other by Jacques-Émile Ruhlmann) at the 1931 Paris 'Exposition Coloniale' in the Musée des Colonies. At the 1937 Paris 'Exposition Internationale des Arts et Techniques dans la Vie Moderne,' he and Étienne Kohlmann designed the general illumination of corridors and vestibules in the Pavilion of Light; Printz showed a table *jardinière* that could be lighted. At the same exposition, he worked on the pavilion of the Société des Artistes Décorateurs.

▶ *Lux*, June 1928:89, Jan. 1929:14, Feb. 1929:34, Feb. 1930:10, Sept. 1931:101–03. G. Henriot, *Luminaire Moderne*, 1937: plate 1. Alastair Duncan, *Art Nouveau and Art Déco Lighting*, New York: Simon and Schuster, 1978:181. Jean-Jacques Dutko, *Eugène Printz*, Paris: Regard, 1986.

Prisunic

▶ French store; located Paris.

▶ Prisunic is the mass-market division of the Au Printemps department store. In 1954, Jacques Gueden hired Denise Fayolle to work for Prisunic. 1954–59, she worked on a new corporate identity. In 1959, the first contemporary furniture, clothing, tableware, and household goods were produced.

▶ Gilles de Bure, *Le mobilier français 1965–1979*, Paris: Regard, 1983:78,82–83.

▶ See Fayolle, Denise

Pritchard, Jack (1899–)

▶ British designer and manufacturer.

▶ Studied engineering and economics at Cambridge University to 1922.

▶ He began working in 1922 for Michelin tires in France and, in 1925, for Venesta Plywood in Britain. After seeing Le Corbusier's 'L'Esprit nouveau' pavilion at the 1925 Paris 'Exposition Internationale des Arts Décoratifs et Industriels Modernes,' he invited the architect to design a stand for Venesta. He also worked with László Moholy-Nagy and hired Wells Coates to design a stand for Venesta at the 1931 'British Empire Trade Exhibition' in Manchester. Attempting to apply 'modern functional design to houses, flats, furniture and fittings,' Pritchard, his wife Molly, and Coates formed Isokon in 1931. Isokon primarily produced furniture in plywood; one of its best known designs was the 1936 bentwood dining table and chaise longue, both by Marcel Breuer, and the *Penguin Donkey* the bookcase designed to hold the paperback books published by Penguin. In 1932, Coates designed Lawn Road Flats, one of the first International Style concrete buildings, on land owned by Pritchard in Hampstead, where refugees Breuer, Moholy-Nagy, and Walter Gropius lived for a time; they all designed for Isokon. Though Pritchard designed furniture pieces himself, his major contribution was the introduction of the International Style to Britain.

▶ Jack Pritchard, *View from a Long Chair: The Memoirs of Jack Pritchard*, London: Routledge and Kegan Paul, 1984. Penny Sparke, *Introduction to Design and Culture in the Twentieth Century*, London: Allen and Unwin, 1986. Peter Dormer (intro.), *The Illustrated Dictionary of 20th-Century Designers: The Key Personalities in Design and the Applied Arts*, New York: Mallard, 1991:120.

Prix, Wolf-Dieter (1942–)

▶ Austrian architect and designer; born and active Vienna.

▶ In 1968, Prix and Helmut Swiczinsky established the architecture studio Coop Himmelblau in Vienna. Prix designed furniture produced by Vitra Edition, including the 1989 *Vodöl* armchair. Vodöl is a play on the Viennese pronunciation of the French *fauteuil* (chair); Prix's design was an askew interpretation of Le Corbusier 1928 *Grand Confort* club chair with its bent metal tube frame partially straightened and resting on an incongruous steel I-beam. Prix and Swiczinsky designed the 1974 mobile kitchen produced by Ewe-Küchen and work for others.

▶ As partner of Coop Himmelblau, his work was included in the 1988 'Deconstructive Architecture' exhibition at the New York Museum of Modern Art.

▶ Günther Feuerstein, *Vienna—Present and Past: Arts and Crafts—Applied Art—Design*, Vienna: Jugend und Volk, 1976: 62,64. Albrecht Bangert and Karl Michael Armer, *80s Style: Designs of the Decade*, New York: Abbeville, 1990:88–89,234. Cat., *Coop Himmelblau, construire le ciel*, Paris: Centre Georges Pompidou, 1992.

▶ See Coop Himmelblau

Procázha, Antonín (1882–1945)

▶ Czech artist and designer; born Važany, near Vyškov.

▶ 1903–04, studied School of Decorative Arts, Prague; 1904–06, Academy of Fine Arts, Prague, under V. Bukovac and H. Schwaigr.

▶ In 1910, he was accepted (after a previous rejection) into Mánes Association of Plastic Artists; became a teacher of drawing in Ostrava. He was one of the first to respond to Cubism through

Cubo-Expressionist paintings and others bordering on analytical Cubism; in c1915, approached Orphism in his painting; designed Cubist architecture and furniture of some note.

▶ In 1907 and 1908, participated in first and second exhibitions of the Group of Eight; 1912 exhibition of Sonderbund in Cologne.

▶ Alexander von Vegesack et al., *Czech Cubism: Architecture, Furniture, and Decorative Arts, 1910–1925*, New York: Princeton Architectural Press, 1992.

Procopé, Ulla (b. Ulrika Procopé 1921–68)

▶ Finnish ceramicist.

▶ Studied Taideteollinen Korkeakoulu, Helsinki, to 1948.

▶ 1948–67, she designed domestic ceramics produced by Arabia, where she worked as a model planner under Kaj Franck. Her designs included the 1957 *Liekki* flameproof stacking dinnerware range with lids for dishes, and 1960 *Ruska* stoneware range in a textured warm brown color.

▶ She received the diploma of honor at the 1957 (XI) Triennale di Milano and gold medals at ceramic exhibitions in Sacramento, California, in 1962 and 1963; in San Francisco in 1963; and Utrecht in 1963. Her work was shown at the 1956–57 West Germany 'Finnish Exhibition,' 1958 'Formes Scandinaves' exhibition at the Paris Musée des Arts Décoratifs, and 1961 USA 'Finlandia' exhibition in Zürich, Amsterdam, and London.

▶ Erik Zahle (ed.), *A Treasury of Scandinavian Design*, New York, 1961:288, Nos. 331,333. Benedict Zilliacus, 'Discreet and Important,' *Ceramics and Glass*, No. 1, 1969:2–3. Leena Maunula, 'A Hundred Years of Arabia Dishes,' *Ceramics and Glass*, Nov. 1973:20. Cat., David Revere McFadden (ed.), *Scandinavian Modern Design 1880–1980*, New York: Abrams, 1982:270, No. 168. Cat., Kathryn B. Hiesinger and George H. Marcus III (eds.), *Design Since 1945*, Philadelphia: Philadelphia Museum of Art, 1983:227,II–50. Jennifer Hawkins Opie, *Scandinavia: Ceramics and Glass in The Twentieth Century*, New York: Rizzoli, 1989.

Proetz, Victor (1897–)

▶ American designer; born St. Louis, Missouri.

▶ Studied School of Architecture of Armour Institute (now Illinois Institute of Technology), Chicago, to 1923.

▶ In 1932, he designed a collection of furniture, furnishings, and lighting for the John Lohmann House in Old Lyme, Connecticut. In 1937, he designed and decorated Lord and Lady Mountbatten's penthouse in London. In 1943, the Lord and Taylor department store in New York appointed Proetz director of its interior decorating department.

▶ Proetz received an award for his work on the Park Plaza Hotel in St. Louis.

Prokop, Miroslav (1896–1954)

▶ Czech designer of lighting fixtures.

▶ Studied electrotechnology, Czech Technical University.

▶ From 1929, he was a member of SČSD (Czechoslovak Werkbund); concentrated on technical problems of lighting; 1927–43, designed a number of lighting fixtures for serial production; collaborated with leading Czech Modern architects; designed lighting for outdoor and neon advertising; in the 1930s, collaborated with Zdeněk Pešánek on lighting sculptures.

▶ A. Adlerová, *České užité umění 1918–1938*, Prague, 1983.

Propst, Robert (1921–)

▶ American designer; born Marino, Colorado.

▶ Studied University of Denver, Colorado, to 1943, and University of Colorado to 1950.

▶ 1946–48, he was head of the department of art at Tarleton College in Dublin, Texas, and, 1950–53, established the firm Propst, where he designed architectural sculpture, ecclesiastical interiors, and playground equipment, and was active with aircraft and institutional equipment companies. In 1960, his firm was incorporated into Herman Miller, forming the research and development segment of its activities in Ann Arbor, Michigan; from

1968, he was president and research director of Herman Miller Research. Propst designed the 1968 *Action Office* system produced by Herman Miller, which catapulted the firm from being a modest producer of seating and tables to the world's second largest office furniture manufacturer. His design work included the 1964 *Action Office 1* concept, 1964 *Perch* chair, 1967 *Pediatrics* bed, 1968 *Action Office 2*, 1969 *Co/Struc* hospital system, and 1970 timber harvester.

▶ He won the 1964 Best Collection of the Year award from *Home Furnishings Daily*, 1970 (XXI) Annual International Design Award of the American Institute of Interior Designers, and 1972 Distinguished Service Citation of the Institute of Business Designers.

▶ 'Nelson, Eames, Girard, Propst: The Design Process at Herman Miller,' *Design Quarterly* 98–99, 1975.

Protière, Régis (1948–)

▶ French furniture designer; active Paris.

▶ Studied École Nationale Supérieure des Arts Décoratifs, Paris.

▶ He was active in the design of public spaces, commercial architecture, exhibitions, objects, and furniture; 1984–85, designed the library and cafeteria of Musée d'Art moderne de la ville de Paris; designed the *Lizie* chair produced by Pallucco; in 1987, set up his own design office and, in 1990, shop.

▶ Received 1988 Prix de la Critique for contemporary furniture (*Frère Jacques* armchair) and 1980 Appel permanent from VIA (*Trois Jeunes Tambours* in cardboard and steel wire).

▶ Cat., *Les années VIA 1980–1990*, Paris: Musée des Arts Décoratifs, 1990:148–49.

Prou, René (1889–1947)

▶ French decorator and furniture designer; active Paris.

▶ Studied painting, École Bernard Palissy, Paris, to 1908.

▶ In 1908, he designed his first work at the furniture manufacturer Gouffé in Paris, where he became chief designer. In 1912, called the first decorator of the *goût moderne* (modern taste), he designed the council room of the Comptoir d'Escompte in Paris and the apartment of the French ambassador in Paraguay. From 1929, his work became more simple, eschewing ornamentation. In his workshop at 80 rue de Rome, Paris, in c1930, he began designing wrought-iron furniture produced by Edgar Brandt, Raymond Subes, and other metalworkers. He received numerous important commissions. He designed a piano for Pleyel; some of his furniture was produced by Henri Lévy. He designed dining rooms on the oceanliner *De Grasse* and other oceanliner interiors, including the 1921 *Paris*, 1926 *Île-de-France*, 1931 *L'Atlantique*, and 1935 *Normandie*. He designed complete interiors for a dozen other oceanliners, including the *Champlain*, *La Fayette*, *Cuba*, and *Florida*. He also designed interiors for railroad cars, including the *Train Bleu*, *Paris-Deauville*, and, in 1929, 500 cars of the Compagnie Internationale des Wagons-Lits; the dining room of the Waldorf Astoria hotel in New York; board room of the League of Nations in Geneva; the Mitsubishi department store in Tokyo; and the oceanliner pier at Le Havre. From 1937, he was associated with his brother Jean-René Prou and worked in his own offices and boutique at 50 rue du Faubourg Saint-Honoré in Paris. In 1928, he succeeded Paul Follot at the Pomone decorating department of the Au Bon Marché department store in Paris and sometimes collaborated with Albert-Lucien Guénot there. In 1932, he became director of Pomone, which produced his limited-production dining room and bedroom furniture. He remained active as a painter and taught at various schools, including, briefly, the École Nationale des Arts Décoratifs.

▶ At the 1925 Paris 'Exposition Internationale des Arts Décoratifs et Industriels Modernes,' Prou designed the boudoir (with Eric Bagge), the 'chambre de Mademoiselle' of 'Une Ambassade française,' in the pavilion of the Société des Artistes Décorateurs.

▶ *Ensembles Mobiliers*, Paris: Charles Moreau, Vol. 6, Nos. 1–7, 27, 1945. Léon Deshairs, *Modern French Decorative Art*, Paris: Albert Lévy. Pierre Kjellberg, *Art Déco: les Maîtres du Mobilier, le décor des Paquebots*, Paris: Amateur, 1986:144–45.

Proun (Project for the Affirmation of the New)
▶ Russian artists' group.
▶ El Lissitsky founded Proun in Titebsk, active 1919–22 as an 'intermediate between painting and architecture.'
▶ Cat., *The Great Utopia: The Russian and Soviet Avant-Garde, 1915–1932*, New York: Guggenheim Museum, 1992.

Prouvé, Jean   (1901–1984)
▶ French metalworker, engineer, builder, and furniture designer; born Paris; son of Victor Prouvé.
▶ 1916–19, trained as an art metalworker in Nancy under Émile Robert and, 1919–21, under the blacksmith Adalbert-Georges Szabó.
▶ Prouvé's early furnishing commissions brought him into contact with avant-garde designers and architects in France, including Le Corbusier, Pierre Jeanneret, Robert Mallet-Stevens, and Paul Herbé. Known for his use of metal in furniture design, he rejected traditional techniques in favor of the electrical welding of sheet metal. He opened his own studio in Nancy in 1923 and received various building commissions. He designed his first furniture in 1923. In 1930, he established Les Ateliers de Jean Prouvé, located in Maxéville, near Nancy, after World War II. His workshop produced furniture for Jacques-Émile Ruhlmann and Charlotte Perriand. In c1930, he developed the 'mur rideau' (curtain wall) replaceable, moveable wall system, the first of its kind; it was based on light metal stanchions. He used it in the 1938 Club House on the Buc airfield and later in the 1958 Lycée at Bagnols-sur-Cèze. His patented system of constructing small metal houses on piles was used in Beaudoin's and Lods's airport in Buc and Maison du Peuple in Clichy. His other structures included 1949 prefabricated houses in Meudon-Bellevue, 1953 temporary school at Villejuif, 1953 apartment block (with Lionel Mirabaud) in Paris, 1956 units with prefabricated concrete cores for Abbée Pierre, 1957 spa building (with Maurice Novarina) in Evian, 1958 school (with Daniel Badani and Marcel Roux-Dorlut) in Bagnols-sur-Cèze, 1959 houses in Meudon-Bellevue, 1958 'Sahara'-type prefabricated houses, 1963 and 1967–69 Free University (with Candilis, Josic and Woods and Manfred Schiedhelm) in Berlin-Dahlem, 1967 Congress Hall in Grenoble, 1967 office tower (with Jean de Mailly and Jacques Depussé) at La Défense, Paris, and 1968 Total service stations. In 1932, he designed furniture for the Université de Nancy. In 1929, he participated in the founding of the UAM (Union des Artistes Modernes), showing at its subsequent exhibitions. He frequently worked with collaborators. To serve a mass culture, he attempted to create lightweight prefabricated components that were easy to transport and erect. All his furniture, with the exceptions of the reproductions from the 1980s, was sold exclusively by Steph Simon in Paris. Active in workshops in Maxéville 1944–54, he opened his own consulting firm in Paris. From the 1980s, reproductions of his *86–3* chair were made by Bermude and the *B 80* chair by Tecta.
▶ From 1930, he showed at UAM exhibitions in Paris and designed the grand staircase for its pavilion at the 1937 Paris 'Exposition Internationale des Arts et Techniques dans la Vie Moderne.' His work was exhibited at the 1949–50 (I) 'Formes Utiles' exhibition at the Pavillon de Marsan in Paris, at the 1957 'Luminaire' exhibition, and 1956–57 (I) 'Triennale d'Art français Contemporain.' His work was the subject of a 1964 exhibition in Paris and included in the 1986 'Der Kragstuhl' exhibition at the Stuhlmuseum Burg Beverungen in Berlin and 1988 exhibition on the UAM at the Paris Musée des Arts Décoratifs.
▶ Jean Prouvé and Pierre Jeanneret, 'Solutions d'Urgence,' *Architecture*, No. 2, 1945. 'Jean Prouvé,' *Architecture*, Nos. 11–12 (special issue), 1954. Cat., *Jean Prouvé*, Paris: Musée des Arts Décoratifs, 1964. B. Huber and J.C. Steinegger (eds.), *Jean Prouvé: Architektur aus der Fabrik*, Zürich, 1971. Dominique Clayssen, *Jean Prouvé: L'Idée Constructive*, Paris: Dunod, 1983. Cat., *Der Kragstuhl*, Stuhlmuseum Burg Beverungen, Berlin: Alexander, 1986:134. Pierre Kjellberg, *Art Déco: les maîtres du Mobilier, le décor des Paquebots*, Paris: Amateur, 1986:144–46. Arlette Barré-

Despond, *UAM*, Paris: Regard, 1986:492–95. Cat., *Les années UAM 1929–1958*, Paris: Musée des Arts Décoratifs, 1988:236–37.

Prouvé, Victor   (1858–1943)
▶ French painter, sculptor and decorator; born Nancy; father of Jean Prouvé.
▶ Working with Louis Majorelle and Émile Gallé, he designed glassware, ceramics, and decorations in wood marquetry. In 1904 when Gallé died, Prouvé assumed the leadership of the École de Nancy. He made jewelry and decorative bronze pieces and produced patterns for lace and embroidery and, working in tooled and polychromed leather, created cushions, *portières*, plaques, caskets, and bindings, embellished with the fauna and flora of Alsace-Lorraine. His best-known binding was *Salammbô* (1893) by Gustave Flaubert; others included *L'Art japonais* (the first volume of L. Gonse's *Histoire de l'art décoratif)*, *L'Art symboliste*, and *La Chanson des gueux*. He and Wiener, another member of the Nancy school, produced innovatory pictorial and figurative bindings.
▶ From 1892, he showed his work in the annual exhibitions of the Champs de Mars, Paris. He participated in the 1894 'Cercle pour l'Art' exhibition of La Libre Esthétique in Brussels.
▶ Yvonne Brunhammer et al., *Art Nouveau Belgium, France*, Houston: Institute for the Arts, Rice University, 1976. Alastair Duncan and Georges de Bartha, *Art Nouveau and Art Déco Bookbinding*, New York: Abrams, 1989:13–14,156,179,195. Thérèse Charpentier, *L'École de Nancy et la reliure d'art*, Paris, 1960:7,15,19,30–33,43,49. Cat., *Le Cuir au musée*, Nancy: Musée de l'École de Nancy, 1985. Cat., *Exposition Lorraine (École de Nancy)*, Paris: Musée de l'Union Centrale des Arts Décoratifs, 2nd series, 1903. 'Modern Bookbindings and Their Designers,' *The Studio*, Special Winter Issue 1899–1900:3–82.

Provinciali, Michele
▶ Italian industrial designer.
▶ 1947, studied in Urbino under Pasquale Rotondi; 1951, Institute of Design, Chicago, under László Moholy-Nagy.
▶ He collaborated with Luigi Moretti. He and Gino Valle produced clock designs for Solari in 1955. He was a graphic designer for magazines *Domus, Qualità, Imago, Casa Novità, Abitare*, and *Edilizia*. He collaborated with Giò Ponti, Alberto Rosselli, Vico Magistretti, the Castiglioni brothers, and the Arbizzoni brothers.
▶ He participated in the 1954 (X) Triennale di Milano. With Moretti, he won the 1955 Compasso d'Oro for Solari clocks. For graphic design for a publication on Charles Rennie Mackintosh, he won a 1975 award from the Art Directors' Club, London.
▶ Alfonso Grassi and Anty Pansera, *Atlante del Design Italiano 1940–80*, Milan: Fabbri, 1980.

Prutscher, Otto   (1880–1949)
▶ Austrian architect, furniture designer, jeweler, and designer; born and active Vienna.
▶ From 1897, studied Kunstgewerbeschule, Vienna, under Josef Hoffmann.
▶ From 1910, he taught at the Kunstgewerbeschule. Soon after its founding in 1903, he became a textile, metalware, book, and glassware designer for the Wiener Werkstätte in a style greatly influenced by Hoffmann. Some of Prutscher's glassware designs were produced by E. Bakalovits.
▶ He showed his work at the 1900 Paris 'Exposition Universelle' and the 1902 Turin 'Esposizione Internazionale d'Arte Decorativa Moderna.'
▶ Max Eisler, *Otto Prutscher*, Leipzig: Friedrich Ernst Hübsch, 1925. Günther Feuerstein, *Vienna—Present and Past: Arts and Crafts—Applied Art—Design*, Vienna: Jugend und Volk, 1976: 35,81. Torsten Bröhan (ed.), *Glaskunst der Moderne*, Munich: Klinkhardt und Biermann, 1992:60,154–61,163,460.

Prydkunstnerlager
▶ Norwegian decorative arts group.
▶ A group of decorative artists organized the Prydkunstnerlager in 1929. They had broken away from the Burkskunst association.

The group wanted to substitute international neo-Classicism with vernacular Norwegian traditionalism and folklore, a recurring theme in Norwegian design throughout the 20th century.

▶ Fredrik Wildhagen, *Norge i Form*, Oslo: Sternersen, 1988.

Prytz, Jacob (1886–1962)

▶ Norwegian designer and metalworker; born and active Kristiania (now Oslo); son of Thorolf Prytz.

▶ Studied Statens Håndverks -og Kunstindustriskole, Kristiania, and in Paris.

▶ He practiced in London and Paris and, in 1912, succeeded his father Thorolf Prytz as director of J. Tostrup in Kristiania; from this time he shaped the development of design in Norway. His Functionalist ideas about form greatly influenced designers in the 1920s and 1930s. From 1914, he was head of Statens Håndverks -og Kunstindustriskole, after the death of Gustav Gaudernack, who taught silversmithing there. From 1945, Prytz was rector there. In 1918, he was co-founder of the Applied Art Association and, 1920–39, its chair. 1946–48, he was chair of the National Applied Art Federation.

▶ He showed his work at the 1938 Salon in Paris.

▶ Cat., David Revere McFadden (ed.), *Scandinavian Modern Design 1880–1980*, New York: Abrams, 1982:270, Nos. 55,125. Fredrik Wildhagen, *Norge i Form*, Oslo: Stenersen, 1988:67–68. Annelies Krekel-Aalberse, *Art Nouveau and Art Déco Silver*, New York: Abrams, 1989:243,258.

Prytz, Thorolf (1858–1938)

▶ Norwegian architect and designer; born and active Kristiania (now Oslo); father of Jacob Prytz.

▶ From 1885, he was associated with family firm J. Tostrup in Kristiania and, in 1890, became its director. In 1912, he was succeeded by his son Jacob. Thorolf Prytz's silver designs were inspired by local fauna and flora.

▶ Cat., David Revere McFadden (ed.), *Scandinavian Modern Design 1880–1980*, New York: Abrams, 1982:270, No. 3. Annelies Krekel-Aalberse, *Art Nouveau and Art Déco Silver*, New York: Abrams, 1989:243,258.

Pryzrembel, Hans (1900–45).

▶ German metalworker.

▶ From 1924, studied Bauhaus under László Moholy-Nagy.

▶ He completed his apprenticeship as a silversmith in 1928. He often produced work for practical uses in hammered silver and brass using semi-precious materials, including ebony. In the 1930s, he worked as a silversmith in Leipzig and designed table and ceiling lamps.

▶ Annelies Krekel-Aalberse, *Art Nouveau and Art Déco Silver*, New York: Abrams, 1989:258. Cat., *Die Metallwerkstatt am Bauhaus*, Berlin: Bauhaus-Archiv, 1992:240–50,319.

Puiforcat, Jean-Émile (1897–1945)

▶ French silversmith; born Paris.

▶ Trained as a silversmith under his father Louis Puiforcat and studied sculpture under Louis-Aimé Lejeune.

▶ He set up his own workshop in Paris in 1921 and rejected traditional decoration in favor of simple geometrical forms. He combined his silverware with lapis lazuli, ivory, jade, rock crystal, and other semi-precious materials; the inlaid stones were cut and handled by Guy de Rougemont. Puiforcat was a founding member of Groupe des Cinq with Pierre Chareau, Pierre Legrain, Dominique, and Raymond Templier from *c*1926; in 1930, became a member of UAM (Union des Artistes Modernes). Interior designers André Domin and Marcel Genevrière of the firm Dominique designed and furnished Puiforcat's residence at Biarritz. Commissions included dining silver for the Maharaja of Indore, the 1935 oceanliner *Normandie*, and religious and sports sculptures. He was influenced by the work of mathematician Matila Ghyka on the Golden Section.

▶ He showed his work at the Salon d'Automne from 1921,

Salons of the Société des Artistes Décorateurs from *c*1921, and in Grenoble, Milan, Madrid, New York, San Francisco, Buenos Aires, and Tokyo. His work was included in the 1925 Paris 'Exposition Internationale des Arts Décoratifs et Industriels Modernes' and in his own stand at the 1937 Paris 'Exposition Internationale des Arts et Techniques dans la Vie Moderne.' In 1926 and 1927 with Groupe des Cinq, he exhibited at Galerie Barbazanges in Paris and, in 1929, independently at the Galerie Renaissance.

▶ *Jean Puiforcat orfèvre sculpteur*, Paris: Flammarion, 1951. Françoise de Bonneville, *Jean Puiforcat*, Paris: Regard, 1986. *Les Carnets du Design*, Paris: Mad-Cap Productions et APCI, 1986. Arlette Barré-Despond, *UAM*, Paris: Regard, 1986:496–99. Cat., *Les années UAM 1929–1958*, Paris: Musée des Arts Décoratifs, 1988:238–39.

Pukebergs Glasbruk

▶ Swedish glass factory.

▶ In 1871, a glass factory was established at Pukeberg, Småland; in 1894, it was bought by lamp manufacturer Arvid Böhlmark and began producing lamps; in the 1930s, under works manager Carl Hermelin, it began to produce glass decorative wares, and in *c*1959, introduced household and decorative glassware by designers including Ann and Göran Wärff. It was acquired in 1984 by Gashbron.

▶ Jennifer Hawkins Opie, *Scandinavia: Ceramics and Glass in the Twentieth Century*, New York: Rizzoli, 1989.

Pulos, Arthur J. (1917–)

▶ American industrial designer; born Vandergrift, Pennsylvania.

▶ 1935–39, studied Carnegie Institute of Technology, Pittsburgh, under Alexander Kostellow, Peter Müller-Munk, and F. Clayter; 1939–41, University of Oregon, Eugene, under Victoria Avakian, Fred Cuthbert, and Robert Motherwell.

▶ From 1958, he was active in Pulos Design Associates, Syracuse, New York; 1946–55, was associate professor of design, University of Illinois, Urbana; from 1982, professor emeritus, Department of Design, Syracuse University, Syracuse, New York, and chair 1955–82. He was a silversmith in the 1940s and 1950s, and published books on industrial design. Designs included instruments for Welch Allyn, power tools for Rockwell, and dictation machines for Dictaphone.

▶ Received design awards from Associated Artists of Pittsburgh, 1939, 1940, 1942; Wichita Art Association, 1947, 1950; Detroit Institute of Arts, 1953; Brooklyn Museum, 1953; Art Institute of Chicago, 1954. Received 1952–53 Ford Foundation Fellowship; 1982 Chancellor's Citation for Achievement, Syracuse University.

▶ Ann Lee Morgan (ed.), *Contemporary Designers*, London: Macmillan, 1984:499–500.

Punt Mobles

▶ Spanish furniture manufacturer.

▶ During the 1970s, Punt Mobles's founders Vicent Martínez and Lola Castello produced their own furniture designs in a workshop in Valencia, making Modern furniture kits. The firm began to produce more sophisticated models at higher prices, such as Martínez's *Halley* table. Pedro Miralles designed its 1988 *Andrews Sisters* three interlocking tables.

▶ Guy Julier, *New Spanish Design*, London: Thames and Hudson, 1991.

Puppa, Daniela (1947–)

▶ Italian architect and designer; born Fiume; active Milan.

▶ Studied Politecnico di Milano to 1970.

▶ 1970–76, she was a writer for and editor of *Casabella*; 1977–83, chief editor for design magazine *Modo*; and consultant to fashion magazine *Donna*. She executed interiors for Driade, Gianfranco Ferrè, Montres and GFF Duty Free, Fontana Arte, Granciclismo sports machines, and Morassutti/Metropolis, and was a consultant to the Croff/Rinascente chain on their image and products. She designed fabrics for Alchimia, Limonta, and Stucchi, and furniture and furnishings for Driade, Vistosi, Kartell, Flos, Carrara, Matta, Fontana Arte, Sisal Collections, Tendentse, Irmel, and Ligne Roset. Her 1984 *Newport* bench for Cappellini International Interiors could be transformed into a table. Her tableware for the Tachikichi department store in Japan included a 1984 cup in porcelain and saucer in melamine. From 1979, she designed accessories for Gianfranco Ferrè. She designed theater sets for the group Magazzini Criminali, including its *Nervous Breakdown* (1981); collaborated on a collection of accessories with Gianfranco Ferrè; taught fashion design at Domus Academy, Milan; was artistic director of Nazareno Fabrielli.

▶ Was co-creator of exhibitions, including 'L'Oggetto Banale' at the 1980 Biennale di Venezia, at 1981 ('Sezione Design') and 1983 (XVII) ('La Casa delle Triennale') Triennali di Milano, 'L'oggetto Naturale' at the 1982 Prato exhibition. Work included in 1982 'Provokationen Design aus Italien' at the 1982 Hanover exhibition, 'La Neomerce' for Montedison at the 1985 (XVII) Triennale di Milano and 1986 Paris exhibition, 'Donne designers italiane' at the 1985 ADI-Takashimaia exhibition in Tokyo, and 1985 'Phoenix' Avanguardia of Italian design at the Toronto exhibition.

▶ Andrea Branzi, *La Casa Calda: Esperienze del Nuovo Disegno Italiano*, Milan: Idea Books, 1982. Fumio Shimizu and Matteo Thun (eds.), *The Descendants of Leonardo: The Italian Design*, Tokyo, 1987:328. Liz McQuiston, *Women in Design: A contemporary View*, New York: Rizzoli, 1988:62–80. *Modo*, No. 148, March–April 1993:125.

Purcell, William F.H.   (1911–)

▶ South African industrial designer; active New York.

▶ Studied engineering, Cambridge University; from 1937, architecture, Massachusetts Institute of Technology, Cambridge, Massachusetts.

▶ During World War II he served in the department of munitions and supply of the Canadian government. In *c*1946, he joined the industrial design office of Henry Dreyfuss and, in 1949, became a partner.

▶ Arthur Pulos, *The American Design Adventure*, Cambridge: MIT, 1988:24.

Purcell, William Gray   (1880–1964)

▶ American architect and furniture designer; active Minneapolis and Philadelphia.

▶ Studied Cornell University.

▶ Purcell was a member of one of the most successful architecture firms practicing in the Prairie School style. In Minnesota, he established the architecture firm Purcell and Feick with George Feick Jr., which was active 1907–09; as Purcell, Feick and Elmslie 1910–13; and Purcell and Elmslie 1913–22. Purcell met George Elmslie in the office of Louis Sullivan in Chicago during his brief employment there. Commissions included banks, many in small towns throughout the upper Midwest. Like Sullivan and Wright, the team avoided obvious Beaux-Arts forms and neoclassical detailing to create a simple, indigenous American style. Their building façades with steel frames, brick facings, and pier-and-lintel articulation incorporated terracotta ornamentation, arched entryways, high clerestory windows, stained-glass windows, and site-specific furniture and furnishings. The firm took on numerous local commissions, including private residences and municipal buildings. Its most successful integration of building and interiors was the 1911–12 Merchants bank in Winona, Minnesota; outside and inside ornamentation was conceived as a whole, including brickwork, terracotta, lighting, stained glass, and furniture; the chair designs were related to Wright's chairs of the 1890s and to similar examples of Koloman Moser of Austria. Unlike Wright, Purcell designed for comfort, and was fond of a modular, geometric type of club chair with narrow vertical splats on three sides; he used the chair in the Winona bank and other interiors, including his own residence on Lake Place, Minneapolis, which he occupied 1913–17; it was turned over to the Minneapolis Institute of Arts and restored in 1990 by MacDonald and Mack, architects, and Alec Wilson.

▶ Anne Yaffe Phillips, *From Architecture to Object*, New York: Hirschl and Adler, 1989:72.

Putman, Andrée   (b. Andrée Aynard 1925–)

▶ French interior designer, furniture designer, and entrepreneur; born Paris.

▶ She was married to Dutch businessman Jacques Putman; worked for the magazines *L'Oeil du Décorateur* and *Femina*. In the 1960s, she was hired as a stylist by Denise Fayolle for Prisunic, the large French store chain, where she became a pioneer in inexpensive, well-designed furniture and housewares. She commissioned artists Matta (aka Roberto Sebastian Matta Echaurren), Bram van Velde, Pierre Alechinsky, and Jean Messagier to design lithographs, tableware, fabric patterns, and housewares for Prisunic. In *c*1963, she decorated the house of Michel Guy, later French minister of culture. In 1968, Putman accompanied Fayolle to the partnership formed by Maimé Arnodin and Fayolle called MAFIA, for which Putman designed interiors, textiles, and furniture. In 1971, she collaborated with Didier Grumbach on clothing and home furnishings in the shop Créateurs et Industriels and promoted young fashion designers. She established the furniture firm Écart International in 1978 and the design firm Écart with Jean-François Bodin. Écart International reproduced the designs of Eileen Gray, Robert Mallet-Stevens, Pierre Chareau, René Herbst, Michel Dufet, and others, including the 1907 projection lamp by Mariano Fortuny and the contemporary designs of Patrick Naggar, Sylvain Dubuisson, and Sacha Kétoff. Putman began Écart's production by weaving the carpet designs of Gray. Putman's own furniture was issued by De Sede, lighting by Baldinger, and fabrics by Stendig. Écart's first commercial interior design assignment was the YSL Rive Gauche boutiques in the USA. Her 1983 layout for the office of French minister of culture Jack Lang was widely published. She designed numerous boutiques, including those for Karl Lagerfeld, Yves Saint-Laurent in 1985, Thierry Mugler 1980–83, Balenciaga, Azzedine Alaïa in 1985, Ebel, and Hémisphères, and the 1987 décors of the Rouen Musée des Beaux-Arts, and Bordeaux Centre d'Art Plastique Contemporain; Saint James Club, Paris; and Hotel Im Wasserturm, Cologne. She designed the Basel Trade Fair, restoration of Le Corbusier's Villa Turque (Ebel's public relations bureau) in La Chaux-de-Fonds (Switzerland), and the 1990 'Les années VIA' exhibition at the Paris Musée des Arts Décoratifs. Putman was best known for her black-and-white palette in interior design, illustrated by the 1985 Morgan Hotel in New York; for the same builders, Ian Schrager and Steve Rubell, she executed the interior design of the 1985 Palladium night club in New York. In *c*1989, she began to incorporate color into her work, illustrated by dinnerware for Sasaki and rugs for Toulemonde Bochart.

▶ Cat., *Design français, 1960–1990: Trois décennies*, Paris: Centre Georges Pompidou/APCI, 1988. 'Andrée Putman, Boutique Ebel, London,' *Domus*, No. 688, Nov. 1987. *Metropolitan Home*, April 1990:86. Jane Delynn, 'Rebel with a Cause,' *Elle Decor*, August 1990:52–64. 'Celebrating Design Innovation,' *Designers West*, April 1991:34. François-Olivier Rousseau, *Andrée Putman*, Paris: Regard, 1989; New York: Rizzoli, 1990. François Mathey, *Au bonheur des formes, design français 1945–1992*, Paris: Regard 1992. Sophie Tasma-Anagyros, *Andrée Putman*, London: Laurence King, 1993.

Pye, Merrill

▶ American theater designer, architect, and furniture designer.

▶ Pye specialized in designing film sets for musicals in Hollywood. Overshadowed by supervising art director Cedric Gibbons, Pye worked under him at MGM. Pye designed *Freaks* (1932), *David Copperfield* (1935), and *North by Northwest* (1959). He was known for his lavish musical numbers in *Dancing Lady* (1933), *Reckless* (1934), *Broadway Melody of 1936* (1935), *The Great Ziegfeld* (1936), and *Born to Dance* (1935). He designed Gibbons' lavish Streamline personal office on the MGM lot. In *Dancing Lady*, Fred Astaire, Joan Crawford, and 41 dancers performed in front of a 20ft (6m) backdrop of clear cellophane draperies.

▶ Howard Mandelbaum and Eric Myers, *Screen Deco: A Celebration of High Style in Hollywood*, New York: St. Martin's, 1985.

Pyrex

▶ A type of heat-resistant glassware.
▶ Pyrex was developed in 1915 by the Corning Glassworks in Corning, New York. A tradename for heat-resistant borosilicate glassware, vessels made from the material could be used for cooking and serving from oven to table. In 1921, James M. Jobling, Sunderland, was assigned a license to produce Pyrex dishes in Britain, some notable examples of which were designed by Milner Gray and Kenneth Lamble in the 1950s.

▶ Jeremy Myerson and Sylvia Katz, *Conran Design Guides: Kitchenware*, London: Conran Octopus, 1990:31.

Q

Quarante, Danielle (1938–)
▶ French furniture designer; active Paris.
▶ 1959–62, studied École Nationale Supérieure des Arts Décoratifs, and André Arbus's workshop, both Paris.
▶ She began her professional career in graphics and designed exhibitions; in 1966, worked on product design (children's furniture, hi-fi systems); was active in research for Saint-Gobain and Usinor; from 1974, was a researcher and teacher, Université de Technologie, Compiègne; 1985–87, was a member of International Congress of Societies of Industrial Design; published the book *Éléments de design industriel* (1984).
▶ Work (*Albatros* polyester and fiberglass chair produced by Airborne and glass table by Saint-Gobain) shown at 1969 Salon of the Société des Artistes Décorateurs. Won 1970 competition sponsored by Prisunic/Shell and managed by Centre de Création Industrielle.
▶ Cat., *Design français 1960–1990*, Paris: Centre Georges Pompidou/APCI, 1988. François Mathey, *Au bonheur des formes, design français 1945–1992*, Paris: Regard, 1992:252.

Quarti, Eugenio (1867–1931)
▶ Italian furniture designer; born near Bergamo; active Milan.
▶ In 1881 at the age of 14, Quarti began working in a furniture factory near Paris. In 1888, he returned to Italy, settling in Milan. After working in Carlo Bugatti's workshop for a few weeks, he set up his own work quarters. Successful at the 1900 exhibition in Paris, he moved to a larger workshop and increased his staff of three. He furnished the 1901–03 Palazzo Castiglioni in Milan by architect Guiseppe Sommaruga, with whom ironworker Alessandro Mazzucotelli and Quarti often collaborated, and the 1908 Casino and 1925 Grand Hotel in Pellegrino. A notable exponent of Art Nouveau in Italy, known as Stile Floreale, inspired by French and Austrian design, his work incorporated wood, silver, mother-of-pearl marquetry, carving, and cast bronze ornamentation. In 1906, he considered mass-production furniture for public buildings, including hotels.
▶ Quarti (collaborating with Bugatti) won a grand prize at the 1900 Paris 'Exposition Universelle,' showed his work at the 1902 Turin 'Esposizione Internazionale d'Arte Decorativa Moderna' and won a prize at the 1906 exhibition in Milan. His work was the subject of a 1980 exhibition in Milan.
▶ Bairati, R. Bossaglia, and M. Roschi, *L'Italia Liberty: Arredamento e arti decorativi*, Milan, 1973. Cat., *Eugenio Quarti*, Milan, 1980. Cat., Gabriel P. Weisberg, *Stile Floreale: The Cult of Nature in Italian Design*, Miami: The Wolfsonian Foundation, 1988. John Fleming and Hugh Honour, *The Penguin Dictionary of Decorative Arts*, London: Viking, 1989.

Quasar (b. Nguyen Manhkhan'n 1934–)
▶ French engineer and furniture and fashion designer.
▶ 1955–58, studied engineering, École Nationale des Ponts et Chaussées, Paris.
▶ In 1964, produced a prototype city automobile in the shape of a transparent cube; in 1969, set up his design office Quasar-France to manufacture foam-rubber seating and designed a series

of inflatable seating, including his *Relax* sofa; *Apollo*, *Satellite*, and *Venus* armchairs; *Chesterfield* sofa; and a transparent lamp; designed a 1971 range of menswear manufactured by Biderman.
▶ Henry de Morant, *Histoire des Arts Décoratifs*, Paris: Hachette 1970:458,460,478. Cat., Milena Lamarová, *Design a Plastické Hmoty*, Prague: Uměleckoprůmyslové Muzeum, 1972:72,74.

Queensberry, David, Marquess of (1930–)
▶ British glassware designer.
▶ Studied Chelsea School of Art; ceramics, Central School of Arts and Crafts, London; design and technology, North Staffordshire College of Technology (now North Staffordshire Polytechnic); and industrial ceramic design, Royal College of Art, London.
▶ He worked in an industrial pottery in Stoke-on-Trent. He was professor of ceramics and glass at the Royal College of Art. He was retained as a consultant designer by Webb Corbett, for whom he produced glassware designs in the early 1960s, including, in stark geometric form and a repetitive pattern, his 1963 *Queensberry–Harlequin* range of cut glass, including tumblers, centerpieces, vases, and bowls. With Martin Hunt, an associate at the Royal College of Art, he formed the Queensberry-Hunt Design Group in 1964. From 1965, Lord Queensberry also worked as a freelance designer for Rosenthal; on other projects, collaborated with Eduardo Paolozzi.
▶ The *Queensberry–Harlequin* glass range won the 1964 Duke of Edinburgh's Prize for Elegant Design.
▶ Frederick Cooke, *Glass: Twentieth-Century Design*, New York: Dutton, 1986:78–79.

Quentin, Bernard (1923–)
▶ French furniture designer; active Paris.
▶ Studied École Nationale des Beaux-Arts, and École Nationale Supérieure des Arts Décoratifs, both Paris.
▶ He designed inflatable objects, including seating in PVC.
▶ Work (inflatable structures) for the French Pavilion at 1970 Osaka 'Universal and International Japanese Exposition (Expo '70).'

Quezel
▶ American glassware factory; located Brooklyn, New York.
▶ Tiffany's former glass mixer and foreman, Martin Bach and Thomas Johnson, founded Quezel Art Glass and Decorating in Brooklyn in 1901. Bach and Johnson produced many pieces of luster and 'favrile'-type glassware. The firm's wide range of glass tableware included bud-vases, compotes, wine glasses, sherbets, bowls, and an obvious copy of Tiffany's *Jack in the Pulpit* model. Its specialty lampshades were non-leaded mouth-blown models up to six inches long in various trumpet, lily, and everted-bowl silhouettes to surround a single electric light bulb. Lacking innovation, the firm did not produce any new designs and techniques of its own. It had difficult financial times in 1905 and 1918, finally closing in 1925.
▶ Alastair Duncan, *Art Nouveau and Art Déco Lighting*, New York: Simon and Schuster, 1978:46.

Quinet, Jacques   (1918–)

▶ French interior architect, furniture designer, and cabinetmaker.

▶ Studied architecture.

▶ From 1946, he worked as an interior architect and decorator. Inspired by the Louis XVI style and working in a style similar to Ardré Arbus, he became known as a perfectionist master cabinetmaker; designed the architectural interior and decoration of the 1953 oceanliner *La Bourdonnais*; collaborated with artists Maxime Adam, Maurice Buché, and André Wogenscky; in his furniture designs, used sycamore, mahogany, oak, and cherry; was associated with metalsmiths Gilbert Poillerat and Raymond Subes in his productions 1945–65.

▶ Yolande Amic, *Intérieurs: Le mobilier français, 1945–1964*, Paris: Regard/VIA, 1983:44–45.

Quistgaard, Jens H.   (1919–)

▶ Danish wood- and metalworker and glassware designer; active Copenhagen.

▶ *c*1935–44, trained as a sculptor, draftsperson, silversmith, ceramicist, and carpenter.

▶ Quistgaard was an apprentice at the Georg Jensen Sølvsmedie. After World War II, he set up his own design studio in Copenhagen. In 1954, he and Ted Nierenberg of the USA founded Dansk International Designs where they were active until 1984. As principal designer for Dansk, Quistgaard designed wooden tableware, silverware, cookware, ceramics, cutlery, and glassware in a sculptural manner.

▶ He was awarded the 1954 Lunning Prize and, for enameled cast-iron cooking pots for De Forenede Jerstøberier and for flatware, received gold and silver medals at the 1954 (X) Triennale di Milano.

▶ Arne Karlsen, *Made in Denmark*, New York, 1960:116–17. 'Thirty-four Lunning Prize-Winners,' *Mobilia*, No. 146, Sept. 1967. Cat., Kathryn B. Hiesinger and George H. Marcus III (eds.), *Design Since 1945*, Philadelphia: Philadelphia Museum of Art, 1983:227,VIII–8–9. Cat., *The Lunning Prize*, Stockholm: Nationalmuseum, 1986:62–65.

R

Raacke, Peter (1928–)
▶ German metalworker and designer.
▶ Studied enamelwork and gold- and silversmithing, Staatliche Zeichenakademie, Hanau, and metalworking and glassware design, Werkschule, Cologne.
▶ He designed cutlery, kitchen tools, and cookware for Hessische Metallwerke, including the 1965 *Mono-a* flatware range in stainless steel and sterling silver. He executed designs for cardboard furniture, including his 1967 *Papp* range of modular seating, tables, stacking easy chairs, and storage units mass-produced by Faltmöbel Ellen Raacke.
▶ His work was included in the 1971 'Gold und Silber, Schmuck und Gerät' exhibition at the Gewerbemuseum in Nuremberg. His *Mono-a* flatware won the 1973 Bundespreis 'Die gute industrieform.'
▶ 'Technologia del Provisorio, Papp, Mobili di Carta,' *Casabella*, No. 323, Feb. 1968:55–56. 'Paper for Parents and Children,' *Design*, No. 232, April 1968:65. Ex. cat., *Gold und silber, Schmuck und Gerät*, Nuremberg: Gewerbemuseum, 1971. Cat., Kathryn B. Hiesinger and George H. Marcus III (eds.), *Design Since 1945*, Philadelphia: Philadelphia Museum of Art, 1983:227,V–33.

Rabanne, Paco (aka Francisco Rabaneva-Cuervo 1934–)
▶ Spanish clothing and furnishings designer.
▶ 1952–64, studied École Nationale Supérieure des Beaux-Arts, Paris.
▶ 1960–64, he designed handbags, shoes, eye glasses, and other accessories for Dior, Givenchy, and Balenciaga. In 1967, he set up his own fashion house in Paris, designing clothing in plastics, paper, leather, strips of knitted fur, and metals. He named his first couture collection and plastic and aluminum dresses *The Unwearables*. In 1966, he produced dresses in plastic disks and coats of neon-colored plastic diamonds sewn onto white crepe. In 1967, his clothing was in chain mail. From 1964, he designed costumes for films, including *Two for the Road* (1967), in which Audrey Hepburn wore his plastic dresses, *Barbarella* (1968), featuring Jane Fonda in revealing futuristic clothing, and *The Last Adventure* (1968). In 1967, he became a founding member of the modern aesthetics association Groupe Verseau in Paris. He is known for his *Calandre* perfume (bottle designed by Ateliers Dinand). His firm markets furniture. Rabanne rendered the 1980 *Dorique* faïence dinnerware in a square, askew-form silhouette produced by Gien Faïencerie.
▶ He won first prize at the 1963 Biennale in Paris; 1967 Tibère d'Or in Capri for fashion design; 1969 Beauté-Industrie Label from the Institut d'Esthétique Industrielle in Paris; 1975 International Oscar for Perfume in New York; 1977 Golden Needle Award in Paris.
▶ *Contemporary Designers*, London: Macmillan, 1984:503. Sophie Manrique, 'Paco Rabanne de la haute couture au prêt à meubler,' *Maison française*, May 1983.

Rabinovich, Isaac Moiseievich (1894–1961)
▶ Russian painter, interior decorator, and designer of film and stage décors.

▶ 1906–12, studied at art school in Kiev; 1912–15, in the studio of A. Murashko.
▶ He produced his first stage designs in 1911.
▶ From 1914, he participated in several exhibitions and was designer of the Soviet pavilion and hall of the State Publishing House at the 1925 Paris 'Exposition Internationale des Arts Décoratifs et Industriels Modernes.'

Race, Ernest (1913–64)
▶ British furniture and industrial designer; born Newcastle.
▶ 1932–35, studied interior design, Bartlett School of Architecture of London University and, 1937–39, weaving in India.
▶ In 1935, he was a model maker, turning to lighting design in *c*1936 under A.B. Read of the lighting manufacturer Troughton and Young. In 1937, he founded Race Fabrics, selling textiles of his own design that were hand woven in India. In 1945, he and J.W. Noel Jordan founded Race Furniture, which, at the time, had to use aircraft metal scrap for its raw material; 1945–54, he was director of the firm. Race used an innovative approach to materials, producing a succession of highly publicized chairs using steel rods. His 1945 *BA* chair of sand-cast aluminum and other furniture in salvaged aluminum were innovations based on the scarcity of raw materials after World War II. Race's firm in Sheerness produced more than 250,000 *BA* chairs using 850 tons of aluminum. His 1951 *Antelope* and *Springbok* chairs popularized the contemporary thin silhouette; reproduction of the former began in 1990. Race also worked in bent plywood, which was incorporated into the *Antelope* chair and influenced by Marcel Breuer and Charles Eames. Other designs included the 1959 *Flamingo* easy chair and 1963 *Sheppey* settee chair. He did some work for Isokon, and contract design work for P&O Orient Lines, Royal Netherland Lines, and the University of Liverpool Medical School. After 1954, he worked as a freelance designer.
▶ The *BA* chair and other furniture was shown for the first time at the 1946 'Britain Can Make It' exhibition at the Victoria and Albert Museum; the chair won a Gold Medal at the 1951 (IX) Triennale di Milano. His 1947 metal-frame wing chair and storage units were included in the 1948 'International Competition for Low Cost Furniture Design' exhibition at the New York Museum of Modern Art. Several of his designs, including *Antelope* and *Springbok* chairs, appeared at the 1951 'Festival of Britain.' He showed his work at the 1954 (X), 1957 (XI), and 1960 (XII) Triennali di Milano, where he won gold and silver medals. He received three Council of Industrial Design awards for furniture. In 1953, elected Royal Designer for Industry.
▶ 'Design Review: Trends in Factory Made Furniture by Ernest Race,' *Architectural Review*, Vol. 103, May 1948:218–20. L. Bruce Archer, 'Theory into Practice: Design and Stress Analysis,' *Design*, No. 101, May 1957:18–21. Gillian Naylor, 'Ernest Race,' *Design*, No. 184, April 1964:54–55. 'Race: Case Histories,' London: Race Furniture Limited (Submitted to the Royal Society of Arts), 1969:3–13. Cat., *Modern Chairs 1918–1970*, London: Lund Humphries, 1971, nos. 26,50. Hazel Conway, *Ernest Race*, London, 1982. Cat., Kathryn B. Hiesinger and George H. Marcus III (eds.), *Design Since 1945*, Philadelphia: Philadelphia Museum of

Art, 1983:227,III—70—71. Fiona MacCarthy and Patrick Nuttgens, *Eye for Industry*, London: Lund Humphries, 1986.

Radice, Barbara   (1943–)
▶ Italian art and design director and writer; born Como.
▶ Studied modern literature, Catholic University, Milan.
▶ 1974—76, she was associate editor of *Data* art magazine in Milan. In 1977 beginning as a freelance journalist, she wrote for *Modo, Domus, Casa Vogue, Japan SD, Wet*, and *Art & Auction*. 1981—88, she was consulting art director to Memphis in charge of exhibition and cultural activities. Her books included *Elogio del Banale* (1980); *Memphis* (1983), *Jewelry by Architects* (1987), *Ettore Sottsass's Design Metaphors* (1987), and *Ettore Sottsass: A Critical Biography* (1993).
▶ Andrea Branzi, *La Casa Calda: Esperienze del Nuovo Disegno Italiano*, Milan: Idea Books, 1982. Liz McQuiston, *Women in Design: A Contemporary View*, New York: Rizzoli, 1988:88.

Radtke, Stefanie   (1963–)
▶ German industrial designer.
▶ Studied industrial design, Gesamthochschule, Essen, to 1983, and, 1986, trained at Lotsch Design, Dortmund.
▶ 1985—86, she developed a typewriter for the blind with the Blindenstudienanstalt (Study Institute for the Blind) in Marburg. 1988—89, she worked on a manual on design for visually handicapped people. Her 1985 hotplate was produced from 1988 by WKM in Lüdenscheid.
▶ She showed her work at the 1986 Hanover Messe and 1987 North Rhine-Westphalia trade exhibition in Moscow. She won second place in the Bob Gutmann prize for her typewriter for the blind at the 1987 (XI) 'Design Börse' in the Haus Industrieform in Essen, first place for the design of a fully automatic focus camera in the 1988 'Nikon promotional prize,' 1988 Glunz Prize for furniture design, and 1988 Düker Design Prize.
▶ Cat., Design Center Stuttgart, *Women in Design: Careers and Life Histories Since 1900*, Stuttgart: Haus der Wirtschaft, 1989:150—53.

Raemisch, Waldemar   (1888–1955)
▶ German metalworker and teacher, active Berlin.
▶ In the early 1920s, studied Kunstgewerbeschule, Berlin, under Josef Wilm.
▶ He taught at the Vereinigte Staatsschulen für freie und angewandte Kunst in Berlin-Charlottenburg and designed metalware, lighting, and medals. From 1939, he taught sculpture at the Rhode Island School of Design, Providence, Rhode Island.
▶ His chased service was shown at the 1922 Munich 'Deutsche Gewerbeschau.'
▶ Annelies Krekel-Aalberse, *Art Nouveau and Art Déco Silver*, New York: Abrams, 1989:144,258. Hans Wichmann, *Deutsche Werkstätten und WK-Verband 1818–1990*, Munich: Prestel, 1992:340.

Raffy, Eric   (1951–)
▶ French designer and architect.
▶ As an architect, he designed many restaurants in Bordeaux, Nantes, and Bayonne, and shops in Tokyo and Paris; designed the *Thèbes* stool produced by Farjon, 1986 *Atlantic* steel furniture by Grange, 1989 rattan furniture by Soca, and 1990 public furniture in granite by Art Mob; from the early 1990s, worked for couturier Paco Rabanne and taught at École d'Architecture, Bordeaux.
▶ Received 1984 Appel permanent (for *Thèbes* stool) from VIA, and 1986 Appel permanent from VIA and 1987 gold medal (for steel furniture by Grange) of the Prix de la critique for contemporary furniture.
▶ Cat., *Les années VIA 1980–1990*, Paris: Musée des Arts Décoratifs, 1990:150.

Raggi, Franco   (1945–)
▶ Italian designer; born Milan.
▶ Studied architecture, Politecnico di Milano, to 1969.

▶ From 1970, he was active as a designer; 1971—75, was an editor of the journal *Casabella* and, 1977—83, of *Modo*; was an organizer and cultural coordinator of the 1973 (XV), 1979 (XVI), 1980 and 1983 (XVII) Triennali di Milano and 1975, 1976, 1977, and 1980 Biennali di Venezia; from 1985, taught architecture, Università di Pescara. His work included architectural structures, environments, interiors, exhibitions, publications, stage designs, and products, including 1991 upholstered seating (with Daniela Puppa) produced by Ligne Roset.
▶ Fumio Shimizu and Matteo Thun (eds.), *The Descendants of Leonardo: The Italian Design*, Tokyo, 1987:338.

Ragot, Christian   (1933–)
▶ French designer and architect.
▶ Studied École Boulle, École Nationale Supérieure des Arts Décoratifs, and Conservatoire National des Arts et Métiers, all Paris.
▶ He set up his own design office in 1970; in 1969, designed the *Elisa* line of seating produced by Ligne Roset in collaboration with Michel Cadestin, *Alcove 2000* adjustable sofa in foam tubes, pasta for Panzani, a bottle for Vittel, an orbital station for the Archepolis competition, and the *Spatial Monument* for the 1989 centenary of the Eiffel Tower.

Ragusa, Mario Augusto   (1938–)
▶ Italian industrial designer; born Trieste; active Milan.
▶ He began his professional career in 1973. His clients included Bialetti (hair dryers), Aifai-Assoluce (lighting), Veca Cesana (bath accessories), M. Bongio (bath accessories), and Tecnogiocattoli (educational toys). Others included De Martino, Valdelsa, Vivi, Vavassori e Priovano, Artime, Coppola e Parodi, and Stanley Works. He was a member of ADI (Associazione per il Disegno Industriale).
▶ *ADI Annual 1976*, Milan: Associazione per il Disegno industriale, 1976.

Raichle, Karl   (1889–1965)
▶ German metalworker.
▶ From 1928, studied Bauhaus, Dessau.
▶ He worked in the Bauhaus metal workshop with Christian Dell, Marianne Brandt, and Hans Pryzembel. Raichle often produced his work in hammered pewter with ebony fittings in the form of teapots, casseroles, and other domestic goods. After the Bauhaus, he founded the Werkgemeinschaft Urach; in 1933, he founded the Meersburger Zinuschmiede. He belonged to a group of Utopian artists in Urach.
▶ Cat., *The Bauhaus: Masters and Students*, New York: Barry Friedman 1988. Cat., *Metalkunst*, Berlin: Bröhan-Museum, 1990:402—12.

Raimondi, Giuseppe   (1941–)
▶ Italian town planner, architect, and industrial designer; born Fiume; active Turin.
▶ Studied architecture, Politecnico di Milano, to 1967.
▶ He began his professional career in 1966; from 1970, he collaborated with architects Sisto Giriodi, Guido Martinero, Alberto Vaccarone in the studio A.BA.CO; designed the *Mozza* foam chair produced by Gufram and the *Cristal System* produced by Cristal Art; had clients including Tarzia; became a member of ADI (Associazione per il Disegno Industriale); wrote for journals including *Casabella, Casa Vogue*, and *Abitare*; designed a project for Museo del Pneumatico in Turin; published the book *Abitare Italia* (Fabbri).
▶ Received 1987 Premio Compasso d'Oro (*Delfina* chair by Bontempi); 1988 gold medal (*Miriade* lighting system by Valenti) in Toronto.
▶ *ADI Annual 1976*, Milan: Associazione per il Disegno Industriale, 1976. *Moderne Klassiker: Möbel, die Geschichte machen*, Hamburg, 1982:75. Hans Wichmann, *Italien Design 1945 bis heute*, Munich: Die Neue Sammlung, 1988. *Modo*, No. 148, March–April 1993:125.

Rajalin, Börje (1933–)
▶ Finnish designer.
▶ Studied, department of metal design, Taideteollinen oppilaitos, Helsinki, to 1955.
▶ Rajalin worked at Bertel Gardberg's silversmithy; from 1952–56, was a designer at Tillander; in 1956, a designer at Kalevala Koru; in 1956, set up his own studio, working as an interior, exhibition, and industrial designer. His design work included technical equipment, plastic fittings, cutlery, stainless-steel table- and cookware, and, with Antti Nurmesniemi in 1972, a train for the Helsinki subway. Rajalin produced silver designs for Bertel Gardberg and jewelry for Kalevala Koru. 1969–71, taught at Taideteollinen oppilaitos and was a director of Taideteollinen ammattikoulu, both Helsinki.
▶ His large silver screen won a gold medal at the 1960 (XII) Triennale di Milano and the 1961 AID International Design Award. He received the 1963 Lunning Prize.
▶ Erik Zahle (ed.), *A Treasury of Scandinavian Design*, New York, 1961:288, nos. 371–72. Graham Hughes, *Modern Silver throughout the World*, New York, 1967, no. 137. Cat., Kathryn B. Hiesinger and George H. Marcus III (eds.), *Design Since 1945*, Philadelphia: Philadelphia Museum of Art, 1983:227,V–34. Cat., *The Lunning Prize*, Stockholm: Nationalmuseum, 1986:142–47.

Ram
▶ Dutch ceramics firm; located Arnhem.
▶ Plateelbakkerij Ram was set up in 1921 to produce fine ceramic bodies. Thomas A.C. Colenbrander, at Ram 1921–25, was the designer for whom, at the age of 80, the company was established. Considered art rather than craft, Ram wares were sold at exhibition auctions. 1924–35, art dealer and artist N. Henri van Lerven and, 1923–27, F. Mansveld experimented with oxide paints; sculptor and designer H.J. Jansen van Galen produced many designs for Ram. Ram's production included Colenbrander ceramics and very hard bodied glazes for utility ware. Colenbrander's designs were supervised after 1925 by Mansveld, who left in 1927. Van Lerven designed most of the products from then on; a highly productive designer, for his utility ware he used single stroke designs of stripes, and for ornamental wares, a broad brush in a watercolor effect produced by oxide paint. After 1931, he used decalcomanias and *zilva* décor, and silver and gold intarsia-like flowers on blue and dark black. Plateelbakkerij Ram lasted until 1935.
▶ *Industry and Design in the Netherlands, 1850–1950*, Amsterdam: Stedelijk Museum, 1985:181–83.

Ramaer, W.G.J.
▶ Dutch fabric manufacturer; located Helmond.
▶ With his mother as partner, W.G.J. Ramaer began as manufacturers of cotton, linen, and woolen goods in 1849. Interior designer Thomas W. Nieuwenhuis of the workshop of Van Wisselingh encouraged Ramaer to produce more sophisticated furnishings goods, which proved successful. He designed for the firm 1909–24. Adding 15 furnishing fabric patterns to its line by 1914, Ramaer sold its wares worldwide. In the Netherlands, its fabrics were used by W. Penaat, H.J.M. Walenkamp, furniture studio De Ploeg, and others. In *c*1924, production of these fabrics was discontinued. 1925–61, the firm was known as Ramaer's Textielfabriek, and was taken over by Van Vlissingen in 1953. It now produces machines and apparatus and supplies services in galvanizing.
▶ *Industry and Design in the Netherlands, 1850–1950*, Amsterdam: Stedelijk Museum, 1985.

Rambusch, Frode Christian Vlademar (1858–1924)
▶ Danish artisan and interior and lighting designer; born Sønde Omme; active New York.
▶ 1871, apprenticed to painter Anderson in Odense; 1875–81, studied Royal Academy, Copenhagen, and under painter Markussen; Kunstgewerbeschule, Berlin and Munich.

▶ He became a journeyman, working in Dresden, Berlin, Paris, Zürich, and Munich. In 1889, he moved to New York, where he worked for the Brooklyn decorating and painting firm Arnold and Locke, becoming a foreman and affectionately known as the 'stencil kid.' He made two unsuccessful attempts at establishing his own workshops: Rambusch and Pettit, Interior Decorators, in 1893 at 120 Court Street in Brooklyn, and in 1896 at 1193 Broadway in Manhattan. In 1899, he established Rambusch Glass and Decorating at 175 Broadway; the production of lighting fixtures began in 1908. Rambusch's early fixtures were made by individual artisans' shops under the firm's supervision, with wiring completed at S.J. O'Brien. In 1919, Rambusch began designing for churches, including candlesticks, chalices, monstrances, crucifixes, tabernacles, and screens. From 1947, the firm was located at 40 West 13th Street. The management of the firm was taken over by Rambusch's sons, Harold William and Viggo; Harold became president in 1924. The firm's patented lighting fixtures included *Lite-Paks*, *Shovelites*, *Pan-a-Lux*, *Annulites*, and *Classic Lanterns*.
▶ Frode Rambusch participated in the 1883–94 Annual Exhibitions of the Architectural League of New York.
▶ Catha Grace Rambush, 'Rambusch Decorating Company: Ninety Years of Art Metal,' *The Journal of Decorative and Propaganda Arts*, Summer 1988:6–43.

Rameckers, Clemens H. B. (1949–)
▶ Dutch designer; active Paris.
▶ Collaborating with Van Geuns in the early 1990s, Rameckers produced hand-made furniture, ceramics, blankets, bed linens, fabrics, and rugs. Their design studio was Ravage in Paris. They were previously fashion designers.
▶ Their work was the subject of a 1990 exhibition at Galerie Néotù in New York.

Ramond, Marcel
▶ French architect and designer; born and active Paris.
▶ From 1968, Ramond was active in research in habitation, working conditions, and means of travel. In 1980, he designed the *Programme 9000* office furniture produced by Strafor.
▶ Won 1983 competition (for *Programme 9000*) sponsored by the Ministère du Culture and Agence pour la Promotion de la Création Industrielle.

Ramos, Charles
▶ French furniture designer and decorator; born Boue (Algeria).
▶ Studied École des Beaux-Arts, Algiers.
▶ After World War II, he lived for two years in New York; primarily active as a designer of hotel, department store, and domestic interiors.
▶ Work shown in salons including those of Société des Artistes Décorateurs, Société des Arts Ménagers, and Salon du Meuble, Paris.
▶ Pascal Renous, *Portraits de créateurs*, Paris: H. Vial, 1969.

Rams, Dieter (1932–)
▶ German designer; born Wiesbaden; active Frankfurt.
▶ 1947–48 and 1951–53, studied architecture and design, Wiesbaden Werkkunstschule.
▶ He was associated with Otto Apel, a Frankfurt architect, and collaborated with the American architecture firm Skidmore, Owings and Merrill, which was involved with the design of US consulate buildings in West Germany in the early 1950s. In 1956, he abandoned architecture in favor of product design. He designed a large number of austere Functionalist forms at Braun, where, in 1955, he became designer and, in 1961, chief designer. His work typified the spare, formal, geometric style associated with postwar German design; he commented, 'I want to make things that recede into the background.' The 1956 *Phonosuper* record player designed with Hans Gugelot was known in Germany as the *Schneewittchensarg* (Snow White's coffin). His 1957 *Atelier 1* unit separated loudspeaker from chassis for the first time. His series of portable radios included the 1956 *Transistor* and 1958 *T3* pocket receiver which, combined with a small record player, became a

portable phonograph-radio combination. His fame was enhanced when, by 1959, the New York Museum of Modern Art placed his designs on exhibition. He designed his first furniture in 1957 for a firm in Eschborn, that was to become Vitsoe. Rams's 1962 *RZ 62 Chair* was produced by Vitsoe, along with other pieces in the line; it was chosen by Florence Knoll for use in her residence in Florida. Vitsoe also produced his 1979 *Dafne* folding chair. With Dietrich Lubs, he designed the 1977 Braun *ET44* pocket calculator, now regarded as a design classic. In 1981, Rams became professor at the Hochschule für Bildenden Künste in Hamburg, and, from 1987, president of Rat für Formgebung.

▶ He shared Grand Prize awards for Braun at the 1957 (XI) and 1960 (XII) Triennali di Milano and was given the 1962 Premio Compasso d'Oro, an award at the 1964 'Bio 1' industrial design biennale in Ljubljana, and the 1966 AID Award in the USA. His *RZ 62 Chair* was included in the 1970 'Modern Chairs, 1918–1970' exhibition at the Whitechapel Gallery in London and was awarded the 1966 Rosenthal Studio Prize and a gold medal at the 1969 Vienna 'International Furniture Exhibition.' In 1968, elected Honorary Royal Designer for Industry, London.

▶ Cat., *Modern Chairs 1918–1970*, London: Lund Humphries, 1971. Dieter Rams, 'And That's How Simple It Is to Be a Good Designer,' *Designer*, Sept. 1978:12–13. Dieter Rams, 'Die Rolle des Designers im Industrieunternehmen,' in *Design ist unsichtbar*, Vienna, 1981:507–16. *Dieter Rams*, Berlin, 1980–81. Cat., Kathryn B. Hiesinger and George H. Marcus III (eds.), *Design Since 1945*, Philadelphia: Philadelphia Museum of Art, 1983:228,I–34–35,III–72. Uta Brandes, *Dieter Rams, Designer: Die leise Ordnung der Dinge*, Güttingen: Steidl, 1990.

Ramsden, Omar (1873–1939)

▶ British silver designer; born Sheffield.

▶ Studied Sheffield School of Art to 1898.

▶ He met Alwyn Carr at the Sheffield School of Art; when he won the open contest to design the ceremonial mace for the city of Sheffield, he turned to Carr for assistance. They went to London and set up a workshop in Stamford Bridge Studios, where they completed the mace in 1899. In the early years of the St. Dunstan Ramsden-Carr workshop, the assistants were Walter Andrews, Leonard Burt, and A.E. Ulyett. Ramsden was recognized as an important silversmith, though it appears that most of the objects credited to him before the war were produced by Carr. Only a few of the workshop's objects were made by hand, though all had a hand-made appearance; labor-saving molding techniques were used. Church plate became a specialty. Some of the objects had Tudor-rose decoration and chased texts. In ornamentation and object type, the workshop's pieces were in 15th- and 16th-century styles, although some of the early work was in the Art Nouveau idiom. Carr and Ramsden produced objects that had wide appeal and became important practitioners in the Arts and Crafts movement. They worked together until 1914; when Carr returned in 1919, he set up his own workshop. In the 1920s and 1930s, Ramsden had a large workshop with many craftsmen, including various designers, chasers, and enamelers; it specialized in embossing and finial, stem, and boss modeling. Ramsden supervised production. The wares during this time were produced in a picturesque Tudor mode.

▶ Cat., Peter Cannon-Brooks, *Omar Ramsden 1873–1973*, City Museum and Art Gallery, Birmingham, 1973. Charlotte Gere, *American and European Jewelry 1830–1914*, New York: Crown, 1975:217. Cat., *Thirties: British art and design before the war*, London: Arts Council of Great Britain, Hayward Gallery, 1979:99,140,299. *British Arts and Design, 1900–1960*, London: Victoria and Albert Museum, 1983. Annelies Krekel-Aalberse, *Art Nouveau and Art Déco Silver*, New York: Abrams, 1989:26,27,258.

Ramstein, Willi (1939–)

▶ Italian industrial designer; born San Gallo; active Milan.

▶ 1958–62, studied Hochschule für Gestaltung, Ulm.

▶ In 1963, he was an assistant in industrial buildings at the Hochschule für Gestaltung. 1963–65, he worked on aluminum structures in Zürich; 1967–72 he participated on a housing project for the Rinascente/Upim group in Milan; in 1973, was a consultant on aluminum panels to Alcan in Montreal; 1963–73, worked on the design of shopping centers; was involved with the design of public swimming pools, including a 1975 pool at Arcore. His clients included Ideal-Standard (sanitary fixtures), Ceramica Laufen, Brionvega, Presbitero (building accessories), Sleeping International System, Vebo-Arredo (stainless-steel furniture), and Kartell (furniture). He was a member of ADI (Associazione per il Disegno Industriale).

▶ He participated in Bayer Leverkursen's 'Visiona 5' project.

▶ *ADI Annual 1976*, Milan: Associazione per il Disegno Industriale, 1976.

Rancillac, Bernard (1931–)

▶ French designer and painter.

▶ Rancillac designed the 1967 *Eléphant Chair* produced by Galerie Lacloche in a sweeping polyester form with a metal base.

▶ Gilles de Bure, *Le mobilier français 1965–1979*, Paris: Regard/VIA, 1983:51.

Randahl, Julius Olaf (1880–1972)

▶ Swedish silversmith; active New York and Chicago.

▶ He moved to New York in 1901, where he worked for Tiffany and Gorham Manufacturing. He settled in Chicago, where he worked in the Kalo Shop in 1907 and, in 1911, opened his own Randahl Shop in Park Ridge, Illinois. Leading department stores including Marshall Field sold its hollow-ware. Production was mechanized; finishing was done by hand. Randahl was influenced by the Kalo Shop and Georg Jensen in Denmark. In 1957, the firm purchased the Cellini Shop and, in 1969, Cellini Craft. In 1965, it was itself was purchased by Reed and Barton.

▶ He showed his silverwares at the 1937 Paris 'Exposition Internationale des Arts et Techniques dans la Vie Moderne,' receiving a silver medal for his fruit stand and candlestick.

▶ Annelies Krekel-Aalberse, *Art Nouveau and Art Déco Silver*, New York: Abrams, 1989:123,258.

Rang, Wolfgang (1949–)

▶ German architect and designer; born Essen.

▶ Studied architecture, Technische Hochschule, Darmstadt, and University of California at Los Angeles.

▶ He set up an architectural practice in 1981 with Michael Landes. In a Post-Modernist style reminiscent of Biedermeier, they designed the 1985 *F1 Frankfurter Schrank* secretary-desk and 1986 *Frankfurter Stuhl FIII* armchair produced by Draenert. 1979–85, he lectured at the Technische Hoschschule in Darmstadt.

▶ Albrecht Bangert and Karl Michael Armer, *80s Style: Designs of the Decade*, New York: Abbeville, 1990:32–33,235.

Ranson, Paul (1862–1909)

▶ French painter and decorator; born Limoges.

▶ 1880, studied Académie Julian, Paris.

▶ At the Académie Julian, he met Paul Sérusier, Jean-Édouard Vuillard, Maurice Denis, Ker-Xavier Roussel, and Pierre Bonnard. Meeting weekly at Ranson's studio, in 1889 the group formed the Nabis, which had a commitment to decorative arts. He worked on stage sets for the Théâtre d'Art in 1892, along with Vuillard, Sérusier, and Bonnard. He also designed sets for Aurélien Lugné-Poë's new Théâtre de l'Oeuvre. Ranson rendered cartoons for tapestries with women and arabesques in the Art Nouveau style. His *Le Tigre* tapestry was woven by the Manufacture des Gobelins. Denis, Maillol, Sérusier, Vallotton, and Bonnard taught at the Académie Ranson in Paris, which Ranson organized with his wife and opened in 1908.

▶ Yvonne Brunhammer et al., *Art Nouveau Belgium, France*, Houston: Institute for the Arts, Rice University 1976.

Ranzo, Patrizia (1953–)
▶ Italian architect and designer; born and active Naples.
▶ Studied architecture in Naples to 1981.
▶ Her work in design began in 1975; from 1983, she collaborated on projects with the department of architecture at the University of Naples. Most of her design and architecture work was done with architect Sergio Cappelli. With Cappelli, she designed the widely published *Agave* table. She was a contributing writer to *Architettura e tecnologia appropriata* (1985); co-author with V. Gangemi of *Il governo del progetto* (1986) and *The Mediterranean sensitivity as a cultural perspective* (1986).
▶ She participated in the 'The city as a theater' with A. Branzi, A. Rossi, L. Thermes, F. Purini, B. Gravagnuolo, and Sergio Cappelli at the 1981 Napoli Centro Zen, the 1982 Paris Biennale, 'Unforeseen consequences: art, fashion, design' at the 1985 Prato and Florence exhibitions, 'South wave' at the 1985 Bari exhibition, 'The wonder wardrobe' at the 1985 Salone del Mobile Italiano, 1986 'New trends in design: the neo-naturalism,' and 1986 Seibu exhibition in Tokyo and Osaka (winning first prize for Italian design). The *Agave* table won the 1987 Compasso d'Oro. She won the 1981 (interiors) and 1983 (design and architecture) awards of Women in Design International competition in California.
▶ Liz McQuiston, *Women in Design: A Contemporary View*, New York: Rizzoli, 1988:90. Andrea Branzi, *La Casa Calda: Esperienze del Nuovo Disegno Italiano*, Milan: Idea Books, 1982.
See **Cappelli, Sergio**

Rapin, Henri (1873–1939)
▶ French artist and decorator.
▶ Studied École des Beaux-Arts under Jean-Léon Gérôme and J. Blanc.
▶ Rapin worked as a painter, illustrator, furniture designer, and decorator. From 1903, his furniture was generally simple; from c1910, he began to produce more elaborate designs using exotic materials and carved wood panels by Eve Le Bourgeois and Charles Hairon. These designs were in response to the challenge from the designers of the Münchner Vereinigte Werkstätten für Kunst in Handwerk exhibiting at the Salon of the same year. In c1924, he became a principal at the Manufacture Nationale de Sèvres and artistic director of École du Comité des Dames de l'Union Centrale des Arts Décoratifs. Some of his furniture was produced by Evrard. He designed numerous interiors of theaters, music halls, and shops in Paris.
▶ He began showing his work at the Salons of the Société des Artistes français from 1900 and the 1910 Salon d'Automne. He designed the stand and dining room of L'Art à l'École, Grand Salon of 'Une Ambassade française' with Pierre Selmersheim, pavilion of Sèvres, and others sections at 1925 Paris 'Exposition Internationale des Arts Décoratifs et Industriels Modernes.'
▶ Léon Deshairs, *Modern French Decorative Art*, Paris: Albert Lévy. Pierre Kjellberg, *Art Déco: les maîtres du Mobilier, le décor des Paquebots*, Paris: Amateur, 1986:148. Maurice Dufrêne, *Ensembles Mobiliers, Exposition Internationale 1925*, Paris: Charles Moreau, 1925, Antique Collectors' Club edition, 1989:60.

Rascaroli, Adelmo (1931–)
▶ Italian architect and designer; born Luzzara; active Milan.
▶ 1956–60, he was active in the studio of architect Renzo Zavanella. He set up his own private practice in 1960. His clients for furniture included Bernini, C.-Nova, Cubina in Barcelona, Driade, Molteni, and Somaschini. He was a member of ADI (Associazione per il Disegno Industriale).
▶ He won three prizes at the VI Internazionale del Mobile in Cantù and seven prizes at the VII event, two prizes at the 1966–67 Nazionale del Mobile in Trieste, and a gold medal at the 1966 MIA in Monza. Participated in the 1966, 1968, 1970, 1972, and 1975 Biennali dello Standard nell'Arredamento in Mariano Comense.
▶ *ADI Annual 1976*, Milan: Associazione per il Disegno Industriale, 1976.

Rasch
▶ German wallpaper manufacturer; located Bramsche.
▶ From 1929, Tapetenfabrik Rasch produced wallpaper designed by students and teachers at the Bauhaus, Dessau; it issued designer papers again in the 1950s; produced the 1992 *Zeitwände* range of wallpapers by designers Nathalie du Pasquier, Alessandro Mendini, Bořek Šípek, Ettore Sottsass, George Sowden, Matteo Thun, and architecture team Norbert Berghof, Michael Landes, and Wolfgang Rang. Šípek's three-dimensional *Zed* pattern was issued in plain paper and blown glass crystal hemispheres.

Rasch, Heinz (1902–) and Bodo Rasch (1903–)
▶ German architects and designers; brothers; born Berlin-Charlottenburg and Elberfield.
▶ Heinz Rasch studied 1916 Kunstgewerbeschule, Bromberg; 1920–23, Technischen Hochschulen, Hanover and Stuttgart.
▶ They founded a factory in Stuttgart in 1922 for household furnishings; became pioneers in the use of thin (3mm) bent plywood. They designed publicity; posters; a 1924 folding chair and bent tubular steel chair models by L. und C. Arnold; *Radio* linking chairs in the orchestral hall, Süddeutscher Rundfunk; 1927 *Sitzgeiststuhl* (Chair of sitting ghost); a stand for the Schonert und Lebrun quilt firm at the 1927 'Werbeschau' (Publicity Show), Stuttgart; Württemberg newspapers stall at the 1927 and 1929 'Pressa Ausstellung,' Cologne. In 1925, Heinz Rasch worked on the editorial staff of *Baugilde*, the journal of the organization of German architects in Berlin, and met Mies van der Rohe and Mart Stam; in 1928, edited the book *Der Stuhl* (*The Chair*); was a pioneer in cantilever chair design; 1937–44, collaborated with Oskar Schlemmer and Franz Krause in Wuppertal; in the 1980s, worked towards establishing the Stuhlmuseum (Chair Museum), Burg Beverungen. Architecture projects included a 1927 filling station, 1927 suspension house, and 1929 low-cost housing. Realized architecture included an office building for Dr. Heberts; flats with furniture (1924–27 chairs, 1927 desk, and adjustable ceiling light) in a building designed by Mies and (bed, wardrobe, night-table, and writing desk) in a building by Stam, both at the 1927 'Weissenhof-Siedlung,' Stuttgart.
▶ 'Heinz Rasch: Bau und Baustoffe des Neuen Hauses,' *Baukunst und Bauhandwerk*, No. 9, Sept. 1927. Heinz and Bodo Rasch, *Der Stuhl*, Stuttgart: Wedekind, 1928. Heinz and Bodo Rasch, *Wie bauen*, Stuttgart: Wedeking, 1928. Heinz and Bodo Rasch, *Zu–offen*, Stuttgart: Wedekind, 1930. Barbie Campbell-Cole and Tim Benton, *Tubular Steel Furniture*, London: The Art Book Company, 1979:11. *Brüder Rasch: Material–Konstruktion–Form 1926–1930*, Düsseldorf: Marzona, 1981. Cat., *Der Kragstuhl*, Stuhlmuseum Burg Beverungen, Berlin: Alexander, 1986:137.

Rasmussen, Ib (1931–)
▶ Danish architect and industrial designer.
▶ Studied architecture, Det Kongelige Danske Kunstakademi, Copenhagen, 1955.
▶ Rasmussen set up an architecture office in 1957 with Jørgen Rasmussen and designed furniture.
▶ Frederik Sieck, *Nutidig Dansk Møbeldesign:–en kortfattet illustreret beskrivelse*, Copenhagen: Bondo Gravesen; 1990 Busck edition in English.

Rasmussen, Jørgen (1931–)
▶ Danish furniture and industrial designer.
▶ Studied architecture, Det Kongelige Danske Kunstakademi, Copenhagen, to 1955.
▶ He designed office furniture and industrial fittings for Kevi in Glastrup. In 1957, Rasmussen set up an architecture office with Ib Rasmussen.
▶ His work was included in the 1972 'Knoll au Louvre,' Paris Musée des Arts Décoratifs, and 1982 'Scandinavian Modern Design 1880–1980,' Cooper-Hewitt Museum, New York, and received the 1969 *ID* prize.
▶ Frederik Sieck, *Nutidig Dansk Møbeldesign:–en kortfattet illustreret beskrivelse*, Copenhagen: Bondo Gravesen; 1990 Busck edi-

tion in English. Cat., David Revere McFadden (ed.), *Scandinavian Modern Design 1880–1980*, New York: Abrams, 1982:270, No. 340.

Rasmussen, Leif Erik (1942–)

▶ Danish architect and furniture designer.
▶ Studied furniture design, Kunsthåndværkerskolen, Copenhagen, to 1968.
▶ From 1968, he was active in the architecture firm Krohn & Hartvig Rasmussen on the project Odense Universitet-Center and, from 1972, with architect Ole Hagen on the Handelsbankens Hovedsæde project. In 1975, he set up his own architecture office and, in 1978, a partnership with Henrik Rolff. Rasmussen's furniture designs were produced by Hyllinge Træindustri.
▶ Frederik Sieck, *Nutidig Dansk Møbeldesign:—en kortfattet illustreret beskrivelse*, Copenhagen: Bondo Gravesen; 1990 Busck edition in English.

Rateau, Armand-Albert (1882–1938)

▶ French furniture designer; active Paris.
▶ Studied drawing and wood carving, École Boulle, Paris.
▶ He worked as a freelance designer for several interior decorators, including, in 1898, Georges Hoentschel, interior decorator and ceramicist. 1905–14, he was the manager of the Maison Alavoine decorating workshop. In 1919 setting up his own workshop in Levallois, he employed cabinetmakers, carpenters, sculptors, ironworkers, painters, gilders, and other craftspeople. He worked in wood at first, later lacquered and patinated metal. His furniture, chairs, lighting, vases, ashtrays, and other domestic objects were influenced by pieces from Pompeii, the Orient, and North Africa; he collaborated with sculptor Paul Plumet on bronze work. Fashion designer Jeanne Lanvin commissioned Rateau to decorate her apartment at 16 rue Barbet-de-Jouy in Paris, for which, 1920–22, he designed some remarkable furniture in *vert-de-gris* bronze, strewn with daisies, butterflies, doves, and pheasants, and all rendered in an antique Pompeiian style. The Lanvin spherical perfume flacon by Rateau was imprinted with Paul Iribe's gold image of Lanvin and her daughter. He designed Lanvin's fashion house and managed the Lanvin-Décoration department of interior design in the rue du Faubourg Saint-Honoré. His clients included the Baron and Baronne Eugène de Rothschild at the Château de la Crôe in Antibes, and American art collectors George and Florence Blumenthal, who arranged for his visit to the USA in 1919. Graduating from ornate to sober, Rateau produced furniture for Dr. Thaleimer and Mlle. Stern in 1929–30. 1921–22, he was manager of Lanvin-Sport. He renovated the Théâtre Daunou in Paris and, in 1926, the bathroom of the duchesse d'Albe in Madrid with gold lacquered walls, Persian decorations, bronze furniture, and fur-covered chairs. His fondness for the overwrought and the sumptuous was usually offset by his good taste.
▶ He hardly ever showed his work at exhibitions and Salons and was not associated with any group. At the 1925 Paris 'Exposition Internationale des Arts Décoratifs et Industriels Modernes,' he participated in the Pavillon de l'Elégance.
▶ Éveline Schlumberger, 'Au 16 rue Barbet-de-Jouy avec Jeanne Lanvin,' *Connaissance des Arts*, No. 138, Aug. 1963:62–71. Yvonne Brunhammer, *Les années 25*, Paris: Musée de Arts Décoratifs, 1966. Yvonne Brunhammer, *Cinquantenaire de l'Exposition de 1925*, Paris: Musée des Arts Décoratifs, 1976:143. Alastair Duncan, *Art Nouveau and Art Déco Lighting*, New York: Simon and Schuster, 1978:182. Jessica Rutherford, *Art Nouveau, Art Deco and the Thirties: The Furniture Collections at Brighton Museum*, Brighton: The Royal Pavilion, Art Gallery and Museums, 1983:40. Pierre Kjellberg, *Art Déco: les maîtres du Mobilier, le décor des Paquebots*, Paris: Amateur, 1986:149–51. Pierre Cabanne, *Encyclopédie Art Déco*, Paris: Somogy, 1986:229–30.

Rath & Doodeheefver

▶ Dutch wallpaper firm; located Amsterdam, Schiebroek, and Duivendrecht.

▶ Originally an upholsterer, Rath & Doodeheefver was a family business established in 1860 in Amsterdam, where it sold curtain and furniture fabrics and wallpaper. By 1890, it became a wallpaper wholesaler and importer. In 1921, a factory was set up in Schiebroek, exporting the bulk of its production. Its first collection in 1924 was designed by J.W. Gidding, A. Klijn, Van Kuyck, F. Oerder, and A.J.J. de Winter. 1924–31 saw the peak of collaboration with freelance artists. Many of the designs were used for a number of years, with color changes and sometimes relief added. Its many designers included H.P. Berlage, who produced small-pattern designs in consultation with the residents of his houses in which the papers were used. Other designers were G.B. Broekema in 1931 and 1939 and Thomas W. Nieuwenhuis, C.A. Lion Cachet, and T. Posthuma 1928–31.
▶ Its products were shown at the 1927 exhibition of curtains by cotton printers Van Vissingen and wallpaper by Rath & Doodeheefver at the Stedelijk Museum in Amsterdam.
▶ *Industry and Design in the Netherlands, 1850/1950*, Amsterdam: Stedelijk Museum, 1985:117–21.

Rath, Hans Harald (1904–68)

▶ Austrian glassware designer; born Vienna.
▶ Studied art history in Munich.
▶ In 1924, he entered the family firm Lobmeyr in Vienna, where he became chief designer in 1938. He helped to revive the glass industry in Austria after World War II and won commissions for chandeliers in public buildings, theaters, and opera houses. Pieces designed by his son Peter Rath were installed in the Metropolitan Opera House in New York in 1966 and the John F. Kennedy Center for the Performing Arts in Washington in 1968. Rath designed the 1952 *Alpha* and 1967 *Montreal* table crystal services produced by Lobmeyr.
▶ *Glass 1959*, Corning, NY: Corning Museum of Glass, 1959: no. 2. Günther Feuerstein, *Vienna—Present and Past: Arts and Crafts—Applied Art—Design*, Vienna: Jugend und Volk, 1976:68,81. Abby Rand, 'The Lights of Lobmeyr,' *Town and Country*, Dec. 1981:266–67,331–34. Cat., Kathryn B. Hiesinger and George H. Marcus III (eds.), *Design Since 1945*, Philadelphia: Philadelphia Museum of Art, 1983:228,II–51.

Rathbone, R. Llewellyn (1864–1939)

▶ British designer and metalworker.
▶ Rathbone was a cousin of Della Robbia pottery head Harold Rathbone and related to W.A.S. Benson. He produced metal fittings and utensils for projects of A.H. Mackmurdo, Heywood Sumner, and C.F.A. Voysey. Active in a workshop in Liverpool, he taught metalworking at the University there c1898–1903. He became head of the Art School of the Sir John Cass Technical Institute, London, taught at the Central School of Arts and Crafts, designed metalwork simpler than in his Liverpool days, and produced some jewelry. He published the books *Simple Jewellery* (1910) and *Unit Jewellery* (1920).
▶ Isabelle Anscombe and Charlotte Gere, *Arts and Crafts in Britain and America*, New York: Rizzoli, 1978:118.

Ratia, Armi (1912–79)

▶ Finnish textile designer.
▶ 1935, studied textile design, Taideteollisuuskeskuskoulu, Helsinki.
▶ She set up a weaving shop in Vyborg, where she designed and produced *rya* rugs until 1939. In 1949, she began working at her husband's company Printex, a producer of oilcloth, which she adapted to the production of silkscreen printing by hand on cotton sheeting. Maija Isola, Vuokko Eskolin, and other designers encouraged Ratia to reproduce their patterns on fabric. She made dresses in the fabrics she produced, first shown in 1951 under the name *Marimekko* ('Mary's frock'). Marimekko later became the name of the entire organization. Small at first, the prints became larger. Primarily in the work of Isola, the designs developed into more intricate abstract patterns with bird and flower motifs being added to the line. In the 1960s and 1970s, Marimekko's products

included jersey, wool, and cotton fabrics, paper products, laminated plastics, and table coverings, successful in northern Europe and the USA. The firm's goods are sold today through franchise shops.
▶ David Davies, 'Fabrics by Marimekko,' *Design*, No. 236, Aug. 1968:28–31. 'The Finn-Tactics,' *Sphere*, March 1975. Ristomatti Ratia, 'The Legacy of Armi Ratia,' *Form Function Finland*, Nos. 1–2, 1980:10–11. Cat., David Revere McFadden (ed.), *Scandinavian Modern Design 1880–1980*, New York: Abrams, 1982:270, No. 210. Cat., Kathryn B. Hiesinger and George H. Marcus III (eds.), *Design Since 1945*, Philadelphia: Philadelphia Museum of Art, 1983:228,VII–51.

Rationalism
▶ Italian architecture and design movement.
▶ Rationalism was an interpretation of European Functionalism known in Italy as MIAR (Movimento Italiano per l'Architettura Razionale). Rationalism was launched France at the turn of the century and in Italy in 1926 with the publication of the four-part manifesto of Gruppo Sette (Group of Seven), formed in Milan by Gino Figini, Guido Frette, Sebastiano Larco, Adalberto Libera, Gino Pollini, Carlo Enrico Rava, and Giuseppe Terragni. They condemned Futurism for its violent ideas and rigid rejection of the past. Their efforts fostered a new architecture based on logic and a distinct strand within the European Modern movement. Constructivists were closer to Functionalists; Rationalists were more romantic, attempting to bring novelty to every project. The positions of the Rationalists and the Traditionalists appeared to be identical, although the two groups argued fruitlessly about technical and formal questions. A proclamation was made at 1928 (I) 'Esposizione Italiana di Architettura Razionale' in Rome, stating, 'We Italians who devote our entire energy to this Movement feel that this is our architecture because the constructive power is our Roman heritage. And Roman architecture was profoundly rational, purposeful, and efficient.' Prolonged and bitter arguments followed with the 1931 (II) 'Esposizione Italiana di Architettura Razionale,' sponsored by the Italian Movement for Modern Architecture. Some examples of Rational architecture appeared in Italy; the earliest included the 1928 apartment house in Como by Giuseppe Terragni and the 1929 Gualino office block in Turin; exhibition buildings at the 1928 'Esposizione di Torino,' both by Giuseppe Pagano and Gino Levi-Montalcini; and drawings and models by Gruppo Sette in Monza and Stuttgart in 1927. In 1933, a group of architects published their comprehensive, nine-point 'Architectural Programme' in the first issue of the new review *Quadrante*. Signed by Piero Bottoni, Cereghini, Luigi Figini, Guido Frette, Enrico Griffini, Pietro Lingeri, Gino Pollini, Gian Luigi Banfi, Ludovico Belgiojoso, Enrico Peressutti, and Ernesto N. Rogers. It affirmed 'Classicism and Mediterraneanism—to be understood as an attitude of mind and not as a mere adoption of forms or as folklore—in contrast to Nordism, Baroquism, or the romantic arbitrariness of some modern European architecture.' The Movement was significantly represented by Terragni's 1936 House of Fascism in Como, Sant'Elia's kindergarten in Como, and the 1935 Corso Sempione. The House of Fascism revealed an essentially intellectual quality and represented the perfection of an architectural idea; Terragni's furniture was a part of the *Gesamtkunstwerk*. The second personality of Italian Rationalism was Giuseppe Pagano, who played a significant part as the theoretician of Rationalism through his writings in *Casabella* 1930–43. Pagano designed the 1932 Institute of Physics (part of the University Precinct in Rome designed by Massimo Piacentini) and the 1938–41 Bocconi University in Milan, with Predaval. The year 1933 was important in the movement's history because of the competitions for the railway station in Florence and the Palazzo del Littorio at the 1932 'Mostra della Rivoluzione Fascista' in the via dell'Impero in Rome. Luigi Figini and Gino Pollini continued the Rationalist tradition after the deaths of Pagano and Terragni in 1943. Figini and Pollini became known at the 1933 (V) Triennale di Milano for their design of an artist's studio and built the Olivetti

industrial park at Ivrea from 1957. At the end of World War II, the enormous problem of reconstruction created an urgent need for standardization and prefabrication. The Rationalists were completely unprepared for the situation, and the building community was confronted with unsuitable structures for industry and a shortage of skilled labor. Reconstruction proceeded by conventional means and without a clearly defined program. Not until the late 1950s was Italian architecture and design on its feet again.
▶ Alberto Galardi, *New Italian Architecture*, New York: Praeger, 1967:12–18. Vittorio Magnago Lampugnani, *Encyclopedia of 20th-Century Architecture*, New York: Abrams, 1986. Richard A. Etlin, *Modernism in Italian Architecture 1890–1940*, Cambridge: MIT, 1991.

Rault, Louis   (1847–1903)
▶ French sculptor, engraver, silversmith, and jewelry designer; active Paris.
▶ 1868–75, Rault worked in the Boucheron workshop on the place Vendôme in Paris. At the end of the century, he set up his own workshop where he produced silver and jewelry in the Art Nouveau style.
▶ Charlotte Gere, *American and European Jewelry 1830–1914*, New York: Crown, 1975:149.

Ravage
▶ French design studio; located Paris.
▶ In 1990, Dutch designers Van Guens and Clemens Rameckers opened the Ravage design studio in Paris. They produced handmade furniture, ceramics, blankets, bed linens, fabrics, and rugs. Rameckers and Guens were previously fashion designers.
▶ Their work was the subject of a 1990 exhibition at Galerie Néotù in New York.

Ravilious, Eric William   (1903–42)
▶ British wood engraver, watercolorist, and ceramics decorator.
▶ 1919–22, studied Eastbourne School of Art and, 1922–25, Royal College of Art, London, under Paul Nash and others.
▶ 1929–39, he taught at the Royal College of Art. His primary activity was the execution of wood engravings for book illustrations. His work appeared in books including *The Elm Angel* (1930) by Walter de la Mare, *Twelfth Night* (1932) by William Shakespeare, *The Kynoch Press Notebook and Diary* (1933), and *The Natural History of Selborne* (1937) by Gilbert White. Influenced by the work of Paul Nash, Ravilious executed printers' ornaments for the Curwen, Golden Cockrel, and Nonesuch presses, decorations for the BBC and London Transport Board publications, advertisements for Austin Reed, and book jackets for the publisher Duckworth. Ravilious, Edward Bawden, and Cyril Mahoney collaborated on the 1928–29 refreshment room mural decorations at Morley College and designed the British pavilion wall decoration at the 1937 Paris 'Exposition Internationale des Arts et Techniques dans la Vie Moderne.' In 1936, he designed a suite of Regency revival furniture for Cecilia Dunbar Kilburn's shop Dunbar Hay in London. In 1935, he received his first commission from Wedgwood; his transfer-printed bucolic vignettes were overpainted in enamel colors on standard ceramic blanks. In 1935, he designed glassware for Stuart Crystal in Stourbridge. In the late 1930s, he became increasingly occupied with watercolor painting. In 1938, he began to pursue color lithography, inaugurated by his illustrations for *High Street* (1938). In 1940, he was appointed an official war artist.
▶ *Eric Ravilious 1903–1942*, Colchester: The Minories, 1972. Cat., *Thirties: British art and design before the war*, London: Arts Council of Great Britain, Hayward Gallery, 1979:43,80,82,83,85, 93,129,151,156,164,165,176,178,299.

Ray, Michael
See Mathieu, Paul

Read, Alfred Burgess   (1899–1973)
▶ British industrial and lighting designer.
▶ 1919–23, studied metalwork, Royal College of Art, London.

▶ In 1923, he worked at the Clement Dane Advertising Studio in London. 1924–35, he worked at French lighting firm Bagnès and subsequently visited Walter Gropius at the Bauhaus in Germany. In 1925, Read became consultant designer and director of Troughton and Young, where he produced pioneering lighting designs after World War II, including fluorescent industrial lighting. Working with architects of the 1920s and 1930s Modern movement, he was instrumental in altering the character of interior lighting. He gave the talk 'Design in Daily Life' on BBC radio before the opening of the 1933 London 'British Industrial Art in Relation to the Home' exhibition at Dorland Hall. His lighting commissions included the 1932 house at Yaffle Hill, Broadstone, Dorset, for Cyril Carter (Edward Maufe, architect). Read was a member of the Society of Industrial Artists. During the 1950s, he was retained as a designer for the ceramics manufacturer Carter in Poole. In 1957, he returned to Troughton and Young.

▶ In 1940, elected Royal Designer for Industry.

▶ Michael Farr, *Design in British Industry: A Mid-Century Survey*, London: Cambridge, 1955:247. Cat., *Thirties: British art and design before the war*, London: Arts Council of Great Britain, Hayward Gallery, 1979:231,233,299. Fiona MacCarthy and Patrick Nuttgens, *Eye for Industry*, London: Lund Humphries, 1986.

Read, Herbert Edward (1893–1968)

▶ British poet, art critic, writer, and historian; born Leeds.

▶ His early poetry collections *Songs of Chaos* (1915) and *Night Warriors* (1919) showed influences of Imagism, the literary movement associated with Ezra Pound. His subsequent works included *The End of the War* (1933). From the 1930s, Read, a friend of T.S. Eliot, became influential in British literary and critical circles. Critical works included *The True Voice in Feeling* (1953) and *Essays in Literary Criticism* (1969). A prolific writer and lecturer, Read helped promote Modernism in Britain in the 1930s. His book *Art and Industry* (1934) in support of the ideas of Walter Gropius and the Bauhaus was influential. He published numerous books on art and aesthetics, including *Art and Society* (1936) and *Education Through Art* (1943), and was supportive of new artistic movements.

▶ T. Duddensieg and H. Rogge, *Industrie-Kultur, Peter Behrens und die AEG, 1907–1914*, Berlin: Mann, 1979. Penny Sparke, *Introduction to Design and Culture in the Twentieth Century*, London: Allen and Unwin, 1986. James King, *The Last Modern: Herbert Read*, London: Weidenfeld and Nicolson, 1990.

Reale Bianca, Bichy

▶ Italian interior and furniture designer; active Vicenza.

▶ In 1967, Reale and Giorgio Manzali set up the studio Bichy in Vicenza, collaborating in interior and furniture design. They were active as architects and interior architects on residences and other structures, including the palazzo Zileri. Reale designed the *Saffo* seating for Art & Form, a furniture range for Amar Collezioni, and Junior Mobili's line. Reale was a member of ADI (Associazione per il Disegno Industriale).

▶ *ADI Annual 1976*, Milan: Associazione per il Disegno Industriale, 1976.

Rebajes, Frank (1907–90)

▶ Dominican craftsperson, designer, artist, and entrepreneur; born Puerto Plata; active New York.

▶ Studied in Barcelona.

▶ He settled in New York in 1922. He produced a collection of animal figures from tin cans, borrowing tools from an engineer friend. In 1932, his animal collection was purchased by Juliana Force, director of the Whitney Museum of American Art; his work was written about by Alden T. Jewel, art critic of *The New York Times*. From the early 1930s in a small workshop on Fourth Street in Greenwich Village, he designed and manufactured costume jewelry and other objects of copper and silver in strong designs with some figuration. He established the crafts firm Rebajes Fifth Avenue in 1942 and Rebajes Craftsmen at 20 West 17th Street with staff in Los Angeles and Chicago. He became internationally known for his cufflinks in coiled wire, African-derived motifs, and simple geometry. In 1960, he moved to Spain and began studying geometry and mysticism.

▶ He exhibited first at the First Washington Square Outdoor Art Exhibition in Greenwich Village, New York. His work was included in the 1937 'Silver, An Exhibition of Contemporary American Design by Manufacturers, Designers and Craftsmen' at New York Metropolitan Museum of Art; 1937 Paris 'Exposition Internationale des Arts et Techniques dans la Vie Moderne,' winning a bronze medal; and 1939 'New York World's Fair,' winning a diploma and gold medal. He was elected a fellow of the Royal Society of Arts, London.

▶ Deanna F. Cera (ed.), *Jewels of Fantasy: Costume Jewelry of the 20th Century*, New York: Abrams, 1992. Matthew L. Burkholz and Linda Lichtenberg Kaplan, *Copper Art Jewelry: A Different Lustre*, West Chester, Pennsylvania: Schiffer, 1992.

Reboldi, Arturo (1958–)

▶ Italian designer.

▶ Studied Accademia di Belle Arti di Brera, Milan, to 1980.

▶ From 1983, he was associated with Studio Alchimia, becoming an associate member.

▶ Fumio Shimizu and Matteo Thun (eds.), *The Descendants of Leonardo: The Italian Design*, Tokyo, 1987:322.

Reboli, Giorgio (1942–)

▶ Italian industrial designer; born and active Milan.

▶ He began his professional career in 1957. He designed trailers and mobile homes for Elnagh, motor homes for Bora, lighting for Candle, and motor boats for Cantieri Sciallino. He was a consultant on building prefabrication systems. His buildings included those for civil and tourist functions; he was also active in interior architecture. He was editor of magazines *Milanocasa* and *Sinaat Italia*. He was a member of ADI (Associazione per il Disegno Industriale).

▶ *ADI Annual 1976*, Milan: Associazione per il Disegno Industriale, 1976.

Reed and Barton

▶ American silversmiths; located Taunton, Massachusetts.

▶ Reed and Barton was founded in 1824; in 1889, began producing flatware and hollow-ware in sterling silver; in 1924, took over the firm Theodore B. Starr of New York; produced Robert Venturi's 1989 silver serving pieces.

▶ Annelies Krekel-Aalberse, *Art Nouveau and Art Déco Silver*, New York: Abrams, 1989:258.

Reeves, Ruth (1892–1966)

▶ American textile designer; active New York.

▶ 1910–11, studied Pratt Institute in Brooklyn, New York; 1911–13, California School of Design, San Francisco; Art Students' League, New York; 1922–28, Académie Moderne, Paris, under Fernand Léger.

▶ She became well known for her handblocked textile, wallpaper, and rug designs that showed strong Cubist influence. From 1930, she was design consultant to W. and J. Slone's furniture store in New York; it produced her 1930 *Manhattan* wallpaper. In 1931, she departed from realistic images in favor of abstract forms and pure textile patterns; was a member of Designer's Gallery from 1929 and American Union of Decorative Artists and Craftsmen 1930–33. She created textiles for the 1932–33 Radio City Music Hall, including the *History of the Theater* fabric covering the rear wall and balcony fascia. In 1934, received Carnegie Traveling Fellowship to Guatemala; in 1936, was appointed national coordinator of the Index of American Design; in 1940, received Guggenheim Fellowship; in 1956, received Fulbright Fellowship to study in India; from 1955–56, documented craft traditions as Advisor in Handicrafts to the Registrar General of India.

▶ Work shown at 1930 'Decorative Metalwork and Cotton Textiles, Third International Exhibition of Contemporary Industrial Art,' New York Metropolitan Museum of Art. Her work was the subject of the 1932 exhibition of her paintings, drawings, and textile designs at the Art Center, New York. In 1935, fabrics shown in Mezzanine Gallery, RCA Building, New York.

▶ Harry V. Anderson, 'Contemporary American Designers,' *Decorators' Digest*, March 1935:42–45,59,68,74,80,82,90. Karen Davies, *At Home in Manhattan: Modern Decorative Arts, 1925 to the Depression*, New Haven: Yale, 1983:54. Jonathan M. Woodham, *Twentieth-Century Ornament*, New York: Rizzoli, 1990: 61,64,178. Whitney Blausen, 'Ruth Reeves' in Mel Byars and Russell Flinchum (eds.), *50 American Designers*, Washington: Preservation, 1994.

Regenspurg, W. Piet (1894–1966)

▶ Dutch silversmith; active Enschede.

▶ Studied Akademie voor Beeldende Kunst, The Hague, under Frans Zwollo Sr.

▶ He founded his own workshop in 1922 in Enschede. Strongly influenced by Zwollo, his work was unoriginal though soundly crafted.

▶ Annelies Krekel-Aalberse, *Art Nouveau and Art Déco Silver*, New York: Abrams, 1989:175,258.

Regondi, Gabriele (1949–)

▶ Italian designer and entrepreneur; active Bovisio.

▶ Studied architecture, Politecnico di Milano.

▶ He taught design at the art school in Monza; in 1975, began working as a freelance designer; from 1978, was active as an independent designer of furniture and furnishings.

▶ Fumio Shimizu and Matteo Thun (eds.), *The Descendants of Leonardo: The Italian Design*, Tokyo, 1987:328.

Regout
See De Sphinx and Kristalunie

Rehm, Wilhelmine (1899–1967)

▶ American ceramicist and glassware designer; active Cincinnati.

▶ Studied Smith College, Northampton, Massachusetts, University of Cincinnati, and Cincinnati Art Academy.

▶ 1927–35, she worked at the Rookwood Pottery in Cincinnati, where she painted others' precast pieces and modeled. 1935–43, she taught and worked as a glassware designer.

▶ Virginia Raymond Cummins, *Rookwood Pottery Potpourri*, Silver Spring, Md.: Cliff R. Leonard and Duke Coleman, 1980:69. Karen Davies, *At Home in Manhattan: Modern Decorative Arts, 1925 to the Depression*, New Haven: Yale, 1983:56

Reich, Lilly (1885–1947)

▶ German interior architect and furniture and exhibition designer; born Berlin.

▶ One of her earliest designs was a rustic metal milk pitcher of c1908. From 1908, Reich worked at the Wiener Werkstätte under Josef Hoffmann. In 1911, she returned to Berlin, where she associated with Anna and Hermann Muthesius and collaborated with Else Oppler-Legband. In 1912, she became a member of the Deutscher Werkbund; in 1920, she became the first woman member of its board of directors. In 1920, she joined the Freie Gruppe für Farbkunst des DWB. She worked for the Atelier für Innenraumgestaltung, Dekorationskunst und Mode (Studio for the Interior Design, Decoration and Fashion) in Berlin until 1924. 1924–26, she worked at the Atelier für Ausstellungsgestaltung und Mode (Studio for Exhibition Design and Fashion) in Frankfurt. Her professional relationship with Mies van der Rohe began with the 1927 'Weissenhof-Siedlung' exhibition; they selected the exhibitors and designed the stands. The glass section had floors in black-and-white linoleum and walls of etched, clear and gray opaque glass, with chairs covered in white chamois and black cowhide and the bench table in rosewood. At the 1927 Berlin 'Mode der Dame' exhibition she showed her expertise with textiles, and she and Mies designed its silk exhibit, at which Mies showed his tubular steel furniture. The silk and velvet fabrics were hung from chromium-plated steel frames, forming black, orange, and red velvet screens that contrasted with gold, silver, black, and lemon-yellow silk ones. In the German section at the 1929

Barcelona exhibition, she was in charge of all the industrial exhibits and designed the stands. The graphics and furniture were designed by Mies. When Mies became head of the Bauhaus in Dessau in 1930, she was already a respected interior designer. Joining the Bauhaus in 1932, she taught in the construction and weaving workshops, subsequently becoming head of the weaving and interior design workshops. Mies took sole credit for their 1930 chaise-couch; the piece may have been from Reich's hand alone. A copy was purchased in 1930 by Philip Johnson for his house in New York; the purchase included Reich's 1930 wood and steel bookcases and 1930 writing table. When the chaise-couch was originally shown at the 1931 Berlin 'Deutsche Bauausstellung' (German Building Exhibition), the tension of the rubber stretched over the frame caused the piece to collapse. It was put into production in the early 1960s by Knoll. Though Mies and Reich officially shared directorship of the 'Deutsche Bauausstellung,' she produced most of the work and showed her own model house along with Mies's. In 1932, Reich moved with the Bauhaus to Berlin-Steglitz but was dismissed by a city official. She designed interiors and some of the furniture for the 1936 apartment of Dr. Facius in Berlin-Dahlem, 1938 furniture for the children's room of the Wolf residence in Guben, 1939 furniture for the Crous residence in Berlin-Südende, and 1939 interior for Dr. Schäppi apartment in Berlin. In 1939, she traveled to Chicago to join Mies, who had settled there in 1937, but returned to Berlin to handle a long-running suit against the molding firm Mauser over her and Mies's furniture designs. During the war, she designed the 1938–40 renovation for the P.A. Büren residence in Berlin-Wannsee and 1942 furniture and the interior for Jürgen Reich's quarters in her house. In 1943, her studio in Genthiner Strasse was destroyed by bombs; she took up temporary residence near Zittau; she was drafted into the Organisation Todt, a forced-labour civil engineering body. From 1945, she worked at the Atelier für Architektur, Design, Textilien und Mode (Studio for Architecture, Design, Textiles, and Fashion) in Berlin. 1945–46, she taught interior design and elementary building construction at the Hochschule für Bildende Künste in Berlin.

▶ She designed interiors at the 1932 'The International Style: Architecture Since 1922' exhibition at the New York Museum of Modern Art, and the German 'Textilindustrie' stand at the 1937 Paris 'Exposition Internationale des Arts et Techniques dans la Vie Moderne.'

▶ Lilly Reich, 'Modefragen,' *Die Form—Monatsschrift für gestaltende Arbeit*, 1922. James Gowan, 'Reflections on the Mies Centennial,' *Architectural Design 56*, March 1956:6. *Mies van der Rohe: European Works*, London: Academy, 1986:48–54. Stephen Calloway, *Twentieth-Century Decoration*, New York: Rizzoli, 1988: 158–59. Cat., *The Bauhaus: Masters and Students*, New York: Barry Friedman, 1988. Sonja Günther, *Lilly Reich 1885–1947, Innenarchitektin, Designerin, Ausstellungsgestalterin*, Stuttgart: Deutsche Verlags-Anstalt, 1988. Otakar Máčel, 'Avant-garde Design and the Law: Litigation over the Cantilever Chair,' *Journal of Design History*, Vol. 3, Nos. 2 and 3, 1990:125–43.

Reichardt, Grete (1907–1984)

▶ German textile designer; born Erfurt.

▶ 1926–31, studied fabric design, Bauhaus, Dessau.

▶ She founded her own handweaving firm in 1934; 1952–77, was a member of the Verband bildender Künstler Deutschlands.

▶ Received a gold medal at the 1940 (VII) Triennale di Milano.

▶ Lionel Richard, *Encyclopédie du Bauhaus*, Paris: Somogy, 1985: 206. Cat., Gunta Stölzl, *Weberei am Bauhaus und ams eigener Werkstatt*, Berlin: Bauhaus-Archiv, 1987:163–64. Cat., *The Bauhaus: Masters and Students*, New York: Barry Friedman, 1988.

Reijmyre Glasbruk

▶ Swedish glass factory.

▶ The factory was established in 1810 at Reijmyra, Östergötland, to produce glassware; by 1900, it had become one of Sweden's leading glass manufacturers of pressed and engraved decorative tablewares; from 1900, produced glass in Art Nouveau styles by

A.E. Boman and Alf Wallander, who were both hired in 1908; in 1930, installed new machinery for pressed glass manufacture; in 1937, hired Monica Bratt as artistic director, who designed colored glassware; after World War II, hired designers including Tom Möller; in 1977, was purchased by Upsala-Ekeby.
▶ Jennifer Hawkins Opie, *Scandinavia: Ceramics and Glass in the Twentieth Century*, New York: Rizzoli, 1989.

Reimann, Albert (1874–1971)

▶ German metalworker and teacher; active Berlin and London.
▶ Stimulated by the British Arts and Crafts movement, Albert and wife Klara Reiman founded the Schülerwerkstätten für Kleinplastik (School for Small Sculpture) in Berlin in 1902. Reiman, a talented craftsperson, produced prototypes for bronze, copper, silver, gold, and pottery production. In 1912, the school expanded into 23 departments, each with its own specialist teacher. Each student took perspective drawing, shadow construction, anatomy, art and costume history, color theory, and tailoring. The original roll of 14 students grew to 500 in 1914. From 1912, the Reimann School was connected with the Höhere Fachschule für Dekorationskunst (Advanced College of the Decorative Arts), an institution set up by the Deutscher Werkbund to educate window decorators in cooperation with the Deutsche Verband für das kaufmännische Unterrichtswesen (German Association for Commercial Education), and the Verband Berliner Spezialgeschäfte (Berlin Association of Specialty Shops). From 1913, the Reimann School was associated with the Kunst- und Kunstgewerbeschule, the only private institution of its kind recognized by the state government. Courses included boutique techniques, ivory carving, painting, clothing design, architecture, spatial arts, and set, packaging, and poster design. Reimann was the only teacher at first. In 1905, he was joined by Karl Heubler, who headed the metalworking studio. Instruction was supervised by a committee that included Hermann Muthesius, Peter Behrens, and Theo Schmuz-Baudiss. By 1927, there were 30 teachers, including Max Hertwig, who taught typography and graphic design, and painters Moriz Melzer and Georg Tappert. Later, the staff included Hans Baluschek and Paul Scheurich. The poster design department was headed by Julius Klinger. In 1916, the first issue of school magazine *Mitteilungen der Schule Reimann* was published; 1920–34, it was called *Farbe und Form*. Heubler's students were encouraged to work independently and in their own personal style. Their work was shown at the 'Grosse Berliner Kunstausstellung' in 1906 at the Kunstgewerbeschule in Berlin, in 1906 in the zoological gardens, in 1908 in their own building, in 1909 in the Kunstgewerbe Museum, and at the 1914 'Deutscher Werkbund-Ausstellung,' where the students decorated a row of shops. The last major exhibition of their work was in 1920 in Schönenberg. The school offered professional training on a par with the Kunstgewerbeschule in Vienna and, in the 1920s, had up to 1,000 students, many from abroad. After 1922, numerous accomplished artists from the Bauhaus were able to continue at the Reimann School. From 1933, Reimann himself produced table-top accessory designs for Chase Copper and Brass, Waterbury, Connecticut, including copper and silver candlesticks and vessels in the Vienna Secession style. In 1935, when the Nazis introduced the antisemitic Nuremberg Laws, Reimann, a Jew, was forced to sell the school to architect Hugo Häring. Reimann settled in London, where he set up a new Reimann School in 1936. In 1936, the Berlin school was renamed the Kunst und Werk-Privatschule für Gestaltung; it was destroyed by bombs in 1943. Reimann's school in London was also bombed.
▶ *Magazine of Art*, Vol. 26, 1902:65–77. A. Reimann, *Kleinplastik; nach originalent wurfen und modellen von bildhauer*, Berlin, p. 40. Albert Reimann, *Farbe und Form*, special issue, 1927:15ff. H. Duve, 'Meisterleistungen aus der Reimann-Schule,' *Die Schaulade* No. 6, 1930:351,364,372,373. *Kunst der 20er und 30er Jahre*, Berlin: Sammlung Bröhan, 1985:463–66. Tilmann Buddensieg (ed.), *Berlin 1900–1933, Architecture and Design*, New York: Cooper–Hewitt Museum and Gebrüder Mann, 1987:110,112. Annelies Krekel-Aalberse, *Art Nouveau and Art Déco Silver*,

Abrams, 1989:144. Cat., *Metallkunst*, Berlin: Bröhan-Museum, 1990:415–18.

Reindl, Hilde (aka Hilde Cieluszek 1909–)

▶ German textile designer.
▶ 1929–31, studied Bauhaus.
▶ In 1931, she designed textiles for Tuchfabrik Meschke, Rummelsberg; 1932–34, instructed weaving teachers; and, from 1955, was active in her own fashion shop in Munich.
▶ Cat., *The Bauhaus: Masters and Students*, New York: Barry Friedman, 1988. Cat., Gunta Stölzl, *Weberei am Bauhaus und ams eigener Werkstatt*, Berlin: Bauhaus-Archiv, 1987:147.

Reiss, Winold (1886–1953)

▶ German artist and designer.
▶ In the early 1920s, Reiss decorated Alamac Hotel's Medieval Grill and Congo Room, New York; in 1920, pioneered an American interior design motif for Crillon Restaurant, New York; 1927 Crillon Restaurant at a new address; in 1928, became a member of American Designers' Gallery, participating in its 1928 exhibition; in 1930, became a member of the American Union of Decorative Artists and Craftsmen, participating in its 1930 and 1931 exhibitions. He designed the exotic 31ft (9.5m) high ballroom of the 1930 addition to St. George Hotel (Emery Roth, addition architect), Brooklyn; 1930–31 Café Bonaparte, Beaux-Arts Apartments, New York; from 1935, a series of Longchamps Restaurants including interior design and decoration (with Albert Charles Schweizer) of its 1938 restaurant (Ely Jacques Kahn, architect), Empire State Building; was an accomplished mosaicist, illustrated by the panaroma at the 1931 Cincinnati Railroad Station (Fellheimer and Wagner, architects).
▶ Robert A.M. Stern et al., *New York 1930*, New York: Rizzoli, 1987:215,277,283–87,338,398. Jonathan M. Woodham, *Twentieth-Century Ornament*, New York: Rizzoli, 1990:145. Mel Byars (intro.), 'What Makes American Design American?' in R.L. Leonard and C.A. Glassgold (eds.), *Modern American Design, by the American Union of Decorative Artists and Craftsmen*, New York: Acanthus Press, 1930, reprinted 1992.

Relling, Ingmar (1920–)

▶ Norwegian furniture and interior designer.
▶ Studied Statens Håndverks -og Kunstindustriskole, Oslo.
▶ He is best known for his 1965 *Siesta* lounge chair and ottoman, and other designs produced by Vestlandske Møbelfabrikk in Ørsta.
▶ His *Siesta* chair and ottoman were shown at the 1980 'Scandinavian Modern Design 1880–1980' exhibition at the Cooper-Hewitt Museum in New York.
▶ Cat., David Revere McFadden (ed.), *Scandinavian Modern Design 1880–1980*, New York: Abrams, 1982:270, No. 264. Fredrik Wildhagen, *Norge i Form*, Oslo: Sternersen, 1988:168.

Renaudot, Lucie (?–1939)

▶ French decorator and furniture designer; born Valenciennes.
▶ She became active in 1918 as a decorator in Paris. Her first commissions were the tearooms Tipperary and Ça Ira. Some of Renaudot's furniture was produced by Maurice Rinck. All of P.A. Dumas's furniture production was designed by her. Some of her models were produced in limited editions. She designed for the 1935 oceanliner *Normandie* and executed a number of assignments in Paris and the provinces, particularly Alsace.
▶ Her work was first shown at the 1919 event of Salon d'Automne. Her rooms in a country house and for a young girl were installed at the 1920 Salon d'Automne. She participated in the 1925 Paris 'Exposition Internationale des Arts Décoratifs et Industriels Modernes,' 1927 competition (a woman's office) of the Union Centrale des Arts Décoratifs, Salons of the Société des Artistes Décorateurs, and 1937 Paris 'Exposition Internationale des Arts et Techniques dans la Vie Moderne' (collaboration of a child's room in 'Une ambassade française'). A retrospective of her work was organized by the Société des Artistes Décorateurs.
▶ *Ensembles Mobiliers*, Vol. II, Paris: Charles Moreau, 1937. Léon Deshairs, *Modern French Decorative Art*, Paris: Albert Lévy. Pierre

Kjellberg, *Art Déco: les maîtres du Mobilier, le décor des Paquebots*, Paris: Amateur, 1986:151–52.

Renk, Alain
See Naço, Studio

Renko, Sandi (1949–)
▶ Italian designer; born Trieste; active Padua.
▶ Renko started in 1972 as a designer of furniture and tabletop accessories. Clients included Lenzi, MAM, Bonaldo, Longato Arredamenti, and Tre Effe. Renko was a member of ADI (Associazione per il Disegno Industriale).
▶ *ADI Annual 1976*, Milan: Associazione per il Disegno Industriale, 1976.

Renoir of California
See Fels, Jerry

Renou, André (1912–80)
▶ French sculptor and furniture designer.
▶ 1923, studied École Boulle, Paris, under Louis Sognot.
▶ He joined La Crémaillère in 1930 and, in 1941, became president and director general. Jean-Pierre Génisset joined the firm in 1933; they collaborated until 1965 and were among the first to produce Modern knick-knacks. In 1941, Renou became a member of UAM (Union des Artistes Modernes); 1954–57, was chair, Société des Artistes Décorateurs.
▶ Work (with Génisset) shown at 1937 Paris 'Exposition Internationale des Arts et Techniques dans la Vie Moderne' and 1958 'Exposition Universelle et Internationale de Bruxelles (Expo '58),' receiving a gold medal.

Renouvin, Georges
▶ French decorator and furniture designer.
▶ From the 1930s, he designed furniture in exotic woods in a style reminiscent of Louis XVI and French Restauration styles. His commissions included government and corporate offices and residences.
▶ Léon Deshairs, *Modern French Decorative Art*, Paris: Albert Lévy. Pierre Kjellberg, *Art Déco: les maîtres du Mobilier, le décor des Paquebots*, Paris: Amateur, 1986:152.

Renwick, William Crosby (1914–92)
▶ American industrial designer.
▶ Studied architecture, Princeton University, to 1940.
▶ 1946–51, he was product designer at Raymond Loewy Associates; 1951–57, vice-president product design at George Nelson, where he designed the *Bubble Lamp* of c1953 for the Howard Miller Clocks, still in production by a different firm; 1957–63, was president, Renwick Thomson and Gove, industrial designers; 1963–66, design director, Dow Corning; 1966–82, design director, Brunswick; 1962–63, he was president of the American Society of Industrial Designers.
▶ 'Design Heads and Tales,' *Innovation*, Winter 1993.

Reumert, Jane (1942–)
▶ Danish ceramicist.
▶ Studied Kunsthåndværkerskolen, Copenhagen.
▶ In 1964, Reumert, Beate Andersen, and Gunhild Åberg set up the workshop Strandstraede Keramik in Copenhagen. Her ceramics were mold cast and individually glazed. Reumert designed for Dansk Designs and the Kosta Boda glassworks.
▶ Her work was the subject of one-person exhibitions, including at Den Permanente in Copenhagen in 1970 and Röhsska Konstslöjdmuseet in Gothenburg in 1977.
▶ Her work was included in the 1971 'Kunst und Kunsthandwerk aus Dänemark' in Wiesbaden, 1974 'Exempla' in Munich, 1975 exhibition at the Hälsingborg Stadsmuseum, and 1981 'Danish Ceramic Design' at Pennsylvania State University.
▶ Cat., David Revere McFadden (ed.), *Scandinavian Modern Design 1880–1980*, New York: Abrams, 1982:270, No. 283.

Revere Copper and Brass
▶ American metalware manufacturer; located Clinton, Illinois, and Rome, New York.
▶ One of its finest designs was Peter Müller-Munk's 1935 chromium-plated *Normandie* pitcher. From the 1930s, it produced other metalware with high design standards. By 1933, W. Archibald Welden was a consultant designer to Revere, where he designed goods in close association with its technicians. He became head of design and created the 1939 *Revere Ware* range of copper-bottomed cookware in stainless steel. The design resulted from extensive study of use, cleaning, heating, tooling, manufacturing, and consumer preferences. In 1954, he designed its range of cookware with heat-resistant metal instead of plastic handles for the institutional market.
▶ The 1954 cookware was included in the 1983–84 'Design Since 1945' exhibition at the Philadelphia Museum of Art.
▶ Don Wallance, *Shaping America's Products*, New York, 1956:41–45. Cat., Kathryn B. Hiesinger and George H. Marcus III (eds.), *Design Since 1945*, Philadelphia: Philadelphia Museum of Art, 1983:236,V–51.

Revere Pottery
See Paul Revere Pottery

Rezek, Ron (1947–)
▶ American industrial designer and entrepreneur; active Los Angeles.
▶ Studied design.
▶ His mentor was Buckminster Fuller. His work was inspired by Antonio Gaudí, and Frank Gehry's innovative approach to raw materials. In 1978, he set up a lighting company. He designed playful, pragmatic lighting fixtures whose sales and distribution were handled by Artemide from 1986. Rezek's inexpensive *Zink* lamp was crudely plated in zinc to produce a deliberately imperfect finish. By 1989, his extensive lighting range included table lamps, sconces, pendant lamps, torchères, and a ceiling fan.
▶ Donna Sapolin, *Metropolitan Home*, August 1989:32E.

Rhead, Frederick Hurten (1880–1942)
▶ British ceramicist; born Hanley, Staffordshire; active Ohio, Missouri, and California.
▶ Rhead was artistic director of the Wardle Art Pottery in Britain. He settled in Ohio in 1902, working for various artware ceramics factories there, including at Vance/Avon with William P. Jervis. From 1903, his wares appeared in the journal *Keramic Studio*. In 1904, he became a designer at Weller Pottery, then artistic director at Roseville Pottery in Zanesville, Ohio, producing some interesting pieces. In 1909, he worked for Jervis Pottery on Long Island. In 1910, he became an instructor on pottery at the University City Pottery near St. Louis, Missouri, where he was associated with Taxile Doat and Adelaide Robineau. In 1911, he settled in California,where he was hired by Philip King Brown, organizer of the pottery at Arequipa Sanatorium in Marin County, as ceramicist and instructor. Leaving Arequipa in 1913, Rhead set up the Rhead Pottery in Santa Barbara, California, producing landscape abstractions with fluid incised lines that reflected the California topography. 1916–17, he published four issues of the magazine *Potter*. He was the most prominent and most productive potter in California at this time. He was known for his squeeze-bag technique for outlining slip and glaze infills. He experimented with over 11,000 formulas for Chinese mirror-black glaze. In 1917, he closed his pottery, calling his work 'a monstrosity.' 1917–27, he became research director of American Encaustic Tiling of Zanesville, Ohio. From 1927, he was artistic director of Homer Laughlin China, where he was responsible for the design of *Fiesta* ware in 1935. He introduced the concept of mixing and matching solid color pieces in one service. In 1920, he organized the art section of the American Ceramic Society and, 1920–25, served as chair of the organization. He was chair of the United States Pottery Association.

▶ Introduced *Fiesta* ware at the 1936 Pittsburgh 'Pottery and Glass Fair.' He won a gold medal at the 1915 San Francisco 'Panama-Pacific International Exposition' and the 1934 Charles F. Binns Medal of the American Ceramic Society. His work was the subject of the 1986 'Frederick Hurten Rhead: An English Potter in America' exhibition at the Erie Art Museum in Erie, Pennsylvania.
▶ Paul Evans in Timothy J. Andersen et al., *California Design 1910*, Salt Lake City: Peregrine Smith, 1980:66,67,72,73,76,77. Cat., Sharon Dale, *Frederick Hurten Rhead: An English Potter in America*, Erie, Pennsylvania: Erie Art Museum, 1986. Garth Clark, *American Ceramics: 1876 to the Present*, New York: Abbeville, 1987:293 et passim.
▶ See Rhead Pottery

Rhead Pottery
▶ American ceramics factory; located Santa Barbara, California.
▶ In 1913, Frederick H. Rhead established the Rhead Pottery in Santa Barbara, California. He brought the inlaid process he had used extensively at the Roseville Pottery in Zanesville, Ohio, in its *Della Robbia* range that Rhead produced while he was artistic director there 1904–08. At Santa Barbara, he produced practical items, including cream and sugar sets and five-piece garniture sets. The firm closed in 1917.
▶ Paul Evans in Timothy J. Andersen et al., *California Design 1910*, Salt Lake City: Peregrine Smith, 1980.
▶ See Rhead, Frederick Hurten

Rhinn, Eric (1960–)
▶ French industrial designer.
▶ Studied École d'Architecture, Strasbourg, and industrial design, École des Arts Décoratifs, Paris.
▶ In 1988, Eric Rhinn with Luc Jozancy established the industrial design and graphics studio Avant-Première, Paris, with offices in Hong Kong and New York, specializing in educational toys, clocks, and plastic accessories; designed the 1988 aluminum chair produced by Mullca and sponsored by VIA. Before co-founding Avant-Première, was the designer for Usus-Solus.
▶ Work (Avant-Première) shown at 1990 'Les années VIA' at the Paris Musée des Arts Décoratifs. (Avant-Première) received 1986 (I) VIA Appel permanent award (lamp and armchair) and 1989 (II) VIA Appel permanent award (side chair and armchair in aluminum).
▶ *Les Carnets du Design*, Paris: Mad-Cap Productions et APCI, 1986:86. Cat., *Les années VIA*, Paris: Musée des Arts Décoratifs, 1990.

Rhode School of Design
See Metcalf, Helen Adelia Rowe

Riart, Carlos (1944–)
▶ Spanish interior, exhibition, and furniture designer; active Barcelona.
▶ 1967 studied industrial design, Escuela de Diseño Eina, Barcelona.
▶ He and Bigas Luna set up interior design shop Gris, Barcelona, in 1968, where they exhibited and sold radical modern objects. Ending the partnership with Luna, Riart began to make his own furniture. He first produced a knock-down wardrobe that he attempted unsuccessfully to sell from a stall outside the football stadium in Barcelona. He designed and produced the 1976 *Colilla* lighting system (a row of neon lighting inside a translucent tube), which he sold by mail order and Santa & Cole reissued in 1979. In the 1970s and 1980s, he designed chairs, tables, cabinets, lighting, and mirrors for clients including Disform, Snark, Tecno, Écart, and Knoll. In the mid-1980s, Riart with Santiago Roqueta, Oleguer Armengol, and Victor Mesalles designed the Snooker bar, and, with Gabriel Ordeig, the 1985 Si-Si-Si bar, both in Barcelona. His work reflectived historical and 1950s models in an individual Post-Modern approach. His 1973 *Desnuda* side chair was produced from 1979 by Tecno. From the 1980s, he worked exclusively for Muebles Casas, producing limited edition models. His

1982 rocking chair for Knoll was widely published. Riart taught at the Escuela de Diseño Eina.
▶ His 1982 rocking chair won the 1983 IBD Award, 1983 Roscoe Award in the USA, and 1987 AFIFAD Award in Barcelona. His 1973 *Desnuda* side chair was included in the 1983–84 'Design Since 1945' exhibition at the Philadelphia Museum of Art.
▶ 'A Barcelona Workshop,' *Domus*, No. 546, May 1975:28. 'Knoll Presents: Three Diverse Furniture Groups,' *Interior Design*, Vol. 53, Dec. 1982:134–35. Cat., Kathryn B. Hiesinger and George H. Marcus III (eds.), *Design Since 1945*, Philadelphia: Philadelphia Museum of Art, 1983:228,III–73. Guy Julier, *New Spanish Design*, London: Thames and Hudson, 1991.

Ribeiro, André (1953–)
▶ French jewelry designer.
▶ Ribeiro is known for his 1982–88 black rubber bracelets with diamond insets produced by Atelier des Bijoux Contemporains.
▶ Cat., David Revere McFadden, *L'Art de Vivre*, New York: Vendome, 1989.

Richard, Alain (1926–)
▶ French furniture designer; husband of Jacqueline Iribe.
▶ Studied École Nationale Supérieure des Arts Décoratifs, Paris, to 1949.
▶ In the 1950s, he lived in the Netherlands with Henri Salomson (former collaborator of Le Corbusier); in 1952, he set up a research firm to study furniture and was color consultant to clients including architects; was active in various fields including lighting, furniture, and interior decoration; collaborated with designer André Monpoix; in the 1950s, designed furniture produced by Vecchione and by Meubles TV.
▶ Yolande Amic, *Intérieurs: Le Mobilier français, 1945–1964*, Paris: Regard/VIA, 1983:100.

Richard, André (1929–)
▶ Spanish designer and writer.
▶ He began designing simple objects in the family pharmaceutical supply firm. Influenced by Raymond Loewy, whom he met in 1956 having read *Ugly Things Don't Sell*, he became Spain's pioneering industrial designer and wrote three books, *Diseño ¿Por qué? (What's Design for?)* (1982), *Diseño y calidad de vida (Design and the quality of life)* (1985), and *Hablando de diseño* (1987) (*Talking of Design*). In 1957, Richard, Antoni de Moragas and others formed the Instituto de Diseño Industrial de Barcelona, suggested by Gio Ponti. Richard attended the 1959 (I) congress of the International Council of Societies of Industrial Design. In 1960, he was one of the founders of Agrupación de Diseño Industrial del Fomento de las Artes Decorativas; 1963–67 and 1976–79, vice-president of ICSID. He designed products for clients including Moulinex, Matalarte, Gaggia, and packaging for Paco Rabanne (1986 perfume bottle by Saint Gobain Desjonquères) and for Puig. His work included the 1966 *Copenhagen* plastic ashtray by Flamagas, 1983 *Pongotodo* waste bin by Plásticos Tatay, 1987 *Oceano* sink by Sangres, 1988 porcelain dinnerware by Porcelanas del Bidasoa, and 1989 *Fichet* alarm by Fichet.
▶ Guy Julier, *New Spanish Design*, London: Thames and Hudson, 1991.

Richardson, Henry Hobson (1838–86)
▶ American architect; born St. James Parish, Louisiana; active Paris, New York, and Brookline, Massachusetts.
▶ 1856–59, studied Harvard University, Cambridge, Massachusetts; 1859, École des Beaux-Arts, Paris.
▶ 1866–78 in Paris, he worked for architects Théodore Labrouste, brother Henri Labrouste, and Jacques-Ignace Hittorff. In 1865, he settled in New York. 1866–67, he practiced with Emlyn Littel; 1867–78, shared an office with partner Charles D. Gambrill, and subsequently began a practice of his own in New York. His clients came from New England, resulting from friendships established in college. In 1874, he moved to Brookline, Massachusetts, keeping an office in New York. Beginning in 1866 with his first commission, the Church of the Unity in Springfield, Massachusetts, he

began designing site-specific furniture, much of it similar to that of William Morris. In the mid-1870s, Richardson's style included Romanesque and Byzantine forms, while characteristic of New England regionalism. He was a member of one of the earliest Arts and Crafts groups in the USA, the American Society of Arts and Crafts in Boston. From 1876, he created masonry buildings that were free of historicism and showed a high degree of sensitity to mass and surface textures. His major architecture projects included the 1871 Winn Memorial Public Library in Woburn, Massachusetts (where his furniture reflected that of E.W. Godwin), 1876 Trinity Church in Boston (built mostly of brick to reflect the adjacent Back Bay houses); 1881 Austin Hall at Harvard University, and 1882 New York State Capitol in Albany, New York. He was proudest of his 1883–88 Allegheny County Courthouse and Jail in Pittsburgh, and 1885–87 Marshall Field Wholesale Store in Chicago. His most lyrical structure was the 1885 John J. Glessner House at 1800 Prairie Avenue in Chicago, finished by Charles Allerton Coolidge of Shepley, Rutan and Coolidge (the architect previously of Richardson's office). Much of the furniture that Isaac Scott designed for his 1875 Glessner residence was installed in Richardson's 1885 residence for the Glessners.

▶ Solo exhibitions included the 1962 'The Furniture of H.H. Richardson' at the Boston Museum of Fine Arts and 1974 'Henry Hobson Richardson and His Office' at the Fogg Art Museum at Harvard University. His work was included in the 1982 'Space and Environment: Furniture by American Architects' at the Whitney Museum of American Art in Fairfield County, Connecticut.

▶ Cat., Henry-Russell Hitchcock, *The Architecture of H. H. Richardson and His Times*, New York: Museum of Modern Art, 1936. Cat., James F. O'Gorman, *Henry Hobson Richardson and His Office*, Cambridge, Massachusetts: Fogg Art Museum, Harvard University, 1974. Cat., Richard H. Randall, Jr., *The Furniture of H.H. Richardson*, Boston: Museum of Fine Arts, 1962. Marian Griswold Van Rensselaer, *Henry Hobson Richardson and His Works*, New York and Boston, 1888. Cat., Lisa Phillips (introduction), *Shape and Environment: Furniture by American Architects*, New York: Whitney Museum of American Art, 1982:50–51. Doreen Bolger Burke et al., *In Pursuit of Beauty: Americans and the Aesthetic Movement*, New York: Metropolitan Museum of Art and Rizzoli, 1986:463–64,467. Jeffrey K Ochsner, *H.H. Richardson: Complete Architectural Works*, Cambridge, Mass. and London, 1982.

Rickert, Franz (1904–91)
▶ German silversmith and enameler; active Munich.
▶ 1921–24, apprenticed in Adolf von Mayrhofer's workshop; 1924–27, studied Staatsschule für angewandte Kunst, Munich.
▶ He worked as a silversmith from 1926 and became one of the most important silversmiths in Munich and an outstanding enameler. 1935–72, he taught at the Staatsschule (later Akademie) für angewandte Kunst in Munich. In the 1950s and 1960s, he designed numerous religious objects.
▶ He showed various designs at the 1937 Paris 'Exposition Internationale des Arts et Techniques dans la Vie Moderne.'
▶ Annelies Krekel-Aalberse, *Art Nouveau and Art Déco Silver*, New York: Abrams, 1989:144,258. Cat., Florain Hufnagel (ed.), *Goldschmiede Silberschmiede, Drei Generationen von der Weimarer Zeit bis heute: In memoriam Franz Rickert*, Munich: Die Neue Sammlung, 1993.

Ricketts, Charles (1866–1931)
▶ Swiss illustrator; born Geneva; active Britain.
▶ He worked in the Art Nouveau style and was active in the private press movement. An admirer of William Morris and Arthur Heygate Mackmurdo, he worked in the same vein as Aubrey Beardsley. Founder with Charles Shannon of the Vale Press, active 1896–1904, he was co-editor with Shannon and chief illustrator of the journal *The Dial* 1889–97, based largely on the Century Guild's magazine *The Hobby Horse*. He executed woodcuts for several books, where the influence of Morris and the Pre-Raphaelites can be seen. From c1906, his chief interest was theatrical design. In addition to painting and sculpture, Ricketts pro-

duced small bronzes and some small pieces of jewelry for his friends, made by Carlo Giuliano.
▶ Yvonne Brunhammer et al., *Art Nouveau Belgium, France*, Houston: Institute for the Arts, Rice University, 1976. Charlotte Gere, *American and European Jewelry 1830–1914*, New York: Crown, 1975:218.

Ridolfi, Francesco (1927–)
▶ Italian designer; born S. Giminiano; active Milan.
▶ Ridolfi was active from 1960 as a designer of furniture and furnishings and interior designer; worked for magazines *Grazia* and *Casa Viva*. He was a member of ADI (Associazione per il Disegno Industriale).
▶ *ADI Annual 1976*, Milan: Associazione per il Disegno Industriale, 1976.

Rie, Lucie (b. Lucie Marie Gomperz 1902–)
▶ Austrian ceramicist; born Vienna, active Austria and Britain.
▶ 1922–26, studied fine art, Kunstgewerbeschule, Vienna, under Michael Powolny.
▶ She first became involved in pottery with Powolny and, 1926–38, was a successful potter in her own studio in Vienna and active in the movement Neue Werkbund Österreichs. She moved to Britain in 1938 and, in 1939, settled in Albion Mews, London. In 1945, her pottery and button-making workshop was reopened after wartime closure. Her unique handmade buttons were made to order, and she developed an extensive range of her own glazes in order to match customers' fabrics. From 1946, German potter Hans Coper joined Rie in the Albion Mews workshop. She became known for her sophisticated domestic wares, including late-1950s coffee services, and for her subtle green, yellow, and pastel pink glazes, often employing cross-hatched sgraffito decoration and rough white tin glaze applied to pots which were only fired once. She taught at the Camberwell School of Art to 1971.
▶ She was awarded a gold medal at the 1935 Brussels international exhibition and a silver medal for work in the Austrian pavilion at the 1937 Paris 'Exposition Internationale des Arts et Techniques dans la Vie Moderne.' As a student, she showed her first pots in 1923 at the Palais Stoclet, Brussels. She participated in the 1925 Paris 'Exposition Internationale des Arts Décoratifs et Industriels Modernes,' 1930 (IV) Monza 'Esposizione Triennale delle Arti Decorative e Industriali Moderne,' 1951 (IX), 1954 (X) Triennali di Milano, 1959 (XX) 'Ceramic International Exhibition' at the Metropolitan Museum of Art, New York, and 1986 'Nine Potters' exhibition at the Fischer Fine Art gallery, London. In 1949, she exhibited for the first time at the Berkeley Gallery, London, and, in 1950 and 1956, shared an exhibition there with Coper. They showed together at the Röhsska Konstslojdmuseet, Gothenburg, in 1955; Boymans Museum, Rotterdam, in 1967; at the Gemeentemuseum, Arnhem; Museum für Künste und Gewerbe, Hamburg, in 1971; and at the Fischer Fine Art gallery, London, in 1984. Retrospectives of her work were mounted at the Arts Council Gallery, London, in 1967 and at the Sainsbury Centre for Visual Arts, Norwich, in 1981, and at the Victoria and Albert Museum, London. She received a CBE in 1981.
▶ Tony Birks, *Lucie Rie*, Dorset: Alphabooks, 1987. R. Craig Miller, *Modern Design 1880–1990*, New York: Abrams, 1990. Cat., *Collection Fina Gomez: 30 ans de céramique contemporaine*, Paris: Musée des Arts Décoratifs, 1991:116.

Riedel, Claus Josef (1925–)
▶ Austrian glassware designer.
▶ 1947–50, studied chemistry in Innsbruck.
▶ He first worked for Richard Ginori at the Cristalleria Nazionale in Naples, where he became technical director. In 1956, Riedel and his father established their own factory, Tiroler Glashütte, in Kufstein. Although he did not consider himself a designer, Riedel's 1958 *Exquisit* and *Monaco* models were widely published. In 1969, a second factory was opened at Schneegattern, notable at the time for its modern production techniques. In 1972, a crystal grinding shop was established in Matrei. Riedel designed for Rosen-

thal. His simple techniques were effectively applied in his *Holdfast* range, where mold-blown glass had vertical cuts through a thick rippled-glass body. He collaborated with Michael Boehm to create the *Calyx* range, where the faint mold lines became a design feature.

▶ Winning his first prize in 1958, his drinking glasses won silver medals at the 1960 (XII) Triennale di Milano; his *Genova* range won the 1982 Bundespreis 'Die gute Industrieform.'

▶ *Glass 1959*, Corning, NY: The Corning Museum of Glass, 1959, No. 5. Cat., *New Glass: A Worldwide Survey*, Corning, NY: The Corning Museum of Glass, 1979, nos. 194−95. 'Moderne Klassiker, pt. 13: Geschirr, Besteck, Glas,' *Schöner Wohnen*, Feb. 1982:183. Cat., Kathryn B. Hiesinger and George H. Marcus III (eds.), *Design Since 1945*, Philadelphia: Philadelphia Museum of Art, 1983:228,II−52.

▶ See Tiroler Glashütte

Riegel, Ernst (1871−1939)

▶ German metalsmith; born Münnerstadt; active Munich, Darmstadt, and Cologne.

▶ 1887−90, apprenticed to silver chaser Otto Pabst in Kempten, Allgäu, and from 1895, to goldsmith Fritz von Miller in Munich.

▶ He worked from 1900−06 as a silversmith in his own workshop in Munich, where he taught at the municipal craft school for goldsmiths. In 1907, he joined the Darmstadt artists' colony of the Grand Duke Louis IV of Hesse-Darmstadt. Of the 23 artists who worked at Darmstadt, only two (Riegel and Theodor Wende) were silversmiths. Riegel produced various mounts for the Grand Duke's collection of nephrite and agate bowls. He was interested in historic silversmithing techniques and ornamentation; his numerous prize cups were covered with embossed and chased foliate scrolls and flowers. Some other objects by him were more Modern, with soldered spiral motifs and semi-precious stones. In 1912, he became a professor at the Städtische Werkschule in Cologne. From 1920, he was in charge of the goldsmithing workshop at the Institute for Religious Art in Cologne.

▶ Annelies Krekel-Aalberse, *Art Nouveau and Art Déco Silver*, New York: Abrams, 1989:132,134,135,142,180,258. Cat., *Ein Dokument Deutscher Kunst*, Vol. 4, Darmstadt: Die Künstler der Mathildenhöhe, 1977:202−10.

Riemerschmid, Richard (1868−1957)

▶ German architect and designer; born Munich.

▶ Studied painting in Munich.

▶ Like a number of other painters of the end of the 19th century, he turned from painting to the applied arts. In the 1910s, he developed a range of standardized furniture for batch production. He designed his own 1896 house in Pasing, Bavaria. He was an early follower of the Arts and Crafts movement in Germany. Following the lead of the Wiener Werkstätte, in 1897, Riemerschmid, Hermann Obrist, Bruno Paul, Bernhard Pankok, and Peter Behrens founded the Münchner Vereinigte Werkstätten für Kunst im Handwerk (The Munich United Workshops for Art in Handwork) to sell everyday objects by Modern artists. About 1899, Riemerschmid and brother-in-law Karl Schmidt began to investigate inexpensive furniture design and production. He designed an 1899 mahogany armchair for his music room at the 1899 art exhibition in Dresden and at the 1900 Paris Exposition; the chair was manufactured by Dunbar Furniture Corp. of Indiana from 1950 through an agreement with the designer. Not until 1904 did he begin to design furniture specifically for serial machine production. In 1901, he designed the interior decorations for the Munich theater. He taught 1902−05 at the art school in Nuremberg. In 1907, he was a founder with Behrens, Mies van der Rohe, Walter Gropius, and others of the Deutscher Werkbund. In 1910, he built several artists' studios in Hellereau. He was director of the Kunstgewerbeschule in Munich 1912−24 and of the Werkschule in Cologne 1926−31. His flatware designs were produced by Bruckmann und Söhne in Heilbronn and Carl Weishaupt in Munich. A Classicist in architecture, his designs ranged eclectically from Arts and Crafts furniture and Art Nouveau ceramics to machine-made objects showing simple proto-Bauhaus geometry. He was one of the most important German designers of the 20th century.

▶ Music room installed at 1899 German art exhibition, Dresden. Furniture (with Karl Schmidt) shown in 1905. Room for an art collector installed at 1900 Paris 'Exposition Universelle.' Work shown at 1910 Brussels 'Exposition Universelle et Internationale.' Work subject of 'Richard Riemerschmid: von Jugendstil zum Werkbund,' exhibition of architecture collection, Technisches Universität München, Münchner Stadtmuseum, and Germanisches Nationalmuseum.

▶ Herwin Schaefer, *Nineteenth Century Modern: The Functional Tradition in Victorian Design*, New York: Praeger, 1970:188−89. Yvonne Brunhammer et al., *Art Nouveau Belgium, France*, Houston: Institute for the Arts, Rice University, 1976. *Dictionnaire de l'Architecture Moderne*, p. 241. Alastair Duncan, *Art Nouveau and Art Déco Lighting*, New York: Simon and Schuster, 1978:125. Cat., *Richard Riemerschmid: Von Jugendstil zum Werkbund*, Munich: Stadtmuseum, 1983. Cat., Kathryn Bloom Hiesinger, *Art Nouveau in Munich*, Munich: Prestel, 1988:107−47. Annelies Krekel-Aalberse, *Art Nouveau and Art Déco Silver*, New York: Abrams, 1989:258.

Rietveld, Gerrit Thomas (1888−1964)

▶ Dutch architect and furniture maker and designer; born Utrecht.

▶ 1899−1906, apprenticed in his father's cabinetmaking workshop in Utrecht; 1906−11, trained as an architectural draftsman.

▶ Rietveld was greatly influenced by Frank Lloyd Wright's portfolio *Ausgeführte Bauten und Entwürfe von Frank Lloyd Wright* (1910). In 1911, he opened his own furniture-making business in Utrecht. 1911−15, he took advanced architectural courses and built several buildings. Rietveld was associated from the time of its formation in 1917 by Theo van Doesburg with the De Stijl group through his friendship with Robert van t'Hoff, and was a member until 1931. The association inspired him to pursue furniture design, conceived as spatial composition with little thought for comfort. His architecture career began with the 1924 Schröder house, Utrecht, which he designed with Truus Schröder-Schräder, a De Stijl member with whom he collaborated from 1921. In partnership with her, Rietveld kept a studio in the house until 1932 and lived there from 1958. Their projects included the 1934 terrace of houses in the Erasmuslaan in Utrecht and 1936 Vreeburg Cinema in Utrecht. Rietveld also designed the 1954 Netherlands Pavilion at the Biennale di Venezia, 1954 sculpture pavilion in the Sonsbeek Park in Arnheim, and 1963−72 Rijkmuseum Vincent van Gogh (with J. van Dillen and J. van Tricht) in Amsterdam. In 1927, Rietveld designed a diagonal bent tubular steel chair. Because of Cassina's reproductions in the 1980s, his best known work became the 1918 *Red Blue* chair incorporating 15 lintels, which explored Piet Mondrian's color use, though it was first produced without color in 1917. Along with this skeletal chair, his 1923 *Berlin* chair and end table and the 1934 *Zig-Zag* chair became icons of 20th-century design. His furniture inspired Marcel Breuer at the Bauhaus in the early 1920s. His furniture could be seen as abstract sculptural objects with a practical function. Like the Futurists, Rietveld preferred houses with scaffolding around them; in his *Red Blue* chair, the 'scaffolding' holds the seat and back in place. One of his chair models of the late 1920s was literally made from scaffolding poles clamped together. Rietveld worked with cardboard from which he made models to develop his ideas, rather than sketching them on paper. Though he worked chiefly in wood, he also produced furniture in bent metal tubing.

▶ His bent tubular steel and wood easy chairs and tables were shown at the 1930 Paris exhibition. His work was the subject of the 1983 'Rietveld als Meubelmaker, Wonen met Experimenten' exhibition at the Central Museum in Utrecht, and included in the 1986 'Der Kragstuhl' exhibition at the Stuhlmuseum Burg Beverungen in Berlin. First major posthumous exhibition at Centre Georges Pompidou, Paris, 23 June−27 Sept. 1993.

▶ Adolf Schenck, *Der Stuhl*, Stuttgart, 1928:56. Theodore M. Brown, *The Works of Gerrit Rietveld, Architect*, Utrecht: A.W. Bruna, 1958. Daniele Baroni and Frits Bless, *The Furniture of Gerrit Thomas Rietveld*, Woodbury, NY: Barron's, 1978. Helma van Rens (ed.), *Gerrit Rietveld Teksten*, Utrecht: Impress, 1979. Barbie Campbell-Cole and Tim Benton (eds.), *Tubular Steel Furniture*, London: The Art Book Company, 1979:30−31. *Rietveld 1888−1964: Een Biografie*, Baam: Bert Bakker/Erven Thomas Rap, 1982. Cat., *Rietveld als Meubelmaker, Wonen met Experimenten 1900−1924*, Central Museum, Utrecht, 1983. Cat., *Der Kragstuhl*, Stuhlmuseum Burg Beverungen, Berlin: Alexander, 1986:137. Marijke Küper and Ida van Lijl, *Gerrit Th. Rietveld: The Complete Works 1888−1964*, Utrecht: Centraal Museum, 1992.

Riffelmacher, Ludwig (1896−)
▶ German metalworker; active Nuremberg,Hamburg, Pforzheim, and Berlin.
▶ Studied metalwork, Gewerbliche Fortbildungsschule, Nuremberg, under Josef Pöhlmann, and Kunstgewerbeschule, Nuremberg.
▶ In 1923, he worked with Otto Stüber in Hamburg and, in 1924, with Karl August Weiss in Pforzheim. 1924−26, he was director of the workshop of H.J. Wilm in Berlin; under his supervision, massive hand-raised pieces were produced with finely engraved ornamentation.
▶ Annelies Krekel-Aalberse, *Art Nouveau and Art Déco Silver*, New York: Abrams, 1989:145,146,258.

Rigot, Gérard
▶ French artist; active Gers region.
▶ He carved furniture in animal and plant shapes, reminiscent of the paintings of Henri Rousseau and evoking, in his own words, 'the imaginary world of childhood.' His fragile painted and varnished furniture was exported worldwide. In 1990, he designed a children's playground in Britain.
▶ In 1980, his work was shown at the Musée des Arts Décoratifs in Paris.
▶ Martine Colombet, 'Gérard Rigot and His Bestiary,' *Vogue Décoration*, No. 26, June/July 1990:134−37.

Riihimäen Lasi
▶ Finnish glass factory.
▶ The factory, established in 1810 for the production of domestic glassware, began production of window glass in 1919; it purchased various small factories, including the factory in which the Finnish Glass Museum is located today; in 1928, sponsored a glass design competition won by Henry Ericsson; in the mid-1930s, was refitted and upgraded; in 1933 and 1936, sponsored competitions entered by Alvar Aalto, Gunnel Nyman, Arttu Brummer, and others; by the late 1930s, had expanded into medical and technical glass. In 1941, the Kauklahti and Ryttylä glassworks merged with Riihimäen. After World War II, new designers included Helena Tynell and Nanny Still. In 1976, the factory was fully automated and discontinued blown-glass production; it now supplies over half of bottles and jars in Finland for food, drink, and technochemical products; in 1985, was purchased by Ahlström.
▶ Jennifer Hawkins Opie, *Scandinavia: Ceramics and Glass in the Twentieth Century*, New York: Rizzoli, 1989.

Rima
▶ Italian furniture manufacturer; located Padua.
▶ Rima was one of the first furniture manufacturers established in Italy after World War II. Gastone Rinaldi designed for the firm, including its 1958 *Saturno* sofa.
▶ Cat., Leslie Jackson, *The New Look: Design in the Fifties*, New York: Thames and Hudson, 1991:126.
▶ See **Rinaldi, Gastone**

Rinaldi, Gastone (1920−)
▶ Italian furniture designer; born and active Padua.
▶ Studied Instituto Tecnico Superior, Padua.

▶ He began as a designer in 1948, specializing in metal furniture produced at first by Rima, Padua, including *S9*, *Linda 1*, *Linda 2*, and *Zeta* chairs; designed a 1955 dual-position chair in steel rods and raffia and 1958 *Saturno* sofa produced by Rima; from 1977, was a partner in the firm Thema, Limena, which produced his *Aurora* stacking chair and 1979 *Daphne* folding chair. He was a member of ADI (Associazione per il Disegno Industriale).
▶ Received 1954 Compasso d'Oro (metal furniture by Rima) and awards at Triennale di Milano. His work was shown at 1951 (XI) Triennale di Milano, and 1979 'Design & design' exhibition at the Palazzo delle Stelline in Milan. The *Daphne* chair was included in the 1983−84 'Design Since 1945' exhibition at the Philadelphia Museum of Art.
▶ Ernst Erik Pfannschmidt, *Metallmöbel*, Stuttgart, 1962:26−28,32,39,44,60,101. *ADI Annual 1976*, Milan: Associazione per il Disegno Industriale, 1976. Cat., *Design & design*, Milan: Palazzo delle Stelline, 1979:28. Hans Wichmann, *Italien Design 1945 bis heute*, Munich: Die Neue Sammlung, 1988.

Rindin, Vadim Feodorovich (1920−74)
▶ Russian stage and film designer.
▶ 1920−22, studied Vkhutemas, Voronezh; 1923−24, Skhutemas, Moscow, under V. Khrakovskii.
▶ 1920−22, he worked in the set and publicity design workshop of the municipal theater in Voronezh; in 1924, became a member of Makovets, of Omkh, and of the Akhr; 1935−53, was a leading set designer of the State Academic Vakhtaganov Theater; and, 1953−74, designer at the Bolshoi Theater in Moscow. 1965−741, he was head of the department of stage design at the College of Art in Moscow, an award-winning artist of the Soviet Russian Socialist Federation, member of the Folk Artists of the Soviet Union, member of the Soviet Academy of Art, and winner of the State Prize of the Soviet Union.
▶ Cat., *Kunst und Revolution: Russische und Sowjetische Kunst 1910−1932*, Vienna: Österreichisches Museum für angewandte Kunst, 1988.

Ripamonti, Roberto (1949−)
▶ Italian designer; born and active Omegna.
▶ Studied architecture, Politecnico di Milano.
▶ He began his professional career in 1972 designing lighting, interiors, and appliances. In 1973, he worked at the Studio Molinari for clients including NPB, Acea, Filab, and Aspaco. He was a member of ADI (Associazione per il Disegno Industriale).
▶ He participated in international competitions including 1972 'Interieur 72' in Belgium, Dupont Italiana in Italy, and the international pottery design competition in Giappone.
▶ *ADI Annual 1976*, Milan: Associazione per il Disegno Industriale, 1976.

Risch, Hildegard (1903−)
▶ German metalsmith; born Halle; active Halle and Cologne.
▶ 1923, studied Kunsthandwerkerschule Burg Giebichenstein, Halle, under Karl Müller.
▶ In 1927, she set up a workshop in Halle with former fellow student Eva Macher-Elsässer. In 1928, Risch worked with architect and designer Fritz Breuhaus de Groot in Düsseldorf. 1929−35, they worked together in partnership as well as for others. From 1935, Risch continued the activities of the workshop alone, devoting herself to jewelry.
▶ Annelies Krekel-Aalberse, *Art Nouveau and Art Déco Silver*, New York: Abrams, 1989:147,258. Cat., *Hildegard Risch: Eine Goldschmiedin der Moderne*, Galerie Mattar, Cologne, 1983.

Risom, Jens (1916−)
▶ Danish furniture designer; born Copenhagen; active in the USA.
▶ Studied Krebs' School to 1928, St. Anne Vester School to 1932, and Niels Brock's Business School, University of Copenhagen, to 1934; 1935−38, furniture and interior design, Kunståndvaerkerskolen, Copenhagen.

▶ 1937—39, he was active as a furniture and interior designer in the office of architect Ernst Kuhn, Copenhagen. In 1939, he settled in the USA. 1939—41, he was design director at Dan Cooper, New York, where he designed furniture, textiles, and interiors. He designed the interiors of the 1940 model home by architect Edward Stone sponsored by *Colliers* magazine in Rockefeller Center, New York. In 1941, he designed Hans Knoll's first chair; 1941—43, he was a freelance designer of furniture, textiles, interiors, and industrial products, with clients including Georg Jensen. His designs for Knoll immediately after World War II reflected the scarcity of raw materials; inexpensive and second-grade woods and upholstery webbing had to be used. 1946—73, his firm in New York was known as Jens Risom Design, where he was the sole designer. From 1973, he was active as chief executive of Design Control in New Canaan, Connecticut. 1970—76, he was a trustee of the Rhode Island School of Design. Unlike other designers at Knoll and Herman Miller after World War II, Risom rejected metal and molded furniture in favor of shaped wood.
▶ Nina Bremer in *Contemporary Designers*, London: Macmillan, 1981:512—13. Nina Bremer, 'Jens Risom' in Mel Byars and Russell Flinchum (eds.), *50 American Designers*, Washington: Preservation, 1994.

Rittweger, Otto (1904—1965)
▶ German designer and metalworker.
▶ 1923—28, studied Bauhaus, Dessau and Weimar.
▶ He was artistic director 1930—31 of the lighting firm Goldschmidt und Schwabe, Berlin.
▶ Cat., *The Bauhaus: Masters and Students*, New York: Barry Friedman, 1988. Annelies Krekel-Aalberse, *Art Nouveau and Art Déco Silver*, New York: Abrams, 1989:258. Cat., *Die Metallwerkstatt am Bauhaus*, Berlin: Bauhaus-Archiv, 1992:252—57,319.

Riva, Eleonore Peduzzi
▶ Italian architect and industrial designer.
▶ Riva first began to work in plastics in 1960, her first design being the *Spyros* ashtray for Artemide. She produced designs for floor coverings and textiles.
▶ Cat., Milena Lamarová, *Design a Plastické Hmoty*, Prague: Uměleckoprůmyslové Muzeum, 1972:150.

Rivier, Mireille (1959—)
▶ French architect and designer; born Lyons.
▶ Studied architecture, École Polytechnique Fédérale, Lausanne.
▶ She moved to Rome, where she collaborated with Paolo Pallucco at Pallucco Design. Rivier and Pallucco designed the witty and culturally critical 1987 *Tankette* table, a miniature tank complete with steel treads.
▶ Albrecht Bangert and Karl Michael Armer, *80s Style: Designs of the Decade*, New York: Abbeville, 1990:82,235.

Rivière, Théodore Louis-Auguste (1857—1912)
▶ French sculptor; born Toulouse.
▶ He lived in Tunis for three years from 1890, teaching drawing at a seminary in Carthage. Returning with some figurines inspired by Gustave Flaubert's historical novel *Salammbô*, he attained some measure of fame. In 1894, he became a member of the Société des Artistes français and, in 1895, his *Salammbô Chez Mathô* sculpture was bought by the French government. Along with large sculptures and public commissions, he was best known for his miniature groups and figurines in bronze, onyx, and ivory, such as *Le Voeu, Charles VI et Odette, Phryné*, and in particular *Loïe Fuller*.
▶ He first showed his work at the 1875 Paris salon. He won a gold medal at the 1900 Paris 'Exposition Universelle.'
▶ Yvonne Brunhammer et al., *Art Nouveau Belgium, France*, Houston: Institute for the Arts, Rice University, 1976.

Rix, Felice (1893—1967) and Kitty Rix (1901—)
▶ Austrian textile and fashion designers; sisters; born Vienna.
▶ Felice Rix studied Kunstgewerbeschule, Vienna, under Oskar Strnad, A. v. Stark, R. Rothansl, and Josef Hoffmann.

▶ As members of the Wiener Werkstätte, they designed textiles and ceramics and contributed to the 1914—15 fashion folder *Die Mode* and 1916 folder *The Life of a Lady*. Felice Rix settled in Japan in 1935. 1939—63, she was a professor at the Kyoto College of Art and was a member of the Vienna women's art association Wiener Frauenkunst and of the Neue Werkbund Österreichs.
▶ Günther Feuerstein, *Vienna—Present and Past: Arts and Crafts—Applied Art—Design*, Vienna: Jugend und Volk, 1976: 35,81. Werner J. Schweiger, *Wiener Werkstätte: Kunst und Handwerk 1902—1932*, Vienna: Brandstaetter, 1982:267. Deanna F. Cera (ed.), *Jewels of Fantasy: Costume Jewelry of the 20th Century*, New York: Abrams, 1992. Cat., *Expressive Keramik der Wiener Werkstätte 1917—1930*, Munich: Bayerische Vereinsbank, 1992:132—33.

Rizzatto, Paolo (1941—)
▶ Italian designer; born and active Milan.
▶ Studied architecture to 1965.
▶ 1969—77, designed for Arteluce; in 1978, founded Luceplan with Riccardo Sarfatti; 1985—87, designed furniture for Busnelli and Molteni and worked on architecture projects with Antonio Monestiroli; with Alberto Meda designed the *Berenice* table lamp, *F3/3 Kit*, and 1990 *Titania* hanging light and, with S. Colbertaldo, *D7* table lamp, all by Luce Plan.
▶ Received 1981 and 1989 Premio Compasso d'Oro and 1992 Design Plus prize at the Frankfurt fair for his *Titania* lamp.
▶ *Modo*, No. 148, March—April 1993:125.

Robeck, Sylvia (1959—)
▶ German designer; born Berlin.
▶ 1971—81, studied graphic design and, 1982—88, studied industrial design, Hochschule der Künste, Berlin.
▶ In 1986, she became an independent consultant designer of household appliances for Product Development Roericht in Ulm. 1988—89, she taught at the Hochschule der Künste in Berlin. From 1989, she worked for Addison Design Consultants in London.
▶ Work included in exhibitions from 1985.
▶ Cat., Design Center Stuttgart, *Women in Design: Careers and Life Histories Since 1900*, Stuttgart: Haus der Wirtschaft, 1989: 156—59.

Robert, Émile
▶ French metalworker.
▶ Robert was apprenticed in the family ironworks and was one of the last to use its forge. He is credited with having revived wrought iron for domestic and architectural metalware, including banisters, consoles, vase mounts, grilles, lighting fixtures, chandeliers, and architectural ironwork. His forms were primarily vegetal, somewhat complicated before 1900, becoming less ornate afterwards. For lighting that included materials other than iron, he turned to Bigot for earthenware reservoirs and Laumonnerie for glass shades.
▶ He showed his work at the Salons of the Société des Artistes français.

Roberts and Belk
▶ British silversmiths; located Sheffield.
▶ The firm was founded in Sheffield in 1908. In the late 1920s and 1930s, architect Walter P. Belk was a designer and silversmith for the firm.
▶ Annelies Krekel-Aalberse, *Art Nouveau and Art Déco Silver*, New York: Abrams, 1989:258.

Robertson, Alexander W. (1840—1925)
▶ British ceramicist; active Chelsea, Massachusetts, San Francisco, and Alberhill, California.
▶ Robertson settled in the USA in 1853. In 1866, he established the Chelsea Keramic Art Works in Chelsea, Massachusetts. In 1884, he settled in California and experimented with local clays. After several unsuccessful attempts to set up an art pottery in San Francisco, he and Linna Irelan founded the Roblin Art Pottery in 1898; it was destroyed in the 1906 San Francisco earthquake.

They relocated the pottery in Los Angeles, where operations continued until 1910, when it was relocated in Halcyon, California, a utopian Theosophist colony. In 1912, Robertson was hired by James H. Hill, president of Alberhill (California) Coal and Clay to experiment with local clays. In 1914, Robertson's last year at Alberhill, he displayed the beginnings of his art range of pottery during a lawsuit between Alberhill and the State of California over a portion of the land that held clay deposits important to the pottery. Having been the only potter at Alberhill, his work remained its sole output. Robertson was briefly a resident potter at Mission Inn, Frank Miller's guest house for early tourists to California; Miller brought in potters and furniture makers.
▶ Work shown at the 1915–16 San Diego 'Panama-California Exposition.'
▶ Paul Evans in Timothy J. Andersen et al., *California Design 1910*, Salt Lake City: Peregrine Smith, 1980:76–77,125.

Robertson, Fred H.   (1869–1952)

▶ American ceramicist; born Massachusetts; active San Francisco and Los Angeles.
▶ In c1900, he joined his father at the Roblin Art Pottery in San Francisco. In 1906, when Roblin relocated in Los Angeles, Robertson joined the Los Angeles Pressed Bricks Works, where he began experimenting with crystalline and luster glazes on artware in c1913. His output was limited. In the early 1920s, he joined Claycraft Potteries, producers of architectural tiles. In c1925, he was joined by son George B. Robertson at Claycraft. In 1934, he established the Robertson Pottery, active until his death.
▶ He won gold medals at the 1915 San Francisco 'Panama-Pacific International Exposition' and 1915–16 San Diego 'Panama-California (International) Exposition.'
▶ Paul Evans in Timothy J. Andersen et al., *California Design 1910*, Salt Lake City: Peregrine Smith, 1980:77.

Robertson Pottery

▶ American ceramics factory; located Los Angeles.
▶ Fred H. Robertson worked around 1906 at Los Angeles Pressed Brick, where he experimented with new clay mixtures. c1913, he became active in producing artware. He sold few of his crystalline vessels; much of his production was luster artware. Some of his pieces with thick, flowing lava glazes were of a higher quality than those of his uncle Hugh C. Robertson of the Dedham Pottery in Massachusetts. In 1914, he developed successful luster and crystalline glazes, while producing other decorative techniques. Though Vase-Krafts was one of the first to introduce all-ceramic lamps with pottery bases, stems, and shades, Robertson was making similar models by 1914 with glass insets provided by the Judson Studios. The Robertson Pottery name was introduced in 1934.
▶ Paul Evans in Timothy J. Andersen et al., *California Design 1910*, Salt Lake City: Peregrine Smith, 1980:71.

Robin, Marie

▶ French fashion and furnishings designer.
▶ She set up Espace Marie Robin in Paris in 1984. She designed and produced glassware, tableware, and sculptures, and issued plates in 1986 in reinforced glass, trimming down Corning glass in order to produce fine household objects.
▶ *Les Carnets du Design*, Paris: Mad-Cap Productions et APCI, 1986:49.

Robineau, Adelaide   (b. Adelaide Alsop   1865–1929)

▶ American ceramicist; born Middletown, Connecticut.
▶ She became a well-known decorator and member of the National League of Mineral Painters. She taught briefly at Saint Mary's in Minnesota and, in 1899, studied painting under William Merritt Chase in New York. She drew watercolors and painted miniatures on ivory. In 1899, she and her husband Samuel and George H. Clark bought the magazine *China Decorator* and, in 1900, began publishing the journal *Keramik Studio*. In 1901, the Robineaus moved to the house 'Four Winds' that they built in Syracuse, New York. Influenced by Royal Copenhagen china at

first and then by sculptural work from the Bing & Grøndahl Porcelænsfabrik in Denmark, she was interested in china painting and studio pottery; in 1901, in the studio of Charles Volkmar, she produced her first pot. She was also influenced by French ceramicist Taxile Doat, whose seminal essay 'Grand Feu Ceramics' she published in 1909. In 1903, she turned from china painting to making fine porcelain. 1910–11, she taught under Doat at the University City Pottery, near St. Louis, Missouri, where she produced the *Scarab Vase*, said to have taken 1,000 hours to produce and shown in 1911 in Turin. 1920–28, she taught at Syracuse University in Syracuse, New York.
▶ She showed her watercolors at annual exhibitions of the National Academy in New York and her experimental slip-cast porcelains at the 1903 Arts and Crafts exhibition in the Craftsman Building, Syracuse. Her work with others was declared 'the finest porcelain in the world' at the 1911 Turin 'Esposizione Internazionale dell'Industria e del Lavoro,' where the American Women's League from University City received the grand prize and Robineau was given the Diploma della Benemerenza. She showed her work at the 1904 St. Louis 'Louisiana Purchase Exposition,' crystalline glazes at the Art Institute of Chicago in 1904, 1911 Salon in Paris, and at the Paris Musée des Arts Décoratifs. She received a medal and prizes from the Art Institute of Chicago and the societies of Arts and Crafts in Boston and Detroit. She won a grand prize at the 1915 San Francisco 'Panama-Pacific International Exposition' and was given an honorary doctorate from Syracuse University. Her work was the subject of the 1929 memorial exhibition at the New York Metropolitan Museum of Art.
▶ *High Fire Porcelains: Adelaide Alsop Robineau, Potter, Syracuse, New York*, San Francisco: Panama-Pacific International Exposition, 1915. Samuel Robineau, 'Adelaide Alsop Robineau,' *Design*, No. 30, April 1929. Cat., Joseph Breck, *A Memorial Exhibition of Porcelain Stoneware by Adelaide Alsop Robineau, 1865–1929*, New York: Metropolitan Museum of Art, 1929. Elaine Levine, 'Pioneers of Contemporary American Ceramics: Charles Binns, Adelaide Robineau,' *Ceramic Monthly*, No. 23, Nov. 1975:22–27. Garth Clark, *American Ceramics: 1876 to the Present*, New York: Abbeville, 1987:293 et passim. *American Art Pottery*, New York: Cooper-Hewitt Museum, 1987.

Robj

▶ French shop and manufacturer; located Paris.
▶ Robj commissioned numerous designers to execute bibelots and curios for his shop in the rue de Paradis, Paris. The shop sold playful but expensive items in sometimes questionable taste, including porcelain Buddhas, native Americans, Japanese geishas, Dutch boys, and Mexican sombreros doubling as lamps, boxes, inkwells, and other tabletop items.
▶ Alastair Duncan, *Art Nouveau and Art Déco Lighting*, New York: Simon and Schuster, 1978:182.

Roblin Art Pottery

▶ American ceramics workshop; located San Francisco.
▶ Roblin Art Pottery was founded in San Francisco by Alexander Robertson before the end of the 1890s. Robertson potted and fired, and his associate Linna Irelan often decorated. Her specialty was modeling, and she applied little mushrooms and lizards liberally. Robertson's work was more severe and classical, often ornamented only with finely rendered feet or handles. He used only Californian materials. The firm closed in 1906 as a result of the San Francisco earthquake.
▶ Paul Evans in Timothy J. Andersen et al., *California Design 1910*, Salt Lake City: Peregrine Smith, 1980:65.

Robots

▶ Italian furniture manufacturer; located Binasco.
▶ Robots was established in 1963 in Binasco. In 1970, Roberto Rebolini set up a department in the firm to concentrate on the development of designs in metal. Its 1971 collection of domestic furnishings was designed by architects Gian Casè and Enrico Panzeri. Bruno Munari designed its 1972 *Abitacolo* (bed/work/play/

living structure), 1972 *Biplano* trolley, 1973 *Bookcase*, 1974 *Vademecum* carrying structure, and 1975 *Divanetta*. Its 1973 table with stool was designed by architects Nani Prina and Enrico Panzeri. Its 1974 domestic furnishings were designed by Guido de Marco and Roberto Rebolini. Its 1975 *Portarobe* was designed by Piero Polato, and 1976 *6 2 X* multiple by Rolando Strati.

▶ Munari's *Abitacolo* unit was shown at the 1972 'Italy: The New Domestic Landscape' exhibition at the New York Museum of Modern Art. Robots was awarded a gold medal at the 1973 'BIO 5' Industrial Design Biennial in Ljubljana.

▶ *ADI Annual 1976*, Milan: Associazione per il Disegno Industriale, 1976. Aldo Tanchis, *Bruno Munari: From Futurism to Post-Industrial Design*, London: Lund Humphries, 1986:142.

Robsjohn-Gibbings, Terence Harold (1905–76)

▶ British interior and furniture designer; born London; active London and New York.

▶ Studied University of Liverpool, and architecture, London University.

▶ He worked briefly as a naval architect, designing passenger ship interiors, and as art director for a film company. In 1936, he worked for Charles of London, the antique dealer and brother of art dealer Joseph Duveen, for clients Elizabeth Arden and Neiman-Marcus department store. In 1929, Duveen moved Robsjohn-Gibbings to New York, where he sold Elizabethan and Jacobean furniture and linen-fold panels. He returned to London in 1933 and rendered interiors for a film company. He disliked the contemporary affinity for an 'indigestible mixture of Queen Anne, Georgian, and Spanish styles.' In 1936 he opened an office in New York with a showroom at 515 Madison Avenue, and started to incorporate touches from his earlier studies of ancient Greek furniture. Culling ideas from his own portfolio of hundreds of drawings, he decorated his showroom with Greek models, mosaic-floor reproductions, and sparse furnishings. His clients included Doris Duke, Mrs. Otto Kahn, and Thelma Chrysler Foy. He copied the 1939 amorphic glass and wood coffee table by Isamu Noguchi designed originally for Congers Goodyear. Devoted to historicist design, Robsjohn-Gibbings considered Modern art a fraud, saying so in his book *Mona Lisa's Moustache: A Dissection of Modern Art* (1947). He wrote *Goodbye, Mr. Chippendale* (1944), a spoof on 20th-century interior decoration in the USA, and *Homes of the Brave* in the 1950s. Robsjohn-Gibbings's two most important projects were houses in Bel Air and Santa Barbara, California. The 1938 'Casa Encantada' house of Mrs. J.O. Weber in Bel Air had neutral rooms with a decidedly classical influence. In 1942, Robsjohn-Gibbings designed a shocking living room with pale blue walls, fuchsia cushions, violet chairs, and dark-gray sofa. In 1944, his red bamboo chairs were upholstered in a tropical-leaf printed fabric. His design ideas were widely emulated. In 1943, he designed a range of furniture for John Widdicomb of Grand Rapids, Michigan, and worked there until 1956. In 1960, he met Greek cabinetmakers Susan and Eleftherios Saridis and created a line of classical Greek furniture still in production by Saridis. The *Klismos* chairs and furniture, with striped linen cushions, were included in Robsjohn-Gibbings's interiors for the apartment of Nicholas and Dolly Goulandris in Athens in the early 1960s. He settled in 1964 in Athens where he became designer to the Goulandrises and Aristotle Onassis. He was effective in promoting Modern furniture and interiors, although he rejected Bauhaus forms and models. Influenced by his work, Charles Pfister's 1990 furniture collection produced by Baker was dedicated to Robsjohn-Gibbings.

▶ He received the 1950 Waters Award and 1962 Elsie De Wolfe Award (with Edward J. Wormley).

▶ Terence Robsjohn-Gibbings, *Goodbye, Mr. Chippendale*, New York, 1944. Terence Robsjohn-Gibbings, *Mona Lisa's Moustache*, New York, 1947. Edmund White, 'America's Classical Modernist,' *House and Garden*, June 1991:100–04,156. Reed Benhamou in *Contemporary Designers*, London: Macmillan, 1981:516–17. Mitchell Owens, 'Terence Robsjohn-Gibbings' in Mel Byars and Rus-

sell Flinchum (eds.), *50 American Designers*, Washington: Preservation, 1994.

Roche, Pierre (1855–1922)

▶ French sculptor, metalworker, and engraver; active Paris.

▶ Interested in ceramics and lead casting, he executed several pieces inspired by the dancer Loïe Fuller and her flowing costumes. The works on Fuller included sketches, statuettes, and a statue for the façade of Henry Sauvage's Théâtre de la Loïe Fuller at the 1900 Paris 'Exposition Universelle.' Roche's architectural sculpture included an image of St. John for the basilica of Montmartre in Paris and comic and tragic medallions for the theater at Tulle.

▶ Roche showed his work at the Musée Galliéra in Paris, the Salons of the Société des Artistes Décorateurs, and the Salons of the Société Nationale des Beaux-Arts.

▶ Yvonne Brunhammer et al., *Art Nouveau Belgium, France*, Houston: Rice University, 1976.

Rochga, Rudolf (1875–1957)

▶ German sculptor and silver designer; active Munich.

▶ In *c*1902, Rochga designed silver hollow-ware produced by Bruckmann und Söhne in Heilbronn. He was one of the first designers of the Münchner Vereinigte Werkstätten für Kunst im Handwerk, active in wall decoration and textiles. From 1903, taught at the Lehr- und Versuchswerk-Stätten, Stuttgart.

▶ Annelies Krekel-Aalberse, *Art Nouveau and Art Déco Silver*, New York: Abrams, 1989:140,258. Cat., *Metallkunst*, Berlin: Bröhan-Museum, 1990:596.

Rodchenko, Aleksandr (1891–1956)

▶ Russian painter, sculptor, and designer; born St. Petersburg; husband of Varvara Stepanova.

▶ 1910–14, Rodchenko studied Kazan Art School under Nikolai Feshin and Georgii Medvedev; and Stroganov Institute, Moscow.

▶ In 1915, Rodchenko was one of the principal organizers of Constructivism in Moscow along with Vladimir Tatlin, Kazimir Malevitch, and other avant-garde Russian artists. A practitioner of Suprematism, in 1917 he produced a series called *Movement of colored plains with one projected on the other*. In 1918, he adopted Linearism. From 1918, he worked at Izo NKP (Department of Fine Arts of Narkompros). With Olga Rozanova, he co-directed the art-industrial subsection of Izo and was head of the purchasing committee for the Museum of Painterly Culture. 1918–26, he taught at the Moscow Proletcult School, and 1918–21, worked on 'spatial constructions.' 1919–20 with Vladimir Krinskii, Alexandr Shevchenko, and Liubov' Popova, he was a member of Zhivskulptarkh (Paintsculptarch). In 1920, he became a member of Inkhuk. 1920–30, he was a professor at Vkhutemas/Vkhutein. 1923–28, he worked with *Lef* and *Novyi lef*, in which some of his photographs and articles appeared; and, in 1927, worked on the Lev Kuleshov film *Zhurnalistka* (*The Journalist*), one of several on which he participated. During the second half of the 1920s, Rodchenko specialized in topographical design and photography. Sympathetic with Tatlin's 'artist engineer' approach, he began more practical pursuits, including the design of furniture and clothing in the 1920s working with his textile-designer wife Varvara Stepanova and others. He was one of the organizers of the Russian pavilion at the 1925 Paris exposition. His Workers' Club at the exposition had all its strictly functional furniture painted black, red and gray; all the objects were plain and utilitarian. In 1930, he joined the October group. From 1924, he specialized in photography and design and, 1930–35, returned to studio painting. In the early 1940s, he produced a series of Abstract Expressionist canvases.

▶ In 1916, ten pieces of his work were included in Tatlin's 'The Store,' including six rendered with a compass and rule. His work was included in the 1921 (III) 'Obmokhu' exhibition and 1921 '5 × 5 = 25' in Moscow. His interior design and furnishings for a Workers' Club was shown in one of the galleries on the Esplanade des Invalides at the 1925 Paris 'Exposition Internationale des Arts Décoratifs et Industriels Modernes.' His work was the subject of the 'Alexander Rodchenko: Photographs' exhibition at the Gantry Arts Centre, Southampton (England), in 1992.

▶ Stephanie Barron and Maurice Tuchman, *The Avant-Garde in Russia, 1910–1930*, Cambridge: MIT, 1980. Pierre Cabanne, *Encyclopédie Art Déco*, Paris: Somogy, 1986:230,233. Selim O. Khan-Magomedov, *Rodchenko: The Complete Work*, Cambridge, MIT, 1987. Selim O. Khan-Magomedov, *Les Vhutemas*, Paris: Regard, 1990: 428–34. Cat., *The Great Utopia: The Russian and Soviet Avant-Garde, 1915–1932*, New York: Guggenheim Museum, 1992.

Roericht, Nick   (1933–)
▶ German designer.
▶ 1955–59, studied Hochschule für Gestaltung, Ulm (Germany).
▶ In 1959, his senior diploma project for stacking dinnerware was widely published and, from 1961 as *Form 11100*, produced by Thomas. He specialized in systems and environments. In 1964, he taught at the Hochschule für Gestaltung. 1967–68, he taught industrial design at Ohio State University in Columbus, Ohio. In 1968, he set up his own studio in Ulm, where he specialized in visual communication and research and developed product design programs. In 1967, he began working for Lufthansa, for which he designed interiors, furnishings, graphics, liveries. He designed stadium seating and desk systems for the 1972 Munich Olympic Games. From 1973, he taught industrial design at the Hochschule der Künste in Berlin.
▶ Cat., Kathryn B. Hiesinger and George H. Marcus III (eds.), *Design Since 1945*, Philadelphia: Philadelphia Museum of Art, 1983:228. Gillo Dorfles, *Il disegno industriale e la sua estetica*, Bologna, 1963: No. 97.

Rogers, Ernesto Nathan   (1909–69)
▶ Italian architect and teacher; born Gardone, Brescia.
▶ Studied Politecnico di Milano.
▶ In 1932, he and others founded the architecture office BBPR. He became well known as an architect and journal editor. 1933–36, he was co-editor of the journal *Quadrante*. 1946–47, he was editor of the journal *Domus*, in which he introduced the ideas of architectural Rationalism, and, 1952–64, of the journal *Casabella-continuità*, which became one of Europe's most influential architecture journals. From 1962, he taught at the Politecnico di Milano, becoming a professor in 1964.
▶ Ernesto N. Rogers, *Esperienze dell'architettura*, Turin, 1958. Ernesto N. Rogers, *Editoriali de architettura*, Turin, 1968. C. De Seta (ed.), *Elementi del fenomeno architettonico*, Naples, 1981. Cat., *Design Process: Olivetti 1903–1983*, Milan, 1983:374.
▶ See BBPR

Roggero, Francesco   (1953–)
▶ Italian designer; born and active Milan.
▶ Studied Liceo Artistico di Brera, Milan, to 1970, and from 1970, architecture, Politecnico di Milano.
▶ In 1970, he established the studio Designers 6R5 in Milan with a group that designed textiles and ceramics. In 1975, Roggero, Maurizio Alberti, Giuseppe Bossi, Pierangelo Marucco, and Bruno Rossio established Original Designers 6R5 in Milan; textile clients included Lanerossi, Sasatex, Taif, and Bassetti in Italy and Griso-Jover in Spain. The group designed tapestries for Printeco and Sirpi in Italy and Le Roi and Griffine Marechal in France. It designed wallpaper for various French firms. Roggero was a member of ADI (Associazione per il Disegno Industriale).
▶ *ADI Annual 1976*, Milan: Associazione per il Disegno Industriale, 1976.

Rohde, Gilbert   (1884–1944)
▶ American industrial designer; born New York.
▶ Studied Art Students' League and Grand Central Galleries, both New York.
▶ By 1923, he was a freelance illustrator for department stores Abraham and Straus, W. and J. Sloane, and Macy's, all New York. In 1927, he traveled to Paris and Germany, where he was inspired by the Modern movement and studied French furniture. In c1928,

he began to design furniture using bakelite and chrome. 1927–28, he decorated the fashion stores of Avedon, Connecticut. In 1928, his interior design and furnishings for the penthouse apartment of Norman Lee at 10 Sheridan Square in Greenwich Village were widely published. 1930–31, he designed two lines of furniture for Heywood-Wakefield of Gardner, Massachusetts, including a renowned bentwood chair that was later reworked for Herman Miller and Kroehler. By 1939, 250,000 copies of the chair had been sold. In c1937, designed a showroom in Chicago for Heywood-Wakefield; designed a showroom for Kroehler and several for Herman Miller; designed the 1942 Executive Office Group by Herman Miller; had other furniture clients including Lloyd, Valley Upholstery, and Brown-Saltzman. From 1931, Rohde designed prolifically for Herman Miller. Rohde designed 1932 tub chairs for Thonet and much furniture in metal for the Troy Sunshade, including 1933 chair in a 'Z' silhouette for which he is well known and a matching stool. For the 1939 'New York World's Fair' he was a design committee member; 1939–43, was head of industrial design, School of Architecture, New York University; designed lighting and consumer appliances, including a large number of electric clocks; lectured throughout the USA; was a member of American Union of Decorative Artists and Craftsmen, and a prolific writer on design.
▶ His work was included in many exhibitions, including the 1932 'Design for the Machine' at the Philadelphia Museum, 1933 Chicago 'Century of Progress' where his interiors for the 'Design for Living' house were shown, 1934 'Machine Art' at the New York Museum of Modern Art, 1934 'Art and Industry Show' of the National Alliance of Art and Industry at the RCA Building, New York, 'Contemporary American Industrial Art: 1940' exhibition at the Metropolitan Museum of Art, and 1939 'New York World's Fair.' His music room was included in the East Gallery of the 1935 'Contemporary American Industrial Art, 1934' exhibition at the New York Metropolitan Museum of Art.
▶ Derek Ostergard and David A. Hanks, 'Gilbert Rohde and the Evolution of Modern Design, 1927–1941,' *Arts Magazine*, October 1981:98–107. Cat., David A. Hanks and Derek Ostergard, *Gilbert Rohde*, New York: Washburn Gallery, 1981. R. Craig Miller, *Modern Design 1890–1990*, New York: Abrams, 1990. Phyllis Ross, 'Gilbert Rohde' in Mel Byars and Russell Flinchum (eds.), *50 American Designers*, Washington: Preservation, 1994.

Rohde, Johan   (1856–1935)
▶ Danish architect, sculptor, metalworker, and textile and furniture designer.
▶ Studied medicine; 1881–82, painting and graphics, Det Kongelige Danske Kunstakademi, Copenhagen.
▶ In 1882, he founded the Kunstnernes Studieskole, where he taught anatomy and, 1908–12, was principal. He designed silver for his own use and had it made at the Georg Jensen Sølvsmedie in 1905. In 1906, he produced his first designs for Jensen, where, from 1913, he worked as a designer. Rohde created many designs still in production today and became one of the firm's most prolific designers. His 1915 *Konge* (*Acorn*) flatware pattern was Jensen's best seller; the motif was later plagiarized by International Silver. His 1920 Streamline pitcher was so advanced that Jensen waited five years before it was put into production. Rohde designed textiles and furniture, and he executed silver designs for A. Dragsted.
▶ He received a bronze medal at the 1900 Paris 'Exposition Universelle,' and the grand prize at the 1925 Paris 'Exposition Internationale des Arts Décoratifs et Industriels Modernes.' His one-person exhibitions included those at Det Danske Kunstindustrimuseum in Copenhagen in 1908 and in Stockholm in 1917. His work was shown in Berlin in 1891, 1893 Chicago 'World's Columbian Exposition,' in Århus in 1909, in Brooklyn, New York, in 1927, and in Helsinki in 1928 and 1931.
▶ Cat., *Georg Jensen Silversmithy: 77 Artists, 75 Years*, Washington: Smithsonian Institution Press, 1980. Cat., David Revere McFadden (ed.), *Scandinavian Modern Design 1880–1980*, New York: Abrams, 1982:270, No. 70. Annelies Krekel-Aalberse, *Art*

Nouveau and Art Déco Silver, New York: Abrams, 1989:218,258.

Rohlfs, Charles (1853–1936)

▶ American furniture designer and craftsman; active Buffalo, New York.

▶ Rohlfs became involved with furniture making when, from his attic studio in Buffalo, he produced furniture mostly for himself and friends. His list of clients expanded and included the Marshall Field department store in Chicago and individuals in Buffalo, New York, Philadelphia, Paris, London, and Bremen. By 1898, he had moved into larger commercial quarters in Buffalo and was making entire rooms of furniture for wealthy clients in other parts of the USA. He used elements of medieval, Moorish, Art Nouveau, and early Norwegian styles, and gave his pieces a distinctly Gothic look. His simple construction and respect for materials associated him with the Arts and Crafts movement. To distinguish his furniture from that of the Stickleys and the simple Mission style, he incorporated ornate surfaces and carving and used exaggerated proportions.

▶ His work was shown at the 1901 Buffalo 'Pan-American Exposition,' 1902 Turin 'Esposizione Internazionale d'Arte Decorativa Moderna,' and 1904 St. Louis 'Louisiana Purchase Exposition,' and included in the 1987–88 ' '"The Art That Is Life"': The Arts and Crafts Movement in America, 1875–1920' traveling exhibition organized by the Boston Museum of Fine Arts.

▶ Cat., Wendy Kaplan, (ed.), ' *"The Art That Is Life"* ': *The Arts and Crafts Movement in America, 1875–1920*, Boston: Museum of Fine Arts, 1987. Cat., Anne Yaffe Phillips, *From Architecture to Object*, New York: Hirschl and Adler, 1989:26.

Rolff, Henrik (1944–)

▶ Danish architect and furniture designer.

▶ Studied furniture design, Kunsthåndværkerskolen, Copenhagen, to 1968.

▶ From 1968, he worked with Krohn & Hartvig Rasmussen on the Hvidovre Hospital project, and, from 1972, with architect Ole Hagen on the Handelbankens project. He set up an architecture office in 1978 with Leif Erik Rasmussen. His furniture designs were produced by Fritz Hansen.

▶ Frederik Sieck, *Nutidig Dansk Møbeldesign:-en kortfattet illustreret beskrivelse*, Copenhagen: Bondo Gravesen; 1990 Busck edition in English.

Roller, Alfred (1864–1935)

▶ Moravian set designer; born Brünn (now Brno, Czech Republic); active Vienna.

▶ He designed sets for the Wiener Werkstätte, subsequently becoming primarily a set designer. He was particularly successful with operas.

▶ Günther Feuerstein, *Vienna—Present and Past: Arts and Crafts—Applied Art—Design*, Vienna: Jugend und Volk, 1976: 42,50,81.

Rollin, Lucien

▶ French designer.

▶ He designed a bedroom in the French pavilion at the 1939 New York World's Fair; was active in the Salons of the Société des Artistes Décorateurs, 1928–37.

▶ Yvonne Brunhammer and Suzanne Tice, *French Decorative Art: The Société des Artistes Décorateurs*, Paris: Flammarion, 1990.

Rolodex

▶ Desktop card file system.

▶ In the 1940s, Zephyr American of Long Island City, New York, produced the *Autodex*, a standard address case the size of an envelope which opened at whichever letter the user chose. The *Rolodex* was invented in 1950 during the process of correcting the *Autodex*'s design flaws. The original model had triangular supports for the wheel which held the file cards. The firm itself was renamed Rolodex in 1974. Some current models hold up to 6,000 cards. Its technology shifted to the computer in the early 1990s.

▶ Diane di Costanzo, *American Home*, October 1990:27.

Romani, Giorgio (1946–)

▶ Italian industrial designer; born and active Milan.

▶ Studied architecture, Politecnico di Milano, to 1968.

▶ He began his industrial design activity in 1968 in association with Riccardo Nava, Duccio Soffientini, and Alessandro Ubertazzi in the studio DA in Milan. From 1970, he collaborated with DA on traditional clocks and electronic equipment for Italora and was a consultant on clock design application and the ergonomics of precision instruments. In 1975 with others at DA, he designed sailboat fittings for Nemo and Comar. His clients included Superband, Sordelli, and Svaba. He was a member of ADI (Associazione per il Disegno Industriale).

▶ He participated in the competition of the magazine *Interni* and the firm Faema, and in the ADI Compasso d'Oro exhibition.

▶ *ADI Annual 1976*, Milan: Associazione per il Disegno Industriale, 1976.

Romanoff, Maya (1941–)

▶ American textile designer.

▶ Studied University of California at Berkeley.

▶ With his wife Rebecca, he began experimenting with resist-dyeing, using the results first for clothing and later furnishings, and developing the process for mass production. During the 1970s, he introduced 'textile environments,' for which unique commissioned pieces, coordinated wall and floor coverings, and upholstery textiles were produced; the first was the 1971 'Garden Room,' created for the magazine *House and Garden*; for the installation, he produced a resist-dyed canvas floor covering, a concept he introduced in 1976. He was the first to use quilting in domestic furnishings and developed methods for resist-dyeing on suede and leather.

▶ His resist-dyed canvas floor covering won the 1976 Resources Council award in the USA for best technological innovation in American domestic furnishings.

▶ Cat., Kathryn B. Hiesinger and George H. Marcus III (eds.), *Design Since 1945*, Philadelphia: Philadelphia Museum of Art, 1983:228,VII–52. *Maya Romanoff: Fabric Impressionist*, New York: The Arsenal, 1979.

Rombaux, Égide

▶ Belgian sculptor and medallist; active Brussels.

▶ Studied under Charles van der Stappen and Joseph Lambeaux.

▶ He worked mainly in ivory, producing portrait busts, statues, and candelabra. Through his collaboration with silversmith Franz Hoosemans he executed work of particular distinction, as illustrated by their table lamps and candelabra.

▶ Rombaux's *Venusberg* ivory group was shown at the 1897 chryselephantine exhibition at the Musée Royal de l'Afrique Centrale in Tervueren.

▶ Alastair Duncan, *Art Nouveau and Art Déco Lighting*, New York: Simon and Schuster, 1978:51.

Ronchi, Carlo (1940–)

▶ Italian designer; born Cinisello Balsamo; active Milan.

▶ Ronchi began his professional career in 1968. His clients included Plan (lighting), First (upholstered furniture), Garavaglia (kitchen systems), and Volani (industrial buildings). He was a member of ADI (Associazione per il Disegno Industriale).

▶ He participated in the 1972 ADI design competition Città.

▶ *ADI Annual 1976*, Milan: Associazione per il Disegno Industriale, 1976.

Ronchi, Domenico (1933–)

▶ Italian architect and designer; born and active Milan.

▶ Studied architecture, Politecnico di Milano, to 1963.

▶ He became associated in 1963 with the group CP & PR, becoming active in design, architecture, and town planning. In 1964, he became a member of Albo. 1963–69, he was assistant professor of elementary construction. From 1964, he worked on interior design magazines published by Mondadori. He designed furniture, shelving systems, ceramics, and lighting; his clients included Fontana Arte, Ideal Standard, Salvarani, Carrara & Matta, G. Pozzi,

and Trigano Italiana. He was a member of ADI (Associazione per il Disegno Industriale).
▶ *ADI Annual 1976*, Milan: Associazione per il Disegno Industriale, 1976.

Rondel, Stéphane   (1962–)
▶ French engineer and furniture designer; active Paris.
▶ Rondel first designed sports equipment; in 1987, turned to furniture, specializing in garden furniture in rusted iron.
▶ Received 1989 Appel permanent sponsorship from VIA for benches and chairs produced by VIA Diffusion and shown at 1990 Salon du Meuble, Paris.
▶ Cat., *Les années VIA 1980–1990*, Paris: Musée des Arts Décoratifs, 1990:189.

Rookwood Pottery
▶ American ceramics manufacturer; located Cincinnati, Ohio.
▶ Maria Longworth Nichols (1849–1932) attended the first china painting classes at the University of Cincinnati School of Design, along with Maria Eggers, in 1874. Competition between Maria Nichols and M. Louise McLaughlin came about when the latter established the Cincinnati Pottery Club in 1879; both worked for Frederick Dallas at his commercial pottery in Cincinnati and experimented with china painting. Nichols established Rookwood Pottery in 1880; it was an event marking the culmination of the Cincinnati women's art movement, and the beginning of art pottery in the USA. Nichols hired Joseph Bailey Jr. in 1880 as superintendent and Joseph Bailey Sr. in 1881; she was its artistic director. 1881–83, with instructors Clara Chipman Newton and Laura Frey, she operated the Rookwood School for Pottery Decoration. China painters working at Rookwood included Frey, Newton, and Lorinda Epply 1904–48, William Henschel 1907–39, Albert R. Valentien from 1881, Matthew A. Daly from 1884, William P. McDonald from 1884, Kataro Shirayamadani from 1887, and William Watts Taylor from 1883 as manager. The pottery became a viable financial operation; it was turned over to Taylor in 1891. Rookwood's painters also included Sara Sax in the 1910s and 1920s, Elizabeth F. McDermott, Edward T. Hurley from the 1900s to 1940s, and Charles J. McLaughlin in the 1910s. Until the 1930s, Rookwood produced artistic ceramics and mass-production pieces in high-glaze and matt finishes. The firm moved in 1960 to Starkville, Missouri, where a few pieces were produced until 1966. In 1982, Arthur J. Townley of Michigan Center, Michigan, purchased the remains of the company and, in 1984, began to produce a limited range of ceramic novelties including paperweights, advertising signs, and bookends with the original master molds.
▶ A full range of Rookwood pottery was shown at the 1893 Chicago 'World's Columbian Exposition.' Rookwood's pieces by Valentien and Shirayamadani won a gold medal at the 1889 Paris 'Exposition Universelle.' The firm won honors at the 1900 Paris 'Exposition Universelle' (grand prize), 1901 Buffalo 'Pan-American Exposition' (gold medal), 1902 Turin 'Esposizione Internazionale d'Arte Decorativa Moderna' (diploma of honor), 1904 St. Louis 'Louisiana Purchase Exposition' (grand prize), 1907 Hampton Roads, Virginia, 'Jamestown Tercentennial Exhibition' (gold medal), and 1909 Seattle 'Alaska-Yukon Pacific Exposition' (grand prize). William Watts Taylor was appointed Chevalier de la Légion d'honneur.
▶ Herbert Peck, *The Book of Rookwood Pottery*, New York: Crown, 1968. Paul Evans, *Art Pottery of the United States: An Encyclopedia of Producers and Their Marks*, New York, 1974:255–60. Cat., *The Ladies, God Bless 'Em: The Women's Art Movement in Cincinnati in the Nineteenth Century*, Cincinnati: Cincinnati Art Museum, 1976. Anthea Callen, *Women Artists of the Arts and Crafts Movement, 1870–1914*, New York, 1979:79–85,226. Garth Clark, *A Century of Ceramics in the United States, 1878–1978*, New York, 1979:255–60. Virginia Raymond Cummins, *Rookwood Pottery Potpourri*, Silver Spring, Md: Cliff R. Leonard and Duke Coleman, 1980. Cat., *Celebrate Cincinnati Art*, Cincinnati: Cincinnati Art Museum, 1982:29–48,49–70. Cat., Kenneth R. Trapp, *Toward the Modern Style: Rookwood Pottery, the Later Years, 1915–1950*, New York: Jordan-Volpe Gallery, 1983. Cat., Doreen Bolger Burke et al., *In Pursuit of Beauty: Americans and the Aesthetic Movement*, New York: Metropolitan Museum of Art and Rizzoli, 1987:464–65. *American Art Pottery*, New York: Cooper-Hewitt Museum, 1987.

Rorimer, Louis   (1872–1939)
▶ American designer; born Cleveland, Ohio.
▶ Studied Manual Training School, Cleveland; Kunstgewerbeschule, Munich; École des Arts Décoratifs, and Académie Julien, Paris.
▶ Variously active as an artist, teacher, and president of the Rorimer Brooks Studios, he was widely known and received numerous interior design commissions, including residences throughout the USA and for the Statler hotel chain. He was a member of the US government commission to visit the 1925 Paris 'Exposition Internationale des Arts Décoratifs et Industriels Modernes.' He was active as a member of the American Union of Decorative Artists and Craftsmen in New York.
▶ *The New York Times*, 1 Dec. 1939:23. Karen Davies, *At Home in Manhattan: Modern Decorative Arts, 1925 to the Depression*, New Haven: Yale, 1983:26.

Rörstrand Porslinsfabrik
▶ Swedish ceramics factory.
▶ The factory was established in 1726 at Rörstrand, Stockholm, as the earliest ceramics production under government-supported management; began production of faïence in cobalt blue; from 1758, began to produce enamel painted and gilded ceramics; in 1783, bought the rival Marieberg factory and began production of cream-colored earthenware, reacting to English competition; in 1895, appointed Alf Wallander artistic director and produced his Art Nouveau designs. From 1917, Edward Hald worked for the firm designing earthenware. In 1926, the firm moved to Gothenburg; in 1931, appointed Gunnar Nylund artistic director; in 1932, expanded to Lidköping, moving there entirely in 1936. Its tradition of hiring innovative designers continued with Signe Persson-Melin and Rolf Sinnemark and Finnish designers Oliva Toikka and Heikki Orvola. In 1983, Rörstrand was purchased by Arabia (of the Wärtsilä group), becoming Rörstrand-Gustavsberg.
▶ Jennifer Hawkins Opie, *Scandinavia: Ceramics and Glass in the Twentieth Century*, New York: Rizzoli, 1989.

Rose, Hajo   (b. Hans-Joachim Rose   1910–)
▶ German textile designer and teacher; born Mannheim; husband of Katja Rose.
▶ 1930–33, studied Bauhaus, Berlin.
▶ He settled in the Netherlands in 1934, and (with Katja Rose) taught in Amsterdam. In 1949, he settled in Dresden, where he taught, and subsequently in Leipzig.
▶ Lionel Richard, *Encyclopédie du Bauhaus*, Paris: Somogy, 1985:207. Hans Wichmann, *Von Morris bis Memphis, Textilien der Neuen Sammlung, Ende 19. bis Ende 20. Jahrhundert*, Basel/Boston/Berlin: Birkhäuser, 1990:14,207,449.

Rose, Katja   (b. Käthe Schmidt   1905–)
▶ German textile designer and teacher; wife of Hajo Rose.
▶ Studied drawing and applied art in Hamburg; 1931–33, Bauhaus, Berlin; textile school, Berlin.
▶ 1936–41, (with Hajo Rose) taught fabric design in Amsterdam and, after World War II, settled in Munich.
▶ Cat., *Katja Rose, Weberei am Bauhaus 1931–33, Bildwebereien 1964–1983*, Berlin: Bauhaus-Archiv, 1983. Lionel Richard, *Encyclopédie du Bauhaus*, Paris: Somogy, 1985:207. Hans Wichmann, *Von Morris bis Memphis, Textilien der Neuen Sammlung, Ende 19. bis Ende 20. Jahrhundert*, Basel/Boston/Berlin: Birkhäuser, 1990:207.

Rose Valley Association
▶ American crafts community; located near Philadelphia.
▶ The Rose Valley Association was begun in 1901 as a community by M. Hawley McLanahan and Philadelphia architect William L. Price in an abandoned mill building at Moylan, near Philadelphia. It was based on the ideals of C.R. Ashbee's Guild of Handicraft and William Morris's *News from Nowhere*; produced pottery and furniture sold in a store in Philadelphia; 1903–07, published the magazine *Artsman* and set up the Village Press. It became bankrupt in 1909.
▶ Isabelle Anscombe and Charlotte Gere, *Arts and Crafts in Britain and America*, New York: Rizzoli, 1978:150.

Rosell, Gemma Bernal   (1949–)
▶ Spanish industrial designer; born Barcelona.
▶ Studied philosophy, University of Barcelona; industrial design, Escuela de Diseño Eina, Barcelona.
▶ Rosell, Ramon Isern, and Beth Galí set up a small studio in Barcelona, designing toys, amplifiers, and other products. From 1971, she was manager of the design department in a metal construction firm and, in 1973, began working once more with Isern; in 1983, (with Isern) set up the studio Bernal-Isern, designing furniture, packaging, stationery products, and bathroom fixtures for clients including Montseny, Concepta, Andreu, Est, Roca Henkel, Miquelrius, Vilagrasa, Blauet, Nova Norma, Dytecma, and Enea; designed the 1984 *Eclipse* table by Disform, Barcelona; 1986 *Biblos* shelving system by Grupo T, Barcelona; and 1988 *Gala* armchair by Sellex, San Sebastian.
▶ Cat., Design Center Stuttgart, *Women in Design: Careers and Life Histories Since 1900*, Stuttgart: Haus der Wirtschaft, 1989: 306–09.

Rosen, Anton   (1858–1928)
▶ Danish architect and designer.
▶ Rosen designed the Palace Hotel in Copenhagen and was principal architect for the 1909 Landsudstillingen (Danish National Exhibition) in Århus. His work for the Georg Jensen Sølvsmedie around this time was noteworthy for its use of silver with amber, coral, malachite, and other semi-precious stones.
▶ Cat., *Georg Jensen Silversmithy: 77 Artists, 75 Years*, Washington: Smithsonian Institution Press, 1980.

Rosenbaum-Ducommun, Wladimir   (1894–1984)
▶ Lithuanian lawyer and art dealer; active Zürich and Ascona.
▶ Studied law in Zürich.
▶ As a lawyer, he was active on behalf of emigrants; he served as lawyer for the construction of the Neubühl settlement in Zürich. 1931–34, he was president of board of directors and stockholder in the Wohnbedarf furniture store. A middleman for various industries, he was a board member of BAG bronzeware and lamp manufacturer in Türgi. He lost his law license and became an antique and art dealer in Ascona.
▶ Friederike Mehlau-Wiebking et al., *Schweizer Typenmöbel 1925–35, Sigfried Giedion und die Wohnbedarf AG*, Zürich: gta, 1989:230.

Rosenberg, Gustav Valdemar   (aka Walle Rosenberg 1891–1919)
▶ Finnish painter and metalworker; active Helsinki.
▶ Studied painting in Helsinki, Paris, and Rome.
▶ Rosenberg designed silver produced by A.A. Alm in Porvoo. His work was influenced by British and Austrian artists, as evident in a jelly bowl of his design and, in his painting, by Post-Impressionists, particularly Henri Matisse.
▶ Cat., David Revere McFadden (ed.), *Scandinavian Modern Design 1880–1980*, New York: Abrams, 1982:270, No. 54. Annelies Krekel-Aalberse, *Art Nouveau and Art Déco Silver*, New York: Abrams, 1989:241,258.

Rosenthal
▶ German ceramics manufacturer.
▶ Philip Rosenthal (1855–1937) settled in the USA in the 1870s, where he worked for a porcelain factory. He returned to Germany in the late 1870s to take over the family business. In 1880, Rosenthal set up a porcelain decorating workshop in Erkersreuth, near Selb. Having difficulty in acquiring plain blanks, he opened a factory at Selb in 1891. Becoming very successful prior to World War II, the firm bought out a number of companies. In 1954, the firm began selling wares through in-store departments, an American technique that assured control over its image and customer relations. Having established Studio Haus throughout Europe, its 'Studio-Line' was launched at the 1961 Hanover trade fair. Designs for the 'Studio-Line' were chosen by a panel of judges (design personalities and lay people). Rosenthal's management encouraged designers through its 'Studio-Line,' including Raymond Loewy (with Richard Latham), Walter Gropius (with Louis A. McMillen and others), and Wilhelm Wagenfeld, and a new generation including Bjørn Wiinblad, Timo Sarpaneva, Tapio Wirkkala, Lino Sabattini, and Michael Boehm. Rosenthal's glass was produced at the factory in Amberg; its design center was located in Selb.
▶ It won numerous awards, including the grand prize at the 1910 Brussels 'Exposition Universelle et Internationale' and 1937 Paris 'Exposition Internationale des Arts et Techniques dans la Vie Moderne.' The Gropius-McMillan *TAC 1* tea set won the 1969 International Vicenza Prize.
▶ Cat., *Hundert Jahre Porzellan*, Hanover: Kestner-Museum, 1982. Frederick Cooke, *Glass: Twentieth-Century Design*, New York: Dutton, 1986:92.

Roseville Pottery
▶ American pottery; located Zanesville, Ohio.
▶ Established in 1892, Roseville was among the largest and most successful Arts and Crafts potteries of its time. Frederick H. Rhead was its artistic director 1904–08; introduced sgraffito there; maintained a stylized English approach. The pottery introduced art ceramics as a sideline. It closed in 1954.
▶ Cat., Anne Yaffe Phillips, *From Architecture to Object*, New York: Hirschl and Adler, 1989:70. Cat., Leslie Greene Bowman, *American Arts & Crafts: Virtue in Design*, Boston: Bulfinch, 1990: 176.

Rosinski, Irena   (1956–)
▶ Polish furniture designer; active France.
▶ Studied School of Applied Arts, Gdansk, and École des Beaux-Arts, Toulouse.
▶ She set up a design office in Toulouse working for furniture companies in the area; designed exhibition stands for the regional council of Midi-Pyrénées, furniture for the airport in Blagnac, and the chamber of commerce and a hospital in Toulouse.
▶ Won 1982 VIA/UNIFA competition for a chair in lacquered wood and steel tubing, 1982 VIA/Conforama competition, and 1983 VIA Carte blanche award for wood and glass dining room furniture.
▶ Cat., *Les années VIA 1980–1990*, Paris: Musée des Arts Décoratifs, 1990:152–53.

Rossari, Ambrogio   (1943–)
▶ Italian industrial designer; born Salò; active Milan.
▶ Studied Corso Superiore di Disegno Industriale, Venice to 1966; received master's degree in product design from Illinois Institute of Technology, Chicago.
▶ Rossari became active in 1971 as a designer of domestic furnishings and lighting, known for his bathroom fittings for Cesame and wares for Guzzini and Cesana. His clients included Rubinetterie Giustina, Armo, Valdadige, Appiani, Pirelli, Veca, and Ceim. He was a member of ADI (Associazione per il Disegno Industriale).
▶ *ADI Annual 1976*, Milan: Associazione per il Disegno Industriale, 1976. *Modo*, No. 148, March–April 1993: 125.

Rosselli, Alberto (1921–76)

▶ Italian architect and industrial designer; born Palermo; active Milan.

▶ 1938–39, studied engineering; 1945–47, architecture, Politecnico di Milano.

▶ In 1950, Rosselli, Gio Ponti, and Antonio Fornaroli established the architecture and design firm Studio PFR; they produced notable structures, including the 1956 Pirelli tower in Milan. Active concurrently, in 1955, he opened his own office in Milan, designing transportation for Fiat-Orlandi, appliances, furniture for Arflex, Bonacina, Kartell, and Saporiti, electric clocks and domestic appliances, bathroom fixtures, lighting for Fontana Arte, metalwork, glassware for Salviati, and ceramics for Cesame. 1963–76, he taught industrial design, Politecnico di Milano; in 1956, was president of ADI (Associazione per il Disegno Industriale); 1961–63, was vice-president of ICSID; and, in 1963, became an industrial design assistant professor at the Politecnico di Milano. In 1957, he developed an interest in plastics, his first design in the medium being a bathroom unit for Montecatini. He was a member of the committee of the 1968 (XIV) Triennale di Milano and a founder of the journal *Stile Industria*, where he was editor 1953–63. One of his best known designs, the colorful and lightweight 1970 one-piece fiberglass *Jumbo Chair* was produced 1970–78 by Saporiti; it looked like a shoe in silhouette and was related to his 1969 *Moby Dick* chaise longue. His architectural works included the *Corriere della Sera* newspaper building.

▶ Received gold medals at 1954 (X), 1957 (XI), and 1960 (XII) Triennali di Milano. The *Jumbo Chair* was shown at the 1967 Milano International Furniture Exhibition, the 1970 'Modern Chairs 1918–1970' exhibition at the Whitechapel Gallery in London, and 1983–84 'Design Since 1945' exhibition at the Philadelphia Museum of Art. Received 1957 Compasso d'Oro for his *Meteor* motor-coach for Fiat-Orlandi.

▶ Cat., *Modern Chairs 1918–1970*, London: Lund Humphries, 1971. Paolo Fossati, *Il design in Italia*, Turin, 1972: 128–38. Cat., Milena Lamarová, *Design a Plastické Hmoty*, Prague: Uměleckoprůmyslové Muzeum, 1972:152. Giovanni Klaus Koenig et al., *Stile Industria: Alberto Rosselli*, Parma, 1981. Cat., Kathryn B. Hiesinger and George H. Marcus III (eds.), *Design Since 1945*, Philadelphia: Philadelphia Museum of Art, 1983:229,III–75.

Rossetti, Dante Gabriel (1828–82)

▶ British painter and poet; born London.

▶ He studied drawing with Cotman and, in 1848, with Holman Hunt.

▶ In 1848, Hunt, John Everett Millais, and Rossetti founded the Pre-Raphaelite Brotherhood. In 1850 with William Morris, he painted frescoes for the Oxford Union debating hall. Morris, G.F. Watts, Edward Burne-Jones, and John Ruskin began supporting the Pre-Raphaelites in 1851 and later became members. In the 1860s, Rossetti, like his friend James Abbot McNeill Whistler, began to collect Chinese porcelain and Japanese woodcuts. Profoundly affected by the death of his wife Elizabeth Siddal in 1862, Rossetti became more and more eccentric and ceased painting in 1877. He published *Poems* (1870) and his last work *Ballads and Sonnets* (1881). Encouraged in the early years by Hunt and Morris, he became involved in the applied arts. Rossetti designed furniture and stained glass and, primarily through his graphic design, was influential on the continent and in the USA. Rossetti was involved in the formation of Morris, Marshall, and Faulkner, the Arts and Crafts decorating firm founded by William Morris and others, and contributed designs.

▶ Yvonne Brunhammer et al., *Art Nouveau Belgium, France*, Houston: Rice University, 1976. Alicia Craig Faxon, *Dante Gabriel Rossetti*; New York: Abbeville, 1989.

Rossi, Aldo (1931–)

▶ Italian architect; born and active Milan.

▶ 1949–59, studied Politecnico di Milano.

▶ He began his career in 1956 in the studio of Ignazio Gardella;

later worked with Marco Zanuso; 1955–64, worked at *Casabella-Continuità* and was its editor 1961–64; in 1963, was an assistant to Ludovico Quaroni in Arezzo; 1963–65, was assistant to Carlo Aymonino at Instituto Universitario di Architettura, Venice; 1969–72, taught at Politecnico di Milano; 1972–74, was guest professor, Eidgenössische Technische Hochschule, Zürich; in 1974, returned to Politecnico di Milano; from 1975, held the chair of architectural composition, Instituto Universitario di Architettura, Venice; in 1977, was visiting professor, Cooper Union School of Architecture, New York; from 1980, visiting professor, Yale University; wrote the book *L'architettura della città* (1966). From 1971, he collaborated with Gianni Braghieri. From 1983, he was director of the architecture section of the Biennale di Venezia. His few buildings included the Teatro del Mondo at the 1980 Biennale di Venezia, a floating wood and steel theater whose form provided the inspiration for his 1983 tea set for Alessi. He was one of the 11 architects and designers to create a service for Alessi's *Tea and Coffee Piazza* project in 1983; Rossi's service was housed in a glass building-like case with a small flag on top and a clock in the frieze. His other coffee pots for Alessi, *90002/6* and *90002/3*, which again reflected the silhouettes of architecture rather than utensils, were highly publicized. His 1985 *Pressofilter* for Alessi incorporated the 1955 Chambord mechanism for pressing coffee grounds. This was followed by the 1986 *Cafetière* for Alessi. The most memorable and refined of Rossi's designs for Alessi was the 1986 *Il Conico* kettle. From the 1980s, some of his furniture was produced by Unifor. He designed the 1983 *Cabina dell'Elba* wardrobe cabinets, *Milano* side chair of c1987, and 1986 *Theatre* seating and bed (with Luca Meda), all by Molteni, and 1986 *Il Rilievo* marble table by Up & Up. For the 1989 hotel Il Palazzo in Japan, he attempted to recreate an Italian castle. He designed marble furniture for Logoni and the 1991 fabric collection for DesignTex. His controversial and much discussed architectural designs included the 1969–73 residential building in Monte Amiata complex, Gallaratese 2, Milan, 1971 competition project for the new cemetery (with Gianni Braghieri) in Modena, 1972 elementary school (with Gianni Braghieri and Arduino Cantafora) in Fagnano Olona, 1977 competition project for the Student House in Chieti, 1981–82 project for the reconstruction of the Teatro Carlo Felice (with Ignazio Gadella and Fabio Reinhart) in Genoa, and 1984 project for an office building (with Gianni Braghieri and others) in Buenos Aires. In 1987, he contributed to Parc de la Villette in Paris; and in 1989, designed the Centre d'Art contemporain à Vassivières in Limousin (France).

▶ He won first prize (with Braghieri, C. Stead, and J. Johnson) in the competition for the 1984 'Südliche Friedrichstadt, Kochstrasse-Friedrichstrasse, IBA 84' in Berlin. He was director of the international architecture division at the 1973 (XV) Triennale di Milano. His work was the subject of the 1979 'Aldo Rossi in America 1976 to 1979' exhibition at the Institute for Architecture and Urban Studies in New York and 1983 exhibition in Modena. His furniture range for Unifor was introduced at the 1989 Salone del Mobile in Milan. His 1980 *Cabina* wardrobe for Molteni, 1986 *Il Rilievo* table for Up & Up, and 1987 *Carteggio* cabinet for Molteni were shown at the 1991 'Mobili Italiani 1961–1991: Le Varie Età dei linguaggi' exhibition in Milan.

▶ Aldo Rossi, *L'architettura della città*, Padua 1966; *The Architecture of the City*, Cambridge, Massachusetts, 1982. Aldo Rossi, *Scritti scelti sull'architettura e la città*, Milan, 1975. 'Aldo Rossi,' *Architecture and Urbanism*, No. 65, 1976. Francesco Moschini (ed.), *Aldo Rossi: Projects and Drawings, 1962–1979*, New York, 1979. Cat., *Aldo Rossi in America 1976 to 1979*, New York: Institute for Architecture and Urban Studies, 1979. Aldo Rossi, *A Scientific Autobiography*, Cambridge, Massachusetts, 1981. Gianni Braghieri, *Aldo Rossi*, Bologna and Barcelona, 1981. Giovanni Klaus Koenig et al., *Stile Industria: Alberto Rosselli*, Parma, 1981. 'Aldo Rossi and 21 works,' *A + U* (special issue), 1982. E.J. Johnson, 'What Remains of Man—Aldo Rossi's Modena Cemetery,' *Journal of the Society of Architectural Historians 41*, No. 1, 1982:38–54. Cat., V. Savi and M. Lupano (eds.), *Aldo Rossi: Opere recenti*,

Modena, 1983. Officina Alessi, *Tea and Coffee Piazza: Il Servizi da tè e caffè*, Milan: Crusinallo, 1983. V. Savi, 'Il cimitero aldorossiano: Traccia di racconto critico,' *Lotus International*, No. 38, 1984:30–43. *Casabella 48*, No. 502, 1984:52ff. *Lotus International*, No. 2, 1984:12–39. H. Piñon, *Arquitectura de las neovanguardias*, Barcelona, 1984:79–116. *Les Carnets du Design*, Paris: Mad-Cap Productions et APCI, 1986:45,79. Fumio Shimizu and Matteo Thun (eds.), *The Descendants of Leonardo: The Italian Design*, Tokyo, 1987:334. Juli Capella and Quim Larrea, *Designed by Architects in the 1980s*, New York, Rizzoli, 1988. Jeremy Myerson and Sylvia Katz, *Conran Design Guides: Tableware*, London: Conran Octopus, 1990:77.

Rossi, Fernando   (1929–)
▶ Italian designer; active Milan.
▶ Rossi began his professional career in 1958. He designed furniture and lighting for clients including O-Luce, Elettronica Trentina, Luigi Colombo, Molteni-Pagani, and Casasei. He was a member of ADI (Associazione per il Disegno Industriale).
▶ *ADI Annual 1976*, Milan: Associazione per il Disegno Industriale, 1976.

Rossi, Pucci De   (1947–)
▶ Italian furniture designer and artist; born Verona; active New York and Paris.
▶ Studied sculpture under H. Brooks Walker.
▶ He began his work as a sculptor in 1971, using metal at first. In 1973, he added wood to his repertoire of materials. His furniture and lighting were designed with a sense of humor. In 1982, he executed works in metal in New York. His 1982 *Tristan Table* and 1985 *Bear Rug* were produced by Galerie Néotù. Other furniture designs included the 1991 *Lido* cocktail side table, *Vizir* console, *Lancelot* candelabra, *Diavola* chair, *Stephanie* mirror, *Parsifal* coffee table, *Battista* table, *Trident* table, and *Maya* étagère.
▶ His one-person exhibitions included those at Galerie Art 3 in Paris in 1973, Galerie Le Métier d'Art in Milan in 1973, Agora gallery in Maastricht in 1974, Galerie Caroline Corre in Paris in 1980, Gallery of Functional Art in Los Angeles in 1986, Galerie Néotù in Paris in 1987 and 1989, Galerie Lechanjour in Nice in 1988, and Institut français de Cologne in 1990. His work was included in the 1973 'Nuovo materiali del fantastico' in Piombino; 1974 'AZ' at the Loggione La Scacchiera in Padua; 1977 exhibition at the Studio Alchimia in Milan; 1978 'Fil de Fer, Fer Blanc' at Centre Georges Pompidou, Paris; 1980 '4+4' exhibition at the Centre Culturel italien in Paris; 1980 'Le Métier d'Art' at the Paris Musée des Arts Décoratifs; 1982 'L'Art vivant' in Paris; 1984 (II) Biennale de Métier d'Art in Villeneuve-les-Avignon; 1985 'Onze Lampes' at Galerie Néotù, and 1986 'Design Beyond Senses' at the Kunstmuseum in Düsseldorf. His *Divola* chair was introduced at the 1991 (III) 'International Contemporary Furniture Fair,' New York.
▶ Sophie Anargyros, *Intérieurs 80*, Paris: Regard, 1983. *Style 85*, Paris: Salon de la Société des Artistes Décorateurs, 1985. Sophie Anargyros, *Les années 80*, Paris: Rivages, 1986. Christine Colin, *Design Aujourd'hui*, Paris: Flammarion, 1989.

Rossin, Antonio
▶ Italian industrial designer; active Monza.
▶ Studied architecture in Venice to 1966.
▶ He worked from 1967 in the studios of Gardella and Morassutti in Milan. 1969–72, he taught at the Scuola Politecnica di Design in Milan. In 1972, he was a consultant to Zanotta in Nova Milanese and to Telbaldi in Monza, setting up industrial prototypes for publication in the magazines *Casabella*, *Domus*, *Ottagono*, and other publications. In 1975, he taught in Bologna. In 1976, he was a consultant designer to Bernini, Bazzani clock works, Cristina Rubinetterie, and others. He was a member of ADI (Associazione per il Disegno Industriale).
▶ *ADI Annual 1976*, Milan: Associazione per il Disegno Industriale, 1976.

Rossio, Bruno   (1953–)
▶ Italian designer; born and active Milan.
▶ From 1970, studied architecture, Politecnico di Milano.
▶ He became associated in 1973 with the studio Designers 6R5 in Milan, which designed textiles and ceramics. In 1975, Rossio, Maurizio Alberti, Giuseppe Bossi, Pierangelo Marucco, and Francesco Roggero established Original Designers 6R5 in Milan; textile clients included Lanerossi, Sasatex, Taif, and Bassetti in Italy and Griso-Jover in Spain. The group designed tapestries for Printeco and Sirpi in Italy and Le Roi and Griffine Marechal in France. It designed wallpaper for various French firms. Rossio was a member of ADI (Associazione per il Disegno Industriale).
▶ *ADI Annual 1976*, Milan: Associazione per il Disegno Industriale, 1976.

Rossmann, Zdeněk   (1905–84)
▶ Czech book designer, architect, set designer, and architectural theoretician; born Mährisch Ostrau (now Moravská Ostrava, Czech Republic).
▶ 1923–28, studied Czech University of Technology, Brno; 1928–29, Bauhaus, Dessau.
▶ He was a member of the Devětsil group from 1923 until its close in 1931, and of the Brno Devětsil group 1923–27. He designed publications including *Pásmo* (1924–27) and the *Fronta* compendium (1927). His work was based on the principles of Bayer and Tschichold. His realized architectural work is not numerous. He criticized Le Corbusier's emotional Functionalism for antisocial excess of form. Rossmann's 1929–32 stage sets for the National Theater in Brno were significant examples of Czech Constructivism.
▶ He designed the pavilion for the newspaper *Právo lidu* at the "Výstava soudobé kultury" exhibition in Brno in the 1920s.
▶ Cat., *Devětsil: Czech Avant-Garde Art, Architecture, and Design of the 1920s and 30s*, Oxford Museum of Modern Art and London Design Museum, 1990.

Rostrup, Stephan   (1947–)
▶ Danish sculptor and painter.
▶ Rostrup began designing silver sculpture and jewelry in 1978 for the Georg Jensen Sølvsmedie.
▶ Cat., *Georg Jensen Silversmithy: 77 Artists, 75 Years*, Washington: Smithsonian Institution Press, 1980.

Rota, Bruno   (1941–)
▶ Italian architect and designer; born Agen (France); active Bergamo.
▶ He designed shelving and office furniture systems produced by Struktura in Ossanesga di Valbrembo, Bergamo; had clients including Kapu, Cose, and Neon/Color; became a member of ADI (Associazione per il Disegno Industriale).
▶ *ADI Annual 1976*, Milan: Associazione per il Disegno Industriale, 1976.

Roth, Alfred   (1903–)
▶ Swiss architect and furniture designer; born Wangen an der Aare; active Zürich.
▶ 1922–26, studied architecture, Eidgenössische Technische Hochschule, Zürich, under Gustav Gull and Karl Moser.
▶ He worked in 1926 in Karl Moser's office, where he got to know Le Corbusier. In 1927, he was hired as contractor for both Le Corbusier houses built at the Weissenhof-Siedlung in Stuttgart. 1928–30, he lived in Sweden, where he set up his own architecture office. In 1930, he returned to Zürich and worked in the construction office of the Neubühl Werkbund settlement. In the early 1930s, furniture designs by Roth were sold at the Wohnbedarf store in Zürich. From 1932, he was active with the CIAM (Congrès Internationaux d'Architecture Moderne) and headed its Swiss group 1950–56. In 1932, he set up his own architectural office. In 1934–39, he and cousin Emil Roth collaborated. In 1935–36, the Roths and Marcel Breuer designed houses in the Doldertal in Zürich for Sigfried Giedion. He became editor of the architecture magazine *Weiterbauen*. In 1932 and 1943–1955, he

was on the editorial staff of the magazine *Werk* and, 1945–52, of the journal *Schweizerischer Baukatalog*. In 1946, he began the publication of his *Civitas* pamphlets. His books include *Die Neue Architektur* (1939), *Das Neue Schulhaus* (1950), and *Begegnung mit Pionieren* (1973). He was a foreign member of UAM (Union des Artistes Modernes) and, 1949–53, lectured at the universities of Washington, St. Louis, and Harvard. In 1956, he became professor at Eidgenössische Technische Hochschule in Zürich.
► In *c*1933, he entered a chair design in the competition of 'Alliance Aluminum CIE France.' Work subject of 'Alfred Roth, Architekt, Lehrer, Publizist,' École Polytechnique Fédérale, Zürich.
► Friederike Mehlau-Wiebking et al., *Schweizer Typenmöbel 1925–35, Sigfried Giedion und die Wohnbedarf AG*, Zürich: gta, 1989:230.

Roth, Emmy (1910–)
► German silversmith; active Berlin and Voorschoten (Netherlands).
► Trained in Düsseldorf under Conrad Anton Beumers.
► She set up her own workshop in 1916 in Berlin-Charlottenburg. Her early work showed Baroque influence, but later work was plain and simple, exemplified by her fruit dish in *The Studio*, 1929. She was a member of the Deutcher Werkbund. Producing functional objects, she hammered metal into versatile objects, including lids that also served as fruit bowls, and extendible candelabra. She was known for imaginative and well-proportioned work. Carl J.A. Begeer met her at the 1927 Leipzig 'Europäisches Kunstgewerbe' exhibition; on his invitation, 1935–38, she worked at in the Netherlands, where she produced austere Modern table silver for industrial production by Zilverfabriek Voorschoten. In 1940, she settled in the USA.
► Her work was shown at exhibitions in Germany and abroad, including the 1927 Leipzig 'Europäisches Kunstgewerbe' exhibition.
► Annelies Krekel-Aalberse, *Art Nouveau and Art Déco Silver*, New York: Abrams, 1989:145,190,259. *Industry and Design in the Netherlands, 1850/1950*, Amsterdam: Stedelijk Museum, 198:211.

Rothschild, Jean-Maurice (1902–)
► French decorator and furniture designer.
► 1917–19, studied École Boulle, Paris.
► He began working in 1921 for Jacques-Émile Ruhlmann in Paris as a designer and artisan, and participated in the design of Ruhlmann's 'Hôtel du collectionneur' at the 1925 Paris 'Exposition Internationale des Arts Décoratifs et Industriels Modernes.' In 1932, Rothschild set up his own workshop at 14 bis rue Marbeuf in Paris. Classical and showing Ruhlmann's influence, some of his furniture was produced by Muro and Ducreuzet. At the end of the 1920s, he rejected Classical forms in favor of the Rationalist approach of the UAM (Union des Artistes Modernes). He worked with architects, particularly Robert Expert, with whom he designed a number of chairs for the 1935 oceanliner *Normandie*, including its smoking room, grill, and first class cabins. In 1937, Rothschild designed the restaurant of the Eiffel Tower. In 1945, he began working as an interior architect. He designed furniture commissioned by the Mobilier National for the Administration de la Monnaie, president of the Assemblée Nationale, and office of President Vincent Auriol in the Palais de l'Élysée.
► *Ensembles Mobiliers*, Vol. II, Paris: Charles Moreau, 1937. *Ensembles Mobiliers*, Paris: Charles Moreau, Nos. 9–11, 1954. Yolande Amic, *Intérieure: Le Mobilier français 1945–1964*, Paris: Regard, 1983:30–33. Pierre Kjellberg, *Art Déco: les maîtres du Mobilier, le décor des Paquebots*, Paris: Amateur, 1986:187–89.

Rouard, Georges
► French glassware and ceramics merchant; active Paris.
► Rouard produced earthenware and porcelain dinner services decorated with flowers, butterflies, and animals. In 1909, having recently opened Maison Rouard in the avenue de l'Opéra in Paris,

he met painter, silversmith, and jewelry designer Marcel Goupy. In 1919, August Heiligenstein enameled glass for Rouard to the specifications of Goupy. Heiligenstein left Rouard in 1923 but showed his work there until 1926, when he switched to the gallery of Edgar Brandt. Serving as Rouard's artistic director until 1954, Goupy designed glassware, much of it enameled inside and out, and porcelain and ceramic dinnerware. Most of Goupy's china was made by Théodore Haviland at Limoges.

Roubíček, René (1922–)
► Czech glassware designer; born Prague.
► Roubíček produced free-blown forms made at the Plastic Art Center of the glassworks in Nový Bor; in the 1950s and 1960s, produced work that showed a sophisticated appreciation for the material; was active at Nový Bor at the same time as Jan Kotík; later designed monumental glass objects.
► Received a grand prize at 1958 'Exposition Universelle et Internationale de Bruxelles.'
► Frederick Cooke, *Glass: Twentieth-Century Design*, New York: Dutton, 1986:90.

Rouchomovskii, Israel
► Russian goldsmith; active Odessa and Paris.
► In 1896, the Louvre purchased the so-called Tiara of Saitapharnes; it turned out not to be antique work, but made in the Odessa workshop of Rouchomovskii. Settling in Paris, he continued producing gold pieces in an antique manner. He was active *c*1870–1906.
► He showed a miniature gold skeleton in a coffin at the 1904 Paris Salon.
► Charlotte Gere, *American and European Jewelry 1830–1914*, New York: Crown, 1975:218.

Rougemont, Guy de (1935–)
► French painter, ceramicist, and designer; active Paris.
► 1954–58, studied École Nationale Supérieure des Arts Décoratifs, Paris, under Marcel Gromaire.
► He was active from 1968 in the design of porcelain for Limoges, furniture, and rugs.
► From 1965, work shown at and subject of numerous exhibitions. Work on permanent display at Galerie Artcurial, Paris.
► Cat., *Rougemont, Espaces publics et arts décoratifs 1965–1990*, Paris: Musée des Arts Décoratifs, 1990.

Rousseau, Clément (1872–1950)
► French sculptor and designer; born Saint-Maurice-la-Fougereuse, Deux-Sèvres; active Neuilly.
► Studied under·Léon Morice.
► From 1912, he executed some highly idiosyncratic furniture for wealthy clients in Neuilly, and other objects. He used rich materials, including inlays of various exotic woods, shagreen, leather, ivory, and mother-of-pearl, designed in a personal interpretation of French styles of the 18th and early 19th centuries; he contributed to the revival and popularization of the use of shagreen. In *c*1925, he participated in the décor of Jacques Doucet's studio in Neuilly.
► From 1921, he showed his work at the Salons of the Société des Artistes français, winning prizes; in 1925, showed his lighting, furniture, clocks, and accessories at the Galerie Charpentier in Paris.
► Pierre Kjellberg, *Art Déco: les maîtres du Mobilier, le décor des Paquebots*, Paris: Amateur, 1986:152–53.

Rousseau, Clément (1948–)
► French industrial designer; active Paris.
► 1971–76, studied École Camondo, Paris.
► 1971–76, he worked at Raymond Loewy's Compagnie de l'Esthétique Industrielle, Paris; 1981–85, at PA Consulting International; in 1985 with Claude Braunstein, set up the design office Plan Créatif/Crabtree Hall.

Rousseau, François-Eugène (1827–91)

▶ French ceramicist and glass designer; born and active Paris.

▶ Rousseau inherited an establishment that specialized in the production of porcelain and faïence at 41 rue Coquillère in Paris. His 1866 *Service Rousseau* earthenware table service was based on Félix Bracquemond's drawings in the style of Hokusai. Rousseau worked for a time with Louis Salon. His own designs showed a distinct Japanese influence and were executed years later, after he had turned to glass production. His designs were applied to clear or palely colored glass engraved with flowers or landscapes by his decorators, including Eugène Michel and Alphonse-Georges Reyen. His glassware was produced by the Appert brothers in Clichy. He also produced cased glass, a Venetian and 18th-century Chinese technique of engraving on an opaque outer layer to expose a translucent inner layer. He became famous for his crackled glass, a 16th-century Venetian technique of immersing glass in cold water between firings. He was associated with Ernest Léveillé from 1885. Rousseau greatly influenced the Modern revival of glassmaking by producing new effects through old techniques.

▶ He showed crackled glass at the 1884 Paris Union Centrale exhibition. His cased glass and imitations of semi-precious stones were shown at the 1878 Paris 'Exposition Universelle.'

▶ Yvonne Brunhammer et al., *Art Nouveau Belgium, France*, Houston: Rice University, 1976.

Roux-Spitz, Michel (1888–1957)

▶ French architect and designer; born Lyons.

▶ Studied under Tony Garnier.

▶ Active from 1925, he designed buildings in the International Style, though he rejected standardization. He designed furniture and interiors, including two apartments in the 1925 house on the rue Guynemer in Paris that he built for himself. His work included the 1932 Centre des Chèques Postaux, Paris; 1933 annex to the Bibliothèque Nationale, Versailles; management of the 1945 reconstruction of Nantes; and the construction of the Hôtel de Ville in Saint-Nazaire.

▶ At the 1925 Paris 'Exposition Internationale des Arts Décoratifs et Industriels Moderns,' Roux-Spitz designed two schemes for the galleries of the Cour des Métiers. His bathroom with lighting by Jean Perzel, silverware by Jean Puiforcat, glassware by Saint-Gobain, and ironwork by Raymond Subes was installed at the 1928 Salon of the Société des Artistes Décorateurs (SAD), and dining room produced by the Société des Glaces in Boussois at its 1929 Salon.

▶ Pierre Kjellberg, *Art Déco: les maîtres du Mobilier, le décor des Paquebots*, Paris: Amateur, 1986:153–54. *Le Petit Robert 2*, Paris, Robert, 1991:1566.

Rowan, Doug

▶ Canadian industrial designer; active Toronto.

▶ Rowan worked independently, and with Frank Dudas and Jan Kuypers. The group's furniture designs included seating for IIL International.

▶ Cat., *Seduced and Abandoned: Modern Furniture designers in Canada, the First Fifty Years*, Toronto: The Art Gallery at Harbourfront, 1986:21.

Rowland, David (1924–)

▶ American industrial designer ; born Los Angeles.

▶ 1940, studied Mills College, Oakland, California, under László Moholy-Nagy; 1950–51, Cranbrook Academy of Art, Bloomfield Hills, Michigan.

▶ 1952–53, he was a design assistant to Norman Bel Geddes in New York. Rowland set up his own design office in New York in 1954. He experimented with the use of steel and plastic finishes in seating. 1956–64, he developed a stacking chair, resulting in the 1964 *40/4* (or *40-in-4*) model produced by General Fireproofing of Youngstown, Ohio; a stack of 40 chairs was only 4ft (122cm) high. It had chromium-plated steel legs, with vinyl-coated seat and back stamped from sheet metal. His 1979 *Sof-Tech*

chair was produced in tubular steel with vinyl-coated springs by Thonet.

▶ Work shown at the 1957 (XI) and 1964 (XIII) Triennali di Milano; he won a gold medal at the latter for the *GF 40/4* chair.

▶ 'United States Steel,' *Industrial Design*, Vol. 12, Nov. 1965:7–9. Cat., *Les Assises du siège contemporain*, Paris: Musée des Arts Décoratifs, 1968. Olga Gueft, 'Thonet Sof-Tech Stacker,' *Interiors*, Vol. 139, Aug. 1979:66–67,84. 'David Rowland Designs the Sof-Tech Chair for Thonet,' *Interior Design*, Vol. 50, Aug. 1979:167. Cat., Kathryn B. Hiesinger and George H. Marcus III (eds.), *Design Since 1945*, Philadelphia: Philadelphia Museum of Art, 1983:229,III–76–77.

Rowlands, Martyn (1920–)

▶ British industrial designer; born Wales.

▶ Studied industrial design, Central School of Arts and Crafts, London.

▶ After working for Bakelite he established the design department of Ekco Plastics. He set up his own practice in 1959. In 1972, he served as vice-president of the Society of Industrial Artists.

▶ He won six Council of Industrial Design Awards, all for plastic products.

▶ Cat., Milena Lamarová, *Design a Plastické Hmoty,* Prague: Uměleckoprůmyslové Muzeum, 1972:154.

Rowley Gallery

▶ British design studio; located London.

▶ A.J. Rowley founded the Rowley Gallery in London in 1898. The firm designed furniture and simple, inexpensive interiors, specializing in picture framing. After World War I, A.J. Rowley hired artists, including William A. Chase, Frank Brangwyn, Robert Anning Bell, and H. Butler to design the marquetry and stained panels produced on the premises. In the 1920s and 1930s, Rowley was known for its marquetry panels, screens, and mirrors, and silver-leaf furniture and interiors. In 1933, Frank Brangwyn redesigned the exterior of the studio's quarters at 140–142 Kensington Church Street, London; three carved wood panels of craftsmen were set over Portland stone. The firm later sold art materials.

▶ Jessica Rutherford, *Art Nouveau, Art Deco and the Thirties: The Furniture Collections at Brighton Museum*, Brighton: The Royal Pavilion, Art Gallery and Museums, 1983:55.

Royal College of Art

▶ British Educational institution; located London.

▶ The School of Design in Ornamental Art, sponsored by the Board of Trade, opened in 1837 and was accommodated at Somerset House on the Strand in three top-floor rooms. It was later transferred to South Kensington and referred to as the Art School or the Art Training School, giving rise to the Victoria and Albert Museum. The school became known as the Royal College of Art and achieved independent status in 1949.

▶ John Physick, *The Victoria and Albert Museum: The history of its building*, Oxford: Phaidon/Christie's, 1982.

Royal Copenhagen Porcelain Manufactory (Den Kongelige Porcelaensfabrik)

▶ Danish porcelain factory.

▶ The first pottery in Copenhagen was established in 1755 under the patronage of King Frederick V; under French manager Louis Fournier, it produced soft paste and Sèvres style porcelain. In 1766, when the King died and Fournier returned to France, the factory closed. A new factory opened at the behest of Queen Juliane Marie under manager Frantz Henrich Mueller was the forerunner of the present Royal Copenhagen Porcelain Manufactory. In 1807, the factory was bombarded by British naval vessels under Lord Nelson. Production was artistically inferior until the factory was taken over by Philip Schou; he moved it from Köbmagergade to Smallegarde and appointed Arnold Krog, who revitalized the firm, artistic manager. Under Krog, the firm's ware showed French and Japanese influence, and its celebrated underglaze decoration in soft grays, pinks, and blues was introduced. In the 20th cen-

tury, new forms and patterns were developed, and workshops for stoneware and special glazes set up. From the 1920s to 1940s, figurines were designed by sculptors Jais Nielsen, Arno Malinowski, Gerhard Henning, Christian Thomsen, and Knud Kyhn, and decorative and table wares by Axel Salto and Nils Thorsson. The 1790–1802 *Flora Danica* pattern designed for Catherine the Great of Russia remains popular today. In 1923, Royal Copenhagen and Holmegård opened joint foreign retail outlets; in 1975, the companies merged. In 1969, the factory began jewelry production with A. Michelsen, jewelers to the Danish court. In 1986, Georg Jensen Sølvsmedie joined the group, which was in turn joined by Bing & Grøndahl. By the 1980s, the group was owned by Carlsberg Tuborg.
▶ Arthur Hayden, *Royal Copenhagen Porcelain: Its history and devleopment from the 18th century to the present day*, London 1911. Jennifer Hawkins Opie, *Scandinavia: Ceramics* and *Glass in the Twentieth Century*, New York: Rizzoli, 1989.

Royal Designer for Industry
▶ British honorary society of industrial designers.
▶ The Royal Society of Arts organized the 1935 'British Art in Industry' exhibition at Burlington House, London, and in 1936 established the Royal Designer for Industry recognition in order to raise the status of professional practitioners of the applied arts in Britain; elects British fellows and honorary fellows from other countries, the first of whom was Edward McKnight Kauffer in 1936.
▶ Fiona MacCarthy and Patrick Nuttgens, *Eye for Industry*, London: Lund Humphries, 1986. Frederick Cooke, *Glass: Twentieth-Century Design*, New York: Dutton, 1986:68.

Royal Worcester Porcelain
▶ British ceramics manufacturer; located Worcester.
▶ Porcelain was produced in Worcester from at least 1751. Royal Worcester Porcelain was established in 1862 as an amalgamation of factories that had been operating in the area since the 18th century, including Kerr and Binns, known for its porcelain figures. In 1862, W.H. Kerr left the firm and R.W. Binns reorganized the firm as Royal Worcester Porcelain and introduced the cream-colored 'ivory' porcelain body, which accepted enamel decoration well. Binns had a large collection of Far Eastern porcelain, and Worcester's Japanesque wares of the 1860s–1880s had enamel, gold, and other raised metallic pastework, widely copied in the USA. Some designs were produced with Persian and Indian-style decorations. Binns left the firm in 1897. Though essentially conservative, Worcester experimented in the 1880s and 1890s with piercing and new glazes. Its 20th-century production focused on historicist models; many of its 19th-century designs remained in production.
▶ The highly decorated dessert service by Kerr and Binns for Queen Victoria was shown at the London 'International Exhibition of 1862.'
▶ R.W. Binns, *Worcester China: A Record of the Work of Forty-five years, 1852–1897*, London, 1897. Geoffrey Godden, *Victorian Porcelain*, London, 1961. Geoffrey Godden, *An Illustrated Encyclopedia of British Pottery and Porcelain*, New York, 1966:365–81. Henry Sandon, *Royal Worcester Porcelain from 1862 to the Present Day*, London, 1973. Paul Atterbury (ed.), *The History of Porcelain*, New York, 1982:155–77. Antoinette Faÿ-Hallé and Barbara Mundt, *Porcelain of the Nineteenth Century*, New York, 1983:216–21,266–67. Doreen Bolger Burke et al., *In Pursuit of Beauty: Americans and the Aesthetic Movement*, New York: Metropolitan Museum of Art and Rizzoli, 1987:486.

Royère, Jean (1902–81)
▶ French decoration and furniture designer.
▶ Studied classics, Cambridge University.
▶ He worked 1934–36 in the design firm Gouffé. He designed the bar of the Hôtel Carlton on the avenue des Champs-Élysées in Paris. He set up his own design office in 1942 and became known as the grand master of decoration in Paris, designing offices

for the Proche-Orient Line in the USA and Europe, and the residences of King Farouk of Egypt, King Hussein of Jordan, and the Shah of Iran. In an eclectic style, he designed palaces, apartments, hotels. By 1954, his studio was located at 234 rue du Faubourg Saint-Honoré; in 1959, with metalworker Gilbert Poillerat and sculptor André Bloc, he designed the Beharestan (Senate) in Teheran. Some of his furniture was serially produced by Galerie Steph Simon.
▶ He designed a bedroom at the 1954 Paris Salon des Arts Ménagers and showed his work at the 1937 Paris 'Exposition Internationale des Arts et Techniques dans le Vie Moderne.'
▶ *Ensembles Mobiliers*, Vol. II, Paris: Charles Moreau, 1937. *Ensembles Mobiliers*, Paris: Charles Moreau, 1954: No. 25. Patrick Favardin, *Le Style 50: Un moment de l'art français*, Paris: Sous Le Vent–Vilo,1987:46–53.

Rozanova, Ol'ga Vladimirovna (1886–1918)
▶ Russian artist, illustrator, and theoretician; born Vladimir.
▶ 1904–10, studied Bolshaov Art College and Stroganov Art School, Moscow; 1912–13, Zvantseva's Art School.
▶ She settled in St. Petersburg in 1911 and made contact with the Union of Youth group and with Vladimir Markov (aka Waldemars Matvjs) and Mikhail Matiushin. From 1912, she illustrated Futurist booklets, including her husband Aleksei Kruchenykh's *Te li le* (1914), *Zaumnaia gniga* (*Trans-rational Book*) (1915), *Balos* (1917), and the important albums *Voina* (*War*) (1916) and *Vselenskaia voina* (*The Universal War*). In 1916, she took up Suprematism, participating with Kazimir Malevich, Mikhail Matiushin, Liubov' Popova, composer Nikolai Roslavets, and others on the first issues of the unrealized journal *Supremus*. In 1918, she became a member of Izo NKP (Department of Fine Arts of Narkompros) and of Proletcult. She co-directed Izo's art-industry section with Aleksandr Rodchenko. She assisted in the organization of Svomas in provincial towns.
▶ Her work was included in the 1913 'Jack of Diamonds,' 1915 'Tramway V,' 1915–16 '0–10,' and other Exhibitions of the Union of Youth. A 1919 exhibition of her work was mounted in Moscow. Her work was included in the 1922 Berlin 'Erste Russische Kunstausstellung.'
▶ Stephanie Barron and Maurice Tuchman, *The Avant-Garde in Russia, 1910–1930*, Cambridge: MIT, 1980:240. Selim O. Khan-Magomedov, *Les Vhutemas*, Paris: Regard, 1990.

Ruban, Petrus (1851–1929)
▶ French bookbinder and gilder; born Villefranche, Rhône.
▶ He rendered Art Nouveau floral patterns that enveloped the entire cover. His later historicist covers were produced in styles including Henri II, Empire, Japanese, and neo-Egyptian. He was known for the high level of his craftsmanship in modeling, incising, tinting, and gold-fillet and blind-tool work. A. Durel, de Piolenc, Belinac, and Bordes collected his bindings. In 1910, the workshop was taken over by Charles Lanoë.
▶ He showed his bindings at the annual Salons of the Société des Artistes français, events of the Salon des Beaux-Arts, and the 1900 Paris 'Exposition Universelle.'
▶ Alastair Duncan and Georges de Bartha, *Art Nouveau and Art Déco Bookbinding*, New York: Abrams, 1989:15,159,195–96. Émile Bosquet, 'La reliure française à l'exposition,' *Art et décoration*, July–Dec. 1900:50–51. Roger Devauchelle, *La Reliure en France de ses origines à nos jours*, Vol. 3, Paris, 1961:84,96–98,105,129. A. Durel (ed.), *Catalogue de cent reliures d'art*, Paris, 1902. Octave Uzanne, *L'Art dans la décoration extérieure des livres en France et à l'étranger*, Paris, 1898:164,167,176,198.

Rubin, Daniel and Patrick
See Canal

Rubliov, Georgii Josifovich (1902–73)
▶ Russian painter and interior designer.
▶ 1919–22, studied Svomas, Lipetsk; 1922–30, Vkhutemas/Vkhutein under A. Osmyorkin, S. Gerasimov, and I. Mashkov.

▶ From the 1930s, he was mainly a monumental painter; in 1931, he was active in the propagandist decoration of Moscow.
▶ From 1927, he participated in exhibitions; designed objects for the 1939 National Agricultural Exhibition.
▶ Cat., *Kunst und Revolution: Russische und Sowjetische Kunst 1910–1932*, Vienna: Österreichisches Museum für angewandte Kunst, 1988.

Rückert, Feodor
▶ Russian goldsmith and jeweler.
▶ Active from the end of the 19th century until the 1917 Revolution, Rückert's workshop was the leading producer of objects in the Old Russian style. Some pieces were decorated with painted enamels in the style of the 17th century; the filigree wire pattern on others used the traditional Russian *skan* technique. Rückert sold some items through Fabergé in Moscow.
▶ Charlotte Gere, *American and European Jewelry 1830–1914*, New York: Crown, 1975:218–19.

Rückert, M.J.
▶ German silversmiths; located Mainz.
▶ The firm was founded in Mainz in 1901. It produced small silver pieces and flatware, some designed by Patriz Huber and Hans Christiansen. The two flatware patterns in the Sezession style that Peter Behrens designed while at Darmstadt were produced by Rückert.
▶ Annelies Krekel-Aalberse, *Art Nouveau and Art Déco Silver*, New York: Abrams, 1989:132,259. Cat., *Metallkunst*, Berlin: Bröhan-Museum, 1990:426–27.

Ruggeri, Cinzia
▶ Italian designer; born Milan.
▶ Studied Academy of Applied Arts, Milan.
▶ She was an apprentice at Carven in Paris. Returning to Italy, she became a stylist in her father's clothing firm, developing the *Bloom* line. She designed costumes for the theater, women's sportswear for Kim, and a range of domestic linens for Castellini. She was art director of the Italian linen board.
▶ She participated in the 1981 Biennale di Venezia, 1983 (XVII) Triennale di Milano, and 1982 'Italian Revolution' exhibition in California.
▶ Andrea Branzi, *La Casa Calda: Esperienze del Nuovo Disegno Italiano*, Milan: Idea Books, 1982.

Ruhlmann, Jacques-Émile (1879–1933)
▶ French designer and decorator; born and active Paris.
▶ He took over the family housepainting business in Paris in 1907. Patronized by architect Charles Plumet and encouraged by couturier Jacques Doucet, Frantz Jourdain, and Tony Selmersheim, he showed his work for the first time in 1911. He moved the business from the rue Marché Saint-Honoré to 10 rue de Maleville (the paint, wallpaper, and mirror workshops) and to 27 rue de Lisbonne (the interior-design and furnishings agency). The first occasion he showed his work alone was the dining room with various 'Classical' pieces in a circular gallery at the 1913 Salon d'Automne, which established him as the primary exponent of luxury furniture. Ruhlmann's work was influenced by the Louis Philippe period and was of the highest quality, elegance, and technical and formal refinement. David David-Weill, a financier and art collector, commissioned a functional desk and cabinet to complement his collection of French 18th-century art. In 1919, he founded the Établissements Ruhlmann et Laurent with painting contractor Pierre Laurent to produce his work. Costly and warm woods were incorporated into simple, elegant forms. Over a year could elapse from receipt of an order to delivery. At his 'hôtel du Collectionneur' pavilion at the 1925 Paris exposition, he showed pieces that blended classical luxury with Parisian Modernism, exemplifying the Art Déco style. By 1928, his work showed a more sumptuous and massive approach. Ruhlmann made a contribution to the avant-garde in the form of standardized macassar-ebony modules, shown at the 1929 Salon of the Société des Artistes Décorateurs and intended for 'a viceroy of India,' in fact the Maharaja of Indore. He decorated the tea room of 1926 oceanliner *Île-de-France*, the meeting room at the Chambre de Commerce in Paris in 1930, interiors for the Palais de l'Élysée, the offices of various government ministers and administrators, the town hall of the 5th arrondissement and of the suburb Puteaux, and numerous private residences. Jean Renouardt commissioned the widely published 1930 *Soleil* bed in rosewood veneer. Towards the end of his relatively short career of about a decade, he began to use chrome plating and silver in his furniture; the combination of metal with luxurious woods can be found in his furniture for the palace of the Maharaja of Indore.
▶ His wallpaper was included in Tony Selmersheim's stand at the 1911 Salon of the Société des Artistes Décorateurs, and other work in its 1919–26, 1928–30, and 1932–34 annual events. He first exhibited alone at the 1913 Salon d'Automne, and again in 1926. His last major display was at the 1932 Salon of the Société des Artistes Décorateurs. With Pierre Patout and a group of artists and ensembliers, at the 1925 Paris 'Exposition Internationale des Arts Décoratifs et Industriels Modernes,' Ruhlmann presented the 'hôtel du Collectionneur'; the group included Jean Puiforcat, Edgar Brandt, Émile Decœur, Jean Dunand, Pierre Legrain, and George Bastard. Ruhlmann exhibited in Madrid and Milan in 1927 and designed one of the salons at the 1931 Paris 'Exposition Coloniale.'
▶ Pierre Cabanne, *Encyclopédie Art Déco*, Paris: Somogy, 1986:233–35. Florence Camard, *Ruhlmann*, Paris: Regard, 1983. Penelope Hunter, *Notable Acquisitions, 1965–75*, New York: Metropolitan Museum of Art, 1975:229. Pierre Kjellberg, *Art Déco: les maîtres du Mobilier, le décor des Paquebots*, Paris: Amateur, 1986:154–167.

Ruskin, John (1819–1900)
▶ British social critic and writer.
▶ 1837–42, studied Oxford University.
▶ His influential books *The Seven Lamps of Architecture* (1849) and *The Stones of Venice* (1851–53) illustrate his interest in architecture and the Gothic style in particular. His writings were the mainspring of inspiration for the Arts and Crafts movement. He persuaded William Morris and Arts and Crafts followers to turn away from industry for aesthetic and social reasons. He abhorred machine-made products such as railway trains, cut glass, iron, and materials that lacked handmade 'truth.' He disparaged the 'fatal newness' of, for example, veneered rosewood furniture, and equated the beauty of medieval craftsmanship and architecture with the joy and artisanal dignity he believed were associated with their creation. The influence of his ideas reached far into 20th-century design; though an ardent historicist, he foreshadowed some of the fundamental tenets of Modernism, particularly by arguing that the forms of things must be faithful to the nature and materials of their construction.
▶ E. T. Cook and A. Wedderburn (eds), *The Complete Works of John Ruskin*, London, 1903–12. Gillian Naylor, *The Arts and Crafts Movement*, London: Trefoil, 1971.

Ruskin Pottery
▶ British ceramics manufacturer; located Smethwick.
▶ William Howson Taylor founded the Ruskin Pottery in Smethwick, near Birmingham, in 1898. Influenced by the Arts and Crafts movement, the pottery was named after John Ruskin and soon became highly regarded. Taylor's style was based on hand-thrown and turned models with unusual glazes. Its three main areas of production were mottled soufflé glazes in single colors, luster finishes, and high-temperature flambé glazes, experimented with from the late 1840s by Grongiart, Salvetat, and others at Sèvres and developed there by Auguste Delaherche, Pierre-Adrien Dalpayrat, Ernest Chaplet, and Théodore Deck. Taylor was the only ceramicist in Britain to match and sometimes exceed the French technique. Mastering the process by 1919, his wares retained their high quality for almost a quarter of a century, and every piece, due to the variety of glazes, was unique. His

glazes in rich tones of green, blue, purple, and red were produced in changing veined, clouded, and mottled patterns. Ruskin Pottery was closed in 1933.

▶ The firm was awarded the grand prize at the 1904 St. Louis 'Louisiana Purchase Exposition' and high awards at international exhibitions in Milan, Brussels, and elsewhere. Its wares were the subject of the 1975 exhibition at the Victoria and Albert Museum in London and, in 1976, at the Birmingham City Museum.

▶ Cat., *Ruskin Pottery*, London: Victoria and Albert Museum, 1975. Haslam and Whiteway, *Ruskin Pottery*, London, 1981. Sales catalogue, *British Decorative Arts from 1880 to the Present Day*, Christie's London, 20 February 1991, lots 212–30.

Russell, Gordon (1892–1980)

▶ British furniture maker and designer; born Cricklewood, London.

▶ In 1908, he worked in his father's small antiques restoration workshop, where he practiced a number of crafts and was in charge of repairs. He began to design furniture in 1910; after World War I, the furniture he made was in the manner of Ernest Gimson. By 1926, his firm was using machinery in an attempt to reconcile the best of the Arts and Crafts tradition with the efficiency of mechanized production, absorbing the theories and ideas of Modernism. He was a member of the Art-Workers' Guild and an early supporter of the Design and Industries Association. In 1929, he set up a shop at 24 Wigmore Street in London with Nikolaus Pevsner as manager. His visit to Gunner Asplund's 1930 Stockholm Exhibition proved a revelation. In 1935, he moved to a large showroom designed by Geoffrey Jellicoe a few doors away from the previous quarters. In *c*1930, Russell, his brother R.D. Russell, and the firm's other designers W.H. Russell (no relation) and Eden Minns began designing furniture in a plain Modern style without ornamentation. From 1931, the firm began producing radio cabinets designed by R.D. Russell for Murphy Radio in Welwyn Garden City; these were starkly Modern and influenced by a combination of the International Style and the Arts and Crafts movement. 1935–39, Nikolaus Pevsner worked at Gordon Russell as a buyer. In 1938, Russell, Crofton Gane (of Gane's in Bristol), and Geoffrey Dunn (of Dunn's of Bromley) initiated the Good Furniture Group for mass-production furniture; this was discontinued with the outbreak of World War II. From 1939, Russell was influential on British domestic furniture through his involvement with the Utility Scheme. He resigned as managing director in 1940 and was succeeded by R.H. Bee. 1943–47, he chaired the Board of Trade Design Panel, responsible for the production of Utility furniture. 1947–59, he was director of the Council of Industrial Design. He was active in the organization of the 1951 London 'Festival of Britain' and was knighted in 1955. He was elected Royal Designer for Industry in 1940 and Fellow of the Society of Arts; 1948–49, was professor of furniture design, Royal College of Art, London.

▶ He showed his furniture first in 1922 at Cheltenham and subsequently at the 1924 Wembley 'British Empire Exhibition' and, winning medals, at the 1925 Paris 'Exposition Internationale des Arts Décoratifs et Industriels Modernes.' His firm showed at the 1935 exhibition at the Royal Academy in London and 1937 Paris 'Exposition Internationale des Arts et Techniques dans la Vie Moderne.' The firm was active at the 1951 'Festival of Britain.' Gordon Russell furniture was included in the 1979–80 'Thirties' exhibition at the Hayward Gallery in London and was the subject of the 1992 centenary exhibition in its London showrooms.

▶ Gordon Russell, *Designer's Trade, Autobiography of Gordon Russell*, London: Allen and Unwin, 1968. Cat., *Thirties: British art and design before the war*, London: Arts Council of Great Britain, Hayward Gallery, 1979:26,73,83,86,149,299. Ken Baynes and Kate Baynes, *Gordon Russell*, London: Design Council, 1980. Jessica Rutherford, *Art Nouveau, Art Deco and the Thirties: The Furniture Collections at Brighton Museum*, Brighton: The Royal Pavilion, Art Gallery and Museums, 1983:57. Fiona MacCarthy and Patrick Nuttgens, *Eye for Industry*, London: Royal Society of Arts, 1986. Jeremy Myerson, *Gordon Russell, Designer of Furniture*, London: Design Council, 1992.

Russell, R.D. (1903–81)

▶ British architect and furniture and industrial designer; brother of Gordon Russell.

▶ Studied Architectural Association, London.

▶ In 1929, he joined his brother's firm Gordon Russell, where he designed dining-room and bedroom furniture, sideboards, chests, and, most notably, radio cabinets for Murphy Radio of Welwyn Garden City. He was staff designer at Murphy 1934–36 and a consultant there in 1936. He produced an influential series of veneered plywood radio cabinets, including the 1932 *AS* model. Continuing in his own practice after World War II, he was also an influential teacher at the Royal College of Art in London, where he was professor of furniture 1949–64. He continued to design Murphy's radio cases after the war. His 1936 square floor model and 1948 tapering concave-frame cabinet with its central speaker have recently been widely published and discussed. In the early 1950s, he worked with Murphy on TV cabinets. In the 1960s with R.Y. Goodden, he designed the remodeled gallery for Greek sculpture at the British Museum and, 1969–71, the Western sculpture and Oriental art galleries and the print room there.

▶ His furniture was included in the 1979–80 'Thirties' exhibition at the Hayward Gallery in London. Was elected Royal Designer for Industry, 1944.

▶ Michael Farr, *Design in British Industry: A Mid-Century Survey*, London: Cambridge, 1955. Fiona MacCarthy and Patrick Nuttgens, *Eye for Industry*, London: Royal Society of Arts, 1986. 'The Radio,' London: Design Museum, 1989. Jeremy Myerson, *Gordon Russell*, Designer of Furniture, London: Design Council, 1992.

rya

▶ Finnish weaving process.

▶ *Rya* (or *ryijy*) is a traditional type of weaving practiced in Finland. Rough yarns are hand-woven into thick tapestries intended for use as carpets, marriage-bed covers, and wall hangings. Eva Brummer set up a studio in Helsinki in 1929 to revive the technique, which involves cutting the pile unevenly in order to create a thick relief effect. As rugs, the weavings became popular in the 1950s and were closely identified with the exuberant Scandinavian Modern style.

▶ Cat., Kathryn B. Hiesinger and George H. Marcus III (eds.), *Design Since 1945*, Philadelphia: Philadelphia Museum of Art, 1983:208. Anja Louhio, *Modern Finnish Rugs*, Helsinki, 1975:42–45.

Ryggen, Hannah (1894–1970)

▶ Swedish textile designer and teacher; born Malmö; active Norway.

▶ She settled on a small farm in Trøndelag (Norway) in 1924 and began weaving. In 1924, she set up her own studio. She did the shearing, carding, spinning, and dyeing herself, and wove without cartoons or sketches. The often political subject matter of her weavings ranged from the Spanish Civil War to the plight of unwed mothers. Her tapestries were akin to Expressionist and late-Cubist paintings.

▶ She showed her work at the 1964 Biennale di Venezia.

▶ Cat., David Revere McFadden (ed.), *Scandinavian Modern Design 1880–1980*, New York: Abrams, 1982:270, No. 109. Cat., Anne Wichstrøm, *Rooms with a View: Women's Art in Norway 1880–1990*, Oslo: The Royal Ministry of Foreign Affairs, 1990:26.

Rykkens, Oddvin (1937–)

▶ Norwegian furniture designer.

▶ Rykkens designed the widely published *Balans Skulptor* ergonomic stool. Along with Peter Opsvik and Svein Gusrud, he was an innovator of the ergonomic seating popular in the early 1980s.

▶ Fredrik Wildhagen, *Norge i Form*, Oslo: Sternersen, 1988:201.

S

Saalburg, Guillaume (1957–)

▶ French glassworker and engraver; active Paris.

▶ Trained in a glass engraver's workshop.

▶ He worked as an architect and designer for business and domestic clients; collaborated with Philippe Starck, Jean-Michel Wilmotte, Gilles Derain, Richard Moyer, and Andrée Putman; participated in the design of the hall of TV company Canal Plus; in 1987, set up his own firm Opaque Diffusion for the production of tabletop objects and glass furniture.

▶ Showed work at Institut français d'Architecture in 1987 and VIA in 1989; showed double glass wall filled with transparent marbles (with Ronald-Cécil Sportes) at 1983 Salon of Société des Artistes Décorateurs. Work shown at 1989 'Le Verre grandeur nature' exhibition, Parc Floral, Vincennes, and 1990 'Les Années VIA 1980–1990,' Musée des Arts Décoratifs.

▶ Cat., *Les années VIA 1980–1990*, Paris: Musée des Arts Décoratifs, 1990:154–55.

Saarinen, Eero (1910–61)

▶ Finnish architect; born Kirkkonummi; active USA; son of Eliel and Loja Saarinen.

▶ 1930, studied fine art, Paris, and architecture, Yale University, to 1934.

▶ He moved with his father to New York in 1923. Intending to become a sculptor, he designed furniture in 1929 in a joint project with his father and mother for the Kingswood School for girls. After 1934, he worked on furniture design with Norman Bel Geddes. In 1936, he returned to his father's Cranbrook Academy in Bloomfield Hills, Michigan, where he taught briefly and, 1937–41, practiced architecture with his father in Ann Arbor, Michigan. 1941–47, he was a partner with his father and J. Robert Swanson in Ann Arbor. From 1950, he was active in his own office in Ann Arbor. For Hans and Florence Knoll's furniture company, beginning his association in 1946, Eero designed the 1946 *Grasshopper* upholstered lounge chair, the 1948 fiberglass-shell *Womb Chair*, and a range of office furniture. The *Womb Chair* became a popular icon of mid-century design; Saarinen created it according to his own account, as a Modern version of the old-fashioned overstuffed club-chair model; it was a direct descendant of the 1940 prize-winning chair entry at the New York Museum of Art competition. Saarinen's position as an accomplished architect was established when he won the 1948 competition for the design of the Jefferson Westward Expansion Memorial in St. Louis, Missouri. Later known as the Gateway Arch, it drew directly on an unrealized project by Italian architect Adalberto Libera (with Di Berardino) for the entrance to the 1942 'Esposizione Universale di Roma.' Saarinen rendered office chairs (produced by Knoll) for the 1948–56 General Motors Technical Center on the artificial lake in Warren, Michigan, a project on which he was the principal architect. His 1955–57 pedestal furniture range (produced by Knoll), including the 1957 *Tulip* chair with its fiberglass seat and aluminum pedestal, pursued his 'one piece, one material' furniture design ideal; their silhouettes were an attempt to rid a room of a forest of furniture legs. He strove to be a designer of sculptural furniture, rejecting the rectilinear forms of the 1920s. His architec-

tural accomplishments were dramatic; he amalgamated architecture, design, and engineering. A lifetime friend of Charles Eames, Saarinen and he designed the innovative seating furniture in the Mary Seaton Room of the Streamline-Modern 1940 Kleinhans Music Hall in Buffalo, New York, of which Saarinen and his father were the architects. In the 1940s, Saarinen worked with Eames in California on various projects, including a sculptural plywood leg splint for the US Navy. Cesar Pelli, Kevin Roche, and John Dinkeloo all began their careers in the architecture office of Saarinen.

▶ His work was shown with that of his father and mother in the 1932 exhibition of their designs at the Detroit Institute of Arts. Eames and Saarinen won the two first prizes at the 1940 'Organic Design in Home Furnishings' competition and exhibition at the New York Museum of Modern Art. His *Tulip* chair was included in the 1968 'Les Assises du siège contemporian' exhibition at the Paris Musée des Arts Décoratifs, 1972 'Knoll au Louvre' exhibition (along with other designs) at the Paris Musée des Arts Décoratifs, and 1970 'Modern Chairs 1918–1970' exhibition at the Whitechapel Gallery in London. Work included in 1982 'Space and Environment: Furniture by American Architects' at the Whitney Museum of American Art in Fairfield County, Connecticut, and 1983–85 'Design in America: The Cranbrook Vision 1925–1950' traveling exhibition. His *Womb Chair* and *Tulip Chair* were included in the 1983–84 'Design Since 1945' exhibition at the Philadelphia Museum of Art. He won the 1962 gold medal of the American Institute of Architects posthumously, and the 1966 American Institute of Architects Honors Award.

▶ His buildings included the 1939 Smithsonian Art Gallery, Washington; 1948–56 General Motors Technical Center (with Eliel Saarinen and architecture firm Smith, Hinchman and Gryllis) in Warren, Michigan; 1953–55 Kresge Auditorium and Chapel at Massachusetts Institute of Technology, Cambridge, Massachusetts; 1956 US Embassy, London; 1956–58 David S. Ingalls Ice Hockey Rink at Yale University, New Haven, Connecticut; 1962 Trans World Airlines Terminal at Idlewild (now John F. Kennedy) airport, New York; 1958–63 Dulles International Airport, Virginia; 1956–63 John Deere administration center, Moline, Illinois; 1964 National Expansion Memorial (Centennial Gateway Arch), St. Louis, Missouri.

▶ Mathew Ginal, *Progressive Architecture*, June 1990:28. Aline Saarinen (ed.), *Eero Saarinen on his Work 1947–64*, New Haven: Yale University, 1962. Eero Saarinen, 'Function, Structure and Beauty,' *Architectural Association Journal*, July–August 1957. Cat., *Modern Chairs 1918–1970*, London: Lund Humphries, 1971. Cat., *Les Assises du siège contemporain*, Paris: Musée des Arts Décoratifs, 1968. Cat., *Knoll au Louvre*, Paris: Musée des Arts Décoratifs, 1972. Cat., Kathryn B. Hiesinger and George H. Marcus III (eds.), *Design Since 1945*, Philadelphia: Philadelphia Museum of Art, 1983:229,III–78,79,80. Allan Temko, *Eero Saarinen*, New York: Braziller, 1962. Robert A. Kuhner, *Eero Saarinen: His Life and Work*, Monticello, Illinois, 1975. Cat., *Cranbrook: The Saarinen Years*, Detroit: Detroit Institute of Arts. Cat., Lisa Phillips (introduction), *Shape and Environment: Furniture by American Architects*, New York: Whitney Museum of American Art,

1982:52—53. Rupert Spade, *Eero Saarinen*, London and New York, 1971. Vittorio Magnago Lampugnani (ed.), *Encyclopedia of 20th-Century Architecture*, New York: Abrams, 1986:291—93. Robert Judson Cark et al., *Design in America: The Cranbrook Vision 1925—1950*, New York: Abrams and Metropolitan Museum of Art, 1983.

Saarinen, Gottlieb Eliel (1873—1950)

▶ Finnish architect and designer; born Rantasalmi; active Helsinki, Kirkkonummi, and Bloomfield Hills, Michigan; husband of Loja Saarinen; father of Eero Saarinen.

▶ Studied painting, Helsinki University; 1893—97, architecture, Helsinki Polytechnic.

▶ Until 1898, Saarinen and former fellow student Herman Gesellius were draftsmen periodically in the office of architect Gustaf Nyström. In 1896, Saarinen formed a productive partnership with Gesellius and another fellow student, Armas Lindgren in Helsinki; and, 1903—05, in the 1901—03 'Hvitträsk' house on Lake Vitträsk, Kirkkonummi, the joint studio and home of the Gesellius, Lindgren, and Saarinen families and employees and, after 1916, the Saarinen residence alone. It became a mecca for artists. Saarinen's furniture at Hvitträsk and Suur-Merijoki of the same year showed the influence of Charles Rennie Mackintosh and Hugh Baillie Scott. His furniture for the 1905 Malchow Haus was lighter and more simple. Saarinen's wife Loja made his architectural models. He was a leader of the National Romantic movement in Finland. In the 1910s, he began designing *rya* rugs. In 1912, he became a member of the Deutscher Werkbund. After winning second prize for the 1922 Chicago Tribune Tower competition, he moved with his family to the USA in 1923, returning to Hvitträsk almost yearly, sometimes with Florence Schust (aka Florence Knoll). He taught architecture at the University of Michigan in Ann Arbor, Michigan, and, in 1924 was invited by George Gough Booth to develop the Cranbrook Educational Community in Bloomfield, Michigan, a preparatory school for boys. In 1925, he designed buildings for the Cranbrook Foundation established in 1927. In 1932, he became president of the Cranbrook Academy of Art. He designed furniture, glass, silver, brass, and other furnishings for his own house. 1929—31, Loja Saarinen (b. Louise Gesellius, sister of Herman Gesellius) (1879—1968) designed and made rugs and textiles at the Cranbrook, including curtains and carpets for the Kingswood School for girls designed by Eliel and the rug for the Frank Lloyd Wright designed office for Edgar Kaufmann in Pittsburgh. Saarinen's sketches for furniture were no more than line drawings, lacking instructions for materials and veneers; construction decisions were made by cabinetmaker Tor Berglund, an instructor at the Cranbrook from Sweden. Saarinen's furniture collection for John Widdicomb was mass produced in bleached wood and steel. During the first half of the 1930s, his silver designs were produced by Arthur Nevill Kirk and Charles Price in the Cranbrook metal workshop and by International Silver, Meriden, Connecticut; his widely published 1934 silver urn and tray set were produced by Wilcox. In 1940 with son Eero, he designed the Streamline-styled Kleinhans Music Hall in Buffalo, New York, which had innovative seating designed by Charles Eames and Eero Saarinen for the Mary Seaton Room. Influential as a teacher, he assembled effective instructors at Cranbrook, who included Eames, Harry Bertoia, his son Eero, and Swedish sculptor Carl Milles. Florence Knoll and Jack Lenor Larsen were among Eliel Saarinen's students. His publications included *The City: Its Growth, Its Decay, Its Future* (1943) and *Search for Form* (1939).

▶ In Finland, Saarinen designed the cupboard and swivel and stationary armchairs for the Pohjola building, 1896—1923; case goods and seating for the 'Suur-Merijoki' house, 1901—03; tables, case goods, seating, and *rya* rugs, 1910s—1920s; numerous furnishing for the 1901—03 Hvitträsk house (statuary in bronze by wife Loja and paintings in dining room by Väinö Blomstedt); tables, case goods, seating, and a piano for the 1901—04 Hvittorp house; lighting, tables, seating, case goods, and shelving for the 1905—07 Remer house; desks, seating, and tables for the Helsinki

Railway Station, 1904—19; and a vast amount of other furniture and furnishings. The majority of Saarinen's furniture designs were site specific. He executed numerous other pieces, resulting from his association with the Friends of Finnish Handicraft, the Finnish Society of Crafts and Design, and the Finnish General Handicraft Society. Private furniture and furnishings commissions came from relatives, friends, and colleagues. Textiles were integral to his interiors, reaching a peak in the 1901—03 Suur-Merijoki house for which he designed a full range of fabrics and textiles, including upholstery fabrics and carpets. He concentrated on curtains and *rya* rugs. He worked on textiles for the Friends of Finnish Handicraft; and his metalwork included candlesticks, tea and coffee services, and compotes. From 1909, he designed banknotes and, from 1917, postage stamps. His graphic design included soap labels, Christmas cards, book illustrations, title pages, company signage and trademarks, emblems, book plates, posters, and cartoons. More than 50 of his paintings and portraits, landscapes, still-lifes, and other art works have been recorded.

▶ Gesellius, Lindgren and Saarinen's executed architectural work included the 1898—1900 Finnish pavilion at the 1900 Paris 'Exposition Universelle'; 1899—1901 Pohjola fire insurance company at Aleksanterinkatu and Mikankatu in Helsinki (with masks by Hilda Flodin); 1897—98 Talberg apartment building, Katajanokka; 1900—01 building in Fabrianinkatu 17, Katojanokka; 1900—02 Olofsborg apartment building; 1901—03 Eol apartment building; 1901—02 Suur-Merijoki house in Merijoki (near Viipuri; now Russia); 1901—03 Hvitträsk house on Lake Vitträsk; 1901—04 Hvittorp house (residence of Robert Emil Westerlund; stone fireplace by Jarl Eklund) on Lake Vitträsk; 1903 Bobrinky house (unrealized) in St. Petersburg or Moscow; 1905—07 house for German poet Paul Remer in Mark Brandenburg (near Alt-Ruppin) on Lake Molchow (Germany); 1902—12 Finnish National Museum (decorations by Armas Lindgren and Emil Wikström, and, in 1928, Akseli Gallen-Kallela fresco); 1903—04 Pohjoismaiden Osakepankki bank (decorations in copper by Lindgren produced by Alpo Sailo) in Helsinki. Metalwork on their buildings was designed and executed by Eric O.W. Ehrström, including that for Pohjola, and Hvitträsk, Hvittorp, Remer house, Finnish National Museum, and Pohjoismaiden Osakepankki bank (with its notable brass doors). Saarinen alone designed the 1904—19 railway station in Helsinki; 1904—13 railway station in Karelia (now Viipuri); 1906 The Hague Peace Palace competition, Saarinen's entry 'L'Homme'; 1908 Parliament House competition (won first prize; unrealized), Helsinki; 1911—12 Town Hall in Lahti; and 1921 Kalevala house (unrealized) in Munkkiniemi. From 1925, Saarinen designed the buildings of the Cranbrook Foundation in Michigan and, with son Eero, 1938 Kleinhans Music Hall in Buffalo, New York; Tanglewood Opera Shed in Stockbridge, Massachusetts, and 1941—42 Tabernacle Church of Christ in Columbus, Indiana.

▶ Saarinen won second prize in a competition for a house for German publisher Wilhelm Girardt in Honnef-am-Rhein, Essen. He showed his furniture at the Salon d'Automne in Paris in the 1910s and the 1914 Cologne 'Deutscher Werkbund-Ausstellung.' The designs of the Saarinen family were shown in the 1932 exhibition at the Detroit Institute of Arts. Saarinen designed a dining room for the 1929 'The Architect and Industrial Art: An Exhibition of Contemporary American Design' at the New York Metropolitan Museum of Art. He and his wife executed 'Room for a Lady' in the Central Gallery of the 1935 (XIII) 'Contemporary American Industrial Art, 1935' exhibition at the New York Metropolitan Museum of Art, where his 1934 silver urn and tray set was shown. His silverwares were shown at the 1937 Paris 'Exposition Internationale des Arts et Techniques dans la Vie Moderne.' Work included in 'Design in America: The Cranbrook Vision 1925—1950' traveling exhibition.

▶ Eliel Saarinen, *The Cranbrook Development*, Bloomfield Hills, Michigan, 1931. Eliel Saarinen, *Search for Form*, New York, 1939. Eliel Saarinen, *The City: Its Growth, Its Decay, Its Future*, New York, 1943. Albert Christ-Janer, *Eliel Saarinen*, Chicago: Chicago University Press, 1948. Marika Jausen, 'Gesellius—Lindgren—Saarinen,' *Arkkitehti*, 9 Nov. 1967. Robert Judson Clark et al., *Design in America: The Cranbrook Vision 1925–1953*, New York: Abrams and Metropolitan Museum of Art, 1983. Marika Mausen et al., *Eliel Saarinen: Projects 1896–1923*, Cambridge: MIT Press, 1990. Gregory M. Wittkopp, 'Eliel Saarinen' in Mel Byars and Russell Flinchum (eds.), *50 American Designers*, Washington: Preservation, 1994.

Saarinen, Loja (b. Louise Gesellius 1879–1968).
See Saarinen, Gottlieb Eliel

Sabattini, Lino (1925–)
▶ Italian metalsmith and designer; born Correggio; active Bregnano and Milan.
▶ Sabattini worked as a silversmith from a very young age. He learned metalworking techniques and became interested in shapes derived from the behavior of natural materials. His early work was exemplified by the 1950 teapot for W. Wolff in Germany. Moving to Milan in 1955, he met Gio Ponti, who encouraged him; included in an exhibition organized by Ponti the next year. Sabattini first came to international attention. 1956–63, he was active in Milan and as director of design at Christofle Orfèvrerie in Paris. His forms were free flowing, simple, and sculptural, as in his 1960 tea service *Como* produced by Christofle 1960–70. He designed ceramics, glassware, and metalwork for Rosenthal, Nava, and Zani & Zani. In 1964, he established his own factory Argenteria Sabattini, Bregnano, near Como. He executed the 1976 *Saucière Estro* sauce bowl. Also produced by his own firm were his 1986 *Insect Legs* silver and black titanium tableware and flatware, and 1987 *Connato* silver-plated brass-alloy vase. He was a member of ADI (Associazione per il Disegno Industriale).
▶ He first showed his work in a 1956 exhibition organized by Ponti. He regularly participated in the Triennali di Milano, including the 1954 (X) and 1957 (XV) events, and various exhibitions. In 1962, he received a gold medal at the 'Fiera Internazionale' in Monaco and at the exhibition of 100 years of avant-garde silver at the Louvre in Paris. He participated in the 1968 'Hemisfair' in San Antonio, Texas, and 1970 international exhibition in Ghent. 1969–75, he participated in the 'Mostra Internazionale dell'Arredamento' in Monza, winning the gold medal in 1971. Other exhibitions included the 'Exempla '73' in Monaco, 1973 'BIO 5' Industrial Design Biennial in Ljubljana, and 'Forme Nuove in Italia' in Tehran. He received a gold medal at the 'World Craft Council' in Munich. He was awarded the 1979 Compasso d'Oro.
▶ *ADI Annual 1976*, Milan: Associazione per il Disegno Industriale, 1976. Enrico Marelli, *Lino Sabattini: Intimations and Craftsmanship*, Mariano Comense, 1980. Enrico Marelli, *Lino Sabattino*, Mariano Comense, 1982. Cat., Kathryn B. Hiesinger and George H. Marcus III (eds.), *Design Since 1945*, Philadelphia: Philadelphia Museum of Art, 1983:229,V–35–36.

Sabino, Ernest-Marius
▶ French designer; active Paris.
▶ Sabino designed his glassware and lighting himself until 1930, when he hired production manager Grivois, whose stated goal was to make lighting transcend banality. Sabino used pressed and molded patterned glass in bas-relief. Ranging from very small to monumental, his lighting models included menu holders, statues, large vases, panels, ceiling tiles, pilasters, columns, stelae, bibelots, doors, and fountains. His commissions included lighting for hotels, restaurants, and the oceanliner *Normandie* of 1935. By 1939, Sabino's work had become more diverse than René Lalique's and Jean Perzel's, although it was of a lesser quality.
▶ He showed his work first at the 1925 event of the Salon d'Automne and the 1925 Paris 'Exposition Internationale des Arts Décoratifs et Industriels Modernes.' He was responsible for all the general illuminations in the halls, passageways, and antechambers of the annual events of the Salon d'Automne.
▶ *Lux*, Nov. 1929:161, June 1928:88, Nov. 1928:155, Jan. 1930:3, Sept. 1931:101–04. G. Henriot, *Luminaire Moderne*, 1937: plate 12. *The Studio Yearbook*, 1930:171. Alastair Duncan,

Art Nouveau and Art Déco Lighting, New York: Simon and Schuster, 1978:183–84.

Saddier, Fernand and Gaston Saddier
▶ French decorators and furniture designers; active Paris.
▶ Active from 1919 to the 1930s in their workshop in the Faubourg Saint-Antoine area in Paris, the Saddier brothers showed their furniture and interior schemes regularly in the Paris Salons.
▶ Pierre Kjellberg, *Art Déco: les maîtres du Mobilier, le décor des Paquebots*, Paris: Amateur, 1986:71.

Saeter, Emil
▶ Norwegian chaser and silversmith; active Oslo.
▶ Saeter was a filigree worker at Tostrup in Oslo, becoming a silversmith.
▶ A number of his standing dishes in the form of transparent flowers were shown by Tostrup at the 1900 Paris 'Exposition Universelle.'
▶ Annelies Krekel-Aalberse, *Art Nouveau and Art Déco Silver*, New York: Abrams, 1989:243.

Sagaidachny, Euveny Yakovlevich (1886–1961)
▶ Russian painter, graphic artist, and stage and decorative designer.
▶ A colleague of Mikhail Larionov, Vladimir Tatlin, M. Boychuk, and M. Le-Dantu, he was art director in 1911 of the performance of *Tsar Maximilian* organized by the Union of Youth. Later in life, he lived in Lvov, active primarily in the decorative arts.
▶ He participated in the 1910 exhibition of the Union of Youth and the 1912 'Donkey's Tail' exhibition.
▶ Cat., *Kunst und Revolution: Russische und Sowjetische Kunst 1910–1932*, Vienna: Österreichisches Museum für angewandte Kunst, 1988.

Saglio, André
See Drésa

Sain, Etienne (1904–)
▶ French decorator and artisan.
▶ Working with an engineer, he developed a synthetic lacquer that was easier to use than Chinese or Béka lacquers. With deep layers of lacquer, his luxurious furniture, panels, and doors often included silver-plated bronze hardware.
▶ Cat., *Decorative Arts 1925 Style*, New York: Didier Aaron, 1979.

Saint-Gaudens, Augustus (1848–1907)
▶ Irish sculptor; born Dublin.
▶ Studied Cooper Union for the Advancement of Science and Art and National Academy of Design, New York; from 1867, École Gratuite de Dessin ('Petite École'), Paris; under François Jouffroy; and from 1868, École des Beaux-Arts, Paris.
▶ His family settled in the USA. He was one of the first Americans to study in Paris rather than Rome or Florence. In 1870, he moved to Rome, where he was deeply influenced by early Renaissance sculpture. In 1875, he returned to New York, where he set up his own studio. As an apprentice, he carved cameos and made copies of antique busts. His decorative work on silver presentation pieces of this period included the medallions on the 1875 William Cullen Bryant Vase designed by James Horton Whitehouse of Tiffany. He joined the Tile Club in 1877, and with John La Farge, Olin Levy Warner, Helena de Kay, Will H. Low and others founded the Society of American Artists, probably in response to the National Academy of Design's rejection of one of his sculptures for an annual exhibition. In collaboration with La Farge, Saint-Gaudens' work was exemplary of the Aesthetic movement and highly respected, including their interior decoration of St. Thomas Church and the 1880 Cornelius Vanderbilt residence, both in New York, the latter designed by George B. Post. Saint-Gaudens was influenced by La Farge and architects Stanford White and Charles Follen McKim. He designed the 1881 Farragut Memorial in Madison Square Park in New York, the beginning of a long career as a sculptor of note. Other monumental statuary

included the 1884–87 standing and 1897–1906 seated versions of Abraham Lincoln in Chicago, 1890–91 John Adams Memorial in Washington, 1897 Memorial to Robert Gould Shaw in Boston, and 1903 statue of General Sherman on the Plaza on the Park in New York.

▶ C. Lewis Hind, *Augustus Saint-Gaudens*, New York, 1908. Homer Saint-Gaudens (ed.), *The Reminiscences of August Saint-Gaudens*, New York, 1913. Cat., John H. Dryfhout and Beverly Cox, *Augustus Saint-Gaudens: The Portrait Reliefs*, Washington, DC: National Portrait Gallery, 1969. Louise H. Tharp, *Saint-Gaudens and the Gilded Era*, Boston, 1969. John H. Dryfhout, *The Work of Augustus Saint-Gaudens*, Hanover, NH, and London, 1982. Kathryn Greenthal, *Augustus Saint-Gaudens: Master Sculptor*, New York, 1985. Burke Wilkinson, *Uncommon Clay: The Life and Works of Augustus Saint-Gaudens*, San Diego: 1985. Doreen Bolger Burke et al., *In Pursuit of Beauty: Americans and the Aesthetic Movement*, New York: Metropolitan Museum of Art and Rizzoli, 1986:465–66,254.

Saint-Gobain
▶ French glass and crystal manufacturer; located Chapelle St.-Mesmin.
▶ Saint-Gobain produced a basic glass design intended for picnics and sold throughout the world for general use. One of its more unusual and widely published products was the 1937 illuminated glass radiator by René Coulon, who was instrumental in establishing the Institut de recherche de la sidérurgie et le laboratoire de recherche de Saint-Gobain (Saint-Gobain Institute of Iron-Steel Research and its research laboratory). In 1948, it began production of the *Duralex* pressed-glass drinking goblets with rims around the middle and bottom.
▶ The Coulon radiator was shown in the Saint-Gobain pavilion at the 1937 Paris 'Exposition Internationale des Art et Techniques dans la Vie Moderne.'
▶ Cat., *Les années UAM 1929–1958*, Paris: Musée des Arts Décoratifs, 1988:166–67. *Les Carnets du Design*, Paris: Mad-Cap Productions et APCI, 1986:44.

Saint-Louis, Cristalleries de
▶ French glass manufacturer.
▶ The Verrerie de Münsthal was established in 1568. In 1767, King Louis XV decreed that the glassworks would be known as Saint-Louis. In 1782, the firm was the first in France to manufacture lead crystal. In 1892, it developed a technique for pressing glassware in colorless and opaque crystal. Known for its paperweights, it began production of opaline glassware in 1844. In c1900, Saint-Louis, under the name Argental, began the production of glassware in the Art Nouveau style. A number of consultant designers worked for the firm, including Michel Dufrêne, Marcel Goupy, Jean Luce, and, from 1930, Jean Sala. It abandoned the production of paperweights after World War II. In 1969, the Castille group (the holding company of Hermès and Pochet) took over the company. In the 1980s, a few outside designers began to be used. The firm is active today.
▶ Gerard Ingold, *Saint-Louis: de l'Art en verre à l'art cristal de 1585 à nos jours*, Paris: Denoël. Cat., *Verriers français contemporains: Art et industrie*, Paris: Musée des Arts Décoratifs, 1982.

Sakier, George (1897–1965)
▶ American industrial designer; born Boston.
▶ From the late 1910s, studied Pratt Institute, Brooklyn, New York; Columbia University Graduate School, New York; and painting in Paris.
▶ In 1913 at the age of 19, he published the textbook *Machine Design and Descriptive Geometry*; began working as an engineer, designing automatic machinery, and was introduced to art through painting camouflage patterns during World War I. After the war, he taught machine design and engineering mathematics. In 1925, he became assistant art director of French *Vogue* and campaigned for the restoration of the Mayan collection stored in

the Trocadéro in Paris; the collection was subsequently put on view. Returning to New York, he became art director of the magazines *Modes and Manners* and *Harper's Bazaar*. From 1927, he was head of the bureau of design development of the American Radiator and Standard Sanitary Corporation, where he designed bathtubs and wash basins, and was simultaneously an independent designer. He was one of the few staff designers in an American company during the 1920s. From 1929, designed for Fostoria Glass in Moundsville, West Virginia, for which he executed a distinctive and extensive collection of domestic glassware. Through Sakier's efforts at Fostoria, American open-stock glassware for the first time became more popular than European. Sakier believed in furnishing the public with what it wanted rather than what it needed; he raised no objection when one of his designs was copied and sold in inexpensive variety-store chains. Sakier designed the first prefabricated bathrooms, available as complete units or as separate components; 233 units were first installed in a Washington apartment building in 1933–34. His freelance-design activities produced $15,000 to $25,000 income a year by the mid-1930s.
▶ In c1918, he showed canvases at the Galerie Julien Lévy in Paris, and a one-person 1949 exhibition at the Philadelphia Art Alliance. Work included in 1934 'The Industrial Arts Exposition,' National Alliance of Art, Rockefeller Center, New York; 1939 'New York World's Fair.'
▶ Harry V. Anderson, 'Contemporary American Designers,' *Decorators Digest*, July 1933:38–41. *Fortune*, Feb. 1934:97–98. Anne-Marie Richard, 'George Sakier' in Mel Byars and Russell Flinchum (eds.), *50 American Designers*, Washington: Preservation, 1994.

Sala, Bienvenu (1869–1939)
▶ Spanish glassmaker and designer; born Arenys-de-Mar, Catalonia; active Paris; father of Jean Sala.
▶ Sala settled in Paris in c1905 and established a glass workshop in the Montparnasse quarter. He produced vases decorated in animal and vegetable motifs.
▶ He showed his work in the Salons in Paris and in various galleries, including Galerie Drouet.
▶ Cat., *Verriers français contemporains: Art et industrie*, Paris: Musée des Arts Décoratifs, 1982.

Sala, Jean (1895–1976)
▶ Spanish glassmaker and designer; born Arenys-de-Mar, Catalonia; active Paris; son of Bienvenu Sala.
▶ Studied École des Beaux-Arts, Paris.
▶ He arrived in Paris in c1905 with his glassmaker father. Active in his father's workshop, he designed vessels and chandeliers for the Cristalleries de Saint-Louis in clear crystal. In c1953, he turned from glassmaking to the antiques trade.
▶ He showed his work regularly in the Salons in Paris, various galleries, and at the 1937 Paris 'Exposition Internationale des Arts et Techniques dans la Vie Moderne.'
▶ Cat., *Verriers français contemporains: Art et industrie*, Paris: Musée des Arts Décoratifs, 1982.

Sala, Pierre (1948–89)
▶ French furniture and stage designer; active Paris.
▶ Sala became active in 1969 as a theater producer; in 1972, opened the Marie Stuart Theater, Paris, and managed the Parisian theater La Potinière; in 1973, set up his own firm Furnitur to produce his designs; designed and produced the 1983 *Clairefontaine* desk of which he sold 5,000 pieces, 1985 *Café* range, and *Piranha, Heure du loup*, and *Mare aux canards* lacquered chairs; in 1985, opened his own shop near the Musée d'Orsay, Paris, and sold furniture, objects, and clothing.
▶ Work (*Mikado* range) shown at VIA in 1984. Won the 1983 VIA/Bloomindale's competition (for *Piscine's memory* table in ceramics and *pâte-de-verre*), and 1985 competition sponsored by Cartier for its headquarters, place Vendôme, Paris.

▶ Cat., *Les années VIA 1980–1990*, Paris: Musée des Arts Décoratifs, 1990:56–57.

Salmenhaara, Kyllikki (1915–81)
▶ Finnish ceramicist and glass designer.
▶ 1943, studied Taideteollinen Korkeakoulu, Helsinki.
▶ 1943–46, she worked at Kauklahti glassworks; 1946–47, at Sakari Vapaavuori Ceramic Studio, Helsinki; 1946–47, at Saxbo; 1947–63, at the Arabia ceramics factory in Helsinki; from 1961–63, taught in Taiwan; 1963–73, taught in the ceramics department at Taideteollinen Korkeakoulu, Helsinki, later becoming head of department; 1973–81, was chief ceramics instructor at Helsingen Teknillinen Korkeakoulu, Helsinki.
▶ She received a silver medal at the 1951 (IX), diploma of honor at the 1954 (X), grand prize at the 1957 (XI), and gold medal at the 1960 (XII) Triennali di Milano; 1960 Pro Finlandia award. Her work was included in the 1954–57 USA 'Design in Scandinavia' traveling exhibition, 1955 'H 55' exhibition in Hälsingborg, 1956–57 West Germany 'Finnish Exhibition,' 1961 'Finlandia' exhibition in Zürich, Amsterdam, and London, and 1980 'Scandinavian Modern Design 1880–1980' exhibition at the Cooper-Hewitt Museum in New York.
▶ Cat., David Revere McFadden (ed.), *Scandinavian Modern Design 1880–1980*, New York: Abrams, 1982:270, No. 184. Cat., *Kyllikki Salmenhaara, 1915–81*, Helsinki: Museum of Applied Arts, 1986. Jennifer Hawkins Opie, *Scandinavia: Ceramics and Glass in the Twentieth Century*, New York: Rizzoli, 1989.

Salmoiraghi, Pietro (1941–)
▶ Italian designer; born and active Milan.
▶ Studied architecture, Politecnico di Milano, to 1966.
▶ He began his professional career in 1965. In 1967, he became a member of ADI (Associazione per il Disegno Industriale) and, in 1973, was its president. His clients in Italy included Cristallerie Imperatore, Cedit, Kartell, and Misal. 1965–70, he taught architecture at the Politecnico di Milano. In 1969, he worked on a project for Ises, the institute for the study of educational architecture. In 1971, he worked on a project for Gescal, the institute for the management of worker housing. He taught courses 1972–73 on ergonomics at the Museo della Scienza e della Tecnica. In 1973, he became a member of Società Italiana di Ergonomia. He was editor of the magazine *Design Italia* and a member of the restructuring committee of the Triennale di Milano. Salmoiraghi, Andries van Onck, Antonio Barrese, Cees Houtzager, and Antonio Locatelli founded Studio Pro, undertaking industrial and visual design, architecture, and town planning. Some of the cultural and political projects were done *pro bono publico*.
▶ Cat., Milena Lamarová, *Design a Plastické Hmoty*, Prague: Uměleckoprůmyslové Muzeum, 1972:148. *ADI Annual 1976*, Milan: Associazione per il Disegno Industriale, 1976.

Salmon, Philip
▶ Canadian furniture designer.
▶ Studied Central Tech, Toronto.
▶ In 1969, Salmon and Hugh Hamilton set up Salmon-Hamilton Design Consultants in Toronto, becoming active as designers of tubular steel and plywood furniture. Their 1971 stool with its one-piece bent tubular steel base was widely published.
▶ Cat., *Seduced and Abandoned: Modern Furniture designers in Canada, the First Fifty Years*, Toronto: The Art Gallery at Harbourfront, 1986:25.

Salo, Markku (1954–)
▶ Finnish glassware designer; born Nokia.
▶ 1972–74, studied Kankaanpää Taidekoulu; 1974–79, Taideteollinen Korkeakoulu, both Helsinki.
▶ 1979–83, he was head of the design department and product designer at Salora; from 1983, glassware, tableware, unique-work, exhibition, and graphic designer at the Hackman Iittala/Nuutajärvi Lasi (glassworks); and, 1982–83 and from 1991, teacher at the Kankaanpää Taidekoulu.

▶ He won the 1976 Extra Prize of Scan Design, 1981 first prize in the Philips Luminaire Design Competition, 1988 Finnish State Award for Industrial Arts, and 1990 Georg Jensen Award. His work was included in Finnish Design Exhibitions, Helsinki, from 1980; 1982 'Finnish Gestaltet,' Hamburg and Düsseldorf; 'The Modern Spirit—Glass Form' in Finland, USA, Canada, Germany from 1985; 1987 'Young Glass' exhibition, Denmark; 1987 'Light and Material,' Helsinki; 1988 'Cold Exhibition,' Sapporo; 1989 'Made in Tavastland,' Stockholm; 1989 'Utopies,' Grand Palais, Paris; and 1900 'Nordform 90,' Malmö.
▶ Cat., *Markku Salo: Lasia/Glass*, Helsinki: Suomen Lasimuseo, 1991. Jennifer Hawkins Opie, *Scandinavia: Ceramics and Glass in the Twentieth Century*, New York: Rizzoli; 1989.

Salocchi, Claudio (1934–)
▶ Italian architect, industrial designer, and teacher; born and active Milan.
▶ Studied architecture, Politecnico di Milano to 1965.
▶ In 1965, he set up his own design office. His first design in plastics was the 1966 *Palla* armchair in soft polyurethane. He designed the plastic 1971 *Apoggio* seat based on ergonomic principles for Sormani. He was associated for a time with the group RNF (Ricerche non finalizzate); became active as an interior architect and organizer of exhibitions and international design events. In 1967, he became a member of ADI (Associazione per il Disegno Industriale) and vice-president; designed the Sormani showrooms in Milan, Bologna, Turin, and Rome. His principal works included the 1966 *Lia* chair in aluminum for Sormani, 1967 *Ellisse* range in aluminum for Sormani, 1967 *Fluo* florescent light for Lumenform, *S 102* kitchen system for Alberti, 1973 *Napoleone* table range for Sormani, 1974 *Free System* seating, beds, and modular components for Skipper, and 1975 *Bankor Office* range of office furniture for Skipper. Other design clients included Besana, Besozzi, Rossi di Albizzate. He taught architecture at the Politecnico di Milano, and furniture and interior design, Instituto Professionale di Stato, Lissone.
▶ Received 1988 Premio Compasso d'Oro. His work was shown in numerous exhibitions, including the 1963 London 'Furniture Exhibition'; 1966 'European Living Art Today' in Kyoto and Tokyo; 1966 'Interior Design Biennale Mariano Corense'; 1966 (I) Genoa 'Eurodomus,' 1968 (II) Turin 'Eurodomus,' 1970 (III) Milan 'Eurodomus'; 1967 Paris 'Présences d'Italie'; 1968 Triennale di Milano; 1968 Zürich 'Domus Design'; 1970 'Modern Chairs 1918–1970' at the Whitechapel Gallery in London; 1972 'Design a Plastické Hmoty' exhibition at the Uměleckoprůmyslové Museum in Prague; and in exhibitions in Paris (1967), Zürich (1969), New York (1970), and London (1971). His *Lia* chair was shown first at the 1966 (V) Biennale dello Standard.
▶ Cat., *Modern Chairs 1918–1970*, London: Lund Humphries, 1971. Cat., Milena Lamarová, *Design a Plastické Hmoty*, Prague: Uměleckoprůmyslové Muzeum, 1972:156. *ADI Annual 1976*, Milan: Associazione per il Disegno Industriale, 1976. Alfonso Grassi and Anty Pansera, *Atlante del design italiano: 1940–1980*, Milan, 1980:310. *Modo*, No. 148, March–April 1993:125.

Salomon, André (1891–1970)
▶ French lighting engineer; active Paris.
▶ Studied École Supérieure d'Électricité.
▶ He was an engineer at Tompson before setting up the small electrical firm Perfécla (Perfectionnement de l'Ecla), working regularly with architects and designers including Pierre Chareau, André Lurçat, René Herbst, and architect Robert Mallet-Stevens. For the latter, he produced the widely published 1929 lighting fixture designed by Francis Jourdain in the form of a suspended concave metal ring projecting rays onto the ceiling and reflecting a soft indirect light elsewhere. This fixture was probably influenced by a 1928 prototype designed by Eugène Printz, called *Couronne lumineuse*. For Herbst, Salomon specified the precise curvature of the two wings of a widely published 1928 ceiling fixture. In 1929, he was a founding member of UAM (Union des Artistes Modernes). With Salomon, Mallet-Stevens executed wall and ceiling lighting

for Paul Poiret's shop in Paris, Casino de Saint Jean-de-Luz, and the entrance hall to the 1930 exhibition of the Union des Artistes Modernes and, for others, Bally and Café du Brésil. With Paul Nelson, he designed the lighting for the American hospital in Neuilly and invented a system of moveable lighting for the 1943 hospital in Saint-Lô. Salomon worked on lighting for the 1935 oceanliner *Normandie*. After World War II, he worked with students of Auguste Perret on the reconstruction of Le Havre and on the lighting of highways and roads, and was in charge of the lighting of harbors. With his friend Georges-Henri Pingusson, he worked on the project of the college in Boulogne-Billancourt and on lighting for its basement theater.

▶ Herbst's double-winged ceiling fixture was shown at the 1928 event of the Salon d'Automne. Collaborating with Francis Jourdain, their illuminated tables appeared at the 1937 Paris 'Exposition Internationale des Arts et Techniques dans la Vie Moderne,' where Salomon contributed to Mallet-Stevens's Pavillon de la Lumière, ten other pavilions, and the giant work of Raoul Dufy, *La Fée électricité*.

▶ Alastair Duncan, *Art Nouveau and Art Déco Lighting*, New York: Simon and Schuster, 1978:153,172,174. Arlette Barré-Despond, *UAM*, Paris: Regard, 1986:502–03.

Salomon, Heike   (1960–)

▶ German industrial designer; born Berlin.

▶ From 1980, studied industrial design, Hochschule der Künste, Berlin; 1984–85, took a practical design course at the firm D-Team Design.

▶ In June 1987, she joined the staff as an industrial designer at the firm D-Team-Design in Schondorf. Her work included the 1988 *Triangle* chair (with Rainer Bohl and Dorothee Hiller) by Drabert.

▶ Cat., Design Center Stuttgart, *Women in Design: Careers and Life Histories Since 1900*, Stuttgart: Haus der Wirtschaft, 1989: 102–03.

Salone del Mobile

▶ Annual exhibition.

▶ The Salone del Mobile was first held in Milan 1961 to exhibit the furniture of Italian manufacturers. It was sponsored by Cosmit (Comitato Organizzatore della manifestazione). Foreign exhibitors were included from the late 1970s. Its 31st national (and 13th international) event was held 1992. Exhibitions of some note took place concurrently with the event: an exhibition of Rationalist furniture of the 1930s was mounted in 1988 and an exhibition of 30 years of Italian furniture and furnishing designs in 1991. Being moved from September to April to coincide with the Euroluce (Salone Internazionale dell'Illuminazione) and Salone del Complemento d'Arredo (Exhibition of Accessories and Furnishings), there was no Salone del Mobile in 1990.

Salto, Axel   (1889–1961)

▶ Danish ceramicist.

▶ Studied painting, Det Kongelige Danske Kunstakademi, Copenhagen.

▶ He co-founded the journal *Klingen* 1917. 1923–25, he worked at Bing & Grøndahl in Copenhagen; from *c*1925–*c*33, worked with Nathalie Krebs at Saxbo; and, from 1933, at the Royal Copenhagen porcelain manufactory. In 1934, he designed patterns for bookbinding papers and, in 1944, printed fabric for L.F. Foght. He headed the restoration project of the 1846 Jørgen Sonne frieze on the Thorvaldsens Museum in Copenhagen.

▶ He received a grand prize at the 1951 (IX) Triennale di Milano.

▶ Axel Salto, *Salto's Keramick*, Copenhagen, 1930. Cat., David Revere McFadden (ed.), *Scandinavian Modern Design 1880–1980*, New York: Abrams, 1982:270, No. 133. Jennifer Hawkins Opie, *Scandinavia: Ceramics and Glass in the Twentieth Century*, New York: Rizzoli, 1989.

Salvati, Alberto   (1935–)

▶ Italian designer; born Milan.

▶ Studied architecture in Milan to 1960.

▶ From 1960, he collaborated with Ambrogio Tresoldi; 1961–64, was an assistant, Faculty of Engineering, Politecnico di Milano; 1962–63, was an assistant, Faculty of Architecture; was active in architecture, interior and industrial design; collaborated with numerous artists; worked for Centro Convenienza for the autostrada Milano–Bergamo and on houses, motels, hotels, and shops; designed furniture and furnishings for clients including Cassina, Delchi, Busnelli, RB Rossana, Saporiti.

▶ With Tresoldi, received 1984 (chair) and 1987 (*Strasburgo* seating system) Compasso d'Oro awards.

▶ Giancarlo Iliprandi and Pierluigi Molinari (eds.), *Industrial Design Italiani*, Fagagma, 1985:202. Alberto Salvati and Ambrogio Tresoldi, *Lo Spazio delle Interazioni*, Milan, 1985. *Modo*, No. 148, March–April 1993:125.

Sambinelli, Flavio   (1949–)

▶ Italian engineer and designer; born Brescia (Italy).

▶ Studied engineering to 1969.

▶ He began his collaboration with Carlo Giannini in 1977.

▶ Received 1984 Design Plus award, Internationale Frankfurter Messe (*Cabiria* expresso machine).

Sambonet

▶ Italian metalware manufacturer.

▶ A factory for manufacturing silverwares was established in 1856 in Piedmont by the Sambonet family. Its designers included Vittorio Bergomi and architects Gio Ponti, Gigi Caccia Dominioni, and Achille and Pier Giacomo Castiglioni. From the 1950s, its designers included Roberto Sambonet, Pieraldo Mortara, Edoardo Brunetti, Piero Fornara, Augusto Salviato, Osvaldo Ferraris, and Ferruccio Vercelloni. Its corporate image was contributed to by Max Huber, Heinz Waibl, Bob Noorda, and Bruno Monguzzi.

▶ Its fish dish by Roberto Sambonet on the 1956 Compasso d'Oro and its entire line won the 1970 Compasso d'Oro. A design by Ponti was shown at the 1963 (XII) Triennale di Milano. Sambonet received the gold medal at the 1960 (XII) Triennale di Milano, and grand prize and gold medal at the 1970 (XV) Triennale. The firm was awarded the 1972 'Domus Inox' prize and 1972 Macef prize.

▶ Jeremy Myerson and Sylvia Katz, *Conran Design Guides: Tableware*, London: Conran Octopus, 1990:77. *ADI Annual 1976*, Milan: Associazione per il Disegno Industriale, 1976.

Sambonet, Roberto   (1924–)

▶ Italian illustrator, painter, and industrial and graphic designer; born Vercelli; active Milan.

▶ 1942–45, studied architecture, Politecnico di Milano.

▶ He was a professional painter; 1948–53, worked at Museo de Arte, São Paulo, and collaborated with P.M. Bardi; 1953, was apprenticed to Alvar Aalto in Helsinki; returning to Italy, was a graphic designer for La Rinascente department store and art director of the journal *Zodiac* from 1957. In 1954, joined the family firm in Vercelli, when it first began producing stainless-steel wares. His designs were streamlined and largely free of decoration; the 1954 fish dish illustrated the full potential of stainless steel as a luxury item. Based on geometrical structures, his notable work included flatware and a series of nesting containers. His 1965 *Center Line* stainless-steel cookware was on a high level of sophistication, function, and aesthetics. He designed glassware for Baccarat in France 1977 and Seguso in Venice 1979, and ceramics for Bing & Grøndahl Porcelænsfabrik in Copenhagen in 1974 and Richard Ginori in Italy in 1979. In 1980, he taught design in Rio de Janeiro, São Paulo, and Carrara. He was a member of ADI (Associazione per il Disegno Industriale).

▶ He showed his paintings and designs at the Museo de São Paulo in 1949, Galleria del Disegno in Milan in 1960, Palazzo dei Centori in Vercelli in 1962, Galleria Profili in Milan in 1963, Pater in 1966, and Il Milione in 1969. His work was the subject of the 1974 retrospective of design, graphics, and painting at the Museo di São Paulo and 1980 exhibition, Palazzo Bagatti-Valsecchi.

▶ Received 1954 (fish-serving dish), 1956, and 1970 (entire Sambonet range) Premio Compasso d'Oro; gold medals 1957 (XI) and 1973 (XV) and a grand prize at 1960 (XII) Triennale di Milano, at which he was a member of the technical jury.

▶ Jeremy Myerson and Sylvia Katz, *Conran Design Guides: Tableware*, London: Conran Octopus, 1990:77. Cat., Kathryn B. Hiesinger and George H. Marcus III (eds.), *Design Since 1945*, Philadelphia: Philadelphia Museum of Art, 1983:229, V–37, II–54. *Roberto Sambonet: Design grafica pittura '74–'79*, Milan: Palazzo Bagatti Valsecchi, 1980. Paolo Fossati, *Il design in Italia*, Turin, 1972:135–40, 239–42, plates 404–49. Alfonso Grassi and Anty Pansera, *Atlante del design italiano: 1940–1980*, Milan, 1980:287. *ADI Annual 1976*, Milan: Associazione per il Disegno Industriale, 1976. Fumio Shimizu and Matteo Thun (eds.), *The Descendants of Leonardo: The Italian Design*, Tokyo, 1987:334.

Sampe, Astrid (1909–)

▶ Swedish textile designer.

▶ Studied Konstfackskolan and Tekniska Skolan, Stockholm, and Royal College of Art, London.

▶ She joined in 1936 and, 1937–72, was head of the textile design workshop of Nordiska in Stockholm, where she was influential as a colorist and pattern designer. She worked with Sven Markelius on the Swedish pavilion at the 1939 'New York World's Fair.' In 1946, she introduced the use of grasscloth in Sweden. At the Wohlbeck and Kasthall rug factories in the 1950s, she was instrumental in reviving industrially woven carpets. In 1955, she executed a number of domestic linens in geometric and folk motifs. In 1972, she set up her own studio in Stockholm, where she designed interiors and textiles. Her clients included Donald of Dundee, Knoll, Svängsta Klädesfabrik, and Almedahl-Dalsjöfors. Sampe and Vera Diurson published the book *Textiles Illustrated* (1948).

▶ Her work was shown at the 1937 Paris 'Exposition Internationale des Arts et Techniques dans la Vie Moderne.' In 1949, elected Honorary Royal Designer for Industry, London. She won a gold medal at the 1954 (X) Triennale di Milano and a silver medal at its 1960 (XII) session, and the 1956 Gregor Paulsson Trophy. Her work was included in the 1980 'Scandinavian Modern Design 1880–1980' exhibition at the Cooper-Hewitt Museum in New York and 1983–84 'Design Since 1945' exhibition at the Philadelphia Museum of Art.

▶ Erik Zahle (ed.), *A Treasury of Scandinavian Design*, New York, 1961:290, Nos. 112,115. Lennart Lindkvist (ed.), *Design in Sweden*, Stockholm, 1972:66–67. Astrid Sampe, *Swedish Textiles*, Stockholm, 1981. Cat., David Revere McFadden (ed.), *Scandinavian Modern Design 1880–1980*, New York: Abrams, 1982:270, No. 212. Cat., Kathryn B. Hiesinger and George H. Marcus III (eds.), *Design Since 1945*, Philadelphia: Philadelphia Museum of Art, 1983:229, VII–53.

Sander-Noske, Sophie (1884–1958)

▶ Austrian designer; born Vienna.

▶ After an apprenticeship in Vienna, she designed for the Wiener Kunstgewerbeschule and worked as a specialist in filigree in Paris and Amsterdam. In 1911, she managed a domestic wares workshop in Cortina d'Ampezzo and, in 1911 and 1912, taught enameling and was head of the jewelry and metalworking departments of the Haarlemsche School voor Kunstnijverheid in Haarlem. She had a workshop at Heuberggasse 13, Vienna. Her earliest designs for children's furniture were published in the pages of her mother's magazine in the late 1920s. In c1923–25, she worked at the Wiener Werkstätte, producing freer and happier forms than those of her earlier years and designing complete interior schemes and individual furniture pieces. Her work included textiles, wallpaper, and decorative-paper designs.

▶ Her work was included in 1909–10, 1910–11, 1911–12, 1912, and 1913–14 exhibitions of the Austrian arts and crafts at the Österreichisches Museum für Kunst und Industrie, Vienna.

▶ Waltrand Neuwirth, *Lexikon Wiener Gold- und Silverschmiede und ihre Punzen 1867–1922*, Vienna, 1977:170–74. Stephen Cal-

loway, *Twentieth-Century Decoration*, New York: Rizzoli, 1988: 151. Annelies Krekel-Aalberse, *Art Nouveau and Art Déco Silver*, New York: Abrams, 1989:259. Deanna F. Cera (ed.), *Jewels of Fantasy: Costume Jewelry of the 20th Century*, New York: Abrams, 1992:104.

Sanderson, Arthur & Sons

▶ British textile and wallpaper firm.

▶ Arthur Sanderson (?–1882) established the firm in 1860. It was incorporated in 1900; set up furnishing fabrics printworks in Uxbridge in 1921 and wove there from 1934.

▶ C. Woods, *Sanderson's 1860–1985*, London: Arthur Sanderson & Sons, 1985. Valerie Mendes, *The Victoria & Albert Museum Textile Collection, British Textiles from 1900 to 1937*, London: Victoria and Albert Museum, 1992.

Sandnes, Eystein (1924–)

▶ Norwegian glassware designer and ceramicist.

▶ 1945–49, studied Statens Håndverks -og Kunstindustriskole, Oslo.

▶ 1951–55, was artistic director at Magnor glassworks and, from 1955, a freelance designer of its tableware and art glass; in c1951, was freelance designer at S & S Helle; from 1955–57, worked at Stavangerflint; from 1957, was artistic director at Porsgrund.

▶ He received a silver medal at the 1960 (XII) Triennale di Milano; 1965 and 1970 Norsk Designcentrum prizes. Work included in numerous exhibitions Norway and abroad.

▶ Cat., David Revere McFadden (ed.), *Scandinavian Modern Design 1880–1980*, New York: Abrams, 1982:270, No. 167. Jennifer Hawkins Opie, *Scandinavia: Ceramics and Glass in the Twentieth Century*, New York: Rizzoli, 1989.

Sandoz, Édouard-Marcel (1881–1971)

▶ French sculptor, metalworker, and ceramics designer.

▶ Studied École des Beaux-Arts, Paris, under Mercié and Injalbert.

▶ He specialized in small animal sculptures and designed a series of polychrome porcelain items such as boxes, bottles, decanters, and tea and coffee sets in animal and other shapes made by Haviland at Limoges.

▶ Work shown at the Salon of the Société Nationale des Beaux-Arts and in Brussels and Barcelona.

Sandoz, Gérard (1902–)

▶ French jeweler, painter, and graphic artist; born Paris.

▶ Trained in his father's workshop as a jeweler and silversmith in Paris.

▶ c1920–30, Sandoz designed mechanistically-inspired jewelry in his father's firm Maison Sandoz, designed posters, and was active in easel painting. He worked for a time for his uncle Paul Follot, who initiated him into the decorative arts. Sandoz produced small enameled and lacquered objects and jewelry with precious and semi-precious stones. Along with Camille Fauré and Jean Goulden, he was known as one of the best enamelers of the 1920s in Paris and an innovator of Modern jewelry along with Jean Fouquet and Raymond Templier. In 1929, he was a founding member of UAM (Union des Artistes Modernes). He abandoned jewelry design in 1928 and closed the family firm in the rue Royale in 1931. Turning to film making in 1931, Sandoz made *Panurge* (1932) with Paul Poiret and Danielle Darrieux, a 1939 documentary film, and wrote for radio and TV. He scripted and designed sets for film and was a poster and cinema house designer. In the 1980s, he returned to jewelry design.

▶ He showed his work at the Salon d'Automne and Salon of the Société des Artistes Décorateurs and the 1925 Paris 'Exposition Internationale des Arts Décoratifs et Industriels Modernes.' He showed at UAM exhibitions from 1930.

▶ Gérard Sandoz, 'Bijoux d'aujourd'hui,' *La Renaissance de l'Art français*, Aug. 1929. Gérard Sandoz, *Objets usuels*, Paris: Charles Moreau. Sylvie Raulet, *Bijoux des Arts Déco*, Paris: Regard, 1984. Sylvie Raulet, 'Gérard Sandoz le Pionnier,' *Harper's Bazaar*, May–June 1985. Arlette Barré-Despond, *UAM*, Paris: Regard, 1986:504–05. Cat., *Les années UAM 1929–1958*, Paris: Musée des Arts Décoratifs, 1988:240–41. Annelies Krekel-Aalberse, *Art Nouveau and Art Déco Silver*, New York: Abrams, 1989:71,259.

Sansoni, Flam (1924–)
▶ Italian designer; born Forano Sabino; active Conegliano.
▶ Sansoni began his professional career in 1949. From 1949, he worked for Dal Vera in Conegliano, designing all its furniture collections in wood, metal, fabric, plastics, and cane. He was a member of ADI (Associazione per il Disegno Industriale).
▶ His furniture was shown in the 1960 Earl's Court Exhibition in London.
▶ *ADI Annual 1976*, Milan: Associazione per il Disegno Industriale, 1976.

Santa & Cole
▶ Spanish furniture manufacturer.
▶ Santa & Cole was established in 1986 by brothers-in-law Gabriel Ordeig (painter, interior designer, and former rock-band promoter) and Javier Nieto (former economist and publisher) in a factory space that had been a part of the 1929–30 'Exposición Internacional de Barcelona.' First as assembly space and subsequently a showroom, the hangar-like building was moved to the hills above Barcelona and renovated by Gariel Ordeig. By 1989, Santa & Cole had ten more showrooms in Spain and was a distributor of Bulthaup German kitchen systems. The firm reissued the 1969 *Zeleste* lamp by Angel Jové and Santiago Roqueta (in 1986), Carlos Riart's 1976 *Colilla* lamp, and Pete Sans's *Lamparaprima* lamp. In 1990, the firm began its *Classic Spanish* line of designs of J.A. Coderch and Jujol. As part of a series of eight decorated lamps, Ordeiga (with painting by Viçenc Viaplana) designed the 1985 *La Bella Durmiente* (*Sleeping Beauty*) floor lamp.
▶ Guy Julier, *New Spanish Design*, London: Thames and Hudson, 1991.

Santachiara, Denis (1950–)
▶ Italian designer; born Campagnola; active Milan.
▶ He began in design on sports cars in Reggio Emilia. In the late 1960s at the time of the Arte Povera movement, he produced analytical and conceptual art, while working in design; in 1966, set up a design office for automobile design. His 1974 project for a communications system (video entertainment and information board) was designed for Milan's city center. In 1974, he duplicated Galileo's telescope as a color-effect amusement. From 1975, he worked on 'soft technology,' midway between art and design. From 1989, he collaborated with Cesare Castelli on multifunctional novelty furniture production, in which little attention was given to traditional values; in 1990 with Castelli, founded Domodinamica, a firm for the production of interactive, experimental design. He designed the 'Habitat' touring exhibition of Italian design and technology, sponsored by the Italian Institute of Foreign Trade. His work addressed the social and philosophical implications of design and incorporated so-called smart materials. He lectured at Università di Firenze; Domus Academy, Milan; Politecnico di Milano; Institute of Design; and Isa, Rome. His work included 1979 stereo earphones by BWA; 1984 *mobile infinito* accessories by Alchimia; 1981 *Maestrale* red-flag lamp; cover design, *Uomo Vogue*, March 1982; 1986 plastic bicycle by Stylresine; 1982 *Ali* lamp by Fontana Arte; 1983 *On-off* lamp (with Raggi and Meda) by LucePlan; 1984 *work Station* (with Meda and Raggi) by Italtel Telematica; 1983 toothbrush by GOG, USA; 1985 *Sparta* lamp stanchions by Oceano Oltreluce; 1986 fast-food restaurant Aquylone, Reggio Emilia; 1988 *Trans* armchair by Campeggi; and an array of objects produced by firms worldwide, including such unorthodox items as a singing doormat. His 1987 *Notturno italiano* bedside lamp in the shape of a large flattened silver lightbulb projected a continuous row of sheep jumping over a fence under a star-filled sky; it was produced by Yamagiwa in 1987 and by Domodinamica in 1990.
▶ Showing his work for the first time, his project 'La casa Telematica' was at 1973 (XV) Triennale di Milano. Work subject of 'La casa onirica,' 1983 (XVII) Triennale and Grand Palais, Paris; 1987

exhibition, Vitra Design Museum, Weil am Rhein, and 'Santachiara: l'estetica dell'uso' exhibition, Civici Musei, Reggio Emilia, 1990.
▶ Cat., François Dagognet and Ezio Manzini, *Santachiara: L'Estetica dell'Uso*, Reggio Emilia, 1990. Fumio Shimizu and Matteo Thun (eds.), *The Descendants of Leonardo: The Italian Design*, Tokyo, 1987.

Santi, Carlo (1925–)
▶ Italian designer; born and active Milan.
▶ He began his professional career in 1949. He designed furniture, lighting, and electronic equipment for clients including Kartell. He was a member of ADI (Associazione per il Disegno Industriale).
▶ *ADI Annual 1976*, Milan: Associazione per il Disegno Industriale, 1976.

Santin, Fabio (1972–)
▶ Italian industrial designer; born Trieste; active Mestre.
▶ Santin began his professional career in 1972. In 1974, he and Giuliano Vido set up a design studio in Mestre. Clients included Genuflex Arredamenti, Bornello Arredamenti, Scarpa Arredamenti, Minotti seating, Nicolini Industria Mobili, and Nason industrial glass. Santin's *Gru* table and floor lamps and *Jojo* suspension lamp were produced by Emil Illuminazione. He was a member of ADI (Associazione per il Disegno Industriale).
▶ *ADI Annual 1976*, Milan: Associazione per il Disegno Industriale, 1976.

Saporiti Industria Arredamenti
▶ Italian furniture manufacturer; located Besnate.
▶ Saporiti Industria Arredamenti produces tables, seating, and bookshelves in both plastics and wood with upholstery. It began manufacturing in plastics in 1967. Alberto Rosselli designed its 1967 *Jumbo* and 1969 *Moby Dick* fiberglass chairs. Its designers included Vittorio Introini, Giovanni Offredi, Giorgio Raimondi, and Antonello Mosca.
▶ Cat., Milena Lamarová, *Design a Plastické Hmoty*, Prague: Uměleckoprůmyslové Muzeum, 1972:74,204.

Sapper, Richard (1932–)
▶ German designer; born Munich; active Munich, Stuttgart, and Milan.
▶ 1952–56, studied mechanical engineering, University of Munich.
▶ 1956–57, he was a designer for Mercedes-Benz in Stuttgart. Settling in Italy, he worked 1958–59 in the studio of Ponti-Rosselli in Milan. He became a member of the design department of La Rinascente department store in Milan before joining Marco Zanuso Sr., with whom he collaborated until 1975. Specializing in high technology products, he is best known for his designs for the housings for consumer electronics and lighting. Sapper and Zanuso designed some of the most recognizable objects of the 1970s, including scales and a timer for Terraillon in the early 1970s. Working for Brionvega from 1962, they designed the 1962 *Doney* and 1964 *Algol 11* TV sets, 1965 *TS 502* folding radio, 1969 *Black 201* black box TV set; and the 1965 *Grillo* folding telephone for Siemens. He was co-organizer of an exhibition of advanced technology at the 1968 (XIV) Triennale di Milano. 1970–76, he was a consultant to Fiat and Pirelli on experimental vehicles and automobile equipment. Setting up his own studio in Germany in 1970, he designed the skeletal low-voltage 1972 *Tizio* lamp and *Tantalo* clock produced by Artemide. The *Tizio* became an ubiquitous cult design object. In 1972, he and Gae Aulenti set up a studio for the development of new systems for urban transportation; the collaboration resulted in an exhibition at the 1979 (XVIII) Triennale di Milano. His 1979 *Cafetière* coffee maker and whistling 1983 *Bollitore* kettles, both produced by Alessi, combined Post-Modernism and the high-tech style. He executed other tablewares and the 1988 *Uri Uri* watch for Alessi and furniture for Castelli, Molteni, and Knoll. He and Zanuso designed the *4000* scales for Terraillon. Industrial design consultant to IBM

from 1981 for all product design work, he also designed a collection of furniture for Unifor for the home office environment. Though he worked largely in his native Germany, he is strongly associated with the postwar Italian design ethic. In his industrial design of the 1970s and 1980s, he successfully married the precision of Germany with the sensual qualities of Italy. He was a member of ADI (Associazione per il Disegno Industriale).

▶ Sapper, Pio Manzù, and William Lansing Plub organized the 'Mostra di Tecnologia' at the 1968 (XIV) Triennale di Milano. Sapper and Zanuso won the 1960, 1962 (Doney TV set), 1964, 1967, and 1970 Compasso d'Oro awards, the gold medals at the 1966 'BIO 2' and 1973 'BIO 5' Industrial Design Biennials in Ljubljana, gold medal and grand prize at the 1964 'BIO 3,' Triennale di Milano, the 1969 Smau prize, and the 1970 Bundespreis 'Die gute Industrieform.' They participated in the 1972 'Italy: The New Domestic Landscape: Achievements and Problems of Italian Design.'

▶ Les Carnets du Design, Paris: Mad-Cap Productions et APCI, 1986:80. Albrecht Bangert and Karl Michael Armer, 80s Style: Designs of the Decade, New York: Abbeville, 1990:131,135, 223,235. Jeremy Myerson and Sylvia Katz, Conran Design Guides: Kitchenware, London: Conran Octopus, 1990:77–78. Cat., Kathryn B. Hiesinger and George H. Marcus III (eds.), Design Since 1945, Philadelphia: Philadelphia Museum of Art, 1983:230, III–96,IV–32,V–39. Paolo Fossati, Il design in Italia, Turin, 1972:219. Alfonso Grassi and Anty Pansera, Atlante del design italiano: 1940–1980, Milan, 1980:289. Jane Lott, 'Interview: Fifties Fantasist Turned Design Houdini,' Design, No. 381, Sept. 1980:37. ADI Annual 1976, Milan: Associazione per il Disegno Industriale, 1976.

Saracino, Titti (1944–)

▶ Italian designer; born and active Milan.

▶ Studied architecture, Politecnico di Milano, to 1968.

▶ She taught in 1971 at the Instituto Europeo di Design. She designed the stand for Flexform of Meda at the 1970 Milan (III) 'Eurodomus' exhibition, and four stands at the 1972 (IV) 'Eurodomus.' She designed the 1973 collection for Boom Line in Florence, 1973 porcelain range for Mangani, 1973 kitchenware and flatware for Valco in Lumezzane, 1974 wooden toys for Furga, 1974 baby's high chair for Isab in Mornago, 1974 jewelry for the Gioielleria Spallanzani, 1975 furniture collection for Gervasoni in Udine, 1976 restoration and interior design of an 18th-century villa in Isola d'Elba, 1976 restoration and interior design of a 17th-century house in Milan, and 1976 tiles for Santagostino. 1969–74, she was director of urban buildings of the Sovraintendenza Regionale Scolastica and, from 1974, director of monuments in Lombardy. She was a member of ADI (Associazione per il Disegno Industriale).

▶ Saracino showed her work at the 1966 jewelry exhibition 'Circolo della Stampa.'

▶ ADI Annual 1976, Milan: Associazione per il Disegno Industriale, 1976.

Sargiani, Franco (1940–)

▶ Italian graphic and industrial designer; born Modena; active Milan.

▶ Studied architecture in Milan.

▶ He was frequently associated with the studio of architect of Bruno Morassutti. From 1963, he worked in design studios in Britain, Denmark, Switzerland, and Finland on the design of industrial buildings and interior architecture. In 1969 under Nino Di Salvatore, he taught a course in industrial design and visualization at the Scuola Politecnica di Design in Novara. From 1970, he designed table metalware and graphics for Alessi, including the Programma 8 range. 1969–70, he designed packaging for Sivam and, 1974–75, wallpaper and packaging for Sipea. He was a member of ADI (Associazione per il Disegno Industriale).

▶ ADI Annual 1976, Milan: Associazione per il Disegno Industriale, 1976.

Sarpaneva, Timo (1926–)

▶ Finnish glassware, ceramics, textile, metalwork, and exhibition designer.

▶ 1941–48, studied graphic arts, Taideteollinen Korkeakoulu, Helsinki.

▶ In 1950, he became head of the exhibition section and artist at Iittala glassworks where, in the 1960s, he developed a process of blowing glass sculpture into wooden molds that, by burning, gave the pieces a textured surface. In the mid-1950s, he designed his first utilitarian domestic glass collection; for this series, he designed the symbol of a small lowercase 'i' in a red circle, which subsequently became the trademark of the Iittala Glasbruk. In the 1950s, he became widely known through his awards at the Triennali di Milano. From 1955–56 he was artistic director of Pori Puuvilla Cotton Mill; from 1959–63, designed cast-iron cookware and wrapping papers at W. Rosenlew; from 1960–62, designed ryijy rugs at Villayhtymä. In 1962, he set up his own studio; in 1963, he designed candles at Juhava; in 1964, metalware at Primo; from 1964–72, worked at Ab Kinnassand textile mill, Sweden; in 1968, designed plastics for Ensto, and glass for Corning, USA, and firms in Venini, Italy. An innovator of techniques and forms, he worked in the factories of his clients in order to gain mastery of the process and learn from the technicians who produced his wares. His 1968 Ambiente fabric range was printed on both sides of the fabric in a process he invented. In 1970, he designed textiles at Tampella; and metalware for Opa; from 1970, was a freelance designer at Rosenthal. From the mid-1950s, he taught textile composition and printing at the Taideteollinen Korkealoulu in Helsinki. Sarpaneva designed the 1955 H 55 exhibition in Hälsingborg, the Finnish section of the 1957 (XI) Triennale di Milano, the 1961 'Finlandia' exhibition in London, and the Finnish section of the 1967 Montreal 'Universal and International Exhibition (Expo '67).'

▶ Received prizes at the 1951 (IX) (silver medal), 1954 (X) (grand prize), 1957 (XI) (two grand prizes), and 1960 (XII) (silver and gold medals) Triennali di Milano, 1956 USA 'American Young Scandinavian Exhibition' (two first-place awards), 1956 Lunning Prize, 1958 Pro Finlandia Prize, 1985 State Award for Industrial Arts, and Eurostar Prize. In 1963, was elected Honorary Royal Designer for Industry; in 1967, honorary doctorate, Royal College of Art, London; in 1976, Academia de Diseno, Mexico City.

▶ Erik Zahle (ed.), A Treasury of Scandinavian Design, New York, 1961:291–92, Nos. 210,212–13,349. 'Timo Sarpaneva,' Interiors, Vol. 128, Jan. 1969:128–31. 'Two Faced Textiles,' Industrial Design, Vol. 16, March 1969:52–53. Geoffrey Beard, International Modern Glass, London, 1976: plates 111,145,271,299. Cat., David Revere McFadden (ed.), Scandinavian Modern Design 1880–1980, New York: Abrams, 1982:270, Nos. 229,232,244,321. Cat., Kathryn B. Hiesinger and George H. Marcus III (eds.), Design Since 1945, Philadelphia: Philadelphia Museum of Art, 1983:230,II–56–57. Cat., The Lunning Prize, Stockholm: Nationalmuseum, 1986:80–85. Jennifer Hawkins Opie, Scandinavia: Ceramics and Glass in the Twentieth Century, New York: Rizzoli, 1989.

Sartori, Franz T. (1927–)

▶ Italian industrial designer; born Milan.

▶ Studied architecture, Trinity Hall College, USA.

▶ Designing furniture for adults and children, glassware, and a range of industrial products, his clients included Arnolfo di Cambio, Vittorio Bonacina, Cristalart, Cea's Carlo Citterio, Colmob Design, Dalmine, Flex Form, Imperial Chemical Industries, Luci, Carlo Parolini, Potocco, Prestige, Ritz Italora, Toiano, Stilux, Saffa, and Zanotta. His Tirangoli foam seating was produced by Delta. He was a professor of industrial design at the London College of Applied Science and taught at the Instituto Statale d'Arte Stagio Stagi in Pietrasanta (Italy). He was president of the Design Collegio Lombardo Pariti Esperti e Consulenti, president of the Accademia Toscana dell'Arte e del Laboro, president of the Associazione Arredatori Progettisti, and member of the Tribunale di Milano.

▶ He won first prize for sculpture at the 1968 Concorso Nazionale Dalmine, 1970 gold medal for civic merit from the Comune di Milano, first prize at the 1973 'Internazionale La Modonnina,' first prize at the 1974 Design, silver medal at the 1974 (XVII) 'Concorso giornalistico Gargagnana,' and 1975 gold medal from the President of the Republic of Italy. He represented Italy at the 1970 Osaka 'Japan World Exposition (Expo '70).'

Sasakura, Soichiro (1949–)
▶ Japanese designer.
▶ Studied Kanazawa College of Art.
▶ He worked for Sasaki Glass, for which he designed the 1988 *San Marino* glassware range.
▶ Albrecht Bangert and Karl Michael Armer, *80s Style: Designs of the Decade*, New York: Abbeville, 1990:150,235.

Sason, Sixten (1912–69)
▶ Swedish industrial designer.
▶ Studied silversmithing.
▶ He was a consultant designer for Electrolux, Hasselblad, and Saab. He designed the Saab *92* automobile body.
▶ Penny Sparke, *Introduction to Design and Culture in the Twentieth Century*, Allen and Unwin, 1986.

Saunders, Brenda (1949–)
▶ British industrial designer; born Newbury, Berkshire; active London.
▶ 1970–73, studied furniture design, Kingston Polytechnic, Surrey, and, 1973–76, Royal College of Art, London.
▶ 1976–77, she was a furniture designer at the architecture and design studio Cini Boeri Associati in Milan. In 1978, she and Peter Bosson set up a design studio in London, designing furniture for clients including Olivetti, International Secretariat, and American Express. 1980–86, she taught furniture and interior design at Kingston Polytechnic; from 1985, furniture and product design at the Royal College of Art; 1985–86, textile and furniture design at Birmingham Polytechnic; 1985–87, at the London College of Furniture; and, 1986–87, furniture at Manchester Polytechnic. Her work included kitchens and bathrooms, computer-related products, housewares, the 1985 *Parasol* chair by Pel in Cooke Mills fabric, 1986 *A Frame Bed* by Sleepeezee, and 1988 leather briefcase by Whitehouse and Cox.
▶ She won the 1974 Burton Group Design Award, 1975 Radford Design Award, 1976 British Council Award, and 1984 David Mitchell Award.
▶ Cat., Design Center Stuttgart, *Women in Design: Careers and Life Histories Since 1900*, Stuttgart: Haus der Wirtschaft, 1989:272–75.

Sauvage, Frédéric-Henri (1873–1932)
▶ French architect and designer.
▶ Studied École des Beaux-Arts, Paris.
▶ 1898–1912, he was associated with the architect Charles Sarazin; in 1903 with Sarazin, founded the Société Anonyme de Logements Hygiéniques à Bon Marché and built a 1912 house in rue Vavin, near Montparnasse, and a house in rue des Amiraux, both Paris; in 1926, was associated with architect Frantz Jourdain on the Samaritaine department store extension; 1900–03, was one of the first French Modern architects; in 1919, set up his own office; from 1928, taught at École Nationale Supérieure des Arts Décoratifs, and from 1931, at École des Beaux-Arts, both Paris; was a practitioner in the Art Nouveau style and was best known for the pavilion for Loïe Fuller at the 1900 Paris 'Exposition Universelle' and 1898 residence for Louis Majorelle in Nancy; designed complete ensembles for the Café de Paris and 1931 Decre department store, Nantes.
▶ *L'Art Décoratif*, June 1902:108. *Allgemeines Lexikon der Bildenden Künstler*, 1955. Alastair Duncan, *Art Nouveau and Art Déco Lighting*, New York: Simon and Schuster, 1978:86. Arlette

Barré-Despond and Suzanne Tise, *Jourdain*, Paris: Regard, 1988:60–68,144,195.

Savini, Augusto (1930–)
▶ Italian architect and designer; born Busto Arsizio.
▶ Studied architecture, Politecnico di Milano, to 1958.
▶ He designed interiors and furniture including the *Pamplona* and *Europa* chairs produced by Pozzi.
▶ *Moderne Klassiker: Möbel, die Geschichte machen*, Hamburg, 1982:28. Hans Wichmann, *Italien Design 1945 bis heute*, Munich: Die Neue Sammlung, 1988.

Saxbo
▶ Danish ceramics factory.
▶ Saxbo pottery was established in 1930 by Nathalie Krebs at Herlev, in collaboration with Eva Staehr-Nielsen, who joined the firm in 1932; it became the most important small independent pottery in Denmark. Krebs developed the glazes, and Staehr-Nielsen designed the shapes. Several generations of potters were employed who helped develop the 'classic Saxbo' style. Saxbo closed in 1968.
▶ Jennifer Hawkins Opie, *Scandinavia: Ceramics and Glass in the Twentieth Century*, New York: Rizzoli, 1989.

Scali, François (1951–)
▶ French designer.
▶ Studied economics to 1974 and architecture to 1979.
▶ Scali collaborated with Alain Domingo in Nemo, established in 1982. They were best known for their furniture designs for the Science Museum at Parc de la Villette in Paris. They designed carpets for Géométrie Variable and Élisée Éditions, graphic design for MBK and Motobécane, pasta for Panzani, furniture for the offices of Caisse Nationale des Monuments Historiques et des Sites in Paris, and packaging for Lesieur. They designed furniture and furnishings for Tébong and the 1983 *Faizzz* chair by Nemo Édition, 1985 computer screen, 1984 *Mediabolo* chair by Nemo Édition, 1984 print lamp by Formica, and 1985 *Marini* and *Moreno* chairs by Nemo Édition.
▶ Juli Capella and Quim Larrea, *Designed by Architects in the 1980s*, New York, Rizzoli, 1988.
See Domingo, Alain.

Scarfatti, Gino (1912–)
▶ Italian lighting designer; born Venice.
▶ Scarfatti established lighting firm Arteluce in 1939; during World War II, lived in Switzerland. He was the most innovative leader in the field of lighting in Italy in the immediate postwar period. He initially produced brass and lacquered metal models in a Rationalist style. Subsequently, he became more daring, incorporating exposed neon, plastics, and moveable parts. In the 1950s, he dominated in his specialty through his own designs and those of others including Franco Albini, Vittoriano Vigano, Ico Parisi, Gianfranco Frattini, and Marco Zanuso. In 1971, he produced the first halogen table lamp. His own work was usually designed for offices, including the Olivetti building in Barcelona, hotels, including the Hilton Hotel in Rome, schools, and ships, including the 1965 *Michelangelo* and *Raffaello*.
▶ He won the 1955 and 1956 Compasso d'Oro and prizes at the Triennali di Milano. Two of his lamps were included in the 1983–84 'Design Since 1945' exhibition at the Philadelphia Museum of Art.
▶ 'Cause for Applause: Lightolier's Italian Lamps and Wormley Decor,' *Interiors*, Vol. 110, Nov. 1950:130–32. Andrea Branzi and Michele de Lucchi (eds.), *Il design italiano degli anni '50*, Milan, 1981:221,223,225–27,229,232. Daniele Baroni, *L'Oggetto lampada*, Milan, 1981:126–27, figs. 268–69,271–72,274–85. *Moderne Klassiker: Möbel, die Geschichte machen*, Hamburg, 1982:52. Cat., Kathryn B. Hiesinger and George H. Marcus III (eds.), *Design Since 1945*, Philadelphia: Philadelphia Museum of Art, 1983:230, IV–33–34.

Scarpa, Carlo (1906–78)

▶ Italian architect and designer; born Venice; father of Tobia Scarpa.

▶ Studied Accademia di Belle Arte, Venice, to 1926.

▶ He set up his own architecture practice in Venice in 1927. His work was influenced by the Gothic-Byzantine style of Venetian architecture, the work of Frank Lloyd Wright, and the De Stijl movement. He admired the Art Nouveau style, including the work of Josef Maria Olbrich. In the late 1920s and early 1930s, he designed exhibitions and elegant interiors. Scarpa produced numerous furniture designs for Gavina and others, designed the Olivetti showroom in Venice, and was best known for his work for the Venini glassworks realized 1933–47 and for interior design. The 1953–54 renovation of the Galleria Nazionale della Sicilia in the Palazzo Abbatellis in Palermo brought him international recognition. He executed a number of museum renovations, including the Accademia in Venice in 1952, Museo Correr in Venice in 1953–60, six rooms in the Uffizi (with Ignazio Gardella and Giovanni Michelucci) in Florence in 1956, annex to the neoclassical Gipsoteca Canoviana in Possegno near Treviso in 1956–57, and interior design of the Museo Castelvecchio in Verona in 1964. He designed the 1970–72 Cimitero a San Vito, Treviso, and 1973–80 Banca Popolare, Verona. He designed the exhibition of Paul Klee at the 1948 Biennale di Venezia 1956, Piet Mondrian exhibition at the Galleria d'Arte Moderna in Rome, Frank Lloyd Wright exhibition at the 1960 (XII) Triennale di Milano, and Erich Mendelsohn exhibition at the 1960 Biennale di Venezia. Other buildings included the 1955–61 Casa Verritti in Udine, 1961–63 Fondazione Querini Stampalia in Venice, 1964 restaurant in the Museo di Castelvecchio in Verona, 1960 Museo Correr in Venice, 1970–78 Brion Cemetery (posthumous), San Vito d'Altivole, 1973–78 Banca Popolare, Verona, 1975 Terrorist Outrage Monument, Brescia, 1975–78 Ottolenghi house, Bardolino, and 1975–78 housing blocks, Vincenza. He designed the Venezuelan pavilion at the 1954–56 Biennale di Venezia, the Italian pavilion at the 1967 Montreal 'Universal and International Exhibition (Expo 67),' the information stand at the 1968 Biennale di Venezia, and the frescoes at the 1969 Florence Exhibition in London. He taught architecture at Instituto Universitario di Architettura, Venice. From 1972–78, he was director of architecture school, Instituto Universitario di Architettura, Venice. In 1955, he received an honorary doctorate from the Accademia di Belle Arti in Venice. In 1969, elected Honorary Royal Designer for Industry, London. Received 1978 posthumous honorary doctorate, Instituto Universitario di Architettura, Venice.

▶ His work was the subject of the 1974 exhibitions in Vicenza and London, and 1983 'Carlo Scarpa et le musée de Vérone' in Paris.

▶ Sergio Los, *Carlo Scarpa—Architetto poeta*, Venice, 1967. Manlio Brusatin, 'Carlo Scarpa Architetto Veneziano,' *Contraspazio*, Nos. 3/4, 1972. Cat., Neri Pozza (ed.), *Carlo Scarpa*, Vicenza, 1974. Louis Kahn and Sheban Cantacuzino, *Carlo Scarpa*, London, 1974. Cat., T. Yokoyama and H. Toyota, 'Carlo Scarpa,' *Space Design*, June 1977. Carlo Scarpa issue, *Progressive Architecture*, Vol. 62, No. 5, 1981. A. Rudi (ed.), 'Carlo Scarpa: Frammenti 1926–1978,' *Rassegna*, No. 7, 1981. L. Magagnato (ed.), *Carlo Scarpa a Castelvecchio*, Milan, 1982. A. Rudi and V. Rossetto (eds.), *La Sede Centrale della Banca Popolare di Verona*, Verona, 1983. Cat., *Carlo Scarpa et le musée de Vérone*, Paris, 1983. A.F. Marcianò, *Carlo Scarpa*, Bologna, 1984. M.A. Crippa, *Scarpa: Il pensiero, il disegno, i progetti*, Milan, 1984.

Scarpa, Tobia (1935–) and **Afra Scarpa** (b. Afra Bianchin 1937–)

▶ Tobia Scarpa: Italian architect and designer; born Venice; son of Carlo Scarpa. Afra Scarpa: Italian architect and designer; born Montebelluna. Active Trevignanó, Treviso. Husband and wife.

▶ Both studied Instituto Universitario di Architettura, Venice, to 1969.

▶ 1957–61, Tobia Scarpa worked for Venini in Murano. He first collaborated with wife at the Venini glassworks 1958–60. In 1960, they they set up their own design studio in Montebelluna, where they occasionally worked as architects. They worked with Gio Ponti at Cassina designing furniture. Tobia Scarpa designed for Gavina from 1960 and for Knoll International. They designed furniture for B&B Italia, glass, cutlery, and exhibition displays. From 1962, they designed the corporate image program for Benetton shops in Europe and the USA. They were best known for their *Torcello* system produced by Stildomus, and *Morna* bed. Tobia Scarpa was a lecturer at the School of Industrial Design in Venice. One of his best-known designs was the 1965 *925 Chair* in Russian leather on plywood by Cassina. The Scarpas' lighting designs for Flos included the 1968 *Biagio*, 1978 *Ballo*, 1982 *Celestia*, and 1982 *Perpetua*; the 1968 *Biagio* lamp produced in white marble by Flos was a sculptural expression of the highest level of Italian design in the 1960s. They designed the 1990 *Vol au Vent* hanging light (similar to a 1920s model by René Herbst) produced by Flos, and monumental objects for a luxury market; they were known for their use of rare hardwoods. Their 1970s flatware was produced by San Lorenzo. In the 1980s, they began designing for firms in Spain; worked on the restoration of the plazas in Veneto and in Emilia. Their other work included the 1960 *Bastiano* divan by Gavina, 1960 *Vanessa* metal bed by Gavina, 1970 *Sonana* armchair by Cassina, 1984 *Poligonon* table series by B&B Italia, 1985 *Bed 8640* by Maxalto, 1986 *Marly* bookshelf by Molteni, 1986 *Mastro* table and chair, *Piediferro* metal and marble table by B&B Italia, 1986 *Veronica* chair by Casas, 1986 *Ronda* armchair by Casas, and 1986 *Manor* bed by Molteni.

▶ Their *Sonana* armchair by Cassina was awarded the 1970 Compasso d'Oro. The *925* armchair, on permanent exhibition in the design gallery of the New York Museum of Modern Art, was first shown at the 1966 Salone del Mobile Italiano, and included in the 1970 'Modern Chairs 1918–1970' exhibition at the Whitechapel Gallery in London. Their work was the subject of a 1985 exhibition, Padiglione d'Arte Contemporanea, Milan.

▶ Cat., *Modern Chairs 1918–1970*, London: Lund Humphries, 1971. Cat., Kathryn B. Hiesinger and George H. Marcus III (eds.), *Design Since 1945*, Philadelphia: Philadelphia Museum of Art, 1983:230,II–55,III–81. *Le Affinità Elettive*, Milan: Electa, 1985. Cat., Antonio Piva, *Afra e Tobia Scarpa*, Milan, 1985. Auction cat., *Asta di Modernariato 1900–1986*, Auction 'Modernariato,' Milan: Semenzato Nuova Geri, 8 Oct. 1986: Lots 119–20. Juli Capella and Quim Larrea, *Designed by Architects in the 1980s*, New York, Rizzoli, 1988. Albrecht Bangert and Karl Michael Armer, *80s Style: Designs of the Decade*, New York: Abbeville, 1990:107,235.

Schaeffer, Rudolph (1886–)

▶ American colorist; born Clare, Michigan.

▶ Studied Thomas Normal Training School, Detroit, Michigan; 1909, studied design under Ernest Batchelder in Minneapolis, Minnesota.

▶ He taught school in Michigan and Ohio before, at ceramicist Ernest Batchelder's instigation, moving to Pasadena, California, where he taught at Troop Polytechnic School, succeeding Douglas Donaldson. In 1914, Schaeffer was appointed by the United States Commissioner of Education to make a study of the role of color in the curriculum of vocational schools in Munich; Germany was a pioneer in new synthetic dyes. Schaeffer quickly introduced new colors (turquoise, chartreuse, magenta, and other prismatic colors) into stage, interior, and crafts design classes in California. He introduced color into warp-dyed weaving goods that had traditionally been white. Dorothy Liebes publicly recognized Schaeffer for his pioneering color ideas, which changed American industrial textile design. Observing the value of color in the environment, he organized courses in flower arrangement, which led to his 1935 book on the subject. In 1926, Schaeffer established the Rhythmo-Chromatic Design School in San Francisco, where students were taught color, textile, and environmental design. The institution continues today.

▶ Bonnie Mattison in Timothy J. Andersen et al., *California Design 1910*, Salt Lake City: Peregrine Smith, 1980:87.

Scharff, Allan (1945–)
▶ Danish metalworker.
▶ Studied Goldsmith School.
▶ From 1978, he was artistic consultant and designer for Hans Hansen Sølvsmedie in Kolding. In 1974, he set up his own silversmithy.
▶ His work was the subject of the 1980 one-person exhibition at Det Danske Kunstindustrimuseum in Copenhangen.
▶ Cat., David Revere McFadden (ed.), *Scandinavian Modern Design 1880–1980*, New York: Abrams, 1982:271.

Schawinsky, Alexander (aka Xanti Schawinsky 1904–79)
▶ Swiss designer; born Basel.
▶ Studied painting and architecture in Zürich, Cologne, and Berlin; 1924–25, Bauhaus, Weimar.
▶ 1926–27, he was a theater designer in Zwickau, and, 1929–31, worked as a graphic designer for the city of Magdeburg. In 1933, he moved to Italy, becoming an illustrator and graphic designer in Milan, notably for Olivetti and Motta. In 1936, invited by Josef Albers, he settled in the USA, teaching at Black Mountain College in North Carolina. Schawinsky collaborated with Walter Gropius and Marcel Breuer on the 1939 'New York World's Fair' and with Luigi Fugini and Gino Pollini on the 1936 *Studio 42* portable typewriter for Olivetti. He taught at several American universities. From 1950, he began to paint and set up a studio near Lake Maggiore (Italy), working in both New York and Italy.
▶ Lionel Richard, *Encyclopédie du Bauhaus*, Paris: Somogy, 1985: 208. Cat., *Xanti Schawinsky*, Berlin: Bauhaus-Archiv, 1986.

Scheid, Georg Anton
▶ Austrian silversmiths and jeweler; located Vienna.
▶ The firm was originally known as the gold and silver jewelry manufacturer Markowitsch und Scheid. In 1862, the firm G.A. Scheid was founded to produce gold- and silver-dross, separation, and plating, and was located at 17 Hofmühlgasse in Vienna in 1876 and in the Gumpendorferstrasse in Vienna 1892–1903. It produced silverwares and jewelry, becoming well known for its high-quality enamel work. Scheid's silverwares were simple in form before 1900, unlike the busily embossed decoration and the Sezession motifs found in the work of contemporary Austrian silversmiths. Before the Wiener Werkstätte was established, Scheid produced the silver designs of Koloman Moser.
▶ The firm's wares were included in the 1889 'Jubilee Exhibition,' 1896–97 'Winter Exhibition,' the Austrian arts and crafts exhibitions at the Österreichisches Museum für Kunst und Industrie 1850–1914, and 1900 Paris 'Exposition Universelle.'
▶ Waltrand Neuwirth, *Lexikon Wiener Gold- und Silberschmiede und ihre Punzen 1867–1922*, Vienna, 1977:178–80. Annelies Krekel-Aalberse, *Art Nouveau and Art Déco Silver*, New York: Abrams, 1989:199,259. Deanna F. Cera (ed.), *Jewels of Fantasy: Costume Jewelry of the 20th Century*, New York: Abrams, 1992: 104.

Scheidecker, Frank
▶ French metalworker and silversmith.
▶ Active *c*1900–10, Scheidecker's silverwares were sold by H. Hébrand in Paris.
▶ Annelies Krekel-Aalberse, *Art Nouveau and Art Déco Silver*, New York: Abrams, 1989:259.

Scheider, Andreas (1861–1931)
▶ Norwegian artist and ceramicist.
▶ Scheider set up the first crafts studio in Norway in 1895. His pottery broke with established traditions. Though not a Modern craftsperson, his work was purely art-based in approach and execution. His wares were produced by skilled potters.
▶ Fredrik Wildhagen, *Norge i Form*, Oslo: Stenersen, 1988:39.

Scheier, Edwin and Mary Scheier
▶ American ceramicists.
▶ The Scheiers were ceramicists in Virginia before becoming teachers at the University of New Hampshire. In 1950, they moved to Oaxaca (Mexico).
▶ Their ceramic work was shown at the 1959 (XX) 'Ceramic International Exhibition' at the Metropolitan Museum of Art, New York.
▶ Miller, *Modern Design 1880–1990*, New York: Abrams.

Schellens & Marto
▶ Dutch fabric manufacturer; located Eindhoven.
▶ Active 1887–1981, Schellens & Marto was directed by J.J. Marto 1887–96 and by members of the Schellens family 1887–1981. It began production as a manufacturer of mock velvet, the process introduced by Huguenot refugees from France in the 17th and 18th centuries. The Dutch firm began with two mechanical test looms but required partial hand production up to 1930. Up to the end of the 1920s, the firm was using printing blocks. By the 1930s, double-weave looms, rather than the earlier rod looms, were used to produce two fabrics simultaneously. From the 1930s, patterns were woven into the fabric in one or more colors and with one or more fabrics on a jacquard loom. Many designs were produced by the firm's staff, while others were purchased from design agencies, including Schnitzler und Vogel and Rudolf in Krefeld. Other design consultants were Chris Lebeau, who designed a fabric in *c*1930 for the Royal Palace, Tilburg; Christiaan de Moor for the Dutch pavilion at the 1937 Paris 'Exposition Internationale des Arts et Techniques dans la Vie Moderne'; C.A. Lion Cachet for various commissions 1910–40 and for oceanliner interiors including the *Stoomvaart Maatschappij Nederland*; and C. van der Sluys 1917–19. Schellens & Marto's fabrics were primarily sold to bus and railway companies and to wholesalers who sold to numerous furniture manufacturers.
▶ *Industry and Design in the Netherlands, 1850/1950*, Amsterdam: Stedelijk Museum, 1985:104–05.

Schenck, Édouard and Marcel Schenck
▶ French metalworkers; active Toulouse; father and son.
▶ Architect Frantz Jourdain built Schenck's 1894 house and workshop in rue Vergniaud, Paris. Édouard Schenck was active from the turn of the century. Schenck, Edgar Brandt, and de Jarny were the best known of the metalworkers at the Salons in Paris around 1900. Schenck produced a wide range of domestic metalware based on insect and vegetal themes, including jardinières, and-irons, screens, lamps, and architectural fittings. In his lamps he sometimes incorporated cabochons of *flambé* earthenware and colored glass panels. In the 1920s, he was joined by his son Marcel. Known for the lightweight metal supports, their work included wrought iron and *repoussé*, silvered, gilded, and patinated copper. Their historicist work was not aesthetically innovative.
▶ They showed their work at the events of the Salon d'Automne and the 1925 Paris 'Exposition Internationale des Arts Décoratifs et Industriels Modernes.'
▶ G. Janneau, *Le Luminaire et les Moyens d'éclairage Nouveaux*, 1st series: plates 37,38; 2nd series: plates 45–46; 3rd series: plates 13–15. *The Studio Yearbook*, 1922:123, 1923:147. Alastair Duncan, *Art Nouveau and Art Déco Lighting*, New York: Simon and Schuster, 1978:86. Pierre Kjellberg, *Art Déco: les maîtres du Mobilier, le décor des Paquebots*, Paris: Amateur, 1986:169. Arlette Barré-Despond and Suzanne Tise, *Jourdain*, Paris: Regard, 1988:44–47.

Schettini, M. Letizia (1961–)
▶ Italian designer; born and active Florence.
▶ Studied Instituto d'Arte, Florence, to 1982.
▶ She founded studio Salotto Dinamico; was active in the design of ceramics, alabaster works, and furnishings.
▶ Work shown in numerous exhibitions. Won competitions including 1982 'Furniture and Its Space' and 1985 'Mainichi International ID Competition.'

▶ Fumio Shimizu and Matteo Thun (eds.), *The Descendants of Leonardo: The Italian Design*, Tokyo, 1987:329.

Schiavina, Angela (1948–)
▶ Italian designer; born and active Ravenna.
▶ Studied Instituto Tecnico per Geometri, Ravenna, to 1968, and, 1972, industrial design, Instituto d'Arte, Florence.
▶ In 1970, she became a member of the Albo Professionale Geometri. She was an interior designer, active in restoration, and a member of the Instituto Superiore Industrie Artistiche and of ADI (Associazione per il Disegno Industriale).
▶ *ADI Annual 1976*, Milan: Associazione per il Disegno Industriale, 1976.

Schiavina, Anna Maria (1945–)
▶ Italian designer; active Bologna.
▶ Schiavina began her professional career in 1970. She designed tabletop accessories for office and domestic use, including for Ny Form. 1972–74, she worked for the magazine *Mia Casa*. She designed theater sets. She was a member of ADI (Associazione per il Disegno Industriale).
▶ *ADI Annual 1976*, Milan: Associazione per il Disegno Industriale, 1976.

Schindler, Rudolph Michael (1887–1953)
▶ Austrian architect; born Vienna; active Vienna and Los Angeles.
▶ 1906–11, studied Technische Hochschule, Vienna, and, 1909–14, Akademie der bildenden Künste, Vienna, under Otto Wagner.
▶ Otto Wagner's Rationalism greatly influenced Schindler. In 1914, he settled in the USA, where he worked for Ottemheimer, Stern and Reichert in Chicago, and 1916–20, for Frank Lloyd Wright. In 1920–21, he was sent to Los Angeles to oversee the construction of Frank Lloyd Wright's Aline Barnsdall houses. From 1921, he was in private practice in Los Angeles. 1925–26, he collaborated loosely with Richard Neutra, whom he had met in Vienna as a student. In the 1930s, he designed 'unit furniture,' a modular system. He built the furniture for his own house on North Kings Road in Hollywood in 1921, and for the 1925–26 Lovell Beach House in Newport Beach, California. The reinforced concrete and wood architecture of the Lovell Beach House, with its spatial treatment, vertical and horizontal play, and structural articulation, showed the influence of De Stijl; its furniture, that of Frank Lloyd Wright.
▶ His work was the subject of the 1967 'Architecture of R.M. Schindler, 1887–1953' exhibition at the Art Galleries of the University of California, and included in the 1982 'Space and Environment: Furniture of American Architects' exhibition at the Whitney Museum of American Art in Fairfield County, Connecticut.
▶ Esther McCoy, *Five California Architects*, New York: Reinhold, 1960. Cat., David Gebhard, *Architecture of R.M. Schindler, 1887–1953*, Santa Barbara, California: University of California, 1967. David Gebhard, *Schindler*, New York: Viking, 1972. Esther McCoy, *Vienna to Los Angeles: Two Journeys*, Santa Monica, California: Arts and Architecture Press, 1979. Cat., Lisa Phillips (introduction), *Space and Environment: Furniture by American Architects*, New York: Whitney Museum of American Art, 1982: 54–55. David Gebhard, 'R.M. Schindler' in Mel Byars and Russell Flinchum (eds.), *50 American Designers*, Washington: Preservation, 1994.

Schirolliares Arredamenti
▶ Italian furniture manufacturer; located Mantua.
▶ Schirolliares was set up by the firm Schirolli to produce office furniture in resin. Its first range was the *Open Space* series of components in ABS Novodur Bayer. Its *Executive Space* series was produced in glass, stainless steel, and resin. It issued the *Delia* swivel chair and *Cris* secretary's chair in bent metal tubing and resin.
▶ *ADI Annual 1976*, Milan: Associazione per il Disegno Industriale, 1976.

Schlegel, Fritz (1896–1965)
▶ Danish architect and furniture designer.
▶ 1916–23, studied Det Kongelige Kunstakademi, Copenhagen.
▶ 1916–34, he worked with architect Edvard Thomsen and, in 1934, set up his own architecture office. His furniture designs were produced by Fritz Hansen.
▶ His work was shown in Stockholm in 1918; Charlottenborg in 1919, 1924, 1927, 1930, 1932, 1933, 1939, and the 1941 retrospective of his work there; The Hague in 1948, Paris in 1949, and London and Edinburgh in 1950.
▶ He received gold medals in 1924 and 1927 at the Danish Academy, 1926 Zacharia Jocobsen award, and 1941 Eckersberg Medal.
▶ Frederik Sieck, *Nutidig Dansk Møbeldesign: — en kortfattet illustreret beskrivelse*, Copenhagen: Bondo Gravesen; 1990 Busck edition in English.

Schlesser, Thomas (1959–)
▶ American furniture designer.
▶ Influenced by Isamu Noguchi, Schlesser designed retro-1950s silhouettes produced by Niedermaier in the early 1990s.
▶ Arlene Hirst, 'World Class at Last,' *American Home*, November 1990:100.

Schlumberger, Jean (1907–)
▶ French jewelry designer; born Mulhouse; active Paris and New York.
▶ Studied art in Paris.
▶ His first designs were produced in semi-precious stones. He collaborated with Elsa Schiaparelli, at first designing buttons for her clothing, then jewelry, including models in motifs such as roller skates and, for her *Circus* collection, various animals. In the late 1930s, one of his best known designs was an articulated cigarette lighter in the form of a fish. In 1940, he left for New York, where he collaborated with Nicolas Bongarde, who produced Schlumberger's designs. In the 1940s and 1950s, he produced distinguished and popular pieces in animal and vegetal forms, including angels, flowers, birds, and hippopotami rendered in enameled gold and precious and semi-precious stones. In 1955, he became the first exclusive designer at Tiffany, where his work was sold in a separate department and where he later became a vice-president.
▶ Melissa Gabardi, *Les Bijoux des Années 50*, Amateur, 1987.

Schlumbohm, Peter (1896–1962)
▶ German inventor; active in the USA.
▶ Studied chemistry, University of Berlin, to 1926.
▶ His early work was in refrigeration, an activity that took him to the USA in 1931. He founded Chemex and is best known for the 1944 *Chemex* hourglass-shaped glass filter coffeemaker. He executed designs for other domestic products, including the 1949 quick water boiler, 1951 air filtering fan, and a frying pan that did not need washing. Schlumbohm executed functionally oriented designs, many of which he engineered, manufactured, and enthusiastically promoted, and sought simple and non-mechanical methods. He held over 300 patents.
▶ His quick water boiler and air filtering fan were included in the 1983–84 'Design Since 1945' exhibition at the Philadelphia Museum of Art.
▶ 'Two Inventors,' *Industrial Design*, Vol. 7, Nov. 1960: 72–75. Ralph Caplan, 'Chemex and Creation,' *Industrial Design*, Vol. 9, Dec. 1962:121–22. Victor Papanek, *Design for the Real World*, New York, 1974:105–06. Cat., Kathryn B. Hiesinger and George H. Marcus III (eds.), *Design Since 1945*, Philadelphia: Philadelphia Museum of Art, 1983:230,I–39,II–59.

Schmid, Carl
▶ Swiss mechanical engineer.
▶ In 1929, he patented a writing device for holding lead in a cartridge. The idea of the holder and a shaft of plastic was already known; Schmid improved the manner in which the lead was held and extended as it wore away. In 1930, Caran d'Ache began mass producing the mechanical *Fixpencil*.

▶ *Unbekannt—Vertraut: 'Anonymes' Design im Schweizer Geb-rauchsgerät seit 1920*, Zürich: Museum für Gestaltung, 1987.

Schmidhuber, Hermann (1878–)
▶ German metalworker; active Cologne.
▶ He produced the designs of Dagobert Peche in Zürich; from 1924, taught metalworking at the Werkschulen in Cologne; in 1931, opened his own workshop.
▶ Annelies Krekel-Aalberse, *Art Nouveau and Art Déco Silver*, New York: Abrams, 1989:259.

Schmid-Riegel, Friedrich
▶ German silversmith; active Nuremberg.
▶ In the late 1920s and 1930s, Schmid-Riegel worked as a silver-smith. In the 1920s, he produced ornate objects in the manner of Viennese designer Dagobert Peche, while his very different 1930s work was influenced by the austerity of the Bauhaus.
▶ Annelies Krekel-Aalberse, *Art Nouveau and Art Déco Silver*, New York: Abrams, 1989:146,259.

Schmidt, Anita (1934–)
▶ German furniture designer; born Bretten.
▶ 1953–56, studied Sorbonne University, Paris.
▶ She trained at the firm C. Staub in Knittlingen and in joineries and weaving mills, including Rohi, Geretsried, and Taunusdruck. In 1965, she set up Waldmann-Gölz-Schmidt with others, with an exclusive arrangement with Straub in Germany, establishing offices in Asco (Finland) and Durlet (Belgium). From 1973, she was an independent designer with clients including WK-ZE Möbel, Kill, Kaufeld, Cor, Rausch, Thörmer, Walter Knoll, Rolf Benz, Draenert, Designo, Maison, Intercane (Spain), Durlet (Belgium), and Artanova (Switzerland). She designed furnishings for prefabrications by Hebel and fabrics and carpet produced in India. Her 1984 *Cushion* sofa was produced by Pro Seda.
▶ Cat., Design Center Stuttgart, *Women in Design: Careers and Life Histories Since 1900*, Stuttgart: Haus der Wirtschaft, 1989:164–65.

Schmidt, Joost (1893–1948)
▶ German woodcarver, sculptor, typographer, and teacher; born Hanover; husband of Helene Schmidt-Nonne.
▶ 1911–14, studied Weimar; from 1919, sculpture and typography, Bauhaus, Weimar.
▶ Schmidt participated in the 1920–21 Sommerfeld house in Berlin-Dahlem by architects Walter Gropius and Adolf Meyer; the building with its interiors was one of the most important early Bauhaus projects. The design of his strongly geometric carved teak door for the vestibule is comparable to the work of Frank Lloyd Wright. He taught at the Bauhaus in Dessau and, until 1932, was an instructor in typography. 1928–32, he was active in graphic design for advertising. From 1933 until after World War II, he was a professor in Berlin.
▶ Cat., *Joost Schmidt: Lehre und Arbeit am Bauhaus 1919–1932*, Düsseldorf, 1984. Lionel Richard, *Encyclopédie du Bauhaus*, Paris: Somogy, 1985:166. Jonathan M. Woodham, *Twentieth-Century Ornament*, New York: Rizzoli, 1990:114.

Schmidt, Karl (1873–1948)
▶ German designer and furniture maker.
▶ In 1898, Schmidt founded the Dresdner Werkstätten für Handwerkkunst. Associated with Richard Riemerschmid, the Dresden factory produced Bruno Paul's furniture designs.
▶ Frederick Cooke, *Glass: Twentieth-Century Design*, New York: Dutton: 1986:39. Hans Wichmann, *Deutsche Werkstätten und WK-Verband 1898–1990*, Munich: Prestel, 1992:315–16.

Schmidt-Nonné, Helene (b. Helene Nonné 1891–1976)
▶ German teacher and journalist; born Magdeburg; wife of Joost Schmidt.
▶ Studied in Magdeburg and Berlin; 1924–30, Bauhaus, Weimar and Dessau.

▶ She became a professor of drawing and, 1919–24, was a sec-ondary-school teacher. After visiting the 1923 'Week at the Bau-haus' exhibition in Weimar, she decided to study there; she worked in the textile workshop. In 1948, she became a journalist and, 1953–61, on Max Bill's invitation, taught color theory at the Hochschule für Gestaltung in Ulm. In 1961, she settled in Darmstadt and published a book on Joost Schmidt.
▶ Lionel Richard, *Encyclopédie du Bauhaus*, Paris: Somogy, 1985: 208. Cat., Gunta Stölzl, *Weberei am Bauhaus und ams eigener Werkstatt*, Berlin: Bauhaus-Archiv, 1987:165.

Schmied, François-Louis (1873–1941)
▶ Swiss designer, painter, engraver, illustrator, book designer, binder, and printer; born Geneva.
▶ Studied wood engraving, School of Industrial Arts, Geneva, under Alfred Martin, to 1895.
▶ He met Jean Dunand at the Geneva school and, in 1895, settled Paris, where he engraved wood blocks for the firm George Auber and worked as an engraver, painter, and illustrator. His first illustrated book, *Sous la Tente* by Édouard Moury, was pub-lished in 1911. He was not recognized until his illustrations appeared in the 1911 edition of the *Jungle Book*, produced by Paul Jouve and commissioned by the exclusive French book club Société du Livre Contemporain. Having lost his right eye in World War I, Schmied returned to Paris and finished the *Jungle Book*. In order to ensure exceptional color reproduction, he set up his own print-ing facility, where he installed a Stanhope platen hand-press oper-ated by Pierre Bouchet. Some illustrations were printed in as many as 25 colors, each from a hand-engraved wood block. Some of his illustrations were colored by pochoir by Suade. A number of the books he produced were illustrated by other artists, including Jean Goulden, Bergue, Paul Jouve, Sureda, and George Barbier. Quickly becoming one of France's best-known illustrators, engravers, and printers, Schmied's fame was allied with that of Dunand, some of whose lacquered panels Schmied designed. He illustrated a number of works in a kind of archaic Orientalism, including *Can-tique des Cantiques, Le Paradis musulman, La Création*, and *Le Livre de la Vérité de la Parole*. Rendered in a geometric and Symbol-ist style, his bookbindings sometimes incorporated lacquered plaques by Dunand. His workshop located at 12 rue Friant in Paris was moved in 1925 to 74 bis rue Halle. His clients included Henri Vever, Miguet, Chouanard, Louis Barthou, and Dr. Mardus. After the stock market crash of 1929, Schmied became bankrupt; his workshop closed in 1935 and his library was sold at the Hôtel Drouot. He settled in Tahanaout in the Moroccan desert, refur-bishing an abandoned fort there.
▶ He exhibited wood engravings at the 1904 Salon of the Société des Beaux-Arts. He showed his graphics, paintings, and books at the annual events of the Salon d'Automne, Société Nationale des Beaux-Arts, Société des Artistes Décorateurs, and Salon de Peintres Orientalistes. With Dunand, Goulden, and Jouve, he parti-cipated in annual shows mounted at the Galerie Georges Petit in Paris. He exhibited as an editor at the 1925 Paris 'Exposition Internationale des Arts Décoratifs et Industriels Modernes.' The 1927 one-person exhibition of his paintings and bindings was held at the Arnold Seligmann Galleries in New York. He showed his paintings and *champlevé* enamel plaques produced for the oceanliner *Normandie* at the 1934 exhibition at the Pavillon de Marsan of the Louvre.
▶ Pierre Cabanne, *Encyclopédie Art Déco*, Paris: Somogy, 1986: 235. Alastair Duncan and Georges de Bartha, *Art Nouveau and Art Déco Bookbinding*, New York: Abrams, 1989:7,8,21,24,61,62,68–71,73,76,89,93,95,131,160–75,196. Louis Barthou, 'L'Évolution artistique de la reliure,' *L'Illustration*, Christmas 1930. Pierre de Bormans, 'Un Artiste du livre: F.-L. Schmied,' *Revue des deux mondes*, 15 May 1932:436–47. Auction cat., *François-Louis Schmied (1873–1941)*, Berne: Schweiz Landebibliothek, Nov. 1976. Cat., Félix Marcilhac, *Des Reliures pour F.-L. Schmied*, Pforzh-eim: Schmuckmuseum, 1975. Georges Rémon, 'F.-L. Schmied,' *Mobilier et décoration*, June 1932:309–10. Ward Ritchie, *François-*

Louis Schmied: Artist, Engraver, Printer, Tucson, Arizona, 1976. Charles Terrasse, 'Les Reliures de Schmied et Dunand,' *Byblis*, Vol. 6, 1927:142–46.

Schmitt, Eric (1955–)

► French furniture designer; active Paris.
► Studied contemporary music.
► In 1986, he created a musical sculpture for the Fondation Charles Jourdain and bronze-patinated door handles for Néotù and Christian Liaigre; in 1989, was commissioned by Philippe Starck to design a chair and small table produced by XO.
► Work (13 furniture and lighting prototypes) subject of 1987 exhibition, VIA gallery, Paris. VIA sponsored exhibition (with En Attendant les Barbares, which produced his lighting fixtures *Nostradamus* and *Louve* and wrought-iron furniture range) at Habiter 87 salon. Work shown at the VIA stand at Art Jonction, Nice, and Illum Boligus stores, Copenhagen.
► Cat., *Les années VIA 1980–1990*, Paris: Musée des Arts Décoratifs, 1990.

Schmitt, Paul (1923–)

► French design entrepreneur; born Bône (Algeria); active Paris.
► Studied law and literature.
► 1948–88, he was president of Le Creuset, manufacturers of enameled cast-iron cookware; in 1958, commissioned Raymond Loewy to design his (Loewy's) first and only kitchen item; in 1973, commissioned Enzo Mari to design *La Mamma* stew pot; in 1978, set up an industrial division of Le Creuset in South Carolina; in 1988, established design centers in ten French provinces; was appointed design consultant to the EEC and, in 1988 and 1990, was a French jury member of European Design Prize.

Schmitz, Ferdinand Hubert (1863–1939)

► German metalworker; active Cologne-Braunsfeld.
► In 1894, he founded the Reunische Broncegiesserei, known as Orivit from 1900. In 1896, he produced objects in a proprietary alloy called Orivit metal. The firm produced pewter dishes and mounts for pottery bowls, as well as candelabra and silvered bronze mounted table lamps. Orivit produced silver by the Huberpresse, a new technique of mass producing stamped hollow-ware and flatware with simple ornamentation by hydraulic press. Its designs were of a high standard. WMF (Württembergische Metallwarenfabrik) took over the firm in 1905.
► *Deutsche Kunst und Dekoration*, 1900–01:17. Cat., *Jugendstil*, Darmstadt: Hessisches Landesmuseum, 1965:247. Cat., *Europa 1900*, Ostend Musée des Arts, Brussels: Connaissance, 1967. *Objekte des Jugendstils*, Bern: Benteli, 1975. Alastair Duncan, *Art Nouveau and Art Déco Lighting*, New York: Simon and Schuster, 1978:126. Annelies Krekel-Aalberse, *Art Nouveau and Art Déco Silver*, New York: Abrams, 1989:141. Cat., *Metallkunst*, Berlin: Bröhan-Museum, 1990:382–87.

Schmoll von Eisenwerth, Fritz (1883–1963)

► Austrian sculptor and silversmith; born Vienna; active Munich.
► Studied in Karlsruhe and Debschitz-Schule, Munich.
► 1909–10, he worked with architect Paul Bonatz in Stuttgart; taught at the Debschitz-Schule, where he was director 1914–20. His silver designs produced by M.T. Wetzlar in Munich were simple and suitable for serial production. Also for serial production, an elaborate silver service was produced by Bruckmann und Söhne in Heilbronn from carved plaster plates; Schmoll von Eisenwerth corrected the steel dies at the factory. His designs included furniture and ceramics. From 1920, he pursued sculpture.
► Annelies Krekel-Aalberse, *Art Nouveau and Art Déco Silver*, New York: Abrams, 1989:130,131,259. Cat., *Münchner Schmuck 1900–1940*, Munich: Bayerisches Nationalmuseum, 1990:37–38.

Schmuz-Baudiss, Theodor Hermann (1859–1942)

► Germany ceramicist; active Munich.
► 1879–82, studied Kunstgewerbschule, Munich; 1882–90, Akademie der bildenden Künste, Munich.

► He designed in the rustic manner of local Diessen pottery; from 1897, decorated wares in a freer manner; supplied brown-glazed stoneware to Jakob Scharvogel, with whom he carried out experiments; in 1898, became a member of Vereinigte Werkstätten für Kunst im Handwerk, Munich, and began a lengthy study of porcelain production at Swaine in Hüttensteinach, Thuringia; in 1902, began working for Königliche Porzellan-Manufaktur, Berlin; 1908–26, was director of the manufactory and established an underglaze department; was regarded as the best ornamental designer of ceramics in Germany of the time.
► Work (vases) shown at 1897 Glaspalast exhibition, Munich. *Pensée* dinner service by Swaine shown at 1900 Paris 'Exposition Universelle.'
► Cat., Kathryn Bloom Hiesinger, *Die Meister des Münchner Jugendstils*, Munich: Stadtmuseum, 1988:154–55.

Schnaidt, Claude (1931–)

► Swiss design theorist; born Geneva; active Paris.
► Schnaidt taught at the Hochschule für Gestaltung in Ulm. He wrote a book on Hannes Meyer, director of the Bauhaus 1928–30.
► Penny Sparke, *Introduction to Design and Culture in the Twentieth Century*, Allen and Unwin, 1986. Cat., *Hochschule für Gestaltung Ulm: Die Moral der Gegenstände*, Berlin: Ernst und Sohn, 1987:274.

Schneck, Adolf G. (1883–1971)

► German architect and designer; born Esslingen.
► 1907–14, studied Kunstgewerbeschule, Stuttgart under Bernhard Pankok.
► From the 1920s, Schneck designed furniture for Thonet. He designed the 1924 'Die Form' exhibition of the Deutscher Werkbund. He contributed to the 1925 Monza 'Art and Design Exhibition' and designed two houses at the 1927 Stuttgart 'Weissenhof-Ausstellung.' He included old and new Thonet bentwood models in his 1928 'Der Stuhl' exhibition at the Werkbund. He designed a range of relatively inexpensive mass-produced furniture made by various manufacturers, including Deutsche Werkstätten and Thonet. 1923–49, he taught at the Kunstgewerbeschule in Stuttgart. In the mid-1950s, he was supportive in the founding of the college of applied and industrial art in Istanbul that opened in 1957. His numerous articles and books included *Das Möbel als Gebrauchsgegenstand* (1928), the exhibition catalogue *Der Stuhl* (1928), and *Neue Möbel vom Jugendstil bis heute* (1962).
► Adolf Schneck, *Das Polstermöbel*, Julius Hoffmann, 1933. Barbie Campbell-Cole and Tim Benton (eds.), *Tubular Steel Furniture*, London: The Art Book Company, 1979:12. *Adolf G. Schneck, 1883–1971, Leben, Lehre, Möbel, Architektur*, Stuttgart: Staatlichen Akademie der bildenden Künste, 1983. Jessica Rutherford, *Art Nouveau, Art Deco and the Thirties: The Furniture Collections at Brighton Museum*, Brighton: The Royal Pavilion, Art Gallery and Museums, 1983:49.

Schneider, Andreas (1867–1931)

► Norwegian painter, ceramicist and furniture and textile designer.
► 1894, studied ceramics in Copenhagen.
► He set up his own workshop for ceramics in 1895 and became a leading figure in the development of studio pottery in Norway. In 1910, he was a designer for the Egersund ceramics factory and, for others, designed textiles and furniture.
► Cat., David Revere McFadden (ed.), *Scandinavian Modern Design 1880–1980*, New York: Abrams, 1982:271, No.44.

Schneider, Cristallerie

► French glassware factory; located Epinay-sur-Seine, later Lorris.
► Brothers Charles (1881–1952) and Ernest Schneider founded the Cristallerie Schneider in 1903. Charles Schneider, born Château-Thierry, studied at the École des Beaux-Arts in Nancy under Émile Gallé, working at the Gallé factory there at the same time. He designed for Daum 1902–08. At Cristallerie Schneider, the elder Ernest Schneider was the administrator, while his brother oversaw production of art glass and was artistic director until

1944. His work was floral with bursts of color, simultaneously refined and crude. The richness of his colors established the reputation of his glassware. The factory produced mostly art glass until production declined in 1925 and was eventually discontinued. In 1962, the firm moved to Lorris, near Orléans.

▶ At the 1925 Paris 'Exposition Internationale des Arts Décoratifs et Industriels Modernes,' he showed an ensemble of glassware and produced three 100m² stained-glass windows for the towers surrounding the Esplanade des Invalides.

▶ Yvonne Brunhammer et al., *Art Nouveau Belgium, France*, Houston: Rice University, 1976. Alastair Duncan, *Art Nouveau and Art Déco Lighting*, New York: Simon and Schuster, 1978:86–87. Cat., *Verriers français contemporains: Art et industrie*, Paris: Musée des Arts Décoratifs, 1982. Pierre Cabanne, *Encyclopédie Art Déco*, Paris: Somogy, 1986:235.

Schoen, Eugene (1880–1957)
▶ American architect and designer; born and active New York.
▶ Studied architecture, Columbia University, New York, to 1901; Akademie der bildenden Künste, Vienna, under Otto Wagner and others.
▶ He set up his own architecture practice in New York in 1905 and, after visiting the 1925 Paris 'Exposition Internationale des Arts Décoratifs et Industriels Modernes,' began offering interior design services. In 1931, he became a professor of interior architecture at New York University. In the gallery he established, he sold his own and imported textiles and furniture and Maurice Heaton's glassware; for several interior schemes, he commissioned Heaton to execute large glass murals, the most impressive of which was *The Flight of Amelia Earhart Across the Atlantic* in the 1932 interior of RKO theater in Rockefeller Center, New York, of which Schoen was interior designer. He designed the interiors of numerous apartments, banks, theaters, and department stores in Manhattan and elsewhere, including Dunhill's interior at Rockefeller Center and an earlier store for Dunhill's. His furniture was rendered in neoclassical forms with exotic wood veneers in an odd amalgamation of various contemporary European styles. Some of his furniture, such as the Chinese-influenced pieces for the apartment of lawyer Henry Root Stern in New York, was produced by Schmieg, Hungate and Kotzian in New York. From the late 1920s, his son Lee was a member of the practice.
▶ He designed a room setting at the 1928 'Exposition of Art in Industry at Macy's' at Macy's department store in New York. His show window, child's nursery, and bedroom were included in the 1929 (XI) 'The Architect and the Industrial Arts: An Exhibition of Contemporary American Design' at the New York Metropolitan Museum of Art. His dining room was included in the Central Gallery of the 1935 'Contemporary American Industrial Art, 1934' at the New York Metropolitan Museum of Art. He designed an exhibition at New York State Building, 1933–34 Chicago 'Century of Progress.' Received a gold medal for crafts from Architectural League of New York for a building entrance.
▶ Marya Mannes, 'Gallery Notes,' *Creative Art*, Feb. 1928:XIII. Eugene Schoen, 'The Design of Modern Interiors,' *Creative Art*, May 1928. Eugene Schoen, 'House and Garden's Modern House,' *House and Garden*, Feb. 1929:94. Harry V. Anderson, 'Contemporary American Designers,' *Decorators' Digest*, June 1935:41–45. Karen Davies, *At Home in Manhattan: Modern Decorative Arts, 1925 to the Depression*, New Haven: Yale, 1983:25. R. Craig Miller, *Modern Design 1890–1990*, New York: Abrams, 1990.

Schofield, Jean (1940–)
▶ British interior and furniture designer.,
▶ Studied Royal College of Art, London.
▶ She opened an office in 1966 with John Wright and Mill Walker in London. She designed domestic and office furniture, lighting, and accessories. Schofield and Wright designed the 1964 knock-down *Chair C1* produced by Anderson Manson Decorations of London.
▶ Her and Wright's *Chair C1* was included in the 1966 'Vijftig Jaar Zitten' exhibition at the Stedelijk Museum, Amsterdam, and

1970 'Modern Chairs 1918–1970' exhibition at the Whitechapel Gallery, London.
▶ Mary Gilliat, *English Style*, London, 1966. Cat., *Modern Chairs 1918–1970*, London: Lund Humphries, 1971.

Schott und Genossen Glaswerke (aka Jenaer Glaswerke Schott und Genossen)
▶ German glassware manufacturer; located Mainz after 1952.
▶ Ernst Schott founded the Jenaer Glaswerke in Jena in 1884. 1930–34, Wilhelm Wagenfeld worked for Jenaer Glaswerke Schott und Genossen, which mass produced his designs in heat-resistant glass, including the 1932 tea infuser, cups and saucers, 1934 coffee percolator, and 1935 kitchenware, much of which remains in production. In the early 1930s, Wagenfeld designed a range of heat-resistant ovenware. Heinz Löffelhardt, a student of Wagenfeld's at the Vereinigte Lausitzer Glaswerke in Zweisel in the 1930s, became Schott's chief designer and was responsible for a number of suites of glasses for domestic and utility use that were considered innovative in the 1950s and 1960s. He continued as consultant designer when the firm moved to Mainz in 1952, working for its utility glass and lighting divisions. He designed its widely published 1957 range of heat-resistant borosilicate glass, including a tea set, cups and saucers, plates, and bowls. With the isolation of Schott und Genossen in East Germany after World War II, the firm was reformed in Mainz by the Vereinigte Lausitzer Glaswerke.
▶ Frederick Cooke, *Glass: Twentieth-Century Design*, New York: Dutton, 1986:92.

Schrager, Ian (1946–)
▶ American entrepreneur; born Bronx, New York.
▶ With Steve Rubell in 1977, he hired architect Scott Bromley to turn an undistinguished old theater on East 54th Street in New York into the discotheque Studio 54. He opened the Palladium discotheque in 1985; its architect was Arata Isozaki, interior designer Andrée Putman, and muralists Kenny Scharf, Keith Haring, and Francesco Clemente. He opened Morgans Hotel in 1984, designed by Putmann in her distinctive black and white style. Having become known for his business ventures that were strongly based on design and extensively promoted in the press, he opened the Royalton Hotel at 44 East 44th Street, New York, in 1988. Schrager commissioned Philippe Starck to design the Royalton as well as the subsequent 1990 Paramount Hotel on West 46th Street, New York. He commissioned Jacques Grange to design interiors for the Barbizon Hotel, New York.
▶ Fred A. Bernstein, 'For Ian Schrager, Design Is Paramount,' *Metropolitan Home*, November 1990:65ff. Esther Henwood, 'Of Love and Accessories,' *Vogue Decoration*, No. 26, June/July 1990:61–63.

Schreckengost, Viktor (1906–)
▶ American ceramicist.
▶ 1924–29, studied Cleveland Institute of Art; Kunstgewerbeschule, Vienna, under Michael Powolny.
▶ In 1930, he began working for the Cowan Pottery Studio in Rocky River, Ohio. In 1931 when Cowan closed, he continued his ceramic sculpture, while also designing mass-production ceramic tablewares for firms including American Limoges Ceramics. His work showed images of popular culture, including cocktail glasses, dancers, skyscrapers and words such as 'follies,' 'café,' and 'jazz.'
▶ Ceramics work shown at the 1947 (XI) traveling 'Ceramic National Exhibition' organized by Syracuse Museum of Fine Art, Syracuse, New York, shown at the Museum of Art, New York. His work was the subject of the 1976 'Victor Schreckengost: Retrospective Exhibition' at the Cleveland Institute of Art.
▶ Cat., Laurence Schmeckebier, *Viktor Schreckengost: Retrospective Exhibition*, Cleveland: Cleveland Institute of Art, 1976. Karen Davies, *At Home in Manhattan: Modern Decorative Arts, 1925 to the Depression*, New Haven: Yale, 1983:81. R. Craig Miller, *Modern Design, 1890–1990*, New York: Abrams, 1990.

Schreiber, Gaby (1912–)
► Austrian designer; active London.
► Studied art and stage and interior design in Florence, Berlin, and Paris.
► She was an interior designer when she arrived in London in the 1930s. In the 1940s, she designed a range of Modern domestic plastic tableware for Runcolite Plastics, including her plastic meat tray of the late 1940s, which was widely published. 1957–63, she was interior design consultant to William Clark in Northern Ireland, National Westminster Bank, Westminster Foreign Bank, GHP Group, Gulf Oil Eastern Hemisphere, Lythe Hill Hotel in Surrey, Anglo-Continental Investment and Finance, Continental Bankers Agents, Myers, Peter Robinson, David Morgan, West Cumberland Hospital, Newcastle Regional Hospital Board, and the Fine Fare Supermarket chain. She was general consultant and designer to Cunard for the oceanliners 1965–68 *Queen Elizabeth II* and *Cunarder*, and to Zarach, the Marquess of Londonderry, Crown Agents, Allen and Hanbury, and the BOAC airline. She was a design consultant on plastics for Marks and Spencer and yachts for Sir Gerard d'Erlanger, Whitney Straight, and others. She designed interiors for oceanliners, department stores, office blocks, hospitals, factories, cinemas, cabin cruisers, restaurants, and conference halls, as well as domestic interiors and conversions. Her work was widely published.
► She designed exhibition pavilions in Europe and the USA and sat on numerous design juries and committees, both national and international.
► Michael Farr, *Design in British Industry: A Mid-Century Survey*, London: Cambridge, 1955:128ff. Penny Sparke, *Introduction to Design and Culture in the Twentieth Century*, Allen and Unwin, 1986. Liz McQuiston, *Women in Design: A Contemporary View*, New York: Rizzoli, 1988:110.

Schröder-Schräder, Truus (b. Truus Schräder 1889–1985)
► Dutch architect; born Deventer.
► Trained as a pharmacist.
► She met architect Gerrit Rietveld when he delivered some Classical furniture copies to her home in Amsterdam, where Bruno Taut, Kurt Schwitters, and others were her frequent guests, beginning a life-long association, though she was given little credit for their mutual accomplishments. The canonical 1924 Schröder house in Utrecht along with its innovative furnishings was the first of a number of collaborations. Dutch painter Theo Van Doesburg pronounced the house an embodiment of the De Stijl ideal of 'the end of art.' Schröder's and Rietveld's other mutual projects ranged from the 1925 glass radio cabinet and 1927 project for standardized housing to the 1936 Vreeburg cinema, 1936 moveable summer houses, and the apartment block opposite the Schröder house. She lived in the Utrecht house for sixty years.
► 'Max van Rooij, Rietveld Schröder Huis De Vorm,' *Maandblad voor Vormgeving*, June–July 1975. Corrie Nagtegaal, *Tr. Schröder-Schräder, Gewoonster van het Rietveld Schröderhuis*, Utrecht: Impress bv, 1987. Marijke Küper and Ida van Lijl, *Gerrit Th. Rietveld: The Complete Works 1888–1964*, Utrecht: Centraal Museum, 1992.

Schroeder, Germaine (1889–1983)
► French bookbinder.
► Often incorporating heart motifs, she used brightly colored leather inlays and vellum for her book covers. Her titles included *Les Amours de Psyché et de Cupidon*. Among her clients were Lecointe, Lazard, Louis Barthou, Dr. Jaltrain, and Marcel Bernard.
► Henri Nicolle, 'La Reliure moderne,' *Les Arts français: la reliure d'art*, No. 36, 1919:199. Gaston Quénioux, *Les Arts décoratifs modernes*, Paris, 1925:339,342. Ernest de Crauzat, *La Reliure française de 1900 à 1925*, Vol. 2, Paris, 1932:141–42. Alastair Duncan and Georges de Bartha, *Art Nouveau and Art Déco Bookbinding*, New York: Abrams, 1989:19,20,196. Ph. Dally, 'Les Techniques modernes de la reliure,' *Art et décoration*, Jan. 1927:18,22.

Schröfer, Joh
► Dutch designer.
► Schröfer designed a 1926 bent tubular steel chair with an upholstered back and seat. In the 1930s, Schröfer and W.H. Gispen independently designed tubular steel furniture for the De Cirkel factory in the Netherlands; became dirctor of De Cirkel; was a member of Raad voor Industriële vormgeving (Council of Industrial Design).
► Barbie Campbell-Cole and Tim Benton (eds.), *Tubular Steel Furniture*, London: The Art Book Company, 1979:31.

Schrutek, Franz
See Siess und Springer

Schultz, Richard (1930–)
► American sculptor and furniture designer.
► Studied Iowa State University; Illinois Institute of Technology, Chicago; Columbia University, New York.
► He joined Knoll in 1951 as a member of its design development group. At first he worked with Harry Bertoia on the wire *Diamond* seating range. For Knoll, Schultz designed the 1960 *Petal* table, 1961 steel-wire lounge chairs, and 1966 outdoor *Leisure Collection* seating and tables. Pursuing outdoor furniture, he executed the design of a 1981 range.
► His *Leisure Collection* chair received the 1967 American Interior Design International Award.
► Cat., *Modern Chairs 1918–1970*, London: Lund Humphries, 1971: No. 84. Cat., *Les Assises du siège contemporain*, Paris: Musée des Arts Décoratifs, 1968. Cat., Kathryn B. Hiesinger and George H. Marcus III (eds.), *Design Since 1945*, Philadelphia: Philadelphia Museum of Art, 1983:230,III–82. Eric Larrabee and Massimo Vignelli, *Knoll Design*, New York, 1981:158–59,292–93.

Schumacher, F.
► American fabric manufacturer; located New York.
► Frederick Schumacher, born in Paris, was associated with Vanoutryve, Paris; he acted as agent for Brown, De Turk; in the early 1880s, traveled to USA to sell European fabrics to distributors; from 1883, was associated with fabric firm Passavant, New York. In 1889, Schumacher founded his own fabric firm, buying out Passavant's stock and opening an office at 935 Broadway, New York; in 1893, he became a partner of Paul Gadebusch in a business at 222 Fourth Avenue. In 1899, Schumacher's nephew Pierre Pozier came from France to succeed Schumacher as stylist and purchasing agent and became president in 1943. Distributing through interior designers, architects and retail stores, Schumacher's best-known designs included fabrics for the Blue Room of the White House, Washington, during presidencies of Theodore Roosevelt, Woodrow Wilson, and Calvin Coolidge; historic restoration prints for Newport and Williamsburg; and fabrics designed by Dorothy Draper, Paul McCobb, James Amster, Vera, William Pahlman, Raymond Loewy, and Frank Lloyd Wright. As early as 1909, Wright ordered fabrics for the Robie and Coonley houses.
► David A. Hanks, *The Decorative Designs of Frank Lloyd Wright*, New York: Dutton, 1979:217–19.

Schumacher-Percy, Ulla (1918–)
► Swedish textile designer.
► 1936–37, studied painting under Otte Sköld; 1938–41, Konstfackskolan, Stockholm.
► From 1947, she was artistic director of the Stockholm Domestic Crafts Association. In 1949, she set up her own workshop, where she produced embroideries and rugs.
► Her work was the subject of 1957 and 1960 one-person exhibitions in Stockholm and was included in the 1958 'Formes Scandinaves' exhibition at the Paris Musée des Arts Décoratifs.
► Cat., David Revere McFadden (ed.), *Scandinavian Modern Design 1880–1980*, New York: Abrams, 1982:271, No. 335.

Schuster, Franz (1892–1976)
▶ Austrian furniture manufacturer.
▶ Studied Kunstgewerbeschule, Vienna, under Heinrich Tessenow.
▶ He was active in Vienna from the 1910s. As part of a municipal program for the construction of workers' homes after World War I, he designed a small row in the Viennese suburb Laaer Berg. At this time he also produced his modular stacking furniture. In 1927, he settled in Frankfurt. Schuster worked with Ernest May to create a furniture range in the Rationalist mode suitable to the small scale of May's housing. Schuster was artistic supervisor of the 'Deutschen Hausratgesellschaften' (Household Furnishings Group) and introduced an installment payment plan for poor home owners and created a range of modular furniture in wood. In c1928, Schuster began to collaborate with the firm Walter Knoll, Stuttgart. By 1930–31, his range of unit furniture for state-supported and owner-occupied homes greatly expanded to include case goods, tables, chairs, and shelving; it was sold by the Hausrat-gesellschaften and subsequently by Edwin Behr in Wendlingen, Stuttgart. This range may have been the basis of Serge Chermayeff's Plan range of unit furniture. Manifesting the more Utopian aspects of the design philosophy of the 1920s and 1930s, Schuster's furniture was lauded as heralding 'a new way of life' in pamphlets and journals of the early 1930s.
▶ Karl Mang, *Geschichte des Modernen Möbels*, Stuttgart: Gerd Hatje, 1978. Franz Schuster, *Ein Möbelbuch 2: Erweitere Auglage*, Stuttgart: Julius Hoffmann, 1932. 'Five Units = One Home,' *Decoration*, Jan. 1934:7–9.

Schütt, Georg (1928–)
▶ Danish metalworker.
▶ Trained as a goldsmith with A. Michelsen and in Stockholm.
▶ In 1951, he joined the design department of the Georg Jensen Sølvsmedie in Copenhagen. He became public relations officer for the Association of Danish Furniture Manufacturers. His fanlike 1958 strainer in stainless steel was distinguished for its simplicity.
▶ Cat., *Georg Jensen Silversmithy: 77 Artists, 75 Years*, Washington: Smithsonian Institution Press, 1980.

Schwab, Harriet (1943–)
▶ German industrial designer; born Breslau (now Wroclaw, Poland).
▶ 1974–78, studied Staatliche Akademie der bildenden Künste, Stuttgart, under Arno Votteler.
▶ From 1979, she worked as a designer at the design office Jürgen Lange in Grafenau on objects, outdoor furniture, and trade fair stands. She designed the 1987 *Facette* hallway range by Schönbuch Collection Möbelmarketing.
▶ She won first prize at the International Design Competition of the Benze Collection and, 1983–89, was represented in the yearly 'Design Section' of the Design Center Stuttgart.
▶ Cat., Design Center Stuttgart, *Women in Design: Careers and Life Histories Since 1900*, Stuttgart: Haus der Wirtschaft, 1989:166–67.

Schwan, Lloyd
▶ American furniture designer; husband of Lyn Godley.
▶ Schwan and Godley designed furniture marketed through their firm Godley-Schwan in New York. They produced their limited-production pieces in a workshop in Brooklyn, New York.
▶ They first showed their sculptural seating and case goods at the 1989 Salone del Mobile in Milan. They showed their *Otto* multi-colored cabinet at the 1991 'International Contemporary Furniture Fair,' New York, and 1991 Salone del Mobile in Milan.

Schwanzer, Karl (1918–75)
▶ Austrian furniture designer; born Vienna.
▶ His chairs were mass produced. He designed the panorama of the Alps at the Austrian pavilion at the 1967 Montreal 'Universal and International Exhibition (Expo '67).'

▶ Günther Feuerstein, *Vienna—Present and Past: Arts and Crafts—Applied Art—Design*, Vienna: Jugend und Volk, 1976:61, 65 ,81.

Schweinberger-Gismondi, Emma
▶ Italian designer.
▶ Active in the 1960s, she was a designer at Artemide, Milan; designed furniture and interiors.
▶ Hans Wichmann, *Industrial Design, Unikate, Serienerzeugnisse: Die Neue Sammlung, Ein neuer Museumtyp des 20. Jahrhunderts*, Munich, 1985:515. Hans Wichmann, *Italien Design 1945 bis heute*, Munich: Die Neue Sammlung, 1988.

Schweizerische Landesausstellung
▶ Swiss National Exposition of 1939.
▶ Its director was Armin Meili, chief architect Hans Hofmann, and chief contractor Heinrich Oetiker. Thirty-two architects and 10 departmental chairmen were part of the design team. The exhibition was based on the the 1930 Stockholm Exposition. Rivalry between the traditional nationalistic 'Heimatstil,' and Modern architecture resulted in the arrangement of the exposition on both banks of the Lake of Zürich. The right bank was reserved for more traditional building styles and included the Halls of Agriculture and a sterotypical Swiss village. The left bank was devoted to more progressive styles, where the Hall of Technology, the Hall of Sport, the Hall of Fashion, and the Halls of Aviation, Press and Intellectual Endeavor were found. The two sides were linked by a cable car. The Kongresshaus built by the architecture firm Haefeli Moser Steiger was examplary of the type of contemporary Modern Swiss architecture found in Zürich. Another manifestation of the Modern movement was found in the perforated aluminum *Landi* chair designed by Hans Coray for outdoor use at the exhibition. A parabolic arch in thin concrete, by the Swiss bridge builder Robert Maillart, was erected as a sculpture in front of the Building Pavilion. Four million visitors were expected to view the exposition; in the event, 10.5 million (or more than double the then population of Switzerland) attended.
▶ Gottlieb Duttwieler (ed.), *Eines Volkes Sein und Schaffen: Die Schweizerische Landesausstellung 1939 Zürich in 300 Bildern*. Jacques Gubler, *Nationalisme et Internationalisme dans L'Architecture Moderne de La Suisse*, Geneva: Archigraphie, 1988:229–35.

Scibillia, Norbert
▶ French architect and designer; active Paris.
▶ Scibillia designed the 1985 *Polyandre* modular furniture (with Serge Guillet) produced by Clen.
▶ Shared first prize (for office furniture) in 1983 competition sponsored by the French ministry of culture.
▶ Agnès Lévitte and Margo Rouard, *100 quotidiens objets made in France*, APCI/Syros-Alteratives, 1987:29.

Scolari, D'Urbino, Lomazzi and De Pas
▶ Collaboration of Italian architects and designers.
▶ Setting up an office in the mid 1960s, they began designing Pop furniture pieces. Their best known designs included the inexpensive 1967 *Blow* chair produced by Zanotta and the 1970 *Joe Sofa*, a parody in the form of an enormous baseball glove. Difficult to keep inflated and considered a gimmick even at the time, the *Blow* was the first Italian inflatable chair successful in mass-production and was offered in four colors.
▶ Cat., *Modern Chairs 1918–1970*, London: Lund Humphries, 1971. Albrecht Bangert, *Italienisches Möbeldesign—Klassiker von 1945 bis heute*, Munich: Bangert, 1989.
▶ See De Pas, Gionatan, D'Urbino, Donato, and Lomazzi, Paolo

Scott Brown, Denise (1932–)
▶ British architect; born in Nkana (Zambia); active Philadelphia; wife of Robert Venturi.
▶ 1952–55, studied Architectural Association, London; 1960 and 1965, University of Pennsylvania.
▶ She moved to the USA in 1956. In 1964, she and Venturi opened an architectural office in Philadelphia called Venturi, Rauch

and Scott Brown from 1967. The firm was known for its Post-Modernist architectural style. She accomplished most of her architecture projects in collaboration with Venturi, as well as their publications, including *Learning from Las Vegas* (1972). 1960–65 and in 1982 and 1983, she taught at the University of Pennsylvania, 1965–68, at the University of California and, 1967–70, at Yale University. Her activities and recognition included several hundred lectures, conferences, juries, selection panels, and awards in Europe, the USA, and Africa. Venturi executed domestic tableware designs produced by Alessi and in 1989 by Reed and Barton; it is difficult to determine Scott Brown's participation in the project.
► Liz McQuiston, *Women in Design: A Contemporary View*, New York: Rizzoli, 1988:24.

Scott, Giles Gilbert (1880–1960)
► British architect.
► He was an apprentice to architect Temple Lushington Moore. In 1903, he set up his own architecture practice. He won the competition for the Liverpool Anglican Cathedral begun in 1903 and unfinished by the time he died in 1960. 1920–21, he was president of the Architectural Association in London and, 1933–35, president of the Royal Institute of British Architects. Scott designed the 1936 *Model K6* red public telephone booth that became known as the *Jubilee Kiosk*. British Telecom's 1988 decision to replace the booths with a new design prompted public opposition, and a number were reprieved. He designed numerous churches and chapels in the Gothic Revival style, including New Court at Clare College, Cambridge. In 1924, he was knighted; 1933–35, was president of the Royal Institute of British Architects. His work in the 1930s included 1934–45 Waterloo Bridge (with engineers Rendel, Palmer and Tritton), 1930–32 Battersea power station (with engineer S.L. Pearce and architect J.H. Halliday), 1928–29 St. Francis Terriers Church in High Wycombe, 1930–32 St. Albans Church in Golders Green, 1932 St. Andrews Church in Luton, 1930–34 University Library at Cambridge University, 1935–46 annex of the Bodleian Library at Oxford University, 1922–60 school houses at Ampleforth College, 1933–51 Guinness factory in Park Royal, and 1935–51 Electricity House in Bristol.
► Adolf K. Placzek (ed.), *Macmillan Encyclopedia of Architects*, Vol. 4, New York: Free Press, 1982. *Issue 2*, London: Design Museum, 1989. Cat., *Thirties: British art and design before the war*, London: Arts Council of Great Britain, Hayward Gallery, 1979:180, 202,235,300.

Scott, Isaac Elwood (1845–1920)
► American furniture designer, wood carver, and ceramicist; born Philadelphia; active Philadelphia, Chicago, New York, and Boston.
► He moved to Chicago in 1873 and became known for his fine wood carving. He modeled architectural ornaments for Chicago Terra Cotta. In 1875, he became a partner of architect Frederick W. Copeland in Scott and Copeland, Designers, Carvers, and Art Wood Workers. Mr. and Mrs. John J. Glessner commissioned him in 1875 to produce furniture for their home at 261 West Washington Boulevard in Chicago. Vases for the house were made by Scott at the Chelsea Keramic Art Works in Massachusetts in 1879. Scott with Asa Lyon, architect and furniture designer, designed the 1878 coach house for the Glessner residence. In the early 1880s, Scott began designing textiles and embroidery patterns. 1882–84, he taught woodcarving at the Chicago Society of Decorative Art. He designed the 1883 Glessner summer villa at The Rocks, near Littleton, New Hampshire. 1882–84, he was in partnership with Henry S. Jaffray, producing interiors and designing the new headquarters of Warder, Bushnell and Glessner at Jefferson and Adams Streets in Chicago. They designed another residence and a six-storey Chicago office building. In 1884, Scott moved to New York and designed interiors at, by 1887, 1129 Broadway. In 1888, he moved to Boston and became active in wood carving and teaching crafts at the Eliot School. When H.H. Richardson designed the 1885 residence of the Glessners at 1800

Prairie Avenue in Chicago, Scott's furniture of the 1870s was installed there.
► His work was included in a display of household furnishing in the 1875 Chicago 'Inter-State Industrial Exposition' and in the 1987 'In Pursuit of Beauty' exhibition at the New York Metropolitan Museum.
► Doreen Bolger Burke et al., *In Pursuit of Beauty: Americans and the Aesthetic Movement*, New York: Metropolitan Museum of Art and Rizzoli, 1987:466–67. David A. Hanks, *Isaac E. Scott: Reform Furniture in Chicago: John Jacob Glessner House*, Chicago, 1974. David A. Hanks, 'Isaac E. Scott, Craftsman and Designer,' *Antiques*, Vol. 105, June 1974:1307–13. Sharon Darling, *Chicago Furniture: Art, Craft, and Industry, 1933–1983*, New York, 1984:159,163–69,194,223,391.

Scott, William Bell (1811–1900)
► British painter, engraver, designer, and book illustrator.
► Scott was a minor member of the Pre-Raphaelite circle. He produced designs for urns, vases, cups, picture frames, scrolls, candelabra, stands, tables, and other furnishings. 1844–64, he taught at the School of Design in Newcastle. He published the illustrated essay *The ornamentist, or artisan's manual in the various branches of ornamental art* (1845).
► W.B. Scott, *The ornamentist, or artisan's manual in the various branches of ornamental art*, London, Dublin and Edinburgh: A. Fullarton, 1845. Jeremy Cooper, 'Victorian Furniture, a guide to sources,' London, Dublin and Edinburgh: A. Fullarton:120. Stuart Durant, *Ornament from the Industrial Revolution to Today*, Woodstock, NY: Overlook, 1986.

SČSD
See Svaz Československého Díla

Secession
See Münchner Sezession and Wiener Sezession

Sedding, George Elton (1882–1915)
► British metalworker and jeweler; son of John Dando Sedding.
► He was apprenticed to Henry Wilson, formerly chief assistant to Sedding's father, in London and Kent. In 1907, Sedding returned to London, opening his own small workshop at 11 Noel Street (near Oxford Circus) and specializing in simple decorative objects and pieces of silver and copper jewelry set with semiprecious stones in a style similar to Wilson's. As his success increased, his production became more ambitious and elaborate. He had mainly ecclesiastical commissions.
► Charlotte Gere, *American and European Jewelry 1830–1914*, New York: Crown, 1975:220.

Sedding, John Dando (1838–1891)
► British artchitect and embroidery, metalwork, and wallpaper designer; father of George Elton Sedding.
► 1853–63, he was apprenticed to architect G.E. Street and became knowledgeable in Gothic ornamentation and architecture. 1863–65, he pursued decorative design and in, 1865, became a partner of his architect brother Edmund Sedding in Penzance, Cornwall. 1868–74, he was active in Bristol. He set up an office in London in 1874 and, in 1876, met John Ruskin. Sedding became interested in the use of natural forms in ornamentation. In 1880, he was appointed architect of the diocese of Bath and Wells. He designed the 1885 Holy Trinity Church in Sloan Street, London, and 1886 Church of the Holy Redeemer, Clerkenwell, London, in the Classical style. His chief assistant Henry Wilson assumed the affairs of the architecture office on Sedding's death and completed his unfinished commissions, including details of the elaborate French Gothic and English Perpendicular Holy Trinity Church.
► Isabelle Anscombe and Charlotte Gere, *Arts and Crafts in Britain and America*, New York: Rizzoli, 1978:140. Adolf K. Placzek (ed.), *Macmillan Encyclopedia of Architects*, Vol. 4, New York: Free Press, 1982.

Seddon, John Pollard   (1827–1906)

▶ British architect.

▶ Seddon was a partner with John Pritchard in Wales (1852–62), with John Coates Carter 1884–1904, and also in own office from 1857. With a largely ecclesiastical clientele, by the mid-1870s he was designing country churches in Herefordshire, rebuilding a church there, and altering another in Norfolk. He applied medievalism to 19th-century values in a sober manner. He is best known for his 1864 Castle House Hotel (now University College of Wales) in Aberystwyth, Dyfed. His apprentice C.F.A. Voysey may have designed some decorative panels in cement at the entrance to its south wing. He lost the 1884 competition for the Law Courts to George Edmund Street. He designed the cabinet *King René's Honeymoon* for William Morris's firm, with painted panels by Ford Madox Brown, Edward Burne-Jones, and Dante Gabriel Rossetti. Some of his furniture showed Pre-Raphaelite influence and that of A.W.N. Pugin. Seddon used decorative hinges boldly and favored plain panels using the grain of the wood as a decorative feature. He executed designs for numerous encaustic floor tiles for leading manufacturers and ecclesiastical embroideries.

▶ In 1874, he showed designs for an orphanage and a chapel interior at the Royal Academy in London. His roll-top desk was shown at the stand of newly-formed Morris, Faulkner, and Marshall at the London 'International Exhibition of 1862.'

▶ Obituary, *Journal of the Royal Institute of British Architects*, 13, 1906:194, 221. Stuart Durant, *The Decorative Designs of C.F.A. Voysey*, London: Lutterworth, 1990:13–14.

Seguso, Archimede   (1909–)

▶ Italian glass designer.

▶ In 1945, he and others established the firm Vetraria Archimede Seguso; Archimede was chief designer and artistic director. He produced tableware and decorative pieces; explored the techniques of Renaissance glassmaking; became known for his engraving techniques; created vessels in thin, transparent glass with pale *latticino* (thin threads). The firm is active today.

▶ Cat., *Venezianisches Glas 19. bis 20. Jahrhundert aus dem Glasmuseum Murano/Venedig*, Berlin: Kunstgewerbemuseum Schloss Köpenick, 1981:51. Cat., *Venini and Murano Renaissance: Italian Art Glass of the 1940s and 50s*, New York: Fifty/50, 1984.

Seguso Vetri d'Arte

▶ Italian glass manufacturers.

▶ 1932, brothers Angelo and Bruno Seguso opened a glass factory. From 1934 to the 1960s, Flavio Poli served as artistic director and incorporated rich color and bubble patterns into his early work; he used strong, simple silhouettes; introduced a style later on in his career known as *vetro astrale*, inspired by outer-space travel and science fiction.

▶ Cat., *Venini & Murano Renaissance: Italian Art Glass of the 1940s and 50s*, New York: Fifty/50, 1984.

Seidelin, Henning   (1904–)

▶ Danish sculptor and designer.

▶ Seidelin worked in silver, steel, porcelain, and faïence. He executed silver designs for the Georg Jensen Sølvsmedie in the 1930s. He was awarded the Eckersberg Medal in 1951.

▶ His work was shown at the 1951 (IX) and 1954 (X) Triennali di Milano.

▶ Cat., *Georg Jensen Silversmithy: 77 Artists, 75 Years*, Washington: Smithsonian Institution Press, 1980.

Seidl, Alfred   (1919–)

▶ Austrian glassware designer; born Vienna.

▶ He worked for Stölzle and for the Tiroler Glashütte Claus Riedl. He was best known for his 1970 *Contra* glass service.

▶ Günther Feuerstein, *Vienna–Present and Past: Arts and Crafts–Applied Art–Design*, Vienna: Jugend und Volk, 1976:66,68,81.

Seiffert, Florian   (1943–)

▶ German industrial designer.

▶ Studied design, Folkwangschule für Gestaltung, Essen.

▶ 1968–72, Seiffert worked for Braun, designing shavers and coffee machines; 1973–78, was active in Milan; and, from 1978, worked in his own design studio in Munich.

Seigneur, François   (1946–)

▶ French architect and designer; active Paris.

▶ Studied École Boulle and École Nationale Supérieure des Arts Décoratifs, both Paris.

▶ In 1970 with architect Jean Nouvel, he opened his first office; was architect of the French pavilion at the 1992 'Exposición universal de Sevilla (Expo '92)'; designed the 1993 'Design miroir du siècle' exhibition, Grand Palais, Paris.

Selmer, Jens   (1911–)

▶ Norwegian furniture designer and architect.

▶ Active from the 1930s, his furniture designs from 1946 were examples of Scandinavian Modern.

▶ Fredrik Wildhagen, *Norge i Form*, Oslo: Sternersen, 1988:102.

Selmersheim, Pierre   (1869–1941)

▶ French architect and decorator; born Paris; brother of Tony Selmersheim.

▶ He and his brother designed lighting and collaborated on the décors of a number of buildings. He decorated an apartment in 1902, that, like the office interior shown at the 1902 Salon in Paris, avoided 'superfluous ornamental forms and acrobatic accomplishments.' He was interested in the design of household goods. By 1910, his designs were being produced by Socard and Gallé. In 1904, he became a founding member of the Société des Artistes Décorateurs. His numerous commissions included the interior design and furnishings of a houseboat in 1919, and automobile designs.

▶ The Selmersheim brothers showed furnishings at the exhibition of the group L'Art dans Tout. They showed their work at Salons of the Société Nationale des Beaux-Arts, Société des Artistes Décorateurs, and the Salons d'Automne.

▶ Yvonne Brunhammer et al., *Art Nouveau Belgium, France*, Houston: Rice University, 1976. Alastair Duncan, *Art Nouveau and Art Déco Lighting*, New York: Simon and Schuster, 1978:87–88.

Selmersheim, Tony   (1871–1971)

▶ French architect and decorator; born Saint-Germain-en-Laye; brother of Pierre Selmersheim.

▶ He was initially in partnership with architect Charles Plumet. Tony and Pierre Selmersheim collaborated on furniture, furnishings, lighting, and the décors of various buildings. In *c*1905, he designed an important range of furniture for the French Embassy in Vienna, the organ gallery of the Church of the Sacré-Coeur in Paris, and a number of offices. He collaborated with his brother on the decoration and furniture for a first-class cabin on the 1935 oceanliner *Normandie*. Until 1935, he worked with L. Monteil and subsequently with his son André Selmersheim in their offices in the boulevard Saint-Marcel in Paris on a number of furniture designs in limited editions. Interested in mechanical objects, he invented a number of tools and some machinery used in his atelier.

▶ He showed his furniture ensembles from 1897, including at the 1900 Paris 'Exposition Universelle.' He won first prize in the 1912 competition for the office of the president of the municipal council of Paris.

▶ Alastair Duncan, *Art Nouveau and Art Déco Lighting*, New York: Simon and Schuster, 1978:87–88. Pierre Kjellberg, *Art Déco: les maîtres du Mobilier, le décor des Paquebots*, Paris: Amateur, 1986:169–70.

Semenzato, Remo   (1934–)

▶ Italian industrial designer; born Mira; active Milan.

▶ 1960–63 and 1967–69, Semenzato collaborated with architect and designer Angelo Mangiarotti and, 1965–67, with architect and designer Mario Bellini. Semenzato designed sound equipment and televisions sets, including the *TP252 CGE, TE355 CGE*, and *TX347 CGE* models produced by Sogetel. He was a member of ADI (Associazione per il Disegno Industriale).

▶ *ADI Annual 1976*, Milan: Associazione per il Disegno Industriale, 1976.

Semet, Marcellin (1894–)

▶ French bookbinder and gilder; active Paris.

▶ During World War I, Semet was apprenticed to René Chambolle. After the war, he worked in the workshop of Léon Gruel, where he met Georges Plumelle. 1925–55, partners Semet and Plumelle took over the firm Pinardon at 19 rue Guisarde in Paris. Their Modernist bindings included *A.O. Barnabooth, Le Siège de Jerusalem*, and *Les Fleurs du mal*. Plumelle continued working to 1980.

▶ Roger Devauchelle, *La Reliure en France de ses origines à nos jours*, Vol. 3, Paris 1961:204,206–07, plate XCII. John F. Fleming and Priscilla Juvelis, *The Book Beautiful and the Binding as Art*, New York, Vol. 1, 1983:113; Vol. 2, 1985:21,24,30. Alastair Duncan and Georges de Bartha, *Art Nouveau and Art Déco Bookbinding*, New York: Abrams, 1989:23,176–7,196–97.

Serini, Rocco (1939–)

▶ Italian designer; born Pavia; active Milan.

▶ Studied Politecnico di Milano to 1967.

▶ He designed furniture, furnishings, glassware, and lighting for clients including Driade, Germa, CBM, Costi, Fiarm, Vistosi, Bilumen, Almo, Valenti, Uvet, and Sintesis. He was a member of ADI (Associazione per il Disegno Industriale).

▶ *ADI Annual 1976*, Milan: Associazione per il Disegno Industriale, 1976.

Serré, Georges (1889–1956)

▶ French ceramicist.

▶ He was an apprentice at Manufacture de Sèvres to 1902 when he traveled to Saigon to study *grès* Kmer ceramics; 1920, set up his own studio in Sèvres, near the plant. He produced sculpture by his friends Dejean, Gimond, Niclausse and Comtesse. Encouraged by Émile Lenoble and Émile Decoeur, from 1922, Serré turned to heavy stoneware and *chamotté* clay. He engraved his pieces with geometrical motifs and simple designs sometimes highlighted with oxides and glazes.

▶ Showed his work at Geo, Rouard, Paris.

▶ Edgar Pelichet, *La Céramique Art Déco*, Lausanne: Grand-Pont, 1988.

Serrurier-Bovy, Gustave (1858–1910)

▶ Belgian architect and designer: born Liège.

▶ Studied architecture Academy of Fine Arts, Liège.

▶ Serrurier-Bovy was influenced by the Arts and Crafts movement and a follower of French architect Eugène-Emmanuel Viollet-le-Duc. During a visit to Britain in 1884, he was introduced to the work of William Morris and the philosophy of John Ruskin and studied the Arts and Crafts movement, becoming an admirer of British design, particularly that of C.F.A. Voysey and A.H. Mackmurdo. He abandoned his architectural practice to devote himself to designing and making furniture. In 1884, Serrurier-Bovy opened a shop in Liège to sell Japanese, Persian, and Indian artifacts in a concession acquired from Liberty of London, and, in 1886, opened a branch in Brussels. In a furniture enterprise in the rue de l'Université, he produced period and Modern American and British interiors and sold Oriental objects and textiles. In 1896, he organized 'L'Oeuvre Artistique' in Liège, the international exposition of decorative arts to which the Glasgow School contributed 110 exhibits. In 1899, he set up a large furniture factory at Liège with a shop in Paris named L'Art dans l'Habitation. A leading Belgian designer, he developed a style of his own showing inspiration from Japanese forms. In his work he typically used the arched truss.

▶ His furnished study interior was installed at the 1894 first event of the Salon de la Libre Esthétique, a worker's house at its 1895 event, and work subsequently included in the 1896 London Arts and Crafts exhibition and, 1896–1903, in the Salons du Champ de Mars of the Société Nationale des Beaux-Arts. He organized and designed the hall that housed the imports sections of the Tervueren colonial section of the 1897 Brussels 'Exposition Internationale.' He participated in the 1900 Paris 'Exposition Universelle' (with architect René Dulong for the Pavillon Bleu) and the 1904 St. Louis 'Louisiana Purchase Exhibition.' He showed his simple and ingeniously designed worker's home in 1905 and created display stands for the 1904, 1905, and 1906 Paris Salons de l'Automobile. He installed his own pavilion at the 1910 Brussels 'Exposition Internationale.'

▶ Jacques-Grégoire Watelet, *Gustave Serrurier-Bovy, architecte et décorateur 1858–1910*, Brussels, Palais des Academies, 1974. Yvonne Brunhammer et al., *Art Nouveau Belgium, France*, Houston: Rice University, 1976. Jessica Rutherford, *Art Nouveau, Art Deco and the Thirties: The Furniture Collections at Brighton Museum*, Brighton: The Royal Pavilion, Art Gallery and Museums, 1983:12.

Sert, Josep Lluís (1902–83)

▶ Spanish architect; born Barcelona.

▶ Studied Escuela Superior de Arquitectura, Barcelona.

▶ 1929–31, he worked in the architecture office of Le Corbusier and Pierre Jeanneret in Paris. 1929–37, he worked in his own architecture office in Barcelona. In 1930, he and Sixt Yllescas founded the GATCPAC group in Barcelona. He designed the Spanish pavilion in the International Style at the 1937 Paris 'Exposition Internationale des Arts et Techniques dans la Vie Moderne.' 1937–39, he was active in Paris. In 1939, he settled in the USA. 1947–56, he was president of CIAM (Congrès Internationaux d'Architecture Moderne). 1944–45, he was professor of Urban Planning at Yale University. 1952–69, he was dean of the Graduate School of Design at Harvard University.

▶ His buildings included the Spanish pavilion at the 1937 Paris Exposition, 1959–64 Fondation Maeght in Saint-Paul-de-Vence, and 1972–75 Fundación Joan Miró in Barcelona.

▶ Maria Llusia Borrás, *Sert: Mediterranean Architecture*, Boston, 1975.

Sert, Mme. J.M.

▶ Designer; wife of painter José Maria Sert (1876–1945).

▶ In the mid-1920s, she designed miniature artificial trees in various combinations of coral, crystal, jade, and cornelian beads on rock-crystal or stone bases, emulating Bonsai tree forms.

▶ She showed her work in *c*1928 at the Bibliothèque Nationale in Paris.

Sessano, Aldo (1931–)

▶ Italian industrial designer; born and active Turin.

▶ Sessano began his professional career in 1971. He designed tabletop objects, sound equipment, film projectors, and automobile bodies for clients including Gruppo Seimart, Bosca, Bencini, and Seat. He was a member of ADI (Associazione per il Disegno Industriale).

▶ *ADI Annual 1976*, Milan: Associazione per il Disegno Industriale, 1976.

Sette, Gruppo

See **Gruppo Sette**

Settepassi

▶ Italian jewelry firm; located Florence.

▶ The Settepassi firm was established in 1850 in a shop on the Ponte Vecchio in Florence. Leopoldo and Cesare Settepassi furnished jewelry to the royal houses of Europe, particularly those of Italy, Greece, and Romania. Settepassi was best known as a specialist in pearls, including its celebrated two-strand necklace for the Ford family of the USA. In 1961, Guido Settepassi took over the firm of friend Raffaele Faraone on the via Montenapoleone in Milan. His son Cesare Settepassi assumed management of the firm, moved in 1985 to the via Tornabuoni in Florence.

▶ Melissa Gabardi, *Les Bijoux des Années 50*, Paris: Amateur, 1987.

Sèvres, Manufacture Nationale de

▶ French ceramics manufactory.

▶ The Vincennes royal porcelain factory moved in 1756 to Sèvres, closer to the royal court at Versailles. By 1758, the workshops employed more than 250 people and, in 1759, were taken over by King Louis XV's administrators. Its first duties were to provide crockery and china pieces for the royal household. Lauth and Vogt developed new and diverse porcelain applications that first appeared in 1880 and were shown at the 1884 exhibition of the Union Centrale des Arts Décoratifs. The new medium allowed for the use of almost every color nuance with certain motifs directly glazed with gold highlights. The factory was known for its range of blue colors, including *céleste, poudré, frotté, soufflé*, and lapis lazuli, as well as yellow and turquoise, and, transcending its original aim of imitating Meissen porcelain, issued gem-like effects and *rocaille* flowers set on metal stems. At the end of the 19th century, the Manufacture de Sèvres underwent structural changes, being divided into artistic and technical departments. Alexandre Sandier was the director of the artistic department. He had available to him four types of materials: soft-paste porcelain, stoneware, hard-paste porcelain, and Sèvres pâte nouvelle (having a lower firing temperature than hard-paste porcelain). Sandier perfected crystalline glazes (known before 1900 but always considered an unfortunate accident.) In 1900, Sèvres showed Sandier glazes. 1903–04, the factory commissioned new forms from Hector Guimard to be completely covered in crystalline glazes. Sandier made unglazed porcelain fashionable with models by Agathon Léonard inspired by Loïe Fuller at the 1900 Paris 'Exposition Universelle.' The spherical Lanvin perfume flacon by Rateau was imprinted with Paul Iribe's gold image of Jeanne Lanvin and her daughter, dressed for a ball. Only from the 1960s did the Sèvres management turn to contemporary designers. In the 1980s, Sèvres extended its business to include private retailers and opened a showroom in Paris. Having become known primarily for its staid historicist patterns, in 1983, an experimental workshop for research in design was organized to include French and foreign artists. Its later products included Bořek Šípek pieces in 1990, Bérnard Guillot's 1989 *Elina* frieze pattern, Christian Genouciat's 1983 trompe-l'oeil box, Serge Poliakoff's 1968 plate, Adrian Saxe's 1984 eccentric lamp, Viola Fry's 1987 figurines, and Garouste et Bonetti's cabinet in wood and Sèvres porcelain. The firm is a member of the Comité Colbert.

▶ New porcelain applications of 1880 were shown at the 1884 exhibition of the Union Centrale des Arts Décoratifs at the Palais de l'Industrie in Paris. Alexandre Sandier's new floral forms were shown at the 1900 Paris 'Exposition Universelle.' The firm's Modern pieces under Lechevalier-Chevignard's direction were shown at the 1925 Paris 'Exposition Internationale des Arts Décoratifs et Industriels Modernes,' including the introduction of a new high-temperature glass applicable to the production of glass lamp shades.

▶ Yvonne Brunhammer et al., *Art Nouveau Belgium, France*, Houston: Rice University, 1976. Cat., *Decorative Arts 1925 Style*, New York: Didier Aaron, 1979. *Les Carnets du Design*, Paris: Mad-Cap Productions et APCI, 1986:13. Françoise Kostolany, 'Everlasting Porcelain: Its Bountiful Past and Dynamic Present,' and Colette Gouvion, 'Porcelain: Today's Creations,' both in *Vogue Décoration*, No. 26, June/July 1990:169,176–77.

Seymour, Richard (1953–)

▶ British designer.

▶ Studied Central School of Arts and Crafts and Royal College of Art, London.

▶ He was creative director for an advertising agency and freelance graphic designer for various advertising and product development accounts. In 1983, he and Dick Powell established the design consultancy Seymour-Powell in London. They were best known for their styling of the Norton 1987 police/military *Commander*

and later *P55 Sport* motorcycles, and designed a successful line of Tefal domestic products, the first being the 1987 *Freeline* cordless electric jug-kettle. They also did work for Yamaha.

▶ Jeremy Myerson and Sylvia Katz, *Conran Design Guides: Tableware*, London: Conran Octopus, 1990:78.

Sezession

See Münchner Sezession and Wiener Sezession

Sghedoni, Alessandro (1947–)

▶ Italian architect and designer; born Venice; active Treviso.

▶ Studied architecture.

▶ Sghedoni began his professional career in 1973. His clients included Archiutti Tullio in 1973, Miniforms in 1974, and Nike in 1975. He was a member of ADI (Associazione per il Disegno Industriale).

▶ *ADI Annual 1976*, Milan: Associazione per il Disegno Industriale, 1976.

Sgubbi, Chrissie (1957–)

▶ British wallpaper and textile designer; born Caerphilly.

▶ Studied wallpaper design, Bournemouth College.

▶ She designed and produced hand-tufted rugs for various clients, including the British Airports Authority. Her 1986 *Ribbons* rug was produced by Tai-Ping.

▶ Albrecht Bangert and Karl Michael Armer, *80s Style: Designs of the Decade*, New York: Abbeville, 1990:180,235.

shagreen

▶ Fish skin used as a veneer to cover furniture and accessories.

▶ Also known as *galuchat* and sharkskin, shagreen is the skin on the belly of the dogfish. As a generic term, it is used to mean untanned animal hides made with pebble-textured surfaces. It was first made in the 17th century by Turkish and Persian herdsmen. *Galuchat* is named after the Parisian craftsman active during the reign of Louis XIV who made sheaths and boxes. British artisan John Paul Cooper specialized in unusual materials, especially shagreen, which he began using in 1903. This was some time before other Arts and Crafts practitioners began using the material and before it became popular in *c*1910, when, after a 200-year hiatus, it was used by Clément Mère on toiletry boxes, sewing cases, and other small objects at the Paris Salons. By the 1920s Jacques-Émile Ruhlmann, Clément Rousseau, André Groult, Dominique, and other French designers used shagreen extensively in combination with exotic woods. Jean-Michel Frank used shagreen to cover whole furniture pieces. When used on furniture, the skin is soaked in a chlorine solution to bleach it, followed by scrubbing with a wire brush and a pumice stone to remove imperfections. The skin is usually stained green by a copper-acetate solution but can be made pink, blue, or gray. Its use is most effective on small objects, like those produced by Tiffany, Asprey, and Dunhill in the 1920s and 1930s. Synthetic shagreen is available, though it is more expensive and less desirable than the real product.

▶ Alastair Duncan, 'Skin-Deep Beauty,' *Elle Decor*, May 1990:40.

Shaker furniture

▶ Furniture produced by Shaker religious communities in the USA.

▶ Originating in England in 1747, the United Society of Believers in Christ's Second Appearance was a Christian sect whose ceremonies of worship included communal dancing, earning them the nicknames 'holy rollers,' 'Shaking Quakers', or simply 'Shakers.' To escape religious persecution, a group led by Mother Ann Lee settled in the USA, establishing their first community in 1787 in New Lebanon, New York. Groups of celibate 'brothers' and 'sisters' spread to Maine, New Hampshire, Massachusetts, Rhode Island, Connecticut, New York, Ohio, Indiana, and Kentucky. New members brought their own belongings, including furniture. The earliest documented Shaker-made furniture is a case of drawers of 1806, although furniture making almost certainly took place earlier. A pine case of drawers, inscribed 'Made by A.B. 1817,' may have been produced by Anthony Brewster (1794–1838). Many of the furniture makers in the community had been trained in cabinet-making before joining the group and were influenced by contemporary styles. The Shaker style, developed from English country and farmhouse models, is known for its simplicity and lack of ornamentation, with built-in cabinets, long trestle tables, wide overhanging table tops, and rocking chairs with thin rockers. Side chairs, when not in use, were hung on pegs attached to wall railings high above the floor, facilitating its cleaning. Shaker cabinetmaker Orren N. Haskins asked in 1887, 'Why patronize the out side [sic] work or gugaws in our manufacture, when they will say we have enough of them abroad? We want a good plain substantial Shaker article, yea, one that bears credit to our profession & tells who and what we are, true and honest before the world, without hypocrisy or any false covering.' Ideas, designs, and furniture pieces were transferred from community to community, and apprentices were trained by masters. Tireless improvers of their material culture, their motto 'hands to work and hearts to God,' their numerous inventions included the circular metal saw, automatic clothes-washing machine, and the apple corer. Industrialization in the outside world, however, meant that the Shakers, who from an early date had made furniture commercially, could no longer produce goods that were competitive in price with machine-made products. The men were enticed into well-paid jobs outside the communities. With a lack of new members, communities began to close in the late 19th and early 20th centuries. When the Mount Lebanon North Family community, the last of the groups, was closed in 1947, Sister Jennie Wells commented, 'Most of our visitors these days are antique collectors, and all they're interested in is buying up what little fine old handmade Shaker furniture we have left. Why, those people would grab the chairs right out from under us if we'd let them. Our furniture is very fashionable all of a sudden, you know ... We're always being told how beautiful our things are. I don't say they aren't but that isn't what they were meant to be ... All our furniture was ever meant to be was strong, light, and, above all, practical.'

▶ Jerry V. Grant and Douglas R. Allen, *Shaker Furniture Makers*, Hanover and London: University Press of New England, 1989. Berton Roueche, 'A Small Family of Seven,' *The New Yorker*, Vol. 23, Aug. 1947:46–57.

Shcekotikhina-Pototskaia, Aleksandra Vasil'evna
(1892–1967)
▶ Russian designer of ceramics, book illustrations, embroidery and traditional crafts; wife of Ivan Bilibin, artist and book illustrator.
▶ Studied Society for the Encouragement of the Arts, St Petersburg, under Nikolai Roerich and Ivan Bilibin.
▶ Shcekotikhina-Pototskaia designed costumes for the theater including for Sergei Diaghilev and Igor Stravinsky; saw Diaghilev's ballet *Russian Seasons* in Paris in 1913; this heightened her enthusiasm for Russian traditional and folk styles. Influenced by Russian ikon art, she disregarded perpective in her porcelain pieces at the State Porcelain Factory, St Petersburg, 1918–23; with her husband and son Mstislav, settled in Alexandria in 1925; visited 1925 Paris Exposition; lived in Paris producing porcelains for Sèvres and firms in Limoges, 1925–36; returned to the Soviet Union in 1936; 1936–53, took up position as artist again at State Porcelain Factory, Leningrad.
▶ Nina Lobanov-Rostovsky, *Revolutionary Ceramics*, London: Studio Vista, 1990. Ian Wardropper et al., *News from a Radiant Future: Soviet Porcelain*, Chicago: Art Institute, 1992.

Shelley Potteries
▶ British ceramics manufacturer; located Longton.
▶ Walter Slater was artistic director at Wileman of Foley Potteries and China Works, owned by the Shelley family, who, in 1925, changed the firm's name to Shelley Potteries. In 1928, Eric Slater succeeded his father as artistic director; his 1935 *Vogue* ceramics dinner set, with its colorful geometric trim on triangular and square silhouettes, and circular-patterned 1935 *Regent* shape were

representative of Shelley's work of the time. In 1966, Allied English Potteries took over Shelley Potteries.
▶ Cat., *Thirties: British art and design before the war*, London: Arts Council of Great Britain, Hayward Gallery, 1979:96,153, 300. *Shelley Potteries*, London: Geffrye Musuem, 1980.

Shérif
See **Chérif**

Sheringham, George   (1884–1937)
▶ British interior and textile designer and decorative painter.
▶ Studied painting, Slade School of Fine Arts and in Paris.
▶ Originally a painter, he was designing fans and silk panels by 1911. He was best known as a theater designer, particularly for his work at the Lyric Theatre in Hammersmith, London, where he designed sets and costumes; produced numerous watercolor designs for fans. He was a successful architectural decorator; Claridges ballroom of 1931 is an example of his work. He was a carpet and textile designer for John Crossley and Seftons, and designed posters, advertising, and book illustrations.
▶ Fiona MacCarthy and Patrick Nuttgens, *An Eye for Industry*, London: Lund Humphries with Royal Society for Arts, 1986. Valerie Mendes, *The Victoria & Albert Museum's Textile Collection, British Textiles from 1900 to 1937*, London: Victoria and Albert Museum, 1992.

Shibasaki, Shintaro   (1946–)
▶ Japanese glass designer.
▶ Studied crafts and industrial design, Musashino Art University, Tokyo, to 1970.
▶ He began working for Kagami Crystal Glass Works, Tokyo, in 1970, becoming chief designer.
▶ Works included in the 1979 three-person exhibition at Matsuyama Crafts Gallery, Tokyo; 1985 'World Glass Now '85,' Hokkaido Museum of Modern Art, Tokyo; 1986 'Japanese Glass–300 years,' Suntory Museum of Art, Tokyo; 1987 and 1990 'Glass in Japan,' Tokyo; and 1991 (V) Triennale of the Japan Glass Art Crafts Association, Heller Gallery, New York. Won Art Scholarship Association Prize of 1982 (XVII) 'Kanagawa Prefectural Exhibition of Fine Arts,' Japan, and Special Achievement Prize of 1983 (XVIII) 'Kanagawa Prefectural Exhibition of Fine Arts.'
▶ Cat., *Glass Japan*, New York: Heller Gallery and Japan Glass Art Crafts Association, 1991: No. 32.

Shibuya, Ryoji   (1956–)
▶ Japanese glass designer.
▶ Studied sculpture, Tama Art University, Tokyo, to 1981; Tokyo Glass Crafts Institute to 1984; and Gerrit Rietveld Akademie, Amsterdam, to 1986.
▶ He set up an independent studio in 1989.
▶ In 1989, his solo exhibition was mounted in Tokyo. His work was included in 1987 'The Art of Contemporary Japanese Studio Glass,' Heller Gallery, New York; 1988 'International Exhibition of Glass Craft,' Industrial Gallery of Ishikawa Prefecture, Kanazawa; 1988 'Arte en Vidro,' São Paulo Art Museum; 1990 'Glass '90 in Japan,' Tokyo; and 1991 (V) Triennale of the Japan Glass Art Crafts Association, Heller Gallery, New York. Included in 1985–87 'Corning Glass Review,' *Neues Glas* magazine.
▶ Cat., *Glass Japan*, New York: Heller Gallery and Japan Glass Art Crafts Association, 1991: No. 33.

Shiner, Cyril James   (1908–)
▶ British craftsperson and teacher; active Birmingham.
▶ Trained under Bernard Cuzner in Birmingham and studied Royal College of Art, London.
▶ He was a liveryman of The Worshipful Company of Goldsmiths, where he rendered a number of formal works, including maces, awards of honor, and church plate. He produced domestic wares, including boxes and small utilitarian objects. Working as a freelance designer and teaching in Birmingham in the 1930s, his hollow-ware designs were produced by Wakely and Wheeler in London.

▶ A 1932 silver fruit bowl and 1935 silver dressing-table set were included in the 1979–80 'Thirties' exhibition at the Hayward Gallery in London.

▶ Annelies Krekel-Aalberse, *Art Nouveau and Art Déco Silver*, New York: Abrams, 1989:35,259. Cat., *Thirties: British art and design before the war*, London: Arts Council of Great Britain, Hayward Gallery, 1979:140,300.

Shirahata, Akira (1948–)

▶ Japanese glass designer.

▶ He began working for Hoya Crystal in Tokyo in 1965.

▶ His work was included in 1977–78 'Traditional Art Craft Musashino Show'; 1983 and 1985 'All Japan Traditional Art Craft Nominated Producers Show,' Tokyo; 1985 'New Glass in Japan,' Badisches Landesmuseum, Karlsruhe; 1985 'World Glass Now '85,' Hokkaido Museum of Modern Art, Sapporo; 1985 'Seibu Art Craft Grand Show,' Tokyo; 1986 'Japan Traditional Crafts,' Mitsukoshi Gallery, Tokyo; 1987 and 1900 'Glass in Japan,' Tokyo; and 1991 (V) Triennale of the Japan Glass Art Crafts Association, Heller Gallery, New York.

▶ Cat., *Glass Japan*, New York: Heller Gallery and Japan Glass Art Crafts Association, 1991: No. 34.

Shire, Peter (1947–)

▶ American designer; active Los Angeles.

▶ Ettore Sottsass invited Shire in 1981 to participate in the Memphis project, for which he designed eccentric, geometrically oriented furniture in Pop Art colors and kinetic shapes. Independently, in 1989, he designed a 63-piece collection of furniture and furnishings made in Italy. Prior to this date, except for Memphis, his pieces were one-offs. His glassware, produced at Mauro Albarelli's Vistosi firm, transformed Murano glass into lively shapes verging on sculpture. He was known for his unusual ceramic teapots. His designs for Memphis included the 1981 *Brazil* table, 1982 *Peninsula* table, 1982 *Anchorage* silver and lacquer teapot, 1983 *Hollywood* side table, 1985 *Cahuenga* floor lamp, 1985 *Laurel* table lamp, 1986 *Big Sur* sofa, and 1987 *Peter* sideboard. His vividly multicolored 1982 *Bel Air* upholstered armchair was widely published as being representative of the Memphis style.

▶ Julie V. Iovine, *Metropolitan Home*, August 1989:33. Auction cat., Memphis: *La Collection Karl Lagerfeld,* Monaco: Sotheby's, 13 Oct. 1991. *Tempest in a Teapot: The Ceramic Art of Peter Shire*, New York: Rizzoli, 1991.

Shirk, Helen (1942–)

▶ American metalworker, born Buffalo, New York.

▶ Studied Indiana University to 1969.

▶ She was known for her metal bowls and vessels and was a professor of art at San Diego State University.

▶ Albrecht Bangert and Karl Michael Armer, *80s Style: Designs of the Decade*, New York: Abbeville, 1990:235.

Shiu-Kay, Kan (1949–)

▶ Hong Kong lighting designer.

▶ Studied architecture, Central London Polytechnic and Architectural Association, London.

▶ He worked for architects Foster Associates and the Fiorucci retail chain. In the mid-1970s, he set up his own lighting design firm SKK Lighting; its first product was the *Kite Light*. The innovative *Mobile Robotic Light*, developed 1983–88, had two remote-controlled spotlights that could be moved along parallel wires hung from the ceiling.

Shop of the Crafters, The

▶ American store and manufacturers; located Cincinnati, Ohio.

▶ The Shop of the Crafters in Cincinnati was founded in 1904 by businessman and philanthropist Oscar Onken (1858–1948). The shop sold an eclectic selection of goods, initially advertising itself as 'Makers of Arts and Crafts Furniture, Hall Clocks, Shaving Stands, Cellarettes, Smokers' Cabinets and Mission Chairs.' By 1906, its inventory was exclusively Mission and Arts and Crafts

furniture in various stained finishes of its own invention, with inlays, applied carving, titles, painted designs, and hardware.

▶ Cat., Anne Yaffe Phillips, *From Architecture to Object*, New York: Hirschl and Adler, 1989:80.

Shreve

▶ American silversmiths and retail shop, located San Francisco.

▶ Founded in 1852, the firm produced its first silver flatware in 1904; it also sold silverware made by Gorham.

▶ Annelies Krekel-Aalberse, *Art Nouveau and Art Déco Silver*, New York: Abrams, 1989:100,104,259.

Siard, Marcello (1939–)

▶ Italian designer; born Trieste; active Padua.

▶ His plastic furniture was produced by Kartell. In 1970, he taught at the Instituto d'Arte in Trieste. His *Ring* table range, department store shelving, and plastic seating were produced by Longato Arredamenti. He was a member of ADI (Associazione per il Disegno Industriale).

▶ He participated in the 1962 (I) 'International Furniture Design Competition' with a project for public furniture. He won first prize in the 1962 national competition 'Domus Inox.' He won the first prize in the 1964 national furniture competition at the Trieste Fair.

▶ *ADI Annual 1976*, Milan: Associazione per il Disegno Industriale, 1976.

Sicard, Jacques (1865–1923)

▶ French ceramicist; active Golfe-Juan, Amiens, and Zanesville, Ohio.

▶ Sicard was associated with potter Clément Massier in Golfe-Juan, near Cannes, where he learned the *reflets métalliques* process. He was hired in 1901 by Weller Pottery, encouraged by the popularity of Tiffany's 'favrile' glass and the iridescent pottery of Europe. He and French assistant Henri Gellie secretly experimented with metallic lusters that were later marketed as thrown and molded *Sicardo Ware* by Weller and sold at Tiffany in 1903. In 1907, when they returned to France, iridescent pottery production was discontinued. Until 1914, Sicard worked in his own pottery in Amiens.

▶ *Sicardo Ware* was shown on the Weller stand at the 1902 St. Louis 'Louisiana Purchase Exposition.' His work was included in the 1972 'The Arts and Crafts Movement in America, 1876–1916' exhibition, Princeton University Art Museum.

▶ Cat., Robert Judson Clark (ed.), *The Arts and Crafts Movement in America, 1876–1916*, Princeton: Princeton University Press, 1976. Diane Chalmers Johnson, *American Art Nouveau*, New York: Abrams, 1979:123, No. 165. *American Art Pottery*, New York: Cooper-Hewitt Museum, 1987:106.

Siècle

▶ French housewares firm; located Paris.

▶ Siècle was established in 1983 by Philippe Chupin (1954–) and his wife Marisa Osorio Farinha. The firm produced domestic goods in Classical and ancient styles.

▶ *Les Carnets du Design*, Paris: Mad-Cap Productions et APCI, 1986:63.

Siegel, Gustav (1880–1970)

▶ Austrian furniture and graphic designer.

▶ Studied cabinetmaking in Vienna, and, from 1897, Kunstgewerbeschule, Vienna.

▶ He was appointed by Felix Kohn, president of J. and J. Kohn, as head of its design department in 1899. He and Otto Wagner were responsible for Kohn's production of early Art Nouveau furniture models. Siegel executed some of Kohn's graphic design, including advertisements appearing in the 1904 and 1908 Vienna Sezession exhibition catalogs. Certain well-known Kohn pieces attributed to others, including Josef Hoffmann, may have been designed by Siegel, particularly the tub chair *728/F*, shell chair *728* used in Hoffmann's Cabaret Fledermaus and settee *728/C*.

His chair *415/F*, settee *415/2*, and plant stand *1015* use the same wooden ball element as the Cabaret Fledermaus furniture.
▶ His designs were shown by Kohn at the 1900 Paris 'Exposition Universelle.'
▶ Graham Day, 'The Development of the Bent-Wood Furniture Industry, 1869–1914,' in Derek E. Ostergard (ed.), *Bent Wood and Metal Furniture 1850–1946*, New York: The American Federation of Arts, 1987.

Siegel, Robert
▶ American architect; active New York.
▶ Siegel joined the architecture partnership of Charles Gwathmey and Richard Henderson in 1970. In 1971, Siegel and Gwathmey established their own practice New York. Their furniture designs were produced by Knoll. From the mid-1980s, the team designed porcelain and silverwares for Swid Powell; designed the 1992 addition to the Guggenheim Museum, New York.
▶ By 1990, the partnership won over 50 design awards and received the 1982 Architecture Firm Award from the American Institute of Architects and 1981 gold medal from the New York American Institute of Architecture.
▶ Stanley Abercrombie: *Gwathmey Siegel*, New York, 1981. Christine Pittel, 'The Hand of Geometry,' *Elle Decor*, Mar. 1991:44–55.
▶ See Gwathmey, Charles

Siégel, Victor-Napoléon   (1870–1958)
▶ Canadian businessman; active Paris.
▶ Siégel, who became known as the 'mannequin king,' established the firm with Fred Stockman that became known as Siégel et Stockman. In the mid-1920s, René Herbst, artistic advisor at Siégel, had an appreciable influence on the firm's work. Lucie Holt Le Son, an American working in Paris, produced mannequin sculptures and panels for the firm in 1927. Other designers included Desmeures. Musician, sculptor, and photographer André Vigneau was artistic director. Its innovations included 'cerolaque' (a wax and lacquer substance) and felt composition used for the construction of mannequins. Its models included likenesses of men, women, and children in realistic and stylized interpretations, as well as abstract sculptural forms and purely functional display racks. From 1927, mannequins in glass and wood were produced. By this date, Siégel owned 67 factories with branch offices in New York, Amsterdam, Copenhagen, Sydney, Stockholm, and Madrid, and a vast workshop operated in Saint-Ouen. In 1927, *Vogue* magazine and its stylists, including Peter Woodruff, designed mannequins for Siégel. The firm is active today.
▶ It showed at the annual Salons of the Société des Artistes Décorateurs and events of the Salon d'Automne. On the Pont Alexandre-III, its pavilion at the 1925 Paris 'Exposition Internationale des Arts Décoratifs et Industriels Modernes' designed by Herbst, included the work of Vigneau, Georges Polez, Léon Leyritz, Fernand Labathe, Camille Liausu, Francis Thomas, Bross, Jean Gougeon, and Herbst himself, and won a first prize.
▶ Alastair Duncan, *Art Nouveau and Art Déco Lighting*, New York: Simon and Schuster, 1978:172. Nicole Parrot, *Mannequins*, Paris: Colona, 1981; London: Academy, 1982.

Sierakowski, Piotr   (1957–)
▶ Polish furniture and lighting designer; born Warsaw.
▶ Studied industrial design, La Cambre National School of Architecture and the Visual Arts, Brussels.
▶ Best known for his lighting, he designed the *Copernicus* sconce, 1986 *Nautilus* floor light, and numerous lighting fixtures and, with Martine Bedin, a collection of tabletop accessories for Koch + Lowy; in 1992 with Bedin and Mathilde Brétillot, opened a small production firm, Manufacture Familiale, near Bordeaux.
▶ Albrecht Bangert and Karl Michael Armer, *80s Style: Designs of the Decade*, New York: Abbeville, 1990:105,236.

Siesbye, Alev Ebüzziya   (1938–)
▶ Turkish ceramicist and glass and metal ware designer; born Istanbul; active Copenhagen and Paris.

▶ 1956–58, studied sculpture, School of Fine Arts, Istanbul, and studied at Füreya'a Ceramic Workshop, Istanbul.
▶ 1958–60, was a production worker at Dümler & Breiden, Höhr-Grenzhausen; 1960–62, worked in Eczacebasi Ceramic Factory in Istanbul and, 1963–68, at Royal Copenhagen porcelain manufactory. He set up his own studio in Copenhagen in 1969, and subsequently in Paris with freelance clients including Rosenthal (from 1975). He was known for his pure forms and rigorously rendered matt enamel surfaces in blues and violets. His work combined Danish forms, the luminous colors of Iznik ceramics, and Middle Eastern textiles.
▶ His work was shown at the Maison du Danemark, Paris, in 1982, at FIAC in 1988, and included in the 1989 'L'Europe des Céramistes' in Auxerre.
▶ Jennifer Hawkins Opie, *Scandinavia: Ceramics and Glass in the Twentieth Century*, New York: Rizzoli, 1989. Cat., *Collection Fina Gomez: 30 ans de céramique contemporaine*, Paris: Musée des Arts Décoratifs, 1991:120.

Siess und Springer
▶ Austrian gold and jewelry firm; located Vienna.
▶ In 1858, Siess und Springer produced jewelry and gold pieces. 1864–65, the firm Josef Siess was located at 34 Mariahilferstrasse, Vienna, and, 1868–1922, at 7 Luftbadgasse, Vienna. With the appointment of Franz Schrutek as head of the workshop in c1900, the firm began producing mass goods as well as individual items and pieces for R. Köchert, Hügler, and Heldwein. Some of its designs were provided by Josef Maria Olbrich, Schrutek, and others. 1908–22, Carl Siess was owner of the firm.
▶ The firm was awarded the progress medal at the 'Welt-Ausstellung 1873 in Wien.'
▶ Deanna F. Cera (ed.), *Jewels of Fantasy: Costume Jewelry of the 20th Century*, New York: Abrams, 1992:104.

Siimes, Aune   (1909–64)
▶ Finnish ceramicist.
▶ Studied Taideteollinen Korkeakoulu, Helsinki, to 1932.
▶ From 1932–64, she worked for Arabia in Helsinki on stoneware and porcelain. Her pieces were known for their delicacy and egg-shell thinness.
▶ She received a silver medal at the 1937 Paris 'Exposition Internationale des Arts et Techniques dans le Vie Moderne' and a gold medal at the 1951 (IX) and silver medal at the 1954 (X) Triennali di Milano. Her work was shown in the 1954–57 USA 'Design in Scandinavia' traveling exhibition, 1955 'H 55' exhibition in Hälsingborg, 1956–57 West Germany 'Finnish Exhibition,' and 1961 'Finlandia' exhibition in Zürich, Amsterdam, and London.
▶ Cat., David Revere McFadden (ed.), *Scandinavian Modern Design 1880–1980*, New York: Abrams, 1982:271, No. 183. Jennifer Hawkins Opie, *Scandinavia: Ceramics and Glass in the Twentieth Century*, New York: Rizzoli, 1989.

Sika, Jutta   (1877–1964)
▶ Austrian ceramicist and glassware designer; born Linz.
▶ Studied under Koloman Moser.
▶ Her porcelain designs were produced by Wiener Porzellan-Manufaktur Josef Böck (with flower decoration by Antoinette Krasnik) in c1901. She designed glassware for E. Bakalovits.
▶ Günther Feuerstien, *Vienna–Present and Past: Arts and Crafts–Applied Art–Design*, Vienna: Jugend und Volk, 1976:35,81. Cat., *Women in Design*, Stuttgart: Design Center, 1989:42–43.

Silver, Arthur   (1853–96)
▶ British designer and silversmith; born Reading; active London; father of Reginald and Harry Silver.
▶ He was apprenticed to H.W. Batley in London in 1872. In 1880, Silver set up his own studio in London. He designed and produced wallpaper, textiles, carpets, and linoleum, and was commissioned by Liberty to provide wallpaper, chintz, and cretonne designs. Other customers included G.P. and J. Baker, Arthur Sanderson, and John Line, into the 1960s.

► Mark Turner and Lesley Hoskins, *Silver Studio of Design: A Design and Source Book for Home Decoration*, London: Webb and Bower, 1988. Alastair Duncan, *Art Nouveau and Art Déco Lighting*, New York: Simon and Schuster, 1978:68.

Silver, Reginald (aka Rex Silver 1879–1964) and Harry Silver (1882–1922)
► British designers and silversmiths; active London; sons of Arthur Silver.
► The Silver Studio was founded in 1880 by Arthur Silver, father of Rex and Harry Silver. In 1896, Harry Napper took over the management of the firm, leaving in 1898 to set up his own business. From 1898, J.R. Houghton managed the studio. Napper and Houghton had sold Silver's wares to American and European manufacturers, including Bergerot, Dupont, Dumas, Florquin, Gros Roman, Zuber, Vanoutryve, Parison, Leborgne, Macy's, and Marshall Field. From 1901, the firm was managed by Rex Silver, who became an important designer of textiles, silver, and pewter for Liberty. The brothers were partners until 1916. In 1899, Rex Silver was one of the first London designers (with Bernard Cuzner and Jessie M. King) to become a member of Liberty's design stable for its *Cymric* range, which he produced until 1910. Harry Silver designed various other silverwares for Liberty. Archibald Knox joined Rex Silver, whose bowls, candlesticks, and silver clocks were very similar to Knox's work. The American market became important in the 1920s. Herbert Crofts worked at the studio; its designers included Frank Price and Lewis Jones, and outside designer H.C. Bareham worked for the studio until it was dissolved in 1963. Designers of the 1930s included John Churton, Edward Bawden, Clifford and Rosemary Ellis, Lucienne Day, John Aldridge, Roger Nicholson, Lawrence Scarfe, and John Line. 1880–1940, no collection was more representative of current middle-of-the-road taste.
► Mark Turner and Lesley Hoskins, *Silver Studio of Design: A Design and Source Book for Home Decoration*, London: Webb and Bower, 1988. Annelies Krekel-Aalberse, *Art Nouveau and Art Déco Silver*, New York: Abrams, 1989:32,259. Alastair Duncan, *Art Nouveau and Art Déco Lighting*, New York: Simon and Schuster, 1978:68. Cat., *Liberty's 1875–1975*, London: Victoria and Albert Museum, 1975.

Simberg-Ehrström, Uhra-Beata (1914–79)
► Finnish textile designer.
► Studied Taideteollinen Korkeakoulu, Helsinki.
► From 1935, she designed rugs for the Friends of Finnish Handicraft. From 1938, she was an industrial designer for Inhemsk U11 (Native Woollens) and, from 1958, for Finlayson-Forssa. 1950–58, she was an artist consultant to Norna Domestic Crafts.
► She received a diploma at the 1937 Paris 'Exposition Internationale des Arts et Techniques dans la Vie Moderne' and awards at the 1954 (X) (diploma of honor), 1957 (XI) (grand prize), and 1960 (XII) (gold medal) Triennali di Milano. Her work was shown at the 1956–57 USA 'Design in Scandinavia' traveling exhibition, 1955 'H 55' exhibition in Hälsingborg, 1961 'Finlandia' exhibition in Zürich, Amsterdam, and London.
► Cat., David Revere McFadden (ed.), *Scandinavian Modern Design 1880–1980*, New York: Abrams, 1982:271, No. 201.

Simeon, Margaret
► British textile designer.
► Studied Chelsea School of Art and Royal College of Art, London.
► She was a teacher of textile printing at the Royal College of Art and a freelance designer of dress and furnishings textiles. Her clients included Allan Walton Textiles, Edinburgh Weavers, Campbell Fabrics, and Fortnum and Mason.
► Cat., *Thirties: British art and design before the war*, London: Arts Council of Great Britain, Hayward Gallery, 1979:91,126, 300.

Simon, Scot (1954–)
► American painter and designer; active San Franciso and New York.
► 1974, studied painting, Carnegie-Mellon University, Pittsburgh, and, 1976, San Francisco Art Institute.
► He painted in San Francisco and New York until 1977, when he began designing jewelry and belts in New York for Accessocraft and independently. He executed embossed wallpaper designs and some fabrics. From 1980, he designed tablewares and table linens for Mikasa and for himself as agent. He began rendering textile designs and wallcoverings, which he pursued exclusively later.
► Cat., Kathryn B. Hiesinger and George H. Marcus III (eds.), *Design Since 1945*, Philadelphia: Philadelphia Museum of Art, 1983:230,VII–55. 'Scot Simon,' *American Fabrics and Fashions*, No. 128, 1983:11–17.

Simon, Steph
► Gallery owner; active Paris.
► In 1956, he opened Galerie Steph Simon, boulevard Saint-Germain, Paris; produced and showed the furniture designs and objects of Charlotte Perriand, Jean Prouvé, Isamu Noguchi, Serge Mouille, Jean Luce, and Jean Royère.

Simonet, Albert and Charles Simonet (?–1929)
► French metalworkers; brothers.
► Albert Simonet was the theoretician and designer, and Henri Dieupart produced his designs in molded glass. Evenness in their work was achieved with a flow of air directed into the mold immediately after pouring. Occasionally using muted gray and violet tints, Dieupart more often left the glass uncolored. Simonet included more glass in his lighting fixtures following his partnership with Dieupart. At first, mostly floral motifs were used (including convolvulus, bracken, honesty, hortensia, lily of the valley, hydrangea, aloe, and thistle). In the 1930s, geometric forms appeared (including rhomboids, squares, and lozenges). By 1933, metal had been almost entirely replaced with glass.
► Albert Simonet showed his work in the 1924 (I) Exposition de l'Art Moderne at the Pavillon Marsan at the Louvre, in Simonets' frères' own stand in the Grand Palais of the 1925 Paris 'Exposition Internationale des Arts Décoratifs et Industriels Modernes,' and the 1934 (II) Salon of Light. In the 1924 Great Lighting Competition organized by the Syndicat de l'Électricité, the Simonets won five of the ten first prizes and numerous honorable mentions for lighting designed for rooms in the houses of families of different incomes.
► Alastair Duncan, *Art Nouveau and Art Déco Lighting*, New York: Simon and Schuster, 1978:184–85. Guillaume Janneau, *Le Luminaire et les Moyens d'éclairage Nouveaux*, first series: plates 16,39.

Simonit, Alfredo (1937–)
► Italian designer; born Romans d'Isonzo; active S. Giovanni al Natisone.
► Simonit began his professional career in 1963. In 1966, he designed furniture for Mobel Italia, where he was artistic director 1967–72. In 1971, he began collaborating with Giorgio Del Piero; in 1974, they set up the design studio A in S. Giovanni al Natisone. He was a member of ADI (Associazione per il Disegno Industriale).
► In 1972 with Del Piero, he showed his work in the Mobel Italia stand at the 1972 (IV) 'Eurodomus.' He participated in the 1963 (V) 'Concorso Internazionale del Mobile' in Cantù, 1965 (II) 'Concorso Nazionale del Mobile Fiera' in Rome, winning a prize, and 1965 'Concorso Nazionale del Mobile' at the fair in Trieste, winning a prize with others.
► *ADI Annual 1976*, Milan: Associazione per il Disegno Industriale, 1976.

Simonson, Lee
► American architect and designer.
► The 1927 'Exposition of Art in Trade at Macy's' at Macy's department store in New York was planned by Simonson. He and

Raymond Loewy designed the designer's office and studio in the 1935 'Contemporary American Industrial Art, 1934' at the New York Metropolitan Museum of Art. Simonson was president of the American Union of Designers, Artists and Craftsmen 1930–32.
▶ R. Craig Miller, *Modern Design 1890–1990*, New York: Abrams, 1990.

Simpson, Edgar
▶ British silversmith and metal worker: active London.
▶ The silver and jewelry designed by Simpson, active from *c*1896–1910, showed the influence of C.R. Ashbee. Simpson's relatively conservative work was admired by contemporary critics. He executed jewelry designs for some commercial smithies, including Charles Horner of Chester, where jewelry in mother-of-pearl and enamel was produced in a style similar to Liberty's *Cymric* range.
▶ Annelies Krekel-Aalberse, *Art Nouveau and Art Déco Silver*, New York: Abrams, 1989:259. Charlotte Gere, *American and European Jewelry 1830–1914*, New York: Crown, 1975:220–21.

Simpson, Ronald, D. (1890–1960)
▶ British textile designer and woodworker.
▶ A woodworker at Kendal, he worked as a textile designer at Alexander Morton from 1908; produced numerous designs for the firm, including advertisements for its non-fading 'Sundour' fabrics.
▶ Valerie Mendes, *The Victoria & Albert Museum's Textile Collection British Textiles from 1900 to 1937*, London: Victoria and Albert Museum, 1992.

Simpson, Hall and Miller
▶ American silversmiths; located Wallingford, Connecticut.
▶ The company was founded in 1866; it began production of sterling silverwares in 1895. In 1898, the firm was incorporated into International Silver. It produced Alfred G. Kintz's successful designs, including dishes and bowls named *Tropical Sunrise, Northern Lights*, and *Ebb Tide*.
▶ Annelies Krekel-Aalberse, *Art Nouveau and Art Déco Silver*, New York: Abrams, 1989:122,259.

Sinclair, Clive (1940–)
▶ British electronic engineer and entrepreneur; born Richmond, Surrey.
▶ He established Sinclair Radionics in 1962. He sold miniature radios and amplifiers by mail before introducing the first pocket calculator, the 1972 *Executive*, designed with brother Iain Sinclair; it was widely published, along with his *Sovereign* calculator and 1976 *Microvision* miniature television set. His firm Sinclair Research launched the *ZX 80*, a small, inexpensive personal computer, in 1980; it sold in greater numbers than any other home computer. Sinclair's 1985 *C5* electric car was a celebrated commercial flop. In 1986, he founded Cambridge Computer, concentrating on research.
▶ The firm won Design Council Awards for its *Executive* calculator in 1972, *Sovereign* calculator in 1977, *Microvision* television set in 1978, and *ZX 81* personal computer in 1982. The *Executive* calculator and *Microvision* television set were included in the 1983–84 'Design Since 1984' exhibition at the Philadelphia Museum of Art.
▶ 'Clive Sinclair's New Leaf,' *Design*, No. 389, May 1981:26–27. Myron Magnet, 'Clive Sinclair's Little Computer That Could,' *Fortune*, Vol. 105, March 8, 1982:78–84. Cat., Kathryn B. Hiesinger and George H. Marcus III (eds.), *Design Since 1945*, Philadelphia: Philadelphia Museum of Art, 1983:230,I–40–41.

Sinel, Joseph (1889 or 1890–1975)
▶ New Zealand commercial artist; active USA.
▶ As a graphic designer, Sinel executed trademarks and package designs; he was active as a freelance designer in New Zealand and, from 1913, Australia; *c*1918 emigrated to the USA; he was one of the wave of consultant designers of the 1930s in the USA who became known as industrial designers; in 1930, became a member of the American Union of Decorative Artists and Craftsmen; was

best known for a late 1920s 1-cent scale, painted bright red; *c*1970, was appointed professor emeritus, California College of Arts and Crafts, San Francisco; was an active member of the Artists Guild and Society of Illustrators and founding member of The American Society of Industrial Design.
▶ *Fortune*, Feb. 1934:88. Wayne Champion, 'Joseph Sinel' in Mel Byars and Russell Flinchum (eds.), *50 American Designers*, Washington: Preservation, 1994.

Singer, Franz (1896–1954)
▶ Austrian architect and furniture designer; born Vienna.
▶ 1914–15, studied painting in Vienna under F.A. Harta; 1917, Open School, Vienna, under Johannes Itten; 1916–17, philosophy; 1919–23, Bauhaus, Weimar, under Itten.
▶ 1920–24, he was active in theater design in Berlin and Dresden with fellow Bauhaus student Friedl Dicker. 1923–25, he and Dicker were active in their Werkstätten bildener Kunstatelier in Berlin. In 1925, he moved to Vienna, where he was active in interior architecture; 1925–26, Dicker and Singer became partners at Wasserburgasse 2 in Vienna, known as the Singer-Dicker workshop 1926–31. In 1927, Singer worked primarily on furniture designs in bent steel tubing produced by firms in Austria, England, and the Netherlands, and was active in the serial production of furniture. In 1930–31, he made his first trip to London and designed nursery and stackable furniture models. In 1930–31, he moved his studio to his original address at Schadekgasse 18 in Vienna, and Dicker-Singer's cooperative efforts were dissolved. He was active in furniture design until 1934, when he moved to London and began working with Wells Coates on a system of modular kitchens, baths, and storage spaces for converted older apartments. After this time, he was active as an architect, specializing in shops, including that (and the restaurant on the top floor) of the John Lewis department store in London. He was in partnership with Hans Biel and subsequently Hedy Schwarz-Abraham. In 1935, he wrote on housing for the London County Council; in 1936, designed children's and nursery furniture; in 1938, closed his studio in Vienna; 1938–54 in England, designed nursery furniture, blackboards for a toy company, the studio of Michael Watkins, a house for W. Foges, a house at 39 Cadogan Gardens, the pavilion of the Hotel Scarborough, the restaurant at Tyrell and Green, and the houses of V. Kraus, the Friedmans, V.F. Evans-Tipping, and the Steanbriges.
▶ 1916–17, he participated in the Kunstschau exhibition at the Vienna Secession and in the Österreichische Ausstellung in Vienna and 1929 'Ausstellung Moderner Inneneinrichtungen' at the Österreichisches Museum für Kunst und Industrie in Vienna. His and Friedl Dicker's works were the subject of the 1988–89 exhibition at the Hochschule für angewandte Kunst in Vienna.
▶ Cat., *Franz Singer/Friedl Dicker: 2X Bauhaus in Wein*, Vienna: Hochschule für angewandte Kunst, 1988.

Singer-Schinnerl, Susi (1891–1965)
▶ Austrian ceramicist; born Vienna.
▶ She was a member of the ceramic workshop of the Wiener Werkstätte; she settled in the USA in 1937.
▶ Günther Feuerstein, *Vienna–Present and Past: Arts and Crafts–Applied Art–Design*, Vienna: Jugend und Volk, 1976:35,81. Cat., *Expressive Keramik der Wiener Werkstätte 1917–1930*, Munich: Bayerische Vereinsbank, 1992:134–35.

Sinnemark, Rolf (1941–)
▶ Swedish designer; born Stockholm.
▶ 1956–63, studied Konstfackskolan and Tekniska Skolan, Stockholm, and, 1956–59, in the silver department; from *c*1963, studied in the USA, Mexico and Europe.
▶ 1967–86, Sinnemark was a designer at the Kosta Boda glassworks; from 1967, at GAB Gense in Rörstrand.
▶ His work was shown in Colorado, Australia, Sweden, and Denmark.
▶ Jennifer Hawkins Opie, *Scandinavia: Ceramics and Glass in the Twentieth Century*, New York: Rizzoli, 1989.

Šípek Bořek (1949–)
▶ Czech designer; born Prague; active Amsterdam.
▶ Studied School of Applied Arts, Prague; 1969, architecture, Hochschule für bildende Künste, Hamburg; philosophy in Stuttgart; architecture, Technische Hogeschool, Delft, to 1979.
▶ 1977–79, he worked as a scientific assistant at the Institute of Industrial Design at the University of Hanover. 1979–83, he taught design theory at the University of Essen. In 1983, he settled in Amsterdam. He was known for his domestic furnishings that merged the functional with the non-functional. His voluptuous objects in glass and metal included the 1984 *Ernst und Geduld* chair and 1988 *Table Satomi San* produced by Galerie Néotù in Paris; 1989 domestic tableware, accessories, and furniture produced by Driade in Italy; and 1990 china produced by Sèvres in France. His widely published 1987 *Sni* chaise longue was produced by Driade. His 1987 range of hand-blown glass was produced by Sawaya e Moroni in Murano and other examples by the glassworks in Nový Bor (Czech Republic). He designed for manufacturers including Moletti, Leitner, Süssmuth, Alter-ego, Alessi, Anthologie Quartett, Cleto Munari, and Vitra.
▶ In the 1983 German Architecture Competition, he won an honorable mention for 'The Glasshouse' in Hamburg. He received the 1988 Kho Liang Ie design award. His work was the subject of the exhibition 'Bořek Šípek—The Nearness of Far' at the Vitra Design Museum, 1992, and Uměleckoprůmyslové Muzeum, Prague, 1993.
▶ Arlene Hirst, *Metropolitan Home*, April 1990:103. Albrecht Bangert and Karl Michael Armer, *80s Style: Designs of the Decade*, New York: Abbeville, 1990:65,156–57,236. Cat., Milena Lamarová and Mel Byars, *Bořek Šípek, The Nearness of Far Architecture and Design*, Amsterdam: Steltman, 1993.

Sirnes, Johan (1883–1966)
▶ Norwegian designer; active Oslo.
▶ 1914–27, Sirnes was a designer for David-Andersen, where he produced expensive, highly ornamental one-off pieces incorporating precious stones. From 1912, he taught at the Royal School of Arts and Crafts in Oslo.
▶ Fredrik Wildhagen, *Norge i Form*, Oslo: Sternersen, 1988:88. Annelies Krekel-Aalberse, *Art Nouveau and Art Déco Silver*, New York: Abrams, 1989:243,259.

Sirrah
▶ Italian lighting manufacturer; located Bologna.
▶ Sirrah was established in Bologna in 1967 to produce public, office, and domestic lighting fixtures. In 1969, it presented a collection of domestic lighting components designed by the team of Franco Albini, Franca Helg, and Antonio Piva. Other designers included Vittorio Balli, Giorgina Castiglioni, Pirro Cuniberti, Salvatore Gregorietti, Glauco Gresleri, Giancarlo Mattioli, Franco Mirenzi, and Paolo Tilche. The *Saori*, *Kaori*, and *Kazuki* lighting ranges designed by Kazuhide Takahama were among its most successful; the fixtures had white fabric stretched over wire frames. Sirrah reproduced Man Ray's *La lune sous le chapeau* table lamp, and Mariyo Yagi and the Studio Simon designed its *Garbo* fixture.
▶ *ADI Annual 1976*, Milan: Associazione per il Disegno Industriale, 1976.

SITE Projects
▶ American architecture firm; located New York.
▶ SITE Projects was established in 1969 by James Wines. SITE stands for 'Sculpture In The Environment.' In 1973, Alison Sky, Michelle Stone, and Emilio Sousa became partners in the firm. They took architectural Deconstructivism to eye-catching extremes with quirky, curious, and amusing structures. SITE was best known for its buildings for the Best chain of stores in the USA, including the first, the 1971–72 Peeling Project in Richmond, Virginia; 1974–75 Indeterminate Façade in Houston, Texas; 1976–78 Tilt Showroom in Towson, Maryland; and Best's business office.

▶ Its work was shown at the New York Museum of Art, Whitney Museum of American Art in New York, Cooper-Hewitt Museum in New York, Centre Georges Pompidou and the Louvre in Paris, and at the Biennale di Venezia. The *Apocalypse/Utopia* chair was shown at the 1985 Triennale di Milano.
▶ *SITE Projects and Theories*, Bari, 1978. Pierre Restany and Bruno Zevi, *SITE, Architecture as Art*, London, 1980. *Le Affinità Elettive* Milan: Electa, 1985. Auction cat., *Asta di Modernariato 1900–1986, Auction 'Modernariato,'* Milan: Semenzato Nuova Geri, 8 Oct. 1986: Lot 102.
▶ See Sky, Alison

Sitte, Camillo (1843–1903)
▶ Austrian architect and town planner; born Vienna.
▶ In his book *Der Städtebau nach seinen künstlerischen Grundsätzen* (1889), Sitte attacked the grid system of urban architecture, the primacy of streets, and untrammeled squares. He was known for his advocacy of the medieval city as an ideal model with its organically developed structure, and the picturesque vistas of the Baroque square. He found wide support in his reversion to Romanticism in opposition to the Rationalism of Otto Wagner.
▶ Camillo Sitte, *Der Städtebau nach seinen künstlerischen Grundsätzen*, Vienna, 1889. Robert Waissenberger, *Vienna 1890–1920*, Secaucus, NJ: Wellfleet 1984:204,269.

Sitterle, Harold and Trudi Sitterle
▶ American ceramic designers; husband and wife.
▶ Previously a graphic designer at the magazine *McCall's*, Harold Sitterle joined his wife's workshop in Croton Falls, New York. From 1949 to the early 1970s, the Sitterles designed and produced a line of porcelain table accessories, including candleholders, sugar bowls, serving utensils, creamers, pitchers, pepper mills, and salt dishes. They developed the 1949 hourglass-shaped pepper mill; widely published, it became a popular item in their newly created porcelain business.
▶ Their pepper mill was shown at the 1950 'Good Design' exhibition at the New York Museum of Modern Art and Chicago Merchandise Mart.
▶ 'Manufacturing in Microcosm: Sitterle Ceramics,' *Industrial Design*, Vol. 2, April 1955:78–81. Don Wallance, *Shaping America's Products*, New York, 1956:159–61. 'Trudi and Harold Sitterle,' *Design Quarterly*, No. 39, 1957:24–27. Cat., Kathryn B. Hiesinger and George H. Marcus III (eds.), *Design Since 1945*, Philadelphia: Philadelphia Museum of Art, 1984:230,II–60–61.

Siune, Svend (1935–)
▶ Danish metalworker and designer.
▶ Studied Kunsthåndvaerkerskolen, Copenhagen, to 1961.
▶ 1961–76, he was a freelance advertising artist and subsequently designed furniture and metal and plastic cutlery. He was best known for his 1965 *Blue Shark* flatware for the Georg Jensen Sølvsmedie in stainless steel, which was widely published and exhibited.
▶ His *Blue Shark* flatware won the 1966 Jensen cutlery contest.
▶ Cat., *Georg Jensen Silversmithy: 77 Artists, 75 Years*, Washington: Smithsonian Institution Press, 1980, No. 137. Cat., Kathryn B. Hiesinger and George H. Marcus III (eds.), *Design Since 1945*, Philadelphia: Philadelphia Museum of Art, 1983:231,V–42.

Siza Vieira, Alvaro (1933–)
▶ Portuguese architect and designer; born Matosinhos.
▶ Studied sculpture, and architecture, School of Fine Arts, Oporto.
▶ He was a professor of architecture at the University of Oporto and visiting professor at the École Polytechnique Fédérale in Lausanne and at the University of Pennsylvania. 1958–60, he worked in the office of architect Fernando Tavora. He designed furniture for the school of architecture at the University of Oporto and the 1985 *Flamingo* halogen lamp produced by B.d Ediciones de Diseño.
▶ He won the invitational competition for the renovation of the Campo di Marte in Venice. One-person exhibitions of his work

were mounted at the Museum of Contemporary Art in Milan in 1979 and at the Alvar Aalto Museum in Finland in 1982.
▶ Juli Capella and Quim Larrea, *Designed by Architects in the 1980s,* New York, Rizzoli, 1988.

Skarland, Henrik (1956–)
▶ Norwegian furniture designer.
▶ Skarland designed the *Sit Stik* stool in c1986 produced by Møre Kalvatn.
▶ Fredrik Wildhagen, *Norge i Form,* Oslo: Sternersen, 1988:203.

Skeaping, John Rattenbury (1901–80)
▶ British sculptor and ceramics designer; husband of Barbara Hepworth.
▶ Studied Royal Academy School, London.
▶ 1926–27, he designed 14 earthenware animal figurines for Wedgwood; at least 12 were produced 1933–39. Norman Wilson's 'straw' glaze was used on Skeaping's figures produced by Doulton. He published the books *Animal Drawing* (1934), *How to Draw Horses* (1938), *The Bay Tree of Mexico* (1952), and *Les Animaux dans l'Art* (1969). 1948–49, he worked on terracotta sculpture assisted by potters in Zapotec (Mexico). 1953–59, he taught sculpture at the Royal College of Art in London.
▶ He showed his sculpture in Mexico City and Oxana (Mexico) and, in London, at the Royal Academy, Leicester Galleries, and Ackermann Galleries.
▶ Cat., *Thirties: British art and design before the war,* London: Arts Council of Great Britain, Hayward Gallery, 1979:154,168, 292,300,303.

Skellern, Victor (1908–66)
▶ British ceramicist and designer.
▶ Studied Royal College of Art, London, to 1933.
▶ He was a painter, stained glass designer, and ceramicist. 1934–36, he was artistic director at Wedgwood, where he designed commemorative wares including characters and images from Gilbert and Sullivan operas, *The Canterbury Tales,* Bayeux tapestries, and Shakespeare's plays. His 1933 *Potland* stained-glass window showed various scenes in the potteries at Staffordshire. Some of his decorations were applied to ceramic shapes designed by Norman Wilson at Wedgwood, including the 1935 *Globe* shaped service.
▶ His work was included in the 1935 London 'British Art in Industry' exhibition at the Royal Academy, 1935 'Exposition Universelle et Internationale de Bruxelles,' and 1937 Paris 'Exposition Internationale des Arts et Techniques dans le Vie Moderne.' The *Potland* window and *Globe* service were included in the 1979–80 'Thirties' exhibition at the Hayward Gallery in London.
▶ Cat., *Thirties: British art and design before the war,* London: Arts Council of Great Britain, Hayward Gallery, 1979:102, 128,136,300.

Skidmore, Owings and Merrill
▶ American architecture firm; located Chicago, New York, San Francisco and London.
▶ The firm was established in 1936 by partners Louis Skidmore (1897–1962) and Nathaniel A. Owings (1903–84) in Chicago. In 1937, they opened an office in New York. In 1939, John Merrill (1896–1975) was taken in as a partner. The office was organized along the principles generally put into place by large corporations in the USA, where individual anonymity was fostered along with efficient work habits. The firm's first significant commission was the 1952 Lever House on Park Avenue in New York. The landmark 21-storey building established a pattern for the postwar office block that was much imitated and much debased. The partnership's subsequent buildings, many distinctive and notable, were designed to solve clients' specific needs. In its own style, SOM took elements from the work of Ludwig Mies van der Rohe, Le Corbusier and other International Style architects. It introduced a new type of corporate headquarters with long, low building complexes placed in park-like settings in the suburbs, of which the 1957 Connecticut General Life Insurance administration build-

ing in Bloomfield, Connecticut, was an example. Through the efforts of staff architect Gordon Bunshaft, it developed the open-plan office with low moveable walls. The firm fostered the reproduction of Modern furniture from the 1920s and 1930s in Europe and encouraged new concepts and designs in office furniture and furnishings with furniture firms Herman Miller and Knoll. Florence Knoll, head of the Knoll firm, was hired as the interior designer for the Connecticut General Life Insurance and Weyerhaeuser buildings. Its staff interior designer was Davis Allen. SOM architects included Bunshaft and Roy Allen in New York; Bruce Graham, Myron Goldsmith and Walter Netsch in Chicago; and Edward Bassett in San Francisco. Netsch in Chicago developed the 'field theory,' applicable to university buildings and hospitals. The firm's use of atrium interior halls was influenced by the 1963–68 Ford Foundation building in New York by architects Kevin Roche and John Dinkeloo. Known for its grandiose gestures, SOM designed the 1974 Sears Tower in Chicago, the world's tallest building. Its 1970 John Hancock Center in Chicago was the first large-scale multiple-purpose building to include residential, office, and retail units in a single structure. Its other buildings included the 1958 Inland Steel building in Chicago; 1961 Upjohn building in Kalamazoo, Michigan; 1962 United Airlines building in Des Plaines, Illinois; 1963 Business Men's Assurance of America building in Kansas City, Missouri; 1965 Brunswick building in Chicago; 1970 American Can building in Greenwich, Connecticut; 1971 Weyerhaeuser building in Tacoma, Washington; 1971 One Shell Plaza in Houston, Texas; 1974 Fourth Financial Center in Wichita, Kansas; 1974 First Wisconsin Plaza in Madison, Wisconsin; 1980 33 Monroe Street in Chicago.
▶ Ernst Danz, *Architecture of Skidmore, Owings and Merrill 1950–1962,* New York, 1962, and London, 1963. Christopher Woodward, *Skidmore, Owings and Merrill,* London and New York, 1970. Nathaniel A. Owings, *The Spaces in Between, an Architect's Journey,* Boston, 1973. Arthur Drexler and Axel Menges, *Architecture of Skidmore, Owings and Merrill 1963–1973,* New York: Museum of Modern Art, 1974. Albert Bush-Brown, *Architecture of Skidmore, Owings and Merrill: Architecture and Urbanism 1973–1983,* London and New York, 1984.
▶ See Allen, Davis

SKK Lighting
See Shiu-Kay, Kan

Skogster-Lehtinen, Greta (1900–)
▶ Finnish textile designer.
▶ 1921–75, she worked in her own studio, where she produced fabrics, carpets, and tapestries. Some of her textiles were intended for furniture upholstery, including fabrications for Lisa Johansson-Pape in the 1930s. Due to the shortages created by World War II, Skogster-Lehtinen used various unusual materials, including birch bark, in her weavings.
▶ Cat., David Revere McFadden (ed.), *Scandinavian Modern Design 1880–1980,* New York: Abrams, 1982:271, Nos. 129,149.

Skrufs Glasbruk
▶ Swedish glass factory.
▶ The glass factory was established in 1897 at Skruv, Småland, as a factory community; began production of simple household glasswares; in 1908, went bankrupt due to unsuccessful experimentation with new kiln types; in 1909, was reorganized as Skrufs Nya Glasbruk; in the 1920s and 1930s, specialized in glass for restaurants; in 1948, changed its name back to Skrufs Glasbruk; in 1953, hired Bengt Edenfalk as its first full-time staff designer and focused production on decorative wares. In 1966, Lars Hellsten was hired, and production expanded into cast, molded, and spun glass. In 1973, the company collaborated with Gullaskruf and Björkshult; 1974–77, merged several times, resulting in the creation of Krona-Bruken. In 1977, Krona-Bruken was bought by Kosta Boda and closed in 1980. It reopened in 1981 as a cooperative producing mouth-blown glass designed by Ingegerd Råman and Anette Krahner.

91 *Moth Balls and Sugar* fabric (in the
American Print series); printed silk, 1927.
Designed by Edward J. Steichen,
produced by Stehli Silk, New York.
(The Metropolitan Museum of Art,
New York, gift of Stehli Silk Corporation, 1927)

92 Corner cabinet (no. 1521 AR/2233 NR);
kingwood veneer on mahogany carcass,
ivory marquetry, 1916.
Designed by Jacques-Émile Ruhlmann,
produced in his workshop in Paris.
(The Brooklyn Museum, Brooklyn, New York)

93 Side chair; oak, loose fabric cushion, 1901. Designed by Charles Rohlfs, produced in his workshop, Buffalo, New York. (Cooper-Hewitt National Museum of Design, Smithsonian Institution/Art Resource, New York, Mary Blackwelder Memorial Fund, photography by John White)

94 *Klismos* side chair; walnut, woven leather thongs, 1961. Designed by Terence Robsjohn-Gibbings, produced by Saridis, Athens. (Cooper-Hewitt National Museum of Design, Smithsonian Institution/Art Resource, New York, gift of Saridis, photography by John White)

95 Flacon; black-violet pressed glass, 1920s. Designed by Louis Süe and André Mare of the Compagnie des Arts français for Parfum d'Orsay, Paris. (Die Neue Sammlung, Staatliches Museum für angewandte Kunst, Munich)

96 Bottles (part of a tea set); glass, 1930. Designed by Ludvika Smrčková, produced by Rückl glassworks, Nižbor, Czech Republic. (Uměleckoprůmyslové Muzeum v Praze)

97 Tea set; glass, 1931. Designed by Ladislav Sutnar, produced by Sklárny Kavalier, Sázava, Czech Republic. (Uměleckoprůmyslové Muzeum v Praze)

98 Tea service; clear mouth-blown heat-resistant glass, 1932. Designed by Wilhelm Wagenfeld, produced by Schott & Gen. Jenaer Glaswerke, Jena, Germany. (Die Neue Sammlung, Staatliches Museum für angewandte Kunst, Munich)

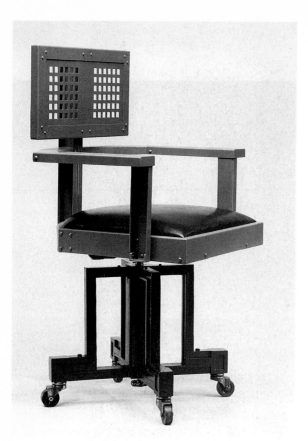

114 Swivel and tilt armchair; terracotta-color painted steel, black leather, 1904.
Designed by Frank Lloyd Wright, produced by Van Doren Iron Works, Cleveland, Ohio. (The Metropolitan Museum of Art, Theodore Robert Gamble Jr gift, in honor of his mother Mrs Theodore Robert Gamble, 1979)

115 *Consumer's Rest* chair; chromed steel, 1990. Designed by Stiletto, produced by Brüder Siegel, Draht- und Metallwarenfabrik, Leipheim/Donau, Germany. (Cooper-Hewitt National Museum of Design, Smithsonian Institution/Art Resource, New York, photography by Steve Tagne)

116 *The Structures Tremble* table; plastic laminate, composition board, painted steel, rubber, glass, 1979.
Designed by Ettore Sottsass. (The Metropolitan Museum of Art, New York, purchase, Theodore Robert Gamble Jr gift, in memory of his mother Mrs Theodore Robert Gamble, 1987)

117 Lamp; copper, mica, c1912–15. Designed and produced by Dirk van Erp, San Francisco. (The Metropolitan Museum of Art, New York, gift of Charles L. and June D. Kaufmann, 1989)

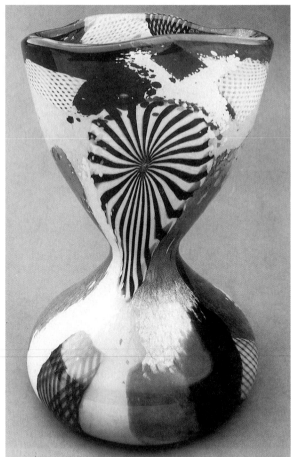

118 *Oriente* vase, mouth-blown glass, 1948. Designed by Dino Martens, produced by Aureliano Toso, Murano, Italy. (Fifty-50, New York)

► Jennifer Hawkins Opie, *Scandinavia: Ceramics and Glass in the Twentieth Century*, New York: Rizzoli, 1989.

Skubic, Peter (1935–)
► Yugoslav jewelry designer; born Gornji-Milanovac (now Serbia).
► His stark jewelry suggested machine parts and pieces.
► Günther Feuerstein, *Vienna—Present and Past: Arts and Crafts— Applied Art—Design*, Vienna: Jugend und Volk, 1976: 66,69, 81.

Sky, Alison
► American designer.
► From 1973, she was project designer and partner in the architecture firm SITE, where she designed the 1982–84 Willi Ware showrooms and displays. Other SITE projects of Sky's included the 1986 Pershing Square Cultural Park in Los Angeles; 1985 Ansel Adams Museum and Center of Photography in Carmel, California; 'Highway 86' at World's Fair Transportation Pavilion and Plaza, 'Expo 86,' Vancouver; 1984 Paz Building, Brooklyn, New York; 1984 Best Products building, Milwaukee, Wisconsin; 1984 Brickwork Design Center, New York; 1985 Museum of the Borough of Brooklyn, New York; and 1986 Theater for The New City, New York. She established the ON SITE books, including *Unbuilt America*, written with Michelle Stone. Her design of 'disappearing' furniture and furnishings in a white-on-white motif for the 1985 Laurie Mallet house renovation in the expansion of an 1820s residence in Greenwich Village, New York was widely published.
► She was a fellow of the American Academy in Rome.
► Liz McQuiston, *Women in Design: A Contemporary View*, New York: Rizzoli, 1988:114. Vittorio Magnago Lampugnani (ed.), *Encyclopedia of 20th-Century Architecture*, 1986:362.

Slang, Gerd (1925–)
► Norwegian glassware designer.
► Studied Statens Håndverks -og Kunstindustriskole, Oslo.
► 1948–52, he was a designer at the Hadelands Glasverk. 1952–63, he was an independent designer, returning to Hadelands 1963–72.
► His work was included in the 1970 'Craftsmen from Norway' exhibition.
► Cat., David Revere McFadden (ed.), *Scandinavian Modern Design 1880–1980*, New York: Abrams, 1982:271. Jennifer Hawkins Opie, *Scandinavia: Ceramics and Glass in the Twentieth Century*, New York: Rizzoli, 1989.

Slany, Erich Hans (1926–)
► German industrial designer.
► 1941–44, studied engineering in Eger (Hungary); 1948, in Esslingen (Germany).
► 1948–55, he worked for Ritter Aluminum in Esslingen, where he was a specialist in metals, plastics, and product development. In 1956, he set up his own studio in Esslingen. Until 1957, he worked in ceramics and glassware design under Heinrich Löffelhardt. From 1957, he executed numerous products, including medical equipment and electronic components for rocket construction, power tools, and plastics. He designed domestic appliances produced by Leifheit and, from 1957, by Progress. In 1959, he became a founding member of VDID, the German designers' association. In 1969 and 1971, he was on the jury of the Bundespreis 'Die gute Industrieform.'
► He was awarded the 1973 Deutsche Ornapreis for his plastic tableware, and the 1975 Bosch prize for his *Panther* and *Dübelblitz* power tools. His work was the subject of the one-person 1965 'E.H. Slany: Auswahl Designarbeiten 1953 bis 1965' exhibition at the Haus Industrieform in Essen. His work was included in the 1977 'Prämiierte Produkte' exhibition at the Rat für Formgebung in Darmstadt, and his domestic appliance for Leifheit was included in the 1983–84 'Design Since 1945' exhibition at the Philadelphia Museum of Art.
► Cat., Kathryn B. Hiesinger and George H. Marcus III (eds.), *Design Since 1945*, Philadelphia: Philadelphia Museum of Art,

1983:231,I–42. Cat., *E.H. Slany: Auswahl Designarbeiten 1953 bis 1965*, Essen: Haus Industrieform, 1965. 'Der Designer E. H. Slany: 10 Fragen,' *Form*, No. 33, March 1966:35–39. Cat., *Prämiierte Produkte*, Darmstadt: Rat für Formgebung, 1977:14,17.

Slater, Eric (1902–)
► British ceramicist.
► Studied modeling and design, Stoke-on-Trent School of Art, design, Burslem School of Art; life classes, Hanley School of Art; 1919–26, under Gordon M. Forsyth.
► 1877–1914, Slater's great-uncle John Slater was the artistic director at Doulton ceramics factory. His father Walter Slater was artistic director at ceramics manufacturer Wileman of Foley Potteries and China Works, Longton, renamed Shelley Potteries in 1925. Eric Slater joined Wileman in 1919. In 1928, he became artistic director at Shelley Potteries, succeeding his father. He was responsible at Shelley for shapes, glazes, and patterns of table and decorative wares. His 1935 *Vogue* dinner set with its colorful geometric trim on triangular and square silhouettes and circular-patterned 1935 *Regent* shape were typical of his Art Déco work. He was secretary of the Staffordshire Artists' and Designers' Society.
► The *Regent* and *Vogue* dinnerwares, and drip-glaze vases, were included in the 1979–80 'Thirties' exhibition at the Hayward Gallery in London.
► Cat., *Thirties: British art and design before the war*, London: Arts Council of Great Britain, Hayward Gallery, 1979: 95,153, 298,300.

Slavik (aka Slavik Vassilieff 1920–)
► Estonian designer; born Tallin.
► Studied École Nationale Supérieure des Arts Décoratifs, Paris.
► He became known in the 1960s for his design and decoration of drugstores in boulevard Saint-Germain and avenue des Champs-Élysées, Paris.

Slott-Møller, Harald (1864–1937)
► Danish painter, ceramicist, and metalworker; active Copenhagen.
► Studied painting.
► His silver designs were produced by A. Michelson. His work showed ornamentation borrowed from Thorvald Bindesbøll. Kaj Bojesen, an apprentice at Georg Jensen Sølvsmedie, produced designs of his own and those of Slott-Møller. Slott-Møller designed ceramics for Aluminia in Copenhagen.
► Michelsen silver by Slott-Møller was shown at the 1900 Paris 'Exposition Universelle.'
► Cat., David Revere McFadden (ed.), *Scandinavian Modern Design 1880–1980*, New York: Abrams, 1982:271, No. 69. Annelies Krekel-Aalberse, *Art Nouveau and Art Déco Silver*, New York: Abrams, 1989:216,217,221,259.

Slutzky, Naum J. (1894–1965)
► Russian designer; born Kiev (now Ukraine); active London.
► Studied in Vienna and Bauhaus, Weimar.
► In the metal workshop at the Bauhaus, he designed alone and collaborated with others at the Bauhaus in Dessau until 1924. He designed lighting, metalware, and jewelry. He was apprenticed as a goldsmith in Vienna and was a goldsmith at the Wiener Werkstätte. Settling in London in 1933, he was active as a jewelry designer. 1935–40, he was a lecturer in jewelry design at the Central School of Arts and Crafts, London, and, 1946–50, in product design at the school of industrial design of the Royal College of Art. 1957–64, he was head of the department of industrial design at the College of Arts and Crafts, Birmingham.
► Sylvie Raulet, *Bijoux Art Déco*, Paris: Regard, 1984. Monika Rudolph, *Naum Slutzky, Meister am Bauhaus: Goldschmied und Designer*, Stuttgart: Arnoldsche, 1990. Deanna F. Cera (ed.), *Jewels of Fantasy: Costume Jewelry of the 20th Century*, New York: Abrams, 1992:108.

Small, Neal (1937–)

▶ American sculptor and designer; active New York and Pine Bush, New York.

▶ He worked in his own studio in New York from c1965 and subsequently in Pine Bush until 1973. He produced furniture, lighting, and glassware, using plastic sheets in bent, folded, and molded forms, sometimes combining them with chromed steel. His designs were produced by his own firm Neal Small Designs and by others, including Nessen lighting. In 1978, he became president of Squire and Small, where he specialized in conceptual sculpture and product designs for clients including Brueton, Kovacs, and Sigma.

▶ His lamp for Nessen was included in the 1983–84 'Design Since 1945' exhibition at the Philadelphia Museum of Art.

▶ Lisa Hammel, 'He's a One-Man Furniture Craft Guild,' *The New York Times*, 7 November 1967. Jocelyn de Noblet, *Design*, Paris, 1974:340–41. Cat., Kathryn B. Hiesinger and George H. Marcus III (eds.), *Design Since 1945*, Philadelphia: Philadelphia Museum of Art, 1983:231,IV–35.

Smart Design

▶ American industrial design consultancy; located New York.

▶ The firm founded in 1978 as Davin Stowell Associates designed a line of fashion eyewear with high-tech glass lenses launched in 1982, but unsuccessful. In 1985, it became Smart Design with partners Davin Stowell, Tom Dair, Tamara Thomsen, and Tucker Viemeister. The firm specialized in industrial and consumer products, packaging, corporate identity, and product graphics, including eyewear for Corning Optics and melamine tableware for Copco. Clients included Kepner-Tregoe (corporate graphics), Knoll Extra (desk accessories), Oxo (kitchen utensils), and Copco (kitchen plastics).

▶ Nicholas Backlund, 'Smart Moves,' *ID*, Sept.–Oct. 1990:29–33.

Smed, Perr (1878–1943)

▶ Danish silversmith.

▶ He set up his own workshop in New York, where he produced handmade silver; in 1937, he produced silver for Tiffany that was typical of Modern Danish work.

▶ Annelies Krekel-Aalberse, *Art Nouveau and Art Déco Silver*, New York: Abrams, 1989:121,259.

Smetana, Pavel (1900–86)

▶ Bohemian architect, furniture designer, and architecture theorist; born Zákupy.

▶ 1918–23, studied School of Industrial Arts, Prague; 1925–26, Academy of Arts, Prague, under Pavel Janák and Josef Gočár.

▶ From 1926 until its close in 1931, he was a member of the Devětsil group. He worked for major design firms in Prague. His 1920s architectural designs presaged the aerodynamic forms of Functionalism of the 1930s, 1940s, and 1950s, and were realized in his 1926 villa shown at the third Devětsil Exhibition and in his competition design for a Catholic church in Prague Vršovice. The only structure from his Devětsil period was the 1926–29 school at 10 Česká St. in Bratislava, designed with Karel Seifert. In 1929, collaborating with Devětsil associate Karel Stránik, Smetana designed the cupboards, armchairs, and bookcases for the converted house of Jan and Jaroslav Novák at 215 Poštovní St. in Prague.

▶ Cat., *Devětsil: Czech Avant-Garde Art, Architecture, and Design of the 1920s and 30s*, Oxford Museum of Modern Art and London Design Museum, 1990.

Smeuninx, Lotte (1964–)

▶ Belgian industrial designer; born Heusden.

▶ 1982–87, studied industrial design in Ghent.

▶ From 1987, her clients included Struktuplas in Belgium, De Gregorio & Simoni architecture and interior design in Belgium, Studio Alchimia in Milan, Randwyck in Maastricht, Jotul Martin in Belgium; participated in the Sottsass Seminar at the Domus Academy in Milan. She was active in the design of furniture, public seating, glassware, and ceramics, and designed the 1988 *Anja* and *Vera* tea set and tea glasses by Randwyck.

▶ Cat., Design Center Stuttgart, *Women in Design: Careers and Life Histories Since 1900*, Stuttgart: Haus der Wirtschaft, 1989:222–23.

Smilow, Judy (1958–)

▶ American furnishings designer; born White Plains, New York.

▶ 1976–78, studied Antioch College, Ohio; 1980–83, communications design, Parsons School of Design, New York; 1982–83, art therapy New School of Social Research, New York.

▶ She was a technical illustrator for United Engineers, Connecticut, 1978–80; an art therapist at Hawthorne Cedar Knolls, New York; and a designer in the art department the New York Museum of Modern Art 1983–85. She set up her own New York studio in 1985, and was in partnership with David Tisdale in a venture called Fresh Design, New York. She specialized in tableware. Her clients included Dansk, Formica, The Limited stores, Marimekko, New York Museum of Modern Art, Paine Webber, Sasaki, and Steuben.

▶ Her work was shown at the 1990 'Art That Works' at the Mint Museum, Charlotte, North Carolina, and 1987 'Pride of Place Setting' at Parsons School of Design, New York.

Smith, Alfred E. (1836–1926) and Harry A. Smith (c1840–1916)

▶ British glass decorators; brothers; born Birmingham; active Birmingham and New Bedford, Massachusetts.

▶ Their father William L. Smith started his career as a glassmaker for Biddle, Lloyd and Summerfield in Birmingham. Before 1851, he worked in his glass decorating workshop. Recruited by Deming Jarves, he settled in the USA and became head of the decorating department of Boston and Sandwich Glass in Massachusetts. The Smith brothers worked for their father in his workshop in Birmingham and for Boston and Sandwich Glass by 1860. William Smith established the Boston China Decorating Works; the brothers settled in New Bedford, Massachusetts, in charge of Mount Washington Glass there. In 1874, they set up their own enterprise on the premises of Mount Washington Glass. Practicing exclusively in glass decoration, they developed a technique for fusing color to the surface of white opal glass blanks they bought from English and American manufacturers. A cylindrical vase produced in Sandwich and New Bedford by various firms, including Smith Brothers, became known as the 'Smith Vase.' In a style associated with the Aesthetic movement, the firm produced wares gilded in red gold, cut, etched, and engraved and lampshades, vases, tiles, salts, and plaques. By 1877, Smith Brothers was located on Prospect Street in New Bedford; by the mid-1880s, at 28–30 William Street in New Bedford; and by c1890, in offices and showrooms in New York. The firm closed in 1899; Alfred Smith opened his own workshop in New Bedford and subsequently returned to the Mount Washington Glass. Harry Smith worked for a time in Meriden, Connecticut.

▶ Smith Brothers wares were shown at the 1876 Philadelphia 'Centennial Exposition.'

▶ Albert Christian Revi, *Nineteenth Century Glass: Its Genesis and Development*, Exton, Pa., 1967:71,73,81–86. Kenneth M. Wilson, *New England Glass and Glassmaking*, New York and Toronto, 1972:344–348. Doreen Bolger Burke et al., *In Pursuit of Beauty: Americans and the Aesthetic Movement*, New York: Metropolitan Museum of Art and Rizzoli, 1986:467.

Smith, John Moyr (1868–94)

▶ British decorative artist; active London.

▶ Trained as an architect in the office of William Salon in Glasgow.

▶ He began working in the 1860s at the design studio of Christopher Dresser. In the 1870s, he executed some designs and lithographs of its wares for furniture maker Collinson and Lock. He published *Ornamental Interiors, Ancient and Modern* (1887), in which he claimed that many of Dresser's designs were his own.

The books he illustrated included works by William Shakespeare, Robert Burns, Plutarch, and fairy tales. His illustrations were published in *Ancient Greek Female Costume* (1882), a version of *Costume of the Ancients* (1809) by Thomas Hope. From c1875 on a freelance basis, he executed designs for tiles for Minton and for W.B. Simpson. Some of his Minton tiles appeared in his *Album of Decorative Figures* (1882). He also published *Legendary Studies and other Sketches for Decorative Figure Panels* (1889).
► Some of his tile designs for Minton were shown at the 1878 Paris 'Exposition Universelle.'
► Julian Barnard, *Victorian Ceramic Tiles*, Greenwich, Conn., 1972:44,83, figs. 16,74,86. Jill Austwick and Brian Austwick, *The Decorated Tile: An Illustrated History of English Tilemaking and Design*, London, 1980:55,91,105−07. Doreen Bolger Burke et al., *In Pursuit of Beauty: Americans and the Aesthetic Movement*, New York: Metropolitan Museum of Art and Rizzoli, 1987:467−68.

Smithson, Alison (1928−93) and Peter Smithson (1923−)
► British architects and designers; husband and wife from 1949.
► 1944−49, both studied architecture, University of Durham, Newcastle upon Tyne.
► Active in London from 1949, Alison Smithson designed for the 1949 schools sections of the London County Council. In practice together from 1950, leading a younger architectural generation towards the Brutalism style, they designed the 1950−54 Hunstanton secondary modern school, Norfolk; private houses; 1960−64 *The Economist* building on St. James's Street, London; 1963−67 Robin Hood Gardens, Tower Hamlets; 1967−69 Garden Building, St. Hilda's College, Oxford; the East India Docks residential project; the Golden Lane municipal building project, London; and University of Bath buildings in the 1980s. Their best known projects were the 1951 Coventry Cathedral, 1957 Sheffield University, 1958 Infant School in Wokingham, 1959 Churchill College, Cambridge, 1964 British Embassy in Brasilia, 1973 Lucas Industries headquarters, and 1984 Maryhill Housing in Glasgow. They designed graphics from 1952, furniture from 1953, and artifacts and clothes. Their chair designs included the 1956 plastic *Egg* chair for 'The House of the Future' and the 1955 tubular steel and Plexiglass *Pogo* dining-room chair for 'Ideal Homes.' Their urban studies included the 1957−58 Hauptstadt in Berlin, 1962 Mehringplatz in Berlin, 1968−70 Old City in Kuwait, 1979 Damascus Gate in Jerusalem, 1980 Lutzowstrasse in Berlin, and 1982 Parc de la Villette, Paris. Alison Smithson's publications include *Young Girl* (1966), *Euston Arch* (1968), *Team 10 Primer* (editor) (1962), *Team 10 at Royaumont* (1975), *Tram Rats* (1976), *Team 10 out of CIAM* (1982), *AS in DS: An Eye on the Road* (1983), *Upper Lawn, Solar Pavilion, Folly* (1986), and, from 1951 numerous essays.
► With Eduardo Paolozzi, Richard Hamilton, Lawrence Alloway, and others, the Smithsons showed their work at the 1954 'This is Tomorrow' exhibition. Their chair design was included in the 1970 'Modern Chairs, 1918−1970' exhibition at the Whitechapel Gallery in London. Their exhibition designs included 1956 'House of Tomorrow' and those at 1968 (XIV) Triennale di Milano, and 1976 Biennale di Venezia.
► Cat., *Modern Chairs 1918−1970*, London: Lund Humphries, 1971. Cat., *Der Kragstuhl*, Stuhlmuseum Burg Beverungen, Berlin: Alexander, 1986:138. Liz McQuiston, *Women in Design: A Contemporary View*, New York: Rizzoli, 1988:118.

Smout-Baeyens, Marie-Christine (1936−)
► Belgian industrial designer; born Ghent.
► 1955−59, studied industrial design, La Cambre-Ensaav, Brussels.
► In 1959, she and husband Frank Smout set up Obei Design. She was a member of the design association UDB in Belgium. 1965−75, she was professor of industrial design at La Cambre-Ensaav and, 1971−80, director of exhibitions at the Brussels Design Center. She designed furniture, lighting, appliances, equipment, machines, vehicles, glassware, ceramics, cutlery, exhibi-

tions, and electronic equipment, including the 1980 kitchen units for the elderly by Resocub, 1987 *Génération 90* central heating boiler by Saint Roch, and 1988 clocks by De Jaeger in Brussels.
► She showed her work first at the 1967 UID design center in Brussels and subsequently at its 1972, 1975, 1976, and 1980 sessions. Her work was included in the 1975 'Selection Interdesign Bruges' ICSID in Brussels, 1983 'Signe d'Or' in Belgium, and 1986 'Belgian Designs' exhibition in Ostend.
► Cat., Design Center Stuttgart, *Women in Design: Careers and Life Histories Since 1900*, Stuttgart: Haus der Wirtschaft, 1989:224−27.

Smrčková, Ludvika (1903−1991)
► Czech glass artist, painter, and graphic designer.
► Studied School of Decorative Arts, Prague, under Emile Dítě, V.H. Brunner, and František Kysela, and Charles University, Prague.
► She began working in glass while studying under Brunner, and designed a collection of book bindings, a subject in which she retained a lifelong interest. 1928−48, she taught at high schools in Příbor, Litomyšl, Kladno, and Prague and, from 1928, was a member of the SČSD (Czechoslovak Werkbund). 1930−48, she worked primarily for the firm Rückel in Nižbor and, after 1948, was a designer for Inwald, Skloexport, and the Center of Glass Industry and Fine Ceramics in Prague. She collaborated with the agency Krásná jizba (The Beautiful Room), introducing simple, dramatic shapes into glass tableware, often incorporating cut edges; she also designed individual crystal pieces. In the 1930s, her vases and bowls in monumental architectural forms were largely geometric, with high-quality cut ornamentation. In the 1960s and 1970s, she experimented with engraved and painted glass.
► Her work was shown at the 1925 Paris 'Exposition Internationale des Arts Décoratifs et Industriels Modernes.' She received the grand prize at the 1935 'Exposition Universelle et Internationale de Bruxelles,' and the grand prize and a gold medal at the 1937 Paris 'Exposition Internationale des Arts et Techniques dans la Vie Moderne.'
► A. Adlerová, *České užité umění 1918−1938*, Prague, 1983. Cat., *Tschechische Kunst der 20+30 Jahre, Avantgarde und Tradition*, Darmstadt: Mathildenhöhe, 1988−89.

Snelling, Douglas
► Australian architect and designer; active Sydney.
► He designed popular webbing chairs in 1946 as part of the Snelling line.
► Cat., *Featherston Chairs*, Victoria, Australia: National Gallery of Victoria, 1988.

Snischek, Max (1891−1968)
► Austrian designer; born Dürnkrut.
► 1912−14, studied Kunstgewerbeschule, Vienna, under R. Rothansl.
► In 1922, when Eduard Josef Wimmer-Wisgrill retired from the Wiener Werkstätte, Snischek became head of its fashion department; he contributed designs for garments, lace, jewelry, tulle covers, and enamelwork, and contributed to the fashion folder *Die Mode* of 1914−15. Subsequently, he was a teacher at the Fashion School of Munich and a member of the Neue Werkbund Österreichs.
► He exhibited in the fashion exhibition at the 1925 Paris 'Exposition Internationale des Arts Décoratifs et Industriels Modernes' and showed his work at the 1929−30 exhibition of Viennese architects.
► Deanna F. Cera (ed.), *Jewels of Fantasy: Costume Jewelry of the 20th Century*, New York: Abrams, 1992.

Société des Artistes Décorateurs
► French decorative arts organization and sponsor of annual exhibitions; active 1900−42.
► One of several artists' and designers' groups in Paris in the first quarter of the 20th century, the Société des Artistes Décorateurs (SAD) was founded in 1900 with the intention of fostering

high standards of production and design in the decorative arts, particularly through its annual so-called salons. Its founder René Guilleré was legal advisor to the Société des Sculptures Modeleurs. The group showed the applied arts and the work of industrial designers, mounting its first Salon exhibition at the Petit-Palais in Paris in 1904 and showing the work of Carrier-Belleuse, Rochegrosse, Grasset, Pierre Selmersheim, Lachenal, and Thesmar. Afterwards its exhibitions appeared at the Pavillon de Marsan of the Louvre until 1923 and subsequently at the Grand-Palais. In 1912, the French Chamber of Deputies voted to mount a major international exhibition that would re-establish French prestige in the decorative arts. Originally planned for 1915 and rescheduled for 1922, the exhibition was finally fixed as the ambitious and highly influential 1925 Paris 'Exposition Internationale des Arts Décoratifs et Industriels Modernes.' The inclusion of industrial design, symptomatic of the weak position of the artists, gave manufacturers and merchants the upper hand. The exhibition was intended to emulate the 1902 Turin 'Esposizione Internazionale d'Arte Decorativa Moderna.' The Paris event might more accurately have been called the 1925 Salon of the Société des Artistes Décorateurs, as all its other annual presentations of members' work were entitled. By the time the 1925 exhibition was mounted, its French members had become divided into two camps: the traditional Baroque style, and the unornamented Modern style. Decorator and designer Jacques-Émile Ruhlmann was a practitioner of the former; architect Le Corbusier of the latter. The traditionalists tended to be the interior design specialists, whereas the Modernists were concentrated in architecture and furniture design. The SAD had its own pavilion, called Une Ambassade française, an imaginary French embassy. The exhibition's title was the origin of the term 'Art Déco,' coined in the 1960s and replacing the more informative 'Art Moderne' and other titles. The seminal exhibition included pavilions from countries and manufacturers from around the world (excluding Germany and the USA). Pride of place was given to traditional design; Le Corbusier's pavilion, called L'Esprit Nouveau, was on the outskirts of the fair grounds. Enthusiasm for the sumptuous traditional approach had faded but was still in place when Le Corbusier, Robert Mallet-Stevens, René Herbst, Eileen Gray, André Lurçat, Francis Jourdain, and others boycotted the Salon of SAD in 1929 and formed the progressive Union des Artistes Modernes, whose exhibitions displayed distinctly utilitarian forms of design and architecture in the International Style. The luxurious 1935 oceanliner *Normandie* was effectively the last gesture of the traditionalists; designers banded together and created opulent and widely published interiors and furnishings in the liner's gigantic spaces. The energy of the traditionalist movement, and the SAD itself, died in 1942 in a society under foreign occupation. Modernism after World War II was translated into a dialect of what had become known as the International Style, whose exponents were Le Corbusier, Mies van der Rohe, and Walter Gropius.

▶ Pierre Cabanne, *Encyclopédie Art Déco*, Paris: Somogy, 1986: 235. Pierre Kjellberg, *Art Déco: les maîtres du Mobilier, le décor des Paquebots*, Paris: Amateur, 1986:170–71. Yvonne Brunhammer and Suzanne Tise, *Les Artistes Décorateurs, 1900–1942*, Paris: Flammarion, 1990. Nancy J. Troy, *Modernism and the Decorative Arts in France: Art Nouveau to Le Corbusier*, New Haven: Yale, 1991.

Society of Industrial Arts
See Chartered Society of Designers

Soénius, Ruth Jeanne   (1969–)
▶ German industrial designer; born Cologne.
▶ 1978–80, trained as a photo-editor and -journalist, Kölnische Rundschau, Cologne; 1980–81, in wood, metal, and plastics processing in Cologne and Aachen; from 1981, studied industrial design, Akademie der bildenden Künste, Stuttgart, under Klaus Lehmann and Richard Sapper.
▶ 1985–86, she was a spokesperson for the Baden-Württemberg VDID regional group. In 1988, she was an independent designer

at 'Fabian Industrie Design' in Mannheim and, 1988–90, lived in the USA, working in the corporate industrial design department of Siemens.
▶ She participated in the 1986 'Enfaltungen' exhibition in Stuttgart and 1987 'Muster und Modelle' exhibition in Rastatt.
▶ Cat., Design Center Stuttgart, *Women in Design: Careers and Life Histories Since 1900*, Stuttgart: Haus der Wirtschaft, 1989:172–73.

Soffientini, Duccio   (1946–)
▶ Italian industrial designer; born and active Milan.
▶ Studied architecture, Politecnico di Milano, to 1968.
▶ Soffientini, Riccardo Nava, Giorgio Romani, and Alessandro Ubertazzi established the studio DA in Milan in 1968. DA designed one of the exhibitions of the Compasso d'Oro award for ADI (Associazione per il Disegno Industriale), of which he was a member. From 1970, he collaborated with DA on traditional clocks and electronic equipment for Italora, consulting on clock design and the ergonomics of precision instruments. In 1975, the DA team designed sailboat fittings for Nemo and Comar. Its clients included Superband, Sordelli, and Svaba.
▶ In association with DA, Soffientini participated in international competitions.
▶ *ADI Annual 1976*, Milan: Associazione per il Disegno Industriale, 1976.

Sognot, Louis   (1892–1970)
▶ French designer and architect; active Paris.
▶ Studied École Bernard Palissy, Paris.
▶ He first worked for furniture manufacturers in the Faubourg Saint-Antoine in Paris. 1920–30, he managed the Primavera decorating studio of the Au Printemps department store in Paris with Charlotte Chauchet-Guilleré, after the death of its founder René Guilleré. From 1926, he was professor of decoration at École Boulle in Paris. He collaborated closely with Charlotte Alix from 1928, and much of their work cannot be individually attributed, although Sognot also designed alone. One of their first commissions was the 1929 library and reception layouts of the Laboratoires Roussel in Paris. This was the time when Sognot began to design furniture in metal and glass. His designs included models in precious and exotic woods, and lighting. Some of his furniture was produced by Bernel. They designed the 1930 office at the journal *La Semaine de Paris* building (of which Robert Mallet-Stevens was architect), the Polo de Bagatelle bar, the first-class doctor's office on the 1935 oceanliner *Normandie*, the 1931 bedroom with furniture and furnishings for the Maharajah of Indore, the interior of poster designer Jean Carlu's atelier, furniture for the syndicate office of the city of Paris, the ticket office of an airline, metal furniture for a naval officer, a room in rattan for a young dancer, and the luxurious décors for Henry Bernstein's theaters. After World War II, Sognot collaborated with Jacques Dumond on bentwood prototype furniture intended for mass production. Their lighting showed strict adherence to the Functionalist aesthetic. Their workshop, Bureau International des Arts français, was located at 15 rue de l'Abbé-Grégoire in Paris. By 1954 and working alone, Sognot's studio was located at 47 avenue Jean-Jaurès in Paris and some of his furniture was produced by Chevallier. From 1929, Sognot was a professor at the École Boulle in Paris. He was an instructor for a number of years at the École de la rue Duperré; from 1938, École des Arts appliqués à l'Industrie, and École Nationale Supérieure des Arts Décoratifs, becoming artist director after the death of René Prou in 1947. He was a founding member of Union des Artistes Décorateurs, Créateurs, Ensembliers and founding member of Jacques Vienot's Institut d'Esthétique Industrielle. He was a member of the Union des Artistes Modernes.
▶ He showed his work for the first time at the 1923 Salon d'Automne and the Salon of the Société des Artistes Décorateurs. Influenced by Cubism, designed the boudoir (with Madeleine Souguez) and bedroom in the pavilion of Primavera at the 1925 Paris 'Exposition Internationale des Arts Décoratifs et Industriels Mod-

ernes.' Sognot and Alix exhibited regularly at the events of the Salon d'Automne in Paris in the 1920s and 1930s, and the first four UAM exhibitions from 1930. His interior design and furniture for the Maharaja of Indore were shown at the 1931 Salon. He won first prize for his rattan furniture at the 1952 Salon of the Société des Artistes Décorateurs; new models of rattan furniture were shown at the 1954 'Formes Utiles' exhibition of the Salon des Arts Ménagers in Paris.

▶ *Lux*, Dec. 1929:183. Raymond Cogniat, 'Louis Sognot et Charlotte Alix, *Art et Décoration*, Vol. LIX, July–Dec. 1930. Louis Sognot, 'L'Art Décoratif Contemporain,' *Cadre de la Vie Contemporaine*, No. 3, Aug. 1935. *Ensembles Mobiliers*, Paris: Charles Moreau, No. 22, 1954. Alastair Duncan, *Art Nouveau and Art Déco Lighting*, New York: Simon and Schuster, 1978:185–86. G. Janneau, *Le Luminaire et les Moyens d'éclairage Nouveaux*, third series: plate 7. Pierre Kjellberg, *Art Déco: les maîtres du Mobilier, le décor des Paquebots*, Paris: Amateur, 1986:172–73. Arlette Barré-Despond, *UAM*, Paris: Regard,1986:506–09. Cat., *Les années UAM 1929–1958*, Paris: Musée des Arts Décoratifs, 1988:247–48. Maurice Dufrêne, *Ensembles Mobiliers, Exposition Internationale 1925*, Paris: Charles Moreau, 1925; Antique Collectors' Club, 1989:84.

Solá, Nona Umbert   (1961–)
▶ Spanish industrial designer; born Barcelona.
▶ Studied painting, crafts, and pottery, Alpe Academy, to 1978, and fashion design, Feli Fashion Institute, Barcelona, to 1979; from 1983, industrial design, Massana Academy, Barcelona.
▶ She worked in fashion design from c1980. 1981–83, she was a painter in a small cartoon film studio with Rodolfo Pastor in Barcelona. In 1988, Solá and two other designers set up the design studio Haz in Barcelona, designing domestic appliances and work tools.
▶ In 1987, she received a medal from the Adifad association for her *Bridge-Seesaw-Toboggan* and second prize at the 1989 'Italy's Cup' in Milan.
▶ Cat., Design Center Stuttgart, *Women in Design: Careers and Life Histories Since 1900*, Stuttgart: Haus der Wirtschaft, 1989:314–17.

Solano, Susana   (1946–)
▶ Spanish sculptor and designer.
▶ She designed the 1989 iron bookcase for Meta-Memphis.
▶ She represented Spain at the 1988 Biennale di Venezia. Her work was the subject of numerous solo exhibitions in European museums.
▶ Albrecht Bangert and Karl Michael Armer, *80s Style: Designs of the Decade*, New York: Abbeville, 1990:85,236.

Solon, Albert L.   (1887–1949)
▶ British ceramicist; active Arequipa, California.
▶ Following Frederick H. Rhead, 1913–16, Solon was the second artistic director of Arequipa Art Pottery in Arequipa, California, where he introduced numerous new glazes, including some Persian faïence examples. Leaving Arequipa, he taught at an institution known today as the California State University at San Jose, California. He established Solon and Schemmel in San Jose, where he produced decorative wall and floor tiles. He later became partners with Paul G. Larkin, renaming the firm Solon and Larkin.
▶ While at Arequipa, he received a gold medal at the 1915 San Francisco 'Panama-Pacific International Exposition.'
▶ Paul Evans in Timothy J. Andersen et al., *California Design 1910*, Salt Lake City: Peregrine Smith, 1980:77.

Solvsten, Harbo   (1915–1980)
▶ Danish furniture designer.
▶ Studied cabinetmaking, Tekniske Skole, Århus, to 1937, and Skolen for Boligindretning to 1942.
▶ In 1935, he was a furniture upholsterer and, in 1945, set up his own firm for furniture manufacturing. In 1972, he taught at the Arkitektskolen in Århus and, in 1976, at the Skolen for Boligindretning.

▶ Frederik Sieck, *Nutidig Dansk Møbeldesign:—en kortfattet illustreret beskrivelse*, Copenhagen: Bondo Gravesen; 1990 Busck edition in English.

Sommaruga, Giuseppe   (1867–1917)
▶ Italian architect; active Milan.
▶ Attended classes, Accademia di Brera, Milan.
▶ His buildings were designed in the *stile floreale* or *stile liberty*, including the 1901–03 Palazzo Castiglioni in Milan. On this structure and others, he collaborated with Alessandro Mazzucotelli, architectural ironworker, and Eugenio Quarti, decorator and furniture designer.
▶ Ugo Monneret de Villard (ed.), *L'Architettura di Giuseppe Sommaruga*, Milan: Preiss & Bestetti; 1908. M. Roschi, *L'Italia Liberty: Arredamento e arti decorativi*, Milan 1973.

Sommers, Inge   (1955–)
▶ German designer; born Paderborn; active Berlin.
▶ 1979–85, studied industrial design, Hochschule der Künste, Berlin.
▶ 1975–78, she was a goldsmith. In 1984, Sommers, John Hirschberg, Susanne Neubohn, and Christof Walther set up the design office Berlinetta in Berlin.
▶ Berlinetta's work was included in numerous exhibitions including the 1987 individual exhibition 'Berlinetta—Furniture 84–86' in Cologne.
▶ Cat., Design Center Stuttgart, *Women in Design: Careers and Life Histories Since 1900*, Stuttgart: Haus der Wirtschaft, 1989:78–81.
▶ See **Berlinetta**

Sony
▶ Japanese electronics products firm.
▶ The company was established in 1946 under the name Tokyo Tsushin Kogyo Kabushikakaika (TTK, or Tokyo Telecommunications Engineering Corporation). It produced the first tape recorder (the 1950 *G* type) in Japan, gaining the firm access to schools and institutions throughout the country. It manufactured the first successful transistor radio (the 1956 *TR-55*) in Japan under license from Western Electric. In 1958, TTK's corporate name was changed to 'Sony.' The first transistorized TV (*TV8-301*) was introduced in 1959, the first transistorized video recorder in 1961, a 5 in (13 cm) micro TV in 1962 (the *TV5-303*), the first domestic video recorder in 1964, the first integrated-circuit radio in 1966, the *Trinitron* color TV tube in 1968, the *U-matic* color video cassette in 1969, the domestic *Betamax* video cassette recorder in 1975, the first *Walkman* personal stereo cassette player in 1978, and the digital audio compact disc in 1980. Its success is attributable to marketing, customer empathy, and product innovation.
▶ The *TV8-301* was awarded a gold medal at the 1960 (XIII) Triennale di Milano. Its products were the subject of the 1982 'Sony Design' exhibition at The Boilerhouse at the Victoria and Albert Museum in London and included in the 1983–84 'Design Since 1945' exhibition at the Philadelphia Museum of Art.
▶ Stephen Bayley (ed.), *The Conran Directory of Design*, London: Conran Octopus, 1985. Cat., Kathryn B. Hiesinger and George H. Marcus III (eds.), *Design Since 1945*, Philadelphia: Philadelphia Museum of Art, 1983:231,I–44–46. Cat., *Sony Design*, London: Victoria and Albert Museum, 1982. Wolfgang Schmittel, *Design Concept Realisation*, Zürich, 1975:169–96.

Sopha Praxis
▶ French industrial design consultancy.
▶ Sopha Praxis was established in 1985 in Paris as part of the Sopha Group, the architecture, interior design, corporate identity, visual communications, and engineering organization.
▶ Agnès Lévitte and Margo Rouard, *100 quotidiens objets made in France*, Paris: APCI/Syros-Alternatives, 1987:82.

Sørensen, Johnny (1944–)

▶ Danish furniture designer.

▶ Studied cabinetmaking, Kunsthåndværkerskolen, Copenhagen, to 1967.

▶ In 1963, he was an apprentice at Helingøor Skibsværft. From 1967, Sørensen and Rud Thygesen collaborated on a major group of seating designs, using lamination and pressure bending of woods, sometimes in cantilever models, for firms including Magnus Olesen and Christensen og Larsen. From 1976, Sørensen taught at Den Permanente.

▶ He and Thygesen received first prize at the 1966 'Society of Cabinetmakers Jubilee Exhibition,' first prize at the 1968 Society of Cabinetmakers Furniture Competition, 1969 and 1975 Central Bank's Jubilee Award, 1971 Society of Furniture Makers Award, third prize at the 1973 Scandinavian Idea Competition, 1976 Alexandor Foss Industrifond-Award. His and Thygesen's work was shown in exhibitions including at Den Permanente in Copenhagen in 1972, Det Danske Kunstindustrimuseum in Copenhagen in 1976, in Chicago in 1977, and 1980 'Scandinavian Modern Design 1880–1980' exhibition at the Cooper-Hewitt Museum in New York.

▶ Cat., David Revere McFadden (ed.), *Scandinavian Modern Design 1880–1980*, New York: Abrams, 1982:271, No. 337. Frederik Sieck, *Nutidig Dansk Møbeldesign:—en kortfattet illustreret beskrivelse*, Copenhagen: Bondo Gravesen; 1990 Busck edition in English.

Sørensen, Oskar (1898–)

▶ Norwegian metalworker.

▶ Sørensen designed simple objects appropriate for mass production in silver and produced by J. Tostrup in Oslo. 1922–65, he taught at the Statens Håndverks -og Kunstindustriskole, Oslo.

▶ His 1937 silver bird decanter for Tostrup was included in the 1980 'Scandinavian Modern Design 1880–1980' exhibition at the Cooper-Hewitt Museum in New York.

▶ Cat., David Revere McFadden (ed.), *Scandinavian Modern Design 1880–1980*, New York: Abrams, 1982:271, No. 110. Annelies Krekel-Aalberse, *Art Nouveau and Art Déco Silver*, New York: Abrams, 1989:243,259.

Sormani

▶ Italian furniture manufacturer.

▶ The firm was founded in 1961 by the Sormani family in Arosio. Its sophisticated factory operation produced furniture in plastics, metal, wood, and upholstery. One of its first designers, Richard Neagle, designed its 1970 *Mini-Madio* wardrobe in ABS plastic, Claudio Salocchi its 1970 *Apoggio* seat, R. Lera its 1970 *Goga* bookshelves, and Studio DA its 1970 *Tomorrow* wine rack. Joe Columbo's 1969 *Roto-Living* unit, and Studio DA's 1970 *DA 35* storage table were widely published.

▶ It won the 1971 Mercurio d'Oro. Seven pieces were included in the 1972 'Design a Plastické Hmoty' exhibition at the Uměleckoprůmyslové Muzeum in Prague.

▶ Cat., Milena Lamarová, *Design a Plastické Hmoty*, Prague: Uměleckoprůmyslové Muzeum, 1972:76,78,206.

Sornay, André (1902–)

▶ French decorator and furniture maker; born Lyons.

▶ Studied École des Beaux-Arts, Lyons.

▶ Abandoning the historicist and ancient styles produced in the family workshop, he designed furniture from 1919 in simple, innovative, and Cubist forms inspired by the work of friends Francis Jourdain and Pierre Chareau and other avant-garde decorators. From 1925, when he opened a factory in Villeurbanne, he decorated numerous apartments in Paris and Lyons, offices, houses, and libraries. 'Le style Sornay' was recognizable for its use of brass nails.

▶ He showed an ensemble in white sycamore at the 1923 Salon d'Automne.

▶ Pierre Kjellberg, *Art Déco: les maîtres du Mobilier, le décor des Paquebots*, Paris: Amateur, 1986:189–90.

Sotavalta, Impi (1885–1964)

▶ Finnish textile designer.

▶ 1917–43, she designed for the Friends of Finnish Handicraft, specializing in rug design, including the low-pile *rya*.

▶ Cat., David Revere McFadden (ed.), *Scandinavian Modern Design 1880–1980*, New York: Abrams, 1982:271, No. 107.

Sottsass Associati

▶ Italian design firm; located Milan.

▶ In 1980, Ettore Sottsass, Aldo Cibic, Matteo Thun, and Marco Zanini founded Sottsass Associati. They participated in industrial and interior design projects ranging from mechanics to electronics and domestic products. Collaborating with Michele De Lucchi, Sottsass Associati designed the Fiorucci shops in Europe. In 1980 for the city of Turin, it designed a multi-purpose kiosk, public toilet, and advertising space. In 1981, it designed graphics for Nava, Mandelli, Ungaro, and Alessi; collaborated with Nathalie du Pasquier, Giovanni Sacchi, and Erminio Rizzotti on various projects; and planned a collection for Memphis.

▶ Andrea Branzi, *La Casa Calda: Esperienze del Nuovo Disegno Italiano*, Milan: Idea Books, 1982.

Sottsass, Ettore (1917–)

▶ Austrian designer; born Innsbruck; active Milan.

▶ 1935–39, studied architecture, Politecnico di Torino.

▶ His father Ettore Sot-Sas studied at the Akademie der bildenden Künste in Vienna under Otto Wagner and moved to Turin in 1928 with his family, where he became a protagonist in the architectural debate between Marcello Piacentini and Giuseppi Pagano over the Railway Station project in Florence in the 1930s. Sottsass Jr. began his career as an architect in 1947, setting up The Studio, Milan. From 1957, he was a consultant designer at Olivetti, where he designed computers, adding machines, typewriters, and systems furniture. He became a father figure of the Anti-Design movement of the 1960s. From 1966, his furniture for Poltronova was influenced by Pop Art and an extended visit to the USA when he worked in the studio of George Nelson in New York for a year in 1966. His subcontinental Indian-inspired ceramics were produced in 1969. He designed the radical, if intentionally plain, 1970 *Grey* furniture range produced by Poltronova; it was inspired by American minimalist sculpture; (with Michele De Lucchi) designed Olivetti's 1982 *Icarus* office-furniture range. His links with Anti-Design became stronger after 1979, when he began to associate with members of Studio Alchimia. In 1980, (with Aldo Cibic, Marco Zanini, and Matteo Thun) he established Sottsass Associati. Sottsass set up the Memphis furniture and furnishings group in 1981, with a highly successful showing at the Salone del Mobile in Milan of that year. Winding up Memphis in 1988, Sottsass continued to include humor and sometimes folly in his designs for clients including Cleto Munari (accessories), Fusital (hardware fittings), Zanotta (furniture), Artemide (lighting), Swid Powell (metalware and ceramics). In 1986 with Christopher Radl and Ambrogio Borsani, established publicity agency Italiana di Communicazione; had more than 100 clients worldwide.

▶ His work for Olivetti included the 1959 *Elea 9003* computer series, 1963 *Praxis* and 1964 *Tekne 3* typewriters, and the 1969 *Valentine* red plastic portable typewriter. His 1988 telephone design was produced by Enorme. His furniture for Memphis included the 1981 *Casablanca* and *Beverly* cabinets, *Carlton* and *Survetta* bookcases, and *Mandarin* table; 1982 *Malabar* console, *Alaska* silver vase, and *Marmansk* silver compote; 1983 *City* and *Park Lane* tables; 1984 *Hyatt* and *Mimosa* side tables, *Palm Spring* and *Holebid* tables; 1985 *Freemont* and *Tartar* consoles and *Ivory* table; 1986 *Manhattan* cart; 1987 *Max* bookcase and *Donald* table. His lighting for Memphis included the 1981 *Treetops* floor lamp, *Tahiti* and *Ashoka* table lamps, 1983 *Bay* table lamp, and 1984 *Diva* table lamp. His Memphis ceramic designs were the 1983 *Tigris*, *Nilo*, and *Euphrates* vases, and 1985 *Indivia*, *Lettuce*, and *Rucola* plates. His fabrics for Memphis included 1983 *Schizzo*, *Rete*, and *Lettraset*. His 1982 glassware collection for Memphis included the *Altair*, *Mizar*, and *Shiro* vases, *Deneb* goblet, and *Sol* compote; the 1983 glassware collection included the *Aldebaran* compote and *Alcor* and *Alioth* vases.

▶ Received 1959, 1969 (*Valentine* portable typewriter), and 1970 Compasso d'Oro; honorable mention, 1973 'BIO 5' Industrial Design Biennial, Ljubljana; and honorary degree, Royal College of Art, London. His environment was included in the 1972 'Italy: The New Domestic Landscape' exhibition at the New York Museum of Modern Art and Work in 1979 'Design Process Olivetti 1908–78' exhibition at the Frederick S. Wight Art Gallery, University of California, Los Angeles, and in exhibitions worldwide. Work subject of 1976 exhibition at the International Design Zentrum, Berlin and Biennale di Venezia; 1977 'Ettore Sottsass, Jr: De l'objet fini à la fin de l'objet' exhibition, Centre Georges Pompidou, Paris; 1987 and 1991 exhibitions, Blum Helman Gallery, New York. *Valentine* typewriter was shown at 1983–84 'Design Since 1945' exhibition, Philadelphia Museum of Art, and 1991 'The Cooper-Hewitt Collections: A Design Resource,' Cooper-Hewitt Museum, New York. The Memphis line was introduced at 1981 Salone del Mobile, Milan. *Esercizio Formale Nr. 3* furniture included in 'Affinità Elettive' exhibition, 1985 Triennale di Milano. *Nairobi* and *Mombasa* cabinets by Zanotta introduced at 1989 Salone del Mobile in Milan. *Casablanca* bookcase included in 1991 'Mobili Italiani 1961–1991: Le Varie Età dei linguaggi' exhibition, Milan.

▶ Federica Di Castro (ed.), *Sottsass's Scrap-Book*, Milan, 1976. Penny Sparke, *Ettore Sottsass Jnr*, London: The Design Council, 1982. *Sottsass Associati*, New York, Rizzoli, 1988. Cat., Kathryn B. Hiesinger and George H. Marcus III (eds.), *Design Since 1945*, Philadelphia: Philadelphia Museum of Art, 1983:231,I–47. *Ettore Sottsass, Jr: De l'objet fini à la fin de l'objet*, Paris: Centre de Création Industrielle, 1977. Paolo Fossati, *Il design in Italia*, Turin, 1972:114–21,220–23, plates 250–74,296–309. Cat., *Design Process Olivetti 1908–1978*, Los Angeles: Frederick S. Wight Art Gallery (University of California, Los Angeles), 1979:267. Marco Zanini, 'A Well Travelled Man,' in *Design ist unsichtbar*, Vienna, 1981:464–74. Christine Colin, 'Memphis a encore frappé,' *Décoration Internationale*, No. 51, Dec. 1982–Jan. 1983:54–57,206. Barbara Radice, *Memphis*, New York: Rizzoli, 1984. Auction cat., *Asta di Modernariato 1900–1986*, Auction 'Modernariato,' Milan: Semenzato Nuova Geri, 8 Oct. 1986: lots 117–18. Paolo Martegani, Andrea Mazzoli, and Riccardo Montenegro, *Memphis una Questione di Stile*, Rome, 1987. Gilles de Bure, *Ettore Sottsass Jr*, Paris, 1987. *Le Affinità Elettive*, Milan: Electa, 1985. Barbara Radice, *Ettore Sottsass: A Critical Biography*, New York: Rizzoli, 1993.

▶ See Memphis

Soudbinine, Seraphin (1870–1944)

▶ Russian artist and sculptor; active Paris.

▶ Soudbinine collaborated on screens with Jean Dunand in Paris. He probably produced the overall design and low-relief images and Dunand the lacquerwork. Soudbinine produced doors and screens for the music room of the Mr. and Mrs. Solomon R. Guggenheim house in Port Washington, New York, in 1925–26; entitled *Crescendo* and *Pianissimo*, they illustrated heroic subjects.

▶ M. Komaneck and V.F. Butera, *The Folding Image Screens by Western Artists of the Nineteenth and Twentieth Centuries*, New Haven: Yale University Art Gallery, 1984:241–42.

Sougez, Madeleine (1891–1945)

▶ French designer.

▶ She designed for the Primavera decorating department of the Au Printemps department store in Paris during the 1920s and 1930s.

▶ She designed the kitchen in the Primavera pavilion at the 1925 Paris 'Exposition Internationale des Arts Décoratifs et Industriels Modernes.' Participated in 1924, 1926 and 1927 Salons of the Société des Artistes Décorateurs.

▶ Alastair Duncan, *Art Nouveau and Art Déco Lighting*, New York: Simon and Schuster, 1978:185.

Souriau, Paul (1852–1926)

▶ French philosopher and theoretician.

▶ In his book *La Beauté rationnelle* he was one of the first to propose that aesthetics and usefulness should be amalgamated, that an object can have a rational beauty, and that its form should be an expression of its function, all propositions presaging industrial aesthetics and Functionalism. His son Étienne Souriau (1892–c1955) was director of the *Revue d'Esthétique*, which had a strong effect on the development of Modern theories of aesthetics and design; published *Pensée vivante et perfection formelle* (1925), *Avenir de l'esthétique* (1929), and *La correspondance des Arts* (1947).

Sowden, George James (1942–)

▶ British designer; born Leeds; active Italy.

▶ 1960–64 and 1966–68, studied architecture, Gloucester College of Arts.

▶ He settled in Milan in 1970, joining the Olivetti studio headed by Ettore Sottsass, where he developed design ideas concerning information technology. In 1981, he was a member of Sottsass's Memphis group and produced objects and furniture for its collections until 1988, when Memphis closed. He subsequently set up his own studio, working independently and with his wife Nathalie du Pasquier. Sowden's tableware designs for Bodum were widely published and popular, including his 1986 stainless-steel fruit bowl, whose pattern was produced by a sophisticated 12-stage stamping process. He had design clients including Lorenz (time pieces with du Pasquier), Olivetti, and Italtel in Italy and Shiznoka in Japan.

▶ His initial 1981 Memphis designs included the *D'Antibes* cabinet, *Pierre* table, *Oberoi* chair, *Chelsea* bed, and *Acapulco*, *Excelsior*, and *American* clocks, and were followed by the 1982 *Metropole* casement clock and *Oriental* bed, 1983 *Palace* armchair, *Savoy* cabinet, and *Quadro* and *Triangolo* fabrics, 1985 *Mamounia* armchair and *Potato* ceramic platter, 1986 *Liverpool* and *Gloucester* armchairs, and 1987 *George* cabinet.

▶ Cat., *Design Process: Olivetti 1981–1983*, Milan, 1983:386. Auction cat., *Memphis: La Collection Karl Lagerfeld*, Monaco: Jeremy Myerson and Sylvia Katz, *Conran Design Guides: Tableware*, London: Conran Octopus, 1990:34,46,78. Sotheby's, 13 Oct. 1991. *Modo*, No. 148, March–April 1993:126.

Spade, Batistin (1891–1969)

▶ French decorator and furniture designer; born Marseilles.

▶ He made a modest beginning in 1919 in his own workshop for cabinetmaking and tapestry design. Working in a sumptuous and refined mode, Spade designed furniture and numerous interiors, including shipping-line offices, banks, and insurance companies, in France and abroad; in 1941 and 1943, he was commissioned by the Mobilier National to design the offices of government officials and ambassadors. He worked on about 30 oceanliners, including the 1926 *Île-de-France*, *Liberté*, *Flandre*, and 1935 *Normandie*.

▶ *Ensembles Mobiliers*, Paris: Charles Moreau, Vol. 5, No. 15, 1945. Yolande Amic, *Le Mobilier français 1945–1964*, Paris: Regard/VIA, 1983:22. Pierre Kjellberg, *Art Déco: les maîtres du Mobilier, le décor des Paquebots*, Paris: Amateur, 1986:172,175.

Spadolini, Pierluigi (1922–)

▶ Italian industrial designer; born and active Florence.

▶ 1947–48, Spadolini designed systems furniture; was a cofounder of Instituto Superiore di Disegno Industriale, Florence; was the architect of Palazzo degli Afari, Florence; Palazzo di Giustizia, Siena; and a university and schools in Messina, Pisa, Rome, and Grosseto. Designs included products from furniture to motor yachts. His plastic furniture was produced by Kartell in Binasco. His clients included Magneti Marelli, ICS, Lesa, Gretz, Autovox, 1 P, Arflex, OTB, and Gandi. He was a member of ADI (Associazione per il Disegno Industriale).

▶ *ADI Annual 1976*, Milan: Associazione per il Disegno Industriale, 1976. Alfonso Grassi and Anty Pansera, *Atlante del design italiano: 1940–1980*, Milan, 1980:291.

Špalek, Josef (1902–42)
▶ Bohemian architect and furniture designer; born Plzěn.
▶ Studied Academy of Arts, Prague, under Josef Gočár.
▶ 1928–34, he worked in the studio of Jaromír Krejcar. In the 1920s, Špalek's most noteworthy project was the 1928–29 monumental Functional villa at 21 Karolíny Světlé St. in Plzěn. He died near Moscow (Russia), a victim of Stalinist repression. Chosen over Karel Stráník, whose furniture was thought to be too snobbish, for the old house in Louny of Marie Bieblová and Konstantin Biebl, Špalek designed a compact combination of bookcase, spacious couch, sideboard, and several cupboards, and included a large round table and various occasional tables from standard models by Thonet. He also produced wooden furniture, including a glass-fronted extension to the sideboard; the walls of the flat were painted white, and its overall style was clearly Bauhaus influenced.
▶ Cat., *Devětsil: Czech Avant-Garde Art, Architecture, and Design of the 1920s and 30s*, Oxford Museum of Modern Art and London Design Museum, 1990.

Spalt, Johannes
See Arbeitsgruppe 4

Sparre, Louis (1866–1964)
▶ Swedish furniture designer and ceramicist; active Finland.
▶ 1886–90, studied painting, Académie Julian, Paris.
▶ 1891–1911, he worked in Finland. In 1897, he founded the Iris factory in Porvoo. He subsequently worked in Stockholm. He designed and illustrated books, and, along with Akseli Gallen-Kallela, Eliel Saarinen, Herman Gesellius, and Armas Lindgren, was considered a pioneer of the revival of design in Finland. His bold furniture designs were rendered in emphatic geometric silhouettes.
▶ He received the first prize in the Friends of Finnish Handicraft's 1894 furniture competition.
▶ Cat., David Revere McFadden (ed.), *Scandinavian Modern Design 1880–1980*, New York: Abrams, 1982:271, No. 61.

Spear, Francis (1902–)
▶ British glass designer and maker; born London.
▶ Studied Central School of Arts and Crafts and Royal College of Art, London, to 1926.
▶ He was an assistant to Martin Travers. Until 1938, he taught lithography at the Central School of Arts and Crafts and Royal College of Art, London. He was a radical exponent of stained glass. In the 1930s, he completed many commissions for church windows, including those at Aldeburgh in 1930, Astley Bridge in 1930, Snaith in 1934, and for the 1957 Cape Town Cathedral, which he considered his best work. Spear was an occasional council member of the Arts and Crafts Exhibition Society.
▶ His 1938 *St. John the Baptist* window in acid-treated flash glass (executed by John Barker) was included in the 1979–80 'Thirties' exhibition at the Hayward Gallery in London.
▶ Cat., *Thirties: British art and design before the war*, London: Arts Council of Great Britain, Hayward Gallery, 1979:102,198,300.

Spear, Laurinda (1951–)
▶ American architect and designer; born Rochester, Minnesota; active Miami, Florida.
▶ Studied Brown University, Providence, Rhode Island, to 1972, and architecture, Columbia University, New York, to 1975.
▶ She is best known for the designs of the Atlantis and Palace buildings in Miami. She designed banks, houses, shopping centers, condominiums, courthouses, and office towers. In 1977 and 1979, she was a part-time faculty member at the University of Miami School of Engineering and Environmental Design. In 1977, she co-founded the architecture firm Arquitectonica with husband Bernardo Fort-Brescia and three associates no longer with the firm.

Their controversial buildings, including the 1979 house (with Rem Koolhaas) for Spear's parents, won numerous design awards and they became one of America's most successful architecture firms. In 1985, Spear and Fort-Brescia established Arquitonica Products. She designed the 1984 *Madonna* red and yellow lacquered table produced by Memphis, 1986 *Miami Beach* dinnerware produced by Swid Powell, and 1990 line of men's neckwear. Spear and Fort-Brescia lived in their own 1990 'Pink House.' She was a co-founding member of the American Institute of Architects National Committee on Design.
▶ She won the 1975 *Progressive Architecture* award with Rem Koolhaas and citations in 1978 and 1980. Other awards included the 1975 New York Society of Architects design award, 1978 Rome Prize in Architecture, 1982 South Florida Chapter of the AIA, 1983 award for the Atlantis building, and 1986 Architectural Record Houses for Casa Los Andes. Her work was included in exhibitions in 1979 at the Cooper-Hewitt Museum, New York, 1979 Florida Chapter of AIA, 1980 Pennsylvania State University, 1980 'Young Architects at Yale University,' 1981 at University of Virginia, 1981 at Columbia University, 1982 at the Biennale de Paris, 1982 at Contemporary Arts Museum in Houston, 1983 Mandeville Arts Gallery/University of California at San Diego, 1983 Hudson River Museum, 1983 Ewald Scholars Symposium/ Sweet Briar College, 1984 Center for the Fine Arts in Miami, 1985 Fort Wayne Museum of Art in Indiana, 1985 Walker Art Center in Minneapolis, 1985 Sarah Campbell Blaffer Gallery in Houston, and 1986 Institute of Contemporary Art in Philadelphia. Work subject of 'Architectonics: Yesterday, Today and Tomorrow' traveling exhibition, USA.
▶ *Les Carnets du Design*, Paris: Mad-Cap Productions et APCI, 1986:15. Robert A.M. Stern (ed.), *The International Design Yearbook*, New York: Abbeville, 1985/1986:272. Patricia Leigh Brown, 'Having a Wonderful Time in Miami,' *The New York Times*, 25 Oct. 1990:C1,6.

Spectre, Jay (1930–92)
▶ American interior and furniture designer; born Louisville, Kentucky; active New York.
▶ He began his interior design career in 1951 in Louisville; in 1968, established the design company Jay Spectre in New York; designed interiors for luxury homes, private jet aircraft, yachts, and offices, which showed Art Déco, Asian, and African influences with high-tech and hand-carved elements; in 1985, (with Geoffrey Bradfield) set up the licensing firm JSPS to sell rights to furniture, china, rugs, and other articles design by the Spectre firm; in 1987, designed the *Neo-Deco* line of furniture for the Century Furniture Industry; executed rug designs for Louis de Poortère, outdoor furniture for Jordan Brown, Filipino wicker furniture for Century, and lighting for Sunset; (with Bradfield) published the book *Point of View: Design by Jay Spectre* (1991).
▶ In 1986, appointed to Interior Design Hall of Fame and received 1987 *Bride's* magazine award for excellence.
▶ *Metropolitan Home*, April 1990:72. 'Jay Spectre, 63: An Interior Designer of Luxurious Homes,' *The New York Times*, 17 Nov. 1992.

Spence, Basil Urwin (1907–76)
▶ British architect and exhibition and interior designer; born Bombay.
▶ Studied architecture in Edinburgh and London.
▶ He was a draftsman during the design of the Viceroy's House in Delhi and worked for architect Rowan Anderson. In 1931, he formed a brief partnership with William Kininmonth in Edinburgh and subsequently moved to London, where he set up a practice. Before World War II, he built large country houses. His designs after the war included housing developments, churches, theaters, schools, civic centers, and educational institutions, including Sussex University. He was best known for his 1954–62 rebuilding of Coventry Cathedral, having won the 1950 competition. He produced designs for Scandinavian-inspired furniture for the Scottish Furniture Manufacturers'

Association and for the Furniture Development Council. His monumental approach was illustrated by his 1971 British Embassy in Rome and 1970 Knightsbridge Barracks in London.

▶ He was the consultant architect to the 1946 'Britain Can Make It' exhibition at the Victoria and Albert Museum in London with James Gardner as chief designer. He designed the Sea and Ships pavilion at the 1951 'Festival of Britain' exposition in London, the British Pavilion at the 1967 'Montreal Universal and International Exposition (Expo '67)', and others.

▶ Michael Farr, *Design in British Industry: A Mid-Century Survey*, London: Cambridge, 1955:216. Vittorio Magnago Lampugnani (ed.), *Encyclopedia of 20th-Century Architecture*, New York: Abrams, 1986:315–16. Charles McKean, *Scottish Thirties: An Architectural Introduction*, Edinburgh: Scottish Academic Press, 1987.

Spenser, Edward   (1872–1938)

▶ British metalworker, silversmith, and jeweler; active London.

▶ Spencer was a junior designer at the Artificers' Guild; when Montague Fordham took over the Guild in 1903, Spenser became chief designer. He designed silver objects with applied shagreen, mother-of-pearl, wood, coconut, and ivory. The craft aspect of his work was emphasized by its visible hammer marks. Part of the success of the Artificers' Guild was due to Spenser's designs, which kept up with the times. In 1905, he founded the short-lived Guild of St. Michael.

▶ He showed his work regularly at the exhibitions of the Arts and Crafts Society and the Artificers' Guild in London.

▶ Annelies Krekel-Aalberse, *Art Nouveau and Art Déco Silver*, New York: Abrams, 1989:22,24,259. Charlotte Gere, *American and European Jewelry 1830–1914*, New York: Crown, 1975:221.

Spindler, Charles   (1865–1938)

▶ German designer.

▶ 1983–89, studied schools of fine art, Düsseldorf, Munich, and Berlin.

▶ In the early 1890s, he became known for figurative marquetry of the type shown in the dining room (produced by Jacquemin) in the Art in Alsace pavilion at the 1925 Paris 'Exposition Internationale des Arts Décoratifs et Industriels Modernes.'

▶ Work (furniture) shown and grand prize and gold medal received at 1900 Paris 'Exposition Universelle.'

▶ Maurice Dufrêne, *Ensembles Mobiliers, Exposition Internationale 1925*, Paris: Charles Moreau, 1925, Antique Collectors' Club, 1989:170.

Spojené Uměleckoprůmyslové Závody   (aka UP)
(United Industrial Art Factories)

▶ Czech furniture firm.

▶ UP was founded in 1921 by Jan Vaněk as a fusion of a number of Moravian furniture factories; in addition to furniture, it produced metal lighting and textiles. It had 600 workers and aimed at the production of standard furniture designed by Jan Grunt, Josef Gočár, Jan Vaněk, and Evžen Wiesner; 1928–35, produced a range of demountable furniture called *E*; 1935–37, produced the 'sector' furniture range *H*; was a member of SČSD (Czechoslovak Werkbund) and participated in all of its exhibitions. It was nationalized in 1947.

▶ A. Adlerová, *České užité umění 1918–1938*, Prague, 1983.

Spook, Per   (1939–)

▶ Norwegian designer; born Oslo; active Paris.

▶ Studied fine art and, 1957, Chambre Syndicale, Paris.

▶ He worked with some of the best known fashion designers for ten years until 1979, when he began designing his own collections; in 1980, established a fashion house; in 1986, created his first ceramic dinner service, produced by Les Porcelaines Lafarge in a series of four bowls with white inside and brown outside; in the early 1990s, opened a shop in Paris.

▶ Received 1978 'Aiguille d'Or de la Haute Couture' award and 1979 'Dé d'Or' award.

▶ *Les Carnets du Design*, Paris: Mad-Cap Productions et APCI, 1986:33.

Sportes, Ronald-Cecil   (1943–)

▶ French architect and designer; born Orléanville (Algeria); active Paris.

▶ Studied École des Arts Appliqués et des Métiers d'Arts, Paris.

▶ He worked with Arne Jacobsen in Copenhagen and returned to Paris, where he worked with French and foreign architects until 1968. He studied inflatable structures, including a multi-directional model for the Kleber-Colombes tire company. He worked at the architecture firm Elsa and subsequently became creative and research director at Marange. In 1975, he set up his own practice in Paris. He designed interiors for Lancôme in New York and its headquarters in Paris, and for the airliner *Concorde*. His commissions included Galerie Artcurial, Arletty cinema, Ministry of Justice, the Cosmair office in New York, Volvo's North African headquarters in Casablanca, the Museum of Science and Technology at Parc de la Villette park in Paris, cultural center and museum of French wines in Osaka, Cherfien des Phosphates office in Morocco, and the interior and furniture of the TGV terminal in the Gare Montparnasse in Paris. He worked with the Beijing Consulting and Engineering Cooperative for Light Industry on the design and production of hardwood furniture and received a commission from the Chinese Ministry for Industry. With design offices in Paris, he designed the interior and furniture for a room in President Mitterrand's suite in the Élysée Palace in 1982–83. Designing interiors, furniture, and lighting, his 22-piece furniture collection was produced by JG Furniture in the USA and designs by Pentalux, Italy. Furniture projects were sponsored by VIA.

▶ His work was included in the 1968 international exhibition on inflatable structures in Paris, 1968 (XIV) Triennale di Milano, 1969 traveling exhibition in the USA, and 1988 exhibitions of contemporary French furniture at the Victoria and Albert Museum, London. The 1987 retrospective of his work was mounted at the International Design Center of New York, Long Island City.

▶ Sophie Anargyros, *Le Mobilier français*, Paris: Regard/VIA, 1980:82–83. Cat., Garth Hall and Margo Rouard Snowman, *Avant Premiere: Contemporary French Furniture*, London: Eprouvé, 1988. Cat., *Les années VIA, 1980–1990*, Paris: Musée des Arts Décoratifs, 1990.

Spratling, William   (1900–67)

▶ American architect and silversmith; born Sonyea, New York; active New Orleans and Taxco (Mexico).

▶ He was instrumental in the emergence of Modern Mexican silver in the 1920s. Spratling taught at Tulane University in New Orleans. In 1925, he settled in Taxco, where he attempted to revive the silversmithing art. He published the book *Little Mexico* (1932). He used artisans in the Taxco area to produce his patterns and shapes, as a result of which Taxco became known as the silver capital of the Americas. He also designed the silver-production tools and molds. In his silverwares and jewelry he incorporated mother-of-pearl, hardwoods, feathers, baroque pearls, tortoiseshell, coral, amber, turquoise, jadeite, rock crystal, obsidian, and malachite. Obviously handcrafted and produced in his workshop known as Las Delicias, his wares were sold at stores including Lord and Taylor, Macy's, Tiffany, and Neiman Marcus in the USA; orders were placed by President Lyndon Johnson and actors Cantinflas, Orson Welles, and Dolores del Rio. At one time, half the silverware sold in Mexico City was from the Spratling workshop. His designs sometimes incorporated ancient Meso-American motifs. His sugar spoon in the shape of a duck's bill was widely published. Known today as William Spratling's Heirs Company, the ranch-workshop was bought by his friend Alberto Ulrich from the former employees. In 1992, the retail store Spratling Silver was opened in San Antonio, Texas, and sold some of Spratling's original designs.

▶ Lucía García-Noriega Nieto (tr. Ahmed Simeón), 'Mexico Silver:

William Spratling and the Taxco Style,' *The Journal of Propaganda and Decorative Arts*, Fall 1988:42–53. Annelies Krekel-Aalberse, *Art Nouveau and Art Déco Silver*, New York: Abrams, 1989:259. Lucia Garcia-Noriega Nieto, 'William Spratling' in Mel Byars and Russell Flinchum (eds.), *50 American Designers*, Washington: Preservation, 1994.

Stabler, Harold (1872–1945)

▶ British ceramicist, enameler, jeweler, and silversmith; born Levens, Westmorland; husband of Phoebe Stabler.

▶ Apprenticed to a woodcarver at Kendal Art School, Cumbria; studied metalworking, Keswick School of Industrial Art, to 1902.

▶ While studying at the Keswick School of Industrial Art, he was appointed director of its metalwork section in 1898. Leaving the school in 1902, he began working for R.L.B. Rathbone in the metalworking department of Liverpool School of Art; Rathbone designed jewelry as a sideline. Arriving in London in the early 1900s, he taught at the Royal College of Art until 1907. 1907–37, he was an instructor and at later head of the art department of the Sir John Cass Technical Institute. In 1915, he became a founding member of the Design and Industries Association. After World War I, his style moved away from the Arts and Crafts idiom to that of British Art Déco. 1912–26, he also taught at the Royal College of Art. In 1921, he became a partner with Charles Carter and John Adams of Carter Pottery, Poole (then known as Carter, Stabler and Adams). An accomplished ceramicist, he worked on war memorials, figurines, tiles, and tableware, including Pyrex glassware and silverware. Setting up his own workshop, he designed silver produced by Adie Bros. and by Wakeley and Wheeler and successfully designed for mass production, introducing die-struck decoration. Despite his crafts orientation, he was an enthusiastic proponent of improvement in the design of everyday, machine-made domestic goods, which alienated him from some of his fellow craftspeople. He and wife Phoebe Stabler designed and modeled a number of decorative figures and garden statues. Many of Stabler's designs showed simple angular stamped ornamentation. His best known silver design was the 1935 tea set for Adie. In the 1930s, Stabler was design consultant to Firth Vickers, the Sheffield stainless steel manufacturer; he also designed stainless-steel hollow-ware for J. and J. Wiggin.

▶ He showed his work at the exhibitions of the Arts and Crafts Society, the New Gallery, and Albert Hall in London, and at exhibitions in Germany and Austria. His covered bowl was shown at the 1929 Buenos Aires exposition. In 1936, elected Royal Designer for Industry. His ceramics, glass, and metalwork were included in the 1979–80 'Thirties' exhibition at the Hayward Gallery in London.

▶ Charlotte Gere, *American and European Jewelry 1830–1914*, New York: Crown, 1975:221. Cat., *Thirties: British art and design before the war*, London: Arts Council of Great Britain, Hayward Gallery, 1979:23,99,100,136,139,156,222, 231,300. Fiona MacCarthy and Patrick Nuttgens, *An Eye for Industry*, London: Lund Humphries with Royal Society for Arts, 1986. Annelies Krekel-Aalberse, *Art Nouveau and Art Déco Silver*, New York: Abrams, 1989:259.

Stabler, Phoebe (?–1955)

▶ British ceramicist, enameler, and silversmith; active London; wife of Harold Stabler.

▶ She worked with husband Harold Stabler and on her own. From c1906, she and he sold designs to Doulton, Worcester, Ashtead, and Harold Stabler's own Carter, Stabler and Adams, Poole. They made opaque *cloisonné* enamel pendants under the guidance of Japanese craftsperson Mr. Kato; some of the items were not wearable. Some of their designs adapted European geometric motifs in a way that exemplified British Art Déco styling.

▶ Toni Lesser Wolf, 'Women Jewelers of the British Arts and Crafts Movement,' *The Journal of Decorative and Propaganda Arts*, No. 14, Fall 1989:34.

Stæhr-Nielsen, Eva (1911–76) and Olaf Stæhr-Nielsen (1896–1969)

▶ Danish ceramicists and metalworkers; wife and husband.

▶ 1930–33, Eva Stæhr-Nielsen studied Kunsthåndværkerskolen, Copenhagen.

▶ 1932–68, she worked with Nathalie Krebs at the ceramics factory Saxbo in Copenhagen and, 1968–76, at the Royal Copenhagen Porcelain manufactory; from 1973, was active in own workshop Designhuser in Lidköping; in the 1950s, designed silver flatware patterns for Georg Jensen Sølvsmedie, including 1958 *Mocha Spoons*. Olaf Stæhr-Nielsen designed ceramics, silver, and furniture, including jewelry for the Georg Jensen Sølvsmedie.

▶ Eva Stæhr-Nielsen received gold medals at 1937 Paris 'Exposition Internationale des Arts et Techniques dans la Vie Moderne' and 1954 (X) and 1957 (XI) Triennali di Milano. Her work shown at 1954–57 USA 'Design in Scandinavia' traveling exhibition, 1956–57 Germany 'Neue Form aus Dänemark' traveling exhibition, Malmö Museum in 1957, 1959 'Formes Scandinaves' exhibition at the Paris Musée des Arts Décoratifs, 1959 Stockholm 'Dansk Form og Miljø' exhibition, 1968 London 'Two Centuries of Danish Design,' and Åborg Kunstmuseum in 1975.

▶ Cat., *Georg Jensen Silversmithy: 77 Artists, 75 Years*, Washington: Smithsonian Institution Press, 1980. Cat., David Revere McFadden (ed.), *Scandinavian Modern Design 1880–1980*, New York: Abrams, 1982:271, No. 162. Jennifer Hawkins Opie, *Scandinavia: Ceramics and Glass in the Twentieth Century*, New York: Rizzoli, 1989.

Stagi, Franca (1937–)

▶ Italian industrial designer and architect; active Modena.

▶ Studied Politecnico di Milano to 1962.

▶ She became a partner in 1962 in the architecture firm of Cesare Leonardi in Modena. Their best known work was the 1967 *Dondolo* rocking chair produced by Elco of Venice; it became a classic of Italian design. They specialized in architecture, town planning, and industrial design, and produced designs for furniture for Bernini, Biarm, and Peguri and lighting for Lumenform.

▶ She showed her furniture at the 1968–69 Milan and Cologne 'International Furniture Exhibitions' and 1970 'Design for Living, Italian Style' exhibition in London. The *Dondolo* rocking chair was first shown at the 1968 Salone del Mobile Italiano in Milan and included in the 1970 'Modern Chairs 1918–1970' exhibition at the Whitechapel Gallery in London and 1983–84 'Design Since 1945' exhibition at the Philadelphia Museum of Art.

▶ Cat., *Modern Chairs 1918–1970*, London: Lund Humphries, 1971. *Casa Arredamento Giardino*, No. 19. Cat., Kathryn B. Hiesinger and George H. Marcus III (eds.), *Design Since 1945*, Philadelphia: Philadelphia Museum of Art, 1983.

Staite Murray, William (1881–1961)

▶ British ceramicist.

▶ Studied Camberwell School of Art, London.

▶ Initially interested in painting, he took up pottery only in 1918 at the age of 37, working first in London and later moving to Bray, Berkshire. In 1925, he began working at the Royal College of Art, London, where, in 1926, he became head of the pottery school; though he offered no formal technical instruction to his students, he was an influential teacher. At odds with Bernard Leach, he considered pottery to be a fine art rather than a craft and did not promote collaboration with industry. Unlike many of his notable contemporaries, the main influence on his work came from Chinese rather than Japanese ceramics. He usually gave titles to his pieces, which like the work of fine artists with whom he exhibited, were expensive. Up to 1939, he worked at the Royal College of Art and in his studio in Bray.

▶ He regularly showed his work (often with painters) at the William Patterson Gallery and at Lefevre Gallery, both in London. In the 1950s, his pottery of the late 1930s was shown at the Leicester Gallery in London.

▶ Cat., *Thirties: British art and design before the war*, London: Arts Council of Great Britain, Hayward Gallery, 1979:97,98,131, 132,291,297.

Stålhane, Carl-Harry (1920–)

▶ Swedish ceramicist.

▶ Studied painting under Isaac Grünewald in Stockholm; at the Académie Colarossi, Paris, under sculptor Ossip Zadkine; and in Spain, Greece, Turkey, the USA, Egypt, and Mexico.

▶ From 1939–73, he worked at the Rörstrand ceramics factory in Lidköping. In 1973, he set up his own workshop in Lidköping. From 1963–71, he taught ceramics at the Konstindustriskolan, Gothenburg.

▶ He received a gold medal at the 1951 (IX) and diploma of honor at the 1954 (X) Triennali di Milano, and 1960 International Design Award of the American Institute of Decorators. His work was the subject of one-person exhibitions in Stockholm in 1951, 1957, and 1960; in Malmö in 1950; and New York in 1960.

▶ Cat., David Revere McFadden (ed.), *Scandinavian Modern Design 1880–1980*, New York: Abrams, 1982:271, No. 163. Jennifer Hawkins Opie, *Scandinavia: Ceramics and Glass in The Twentieth Century*, New York: Rizzoli, 1989.

Stam, Martinus Adrianus (aka Mart Stam 1899–1986)

▶ Dutch designer; born Purmerend; active the Netherlands, Germany, and Russia.

▶ Studied Design Academy, Amsterdam, and under M. J. Granpré Molière in Verhagen (Netherlands); under Kok in Rotterdam.

▶ Stam's career documents the interchange between the Bauhaus, Dutch Rationalism, and Constructivism. Stam was chair of 'de Opbouw' ('Construction'), the Dutch architecture group founded in 1920, whose members included W.H. Gispen, Willem Kromhout, J.J.P. Oud, Granprè Moliere, and L.C. van der Vlught. While in Switzerland and Germany, he met German Constructivists, El Lissitzky, Theo van Doesburg, and Ludwig Mies van der Rohe. Stam entered the 1923 competition for Königsberg, in which he used reinforced concrete and glass for the design of an office-building project. He worked with Lissitzky on the 1924–25 Wolkenbügel (or 'Cloud Props') project, using Constructivist principles that he later applied to the 1925 redevelopment project for the Rokin and the dam in Amsterdam. In 1914, Stam worked with Dutch architects J.A. Brinkman and van der Vlught on the mammoth 1926–30 Van Nelle tobacco factory in Rotterdam, for which he rendered interior decoration and furniture designs. The complex was an ambitious pioneering work of Modern industrial architecture. He worked in collaboration with other architects, including Hans Poelzig and Max Taut in 1922. Stam is best known for his 1924 design of one of the first cantilever tubular steel chairs, initially constructed from ten pieces of gas-pipe tubing and ten elbow joints, but not realized until 1926, by which time Marcel Breuer and Le Corbusier had also arrived at the cantilever solution. Stam's houses for the 1927 Stuttgart 'Weissenhofsiedlung' were among the most interesting examples of domestic interior design and architecture there. 1925–28, he worked in the office of van der Vlught and Brickmann. 1928–29, he was a guest lecturer for elementary construction and town planning at the Bauhaus in Dessau, where association with those working in town planning there contributed to his inspiration for the Hellerhof garden-city complex. 1929–35, he worked in several countries; important during this time were his activities in housing and town planning with German architect Ernst May in the Soviet Union. He designed the 1932 house and furnishings (including dining and easy chairs in bent tubular steel) of W. Schwagenscheidt in Moscow. In 1932, he designed a stackable chair. 1935–48, he lived in Amsterdam, where, from 1939, was director of the Institute for Teaching Industrial Art. In 1948, he became director of the Akademie der bildenden Künste in Dresden. In 1950, he became head of the Kunsthochschule Berlin-Weissensee.

▶ Stam furnished three houses with steel tables, desks, and shelving (produced by F. Ulmer in Möhringen [Netherlands]) at the 1927 'Die Wohnung' exhibition at the Deutscher Werkbund, Stuttgart; his furniture for the exhibition was commercially produced by L. und C. Arnold in Schorndorf, near Stuttgart, from 1927.

▶ Giovanni Fanelli, *Architettura Moderna in Olanda, 1900–1940*, Marchi e Bertolli, 1968:359–60. G. Dorthuys, *Mart Stam*, London, 1970. Barbie Campbell-Cole and Tim Benton (eds.), *Tubular Steel Furniture*, London: The Art Book Company, 1979:29. Otakar Máčel, 'Avant-garde Design and the Law: Litigation over the Cantilever Chair,' *Journal of Design History*, Vol. 3, Nos. 2 and 3, 1990:125–43.

Standardmöbel Lengyel (Standard-Möbel)

▶ German furniture manufacturer.

▶ Standardmöbel was established in 1926 or 1927 to produce bent tubular steel furniture by Kálmán Lengyel and Marcel Breuer at Teltowerstrasse 47–48 in Berlin. The venture proving unsuccessful, Breuer sold the rights to his tubular steel furniture in 1928 to Hungarian businessman Anton Lorenz, who took over the production of Breuer's furniture from Standardmöbel Lengyel. Breuer's 1927–28 designs were not transferred to the firm. Because the famous *B33* and *B34* chairs had been stored as prototypes on Standardmöbel's premises until 1929, both Standardmöbel and Thonet, with which Breuer had entered into an agreement in 1928, produced the chairs in slightly different versions simultaneously. In 1929, Thonet bought Standardmöbel with the exception of its factory. Lorenz had in the meantime become director of Standardmöbel, and, in 1929, he signed an agreement with Mart Stam to produce his cantilever chair. Since Thonet asserted that the cantilever chair was a Breuer design, rights to which had transferred to Thonet through the Standardmöbel sale, it filed suit against Lorenz. Included in the suit was Lorenz's firm Deutsche Stahlmöbel (DESTA). Lorenz won in 1930 and again on appeal in 1932; Thonet had to stop production of the *L33* and *L34* cantilever chairs.

▶ Barbie Campbell-Cole and Tim Benton, *Tubular Steel Furniture*, London: The Art Book Company, 1979:13,20. Otakar Máčel, 'Avant-Garde Design and the Law: Litigation over the Cantilever Chair,' *Journal of Design History*, Vol. 3, Nos. 2 and 3, 1990:129.

Starck, Philippe (1949–)

▶ French product, furniture, and interior designer; born Paris.

▶ 1968, studied École Camondo, Paris.

▶ He produced his first piece of furniture, the 1968 folding *Francesca Spanish Chair*, at the age of 18. In 1969, he became artistic director of the firm Pierre Cardin. His career as an independent designer was largely undistinguished during the 1970s, although, in 1976–78, he was the interior architect of La Main Bleue and Les Bains-Douches nightclubs, Paris. 1982–83, along with four other designers, Starck designed and laid out a room in the quarters of President François Mitterand in the Élysée Palace. In 1984, the owner of Café Costes saw the designer's curved-back chair with spiky-metal legs at Galerie VIA; in Paris; the chair was sponsored by VIA. Starck was hired to design Café Costes, and the Paris restaurant and its designer became famous almost overnight. By 1990, 400,000 copies had been sold of the *Café Costes* chair, as it came to be known. Starck was appointed artistic director of the newly formed firm XO and created the 1984 furniture collection for 3 Suisses, a mail-order home furnishings operation outside Paris. His La Cigale discotheque was built in 1988 in Paris. He designed furniture for Driade, Idée, Rateri, Baleri, and Disform, 1990 domestic goods for Alessi, 1988 crystal for Daum, a 1989 clock for Spirale, 1986 cutlery for Sasaki, a boat interior for Beneteau, a 1991 plastic bottle for Vittel, and lamp models for Flos, including the 1988 *Ara* table lamp and 1989 *Lucifair* phallic sconce. In 1987, he designed Restaurants Castel in Paris, Dijon, and Nice, Hôtel Costes in Paris, the Bathmann drugstore in Zürich, and restaurants, offices, and residences in Tokyo. Starck assigned catchy titles to his furniture, such as chairs named *Dr. Glob*, *Mickville*, *Miss Dorn*, *Tippy Jackson*, and, after a dirigible pilot, *Dr. Sonderbar*. For Driade, the names of items in his Ubik line were taken from Philip K. Dicks's science fiction novel *Ubik*. Starck was the artistic director of the 1987 *International Design Yearbook*. He designed the 1988 exhibition of French design at Centre Georges Pompidou, later more modestly remounted in London. His design and decoration for Ian Schrager's and Steve Rubell's 1988 Hotel Royalton in New York and 1990 Paramount Hotel for Schrager were widely published; his 1991 *Royalton* chair was produced by Driade. His first domestic architecture was the 1989 narrow-lot residence of Bruno Le Moult on Île St.-Germain, Paris. Buildings (with various architects) included the 1989 Nani Nani café in Tokyo, 1990 Asahi brasserie in Tokyo, and 1990 Teatriz Restaurant in Madrid. With his talent for self-promotion and a supportive press and wife (who died in 1992), Starck was the standard-bearer for the French design community in the 1980s. His 1989 Fluocaril toothbrush and stand, produced by Laboratoires Pharmaceutiques, Groupil in France, was labeled, perhaps jokingly, 'the ultimate designer toothbrush.'

▶ Starck's 1982 *Miss Dorn* chair won the 1982 VIA 'Carte blanche' award. By 1987, he had already shown his work in 30 exhibitions in the USA, Europe, and Japan, followed by the 1988 French contemporary furniture exhibition at the Victoria and Albert Museum, London, 1989 'L'Art de Vivre' exhibition at the Cooper-Hewitt Museum, New York, and 1990 'Les années VIA' exhibition at the Paris Musée des Art Décoratifs. He designed the 1988 exhibition of French design at Centre Georges Pompidou. His *Bob Dubois* wooden dining chair produced by Aleph was introduced at the 1989 Salone del Mobile in Milan. His 1991 *Super Glob* plastic chair for Kartell and 1985 *Café Costes* chair for Aleph (Driade) were included in the 1991 'Mobili Italiani 1961–1991: Le Varie Età dei linguaggi' exhibition at the Salone del Mobile in Milan.

▶ Sophie Anargyros, *Le Mobilier français*, Paris: Regard/VIA, 1980:26–32. Gilles de Bure, *Le Mobilier français 1965–1979*, Paris: Regard/VIA, 1983:125. *Nouvelles Tendances: les avant-gardes de la fin du XXe siècle*, Paris: Centre Georges Pompidou, 1986. Cat., *Les années VIA*, Paris: Musée des Arts Décoratifs, 1990. *Issue 5*, London: Design Museum, Winter 1990. Olivier Boissière, *Philippe Starck*, Cologne: Taschen, 1991. François Mathey, *Au bonheur des formes, le design français 1945–1992*, Paris: Regard, 1992.

Starr, Theodore B.
▶ American silversmiths; located New York.
▶ The firm was one of the oldest American silversmithies and active *c*1885–1924, when it was incorporated into Reed and Barton.
▶ Annelies Krekel-Aalberse, *Art Nouveau and Art Déco Silver*, New York: Abrams, 1989:98,259.

Stavangerflint
▶ Norwegian ceramics factory.
▶ Stavangerflint was established in 1949 at Stavanger; it soon had a design department that was concerned with both serial production and decorative wares; hired freelance designer Kari Nyquist, who worked for the firm from *c*1955; in 1957, appointed Kaare Fjeldsaa chief designer and artistic director, who remained until after the merger with Figgjo Fajanse in 1968. The firm closed in 1979.
▶ Jennifer Hawkins Opie, *Scandinavia: Ceramics and Glass in the Twentieth Century*, New York: Rizzoli, 1989.

Stead McAlpin and Company
▶ British textile firm.
▶ The dye-works were founded in 1745 by Kenneth McAlpin at Wigton, Cumberland; took over local printworks; became one of the earliest firms to produce glazed chintz by engraved copper roller; discontinued its block printing in 1978; produces goods for Liberty's and John Lewis.
▶ Received gold medal at 1862 London 'International Exhibition on Industry and Art.'

▶ Valerie Mendes, *The Victoria & Albert Museum's Textile Collection. British Textiles from 1900 to 1937*, London: Victoria and Albert Museum, 1992.

steel furniture
See tubular steel furniture

Steelcase
▶ American furniture manufacturer; located Grand Rapids, Michigan.
▶ The largest furniture manufacturer in the world by 1993, Steelcase was founded in 1912 by Grand Rapids engineer Peter M. Wege Sr. (1879–1947) and 11 associates; they initially named the firm Metal Office Furniture. It produced fireproof office safes, gradually expanding its operations to include steel desks and filing cabinets. The firm's claim to design distinction was its 1937 commission to produce the metal office furniture designed by Frank Lloyd Wright for the Johnson Wax administration building, Racine, Wisconsin. Steelcase and Warren MacArthur submitted prototypes; MacArthur's version was in aluminum. Named Steelcase from 1954, the company was perceived as a producer of durable products made in large quantities. It largely ignored the design community; as chairman Robert Pew admitted, 'I hate to tell you how it was done in the 1950s. We'd take an arm from one chair, a base from another, a back from another.' Despite its lack of design sophistication, Steelcase dominated the office furniture market because of its client base (IBM, AT&T, and others) and tightly coordinated distribution system. Steelcase sought design respectability through the Steelcase Design Partnership, a consortium of design-oriented companies associated with the industry's elite and intended to reach designers rather than end-users; it was headed by William Crawford. Creative director and senior advisor to the Partnership was George Beylerian, who in the 1960s was an importer from Europe of domestic goods of high design standard. Steelcase's status was enhanced by the Partnership's acquisition of Atelier International (lighting and licensed Wright, Le Corbusier, and Rietveld furniture made by Cassina in Italy), Brayton International (executive and lounge seating), DesignTex Fabrics (office textiles), Metropolitan Furniture (lounge seating and conference room tables), Vecta Contract (executive furnishings, including Beylerian Collection), and its largest start-up company, Details, producing, it claims, 'tools for a better day at work.'
▶ David A. Hanks, *The Decorative Designs of Frank Lloyd Wright*, New York: Dutton, 1979:220–21. *Steelcase, The First 75 Years*, Grand Rapids: Steelcase, 1987. Margery B. Stein, 'Teaching Steelcase to Dance,' *The New York Times Magazine, The Business World* section, 1 April 1990.

Steelchrome
▶ British furniture manufacturer; located London.
▶ Phillip Braham established the firm in 1932 with offices on Portland Street, London. Braham had earlier trained in the coach-building industry, where he acquired a knowledge of upholstery and metalworking. He was the firm's administrator, controller, and designer. Bending and welding in its own factories, Steelchrome purchased its steel tubing from Tube Products, the sister firm of Steelchrome's competitor Pel. Steelchrome specialized in furniture for hairdressing and beauty salons and hospitals. Its *DC111* chair was a commercial success. In 1964, Braham sold the firm; it still operates.
▶ Cat., Dennis Sharp et al., *Pel and Tubular Steel Furniture in the Thirties*, London: Architectural Association, 1977.

Stefani, Stefano (1953–)
▶ Italian architect and designer; born Rome.
▶ Studied architecture to 1977.
▶ From 1978, he collaborated with architect Laura de Lorenzo on industrial and interior design and visual communication; in 1985, founded Grifite with architects de Lorenzo, L. Leonori, and F. Piferi.

► Fumio Shimizu and Matteo Thun (eds.), *The Descendants of Leonardo: The Italian Design*, Tokyo, 1987:329.

Stefanoni, Franco (1926–)

► Italian designer; born and active Lecco.

► Stefanoni began his professional career in 1952. His *Stalagmite* lamp was produced by Stilnovo in Milan and *Martina* drawer pull by B. Olivari in Borgomanero. He designed lighting produced by Candle in Milan, seating for Base Interiors, and a metal furniture range for Farina in Lissone. He was a member of ADI (Associazione per il Disegno Industriale).

► Participated in numerous competitions and exhibitions including 1985 'Uhr und Mode, Deutsche Uhrenindustrie,' Pforzheim; 1986 'Itinerari Manzoniani,' Milan.

► *ADI Annual 1976*, Milan: Associazione per il Disegno Industriale, 1976.

Stefanoni, Guido (1957–)

► Italian designer; born Lecco.

► Studied architecture, Politecnico di Milano, to 1982.

► In 1980, he worked with Marco Zanuso in a design studio; 1981–82, was assistant art director at the Young and Rubicam advertising agency, Milan; from 1982, was active in a design studio with Leopoldo Freyrie.

► Participated in numerous competitions and exhibitions including 1985 'Uhr und Mode, Deutsche Uhrenindustrie,' Pforzheim; 1986 'Itinerari Manzoniani,' Milan.

► Hans Wichmann, *Italien Design 1945 bis heute*, Munich: Die Neue Sammlung, 1988.

Steichen, Edward Jean (1879–1973)

► Luxembourgian photographer, painter, and designer; active New York.

► Studied fine art.

► He began his career in fine art, and, in 1881, moved to the USA. In 1894 with George Niedecken and others, he organized the Art Students' League in Milwaukee, Wisconsin. His first photographs appeared in 1889; in 1902, he became a founding member of the Photo-Secession in New York. In 1911, his activities in fashion photography began. Influenced initially by Impressionism, he began photographing nature, which gave way to portraiture. 1914–18, he was commander of the photographic division of the US Expeditionary Forces. 1923–28, he was director of photography for the magazines *Vogue* and *Vanity Fair*, making numerous portraits of the *beau monde*. His abstract photographs of matchsticks (*Matches and Match Boxes*), sugar cubes, and other small items, which appeared in *Vogue* in the 1920s, were converted into printed fabrics by Stehli Silk in *c*1928. In the 1920s, he designed graphics, book jackets, and glassware produced by Steuben. In 1928, he designed two pianos for Hardman and Peck as part of its *Modernique* range. 1945–46, he served in the US Marine Corps as a war photographer. 1947–62, he was head of the photography department of the New York Museum of Modern Art. His work mirrored the trends in 20th-century photography.

► His photography was shown in the 1954 'The Family of Man' exhibition at the New York Museum of Modern Art.

► Paul Frank, *New Dimensions*, New York: Payson and Clarke, 1928. Pierre Migennes, 'Ombres Portés et Décor de Tissus,' *Art et Décoration*, Vol. 51, Jan.–June 1927:140–42. Stuart Durant, *Ornament from the Industrial Revolution to Today*, Woodstock, NY: Overlook, 1986:256,329.

Steiger, Carl (1857–1946)

► Swiss engineer, painter, and furniture designer; father of architect Rudolf Steiger.

► Studied engineering, at Technische Hochschule, Munich.

► He became a painter and was interested in aviation, executing airplane prototypes; as an aviation pioneer, he wrote the theoretical work *Technologie des Menschenflugs* (*The Technology of Human Flight*); experimented with furniture design, resulting in a chair model in the early 1930s.

► Friederike Mehlau-Wiebking et al., *Schweizer Typenmöbel 1925–35, Sigfried Giedion und die Wohnbedarf AG*, Zürich: gta, 1989:230.

Steiger, Rudolf (1900–82)

► Swiss architect; active Basel and Zürich; son of Carl Steiger; husband of Flora Steiger-Crawford.

► 1919–23, studied architecture, Eidgenössische Technische Hochschule, Zürich, under Karl Moser.

► 1923–24, he worked for the firms Dumont in Brussels and A. Korn in Berlin. In 1924, he and wife Flora Steiger-Crawford opened their own architecture practice in Basel, moving to Zürich in 1925. In 1927, he became a member of Swiss collective that furnished Mies van der Rohe's buildings at the Weissenhof-Siedlung in Stuttgart. In 1928, he became a founding member of CIAM (Congrès Internationaux d'Architecture Moderne). Specializing in town and regional planning, 1928–31, he served on the planning team for Neubühl Werkbund settlement in Zürich. He and his wife created some of the furniture designs included in the basic inventory of the Wohnbedarf furniture store from its founding in Zürich in 1931. He was also a bookkeeper at Wohnbedarf. Partners 1929–37, he and Carlo Hubacher designed the 1930–32 restaurant in Zett-Haus, furnished with Steiger's stackable chairs. In 1937, Steiger, Werner Max Moser, and Max Ernst Haefeli founded the cooperative-office HMS for the construction of the Kongresshaus in Zürich. In the Architektengruppe Kantonsspital Zürich, of which HMS was a part, Steiger and H. Fietz directed the construction of Cantonal Hospital in Zürich 1939–51. From 1957, he specialized in hospital architecture. In 1973, he became active in the founding of Schweizerische Vereinigung für Landesplanung (Swiss Union for National Planning). In 1964, he became president of a professional group for regional planning in and around Zürich and was a member of the board of directors of the Bund Schweizer Planer (Association of Swiss Planners).

► For his achievements in hospital architecture, he was awarded an honorary doctorate of the medical faculty at the University of Zürich.

► Friederike Mehlau-Wiebking et al., *Schweizer Typenmöbel 1925–35, Sigfried Giedion und die Wohnbedarf AG*, Zürich: gta, 1989:231. Gilbert Frey, *Schweizer Möbeldesign 1927–1989*, Bern: Benteli, 1986.

Steiger-Crawford, Flora (b. Flora Crawford 1899–)

► Swiss architect and furniture designer; born Bombay; active Basel and Zürich; wife of Rudolf Steiger.

► Studied architecture, Eidgenössische Technische Hochschule, Zürich, under Karl Moser, to 1923.

► 1923–24, she worked in the architecture office of Pfleghard und Haefeli in Zürich. In 1924, she and husband Rudolf Steiger opened an architecture office in Basel; they moved the office to Zürich in 1925. She rendered architectural plans and executed furniture designs. Steiger-Crawford and weaver sister Lilly Humm-Crawford designed the 1931 weaving studio at the Neubühl Werkbund settlement in Zürich and furnished a small apartment for a family of six and an inexpensive one-family house. Her furniture was sold by the Wohnbedarf furniture store in Switzerland. From 1931, she worked as a sculptor in her own studio, creating portrait busts, nudes, and some draped figures in bronze, plaster and artificial stone. In 1932, she became active as a landscape painter.

► Friederike Mehlau-Wiebking et al., *Schweizer Typenmöbel 1925–35, Sigfried Giedion und die Wohnbedarf AG*, Zürich: gta, 1989:230–31.

Steiner, F., and Co

► British textile firm.

► Frederick Steiner emigrated to Britain in the early 19th century; took over a printworks (founded in 1722) in Church (near Accrington), Lancashire, printing calico and dyeing. The firm used known designers, producing important Art Nouveau fabrics. When others joined the Calico Printers' Association in 1899, Steiner remained independent; was voluntarily liquidated in 1955.

▶ Valerie Mendes, *The Victoria & Albert Museum's Textile Collection, British Textiles from 1900 to 1937*, British Textiles from 1900 to 1937, London: Victoria and Albert Museum, 1992.

Steltman, Johannes (1891–1961)

▶ Dutch jeweler and silversmith; active The Hague.

▶ Studied Königliche Preussische Zeichenakademie, Hanau.

▶ In 1917, he set up the jewelry shop Joaillerie Artistique in The Hague. When silversmith Robert Mack became one of the jewelers at the shop a few years later, Steltman began producing hollow-ware in the fluid silhouettes of the Art Nouveau style. Reminiscent of the organic work of 17th-century Dutch silversmiths, the tea service shown at the 1925 Paris 'Exposition Internationale des Arts Décoratifs et Industriels Modernes' was inspired by Malcolm Campbell's racing car that broke the world speed record in 1923. (Johannes Rohde's Streamline silver pitcher of *c*1925 was of an entirely different genre.) Becoming more subdued, Steltman's later work was smooth and severely Modern. Sometimes the work of the workshop included services in the Danish style, influenced by Georg Jensen.

▶ Steltman's tea service shown at the 1925 Paris 'Exposition Internationale des Arts Décoratifs et Industriels Modernes' won the gold prize.

▶ Annelies Krekel-Aalberse, *Art Nouveau and Art Déco Silver*, New York: Abrams, 1989:173,175,219,259.

Stelton

▶ Danish metalware and plastics manufacturer.

▶ Stelton was established in 1960, to make and sell stainless-steel hollow-ware primarily for the Danish market; in 1964, commissioned freelance designer Arne Jacobsen to design its tablewares and serving pieces; in 1967, introduced his successful *Cylinda-Line* of stainless-steel hollow-ware. Stelton posthumously produced Jacobsen's *Multi-Set* range of serving pieces from his drawings. In 1975, owner-manager Peter Holmblad hired freelance designer Erik Magnussen to design for metal and plastic production.

▶ Jennifer Hawkins Opie, *Scandinavia: Ceramics and Glass in the Twentieth Century*, New York: Rizzoli, 1989.

Stenberg, Georgii Avgustovich (1990–1933) and Vladimir Avgustovich Stenberg (1899–)

▶ Russian graphic, theater set, and interior designers and ceramicists; born Moscow; brothers.

▶ 1912–17, studied Stroganov Art School, Moscow; 1917–20, Svomas, in the Studio Without a Supervisor with fellow students Nikolai Denisovskii, Vasilii Komardenkov, Konstantin Medunetskii, Nikolai Prusakov, and Sergei Y. Svetlov.

▶ They contributed to the 1918 May Day agitprop decorations in Moscow, worked on designs for the Napoleon cinema and the Railroad Workers' Club, and produced agitprop decorations for the 1919 anniversary of the Bolshevik Revolution. 1919–21, they were members of the group Obmokhu and, in 1920, became members of Inkhuk, where they organized an exhibition of constructions. In 1921, with Alexei Gan, Aleksandr Rodchenko, Varvara Stepanova, and others, they opposed the *veshch* (object) group at Inkhuk, rejecting pure art for industrial Constructivism. From 1923, they produced film poster designs. 1923–25, they were closely associated with the journal *Lef*. 1924–31, they produced set designs and costumes for Aleksandr Tairov's Chamber Theater productions, including Aleksandr Ostrovskii's *Groza* (*Storm*), George, Bernard Shaw's *Saint Joan*, and Bertholt Brecht's *Three-penny Opera*, and thereafter for theatrical productions in Russia and abroad. 1929–32, they taught at the Architecture-Construction Institute in Moscow.

▶ Vladimir Stenberg's work was included in the 1922 Berlin 'Erste Russische Kunstausstellung.' With Aleksandra Exter, Ignatii Nivinskii, Vera Mukhina, and others, they worked on the design and decoration of the 1923 'First Agricultural and Handicraft-Industrial Exhibition.' With Medunetskii, they showed their work as 'Constructivists' at the 1924 Moscow 'First Discussional Exhibi-

tion of Associations of Active Revolutionary Art.' They received a gold medal at the 1925 Paris 'Exposition Internationale des Arts Décoratifs et Industriels Modernes.'

▶ Stephanie Barron and Maurice Tuchman, *The Avant-Garde in Russia, 1910–1930*, Cambridge: MIT, 1980:244. Cat., *The Great Utopia: The Russian and Soviet Avant-Garde, 1915–1932*, New York: Guggenheim Museum, 1992.

Stene, John

▶ Norwegian furniture designer; active Canada.

▶ Studied chemical engineering in Norway to 1938.

▶ After World War II in Toronto, he and Sheilagh Vansittart established the furniture shop Shelagh's, specializing in high-quality Scandinavian imports. He subsequently established the furniture producer Brunswick Manufacturing in Toronto.

▶ Cat., *Seduced and Abandoned: Modern Furniture designers in Canada, the First Fifty Years*, Toronto: The Art Gallery at Harbourfront, 1986:18.

Stepanova, Varvara Fedorvna (aka Agrarykh; Varst 1894–1958)

▶ Russian graphic, set, and costume designer; born in Kovno; wife of Aleksandr Rodchenko.

▶ From 1911, studied Kazan Art School; in 1912, under Il'ia Mashjkov and Konstantin Yuon in Moscow; from 1918, Izo NKP (School of Fine Arts of Narkompros); 1913–14, Stroganov Art School.

▶ She became a member of Inkhuk in 1920 and, in 1922, designed sets and costumes for Vsevolod Ermilievitch Meyerhold's production of Tarelkin's *Death*. Many of her designs drew on the imagery of technology. She and others argued that artists should work for the benefit of society as a whole by pursuing direct utilitarian and social applications of their efforts aligned with mass production through advanced technology. In 1923 with Liubov' Popova. Rodchenko, and others, she worked as a designer at the First State Textile Factory (Tsindel Works) near Moscow and, 1923–28, was closely associated with the journals *Lef* and *Novyi lef*. 1924–25, she was professor in the textile department of Vkhutemas. From the mid-1920s, she produced designs for typography, posters, and stage sets. In the 1930s, she worked on the magazine *USSR in Construction*.

▶ Her work was included in the 1914 Moscow Salon and was shown in exhibitions in the Soviet Union and abroad, including the 1918 (V) 'Fifth State Exhibition,' 1919 (X) 'Tenth State Exhibition,' the 1925 Paris 'Exposition Internationale des Arts Décoratifs et Industriels Modernes,' and 1927 Leningrad (now St. Petersburg) 'Russian Xylography of the Past Ten Years.' Her work was included in the 1921 '5 × 5 = 25' exhibition and 1922 Berlin 'Erste Russische Kunstausstellung.'

▶ Stephanie Barron and Maurice Tuchman, *The Avant-Garde in Russia, 1910–1930*, Cambridge: MIT, 1980:246. Selim Om Khan-Magomedov, *Les Vhutemas*, Paris: Regard, 1990:435–38. Cat., *The Great Utopia: The Russian and Soviet Avant-Garde, 1915–1932*, New York: Guggenheim Museum, 1992.

Stephensen, Magnus (1903–)

▶ Danish architect, metalworker, ceramicist, and furniture designer.

▶ Studied Teknisk Skole to 1924; architecture, Det Kongelige Danske Kunstakademi, Copenhagen, to 1931; 1931, French School, Athens.

▶ In a long career, he designed apartment buildings, terrace houses, schools, and waterworks, rejecting decoration and emphasizing the outlines of his structures. In tableware, his work showed a Chinese influence. 1938–52, he designed for Kay Bojesen and, in 1950, began producing designs for the Georg Jensen Sølvsmedie, including silver hollow-ware and the stainless-steel patterns *Tanaquil* and *Frigate*. He designed furniture for Fritz Hansen and ceramics for the Royal Copenhagen Porcelain Manufactory and Aluminia, both in Copenhagen. His oven-to-table ceramics began the trend in Denmark towards multi-use and interchangeable dinnerware.

▶ He won the 1948 Eckersberg Medal, 1971 medal of Industrielle Designere Danmark, and awards at the 1951 (IX) (three gold medals), 1954 (X) (two grand prizes), 1957 (XI) (three gold medals) and 1960 (XII) (silver medal) Triennali di Milano. His work was included in the 1948 exhibition of the Kunsthåndværker-skolen, Copenhagen, 1954–57 USA 'Design in Scandinavia' traveling exhibition, 1956–59 Germany 'Neue Form aus Dänem-ark' traveling exhibition, 1958 'Formes Scandinaves' at the Paris Musée des Arts Décoratifs, and 1960–61 USA 'The Arts of Denmark.'

▶ Cat., *Georg Jensen Silversmithy: 77 Artists, 75 Years*, Washington: Smithsonian Institution Press, 1980, No. 140. Cat., Kathryn B. Hiesinger and George H. Marcus III (eds.), *Design Since 1945*, Philadelphia: Philadelphia Museum of Art, 1984:231,II–62,V–43. Arne Karlsen, *Made in Denmark*, New York, 1960:114–15,119,122. Erik Zahle (ed.), *A Treasury of Scandinavian Design*, New York, 1961:292, Nos. 275,387,412. Cat., David Revere McFadden (ed.), *Scandinavian Modern Design 1880–1980*, New York: Abrams, 1982:271, No. 190.

Sterlé, Pierre
▶ French jeweler; located Paris.
▶ Pierre Sterlé founded the jewelry store in 1934 at 43 avenue de l'Opéra in Paris, where it is located today. In the 1950s, Sterlé was known for his collaboration with clothing designer Jacques Fath. His best known designs included brooches in the forms of roses and arrows, produced in platinum, diamonds, and rubies.
▶ Melissa Gabardi, *Les Bijoux des Années 50*, Paris: Amateur, 1987.

Stern, Robert A.M. (1939–)
▶ American architect and designer; born and active New York.
▶ Studied fine arts, Columbia University, New York, to 1960, and architecture, Yale University, to 1965.
▶ He worked briefly as a designer in the office of architect Richard Meier. He was a planner for New York City until 1969, when he opened an architecture office with associate John S. Hagmann. In 1977, he set up his own architecture practice in New York. From 1977, he was professor at Columbia University. He amalgamated historical American and classical forms into a kind of Post-Modernism, manifested in his furniture produced by Sunar-Hauserman, bed linens by various mills, and the 1989 hotel for Walt Disney World in Orlando, Florida, that echoed Victorian beach resorts. He designed domestic tableware produced Alessi, the 1985 *Dinner at Eight* rug by B.d Ediciones de Diseño, 1986 jewelry by Acme Jewelry, 1984 ceramics and metalware by Swid Powell, and a 1990 furniture collection in a retro-neoclassical style by Hickory Business Furniture. Stern, Robert Graves, Frank Gehry, Tigerman-McCurry, and Venturi-Scott-Brown developed the resort site plan at Euro Disney near Paris, designed the Newport Bay Hotel, inspired by his favored Shingle style, and the Cheyenne Hotel at Disney World in Florida. Stern's theoretical views were published in the journal *Perspecta* in 1965, in which, rejecting the International Style, he espoused a return to history with an eclectic romantic style. He achieved some recognition with a highly personal view of architecture in his 1986 television series produced in the USA and the accompanying book. Architects who worked in his office included Thomas P. Catalano of Boston; Thomas A. Kligerman of Ike and Kligerman in New York; and Peter Pennoyer of New York. Stern's books included *New Directions in American Architecture* (1969), *George Howe: Toward a Modern American Architecture* (1975), *New York 1900* (1983), *The International Design Yearbook* (editor, 1986), and *New York 1930* (1987).
▶ His other buildings included the 1967 Wiseman house in Montauk, New York; 1974 Lang house in Washington, Connecticut; 1975 Ehrman house in Armonk, New York; 1975 competition entry for the Roosevelt Island development in New York; 1988 house on Mecox Bay, Bridgehampton, New York; and 1993 Norman Rockwell Museum, Lenox, Massachusetts.

▶ He represented the USA at the 1976 and 1980 Biennali di Venezia. He received the 1980 and 1985 National Honor Awards, 1982 Distinguished Architecture Award, and 1984 Medal of Honor of the New York Chapter, all from the American Institute of Architects. His work was the subject of the 1982 one-person exhibition at the Newberger Museum of New York. His work was included in exhibitions at the New York Museum of Modern Art, The Drawing Center, The Cooper-Hewitt Museum in New York, Whitney Museum of American Art in New York, Art Institute of Chicago, and Walker Art Center in Minneapolis, Minnesota.
▶ Robert A.M. Stern, *Perspecta, the Yale Architectural Journal*, Nos. 9–10, 1965. Robert A.M. Stern, *New Directions in American Architecture*, New York, 1969. 'The Work of Robert A.M. Stern and John S. Hagmann,' *Architecture and Urbanism*, Oct. 1975. *Robert Stern*, London, 1981. Peter Arnell and Ted Bickford (eds.), *Robert A.M. Stern, Buildings and Projects 1965–1980*, New York, 1981. Juli Capella and Quim Larrea, *Designed by Architects in the 1980s*, New York, Rizzoli, 1988. Paul Goldberger, 'Beyond the Master's Voice,' *Home Design, The New York Times Magazine*, 13 Oct. 1991:34.

Steuben Glass Works
▶ American glassware manufacturer; located Corning, New York.
▶ The Steuben Glass Works was incorporated in 1903 in Corning, New York. In the beginning it was established to produce glass blanks and crystal ware for T.G. Hawkes, a glass-cutting firm. When British glass designer Frederick Carder became its artistic director, the firm's range was extended to include domestic glassware, including vases, millefiori paperweights, candlesticks, goblets, and lampshades. After World War II, Steuben continued to be the major manufacturer of quality glassware. By the 1950s, it became known as a manufacturer of crystal glassware and ornamental art glass of the highest quality and design. Its high lead content tended to make the objects, particular the utilitarian ware, brittle and easy to chip. During the 1950s, George Thompson was a skilled designer at Steuben of domestic glassware in the type of heavy, free-form crystal for which the firm became known. Steuben issued one-off commemorative pieces that were given to heads of state and their representatives. Its unique 1947 *Merry-Go-Round Bowl* by Sidney Waugh was given by President Harry Truman to Britain's Princess Elizabeth as a wedding present. In 1954, Steuben began commissioning British designers, including Graham Sutherland, John Piper, Mathew Smith, and engraver Laurence Whistler, as part of its 'British Artists in Glass' traveling exhibition. Its 'New Glass' annual exhibitions began in 1959. The Corning Institute is one of the world's most important contributors to glassmaking and its study. As part of Owens-Corning, Steuben, a flagship operation, is not profitable; in 1993, began producing more inexpensive glassware, with the designs of Massimo Vignelli.
▶ Alastair Duncan, *Art Nouveau and Art Déco Lighting*, New York: Simon and Schuster, 1978:46–47. Mary Jean Madigan, *Steuben Glass: An American Tradition in Crystal*, New York: Abrams, 1982. Frederick Cooke, *Glass: Twentieth-Century Design*, New York: Dutton, 1986:103.
▶ See **Carder, Frederick**

Stevens and Williams
▶ British glassware manufacturer.
▶ In the 1880s, cameo glass was being made at three major companies in Britain: Thomas Webb, Stevens and Williams, and Richardsons. In 1931, the proprietor of Stevens and Williams, Hubert Williams-Thomas, sought a designer to render work in the Modern style. On the advice of Ambrose Heal and Gordon Russell, the services of designer Keith Murray were retained. In 1932, Stevens and Williams held an exhibition of Murray's prototypes. Murray's designs were for table glass and vases. Presented to Princess Elizabeth, the 1946 *Royalty* range was designed by Tom Jones; it went into production in the 1950s. In 1951, when the John Walsh firm closed, Clyne Farquharson was hired as Stevens

and Williams's chief designer to replace Murray. In 1956, Farquharson left and was replaced by Jones as chief designer.

▶ Frederick Cooke, *Glass: Twentieth-Century Design*, New York: Dutton, 1986:32,68.

Stevens, Brooks (1911–)

▶ American industrial designer; born Wisconsin; active Milwaukee, Wisconsin.

▶ Studied Cornell University, Utica, New York, to 1933.

▶ Stevens set up his own studio in 1933 to redesign machinery in Milwaukee, Wisconsin. In 1936, he designed the first electric clothes drier; he transformed it from the manufacturer's concept of a simple heated box into an apparatus that had a glass window incorporated into its door. He designed the first snowmobile, outboard motor, mass-marketed Jeep, and the housing for the 1941 *Petipoint* iron (with Edward P. Schreyer), 1950 Harley-Davidson motorcycle (with the twin engine still used today), 1958 Oscar Mayer Wienermobile (a promotional gimmick) in fiberglass, and 1959 *Lawn-Boy* power lawn mower. Stevens designed automobile bodies for Volkswagen and Alfa Romeo, the 1940 Packard and 1980 AMC Cherokee, and perfected the first wide-mouth peanut butter glass jar, allowing access to the bottom. He worked with Formica in the late 1940s to create *Luxwood*, the wood-grain laminate used on much of the furniture of the time. He was the first to use color in kitchen appliances, being responsible for the ubiquitous avocado green of the 1950s and 1960s. He taught at the Milwaukee Institute of Art and Design and directed the Brooks Stevens Automotive Museum. In 1991, the Brooks Stevens Design Center was built at the Milwaukee Institute of Art and Design.

▶ Isabel Wilkerson, 'The Man Who Put Steam in Your Iron,' *The New York Times*, 11 July 1991:C1,C6. Susan Grant Lewin (ed.), *Formica and Design: From the Counter Top to High Art*, New York: Rizzoli, 1991:91–97. Michael Bersch, 'Brooks Stevens' in Mel Byars and Russell Flinchum (eds.), *50 American Designers*, Washington: Preservation, 1994.

Stevens, Irene

▶ British designer.

▶ In 1946, Stevens joined Webb Corbett of Stourbridge. She produced designs in cut blown glassware for the firm in 1949, produced in 1953. The range included a pitcher, drinking glasses, and a fruit bowl. Her designs of the 1950s were influenced by Clyne Farquharson at Stevens and Williams. She taught at the Royal College of Art and at Foley College.

▶ Kenneth Farr, *Design in British Industry: A Mid-Century Survey*, London: Cambridge, 1955. Frederick Cooke, *Glass: Twentieth-Century Design*, New York: Dutton, 1986:71–72.

Stewart, Michael

▶ Canadian furniture designer.

▶ Studied art, Ontario College of Art.

▶ He designed a number of popular furniture items, including the *7000 Series* public outdoor furniture. Stewart and Keith Muller designed the successful *Image* sofa and chair of the late 1960s, and their 1968 molded plywood stacking chair was produced by Ambient Systems in Toronto.

▶ Cat., *Seduced and Abandoned: Modern Furniture designers in Canada, the First Fifty Years*, Toronto: The Art Gallery at Harbourfront, 1986:21.

Stickley, Albert, Charles Stickley, John George Stickley (1871–1921), and Leopold Stickley (1869–1957)

▶ American furniture designers; brothers of Gustav Stickley.

▶ The Stickley brothers were concerned with the design and production of furniture. In the 1880s, Charles, Albert, and Gustav Stickley established Stickley Brothers, their first firm, in Binghamton, New York. At first they sold popular furniture by others and then designs of their own production. Their style became known as Craftsman or Mission furniture. In 1891, Albert and John George Stickley set up Stickley Brothers Furniture in Grand Rapids, Michigan. John George Stickley left the firm, setting up his own Onondaga Shop with Leopold Stickley in Fayetteville,

New York. Gustav Stickley now came into competition with his brothers. Good at business and excellent furniture makers, the success of Leopold and John George Stickley was illustrated in the rapid growth of their firm; incorporated in 1904 as L. and J.G. Stickley, which is still active today.

▶ Anne Yaffe Phillips, *From Architecture to Object*, New York: Hirschl and Adler, 1989:23–24. David M. Cathers, *Furniture of the American Arts and Crafts Movement*, New York: The New American Library, 1981.

Stickley, Gustav (b. Gustave Stickley 1858–1942)

▶ American craftsman, furniture designer, manufacturer, and entrepreneur; born Osceola, Wisconsin; brother of Albert, Charles, John George, and Leopold Stickley.

▶ Trained under his father as a stonemason.

▶ His émigré parents anglicized their German name from Stoeckel to Stickley. He worked with his brothers in his uncle's chair factory in Pennsylvania. Gustav, Charles, Albert, Leopold, and John George Stickley were all active in furniture making. Over the years, separate companies were set up for production of what became known as Craftsman or Mission furniture. In the 1880s, Charles, Albert, and Gustav Stickley established the first firm, Stickley Brothers, in Binghamton, New York. They sold popular furniture at first, and later pieces that they designed and made. Gustav Stickley found himself in competition with his brothers. His *Craftsman* oak electric chair for state corporal punishment was installed at the New York State prison, Auburn, in 1890. Through the magazine *The Craftsman* and his furniture production early in the 20th century, he became the greatest single influence on the American Arts and Crafts movement. Begun in 1901, the magazine expounded Stickley's philosophy documenting his own home in Syracuse, New York, in 1902, and, from 1908, his Craftsman Farms project in Morris Plains, New Jersey. Architect and designer Harvey Ellis designed the houses, furniture, and wall decorations for Stickley's United Crafts Workshop in Eastwood, New York. The Craftsman Farms project was a Utopian farm and school community, designed in 1907 and first introduced in 1908 in the form of plans and elevations for the Log House and the cottages. The project was probably finished in 1909. 1910–12, the farm and school were discussed in five successive issues of *The Craftsman*. In 1910, Stickley moved his family into the new Log House with furniture from his earlier Syracuse interior. He sold franchises from Los Angeles to Boston, and in 1913 bought a large building in New York City, where he set up showrooms, offices, and a restaurant. Craftsman Farms was short lived and his move to New York City proved over-ambitious, with the bankruptcy of his furniture empire in 1915 and the closing of *The Craftsman* in 1916. The full plan for the farm was never realized. In 1917, the 650-acre estate with all its furnishings were sold at public auction; in 1989, it became publicly owned. The furniture was dispersed. The advent of Modernism and the change of public taste brought Stickley's venture to an end, although he was a central figure in the development of Modern design. Though his commitment to solid construction, 'truth in materials,' and high-quality handicraft aligned him with the Arts and Crafts movement, his emphasis on simplicity and purity of form anticipated European Functionalism.

▶ He showed his work at the 1904 St. Louis 'Louisiana Purchase Exposition.' Along with the ceramics of William Greuby's designers, George P. Kendrick and later Addison LeBoutillier, Stickley often exhibited his furniture at international exhibitions.

▶ David M. Cathers, *Furniture of the American Arts and Crafts Movement*, New York: The New American Library, 1981. Anne Yaffe Phillips, *From Architecture to Object*, New York: Hirschl and Adler, 1989:23–25. Mary Ann Smith, *Gustav Stickley, The Craftsman*, Syracuse: Syracuse University, 1983.

Stiepevich, Vincent G. (1841–)

▶ Italian decorative painter; born Florence or Venice; active New York.

▶ Studied Royal Academy of Venice under Karl von Blaas.

▶ Stiepevich became a muralist in Milan in 1868. When he received the commission to decorate the main hall of the St. Louis Chamber of Commerce in St. Louis, Missouri, in 1872, he settled in the USA. From 1878 to at least 1894, he ran a mural painting workshop at 1193 Broadway in New York in partnership with Brooklyn artist Robert J. Pattison. Besides murals, the firm produced oil and watercolor genre paintings and drawings of Venetian scenes, peasants, and harems. In the early 1880s, he became a member of the Committee on Art Schools and Industrial Art of the Metropolitan Museum of Art, where he taught 'Water Color, Window and Wall Decoration' 1885–92. 1900–10, he was a member of the Artists' Fund Society and, 1903–04, its secretary.

▶ In 1862, he won a bronze medal at the Royal Academy of Venice and, in 1865, a grand prize for watercolor. In 1869, he showed paintings in Vienna. From 1878 in the USA, he showed his paintings at the National Academy of Design in New York City and at the Brooklyn Art Association exhibitions.

▶ Doreen Bolger Burke et al., *In Pursuit of Beauty: Americans and the Aesthetic Movement*, New York: Metropolitan Museum of Art and Rizzoli, 1987:468–69.

Stijl, De
See De Stijl

stile liberty
See Art Nouveau

Stiletto (1959–)
▶ German designer, born Rüsselsheim; active Berlin.

▶ 1980–81, attended engineering school, Technische Hochschule, Berlin; in 1982, studied visual communication, Hochschule der Künste, Berlin; from 1987, studied sculpture, Kunstakademie, Düsseldorf.

▶ From 1979–80, Stiletto was a metal- and locksmith in the German Federal Armed Forces; in 1981, was a video and super 8 artist; in 1982, designed furniture objects; in 1983, was active in holography; designed cutlery sets; 1983–84 furniture was based on large wire-grid waste baskets; 1985 *Consumer's Rest*, 1990 *Consumer's Rest* and 1990 *Short Rest* chairs were based on a wire-grid grocery-store cart.

▶ Participated in exhibitions: 1984 'Der elektronische Raum,' Berlin; 1984 'Kaufhaus des Ostens,' Berlin, Munich, and Hamburg; 1986 'Prototypen: Avant garde uit Belijn,' Rotterdam; 1986 'Gefühlschollagen,' Kunstmuseum, Düsseldorf; 1987 'Animal Art,' Steirischer Herbst, Graz; 1987 'Möbel als Kunstobjekt,' Munich; 1987 'Kraft durch Design,' Promodo, Vienna; 1987 'Trojanische Pferde,' Galerie Margine, Zürich; 1988 'Berlin: Les Avant-Gardes du Mobilier,' at Centre Georges Pompidou, VIA, and Galerie Néotù, both Paris.

▶ Christian Borngraeber, *Prototypen: Avantgarde Design uit/aus Berlin*, Rotterdam: Uitgeverij 010, 1986. Cat., *Berlin: Les Avant-Gardes du Mobilier*, Berlin: Design Zentrum, 1988.

Still McKinney, Nanny (b. Nanny Still 1926–)
▶ Finnish designer.

▶ Studied Taideteollinen oppilaitos, Helsinki, to 1949.

▶ 1949–76, she worked at the glass factory Riihimäen Lasi, where she produced her first glassware; in 1959, moved to Belgium; in 1962, designed ceramics for Cerabel-Porcelain, Baudour; from 1965–76, ceramics for Heinrich Porzellan, Germany; in 1966 and 1968, glassware for Val Saint-Lambert, Belgium. She created both mouth-blown and molded decorative and utility glassware, often in unusual shapes with textured surfaces. Subsequently executing handcrafted and industrial objects, she designed wooden objects, jewelry, ceramics, lighting for Raak, and cutlery for Hackman. From 1977, she designed glassware and ceramics for the Rosenthal Studio Line; from 1986, plastics for Sarvis; in 1987, cookware for Hackman.

▶ Her wooden objects won a diploma of honor at the 1954 (X) Triennale di Milano. Received 1972 Pro Finlandia prize. Her work

was the subject of the 1963 'Nanny Still Design' exhibition at the Huidevettershuis in Bruges.

▶ Cat., Kathryn B. Hiesinger and George H. Marcus III (eds.), *Design Since 1945*, Philadelphia: Philadelphia Museum of Art, 1983:232, II–63. Cat., *Nanny Still Design*, Bruges: Huidevettershuis, 1963. Erik Zahle (ed.), *A Treasury of Scandinavian Design*, New York, 1961:292, Nos. 242–43. Geoffrey Beard, *International Modern Glass*, London, 1976, plates 97,119,137. Jennifer Hawkins Opie, *Scandinavia: Ceramics and Glass in the Twentieth Century*, New York: Rizzoli, 1989.

Stock, Carl (1876–1945)
▶ German sculptor and designer.

▶ Trained at Bruckmann und Söhne, Heilbronn.

▶ From 1908, he collaborated with architect Eberhardt in Frankfurt.

▶ Annelies Krekel-Aalberse, *Art Nouveau and Art Déco Silver*, New York: Abrams, 1989:259.

Stockar, Rudolf (1886–1957)
▶ Czech architect and designer; born Dolnoplazy.

▶ 1904–09, studied architecture, Czech Technical University, Prague.

▶ He worked as a freelance architect and designed furniture, interiors, and utilitarian objects; 1915–30, was director of the Artěl Cooperative and commissioner of the 1923 (I) 'Esposizione Biennale delle Arti Decorative e Industriali Moderne,' Monza. His work was somewhat influenced by Cubism and increasingly in the Art Déco style.

▶ Alexander von Vegesack et al., *Czech Cubism: Architecture, Furniture, and Decorative Arts, 1910–1925*, New York: Princeton Architectural Press, 1992.

Stockholm, Marianne (1946–)
▶ Danish industrial designer; born Copenhagen.

▶ 1967–73, studied School of Architecture, Århus.

▶ 1974–75, she worked as an architect. 1975–78, she taught at the School of Architecture in Århus and was a freelance architect designing for the handicapped, houses, and exhibitions. She published *Workplace and Working Movements* (1982) on ergonomic design in the workplace. In 1983, she became a partner in the firm Stockholm/Zorea Design and set up an industrial design course at the School of Architecture at Århus. Her work included furniture, invalid vehicles, tableware, the 1988 *Skyline* graphic computer by Stantex, 1986 *Kirk Plus* wall telephone by Alcatel Kirk, 1986 *Kirk Delta* desktop telephone by Alcatel Kirk, and a 1988 control unit for concrete pipe machines by Pedershaab Maskinfabrik.

▶ She received the 1988 'if-Preis' in Hanover for the graphic computer.

▶ Cat., Design Center Stuttgart, *Women in Design: Careers and Life Histories Since 1900*, Stuttgart: Haus der Wirtschaft, 1989:234–37.

Stockman, Fred
▶ Belgian artist, mannequin designer, and entrepreneur; active France.

▶ Studied tailoring in Paris under Lavigne.

▶ In 1898, he founded 'Stockman Brothers, Busts and Mannequins,' and became one of the first to show the complete female torso in shop windows rather than partial figures. In 1922, Jérôme Le Maréchal, the director of the Galeries Lafayette department store in Paris, asked Stockman's artisans to work from fashion drawings rather than live models.

▶ From 1878, he showed his work at exhibitions in Tunis, London, Moscow, Chicago, Amsterdam, Antwerp, Brussels, and Hanoi, and won a medal at the 1849 'Trade and Industry Exposition' for his patented 'trunk-mannequin.' He was a juror and exhibitor at the 1900 Paris 'Exposition Universelle.'

▶ Nicole Parrot, *Mannequins*, Paris: Colona, 1981; London: Academy, 1982.

▶ See Siégel, Victor-Napoléon.

Stockton Art Pottery

▶ American ceramics firm; located Stockton, California.

▶ The firm was founded in 1881 in Stockton, California, where, in 1895, it introduced *Rekston* art pottery, similar in treatment to Rookwood's *Standard* ware and the *Lonhuda* ware of Stubenville. *Rekston* was an adaptation of Haviland's *Cincinnati faience*. From 1897, ten women worked at Stockton as artists, producing about 100 pieces of art pottery a day. Stockton ware without underglaze resembled Bennington's flint-enamel glazed work produced in the mid-19th century. Plastic yellow California clay from the Valley Springs region was used. The firm closed in 1900.

▶ Paul Evans in Timothy J. Andersen et al., *California Design 1910*, Salt Lake City: Peregrine Smith, 1980:64.

Stojan, Fabio (1953–)

▶ Italian industrial designer; born and active Milan.

▶ Studied Scuola Politecnica di Design, Milan.

▶ From 1974, he collaborated with Anna Castelli, Giorgio Brambilia, and Lorenzo Tosi in a studio in Milan. Stojan specialized in aspects of safety and ergonomics in town planning, working with the accident-prevention department of Montedison in Milan. He was a member of ADI (Associazione per il Disegno Industriale).

▶ *ADI Annual 1976*, Milan: Associazione per il Disegno Industriale, 1976.

Stölzl, Adelgunde 'Gunta' (from 1929, Gunta Sharon-Stölzl; from 1942, Gunta Stadler-Stölzl   1897–1983)

▶ German textile designer; born Munich; active Weimar, Dessau, and Zürich.

▶ 1914–16, studied decorative art, painting on glass, and ceramics, Kunstgewerbeschule, Munich; Textil- und Färbereifachschule (Professional School for Textiles and Dyeing), Krefeld; from 1919, Bauhaus, Weimar.

▶ As the first weaver at the Bauhaus, she produced chair seats for Marcel Breuer and others and contributed textiles to Walter Gropius's 1921–22 Sommerfeld house. 1922–23, she passed the journeyman's examination at the Bauhaus with a large Smyrna carpet. In 1924, encouraged by Johannes Itten, she set up a studio in Switzerland; 1925–26, she taught at the Bauhaus in Dessau, where she was one of two women master instructors. Succeeding Georg Muche, 1927–31, she was in charge of the Bauhaus weaving department. Under Stölzl's leadership, Bauhaus textiles were marketed through firms in Berlin, Dresden, and Stuttgart. In 1931, she and former students Gertrud Dirks-Preiswerk and Heinrich Otto Hürlimann established the firm SPH, a handweaving studio and workshop for textile design in Zürich. At this time, she began working with the Wohnbedarf furniture store in Zürich. A commission by Wohnbedarf, however, led to financial problems: a large number of textiles were lost, forcing her to dissolve the SPH partnership. She and Hürlimann set up the weaving-workshop S+H Stoffe, where she continued to work after Hürlimann left to form his own firm.

▶ Lionel Richard, *Encyclopédie du Bauhaus*, Paris: Somogy, 1985: 166–67. Cat., Gunta Stölzl, *Weberei am Bauhaus und ams eigener Werkstatt*, Berlin: Bauhaus-Archiv, 1987. Cat., *The Bauhaus: Masters and Students*, New York: Barry Friedman, 1988. Friederike Mehlau-Wiebking et al., *Schweizer Typenmöbel 1925–35*, Sigfried Giedion und die Wohnbedarf AG, Zürich: gta, 1989:231.

Stone, Arthur J. (1847–1948)

▶ English designer and silversmith; born Sheffield; active USA.

▶ 1861–68, apprenticed to a silversmith in Sheffield; studied National School of Design, New York.

▶ Setting in the USA in 1884, he was first employed by the firm William B. Durgin in Concord, New Hampshire. In 1887, he moved to Gardner, Massachusetts, where he worked for Frank W. Smith Silver as designer and head of the hollow-ware department. In 1895, he became a partner in J.P. Howard in New York. In 1886, he returned to Gardner and set up his own workshop. In 1901, he opened a shop and joined the Society of Arts and Crafts in Boston (founded in 1898), in which he was active until 1937.

Stone produced historicist, traditional presentation silver from 1904, ecclesiastical silver from 1905, and domestic tableware, sometimes collaborating with Hollis French and often modifying and reinterpreting 17th- and 18th-century American and English forms. His flatware handles were often chased with flowers or initials. The firm produced toys, miniatures, boxes, vases, porringers, tankards, tea sets, flatware, and items for children. Stone was one of the last independent designer-silversmiths in New England to train apprentices.

▶ He won the 1903 and 1906 Master Craftsman and 1913 Medallist awards of the Society of Arts and Crafts of Boston and a silver medal for his four-piece entry at the stand of the Boston group at the 1904 St. Louis 'Louisiana Purchase Exposition.' He showed his work at Arts and Crafts shows in Chicago, Detroit, Cincinnati, and Philadelphia.

▶ Elenita C. Chickering, 'Arthur J. Stone, silversmith,' *Antiques*, January 1986:274–83.

Stone, Robert E. (1903–)

▶ British silversmith; active London.

▶ Studied Central School of Arts and Crafts, London.

▶ He set up his own workshop in 1930.

▶ Annelies Krekel-Aalberse, *Art Nouveau and Art Déco Silver*, New York: Abrams, 1989:259.

Stoppino, Giotto (b. Luigi Stoppino   1926–)

▶ Italian architect and industrial designer; born Vigevano, Pavia.

▶ 1945–50, studied architecture, Milan; 1955–57, Università di Venezia.

▶ 1953–63, he was a partner in the Stoppino Gregotti Meneghetti design firm in Novara and, 1964–68, in Milan; from 1968, was an independent designer in Milan; in 1963, was a visiting lecturer at Oregon University, Pavia, and, in 1972, at the Scuola Cantonale Superiore in Lugano. In 1954, he became a member of the Movimento Studi per l'Architettura in Milan and, in 1960, of ADI (Associazione per il Disegno Industriale), of which he was a director 1966–68 and 1971–73, president 1982–84, and its delegate to the 1967 (V) Congress of ICSID in Montreal (Canada). In 1983, he was president of the development committee of the International Congress of ICSID in Milan. He began designing in plastics in 1967. His first design was the 1968 group of three folding tables. He designed the 1969 *537* table lamps (with V. Gregotti and L. Meneghetti) produced by Arteluce, 1970 *Alessia* fiberglass chair by Driade, 1971 stacking tables by Kartell, and 1984 champagne and ice bucket by Cleto Munari. For Acerbis International with Ludovico Acerbis, with whom he developed a special collaborative relationship, he designed the 1981 *Madison* shelving system, 1983 *Solemio* mirror, 1983 *Menhir* table system in marble, 1985 *Playbox* system, and 1986 *Soffio di Vento* shelving system. Other clients included Arnolfo di Cambio, Astheria, Bacci, Bellato, Bernini, Brambilla, Candle, Elco, Interior, Joint, La Rinascente, Moroni Mobili, Nicolini, Rexite, Tronconi, and Zanotta in Italy; Heller in the USA; and Raak in the Netherlands.

▶ His work was the subject of the 1983 exhibition at the Galleria Arte Borgogna, Milan. He participated in numerous exhibitions, including the 1950 (IX), 1954 (X), 1960 (XII), 1964 (XIII) (grand prize for the entrance hall) Triennali di Milano; 1963 'Aspetti dell'arte contemporanea' in Aguila; 1965 'La Casa Abitata' exhibition in Florence; 1966 'Prima Triennale Itinerate di Architettura Contemporanea Italiana' exhibition; 1968 'Italian Style' exhibition at the Hallmark Gallery in New York; exhibition of Italian design at the 1968 'Hemisfair' in San Antonio, Texas; 1970 'Design aus Italien' at the Deutscher Werkbund in Karlsruhe and other German cities; 1972 'Italy: The New Domestic Landscape' at the New York Museum of Modern Art; and others. The 1968 stacking tables for Kartell won first prize at the 1968 (VIII) 'Mobile accessorio da vendere nei grandi magazzini' competition in Trieste; other prizes included the grand prize at the 1964 (VIII) Triennale di Milano; Compasso d'Oro in 1960 (for the *Cavour* armchair), 1970 (for the *Tic-Tac* lamp and small circular ABS tables, both by Kartell), and 1979 (for *Sheraton* furniture by Acerbis); gold medal,

1981 'BIO 9' Industrial Design Biennial, Ljubljana; and 1981 Product Design Award, IBD, New York.
▶ Cat., Milena Lamarová, *Design a Plastické Hmoty*, Prague: Uměleckoprůmyslové Muzeum, 1972:158. *ADI Annual 1976*, Milan: Associazione per il Disegno Industriale, 1976. Daniele Baroni, *Giotto Stoppino: dall'architettura al design*, Milan: Electa, 1983. Juli Capella and Quim Larrea, *Designed by Architects in the 1980s*, New York, Rizzoli, 1988.

Storck, Josef Ritter von (1830–1902)
▶ Austrian metalworker; born Vienna.
▶ He was known for his delicate jewelry designs; was director of the Kunstgewerbeschule, Vienna. He designed historicist furniture in Renaissance and other styles.
▶ Günther Feuerstein, *Vienna—Present and Past: Arts and Crafts—Applied Art—Design,* Vienna: Jugend und Volk, 1976:13, 81. Ulrike Scholda, *Theorie und Praxis in Wiener Kunst-gewerbe des Historismus am Beispiel von Josef Ritter von Storck*, dissertation, Salzburg, 1992.

Storck und Sinsheimer
▶ German silversmiths; located Hanau.
▶ The firm was founded in Hanau in 1874. It produced hollowware in the Art Nouveau style.
▶ Annelies Krekel-Aalberse, *Art Nouveau and Art Déco Silver*, New York: Abrams, 1989:259.

Stourbridge Glass
▶ American glassware manufacturer; located Corona, New York.
▶ The firm was founded in 1902 by British glassmaker Arthur Nash. It was incorporated into Tiffany Glass, thereafter being known as Tiffany Furnaces, and issued a number of 'favrile' glass variants and new ranges of internal-luster glass.
▶ Frederick Cooke, *Glass: Twentieth-Century Design*, New York: Dutton, 1986:52.

Stowell, Davin (1953–)
▶ American industrial designer; born Corning, New York.
▶ Studied industrial design, Syracuse University, Syracuse, New York, to 1976.
▶ He first worked for Corning Glass Works consumer products division, Corning, New York, and, in 1978, set up his first firm, Davin Stowell Associates, a consultant to Corning Glass Works, designing consumer products and exhibitions. Employees included Tucker Viemeister and Tom Dair. In 1985, the company became known as Smart Design, located in New York. Stowell specialized in consumer product design, product planning, marketing communications, and graphic identity for clients including Oxo, Copco, Corning, International Playtex, Kepner-Tregoe, and 3M. He holds dozens of utility and design patents for consumer products and was a member of the Industrial Designers Society of America.
▶ He received numerous 'IDEA' awards and five annual *ID* Design Review awards.

Stramitz, Leonhard (1945–)
▶ Austrian jewelry designer; born Vienna.
▶ Stramitz was known for his machine-aesthetic jewelry, which incorporated various metals, acrylic, glass, bone, and rubber.
▶ Günther Feuerstein, *Vienna—Present and Past: Arts and Crafts—Applied Art—Design,* Vienna: Jugend und Volk, 1976:66, 69,81.

Stráník, Karel (1899–1978)
▶ Bohemian architect and furniture designer; born Prague; active Prague and Paris.
▶ 1918–23, studied University of Technology, Prague.
▶ From 1925 until its close in 1931, he was a Devětsil group member. He assisted Le Corbusier on the L'Esprit Nouveau pavilion at the 1925 Paris 'Exposition Internationale des Arts Décoratifs et Industriels Modernes' and on plans for the Cook House where he was working in 1925–26 in Le Corbusier's office in Paris. Returning to Prague, his 1925 competition entry for a

museum adjacent to the Liberation Movement monument in Prague was noteworthy; it incorporated a classical layout with Functionalist volume and detail. He designed the 1926–29 conversion of an older ground-floor building at 215 Poštovní St. in Černošice for Jaroslav and Jan Novák, stockbrokers and collectors of Czech Modern art. Like Le Corbusier, Stráník incorporated alternating white and colored spray-coated walls, setting off standard Thonet furniture and tubular metal banisters. Collaborating with Devětsil-friend Smetana, Stráník designed simple cupboards, armchairs, and bookcases for the house.
▶ Cat., *Devětsil: Czech Avant-Garde Art, Architecture, and Design of the 1920s and 30s*, Oxford Museum of Modern Art and London Design Museum, 1990.

Straub, Marianne (1909–)
▶ Swiss weaver and designer; born Amriswil; active Britain.
▶ 1928–31, studied Kunstgewerbeschule, Zürich, and 1932–33, machine production, Bradford Technical College.
▶ An experimenter, Straub used vegetable dyes in her fabrications of the 1920s and 1930s. She worked in a Swiss cotton mill and under weaver Ethel Mairet in Britain. 1934–37, she revitalized the flagging production of the Rural Industries Bureau for the 77 Welsh Woollen Mills, including upholstery fabrics used by Gordon Russell. She began weaving in her own home, simultaneously working in industrial methods in a small cotton mill. 1937–50, she was a designer at Helios, a division of Barlow and Jones, and, in the late 1940s, its managing director. At Helios, she worked on a dobby loom and was responsible for important advances in the production of contemporary fabrics on power looms and set a precedent for hand weaves for mass production. 1950–70, she designed contemporary fabrics for Warner, the successor to Helios, including for the 1951 *Festival Pattern Group*, a program established by the Council of Industrial Design for materials for the 1951 'Festival of Britain' exposition. Her 1951 *Surrey* curtain fabric for the program (originally installed in the Regatta Restaurant at the Festival) was printed under license by 26 manufacturers. Straub was a consultant designer to Tamesa Fabrics and Heal Fabrics. She taught widely, including at the Central School of Arts and Crafts and the Royal College of Art, both in London. Up to the 1980s, she was active as designer and teacher. She published the book *Hand Weaving and Cloth Design* (1977). Her *Tamesa* range was used on oceanliners 1934 *Queen Mary* and 1965–68 *Queen Elizabeth II*.
▶ Michael Farr, *Design in British Industry: A Mid-Century Survey*, London: Cambridge: Cambridge University Press, 1955. Marianne Straub, *Hand Weaving and Cloth Design*, London, 1977. Cat., *Thirties: British art and design before the war*, London: Arts Council of Great Britain, Hayward Gallery, 1979:90,92, 126,144,301. *A Choice of Design: 1950–1980*, London: Warner and Sons, 1981:64–65, nos. 244,248. Cat., Kathryn B. Hiesinger and George H. Marcus III (eds.), *Design Since 1945*, Philadelphia: Philadelphia Museum of Art, 1983:232,VII–56. Mary Schoeser, *Marianne Straub*, London: Design Council, 1984.

Strauss, Paula (1894–1943)
▶ German silversmith.
▶ Studied Kunstgewerbeschule, Stuttgart, under Paul Haustein.
▶ She was active in the 1920s and 1930s. From 1925, she designed silver produced by Bruckmann und Söhne in Heilbronn. She died at Auschwitz.
▶ Annelies Krekel-Aalberse, *Art Nouveau and Art Déco Silver*, New York: Abrams, 1989:150,259. Cat., *Metallkunst*, Berlin: Bröhan-Museum, 1990:577.

Streamline
▶ A form of styling popular in the 1930s.
▶ With prices in the USA fixed by the 1932 National Recovery Act, the need for product differentiation in the fiercely competitive Depression-hit market meant that unprecedented focus was placed on the way a product looked. The advertising industry was developing new techniques, and consumers often saw pictures of

goods before they were exposed to them in stores. The fledgling freelance designers jumped at the opportunity to sell their services; they came from backgrounds in commercial art, graphic design, advertising, and stage design, and promised commercial benefits for 'styling.' Designers included Norman Bel Geddes, Raymond Loewy, Henry Dreyfuss, and Walter Dorwin Teague Sr.; they all wrote books advocating their services. By the mid-1940s, Streamline household products were commonplace. Edgar Kaufmann Jr., director of the Department of Industrial Design at the New York Museum of Modern Art, considered Streamline an anathema and saw it as a 'widespread and superficial kind of design . . . used to style nearly any object from automobiles to toasters. Its theme is the magic of speed expressed in teardrop shapes, fairings and a curious ornament of parallel lines—sometimes called speed whiskers. The continued misuse of these devices has spoiled them for most designers . . . '
▶ 'Styling,' London: Design Museum, 1989. Edgar Kaufmann, *What is Modern Design?*, New York: Museum of Modern Art, 1950.

Strengell, Marianne (1909–)
▶ Finnish textile designer; active Bloomfield Hills, Michigan.
▶ 1929, studied Atheneum, Helsinki.
▶ 1930–36, she designed rugs and furnishing fabrics for Hemflit-Kotiahkeruus and, 1934–36, for Bo Atieselskab in Copenhagen. 1930–36, she was co-owner of Koti-Hemmet, which specialized in fabrics, furniture, and interior design. In 1937, she settled in Bloomfield Hills, Michigan, and was an instructor at the Cranbrook Academy of Art there. 1942–61, she was head of the Cranbrook's weaving and textile design department. Strengell used hand and power looms at the school, where she developed prototypes for machine-woven fabrics. These fabrications emphasized textures created with new synthetic materials and combinations of synthetic and natural fibers. Her work made hand-woven fabrics commercially popular in the USA in the 1940s. From 1947, she designed drapery and upholstery fabrics for Knoll and tweed and jacquard-filament automobile upholstery fabrics for Catham. Eero Saarinen used her textured materials at his 1948–56 General Motors Technical Center in Warren, Michigan. Her fiberglass fabrics were used in the Owens Corning Fiberglass building in New York. She was a consultant to government weaving programs to agencies in Jamaica in 1966, the Appalachia area of the USA, and St. Croix in the Virgin Islands 1969–71.
▶ Don Wallance, *Shaping America's Products*, New York 1956: 183. Eric Larrabee and Massimo Vignelli, *Knoll Design*, New York, 1981:91,272. Cat., Kathryn B. Hiesinger and George H. Marcus III (eds.), *Design Since 1945*, Philadelphia: Philadelphia Museum of Art, 1983: 232,VII–57. Gillian Moss, 'Marianne Strengell' in Mel Byars and Russell Flinchum (eds.), *50 American Designers*, Washington: Preservation, 1994.

Strnad, Oskar (1879–1935)
▶ Austrian architect and furniture and interior designer; born Vienna.
▶ From 1909, he was a highly influential teacher at the Kunstgewerbeschule in Vienna. The Wiener Möbel (Viennese furniture) was a new style, developed in the 1920s, that offered solid craftsmanship without historicism. Along with Josef Frank, Strnad was the main representative of this style of interior design. He was also known for his theater set designs and, in 1924, became chief designer for the Deutsches Volkstheater, which presented the works of avant-garde Expressionist playwrights. His sets included Ernst Křenek's *Jonny spielt auf* (1927) and František Langer's *Peripherie* (1930).
▶ His Österreichischer Edelraum (Austrian nobleman's room) was installed at 1922 'Gewerbeschau,' Munich. His work was included in the Austrian pavilion at the 1925 Paris 'Exposition Internationale des Arts Décoratifs et Industriels Modernes.'
▶ Günther Feuerstein, *Vienna—Present and Past: Arts and Crafts—Applied Art—Design*, Vienna: Jugend und Volk, 1976:

49,50,81. Otto Niedermoser, *Oskar Strnad 1879–1935*, Vienna: Bergland, 1965.

Strobl, Max (1861–1946)
▶ German silversmith; active Munich.
▶ In 1891 or 1892, Strobl bought the goldsmith firm Georg Sanktjohannsens Erben. He began specializing in the design of religious objects and later jewelry. His ornamentation derived from early medieval patterns, including Carolingian, Merovingian, and Romanesque.
▶ Cat., *Müncher, Schmuck 1900–1940*, Munich: Bayerisches Nationalmuseum, 1990:76–78.

Strömbergshyttan
▶ Swedish glass factory.
▶ The Lindfors Glasbruk at Hovmantorp, Småland, was founded in 1876. In 1933, it was leased by Edward Strömberg, formerly head of Orrefors and Eda. He renamed it Strömbergshyttan and began production of decorative glasswares designed by Gerda Strömberg and blown by Knut Bergqvist, also formerly of Orrefors. In c1943, Strömberg bought the facility and, in 1944, sold it to his son Erik. In 1954, Gunnar Nyland became artistic director. In 1975, it was bought by Orrefors and closed in 1979.
▶ Jennifer Hawkins Opie, *Scandinavia: Ceramics and Glass in the Twentieth Century*, New York: Rizzoli, 1989.

Strum, Gruppo
See Gruppo Strum

Stuart
▶ British glassware manufacturer.
▶ Producing simple straightforward forms and motifs, the firm's designers included F.H. Stuart and E.N. Khouri. John Luxton designed various pieces of glassware for the firm, including drinking glasses in a robust silhouette.
▶ It showed designs by Graham Sutherland, Paul Nash, Eric Ravilious, Dod Proctor, and Laura Knight at the 1935 'British Art in Industry' exhibition of the Royal Society of Arts in London.
▶ Frederick Cooke, *Glass: Twentieth-Century Design*, New York: Dutton, 1986:70,78.

Stüber, Otto
▶ German silversmith; active Scandinavia and Hamburg.
▶ Trained under Fritz von Miller in Munich.
▶ He worked for a time in Scandinavia. In 1910 with Christoph Kay, he set up a workshop in Hamburg.
▶ Annelies Krekel-Aalberse, *Art Nouveau and Art Déco Silver*, New York: Abrams, 1989:259.

Stuck, Franz von (1863–1928)
▶ German painter, sculptor, architect, and designer, born Tettenweis Lower Bavaria.
▶ Studied Kunstgewerbeschule 1878–81 and Akademie 1881–85, both Munich.
▶ Stuck received his first public notice as an illustrator for *Fliegende Blätter*, the Munich satirical magazine. Primarily a painter and illustrator, in the 1890s, he turned to sculpture and became one of the important artists of the Munich Jugendstil style; 1892, co-founded the Münchener Sezession; 1895, was appointed professor at the Akademie, Munich; 1897–98 (with Jakob Heilmann and Max Littmann), designed his Villa Stuck with architecture, interior design, furniture, painting and sculpture as a *Gesamtkunstwerk*.
▶ Grecian-style furniture for his own house won a gold medal at the 1900 Paris 'Exposition Universelle.'
▶ *Franz von Stuck: Persönlickkeit und Werk*, Museum Villa Stuck, 1977. Kathryn Bloom Hiesinger, *Die Meister des Münchner Jugendstil*, Munich: Stadtmuseum, 1988:160–61. Auction cat., Christie's, 9 Dec. 1989.

Studio Alchimia (aka Studio Alchymia)
See Alchimia

Studio DA
▶ Italian consultant design group.
▶ In the mid-1960s, architects and designers Cesare M. Casati and C. Emanuele Ponzio established the design partnership Studio DA. In 1965, they began experimenting with plastics, producing the 1965 *Alda* lounge chair produced by Confort. They were on the editorial board of Domus and designed its headquarters in Rozzano. Their furniture and furnishings were produced by manufacturers in Italy and abroad.
▶ From 1966, they showed their work at the major international expositions, including the 'Eurodomus' events and the Triennali di Milano.
▶ Cat., Milena Lamarová, *Design a Plastické Hmoty*, Prague: Uměleckoprůmyslové Muzeum, 1972:110.

Studio Naço
See Naço, Studio

Studio OPI
See OPI, Studio

Studio PER
See PER, Studio

Studio Pro
▶ Italian consultant-design group.
▶ Studio Pro was founded in the 1970s by Andries van Onck, Antonio Barrese, Cees Houtzager, Antonio Locatelli, and Pietro Salmoiraghi. They produced industrial design, visual design, architecture, and town planning. Their work included cultural and political projects.
▶ Cat., Milena Lamarová, *Design a Plastické Hmoty*, Prague: Uměleckoprůmyslové Muzeum, 1972:148.

Studiodada Associati
▶ Italian design cooperative; located Milan.
▶ Studiodada was founded in 1977 by partners Ada Alberti, Marco Piva, Paolo Francesso Piva, Dario Ferrari, and Maurizio Maggi; was active in architecture, video production, and interior, product, and graphic design.
▶ Participated in numerous exhibitions.
▶ Fumio Shimizu and Matteo Thun (eds.), *The Descendants of Leonardo: The Italian Design*, Tokyo, 1987:329.

Studium (aka Studium-Louvre)
▶ French decorating and design workshop; located Paris.
▶ The Studium decorating workshop was established in 1923 by Grands Magasins du Louvre in Paris. Until 1938, its director was Étienne Kohlmann, who collaborated regularly with consultant designers, including avant-garde designer Édouard-Joseph Bourgeois (Djo-Bourgeois) and more traditional designers André Fréchet, Pierre Lahalle, Georges Levard, and Maurice Matet. The workshop is sometimes referred to as the Studium-Louvre.
▶ The pavilion of the Studium was built at the 1925 Paris 'Exposition Internationale des Arts Décoratifs et Industriels Modernes.'
▶ 'Studium Louvre,' *Mobilier et Décoration*, Sept. 1925:173–77. Pierre Kjellberg, *Art Déco: les maîtres du Mobilier, le décor des Paquebots*, Paris: Amateur, 1986:175.

Stumpf, Axel (1957–)
▶ German designer; born Seigertshausen; active Berlin.
▶ 1981–84, studied Hochschule der Künste, Berlin.
▶ Stumpf was an exponent of German avant-garde design of the 1980s and a designer in the Berlin Design Workshop. The 1986 *Kumpel 1* and *Kumpel II* tables were constructed from three pickaxes and plate glass; designed 1985 strainer; and 1984 *Die Rache der Kellnerin* hanging lighting.
▶ Participated in 1984–85 'Kaufhaus des Ostens,' Berlin, Munich, and Hamburg; 1986 'Wohnen von Sinnen,' Kunstmuseum, Düsseldorf; 1986 'Erkundungen,' Stuttgart; 1988 'Berlin:

Les Avant-Gardes du Mobilier,' at Centre Georges Pompidou, VIA, and Galerie Néotù, Paris.
▶ Christian Borngraeber, *Prototypen: Avantgarde Design uit/aus Berlin*, Rotterdam: Uitgeverij 010, 1986. Cat., *Berlin: Les Avant-Gardes du Mobilier*, Berlin: Design Zentrum, 1988. Albrecht Bangert and Karl Michael Armer, *80s Style: Designs of the Decade*, New York: Abbeville, 1990:73,235.

Stumpf, Bill (b. William Stumpf 1936–)
▶ American industrial designer.
▶ Studied industrial design, University of Illinois, and, environmental design, University of Wisconsin, to 1968.
▶ He designed and produced the 1966 (first version) *Ergon* chair. 1970–73, he was a vice-president in charge of research at Herman Miller and became best known for office systems furniture. In 1973, he set up his own consulting firm in Winona, Minnesota. In 1977 with Donald Chadwick, he set up a design partnership and designed the 1979–84 *Equa* flexing plastic chair (with Don Chadwick) and 1984 *Ethospace* open-plan office system, both produced by Herman Miller.
▶ He was voted designer of the 1970s by the magazine *Industrial Design*.

Sture, Alf (1915–)
▶ Norwegian furniture and interior designer.
▶ Studied Statens Håndverks -og Kunstindustriskole, Oslo.
▶ 1940–50, he was an apprentice cabinetmaker and designer at Hiorth & Østlynsen in Oslo. In 1950, he set up his own design studio, continuing to design for Hjort & Østlynsen.
▶ Cat., David Revere McFadden (ed.) *Scandinavian Modern Design 1880–1980*, New York: Abrams, 1982:271, No. 153. Fredrik Wildhagen, *Norge i Form*, Oslo: Sternersen, 1988:120.

Sturm, Alexander
▶ Austrian silversmiths; located Vienna.
▶ The firm was founded in Vienna in 1882. In *c*1902, it produced the silver designs of Josef Hoffmann. When the silver workshop of the Wiener Werkstätte closed *c*1930, Strum again produced Hoffman's silver designs. Its production of the 1902 cigarette case with a stylized *plique-à-jour* enamel dragonfly designed by Antoinette Krasnik was noteworthy.
▶ The Krasnik cigarette case was shown at the 1902–03 winter exhibition at the Österreichisches Museum für Kunst und Industrie.
▶ Annelies Krekel-Aalberse, *Art Nouveau and Art Déco Silver*, New York: Abrams, 1989:194,202,259. Waltrand Neuwirth, *Wiener Gold- und Silberschmiede und ihre Punzen 1867–1922*, Vol. 2, Vienna, 1977:238–39.

Stuttgart Design Center
▶ German organization for the promotion of design in industry.
▶ As an organ of the Baden-Württemberg Office for the Promotion of Trade and Industry, the Design Center Stuttgart is the oldest established institution of its kind and the only government-operated design center in Germany. The center originated with the collection of the Royal Center for Trade and Crafts, as the Office for the Promotion of Trade and Industry was known in the 19th century. In 1850, Ferdinand von Steinbeis, the first president of the Royal Center, set up a collection of products, which eventually included textiles, clocks, jewelry, appliances, toys, and commercial graphic design, organized 'to provide craftsmen in the Kingdom of Württemberg with the opportunity to observe and copy exemplary pieces of work, and at the same time, to make trades both in the Kingdom of Baden-Württemberg and elsewhere aware of the competent craft products in this land.' In 1896, the collection was housed in the new Museum of Trade and Industry, known today as the Haus der Wirtschaft. Though the collection was undamaged during World War II, the museum never reopened. Postwar exhibitions on contemporary themes, such as the 1949 'Living' and 1953 'The Beauty of Technology,' were organized, placing a greater emphasis on the subject of design. With the need for a new institution, the Federal State of Baden-

Württemberg established the LGA-Zentrum Form in 1962, renamed the Design Center Stuttgart in 1969.
▶ Cat., *Design Selection 92*, Stuttgart: Design Center Stuttgart, 1992.

Stüttgen, Gerhard (1878–1952)
▶ German metalworker; active Cologne.
▶ Stüttgen taught at the Kunstgewerbeschule in Cologne. He instructed his students in bending steel tubing and became involved for a time in creating a chair frame with no back legs. His design was revealed at the hearings in 1938 of the famous court case between Mauser and Mies van der Rohe as, in 1937, Stüttgen had sold rights to the frame design to Mauser.
▶ With little significance at the time, his tube frame was shown at the 1923–24 exhibition of the work of the Kunstgewerbeschule in Cologne.
▶ Otakar Máčel, 'Avant-garde Design and the Law: Litigation over the Cantilever Chair,' *Journal of Design History*, Vol. 3, Nos. 2 and 3, 1990.

Stuyfzand, Jos (1958–)
▶ Dutch industrial designer.
▶ Studied Akademie Industriële Vormgeving, Eindhoven.
▶ 1983–89, he worked for Océ van de Grinten and, in 1989, joined the Lumiance Design Team.

Subes, Raymond (1893–1970)
▶ French metalsmith; active Paris.
▶ Studied École Boulle and École des Arts Décoratifs, both Paris, and under wrought iron designer Émile Robert.
▶ From 1916, he worked in the small workshop set up by Émile Robert in Enghien-les-Bains. In 1919, he began working for Robert's metal contracting firm Borderel et Robert at 131 rue Damrémont in Paris and became chief of the design department and subsequently director of the wrought iron workshop. Collaborating with a number of architects, he quickly became a leading designer and maker of metalworks. Prolific in the 1920s, he produced a considerable number of works in wrought iron, including the pulpit of the cathedral in Rouen; the grilles of the choir entry at the church of Saint-Germain-des-Prés; the telescoping lighting fixtures on the Carousel bridge in Paris; with sculptor R. Martin, the monument to General Leclerc at Porte d'Orléans; and, with architect Laprade, the tomb of Marshal Lyautey at Esplanade des Invalides in Paris. In the 1930s, he produced furniture for Jacques-Émile Ruhlmann's nephew and architect Alfred Porteneuve, using chromium-plated tubular metal. He designed a grille for the Permanent Colonial Museum in 1931; large amounts of ironwork for the oceanliners 1931 *Atlantique*, 1926 *Île-de-France*, *Pasteur*, and 1935 *Normandie*; and ironwork for the Banque de France and National City Bank, both on the avenue des Champs-Élysées, Institut Pasteur, Caisse des Dépôts et Consignations, Musée de la France d'Outre-Mer, and Église du Saint-Esprit (doors) in Paris. His works were mainly in wrought iron (patinated, chromed, or gilded), and in polished steel, bronze, and *repoussé* copper. He used alabaster, levantine marble, frosted glass, and (produced for him by Mme. Luhuché-Méry in the early 1920s) embroidered silk shades in his lighting. After World War II, he became director of Borderel et Robert, while active as a metalworker.
▶ He first showed his work in 1919. He designed and produced a lacquered metal bookcase and console with Ruhlmann for the 'Hôtel du collectionneur' at the 1925 Paris 'Exposition Internationale des Arts Décoratifs et Industriels Modernes.' At the 1937 Paris 'Exposition Internationale des Arts et Techniques dans la Vie Moderne,' he produced the fountains for the Radio pavilion and a madonna and child for the papal pavilion, and numerous screens, consoles, and grilles for other sections. In 1958, he became a member of the Académie des Beaux-Arts.
▶ Alastair Duncan, *Art Nouveau and Art Déco Lighting*, New York: Simon and Schuster, 1978:187–88. Victor Arwas, *Art Déco*, Abrams, 1980. Pierre Cabanne, *Encyclopédie Art Déco*, Paris:

Somogy, 1986:235. Pierre Kjellberg, *Art Déco: les maîtres du Mobilier, le décor des Paquebots*, Paris: Amateur, 1986:175–76.

Südfeld, Hermann
▶ Austrian silversmiths; located Vienna.
▶ The firm was founded in Vienna in 1835. It produced silver in decorative and geometric Viennese styles of the first decade of the 20th century.
▶ Annelies Krekel-Aalberse, *Art Nouveau and Art Déco Silver*, New York: Abrams, 1989:259. Waltrand Neuwirth, *Wiener Gold- und Silberschmiede und ihre Punzen 1867–1922*, Vol. 2, Vienna, 1977:240–41.

Sudo, Reiko (1953–)
▶ Japanese textile designer; born Ibaraki Prefecture.
▶ Studied textiles, Musashino Art University.
▶ She set up a textile design workshop in 1978. In 1984, she was instrumental in founding the Nuno Corporation.
▶ Albrecht Bangert and Karl Michael Armer, *80s Style: Designs of the Decade*, New York: Abbeville, 1990:168,235.

Süe, Louis (1875–1968)
▶ French architect, painter, and decorator; born Bordeaux; active Paris.
▶ Studied painting, École National des Beaux-Arts, Paris.
▶ He settled in Paris in 1895, where he became an architect but continued painting, showing his canvases at the Salon des Indépendants and Salon d'Automne. 1905–07, collaborating with Paul Huillard, he built his first houses on the rue Cassini, near the observatory in Paris. Süe's furniture at this time was marked by a German influence. He was a friend of Pierre Louÿs, André Gide, and Claude Debussy. In 1910 with painter André Mare, he began designing furniture in a workshop called Atelier français on the rue de Courcelles in Paris. Mare and Süe set themselves up as interior designers in 1919 in the firm they called Compagnie des Arts français at 116 rue du Faubourg Saint-Honoré in Paris. Collaborators included Marie Laurencin, André Derain, Maurice Marinot, Aristide Maillol, Charles-Georges Dufresne, Gustave-Louis Jaulmes, Paul Vera, Richard Desvallières, and Raoul Dufy. Their approach was inspired by the style of the Louis Philippe period and encouraged the use of massive, theatrical forms with a great amount of gilding. They designed lighting and *objets d'art*. In 1921, a portfolio of their work and projects, with text by Paul Valéry, was published under the title *Architecture*. In 1923, Süe published with Léandre Vaillat *Rythme de l'Architecture*, and, in 1924, Jean Badovici issued *Intérieurs de Süe et Mare*. Süe designed silver produced by Orfèvrerie Christofle. The team designed interiors for several oceanliners, including the lounge of the 1926 *Île-de-France*, and the 1925 d'Orsay perfume shop in Paris and its flacon. 1927–28, they constructed and furnished the Art Déco villa of comedienne Jane Renouard at Saint-Cloud and designed couturier Jean Patou's apartment in the rue de la Faisanderie, Paris, and his country house, Ustaritz. In 1928, Jacques Adnet took over as director of design at Compagnie des Arts français, at which time Süe returned to architecture, though continuing to decorate, including the *c*1929 townhouse of Bernard Bouvet de Monvel and 1938 apartment of Helena Rubinstein, both Paris, and Mare to painting. In 1939, Süe left for Istanbul, where he taught at the academy of fine arts until 1944; in 1950, he was commissioned by collector Georges Grammont to transform the chapel in Annonciade in Saint-Tropez.
▶ Süe first showed a massive desk-bookcase (with Paul Huillard) at the 1911 Salon d'Automne and subsequently chairs (with Jacques Palyart). Süe and Mare designed two pavilions for the 1925 Paris 'Exposition Internationale des Arts Décoratifs et Industriels Modernes,' one for their firm (CAF) and the other for the Musée des Arts Contemporains. Süe showed without Mare at the 1937 Paris 'Exposition Internationale des Arts et Techniques dans la Vie Moderne.' Work subject of the exhibition 'André Mare et la Compagnie des Arts français (Süe et Mare),' Ancienne Douane Strasbourg, 1971.

▶ Raymond Foulk, *The Extraordinary Work of Süe and Mare*, London: The Foulk Lewis Collection, 1979. Victor Arwas, *Art Déco*, Abrams, 1980. Jessica Rutherford, *Art Nouveau, Art Deco and the Thirties: The Furniture Collections at Brighton Museum*, Brighton: The Royal Pavilion, Art Gallery and Museums, 1983:44—45. Pierre Cabanne, *Encyclopédie Art Déco*, Paris: Somogy, 1986:235—39.

Suetin, Nikolai Mikhailovich (1897–1954)
▶ Russian artist, ceramicist, and designer; born Metlevsk Station, Kaluga; husband of Anna Leporskaia.
▶ 1918—22, studied Vitebsk Art School.
▶ He became a member of Kazimir Malevich's Posnovis/Unovis group in 1919, and, with Il'ia Chashnik, was one of Malevich's closest collaborators. In 1922 with Malevich, Chashnik, Vera Ermolaeva, Lev Yudin, and others, he settled in Petrograd, working with Malevich on Suprematist architectural constructions known as *arkhitektony* and *planity* and entering the Inkhuk affiliation there. From 1923, Suetin worked at the Lomonosov State Porcelain Factory in Petrograd, where he decorated much porcelain (including tea sets), in Suprematist designs at first, and where Eva Zeisel was one of his student workers. By 1930, his approach was a sort of stylized folk realism. He became artistic director of Lomonosov in Leningrad (now St. Petersburg) in 1932, remaining there until 1952.
▶ With Anna Leporskaia, he rendered the interior design for the 1928 Leningrad 'The Construction of the NKVD House.' His work was included in the 1930 (I) 'First All-City Exhibition of Visual Arts' at the Academy of Arts in Leningrad, 1932 jubilee 'Artists of the RSFSR During the Last 15 Years' at the Academy of Arts in Leningrad, and, during the 1930s, in several exhibitions abroad including the 1937 Paris 'Exposition Internationale des Arts et Techniques dans la Vie Moderne,' where he helped design the Soviet pavilion.
▶ L. Zhadova, 'O farfore N.M. Suetina,' in K. Rozhdestvenskii (ed.), *Sovetskow dekorativnoe iskusstvo 73/74*, Moscow, 1975:211. I. Riazantsev, *Iskusstvo sovetskogo vystavochynogo ansamblia 1917–1970*, Moscow, 1976:353 et passim. L. Zhadova, 'Blokadnaia grafika N.M. Suetina,' in M. Nemirovskais (ed.), *Sovetskaia grafika 74*, Moscow, 1976:185—90. Stephanie Barron and Maurice Tuchman, *The Avant-Garde in Russia, 1910–1930*, Cambridge: MIT, 1980:250. Cat., *The Great Utopia: The Russian and Soviet Avant-Garde, 1915–1932*, New York: Guggenheim Museum, 1992.

Sugahara, Minoru (1940–)
▶ Japanese glassware designer; born Tokyo.
▶ Studied Wasada University.
▶ He joined the design staff of the family's firm Sugahara Glass in 1963 and, in 1973, became its design team head. He designed its 1988 *Indigo* and *Clear Frost* square-format glass dinnerware.
▶ His *BK & WH* glassware designs won a 1989 Japanese design award.
▶ Albrecht Bangert and Karl Michael Armer, *80s Style: Designs of the Decade*, New York: Abbeville, 1990:142,235.

Sugasawa, Toshio (1940–)
▶ Japanese glass designer.
▶ Studied crafts, Tokyo University of Arts, to 1965.
▶ He began working for Hoya Crystal in Tokyo in 1965, becoming chief of planning and design in its department of crystal glass.
▶ Solo exhibition at 1979 'Another World,' Matsuya Gallery, Ginza, Tokyo. Work included in 1983 'Modern Japan Craft,' Fukui Prefectural Museum, Japan; 1984, 1987, and 1900 'Glass in Japan,' Tokyo; 1985 'New Glass in Japan,' Badisches Landesmuseum, Karlsruhe; 1986 'Crafts, Standard-Bearers of the End of This Century,' Suntory Museum of Art, Tokyo; 1986 'Asahi Annual Modern Craft Exhibition,' Tokyo; 1986 'Japanese Glass — 300 Years,' Suntory Museum, Tokyo; and 1991 (V) Triennale of the Japan Glass Art Crafts Association, Heller Gallery, New York.

Won the Asahi Shimbun Prize at the 1982 'World Glass Now '82,' Hokkaido Museum of Art, Sapporo.
▶ Cat., *Glass Japan*, New York: Heller Gallery and Japan Glass Art Crafts, Association, 1991: No. 35.

Sugawara, Seizo
▶ Japanese lacquerer; active Paris.
▶ He arrived in Paris in 1900 with the Japanese delegation to the 'Exposition Universelle' and decided to stay in France. In his own studio, he produced lacquer works that showed a synthesis of traditional Japanese techniques and geometric motifs, while experimenting with unprecentedly opulent materials. He imported his raw materials from Japan. In 1907, his work attracted the attention of Eileen Gray, who, having worked in lacquer in Britain, was trained by Sugawara. She showed his wooden sculptures in her shop Jean Désert in Paris: he produced some of her lacquerwork in his workshop in the rue Guénégaud. In 1912, he taught Jean Dunand the ancient and traditional procedures; in exchange, Dunand showed him various metalwork techniques. In the late 1920s, Sugawara assisted Evelyn Wyld (an earlier associate of Gray) and Eyre de Lanux on lacquered furniture.
▶ Peter Adam, *Eileen Gray, Architect/Designer*, New York: Abrams, 1987:157,182. Félix Marcilhac, *Jean Dunand: His Life and Work*, New York: Abrams, 1991:28ff,170.

Sullivan, Louis Henri (1856–1924)
▶ American architect; born Boston; active Philadelphia and Chicago.
▶ 1872—73 studied architecture, Massachusetts Institute of Technology in Cambridge, Massachusetts, under William Robert Ware; 1874—75, École des Beaux-Arts, Paris, under Auguste-Émile Vaudremer.
▶ In 1873, he moved to Philadelphia, working briefly in the office of Frank Furness and George W. Hewitt. The stock market crash of 1873 sent Sullivan to Chicago, where he worked for skyscraper pioneer William Le Baron Jenney. Returning from his Paris studies to the USA in 1875, he held a number of jobs. Chief draftsman in the Chicago office of Dankmar Adler from 1879, he became a full partner in 1883 and was mentor to the three most prominent Prairie School architects: Frank Lloyd Wright, George Grant Elmslie, and George Washington Mahler. Undistinguished at first, Adler and Sullivan's work was influenced by Richard Morris Hunt of New York, Furness of Philadelphia, English High Victorian Gothic, and popular French neoclassical styles. Their first major commission was the 1887—89 Auditorium Building in Chicago; his interiors of the 1890s illustrate the sureness his mature ornamental style, and the building, restored in the late 1980s, is dramatic in its use of the ornamentation that crawls over every surface. The 1890 Getty Tomb in Chicago was the first essay in his monumental geometric exterior forms and ornamentation, and the 1890 Wainwright Building in St. Louis, Missouri, illustrated a full blossoming of the expression. His last major building was the 1898—1902 Schlesinger and Mayer building (now Carson, Pirie and Scott department store) in Chicago. His partnership with Adler was discontinued in 1895. Sullivan became the pioneer of the modern office block and father of Prairie School architecture. He published the 'Kindergarten Chats' essays (including, in 1896, his famous dictum, 'Form ever follows function. This is the law.') and *The Autobiography of an Idea* (1924). Though Sullivan did not design moveable furniture, he had considerable influence on the decorative arts in the USA through his writings, in the development of an individual style of ornament that used finely drawn plant forms and ideas from 19th-century sources anticipating Art Nouveau, and through his influence on assistants Frank Lloyd Wright and George Grant Elmslie. Though uniquely his own, his ornamentation was akin to that of Christopher Dresser, A.W.N. Pugin, and James Kellaway Colling. He was not commercially successful in his later years, although he built a group of small distinguished banks in the Midwest that were among his best designs. The 1913 Land and Loan Office (later the Adams building), 1914

Merchant's National Bank in Grinnel, Iowa, and 1917–18 People's Savings and Loan Association Bank in Sidney, Ohio, are outstanding among the six banks designed 1913–19. The Adams building has leaded-glass windows in ochre and cream with counterpoints of turquoise, azure, burgundy, green, and yellow against an opalescent sky-blue ground with upper and lower horizontal geometric borders of blue-green banded by rectangles of green and ochre centering rectangles of randomly placed bright colors. The building's large urns were made of glazed terracotta, a material used throughout the building. The elaborate organic ornamentation on the urns, originally used for greenery, recalls Sullivan's motifs from earlier commissions. His other buildings included 1885–87 Marshall Field Wholesale Store in Chicago; 1887 Selz, Schwab factory in Chicago; 1889 Walker Warehouse in Chicago; 1892 Schiller building in Chicago; 1894 Stock Exchange in Chicago; 1895 Guaranty building in Buffalo, New York; 1898 Bayer building in New York; 1898–99 Gage building in Chicago; and 1907–08 National Farmers' Bank in Owatonna, Minnesota.

▶ Louis Sullivan, 'Kindergarten Chats,' *Interstate Architect*, Vols. 2–3, Feb. 16, 1910–Feb. 8, 1912. Hugh Morrison, *Louis Sullivan, Prophet of Modern Architecture*, New York: Norton, 1935. George G. Elmslie, 'Sullivan Ornamentation,' *Monthly Bulletin, Illinois Society of Architects*, June-July 1935; reprinted in *Journal of the American Institute of Architect*, Vol. 6, Oct. 1946:155–58. Edgar Kaufmann Jr. (ed.), *Louis Sullivan and the Architecture of Free Enterprise*, Chicago, 1956. John Szarkowski, *The Idea of Louis Sullivan*, Minneapolis, 1956. Vincent Scully Jr., 'Louis Sullivan's Architectural Ornament,' *Perspecta* 5, 1959, pp. 73–80. Albert Bush-Brown, *Louis Sullivan*, New York, 1960. Willard Connely, *Louis Sullivan as He Lived*, New York, 1960. Paul Sherman, *Louis Sullivan: An Architect in American Thought*, Englewood Cliffs, NJ: Prentice-Hall, 1962. Paul Sprague, *The Drawings of Louis Henry Sullivan*, Princeton, 1979. Narciso G. Menocal, *Architecture as Nature: The Transcendentalist Idea of Louis Sullivan*, Madison, Wis., 1981. Linda L. Chapman et al., *Louis H. Sullivan Architectural Ornament Collection*, Edwardsville, Ill.: Southern Illinois University, 1981. Robert Twombly, *Louis Sullivan: His Life and Work*, New York, 1986. Stuart Durant, *Ornament from the Industrial Revolution to Today*, Woodstock, NY: Overlook, 1986.

Summers, Gerald (1899–1967)
▶ British furniture designer.
▶ Summers was the only Briton in the 1930s whose furniture designs rivalled those of the continent as a contribution to the development to Modern design. Comparable to Marcel Breuer and Alvar Aalto, Summers's chair designs in bent plywood represent milestones in the evolution of the Modern aesthetic in seating, although little of his furniture was made. In *c*1931, he founded the firm Makers of Simple Furniture. With a distaste for self promotion, he was overshadowed by Gordon Russell and Ambrose Heal, whose larger and well-established firms assured their fame. Only a handful of his designs had been published widely by the early 1990s, except in auction catalogs. The austere forms of his early painted-plywood furniture rejected his industrial apprenticeship. His furniture was characterized by an emphasis on function, absence of ornament, and the exploration of new, efficient materials and construction techniques. The first phase of his designs from 1933 had few parallels with other British designers. He showed a preference for plain flat and curved forms in plywood. Summers was one of the first Modernists to adopt Alvar Aalto's bent plywood and organic forms for seating design. Reaching his stride by the mid-1930s, Summers produced two of his best-known designs: the one-piece 1934 *Bent Plywood Lounge Chair* and the curved 1934 *High-Back Chair*. The *Bent Plywood Lounge Chair* was a formal and technical advance over Aalto's less integrated chair designs. Summers's Functionalist aesthetic was applied to a wide range of pieces 1935–37, including tables, beds, desks, chairs, trolleys, case goods, vases, coal bins, a gramophone, and children's furniture. 1938–40, Summers produced purpose-shaped pieces. The firm closed in 1940.

▶ Martha Hart Deese, *Gerald Summers and Makers of Simple Furniture*, thesis New York: Cooper-Hewitt/Parsons School of Design, New York.

Sumner, George Heywood Maunoir (1853–1940)
▶ British designer, artist, and archeologist.
▶ Sharing quarters with Arts and Crafts architect W.A.S. Benson, Sumner turned to art. In 1894, he became Master of the Art-Workers' Guild. He was associated with A.H. Mackmurdo's Century Guild. He became a painter, etcher, book designer, and archeologist. Best known for his decoration of several churches, he used the sgraffito (scratched) technique in his artwork.
▶ Stuart Durant, *Ornament from the Industrial Revolution to Today*, Woodstock, NY: Overlook, 1986:126,222,232.

Suomen Kultaseppät
▶ Finnish silversmiths; located Turku.
▶ The firm produced the silver designs of Gunilla Jung in the 1930s.
▶ Annelies Krekel-Aalberse, *Art Nouveau and Art Déco Silver*, New York: Abrams, 1989:241,259.

Superstudio
▶ Italian architecture and design cooperative; located Florence.
▶ Superstudio was established in 1966 in Florence by Adolfo Natalini and Cristano Toraldo di Francia. 1970–72, Gian Pietro Frassinelli, Alessandro Magris, Roberto Magris, and Alessandro Poli joined the group. From 1973, its members were teachers, mostly from the Università di Firenze. The group rebelled against the postwar orthodoxies of architecture and design, as did its sister group, Archizoom, formed the same year. Aligned with student unrest and expressing metaphors with a Marxist slant, Superstudio and Archizoom were part of the Anti-Design (or Counter-Design) movement of the late 1960s and early 1970s. Superstudio took a conceptual approach to Anti-Design and became prominent through its projects in the late 1960s that fell midway between architecture and fine art, in a manner similar to the work of Hans Hollein. Superstudio wanted to replace product design with 'evasion design.' A manifestation of Superstudio's production was its grid-design 1970 *Quaderna* laminate table range produced by Zanotta. Their 1969 project 'Il monumento continuo' proposed an endless framework covering the entire surface of the earth, in a mocking critique of contemporary planning. 1971–73, the group produced a series of films on the philosophical and anthropological aspects of 're-building.' Their 1972 proposal to submerge the city of Florence so that only the dome of the cathedral was exposed as a tourist attraction was their subversive contribution to the 'Save the Historic Centers' campaign of the time. Their 1973 'Fragments from a personal museum' exhibition proposed a 'radical architecture' through the use of Surrealist graphics. 1973–75, the studio joined Global Tools and, from 1973, was active in research and teaching at the Università di Firenze and other institutions. It abandoned its critique of architecture in a capitalist society in 1978. Reverberations of the group's work appeared later in the projects of member Adolfo Natalini, including the 1979 unrealized project for the design of a building on the Römerberg in Frankfurt.
▶ The studio participated in the 1972 'Italy: The New Domestic Landscape' exhibition at the New York Museum of Modern Art, 1973 (XV) and 1979 (XVI) Triennali di Milano, 1978 and 1980 Biennali di Venezia, and other important exhibitions from 1968. The group's work was the subject of the 1973–74 'Superstudio: Fragmente aus einem persönlichen Museum' European touring exhibition, 1973–75 'Sottsass and Superstudio: Mindscapes' USA touring exhibition, and 1982 exhibition in Milan.
▶ *Superstudio: Italia vostra, Salvataggi di centri storici*, Florence, 1972. Superstudio, 'Drei Warnungen vor einer mystischen Widergeburt des Urbanismus,' *Archithese (Niederteufen)*, No. 1, 1972. F. Raggi, 'Radical Story,' *Casabella*, No. 382, 1973:40. Lara Vinca Masini (ed.), *Topologia e morfogenesi, Utopia e crisi dell'antinatura; Momenti delle intenzioni architettoniche in Italia*, Venice,

1978. Penny Sparke, *Ettore Sottsass Jnr*, London: Design Council, 1982. Cat., G. Pettena (ed.), *Superstudio 1966–1982: Storia, figure, architettura*, Florence: Electa, 1982. Andrea Branzi, *La Casa Calda: Esperienze del Nuovo Disegno Italiano*, Milan: Idea Books, 1982. Vittorio Magnago Lampugnani in Vittorio Magnago Lampugnani (ed.), *Encyclopedia of 20th-Century Architecture*, New York: Abrams, 1986:326.

Suprematism
▶ Russian abstract art style.
▶ 'Suprematism' was the term coined by Russian artist Kazimir Malevich for a purely abstract art image, meaning, according to him, 'supremacy of pure sensation in the fine arts.' He first used the term in reference to his painting *Black Square on White Group* (1913). He and followers, including Nikolai Suetin, furthered the concept in architecture-related compositions and in the forms of and decorations on ceramics at the Lomonossov porcelain factory in St. Petersburg. There are parallels with the work and ideas of the contemporary De Stijl group in the Netherlands. In 1916, Kazimir Malevich founded and led the artists' group Supremus, which published a journal by the same name.
▶ Cat., *Kunst und Revolution: Russische und Sowjetische Kunst 1910–1932*, Vienna: Österreichisches Museum für angewandte Kunst, 1988. Jaroslav Andel et al., *Art into Life: Russian Constructivism 1914–1932*, New York: Rizzoli, 1990. Cat., *The Great Utopia: The Russian and Soviet Avant-Garde, 1915–1932*, New York: Guggenheim Musem, 1992.

Survage, Léopold   (1879–1958)
▶ Russian architect; born Moscow.
▶ Studied School of Fine Arts, Moscow, and under Henri Matisse in Paris.
▶ Survage settled in Paris in 1908 and was actively involved in the emergence of Cubism. He was instrumental in the revival of the art mural. In 1937, he became a member of UAM (Union des Artistes Modernes).
▶ In Russia, he showed his work with the small group The Blue Rose. He painted three murals for the Palais des Chemins de Fer, and worked with Albert-Léon Gleizes and Fernand Léger on the mural *Accompagnement d'Architecture* in the grand hall of the UAM pavilion, both at the 1937 Paris 'Exposition Internationale des Arts et Techniques dans la Vie Moderne.' His work was the subject of the 1966 'Survage' exhibition at the Musée Galliéra in Paris.
▶ Cat., Waldemar George, 'Présence de Léopold Survage,' in *Survage*, Paris: Musée Galliéra, 1966. Cat., *Les années UAM 1929–1958*, Paris: Musée des Arts Décoratifs, 1988.

Süssmuth, Richard   (1900–74)
▶ German glassware designer.
▶ Studied Akademie für Kunsthandwerk, Dresden.
▶ He founded a glass factory in Penzig in 1924. Re-establishing a factory in Immenhausen after World War II, he produced art- and stained-glass works and glass tablewares. His tableware designs included the 1948 *Capitol* range.
▶ His work was shown at the 'Good Design' exhibition at the New York Museum of Modern Art and Chicago Merchandise Mart in the 1950s.
▶ Cat., Kathryn B. Hiesinger and George H. Marcus III (eds.), *Design Since 1945*, Philadelphia: Philadelphia Museum of Art, 1983:232. *Glass 1959*, Corning, NY.: The Corning Museum of Glass, 1959: No. 147.

Sutherland, Graham Vivian   (1903–80)
▶ British artist, graphic artist, and designer; born London.
▶ 1920–26, studied engraving and etching, Goldsmiths' College School of Art, London.
▶ Up to 1930, he worked as a graphic artist, producing etchings in a Romantic style reminiscent of Samuel Palmer. 1926–35, he taught engraving at the Chelsea College of Art. 1933–34, he produced decorations for tableware for ceramics manufacturer E.

Brain, Fenton, under artistic director T.A. Fennemore, and ceramics manufacturer Arthur J. Wilkinson in Burslem, under artistic director Clarice Cliff, and glassware designs for Stuart in Stourbridge. Experimenting with oils in the early 1930s, he returned to painting 1934–35. 1941–44, he worked as an official war artist, achieving maturity in his work. In the 1940s, he created fabric designs for Helios and, after World War II, became known for his paintings of landscapes, religious subjects, and portraiture, including *The Crucifixion* (1946) for St. Matthew's Church in Northampton and *Somerset Maugham* (1949). Incorporating a slight caricature into his work, his *Winston Churchill* (1954) was not liked by Lady Churchill, who destroyed it. His most popular work was the 1962 *Christ in Glory* tapestry hanging in Coventry Cathedral. In the 1950s, Sutherland created designs for textiles for Cresta Silks and wallpaper for Cole. He designed crystal for Steuben, glassware for Stuart, stage costumes, and interiors.
▶ 1923–29, he showed his etchings at the Royal Academy in London. His china and glassware were included in the 1934 'Modern Art for the Table' at Harrods department store in London. His work was included in the 1936 London 'International Surrealist Exhibition.' His 1938 first one-person exhibition was mounted at the Rosenberg and Helft gallery, followed by the 1940 exhibition at the Leicester Galleries, both in London. His glassware for Stuart was shown at the 1935 London 'British Art in Industry' exhibition of the Royal Society of Arts. His fabric patterns for Helios were shown at the 1946 'Britain Can Make It' exhibition at the Victoria and Albert Museum in London. He won the São Paulo prize at the 1952 Biennale di Venezia. In 1960, he received the Order of Merit. Examples of his glassware, china, graphic design, and artwork were included in the 1979 'Thirties' exhibition at the Hayward Gallery in London. His work was the subject of the 1992 'Graham Sutherland: Portraits' exhibition at the Villa Mirabello, Varese (Italy).
▶ Michael Farr, *Design in British Industry: A Mid-Century Survey*, London: Cambridge, 1955. Cat., *Thirties: British art and design before the war*, London: Arts Council of Great Britain, Hayward Gallery, 1979:80, 95, 133, 155, 172, 203, 211, 212, 220, 280, 301. Frederick Cooke, *Glass: Twentieth-Century Design*, New York: Dutton: 1986:70,78,103. Chivers et al., *The Oxford Dictionary of Art*, Oxford: Oxford University Press, 1988:483.

Sutnar, Ladislav   (1897–1969)
▶ Bohemian painter and advertising, display, and industrial designer; born Pilsen (now Plzeň, Czech Republic).
▶ 1915–23, studied School of Applied Arts and Charles University, and Technical University, all Prague.
▶ 1923–36, he was professor of design at the State School of Graphic Arts in Prague; from 1926, was the designer of exhibitions of SČSD (Czechoslovak Werkbund) in Czechoslavakia and abroad; from 1929, was artistic director of Krásná jizba (The Beautiful Room); was a board member of the magazine *Panorama*, promoting good design and the Modern aesthetic. His most important designs included 1930–32 glass drinking set, 1928–32 china table set, and cutlery. In 1930, Sutnar produced designs for porcelain dinnerware and, in 1931, heat-resistant cups, tea sets, and containers for Schöne Stube in Prague. As the exhibition architect of the Czechoslovak government, he was chief designer of the Czechoslovak Hall at the International Book Design Exhibition in Leipzig, and the Czech pavilion at the 1939–40 'New York World's Fair.' A pioneering designer, he worked as a painter and stage designer, becoming one of the most notable exhibition designers of the 1930s. In 1939, he settled in the USA; from 1942, was designer and consulting art director to several firms; 1941–60, was director, Sweet's Catalogue Service. In 1951, he established his own design firm and was a fellow of the Institut International des Arts et Lettres. He wrote numerous articles and books including *Design for Point of Sale* (1952), *Package Design: The Force of Visual Selling* (1953), and *Visual Design in Action: Principles, Purposes* (1961).

▶ He won a gold medal at the 1929–30 Exposición Internacional de Barcelona, grand prize at the 1936 (VI) Triennale di Milano, and 14 grand prizes and gold medals at the 1937 'Exposition Internationale des Arts et Techniques dans la Vie Moderne.'
▶ R. Roger Remington in *Contemporary Designers*, London: Macmillan, 1981:572. A. Adlerová, *České užité umění 1918–1938*, Prague, 1983. Vladimír Šlapeta (essay), *Czech Functionalism*, London: Architectural Association, 1987:80,96. Sylva Petrová and Jean-Luc Olivié, *Verre de Bohême 1400–1989*, Paris: Flammarion, 1989.

Svarth, Dan (1942–)
▶ Danish designer.
▶ Studied Kunsthåndværkerskolen, Copenhagen, to 1967, furniture design, Det Kongelige Danske Kunstakademi, to 1969.
▶ In 1962, he was a cabinetmaker's apprentice; in 1969, worked with Herman Olsen; and, in 1971, set up his own design studio. From 1973, he taught furniture design at the Skolen for Brugskunst (formerly Det Tekniske Selskabs Skoler) and, from 1974, in the furniture school of Det Kongelige Danske Kunstakademi. His furniture designs were produced by Jørgen V. Hansen.
▶ He received the 1966 Johannes Krøiers award, 1966 L.F. Foghts award (of the Kunsthåndværkerskolen), and 1970 and 1973 Danish State art award.
▶ Frederik Sieck, *Nutidig Dansk Møbeldesign:-en kortfattet illustreret beskrivelse*, Copenhagen: Bondo Gravesen; 1990 Busck edition in English.

Svaz Československého Díla (SČSD) (Czechoslovak Werkbund)
▶ Czechoslovak artistic-industrial association; located Prague.
▶ Jan Kotěra founded the Czech Werkbund in 1914, revived in 1920 as the SČSD (Czechoslovak Werkbund); it issued a program for the support of art and folk art that set out to enrich industrial production, improve arts and crafts education, and organize exhibitions, lectures, and consultation. It turned to Modernism in 1931, and became more concerned with introducing good design into industrial production and 'collaboration between engineers and artists'; its chairpeople were Josef Gočár, followed by Pavel Janák, and Otakar Starý. It had about 500 members in 1930; 1921–23 in Prague, it mounted two exhibitions that focused debate on the choice between Arts and Crafts production and Modernism. It broke away from national decorativism in favor of Modernism with its participation in the 1925 Paris 'Exposition Internationale des Arts Décoratifs et Industriels Modernes' and 1928 'Contemporary Culture' exhibition in Brno; organized the 1930–31 exhibition of Czech architecture and art traveling to Geneva, Budapest, Strasbourg, and Stockholm; organized the 1928–32 Dejvice housing project in Prague with 33 family houses as examples of Modern housing. It provided grants to artists to work in factories and workshops, and organized design competitions; published catalogs, books, and periodicals, including the magazines *Výtvarná práce* (*Creative Work*) in 1921–22 and *Žijeme* (*We Live*) 1931–33; in 1936, completed the construction of its own administrative and exhibition center, the House of Art Industry, 36 Národí St. Prague, designed by Oldřich Starý in a purely Modern style. In 1948, SČSD was incorporated into the Center of Folk Art Production and discontinued its separate activities.

Sveinsdottir, Juliana (1889–1966)
▶ Icelandic textile designer.
▶ 1912–17, studied Det Kongelige Danske Kunstakademi, Copenhagen.
▶ With her interior fabrics first appearing in 1921, she was an accomplished designer of non-figurative textiles. Her textiles were used in the chambers of the Supreme Court of Denmark.
▶ She received the 1947 Eckersberg Medal and gold medal at the 1951 (IX) Triennale di Milano. Her work was shown at the Triennali di Milano, 1954–57 USA 'Design in Scandinavia' traveling exhibition, and 1958 'Formes Scandinaves' at the Paris Musée des Arts Décoratifs.
▶ Cat., David Revere McFadden (ed.), *Scandinavian Modern Design 1880–1980*, New York: Abrams, 1982:271, No. 200.

Svensson, Inez (1923–)
▶ Swedish textile designer.
▶ From 1957, Svensson was artistic director of Borås Wäfveri. She was a member of 10-Gruppen in Stockholm in the early 1970s and worked on design projects for UNESCO, including in Afghanistan.
▶ Cat., David Revere McFadden (ed.), *Scandinavian Modern Design 1880–1980*, New York: Abrams, 1982:271, No. 295.

SVOMAS
See **Vhutemas**

Swarovski
▶ Austrian producers of cut crystal stones.
▶ In 1895, Daniel Swarovski I, son of a skilled stone craftsperson, founded Swarovski in Bohemia to protect an invention. He had developed a machine for cutting crystal to be used as stones in jewelry and thereby revolutionized the fashion industry. He settled at Wattens where he was able to use hydraulic power and soon became a major supplier to costume jewelers in Europe and the USA. Becoming the leading source and creator of cut crystal today, the Swarovski firm is one of Austria's largest privately owned companies, managed by descendants of the founder. It became a major supplier of iron-on rhinestones and patented the brand name Swarogem for green-agate and marcasite natural stones. In 1976, the Swarovski Silver Crystal line of giftware and collectibles was launched. In the early 1990s, the design of an expensive group of crystal objects and vessels was commissioned from Ettore Sottsass, Alessandro Mendini, Matteo Thun, and others.

Swiczinsky, Helmut (1945–)
▶ Austrian architect and designer; active Vienna.
▶ Swinczinsky and Wolf D. Prix founded the architecture firm Coop Himmelblau in Vienna in 1968. They designed the 1974 mobile kitchen produced by Ewe-Küchen. Their Deconstructivist 1989 *Vodöl* armchair produced by Vitra was a version of Le Corbusier's 1928 *Grand Confort* armchair that they dissected; *Vodöl* was based on the Austrian mispronunciation of the French word *fauteuil*.
▶ Their work was included in the 1988 'Decontructivist Architecture' exhibition organized by Philip Johnson at the New York Museum of Modern Art.
▶ Günther Feuerstein, *Vienna—Present and Past: Arts and Crafts—Applied Art—Design,* Vienna: Jugend und Volk, 1976: 62,64,80. Albrecht Bangert and Karl Michael Armer, *80s Style: Designs of the Decade*, New York: Abbeville, 1990:88–89,236. Cat., *Coop Himmelblau, Construire le ciel*, Paris: Centre Georges Pompidou, 1992.

Swid Powell
▶ American metalware and ceramics manufacturer.
▶ Swid Powell was originally set up as a branch of Knoll International by Addie Powell and Nan Swid; the two principals were wives of Knoll International executives. It presented its first tableware collection in 1984. The marketing strategy was to appeal to many of the best known names in architecture worldwide to render domestic designs, particularly for accessories and tableware. In the beginning it commissioned Richard Meier, Robert Stern, Charles Gwathmey, Arata Isozaki, Laurinda Spear, and Stanley Tigerman with Margaret McCurry. Later the works of Hans Hollein, Javier Bellosito, Trix and Robert Haussmann, Paolo Portoghesi, and Steven Holl were added to the line. The firm produced porcelain dinner services, crystal, linens, and some silver pieces, including Robert Mapplethorpe's photographic images of flowers on porcelain plates. Swid Powell's wares came to be known irreverently as the 'architects' plates.'

▶ *Les Carnets du Design*, Paris: Mad-Cap Productions et APCI, 1986:13. Arlene Hirst, *Metropolitan Home*, April 1990:115.

Swiss National Exhibition
See Schweizerische Landesausstellung

Sylve, Le
▶ French design and decoration department; located Paris.
▶ Le Sylve was established by the Le Bûcheron store shortly before the 1925 Paris 'Exposition Internationale des Arts Décoratifs et Industriels Modernes,' though the shop had commissioned some Art Nouveau furniture at the turn of the century. Its director M. Boutillier ordered a Modern interior to be designed for its stand at the exhibition. When the staff of the atelier designed the second-class dining room of 1926 oceanliner *Île-de-France*, Boutillier was encouraged to set up the studio under the direction of Michel Dufet and art critic Léandre Vaillat. The furniture was designed by Guérin, Sénéchal, and Michel Dufet, with sculpture by Antoine Bourdelle, Chana Orloff, Pierre Traverse, Drivier, Guénot, Yvonne Serruys, and Albert Marque, glass by Jean Sala and Chappellin, ceramics by Georges Serré and Marcel Goupy, silver by Georg Jensen, metalwork by Jean Dunand, and paintings by Maurice Utrillo, Maurice de Vlaminck, Van Dongen, Albert Marquet, Edouard Goerg, and others. The studio had its own doorway on rue de Rivoli, Paris, made by Binquet using the motif by Cassandre in his first poster. Dufet was director until 1939.
▶ Victor Arwas, *Art Déco*, New York: Abrams, 1980. Pierre Kjellberg, *Art Déco: les maîtres du Mobilier, le décor des Paquebots*, Paris: Amateur, 1986:181.

Symonds, David   (1952–)
▶ British designer; born London.
▶ Symonds designed tableware with Hilary Watter. Their 1983 teapot design was produced by Axis.
▶ *Les Carnets du Design*, Paris: Mad-Cap Productions et APCI, 1986:30.

Synthèse
▶ French decorating firm; located Paris.
▶ From the 1930s (possibly before), Robert Le Manach was a decorator in the decorating firm Synthèse, which produced his furniture.
▶ *Ensembles Mobiliers*, Paris: Charles Moreau, Vol. 5, Nos. 1–4, 1945.

Synthez
▶ French design studio; located Paris.
▶ Synthez was headed by Jacques Macaire and Hervé Dumoitier. The group designed a widely published picnic tableware set.
▶ The picnic tableware set won recognition in the 1986 competition of APCI (Agence pour la Promotion de la Création Industrielle) and UGAP (Union des Groupements d'Achats Publics).
▶ *Les Carnets du Design*, Paris: Mad-Cap Productions et Agence pour la Promotion de la Création Industrielle (APCI), 1986:87.

Szabó, Adalbert-Georges
▶ Hungarian metalsmith; active Paris.
▶ In 1907, he became a member of the Société des Artistes Décorateurs. His work before World War I was historicist; from 1918, closer to Art Déco. His models included table lamps, sconces, chandeliers, balustrades, doors, and firescreens. He produced the chased and gilded bronze door of the dining room on the 1935 oceanliner *Normandie*. Opposed to industrial techniques, particularly arc welding, he pursued traditional blacksmithing.
▶ As early as 1906 and as late as 1938, he showed his metalwork at the Salons of the Société des Artistes français and at 25 Salons of the Société des Artistes Décorateurs from 1907–40.

▶ G. Janneau, *Le Luminaire et les Moyens d'éclairage Nouveaux*, first series: plates 27, 28, 35; second series: plates 47–48; third series: plate 46. G. Henriot, *Luminaire Moderne*, 1937: plate 14. Alastair Duncan, *Art Nouveau and Art Déco Lighting*, New York: Simon and Schuster, 1978:187–88. Pierre Kjellberg, *Art Déco: les maîtres du Mobilier, le décor des Paquebots*, Paris: Amateur, 1986:181–82.

Szekely, Martin   (1956–)
▶ French furniture designer; born and active Paris.
▶ Studied École Estienne and École Boulle, both Paris, and metalworking under a Chinese artisan.
▶ He began as a copper-plate engraver. 1977–78, he designed furniture, including the *Ar* stool; some of his early projects were sponsored by VIA. His first success was the 25-piece collection of furniture for the Sauvagnat company, shown at the 1979 Salon du Meuble in Paris. His 1980 *Coin* furniture collection in wood and aluminum for Skina was shown at the 1981 Salon du Meuble in Paris and Salon del Mobile in Milan. Widely published, some of his stark and unadorned furniture models were produced in black carbon-steel by Galerie Néotù, Paris, including his 1980 *Cornette* chair and 1983 *Pi* range. He studied in Italy in 1984 and met Ettore Sottsass, Paolo Deganello, and Michele De Lucchi. He designed the 1986 *Carbone* chair produced by Tribu. He produced case goods in MDF and upholstered seating, including the 1987 *Haut Ouvert*, 1987 *Presse Papiers*, and 1987 *Stoleru* armchair and sofa. Néotù produced his 1987 *Chaise Toro* (later mass produced), 1989 *Table Liberata*, 1989 *Armoire Leone*, 1989 *Chaise Longue Lysistrata*, and 1989 *Chauffeuse Marie France*. In 1987, he restored the Musée de Picardie in Amiens and designed the entrance hall of the house of George Sand in Nohant, the 1988 office of the president of the General Council of Belfort, and the 1988–89 shop and 1990 park of the Musée de Villeneuve d'Asq. His *Pi* bookshelves were produced by Mega Éditions of France. In 1989, he began to move away from the black metal forms for which he had earlier gained recognition. His small editions represented a successful collaboration between designer and producer, in this case Pierre Staudemeyer of Galerie Néotù in Paris.
▶ He received the 1982 VIA 'Carte Blanche' award from VIA. In 1982, his work was first shown at the VIA gallery in Paris. His work was included the the 1982 Salon du Meuble in Paris and 1984 Biennale des Métiers d'Art in Villeneuve-les-Avignon. In 1985, his work was the subject of one-person exhibitions at Galerie Néotù in Paris and the Galerie Théorème in Brussels. He won the 1984 Agora award. In 1987, his *Containers* collection in MDF was shown and, in 1989, the *Pour fair salon* collection in lacquer, bronze and exotic wood, velour, and crystal, both at Galerie Néotù. He was selected as designer of the year at the 1987 Paris Salon du Meuble and, in 1988, received first prize from the French art critics and VIA. His work was shown at the 1988 'Avant Premiere: Contemporary French Furniture,' at the Victoria and Albert Museum, 1989 Paris Salon du Meuble, 1989 'L'Art de Vivre' at the Cooper-Hewitt Museum in New York, and 1990 'Les années VIA' exhibition at the Paris Musée des Arts Décoratifs.
▶ Sophie Anargyros, *Le Mobilier français*, Paris: Regard/VIA, 1980:52–54. Cat., Garth Hall and Margo Rouard Snowman, *Avant Premiere: Contemporary French Furniture*, London: Eprouvé, 1988. Suzanne Tise, 'Innovators at the Museum,' *Vogue Décoration*, No. 26, June/July 1990:46. Cat., *Les années VIA, 1980–1990*, Paris: Musée des Arts Décoratifs, 1990. François Mathey, *Au bonheur des formes, design français 1845–1992*, Paris: Regard, 1992:156,230.

Szekely, Pierre   (1923–)
▶ Interior and furniture designer; active Paris.
▶ He collaborated in the 1950s with Jean Royère on the decoration of the home of singer Henri Salvador in Paris.
▶ Furniture from the Salvador home was shown at Galerie 1950 in Paris in a setting designed for the exhibition by Matia Bonetti and Elizabeth Garouste.
▶ *Blueprint*, June 1989:68.

T

Tackett, La Gardo (1911–)
▶ American ceramicist; active Los Angeles.
▶ Studied sculpture and art history, Claremont College, California.
▶ He maintained a pottery studio *c*1946–54. He was a teacher at the California School of Design in Los Angeles, where he and his students developed outdoor pottery planters, leading to the establishment of the Architectural Pottery in 1950. He subsequently executed glazed and unglazed hemispherical, cylindrical, and hourglass-shaped planters for indoor and outdoor use. He designed the 1957 range of ceramic dinnerware for Schmid International, produced in Japan. From 1963, he was manager of the object division of Herman Miller.
▶ La Gardo Tackett, 'A New Casual Structure for Ceramic Design,' *Art and Architecture*, Vol. 72, April 1955:14–15,30 'New Solutions to Planting Problems,' *Interiors*, Vol. 115, Feb. 1956:114–15. Norbert Nelson, 'The Marketplace,' *Industrial Design*, Vol. 10, March 1963:74–76. Cat., Kathryn B. Hiesinger and George H. Marcus III (eds.), *Design Since 1945*, Philadelphia: Philadelphia Museum of Art, 1983:232, II–65.

Taeuber-Arp, Sophie (b. Sophie Taeuber 1889–1943)
▶ Swiss artist and designer; wife of Jean Arp.
▶ She executed collages, embroideries, sculpture, paintings, stage designs, and puppets. Her work was mostly abstract. From 1916, she and Jean Arp collaborated with the Zürich Dada group and on joint paintings and compositions in a kind of Constructivist style. 1927–40, they lived in Meudon, near Paris, joining the Cercle et Carré in 1939 and Abstract-Création in 1931 or 1932. While in Meudon, she established and edited the trilingual (French, German, and English) abstract art periodical *Plastique*, published in five issues 1937–39. 1941–43, she and Arp lived at Grasse in a community of artists including Sonia Delaunay and Alberto Magnelli.
▶ Ian Chilvers et al., *The Oxford Dictionary of Art*, Oxford and New York: Oxford, 1988:486–87.

Tagini, Giorgi (1940–)
▶ Italian industrial designer; born Asti; active Milan.
▶ Tagini began his professional career in 1966, becoming a member of ADI (Associazione per il Disegno Industriale).
▶ *ADI Annual 1976*, Milan: Associazione per il Disegno Industriale, 1976.

Tagliapietra, Lino (1934–)
▶ Italian glassworker and teacher; born Murano.
▶ From 1956, Tagliapietra taught glassmaking with Archimede Seguso and Nane Ferro; 1966–68, designed glass for Venini, Murano; until 1968, for Murrina; from 1968, taught glassmaking at Haystack School and Pilchuck School, Stanwood, Washington.
▶ Participated in exhibitions in Venice, Hamburg, San Francisco, and New York.
▶ Hans Wichmann, *Italien Design 1945 bis heute*, Munich: Die Neue Sammlung, 1988.

Takahashi, Yukio (1930–)
▶ Japanese glass designer.
▶ Studied painting, Tokyo University of Arts, to 1955.
▶ In 1961, Takahashi began working for Joetsu Crystal, Gumma, becoming section chief of design.
▶ Work shown at 1978, 1981, 1984, 1987, and 1990 'Glass in Japan,' Tokyo, and 1991 (V) Triennale of the Japan Glass Art Crafts Association, Heller Gallery, New York.
▶ Cat., *Glass Japan*, New York: Heller Gallery and Japan Glass Art Crafts Association, 1991: No. 36.

Talbert, Bruce J. (1838–81)
▶ British architect and designer; born Dundee.
▶ He was apprenticed to cabinet-carver Millar and subsequently to Charles Edwards, an architect in Dundee, who worked on the Corn Exchange Hall. In 1856, he settled in Glasgow, working in the architecture office of W.H. Tait and Cambell Douglas. In the early 1860s, he began to design furniture and execute some decorative work in a simple Gothic style. In *c*1862, he began working for Doveston, Bird and Hull in Manchester, and shortly after began designing silver and wrought-iron work for Francis Skidmore's firm Art Manufacturers in Coventry. Settling in London in 1865 or 1866, he began designing furniture for Holland and Sons. He published *Gothic Forms Applied to Furniture, Metal Work, and Decoration for Domestic Purposes* (1867), which influenced cabinetmaking in England and the USA. Preferring 12th- and 13th-century Gothic styles, he designed furniture based on framed construction with low relief work, inlay and piercing, attempting to integrate it with its architectural environment. His ecclesiastical metalwork was produced by Cox, wallpaper by Jeffrey, carpets by Brinton, ironwork by Coalbrookdale, and textiles by Cowlishaw and Nicol, Barbone and Miller, and Warner. His work by 1876 had become more Jacobean in style. He published *Examples of Ancient and Modern Furniture, Metal Work, Tapestries, Decorations, Etc.* (1876). By the 1860s, he had become one of the most influential industrial designers of the Aesthetic movement in Britain.
▶ He received gold medal for architectural design, 1860; gold medal for drawing 1862, Edinburgh Architectural Association. 1870–76, he showed architectural drawings regularly at the Royal Academy of Arts, London. Talbert's furniture for Holland and Sons was shown at the 1867 Paris 'Exposition Universelle.' His *Pet Sideboard* for Gillow was shown at the 1873 'Weltausstellung Wien.' His *Juno* cabinet for Jackson and Graham was shown at the 1878 Paris 'Exposition Universelle'.
▶ Elizabeth Aslin, *The Aesthetic Movement: Prelude to Art Nouveau*, New York and Washington, 1969:63,66–67, plates 7–9,12–13,70–71. Doreen Bolger Burke *et al.*, *In Pursuit of Beauty: Americans and the Aesthetic Movement*, New York: Metropolitan Museum of Art and Rizzoli, 1986:470–71.

Tallon, Roger (1929–)
▶ French industrial designer.
▶ Trained in Paris.
▶ In 1953, he joined Technès in Paris, becoming director of research in 1960. His range of objects included furniture, indus-

trial machinery, and lighting. He designed 1957 and 1961 cameras produced by SEM, a 1957–58 coffee grinder by Peugeot, 1960 typewriter by Japy, 1964 television set for Thomson Téléavia, and 1970 drinking glasses for Daum. French industry was slow to use the services of professional designers, and most of his commissions were foreign; 1957–64, he was a consultant designer to General Motors' Frigidaire refrigerators. His experimentation with new techniques and materials resulted in one of his best known pieces, the 1965 *High-Back* chair in aluminum with its textured, spiky polyether-foam upholstery produced by Galerie Jacques Lacloche of Paris. His 1965 *TS Chair* was produced by Archigram in a folding-wood configuration. His 1973 watches for Lip were widely published. His 1977 lighting was produced by Erco. From 1970, he was a consultant designer to SNCF, designing the carriage for the 1988 high-speed TGV train produced by Alsthom Atlantique, and Corail locomotives. He taught at École Nationale Supérieure des Arts Décoratifs, Paris; and was a founding member of the design consultancy ADSA.

► Received silver medal (typewriter for Japy), 1960 (XII) Triennale di Milano, and 1985 French national grand prize for industrial design. In 1973, elected Honorary Royal Designer for Industry, London. Work shown at the 1966 'L'Objet' and 1968 'Les Assises du siège contemporain' exhibitions, Paris Musée des Arts Décoratifs; 1981 'Paris 1937–57,' 1988 'Les années 50,' Centre Georges Pompidou, Paris; 1989 'L'Art de Vivre,' Cooper-Hewitt Museum, New York.

► 'Da Parigi: Design e idee di Roger Tallon,' *Domus*, No. 452, July 1967:40–45. Cat., *Qu'est-ce que ce le design?*, Paris: Centre de Création Industrielle, 1969. Cat., *Modern Chairs 1918–1970*, London: Lund Humphries, 1971. Xavier Gilles, 'Le Design selon Tallon,' *L'Oeil*, No. 244, Nov. 1975:57–59. Catherine Millet, 'Un Designer à Paris,' in *Paris 1937–1957*, Paris: Centre Georges Pompidou, 1981:445–52. Cat., Kathryn B. Hiesinger and George H. Mercus III (eds.) *Design Since 1945*, Philadelphia: Philadelphia Museum of Art, 1983:III–85. François Mathey, *Au bonheur des formes, design français 1945–1992*, Paris: Regard, 1992:86,90, 117, 121,133,241,268,322,333.

Tanaka, Kimiko (1945–)

► Japanese glass designer.
► Studied fine arts, Osaka University of Education, to 1967.
► Tanaka was a lecturer at Osaka Prefectural Takatsu High School.
► Solo exhibitions 1980–85 at Shinanobashi Gallery, Osaka. Work included in 1986 'Crafts Salon Exhibition,' Seibu department store, Tokyo; 1990 'Glass '90 in Japan,' Tokyo; and 1991 (V) Triennale of the Japan Glass Art Crafts Association, Heller Gallery, New York.
► Cat., *Glass Japan*, New York: Heller Gallery and Japan Glass Art Crafts Association, 1991: No. 37.

Tani, Shoichi (1949–)

► Japanese glass designer.
► In 1970, Tani became a designer for Glass Maker Studio. In 1980, he set up his own glass studio.
► Work included in 1990 'Glass '90 in Japan,' Tokyo; 1991 (V) Triennale of the Japan Glass Art Crafts Association, Heller Gallery, New York.
► Cat., *Glass Japan*, New York: Heller Gallery and Japan Glass Art Crafts Association, 1991: No. 38.

Tapiovaara, Ilmari (1914–)

► Finnish interior and furniture designer.
► 1937, studied industrial and interior design, Taideteollisuuskeskuskoulu, Helsinki.
► 1935–36, he worked for Alvar Aalto in the London office of Artek; in 1937, for Le Corbusier in Paris; and 1952–53, for Mies van der Rohe in Chicago. In the 1940s and 1950s, he was one of the pioneers of knock-down furniture design. He was a Functionalist who approached construction so that it should be readily seen. He set up his own design office in 1950 with Annikki Tapiovaara.

1937–40, he was artistic director at Askon Tehtaat and was founder and artistic and managing director of Keravan Puuteollisuus in Kervo 1941–50. 1950–52, he was department head at the Institute of Design in Helsinki and, 1952–53, visiting instructor at the Illinois Institute of Design in Chicago. He designed for Merva, Knoll, Thonet, Schauman, and Hackman. His work included furniture, carpets, lighting, glassware, stainless-steel flatware, toys, and interiors. For the 1952 Olivetti showroom in Helsinki, Tapiovaara's stacking *Lukki I* chair, produced by Lukkiseppo in Rekola, was designated the 'universal chair.' He also designed a stacking chair for Knoll in wood, cloth, tape, and upholstery. He designed the *Polar* cutlery produced by Hackman, 1972–74 radio and stereo equipment produced by Centrum, 1972–74 color-planning program for paint manufacturer Winter, wall paintings, and tapestries. His 'stabile' constructions of the 1970s were installed in Udine (Italy); Quatre Bornes (Mauritius); and Rauma-Repola (Finland). Interior design work included the 1947 and 1949 student hostels, Helsinki; 1955–73 offices, cinemas, and theaters, including a concert hall, Leningrad (now St. Petersburg); 1960s aircraft interiors for Finnair; and 1973 Intercontinental Hotel, Helsinki.

► His knock-down fabric or leather chair was shown at the exhibition of the 1948 'International Competition for Low Cost Furniture Design,' New York Museum of Modern Art. His work shown at 1953–57 Cantù 'International Furniture Competition' (receiving three first prizes); 1951 (IX), 1954 (X), 1957 (XI), and 1960 (XII) Triennali di Milano (receiving six gold medals); 1963 'International Furniture Competition' (received first prize), Mariano Comense; 1968 'Les Assises du siège contemporain' exhibition, Paris Musée des Arts Décoratifs; 1970 'Modern Chairs 1918–1970' exhibition, Whitechapel Gallery, London; and one-person exhibitions, Helsinki (1949), Chicago (1952), Stockholm (1961), and Buenos Aires (1964). In 1969, elected Honorary Royal Designer for Industry, London.

► Benedict Zilliacus, *Finnish Designer*, Helsinki, 1954. Erik Zahle (ed.), *A Treasury of Scandinavian Design*, New York, 1961:293, nos. 21–24. Cat., *Les Assises du siège contemporain*, Paris: Musée des Arts Décoratifs, 1968. Cat., *Modern Chairs 1918–1970*, London: Lund Humphries, 1971. Ilmari Tapiovaara, 'The Idea was more Important than the Product,' *Form Function Finland*, 1983:17–19. Cat., Kathryn B. Hiesinger and George H. Marcus III (eds.) *Design Since 1945*, Philadelphia: Philadelphia Museum of Art, 1983:232,V–45.

Tatlin, Vladimir Evgrafovich (1885–1953)

► Russian artist; born Moscow.
► 1902–04, studied Moscow Institute for Painting, Sculpture and Architecture; 1904–09, Penza Art School; 1909–10, Moscow Institute, under Konstantin Korovin, Valentin Serov, and others.
► From 1908, he was associated with painters Mikhail Larionov and Nataliya Goncharova, and, from 1911, with Kazimir Malevich. In 1911, he designed costumes for the folk drama *The Emperor Maximilian and His Son Adolph* produced in Moscow. Around 1912, his work showed a preoccupation with compositional structure and revealed his interest in the the Russian icon and Russian folk art. When the 1913 'Jack of Diamonds' exhibition traveled to Paris, Tatlin met Pablo Picasso, who inspired him to begin his Painterly Reliefs. From 1914, he pursued work on his Painterly and Counter Reliefs and became close to Aleksei Grishchenko, Aleksei Morgunov, Liubov' Popova, Nadezhda Udal'tsova, and Aleksandr Vesnin. He collaborated to a minor degree with Aleksandr Rodchenko and Georgii Yakulov on the Dada-Constructivist furnishings for the 1917 Café Pittoresque, Moscow, under Yakulov's guidance. From 1918, he was head of the Moscow Izo NKP (Department of Fine Arts of Narkompros). 1918–20, he was professor at the Freie Werkstätten. 1919–20, he was director of the painting department of the Svomas/Vkhutemas, Moscow; worked in Petrograd on his famous 1918 model for the *Monument to the Third International*, shown in Moscow and Petrograd. Moving to Petrograd in 1919 or 1921, he set up a studio to pursue work

focusing on 'volume, material and construction' and, in 1921, became head of the department of sculpture at the reorganized Academy of Arts there. In 1923, he organized the stage production of Khlebnikov's poem *Zangezi* at the Petrograd Inkhuk. 1923–24, he attempted to reform design especially for clothing and for ovens and from this time was interested in practical design. 1925–27, he taught courses in the 'culture of materials' at the theater and cinema section of NKP, Kiev. In 1927, he began teaching woodwork, metalwork, and ceramics at the Moscow Vkhutein. With N.N. Rogzhin in 1927, he designed a cantilever bentwood chair with a molded seat and supporting legs at the back and also produced designs for milk-jug containers in a hand-sculptured form. Both appear to have been influenced by a similar Bauhaus language. After working on the human-powered glider *Letatlin* 1929–32, he returned to painting, adopting a figurative style. During the 1930s and 1940s, he executed several theatrical designs.
▶ Work included in Izdebskii's 1911 (II) Salon in Odessa, 1911 Union of Youth exhibition, 1911 Moscow 'Contemporary Painting,' Larionov's 'Donkey's Tail' exhibition, 1912 Union of Youth exhibition, 1912 Moscow 'Contemporary Painting,' 1913 Moscow and St. Petersburg 'Jack of Diamonds' exhibition traveling to Berlin and Paris, one-person 1914 Moscow exhibition, 1915 'Tramway V' exhibition (seven Painterly Reliefs), 1915 'Exhibition of Painting,' 1915–16 '0–10' exhibition, 1922 Berlin 'Erste Russische Kunstausstellung.' He organized his own 1916 'The Store' exhibition, which included the three-dimensional works of Lev Bruni and Sofia Dymshits-Tol'staia. Tatlin's canvases entirely in pink were included in 1922 'Union of New Trends in Art' exhibition, Museum of Artistic Culture, Petrograd.
▶ Stephanie Barron and Maurice Tuchman, *The Avant-Garde in Russia, 1910–1930*, Cambridge: MIT, 1980:244. Cat., *Der Kragstuhl*, Stuhlmuseum Burg Beverungen, Berlin: Alexander, 1986: 139. Selim O. Khan-Megomedov, *Les Vhutemas*, Paris: Regard, 1990:638–42. Cat., *The Great Utopia: The Russian and Soviet Avant-Garde, 1915–1932*, New York: Guggenheim Museum, 1992.

Tattersfield, Brian (1936–)
▶ British designer; born Heckmondwike, Yorkshire.
▶ 1953–57, studied Batley School of Art, Yorkshire; 1959–61, Royal College of Art, London.
▶ See Minale, Marcello

Taylor, Gerard
▶ British designer; active London.
▶ Studied industrial design, Royal College of Art, London; to 1981.
▶ For the Memphis group's second collection, Taylor designed the 1982 *Piccadilly* lamp and, in 1985, became associated with Daniel Weil. Clients included Driade, Yamagiwa, Knoll, and Alessi.
▶ *Acquisitions 1982–1990 arts décoratifs*, Paris: Fond National d'Art Contemporain, 1991. Cat., *Londres, images et objets du nouveau design*, Paris: CCI/Centre Georges Pompidou, 1990.

Taylor, Michael (1927–86)
▶ American interior and furniture designer; born Santa Rosa, California; active San Francisco.
▶ Studied Rudolf Schaeffer School of Interior Design, San Francisco.
▶ Taylor frequently used logs and wicker in his furniture designs for his beige-on-beige interiors, often incorporating natural stone. After a partnership with Frances Milhailoff in San Francisco beginning in 1951, he set up his own practice in 1956 with initial clients including Maryon Lewis and her father Ralph Davies. His early interiors were influenced by Syrie Maugham and Frances Elkins. Some of his clients were people in showbusiness, including Maryon Lewis, Gorham and Diana Knowles, Nan Kempner, Douglas S. Cramer, Steve Martin, Donald Bren, Martha Hyer, and Hal Wallis. Projects included Norton Simon's and Jennifer Jones's

Malibu house, the Bernard Maybeck-designed house of John and Frances Bowes, architect John Lautner's Malibu house, and the Arizona villa of Jimmy Wilson. Typical Taylor designs included ball-shaped pillows (derived from ancient China), and he has been credited with rediscovering the lamps and furniture of Diego Giacometti. He was frequently copied. His retail shop was on Sutter Street, San Francisco.
▶ Mary Chesterfield, 'California Classics,' *Elle Decor*, Winter 1990:30,32. Mark Hampton, *The Legendary Decorators of the Twentieth Century*, New York: Doubleday, 1992.

Taylor, William Howson (1876–1935)
▶ British ceramicist.
▶ In 1898, Taylor founded the Ruskin Pottery (named after John Ruskin), Smethwick, with his father Edward Richard Taylor. One of the few British potters to work with high-temperature *flambé* glazes. Taylor developed an impressive range and worked at the pottery until 1935.
▶ Before World War I, the pottery received grand prizes at six major international exhibitions.
▶ *British Arts and Design, 1900–1960*, 1983.
▶ See Ruskin Pottery

Tcherniack, Malvine
▶ French decorator.
▶ Studied painting and sculpture, École des Beaux-Arts, Bordeaux and Paris.
▶ In the 1920s, she designed ceramics, textiles, wallpaper, and domestic items for the Primavera department of the Au Printemps department store, Paris.
▶ Exhibited paintings and sculpture. Designed a country dining room for La Maîtrise pavilion at 1925 Paris 'Exposition Internationale des Arts Décoratifs et Industriels Modernes.'
▶ Maurice Dufrêne, *Ensembles Mobiliers, Exposition Internationale 1925*, Paris: Charles Moreau, 1925; Antique Collectors' Club 1989:136.

Teague Jr., Walter Dorwin (1910–)
▶ American industrial designer; born Garden City, New York; son of Walter Teague.
▶ 1928–31, studied Massachusetts Institute of Technology, Cambridge, Massachusetts.
▶ 1935–42, he was head of product design at his father's design firm in New York. He designed the widely published *c*1939 desk lamp for Polaroid with its overhanging bakelite hood on a spun-aluminum stem, and Marmon 16 and 1932 12 bodies. 1942–52, he was head of the research engineering department of Bendix Aviation, Teterboro, New Jersey. 1952–67, he was a partner at Walter Dorwin Teague Associates and, from 1967, president of Dorwin Teague, Nyack, New York. His clients included Caterpillar Tractor, National Cash Register, Dresser Industries, Ford, A.B. Dick, Montgomery Ward, Sears Roebuck, Ritter Dental, Steinway, Remington Arms, Boeing, Du Pont, Corning Glass, Tappan, Volkswagen of America, Pearson Boat, Bristol Myers, and the US Atomic Energy Commission. More than 90 patents were assigned to him. He wrote many articles and designed several hundred products including sports equipment, chairs, tables, settees, folding beds, boats, ski bindings, vacuum cleaners, bicycles, cash registers, glassware, radios, telephones, cameras, packaging, aircraft accessories, automobiles, buildings in Austria, Yugoslavia, and the USA, and exhibitions in seven countries. In 1952, he became associate fellow, American Institute of Aeronautics and Astronautics.
▶ He received the 1960 (X) Annual Industrial Design Award, 1969 American Iron and Steel Award for best consumer product, 1969 IDSA Design Review Award, 1980 Pioneer Award for Advancement of Space Exploration Through Rocket Pioneering of the American Institute of Aeronautics and Astronautics, and, in 1980, became honorary member, Classic Car Club of America, for design of the Marmon 15 automobile.

► Russell Flinchum, 'Walter Dorwin Teague, Sr. and Jr.,' in Mel Byars and Russell Flinchum (eds.), *50 American Designers*, Washington: Preservation, 1994.

Teague Sr., Walter Dorwin　(1883–1960)
► American industrial designer; born Indiana; father of Walter Teague Jr.
► Studied Art Students' League, New York.
► Moving to New York in 1903, from 1908 he worked in the art department of advertising agency Calkins and Holden. In the 1910s, his affection for Neo-Classical forms was reflected in his study of 19th-century French culture. In 1911, he opened his own studio, specializing in book design and advertisements, including illustrations for Community Plate and Phoenix Hosiery campaigns. In the mid-1920s, Teague expanded his range, designing piano cases for Steinway and packaging for consumer goods. His first major client was Eastman Kodak. He became one of the small coterie of highly paid industrial designers of the mid-1930s. His studio's design work included a 1930 Marmon car, 1936 *Baby Brownie* camera, 1952 *Scripto* pen, New Haven Railroad Pullman coaches, 1937 Ford showroom in New York, Texaco service stations, and 1932 crystal for Steuben (with bowl incorporating an adaptation of the *cyma recta* molding found in classical architecture). In 1932, Corning Glassworks president Amory Houghton hired Teague to help improve the firm's Depression-hit sales. On large kitchen appliances, he eliminated the clumsy apron at the foot and dropped the machinery into the legs. He designed the 1932 'Design for the Machine' exhibition at the Philadelphia Museum of Art. He was head of the 1939 World's Fair design committee and designed many exhibitions. Teague wrote *Design This Day: The Technique of Order in the Machine Age* (1940). Profoundly influenced by Le Corbusier, Teague argued that geometry rules all design and analyzed the Parthenon as a paradigm of good design. With Frank del Giudice, his successor in 1946, he designed the Boeing 707 and 727 airliner interiors. Like Raymond Loewy, Teague was not personally involved with every project undertaken by his office. His firm in name only, Walter Dorwin Teague Associates is still in operation with David Provan as president, having merged in 1989 with Gad Shanaan of Montreal.
► Exhibition work included 1934 San Diego 'Pacific International Exposition' and Ford, Dupont (with Robert J. Harper and A.M. Erikson) and National Cash Register building at 1939 'New York World's Fair'; atop the NCR building was an enormous replica of a cash register that showed the Fair's attendance figures. In 1951, elected Honorary Royal Designer for Industry, London.
► Karen Davies, *At Home in Manhattan: Modern Decorative Arts, 1925 to the Depression*, New Haven: Yale, 1983:27. Mary Siff, 'A Realist in Industrial Design,' *Arts and Decoration*, Oct. 1934:46–47. Jeffrey L. Meikle, *Twentieth Century Limited: Industrial Design in America, 1925–1939*, Philadelphia: Temple, 1979:43–46. Russell Flinchum, 'Walter Dorwin Teague, Sr. and Jr.,' in Mel Byars and Russell Flinchum (eds.), *50 American Designers*, Washington: Preservation, 1994.

Tébong
See **Domingo, Alain**

Tecno
► Italian furniture manufacturer.
► Designer Osvaldo Borsani established the furniture company Tecno in 1954 with brother Fulgenzio Borsani. The operation had evolved from Atelier Varedo, the workshop of the father in Varedo, and the subsequent small firm Arredamento Borsani. Among other models, it produced Osvaldo Borsani's successful 1953 *P40* chair and 1953 *D70*.
► Cat., *Modern Chairs 1918–1970*, London: Lund Humphries, 1971. Charlotte Fiell and Peter Fiell, *Modern Furniture Classics Since 1945*, London: Thames and Hudson, 1991:54,73,75, Nos. 25,41.
► See **Borsani, Osvaldo**

Teco
See **Gates Potteries, The**

Tedioli, Giorgio　(1947–)
► Italian industrial designer; born Casalbuttano; active Anzano del Parco.
► Studied Liceo Artistico di Brera, Milan.
► He began his professional career in 1968 in the office of domestic appliance manufacturer Candy, for which he (with Joe Columbo) designed an air-conditioner. From 1971, clients included Giogenzana Style, Prima, Fonderie Toni, and Fondomini. He was a member of ADI (Associazione per il Disegno Industriale).
► *ADI Annual 1976*, Milan: Associazione per il Disegno Indsutriale, 1976.

Teige, Karel　(1900–51)
► Czech art critic, painter, typographic artist, and collagist; born Prague.
► Studied art history, Charles University, Prague.
► Teige was a leading figure in Czech art and architecture between the wars. He wrote on art and was editor of several avant-garde magazines, including *Disk, Stavba*, and *ReD*. At the first Devětsil exhibitions, he showed pictures and paintings in a Cubist style; in 1923, fusing art and poetry, he produced the new medium of Pictorial Poems; influenced by Soviet Constructivism, he espoused 'proletarian' art; in 1929, delivered a presentation at the Bauhaus in Dessau on new forms in Czech art and was invited by Hannes Meyer to organize conferences on the theme of 'Sociology and Architecture,' a summary of which appeared in 1929 in the revue *ReD*. Later specializing in typography, photomontage, and stage design, his photomontage book covers, posters and typography were noteworthy. 1935–41, turning to Surrealism, he created complex collages based on the metamorphosis of the female body.
► Photomontage book covers, typography, and posters were shown at a number of avant-garde European exhibitions.
► Lionel Richard, *Encyclopédie du Bauhaus*, Paris: Somogy, 1985: 173. Cat., *Devětsil: Czech Avant-Garde Art, Architecture, and Design of the 1920s and 30s*, Oxford Museum of Modern Art and London Design Museum, 1990.

Teinitzerová, Marie　(1879–1960)
► Czech textile artist and producer; born Čížkov u Pelhřimova.
► Studied painting in Vienna and Brno; 1905–06, School of Applied Arts, Prague; 1906, Weaving School, Berlin.
► She was a co-founder of Artěl; in 1910, set up her own textile studio in Jindřichův Hradec; 1911–60, created a number of monumental tapestries, designed primarily by painters. Her most fruitful collaboration was with František Kysela. She designed and produced handmade textiles for domestic furnishings; collaborated with Czech Cubist architects; and designed upholstery materials. She prepared most of the natural fibers and devised new weaving techniques.
► Received a grand prize (*The Crafts* tapestry) at 1925 Paris 'Exposition Internationale des Arts Décoratifs et Industriels Modernes.' Work (*The Czech Linen* designed by Karl Putz) shown at 1939 'New York World's Fair.'
► A. Adlerová, *České užité umění 1918–1938*, Prague, 1983.

Templier, Raymond　(1891–1968)
► French jewelry designer and metalworker; born Paris.
► 1909–12, studied École des Beaux-Arts, Paris.
► He joined the long-established family firm in 1912. With Georges Fouquet and Gérard Sandoz, he was known for his Art Déco designs produced in gold, lacquer, silver, eggshells, and semi-precious and precious stones, including diamonds, and executed without ornamentation in pure geometric forms reflecting the machine aesthetic. His designs, particularly for cigarette cases and boxes, were inspired by automobiles, airplanes, and sport. He was a friend of poet Blaise Cendrars and poster artist Cassandre, both of whom worked together and illustrated advertising literature for Templier's firm. He was a member of Groupe des Cinq with Pierre

Chareau, Dominique, Pierre Legrain, and Jean Puiforcat. He designed jewelry for the Marcel L'Herbier films *L'Inhumaine* (1923) and *L'Argent* (1928); was a member of the superior council of instruction at the École Nationale Supérieure des Arts Décoratifs, and 1929 founding member of UAM (Union des Artistes Modernes). In 1929, Marcel Percheron joined the firm as a sketch artist, fastidiously executing details of Templier's work for 36 years. Templier's son assumed the directorship in 1935; Percheron followed in 1965.

▶ First showed his work at the 1911 Salon of the Société des Artistes Décorateurs, and subsequently at important exhibitions in France and abroad; 1926 and 1927 exhibitions (with Le Cinq), Galerie Barbazanges, Paris; and at UAM exhibitions from 1930.

▶ Gaston Varenne, 'Raymond Templier et le Bijou Moderne,' *Art et Décoration*, Vol. LIX, 1930. Paul Sentenac, 'L'Esprit Moderne dans les Bijoux de Raymond Templier,' *La Renaissance de l'Art français*, No. 1, Jan. 1932. Sylvie Raulet, *Bijoux des Art Déco*, Paris: Regard, 1984. Pierre Cabanne, *Encyclopédie Art Déco*, Paris: Somogy, 1986:239. Arlette Barré-Despond, *UAM*, Paris: Regard, 1986:510–13. Cat., *Les années UAM 1929–1958*, Paris: Musée des Arts Décoratifs, 1988:250. Annelies Krekel-Aalberse, *Art Nouveau and Art Déco Silver*, New York: Abrams, 1989:71,260.

Terragni, Giuseppe (1904–43)

▶ Italian architect; born Meda.

▶ 1917–21, studied technical school, Como; 1921–26, Politecnico di Milano.

▶ 1927–39, he and brother Attilio worked in their own architecture office. His first notable architecture was a 1927 gasworks, shown at the 1927 (III) Biennale di Monza. He was a co-founder of Gruppo 7. In 1928 with Gio Ponti, he joined the Italian Rationalist movement. As one of the protagonists of Rationalism, his work exemplified Italian design's move into the mainstream of the European Modern movement. Known for his uncompromising consistency, Terragni successfully combined academic Neo-Classicism, orthodox Rationalism, the basics of the Novecento Italiano, and the *Pittura metafisica* of Giorgio de Chirico. His 1927–28 five-storey apartment block 'Novocomum' in Como, with its simplicity and bold volumetric solutions, showed clear influences from Constructivism, and promoted controversy. Como was the center of experimental architecture in Italy in the 1920s and 1930s. Due to postwar reissues, he became known for the 1930 cantilever furniture designs in tubular steel and leather installed in his Fascist headquarters Casa del Popolo (originally Casa del Fascio), Como. His architecture included 1936–37 Casa Bianca, Seveso, influenced by Ludwig Mies van der Rohe, and 1936–37 Novocomum house, Como. From 1936, he designed the Danteum (with Pietro Lingeri) in Rome and worked on the kindergarten of Antonio Sant'Elia in Como. Others of his structures included the 1938–39 Casa del Fascio (with A. Carminati), Lissone, and his last work of consequence, 1939–40 Casa Giuliani Frigerio in Como. He participated in the 1933 CIAM (Congrès Internationaux d'Architecture Moderne) and in discussions leading to the Athens Charter. Posthumously, his work was influential on that of the New York Five, especially Peter Eisenman.

▶ Work included in 1927 Stuttgart 'Werkbundausstellung' (with Gruppo 7) and projects at 1927 (III) 'Esposizione Biennale delle Arti Decorative e Industriali Moderne,' 1933 (V) Triennale di Milano (with others, Artist's House on a Lake).

▶ G. Labò, *Giuseppe Terragni*, Milan: Il Calcone, 1947. P. Koulermos (ed.), 'The Work of Terragni, Lingeri and Italian Rationalism,' *Architectural Design*, Special No., March 1963. 'Omaggio a Terragni,' No. 153, Special Issue, *Arte e architettura*, July 1968. Enrico Mantero (ed.), *Giuseppe Terragni e la città del razionalismo italiano*, Bari: Dedalo, 1969. Sembach, *Style 1930*, Berlin: Wasmuth, 1971. Peter Eisenman, *Giuseppe Terragni*, Cambridge, 1978. B. Levi (ed.), *Giuseppe Terragni*, Bologna: Zanichelli, 1980.

Terry, Emilio (1890–1969)

▶ French furniture designer and architect; active Paris.

▶ In the 1920s and 1930s, he was known for his collaboration with Jean-Michel Frank and others in Frank's stable, including Christian Gérard and Diego and Alberto Giacometti; from the 1920s, wrote and lectured on architecture from an anti-Functional standpoint which fascinated the Surrealists (Salvador Dalí painted his portrait); was invited by Charles de Bestegui and vicomte Charles de Noailles to work on their houses after they became disenchanted with Modern architecture.

▶ Work (drawings and models) shown at 1939 exhibition 'Fantastic Arts, Dada and Surrealism,' New York Museum of Modern Art.

Testa, Angelo (1921–)

▶ American fabric designer.

▶ Studied Institute of Design, Chicago, to 1945.

▶ As well as being a fabric designer, he was a painter and sculptor. He designed the 1941 *Little Man* abstract floral fabric, widely published and hailed as a new direction in textile design; introduced abstract and non-objective motifs into commercial textile design in the USA; produced motifs included in *Diagonals, Space Dashes, Forms within Forms, Line in Act*, and *Experiment in Space*. Some of these had matching wallpapers. Clients included Greeff, Forster, Cohn-Hall-Marx, and Knoll. He executed patterns for plastic laminates, vinyls, and fiberglass panels.

▶ Work subject of 1983 'Angelo Testa' exhibition, College of Architecture, Chicago. Fabric designs included in 1984 'Design Since 1945' exhibition at the Philadelphia Museum of Art.

▶ 'Textiles,' *Arts and Architecture*, Vol. 62, Oct. 1945:42–43. 'Angelo Testa,' *Arts and Architecture*, Vol. 63, July 1946:42–43. 'Angelo Testa,' *Everyday Art Quarterly*, No. 25, 1953:16–17. Cat., Kathryn B. Hiesinger and George H. Marcus III (eds.), *Design Since 1945*, Philadelphia: Philadelphia Museum of Art, 1983: 233,VII–58. Cat., *Angelo Testa*, Chicago: College of Architecture, 1983.

Tétard

▶ French silversmiths; located Paris.

▶ Maison Tétard was founded in 1880. It produced the distinctive designs of founder's son Louis Tétard (1907–), Valéry Bizouard, and, from the 1920s, Jean Tétard. 1902–37, Bizouard pursued all phases of French silver design.

▶ Maison Tétard showed its wares at the 1925 Paris 'Exposition Internationale des Arts Décoratifs et Industriels Modernes,' including Bizouard's austere ten-sided vase. Jean Tétard's objects first shown at the 1930 'Décor de la Table' exhibition at the Musée Galliéra in Paris.

▶ Annelies Krekel-Aalberse, *Art Nouveau and Art Déco Silver*, New York: Abrams, 1989:66,67,69,260.

Thames, Gösta (1916–)

▶ Swedish engineer and designer.

▶ 1938–81, Thames worked as deputy technical manager of the Ericsson telephone instrument engineering department. Hugo Blomberg and Ralph Lysell conceived the *Ericofon* telephone set from 1940; 1949–54, Thames was responsible for the telephone's design and construction.

▶ Work (*Ericofon*) shown at 1984 'Design Since 1945' exhibition, Philadelphia Museum of Art.

▶ Hugo Blomberg, 'The Ericofon—The New Telephone Set,' *Ericsson Review*, Vol. 33, No. 4, 1956:99–109. Cat., Kathryn B. Hiesinger and George H. Marcus III (eds.), *Design Since 1945*, Philadelphia: Philadelphia Museum of Art, 1983.

Theill, Christian (1954–)

▶ German designer; born Remscheid; active Florence.

▶ Studied industrial design, ISIA, Florence.

▶ He settled in Italy in 1975; worked with several consultant designers, including Antonio Citterio in 1983; in 1981, set up his own industrial and interior design studio with various clients, including Poltronova (furniture), Eleusi (lighting), Nova (Zeus collection), Domus, and Intermezzo; 1981–83, taught at Università Internazionale dell'Arte, Florence; 1986–87, at Scuola Lorenzo de Medici, Florence; 1988–89, at Scuola Internazionale di Design, Bologna; designed the 1986 *Antenna* table lamp produced by Targetti Sankey; in 1988, with Paolo Targetti, established Theill-Targetti studio, designing furniture, furnishings, objects, lighting, graphics, and packaging.

▶ Received 1981 young industrial designer award, ADI (Associazione per il Disegno Industriale).

▶ Fumio Shimizu and Matteo Thun (eds.), *The Descendants of Leonardo: The Italian Design*, Tokyo, 1987:329. Albrecht Bangert and Karl Michael Armer, *80s Style: Designs of the Decade*, New York: Abbeville, 1990:109,236. *Modo*, No. 148, March–April 1993:126.

Thesmar, André Fernand (1843–1912)

▶ French enamelist; active Neuilly.

▶ *Cloisonné* enamel was popular in Paris in the 1870s, when Thesmar learned the technique as an apprentice at Barbedienne. He settled in Neuilly, where, in 1888, he rediscovered *plique-à-jour* enamel, applying it for the first time on small objects, and collaborated with Hirné on mounts. He experimented with other enamel processes.

▶ Annelies Krekel-Aalberse, *Art Nouveau and Art Déco Silver*, New York: Abrams, 1989:59,60,260.

Thielemann, A.

▶ Russian goldsmith and silversmith; active St. Petersburg.

▶ Thielemann and A. W. Holström were the chief jewelers in the workshop of Fabergé in St. Petersburg. Theilemann's specialties included small round asymmetrical brooches with single colored stones, diamond and enamel jewelry pieces, and miniature Easter eggs, incorporating Siberian and other hardstones, sold as tourists' souvenirs. The eggs were intended to be worn as bracelet or necklace pendants.

▶ Charlotte Gere, *American and European Jewelry 1830–1914*, New York: Crown, 1975:222.

Thiers

See Coutellerie à Thiers, La

Thomas

▶ German ceramics firm.

▶ The firm was founded in 1903 by Fritz Thomas in Marktredwitz; in 1908, became part of Rosenthal. Its designers included Wolfgang von Wersin, Tapio Wirkkala, Hans Theo Baumann, and Nick Roerich.

▶ See Rosenthal and Roericht, Nick

Thomas, Rodney (1902–)

▶ British painter, architect, and interior and exhibition designer.

▶ Studied painting and sculpture, Byam Shaw Art School and Slade School of Art, and under Leon Underwood; c1922–24, architecture, Bartlett School of Architecture, London University.

▶ In c1924, he worked in the offices of architect Giles Gilbert Scott in London and subsequently with his uncle Brummell Thomas, after which he entered the architects' department of the Southern Railways, working on station buildings; E. Maxwell Fry and Guy Morgan worked in the railway offices alongside him. In 1930, Thomas designed the studio interiors of painter Eileen Agar in Bramham Gardens, London, and, in the 1930s, of painter and designer Ashley Havinden, and office interiors for William Crawford London; c1935–39, was consulting architect and designer for the showrooms and exhibition stands of the water heater firm Ascot. After World War II, Thomas, Edric Neal, Raglan Squire, and Jim Gear formed the firm Arcon to design prefabricated factory-produced housing. He designed the Transport Pavilion at the 1951 London 'Festival of Britain' exhibition.

▶ Cat., *Thirties: British art and design before the war*, London: Arts Council of Great Britain, Hayward Gallery, 1980:150,301.

Thompson, Jim (1906–67)

▶ American architect and entrepreneur; active Bangkok.

▶ Thompson settled in Thailand after World War II, and established the firm Thai Silk in Bangkok in 1948; having abandoned architecture, was responsible for developing the technologically advanced silk industry in Thailand, where he replaced the traditional vegetable dyes with high-quality colorfast dyes from Switzerland; made it possible for the weavers to use faster, foot-operated looms and was responsible for introducing the bright, iridescent color palette Thai silk is known for today. Sales soared in the 1950s and 1960s and by 1967 he had established a cottage industry of 20,000 weavers with export sales exceeding $6 million.

▶ William Warren, *The Legendary American: The Remarkable Career and strange Disappearance of Jim Thompson*, Boston, 1970. Cat., Kathryn B. Hiesinger and George H. Marcus III (eds.), *Design Since 1945*, Philadelphia: Philadelphia Museum of Art, 1983:233.

Thomsen, Tamara (1953–)

▶ American painter and industrial designer; born Sioux Falls, South Dakota.

▶ Studied fine arts, Syracuse University, Syracuse, New York, to 1976, and Virginia Commonwealth University. Richmond, Virginia, to 1980.

▶ She taught painting at the Virginia Commonwealth University and, in 1981, became a founding partner with David Stowell, Tom Dair, and Tucker Viemeister of the industrial design practice that became Smart Design in 1985. She was vice-president of graphic design and managed design programs for Citibank, Polder, Sam Flax, American Institute of Architects, Prodigy Services, University of Southern California, Kepner-Tregoe, Family Care International.

▶ She exhibited her painting in group and one-person shows in New York, Syracuse, and Richmond.

Thonet, Michael (1796–1871)

▶ German entrepreneur; born Boppard am Rhein.

▶ Thonet was born a few miles up the Rhine river from where renowned cabinetmaker David Roentgen's workshop was active. In 1841, he was invited to Vienna by Count Metternich, the chancellor of Austria, who had seen Thonet's furniture on a trip to Germany; he sold his furniture to members of the imperial court and to the nobility, although he was primarily interested in a wider market, with mass production as his goal; by 1856, had designed his own factory, from machinery to architecture, in the Moravian forests near a supply of the beechwood used for his bentwood furniture. He was the most innovative of 19th-century German furniture makers and designers. His bentwood process for making chairs resulted in low costs, durability, lightness, and flexibility, and eliminated the need for hand-carved joints and, notably, ornamentation. Thonet began experimenting by bending wood, initially gluing together veneers to make sections of furniture, and later inventing a new process where solid lengths of beechwood were steamed or boiled in water and glue, allowing long pieces to be bent to make chair frames, in some cases in fantastic forms; in 1841, took out patents in France, Britain, and Belgium for his bentwood process, and exhibited bentwood chairs at Coblenz. In 1888, the folding theater seat was invented by the firm Gebrüder Thonet, by then operated by Thonet's sons. Some 50 million copies of *Chair No. 4* have been made; found in cafés worldwide, it is still in production. Le Corbusier admired Thonet's *B9* chair (made from six pieces of bentwood, with caning for the seat) and used it frequently in his interiors. The French branch of Thonet was founded in 1929 to produce Modern chromium-plated tubular steel furniture, including the designs of Marcel Breuer and the team of Le Corbusier, Pierre Jeanneret, and Charlotte Perriand. When this subsidiary closed, the entire production of tubular steel furniture was moved to Frankenberg (Germany) under the directorship of Bruno Weill. In 1932 in America, Gilbert Rohde designed bent tubular metal chairs produced by Thonet. The firm continues today, using contemporary designers and reissuing earlier models.

▶ Yvonne Brunhammer et al., *Art Nouveau Belgium, France*, Houston: Rice University, 1976. Christopher Wilk, *Thonet: 150 Years of Furniture*, Woodbury, NY: Barron's, 1980. Derek E. Ostergard,

Bent Wood and Metal Furniture, 1850–1946, New York: The American Federation of Arts, 1987. Alexander von Vegesack, *Das Thonet Buch*, Munich: Bangert, 1987.

Thorup, Torsten (1944–)
▶ Danish architect and industrial designer.
▶ 1965–69, studied architecture and planning, Det Kongelige Danske Kunstakademi, Copenhagen, under Henning Larsen; 1969–73, psychology, University of Copenhagen.
▶ He was a senior architect in the office of Henning Larsen; in 1968, set up an office in collaboration with architect Claus Bonderup; became a member of the Federation of Danish Architects and Federation of Industrial Designers in Denmark; from 1969, designed lighting, furniture, and ski equipment. After his association with Larsen, his design and architecture commissions included 1981 Café Brix in Ålborg, 1981 signage for Jan-Flex in Copenhagen, and 1982 leather and cotton clothing for Clemme in Ålborg.
▶ Awarded 1974 Bundespreis 'Die gute Industrieform' for *Semi* lamp for Fog & Mørup, 1976 'Form Utile' prize in France for *Calot* lamp for Focus Belysning, and 1982 Swedish Design Prize gold medal for *Pendel No. 1* lamp for Focus Belysning. Work shown at the 'Euroluce' fair in Milan from 1972; 1979 exhibition of lighting and furniture, Louisiana Museum, Copenhagen; 1980 'Industriforeningen,' Copenhagen; 1981 and 1982 exhibitions, Gothenburg; 1981 'Lumière,' Paris; and 1982 exhibition of industrial design sponsored by Federation of Danish Architects, Ålborg.

Thun, Matteo (Count Matteo Thun-Hohenstein 1952–)
▶ Italian ceramicist and designer; born Bolzano; active Brera, Milan.
▶ Studied architecture, Università di Firenze, to 1975; studied sculpture, Academy of Oskar Kokoschka, Salzburg; University of California, Los Angeles.
▶ A founder of the Memphis group in 1981 and best known for his work there, he was a prolific designer of ceramics, including the *Teje* and *Tuja* vases, *Nefretiti* tea set, *Api* ashtray, and *Palma* bud vase for the initial 1981 collection; and the *Manitoga* tray, *Ontario*, *Erie*, *Superior*, and *Michigan*, bud vases, and *Kariba* compote, *Garda* amphora, and *Lodoga*, *Titicaca*, *Onega*, and *Chad* vases for the 1982 collection. From 1982, taught product design and ceramics, Kunstgewerbeschule, Vienna, where his students produced projects for his 'In the Spirit of the USA' assignment; dinnerware sets by students (including Renate Hattinger, Margit Denz, Klara Obereder, Maria Wiala, and Michaela Lange) were produced by Villeroy et Boch in limited editions. Thun worked with Ettore Sottsass in Sottsass Associati; in 1985, published the manifesto *The Baroque Bauhaus*, encouraging use of the styles from the past available to designers today. He designed 1986 *Via Col Vento* blown and formed vase produced by Lobmeyr, 1985 *Settimana* metal chest by Bieffeplast, 1988 rug designs for the Dialog collection of Vorwerk, 1983 range of ceramic hanging light fixtures, including *Santa Monica*, *Santa Ana*, and *Santa Fe*, and architectonic *Stillight* range of table lamps produced by Bieffeplast in the 1980s. The 1967 *Fantasia* porcelain series was produced by Arzberg. He designed domestic products for Thonet, Villeroy et Boch, WMF (Württembergische Metallwarenfabrik), Tiffany, Campari, Swatch, Cleto Munari, and Alessi is active in his own studio today.
▶ Participated in numerous exhibitions including with Memphis from 1981 and Triennali di Milano.
▶ Andrea Branzi, *La Casa Calda: Esperienze del Nuovo Disegno Italiano*, Milan: Idea Books, 1982. *Les Carnets du Design*, Paris: Mad-Cap Productions et APCI, 1986:55. Fumio Shimizu and Matteo Thun (eds.), *The Descendants of Leonardo: The Italian Design*, Tokyo, 1987. Volker Fischer, *Bodenreform: Teppichboden von Künstlern und Architekten*, Berlin: Ernst und Sohn, 1989. Albrecht Bangert and Karl Michael Armer, *80s Style: Designs of the Decade*, New York: Abbeville, 1990:140.

Thuret, André (1898–1965)
▶ French glassware designer and glass engineer; active Paris.
▶ He was a research worker and teacher at the Conservatoire National des Arts et Métiers, and consultant, Institut du Verre; in 1924 with friend Henri Navarre, created his first glass; in 1949, was sponsored by Jean Fouquet for membership of UAM (Union des Artistes Modernes). He suspended colored pigments, pinching glass by fusion; was the most creative 1940–50; until 1958, worked in a glass factory, aided by glass blowers.
▶ He participated in the 1956–57 (I) Triennale d'Art français Contemporain in the Pavillon de Marsan in Paris.
▶ René Chavance, 'André Thuret, Artiste et Technicien du Verre,' *Mobilier et Décoration*, No. 1, 1955. Sylvie Raulet, *Bijoux Art Déco*, Paris: Regard, 1984. Arlette Barré-Despond, *UAM*, Paris: Regard, 1986:514–15. Cat., *Les années UAM 1929–1958*, Paris: Musée des Arts Décoratifs, 1988:251.

Thwaites, A.F.
▶ British industrial designer.
▶ From 1945, Thwaites produced designs for Murphy Radio cabinets in wood-veneer models, followed in the 1950s by plastic forms.
▶ Work (baffle-board radio sets) shown at 1946 'Britain Can Make It' exhibition, Victoria and Albert Museum, London.
▶ Michael Farr, *Design in British Industry: A Mid-Century Survey*, London: Cambridge, 1955. 'The Radio,' London: Design Museum, 1989.

Thygesen, Rud (1932–)
▶ Danish furniture designer.
▶ Studied Kunsthåndværkerskolen, Copenhagen, to 1966.
▶ He set up his own design studio in 1966 with Johnny Sørensen. 1970–74, he taught at the Kunsthåndværkerskolen and, from 1971, at Den Permanente. His furniture designs (with Olesen) were produced by Erik Boisens Møbelfabrik.
▶ Henrik Sten Møller, *Rud Thygesen—Johnny Sørensen Industri & Design*, Copenhagen: Rhodos, 1976. Frederik Sieck, *Nutidig Dansk Møbeldesign:—en kortfattet illustreret beskrivelse*, Copenhagen: Bondo Gravesen; 1990 Busck edition in English.

Tiffany, Charles Louis (1812–1902)
▶ American entrepreneur; born Connecticut; active New York; father of Louis Comfort Tiffany.
▶ In 1837, Tiffany and John B. Young opened a fancy goods and stationery store at 259 Broadway, New York. Enlarged in 1841, the store's stock of accessories and stationery was augmented with cutlery and clocks, jewelry from Paris, glass from Bohemia, and porcelain from France and Dresden; J.L. Ellis became a partner, and the firm moved to 271 Broadway and became known as Tiffany, Young and Ellis. Better-quality English jewelry, mosaic jewelry from Florence and Rome, and good quality stock from Paris replaced the originally stocked cheap goods from Hanau and Paris. In 1848, the firm began manufacturing its own jewelry and, by 1850, had set up a shop on rue de Richelieu in Paris. When Charles Tiffany took over in 1853, the firm became known as Tiffany. A Boston jeweler, Gideon F.T. Reed, became Tiffany's partner to direct the Paris branch, known as Tiffany and Reed. From 1848, the firm made large purchases of diamonds in Paris; in 1850, it bought the reputed diamonds of Marie Antoinette, purchased $100,000 worth of jewelry at the Eszterházy sale, and spent $500,000 at the sale of the French crown jewels. In 1854, the firm moved to 550 Broadway and, in 1870, to 15th Street on Union Square. One of its first designers was Gustave Herter, although most of its silverwares were bought from independent artisans in New York. In 1851, John Chandler Moore, who had previously made silver for Tiffany's, was hired to produce silver hollow-ware. Though the firm sold silverplate from 1868, it became known for its sterling silver. Most of its silver cannot be assigned to a specific designer, although goods in the Japanese taste can be credited to Moore. In 1852, Moore saw to it that Tiffany became the first firm to adopt the English sterling standard

(92.5 per cent pure silver). In 1868, Moore became an officer and silver department director; he worked at Tiffany for 40 years. A London branch was opened the same year. Tiffany was at the forefront of exploiting the European and American enthusiasm for *japonisme*, probably thanks to Moore, a knowledgeable collector of Japanese art. In 1876, Tiffany hired Christopher Dresser to bring back *objets d'art* from Japan; the collection of almost 2,000 pieces was sold in 1878. As early as 1871, the firm produced silverwares in the Japanese style. Tiffany's artisans practiced damascening and inlaying techniques for small *bibelots* and jewels in the *japoniste* style; Japanese technicians executed some of its production. By 1873, the firm was producing hollow-ware; it became well known for the 1875 *William Cullen Bryant Vase* designed by James Horton Whitehouse with medallions by Augustus Saint-Gaudens. Another distinguished vase was commissioned in 1877 as a gift to Cincinnati-philanthropist Reuben R. Springer. Louis Comfort Tiffany joined his father in the firm, and, on the latter's death, became director of the jewelry workshops in 1902. 1952–78, Van Day Truex, hired by Walter Hoving, was a prolific designer for the firm; many of his designs are still in production. From 1978, John Loring was the design director.

▶ Tiffany exhibited at 1867 Paris 'Exposition Universelle' (silver medal), 1876 Philadelphia 'Centennial Exposition' (award of merit), 1878 Paris 'Exposition Universelle' (gold medals), its precious stones of North America at the 1889 Paris 'Exposition Universelle,' 1893 Chicago 'World's Columbian Exposition,' and 1900 Paris 'Exposition Universelle.' Charles Louis Tiffany in 1878 and Edward Chandler Moore in 1889 were appointed Chevaliers of the Légion d'honneur.

▶ George Frederick Heydt, *Charles L. Tiffany and the House of Tiffany and Company*, New York, 1893. 'The Edward C. Moore Collection,' *Bulletin of The Metropolitan Museum of Art*, Vol. 2, June 1902:105–06. Charlotte Gere, *American and European Jewelry 1830–1914*, New York: Crown, 1975:222–24. Henry H. Hawley, 'Tiffany's Silver in the Japanese Taste,' *Bulletin of the Cleveland Museum of Art*, Vol. 63, Oct. 1976:236–45. Charles H. Carpenter Jr. and Mary Grace Carpenter, *Tiffany Silver*, New York, 1978. Doreen Bolger Burke et al., *In Pursuit of Beauty: Americans and the Aesthetic Movement*, New York: Metropolitan Museum of Art and Rizzoli, 1987:472–73.

Tiffany, Louis Comfort (1848–1933)

▶ American glassmaker, jeweler, painter, designer, and interior decorator; born New York; son of Charles L. Tiffany.

▶ Studied painting in New Jersey under George Innes; 1866–68, under Samuel Colman; and in Paris under Léon Bailly to 1869.

▶ In 1870, he traveled through Spain, North Africa, and Egypt in the company of Samuel Colman; his later glasswork was influenced by the Hispano-Moresque and Roman glass he saw on the trip. In 1878, he became influenced by the French decorative arts he saw at the Paris 'Exposition Universelle' and by Edward C. Moore (chief designer and silver department director at his father's firm), who encouraged him to pursue Orientalism. In 1876, he began designing stained glass for the Thills Glass House in Brooklyn, New York; in 1877, after the 1876 Philadelphia 'Centennial Exposition,' founded the Society of American Artists with Innes, Colman, and John La Farge, which led, in 1878, to the formation of Louis C. Tiffany and Associated Artists. The new company received many commissions, including the red and blue rooms in the White House in Washington of 1882–83. In the 1870s, Tiffany began producing distinctive designs in stained glass and, in 1880, made art glass for the Heidt Glass House in Brooklyn, using a Venetian glass-blower and experimenting with color, luster, and opacity. In 1881, his first patent for luster-glass was taken out and, in 1886, one for the process of spraying metallic chloride onto hot glass, producing a product to become known as carnival glass. In 1885, he founded Tiffany Glass. In 1895, Siegfried Bing asked Tiffany to make ten stained-glass windows for Bing's shop L'Art Nouveau in Paris; they were designed by Pierre Bonnard, Édouard Vuillard, Paul Sérusier, and Henri de Toulouse-Lautrec.

Bing had furnished Tiffany with Oriental objects as early as the 1870s; the collaboration placed Tiffany in touch with European artists, spurring him on to greater creativity. Encouraged by his success at the 1893 Chicago 'World's Columbian Exposition,' Tiffany established a furnace at Corona, Long Island, New York, for the production of blown glass pieces, inspired by Émile Gallé's work in Nancy; in 1894, registered the 'favrile' trademark. In 1895, achieving immediate success after showing his 'favrile' glass at the opening of Bing's Paris shop and in the Salon of that year, Tiffany glassware was bought by European museums and widely imitated. In 1890, Tiffany established Tiffany Studios to make bronze and lamps; in 1900, began producing metalwork and jewelry; when his father died in 1902, became artistic director of Tiffany and Co; 1902–04, spent over two million dollars building his artists' colony at Laurelton Hall in Oyster Bay, Long Island, New York. Best known for his stained glass and art glass, he also designed and produced mosaics, jewelry, furniture, textiles, and metalwork. His *Wisteria* lamp epitomized his skill in combining colored glass and metal to create a delicate illusion. Tiffany Studios closed in 1932. He had been responsible for persuading rich Americans, who had bought luxury goods in Europe almost exclusively, to recognize that interior decoration accoutrements and fancy art-glass goods could be designed and produced with the same high quality in the USA.

▶ Tiffany showed his work at 1893 Chicago 'World's Columbian Exposition.' In 1895, showed 'favrile' glass at the opening of Bing's shop L'Art Nouveau in Paris; in 1885, stained-glass windows at the Salon of the Société Nationale des Beaux-Arts; lily-cluster lamp (gold medal) at 1902 Turin 'Esposizione Internazionale d'Arte Decorativa Moderna.'

▶ Gertrude Speenburgh, *The Arts of the Tiffanys*, Chicago, 1956. Robert Koch, 'The Stained Glass Decades: A Study of Louis Comfort Tiffany (1848–1933) and the Art Nouveau in America,' doctoral thesis, Yale University, 1957. Cat., Robert Koch, *Louis Comfort Tiffany, 1848–1933*, New York, Museum of Contemporary Crafts of the American Craftsmen's Council, 1958. Stuart P. Feld, ' "Nature in Her Most Seductive Aspects": Louis Comfort Tiffany's Favrile Glass,' *Bulletin of the Metropolitan Museum of Art*, Nov. 1962. Robert Koch, *Louis C. Tiffany: Rebel in Glass*, New York, 1964. Siegfried Bing, *Artistic America, Tiffany Glass, and Art Nouveau*, Cambridge: MIT, 1970. Cat., Gary A. Reynolds and Robert Littman, *Louis Comfort Tiffany: The Paintings*, New York: Grey Art Gallery and Study Center, 1979. Alastair Duncan, *Tiffany Windows*, New York, 1980. Cat., Donald L. Stover, *The Art of Louis Comfort Tiffany*, San Francisco: M.H. de Young Memorial Museum, 1981.

Tiffany Pottery

▶ American pottery firm; located Corona, New York.

▶ Louis Comfort Tiffany produced experimental pottery pieces by 1900. The public saw the results at the Tiffany Studios stand at the 1904 St. Louis 'Louisiana Purchase Exposition,' where three vases were on display. In 1905, pottery went into full production at Tiffany's Corona works, and, by 1906, Tiffany 'favrile' pottery was being offered. Most of the pots were slip-cast in molds. Each pot was hand finished and glazed, producing a unique piece. The glazes included matt, crystalline, and iridescent, primarily a transparent yellow-green. Some of the pieces were left unglazed on the outside. In *c*1910, Tiffany added to the line 'Favrile Bronze' produced by electroplating a metal coating onto the outside of the pottery, which was then patinated. In 1919, the pottery was discontinued; limited in output, it was never commercially successful.

▶ Tiffany Pottery pieces were shown at 1904 St. Louis 'Louisiana Purchase Exposition' and at 1915 San Francisco 'Panama-Pacific International Exposition.'

▶ Robert Koch, *Louis C. Tiffany, Rebel in Glass*, New York: Crown, 1964. Martin Eidelberg, 'Tiffany Favrile Pottery: A New Study of a Few Known Facts,' *Connoisseur*, No. 169, Sept. 1968:57–61. Hugh F. McKean, *The 'Lost' Treasures of Louis Comfort Tiffany*,

Garden City: Doubleday, 1980. Donald L. Stove, *The Art of Louis Comfort Tiffany*, San Francisco: M.H. de Young Memorial Museum, 1981. *American Art Pottery*, New York: Cooper Hewitt Museum, 1987:100.

Tigerman, Stanley (1931–) and Margaret McCurry (1943–)

▶ American architects; active Chicago.
▶ Tigerman studied Massachusetts Institute of Technology, Cambridge, Massachusetts; Institute of Design, Chicago; and Yale University, under Paul Rudolph.
▶ 1961–62, he was head designer at Skidmore, Owings and Merrill, Chicago, under Harry M. Weese; subsequently a partner with Norman Koglin, Chicago; in 1964, opened his own practice in Chicago; 1965–71, taught at the University of Illinois, Chicago Circle; in the 1960s, was known for designing extremely large structures, including the 1968 'Instant City.' As an example of an old building converted to new use, he designed the 1970–73 vacation house in Burlington, Wisconsin. His later Post-Modernist buildings included the 1977 Daisy house in Porter, Indiana, and the 1976 Hot Dog House. He and wife Margaret McCurry are outspoken voices on contemporary architecture. They designed domestic tableware for Swid Powell and a tea set for Alessi's 1983 *Tea and Coffee Piazza* project. His later, lighthearted, assignments included the 1985 Hard Rock Café, and 1987 One Pool House, both Chicago. In c1990, Tigerman-McCurry participated in the resort site plan and designed buildings at Euro Disney, near Paris.
▶ Images of Tigerman's architecture were included in 1976 'Seven Chicago Architects' exhibition, Chicago.
▶ *Seven Chicago Architects*, Chicago, 1976. Stanley Tigerman, *Versus: An American Architect's Alternatives*, New York, 1981. Officina Alessi, *Tea and Coffee Piazza: 11 Servizi da tè e caffè*, Milan: Crusinallo, 1983. Stanley Tigerman, *The Architecture of Exile*, New York: Rizzoli, 1988.

Tiliche, Paolo (1925–)

▶ Italian architect and designer; born Alexandria; active Milan.
▶ Studied architecture, Politecnico di Milano, to 1949.
▶ He began his career as an architect in 1950. He was a prolific designer of residences, industrial plants, and offices; became a member of ADI (Associazione per il Disegno Industriale); was known for his inventive shapes and multi-function combinations; designed lighting, glassware, plastic and wooden furniture, domestic kitchenware, and wallpaper for numerous clients, including furniture for Arform, sanitary equipment for Ideal Standard, blown-glass lighting for Barbini, plastic tabletop objects for Fratelli Guzzini, glass tableware, and ceramics.
▶ Work included in 1979 'Design & design' exhibition, Palazzo delle Stelline, Milan; 1984 'Design Since 1945' exhibition, Philadelphia Museum of Art.
▶ *ADI Annual 1976*, Milan: Associazione per il Disegno Industriale, 1976. Cat., *Design & design*, Milan: Palazzo delle Stelline, 1979:150. Cat., Kathryn B. Hiesinger and George H. Marcus III (eds.), *Design Since 1945*, Philadelphia: Philadelphia Museum of Art, 1983:233, VI–18. Giancarlo Iliprandi and Pierluigi Molinari (eds.), *Industrial Designers Italiani*, Fagagna, 1985:224.

Tillander Jr., Alexander

▶ Finnish jeweler and silversmith; active St. Petersburg and Helsinki.
▶ In 1860, he established the jewelry firm A. Tillander, St. Petersburg, where he produced jewelry, eggs, small objects, including letter-openers, photography frames, and cigarette cases. Later, the workshop produced silver in the Art Nouveau style, engraved rather than chased as in Western Europe. As holder of the royal Russian warrant, the jewelry firm Karl Karlovitch Hahn produced the diadem worn by Czarina Alexandra at the 1896 coronation; the crown was marked 'T.A.' for A. Tillander. After the 1917 Revolution, he returned to Helsinki and set up a new firm there.
▶ Annelies Krekel-Aalberse, *Art Nouveau and Art Déco Silver*, New York: Abrams, 1989:241,249,260. Charlotte Gere, *American and European Jewelry 1830–1914*, New York: Crown, 1975:189.

Tillett, D.D. (aka Doris Tillett)

▶ American textile designer.
▶ With husband Leslie Tillett, who had experience in textile production and color technology, she established a laboratory and studio where printed textiles were designed and produced in New York City. Designing by dyeing straight onto fabric, rather than the traditional procedure of first drawing with watercolors on paper, the Tilletts designed textiles for both custom and mass production. Industrial clients included J.C. Penney, Covington, and Leacock. Some of the Tillett designs were adapted from nature, including the 1950 *Queen Anne's Lace* produced by the firm for more than 30 years. Some of Doris Tillett's designs were inspired by Peruvian art, ancient tapestries, and 19th-century sporting prints. In 1954, they executed designs for printed fiberglass for Owens Corning.
▶ *Queen Anne's Lace* fabric was included in 1984 'Design Since 1945' exhibition, Philadelphia Museum of Art.
▶ 'Pilot Printing Plant,' *Interiors*, Vol. 108, June 1949. Don Wallance, *Shaping America's Products*, New York, 1956:99–101. Cat., Kathryn B. Hiesinger and George H. Marcus III (eds.), *Design Since 1945*, Philadelphia: Philadelphia Museum of Art, 1983:233, VII–60.

Tiroler Glashütte

▶ Austrian glassware manufacturer; located Kufstein.
▶ Glassmaster Johann Leopold Riedel built a glass factory in northern Bohemia in 1756. By 1860, Josef Riedel employed over a thousand workers at the plant. Josef Riedel the Younger (1862–1924) discovered that selen dyes glass a ruby-red color. Walter Riedel (1895–) managed the Tiroler Glashütte in Kufstein from the second quarter of the 20th century. In 1957, Claus Josef Riedel re-established the factory in Kufstein. He had previously been manager of a glassworks in Naples and designed for Rosenthal. At the Tiroler Glashütte, he applied his simple techniques in the *Holdfast* range, and collaborated with Michael Boehm to create the *Calyx* range, with faint mold lines as a design feature.
▶ Received grand prize (*Bruxelles* service) at 1958 'Exposition Universelle et Internationale de Bruxelles (Expo '58)'; 1959 Österreichischer Staatspreis (*Special Sizes* range), Vienna; medals for 'good design' (*Tevevisionglas*, *Equisit*, and *Monaco* ranges), 1960 (XII) Triennale di Milano; Deutscher Staatspreis (candleholders), 1961 Handwerksmesse, Munich; 1962 Österreichischer Staatspreis (*Burg* and *Bridge* series) in Vienna.
▶ Frederick Cooke, *Glass: Twentieth-Century Design*, New York: Dutton, 1986:96. Cat., Kathryn B. Hiesinger and George H. Marcus III (eds.), *Design Since 1945*, Philadelphia: Philadelphia Museum of Art, 1983.

Tisdale, David (1956–)

▶ American metalworker; born San Diego, California.
▶ Studied University of California, Berkeley, and University of California, Davis; art, San Diego State University.
▶ David Tisdale Jewelry Design, New York, was active 1981–86. Tisdale was owner of Livewires! 1985–86, when he set up David Tisdale Design, was concurrently a partner in Fresh Design, New York, with Judy Smilow, established in 1989. His work has been widely published.
▶ From 1978, work included in numerous jewelry and metalworking exhibitions.

Tisdall, Hans (b. Hans Aufseeser 1910–)

▶ German painter and designer; active Munich, Paris, and London.
▶ Studied Academy of Fine Art, Munich.
▶ He set up a studio in 1930 in Fitzroy Street, London, and began designing mural paintings, book jackets, and textiles. His 1938 *Athene* jacquard woven cotton fabric was produced by Edinburgh Weavers in Carlisle, as well as other patterns 1938–39. He rendered large-scale paintings, mosaics and tapestries for public buildings, including English Electric, Manchester University, and

the Ionian Bank; by the 1980s, lectured in fine art at London Central School of Arts and Crafts, Dartington Summer School, and in Venice.

▶ Work shown at 1937 Paris 'Exposition Internationale des Arts et Techniques dans la Vie Moderne' (medal of honor); was subject of 1945 one-person exhibition; included in 1979–80 'Thirties' exhibition at the Hayward Gallery in London.

▶ Cat., *Thirties: British art and design before the war*, London: Arts Council of Great Britain, Hayward Gallery, 1979:90, 144,301.

Toffoloni, Werther (1930–)

▶ Italian designer; born Udine; active Manzano.

▶ Toffoloni designed ceramics, furniture, accessories, and fabrics (in collaboration with Piero Palange until 1975) for various firms in Italy, including the *G 54* wooden table and a rocking chair produced by Germa in Pavia. Clients in Italy included Malobbia, Fratelli Montina (furniture), Tonon, A. Barbini (glassware), Gervasoni, Mobel Italia, E. & C. Pecci, Gabbianelli Ceramiche, Moretuzzo, Iterby Italiana Mobili, and Ibisi and, in Germany, Schieder Möbel. He was a member of ADI (Associazione per il Disegno Industriale).

▶ *ADI Annual 1976*, Milan: Associazione per il Disegno Industriale, 1976.

Toikka, Oiva (1931–)

▶ Finnish ceramicist and glass, stage, and textile designer.

▶ 1953–60, studied ceramics at Taideteollinen Korkeakoulu, Helsinki.

▶ 1956–59, worked at Arabia ceramics works; in 1959, at Marimekko textiles; from 1960–63, taught at Taideteollinen Korkeakoulu, Helsinki; from 1959–63, at Sodankylä Secondary High School; from 1963, was artistic director at Nuutajärvi; from 1985, visiting designer at Rörstrand, Sweden. From the 1960s, he was costume and scenery designer for Tampere and for Savonlinna Theaters and Opera Houses, including set decorations for 1984 *Silkdrum* ballet.

▶ Received 1970 Lunning Prize, 1975 Finnish State Award for Industrial Art, 1980 Pro Finlandia prize.

▶ Jennifer Hawkins Opie, *Scandinavia: Ceramics and Glass in the Twentieth Century*, New York: Rizzoli, 1989.

Tonucci, Enrico (1946–)

▶ Italian industrial and graphic designer; born and active Pesaro.

▶ Studied at the Mistero d'Arte in Florence; took course in scenographics, Accademia d'Arte, Urbino.

▶ From 1970, he designed furniture, lighting, accessories, and furnishings; clients included, in Germany, Schönbuch and Walter Knoll, and, in Italy, Novalinea and La Bottega. He was a member of ADI (Associazione per il Disegno Industriale).

▶ *ADI Annual 1976*, Milan: Associazione per il Disegno Industriale, 1976. *Modo*, No. 148, March–April 1993:126–27.

Toraldo di Francia, Cristiano (1941–)

▶ Italian designer; born and active Florence.

▶ Studied architecture, Florence, to 1968.

▶ He began his professional career in Florence in 1966. From 1966 as cofounder of Superstudio in Florence, he was a partner there with Adolfo Natalini, Roberto Magris, Piero Frassinelli, and Alessandro Magris; designed furniture systems, furnishings, lighting, and accessories; taught industrial design at the Università Internazionale d'Arte, Florence; lectured in the USA; in 1970, began to collaborate with Gruppo 9999 and Scuola Separata per l'Architettura Concettuale Espansa (S-Space); 1973–75, as cofounder of the designers' collective Global Tools, designed there. His *Bazaar* seating system and *Teso* knock-down table were produced by Giovanetti. He produced films on architecture.

▶ Work included in 1972 'Italy: The New Domestic Landscape,' New York Museum of Modern Art; 1973 (XV) Triennale di Milano; and 1973–75 traveling exhibition of Superstudio's work in Europe and the USA.

Torck, Emmanuelle (1963–) and Emmanuelle Noirot (1961–)

▶ French furniture designers; active Paris.

▶ Studied École Nationale Supérieure des Arts Décoratifs, Paris.

▶ Their first work of note was the 1989 *Pilo Tole* lounge chair and 1989 *Pilo Pilo* chair produced by Christian Farjon and Idée; designed 1992 furniture range produced by Ligne Roset.

▶ Received the 1988 Agora award, 1989 VIA sponsorship, 1991 VIA Carte Blanche award, and 1989 Art Critics Prize.

▶ François Mathey, *Au bonheur des formes, design français 1945–1992*, Paris: Regard, 1992:255.

Torres Tur, Elias (1944–)

▶ Spanish architect and designer; born Ibiza.

▶ Studied Escuela Técnica Superior de Arquitectura, Barcelona, to 1968.

▶ He set up an architecture practice in 1968 with José Antonio Martínez Lapeña; 1973–77, was town architect of Ibiza; 1969–78, was professor of design and composition at the Escuela Técnica Superior de Arquitectura and, from 1979, professor of landscape architecture and drawing there; in 1977, 1981, and 1984, was guest professor, University of California at Los Angeles; published the book *Guía de Arquitectos de Ibiza y Formentera* (1980); (with Martínez) designed the 1986 *Lampelunas* street light produced by Cemusa, 1986 *Barcelona* and 1986 *Hollywood* rugs by BVD, and 1987 bus shelter (with José Luís Canosa) by Cemusa.

▶ Received 1986 Delta de Oro of ADI/FAD de Diseño Industrial and 1987 Premio FAD de Arquitectura.

▶ Juli Capella and Quim Larrea, *Designed by Architects in the 1980s*, New York: Rizzoli, 1988.

Torricelli, Eugenio (1948–)

▶ Italian designer; born and active Milan.

▶ Studied architecture to 1971.

▶ He began his professional career in 1972. Clients included Sormani (furniture, accessories, and lighting) in 1972, Brevetto (mechanical equipment) in 1972, Mopoa Milano (clocks) in 1974, Velca Legnano (furniture), and Gabbianelli (tableware). In 1973, he designed graphics for the magazine *Nuovi Orizzonti* for the Italian Tourist Bureau; taught at the Liceo Artistico di Brera in Milan; became a member of ADI (Associazione per il Disegno Industriale).

▶ He participated in the 'Interieur 72' exhibition.

▶ He won a prize at the 1973 'International Pottery Design Competition.'

▶ *ADI Annual 1976*, Milan: Associazione per il Disegno Industriale, 1976.

Torrigiani, Carlo (1928–)

▶ Italian designer; born Modena; active Milan.

▶ 1947–55, studied architecture, Politecnico di Milano.

▶ He designed interiors and housing, and was active in industrial design; became a member of ADI (Associazione per il Disegno Industriale).

▶ *ADI Annual 1976*, Milan: Associazione per il Disegno Industriale, 1976.

Tosi, Lorenzo (1948–)

▶ Italian designer; born Cortemaggiore; active Milan.

▶ Studied chemistry to 1974, and industrial design, Scuola Politecnica di Design, Milan.

▶ He was associated with the studio Gruppo, the design and communication collaborative in Milan, whose partners included Giorgio Brambilla, Anna Castelli, and Fabio Stojan; was active in the office of prevention and safety of Montedison in Milan; became a member of ADI (Associazione per il Disegno Industriale).

▶ *ADI Annual 1976*, Milan: Associazione per il Disegno Industriale, 1976.

Toso, Aureliano (1894–1979), Giani Toso, and Renato Toso (1940–)

▶ Italian glass designers.

► In the 1950s, Aureliano Toso was active as a glass designer in Murano in the family glass firm established in the 19th century. In 1962, Giani Toso became active in the family firm. Renato Toso and Noti Massari, husband and wife, collaborated at the factory. Massari also designed furnishings, ceramics, and textiles. Renato Toso designed furniture and lighting (with Roberto Pamio).
► *Moderne Klassiker: Möbel, die Geschichte machen*, Hamburg, 1982:139. Robert A.M. Stern (ed.), *The International Design Yearbook*, New York: Abbeville, 1985/1986: No. 323. Hans Wichman, *Italien Design 1945 bis heute*, Munich: Die Neue Sammlung, 1988.

Tostrup, J.

► Norwegian silversmiths; located Christiania (now Oslo).
► The firm J. Tostrup, founded in 1832, was best known for its enamel work. Working in *champlevé* and *cloisonné* from the 1880s, it began specializing in the 1890s in the *plique-à-jour* technique, achieving elegant effects after 1900. The firm also produced flatware and hollow-ware. 1890–1912, Thorolf Prytz was director, with designs inspired by local fauna and flora; in 1912, he was succeeded by son Jakob Prytz. In the 1920s, Oskar Sørensen designed simple forms suitable for mass production by machinery.
► Work shown at 1900 Paris 'Exposition Universelle,' including a number of standing dishes by Emil Saeter.
► Annelies Krekel-Aalberse, *Art Nouveau and Art Déco Silver*, New York: Abrams, 1989:242,243,260.

Totem

► French design collaborative; located Lyons.
► Totem was established in 1980 by cabinetmakers Jacques Bonnet, Frédérich du Chayla, Vincent Lemarchand, and Claire Olives. Their furniture hovered between art and utility; 1980–90, they produced *c*100 furniture pieces for the town hall of Villeurbanne, near Lyons, and for the Musée d'Art moderne, Saint-Étienne, including signage; designed tableware produced by Manufacture de Sèvres and rugs, furniture, and objects for Archimia produced by Zabro; organized the association Caravelles to manage the Quadriennale Internationale de design.
► Gilles de Bure, *Le Mobilier français 1965–1979*, Paris: Regard, 1983:130–31.

Toulemonde Bochard

► French carpet factory.
► The firm was established in 1945 and, in the 1970s, began to pursue design research, hiring contemporary designers and textile artisans including Andrée Putman, Christian Duc, Hilton McConnico, Jean-Michel Wilmotte, and Didier Gomez.
► Received 1992 European Community Design Prize.

Toulouse-Lautrec, Henri de (1864–1901)

► French painter and graphic artist; born Albi.
► He executed his first poster in 1891 for the Moulin Rouge cabaret in Paris. By 1900, he had created 31 posters. His work was influenced by Japanese *ukio-e* prints, particularly in its layout, areas of flat color, outlined figures, and blank areas within the composition. He was associated with both French and Belgian Art Nouveau practitioners. He designed stained-glass windows for Siegfried Bing's shop L'Art Nouveau, Paris, made by Louis Comfort Tiffany.
► Work shown at 1888 Salon des Vingt.
► Yvonne Brunhammer et al., *Art Nouveau Belgium, France*, Houston: Rice University, 1976.

Tourette, Étienne

► French enameler; active Paris.
► Trained under Louis Houillon.
► He produced jewelry for Georges Fouquet, Lalique, and other jewelers in Paris; after 1900, used *paillons* in his enamel work to lend brilliance to his jewelry, boxes, and vases.
► Work shown (jointly with Houillon) from 1878; work shown alone from 1893, including at 1902 Salon.
► Léonard Penicaud, 'L'émail aux Salons de 1902,' *Revue de la Bijouterie Joaillerie et Orfèvrerie*, 1902:165. Annelies Krekel-

Aalberse, *Art Nouveau and Art Déco Silver*, New York: Abrams, 1989:60,91,260.

Toussaint, Jeanne

► French designer.
► She worked until 1923 for Cartier in Paris; in 1930, directed the Haute Joaillerie; was nicknamed 'La Panthère' and used panther fur on the walls of her Paris apartment; designed a cigarette case with the appliqué figure of a panther in diamonds by Cartier. Louis Cartier joined his brother Pierre in New York in 1942 and Jacques Cartier lived in Saint-Moritz during the war, while the Cartier shop in Paris was left in the hands of Toussaint.
► *Ensembles Mobiliers*, Paris: Charles Moreau, 1927.

Tram Design

► French design workshop.
► Tram Design was established in 1983, by Jean-François Mermillot (1951–); it specialized in general consumer products, mechanical equipment, visual-identity programs, and packaging; designed Salomon *SX91* shoes, 1983 *747* ski bindings, and 1984 *Profila* roller-cutter system.

Tranchant, Jean

► French designer and singer.
► Not a prolific designer, he designed notable clocks and jewelry from the 1920s. Examples of his work appeared in *La Revue d'Industrie d'Art*.

Tranchant, Madame Jean

► French designer; wife of Jean Tranchant.
► From the 1920s, she was known for her widely published pillows and metal flower arrangements, among other furnishings.

Traquair, Phoebe Anna (b. Phoebe Anna Moss 1852–1936)

► British enameler and jeweler; born Dublin; active Scotland.
► Studied Royal Dublin Society.
► Working at first on domestic embroidery, she later specialized in large embroidered panels and enameling in a medieval manner; was influenced by medieval manuscripts that she studied in Dublin and sent to her by John Ruskin, medieval metalwork at the Royal Museum of Scotland, and Edward Burne-Jones and other Pre-Raphaelites. She learned enameling from Lady Gibson Carmichael, a pupil of Alexander Fisher; 1902–03, produced enamels that were pale and occasionally executed on silver rather than copper, and were brighter and deeper from 1905; in 1920, became the first honorary woman member of the Royal Scottish Academy.
► Showed work at the Arts and Crafts Exhibition Society, London; Edinburgh Arts and Crafts Club; and the Royal Scottish Academy.
► Toni Lesser Wolf, 'Women Jewelers of the British Arts and Crafts Movement,' *Journal of Decorative and Propaganda Arts*, No. 14, Fall 1989:43–44.

Trassinelli, Duccio (1945–)

► Italian designer; born Florence; active S. Casciano.
► Trassinelli began his professional career in 1970, designing furniture and lighting. He collaborated with Alessandro Mazzoni delle Stelle and was a member of ADI (Associazione per il Disegno Industriale).
► *ADI Annual 1976*, Milan: Associazione per il Disegno Industriale, 1976.

Trautmann, George H.

► American metalworker; active Chicago.
► Trautmann established his workshop at 4602 N. Hermitage, Chicago; *c*1910 produced lighting in the Arts and Crafts style, including lanterns, chandeliers, wall sconces, and copper desk lamps with colorful art-glass shades.
► 1910–14, showed work at Chicago Arts and Crafts exhibitions at the Art Institute of Chicago.
► Sharon S. Darling with Gail Farr Casterline, *Chicago Metalsmiths*, Chicago Historical Society, 1977.

Tresoldi, Ambrogio   (1933–)
▶ Italian architect, designer, and teacher.
▶ From 1960, studied architecture in Milan.
▶ He collaborated from 1960 with Alberto Salvati; 1961–62, was assistant at the Facoltà di Architettura, Politecnico di Milano; was active as an architect and interior and industrial designer.
▶ See Salvati, Alberto

Tressera, Jaime
▶ Spanish designer; active Barcelona.
▶ Beginning as a silversmith, he was subsequently active in publicity, interior design, and architecture, before pursuing furniture design; set up a firm in 1968 to produce his own furniture models. Following Carlos Riart's high-quality approach to cabinetmaking, Tressera was prolific during the first three years. His *Spinnacker* chair, *Butterfly* desk, and *Elliptic* cabinet, all of 1988, were noteworthy.
▶ His furniture was featured in the film *Batman* (1989). He showed his work at Mary Fox Linton in London and at the Salone del Mobile in Milan.
▶ Guy Julier, *New Spanish Design*, London: Thames and Hudson, 1991.

Tribel, Annie   (1933–)
▶ French furniture designer; active Paris.
▶ 1952–56, studied École Nationale Supérieure des Arts Décoratifs, Paris.
▶ She joined Atelier d'Urbanisme et d'Architecture, Paris, in 1962; 1962–68, designed interiors and furniture for youth clubs, rest homes, theaters (Le Théâtre de la Ville, Paris), and conference rooms; designed public institutions including the French Embassy in New Delhi, and, in 1983, guest rooms in the private apartments of the Palais de l'Élysée; taught at École Camondo, Paris.
▶ Cat., *Design français 1960–1990*, Paris: Centre Georges Pompidou/APCI, 1988. Gilles de Bure, *Le Mobilier français 1965–1979*, Paris: Regard/VIA, 1983:70–71.

Triboy, Maurice   (1890–1974)
▶ French cabinetmaker; born Bordeaux.
▶ He was active 1922–54 as a cabinetmaker in Bordeaux. His production was very traditional, as illustrated by a rosewood living-room ensemble of c1930–35 for the woman who founded the *Quincaillerie d'art*.

Triennale di Milano
▶ Italian exhibition.
▶ In 1923, 1925, and 1927, the 'Biennale Internazionale dell'Arte di Decorativa' was held in Monza. In 1930, it became the 'Triennale Internazionale dell'Arte di Decorativa.' In 1933, it was moved to Milan, where it continues to be held, and became known as the 'Triennale di Milano.'
▶ Pier Maria Bardi, 'Biennale e Triennale,' *L'Italia Letteraria*, 7 June 1936.

Trifari, Krussman and Fishel
▶ American costume jewelry firm; located Providence, Rhode Island.
▶ Gustavo Trifari began to design and make jewelry in 1900 in the workshop established by his grandfather in Naples; in 1904, emigrated to New York; became office supervisor and designer at the jewelry firm Weinberg and Sudzen; 1909–12, he was in partnership with uncle Ludovico Trifari in the firm Trifari and Trifari, producing imitation jewelry; in 1912, set up his own firm to produce hair ornaments in sterling silver and metal set with rhinestones and buckles, and covers for shoe heels. In 1917, Leo Krussman, formerly at hair ornament producer Rice and Hochster, joined the firm as administrative and sales director and partner; in 1925, salesperson Carl M. Fishel became a third partner. Its designer was Alfred Philippe, a student of the École Boulle in Paris and formerly designer at William Scheer. His widely admired designs contributed to Trifari, Krussman and Fishel's success. From 1933, the firm designed costume jewelry for Broadway musicals, including *Roberta* (1933), *The Great Waltz* (1934), and *Jubilee* (1935); in 1938, it became the first costume jeweler to advertise nationally, promoting the idea that costume jewelry was an acceptable alternative to precious jewelry. In 1939, it moved its manufacturing facility to Providence, Rhode Island, with executive and design offices remaining in New York; during World War II, produced jewelry in sterling silver, models incorporating Lucite for animal motifs, a line of patriotic brooches for the USA and Britain, and components for the US Navy. After the war, it developed an alloy, 'Trifanium,' a good medium for plating rhodium and gold. In 1950, Philippe created jewelry that featured rhinestone and held its popularity for 15 years, and the Countess de Polignac (daughter of Jeanne Lanvin) showed the new Trifari collection in Paris; in 1953, Norman Hartnell showed Trifari jewelry in his salon in London; in 1952 and 1956, fist lady Mamie Eisenhower wore Trifari jewelry at the presidency inaugural balls. In the 1950s–60s, the firm's glass bead and multicolor parure pieces were widely acclaimed. In the late 1950s and during the 1960s, its designers included Jean Paris (formerly of Cartier in Paris, and Van Cleef and Arpels) who worked at Trifari until 1965. 1967–79, André Boeuf, also formerly of Cartier in Paris, was a designer at Trifari. The designer of the highly successful 1966 *Jewels of India* collection, Philippe retired in 1968. In 1964, sons of the founders Gustavo Trifari Jr., Louis Krussman, and Carlton Fishel took over management of the firm. In the late 1960s and early 1970s, costume jewelry fell from favor and was replaced by gold chains and molten-gold pieces. Diane Love, formerly a designer at Bergdorf Goodman, designed new collections for Trifari; 1971–74, she created classically-inspired Modern pieces. In 1975, Trifari was bought by Hallmark Cards and, in 1982, by Crystal Brands. In 1978, Barbara Raleigh, assisted by Kunio Matsumoto, became design director.
▶ Deanna F. Cera (ed.), *Jewels of Fantasy: Costume Jewelry of the 20th Century*, New York: Abrams, 1992:220.

Trock, Paula   (1889–1979)
▶ Danish textile designer.
▶ Studied in Denmark, Sweden, and Finland.
▶ Her weaving school and workshop was active 1928–34 in Askov and, 1932–42, in Sønderborg. In 1948, she established the Spindegarden in Askov, where handweaving production was achieved with lighter, textured yarns and with experimental plastic threads and open weaves. In c1950, she began to design for mass production for clients including for Unika-Vaev.
▶ Received gold medals at the 1954 (X), 1957 (XI), and 1960 (XII) Triennali di Milano.
▶ Cat., Kathryn B. Hiesinger and George H. Marcus III (eds.), *Design Since 1945*, Philadelphia: Philadelphia Museum of Art, 1983:233, VII–61. Bent Salicath and Arne Karlsen (eds.), *Modern Danish Textiles*, Copenhagen, 1959:18. Arne Karlsen, *Made in Denmark*, New York:1960:160–61.

Trois Suisses
▶ French mail order firm.
▶ Trois Suisses was established in 1938, and, by 1993, was number two in the mail order business in France. From 1977, it sold items designed for the firm by Philippe Starck, Andrée Putman, and other well-known designers.

Truex, Van Day   (?–1979)
▶ American teacher, interior designer, and furnishings designer; born Kansas; active New York and Paris.
▶ From 1925, studied Parsons School of Design, Paris, under William Odom.
▶ His Paris apartment was decorated entirely with mattress ticking. 1942–52, Truex was president of Parsons School of Design in New York and Paris as William Odom's chosen successor. Among Truex's architecture students were Mrs. Archibald Brown, founder of McMillen, and Albert Hadley; in 1941, Truex arranged McMillen's backing for Jean-Michel Frank's refuge in New York. In 1952, Walter Hoving hired Truex as design director of Tiffany, with the

request that nothing should be sold by the store that the designer himself would not own. Truex brought in the talents of freelance designers for the production of crystal and metalwares; designed the *Bamboo* flatware and *Rock Crystal* candlesticks of the 1950s by Tiffany, and the 1954 *Dionysos* crystal decanter by Baccarat in the shape of a wine bottle with the designer's sobriquet 'Van ordinaire'; designed hardware (door pulls and push plates) and supervised the work of others, including Fernand Léger, Joan Miró, Isamu Noguchi, and others, for Yale and Towne.

▶ Van Day Truex, 'Jean-Michel Frank Remembered,' *Architectural Digest*, Sept.–Oct. 1976. John Esten and Rose Bennett Gilbert, *Manhattan Style*, Boston: Little, Brown, 1990:7–8. Mark Hampton, *The Legendary Decorators of the Twentieth Century*, New York: Doubleday, 1992. Christopher Petkanas, 'Van Day Truex: Master of Understatement,' *House and Garden*, Jan. 1993:72–75,119. Mitchel Owens, 'Van Day Truex' in Mel Byars and Russell Flinchum (eds.), *50 American Designers*, Washington: Preservation, 1994.

tubular steel furniture

▶ Technique and material used in furniture making.

▶ The tubular metal chair, quintessentially associated with avant garde design in the 1920s in Europe, had 19th-century antecedents. Cast-iron furniture arrived with the Industrial Revolution; from 1825, architect Karl Friedrich Schinkel was one of the first to produce tables, benches, and chairs at an iron foundry in Berlin. Iron tubing was used from *c*1830 for bed frames in Britain, though with awkward solutions to the joining of vertical and horizontal elements. 1827–41, British manufacturer Robert Walter Wingfield patented metal furniture of various designs. Cheap iron bedsteads were shown at the 1867 Paris 'Exposition Universelle.' Marble-topped cast-iron tables became ubiquitous fixtures in cafés. French manufacturers welded iron tubes with some success; hollow-tube chairs were produced in Paris as early as 1844, with glue and plaster pumped in for reinforcement. In 1911 in Germany, Bernhard Pankok designed a tubular aluminum chair for the Zeppelin. Whereas Siegfried Giedion claimed that the bent tubular steel chairs developed at the Bauhaus were a totally new concept, Marcel Breuer pointed out that his first 1925 model was suggested by bicycle handlebars, and the 19th-century bentwood chairs of Michael Thonet. Though bent steel had been used in furniture earlier, its resilience making possible sprung cantilever construction, Mart Stam in the Netherlands used gas pipes and plumber's elbow joints in a 1924 prototype now regarded as the first tubular steel cantilever chair. Another Dutchman, J.J.P. Oud, incorporated his own designs for bent tubular steel furniture in the dining room of his 1926–27 Villa Allegonda, Katwijk. Ludwig Mies van der Rohe brought back sketches of the Stam chair to Berlin, where he developed his own elegant 1927 version of the cantilever chair. Like Stam's, it was designed in an office-dining version and arm chair version. The US patent office refused to issue Mies a patent for his chair, referring him to Harry Nolan's patent of 1922, although the Mies model was produced in tubular steel, unlike Nolan's solid steel rods, and was intended for indoor use, in contrast to Nolan's 'lawn chair.' When Mies built a model on American specifications, a patent was granted. Contemporary attribution to designers in manufacturers' catalogs cannot be relied upon. Tubular steel furniture resulted in two famous lawsuits: the 1929 action between Anton Lorenz and manufacturer Thonet, and the lengthy dispute, starting in 1936, between Mies van der Rohe and manufacturer Mauser. The outcome was that only Thonet and Mauser in Germany had rights to the *Freischwinger*; other manufacturers had to pay them royalties until the year 2036, the 50th anniversary of Stam's death. Robert Cromie was the first in Britain to use tubular steel furniture on a large public scale, in the restaurant of the 1929 Capital Cinema in Epsom. In the 1930s in the USA, the bent tubular metal chairs of Gilbert Rohde and Wolfgang Hoffmann were produced by Lloyd, Troy, and others. Mass production of Marcel Breuer's innovative models began in the early 1950s and has continued ever since.

▶ Oud's, Stam's, and Breuer's bent tubular steel chairs were shown in interiors at the 1927 'Weissenhof-Siedlung' exhibition in Stuttgart.

▶ P.R. d'Yvay, 'Le meuble de l'avenir sera-t-il métallique?,' *Les Échos des Industries d'Art*, No. 33, April 1928:32–33, Charlotte Benton translation in *Journal of Design History*, Vol. 3, Nos. 2 and 3, 1990:166–67. Ernö Goldfinger and André Szivessy, 'Meubles,' *L'Organisation Ménagère*, June 1928. Ernö Goldfinger and André Szivessy, 'Meubles: les sièges,' *L'Organisation Ménagère*, Oct. 1928. Marcel Breuer, 'Metallmöbel' in W. Gräff, *Innenräume*, Stuttgart, 1928:133–34. Charlotte Perriand, 'Wood or Metal?,' *The Studio*, Vol. 97, 1929. Siegfried Giedion, *Mechanization Takes Command*, Oxford: Oxford University Press, 1948:490–91. Barbie Campbell-Cole and Tim Benton (eds.), *Tubular Steel Furniture*, London: The Art Book Company, 1979:14,29,53. Cat., *Der Kragstuhl*, Stuhlmusuem Burg Beverungen, Berlin: Alexander, 1986: 135. Sonia Günther (introduction), *Thonet Tubular Steel Furniture Card Catalogue*, Weil am Rhein: Vitra Design Publications, 1989. Otakar Máčel, 'Avant-garde Design and the Law: Litigation over the Cantilever Chair,' *Journal of Design History*, Vol. 3, Nos. 2 and 3, 1990:125–43.

Tümpel, Wolfgang   (1903–1978)

▶ German metalworker; born Bielefeld active Halle, Cologne, and Bielefeld.

▶ Trained as a silversmith; 1922–25, studied Bauhaus, Dessau; Burg Giebichenstein, Halle, under Karl Müller.

▶ In 1927, he produced a silver and ivory tea set for Dr. Erich Bohn, Breslau (now Wroclaw, Poland), on the recommendation of Bauhaus director Walter Gropius. His cylinder table lamp of *c*1927 was produced by Goldschmidt and Schwabe, Berlin. Tümpel was a member of the Gesellschaft für Goldschmiedekunst; in 1927, set up his own workshop in Halle; in 1929, moved to Cologne; in 1934, moved to Bielefeld; from 1951, taught in Hamburg, where he managed the metalworking department of the Landeskunstschule.

▶ His 1924 set of four silver and bronze tea infusers and holder was included in the 'Neue Arbeiten der Bauhaus-Werkstätten' section of *Bauhausbücher 7*. Hand-raised objects shown at 1937 Paris 'Exposition Internationale des Arts et Techniques dans la Vie Moderne.'

▶ Heinz Spielmann, *Wolfgang Tümpel und seine Schüler, Goldschmiedekunst und Design*, Hamburg: Museum für Kunst und Gewerbe, 1978. *Collection Catalog*, Bauhaus Archiv Museum für Gestaltung, Berlin, 1981, plate 187. Lionel Richard, *Encyclopédie du Bauhaus*, Paris: Somogy, 1985:210. Cat., *The Bauhaus: Masters and Students*, New York: Barry Friedman, 1988. Annelies Krekel-Aalberse, *Art Nouveau and Art Déco Silver*, New York: Abrams, 1989:149,260. Cat., *Die Metallwerkstatt am Bauhaus*, Berlin: Bauhaus-Archiv, 1992:278–91,320–21. Katja Schneider, *Burg Giebichenstein*, Weinheim: VCH, Acta Humaniora, 1992:481–82 passim.

Tupper, Earl   (1907–83)

▶ American inventor, chemist, and engineer; born Massachusetts.

▶ Invented by ICI in Britain in 1939, polyethylene became commercially available soon after. In 1942, Tupper stumbled upon a technique for injection molding the material, enabling him to produce air-tight, lightweight, unbreakable, and hygienic kitchen containers. He founded Tupper Plastics in 1942, with its first manufacturing facility in South Grafton, Massachusetts. Tupper's products were sold in vast numbers by housewives who gave 'Tupperware home parties' where neighbors placed orders, shipped later. In 1955, after making plans to move his factory to larger quarters, Tupper abruptly changed his mind and sold his business to Rexall Drug. The firm's plant is today located in Kissimmee, Florida.

▶ Included in the permanent collection of the New York Museum of Modern Art, and in 1983–84 'Design Since 1945' exhibition at the Philadelphia Museum of Art.

▶ 'Tupperware,' *Time*, Sept. 1947:90. Elizabeth Gordon, 'Fine Art for 39¢,' *House Beautiful*, Vol. 89, Oct. 1947:130–31. Cat., Kathryn B. Hiesinger and George H. Marcus III (eds.), *Design Since*

1945, Philadelphia: Philadelphia Museum of Art, 1983:233,VI–19–20. Jeremy Myerson and Sylvia Katz, *Conran Design Guides: Tableware*, London: Conran Octopus, 1990:17–18,49,78.

Turin 6
▶ Italian design group.
▶ The group of designers active in Turin included Gigi Chessa, Carlo Levi, and Enrico Paolucci; for wealthy clients, they produced Rationalist designs in tubular steel.
▶ Penny Sparke, *Design in Italy, 1870 to the Present*, New York: Abbeville, 1988.

Turnbull and Stockdale
▶ British textile firm.
▶ The textile printers, dyers, bleachers, and finishers was founded in 1881, the year Lewis F. Day was appointed artistic director; produced some of the most interesting printed and hand-blocked fabrics of the late 19th and early 20th century; is one of the few hand-block printers in Britain today.
▶ Valerie Mendes, *The Victoria & Albert Museum's Textile Collection, British Textiles from 1900 to 1937*. London: Victoria and Albert Museum, 1992.

Tusquets Blanca, Oscar (1941–)
▶ Spanish painter, architect, and designer; born and active Barcelona.
▶ 1954–60, trained as a painter, architect, and designer, Escuela de Artes y Oficios de la Llotja, Barcelona; 1958–65, studied Escuela Técnica Superior de Arquitectura, Barcelona, under Oriol Bohigas and Federico Correa.
▶ 1961–64, he worked in the studio of architects Frederico Correa and Alfonso Milá; in 1964, (with fellow Escuela de Arquitectura graduates Pep Bonet, Cristian Cirici, and Lluís Clotet) founded Studio PER. In 1972, Studio PER members with others (in particular Xavier Carulla) formed B.d Ediciones de Diseño, which produced many of Tusquets's furniture and product designs and those of others considered too risky by Spanish manufacturers at the time. In 1983, he was one of the 11 architects to design a coffee and tea set by Alessi. Collaborating with Lluís Clotet until 1985, his controversial 1972 Belvedere Regás building was one of the first Post-Modernist structures, widely published, and highly controversial; Tusquets had been strongly influenced by the writings of Robert Venturi. 1975–76 as adjunct professor of the design chairmanship, he was in charge of projects at the Escuela Técnica Superior de Arquitectura; a visiting professor at the Rhode Island School of Design; in 1980, lecturer at Harvard and Yale Universities; in 1984, at University of Southern California and University of California at Berkeley; in 1981, at École Polytechnique Fédérale, Lausanne; in 1983, at Kunstakademie, Düsseldorf; in 1983, at the architecture faculty, Karlsruhe; in 1984, at Institut français d'Architecture; in 1982, 1984, and 1985, at Universidad Internacional Menéndez y Pelayo. He was a partner in the publishing firm Tusquets Editores, which issued the Spanish edition of Venturi's *Learning from Las Vegas* (1972); in 1985, formed a partnership with Carlos Diaz, designing the 1991 pavilion and entrance, Parc de la Villette, Paris, apartment house for Nexus World Kashil, Fukuoka, and 1989 restoration and addition, Palau de la Musica Catalana (by Domènech i Montaner in the early 20th century). His 1986 *Gaulino* chair and stool by Carlos Jané were widely published. Designs included 1980 *Hypóstila* shelving system by B.d Ediciones de Diseño, *Cuc* lamp (with Clotet) of the early 1970s, 1983 *Varius* armchair by Casas Mobilplast, 1989 *Teulada* TV cart, 1987 *Suono/Pico/Proto* carts (with Clotet) by Zanotta, 1988 *Carrito* trolley/reading-stand by Zanotta, *Vaivén* chair-table combination by Casas, *Astrolabio* table, 1980 *Bourgeois* coffee table by B.d Ediciones de Diseño, 1984 *Varius* chair by Casas, 1985 *Talaya* shelving by B.d Ediciones de Diseño, 1986 *Bib-Luz* book lamp by B.d Ediciones de Diseño, 1986 jewelry collection by Cleto Munari, 1986 winged table by Casas, 1987 electronic components cabinet by Artespaña, 1987 *Earth* and *Moon* rugs by

B.d Ediciones de Diseño, 1988 *Sofanco* public seating for Hijo de E.F. Escofet, 1988 rattan-and-metal *Abanica* stacking chair by Driade, 1989 *Vortice* table by Carlos Jané, 1990 *Ali Baba* divan by Casas, and 1991 *Victoria* porcelain dinnerware and stainless-steel flatware range (with wife Roqué) by Follies.
▶ Showed regularly at the Triennale di Milano and at international exhibitions; participated (with Clotet) in the 1980 'Design Forum' in Linz. Awards included 1965, 1972, and 1983 Premio FAD de Interiorismo; 1979 Premio FAD de Arquitectura; 1980 Premio FAD and Premio Nacional de Restauración; 1974, 1979, and 1980 Delta de Oro ADI/FAD de Diseño Industrial; and 1984 Critica and Leon de Oro for best illustrated book at the XII Biennale di Venezia.
▶ *Les Carnets du Design*, Paris: Mad-Cap Productions et APCI, 1986:70–71. *International Design Yearbook*, 1989/1990:228, Nos. 42–45. Officina Alessi, *Tea and Coffee Piazza: 11 Servizi da tè e caffè*, Milan: Crusinallo, 1983. Juli Capella and Quim Larrea, *Designed by Architects in the 1980s*, New York: Rizzoli, 1988. Guy Julier, *New Spanish Design*, New York: Rizzoli, 1991. Marisa Bartolucci, 'Oscar Tusquets,' *Metropolis*, June 1992:37–42,56–57.

Tuttle, Paul (1918–)
▶ American designer; born Springfield, Missouri.
▶ Studied Art Center School, Los Angeles, and Taliesen West, Phoenix, Arizona.
▶ He was associated with Alvin Lustig, Los Angeles; Knoll Associates, New York; Welton Becket and Associates, Los Angeles; architect Thornton Ladd, Pasadena, California; Doetsch und Grether, Basel; Strassle International, Kirchberg (Switzerland); and Atelier International, New York.
▶ Received 1966 Carson-Pirie-Scott award in Chicago, 1980 Pacifica Award (first prize) in Los Angeles, 1980 International Design Products Award from the ASID, 1980 award from IBD in New York, 1982–93 design grant from USA National Endowment for the Arts, 1987 Resource Council Award. Work subject of 1966–67 retrospective at the Pasadena Museum of Art; Trudel House Gallery, Baden; 1973 Santa Barbara Museum of Art, Santa Barbara, California; 1987 University Art Museum, Santa Barbara; 1991 Westmount College, Santa Barbara; and 1992 Anthony Ralph Gallery, New York. Group exhibitions included 1951 'Good Design,' New York Museum of Modern Art; 1955–56 'California Design,' Long Beach Art Museum and M.H. de Young Museum, San Francisco; 1962, 1965, 1968, and 1976 'California Design,' Pasadena Art Museum; 1966 'Design from California,' Carson-Pirie-Scott, Chicago; 1977 'Furniture Designs of Architects, 1900–1976,' Los Angeles County Museum of Art; 1981 'Innovative Furniture in America, 1800 to the Present,' Cooper-Hewitt Museum, New York; and 1986 ' "21" Tools for Relaxing' traveling exhibition organized by the Copenhagen Fair.
▶ 'Young Man on a Mountain,' *House Beautiful*, No. 108, Oct. 1966:62–63. Cat., Eudorah M. Moore, *The Furniture Designs of Paul Tuttle*, Pasadena: Pasadena Art Museum, 1966. Cat., Eudorah M. Moore, *Paul Tuttle, Designer*, Santa Barbara Museum of Art, 1978. Maeve Slavin, 'Paul Tuttle Out in the Open,' *Interiors*, Aug. 1980:52–53,82. David A. Hanks, *Innovative Furniture in America, 1800 to the Present*, New York: Horizon, 1981:119–20. Kay Wettstein Szakall, 'Architekt und Designer Paul Tuttle,' *Ideales Heim*, Jan. 1986:18–23.

Tynell, Helena (1918–)
▶ Finnish glassware designer and ceramicist.
▶ Studied Taideteollinen Korkeakoulu, Helsinki, to 1943.
▶ 1943–46, she designed ceramics for Arabia in Helsinki; 1943–53, lighting for Taito; from 1946, glassware for Riihimäki. From 1957, she worked with Nord in New York.
▶ Work shown at Triennali di Milano from 1954 (X) to 1960 (XII), 1955 'H 55' exhibition in Hälsingborg, 1961 'Finlandia' exhibition in Zürich, Amsterdam, and London.
▶ Cat., David Revere McFadden (ed.), *Scandinavian Modern Design 1880–1980*, New York: Abrams, 1982:272, No. 137.

UAM (Union des Artistes Modernes)

▶ French organization for the promotion of the arts.

▶ The 1925 Paris 'Exposition Internationale des Arts Décoratifs et Industriels Modernes' was realized through the efforts of the Société des Artistes Décorateurs. Enthusiasm for the sumptuous traditional approach had faded by 1927, when Le Corbusier and others broke with the Salon of the Société des Artistes Décorateurs. Robert Mallet-Stevens proposed a secession and organized a Parisian group equivalent of the Deutscher Werkbund; the Union des Artistes Modernes was formed in 1929 by a group of artists, designers, architects, and sculptors, with its first offices at Hélène Henry's apartment, 7 rue des Grands Augustins. Robert Mallet-Stevens was its first president, René Herbst its second. Searching for a kind of universality, the members based their work on stark spareness and an absence of ornamentation, dubbed the 'great nudity.' In addition to Mallet-Stevens, founding members included Jan and Joël Martel, Charlotte Perriand, Jean Puiforcat, Pierre Chareau, Eileen Gray, and André Lurçat. In 1930 at the Musée des Arts Décoratifs, members showed their work at the UAM's first exhibition. Through the years, a large number of artists joined the group; by 1932, membership numbered 60. Its first foreign members included Alfred Gelhorn, Emanuel Josef Margold, Van der Leck, Josep Nicolas, William Penaat, and Gerrit Rietveld. The UAM's first manifesto, published in 1934, was written by Louis Chéronnet and designed by Jean Carlu, as a partial response to Paul Iribe's attacks against Modernism. In 1949, George-Henri Pingusson wrote its second manifesto and the UAM gave birth to the movement Formes Utiles.

▶ Jean-Louis Cohen, 'Mallet-Stevens et l'UAM, Comment frapper les masses,' *AMC*, No. 41. *Union des Artistes Modernes*, Paris: Charles Moreau, 1929. Pierre Cabanne, *Encyclopédie Art Déco*, Paris: Somogy, 1986:239. Arlette Barré-Despond, *UAM*, Paris: Regard, 1986. Cat., *Les années UAM 1929–1958*, Paris: Musée des Arts Décoratifs, 1988.

Ubertazzi, Alessandro (1944–)

▶ Italian industrial designer; born Bibbiena; active Milan.

▶ Studied architecture, Politecnico di Milano, to 1968.

▶ Ubertazzi, Duccio Soffientini, Riccardo Nava, and Giorgio Romani established the studio DA in Milan in 1968. The staff of DA designed the exhibition of the Premio Compasso d'Oro for ADI (Associazione per il Disegno Industriale), of which Ubertazzi was a member. From 1970, he collaborated with the studio DA on clocks and electronic equipment for Italora, consulting on clock design and the ergonomics of precision instruments. In 1975, the DA team designed sailboat fittings for Nemo in Sarsina and Comar in Forlì. Its clients in Italy included Superband, Sordelli, and Svaba.

▶ In association with DA, Ubertazzi participated in international competitions.

▶ *ADI Annual 1976*, Milan: Associazione per il Disegno Industriale, 1976.

Udal'tsova, Nadezhda Andreevna (1886–1961)

▶ Russian artist and designer; born Orel.

▶ 1905–09, studied Institute of Painting, Sculpture, and Architecture, Moscow; 1906, Konstantin Yuon's private art school under Yuon, Ivan Dudin, Nikolai Ulianov; 1906, Kim's private school.

▶ 1911–12, she lived in Paris, where she worked under Jean Metzinger, Henri Le Fauconnier, and André Dunoyer de Segonzac, becoming familiar with the principles of Cubism; in 1913 returning to Moscow, worked in Vladimir Tatlin's studio 'The Tower' and came into contact with Alexei Grishchenko, Liubov' Popova, and Alekandr Vesnin; 1913–14, was interested in the art theory Rayonism, painting some pictures in this style; 1915–16, was briefly attracted to Suprematism but returned to Cubism and subsequently to naturalism; 1917–18, assisted Georgii Yakulov, Valdimir Tatlin, and others with the interior design of the Café Pittoresque in Moscow, worked in Izo NKP, and was a professor at Svomas; from c1920, was associated with Aleksandr Drevin; 1921–34, was a professor at Vkhutemas/Vkhutein.

▶ Work included in 1914 Moscow 'Jack of Diamonds' exhibition and afterwards in many exhibitions in the USSR and abroad, including 1915 'Tramway,' 1915–16 '0–10,' and 1916 'The Store' of the Union of Youth, 1922 Berlin 'Erste Russische Kunstausstellung,' and regularly in the 1930s and 1940s.

▶ M. Miasina (ed.), *Stareishie sovetskie khudozhniki o Srednei Azii i Kavkaze*, Moscow, 1973:220–22. Cat., 'Nadezhda Udaltsova's Cubist Period,' *Women Artists of the Russian Avant-Garde 1910–1930*, Cologne: Galerie Gmurzynska, 1979:288–308. Stephanie Barron and Maurice Tuchman, *The Avant-Garde in Russia, 1910–1930*, Cambridge: MIT, 1980:258. Selim Om Khan Magomedov, *Les Vhutemas*, Paris: Regard, 1990:411–13. Cat., *The Great Utopia: The Russian and Soviet Avant-Garde, 1915–1932*, New York: Guggenheim Musem, 1992.

Ueno, Yukio (1949–)

▶ Japanese glass designer.

▶ Studied Kuwazawa Design Institute, Tokyo, to 1976.

▶ In 1977, Ueno began working for Iwata Glass, Tokyo, becoming section chief of design; was a member of the Japan Traditional Crafts Association.

▶ Work included in 1981 and 1990 'Glass in Japan,' Tokyo; 1983 'Japan Traditional Crafts,' Tokyo; 1985 'New Glass in Japan,' Badisches Landesmuseum, Karlsruhe; and 1991 (V) Triennale of the Japan Glass Art Crafts Association, Heller Gallery, New York.

▶ Cat., *Glass Japan*, New York: Heller Gallery and Japan Glass Art Crafts Association, 1991: No. 39.

Ueshima, Aiko (1957–)

▶ Japanese glass designer.

▶ Studied crafts design, Musashino Art Junior College, Tokyo, to 1977.

▶ Solo exhibitions at 1983 and 1985 Sembikiya Gallery, Tokyo, and 1984–88 at Matsuya Crafts Gallery, Tokyo. Work included in 1986 'Jugend Gestaltet,' Munich; 1987 and 1990 'Glass in Japan,' Tokyo; 1988 'Arte en Vidro,' São Paulo Art Museum; 1991 (V) Triennale of the Japan Glass Art Crafts Association, Heller Gallery, New York. Received President's Prize at 1988 'International Exhibition of Glass Crafts,' Industrial Gallery of Ishikawa Prefecture, Kanazawa.

▶ Cat., *Glass Japan*, New York: Heller Gallery and Japan Glass Art Crafts Association, 1991: No. 39.

UFO
▶ Italian radical group of architects; active in the late 1960s.
▶ UFO was founded in 1967 by Lapo Binazzi, Carlo Bachi, Riccardo Foresi, Patrizia Cammeo, Vittorio Maschietto, and Sandro Gioli (who left soon after) as a radical architecture group in Florence. From the beginning, the group collaborated with writer Umberto Eco. Its theme of town 'happenings' was demonstrated in Florence through interior decoration and shop designs. The group used *papier mâché*, polyurethane, blow-ups, literary quotations, and linguistic configurations. Typical examples of the group's work were the design of the Sherwood Restaurant, Florence, and the 1969 Bamba Issa discotheque, Forte dei Marmi. Members of the group went on to found Global Tools. Three covers of the journal *Domus* featured the ideas of UFO. From 1972, Binazzi was director of the group's activities.
▶ The group documented its urban 'blow-ups' at the 1968 (XIV) Triennale di Milano and participated in the 1971 Youth Biennale in Paris, 1976 International Graphic Biennale in Florence, and 1978 Biennale di Venezia.
▶ Andrea Branzi, *La Casa Calda: Experienze del Nuovo Disegno Italiano*, Milan: Idea Books, 1982.

UGAP (Union des Groupements d'Achats Publics)
▶ French government design association; located Paris.
▶ Formerly SGAM (Service généraux d'achats de mobilier), UGAP was under direction of the ministries of finance and education before 1986; it published an annual catalog of furniture designs for schools, universities, and local institutions. UGAP and APCI (Agence pour la promotion de la création industrielle) sponsor design competitions in which young designers participate. Marc Berthier and Daniel Pigeon won the 1975 'K2000' school-furniture competition, Norbert Scibilla and Serge Guillet won the 1982 office furniture competition, Sacha Kétoff the 1984 lighting competition, and Sylvain Dubuisson the 1992 hospital furniture competition. All winners' work sells through the catalog.

Ulm
See Hochschule für Gestaltung

Umeda, Masanori
▶ Japanese designer.
▶ His 1983 *Orinoco* ceramic vase and 1983 *Parana* ceramic compote were produced by Memphis; he became known for his 1981 *Tawaraya* boxing-ring bed, part of the first Memphis collection and widely published in photographs of Karl Lagerfeld's apartment in Monte Carlo of c1982.
▶ Penny Sparke, *Design in Italy, 1870 to the Present*, New York: Abbeville, 1988. Auction cat., *Memphis: La Collection Karl Lagerfeld*, Monaco: Sotheby's 13 Oct. 1991.

UMS (Utrechtsche Machinale Stoel- en Meubelfabriek)
▶ Dutch furniture firm; located Utrecht.
▶ In 1908, Fritz Loeb inherited a department store in Utrecht that sold furniture and other items, and began to produce his own furniture. In 1913, Loeb's UMS workshop produced furniture for wholesalers. Cabinetmaker D.L. Braakman was hired in 1915 as manager responsible for technical operations. The wide range and high quality of the firm's products made it one of the most important in the Netherlands by the 1920s. In c1938, the factory began to sell directly to the public. Its Modern furniture models from c1923 were not particularly successful, and UMS returned to more saleable historicist suites. Modern pieces were shown again at the 1930 Jaarbeurs (industries fair), with sober models probably designed by W. Barnasconi. Working with the HOPMI bicycle firm in Utrecht, UMS offered demountable bent tubular steel furniture designed by H.F. Mertens; it did not sell well and was transferred to HOPMI in 1934. Interior architect A.K. Grimmon of Amsterdam also designed metal furniture for UMS; its stand at Jaarbeurs included his varnished oak cabinets. Barnasconi, Grimmon, and Mertens were freelance designers. In 1955, the firm was merged, becoming UMS Pastoe, producing Cees Braakman's 1954 *SM 01* chair with its biomorphic seat and back supported by spindly bent iron legs. Succeeding his father, C. Braakman designed contemporary serially-produced furniture. From the end of the 1970s, the firm worked with freelance designers.
▶ From 1917, UMS showed furniture at the Jaarbeurs fairs.
▶ *Industry and Design in the Netherlands, 1850/1950*, Amsterdam: Stedelijk Museum, 1985:276–78.

Unger
▶ American silversmiths and jewelers; located Newark, New Jersey.
▶ The firm was founded in 1872 in Newark, New Jersey, by brothers Herman, Eugene, and Frederick Unger. In 1903, patents were taken out by Philomen Dickinson, chief designer and brother-in-law of Eugene Unger, for Art Nouveau designs applied to various silver articles, including clasps, brooches, buckles, and pendants. From 1904, Unger produced a large amount of jewelry in an imitation *repoussé* finish. Incorporating flowers, leaves, and idealized female heads, the inexpensive jewelry mimicked French Art Nouveau, From 1900, Unger's Art Nouveau range included vases, dishes, desk and toilet sets, and other small objects. Eugene Unger died in 1909; production of Art Nouveau silver ceased a year later. Continuing with its silverwares until 1914, the firm turned to the production of airplane parts and components during World War I.
▶ Charlotte Gere, *American and European Jewelry 1830–1914*, New York: Crown, 1975:225. Annelies Krekel-Aalberse, *Art Nouveau and Art Déco Silver*, New York: Abrams, 1989:98,101,260.

Ungerer, Alfons (1884–1961)
▶ German silversmith; active Dresden, Berlin, and Pforzheim.
▶ Trained with Theodor Heiden, Munich; studied Kunstgewerbeschule, Pforzheim and Dresden.
▶ He set up his own workshop in Berlin in 1910; from 1918, taught at Kunstgewerbeschule, Pforzheim.
▶ Annelies Krekel-Aalberse, *Art Nouveau and Art Déco Silver*, New York: Abrams, 1989:260.

Ungers, Oswald Mathias (1926–)
▶ German architect and designer; born Kaiseresch, Eifel.
▶ Studied architecture, Technische Hochschule, Karlsruhe, under Egon Eiermann, to 1950.
▶ His designs were based on geommetric forms and variations on the square. His work in the decorative arts included furniture for Sawaya & Moroni, Italy, and 1988 rugs for the Dialog collection of Vorwerk, Germany. His architecture included 1979–84 Deutsches Architekturmuseum, Frankfurt; 1980–84 Landesbibliothek, Karlsruhe; Ozeanographisches Institut, Bremerhaven; 'Tor' highrise, Frankfurt Fair; and 1986 City-West plan for Frankfurt.
▶ Participated in numerous architecture exhibitions including 1957 Biennale di São Paulo; 1976 Rationalist architecture exhibition, London; 1976 'Man-trans-Forms' exhibition, Cooper-Hewitt Museum, New York; and 1978 and 1980 Biennali di Venezia. His 'Cabinet Tower' was shown at the 1985 Triennale di Milano.
▶ *Le Affinità Elettive*, Milan: Electa, 1985. Auction cat., *Asta di Modernariato 1900–1986, Auction 'Modernariato,'* Milan: Semenzato Nuova Geri, 8 Oct. 1986: lots 99–100. Volker Fischer, *Bodenreform: Teppichboden von Künstlern und Architekten*, Berlin: Ernst und Sohn, 1989.

UNIFA (Union Nationale des Industries français)
▶ French government organization.
▶ UNIFA was set up in the 1960s to promote the French furniture industry through Salons, including those of the Société des Artistes Décorateurs (SAD). In 1966, it established CREAC (Centre de Recherches Esthétiques de l'Ameublement Contemporain) to assist young designers and sponsor open competitions such as 1965 'Premiers Pas' at the Salon of SAD and 1967–69 and 1972 'Révélation'; organized exhibitions in France and abroad for contemporary French furniture; in 1979, participated with the ministry of industry in the formation of VIA.

Unimark
See Vignelli, Massimo

Union des Artistes Modernes
See UAM

Union Porcelain Works
▶ American ceramics manufacturer; located Greenpoint, New York.
▶ In 1850, William Boch and Brothers founded a factory on Eckford Street in Greenpoint (now the Greenpoint section of Brooklyn), New York, where soft-paste porcelain was produced. The firm was also known as the Empire Porcelain Works and Union Porcelain Works. In 1861, a major interest in the firm was acquired by Thomas Carll Smith (1851–?), a builder, architect, and native of Bridgehampton, New York, on Long Island. In 1862, he purchased the balance of the firm's shares; in 1863, traveled to Europe and visited the factories of Staffordshire and Sèvres; began producing hard-paste porcelain (porcelain with a kaolinic body); became the first manufacturer to produce true porcelain in the USA, encouraged by high tariffs on imported ceramics. Selling hard porcelain by 1868, Smith's quartz and feldspar came from a quarry in Branchfield, Connecticut, and kaolin from Pennsylvania. He was the first American to produce vessels with an underglaze decoration on a body of hard porcelain. 1864–69, the firm was named Thomas C. Smith and Co, 300 Eckford Street, although still known as the Union Porcelain Works. Smith's financial partner was John W. Mersereau. In 1869 when son Charles H.L. Smith joined the firm, it was renamed Thomas C. Smith and Son. Its wares were primarily white hotel china, hardware, electrical insulators, and tiles. In 1874, Karl L.H. Mueller joined the firm as chief designer, inaugurating genre-type figure porcelain and portrait medallions of famous Americans, including George Washington, Noah Webster, and Samuel Morse. The firm was best known for its large urn-shaped 1876 *Century Vase*, produced under Mueller's direction; it was applied with a relief of George Washington, panels illustrating events in American history, and emblems representing industry. Smith offered amateur artists studio space at the factory; it closed in 1922.
▶ *Century Vase* shown at 1876 Philadelphia 'Centennial Exposition'; other works in 1878 loan exhibition benefiting New York Society of Decorative Art.
▶ Edwin AtLee Barber, *The Pottery and Porcelain of the United States*, New York, 1909:162–64,252–58,276,406. Marvin D. Schwartz and Richard Wolfe, *A History of American Art Porcelain*, New York, 1967:43, plates 24–30,32–34,36. Cat., *Nineteenth-Century America: Furniture and Other Decorative Arts*, 1970: Nos. 196,199–201,203–04,240. Cat., *The Quest for Unity: American Art Between World's Fairs, 1876–1893*, 1983:80–81, 209. Doreen Bolger Burke et al., *In Pursuit of Beauty: Americans and the Aesthetic Movement*, New York: Metropolitan Museum of Art and Rizzoli, 1987:475–76.

United Glass Bottle Manufacturers (UGBM)
▶ British glassware manufacturer.
▶ UGBM were makers of glass at the Ravenhead and Sherdley glassworks; produced new ranges of domestic table glass from 1945. A lecturer in the department of industrial glass at the Royal College of Art in London, A.H. Williamson was hired to design certain models; previously, new products had been designed by managers. Williamson advised the technical and production staff at UGBM and its distributors, Johnsen and Jorgensen Flint Glass.
▶ Frederick Cooke, *Glass: Twentieth-Century Design*, New York: Dutton, 1986:76.

University City Pottery
▶ American ceramics factory; located University City, Missouri.
▶ The American Women's League, established in Missouri in 1907, provided members with a program of correspondence courses from the People's University. By 1901, there were 50,000 enrollments. A few of the best students were invited to study at University City, near St. Louis, Missouri, where the faculty was located. Founder of the League and the People's University Edward G. Lewis had an interest in art, and the Art Institute in University City was the most developed of the departments. Painting, metal and leatherwork, handicrafts, and ceramics courses were offered. Familiar with Taxile Doat's technical book *Grand Feu Ceramics*, Lewis invited Doat in 1909 to become director of the School of Ceramic Art. Doat arrived with assistants Eugène Labarrière and Émile Diffloth, who set up the first kiln the next year. The distinguished faculty of the school included Frederick Rhead, Frank J. Fuhrmann, Kathryn E. Cherry, Edward Dahlquist, Labarrière, Diffloth, and Adelaide Alsop Robineau. They taught about 30 students by correspondence and about 10 at University City. Using native clays, ceramics were developed there based on designs rendered earlier by Doat at Sèvres; the range of glazes included matt, gloss, crystalline, Oriental crackle, and alligator skin. Rhead and the Robineaus left in 1911, along with Diffloth and Labarrière. Concentrating on *flambé*, crystalline, and metallic glazes, Doat stayed on with ceramic chemist William V. Bragdon (subsequently founder of California Faience) until production was discontinued in 1915, when Doat returned to France. Lewis sent the pottery equipment of University City to Atascadero, with the intention of establishing the Art Institute there; these plans were never realized.
▶ The school's work received a grand prize at 1900 Turin 'Esposizione Internazionale dell'Arte Decorativa Moderna.'
▶ William P. Jervis, 'Taxile Doat,' *Keramic Studio*, No. 4, July 1902:54–55. M.P. Verneuil, 'Taxile Doat, Céramiste,' *Art et Décoration*, No. 16, Sept. 1904:77–86. Taxile Doat, *Grand Feu Ceramics*, Syracuse: Keramic Studio, 1905. Yvonne Brunhammer et al., *Art Nouveau Belgium, France*, Houston: Rice University, 1976. *American Art Pottery*, New York: Cooper-Hewitt Museum, 1987:134.

Uno A Erre
▶ Italian jeweler.
▶ Leopoldo Gori and Carlo Zucchi established the jewelry firm of Gori e Zucchi in 1926, but did not introduce their own wares until 1934. Its craftspeople mastered industrial production, issuing fine jewelry and medals on a large scale. The firm is known today as Uno A Erre.
▶ Melissa Gabardi, *Les Bijoux des Années 50*, Paris: Amateur, 1987.

Unovis (Posnovis)
▶ Russian art institution.
▶ Active 1919–23, Unovis (Utverditeli novogo iskussetvo; Affirmers of the New Art), also known as Posnovis earlier on, was the artistic group in Vitebsk founded and led by Kazimir Malevich.
▶ Cat., *Kunst und Revolution: Russische und Sowjetische Kunst 1910–1932*, Vienna: Österreichisches Museum für angewandte Kunst, 1988. Cat., *The Great Utopia: The Russian and Soviet Avant-Garde, 1915–1932*, New York: Guggenheim Museum, 1992.

Urban, Joseph (1872–1933)
▶ Austrian designer, painter, sculptor, architect, and interior and scenic designer; born Vienna; active Vienna and USA.
▶ 1890–93, studied Akademie der bildenden Künste under Karl von Hasenaurer; subsequently, Polytechnicum, both Vienna.
▶ A member of the Wiener Werkstätte, Urban designed bridges, villas, and the interiors of castles. He and brother-in-law Heinrich Lefler designed a room at the 1897 winter exhibition at the Österreichisches Museum für Kunst und Industrie. Though he employed Secession motifs, he was clearly crafts oriented. His work in the Austrian pavilion at the 1904 St. Louis 'Louisiana Purchase Exposition' and his talent for stage design brought him many commissions for theaters, from Budapest to Paris. He designed architectural features at the 1908 60th anniversary pageant in Vienna of Emperor Franz Josef 's coronation. In the last decade of the 19th century, Urban's illustrations adopted an English style, showing the influence of Aubrey Beardsley's work, as in *Rolands Knappen* by Johann Musäus (c1897), and in 'Playing Card.' In 1900, he

and Lefler founded the Künstlerbund Hagen (better known as the Hagenbund). He settled in the USA in 1911, and became scenic designer for the short-lived Boston Opera Company, designing 34 productions. In New York, he became house designer for Florenz Ziegfeld's *Follies* (12 editions) and created spectacular yet tasteful productions that presaged and influenced Hollywood film designs and other Ziegfeld productions. From 1917, he was artistic director of the Metropolitan Opera, New York, designing 55 productions. He designed the interior of the nightclub 1931 Park Avenue Club, New York, and sets for 18 Broadway shows. The first art director in American films to use Modern décors, Urban designed 25 film sets for William Randolph Hearst's Cosmopolitan Productions, including *Enchantment* (1921), followed by *Photoplay* and *The Young Diana* (1922), *Murder at the Vanities* (1934), and *Fashions of 1934* (1934); in most of them his Wiener Werkstätte background was in evidence. The Hearst film *When Knighthood Was in Flower* (1922), on which Urban worked, cost $1,500,000, an enormous sum at the time. His creations anticipated the best of 1920s design and presaged the Art Déco style of the 1930s, although immobile cameras and flat direction often undermined his efforts. In 1921, Urban founded Wiener Werkstätte of America, New York, which soon closed due to lack of sales; in 1925, he returned to architecture. His buildings included the 1927 Ziegfeld Theatre (with Thomas W. Lamb), 1927 Hearst International Building, and 1929–30 New School for Social Research (the first International Style building in the USA) and its auditorium (named Tishman Auditorium, restored 1993), all in New York, and the 1926 Mar-a-Lago house for Marjorie Merriweather Post (today owned by Donald J. Trump), Palm Beach, Florida.

▶ Interiors installed at Austrian pavilion at 1904 St. Louis 'Louisiana Purchase Exposition' (gold medal); conservatory and man's den settings at 1929 (XI) 'The Architect and the Industrial Arts: An Exhibition of Contemporary American Design,' New York Metropolitan Museum of Art; color-coded orientation system for 1933 Chicago 'Century of Progress.' Work was subject of 1987 retrospective, Cooper-Hewitt Museum, New York.

▶ Günther Feuerstein, *Vienna—Present and Past: Arts and Crafts—Applied Art—Design*, Vienna: Jugend und Volk, 1976:23,35,81. Howard Mandelbaum and Eric Myers, *Screen Deco: A Celebration of High Style in Hollywood*, New York: St. Martin's, 1985. John Morris Dixon, *Progressive Architecture*, January 1988:28–29. Robert Waissenberger, *Vienna 1890–1920*, Secaucus, NJ: Wellfleet 1984:136,148,149,191,270. Suzanne Stephens, 'Eggs to Igloos, at the New School,' *The New York Times*, 1 Oct. 1992:C3. Randolph Carter and Robert Reed Cole, *Joseph Urban: Architecture/Theatre/Opera/Film*, New York: Abbeville, 1992. Mary Beth Betts, 'Joseph Urban' in Mel Byars and Russell Flinchum (eds.), *50 American Designers*, Washington: Preservation, 1994.

Urbinati, Carlo   (1949–)

▶ Italian industrial designer; born and active Rome.
▶ Urbinati began his professional career in 1970. His clients for lighting, domestic accessories, and sanitary fittings included Teuco Guzzini, Fratelli Guzzini, Ellisse, Tulli Zuccari, Incom Sud, and Sis. He became a member of ADI (Associazione per il Disegno Industriale).
▶ *ADI Annual 1976*, Milan: Associazione per il Disegno Industriale, 1976.

Ústav Bytové a Oděvní Kultury (ÚBOK)
(Institute of Housing and Clothing Culture)

▶ Czechoslovak association; located Prague.
▶ ÚBOK was originally founded in 1947 as Textilní tvorba (Textile Art); was later active in interior design and fashion; attempted to improve the aesthetics of industrial design and to involve architects and artists in the process of industrial production; in the 1950s–60s, was active in Czechoslovakia's participation in exhibitions including 1958 'Exposition Universelle et Inter-nationale de Bruxelles (Expo '58)' and 1961 (XII) Triennale di Milano; it included some of the best glass designers; organized lectures and seminars; published catalogs. Pavel Hlava, Adolf Matura, Jiří Šuhájek, Václav Dolejš, and Václav Šerák worked in the ceramics department, and Jindřich Vašut, Jiří Mrásekz, Zora Smetanová, Jaroslava Hrušková, and Olga Karlíková designed textiles. ÚBOK's involvement with industry was not successful, and its members were unwilling or unable to realize high-quality design in quantity.

Utility furniture

▶ British program of furniture production; active 1943–52.
▶ Furniture manufacture in Britain during World War II was subject to severe restrictions. By 1941, timber shortages were acute, while damage from bombing boosted demand for furniture, raising prices; the government announced the establishment of a program to produce 'Standard Emergency Furniture' and registered the utility mark 'CC41,' which had to appear on every piece of new furniture. A system for rationing furniture was devised, and the President of the Board of Trade appointed a committee headed by Charles Tennyson, vice-president of the Council for Art and Industry and chair of the board of governors of the National Register of Art and Design. Members of the Utility Furniture Advisory Committee included Elizabeth Denby, John Gloag, W. Johnstone, the Reverend Charles Jenkinson, Herman Lebus, Gordon Russell, V. Welsford, and E. Winborn. The group was to advise Tennyson 'on specifications for the production of utility furniture of good sound construction in simple but agreeable designs, for sale at reasonable prices, having due regard to the necessity for the maximum economy of raw materials and labor.' The committee hired designers Edwin Clinch and H.T. Cutler of High Wycombe to design the first series, the *Cotswold* collection (about 30 pieces); Gordon Russell had final approval of their designs. Introduced in 1943 through the first Utility catalog and arriving in shops early that year, the *Cotswold* collection, too austere for popular tastes, was manufactured by firms in all sectors of the furniture trade. The Utility Furniture Advisory Panel dictated the composition employed and the nature of the designs produced. The *Chiltern* collection, introduced in 1945, was designed to be produced by both hand and machine, because all the best-tooled firms had been transferred to the war effort; *Chiltern*, combining traditional joinery and contemporary Swedish influence, was produced in more expensive veneered and paneled models in a broader range. The *Cockaigne* (later called *Cheviot*) range was never put into production. New furniture was available only to newlyweds and people whose furniture had been destroyed by bombing; others had to choose from a restricted range or purchase second hand. Booth and Ledeboer produced other designs made by a team of firms. Enid Marx designed most of the Utility furniture, furnishings, and fabrics sold in Britain in the late war years and through the early postwar period, working with very limited raw materials; until 1946, there were only four colors available in two types of cotton yarn; patterns were selvage pieced. In 1944, two radio models were introduced using minimum labor and materials. Regulations controlling the appearance of Utility furniture were rescinded in 1948, though price regulation of furniture made to the Board of Trade's general specification remained. The Utility program ended in 1953, when there were about 2,500 firms making the tax-free furniture.

▶ Subject of 1974 'CC41: Utility Furniture and Fashion' exhibition, Geffrye Museum, London. *Cotswold* pieces included in 1984 'Design Since 1945' exhibition, Philadelphia Museum of Art.

▶ Michael Farr, *Design in British Industry: A Mid-Century Survey*, London: Cambridge, 1955. Cat., *CC41: Utility Furniture and Fashion*, London: Geffrye Museum, 1974. 'Utility CC41,' *Design*, No. 309, Sept. 1974:62–71. Cat., Kathryn B. Hiesinger and George H. Marcus III (eds.), *Design Since 1945*, Philadelphia: Philadelphia Museum of Art, 1983:233,III–86. 'The Radio,' London: Design Museum, 1989. Harriet Dover, *Home Front Furniture: British Utility Design 1941–1951*, Hampshire: Scolar Press, 1991.

Utzon, Jørn (1918–)

▶ Danish architect, urban planner, and industrial designer; born Copenhagen.

▶ 1937–42, studied Det Kongelige Danske Kunstakademi, Copenhagen, under Kay Fisker and Steen Eiler Rasmussen.

▶ In the mid-1940s for three years, he worked in the office of Gunnar Asplundin Stockholm; in 1947, opened his own offices in Zürich and Ålsgårde; early on, showed a fondness for the organic architecture of Frank Lloyd Wright and Alvar Aalto; won major international architectural competitions, including the Sydney Opera House (first prize in 1956) and Zürich State Theater; produced furniture designs in the late 1960s and early 1970s, made by Fritz Hansen of Allerod. The 1967 furniture line for Hansen was based on a system of component arcs locking at 45-degree angles.

▶ Received 1947 gold medal of the Royal Academy in Copenhagen, 1947 Bissen prize, 1949 Zacharia Jacobsen Award, 1957 Eckersberg Medal, 1965 German Institute of Architects Medal, 1967 C.F. Hansen Medal, 1970 Danish Furniture Prize (for *8108* chair), 1970 recognition from the American Institute of Architects, 1978 gold medal from the Royal Institute of British Architects, Thorvaldsen Medal. Hansen furniture collection first shown at 1968 Cologne International Furniture Exhibition; his chairs in 1968 'Les Assises du siège contemporain' at the Paris Musée des Arts Décoratifs; 1970 'Modern Chairs, 1918–1970' exhibition, the Whitechapel Gallery in London.

▶ Cat., *Les Assises du siège contemporain*, Paris: Musée des Arts Décoratifs, 1968. Cat., *Modern Chairs 1918–1970*, London: Lund Humphries, 1971. Philip Drew, *The Third Generation: the changing meaning of architecture*, New York, 1972. Frederik Sieck, *Nutidig Dansk Møbeldesign:—en kortfattet illustreret beskrivelse*, Copenhagen: Bondo Gravesen; 1990 Busck edition in English.

V

V mire iskusstv (mir ikusstva)
See World of Art, The

Vaccarone, Alberto (1939–)
▶ Italian architect and designer; born Casale Monterrato; active Turin.
▶ He began his professional career in 1970, as an architect, town planner, and industrial designer, collaborating with architect Giuseppe Raimondi in the studio A.BA.CO; designed 1973 shelving unit for Tarzia and 1975 glassware for Cristal Art; became a member of ADI (Associazione per il Disegno Industriale).
▶ *ADI Annual 1976*, Milan: Associazione per il Disegno Industriale, 1976.

Vaghi, Luigi (1938–)
▶ Italian designer; born Carimate; active Cantù.
▶ He began his professional career in 1962; designed furniture for Former, Cattadori, Gasparello, and Gilberto Cassina; became a member of ADI (Associazione per il Disegno Industriale).
▶ *ADI Annual 1976*, Milan: Associazione per il Disegno Industriale, 1976.

Vágó, Pierre (1910–)
▶ Hungarian architect and designer.
▶ Studied École Spéciale d'Architecture, Paris.
▶ He settled in France in 1928, where he was editor-in-chief on three issues of the review *L'Architecture d'aujourd'hui*; after World War II, was active in reviving the journal and set up his own architecture office; in 1948, he left the journal; in 1946, became a member of UAM (Union des Artistes Modernes); built 1955–58 Basilica de Saint-Pie X (with architect Pierre Pinsard and engineer Eugène Freysinnet) in Lourdes.
▶ His 1934 dining room with aluminum furniture in his all-metal house was installed at the 1935 Paris Salon d'Habitation.
▶ 'La Maison Métallique Présentée à l'Exposition de l'Habitation,' *L'Architecture d'aujourd'hui*, No. 1, Feb. 1934. 'Les Nouveaux Aménagements de Lourdes,' *L'Architecture d'aujourd'hui*, No. 71, 1957. Cat., *Les années UAM 1929–1958*, Paris: Musée des Arts Décoratifs, 1988:254.

Val Saint Lambert, Verreries et Establissements du
▶ Belgian glass factory; located near Liège.
▶ The firm was established in 1826 in a former Cistercian abbey near Liège. Its original workers came from the old Vonèche factory. It soon took over the glassworks at Vaux-sous-Chèvremont, Herbatte, and Mariemont; in 1861, opened a shop in London. In a factory founded by Léon Ledru, its most creative period was 1880–1914, when its huge and varied output included the glass designs of Henry van de Velde, Philippe Wolfers, Léon Ledru, Dieudonné Masson, Camille Renard-Steinbach, and Gustave Serrurier-Bovy, including pieces with etched decorations by brothers Desiré and Henri Muller, students of Gallé. Horta's reflecting crystal plates for the 1903 Hôtel Solvay chandeliers, and possibly the shades for Serrurier-Bovy's lamps, were made by Val Saint Lambert. In 1906, the Muller brothers worked there to teach the glassmakers the 'fluogravure' technique. In the 1980s, the firm renewed its tradition of working with contemporary designers, commissioning Martin Szekeley.
▶ Work shown at 1835 Brussels 'Exposition de l'Industrie.'
▶ G.P. Woeckel, *Jugendstilsammlung*, Kassel: Staatliche Kunstsammlungen, 1968. H. Hilschenz, *Das Glas des Jugendstils*, Munich: 1973:69–76. Jacob Philippe, *Le Val St Lambert*, Liège: Halbert, 1974. Yvonne Brunhammer et al., *Art Nouveau Belgium, France*, Houston: Rice University, 1976. Alastair Duncan, *Art Nouveau and Art Déco Lighting*, New York: Simon and Schuster, 1978:52–53.

Valabrega, Vittorio (1861–1952)
▶ Italian furniture manufacturer; active Turin.
▶ Valabrega and his brother established a furniture manufacturing firm in the late 19th century, producing historicist styles. When home decoration became popular in the 1890s, the firm grew, with more than 50 craftsmen specializing in woodworking and upholstery; by 1898, began to turn towards the prevailing popular *stile floreale*; became known for understated pieces, pointing the way in Italy towards Modern furniture design.
▶ Showed at 1884 Turin exhibition (bronze medal), 1898 Turin exhibition (*stile floreale* small salon with wrought-iron decoration), 1900 Paris 'Exposition Universelle' (gold medal), and 1902 Turin 'Esposizione Internazionale d'Arte Decorativa Moderna' (silver medal).
▶ Cat., Gabriel P. Weisberg, *Stile Floreale: The Cult of Nature in Italian Design*, Miami: The Wolfsonian Foundation, 1988.

Valboni, Luciano (1948–)
▶ Italian industrial designer; born Florence; active Bergamo.
▶ Valboni began his professional career in 1970, became a designer at Zanussi and member of ADI (Associazione per il Disegno Industriale).
▶ *ADI Annual 1976*, Milan: Associazione per il Disegno Industriale, 1976.

Valentien, Anna Marie (b. Anna Marie Bookprinter 1862–1950) and **Albert R. Valentien** (1847–1925)
▶ American ceramicists; born Cincinnati; wife and husband.
▶ Anna Marie Valentien studied Cincinnati Art Academy and under Auguste Rodin in Paris.
▶ Anna Marie Bookprinter worked in the decorating department at the Rookwood Pottery, where Albert Valentien was in charge. Unable to incorporate sculptural form into Rookwood production, the Valentiens left the firm in 1905 but stayed in Cincinnati until 1907, when Albert received a commission from Ellen Scripps to paint California's wild flowers; they left for San Diego, where they set up Valentien Pottery with funding from local banker J.W. Sefton Jr., who had the pottery designed in 1911 by Irving Gill. The pottery was probably in operation 1911–14.
▶ Yvonne Brunhammer et al., *Art Nouveau Belgium, France*, Houston: Rice University, 1976. Paul Evans in Timothy J. Andersen et al., *California Design 1910*, Salt Lake City: Peregrine Smith, 1980:77.

Valeur, Torben (1920–)

▶ Danish architect and furniture designer.
▶ Studied architecture, Det Kongelige Danske Kunstakademi, Copenhagen, to 1944.
▶ 1958–64, he taught at Det Kongelige Danske Kunstakademi; in 1960, set up a design studio with Henning Jensen; from 1963, was associated with Den Permanente; designed furniture produced by Magnus Olesen.
▶ Participated (with Hanne Valeur) in 1957 (XI) Triennale di Milano; 1962 'Unga nordiska formgivare,' Röhsska Konstslöjdmuseet, Gothenburg, 1962 'Moderne Dänische Wohnkultur,' Vienna.
▶ Received 1963 Eckersberg Medal; became Design Associate, American Institute of Interior Design, 1963.
▶ Frederik Sieck, *Nutidig Dansk Møbeldesign:— en kortfattet illustreret beskrivelse*, Copenhagen: Bondo Gravesen; 1990 Busck edition in English.

Valle, Gino (1923–)

▶ Italian architect, designer, and town planner; born Udine.
▶ Studied Instituto Universitario di Architettura, Venice, to 1948; 1951, Harvard Graduate School of Design, Cambridge, Massachusetts.
▶ He began working in 1948 in the architect's office of his father Provino Valle in Udine. Subsequently, Gino and brother Nani Valle took over the firm. From 1977, he was professor at the Instituto Universitario di Architettura, Venice. He collaborated on numerous industrial and commercial buildings in northern Italy, including Udine, and the 1961 Zanussi administration building, Pordenone. His buildings related both to Brutalism and Rationalism. His 1965–66 double house in Udine reflected regional styles. He was best known for his automated schedule boards in train stations and airports, produced by Solari; his systems used modular flaps, as, on a more modest scale, did his domestic table clocks. In the 1980s, Valle (with others) designed IBM buildings, La Défense, Paris.
▶ Received 1956 (*Cifa 5* clock), 1953 (indicator board), 1956, and 1963 Compasso d'Oro. Work subject of one-person 1979 'Gino Valle: Architetto 1950–1978' exhibition, Padiglione d'Arte Contemporanea di Milano. Cylindrical table clock included in 1984 'Design Since 1945' exhibition, Philadelphia Museum of Art.
▶ 'Fewer Queues, Fewer Questions,' *Design*, No. 215, Nov. 1966:66. 'Gino Valle,' *Zodiac*, No. 20, 1970:82–115. Jocelyn de Noblet, *Design*, Paris, 1974:347, Nos. 291–93. *Gino Valle 1950–1978*, Milan: Padiglione d'Arte Contemporanea di Milano, 1979. G. Polin, 'Nuove abitazioni popolari a Venezia,' *Casabella 46*, No. 478, 1982:50–61. Vittorio Gregotti, *Il disegno del prodotto industriale*, Milan, 1982:342–43. P.-A. Croset, 'Centro direzionale a Pordenone,' *Casabella 47*, No. 485, 1983:60–61. S. Marpillero, 'Grattacielo a metà. Gino Valle: uffici della Banca Commerciale Italiana a Manhattan,' *Lotus International*, No. 37, 1983:96–119. Cat., Kathryn B. Hiesinger and George H. Marcus III (eds.), *Design Since 1945*, Philadelphia: Philadelphia Museum of Art, 1983: 223,I–48. P.-A. Croset and G. Polin, 'IBM Distribution Center a Basiano,' *Casabella 49*, No. 500, 1984:52–63. P.-A. Croset, 'Gino Valle: Edifico per uffici alla Défense a Parigi,' *Casabella 49*, No. 519, 1985:4–15. Gino Valle, 'Una conversazione con Gino Valle,' *Casabella 49*, No. 519, 1985:16–17.

Vallien, Bertil (1936–)

▶ Swedish designer; born Stockholm; husband of Ulrica Hydman.
▶ 1956–61, studied Konstfackskolan and Tekniska Skolan, Stockholm; 1961–63, studied and worked in the USA and Mexico on Royal Scholarship.
▶ From 1963, Vallien was a designer at Kosta Boda Glassworks, Åfors factory; from 1963, was active in own workshop in Åfors; from 1967–84, was head of glass department at Konstfackskolan and Tekniska Skolan, Stockholm; from 1974, lectured and taught at art conferences and art schools internationally and was artist-in-residence at Rhode Island School of Design, Providence, Rhode

Island; from 1980, was visiting professor, at Pilchuk Glass Center, Stanwood, Washington.
▶ Work shown in Los Angeles, California, New York, Montreal, Sydney, Amsterdam, Denmark, and Sweden.
▶ Jennifer Hawkins Opie, *Scandinavia: Ceramics and Glass in the Twentieth Century*, New York: Rizzoli, 1989.

Valorisation de l'Innovation dans l'Ameublement

See VIA.

Valsecchi, Gastone Beppe (1930–)

▶ Italian designer; born Falconara Marittima; active Calolziocorte.
▶ He began his professional career in 1955 designing furniture and furnishings. Clients in Italy included Nespoli, Galbiati, Vom, and Miù. His *Programma M 186* range of furniture was produced by Composit in Montecchio. He became a member of ADI (Associazione per il Disegno Industriale).
▶ *ADI Annual 1976*, Milan: Associazione per il Disegno Industriale, 1976.

Van Alen, William (1883–1954)

▶ American architect; born Brooklyn, New York; active New York.
▶ Studied Pratt Institute, Brooklyn; 1908, École des Beaux-Arts, Paris, under Victor-A.-F. Laloux.
▶ He was office boy in the architecture office of Clarence True in New York; worked for architecture firms Copeland and Dole, and Clinton and Russell; became partner of H. Craig Severance and known for distinctive multi-storey commercial buildings that abandoned traditional base, shaft, and capital arrangement; from *c*1925, he practiced alone. His architecture included 1926 Child's Restaurant Building, 1928 Reynolds Building, both in New York. Van Alen was best known for his 1928–31 Chrysler Building, 42nd Street and Lexington Avenue, New York. Distinctive features included the decorative brickwork frieze of automobile wheels and radiator caps, and stainless-steel gargoyles at the 31st floor level, with other notable work on the 63rd floor façade. The decoration was derived from the 1929 Chrysler automobile hood ornamentation. The building's lobby was one of the most striking examples of Art Déco in the USA and incorporated dramatic murals, beige and red marble walls, and other walls and elevator doors inlaid with African woods based on floral abstraction.
▶ F.S. Swales, 'Draftsmanship and Architecture V: Exemplified by the Work of William Van Alen,' *Pencil Points*, Vol. 10:514–26. Jonathan M. Woodham, *Twentieth-Century Ornament*, New York: Rizzoli, 1990:61–62,95.

Van Briggle, Artus (1869–1904)

▶ American studio potter; born Felicity, Ohio.
▶ Studied painting, Art Academy, Cincinnati, under Frank Duveneck; 1893–96, easel and mural painting, Académie Julian, and sculpture and clay modeling, École des Beaux-Arts, Paris.
▶ When Avon Pottery closed in 1887, Maria Storer hired Van Briggle to work at Rookwood Pottery, where he became senior decorator by 1891. Concurrently, he had his own studio on Mt. Adams; when not at Rookwood, he was an easel painter. In 1893, Rookwood paid for him to study in Paris for three years. He became interested in Chinese glazes, particularly Ming dynasty matt glazes which he researched after returning to Rookwood in 1896. He produced a few vases in his matt glazes at Rookwood; suffering from tuberculosis and forced to live in a more healthful climate, he set up his own pottery in 1899 in Colorado Springs, Colorado, with financial support from Storer; began experimenting with local clays in a small kiln at Colorado College; from 1902, in less than a year, Van Briggle (with thrower Harry Bangs, a young male assistant, and fiancée Anne Lawrence Gregory) produced 300 pieces for exhibition. The pottery became successful; in 1903, increased its staff to 14, including German thrower Ambrose Schlegel. His widow Anne took over the pottery in 1904 but sold it in 1913. 1900–12, the pottery designed at least 904 patterns of art ware; it is still in operation, producing early designs.

► Showed a painting at the 1893 Chicago 'World's Columbian Exposition.' Some of his Rookwood matt glazes shown at 1900 Paris 'Exposition Universelle.' Van Briggle wares shown at 1903 Paris Salon of the Société des Artistes français (two gold, one silver, and 12 bronze medals), 1904 St. Louis 'Louisiana Purchase Exposition,' and 1905 Portland (Oregon) 'Lewis and Clark Centennial Exposition.'

► Anna Gregory Van Briggle, 'Chinese Pots and Modern Faience,' *Craftsman*, No. 4, Sept. 1903:415–25. Dorothy McGraw Bogue, *The Van Briggle Story*, Colorado Springs: Dentan-Berkeland, 1968. Barbara M. Arnest (ed.), *Van Briggle Pottery: The Early Years*, Colorado Springs: Colorado Springs Fine Art Center, 1975. Yvonne Brunhammer et al., *Art Nouveau Belgium, France*, Houston: Rice University, 1976. Scot H. Nelson et al., *A Collector's Guide to Van Briggle Pottery*, Indiana, Pennsylvania: Halldin, 1986. *American Art Pottery*, New York: Cooper-Hewitt Museum, 1987.

Van Cleef et Arpels
► French jeweler; initially located Paris.
► Brothers Julien, Louis, and Charles Arpels and brother-in-law Alfred Van Cleef transformed a small store on place Vendôme, Paris, in 1904 or 1906 into the firm of Van Cleef et Arpels. A branch was opened c1924 in Cannes, followed by Deauville, Monte Carlo, and, in 1938, New York. In 1930, Louis Arpels created for Florence J. Gould the first *minaudière*, a kind of small hard metal purse in gold, studded with gems and carried on formal evening occasions. Characterized by innovative techniques, the firm introduced in 1935 the *serti mystérieux* or *serti invisible*: stones are cut with a trough, allowing them to be slid onto a hidden track, eliminating prong mounting and creating an unobstructed *pavé* effect. A member of the Comité Colbert, the firm is managed today by Jacques Arpels.
► Work shown at 1925 Paris 'Exposition Internationale des Arts Décoratifs et Industriels Modernes.'
► Sylvie Raulet, *Bijoux Art Déco*, Paris: Regard, 1984. Sylvie Raulet, *Van Cleef & Arpels*, Paris: Regard, 1986. Melissa Gabardi, *Les Bijoux des Années 50*, Paris: Amateur, 1987.

van de Groenekan, Gerald A.
► Dutch furniture maker.
► Assistant to architect Gerrit Rietveld, de Groenekan made built-in furniture for the Schröder house, Utrecht, from 1924, when Rietveld handed his furniture business over to van de Groenekan. He produced Rietveld furniture models until 1971, when he sold the rights to Cassina. By the late 1980s, de Groenekan was a restorer of Rietveld furniture, making pieces on commission for museums.

van de Velde, Henry Clemens (1863–1957)
► Belgian architect, industrial designer, painter, and art critic; born Antwerp; active Belgium, Germany, and the Netherlands.
► 1881–84, studied painting, Académie des Beaux-Arts, Antwerp; 1884–85, in Paris under Carolus Duran.
► Initially a Post-Impressionist and Symbolist *pointilliste* painter, he became an architect and, subsequently, decorative designer. His early style was strongly influenced by William Morris and the British Arts and Crafts movement. Returning to Antwerp, he co-founded the cultural circle Als ik Kan (after Jan van Eyck's motto) in 1886 and, in 1887, L'Art indépendant, the association of young neo-Impressionist painters; from 1889, took part in the activities of the Brussels avant-garde group Les Vingt; in 1894, wrote his famous treatise *Déblaiements d'Art*, opening his campaign to purify the architectural vocabulary of historicist references; became known as an avant-garde designer with Victor Horta in Belgium; designed his own 1895 Art Nouveau house, 'Bloemenwerf,' Uccle. The house was designed as an organic whole from architecture to furniture, furnishings, and fittings. Upon seeing the house, Siegfried Bing asked him to design four rooms for his shop L'Art Nouveau, Paris. Julius Meier-Graefe commissioned van de Velde to furnish his shop La Maison Moderne

in 1899, the year van de Velde settled in Germany, where he remained until 1917. Meier-Graefe arranged for van de Velde to meet German designers associated with the Art Nouveau magazine *Pan*. In Germany, he became a prolific designer, with commissions including the 1900–02 interior of the Folkwang Museum, Hagen; silver for the court jewelers of the Grand Duke of Saxe-Weimar from 1901; and other silver designs produced by A. Debain, Koch und Bergfeld, Theodor Müller, and his pupil Albert Feinauer. Designing the Kunstgewerbeschule building in Weimar in 1906, he became director of the school upon its completion in 1908; was a co-founder of the Deutscher Werkbund in 1907 but, disagreeing profoundly with Hermann Muthesius's insistence on standardization, left the organization; with the start of World War I, was forced to give up teaching at the Kunstgewerbeschule due to his Belgian citizenship; recommended Walter Gropius as his replacement as the head of the Kunsgewerbeschule; continued as artist and author; in 1917, moved to Switzerland; lived in the Netherlands 1921–24 and in Belgium 1925–47; in c1921, was commissioned by the Kröller-Müller family to build a museum 1937–54 in Otterlo (Netherlands); founded the Instituts des Arts Décoratifs de La Cambrai in 1926 and was its director until 1935; occupied the chair of architecture, University of Ghent, 1926–36.
► Work (robust and curvilinear furniture) shown at 1897 'Exhibition of Applied Arts,' Dresden. Work included in Colonial Museum pavilion (with Hobé, Serrurier-Bovy, and Hankar) at 1897 Brussels exposition; 1899 Hohenzollern Craftwork Shop, Berlin; 1901 Hoby's barber shop, Berlin; 1900 premises for Habana Tobacco Co; 1900–02 interior decoration, Folkwang Museum, Hagen; 1906 Kunstgewerbeschule, Weimar; house at 1913 Ghent 'Exposition Universelle et Industrielle'; Werkbund theater at 1914 Cologne 'Werkbund-Ausstellung'; Belgian pavilion (with Eggericx and Verweighen) at 1937 Paris 'Exposition Internationale des Arts et Techniques dans la Vie Moderne.'
► Ernst Karl, *Henry van de Velde: Leben und Schaffen des Künstlers*, Hagen, 1920. Maurice Casteels, *Henry van de Velde*, Brussels, 1932. Herman Teirlinck, *Henry van de Velde*, Brussels, 1959. A.M. Hammacher, *Die Welt Henry van de Veldes*, Cologne, 1967. K.-H. Hüter, *Henry van de Velde: Sein Werk bis zum Ende seiner Tätigkeit in Deutschland*, East Berlin, 1967. Charlotte Gere, *American and European Jewelry 1830–1914*, New York: Crown, 1975:226. Robert L. Delevoy in Vittorio Magnago Lampugnani, *Encyclopedia of 20th-Century Architecture*, New York: Abrams, 1986:355–57. Léon Ploegaerts and Pierre Puttemans, *Henry van de Velde*, Brussels: Atelier Vokaer, 1987. Annelies Krekel-Aalberse, *Art Nouveau and Art Déco Silver*, New York: Abrams, 1989:260 passim. Klaus-Jurgen Sembach, *Henry van de Velde*, London: Thames and Hudson, 1989.

van den Broeke, Floris (1945–)
► Dutch furniture designer; active London.
► 1961–66, studied painting, Academy of Art, Arnhem; furniture design, Royal College of Art, London, to 1969.
► He was one of the 'designer-makers' of the 1960s in Britain.
► Work shown at the Whitechapel Gallery, London, 1974; Crafts Council, London, 1980; 1989 'British Design,' Museum Boymans-van Beuningen, Rotterdam; 1990 'Dutch Design,' New York; and Design Museum, London, 1991.
► Frederique Huygen, 'The Britishness of British Design: Een interview met Floris van den Broecke,' *Items*, No. 15, 1985:21–25. Frederique Huygen, *British Design, Image and Identity*, London: Thames and Hudson, 1989.

van den Nieuwelaar, Aldo (1944–)
► Dutch architect and designer; active Amsterdam.
► Studied Akademie van Beeldende Kunsten, St. Joost, Breda.
► He worked for various architecture and design offices in Amsterdam; in 1969, set up his own office in Amsterdam; during the 1970s, designed furniture, lighting, and exhibitions; was consultant to the Dutch lighting industry; in 1974, designed lighting for the courtyard of the Frans Hals Museum, Haarlem, and, 1978–

79, lighting for the Bijenkorf company in Amsterdam. His designs were based on pure geometric forms.

▶ Cat., Kathryn B. Hiesinger and George H. Marcus III (eds), *Design Since 1945*, Philadelphia: Philadelphia Museum of Art, 1983:224,III—59. *Design from the Netherlands*, Amsterdam: Visual Arts Office for Abroad, 1981:38—41.

Van der Hurd, Christine   (1951–)
▶ British designer; active New York.
▶ Studied Winchester School of Art, Hampshire, to 1973.
▶ She settled in the USA in 1977; designed textiles for clients including Jack Lenor Larsen, Donghia, and Kenzo; wallcoverings for Osborne and Little; scarves for Liberty of London; and bedding for J.P. Stevens and Wamsutta. In 1981, she set up her own textile business for rugs; in 1991, became active in designing and producing furnishings and rugs for her own firm All Elements; in 1993, collaborated with Annie Walwyn-Jones on clothing and began designing home furnishings accessories.

van der Leck, Bart A.   (1876–1958)
▶ Dutch designer; born Utrecht.
▶ He collaborated in 1905 with P.J.C. Klaarhamer on book illustration and was in contact with H.P. Berlage; in 1912, began his studies of forms and flat color planes; in 1916, settled in Laren, met Piet Mondriaan, Theo van Doesburg, Vilmos Huszár, and philosopher M.H.J. Schoenmaekers, painted the nearly abstract *Mine Triptych*, and designed an interior color scheme for the Villa Kröller-Müller, Otterlo; in 1917, co-founded De Stijl and painted nonobjective 'compositions'; in 1918, left De Stijl and returned to abstract painting based on observed subjects; from 1928, designed textiles for Metz in Amsterdam.
▶ Work subject of 1949 retrospective exhibition, Stedelijk Museum, Amsterdam.
▶ W.C. Feltkamp, *B.A. van der Leck, Leven en Werken*, Leiden: Spruyt, Van Mantem Y De Does, 1956. Rudolf Willem Daan Oxenaar, *Bart van der Leck, 1876–1958*, Otterlo: Rijksmuseum Kröller-Müller, 1976. Cat., *Bart van der Leck*, Amsterdam: Stedelijk Museum, 1980. *Bart van der Leck, à la recherche de l'image des temps*, Paris: Institut Néerlandais, 1980. Hans L.C. Jaffé et al., De Stijl: 1917–31, Visions of Utopia, Abbeville, 1982:238 passim.

van der Stappen, Charles   (1843–1910)
▶ Belgian sculptor; born Brussels.
▶ Studied sculpture, Brussels Academy.
▶ In *c*1875, he produced several pieces of decorative art; set up his own studio before becoming professor of sculpture at the Brussels Academy; incongruously, showed rather classical work at the salons of Les Vingt group. In 1891, Art Nouveau tendencies began to appear in his work, as in the table centerpiece he designed for the city of Brussels, and particularly in his smaller pieces.
▶ His *Sphinx Mystérieux* in silver and ivory, with other objects, shown at the Colonial pavilion in Tervueren at the 1897 Brussels 'Exposition Internationale.'
▶ Yvonne Brunhammer et al., *Art Nouveau Belgium, France*, Houston: Rice University, 1976.

van Dissel
▶ Dutch fabrics firm; located Eindhoven.
▶ 1871–1971, Linenfabrieken E.J.F. van Dissel & Zonen was a fabric manufacturer in Eindhoven; until 1903, wove only domestic linens in simple checks, huckaback patterns, and stripes. Succeeding his father, W.P.J. van Dissel became manager of the firm; he was behind the production of high quality damask table linens for which three plants were set up. Van Dissel was only mechanized *c*1920, although by this time almost no fine linens were being produced. In order to produce up-to-date fabrications, the firm hired Chris Lebeau, who worked there *c*1905–43; his first damask designs appeared in a 1906 catalog. 1936–66, Kitty van der Mijll Dekker designed for van Dissel. Its linens were sold to institutions with their names woven into the design, at times combined with Lebeau's borders.

▶ *Industry and Design in the Netherlands, 1850–1950*, Amsterdam: Stedelijk Museum, 1985:98—101.

van Doesburg, Theo   (b. Christiaan Emil Marie Küpper 1883–1931)
▶ Dutch architect, painter, stained glass artist, and theoretician; born Utrecht.
▶ Active as a conventional painter at first, he became a follower of Vasilii Kandinskii in 1912; as early as 1915, planned a journal with Piet Mondriaan to disseminate Neo-Plasticism in an effort to transfer two-dimensional art into architecture, collaborating with J. J. P. Oud and Jan Wils; in 1916, (with Oud) founded the artists' group Sphinx in Leiden, which shut down in 1917; in 1917, established the journal *De Stijl*, which gave its name to the group of architects and artists seeking a 'radical renewal of art,' for which he became spokesperson. He was known for his use of primary colors, stained-glass windows, and tile floors; designed the distinctive *Composition IV* triptych window (executed by Vennootschap Crabeth of The Hague), 1917 townhouse by Jan Wils, Alkmaar, and for others, designed the 1917 hallway of Oud's residence, Noordwijkerhout, near Leiden, where he used painting to emphasize the structural elements of the architecture; traveled to Berlin and Dessau, lecturing on De Stijl principles at the Bauhaus, Dessau; published his book *Grundbegriffe der bildenden Kunst* in the 'Bauhausbücher' series (published earlier in Dutch in Amsterdam); was in contact with El Lissitzky and László Moholy-Nagy, resulting in a 1922 issue of *De Stijl* on Suprematism and Lissitzky. He emphasized the importance of fine art over architecture, which led to his alienation from Oud; from the 1920s, collaborated with Cornelis van Eesteren on models and architectural drawings for the De Stijl architecture exhibition at Léonce Rosenberg's Galerie L'Effort Moderne, Paris, which began the organization's 'international phase' resulting in Mondriaan's final withdrawal from De Stijl in 1925. He designed the color scheme for a 'little flower room' in the 1923 de Noailles villa, Hyères; (with Hans Arp) designed the 1926—28 interior renovation of Café L'Aubette, Strasbourg; as the antithesis of De Stijl ideas, designed his own 1929—30 residence, Meudon-Val-Fleury; (with Eesteren) became active in town planning, applying De Stijl principles; published *De Nieuwe Beweging in de Schilderkunst* (1917), *Drie voordrachten over de nieuwe bildende Kunst* (1919), *Klassiek, barok, modern* (1920). His death marked the end of De Stijl.
▶ Cat., *Theo van Doesburg 1883–1931*, Eidhoven, 1968. Joost Balieu, *Theo van Doesburg*, London, 1974. Jacob Jahannes Vriend in Vittorio Magnago Lampugnani (ed.), *Encyclopedia of 20th-Century Architecture*, New York: Abrams, 1986:83—84. Evert van Straaten, *Theo van Doesburg: Painter and Architect*, The Hague: SDU, 1988.

van Doren, Harold L.   (1895–1957)
▶ American industrial designer; born Chicago; active Philadelphia.
▶ He worked at the Minneapolis Institute of Arts before setting up a design office in Philadelphia, where he took on the Toledo Scale account for equipment design subsequent to Norman Bel Geddes. Van Doren's and J.G. Rideout's widely published 1930—31 green plastic radio in the image of a skyscraper was produced by Air-king Products. Van Doren's patents included the 1936 child's scooter (with Rideout). Clients included Swartzbaugh, DeVilbiss, and Philco. He was widely known for his book *Industrial Design* (1940).
▶ *Fortune*, Feb. 1934:88. Harold van Doren, *Industrial Design: A Practical Guide to Product Design and Development*, New York: McGraw-Hill 1940. Jonathan M. Woodham, *Twentieth-Century Ornament*, New York: Rizzoli, 1990:150—51,224. Eric Baker, *Great Inventions, Good Intentions*, San Francisco: Chronicle, 1990:129.

Van Erp, Dirk   (1859–1933)
▶ Dutch metalwork designer; born Leeuwarden; active California.

▶ He emigrated to the USA in 1886; in 1900, worked as a coppersmith in the US Navy shipyards on Mare Island, near San Francisco. The spent brass shell casings he acquired were made into vases, an activity that developed into a profitable business. By 1906, a fashionable shop in San Francisco, Vickery Atkins and Torrey, was carrying his wares. With public interest in his work, he opened his own shop in 1908 in Oakland and devoted himself to art metalwork. Two of his apprentices at this time were Harry Dixon and his daughter Agatha Van Erp. 1910–11, he was in partnership with designer D'Arcy Gaw, moving the business to Sutter Street, San Francisco. Previously a weaver with the New York firm Herter Looms, Gaw designed several early mica-shade lamps, a type that Van Erp had earlier initiated. At its zenith in 1915, the Van Erp shop produced a variety of decorative objects, including vases, planters, bowls, smoking accoutrements, and copper electric lamps with mica shades. Some of Van Erp's and Gaw's work incorporated Grueby tiles. When Van Erp joined the war effort in 1916 by returning to the shipyards, the shop was attended by his daughter with some assistance from his son William and from Harry St. John Dixon, who apprenticed under Van Erp and later set up his own shop. Retiring in 1929, Van Erp left the shop to son William.
▶ Bonnie Mattison in Timothy J. Andersen et al., *California Design 1910*, Salt Lake City: Peregrine Smith, 1980:87. Cat., Ann Yaffe Phillips, *From Architecture to Object*, New York: Hirschl and Adler, 1989:106ff.

van Goor, J.J.   (1874–1956)
▶ Dutch silversmith; active Utrecht.
▶ Studied Königliche Preussische Zeichenakademie, Hanau.
▶ He was a designer and modeler at the Koninklijke Utrechtsche Fabriek van Zilverwerk C.J. Begeer.
▶ Annelies Krekel-Aalberse, *Art Nouveau and Art Déco Silver*, New York: Abrams, 1989:254.

van Hoe, Marc   (1945–)
▶ Belgian designer; born Zulte.
▶ Studied Royal Academy of Fine Arts, Kortrijk.
▶ From 1975, he was a freelance designer and researcher, specializing in industrial textiles and tapestry; taught at Royal Academy of Fine Arts, Kortrijk; was a docent at Academie voor Beeldende Vorming, Tilburg.
▶ Work shown in Belgium, France, Switzerland, Poland, Hungary, and Britain.

van Kempen, J.M.
▶ Dutch silversmiths; located Utrecht and later Voorschoten.
▶ In 1835, J.M. van Kempen (1814–77) established the silver factory J.M. van Kempen in Utrecht. With quality as its priority, it was run along traditional lines; in 1858, it moved to Voorschoten. English craftsmen were hired to instruct Dutch workers in the production of forks and spoons in the new techniques. Under manager L.J.S. van Kempen (1838–1910), a separate studio was set up to produce both large and small sculpture along with mechanically made silverwork components. It became the largest and oldest manufacturer of silver in the Netherlands. 1845–1903, G.W. van Dokkum worked as a draftsman and modeler. Becoming chief draftsperson, J.L. Bernhardie worked at the firm 1858–86; he was succeeded by H.J. Valk, who worked at van Kempen 1886–1924. Not until the 19th century did the firm hire outside artists, notably Th. K.L. Sluyterman, who designed Art Nouveau ware in *c*1900. The firm's high-quality objects around 1900 showed Art Nouveau characteristics, although it specialized in uninspired classical models. In 1919, the firm C.J. Begeer merged with former competitor J.M. van Kempen en Zoon and jeweler J. Vos, becoming Van Kempen, Begeer en Vos.
▶ Van Kempen displayed silverware designed by van Dokkum at 1851 London 'Great Exhibition of the Works of Industry of All Nations'; did not participate in exhibitions after 1900 Paris 'Exposition Universelle' where its Art Nouveau dinner service by A.F. Gips for Begeer was shown.

▶ Annelies Krekel-Aalberse, *Art Nouveau and Art Déco Silver*, New York: Abrams, 1989:18,91,177,178,179,251,256.
▶ See Begeer

Van Keppel, Hendrik   (1914–)
▶ American interior designer; active Los Angeles.
▶ Van Keppel and Taylor Green set up an interior design office in Los Angeles in 1938; in 1939, established a retail shop for custom production of their furniture; became known for their Modern limited-edition furniture with its clean lines, including metal frame outdoor furniture strung with yacht cord in place of upholstery; after World War II, began producing furniture commercially using industrial raw materials. The gas piping used in their earlier models was replaced with enameled steel; booming sales led to the expansion of their operation in 1948. In the 1950s their clients for mass-produced goods included Balboa Chrome, Brown-Saltman, and Mueller. In the 1960s, Brown Jourdan became a client.
▶ Postwar furniture included in 1984 'Design Since 1945' exhibition, Philadelphia Museum of Art.
▶ James J. Cowen, 'Van Keppel-Green . . . Design Team,' *Furniture Field*, 1951. *Design Since 1945*, Philadelphia: Philadelphia Museum of Art, 1983:234,III–87. Cat., Kathryn B. Hiesinger and George H. Marcus III (eds.),

van Leersum, Emmy
See Bakker, Gijs

van Onck, Andries   (1928–)
▶ Dutch architect and industrial designer; born Amsterdam; active Milan.
▶ Studied Hochschule für Gestaltung, Ulm.
▶ He began his professional career in 1959, settling in Italy and working for Olivetti on electronic office equipment; in 1965, set up his own design studio in Milan; collaborated with Hiroko Takeda on products for industries in Italy and abroad. He collaborated with industrial designer Peppe Di Giuli at Studio Pro; designed industrial equipment and electronics for clients including Philips Italiana, Società Fisica Applicata, Dielectrix, and Colussi, and domestic electrical appliances and sound equipment for La Rinascente, Flash, and Varom. His designs for domestic furniture, accessories, and glassware were produced by Upim, Cristallerie, Imperatore, Caminda, Metaltex, Arosio Lissone, and Appiani. He taught at the Corso Superiore Disegno Industriale e Comunicazioni Visive in Rome; became a member of Società Italiana Ergonomic, Kio Kring Industriele in Antwerp, and ADI (Associazione per il Disegno Industriale) in Milan.
▶ Received 1979 Premio Compasso d'Oro.
▶ *ADI Annual 1976*, Milan: Associazione per il Disegno Industriale, 1976. *Modo*, No. 148, March–April 1993:127.

van Schouwen, J.
▶ Dutch metalworker; active Haarlem and The Hague.
▶ Studied Haarlemsche School voor Kunstnijverheid under Frans Zwollo Sr. and A. Peddemors.
▶ 1916–26, he worked in his own workshop in Haarlem; 1932–35, in The Hague. Although his work was of a high quality, his designs did not show originality.
▶ Annelies Krekel-Aalberse, *Art Nouveau and Art Déco Silver*, New York: Abrams, 1989:175,259.

van Vlissingen
▶ Dutch textile firm; located Helmond.
▶ The firm of P. Fentener van Vlissingen was established in 1846 in Helmond, taking over PA Sutorius, also in Helmond. In 1863, it purchased a rouleau printing machine; from 1873, began using synthetic dyes; in 1905, changed to *Indanthren* dyes. Having exported worldwide for some time, its cretonne ware (drapery fabrics, cushion covers, and bedspreads) were sold in Britain 1900–12; some, in nature-inspired motifs, were designed by M. Duco Crop, who designed for the firm 1894–99. 1914–27, van Vlissingen's export markets were Singapore and Bangkok, until

1931 India, and, most importantly, Africa and the Dutch West Indies. In 1927, the successful 'Vlisco' range of fabrics, based on modern designs and advanced mechanized methods, was introduced. J.W. Gidding and A. van der Plas designed curtains and tablecloths for the firm. With wallpaper manufacturer Rath en Doodeheefver, van Vlissingen set up the association Teentoonstelling het Behang en het Gordijn (as a successor to Het Behang en het Gordijn) with the aim of fostering new design work from Dutch artists. This organization led to the formation of Samenwerkende Industrie en Ambacht (Association for Cooperation of Industry and Crafts), with its publication *Ensemble*. Van Vlissingen's postwar production was, and continues to be, for African markets.
▶ Wares shown at 1927 'Het Behang en het Gordijn' ('Wallpaper and Curtains') exhibition, Stedelijk Museum, Amsterdam, and traveling.
▶ *Industry and Design in the Netherlands, 1850–1950*, Amsterdam: Stedelijk Museum, 1985:90–93.

Vaněk, Jan (1891–1962)
▶ Czech architect, designer, entrepreneur, and publicist; born Třebíč.
▶ Studied School of Woodwork, Chrudim.
▶ He began working for leading furniture manufacturers in Munich, Stuttgart, and Heilbronn; in 1921, organized Spojené Uměleckoprůmyslové závody (United Industrial Arts Factories); initiated the production of standard furniture and collaborated with leading foreign architects; in 1925, became a founder of and, until 1932, directed Standard, a housing society in Brno that produced furniture and furnished standardized family houses; in 1933, moved to Prague and founded the Consulting Center for Housing, the House and Garden workshop, and the textile firm Vatex; published the magazine *Bytová kultura*; organized the 1929 'The Civilized Woman' exhibition and published a book of same title advocating women's clothing reform; designed a number of domestic, school, and public interiors.
▶ A. Adlerová, *České užité umění 1918–1938*, Prague, 1983.

Varley, Fleetwood C.
▶ British enameler; active Chipping Campden.
▶ Varley was a member of C.R. Ashbee's Guild of Handicraft, where he and Arthur Cameron used copious amounts of enamel on the silverwares produced in its workshop; later produced the pictorial enamels for cigarette boxes and other items for W.H. Haseler, Birmingham, and Connell, London.
▶ Annelies Krekel-Aalberse, *Art Nouveau and Art Déco Silver*, New York: Abrams, 1989:24,260.

Vasegaard, Gertrud (1913–)
▶ Danish ceramicist; born Bornholm, Denmark.
▶ 1930–32, studied Kunsthåndvaerkerskolen, Copenhagen; 1932–33, studied in the studio of Axel Salto and Bode Willumsen, Saxbo.
▶ She was active with her sister Lisbeth Munch-Petersen 1933–35 in her own studio, in Gudhjem, Bornholm, and, 1936–48, alone in Holkadalen, Bornholm; was known for her high standards of production and her designs of handmade stoneware; 1945–59, designed bowls, vases, and the 1957 Chinese-influenced porcelain tea service for Bing & Grøndahl Porcelænsfabrik (working there freelance and full-time from 1949–59); subsequently, designed tea services for Royal Copenhagen (where she was freelance from 1959–75); in 1959, (with daughter Myre Vasegaard) set up a studio in Frederiksberg; collaborated with Aksel Rode.
▶ Received gold medal at the 1957 (XI) Triennale di Milano. Work shown at 1982 'Danish Ceramic Design' exhibition, Pennsylvania State University.
▶ Erik Zahle (ed.), *A Treasury of Scandinavian Design*, New York, 1961:294, Nos. 262,321. *Danish Ceramic Design*, University Park, Pa.: Pennsylvania State University, 1981. Jennifer Hawkins Opie, *Scandinavia: Ceramics and Glass in the Twentieth Century*, New York, Rizzoli, 1989. Cat., Kathryn B. Hiesinger and George H.

Marcus III (eds.), *Design Since 1945*, Philadelphia: Philadelphia Museum of Art, 1983:234, II–66.

Vasil'eva, Mariia (1884–1957)
▶ Russian artist and designer.
▶ 1902, studied School of Art, St. Petersburg.
▶ In 1908, she established The Russian Academy, which became a center for writers and artists.
▶ In 1920, she showed her celebrated doll-portraits in Paris and London and, 1924–37, costumes and sets for Rolf de Mare's ballet troupe of Sweden.
▶ Cat., *The Great Utopia: The Russian and Soviet Avant-Garde, 1915–1932*, New York: Guggenheim Museum, 1992.

Vassos, John (1898–1985)
▶ Greek illustrator and designer, born Bucharest; active Boston.
▶ Studied Boston Museum of Fine Arts School and Art Students' League, New York.
▶ He produced graphic design for labels, packages, and occasionally small appliances, and illustrated many publications of the 1920s–1950s; a marketing pioneer, he used applied psychology to analyze buying habits and motivations. For Coca-Cola, he designed bottle dispensers with aluminum coils on the bottom of the barrel that sat on the counter to suggest coolness, with red and green bands on the body of the barrel to lend a sense of guarded treasure; 1930s–1960s, designed sound equipment for RCA, including the portable *RCA Phonograph Special* in aluminum of c1935, which was widely published, and the first (1939) tv set (*TRK-11*). Perey Manufacturing produced his turnstile design. In 1939, he patented a design for a Streamline child's tricycle and a harmonica; c1933, designed the interior of photographer Margaret Bourke-White's studio-office on the 61st floor of the Chrysler building, and, 1931, of the Rismont Tea Room, Broadway, both New York. He wrote and illustrated 14 books published by Dutton, New York.
▶ *Fortune*, Feb. 1934:88. Eric Baker, *Great Inventions, Good Intentions*, San Francisco: Chronicle, 1990:121. Robert A.M. Stern et al., *New York 1930: Architecture and Urbanism Between the Two World Wars*, New York: Rizzoli, 1987. Arthur Pulas, 'John Vassos,' in Mel Byars and Russell Flinchum (eds.), *50 American Designers*, Washington, DC: Preservation, 1994.

Vchtemas and Vchutein
See **Vhutemas**

Vedel, Kristian (1923–)
▶ Danish furniture designer.
▶ 1944–45, studied architecture, Det Kongelige Danske Kunstakademi, Copenhagen, under Kaare Klint; 1946, furniture design, Kunsthåndværkerskolen.
▶ He was strongly influenced by Klint's simple, functional approach to furniture design and production; in 1955, set up his own design studio in Copenhagen and soon after rendered two innovative pieces: the 1956 slotted child's chair (produced by Torben Ørskov) formed from curved plywood, and a melamine-plastic range of vessels; designed the popular 1963 *Modus* range of furniture produced by Søren Willadsen; 1952–53, taught at Askov Køjskole and, 1953–56, furniture design at Kunsthåndværkerskolen; in 1961, set up (with Ane Vedel) design studio, from 1972, in Hvidberg, northern Jutland; in 1968, led department of industrial design, The East African University in Nairobi (Kenya) and, 1969–71 and in 1975, was professor of industrial design there; 1966–68, was chair of IDD (Industrielle Designere Danmark); in 1974, was a juror on Danish Design Prize.
▶ Received 1962 Lunning Prize and silver medal (for child's chair) at 1957 (XI) and gold medal at 1960 (XII) Triennali di Milano. His child's chair was included in 1969 'Sitzen 69' exhibition, Österreichisches Museum für Angewandte Kunst, Vienna, and 1984 'Design Since 1945' exhibition at the Philadelphia Museum of Art. Work included in the 1958 'Formes Scandinaves,' Paris Musée des Arts Décoratifs; 1960–61 USA 'The Arts of Denmark'; and furniture exhibition, Copenhagen Cabinetmaker's Guild.

▶ 'Thirty-four Lunning Prize-Winners,' *Mobilia*, No. 146, Sept. 1967. Cat., *Sitzen 69*, Vienna: Österreichisches Museum für Angewandte Kunst, 1969, No. 10. Frederik Sieck, *Nutidig Dansk Møbeldesign:—en kortfattet illustreret beskrivelse*, Copenhagen: Bondo Gravesen; 1990 Busck edition in English. Cat., Kathryn B. Hiesinger and George H. Marcus III (eds.), *Design Since 1945*, Philadelphia: Philadelphia Museum of Art, 1983:234,VI-21. Cat., *The Lunning Prize*, Stockholm: Nationalmuseum, 1986:134—37.

Vedel-Rieper, John (1929–)
▶ Danish furniture designer.
▶ Studied Skolen for Boligindretning to 1949.
▶ 1954–60, he worked with Børge Mogensen; 1971–75, was associated with Skolen for Brugskunst (formerly Det Tekniske Selskabs Skoler) and, in 1974 and 1975, taught there; from 1972, taught in the furniture laboratory of Det Kongelige Danske Kunstakademi, Copenhagen. His furniture was produced by Hakon Stephensen.
▶ From 1977, work included in exhibitions of furniture laboratory of the Danish Academy and in furniture exhibitions in Stockholm, Gothenburg, Malmö, Copenhagen, and Århus.
▶ Frederik Sieck, *Nutidig Dansk Møbeldesign:—en kortfattet illustreret beskrivelse*, Copenhagen: Bondo Gravesen; 1990 Busck edition in English.

Velcro
See de Mestral, Georges

Venini, Paolo (1895–1959)
▶ Italian glassware designer and maker; active Murano.
▶ A glassmaker from 1921, he became a partner with Venetian antique dealer Giacomo Cappelin, Andrea Rioda, and Vittorio Zecchin in Vetri Soffiati Muranesi Cappelin-Venini. A distinguished painter, decorator, and glass designer, Zecchin became its artistic and technical director. In 1925, Venini opened his own glass factory in Murano with sculptor Napoleone Martinuzzi; designed in a simple, functional style early on; later interpreted Modernism (or *Novecento*) in a livelier and more novel manner than in northern Europe, developing the first Modern style in glass. Murano glasswares were traditionally rendered in gaudy ruby and gold along with playful forms in bright colors. He commissioned various designers, including Gio Ponti from 1927, Carlo Scarpa from 1932, Eugene Berman from 1951, Ken Scott from 1951, Franco Albini from 1954, and Massimo Vignelli from 1956; made a practice of hiring freelance designers, including Martinuzzi and Fulvio Bianconi; at the 1956 Biennale di Venezia, showed bottles by Ponti and Bianconi called *Morandiennes*, made of double-colored cane, an element of extruded glass. Another favored technique was *vetro a fili* (glass with lines), where rods of colored glass were embedded to create stripes in a technique called *zanfirico*. His 1950 *vetro pezzato* process had a patchwork effect of squares in various colors. One of the Venini firm's best-known 1950s forms was the *vaso fassoletto* (handkerchief vase) by Bianconi, where a square of thin glass was melted over a form, creating a wavy-edged vessel. Its humorous figurines were developed spontaneously through hot-glass experiments. Paolo Venini's own glassware achieved a vitality attained through direct contact with glassmaking, an approach not generally employed in northern Europe, where designers' ideas were realized through craftsmen. His widow Ginette Venini and son-in-law Ludovico de Santillana assumed management of the firm upon his death and commissioned designers including Tobia Scarpa and Tapio Wirkkala.
▶ Achieved initial success at 1925 Paris 'Exposition Internationale des Arts Décoratifs et Industriels Modernes.' Work shown at 1923 (I) Monza Biennale, 1933 (V) Triennale di Milano, and at 1956 Biennale di Venezia. Work subject of the 1981 'Venini Glass' exhibition, Smithsonian Institution, Washington. The *vetro pezzato* glassware and vessels by Tobia Scarpa and Wirkkala included in 1983–84 'Design Since 1945' exhibition, Philadelphia Museum of Art.

▶ Ada Polak, *Modern Glass*, London, 1962:55—56,66—67, plates 50A,50B,52,64A,64B. *Venini Glass*, Washington: Smithsonian Institution, 1981. Cat., Kathryn B. Hiesinger and George H. Marcus III (eds.), *Design Since 1945*, Philadelphia: Philadelphia Museum of Art, 1983:234, II—67—68, II—55, II—73—74. Cat., *Venini and Murano Renaissance: Italian Art Glass of the 1940s and 50s*, New York: Fifty/50, 1984. Franco Deboni, *Venini Glass*, Basel: Wiese, 1990.

Venosta, Carla (1965–)
▶ Italian designer; born Monza; active Milan.
▶ Venosta began her professional career in 1965. She designed furniture, shelving, and accessories, for clients including Arflex, Full, Nazzareno, Gabrielli, Cinova, Zanotta, Italidea, Bacci, Oggett, and Siv. She was a member of ADI (Associazione per il Disegno Industriale); occupied with problems of urban living; designed objects and furniture for Busnelli, Calderoni, Fabbianelli and fittings for Nicola Trussardi, piazza of Duomo in Milan, PAC, Triennale di Milano; designed offices, lofts, shops, and apartments.
▶ Received 1979 and 1981 Premio Compasso d'Oro. Participated in exhibitions in Italy and abroad.
▶ *ADI Annual 1976*, Milan: Associazione per il Disegno Industriale, 1976. *Modo*, No.148, March—April 1993:127.

Venturi, Robert (1925–)
▶ American architect; born and active Philadelphia; husband of Denise Scott Brown.
▶ 1943–50, studied architecture, Princeton University.
▶ He worked in the offices of Eero Saarinen and Louis Kahn; 1954–56, was at the American Academy in Rome on a Prix de Rome fellowship; 1957–65, taught architecture at the University of Pennsylvania, his work there forming the basis of his 1966 book *Complexity and Contradiction in Architecture*, which heralded Post-Modernism. Through a graduate seminar at Yale University, taught with future wife Denise Scott Brown and Stephen Izenour in 1966, he gathered material for his second book, *Learning from Las Vegas* (1972); in 1964, opened an architecture office in Philadelphia, known as Venturi, Rauch and Scott Brown from 1967. He was known for his Post-Modernism and Post-Modern classicism, examples of which can been seen in his design of his mother's split-gabled 1962 Chestnut Hill House, Pennsylvania, and in the 1982 stucco-and-wood house, New Castle County, Delaware. The Chestnut Hill House became an immediately recognizable symbol of the Post-Modern movement. Venturi was the designer of Wu Hall in Princeton, New Jersey. For Formica's 1982 Colorcore competition, he designed *Mirror in the Greek revival manner*; for Alessi's 1983 *Tea and Coffee Piazza* project, a coffee and tea set based on Georgian column forms; a 1984 furniture group (nine chairs, two tables, a low table, and a sofa) for Knoll, including the widely published *Chippendale* chair in bentwood and Formica, and a *Grandmother*; 1989 flatware for Reed and Barton; and 1990 house-shaped mail box.
▶ The Chestnut Hill house won the first (1989) AIA '25 Year Award.'
▶ Officina Alessi, *Tea and Coffee Piazza: 11 Servizi da tè e caffè*, Milan: Crusinallo, 1983. Stanislaus von Moss, *Venturi, Rauch and Scott Brown*, Fribourg: Office du Livre, 1987. *Progressive Architecture*, May 1989:25.

Vera, Paul (1882–1958)
▶ French painter and decorator; active Paris.
▶ Vera produced painted panels, bas-reliefs, printed fabrics, rugs, and illustrations; worked for Louis Süe and André Mare at their Compagnie des Arts français, Paris, where he executed models for painted and sculpted décors, and for the Manufacture Nationale de Sèvres.
▶ Participated in several installations at 1925 Paris 'Exposition Internationale des Arts Décoratifs et Industriels Modernes.'
▶ Pierre Cabanne, *Encyclopédie Art Déco*, Paris: Somogy, 1986:240.

Verdura, Fulco Santostefano della Ceraa, Duke of
(1900–)
▶ Italian jewelry designer; born Palermo.
▶ Verdura settled in Paris in c1927; began designing jewelry in 1931 for Coco Chanel, using semi-precious stones and enamel; in 1937, settled in New York; designed jewelry for Paul Flato; in 1939, opened his own shop at 712 Fifth Avenue.
▶ Sylvie Raulet, *Bijoux Art Déco*, Paris: Regard, 1984.

Vereinigte Lausitzer Glaswerke
▶ German glassware manufacturer; located Weisswasser.
▶ The firm was founded in 1899. From 1935, Wilhelm Wagenfeld was its artistic director; he designed pressed glass (utility wares and table glass) 1935–38, when the firm employed 3,500 people. Its best-known designs were Wagenfeld's 1938 *Kubus* modular stacking containers and glass coffee pot. Wagenfeld's goal there was to make glass that was cheap enough for the working class and good enough for the rich. In 1936, Dr. Mey, co-chair of Lausitzer, set up Wagenfeld in a ten-person design department, with Heinrich Löffelhardt as his student. Among the first of its kind, the studio had modeling rooms and a grinding shop. Wagenfeld's *Oberweimar* set of glasses, at first considered elitist, reached the highest production figure of any set of glasses ever made. Löffelhardt became chief designer and was responsible for a number of suites of glasses, for both domestic and utility use, that were quite innovative in the 1950s and 1960s. When Jenear Glaswerke Schott und Genossen was nationalized in East Germany after World War II, the firm was re-established in the West by Vereinigte Lausitzer.
▶ Frederick Cooke, *Glass: Twentieth-Century Design*, New York: Dutton, 1986:92. Cat., *Lausitzer Glas*, Dresden: Museum für Kunsthandwerk, 1987.

Vereinigte Silberwaren-Fabriken
▶ German silversmith; located Düsseldorf.
▶ Franz Bahner founded a metalwork firm in 1895 that in 1901 became the Vereinigte Silberwaren-Fabriken. It produced silver flatware and hollow-ware. Henry van de Velde's contemporary adaptation of a classic flatware design was produced by the firm. Its designers of flatware included Peter Behrens in 1904, and Gerhard Duve and Emil Lettré in the 1930s.
▶ Annelies Krekel-Aalberse, *Art Nouveau and Art Déco Silver*, New York: Abrams, 1989:136,260. Cat., *Metallkunst*, Berlin: Bröhan-Museum, 1990:2–11.

Vereinigte Werkstätten für Kunst im Handwerk
See Münchner Vereinigte Werkstätte

Verga, Adriano   (1950–)
▶ Italian designer; born and active Milan.
▶ Verga began his professional career in 1973; became a member of ADI (Associazione per il Disegno Industriale); had clients including Studio Zerbi, Vergafil, and Luisella Pennati.
▶ *ADI Annual 1976*, Milan: Associazione per il Disegno Industriale, 1976.

Verga, Sandro   (1950–)
▶ Italian architect and designer; born and active Milan.
▶ Studied architecture, Politecnico di Milano.
▶ He began his professional career in 1973; designed domestic furniture and accessories produced by Crystal Art, New Land, and Bilumen; became a member of ADI (Associazione per il Disegno Industriale).
▶ *ADI Annual 1976*, Milan: Associazone per il Disegno Industriale, 1976.

Vergottini, Bruno   (1935–)
▶ Italian industrial designer; born Genoa; active Milan.
▶ Vergottini began his professional career in 1968 in fashion as well as industrial and interior design; (with Elena Spagnol) published the book *Uomini in Cucina* (1975), illustrated by Milton Glaser. Clients included G. Appiani (ceramic tiles), Mazzucchelli, SILT (textiles), Vincenzo Zucchi, Wella Mobili (furniture),

Alemagna, Vanessa (fabrics and linens), Esse (umbrellas), Inco (bathroom fixtures), Innocenti (automobile coloring), Upim/Rinascente (handbags and purses), and Valigeria Brocchi (handbags and purses). He became a member of ADI (Associazione per il Disegno Industriale).
▶ *ADI Annual 1976*, Milan: Associazione per il Disegno Industriale, 1976.

Vermorel   (?–1925)
▶ French bookbinder; born Lyons; active Paris.
▶ Vermorel settled in Paris in 1887, where he became an apprentice to Édouard Pagnant; in 1894, set up his own workshop in the rue du Faubourg St.-Honoré; in 1912, moved to the place de l'Étoile; produced liturgical bindings and was subsequently assisted by his son, who was killed during World War I in 1914. Vermorel produced bindings in a Modern linear style. His popular bindings included *Mireille, Le Livre de la jungle, Antar*, and *Autour de nos moulins*.
▶ Showed work at the annual Salons in Paris.
▶ Alastair Duncan and Georges de Bartha, *Art Nouveau and Art Déco Bookbinding*, New York: Abrams, 1989:178,197. Roger Devauchelle, *La Reliure en France de ses origines à nos jours*, Vol. 3, Paris, 1961:278–79. Ernest de Crauzat, *La Reliure française de 1900 à 1925*, Vol. 1, Paris, 1932:69–70.

Vernizzi, Alberto   (1954–)
▶ Italian industrial and interior designer; born and active Suzzara.
▶ Vernizzi began his professional career in 1975; designed public and domestic lighting, interiors (on occasion with Scaravelli e Baraldi) and theater sets in Suzzara; became a member of ADI (Associazione per il Disegno Industriale).
▶ *ADI Annual 1976*, Milan: Associazione per il Disegno Industriale, 1976.

Versen, Kurt   (1901–)
▶ Swedish consultant, lighting designer, and manufacturer; active USA.
▶ Studied in Germany.
▶ He settled in 1930 in the USA, where he produced lighting for stores, offices, and public buildings, including an early version of indirect lighting for the 1931 Philadelphia Saving Fund Society building, on which Lescaze and Howe were architects, and a commission at the 1939 'New York World's Fair'; in the 1940s and 1950s, executed many assignments from architects for flexible lighting appropriate to Modern interiors. His swivel floor lamp of c1946 could be used for direct or indirect lighting.
▶ Lamps shown at 1951 'Good Design' exhibition, New York Museum of Modern Art and Chicago Merchandise Mart.
▶ *Good Design Is Your Business*, Buffalo, NY: Buffalo Fine Arts Academy, Albright Art Gallery, 1947: figs. 33–37. Eliot Noyes, 'The Shape of Things: Lamps,' *Consumer Reports*, Nov. 1948:506–08. Edgar Kaufmann, Jr., *What Is Modern Design?*, New York: Museum of Modern Art, 1950: fig. 59. Jay Doblin, *One Hundred Great Product Designs*, New York, 1970: No. 25. Cat., Kathryn B. Hiesinger and George H. Marcus III (eds.), *Design Since 1945*, Philadelphia: Philadelphia Museum of Art, 1983:234, IV–36.

Vertemati, Gianni   (1946–)
▶ Italian architect and designer; born and active Bernareggio.
▶ Studied architecture, Politecnico di Milano, to 1975.
▶ He began his professional career in 1971; was artistic director of the furniture store Galliani Höst; designed seating furniture and tables for Vertemati; worked on the design of buildings with brother and architect Angelo Vertemati; became a member of ADI (Associazione per il Disegno Industriale).
▶ *ADI Annual 1976*, Milan: Associazione per il Disegno Industriale, 1976.

Vesnin, Aleksandr Aleksandrovich   (1883–1959)
▶ Russian engineer, architect, and set and costume designer; born Yurevets, Volga Province.

▶ Studied Moscow Practical Academy; 1901–12, Institute of Civil Engineers, St. Petersburg.

▶ 1912–14, he worked in Vladimir Tatlin's studio 'The Tower,' with Liubov' Popova, Nadezhda Udal'tsova, and others; in 1918, produced agitprop decorations for streets and squares in Petrograd and Moscow; in 1920, designed sets and costumes for Claudel's *L'Annonce faite à Marie* produced by Aleksandr Tairov at the Chamber Theatre, Moscow; was involved in subsequent theatrical productions, including *The Man Who Was Thursday*, the 1923 production for which he is best known, produced by Tairov; was a member of Inkhuk; 1923–33, was involved with the journal *Lef* and a supporter of Contructivism; 1923–33, worked with brothers Leonid and Viktor on architecture and industrial design projects, including the Lenin Library and Palace of Soviets in Moscow, and communal housing in Kuznets and elsewhere; was cofounder of Osa (Association of Contemporary Architects). From 1933, when Leonid Vesnin died, and with the official condemnation of Constructivism, Vesnin's architecture activities diminished greatly.

▶ Work included in the 1921 '5 × 5 = 25' exhibition.

▶ Stephanie Barron and Maurice Tuchman, *The Avant-Garde in Russia, 1910–1930*, Cambridge: MIT, 1980:260. Selim Om Khan-Magomedov, *Les Vhutemas*, Paris: Regard, 1990:450–55. Jaroslav Andel, *Art into Life: Russian Constructivism 1914–1932*, New York: Rizzoli, 1990. Cat., *The Great Utopia: The Russian and Soviet Avant-Garde, 1915–1932*, New York: Guggenheim Musem, 1992.

Vever, Paul (1851–1915) and Henri Vever (1854–1942)

▶ French jewelry designers; born Metz; brothers.

▶ Paul Vever founded a goldsmiths and jewelry firm in Metz in 1821. In 1848, his son Ernest Vever joined the firm. In 1871, when Alsace-Lorraine was annexed by Germany following the Franco-Prussian War, Vever went to Paris, where he bought the Maison Marrett et Baugrand at 19 rue de la Paix. In 1881, brothers Paul and Henri Vever (working at the firm from 1874) succeeded their father Ernest as directors. Representing the most advanced trends in jewelry design and favorably compared to René Lalique and Alphonse Fouquet, and in sharp contrast to Vever's conventional work of the 1870s, the firm's originality and Modern approach won them an enviable reputation. In 1904, the Vever brothers set up a specially designed and built shop at 14 rue de la Paix. Their jewelry was designed by Henri Vever, Edward Colonna, and Eugène Grasset. At one time, enamelist Tourrette and L. Gautrait (chief engraver at Léon Gariod) worked for Vever. Henri Vever wrote the standard, comprehensive history of 19th-century French jewelry *La bijouterie française au XIXe siècle* (1906–08). Henri Vever's sons André and Pierre Vever took over the firm.

▶ Vever's work shown at 1878 and 1889 expositions; established the firm's reputation at the 1900 Paris 'Exposition Universelle.'

▶ Yvonne Brunhammer et al., *Art Nouveau Belgium, France,* Houston: Rice University, 1976. Charlotte Gere, *American and European Jewelry 1830–1914*, New York: Crown, 1975.

Vhutemas

▶ Russian design school

▶ Svomas (Free State Art Studios) was founded in 1918 in Moscow as an amalgamation of the Academy of Fine Arts in Petrograd (now St. Petersburg), the Stroganov School of Decorative and Applied Art, and the Muzhyz (Moscow School of Painting, Sculpture and Architecture), founded in 1832. Active 1920–27, Vhutemas (Higher State Artistic and Technical Workshops) succeeded Svomas. Active 1927–30, Vhutein (Higher State Artistic and Technical Institute) in turn succeeded Vhutemas. It was particularly active in developing advanced teaching techniques and training a large number of Soviet artists of some renown. The most influential teachers were artists and architects including Aleksandr Rodchenko, Naum Gabo, Antoine Pevsner, Liubov' Popova, Anton Lavinskii and Viktor and Aleksandr Vesnin. The institution, along with Karkompros, Izo, and Inkhuk, completely dominated artistic

ideology, education, and administration in the Soviet Union. Vhutemas was the corollary to the Bauhaus; Walter Gropius wrote, in the year of its founding, 'Since we now have no culture whatever, merely a civilization, I am convinced that for all its evil concomitants Bolshevism is probably the only way of creating the preconditions for a new culture in the foreseeable future.' Links were forged with the Bauhaus through El Lissitzky, Kazimir Malevich, Erhrenburg, and Vassilii Kandinskii, although Vhutemas lacked anyone with Gropius's professionalism, broad-mindedness, and political tolerance. In 1932, a year before the Nazis shut down the Bauhaus, a Soviet Central Committee decree abolished all the architectural organizations and groups which had grown up in the 1920s and replaced them with professional unions under rigid Party control; Vhutein became the Union of Soviet Architects.

▶ J. Willet, *The New Sobriety 1917–33: Art and Politics in the Weimar Period,* London, 1978:70. Cat., *Kunst und Revolution: Russische und Sowjetische Kunst 1910–1932*, Vienna: Österreichisches Museum für angewandte Kunst, 1988. Selim Om Khan-Magomedov, *Les Vhutemas*, Paris: Regard, 1990.

VIA (Valorisation de l'Innovation dans l'Ameublement)

▶ French semi-public organization supporting furniture designers; located Paris.

▶ VIA was established in 1979 under the patronage of the ministry of industry and financed by CODIFA and UNIFA. Its goal was to promote contemporary French furniture design. Its first gallery was located on place Sainte-Opportune, Paris. Its traveling exhibitions, extensive promotional activities, and production were supported by the French furniture and furnishings manufacturing syndicate. It revitalized an industry flagging in the 1970s in the face of stiff competition from Italy. Its competitions were open to all tendencies, under its broad-minded president Jean-Claude Maugirard. VIA financed prototypes for more than 100 projects each year and staged worldwide exhibitions to show them; it established the 'Carte Blanche' and 'Appel Permanant' awards; gave technical and financial support to manufacturers participating in the realization of artists' works. Holding numerous exhibitions at its Paris gallery, it participated with Bloomingdale's (1983) and Habitat (1985) on competitions. Roche-Bobois, Cinna, and Ligne Roset distributed some VIA-label designs. Designers supported by VIA included Philippe Starck, Pascal Mourgue, Bruno Savatte and Guillaume Parent, Sylvain Dubuisson, Xavier Mategot, Rena Dumas, and Olivier Gagnère.

▶ Subject of 1990 'Les Années VIA' exhibition at the Musée des Arts Décoratifs, Paris. Lacquered plywood chairs by François Bauchet won the first 'Appel Permanant' award in 1982; Martin Szekely received the first 'Carte Blanche' award in 1982 for his *Pi* lounge chair of black metal and leather; Garouste and Bonetti had an exhibition at the VIA gallery in 1984; and Pascal Mourgue's *Arc* armchair won the first prize in the 1983 VIA/Bloomingdale's competition.

▶ Suzanne Tise, *Vogue Décoration*, No. 26, 1990:46,47. Cat., *Les années VIA 1980–1990*, Paris: Musée des Arts Décoratifs, 1990.

Vialov, Konstantin Alexandrovich (1900–)

▶ Russian artist, illustrator, and textile, graphic, and set designer; born Moscow.

▶ 1914–17, studied textile design, Stroganov Art Institute, Moscow; 1917–24, Svomas/Vkhutemas under Aristarkh Lentulov and Aleksei Morgunov.

▶ During the mid-1920s, his style was Expressionist and Surrealist before Soviet politics dictated a return to more traditional forms of artistic expression. At this time, he was a studio painter and theatrical designer, rendering stage sets for productions, including the 1924 Vasilii Kamenskii's staging of *Stenka Razin*. His 1923 painting *Worker*, with its geometric shapes and bold forms, pointed towards Social Realism. In 1925, he became a founding member of Ost (Society of Easel Painters); designed posters, including for the film *When the Dead Awaken* (1927), and illustrated books, including the Russian version of L. Mitchell's *Skyscraper*

(1930). After the 1930s, landscapes were a favorite subject. Vialov continued to paint up to the 1960s.

▶ In 1923, showed work and contributed to Ost 1925, 1926, 1927, and 1928 exhibitions; up to the 1960s, showed work regularly.

▶ Stephanie Barron and Maurice Tuchman, *The Avant-Garde in Russia, 1910–1930*, Cambridge: MIT, 1980:262.

Vibert, Max

▶ French designer.

▶ She designed rugs for the decorating atelier Studium of the Grands Magasins du Louvre, Paris.

▶ Her rug was including in the office designed by Maurice Matet for the Studium at 1928 Salon of Société des Artistes Décorateurs.

▶ Pierre Kjellberg, *Art Déco: les maîtres du Mobilier, le décor des Paquebots*, Paris: Amateur, 1986:125.

Vida, Beppe (1933–)

▶ Italian interior, graphic, and industrial designer; born Cremona; active Bologna.

▶ 1960–75, he was active as an interior architect and graphic and interior designer; designed the 1960 furniture range (with Giovanni Ausenda) produced by Ny Form; designed the 1965 *Asteria* furniture range (with Vittorio Gregotti, Giotto Stoppino, and Renato Meneghetti); designed the 1967 *Expansion Design* group of fabrics (with Gaetano Pesce), 1972 seating furniture, and 1972 corporate identity of Le Coquelicot; in 1969, designed accessories, lighting, and inflatable seating (with Gaetano Pesce and Xavier David); 1969–75, participated in the preparation of the catalogs of the Salone del Mobile in Milan and of the Bologna art fair, of Ny Form Expansion Design, Le Coquelicot, and others; became a member of ADI (Associazione per il Disegno Industriale).

▶ *ADI Annual 1976*, Milan: Associazione per il Disegno Industriale, 1976.

Viemeister, Tucker (1948–)

▶ American product designer; born Yellow Springs, Ohio; active New York; son of industrial designer Read Viemeister (1923–93).

▶ Studied industrial design, Pratt Institute, Brooklyn, New York.

▶ He worked in his father Read Viemeister's industrial design firm Vie Design Studios, managed today by his sister; subsequently, designed jewelry with his brother and later with Ted Muehling. In 1979, Viemeister, Davin Stowell, Tom Dair, and Tamara Thomsen were partners in the New York industrial design firm David Stowell Associates, known as Smart Design from 1985. Viemeister designed eyeglasses for Serengeti, travel irons for Sanyei, and dinnerware for Copco and Corning Ware. For Oxo, Smart Design produced the designs for 22 kitchen products for the handicapped. He was at-large director of the Industrial Designers' Society of America, member of the American Institute of Graphic Arts, and trustee of the Rowena Reed Kostellow Fund at Pratt Institute.

▶ Received the Presidential Design Achievement Award and two IDEA awards; work chosen 10 times for the Annual ID Design Review.

▶ *Metropolitan Home*, September 1990:89–92.

Vienna Secession
see Wiener Sezession

Viénot, Jacques (1893–1959)

▶ French industrial designer and theoretician; active Paris.

▶ In 1929, Viénot set up his own office DIM (Décore Installe Meuble); in 1930, established the association Porza, precursor of ICSID (International Council of the Societies of Industrial Design); in 1933, became director of the Au Printemps department store, Paris; designed low-cost industrial furniture known as 'Stylnet'; published the influential book *La République des Arts*; in 1951, established the Institut d'Esthétique Industrielle 'to increase the attractive power of French production'; in 1953, with the assistance of the French ministries of commerce and industry, created the 'Beauté-France' label of recognition on products; promoted design teaching at the École des Arts Appliqués, Paris.

▶ Georges Patrix and Denis Huisman, *L'Esthétique Industrielle*, Paris: Presses Universitaires de France, 1965:32–40.

Viezzoli, Mario (1948–)

▶ Italian designer; born Trieste; active Padua.

▶ Viezzoli began his professional career in 1972; designed furniture for children and adults in ABS plastic; worked for furniture manufacturer Longato Arredamenti; became a member of ADI (Associazione per il Disegno Industriale).

▶ *ADI Annual 1976*, Milan: Associazione per il Disegno Industriale, 1976.

Viganò, Vittoriano (1919–)

▶ Italian architect, town planner, and exhibition and industrial designer; born and active Milan.

▶ Studied architecture, Politecnico di Milano, to 1944.

▶ He began his professional career in 1944, first working in the studio of architect and designer Gio Ponti; subsequently in the architecture office BBPR; in 1947, set up his own architecture firm and became a prominent member of the Brutalist school; early on, designed furniture in molded plywood produced by Rima, and glassware and metalwork by others. His lighting for Arteluce in Milan included the 1960 three-direction floor lamp. Clients in Italy included Conpensati Curvati, Vecchi, Alpha, and Adreani Materie Plastiche. From the 1960s, he largely abandoned design, teaching architecture at the Politecnico di Milano; became a member of ADI (Associazione per il Disegno Industriale).

▶ Work (three-direction lamp) shown at 1983–84 'Design Since 1945' exhibition, Philadelphia Museum of Art.

▶ 'Nuovo disegno per due lampade,' *Domus*, No. 389, April 1962:49. L. Rubino, *Joe Colombo, Afra Carlo, Tobia Scarpa, Vittoriano Vigano: Chiamali Totem*, Verona, 1973. *ADI Annual 1976*, Milan: Associazione per il Disegno Industriale, 1976. Andrea Branzi and Michele De Lucchi (eds.), *Il design italiano degli anni '50*, Milan, 1981:45,54,132–33,144,153,159,205. Cat., Kathryn B. Hiesinger and George H. Marcus III (eds.), *Design Since 1945*, Philadelphia: Philadelphia Museum of Art, 1983:234, IV–37.

Vigeland, Tone (1938–)

▶ Norwegian jewelry designer; born Oslo.

▶ Studied Statens Håndverks -og Kunstindustriskole, Oslo, to 1955, and, 1957, Oslo Technical College.

▶ 1958–61, she was a designer at the Plus art and craft center in Fredrikstad; for a time, worked for Norway Silver Designs; in 1961, set up her own workshop in Oslo, becoming known as Norway's foremost contemporary jewelry designer; from 1975, taught at the Statens Håndverks -og Kunstindustriskole; became known for fantastic designs in various materials, including feathers, quills, and metal, particularly in the 1980s.

▶ Received four prizes in the Goldsmiths' Guild competition. Work included in 1970 New York City 'Craftsmen from Norway' exhibition and the subject of exhibitions at Kunstnernes Hus, Oslo, 1967; Galleri 71, Tromsø, 1973; Smykkegalleriet Dahlsveen, Trondheim, 1975; Kunstnerforbundet, Oslo, 1978 and 1989; Electrum Gallery, London, 1970 and 1981; Galleri Ingeleiv, Bergen, 1982; Artwear, New York, 1983 and 1987; Kunstindustrimuseet, Oslo, 1986.

▶ Cat., David Revere McFadden (ed.), *Scandinavian Modern Design 1880–1980*, New York: Abrams, 1982:272, Nos. 316,317. Fredrik Wildhagen, *Norge i Form*, Oslo: Sternersen, 1988:152.

Vigneau, André

▶ French designer, sculptor, photographer, and musician; active Paris.

▶ From the 1920s, Vigneau designed mannequins and store decorations for Siégel, Paris, and was its artistic advisor.

▶ Work (with that of others in the Siégel stable) shown at the pavilion (designed by Siégel artistic advisor René Herbst) on the Pont Alexandre-III, 1925 Paris 'Exposition Internationale des Arts Décoratifs et Industriels Modernes.'

▶ Nicole Parrot, *Mannequins*, Paris: Colone, 1981; London: Academy, 1982.

Vignelli, Lella   (b. Lella Elena Valle   1934–)

▶ Italian architect and designer; born Udine; active Udine, Milan, Chicago, and New York; wife of Massimo Vignelli.

▶ Studied Università di Architettura, Venezia; 1958, School of Architecture, Massachusetts Institute of Technology, Cambridge, Massachusetts.

▶ She joined the architecture firm Skidmore, Owings and Merrill in Chicago in 1959 as a junior designer in the interiors department; in 1960 in Milan, (with her husband) established the Lella and Massimo Office of Design and Architecture; in 1965, became head of the interior design department at Unimark International in Milan and, in 1966, in New York; in 1971, (with her husband) set up the design firm Vignelli Associates in New York, of which she was executive vice-president. She specialized in interiors, furniture, lighting, products, and exhibition design for clients including Rosenthal, San Lorenzo, Sunar, Poltronova, Heller, Casigliani, Poltrona Frau, and Knoll.

▶ Liz McQuiston, *Women in Design: A Contemporary View*, New York: Rizzoli, 1988:126.

▶ See Vignelli, Massimo

Vignelli, Massimo   (1931–)

▶ Italian graphic, industrial, interior, and furniture designer; born Milan; active Milan, New York, and Chicago; husband of Lella Vignelli.

▶ 1950–53, studied architecture, Politecnico di Milano; 1953–57, Università di Architettura, Venice.

▶ 1958–60, he taught at the Institute of Design, Illinois Institute of Technology, Chicago. In 1960, the Vignellis settled in Milan and set up the Lella and Massimo Vignelli Office of Design and Architecture. In 1965 in Chicago, he co-founded Unimark International, a design firm with offices worldwide; 1966–71, having moved to New York, was active in the design office he established there. During this time, corporate identity programs were designed for American Airlines, Knoll, Ford, and others, and signage for the New York City and Washington, DC, subway systems. In 1971, the Vignellis set up the design firm Vignelli Associates in New York with a staff of designers. He became a member of ADI (Associazione per il Disegno Industriale). The Vignellis' work included corporate identity programs for Xerox, Lancia, Cinzano, Bloomingdale's, USA National Parks Services Publications, and International Design Center of New York; book design for Chanticleer Press, Rizzoli, and Fodor Travel Guides; graphic formats for magazines *Architectural Record*, *American Ceramics*, *Opposition*, *A+U Zodiac*, and others; graphics for Knoll; glassware for Venini and Steuben; and silverware for San Lorenzo and Calegaro. Their designs included the 1964 *Saratoga* chair and sofa for Poltronova, 1966 logos for True Cigarette, 1964–71 furniture for Poltronova, from 1987 furniture for Poltrona Frau, 1971 furniture for Sunar, 1974 interiors at the Minneapolis Institute of Fine Arts, 1975 interior designs for St. Peter's Church in New York, 1972 shopping bag for Bloomingdale's department store, 1972–87 showrooms worldwide of Artemide, 1974 and 1990 jewelry for San Lorenzo, 1979 furniture for Rosenthal, 1979 goblets and flatware produced by Venini for Ciga Hotels, 1979 *Acorn* chair and *Rotunda* for Sunar, 1979 shopping bag for Saks Fifth Avenue store, 1981 showrooms of Hauserman in Chicago, 1985 *Serenissimo* table for Acerbis, 1985 jewelry for Cleto Munari, 1985–87 ceramics, flatware, and glassware for Sasaki, 1982–87 *Handkerchief* chair (produced from 1991, designed with David B. Law) by Knoll, 1990 *Magie* illuminated coffee table produced by Morphos, and 1993 range of crystal vessels by Steuben.

▶ The retrospective from 1990 of the Vignellis' work traveled to museums in Moscow, St. Petersburg, Helsinki, London, Budapest, Barcelona, Copenhagen, Munich, Prague, and Paris. Their awards included grand prize at 1964 (XIII) Triennale di Milano; 1964 Premio Compasso d'Oro; 1973 American Institute of Architects

Industrial Arts Medal; honorary doctorates from Parsons School of Design in New York, Pratt Institute in Brooklyn, New York, and Rhode Island School of Design in Providence; 1982 Hall of Fame award of the Art Directors' Club, New York; 1983 AIGA gold medal; 1985 (first) Presidential Design Achievement Award; 1988 *Interior Design* magazine Hall of Fame; 1991 National Arts Club Gold Medal for Design; and 1992 Interior Product Designers Fellowship of Excellence.

▶ *Design Vignelli*, New York, 1981, Stephen Kliment, 'The Vignellis—Profile of a Design Team,' in *Designer's Choice*, New York, 1981:6–12. Barbaralee Diamonstein, *Interior Design: The New Freedom*, New York, 1982:176–91. Stan Pinkwas, 'King and Queen of Cups,' *Metropolis*, Jan.–Feb. 1983:12–17. *ADI Annual 1976*, Milan: Associazione per il Disegno Industriale, 1976. Cat., Kathryn B. Hiesinger and George H. Marcus III (eds.), *Design Since 1945*, Philadelphia: Philadelphia Museum of Art, 1983:234, VI–22, V–46. *Design: Vignelli*, New York: Rizzoli, 1990.

▶ See Vignelli, Lella

Vigo, Nanda

▶ Italian architect, designer, and environmental artist; born and active Milan.

▶ Studied architecture, École Polytecnique Fédérale, Lausanne, to 1956, then studied in San Francisco.

▶ She worked with Lucio Fontana and Gio Ponti; opened her own studio in Milan in 1959; using her architecture and design training, in the 1960s developed her 'chronotopical theory of space and time'; subsequently, in aesthetic research with Zero Group, Aktuel Group, and Light & Bewegung, explored the possibilities of sensory stimuli obtained by using industrial materials, such as glass, mirrors, and neon lights; collaborated with Gio Ponti, Lucio Fontana, and Piero Manzoni. Her 1968 *Golden Gate* and 1969 *Iceberg* lamps were produced by Arredoluce, 1968 glass and mirror chairs and tables by FAI International, 1985 *Light Tree* lamp by Quartet, and 1986 *Null* table by Glass Design. Her architectural projects included 1967–71 Brindisi Museum and the private house Lido di Spina in Ferrara. She taught at the École Polytecnique Fédérale and at the Academy of Fine Art, Macerata; had design clients including Driade, and Gabbianelli.

▶ First showed work in 1959; work included in 1964 (XIII) and 1973 (XV) Triennali di Milano; 1982 Biennale di Venezia. Received 1971 New York Award for Industrial Design (*Golden Gate* lamp); St. Gobain Award for Industrial Design, Milan.

▶ Andrea Branzi, *La Casa Calda: Esperienze del Nuovo Disegno Italiano*, Milan: Idea Books, 1982. Liz McQuiston, *Women in Design: A Contemporary View*, New York: Rizzoli, 1988:130. *Modo*, No. 148, March–April 1993:127.

Villeroy et Boch

▶ German ceramics and glassware manufacturer; located Mettlach.

▶ In the 18th century, François Boch and members of the Villeroy family founded separate factories. In 1936, these were amalgamated to form Villeroy et Boch, where today ceramic tiles, sanitary fittings, and ceramics and glassware for the table are produced. Although previously known for its traditional wares, from the late 1960s, the firm began issuing designs in contemporary shapes, colors, and functions, including stacking features. In the early 1970s, Helen von Boch with Federigo Fabbrini designed its *Sphere* stoneware and 1973 *Bomba* melamine dinnerwares in a one-unit portable design. In 1982, limited editions of the work of students of Matteo Thun at the Kunstgewerbeschule in Vienna were issued. The firm produced the designs of Matteo Thun and frogdesign, and Paloma Picasso's 1991 range of flatware, glassware, and ceramics, and Keith Haring motifs in limited editions from c1992.

▶ 'Design in Action: Inner Beauty,' *Industrial Design*, Vol. 18, May 1971:34. Sylvia Katz, *Plastics: Designs and Materials*, London, 1978:71–72. Cat., Kathryn B. Hiesinger and George H. Marcus III (eds.), *Design Since 1945*, Philadelphia: Philadelphia Museum of Art, 1983:234, VI–3.

Vincent, René (aka René Maël 1879–1936)
▶ French ceramicist, illustrator, and designer.
▶ Studied architecture, École des Beaux-Art, Paris.
▶ He rendered illustrations for *La Vie Parisienne* and *L'Illustration*; in 1905, published his first illustrated book; moving from an Art Nouveau style to the angularity of Art Déco, he designed vases, table services, clocks, and other objects, some of which were made in ceramics by Jean Besnard, Ivry; in 1924, opened Vinsard, his workshop at Sèvres.
▶ Victor Arwas, *Art Déco*, Abrams, 1980.

Vinçon
▶ Spanish shop; located Barcelona.
▶ In 1940, Jacinto Amat set up the shop Vinçon in Passeig de Gràcia, Barcelona, to sell German porcelain. From the 1960s, his son Fernando Amat took over direction of the shop and, in 1967, began to sell avant-garde design. Its exhibition hall La Sala Vinçon was reopened with the 1973 exhibition of Bigas Luna's Post-Modern tables; Oscar Tusquet's *Gaulino* chair was shown there in 1987. In 1986, the gallery launched the work of manufacturer Santa & Cole.
▶ Guy Julier, *New Spanish Design*, New York: Rizzoli, 1991.

Viollet, Jean-Paul
▶ French furniture designer and maker; born Rhône Valley; active Brooklyn, New York.
▶ He settled in New York in 1978; in 1984, set up a furniture design and production workshop in a loft in Brooklyn; designed furniture reflective of 1920s, and 1930s French styles in exotic woods and veneers inlaid with shagreen, silver, parchment, bone, mother-of-pearl, and abalone.
▶ Cathy Cook, 'John-Paul Viollet Bring Back Soul,' *Elle Decor*, Aug. 1991:26.

Vitha, Norbert (1952–)
▶ Dutch industrial designer.
▶ Studied Akademie Industriële Vormgeving Eindhoven.
▶ 1979–84, he worked as an industrial designer for the Heykop fastening factory; in 1984, joined the Lumiance Design Team.

Vitrac, Jean-Pierre (1944–)
▶ French industrial designer.
▶ Vitrac established his own studio in Paris in 1974. His firm pursued speculative research and new concepts in product design with offices in New York, Milan, and Tokyo. A commercial failure yet his favorite design, Vitrac designed the inexpensive 1979 *Plack* picnic set for Diam Polystrène; its knife, fork, spoon, cup, and plate were thermoformed as a single piece to be separated by the user. His 1970 variable floor lamp for Verre Lumière illustrated his commitment to 'radically new products.' His other designs included a 1984 suitcase for Superior PVC, and designs for furniture, tableware, sports equipment, and scientific instruments.
▶ Cat., Kathryn B. Hiesinger and George H. Marcus III (eds.), *Design Since 1945*, Philadelphia: Philadelphia Museum of Art, 1983:234, IV–38, VI–23. *Les Carnets du Design*, Paris: Mad-Cap Productions et APCI, 1986:88. François Mathey, *Au bonheur des formes*, *design français 1945–1992*, Paris; Regard, 1992:274.

Vízner, František (1936–)
▶ Czech glassware designer.
▶ 1951–53, Studied glassmaking in Nový Bor; 1953–56, in Železný Brod; 1956–62, Academy of Applied Arts, Prague.
▶ 1962–67, he designed pressed-glass decorative objects produced by the Dubí glassworks; 1967–77, free-blown glass by the Škrdlovice glassworks; from 1977, heavy colored glass pieces with sandblasted surfaces.
▶ *František Vízner—Sklo 1961–1971*, Prague, 1971. *František Vízner: Sklo*, Prague, 1982. Cat., *Czechoslovakian Glass: 1930–1980*, Corning, NY: The Corning Museum of Glass, 1981: Nos. 132–33. Cat., Kathryn B. Hiesinger and George H. Marcus III (eds.), *Design Since 1945*, Philadelphia: Philadelphia Museum of Art, 1983:235, II-69.

Vkhutemas
▶ See Vhutemas

Vodder, Arne (1926–)
▶ Danish architect and furniture designer.
▶ Vodder set up a design office in 1951 with Anton Borg. His furniture designs were produced by Sibast Møbler and Cado.
▶ Work shown in exhibitions in Stockholm, Brussels, London, Zürich, and New York, and at Triennali di Milano.
▶ Frederik Sieck, *Nutidig Dansk Møbeldesign: – en kortfattet illustreret beskrivelse*, Copenhagen: Bondo Gravesen; 1990 Busck edition in English.

Vogeler, Heinrich (1872–1942)
▶ German painter, graphic designer, and silversmith; active Worpswede (Germany) and Karaganda (Russia).
▶ Vogeler designed silverwares for M.H. Wilkens und Söhne, Bremen-Hemelingen; its best-known consultant designer, he executed designs for candelabra, other tablewares, and accessories c1900. His *Tulip* pattern silver was sold at Julius Meier-Graefe's La Maison Moderne in Paris. His design work included books, ceramics, and furniture. In 1932, he settled in the Soviet Union.
▶ His work was shown at the 1910 Brussels 'Exposition Universelle et Internationale.'
▶ Annelies Krekel-Aalberse, *Art Nouveau and Art Déco Silver*, New York: Abrams, 1989:141,260.

Vogtherr, Burkhard (1942–)
▶ German industrial designer; active Karden-Holzen.
▶ Studied industrial design, Werkkunstschulen, Kassel and Wuppertal.
▶ He served as an apprentice for three years before he became a freelance designer in 1970. His 1984 *T-Line* metal and polyethane-foam chair was produced by Arflex.
▶ He received the 1969 Bundespreis 'Die gute Industrieform.'
▶ Albrecht Bangert and Karl Michael Armer, *80s Style: Designs of the Decade*, New York: Abbeville, 1990:44,236.

Volonterio, Roberto (1944–)
▶ Italian architect and designer; born Taranto; active Milan.
▶ Studied Politecnico di Milano to 1971, under Marco Zanuso and Renzo Piano.
▶ Volonterio began his professional career in 1971; designed houses, apartment buildings, and interior architecture for offices and residences; became a member of ADI (Associazione per il Disegno Industriale). Clients for furniture, lighting, and industrial design included Sormani, Zanotta, La Linea, Maisa, Flumen, Elam, Quattrifolio, Ginova, Saporiti, and Bernini; in 1990, worked on urban décor for Azienda Energetica Municipale in Milan.
▶ Received a prize at the 1973 (I) Grandecoro national ceramic competition, Reggio Emilia; showed accessories and lighting at 1975 Salone di Bari, and wooden furniture at Salone del Mobile in Milan.
▶ *ADI Annual 1976*, Milan: Associazione per il Disegno Industriale, 1976. *Modo*, No. 148, March–April 1993:127.

Von Bohr, Olaf (1927–)
▶ Austrian industrial designer; born Salzburg; active Milan.
▶ Von Bohr began his professional career in 1954; 1953–55, worked in the studio of Gio Ponti and, 1954–64, in the studio of Alberto Rosselli; in 1955, designed the office development of La Rinascente; from 1966, designed for Kartell (plastic furniture and accessories, including the 1970 *4930–7* modular bookshelves), Velca, and Valenti (lighting) and, from 1974, for Gedy and Bilumen. His shelving system in plastic and articulated table lamp were produced by Kartell in Binasco, and furniture, including the stool *Trio*, by Gedy in Varedo. He became a member of ADI (Associazione per il Disegno Industriale).
▶ *ADI Annual 1976*, Milan: Associazione per il Disegno Industriale, 1976.

von Brauchitsch, Margarethe　(1865–1957)

▶ German embroiderer.

▶ Studied painting in Leipzig under Max Klinger, and in Vienna under Koloman Moser.

▶ Active at the turn of the century, von Brauchitsch may have been associated with the embroidery studio founded in Munich in 1895 by Hermann Obrist, whose influence showed in her work. She became an important Art Nouveau textile designer and a founding member of the Vereinigte Werkstätten für Kunst im Handwerk, Munich. Her embroidery designs were published in the journal *Dekorative Kunst* in 1900.

▶ Stuart Durant, *Ornament from the Industrial Revolution to Today*, Woodstock, NY, 1986:52. Cat., Kathryn Bloom Hiesinger, *Die Meister des Münchner Jugendstils*, Munich: Stadtmuseum, 1988:42–43.

von Brevern, Renate　(1942–)

▶ German designer, born Wiesbaden.

▶ 1963–67, studied ceramics, Werkkunstschule, Wiesbaden, under Margot Münster.

▶ She and Neike Mühlhaus formed the design studio Projekt Cocktail in 1981; from 1984, participated in various design exhibitions. Their work included the 1988 mirror and 1986 *Sisters* vases, marketed by Herbert Jakob Weinand in limited editions.

▶ Their work was the subject of numerous exhibitions and included in various group shows.

▶ Cat., Design Center Stuttgart, *Women in Design: Careers and Life Histories Since 1900*, Stuttgart: Haus der Wirtschaft, 1989:94–95.

von Klier, Hans　(1934–)

▶ Czech industrial designer; born Děčín; active Milan.

▶ Studied Hochschule für Gestaltung, Ulm, to 1959.

▶ After working in Sessanta, he settled in Milan and was a consultant designer to La Rinascente department store; collaborated with Rodolfo Bonetto; 1960–68, worked in the design office of Ettore Sottsass as a designer of furniture and equipment by Olivetti, including the *Tekne 3* and *Praxis 48* typewriters, *TE 300* teletyper, and *Summa 19R* adding machine; from 1969, was in charge of corporate identity at Olivetti; 1973–75, was jury member of the German Bundespreis 'Die gute Industrieform'; taught in Britain, Germany, and the USA; became known for distinctive lighting design, including his 1987 *Grillo* table lamp. Clients in Italy included Bilumen, Foemm, Planula, Rossi-Arredamenti, Skipper, Valsodo, Viennaline, and Gavazzi, and German firms Wirus and Drabert. He was a member of ADI (Associazione per il Disegno Industriale).

▶ Work (educational toys) subject of 1962 exhibition, gallery Il Sestante, Milan. Participated in Triennali di Milano.

▶ Cat., Milena Lamarová, *Design a Plastické Hmoty*, Prague: Uměleckoprůmyslové Muzeum, 1972:118. *ADI Annual 1976*, Milan: Associazione per il Disegno Industriale, 1976. Alfonso Grassi and Anty Pansera, *Atlante del Design Italiano 1940–80*, Milan: Fabbri, 1980:331. Cat., *Donation Olivetti: Die Neue Sammlung*, Munich, 1986:39. Fumio Shimizu and Matteo Thun (eds.), *The Descendants of Leonardo: The Italian Design*, Tokyo, 1987:339. Hans Wichmann, *Italien Design 1945 bis heute*, Munich: Die Neue Sammlung, 1988.

von Nessen, Margaretta 'Greta'　(c1900–c1978)

▶ Swedish designer; active New York; wife of Walter von Nessen.

▶ She collaborated with her husband Walter von Nessen in his New York lighting and metalworking firm, established in 1927. In the 1950s, she and her son revived the Nessen Studio following her husband's death in 1943. She executed her own designs and continued production of her husband's earlier work, including his 1927 swing-arm lighting range, and introduced the work of other designers. Her 1952 *Anywhere* lamp was economical and popular; its versatility permitted it to be hung, wall mounted, and set on a table. In 1954, the Nessen Studio was sold to Stanley Wolf, who had joined the firm two years earlier, and, in the 1980s, was acquired by Luxo.

▶ *Anywhere* lamp shown at 1952 'Good Design' exhibition, New York Museum of Modern Art and Chicago Merchandise Mart, and at 'Design Since 1945' Philadelphia Museum of Art.

▶ 'von Nessen, Walter' in *Who's Who in American Art*, 1936–37. *The New York Times*, 5 Sept. 1943:28. 'Market Spotlight,' *Interior Design*, Vol. 42, March 1971:68. Cat., Kathryn B. Hiesinger and George H. Marcus III (eds.), *Design Since 1945*, Philadelphia: Philadelphia Museum of Art, 1983:224,IV–28. *Lighting and Accessories*, April 1988:22–26.

von Nessen, Walter　(1889–1943)

▶ German metalworker; born Berlin; active New York; husband of Greta von Nessen.

▶ Studied Vereinigte Staatsschulen für freie und angewandte Kunst (Kunstgewerbeschule), Berlin-Charlottenburg, under Bruno Paul.

▶ Paul taught von Nessen the importance of careful workmanship in the tradition of the Werkbund and Vienna Secession. Von Nessen redesigned the interiors of the Berlin subway stations and taught at the Kunstgewerbeschule, Charlottenburg; 1919–23, designed furniture in Stockholm. He settled in the USA in 1923; during his first years in New York, created furniture and furnishings for Manhattan homes and apartments; in 1927, founded Nessen Studio for design and manufacture in New York, where his famous 1927 swing-arm lamp was created; in various configurations, it is in production today. In 1930, when many other businesses were facing bankruptcy, the Nessen Studio announced its expansion; its 1930 catalog showed 30 lamps, mirrors, and tables. Its customers included architects, designers, and retailers. Von Nessen was a prolific designer for various American firms, including Chase Brass and Copper, one of his biggest commissions. His first Chase contribution was a collection of ten pieces in 1930. For his Chase metalwares, he used preexisting extruded industrial metal parts for ashtrays, bowls, and other items such as the mid-1930s *Diplomat* coffee service that was among his finest work. His approach in the mid-1930s was more Functionalist than the revival styles in luxurious materials he had produced in the late 1920s. He did much of his work in metal, though he also designed some wooden furniture. Despite a fondness for *torchère* lamps, he did not mimic the forms of pre-electric lighting, but borrowed techniques of indirect illumination from theater designers. Eliel Saarinen, Skidmore, Owings and Merrill, and Florence Knoll all incorporated von Nessen lamps into their interiors, and his lighting fixtures became ubiquitous in tasteful settings of the 1950s and 1960s. Von Nessen innovatively incorporated brass with satin chrome, spun aluminum, Bakelite, fiberglass, and natural cherry and rosewood into his work. The Nessen Studio, later Nessen Lamps, was bought from the von Nessen family by Stanley Wolf in 1952 and acquired by Luxo in the 1980s.

▶ His work was shown in the influential 1929 'Modern American Design in Metal' exhibition at the Newark Museum in Newark, New Jersey, where von Nessen's chair was shown alongside one by Mies van der Rohe. *Torchère* lamp shown at 1930 'Modern Age Furniture' exhibition at W. and J. Sloane, and at 1931 exhibition of the AUDAC (American Union of Decorative Arts and Craftsmen), New York. Work shown at 1930 New York 'Third International Exhibition of Contemporary Industrial Design' sponsored by the American Federation of Arts (adjustable ball-bearing lamp); 1932 New York 'Design and Industry Exhibition' (wall sconces, glassware, tables, and other accessories); 1937 Paris 'Exposition Internationale des Arts et Techniques dans la Vie Moderne' (gold medal); 1935 'Contemporary American Industrial Art, 1934' (metal, ceramic, and glass objects) and 'Contemporary American Industrial Art: 1940, 15th Exhibition,' both at the New York Metropolitan Museum of Art; and other exhibitions in New York.

▶ Karen Davies, *At Home in Manhattan: Modern Decorative Arts, 1925 to the Depression*, New Haven: Yale, 1983:24. Kimberly Sichel, *Industrial Design*, May—June 1984:38—42. *Home Lighting and Accessories*, April 1988:22—26. Anne-Marie Richard, 'Walter von Nessen' in Mel Byars and Russell Flinchum (eds.), *50 American Designers*, Washington: Preservation, 1994.

von Savigny, Christiane (1958–)
▶ German furniture designer; born Frankfurt am Main.
▶ Studied law, Maximilian-Universität, Würzburg; 1977—82, product design in Germany, and subsequently woodworking in Germany and Italy.
▶ She worked in 1980 at the home decorating firm House and Garden, Munich; in 1981, the design office of Rodolfo Bonetto in Milan; briefly at the Freien Kunstschule, Zürich. In 1983, she worked in a cabinetmaking workshop in Schauenburg, near Kassel; 1983—88, was a furniture and interior designer at Thonet, designing its *Programm 400* stacking chair; from 1988, was an independent consultant designer in Stuttgart.
▶ Cat., Design Center Stuttgart, *Women in Design: Careers and Life Histories Since 1900*, Stuttgart: Haus der Wirtschaft, 1989:162—63.

von Schnellenbühel, Gertraud (1878–1959)
▶ German metalworker; active Munich and Weimar.
▶ Studied metal work Debschitz-Schule, Munich.
▶ From 1911, she worked in the workshop of Adalbert Kinzinger, Munich; in the 1930s, worked in Weimar.
▶ Work shown at 1914 'Werkbund-Ausstellung,' Cologne.
▶ Annelies Krekel-Aalberse, *Art Nouveau and Art Déco Silver*, New York: Abrams, 1989:130,142,259. Cat., Kathryn Bloom Hiesinger, *Die Meister des Münchner Jugendstils*, Munich: Stadtmuseum, 1988:156—57.

von Sydow, Christian (1950–)
▶ Swedish designer.
▶ Von Sydow was a designer at the Kosta Boda glassworks.
▶ Work shown in Sweden and Italy.

Vondráčková, Jaroslava (1894–1989)
▶ Czech textile designer, producer, and publicist; born Prague.
▶ Studied painting in Prague, Paris, and Berlin.
▶ In 1923, he set up his own workshop and, in 1929 with Božena Pošepná, a studio; in 1926, became a member of SČSD (Czechoslovak Werkbund); belonged to the Devětsil circle; visited the Bauhaus several times, becoming friends with Otti Berger, experimented with artificial fibers and worked at Rodier, Paris; traveled to Scotland to study Harris tweed; in the 1930s, collaborated with leading Modern Czech architects; designed simple textiles in a Functionalist style.
▶ A. Adlerová, *České užité umění 1918–1938*, Prague, 1983.

Voulkos, Peter (1924–)
▶ American ceramicist and glassware designer; born Bozeman, Montana; active California.
▶ Studied Montana State University, Bozeman, to 1949; California College of Arts and Crafts, Oakland, California, to 1952; and Cranbrook Academy of Art, Bloomfield, Michigan, under Maija Grotell.
▶ He became head of ceramics at Berkeley, California; from 1951, worked at the Archie Bray foundation in Montana under resident sculptor Rudy Autio.
▶ Work shown at 1959 (XX) 'Ceramic International Exhibition,' Metropolitan Museum of Art, New York; one of six artists in 1981—82 ceramic sculpture exhibition, Whitney Museum of American Art, New York.
▶ R. Craig Miller, *Modern Design 1880–1990*, New York: Abrams. Frederick Cooke, *Glass: Twentieth-Century Design*, New York: Dutton, 1986:104—05.

Voysey, Charles Francis Annesley (1857–1941)
▶ British architect and designer; born Hessle, Yorkshire.
▶ Voysey was apprenticed to several prominent architects including, 1874—78, John Pollard Seddon. Seddon's imprint appeared in his furniture, and in the bold use of decoration in his architecture. In 1878 or 1879, he joined the office of architect Saxon Snell, who specialized in the design of charitable institutions and hospitals; 1880—82, worked in the office of architect George Devey in London. Devey was a designer of country houses for wealthy clients, including Lord Lytton, the Marquis of Lorne, Lord Granville, the Rothschilds, the Duke of Westminster, and Mrs. Henrietta Montefiore. In 1882, Voysey set up his own practice at Queen Anne's Gate in London. His strong original style was infused with an original interpretation of traditional vernacular details. Influenced by the Arts and Crafts movement, Voysey began in 1888 to design furniture, wallpaper, and textiles. Art Nouveau characteristics were expressed in his metal vessels. His textiles and wallpapers reflected the influence of A.H. Mackmurdo, with whom he worked. A skilful self-publicist, his work was exposed internationally through *The Studio* journal, in which he was frequently featured; his interview published in its September 1893 issue may have been the earliest of its kind with a designer. In the 1890s, he designed wallpapers produced by Essex and Co as well as its advertisement in magazines. Some of his patterns may have inspired the images of Walter Crane. Voysey was also influenced by Japanese art; like many contemporaries, such as Frank Lloyd Wright, he believed that furniture and furnishings should be specific to each architectural commission. Some of his designs were intended for mass production and among the most commercially successful of their time. Voysey designed numerous small and medium-sized houses in England including the 1891 Forster house, Bedford Park, London; 1899 Julian Sturgis house, Surrey; 1899 H.G. Wells's Spade House, Sandgate, Kent; 1905–06 Burke house, Hollymount; and Broadleys, Lake District. Most of Voysey's furniture was in oak and often unstained and unpolished, making features of joints and pegs. He is linked to the Modern movement through his concern for function and the reduction of ornamental details. Unwillingness to alter his Arts and Crafts allegiance, he did little work after World War I. His textiles were used extensively by Gustav Stickley in the USA.
▶ His architecture was represented in 1894 and 1897 events of the Salon de la Libre Esthétique, at Liège in 1895 with the Glasgow School, and at 1902 Turin 'Esposizione Internazionale d'Arte Decorativa Moderna.' Work subject of 1978 'C.F.A. Voysey: Architect and Designer, 1857–1941' exhibition, Brighton, and 1970 'Charles F.A. Voysey' exhibition, Santa Barbara, California; included in the 1959 'Art Nouveau: Art and Design at the Turn of the Century,' New York Museum of Modern Art, and 1981 'Architect-Designers, Pugin to Mackintosh' exhibition, London. In 1936, elected Royal Designer for Industry. Received 1940 gold medal, Royal Institute of British Architects.
▶ Yvonne Brunhammer et al., *Art Nouveau Belgium, France*, Houston: Rice University, 1976. *British Arts and Design, 1900–1960*, London: Victoria and Albert Museum, 1983. John Brandon-Jones, *C.F.A. Voysey: A Memoir*, London, 1957. David Gebhard, *Charles F. A. Voysey: Architect*, Los Angeles, 1957. Cat., *Charles F.A. Voysey*, Santa Barbara, California, 1970. Raymond McGrath, *Twentieth-Century Houses*, London, 1934. Charles Marriott, *Modern English Architecture*, London, 1924. Duncan Simpson, *C.F.A. Voysey: An Architect of Individuality*, London, 1979. Alan Victor Sugden and John Ludlam Edmundson, *A History of British Wallpaper, 1509–1914*, London, 1925. Stuart Durant, *The Decorative Designs of C.F.A. Voysey*, London: Lutterworth, 1990. Cat., *Architect-Designers, Pugin to Mackintosh*, London, 1981. Cat., John Brandon-Jones et al., *C.F.A. Voysey: Architect and Designer, 1857–1941*, Brighton, 1978.

Vretzaki, Helen (1960–)
▶ Greek industrial designer; born Edessa.
▶ 1977–83, studied architecture, Aristotelian University, Thessalonica, under Lavas George.
▶ From 1983, she was active as an interior designer of homes and shops and designer of the hall and pavilions for the International Fair, Thessalonica; in 1984, became a member of the Tetras

group; in 1986, began designing objects for various domestic uses and for industry and business, including stoves, bathroom fixtures, and furniture. She designed the 1986 'Ktenion' clothes stand for Studio Epsilon, Thessalonica.

▶ Work included in 1986 (VIII) Biennale of young artists from the Mediterranean, Thessalonica; 1987 (III) 'European Exhibition of Creation — SAD '87,' Grand Palais, Paris 1987 (V) and 1988 (VI) 'Panhellenic Competition of Furniture Design- Furnidec' (third prize for *Pyramis* furniture system, first prize for *Nautilus* furniture group), Thessalonica; 1988 Biennale de la Création, Namur; 1989 'Design Objects II,' Gallery Popi K, Athens.

▶ Cat., Design Center Stuttgart, *Women in Design: Careers and Life Histories Since 1900*, Stuttgart: Haus der Wirtschaft, 1989:260–63.

V'Soske, Stanislav   (1900–83)

▶ Polish textile designer and manufacturer; active USA.

▶ With his brother, V'Soske established a factory in Grand Rapids, Michigan; in 1924, designed and wove the first hand-tufted rugs in the USA; in the late 1930s, opened an additional manufacturing facility in Puerto Rico; in addition to producing fine quality, hand-finished rugs of his own designs in vibrant colors, occasionally with figurative motifs, commissioned other designers and artists, including Stuart Davis, George Nelson, and Michael Graves; in the 1950s, produced the rug for the Green Room of the White House, Washington; was best known for his high-pile sculptured and molded rugs. His own designs had titles such as *Riders in the Spring*.

▶ His 1955–60 *Romanesque* area rug shown at 1983–84 'Design Since 1945' exhibition, Philadelphia Museum of Art.

▶ 'V'Soske 1959 Exhibition of Rugs,' *Interiors*, Vol. 118, April 1959:134–35. 'The V'Soske Rugmakers,' *American Fabrics*, No. 51, Fall 1960:83–86. Cat., Kathryn B. Hiesinger and George H. Marcus III (eds.), *Design Since 1945*, Philadelphia: Philadelphia Museum of Art, 1983:235,VII–62.

Vuitton, Louis

▶ French luggage manufacturer; located Asnières from 1860.

▶ Louis Vuitton (1821–92) began in 1854 to design trunks with flat tops which made them stackable in the holds of oceanliners and in the baggage compartments of trains, covering them in elegant gray Trianon canvas. So successful was Vuitton that he was in the service of Empress Eugénie, becoming her favorite 'packer.' In 1890, his son Georges Vuitton (1857–1936) created a special lock featuring five prick-proof tumblers; in 1892, began

a study of the evolution of transportation and luggage, that led to the book *Le Voyage* (1894). To discourage counterfeiters of the luggage, the 'LV' symbol imprinted on paint impregnated canvas was introduced in 1896. The wardrobe trunk was introduced in 1875. Explorer Savorgnan de Brazza ordered the special trunk bed for a trip to the Congo in 1876. Georges Vuitton's son Gaston (1883–1970) began to establish branches throughout the world. In 1924, he designed the *Keepall* bag, a soft satchel with handles on the top, suitable for short trips. He assembled a rather large collection of antique traveling cases displayed in the London, Boston, New York, and Paris shops in 1926. The writing desk trunk first produced for Leopold Stokowski is still available today. In 1959, the company added dressing tables, manicure sets, glass scent bottles, and silver accessories to its range. In the 1980s, the *Epi* non-monogrammed series in six brightly colored leathers was introduced. In 1991, Christian Liaigre designed a leather and sycamore travel furniture set. From the 1980s, Françoise Jollant was coordinator of design.

▶ Vuitton won its first awards at the 1867 'Exposition Universelle' in Paris. Work subject of 1987 'L'invitation au voyage: Autour de la Donation Louis Vuitton,' Paris Musée des Arts Décoratifs.

▶ Cat., *L'invitation au voyage: Autour de la Donation Louis Vuitton*, Paris: Musée des Arts Décoratifs, 1987.

Vuokko
See Eskolin-Nurmesniemi, Vuokko

Vyse, Charles   (1882–1971)

▶ British ceramicist; born Staffordshire.

▶ Apprenticed to a pottery firm in Staffordshire; from 1896, studied sculpture, Royal College of Art, London.

▶ In 1920, he and wife Nell Vyse began production of ceramic figures in a studio in Cheyne Row, Chelsea; were members of a colony of various types of potters, including Reginald Wells and Gwendolen Parnell; produced figurines, a specialty of Chelsea, as well as attractive pots in sophisticated glazes (including experiments with wood-ash glazes) and ceramics based on celadon and other wares. In the 1930s, he experimented by applying drawn brushwork to pottery. He became a modeler and instructor in pottery at Farnham School of Art, Surrey.

▶ Beginning in 1922, showed his work regularly at BIIA exhibitions, Victoria and Albert Museum, London.

▶ *British Arts and Design, 1900–1960*, 1983. Cat., *Thirties: British art and design before the war*, London: Arts Council of Great Britain, Hayward Gallery, 1979:98,132,302.

W

Waals, Peter van der (1870–1937)
▶ Dutch furniture designer and maker; active Britain.
▶ Studied in The Hague, Brussels, Berlin, and Vienna; from 1899, London.
▶ In 1901, he joined cabinetmakers Ernest Barnsley and Ernest Gimson as foreman and cabinetmaker in their workshop at Daneway House, near Sapperton, Gloucestershire; subsequently, became an important member of the group, supervising production of Gimson's designs and training the craftspeople in the workshop. In 1926 when Gimson died, Waals moved the workshop facility to Chalford, Gloucestershire; continued his furniture production in the manner of Gimson.
▶ Cat., *Thirties: British art and design before the war*, London: Arts Council of Great Britain, Hayward Gallery, 1979:72,83,128,302.

Wagenfeld, Wilhelm (1900–90)
▶ German architect and industrial designer; born Bremen.
▶ 1915–18, apprenticed at Koch und Bergfeld silverware factory, Bremen; concurrently, studied Kunstgewerbeschule, Bremen; 1919–21, Staatliche Zeichenakademie, Hanau; 1921–22, privately in Bremen and Worpswede; 1923–24, Bauhaus, Weimar, under László Moholy-Nagy.
▶ 1925–29, he was an assistant instructor at the Bauhaus, Weimar, where he designed primarily lighting fixtures, including the *MT8* table lamp of *c*1923 in nickel-plated brass with a disk base resting on three small hemispherical padded feet and a cylindrical column surmounted by a metal ring on which rested a hemispherical shade. The lamp was one of the earliest examples of the Bauhaus design philosophy. It was produced in two versions: one with a glass disk base, and one with a metal one. Until 1928, it was produced in both versions by Schwintzer und Gräff, Berlin; by 1930, made in a variant model by Bünter und Remmeler in Frankfurt; in 1931, further adapted by Wagenfeld in the model by Architekturbedarf in Dresden; an icon of 20th-century design, is still in production today. In 1929, was director of the Bauhaus metalworking department; best known for his glasswork, he also designed metalwork and carved and printed woodcuts while at the Bauhaus; became director of the metal workshop of the Staatliche Hochschule für Baukunst und Handwerk, Weimar; moving to Berlin, 1931–35, taught at the Kunsthochschule; in 1942, was director of the glassworking department. 1930–34, he worked for Jenaer Glaswerke Schott und Genossen; there designed mass-produced heat-resistant glass kitchenware, including the 1932 tea pot and diffuser, cups and saucers, 1934 coffee percolator, and 1935 kitchenware, much of which is still in production today; designed pressed-glass utility wares and table glass for Vereinigte Lausitzer Glaswerke of which he was artistic director, 1935–38. His best-known designs were the 1938 *Kubus-Geschirr* (*Cube-formed Dishes*) modular stacking containers (nine pressed-glass sections forming a cube shape when assembled) for Lausitzer and 1938 zig-zag shaped ink bottle for the Pelikan ink company. His stated goal at Lausitzer was to make glass cheap enough for the working class, and good enough for the rich. Dr. Mey, co-chair Lausitzer, set up Wagenfeld in a ten-person design department in 1936. Wagenfeld's *Oberweimar* set of glasses, at first considered eli-

tist, outsold every set of glasses ever made worldwide. He produced severe Bauhaus forms throughout the Nazi period and continued to work at Lausitzer after World War II; in 1947, became a professor of design at the Hochschule für Bildenden Kunste in Berlin; in 1954, set up his own studio in Stuttgart; became a consultant designer to Württembergische Metallwarenfabrik (WMF), and designed inflight hospitality packs for Lufthansa airlines, porcelain for Rosenthal, appliances for Braun, and lighting for WMF and for Schott. His porcelain designs were produced by Porzellanmanufaktur Fürstenberg in 1934. His work was widely published, including through editions of journals *Die Form* and *Kunst und Handwerk*. He wrote articles on industrial design theory, stressing a Functional approach as a prerequisite to good design.
▶ Jena and Lausitzer designs shown at 1937 Paris 'Exposition Internationale des Arts et Techniques dans la Vie Moderne' (two grand prizes). Other awards included bronze medal at 1936 (VI) and grand prizes at 1940 (VII) and 1957 (XI) Triennali di Milano; 1968 'Berliner Kunstpreis,' Bonn; 1969 Heinrich Tessenow Medal at the Technische Universität, Hanover; 1969 Bundespreis 'Die gute Industrieform,' Bonn. Work was subject of 1960 'Industrieware von Wilhelm Wagenfeld' exhibition, Kunstgewerbemuseum, Zürich; 'Wilhelm Wagenfeld: 50 Jahre Mitarbeit in Fabriken' exhibition, Kunstgewerbemuseum, Cologne, 1973, and Die Neue Sammlung, Munich, 1974; 1980 'Wilhelm Wagenfeld: Schöne Form, Gute Ware' exhibition, Württembergisches Landesmuseum, Stuttgart. Glassware and metalwork for WMF included in 1983–84 'Design Since 1945' exhibition at the Philadelphia Museum of Art.
▶ Michael Farr, *Design in British Industry: A Mid-Century Survey*, London: Cambridge, 1955:145. Cat., *Industrieware von Wilhelm Wagenfeld*, Zürich; Kunstgewerbemuseum, 1960. Cat., *Wilhelm Wagenfeld: 50 Jahre Mitarbeit in Fabriken*, Cologne: Kunstgewerbemuseum and Munich: Die Neue Sammlung, 1973. Carl-Wolfgang Schümann, *Wilhelm Wagenfeld: Du Bauhaus à l'Industrie*, Cologne: Kunstgewerbemuseum der Stadt Köln, 1973–75. Cat., *Wilhelm Wagenfeld: Schöne Form, Gute Ware*, Stuttgart: Württembergisches Landesmuseum, 1980. *Sammlung Katalog*, Berlin: Bauhaus Archiv, Museum für Gestaltung, 1981. Magdalena Droste in *Contemporary Designers*, London: Macmillan, 1981:616–17. Cat., Kathryn B. Hiesinger and George H. Marcus III (eds.), *Design Since 1945*, Philadelphia: Philadelphia Museum of Art, 1983:235,II–70–71,V–47–48. Lionel Richard, *Encyclopédie du Bauhaus*, Paris: Somogy, 1985:210–11. Frederick Cooke, *Glass: Twentieth-Century Design*, New York: Dutton, 1986:43,92. Beate Manske and Gudrun Scholz (eds.), *Täglich in der Hand: Industrieformen von Wilhelm Wagenfeld aus sechs Jahrzehnten*, Bremen: Worpsweder, 1987. Annelies Krekel-Aalberse, *Art Nouveau and Art Déco Silver*, New York: Abrams, 1989:141,150,260. Jeremy Myerson and Sylvia Katz, *Conran Design Guides: Tableware*, London: Conran Octopus, 1990:79.

Wagner, Otto (1841–1918)
▶ Austrian architect and designer; born and active Vienna.
▶ 1857, studied at Technische Hochschule, Vienna; 1860, Bauenakademie, Berlin; 1861–63, Akademie der bildenden

Künste, Vienna, under Eduard van der Null and August Sicard von Sicardsburg.

▶ His historicist early work was mainly confined to the design of apartment houses. One of the buildings for which he became best known, and for which he designed distinctive furniture still reproduced today, was the 1904–06 Postsparkasse (Postal Savings Bank) in Vienna. In 1894, he became head of and an influential professor at the Akademie der bildenden Künste, Vienna; Josef Hoffman and Josef Maria Olbrich were among his pupils. In the 1890s, he worked on the periphery of the Art Nouveau style, showing more classical tendencies by the turn of the century; published the book *Moderne Architektur* (1894), marking a turning-point in his career and arguing that Modern life was the single point of departure for the creative artist. Responsible for design of the Vienna city railway project in the last decade of the 19th century, he established a large drawing office where there were some 70 collaborators, including Hoffmann, Jože Plečnik, Max Fabiani, Leopold Bauer, and the office's chief draftsman and manager Olbrich. In 1902, he designed silver for J.C. Klinkosch. He was a member of the Deutscher Werkbund, along with his pupils Adolf Loos and Olbrich. His architecture included the 1898 Stadtbahn station in the Karlsplatz, Vienna: 1898 Majolika house, Vienna; 1906–07 sluice-house of the Kaiserbad dam, Danube Canal; and 1908–13 Lupus Hospital, Vienna.

▶ Work shown in Austrian stand at 1902 Turin 'Esposizione Internazionale d'Arte Decorativa Moderna' (including silver designs for Klinkosch), and in 1902 winter exhibition of the Österreichisches Museum für Kunst und Industrie, Vienna; subject of 1963 'Otto Wagner: Das Werk des Architekten' exhibition, Vienna.

▶ Otto Wagner, *Moderne Architektur*, Vienna, 1896. Joseph August Lux, *Otto Wagner*, Munich, 1914. Hans Tietze, *Otto Wagner*, Vienna, 1922. Cat., *Otto Wagner: Das Werk des Architekten*, Vienna, 1963. H. Geretsegger and M Peintner, *Otto Wagner, 1841–1918: The Expanding City and the Beginning of Modern Architecture*, New York, 1979. Robert Waissenberger et al., *Vienna 1890–1920*, Secaucus, NJ: Wellfleet, 1984:172–83. Cat., *Otto Wagner, Vienna 1841–1918: Designs for Architecture*, Oxford: Museum of Modern Art, 1985. Annelies Krekel-Aalberse, *Art Nouveau and Art Déco Silver*, New York: Abrams, 1989:191,195,199,260.

Wagner, Seigfried (1874–1952)

▶ Danish sculptor and metalworker.

▶ In the 1910s, Wagner designed flatware for the Georg Jensen Sølvsmedie, including 1912 *Dahlia* pattern.

▶ Cat., *Georg Jensen Silversmithy: 77 Artists, 75 Years*, Washington: Smithsonian Institution Press, 1980.

Wainwright, Colbran Joseph (1867–1948)

▶ British silversmith and jeweler.

▶ In the early 1890s, Wainwright joined his father's jewelry firm; produced fine-quality enameled jewelry in the Arts and Crafts manner. In 1896, he became a shareholder in the Birmingham Guild of Handicrafts; in 1917, sold his shares to R. Hugh Roberts, director of jewelry firm E.R. Gittins, which amalgamated with the Guild in 1910.

▶ Charlotte Gere, *American and European Jewelry 1830–1914*, New York: Crown, 1975:227.

Wakefield Rattan

▶ American furniture manufacturer; located Wakefield, Massachusetts.

▶ Cyrus Wakefield Sr. (1811–73), a Boston grocer, began experimenting c1844 with discarded bundles of raffia, wrapping ordinary chairs in cane strips. Selling cane to furniture manufacturers, he became a major supplier and imported split rattan from China. In 1855, Wakefield moved his facilities to Mill River, South Reading, near Boston, and set up Wakefield Rattan. In 1856, the Opium War disrupted his supplies, and he turned to a by-product of the reeds used to make skirt hoops and baskets, devising furni-

ture made from the inner reed, which could be stained and painted, whereas natural rattan could only be varnished. His early models from rattan cane and domestic willow were in the kind of baroque forms popular at the time. In 1870, his assistant William Houston invented a process for weaving cane to make railroad and streetcar seat upholstery. In 1868, the town of South Reading was renamed Wakefield; the plant by the 1870s covered ten acres (4ha). In c1875, nephew and successor Cyrus Wakefield purchased several small competitors, including American Rattan. In 1883, a West Coast branch and Chicago factory were set up. The firm was bought in 1889 by competitor Heywood Brothers of Gardner, Massachusetts, and became known as Heywood Brothers and Wakefield.

▶ Received award for design and workmanship at 1876 Philadelphia 'Centennial Exposition.'

▶ Constance Cary Harrison, *Woman's Handiwork in Modern Homes*, New York, 1881:191,193–94. Esther Gilman Moore, *History of Gardner, Massachusetts, 1785–1967*, Gardner, Mass., 1967:222–28. Ruth A. Woodbury, *Wakefield's Century of Progress*, Wakefield, Mass., 1968:3–7. Doreen Bolger Burke et al., *In Pursuit of Beauty: Americans and the Aesthetic Movement*, New York: Metropolitan Museum of Art and Rizzoli, 1987:478–79.

Wakeley and Wheeler

▶ British silversmiths; located London.

▶ The firm was founded in 1891 by Arthur Wakely and partner Wheeler. In the 1920s and 1930s, its artisans included W.E. King, F.S. Beck, chaser B.J. Colson, and designers James Warwick, Leslie Auld, R.M.Y. Gleadowe, Reginald Hill, Harold Stabler, Kenneth Mosley, Cyril Shiner, and Arthur Wakely himself. It produced silver in Art Nouveau and Arts and Crafts styles, although most of its production was in historicist forms.

▶ Annelies Krekel-Aalberse, *Art Nouveau and Art Déco Silver*, New York: Abrams, 1989:32,33,35,260.

Wakisaka, Katsuji (1944–)

▶ Japanese textile designer.

▶ 1960–63, studied textile design in Kyoto.

▶ 1963–65, he worked for Itoh, Osaka and, 1965–68, for Samejima, Kyoto; 1968–76, designed printed fabrics for Marimekko in Helsinki; from 1976, executed patterns for printed and woven fabrications for Larsen, New York, and Wacoal, Tokyo.

▶ Wacoal fabric was the subject of a 1980 exhibition sponsored by the Japan Design Committee, and included in the 1983–84 'Design Since 1945' exhibition, Philadelphia Museum of Art.

▶ 'Bright Spell Forecast,' *Design*, No. 289, Oct. 1973:58–61. Cat., Kathryn B. Hiesinger and George H. Marcus III (eds.), *Design Since 1945*, Philadelphia: Philadelphia Museum of Art, 1983:235, VII–63.

Wall, James E. (?–1917)

▶ American furniture manufacturer; active Boston.

▶ Wall produced furniture and furnishings made from imported bamboo and lacquered panels. His bamboo wares included stands, tables, curtain poles, fire screens, and chairs. From c1881, he was active as a bamboo worker in Boston; after 1896, was a stockbroker; in 1901, returned to furniture making and became a partner of wallpaper hangers Wall and Brackett. In 1910 at 43 Cornhill Street, the firm imported wallpaper from Britain, France, and Germany, and grasscloth and leather from Japan.

▶ Doreen Bolger Burke et al., *In Pursuit of Beauty: Americans and the Aesthetic Movement*, New York: Metropolitan Museum of Art and Rizzoli, 1987:479.

Wall, James (1877–1952) and Gertrude Wall (1881–1971)

▶ British ceramists.

▶ James Wall worked for the Royal Doulton works before settling in the USA. In 1922 in California, the Walls established the Walrich Pottery, after their son's name Richard Wall. The spirit of their work was akin to that of neighbor California Faience, and Marblehead Pottery in Massachusetts. Their wares had the simplicity of which Gustav Stickley was so fond: monochrome glazes applied to simple silhouettes, with one color complementing the other. Many of the glazes were developed by James Wall. Its production ended in the 1930s. Subsequently, Gertrude Wall was an instructor in various arts and crafts programs. Richard Wall worked for Westinghouse in Emeryville, California, where high-voltage porcelain insulators were produced, and later taught firing to art students in San Francisco schools.

▶ Paul Evans in Timothy J. Andersen et al., *California Design 1910*, Salt Lake City: Peregrine Smith, 1980:74,77.

Wallance, Donald A. (1909–90)
▶ American metalworker and furniture designer; born New York City; active Croton, near New York.
▶ Studied New York University to 1930; 1936–40, Design Laboratory, New York.
▶ 1940–41, he was design and technical director of the National Youth Administration, Louisiana; during World War II, was active in the Office of the Quartermaster General, Washington, participating in a variety of design projects; subsequently, became a consultant on the design of mass-produced furniture for servicemen's families living abroad; discharged in 1944, continued to work for Quartermaster Corps until 1948; in 1949, set up a small studio in Croton-on-Hudson, New York, where he worked alone and occasionally collaborated on graphic design projects with wife Shula. Influenced by the Arts and Crafts movement of the turn of the century, he labeled himself an 'industrial craftsman'; is best known for his book *Shaping America's Products* (1956) rather than for his design work. In 1951, he began executing designs for tableware, cutlery, and accessories for H.E. Lauffer. His 1953 *Design 1* brushed stainless-steel flatware was designed for Lauffer and produced by Pott in Germany. From 1958–64, he designed hospital furniture for Hard Manufacturing, Buffalo, New York, and, in 1959, a range of cooking and serving pieces for Kensington (Aluminum Company of America); in c1960, was a consultant and designer on Philharmonic Hall, Lincoln Center, New York, where his widely praised 1964 auditorium seating was installed. Later designs included his 1978–79 *Design 10* plastic flatware for Lauffer.
▶ Received Golden Form award (*Bedford* stainless-steel flatware), Utrecht Fair, Netherlands.
▶ Donald A. Wallance, 'Design in Plastics,' *Everyday Art Quarterly*, Vol. 6, 1947:3–4,15. Cat., Kathryn B. Hiesinger and George H. Marcus III (eds.), *Design Since 1945*, Philadelphia: Philadelphia Museum of Art, 1983:235, V–49. Don Wallance, *Shaping America's Products*, New York: Reinhold, 1956. Ada Louise Huxtable, 'Stainless Comes to Dinner,' *Industrial Design*, Vol. 1, Aug. 1954:30–38. James Elliott Benjamin, 'Don Wallance' in Mel Byars and Russell Flinchum (eds.), *50 American Designers*, Washington: Preservation, 1994.

Wallander, Alf (1862–1914)
▶ Swedish ceramicist, metalworker and glassware, furniture, and textile designer.
▶ 1879–85, studied Konstfackskolan, Stockholm; 1885–89, Academie Morot & Constant, Paris.
▶ From 1895–1910, he worked at Rörstrand in Lidköping, where he was artistic director from 1900; designed furniture and textiles for Svensk Konstslöjdsutställning Selma Giöbel, where he was director from 1899; 1908–09, designed glassware for the Kosta glassworks and, 1908–14, for Reijmyre glassworks; from 1908, was a senior tutor Konstfackskolan, Stockholm.
▶ Work shown at 1897 Stockholm 'Konst- och Industriutställningen' and 1900 Paris 'Exposition Universelle.'
▶ Cat., David Revere McFadden (ed.) *Scandinavian Modern Design 1880–1980*, New York: Abrams, 1982:272, Nos. 11,12,15,49,62. Jennifer Hawkins Opie, *Scandinavia: Ceramics and Glass in the Twentieth Century*, New York: Rizzoli, 1989.

Walrich Pottery
See Wall, James and Gertrude Wall

Walsh Walsh, John
▶ British glassware manufacturer; located Birmingham.
▶ The firm's cut and engraved crystal range was extended in 1929 to include their new *Pompeian* range of colored iridescent Venetian-style tableware. Of the glasshouses in the Midlands, Walsh Walsh was the only firm to advertise blown iridescent glass. Clyde Farquharson was a designer there from 1935 until the firm closed in 1951.
▶ *Pompeian* ware shown at 1929 British Industries Fair.
▶ Frederick Cooke, *Glass: Twentieth-Century Design*, New York: Dutton, 1986:60,67–68.

Walter, Almaric (1859–1942)
▶ French glassmaker and ceramicist; born Sèvres.
▶ Studied École Nationale de la Manufacture de Sèvres.
▶ He began working in 1902 with *pâte-de-verre*; 1908–14 at Daum, executed glass sculptures based on models by Henri Bergé, the firm's artistic director; in 1919, set up his own workshop, where he produced *pâte-de-verre* objects; by 1925, had ten employees; made windows and objects based on models, including the Tanagra figurines in the Louvre and 18th-century reliefs.
▶ Yvonne Brunhammer et al., *Art Nouveau Belgium, France*, Houston: Rice University, 1976.

Walters, Carl (1883–1955)
▶ American ceramicist; active Woodstock, New York.
▶ 1905–07, studied Minneapolis School of Art; 1908–11, Chase School, New York, under Robert Henri.
▶ He set up a workshop in 1919 in Cornish, New Hampshire; in 1920, moved to Woodstock, New York; at first, produced ceramic candlesticks, bowls, plates, and vases with applied calligraphic motifs inspired by Persian pottery; began producing whimsical ceramic animals based on hollow clay forms.
▶ Garth Clark, *A Century of Ceramics in the United States, 1878–1978*, New York: Dutton with Everson Museum of Art, 1979:338. 'Carl Walters—Sculptor of Ceramics,' *Index of Twentieth-Century Artists*, June 1936:305.

Walton, Allan (1891–1948)
▶ British painter, decorator, architect, and textile designer and manufacturer; active London.
▶ Trained with an architect in London; studied painting, Slade School of Art, London; Westminster School of Art under W.R. Sickert; Académie de la Grande Chaumière, Paris.
▶ He was a member of the London Group of artists; in 1925, set up Allan Walton Textiles with his brother in London; as a principal of Allan Walton Fabrics, commissioned some of the most enterprising screen prints of the 1930s, designed by Vanessa Bell and Duncan Grant; designed carpets, embroideries, and printed fabrics; in the late 1920s, became head of the decorating department of the Fortnum and Mason department store in London, for whose clients he produced fashionable and stylish rooms, occasionally with wall decorations painted by John Armstrong; decorated the 1925 Restaurant Français, Leicester Square, London, and 1927 Restaurant Boulestin in Covent Garden, London, both with Clough Williams-Ellis overseen by X. Marcel Boulestin. Their design for Restaurant Français was innovative, attracting a clientele who came there as much for the décor as for the food. He was an influential propagandist of good design and a member of most of the British industrial design and art education organizations; 1943–45, was director of Glasgow School of Art.
▶ Frequently showed paintings and watercolors. Allan Walton Fabric's textiles included in 1979–80 'Thirties' exhibition, Hayward Gallery, London.
▶ Cat., *Thirties: British art and design before the war*, London: Arts Council of Great Britain, Hayward Gallery, 1979:70, 87,91,126,127,143,145,302. Stephen Calloway, *Twentieth-Century Decoration*, New York: Rizzoli, 1988:167,235. Valerie Meads, *The Victoria & Albert Museum's Textile Collection, British Textiles from 1900 to 1937*, London: Victoria and Albert Museum, 1992.

Walton, George Henry   (1867–1933)

▶ Scottish architect and designer; active Glasgow.

▶ He spent the first ten years of his career in Glasgow; in 1888, set up retail quarters and a decorating workshop in Glasgow. His commissions included Clutha Clagg for James Couper, stained-glass panels for William Burrell, furniture and interiors for Liberty, and the refurbishment of Miss Cranston's tea rooms, Argyll and Buchanan Streets, Glasgow; in 1898, settled in London; designed interiors for Kodak in Glasgow, Brussels, Vienna, Milan, London, Moscow, and Leningrad (now St. Petersburg). Closely associated with the Arts and Crafts movement, Walton's designs were quieter than those of Charles Rennie Mackintosh. Working in a rectilinear manner, his exaggeratedly vertical interiors incorporated white-painted full-length wall panels. His furniture was influenced by Sheraton and Chippendale. Later in his career he designed and built houses in Wales, London, Oxfordshire, and France; in his interiors, incorporated inglenooks with built-in settles, and sideboards at the ends of rooms. The 1901 'The Leys' house near Elstree, Hertfordshire, exemplified his mature style.

▶ Stephen Calloway, *Twentieth-Century Decoration*, New York: Rizzoli, 1988:66.

Wanscher, Ole   (1903–)

▶ Danish architect, furniture designer, and writer.

▶ 1944, studied Bygningsteknisk Skole; subsequently, architecture, Det Kongelige Danske Kunstakademi, Copenhagen.

▶ He set up his own office in 1928; designed furniture showing high standards of woodworking and cabinetmaking, and worked for several furniture firms in Copenhagen; was one of the founders of the Cabinetmakers' Guild in Copenhagen; 1953–73, taught architecture at Det Kongelige Danske Kunstakademi. His furniture designs were produced by A.J. Iversen and P. Jeppesen Møbelfabrik. His books included *Furniture Types* (1932), *Outline History of Furniture* (1941), *English Furniture c1680–1800* (1944), and *History of the Art of Furniture* (1946–56).

▶ Received gold medal at 1960 (XI) Triennale di Milano and 1966 Georg Jensen Sølvsmedie design competition (silver flatware). Work included in 1937 Paris 'Exposition Internationale des Arts et Techniques dans la Vie Moderne'; 1942 'Dansk Kunsthåndværk,' Nationalmuseet, Stockholm; 1964–67 USA 'Design in Scandinavia' traveling exhibition; 1956–59 Germany 'Neue Form aus Dänemark' traveling exhibition; 1958 'Formes Scandinaves' exhibition, Paris Musée des Arts Décoratifs; 1960–61 USA 'The Arts of Denmark' traveling exhibition; and 1964–65 'Formes Danoises,' France.

▶ Cat., *Georg Jensen Silversmithy: 77 Artists, 75 Years*, Washington: Smithsonian Institution Press, 1980. Frederik Sieck, *Nutidig Dansk Møbeldesign:—en kortfattet illustreret beskrivelse*, Copenhagen: Bondo Gravesen; 1990 Busck edition in English. Cat., David Revere McFadden (ed.), *Scandinavian Modern Design 1880–1980*, New York: Abrams, 1982:272, No. 219.

Ward, Neville   (1922–)

▶ British interior designer.

▶ Studied architecture, Liverpool University and Edinburgh College of Art.

▶ In 1948, he established the practice Ward and Austin, now called Ward Associates; designed the original façade for the Design Centre in the Haymarket, London, a Thames-side restaurant for the 1951 'Festival of Britain,' interiors for Sealink ferries, the oceanliner *Oriana*, and other ships, numerous exhibitions, and products ranging from pianos to decorative laminates.

Ware, Alice Hathaway Cunningham   (b. Alice Hathaway Cunningham   1851–1937)

▶ American amateur ceramicist and wood carver; born Cambridge, Massachusetts; active Boston and Milton, Massachusetts.

▶ From 1905, studied drawing, Museum of Fine Arts, Boston, under Philip Hale.

▶ She became a ceramicist in the 1870s. Her work was compared to that of Hannah Barlow of Doulton in England and Laura Fry in Cincinnati. Ware's interest in Japanese motifs was fostered by her father's involvement in the China trade. She was in charge of the porcelain painting classes at the Museum of Fine Arts, Boston; painted oils, watercolors, and pastels. Her painted tiles applied to fireplaces can be seen today on some homes in Milton, Massachusetts.

▶ Work included in Women's Pavilion, 1876 Philadelphia 'Centennial Exhibition'; exhibited wood carving at 1899 Boston Society of Arts and Crafts exhibition.

▶ Emma Forbes Ware, *Robert Ware of Dedham, Massachusetts (1642–99), and His Lineal Descendants*, Boston, 1901:286. 'Mrs. William R. Ware,' *The New York Times*, Apr. 2, 1937:23. Doreen Bolger Burke et al., *In Pursuit of Beauty: Americans and the Aesthetic Movement*, New York: Metropolitan Museum of Art and Rizzoli, 1987:479.

Wärff, Ann

See Wolff, Ann

Warnaar, J.J.   (1868–1960)

▶ Dutch silversmith; active Voorschoten and Haarlem.

▶ From 1880, trained as an engraver at H.M. Van Kempen en Zoon in Voorschoten.

▶ 1880–1922, he worked at Van Kempen, subsequently becoming a designer; after World War I, designed a number of expensive one-off pieces; from 1922, was an engraver in Haarlem. Often applied with semi-precious stones, his work showed luxurious ornamentation influenced by the Orient.

▶ Annelies Krekel-Aalberse, *Art Nouveau and Art Déco Silver*, New York: Abrams, 1989:178,260.

Warner and Sons

▶ British textile manufacturer; located Braintree, Essex.

▶ Warner's was founded in 1850 by Benjamin Warner; became the leading 19th- and 20th-century silk weavers and cotton printers; was known as Warner, Sillett and Ramm (before 1875), Warner and Ramm (1875–92), Warner and Sons (after 1892); was noted for high-quality technical achievement and design; hired leading designers of the day. In the 1930s, its designers included Eileen Hunter, Theo Moorman, Alec Hunter; Moorman and Hunter were responsible for hand-woven prototypes intended for power-loom production. As production manager 1932–58, Hunter oversaw style and design. Warner's weavings included natural yarns, sometimes with trial rayons, metallic strips, and cellophane. Hunter worked with the freelance designers, who were often not weavers, to translate their motifs into machine-woven goods.

▶ Cat., *A Century of Warner Fabrics, 1870 to 1970*, London: Victoria and Albert Museum, 1973. Cat., *Thirties: British art and design before the war*, London: Arts Council of Great Britain, Hayward Gallery, 1979:88,127,144,145. *A Choice of Design 1850–1980: Fabrics by Warner and Sons Ltd*, Braintree: Warner, 1981.

Warren and Fuller

▶ American wallpaper manufacturer; located New York.

▶ The firm of J.S. Warren was established in 1855, subsequently producing patterns in the mode of the Aesthetic movement. In 1882, John H. Lange joined J.S. Warren and William H. Fuller as a partner. Clarence Cook was engaged to write the history of the firm and describe its papers; the resulting small book was published as *What Shall We Do with Out Walls?* (1880). Louis Comfort Tiffany's and Samuel Colman's designs illustrated in the book were produced by the firm. In its 1881 design competition, Warren and Fuller received entries from Britain, Germany, France, and the USA; the judges were furniture maker Christian Herter, metalworker Edward C. Moore, and painter Francis Lathrop. The four prizes went to Americans, including Candace Wheeler (first prize for her bee-motif wallpaper) and daughter Dora Wheeler (fourth prize). The firm produced a full range of papers, including plain and embossed, bronzed and iridescent, washable tile, fireproof asbestos, and flocked.

▶ Showed papers at 1893 Chicago 'World's Columbia Exposition.'
▶ Catherine Lynn, *Wallpaper in America: From the Seventeenth Century to World War I*, New York, 1980:387,389,398,402–03,412–13,420,475,513. Charles C. Oman and Jean Hamilton, *Wallpapers: A History and Illustrated Catalogue of the Collection of the Victoria and Albert Museum*, London, 1982:73,77. Doreen Bolger Burke et al., *In Pursuit of Beauty: Americans and the Aesthetic Movement*, New York: Metropolitan Museum of Art and Rizzoli, 1987:479–80.

Washington, Robert Johnson (1913–)
▶ British ceramicist and teacher.
▶ 1930–33, studied Goldsmiths' School of Art; 1933–37, Royal College of Art, London; 1937–38, pottery under William Staite Murray.
▶ From 1938, he taught painting and pottery at the Derby School of Art, where he returned after World War II; 1946–48, was deputy principal at Margate; 1948–49, was principal of Dewsbury School of Art; became art advisor to Essex Education Committee; although retired by the 1980s, continued potting at his residence near Chelmsford.
▶ 1938 stoneware vase included in 1979–80 'Thirties' exhibition at the Hayward Gallery in London.
▶ Cat., *Thirties: British art and design before the war*, London: Arts Council of Great Britain, Hayward Gallery, 1979:132,301.

Watanabe, Suzuya (1934–)
▶ Japanese glass designer.
▶ Studied Women's College of Art, Tokyo, to 1957.
▶ She began working in 1957 for Otake Stained Glass; in 1982, became its director.
▶ Work included 1990 'Glass '90 in Japan,' Tokyo, and 1991 (V) Triennale of the Japan Glass Art Crafts Association, Heller Gallery, New York.
▶ Cat., *Glass Japan*, New York: Heller Gallery and Japan Glass Art Crafts Association, 1991: No. 41.

Waterer, John (1892–1977)
▶ British leather goods designer.
▶ Waterer was managing director of S. Clark; designed and produced luggage and other domestic leather products; was the instigator of the use of the zipper for luggage, and the inventor of the lightweight suitcase.

Watrous, Gilbert (1919–)
▶ American industrial designer; active San Diego, California.
▶ Studied industrial design, Illinois Institute of Technology, Chicago.
▶ 1957–c1962, he was a partner in the design studio Visual and Industrial Design, San Diego, where he designed products for various clients, including Convair air conditioning and Stromberg-Carlson sound equipment.
▶ Received special prize in 1950 international competition for floor-lamp design, New York Museum of Modern Art. His winning entry (1950 floor lamp with a fully-articulated adjustable arm on a low tripod base) included in 1983–84 'Design Since 1945' exhibition, Philadelphia Museum of Art.
▶ Cat., Kathryn B. Hiesinger and George H. Marcus III (eds.), *Design Since 1945*, Philadelphia: Philadelphia Museum of Art, 1983:235,IV–39. W.J. Hennessey, *Modern Furnishing for the Home*, Vol. 1, New York, 1952:245.

Waugh, Sidney (?–1963)
▶ American sculptor and glassware designer; born Amherst, Massachusetts.
▶ Studied Amherst College; School of Architecture, Massachusetts Institute of Technology; École des Beaux-Arts, Paris.
▶ He was an apprentice of and assistant to Henri Bouchard;

designed monuments worldwide; 1942–57, was director, Rhinehart School of Sculpture, Baltimore; wrote books *The Art of Glassmaking* (1938) and *The Making of Fine Glass* (1947); 1933 (with Arthur Houghton), reorganized Steuben Glass, where he was chief associate designer until his death; designed both form and engraved motifs for Steuben pieces.
▶ Received Prix de Rome and Herbert Adams Memorial Award for sculpture.
▶ Mary Jean Madigan, *Steuben Glass; An American Tradition in Crystal*, New York: Abrams, 1982.

Webb Corbett
▶ British glassware manufacturer; located Stourbridge.
▶ Irene Stevens joined Webb Corbett as designer in 1946. L. Green designed its 1958 *Bouquet* range of cut glass. David, Marquess of Queensberry was retained as a consultant designer in the early 1960s; he designed its 1963 *Queensberry-Harlequin* range, including centerpieces, bowls, vases, and tumblers, decorated in a stark geometrical pattern in clear cut glass.
▶ The *Queensberry-Harlequin* range won the 1964 Duke of Edinburgh's Prize for Elegant Design.
▶ Frederick Cooke, *Glass: Twentieth-Century Design*, New York: Dutton, 1986:77,78–79.

Webb, Philip (1831–1915)
▶ British architect and designer; born Oxford.
▶ 1849–52. Trained under architect John Billing in Reading.
▶ He joined architect G.E. Street's office in Oxford as principal assistant; while there in 1856, met William Morris and became greatly influenced by the writings of John Ruskin; in 1858, set up his own office and began to design Morris's 1859 Red House, Bexleyheath. With its asymmetrical and free ground plan and its inter-related interior and exterior, the house, built in unpretentious red brick, was an influential early example of a new type of domestic architecture in the Gothic Revival style, and the first full manifestation of the Arts and Crafts movement. In 1861, Webb became a partner in Morris, Marshall, and Faulkner, for which he designed solid furniture in oak in a simplified and austere Gothic style; produced stained glass and book covers and designed simple small glass items and metalwork with medieval references. His town and country houses combined medieval and 19th-century elements in an unconventional manner; one of the best known is the 1891 house, Standen, East Grinstead.
▶ W.R. Lethaby, *Philip Webb and His Work*, London: Oxford, 1935 (reprinted, London: Raven Oak, 1979). John Brandon-Jones, 'Philip Webb' in Peter Ferriday (ed.), *Victorian Architecture*, London, 1964. Robert Macleod, *Style and Society*, London, 1971.

Webb and Sons, Thomas
▶ British glassware manufacturer.
▶ Thomas Webb (?–1869) went into partnership with William Haden Richardson and Benjamin Richardson, taking over the Wordsley Flint Glassworks from the Wainwright Brothers. Dissolved in 1836, the firm became W. H., B. and J. Richardson. When Webb died, the business was assumed by his sons. In 1876, John Northwood produced Webb's *Denis* or *Pegasus* vase. Webb's famous craftsmen were brothers Thomas (1849–1926) and George Woodall (1850–1925); soon after 1878, it began cameo-glass production. In 1877, a patent was taken out by Thomas Webb for the *Iris* range. Noted Bohemian engraver, William Fritsche (c1853–1924) was at Webb's for 50 years. The firm was known for its bronze glass from 1873, Peach Bloom glass from 1885, Old Roman from 1888, and Tricolour from 1889. In the 1960s, David Hannmond designed it *Bodiam* cut-glass range.
▶ Victor Arwas, *Glass: Art Nouveau to Art Deco*, New York: Rizzoli, 1977.

Weber, Karl Emanuel Martin (Kem Weber 1889–1963)
▶ German designer; born Berlin; active Hollywood, California.
▶ 1904, apprenticed to Eduard Schultz, the royal cabinetmaker at Potsdam; 1908–10, studied Vereinigte Staatsschulen für freie und angewandte Kunst (Kunstgewerbeschule), Berlin-Charlottenburg (Germany), under Bruno Paul.
▶ In 1914, he traveled to California to design the German segment of the 1915 San Francisco 'Panama-Pacific International Exposition'; becoming trapped there by the events of World War I, he was refused permission to return to his homeland after the war's end, settling finally in Los Angeles; joined the design studio of Barker Bros., as a draftsperson; in 1927, opened his own studio in Hollywood, dubbing himself 'industrial designer'; was unable to work in a Modern idiom due to postwar anti-German prejudice, although he continued to find commissions. By 1926, the cultural climate became more sympathetic to Modernism. Virtually the only decorative arts designer to carry the Modern movement to the West Coast, his style was nevertheless his own. In 1929, he designed two cocktail-shakers with ebony handles for Friedman Silver, New York; silversmith Porter Blanchard of Pacioma, California, may have produced some tea sets after Weber designs. His designs for various silver vessels were simple and undecorated and were, like all of his work, intended for industrial production. Though Weber lived in California throughout the 1920s, his effect on design in New York was as great as if he had been a resident of Manhattan. He was an innovator of multi-functional furniture, and his pieces often mimicked the soaring skyscraper silhouette, with which Paul Frankl was likewise identified. A widely published assignment of his was the Bissinger residence in San Francisco. His c1934–35 *Airline* chair was widely published; with its sweeping arms, it had a powerful sculptured form and was reproduced from 1993. Weber published numerous articles on the new Streamline aesthetic.
▶ Room setting at 1928 'Exposition of Art in Industry at Macy's,' Macy's department store, New York; *Airline* chair included in 1991 'What Modern Was' traveling exhibition. Work subject of 1969 'Kem Weber: The Moderne in Southern California 1920 through 1941' exhibition, Art Galleries of the University of California at Santa Barbara, California.
▶ Kem Weber, 'What about Modern Art?,' *Retailing*, 23 Nov. 1929:20. Cat., David Gebhard and Harriette von Breton, *Kem Weber: The Moderne in Southern California 1920 through 1941*, Santa Barbara: University of California, 1969. Karen Davies, *At Home in Manhattan: Modern Decorative Arts, 1925 to the Depression*, New Haven: Yale, 1983:72–73. Annelies Krekel-Aalberse, *Art Nouveau and Art Déco Silver*, New York: Abrams, 1989:124–25,144,260. David Gebhard, 'Kem Weber' in Mel Byars and Russell Flinchum (eds.), *50 American Designers*, Washington: Preservation, 1994.

Weckström, Björn (1935–)
▶ Finnish metalworker and jewelry and glassware designer.
▶ Studied Kultaseppäkoulu, Helsinki, to 1956.
▶ 1956–63, he was a freelance designer; in 1957, a designer for Hopeakontu; from 1963, for Lapponia Jewelry in Helsinki; and, from 1964, for Kruunukoru. He was a furniture designer and sculptor in various media. In 1981, he settled in Italy and became a sculptor.
▶ Received awards at 1960 (XII) Triennale di Milano; 1968 Lunning Prize; 1972 Illum Prize; 1962 second prize and 1967 medal of merit, Finnish Jewelry Society event; and 1971 Pro Finlandia medal. Work subject of one-person exhibitions in Finland and abroad.
▶ Cat., David Revere McFadden (ed.), *Scandinavian Modern Design 1880–1980*, New York: Abrams, 1982:272, No. 299. Cat., *The Lunning Prize*, Stockholm: Nationalmuseum, 1986:184–89.

Wedgwood, Josiah
▶ British ceramics manufacturer; located Burslem and Barlaston, Staffordshire.

▶ At a young age, Josiah Wedgwood (1730–95) worked as an apprentice in various factories; by 1754, experimented with clay bodies and glazes; in 1759, founded the ceramics factory that is still in operation today; in the beginning, produced ordinary tableware; by 1759, had included ornamental wares, including classical vases and portrait busts; became one of the first manufacturers to use artists to design its range of goods. By the early 19th century, consultant designers John Flaxman and George Stubbs had been commissioned to do work for the firm, a practice subsequently emulated by other companies. Success in the 1860s was achieved through the firm's creation of an inexpensive, lightweight earthenware known as creamware or Queen's ware, and of fine-grained matt earthenware in black, blue, and other colors, known as jasperware or, in black, as basalt ware. From the 1840s until c1860, it produced copies of Classical antique pottery. 1860–c1910, its range included brightly colored majolica in relief molds (revived earlier by Minton). In 1859, Josiah Wedgwood's grandson Godfrey Wedgwood (1833–1905) joined the firm, becoming director at the turn of the century. The firm's freelance designers included French painter Émile Lessore from 1858, who continued to paint Wedgwood's pieces when he returned to France in 1863; Walter Crane 1867–c1888; and Christopher Dresser c1866–68. One of Dresser's best-known designs was the 1867 two-handled vase, transfer printed on unglazed earthenware (illustrated in Dresser, *Principles of Decorative Design*, 1873). In 1880, Thomas Allen, at Minton for 27 years, became Wedgwood's artistic director. Under Allen, Wedgwood set up a design department, where Allen instigated a range of ivory-bodied porcelain (like that of Royal Worcester) in the Japanese taste, along with less expensive transfer-printed earthenware of the 1870s and 1880s. In 1940, Wedgwood moved to Barlaston, Staffordshire. Its 20th-century designers, who were actively promoted by the firm, included Walter Crane, C.F.A. Voysey, Susie Cooper, Keith Murray, Eric Ravilious, and John Skeaping.
▶ Harry Barnard, *Chats on Wedgwood Ware*, London, 1920. William Burton, *Josiah Wedgwood and His Pottery*, London, 1922. Alison Kelly, *Decorative Wedgwood in Architecture and Furniture*, London, 1965. Alison Kelly, *The Story of Wedgwood*, London, 1975. David Buten and Patricia Pelehach, *Émile Lessore, 1805–1876: His Life*, Philadelphia, 1979. Robin Reilly and George Savage, *The Dictionary of Wedgwood*, Woodbridge, 1980. Maureen Batkin, *Wedgwood Ceramics, 1846–1959: A New Appraisal*, London, 1982. Doreen Bolger Burke et al., *In Pursuit of Beauty: Americans and the Aesthetic Movement*, New York: Metropolitan Museum of Art and Rizzoli, 1987:480–81.

Weedon, Harry W. (1887–1970)
▶ British architect.
▶ 1904, studied architecture in Birmingham; 1907–12, Royal Academy School, London.
▶ 1907–8, he worked for various architecture firms; 1908–12, was apprenticed to architect R.F. Atkinson; in 1912, set up his own architecture practice, where he designed cinemas at first, including the 1912–13 cinema at Perry Barr; in the 1920s, designed industrial and public buildings, housing developments in Birmingham, and houses in Warwickshire; designed the renovation of the Deutsch and Brenner factory in Hockley; was interior design consultant to Oscar Deutsch's Odeon Theatres, serving as its consultant architect from c1934. His Odeon designs included the 1935 cinema (with J.C. Clavering) in Kingstanding, Birmingham; 1936 cinema (with J.C. Clavering and R. Bullivant) in Scarborough; 1936 cinema (with J.C. Clavering) in Sutton Coldfield; 1937 cinema (with R. Bullivant) in Burnley; 1937 cinema (with Budge Reid) in Crewe; 1937 cinema (with Andrew Mather) in Leicester Square, London; and 1938 cinema (with P.J. Price) in Chorley. He executed a design program for the theater chain and oversaw its other architects; 1934–39, was involved in commissions for over 250 cinemas. After World War II, Weedon's firm's work included industrial buildings, such as those for car makers Austin at Longbridge, Birmingham, and for schools.

▶ Cat., *Thirties: British art and design before the war*, London: Arts Council of Great Britain, Hayward Gallery, 1979:27,30–74,302.

Wegner, Hans J. (1914–)

▶ Danish designer; born Tønder, Jutland.

▶ 1931, apprenticed to a cabinetmaker in Tønder and at Teknologisk Institut; 1936–38, studied Akademiets Arkitektskole; 1938, Kunsthåndværkerskolen, both Copenhagen.

▶ 1938–43, he was an assistant to Arne Jacobsen and Erik Møller; in 1943, opened his own office in Gentofte; 1946–53, was a lecturer at the Kunsthåndværkerskolen, Copenhagen. His meeting Johannes Hansen in 1940 or 1941 resulted in his numerous designs for Hansen in Copenhagen, including 1949 *The Chair*. Later, he designed for AP-stolen, FDB, Danish CWS, Getama, Carl Hansen, Fritz Hansen, CM Furniture, Planmøbel, P.P. Møbler, and Ry Møbler, producing more than 500 models; designed the interiors of headquarters of major companies. Best known for his early wood pieces, many of which are still in production today, he designed tubular steel furniture later on, and the 1960 *Bull* chair and ottoman in leather upholstery. His range of objects included furniture, silverware, lighting, and wallpaper. His 1947 *Påfuglestolen* (Peacock) chair by Johannes Hansens Møbelsnedkeri featured a dramatic bentwood back.

▶ Showed work at Cabinetmakers' Guild of Copenhagen; 1949–52, was involved in the mounting and arrangement of the Danish art and handicraft exhibitions. Received 1951 Lunning Prize; awards at the 1951 (IX) (grand prize), 1954 (X) (diploma of honor and gold medal), and 1957 (XI) (silver medal) at the Triennali di Milano; 1956 Eckersberg Medal; 1959 and 1965 Copenhagen Cabinetmakers' Guild prize; 1959 Citation of Merit from Pratt Institute, Brooklyn, New York; 1961 and 1968 International Design Award of the American Institute of Designers; 1961 Prince Eugen Medal; and 1967 and 1968 Citation of Merit from the American Institute of Interior Designers. In 1959, elected Honorary Royal Designer for Industry, London. *Påfuglestolen* (Peacock) chair shown 1947 exhibition of the Copenhagen Cabinetmakers' Guild and round table and chairs at its 1949 event. Work included in 1948 'Deense Kunsthandwerk,' Gemeente Museum, The Hague; 1954–57 USA 'Design in Scandinavia' traveling exhibition; 1956–59 Germany 'Neue Form aus Dänemark' traveling exhibition; 1958 'Formes Scandinaves' exhibition, Paris Musée des Arts Décoratifs; 1959 'Dansk Form og Miljø,' Kiljevalchs Konsthall, Stockholm; 1960–61 USA 'The Arts of Denmark' traveling exhibition; 1962 New York 'Creative Craft in Denmark Today'; 1964 'New York World's Fair'; 1964–65 'Formes Danoises' in France; 1968 'Two Centuries of Danish Design,' Victoria and Albert Museum, London; 1975–77 Eastern Europe 'Dansk Miljø' traveling exhibition; 1977 'Dänische Formgestaltung,' Berlin; and 1978 'Danish Design,' Dublin. Work was subject of exhibition in Zürich, 1958; at Georg Jensen, New York, 1959 and 1965; in Stockholm, 1962; Kunstindustrimuseet, Copenhagen, 1965; and Röhsska Konstslöjdmuseet, Gothenburg, 1967.

▶ George Nelson, *Chairs*, New York: Whitney Library of Ideas, 1952. Arne Karlsen, *Made in Denmark*, New York, 1960:56–63. Erik Zahle, *Scandinavian Domestic Design*, London, 1963. Johan Møller-Nielsen, *Wegner: En Dansk Møbelkunstner*, Copenhagen, 1965. Cat., *Modern Chairs 1918–1970*, London: Lund Humphries, 1971. Henrik Sten Møller, *Tema med Variationer: Hans J. Wegner's Møbler*, Tønder, 1979. Irving Sloane, 'Hans Wegner: A Modern Master of Furniture Design,' *Fine Woodworking*, No. 20, Jan.–Feb. 1980:36–42. Frederik Sieck, *Nutidig Dansk Møbeldesign:—en kortfattet illustreret beskrivelse*, Copenhagen: Bondo Gravesen; 1990 Busck edition in English. Cat., David Revere McFadden (ed.), *Scandinavian Modern Design 1880–1980*, New York: Abrams, 1982:272, Nos. 155,156. Cat., Kathryn B. Hiesinger and George H. Marcus III (eds.), *Design Since 1945*, Philadelphia: Philadelphia Museum of Art, 1983:235,II–89,II–90–91. Cat., *The Lunning Prize*, Stockholm: Nationalmuseum, 1986:202–05.

Weihrauch, Svend (1899–)

▶ Danish silversmith; active Århus.

▶ Weihrauch worked from 1928 as a silversmith and designer for the firm Frantz Hingelberg, Århus; often incorporated wood handles and bases on vessels for hot liquids.

▶ Weihrauch's Hingelberg silverwares shown first abroad at 1935 'Exposition Universelle et Internationale de Bruxelles.'

▶ Annelies Krekel-Aalberse, *Art Nouveau and Art Déco Silver*, New York: Abrams, 1989:220,260.

Weil, Bruno (aka Béwé)

▶ Austrian architect.

▶ Studied architecture.

▶ He used the pseudonym Béwé (the German pronunciation of his initials) as a furniture designer; produced the designs of German and French architects and designers including Le Corbusier, Charlotte Perriand, and André Lurçat; was director of the French branch of Thonet; designed furniture that included the 1928–29 *B282* table and 1928–29 *B250* office cabinet; under Charles Eames's influence, began the *Bently* chair program first produced in New York and subsequently in France.

▶ Jan van Geest and Otakar Máčel, *Stühle aus Stahl, Metallmöbel 1925–1940*, Cologne: König, 1980. Cat., *Pioneers of Modern Furniture*, London: Fischer Fine Art, 1991: Nos. 10–11.

Weil, Daniel (1953–)

▶ Argentine architect and designer; born Buenos Aires; active London.

▶ Studied architecture, University of Buenos Aires, to 1977; 1978–81, industrial design, Royal College of Art, London.

▶ From 1981, he designed a series of digital clocks, radios, and lighting for his own firm Parenthesis. His 1984 *Andante* deconstructed radio was executed with colorful separate parts housed in a clear plastic bag to be wall-hung; it was part of the *Anthologie* collection for Quartett. Viewed both as art and utilitarian objects, various radio designs screen-printed in colorful motifs and with exposed wiring and electronic parts were sold both as inexpensive production pieces and as limited-edition items in galleries. Weil believes that design should be not only technical and stylistic but also intellectual; (with Gerald Taylor) founded the design and manufacturing firm Parenthesis; in 1985, formed a design partnership with Taylor; became of partner in the Pentagram group; from 1991, was professor of industrial design, Royal College of Art. Parenthesis work included the 1981–83 *Bag Radio*, 1982 *Walking Radio*, 1982 *Cambalache Radio*, 1982 *China Wall Radio*, 1984 *Walter* flower vase, 1984 *Small Door Radio*, and 1984 *Claire* fruit bowl.

▶ Work shown in London, Milan, San Francisco, Dallas, Philadelphia, Hanover, and Venice. *Andante* radio included in 1983–84 'Design Since 1945' exhibition, Philadelphia Museum of Art.

▶ Cat., Kathryn B. Hiesinger and George H. Marcus III (eds.), *Design Since 1945*, Philadelphia: Philadelphia Museum of Art, 1983:235, I–49. Terry Ilott, 'Martian Crafts,' *Crafts*, No. 62, May–June 1983:30–33. Juli Capella and Quim Larrea, *Designed by Architects in the 1980s*, New York: Rizzoli, 1988. Albrecht Bangert and Karl Michael Armer, *80s Style: Designs of the Decade*, New York, Abbeville, 1990:196,236.

Weill, Lucie (1901–)

▶ French bookbinder and illustrator; born and active Paris.

▶ She produced Modern illustrated books in her own workshop, 6 rue Bonaparte, Paris, 1930–78.

▶ Showed work in France and abroad; participated in 1937 Paris 'Exposition Internationale des Arts et Techniques dans la Vie Moderne' and 1949 'The French Art of the Book' exhibition, California Palace of the Legion of Honor, San Francisco.

▶ Alastair Duncan and Georges de Bartha, *Art Nouveau and Art Déco Bookbinding*, New York: Abrams, 1989:23,176–7,196–97. Roger Devauchelle, *La Reliure en France de ses origines à nos jours*, Vol. 3, Paris 1961:206–07,279. Georges Lecomte, 'Les Relieurs d'art français à l'exposition de Paris,' *La Chronique graphique*, Brussels, 1938.

Weinand, Herbert (1953–)
▶ German designer; born Wittlich, Eifel.
▶ Apprenticed to a cabinetmaker; studied interior, furniture, and product design in Germany and Italy.
▶ From 1984, he designed numerous interiors for shops and restaurants in Berlin, Mainz, and Luxembourg; established his own gallery; was a participant in the German avant-garde movement of the 1980s. His 1988 *Karajan I* desk and *Karajan II* typewriter table for Designwerkstatt were shaped as grand pianos in black lacquer with silkscreened keys.
▶ Showed work in Germany, Austria, and Italy.
▶ Albrecht Bangert and Karl Michael Armer, *80s Style: Designs of the Decade*, New York: Abbeville, 1990:236.

Weininger, András (1899–)
▶ Hungarian designer; born Pécs.
▶ Studied architecture in Budapest; 1921–28, Bauhaus, Weimar and Dessau.
▶ From 1928, he was active as a decorator in Berlin; in 1939, moved to the Netherlands, participating in numerous painting exhibitions; in 1951, left for Canada; from 1958, lived in New York.
▶ Lionel Richard, *Encyclopédie du Bauhaus*, Paris: Somogy, 1985:212.

Weishaupt, Carl
▶ German firm of silversmiths; located Munich.
▶ One of the oldest German silversmithies, it was founded in the 17th century; produced the 1911 flatware designed by Richard Riemerschmid, who executed very few silver designs; also produced silverware based on Carl Weishaupt's own and others' ornamental sources. A box made in the workshops had an angular, spiral motif borrowed from designs by Patriz Huber of the Darmstadt artists' colony.
▶ Wares shown at 1914 Cologne 'Werkbund-Ausstellung' and 1922 Munich 'Deutsche Gewerbeschau.'
▶ Annelies Krekel-Aalberse, *Art Nouveau and Art Déco Silver*, New York: Abrams, 1989:129,131,142,143,260. Cat., *Metallkunst*, Berlin: Bröhan-Museum, 1990:500–01.

Weiss, Ivan (1946–)
▶ Danish ceramicist.
▶ 1962–66, Weiss worked as a painter at the Royal Copenhagen Porcelain Manufactory; 1966–70, as designer there, and subsequently as artist-in-residence. He taught at the College of Arts and Crafts in Kolding.
▶ Work subject of exhibitions at Royal Copenhagen Porcelain Manufactory, 1973; in Kyushu, 1977; at the Dordrecht Museum in 1979; in Sopot (Poland) in 1970, and at Det Danske Kunstindustrimuseum in Copenhagen in 1979. Work included in exhibitions including the 1981 'Danish Ceramic Design' at Pennsylvania State University.
▶ Cat., David Revere McFadden (ed.), *Scandinavian Modern Design 1880–1980*, New York: Abrams, 1982:272, No. 276.

Weiss, Reinhold (1934–)
▶ German industrial designer; active USA.
▶ 1959, studied Hochschule für Gestaltung, Ulm.
▶ While at Ulm, he worked with Hans Gugelot; in 1959 at Ulm, became associate director of the product design department and executive designer of the appliance division. His 1961 table fan (produced until 1970) by Braun was austerely Functionalist and epitomized the aesthetics of Braun and the Ulm school. In 1967, he settled in Chicago, where he joined the staff of Unimark; in 1970, set up his own office in Chicago, producing award-winning graphic and product designs.
▶ Received 1972 American Institute of Graphic Arts award (package design); gold medal at 1982 Industry Fair, Brno; 1970 Bundespreis 'Die gute Industrieform' (1961 fan). Work included

in 1983–84 'Design Since 1945' exhibition, Philadelphia Museum of Art.
▶ Cat., Kathryn B. Hiesinger and George H. Marcus III (eds.), *Design Since 1945*, Philadelphia: Philadelphia Museum of Art, 1983:235,I–50. Tomás Maldonado and Gui Bonsiepe, 'Science and Design,' *Ulm*, Vols. 10–11, May 1964:16–18.

Welch, Robert Radford (1929–)
▶ British product designer and silversmith; born Hereford.
▶ 1946–47 and 1949–50, studied painting, Malvern School of Art, under Victor Moody; 1950–52, silversmithing, Birmingham College of Art, under C.J. Shiner and R. Baxendale; 1952–55, silversmithing, Royal College of Art, London, under Robert Gooden.
▶ He set up his own workshop in 1955, in Chipping Campden, where he pursued the tradition of the Arts and Crafts designers who had worked there at C.R. Ashbee's Guild of Handicrafts; from 1955, was consultant designer to Old Hall Tableware, for which he designed a stainless-steel toast rack. He specialized in stainless-steel designs and products, including flatware, enamel-steel objects, lighting, door furniture, alarm clocks, bathroom fixtures, and cast-iron cooking utensils; after his visit to Sweden and Norway in 1953–54, became influenced by Scandinavian design; taught at London Central School of Arts and Crafts 1956–59 and Royal College of Art, London, 1960–71. He designed products for private commissions and manufacturers, including the cast-iron and enamel cookware produced by Prinz in 1966 and Lauffer in 1970, stoneware by Brixham Pottery in 1970, clocks by Westclox, and lamps by Lumitron; in 1969, added a retail shop to his studio. His 1979 professional knife range produced by Kitchen Devil was widely published.
▶ Received British Design Centre Awards (stainless-steel toast rack for Old Hall Tableware, 1958; electric alarm clock for Westclox, 1964; *Alveston* flatware, 1965); silver medal (with David Mellor) at 1957 (IX) Triennale di Milano; silver medal, Biennial International Art Book Prize (*Robert Welch: Design in a Cotswold Workshop*); 1975 Jerusalem Book Fair. In 1965, elected Royal Designer for Industry; in 1972, fellow of the Royal College of Art. Work included in 1956 exhibition, Foyles Art Gallery, London; 1964 exhibition at Heal's, London; 1967 exhibition, Skjalm Petersen Shop, Copenhagen; 1969 exhibition, Leeds Art Gallery; 1974 exhibition, Crafts Advisory Council, London; 1983–84 'Design Since 1945' exhibition, Philadelphia Museum of Art.
▶ Fiona MacCarthy and Patrick Nuttgens, *An Eye for Industry*, London: Lund Humphries with Royal Society for Arts, 1986. Jeremy Myerson and Sylvia Katz, *Conran Design Guides: Tableware*, London: Conran Octopus, 1990:79. Cat., Kathryn B. Hiesinger and George H. Marcus III (eds.), *Design Since 1945*, Philadelphia: Philadelphia Museum of Art, 1983:236, V–50. Colin Forbes (ed.), *Robert Welch: Design in a Cotswold Workshop*, London: Lund Hmphries 1973. Graham Hughes, *Modern Silver throughout the World*, New York, 1967, Nos. 144–146–49,389–91,393. Fiona MacCarthy, *British Design since 1880*, London, 1982, figs. 151,155–56,187,190,200,217.

Welden, W. Archibald
▶ American metalworker.
▶ By 1933, he was a consultant designer to Revere Copper and Brass, where he produced goods in close association with its technicians; later, as head of design at Revere, created the 1939 *Revere Ware* range of copper-bottomed cookware in stainless steel. He designed a 1954 range of cookware for Revere with heat-resistant metal instead of plastic handles for the institutional market. He also designed architectural ornaments and decorative metalwork.
▶ 1954 cookware included in 1983–84 'Design Since 1945' exhibition, Philadelphia Museum of Art.
▶ Don Wallance, *Shaping America's Products*, New York: Reinhold, 1956:41–45. Cat., Kathryn B. Hiesinger and George H. Marcus III (eds.), *Design Since 1945*, Philadelphia: Philadelphia Museum of Art, 1983:236, V–51.

Weller Pottery
► American commercial art pottery; located Fultonham and Putnam, Ohio.
► Samuel A. Weller (1851–1925) established a small pottery in c1872 in Fultonham, near Zanesville, Ohio, to produce plain and decorated crocks and flowerpots using local common red clay; relocated the works in Putnam (now part of Zanesville), Ohio; by 1880, had set up another pottery in Zanesville itself; in 1891, occupied the plant previously housing American Encaustic Tiling to produce ornamental pottery; encouraged by a visit to the stand of William A. Long's Lonhuda Pottery of Steubenville, Ohio, at the 1892 Chicago 'World's Columbian Exposition'; became a partner with Long in 1894, moving the latter's pottery to Zanesville. Lonhuda Faience lasted only 1895–96. Long left and began working for the pottery J.B. Owens in Zanesville. Weller continued with brown-shaded, high-glazed ware, renamed *Louwelsa*, in production until 1918; produced the *Aurelian*, *Samantha*, and *Tourada* wares with solid brushed grounds. Weller's blue-gray and pale-green *Eocean* ware imitated Rookwood's *Iris* ware. By 1902, Weller was able to offer a wide range of art ware. 1902–04, Frederick H. Rhead developed Weller's *Jap Birdimal*, using the squeeze-bag technique, and *L'Art Nouveau* ranges. From 1901, Jacques Sicard worked at the pottery and produced its *Sicardo* line with metal lusters on iridescent grounds. Weller became one of the largest producers of art pottery in the USA. By 1906, it ran 25 kilns and used the most modern machinery; after World War I, production of art ware ended, though, in the early 1920s, artistic director John Lessell produced several new art ranges, including *Lamar* ware and the lustrous *LaSa* decorated with landscapes and trees. After Weller's death, the pottery became known as S.A. Weller. With much reduced production, the firm survived until 1948.
► Kenneth H. Markham, 'Weller Sicardo Art Pottery,' *Antiques Journal*, No. 19, Sept. 1964:18. Louise Purviance et al., *Weller Art Pottery in Color*, Des Moines: Wallace-Homestead, 1971. Sharon Huxford and Bob Huxford, *The Collector's Encyclopedia of Weller Pottery*, Paducah, Kentucky: Collector's Books, 1979. *American Art Pottery*, New York: Cooper-Hewitt Museum, 1987:104–05.

Welles, Clara Barck (1868–1965)
► American metalworker and entrepreneur; born Oregon; active Chicago.
► Studied School of the Art Institute of Chicago.
► Welles was primarily responsible in 1900 for establishing the Kalo Shop, the largest Chicago producer of hand-wrought silverware, at 175 Dearborn Street. (*Kalo* is Greek for 'beautiful.') It was the first of a series of Arts and Crafts shops to be set up in Chicago. At first, all designs were by Welles, who produced classic round and curving forms. Later designs were executed by Yngve Olsson, émigré to Chicago before World War I and engraver and chaser of most of Kalo's wares. After 1905, Welles employed up to 25 silversmiths, whom she trained herself, and who also produced copper pieces; they included Arne Myhre, Einar Johansen, Bjorne O. Axness, Daniel P. Pederson, Robert P. Bower, and Julius Randahl. Kalo continued to be the most important producer of handmade silver in Chicago after World War I, rendering rounded forms and hammered surfaces. Welles was active in the Cordon Club, a group of professional women in the arts, and was known for giving women opportunities in the metalsmithing trade; frequently lectured on silversmithing to labor groups; in 1959, turned over Kalo to employees Bower, Pederson, Olsson, and Myhre; it closed in 1970, after the deaths of Pederson and Olsson.
► Sharon S. Darling with Gail Farr Casterline, *Chicago Metalsmiths*, Chicago Historical Society, 1977. Annelies Krekel-Aalberse, *Art Nouveau and Art Déco Silver*, New York: Abrams, 1989:103,122,260.

Wells, Reginald (1877–1951)
► British ceramicist.
► Studied sculpture, Royal College of Art, London.

► Wells learned to pot in 1909 at the Coldrum Pottery near Wrotham, Kent. Wells was one of the first to revive traditional slipware techniques, also working with Chinese-style glazes on what he called 'soon' (meaning Sung) pottery; made stoneware figures.
► *British Arts and Design, 1900–1960*, London: Victoria and Albert Museum, 1983.

Wende, Theodor (1883–1968)
► German silversmith; active Berlin, Darmstadt, and Pforzheim.
► Trained at jewelry firms in Berlin and Dresden; studied Königliche Preussische Zeichenakademie, Hanau, and Vereinigte Staatsschulen für freie und angewandte Kunst (Kunstgewerbeschule), Berlin-Charlottenburg, under Bruno Paul.
► Wende became a member in 1913 of the Darmstadt artists' colony of the Grand Duke Louis IV of Hesse-Darmstadt. Of the 23 artists who worked at Darmstadt during its 15 years of activity, Ernst Riegel and his successor Wende were the only silversmiths. Wende had a preference for large hammered surfaces with Cubist-influenced abstract ornamentation. In 1921, he became professor at Badische Kunstgewerbeschule, Pforzheim.
► Annelies Krekel-Aalberse, *Art Nouveau and Art Déco Silver*, New York: Abrams, 1989:132,135,260. Cat., *Metallkunst*, Berlin: Bröhan-Museum, 1990:512–13.

Wendingen
See **Wijdeveld, Hendrik Theodore**

Wendt, Ove (1907–)
► Danish metalworker.
► Wendt set up his own workshop in 1959; 1970–78, worked for Andreas Mikkelsen; in 1978, began designing jewelry for Georg Jensen Sølvsmedie, including 1948 *Armring* and *Neckring*.
► Work included in 1980 'Georg Jensen Silversmithy: 77 Artists, 75 Years' exhibition at the Smithsonian Institution, Washington.
► Cat., *Georg Jensen Silversmithy: 77 Artists, 75 Years*, Washington: Smithsonian Institution Press, 1980.

Wennerberg, Gunnar Gison (1863–1914)
► Swedish painter, ceramicist, and textile and glassware designer.
► Studied in Uppsala; 1886–1908, painting in Paris; and at Sèvres.
► 1895–1908, he was artistic director of the Gustavsberg ceramics factory, bringing a fresh new style to its goods and incorporating motifs from nature; was at Gustavsberg when imitation Wedgwood Jasperware was being made there and, in 1908, left the firm; 1898–1909, designed for the Kosta glassworks; in c1900, designed carved cameo-glass vessels for Kosta and blown glass for Orrefors; 1902–08, taught painting Konstfackskolan, Stockholm; from 1908, worked at Sèvres and drew cartoons and designed woven textiles at Handarbetets Vänner.
► Work shown in numerous exhibitions; subject of 1981 retrospective at Waldemarsudde, Stockholm.
► Cat., *Gunnar Gison Wennerberg*, Stockholm: Prins Eugens Waldemarsudde, 1981. Cat., David Revere McFadden (ed.), *Scandinavian Modern Design 1880–1980*, New York: Abrams, 1982:272–73, Nos. 10,24,33–36. Jennifer Hawkins Opie, *Scandinavia: Ceramics and Glass in the Twentieth Century*, New York: Rizzoli, 1989.

West, Franz (1947–)
► Austrian artist and designer; active Vienna.
► He designed lighting and furniture for Meta-Memphis, including his 1989 welded iron chain and 1989 *Privatlampe des Künstlers I* floor lamp.
► Work subject of exhibitions in New York, Frankfurt, Krefeld, and Milan, and shown at 1990 Biennale di Venezia.
► Albrecht Bangert and Karl Michael Armer, *80s Style: Designs of the Decade*, New York: Abbeville, 1990:123,236.

Westman, Carl (1866–1936)
► Swedish architect and furniture and interior designer.
► 1900, studied in England.

▶ Highly influenced by C.F.A. Voysey, Hugh Baillie Scott, and the Arts and Crafts movement, Westman's furniture was primarily simple, expressive in form, and decidedly Swedish.
▶ Cat., David Revere McFadden (ed.), *Scandinavian Modern Design 1880–1980*, New York: Abrams, 1982:273, No. 60.

Wetzler, M.T.
▶ German silversmiths; active Munich.
▶ From *c*1905, Wetzler was a silversmith in Munich, where he produced the designs of Debschitz-Schule pupils. The school's director Fritz Schmoll von Eisenwerth supplied simple and practical silver designs intended for serial production. The workshop closed during World War II.
▶ Wares shown at 1914 Cologne 'Werkbund-Ausstellung' and 1922 Munich 'Deutsche Gewerbeschau.'
▶ Annelies Krekel-Aalberse, *Art Nouveau and Art Déco Silver*, New York: Abrams, 1989:130,131,142,143,260.

Wewerka, Stefan (1928–)
▶ German architect and designer; born Magdeburg; active Cologne and Berlin.
▶ Studied architecture and town planning to 1947; earth architecture to 1954; sculpture and painting to 1961.
▶ He designed the 1974 *Classroom* chair for Tecta, where he worked from 1977; in 1979, began designing clothing; in 1981, executed jewelry designs for Cleto Munari of Vicenza; from 1975, developed a 'sitting tool' with multiple seating positions. His Tecta work included the 1971 *B1* chair, 1982 *B5* one-piece bent steel tube chair, 1982 *M 5/1* table, 1982 *D2* armchair, 1982 *L30* lamp, 1983 *L6* table, and 1984 kitchen unit.
▶ Cat., *Der Kragstuhl*, Stuhlmuseum Burg Beverungen, Berlin: Alexander, 1986:140. Juli Capella and Quim Larrea, *Designed by Architects in the 1980s*, New York: Rizzoli, 1988.

Wharton, Edith Newbold (1862–1937)
▶ American writer and interior designer; active New York.
▶ Wharton collaborated with Ogden Codman on interiors and on the influential book *The Decoration of Houses (1897)*, observing 'We have passed from the golden age of architecture to the gilded age of decoration.' They began working together when Codman designed her house 'Land's End' in Newport, Rhode Island. After an extensive collaboration, Wharton hired another architect to build her most important house.
▶ John Esten and Rose Bennett Gilbert, *Manhattan Style*, Boston: Little, Brown, 1990:2. Edith Wharton and Ogden Codman Jr., *The Decoration of Houses*, New York: Scribner's, 1897.
▶ See Codman Jr., Ogden

Wheeler, Candace (b. Candace Thurber 1827–1923)
▶ American textile and wallpaper designer; born Delhi, New York; active New York.
▶ An amateur artist who painted china and rendered needlework, she was greatly influenced by the embroideries of the Royal School of Art Needlework in London that she saw at the 1876 Philadelphia 'Centennial Exposition.' In 1877, she became vice-president and corresponding secretary of the New York Society of Decorative Art, where classes were taught by Louis Comfort Tiffany, John La Farge, Lockwood de Forest, and Samuel Colman. In 1878, she founded the Women's Exchange, which, until the 1980s, sold goods, crafts, and foodstuffs on Madison Avenue. In 1879, she was hired by Louis Comfort Tiffany as a textile specialist in his new decorating firm Associated Artists, where, until it was dissolved in 1883, she designed wallpaper. She continued designing textiles for a firm managed by her son and assisted by her daughter Dora until 1907. She invented new techniques in textile production; designed fabrics for silk mill Cheney Brothers of Connecticut; was appointed director of the Bureau of Applied Arts for the New York State stand at the 1892 Chicago 'World's Columbian Exposition,' and was interior decorator of the Women's Building there. She wrote *Household Art* (1893), *Content in a Garden* (1901), *How to Make Rugs* (1902), *Principles of Home Decoration* (1903),

The Development of Embroidery in America (1921), and the autobiography *Yesterdays in a Busy Life* (1918).
▶ Received first prize at 1879 New York Society of Decorative Art exhibition (portiere design) and 1881 design competition (first prize; her daughter Dora won fourth prize) sponsored by wallpaper manufacturer Warren and Fuller.
▶ 'Candace Wheeler, Textile Designer,' *Antiques 112*, Aug. 1977:258–61. Karal Ann Marling, 'Portrait of the Artist as a Young Woman: Miss Dora Wheeler,' *Bulletin of the Cleveland Museum of Art 65*, Feb. 1978:47–57. Catherine Lynn, *Wallpaper in America: From the Seventeenth Century to World War I*, New York, 1980:412–13. Virginia Williams, 'Candace Wheeler, Textile Designer for Associated Artists,' *Nineteenth Century 6*, Summer 1980:60–61. Doreen Bolger Burke et al., *In Pursuit of Beauty: Americans and the Aesthetic Movement*, New York: Metropolitan Museum of Art and Rizzoli, 1987:481–82.

Whistler, James Abbott McNeill (1843–1903)
▶ American painter; born Lowell, Massachusetts; active Europe.
▶ Studied drawing, Imperial Academy of Science, St. Petersburg; from 1851, West Point Military Academy, New York; 1855 or 1856, École Impériale et Spéciale du Dessin, Paris; 1856, under Swiss painter Charles Gleyre.
▶ Expelled from West Point, he worked briefly in Baltimore as an etcher in the drawings division of the US Coast and Geodetic Survey before deciding to become an artist and moving to Paris. He produced his first set of etchings in 1858. His prolific activity in printmaking encouraged the medium in Britain, France, and the USA in the 1860s and 1870s. In 1858–59, he produced his first major painting *At the Piano* and settled in Wapping, London. Visiting France often, he painted with Gustave Courbet, Charles-François Daubigny and Claude Monet. His early work was influenced by the Pre-Raphaelites; Oriental influences showed up in his work of the 1860s, when he produced the first of his purely decorative compositions. In the 1870s, he became interested in furniture, picture-frame design, exhibitions, and interior decoration; decorated the 1876–77 'Peacock Room' (dining room) of Frederick Richards Leyland (designed by Thomas Jeckyll; installed today at Freer Gallery, Washington DC). A widely publicized altercation between Leyland and Whistler overshadowed the ambitious decoration. John Ruskin's remarks on Whistler's *Nocturne in Black* and *Gold: The Falling Rocket* resulted in a 1878 libel suit, which Whistler won. Declared bankrupt in 1879, he went to Venice but returned to London, producing the *Set of Twenty-six Etchings* (1886) of Venice and *Notes* (1887) lithographs. His 1885 lecture 'Ten O'Clock' expounded his theories and attacked the aesthetics of Ruskin. In the 1880s and 1890s, Whistler's influence began to show up in the works of artists William Merritt Chase, Thomas Wilmer Dewing, and John H. Twachtman. In 1890, he met Charles Lang Freer of Detroit, who became his chief patron in the USA. From 1898, Whistler's own Company of the Butterfly sold his works. In 1898, he became president of the International Society of Sculptors, Painters, and Gravers.
▶ Rejected by 1859 Paris Salon, *At the Piano* was shown at Royal Academy of Arts, London. Rejected by the 1862 Royal Academy event and 1863 Paris Salon, *The White Girl, No. 1 (Symphony in White)* (1862) shown with Édouard Manet's *Déjeuner sur L'herbe* in 1863 Salon des Refusés, Paris. E.W. Godwin's and Whistler's furniture suite produced by William Watt shown at 1878 Paris 'Exposition Universelle.' Work subject of 1889 exhibition, Wunderlich Gallery, New York, and memorial exhibition in Boston, 1904; International Society in London, 1905; and École des Beaux-Arts, Paris, 1905.
▶ Cat., *Notes—Harmonies—Nocturnes*, London, 1884. Denys Sutton, *Nocturne: The Art of James McNeill Whistler*, Philadelphia and New York, 1964. Cat., Allen Staley, *From Realism to Symbolism: Whistler and his World*, New York: Wildenstein, 1971. Cat., Robert H. Getscher and Allen Staley, *The Stamp of Whistler*, Oberlin, Ohio: Allen Memorial Art Museum, 1977. Andrew McLaren Young et al., *The Paintings of James McNeill Whistler*, New Haven,

1980. Cat., David Park Curry, *James McNeill Whistler at the Freer Gallery of Art*, Washington: Freer Gallery of Art, 1984. Katharine A. Lochnan, *The Etchings of James McNeill Whistler*, New Haven, 1984. Doreen Bolger Burke et al., *In Pursuit of Beauty: Americans and the Aesthetic Movement*, New York: Metropolitan Museum of Art and Rizzoli, 1987:483–85.

Whistler, Laurence   (1912–)
▶ British glass engraver, glassware designer, and writer; brother of Rex Whistler.
▶ Studied Oxford University.
▶ His brother Rex Whistler and Edwin Lutyens encouraged him to take up glass engraving. Lutyens and his daughter Lady Ridley became important contacts and patrons. Whistler began glass-working with what he termed 'window writing,' followed by the production of bottles, decanters, panels, goblets, and commissioned caskets and windows; designed some historicist (mostly neo-Georgian) glass tableware, blown by others including Whitefriars Glassworks; was a reviver of stipple engraving along with John Hutton; became the first of many British artists to have glassware designs produced by Steuben. His designs included the 1947–48 King George's Casket; windows at Sherborne Abbey, Eastbury, Bedfordshire; Guards' Chapel, St. Hugh's College, Oxford.
▶ Received 1935 (first award) King's Medal for Poetry (England). Work shown at Agnews, London, 1969; Marble Hill, 1972; Corning Museum, New York, 1974; Ashmolean Museum, Oxford, 1976; Fine Art Society, London, and 1977; and included in 1979–80 'Thirties' exhibition, Hayward Gallery, London. Appointed CBE (Companion of the British Empire).
▶ Frederick Cooke, *Glass: Twentieth-Century Design*, New York: Dutton, 1986:75,103. Cat., *Thirties: British art and design before the war*, London: Arts Council of Great Britain, Hayward Gallery, 1979:134,302.

Whistler, Rex John   (1904–44)
▶ British painter, theater designer, and book illustrator; brother of Laurence Whistler.
▶ 1922–25, studied Slade School of Art, London, under Henry Tonks, and in Rome.
▶ He was probably best known for his 1926–27 decorations in the refreshment room of the Tate Gallery, London. His many private commissions included the 1936–38 decorations for Sir Philip Sassoon's stately home at Plas Newydd. He designed the 160-inch (4m) 1932 *Nine Samuels* pair of carved-wood urns for Samuel Courtauld (commemorating Courtauld and eight other Samuels: Scott, Pepys, Rogers, the Prophet, Johnson, Richards, Butler, and Coleridge). He designed costumes for the 1934 production of *The Tempest* at Stratford-upon-Avon; poster, program, scenery, and costumes for *Pride and Prejudice* at St. James's Theatre, London, in 1936, and for *Victoria Regina* at the Lyric Theatre, London, in 1937; scenery for *Fidelio* at Covent Garden, London, in 1934; and scenery and costumes for *The Marriage of Figaro* at Sadler's Wells, London, in 1934. He illustrated the books *Gulliver's Travels* (Cressent Press 1930), *The Next Volume* (The James Press 1932) by Edward James; *The Lord Fish* (Faber and Faber 1933) by Walter de la Mare, and *Fairy Tales and Legends* (Cobden-Sanderson 1935) by Hans Christian Andersen; designed stamps, bookplates, and ephemera, including a 1930 envelope for the National Trust, 1935 Valentine's Day Greeting Telegram, 1932–36 Christmas catalogs (filled with witty drawings) for the Fortnum and Mason store, London. In 1932, he designed earthenware for Wedgwood, a 1935 carpet for Edward James woven by Wilton Royal Carpet Factory, and monuments. He died in action during World War II.
▶ Work included in 1979–80 'Thirties' exhibition, Hayward Gallery, London.
▶ Cat., *Thirties: British art and design before the war*, London: Arts Council of Great Britain, Hayward Gallery, 1979:38,43, 79,130,161,203,204,211,214,302.

White, Gleeson   (1852–98)
▶ British publisher.
▶ White was editor from 1893 of the art journal *The Studio*, which promoted the Arts and Crafts movement; publicized the works of C.F.A. Voysey, Hugh Baillie Scott, and members of the Glasgow School, including Mackintosh and the Macdonald sisters.

White, William Stamford
See **McKim, Mead and White**

Whitefriars Glass
▶ British glassware manufacturer.
▶ Whitefriars was built in 1680 on a former Carmelite monastery site; in 1834, it was taken over by James Powell; remained in the family until 1919, when it became James Powell and Sons; from the 1850s, it produced Venetian-style glassware; employed leading craftsman Joseph Leicester and, from c1840, Charles Winston who returned its wares to a purer ancient style; was directed by Harry J. Powell (1835–1922) from 1880–1920; was long associated with aesthetic reforms and active in raising design standards. In the late 19th century Philip Webb's designs for the Powell glasshouse of Whitefriars prefigured 20th century forms. Playing a significant role in the revival of diamond-point engraving, William Wilson was managing director 1950–73, and hired George Baxter as staff designer. The firm engaged the services of John Hutton, one of the best postwar engravers and etchers of glass and a reviver of stipple engraving along with Laurence Whistler, for whom Whitefriars produced forms.
▶ Frederick Cooke, *Glass: Twentieth-Century Design*, New York: Dutton, 1986:73–74,75.
▶ See **Powell, Edmund Barnaby** and **Powell, James**

Whiting
▶ American silver manufacturer; located North Attleboro, Massachusetts, and New York.
▶ William Dean Whiting (1815–91) first began working with precious metals during a seven-year apprenticeship in his uncle's jewelry firm Draper and Tifft; in Attleboro, Massachusetts, he worked for R. and W. Robinson, Draper and Blackington, and H. M. Richards. When the latter moved to Philadelphia, Whiting followed, becoming superintendent for a short time. In 1840, Whiting and partner Albert Tifft set up a firm in North Attleboro, where for 13 years they made jewelry and small silver toilet articles; in 1847, built a factory for the Whiting Manufacturing Company. 1853–54, M. Whiting Jeweler was operated as a retail outlet in New York. 1865–67, Whiting was a partner in Whiting, Cowan and Bowen. In 1866, the Whiting firm moved to New York; from the late 1860s, became one of the most important producers of silver in the USA. Chief designer in the 1870s, Charles Osborne tried to get the William Cullen Bryant Vase commission; it was won by Tiffany's. Ogden Goelet commissioned the trophy for an 1882 New York Yacht Club schooner race. Whiting's son Frank Mortimer joined the firm, later setting up his own firm, Holbrook, Whiting and Albee, which produced plated jewelry and novelties on the premises of the Whiting plant until the late 1870s, when father and son set up F. M. Whiting (later Frank M. Whiting); 1891–95, it was managed by their wives and Frank's two sisters. The firm was absorbed by Gorham in 1924 and bought by Ellmore Silver, Meriden, Connecticut, in 1940.
▶ Doreen Bolger Burke et al., *In Pursuit of Beauty: Americans and the Aesthetic Movement*, New York: Metropolitan Museum of Art and Rizzoli, 1987:485. Charles H. Carpenter Jr., *Gorham Silver, 1831–1981*, New York, 1982:91,200,254. Dorothy T. Rainwater, *Encyclopedia of American Silver Manufacturers*, New York, 1975:51–52,60–61,169,187.

Wibo, G.
▶ French architect.
▶ He collaborated in the late 1920s with designers Louis Sognot and Marcelle Guillemard on rooms of the Au Printemps department store in Paris. With Guillemard, he was the architect of its tea room, where the paintings of Robert Bonfils were installed.

▶ *Restaurants, dancing, cafés, bars*, Paris: Charles Moreau, Nos. 15–16, 1929.

Wichman, Erich (1890–1929)
▶ Dutch sculptor, painter, and silversmith; active Utrecht.
▶ 1917–19, Wichman executed models for silverware produced by C. J. Begeer, Utrecht.
▶ Annelies Krekel-Aalberse, *Art Nouveau and Art Déco Silver*, New York: Abrams, 1989:260.

wicker
▶ Vegetable fiber used in furniture and utility-goods manufacture.
▶ Woven furniture has been produced since ancient times. The term derives from *vikker*, the Scandinavian word for willow, and denotes woven furniture rather than a specific material. Wicker furniture has been produced from swamp reed, raffia, willow, thin bamboo, thin wood strips, and even twisted paper. Most wicker furniture is produced from flexible and water-resistant rattan, a palm-vine variety that grows in Malaysia and elsewhere in the Far East. Cane (a rattan bark by-product) is woven for the seats and backs of chairs. Light and weather-resistant furniture in wicker was popular from the 1850s, peaking 1865–80 first in America, then in the Orient and Europe. From *c*1880, reed furniture was used indoors and usually painted gold, brown, green, and white; rectilinear in form, it reflected Oriental furniture designs. In 1917, Marshall Burns Lloyd patented a method of producing wicker from paper twisted into strands, used for furniture manufactured by Lloyd Looms.
▶ Richard Saunders, *Collecting and Restoring Wicker Furniture*, New York, 1976. Richard Saunders, *Collector's Guide to American Wicker Furniture*, New York, 1983. Doreen Bolger Burke et al., *In Pursuit of Beauty: Americans and the Aesthetic Movement*, New York: Metropolitan Museum of Art and Rizzoli, 1986:478. Lee J. Curtis, *Lloyd Loom Woven Fiber Furniture*, New York: Rizzoli, 1991.

Wiener, René (1855–1940)
▶ French bookbinder; active Nancy.
▶ Inheriting the family printing shop in Nancy, he became involved in bookbinding when, in 1883, Camille Martin and Victor Prouvé of the École de Nancy commissioned him to produce their book covers. Wiener's work included leather screens, buckles, box covers, and purses. The disparaging term 'wienerism' referred to highly commercial book covers designed by others and produced by Wiener.
▶ Alastair Duncan and Georges de Bartha, *Art Nouveau and Art Déco Bookbinding*, New York: Abrams, 1989:13,14,159,179,197. Thérèse Charpentier, *L'École de Nancy et la reliure d'art*, Paris, 1960:6,8–10,12–14,21,24,38–39,42. 'Modern Bookbindings and Their Designers,' *The Studio*, Special Winter Issue 1899–1900:57,60,61,64. Octave Uzanne, *L'Art dans la décoration extérieure des livres en France et à l'étranger*, Paris, 1898:202–09.

Wiener Kunstgewerbeschule
▶ Austrian applied arts school; located Vienna.
▶ Affiliated with the Österreichisches Museum für Kunst und Industrie, the Kunstgewerbeschule was founded in Vienna in 1867; in 1899, Felician von Myrbach became director, with Koloman Moser as professor of painting, and Josef Hoffmann as professor of architecture; Rudolf Hammel became a teacher. The school's teaching staff and curriculum were radically changed, and it became a center for the study of contemporary movements. Emphasis was placed on producing artistic 'masters' rather than trade-oriented artisans to meet demands of the art industry. The curriculum emphasized British design and William Morris's and John Ruskin's theories. Chasing and embossing were under the direction of professor H. Schwarts, enameling under Adèle von Stark. The school made it possible for young creative artists and artisans to reject the historicist style prevalent at the time and it became a gathering place for the avant-garde. Hoffmann taught

at the school longer than any other instructor, retiring in 1936; some 400 students from Austria and elsewhere matriculated in his courses. Students were taught fine art as well as weaving, pottery, metalwork, and fabric printing; this multi-disciplinary approach anticipated the teaching methods of the Bauhaus. Annual winter exhibitions up to 1914 were organized by the Österreichisches Museum für Kunst und Industrie to promote public interest in Modern decorative arts. The school also participated in international exhibitions, first at the 1900 Paris 'Exposition Universelle.' Some manufacturers in Vienna purchased designs from the school's students. A tea-kettle and stand designed by Oskar Thiede was produced by Brüder Frank; the glass and porcelain designs of Moser student Antoinette Krasnik were produced, along with her silverwares and jewelry; her cigarette case with a dramatic blue *plique-à-jour* dragonfly was produced by the firm Alexander Sturm. Because it was difficult to persuade manufacturers to issue Modern designs, designers began producing their own furniture and furnishings, resulting in the formation of Wiener Werkstätte in 1903, which was financially supported by Moser, Hoffmann, and Fritz Wärndorfer; it became a place of continuing education for producing goods, both artistic and craft oriented. In 1970, the Wiener Kunstgewerbeschule changed its name to the Hochschule für angewandte Kunst.
▶ Hoffmann's Secessionist room and student work shown at 1900 Paris 'Exposition Universelle.' Students' silver designs produced by Alfred Pollak of Vienna and Rudolf Hammel silver produced by Josef Bannert shown at 1902 Turin 'Esposizione Internazionale d'Arte Decorativa Moderna.' Student Antoinette Krasnik's cigarette case shown at 1902–03 winter exhibition, Österreichisches Museum für Kunst und Industrie.
▶ Jessica Rutherford, *Art Nouveau, Art Deco and the Thirties: The Furniture Collections at Brighton Museum*, Brighton: The Royal Pavilion, Art Gallery and Museums, 1983:6. Annelies Krekel-Aalberse, *Art Nouveau and Art Déco Silver*, New York: Abrams, 1989:192–94. Deanna F. Cera (ed.), *Jewels of Fantasy: Costume Jewelry of the 20th Century*, New York: Abrams, 1992.

Wiener Sezession (Vienna Secession)
▶ Group of Austrian artists and architects.
▶ In 1897, a number of artists in Vienna, led by Gustav Klimt (along with Josef Maria Olbrich, Josef Hoffmann, and Koloman Moser), made a radical break with the academic style of painting pursued at the time in Vienna and founded the Vereinigung bildender Künstler Österreichs-Sezessions, generally known as the Wiener Sezession. Many of its proponents taught at the Akademie der bildenden Künste in Vienna. Emulating a group of artists in Munich and Berlin, members sought an alternative to Art Nouveau, believing it to be decadent. In 1898, the group published the first issue of their journal *Ver Sacrum* (*Sacred Spring*), where they vented their ideas. In the same year, they built an exhibition gallery on the Karlsplatz, Vienna, after a design by member Olbrich. The stained glass and interior decorations were designed by Moser, and the inscription by Ludwig Hevesi placed over the door read: *Die Zeit ihre Kunst, der Kunst ihre Freiheit* (To the age its art, to art its freedom). The organization sought to introduce the Viennese public to the best of Modern decorative art from around Europe. In 1899, Olbrich left for the artists' colony in Darmstadt. At the gallery, members showed their works, together with those of foreign honorary members, several times a year; fine and applied art were shown together. In 1902, Hoffmann invited C.R. Ashbee and Charles Rennie Mackintosh to show their work at the great 1900 (VIII) Wiener Sezession exhibition, which included the work of Henry van de Velde and pieces from Julius Meier-Graefe's La Maison Moderne shop in Paris. Ashbee's jewels and silver objects were included in the 1906 (XXVII) exhibition. The Sezession members' commercial venture, the Wiener Werkstätte, was based on Ashbee's Guild of Handicrafts.
▶ Frederick Cooke, *Glass: Twentieth-Century Design*, New York: Dutton, 1986. Annelies Krekel-Aalberse, *Art Nouveau and Art Déco Silver*, New York: Abrams, 1989:191–92.

Wiener Werkstätte

▶ Austrian art and crafts studio; located Vienna.

▶ The Werkstätte-Produktiv-Genossenschaft von Kunsthandwer-kern in Wien (Art-Craft Workshop Cooperative in Vienna) was founded in 1903 by Secession members Josef Hoffmann and Kolo-man Moser, and financial backer Fritz Wärndorfer, later joined by C.O. Czeschka. As much a movement as a financial enterprise, the Wiener Werkstätte (as it was generally called) had support from artist Gustav Klimt and architect Otto Wagner. The work-shop was founded on the work of Charles Rennie Mackintosh and the principles of C. R. Ashbee's Guild of Handicraft, both of which Hoffmann admired. The exponents of the British counterpart organizations were not required to have formal training, whereas Werkstätte employees had to show their *Befähigungsnachweis*—evidence of their apprenticeship and journeymanship and the acquisition of a master's certificate. The Werkstätte's goals were to fulfill the ideals of the guild system; to establish a direct relation-ship between designers, craftspeople, and the public by producing well-designed domestic goods; and to reverse the decline in the quality of handmade objects. The Werkstätte's rejection of the machine in fact resulted in costly products that ultimately pre-vented wide public access. Its silver designers included Carl Otto Czeschka, Dagobert Peche, Otto Prutscher, Eduard Josef Wimmer-Wisgrill, Hoffmann, and Moser. Its silversmiths included Arthur Berger, Josef Wagner, Adolf Erbrich, J. Sedlicky, Augustin Grötz-bach, Josef Hossfeld, Karl Ponocny, Eugen Pflaumer, Anton Pribit, Alfred Mayer, Josef Czech, Josef Husnik, and Karl Kallert. Within ten years, 100 workmen were employed. With no facilities of its own for manufacturing glass, it used the Bohemian glass houses Johann Oertl, Karl Schappel, Meyrs Neffe, Ludwig Moser, Johann Loetz Witwe, and E. Bakalowitz. Bakalowitz was effective in pro-motion and distribution; J. und L. Lobmeyr joined the forces of the Werkstätte once its products had been established in European markets. Its success prompted the formation of Werkstätten organ-ized along similar lines in other cities, notably Munich and Dresden. In 1932, when Wiener Werkstätte was dissolved, its 212 members included 139 students and 20 professors from the Kunstgewerbeschule.

▶ Werner J. Schweiger, *Wiener Werkstätte: Kunst und Handwerk 1903–1932*, Vienna: Brandstaetter, 1982. Jessica Rutherford, *Art Nouveau, Art Deco and the Thirties: The Furniture Collections at Brighton Museum*, Brighton: The Royal Pavilion, Art Gallery and Museums, 1983:6. Annelies Krekel-Aalberse, *Art Nouveau and Art Déco Silver*, New York: Abrams, 1989:260.

Wièse, Jules   (1818–1890)

▶ German goldsmith and jeweler; active London.

▶ Wièse was the principal artist at the firm F.-D. Froment-Meurice until c1860, when he set up his own workshop; worked in the sculptural form of the archeological style that Froment-Meurice had developed, although not in the elaborate manner of Fontenay's work; in the years immediately before his retirement in 1880, also produced pieces in the *japoniste* taste.

▶ Showed work at London 'International Exhibition of 1862.'

▶ Charlotte Gere, *American and European Jewelry 1830–1914*, New York: Crown, 1975:227.

Wieselthier, Valerie   (1895–1945)

▶ Austrian designer.

▶ 1914–18, studied Kunstgewerbeschule, Vienna, under Michael Powolny, Koloman Moser, Josef Hoffmann, and others.

▶ She was head of the ceramic workshop of the Wiener Werk-stätte and worked in a highly idiosyncratic style with coarse modeling and drip-glass effects; in 1924, when the Ausgarten por-celain factory was reopened, contributed designs to ceramics as well as fabrics; in 1922, set up her own workshop. In 1929, she moved to the USA, where she produced ceramic designs for Contempora, New York, and Sebring Pottery, Ohio; was also active in the design of glassware, textiles, and *papier-mâché* mannequins; designed the metal elevator doors of the 1929–30 Squibb building (architect Ely Jacques Kahn), New York.

▶ First showed work in Germany in 1922. Work shown at 1925 Paris 'Exposition Internationale des Arts Décoratifs et Industriels Modernes' (gold and silver medals); 1928–29 ceramic exhibition, American Federation of Arts, New York; subject of exhibitions at Art Center, 1928, and Weyhe Galleries, 1930, both from New York.

▶ Ruth Canfield, 'The Pottery of Vally Wieselthier,' *Design*, Nov. 1929:104. *The New York Times*, 3 Sept. 1945:23. Günther Feu-erstein, *Vienna—Present and Past: Arts and Crafts—Applied Art—Design*, Vienna: Jugend und Volk, 1976:34–35,48,81. Garth Clark, *A Century of Ceramics in the United States, 1878–1978*, New York: Dutton, 1979:339. Karen Davies, *At Home in Manhat-tan: Modern Decorative Arts, 1925 to the Depression*, New Haven: Yale, 1983:93. Cat., *Expressive Keramik der Wiener Werkstätte 1817–1930*, Munich: Bayerische Vereinsbank, 1992:135–36 passim.

Wight, Don   (1924–)

▶ American artist, photographer, and textile designer; active San Francisco and New York.

▶ 1942–43, studied Alfred University, New York; 1945–47, Black Mountain College, North Carolina, under Josef and Anni Albers.

▶ In 1947, he was an apprentice weaver in the Dorothy Liebes studio, San Francisco; 1948–66 in New York and from 1977 abroad, executed textile print patterns for numerous firms, includ-ing Liebes, Jack Lenor Larsen, Schumacher, Bates, and Brunschwig.

▶ *Garden of Glass* printed fabric shown at 1951 and 1954 'Good Design' exhibitions, New York Museum of Modern Art and Chicago Merchandise Mart; a fabric for Larsen included in 1983–84 'Design Since 1945' exhibition, Philadelphia Museum of Art.

▶ Cat., Kathryn B. Hiesinger and George H. Marcus III (eds.), *Design Since 1945*, Philadelphia: Philadelphia Museum of Art, 1983:236, VII–64.

Wiherheimo, Yrjö   (1941–)

▶ Finnish furniture and industrial designer.

▶ Wiherheimo designed furniture for Vivero, Asko, and Haimi, all in Helsinki; from the late 1970s, he collaborated with Simo Heikkilä on furniture. His designs for plastics were produced by Nokia.

▶ Cat., David Revere McFadden (ed.), *Scandinavian Modern Design 1880–1980*, New York: Abrams, 1982:273, No. 339.

Wiinblad, Björn   (1918–)

▶ Danish ceramicist, glassware and textile designer, and graphic artist.

▶ 1936–39, studied Technical High School, Copenhagen; 1940–43, studied illustration, Det Kongelige Danske Kuntakademi, Copenhagen; 1943–46, ceramics under Lars Syberg at Taastrup.

▶ 1946–56, he was a designer for the Nymølle faïence factory; from 1952, was active in his own studio at Kongens Lyngby; from 1957, worked for Rosenthal, and on numerous commissions for decorations and designs in the USA, Japan, and Europe. In 1965, he was a theater designer for the Dallas Theater Center and sub-sequently the Pantomime Theater, Tivoli Gardens, Copenhagen; received commissions for the decoration of hotels and restaurants in Japan, Britain, and the USA; designed silver sculpture produced by Hans Hansen Sølvsmedie, Kolding; designed metalwork and furniture.

▶ *Björn Wiinblad*, Copenhagen: Det Danske Kunstindustrimu-seum, 1981. Cat., David Revere McFadden (ed.), *Scandinavian Modern Design 1880–1980*, New York: Abrams, 1982:272, No. 160. Jennifer Hawkins Opie, *Scandinavia: Ceramics and Glass in the Twentieth Century*, New York: Rizzoli, 1989.

Wijdeveld, Hendrik Theodore   (1885–)

▶ Dutch architect and publisher; active Amsterdam.

▶ Studied architecture and decoration in London.

▶ Wijdeveld was editor of *Wendigen* (*Turns*), the sophisticated avant-garde art and architecture journal that explored innovative typographic design and was an organ of the Architectura et Amicitia group in Amsterdam; he designed the typography and covers and sometimes commissioned graphic designers, including El Lissitsky. *Wendigen* was published 1918–31 and played an important role in promoting the ideas of the Amsterdam School. It also published articles on African sculpture, Far Eastern art, and Native-American basketwork. Wijdeveld left the journal in 1926. In 1924, he designed the exhibition stand for Philips at the Utrecht Industries Fair. As an architect, he was interested in utopian design, and known for his contact with Frank Lloyd Wright and with Expressionist architects including Erich Mendelsohn, Bruno Taut, and Hermann Finsterlin.

▶ Giovanni Fanelli and Eziuo Godoli (eds.), *Wendigen 1918–1931: Documenti dell'arte olandese del Novecento*, Florence: Centro Di, 1982. Wim de Wit (ed.), *The Amsterdam School: Dutch Expressionist Architecture, 1915–1930*, Cambridge: MIT, 1983. Stuart Durant, *Ornament from the Industrial Revolution to Today*, Woodstock, NY: Overlook, 1986:137,331.

Wikkelsø, Illum (1919–)
▶ Danish furniture designer.
▶ Studied Kunsthåndværkerskolen, Copenhagen, to 1941.
▶ He was apprenticed to a cabinetmaker in 1938; worked with architects Jacob Kjær, Peter Hvidt, and Orla Mølgård-Nielsen; in 1954, set up his own design studio; designed furniture produced by P. Schultz.
▶ Frederik Sieck, *Nutidig Dansk Møbeldesign: — en kortfattet illustreret beskrivelse*, Copenhagen: Bondo Gravesen; 1990 Busck edition in English.

Wilde, Fred H.
▶ British ceramicist.
▶ He settled in 1885 in the USA, where he was associated with several tile firms, including Robertson Art Tile, Morrisville, Pennsylvania, and Pacific Art Tile (later Western Art Tile), Tropico, California; 1916–18, was third artistic director at the Arequipa Art Pottery, succeeding Frederick H. Rhead and Albert L. Solon; when Pomona Tile in Los Angeles was formed in 1923, became ceramics engineer there, remaining until 1940.
▶ Paul Evans in Timothy J. Andersen et al., *California Design 1910*, Salt Lake City: Peregrine Smith, 1980:71,77.

Wildenhain, Franz Rudolf (1905–81)
▶ German ceramicist; born Leipzig; husband of Marguerite Wildenhain.
▶ Trained as a lithographer; 1924–25, studied ceramics, Bauhaus, Dornburg; from 1925, Burg Giebichenstein (later Kunstgewerbeschule), Halle.
▶ In 1933, he and his wife set up a workshop in the Netherlands. He joined his wife in the USA in 1942. 1950–56, he taught pottery in Rochester, New York; in 1958, was awarded a Guggenheim Fellowship.
▶ Lionel Richard, *Encyclopédie du Bauhaus*, Paris: Somogy, 1985. Cat., *Keramik und Bauhaus*, Berlin: Bauhaus-Archiv, 1989:154–200,264.

Wildenhain, Marguerite (b. Marguerite Friedländer 1896–1985)
▶ French ceramicist; born Lyons; wife of Franz Wildenhain.
▶ 1919–25, studied ceramics, Bauhaus, Dornburg; from 1925, Burg Giebichenstein (later Kunstgewerbeschule), Halle.
▶ From 1926, she was director of the ceramics workshop at Burg Giebichenstein. In 1929, (with Franz Wildenhain) worked with KPM; in 1933, settled in the Netherlands and set up a workshop with her husband; in 1940, emigrated to the USA and taught and worked in her own workshop, where her husband joined her in 1942. A notable ceramicist, she established her own school in Guerneville, California.
▶ Ceramics work shown at 1947 (XI) 'Ceramic National Exhibition' (traveling), organized by Syracuse Museum of Fine Art, Syracuse, New York; New York Museum of Art; 1959 (XX) 'Ceramic

International Exhibition,' New York Metropolitan Museum of Art.
▶ Lionel Richard, *Encyclopédie du Bauhaus*, Paris: Somogy, 1985: 212. Cat., *Keramik und Bauhaus*, Berlin: Bauhaus-Archiv, 1989:154–200,268. R. Craig, Miller, *Modern Design 1890–1990*, New York: Abrams, 1990.

Wilkens, M.H.
▶ German silversmiths; located Bremen-Hemelingen.
▶ The firm M.H. Wilkens und Söhne was founded in 1810 by Martin Heinrich Wilkens (1782–1869); at the turn of the century, it was the leading silverware producer in Germany along with Bruckmann und Söhne; hired designers including Peter Behrens, Heinrich Vogeler, and Albin Müller, and, 1910–40, A. Donant, H. Bulling. C. Krauss, and Karl Müller. Modern silver remained a sideline. It gave little importance to the use of well-known independent artists, and painter and graphic designer Heinrich Vogeler was its best known freelancer. In c1900, he designed candelabra, table ornaments, and cutlery for the firm. His *Tulip* pattern for Wilkens was sold by Julius Meier-Graefe's La Maison Moderne, Paris. Some of Wilkens's designs, like those at the 1922 Munich exhibition, showed Viennese influence; others had Art Déco characteristics.
▶ Silverwares designed by Bulling and Karl Müller shown at 1922 Munich 'Deutsche Gewerbeschau.'
▶ Annelies Krekel-Aalberse, *Art Nouveau and Art Déco Silver*, New York: Abrams, 1989:18,134,140,141,150,260. Cat., *Metallkunst*, Berlin: Bröhan, 1990:534–42.

Willers, Margarete (1883–1977)
▶ German textile designer.
▶ From 1905, studied painting and drawing, Düsseldorf and Munich, and under Maurice Denis, Paris; 1921–22, studied Bauhaus, Weimar.
▶ In 1927–28, she had her own workshop at the Bauhaus; 1928–43, was director, handweaving and embroidery studio, Folkwangschule, Essen, 1943–55, taught at the Handweaving Studio in Bückeburg; 1955–60, ran independent studio.
▶ Cat., *The Bauhaus: Masters and Students*, New York: Barry Friedman, 1988. Cat., Gunta Stölzl, *Weberei am Bauhaus und ams eigener Werkstätt*, Berlin: Bauhaus-Archiv, 1987:167. Sigrid Wortmann Weltge, *Women's Work: Textile Art from The Bauhaus*, San Francisco: Chronicle, 1993.

Williamson, A.H.
▶ British industrial designer.
▶ In the early 1950s, he designed machine-pressed glassware vessels for United Glass Bottle Manufacturers (UGBM), makers of Ravenhead and Sherdley glass. UGBM's hiring of Williamson as its consultant designer represented a major change in the firm's approach to product design. He taught industrial glass at the Royal College of Art, London.
▶ Michael Farr, *Design in British Industry: A Mid-Century Survey*, London: Cambridge, 1955:145.

Willumsen, Jens Ferdinand (1863–1958)
▶ Danish sculptor and ceramicist.
▶ Studied at technical school; 1881–85, architecture, Det Kongelige Danske Kunstakademi, Copenhagen.
▶ 1897–1900, he was artistic director of Bing & Grøndahl, Copenhagen.
▶ Work shown at 1889 Paris 'Exposition Universelle' (honorable mention award) and 1900 Paris 'Exposition Universelle'; received 1947 Thorvaldsens Medal.
▶ Cat., David Revere McFadden (ed.), *Scandinavian Modern Design 1880–1980*, New York: Abrams, 1982:273, No. 1.

Wilm, Ferdinand Richard (1880–1972)
▶ German silversmith; active Berlin.
▶ Studied Königliche Preussische Zeichenakademie, Hanau.
▶ From 1911, he worked in the family firm founded in 1767; used sterling silver in the production of handmade silverwares; in

1932, founded the Deutsche Gesellschaft für Goldschmiedekunst with Ludwig Roselius, Peter Behrens, and Wilhelm Wätzoldt (director of the Staatliche Museen in Berlin), of which almost all the independent silversmiths in Germany became members. In the 1920s, Peter Behrens's silver designs were produced in Wilm's workshop.

▶ Annelies Krekel-Aalberse, *Art Nouveau and Art Déco Silver*, New York: Abrams, 1989:144,260. Cat., *Metallkunst*, Berlin: Bröhan-Museum, 1990:543–45.

Wilm, H.J.

▶ German silversmiths; located Berlin.

▶ The firm was founded in 1767. From 1911, Ferdinand Richard Wilm worked at the firm, furthering the development and improvement of silversmithing. From 1924, the firm was directed by Ludwig Riffelmacher, who encouraged massive, carefully detailed hand-raised pieces. In the early 1930s, Erna Zarges-Dürr worked at Wilm. From 1945, it was located in Hamburg and directed by Johann Renatus Wilm.

▶ Annelies Krekel-Aalberse, *Art Nouveau and Art Déco Silver*, New York: Abrams, 1989:144,146,260. Cat., *Metallkunst*, Berlin: Bröhan-Museum, 1990:543–45.

Wilm, Josef   (1880–1924)

▶ German silversmith; active Berlin.

▶ Trained under his father in Dorfen and Fritz von Miller in Munich.

▶ From 1909, he taught metalworking and enameling at the Vereinigte Staatsschulen für freie und angewandte Kunst (Kunstgewerbeschule), Berlin-Charlottenburg.

▶ Annelies Krekel-Aalberse, *Art Nouveau and Art Déco Silver*, New York: Abrams, 1989:144,261.

Wilmotte, Jean-Michel   (1948–)

▶ French interior architect and designer of furniture, lighting, and accessories; born Soissons; active Paris.

▶ From 1968, studied architecture, École Camondo, Paris.

▶ In 1975, he set up the office Governor in Paris which, by the late 1980s, employed a large staff; in 1977, opened the furniture showroom Academy on place de l'Odéon, Paris, to show his own work. He undertook major interior design projects, including the 1982–83 bedroom for President Mitterand in the Palais de l'Élysée, and the 1984 office of the French ambassador in Washington; designed furniture for Nobilis and Mobilier International; fabrics for Nobilis, Casal, and Suzanne Fontan; carpets for Toulemonde Bochart, Tisca, and Flipo; and a faïence dinner service for Gien. Some of his furniture projects were sponsored by VIA, of which he was a founding member. He designed the 1983 *Washington* lamp, originally for the ambassador's offices, produced by Lumen Center; 1986 outdoor chair for the Palais Royal park, Paris; interiors beneath the 1989 Pyramid (I.M. Pei, architect) at the Louvre, Paris; and the 1989 shop Jumbo. In 1986, he set up an office and showroom in Tokyo and, in 1987, offices in Nîmes and Cannes; in the late 1980s, designed the Musée des Beaux-Arts and town hall in Nîmes, a reception-conference room and projection facilities for the Canal + TV network, and the Bunka Mura cultural center in Tokyo. His team of over 30 designers worked on more than 100 projects, including those involving the Palais des Congrès, Grasse and Lyons, and offices and apartments in Tokyo. His furniture designs included the 1983 *Cylindre* chair, 1984 *Élysée* stool, 1986 Palais Royal park chair, 1987 *Etalon* table base, 1988 *La Fontaine* chair, and 1988 *Palmer* chest (sponsored by VIA) in various models.

▶ Work shown at 1989 'L'Art de Vivre' exhibition, Cooper-Hewitt Museum, New York, and 1990 'Les années VIA,' Paris Musée des Art Décoratifs. Appointed Designer of the Year (interiors for 1990 Louvre installation) at 1989 Paris Salon du Meuble.

▶ Jean-Louis Pradel, *Wilmotte*, Paris: Electa Moniteur, 1988. Cat., Garth Hall and Margo Rouard Snowman, *Avant-Première: Contemporary French Furniture*, London: Eprouvé, 1988:84–89.

François Mathey, *Au bonheur des formes, design français 1945–1992*, Paris: Regard, 1992:64,143,182,197,233,244,259.

Wilson, Elsie Cobb   (1877–)

▶ American interior decorator; born Washington, DC.

▶ Attended Parsons School of Design, New York.

▶ First worked for a decorator; by 1919, Wilson had decorated offices in New York and Washington. If Elsie de Wolfe was the first American interior designer, Wilson was the second. She decorated great houses and apartments along America's Eastern seaboard as well as US embassies in Paris, Peking, and Tokyo; helped to restore the Marine commandant's house in Washington for the parents of Lady Brooke Astor. Her taste expressed the new refinement and restraint of post-Victorian decoration. She arranged furniture for conversation rather than for style; worked in a narrow, strict range of austere taste, blending European tradition with American discipline. In a conservative style, she decorated the apartment of her sister Mrs. Cornelius Bliss on Fifth Avenue, New York, and her house on Long Island. She hired as an assistant decorator Eleanor McMillen (later Eleanor Brown), who went on to found the distinguished interior design firm McMillen.

▶ Mark Hampton, *House and Garden*, May 1990. Mark Hampton, *Legendary Decorators of the Twentieth Century*, New York: Doubleday, 1992.

Wilson, Henry   (1864–1934)

▶ British architect, sculptor, and silversmith.

▶ Studied Kidderminster School of Art.

▶ He became the chief assistant to the architect J.D. Sedding; when Sedding died in 1891, took over the firm and completed Sedding's unfinished work; after 1890, became interested in metalworking, setting up a workshop in c1895. In 1892, he joined the Art-Workers' Guild; from 1896, taught metalworking at the London Central School of Arts and Crafts under W.R. Lethaby; having met Alexander Fisher at the Central School, collaborated with him for a short time; taught at Royal College of Art, London; from c1902, taught at Vittoria Street School of Jewellers and Silversmiths, Birmingham; published the design and technique manual *Silverwork and Jewellery* (1903), still considered one of the best handbooks on the subject; in the 1912 second edition, included a chapter on Japanese metalworking techniques, based on lectures and demonstrations of instructors Unno Bisei of Tokyo Fine Art College and R. Kobayashi; in 1915, succeeded Walter Crane as president of the Arts and Crafts Exhibition Society; in 1917, became master of Art-Workers' Guild. J. Paul Cooper, who later set up his own workshop, worked with Wilson. In 1898, H.G. Murphy was apprenticed to Wilson before serving as his assistant.

▶ From 1889, work shown regularly at Arts and Crafts Exhibition Society; included in British pavilion, 1925 'Exposition Internationale des Arts Décoratifs et Industriels Modernes.'

▶ Annelies Krekel-Aalberse, *Art Nouveau and Art Déco Silver*, New York: Abrams, 1989:25,27,260. Charlotte Gere, *American and European Jewelry 1830–1914*, New York: Crown, 1975:227–29.

Wilson, Lynne   (1952–)

▶ British furniture and textile designer; born Epsom, Surrey; active Milan.

▶ Studied Kingston Polytechnic to 1975, and Royal College of Art, London, to 1979.

▶ She was a design apprentice for three months in Centro Design Prototipo at Cassina in Meda; 1979–80, worked with Mario Bellini on projects for Rosenthal and Cleto Munari; in 1982, began working as a freelance designer for Italian furniture clients; for Mobilia Italia, produced her first commercial product, the *Lotto* knock-down chair; from 1984, designed textiles for Centro Design e Comunicazione, Milan; designed the 1985 textile collection *Oltre il Giardino* for Assia, 1985 prototype *Felice* metal tube and polyurethane divan for Centro Design e Comunicazione, 1979 *Toba* knock-down table for Gemini, 1986 *Il Risveglio* textile collection for

Assia, and 1987 *Paradiso ritrovato* curtains for Fanair of Florence.
▶ *Lotto* chair and 1983 *Felice* divan shown at 1985 Salone del Mobile, Milan; *Il Risveglio* fabrics at 1986 Milan textile fair Star; *Paradiso ritrovato* curtains at 1987 Incontri Venezia.
▶ Liz McQuiston, *Women in Design: A Contemporary View*, New York: Rizzoli, 1988:136.

Wilson, Norman   (1902–)
▶ British ceramicist.
▶ Studied North Staffordshire Technical College.
▶ He began working for Wedgwood in Etruria, where, in 1927, he became works manager; in 1928, developed the gas-fired china glost tunnel kiln; in 1931, developed the oil-fired earthenware glost tunnel kiln; 1928–62, produced *NW Unique Pieces*, usually turned and thrown, in three or four glazes; in 1933, introduced the two color bodies and the *Moonstone* matt glaze used on the 1932–33 *Annular* dinner service by John Goodwin, Tom Wedgwood, and others; in 1934, introduced 'Alpine Pink' glaze. In 1935, his 'Matt Green' and 'Straw' glazes were applied to Keith Murray's wares and John Skeaping's animal figurines. In 1935, he designed the *Globe* shape, decorated by artists including Victor Skellern; 1932–39, produced numerous decorative shapes glazed in 'Veronese,' in other glazes, and with silver luster; in 1946, became production manager of Wedgwood at Barlaston; in 1955, rendered the *Barlaston* shape; in 1961, became joint managing director.
▶ Wares included in 1979–80 'Thirties' exhibition, Hayward Gallery, London.
▶ Cat., *Thirties: British art and design before the war*, London: Arts Council of Great Britain, Hayward Gallery, 1979:135, 136,153,303.

Wilson, William   (1914–)
▶ British glassware designer; active Wealdstone.
▶ 1930–33, studied St. Martin's School of Art, London; subsequently, Central School of Arts and Crafts.
▶ At the age of 14, Wilson joined the stained glass department of James Powell (Whitefriars Glassworks) on Wigmore Street as an errand boy; studied at nights and some days while at Powell; in 1933, transferred to the works at Wealdstone, where he designed domestic glassware and executed some diamond-point engraving; encouraged fashionable Modern glass in the Scandinavian style; in 1940, became works manager and, subsequently, general manager, director, and 1950–73, managing director, working as a designer throughout; hired George Baxter as staff designer; played a significant role in the revival of diamond-point engraving.
▶ 1939 bowl and vase shown at 1979–80 'Thirties' exhibition, Hayward Gallery, London.
▶ Frederick Cooke, *Glass: Twentieth-Century Design*, New York: Dutton, 1986:73–75. Cat., *Thirties: British art and design before the war*, London: Arts Council of Great Britain, Hayward Gallery, 1979:94,95,156,303.

Wimmer-Wisgrill, Eduard Josef   (aka Eduard Josef Wimmer   1882–1961)
▶ Austrian fashion, costume, and set designer and metalworker; born Vienna.
▶ 1901–07, studied School of Commerce; and Akademie für angewandte Kunst (Kunstgewerbeschule), both in Vienna.
▶ He was director 1910–22 of the Wiener Werkstätte fashion department and produced designs for silverwares there, including jewelry. Partially due to the influence of Wimmer-Wisgrill the geometric forms of the Wiener Werkstätte became less austere, and bell-flowers, heart-shaped leaves, and spiraling tendrils appeared. In 1912–13, 1918–21, and 1925–53, Wimmer-Wisgrill was professor at the Akademie für angewandte Kunst (Kunstgewerbeschule), Vienna. He was at the Wiener Werkstätte until it closed in 1932.
▶ Charlotte Gere, *American and European Jewelry 1830–1914*, New York: Crown, 1975:229. Werner J. Schweiger, *Wiener Werkstätte*, Vienna: Christian Brandstaetter, 1982:269. Annelies

Krekel-Aalberse, *Art Nouveau and Art Déco Silver*, New York: Abrams, 1989:198,200,261.

Winckler, Ida   (1930–)
▶ Danish textile designer.
▶ She was a textile artist for the Danish Handicraft Guild and became known for her cross-stitch embroideries.
▶ Cat., David Revere McFadden (ed.), *Scandinavian Modern Design 1880–1980*, New York: Abrams, 1982:272, No. 333.

Winn, James H.   (1866–c1940)
▶ Américan jeweler; active Pasadena, California.
▶ Winn's jewelry was rendered in both Art Nouveau and Arts and Crafts idioms; in 1929, he moved to Pasadena, and turned to painting and sculpture.
▶ Sharon S. Darling with Gail Farr Casterline, *Chicago Metalsmiths*, Chicago Historical Society, 1977.

Wirkkala, Tapio Veli Ilmaari   (1915–85)
▶ Finnish glassware, wood, graphic and exhibition designer and metalworker; born Hanko.
▶ 1933–36, studied sculpture, Taideteollinen Korkeakoulu, Helsinki.
▶ Wirkkala was one of the most celebrated postwar Finnish designers. In 1947, he began designing for Iittala glassworks and was concurrently active as a freelance designer. His 1947 *Kanttrelli* vase for Iittala was widely published and, along with his remarkable 1951 laminated wooden dishes by Soinne, gained him recognition. Venini produced his 1970 *Coreano* dish and 1970 *Bolla* bottle-vase. From the 1950s, he was a highly influential designer of glass. He designed the Finnish pavilions at 1952 (IX) and 1954 (X) Triennali di Milano and 1958 Brussels 'Exposition Universelle et Internationale de Bruxelles (Expo '58)'; 1951–54, was artistic director of Taideteollinen Korkeakoulu; in 1955, established his own workshop in Helsinki. 1955–56, he worked in the studio of Raymond Loewy in New York; 1956–85, for Rosenthal; 1959–85, for the Venini glassworks; and for Orfèvrerie Christofle, France. His clients included Airam and Hackman. His stacking glasses of the mid-1960s set a trend. His 1963 *Puukko* knife was produced by Hackman. His 1965 *Karelia* suite of drinking glasses was an instant success.
▶ Received first prize in 1946 Iittala glass competition. Sharing with Kaj Franck, received three gold medals and a grand prize at the 1947 (VIII) Triennale di Milano and alone: three grand prizes (design, glass, carving) at 1951 (IX), three grand prizes (design, glass, sculpture) at 1954 (X), grand prize and gold medal at 1960 (XI), silver medal at 1963 (XII) Triennali di Milano. Received 1951 Lunning Prize; 1963, 1966, 1967, 1969 and 1973 gold medals at Faenza; 1980 Prince Eugen Medal. Work shown in numerous exhibitions, including 1970–72 USA 'Contemporary Finnish Design,' Smithsonian Institution traveling exhibition; 1980 'Scandinavian Modern Design 1880–1980' exhibition, Cooper-Hewitt Museum, New York; 1983–84 'Design Since 1945' exhibition, Philadelphia Museum of Art. Work subject of 1981–82 exhibition, traveling worldwide. Appointed honorary member of the Royal Society of Arts, London, in 1961, becoming Academician in 1972; received honorary doctorate from the Royal College of Art, London. Elected Honorary Royal Designer for Industry, London, in 1964; honorary member Diseñadores industriales, Instituto Politécnico Nacional, Mexico City, in 1975; honorary academician, Académie de l'Architecture, silver medal, in 1983.
▶ Frederick Cooke, *Glass: Twentieth-Century Design*, New York: Dutton, 1986:83–84,92. Cat., Kathryn B. Hiesinger and George H. Marcus III (eds.), *Design Since 1945*, Philadelphia: Philadelphia Museum of Art., 1983:236,II–73–74,V–52–53. Rut Bryk, *Tapio Wirkkala*, Washington: Smithsonian Institution, 1956–59. Cat., David Revere McFadden (ed.), *Scandinavian Modern Design 1880–1980*, New York: Abrams, 1982:272, Nos. 143,178,179,199, 222,237,312. *Tapio Wirkkala*, Helsinki: The Finnish Society of Crafts and Design, 1981. 'Interview with Tapio Wirkkala,' *Domus*, No. 619, July–Aug. 1981:6–7. Pekka Suhonen, 'Counter-

points in Tapio Wirkkala's Output,' *Form Function Finland*, No. 2, 1981:38–43. Cat., *The Lunning Prize*, Stockholm: Nationalmuseum, 1986:36–41. Jennifer Hawkins Opie, *Scandinavia: Ceramics and Glass in the Twentieth Century*, New York: Rizzoli, 1989.

Wittmann, Ludwig (1877–1961)
▶ German silversmith; active Munich and Oslo.
▶ Until 1910, Wittmann worked with Theodor Heiden in Munich; 1910–28, was a designer at David-Andersen in Oslo, where his designs were produced with heavy, abstract ornamentation with applied precious stones.
▶ Annelies Krekel-Aalberse, *Art Nouveau and Art Déco Silver*, New York: Abrams, 1989:243,261.

Wkhotemas
See Vhutemas

Wlach, Oskar (1881–?)
▶ Austrian architect and furniture and interior designer; born Vienna.
▶ Active in Austria and contributing to the 'Viennese element,' his output was rather modest; (with Josef Frank) founded the interior design cooperative Haus und Garten, Vienna, which produced furniture, textiles, and utensils.
▶ Günther Feuerstein, *Vienna—Present and Past: Arts and Crafts—Applied Art—Design*, Vienna: Jugend und Volk, 1976: 49,80.

WMF
See Württembergische Metallwarenfabrik

Wohlert, William (1920–)
▶ Danish architect and furniture designer.
▶ Studied architecture, Det Kongelige Danske Akademi, Copenhagen, to 1944.
▶ He set up his own architecture office in 1948; 1951–53, taught at the University of California; 1944–46 and 1953–59, at Det Kongelige Danske Akademi.
▶ Work shown in Danish architecture and design exhibitions in London, New York, and Stockholm.
▶ He was awarded the 1958 Eckersberg Medal and Bundespreis 'Die gute Industrieform.'
▶ Frederik Sieck, *Nutidig Dansk Møbeldesign: - en kortfattet illustreret beskrivelse*, Copenhagen: Bondo Gravesen; 1990 Busck edition in English.

Wohnbedarf
▶ Swiss furniture and furnishings store; initially located Zürich.
▶ Wohnbedarf ('household requirements') was founded in 1931 by Sigfried Giedion, Rudolf Graber, and Werner M. Moser, in an effort to sell Modern design to middle-class customers. The first store was at Claridenstrasse 47, Zürich; its interior was designed by architect and designer Ernst F. Burckhardt. A standardized basic model of furniture was mass produced, including cabinets, chairs with and without arms (covered in a range of upholstery fabrics), and other modular configurations. Max Bill, while working on the Neubühl settlement near Zürich in the early 1930s, designed the firm's letterhead, advertisements, flyers, invitation cards, and the first Wohnendarf logo of 1931. From 1934 for a number of years, Herbert Bayer designed most of the store's printed advertising and promotion. Alvar Aalto's bentwood furniture was sold at Wohnbedarf before his Artek firm was founded in 1935. An active and important designer for Wohnbedarf, Aalto's entire collection of bentwood furniture was included in the catalog *New Wooden Furniture: Aalto, Wohnbedarf* (1934) designed by Herbert Bayer. Marcel Breuer's convertible sofa was produced by the firm. In 1935, the enterprise became wholly owned by Graber and his mother. Selling furniture and furnishings from other manufacturers, the firm is still in business today, with branch stores in various Swiss cities.
▶ Stanislaus von Moos, 'Wohnbedarf und Lebensform, *Archithese*, No. 2, 1980. Friederike Mehlau-Wiebking et al., *Schweizer Typenmöbel 1925–35, Sigfried Giedion und die Wohnbedarf AG*, Zürich: gta, 1989.

Wojtech, Karl
▶ Swedish silversmith; active Stockholm.
▶ Wojtech sometimes collaborated with Wolter Gahn and Anna Petrus; produced wares in severe, matt-finished, almost Romanesque forms and ornamentation.
▶ His silver designs were included in the Swedish pavilion at the 1925 Paris 'Exposition Internationale des Arts Décoratifs et Industriels Modernes.'
▶ Annelies Krekel-Aalberse, *Art Nouveau and Art Déco Silver*, New York: Abrams, 1989:245,261.

Wold-Torne, Oluf (1867–1919)
▶ Norwegian ceramicist.
▶ Wold-Torne produced the 1907 dinner service design in a berry and leaf pattern for Porsgrunds Porselænsfabrik.
▶ Fredrik Wildhagen, *Norge i Form*, Oslo: Stenersen, 1988:66–67.

Wolfers Frères
▶ Belgian jeweler; located Brussels.
▶ The firm was founded in 1812 as a jewelry business in Brussels; in the early 19th century, was known for its ivory carving, popular due to King Léopold II's interests in the Congo (now Zaïre), from where the material was obtained. Ivory in sculptural forms was usually combined with precious or base metals. Upon his father's death in 1892, Philippe Wolfers became artistic director of the firm and its best-known member, to whom the Modern development there was owed; produced pieces in an imaginative Art Nouveau style, even through the period of its decadence at the turn of the century. From 1910, the firm's shop and studios were housed in the building designed for the firm by Victor Horta on the rue d'Arenenburg, Brussels. In 1929, Philippe was succeeded by his sons, sculptor and lacquerer Marcel (1886–1976) and Lucien. Wolfers silver was sold at Bonebakker, Amsterdam, and Begeer, Utrecht. In the 1950s, firm was located at 82 avenue Louise, Brussels, under the management of Willy Wolfers, a nephew of Philippe Wolfers. He was succeeded by son Freddy Wolfers. In 1983, the firm became part of Chaumet.
▶ Philippe Wolfers's jewelry shown at 1899 Munich Secession exhibition; colonial section, 1897 Brussels 'Exposition Internationale'; 1902 Turin 'Esposizione Internazionale d'Arte Decorativa Moderna'; and 1903 Paris Salon. Willy Wolfers's pieces shown at various exhibitions, including 1958 Brussels 'Exposition Universelle et Internationale de Bruxelles (Expo 58).'
▶ Charlotte Gere, *American and European Jewelry 1830–1914*, New York: Crown, 1975:229. Melissa Gabardi, *Les Bijoux des Années 50*, Paris: Amateur, 1987. Annelies Krekel-Aalberse, *Art Nouveau and Art Déco Silver*, New York: Abrams, 1989:91, 93,261.
▶ See Wolfers, Philippe

Wolfers, Philippe (1858–1929)
▶ Belgian jeweler and sculptor; born and active Brussels.
▶ Studied drawing and sculpture, Académie Royale des Beaux-Arts, Brussels, under sculptor Isidore de Rudder, and enameling in Paris under Louis Houillon.
▶ Wolfers worked from 1876 in his father's gold and silver workshop in Brussels, where he learned modeling, casting, burnishing, chasing, and stone-setting. The jewelry he designed 1880–85 was in the Louis XV style, although Japanese influence began to appear in c1882. In c1890, motifs from orchids, lilies, irises, and wild flowers began to appear on Wolfers's silverwares. In 1892, when his father died, he became artistic director of the firm; in 1890, he created his first sculpture pieces and made thousands of drawings of flora, fauna, and the human body throughout his career; used baroque pearls and opaque or translucent enamels; in c1893, set up a workshop of his own in the place Marie-Louise, Brussels, separate from the family firm, where he personally directed a modeler, enameler, chaser, diamond-setter, and ivory carver;

issued the separate catalog *Exemplaires Uniques*, in which 136 one-off items were shown, including silver pieces with enamel and stones, ivory and crystal vases, and jewelry similar to René Lalique's designs; in 1893 or 1894, began using ivory from the Congo (now Zaïre). Paul Hankar designed the house and workshop that Wolfers built in La Hupe; his associates were housed nearby. In 1905 or 1908 with the appearance of his last jewelry pieces, he turned almost exclusively to bronze and marble sculptures inlaid with precious materials; later returning to design, produced the ten-sided geometrically patterned *Gioconda* silver range, augmented by a completely outfitted dining room (tea set, flatware, furniture, and furnishings) shown at the 1925 Paris Exposition.
▶ Sculpture shown at 1894 Antwerp 'Exposition Internationale d'Anvers'; chryselephantine exposition, colonial section, 1897 Brussels 'Exposition Internationale'; 1899 Munich Secession exhibition; 1902 Turin 'Esposizione Internazionale d'Arte Decorativa Moderna'; and 1903 Paris Salon. *Gioconda* range and dining room shown at 1925 Paris 'Exposition Internationale des Arts Décoratifs et Industriels Modernes.'
▶ *The Studio*, 15 November 1898. Yvonne Brunhammer et al., *Art Nouveau Belgium, France*, Houston: Rice University, 1976. Melissa Gabardi, *Les Bijoux des Années 50*, Paris: Amateur, 1987. Annelies Krekel-Aalberse, *Art Nouveau and Art Déco Silver*, New York: Abrams, 1989:91–92,261. Charlotte Gere, *American and European Jewelry 1830–1914*, New York: Crown, 1975:229. M. Wolfers, *Philippe Wolfers*, Brussels, 1965. Tardy, *Les Ivoires: Évolution décorative du Ier siècle à nos jours*, Paris, 1966:204.

Wolff, Ann   (b. Ann Wärff   1937–)
▶ German glassware designer; born Lübeck; active Sweden.
▶ Studied graphic design in Hamburg; 1956–59, studied Hochschule für Gestaltung, Ulm; and in Zürich.
▶ From 1960–64, she was a designer for Pukebergs Glasbruk; 1964–79, designer at the Kosta Boda glassworks; in 1978, set up her own studio in Transjö; lectured in Europe, the USA, Japan; in 1977, 1979, and 1984, was guest lecturer at the Pilchuck School of Glass, Stanwood, Washington. Designed 1983 *My red thread* bowl.
▶ Received 1967 Swedish State traveling scholarship and 1968 Lunning Prize (with Göran Wärff).
▶ Cat., *The Lunning Prize*, Stockholm: Nationalmuseum, 1986:190–93.

Wolff Olins
▶ British design studio.
▶ Wolff Olins was established in London in 1955. Its work ranged from graphics to interiors, with a specialization in corporate identity programs. Wally Olins and Michael Wolff were the original principals; though the partnership was dissolved, the name was retained. The firm designed the British Telecom corporate identity.
▶ Penny Sparke, *Introduction to Design and Culture in the Twentieth Century*, Allen and Unwin, 1986.

Wollenweber, Eduard
▶ German silversmiths; located Munich.
▶ Wollenweber set up his workshop in Munich in the first half of the 19th century and was a silversmith to the Bavarian court. After an apprenticeship in the workshop of F. Harrach, Munich, Adolf von Mayrhofer worked c1891–1903 as assistant to Wollenweber. The workshop produced the silver designs of A. Strobl in c1900 and Adelbert Niemeyer in c1912; it went out of business during World War II.
▶ Silverwares shown at 1922 Munich 'Deutsche Gewerbeschau.'
▶ Annelies Krekel-Aalberse, *Art Nouveau and Art Déco Silver*, New York: Abrams, 1989:131,143,261.

Wollner, Leo   (1932–) and **Grete Wollner**   (1934–)
▶ Austrian textile designers; born Vienna.
▶ Known for their high quality fabrications in limited production, the Wollners settled in Germany.

▶ Günther Feuerstein, *Vienna—Present and Past: Arts and Crafts—Applied Art—Design*, Vienna: Jugend und Volk, 1976: 41,49,50,81.

Woloch, Rose
See Idée, Rose

Wolter, Erna   (1885–1973)
▶ German sculptor and silversmith; active Magdeburg.
▶ Studied Kunstgewerbeschule, Magdeburg.
▶ She set up her metalworking facility in Magdeburg in 1907.
▶ Annelies Krekel-Aalberse, *Art Nouveau and Art Déco Silver*, New York: Abrams, 1989:261.

Wood, Beatrice   (1893–)
▶ American ceramicist; born San Francisco.
▶ Studied under Glen Lukens, Gertrud and Otto Natzler, Viveka, and Otto Heino; 1938, University of Southern California, Los Angeles.
▶ Ceramics shown at 1947 (XI) traveling 'Ceramic National Exhibition' organized by Syracuse Museum of Fine Art, Syracuse, New York, and at New York Metropolitan Museum of Art.
▶ R. Craig Miller, *Modern Design, 1890–1990*, New York: Abrams, 1990. Auction cat., 'Contemporary Works of Art,' Sotheby's New York, 14 March 1992.

Wood, Kenneth
See Kenwood

Wood, Ruby Ross   (b. Ruby Ross Goodnough   1880–1950)
▶ American interior decorator; born Monticello, Georgia.
▶ Settling in New York, Wood worked on a farming journal; became a freelance writer; was a ghostwriter for interior decorator Elsie de Wolfe, at first writing for Theodore Dreiser's *Delineator* magazine under de Wolfe's name, and writing magazine articles and the book *The House in Good Taste* (1913); under her own name wrote the book *The Honest Home* (1914). In 1914, she began working at the Wanamaker's department store's Au Quatrième decorating studio; in 1918, when Nancy Vincent McClelland left, became its director. She was known briefly as Ruby Rose Goodenough and soon after married Chalmers Wood. She opened her own shop and, by the 1920s, was a leading society decorator in a distinctively American style that was less formal and less luxurious than that of her predecessors, and less grandiose than its European counterpart. She persuaded decorator Billy Baldwin, a fellow Southerner, to move to New York to work with her from 1935–50. Wood's interiors for the David Adler-designed house in Palm Beach for Mr. and Mrs. Wolcott Blair were typical of her style: the house was decorated in cream leather, Elsie de Wolfe's leopard chintz, and off-white textured cotton from Sweden; there were tubs of tall white flowering plants between monumental windows. The geometric floor was paved with old Cuban marble in a parchment color. The architect for Wood's own house on Long Island, New York, was William Delano; its furniture was eclectic, diffident, and unselfconsciously combined with no particular interest for value.
▶ Robert L. Green, 'The Legendary Ruby Ross Wood, *Architectural Digest*, Oct. 1979, Mark Hampton, *House and Garden*, May 1990. John Esten and Rose Bennett Gilbert, *Manhattan Style*, Boston: Little, Brown, 1990:4. Mark Hampton, *Legendary Decorators of the Twentieth Century*, New York: Doubleday, 1992.

World of Art, The   (V mire iskusstv)
▶ Russian arts society and magazine; located St. Petersburg.
▶ 'The World of Art' or, more accurately, 'In the World of Art' was founded in 1898 by a group of artists, critics, and aesthetes, including Serge Diaghilev and Aleksandra Exter. Valentin Serov's name was linked with its activities. B. Kustodiev was one of its most distinctive artists. Until 1905, it published a magazine by the same name; like its sponsoring organization, the journal's goal was to arouse interest in Russian folklore; revived 1910–24, it also documented contemporary developments in the applied arts

elsewhere in Europe. The combination of the old with the new was peculiar to Russia and reflected the nationalist mood in Europe with its interest in traditional crafts. Léon Bakst and Aleksandr Benois were contributors to the journal, whose name has come to represent an entire movement parallel to Art Nouveau in Western Europe. Many of the articles printed in *V mire iskusstv* had been previously published in journals in the West. Artists in the group were chiefly identified with the sets and costumes for ballets produced by Diaghilev, who first brought them to Paris in 1909. *V mire iskusstv* reflected the Westward-looking artistic culture of St. Petersburg and its Artists' Association, whose chief rival was the more nationalistic and conservative League of Russian Artists in Moscow. In *c*1910, other notable participants included Nokolai Roerich, Aleksandr Benois, Mstivlav Dobuzhinskii, Anna Ostroumova-Lebedeva, Igor Grabar, Kuzma Petrov-Vodkin, Aleksandr Golovin, Zinaida Serebriakova, Konstantin Bogaevskii, Sergei Sudeikin, Sapunov, Boris Grigoriev, Pavel Kuznetsov, Martiros Saryan, and Aleksandr Matveev. From 1911, *V mire iskusstv* held its famous Russian Festivals led by Diaghilev in Paris and other cities in Western Europe.

▶ Gabriella di Milia, *Mir Iskusstva–Il Mando dell' Arte: Artisti Russi dal 1898 al 1924*, Naples: Società Napoletana, 1982. Nina Lobanov-Rostovsky, *Revolutionary Ceramics*, London: Studio Vista, 1990.

Wormley, Edward (1907–)

▶ American furniture designer; active Chicago and New York.

▶ 1926–27, studied Art Institute of Chicago.

▶ 1928–31, he worked in the design studio of the Marshall Field department store in Chicago; 1931–41 in New York, was a designer for Dunbar Furniture of Indiana, refining its range of wood and upholstered furniture to appeal to a wide range of tastes. In 1945, he opened his own office in New York, continuing with Dunbar as his client for furniture, Alexander Smith for carpets, and others for textiles. His postwar work showed Scandinavian and Italian influences. One of his highly regarded designs was the 1947 *Listen to Me* chaise for Dunbar.

▶ Work included in 1951 and 1952 (six pieces of furniture) 'Good Design' exhibition at the New York Museum of Modern Art.

▶ George Nelson (ed.), *Chairs*, New York: Whitney Library of Ideas, 1953:41,62–63,73,93,158,161. W.J. Hennessey and E.D. Hennessey, *Modern Furnishings for the Home*, Vol. 2, New York, 1956. Edgar Kaufmann Jr., 'Edward Wormley: 30 Years of Design,' *Interior Design*, Vol. 32, March 1961:190. Cat., Kathryn B. Hiesinger and George H. Marcus III (eds.), *Design Since 1945*, Philadelphia: Philadelphia Museum of Art, 1983:236,III–92. Cherie Fehrman and Kenneth Fehrman, *Postwar Interior Design, 1945–1960*, New York: Van Nostrand Reinhold, 1987. Alexander Polakov, 'Edward Wormley' in Mel Byars and Russell Flinchum (eds.), *50 American Designers*, Washington: Preservation, 1994.

Wright, Frank Lloyd (1867–1959)

▶ American architect, designer, and theorist; born Richland Center, Wisconsin; active Chicago; Spring Green, Wisconsin; Chandler and Paradise, Arizona; and Tokyo.

▶ 1885–87, studied engineering, University of Wisconsin, Madison, Wisconsin.

▶ From 1887, he worked for architect Lyman Silsbee in Chicago; 1889–92, in the architecture firm of Dankmar Adler and Louis Sullivan in Chicago; 1893–96, in partnership with architect Cecil Corwin in Chicago; 1896–97, in private practice in the Oak Park suburb of Chicago; and, 1897–1909, in his own practice in Chicago. 1909–11, he traveled in Europe; in 1911, built his first Taliesin (Gaelic for 'shining brow') house and studio and resumed his private practice in Spring Green, Wisconsin; in 1912, opened an office again in Chicago. In 1914, Taliesin was partially destroyed by fire, and Wright built the 1914 Taliesin II. 1915–20, he was active in an office in Tokyo, while designing the Imperial Hotel; 1921–24, produced the world's first concrete 'texture block' (cinder block) houses. In 1925, Taliesin II was partially

destroyed by another fire, resulting in Taliesin III. In 1928, he worked in La Jolla, California; 1928–29, was active in an office (a temporary desert camp that he called 'Ocatillo') in Chandler, Arizona; and, in 1932, founded the Wright Foundation Fellowship at Taliesin; in 1938, built Taliesin West in Paradise near Scottsdale, Arizona; was active in both Wisconsin and Arizona for the rest of his life. Wright exerted a profound influence on the decorative arts and became known as the greatest American architect; worked beside G.G. Elmslie in the offices of Lyman Silsbee and of Louis Henry Sullivan in Chicago. In *c*1885, Wright's first furniture appeared, designed for his Oak Park residence. The furniture's most marked characteristic was its angularity and exaggerated verticality, with long, narrow spindles on his famous tall chairs. (Influenced by Victorian design, the first spindles were round, later replaced by square ones.) Wright's work was not only crucial to architectural development in the 20th century but also an important source of Arts and Crafts design 1898–1915. Many of his designs showed a kinship to the Mission furniture being produced by the Stickley brothers, Elbert Hubbard, and others, and their philosophies of incorporating art into everyday life were akin. 1900–14, as a leader of the Prairie School of architectural design, Wright held that the furniture of a house should reflect the entire structure, and designed furniture for almost all of his buildings. He regarded built-in furniture as the link between the interior space and moveable furniture pieces. His early clients used Stickley furniture in his houses. Though he never insisted on handcrafted objects, he maintained a close relationship with the firms and people who produced his designs, such as with George Niedecken of Niedecken-Walbridge, a firm specializing in interior design that supervised the interiors of some of Wright's most important Prairie houses in Oak Park, Illinois. In 1901, he delivered his seminal lecture 'The Art and Craft of the Machine' at Jane Addams's Hull House in Chicago. He designed the 1904 Larkin office building in Buffalo, New York, considered by many to be his most important contribution to design; the building was fitted with the world's first metal office chairs and desks that did not imitate wood. In 1904, wooden-frame chairs with slab-like seats and backs (also designed for his own house) were designed for the Larkin building and elsewhere; they had a great influence on furniture design through Gerrit Rietveld in the Netherlands. Wright designed the 1907–09 Robie house in Chicago with many notable stained-glass windows. His essay 'In the Cause of Architecture' in the 1908 issue of the journal *Architectural Record* was influential on architecture and industrial design in Europe. It was often quoted by C.R. Ashbee, the British proponent of the Arts and Crafts movement. In 1910, a two-volume portfolio of Wright's work was published in Berlin as *Ausgeführte Bauten und Entwürfe von Frank Lloyd Wright (The Buildings and Projects of Frank Lloyd Wright)*; it had a powerful impact on European architecture and design. Jan Kotera's 1908–12 municipal museum in Hradec Kralove (now Czech Republic) was the first structure in Europe clearly influenced by Wright. Walter Gropius's work at the 1914 Cologne Werkbund-Ausstellung was indebted to Wright's 1909–10 Park Inn Hotel in Mason City, Iowa, and Ludwig Mies van der Rohe's 1923 brick house paraphrased the Wright Prairie House type. Wright's 1915–22 Imperial Hotel in Tokyo was heavily decorated and exemplified his fondness at the time for sharply-angled polygonal forms, found also in its furniture which, along with tableware, textiles, and other furnishings, was designed and made for the hotel. The architecture and furniture of the 1920 Barnsdall house in Los Angeles illustrated his interest in Pre-Columbian Meso-American structures and forms. In the 1950s, Wright's domestic wares were mass produced; his furniture for Henredon-Heritage was commercially unsuccessful. His plywood furniture for 1950s Usonian houses was designed to be produced by the house's carpenter, local craftsperson, or its owner. From the late 1980s, reproductions of Wright's earlier furniture designs began to be manufactured under Taliesen Foundation licenses by Cassina, silver and crystal by Tiffany, textiles by Schumacher, and stained-glass windows by Oakbrook Esser Studios. Most of the reissued textile designs were not original but rather interpretations of Wright's recurring motifs, although the originals of the 1950s were not by Wright but by the students at Taliesin West.

▶ Architectural works included 1894 Winslow house in River Forest, Illinois; 1904–5 Larkin building in Buffalo, New York; 1905–07 Unitarian Church in Oak Park, Illinois; 1907 Tomek house in Riverside, Illinois; 1907–09 Robie house in Chicago; 1907–11 Avery Coonley house in Riverside, Illinois; 1911 Taliesin (and others after two fires) in Spring Green, Wisconsin; 1915–22 Imperial Hotel in Tokyo; 1917–20 Barnsdall House in Los Angeles; 1928 Ocatillo Desert Camp (temporary) near Chandler, Arizona; 1935–39 Kaufmann house ('Fallingwater') near Bear Run, Pennsylvania; 1935–39 S.C. Johnson administration building and 1944–50 laboratory tower in Racine, Wisconsin; 1934 Willey house in Minneapolis, Minnesota; 1937 onwards Taliesin West near Scottsdale, Arizona; 1953–56 Price Tower in Bartlesville, Oklahoma; 1957–66 Marin County Civic Center in San Rafael, California; 1958–59 Beth Sholom Synagogue in Elkins Park, Pennsylvania; 1943–46 and 1956–59 Solomon R. Guggenheim Museum in New York; 1956 'Illinois' project for a mile-high skyscraper for 130,000 inhabitants on 528 floors.

▶ Major exhibitions included 1910 exhibition in Berlin; 1991–92 'Frank Lloyd Wright: Preserving an Architectural Heritage' traveling exhibition in the USA; 1993 retrospective, New York Museum of Modern Art. Living room of 1913 Francis W. Little House, Wayzata, Minnesota, installed in New York Metropolitan Museum of Art, and 1935–37 office of Edgar J. Kaufmann Sr. installed in Victoria and Albert Museum, London, in 1993.

▶ Frederich Gutheim (ed.), *Frank Lloyd Wright on Architecture: Selected Writings 1894–1940*, New York: Duell, Sloan and Pearce, 1941. Henry Russell-Hitchcock, *In the Nature of Materials, 1887–1941: The Buildings of Frank Lloyd Wright*, New York: Duell, Sloan and Pearce, 1942. Frank Lloyd Wright, *An Autobiography*, New York, 1943. Frank Lloyd Wright, *The Future of Architecture*, New York: Horizon, 1953. Vincent Scully, *Frank Lloyd Wright*, New York: Braziller, 1960. William Allin Storrer, *The Architecture of Frank Lloyd Wright: A Complete Catalogue*, Cambridge, Massachusetts: MIT, 1974. H. Allen Brooks, *The Prairie School: Frank Lloyd Wright and his Midwest Contemporaries*, New York: Norton, 1976. Robert L. Sweeney, *Frank Lloyd Wright: An Annotated Bibliography*, Los Angeles, 1978. Robert C. Twombly, *Frank Lloyd Wright: His Life and Architecture*, New York: Wiley, 1979. David A. Hanks, *The Decorative Designs of Frank Lloyd Wright*, New York: Dutton, 1979. Cat., Lisa Phillips (introduction), *Space and Environment: Furniture by American Architects*, New York: Whitney Museum of American Art, 1982:56–57.

Wright, John (1940–)
▶ British interior and furniture designer.
▶ Studied Royal College of Art, London.
▶ He opened an office in 1966 with Jean Schofield and Jill Walker in London. His range of objects included domestic and office furniture, lighting, and accessories. Wright and Jean Schofield designed the 1964 knock-down *Chair C1* produced by Anderson Manson Decorations, London.
▶ Wright's and Schofield's chairs included in 1966 'Vijftig Jaar Zitten,' Stedelijk Museum, Amsterdam; 1970 'Modern Chairs 1918–1970' exhibition, Whitechapel Gallery, London.
▶ Mary Gilliat, *English Style*, London 1966. Cat., *Modern Chairs 1918–1970*, London: Lund Humphries, 1971.

Wright, Russel (1904–76)
▶ American designer of domestic goods; born Lebanon, Ohio; active New York.
▶ Studied painting, Cincinnati Art Academy, under Frank Duveneck; 1920, Art Students' League, New York; 1922, law, Princeton University; from 1923, architecture, Columbia University, New York.
▶ He was the first designer of home products to have his name mentioned in the manufacturers' advertising. He managed to balance in a peculiar manner Functionalism, Art Déco, and the verna-

cular Mission Style. Raised as a Quaker, his puritanism and Midwest practicality informed his designs. His work reflected a change in lifestyles in America after the Depression. He was drawn to the theater through his friendship with playwright Thornton Wilder, and Norman Bel Geddes offered him a job designing theater sets in 1924. In 1927, he became involved in the decorative arts by casting miniature versions of his *papier-mâché* stage props; under the influence of his wife Mary, moved away from theater design, producing household accessories in spun aluminum that sold well and launched his career; in 1930, established a workshop in New York and began producing metalware, including 1930 flatware in sterling silver that echoed the designs of Jean Puiforcat and Josef Hoffmann, though the pieces have a signature of their own; from 1933–34, executed designs for chromium-plated wares by Chase Brass and Copper. In 1935, his enormously successful *Modern Living* furniture line from Conant-Ball was introduced at Macy's department store in New York. Mary Wright, his sales representative, coined the word 'blonde' for the bleached finish of maple wood used in his furniture. In 1937, Wright concentrated on ceramics, resulting in *American Modern* by Steubenville Pottery, the highly successful line of dinnerware produced 1939–59. He patented a wooden chair with an adjustable back. There was hardly a household in America that did not, at one time, have a piece of Russel Wright's china; curvaceous and witty, the pieces became classics of popular design. In 1955, as a consultant to the US State Department, he developed ideas for cottage industries in Southeast Asia; in 1965, designed over 100 products for manufacture in Japan; in 1967, abandoned most of his design activities and became a consultant to the National Parks Service on programming and planning; disappointed by the failure of his 'American Way' home furnishings venture and devastated by his wife's death at the peak of his fame, he retreated to 'Manitoga,' his country home near Garrison, New York, and worked only occasionally thereafter. His designs included a 1932 Wurlitzer radio cabinet; 1934 60-piece furniture range for Heywood-Wakefield; 1943–46 Bauer Pottery freeform art ceramics; 1946 *Casual China*, Iroquois; glassware from 1945 for Century Metalcraft and subsequently numerous firms; 1951 *Highlight* glassware and pottery; 1949 *Flair* glassware; 1950 *Easier Living* 50-piece furniture range for Stratton; 1950 range of metal furniture for Samsonite; and 1945 *Melmac* dinnerware range for Northern Industrial Chemical.

▶ Work (cocktail shaker of *c*1931) included in 1931 exhibition of the American Union of Decorative Arts and Craftsmen, and other work in 1934 'Machine Art' exhibition, New York Museum of Modern Art; 1985 'High Styles' exhibition, Whitney Museum of American Art; and 1983–84 'Design Since 1945' exhibition, Philadelphia Museum of Art.

▶ Russel and Mary Wright, *A Guide for Easier Living*, New York, 1951. Diane Cochrane, 'Designer for All Seasons,' *Industrial Design*, Vol. 23, March–April 1976:46–51. William J. Hennessey, *Russel Wright: American Designer*, Cambridge, Mass.: MIT Press, 1983. Cat., Kathryn B. Hiesinger and George H. Marcus III (eds.), *Design Since 1945*, Philadelphia: Philadelphia Museum of Art, 1983: II–75–76. Lisa Phillips et al., *High Styles: Twentieth Century American Design*, New York: Whitney Museum of American Art with Summit Books, 1985. William J. Hennessey, 'Russel Wright,' in Mel Byars and Russell Flinchum (eds.), *50 American Designers*, Washington: Preservation, 1994.

Würbel und Czokally
▶ Austrian silversmiths; located Vienna.
▶ The firm was founded in 1860 or 1862; in 1902, produced the silver designs of Josef Hoffmann.
▶ Annelies Krekel-Aalberse, *Art Nouveau and Art Déco Silver*, New York: Abrams, 1989:199,261.

Württembergische Metallwarenfabrik (WMF)
▶ German manufacturer; located Geislingen.
▶ The firm was founded in 1853 by Daniel Straub and the brothers Schweizer. In 1880, Straub und Schweizer was amalgamated with competitor A. Ritter, Esslingen, forming Württembergische

Metallwarenfabrik (usually abbreviated to WMF). In c1900, with a staff of 3,000, it specialized in domestic metalwares, including silver-plated flatware and hollow-ware, pewter, copper, and brass. Its products were sold in sales outlets in Cologne, Berlin, Vienna, Warsaw, and elsewhere. Up to 1900, its styles were neo-Renaissance and Rococo. After 1900, it concentrated on Jugendstil forms. In 1905, WMF took over Orivit, manufacturers of machine-pressed hollow-ware and flatware. In the 1920s, WMF developed the new glass techniques Myra, Lava-luna, and Ikova; in c1928, began producing silverwares, some of which were designed by F.A. Breuhaus. It grew into a diversified industrial giant. In 1950, it hired Wilhelm Wagenfeld as consultant designer; his glass for the firm was worked out precisely with models and measured drawings, even though the models were mouth blown. He also executed some of its lighting designs. Active today, WMF's facilities include glass and crystal works in Göppingen.

▶ *Objekte des Jugendstils*, Bern: Beneli, 1975:261. Alastair Duncan, *Art Nouveau and Art Déco Lighting*, New York: Simon and Schuster, 1978:126. Cat., *WMF Glas, Keramik, Metall, 1925–50*, Berlin: Kunstgewerbemuseum, 1980. Frederick Cooke, *Glass: Twentieth-Century Design*, New York: Dutton, 1986:92. Annelies Krekel-Aalberse, *Art Nouveau and Art Déco Silver*, New York: Abrams, 1989:141,261. Cat., *Metallkunst*, Berlin: Bröhan-Museum, 1990:546–79.

Wyld, Evelyn

▶ American designer; active Paris.
▶ Studied Royal College of Music, London.
▶ She settled in Paris in c1907. She and Eileen Gray traveled to North Africa, where they learned weaving and wool dyeing with natural colors from Arab women. In 1909, Wyld returned to Britain, where she studied weaving and rug knotting, while Gray tried her hand at designing rugs; Wyld brought back to Paris looms and a teacher from the National School of Weavers. In 1927, she and Eyre de Lanux began living together and first worked on the rue Visconti, Paris, where in the 1920s Wyld supervised the weaving of rugs designed by Gray; at one point, eight women worked in the three rooms on the top floor of the building where Honoré de Balzac had earlier run a printshop. The wool came from the Auvergne, was dyed in Paris, and had labels attached that read 'Designed by Eileen Gray at the workshop of Evelyn Wyld.' The rugs were given names, including *Héliogabale*, *Ulysse*, *Hannibal*, *Macédoine*, *Pénélope*, *Fidèle*, *Casimir*, *Biribi*, *D* (for Darnia) and *E* (for Eileen). The best seller was *Footit*, named for the clowns Chocolat et Footit. Gray's rugs were severely geometric; Wyld's tended to be flowery. In 1929, Wyld and Eyre de Lanux moved to Saint-Tropez, then to La Roquette-sur-Siagne, and opened the shop Décor in Cannes, which soon closed. They designed interiors and lacquered furniture, some with the assistance of Seizo Sugawara.

▶ Wyld and de Lanux showed furniture and rugs at 1927, 1929, and 1932 Salons of the Société des Artistes Décorateurs and 1930 (I) UAM (Union des Artistes Modernes). Wyld's rugs shown at 1931 rug exhibition, Curtis Moffat Gallery, London.

▶ Peter Adam, *Eileen Gray, Architect/Designer*, New York: Abrams, 1987. Philippe Garner, *Eileen Gray: Design and Architecture, 1878–1976*, Cologne: Taschen, 1993.

Wynne, Madeline Yale (1847–1918)

▶ American amateur jeweler and silversmith; active Chicago.
▶ Wynne practiced in the Arts and Crafts style; was a mentor to Frances M. Glessner, also engaged in silversmithing as a hobby.
▶ Annelies Krekel-Aalberse, *Art Nouveau and Art Déco Silver*, New York: Abrams, 1989:104,254.

Y

Yakulov, Georgii Bogdanovich (1882–1928)
▶ Russian set designer and decorator; born Tiflis (now Tbilisi, Georgia).
▶ 1901–03, studied Institute of Painting, Sculpture, and Architecture, Moscow.
▶ From 1905, he developed his theory of light; after 1907, became associated with Moscow Association of Artists; 1910–11, was active as the decorator of balls, spectacles, and other public events; in 1913, was among a group of Russian artists including Aleksandra Exter, Liubov' Popova, Nadezhda Udal'tsova, Marc Chagall, Ivan Puni, and Natan Al'tman, who traveled to Paris, where he met Robert and Sonya Delaunay, whose theory of Simultanism corresponded to his own ideas; assisted by Aleksandr Rodchenko, Vladimir Tatlin, and others, rendered the interior design of the 1917 Café Pittoresque, Moscow; from 1918, was active in set design; in 1919, co-signed the *Imagist Manifesto*; became a professor at Vkhutemas, Moscow; joined the Obmokhu (Society of Young Artists); in the early 1920s, primarily designed sets; designed the 1923–26 Baku Commissars monument; traveled to Paris again in 1925, where he designed the set for *Le Pas d'Acier* of the Ballets Russes de Monte Carlo (production realized in 1927, when he returned to Moscow).
▶ Work first shown at 1907 events of the Moscow Association of Artists; subsequently, included in exhibitions in USSR and abroad.
▶ *Notes et Documents Édités par la Société des Amis de Georges Yakoulov*, Paris, 1967–75. S. Aladzhalov, *Georgii Yakulov*, Yerevan, 1971. E. Kostina, *Georgii Yakulov*, Moscow, 1979. Stephanie Barron and Maurice Tuchman, *The Avant-Garde in Russia, 1910–1930*, Cambridge: MIT, 1980:264.

Yamada, Teruo (1945–)
▶ Japanese glass designer.
▶ Yamada was a member of the Japan Traditional Crafts Association.
▶ Work shown at 1980 'Japan Traditional Crafts Exhibition,' Tokyo; 1981 and 1990 'Glass in Japan,' Tokyo; 1985 'New Glass in Japan,' Badisches Landesmuseum, Karlsruhe; 1987 'The Art of Contemporary Japanese Studio Glass,' Heller Gallery, New York; 1991 (V) Triennale of the Japan Glass Art Crafts Association, Heller Gallery.
▶ Cat., *Glass Japan*, New York: Heller Gallery and Japan Glass Art Crafts Association, 1991: No. 41.

Yamaguchi, Kazuma (1946–)
▶ Japanese industrial designer; born Osaka; active Milan.
▶ Yamaguchi began his professional career in 1970; became known for lighting and vehicle body designs; was a member of ADI (Associazione per il Disegno Industriale). Clients included Bon Marché, Leonardo Auto, and Stilnovo.
▶ He participated in the 1973 bicycle competion of the ICSID in Kyoto.
▶ *ADI Annual 1976*, Milan: Associazione per il Disegno Industriale, 1976.

Yamano, Kiroshi (1956–)
▶ Japanese glass designer.
▶ Studied Tokyo Glass Crafts Institute to 1984 and Rochester Institute of Technology, Rochester, New York, to 1989.
▶ In 1988, Yamano was an assistant at Penland School, Penland, North Carolina.
▶ Work was subject of exhibition at 1990 Grohë Glass Gallery, Boston; included in 1986 'Japan Modern Decorative Art,' Tokyo; 1986 'New Glass from Japan and America,' Switzerland; 1987 and 1990 'Glass in Japan,' Tokyo; 1991 (V) Triennale of the Japan Glass Art Crafts Association, Heller Gallery, New York. Received 1989 fellowship of Creative Glass Center of America, Millville, New Jersey.
▶ Cat., *Glass Japan*, New York: Heller Gallery and Japan Glass Art Crafts Association, 1991: No. 43.

Yamashita, Kari (1959–)
▶ Japanese glass designer.
▶ 1989, studied Pilchuck Glass School, Stanwood, Washington.
▶ Work included in 1990 'Glass '90 in Japan,' Tokyo, and 1991 (V) Triennale of the Japan Glass Art Crafts Association, Heller Gallery, New York. Received 1987 award of excellence, 'Japan Stained Glass Exhibition,' and achievement award, 1989 (V) 'Stained Glass Art Competition.'
▶ Cat., *Glass Japan*, New York: Heller Gallery and Japan Glass Art Crafts Association, 1991: No. 44.

Yamashita, Kasumasa (1937–)
▶ Japanese architect and designer, born Tokyo.
▶ Yamashita taught at the Institute of Art and Design in Tokyo. In 1977, he was awarded the most prestigious prize available in architecture in Japan. Working as a designer, he was one of 11 to render a service for Alessi's 1983 *Tea and Coffee Piazza* project.
▶ *Les Carnets du Design*, Paris: Mad-Cap Productions et APCI, 1986:71. Officina Alessi, *Tea and Coffee Piazza: 11 Servizi da tè e caffè*, Milan: Crusinallo, 1983.

Yamo (1959–)
▶ Algerian designer; born Algiers.
▶ Studied École Nationale des Beaux-Arts, Algiers; 1986, École Nationale des Arts Décoratifs, Paris.
▶ Active in Paris, he was particularly interested in Japan, where he worked on a lighting project, illustrating kites in glass, for a palace in Osaka. He designed the interior architecture of the apartment of Gladys Fabre, sofa for Anne de Lierville, a metal and glass collection (with Sabrina), numerous glass designs (with Bernard Pictet), jewelry, and paintings. Established the prototype workshop in the furniture department at the École Nationale Supérieure des Arts Décoratifs, Paris. Designs included 1988 *La flèche* lighting fixture for Drimmer, 1989 *Wacapou* furniture collection for Roche-Bobois, objects for Techniland, and 1990 table service for Christofle. Clients included KL Luminaires, Artistes et Modèles, and Pictet.
▶ He exhibited for the first time in 1988 at VIA in Paris. Won 1987 Drimmer-sponsored competition (*Le fourmilier* and *Teyla*

lighting fixtures, prototype realized through VIA Appel permanent). Received 1989 gold Salon du Meuble award and 1989 Palme d'or award for young designers (1989 *Cynitia* furniture range).
► Cat., *Les années VIA 1980–1990,* Paris: Musée des Arts Décoratifs, 1990: 182–83. 'Les Designers du Soleil,' *Maison française décoration internationale,* June 1992.

Yanagi, Sori (1915–)
► Japanese industrial designer.
► Studied painting and architecture in Tokyo.
► He worked in the Tokyo design office of Charlotte Perriand; in the 1940s, was active as a product design advisor in Japan. He retained a traditional Japanese sensibility towards materials and forms, and concentrated on efficiency, structure, and logic in products; designed wooden furniture, including his best-known design, the *Butterfly* stool of c1955; was known for his ceramics.
► Received first prize, 1951 (I) Japanese Competition for Industrial Design. Work (wooden furniture) included in 1982 'Contemporary Vessels: How to Pour,' Tokyo National Museum of Modern Art.
► 'Produzione recente di Sori Yanagi,' *Stile Industria,* No. 28, Aug. 1960:42–45. Bruno Munari, 'Design According to Yanagi,' *Domus,* No. 609, Sept. 1980:40–41. Cat., *Contemporary Vessels: How to Pour,* Tokyo: National Museum of Modern Art, 1982: Nos. 192–99. Cat., Kathryn B. Hiesinger and George H. Marcus III (eds.), *Design Since 1945,* Philadelphia: Philadelphia Museum of Art, 1983:236, III–93.

Yellin, Samuel (1885–1940)
► Polish metalworker; active Philadelphia.
► Yellin learned the metalsmithing trade in Germany, Belgium, and Britain before moving to Philadelphia in 1906; in 1909, opened a shop there, becoming successful by designing for architects, particularly the firm of McKim, Mead, and White. In expanded facilities, his Metalworker's studio (completed 1915) on Arch Street was designed by Walter Mellor and Arthur Meigs; it included a showroom, drafting room, museum, library, and vast work space with 60 forges and more than 200 workers. Yellin's workers specialized in the areas of chisel decoration, *repoussé,* and polishing. He believed in forging with hammer and anvil in the traditions of the Arts and Crafts movement, although he used standard rods, bars, and plates and employed electronically controlled blowers for even temperatures during forging. He lectured on the history of metalworking.
► Anne Yaffe Phillips, *From Architecture to Object,* New York: Hirschl and Adler, 1989:66.

Yokoyama, Naoto (1937–)
► Japanese glass designer.
► Studied crafts, Tokyo University of Arts, to 1962.
► Work was subject of 1988 exhibition at Clara Scremini Gallery, Paris, and 1989 (IV) 'Annual Glass Decor by Naoto Yokoyama,' Takashimaya department store, Tokyo. Work included in 1985 'World Glass Now '85,' Hokkaido Museum of Art, Sapporo; 1985 'New Glass in Japan,' Badisches Landesmuseum, Karlsruhe; 1987 'The Art of Contemporary Japanese Studio Glass,' Heller Gallery, New York; 1990 'Glass '90 in Japan,' Tokyo; 1991 (V) Triennale of the Japan Glass Art Crafts Association, Heller Gallery. Received 1984 achievement award at 'Glass '84 in Japan,' Tokyo.
► Cat., *Glass Japan,* New York: Heller Gallery and Japan Glass Art Crafts Association, 1991: No. 45.

Yonehara, Shinji (1961–)
► Japanese glass designer.
► Studied glassmaking, Tama Art University, Tokyo, to 1986.
► In 1988, Yonehara joined the Examination Office of Industry, Hokkaido.
► Work included in 1989 'Crafts Competition of Art Forest,' Sapporo; 1990 'Glass '90 in Japan,' Tokyo; 1991 (V) Triennale of the Japan Glass Art Crafts Association, Heller Gallery, New York. Received award of excellence at 1989 'Hokkaido Glass Art,' Japan.
► Cat., *Glass Japan,* New York: Heller Gallery and Japan Glass Art Crafts Association, 1991: No. 47.

Yoshimoto, Yumiko (1944–)
► Japanese glass designer.
► Studied design, Women's College of Art, Tokyo, to 1967.
► She was a lecturer at the Kanazawa Utatsuyama Crafts Studio, and a member of Japan Crafts Design Association.
► Work subject of 1988 exhibition at Gallery Humanite, Tokyo. Work included in 1985 'Five Artists in Miyagi,' Miyagi Prefectural Museum of Art, Sendai; 1986 'Japanese Glass—300 Years,' Suntory Museum of Art, Tokyo; 1986 'Crafts-Standard-Bearers of the End of This Century,' Suntory Museum of Art; 1987 'The Art of Contemporary Japanese Studio Glass,' Heller Gallery, New York; 1990 'Glass '90 in Japan,' Tokyo; 1991 (V) Triennale of the Japan Glass Art Crafts Association, Heller Gallery. Received 1978 Shiseido Award, World Crafts Council, Kyoto; Japan Glass Art Crafts Association Award, 1984 'Glass '84 in Japan,' Tokyo. Participated in 1988 (III) 'Interglas Symposium,' Crystalex, Nový Bor (Czech Republic).
► Cat., *Glass Japan,* New York: Heller Gallery and Japan Glass Art Crafts Association, 1991: No. 46.

Young, Dennis (1917–)
► British furniture, interior, and industrial designer.
► Studied Royal College of Art, London.
► He opened his own office in London in 1946; became chief designer at the Isotype Institute of Visual Education and a consultant designer to Baume, the Natural Rubber Bureau, and British Vita; designed fiberglass furniture for Gaeltarra Eireann; lectured on furniture and interior design at Camberwell School of Art. His 1947–48 *Shell Chair* for Design London was an early manifestation of ergonomic furniture; during its design he used a 'sitting box' to record the body shapes of 67 individuals with modeling clay.
► Work shown at 1951 'Festival of Britain,' 1965 Moscow 'International Exhibition,' 1966 Paris 'Europlastic Exhibition,' and 1967 Ireland 'Furniture Exhibition.'
► Ernö Goldfinger, *British Furniture Today,* 1951. S.H. Glenister, *Contemporary Design in Woodwork.* Ulfrico Hoepli, *Mobili Tipo,* Milan, 1956. Dennis and Barbara Young, *Furniture in Britain Today,* London: Alec Tiranti, 1964. Cat., *Modern Chairs 1918–1970,* London: Lund Humphries, 1971.

Yseux (?–1951)
► French bookbinder; active Paris (France).
► Yseux worked for some time for Durvand; from 1908, was associated with Thierry, who took over in 1916 the workshop of Petit-Simier, 7 quai de Conti, Paris; moved to 18 rue Dauphine, Paris; worked with the tools he acquired from Thierry, in c1919, produced bindings in leather and white vellum with oils painted by Théophile Gautier. Barbance assumed Yseux's workshop when he retired.
► Ernest de Crauzat, *La Reliure française de 1900 à 1925,* Vol. 2, Paris, 1932:59–60. Alastair Duncan and Georges de Bartha, *Art Nouveau and Art Déco Bookbinding,* New York: Abrams, 1989:180.

Z

Zadikian, Zadik (1948–)
▶ Armenian sculptor and furniture designer.
▶ Studied sculpture in Yerevan and Academy in Rome.
▶ In 1967 he escaped from the USSR by swimming the Araks River; lived for a time in Istanbul and Beirut; in 1974, settled in New York. His early work suggested sculptural clay fragments found in archeological digs. His 1975 installation *1,000 Bricks Gilded in 22 Carat Gold Leaf* at P.S. 1 in Long Island City, New York, showed an interest in gold leaf, later used on his furniture pieces. In *c*1987 he began to design utilitarian objects, including the massive *Nina* sofa and *Regina* chairs in voluptuous rounded forms. The furniture was made in cast plaster from a clay original and finished in a marbleized gilding.
▶ Alice Feiring, 'Casting Chrones,' *Metropolis*, Oct. 1991:45.

Žák, Ladislav (1900–1973)
▶ Czech architect, designer, painter, and writer.
▶ 1919–24, studied painting, Academy of Fine Arts, Prague, under Karel Krattner; 1924–27, architecture under Josef Gočár.
▶ From 1927, he was a member of SVU Aleš (Association of Fine Arts) in Brno; in 1928, joined the SČSD (Czechoslovak Werkbund); from 1933, was a member of Svaz socialistických architektů (Union of Socialist Architects); until 1930, taught at high schools in Prague, Brno, and Plzeň; 1946–73, was associate professor, Academy of Fine Arts, Prague, where he taught landscape architecture and town planning; specialized in the interior design of Functional housing, particularly small flats; based on functional flexibility, designed a 1931 collection of tubular furniture named *Malý byt* (*Small Flat*). His tubular metal easy chair produced by Gottwald was comparable with the best of the European models of a similar aesthetic. He incorporated these tubular furniture models into family houses designed in the 1930s in Prague Vysočany, Prague Hodkovičky, and three villas in Prague Baba; was interested in social and collective housing; designed a 1937 collection of furniture named *Lidový byt* (*Popular Flat*); writing for various periodicals, supported the ideas of functional housing; after World War II, was active primarily as a landscape architect; published the book *Obytná krajina* (*A Living Landscape*).
▶ A. Adlerová, *České užité umění 1918–1938*, Prague, 1983. V. Šlapeta in *Czech Functionalism*, London: Architectural Association, 1987:84.

Zambusi, Antonio (1937–)
▶ Italian designer; born and active in Padua.
▶ Zambusi began his professional career in 1962; designing lighting and accessories, collaborated with architects Marilena Boccato and Gian Nicola Gigante; became a member of ADI (Associazione per il Disegno Industriale).
▶ *ADI Annual 1976*, Milan: Associazione per il Disegno Industriale, 1976.

Zanello, Gastone (1931–)
▶ Italian industrial designer; born Tarcento; active Pordenone.
▶ Zanello began his professional career in 1958, working for Industrie Zanussi, Pordenone, and responsible for the design of its domestic electrical appliances. His designs included the *Rex 700* kitchen, *P5 Rex* washing machine, and *Naonis* range of kitchen appliances. He became a member of ADI (Associazione per il Disegno Industriale).
▶ *ADI Annual 1976*, Milan: Associazione per il Disegno Industriale, 1976.

Zani e Zani
▶ Italian silversmiths.
▶ In the second half of the 19th century, Serafino Zani founded the silversmithy and metalworkers Zani, now Zani e Zani. Its postwar designers included Achille Castiglioni.
▶ Hans Wichmann, *Italien Design 1945 bis heute*, Munich: Die Neue Sammlung, 1988.

Zanier, Mario (1942–)
▶ Italian industrial designer; born Vivaro; active Pordenone.
▶ Zanier began his professional career in 1963; occasionally collaborated with A. Foschia, and designed sound equipment for Industrie Zanussi, including television sets, videophones, tape-editing machines, and video intercoms; became a member of ADI (Associazione per il Disegno Industriale).
▶ *ADI Annual 1976*, Milan: Associazione per il Disegno Industriale, 1976.

Zanine, José (1919–)
▶ Brazilian architect.
▶ He began his career as an architectural model maker and furniture designer; in *c*1965, began designing and building houses for clients, including composer Antonio Carlos Jobim, pianist Nelson Freire, and actor Florinda Bolkan. His furniture consisted of solid-hewn wood chairs and chaises and tribal drum-like wooden tables. He built houses on stilts to encourage air circulation, and with visible solid timber framing elements. He founded DAM (Foundation for the Development and Application of Brazilian Woods) to foster sound forestry and logging methods and encourage the use of wood for low-cost public housing.
▶ Elisabeth de Portzamparc, 'Brazil's Maverick Architect Zanine's Rich Woodwork,' *Elle Decor*, Aug. 1991:64–67.

Zanini, Marco (1954–)
▶ Italian architect; born Trento.
▶ Studied architecture, Università di Firenze, under Adolfo Natalini, to 1978.
▶ 1975–77, he worked for the Argonaut Company, California; did freelance work in San Francisco; from 1978, worked with Ettore Sottsass in Milan, initially as assistant in Sottsass's studio; in 1980, joined the design consultancy Sottsass Associati, Milan, where he designed for its first two collections; 1981–88, designed furniture, lighting, and glass designs produced by Memphis. His Memphis pieces included 1981 *Dublin* sofa; 1982 *Rigel* glass container, *Arturo* and *Vega* glass goblets, *Alpha Centauri* glass vase, *Cassiopea* glass goblet, and *Victoria* and *Baykal* ceramic vases; 1983 *Colorado* ceramic teapot and *Beltegeuse* glass goblet; 1984 *Lucrezia* armchair; 1985 *Amazon* cabinet, *Rossella* hanging light, and *Broccoli* compote; 1986 *Roma* iridescent fiberglass armchair;

and 1987 *Juan* chaise longue. He also designed graphics and industrial machinery.

▶ Marco Zanini, 'A Well Traveled Man,' in *Design ist unsichtbar*, Vienna, 1981:464–74. Barbara Radice (ed.), *Memphis: The New International Style*, Milan, 1981:65–66. Christine Colin, 'Memphis a encore frappé,' *Décoration Internationale*, No. 51, Dec. 1982–Jan. 1983:54–57,206. Cat., Kathryn B. Hiesinger and George H. Marcus III (eds.), *Design Since 1945*, Philadelphia: Philadelphia Museum of Art, 1983:236. Fumio Shimizu and Matteo Thun (eds.), *The Descendants of Leonardo: The Italian Design*, Tokyo, 1987:329.

Zanotta

▶ Italian furniture manufacturer.

▶ Established in 1932, the firm was particularly innovative and daring in Italy after World War II, and supportive of Anti-Design groups. Its early designs, still in production today, included the 1929 *Lira* armchair and *Comacina* desk of 1930 (originally produced by Thonet as *B36*) by Piero Bottoni; 1934 *Follia* side chair, 1936 *Sant'Elia* armchair, and 1936 *Lariana* side chair by Giuseppe Terragni; 1947 *Maggiolina* armchair by Marco Zanuso; 1935 *Susanna* and 1935 *Genni* armchairs by Gabriele Mucchi; 1947 *Pontina* side chair by Gio Ponti; 1946 *Reale* table, 1937 *Milo* mirror, and 1959 *Fennis* side chair by Carlo Molino; 1938 *Spartana* chair (production from the 1970s of a version of the original *Landi* aluminum chair) by Hans Coray; 1940 *Leonardo* table base by Achille Castiglioni; 1950 *Bramante* table base by the Castiglionis; 1950 *Sgabillo* stool by Max Bill; and various models by unidentified designers. Its landmark Anti-Design models included the 1967 *Blow* clear plastic inflatable chair by De Pas, D'Urbino and Lomazzi; the Castiglionis' 1970 *Messandro* tractor seat stool (designed in 1957); Superstudio's 1970 *Quaderna* laminate table range; and the 1970 *Sacco* bean bag chair by Gatti, Paolini, and Teodora. By 1990, its stable of 59 designers worldwide included Max Bill, Switzerland; Liisi Beckmann, Finland; Gilles Derain, France; Oscar Blanca Tusquets and Lluis Clotet, Spain; and Willie Landels, Britain. In Italy, designers included Gae Aulenti, Riccardo Dalisi, Ugo La Pietra, Alessandro Mendini, Gio Ponti, Ettore Sottsass, and Giotto Stoppino. Founder Aurelio Zanotta's daughter Eleanora Zanotta manages the firm today.

▶ Received three Premi Compasso d'Oro (1968, for *Guscio* shelter by Roberto Menghi; 1979, for *Sciangai* clothes stand by De Pas, D'Urbino and Lomazzi; 1987, for *Tonietta* chair by Enzo Mari). Received gold medals at 1948 (VII) and 1951 (IX) Triennali di Milano; prizes at 1973 'BIO 5,' 1977 'BIO 7,' and 1988 'BIO 12' Industrial Design Biennials, Ljubljana; first prize at 1986 (V) Stelle Technhotel. Products subject of 1985 '1932–1985 Histoire du Design Zanotta,' Instituto Italiano di Cultura, Paris; 1986, Strasbourg; 1987, Cologne. Products included in 1972 'Italy: The New Domestic Landscape,' New York Museum of Modern Art; 1982 'Anni Trenta: Arte e Cultura in Italia,' Palazzo Reale, Milan; 1983 'Möbel aus Italien,' Design Center, Stuttgart; 1985 'La Chaise Objet de Design ou d'Architecture,' Centre de Création et de Diffusion, Montreal; 1987 'Design-Dasein,' Museum für Kunst und Gewerbe, Hamburg; 1988 'Nouveaux Projets pour l'Habitat,' Salon du Meuble, Paris; 1988 'Furniture Follows Function,' Bella Center's Hall, Copenhagen; 1988 'Forum Design '88,' International Design Center, New York; and 1988 'Italia 2000,' Moscow.

▶ Stefano Cascani, *Mobile come architettura il disegno della produzione Zanotta*, Milan: Arcadia, 1984. *Maison et Jardin*, April 1992.

Zanuso Jr., Marco (1954–)

▶ Italian architect and designer; active Milan; son of Marco Zanuso Sr.

▶ Studied architecture in Florence.

▶ Zanuso worked with his father and Adolfo Natalini; was assistant lecturer at Politecnico di Milano; from 1980, specialized in architecture and industrial design in his own studio; in 1981, (with Luigi Greppi, Pietro Greppi, and Bepi Maggiori) founded the lighting firm Oceano Oltreluce.

▶ Fumio Shimizu and Matteo Thun (eds.), *The Descendants of Leonardo: The Italian Design*, Tokyo, 1987:330.

Zanuso Sr., Marco (1916–)

▶ Italian architect and designer; born Milan.

▶ Studied architecture, Politecnico di Milano, to 1939.

▶ After World War II, he practiced as a member of the Italian Modern movement; from 1945–86, was a professor of architecture, design, and town planning, Politecnico di Milano; from 1949, was professor, Instituto di Tecnologia della Facoltà di Architettura del Politecnico di Milano, where he became director in 1970. He set up his own design office in Milan in 1945; was an editor of the architecture and design journals *Domus* and *Casabella*; in the early 1950s, began designing furniture in bent metal tubing, organized theoretical debates, and designed several Triennali di Milano. His chair design for the 1948 low-cost furniture competition sponsored by the New York Museum of Modern Art included a new joining mechanism for the fabric seat to be suspended from the tubular steel frame. He designed the 1956–58 Olivetti factory and offices in São Paulo with honeycomb cells covered with a thin shell vault roof. His 1951 *Lady* armchair for Arlex featured the innovative application of foam-rubber upholstery; his 1962 *Lambda* chair, sheet-metal construction; and his 1964 child's stacking chair, the first use of polyethylene in a piece of furniture. His 1955 sofabed for Arflex incorporated an innovative mechanism for converting sofa to bed. 1958–77, he and Richard Sapper designed numerous works that subsequently became cult objects, including scales and timer for Terraillon in the early 1970s, 1964 *TS 502*, 1962 *Doney 14* and 1969 *Black 201* TV sets by Brionvega, and 1966 *Grillo* folding telephone by Siemens. Working for Brionvega from 1962, their work was noted for elegant visual solutions. 1956–58, he was a member of the CIAM (Congrès Internationaux d'Architecture Moderne); member of the Instituto Nazionale Urbanistica; in 1956, a founder of ADI (Associazione per il Disegno Industriale) and Premio Compasso d'Oro; served on international juries; and was one of the guiding forces behind the formation of the Triennale di Milano and of Milan's urban planning program. For Ettore Sottsass, he designed the 1987 *Cleopatra* and *Antonio* side tables for Memphis, Milan. His 1989 *I Buoni Sentimenti* table was produced by Galerie Néotù, Paris. Other designs included the 1983 *Caraffa* teapot by Cleto Munari, 1985 *Due Z* hardware fittings by Fusital, and 1986 *Laveno* table by Zanotta. Projects from the late 1980s included the restoration of the Fossati theater and corso del Piccolo Teatro in Milan.

▶ Chair shown at 1948 'International Competition for Low Cost Furniture Design' exhibition, New York Museum of Modern Art. Sewing machine for Borletti shown at 1957 (XI) Triennale. *Lady* armchair, *Grillo* telephone, and *Doney 14* and *Black 201* TV sets shown at 1983–84 'Design Since 1945' exhibition, Philadelphia Museum of Art. Received grand prizes and two gold medals at 1948 (VIII), grand prize and two gold medals at 1951 (IX), grand prize and gold medal at 1954 (X), gold medal at 1957 (XI), silver medal at 1960 (XII), and gold medal at 1964 (XIII) Triennali di Milano; 1953, 1956 (Borletti sewing machine), 1962 (*Doney 14* TV set), 1964, and 1967 Compasso d'Oro; gold seal prize (*Lambda* chair) at 1965 'Mostra La casa abitata,' Florence; Interplas prize (Kartell chair); gold medal (Necchi knife sharpener), 1966 'BIO 2' Industrial Design Biennial, Ljubljana; 1966 gold medal, Italian Ministry of Trade and Industry; 1971 SAIE prize; and 1972 Bolaffi prize.

▶ Gillo Dorfles, *Marco Zanuso: Designer*, Rome: Editalia, 1971. Cat., Milena Lamarová, *Design a Plastické Hmoty*, Prague: Uměleckoprůmyslové Muzeum, 1972:160. Paolo Fossati, *Il design in Italia*, Turin, 1972:107–13,207–19, plates 177–235. *ADI Annual 1976*, Milan: Associazione per il Disegno Industriale, 1976. Andrea Branzi and Michele De Lucchi (eds.), *Il design italiano degli anni '50*, Milan: Fabbri, 1981:203–04. Cat., Kathryn B. Hiesinger and George H. Marcus III (eds.), *Design Since 1945*, Philadelphia: Philadelphia Museum of Art, 1983:236–37, I–51–53–54, III–

94–96. S. Brandolin and G. Polin, 'Studio Associato Marco Zanuso e Pietro Crescini: Un nuovo complesso teatrale a Milano,' *Casabella 48*, No. 508, 1984:4–15. Fumio Shimizu and Matteo Thun (eds.), *The Descendants of Leonardo: The Italian Design*, Tokyo, 1987:335. Juli Capella and Quim Larrea, *Designed by Architects in the 1980s*, New York: Rizzoli, 1988.

Zanussi
▶ Italian manufacturer located Pordenone.
▶ Antonio Zanussi established the household appliance firm in Pordenone in 1916. It was initially a workshop for repairing stoves. Its prewar cookers, refrigerators, and vacuum cleaners had Streamline styling. The firm set up a design department in the 1950s. Its innovative designs included an 18-inch (45cm) wide dishwasher. Gino Valle designed its 1958 cooker and kitchen appliances in the 1950s that he grouped together into units and designed with neat housings and controls. The firm's designs up to the mid-1980s tried to be inobtrusive; its late 1980s *Wizard* collection included more visually assertive objects for the kitchen. Designed by head designer Roberto Pezetta, the *Wizard* refrigerator was unsuccessful in Britain and withdrawn. In 1984, Zanussi merged with Electrolux.
▶ *Issue 2*, London: Design Museum, 1989.

Zapf, Otto (1931–)
▶ German designer.
▶ Zapf created important system furniture designs, including the *Zapf Office System* by Knoll and *7500* workstations for Pacific Telesis; (with Dieter Rams) designed his first furniture in the 1960s and 1970s.

Zarges-Dürr, Erna (1907–)
▶ German silversmith; active Pforzheim, Leipzig, Berlin, and Stuttgart.
▶ 1924–27, trained at Bruckmann und Söhne, Heilbronn, as the first women in the silversmiths' department; from 1927, studied Kunstgewerbeschule, Pforzheim, under Theodor Wende and others.
▶ 1931–33, she worked in the workshops of Ernst Treusch, Leipzig, and of H.J. Wilm, Berlin; in 1933, set up her own workshop in Heilbronn; 1936–39, relocated to Stuttgart. Her work showed carefully worked out proportions with original, Modern ornamentation.
▶ Received numerous awards, including a gold medal for her 1932 silver wine jug shown at the 1937 Paris 'Exposition Internationale des Arts et Techniques dans la Vie Moderne.' Work shown at international exhibitions.
▶ Annelies Krekel-Aalberse, *Art Nouveau and Art Déco Silver*, New York: Abrams, 1989:146,261.

Zecchin, Vittorio (1878–1947)
▶ Italian painter and decorator.
▶ In 1921, the partnership of lawyer Paolo Venini, antiques dealer Giacomo Cappelin, Andrea Rioda, and Vittorio Zecchin resulted in the formation of Vetri Soffiati Muranesi Cappelin-Venini. A distinguished painter, decorator, and glass designer in Murano, Zecchin became the firm's artistic and technical director. In 1925, Venini opened his own glass factory in Murano.
▶ F. Deboni, *Venini Glass*, Basel: Wiese, 1990:34.
▶ See Venini, Paolo

Zeisel, Eva (1906–)
▶ Hungarian designer and ceramicist; born Budapest, active Germany, Russia, Austria, and USA.
▶ 1923–24, studied painting, Képzömüvészeti Akadémia (Academy of Art), Budapest, under Vaszari; subsequently, apprenticed in pottery.
▶ 1927–32, she worked first for the Kispest earthenware factory, Budapest, and for various ceramics factories in Germany, including as a ceramics designer at Schramberg Majolika Fabrik and at the Carsten ceramics factory; was familiar with Werkbund and Bauhaus forms and, in 1932, went to the Soviet Union, where she worked in various ceramics factories including a sanitary ceramics plant and at Lomonosov porcelain factory in St. Petersburg under Nikolai Suetin. Suetin applied motifs to some of her forms. From 1934, she worked for the Deulevo ceramics factory, Moscow; became artistic director, Central Administration of the Glass and China Industry of the USSR, Moscow; during the Stalin Purges, was imprisoned 1936–37, released, and deported; via Vienna and Britain, settled in the USA; 1939–53, taught at Pratt Institute, Brooklyn, New York, and, 1959–60, at the Rhode Island School of Design in Providence, Rhode Island, while also designing for clients. Her ceramic designs of the 1940s reflected the organic furniture of the time. Her classic 1942–45 *Museum White* dinnerware, designed in collaboration with the New York Museum of Modern Art, was produced by Castleton China, New Castle, Pennsylvania; it emulated the Functionalist ceramics produced by major factories in Europe, especially those in Arzberg and Berlin. She designed the 1950 knock-down chair with a zippered plastic cover for Richards-Morgenthau, wooden pieces for Salisbury Artisans from 1951, and 1952 dinnerware for Hall China.
▶ *Museum White* china subject of 1946 'Modern China by Eva Zeisel' exhibition, New York Museum of Modern Art. Work included in 1991 USA 'Design 1935–1965: What Modern Was' traveling exhibition. Work was subject of 1984 'Eva Zeisel: Designer for Industry' traveling exhibition organized by Musée des Arts Décoratifs, Montreal. Received 1983 Senior Fellowship, National Endowment for the Arts.
▶ Cat., Kathryn B. Hiesinger and George H. Marcus III (eds), *Design Since 1945*, Philadelphia: Philadelphia Museum of Art, 1983:237, II–78. Cat., *Eva Zeisel: Designer to Industry*, Musée des Arts Décoratifs de Montréal, Chicago: University of Chicago Press, 1984. 'In the Showrooms: Furniture,' *Interiors*, Vol. 109, March 1950:122.'Merchandise Cues,' *Interiors*, Vol. 111, Feb. 1952:114. Jay Doblin, *One Hundred Great Product Designs*, New York, 1970:62. Mark Rabun, 'Eva Zeisel' in Mel Byars and Russell Flinchum (eds.), *50 American Designers*, Washington: Preservation, 1994.

Zeitner, Herbert (1900–88)
▶ German silversmith; active Berlin.
▶ Studied Königliche Preussische Zeichenakademie, Hanau.
▶ He set up his own workshop in 1924 in Berlin; taught at the Vereinigte Staatsschulen für freie und angewandte Kunst (Kunstgewerbeschule), Berlin-Charlottenburg; in 1939, became director of the goldsmiths' master workshop at Preussische Akademie der Künste.
▶ Annelies Krekel-Aalberse, *Art Nouveau and Art Déco Silver*, New York: Abrams, 1989:261. Cat., *Metallkunst*, Berlin Bröhan-Museum, 1990:580–81,600.

Zelenka, František (1896–1942)
▶ Czech architect and stage and graphic designer; born Prague.
▶ Studied České vysoké učení technické (Czech Technical University), Prague.
▶ In 1930, he became a member of SČSD (Czechoslovak Werkbund); designed a number of interiors, among them the flat (with its 'blue room') for composer Jaroslav Ježek; wrote for various magazines; 1929–32, was active as a stage designer at Osvobozené divadlo (The Liberated Theater) and, subsequently, for the National and Stavovské theaters, both Prague; 1926–37, designed a number of posters for theaters and films. He was killed at the Auschwitz-Birkenau extermination camp.
▶ A. Adlerová, *České užité umění 198–1938*, Prague, 1983.

Zemp, Werner (1940–)
▶ Swiss designer; active Cabiate (Italy).
▶ He began his professional career in 1967 in Germany; in 1973, settled in Italy, becoming active as an environmental designer for department stores, sports stadia, and playgrounds; became a member of ADI (Associazione per il Disegno Industriale). Clients included the La Rinascente department store, Milan; Intec

(Instituto de Investigaciones Tecnológicas), Corfo; Institut für Räumichen Stadtebau, Bern; and Karl Steiner, Limbiate.

▶ *ADI Annual 1976*, Milan: Associazione per il Disegno Industriale, 1976.

Zen, Carlo (1851–1918)

▶ Italian cabinetmaker; active Milan; father of Piero Zen.

▶ From *c*1880, Zen directed the most important furniture workshop in Milan; active in the *stile floreale*, continued after the 1902 Turin 'Esposizione Internazionale d'Arte Decorativa Moderna' to be known for his Art Nouveau and Symbolist motifs; was not a designer himself but rather factory owner and manager. From 1898, his firm was associated with the firm Haas of Vienna, whose designers included Otto Eckmann. Using inlays of mother-of-pearl, his artisans' elegant, asymmetrical patterns became more geometric towards 1910 and showed the simplification typical of German and Austrian forms.

▶ E. Bairati, R. Bossaglia, and M. Roschi, *L'Italia Liberty: Arredamento e arti decorativi*, Milan, 1973. Cat., Gabriel P. Weisberg, *Stile Floreale: The Cult of Nature in Italian Design*, Miami: The Wolfsonian Foundation, 1988.

Zen, Piero (1879–1950)

▶ Italian furniture designer; active Milan; son of Carlo Zen.

▶ In 1906, Piero Zen became active in the family firm known for its elegant *stile floreale*; he designed in a Modernist mode.

▶ E. Bairati, R. Bossaglia, and M. Roschi, *L'Italia Liberty: Arredamento e arti decorativi*, Milan, 1973.

Zena

▶ Swiss manufacturer.

▶ Zena was founded by Alfred Neweczerzal, inventor of the 1947 *Rex* vegetable peeler, that by 1990 sold for one-fifth of its 1947 price. The moveable blade portion of the device was a patented invention.

▶ Cat., *Unbekannt–Vertraut: 'Anonymes' Design im Schweizer Gebrauchsgerät seit 1920*, Zürich: Museum für Gestaltung, 1987. 'Schweizer Erfindungen' exhibition, Globus department store, Basel 1991.

Zeppelin

▶ German airship.

▶ The Zeppelin airship was named after Count Ferdinand von Zeppelin, head of the Luftschiffbau-Zeppelin, who was succeeded by Hugo Eckener. Most notable among the German Zeppelins was the 1936 *Hindenburg*. Its predecessor was the 1928 *Graf Zeppelin*. Interior architect Fritz Breuhaus de Groot designed, laid out, and decorated (with artist Arpke and chief constructor Ludwig Dürr at Luftschiffbau-Zeppelin) the *Hindenburg*, making innovatory use of aluminum in the brown fabric-upholstered furniture and even for the Bluthner grand piano.

▶ J. Gordon Vaeth, 'Zeppelin Decor: The Graf Zeppelin and the Hindenburg,' *Journal of Decorative and Propaganda Art*, No. 15, Winter/Spring 1990:53.

Zerbi, Giorgio (1940–)

▶ Italian designer; born Genoa; active Milan.

▶ Zerbi began his professional career in 1969. He designed furniture and furnishings for clients including Babyterraneo, Brevi, Rigamonti, Stilnovo, Pozzi, Martini, and Merati. He became a member of ADI (Associazione per il Disegno Industriale).

▶ *ADI Annual 1976*, Milan: Associazione per il Disegno Industriale, 1976.

Zeus

▶ Italian design group; located Milan.

▶ Zeus was founded in 1984 by Sergio Calatroni, Roberto Marcatti, Ruben Mochi, and Maurizio Peregalli. Peregalli designed a chair and table collection for Zeus; he was artistic director and partner of Noto, which produced Zeus's collections and interior designs.

▶ Fumio Shimizu and Matteo Thun (eds.), *The Descendants of Leonardo: The Italian Design*, Tokyo, 1987:330.

Zimmerman, Marie (1878–1972)

▶ American metalworker and artist.

▶ Studied Art Students' League, New York.

▶ She became known for her metalwork and jewelry; she used Egyptian, Far Eastern, and Greek art as inspiration for her Modern styles; studied ancient patination methods and used various chemicals, gildings, and platings to achieve the appearance of antique models in her own work. In the 1920s, her work was widely published in periodicals, including *The International Studio*, *Art et Décoration*, *House and Garden*, and *Vogue*. Her vessels were elegant, naturalistic, and highly stylized.

▶ Work included in 1903 exhibition, Art Institute of Chicago, and in 1915 and 1916 exhibitions, Ehrich Galleries, New York.

▶ Anne Yaffe Phillips, *From Architecture to Object*, New York: Hirschl and Adler, 1989:67.

Zimpel, Julius (1896–1925)

▶ Austrian silversmith; active Vienna.

▶ Studied Kunstgewerbeschule, Vienna, under Koloman Moser.

▶ He was a designer (including of silverware) at the Wiener Werkstätte, and a follower of Dagobert Peche, its artistic director.

▶ Günther Feurstein, *Vienna—Present and Past: Arts and Crafts—Applied Art—Design*, Vienna: Jugend und Volk, 1976:49,81. Werner J. Schweiger, *Wiener Werkstätte*, Vienna: Brandstaeter, 1982:269. Annelies Krekel-Aalberse, *Art Nouveau and Art Déco Silver*, New York: Abrams, 1989:261.

Zolotas

▶ Greek group of jewelry designers; active Athens.

▶ The Zolotas group of jewelers was founded in Athens in 1957 and headed by Ilias Llaounis; taking its inspiration from antique Greek models, it became internationally known.

▶ Melissa Gabardi, *Les Bijoux des Années 50*, Paris: Amateur, 1987.

Zoritchak, Yan (1944–) and Catherine Zoritchak (1947–)

▶ Czech industrial designers; active Paris; husband and wife.

▶ Yan Zoritchak was director of the Centre International de Recherche sur le Verre et les Arts Plastiques. He and his wife, Catherine designed the 1984 *Espace 2000* dinner plate in a geometric motif in Corning industrial glass.

▶ *Les Carnets du Design*, Paris: Mad-Cap Productions et APCI, 1986:49.

Zotta, Marco (1945–)

▶ Italian designer; born Padua; active Milan.

▶ Studied architecture to 1973.

▶ He designed furniture, furnishings, and lighting for clients including Fargas, Le Cose, Studio Grando, Stilnovo, and Evoluzione. He became a member of ADI (Associazione per il Disegno Industriale).

▶ *ADI Annual 1976*, Milan: Associazione per il Disegno Industriale, 1976.

Zschaler, Othmar (1930–)

▶ Swiss jewelry designer.

▶ In his workshop in Switzerland in the 1960s, Zschaler designed jewelry for Georg Jensen Sølvsmedie, Copenhagen.

▶ Work included in 1980 'Georg Jensen Silversmithy: 77 Artists, 75 Years' exhibition, Smithsonian Institution, Washington.

▶ Cat., *Georg Jensen Silversmithy: 77 Artists, 75 Years*, Washington: Smithsonian Institution Press, 1980.

Zsolnay (Pécs pottery)

▶ Hungarian pottery; located Pécs.

▶ Ignaz Zsolnay set up a pottery in Pécs in 1862. In 1865, Vilmos Zsolnay (1828–1900) took over as director. Small at first, the pottery grew to 450 employees by 1883 and 1,000 by 1900. Its early production was stoneware decorated in Hungarian folk styles. In the 1870s, the factory began producing luster wares in a Neo-Renaissance style and imitation Iznik, known as *ivoir-fayence*, applied with high-temperature colors and a porcelain glaze. In the

1890s, numerous pieces of its wares in the Art Nouveau style were designed by József Rippl-Rónai. By this time, much of the factory's production was architectural and industrial. Mikløs Zsolnay (1857–1925) succeeded his father as director of the factory, which is still active today.

▶ K. Csány, *Geschichte der Ungarischen Keramik, der Porzellane und ihre Marken*, Budapest, 1954. Cat., *Zsolnay: Ungarische Jugendstilkeramik*, Budapest and Vienna, 1986.

Zuber

▶ French wallpaper firm; located Rixheim.
▶ Jean Zuber was a salesperson for a textile and wallpaper printer in Mulhouse; in 1802, became director and controller of the firm; established his own firm as the first producer of scenic wallpaper and, along with J. Dufor, the best; in 1804, produced his first dated scenic paper *Vues de Suisse*; at this time, specialized in Empire-style textured papers, and hired accomplished designers. In 1850, the firm adopted mechanical printing. Designs were kept in active production for many years, in some cases into the 20th century. Zuber's wares were exported worldwide, including to the USA in the mid-19th century. Its papers were installed in the White House, Washington, when it was initially constructed and decorated in the early 19th century, and in the diplomatic reception rooms in the 20th century. Zuber's scenic papers depicting horse racing and views of Boston and Niagara Falls were widely published. In *c*1925, André Marty painted scenes for the firm, and his image of the updated *déjeuner sur l'herbe* motif was used by Louis Süe and André Mare in their interior designs. The business is still active today.

▶ E.A. Entwistle, *French Scenic Wallpaper 1800–1860*, Leigh-on-Sea, 1972. O. Nouvel, *Wall-papers of France, 1800–1850*, London, 1981. Patricia Bayer, *Art Deco Interiors*, London: Thames and Hudson, 1990:51.

Zuid-Holland

▶ Dutch ceramics factory; located Gouda.
▶ Having been a co-founder of the Firma Weduwe Brantjes Purmerend, E. Estié established his own company in Gouda in 1898 in the former earthenware factory Het Hert owned by A. Jonker Krjnszoon, with whom Estié became a partner. Both delft blue and colored pottery in figurative designs was produced there, and some products were decorated with linear floral décors similar to eggshell porcelain by Rozenburg. Its limited production of the *Gouda* décor may have been designed by W.G.F. Jànsen, who was at the firm 1898–99. In 1903, the firm became incorporated as Plateelbakkerij Zuid-Holland. Commissioned by De Woning, its utility ware, known as *duizendjes motif* (a thousand motifs) was designed by C.J. van der Hoef and produced from 1904. These designs were geometric. W.P. Hartgring designed new decorations for the *New-P* line. Putting into place new techniques, industrial artists were hired to produce new decorations, including Thomas A.C. Colenbrander, who stayed 1912–13, and H.L.A. Breetvelt, who worked at the firm 1916–23. They and painters executed Zuid-Holland's motifs. By the time it closed in 1965, the Koninklijke Plateelbakkerij Zuid Holland had become Gouda's largest and best-known ceramics factory.

▶ *Industry and Design in the Netherlands, 1850–1950*, Amsterdam: Stedelijk Museum, 1985.

Zwart, Piet (1885–1977)

▶ Dutch architect and designer; born Zaandijk.
▶ In 1919, Zwart met Vilmos Huszár and Jan Wils and became acquainted with De Stijl principles; 1920–21, (with Huszár) collaborated on furniture designs; 1920–22, (with Wils and Huszár) collaborated on architecture; from 1921, worked in the architecture firm of H.P. Berlage, becoming chief assistant in 1925; from 1923, designed publicity for NKF (Dutch cable works); in 1923, met El Lissitzky and Kurt Schwitters; designed the 1925–26 interiors of the restaurant Leo Faust, Paris; in 1927, joined the design

group Ring neuer Werbegestalter and left Berlage's firm; in 1929, became designer for the Netherlands postal, telegraph, and telephone service.
▶ In 1966, elected Honorary Royal Designer for Industry, London.
▶ Herbert Spencer, *Pioneers of Modern Typography*, New York: Hastings House, 1969:110–21. Kees Broos, *Piet Zwart*, The Hague: Haags Gemeentemuseum, 1973. 'Piet Zwart,' *Studio International*, April 1973:176–80. Hans L.C. Jaffé et al., *De Stijl: 1917–31, Visions of Utopia*, Abbeville, 1982:244–45 passim.

Zwerger, Reinhold (1924–)

▶ Austrian industrial designer; born Kirchberg.
▶ Zwerger was a designer at Eumig of Austria, which produced his 1974 film projector and video camera.
▶ Günther Feuerstein, *Vienna—Present and Past: Arts and Crafts—Applied Art—Design*, Vienna: Jugend und Volk, 1976:77, 81.

Zwicky, Stefan (1952–)

▶ Swiss interior and furniture designer; active Zürich.
▶ He was a member of the PD Beroulli interior design studio, Zürich, and Studio Olivetti, Milan; in 1983, set up his own studio in Zürich. His 1980 *Grand Confort, Sans Confort—Homage à Corbu* furniture sculpture, a parody of Le Corbusier's 1927 *Grand Confort* armchair, was made of solid concrete for the cushions and reinforcing iron rods for the frame.
▶ Work included in 1989 'Mobilier suisse,' Galerie des brèves du CCI, Centre Georges Pompidou, Paris.
▶ Albrecht Bangert and Karl Michael Armer, *80s Style: Designs of the Decade*, New York: Abbeville, 1990:83,236.

Zwollo Jr., Frans (1896–)

▶ Dutch silversmith; active Oosterbeek; son of Frans Zwollo Sr.
▶ Zwollo trained with his father; in 1931, set up his own workshop in Oosterbeek.
▶ Annelies Krekel-Aalberse, *Art Nouveau and Art Déco Silver*, New York: Abrams, 1989:261.

Zwollo Sr., Frans (1872–1945)

▶ Dutch silversmith; active Amsterdam, The Hague, and Hagen (Germany); father of Frans Zwollo Jr.
▶ Trained at Bonebakker, Amsterdam, and Delheid, Brussels.
▶ 1897–1907, he was the first teacher of metalworking at Haarlemsche School voor Kunstnijverheid; on the recommendation of architect J.L.M. Lauweriks, was director 1910–14 of Hagener Silverschmiede, intending 'to execute chasing and embossing perfectly after designs by our best artists and in this way to create an institute capable of equaling the Wiener Werkstätte.' Most of the silver designs executed under Zwollo at Hagener Silverschmiede were produced by Lauweriks and attracted little interest. Karl Ernst Osthaus, who was behind the workshop, was unable to obtain commissions despite publicity and exhibitions. Returning to the Netherlands in 1914, Zwollo settled in The Hague, where he taught metalworking at the Haagsche Akademie voor Beeldende Kunst until 1932.
▶ Work subject of 1982 'Franz Zwollo en zihn tijd' exhibition, Museum Boymans-van Beuningen, Rotterdam.
▶ Annelies Krekel-Aalberse, *Art Nouveau and Art Déco Silver*, New York: Abrams, 1989:138,261. Cat., *Franz Zwollo en zijn tijd*, Rotterdam: Museum Boymans-van Beuningen, 1982:53.

Zzigurat

▶ Italian design group.
▶ Organized in 1967, Zziggurat's members included Alberto Breschi, Giuliano Fiorenzuoli, Gigi Gavini, and Roberto Pecchioli, who explored architectural semiotics, with its references to myth, history, and the subconscious; organized the seminar 'Life, death and miracles of Architecture' at the Electronic Space, Florence. Its members participated in the formation of Global Tools.
▶ Andrea Branzi, *La Casa Calda: Esperienze del Nuovo Disegno Italiano*, Milan: Idea Books, 1982.

International Exhibitions

1851 'Great Exhibition of the Works of Industry of All Nations (Crystal Palace Exhibition),' London, 1 May–11 October
1853 'Great Industrial Exhibition,' Dublin
1853–54 'World's Fair of the Works of Industry of All Nations,' New York
1855 'Exposition Universelle des produits de l'agriculture, de l'industrie et des beaux-arts de Paris, 1855,' 15 May–15 November
1862 'London International Exhibition on Industry and Art 1862,' 1 May–1 November
1865 'International Exhibition of Arts and Manufacturers,' Dublin
1867 'Exposition Universelle de Paris 1867,' 1 April–1 November
1871 'First Annual International Exhibition,' London
1872 'Second Annual International Exhibition,' London
1873 'Third Annual International Exhibition,' London
1873 'Welt-Ausstellung 1873 in Wien,' Vienna, 1 May–31 October
1874 'Fourth Annual International Exhibition,' London
1875 'Exposición Internacional de 1875,' Santiago (Chile)
1876 'Centennial Exposition (International Exhibition of Arts, Manufacturers and Products of the Soil and Mine,' Philadelphia, 10 May–10 November
1877 'South African International Exhibition,' Cape Town
1878 'Exposition Universelle de 1878,' Paris, 10 May–19 November
1879–80 'Sydney International Exhibition'
1880–81 'International Exhibition of Arts, Manufactures and Agricultural and Industrial Products of All Nations,' Melbourne, 1 October 1880–30 April 1881
1883 'Internationale Koloniale en Uitvoerhandel Tentoonstelling te Amsterdam'
1883 'American Exhibition of the Products, Arts and Manufactures of Foreign Nations,' Boston
1883–84 'International Exhibition,' Calcutta
1884–85 'World's Industrial and Cotton Centennial Exhibition,' New Orleans
1885 'Exposition Universelle d'Anvers,' Antwerp
1886 'Colonial and Indian Exhibition,' London
1886 'International Exhibition,' Liverpool
1887 'Jubilee International Exhibition,' Adelaide
1888 'Exposición universal de Barcelona, 1888,' 10 April–10 December
1888 'Grand Concours International des Sciences et d'Industrie,' Brussels
1888 'International Exhibition,' Glasgow
1888–89 'Centennial International Exhibition,' Melbourne
1889 'Exposition Universelle de 1889,' Paris, 5 May–31 October
1891 'International Exhibition,' Kingston (Jamaica)
1891–92 'Tasmania International Exhibition,' Launceston (Australia)
1893 'South Africa and International Exhibition,' Kimberley
1893 'World's Columbian Exposition,' Chicago, 1 May–3 October
1894 'California Midwinter International Exposition,' San Francisco
1894 'Exposition Internationale d'Anvers, Antwerp
1894–95 'Tasmania International Exhibition,' Hobart (Australia)
1897 'Konst- och Industriutställningen,' Stockholm
1897 'Exposición Centro-Americana,' Guatemala City
1897 'Queensland International Exhibition,' Brisbane

1897 'Exposition Internationale de Bruxelles, 1897,' Brussels, 10 May–8 November
1898 'Trans-Mississippi and International Exposition,' Omaha, Nebraska
1900 'Exposition Universelle et Internationale de Paris, 1900,' 15 April–12 November
1901 'Glasgow International Exhibition'
1901 'Pan-American Exposition,' Buffalo, New York
1902 'Esposizione Internazionale d'Arte Decorativa Moderna,' Turin
1902–03 'Exposition Française et Internationale,' Tonkin (now Hanoi, Vietnam)
1904 'Louisiana Purchase Exposition,' St. Louis, 30 April–1 December
1905 'Exposition Universelle et Internationale de Liège, 1905,' 27 April–6 November
1905 'Lewis and Clark Exposition,' Portland, Oregon
1906 'Esposizione Internazionale del Sempione,' Milan, 28 April–11 November
1906–07 'New Zealand International Exhibition of Arts and Industries,' Christchurch
1907 'Irish International Exhibition of 1907,' Dublin
1907 'Jamestown Tercentennial Exhibition,' Hampton Roads, Virginia
1909 'Alaska-Yukon Pacific Exposition,' Seattle
1910 'Exposition Universelle et Internationale de Bruxelles, 1910,' Brussels, 23 April–8 November
1911 'Esposizione Internazionale dell' Industria e del Lavoro,' Turin
1913 'Exposition Universelle et Industrielle de Gand (Wereldtentoonstelling Gent) 1913,' Ghent, 26 April–3 November
1915 'Panama-Pacific International Exposition, 1915,' San Francisco, 20 February–4 December
1922–23 'Exposicao Internacional do Centenario do Rio de Janeiro'
1924–25 'British Empire Exhibition,' London
1924 'Esposizione Internazionale,' Venice
1924–26 'New Zealand and South Seas International Exhibition,' Dunedin
1925 'Exposition Internationale des Arts Décoratifs et Industriels Modernes,' Paris
1926 'Sesqui-Centennial Exposition,' Philadelphia
1929–30 'Exposición Internacional de Barcelona,' 20 May 1929–15 January 1930
1930 'Exposición Ibero Americana,' Seville
1930 'Stockholmsutstäliningen,' Stockholm
1930 'Exposition Internationale, Coloniale, Maritime et d'Art Flammand,' Antwerp
1930 'Exposition Internationale de la Grande Industrie, Science et Application Art Wallon,' Liège
1931 'Exposition Coloniale Internationale,' Paris
1933–34 'International Exposition (A Century of Progress),' Chicago, 27 May–12 November 1933 and 1 June–31 October 1934
1935 'Exposition Universelle et Internationale de Bruxelles, 1935,' Brussels, 27 April–6 November
1936 'British Empire Exhibition,' Johannesburg
1937 'Exposition internationale des Arts et Techniques dans la Vie Moderne,' Paris, 25 May–25 November
1938 'British Empire Exhibition,' Glasgow
1939 'Golden Gate International Exposition,' San Francisco
1939–40 'New York World's Fair,' 30 April–31 October 1939 and 11 May–27 October 1940
1958 'Exposition Universelle et Internationale de Bruxelles

(Wereldtentoonstelling Brussels) (Expo '58),' 17 April–19 October
1959 'International Exposition,' Copenhagen
1961 'International Exhibition,' Moscow
1962 'Century 21 Exposition,' Seattle, 21 April–21 October
1964–65 'New York World's Fair,' 22 April–18 October 1964, 21 April–17 October 1965
1967 'Exposition Universelle et Internationale Montréal (Universal and International Exposition) (Expo '67),' 28 April–27 October
1968 'HemisFair '68,' San Antonio, Texas
1970 'Nippon Bankoku Hakurankai (Universal and International Japanese Exposition) (Expo '70),' Osaka, 15 March–13 September
1974 'Expo '74 World's Fair,' Spokane, Washington
1975 'International Ocean Exposition (Expo '75),' Okinawa
1984 'Louisiana World Exposition,' New Orleans
1986 'World's Fair Transportation Pavilion and Plaza (Expo '86),' Vancouver
1992 'Exposición Universal de Sevilla (Expo '92),' Seville, 20 April–12 October

Specialized Exhibitions

1882 'Pan-Russian Exhibition,' Moscow
1884 'Esposizione Nazionale Italiana,' Turin
1885 'International Goldsmiths' Exhibition,' Nuremberg
1888 'Scandinavian Exhibition of Industry, Agriculture and Art,' Copenhagen
1890 'Prima Esposizione Italiana di Architettura,' Turin
1896 'Pan-Russian Exhibition,' Nijny Novgorod
1896 'L'Oeuvre Artistique,' Liège
1897 'Tervueren, Musée Royal de l'Afrique Centrale,' part of the 1897 'Exposition Internationale,' Brussels
1897 'Exhibition of Art and Industry,' Stockholm
1900 (VII) Secession exhibition, Vienna
1902–03 'Esposizione Promotrice di Belle Arti,' Palermo
1902 'Comité Français des Expositions à l'Étranger,' St. Petersburg
1903 'Handicraft Exhibition,' Chicago Art Institute
1906 'Deutsche Kunstgewerbe Ausstellung,' Dresden
1907 'Austro-Hungarian Exhibition,' London
1908 'Franco-British Exhibition,' London
1908 'Exposition Internationale des Applications de l'Électricité,' Marseilles
1909 'Landsudstillingen (Danish National Exhibition),' Århus
1911 'Esposizione Nazionale per il Cinquantenario dell'Unità d'Italia,' Rome
1911 'House and Home,' London
1912 'Modern German Applied Arts,' Newark Museum, Newark, New Jersey
1912 (I) 'Art Exhibition of the Union of Plastic Artists,' Mánes Association of Plastic Artists, and Group of Plastic Artists, Municipal Hall, Prague
1912 (II) 'Exhibition of the Group of Plastic Artists,' Municipal Hall, Prague
1913 (III) 'Exhibition of the Group of Plastic Artists,' Municipal Hall, Prague
1913 'Internationale Baufachausstellung,' Leipzig
1913 'Ideal Home Exhibition,' Prague
1913 'Österreichische Tapeten-Linkrusta und Linoleum-Industrie,' Österreichisches Museum für Kunst und Industrie, Vienna
1914 (IV) 'Exhibition of the Group of Plastic Artists,' Municipal Hall, Prague

1914 'Centenary Exhibition,' Frogner, Oslo
1914 'Deutsche Werkbundausstellung,' Cologne
1914 'Baltic Exhibition,' Malmö
1914 'British Arts and Crafts Exhibition,' Paris
1914 'Jack of Diamonds,' Moscow
1915–16 '0–10,' Moscow
1916 'Jack of Diamonds,' Moscow
1916 'The Store' of the Union of Youth, Moscow
1916 'The Store' of the Union of Youth, Moscow
1917 'Home Exhibition,' Liljevalch's Gallery, Stockholm
1918 'Exhibition of Paintings and Sculpture by Jewish Artists,' Moscow
1919 'First State Free Exhibition of Works of Art,' Petrograd (now St. Petersburg)
1920 'Ideal Home Exhibition,' Olympia, London
1921 'Vornehme Wohnungseinrichtungen,' Österreichisches Museum für Kunst und Industrie, Vienna
1921–22 (first) 'Exhibition of the Czechoslovak Artistic Industry,' Uměleckoprůmyslové Muzeum, Prague
1921 '5 x 5 = 25,' Moscow
1922 'Deutsche Gewerbeschau,' Munich
1922 'Erste Russische Kunstausstellung,' Galerie van Diemen, Berlin
1922 Exhibition of the work of the Deutscher Werkbund, Newark Museum, Newark, New Jersey
1923 'First Agricultural and Handicraft-Industrial Exhibition,' Moscow
1923 'Esposizione Italiana d'Arte Decorativa e Popolare,' Stockholm
1924 'First Discussional Exhibition of Associations of Active Revolutionary Art,' Moscow
1924 'Die Form,' exhibition of the Deutsche Werkbund, Stuttgart
1924 '40th Jubilee Exhibition of the Wiener Kunstgewerbeverein,' Vienna
1925 'Art and Design Exhibition,' Monza
1926–27 'Exhibition of Northern Bohemia,' Mlada Boleslav
1926–27 'American Industrial Art, Tenth Annual Exhibition of Current Manufactures Designed and Made in the United States,' Metropolitan Museum of Art, New York, 4 December 1926–5 January 1927
1926–28 'Novy Dum Exhibition,' Brno
1927 'Art in Industry,' Halle Brothers department store, Cleveland, Ohio
1927–28 'Exhibition of Contemporary Culture,' Brno
1927 'Europäisches Kunstgewerbe,' Grassi Museum, Leipzig
1927 'Art and Design Exhibition,' Monza
1927 'Exposition de la Mode,' Berlin
1927 Exhibition sponsored by the Norwegian Society of Arts and Crafts, Bergen
1927 'Swedish Contemporary Decorative Arts,' Metropolitan Museum of Art, New York
1927 Exhibition of Danish wares, Metropolitan Museum of Art, New York
1927 'Exposition of Art in Trade at Macy's,' Macy's department store, New York, 2–7 May
1927 'Russian Xylography of the Past Ten Years,' Leningrad (now St. Petersburg)
1927 'Werkbund-Ausstellung/Die Wohnung,' 'Weissenhof-siedlung,' Stuttgart, July–September
1927 'Het Behang en het Gordijn,' Stedelijk Museum, Amsterdam
1928 'Die neuzeitliche Wohnung (The Modern Apartment),' Österreichisches Museum für Kunst und Industrie, Vienna
1928 'Esposizione di Torino,' Turin
1928 'Bytovoi sovetskii tekstil,' Vkhutein, Moscow
1928 (I) 'Esposizione Italiana di Architettura Razionale,' Palazzo delle Esposizioni, Rome
1928 'Press and Book Exposition,' Cologne

magazine, Metropolitan Museum of Art, New York, 28 October–24 November

1947 (XI) 'Ceramic National Exhibition' (traveling), organized by Syracuse Museum of Fine Art, Syracuse, New York, mounted at Metropolitan Museum of Art, New York

1947 'British Architecture Yesterday and Tomorrow,' Prague

1947 'French Tapestries: Medieval Renaissance, and Modern,' Metropolitan Museum of Art, New York, 21 November–29 February

1948 'Photography in Design,' Design and Industries Association and Royal Photographic Society, London

1948 'Deense Kunsthandwerk,' Gemeentemuseum, The Hague

1949 'For Modern Living,' Detroit Institute of Arts

1949 (I) 'Die gute Form,' Munstermesse Basel

1949–50 (I) 'Formes Utiles,' Pavillon de Marsan, Paris

1950 'Design for Modern Use, made in the USA,' traveling exhibition to Europe organized by the New York Museum of Modern Art

1950–55 'Good Design' exhibitions, New York Museum of Modern Art and Chicago Merchandise Mart

1951 'An Exhibition of Cotswold Craftsmanship,' Art Gallery and Museum, Cheltenham

1951 'Constructa,' Berlin

1951 'Exhibition of Finnish Design,' Kunstgewerbeschule, Zürich

1952 'Um 1990: Art Nouveau und Jugendstil,' Kunstgewerbemuseum, Zürich

1952 'Register Your Vote,' Design and Industries Association, London

1953 'Engelse Ceramiek,' Stedelijk Museum, Amsterdam

1953 'Exposition française,' Paris

1954 'This Is Tomorrow,' London

1954–57 'Design in Scandinavia' (traveling), USA

1955 'H 55,' Hälsingborg (Sweden)

1955 'Svensk Form,' Copenhagen

1955 'Die gute Industrieform,' Die Neue Sammlung, Munich

1955 'Das Bild im Wohnraum unserer Zeit,' Kunstgewerbemuseum, Saint-Gall (Switzerland)

1956 'Modern Italian Design,' Manchester City Art Galleries

1956 'Möbel aus Holz und Stahl,' Gewerbemuseum, Basel

1956 'This Is Tomorrow,' Whitechapel Gallery, London

1956 (I) 'Triennale d'Art Français Contemporain,' Pavillon de Marsan, Paris

1956 'American Young Scandinavian Exhibition' (traveling), USA

1956–57 'Finnish Exhibition' (traveling), Germany

1956–59 'Neue Form aus Dänemark' (traveling), Germany

1957 'Make or Mar,' Design and Industries Association, London

1957 'Good Design in Switzerland' (traveling), USA and Canada

1958 'Formes Scandinaves,' Musée des Arts Décoratifs, Paris

1959 'Dansk Form og Miljø,' Liljevalchs Konsthall, Stockholm

1959 (XX) 'Ceramic International Exhibition,' Metropolitan Museum of Art, New York, 23 January–8 March

1959 'Form Givers at Mid-Century,' Metropolitan Museum of Art, New York, 12 March–19 October

1959 'Glas, Gebrauchs- und Zierformen aus vier Jahrtausender,' Die Neue Sammlung, Munich

1959–60 'Glass 1959' organized by the Corning Museum of Glass, Metropolitan Museum of Art, New York, 19 November–3 January

1959 'The Face of the Firm,' Design and Industries Association, London

1960 'Wohnen heute,' Kunsthaus, Lucerne

1960 'Der Stuhl: Seine Funktion und Konstruktion,' Die Neue Sammlung, Munich

1960–61 'The Arts of Denmark' (traveling), USA, originating New York Metropolitan Museum of Art

1960–61 'Les Sources du XXè siècle: Les Arts

en Europe de 1884 à 1914,' Musée Nationale d'Art Moderne, Paris

1961 (I) 'Salone del Mobile Italiano,' Milan, 24 September–1 October

1961 'Gute Möbel,' Kunstgewerbemuseum, Zürich

1961 'Wohnen mit Holz,' Globus department store, Zürich

1961 'Finlandia,' Zürich, Amsterdam, and London

1962 'Creative Craft in Denmark Today,' New York

1962 'Unga nordiska formgivare,' Röhsska Konstslöjdmuseet, Gothenburg

1962 'Moderne Dänische Wohnkultur,' Vienna

1961 'The Arts of Denmark, Viking to Modern,' Metropolitan Museum of Art, New York

1963 'New Forms,' Charlottenborg Museum, Copenhagen

1963 'Czech Cubism,' V. Kramář Gallery, Prague

1964 'Formes Danoises,' Paris

1964 'Wien um 1900,' Historisches Museum, Vienna

1964 'Exhibition of Stained Glass and Mosaics,' Victoria and Albert Museum, London

1964 'Cents ans: Cent chefs-d'œuvre, Cent collections,' Musée des Arts Décoratifs, Paris, 16 October 1964–15 January 1965

1964 Photographic exhibition on international exhibitions 1851–1939, Metropolitan Museum of Art, New York

1964 'Schweizerische Landesausstellung,' Lausanne

1965 'La Casa Abitata,' Palazzo Strozzi, Florence, 6 March–25 April

1965 'International Exhibition of Ceramics,' Vicenza

1966 'Vijftig Jaar Zitten,' Stedelijk Museum, Amsterdam

1966 'Prima Triennale Itinerante di Architettura Contemporanea Italiana,' Italy

1966 'Paris–Prague,' Musée National d'Art Moderne, Paris

1966 'Les Années 25: Art Déco/Bauhaus/Stijl/Esprit Nouveau,' Musée des Arts Décoratifs, Paris, 3 March–16 May

1967 'Domus Formes italiennes,' Galeries Lafayette, Paris, 13 March–1 April

1967 'Design in Czechoslovakia,' London

1967 'Europa 1900,' Musée des Beaux-Arts, Ostend, 3 June–30 September

1967 'Die Wiener Werkstätte: Modernes Kunsthandwerk 1903–1932,' Österreichisches Museum für Kunst und Industrie, Vienna

1967 'Stapelstühle.' Gewerbemuseum, Basel

1968 'Design Italian Style,' Hallmark Gallery, New York

1968 'Les Assises du siège contemporain,' Musée des Arts Décoratifs, Paris, 3 May–29 July

1968 '50 Years Bauhaus,' Royal Academy of Art, London, 21 September–27 October

1968 'Two Centuries of Danish Design,' London, Manchester, and Glasgow

1969 'Plastic as Plastic,' Museum of Contemporary Crafts, New York

1968 'Seit Langem Bewährt: Klassische Produkte Moderne Formgebung,' Die Neue Sammlung, Munich

1968 'Bauzentrum Wien,' Vienna

1969 'Qu'est-ce que le design?,' Centre Georges Pompidou, Paris, 24 October–31 December

1969 'Visiona,' Germany

1969 'Czech Cubism,' V. Kramář, Prague

1969 'Modern Danish Design,' Moscow

1969 'Sitzen 69,' Österreichisches Museum für Angewandte Kunst, Vienna

1969 'Um 1930: Bauten, Möbel, Geräte, Plakate, Fotos,' Die Neue Sammlung, Munich

1970 'Designs aus Italien,' Deutsche Werkbund, Karlsruhe and other cities in Germany

1970 'Modern Chairs: 1918–1970,' Whitechapel Gallery, London, 22 July–30 August

1970 'Craftsmen from Norway,' New York

1970 'Ideal Home,' London

1970 'Design for Living, Italian Style,' London

1970–71   'Vitalità del Negativo,' Palazzo delle Esposizioni,'
Rome, November 1970–January 1971

1971   'Kunst und Kunsthandwerk aus Dänemark,' Wiesbaden

1971   'Gold und Silber, Schmuck und Gerät,'
Gewerbemuseum, Nuremberg, 19 March–22 August

1971   'Milano 70/70: Un secolo d'arte, dal 1915 al 1945,'
Museo Poldi Pezzoli, Milan, 28 April–10 June

1971   'L'Art de la Poterie en France de Rodin à Dufy,' Musée
National de Céramique, Paris

1971   'Design Français,' Centre de Création Industrielle, Centre
Georges Pompidou, Paris

1971   'The World of Art Deco' (traveling), originating at
Minneapolis Institute of Arts

1971   'Art Nouveau,' Virginia Museum, Richmond, Virginia,
22 November–26 December

1971   'Die Vergorgene Vernunft: Funktionale Gestaltung im
19. Jahrhundert,' Die Neue Sammlung, Munich

1972   'Italy: the new domestic landscape,' Museum of Modern
Art, New York, 26 May–11 September

1973   '1928–1973 Domus: 45 ans d'architecture, design,
art,' Musée des Arts Décoratifs, Paris, 31 May–23
September

1972   Exhibition on art in the Soviet Union, Metropolitan
Museum of Art, New York, 7–31 October

1972   'Design a Plastické Hmoty,' Uměleckoprůmyslové
Muzeum, Prague

1972   'Milano 70/70: Un secolo d'arte, dal 1946 al 1970,
Milan

1973   'The Arts and Crafts Movement: Artists Craftsmen and
Designers 1890–1930,' Fine Arts Society, London

1973   'New Form in Italy,' Teheran

1973   'Italy Today,' Pittsburgh

1973   'Gold' (on gold in the Soviet Union), Metropolitan
Museum of Art, New York, 14 April–9 September

1973   'Frank Lloyd Wright and the Francis W. Little House,'
Metropolitan Museum of Art, New York

1973   'Weltausstellungen im 19. Jahrhundert,' Die Neue
Sammlung, Munich

1974   'Exempla,' Munich

1974   'CC 41: Utility Furniture and Fashion, 1941–1951,'
Geffrye Museum, London, 24 September–29 December

1974   'Die Shaker: Leben und Produktion einer Commune in
der Pionierzeit Amerikas,' Die Neue Sammlung, Munich

1975   'Akari Lampen aus Japan,' Kunstgewerbemuseum,
Zürich

1975   'Bauen–Wohnen–Leben,' Olma, Saint-Gall (Switzerland)

1975   'Italian Industrial Design,' Porto Alegre, Brasilia, and São
Paulo

1975   'Adventures in Swedish Glass,' Australia

1975   '50 Anni di Design,' Italian design, Paris

1975   'La Sedia in Materiale Plasico,' Centrokappa, Noviglio
(Milano), 10 September–30 October

1975   'A Modern Consciousness: D. J. DePree, Florence Knoll,'
Renwick Gallery, Washington, 11 April–9 November

1975   'Un Siècle de Bronzes Animaliers,' Galerie P. Ambroise,
Paris

1975   'Zwischen Kunst und Industrie: Der Deutsche
Werkbund,' Die Neue Sammlung, Munich

1975–77   'Dansk Miljø' (traveling), Europe

1975   'Danske Fyrretræsmøbler,' Berlin

1976   'Czech Cubist Interiors,' Uměleckoprůmyslové Muzeum,
Prague

1976   'Gestaltung von Kindertagesstätten,' IDZ, Berlin

1976   'The Pre-Raphaelite Era 1848–1914,' Delaware Art
Museum

1976   'Italian Industrial Design,' Rio de Janeiro

1976   'Acht Deense Ceramisten,' Rotterdam

1976   'Modernes Glas,' Museum für Kunsthandwerk,
Frankfurt, 15 May–27 June

1976   'Il Werkbund 1907, alle origini del design,' 1976

(XXXVII) Biennale di Venezia, Ca' Pesaro

1976   'Art Nouveau, Belgium, France,' Rice University
Museum, Houston, Texas, 26 March–27 June

1976   'SCAN,' Washington

1976–77   'Industrieform,' Hanover

1976–77   'Cinquantenaire de l'Exposition de 1925,' Musée des
Arts Décoratifs, Paris, 15 October 1976–2 February
1977

1977   'Um 1930 in Zürich,' Kunstgewerbemuseum, Zürich

1977   'Dänische Formgestaltung,' Berlin

1977   'Il Design Italiano negli Anni '50,' Centrokappa,
Noviglio (Italy)

1977   'Prämiierte Produkte,' Rat für Formgebung, Darmstadt,
19 June–24 July

1978   '28–78 Architettura, Cinquant'anni di architettura
italiana,' Palazzo delle Stelline, Milan, 28 March–13 May

1978   'Danish Design,' Dublin

1978   '100 Jahre Kunstgewerbemuseum der Stadt Zürich,'
Zürich

1979   'Paesaggio Casalingo: La Produzione Alessi nell'industria
dei casalinghi dal 1921 al 1980,' originating at the 1979
(XVI) Triennale di Milano

1979   'Design Process Olivetti 1908–1978,' University of
California, Frederick S. Wight Art Gallery, Los Angeles,
27 March–6 May

1979   'New Glass: A Worldwide Survey,' The Corning
Museum of Glass, Corning, New York, 26 April–1
October

1979   'Design & design,' Palazzo delle Stelline, Milan, 29
May–31 July, and to Palazzo Grassi, Venice

1979   'Jewelry Arts Exhibition,' Tokyo

1979   'Paris-Moscou,' Centre Georges Pompidou, Paris

1979–80   'Thirties: British Art and Design before the War,'
Hayward Gallery, London, 25 October 1979–13 January
1980

1980   'Georg Jensen–Silversmithy: 77 Artists 75 Years,'
Renwick Gallery, Washington, 29 February–6 July

1980   'Arte e design,' Palazzo delle Esposizioni, Faenza

1980   'Forum Design,' Hochschule für künstlerische und
industrielle Gestaltung, Linz, 27 August–5 October

1980   'Speed, Style, Symbol,' Cooper-Hewitt Museum, New
York

1980   'Der Sport formt sein Gerät,' Die Neue Sammlung,
Munich

1980–81   'Kultur und Technologie im italienisches Möbel
1950–1980,' Stadtmuseum, Cologne, 29 November
1980–25 January 1981

1981   'Italienische Möbel Design 1950–80,' Stadtmuseum,
Cologne

1981   'Stühle aus Stahl: Metallmöbel in Europa, 1925–1940,'
Kunstgewerbemuseum, Zürich

1981   'Czechoslovakian Glass: 1350–1980,' The Corning
Museum of Glass, Corning, New York, 2 May–1
November

1981   'Paris 1937–57,' Centre Georges Pompidou, Paris, 28
May–2 November

1981   'Danskt 50 Tal: Scandinavian Design,' Nationalmuseum,
Stockholm, 7 October–29 November

1981   'New Glass: A Worldwide Survey,' organized by Corning
Museum of Glass, Metropolitan Museum of Art, New
York

1981   '1900 en France,' Mitsukoshi, Tokyo, 11–30 August

1981   'Warenplakate: Meisterplakate von der
Jahrhundertwende bis heute,' Die Neue Sammlung,
Munich

1981–82   'Danish Ceramic Design,' Pennsylvania State
University, 18 October 1981–24 January 1982

1982   'Art and Industry,' Boilerhouse Project, Victoria and
Albert Museum, London, 18 January–2 March

1982   '1, 2, 3, . . . Egg cup,' London and Berlin

1982 'Contemporary Vessels: How to Pour,' National Museum of Modern Art, Tokyo, 10 February–22 March

1982 'L'Interno Dopo la Forma dell'Utile,' Palazzo dell'Arte Triennale, Milan

1982 'Re-Evolution: Design in Italian Society in the 80's,' La Jolla Museum of Art, La Jolla, California

1982 'Verriers français contemporains: Art et industrie,' Musée des Arts Décoratifs, Paris, 2 April–5 July

1982 'Aktuel Svensk Form,' Ibsenhuset, Skien (Sweden), 3–21 October

1982 'Anni Trenta: Arte e Cultura in Italia,' Palazzo Reale, Milan

1982–83 'Scandinavia Modern: 1880–1980,' Cooper-Hewitt Museum, New York, 14 September 1982–2 January 1983

1982–83 'Fila, Gutfreund, Kubka och tjeckisk kubism,' Konsthall, Malmö

1983 'Design,' Kunstgewerbemuseum, Zürich

1983 '70 Jahre Schweizerischer Werkbund,' Kunstgewerbemuseum, Zürich

1983 'Möbel aus Italien,' Design Center, Stuttgart

1983 'Works of Art in Glass from the Museum's Collections,' Metropolitan Museum of Art, New York

1983 'Mostra del Disegno Industriale Italiano,' Shanghai

1983 'Dal Cucchiaio alla Città nell'Itinerario,' Palazzo dell'Arte, Milan

1983 'La Casa della Triennale,' Palazzo dell'Arte, Milan

1983–84 'At Home in Manhattan: Modern Decorative Arts, 1925 to the Depression,' Yale University Art Gallery, New Haven, Connecticut, 10 November 1983–5 February 1984

1983–84 'Design Since 1945,' Philadelphia Museum of Art, 16 October 1983–8 January 1984

1984 'Pionniers du Meuble,' Musée d'Art et d'Histoire,' Geneva

1984 'Schweizer Design für Innenräume 1925–1975,' Ornaris, Zürich

1984 'L'Empire du Bureau 1900–2000,' CNAP, Paris

1984 'Exhibition of Italian Design,' Sogetsu Kaikan Palace, Tokyo, 8–16 February

1984 'Mobilier national: 20 ans de création,' CNACGP, CCI, CNAP, Paris

1984 'Design in America: The Cranbrook Vision, 1925–1950,' Metropolitan Museum of Art, New York, 18 April–17 June and traveling

1984 'Italian Design,' Sogetsu Kaikan Palace, Tokyo

1984 'Czechoslovakian Cubism–the World of Architecture, Furniture, and Craft,' Parco, Tokyo

1984–85 'Shop of the East,' Berlin, Munich, and Hamburg

1985 'Contemporary Landscape,' Kyoto and Tokyo

1985 '16 Italian Women Designers,' ADI, Milan, and Takshimaya department store, Tokyo

1985 'Le Affinità Elettive,' Palazzo dell'Arte

1985 'La Neomerce,' Palazzo dell'Arte

1985 'Les Immatériaux,' Centre Georges Pompidou, Paris

1985 'High Styles,' Whitney Museum of American Art, New York

1985 'New Glass in Japan,' Badisches Landesmuseum, Karlsruhe

1985 'La Chaise: Objet du Design ou d'Architecture,' Centre de Création et de Diffusion, Montreal

1985 'Radical Design,' Maison de la Culture, Rennes

1985 'Lumière je pense à vous,' Centre Georges Pompidou, Paris, 3 June–5 August

1985 'Uhr und Mode, Deutsche Uhrenindustrie,' Pforzheim

1985–86 'Industry and Design in the Netherlands 1850–1950,' Stedelijk Museum, Amsterdam, 21 December 1985–6 February 1986

1986 'Il Progetto Domestico,' Palazzo dell'Arte Triennale, Milan, 19 January–23 March

1986 'Italia Deseño 1946–1986,' Museo Rufino Tamayo, Mexico City

1986 'Caravelles,' Quadriannale Internationale de Design, Musée Saint-Pierre, Lyons

1986 'Expression en Verre,' Musée des Arts Décoratifs, Lausanne

1986 'Itinerari Manzoniani,' Milan

1986 'Seduced and Abandoned: Modern Furniture Design in Canada, the First Fifty Years,' Art Gallery at Harbourfront, Toronto

1986 'Design–Process–Auto: Zum Beispiel BMW,' Die Neue Sammlung, Munich

1986 'Der Kragstuhl,' Stuhlmuseum Burg Beverungen

1986–87 'In Pursuit of Beauty: Americans and the Aesthetic Movement,' Metropolitan Museum of Art, New York, 23 October 1986–11 January 1987

1986–88 'The Machine Age,' traveling USA, originating Brooklyn Museum, New York

1987–88 'Berlin Ways–Products and Design from Berlin,' traveling Berlin, Stuttgart, Stockholm, and Barcelona

1987 'Nouvelles Tendances: avante-gardes de la fin du 20ème siècle,' Centre Georges Pompidou, Paris, 14 April–18 September

1987 'Design-Dasein,' Museum für Kunst und Gewerbe, Hamburg

1987 'Le Città Immaginate,' Palazzo dell'Arte Triennale, Milan

1987 'I Modi del Design,' Palazzo dell'Arte Triennale, Milan

1987 'Reiz und Hülle: Gestaltete Warenverpackungen des 19. and 20. Jahrhunderts,' Die Neue Sammlung, Munich

1987 'A Material World,' National Museum of American History, Washington

1987–88 '"The Art that Is Life": The Arts and Crafts Movement in America, 1875–1920' (traveling), originating Museum of Fine Arts, Boston, 4 May 1987–2 June 1988

1988 'Le Japonisme,' Galeries Nationales du Grand Palais, Paris, 17 May–15 August

1988 'Abitare il Tempo,' Verona

1988 'Nouveaux Projets pour l'Habitat,' Salon du Meuble, Paris

1988 'Furniture Follows Function,' Bella Center's Hall, Copenhagen

1988 'Design from Europa . . . for the world,' Interieur '88, Kortrijk (Belgium)

1988 'Les Avantgardes du Mobilier: Berlin,' Centre de Creation Industrielle (CCI) at Centre Georges Pompidou and Galerie Néotù, Paris

1988 'Arte en Vidro,' Saõ Paulo Art Museum

1988 'Italia 2000,' ADI/ICE, Moscow

1988–90 'Design français 1960–1990: Trois décennies,' Galerie du CCI, Centre Georges Pompidou, Paris, October–December 1988, and London, 31 October 1989–2 January 1990

1988 'Kunst und Revolution: Russische und Sowjetische Kunst 1910–1932,' Mücsarnok, Budapest, 5 November 1987–17 January 1988, and Österreichisches Museum für angewandte Kunst, Vienna, 11 March–15 May 1988

1988 'Les Années 50,' Centre Georges Pompidou, 30 June–17 October

1988 'The Most Contemporary French Design,' Victoria and Albert Museum, London

1988 'Deconstructivist Architecture,' Museum of Modern Art, New York

1988 'Trentacinque Mobili del Razionalismo Italiano,' Salone del Mobile, Milan

1988 'Hahen: Design 1945 bis heute,' Die Neue Sammlung, Munich

1989 'Mobilier suisse,' Galerie des brèves du CCI, Centre Georges Pompidou, Paris, 1 November–4 December

1989 'L'Art de Vivre: Decorative Arts and Design in France,

1789–1989,' Cooper-Hewitt Museum, New York

1989 'Remembering the Future: The New York World's Fairs from 1939 to 1964,' Queens Museum, New York

1989–90 'From Architecture to Object: Masterworks of the American Arts and Crafts Movement,' Hirschl and Adler Galleries, New York, 7 October–18 November 1989, and Struve Gallery, Chicago, 15 December 1989–22 January 1990

1989–90 'Scandinavian Ceramics and Glass in the Twentieth Century,' Victoria and Albert Museum, London, 20 September 1989–7 January 1990

1989 'La Città del Mondo e il Futuro delle Metropoli,' Palazzo dell'Arte Triennale, Milan, 21 September–18 December

1989 'British Design, Image and Identity,' Museum Boymans-van Beuningen, Netherlands

1990 'Creativitalia, the Joy of Italian Design,' Railcity Shiodome, Tokyo, 7 April–13 May 1990

1990 'Nordform 90,' Scandinavian craft, industrial design, and architecture, Malmö, 1 June–2 September

1990 'Civiltà delle Macchine,' Lingotto, Turin, 20 September–30 December

1990 'Les Années VIA,' Musée des Arts Décoratifs, Paris

1990 'Londres, images et objets du nouveau design,' Galerie du CCI, Centre Georges Pompidou, Paris

1991 'Mobili Italiana 1961–1991: Le Varie Età dei linguaggi,' Salone del Mobile, Milan, 12 April–12 May

1991 'What Modern Was,' traveling exhibition sponsored by the Château Dufresne, Montreal

1991 'Design und Kunst, Burg Gebichenstein 1945–1990,' Die Neue Sammlung, Munich

1991–92 'The New Look–Design in the Fifties,' originating Manchester City Art Galleries, 13 October 1991–5 January 1992

1991–93 'Czech Design 1910–1925,' originating Uměleckoprůmyslové Muzeum, Prague

1992 'Futurism 1909–44,' Hokkaido Museum of Art, Sapporo

1992 'Russian Avant-Garde 1915–32,' Stedelijk Museum, Amsterdam, 5 June–31 August

1992 '20th-Century Costume Jewelry,' Victoria and Albert Museum, London

1992 'World's Fair and Modern Life,' National Gallery of Art, Washington

1992 'The Great Utopia: The Russian and Soviet Avant-Garde, 1915–1932,' originating Schirn Kunsthalle, Frankfurt

1992–93 'Japan: Hülle und Gefass,' Die Neue Sammlung, Munich

1992–93 'News from a Radiant Future: Soviet Porcelain from the Collection of Craig H. & Kay A. Tuber,' The Art Institute of Chicago, 25 October 1992–31 January 1993

1993 'The Cutting Edge: 200 Years of Cut Crystal,' Smithsonian Institute, F. Dillon Ripley, Washington

1993 'Revolution, Life, and Labor: Soviet Porcelains 1918–1985,' Cooper-Hewitt Museum, New York

1993 'Design, Mirror du Siècle,' Grand Palais, Paris, 15 May–25 July

1993 'Citizen Office,' Vitra Design Museum, Weil am Rhein, April–September

Fairs

Concorso Internazionale del Mobile, Cantù (Italy), from 1955

'Eurodomus,' Genoa, 1966 (I); Turin, 1968 (II); Palazzo dell'Arte, Milan, 1970 (III); Turin, 1972 (IV)

'Interbau' international construction fair, Berlin

'BIO' (Biennial of Industrial Design/Bienale Industrijskega Oblikovanja), Ljubljana, 1964 (BIO 1), 1966 (BIO 2), 1968 (BIO 3), 1971 (BIO 4), 1973 (BIO 5), 1975 (BIO 6), 1977 (BIO 7), 1979 (BIO 8), 1981 (BIO 9), 1984 (BIO 10), 1986 (BIO 11), 1988 (BIO 12), 1992 (BIO 13), 1994 (BIO 14)

Feria International del Meuble, Valencia, from 1963

'Interior/1978,' Courtrai (Belgium)

Kölner Möbelmesse, Cologne, from 1929; Internationale Kölner Möbelmesse from 1983

Salone del Mobile, Milan, from 1961

Salon du Meuble, Paris

International Furniture Fair, New York, from 1990

Biennali di Monza and Triennali di Milano

Monza 'Esposizione Biennale delle Arti Decorative e Industriali Moderne': 1923 (I), 1925 (II), 1927 (III), 1930 (IV)

Milan 'Triennale di Milano,' 1933 (V), 1936 (VI), 1940 (VII), 1947 (VIII), 1951 (IX), 1954 (X), 1957 (XI), 1960 (XII), 1964 (XIII), 1968 (XIV), 1973 (XV), 1979 (XVI), 1983–88 (XVII), 1990 (XVIII) (continuing), 1995 (XIX) (forthcoming)